HARRAP'S
Concise
FRENCH AND ENGLISH
DICTIONARY

HARRAP'S
Concise
FRENCH AND ENGLISH DICTIONARY

FRENCH-ENGLISH/ENGLISH-FRENCH
IN ONE VOLUME

EDITED BY
Patricia Forbes & Muriel Holland Smith
GENERAL EDITOR P. H. Collin

HARRAP · LONDON

First published in Great Britain
by GEORGE G. HARRAP & CO. LTD
182–184 High Holborn, London WC1V 7AX

© *George G. Harrap & Co. Ltd* 1978
Copyright. All rights reserved.

ISBN 0 245 52829 6

Printed in Great Britain by offset lithography by
Billing & Sons Ltd, Guildford, London and Worcester

PREFACE

This work is a completely new version, revised and enlarged, of *Harrap's Concise French and English Dictionary,* originally compiled by the late R. P. Jago and published by Harrap in London in 1949. The aim of the present publication is to offer the user, whether businessman, tourist or student, an up-to-date and practical work of reference giving translations of modern French and English vocabulary, including Americanisms and French-Canadianisms.

As far as the English language is concerned, the standard spellings current in England have been used throughout. Common alternative spellings are given in the English–French part, though it should be noted that for words with the alternative suffixes -**ise** or -**ize** and -**isation** or -**ization**, -**ize** and -**ization** have been adopted throughout.

The attention of the North-American user is directed towards a few salient differences in spelling:

(a) the English use of -**our** in words which in American usage are spelt with -**or** (*e.g. Eng:* col**our**, *N.Am:* color).

(b) the use of the final -**re** in words where American usage favours -**er** (*e.g. Eng:* theat**re**, *N.Am:* theater).

(c) the doubling of the l before an ending beginning with a vowel, irrespective of accentuation (*e.g. Eng:* woo**ll**en, *N.Am:* woolen; *Eng:* trave**ll**ing, *N.Am:* traveling).

(d) the single l before a final syllable beginning with a consonant, where the American usage is **ll** (*e.g. Eng:* ski**l**ful, *N.Am:* skillful; *Eng:* enro**l**ment, *N.Am:* enrollment).

(e) the use of a **c** in certain words where American usage favours an **s** (*e.g. Eng:* defen**c**e, *N.Am:* defense).

The phonetics of both French and English words are given according to the symbols of the International Phonetic Association.

The particular feature of this dictionary as of all Harrap's dictionaries is the number of examples given to show the various uses of the more important words. In order to do this and to keep the length to reasonable dimensions a number of space-saving devices have been adopted:

1. When in an example a headword is repeated in exactly the same form it is represented by the initial letter, though plural nouns or verb conjugations in which the form differs from the infinitive are given in full, *e.g.* **pave,** *v.tr.* paver (une rue) . . . **to p. the way,** préparer le terrain.

2. In the French–English part a certain number of adverbs and simple derivatives follow the headword; the form of these is indicated simply by the ending, *e.g.* **prison,** *s.f.* prison, *s.* -**nier,** -**nière,** prisoner; **observ/er,** *v.tr.* to observe . . . *s.f.* -**ation,** observation.

3. In the English–French part nouns, verbs, adjectives or adverbs which have the same form are shown together under one headword, with the distinguishing divisions **I, II, III**, etc. Derivatives, whether hyphenated or not, are listed under the main headword, but the words appear in full in order that the stressed syllable may be shown. Where phonetic changes occur in derivatives, these are indicated, *e.g.* **peel, I.** *s.* pelure *f*. . . **II.** *v*. **1.** *v.tr.* peler (un fruit) . . . *'***peeler,** *s.* éplucheur *m* . . . *'***peelings,** *s. pl.* épluchures *f*.

The following conventions have also been observed:
  (a) Nouns have been described as 'substantives', being listed as *s.m.* or *s.f.* in the French–English part. In the English–French part the gender is given after the French word. Irregular plurals of nouns, irregular feminine forms of adjectives, irregular conjugations of verbs are also indicated. The user is therefore advised to consult the French or English headword for information on irregular forms.
  (b) Owing to the different systems of administration, etc., in the different countries it is not always possible to give true translations for different functions or offices. In such cases the sign = has been used to indicate the nearest equivalent.

We should like to thank all who have helped us in our revision work and in the reading of the proofs, notably Mr C. B. Johnson, M.A., Mrs Margaret Ledésert, M.A., Madame S. Chandless and Mrs F. Collin, M.A. (Montréal).

Patricia Forbes
Muriel Holland Smith
Peter H. Collin

PRÉFACE

Cet ouvrage est une version tout à fait nouvelle, revue et augmentée, du *Harrap's Concise French and English Dictionary,* par M. R. P. Jago, maintenant décédé, et publié par Harrap à Londres en 1949. Le but de la nouvelle publication est d'offrir à son utilisateur, qu'il soit homme d'affaires, touriste ou étudiant, un ouvrage de référence pratique et à jour qui donne les traductions d'un vocabulaire moderne anglais et français, y compris des américanismes et des canadianismes français.

L'orthographic des mots anglais respecte l'usage britannique. Les variantes usuelles figurent dans la partie anglais-français; il faut cependant signaler que pour la double forme des suffixes -ise ou -ize, et -isation ou -ization l'orthographe -ize et -ization a été adoptée dans les deux parties du dictionnaire.

Nous attirons l'attention du lecteur habitué à l'usage américain sur quelques différences particulièrement frappantes:

(*a*) l'emploi anglais de -our dans des mots pour lesquels l'américain emploierait l'orthographe -or (*ex. angl:* colour, *N.Am:* color).

(*b*) l'emploi de la finale -re dans des mots pour lesquels l'usage américain donne la préférence à la forme -er (*ex. angl:* thèatre, *N.Am:* theater).

(*c*) le redoublement de la lettre l devant une voyelle (*ex. angl:* woollen, *N.Am:* woolen; *angl:* travelling, *N.Am:* traveling).

(*d*) l'emploi de l'i simple devant une syllabe finale commençant par une consonne, alors que l'usage américain est ll (*ex. angl:* skilful, *N.Am:* skillful; *angl:* enrolment, *N.Am:* enrollment).

(*e*) l'emploi d'un c dans certains mots pour lesquels l'américain donne la préférence à l's (*ex. angl:* defence, *N.Am:* defense).

Pour la transcription phonétique des mots français et anglais, nous employons les signes de l'Association phonétique internationale.

L'intérêt particulier de ce dictionnaire, ainsi que de tous les dictionnaires Harrap, réside dans le nombre des exemples donnés afin de montrer les usages variés des mots les plus importants. Cependant, afin d'éviter d'accroître démesurément le volume de l'ouvrage un certain nombre de règles typographiques ont été adoptées pour gagner de la place.

1. Quand, dans un exemple, un mot principal est répété sans changement il est représenté par la lettre initiale, alors que les noms au pluriel ou les formes des verbes pour lesquels l'orthographe change (ce qui n'est pas toujours le cas en anglais) sont écrits en toutes lettres, *ex.* pave, *v.tr.* paver (une rue) . . . to p. the way, préparer le terrain.

2. Dans la partie français-anglais un certain nombre d'adverbes et de dérivés simples sont insérés à la suite du mot principal, *e.g.* prison, *s.f.* prison, *s.* -nier, -nière, prisoner; observ/er, *v.tr.* to observe . . . *s.f.* -ation, observation.

3. Dans la partie anglais–français les noms, verbes, adjectifs ou adverbes ayant la même forme sont groupés sous le même mot principal, et séparés par les sous-titres **I, II, III**, etc. Les dérivés écrits avec ou sans trait d'union suivent le mot principal; ils sont écrits en toutes lettres afin de pouvoir indiquer la syllabe accentuée. Quand des changements phonétiques interviennent dans les dérivés, ceux-ci sont indiqués, *ex.* **peel. I.** *s.* pelure *f.* . . **II.** *v.tr.* peler (un fruit). . . **'peeler,** *s.* éplucheur *m* . . . **'peelings,** *s.pl.* épluchures *f.*

En outre, les conventions suivantes ont été respectées:

 (*a*) Les noms ont été classés comme substantifs et leur genre défini *s.m.* ou *s.f.* dans la partie français-anglais. Dans la partie anglais-français le genre est indiqué après le mot français. Les pluriels irréguliers des noms, les formes féminines irrégulières des adjectifs, les conjugaisons irrégulières des verbes sont également indiqués. Pour les informations grammaticales, le lecteur est donc renvoyé à chaque mot principal des deux parties de l'ouvrage.

 (*b*) Étant donné différences dans les structures administratives et autres des deux pays, il n'est pas toujours possible de traduire exactement les diverses charges, fonctions, etc. Dans de tels cas, le signe = a été utilisé pour indiquer l'équivalent le plus proche.

Nous tenons à remercier tous ceux qui nous ont aidés au travail de révision et à la lecture des épreuves et plus particulièrement: Mr C. B. Johnson, M.A., Mrs Margaret Ledésert, M.A., Madame S. Chandless et Mrs F. Collin, M.A. (Montréal).

Patricia Forbes
Muriel Holland Smith
Peter H. Collin

ABBREVIATIONS USED IN THE DICTIONARY

ABREVIATIONS UTILISÉES DANS LE DICTIONNAIRE

a.	adjective	adjectif
A:	archaism	désuet
abbr.	abbreviation	abréviation
abs.	absolute use of verb	emploi absolu du verbe
acc.	accusative	accusatif
adj.	adjective; adjectival	adjectif
adj. phr.	adjectival phrase	locution adjective
Adm:	administration; civil service	administration
adv.	adverb	adverbe
adv. phr.	adverbial phrase	locution adverbiale
Aer:	aeronautics	aéronautique
Agr:	agriculture	agriculture
Anat:	anatomy	anatomie
approx.	approximately	sens approché
Arach:	Arachnida	arachnides
Arch:	architecture	architecture
Archeol:	archaeology	archéologie
art.	article	article
Art:	art	beaux-arts
Artil:	artillery	artillerie
Astr:	astronomy	astronomie
Atom. Ph:	atomic physics	sciences atomiques
attrib.	attributive	attributif
Austr:	Australia; Australian	Australie; australien
Aut:	motoring; automobile industry	automobilisme; industrie automobile
aux.	auxiliary	auxiliaire
Av:	aviation; aircraft	aviation; avions
B:	Bible; biblical	Bible; biblique
Bank:	banking	opérations de banque
B. Hist:	Bible history	histoire sainte
Bill:	billiards	jeu de billard
Bio-Ch:	biochemistry	biochimie
Biol:	biology	biologie
B. Lit:	Bible literature	littérature biblique
Bookb:	bookbinding	reliure
Book-k:	book-keeping	comptabilité
Bot:	botany	botanique

Box:	boxing	boxe
Breed:	breeding	élevage
card.a.	cardinal adjective	adjectif cardinal
Carp:	carpentry	charpenterie; menuiserie du bâtiment
Ch:	chemistry	chimie
Cin:	cinema	cinéma
Civ. E:	civil engineering	génie civil
Cl:	clothing	vêtements
Coel:	Coelenterata	cœlentérés
cogn.acc.	cognate accusative	accusatif de l'objet interne
coll.	collective	collectif
Com:	commerce; business term	(terme du) commerce
Comest:	comestibles, food	comestibles
comp.	comparative	comparatif
condit.	conditional	conditionnel
conj.	conjunction	conjonction
conj. like	conjugated like	se conjugue comme
const.	(grammatical) construction	construction (grammaticale)
Const:	construction, building industry	industrie du bâtiment
Corr:	correspondence, letters	correspondance, lettres
Cost:	costume	costume
Crust:	Crustacea	crustacés
Cu:	culinary; cooking	culinaire; cuisine
Cust:	customs	douane
Danc:	dancing	danse
dat.	dative	datif
def.	(i) definite; (ii) defective (verb)	(i) défini; (ii) (verbe) défectif
dem.	demonstrative	démonstratif
Dent:	dentistry	art dentaire
Dom. Ec:	domestic economy; household equipment	économie domestique; ménage
Dressm:	dressmaking	couture (mode)
Dy:	dyeing	teinture
E:	engineering	industries mécaniques
Ecc:	ecclesiastical	église et clergé
Economics:	economics	science économique, économie politique

El:	electricity; electrical	électricité; électrique
El. E:	electrical engineering	électrotechnique
El. Meas:	electrical measurement	mesure en électricité
Eng:	England; English	Angleterre; anglais, britannique
Engr:	engraving	gravure
Ent:	entomology	entomologie
Equit:	equitation	équitation
esp.	especially	surtout
Ethn:	ethnology	ethnologie
exclam.	exclamation; exclamatory	exclamation; exclamatif
Exp:	explosives	explosifs
expr.	expression	expression, locution
f.	feminine	féminin
F:	colloquial(ism)	familier; style de la conversation
Fb:	(Association) football	football
Fenc:	fencing	escrime
Fin:	finance	finances
Fireworks:	fireworks	pyrotechnie
Fish:	fishing	pêche
Fort:	fortification	fortification
Fr.	France; French	France; français
Fr. C:	French Canadian	canadien français
fu.	future	futur
Furn:	furniture	mobilier
Gaming:	gaming; gambling	le jeu; jeux d'argent
Geog:	geography	géographie
Geol:	geology	géologie
Geom:	geometry	géométrie
ger.	gerund	gérondif
Golf:	golf	golf
Gram:	grammar	grammaire
Gym:	gymnastics	gymnastique
H:	household	économie domestique
Hairdr:	hairdressing	coiffure
Her:	heraldry	blason
Hist:	history; historical	histoire; historique
Hort:	horticulture	horticulture
Hyg:	hygiene; sanitation	hygiène; installations
i.	intransitive	intransitif

I.C.E:	internal combustion engines	moteurs à combustion interne
Ich:	ichthyology; fish	ichtyologie; poissons
imp.	imperative	impératif
impers.	impersonal	impersonnel
ind.	indicative	indicatif
Ind:	industry; industrial	industrie; industriel
indef.	indefinite	indéfini
inf.	infinitive	infinitif
Ins:	insurance	assurance
int.	interjection	interjection
interr.	interrogative	interrogatif
intr.	intransitive	intransitif
inv.	invariable	invariable
Iron:	ironic(ally)	ironique(ment)
irreg.	irregular	irrégulier
Jewel:	jewellery	bijouterie
Journ:	journalism; journalistic	journalisme; style journalistique
Jur:	jurisprudence; legal term	droit, terme de palais
Knitting:	knitting	tricot
Laund:	laundering	blanchissage
Ling:	linguistics; language	linguistique; langue
Lit:	literary use; literature; literary	forme littéraire; littérature; littéraire
m., masc.	masculine	masculin
Mch:	machines; machinery	machines; machines à vapeur
Meas:	weights and measures	poids et mesures
Mec:	mechanics	mécanique
Mec.E:	mechanical engineering	industries mécaniques
Med:	medicine; illnesses	médecine; maladies
Metalw:	metalworking	travail des métaux
Meteor:	meteorology	météorologie
Mil:	military; army	militaire; armée de terre
Mil.Av:	military aviation	aviation militaire
Min:	mining and quarrying	exploitation des mines et carrières
Miner:	mineralogy	minéralogie
Moll:	molluscs	mollusques
Mount:	mountaineering	alpinisme

Mth:	mathematics	mathématiques
Mus:	music	musique
Myth:	mythology; myths and legends	mythologie; mythes et légendes
n.		nous
N.Am:	North American	nord-américain
Nau:	nautical	terme de marine
Nau.Meas:	nautical measurement	mesure de navigation
Navy:	Navy	marine militaire
Needlew:	needlework	couture (travaux d'aiguille)
neg.	negative	négatif
neut.	neuter	neutre
nom.	nominative	nominatif
num.a.	numeral adjective	adjectif numéral
occ.	occasionally	parfois
Opt:	optics	optique
Orn:	ornithology; birds	ornithologie; oiseaux
P:	uneducated speech; slang	expression populaire; argot
Paint:	painting trade	peinture en bâtiment
Parl:	Parliament	parlement
p.d.	imperfect, past descriptive (tense)	imparfait (de l'indicatif), passé descriptif
Pej:	pejorative	péjoratif
perf.	perfect	passé composé
pers.	person(s); personal	personne(s); personnel
Ph:	physics	physique
p.h.	past historic, past definite (tense)	passé historique, passé simple
Pharm:	pharmacy	pharmacie
Ph.Meas:	physical measurement	mesure en physique
Phon:	phonetics	phonétique
Phot:	photography	photographie
phr.	phrase	locution
Physiol:	physiology	physiologie
pl.	plural	pluriel
Plumb:	plumbing	plomberie
P.N:	public notice	affichage; avis au public
Pol:	politics; political	politique

Pol. Ec:	political economy; economics	économie politique
poss.	possessive	possessif
Post:	postal services	postes et télécommunications
p.p.	past participle	participe passé
pr.	(i) present (tense); (ii) pronominal	(i) présent (de l'indicatif); (ii) pronominal
pred.	predicate	attribut
pref.	prefix	préfixe
prep.	preposition	préposition
prep. phr.	prepositional phrase	locution prépositive
Pr.n.	proper noun	nom propre
pron.	pronoun	pronom
pronom.	pronominal	pronominal
pr.p.	present participle	participe présent
Psy:	psychology	psychologie
Psychics:	psychics	métapsychisme
p.t.	past tense	passé
P.T.T:	post, telegraph, telephone	postes et télécommunications
Pub:	publishing	édition
qch.		quelque chose
qn		quelqu'un
Rac:	racing	courses
Rad:	radio	radio
Rail:	railways, railroads	chemins de fer
R.C.Ch:	Roman Catholic Church	Église catholique
Rec:	tape recorders; record players	magnétophones; tourne-disques
refl.	reflexive	réfléchi
rel.	relative	relatif
Rel:	religion(s)	religion(s)
Rept:	reptiles	reptiles
R.t.m:	registered trade mark	marque déposée
Rugby Fb:	Rugby football	le rugby
s.	substantive, noun	substantif, nom
Sailing:	sailing	navigation à voile
sb.	substantive, noun	substantif, nom
Sch:	schools and universities; students' (slang, etc.)	université; écoles; (argot, etc.) scolaire

Scot:	Scotland, Scottish	Écosse, écossais
Scouting:	Scout and Guide Movements	scoutisme
Sculp:	sculpture	sculpture
sg., sing.	singular	singulier
Ski:	skiing	le ski
Sm.a:	small arms	armes portatives
s.o.	someone	quelqu'un
Sp:	sport	sport
Space:	astronautics; space travel	astronautique; voyages interplanétaires
St. Exch:	Stock Exchange	terme de Bourse
sth.	something	quelque chose
sub.	subjunctive	subjonctif
sup.	superlative	superlatif
Surg:	surgery	chirurgie
Surv:	surveying	géodésie et levé de plans
Tail:	tailoring	mode masculine
Tchn:	technical	terme technique, terme de métier
temp.	temporary	temporaire
Ten:	tennis	tennis
Tex:	textiles; textile industry	industries textiles
Th:	theatre; theatrical	théâtre
Theol:	theology	théologie
thg	thing	
Tls:	tools	outils
Toil:	toilet; make-up	toilette; maquillage
tr.	transitive	transitif
T.V:	television	télévision
Typ:	typography	typographie
Typew:	typing; typewriters	dactylographie; machines à écrire
U.S:	United States; American	États-Unis; américain
usu.	usually	d'ordinaire
v.	verb: verbal	verbe; verbal
var.	variable	variable
vb.	verb	verbe
Veh:	vehicles	véhicules
Ven:	venery; hunting	la chasse

Vet:	veterinary science	art vétérinaire
v.i.	intransitive verb	verbe intransitif
v.impers.	impersonal verb	verbe impersonnel
v.ind.tr.	indirectly transitive verb	verbe transitif indirect
Vit:	viticulture	viticulture
v.pr.	pronominal verb	verbe pronominal
v.pred.	predicative verb	verbe prédicat
v.tr.	transitive verb	verbe transitif
Z:	zoology; mammals	zoologie; mammifères
=	nearest equivalent (of an institution, an office, etc., when systems vary in the different countries)	équivalent le plus proche (d'un terme désignant une institution, une charge, etc., dans les cas où les systèmes varient dans les différents pays)

PART I

FRENCH–ENGLISH

FRANÇAIS–ANGLAIS

PRONUNCIATION

A table of the phonetic symbols used to represent the pronunciation of the French words is given below, with examples of the words in which they occur. The following consonants, for which the phonetic symbol is the same as the letter of the written word, and which therefore cause no pronunciation difficulties, have not been listed:

b, d, l, m, n, r, t, v.

The stressed syllables are not indicated; the general rule is that in a word of more than one syllable the stress falls on the last syllable except where the vowel of that syllable is a mute e, when the stress is on the preceding syllable. But it must be borne in mind that the stress is much lighter than in English.

TABLE OF PHONETIC SYMBOLS

VOWELS

[i]	vite, cygne	[y:]	mur, sûr
[i:]	rire, lyre	[ø]	feu, ceux, nœud
[e]	été, donner, j'ai	[ø:]	meule, jeûne
[ɛ]	elle, très, peine, mais, Noël	[œ]	jeune, œuf, cueillir
[ɛ:]	terre, père, paire	[œ:]	fleur, sœur, œuvre
[a]	chat, là, femme, toit [twa]	[ə]	le, ce, entremets
[a:]	rare, tard, noir [nwa:r]	[ɛ̃]	vin, plein, main, chien, examen,
[ɑ]	pas, âgé, le bois [bwɑ]		faim, thym
[ɑ:]	sable, âge, tâche	[ɛ̃:]	prince, ceindre, plaindre
[ɔ]	donne, album	[ɑ̃]	enfant, temps, paon
[ɔ:]	fort	[ɑ̃:]	danse, centre, ample
[o]	dos, impôt, chaud	[ɔ̃]	mon, plomb, nom
[o:]	fosse, fausse, rôle	[ɔ̃:]	honte, nombre, comte
[u]	tout, goût, août	[œ̃]	lundi, à jeun, parfum
[u:]	cour, autour	[œ̃:]	humble
[y]	cru, eu		

CONSONANTS

[f]	feu, bref, phrase	[k]	camp, képi, quatre, écho
[p]	pain, absolu	[g]	grade, guerre, second
[s]	sou, rébus, cire, scène, action, six	[ɲ]	campagne
[z]	cousin, zéro, deuxième	[ks]	accident, extrême
[ʃ]	chose, chercher, schisme	[gz]	exister
[ʒ]	gilet, manger, jeter		

SEMI-CONSONANTS

[j]	yacht, piano, ration, voyage, travailler, cahier	[w]	ouate, ouest, noir [nwa:r], pingouin
		[ɥ]	muet, huit, lui

DIPHTHONGS

[i:]	fille, famille	[a:j]	ferraille
[ɛ:j]	soleil, veille, paye	[ɑ:j]	il bâille, rail
[aj]	bail, travail, médaille	[œj]	fauteuil, œil, je cueille

A

A, a [ɑ], *s.m.* (the letter) A, a.

à [a], *prep.* (*contracts with* **le** *into* **au**, *with* **les** *into* **aux**). **I. 1.** (*a*) (*direction*) **aller à l'école**, to go to school; **voyage à Paris**, journey to Paris; **au voleur!** stop thief! **à l'assassin!** murder! (*b*) **on se battit homme à homme**, they fought man to man; *Ten:* **quinze à**, fifteen all. **2.** (*time*) **du matin au soir**, from morning to night; **à jeudi!** see you (on) Thursday. **3.** (*point in space*) **au jardin**, in the garden; **à la gare**, at the station; **à deux kilomètres d'ici**, two kilometres away; **avoir qch. à la main**, to have sth. in one's hand. **4.** (*point in time*) **à deux heures**, at two o'clock; **à mon arrivée**, on my arrival, when I arrived; **au mois de juillet**, in (the month of) July. **5.** **vendre des marchandises à la douzaine**, to sell goods by the dozen; **à la main**, by hand; **à pied**, on foot; **à cheval**, on horseback; **louer une maison à l'année**, to let a house on a yearly basis; **manger à sa faim**, to eat one's fill; **recevoir qn à bras ouverts**, to receive s.o. with open arms; **à la française**, (in the) French fashion; **nager à la chien**, to dog-paddle; **on le voit à votre visage**, I can tell it by your face. **6.** (*indirect object*) **donner qch. à qn**, to give sth. to s.o.; **parler à qn**, to speak to s.o.; **penser à qch.**, to think of sth. **7.** (*a*) **tasse à thé**, teacup; (*b*) **moulin à vent**, windmill; (*c*) **homme à barbe noire**, man with a black beard; **chambre à deux lits**, double(-bedded) room; (*d*) (*possessive*) **un livre à moi**, a book of mine; **ce stylo est à Jean**, this pen is John's. **8.** **c'est à vous de décider**, it's for you to decide; (**c'est**) **à vous!** your turn! *W.Tel:* **à vous**, over (to you).
II. (*introducing inf.*). **1.** **il me reste à vous remercier**, I still have to thank you. **2.** **apprendre à lire**, to learn to read; **j'ai à faire**, I've got some work to do. **3.** **j'ai une lettre à écrire**, I've got a letter to write; **il est homme à se défendre**, he's the kind of man who will hit back; **machine à coudre**, sewing machine. **4.** **je suis prêt à vous écouter**, I'm ready to listen to you. **5.** (*a*) **il est à travailler**, he's (busy) working; (*b*) **à les en croire**, if they are to be believed; **à partager les mêmes périls . . .**, by sharing the same dangers . . . **6.** **laid à faire peur**, frightfully ugly, as ugly as sin; **un bruit à tout casser**, a shattering noise.

abaissant [abɛsɑ̃], *a.* degrading, humiliating.

abaissement [abɛsmɑ̃], *s.m.* **1.** lowering (of a blind, of prices, etc.). **2.** falling, subsidence,

sinking; fall (in temperature).

abaisser [abɛse], *v.tr.* **1.** to lower; **a. les yeux sur la foule**, to look down on the crowd. **2.** to lower (one's voice); to reduce (prices). **3.** to humble, to humiliate (s.o.)
s'abaisser. **1.** to slope down, go down, dip down. **2.** to humble oneself; **s'a. à faire qch.**, to stoop to doing sth.

abandon [abɑ̃dɔ̃], *s.m.* **1.** (*a*) surrender, renunciation; (*b*) *Sp:* giving up, withdrawal. **2.** desertion; neglect (of children, duty). **3.** neglect; **jardin à l'a.**, neglected, overrun, garden. **4.** abandon, lack of restraint.

abandonné [abɑ̃dɔne], *a.* abandoned; deserted; derelict (ship, etc.).

abandonner [abɑ̃dɔne], *v.tr.* **1.** to desert, abandon; to leave; **a. sa famille**, to desert one's family; **mes forces m'abandonnent**, my strength is failing; **abandonné par les médecins**, given up by the doctors; **a. la partie**, to throw in one's hand. **2.** to renounce, abandon, give up (plan, etc.). **3.** to let go (a rope).
s'abandonner. **1.** (*a*) to neglect oneself; (*b*) to give way (to grief, etc.). **2.** to be unconstrained; to let oneself go. **3.** **s'a. à qch.**, to give oneself up to sth.; to become addicted to (vice, etc.); **s'a. au sommeil**, to give way to sleep.

abasourd‖ir [abazurdiːr], *v.tr.* to astound, bewilder, stun, flabbergast; *s.m.* **-issement**.

abasourdissant [abazurdisɑ̃], *a.* astounding, bewildering, flabbergasting, staggering.

abat-jour [abaʒuːr], *s.m.inv.* (*a*) lampshade; (*b*) eyeshade; (*c*) sun-blind, awning.

abattage [abataːʒ], *s.m.* **1.** (*a*) knocking down; (*b*) felling (of trees). **2.** slaughtering.

abattant [abatɑ̃]. **1.** *a.* (*a*) depressing; (*b*) **siège a.**, tip-up seat (of car, etc.). **2.** *s.m.* flap (of table, envelope, etc.).

abattement [abatmɑ̃], *s.m.* **1.** (*a*) exhaustion, prostration; (*b*) despondency, depression, low spirits. **2.** *Fin:* (*income tax*) abatement, allowance.

abatteur [abatœːr], *s.m.* *F:* **a. de besogne**, hard worker, slogger.

abattis [abati], *s.m.* **1.** (*a*) felled timber; (*b*) *Mil:* abat(t)is. **2.** *pl.* (*a*) *Cu:* giblets; (*b*) *P:* limbs, hands and feet.

abattoir [abatwaːr], *s.m.* slaughter-house; abattoir.

abattre [abatr], *v.tr.* (*conj. like* BATTRE). **1.** (*a*) to knock down, to demolish; (*b*) to fell, cut down (trees); (*c*) to cut off. **2.** to slaughter, kill. **3.** to bring down; to shoot down. **4.** to lower; to strike (tents). **5.** to lay (dust). **6.** to blow down (trees, etc.). **7.** to dishearten, depress (s.o.); **ne vous laissez pas a.!** don't let it get you down!

s'abattre (sur). 1. to fall, crash down (on sth.). **2.** to pounce, swoop down (on sth.). **3.** to abate, subside. **4.** to become depressed, discouraged.

abattu [abaty], *a.* dejected, discouraged, depressed.

abbatial, -ale, -aux [abasjal, -o]. **1.** *a.* abbey (lands, etc.). **2.** *a. & s.f.* **(église) abbatiale,** abbey church.

abbaye [abei], *s.f.* abbey, monastery.

abbé [abe], *s.m.* **1.** abbot. **2.** *R.C.Ch:* priest.

abbesse [abɛs], *s.f.* abbess.

abcès [apsɛ], *s.m.* abscess, gathering.

abdication [abdikasjɔ̃], *s.f.* (a) abdication; (b) renunciation, surrender (of authority).

abdiquer [abdike], *v.tr.* to abdicate (throne); to renounce, surrender (rights).

abdomen [abdɔmɛn], *s.m.* abdomen.

abdominal, -aux [abdɔminal, -o], *a.* abdominal.

abeille [abɛːj], *s.f.* bee; **a. domestique,** honey bee; **a. mâle,** drone; **a. mère,** queen-bee.

abêtir(s') [sabetiːr, -be-], *v.i. & pr.* to grow dull, stupid; *s.m.* **-issement.**

abîme [abiːm], *s.m.* abyss, chasm, depth(s).

abîmer [abime], *v.tr.* to spoil, damage, injure.

s'abîmer. 1. (a) **s'a. dans les flots,** to be swallowed up by the sea; (b) **s'a. dans la douleur,** to be sunk in grief. **2.** to get spoiled.

abject [abʒɛkt], *a.* abject (poverty); mean, contemptible, despicable (person, conduct); *adv.* **-ement.**

abjurer [abʒyre], *v.tr.* to abjure; to recant.

aboi [abwa], *s.m.* **aux abois,** at bay; hard pressed.

aboiement [abwamɑ̃], *s.m.* bark, barking.

abolir [abɔliːr], *v.tr.* to abolish, suppress.

abolition [abɔlisjɔ̃], *s.f.* abolition, suppression.

abominable [abɔminabl], *a.* abominable, loathsome; *adv.* **-ment.**

abominer [abɔmine], *v.tr.* to abominate, loathe.

abondamment [abɔ̃damɑ̃], *adv.* abundantly.

abondance [abɔ̃dɑ̃ːs], *s.f.* **1.** abundance, plenty. **2.** wealth (of details); **parler avec a.,** to have a great flow of words; **parler d'a.,** to speak extempore.

abondant [abɔ̃dɑ̃], *a.* abundant, copious, plentiful; rich (style); **a. en qch.,** abounding in sth.

abonder [abɔ̃de], *v.i.* **1.** to abound (**en,** in); to be plentiful. **2. a. dans le sens de qn,** to be entirely of s.o.'s opinion.

abonné, -ée [abɔne], *s.* **1.** subscriber (to paper). **2.** season-ticket holder. **3. abonnés du gaz,** gas consumers.

abonnement [abɔnmɑ̃], *s.m.* **1.** subscription (to paper). **2. (carte d')a.,** season-ticket. **3.** *Adm:* (water) rate; (telephone) rental; **payer par a.,**

to pay by instalments.

abonner(s') [sabɔne], *v.pr.* **1. s'a. à un journal,** to subscribe to a paper. **2.** to take a season-ticket.

abord [abɔːr], *s.m.* **1.** access, approach (to land); **île d'un a. difficile,** island difficult of access. **2.** *pl.* approaches (**d'un endroit,** to a place); surroundings. **3.** (a) manner in which a person approaches another; **son a. fut respectueux,** he greeted me respectfully; (b) manner in which a person receives others; **avoir l'a. facile,** to be approachable. **4.** *Adv. phr.* **d'a., tout d'a.,** first, at first, in the first place; **dès l'a.,** from the outset; **à l'a.,** at first sight, to begin with.

abordable [abɔrdabl], *a.* **1.** easy to land on; easy of access; accessible. **2.** easily approached; accessible, affable; **peu a.,** stand-offish; grumpy.

aborder [abɔrde]. **1.** *v.i.* to land; **a. à quai,** to berth. **2.** *v.tr.* (a) to accost, approach (s.o.); (b) **a. une question,** to approach, tackle, a question; (c) to board (ship in a fight); to come alongside (a ship); (d) to collide with (ship).

aborigène [abɔriʒɛːn]. **1.** *a.* aboriginal, native. **2.** *s.* aboriginal.

aboutir [abutiːr], *v.i.* **1. a. à, dans, en, qch.,** to end at, in, sth.; to lead to sth.; to result in sth.; **n'a. à rien,** to come to nothing. **2.** *abs.* (of plan, etc.) to succeed; **faire a. qch.,** to bring sth. to a successful issue; **ne pas a.,** to fail; to fall through; *s.m.* **-issement,** issue, outcome.

aboutissant [abutisɑ̃], *a.* bordering, abutting (**à, on**).

aboyer [abwaje], *v.i.* **(j'aboie)** (of dog) to bark; (of hound) to bay.

aboyeur, -euse [abwajœːr, -øːz]. **1.** *a.* barking (dog). **2.** *s. F:* (a) carper; (b) tout (in front of booth).

abrégé [abreʒe], *s.m.* précis, summary; **en a.,** in abbreviated form; **faire un a.,** to make a précis.

abréger, *v.tr.* **(j'abrège; n. abrégeons; j'abrégerai). 1.** to shorten, to cut short; **pour a. . . .,** to be brief . . .. **2.** to abridge, cut down (article); to abbreviate; *s.m.* **-ement.**

s'abréger, (of days) to grow shorter.

abreuvage [abrœvaːʒ], **abreuvement** [abrœvmɑ̃], *s.m.* **1.** watering (of horses). **2.** drenching (of meadow).

abreuver [abrœve], *v.tr.* **1.** to water (horses). **2.** to flood, irrigate; **l'Égypte est abreuvée par le Nil,** Egypt is watered by the Nile.

s'abreuver, (of horse) to drink; (of pers.) to quench one's thirst.

abreuvoir [abrœvwaːr], *s.m.* (a) watering-place (in river, etc.); horse-pond; (b) drinking-trough.

abréviation [abrevjasjɔ̃], *s.f.* abbreviation.

abri [abri], *s.m.* shelter, cover; **a. public,** public shelter; **a. bétonné,** bunker; **prendre a.,** to take cover; à l'a., sheltered, under cover; se mettre à l'a., to take shelter; à l'a. de qch., sheltered, screened, from sth.; *Nau:* à l'a. de la côte, under the lee of the shore.

abricot |abriko|, *s.m.* apricot.

abricotier |abrikɔtje|, *s.m.* apricot-tree.

abri-garage [abrigara:ʒ], *s.m.* car port; *pl. abris-garages.*

abriter |abrite|, *v.tr.* to shelter, screen, shield. **s'abriter**, to take shelter (**contre, de,** from).

abrogation |abrɔgasjɔ̃|, *s.f.* repeal (of law).

abroger |abrɔʒe|, *v.tr.* (*n.* **abrogeons**) to rescind, repeal (law).

abrupt |abrypt|, *a.* **1.** abrupt, steep (descent). **2.** abrupt, blunt; *adv.* **-ement.**

abruti |abryti|, *s.m.* **1.** *F:* boozer. **2.** *P:* fool.

abrutir |abryti:r|, *v.tr.* to brutalize, stupefy; **abruti par la boisson,** sodden with drink; **être a.,** to be exhausted. **s'abrutir**, to become stupid.

abrutissant |abrytisɑ̃|, *a.* stupefying; deadly dull.

abrutissement |abrytismɑ̃|, *s.m.* **1.** degradation. **2.** sottishness.

absence |apsɑ̃:s|, *s.f.* **1.** absence; **remarquer l'a. de qn,** to miss s.o. **2. a. d'imagination,** lack, want, of imagination.

absent |apsɑ̃|. **1.** *a.* (*a*) absent, away (**de,** from); (*b*) missing, wanting, absent; (*c*) **son esprit est a.,** his thoughts are far away. **2.** *s.* (*a*) (the) absent one; (*b*) absentee.

absentéisme |apsɑ̃teism|, *s.m.* absenteeism.

absenter (s') |sapsɑ̃te|, *v.pr.* **1.** to absent oneself; to go away (from home). **2. s'a. de l'école,** to stay away from school.

abside |apsid|, *s.f. Ecc.Arch:* apse.

absolu |apsɔly|, *a.* absolute; (*a*) **refus a.,** flat refusal; (*b*) **pouvoir a.,** absolute power; **caractère a.,** autocratic nature; (*c*) positive, peremptory (tone); *adv.* **-ment.**

absolution |apsɔlysjɔ̃|, *s.f. Theol:* absolution.

absorbant |apsɔrbɑ̃|, *a.* **1.** absorbent (substance). **2.** absorbing, engrossing (book).

absorber |apsɔrbe|, *v.tr.* **1.** to absorb, soak up. **2.** to imbibe. **3.** to absorb, engross. **s'absorber**, to become absorbed, engrossed (**dans,** in).

absoudre |apsudr|, *v.tr.* (*pr.p.* **absolvant;** *p.p.* **absous,** *f.* **absoute;** *pr. ind.* **j'absous**) (*a*) to forgive (s.o. sth.); to exonerate (s.o. from sth.); (*b*) to absolve (s.o. from a sin).

abstenir (s') |sapstəni:r|, *v.pr.* (*conj. like* TENIR) **s'a. de qch.,** to abstain from sth.; to forgo sth.

abstention |apstɑ̃sjɔ̃|, *s.f.* abstaining, abstention.

abstentionnisme |apstɑ̃sjɔnism|, *s.m. Pol:* abstention; *s.* **-iste.**

abstinence |apstinɑ̃:s|, *s.f.* abstinence. **1.** abstemiousness. **2.** abstention (**de,** from).

abstraction |apstraksjɔ̃|, *s.f.* abstraction; (*a*) **faire a. de qch.,** to leave sth. out of account; (*b*) **dans un moment d'a.,** in a moment of abstraction.

abstraire |apstrɛ:r|, *v.tr.* (*conj. like* TRAIRE) to abstract; to separate.

abstrait |apstrɛ|, *a.* **1.** abstracted. **2.** abstract (idea); abstruse (question); *adv.* **-ement.**

absurde |apsyrd|. **1.** *a.* absurd, nonsensical. **2.** *s.m.* **l'a.,** absurdity, the absurd; *adv.* **-ment.**

absurdité |apsyrdite|, *s.f.* **1.** absurdity. **2.** **dire des absurdités,** to talk nonsense.

abus |aby|, *s.m.* **1.** (*a*) abuse, misuse (**de,** of); **employer un terme par a.,** to misuse a term; (*b*) over-indulgence (**de,** in); (*c*) violation (of rights); **a. de confiance,** breach of trust. **2.** abuse; corrupt practice. **3.** error, mistake.

abuser |abyze|. **1.** *v.i.* **a. de qch.** (*a*) to misuse sth.; **vous abusez de vos forces,** you are overexerting yourself; (*b*) to take (an unfair) advantage of sth.; **a. de l'amabilité de qn,** to impose upon s.o.'s kindness. **2.** *v.tr.* to deceive, delude. **s'abuser**, to delude oneself; to be mistaken.

abusif, -ive |abyzif, -i:v|, *a.* **1.** contrary to usage; **emploi a.,** wrong use, misuse. **2.** excessive; **une mère abusive,** a possessive mother; *adv.* **-ivement.**

Abyssinie (l') [labis(s)ini]. *Pr.n.f. Geog:* Abyssinia.

acacia |akasja|, *s.m. Bot:* acacia.

académicien |akademisjɛ̃|, *s.m.* academician; *esp.* member of the **Académie française.**

académie |akademi|, *s.f.* academy. **1.** university, college or centre. **2.** society (of letters, science, art); **l'A. française,** the French Academy (of letters). **3.** (*a*) riding school; (*b*) **a. de musique,** school of music.

académique |akademik|, *a.* academic; *adv.* **-ment.**

acajou |akaʒu|, *s.m.* mahogany.

acariâtre |akarjɑ:tr|, *a.* (*esp. of women*) bad-tempered, shrewish.

accablant |akablɑ̃|, *a.* **1.** overwhelming (proof). **2.** overpowering (heat).

accablé |akable|, *a.* **1.** overwhelmed (with work); overcome (with grief); tired out. **2. a. par la chaleur,** prostrated by the heat.

accablement |akabləmɑ̃|, *s.m.* dejection, despondency; depression.

accabler |akable|, *v.tr.* **1.** to overpower, overwhelm, crush. **2.** to load (s.o. with gifts, etc.).

accalmie |akalmi|, *s.f.* lull (in the storm).

accaparer |akapare|, *v.tr.* to corner, hoard (wheat); *F:* **a. la conversation,** to monopolize the conversation.

accapareur, -euse |akaparœ:r, -ø:z|, *s.* (*a*) monopolist; (*b*) *Pej:* grabber, shark.

accéder |aksede|, *v.i.* (**j'accède; j'accéderai**). **1.**

to have access (à, to). **2. a. à une requête,** to comply with a request. **3. a. au trône,** to accede to the throne.

accélérateur, -trice [akseleratœ:r, -tris]. **1.** *a.* accelerative, accelerating. **2.** *s.m.* accelerator.

accélération [akselerasjɔ̃], *s.f.* (a) acceleration; *Aut:* **pédale d'a,** accelerator (pedal); (b) hastening, speeding up (of work).

accéléré [akselere], *a.* **1.** accelerated (motion). **2.** quick, fast.

accélérer [akselere], *v.tr.* (**j'accélère; j'accélérerai**) to accelerate, quicken; to speed up.

s'accélérer, to become faster; to accelerate.

accent [aksɑ̃], *s.m.* accent. **1.** stress. **2. a. aigu,** acute accent. **3.** pronunciation. **4.** tone of voice. **5.** *pl.* (a) **les accents du désespoir,** the accents of despair; (b) **les accents de la Marseillaise,** the strains of the Marseillaise.

accentu|er [aksãtye], *v.tr.* **1.** to stress (syllable). **2.** to mark (vowel) with an accent; to accentuate. **3.** to emphasize; **traits fortement accentués,** strongly marked features; **a. le chômage,** to increase unemployment; *s.f.* **-ation.**

s'accentuer, to become accentuated, more pronounced, more marked.

acceptabilité [akseptabilite], *s.f.* acceptability.

acceptable [akseptabl], *a.* **1.** acceptable (à, to); **offre a.,** reasonable offer; **cadeau a.,** welcome gift. **2.** in fair condition; *adv.* **-ment.**

acceptation [akseptasjɔ̃], *s.f.* acceptance.

accepter [aksepte], *v.tr.* to accept; **a. que qch. se fasse,** to agree to sth. being done.

accès [akse], *s.m.* **1.** access, approach; **trouver a. auprès de qn,** to gain admission to s.o.; *P.N:* **a. aux quais,** to the trains. **2.** fit, attack, outburst; *Med:* fit; **travailler par a.,** to work by fits and starts.

accessibilité [aksesibilite], *s.f.* accessibility.

accessible [aksesibl], *a.* **1.** accessible; **endroit a.,** *F:* get-at-able place. **2.** (a) approachable; (b) **a. à la pitié,** open to pity.

accession [aksesjɔ̃], *s.f.* **1.** accession. **2.** union. **3.** adherence, adhesion (to a party).

accessoire [akseswa:r]. **1.** *a.* accessory; subordinate (part). **2.** *s.m.* accessory, appurtenance; *pl. Th:* properties, *F:* props.

accident [aksidã], *s.m.* **1.** accident; (a) **je l'ai retrouvé par a.,** I found it accidentally; (b) mishap; **a. mortel,** fatality; **a. d'avion,** air crash; **nous sommes arrivés sans a.,** we arrived safely. **2.** *Mus:* accidental. **3. a. de terrain,** undulation of the ground.

accidenté, -ée [aksidãte]. **1.** *a.* (a) eventful (life); (b) uneven, broken (ground); (c) damaged (car). **2.** *s.* victim of an accident; **les accidentés,** the injured.

accident|el, -elle [aksidãtel], *a.* **1.** accidental, undesigned. **2.** *Mus:* **signes accidentels,** (i) ac-

cidentals; (ii) key-signature; *adv.* **-ellement.**

acclamation [aklamasjɔ̃], *s.f.* acclamation, cheering.

acclamer [aklame], *v.tr.* (a) to acclaim, applaud, cheer; (b) *pred.* **a. qn empereur,** to hail s.o. as emperor.

acclimatation [aklimatasjɔ̃], *s.f.* acclimatization; **le Jardin d'A.,** *F:* the (Paris) zoo.

acclimatement [aklimatmã], *s.m.* acclimatization.

acclimater [aklimate], *v.tr.* to acclimatize (à, to).

s'acclimater, to become acclimatized.

accolade [akɔlad], *s.f.* **1.** (a) embrace; (b) *F:* hug, kiss. **2. recevoir l'a.,** to be knighted. **3.** *Mus: Typ:* bracket. **4.** *Arch:* **arc en a.,** ogee arch.

accommodage [akɔmɔda:ʒ], *s.m. Cu:* dressing, preparing.

accommodant [akɔmɔdã], *a.* good-natured, easy-going, accommodating.

accommodement [akɔmɔdmã], *s.m.* compromise, arrangement; **politique d'a.,** give and take policy.

accommoder [akɔmɔde], *v.tr.* **1.** (a) to make (s.o.) comfortable; (b) to suit (s.o.); **difficile à a.,** difficult to please. **2.** to cook, dress (food). **3. a. qch. à qch.,** to fit, adapt, sth. to sth.

s'accommoder. 1. to make oneself comfortable; **il s'accommode partout,** he is very adaptable. **2. s'a. de qch.,** to make the best of sth. **3. s'a. à qch.,** to adapt, accommodate, oneself to sth. **4. s'a. avec qn,** to come to an agreement with s.o.

accompagnateur, -trice [akɔ̃paɲatœ:r, -tris], *s. Mus:* accompanist.

accompagnement [akɔ̃paɲmã], *s.m.* **1.** (action of) accompanying (s.o.). **2.** *Mus:* accompaniment.

accompagner [akɔ̃paɲe], *v.tr.* to accompany; (a) to go, come, with (s.o.); (b) to escort (s.o.); (c) **a. qn au piano,** to accompany s.o. on the piano.

accompli [akɔ̃pli], *a.* accomplished (musician).

accomplir [akɔ̃pli:r], *v.tr.* **1.** to accomplish, achieve (purpose, etc.); to carry out, perform, fulfil (order, promise). **2.** to complete, finish; **il a quarante ans accomplis,** he's turned forty.

accomplissement [akɔ̃plismã], *s.m.* **1.** accomplishment, performance (of duty); fulfilment (of wish). **2.** completion.

accord [akɔ:r], *s.m.* **1.** agreement; (a) settlement; (b) harmony; **d'a.,** in agreement, in accordance (**avec,** with); **se mettre d'a. avec qn,** to come to an agreement with s.o.; **d'a.!** agreed! quite so! (c) *Gram:* concordance; **les règles d'a.,** the concords. **2.** *Mus:* chord. **3.** *Mus:* pitch, tune; **être d'a.,** to be in tune; *Rad:* to be tuned in.

accordéon |akɔrdeɔ̃|, *s.m.* accordion; **en a.,** (i) pleated (skirt); (ii) *F:* crumpled (mudguard).

accorder |akɔrde|, *v.tr.* **1.** to reconcile. **2.** *Mus:* to tune. **3.** to grant, concede; to award.

s'accorder. 1. (*a*) to agree, come to an agreement; (*b*) to get on (**avec qn,** with s.o.). **2.** to accord, harmonize; to be in keeping. **3.** *Gram:* to agree. **4.** (*of dress*) to go (**avec,** with). **5.** (*of instruments*) to tune (up).

accordeur |akɔrdœ:r|, *s.m.* tuner.

accost|er |akɔste|, *v.tr.* **1.** to accost (s.o.); to go, come, up to (s.o.). **2.** to berth (a boat). **3.** *Nau:* to come on board; *s.m.* **-age.**

accoter (s') |sakɔte|, *v.pr.* **s'a. à, contre, un mur,** to lean against a wall.

accouch|er |akuʃe|, *v.i.* to be confined; **a. d'un garçon,** to give birth to a boy, *s.m.* **-ement.**

accoucheur, -euse |akuʃœ:r, -ø:z|, *s.* obstetrician; *f.* midwife.

accouder (s') |sakude|, *v.pr.* to lean on one's elbows.

accoupl|er |akuple|, *v.tr.* (*a*) to couple; to yoke (oxen); (*b*) to couple (up) (parts); (*c*) *El:* to connect (batteries); *s.m.* **-ement.**

accourir |akuri:r|, *v.i.* (*conj. like* COURIR; *aux.* avoir *or* être); to hasten (up); **ils ont accouru, sont accourus, à mon secours,** they came running to my help.

accoutrement |akutrəmã|, *s.m. usu. Pej:* dress, garb; *F:* get-up.

accoutrer |akutre|, *v.tr. usu. Pej:* to rig (s.o.) out, get (s.o.) up (**de,** in).

accoutumance |akutymã:s|, *s.f.* **1.** (*a*) familiarization (**à,** with); (*b*) *Med:* **a.** (**à une drogue**), tolerance (to a drug). **2.** habit.

accoutumé |akutyme|, *a.* (*a*) accustomed, used (**à,** to); (*b*) accustomed, customary, usual; *adv. phr.* **comme à l'accoutumée,** as usual.

accoutumer |akutyme|, *v.tr.* **a. qn à qch.,** to accustom s.o. to sth.; to inure s.o. (to hunger).

s'accoutumer à qch., to get accustomed to sth.; to become inured to sth.

accréditer |akredite|, *v.tr.* **1.** (*a*) to accredit (an ambassador); (*b*) to cause (sth.) to be credited. **2.** to credit, believe (sth.).

s'accréditer, (*of news*) to gain credence.

accroc |akro|, *s.m.* **1.** tear, rent (in clothes). **2.** hitch, difficulty.

accroch|er |akrɔʃe|, *v.tr.* (*a*) to hook; **a. sa robe à un clou,** to catch one's dress on a nail; **a. une voiture,** to run into a car; (*b*) **a. une voiture au train,** to hitch, couple, a carriage on to the train; (*c*) **a. sa robe à un clou,** to hang (up) one's dress on a nail; *s.m.* **-age.**

s'accrocher. 1. s'a. à qch., to fasten on to, cling to, sth. **2.** to get caught (**à,** on). **3.** *F:* to have a set-to.

accroire |akrwa:r|, *v.tr.* (*used only in*) **faire a. à qn que . . .,** to cause s.o. to believe that . . .;

en faire a. à qn, to delude s.o.; **s'en faire a.,** to think too much of oneself.

accroissement |akrwasmã|, *s.m.* **1.** (*a*) growth (of plant); (*b*) increase. **2.** (amount of) increase, growth; **taux d'a.,** rate of increase.

accroître |akrwa:tr|, *v.tr.* (*pr.p.* **accroissant;** *p.p.* **accru;** *pr.ind.* **j'accrois, il accroît**) to increase, augment; to enhance (reputation).

s'accroître, to increase, grow.

accroupir (s') |sakrupi:r|, *v.pr.* to squat, to crouch (down); **accroupi,** squatting, crouching.

accu |aky|, *s.m. El: F:* (car) battery.

accueil |akœj|, *s.m.* reception, welcome; **faire bon a. à qn,** to welcome s.o.

accueillant |akœjã|, *a.* gracious, affable.

accueillir |akœji:r|, *v.tr.* (*conj. like* CUEILLIR) to receive, greet.

acculer |akyle|, *v.tr.* to drive s.o. back (**contre,** against).

s'acculer à, contre, qch., to set one's back against sth., to stand at bay.

accumulateur, -trice |akymylatœ:r, -tris|, *s.* **1.** accumulator, hoarder. **2.** *s.m. El:* accumulator; storage-cell, battery.

accumul|er |akymyle|, *v.tr.* to accumulate, amass; to hoard; to heap up; *s.f.* **-ation.**

accusateur, -trice |akyzatœ:r, -tris|. **1.** *a.* accusatory, incriminating. **2.** *s.* accuser, impeacher.

accusatif |akyzatif|, *a. & s.m. Gram:* accusative.

accusation |akyzasjɔ̃|, *s.f.* **1.** accusation, charge. **2.** *Pol:* impeachment, arraignment.

accusé, -ée |akyze|. **1.** *a.* prominent, pronounced, bold (features). **2.** *s.* accused (person); (*in court*) defendant. **3.** *s.m.* **a. de réception d'une lettre,** acknowledgment (of receipt) of a letter.

accuser |akyze|, *v.tr.* **1. a. qn de qch.,** to accuse s.o. of sth., to charge, tax, s.o. with sth. **2. a. qch.,** to own to, profess, sth.; *Fenc:* **a. un coup,** to acknowledge a hit. **3.** to define, show up, accentuate; **l'indicateur accuse une vitesse de . . .,** the speedometer shows a speed of. . . . **4. a. réception de qch.,** to acknowledge receipt of sth.

acerbe |asɛrb|, *a.* **1.** tart, sour. **2.** sharp, harsh.

acerbité |asɛrbite|, *s.f.* acerbity. **1.** tartness, sourness. **2.** sharpness, harshness.

acéré |asere|, *a.* (*a*) sharp(-pointed); (*b*) sharp-edged, keen (blade).

acérer, *v.tr.* (**j'acère; j'acérerai**) to point; to give a keen edge to (sth.).

acétate |asetat|, *s.m. Ch:* acetate.

acétique |asetik|, *a. Ch:* acetic.

acétocellulose |asetɔsɛlylo:z|, *s.f. Ind:* cellulose acetate.

acétylène |asetilɛ(:)n|, *s.m.* acetylene.

achalandé |aʃalɑ̃de|, *a*. **magasin bien a.**, (i) shop with a large custom; (ii) well-stocked shop.
achalandier |aʃalɑ̃de|, *v.tr.* to provide (shop) with custom; *s.m.* **-age.**
acharné |aʃarne|, *a*. **1.** eager in pursuit; **hommes acharnés les uns contre les autres,** men fighting desperately against each other. **2. joueur a.,** inveterate, keen, gambler. **3. lutte acharnée,** stubborn, desperate, contest.
acharnement |aʃarnəmɑ̃|, *s.m.* (*a*) desperate eagerness; (*b*) relentlessness; **a. au travail, pour le travail,** passion for work; **travailler avec a.,** to work (desperately) hard.
acharner (s') |saʃarne|, *v.pr.* **1. s'a après, contre, sur, qn,** to be dead set against s.o.; **le malheur s'acharne après lui,** misfortune dogs his footsteps. **2. s'a. à, sur, qch.,** to work unceasingly at sth.
achat |aʃa|, *s.m.* purchase. **1.** buying. **2.** thing bought.
acheminer (s') |saʃmine|, *v.pr.* **s'a. vers sa maison,** to proceed, to wend one's way, homeward.
acheter |aʃte|, *v.tr.* (**j'achète**) (*a*) **a. qch.,** to buy, purchase, sth.; (*b*) **a. qch. à qn,** to buy sth. from s.o.; (*c*) **je vais lui a. un livre,** I am going to buy him a book; *s.* **-eur, -euse.**
achevé |aʃve|. **1.** *a*. (*a*) accomplished (horseman); perfect (piece of work); (*b*) *F:* **sot a.,** downright fool. **2.** *s.m.* finish, perfection (of work of art).
achèvement |aʃɛvmɑ̃|, *s.m.* completion, finishing.
achever |aʃve|, *v.tr.* (**j'achève**). **1.** to end, finish (off), complete; **a. de faire qch.,** to finish doing sth.; **achève de boire ton café,** drink up your coffee. **2.** to put (animal) out of pain; *F:* **cette perte l'a achevé,** this loss finished him (off).
s'achever. 1. to draw to a close; to end. **2.** (*of work*) to reach completion.
acide |asid|. **1.** *a*. acid, sharp, sour. **2.** *s.m.* acid.
acidité |asidite|, *s.f.* acidity, sourness, tartness.
acier |asje|, *s.m.* steel; **lame d'a., en a.,** steel blade; **regard d'a.,** steely glance.
aciérie |asjeri|, *s.f.* steelworks.
acompte |akɔ̃:t|, *s.m.* instalment, payment on account.
aconit |akɔnit|, *s.m. Bot:* aconite.
Açores (les) |lezasɔ:r|. *Pr.n.f. pl. Geog:* the Azores.
à-côté |akote|, *s.m.* **1.** aside (remark). **2.** (*a*) *usu. pl.* side issues; sidelights on, by-ways of, history, etc.; (*b*) *F:* extras; perks; **avoir des à-côtés,** to make a little on the side.
à-coup |aku|, *s.m.* jerk; sudden stoppage; **il travaille par à-coups,** he works by fits and starts; *El:* surge (of current); **sans à-coups,** smoothly.
acoustique |akustik|. **1.** *a*. acoustic; **voûte a.,**

whispering gallery. **2.** *s.f.* acoustics.
acquéreur, -euse |akerœ:r, -ø:z|, *s.* acquirer, purchaser.
acquérir |akeri:r|, *v.tr.* (*pr.p.* **acquérant;** *p.p.* **acquis;** *pr.ind.* **j'acquiers, n. acquérons, ils acquièrent;** *pr.sub.* **j'acquière, n. acquérions;** *p.h.* **j'acquis;** *fu.* **j'acquerrai**) to acquire, obtain, get, win, gain, secure; **sa protection m'est acquise,** I can count on his protection.
acquiescement |akjɛsmɑ̃|, *s.m.* acquiescence, assent.
acquiescer |akjese, -kiɛ-|, *v.ind.tr.* (**n. acquiesçons**) **a. à qch.,** to acquiesce in sth., to agree to sth.
acquis |aki|. **1.** *a*. (*a*) acquired (knowledge, etc.); (*b*) **droits a.,** vested interests. **2.** *s.m.* acquired knowledge; experience.
acquisition |akizisjɔ̃|, *s.f.* acquisition. **1.** acquiring. **2.** thing bought or obtained; purchase.
acquit |aki|, *s.m.* **1.** *Com:* receipt, acquittance; **"pour a.,"** 'paid.' **2.** release (from promise); **faire qch. par manière d'a.,** to do sth. as a matter of form.
acquit-à-caution |akiakosjɔ̃|, *s.m. Cust:* permit; excise bond; *pl.* **acquits-à-caution.**
acquittement |akitmɑ̃|, *s.m.* **1.** discharge, payment (of debt). **2.** *Jur:* acquittal.
acquitter |akite|, *v.tr.* **1.** (*a*) **a. qn (d'une obligation),** to release s.o. (from an obligation); (*b*) **a. un accusé,** to acquit an accused person. **2.** (*a*) **a. une dette,** to discharge a debt; (*b*) **a. une facture,** to receipt a bill.
s'acquitter. 1. s'a. d'un devoir, to discharge a duty. **2. se bien a.,** to acquit oneself well.
âcre |ɑ:kr|, *a*. acrid, bitter, tart, pungent; *adv.* **-ment.**
âcreté |ɑkrəte|, *s.f.* acidity, bitterness, pungency.
acrimonie |akrimɔni|, *s.f.* acrimony, acrimoniousness.
acrimonieu|x, -euse |akrimɔnjø, -ø:z|, *a*. acrimonious; *adv.* **-sement.**
acrobate |akrɔbat|, *s.m. & f.* acrobat, tumbler.
acrobatie |akrɔbasi|, *s.f.* **1.** (*a*) acrobatics; (*b*) acrobatic feat. **2.** *Av:* **a. aérienne,** aerobatics.
acrobatique |akrɔbatik|, *a*. acrobatic.
acte |akt|, *s.m.* **1.** action, act, deed; **faire a. de bonne volonté,** to give proof of good will. **2.** *Jur:* (*a*) deed, title; **a. de vente,** bill of sale; (*b*) **a. judiciaire,** writ; **a. d'accusation,** bill of indictment; (*c*) record; **a. de décès,** death-certificate; **a. de dernière volonté,** last will and testament; **prendre a. de qch.,** to record, note, sth. **3.** *Th:* act.
acteur |aktœ:r|, *s.m.* actor.
actif, -ive |aktif, -i:v|. **1.** *a*. (*a*) active; **armée active,** regular army; *Pol.Ec:* **population active,** working population; (*b*) active, brisk, alert. **2.**

s.m. (*a*) *Com:* assets; credit (account); (*b*) *Gram:* verbe à l'a., verb in the active voice.

action |aksjɔ̃|, *s.f.* **1.** (*a*) action, act; (*b*) action, deed, exploit. **2.** (*a*) (i) **a. sur qch.**, effect on sth.; (ii) **a. sur qn**, influence over s.o.; **sans a.**, ineffective; (*b*) **a. de l'eau**, agency of water; (*c*) action, motion, working (of machine, etc.). **3.** (*a*) action, gesture; (*b*) *Th:* action. **4.** *Fin:* share; **compagnie par actions**, joint-stock company. **5.** *Jur:* action, lawsuit, trial. **6.** *Mil:* action, engagement.

actionnaire |aksjɔnɛːr|, *s.m. & f.* shareholder.

actionner |aksjɔne|, *v.tr.* **1.** *Jur:* to sue. **2.** *Mec.E:* to set in action; **actionné à la main**, hand-operated.

s'actionner, to get cracking.

activement [aktivmɑ̃], *adv.* actively, briskly.

activer |aktive|, *v.tr.* to quicken, stir (up), urge on; **a. un travail**, to expedite a piece of work.

s'activer, to hurry, get a move on.

activité |aktivite|, *s.f.* activity. **1. a. chimique d'un corps**, chemical activity of a body. **2.** quickness, dispatch. **3. en a.**, in progress, at work; **l'usine est en a.**, the factory is in production.

actrice |aktris|, *s.f.* actress.

actuaire |aktɥɛːr|, *s.m. Ins:* actuary.

actualité |aktɥalite|, *s.f.* **1.** actuality, reality. **2.** question, event, of the moment; **les actualités**, current events; *T.V:* news.

actuel, -elle |aktɥɛl|, *a.* of the present day; existing, current; **à l'heure actuelle**, at the present time; *adv.* **-lement.**

acuité |akɥite|, *s.f.* acuteness, sharpness (of point); **a. d'un son**, high pitch of a sound; **a. visuelle**, keenness of sight.

acuponcture |akypɔ̃ktyːr|, *s.f. Surg:* acupuncture.

adaptation |adaptasjɔ̃|, *s.f.* adaptation, adjustment (à, to); *Rad:* matching.

adapter |adapte|, *v.tr.* **a. qch. à qch.**, (i) to fit, adjust, sth. to sth.; (ii) to adapt sth. to sth.; *a.* **-able.**

s'adapter. 1. s'a. à qch., to fit, suit, sth. **2. s'a. aux circonstances**, to adapt oneself to circumstances.

addenda |adɛ̃da|, *s.m.inv.* addendum, addenda (à, to).

addition |ad(d)isjɔ̃|, *s.f.* **1.** addition, (i) adding (à, to); (ii) adding up, totting up. **2.** (*a*) accession, accretion; (*b*) *Mth:* addition; (*c*) (*in restaurant, etc.*) bill, *N.Am:* check.

additionnel, -elle |ad(d)isjɔnɛl|, *a.* additional.

additionner |ad(d)isjɔne|, *v.tr.* **1.** to add up, tot up (sum). **2. lait additionné d'eau**, watered milk.

adénoïde |adenɔid|, *a. Med:* **végétations adénoïdes**, adenoids.

adhérent, -ente [aderɑ̃, -ɑ̃ːt]. **1.** *a.* adherent (à,

to); adhesive. **2.** *s.* **a. d'un parti**, member, supporter, of a party.

adhérer |adere|, *v.i.* (**j'adhère; j'adhérerai**). **1.** to adhere, stick; (*of wheels*) **a. à la route**, to grip the road. **2.** to adhere (to opinion). **3. a. à un parti**, to join (a party); *s.f.* **-ence.**

adhésif, -ive |adezif, -iːv|, *a. & s.m.* adhesive.

adhésion |adezjɔ̃|, *s.f.* **1.** adhesion, sticking. **2.** adhesion, adherence (à, to); **a. à un parti**, joining of a party.

adieu, *pl.* **-eux** |adjø|. **1.** *adv.* good-bye, farewell. **2.** *s.m.* farewell, parting, leave-taking; **faire ses adieux à qn**, to take leave of s.o.

adipeux, -euse |adipø, -øːz|, *a.* adipose, fatty (tissue).

adjacent |adʒasɑ̃|, *a.* adjacent, contiguous (à, to); adjoining; bordering (à, on).

adjectif, -ive |adʒɛktif, -iːv|. **1.** *a.* adjectival. **2.** *s.m.* adjective.

adjoindre |adʒwɛ̃ːdr|, *v.tr.* (*conj. like* JOINDRE). **1. a. qch. à qch.**, to unite sth. with sth. **2. a. qn à un comité**, to add s.o. to a committee.

s'adjoindre à d'autres, to join (in) with others.

adjoint, -ointe [adʒwɛ̃, -wɛ̃t]. **1.** *a.* assistant (professor). **2.** *s.* assistant; deputy.

adjudant |adʒydɑ̃|, *s.m.* **1.** *Mil:* (*a*) company sergeant-major; (*b*) **a.-major**, adjutant. **2.** *Orn:* adjutant-bird.

adjudicataire |adʒydikatɛːr|. **1.** *a.* **partie a.**, contracting party. **2.** *s.* highest bidder (at auction).

adjudicateur, -trice [adʒydikatœːr, -tris], *s.* adjudicator, awarder (of contract).

adjudication |adʒydikasjɔ̃|, *s.f.* (*a*) adjudication, award; allocation (of contract); (*b*) knocking-down (of sth. to s.o.); **par voie d'a.**, (i) by tender; (ii) by auction.

adjuger |adʒyʒe|, *v.tr.* (*n.* **adjugeons**) **a. qch. à qn**, (i) to adjudge, award, allocate, sth. to s.o.; (ii) to knock down sth. to s.o.

adjurer |adʒyre|, *v.tr.* **a. qn de faire qch.**, to adjure, beseech, s.o. to do sth.

admettre |admɛtr|, *v.tr.* (*conj. like* METTRE). **1.** to admit; to let (s.o.) in; **être admis à un examen**, to pass an examination. **2. a. qn à faire qch.**, to permit s.o. to do sth. **3.** (*a*) **a. qch.**, to allow, permit, sth.; **l'usage admis**, the accepted custom; (*b*) **j'admets que j'ai tort**, I admit that I am in the wrong.

administrateur, -trice [administratœːr, -tris], *s.* **1.** administrator (of charity). **2.** director (of bank, company). **3.** trustee (of estate).

administratif, -ive |administratif, -iːv|, *a.* administrative; *adv.* **-ivement.**

administration |administrasjɔ̃|, *s.f.* **1.** administering (of justice). **2.** (*a*) administration, management (of business); **conseil d'a.**, board of directors; (*b*) governing (of country). **3.** (*a*) governing body; (*b*) government service; (*c*) the officials.

administré, -ée |administre|, *s.* person under s.o.'s administration or jurisdiction.

administrer |administre|, *v.tr.* 1. to administer, conduct (business); to govern (country). 2. **a. qch. à qn**, to administer sth. to s.o.

admirable |admirabl|, *a.* admirable, wonderful; *adv.* **-ment.**

admirateur, -trice |admiratœ:r, -tris|. 1. *a.* admiring. 2. *s.* admirer.

admirat|if, -ive |admiratif, -i:v|, *a.* admiring (gesture); *adv.* **-ivement.**

admiration |admirasjɔ̃|, *s.f.* admiration; **être, faire, l'a. de qn**, to be admired by s.o.

admirer |admire|, *v.tr.* to admire.

admissibilité |admisibilite|, *s.f.* admissibility; *Sch:* **épreuves d'a.**, written examination.

admissible |admisibl|, *a.* (*a*) admissible (excuse, etc.); (*b*) **a. à un emploi**, eligible for an occupation.

admission |admisjɔ̃|, *s.f.* admission (**à, dans,** to); **cotisation d'a.**, entrance fee.

admonest|er |admɔneste|, *v.tr.* to admonish, censure; *s.f.* **-ation.**

adolescence |adɔlessɑ̃:s|, *s.f.* adolescence, youth.

adolescent, -ente |adɔlessɑ̃, -ɑ̃:t|. 1. *a.* adolescent; *F:* teenage. 2. *s.* adolescent; *F:* teenager.

adonner (s') |sadɔne|, *v.pr.* **s'a. à qch.**, to devote oneself to sth.; **s'a. aux sports**, to go in for, to take up, sport.

adopter |adɔpte|, *v.tr.* 1. **a. un enfant**, to adopt a child. 2. **a. un projet de loi**, to pass a bill.

adoptif, -ive |adɔptif, -i:v|, *a.* adopted, adoptive (child).

adoption |adɔpsjɔ̃|, *s.f.* adoption (of child); *Parl:* passage, carrying (of bill).

adorable |adɔrabl|, *a.* adorable; charming; *adv.* **-ment.**

adorateur, -trice |adɔratœ:r, -tris|, *s.* adorer, worshipper.

ador|er |adɔre|, *v.tr.* to adore, worship (s.o., sth.); *s.f.* **-ation.**

adossé |adose|, *a.* (*a*) back to back; (*b*) **a. à qch.**, with one's back against sth.

adosser |adose|, *v.tr.* to place (two things) back to back.

s'adosser à, contre, qch., to set, lean, one's back against sth.

adoucir |adusi:r|, *v.tr.* 1. to soften; to tone down; to subdue; to sweeten. 2. to alleviate, relieve. 3. to pacify, mollify. 4. to temper (steel).

s'adoucir. 1. (*of voice*) to grow softer. 2. (*of weather*) to grow milder. 3. (*of pain*) to grow less.

adouciss|ement |adusismɑ̃|, *s.m.* 1. softening (of voice). 2. alleviation (of pain); *s.m.* **-age;**

s.m. **-eur,** water-softener.

adrénaline |adrenalin|, *s.f. Med:* adrenalin.

adresse |adrɛs|, *s.f.* 1. address, destination; **let tre à l'a. de qn**, letter addressed to s.o.; **un observation à votre a.**, a hit at you. 2. (*a*) skill dexterity; (*b*) shrewdness, adroitness; **dénu d'a.**, tactless (person); (*c*) craftiness, cunning.

adresser |adrɛse|, *v.tr.* 1. to address, direc (letter). 2. **on m'a adressé à vous**, I have bee recommended to come to you. 3. to aim, ad dress (remarks).

s'adresser. 1. to apply (**à**, to); **"s'a. ici,"** 'apply enquire, here.' 2. **s'a. à qn**, to address s.o., t speak to s.o.

adroit |adrwa|, *a.* 1. (*a*) dexterous, deft, skilful handy; (*b*) **phrase adroite**, neat way of puttin it. 2. shrewd, adroit (answer); *adv.* **-ement.**

adulateur, -trice |adylatœ:r, -tris|. 1. *a* adulatory, flattering, sycophantic. 2. *s* sycophant; flatterer.

adulation |adylasjɔ̃|, *s.f.* adulation sycophancy.

adulte |adylt|, *a. & s.m. & f.* adult, grown-up.

adultération |adylterasjɔ̃|, *s.f.* adulteration (o food); falsification (of document).

adultère |adylte:r|. 1. *a.* adulterous. 2. *s* adulterer, *f.* adulteress. 3. *s.m.* adultery.

adultérer |adyltere|, *v.tr.* (**j'adultère j'adultérerai**) to adulterate (food, etc.); t falsify (document).

advenir |advəni:r|, *v.* (*conj. like* VENIR; *used onl in the 3rd pers.*) to occur, happen; to com (about). 1. *v.i.* **je ne sais ce qui en adviendra,** don't know what will come of it; **le cas adve nant que** + *sub.*, in the event of (somethin happening). 2. *v.impers.* **or, il advint**, now happened (**que**, that); **advienne que pourra** come what may.

adverbe |adverb|, *s.m.* adverb.

adverbial, -aux |adverbjal, -o|, *a.* adverbial **locution adverbiale**, adverbial phrase; *adv* **-ement.**

adversaire |adverse:r|, *s.m.* adversary opponent.

adverse |advers|, *a.* (*a*) *Jur:* **la partie a.**, the other side; (*b*) adverse, unfavourable; **fortune a.**, bad luck.

adversité |adversite|, *s.f.* 1. adversity; **être dan l'a.**, to be in straitened circumstances. 2. mis fortune, trial.

aérage |aera:ʒ|, *s.m.,* **aération** |aerasjɔ̃|, *s.f.* 1 ventilation (of room). 2. aeration (of water etc.).

aérer |aere|, *v.tr.* (**j'aère, j'aérerai**). 1. (*a*) to ven tilate; (*b*) to air (clothes, etc.). 2. to aerate.

aérien, -ienne |aerjɛ̃, -jɛn|, *a.* 1. aeria (phenomenon); overhead (cable); elevate (railway); **raid a.**, air-raid; **ligne, base aérienne**, air-line, -base. 2. (light and) airy (footstep).

aéro-club [aerɔklyb, -klœb], s.m. flying-club.

aérodrome [aerɔdroːm], s.m. aerodrome.

aérodynamique [aerɔdinamik]. **1.** *a.* aerodynamic; F: streamlined. **2.** *s.f.* aerodynamics.

aérogare [aerɔgaːr], s.f. air(ways) terminal.

aéroglisseur [aerɔglisœːr], s.m. hovercraft.

aérogramme [aerɔgram], s.m. air letter.

aéronaute [aerɔnoːt], s.m. & f. aeronaut.

aéronautique [aerɔnɔtik]. **1.** *a.* aeronautical; air (service). **2.** *s.f.* aeronautics.

aéronaval, -ale, -als [aerɔnaval]. **1.** *a.* air and sea (manœuvres, etc.). **2.** *s.f.* l'Aéronavale = the Fleet Air Arm.

aéroport [aerɔpɔːr], s.m. airport.

aéroporté [aerɔpɔrte], *a.* airborne (troops, forces).

aéropostal, -aux [aerɔpɔstal, -o], *a.* airmail.

aérosol [aerɔsɔl], s.m. aerosol.

aérotransporter [aerɔtrɑ̃spɔrte], *v.tr.* to fly (goods, passengers).

affabilité [afabilite], s.f. graciousness, affability.

affable [afaːbl], *a.* gracious, affable; adv. **-ment.**

affaibl\|ir [afɛbliːr], *v.tr.* to weaken; (*a*) to enfeeble; (*b*) to lessen; **a. le courage de qn,** to damp s.o.'s courage; s.m. **-issement.**

s'affaiblir, to become weak(er); to lose one's strength.

affaire [afɛːr], s.f. **1.** (*a*) business, affair; **ce n'est pas votre a.,** it's no business of yours; **j'en fais mon a.,** leave it to me; I will deal with it; **savoir son a.,** to know what one is about; (*b*) question, matter, affair; **a. de cœur,** love-affair; **a. de goût,** matter of taste; **ce n'est que l'a. d'un instant,** it won't take a minute; (*c*) thing (required); **j'ai votre a.,** I have the very thing you want; **faire l'a. de qn,** to answer the purpose of s.o.; **son a. est faite,** he is done for; (*d*) (i) business, matter; **vilaine a.,** ugly business; **ce n'est pas une a.,** it's no great matter; **la belle a.!** is that all? that's nothing! **en voici une a.!** here's a pretty kettle of fish! (ii) **s'attirer une (mauvaise) a.,** to get into trouble. **2.** (*a*) business, deal; **faire une bonne a.,** to do a good stroke of business; **c'est une a. d'or,** it will be a gold mine; **venir pour affaire(s),** to come on business; **c'est une a. faite!** done! that's settled! (*b*) **avoir a. à, avec, qn,** to have to deal with s.o.; **c'est a. à vous de . . .,** F: it's up to you to; . . . **3.** *pl.* (*a*) things, belongings; **serrer ses affaires,** to put away one's things; (*b*) business, trade; **faire de bonnes affaires,** to be successful in business; **homme d'affaires,** (i) business man; (ii) agent; (iii) steward; (iv) lawyer; (*c*) **les affaires de l'État,** affairs of State; **le Ministère des affaires étrangères,** (*in Britain*) the Foreign Office; *U.S:* the State Department. **4.** *Jur:* case, lawsuit. **5.** (*a*) **a. d'honneur,** duel; (*b*) *Mil:*

engagement.

affairé [afɛre], *a.* busy; **faire l'a.,** to pretend to be busy, to fuss around.

affaissement [afɛsmɑ̃], s.m. **1.** subsidence; collapse (of floor, etc.). **2.** depression, despondency.

affaisser (s') [safɛse], *v.pr.* (*a*) (*of thg*) to subside, give way, collapse; (*of material*) to give, yield; (*b*) (*of pers.*) to collapse.

affamé [afame], *a.* hungry, starving, famished; **être a. de qch.,** to hunger after sth.; to long for sth.

affectation [afɛktasjɔ̃], s.f. **1.** affectation; (*a*) affectedness; **sans a.,** unaffectedly; (*b*) simulation, pretence. **2. a. de qch. à qch.,** assignment of sth. to a purpose; appropriation of sth. for a purpose.

affecté [afɛkte]. **1.** *a.* affected (manners). **2.** *s.m. Mil:* **a. spécial** = man in a reserved occupation.

affecter [afɛkte], *v.tr.* **1. a. qch. à un certain usage,** to assign sth. to a certain use. **2.** to affect, simulate; **a. la mort,** to pretend to be dead. **3.** to affect; to have a partiality for; **a. les grands mots,** to affect big words. **4.** to assume, take on (shape). **5.** (*a*) to affect, move, touch (s.o.); (*b*) to affect (career).

affection [afɛksjɔ̃], s.f. affection. **1.** fondness, attachment, liking (**pour,** for); **avoir qn en a.,** to be fond of s.o. **2.** *Med:* complaint.

affectionné [afɛksjɔne], *a.* affectionate, loving.

affectionner [afɛksjɔne], *v.tr.* **a. qn,** to have an affection for s.o.

affectu\|eux, -euse [afɛktɥø, -øːz], *a.* affectionate, loving; adv. **-eusement.**

afférent [aferɑ̃], *a.* **1.** assignable (à, to); **traitement à un emploi,** salary attaching to a post. **2.** relating (à, to).

afferm\|ir [afɛrmiːr], *v.tr.* **1.** to strengthen, steady, make firm. **2.** to strengthen, consolidate; s.m. **-issement.**

s'affermir, to become stronger, firmer.

affiche [afiʃ], s.f. (*a*) **a. murale,** placard, poster, bill; **a. de théâtre,** play-bill; (*b*) stamp, mark, sign (of quality).

affich\|er [afiʃe], *v.tr.* **1.** to stick (up), placard, display (notice); **a. une vente,** to advertise a sale; *P.N:* **défense d'a.,** stick no bills. **2.** to parade; to make a show of (sth.); **a. ses opinions,** to flaunt one's opinions; s.m. **-age.**

s'afficher, to show off; to seek notoriety.

afficheur [afiʃœːr], s.m. bill-sticker, bill-poster.

affilé [afile], *a.* sharp.

affilée [afile], s.f. F: (*used only in the adv. phr.* d'a.) **cinq heures d'a.,** five hours at a stretch, on end.

affil\|er [afile], *v.tr.* to sharpen, set, whet (blade); s.m. **-age.**

affilié, -ée [afilje]. **1.** *a.* affiliated. **2.** *s.* affiliated member.

affili|er [afilje], *v.tr.* to affiliate (à, to, with); *s.f.* -**ation**.

affin|er [afine], *v.tr.* 1. to improve, refine. 2. to sharpen (the intelligence); to ripen (cheese). 3. to thin, fine down; *s.m.* -**age**; *s.m.* -**ement**. **s'affiner.** 1. to gain in refinement. 2. (*of cheese*) to ripen.

affinité [afinite], *s.f.* affinity; (*a*) relationship by marriage; (*b*) resemblance; similarity of character; (*c*) *Ch:* **a. pour un corps**, affinity for a body.

affirmat|if, -ive [afirmatif, -i:v]. 1. *a.* affirmative, positive; **signe a.**, nod. 2. *s.f.* **l'affirmative**, the affirmative; *adv.* -**ivement**.

affirmation [afirmasjɔ̃], *s.f.* affirmation; assertion.

affirmer [afirme], *v.tr.* (*a*) to affirm, assert; (*b*) **théorie affirmée par l'expérience**, theory supported by experience.

affixe [afiks]. *Ling:* 1. *a.* affixed. 2. *s.m.* affix.

affleur|er [aflœre]. 1. *v.tr. Carp:* to bring (timbers, etc.) to the same level. 2. *v.i.* (*a*) to be level, flush; (*b*) *Geol:* (*of lode*) to outcrop; *s.m.* -**ement**.

affliction [afliksjɔ̃], *s.f.* tribulation, sorrow.

affligé [afliʒe], *a.* afflicted; **être a. d'une infirmité**, to suffer from an infirmity; **être a. d'une nouvelle**, to be grieved at a piece of news.

affligeant [afliʒɑ̃], *a.* distressing, sad (news).

affliger [afliʒe], *v.tr.* (**n. affligeons**). 1. to afflict (**de**, with). 2. to pain, distress, grieve. **s'affliger**, to grieve, to sorrow (**de**, at, about, over).

affluence [aflyɑ̃:s], *s.f.* 1. flow, flood. 2. affluence, abundance. 3. crowd, concourse; **heures d'a.**, rush hours.

affluent [aflyɑ̃], *s.m.* tributary (of river).

affluer [aflye], *v.i.* 1. (*of water*) to flow. 2. to abound; to be plentiful. 3. **a. à, dans, un endroit**, to crowd to a place.

affolé [afɔle], *a.* crazy, distracted, panic-stricken; (*of engine*) racing.

affolement [afɔlmɑ̃], *s.m.* 1. distraction, panic. 2. racing (of engine).

affoler [afɔle], *v.tr.* 1. to madden, distract. 2. *Mch:* to let (machine) race. **s'affoler**, to get into a panic; to stampede.

affranchi, -ie [afrɑ̃ʃi], *a.* (*a*) freed, emancipated (slave); (*b*) free (**de**, of, from).

affranch|ir [afrɑ̃ʃi:r], *v.tr.* 1. to free; to set free; to emancipate. 2. to pay the postage on; to stamp (letter); *s.m.* -**issement**. **s'affranchir**, to become free, independent; **s'a. de qch.**, to shake off sth.

affranchisseur [afrɑ̃ʃisœ:r], *s.m.* liberator.

affr|éter [afrete], *v.tr.* (**j'affrète**; **j'affréterai**) to charter (ship, plane); *s.m.* -**ètement**; *s.m.* -**éteur**.

affr|eux, -euse [afrø, -ø:z], *a.* 1. frightful, hideous. 2. frightful, shocking (crime); *adv.* -**eusement**.

affront [afrɔ̃], *s.m.* insult, snub.

affront|er [afrɔ̃te], *v.tr.* to face, confront (s.o.); to affront (danger); **a. les périls d'un voyage**, to face the perils of a journey; *s.m.* -**ement**.

affublement [afyblǝmɑ̃], *s.m. Pej:* get-up, rig out.

affubler [afyble], *v.tr. Pej:* **a. qn de qch.**, to dress s.o. up in sth.; to rig s.o. out in sth. **s'affubler**, to rig oneself out (in sth.).

affût [afy], *s.m.* 1. hiding-place; **chasser un animal à l'a.**, to stalk an animal; **être, se mettre, à l'a. de qn**, to lie in wait for s.o.; **à l'a. de nouvelles**, on the look-out for news. 2. gun carriage.

affûter [afyte], *v.tr.* to sharpen (tool); to set (saw).

afin [afɛ̃], *adv.* 1. **a. de (faire qch.)**, to, in order to, so as to (do sth.). 2. **a. que** + *sub.*, so that, in order that.

africain, -aine [afrikɛ̃, -ɛn], *a. & s.* African.

Afrique (**l'**) [lafrik]. *Pr.n.f.* Africa.

agaçant [agasɑ̃], *a.* 1. annoying, irritating. 2 provocative.

agac|er [agase], *v.tr.* (**n. agaçons**). 1. to set (teeth) on edge; to jar, grate, upon (nerves). 2 **a. qn**, to provoke s.o.; *s.m.* -**ement**; *s.f.* -**erie**. **s'agacer**, to become irritated.

agate [agat], *s.f. Miner:* agate.

âge [ɑ:ʒ], *s.m.* 1. age; (*a*) **quel â. avez-vous?** how old are you? **être d'â. à faire qch.**, to be old enough to do sth.; **mourir avant l'â.**, to die before one's time; (*b*) **le bas â.**, infancy; **d'un certain â.**, entre deux âges, middle-aged; **getting on**; **être à l'â. de raison**, to have reached the age of discretion; (*c*) old age; **prendre de l'â.**, to be getting on in years. 2. generation. 3. period epoch; *Hist:* **le moyen â.**, the Middle Ages.

âgé [aʒe], *a.* old, aged. 1. **â. de dix ans**, aged ten years old. 2. advanced in years, elderly.

agence [aʒɑ̃:s], *s.f.* agency; **a. de placement** registry office, employment bureau; **a. de voyages**, travel agency.

agencement [aʒɑ̃smɑ̃], *s.m.* 1. arrangement (of a house); fitting up (of parts of machine). 2. fixtures, fittings (of house, machine, etc.).

agencer [aʒɑ̃se], *v.tr.* (**n. agençons**) to arrange (house); to adjust (parts of machine); **local bien agencé**, well-designed, -equipped premises.

agenda [aʒɛ̃da], *s.m.* memorandum-book engagement-book; diary.

agenouill|er (**s'**) [saʒnuje], *v.pr.* to kneel (down); *s.m.* -**ement**.

agent [aʒɑ̃], *s.m.* 1. agent, agency. 2. (*a*) agent; **a. d'affaires**, man of business; (*b*) **a. (de police)** policeman; (*c*) **a. de change**, (i) stock-broker

(ii) mercantile broker.

agglomération [aglɔmerasjɔ̃], *s.f.* agglomeration. **1.** caking, packing (of snow, etc.). **2.** mass, cluster. **3.** built-up area.

aggloméré [aglɔmere], *s.m.* **1.** compressed fuel, (coal-dust) briquette. **2.** breezeblock.

agglutiner (s') [saglytine], *v.pr.* to bind; to cake.

aggravl er [agrave], *v.tr.* **1.** to aggravate (disease); to worsen. **2.** to increase, augment (penalty); *s.f.* **-ation.**

s'aggraver, to worsen; to grow worse.

agile [aʒil], *a.* agile, nimble; active; *adv.* **-ment.**

agilité [aʒilite], *s.f.* agility, nimbleness, litheness.

agiotage [aʒjɔtaːʒ], *s.m. Pej:* gambling (on the Stock Exchange).

agiotl er [aʒjɔte], *v.i.* to speculate; *s.m.* **-eur.**

agir [aʒiːr], *v.i.* to act. **1. a.** de soi-même, to act on one's own initiative; **faire a. qch.,** to set sth. going, working; **est-ce ainsi que vous en agissez avec moi?** is that how you treat me? **2.** to act, operate, take effect; **a. sur qn,** to bring an influence to bear upon s.o. **3.** *Jur:* to take proceedings.

s'agir (de), *v.impers.* (a) to concern; to be in question; to be the matter; **de quoi s'agit-il?** what is the question? what is it all about? **voici de quoi il s'agit,** the thing is this; **il s'agit de votre avenir,** your future is at stake; **il ne s'agit pas de cela,** that is not the question; (b) **s'a. de faire qch.,** to be a matter of doing sth.

agissant [aʒisɑ̃], *a.* **1.** active, busy, bustling. **2.** efficacious (medicine, etc.).

agitateur, -trice [aʒitatœːr, -tris]. **1.** *s.* (political) agitator. **2.** *s.m.* stirrer, stirring-rod.

agitation [aʒitasjɔ̃], *s.f.* agitation. **1.** (a) shaking, stirring; waving (of flag); wagging (of tail); (b) discussing (of question); (c) **l'a. ouvrière,** labour unrest. **2.** (a) (state of) perturbation; (b) restlessness; (c) roughness (of sea).

agité [aʒite], *a.* **1.** choppy, rough (sea). **2.** agitated, restless (night); troubled (sleep). **3.** excited.

agiter [aʒite], *v.tr.* **1.** (a) to agitate; to wave (handkerchief); **le chien agite sa queue,** the dog wags its tail; (b) to shake (bottle); (c) to stir (mixture). **2.** to agitate, excite (the people). **3.** to debate (question).

s'agiter, (a) to be agitated, in movement; **s'a. dans son sommeil,** to toss in one's sleep; (b) to become agitated, excited.

agneau, -eaux [aɲo], *s.m.* lamb.

agonie [agɔni] *s.f.* death agony; pangs of death; **être à l'a.,** to be at one's last gasp.

agonisant, -ante [agɔnizɑ̃, -ɑ̃ːt]. **1.** *a.* dying; in the throes of death. **2.** *s.* dying person.

agoniser [agɔnize], *v.i.* to be dying.

agrafe [agraf], *s.f.* hook, fastener; clasp; buckle (of strap); clip, staple (for papers); **agrafes et portes (de couturière),** hooks and eyes.

agrafer [agrafe], *v.tr.* to fasten by means of a hook, clasp, or clip.

agrafeuse [agraføːz], *s.f.* stapler.

agrandir [agrɑ̃diːr], *v.tr.* (a) to make (sth.) larger; to enlarge; (b) to magnify.

s'agrandir. 1. to grow larger; to become greater; to increase; to expand. **2.** to become richer, more powerful.

agrandissement [agrɑ̃dismɑ̃], *s.m.* **1.** (a) enlarging, extending; (b) enlargement, extension (of factory); *Phot:* enlargement. **2.** increase in power; aggrandizement.

agréable [agreabl], *a.* agreeable, pleasant, nice; **si cela peut vous être a.,** if you like; **faire l'a.,** to make oneself pleasant (**auprès de,** to); **pour vous être a.,** to oblige you; *adv.* **-ment.**

agréer [agree]. **1.** *v.tr.* to accept, approve (of), agree to; **a. un contrat,** to approve an agreement; **agréez mes salutations empressées,** (I am) yours sincerely. **2.** *v.ind.tr.* to suit, please; **si cela lui agrée,** if that suits him, his convenience.

agrégation [agregasjɔ̃], *s.f.* (**concours d')a.,** State competitive examination for admission to teaching posts in the **Lycées.**

agrégé, -ée [agreʒe], *a. & s. Sch:* (**professeur**) **a.,** schoolmaster, -mistress, who has passed the **agrégation** examination.

agrément [agremɑ̃], *s.m.* **1.** (a) pleasure, amusement; **voyage d'a.,** pleasure-trip; **ouvrages d'a.,** fancy work; (b) attractiveness, charm. **2.** *usu. pl.* amenities (of place); charms (of person). **3. a. donné à qch.,** assent, consent, to sth.

agrémenter [agremɑ̃te], *v.tr.* to embellish, ornament, adorn (**de,** with).

agrès [agrɛ], *s.m.pl.* tackle, gear, rigging (of ship); apparatus (of gymnasium).

agresseur [agresœːr], *s.m.* aggressor.

agressl if, -ive [agresif, -iːv], *a.* aggressive, provocative; *adv.* **-ivement.**

agression [agresjɔ̃], *s.f.* aggression.

agricole [agrikɔl], *a.* agricultural (produce); **comices agricoles,** agricultural show.

agriculteur [agrikyltœːr], *s.m.* farmer.

agriculture [agrikyltyːr], *s.f.* agriculture, farming.

agripper [agripe], *v.tr.* to clutch, grip.

s'agripper à qch., to cling to sth.

agronomie [agrɔnɔmi], *s.f. Agr:* agronomics.

agrumes [agrym], *s.m.pl.* citrus fruit.

aguerri [ageri], *a.* seasoned, trained (army); **peu a.,** raw (soldier, etc.).

aguets [agɛ], *s.m.pl.* **aux a.,** watchful (**de,** for); **être aux a.,** to be on the watch; **avoir l'oreille aux a.,** to keep one's ears open.

ahuri [ayri], *a.* bewildered; flabbergasted; confused, dazed.

ahurl ir [ayriːr], *v.tr.* to bewilder. **1.** to dumb-

found. **2.** to confuse, daze; *s.m.* **-issement.**
ahurissant [ayrisɑ̃], *a.* bewildering,
breathtaking, staggering.
aide[1] [ɛ(:)d], *s.f.* (*a*) help, assistance, aid; **venir
en a. à qn,** to help s.o.; **à l'a.!** help! *prep.phr.* **à
l'a. de qch.,** with the help, assistance, of sth.;
(*b*) relief, succour.
aide[2], *s.m. & f.* assistant, helper; **a. de camp,**
aide-de-camp.
aide-mémoire [ɛdmemwa:r], *s.m.inv.* manual,
memorandum.
aide-ouïe [ɛdwi], *s.m.inv.* hearing-aid.
aider [ɛde]. **1.** *v.tr.* **a. qn,** to help, assist, aid, s.o.;
je me suis fait a., I got some help; **s'a. de qch.,**
to make use of sth.; **le temps aidant,** with the
help of time. **2.** *v.ind.tr.* **a. à qch.,** to help
towards sth.
aïe [aj] *int.* (*indicating twinge of pain*) ow! ouch!
aïeul [ajœl], *s.m.* **1.** (*pl.* **aïeuls**) grandfather. **2.**
(*pl.* **aïeux** [ajø]) ancestor.
aïeule [ajœl], *s.f.* **1.** grandmother. **2.** ancestress.
aigle [ɛgl]. **1.** (*a*) *s.m. & f. Orn:* eagle; **regard
d'a.,** keen glance; (*b*) *s.m. Lit:* genius; **ce n'est
pas un a.,** he's not brilliant. **2.** *s.m.* lectern,
reading-desk. **3.** *s.m. & f. Mil:* eagle, standard.
aiglefin [ɛgləfɛ̃], *s.m. Ich:* haddock.
aiglon, -onne [ɛglɔ̃, -ɔn], *s.* eaglet; young eagle.
aigre [ɛ:gr], *a.* (*a*) sour, acid, tart; *s.m.* **tourner à
l'a.,** to turn sour; (*b*) sour(-tempered), crabbed;
(*c*) shrill, sharp (sound); *adv.* **-ment.**
aigre-doux, -douce [ɛgrədu, -dus], *a.* bitter-
sweet (fruit); **ton a.-d.,** subacid tone.
aigrefin[1] [ɛgrəfɛ̃], *s.m. Ich:* haddock.
aigrefin[2], *s.m.* sharper, swindler.
aigrelet, -ette [ɛgrələ, -ɛt], *a.* sourish, tart.
aigrette [ɛgrɛt], *s.f.* **1.** (*a*) aigrette (of heron);
tuft; (*b*) *Cost:* aigrette, plume. **2.** *Orn:* egret.
aigreur [ɛgrœ:r], *s.f.* sourness, tartness, acidity.
aigrir [ɛgri:r]. **1.** *v.tr.* (*a*) to make sour; (*b*) to
sour, embitter. **2.** *v.i.* to turn sour; *s.m.*
-issement.
s'aigrir. 1. to turn sour. **2.** to become soured,
embittered.
aigu, -uë [ɛgy], *a.* **1.** sharp, pointed (instrument);
Geom: **angle a.,** acute angle. **2.** acute, sharp;
keen. **3.** shrill, piercing, high-pitched. **4. accent
a.,** acute accent.
aiguille [egɥi:j], *s.f.* **1.** needle; **a. à coudre,** sewing
needle; **travailler à l'a.,** to do needlework. **2.** (*a*)
a. de pin, pine-needle; (*b*) *Rail:* point. **3.** needle,
point; **a. d'un clocher d'église,** church spire. **4.**
(*a*) (swinging) needle (of compass); (*b*) index,
pointer (of balance); (*c*) hand (of clock); **petite
a.,** hour hand; **grande a.,** minute hand; **a.
trotteuse,** second hand.
aiguilleur [egɥijœ:r], *s.m. Rail:* pointsman.
aiguillon [egɥijɔ̃], *s.m.* **1.** (*a*) goad; **l'a. du
remords,** the pricks of remorse; (*b*) spur, incentive. **2.** (*a*) *Bot:* prickle, thorn; (*b*) sting (of

wasp).
aiguillonner [egɥijɔne], *v.tr.* **1.** to goad. **2.** to
urge on, incite; to rouse; to whet (appetite);
s.m. **-ement.**
aiguiser [eg(ɥ)ize], *v.tr.* **1.** (*a*) to whet; to
sharpen; (*b*) to point, to sharpen (tool) to a
point; **a. un crayon,** to sharpen a pencil. **2.** to
make keen; to whet (appetite).
s'aiguiser, (*of wits*) to become keen.
ail [a:j], *s.m.* garlic.
aile [ɛl], *s.f.* **1.** wing, pinion; **battre de l'a.,** (i) to
flutter; (ii) to be exhausted; **ne (plus) battre que
d'une a.,** (*of pers.*) to be on his last legs. **2.** wing
(of aeroplane); sail (of windmill); arm (of
semaphore); blade (of propeller); *Aut:* wing.
ailé [ɛle], *a.* winged, feathered.
aileron [ɛlrɔ̃], *s.m.* **1.** (*a*) pinion (of bird); (*b*) fin
(of shark). **2.** *Av:* aileron, wing-tip.
ailier [ɛlje], *s.m. Sp:* (*player*) wing.
ailleurs [ajœ:r], *adv.* **1.** elsewhere, somewhere
else. **2.** *adv. phr.* (*a*) **d'a.,** (i) besides, moreover;
(ii) from another place; (*b*) **par a.,** (i) by
another route; (ii) in other respects.
aimable [ɛmabl], *a.* **1.** amiable, agreeable; kind;
nice; **vous êtes bien a., c'est très a. à vous,** that
is very kind of you; **peu a.,** ungracious. **2.**
lovable, attractive; *adv.* **-ment.**
aimant[1] [ɛmɑ̃], *a.* loving, affectionate.
aimant[2], *s.m.* magnet.
aimanter [ɛmɑ̃te], *v.tr.* to magnetize; **aiguille
aimantée,** magnetic needle.
Aimée [ɛme]. *Pr.n.f.* Amy.
aimer [ɛme], *v.tr.* **1.** (*a*) to like, care for, to be
fond of; **se faire a. de qn,** to win s.o.'s affection;
a. faire qch., to like to do sth.; (*b*) **a. autant:
j'aime(rais) autant rester ici (que de . . .),** I
would just as soon stay here (as . . .); (*c*) **a.
mieux: j'aime mieux qu'il vienne,** I would
rather he came. **2. a. qn (d'amour),** to love s.o.
aine [ɛn], *s.f. Anat:* groin.
aîné [ɛne], *a.* (*a*) elder (of two); eldest; *s.* **il est
mon a.,** he is older than I am; (*b*) senior; **M. Dumont a.,** Mr Dumont senior.
aînesse [ɛnɛs], *s.f.* **1.** primogeniture; **droit d'a.,**
(i) law of primogeniture; (ii) birthright. **2.**
seniority.
ainsi [ɛ̃si]. **1.** *adv.* thus; so; in a like manner; **s'il
en est a.,** if such is the case, if (it is) so; **et a. de
suite,** and so on; **pour a. dire,** so to speak, as it
were; **a. soit-il,** (i) so be it; (ii) *Ecc:* amen. **2.**
conj. so, thus; **a. vous ne venez pas?** so you are
not coming? **3.** *conj.phr.* **a. que,** (just) as; **cette
règle a. que la suivante me paraît, me parais-
sent, inutile(s),** this rule, as also the next one
seems to me to be unnecessary; (*the concord is
usu. in the pl.*).
air [ɛ:r], *s.m.* **I. 1.** (*a*) air, atmosphere; **École de
l'A.** = R.A.F. College; **sortir prendre l'a.,** to go
for a breath of fresh air; **à a. conditionné,** air-

conditioned; **vivre de l'a. du temps,** to live on (next to) nothing, on air; **au grand a., en plein a.,** in the open air; **jeux de plein a.,** outdoor games; (*b*) **en l'a.,** in the air; **être en l'a.,** to be in a state of confusion; **paroles en l'a.,** idle talk. **2.** wind, draught; **il fait de l'a.,** it is breezy; **courant d'a.,** draught.
II. air. (*a*) appearance, look; **avoir bon a.,** (i) to look distinguished; (ii) (*of dress*) to look well; **a. de famille,** family likeness; (*b*) **avoir l'a.,** to look, seem; (*the predicative adj. may agree either with air or with the subject*) **elle a l'a. fatigué(e),** she looks tired; **cela en a tout l'a.,** it looks like it. **2.** manner, way; **se donner des airs,** to give oneself airs.
III. air, tune, air, melody; **je connais des paroles sur cet a.-là,** I've heard that tale before.
airain |ɛrɛ̃|, *s.m.* bronze, brass; **avoir un cœur d'a.,** to have a heart of stone; **avoir un front d'a.,** to be brazen-faced.
aire |ɛ:r| *s.f.* **1.** surface; flat space; floor; *Av:* **a. d'embarquement,** tarmac; **a. d'atterrissage,** landing area; **a. de lavage,** wash-down, *N.Am:* wash-rack. **2.** area (of field, triangle). **3.** eyrie (of eagle). **4.** *Nau:* **les aires du vent,** the points of the compass; *F:* **prendre l'a. du vent,** to see which way the wind is blowing.
airelle |ɛrɛl|, *s.f. Bot:* whortleberry, bilberry; *N.Am:* blueberry; huckleberry.
aisance |ɛzã:s|, *s.f.* ease; (*a*) freedom (of movement); **donner de l'a. à qch.,** to ease sth.; **a. des coudes,** elbow-room; (*b*) **jouir de l'a.,** to be in easy circumstances.
aise |ɛ:z|. **1.** *s.f.* ease, comfort; **être à l'a., à son a.,** (i) to be comfortable; (ii) to be well-off; **ne pas être à son a.,** (i) to feel uncomfortable; (ii) to feel ill; **il en prend à son a.,** (i) he takes it easy; (ii) he is a cool customer; **à votre a.!** just as you like! **2.** *a.* **bien a.,** very glad.
aisé |ɛze|, *a.* **1.** (*a*) easy, free (manner); comfortable (clothes); (*b*) well-to-do (person). **2.** easy (task); **c'est plus a. à dire qu'à faire,** it is more easily said than done; *adv.* **-ment.**
aisselle |ɛsɛl|, *s.f.* armpit.
ajonc |aʒɔ̃|, *s.m. Bot:* furze, gorse, whin.
ajour |aʒu:r|, *s.m.* **1.** opening (which lets the light through). **2.** openwork (in wood-carving, etc.).
ajouré |aʒure|, *a.* perforated, pierced; *Carp:* **travail a.,** fretwork.
ajourner |aʒurne|, *v.tr.* (*a*) to postpone, put off, adjourn, defer; (*b*) *Sch:* to refer (candidate); to grant deferment to (s.o.); *s.m.* **-ement.**
s'ajourner, (*of Parliament, etc.*) to adjourn.
ajouter |aʒute|, *v.tr.* to add. **1. a. des chiffres,** to add up figures; **a. l'action aux paroles,** to suit the action to the word. **2. "venez aussi,"** **ajouta-t-il,** "you come too," he added. **3. a. foi à qch.,** to believe sth.

ajustage |aʒysta:ʒ|, *s.m.* **1.** fitting (of dress). **2.** assembly (of machine).
ajuster |aʒyste|, *v.tr.* **1.** (*a*) to adjust, set (tool); to true up (sth.); (*b*) to fit together (machine); (*c*) **a. son fusil,** to take aim with one's gun; **a. qn (avec un fusil),** to aim (a gun) at s.o.; (*d*) **a. qch. à qch.,** to fit, adapt, sth. to sth. **2.** to put (sth.) right, straight; to settle (sth.); *a.* **-able;** *s.m.* **-ement.**
alanguir (s') |salãgi:r|, to languish, droop.
alanguissement |alãgismã|, *s.m.* languor, weakness; drooping, decline.
alarmant |alarmã|, *a.* alarming; startling.
alarme |alarm|, *s.f.* alarm; **donner, sonner, l'a.,** to give, sound, the alarm; *Rail:* **tirer la sonnette d'a.,** to pull the communication-cord.
alarmer |alarme|, *v.tr.* **1.** to give the alarm to (s.o.). **2.** to frighten, startle, alarm (s.o.).
s'alarmer, to take fright (**de,** at).
alarmiste |alarmist|, *a. & s.* alarmist; scaremonger.
albanais, -aise |albanɛ, -ɛ:z|, *a. & s.* Albanian.
Albanie (l') |albani|. *Pr.n.f.* Albania.
albatros |albatrɔs|, *s.m. Orn:* albatross.
albinos |albino:s|, *s. & a. inv.* albino.
album |albɔm|, *s.m.* **1.** album, sketch-book. **2.** trade catalogue.
albumine |albymin|, *s.f. Ch:* albumin.
alcali |alkali|, *s.m.* alkali.
alcalin |alkalɛ̃|, *a.* alkaline.
alcaliniser |alkalinize|, *v.tr. Ch:* to alkalize.
alcool |alkɔl|, *s.m.* alcohol, *F:* spirit(s); **vins et alcools,** wines and spirits; **a. à brûler,** methylated spirit; *s.m.* **-isme.**
alcoolique |alkɔlik|. **1.** *a.* alcoholic, spirituous. **2.** *s.* drunkard.
alcootest |alkɔtest|, *s.m.* breathalyser (test).
alcôve |alko:v|, *s.f.* alcove.
aléa |alea|, *s.m.* risk, hazard, chance; *a.* **-toire,** risky; random.
alène |alɛn|, *s.f. Tls:* awl; **a. plate,** bradawl.
alentour |alãtu:r|. **1.** *adv.* around, round about; **le pays d'a.,** the neighbouring countryside. **2.** *s.m.pl.* **alentours (d'une ville),** environs, surroundings (of a town).
alerte |alɛrt|. **1.** *int.* to arms! **2.** *s.f.* alarm, warning; **fin d'a.** all clear; **fausse a.,** false alarm. **3.** *a.* (*a*) alert, brisk; (*b*) vigilant.
alerter |alɛrte|, *v.tr.* to alert, warn (police, etc.).
alezan, -ane |alzã, -an|, *a. & s.* chestnut (horse).
alfa |alfa|, *s.m. Bot:* alfa(-grass), esparto.
algèbre |alʒɛbr|, *s.f.* algebra; *a.* **-gébrique,** algebraic.
Alger |alʒe|. *Pr.n.* Algiers.
Algérie (l') |lalʒeri|. *Pr.n.f.* Algeria.
algérien, -ienne |alʒerjɛ̃, -jɛn|, *a. & s.* Algerian.
algérois, -oise |alʒerwa, -wa:z|, *a. & s.* (native, inhabitant) of Algiers.

algue |alg|, *s.f. Bot:* seaweed.

aliénation |aljenasjɔ̃|, *s.f.* alienation. **1.** *Jur:* transfer (of property). **2.** estrangement. **3. a. mentale,** insanity.

aliéné, -ée |aljene|, *a. & s.* lunatic, madman, -woman.

aliénler |aljene|, *v.tr.* (j'aliène; j'aliénerai). **1.** *Jur:* to alienate, part with (property). **2.** to alienate, estrange (a friend); *s.m. & f.* **-iste,** mental specialist.

alignler |aliɲe|, *v.tr.* to align, draw up; to put (thgs) in a line, in a row; *s.m.* **-ement.**

s'aligner, to fall into line.

aliment |alimã|, *s.m.* food.

alimentaire |alimãtɛːr|, *a.* **1.** *Jur:* pension a., alimony. **2.** alimentary, nourishing (product); **conserves alimentaires,** tinned, canned, foods; **pâtes alimentaires,** pasta, noodles.

alimentler |alimãte|, *v.tr.* to feed, nourish (s.o.); to supply (market) with food; *s.f.* **-ation.**

alinéa |alinea|, *s.m. Typ:* **1.** first line of paragraph; **en a.,** indented. **2.** paragraph.

alité |alite|, *a.* confined to (one's) bed; *F:* laid up.

alitler |alite|, *v.tr.* to keep (s.o.) in bed; *s.m.* **-ement.**

s'aliter, to take to one's bed.

alizé |alize|, *a. & s.m.* **les (vents) alizés,** the tradewinds.

allaitler |alɛte|, *v.tr.* to suckle (child); *s.m.* **-ement.**

allant |alã|. **1.** *a.* active; spirited; *s.m.* **avoir de l'a.,** to have plenty of go. **2.** *s.m.pl.* **allants et venants,** passers-by.

alllécher |al(l)eʃe|, *v.tr.* (j'allèche; j'allécherai) to allure, attract, entice, tempt; *s.m.* **-èchement.**

allée |ale|, *s.f.* **1.** (action of) going; **allées et venues,** coming and going. **2.** (*a*) walk (*esp.* lined with trees); (*b*) path (in garden); (*c*) passage, alley; drive (for cars).

allléger |al(l)eʒe|, *v.tr.* (j'allège, n. **allégeons;** j'allégerai) (*a*) to lighten (ships, taxes); (*b*) to relieve (pain); *s.m.* **-ègement.**

s'alléger, to become lighter, easier.

allégorlie |al(l)egɔri|, *s.f.* allegory; *a.* **-ique.**

allègre |al(l)ɛːgr|, *a.* lively, gay, cheerful.

allégresse |al(l)egrɛs|, *s.f.* gladness, liveliness.

alléguer |al(l)ege|, *v.tr.* (j'allègue; j'alléguerai). **1.** to allege, urge; **a. l'ignorance,** to plead ignorance. **2.** to quote (author).

Allemagne (l') |lalmaɲ|. *Pr.n.f.* Germany.

allemand, -ande |almã, -ãːd|. **1.** *a. & s.* German. **2.** *s.m.* **l'a.,** (the) German (language).

aller |ale|. **I.** *v.i.* (*pr. ind.* je vais, tu vas, il va, n. **allons, ils vont;** *pr. sub.* j'aille; *imp.* va (vas-y), **allons;** *fu.* j'irai; *aux.* être). **1.** to go; (*a*) **a. et venir,** to come and go; **je ne ferai qu'a. et revenir,** I shall come straight back; **il va sur ses dix ans,** he is nearly ten (years old); *F:* **faire a. qn,** to

order s.o. about; (*b*) **allez, je vous écoute,** go on, I'm listening; (*c*) **sentier qui va à la gare,** path leading to the station. **2.** (*a*) to go, be going (well); **les affaires vont,** business is brisk; **ça ira!** we'll manage it! **je vous en offre cinq francs—va pour cinq francs!** I'll give you five francs for it—all right, five francs! **cela va sans dire, cela va de soi,** that's understood, that's a matter of course; (*b*) (*of machine*) to go, work, run; **la pendule va bien,** the clock is right; (*c*) **comment allez-vous?** *F:* **comment cela va-t-il?** how are you? how do you do? **je vais bien,** *F:* **ça va,** I'm well, I'm all right. **3. a. à qn,** (*a*) (*of clothes*) to suit, become, s.o.; (*b*) (*of food*) to agree with s.o.; (*c*) (*of clothes*) to fit s.o.; (*d*) to be to s.o.'s liking; *F:* **ça va!** all right! O.K.! **4. plat allant au four,** oven-proof dish. **5.** (*of colours*) **a. avec qch.,** to go well with sth.; to match sth. **6.** (*a*) **a. voir qn,** to go and see s.o.; to call on s.o.; **a. trouver qn,** to go to s.o.; (*b*) to be going, to be about (to do sth.); **il va s'en occuper,** he is going to see about it; **elle allait tout avouer,** she was about to confess everything; **a. en augmentant,** to increase. **7.** y a. (*a*) **j'y vais!** on y va! coming! (*b*) **y a. de tout son cœur,** to put one's back into it; **allons-y!** well, here goes! **vas-y! allez-y!** go it! go on! (*c*) **y a. de sa personne,** to take a hand in it oneself. **8.** *v.impers.* **il va de soi,** it stands to reason, it goes without saying; **il en va de même pour lui,** it's the same with him; **il y allait de la vie,** it was a matter of life and death; *int.* **allons, dépêchez-vous!** come on, hurry up! **allons donc!** (i) come along! (ii) nonsense! **allons bon!** there now! **mais va donc!** get on with it! **j'ai bien souffert, allez!** I've been through a lot, believe me!

II. aller, *s.m.* **1.** going; outward journey; **billet d'a. (et) retour,** return ticket, *N.Am:* round trip ticket; *Sp:* **match a.,** away match. **2. pis a.,** last resort; makeshift; **au pis a.,** if the worst comes to the worst.

s'en aller (*pr. ind.* je m'en vais; *imp.* va-t-en, allons-nous-en; *perf.* je m'en suis allé(e)). **1.** to go away, to depart; **il faut que je m'en aille,** I must be going; **le malade s'en va,** the patient is sinking. **2.** *F:* **je m'en vais vous raconter ça,** I'll tell you about it.

allergie |alɛrʒi|, *s.f. Med:* allergy.

allergique |alɛrʒik|, *a.* allergic.

alliage |alja:ʒ|, *s.m.* **1.** alloying, blending. **2.** alloy.

alliance |aljɑ̃ːs|, *s.f.* **1.** alliance; (*a*) match, marriage, union; (*b*) union, blending. **2.** wedding ring.

allié, -ée |alje|. **1.** *a.* (*a*) allied (nation, etc.); (*b*) related (by marriage). **2.** *s.* (*a*) ally; (*b*) relation by marriage.

allier |alje|, *v.tr.* **1.** to ally, unite. **2.** to alloy, mix to match (colours) (**à,** with).

s'allier, (*a*) to form an alliance; (*b*) **s'a. à une famille,** to marry into a family.

alligator [al(l)igatɔːr], *s.m. Z:* alligator.

allô, allo [alo], *int. P.T.T:* hullo! hallo!

allocation [allɔkasjɔ̃], *s.f.* 1. allocation, assignment (of supplies). 2. allowance, grant; **allocations familiales,** family allowances.

allocution [allɔkysjɔ̃], *s.f.* short speech; address.

allonger [alɔ̃ʒe], *v.tr.* (**n. allongeons**). 1. to lengthen (garment). 2. to stretch out (one's arm). 3. to protract, prolong; *a.* **-eable;** *s.m.* **-ement.**

s'allonger. 1. (*of days*) to grow longer; **son visage s'allongea,** he pulled a long face. 2. **s'a. par terre,** to come a cropper.

allumer [alyme], *v.tr.* 1. to light; to kindle; *abs.* to switch on the light; to light up. 2. to inflame, excite (passion); *s.m.* **-age,** ignition.

s'allumer. 1. to kindle, to take fire. 2. to warm up to one's subject.

allumette [alymɛt], *s.f.* match; **a. de sûreté,** safety match.

allumeur, -euse [alymœːr, -øːz], *s.* 1. lighter; igniter. 2. *s.m.* igniting device; *El:* contactmaker. 3. *s.f.* **allumeuse,** flirt.

allure [alyːr], *s.f.* 1. (*a*) walk, bearing; (*b*) pace; **marcher à une vive a.,** to walk at a brisk pace; (*c*) speed; **à toute a.,** at full speed; (*d*) working (of engine). 2. (*a*) demeanour, behaviour; (*b*) aspect, look; **avoir l'a. d'un paysan,** to look like a farmer.

allusion [allyzjɔ̃], *s.f.* allusion; hint, innuendo.

alluvial, -iaux [allyvjal, -jo], *a.* alluvial.

almanach [almana], *s.m.* almanac; calendar.

aloi [alwa], *s.m.* standard, quality; fineness (of gold); **de bon a.,** genuine.

alors [alɔːr], *adv.* 1. then; at that, the, time. 2. (*a*) then; **a. vous viendrez?** well then, you're coming? (*b*) therefore, so; **il n'était pas là, a. je suis revenu,** he wasn't there, so I came back again. 3. *conj.phr.* **a. que,** when; **a. même que,** even though. 4. (= ENSUITE) then, next.

alouette [alwɛt], *s.f. Orn:* lark.

alourdir [alurdiːr], *v.tr.* 1. to make (sth.) heavy. 2. to make (s.o.) dull. 3. to weigh down (s.o.); *s.m.* **-issement.**

s'alourdir, to grow (i) heavy, (ii) stupid.

alourdissant [alurdisɑ̃], *a.* oppressive (heat).

aloyau [alwajo], *s.m.* sirloin (of beef).

alpaga [alpaga], *s.m.* alpaca.

alpe [alp], *s.f.* 1. alp, mountain. 2. *Geog:* **les Alpes,** the Alps.

alpestre [alpɛstr], *a.* alpine (scenery).

alphabet [alfabɛ], *s.m.* 1. alphabet. 2. *Sch:* spelling book, primer; *a.* **-bétique.**

alpin [alpɛ̃], *a.* alpine.

alpinisme [alpinism], *s.m.* mountaineering;

s.m. & f. **-iste.**

alsacien, -ienne [alzasjɛ̃, -jɛn], *a. & s.* Alsatian.

altérable [alterabl], *a.* liable to deterioration.

altérant [alterɑ̃], *a.* thirst-producing.

altercation [alterkasjɔ̃], *s.f.* dispute.

altéré [altere], *a.* 1. faded (colour); broken (voice); drawn (face). 2. thirsty.

altérer [altere], *v.tr.* (**j'altère; j'altérerai**). 1. to change (for the worse); to impair (health). 2. to tamper with (sth.); to adulterate (food); to falsify (document). 3. to make (s.o.) thirsty; *s.f.* **-ation.**

alternatif, -ive [alternatif, -iːv], *a.* 1. (*a*) alternate; (*b*) *El:* alternating (current). 2. alternative. 3. *s.f.* **alternative,** alternative; *adv.* **-ivement.**

alterne [altern], *a.* alternate (angles).

alterner [alterne], *v.i.* (*a*) to alternate; (*b*) to take turns (**pour,** in + *ger.*); to take it in turns (**pour,** to + *inf.*); **ils alternent pour veiller,** they take it in turns to sit up; *s.f.* **-ance,** alternation.

altesse [altɛs], *s.f.* (Royal, etc.) Highness.

altier, -ière [altje, -jɛːr], haughty, proud; *adv.* **-ièrement.**

altitude [altityd], *s.f.* altitude, height.

alto [alto], *s.m. Mus:* 1. alto (voice). 2. viola.

altruisme [altryism], *s.m.* altruism; *a. & s.* **-iste.**

aluminium [alyminjɔm], *s.m.* aluminium.

alun [alœ̃], *s.m.* alum.

alunir [alyniːr], *v.i.* to land on the moon.

alunissage [alynisaːʒ], *s.m.* moon landing.

alvéole [alveɔl], *s.m. or f.* 1. (*a*) alveole; cell (of honeycomb); (*b*) pigeonhole (of desk). 2. socket (of tooth). 3. cavity (in stone).

alvéolé [alveɔle], *a.* 1. honeycombed. 2. pitted.

amabilité [amabilite], *s.f.* 1. amiability; kindness. 2. *pl.* civilities.

amadouer [amadwe], *v.tr.* 1. to coax, wheedle, persuade. 2. to soften.

amaigrir [amɛgriːr], *v.tr.* to make thin; to emaciate; *s.m.* **-issement.**

s'amaigrir, to grow thin, slim, to lose flesh.

amalgame [amalgam], *s.m.* amalgam; *s.f.* **-ation,** *Fin:* merger.

amalgamer [amalgame], *v.tr.* to amalgamate; to merge.

s'amalgamer, to amalgamate; to blend; to merge.

amande [amɑ̃ːd], *s.f.* almond; *s.m.* **-ier,** almond-tree.

amant, -ante [amɑ̃, -ɑ̃ːt], *s.* lover, *f.* mistress.

amarrage [amaraːʒ], *s.m.* (*a*) mooring; **droits d'a.,** berthage; (*b*) berth, moorings.

amarre [amaːr], *s.f.* (*a*) (mooring) rope; painter; *pl.* moorings; (*b*) cable, hawser.

amarrer [amare], *v.tr.* to make fast, to moor.

s'amarrer, to make fast, to moor.

amas [amɑ], *s.m.* heap, pile, accumulation.

amass|er [amase], *v.tr.* **1.** to heap up, pile up. **2.** to hoard up, to store up; to amass (a fortune). **3.** to gather (troops) together; *s.m.* **-age**.

s'amasser, to pile up, accumulate.

amateur [amatœːr], *s.m.* **1.** lover (of sth.); **a. d'art,** art lover; **a. de chiens,** dog-fancier. **2.** (*a*) amateur; **championnat d'amateurs,** amateur championship; (*b*) dilettante. **3.** buyer; **est-ce qu'il y a des amateurs?** any takers?

amazone [amaʒɔn], *s.f.* **1.** (*a*) *Myth:* Amazon; *Geog:* **l'A.,** the (River) Amazon; (*b*) horsewoman. **2.** (lady's) riding-habit.

ambages [ɑ̃baːʒ], *s.f.pl.* circumlocution; **parler sans a.,** to speak to the point.

ambassade [ɑ̃basad], *s.f.* **1.** embassy. **2.** errand, mission.

ambassadeur [ɑ̃basadœːr], *s.m.* **1.** ambassador. **2.** messenger.

ambassadrice [ɑ̃basadris], *s.f.* **1.** ambassadress; (*a*) woman ambassador; (*b*) ambassador's wife. **2.** (woman) messenger.

ambiance [ɑ̃bjɑ̃ːs], *s.f.* (*a*) surroundings, environment; (*b*) atmosphere, tone.

ambigu, -uë, [ɑ̃bigy], *a.* ambiguous; cryptic; *adv.* **-ment**; *s.f.* **-ité**.

ambit|ieux, -ieuse [ɑ̃bisjø, øz]. **1.** *a.* ambitious. **2.** *s.* ambitious person; *adv.* **-ieusement**.

ambition [ɑ̃bisjɔ̃], *s.f.* ambition (**de,** of, for).

ambitionner [ɑ̃bisjɔne], *v.tr.* to be ambitious of; to covet (sth.).

amble [ɑ̃:bl], *s.m. Equit:* amble; ambling pace.

ambre [ɑ̃:br], *s.m.* **1. a. gris,** ambergris. **2. a. jaune,** yellow amber.

ambré [ɑ̃bre], *a.* **1.** perfumed with amber(gris). **2.** warm (complexion).

ambulance [ɑ̃bylɑ̃:s], *s.f.* ambulance.

ambulancier, -ière [ɑ̃bylɑ̃sje, -jɛːr], *s.* (*a*) *Mil:* hospital orderly; *f.* nurse; (*b*) stretcher-bearer; ambulance man.

ambulant [ɑ̃bylɑ̃], *a.* itinerant, peripatetic; **marchand a.,** pedlar, hawker.

âme [ɑ:m] *s.f.* **1.** soul; (*a*) **rendre l'â.,** to give up the ghost; (*b*) (departed) soul, spirit; (*c*) heart, feeling. **2.** (*a*) bore (of gun); (*b*) sound-post (of violin).

amélior|er [ameljɔre], *v.tr.* to ameliorate, to improve; *a.* **-ant**; *s.f.* **-ation**.

s'améliorer, to get better; to improve.

amen [amɛn], *int. & s.m.inv.* amen.

aménag|er [amenaʒe], *v.tr.* (**n. aménageons**) to fit up; *s.m.* **-ement**, (office, etc.) fittings.

amende [amɑ̃:d], *s.f.* **1. être condamné à une a.,** to be fined; *Games:* **être mis à l'a.,** to have to pay a forfeit. **2. faire a honorable,** to apologize.

amend|er [amɑ̃de], *v.tr.* (*a*) to improve (soil); (*b*) *Pol:* to amend (bill); *a.* **-able**; *s.m.* **-ement**.

s'amender, to improve.

amener [amne], *v.tr.* (**j'amène**). **1.** to bring; to lead; **amenez votre ami,** bring your friend along; **a. qn à faire qch.,** to get, induce, s.o. to do sth. **2. a. une mode,** to bring in a fashion. **3.** *Nau:* to strike (colours); to lower (sail).

aménité [amenite], *s.f.* **1.** amenity, charm (of manners); grace (of style). **2.** *pl.* compliments.

am|er¹, -ère [amɛːr]. **1.** *a.* (*a*) bitter; (*b*) **ironie amère,** bitter irony. **2.** *s.m.* bitter(s); *adv.* **-èrement**.

amer², *s.m. Nau:* sea-mark, landmark.

américain, -aine [amerikɛ̃, -kɛn], *a. & s.* **1.** American; *F:* Yank(ee). **2.** *s.m.* **l'a.,** American English.

américan|iser [amerikanize], *v.tr.* to Americanize; *s.m.* **-isme**; *s.f.* **-isation**.

s'américaniser, to become Americanized.

Amérique (**l'**) [amerik]. *Pr.n.f.* America.

amer|rir [ameriːr], *v.i. Av:* to land (on the sea), to splash down; *s.m.* **-rissage**.

amertume [amɛrtym], *s.f.* bitterness.

améthyste [ametist], *s.f.* amethyst.

ameublement [amœbləmɑ̃], *s.m.* **1.** furnishing (of house). **2.** furniture; **tissu d'a.,** furnishing fabric.

ameublir [amœbliːr], *v.tr.* to loosen, break up (soil).

ameuter [amøte], *v.tr.* to collect (riotous crowd) to stir up (a mob).

s'ameuter, to gather into a mob.

ami [ami]. **1.** *s.* friend; **sans amis,** friendless; **mon a.,** (i) my dear fellow; (ii) my good man; (iii) my dear; **mon amie,** my dear, my love; *adv.phr.* **en ami(e),** in a friendly manner. **2.** *a.* friendly (**de,** to).

amiable [amjabl], *a. Jur:* friendly, amicable; **arrangement à l'a.,** amicable arrangement; **vente à l'a.,** private sale.

amiante [amjɑ̃:t], *s.m. Miner:* asbestos; **carton d'a.,** asbestos-board.

amibe [amib], *s.f.* amœba.

amical, -aux [amikal, -o], *a.* friendly; *adv.* **-ement**.

amidon [amidɔ̃], *s.m.* starch.

amidonner [amidɔne], *v.tr.* to starch.

aminc|ir [amɛ̃siːr], *v.tr.* to make thinner; to slim; **taille amincie,** slender figure; *a.* **-issant**, slimming; *s.m.* **-issement**.

s'amincir, to grow thinner, more slender.

amiral, pl. -aux [amiral, -o], *s.m.* **1.** admiral. **2.** (**navire**) **a.,** flagship.

amirauté [amirote], *s.f.* **l'A.,** the Admiralty.

amitié [amitje], *s.f.* **1.** friendship, friendliness affection; **prendre qn en a.,** to take to s.o.; **se lier d'a. avec qn,** to strike up a friendship with s.o.; **par a.,** out of friendliness. **2.** (*a*) kindness favour; (*b*) *pl.* **avec les sincères amitiés de,** with kind regards from.

ammoniaque [amɔnjak], *s.f. Ch:* ammonia.

amnés|ie [amnezi], *s.f. Med:* amnesia; *a. & s.*
-**ique,** amnesic (patient).
amnistie [amnisti], *s.f.* amnesty; general
pardon.
amnistier [amnistje], *v.tr.* to amnesty, pardon.
amocher [amɔʃe], *v.tr. F:* to damage (sth.); *P:* to
beat (s.o.) up.
s'amocher, *P:* to grow slack, to deteriorate.
amoindr|ir [amwɛ̃dri:r] **1.** *v.tr.* to reduce,
diminish, belittle; **a. un mal,** to mitigate an evil.
2. *v.i. & pr.* to diminish, to grow less; *s.m.*
-**issement,** reduction.
amoll|ir [amɔli:r], *v.tr.* **1.** to soften. **2.** to weaken,
enervate; *s.m.* -**issement.**
s'amollir. 1. to become soft. **2.** to grow weak,
effeminate.
amonc|eler [amɔ̃sle], *v.tr.* (**j'amoncelle**) to pile
up, heap up, bank up; *s.m.* -**ellement,** heap.
s'amonceler, to pile up; (*of snow*) to drift.
amont [amɔ̃], *s.m.* upper waters (of river); **en a.,**
upstream; **en a. du pont,** above the bridge.
amorce [amɔrs], *s.f.* **1.** beginning; *Civ.E:* **a. d'un
tunnel,** beginning (of the cutting) of a tunnel. **2.**
(*a*) *Exp:* detonator; (*b*) *Sm.a:* percussion cap;
(*c*) priming (of pump). **3.** bait; **se laisser prendre à l'a.,** to swallow the bait.
amor|cer [amɔrse], *v.tr.* (**n. amorçons**). **1.** to
begin (building, negotiations, etc.). **2.** (*a*) to
prime (pump); to start (dynamo); (*b*) to bait
(trap); to decoy, entice (animal); *s.m.* -**çage.**
amorphe [amɔrf], *a.* (*a*) amorphous; (*b*) flabby.
amort|ir [amɔrti:r], *v.tr.* **1.** to deaden (pain,
sound); to damp (ardour); to break (fall). **2.** to
slake (lime). **3.** to redeem, pay off (debt); to
allow for depreciation of (house, car, etc.); *a.*
-**issable;** *s.m.* -**issement.**
s'amortir, to become deadened; *Ph:* to damp
down.
amortisseur [amɔrtisœ:r], *s.m.* **1.** damping
device. **2.** *Av: Aut:* shock-absorber.
amour [amu:r], *s.m.* (*occ.f. in poetry, often f. in
pl. in 1 & 2*). **1.** love, affection, passion; **les
premières amours,** first love; *F:* calf love;
mariage d'a., love match; **pour l'a. de qn,** for
the sake of, for love of, s.o.; **faire l'a.,** to make
love. **2. mon a.,** my love, my sweetheart. **3.
quel a. d'enfant!** what a darling child! **quel a.
de bijou!** what a lovely jewel! **tu es un a.!**
you're an angel!
amoureu|x, -euse [amurø, -ø:z]. **1.** *a.* loving
(look); **être a. de qn,** to be in love with s.o. **2.** *s.*
lover, sweetheart; *adv.* -**sement.**
amour-propre [amurprɔpr], *s.m.* (*a*) self-
respect; pride; (*b*) self-esteem, vanity.
amov|ible [amɔvibl], *a.* **1.** (*of official*)
removable. **2.** (*of parts of machine*)
detachable, interchangeable; *s.f.* -**ibilité.**
ampère [ɑ̃pɛ:r], *s.m. El:* ampere.
ampèremètre [ɑ̃pɛrmɛtr], *s.m. El:* ammeter.

amphibie [ɑ̃fibi]. **1.** *a.* amphibious; *Mil: etc:*
opération a., combined operation. **2.** *s.m.* Z:
amphibian.
amphithéâtre [ɑ̃fitea:tr], *s.m.* amphitheatre.
amphore [ɑ̃fɔ:r], *s.f.* **1.** *Archeol:* amphora. **2.**
jar.
ample [ɑ̃:pl], *a.* **1.** ample; full (dress). **2.** roomy,
spacious. **3.** full (account); *adv.* -**ment.**
ampleur [ɑ̃plœ:r], *s.f.* fullness (of garment);
copiousness (of meal); volume (of voice).
amplificateur, -trice [ɑ̃plifikatœ:r, -tris]. **1.** (*a*)
a. magnifying; (*b*) *s.* magnifier (of trifles). **2.**
s.m. (*a*) *Phot:* enlarger; (*b*) *Rad:* amplifier.
amplifi|er [ɑ̃plifje], *v.tr.* **1.** to amplify; to expand
(thought). **2.** to magnify; *s.f.* -**cation.**
ampoule [ɑ̃pul], *s.f.* **1.** (electric) bulb. **2.** blister.
3. *Med:* ampoule.
amput|er [ɑ̃pyte], *v.tr.* to amputate (limb); *s.f.*
-**ation.**
amusant [amyzɑ̃], *a.* amusing, funny.
amuse-gueule [amy:zɡœl], *s.m. F:* cocktail
snack; *pl. amuse-gueules.*
amus|er [amyze], *v.tr.* to amuse, entertain; *s.m.*
-**ement.**
s'amuser, to amuse, enjoy, oneself; **bien s'a.,** to
have a good time.
amygdal|e [ami(g)dal], *s.f.* tonsil; *s.f.* -**ite,**
tonsillitis.
an [ɑ̃], *s.m.* year; **tous les ans,** every year; **avoir
dix ans,** to be ten years old; **en l'an 1200,** in the
year 1200; **le jour de l'an,** New Year's day.
anachronisme [anakrɔnism], *s.m.*
anachronism.
anagramme [anagram], *s.f.* anagram.
analo|gie [analɔʒi], *s.f.* analogy; *a.* -**gue,**
similar.
analphabète [analfabɛt], *a. & s.* illiterate.
analyse [anali:z], *s.f.* analysis. **1.** (*a*) **a. gram-
maticale,** parsing; (*b*) *Ch:* **a. quantitative,**
quantitative analysis. **2.** abstract, précis.
analys|er [analize], *v.tr.* to analyse; **a. une
phrase,** (i) to parse, (ii) to analyse, a sentence;
a. -**able.**
analytique [analitik], *a.* analytical; *adv.* -**ment.**
ananas [anana(:s)], *s.m.* pineapple.
anarch|ie [anarʃi], *s.f.* anarchy; *a.* -**ique;** *a. & s.*
-**iste.**
anathématiser [anatematize], *v.tr.* to curse
(s.o.).
anathème [anatɛm], *s.m.* anathema; ban, curse.
anatife [anatif], *s.m. Crust:* barnacle.
anatom|ie [anatɔmi], *s.f.* anatomy; *a.* -**ique;**
s.m. -**iste.**
ancestral, -aux [ɑ̃sɛstral, -o], *a.* ancestral.
ancêtre [ɑ̃sɛ:tr], *s.m. & f.* ancestor, ancestress.
anchois [ɑ̃ʃwa], *s.m.* anchovy; **beurre d'a.,**
anchovy paste.
ancien, -ienne [ɑ̃sjɛ̃, -jɛn], *a.* **1.** ancient, old;
amitié ancienne, friendship of long standing. **2.**

ancient, old(en), early; **l'A. Testament,** the Old Testament; *s.m.pl.* **les anciens,** the ancients. **3.** former, old; ex-; **a. élève,** old boy (of a school); **anciens combattants,** ex-servicemen. **4.** senior (officer); **les (élèves) anciens,** the senior boys; **il est votre a.,** he is senior to you; *adv.* -**nement.**

ancienneté [ɑ̃sjɛnte], *s.f.* **1.** antiquity (of monument). **2.** seniority; length of service.

ancr│e [ɑ̃:kr], *s.f.* anchor; **jeter, mouiller, l'a.,** to anchor; *s.m.* -**age,** anchorage.

ancrer (s') [sɑ̃kre], *v.pr.* to establish oneself, to get a firm footing.

Andorre [ɑ̃dɔ:r]. *Pr.n.* (Republic of) Andorra.

andouille [ɑ̃du:j], *s.f. Cu:* chitterlings.

andouiller [ɑ̃duje], *s.m. Ven:* tine (of antler).

André [ɑ̃dre]. *Pr.n.m.* Andrew.

âne [ɑ:n], *s.m.* **1.** ass; donkey; (*a*) **faire une promenade à dos d'â.,** to go for a donkey ride; (*b*) **en dos d'â.,** ridged, razor-backed; **pont en dos d'â.,** hump-backed bridge. **2.** fool, ass, dunce; **bonnet d'â.,** dunce's cap. **3.** *Ich:* **tête d'â.,** bullhead, miller's thumb. **4.** *Tchn:* bench-vice.

anéant│ir [aneɑ̃ti:r], *v.tr.* to destroy; **je suis anéanti,** I'm exhausted, *F:* dead-beat; *s.m.* -**issement,** destruction.

s'anéantir. 1. to melt into thin air. **2.** to humble oneself.

anecdote [anɛgdɔt], *s.f.* anecdote.

aném│ie [anemi], *s.f. Med:* anaemia; *a.* -**ique.**

anémier (s') [sanemje], *v.pr.* to become anaemic.

anémone [anemɔn], *s.f.* **1.** anemone, wind-flower. **2.** *Coel:* **a. de mer,** sea-anemone.

ânerie [ɑnri], *s.f.* foolish act or remark.

ânesse [ɑnɛs], *s.f.* she-ass.

anesthés│ie [anɛstezi], *s.f. Med:* anaesthesia; *a. & s.m.* -**ique,** anaesthetic.

anesthés│ier [anɛstezje], *v.tr.* to anaesthetize; *s.m. & f.* -**iste.**

ange [ɑ̃:ʒ], *s.m.* **1.** angel; *F:* **être aux anges,** to walk on air. **2. a. (de mer),** angel-fish.

angélique [ɑ̃ʒelik]. **1.** *a.* angelic(al). **2.** *s.f. Bot: Cu:* angelica; *adv.* -**ment.**

angélus [ɑ̃ʒely:s], *s.m.* angelus(-bell); ave-bell.

angine [ɑ̃ʒin], *s.f. Med:* **1.** quinsy; tonsillitis. **2. a. de poitrine,** angina pectoris.

anglais, -aise [ɑ̃glɛ, -ɛ:z]. **1.** *a.* English (language); British (army); *F:* **filer à l'anglaise,** to take French leave. **2.** *s.* Englishman, -woman; Briton. **3.** *s.m.* **l'a.,** (the) English (language).

angle [ɑ̃:gl], *s.m.* **1.** angle; **a. droit,** right angle; **à angles droits,** rectangular. **2.** corner, angle (of wall).

Angleterre (l') [lɑ̃glətɛ:r]. *Pr.n.f.* England.

anglican, -ane [ɑ̃glikɑ̃, -an], *a. & s. Rel:* Anglican; **l'église anglicane,** the Church of England.

anglic│isme [ɑ̃glisism], *s.m.* anglicism; English

idiom; *s.m. & f.* -**iste,** student of, authority on, English.

anglo-normand, -ande [ɑ̃glonɔrmɑ̃, -ɑ̃:d], *a. & s.* **les îles Anglo-Normandes,** the Channel Islands.

anglophile [ɑ̃glɔfil], *a. & s.* anglophil(e), pro-English.

anglophobe [ɑ̃glɔfɔb]. **1.** *a.* anglophobic. **2.** *s.* anglophobe.

anglophone [ɑ̃glɔfɔn], *a.* English-speaking.

anglo-saxon, -onne [ɑ̃glosaksɔ̃, -ɔn]. **1.** *a. & s.* Anglo-Saxon. **2.** *a.* English-speaking.

angoissant [ɑ̃gwasɑ̃], *a.* distressing (news); tense.

angoisse [ɑ̃gwas], *s.f.* anguish; distress; agony.

angoisser [ɑ̃gwase], *v.tr.* to distress; **angoissé,** (i) anguished; (ii) anxious.

anguille [ɑ̃gi:j], *s.f. Ich:* (*a*) eel; **soupçonner a. sous roche,** *F:* to smell a rat; (*b*) **a. de mer,** conger-eel.

angulaire [ɑ̃gylɛ:r]. **1.** *a.* angular; **pierre a.,** corner-stone. **2.** *s.m. Phot:* **grand a.,** wide-angle lens.

angularité [ɑ̃gylarite], *s.f.* angularity.

anguleux, -euse [ɑ̃gylø, -ø:z], *a.* angular, bony (face); rugged (outline).

anicroche [anikrɔʃ], *s.f. F:* difficulty, hitch, snag.

aniline [anilin], *s.f. Dy:* aniline.

animal, -aux [animal, -o]. **1.** *a.* (*a*) animal (kingdom, etc.); (*b*) sensual, brutal (instinct). **2.** *s.m.* (*a*) animal; (*b*) *F:* **quel a.!** what a brute!

animé [anime], *a.* bright, lively; busy; **marché a.,** brisk market.

anim│er [anime], *v.tr.* **1.** to animate, quicken. **2.** to actuate; to move, propel. **3.** to enliven (conversation); *a. & s.* -**ateur,** *f.* -**atrice,** (*a*) *a.* animating, stimulating; (*b*) *s.* stimulating person, *F:* live wire; *T.V:* question master; *s.f.* -**ation.**

s'animer. 1. to come to life. **2.** to become animated, lively.

animosité [animɔzite], *s.f.* animosity, spite (contre, against).

anis [ani(s)], *s.m.* (*a*) *Bot:* anise; (*b*) (*,* raine d')a., aniseed.

anisette [anizɛt], *s.f.* anisette (liqueur).

ankyloser (s') [sɑ̃kiloze], *v.pr. Med:* to anchylose; to stiffen, to become, get, stiff.

annales [anal], *s.f.pl.* annals; (public) records.

annaliste [analist], *s.m.* annalist.

anneau, -eaux [ano], *s.m.* **1.** ring. **2.** (*a*) link (of chain); (*b*) coil (of serpent).

année [ane], *s.f.* year, twelvemonth; **pendant toute une a.,** for a whole year; **à l'a.,** by the year; **étudiants de première a.,** first year students; **d'a. en a.,** from year to year.

année-lumière [anelymjɛ:r], *s.f.* light-year; *pl.* *années-lumière.*

annexe [an(n)ɛks], *s.f.* **1.** annexe (to building). **2.** (*a*) rider; schedule; appendix; (*b*) enclosure (with letter). **3.** *a.* **lettre a.,** covering letter.

annexier [an(n)ɛkse], *v.tr.* **1.** to annex (territory). **2.** to append, attach, enclose; *s.f.* **-ion,** annexation.

annihiler [an(n)iile], *v.tr.* to destroy; *s.f.* **-ation.**

anniversaire [aniverse:r]. **1.** *a. & s.m.* anniversary. **2.** *s.m.* birthday.

annonce [anɔ̃:s], *s.f.* **1.** (*a*) announcement, notice; (*b*) (*at cards*) declaration; call; (*c*) sign, indication. **2.** advertisement; **petites annonces,** classified advertisements.

annoncer [anɔ̃se], *v.tr.* (**n. annonçons**). **1.** to announce, give notice of, give out; (*at cards*) **a. son jeu,** to declare. **2.** to advertise. **3.** (*a*) to promise, foretell; **cela n'annonce rien de bon,** it doesn't look promising; (*b*) to show; **visage qui annonce l'énergie,** face that reveals energy. **4.** to announce (s.o.).

s'annoncer. 1. to announce oneself. **2.** to augur (well, ill); **le temps s'annonce beau,** the weather promises to be fine.

annonceur, -euse [anɔ̃sœ:r, -ø:z], *s.* **1.** advertiser. **2.** *Rad: T.V:* announcer.

annonciateur, -trice [anɔ̃sjatœ:r, -tris], *s.* **1.** announcer; messenger. **2.** *s.m. P.T.T: etc:* indicator-board.

annonciation [anɔ̃sjasjɔ̃], *s.f.* **Fête de l'A.,** Feast of the Annunciation; Lady day.

annoter [an(n)ɔte], *v.tr.* to annotate (text); *s.* **-ateur, -atrice;** *s.f.* **-ation.**

annuaire [an(n)ɥe:r], *s.m.* **1.** annual, year-book. **2.** calendar. **3.** (yearly) list; (telephone) directory.

annuel, -elle [an(n)ɥɛl], *a.* annual, yearly; *adv.* **-lement.**

annuité [an(n)ɥite], *s.f.* **1.** annual instalment (in repayment of debt). **2.** (terminable) annuity.

annulaire [an(n)ylɛ:r]. **1.** *a.* annular, ring-shaped. **2.** *s.m.* the ring-finger.

annuller [an(n)yle], *v.tr.* to annul; to render void; to repeal (law), quash (judgment), set aside; to cancel (contract); *s.f.* **-ation;** *s.m.* **-ement.**

anoblir [anɔbli:r], *v.tr.* to ennoble; to raise (s.o.) to the peerage; *s.m.* **-issement.**

anode [anɔd], *s.f. El:* anode; positive pole.

anodin [anɔdɛ̃]. **1.** *a.* anodyne, soothing. **2.** *s.m.* palliative; pain-killer.

anomalie [anɔmali], *s.f.* anomaly.

ânon [anɔ̃], *s.m.* ass's foal, ass's colt.

ânonner [anɔne], *v.tr.* to stumble through (speech); to hum and haw; to mumble.

anonymat [anɔnima], *s.m.* anonymity.

anonyme [anɔnim]. **1.** *a.* (*a*) anonymous (letter); (*b*) *Com:* **société a.,** limited(-liability) company. **2.** *s.m.* anonymity; *adv.* **-ment.**

anorak [anɔrak], *s.m.* anorak, windcheater.

anormal, -aux [anɔrmal, -o], *a.* abnormal, irregular; *a. & s.* (**enfant**) **a.,** mentally deficient child; *adv.* **-ement.**

anse [ã:s], *s.f.* **1.** handle (of basket). **2.** *Geog:* bight, bay.

antagonisme [ãtagɔnism], *s.m.* antagonism.

antagoniste [ãtagɔnist]. **1.** *a.* antagonistic, opposed. **2.** *s.* antagonist, opponent.

antarctique [ãtar(k)tik]. **1.** *a.* Antarctic. **2.** *Pr.n.m. Geog:* **l'A.,** Antarctica, the Antarctic.

antécédent [ãtesedã]. **1.** *a.* antecedent, previous. **2.** *s.m.* (*a*) *Gram:* antecedent; (*b*) *pl.* previous history; antecedents.

antédiluvien, -ienne [ãtedilyvjɛ̃, -jɛn], *a.* antediluvian.

antenne [ãtɛn], *s.f. Rad: T.V: etc:* aerial (wire); **a. (de) radar,** radar scanner. **2.** antenna, feeler (of insect).

antérieur [ãterjœ:r], *a.* **1.** (*a*) anterior (**à,** to); former (period); earlier (date); prior (engagement). **2.** fore-(limb); front-(wall); *adv.* **-ement,** previously.

antériorité [ãterjɔrite], *s.f.* priority.

anthologie [ãtɔlɔʒi], *s.f.* anthology.

anthracite [ãtrasit], *s.m.* anthracite.

anthropoïde [ãtrɔpɔid], *a. & s.m.* anthropoid.

anthropologie [ãtrɔpɔlɔʒi], *s.f.* anthropology; *s.m.* **-ogiste, -ogue,** anthropologist.

anti-aérien, -ienne [ãtiaerjɛ̃, -jɛn], *a.* anti-aircraft (gun, etc.).

antialcoolique [ãtialkɔlik]. **1.** *a.* anti-alcohol; teetotal. **2.** *s.* teetotaller; *s.m.* **-isme.**

anti-atomique [ãtiatɔmik], *a.* antinuclear.

antibiotique [ãtibjɔtik], *a. & s.m.* antibiotic.

antibrouillard [ãtibruja:r], *a. & s.m. Aut:* (**phare**) **a.,** fog-lamp.

antibuée [ãtibɥe], *a. & s.m.* (**dispositif**) **a.,** demister.

anticancéreux, -euse [ãtikãserø, -ø:z], *a.* **centre a.,** cancer hospital.

antichambre [ãtiʃã:mbr], *s.f.* anteroom; waiting-room; **pilier d'a.,** hanger-on.

antichoc [ãtiʃɔk], *a. inv.* shock-proof.

anticiper [ãtisipe]. **1.** *v.tr.* to anticipate (sth.); to forestall (s.o.). **2.** *v.i.* **a. sur les événements,** to anticipate events; *a.* **-atif, -ative,** anticipatory, *s.f.* **-ation.**

anticlérical, -aux [ãtiklerikal, -o], *a.* anti-clerical.

anticoagulant [ãtikɔagylã], *a. & s.m.* anticoagulant.

antidater [ãtidate], *v.tr.* to antedate.

antidérapant [ãtiderapã], *a. Aut: etc:* non-skid(ding) (tyre, etc.).

antidétonant [ãtidetɔnã], *a. & s.m. Aut: etc:* anti-knock (petrol).

antidote [ãtidɔt], *s.m.* **a. d'un poison, contre un poison,** antidote for, against, a poison.

antigel [ãtiʒɛl], *a. & s.m. inv.* anti-freeze.

antigivrage [ãtiʒivra:ʒ], *s.m.* anti-icing.

antigrippal [ãtigripal], *a.* anti-flu.

antihygiénique [ãtiiʒjenik], *a.* unhygienic, insanitary.

antillais, -aise [ãtijɛ, -ɛ:z], *a. & s.* West Indian.

Antilles [ãti:j]. *Pr.n.f.pl.* **les A.**, the West Indies; **la mer des A.**, the Caribbean.

antilope [ãtilɔp], *s.f. Z:* antelope.

antimite(s) [ãtimit], *(a) a.* moth-proof; *(b) a.* moth-destroying; *s.m.* moth-killer.

antimoine [ãtimwan], *s.m. Ch:* antimony.

antiparasite [ãtiparazit], *s.m. El:* suppressor.

antipath|ie [ãtipati], *s.f.* **a. pour qn,** antipathy to s.o.; aversion to s.o.; *a.* **-ique,** antipathetic.

antipodes [ãtipɔd], *s.m.pl.* **les a.**, the antipodes.

antiquaire [ãtikɛ:r], *s.m.* antiquary, antiquarian; antique dealer.

antique [ãtik], **1.** *a. (a)* ancient; pertaining to the ancients; *(b)* antique (furniture). **2.** *s.f.* antique (work of art).

antiquité [ãtikite], *s.f.* **1.** antiquity (of race, etc.). **2.** ancient times. **3.** *pl.* antiques; **magasin d'antiquités,** antique shop.

antirouille [ãtiru:j], *s.m.* rust preventive.

antisept|iser [ãtisɛptize], *v.tr. Med:* to antisepticize; *a. & s.m.* **-ique.**

antisportif, -ive [ãtispɔrtif, -i:v], *a.* unsporting, unsportsmanlike.

antitank [ãtitã:k], *a. Mil:* anti-tank.

antithèse [ãtitɛ:z], *s.f.* antithesis.

antitox|ine [ãtitɔksin], *s.f. Med:* antitoxin; *a. & s.m.* **-ique.**

antituberculeux, -euse [ãtityberkylø, -ø:z], *a.* antitubercular; **centre a.,** tuberculosis centre.

antivol [ãtivɔl]. **1.** *a. inv.* theft-proof. **2.** *s.m.* anti-theft device.

Antoine [ãtwan]. *Pr.n.m.* Ant(h)ony.

antre [ã:tr], *s.m.* cave; den, lair.

Anvers [ãvɛ:r, ãvɛrs]. *Pr.n.m. Geog:* Antwerp.

anxiété [ãksjete], *s.f.* anxiety, concern.

anxieu|x, -euse [ãksjø, -ø:z], *a.* anxious, uneasy; *adv.* **-sement.**

aorte [aɔrt], *s.f. Anat:* aorta.

août [u, ut], *s.m.* August; **au mois d'a., en a.,** in (the month of) August; **le premier, le sept, a.,** (on) the first, the seventh, of August.

apais|er [apɛze], *v.tr.* **1. a. qn,** to appease, pacify, calm, s.o. **2.** to allay; to quell; *s.m.* **-ement.**

s'apaiser, to calm down.

apanage [apana:ʒ], *s.m.* attribute, prerogative (de, of).

aparté [aparte], *s.m. Th:* aside: stage-whisper.

apathie [apati], *s.f.* apathy; listlessness.

apathique [apatik], *a.* apathetic; listless; *adv.* **-ment.**

apatri|de [apatrid], *s.m. & f. Jur:* stateless person; *s.f.* **-die,** statelessness.

aperce|voir [apɛrsǝvwa:r], *v.tr. (conj. like* RECEVOIR) to perceive, see; to catch sight of (s.o., sth.); **je n'ai fait que l'a.,** I only caught a glimpse of him; *a.* **-vable.**

s'apercevoir de qch., to perceive, notice, sth.; to become aware of sth.; **sans s'en a.,** without noticing it.

aperçu [apɛrsy], *s.m.* **1.** glimpse. **2.** outline, sketch, summary; **par a.,** at a rough guess.

apéritif [aperitif], *s.m.* drink, aperitif.

à-peu-près [apøprɛ], *s.m.inv.* approximation; imprecise statement; vague answer.

à-pic [apik], *s.m.* cliff, bluff, steep (place); *pl. à-pics.*

apicult|ure [apikylty:r], *s.f.* bee-keeping; *s.m.* **-eur,** bee-keeper.

apitoyer [apitwaje], *v.tr.* **(j'apitoie)** to move (to pity); to incite to pity.

s'apitoyer sur le sort de qn, to commiserate with s.o.

aplan|ir [aplani:r], *v.tr.* **1.** to flatten (surface); to plane (wood); to smooth away (difficulties). **2.** to level (road); *s.m.* **-issement;** *s.m.* **-isseur.**

s'aplanir. 1. to grow smoother; *(of difficulties)* to disappear. **2.** to become level.

aplati [aplati], *a. (a)* flattened; *(b)* deflated.

aplat|ir [aplati:r], *v.tr.* to flatten; to hammer down (rivet); *F:* **a. qn,** to flatten s.o. (by rebuff); *s.m.* **-issement.**

s'aplatir. 1. to become flat; to collapse; *(of tyre)* to go flat. **2. s'a. devant qn,** to grovel before s.o.

aplomb [aplɔ̃], *s.m.* **1.** perpendicularity; uprightness; balance *(of pers.);* **d'a.,** upright; vertical(ly); plumb; **voilà qui vous remettra d'a.,** that will set you up. **2.** (self-)assurance; **perdre son a.,** to lose one's self-possession.

apogée [apɔʒe], *s.m. (a) Astr:* apogee; height, zenith (of one's glory); *(b) Mth:* peak (of a curve).

apolo|gie [apɔlɔʒi], *s.f.* defence, vindication. (NOTE: *never* = EXCUSE, *q.v.*) *s.m.* **-giste.**

apoplectique [apɔplɛktik], *a. & s. Med:* apoplectic.

apoplexie [apɔplɛksi], *s.f. Med:* apoplexy.

apostat, -ate [apɔsta, -at], *a. & s.* apostate; turncoat.

apostolique [apɔstɔlik], *a.* apostolic.

apostrophe [apɔstrɔf], *s.f.* apostrophe.

apothéose [apɔteo:z], *s.f.* **1.** apotheosis; deification. **2.** *Th:* grand finale.

apôtre [apo:tr], *s.m.* apostle.

apparaître [aparɛ:tr], *v.i. (conj. like* CONNAÎTRE; *aux. usu.* être, *occ.* avoir). **1.** to appear; to become visible; to come into sight. **2.** to become evident.

apparat [apara], *s.m.* state, pomp, display.

appareil [aparɛ:j], *s.m.* **1.** display, pomp. **2.** *(a)* apparatus, outfit; **a. de pêche,** fishing-tackle;

l'a. **digestif,** the digestive system; (b) device, appliance; mechanism; a. **à gaz,** gas-appliance; (c) machine, instrument; *P.T.T:* F: **être à l'a.,** to be on the phone; **qui est à l'a.?** who's speaking? *Phot:* a. **(photographique),** camera.

appareill|er[1] [apareje], v.tr. 1. to install, fit up (workshop). 2. *Nau:* (a) a. **une voile,** to trim a sail; (b) abs. to get under way; s.m. **-age**[1].

appareill|er[2], v.tr. to match (gloves, colours); s.m. **-age**[2]; s.m. **-ement.**

apparence [aparã:s], s.f. 1. (a) appearance; look; **selon toute a.,** to all appearances; (b) **(fausse) a.,** false, fallacious, appearance; **en a.,** outwardly; on the surface. 2. **avoir de l'a.,** to look well; **sauver les apparences,** to keep up appearances.

appar|ent [aparã], a. 1. (a) visible, conspicuous, apparent; **peu a.,** inconspicuous; (b) obvious, evident. 2. apparent, not real; adv. **-emment.**

apparenté [aparãte], a. related, akin (**à, avec,** to); **bien a.,** well connected.

appari|er [aparje], v.tr. to match (socks); to pair off (opponents); s.m. **-ement.**

apparition [aparisjõ], s.f. 1. appearance; coming out; publication (of book). 2. apparition, ghost.

appartement [apartəmã], s.m. flat, *N.Am:* apartment.

appartenir [apartəni:r], v.i. (conj. like TENIR). 1. to belong (**à, to**). 2. v. impers. **il lui appartient de . . .,** it falls to him to. . . .

s'appartenir, to be one's own master.

appât [apɑ], s.m. (a) bait; (b) lure (of success); attraction (of pleasure).

appauvr|ir [apovri:r], v.tr. to impoverish; s.m. **-issement.**

s'appauvrir, to grow poor(er).

appel [apɛl], s.m. 1. appeal; (a) **faire a. à qn,** to appeal to s.o.; (b) *Jur:* appeal at law. 2. call; (vocal) summons; **cri d'a.,** call for help; a. **d'incendie,** fire-alarm; *P.T.T:* a. **du téléphone,** the phone bell; a. **téléphonique,** phone call; a. **avec préavis,** personal call. 3. roll-call, call-over; **faire l'a.,** to call (over) the roll; **répondre à l'a.,** to answer (to) one's name.

appelant, -ante [aplã, -ã:t], *Jur:* (a) a. appealing (party); (b) s. a. **d'un jugement,** appellant against a judgment.

appeler [aple], v.tr. (**j'appelle**). 1. (a) to call, call to (s.o.); (b) a. **qn de la main,** to beckon (to) s.o.; (c) *P.T.T:* a. **qn,** to phone s.o., to ring s.o. up; a. **à l'automatique,** to dial (s.o.). 2. (a) to call in, send for, summon; **faire a. un médecin,** to call in a doctor; *Mil:* a. **une classe,** to call up a class; **les appelés,** servicemen; *Jur:* a. **qn en justice,** to summons s.o., to sue s.o.; (b) **être appelé à qch.,** to be destined for sth. 3. to call (by name); to name; **on l'appelle Jean,** he's

called John. 4. (a) to appeal to, call on (s.o., sth.); (b) to call for; **ce problème appelle une solution immédiate,** the problem calls for an immediate solution. 5. (a) to provoke, arouse; (b) **corps appelé par une force,** body attracted by a force. 6. v.i. (a) *Jur:* a. **d'un jugement,** to appeal against a sentence; (b) **en a. à qn,** to appeal to s.o.

s'appeler, to be called, named; **comment vous appelez-vous?** what is your name?

appellation [apɛllasjõ], s.f. (a) name, (abusive) term; (b) trade name; (c) *Vit:* **bourgogne d'a.,** vintage burgundy; a. **contrôlée,** guaranteed vintage.

appendice [apɛ̃dis], s.m. 1. appendix (of book). 2. annexe (of building). 3. *Anat:* appendix.

appendicite [apɛ̃disit], s.f. appendicitis.

appentis [apãti], s.m. (a) penthouse; **toit en a.,** lean-to roof; (b) outhouse.

appesant|ir [apəzãti:r], v.tr. 1. to make (sth.) heavy; to weigh down. 2. to dull (the mind); s.m. **-issement.**

s'appesantir. 1. to become heavy. 2. **s'a. sur un sujet,** to dwell on a subject.

appétissant [apetisã], a. tempting, appetizing.

appétit [apeti], s.m. 1. appetite; **avoir bon a.,** to have a hearty appetite. 2. desire, craving; a. **du gain,** lust for gold.

applaud|ir [aplodi:r]. 1. v.tr. (a) to applaud, clap; F: **se faire a. à rout casser,** to bring the house down; (b) to applaud, commend. 2. v.ind.tr. a. **à qch.,** to approve sth.; s.m. (usu. pl.) **-issement(s),** applause.

s'applaudir de qch., to congratulate oneself on sth.

applic|able [aplikabl], a. applicable; **mot a.,** appropriate word.

application [aplikasjõ], s.f. application. 1. (a) a. **d'un bandage à une blessure,** applying of a bandage to a wound; (b) a. **de peinture,** coat of paint. 2. diligence (in work).

applique [aplik], s.f. (a) (wall-)bracket (for lamps); (b) bracket-lamp.

appliqué [aplike], a. 1. studious, hard-working (person). 2. **sciences appliquées,** applied sciences.

appliquer [aplike], v.tr. 1. to apply (sth.) (**sur, à,** on, to (sth.)). 2. a. **la loi,** to enforce the law.

s'appliquer. 1. **s'a. à qch.,** to apply oneself to sth.; to work hard at sth. 2. **à qui s'applique cette remarque?** to whom does this remark apply?

appointements [apwɛ̃tmã], s.m.pl. salary.

appontement [apõtmã], s.m. 1. gangplank. 2. (wooden) wharf; landing-stage.

appont|er [apõte], v.i. *Av:* to land (on deck of aircraft-carrier); s.m. **-age.**

apport [apɔ:r], s.m. contribution (of capital, etc.); *Com:* initial share (in undertaking).

apport|er [apɔrte], v.tr. to bring. **1. a. des nouvelles,** to bring news (à, to). **2. a. du soin à faire qch.,** to exercise care in doing sth. **3.** to bring in, supply; s. **-eur, -euse.**

apposer [apoze], v.tr. to affix, place, put.

appréciable [apresjabl], a. appreciable.

appréciateur, -trice [apresjatœːr, -tris]. **1.** a. appreciative. **2.** s. appreciator **(de, of).**

appréciation [apresjasjɔ̃], s.f. **1.** valuation, estimate, appraising. **2.** appreciation (of work of art, etc.); **une affaire d'a.,** a matter of opinion, of taste. **3.** rise in value.

apprécier [apresje], v.tr. **1.** (a) to appraise; to value (sth.); (b) to determine, estimate (distance). **2.** to appreciate (good thing).

appréhender [apreɑ̃de], v.tr. **1. a. qn (au corps),** to arrest s.o. **2.** to dread, fear (sth.).

appréhensif, -ive [apreɑ̃sif, -iːv], a. apprehensive **(de, of);** fearful, timid.

appréhension [apreɑ̃sjɔ̃], s.f. **1.** understanding. **2.** dread **(de, of).**

apprendre [aprɑ̃ːdr], v.tr. (conj. like PRENDRE). **1.** (a) to learn (lesson); **a. à faire qch.,** to learn (how) to do sth.; (b) to learn, hear of, F: get to know of (sth.). **2. a. qch. à qn,** (a) to teach s.o. sth.; (b) to tell s.o. sth.

apprent|i, -ie [aprɑ̃ti], s. (a) apprentice; (b) Jur: etc: articled clerk; (c) F: novice, tyro; s.m. **-issage,** apprenticeship; articles.

apprêté [aprɛte], a. affected, stiff (style, manner).

apprêt|er [aprɛte], v.tr. **1.** to prepare; to make ready. **2.** to dress, finish (fabrics, etc.); s.m. **-age;** s. Ind: **-eur, -euse,** finisher.

s'apprêter. 1. to prepare oneself, get ready. **2.** (of trouble) to be brewing.

apprivoisé [aprivwaze], a. tame.

apprivois|er [aprivwaze], v.tr. to tame (animal); to win (s.o.) over; a. **-able;** s.m. **-ement;** s. **-eur, -euse,** tamer.

s'apprivoiser, to become tame.

approbateur, -trice [aprɔbatœːr, -tris]. **1.** a. approving (gesture). **2.** s. approver.

approbat|if, -ive [aprɔbatif, -iːv], a. approving (gesture); adv. **-ivement.**

approbation [aprɔbasjɔ̃], s.f. approval, approbation.

approchant [aprɔʃɑ̃], a. approximating, similar **(de, to); couleur approchante du bleu,** colour approximating to blue.

approche [aprɔʃ], s.f. **1.** approach, drawing near; **à son a.,** as he came up; **d'une a. difficile,** difficult of access. **2.** pl. **approaches,** approaches (of a town).

approch|er [aprɔʃe]. **1.** v.tr. (a) **a. qch. de qch.,** to bring, draw, sth. near (to) sth.; **approchez votre chaise,** draw up your chair; (b) to approach, come near; to come close to. **2.** v.i. (a) to approach, draw near; (b) **a. de qn,** to ap-

proach s.o.; **nous approchons de Paris,** we are getting near Paris; (c) **a. de qch.,** to resemble sth.; to approximate to sth.; a. **-able.**

s'approcher, to come near; to approach; **s'a. de qch.,** to come up to sth.

approfondi [aprɔfɔ̃di], a. careful (study); **connaissance approfondie du français,** thorough command of French.

approfond|ir [aprɔfɔ̃diːr], v.tr. **1.** to deepen, excavate (river-bed). **2.** to go thoroughly into (sth.); s.m. **-issement.**

s'approfondir, to grow deeper; to deepen.

approprié [aprɔprie], a. appropriate, adapted **(à, to);** suitable (reply).

appropri|er [aprɔprie], v.tr. to make appropriate; to adapt (sth.) to fit (sth.); s.f. **-ation.**

s'approprier, to appropriate (sth.).

approuver [apruve], v.tr. **1. a. qch.,** to approve of, be pleased with, sth.; **a. de la tête,** to nod approval. **2.** to agree to, sanction (expenditure); **a. un contrat,** to ratify a contract; **lu et approuvé,** read and approved.

approvisionné [aprɔvizjɔne], a. stocked **(de, with); bien a.,** well stocked.

approvisionn|er [aprɔvizjɔne], v.tr. to supply **(de,** with); to furnish with supplies; to provision; s.m. **-ement,** stock; stocking.

s'approvisionner, to take in, lay in, a supply **(en, de,** of); to lay in stores.

approximat|if, -ive [aprɔksimatif, -iːv], a. approximate; rough (estimate); adv. **-ivement.**

approximation [aprɔksimasjɔ̃], s.f. approximation.

appui [apɥi], s.m. **1.** (a) prop, stay; (b) rest; Arch: balustrade; **a. de fenêtre,** window-ledge; **a. d'escalier,** banisters. **2.** support; (a) **mur d'a.,** supporting wall; **barre d'a.,** hand-rail; **à hauteur d'a.,** breast-high; (b) **a. moral,** moral support; **être sans a.,** to be friendless. **3. a. de la voix sur une syllabe,** stress on a syllable.

appui(e)-tête [apɥitɛːt], s.m. head-rest; pl. **appuis-tête, appuie-tête.**

appuyer [apɥije], v.tr. **(j'appuie). 1.** to support; (a) to prop (up); (b) **a. une pétition,** to support a petition. **2.** (a) **a. qch. contre qch.,** to lean sth. against sth.; **a. son opinion sur qch.,** to base one's opinion on sth.; (b) Mus: **a. (sur) une note,** to dwell on, sustain, a note. **3.** abs. **a. sur le bouton,** to press the button; **a. sur une syllabe,** to stress a syllable; **a. à droite,** to bear (to the) right.

s'appuyer sur, contre, à, qch., to lean, rest, on, against, sth.

âpre [ɑːpr], a. **1.** rough, harsh. **2.** biting, sharp (rebuke); **temps â.,** raw weather. **3.** keen (competition); **â. au gain,** grasping (man); adv. **-ment.**

après [aprɛ]. **I.** prep. **1.** (order in time, space) (a) after; **jour a. jour,** day after day; (b) **je viens a**

lui, I come next to him. 2. **courir a. qn**, to run after s.o.; **il est toujours a. moi**, he is always nagging at me. 3. *prep.phr.* **d'a.**, according to; after; from; **paysage d'a.** Turner, landscape after Turner. 4. **a. avoir dîné, il sortit**, after dining he went out.
II. après, *adv.* 1. (*a*) afterwards, later; **le jour (d')a.**, the next day; the day after; **et a.?** what then? (*b*) *conj.phr.* **a. que**, after, when. 2. *F:* **tout le monde leur court a.**, everybody runs after them.

après-demain [apredmɛ̃], *adv.* the day after tomorrow.

après-guerre [apregɛːr], *s.m.* post-war period; *pl.* **après-guerres**.

après-midi [apremidi], *s.m. inv.* afternoon.

après-ski [apreski], *s.m. inv.* **des a.-s.**, snow-boots; **tenue d'a.-s.**, après-ski outfit.

à-propos [apropo], *s.m.* 1. aptness, suitability (of an expression). 2. opportuneness; **manque d'à-p.**, untimeliness.

apte [apt], *a.* 1. **a. à qch.**, fitted, qualified, for sth. 2. apt, suitable (example).

aptitude [aptityd], *s.f.* aptitude, fitness (**à, pour**, for); **il a des aptitudes**, he is naturally gifted.

aquaplane [akwaplan], *s.m. Sp:* surf-board; aquaplane.

aquarelle [akwarɛl], *s.f.* water-colour.

aquarium [akwarjɔm], *s.m.* aquarium.

aquatique [akwatik], *a.* aquatic (bird, sport).

aqueduc [ak(ə)dyk], *s.m.* aqueduct.

aquilin [akilɛ̃], *a.* aquiline; **nez a.**, Roman nose.

arabe [arab]. 1. (*a*) *a. & s.* Arab (person, horse); (*b*) *a.* Arabian (customs). 2. (*a*) *a.* Arabic (language, numerals); (*b*) *s.m.* Arabic.

arabesque [arabɛsk], *s.f.* arabesque.

Arabie (**l'**) [larabi]. *Pr.n.f. Geog:* Arabia; **l'A. Séoudite**, Saudi Arabia.

arable [arabl], *a.* arable, tillable (land).

arachide [araʃid], *s.f. Bot:* peanut, groundnut; **huile d'a.**, peanut oil; *Fr.C:* **beurre d'a.**, peanut butter.

araignée [arɛɲe], *s.f.* spider; **toile d'a.**, cobweb, spider's web; *F:* **avoir une a. au plafond**, to have a bee in one's bonnet.

aratoire [aratwaːr], *a.* agricultural.

arbitraire [arbitrɛːr], *a.* 1. arbitrary; discretionary. 2. arbitrary, despotic; high-handed (government, action); *adv.* -**ment**.

arbitre [arbiːtr], *s.m.* (*a*) *Jur:* arbitrator, referee; (*b*) *Games:* referee, umpire; (*c*) arbiter.

arbitrer [arbitre], *v.tr.* (*a*) *Jur:* to arbitrate; (*b*) *Games:* to referee, umpire (match); *s.m.* -**age**, arbitration.

arborer [arbɔre], *v.tr.* to hoist (flag); **a. une cravate rouge**, to sport a red tie.

arbre [arbr], *s.m.* 1. (*a*) tree; **a. fruitier**, fruit-tree; **a. vert**, evergreen (tree); (*b*) **a. généalogique**, genealogical tree; (*c*) **a. de Noël**, Christmas-

tree. 2. *E:* shaft, axle.

arbrisseau [arbriso], *s.m.* shrubby tree.

arbuste [arbyst], *s.m.* bush; shrub.

arc [ark], *s.m.* 1. bow; **tir à l'a.**, archery. 2. arch. 3. *Mth:* El: arc.

arcade [arkad], *s.f.* (*a*) archway; (*b*) *pl.* **arcades**, arcade.

arc-boutant [arkbutã], *s.m.* 1. flying-buttress. 2. strut, stay, spur; *pl.* **arcs-boutants**.

arc-bouter [arkbute], *v.tr.* to buttress, shore up. **s'arc-bouter**, to brace oneself (to resist a shock).

arceau [arso], *s.m.* 1. arch (of vault). 2. ring bow (of padlock); (croquet) hoop.

arc-en-ciel [arkãsjɛl], *s.m.* rainbow; *pl.* **arcs-en-ciel** [arkãsjɛl].

archaïsme [arkaism], *s.m.* archaism; *a.* -**ique**, archaic.

archange [arkãːʒ], *s.m.* archangel.

arche[1] [arʃ], *s.f.* **l'a. de Noé**, Noah's ark.

arche[2], *s.f.* arch (of bridge); (croquet) hoop.

archéologie [arkeɔlɔʒi], *s.f.* archaeology; *a.* -**logique**, archaeological; *s.m.* -**logue**, archaeologist.

archer [arʃe], *s.m.* archer, bowman.

archet [arʃɛ], *s.m.* bow; **a. de violon**, violin bow.

archevêque [arʃəvek], *s.m.* archbishop; *s.m.* -**vêché**, archbishopric.

archi- [arʃi], *pref.* (*intensive*) **archifou**, stark mad; **archiplein, archibondé**, packed tight, crammed.

archiduc [arʃidyk], *s.m.* archduke; *s.f.* -**duchesse**, archduchess.

archipel [arʃipɛl], *s.m. Geog:* archipelago.

architecte [arʃitɛkt], *s.m.* architect; **a. urbaniste**, town-planner.

architecture [arʃitektyːr], *s.f.* architecture.

archives [arʃiːv], *s.f.pl.* archives; records.

archiviste [arʃivist], *s.m. & f.* 1. archivist; keeper of public records. 2. filing clerk.

arçon [arsɔ̃], *s.m. Equit:* saddle-bow; **vider les arçons**, to be thrown.

arctique [arktik]. **I.** *a.* arctic. **II.** *Pr.n.m.* **l'A.**, the Arctic.

ardent [ardã], *a.* burning, scorching; blazing (fire); **charbons ardents**, live coals. 2. ardent, passionate, eager; *adv.* -**emment**.

ardeur [ardœːr], *s.f.* 1. heat. 2. eagerness.

ardoise [ardwaːz], *s.f.* slate; *s.m.* -**ier**, slate quarry owner, worker; *s.f.* -**ière**, slate quarry.

ardu [ardy], *a.* 1. steep, difficult (path). 2. arduous, difficult (task).

are [aːr], *s.m.* 100 square metres.

arène [arɛn], *s.f.* arena; *esp.* bullring; **descendre dans l'a.**, to enter the lists; **les arènes d'Arles**, the amphitheatre of Arles.

aréole [areɔl], *s.f. Anat: Bot:* areola.

arête [arɛt], *s.f.* 1. (fish-)bone; **grande a.**, backbone (of fish). 2. line; edge; **a. vive**, sharp edge; *Geog:* arête, (serrated) ridge; **a. d'un comble,** hip of a roof; **a. du nez,** bridge of the nose.

argent [arʒɑ̃], *s.m.* **1.** silver; **vaisselle d'a.,** (silver-)plate; *Geog:* **Côte d'A.,** the Gascony coast. **2.** money, cash; **a. liquide,** ready money, cash (in hand); **gagner de l'a.,** to make money; *F:* **avoir un a. fou,** to be rolling in money; **en avoir pour son a.,** to have one's money's worth; **avoir toujours de l'a. à la main,** to be always paying out.

argenté [arʒɑ̃te], *a.* **1.** silver-plated. **2.** *F:* **se trouver bien a.,** to be very flush (of money).

argent|er [arʒɑ̃te], *v.tr.* to silver; *s.f.* **-erie,** (silver-)plate; *a.* **-in, -ine,** silvery (colour, tone); *Pr.n.f. Geog:* **l'Argentine,** Argentina.

argil|e [arʒil], *s.f.* (*a*) clay; (*b*) **a. cuite,** terracotta, earthenware; *a.* **-eux, -euse,** clayey (soil).

argot [argo], *s.m.* slang.

arguer [argɥe], *v.* (**j'arguë**). **1.** *v.tr.* to infer, assert, deduce. **2.** *v.i.* to argue.

argument [argymɑ̃], *s.m.* **1.** argument. **2.** outline, summary (of book).

argument|er [argymɑ̃te], *v.i.* (*a*) to argue (**contre,** against); (*b*) *F:* to argufy; *s.* **-ateur, -atrice;** *s.f.* **-ation.**

arid|e [arid], *a.* arid, dry, barren; *s.f.* **-ité.**

aristocrat|e [aristɔkrat], *s.m. & f.* aristocrat; *a.* **-ique.**

aristocratie [aristɔkrasi], *s.f.* aristocracy.

arithmét|ique [aritmetik]. **1.** *a.* arithmetical. **2.** *s.f.* arithmetic; *s.* **-icien, -icienne,** arithmetician.

Arlequin [arləkɛ̃], *s.m.* Harlequin.

armateur [armatœːr], *s.m. Nau:* (*a*) fitter-out (of ship); (*b*) (ship)owner.

armature [armatyːr], *s.f.* **1.** framework (of window); (*concrete-work*) reinforcements; truss (of girder); **a. d'une raquette,** frame of a racquet. **2.** *El:* armature. **3.** *Mus:* key-signature.

arme [arm], *s.f.* **1.** arm, weapon; **armes à feu,** fire-arms; **armes portatives,** small-arms; **armes blanches,** side-arms; **faire des armes,** to fence; **salle d'armes,** (i) armoury; (ii) fencing-school; **maître d'armes,** fencing-master; **faire ses premières armes,** to go through one's first campaign; **place d'armes,** parade-ground; **passer (qn) par les armes,** to (court-martial and) shoot (s.o.). **2.** arm (as a branch of the army). **3.** *pl. Her:* arms.

armée [arme], *s.f.* army; **a. de l'air,** Air Force; **a. navale,** naval forces.

armement [arməmɑ̃], *s.m.* **1.** (*a*) arming; war preparations; (*b*) *pl.* armaments. **2.** fortifying, strengthening. **3.** *Nau:* commissioning, fitting out; **port d'a.,** port of registry. **4.** loading (of gun); setting (of camera). **5.** fittings, moun-

tings, gear.

armer [arme]. **I.** *v.tr.* **1.** to arm (**de,** with). **2.** to fortify, strengthen; **béton armé,** reinforced concrete. **3.** *Nau:* to equip, commission (ship). **4.** (*a*) **a. un canon,** to load a gun; (*b*) to set (camera); (*c*) to cock (fire-arm). **II. armer,** *v.i.* to arm, prepare for war.

armistice [armistis], *s.m.* armistice.

armoire [armwaːr], *s.f.* **1.** wardrobe. **2.** cupboard.

armoiries [armwari], *s.f.pl. Her:* (coat of) arms; armorial bearings.

armorier [armɔrje], *v.tr.* to (em)blazon; to adorn (sth.) with a coat-of-arms.

armur|e [armyːr], *s.f.* armour; *s.f.* **-erie,** arms factory; *s.m.* **-ier,** gunsmith, armourer.

arnica [arnika], *s.f. Bot: Pharm:* arnica.

aromate [arɔmat], *s.m.* aromatic; spice.

aromatique [arɔmatik], *a.* aromatic; *adv.* **-ment.**

arôme [aroːm], *s.m.* **1.** aroma. **2.** *Cu:* flavouring.

aronde [arɔ̃ːd], *s.f. Carp:* **queue d'a.,** dovetail.

arpège [arpɛːʒ], *s.m. Mus:* arpeggio; spread chord.

arpent|er [arpɑ̃te], *v.tr.* **1.** to survey, measure (land). **2.** **a. le terrain,** to stride over the ground; **a. le quai,** to pace up and down the platform; *s.m.* **-age,** (land-)surveying; *s.m.* **-eur,** (land-)surveyor.

arqué [arke], *a.* arched, curved; cambered; high-bridged (nose).

arquer [arke]. **1.** *v.tr.* to bend, curve (wood); **a. le dos,** to hump the back; (*of cat*) to arch its back. **2.** *v.i.* to bend.

s'arquer, (*of the legs*) to become bent.

arrache-pied (d') [daraʃpje], *adv.phr.* without interruption; **travailler d'a.-p.,** to work steadily.

arracher [araʃe], *v.tr.* to tear (out); to pull (up); **a. qch. à qn,** to snatch sth. from s.o.; **se faire a. une dent,** to have a tooth out; **s'a. les cheveux,** to tear one's hair.

arrang|er [arɑ̃ʒe], *v.tr.* (n. **arrangeons**) to arrange. **1.** to set in order; to alter (a dress); **a. une chambre,** to tidy up a room. **2.** to contrive; **a. une fête,** to get up an entertainment. **3.** to settle (quarrel); *a.* **-eant, -e,** obliging; *a.* **-cable;** *s.m.* **-ement.**

s'arranger. 1. to manage, contrive; **il s'arrange de tout,** he is very adaptable; **qu'il s'arrange!** that's his look-out! **2. s'a. avec qn,** to come to an agreement with s.o.

arrérages [arera:ʒ], *s.m.pl.* arrears.

arrestation [arɛstasjɔ̃], *s.f.* arrest; **en état d'a.,** under arrest.

arrêt [arɛ], *s.m.* **1.** stop, stoppage; stopping; **cran d'a.,** safety catch; **point d'a.,** stopping place; **trajet sans a.,** non-stop journey; **dix minutes d'a.,** ten minutes' stop; *Rail:* **signal à l'a.,**

signal at danger; *P.N:* **a. fixe,** bus stop. **2.** (*a*) decree; (*b*) *Jur:* judgment; **a. de mort,** sentence of death. **3.** seizure; **mettre a. sur un navire,** to put an embargo on a ship. **4.** arrest; **mandat d'a.,** warrant (for arrest); **maison d'a.,** gaol. **5. chien d'a.,** setter, pointer.

arrêté [arɛte], *a.* fixed, decided (ideas); **dessein a.,** settled plan. **2.** *s.m.* decision, order, decree.

arrêter [arɛte]. I. *v.tr.* **1.** to stop (s.o., sth.); to check; to hinder; to detain; **a. qn tout court,** to stop s.o. short; *Aut:* **a. le moteur,** to switch off the engine. **2.** to fix, fasten (shutter); **a. l'attention,** to arrest attention. **3.** to arrest, seize; **faire a. qn,** to have s.o. arrested. **4.** (*a*) to engage, hire (a room); (*b*) to decide; **a. un jour,** to fix a day. II. **arrêter,** *v.i.* to stop, halt; **arrêtez un moment,** stop a moment.

s'arrêter. 1. to stop; to come to a stop, to a standstill; **s'a. en route,** to break one's journey. **2.** (*a*) **s'a. à un sujet,** to dwell on a subject; (*b*) **son regard s'arrêta sur moi,** he eyed me intently.

arrhes [aːr], *s.f.pl.* (*money*) deposit.

arrière [arjɛːr]. **1.** *adv.* (**en**) **a.,** (*a*) behind; **rester en a.,** to lag behind; *prep.phr.* **en a. de qch.,** behind sth.; **en a. de son siècle,** behind the times; (*b*) in arrears; (*c*) backwards; backward (motion); **a.!** back! **faire marche a.,** to back; *Aut:* to reverse; *N.Am:* to back up. **2.** *a.inv.* back; *Aut:* **feu a.,** rear light. **3.** *s.m.* (*a*) back (part) (of house); (*b*) stern (of ship). **4.** *s.m. Fb:* back.

arriéré [arjere], *a.* **1.** in arrears; overdue (payment). **2.** backward (child); (person) behind the times; **pays arriérés,** underdeveloped countries.

NOTE. *In all the following compounds* ARRIÈRE *is inv., the noun takes the plural; for phonetics consult the second component.*

arrière-boutique, *s.f.* back of the shop.

arrière-cour, *s.f.* back-yard.

arrière-cousin, -ine, *s.* distant cousin.

arrière-garde, *s.f.* **1.** *Mil:* rear-guard. **2.** *Navy:* rear-division (of squadron).

arrière-goût, *s.m.* after-taste, faint taste.

arrière-grand-mère, -grand-père, *s.* greatgrandmother, -grandfather.

arrière-grands-parents, *s.m.pl.* greatgrandparents.

arrière-pensée, *s.f.* (*a*) mental reservation; (*b*) ulterior motive.

arrière-petite-fille, -petit-fils, *s.* greatgranddaughter, -grandson.

arrière-plan, *s.m.* background; *Th:* **à l'a.-p.,** upstage, at the back.

arrière-port, *s.m.* inner harbour.

arrière-saison, *s.f.* late season, end of autumn.

arrière-scène, *s.f. Th:* back of the stage.

arrière-train, *s.m.* (hind)quarters (of animal).

arrimer [arime], *v.tr.* (*a*) to stow (cargo); (*b*) to trim (ship); *s.m.* **-age;** *s.m.* **-eur,** stower; stevedore.

arrivant [arivɑ̃], *s.m.* person arriving; arrival; **le dernier a.,** the last comer.

arrivée [arive], *s.f.* (*a*) arrival, coming, advent; **à mon a.,** on my arrival; (*b*) *Sp:* (winning-)post, finishing-post.

arriver [arive], *v.i.* (*aux.* être). **1.** (*a*) to arrive, come; **il arriva en courant,** he came running up; *F:* **j'arrive!** (I'm) coming! **la nuit arriva,** night came on; *impers.* **il arriva un soldat,** there came a soldier; (*b*) **a. à un endroit,** to reach a place; **a. à bon port,** to arrive safely; (*c*) **il faudra bien en a. là,** it must come to that. **2.** to succeed; (*a*) **il n'arrivera jamais à rien,** he will never achieve anything; (*b*) **a. à faire qch.,** to manage to do sth. **3.** to happen; **cela arrive tous les jours,** it happens every day; *impers.* **il lui est arrivé un accident,** he has met with an accident; **faire a. un accident,** to cause an accident; *s.m.* **-age,** arrival, new consignment (of goods); *s.m. & f.* **-iste,** thruster.

arrogance [arɔgɑ̃ːs], *s.f.* arrogance.

arrogant [arɔgɑ̃], *a.* arrogant, overbearing.

arroger (s') [sarɔʒe], *v.pr.* (n.n. **arrogeons**) **s'a. un droit,** to arrogate, assume, a right to oneself.

arrondi [arɔ̃di], *a.* round, rounded (chin, etc.).

arrondir [arɔ̃diːr], *v.tr.* (*a*) to round (off); to make round; (*b*) **phrase bien arrondie,** wellrounded sentence; **bouche arrondie,** mouth agape.

s'arrondir, to become round; to fill out.

arrondissement [arɔ̃dismɑ̃], *s.m.* **1.** rounding (off). **2.** *Fr. Adm:* administrative area; ward (in Paris).

arroser [aroze], *v.tr.* (*a*) to water (plants); **a. un rôti,** to baste a joint; **yeux arrosés de larmes,** eyes bathed in tears; (*b*) **a. une prairie,** to irrigate a meadow; *s.m.* **-age;** *s.m.* **-ement.**

arroseur, -euse [arozœːr, -øːz]. **1.** *s.* person who waters (plants, grass); *Adm:* watercartman. **2.** *s.f.* watering machine; **arroseuse à jet tournant,** lawn-sprinkler.

arrosoir [arozwaːr], *s.m.* watering-can.

arsenal, -aux [arsənal, -o], *s.m.* arsenal.

arsenic [arsənik], *s.m.* arsenic.

art [aːr], *s.m.* **1.** art; (*a*) **arts d'agrément,** artistic hobbies; (*b*) **beaux-arts,** fine arts; **œuvre d'a.,** work of art. **2.** skill; artistry; *Civ. E:* **travaux, ouvrages, d'a.,** constructive works.

artère [artɛːr], *s.f.* **1.** *Anat:* artery. **2.** main road; thoroughfare (in town).

artériel, -elle [arterjɛl], *a.* arterial; **tension artérielle,** blood pressure.

arthrite [artrit], *s.f. Med:* arthritis; *a. & s.* **-ique.**

artichaut [artiʃo], *s.m.* (globe) artichoke.
article [artikl], *s.m.* **1.** critical point, moment; **être à l'a. de la mort,** to be at the point of death. **2.** (*a*) article, clause (of treaty); **a. de foi,** article of faith; (*b*) **articles de dépense,** items of expenditure; (*c*) article (in newspaper). **3.** *Com:* article, commodity; *pl.* goods, wares; **articles de Paris,** fancy goods; **articles de ménage,** household goods. **4.** *Gram:* article.
article-réclame [artikləreklam], *s.m. Com:* special offer; *pl. articles-réclame.*
articulé [artikyle], *a.* (*a*) articulate(d); jointed; hinged; (*b*) articulate; distinct (utterance).
articuller [artikyle], *v.tr.* **1.** to articulate, to hinge. **2.** to articulate; to pronounce distinctly; *s.f.* **-ation.**
artifice [artifis], *s.m.* **1.** artifice; guile; contrivance. **2. feu d'a.,** fireworks (display).
artificillel, -elle [artifisjɛl], *a.* artificial. **1.** (*a*) **lumière artificielle,** artificial light; (*b*) **rire a.,** forced laugh. **2.** imitation (pearl); *adv.* **-ellement.**
artificieulx, -euse [artifisjø, -ø:z], *a.* crafty, cunning, artful; *adv.* **-sement.**
artilllerie [artijri], *s.f.* **1.** artillery. **2.** gunnery; *s.m.* **-eur.**
artisan [artizã], *s.m.* **1.** artisan, craftsman. **2.** maker, contriver; **il a été l'a. de sa fortune,** he's a self-made man.
artiste [artist]. **1.** *s.m. & f.* (*a*) artist (including musician, etc.); (*b*) *Th: Mus:* performer; (*c*) *Th:* artiste. **2.** *a.* artistic.
artistique [artistik], *a.* artistic (furniture, arrangement, etc.); *adv.* **-ment.**
aryen, -yenne [arjɛ̃, -jɛn], *a. & s. Geog: Ling:* Aryan; Indo-European.
as [ɑːs], *s.m.* **1.** ace; **as de pique,** ace of spades. **2.** *Games:* ace; star; *Aut:* **as du volant,** crack racing driver, driving ace.
ascendlant [as(s)ãdã]. **1.** *a.* ascending, upward; *Av:* **vol a.,** climbing flight. **2.** *s.m.* (*a*) ascendancy, influence; (*b*) *pl.* **ascendants,** ancestry; *s.f.* **-ance,** ancestry, lineage.
ascenseur [asãsœːr], *s.m.* lift; *N.Am:* elevator.
ascension [asãsjõ], *s.f.* ascent, ascension; rising (of sap); **faire l'a. d'une montagne,** to climb a mountain; *Ecc:* **Fête de l'A.,** Ascension Day; *s.m. & f.* **-niste,** mountaineer.
ascensionnel, -elle [asãsjɔnɛl], *a.* ascensional; upward (motion); *Av:* **force ascensionnelle,** lift.
ascète [asɛt], *s.m. & f.* ascetic.
ascétlique [asetik], *a. & s.* ascetic; *s.m.* **-isme,** asceticism.
ascorbique [askɔrbik], *a.* **acide a.,** vitamin C.
asdic [asdik], *s.m. Nau:* asdic.
aseptique [asɛptik], *a. Med:* aseptic.
asiate [azjat], *a. & s.* (*of pers.*) Asian.
asiatique [azjatik], *a. Geog:* Asiatic, Asian.

Asie (l') [lazi]. *Pr.n.f. Geog:* Asia.
asile [azil], *s.m.* shelter, home, refuge; **sans a.,** homeless; **a. des marins,** Sailors' Home; **donner a. à qn,** to shelter s.o.
aspect [aspɛ], *s.m.* **1.** sight, aspect; **au premier a.,** at first sight. **2.** aspect, appearance, look; **être d'un a. repoussant,** to be repulsive-looking; **considérer une affaire sous tous ses aspects,** to look at a thing from all points of view.
asperge [aspɛrʒ], *s.f.* asparagus.
asperger [aspɛrʒe], *v.tr.* (**n. aspergeons**) to sprinkle with water.
aspérité [asperite], *s.f.* asperity. **1.** ruggedness, roughness (of surface). **2.** harshness (of voice, etc.).
asphalte [asfalt], *s.m.* asphalt; **a. minéral,** bitumen.
asphyxlier [asfiksje], *v.tr.* to asphyxiate, suffocate; *Min:* to gas; *a.* **-iant,** suffocating, asphyxiating (gas, etc.); *s.f.* **-ie,** suffocation, asphyxiation.
aspic [aspik], *s.m. Cu:* aspic(-jelly).
aspirant, -ante [aspirã, -ã:t]. **1.** *a.* sucking; **pompe aspirante,** suction pump. **2.** *s.* (*a*) aspirant (à, to); candidate; (*b*) *Navy:* midshipman, naval cadet; *Mil:* = officer cadet; *Mil.Av:* acting pilot-officer.
aspirateur, -trice [aspiratœːr, -tris]. **1.** *a.* suction(-device). **2.** *s.m.* vacuum-cleaner.
aspirler [aspire]. **1.** *v.ind.tr.* to aspire (à, to). **2.** *v.tr.* (*a*) to inhale, breathe in; (*b*) to suck up (water); (*c*) *Ling:* to aspirate, breathe (a sound); *s.f.* **-ation.**
aspirine [aspirin], *s.f. Pharm:* aspirin.
assaglir [asaʒiːr], *v.tr.* to make wiser; to sober; *s.m.* **-issement.**
s'assagir, to become wiser.
assailllir [as(s)ajiːr], *v.tr.* (*pr.p.* **assaillant;** *pr.ind.* **j'assaille**) to assail, assault, attack; *s.m.* **-ant,** assailant.
assainlir [asɛniːr], *v.tr.* to make healthier; to purify (atmosphere); *s.m.* **-issement,** cleansing.
assaisonnler [asɛzɔne], *v.tr.* to season (food) (**de,** with); *s.m.* **-ement,** seasoning.
assassin, -ine [asasɛ̃, -in]. **1.** *s.* assassin, murderer, *f.* murderess. **2.** *a.* (*a*) murderous (horde); (*b*) provocative (smile).
assassinler [asasine], *v.tr.* **1.** to assassinate, murder. **2.** to pester (s.o.) to death (**de,** with); *s.m.* **-at,** murder, assassination.
assaut [aso], *s.m.* **1.** assault, attack, onslaught; **troupes d'a.,** storm-troops, shock troops. **2.** match, bout.
asslécher [aseʃe], *v.* (**j'assèche; j'assécherai**). **1.** *v.tr.* to dry, drain (marsh). **2.** *v.i. & pr.* to dry up; **-èchement,** draining, drainage.
assemblée [asãble], *s.f.* assembly; (*a*) **a. d**

famille, family gathering; (*b*) (public, political) meeting.
assembl|er [asɑ̃ble], *v.tr.* **1.** to assemble; to convene (committee, etc.); to collect, gather. **2.** to assemble, fit together (machine); *s.m.* **-age,** assembly; assemblage; *s.* **-eur, -euse.**
s'assembler, to assemble, meet together.
assentiment [asɑ̃timɑ̃], *s.m.* assent, consent.
asseoir [aswa:r], *v.tr.* (*pr.p.* asseyant, assoyant; *p.p.* assis; *pr.ind.* j'assieds, ils asseyent, *or* j'assois, ils assoient; *pr.sub.* j'asseye, *or* j'assoie; *p.h.* j'assis; *fu.* j'assiérai, j'asseyerai, j'assoirai). **1.** to set, seat. **2.** to lay (foundations); **a. un camp,** to pitch a camp; *Av:* **a. l'appareil,** to pancake.
s'asseoir, to sit down.
assermenté [asɛrmɑ̃te], *a.* sworn (in).
asserment|er [asɛrmɑ̃te], *v.tr.* to swear (s.o.) in; to administer the oath to (s.o.); *s.f.* **-ation,** swearing in.
asserv|ir [asɛrvi:r], *v.tr.* to enslave; *s.m.* **-issement,** bondage.
assesseur [asɛsœ:r], *s.m.* assessor (to magistrate); assistant, advisor.
assez [ase], *adv.* **1.** enough, sufficient, sufficiently; (*a*) **j'aurai a. de cent francs,** I shall have enough with a hundred francs; (*b*) **avez-vous a. d'argent?** have you enough money? **oui, j'en ai a.,** yes, I have enough; *F:* **j'en ai a.!** I've had enough of it! I'm sick of it! (*c*) **c'est a. parler,** I, you, have said enough; (*d*) **être a. près pour voir,** to be near enough to see. **2.** rather, fairly; **elle est a. jolie,** she is quite pretty. **3. est-il a. enfant!** how childish of him!
assid|u [asidy], *a.* assiduous; (*a*) industrious, hardworking, steady; **être a. à qch.,** to be persevering in sth.; (*b*) unremitting, unceasing (care, etc.); (*c*) regular (visitor); *adv.* **-ûment.**
assiduité [asidɥite], *s.f.* assiduity. **1.** (*a*) steadiness (at work); *Sch:* **prix d'a.,** attendance prize. **2.** constant care.
assiég|er [asjeʒe], *v.tr.* (**j'assiège, n. assiégeons; j'assiégerai**). **1.** (*a*) to besiege, lay siege to (a town); (*b*) **a. qn de questions,** to bombard s.o. with questions. **2.** to beset, crowd round (s.o., sth.); *a. & s.m.* **-eant,** besieging (army); besieger.
assiette [asjɛt], *s.f.* **1.** stable position (of sth.); (*a*) *F:* **ne pas être dans son a.,** to be out of sorts; (*b*) *Golf:* **a. d'une balle,** lie of a ball; (*of foundation*) **prendre son a.,** to set, to settle. **2.** support, basis. **3.** plate; **a. creuse,** soup-plate; *F:* **l'a. au beurre,** cushy job, *N.Am:* the gravy-train.
assiettée [asjete], *s.f.* plate(ful).
assign|er [asiɲe], *v.tr.* **1.** to assign; (*a*) to fix, appoint (time, etc.); (*b*) to earmark (a sum of money). **2.** *Jur:* (*a*) to summon, subpoena (witness); (*b*) to issue a writ against (s.o.); *s.f.*

-ation, writ.
assimil|er [asimile], *v.tr.* **1.** to assimilate. **2.** to liken, compare (à, to, with); *s.f.* **-ation.**
assis [asi], *a.* seated, sitting; **demeurer a.,** to remain seated.
assise [asi:z], *s.f.* **1.** laying (of foundation). **2.** (*a*) **les assises de la société,** the foundations of society; (*b*) seat (on horseback). **3.** *pl. Jur:* **Cour d'assises,** Assize Court.
assistance [asistɑ̃:s], *s.f.* **1.** presence, attendance (of magistrate). **2.** (*a*) audience, company; *Ecc:* congregation; (*b*) spectators, onlookers. **3.** assistance, help; **a. aux vieillards,** old people's welfare.
assistant, -ante [asistɑ̃, -ɑ̃:t], *s.* **1.** *usu. pl.* (*a*) bystander, onlooker, spectator; (*b*) member of the audience. **2.** (*a*) assistant (professor); (*b*) foreign assistant (in school); laboratory assistant, demonstrator.
assister [asiste]. **1.** *v.i.* **a. à qch.,** to attend sth.; to be present at sth. **2.** *v.tr.* to help, assist.
associé, -ée [asɔsje], *s.* (*a*) *Com:* partner; (*b*) associate member (of learned body).
associ|er [asɔsje], *v.tr.* to associate, unite, join; **a. des idées,** to connect ideas; *s.f.* **-ation,** association; partnership.
s'associer. 1. s'a. à qch., to share in, join in, sth. **2. s'a. à, avec, qn,** (*a*) to enter into partnership with s.o.; (*b*) to associate with s.o.
assoiffé [aswafe], *a.* **être a. de qch.,** to be thirsty, thirsting, eager, for sth.
assombr|ir [asɔ̃bri:r], *v.tr.* (*a*) to darken, obscure; (*b*) to cast a gloom over (company); *s.m.* **-issement.**
s'assombrir. (*a*) to darken; to cloud over; (*b*) to become gloomy, sad.
assomm|er [asome], *v.tr.* **1. a. un bœuf,** to fell an ox. **2.** *F:* to bore (s.o.); to pester (s.o.); *a.* **-ant,** *F:* boring.
assommeur [asomœ:r], *s.m.* slaughterman.
assommoir [asɔmwa:r], *s.m.* **1.** (*a*) pole-axe; (*b*) club, bludgeon. **2.** *F:* low pub.
assomption [asɔ̃psjɔ̃], *s.f.* **1.** assumption. **2.** *Ecc:* **l'A.,** (feast of) the Assumption.
assorti, -ie [asɔrti], *a.* **1.** matched, paired; **bien, mal, a.,** well-, ill-matched. **2.** assorted, mixed. **3. bien a.,** well stocked (shop).
assort|ir [asɔrti:r], *v.tr.* (*a*) to assort, sort, match (colours); (*b*) to stock (shop); *s.m.* **-iment,** match(ing); assortment; set.
s'assortir, to match; to harmonize.
assoupi [asupi], *a.* **1.** dozing. **2.** dormant.
assoup|ir [asupi:r], *v.tr.* (*a*) to make drowsy; (*b*) to allay, lull (pain); *a.* **-issant,** soporific; *s.m.* **-issement.**
s'assoupir. 1. to drop off to sleep; to doze off. **2.** (*of pain*) to ease off.
assoupl|ir [asupli:r], *v.tr.* to make supple; *s.m.* **-issement.**

s'assouplir, to become supple.

assourd|ir [asurdiːr], *v.tr.* **1.** to make (s.o.) deaf; to deafen. **2.** (*a*) to deaden (sound); (*b*) to soften, tone down (colour); *a.* **-issant,** deafening; *s.m.* **-issement,** muffling, deadening.

s'assourdir, (*of sound*) to grow fainter.

assouv|ir [asuviːr], *v.tr.* to appease (hunger); *s.m.* **-issement.**

s'assouvir, to gorge oneself.

assujetti, -ie [asyʒeti], *a.* subject (à, to).

assujett|ir [asyʒetiːr], *v.tr.* **1.** to subdue, subjugate (province); *a.* **ses passions,** to curb one's passions. **2.** to fix, fasten (à, to); to make (sth.) fast; *s.m.* **-issement,** subjection.

assumer [asyme], *v.tr.* to assume, take upon oneself.

assurance [asyrɑ̃ːs], *s.f.* **1.** assurance; (self-) confidence. **2.** (*a*) making sure or safe; (*b*) *Com:* insurance, assurance; **a. sur la vie,** life-insurance; **assurances sociales,** national, state, insurance.

assuré [asyre]. **1.** *a.* firm, sure (step); assured, confident (air); certain (cure); **voix mal assurée,** unsteady voice. **2.** *s.* insured person; *adv.* **-ment,** certainly.

assur|er [asyre], *v.tr.* **1.** (*a*) to make firm; to fix, secure; (*b*) **a. un résultat,** to ensure a result; **a. le service,** to ensure good service. **2. a. qn de son affection,** to assure s.o. of one's affection. **3.** *Com:* to insure; **se faire a. sur la vie,** to have one's life insured; *s.m.* **-eur,** insurer.

s'assurer. 1. s'a. sur ses pieds, to take a firm stand. **2. s'a. de qch.,** to make sure, certain, of sth.; **s'a. que** + *ind.,* to make sure, ascertain, that. . . . **3. s'a. de qch.,** to make sure of, to secure, sth. **4.** *Com:* to take out an insurance (**contre,** against).

astérisque [asterisk], *s.m.* asterisk.

asthmatique [asmatik], *a. & s.* asthmatic.

asthme [asm], *s.m.* asthma.

asticot [astiko], *s.m.* maggot; *Fish:* gentle.

astiqu|er [astike], *v.tr.* to polish, furbish (belt, brass, etc.); *s.m.* **-age.**

astral, -aux [astral, -o], *a.* astral (body).

astre [astr], *s.m.* heavenly body; star.

astreindre [astrɛ̃ːdr], *v.tr.* (*conj. like* PEINDRE) to compel, oblige; to tie down (**à un devoir,** to a duty).

astringent [astrɛ̃ʒɑ̃], *a. & s.m.* astringent.

astro|logie [astrɔlɔʒi], *s.f.* astrology; *a.* **-logique;** *adv.* **-logiquement;** *s.m.* **-logue,** astrologer.

astronaut|e [astronoːt], *s.m.* astronaut; *s.f.* **-ique,** space-travel.

astronef [astronɛf], *s.m.* space-ship.

astro|nome [astronɔm], *s.m.* astronomer; *s.f.* **-nomie,** astronomy; *a.* **-nomique,**

astronomical; *adv.* **-nomiquement.**

astuce [astys], *s.f.* **1.** astuteness; artfulness. **2.** wile. **3.** witticism, joke. **4.** *F:* gadget.

astucieu|x, -euse [astysjø, -øːz], *a.* astute, artful, wily, crafty; *adv.* **-sement.**

asymétrique [asimetrik], *a.* asymmetrical.

atelier [atəlje], *s.m.* **1.** (*a*) (work)shop, workroom; (*b*) studio (of artist). **2.** staff (of shop, workroom).

athé|e [ate]. **1.** *a.* atheistic. **2.** *s.* atheist; *s.m.* **-isme.**

athénée [atene], *s.m.* **1.** athenaeum. **2.** (*in Switzerland and Belgium*) public secondary school.

Athènes [atɛn]. *Pr.n.f. Geog:* Athens.

ath|lète [atlɛt], *s.m. & f.* athlete; *a.* **-létique,** athletic; *adv.* **-létiquement;** *s.m.* **-létisme,** athletics.

atlantique [atlɑ̃tik], *a.* **l'océan A.,** *s.m.* **l'A.,** the Atlantic (Ocean).

atlas [atlɑːs]. *Pr.n.m. Geog:* **l'A.,** Atlas (mountains). **2.** *s.m.* atlas, book of maps.

atmos|phère [atmosfɛːr], *s.f.* atmosphere; *a.* **-phérique.**

atoll [atɔl], *s.m. Geog:* atoll; coral island.

atome [atoːm], *s.m. Ph:* atom.

atomique [atɔmik], *a.* atomic; **pile a.,** atomic pile; **bombe a.,** atomic bomb, atom bomb; **sous-marin a.,** nuclear submarine.

atomis|er [atɔmize], *v.tr.* to atomize, to spray (liquid); *s.m.* **-eur,** (scent, etc.) spray.

atout [atu], *s.m. Cards:* trump.

âtre [ɑːtr], *s.m.* fireplace, hearth(-stone).

atroce [atrɔs], *a.* atrocious, heinous (crime); **douleur a.,** agonizing pain; *adv.* **-ment.**

atrocité [atrɔsite], *s.f.* **1.** atrociousness. **2.** atrocity.

atrophier [atrɔfje], *v.tr.* to atrophy.

s'atrophier, to atrophy; to waste (away).

attabler (s') [satable], *v.pr.* to sit down to table.

attachant [ataʃɑ̃], *a.* **1.** interesting (book), arresting (spectacle). **2.** engaging (personality).

attache [ataʃ], *s.f.* **1.** fastening; tying up; *Nau:* **port d'a.,** home port. **2.** tie, fastener, fastening; (*a*) head-rope (of horse); leash (of dog); (*b*) paper-fastener, clip.

attaché [ataʃe]. **1.** *a.* (*a*) fastened, tied up; (*b*) **être a. à qn,** to be attached, devoted, to s.o.; (*c*) **il est a. à mes pas,** he dogs my footsteps. **2.** *s.m.* **a. militaire,** military attaché.

attache-lettre [ataʃlɛtr], *s.f.* paper-clip; *pl.* **attache-lettres.**

attach|er [ataʃe]. **1.** *v.tr.* to attach; (*a*) to fasten, bind; to tie (up); (*b*) **spectacle qui attache l'attention,** spectacle that rivets the attention. **2.** *v.i. Cu:* (*of rice, etc.*) *F:* to catch, stick; *s.m.* **-ement,** affection.

s'attacher. 1. to attach oneself, to cling, stick;

s'a. aux pas de qn, to dog s.o.'s footsteps.
2. s'a. à une tâche, to apply oneself to a task.

attaque [atak], *s.f.* 1. (*a*) attack, onslaught; *Mil:* a. aérienne, air-raid; (*b*) *Med:* a. de goutte, attack of gout. 2. *Mec:* a. directe, direct drive (of motor).

attaquer [atake], *v.tr.* 1. to attack, assail. 2. to begin, *F:* to tackle (piece of work). 3. (*of piece of mechanism*) to drive, operate (another piece).
s'**attaquer** à qn, to attack s.o.; s'a. à une difficulté, to grapple with a difficulty.

attardé [atarde], *a.* 1. belated (traveller); late; behindhand. 2. behind the times. 3. *s.m.* mentally retarded (child).

attarder [atarde], *v.tr.* to keep, make, (s.o.) late, to delay (s.o.).
s'**attarder**, to linger, dally, loiter; to stay late.

atteindre [atɛ̃:dr], *v.* (*conj. like* PEINDRE). 1. *v.tr.* to reach; to overtake; to attain; (*a*) a. la ville, to reach the town; a. son but, to attain one's end; (*b*) a. le but, to hit the target; le poumon est atteint, the lung is affected. 2. *v.ind.tr.* a. à qch., to reach, attain (to) sth.

atteinte [atɛ̃:t], *s.f.* 1. reach; hors d'a., out of reach. 2. blow, hit; porter a. aux intérêts de qn, to injure s.o.'s interests.

attelage [atla:ʒ], *s.m.* 1. (*a*) harnessing; (*b*) way of harnessing; a. à quatre, four-in-hand. 2. team; yoke (of oxen). 3. *Rail:* coupling.

atteler [atle], *v.tr.* (j'attelle). 1. to harness (horses); to yoke (oxen). 2. a. une voiture, to put horses to a carriage. 3. *Rail:* a. des wagons, to couple (up) waggons.
s'**atteler à une tâche**, to settle down to a task.

attelle [atɛl], *s.f. Surg:* splint.

attenant [atnɑ̃], *a.* contiguous (à, to); adjoining.

attendre [atɑ̃:dr], *v.tr.* 1. to wait for, to await; faire a. qn, to keep s.o. waiting; se faire a., to be late; attendez donc! wait a bit! en attendant, meanwhile, in the meantime; *conj.phr.* en attendant que + *sub.*, till, until. 2. to expect.
s'**attendre à qch.**, to expect sth.; je m'y attendais, I thought as much.

attendri [atɑ̃dri], *a.* fond, compassionate (look); full of pity.

attendrir [atɑ̃dri:r], *v.tr.* 1. to make (meat) tender. 2. to soften (s.o.'s heart); *a.* -issant, moving, affecting; *s.m.* -issement, pity.
s'**attendrir**, to be moved (to pity).

attendu [atɑ̃dy]. 1. *prep.* considering (the circumstances); owing to (the events). 2. *conj. phr.* a. que + *ind.*, considering that . . ., seeing that. . . .

attentat [atɑ̃ta], *s.m.* (criminal) attempt; outrage.

attente [atɑ̃:t], *s.f.* 1. wait(ing); salle d'a., waiting-room. 2. expectation(s), anticipation;

contre toute a., contrary to all expectations; dans l'a. de votre réponse, awaiting your reply.

attenter [atɑ̃te], *v.ind.tr.* to make an attempt (à, on).

attent|if, -ive [atɑ̃tif, -i:v], *a.* attentive (à, to); heedful (à, of); careful; *adv.* -ivement.

attention [atɑ̃sjɔ̃], *s.f. adv.* attention, care; (*a*) a. suivie, close attention; attirer l'a., to catch the eye; faites a.! take care! a.! look out! (*b*) être plein d'attentions pour qn, to show s.o. much attention.

attentionné [atɑ̃sjɔne], *a.* attentive; être a. pour qn, to be considerate towards s.o.

atténu|er [atenɥe], *v.tr.* 1. (*a*) to attenuate, lessen; to subdue (light); to mitigate (punishment); a. une chute, to break a fall; (*b*) *Phot:* to reduce (negative). 2. to extenuate (offence); *a. Jur:* -ant, extenuating (circumstance); *s.f.* -ation.
s'**atténuer**, to lessen; to diminish.

atterré [atere], *a.* (utterly) crushed, stunned (by news).

atterr|er [atere], *v.tr.* to overwhelm, astound; to strike with consternation; *a.* -ant, crushing, staggering (news); *s.m.* -ement, stupefaction, consternation.

atterr|ir [ateri:r], *v.i.* (*a*) *Nau:* to make a landfall; (*b*) (*of boat*) to ground; (*c*) *Av:* to land; *s.m.* -issage.

attest|er [ateste], *v.tr.* 1. a. qch., to attest sth.; to testify to sth. 2. a. qn (de qch.), to call s.o. to witness (to sth.); *s.f.* -ation.

attiéd|ir [atjedi:r], *v.tr.* to make tepid, lukewarm; *s.m.* -issement, cooling (off).
s'**attiédir**, to grow lukewarm, to cool (off).

attif|er (s') [satife], *v.pr. usu. Pej:* to dress, *F:* get, oneself up; *s.m.* -age; *s.m.* -ement.

attirail [atira:j], *s.m.* apparatus, gear; outfit.

attir|er [atire], *v.tr.* 1. (*a*) (*of magnet*) to attract, draw; (*b*) a. qch. à, sur, qn, to bring sth. on s.o.; s'a. un blâme, to incur a reprimand. 2. a. qn dans un piège, to lure s.o. into a trap; *a.* -ant, attractive.

attisée [atize], *s.f. Fr.C:* (bright) fire.

attiser [atize], *v.tr.* to stir (up), poke (fire).

attitré [atitre], *a.* regular, appointed (agent).

attitude [atityd], *s.f.* 1. attitude, posture; être toujours en a., to be always posing. 2. behaviour.

attraction [atraksjɔ̃], *s.f.* 1. (*a*) attraction (of magnet); (*b*) attractiveness (of person). 2. *pl. Th:* music-hall show.

attrait [atrɛ], *s.m.* attraction, lure; allurement.

attrape [atrap], *s.f.* (*a*) trap, snare (for birds); (*b*) *F:* trick, catch, hoax.

attrape-nigaud [atrapnigo], *s.m. F:* boobytrap; *pl. attrape-nigauds.*

attraper [atrape], *v.tr.* to catch. 1. (*a*) to trap, (en)snare; (*b*) a. qn, to trick, cheat, s.o.;

attrapé! sold again! **2.** (*a*) to seize (ball, thief); **attrape!** take that! (*b*) **une pierre l'a attrapé au front,** a stone hit him on the forehead; (*c*) **a. un rhume,** to catch (a) cold.

attrayant [atrɛjɑ̃], *a.* attractive, engaging, alluring; **peu a.,** unattractive.

attribu|er [atribɥe], *v.tr.* **1.** to assign, allot (à, to). **2.** to attribute, ascribe (fact); to impute (crime). **3. s'a. qch.,** to lay claim to sth.; *a.* **-able,** attributable.

attribut [atriby], *s.m.* **1.** attribute. **2.** *Gram:* predicate; complement.

attributif, -ive [atribytif, -i:v], *a.* predicative.

attribution [atribysjɔ̃], *s.f.* **1.** assigning, attribution; allocation. **2.** *usu. pl.* (*a*) prerogative; powers; (*b*) sphere of duties; functions. **3.** *Gram:* **complément d'a.,** predicative complement.

attrister [atriste], *v.tr.* (*a*) to sadden, grieve; (*b*) to give a gloomy appearance to (sth.).

s'attrister, to grow sad.

attroup|er [atrupe], *v.tr.* to gather (mob) together; *s.m.* **-ement,** (unlawful) assembly; mob.

s'attrouper, to gather into a mob.

au [o] = **à le;** *see* À *and* LE.

aubaine [obɛn], *s.f.* windfall, godsend; *Fr.C: F:* bargain.

aube¹ [o:b], *s.f.* **1.** dawn. **2.** *Ecc:* alb.

aube², *s.f.* paddle, blade (of wheel, of turbine); vane (of fan).

aubépine [obepin], *s.f.* hawthorn, may(tree).

auberg|e [obɛrʒ], *s.f.* inn; *s.m. & f.* **-iste,** innkeeper.

aubergine [obɛrʒin], *s.f.* **1.** *Bot:* aubergine, eggplant. **2.** *F:* traffic warden.

aucun, -une [okœ̃, -yn]. **1.** *pron.* (*a*) anyone, any; (*b*) (*with negation expressed or understood*) (i) no one, nobody; (ii) none, not any; **je n'ai a. soupçon,** I haven't the slightest suspicion; (*c*) *pl. Lit:* some, some people. **2.** *a.* (*a*) any; (*b*) (*with negation expressed or understood*) **le fait n'a aucune importance,** the fact is of no importance.

aucunement [okynmɑ̃], *adv.* **1.** (*with implied negation*) in any way, at all; **le connaissez-vous a.?** do you know him at all? **2.** (*with negation expressed or understood*) in no way, in no wise; not at all; **je ne le connais a.,** I don't know him at all.

audace [odas], *s.f.* audacity, audaciousness. **1.** boldness, daring; **n'ayez pas l'a. de le toucher!** don't you dare touch him! **2.** impudence; **vous avez l'a. de me dire cela!** you have the face to tell me that!

audacieu|x, -euse [odasjø, -ø:z], *a.* audacious. **1.** bold, daring. **2.** impudent; brazen (lie); *adv.* **-sement.**

au-dessous [odsu], *adv.* **1.** (*a*) below (it); underneath; **les locataires a.-d.,** the tenants below; (*b*) **les enfants âgés de sept ans et a.-d.,** children of seven years and under. **2.** *prep. phr.* **a.-d. de,** (*a*) below, under; **a.-d. du genou,** below the knee; **il est a.-d. de lui de se plaindre,** it is beneath him to complain; (*b*) **épouser qn a.-d. de soi,** to marry beneath one; (*c*) **a.-d. de cinq ans,** under five (years of age).

au-dessus [odsy], *adv.* **1.** (*a*) above (it); (*b*) **mille francs et a.-d.,** a thousand francs and upwards. **2.** *prep. phr.* **a.-d. de;** (*a*) above; **il est a.-d. de cela,** he is above doing such a thing; (*b*) **a.-d. de cinq ans,** over five (years of age); (*c*) **a.-d. de tout éloge,** beyond all praise.

au-devant [odvɑ̃], *adv. used only in such phrases as:* **aller, courir, a.-d. 1. quand il y a un problème, je vais a.-d.,** when there's a problem, I anticipate it. **2.** *prep. phr.* **aller a.-d. de qn,** to go to meet s.o.; **aller a.-d. des désirs de qn,** to anticipate s.o.'s wishes.

aud|ible [odibl], *a.* audible; *s.f.* **-ibilité.**

audience [odjɑ̃:s], *s.f.* (*a*) hearing; (*of King*) **tenir une a.,** to hold an audience; (*b*) *Jur:* hearing (by the court); sitting, court; **lever l'a.,** to close the session.

audio-visuel, -elle [odjovizɥɛl], *a.* audio-visual.

audit [odi], *see* LEDIT.

auditeur, -trice [oditœ:r, -tris], *s.* hearer, listener; *Rad: T.V:* **les auditeurs,** the audience; **programme des auditeurs,** request programme.

audition [odisjɔ̃], *s.f.* **1.** hearing (of sounds); audition. **2.** (*a*) audition, trial hearing (of singer); (*b*) *Jur:* **a. des témoins,** hearing of the witnesses.

auditionner [odisjone], *v.tr.* to audition (singer); *v.i.* to have an audition.

auditoire [oditwa:r], *s.m.* **1.** auditorium. **2.** audience; *Ecc:* congregation.

auge [o:ʒ], *s.f.* feeding-trough.

augment|er [ɔgmɑ̃te]. **1.** *v.tr.* to increase, augment; **édition augmentée,** enlarged edition; **a. qn,** to raise s.o.'s salary or rent. **2.** *v.i.* to increase; **la rivière a augmenté,** the river has risen; **les prix augmentent,** prices are going up; *s.f.* **-ation.**

augure [ogy:r], *s.m.* augury, omen; **oiseau de mauvais a.,** bird of ill omen.

augurer [ogyre], *v.tr.* to augur, forecast.

auguste [ogyst], *a.* august, majestic.

aujourd'hui [oʒurdɥi], *adv.* today; **cela ne se pratique plus a.,** this is not done nowadays; **d'a. en huit, en quinze,** today week, fortnight; **il y a a. huit jours,** a week ago today.

aumône [omo:n], *s.f.* alms.

aumônier [omonje], *s.m.* chaplain.

aune [o:n], *s.f. Bot:* alder.

auparavant [oparavɑ̃], *adv.* before(hand), previously; **un moment a.,** a moment before.

auprès [oprɛ], *adv.* **1.** close to. **2.** *prep.phr.* **a. de,** *(a)* close to, by, beside, near; **il vit a. de ses parents,** he lives with his parents; *(b)* **être bien a. de qn,** to be in favour with s.o.; *(c)* compared with; **nous ne sommes rien a. de lui,** we are nothing beside him.

auquel [okɛl], *see* LEQUEL.

auréole [ɔreɔl], *s.f.* *(a)* aureole, halo (of saint); *(b)* halo (of moon).

auriculaire [ɔrikylɛːr]. **1.** *a.* auricular (confession, etc.); **témoin a.,** ear-witness. **2.** *s.m.* the little finger.

Aurigny [ɔriɲi]. *Pr.n.m. Geog:* Alderney.

aurore [ɔrɔːr], *s.f.* *(a)* dawn, day-break; break of day; *(b)* **a. boréale,** aurora borealis; northern lights.

auscult|er [ɔskylte]. *v.tr. Med:* to examine, sound (patient); *s.f.* **-ation.**

auspices [ɔspis], *s.m.pl.* omen, presage; **faire qch. sous les a. de qn,** to do sth. under s.o.'s patronage.

aussi [osi]. **1.** *adv.* *(a)* *(in comparisons)* as; **il est a. grand que son frère,** he is as tall as his brother; *(b)* so; **après avoir attendu a. longtemps,** after waiting so long; *(c)* (i) also, too; (ii) so; **j'ai froid—moi a.,** I am cold—so am I; *(d)* *conj.phr.* **a. bien que,** as well as. **2.** *conj.* *(a)* therefore, consequently, so; *(b)* **a. bien,** moreover, for that matter, besides.

aussitôt [osito]. **1.** *adv.* *(a)* immediately, directly, at once; **a. dit, a. fait,** no sooner said than done; *(b)* *conj.phr.* **a. que** + *ind.,* as soon as. **2.** *prep.* **a. son départ, je reviens,** as soon as he is gone I shall come back.

austère [ɔstɛːr], *a.* austere (life); severe (style); *adv.* **-ment.**

austérité [ɔsterite], *s.f.* austerity.

Australie (l') [lɔstrali]. *Pr.n.f.* Australia.

australien, -ienne [ɔstraljɛ̃, -jɛn], *a. & s.* Australian.

autant [otɑ̃], *adv.* **1.** *(a)* as much, so much; as many, so many; **a. vous l'aimez, a. il vous hait,** he hates you as much as you love him; **encore a., une fois a.,** twice as much; as much again; **il se leva, j'en fis a.,** he got up and I did the same; *(b)* (i) **a. vaut; le travail est fini ou a. vaut,** the work is as good as finished; **a. vaut rester ici,** we may as well stay here; **a. vaudrait dire que . . .,** one might as well say that . . .; (ii) *(with ellipsis of valoir);* **a. dire mille francs,** we might as well say a thousand francs. **2. a. que;** *(a)* as much as, as many as; *(b)* as far as, as near as; **a. qu'il m'en souvienne,** as far as I can remember. **3. a. de,** as much, as many, so much, so many; **ils ont a. d'amis que vous,** they have as many friends as you; **c'est a. de fait,** it is so much done. **4.** *(a)* *conj.phr.* **d'a. que,** more especially as; *(b)* **d'a. plus,** (all, so much) the more; **je l'en aime d'a. plus,** I like

him (all) the better for it; *(c)* **d'autant plus, moins, . . . que,** (all) the more, the less, . . . as. **5. pour a.,** for all that.

autel [otɛl], *s.m.* altar; **maître a.,** high altar.

auteur [otœːr], *s.m.* **1.** author, perpetrator (of crime); promoter (of scheme); **a. d'un accident,** party at fault in an accident. **2.** author, writer; **droit d'a.,** copyright; **droits d'a.,** royalties.

authenti|cité [otɑ̃tisite], *s.f.* authenticity, genuineness; *a.* **-que,** authentic.

auto [ɔto, o-], *s.f.* F: (motor) car; **faire de l'a.,** to go in for motoring.

auto-allumage [otoalymaːʒ], *s.m. Aut:* pre-ignition, *F:* pinking.

autobiograph|ie [otobjɔgrafi], *s.f.* autobiography; *a.* **-ique,** autobiographic(al).

autobus [otɔbyːs], *s.m.* bus.

autocar [otokaːr], *s.m.* (motor) coach; (country) bus.

autochenille [otoʃniːj], *s.f.* *(a)* caterpillar tractor; *(b)* half-track vehicle.

autocopier [otokɔpje], *v.tr.* to duplicate (circulars, etc.).

autocrate [otokrat]. **1.** *s.m.* autocrat. **2.** *a.* autocratic.

autocratie [otokrasi], *s.f.* autocracy.

autocratique [otokratik], *a.* autocratic; *adv.* **-ment.**

autocritique [otokritik], *s.f.* self-criticism.

autocuiseur [otokɥizœːr], *s.m. Cu:* pressure-cooker.

autodébrayage [otodebrejaːʒ], *s.m. Aut:* automatic clutch.

autodétermination [otodeterminasjɔ̃], *s.f. Pol:* self-determination.

auto-école [otoekɔl], *s.f.* school of motoring, driving school; *pl.* **auto-écoles.**

autogare [otogaːr], *s.f.* coach-, bus-station.

autographe [otograf]. **1.** *a.* autograph(ic) (letter). **2.** *s.m.* autograph.

autographier [otɔgrafje], *v.tr.* to autograph.

automate [otɔmat], *s.m.* automaton.

automation [otɔmasjɔ̃], *s.f.* automation.

automatique [otɔmatik]. **1.** *a.* automatic; self-acting. **2.** *s.m.* dial telephone; *adv.* **-ment.**

automnal, -aux [otɔmnal, -o], *a.* autumnal, *N.Am:* fall.

automne [otɔn], *s.m.* autumn; *N.Am:* fall.

automobile [otɔmɔbil]. **1.** *a.* *(a)* self-propelling; **voiture a.,** motor vehicle; **canot a.,** motor boat; *(b)* **salon a.,** motor show. **2.** *s.f.* (motor) car, *N.Am:* automobile.

automobil|isme [otɔmɔbilism], *s.m.* motoring; *s.m. & f.* **-iste,** motorist.

automoteur, -trice [otɔmɔtœːr, -tris]. **1.** *a.* self-propelling (vehicle). **2.** *s.f.* **automotrice,** rail-car.

autonome [otɔnɔm], *a.* autonomous, self-governing.

autonomie [otɔnɔmi], *s.f.* autonomy. self-government.

autopropulsé [otopropylse], *a.* self-propelled.

autopsie [otɔpsi], *s.f.* autopsy; post-mortem (examination).

autorail [otɔraːj], *s.m.* rail-car.

autorisé [otɔrize], *a.* authorized, authoritative.

autoris|er [otɔrize], *v.tr.* to authorize. **1.** to invest with authority; **a. qn à faire qch.,** to authorize s.o. to do sth. **2.** to sanction; *s.f.* **-ation,** authority; permit.

autoritaire [otɔriteːr], *a.* authoritative, dictatorial; *F:* bossy; *adv.* **-ment.**

autorité [otɔrite], *s.f.* **1.** (*a*) authority; **il veut tout emporter d'a.,** he wants his own way in everything; (*b*) **faire a. en matière de faïence,** to be an authority on china; **sa parole a de l'a.,** his word carries weight. **2. les autorités,** the authorities (of a town).

autoroute [otorut], *s.f.* motorway, *N.Am:* superhighway, expressway.

auto-stop [otostɔp], *s.m.* hitch-hiking; **faire de l'a.-s.,** to hitch-hike; *s.* **-peur, -peuse,** hitch-hiker.

autour [otuːr], *adv.* **1.** round; about. **2.** *prep.phr.* **a. de,** round, about; **assis a. de la table,** seated round the table; **tourner a. du pot,** to beat about the bush.

autre [oːtr], *a. & pron.* **1.** (*a*) other, further; **d'autres vous diront que,** others will tell you that; **sans a. perte de temps,** without further loss of time; **parler de choses et d'autres,** to talk about one thing and another; **c'est une raison comme une a.,** it's a good enough reason; (*b*) **nous autres Anglais,** we English; (*c*) **cela peut arriver d'un jour à l'a.,** it may happen any day; **je le vois de temps à a.,** I see him now and then; (*d*) **l'un et l'a.,** both; **les uns et les autres,** (i) all and sundry; (ii) both parties; (*e*) **l'un ou l'a.,** either; **ni l'un ni l'a.,** neither; (*f*) **l'un dit ceci, l'a. dit cela,** one says this and the other says that; **les uns . . ., les autres . . .,** some . . ., some . . .; (*g*) **l'un l'a.,** each other, one another; **elles se moquent les unes des autres,** they make fun of each other; (*h*) **l'un dans l'a.,** on se fait trente francs, one thing with another, on an average, we earn thirty francs. **2.** (*a*) other, different; **une tout(e) a. femme,** quite a different woman; **j'ai des idées autres,** my ideas are different; **j'en ai vu bien d'autres,** that's nothing; I've been through worse than that; **il n'en fait jamais d'autres!** that's just like him! (*b*) (someone, something) else; **adressez-vous à quelqu'un d'a.,** ask someone else; **nul a., personne (d')a.,** ne l'a vu, no one else, nobody else, saw him; **(dites cela) à d'autres!** nonsense! tell that to the marines! (*c*) *indef.pron.m.* **a. chose,** something else; **c'est tout a. chose!** that's quite a different

matter!

autrefois [otrəfwa], *adv.* formerly; in the past; **livre a. si populaire,** book once so popular; **les hommes d'a.,** the men of old.

autrement [otrəmã], *adv.* otherwise. **1.** (*a*) differently; (*b*) **c'est bien a. sérieux,** that is far more serious. **2. venez demain, a. il sera trop tard,** come tomorrow, or else it will be too late.

Autriche (l') [lotriʃ]. *Pr.n.f. Geog:* Austria.

autrichien, -ienne [otriʃjɛ̃, -jɛn], *a. & s.* Austrian.

autruche [otryʃ], *s.f. Orn:* ostrich.

autrui [otrɥi], *pron.indef.* others; other people.

auvent [ovã], *s.m.* (*a*) penthouse, open shed; (*b*) porch roof.

auvergnat, -ate [ovɛrɲa, -at], *a. & s.* (native) of Auvergne, Auvergnat.

aux [o] = **à les;** *see* À *and* LE.

auxiliaire [ɔksiljɛːr]. **1.** *a.* auxiliary (verb); **bureau a.,** sub-office. **2.** *s.* auxiliary; (*a*) aid, assistant; (*b*) *s.m.pl.* auxiliaries; **auxiliaires médicaux,** (*general term for*) nursing and midwife services, masseurs, etc.

auxquels, -elles [okɛl], *see* LEQUEL.

avachi [avaʃi], *a.* slack, sloppy; flabby.

avach|ir (s') [savaʃiːr], *v.pr.* **elle s'est avachie,** she's gone to seed, she's got sloppy; *s.m.* **-issement.**

aval [aval], *s.m.* lower part (of stream); **en a.,** down-stream; **en a. du pont,** below the bridge.

avalanche [avalãːʃ], *s.f.* avalanche.

avaler [avale], *v.tr.* to swallow (down); to drink up; to devour; **c'est dur à a.,** that's a bitter pill; I can hardly stomach that.

avale-tout [avaltu], *s.m.inv.* **1.** *F:* glutton. **2.** *F:* credulous person.

avance [avãːs], *s.f.* **1.** advance, lead; **avoir de l'a. sur qn,** to be ahead of s.o.; **arriver avec cinq minutes d'a.,** to arrive five minutes before time; *F:* **la belle a.!** much good that will do you! **2.** projection; **balcon qui forme a.,** balcony that juts out. **3.** (*a*) **a. de fonds,** advance, loan; (*b*) *pl.* **faire des avances à qn,** to make advances to s.o.; to make up to s.o. **4.** *adv.phr.* (*a*) **payer qn d'a.,** to pay s.o. in advance; (*b*) **se réjouir par a.,** to rejoice beforehand; (*c*) **payable à l'a.,** payable in advance; (*d*) **l'horloge est en a.,** the clock is fast; **nous sommes en a.,** we are early.

avancé [avãse], *a.* (*a*) **position avancée,** advanced position; (*b*) **opinions avancées,** advanced ideas; (*c*) **élève a.,** forward pupil; (*d*) **à une heure avancée de la nuit,** at a late hour of the night; (*e*) **a. en âge,** well on in years; (*f*) *F:* **vous voilà bien a.!** a lot of good that has done you!

avanc|er [avãse], *v.* (*n.* **avançons**). **I.** *v.tr.* **1.** (*a*) to advance, put forward (one's hand); (*b*) **a. une**

proposition, to put forward a proposal. 2. to make (sth.) earlier; to hasten (sth.) on. 3. **a. de l'argent à qn,** to advance money to s.o. 4. to promote; **à quoi cela vous avancera-t-il?** what good will that do you?
II. **avancer,** *v.i.* 1. to advance; (*a*) to move forward; **montre qui avance d'une minute par jour,** watch that gains a minute a day; (*b*) to progress; to make headway. 2. (*a*) to be ahead of time; **l'horloge avance,** the clock is fast; (*b*) to jut out, project; *s.m.* -**ement.**
'avancer. 1. to move forward, to advance. 2. to progress. 3. to jut out.
avanie [avani], *s.f. F:* insult, snub.
avant [avɑ̃]. I. 1. *prep.* before; (**surtout et**) **a. tout,** first of all; above all. 2. (*a*) *prep.phr.* **a. de** + *inf.*; **je vous reverrai a. de partir,** I shall see you before leaving; (*b*) *conj.phr.* **a. que** + *sub*; **je vous reverrai a. que vous (ne) partiez,** I shall see you again before you leave; (*c*) **pas a. de, que,** not before, not until. 3. *adv.* **il était arrivé quelques mois a.,** he had arrived some months before. 4. *adv.* (*a*) far, deep; **pénétrer très a. dans les terres,** to penetrate far inland; (*b*) far, late; **bien a. dans la nuit,** far into the night. 5. *adv.phr.* **en a.,** in front; before; forward; *Nau:* **en a. à toute vitesse,** full steam ahead; *prep.phr.* **en a. de,** in front of, ahead of. 6. (*in adj. relation to sb.*) (*a*) fore, forward, front; **essieu a.,** front axle; (*b*) **la nuit d'a.,** the night before.
II. **avant,** *s.m.* 1. *Nau:* bow; **le logement de l'équipage est à l'a.,** the crew's quarters are forward; **aller de l'a.,** to go ahead; (*b*) front. 2. *Fb:* forward.
avantage [avɑ̃taːʒ], *s.m.* 1. advantage; **tirer a. de qch.,** to turn sth. to account; **il y a a. à + *inf.*,** it is best to + *inf.*; **avoir l'a.,** to have the best of it. 2. *Ten:* (ad)vantage.
avantager [avɑ̃taʒe], *v.tr.* (**n. avantageons**) (*a*) to favour; to give an advantage to; (*b*) **l'uniforme l'avantage,** he looks well in uniform.
avantageu|x, -euse [avɑ̃taʒø, -øːz], *a.* advantageous, favourable; **cet article est a.,** this article is good value; **prix a.,** reasonable price; *adv.* -**sement.**
NOTE. *In all the following compounds* AVANT *is inv., the noun or adj. takes the plural. For phonetics, consult the second component.*
avant-bras, *s.m.* forearm.
avant-centre, *s.m. Sp:* centre-forward.
avant-cour, *s.f.* forecourt.
avant-coureur. 1. *s.m.* forerunner. 2. *a.m.* premonitory (symptom).
avant-dernier, -ière, *a. & s.* last but one.
avant-garde, *s.f.* advanced guard; *Art: etc:* avant-garde; **théâtre d'a.-g.,** avant-garde theatre.
avant-goût, *s.m.* foretaste.
avant-guerre, *s.m.* pre-war period.

avant-hier, *adv.* the day before yesterday.
avant-plan, *s.m.* foreground.
avant-première, *s.f. Cin: etc:* preview.
avant-projet, *s.m.* preliminary plan; draft.
avant-propos, *s.m.* preface, foreword (to book); preliminary remarks.
avant-veille, *s.f.* two days before.
avar|e [avaːr]. 1. *a.* (*a*) miserly; (*b*) **être a. de paroles,** to be sparing of words. 2. *s.* miser; *s.f.* -**ice,** avarice.
avaricieu|x, -ieuse [avarisjø, -jøːz], *a.* avaricious, stingy; *adv.* -**sement.**
avarie [avari], *s.f.* damage, injury.
avarier [avarje], *v.tr.* to damage, injure, spoil (goods, etc.).
s'avarier, to deteriorate, go bad.
avec [avɛk]. 1. *prep.* (*a*) with; **et a. cela, madame?** anything else, madam? (*b*) **cabane construite a. quelques planches,** hut built out of a few boards; (*c*) **cela viendra a. le temps,** that will come in time; (*d*) **combattre a. courage,** to fight with courage; (*e*) **avec cela,** *F:* **avec ça; je suis grande et a. ça mince,** I am tall, and slender as well; (*f*) **d'a.,** from; **séparer le bon d'a. le mauvais,** to separate the good from the bad. 2. *adv.* with it, with them.
aven [avɛn], *s.m. Geol:* swallow-hole, aven.
avenant [avnɑ̃], *a.* 1. comely, pleasing, prepossessing. 2. **à l'a.,** in keeping, correspondingly; **et un chapeau à l'a,** and a hat to match.
avènement [avɛnmɑ̃], *s.m.* (*a*) advent (of Christ); (*b*) accession (to the throne).
avenir [avniːr], *s.m.* future; **jeune homme d'un grand a.,** youth of great promise; **dans l'a.,** at some future date; **à l'a.,** in (the) future, henceforth.
Avent [avɑ̃], *s.m. Ecc:* Advent.
aventure [avɑ̃tyːr], *s.f.* 1. adventure. 2. chance, luck, venture; **tenter l'a.,** to try one's luck; **à l'a.,** at random; at a venture; **par a., d'a.,** by chance, perchance. 3. **dire la bonne a. (à qn),** to tell fortunes; to tell (s.o.'s) fortune.
aventur|er [avɑ̃tyre], *v.tr.* to venture, risk (one's life); *s.* -**ier, -ière,** adventurer, *f.* -**uress.**
s'aventurer, to venture; to take risks.
aventureu|x, -euse [avɑ̃tyrø, -øːz], *a.* adventurous, venturesome; rash; reckless; *adv.* -**sement.**
avenue [avny], *s.f.* avenue; (carriage) drive.
avéré [avere], *a.* authenticated, established (fact); **ennemi a.,** avowed enemy.
avérer (s') [savere], *v.pr.* **l'entreprise s'avère improductive,** the undertaking is proving unproductive.
averse [avɛrs], *s.f.* sudden shower; downpour.
aversion [avɛrsjɔ̃], *s.f.* aversion (**envers, pour,** to, for, from); dislike (**pour,** to, for, of); **prendre qn en a.,** to take a dislike to s.o.
averti [avɛrti], *a.* experienced; wide-awake;

well-informed.

avert|ir [averti:r], *v.tr.* **a. qn de qch.**, to warn, notify, s.o. of sth.; **se tenir pour averti**, to be on one's guard; *s.m.* **-issement**, warning.

avertisseur, -euse [avertisœ:r, -ø:z]. **1.** *a.* **toux avertisseuse**, warning cough. **2.** *s.m.* alarm; *Aut:* horn; **a. d'incendie**, fire-alarm.

aveu, -eux [avø], *s.m.* avowal, confession.

aveuglant [avœglɑ̃], *a.* blinding; dazzling.

aveugl|e [avœgl], *a.* blind, sightless. **1.** (*a*) **devenir a.**, to go blind; (*b*) *s.* **un a.**, a blind man. **2.** *Arch:* **fenêtre a.**, blind window. **3.** blind, unreasoning (hatred); implicit (confidence); *adv.* **-ément**, blindly.

aveugle-né, -née [avœgləne], *a. & s.* (man, woman) blind from birth.

aveugl|er [avœgle], *v.tr.* **1.** (*a*) to blind (s.o.); (*b*) to dazzle, blind. **2.** *Nau:* **a. une voie d'eau**, to stop a leak; *s.m.* **-ement**, blinding; blindness.

aveuglette (à l') [alavœglɛt], *adv.phr.* blindly; **avancer à l'a.**, to grope one's way.

aveull|ir (s') [savœli:r], *v.pr.* to become mentally lazy; to become indifferent to everything; *s.m.* **-issement**.

aviateur, -trice [avjatœ:r, -tris], *s.* aviator; airman, -woman.

aviation [avjasjɔ̃], *s.f.* aviation.

aviculture [avikylty:r], *s.f.* poultry-farming.

avid|e [avid], *a.* greedy; **a. de qch.**, (i) greedy for sth.; (ii) eager for sth.; *s.f.* **-ité**, greed; *adv.* **-ement**, greedily.

avil|ir [avili:r], *v.tr.* **1.** to render vile; to degrade. **2.** *Com:* to depreciate (prices); *a.* **-issant**; *s.m.* **-issement**.

avion [avjɔ̃], *s.m.* aircraft, *F:* plane; **a. de chasse**, fighter; **par a.**, by air-mail.

avion-taxi [avjɔ̃taksi], *s.m.* charter plane; *pl.* **avions-taxis.**

aviron [avirɔ̃], *s.m.* **1.** oar; scull; *Fr.C:* paddle (of canoe); **armer les avirons**, to ship the oars. **2.** **l'a.**, rowing; **cercle d'a.**, rowing club.

avis [avi], *s.m.* **1.** (*a*) opinion, judgment; **à, selon, mon a.**, in my opinion; **de l'a. de tous**, in the opinion of all; **j'ai changé d'a.**, I have changed my mind; **je suis d'a. qu'il vienne**, in my opinion he ought to come; (*b*) advice, counsel; **demander l'a. de qn**, to ask s.o.'s advice. **2.** notice, warning, announcement; **a. au public**, notice to the public; **a. au lecteur**, foreword (to book); **jusqu'à nouvel a.**, until further notice.

avisé [avize], *a.* prudent, circumspect; farseeing; **bien a.**, well-advised.

aviser [avize]. **1.** *v.tr.* (*a*) to perceive, *F:* to spot (s.o.); (*b*) **a. qn de qch.**, to inform s.o. of sth. **2.** *v.i.* **a. à qch.**, to deal with (situation).

s'aviser de qch., to think of sth.; **ne vous en avisez pas!** you'd better not!

avitaminose [avitamino:z], *s.f. Med:* vitamin deficiency.

aviver [avive], *v.tr.* **1.** to quicken; to revive, brighten (colours); to irritate (wound). **2.** to put a keen edge on (tool).

avocat, -ate [avɔka, -at], *s.* **1.** barrister; counsel; *N.Am:* lawyer; **être reçu a.**, to be called to the bar. **2.** advocate, intercessor.

avoine [avwan], *s.f.* oat(s); **farine d'a.**, oatmeal.

avoir [avwa:r]. **I.** *v.tr.* (*pr.p.* **ayant**; *p.p.* **eu**; *pr.ind.* **j'ai, tu as, il a, n. avons, ils ont**; *pr.sub.* **j'aie, il ait**; *p.d.* **j'avais**; *fu.* **j'aurai**; avoir *is the aux. of all tr. and many intr. vbs.*). **1.** (*a*) to have, possess; (*b*) **elle avait une robe bleue**, she had a blue dress on; (*c*) **a. les yeux bleus**, to have blue eyes; (*d*) **a. dix ans**, to be ten years old. **2.** to get, obtain; **a. le prix**, to get the prize; **a. Paris**, to get Paris (i) on the phone, (ii) on the radio. **3.** *F:* to get the better of (s.o.); **on vous a eu!** you've been had! **4.** (= FAIRE, *esp. in p.h.*); **il eut un mouvement brusque**, he made a sudden gesture. **5.** to feel unwell; **qu'avez-vous? qu'est-ce que vous avez?** what's the matter with you? **6.** **en a.**; (*a*) **nous en avons pour deux heures**, it will take us two hours; (*b*) **en a. à, contre, qn**, to have a grudge against s.o.; **quoi qu'il en ait**, whatever he may say. **7.** **a. qch. à faire**, to have sth. to do; **vous n'avez pas à vous inquiéter**, you have no need to feel anxious. **8.** *impers.* **il y a**; (*a*) **combien y a-t-il de blessés?** how many wounded are there? **il y en a qui disent**, there are some who say; **il n'y a pas de quoi**, pray don't mention it; (*b*) **qu'est-ce qu'il y a?** what is the matter? (*c*) **il y a deux ans**, two years ago; **il y avait six mois que j'attendais**, I had been waiting for the last six months; (*d*) **combien y a-t-il d'ici à Londres?** how far is it (from here) to London? **9.** *aux. use.* **j'ai fini**, I have done; **quand il eut fini de parler, il vint à moi**, when he had finished speaking he came to me.

II. avoir, *s.m.* property; **tout mon a.**, all I possess; *Com:* **doit et a.**, debit and credit.

avoisinant [avwazinɑ̃], *a.* neighbouring; nearby.

avoisiner [avwazine], *v.tr.* **a. qch.**, to be near sth., close, adjacent, to sth.; to border on sth.

avort|er [avɔrte], *v.i.* to miscarry; **faire a. un dessein**, to frustrate a plan; *s.m.* **-ement**, (*a*) a. spontané, miscarriage; (*b*) a. provoqué, abortion.

avorton [avɔrtɔ̃], *s.m.* puny, stunted, man; *F:* runt.

avoué [avwe], *s.m. Jur:* = solicitor, *N.Am:* attorney.

avouer [avwe], *v.tr.* **1.** to acknowledge; **s'a. coupable**, to admit one's guilt. **2.** to confess, to own (a misdeed).

avril [avril], *s.m.* April; **en a.**, in April; **au mois d'a.**, in the month of April; **le sept a.**, (on) April the seventh; **le premier a.**, (i) the first of April;

(ii) April Fool's day; **donner un poisson d'a. à qn**, to make an April fool of s.o.

axe [aks], *s.m.* **1.** axis (of ellipse). **2.** axle, spindle.

axiom|e [aksjo:m], *s.m.* axiom; *a.* -**atique**, axiomatic.

ayant [ɛjã]. **1.** *see* AVOIR. **2.** *s.m. Jur:* **a. droit**, rightful claimant or owner; interested party; beneficiary; *pl. ayants droit*.

azalée [azale], *s.f. Bot:* azalea.

azotate [azɔtat], *s.m. Ch:* nitrate.

azote [azɔt], *s.m. Ch:* nitrogen.

azoté [azɔte], *a.* nitrogenous.

azoteux, -euse [azɔtø, -ø:z], *a. Ch:* nitrous.

azotique [azɔtik], *a. Ch:* nitric.

aztèque [aztɛk], *a. & s. Ethn:* Aztec.

azur [azy:r], *s.m.* azure, blue; *Geog:* **la Côte d'A.**, the (French) Riviera.

azyme [azim], *a.* unleavened (bread).

B

B, b [be], *s.m.* (the letter) B, b.
baba [baba], *s.m. Cu:* baba.
babill|er [babije], *v.i.* to prattle; to chatter; (*of brook*) to babble; *s.m.* **-age; s. -ard, -arde,** chatterbox.
bâbord [babɔːr], *s.m. Nau:* port (side).
babouin [babwɛ̃], *s.m.* baboon.
bac¹ [bak], *s.m.* **1.** (*a*) ferry-boat; (*b*) ferry; **passer le b.,** to cross the ferry. **2.** tank, vat.
bac², *s.m. Sch: F:* = G.C.E.
baccalauréat [bakalɔrea], *s.m.* = General Certificate of Education.
bâche [baːʃ], *s.f.* canvas cover; tarpaulin.
bachelier, -ière [baʃəlje, -jɛːr], *s. Sch:* one who has passed the **baccalauréat.**
bachot [baʃo], *s.m. Sch: F:* = G.C.E.; **boîte à b.,** crammer's.
bachot|er [baʃɔte], *v.i. Sch: F:* to cram, to grind; *s.m.* **-age; s. -eur, -euse.**
bacille [basil], *s.m. Biol:* bacillus.
bacl|er [bakle], *v.tr.* **1.** to bar, bolt (door). **2.** *Nau:* to close (harbour). **3.** *F:* to scamp (work); *s.m.* **-age,** scamping (of work).
bactér|ie [bakteri], *s.f.* bacterium, *pl.* **-ia;** *s.m.* **-icide.**
bactérien, -ienne [bakterjɛ̃, -jɛn], *a.* bacterial.
bactériolog|ie [bakterjɔlɔʒi], *s.f.* bacteriology; *a.* **-ique;** *s.* **-iste.**
badaud [bado], *s.m.* saunterer, stroller.
badigeon [badiʒɔ̃], *s.m.* distemper (for walls, etc.); **b. à la chaux,** whitewash.
badigeonn|er [badiʒɔne], *v.tr.* to distemper (a wall); *s.m.* **-age,** distempering.
badin|er [badine]. **1.** *v.i.* to jest. **2.** *v.tr.* to tease; *s.m.* **-age.**
bafouer [bafwe], *v.tr.* to scoff, jeer, at (s.o.).
bafouill|er [bafuje], *v.tr. & i. F:* to splutter, stammer; (*of engine*) to miss, to sputter; *s.m.* **-age; s. -eur, -euse.**
bâfrer [bɑfre], *F:* **1.** *v.i.* to guzzle. **2.** *v.tr.* to stuff, guzzle, wolf (food).
bagage [bagaːʒ], *s.m.* **1.** baggage; **plier b.,** to decamp. **2.** *pl.* luggage.
bagarre [bagaːr], *s.f.* scuffle, brawl; free fight.
bagarrer (se) [səbagare], *v.pr.* to scuffle, to brawl.
bagatelle [bagatɛl], *s.f.* trifle; **acheter qch. pour une b.,** to buy sth. for a song.
bagne [baɲ], *s.m. A:* convict prison.
bagnole [baɲɔl], *s.f. F:* (motor) car, automobile.
bague [bag], *s.f.* (jewelled) ring.

baguenauder [bagnode], *v.i. & pr. F:* to foo around.
baguette [bagɛt], *s.f.* rod, wand, stick; long, thin loaf of French bread.
bah [ba], *int.* nonsense! rubbish!
bahut [bay], *s.m.* cupboard, buffet, sideboard.
bai [bɛ], *a.* bay (horse); **b. châtain,** chestnut-bay.
baie¹ [bɛ], *s.f. Geog:* bay, bight.
baie², *s.f. Arch:* bay (window).
baie³, *s.f. Bot:* berry.
baignade [bɛɲaːd], *s.f.* **1.** bathe. **2.** bathing place.
baign|er [bɛɲe]. **1.** *v.tr.* (*a*) to bathe; to dip; (*b* (*of sea*) to wash (coast); (*of river*) to water (a district); (*c*) to bath (baby). **2.** *v.i.* to soak, steep (in sth.); *s.* **-eur, -euse,** bather.
se baigner. 1. to take a bath. **2.** to bathe; to have a bathe.
baignoire [bɛɲwaːr], *s.f.* **1.** bath; (bath-)tub. **2.** *Th:* ground-floor box.
bail, *pl.* **baux** [baːj, bo], *s.m.* lease (to tenant) **prendre une maison à b.,** to lease a house.
bâillant [bɑjɑ̃], *a.* gaping; yawning.
bâill|er [bɑːje], *v.i.* **1.** to yawn. **2.** to gape; *s.m.* **-ement.**
bâillon [bɑjɔ̃], *s.m.* gag.
bâillonn|er [bɑjɔne], *v.tr.* to gag; *s.m.* **-ement.**
bain [bɛ̃], *s.m.* bath; (*a*) **salle de bains,** bathroom (*b*) **bains publics,** public baths; (*c*) *pl.* watering-place; spa; (*d*) bathing; **bains de mer,** (i) sea-bathing; (ii) seaside resort.
bain-marie [bɛ̃mari], *s.m. Cu:* double saucepan *pl.* **bains-marié.**
baïonnette [bajɔnɛt], *s.f.* bayonet.
baiser [bɛze]. **I.** *v.tr.* to kiss (s.o.); **b. qn sur, à, la joue,** to kiss s.o. on the cheek.
II. baiser, *s.m.* kiss.
baissant [bɛsɑ̃], *a.* declining; setting (sun); failing (sight).
baisse [bɛs], *s.f.* **1.** subsidence (of water); ebb (of tide). **2.** fall, drop (in prices).
baisser [bɛse]. **I.** *v.* **1.** *v.tr.* to lower (price); to let down (window); **b. les lumières,** to lower the lights; **donner tête baissée dans un piège,** to fall headlong into a trap; **b. les yeux,** to cast down one's eyes; to look down. **2.** *v.i.* (*a*) to be on the decline; to ebb; (*of flood*) to abate; **le soleil baisse,** the sun is sinking; **sa vue baisse,** his sight is failing; (*b*) (*of prices*) to fall.
II. baisser, *s.m. Th:* **b. du rideau,** fall of the curtain.

se baisser, to stoop; to bend down.

bal, *pl.* bals [bal], *s.m.* ball, dance.

balader [balade], *F:* 1. *v.i. & pr.* to stroll, saunter; se b. en auto, to go for a drive. 2. *v.tr.* to take (s.o., the dog) for a walk.

baladeur, -euse [baladœ:r, -ø:z], *s.* 1. *F:* stroller, saunterer. 2. *s.f.* baladeuse, (*a*) trailer (of car); (*b*) costermonger's barrow; (*c*) inspection lamp.

balafre [balafr], *s.f.* 1. slash, gash (*esp. in face*). 2. scar.

balafrer [balafre], *v.tr.* 1. to gash, slash (*esp. the face*). 2. visage balafré, scarred face.

balai [balɛ], *s.m.* broom; b. mécanique, carpet-sweeper; b. électrique, vacuum-cleaner; manche à b., broom-stick.

balance [balɑ̃:s], *s.f.* 1. (*a*) balance; (pair of) scales; b. romaine, steelyard; faire pencher la b., to turn the scale; (*b*) scale(-pan). 2. b. d'un compte, balancing of an account; faire la b., to strike the balance. 3. *Astr:* la B., Libra.

balancé [balɑ̃se], *a.* 1. well-balanced; well-poised. 2. swinging (blow).

balancer [balɑ̃se], *v.* (n. balançons). I. *v.tr.* 1. to balance; (*a*) b. un compte, to balance an account; (*b*) to poise. 2. to swing, rock. 3. *F:* to fire, sack (employee); *s.m.* -ement. II. balancer, *v.i.* to swing.

se balancer, to swing; to sway, rock.

balançoire [balɑ̃swa:r], *s.f.* (*a*) see-saw, *N.Am:* teeter-totter; (*b*) (child's) swing.

balayer [balɛje], *v.tr.* (je balaie, je balaye). 1. to sweep; to sweep out (room); to sweep up (dirt); b. la mer, to scour the sea. 2. *T.V:* to scan (image). 3. *F:* to fire, sack (staff).

balayeur, -euse [balɛjœ:r, -ø:z], *s.* 1. sweeper. 2. *s.f.* balayeuse, (i) carpet-sweeper; (ii) (*machine*) street-sweeper.

balayures [balɛjy:r], *s.f.pl.* sweepings.

balbutier [balbysje]. 1. *v.i.* to stammer, mumble. 2. *v.tr.* to stammer out (sth.); *s.m.* -ement, stammering.

balcon [balkɔ̃], *s.m.* 1. balcony. 2. *Th:* dress-circle.

Bâle [bɑ:l]. *Pr.n.f. Geog:* Basel, Basle.

baléare [balea:r], *a. Geog:* les (îles) Baléares, the Balearic Islands.

baleine [balɛn], *s.f.* 1. whale; blanc de b., spermaceti. 2. whalebone; baleines d'un parapluie, ribs of an umbrella.

baleinier, -ière [balɛnje, -jɛ:r]. 1. *a.* whaling (industry). 2. *s.m.* whaler. 3. *s.f.* whale-boat.

balise [bali:z], *s.f.* (*a*) *Nau:* beacon; sea-mark; b. flottante, buoy; (*b*) *Av:* ground light.

baliser [balize], *v.tr.* to buoy, mark out, (i) *Nau:* channel, (ii) *Av:* runway; piste balisée, flarepath; *s.m.* -age.

balistique [balistik]. 1. *a.* ballistic. 2. *s.f.* ballistics; gunnery.

baliverne [balivɛrn], *s.f.* futile remark, occupation; débiter des balivernes, to talk nonsense.

ballade [balad], *s.f.* ballad.

ballant [balɑ̃], *a.* swinging, dangling (arms, etc.).

ballast [balast], *s.m.* 1. *Civ.E:* etc: ballast, bottom (of road). 2. *Nau:* ballast-tank (of submarine).

balle [bal], *s.f.* 1. ball; b. de tennis, tennis-ball; renvoyer la b. à qn, (i) to return the ball to s.o.; (ii) to return the compliment; *Games:* b. au camp, rounders; b. au mur, fives. 2. bullet; shot; b. perdue, stray bullet. 3. *Com:* bale (of cotton); mettre en b., to bale.

ballerine [balrin], *s.f. Th:* ballerina, ballet-dancer.

ballet [balɛ], *s.m. Th:* ballet.

ballon [balɔ̃], *s.m.* 1. balloon; b. de sondage, pilot balloon; *Aut:* pneu b., balloon tyre. 2. ball; football.

ballonner [balɔne], *v.i. & pr.* to swell (out); (*of skirt*) to balloon out; *a.* -ant, distended (stomach, etc.); *s.m.* -ement.

ballot [balo], *s.m.* 1. bundle, bale; (pedlar's) pack. 2. *P:* nit(wit), clot.

ballottage [balɔtaʒ], *s.m.* 1. shaking, jolting. 2. (*a*) voting; (*b*) second ballot (at election).

ballotter [balɔte]. 1. *v.tr.* to toss (about), shake (about). 2. *v.i.* (*a*) (*of door*) to rattle; (*b*) to toss (on the water); *s.m.* -ement.

balnéaire [balneɛ:r], *a.* station b., (i) seaside resort; (ii) spa.

balourd, -ourde [balu:r, -urd]. 1. *a.* awkward, lumpish. 2. *s.* awkward person; yokel; *s.f.* -ise, awkwardness.

baltique [baltik]. *Geog:* 1. *a.* Baltic. 2. *Pr.n.f.* la B., the Baltic (Sea).

balustrade [balystrad], *s.f.* 1. balustrade. 2. (hand-)rail; railing.

balustre [balystr], *s.m.* (*a*) baluster; (*b*) *pl.* banisters.

bambin, -ine [bɑ̃bɛ̃, -in], *s. F:* little child.

bambou [bɑ̃bu], *s.m. Bot:* bamboo(-cane).

banal, -als [banal], *a.* commonplace, trite; *F:* pas b., unusual, out of the ordinary.

banaliser [banalize], *v.tr.* to make (sth.) commonplace; voiture banalisée, unmarked (police) car.

banalité [banalite], *s.f.* 1. banality, triteness. 2. commonplace remark.

banane [banan], *s.f.* banana; *s.m.* -ier, banana-tree.

banc [bɑ̃], *s.m.* 1. bench, seat, form; b. d'église, pew; *Jur:* b. des prévenus, dock; b. du jury, jury-box. 2. b. de sable, sand-bank; b. d'huîtres, oyster-bed. 3. shoal (of fish).

bancaire [bɑ̃kɛ:r], *a.* (concerning) banking.

bancal, *pl.* -als [bɑ̃kal], *a.* (*a*) bandy-legged; (*b*) rickety (furniture).

bandage [bɑ̃daːʒ], *s.m.* 1. bandage. 2. (rubber) tyre.

bande[1] [bɑ̃ːd], *s.f.* 1. (*a*) band, strip (of cloth); **envoyer qch. sous b.,** to send sth. by book post; *Rad:* **b. de fréquence,** frequency band; (*b*) *Cin:* reel (of film); film; **b. sonore,** sound track; **b. magnétique,** (recording) tape; **b. dessinée,** strip cartoon; (*c*) (metal) tyre; (*d*) *Bill:* cushion. 2. *Nau:* (*a*) side (of ship); (*b*) heel, list(ing).

bande[2], *s.f.* 1. band, party, troop. 2. flight, flock; pack; school (of porpoises).

bandeau, -eaux [bɑ̃do], *s.m.* 1. bandeau, headband. 2. bandage (over the eyes).

bander [bɑ̃de], *v.tr.* 1. to bandage, bind (up) (wound); **b. les yeux à qn,** to blindfold s.o. 2. **b. une roue,** to put a (metal) tyre on a wheel. 3. **b. un arc,** (i) to bend, (ii) to string, a bow.

banderole [bɑ̃drɔl], *s.f.* banderole, streamer.

bandit [bɑ̃di], *s.m.* (*a*) bandit; (*b*) ruffian.

bandoulière [bɑ̃duljɛːr], *s.f.* shoulder-strap; **porter qch. en b.,** to carry sth. slung across one's back.

banlieu|e [bɑ̃ljø], *s.f.* suburbs; outskirts; *s.m.* **-sard,** suburbanite.

banni, -e [bani]. 1. *a.* banished, outlawed. 2. *s.* exile, outlaw.

bannière [banjɛːr], *s.f.* banner.

bann|ir [baniːr], *v.tr.* to banish; to exile; to outlaw; *s.m.* **-issement.**

banque [bɑ̃k], *s.f.* 1. (*a*) bank; (*b*) banking; (*c*) *Med:* **b. du sang,** blood bank. 2. *Cards:* bank; **faire sauter la b.,** to break the bank; *s.f.* **-route,** bankruptcy; *a. & s.m.* **-routier,** fraudulent bankrupt.

banquet [bɑ̃kɛ], *s.m.* banquet, feast.

banquette [bɑ̃kɛt], *s.f.* 1. bench, seat, form; wall-sofa (in restaurant); *Th:* **jouer devant les banquettes,** to play to empty benches. 2. *Golf:* bunker.

banquier, -ière [bɑ̃kje, -jɛːr]. 1. *a.* banking (house). 2. *s.* banker.

banquise [bɑ̃kiːz], *s.f.* ice-floe, ice-pack.

bans [bɑ̃], *s.m.pl.* banns (of marriage).

baptême [batɛːm], *s.m.* baptism, christening; **nom de b.,** Christian name.

baptiser [batize], *v.tr.* to baptize; to christen; **b. son vin,** to water down one's wine.

baquet [bakɛ], *s.m.* tub, bucket.

bar [baːr], *s.m.* (public) bar; bar (counter).

baragouin|er [baragwine], *v.tr. & i. F:* (*a*) to speak a language badly; **b. l'anglais,** to speak broken English; (*b*) to talk gibberish, to jabber; *s.m.* **-age; s.** **-eur, -euse.**

baraque [barak], *s.f.* (*a*) hut, shanty; *pl. Mil:* huts, hutments; *P:* **toute la b.,** the whole lot; (*b*) booth (at fair).

baratte [barat], *s.f.* churn.

baratter [barate], *v.tr.* to churn.

Barbade (la) [labarbad]. *Pr.n.f.* Barbados.

barbant [barbɑ̃], *a. P:* tiresome, boring.

barbare [barbaːr]. 1. *a.* (*a*) barbaric; uncouth (*b*) barbarous, inhuman. 2. *s.m.* barbarian *adv.* **-ment.**

barbarie [barbari], *s.f.* 1. barbarism. 2. barbarity, cruelty.

barbarisme [barbarism], *s.m. Gram:* barbarism.

barbe [barb], *s.f.* beard; *F:* **rire dans sa b.,** tc laugh up one's sleeve; **se faire la b.,** to shave *P:* **quelle b.!** what a bore! **la b.!** shut up!

barbeau, -eaux [barbo], *s.m.* cornflower.

barbelé [barbəle], *a.* barbed; **fil de fer b.,** *s.m.* **b.** barbed wire.

barbiche [barbiʃ], *s.f.* (*a*) short beard; (*b* goatee.

barbier [barbje], *s.m.* barber.

barboter [barbote], *v.i.* to paddle, splash (about).

barbouill|er [barbuje], *v.tr.* 1. (*a*) to daub; tc smear (**de,** with); (*b*) to smear (one's face); tc blur (printing). 2. **avoir le cœur barbouillé,** tc feel sick, squeamish; *s.m.* **-age; s. -eur, -euse** (i) dauber; (ii) scribbler.

se barbouiller, to dirty one's face.

barbu [barby]. 1. *a.* bearded. 2. *s.f. Fish:* **bar bue,** brill.

barde[1] [bard], *s.f. Cu:* slice of bacon (used tc cover fowl, joint), bard.

barde[2], *s.m.* bard, poet.

barème [barɛːm], *s.m.* 1. ready-reckoner. 2 scale (of salaries). 3. printed table (of fares).

barguign|er [bargiɲe], *v.i. F:* to shilly-shally *s.m.* **-age; s. -eur, -euse.**

baril [baril], *s.m.* barrel, cask, keg.

bariolé [barjɔle], *a.* gaudy, motley; of man colours; splashed with colour.

bariol|er [barjɔle], *v.tr.* to variegate; to pain (sth.) in gaudy colours; *s.m.* **-age.**

baro|mètre [barɔmɛtr], *s.m.* barometer; *a* **-métrique,** barometric.

baron, -onne [barɔ̃, -ɔn], *s.* baron; baroness.

baronnet [barɔnɛ], *s.m.* baronet.

baroque [barɔk], *a.* 1. quaint, odd. 2. *a. & s.m* baroque (style).

barque [bark], *s.f.* boat.

barrage [baraːʒ, ba-], *s.m.* 1. (*a*) barring, stop ping (of road); damming (of valley); (*b* crossing (of cheque). 2. (*a*) barrier, obstruc tion; dam, weir; (*b*) *Mil:* barrage.

barre [baːr], *s.f.* 1. (*a*) bar, rod (of metal); (*b* bar, barrier; **b. d'appui,** hand-rail; *Ju* **paraître à la b.,** to appear before the court, ε the bar; (*c*) (harbour) boom; (*d*) bar (of rive or harbour); **b. d'eau,** (tidal) bore. 2. *Nau:* ba tiller (of boat); helm (of ship); (*of ship*) **sentir** **b.,** to answer to the helm; **homme de b.,** man ε the wheel; helmsman. 3. line, dash, stroke, ba

4. stripe; étoffe à barres, striped cloth. 5. *Games:* jeu de barres, prisoners' base.

arreau, -eaux [baro], *s.m.* 1. (*a*) small bar; rail; barreaux d'une échelle, rungs of a ladder; (*b*) grate-bar, fire-bar. 2. *Jur:* bar; être reçu au b., to be called to the bar.

arrier [bare], *v.tr.* 1. to strengthen by means of a bar or bars. 2. (*a*) to fasten with a bar; to bar; (*b*) to bar, obstruct; to dam; rue barrée, no thoroughfare. 3. to cross (a t, an A); **b. un chèque,** to cross a cheque. 4. to cross out, strike out (word). 5. *Nau:* to steer; to cox; *s.m.* -eur, (*a*) steersman; (*b*) cox.

arrette [baret], *s.f.* biretta; (cardinal's) cap.

arricade [barikad], *s.f.* barricade.

arricader [barikade], *v.tr.* to barricade.

arrière [barje:r], *s.f.* 1. barrier. 2. gate; tollgate.

arrique [barik], *s.f.* large barrel; cask.

arrir [bari:r], *v.i.* (*of elephant*) to trumpet; *s.m.* -issement; *s.m.* -it, trumpeting.

aryton [baritɔ̃], *a. & s.m.* baritone (voice).

aryum [barjɔm], *s.m. Min:* barium.

as, basse [ba, ba:s]. I. *a.* 1. low; **voix basse,** deep voice; **conversation à voix basse,** whispered conversation; **enfant en b. âge,** child of tender years; **avoir la vue basse,** to be short-sighted. 2. mean, base, low. 3. low(er); **au b. mot,** at the lowest estimate; *adv.* -sement, basely, contemptibly. II. **bas,** *adv.* 1. low (down); *Nau:* **haler b. une voile,** to haul down a sail. 2. **mettre b.,** (*a*) to take off (one's hat); (*b*) to overthrow; (*c*) **mettre b. les armes,** to lay down one's arms. 3. **parler tout b.,** to speak in a whisper. III. **bas,** *s.m.* 1. lower part (of sth.); *F:* **les hauts et les b. de la vie,** life's ups and downs; *adv.phr.* **en b.,** (down) below; **aller en b.,** to go downstairs; **tomber la tête en b.,** to fall head foremost; *prep.phr.* **en b. de,** at the foot of; **en b. de l'escalier,** downstairs; *adv.phr.* **à b.,** down; **à b. les mains!** hands off! **à b. les dictateurs!** down with dictators! **tomber à b. de son cheval,** to fall off one's horse. 2. **b. de l'eau,** low water. 3. stocking. IV. **basse,** *s.f. Mus:* bass.

asalte [bazalt], *s.m.* basalt.

asané [bazane], *a.* sunburnt, tanned; swarthy.

asaner [bazane], *v.tr.* to bronze, tan.

as-bleu [bablø], *s.m.* blue-stocking; *pl. bas-bleus.*

as-côté [bakote], *s.m.* 1. (side-)aisle (of church). 2. shoulder, side (of road); *pl. bas-côtés.*

asculant [baskylɑ̃], *a.* rocking, tilting; **siège b.,** tip-up seat.

ascule [baskyl], *s.f.* rocker; see-saw; **chaise à b.,** rocking-chair; **wagon à b.,** tip-waggon.

asculer [baskyle], *v.tr. & i.* 1. (*a*) to rock, swing; to see-saw; (*b*) to tip (up); (**faire**) **b. une**

charrette, to tip a cart. 2. to topple over; *s.m.* -age.

base [ba:z], *s.f.* 1. base (of triangle); **b. d'aviation,** air base; **b. de lancement (de fusées),** launching pad. 2. lower part, foot, base (of mountain). 3. basis, foundation; **sans b.,** ungrounded (suspicions). 4. radix, root, basis (of logarithm). 5. *Ch:* base (of salt).

base-ball [bɛzbo:l], *s.m. Sp:* baseball; *s.m.* -eur.

baser [baze], *v.tr.* to found upon (a principle). **se baser sur qch.,** to take sth. as a basis.

bas-fond [bafɔ̃], *s.m.* 1. low ground, hollow; swamp. 2. shallow, shoal; *pl. bas-fonds.*

basilique [bazilik], *s.f. Arch:* basilica.

basket(-ball) [basket(bo:l)], *s.m. Sp:* basketball.

basketteur, -euse [basketœ:r, -ø:z], *s.* basketball player.

basquais, -aise [baskɛ, -ɛ:z], *a.* Basque.

basque[1] [bask], *a. & s. Ethn:* Basque.

basque[2], *s.f.* skirt, tail (of coat).

bas-relief [barəljɛf], *s.m.* bas-relief, low-relief; *pl. bas-reliefs.*

basse-cour [basku:r], *s.f.* farm-yard, poultry-yard; *pl. basses-cours.*

basse-fosse [basfo:s], *s.f.* dungeon; *pl. basses-fosses.*

bassesse [bases], *s.f.* 1. baseness, lowness. 2. low, mean, contemptible, action.

bassin [basɛ̃], *s.m.* 1. basin, bowl, pan. 2. (*a*) ornamental lake; (*b*) reservoir, tank. 3. dock, basin. 4. (*a*) **b. d'un fleuve,** drainage basin of a river; (*b*) **b. houiller,** coal-field. 5. *Anat:* pelvis.

basson [basɔ̃], *s.m. Mus:* 1. bassoon. 2. bassoonist.

bastingages [bastɛ̃ga:ʒ], *s.m.pl. Nau:* bulwarks, topsides; rails; **accoudé aux b.,** leaning over the rails.

bât [ba], *s.m.* 1. pack-saddle; **cheval de b.,** pack-horse; *F:* **c'est là que le b. le blesse,** that's where the shoe pinches. 2. pack.

bataclan [bataklɑ̃], *s.m. F:* belongings, paraphernalia; **vendez tout le b.!** sell the whole caboodle!

bataille [bata:j], *s.f.* battle; **le fort de la b.,** the thick of the fight; **champ de b.,** battlefield.

batailler [bataje], *v.i.* to fight, battle (**contre,** with, against); *a.* -eur, -euse, fighting, quarrelsome.

bataillon [batajɔ̃], *s.m. Mil:* battalion.

bâtard, -arde [bata:r, -ard], *a. & s.* bastard; (*a*) illegitimate; (*b*) mongrel; (*c*) **race bâtarde,** degenerate race; *s.f.* -ise, bastardy.

bateau, -eaux [bato], *s.m.* boat; vessel; **grands, petits, bateaux,** large, small, craft; **pont de bateaux,** pontoon-bridge; *Rail:* **le train du b.,** the boat-train; **aller en b.,** to go boating; to boat.

bateau-citerne [batositɛrn], *s.m.* tanker; *pl. bateaux-citernes.*

bateau-mouche [batomuʃ], *s.m.* river passenger boat (in Paris); water bus; *pl. bateaux-mouches.*

bateau-phare [batofaːr], *s.m.* lightship; *pl. bateaux-phares.*

bateleur, -euse [batlœːr, -øːz], *s.* juggler, tumbler.

batelier, -ière [batəlje, -jεːr], *s.* boatman, -woman; waterman; ferryman, -woman.

bathyscaphe [batiskaf], *s.m.* bathyscaph.

bâti [bati], *s.m.* frame(-work), structure, support.

batifol|er [batifɔle], *v.i. F:* to frolic, to fool about; *s.m.* -age; *s.* -eur, -euse.

bâtiment [batimã], *s.m.* 1. building trade. 2. building, edifice, structure. 3. ship, vessel; **b. de guerre,** warship.

bâtir [batiːr], *v.tr.* to build, erect, construct; **homme bien bâti,** well-built man; **terrain à b.,** building-site.

bâtisse [batis], *s.f.* 1. masonry; bricks and mortar. 2. *F:* ramshackle building.

batiste [batist], *s.f. Tex:* batiste, cambric.

bâton [batɔ̃], *s.m.* 1. stick, staff, rod; (*a*) **b. ferré,** iron-shod stick; **b. de vieillesse,** support, prop, of old age; **coup de b.,** blow with a stick; **mettre des bâtons dans les roues,** to put a spoke in s.o.'s wheel; to throw a spanner in the works; (*b*) **conversation à bâtons rompus,** desultory conversation; (*c*) staff, pole; **b. de pavillon,** flagstaff; (*d*) (*wand of office*) **b. pastoral,** pastoral staff, crozier; **b. de chef d'orchestre,** conductor's baton. 2. stick, roll; **b. de cannelle,** roll of cinnamon. 3. stroke (of the pen).

bâtonner [batɔne], *v.tr.* to beat, cudgel, cane.

bâtonnet [batɔnε], *s.m.* (*a*) square ruler; (*b*) *Biol:* rod-bacterium; (*c*) *pl. Anat:* rods (of the retina).

battant [batã]. I. *a.* beating; **pluie battante,** driving rain; downpour; **mener les choses tambour b.,** to hustle things on; *F:* **tout b. neuf,** brand-new.

II. **battant,** *s.m.* 1. clapper, tongue (of bell). 2. (*a*) leaf, flap (of table); **porte à deux battants,** folding doors; (*b*) door (of cupboard).

batterie [batri], *s.f.* 1. beat (of drum). 2. *Artil:* battery; **pièces en b.,** guns in action; **montrer, démasquer, ses batteries,** to show one's hand. 3. (*a*) set, collection; **b. de cuisine,** (set of) kitchen utensils; (*b*) **b. électrique,** electric battery. 4. *Agr:* battery (for chickens).

batteur, -euse [batœːr, -øːz], *s.* 1. (*a*) **b. en grange,** thresher; (*b*) *Ven:* beater; (*c*) *F:* **batteurs de pavé,** loafers, idlers; (*d*) *Cricket:* batsman; *Baseball:* batter. 2. *s.f.* **batteuse,** threshing-machine; thresher.

batt|re [batr], *v.* (*pr.ind.* **je bats, il bat**) to beat. 1. *v.tr.* (*a*) to beat, thrash, flog; **b. du blé,** to thresh corn; **b. monnaie,** (i) to mint money; (ii) *F:* to

raise the wind; (*b*) to beat, defeat; (*c*) **b. la campagne,** (i) to scour the country; (ii) *F:* to b delirious; *Ven:* **b. un bois,** to beat a wood; (*a* *Nau:* **b. un pavillon,** to fly a flag; (*e*) **b. le cartes,** to shuffle the cards. 2. *v.tr. & i.* (*a*) **b.** **mesure,** to beat time; **la montre bat,** the watc ticks; (*b*) **b. l'alarme,** to beat the alarm; **le tan bour bat,** the drum is beating; **le cœur lui ba tait,** his heart was going pit-a-pat; (*c*) **porte q** **bat,** banging door; (*d*) **b. des mains,** to cla one's hands; **b. du pied,** to stamp one's foo *s.m.* -**age,** threshing; *s.m.* -**ement.**

se battre, to fight.

battu [baty], *a.* 1. **avoir les yeux battus,** to hav rings, circles, round one's eyes. 2. *Metalw:* f **b.,** wrought iron. 3. **suivre le chemin b.,** t follow the beaten track.

battue [baty], *s.f. Ven:* battue, beat.

baume [boːm], *s.m.* balm, balsam.

bauxite [boksit], *s.f. Miner:* bauxite.

bavard, -arde [bavaːr, -ard]. 1. *a.* (*a*) talkativ garrulous; (*b*) tale-bearing, gossiping. 2. chatterbox.

bavard|er [bavarde], *v.i.* 1. to chatter. 2. gossip. 3. to blab, to tell tales; *s.m.* -**age.**

bavarois, -oise [bavarwa, -waːz], *a. &* Bavarian.

bave [baːv], *s.f.* slaver, dribble.

bav|er [bave], *v.i.* to slaver; to slobber; *a. &* -**eur, -euse;** *a.* -**eux, -euse.**

bavette [bavεt], *s.f.* 1. bib. 2. *Cu:* top of tl sirloin.

Bavière [bavjεːr]. *Pr.n.f. Geog:* Bavaria.

bazar [bazaːr], *s.m.* bazaar; cheap stores; **tout le b.,** the whole caboodle.

béant [beã], *a.* gaping (wound); yawnir (chasm).

béat, -ate [bea, -at], *a.* 1. **optimisme b.,** compl cent optimism. 2. sanctimonious, smug; *a* -**ement.**

béatifi|er [beatifje], *v.tr. Ecc:* to beatify; *s.* -**cation;** *a.* -**que,** beatific.

béatitude [beatityd], *s.f.* 1. (*a*) beatitude; (bliss. 2. smugness, complacency.

beau [bo], **bel,** *f.* **belle** [bεl], *pl.* **beaux, bell** (*The form* **bel** *is used before m.sg. sbs begi ning with a vowel or a 'mute' h*). I. *a.* beautiful, handsome, fair; **un bel homme,** good-looking man; **le b. sexe,** the fair sex; **beaux arbres,** handsome, fine, trees. 2. fine; (*a* **de beaux sentiments,** fine, noble, loft feelings; (*b*) **b. danseur,** fine dancer; **un b** **esprit,** a wit; **belle occasion,** fine opportunit avoir **b. jeu à faire qch.,** to have every oppc tunity to do sth.; **un b. joueur,** a good lose **voir tout du b. côté,** to see the bright side everything; (*c*) smart, spruce; **le b. mon** society; the fashionable set; **se faire b.,** smarten oneself up; (*d*) **b. temps,** fine weathe (*e*) **tout cela est bel et bon,** that is all well and good; **il en a fait de belles,** pretty things he's been up to! **en voici d'une belle!** here's a fine state of affairs! (*f*) **j'ai eu une belle peur!** I got an awful fright! **au b. milieu de la rue,** right in the middle of the street; **il y a b. jour qu'il est parti,** it's many a long day since he went away. **3.** *adv.phrs.* **bel et bien,** entirely, fairly, quite; **tout b.!** steady! gently! **de plus belle,** more than ever. **4.** *v.phrs.* (*a*) **l'échapper belle,** to have a narrow escape; **la manquer belle,** to miss a brilliant opportunity; (*b*) **il ferait b. voir cela,** that would be a fine thing to see; (*c*) **il fait b. (temps),** it is fine (weather); (*d*) **avoir b. faire qch.,** to do sth. in vain; **j'avais b. chercher, je ne trouvais rien,** search as I might, I found nothing. **II. beau, belle,** *s.* **1.** (*a*) fair one, beauty; **la Belle au bois dormant,** the Sleeping Beauty; (*b*) **un vieux b.,** an old beau. **2.** *s.m.* (*a*) **le b.,** the beautiful; (*b*) **le b. de l'histoire c'est que . . .,** the best part of the story is that . . .; (*c*) fine weather; **le temps est au b. (fixe),** the weather is set fair. **3.** *s.f.* **belle; jouer la belle,** to play the deciding game or set.

beaucoup [boku]. **1.** *s.m.inv.* (*a*) much, a great deal; *F:* a lot; (*b*) (a great) many; *F:* a lot; **b. de,** much; (a great) many; a great deal of; *F:* lots of; **avec b. de soin,** with much care; **b. d'entre nous,** many of us; (*c*) *adv.phr.* **de b.,** much, by far, by a great deal; **c'est de b. le meilleur,** it is far and away the best. **2.** *adv.* much; **elle parle b.,** she talks a great deal.

beau-fils [bofis], *s.m.* **1.** son-in-law. **2.** stepson; *pl. beaux-fils.*

beau-frère [bofrɛːr], *s.m.* brother-in-law; *pl. beaux-frères.*

beau-père [bopɛːr], *s.m.* **1.** father-in-law. **2.** stepfather; *pl. beaux-pères.*

beauté [bote], *s.f.* **1.** beauty, loveliness; **grain, tache, de b.,** beauty spot; **de toute b.,** extremely beautiful; **institut de b.,** beauty parlour; **soins de b.,** beauty treatment. **2.** beauty; beautiful woman.

beaux-arts [bozaːr], *s.m.pl.* fine arts; **école des b.-a.,** art-school.

beaux-parents [boparɑ̃], *s.m.pl.* parents-in-law.

bébé [bebe], *s.m.* baby.

bec [bɛk], *s.m.* **1.** beak; bill (of bird); **coup de b.,** peck; **attaquer qn du b. et des ongles,** to go for s.o. tooth and nail. **2.** *F:* mouth or nose; **fin b.,** gourmet; *F:* **tenir qn le b. dans l'eau,** to keep s.o. in suspense; **laisser qn le b. dans l'eau,** to leave s.o. in the lurch; **prise de b.,** altercation, squabble. **3.** (*a*) nose (of tool); spout (of coffee-pot); cut-water (of bridge pier); (*b*) **b. de gaz,** gas burner.

bécane [bekan], *s.f. F:* bicycle; *F:* bike.

bécasse [bekas], *s.f. Orn:* woodcock.

bécassine [bekasin], *s.f. Orn:* snipe.

bêche [bɛʃ], *s.f.* spade.

bêch|er [beʃe], *v.tr.* to dig; *s.m.* **-age,** digging; *s.* **-eur, -euse,** digger.

bécoter [bekɔte], *v.tr. F:* to give (s.o.) a little kiss, a peck.

becquée [beke], *s.f.* **1.** beakful. **2.** **l'oiseau donne la b. à ses petits,** the bird feeds its young.

becquet|er [bɛkte], *v.tr.* (**je becquète**). **1.** (*of birds*) (*a*) to pick up (crumbs); (*b*) to peck at (sth.). **2.** *F:* to kiss; *s.m.* **-age.**

bedeau, -eaux [bədo], *s.m. Ecc:* verger.

bédouin, -ine [bedwɛ̃, -in], *a. & s.* bedouin.

bée [be], *a.f.* gaping; *used in* **bouche b.,** agape.

beffroi [befrwa], *s.m.* belfry.

bég|ayer [begɛje], *v.* (**je bégaye, bégaie**). **1.** *v.i.* to stutter, stammer. **2.** *v.tr.* to stammer out (one's lesson); *s.m.* **-aiement,** stammering; *a. & s.* **-ayeur, -ayeuse. 1.** stammering. **2.** stammerer.

bègue [bɛg]. **1.** *a.* stammering; **il est b.,** he stammers. **2.** *s.* stammerer.

béguin [begɛ̃], *s.m. F:* **avoir un b. pour qn,** to have an infatuation for s.o., to be in love with s.o.

beige [bɛːʒ], *a.* beige.

beignet [bɛɲɛ], *s.m. Cu:* fritter.

bel [bɛl], *see* BEAU.

bêl|er [bɛle], *v.i.* to bleat; *s.m.* **-ement.**

belette [bəlɛt], *s.f.* weasel.

belge [bɛlʒ], *a. & s.* Belgian.

Belgique (la) [labɛlʒik]. *Pr.n.f.* Belgium.

bélier [belje], *s.m.* **1.** *Z:* ram. **2.** *Civ.E:* **b. à pilotage,** pile-driver. **3.** *Astr:* **le B.,** Aries.

belladone [bɛl(l)adɔn], *s.f. Bot:* belladonna, deadly nightshade.

belle [bɛl], *see* BEAU.

belle-famille [bɛlfami:j], *s.f. F:* the 'in-laws'; *pl. belles-familles.*

belle-fille [bɛlfi:j], *s.f.* **1.** stepdaughter. **2.** daughter-in-law; *pl. belles-filles.*

belle-mère [bɛlmɛːr], *s.f.* **1.** stepmother. **2.** mother-in-law; *pl. belles-mères.*

belles-lettres [bɛlletr], *s.f.pl.* humanities, belles-lettres.

belle-sœur [bɛlsœːr], *s.f.* sister-in-law; *pl. belles-sœurs.*

belligér|ant, -ante [bɛl(l)iʒerɑ̃, -ãːt], *a. & s.m.* belligerent; *s.f.* **-ance.**

belliqueux, -euse [bɛl(l)ikø, -øːz], *a.* warlike, bellicose.

belvédère [bɛlvedɛːr], *s.m.* **1.** belvedere; view-point; observation tower. **2.** summer-house.

bémol [bemɔl], *s.m. Mus:* flat.

bénédicité [benedisite], *s.m.* grace (at a meal).

bénédictin, -ine [benediktɛ̃, -in], *a. & s.* **1.** Benedictine (monk, nun). **2.** *s.f.* **bénédictine,** benedictine (liqueur).

bénédiction [benediksjɔ̃], *s.f.* blessing, benediction; **quelle b.!** what a blessing!

bénéfice [benefis], *s.m.* **1.** profit, gain; **je suis en b.,** I am in pocket. **2.** benefit; **faire qch. au b. de qn,** to do sth. for s.o.'s benefit. **3.** *Ecc:* living, benefice.

bénéficier [benefisje], *v.i.* (*a*) to profit (**de,** by); (*b*) to make a profit (**sur,** on).

Bénélux (le) [ləbenelyks]. *Pr.n.m.* Benelux.

bénévole [benevɔl], *a.* **1.** benevolent; kindly; indulgent. **2.** gratuitous, unpaid (service); *adv.* **-ment.**

bénignité [beniɲite], *s.f.* (*a*) benignity, kindness; (*b*) mildness.

bén|in, -igne [benɛ̃, -iɲ], *a.* (*a*) benign, kindly; (*b*) mild, gentle (remedy); **hiver b.,** mild winter; *adv.* **-ignement.**

bénir [beniːr], *v.tr.* (*p.p.* **béni, bénit;** *the latter used chiefly as an adj.*) **1.** (*a*) to bless; (**que**) **Dieu vous bénisse!** God bless you! (*b*) to pronounce a blessing on; (*c*) **le ciel en soit béni!** heaven be thanked for it! **2.** to consecrate.

bénit [beni], *a.* consecrated, blessed; **eau bénite,** holy water; *s.m.* **-ier,** (holy water) stoup.

benne [bɛn], *s.f.* **1.** flat hamper, basket. **2.** *Min:* skip, tub; **camion à b. basculante,** tip-truck.

benzine [bɛ̃zin], *s.f.* benzine.

béquille [bekiːj], *s.f.* **1.** crutch. **2.** (motor cycle) stand.

berceau, -eaux [bɛrso], *s.m.* **1.** cradle; (swing-)cot. **2.** *Hort:* arbour, bower.

berc|er [bɛrse], *v.tr.* (**n. berçons**). **1.** to rock. **2.** to lull; to send (s.o.) to sleep; *s.m.* **-ement.**

se bercer. 1. to rock, swing, sway. **2. se b. d'une illusion,** to cherish an illusion.

berceuse [bɛrsøːz], *s.f.* **1.** (*a*) swing-cot; (*b*) rocking-chair. **2.** lullaby, cradle-song.

béret [berɛ], *s.m.* beret; **les bérets rouges,** the parachutists.

berge [bɛrʒ], *s.f.* (steep) bank (of river); banked edge (of road).

berg|er, -ère [bɛrʒe, -ɛːr], *s.* **1.** shepherd, shepherdess, herdsman; **l'heure du b.,** the gloaming. **2.** *s.f.* **bergère,** (*a*) easy-chair; (*b*) *Orn:* wagtail; *s.f.* **-erie,** sheepfold.

bergeronnette [bɛrʒərɔnɛt], *s.f.* *Orn:* wagtail.

berline [bɛrlin], *s.f.* *Aut:* limousine.

berlinois, -oise [bɛrlinwa, -waːz]. **1.** *a.* of Berlin. **2.** *s.* Berliner.

Bermudes [bɛrmyd]. *Pr.n.f.pl.* **les (îles) B.,** Bermuda.

bernard-l'ermite [bɛrnarlɛrmit], *s.m. inv.* hermit-crab.

berner [bɛrne], *v.tr.* to ridicule, to laugh at (s.o.); to hoax (s.o.).

bernique [bɛrnik], *int.* *F:* not a bit of use! no go!

béryl [beril], *s.m.* *Miner:* beryl.

besicles [bəzikl], *s.f.pl.* *F:* glasses, specs.

besogne [b(ə)zɔɲ], *s.f.* work; task, job; **se mettre à la b.,** to set to work; **une rude b.,** a stiff piece of work.

besogneux, -euse [bəzɔɲø, -øːz], *a.* needy, impecunious; *F:* hard up.

besoin [bəzwɛ̃], *s.m.* want, need. **1.** necessity requirement; (*a*) **pourvoir aux besoins de qn** to provide for s.o.'s needs; **au b., en cas de b.** in case of need; if necessary; when required (*b*) **avoir b. de qch.,** to need, want, sth.; **je n'a pas b. qu'on me le rappelle,** I don't need to b reminded of it; (*c*) *impers.* **il n'est pas b.,** ther is no need; **si b. est,** if need be. **2.** poverty, in digence; **être dans le b.,** to be in need.

bestial, -aux[1] [bɛstjal, -o], *a.* bestial, beastly brutish; *adv.* **-ement;** *s.f.* **-ité,** bestiality.

bestiaux[2] [bɛstjo], *s.m.pl.* cattle, beasts.

bestiole [bɛstjɔl], *s.f.* tiny insect, animal.

bétail [betaːj], *s.m. coll:* (*no pl.*) cattle; live stock; **gros b.,** cattle; **menu b.,** smaller live stock.

bête [bɛːt], *s.f.* **1.** beast, animal; dumb creature (*a*) **b. à cornes,** horned beast; (*b*) *F:* **chercher l petite b.,** to be over-critical; **b. à bon Dieu** ladybird. **2.** *F:* (*a*) fool, simpleton; (*b*) *a.* stupid foolish; **pas si b.!** I'm not such a fool! *ad* **-ment,** stupidly.

Bethléem [bɛtleɛm]. *Pr.n.m.* *B.Hist:* Bethlehem

bêtise [betiːz], *s.f.* **1.** stupidity, silliness. **2.** non sense, absurdity; **dire des bêtises,** to talk non sense; **faire des bêtises,** to play the fool. **3** blunder; piece of stupidity.

béton [betɔ̃], *s.m.* concrete; **b. armé,** reinforce concrete.

bétonn|er [betɔne], *v.tr.* to concrete; to con struct (sth.) with, in, concrete; *s.m.* **-age;** *s.* **-ière,** concrete-mixer.

betterave [bɛtraːv], *s.f.* beet(root); **b. à sucr** sugar-beet.

beugl|er [bøgle], *v.i.* to low; to bellow; *s.n* **-ement.**

beurre [bœːr], *s.m.* butter; *Cu:* **au b.,** cooked butter.

beurrer [bœre], *v.tr.* to butter.

beurrier, -ière [bœrje, -jɛːr]. **1.** *a.* butte producing (district, etc.). **2.** *s.* butter-dealer. *s.m.* butter-dish.

bévue [bevy], *s.f.* blunder, mistake; *Sch:* howle

biais [bjɛ]. **1.** *a.* oblique, slanting, bevelled. *s.m.* (*a*) slant (of wall); **en b.,** on the slan slantwise; askew; **regarder qn de b.,** to loc sideways at s.o.; (*b*) indirect means, expedien **prendre une affaire du bon b.,** to go the rig way to work.

biaiser [bjeze], *v.i.* **1.** to slant; to lean over. **2.** use evasions; to shuffle.

bibelot [biblo], *s.m.* **1.** curio, knick-knac trinket. **2.** *pl.* odds and ends.

bibelot|er [biblɔte], *v.i.* *F:* (*a*) to collect curic (*b*) to do odd jobs; *s.m.* **-age;** *s.* **-eur, -eus**

biberon [bibrɔ̃], *s.m.* feeding-bottle.

Bible [bibl], *s.f.* la Bible, the Bible.
bibliobus [biblɔbys], *s.m.* mobile library.
biblio|graphe [bibliɔgraf], *s.m. & f.* bibliographer; *s.f.* -**graphie**, bibliography; *a.* -**graphique**, bibliographical.
biblio|mane [bibliɔman], *s.m. & f.* book-collector; *s.f.* -**manie**, book-collecting.
bibliophile [bibliɔfil], *s.m. & f.* bibliophile, book-lover.
bibliothécaire [bibliɔtekɛːr], *s.m. & f.* librarian.
bibliothèque [bibliɔtɛk], *s.f.* 1. (*a*) library (building); (*b*) library (room). 2. bookcase, book-stand. 3. library; collection of books. 4. b. de gare, railway bookstall.
biblique [biblik], *a.* biblical.
biche [biʃ], *s.f.* 1. *Z:* hind, doe. 2. *F:* ma b., darling, dear.
bicolore [bikɔlɔːr], *a.* two-coloured.
bicoque [bikɔk], *s.f. F:* poky little house; shanty.
bicyclette [bisiklɛt], *s.f.* bicycle, cycle.
bidet [bidɛ], *s.m.* 1. nag; pony. 2. *Hyg:* bidet. 3. sawing-horse; trestle.
bidon [bidɔ̃], *s.m.* (*a*) can, drum (for oil); (*b*) *Mil:* water-bottle.
bidonville [bidɔ̃vil], *s.m.* shantytown.
bief [bjɛf], *s.m.* 1. (canal) reach, level. 2. mill-course, (mill-)race.
bielle [bjɛl], *s.f. Aut: etc:* crank-arm; tête de b., big end.
bien [bjɛ̃]. I. *adv.* 1. well; il faut b., les soigner, we must look after them well; vous avez b. fait, you did right; tout va b., all's well; aller, se porter, b., to be well, in good health; bien! (i) good! (ii) that's enough! (iii) all right! très b.! very good! well done! 2. (*with adj. function*) (*a*) right, proper; comme c'est b. à vous d'être venu! how nice of you to come! (*b*) comfortable; vous ne savez pas quand vous êtes b., you don't know when you are well off; *F:* vous voilà b.! now you're in a fine fix! (*c*) je ne me sens pas b., I don't feel well; (*d*) être b. avec qn, to be on good terms with s.o.; (*e*) of good appearance, position, etc.; il est très b., he is very gentlemanly; ce sont des gens b., they are people of good position; donnez-moi quelque chose de b., give me something good. 3. (*emphatic*) (*a*) indeed, really, quite; je l'ai regardé b. en face, I looked him full in the face; est-ce b. vous? is it really you? je l'avais b. dit! didn't I say so! j'espère b. qu'il viendra, I do hope he will come; b. entendu, of course; il est b. venu, mais j'étais occupé, he did come, but I was busy; (*b*) very; b. malheureux, very unhappy; (*c*) much, many, a great deal, a great many; (i) j'ai b. envie de lui écrire, I have a good mind to write to him; (ii) je l'ai vu b. des fois, I have seen him many times; b. d'autres, many others. 4. *adv.phr.* (*a*) tant b. que mal, somehow (or other); (*b*) b. plus, besides, moreover. 5. *conj.phr.* (*a*) b. que + *sub.*, though, although; (*b*) si b. que + *ind.*, so that, and so; il ne reparut plus, si b. qu'on le crut mort, he failed to reappear and so he was thought dead; (*c*) ou b., or else. 6. *int.* eh b.! well!
II. **bien**, *s.m.* 1. le b. et le mal, good and evil; homme de b., good, upright, man; c'est pour votre b., it is for your good; grand b. vous fasse! much good may it do you! 2. (*a*) possession, property, wealth; *F:* avoir du b. au soleil, to be a man of property; (*b*) *Jur:* biens mobiliers, personal estate; biens immobiliers, real estate; *Com:* biens de consommation, consumer goods. 3. *adv.phr.* (*a*) prendre la chose en b., to take the matter in good part; changement en b., change for the better; (*b*) mener une affaire à b., to bring a matter to a successful issue.
bien-aimé [bjɛ̃neme], *a. & s.* (well-)beloved; *pl.* bien-aimés.
bien-être [bjɛ̃nɛːtr], *s.m.* (*no pl.*) (*a*) well-being; comfort; (*b*) welfare.
bienfaisance [bjɛ̃fəzãːs], *s.f.* charity; bureau de b., relief committee.
bienfaisant [bjɛ̃fəzã], *a.* 1. beneficent, charitable. 2. beneficial, salutary.
bienfait [bjɛ̃fɛ], *s.m.* 1. benefit, kindness, service, good turn. 2. gift; *s.* -**eur**, -**rice**, benefactor, -factress.
bienheureux, -euse [bjɛ̃nœrø, -øːz], *a.* 1. blissful, happy. 2. *Ecc:* blessed; *s.* les b., the Blest.
biennal, -aux [bien(n)al, -o], *a.* biennial, two-yearly.
bienséance [bjɛ̃seãːs], *s.f.* propriety, decency; manquer aux bienséances, tò fail in good manners.
bientôt [bjɛ̃to], *adv.* (very) soon; before long; *F:* à b.! good-bye, see you again soon! c'est b. dit! it is easier said than done!
bienveill|ant [bjɛ̃vɛjã], *a.* kind, kindly, benevolent (envers, pour, to); *s.f.* -**ance**, kindness.
bienvenu, -e [bjɛ̃vəny]. 1. *a. & s.* welcome; soyez le b., la bienvenue! welcome! 2. *s.f.* welcome; souhaiter la bienvenue à qn., to welcome s.o., to bid s.o. welcome.
bière¹ [bjɛːr], *s.f.* beer; b. blonde = light ale.
bière², *s.f.* coffin.
biff|er [bife], *v.tr.* to cross out, cancel (word); *s.f.* -**ure**, cancelling stroke.
bifteck [biftɛk], *s.m.* (beef) steak; *F:* la course au b., the rat race.
bifur|quer [bifyrke], *v.tr. & i.* to fork, bifurcate, divide; to branch off; *s.f.* -**cation**, fork, junction.
bigamie [bigami], *s.f.* bigamy.

bigarré [bigare], *a.* variegated, mottled, parti-coloured.

bigarreau, -eaux [bigaro], *s.m.* white-heart cherry.

bigarrier [bigare], *v.tr.* to variegate, mottle; *s.f.* -ure, (colour-)medley.

bigorneau, -eaux [bigɔrno], *s.m. Moll:* winkle.

bigot, -ote [bigo, -ɔt]. 1. *a.* (over-)devout. 2. *s.* bigot; *s.f.* -erie, bigotry.

bigre [bigr], *int. F:* **b.!** qu'il fait froid! my God, it's cold!

bigrement [bigrəmã], *adv. F:* vous avez b. raison! you're dead right!

bijou, -oux [biʒu], *s.m.* piece of jewellery; jewel, gem; *F:* mon b.! my pet! *s.f.* -terie, jeweller's shop; jewellery; *s.* -tier, -tière, jeweller.

bikini [bikini], *s.m.* bikini.

bilan [bilã], *s.m. Com:* 1. balance-sheet. 2. déposer son b., to file one's petition (in bankruptcy).

bilatéral, -aux [bilateral, -o], *a.* bilateral, two-sided (contract).

bille [bil], *s.f. (a)* bile, gall; *(b)* bile; bad temper; s'échauffer la b., to worry, fret, get angry; ne te fais pas de b.! don't worry! *a. F:* -eux, -euse, easily upset.

bilieux, -euse [biljø, -ø:z], *a.* 1. bilious. 2. *(a)* short-tempered, irascible, testy; *(b)* morose.

bilingue [bilɛ̃:g], *a.* bilingual.

billard [bija:r], *s.m.* 1. (game of) billiards. 2. billiard-table; *Med: F:* operating table. 3. billiard-room.

bille [bi:j], *s.f.* (small) ball. 1. billiard-ball. 2. marble. 3. ballpoint (pen). 4. *Mec.E:* roulement à billes, ball-bearing(s).

billet [bijɛ], *s.m.* 1. note, short letter; **b. doux**, love-letter. 2. notice, invitation-card, circular; **b. de faire-part**, notice announcing a family event (birth, marriage, death). 3. ticket; **b. simple**, single ticket; **b. d'aller (et) retour**, return ticket; *N.Am:* round trip ticket; **b. de quai**, platform ticket; *(in lottery)* tirer un b. blanc, to draw a blank. 4. *Com: (a)* promissory note, bill; *(b)* **b. de banque**, bank-note. 5. **b. de santé**, health certificate. 6. permit, permission; *Sch:* **b. de sortie**, exeat.

billevesée [bilvəze, bij-], *s.f.* crack-brained notion; nonsense.

billion [biljõ], *s.m.* billion.

billot [bijo], *s.m.* block (of wood); chopping-log; (butcher's, executioner's) block.

bimbelot [bɛ̃blo], *s.m.* (cheap) knick-knack; *s.f.* -erie, toy business.

bimensuel, -elle [bimãsɥɛl], *a.* fortnightly; *adv.* -ellement.

bimoteur [bimɔtœ:r], *a.m. Av:* appareil b., twin-engine aircraft.

biner [bine], *v.tr. Agr:* to hoe; *s.m.* -age, hoeing; *s.f.* -ette, hoe; *s.f.* -euse, (motor)

cultivator.

binôme [bino:m], *a. & s.m.* binomial; **le b. de Newton**, the binomial theorem.

biochimie [bjoʃimi], *s.f.* biochemistry.

biographe [bjɔgraf], *s.m. & f.* biographer; *s.f.* -graphie, biography; *a.* -graphique, biographical.

biologie [bjɔlɔʒi], *s.f.* biology; *a.* -logique, biological; *s.m.* -logiste, -logue, biologist.

bioxyde [biɔksid], *s.m. Ch:* dioxide.

biparti, -ite [biparti, -it], *a.* bipartite.

bipède [bipɛd]. 1. *a.* two-legged. 2. *s.m.* biped.

biphasé [bifaze], *a. El:* two-phase (current).

biplace [biplas], *a. & s.m. Aut: Av:* two-seater.

bique [bik], *s.f. F:* she-goat, nanny-goat; *P: (of woman)* old cow.

birman, -ane [birmã, -an], *a. & s.* Burmese.

Birmanie (la) [labirmani]. *Pr.n.f.* Burma.

bis¹, bise¹ [bi, bi:z], *a.* greyish-brown; toile bise, unbleached linen; pain b., wholemeal bread.

bis² [bi:s], *adv.* twice. 1. no. 10 bis = No. 10A (of street). 2. *(after a line of a song)* repeat. 3. *Th:* encore!

bisaïeul, -eule [bizajœl], *s.* great-grandfather, -grandmother.

bisannuel, -elle [bizanɥɛl], *a.* biennial.

biscornu [biskɔrny], *a. F:* 1. mis-shapen; irregular (building). 2. distorted; crotchety, queer (mind).

biscotte [biskɔt], *s.f.* rusk.

biscuit [biskɥi], *s.m.* biscuit, *N.Am:* cookie, plain cake; **b. de Savoie**, sponge-cake; *s.f.* -erie, biscuit factory or trade.

bise² [bi:z], see BIS¹.

bise³, *s.f.* north wind.

bise⁴, *s.f. P:* kiss; fais b. à maman, give Mummy a kiss.

bismuth [bismyt], *s.m. Ch:* bismuth.

bisséqué [biseke], *a.* bisected.

bissextile [bisɛkstil], *a.f.* année b., leap-year.

bistro(t) [bistro], *s.m. F:* pub.

bitume [bitym], *s.m. Miner:* bitumen, asphalt.

bitumer [bityme], *v.tr.* 1. to asphalt (road). 2. to tar; carton bitumé, tarred felt; *s.m.* -age, tarring; *a.* -ineux, -ineuse, tarry.

bivouac [bivwak], *s.m. Mil:* bivouac.

bivouaquer [bivwake], *v.i.* to bivouac.

bizarre [biza:r], *a.* peculiar, odd, queer, bizarre *adv.* -ment.

bizarrerie [bizarri], *s.f.* 1. peculiarity, oddness 2. whimsicalness; extravagance; oddity.

black-out [blakaut], *s.m.* black-out; faire le b.-out sur qch., to hush sth. up.

blafard, -arde [blafar, -ard], *a.* pallid, wan; lambent (flame).

blague [blag], *s.f.* 1. **b. à tabac**, tobacco-pouch 2. *F: (a)* tall story, humbug; sans b.? really? *(b)* joke; quelle b.! what a joke! une sale b., a dirty trick.

blagu|**er** [blage], F: **1.** v.i. to joke. **2.** v.tr. to chaff, banter (s.o.); to make fun of (s.o., sth.); a. & s. -**eur**, -**euse**.

blaireau, -**eaux** [blɛro], s.m. **1.** badger. **2.** shaving-brush.

blâme [blɑːm], s.m. **1.** blame, disapprobation; **vote de b.**, vote of censure. **2.** Adm: **s'attirer un b.**, to incur a reprimand.

blâm|**er** [blɑme], v.tr. **1.** to blame; to find fault with. **2.** Adm: to reprimand; a. -**able**, blameworthy.

blanc, blanche [blɑ̃, blɑ̃ːʃ]. **I.** a. **1.** white; **vieillard à cheveux blancs**, white-haired old man. **2.** light-coloured; pale; s. **un b.**, a white man; **b. comme un linge**, as white as a sheet. **3.** clean, white, pure, stainless; **linge b.**, clean, un-soiled, linen; F: **c'est bonnet b. et b. bonnet**, it is six of one and half a dozen of the other; **montrer patte blanche**, to show one's credentials. **4.** blank (paper); **nuit blanche**, sleepless night; **voix blanche**, toneless voice; **vers blancs**, blank verse. **5. fer b.**, tin-plate; **boîte en fer b.**, tin, can.
II. blanc, s.m. white. **1. robe d'un b. sale**, dingy white dress. **2.** (a) **le b. des yeux**, the white of the eyes; (b) **b. d'une cible**, bull's-eye of a target; (c) blank; **chèque en b.**, blank cheque. **3.** (a) **saigner qn à b.**, to bleed s.o. white; (b) **cartouche à b.**, blank cartridge. **4.** (a) **b. de volaille**, breast of chicken; **un b. d'œuf**, the white of an egg; (b) **b. d'Espagne**, whiting; (c) **(articles de) b.**, linen drapery; **vente de b.**, white sale.
III. blanche, s.f. **1.** Bill: white ball. **2.** Mus: minim.

blanchaille [blɑ̃ʃɑːj], s.f. **1.** Fish: small fry. **2.** Cu: whitebait.

blanchâtre [blɑ̃ʃɑːtr], a. whitish, whity.

blancheur [blɑ̃ʃœːr], s.f. **1.** whiteness, paleness. **2.** purity, spotlessness.

blanch|**ir** [blɑ̃ʃiːr]. **1.** v.tr. (a) to whiten; to make white; (b) Tex: to bleach; (c) to wash, launder; **donner du linge à b.**, to send clothes to the wash; (d) to whitewash; (e) Cu: to blanch. **2.** v.i. to whiten; to turn white; **il commence à b.**, he is going white; s.m. -**issage**, washing, laundry; s.f. -**isserie**, (a) laundering; (b) laundry; s. -**isseur**, -**isseuse**, laundryman, f. laundress; washer-woman.

blanchisserie [blɑ̃ʃisri], s.f. (a) laundering; (b) laundry; **b. automatique**, launderette.

blanquette [blɑ̃kɛt], s.f. **1.** Cu: white (veal) stew. **2.** (varieties of) white wine.

blasé [blaze], a. blasé; surfeited.

blaser [blaze], v.tr. to surfeit.

se blaser, to become blasé, indifferent.

blason [blazɔ̃] s.m. (a) coat of arms; (b) heraldry.

blasphème [blasfɛːm], s.m. blasphemy.

blasphém|**er** [blasfeme], v.tr. & i. (**je blasphème; je blasphémerai**) to blaspheme; -**ateur**, -**atrice**. **1.** a. blasphemous. **2.** s. blasphemer.

blatte [blat], s.f. Ent: cockroach, black-beetle.

blé [ble], s.m. **1.** (a) corn; **halle aux blés**, corn-exchange; **manger son b. en herbe**, to live on capital; (b) corn-field; **faire les blés**, to cut the corn. **2. b. (froment)**, wheat; **b. d'Inde**, maize, N.Am: corn.

bled [blɛd], s.m. F: **dans le b.**, up country; **un sale b.**, a rotten place.

blême [blɛm], a. **1.** (a) livid, ghastly; (b) cadaverous (face). **2.** pale; wan (light).

blêm|**ir** [blemiːr], v.i. **1.** to turn pale, livid. **2.** (of light) to grow faint; s.m. -**issement**.

blessant [blɛsɑ̃], a. offensive, cutting (remark).

blessé, -ée [blese], s. wounded, injured, person.

bless|**er** [blese], v.tr. **1.** (a) to wound, hurt; **blessé à mort**, mortally wounded; (b) (of saddle) to gall (horse). **2.** to offend (the eye, etc.); to wound the feelings of (s.o.). **3.** to hurt (s.o.'s interests); s.f. -**ure**, wound, hurt.

se blesser. 1. to injure, wound, oneself. **2.** to take offence (**de**, at).

blet, blette [blɛ, blɛt], a. over-ripe, soft (fruit).

bleu, pl. **bleus** [blø]. **1.** a. blue; **conte b.**, fairy tale; **j'en suis resté b.**, I was flabbergasted; **il en a vu de bleues**, he has had some queer experiences. **2.** s.m. (a) blue (colour); F: **mon bras est couvert de bleus**, my arm is all black and blue; (b) F: **tout cet argent a passé au b.**, all this money has vanished; **n'y voir que du b.**, (i) to be puzzled, all at sea; (ii) to remain blissfully unconscious of sth. **3.** s. F: tyro, novice; Mil: recruit. **4.** s.m. (a) Tchn: blue-print; (b) pl. bleus, dungarees; **un b. de chauffe**, a boiler-suit; a. -**âtre**, bluish.

bleuet [bløɛ], s.m. Bot: (a) cornflower; (b) Fr.C: blueberry.

bleu|**ir** [bløiːr]. **1.** v.tr. to blue; to make (sth.) blue. **2.** v.i. to become blue; s.m. -**issage**; s.m. -**issement**.

blindé [blɛ̃de], a. Mil: armour-plated. **1. abri b.**, bomb-proof shelter; **division blindée**, armoured division. **2.** s.m. **les blindés**, the armour.

blind|**er** [blɛ̃de], v.tr. **1.** to armour-plate (ship, tank, car, etc.). **2.** El: to screen, shroud (parts); s.m. -**age**.

bloc [blɔk], s.m. **1.** block, lump (of wood); **acheter qch. en b.**, to buy sth. in the lump; to buy the whole stock of sth. **2.** Pol: coalition; **faire b.**, to unite. **3.** pad (of writing-paper); **b. dessin**, drawing-block. **4.** unit; Cin: **b. sonore**, sound unit; H: **b. cuisine**, kitchen unit; Aut: Av: **b. moteur**, engine block.

blocage [blɔkaːʒ], s.m. **1.** clamping; locking (of part). **2.** Mch: sticking, jamming. **3.** Pol.Ec:

pegging; freezing (of prices, wages).
bloc-notes [blɔknɔt], *s.m.* memo-pad, writing-pad; *pl. blocs-notes.*
blocus [blɔkys], *s.m.* blackade; **forcer le b.,** to run the blockade.
blond, -onde [blɔ̃, -ɔ̃:d]. **1.** *a.* fair, flaxen (hair); blond (person); **bière blonde** = light ale. **2.** *s.* fair(-haired) man, woman; blond(e). **3.** *s.m.* blond, flaxen (colour); **cheveux (d'un) b. doré,** golden hair.
blondin, -ine [blɔ̃dɛ̃, -in], *a. & s.* fair-haired (person).
bloquer [blɔke], *v.tr.* **1.** to jam on (brake); **b. les roues,** to lock the wheels. **2.** (*a*) to block, obstruct; to stop (cheque); (*b*) to blockade (a port); (*c*) *Pol.Ec:* to freeze (wages).
se bloquer, to jam; to get jammed.
blottir (se) [səblɔti:r], *v.pr.* to cower, crouch; **blotti dans un coin,** huddled in a corner.
blouse [blu:z], *s.f.* loose overgarment; overall, smock; blouse.
blouson [bluzɔ̃], *s.m.* (lumber-)jacket, wind-cheater; *F:* **b. noir,** teddy-boy.
bluet [blyɛ], *s.m. Bot:* cornflower.
bluff [blœf], *s.m. F:* bluff; **coup de b.,** piece of bluff.
bluffer [blœfe]. **1.** *v.tr. F:* to bluff. **2.** *v.i. F:* to try it on; *s.m.* **-eur.**
bobine [bɔbin], *s.f.* (*a*) bobbin, spool, reel; (*b*) reel, drum (for wire); *Phot:* spool, roll of film; (*c*) *El:* **b. d'induction,** induction coil.
bocage [bɔka:ʒ], *s.m.* small wood, copse.
bocal, -aux [bɔkal, -o], *s.m.* (*a*) wide-mouthed bottle; (*b*) goldfish bowl.
bock [bɔk], *s.m.* glass of beer.
bœuf, *pl.* **bœufs** [bœf, bø], *s.m.* **1.** ox, bullock; **jeune b.,** steer. **2.** beef; **b. à la mode,** stewed beef.
bohème [bɔɛm], *a. & s.* Bohemian; **mener une vie de b.,** to lead a free and easy existence.
bohémien, -ienne [bɔemjɛ̃, jɛn], *a. & s.* **1.** *Geog:* Bohemian. **2.** gipsy.
boire [bwa:r]. **I.** *v.tr.* (*pr.p.* **buvant;** *p.p.* **bu;** *pr.ind.* **ils boivent;** *pr.sub.* **je boive**). **1.** to drink; **b. qch. à petits coups,** to sip sth.; **b. un coup,** to have a drink; **b. un affront,** to swallow, pocket, an insult. **2.** (*of plants*) to absorb, drink up (moisture); (*of boots*) to take in (water). **3.** to drink (alcoholic beverages); **il a trop bu,** he is the worse for drink; *abs.* **il boit,** he drinks. **4.** to drink in (with one's eyes, ears); **b. qn des yeux,** to devour s.o. with one's eyes.
II. boire, *s.m.* drink, drinking; **le b. et le manger,** food and drink.
bois [bwa], *s.m.* **1.** wood, forest; **petit b.,** spinney. **2.** timber(-tree); **b. en état,** *Fr.C:* **b. debout,** standing timber; *F:* **abattre du b.,** to work hard. **3.** wood, timber, *N.Am:* lumber; **b. de chauffage,** firewood; **chantier de b.,** timber-

yard, *N.Am:* lumberyard; *Fr.C:* **b. franc,** hardwood; **maison en b. rond,** log house; **gravure sur b.,** woodcut; **je leur ferai voir de quel b. je me chauffe,** I'll show them what I'm made of. **4.** *Engr:* woodcut. **5.** *pl.* **de cerf,** horns, antlers, of a stag. **6. b. de lit,** bedstead; *Mus:* **les b.,** the woodwind instruments.
boisé [bwaze], *a.* **1.** (well-)wooded (country). **2.** panelled (room).
boiser [bwaze], *v.tr.* **1.** (*a*) to panel (room); (*b*) to prop (mine). **2.** to afforest; *s.m.* **-age,** timbering; afforestation; *s.f.* **-erie,** woodwork; panelling.
boisson [bwasɔ̃], *s.f.* beverage, drink; *Fr.C:* spirits, hard liquor; **pris de b.,** the worse for drink.
boîte [bwat], *s.f.* **1.** box; **b. de, en, fer blanc,** tin box; canister; tin, can; **conserves en b.,** tinned, canned, foods; **en b.,** boxed; **b. aux lettres,** letter-box; **b. à outils,** tool-chest; *Anat:* **b. du crâne,** brain-pan. **2.** *Aut:* **b. de vitesses,** gear-box; *El:* **b. à fusible,** fuse-box. **3.** *P:* (*a*) one's office, shop, school; **sale b.,** rotten firm, school, etc.; (*b*) **b. de nuit,** night-club; (*c*) *Mil:* guard-room, cells.
boiter [bwate], *v.i.* to limp; **b. d'un pied,** to be lame in one foot; *Lit:* **vers qui boitent,** halting verse; *a. & s.* **-eux, -euse. 1.** lame. **2.** lame man, woman.
boîtier [bwatje], *s.m.* case; **b. de montre,** watch-case.
bol [bɔl], *s.m.* (*a*) bowl, basin; (*b*) finger-bowl.
bolide [bɔlid], *s.m.* meteor; *F:* racing car; **lancé comme un b. sur la route,** hurtling along the road.
Bolivie (la) [labɔlivi]. *Pr.n.f. Geog:* Bolivia.
bolivien, -ienne [bɔlivjɛ̃, -jɛn], *a. & s. Geog:* Bolivian.
bombance [bɔ̃bɑ̃:s], *s.f. F:* feast(ing); carousing; **faire b.,** to have a good blow-out.
bombarder [bɔ̃barde], *v.tr.* to bombard, shell; **b. qn de demandes d'argent,** to pester s.o. for money; *s.m.* **-ement,** bombing; *s.m. Av:* **-ier,** bomber.
bombe [bɔ̃:b], *s.f.* **1.** bomb; **b. volante,** flying bomb; *F:* doodlebug; **entrer en b.,** to come bursting in. **2.** *Cu:* **b. glacée,** ice-pudding. **3.** **faire la b.,** to go, to be, on the binge.
bombé [bɔ̃be], *a.* convex, bulging; **avoir le dos b.,** to be round-shouldered.
bomber [bɔ̃be]. **1.** *v.tr.* (*a*) to cause (sth.) to bulge; **b. la poitrine,** to throw out one's chest; (*b*) to bend, arch (one's back); (*c*) to camber (road). **2.** *v.i.* to bulge (out).
bon, bonne [bɔ̃, bɔn]. **I.** *a.* **1.** good, upright, honest. **2.** good, nice, pleasing; **la bonne société,** well-bred people; *F:* **cela est b. à dire,** it's easier said than done. **3.** (*of pers.*) clever,

capable. 4. right, correct, proper; **suis-je dans le b. train?** am I on the right train? *Typ:* **b.,** stet. 5. good, kind (**pour, envers,** to); **vous êtes bien b. de m'inviter,** it is very kind of you to invite me; **faire b. visage à qn,** to be gracious to s.o.; **une bonne âme,** a simple soul. 6. good, advantageous; **c'est b. à savoir,** it is worth knowing; **acheter qch. à b. marché,** to buy sth. cheap; **à quoi b.?** what's the good of it? **puis-je vous être b. à quelque chose?** can I do anything for you? 7. good, fit, suitable; **être b. à qch.,** to be good for sth.; *Mil:* **b. pour le service,** fit for duty; **je ferai comme b. me semblera,** I shall do as I think fit. 8. good, favourable; **souhaiter la bonne année à qn,** to wish s.o. a happy New Year; *Nau:* **b. vent,** fair wind. 9. good, sound, safe; **en b. état,** sound; in working order; **billet b. pour trois mois,** ticket valid for three months; *F:* **son affaire est bonne!** he's in for it! 10. *F:* **j'ai attendu deux bonnes heures,** I waited a full two hours. 11. *adv.* **tenir b.,** to stand fast, to hold one's own; **sentir b.,** to smell nice; **il fait b. ici,** it is pleasant, comfortable, here. 12. **pour de b.,** for good (and all); **il pleut pour de b.,** it is raining in real earnest; **est-ce pour de b.?** are you in earnest? **en voilà une bonne!** that's a good one! **c'est b.!** that will do! 13. *int.* **b.!** good! agreed! 14. *s. F:* **mon b.,** my dear fellow; **ma bonne,** my dear. II. **bon,** *s.m.* 1. order, voucher, ticket; **b. de caisse,** cash voucher. 2. *Fin:* bond, bill, draft. III. **bonne,** *s.f.* (*a*) maid(servant), servant; (*b*) **b. d'enfants,** nursery-maid, nanny; (*c*) waitress.

bonbon [bɔ̃bɔ̃], *s.m.* sweet, *N.Am:* candy.

bonbonnière [bɔ̃bɔnjɛːr], *s.f.* 1. sweet-box. 2. neat little house or flat.

bond [bɔ̃], *s.m.* 1. bound, leap, jump, spring; **franchir qch. d'un b.,** to clear sth. at one jump. 2. (*of ball*) bounce; **faire faux b.,** (*of ball*) to break.

bonde [bɔ̃ːd], *s.f.* 1. (*a*) bung (of cask); (*b*) plug (of sink). 2. bung-hole, plug-hole.

bondé [bɔ̃de], *a.* chock-full, crammed, packed.

bondir [bɔ̃diːr], *v.i.* 1. (*a*) to leap, bound; to spring up; **b. sur qch.,** to spring at, pounce on, sth.; (*b*) to gambol, skip, caper. 2. (*of ball*) to bounce; *a.* **-issant;** *s.m.* **-issement.**

bonheur [bɔnœːr], *s.m.* 1. good fortune, good luck, success; **être en b.,** to be in luck; **porter b.,** to bring (good) luck; **quel b.!** what a blessing! **jouer de b.,** to be lucky, in luck. 2. happiness; **faire le b. de qn,** to be the source of s.o.'s happiness.

bonhomie [bɔnɔmi], *s.f.* simple good-heartedness; good nature.

bonhomme [bɔnɔm], *s.m.* (*a*) simple, good-natured, man; **faux b.,** sly, shifty, customer; **pourquoi pleures-tu, mon b.?** why are you

crying, my little man? **il va son petit b. de chemin,** he is jogging quietly along; *a.* **prendre un air b.,** to put on an air of simplicity, of good nature; (*b*) **b. en pain d'épice,** gingerbread man; **b. de neige,** snowman; *pl.* **bonshommes** [bɔ̃zom].

boniment [bɔnimã], *s.m.* (showman's) patter; **faire du b.** (à qn), to butter (s.o.) up.

bonjour [bɔ̃ʒuːr], *s.m.* good day, good morning, good afternoon.

Bonne-Espérance [bɔnɛsperã:s]. *Pr.n.f.* **le Cap de B.-E.,** the Cape of Good Hope.

bonne femme [bɔnfam], *s.f.* simple, good-natured woman; **une petite b. f.,** a little old woman; **contes, remèdes, de b. f.,** old wives' tales, remedies; **quelle sale b. f.!** what an unpleasant woman! **rideaux b. f.,** draped curtains.

bonne-maman [bɔnmamã], *s.f. F:* granny; *pl.* **bonnes-mamans.**

bonnement [bɔnmã], *adv.* (*only in*) **tout b.,** simply, plainly.

bonnet [bɔnɛ], *s.m.* (*a*) (*close-fitting and brimless*) cap; **donner un coup de b. à qn,** to touch one's cap to s.o.; *F:* **avoir la tête près du b.,** to be hot-tempered; **avoir mis son b. de travers,** to be in a bad mood; *Mil:* **b. de police,** forage cap; *F:* **gros b.,** bigwig, big shot; **b. de bain,** bathing-cap; *F:* **elle a jeté son b. par-dessus les moulins,** she has kicked over the traces; (*b*) cup (of brassière).

bonnet|erie [bɔntri], *s.f.* hosiery; knitted goods; *s.* **-ier, -ière,** hosier.

bon-papa [bɔ̃papa], *s.m. F:* grand(pa)pa, grandad; *pl.* **bons-papas.**

bonsoir [bɔ̃swaːr], *s.m.* good evening, good night.

bonté [bɔ̃te], *s.f.* 1. (*a*) goodness, kindness; kindly feeling; (*b*) *pl.* kindnesses, kind actions. 2. goodness, excellence (of things).

borax [bɔraks], *s.m. Ch:* borax.

bord [bɔːr], *s.m.* 1. *Nau:* (*a*) side (of ship); **moteur hors b.,** outboard motor; **le b. du vent,** the weather-side; **le b. sous le vent,** the lee-side; **faux b.,** list; **le long du b.,** alongside; (*b*) tack, leg; **courir un b.,** to make a tack; (*c*) les **hommes du b.,** the ship's company. 2. edge, border, hem; brink, verge; brim; **remplir les verres à pleins bords,** to fill the glasses brimfull. 3. shore, strand; bank (of river); **aller au b. de la mer,** to go to the seaside.

bordeaux [bɔrdo], *s.m.* Bordeaux (wine); **b. rouge,** claret.

bordée [bɔrde], *s.f. Nau:* 1. broadside; *F:* **lâcher une b. de jurons,** to let fly a volley of oaths. 2. board, tack; **tirer des bordées,** to tack; to beat up to windward. 3. watch; **b. de tribord, de bâbord,** starboard watch, port watch. 4. *Fr.C:* **b. (de neige),** heavy snowfall.

bordel [bɔrdɛl], *s.m.* brothel.

bordelais, -aise [bɔrdəlɛ, -ɛːz], *a. & s.* (native, inhabitant) of Bordeaux.

border [bɔrde], *v.tr.* (*a*) to border; (*b*) **b. qch. de qch., avec qch.,** to edge, fringe, sth. with sth.; (*c*) **b. un lit,** to tuck in the bed-clothes.

bordereau, -eaux [bɔrdəro], *s.m. Com:* memo, consignment note; schedule; **b. de paie,** wages docket; **b. de crédit,** credit note.

bordure [bɔrdyːr], *s.f.* 1. (*a*) border, rim; edge; fringe; kerb; skirt (of a wood). 2. frame.

bore [bɔːr], *s.m. Ch:* boron.

borgne [bɔrɲ], *a.* 1. (*a*) one-eyed; blind in one eye; (*b*) **rue b.,** blind alley. 2. disreputable, shady (public house).

borique [bɔrik], *a.* boric; *F:* boracic (acid).

borne [bɔrn], *s.f.* 1. (*a*) boundary-mark, -stone; **b. kilométrique** = milestone; (*b*) *pl.* boundaries, limits; **cela passe les bornes,** that is going too far, beyond a joke. 2. (stone) corner-post. 3. *El:* terminal.

borné [bɔrne], *a.* limited, restricted; **homme (d'un esprit) b.,** narrow-minded man.

borner [bɔrne], *v.tr.* 1. (*a*) to mark out the boundary of (field); to stake (claim); (*b*) to form the boundary of (country). 2. to limit, restrict (power); to set limits, bounds, to (ambition). **se borner,** to restrict oneself, to exercise self-restraint; **je me suis borné à (vous) faire remarquer que . . .,** I merely observed that . . .; **leur science se borne à . . .,** their knowledge amounts to, *F:* boils down to . . . .

bosquet [bɔskɛ], *s.m.* grove, thicket.

bosse [bɔs], *s.f.* 1. hump (of camel). 2. (*a*) bump, swelling, lump; (*b*) unevenness, bump. 3. dent. 4. boss; **en b.,** in relief, in the round.

bosseler [bɔsle], *v.tr.* (**je bosselle**). 1. to emboss (plate). 2. to dent; **théière toute bosselée,** battered teapot; *s.m.* **-age,** embossing; *s.m.* **-lement,** denting, bruising; *s.f.* **-ure,** dent, bruise.

bossu [bɔsy]. 1. *a.* hunch-backed (person); humped (animal). 2. *s.* hunchback.

bot [bo], *a.* **pied b.,** club foot.

botanique [bɔtanik]. 1. *a.* botanical. 2. *s.f.* botany.

botaniste [bɔtanist], *s.m. & f.* botanist.

botte[1] [bɔt], *s.f.* bunch (of carrots); truss, bundle (of hay).

botte[2], *s.f.* (high) boot, wellington (boot); *s.m.* **-tier,** bootmaker; *s.f.* **-tine,** (ankle-)boot.

botter [bɔte], *v.tr.* 1. (*a*) to put boots, shoes, on (s.o.); (*b*) **être bien botté,** to be well shod. 2. to kick; *Fb:* **b. le ballon,** to kick the ball; *F:* **b. qn,** to boot s.o.

Bottin [bɔtɛ̃], *s.m. R.t.m:* (the best known) French street and trade directory.

bouc [buk], *s.m.* billy-goat; (**barbe de) b.,** goatee (beard); **b. émissaire,** scapegoat.

bouche [buʃ], *s.f.* mouth. 1. **garder qch. pour la bonne b.,** to keep something as a tit-bit; **faire la petite b.,** to pick at one's food; **manger à pleine b.,** to eat greedily; **c'est une fine b.,** he is a gourmet; **b. bée,** open-mouthed. 2. mouth (of horse, cattle, fish). (NOTE: *of a dog and carnivorous animals* **gueule** *is used*.) 3. mouth, opening, aperture (of well); muzzle (of gun); **b. à feu,** gun, piece of artillery; **b. d'eau,** hydrant; **b. d'incendie,** hydrant; **les Bouches du Gange,** the mouths of the Ganges.

bouche-à-bouche [buʃabuʃ], *s.m.inv.* kiss of life.

bouché [buʃe], *a.* 1. plugged (up); **avoir l'esprit b.,** to be dull-witted; **temps b.,** overcast weather. 2. **cidre b.,** bottled cider.

bouchée [buʃe], *s.f.* 1. mouthful. 2. *Cu:* **b. aux huîtres,** oyster patty; **b. à la reine,** vol-au-vent.

boucher[1] [buʃe], *v.tr.* **b. un trou,** to stop (up), to plug, a hole; **cela servira à b. un trou,** it will serve as a stop-gap; **se b. le nez,** to hold one's nose; **se b. les oreilles,** to stop one's ears, to refuse to hear; *s.m.* **-age.**

boucher[2], *s.m.* butcher; *s.f.* **-erie,** butcher's shop, -trade.

bouche-trou [buʃtru], *s.m.* stop-gap, substitute; makeshift; *pl.* **bouche-trous.**

bouchon [buʃɔ̃], *s.m.* 1. wisp, handful (of straw). 2. stopper, plug, bung; **b. de liège,** cork; **b. de verre,** glass stopper.

boucle [bukl], *s.f.* 1. buckle; **b. de ceinture,** belt-buckle. 2. (*a*) loop, bow (of ribbon); (*b*) loop, sweep (of river). 3. ring; **boucles d'oreilles,** earrings. 4. curl, ringlet (of hair). 5. *Sp:* lap.

boucler [bukle]. 1. *v.tr.* (*a*) to buckle (belt); to fasten (strap); *F:* **b. une affaire,** to clinch a matter; (*b*) to loop, tie up, knot (ribbon); *Av:* **la boucle,** to loop the loop; (*c*) to lock up, imprison; (*d*) **b. (les cheveux de) qn,** to curl s.o.'s hair. 2. *v.i.* (*u*) (*of metal*) to buckle; (*b*) (*of hair*) to curl, to be curly.

bouclier [bukli(j)e], *s.m.* buckler, shield.

bouddhiste [budist], *a. & s.* Buddhist.

bouder [bude]. 1. *v.i.* to sulk; **b. contre qn,** to be sulky with s.o. 2. *v.tr.* **b. qn,** to be sulky, in the sulks, with s.o.; *s.f.* **-erie,** sulkiness; *a. & s.* **-eur, -euse,** sulky (person).

boudin [budɛ̃], *s.m.* 1. (*a*) *Cu:* black-pudding, *N.Am:* blood sausage; (*b*) *F:* **boudins,** fat, podgy, fingers. 2. (*a*) corkscrew curl; roll, twist (of tobacco); (*b*) *Mec.E:* flange (on wheel).

boue [bu], *s.f.* 1. mud, mire; filth, dirt; **tirer qn de la b.,** to raise s.o. from the gutter. 2. (building) mud, clay. 3. sediment, mud, deposit; **bain de boues,** mud-bath; *s.m.* **-eur,** dustman; *a.* **-eux, -euse,** muddy.

bouée [bue], *s.f. Nau:* buoy. 1. **b. à cloche,** bell-buoy. 2. **b. de sauvetage,** life-buoy.

bouffée [bufe], *s.f.* puff (of smoke); whiff (of scent); gust (of air).

bouffer [bufe]. **1.** *v.i.* (*of dress*) to puff (out), swell out. **2.** *v.tr.* **b. les joues,** to puff out one's cheeks. **3.** *v.tr. P:* to eat greedily; **b. son dîner,** to bolt one's dinner.

bouffi [bufi], *a.* puffy, swollen (eyes); bloated (face).

bouffir [bufiːr]. **1.** *v.tr.* to swell, blow out. **2.** *v.i.* to become swollen, puffed up, bloated; *s.f.* **-issure,** swelling, puffiness.

bouffon [bufɔ̃]. **1.** *s.m.* buffoon, clown. **2.** *a.* (*f.* **bouffonne** [bufɔn]) farcical; *s.f.* **-nerie,** buffoonery.

bouger [buʒe], *v.* (*n.* **bougeons**). **1.** *v.i.* to budge, stir, move. **2.** *v.tr. F:* **il ne faut rien b.,** you must not move anything.

bougie [buʒi], *s.f.* candle; **à la b.,** by candlelight. **2.** *Ph.Meas:* candle-power. **3.** *I.C.E:* **b. (d'allumage),** sparking-plug; *s.m.* **-oir,** (flat) candlestick.

bougon, -onne [bugɔ̃, -ɔn], *F:* **1.** *s.* grumbler, grouser. **2.** *a.* grumpy.

bougonner [bugɔne], *v.i. F:* to grumble.

bouillabaisse [bujabɛs], *s.f. Cu:* Provençal fish-soup; bouillabaisse.

bouillant [bujɑ̃], *a.* **1.** boiling. **2.** fiery, hot-headed, impetuous.

bouillie [buji], *s.f.* gruel, porridge.

bouillir [bujiːr], *v.i.* (*pr.p.* **bouillant;** *pr.ind.* **je bous**) to boil; **faire b. qch.,** to boil sth., bring sth. to the boil; *s.f.* **-oire,** kettle.

bouillon [bujɔ̃], *s.m.* **1.** bubble; **bouillir à gros bouillons,** to boil fast; **cuire à petits bouillons,** to simmer. **2.** *Cu:* **b. gras,** beef-tea; stock.

bouillonner [bujɔne], *v.i.* to bubble, boil up, seethe; *s.m.* **-ement.**

boulanger [bulɑ̃ʒe], *s.m.* baker; *s.f.* **-erie,** baker's shop.

boule [bul], *s.f.* **1.** (*a*) ball, sphere, globe; **b. de hockey,** hockey ball; (*b*) **b. de scrutin,** ballot-ball. **2.** *Games:* **jouer aux boules,** to play bowls; **jeu de boules,** bowling-green; **partie de boules,** game of bowls.

bouleau, -eaux [bulo], *s.m.* birch(-tree).

bouledogue [buldɔg], *s.m.* bulldog.

boulette [bulɛt], *s.f.* **1.** pellet (of paper, etc.). **2.** *Cu:* force-meat ball; rissole. **3.** *F:* **faire une b.,** to drop a brick.

boulevard [bulvaːr], *s.m.* boulevard.

bouleversant [bulversɑ̃], *a.* upsetting, bewildering.

bouleverser [bulverse], *v.tr.* (*a*) to upset, overthrow; to throw into confusion; (*b*) to upset, discompose (s.o.); *s.m.* **-ement,** overthrow; confusion.

boulon [bulɔ̃], *s.m.* bolt, pin; **b. à écrou,** screw-bolt.

boulot [bulo], *s.m. F:* work; **quel est son b.?**

what's his job?

bouquet [bukɛ], *s.m.* **1.** (*a*) bunch of flowers, posy, bouquet; (*b*) cluster, clump (of trees); plume, tuft (of feathers). **2.** aroma (of cigar); bouquet (of wine). **3.** *F:* **réserver qch. pour le b.,** to keep sth. for the last; **ça, c'est le b.!** that's the last straw!

bouquetier, -ière [buktje, -jɛːr], *s.* flower-seller; *esp.f.* flower-girl.

bouquin [bukɛ̃], *s.m.* old book; *F:* book.

bouquiner [bukine], *v.i.* **1.** to hunt after old books. **2.** (*a*) to pore over old books; (*b*) *F:* to read; *s.m.* **-eur,** lover of old books; *s.m.* **-iste,** second-hand bookseller.

bourbe [burb], *s.f.* mud (of pond); mire; *a.* **-eux, -euse,** muddy, miry; *s.m.* **-ier,** slough, mud-pit, -mire.

bourde [burd], *s.f. F:* **1.** fib, falsehood; **débiter des bourdes,** to tell fibs. **2.** blunder, bloomer; **faire une b.,** to put one's foot in it, to drop a brick.

bourdon [burdɔ̃], *s.m.* **1.** *Mus:* drone (of bagpipes). **2.** great bell. **3.** *Ent:* humble-bee; *F:* bumble-bee.

bourdonner [burdɔne]. **1.** *v.i.* (*of insects*) to buzz, hum. **2.** *v.tr.* to hum (tune); *s.m.* **-ement,** buzzing, humming; booming (of bell).

bourg [buːr], *s.m.* small market-town.

bourgade [burgad], *s.f.* large village.

bourgeois, -oise [burʒwa, -waːz]. **I.** *s.* **1.** civilian, townsman; **en b.;** *F:* in civvies; **agent de police en b.,** plain-clothes detective. **2.** middle-class man, woman; *Pej:* bourgeois; *P:* **la bourgeoise,** the missis; **les petits b.,** the lower middle class; small shopkeepers. **3.** *P:* (*as used by workmen*) boss. **II.** *a.* **1.** middle-class (family). **2.** homely, simple, plain (cooking, tastes, etc.); **pension bourgeoise,** private boarding-house. **3.** common, unrefined, vulgar; *s.m.* **c'est du dernier b.!** it's horribly middle-class! *adv.* **-ement.**

bourgeoisie [burʒwazi], *s.f.* the middle class.

bourgeon [burʒɔ̃], *s.m.* **1.** bud. **2.** *F:* pimple (on the nose, etc.).

bourgeonner [burʒɔne], *v.i.* **1.** *Bot:* to bud, shoot. **2.** *F:* to become pimply; *s.m.* **-ement.**

Bourgogne [burgɔɲ]. **1.** *Pr.n.f. Geog:* Burgundy. **2.** *s.m.* (**vin de**) **B.,** Burgundy (wine).

bourguignon, -onne [burgiɲɔ̃, -ɔn], *a. & s.* Burgundian.

bourrade [burad], *s.f.* blow; thrust; thump (on the back).

bourrasque [burask], *s.f.* squall; gust of wind.

bourreau, -eaux [buro], *s.m.* executioner; hangman; inhuman wretch; **b. de travail,** glutton for work.

bourreler [burle], *v.tr.* (**je bourrèle**) to torment (s.o. mentally); *s.m.* **-èlement,** pangs of remorse.

bourrelet [burlɛ], *s.m.* 1. pad, wad, cushion; **b. de porte,** draught-excluder; **b. de graisse,** roll of fat. 2. rim, flange (of wheel).

bourr|er [bure], *v.tr.* 1. to stuff, pad (cushion); to fill (pipe with tobacco); *F:* **b. le crâne à qn,** to stuff s.o. with false stories. 2. **b. qn (de coups),** to beat s.o. up; *s.m.* **-elier,** harness-maker.

se bourrer, *v.pr.* to stuff oneself (with food).

bourricot [buriko], *s.m.* small donkey.

bourri|que [burik], *s.f.* (a) she-ass; donkey; (b) *F:* dunce, duffer, ignoramus; *s.m.* **-quet,** baby donkey.

bourru [bury], *a.* rough, rude, surly.

bourse [burs], *s.f.* 1. (a) purse, bag, pouch; **sans b. délier,** without spending a penny; **faire b. commune,** to share expenses; (b) *Z:* pouch (of marsupial). 2. *Sch:* scholarship; **b. d'entretien,** maintenance grant. 3. stock exchange; **jouer à la B.,** to speculate; **b. du Travail,** Labour Exchange.

boursier, -ière [bursje, -jɛːr], *s.* scholarship holder.

boursouflé [bursufle], *a.* swollen, bloated; **style b.,** inflated, turgid, style.

boursoufl|er [bursufle], *v.tr.* to puff up, swell (flesh); to blister (paint); *s.f.* **-ure,** swelling; blister.

se boursoufler, to rise, swell; to increase in volume; (*of paint*) to blister.

bouscul|er [buskyle], *v.tr.* 1. **b. des objets,** to up-set things. 2. **b. qn,** to jostle, hustle, s.o.; *s.f.* **-ade,** scuffle; hustle.

bouse [buːz], *s.f.* **b. de vache,** cow-dung.

bousill|er [buzije], *v.tr. F:* **b. un ouvrage,** to bungle, botch, scamp, a piece of work; *Av:* **b. son appareil,** to crash one's plane; *s.m.* **-age;** *s.m.* **-eur.**

boussole [busɔl], *s.f.* compass.

bout [bu], *s.m.* 1. extremity, end; **au b. de la rue,** at the end of the street; **le haut b. de la table,** the head of the table; **écouter qn jusqu'au b.,** to hear s.o. through; **au b. du compte,** after all; *adv.phr.* **de b. en b.,** from beginning to end, from end to end; **être à b.,** to be exhausted; **pousser à b. la patience de qn,** to exhaust s.o.'s patience; **nous sommes à b. d'essence,** we have run out of petrol; **venir à b. de faire qch.,** to succeed in doing sth. 2. end, tip, end-piece; **b. de pipe,** mouthpiece of a pipe; **à b. portant,** point-blank; *F:* **prendre qch. par le bon b.,** to tackle sth. the right way. 3. bit, fragment; **nous avons un b. de jardin,** we have a bit of garden; **b. de papier,** scrap of paper; **c'est un bon b. de chemin,** it's a good step to go.

boutade [butad], *s.f.* 1. whim, caprice. 2. sudden outburst (of ill-temper). 3. sally; flash of wit.

boute-en-train [butãtrɛ̃], *s.m.inv.* **le b.-en-t. d'une société,** the life and soul of a party.

bouteille [butɛːj], *s.f.* bottle; **b. isolante, b. Thermos** [tɛrmɔs], vacuum, Thermos (*R.t.m.*), flask; **b. à gaz,** gas cylinder.

bouti|que [butik], *s.f.* (a) shop; **tenir b.,** to keep a shop; **fermer b.,** (i) to shut up shop; (ii) to give up one's shop; *F:* **parler b.,** to talk shop; (b) market stall; (c) boutique; *s.* **-quier, -quière,** shop-keeper.

bouton [butɔ̃], *s.m.* 1. bud; **en b.,** budding, in bud. 2. button; **b. de plastron,** stud; **b. de col,** collar-stud; **boutons de manchettes,** cuff-links. 3. (a) knob, handle (of door); button (of foil); **tourner le b.,** to switch (the wireless) on or off; (b) *P.N:* **appuyez sur le b.,** press the button. 4. pimple (on face). 5. *Bot:* **b. d'or,** buttercup.

boutonn|er [butɔne]. 1. *v.i. Bot:* to bud. 2. *v.tr.* to button (up) (coat, dress); *s.f.* **-ière,** button-hole.

bouture [butyːr], *s.f. Hort:* slip, cutting.

bouturer [butyre], *v.tr.* to propagate (plants) by cuttings.

bouvier [buvje], *s.m.* (a) cowman; (b) drover.

bouvreuil [buvrœːj], *s.m. Orn:* bullfinch.

bovin [bɔvɛ̃], *a.* bovine.

box [bɔks], *s.m.* 1. horse-box, loose-box. 2. *Aut:* lock-up garage. 3. *Jur:* **le b. des accusés,** the dock.

box|e [bɔks], *s.f.* boxing; *s.m.* **-eur,** boxer.

boyau, -aux [bwajo]. 1. *F:* bowel, gut; **corde de b.,** (cat) gut. 2. hose-pipe. 3. narrow thoroughfare.

brabançon, -onne [brabãsɔ̃, -ɔn], *a. & s.* Brabantine, Belgian; **la Brabançonne,** the Belgian national anthem.

bracelet [braslɛ], *s.m.* 1. bracelet, bangle; watchstrap. 2. metal band, ring.

braconn|er [brakɔne], *v.tr. & i.* to poach; *s.m.* **-age,** poaching; *s.m.* **-ier,** poacher.

brai [brɛ], *s.m.* pitch, tar.

braill|er [brɑje], *v.i. F:* to bawl, shout; *a. & s.* **-ard, -arde,** bawling; bawler; *s.f.* **-erie,** shouting, bawling.

brai|re [brɛːr], *v.i.def.* to bray; *s.m.* **-ment,** braying.

braise [brɛːz], *s.f.* 1. (glowing) embers. 2. small cinders; small coke.

braiser [brɛze], *v.tr. Cu:* to braise.

brancard [brɑkaːr], *s.m.* stretcher; *s.m.* **-ier,** stretcher-bearer.

branchage [brɑ̃ʃaːz], *s.m. coll.* branches, boughs (of trees).

branche [brɑ̃ʃ], *s.f.* 1. (a) branch, bough; (b) **notre b. de la famille,** our branch of the family; (c) **b. d'un fleuve,** branch of a river; (d) **les différentes branches des sciences,** the various branches of learning. 2. leg (of compasses); blade (of propeller).

branch|er [brɑ̃ʃe], *v.tr. El:* to plug in; *P.T.T:* to put (s.o.) through (on phone); *s.m.* **-ement.**

branchies [brãʃi], *s.f.pl.* gills (of fish).
brandl ir [brãdi:r], *v.tr.* to brandish, flourish (stick, weapon); *s.m.* -**issement.**
branle [brã:l], *s.m.* (*a*) oscillation, swing (motion); (*b*) impulse, impetus; **mettre qch. en b.,** to set sth. going.
branll er [brãle]. **1.** *v.tr.* to swing, shake (one's legs); to wag (one's head). **2.** *v.i.* to shake; to be loose; **dent qui branle,** loose tooth; *a.* -**ant,** shaky, rickety; *s.m.* -**ement,** oscillation.
braqul er [brake], *v.tr.* (*a*) **b. un fusil sur qch.,** to point a gun at sth.; (*b*) **b. les yeux sur qn,** to fix one's eye(s) on s.o.; (*c*) *v.i.* **voiture qui braque bien,** car with a good lock; *s.m.* -**age,** (*a*) aiming; (*b*) lock (of car).
bras [bra], *s.m.* arm. **1.** (*a*) **il a le(s) b. long(s),** he is long in the arm; **avoir le b. long,** to have a wide influence; **les b. m'en tombent,** I am dumbfounded; **cette nouvelle m'a cassé b. et jambes,** this piece of news stunned me; **avoir qn sur les b.,** to have s.o. on one's hands; **voiture à b.,** handcart; **prendre qn à pleins b.,** to hug s.o.; **saisir qn à b.-le-corps,** to grapple with s.o.; **b. dessus b. dessous,** arm in arm; (*b*) *pl.* hands, workmen; **manquer de b.,** to be shorthanded. **2. b. d'une chaise,** arm of a chair.
brasl er [braze], *v.tr.* to braze; to hard-solder; *s.m.* -**age.**
brasier [brazje], *s.m.* (*a*) fire of live coals; (*b*) source of intense heat.
brassard [brasa:r], *s.m.* armlet, arm-badge; **b. de deuil,** mourning-band; arm-band.
brasse [brɑ:s], *s.f.* **1.** span (of the arms); *Nau:* fathom. **2.** *Swimming:* stroke; **nager (à) la b.,** to swim breast-stroke.
brassée [brase], *s.f.* armful.
brassl er [brase], *v.tr.* **1.** to brew (beer). **2.** to mix, stir (up); **b. des affaires,** to handle a lot of business; *s.m.* -**age.**
brasserie [brasri], *s.f.* **1.** brewery. **2.** brewing. **3.** = restaurant (with bar).
brasseur [brasœ:r], *s.m.* **1.** brewer. **2.** *Metall:* mixer; *F:* **b. d'affaires,** (i) *F:* tycoon; (ii) shady financier.
bravade [bravad], *s.f.* bravado, bluster.
brave [bra:v], *a.* **1.** brave, bold, gallant; **un (homme) brave,** a brave, courageous, man. **2.** good, honest, worthy; **c'est un b. homme,** *F:* **un b. type,** he's a decent sort, a good chap; *s.m.* **je vous félicite, mon b.,** I congratulate you, my good man; *adv.* -**ment.**
braver [brave], *v.tr.* to brave. **1.** to face (sth.) bravely. **2.** to defy, dare.
bravo [bravo]. **1.** *int.* bravo! well done! hear, hear! **2.** *s.m.* cheer, cheering.
bravoure [bravu:r], *s.f.* bravery, gallantry.
brebis [brəbi], *s.f.* **1.** ewe. **2.** sheep.
brèche [breʃ], *s.f.* breach, opening, gap, break (in hedge, wall, etc.); *F:* **battre qn en b.,** to run

s.o. down.
bredouille [brədu:j], *a.inv. F:* **être b.,** to have failed completely (in sth.).
bredouilll er [brəduje], *v.i.* to mumble; *v.tr.* **b. une excuse,** to stammer out an excuse; *s.* -**eur,** -**euse.**
bref, *f.* **brève** [bref, bre:v]. **1.** *a.* brief, short; **raconter qch. en b.,** to relate sth. in a few words. **2.** *adv.* briefly, in short; **parler b.,** to speak curtly. **3.** *s.m.* (papal) brief. **4.** *s.f.* **brève,** short syllable.
brème [brem], *s.f. Ich:* bream.
Brême [brem]. *Pr.n.f. Geog:* Bremen.
Brésil (le) [ləbrezil]. *Pr.n.m. Geog:* Brazil.
brésilien, -**ienne** [breziljẽ, -jɛn], *a. & s.* Brazilian.
Bretagne (la) [labrətaɲ]. *Pr.n.f. Geog:* **1.**Britanny. **2.** Britain (*in* GRANDE-BRETAGNE).
bretelle [brətɛl], *s.f.* **1.** strap, sling; shoulder-strap. **2.** (**paire de) bretelles,** (pair of) braces, *N.Am:* suspenders.
breton, -**onne** [brətɔ̃, -ɔn], *a. & s.* Breton.
breuvage [brœva:ʒ], *s.m.* **1.** beverage, drink. **2.** *Med:* draught, potion.
brevet [brəve], *s.m.* **1. b. d'invention,** (letters) patent. **2.** diploma, certificate.
breveté [brəvte]. **1.** (*a*) *s.* patentee; (*b*) *a.* (i) **fournisseur b. de sa Majesté,** (tradesman) by special appointment to His, Her, Majesty; (ii) patent. **2.** *a.* certificated.
breveter [brəvte], *v.tr.* (**je brevète, je brevette)** to patent (invention).
bréviaire [brevjɛ:r], *s.m. Ecc:* breviary.
brévité [brevite], *s.f.* shortness (of vowel, speech).
bribes [brib], *s.f.pl.* scraps, fragments; **b. de conversation,** snatches of conversation.
bricole [brikɔl], *s.f.* usu. *pl. F:* odd jobs; odds and ends; **s'occuper de bricoles,** to do odd jobs.
bricoll er [brikɔle], *F:* (*a*) *v.tr.* **c'est une affaire bricolée,** it's a put-up job; (*b*) *v.i.* (i) to do odd jobs; (ii) to do it yourself; *s.m.* -**age,** doing odd jobs; *s.* -**eur,** -**euse,** (i) odd-job man, woman; (ii) do-it-yourself man.
bride [brid], *s.f.* (*a*) bridle; (*b*) rein(s); **aller à b. abattue,** to ride at full speed; **lâcher la b. à sa colère,** to give vent to one's anger; **tenir qn en b.,** to keep a tight hand over s.o.
brider [bride], *v.tr.* **1.** (*a*) to bridle (horse); (*b*) **b. ses passions,** to curb one's passions. **2.** to tie up, fasten (up); *Cu:* to truss (fowl).
bridge [bridʒ], *s.m. Games:* bridge.
bridgl er [bridʒe], *v.i.* to play bridge; *s.* -**eur,** -**euse,** bridge-player.
brièvel té [brievte], *s.f.* **1.** shortness, brevity (of time). **2.** brevity, conciseness; *adv.* -**ment.**
brigade [brigad], *s.f.* **1.** *Mil:* brigade; *Av:* **b. aérienne,** group, *N.Am:* wing. **2.** squad,

detachment (of gendarmes).

brigadier [brigadje], *s.m.* (*a*) corporal (of mounted arms); (*b*) b. de police, police sergeant.

brigand [brigɑ̃], *s.m.* brigand; ruffian; *s.m.* -age.

briguer [brige], *v.tr.* 1. to solicit, to court (s.o.'s favour); b. des voix, to canvass (for votes). 2. b. un poste, to intrigue for a job; *s.* -eur, -euse, intriguer.

brillant [brijɑ̃]. 1. *a.* brilliant; (*a*) sparkling, glittering (gem); glossy; (*b*) spectacle b., splendid sight; (*c*) b. de santé, radiant with health. 2. *s.m.* (*a*) brilliancy, brilliance, brightness; (*b*) polish, shine (on boots). 3. *s.m.* brilliant (diamond); *adv.* -amment.

briller [brije], *v.i.* to shine, sparkle, glitter, glisten; b. par son absence, to be conspicuous by one's absence.

brin [brɛ̃], *s.m.* 1. blade (of grass). 2. *F:* bit, fragment; b. de consolation, crumb of comfort; b. de malice, touch of malice. 3. strand (of rope); ply (of wool).

brindille [brɛ̃di:j], *s.f.* sprig, twig.

brioche [briɔʃ], *s.f. Cu:* brioche.

brique [brik], *s.f.* brick; b. à paver, flag, tile; *s.f.* -terie, brick-field.

briquet [brikɛ], *s.m.* (cigarette-)lighter.

brisant [brizɑ̃]. 1. *a.* shattering, disruptive. 2. *s.m.* (*a*) reef, shoal; (*b*) breaker.

brise [bri:z], *s.f.* breeze.

brisé [brize], *a.* b. de fatigue, tired out.

brise-lames [brizlam], *s.m.inv.* breakwater.

briser [brize], *v.tr.* to break, smash, shatter; (*a*) b. une porte, to break open a door; (*b*) to crush (ore); brisé par la douleur, crushed by grief; (*c*) to break (treaty); b. toute résistance, to break down all resistance; (*d*) to break off (conversation); *abs.* brisons là, let's say no more about it; *s.f.* -ure, break.

se briser, to break.

brise-vent [brizvɑ̃], *s.m.inv.* windbreak.

britannique [britanik], *a.* British; les Iles Britanniques, the British Isles.

broc [bro], *s.m.* pitcher; (large) jug.

brocanter [brokɑ̃te], *v.i.* to deal in second-hand goods; to buy and sell; *s.m.* -age; *s.* -eur, -euse, second-hand dealer.

brocart [broka:r], *s.m. Tex:* brocade.

broche [broʃ], *s.f.* 1. *Cu:* (*a*) spit; (*b*) meat skewer. 2. peg, pin; b. de charnière, hinge-pin. 3. *Tex:* spindle. 4. *Cost:* brooch; *s.f.* -ette, skewer.

brocher [broʃe], *v.tr. Bookb:* to stitch, sew (book); livre broché, paper-bound book; *s.m.* -age; *s.* -eur, -euse, (book) stitcher; *s.f.* -ure, pamphlet, brochure.

brochet [broʃɛ], *s.m. Ich:* pike.

broder [brode], *v.tr.* to embroider; *s.f.* -erie, embroidery; *s.* -eur, -euse, embroiderer.

broiement [brwamɑ̃], *s.m.* grinding, crushing.

bromure [bromy:r], *s.m. Ch:* bromide; *Phot:* (papier au) b., bromide paper.

broncher [brɔ̃ʃe], *v.i.* 1. (*of horse*) (*a*) to stumble; (*b*) to shy. 2. *F:* (*a*) sans b., without flinching; (*b*) to budge, stir.

bronchial, -aux [brɔ̃ʃjal,-o], *a.* bronchial.

bronchite [brɔ̃ʃit], *s.f. Med:* bronchitis.

bronze [brɔ̃:z], *s.m.* 1. bronze. 2. b. à canon, gun-metal.

bronzer [brɔ̃ze], *v.tr.* to bronze (statue); to tan; teint bronzé, sunburnt complexion.

se bronzer, to tan, to become bronzed, sunburnt.

brosse [brɔs], *s.f.* 1. brush; (*a*) donner un coup de b. à qn, to give s.o. a brush-down; *Hairdr:* cheveux taillés en b., crew cut; (*b*) paint-brush; passer la b. sur qch., to paint sth. out. 2. *pl.* brushwood.

brosser [brose], *v.tr.* to brush; to paint (boldly); b. un tableau général de la situation, to give a general picture of the situation; se b. les dents, to clean one's teeth; *s.m.* -age.

brouette [bruet], *s.f.* wheelbarrow.

brouhaha [bruaa], *s.m. F:* hubbub; uproar; hum (of conversation).

brouillard [bruja:r], *s.m.* 1. fog, mist, haze. 2. *Com:* day-book.

brouillé [bruje], *a.* 1. jumbled, mixed, confused; œufs brouillés, scrambled eggs. 2. être b. avec qn, to have fallen out with s.o.

brouiller [bruje], *v.tr.* 1. to mix up, jumble; b. des œufs, to scramble eggs; b. les cartes, (i) to shuffle the cards; (ii) to spread confusion; *Rad:* b. un message, to jam a message. 2. to set (people) at loggerheads; *s.m. Rad:* -age, jamming, interference.

se brouiller. 1. to become mixed, confused; le temps se brouille, the weather is breaking up. 2. to quarrel, to fall out.

brouillon, -onne [brujɔ̃, -ɔn]. 1. *a.* muddle-headed. 2. *s.m.* (rough) draft; rough paper.

broussaille [brusa:j], *s.f. usu. pl.* brushwood, scrub; cheveux en b., unkempt hair.

brousse [brus], *s.f.* (*in Africa, etc.*) (the) bush; (*in Australia*) the outback.

brouter [brute], *v.tr.* b. l'herbe, to browse on the grass; to graze.

broyer [brwaje], *v.tr.* (je broie) to pound, grind, pulverize; *F:* b. du noir, to have the blues; *s.m.* -age, grinding; *s.* -eur, -euse, crusher, grinder.

bru [bry], *s.f.* daughter-in-law.

brugnon [brynɔ̃], *s.m. Hort:* nectarine.

bruine [brɥin], *s.f.* fine rain; drizzle.

bruiner [brɥine], *v.impers.* to drizzle; *a.* -eux, -euse, drizzly.

bruire [brɥi:r], *v.i.def.* (*pr.p.* bruissant; *pr.ind.* bruit, ils bruissent; *p.d.* il bruyait, il bruissait *the pr.p.* **bruyant** *is now used only as an adj.*) to rustle; to rumble; to hum; (*of brook*) to murmur.

bruissement [brɥismã], *s.m.* rumbling; humming (of machinery); murmuring (of brook); surging (of sea); rustling; *Rad:* **bruissements parasites**, strays.

bruit [brɥi], *s.m.* **1.** (*a*) noise; din; report (of a gun); **faire du b.**, to make a noise; (*b*) noise, fuss; **beaucoup de b. pour rien**, much ado about nothing; **sans b.**, quietly. **2.** rumour, report; **faire courir un b.**, to set a rumour afloat; *s.m.* -**age**, *Th:* sound effects; *s.m.* -**eur**, *Th:* (*pers.*) noises off, sound effects man.

brûlant [brylã], *a.* burning; on fire; **larmes brûlantes**, scalding tears.

brûlé [bryle]. **1.** *a.* burnt; *Cu:* **crème brûlée**, caramel custard; **cerveau b.**, daredevil. **2.** *s.m.* **odeur de b.**, smell of burning; **sentir le b.**, (*of opinions*) to smack of heresy. **3.** *s.m. Fr.C:* burnt-out forest area, *N.Am:* brulé(e).

brûle-pourpoint (à) [abrylpurpwẽ], *adv.phr.* point-blank.

brûler [bryle]. **I.** *v.tr.* to burn. **1.** to burn (down) (house); to burn (up) (rubbish). **2.** to scorch; (*a*) **le lait est brûlé**, the milk has caught; **b. le pavé, la route**, to tear along the road; (*b*) *Aut:* **b. un village**, to pass through a village without stopping; **b. les feux**, to shoot the (traffic) lights; (*c*) (*of frost*) to bite, nip (buds); **la fumée me brûlait les yeux**, the smoke made my eyes smart; *s.m.* -**age**. **II.** **brûler**, *v.i.* **1.** to burn; to be on fire; *Games:* **tu brûles**, you are getting hot. **2. b. de curiosité**, to be aflame with curiosity; **les mains lui brûlent**, (i) his hands are hot; (ii) *F:* he's itching to get on with the job. **3.** (*of meat*) to burn; (*of milk*) to catch.

brûlure [brylyːr], *s.f.* **1.** burn, scald; **b. d'estomac**, heart-burn. **2.** (*a*) frost-nip; (*b*) blight, smut (on corn).

brume [brym], *s.f.* thick fog, haze, or mist; *a.* -**eux**, -**euse**, foggy.

brun, -e [brœ̃, bryn]. **1.** *a.* brown; dark (complexion). **2.** *s.m.* brown (colour). **3.** *s.f.* à **la brune**, at dusk; *a.* -**âtre**, brownish.

brunet, -ette [brynɛ, -ɛt]. **1.** *a.* brownish. **2.** *s.f.* **jolie brunette**, pretty brunette.

brunir [bryniːr]. **1.** *v.i. & pr.* to become dark. **2.** *v.tr.* (*a*) to brown, darken; *s.m.* -**issement**; (*b*) to burnish (gold); (*c*) to polish (metal); *s.m.* -**issage**; *s.* (*pers.*) -**isseur**, -**isseuse**, burnisher; *s.m. Tls:* -**issoir**, burnisher.

brusque [brysk], *a.* **1.** abrupt, blunt, brusque (manner). **2.** sudden; *Aut:* **tournant b.**, sharp turn; *adv.* -**ment**.

brusquer [bryske], *v.tr.* **1. b. qn**, to be abrupt with s.o. **2. b. les choses**, to precipitate, rush, matters; *s.f.* -**erie**, abruptness.

brut [bryt], *a.* **1. force brute**, brute force. **2.** raw, unmanufactured (material); unpolished; unrefined; crude (oil); dry (champagne); rough, uncut (diamond). **3.** *Com:* gross (weight). **4.** *s.f.* **brute**, (*a*) brute beast; (*b*) ruffian.

brutal, -aux [brytal, -o], *a.* (*a*) brutal, brutish; (*b*) coarse, rough; **force brutale**, brute force; **coup b.**, savage blow; **vérité brutale**, unvarnished truth; *Aut:* **frein b.**, fierce brake; *adv.* -**ement**.

brutaliser [brytalize], *v.tr.* to ill-treat; to bully.

brutalité [brytalite], *s.f.* **1.** (*a*) brutality, brutishness; (*b*) brutality, savage cruelty. **2.** brutal act.

Bruxelles [brysɛl]. *Pr.n.f.* Brussels.

bruyant [brɥijã], *a.* **1.** noisy; resounding (success). **2.** loud; boisterous (laughter); *adv.* -**amment**, noisily.

bruyère [brɥijɛːr], *s.f.* **1.** (*a*) heather, heath; (*b*) heath(-land). **2.** briar; **pipe en b.**, briar pipe.

buanderie [bɥãdri], *s.f.* wash-house.

bûche [byʃ], *s.f.* (*a*) (fire-)log; **b. de Noël**, yule-log; (*b*) *F:* fool, blockhead.

bûcher¹ [byʃe], *s.m.* **1.** wood-shed. **2.** (*a*) **mourir sur le b.**, to be burnt at the stake; (*b*) funeral-pyre.

bûcher², *v.tr. & i. F:* to work hard; to swot.

bûcheron [byʃrɔ̃], *s.m.* (*a*) woodcutter; (*b*) lumberman.

bûcheur, -euse [byʃœːr, -øːz], *s. F:* plodder, hard worker, swot.

budget [bydʒɛ], *s.m.* budget; (government, etc.) estimates; *a.* -**étaire**, budgetary; fiscal.

buée [bɥe], *s.f.* steam, vapour; mist (on windscreen).

buffet [byfɛ], *s.m.* **1.** sideboard; **b. de cuisine**, dresser. **2.** buffet (at ball, etc.); *Rail:* refreshment room.

buffle [byfl], *s.m. Z:* buffalo.

buis [bɥi], *s.m.* **1.** *Bot:* box(-tree). **2.** box(-wood).

buisson [bɥisɔ̃], *s.m.* **1.** bush. **2.** brake, spinney; *a.* -**neux**, -**neuse**, bushy.

bulbe [bylb]. **1.** *s.m. or f. Bot:* bulb. **2.** *s.m. Anat:* bulb; **b. pileux**, root of a hair; *a.* -**eux**, -**euse**, bulbous.

bulgare [bylgaːr], *a. & s.* Bulgarian.

Bulgarie (la) [labylgari]. *Pr.n.f.* Bulgaria.

bulldozer [byldozɛːr], *s.m.* bulldozer.

bulletin [byltɛ̃], *s.m.* **1.** bulletin; report; **b. météo(rologique)**, weather report. **2.** ticket; receipt; certificate; (telegraph) form; **b. de vote**, voting paper; **b. de commande**, order form.

buraliste [byralist], *s.m. & f.* (*a*) clerk (in post office, etc.); (*b*) receiver of taxes; (*c*) tobacconist (in country districts).

bureau, -eaux [byro], *s.m.* **1.** writing-table, -desk; bureau; **b. ministre**, knee-hole writing-table; **b. américain**, roll-top desk. **2.** (*a*) office; **b.**

personnel, private office; *Th:* **b. de location,** box-office; **b. de tabac,** tobacconist's shop; (*b*) board, committee.

bureaucrate [byrɔkrat], *s.m.* bureaucrat.

bureaucratie [byrɔkrasi], *s.f.* bureaucracy; *F:* red tape.

burette [byrɛt], *s.f.* 1. cruet. 2. oil-can; oiler.

burlesque [byrlɛsk], *a.* 1. burlesque. 2. comical, ludicrous.

buse¹ [by:z], *s.f.* 1. *Orn:* buzzard. 2. *F:* blockhead, dolt, fool.

buse², *s.f.* nose-piece, nozzle (of tube).

busqué [byske], *a.* aquiline, hooked (nose).

buste [byst], *s.m.* bust.

bustier [bystje], *s.m.* strapless brassière.

but [by(t)], *s.m.* 1. mark (to aim at); target, objective. 2. goal; **marquer un b.,** to score a goal; *F:* **aller droit au b.,** to go straight to the point. 3. object, aim, purpose; **dans le b. de faire qch.,** with the object of doing sth.; **errer sans b.,** to wander about aimlessly. 4. *adv.phr.* (*a*) **b. à b.,** even; without any advantage to either party; (*b*) **tirer de b. en blanc,** to fire

point-blank; **faire qch. de b. en blanc,** to do sth. on the spur of the moment.

butan|e [bytan], *s.m. Ch:* butane; *s.m.* -ier, tanker.

buté [byte], *a.* obstinate.

buter [byte], *v.i.* to strike, knock (**contre,** against); to stumble (**contre,** over); (*of beams*) to abut, rest (**contre,** against).

se buter. (*a*) **se b. à un obstacle,** to come up against an obstacle; (*b*) **se b. à faire qch.,** to be set on doing sth.

butin [bytɛ̃], *s.m.* booty, plunder, loot.

butiner [bytine], *v.tr. & i.* (*of bees*) **b. (sur) les fleurs,** to gather pollen from the flowers.

butte [byt], *s.f.* 1. knoll, hillock, mound. 2. *F:* être en **b. à,** to be exposed to (ridicule, etc.).

buvard [byva:r]. 1. *a.* **papier b.,** blotting-paper. 2. *s.m.* blotter; blotting-pad.

buvette [byvɛt], *s.f.* refreshment bar.

buveur, -euse [byvœ:r, -ø:z], *s.* 1. drinker. 2. toper, drunkard.

byzantin, -ine [bizɑ̃tɛ̃, -in], *a. & s.* Byzantine.

C

C, c [se], *s.m.* (the letter) C, c.
c', *see* CE[1].
ça, *see* CELA.
çà [sa]. **1.** *adv.* hither; **çà et là,** here and there, this way and that. **2.** *int.* **ah çà!** now then!
cabane [kaban], *s.f.* (*a*) (i) hut, shanty; (ii) (rabbit-)hutch; (*b*) *Fr.C:* **c. à sucre,** saphouse.
cabaret [kabarɛ], *s.m.* **1.** (*a*) =public-house; (*b*) night club; cabaret. **2.** *Fr.C:* tray; *s.* **-ier, -ière,** publican; inn-keeper.
cabestan [kabɛstɑ̃], *s.m.* capstan, windlass, winch.
cabillau(d) [kabijo], *s.m.* codfish; fresh cod.
cabine [kabin], *s.f.* cabin; (*a*) beach-hut, bathing hut; **c. (téléphonique),** phone box; *Rail:* **c. d'aiguillage,** signal box; *Av:* **c. étanche,** pressure cabin; *Cin:* **c. de projection,** projection room; (*b*) *Nau:* **la c.,** the saloon; **c. de luxe,** stateroom; (*c*) cage (of lift); cab (of locomotive, crane).
cabinet [kabinɛ], *s.m.* **1.** closet; small room; **c. de toilette,** dressing room; *F:* **les cabinets,** the lavatory, *F:* the loo, *U.S:* *F:* the john; **c. de travail,** study; *Phot:* **c. noir,** dark-room. **2.** office, (doctor's) consulting-room. **3.** collection (of works of art). **4.** (*a*) *Pol:* cabinet; (*b*) **c. d'un ministre,** minister's departmental staff; **chef de c.** = principal private secretary.
câble [kɑ:bl], *s.m.* (*a*) cable, rope; (*b*) *El:* *P.T.T:* cable.
câbl|er [kɑble], *v.tr.* (*a*) to cable (message); (*b*) *El:* to connect up; *s.m.* **-age,** wiring.
cabosser [kabɔse], *v.tr.* *F:* to dent (silverware); to bash (sth.) in.
cabot|age [kabɔta:ʒ], *s.m.* coastal trade; *s.m.* **-eur,** coaster.
cabrer (se) [səkɑbre], *v.pr.* (*of horse, etc.*) to rear; *Av:* to pull up, nose up; *F:* (*of pers.*) to jib (at sth.).
cacah(o)uète [kakawɛt], *s.f.* peanut.
cacao [kakao], *s.m.* *Bot:* cacao; *Com:* cocoa.
cacatoès [kakatɔɛ:s], *s.m.* *Orn:* cockatoo.
cache [kaʃ], *s.f.* hiding-place; cache.
cache-cache [kaʃkaʃ], *s.m.* hide-and-seek.
Cachemire [kaʃmi:r]. **1.** *Pr.n.m.* *Geog:* Kashmir. **2.** *s.m.* *Tex:* cashmere.
cache-nez [kaʃne], *s.m.inv.* muffler, scarf.
cacher [kaʃe], *v.tr.* (*a*) to hide, secrete; (*b*) to hide (one's face) from view; to mask (one's feelings); **c. qch. à qn,** to hide sth. from s.o.
se cacher. **1.** to hide, lie in hiding. **2.** (*a*) se c. de

qn, to keep out of s.o.'s way; (*b*) je ne m'en cache pas, I make no secret of it.
cachet [kaʃɛ], *s.m.* **1.** (*a*) seal; (*b*) (trade) mark, stamp; **c. de la poste,** postmark; **œuvre qui manque de c.,** work that lacks character. **2.** *Med:* cachet. **3.** (*of clothes*) avoir du c., to be smart, stylish.
cacheter [kaʃte], *v.tr.* (je cachette) to seal (up).
cachette [kaʃɛt], *s.f.* hiding-place; en c., secretly; on the sly; on the quiet.
cachot [kaʃo], *s.m.* dungeon.
cactus [kaktys], *s.m.* *Bot:* cactus.
cadastre [kadastr], *s.m.* *Adm:* national land survey service.
cadavre [kadɑ:vr], *s.m.* (*a*) corpse; dead body; (*b*) carcase (of animal).
cadeau, -eaux [kado], *s.m.* present; gift.
cadenas [kadna], *s.m.* **1.** padlock. **2.** clasp, snap (of bracelet).
cadence [kadɑ̃:s], *s.f.* **1.** cadence, rhythm (of verse, etc.); **en c.,** rhythmically. **2.** (*a*) *Mus:* cadence; (*b*) intonation (of voice).
cadet, -ette [kadɛ, -ɛt], *s.* (*a*) (the) younger, junior; **il est mon c.,** he's my junior; *a.* avoir trois frères cadets, to have three younger brothers; (*b*) junior (in rank); (*c*) the youngest (of a family).
cadran [kadrɑ̃], *s.m.* **1.** dial; **c. solaire,** sundial. **2.** face (of clock, barometer, etc.).
cadre [kɑ:dr], *s.m.* **1.** (*a*) frame (of picture, door, etc.); (*b*) border (of map); setting (of scene); (*c*) compass, limits; **dans le c. des Nations Unies,** within the framework of the United Nations. **2.** frame(work) (of bicycle). **3.** *Mil:* cadre; **c. de réserve,** reserve list; *Ind:* (*usu. in pl.*) trained personnel; managerial staff.
caduc, -uque [kadyk], *a.* **1.** (*a*) decaying (house); (*b*) (*of pers.*) decrepit. **2.** *Bot:* deciduous. **3.** null and void (legacy).
cafard [kafa:r]. **1.** *s.* *Sch:* sneak. **2.** *s.m.* (*a*) cockroach; (*b*) *F:* avoir le cafard, to be fed up; *a.* **-eux, -euse,** depressed, *F:* browned off.
caf|é [kafe], *s.m.* **1.** coffee; (*a*) grain de c., coffee-bean; (*b*) **c. noir, c. nature,** black coffee; **c. complet,** continental breakfast; (*c*) *a.inv.* coffee-coloured. **2.** café; *s.* **-etier, -etière,** café-owner; *s.f.* **-etière,** coffee-pot.
caféine [kafein], *s.f.* *Ch:* caffein(e).
cage [ka:ʒ], *s.f.* **1.** cage. **2.** cover, case (for protection). **3.** well(-hole) (of stairs); shaft (of lift). **4.** *Mec:* **c. à billes,** ball-race.

cagneux, -euse [kaɲø, -ø:z], *a. & s.* knock-kneed (person); crooked (legs).

cagnotte [kaɲɔt], *s.f. Games:* pool, kitty, pot.

cahier [kaje], *s.m.* exercise book.

cahot [kao], *s.m.* jolt; bump (of vehicle).

cahot|er [kaɔte], *v.tr. & i.* to bump along (in cart, etc.); *s.m.* **-ement,** bumping; *a.* **-eux, -euse,** bumpy (road).

caille [kɑ:j], *s.f. Orn:* quail.

cailler [kɑje], *v.tr., i. & pr.* to clot, curdle; (*of blood*) to congeal.

caillou, *pl.* **-oux** [kaju], *s.m.* (*a*) pebble; (*b*) boulder; (*c*) *pl.* cobble-stones.

caillout|er [kajute], *v.tr.* (*a*) to ballast, metal (road); (*b*) to pave (with pebbles, cobbles); *s.m.* **-age;** *a.* **-eux, -euse,** stony; *s.m.* **-is,** road-metal.

Caire (le) [ləkɛ:r]. *Pr.n.* Cairo.

caiss|e [kɛs], *s.f.* **1.** (*a*) (packing-)case; (*b*) box, chest. **2.** body (of vehicle). **3.** *Com:* (*a*) cash-box; till; **c. enregistreuse,** cash-register; (*b*) pay-desk; (*c*) **petite c.,** petty cash; **livre de c.,** cash-book; (*d*) fund; **c. d'amortissement,** sinking-fund; (*e*) bank; **c. d'épargne,** savings-bank. **4. grosse c.,** big drum; *s.* **-ier, -ière,** cashier.

caisson [kɛsɔ̃], *s.m.* box. **1.** *Nau:* locker, bin. 2. *Arch:* **plafond en caissons,** coffered ceiling. **3.** *Civ.E:* caisson, coffer-dam; *Med:* **mal des caissons,** *F:* the bends.

cajol|er [kaʒɔle], *v.tr.* to cajole, coax; *s.* **-eur, -euse;** *s.f.* **-erie.**

calam|ité [kalamite], *s.f.* calamity, disaster; *a.* **-iteux, -iteuse,** disastrous.

calandre [kalɑ̃:dr], *s.f.* (*a*) roller; (*b*) mangle; (*c*) *Aut:* radiator grill.

calandr|er [kalɑ̃dre], *v.tr.* (*a*) to calender, roll; (*b*) *Laund:* to mangle (clothes); *s.m.* **-age;** *s.* **-eur, -euse.**

calcaire [kalkɛ:r]. **1.** *a.* calcareous; **sol c.,** chalky soil; **eau c.,** hard water. **2.** *s.m.* limestone.

calciner [kalsine], *v.tr.* (*a*) to char; (*b*) **être calciné,** to be burnt to death.

calcium [kalsjɔm], *s.m. Ch:* calcium.

calcul [kalkyl], *s.m.* **1.** (*a*) calculation, reckoning; **tout c. fait,** taking everything into account; (*b*) arithmetic. **2.** *Med:* stone (in bladder).

calculateur, -trice [kalkylatœ:r, -tris], *s.* **1.** (*pers.*) calculator; statistical assistant. **2.** calculating machine; computer.

calculé [kalkyle], *a.* premeditated, calculated (insult, etc.).

calculer [kalkyle], *v.tr.* to calculate, compute.

cale [kal], *s.f.* **1.** hold (of ship). **2.** (*a*) wedge, chock; (*b*) prop, strut. **3. c. sèche,** dry dock.

caleçon [kalsɔ̃], *s.m.* underpants; *Sp:* trunks.

calendrier [kalɑ̃dri(j)e], *s.m.* calendar; **bloc c.,** desk diary.

calepin [kalpɛ̃], *s.m.* note-book.

caler [kale], *v.tr.* **1.** to chock (up) (piece of furniture). **2.** *Aut:* to stall (the engine); *v.i.* (*of engine*) to stall.

calibre [kalibr], *s.m.* **1.** calibre, bore (of fire-arm). **2.** *Tls:* gauge.

calibr|er [kalibre], *v.tr.* to gauge; *s.m.* **-age.**

calice [kalis], *s.m.* **1.** chalice. **2.** *Bot:* calyx.

califourchon (à) [kalifurʃɔ̃], *adv.phr.* astride.

câlin, -ine [kɑlɛ̃, -in], *a.* caressing, winning (ways); *s.f.* **-erie,** caress(ing).

call|eux, -euse [kalø, -ø:z], *a.* horny, callous; *s.f.* **-osité,** callosity.

calmant [kalmɑ̃]. **1.** *a.* calming; soothing. **2.** *s.m. Med:* sedative.

calme [kalm], *a. & s.m.* calm; *adv.* **-ment.**

calmer [kalme], *v.tr.* to calm, to quieten, allay (fears); to soothe (pain).

se calmer, to become calm; (*of storm*) to abate.

calomnie [kalɔmni], *s.f.* calumny, slander, libel.

calomni|er [kalɔmnje], *v.tr.* to slander, libel; *a. & s.* **-ateur, -atrice.**

calomnieu|x, -euse [kalɔmnjø, -ø:z], *a.* slanderous, libellous; *adv.* **-sement.**

calorie [kalɔri], *s.f. Ph.Meas:* calorie.

calorifug|er [kalɔrifyʒe], *v.tr.* (**n. calorifugeons**) to insulate, lag (pipe, etc.); *s.m.* **-eage,** insulation.

calotte [kalɔt], *s.f.* skull-cap; **c. glaciaire,** ice-cap.

calque [kalk], *s.m.* tracing; traced design.

calqu|er [kalke], *v.tr.* to trace (**sur,** from); to make a tracing of (drawing); *s.m.* **-age.**

calvaire [kalvɛ:r], *s.m.* calvary.

calvin|isme [kalvinism], *s.m. Ecc:* Calvinism; *s.* **-iste,** Calvinist.

calvitie [kalvisi], *s.f.* baldness.

camarad|e [kamarad], *s.m. & f.* comrade; *F:* chum; *s.f.* **-erie,** comradeship.

Cambodge (le) [ləkɑ̃bɔdʒ]. *Pr.n. Geog:* Cambodia.

cambré [kɑ̃bre], *a.* **1.** cambered, arched. **2.** bent, warped, crooked.

cambrer (se) [səkɑ̃bre], *v.pr.* to brace oneself back; to draw oneself up.

cambriol|er [kɑ̃briɔle], *v.tr.* to break into (house), *F:* to burgle; *s.m.* **-age,** burglary; *s.* **-eur, -euse,** burglar.

caméléon [kameleɔ̃], *s.m. Rept:* chameleon.

camélia [kamelja], *s.m. Bot:* camellia.

camelot [kamlo], *s.m. F:* cheapjack; street hawker.

camelote [kamlɔt], *s.f.* (*a*) cheap, shoddy goods, junk; **c'est de la c.,** it's trash; (*b*) *P:* goods; **fais voir ta c.,** let's see your stuff.

caméra [kamera], *s.f.* cine-camera; *T.V* camera; *s.m.* **-man,** cameraman.

Cameroun (le) [ləkamrun]. *Pr.n.m. Geog:* the Cameroon Republic.

camion [kamjɔ̃], s.m. lorry, N.Am: truck; s.m. -**nage**, haulage; s.m. -**neur**, lorry-, N.Am: truck-, driver.

camion-citerne [kamjɔ̃sitɛrn], s.m. tanker (-lorry); pl. camions-citernes.

camionnette [kamjɔnɛt], s.f. (delivery) van, N.Am: light truck.

camisole [kamizɔl], s.f. 1. Fr.C: vest, N.Am: undershirt. 2. c. de force, strait-jacket.

camomille [kamɔmiːj], s.f. camomile.

camoufl|er [kamufle], v.tr. to camouflage; c. les lumières, to black out; s.m. -**age**.

camp [kɑ̃], s.m. 1. établir le c., to pitch camp; lever le c., to strike camp; c. de vacances, holiday camp; Fr.C: c. d'été, summer cottage; F: fiche(r) le c., to clear out. 2. party, faction; Games: side.

campagnard, -**arde** [kɑ̃paɲaːr, -ard]. 1. a. country (gentleman); rustic. 2. s. countryman, -woman.

campagne [kɑ̃paɲ], s.f. 1. (a) plain; open country; en pleine c., in the open (country); (b) country(-side); partie de c., picnic. 2. Mil: (the) field; entrer en c., to take the field. 3. campaign.

campanule [kɑ̃panyl], s.f. Bot: campanula.

camp|er [kɑ̃pe]. 1. v.i. to camp. 2. v.tr. to encamp (troops); s.m. -**ement**, (i) camp; (ii) camping ground; s. -**eur**, -**euse**, camper. se camper. 1. to pitch one's camp. 2. se c. devant qn, to plant oneself in front of s.o.

camphre [kɑ̃ːfr], s.m. camphor.

camping [kɑ̃piŋ], s.m. 1. camping. 2. camp site; holiday camp.

campus [kɑ̃pys], s.m. c. (universitaire), (university) campus.

camus [kamy], a. flat-, snub-nosed (person).

Canada (**le**) [ləkanada]. Pr.n.m. Canada; au C., in Canada.

canadien, -**ienne** [kanadjɛ̃, -jɛn], a. & s. 1. Canadian. 2. s.f. lumber jacket.

canaill|e [kanɑːj], s.f. rabble; s.f. -**erie**, dirty trick.

canal, -**aux** [kanal, -o], s.m. 1. channel. 2. canal.

canalis|er [kanalize], v.tr. 1. to canalize (river). 2. to shepherd (crowd); to channel (correspondence); s.f. -**ation**, (water) mains; pipeline.

canapé [kanape], s.m. 1. sofa, couch, settee. 2. Cu: (i) c. d'anchois, anchovy on toast; (ii) (cocktail) canapé.

canard [kanaːr], s.m. 1. duck; drake; c. sauvage, wild duck. 2. F: false report, hoax.

canard|er [kanarde], v.tr. Mil: to snipe at (s.o.).

canari [kanari], s.m. 1. Orn: canary. 2. f. pl. les (îles) Canaries, the Canary Islands, the Canaries.

cancan [kɑ̃kɑ̃], s.m. 1. F: pl. gossip. 2. cancan (dance); s. -**ier**, -**ière**, scandalmonger.

cancer [kɑ̃sɛːr], s.m. 1. Med: cancer; c. du sang, leukaemia. 2. Astr: le C., Cancer; a. & s. -**éreux**, -**éreuse**, (a) cancerous; (b) cancer patient; a. -**érigène**, carcinogenic; s.m. -**érologue**, cancer specialist.

candeur [kɑ̃dœːr], s.f. ingenuousness, artlessness.

candidat [kɑ̃dida], s.m. candidate, applicant (à une place, for a job); examinee; s.f. -**ure**, candidature.

candide [kɑ̃did], a. ingenuous, guileless, artless; adv. -**ment**.

can|e [kan], s.f. duck (as opposed to drake); s.m. -**eton**, s.f. -**ette**, duckling.

canevas [kanva], s.m. canvas.

caniche [kaniʃ], s.m. & f. poodle.

canicul|e [kanikyl], s.f. the dog-days; a. -**aire**, sultry (heat).

canif [kanif], s.m. penknife.

canin, -**ine** [kanɛ̃, -in]. 1. a. canine; exposition canine, dog-show. 2. s.f. canine, canine (tooth).

caniveau [kanivo], s.m. gutter.

canne [kan], s.f. 1. cane, reed; c. à sucre, sugar-cane. 2. walking-stick; cane. 3. c. à pêche, fishing-rod.

cannelle [kanɛl], s.f. cinnamon.

cannelure [kanlyːr], s.f. (a) groove, channel, slot; Arch: fluting; (b) corrugation.

cannibal|e [kanibal], s.m. cannibal; s.m. -**isme**.

cano|ë [kanɔe], s.m. canoe; s.m. -**éisme**, canoeing; s. -**éiste**, canoeist.

canon[1] [kanɔ̃], s.m. 1. gun, cannon. 2. barrel (of rifle); s.f. -**nade**, gunfire; s.m. -**nier**, gunner; s.f. -**nière**, (a) loop-hole; (b) (naval) gunboat.

canon[2], s.m. 1. Ecc: canon, rule (of an order). 2. Mus: canon, round, catch.

canot [kano], s.m. (open) boat; dinghy; s.m. -**age**, boating.

canotier [kanɔtje], s.m. 1. oarsman. 2. straw hat; boater.

cantat|e [kɑ̃tat], s.f. Mus: cantata; s.f. -**rice**, (professional) singer.

cantin|e [kɑ̃tin], s.f. canteen; s.m. -**ier**, canteen-keeper.

cantique [kɑ̃tik], s.m. Ecc: (a) canticle; le C. des cantiques, the Song of Songs; (b) hymn.

canton [kɑ̃tɔ̃], s.m. canton, district.

cantonade [kɑ̃tɔnad], s.f. Th: (the) wings; parler à la c., to speak to nobody in particular.

cantonn|er [kɑ̃tɔne], v.tr. to quarter, billet (troops); s.m. -**ement**, billeting; billet.

cantonnier [kɑ̃tɔnje], s.m. roadman, road-mender.

caoutchouc [kautʃu], s.m. 1. (india-)rubber; c. mousse, foam rubber. 2. (i) waterproof, rain-coat; (ii) pl. rubber overshoes. 3. elastic; rubber band.

caoutchouter [kautʃute], v.tr. to treat (sth.) with rubber, to rubberize (sth.).

cap [kap], *s.m.* 1. cape, headland; **le C.,** Capetown. 2. head (of ship); **changement de c.,** change of course.

capable [kapabl], *a.* capable; *adv.* **-ment.**

capacité [kapasite], *s.f.* 1. capacity (of vase, etc.). 2. capacity, ability, capability.

cape [kap], *s.f.* (hooded) cape, cloak; **rire sous c.,** to laugh up one's sleeve.

capitaine [kapitɛn], *s.m.* (*a*) captain; *Nau:* **c. de port,** harbour-master; **c. de vaisseau,** captain; **certificat de c.,** master's certificate; *Mil:* captain; *Av:* **c. (aviateur)** = flight-lieutenant, *N.Am:* (air) captain; (*b*) chief, leader; **un grand c.,** a great (military) leader; **un c. d'industrie,** a captain of industry.

capital, -aux [kapital, -o]. 1. *a.* (*a*) capital (punishment); (*b*) essential, principal; **la ville capitale,** *s.f.* **la capitale,** the capital; (*c*) **lettre capitale,** *s.f.* **une capitale,** capital (letter). 2. *s.m.* capital, assets; **c. social,** registered capital; *s.m.* **-isme;** *s.m. & f.* **-iste.**

capitonner [kapitɔne], *v.tr.* to upholster (furniture).

capituller [kapityle], *v.i.* to capitulate; to surrender; *s.f.* **-ation.**

caporal, -aux [kapɔral, -o], *s.m.* 1. corporal; *Av:* leading aircraftman. 2. caporal, standard French cut tobacco.

capot [kapo], *s.m.* 1. cover, hood, casing; *Aut:* bonnet (of car), *N.Am:* hood; *Nau:* tarpaulin. 2. *Nau:* companion hatch.

capote [kapɔt], *s.f.* 1. *Mil:* great-coat. 2. (baby's) bonnet. 3. *Veh:* hood, *N.Am:* top. 4. cowl (of chimney).

capotler [kapɔte], *v.i.* 1. *Nau:* to capsize; to turn turtle. 2. *Aut:* to overturn; *s.m.* **-age.**

câpre [kɑːpr], *s.f. Bot:* caper.

caprice [kapris], *s.m.* caprice, whim.

capricieulx, -euse [kaprisjø, -øːz], *a.* capricious, whimsical; *adv.* **-sement.**

Capricorne [kaprikɔrn]. *Astr:* **le C.,** Capricorn.

capsule [kapsyl], *s.f.* capsule.

captler [kapte], *v.tr.* 1. to obtain (by undue influence); to pick up (transmission); to intercept; *P.T.T:* to tap (a telephone call). 2. to harness (river); *El:* to pick up, collect (current); *s.m.* **-age.**

captilf, -ive [kaptif, -iːv], *a. & s.* captive; prisoner; *s.f.* **-vité,** captivity.

captivler [kaptive], *v.tr.* to captivate, charm; *a.* **-ant,** captivating, charming.

capture [kaptyːr], *s.f.* 1. capture, seizure (of ship, etc.). 2. capture, prize.

capturer [kaptyre], *v.tr.* to capture, to catch.

capuchon [kapyʃɔ̃], *s.m.* 1. (*a*) hood; (*b*) *Ecc:* cowl. 2. cap (of fountain-pen); chimney-cowl.

capucine [kapysin], *s.f. Bot:* nasturtium.

caquet [kakɛ], *s.m.* cackling (of hens); chatter.

caquetler [kakte], *v.i.* (**je caquète, je caquette**).

1. (*of hen*) to cackle. 2. *F:* to chatter; *s.m.* **-age;** *s.* **-eur, -euse.**

car¹ [kaːr], *conj.* for, because.

car² *s.m.* 1. (tram-)car. 2. (motor-)coach; (country-)bus; *Rad:* **c. de radio-reportage,** outside broadcasting van; **c. sonore,** mobile sound unit.

carabine [karabin], *s.f.* rifle; **c. de salon,** gallery rifle.

caractère [karaktɛːr], *s.m.* 1. character; graphic symbol; *Typ:* (metal) type; **imprimé en gros caractères,** printed in large type. 2. characteristic, feature; **l'affaire a pris un c. grave,** the matter has taken a serious turn. 3. (*a*) nature, disposition; **homme au c. emporté,** hot-tempered man; (*b*) personality, character; **montrer du c.,** to show spirit.

caractérisler [karakterize], *v.tr.* to characterize; *a. & s.f.* **-tique,** characteristic.

se caractériser. 1. to assume character, to become clearly marked. 2. to be distinguished (**par, by**).

carafe [karaf], *s.f.* decanter; carafe; **vin par c.** = wine by the glass.

caraïbe [karaib], *a. & s. Geog: Ling:* Caribbean; **la mer des Caraïbes,** the Caribbean (Sea).

carambolage [karɑ̃bɔlaːʒ], *s.m.* 1. cannon (at billiards). 2. *Aut: F:* pile-up (in a road smash).

caramboler [karɑ̃bɔle], *v.i.* 1. to cannon. 2. *v.tr.* **c. une voiture,** to run into a car; **plusieurs voitures se sont carambolées,** there was a pile-up.

caramel [karamɛl], *s.m.* caramel; burnt sugar.

carat [kara], *s.m.* carat.

caravanle [karavan], *s.f.* caravan; *s.m.* **-ier,** caravaner; *s.m.* **-(n)ing,** caravan(n)ing.

carbonate [karbɔnat], *s.m. Ch:* carbonate; **c. de soude,** washing soda.

carbone [karbɔn], *s.m.* carbon; **papier c.,** carbon paper.

carbonique [karbɔnik], *a. Ch:* carbonic; **acide c.,** carbon dioxide; **neige c.,** dry ice.

carbonisler [karbɔnize], *v.tr.* to burn, to char; **être carbonisé,** to be burnt to death (in an accident); *s.f.* **-ation.**

carburant [karbyrɑ̃], *s.m.* motor-fuel.

carburateur [karbyratœːr], *s.m.* carburettor.

carcasse [karkas], *s.f.* 1. carcase. 2. framework.

cardiaque [kardjak]. 1. *a.* cardiac (murmur); **crise c.,** heart-attack. 2. *s.* heart patient, case.

cardinal, -aux [kardinal, -o]. 1. *a.* cardinal (number). 2. *s.m. Ecc:* cardinal.

cardiollogie [kardjɔlɔʒi], *s.f. Med:* cardiology; *s.m.* **-logue,** cardiologist.

carême [karɛm], *s.m.* Lent; *F:* **figure de c.,** dismal face.

carène [karɛn], *s.f.* hull (of ship, aircraft).

carénler [karene], *v.tr.* (**je carène, je carénerai**) 1. to careen (ship). 2. *Av: Aut:* to streamline *s.m.* **-age.**

caresse [karɛs], *s.f.* caress.

caresser [karɛse], *v.tr.* 1. to caress, fondle; **c. qn du regard,** to look fondly at s.o. 2. to cherish (hope).

carg|o [kargo], *s.m.* cargo-boat; tramp (steamer); *s.f.* **-aison,** cargo, freight.

caricature [karikaty:r], *s.f.* caricature.

caricatur|er [karikatyre], *v.tr.* to caricature; *s.m.* **-iste.**

carié [karie], *a.* decayed; **dent cariée,** bad tooth.

carillon [karijɔ̃], *s.m.* chime(s).

carillonn|er [karijɔne], *v.i.* (*a*) to ring a peal; (*b*) to chime; *s.m.* **-ement;** *s.m.* **-eur,** bell-ringer.

carmin [karmɛ̃], *s.m.* carmine (colour).

carnassier, -ière [karnasje, -jɛːr]. 1. *a.* carnivorous. 2. *s.m.* carnivore. 3. *s.f.* **carnassière,** game-bag.

carnation [karnasjɔ̃], *s.f.* *Art:* (*a*) flesh-tint; (*b*) rendering of flesh-tints.

carnaval, *pl.* **-als** [karnaval], *s.m.* carnival; *a.* **-esque,** carnival-like.

carnet [karnɛ], *s.m.* note-book; **c. de banque,** passbook; **c. de chèques,** cheque-book.

carnivore [karnivɔ:r], *a. & s.* carnivorous (animal).

carotte [karɔt], *s.f.* 1. *Bot:* carrot; *a.inv. F:* **cheveux (rouge) c.,** carroty, ginger, hair. 2. *Min:* core (sample). 3. *F:* trick, sell.

carpe [karp], *s.f. Ich:* carp; *F:* **saut de c.,** jack-knife (dive); **faire des sauts de c.,** to flop about, to somersault.

carpette [karpɛt], *s.f.* rug.

carré [kare]. 1. *a.* (*a*) square; *Mth:* **nombre c.,** square number; **partie carrée,** foursome; **tête carrée,** (i) level-headed man; (ii) stubborn man; (*b*) *F:* plain, blunt (answer). 2. *s.m.* (*a*) *Mth:* square; (*b*) landing (of staircase); **c. de choux,** cabbage-patch; *Navy:* **c. des officiers,** ward-room; *Cl:* **c. de soie,** silk square; *adv.* **-ment.**

carreau, -eaux [karo], *s.m.* 1. small square; **tissu à carreaux,** check material. 2. (*a*) (flooring) tile; (*b*) **c. (de vitre),** window-pane. 3. floor (of room); **c. de mine,** pithead. 4. *Cards:* diamonds.

carrefour [karfu:r], *s.m.* cross-roads, *N.Am:* intersection; square, circus.

carrel|er [karle], *v.tr.* (**je carrelle**). 1. to lay (floor) with tiles; to pave. 2. **tissu carrelé,** check material; *s.m.* **-age.**

carrelet [karlɛ], *s.m. Ich:* plaice.

carrière[1] [karjɛ:r], *s.f.* 1. career; **soldat de c.,** regular (soldier). 2. *F:* **donner libre c. à son imagination,** to give free play to one's fancy.

carrière[2], *s.f.* stone-pit, quarry.

carrossable [karɔsabl], *a.* **route c.,** road suitable for motor vehicles.

carross|erie [karɔsri], *s.f. Aut:* body,

coachwork (of car, etc.); *s.m.* **-ier,** *Aut:* coach-, body-builder.

carrure [kary:r], *s.f.* breadth across the shoulders; **homme d'une belle c.,** well-built man.

cartable [kartabl], *s.m.* 1. writing-pad. 2. (cardboard) portfolio. 3. school satchel.

carte [kart], *s.f.* 1. (piece of) cardboard; **c. à jouer,** playing card; **c. d'identité,** identity card; **c. de lecteur,** reader's ticket; **c. d'abonnement,** season ticket; **donner c. blanche à qn,** to give s.o. a free hand; **c. postale,** postcard; *Aut:* **c. grise,** logbook. 2. map; **c. d'état-major,** ordnance survey map; **c. routière,** road-map; **perdre la c.,** to lose one's bearings. 3. **c. (de restaurant),** menu; **c. du jour,** menu for the day; **c. des vins,** wine-list.

carter [kartɛ:r], *s.m. Mch:* casing, housing (of small machine, crank, gear, etc.); *Aut:* crank-case; **fond de c.,** sump; *Cin:* spool-box.

cartograph|e [kartɔgraf], *s.m.* cartographer, map-maker; *s.f.* **-ie,** cartography, mapping.

carton [kartɔ̃], *s.m.* 1. cardboard; pasteboard. 2. cardboard box, carton; *s.m. coll.* **-nage,** (cardboard) boxes.

carton-pâte [kartɔ̃pɑ:t], *s.m.* papier mâché.

cartouch|e [kartuʃ]. 1. *s.m.* scroll (round coat-of-arms, etc.); cartouche. 2. *s.f.* cartridge; **cent cartouches,** a hundred rounds (of ammunition); *s.f.* **-ière,** cartridge-belt.

cas [kɑ], *s.m.* 1. case, instance; **c. limite,** border-line case; **c. imprévu,** emergency; *F:* **c'est bien le c. de le dire,** ... and no mistake. 2. case, matter, affair; **c. de conscience,** matter of conscience. 3. **faire c. de qch.,** to value sth. 4. *Gram:* case. 5. **en ce c.,** in that case; **dans, en, aucun c.,** in no circumstances, on no account; **en tout c.,** in any case, at all events; **le c. échéant,** should the occasion arise.

casanier, -ière [kazanje, -jɛ:r], *a.* home-loving; stay-at-home.

cascade [kaskad], *s.f.* cascade, waterfall.

case [kɑ:z], *s.f.* 1. hut, cabin. 2. (*a*) compartment; pigeon-hole; **c. postale,** P.O. box; (*b*) division, space to be filled in (on printed form); (*c*) square (on chessboard).

caser [kaze], *v.tr.* to put away; to file (papers); **c. qn,** to find a job for s.o.

se caser, to settle down; to marry.

caserne [kazɛrn], *s.f.* (*a*) barracks; (*b*) **c. de pompiers,** fire station.

casier [kazje], *s.m.* 1. set of pigeon-holes. 2. (*a*) (wine) bin, rack; (*b*) **c. à outils,** tool-cabinet.

casino [kazino], *s.m.* casino.

caspien, -ienne [kaspjɛ̃, -jɛn], *a.* **la mer Caspienne,** the Caspian (Sea).

casque [kask], *s.m.* (*a*) helmet; **c. blindé,** crash-helmet; **Casques bleus,** United Nations troops; (*b*) *P.T.T:* **c. téléphonique,** head-phones.

casquette [kaskɛt], *s.f.* (peaked) cap.

cassant [kasã], *a.* **1.** (*a*) brittle; (*b*) crisp (biscuit). **2.** curt, abrupt (tone of voice).

cassation [kasasjɔ̃], *s.f.* annulment. **1.** *Jur:* Cour de c., Supreme Court of Appeal. **2.** *Mil:* reduction (of N.C.O.) to the ranks.

casse [kɑːs], *s.f.* breakage, damage; *F:* il y aura de la c., there will be trouble.

cassé [kase], *a.* broken, worn out (person); cracked (voice).

casse-cou [kasku], *s.m.inv.* **1.** death-trap. **2.** daredevil.

casse-croûte [kaskrut], *s.m.inv.* snack.

casse-noisettes [kasnwazɛt], *s.m.inv.* **1.** (pair of) nutcrackers. **2.** *Orn:* nuthatch.

casse-pieds [kaspje]. **1.** *s.m.inv.* (*of pers.*) bore, nuisance; *F:* pain in the neck. **2.** *a. inv.* boring, tiresome.

cass‖er [kase], *v.tr.* **1.** to break, snap; to crack (nuts); **se c. la tête,** (i) to crack one's skull; (ii) to rack one's brains; **applaudir à tout c.,** to bring the house down (with applause); *P:* **c. les pieds à (qn),** to plague (s.o.); **c. sa pipe,** to kick the bucket; **il ne se casse rien,** he doesn't overwork. **2.** to cashire, break (s.o.). **3.** *Jur:* to quash, set aside (verdict); *s.m.* **-age,** breaking; *s.* **-eur,** **-euse,** breaker; *s.f.* **-ure,** fracture.

se casser, to break, snap, give way.

casserole [kasrɔl], *s.f.* **1.** (sauce)pan, stewpan. **2.** *Cu:* stew.

casse-tête [kastɛt], *s.m.inv.* **1.** club; loaded stick; truncheon. **2.** (*a*) puzzling task; headache; (*b*) puzzle.

cassette [kasɛt], *s.f.* (*a*) casket; (*b*) money-box; (*c*) cassette.

cassis [kasis], *s.m.* **1.** black-currant (fruit, bush). **2.** black-currant liqueur.

cassonade [kasɔnad], *s.f.* brown sugar, moist sugar.

caste [kast], *s.f.* caste; **esprit de c.,** class consciousness; **hors c.,** outcast.

castor [kastɔːr], *s.m.* *Z: Com:* beaver.

casu‖el, -elle [kazɥɛl]. **1.** *a.* (*a*) accidental, casual; (*b*) *Gram:* flexions casuelles, case-endings. **2.** *s.m.* perquisites; *adv.* **-ellement.**

cataclysme [kataklism], *s.m.* disaster.

catacombes [katakɔ̃ːb], *s.f.pl.* catacombs.

catadioptre [katadiɔptr], *s.m.* reflector; (*in middle of road*) cat's-eye.

catalan, -ane [katalã, -an], *a. & s.* Catalan, Catalonian.

Catalogne (la) [lakatalɔɲ]. *Pr.n.f.* Catalonia.

catalogue [katalɔg], *s.m.* catalogue, list.

catalogu‖er [katalɔge], *v.tr.* to catalogue; to list; *s.m.* **-age,** cataloguing; *s.m.* **-eur,** cataloguer.

cata‖lyse [kataliːz], *s.f.* *Ch:* catalysis; *s.m.* **-lyseur,** catalyst; *a.* **-lytique,** catalytic.

cataphote [katafɔt], *s.m.* *R.t.m:* cat's-eye.

cataplasme [kataplasm], *s.m.* poultice.

catapulte [katapylt], *s.f.* catapult; *Av:* **c. (de lancement),** (launching) catapult; **lancer par c.,** to catapult off.

catapult‖er [katapylte], *v.tr.* (*a*) *Av:* to catapult; (*b*) to send (s.o., sth.) hurtling off; *a.* **-able,** catapult-launched (aircraft); *s.m.* **-age,** catapult-launching.

cataracte [katarakt], *s.f.* **1.** cataract, falls. **2.** *Med:* cataract.

catarrhe [kataːr], *s.m.* *Med:* catarrh.

catastrophe [katastrɔf], *s.f.* catastrophe.

catastrophé [katastrɔfe], *a.* *F:* (*a*) wrecked; (*b*) dumbfounded.

catch [katʃ], *s.m.* all-in wrestling; *s.m.* **-eur,** all-in wrestler.

caté‖chiser [kateʃize], *v.tr.* **1.** (*a*) *Ecc:* to catechize; (*b*) *F:* to tell (s.o.) what to say. **2.** (*a*) to reason with (s.o.); (*b*) to lecture (s.o.); *s.m.* **-chisme,** catechism; *s.m. & f.* **-chiste,** catechist.

catégorie [kategɔri], *s.f.* category.

catégorique [kategɔrik], *a.* categorical; **refus c.,** flat refusal; *adv.* **-ment,** categorically, clearly.

cathédrale [katedral], *s.f.* cathedral.

cathod‖e [katɔd], *s.f.* *El:* cathode; *a.* **-ique.**

catholicisme [katɔlisism], *s.m.* (Roman) Catholicism.

catholique [katɔlik]. **1.** *a.* orthodox; *F:* **ce n'est pas c.,** it sounds fishy. **2.** *a. & s.* (Roman) Catholic.

Caucase (le) [ləkokaːz]. *Pr.n.* *Geog:* the Caucasus.

cauchemar [koʃmaːr, ko-], *s.m.* nightmare; *a.* **-desque,** nightmarish.

cause [koːz], *s.f.* **1.** cause; **être c. de qch.,** to be the cause of sth.; **il ne viendra pas et pour c.,** he will not come and for a very good reason; *prep.phr.* **à c. de,** on account of; owing to. **2** (*a*) *Jur:* cause, suit, action; **avocat sans c.,** briefless barrister; **être en c.,** (i) to be a party to a suit; (ii) *F:* to be concerned in sth.; **mettre en c. la probité de qn,** to question s.o.'s honesty; **questions hors de c.,** irrelevant questions; **mettre qn hors de c.,** to exonerate s.o.; **agir en connaissance de c.,** to act with full knowledge of the case; (*b*) **c'est pour une bonne c.,** it's for a good cause; **faire c. commune avec qn,** to make common cause with s.o.; to side with s.o.

causer¹ [koze], *v.tr.* to cause; to bring about.

caus‖er², *v.i.* to converse, chat; **c. de la pluie et du beau temps,** to indulge in small talk; **c. musique,** to talk music; **faire c. qn,,** to pump s.o.; *a.* **-ant, -ante,** chatty (person); *s.f.* **-erie,** chat; chatty talk; *s.f.* **-ette,** *F:* little chat; *s.* **-eur, -euse,** talker; tattler.

caustique [kostik]. **1.** *a.* (*a*) *Ch:* caustic; (*b*) caustic, cutting (remark); **2.** *s.m.* *Pharm:* caustic; *adv.* **-ment.**

cautériser [koterize], *v.tr.* to cauterize (wound).
caution [kosjɔ̃], *s.f.* **1.** security, guarantee; **donner c. pour qn,** to go bail for s.o.; **mettre qn en liberté sous c.,** to let s.o. out on bail; *Com:* **verser une c.,** to pay a deposit; *F:* **sujet à c.,** unconfirmed (news). **2.** surety, guaranty; **se rendre c. de qn,** (i) to go bail for s.o.; (ii) *Com:* to stand surety for s.o.; *s.m. Com:* **-nement,** surety-bond.
cavalcade [kavalkad], *s.f.* **1.** cavalcade. **2.** pageant(-procession).
cavalerie [kavalri], *s.f.* cavalry.
cavallier, -ière [kavalje, -jɛːr]. **1.** *s.* rider; horseman, horsewoman; *a.* **piste cavalière,** bridle path. **2.** *s.m.* (*a*) *Mil:* trooper; (*b*) *Chess:* knight; (*c*) gentleman, gallant; (*d*) partner (to lady at ball). **3.** *s.m. Tchn;* (*a*) staple; (*b*) rider (of balance). **4.** *a.* cavalier, off-hand (manner); *adv.* **-ièrement.**
cavle [kaːv], *s.f.* cellar, vault; **avoir une bonne c.,** to keep a good cellar (of wine); *s.m.* **-eau,** (burial) vault.
cavernle [kavɛrn], *s.f.* cave, cavern; *a.* **-eux, -euse,** hollow (voice).
caviar [kavjaːr], *s.m.* caviar.
cavité [kavite], *s.f.* cavity, hollow.
ce[1] [s(ə)], *dem.pron.neut.* (**c'** before parts of **être** beginning with a vowel); it, that. **1.** (*as neuter subject of* être, devoir être, pouvoir être) (*a*) (*with adj. or adv. complement*) **c'est faux!** it's untrue! **est-ce assez?** is that enough? (*b*) (*with s. or pron. as complement*) (*with a 3rd pers. pl. complement, colloquial usage allows the sing.*) **c'est moi, c'est nous, ce sont eux;** *F:* **c'est eux,** it's I, we, they, *F:* me, us, them; (*inv.phr.*) **si ce n'est,** except, unless; (*c*) **ce . . . ici** = CECI; (*d*) **ce . . . là** = CELA; (*e*) (*subject isolated for the sake of stress*) **Paris, c'est bien loin!** it's a far cry to Paris! (*f*) (*anticipating the subject*) **c'est demain dimanche,** tomorrow's Sunday; (*g*) (i) *F:* (*as temp. subject when an adj. is followed by a sb. clause or an inf. subject*) **c'était inutile de sonner,** you need not have rung; (ii) **c'est assez qu'il veuille bien pardonner,** that's willing to forgive is enough; (*h*) (**c'est . . . que** *used to bring a word into prominence*) **c'est un bon petit garçon que Jean!** what a fine little chap John is! (*i*) (**c'est que** *introducing a statement*) **c'est qu'il fait froid!** it's cold and no mistake! (*j*) (**est-ce que** [ɛskə] *introducing a question*) **est-ce que je peux entrer?** may I come in? **2.** (*used as object to* dire, faire, *etc.*) **ce disant,** so saying. **3.** (*a*) (*used as neuter antecedent to a rel. pron.*) **ce qui, ce que,** *etc.* = what; **je sais ce qui est arrivé,** I know what has happened; (*b*) **ce qui, ce que,** *etc.* = which; **il est parti, ce que je ne savais pas,** he has gone, which I didn't know; (*c*) **tout ce qui, que,** everything, all (that); **tout ce que vous voudrez,** whatever you

like; (*d*) *F:* **ce que** = how; **ce qu'elle a changé!** how she has changed! **4. sur ce,** thereupon. **5.** *conj.phr.* **tenez-vous beaucoup à ce qu'il vienne?** are you very anxious for him to come? **6.** *prep.phr.* **pour ce qui est de cela,** for that matter.
ce[2] (**cet**), **cette, ces** [sə, (sɛt), sɛt, se *or* sɛ], *unstressed dem.a.* (*the form* **cet** *is used before a s. or adj. beginning with a vowel or h 'mute'.*) this, that, *pl.* these, those. **1. un de ces jours,** one of these days; **ce dernier,** the latter. **2.** *pl.* (*deferential use*) **ces dames sont au salon,** the ladies are in the drawing-room. **3. ce . . . -ci,** this; **ce . . . -là,** that; **prenez cette tasse-ci,** take this cup.
ceci [səsi], *dem. pron. neut. inv.* this (thing, fact, etc.); **écoutez bien c.,** now listen to this; **le cas offre c. de particulier, que . . .,** the case is peculiar in this, that. . . .
cécité [sesite], *s.f.* blindness.
céder [sede], *v.* (**je cède; je céderai**). **1.** *v.tr.* (*a*) (i) to give up, yield (à, to), to surrender (right); **c. le pas à qn,** to give way to s.o.; (ii) to transfer, assign; **maison à c.,** business for sale; (*b*) **le c. à qn en qch.,** to be inferior to s.o. in sth. **2.** *v.i.* to yield, give way; **le câble céda sous l'effort,** the rope parted under the strain; **c. aux circonstances,** to yield to circumstances.
cédille [sediːj], *s.f. Gram:* cedilla.
cèdre [sɛːdr], *s.m.* cedar(-tree, -wood).
ceindre [sɛ̃ːdr], *v.tr.* (*conj. like* ATTEINDRE). **1.** to gird; (*a*) **c. une épée,** to buckle on a sword; (*b*) **c. qn de qch.,** to gird, encircle, s.o. with sth. **2.** to encompass (a town with walls).
ceinture [sɛ̃tyːr], *s.f.* **1.** (*a*) girdle; (leather) belt; (silk) sash; waistband; **c. de sauvetage,** lifebelt; *Aut: Av:* **c. de sécurité,** safety belt; (*b*) waist, middle (of the body). **2.** girdle, circle (of walls); belt (of hills). **3.** *Rail:* **chemin de fer de petite, grande, c.,** inner-, outer-circle railway.
ceinturer [sɛ̃tyre], *v.tr.* **1.** to girdle, surround. **2.** *Rugby Fb:* **c. un joueur,** to tackle a player low.
ceinturon [sɛ̃tyrɔ̃], *s.m. Mil:* belt.
cela [səla, sla], *F:* **ça** [sa], *dem. pron. neut.* (*a*) that (thing); **qu'est-ce que c'est que c.,** *F:* **que ça?** what is that? NOTE. *an adj. qualifying* **cela** *is partitive;* **s'il n'y a que c. de nouveau,** if that is all that is new; (*b*) that, it (**cela** *is the pron. used as neuter subject to all vbs. other than* être; *used with* être, *is more emphatic than* ce) **c. ne vous regarde pas,** it is no business of yours; (*c*) *F:* **comment allez-vous?—comme (ci comme) ça,** how are you?—so-so; (*d*) **c'est ça,** that's it, that's right; **c'est c. même!** the very thing! **il n'y a que ça,** there's nothing like it; **et avec c., madame?** and what else, madam? *F:* **allons, pas de ça!** come on, none of that! **où ça?** where? **comment ça?** how?
célèbre [selɛbr], *a.* celebrated, famous (**par,** for).

célébr|er [selebre], *v.tr.* (**je célèbre; je célébrerai**). **1.** to celebrate; (i) to solemnize (rite); (ii) to observe, keep (feast). **2.** to praise (s.o.); **c. les louanges de qn**, to sing s.o.'s praises; *s.f.* **-ation;** *s.f.* **-ité,** celebrity.

céleri [selri], *s.m.* celery; **pied de c.,** head of celery.

célérité [selerite], *s.f.* speed.

céleste [selɛst], *a.* celestial, heavenly; **bleu c.,** sky blue.

célibat [seliba], *s.m.* celibacy.

célibataire [selibatɛ:r], *a. & s.* unmarried, single (man, woman); *s.m.* bachelor; *s.f.* spinster.

celle, celle-ci, celle-là, *see* CELUI.

Cellophane [selɔfan], *s.f. R.t.m:* Cellophane.

cellulaire [selylɛ:r], *a.* **1.** cellular (tissue). **2. voiture c.,** police-van, *F:* Black Maria.

cellul|e [selyl], *s.f.* cell; *s.f. Med:* **-ite,** cellulitis.

celluloïd [selylɔid], *s.m. Ind:* celluloid.

cellulose [selylo:z], *s.f. Ch: Com:* cellulose.

celt|e [sɛlt]. **1.** *a. & s.m. Ling:* Celtic. **2.** *s.m. & f.* Celt; *a. & s.m.* **-ique,** Celtic (language).

celui, celle, *pl.* **ceux, celles** [səlɥi, sɛl, sø, sɛl], *dem. pron.* **1.** (*a*) (*completed by an adj. clause*) the one; those; **celui qui était parti le dernier,** the one who started last; (*b*) he, she, those; **c. qui mange peu dort bien,** he who eats little sleeps well. **2.** (*followed by* de) **mes livres et ceux de Jean,** my books and John's. **3.** (*completed by an adj. equivalent*) **les rails en acier et ceux en fer,** steel rails and iron ones. **4. celui-ci, ceux-ci,** this (one), these; the latter; **celui-là, ceux-là,** that (one); those; the former. **5. celui-là** *is used for* **celui** 1, *when the rel. pron. does not follow at once:* **celui-là est heureux qui . . .,** he is happy who. . . .

cément|er [semɑ̃te], *v.tr. Ind:* to case-harden (steel); *s.f.* **-ation.**

cendre [sɑ̃:dr], *s.f.* ash(es), cinders; **mercredi des Cendres,** Ash-Wednesday; **visage couleur de c.,** ashen face.

cendré [sɑ̃dre], *a.* (ash-)grey; ashy; **cheveux blond c.,** ash blond hair.

cendrée [sɑ̃dre], *s.f. Sp:* **piste en c.,** (i) cinder-track; (ii) dirt-track.

cendrier [sɑ̃drie], *s.m.* (*a*) ashpan; (*b*) ash-tray.

cénotaphe [senɔtaf], *s.m.* cenotaph.

censé [sɑ̃se], *a.* supposed; **je ne suis pas c. le savoir,** I am not supposed to know; *adv.* **-ment,** supposedly.

censeur [sɑ̃sœ:r], *s.m.* **1.** critic, fault-finder; *a.* **esprit c.,** carping spirit. **2.** (*a*) *Adm:* censor; (*b*) *Fin:* auditor. **3.** *Sch:* vice-principal (of lycée).

censure [sɑ̃sy:r], *s.f.* **1.** (*a*) censorship; (*b*) audit (of accounts). **2.** censure, blame.

censur|er [sɑ̃syre], *v.tr.* **1.** to censure, to find fault with (sth.). **2.** to censor (a film); *a.* **-able,** open to censure.

cent [sɑ̃]. **1.** (*a*) *num.a.* (*takes a pl. s when multiplied by a preceding numeral but not followed by another numeral; inv. when used as an ordinal*) (a, one) hundred; **deux cents hommes,** two hundred men; **deux c. cinquante hommes,** two hundred and fifty men; **la page deux c.,** page two hundred; **faire les c. pas,** to pace up and down; (*b*) *s.m.inv.* a hundred; **sept pour c.,** seven per cent. **2.** *s.m.var.* **un c. d'œufs,** a hundred eggs.

centaine [sɑ̃tɛn], *s.f.* **une c. de francs,** a hundred francs or so; **atteindre la c.,** to live to be a hundred.

centenaire [sɑ̃tnɛ:r]. **1.** *a.* age-old; **chêne c.,** ancient oak. **2.** *s.m. & f.* centenarian. **3.** *s.m.* centenary (anniversary).

centième [sɑ̃tjɛm]. **1.** *num. a. & s.* hundredth. **2.** *s.m.* hundredth (part).

centigrade [sɑ̃tigrad], *a.* centigrade.

centigramme [sɑ̃tigram], *s.m.* centigramme.

centilitre [sɑ̃tilitr], *s.m.* centilitre.

centime [sɑ̃tim], *s.m.* centime.

centimètre [sɑ̃timɛtr], *s.m.* **1.** centimetre. **2.** tape-measure.

centrafricain [sɑ̃trafrikɛ̃], *a. Geog:* Central African; **République Centrafricaine,** Central African Republic.

central, -aux [sɑ̃tral, -o]. **1.** *a.* central; (*a*) middle (point); (*b*) principal, head (office). **2.** (*a*) *s.m.* **c. téléphonique,** telephone exchange; (*b*) *s.f.* **centrale (électrique),** power-station; **centrale thermique, nucléaire, marémotrice,** thermal, nuclear, tidal, power-station; *adv.* **-ement.**

centralis|er [sɑ̃tralize], *v.tr.* to centralize; *s.f.* **-ation.**

centre [sɑ̃:tr], *s.m.* centre; middle; **c. politique,** political centre; **c. commercial,** (i) shopping centre, precinct; (ii) business centre; **c. de villégiature,** holiday resort; *Fb: etc:* centre (player).

centr|er [sɑ̃tre], *v.tr.* to centre (**sur,** on); to adjust (tool, etc.); *Sp:* **c. le ballon,** to centre the ball; *s.m.* **-age;** *s.m.* **-eur.**

centuple [sɑ̃typl], *a. & s.m.* centuple; hundred-fold.

cep [sɛp], *s.m.* vine-stock.

cépage [sepa:ʒ], *s.m.* vine-plant.

cèpe [sɛp], *s.m. Bot:* boletus, *F:* penny-bun mushroom.

cependant [s(ə)pɑ̃dɑ̃]. **1.** *adv.* meanwhile; in the meantime. **2.** *conj.* yet, still, nevertheless.

céramique [seramik], *s.f.* ceramics; pottery.

cercle [sɛrkl], *s.m.* **1.** circle; (*a*) **c. d'activités,** circle, sphere, of activities; (*b*) circle, set (of friends); (*c*) club. **2.** (binding) hoop, ring, (iron) tyre. **3.** (*a*) dial; (*b*) **quart de c.,** quadrant.

cercl|er [sɛrkle], *v.tr.* **1.** to encircle, to ring. **2.** to hoop (barrel); to tyre (wheel); *s.m.* **-age.**

cercueil [sɛrkœ:j], *s.m.* coffin, *N.Am:* casket.

céréale [sereal], *a.f. & s.f.* **plantes céréales,** *s.f.pl.* **céréales,** cereal plants; cereals; **commerce des céréales,** corn trade; **céréales (en flocons),** (breakfast) cereals.

cérémon|ie [seremɔni], *s.f.* ceremony; **visite de c.,** formal call; *F:* **faire des cérémonies,** to stand on ceremony; *a. & s.m.* **-ial, -iaux,** ceremonial.

cérémonieu|x, -euse [seremɔnjø, -ø:z], *a.* ceremonious, formal; *adv.* **-sement.**

cerf [sɛːr, sɛrf, *pl.* sɛːr], *s.m.* stag, hart.

cerf-volant [sɛrvɔlɑ̃], *s.m.* **1.** *Ent:* stag-beetle. **2.** (paper) kite; *pl.* **cerfs-volants.**

cerisaie [s(ə)rizɛ], *s.f.* cherry-orchard.

ceris|e [s(ə)riːz]. **1.** *s.f.* cherry. **2.** *s.m. & a.inv.* cherry-red, cerise; *s.m.* **-ier,** cherry-tree.

cern|er [sɛrne], *v.tr.* **1.** to encircle, surround (army); to invest (town); **avoir les yeux cernés,** to have rings round the eyes. **2.** to girdle, ring (tree); *s.m.* **-ement.**

certain [sɛrtɛ̃]. **1.** *a.* (*a*) certain, sure; **tenir qch. pour c.,** to look on sth. as a certainty; (*b*) **il est c. de réussir,** he is sure to succeed; (*c*) fixed, stated (date, price). **2.** *indef. a. & pron.* some, certain; **certains affirment que . . .,** some people maintain that . . .; **après un c. temps,** after a certain time; **d'un c. âge,** getting on; *adv.* **-ement.**

certes [sɛrt], *adv.* (oui) **c.!** yes indeed!

certificat [sɛrtifika], *s.m.* certificate, testimonial; **c. d'origine,** pedigree (of dog, etc.).

certifier [sɛrtifje], *v.tr.* to certify, attest; to witness (signature).

certitude [sɛrtityd], *s.f.* certainty; **j'en ai la c.,** I am sure of it.

cerveau, -eaux [sɛrvo], *s.m.* (*a*) brain; **rhume de c.,** cold in the head; *F:* **vous me rompez le c.,** you give me a headache; (*b*) mind, intellect, brains; **c. creux,** dreamer; **c. brûlé,** hot-head.

cervelas [sɛrvəla], *s.m. Cu:* saveloy.

cervelle [sɛrvɛl], *s.f.* **1.** *Anat:* brain(s) (as matter); **brûler la c. à qn,** to blow s.o.'s brains out; *Cu:* **c. de veau,** calves' brains. **2.** mind, brains; **se creuser la c.,** to rack one's brains (pour, to).

ces [se], *see* CE[2].

césarienne [sezarjɛn], *a.f. & s.f. Med:* caesarean (operation).

cesse [sɛs], *s.f.* cease, ceasing; **sans c.,** unceasingly.

cess|er [sɛse], *v.* to cease, leave off, stop. **1.** *v.i.* **faire c. (qch.),** to put a stop to (sth.); **c. de faire qch.,** to cease doing sth. **2.** *v.tr.* **c. le travail,** to cease, leave off, work; *s.f.* **-ation,** cessation; suspension.

cession [sɛsjɔ̃], *s.f.* **1.** *Jur:* transfer, assignment. **2.** *Mch:* delivery (of heat); supply (of power); *s.m.* **-naire,** transferee, assignee.

c'est-à-dire [sɛtadiːr], *conj.phr.* **1.** that is (to say). **2.** **c'est-à-dire que** + *ind.,* the fact is that. . . .

cet, cette [sɛt], *see* CE[2].

ceux [sø], *see* CELUI.

Ceylan (le) [ləsɛlɑ̃]. *Pr.n.m. Geog:* Ceylon.

chablis [ʃabli], *s.m.* chablis (wine).

chacun, -une [ʃakœ̃, -yn], *pron.* **1.** each; every one; each one; **trois francs c.,** three francs each. **2.** everybody, everyone; **c. (à) son goût,** every man to his taste.

chagrin [ʃagrɛ̃]. **1.** *a.* sad, troubled (**de,** at); morose; embittered. **2.** *s.m.* (*a*) grief, sorrow, trouble; (*b*) vexation, annoyance.

chagrin|er [ʃagrine], *v.tr.* **1.** to grieve, distress. **2.** to vex, annoy; *a.* **-ant.**

chahut [ʃay], *s.m. F:* rag; rowdyism; **faire du c.,** to kick up a shindy.

chahut|er [ʃayte]. **1.** *v.i. F:* to kick up a shindy; to lark about. **2.** *v.tr.* to rag (s.o.); *s.m.* **-age.**

chai [ʃɛ], *s.m.* **1.** wine and spirits warehouse. **2.** (wine-grower's) wine-press and plant.

chaîne [ʃɛn], *s.f.* **1.** (*a*) chain; *Nau:* cable; *Ind:* **travail à la c.,** work on an assembly line; (*b*) shackles, fetters, bonds. **2.** **c. de montagnes,** mountain range; **c. d'idées,** train of thought. **3.** *Tex:* warp.

chaînon [ʃɛnɔ̃], *s.m.* link (of chain).

chair [ʃɛːr], *s.f.* flesh. **1.** **voir qn en c. et en os,** to see s.o. in the flesh; **être (bien) en c.,** (i) to be plump; (ii) to be beefy; **c. de poule,** goose-flesh. **2.** (*a*) meat; **c. à pâté, mince; c. à saucisse,** sausage meat; **c. à canon,** cannon-fodder; (*b*) pulp (of fruit).

chaire [ʃɛːr], *s.f.* **1.** pulpit. **2.** (*a*) chair, desk, rostrum (of lecturer); (*b*) professorship, chair.

chaise [ʃɛːz], *s.f.* chair, seat; **c. de paille, c. cannée,** straw-, cane-bottomed, chair; **c. pliante,** folding chair; **c. haute, c. d'enfant,** high chair; **c. longue,** reclining chair, couch; *Jur: U.S:* **c. électrique,** (electric) chair.

chaland [ʃalɑ̃], *s.m.* lighter, barge.

châle [ʃɑːl], *s.m.* shawl.

chalet [ʃalɛ], *s.m.* (*a*) chalet; (*b*) country cottage.

chaleur [ʃalœːr], *s.f.* (*a*) heat, warmth; **vague de c.,** heat wave; **craint la c.,** to be kept in a cool place; *pl.* **les chaleurs,** the hot weather; (*b*) ardour, zeal; **parler avec c.,** to speak warmly.

chaleureu|x, -euse [ʃalørø, -ø:z], *a.* warm (thanks); cordial (welcome); profuse (compliments); glowing (colour); *adv.* **-sement.**

chaloupe [ʃalup], *s.f.* launch; long-boat; *Fr.C:* rowing-boat.

chalumeau, -eaux [ʃalymo], *s.m.* **1.** straw (for drinking). **2.** *Mus:* pipe. **3.** blow-lamp; *Ind:* **c. de découpage,** oxyacetylene cutting torch.

chalut [ʃaly], *s.m.* drag-net; trawl; *s.m.* **-ier,** trawler.

chalut|er [ʃalyte], *v.i.* to trawl; *s.m.* -age, trawling.

chamaill|er (se) [səʃɑmɑje], *v.pr. F:* to squabble, to bicker; *s.f.* -erie.

chambard|er [ʃɑbarde], *F:* 1. *v.tr.* (*a*) to sack, rifle (room); (*b*) to smash up (furniture). 2. *v.i.* to make a racket; *s.m.* -ement; *s.* -eur, -euse, rowdy, hooligan.

chambranle [ʃɑbrɑ:l], *s.m.* frame (of door); c. de cheminée, mantelpiece.

chambre [ʃɑ̃:br], *s.f.* 1. room; (*a*) c. à coucher, bedroom; c. à deux lits, double(-bedded) room; c. d'ami, spare (bed)room; c. d'enfants, nursery; faire une c., to clean out, tidy, a room; (*b*) c. de chauffe, boiler-house. 2. *Adm:* chamber, house; c. de commerce, chamber of commerce; C. des Députés, Chamber of Deputies. 3. *Tchn:* chamber, cavity, space; c. à air, inner tube (of tyre); *Phot:* c. noire, (i) camera (body); (ii) dark-room.

chambrée [ʃɑbre], *s.f. Mil:* barrack-room.

chambrer [ʃɑbre], *v.tr.* to take the chill off (red wine).

chameau, -eaux [ʃamo], *s.m.* 1. (*a*) camel; (*b*) *P:* (*of man*) quel c.! what a brute! 2. shunting engine.

chamois [ʃamwa], *s.m.* chamois; (peau de) c., wash-leather, chamois leather, shammy.

champ [ʃɑ̃], *s.m.* field. 1. (*a*) prendre, couper, à travers champs, to go, cut, across country; *F:* prendre la clef des champs, to decamp, abscond; à tout bout de c., repeatedly; at every turn; (*b*) c. de foire, fair ground; c. d'aviation, airfield; c. de tir, rifle-range. 2. (*a*) field of action; range, scope; le c. est libre, the coast is clear; (*b*) c. d'une lunette, field of a telescope; (*c*) c. magnétique, magnetic field.

champagne [ʃɑpaɲ]. 1. *Pr.n.f. Geog:* Champagne. 2. *s.m.* (*also* vin de C.) champagne; c. brut, dry champagne. 3. *s.f.* fine c., liquer brandy.

champenois, -oise [ʃɑpənwa, -wa:z], *a. & s.* (native) of Champagne.

champêtre [ʃɑpɛ:tr], *a.* rustic, rural; garde c., country policeman.

champignon [ʃɑpiɲɔ̃], *s.m.* (*a*) c. comestible, (i) edible fungus; (ii) mushroom; (*b*) c. vénéneux, poisonous fungus, toadstool.

champion, -ionne [ʃɑpjɔ̃, -jɔn], *s.* champion; *s.m.* -nat, championship.

chance [ʃɑ̃:s], *s.f.* 1. chance, likelihood; il a peu de chances de réussir, he has little chance of succeeding; c. aléatoire, douteuse, off-chance. 2. luck, fortune; souhaiter bonne c. à qn, to wish s.o. good luck; pas de c.! hard luck! avoir de la c., to be lucky.

chancelant [ʃɑslɑ̃], *a.* staggering, tottering; santé chancelante, delicate health.

chanceller [ʃɑsle], *v.i.* (je chancelle) to stagger, totter; *s.m.* -lement.

chancel|ier [ʃɑsəlje], *s.m.* Chancellor; (in Britain) Grand C., Lord Chancellor; C. de l'Échiquier, Chancellor of the Exchequer; *s.f.* -lerie, (i) chancellery; (ii) chancery (of embassy).

chanceux, -euse [ʃɑsø, -ø:z], *a. F:* 1. hazardous. 2. lucky.

chandail [ʃɑda:j], *s.m. Cl:* sweater, pullover.

chandel|le [ʃɑdɛl], *s.f.* 1. (*a*) (tallow) candle; *F:* économies de bouts de c., cheeseparing economy; voir trente-six chandelles, to see stars; (*b*) (church) candle, taper; *F:* je vous dois une fière c., I owe you more than I can repay. 2. *P:* snot; drop (on the end of the nose). 3. (*of aircraft, prices*) monter en c., to zoom, rocket; *s.m.* -ier, candlestick.

change [ʃɑ̃:ʒ], *s.m.* 1. *Fin:* exchange; contrôle des changes, exchange control; bureau de c., foreign exchange office; lettre de c., bill of exchange. 2. donner le c. à qn, to sidetrack s.o.

changeable [ʃɑʒabl], *a.* 1. changeable. 2. exchangeable.

changeant [ʃɑʒɑ̃], *a.* changing; fickle; taffetas c., shot silk.

chang|er [ʃɑʒe], *v.* (n. changeons). 1. *v.tr.* to change, to exchange. 2. *v.tr.* to change, alter; la campagne me changera, the country will be a change for me. 3. *v.i.* to (undergo a) change; le temps va c., the weather is going to change; *s.m.* -ement, change, alteration; *s.m.* -eur. 1. money changer. 2. record-changer.

se changer. 1. to change; to alter. 2. to change one's clothes, *F:* to change.

Changhaï [ʃɑgaj]. *Pr.n.m. Geog:* Shanghai.

chanoine [ʃanwan], *s.m. Ecc:* canon.

chanson [ʃɑsɔ̃], *s.f.* song; *F:* c'est toujours la même c.! it's the same old story; *s.f.* -nette, little song; *s.* -nier, chansonnier.

chant [ʃɑ̃], *s.m.* 1. singing; song; leçon de c., singing lesson; c. du coq, crowing of the cock. 2. melody, air; c. funèbre, dirge.

chantant [ʃɑtɑ̃], *a.* (*a*) sing-song (accent); (*b*) soirée chantante, musical evening; (*c*) melodious, tuneful.

chant|er [ʃɑte], *v.* to sing. 1. *v.tr.* c. victoire sur qn, to crow over s.o.; qu'est-ce que vous me chantez? what story is this you are telling me? 2. *v.i.* (*of birds*) to sing; (*of cock*) to crow; (*of cricket*) to chirp; faire c. qn, to blackmail s.o.; si ça me chante, if it suits me; *s.m.* -age, blackmail.

chanteur, -euse [ʃɑtœ:r, -ø:z], *s.* singer, vocalist; c. de charme, crooner; maître c., *F:* blackmailer.

chantier [ʃɑtje], *s.m.* yard, work(ing) site; depot; *P.N:* road works; (*a*) c. de construction, (i) building site; works site; (ii) builder's yard; *P.N:* c. interdit au public, no admittance

except on business; (*b*) **c. naval, shipyard;
vaisseau sur le c.,** vessel on the slips; (*c*) *Min:*
c. d'exploitation, mine working.

chantonn|er [ʃɑ̃tɔne], *v.tr. & i.* to hum; to sing
softly; *s.m.* **-ement.**

chantre [ʃɑ̃:tr], *s.m. Ecc:* cantor; chorister;
grand c., precentor.

chanvre [ʃɑ̃:vr], *s.m.* hemp; **cheveux couleur de
c.,** flaxen hair.

chao|s [kao], *s.m.* chaos, confusion; *a.* **-tique,**
chaotic.

chapard|er [ʃaparde], *v.tr. F:* to scrounge, to
pinch; *s.m.* **-age.**

chap|eau, -eaux [ʃapo], *s.m.* **1.** hat; *int. F:* well
done! **c. mou,** soft felt hat; **c. gibus, c. claque,**
opera-hat; **saluer qn d'un coup de c.,** to raise
one's hat to s.o.; **c. bas,** hat in hand. **2.** cover, lid;
(*a*) *Cu:* piecrust; (*b*) cap (of pen); (*c*) hood, cowl
(of chimney); *s.m.* **-elier,** hatter; *s.f.* **-ellerie,**
hat-trade, -shop.

chapelet [ʃaplɛ], *s.m.* (lesser) rosary; **égrener
son c.,** to tell one's beads; **c. d'oignons,** string
of onions.

chapelle [ʃapɛl], *s.f.* (*a*) chapel; **c. de la Vierge,**
Lady chapel; (*b*) *Ecc:* **maître de c.,** choir-
master.

chapelure [ʃaply:r], *s.f. Cu:* breadcrumbs.

chaperonner [ʃaprɔne], *v.tr.* to chaperon (a
girl).

chapit|eau, -eaux [ʃapito], *s.m. Arch:* capital (of
column).

chapitre [ʃapitr], *s.m.* **1.** *Ecc:* chapter; **salle du
c.,** chapter-house. **2.** (*a*) chapter (of book); (*b*)
head(ing); item (of expenditure).

chapon [ʃapɔ̃], *s.m. Cu:* capon.

chaque [ʃak], *a.* each, every.

char [ʃa:r], *s.m.* **1.** waggon, cart; **c. à bœufs,**
bullock cart; **c. funèbre,** hearse; **c. de carnaval,**
float; *Mil:* **c. de combat, d'assaut,** tank. **2.**
Fr.C: car.

charbon [ʃarbɔ̃], *s.m.* (*a*) **c. de bois,** charcoal;
être sur des charbons ardents, to be on tenterhooks; (*b*) *Ch:* carbon; (*c*) coal; *s.m.* **-nage,**
coal-mining; *pl.* collieries.

charbonnier, -ière [ʃarbɔnje, -jɛ:r]. **1.** *s.m.*
Nau: collier. **2.** *s.* coal-merchant. **3.** *a.* coal-
mining (industry).

charcut|er [ʃarkyte], *v.tr.* to cut up (meat); *F:*
Med: to operate clumsily upon, to butcher (a
patient); *s.f.* **-erie. 1.** pork-butcher's trade,
shop. **2.** delicatessen; *s.* **-ier, -ière. 1.** pork-
butcher. **2.** bungling surgeon, saw-bones.

chardon [ʃardɔ̃], *s.m.* thistle.

chardonneret [ʃardɔnrɛ], *s.m.* goldfinch.

charge [ʃarʒ], *s.f.* **1.** load, burden; **être à c. à qn,**
to be a burden to s.o. **2.** *Tchn:* **c. admissible,**
safe load; *El:* charge. **3.** charge (of furnace,
projectile). **4.** (*a*) charge, responsibility; trust;
cela est à votre c., that is part of your duty;

femme de c., housekeeper; (*b*) office; **charges
publiques,** public offices. **5.** charge, expense;
charges de famille, dependents; *prep.phr.* **à (la)
c. de,** on condition of; **à c. de revanche,** on condition that I may do as much for you. **6.**
loading, charging; **c. utile,** *Aut:* carrying
capacity, *Av:* commercial load; *Av:* **c. en vol,**
flight load. **7.** *Mil:* charge. **8.** *Jur:* charge, indictment; **témoin à c.,** witness for the
prosecution.

chargé [ʃarʒe], *a.* **1.** loaded, laden; **jour c.,** busy
day; **temps c.,** heavy, overcast, weather. **2.** lettre **chargée,** registered letter. **3.** *s.* **c. d'affaires,**
chargé d'affaires; *Sch:* **c. de cours** = (university) assistant lecturer.

charg|er [ʃarʒe], *v.tr.* (n. **chargeons**). **1.** to load
(**de,** with); (*a*) **c. qn de reproches,** to heap
reproaches on s.o.; (*b*) **c. qch. sur son dos,** to
take sth. on one's back; (*c*) to fill (pipe); to load
(gun); to charge (accumulator). **2. c. qn de
(faire) qch.,** to instruct s.o. to do sth. **3.** *Mil:*
to charge (the enemy). **4.** *Jur:* to indict (s.o.);
s.m. **-ement,** cargo, load, freight.

se charger. 1. le temps se charge, the weather is
becoming overcast. **2.** (*a*) **se c. d'un fardeau,** to
shoulder a burden; (*b*) **se c. de qch.,** to undertake sth.

chariot [ʃarjo], *s.m.* **1.** (*a*) waggon; (*b*) truck,
trolley; (*c*) *Cin:* dolly. **2.** (*a*) carriage (of
typewriter); (*b*) *Av:* **c. d'atterrissage,** undercarriage; landing gear.

charitable [ʃaritabl], *a.* charitable (**envers,** to,
towards); *adv.* **-ment.**

charité [ʃarite], *s.f.* **1.** charity, love. **2.** act of
charity; alms(-giving).

charlatan [ʃarlatɑ̃], *s.* charlatan, quack; *s.m.*
-isme.

charme [ʃarm], *s.m.* **1.** charm, spell. **2.** charm,
attraction, seductiveness; **faire du c.,** to make
oneself pleasant.

charm|er [ʃarme], *v.tr.* **1.** to charm, bewitch. **2.**
to charm, please, delight; *a.* **-ant,** charming; *s.*
-eur, -euse, (*a*) sorcerer, *f.* sorceress; (*b*)
(snake) charmer; (*c*) charming person.

charnel, -elle [ʃarnɛl], *a.* carnal; sensual; *adv.*
-lement.

charnière [ʃarnjɛ:r], *s.f.* hinge; **nom à c.,**
double-barrelled name.

charnu [ʃarny], *a.* fleshy; **bras c.,** plump arm.

charpente [ʃarpɑ̃:t], *s.f.* frame(work), framing;
bois de c., timber; (*of pers.*) **avoir la c. solide,** to
be solidly built.

charpenté [ʃarpɑ̃te], *a.* built, framed; **homme
solidement c.,** sturdily-built man.

charpent|er [ʃarpɑ̃te], *v.tr.* **1.** to cut (timber)
into shape. **2.** to frame (up) (roof); *s.f.* **-erie,**
carpentry; *s.m.* **-ier,** carpenter.

charretée [ʃarte], *s.f.* cart-load, cartful.

charret|te [ʃarɛt], *s.f.* cart; **c. à bras,** hand-cart;

barrow; *s.m.* **-ier,** carter.

charri|er [ʃarje], *v.tr.* to cart, carry, transport; (*of river, etc.*) to carry, wash down (sand, etc.); *a.* **-able,** transportable; *s.m.* **-age,** haulage.

charron [ʃarɔ̃], *s.m.* cartwright; wheelwright.

charrue [ʃary], *s.f.* plough; *F:* **mettre la c. devant les bœufs,** to put the cart before the horse.

charte [ʃart], *s.f.* 1. charter; **compagnie à c.,** chartered company. 2. (ancient) deed; title; **l'École des chartes,** the School of Palaeography and Librarianship (in Paris).

chartreux, -euse [ʃartrø, -øːz]. 1. *s.* Carthusian (monk, nun). 2. *s.f.* **chartreuse,** (*a*) Carthusian monastery, charterhouse; (*b*) chartreuse (liqueur).

chas [ʃa], *s.m.* eye (of needle).

chasse [ʃas], *s.f.* 1. (*a*) hunting; **c. au tir,** (game) shooting; **aller à la c.,** to go hunting or shooting; **c. sous-marine,** underwater fishing; (*b*) **louer une c.,** to rent a shoot; (*c*) *Nau:* **donner c. à un navire,** to give chase to a ship. 2. **c. d'eau,** (*in W.C.*) flush. 3. *Mec.E:* play (of wheels).

châsse [ʃɑːs], *s.f.* 1. reliquary, shrine. 2. mounting; frame (of spectacles).

chasse-neige [ʃasnɛːʒ], *s.m.inv.* 1. snowplough. 2. (*skiing*) virage en c.-n., stern-turn.

chasser [ʃase]. 1. *v.tr.* (*a*) to chase, hunt; **c. à courre,** to ride to hounds; to hunt; **c. au fusil,** to shoot; (*b*) to drive (s.o.) out, away; to expel; to dismiss, to fire (s.o.); **nuages chassés par le vent,** wind-driven clouds; **c. un clou,** to drive a nail in or out. 2. *v.i.* (*a*) to hunt; to shoot; **c. au lion,** to hunt lions; (*b*) to drive; **nuages qui chassent du nord,** clouds driving from the north; (*c*) *Nau:* (*of anchor*) to drag.

chasseur, -euse [ʃasœːr, -øːz], *s.* 1. (*a*) huntsman; hunter; (*b*) sportsman with gun. 2. *s.m.* (*in hotel*) messenger; porter; page-boy, *N.Am:* bell boy, bellhop. 2. *s.m.Mil:Av:* fighter; *Navy:* **c. de sous-marins,** submarine chaser.

châssis [ʃɑsi], *s.m.* (*a*) frame; **c. de porte, de fenêtre,** door-, window-frame; (*b*) *Aut:* chassis; *Av:* under-carriage; **c. d'atterrissage,** landing-gear.

chaste [ʃast], *a.* chaste, pure; *adv.* **-ment;** *s.f.* **-té,** chastity, purity.

chat, f. chatte [ʃa, ʃat], *s.* cat; *m.* tom-cat, *f.* female cat; **c. de gouttlère,** ordinary domestic cat, *F:* alley cat; *F:* **mon petit c., ma petite chatte,** darling; **acheter c. en poche,** to buy a pig in a poke; **à bon c. bon rat,** tit for tat.

châtaign|e [ʃatɛɲ], *s.f. Bot:* (sweet) chestnut; *s.f.* **-eraie,** chestnut plantation; *s.m.* **-ier,** chestnut-tree, -wood.

châtain [ʃatɛ̃], *a. usu. inv. inf.* (chestnut-)brown; **cheveux c. clair,** light brown hair.

château, -eaux [ʃato], *s.m.* 1. **c. (fort),** castle; **bâtir des châteaux en Espagne,** to build castles

in the air. 2. (*a*) country seat; manor, hall; (*b*) (royal) palace. 3. **c. d'eau,** water-tower; *Rail:* tank.

châteaubriand, -briant [ʃatobriɑ̃], *s.m. Cu:* porterhouse steak.

châtelain, -aine [ʃatlɛ̃, -ɛn], *s.* 1. owner, tenant, of a château. 2. *s.f.* (*a*) wife of owner, tenant, of a château; (*b*) woman owner, tenant, of a château; (*c*) chatelaine (for keys).

chat-huant [ʃaɥɑ̃], *s.m.* tawny owl, brown owl; *pl. chats-huants.*

châti|er [ʃatje], *v.tr.* to punish, chastise; to chasten; *s.m.* **-ment.**

chatoiement [ʃatwamɑ̃], *s.m.* (*a*) shimmer; sheen; (*b*) glistening.

chaton [ʃatɔ̃], *s.* 1. kitten. 2. *s.m. Bot:* catkin.

chatouill|er [ʃatuje], *v.tr.* to tickle; **c. la curiosité de qn,** to arouse s.o.'s curiosity; *s.m.* **-ement,** tickling; *a.* **-eux, -euse,** ticklish; touchy; sore (point).

chatoy|er [ʃatwaje], *v.i.* (**il chatoie**) (*a*) to shimmer; (*b*) to glisten, sparkle; *a.* **-ant,** iridescent.

chatte [ʃat], *see* CHAT.

chaud [ʃo]. 1. *a.* warm; hot; *F:* **avoir la tête chaude,** to be hot-headed; **affaire chaude,** brisk engagement; **guerre chaude,** shooting war; **pleurer à chaudes larmes,** to weep bitterly; *v.phr.* **il fait c.,** it's warm (weather). 2. *s.m.* (*on label*) **tenir au c.,** to be kept in a warm place; **cela ne me fait ni c. ni froid,** it's all the same to me; **attraper un c. et froid,** to catch a chill; **avoir c.,** (*of pers.*) to be warm; *adv.* **-ement,** warmly.

chaudière [ʃodjɛːr], *s.f.* 1. copper (for washing). 2. boiler.

chaudron [ʃodrɔ̃], *s.m.* cauldron; *s.m.* **-nier,** boiler-maker.

chauffage [ʃofaːʒ], *s.m.* (*a*) warming, heating (of room); (*b*) heating apparatus; *Aut:* car heater; **c. central,** central heating; **c. au mazout,** oil heating; (*c*) firing, stoking (of boiler).

chauffard [ʃofaːr], *s.m. F:* road-hog, speed merchant.

chauffe [ʃoːf], *s.f.* 1. heating. 2. *Mch:* stoking.

chauffe-eau [ʃofo], *s.m.inv.* (electric) waterheater.

chauffer [ʃofe]. 1. *v.tr.* (*a*) to warm, heat; **c. une maison au gaz,** to heat a house with gas; **se c. les mains,** to warm one's hands; **c. du linge,** to air linen; (*b*) **chauffé au rouge,** red-hot; **c. une chaudière,** to stoke up a boiler; *F:* **c. un examen,** to swot for an examination. 2. *v.i.* to get, become, warm, hot; *P:* **ça va c.,** things are getting hot.

chauffeur, -euse [ʃofœːr, -øːz], *s.* 1. (*a*) stoker, fireman; (*b*) *Sch: F:* crammer. 2. *Aut:* driver; chauffeur; **elle est c. de taxi,** she's a taxi-driver.

chaum|e [ʃoːm], *s.m.* (*a*) straw; (*b*) thatch; **toit de c.,** thatched roof; (*c*) stubble; *s.f.* **-ière,** thatched cottage.

chaussée [ʃose], s.f. **1.** (a) sea-wall; (b) causeway (across marsh). **2.** (a) roadway; carriageway; (b) road; high road; (c) (on motorway) carriageway.

chausse-pied [ʃospje], s.m. shoe-horn; pl. chausse-pieds.

chausser [ʃose], v.tr. **1.** to put on (footwear); chaussé de pantoufles, wearing slippers. **2.** (a) to put shoes on (s.o.); (b) to supply, fit, (s.o.) with footwear; être bien chaussé, to be well shod; F: cela me chausse, that suits me (down to the ground); s.f. -ette, sock.

chausson [ʃosɔ̃], s.m. **1.** (a) slipper; (b) ballet shoe; (c) c. de bébé, bootee; (d) bed-sock; (e) Fr.C: thick woollen sock. **2.** Cu: c. aux pommes, apple turnover.

chaussure [ʃosyːr], s.f. footwear; fabricant de chaussures, boot and shoe manufacturer.

chauve [ʃoːv]. **1.** a. (a) bald; (b) bare, denuded (mountain). **2.** s.m. bald person.

chauve-souris [ʃoːvsuri], s.f. Z: bat; pl. chauves-souris.

chauvin, -ine [ʃovɛ̃, -in]. **1.** s. chauvinist. **2.** a. chauvinist(ic), jingoist(ic); s.m. -isme, chauvinism, jingoism.

chaux [ʃo], s.f. lime; c. vive, quicklime; c. éteinte, slaked lime; blanchir un mur à la c., to whitewash a wall.

chavirer [ʃavire]. **1.** v.i. (of boat) to capsize, turn turtle, upset. **2.** v.tr. to turn (sth.) upside down; to upset, capsize (boat); s.m. -ement.

chef [ʃɛf], s.m. **1.** head (of family); chief (of tribe); principal, head, chief (of business house); leader; scoutmaster; c. de bureau, head clerk; c. de bande, ring-leader; c. (de cuisine), chef; c. de musique, bandmaster; Sp: c. d'équipe, captain; Rail: c. de gare, stationmaster; c. de train, guard. **2.** authority, right; faire qch. de son (propre) c., to do sth. on one's own (authority). **3.** head(ing) Jur: c. d'accusation, count of an indictment, charge.

chef-d'œuvre [ʃedœːvr], s.m. masterpiece; pl. chefs-d'œuvre.

chef-lieu [ʃefljø], s.m. chief town (of department); pl. chefs-lieux.

cheftaine [ʃeftɛn], s.f. (guide) captain; Brown Owl; (woman) cubmaster.

chemin [ʃmɛ̃], s.m. **1.** (a) way, road; il y a dix minutes de c., it is ten minutes away; faire son c., to make one's way; c. faisant, on the way; faire un bout de c. avec qn, to accompany s.o. a little way; se mettre en c., to set out; demeurer en c., to stop on the way; ne pas y aller par quatre chemins, to go straight to the point; (b) road, path, track; c. vicinal, by-road; c. piéton, footpath; grand c., highway, high road. **2.** c. de fer, railway, N.Am: railroad.

chemineau, -eaux [ʃmino], s.m. tramp, vagrant.

cheminée [ʃmine], s.f. **1.** (a) fireplace; pierre de c., hearthstone; (b) (manteau de) c., chimney-piece, mantelpiece. **2.** (a) chimney (flue, stack); (b) funnel (of locomotive).

cheminer [ʃmine], v.i. to tramp, walk; to proceed; s.m. -ement, tramping; progress.

cheminot [ʃmino], s.m. railwayman.

chemise [ʃmiːz], s.f. **1.** (a) shirt; toile à c., shirting; (b) c. de nuit, night-dress; (c) c. américaine, (woman's) vest. **2.** (a) folder; portfolio; (b) dust-jacket (of book); s.f. -erie, shirt factory, shop.

chenal, -aux [ʃ(ə)nal, -o], s.m. **1.** channel, fairway (of river). **2.** mill-race.

chêne [ʃɛn], s.m. oak; c. vert, holm-oak; s.f. -aie, oak plantation.

chêne-liège [ʃɛnljɛːʒ], s.m. cork-oak; pl. chênes-lièges.

chenet [ʃ(ə)nɛ], s.m. fire-dog; andiron.

chenil [ʃ(ə)ni], s.m. kennels.

chenille [ʃ(ə)niːj], s.f. **1.** (a) caterpillar; (b) track (of tracked vehicle). **2.** Tex: chenille.

cheptel [ʃeptɛl], s.m. (live-)stock; c. bovin, population in cattle (of a region).

chèque [ʃɛk], s.m. cheque, N.Am: check; c. barré, crossed cheque; c. de voyage, traveller's cheque; c. sans provision, dud cheque, F: bouncer.

chèque-fleurs [ʃɛkflœːr], s.m. flower-token; pl. chèques-fleurs.

chèque-repas [ʃɛkrəpa], s.m. luncheon-voucher; pl. chèques-repas.

cher, chère[1] [ʃɛːr], a. **1.** dear, beloved; s. mon c., my dear fellow; ma chère, my dear. **2.** dear, expensive, costly; la vie chère, the high cost of living; adv. il me le payera c., I will make him pay dearly for it; je l'ai eu pour pas c., I got it cheap; s.f. -té, expensiveness.

chercher [ʃɛrʃe], v.tr. **1.** to search for, look for; to seek; je l'ai cherché partout, I have hunted for it everywhere; c. aventure, to seek adventure. **2.** aller c. qn, to (go and) fetch s.o.; allez c. le médecin, go for a doctor; envoyer c. qn, to send for s.o. **3.** c. à faire qch., to endeavour, attempt, to do sth.

chercheur, -euse [ʃɛrʃœːr, -øːz], s. seeker, searcher; investigator; (scientific) research-worker; a. esprit c., enquiring mind.

chère[2] [ʃɛːr], s.f. cheer, fare, living; bonne c., good food; faire maigre c., to go short.

chèrement [ʃɛrmã], adv. **1.** dearly, lovingly. **2.** dearly; at a high price.

chéri, -ie [ʃeri]. **1.** a. cherished, dear. **2.** s. darling.

chérir [ʃeriːr], v.tr. to cherish; to love dearly.

chérubin [ʃerybɛ̃], s.m. cherub.

chétif, -ive [ʃetif, -iːv], a. **1.** weak, puny, sickly (person). **2.** poor, miserable, wretched; adv. -ivement.

cheval, -aux [ʃ(ə)val, -o], s.m. **1.** horse; (a) c. de selle, saddle horse; **c. de chasse**, hunter; **c. de course**, race-horse; **à c.**, on horseback; **monter à c.**, to ride; **être à c. sur qch.**, (i) to sit astride sth.; (ii) **être à c. sur l'algèbre**, to be well up in algebra; **fièvre de c.**, raging fever; (b) *Ich:* **c. marin**, sea-horse. 2. **c. de bois**, vaulting horse; **chevaux de bois**, roundabout, merry-go-round. 3. *Mch:* horse-power.

chevaler|ie [ʃ(ə)valri], *s.f.* 1. knighthood. 2. chivalry; a. **-esque**, chivalrous, knightly; adv. **-esquement**, chivalrously.

chevalet [ʃ(ə)valɛ], *s.m.* support, stand; (a) trestle, frame, stand; (b) **c. de peintre**, easel; (c) clothes-horse; (d) bridge (of violin).

cheval|ier [ʃ(ə)valje], *s.m.* 1. (a) knight; **c. d'industrie**, adventurer, sharper; (b) rider, horseman. 2. *Orn:* sandpiper; *s.f.* **-ière**, signet-ring.

chevalin [ʃəvalɛ̃], a. equine; **boucherie chevaline**, horse-butcher's shop.

cheval-vapeur [ʃəvalvapœ:r], *s.m. Mch:* horse-power; pl. *chevaux-vapeur*.

chevauchant [ʃ(ə)voʃɑ̃], a. overlapping.

chevauchée [ʃ(ə)voʃe], *s.f.* 1. ride. 2. cavalcade.

chevauch|er [ʃ(ə)voʃe]. 1. *v.i.* (a) to ride (on horse); (b) **c. sur un mur**, to sit astride a wall; (c) to overlap. 2. *v.tr.* (a) to ride (on), straddle, to be astride (horse, etc.); (b) to span; *s.m.* **-age**, riding; *s.m.* **-ement**, riding; overlapping; spanning.

chevet [ʃ(ə)vɛ], *s.m.* bed-head; **livre de c.**, bedside book.

chev|eu, -eux [ʃ(ə)vø], *s.m.* 1. (a single) hair; **couper un c. en quatre**, to split hairs; **comme un c. sur la soupe**, very inappropriately. 2. **les cheveux**, the hair; a. **-elu**, long-haired; hairy; **cuir c.**, scalp; *s.f.* **-elure**, (head of) hair.

cheville [ʃ(ə)vi:j], *s.f.* 1. peg, pin; **c. en fer**, bolt; **c. ouvrière**, (i) king-bolt, -pin (of vehicle); (ii) mainspring (of enterprise). 2. peg, plug. 3. *Anat:* ankle; **il ne vous vient pas à la c.**, he can't hold a candle to you.

chevill|er [ʃəvije], *v.tr.* 1. to pin, bolt, peg, together; **avoir l'âme chevillée au corps**, to be hard to kill. 2. to peg, plug (up); *s.m.* **-age**, pegging; bolting; plugging.

chèvre [ʃɛːvr], *s.f.* 1. goat, *esp.* she-goat, *F:* nanny-goat; **barbe de c.**, goatee; **ménager la c. et le chou**, to run with the hare and hunt with the hounds. 2. (a) *Mec.E:* derrick; (b) saw-horse.

chevreau, -eaux [ʃəvro], *s.m.* kid.

chèvrefeuille [ʃɛvrfœːj], *s.m. Bot:* honeysuckle.

chevreuil [ʃəvrœːj], *s.m.* roe-deer; *Cu:* venison.

chevron [ʃəvrɔ̃], *s.m.* 1. rafter. 2. *Her:* chevron; *Tex:* **en c.**, in herring-bone pattern. 3. *Mil:* long-service stripe.

chevrot|er [ʃəvrɔte], *v.i.* to sing, speak, in a quavering voice; to quaver; a. **-ant**, quavering; *s.m.* **-ement**, quaver, tremulousness (of voice).

chevrotine [ʃəvrɔtin], *s.f.* buck-shot.

chez [ʃe], *prep.* 1. (a) **c. qn**, at s.o.'s house, home; **je vais c. moi**, I'm going home; **acheter qch. c. l'épicier**, to buy sth. at the grocer's; (on letters) **c. . . .**, care of, c/o . . .; **faire comme c. soi**, to make oneself at home; (b) **son c.-soi**, one's home, one's house. 2. with, among; **il en est ainsi c. les Français**, it's so among Frenchmen; **c. les animaux**, in the animal kingdom.

chic [ʃik]. 1. *s.m.* (a) skill, knack; **il a le c. pour (faire) cela**, he has the knack of doing that; (b) smartness, stylishness; **il a du c.**, he has style. 2. a. *inv. in f., var. in pl.* (a) smart, stylish; **les gens chics**, the smart set; (b) *F:* fine, first-rate; **sois c.!** come on, be a sport!

chicane [ʃikan], *s.f.* 1. (a) chicanery, pettifogging; (b) quibbling, wrangling; (c) (at bridge) chicane. 2. *Tchn:* (a) baffle(-plate); (b) joints en c., staggered joints.

chican|er [ʃikane]. 1. *v.i.* to chicane; to quibble; to haggle. 2. *v.tr.* **c. qn**, to wrangle with s.o. (sur, about); *s.f.* **-erie**, quibbling; a. & s. **-eur, -euse**. 1. a. quibbling. 2. s. quibbler; a. & s. **-ier, -ière**. 1. a. quibbling. 2. s. quibbler.

chiche [ʃiʃ], a. (a) (of thg) scanty, poor; (b) (of pers.) stingy, niggardly; adv. **-ment**.

chicorée [ʃikɔre], *s.f.* 1. chicory (for coffee). 2. endive.

chien, f. chienne [ʃjɛ̃, ʃjɛn], s. 1. dog; f. bitch; **c. de berger**, sheep-dog; **c. de garde**, watch-dog; **c. courant**, hound; **se regarder en chiens de faïence**, to glare at one another; **avoir d'autres chiens à fouetter**, to have other fish to fry; **entre c. et loup**, in the twilight; **quel temps de c.!** what beastly weather! 2. (a) hammer (of gun); (b) **c. d'arrêt**, pawl, catch.

chiendent [ʃjɛ̃dɑ̃], *s.m. Bot:* couch-grass; **brosse en c.**, scrubbing-brush.

chien-loup [ʃjɛ̃lu], *s.m.* Alsatian (dog); pl. *chiens-loups*.

chiffon [ʃifɔ̃], *s.m.* 1. rag. 2. *Tex:* chiffon.

chiffonn|er [ʃifɔne], *v.tr.* (a) to rumple (dress); to crumple (piece of paper); (b) to annoy, vex (s.o.); *s.m.* **-ier**. 1. rag-and-bone man. 2. small chest of drawers.

chiffre [ʃifr], *s.m.* 1. (a) figure, number, numeral; *Com:* **marqué en chiffres connus**, marked in plain figures; (b) amount, total; *Com:* **c. d'affaires**, turnover. 2. cipher, code. 3. (a) monogram; (b) *Typ:* colophon.

chiffr|er [ʃifre]. 1. *v.i.* to calculate, reckon. 2. *v.tr.* (a) to number (pages of book); (b) to work out (amount); **détails chiffrés**, figures (of scheme); (c) to cipher; to write (despatch) in code; **mot chiffré**, code word; (d) to mark (linen); (e) *Mus:* to figure (the bass); *s.m.* **-age**, reckoning; numbering; coding.

chiffre-taxe [ʃifrətaks], *s.m.* postage-due stamp; *pl. chiffres-taxes.*

chignon [ʃiɲɔ̃], *s.m.* knot of hair; chignon, bun.

Chili (le) [ləʃili]. *Pr.n.m. Geog:* Chile.

chimie [ʃimi], *s.f.* chemistry.

chimique [ʃimik], *a.* chemical; **un produit c.**, a chemical; *adv.* -ment.

chimiste [ʃimist], *s.m.* research chemist; **c. analyste**, analytical chemist.

chimpanzé [ʃɛ̃pɑ̃ze], *s.m. Z:* chimpanzee.

Chine (la) [laʃin]. *Pr.n.f. Geog:* China; **encre de C.**, Indian ink; **papier de C.**, rice-paper.

chinois, -oise [ʃinwa, -waːz]. 1. *a.* Chinese. 2. *s.* Chinese (man, woman); **les C.**, the Chinese. 3. *s.m. Ling:* Chinese.

chinoiserie [ʃinwazri], *s.f.* 1. Chinese curio. 2. *F:* monkey trick; **chinoiseries administratives**, red tape.

chiot [ʃjo], *s.m.* puppy.

chiper [ʃipe], *v.tr. F:* to pinch, to swipe (sth.); *s.m.* -age; *s.* -eur, -euse.

chipoter [ʃipote]. 1. *v.i.* (a) to waste time; (b) to haggle. 2. *v.tr.* to peck at (food); *s.m.* -age; *a. & s.* -eur, -euse.

chips [ʃips], *s.m. pl. Cu:* potato crisps.

chiquement [ʃikmɑ̃], *adv. F:* 1. smartly, stylishly. 2. like a sport.

chiquenaude [ʃiknoːd], *s.f.* fillip, flick (of the finger).

chiroman|cie [kiromɑ̃si], *s.f.* palmistry; *s.* -cien, -cienne, fortune-teller, palmist.

chirurg|ie [ʃiryrʒi], *s.f.* surgery; *a.* -ical, -icaux, surgical; *a.* -ique, surgical.

chirurgien, -ienne [ʃiryrʒjɛ̃, -jɛn], *s.* surgeon; **c. dentiste**, dental surgeon.

chiure [ʃjyːr], *s.f.* fly-speck, -mark.

chlor|e [kloːr], *s.m. Ch:* chlorine.

chlorhydrique [kloridrik], *a. Ch:* hydrochloric (acid).

chloroforme [klorofɔrm], *s.m.* chloroform.

chloromycétine [kloromisetin], *s.f. Med:* chloromycetin.

chlorophylle [klorofil], *s.f.* chlorophyll.

chlorure [kloryːr], *s.m. Ch:* chloride; **c. de chaux**, bleaching powder, bleach.

choc [ʃɔk], *s.m.* 1. shock, impact; **c. des verres**, clink of glasses; **c. des opinions**, clash of opinions; *Com:* **prix c.**, drastic reductions. 2. shock (to nervous system); *Med:* **c. opératoire**, post-operative shock.

chocolat [ʃɔkɔla], *s.m.* chocolate; **c. à croquer**, plain chocolate; **c. au lait**, milk chocolate.

chœur [kœːr], *s.m.* 1. **chanter en c.**, to sing in chorus. 2. choir.

choisi [ʃwazi], *a.* 1. selected. 2. select, choice.

choisir [ʃwaziːr], *v.tr.* to choose, select; **c. ses mots**, to pick one's words.

choix [ʃwa], *s.m.* choice, selection; **je vous laisse le c.**, choose for yourself; **nous n'avons pas le c.**, we have no option; **avancer au c.**, to be promoted by selection; *Com:* **au c.**, all one price.

choléra [kolera], *s.m. Med:* cholera.

cholestérol [kolesterol], *s.m. Med:* cholesterol.

chôm|er [ʃome], *v.i.* 1. to take a holiday (on public holidays); **fête chômée**, public holiday. 2. to be unemployed; **les usines chôment**, the works are at a standstill; *s.m.* -age, unemployment; *s.* -eur, -euse, unemployed person.

chopine [ʃopin], *s.f.* half-litre mug.

choquant [ʃɔkɑ̃], *a.* shocking, offensive.

choquer [ʃɔke], *v.tr.* 1. to strike, knock (sth. against sth.); **c. les verres**, to clink glasses. 2. to shock; (a) to displease, offend; **idée qui choque le bon sens**, idea that offends common sense; (b) to distress (s.o.).

se choquer. 1. to collide (**contre**, with). 2. to be shocked; to take offence (**de**, at).

choral, *pl.* -als [kɔral]. 1. *a.* choral. 2. *s.m.* choral(e). 3. *s.f.* **chorale**, choral society.

chorégraphe [kɔregraf], *s.* choreographer.

chorégraph|ie [kɔregrafi], *s.f. Th:* choreography; *a.* -ique, choreographic.

choriste [kɔrist], *s.m.* chorus-singer (in opera); (church) chorister.

chose [ʃoːz]. 1. *s.f.* thing; **dites bien des choses de ma part à . . .**, remember me kindly to . . .; **la c. en question**, the case in point; **je vois la c.**, I see how matters stand. 2. *s.m. & f.* Monsieur C., Mr. What's-his-name. 3. *a.inv. F:* **être tout c.**, to feel queer.

chou, *pl.* -oux [ʃu], *s.m.* 1. cabbage, **choux de Bruxelles**, Brussels sprouts; **planter ses choux**, to live retired in the country; **mon petit c.**, my dear. 2. *Cu:* **c. à la crème**, cream bun, chou.

choucas [ʃuka], *s.m. Orn:* jackdaw.

choucroute [ʃukrut], *s.f. Cu:* sauerkraut.

chouette[1] [ʃwet], *s.f.* owl; **c. des clochers**, barn owl; **c. des bois**, tawny owl.

chouette[2], *a. & int. F:* fine, stunning; **c. alors!** splendid!

chou-fleur [ʃuflœːr], *s.m.* cauliflower; *pl. choux fleurs.*

chow-chow [tʃoutʃou], *s.m. Z:* chow; *pl. chow-chows.*

chrétien, -ienne [kretjɛ̃, -jɛn], *a. & s.* Christian; *s.f.* -té, Christendom.

Christ [krist], *s.m.* **le Christ**, Christ; **Jésus-C.** [ʒezykri], Jesus Christ.

christianisme [kristjanism], *s.m.* Christianity.

chromatique [krɔmatik], *a. Mus: Opt:* chromatic (scale, aberration).

chrome [kroːm], *s.m.* 1. *Ch:* chromium. 2. *Com:* chrome (yellow).

chrom|er [krome], *v.tr. Ind:* to chrome; *s.m.*

-age, chromium-plating.
chromo [krɔmo], *s.m. F:* chromo(lithograph); colour print.
chronique[1] [krɔnik], *a.* chronic (disease).
chronique[2] *s.f.* **1.** chronicle. **2.** *Journ:* news, reports; *s.* -eur, -euse, reporter.
chronologie [krɔnɔlɔʒi], *s.f.* chronology.
chronologique [krɔnɔlɔʒik], *a.* chronological; *adv.* -ment.
chronomètre [krɔnɔmɛtr], *s.m.* (*a*) chronometer; (*b*) stop-watch.
chronométr|er [krɔnɔmetre], *v.tr.* (je chronomètre, je chronométrerai) *Sp:* to time (race, etc.); *s.m.* -age, timing; *s.m.* -eur, timekeeper.
chrysalide [krizalid], *s.f. Ent:* chrysalis, pupa.
chrysanthème [krizɑ̃tɛ(:)m], *s.m. Bot:* chrysanthemum.
chuchot|er [ʃyʃɔte], *v.i. & tr.* to whisper; *s.m.* -ement, whisper(ing); *s.f.* -erie, whispered conversation.
chut [ʃyt, ʃt], *int.* hush! ssh!
chute [ʃyt], *s.f.* **1.** (*a*) fall; **faire une c.,** to have a fall; **c. du jour,** nightfall; **c. d'eau,** waterfall; *Com:* **c. de prix,** fall, drop, in prices; (*b*) (down)fall. **2. c. des reins,** small of the back. **3.** *Min: Ind:* shoot.
Chypre [ʃipr]. *Pr.n.f.* (**l'île de**) **C.,** Cyprus.
ci[1] [si], *adv.* **par-ci par-là,** here and there.
ci[2], *dem. pron. inv.* (*still used in*) **comme ci, comme ça,** so-so.
cible [sibl], *s.f.* target.
ciboul|e [sibul], *s.f.* spring onion; *s.f. Cu:* -ette, chives.
cicatrice [sikatris], *s.f.* scar.
cicatriser [sikatrize]. **1.** *v.tr.* (*a*) to heal (wound); (*b*) to scar (face). **2.** *v.i. & pr.* (*of wound*) to heal (up).
ci-contre [sikɔ̃tr], *adv.* (*a*) opposite; in the margin; *Book-k:* **porté ci-c.,** as per contra; (*b*) annexed (circular); (*c*) on the other side (of page).
ci-dessous [sidsu], *adv.* hereunder; under-mentioned, below.
ci-dessus [sidsy], *adv.* above(-mentioned).
cidre [si(:)dr], *s.m.* cider.
ciel, *pl.* **cieux** [sjɛl, sjø], *s.m.* **1.** (*a*) sky, heaven; **à c. ouvert,** out of doors; (*b*) (*pl. often* **ciels**) climate, sky. **2.** heaven; *F:* **tomber du c.,** to come as a godsend; (**juste**) **c.!** (good) heavens!
cierge [sjɛrʒ], *s.m. Ecc:* wax candle; taper.
cieux [sjø], *see* CIEL.
cigale [sigal], *s.f. Ent:* cicada.
cigar|e [siga:r], *s.m.* cigar; *s.f.* -ette, cigarette.
ci-gisent, ci-gît [siʒi:z, siʒi], (*on gravestone*) here lie(s) . . ..
cigogne [sigɔɲ], *s.f.* stork.
ci-inclus [siɛ̃kly], *a.* (*inv. when it precedes the s.*) **la copie ci-incluse,** the enclosed copy; **ci-i.**

copie . . ., herewith copy . . ..
ci-joint [siʒwɛ̃], *a.* (*inv. when it precedes the s.*) herewith.
cil [sil], *s.m.* (eye-)lash.
cime [sim], *s.f.* summit (of hill); top (of tree).
ciment [simɑ̃], *s.m.* cement; **c. armé,** reinforced concrete.
ciment|er [simɑ̃te], *v.tr.* to cement; *s.m.* -age.
cimetière [simtjɛ:r], *s.m.* cemetery, graveyard.
cinéaste [sineast], *s.m. Cin:* (*a*) film director; (*b*) scenario-writer; (*c*) film technician.
cinéma [sinema], *s.m.* cinema.
cinémascope [sinemaskɔp], *s.m.* cinemascope.
cinémathèque [sinematɛk], *s.f.* film library.
cinérama [sinerama], *s.m. R.t.m:* Cinerama.
cinglant [sɛ̃glɑ̃], *a.* lashing (rain); cutting, biting (wind); bitter (cold); scathing (remark).
cinglé [sɛ̃gle], *a. P:* cracked, daft; **il est complètement c.,** he's quite nuts.
cingler [sɛ̃gle], *v.tr.* to lash, cut (horse with a whip); **la grêle lui cinglait le visage,** the hail stung his face.
cinq [sɛ̃k], *num. a. inv. and s.m. inv.* (*as cardinal a. before a. or s. beginning with a consonant pronounced* [sɛ̃]), five; **c. garçons** [sɛ̃garsɔ̃] five boys; (*but*) **c. hommes** [sɛ̃kɔm], five men; **le c. mars** [ləsɛ̃kmars], the fifth of March; *F:* **il était moins c.,** it was a near thing.
cinquantaine [sɛ̃kɑ̃tɛn], *s.f.* (about) fifty; **avoir passé la c.,** to be in the fifties.
cinquante [sɛ̃kɑ̃:t], *num. a. inv.* fifty.
cinquantième [sɛ̃kɑ̃tjɛm], *num. a. & s.* fiftieth.
cinquième [sɛ̃kjɛm]. **1.** *num. a. & s.* fifth. **2.** *s.m.* fifth (part).
cintre [sɛ̃:tr], *s.m.* **1.** curve, bend. **2.** arch (of tunnel). **3.** coat-hanger.
cintré [sɛ̃tre], *a.* (*a*) arched (window); (*b*) curved; (*c*) **taille cintrée,** nipped-in waist.
cirage [sira:ʒ], *s.m.* shoe-, floor-, polish.
circon|cire [sirkɔ̃si:r], *v.tr.* (*pr.p.* **circoncisant** *p.p.* **circoncis;** *p.h.* **je circoncis**) to circumcise *s.f.* -cision, circumcision.
circonférence [sirkɔ̃ferɑ̃:s], *s.f.* circumference
circonflexe [sirkɔ̃flɛks], *a.* circumflex (accent)
circonlocution [sirkɔ̃lɔkysjɔ̃], *s.f.* circumlocution.
circonscri|re [sirkɔ̃skri:r], *v.tr.* (*conj. like* ÉCRIRE) to circumscribe; *s.f.* -ption, (electoral) district.
circonstanc|e [sirkɔ̃stɑ̃:s], *s.f.* **1.** circumstance event; **en pareille c.,** in such a case; **à la hauteur des circonstances,** equal to the occasion. **2.** *Jur:* **circonstances atténuantes** extenuating circumstances; *a.* -iel, -ielle circumstantial.
circonvenir [sirkɔ̃vni:r], *v.tr.* (*conj. like* VENIR) to circumvent, thwart; to outwit (s.o.).
circuit [sirkɥi], *s.m.* circuit. **1.** (*a*) circumference (of a town); (*b*) *Sp:* lap; circuit; (*c*) a

touristique, organized tour. **2.** deviation; **circuits d'une rivière**, windings of a river. **3.** *El:* **mettre (une lampe) en c.**, to switch (a lamp) on; **mettre l'accu hors c.**, to cut out the battery.

circuler [sirkyle], *v.i.* **1.** (*of blood, etc.*) to circulate, flow. **2.** to circulate, move about; **circulez! pass along!** *a. & s.f.* **-aire**, circular; *s.f.* **-ation**, traffic.

cire [siːr], *s.f.* wax.

ciré [sire], *a.* **1.** waxed, polished; **toile cirée**, oil cloth. **2.** *s.m. Nau:* oilskins.

cirer [sire], *v.tr.* to wax; to polish (floors); **c. des chaussures**, to polish shoes; *s.f.* **-euse**, electric polisher.

cirque [sirk], *s.m.* **1.** circus. **2.** *Geol:* cirque, cwm, corrie.

cisaille(s) [sizɑːj], *s.f. sg. or pl.* shears; nippers; wire-cutter; *Hort:* **c. à bordures**, edging-shears.

ciseau, -eaux [sizo], *s.m.* **1.** chisel. **2.** *pl.* (*a*) scissors; (*b*) shears.

ciseler [sizle], *v.tr.* (**je cisèle, je ciselle**) to chase (gold); to chisel, carve (wood); *s.m.* **-age**; *s.m.* **-eur**; *s.f.* **-ure**, chased, chiselled, work.

citadelle [sitadɛl], *s.f.* citadel, stronghold.

citadin [sitadɛ̃], *s.* townsman, town-dweller.

cité [site], *s.f.* city; (*a*) (large) town; ancient part of a town; **la C. (de Londres)**, the City (of London); (*b*) housing estate; **c. universitaire**, students' halls of residence.

citer [site], *v.tr.* **1.** to quote, cite. **2.** *Jur:* to summon; to subpoena (a witness). **3.** *Mil:* **c. qn (à l'ordre du jour)** = to mention s.o. in dispatches; *s.f.* **-ation**, (*a*) quotation; (*b*) *Jur:* summons; subpoena.

citerne [sitɛrn], *s.f.* cistern, tank.

citoyen, -enne [sitwajɛ̃, -ɛn], *s.* citizen.

citrique [sitrik], *a. Ch:* citric (acid).

citron [sitrɔ̃], *s.m.* lemon; lime; citron; **c. pressé**, lemon juice; *s.f.* **-nade**, lemon drink; *s.m.* **-nier**, lemon tree.

citrouille [sitruːj], *s.f.* pumpkin.

civet [sive], *s.m. Cu:* stew (of game); **c. de lièvre** = jugged hare.

civière [sivjɛːr], *s.f.* **1.** hand-barrow. **2.** stretcher. **3.** bier (for coffin).

civil [sivil], *a.* civil; (*a*) civic (rights); **guerre civile**, civil war; (*b*) *Jur:* **droit c.**, common law; (*c*) lay, secular; civilian; *s.m.* **un c.**, a civilian; **en c.**, in plain clothes; *s.f.* **-ité**, courtesy.

civilement [sivilmɑ̃], *adv.* **se marier c.**, to be married in a registry office; *Jur:* **c. responsable**, liable for damages.

civiliser [sivilize], *v.tr.* to civilize; *a. & s.* **-ateur, -atrice**, (*a*) civilizing; (*b*) civilizer; *s.f.* **-ation**, civilization.

civique [sivik], *a.* civic (duties); civil (rights); *Sch:* **instruction c.**, civics; **centre c.**, civic centre (of a town).

civisme [sivism], *s.m.* good citizenship.

claie [klɛ], *s.f.* **1.** (*a*) hurdle; (*b*) **c.** (wicker) fruit-tray. **2.** screen, riddle.

clair [klɛːr]. **1.** *a.* clear; (*a*) unclouded, limpid, obvious, plain (meaning); **explication claire**, lucid explanation; (*c*) bright, light (room); **il fait pas c. ici**, you can't see here; (*d*) light (colour). **2.** *adv.* plainly, clearly; **y voir c.**, (i) to be clear-sighted; (ii) to be able to see clearly. **3.** *s.m.* (*a*) light; **au c. de (la) lune**, in the moonlight; (*b*) **message en c.**, message in plain language (not in cipher); **sabre au c.**, with drawn sword; *adv.* **-ement**, clearly, plainly.

claire-voie [klɛrvwa], *s.f.* lattice-work (fence, gate); **caisse à c.-v.**, crate; *pl.* **claires-voies**.

clairière [klɛrjɛːr], *s.f.* clearing, glade.

clairon [klɛrɔ̃], *s.m.* (*a*) bugle; (*b*) bugler; *a.* **-nant**; **voix claironnante**, loud, brassy voice.

clairsemé [klɛrsəme], *a.* scattered, sparse (vegetation, etc.); thin (hair).

clairvoyant, -ante [klɛrvwajɑ̃, -ɑ̃t]. **1.** *a.* perspicacious, clear-sighted, shrewd. **2.** *a. & s.* clairvoyant; *s.f.* **-ance**, perspicacity; clairvoyance.

clameur [klamœːr], *s.f.* clamour, outcry.

clandestin [klɑ̃dɛstɛ̃], *a.* clandestine, secret; *adv.* **-ement**, secretly.

clapet [klapɛ], *s.m.* valve; **c. à charnière**, clack-valve.

clapier [klapje], *s.m.* rabbit-hutch; **lapin de c.**, tame rabbit.

clapoter [klapɔte], *v.i.* (*of sea*) to be choppy; to lap (against sth.); *s.m.* **-ement**, *s.m.* **-is**, lap(ping) (of waves).

claque [klak], *s.f.* **1.** smack, slap. **2.** *Th:* hired clappers. **3.** *pl. Fr.C:* galoshes; *N.Am:* rubbers.

claqué [klake], *a.* (*a*) strained, snapped (tendon); (*b*) worn out, dog-tired.

claquer [klake]. **1.** *v.i.* (*a*) to clap; (*of door*) to bang; **il claque des dents**, his teeth are chattering; (*b*) *F:* to die; (*of engine, etc.*) to conk out. **2.** *v.tr. & i.* (**faire**) **c.**, to slam (the door); to crack (a whip). **3.** *v.tr.* (*a*) to slap (child); (*b*) to burst (tyre); (*c*) to tear (muscle); *s.m.* **-ement**.

clarifier [klarifje], *v.tr.* to clarify.

clarinette [klarinɛt], *s.f.* (*a*) clarinet; (*b*) clarinettist.

clarté [klarte], *s.f.* **1.** clearness, clarity; (*a*) limpidity (of water); transparency; (*b*) lucidity (of mind, style); (*c*) **avoir des clartés sur un sujet**, to have *some* knowledge of a subject. **2.** light, brightness.

classe [klaːs], *s.f.* **1.** class, division; **billet de première c.**, first-class ticket. **2.** *Sch:* (*a*) class, form; **les hautes classes**, the top forms; **livre de c.**, schoolbook; **salle de c.**, class-room; (*b*) **aller en c.**, to go to school. **3.** *Mil:* annual contingent (of recruits); age-group.

classe], *v.tr.* 1. to class(ify). 2. (*a*) to sort ...es); (*b*) to file (documents); **c. une** ...shelve a matter; *s.m.* **-ement;** *s.m.* ...ng cabinet, file.

...r [klasifje], *v.tr.* 1. to classify (plant). 2. ...t (out) (articles); *s.f.* **-cation.**

...ue [klasik]. 1. *a.* (*a*) classic(al); (*b*) stan-...d (work); *F:* **c'est un coup c.,** that's an old ...dge. 2. *s.m.* **les classiques grecs,** the Greek classics.

clause [klo:z], *s.f. Jur:* clause (in a contract, etc.); **c. additionnelle,** rider.

clavicule [klavikyl], *s.f.* collar-bone.

clavier [klavje], *s.m.* 1. keyboard (of piano, typewriter); manual (of organ). 2. range, compass (of clarinet).

clé, clef [kle], *s.f.* 1. key; (*a*) **fermer une porte à c.,** to lock a door; **tenir qch. sous c.,** to keep sth. under lock and key; (*b*) **position c.,** key position; **industrie c.,** key industry; (*c*) key (to a cipher). 2. *Mus:* (*a*) clef; (*b*) key-signature. 3. *Arch:* **c. de voûte,** keystone. 4. *Tls:* key, wrench, spanner; **c. anglaise,** monkey-wrench.

clématite [klematit], *s.f. Bot:* clematis.

clémence [klemã:s], *s.f.* 1. clemency (**pour, envers,** to, towards). 2. mildness (of the weather).

clément [klemã], *a.* 1. clement (**pour, envers,** to, towards). 2. mild (weather).

cleptoman|e [kleptoman], *s.m. & f.* kleptomaniac; *s.f.* **-ie,** kleptomania.

clerc [klɛ:r], *s.m.* clerk (in lawyer's office).

clergé [klerʒe], *s.m.* (the) clergy, priesthood.

clérical, *pl.* **-aux** [klerikal, -o], *a.* clerical.

cliché [kliʃe], *s.m.* 1. *Phot:* negative. 2. cliché, hackneyed expression, tag.

client, -ente [kliã, -ã:t], *s.* client, customer; (hotel) visitor.

clientèle [kliãtɛl], *s.f.* (*a*) (doctor's, lawyer's) practice; (*b*) *Com:* customers; custom.

clign|er [kliɲe], *v.tr. & i.* 1. **c. les yeux,** (i) to screw up one's eyes; (ii) to blink. 2. **c. de l'œil à qn,** to wink at s.o.; *s.m.* **-ement.**

clignotant [kliɲɔtã]. 1. *a.* blinking; twinkling (star). 2. *s.m. Aut:* (direction) indicator, *F:* winker.

clignot|er [kliɲɔte], *v.i.* (*a*) **c. des yeux,** to blink; (*b*) (*of star*) to twinkle; (*c*) (*of eyelid*) to twitch; (*d*) (*of light*) to flicker; (*e*) (*of signal light*) to flash; *s.m.* **-ement.**

climat [klima], *s.m.* 1. climate. 2. region, climate; *a.* **-ique,** climatic (conditions, etc.).

climatis|er [klimatize], *v.tr.* to air-condition; *s.f.* **-ation,** air-conditioning.

clin d'œil [klɛ̃dœ:j], *s.m.* wink; *esp.* **en un c. d'œil,** in the twinkling of an eye.

clinique [klinik]. 1. *a.* clinical (instruction). 2. *s.f.* nursing-home; surgery.

clinquant [klɛ̃kã], *s.m.* tinsel.

clique [klik], *s.f.* clique, gang, set.

cliquet [klikɛ], *s.m. Mec:* catch, pawl.

cliquet|er [klikte], *v.i.* (**il cliquette**) (*of chains*) t... clank; (*of keys*) to jingle; *s.m.* **-is,** rattling chinking, jingling.

clochard [klɔʃa:r], *s.m. F:* tramp, *N.Am:* hobo.

cloche [klɔʃ], *s.f.* 1. bell. 2. *Ch:* bell-jar; *Hor...* bell-glass, cloche; *H:* dish-cover.

clocher[1] [klɔʃe], *s.m.* belfry, bell-tower; steeple **esprit de c.,** parochialism; **course au c.,** poin... to-point race.

clocher[2], *v.i.* to limp, hobble; *F:* **il y a quelqu... chose qui cloche,** there's something wrong.

clochette [klɔʃɛt], *s.f.* small bell; hand-bell.

cloison [klwazɔ̃], *s.f.* 1. partition, division; (m... de) c., dividing wall. 2. *Nau:* bulkhead.

cloisonner [klwazɔne], *v.tr.* to partition (of... (room).

cloître [klwa:tr], *s.m.* cloister(s).

clopin-clopant [klɔpɛ̃klɔpã], *adv. F:* **aller c.-c** to limp along, hobble about.

clopiner [klɔpine], *v.i.* to hobble, limp.

cloque [klɔk], *s.f.* 1. swelling, blister. 2. *Ag* rust, blight.

clos [klo]. 1. *a.* (*a*) closed; shut up; **à la nuit clos...** after dark; (*b*) concluded. 2. *s.m.* enclosure; **de vigne,** vineyard.

clôture [kloty:r], *s.f.* 1. enclosure, fence, fe... cing. 2. (*a*) closing (of offices); (*b*) conclusio... (of sitting); *St.Exch:* **cours de c.,** closing pric... *Com:* winding up (of account).

clôtur|er [klotyre], *v.tr.* 1. to enclose (field). 2. (... to close down (factory); (*b*) to end (session). to wind up, close (accounts).

clou, *pl.* **-s** [klu], *s.m.* 1. (*a*) nail; (*b*) **c. à croch...** hook; **c. cavalier,** staple; (*c*) stud (at pedestri... crossing); (*d*) star turn, chief attraction (... entertainment). 2. **c. de girofle,** clove.

clouer [klue], *v.tr.* 1. to nail (sth.). 2. **rester clo... sur place,** to stand rooted to the spot; ê... **cloué à son lit,** to be bed-ridden.

clout|er [klute], *v.tr.* to stud (boot); to fix (hors... shoe); **passage clouté,** pedestrian crossin... *s.m.* **-age.**

clown [klun], *s.m.* clown, buffoon.

coagul|er (se) [sɔkoagyle], *v.pr.* to coagula... clot; to curdle; *s.f.* **-ation.**

coali|ser (se) [sɔkoalize], *v.pr.* to form... coalition; to unite; *s.f.* **-tion.**

coass|er [koase], *v.i.* (*of frog*) to croak; *s...* **-ement,** croaking.

cobalt [kɔbalt], *s.m.* cobalt; **bombe au c.,** cob... bomb.

cobaye [kɔba:j], *s.m. Z:* guinea-pig; cavy; **ser... de c.,** to be a guinea-pig.

Coblence [kɔblã:s]. *Pr.n.f. Geog:* Coblentz.

cocaïne [kɔkaïn], *s.f. Pharm:* cocaine.

cocarde [kɔkard], *s.f.* cockade, rosette; ... company crest (on airliners).

cocasse [kɔkas], a. F: droll, laughable.
coche [kɔʃ], s.f. notch, nick.
cochère [kɔʃɛːr], a.f. porte c., main gateway.
cochon [kɔʃɔ̃], s.m. 1. (a) pig, hog; (b) (of pers.) swine. 2. c. d'Inde, guinea-pig.
cocktail [kɔktɛl], s.m. (a) cocktail; (b) cocktail party.
coco koko, kɔ-], s.m. 1. noix de c., coconut. 2. F: liquorice water; s.m. -tier, coconut palm.
cocon [kɔkɔ̃], s.m. cocoon.
cocotte-minute [kɔkɔtminyt], s.f. R.t.m: pressure-cooker; pl. cocottes-minute.
code [kɔd], s.m. 1. code, system of laws; statute-book; c. civil = Common Law; c. pénal, penal code; Aut: c. de la route, (i) Highway Code; (ii) rule of the road; se mettre en c., to dip one's headlights. 2. code, cipher; c. télégraphique, telegraphic code; Nau: c. international de signaux, International Code; Mil: c. de chiffrement, cipher book.
codicille [kɔdisil], s.m. codicil.
codifi|er [kɔdifje], v.tr. 1. to codify (laws). 2. to code (message); s.f. -cation.
codirecteur, -trice [kodirɛktœːr, -tris], s. codirector; joint manager, manageress.
coefficient [koefisjɑ̃], s.m. coefficient; Ind: c. de sécurité, safety factor.
coéquipier [koekipje], s.m. Sp: fellow-member (of team, crew).
cœur [kœːr], s.m. heart. 1. (a) en c., heart-shaped; (b) maladie de c., heart disease; avoir mal au c., to feel sick; cela soulève le c., it's sickening, nauseating; opération à c. ouvert, open-heart surgery. 2. soul, feelings, mind; (a) avoir qch. sur le c., to have sth. on one's mind; en avoir le c. net, to clear the matter up; parler à c. ouvert, to speak freely; avoir le c. gros, to be sad at heart; avoir trop de c., to be too tender-hearted; si le c. vous en dit, if you feel like it; je n'ai pas le c. à faire cela, I am not in the mood to do that; avoir à c. de faire qch., to be bent, set, on doing sth.; (b) apprendre qch. par c., to learn sth. by heart. 3. courage, spirit, pluck; donner du c. à qn, to hearten s.o.; F: avoir du c. au ventre, to have plenty of guts; faire contre mauvaise fortune bon c., to put a brave face on things. 4. (a) avoir le c. à l'ouvrage, to have one's heart in one's work; travailler, y aller, de bon c., to work with a will; (b) à vous de tout c., yours affectionately. 5. middle, midst; au c. de l'hiver, in the depth of winter. 6. Cards: hearts.
offr|e [kɔfr], s.m. (a) chest, bin; (b) boot, N.Am: trunk (of car); s.m. -age, framework, shuttering (for concrete work); s.m. -et, small box.
offre-fort [kɔfrəfɔːr], s.m. safe; pl. coffres-forts.
co|gérer [koʒere], v.tr. to manage (a business) jointly; s. -gérant, -gérante, joint manager,

manageress; s.f. -gestion, joint management.
cognac [kɔɲak], s.m. cognac; brandy.
cognée [kɔɲe], s.f. (woodman's) axe, hatchet.
cogn|er [kɔɲe]. 1. v.tr. (a) to drive in, hammer in (sth.); (b) to knock, thump (s.o., sth.); to hit (s.o.). 2. v.i. to knock, thump (sur, on); to bump (contre, against); (of engine) to knock.
cohérence [kɔerɑ̃ːs], s.f. coherence.
cohérent [kɔerɑ̃], a. coherent.
cohésion [kɔezjɔ̃], s.f. cohesion, cohesiveness.
cohue [kɔy], s.f. crowd, mob, throng.
coiffé [kwafe], a. 1. être c. d'un chapeau, to be wearing a hat; il est né c., he was born with a silver spoon in his mouth. 2. être bien c., to have one's hair well done.
coiffer [kwafe], v.tr. 1. (a) to cover (the head); montagne coiffée de neige, snow-capped mountain; (b) c. un chapeau, to put on a hat. 2. c. qn, to do s.o.'s hair. se coiffer. 1. to put one's hat on. 2. to do one's hair.
coiffeur, -euse [kwafœːr, -øːz], s. 1. hairdresser. 2. s.f. coiffeuse, dressing-table.
coiffure [kwafyːr], s.f. 1. head-gear. 2. hair style. 3. hairdressing.
coin [kwɛ̃], s.m. 1. (a) corner; maison du c., corner house; l'épicier du c., the local grocer; (b) petit c. rustique, small country place; (c) Furn: corner cupboard; (d) c. du feu, ingle-nook; au c. du feu, by the fireside; (e) patch (of land). 2. wedge. 3. stamp, die; hall-mark.
coin|cer [kwɛ̃se], v. (n. coinçons). 1. v.tr. to wedge (up), chock (up) (rails); F: c. qn, to corner s.o.; to arrest s.o.; s.m. -çage. 2. v.i. & pr. (of machine parts) to jam, to stick, to bind; s.m. -cement.
coïncid|er [kɔɛ̃side], v.i. to coincide; s.f. -ence; a. -ent.
coing [kwɛ̃], s.m. Bot: quince.
coke [kɔk], s.m. Ind: coke.
col [kɔl], s.m. 1. neck (of bottle). 2. Cost: collar; faux c., (i) detachable collar; (ii) F: head (of froth on glass of beer); c. raide, mou, hard, soft, collar. 3. Geog: pass, col.
coléoptère [kɔleɔptɛːr], s.m. beetle.
col|ère [kɔlɛːr]. 1. s.f. anger; F: c. bleue, towering passion; se mettre en c., to lose one's temper. 2. a. angry (voice); irascible (pers.); a. -éreux, -euse, quick-tempered (pers.); a. -érique, fiery (disposition).
colimaçon [kɔlimasɔ̃], s.m. snail; escalier en c., spiral staircase.
colique [kɔlik], s.f. colic, stomach-ache.
colis [kɔli], s.m. parcel, package; c. postal, postal packet; par c. postal, by parcel post.
collabor|er [kɔlabɔre], v.i. to collaborate; s. -ateur, -atrice, collaborator; s.f. -ation, collaboration.
collant [kɔlɑ̃]. 1. a. (a) sticky; (b) close-fitting,

skin-tight (garment). **2.** *s.m.* (pair of) tights.
collatéral, *pl.* **-aux** [kɔlateral, -o], *a.* collateral.
colle [kɔl], *s.f.* **1.** (i) paste; (ii) glue; (iii) size. **2.** *F:*
Sch: (i) poser; (ii) oral test; (iii) detention; **poser
une c.,** to ask a tricky question.
collectif, -ive [kɔlɛktif, -iːv], *a.* collective, joint
(action); *adv.* **-ivement,** collectively, jointly;
s.f. **-ivité,** community.
collection [kɔlɛksjɔ̃], *s.f.* **1.** collecting. **2.** collection (of stamps, etc.); *Dressm:* **présentation de
collections,** fashion show.
collectionner [kɔlɛksjɔne], *v.tr.* to collect
(stamps, curios, etc.); *s.m.* **-ement,** collecting
(of curios, etc.); *s.* **-eur, -euse,** collector.
collège [kɔlɛːʒ], *s.m.* **1.** college. **2.** school; *s.*
-légien, -légienne, schoolboy, -girl.
collègue [kɔlɛg], *s.m. & f.* colleague.
coller [kɔle]. **1.** *v.tr.* to paste, stick, glue (à, to,
on); *F:* to stump, floor (s.o.); **c. un candidat,** to
fail, plough, a candidate. **2.** *v.i.* to stick, adhere,
cling; **vêtement qui colle,** clinging garment; *F:*
ça ne colle pas, it doesn't work.
se coller, to stick, adhere closely; **se c. contre un
mur,** to stand close to a wall.
collet [kɔlɛ], *s.m.* **1.** collar (of coat); *a.inv.* **elle est
très c. monté,** she is very prim (and proper),
very formal. **2.** flange, collar (of pipe). **3.** snare,
noose; **prendre des lapins au c.,** to snare
rabbits.
collier [kɔlje], *s.m.* **1.** necklace. **2. c. de chien, de
cheval,** dog-collar, horse-collar; **donner un
coup de c.,** to put one's back into it.
colline [kɔlin], *s.f.* hill.
collision [kɔl(l)izjɔ̃], *s.f.* collision; **entrer en c.
avec qch.,** to collide with sth.; *Atom.Ph:* **c. de
neutrons,** knock-on; **c. nucléaire,** nuclear
collision.
colloque [kɔlɔk], *s.m.* (formal) conversation;
conference.
collusion [kɔlyzjɔ̃], *s.f. Jur:* collusion.
colombe [kɔlɔ̃b], *s.f. Orn:* pigeon, dove; *s.m.*
-ier, dovecote.
Colombie (la) [lakɔlɔ̃bi]. *Pr.n.f. Geog:* Colombia. **2. la C. britannique,** British Columbia.
colon [kɔlɔ̃], *s.m.* colonist, settler; *a. & s.m.* **-ial,**
pl. **-iaux.**
colonel [kɔlɔnɛl], *s.m.* colonel; *Mil.Av:* group
captain.
colonialisme [kɔlɔnjalism], *s.m. Pol:* (a) im-
perialism; (b) colonialism; *a.* **-iste.**
colonie [kɔlɔni], *s.f.* colony, settlement; **c.
pénitentiaire,** reformatory school; **c. de
vacances,** (children's) holiday camp; **la c.
anglaise à Paris,** the English colony in Paris.
coloniser [kɔlɔnize], *v.tr.* to colonize; *a. & s.*
-ateur, -atrice, colonizing; colonizer; *s.f.*
-ation.
colonne [kɔlɔn], *s.f.* **1.** column, pillar; **c. d'un
journal,** column of a newspaper; *Anat:* **c.**

vertébrale, spine, backbone. **2.** *Mil:* column. 3
Pol: **cinquième c.,** fifth column.
colorer [kɔlɔre], *v.tr.* to colour, tint; **tein
coloré,** florid complexion; **c. un récit,** to lenc
colour to a tale; *s.f.* **-ation,** colouring; colour.
colorier [kɔlɔrje], *v.tr.* to colour (drawing)
colorié à la main, hand-coloured.
coloris [kɔlɔri], *s.m.* colour(ing) (of painting)
Com: **carte de c.,** shade card.
colossal, *pl.* **-aux** [kɔlɔsal, -o], *a.* colossal, gigantic, huge; *adv.* **-ement.**
colporter [kɔlpɔrte], *v.tr.* (a) to hawk (goods)
(b) to spread abroad (news); *s.m.* **-age.**
colporteur, -euse [kɔlpɔrtœːr, -øːz], *s.* (a) door
to-door salesman; (b) **c. de nouvelles**
newsmonger.
coma [kɔma], *s.m.* coma.
combat [kɔ̃ba], *s.m.* **1.** combat, fight, contest
engager le c., to go into action; **hors de c.,** dis
abled; out of action. **2.** conflict; battle (o
wits).
combattant [kɔ̃batɑ̃], *s.m.* fighting man; com
batant; **anciens combattants,** ex-servicemen.
combattre [kɔ̃batr], *v.* (*conj. like* BATTRE) **1**
v.tr. to combat, to fight (against) (enemy
temptation, etc.). **2.** *v.i.* to fight, strive; *a.* -i
-ive, pugnacious.
combien [kɔ̃bjɛ̃], *adv.* **1.** (*exclamative*) (a) hov
(much)! (b) how many! **c. de gens!** what a lo
of people! **2.** (*interrogative*) (a) how much? c
vous dois-je? how much do I owe you? **c'es
c.?** how much is it? (b) **c. de fois?** how man
times? how often? *F:* **le c. sommes-nous?** wha
day of the month is it? **il y a un car tous les c.**
how often does the bus run?
combinaison [kɔ̃binɛzɔ̃], *s.f.* **1.** (a) combina
tion, arrangement; (b) plan, scheme; (c) *Ch*
combination. **2.** *Cl:* overalls, dungarees, flyin
suit; (woman's) slip.
combinard [kɔ̃binaːr], *s.m.* *P:* grafter
racketeer; slick customer.
combine [kɔ̃bin], *s.f.* scheme, racket, fiddle;
faut savoir la c., you have to know the trick.
combiner [kɔ̃bine], *v.tr.* **1.** (a) to combine, uni
(forces); to arrange (ideas); (b) *Ch:* to com
bine. **2.** to contrive (plan).
comble[1] [kɔ̃bl], *s.m.* **1.** heaped measure; **pour**
de malheur, as a crowning misfortune; *F:* **c**
c'est le c.! that's the limit, the end! **2.** (
roofing; **de fond en c.,** from top to bottom; (
F: highest point; height (of happiness).
comble[2], *a.* (a) (*of measure*) heaped u
overflowing; (b) (*of hall*) packed; **salle c.,** fu
house.
combler [kɔ̃ble], *v.tr.* **1.** to fill in (ditch); to mak
good (a loss); to fill (a vacancy). **2.** to fi
(measure) to overflowing; **c. qn de bienfaits,**
heap kindness on s.o.; **il est comblé,** he's e
tirely happy.

combustible [kɔ̃bystibl]. **1.** *a.* combustible. **2.** *s.m.* fuel; *Rockets:* propellant.

combustion [kɔ̃bystjɔ̃], *s.f.* combustion, burning.

coméd|ie [kɔmedi], *s.f.* (*a*) comedy; **c'était une vraie c.!** it was as good as a play; (*b*) (*to child*) **pas de c.**, behave yourself; *s.* **-ien, -ienne,** actor, actress.

comestible [kɔmɛstibl]. **1.** *a.* edible, eatable. **2.** *s.m.* article of food.

comète [kɔmɛt], *s.f.* comet.

comice [kɔmis], *s.m. usu. pl.* **comices agricoles** = agricultural show.

comique [kɔmik]. **1.** *Th: Lit:* (*a*) *a.* comic (actor, part, etc.); **le genre c.,** comedy; (*b*) *s.m.* (i) comedy; (ii) comedian. **2.** (*a*) *a.* comical, funny; (*b*) *s.m.* **le c. de l'histoire c'est que . . .,** the funny part, the joke, is that . . .; *adv.* **-ment.**

omité [kɔmite], *s.m.* committee, board; **c. d'entreprise,** joint production committee; **être en petit c.,** to be an informal gathering.

ommandant [kɔmɑ̃dɑ̃]. **1.** *a.* commanding (officer). **2.** *s.m. Nau:* Commander; *Mil:* Major; *Av:* Squadron-leader.

ommande [kɔmɑ̃:d], *s.f.* **1.** *Com:* order; **fait sur c.,** made to order; **payable à la c.,** cash with order. **2.** *Mec:* (*a*) control, operation; **organes de c.,** controls; **levier de c.,** operating lever; *Av:* control column; *Aut:* **c. du changement de vitesse,** gear lever.

ommandement [kɔmɑ̃dmɑ̃], *s.m.* **1.** command, order. **2.** (position of) command, authority.

ommander [kɔmɑ̃de]. **1.** *v.tr.* (*a*) to command, order; **c. un dîner,** to order a dinner; **c. à qn de faire qch.,** to command, order, s.o. to do sth.; **apprendre à se c.,** to learn to control oneself; (*b*) to govern (province, etc.); to be in command of (army); (*c*) **c. le respect,** to command respect; (*d*) (*of fort*) to command, dominate (town); (*e*) *Mec:* to drive (machine). **2.** *v.ind.tr.* **c. à son impatience,** to control one's patience.

ommandit|er [kɔmɑ̃dite], *v.tr.* to finance (enterprise); *s.m. Com:* **-aire,** sleeping partner.

ommando [kɔmɑ̃do], *s.m. Mil:* commando.

omme [kɔm]. **I.** *adv.* **1.** (*a*) as, like; **faites c. moi,** do as I do; **tout c. un autre,** (just) like anyone else; **c. ça vous venez de Paris?** and so you come from Paris? (*b*) **blanc c. neige,** snow-white; (*c*) **c. (si),** as if, as though; **il resta c. pétrifié,** he stood as if petrified; *F:* **c'est tout c.,** it amounts to the same thing. **2.** (*before verbs*) as; **faites c. il vous plaira,** do as you please. **3.** as; in the way of; **qu'est-ce que vous avez c. légumes?** what have you got in the way of vegetables? **4.** (*exclamative*) how! **c. il est maigre!** how thin he is!

II. *conj.* **1.** as; seeing that; **c. vous êtes là,**

since you are here. **2.** (just) as; **c. il allait frapper, on l'arrêta,** (just) as he was about to strike he was arrested.

commémor|er [kɔmemɔre], *v.tr.* to commemorate; *a.* **-atif, -ative,** commemorative; *s.f.* **-ation.**

commenc|er [kɔmɑ̃se], *v.tr. & i.* (**n. commençons**) to begin, commence, start; *abs.* **pour c.,** to begin with; *s.m.* **-ement,** beginning.

comment [kɔmɑ̃], *adv.* **1.** (*interrogative*) how; **c. allez-vous?** how are you? **c. cela?** how so? **c. (dites-vous)?** what (did you say)? I beg your pardon? **c. faire?** what is to be done? **2.** (*exclamative*) what! why! **c.! vous n'êtes pas encore parti!** what, haven't you gone yet! **mais c. donc!** why, of course!

commentaire [kɔmɑ̃tɛ:r], *s.m.* **1.** commentary (sur, on). **2.** comment; **voilà qui se passe de c.,** comment is needless.

comment|er [kɔmɑ̃te], *v.tr. & i.* **1.** to comment (up)on, annotate (text). **2.** **c.** (sur) qn, qch., to pass remarks upon s.o., sth.; *s.* **-ateur, -atrice,** commentator.

commerçant, -ante [kɔmɛrsɑ̃, -ɑ̃:t]. **1.** *a.* commercial, business; **rue commerçante,** shopping street; **peu c.,** (i) unbusinesslike; (ii) (town) that does little trade. **2.** *s.* merchant, tradesman; **être c.,** to be in business.

commerce [kɔmɛrs], *s.m.* **1.** commerce; trade; **c. en gros, en détail,** wholesale, retail, trade; **faire le c. du thé,** to deal in tea. **2.** intercourse, dealings; **c. du monde,** human intercourse; **être en c. avec qn,** to be in touch with s.o.

commercial, *pl.* **-aux** [kɔmɛrsjal, -o]. **1.** *a.* commercial; trading, business (relations). **2.** *s.f.* estate car, station-wagon.

com|mère [kɔmɛ:r], *s.f.* (*a*) gossip, busybody; (*b*) crony; *s.m.* **-mérage,** gossip.

commettre [kɔmɛtr], *v.tr.* (*conj. like* METTRE). **1.** **c. qch. à qn,** to entrust sth. to s.o. **2.** to commit, perpetrate (crime).

commis [kɔmi], *s.m.* **1.** clerk; book-keeper. **2.** (*a*) (shop-)assistant; (*b*) **c. voyageur,** commercial traveller.

commisération [kɔmizerasjɔ̃], *s.f.* commiseration, pity.

commis|saire [kɔmisɛ:r], *s.m.* commissioner; steward (of meeting); purser (of ship); **c. de police** = police inspector; *s.m.* **-sariat (de police),** central police station.

commission [kɔmisjɔ̃], *s.f.* commission. **1.** vente à c., sale on commission; **c. de deux pour cent,** commission of two per cent. **2.** message, errand; **j'ai fait toutes mes commissions,** I've done all my shopping. **3.** committee, board; **c. d'enquête,** court of inquiry; *s.m.* **-naire,** (i) (commission) agent; (ii) commissionaire; (iii) errand boy.

commod|e [kɔmɔd]. **1.** *a.* (*a*) convenient

(moment); handy (tool, etc.); (*b*) convenient, comfortable (house); (*c*) accommodating (disposition); **c. à vivre,** easy to live with. **2.** *s.f.* chest of drawers; *adv.* **-ément;** *s.f.* **-ité,** convenience, comfort.

Commonwealth [kɔmœnwelθ], *s.m.* **le C. britannique,** the British Commonwealth of Nations.

commoltion [kɔmosjɔ̃], *s.f.* **1.** commotion, disturbance, upheaval; **c. électrique,** electric shock. **2.** *Med:* concussion; *a.* **-tionné,** *Med:* shocked, *F:* concussed.

commun, -une [kɔmœ̃, -yn]. **1.** *a.* (*a*) common (à, to); **amis communs,** mutual friends; **faire bourse commune,** to share expenses; **d'un c. accord,** with one accord; (*b*) universal, general (custom); **le sens c.,** common sense; (*c*) usual, everyday (occurrence); (*d*) vulgar. **2.** *s.m.* common run (of persons); **œuvre au-dessus du c.,** work above the average; *adv.* **-ément.**

communal, *pl.* **-aux** [kɔmynal, -o], *a.* **1.** common (land). **2.** communal (council, etc.).

communauté [kɔmynote], *s.f.* **1.** community (of interests); **c. de vues,** likemindedness; **2.** society; (religious) community, order.

commune [kɔmyn], *s.f.* **1.** (*in Eng.*) **la Chambre des Communes,** the House of Commons. **2.** *Fr.Adm:* (*smallest territorial division*) commune; *approx.* = parish.

communicaltion [kɔmynikasjɔ̃], *s.f.* communication. **1.** (*a*) **donner c. de qch. à qn,** to communicate sth. to s.o.; (*b*) **entrer en c. avec qn,** to get into communication with s.o.; *P.T.T:* **fausse c.,** wrong number; **vous avez la c.,** you're through; **c. avec P.C.V.,** reverse charge, *N.Am:* collect, call; (*c*) *Med:* **c. interauriculaire, interventriculaire,** (abnormal congenital) interauricular, interventricular communication, *F:* hole in the heart. **2.** message; *a.* **-tif, -tive,** talkative.

communiler [kɔmynje], *v.i. Ecc:* to communicate, to receive Holy Communion; *s.* **-ant, -ante,** communicant.

communion [kɔmynjɔ̃], *s.f.* communion.

communiqué [kɔmynike], *s.m.* official statement; **c. de presse,** press release.

communiler [kɔmynike], *v.* to communicate. **1.** *v.tr.* to impart, convey (information). **2.** *v.i.* **porte qui communique au, avec le, jardin,** door that communicates with the garden; *a.* **-cant,** communicating (rooms).

communlisme [kɔmynism], *s.m.* communism; *s.* **-isant, -isante,** fellow-traveller; *s.m. & f.* **-iste,** communist.

commutateur [kɔmytatœ:r], *s.m.* (electric-light) switch.

compact [kɔpakt], *a.* compact, close, dense.

compagne [kɔ̃paɲ], *s.f.* (female) companion.

compagnie [kɔ̃paɲi], *s.f.* **1.** company; **tenir c. à**

qn, to keep s.o. company; **fausser c. à qn,** to give s.o. the slip. **2.** company; party; **une nombreuse c.,** a large party. **3.** *Com:* **la maison Durand et C.** (*usu.* et Cie), the firm of Durand and Company (*usu.* & Co.). **4.** *Mil:* company. **5.** herd (of deer); covey (of partridges).

compagnon [kɔ̃paɲɔ̃], *s.m.* companion, comrade; **c. de bord,** shipmate.

comparaison [kɔ̃parɛzɔ̃], *s.f.* comparison *prep.phr.* **en c. de qch.,** in comparison with sth.

comparaître [kɔ̃parɛ:tr], *v.i.* (*conj. like* CONNAÎTRE) *Jur:* **c.** (**en justice**), to appear before a court of justice.

comparatlif, -ive [kɔ̃paratif, -i:v], *a. & s.m.* comparative; *adv.* **-ivement.**

comparler [kɔ̃pare], *v.tr.* to compare; *a.* **-able.**

compartiment [kɔ̃partimɑ̃], *s.m.* compartmen (of railway carriage, etc.); partition (of box etc.).

compas [kɔ̃pɑ], *s.m.* **1.** (pair of) compasses; **c. à pointes sèches,** dividers; **c. à calibrer** cal(l)ipers. **2. c. de mer,** mariner's compass.

compassion [kɔ̃pasjɔ̃], *s.f.* compassion, pity.

compatlible [kɔ̃patibl], *a.* compatible; *s.f.* **-ibilité.**

compatissant [kɔ̃patisɑ̃], *a.* compassionat (**pour,** to, towards); tender-hearted.

compatriote [kɔ̃patriɔt], *s.m. & f.* compatriot.

compensation [kɔ̃pɑ̃sasjɔ̃], *s.f.* (*a*) compen sation; set-off; **cela fait c.,** that makes up for i **Bank: chambre de c.,** clearing-house; (*b* equalization (of forces); *Sp:* handicapping.

compensler [kɔ̃pɑ̃se], *v.tr.* (*a*) to compensate; t offset (a fault, etc.); to make up for (sth.); (*a*) **une perte,** to make good a loss; (*b*) to compen sate, set off (debts); *a.* **-ateur, -atrice,** con pensating; *s.m.* **-ateur,** compensator.

compère [kɔ̃pɛ:r], *s.m.* **1.** *Th:* compère (i revue). **2. un bon c.,** a pleasant companion, good sort.

compétlence [kɔ̃petɑ̃:s], *s.f.* **1.** competenc jurisdiction (of court); **sortir de sa c.,** to excee one's powers. **2.** competence, abilit; proficiency; *a.* **-ent.**

compiller [kɔ̃pile], *v.tr.* to compile; *s.* **-ateu -atrice,** compiler; *s.f.* **-ation,** compilin compilation.

complaire [kɔ̃plɛ:r], *v.ind.tr.* (*conj. like* plai *Lit:* **c. à qn,** to please, humour, s.o.

se complaire à faire qch., to take pleasure doing sth.

complaisance [kɔ̃plɛzɑ̃:s], *s.f.* **1.** oblignes willingness; **auriez-vous la c. de . . .,** wou you be so kind as to . . .. **2.** complacenc (self-)satisfaction.

complaislant [kɔ̃plɛzɑ̃], *a.* (*a*) obliging (pers. (*b*) complacent, self-satisfied; *adv.* **-ammen**

complément [kɔ̃plemɑ̃], *s.m.* complement;

-aire, complementary.
complet, -ète [kɔ̃plɛ, -ɛt]. **1.** *a.* (*a*) complete, entire; (*b*) full (bus, *Th:* house, etc.). **2.** *s.m.* (*a*) suit (of clothes); (*b*) *adj.phr.* **au c.,** full (up); *adv.* **-ètement,** completely, entirely.
compléter [kɔ̃plete], *v.tr.* (**je complète; je compléterai**) to complete; to finish off; to make up (a sum of money).
complexe [kɔ̃plɛks]. **1.** *a.* complex; complicated; **nombre c.,** compound number. **2.** *s.m.* (*a*) *Psy:* complex; (*b*) **un c. industriel,** an industrial complex; *s.f.* **-ité.**
complexion [kɔ̃plɛksjɔ̃], *s.f.* constitution, temperament.
complication [kɔ̃plikasjɔ̃], *s.f.* **1.** complication. **2.** intricacy.
complice [kɔ̃plis], *a. & s.* (*a*) accessory (**de,** to); (*b*) accomplice, abettor (**de,** of); *s.f.* **-ité,** complicity.
compliment [kɔ̃plimã], *s.m.* **1.** compliment. **2.** *pl.* compliments, greetings; **mes compliments à . . .,** my kind regards to . . . . **3.** *pl.* congratulations.
complimenter [kɔ̃plimãte], *v.tr.* to compliment; to congratulate (**de, sur,** on).
compliqué [kɔ̃plike], *a.* complicated, elaborate (plans); intricate (mechanism).
compliquer [kɔ̃plike], *v.tr.* to complicate.
se compliquer, to become complicated; (*of plot*) to thicken.
complot [kɔ̃plo], *s.m.* plot, conspiracy.
comploter [kɔ̃plote], *v.tr.* to plot, to scheme.
componction [kɔ̃pɔ̃ksjɔ̃], *s.f.* compunction; scruple, regret.
comporter [kɔ̃pɔrte], *v.tr.* **1.** to allow (of), to admit of (sth.). **2.** to call for, require (sth.). **3.** to comprise (sth.); **les fatigues que comporte un voyage,** the fatigue incidental to a journey; *s.m.* **-ement,** behaviour.
se comporter, to behave; **se c. bien, mal,** to behave well, badly.
composant, -ante [kɔ̃pozã, -ã:t], *a. & s.m.* component, constituent (part).
composé [kɔ̃poze]. **1.** *a.* (*a*) *Ch:* compound; (*b*) *Bot:* composite (flower); (*c*) composed, demure (behaviour). **2.** *s.m.* compound.
composer [kɔ̃poze]. **1.** *v.tr.* (*a*) to compose (music); to form (a ministry); (*b*) to set (type); *P. T. T:* **c. le numéro,** to dial the number; (*c*) **c. son visage,** to compose one's features. **2.** *v.i.* to compound, come to terms (**avec,** with); *s.* **-iteur, -itrice,** (i) composer; (ii) compositor; *s.f.* **-ition.**
se composer de, to consist of.
compote [kɔ̃pɔt], *s.f.* stewed fruit; *s.m.* **-ier,** fruit-dish.
compréhensif, -ive [kɔ̃preãsif, -i:v], *a.* **1.** comprehensive (statement). **2.** understanding (mind).

compréhension [kɔ̃preãsjɔ̃], *s.f.* understanding; *a.* **-sible.**
comprendre [kɔ̃prã:dr], *v.tr.* (*conj. like* PRENDRE). **1.** to comprise, include; **emballage non compris,** exclusive of packing; **y compris . . .,** including . . . . **2.** to understand, comprehend; **je n'y comprends rien,** I can't make it out; **se faire c.,** to make oneself understood; **cela se comprend,** of course, naturally.
compression [kɔ̃presjɔ̃], *s.f.* **1.** compression; squeezing; crushing. **2.** **c. du personnel,** reduction of staff.
comprimé [kɔ̃prime]. **1.** *a.* compressed (air); **outil à air c.,** pneumatic tool. **2.** *s.m. Pharm:* tablet.
comprimer [kɔ̃prime], *v.tr.* **1.** to compress. **2.** to repress, restrain (tears, etc.).
compromettre [kɔ̃prɔmɛtr], *v.* (*conj. like* METTRE). **1.** *v.tr.* (*a*) to compromise (s.o.); **être compromis,** to be implicated; (*b*) to endanger (life). **2.** *v.i.* to compromise.
se compromettre, to compromise oneself; to commit oneself.
compromis [kɔ̃prɔmi], *s.m. Jur:* compromise; **mettre une affaire en c.,** to submit a matter for arbitration.
comptabilité [kɔ̃tabilite], *s.f.* **1.** book-keeping; accountancy. **2.** accounts department; *Com:* counting-house.
comptable [kɔ̃tabl], *s.m.* accountant; book-keeper; **expert c.** = chartered accountant.
comptant [kɔ̃tã]. **1.** *a.* **argent c.,** ready money. **2.** *adv.* **payer c.,** to pay (in) cash. **3.** *s.m.* **vendre au c.,** to sell for cash.
compte [kɔ̃:t], *s.m.* account; (*a*) reckoning; **faire son c. de qch.,** to count on sth.; **cela fait mon c.,** that is the very thing I wanted; **y trouver son c.,** to get sth. out of it; **le c. y est,** the account is correct; *F:* **il a son c.,** he is done for; **son c. est bon,** I'll sort him out; **en fin de c. . . .,** **tout c. fait . . .,** all things considered . . .; (*b*) *Box:* count; (*missiles*) **c. à rebours,** countdown; (*c*) **régler de vieux comptes,** to pay off old scores; **c. en banque,** bank account; **donner son c. à qn,** to pay s.o. off (on dismissal); **pour mon c. . . .,** for my part . . .; (*d*) **c. rendu,** report, review; **se rendre c. de qch.,** to realize sth.
compter [kɔ̃te]. **1.** *v.tr.* (*a*) to count (up), reckon (up); **dix-neuf tous comptés,** nineteen all told; **marcher à pas comptés,** to walk with measured tread; **sans c. que . . .,** not to mention that . . .; *prep.phr.* **à c. de . . .,** (reckoning) from . . .; (*b*) **c. cent francs à qn,** to pay s.o. a hundred francs; (*c*) *Com:* to charge; (*d*) to value; **c. sa vie pour rien,** to hold one's life cheap; (*e*) **c. faire qch.,** to count on, to reckon on, doing sth. **2.** *v.i.* (*a*) **c. sur qn,** to count, depend, rely, on s.o.; **vous pouvez y c.,**

you may depend on it; (*b*) **c. avec qn**, to reckon with s.o.; (*c*) **ne c. pour rien**, to stand, count, for nothing.

compte-tours [kɔ̃ttuːr], *s.m.inv. Aut:* revolution counter.

compteur [kɔ̃tœːr], *s.m.* meter; **c. kilométrique**, mileage indicator, *F:* clock; **c. de trajet**, triprecorder; **c. de vitesse**, speedometer; *Fr.C:* **c. de stationnement**, parking meter.

comptoir [kɔ̃twaːr], *s.m.* **1.** *Com:* counter; **garçon de c.**, bartender. **2.** *Fin:* **c. d'escompte**, discount bank.

comput|er [kɔ̃pyte], *v.tr.* to compute, to calculate; *s.f.* **-ation**.

comte [kɔ̃ːt], *s.m.* count; (*in Eng.*) earl.

comté [kɔ̃te], *s.m.* county.

comtesse [kɔ̃tɛs], *s.f.* countess.

concass|er [kɔ̃kase], *v.tr.* to crush, grind (ore); *s.m.* **-age**; *s.m.* **-eur**, crushing mill.

concav|e [kɔ̃kaːv], *a.* concave; *s.f.* **-ité**, concavity.

concéder [kɔ̃sede], *v.tr.* (**je concède; je concéderai**). **1.** to concede (privilege). **2. c. qu'on a tort**, to admit that one is wrong.

concentr|er [kɔ̃sɑ̃tre], *v.tr.* to concentrate; to focus (rays, etc.); to centre; *s.f.* **-ation; camp de c.**, concentration camp.

se concentrer, to concentrate, to centre (**sur, dans**, in, on, round).

conception [kɔ̃sɛpsjɔ̃], *s.f.* **1.** conception, conceiving; **c. dirigée**, birth control. **2.** conception, idea.

concerner [kɔ̃sɛrne], *v.tr.* (*used in third pers. only*) to concern, affect; **cela vous concerne**, it concerns you.

concert [kɔ̃sɛːr], *s.m.* concert. **1.** harmony, agreement. **2.** musical entertainment; **salle de c.**, concert hall; *s.m. & f.* **-iste**, concert performer.

concerter (se) [səkɔ̃sɛrte], *v.pr.* **se c. (avec qn)**, to take counsel, to consult (with s.o.); *Pej:* to connive (**avec qn**, with s.o.).

concerto [kɔ̃sɛrto], *s.m. Mus:* concerto.

concession [kɔ̃sɛsjɔ̃], *s.f.* concession; *s.* **-naire**, licence-holder, concessionaire.

concev|oir [kɔ̃səvwaːr], *v.tr.* (*conj. like* RECEVOIR). **1.** to conceive (child). **2.** (*a*) to imagine (idea, etc.); to form (plan); (*b*) to understand; **cela se conçoit facilement**, that's easily understood; (*c*) **ainsi conçu**, (letter, etc.) worded as follows; *a.* **-able**, conceivable.

concierge [kɔ̃sjɛrʒ], *s.m. & f.* (house-)porter; caretaker (of flats); keeper (of prison).

concile [kɔ̃sil], *s.m. Ecc:* council, synod.

concil|ier [kɔ̃silje], *v.tr.* **1.** to conciliate, reconcile (two parties); **c. un différend**, to adjust a difference. **2.** to win over, gain (esteem, etc.); **se c. qn**, to gain s.o.'s goodwill; *a.* **-iant**, conciliating, conciliatory; *s.f.* **-iation**.

se concilier, to agree (**avec**, with).

concis [kɔ̃si], *a.* concise, terse.

concision [kɔ̃sizjɔ̃], *s.f.* conciseness, brevity.

concitoyen, -enne [kɔ̃sitwajɛ̃, -ɛn], *s.* fellow citizen.

conclu|re [kɔ̃klyːr], *v.tr.* (*p.p.* **conclu**) to conclude. **1.** (*a*) to end, finish; (*b*) **c. un marché**, to drive a bargain. **2.** (*a*) to decide, infer; (*b*) **c. à qch.**, to conclude in favour of sth.; *a.* **-ant** conclusive, decisive; *a.* **-sif, -sive**, conclusive *s.f.* **-sion**.

concombre [kɔ̃kɔ̃ːbr], *s.m.* cucumber.

concorde [kɔ̃kɔrd], *s.f.* concord, harmony.

concord|er [kɔ̃kɔrde], *v.i.* to agree, to tally (**avec** with); *s.f.* **-ance**, agreement.

concourir [kɔ̃kuriːr], *v.i.* (*conj. like* COURIR) to converge; to coincide. **2.** to combine, unite **c. avec qn**, to co-operate with s.o. **3. c. pour u prix**, to compete for a prize.

concours [kɔ̃kuːr], *s.m.* **1.** (*a*) concourse (o people); (*b*) coincidence (of events). **2.** co operation, help. **3.** (*a*) *Sp: etc:* competition **hors concours**, not for competition; hors con cours; not competing; (*b*) **c. hippique**, horse show.

concret, -ète [kɔ̃krɛ, -ɛt], *a.* concrete, solid; **c.**, actual case, concrete example.

concrètis|er [kɔ̃kretize], *v.tr.* to put (idea) int concrete form; *s.f.* **-ation**.

concurrence [kɔ̃kyrɑ̃ːs], *s.f.* **1.** concurrence coincidence (of events). **2.** competition rivalry.

concurr|ent, -ente [kɔ̃kyrɑ̃, -ɑ̃ːt]. **1.** *a.* (*a*) co operative; (*b*) competitive. **2.** *s.* competitor candidate; *adv.* **-emment**.

condamné, -ée [kɔ̃dane], *s.* condemned mar woman.

condamn|er [kɔ̃dane], *v.tr.* to condemn. **1.** *Jur* (*a*) to convict, sentence; **le médecin l'a con damné**, the doctor has given him up; (*b*) **c. un porte**, to block up a door; (*c*) **c. sa porte**, to b not at home to visitors. **2.** to censure, reprov (s.o.'s conduct, etc.); *a.* **-able**, blameworthy *s.f.* **-ation**.

condens|er [kɔ̃dɑ̃se], *v.tr.* to condense (gas, lec ture, etc.) (**en**, into); **lait condensé**, condense milk; *s.m. Techn:* **-ateur**, condenser; *s.* **-ation**.

condescend|re [kɔ̃desɑ̃ːdr], *v.i.* to condescen (**à faire qch.**, to do sth.); *s.f.* **-ance** condescension.

condiment [kɔ̃dimɑ̃], *s.m.* condiment seasoning.

condition [kɔ̃disjɔ̃], *s.f.* condition. **1.** (*a*) state **en c.**, in (good) condition; (*b*) *pl.* condition circumstances; **dans ces conditions . . .**, thi being so . . .. **2.** condition, stipulation; *p* terms; **conditions de faveur**, preferentia terms; **offre sans conditions**, unconditiona offer; **marchandises à c.,** goods on approval; **à condition que** + *sub.,* provided that . . ..

conditionnel, -elle [kɔ̃disjɔnɛl]. **1.** *a.* conditional. **2.** *s.m. Gram:* conditional (tense).

conditionn|er [kɔ̃disjɔne], *v.tr.* **1.** to condition (wool); to season (wood). **2.** *Com:* to pack(age) (goods); *s.m.* **-ement,** (i) packaging; (ii) air-conditioning; *s.m.* **-eur,** air-conditioner; *s.* **-eur, -euse,** packer.

condoléance [kɔ̃dɔleɑ̃:s], *s.f.* condolence; (expression of) sympathy.

conducteur, -trice [kɔ̃dyktœ:r, -tris]. **1.** *s.* (*a*) leader, guide; (*b*) driver. **2.** *a. El: Ph:* conducting, transmitting. **3.** *s.m. El: Ph:* (*a*) conductor (of heat); **mauvais c.,** non-conductor; (*b*) *El:* lead, main; **c. souple,** flex.

conduire [kɔ̃dɥi:r], *v.tr.* (*pr.p.* **conduisant;** *p.p.* **conduit;** *p.h.* **je conduisis**). **1.** (*a*) to conduct; to lead; to guide; **c. à bien une affaire,** to bring off a deal successfully; (*b*) **c. qn à faire qch.,** to induce s.o. to do sth. **2.** to drive (car); to steer (boat). **3.** to convey, conduct (water, electricity). **4.** to conduct, manage; **c. une maison,** to run a house; **c. un orchestre,** to conduct an orchestra.

se conduire, to behave.

conduit [kɔ̃dɥi], *s.m.* passage, conduit, pipe; **c. principal,** main.

conduite [kɔ̃dɥit], *s.f.* **1.** (*a*) conducting, leading (of s.o.); (*b*) driving (of car); navigation (of boat); (*c*) *Aut:* **c. intérieure,** saloon. **2.** direction (of affairs). **3.** conduct, behaviour; **avoir de la c.,** to be well-behaved; **changer de c.,** to turn over a new leaf. **4.** piping, tubing; **c. d'eau,** water main.

cône [ko:n], *s.m.* cone; **c. de pin,** pine cone.

confection [kɔ̃fɛksjɔ̃], *s.f.* **1.** making (of machine); manufacture (of goods). **2.** ready-made clothes; **maison de c.,** (ready-made) dress shop; **être dans la c.,** *F:* to be in the rag trade.

confectionné [kɔ̃fɛksjɔne], *a.* ready-made (article, goods); ready-to-wear (clothes).

confectionn|er [kɔ̃fɛksjɔne], *v.tr.* to make (up) (dress); to construct (machine); to manufacture (goods); *s.m.* **-ement,** manufacture (of goods, machinery, clothing).

confédéré [kɔ̃federe], *a.* confederate.

confédér|er [kɔ̃federe], *v.tr.* (**je confédère; je confédérerai**) to confederate, unite; *s.f.* **-ation.**

confér|er [kɔ̃fere], *v.* (**je confère; je conférerai**). **1.** *v.tr.* to confer, award (privileges). **2.** *v.i.* to confer (**avec,** with); *s.f.* **-ence,** lecture; *s.* **-encier, -encière,** lecturer.

confesse [kɔ̃fɛs], *s.f. usu. in phrase* **aller à c.,** to go to confession.

confess|er [kɔ̃fese], *v.tr.* **1.** to confess; to own up to (sth.). **2.** to confess (one's sins). **3.** (*of*

priest) to confess (penitent); *s.m.* **-eur,** (Father-)confessor.

se confesser, to confess one's sins.

confession [kɔ̃fɛsjɔ̃], *s.f.* confession; *s.m.* **-nal,** *pl.* **-naux,** confessional(-box).

confiance [kɔ̃fjɑ̃:s], *s.f.* **1.** confidence, trust, reliance; **avoir c. en qn,** to trust s.o.; **acheter qch. de c.,** to buy sth. on trust; **abus de c.,** breach of trust; **maison de c.,** reliable firm; **commis de c.,** confidential clerk. **2.** confidence, sense of security; **c. en soi,** self-confidence.

confiant [kɔ̃fjɑ̃], *a.* **1.** confiding, trustful (**dans,** in). **2.** confident. **3.** self-confident (manner, etc.).

confidence [kɔ̃fidɑ̃:s], *s.f.* confidence; **dire qch. en c.,** to say sth. in confidence.

confident, -ente [kɔ̃fidɑ̃, -ɑ:t], *s.* confidant, *f.* confidante; *a.* **-iel, -ielle,** confidential; *adv.* **-iellement.**

confier [kɔ̃fje], *v.tr.* **1.** to trust, entrust (s.o. with sth.). **2.** to confide, disclose (sth.).

se confier à qn, (i) to put one's trust in s.o.; (ii) to take s.o. into one's confidence.

configuration [kɔ̃figyrasjɔ̃], *s.f.* configuration; lie of the land.

confiner [kɔ̃fine]. **1.** *v.i.* **c. à un pays,** to border (up)on a country. **2.** *v.tr.* to confine, imprison.

confirm|er [kɔ̃firme], *v.tr.* to confirm (news); to ratify (treaty); *a.* **-atif, -ative,** confirmative; *s.f.* **-ation.**

confis|erie [kɔ̃fizri], *s.f.* (*a*) confectioner's shop; (*b*) confectionery; *s.* **-eur, -euse,** confectioner.

confis|quer [kɔ̃fiske], *v.tr.* to confiscate, seize; *s.f.* **-cation.**

confit [kɔ̃fi]. **1.** *a.* crystallized (fruit). **2.** *s.m.* conserve (of goose, etc.).

confiture [kɔ̃fity:r], *s.f.* jam.

conflagration [kɔ̃flagrasjɔ̃], *s.f.* conflagration, blaze.

conflit [kɔ̃fli], *s.m.* conflict; clash (of interests).

confluent [kɔ̃flyɑ̃], *s.m.* confluence (of rivers).

confondre [kɔ̃fɔ̃:dr], *v.tr.* to confound. **1.** (*a*) to mingle; (*b*) to mistake, confuse. **2.** to disconcert (s.o.); **c. la calomnie,** to silence calumny.

se confondre. 1. (*a*) to blend (**en,** into); (*b*) (*of* streams) to intermingle. **2. se c. en excuses,** to apologize profusely.

confondu [kɔ̃fɔ̃dy], *a.* **1.** disconcerted. **2.** dumbfounded (**de,** at).

conformation [kɔ̃fɔrmasjɔ̃], *s.f.* conformation, structure.

conforme [kɔ̃fɔrm], *a.* conformable; consistent (**à,** with); identical; **copie c.,** true copy; *adv.* **-ément,** according (**à,** to).

conform|er [kɔ̃fɔrme], *v.tr.* (*a*) to form, shape; (*b*) **c. qch. à qch.,** to conform sth. to sth.; *s.f.* **-ité,** conformity.

se conformer à qch., to conform to sth.; to comply with (an order).
confort [kɔ̃fɔːr], *s.m.* comfort; **tout c. moderne,** all modern conveniences.
confortable [kɔ̃fɔrtabl], *a.* comfortable, snug, cosy; *adv.* **-ment.**
confrère [kɔ̃frɛːr], *s.m.* colleague, fellow-member (of profession, society).
confrérie [kɔ̃freri], *s.f.* (*usu.* religious). confraternity.
confront|**er** [kɔ̃frɔ̃te], *v.tr.* to confront (**avec,** with); *s.f.* **-ation.**
confus [kɔ̃fy], *a.* **1.** confused (heap); indistinct (noise); obscure (style). **2.** confused; *adv.* **-ément,** confusedly, vaguely.
confusion [kɔ̃fyzjɔ̃], *s.f.* confusion. **1.** (*a*) disorder, muddle; **mettre tout en c.,** to upset everything; *Med:* **c. mentale,** mental derangement; (*b*) mistake, error; **c. de dates,** confusion of dates. **2.** confusion, embarrassment.
congé [kɔ̃ʒe], *s.m.* **1.** (*a*) leave (to depart); **prendre c. de qn,** to take leave of s.o.; (*b*) leave (of absence); **être en c.,** to be on holiday, *N.Am:* on vacation; *Ind:* **congé(s) payé(s),** holidays with pay. **2.** (*a*) (notice of) dismissal; **donner c. à qn.,** to give s.o. notice, *F:* the sack; **demander son c.,** to give notice, *N.Am:* to quit; (*b*) **donner c. à un locataire,** to give a tenant notice (to quit).
congédi|**er** [kɔ̃ʒedje], *v.tr.* to dismiss (s.o.); *s.m.* **-ement,** dismissal.
congelé [kɔ̃ʒle]. **1.** *a.* frozen, deep-frozen (food, etc.). **2.** *s.m.* **du c.** (deep-)frozen food.
cong|**eler** [kɔ̃ʒle], *v.tr.* (**il congèle**) to congeal; to freeze (water); to deep-freeze (food); **viande congelée,** frozen meat; *s.m.* **-élateur,** deep-freeze; *s.f.* **-élation,** (*a*) freezing; (*b*) cold storage.
congestion [kɔ̃ʒɛstjɔ̃], *s.f. Med:* congestion; **c. cérébrale,** apoplexy, *F:* stroke.
congestionné [kɔ̃ʒɛstjɔne], *a.* flushed, red (face).
Congo (**le**) [ləkɔ̃go]. *Pr.n.m.* **1.** *Geog:* the (river) Congo. **2. la république du C.,** the Republic of the Congo.
congolais, -aise [kɔ̃gɔlɛ, -ɛːz], *a. & s.* Congolese.
congre [kɔ̃ːgr], *s.m.* conger-eel.
congr|**ès** [kɔ̃grɛ], *s.m.* congress; *s.m.* **-essiste,** member of congress.
conifère [kɔnifɛːr], *Bot:* **1.** *a.* coniferous, cone-bearing. **2.** *s.m.pl.* **conifères,** conifers.
conique [kɔnik], *a.* cone-shaped, conical.
conjecture [kɔ̃ʒɛkty:r], *s.f.* conjecture, surmise, guess.
conjectur|**er** [kɔ̃ʒɛktyre], *v.tr.* to conjecture, surmise, guess; *a.* **-al,** *pl.* **-aux,** conjectural; *adv.* **-alement,** by guesswork.

conjoint [kɔ̃ʒwɛ̃], *a.* **1.** united, joint. **2.** married; *s.m. Jur:* **les conjoints,** husband and wife; *adv.* **-ement,** (con)jointly.
conjonction [kɔ̃ʒɔ̃ksjɔ̃], *s.f.* **1.** union, connection. **2.** *Gram:* conjunction.
conjoncture [kɔ̃ʒɔ̃kty:r], *s.f.* conjuncture.
conjugal, *pl.* **-aux** [kɔ̃ʒygal, -o], *a.* conjugal; **vie conjugale,** married life; *adv.* **-ement.**
conjug|**uer** [kɔ̃ʒyge], *v.tr.* **1.** *Gram:* to conjugate. **2.** (*a*) to combine; (*b*) to pair (off); *s.f.* **-aison,** conjugation.
conjuré [kɔ̃ʒyre], *s.m.* conspirator.
conjur|**er** [kɔ̃ʒyre], *v.tr. & i.* **1.** to plot. **2.** (*a*) to conjure up (spirits); to exorcise (the devil); (*b*) to ward off (danger). **3. c. qn de faire qch.,** entreat s.o. to do sth.; *s.f.* **-ation,** conspiracy, plot.
connaiss|**ance** [kɔnɛsɑ̃ːs], *s.f.* **1.** (*a*) acquaintance, knowledge; **avoir c. de qch.,** to be aware of sth.; **en c. de cause,** with full knowledge of the facts; **une personne de ma c.,** someone I know; **une figure de c.,** a familiar face; (*b*) **c'est une de mes connaissances,** he is an acquaintance of mine. **2.** knowledge, understanding. **3.** consciousness; **perdre c.,** to faint; *s.* **-eur, -euse,** expert, authority (on sth.); connoisseur (of sth.); (good) judge (of wine, art).
connaissement [kɔnɛsmɑ̃], *s.m. Com:* bill of lading.
connaître [kɔnɛ:tr], *v.tr.* (*pr.p.* **connaissant;** *p.p.* **connu;** *pr.ind.* **je connais, il connaît**) to know **1.** to be acquainted with (sth.); **il en connaît bien d'autres,** he has plenty more tricks up his sleeve. **2.** to be acquainted with (s.o.); **gagner à être connu,** to improve on acquaintance; **ça me connaît,** you can't teach me anything about that; **connu!** I've heard that one before. **3.** to be versed in, to have a thorough knowledge of (sth.).
se connaître. 1. se c. à, en, qch., to know all about sth.; **il s'y connaît,** he's an expert; **je ne m'y connais plus,** I am all adrift, all at sea. **2. il ne se connaît plus,** he has lost control of himself; **il ne se connaît plus de joie,** he is beside himself with joy.
connexion [kɔn(n)ɛksjɔ̃], *s.f.* **1.** connection (of parts, of ideas); *Mec:* **c. directe,** positive drive. **2.** connecting organ or part; *El:* lead.
connivence [kɔnivɑ̃ːs], *s.f.* connivance, complicity.
conquérant [kɔ̃kerɑ̃], *a.* conquering; **air c.,** swagger; *s.* **Guillaume le C.,** William the Conqueror.
conquérir [kɔ̃keri:r], *v.tr.* (*conj. like* ACQUÉRIR) (*a*) to conquer, subdue (country); (*b*) to win (over) (s.o.).
conquête [kɔ̃kɛt], *s.f.* **1.** (act of) conquest. **2.** conquered territory.

consacrer [kɔ̃sakre], v.tr. 1. (a) to consecrate; **c. toute son énergie à une tâche,** to devote (all) one's energies to a task. 2. to sanctify; **expression consacrée,** stock phrase.

conscience [kɔ̃sjɑ̃:s], s.f. 1. consciousness; **avoir c. de qch.,** to be aware of sth. 2. (a) conscience; **c. nette,** clear conscience; **c. large,** accommodating conscience; **faire qch. par acquit de c.,** to do sth. for conscience' sake; (b) conscientiousness; **faire qch. en c.,** to do sth. conscientiously.

consciencieu|x, -euse [kɔ̃sjɑ̃sjø, -ø:z], a. conscientious; adv. **-sement.**

consci|ent [kɔ̃sjɑ̃], a. conscious; fully aware (**de,** of); adv. **-emment.**

conscription [kɔ̃skripsjɔ̃], s.f. conscription.

conscrit [kɔ̃skri], s.m. Mil: conscript.

consécration [kɔ̃sekrasjɔ̃], s.f. consecration; dedication.

consécut|if, -ive [kɔ̃sekytif, -i:v], a. consecutive; adv. **-ivement.**

conseil [kɔ̃sɛ:j], s.m. 1. counsel; (piece of) advice; **homme de bon c.,** man worth consulting. 2. (a) Jur: counsellor, counsel; (b) **ingénieur c.,** consulting engineer. 3. council, committee; **tenir c.,** to hold a council; **le c. des ministres,** the Cabinet; Com: **c. d'administration,** board of directors; **c. de guerre,** (i) war-council; (ii) court-martial; **c. d'enquête,** court of enquiry.

conseiller[1] [kɔ̃sɛje], v.tr. to advise; to recommend.

conseiller[2], **-ère** [kɔ̃sɛje, -ɛ:r], s. 1. counsellor, adviser. 2. **c. municipal,** town-councillor; **c. fiscal** = chartered accountant; **c. général** = county councillor.

consent|ir [kɔ̃sɑ̃ti:r], v. (conj. like MENTIR). 1. v.i. to consent, agree. 2. v.tr. **c. un prêt,** to grant a loan; s.m. **-ement.**

conséquence [kɔ̃sekɑ̃:s], s.f. (a) consequence, result; **en c.,** accordingly; (b) inference; **tirer une c. de qch.,** to draw an inference from sth.; (c) importance, consequence; **affaires de la dernière c.,** matters of the highest moment; **tirer à c.,** to be of importance.

conséqu|ent [kɔ̃sekɑ̃]. 1. a. (a) consistent, rational (mind); (b) following. 2. s.m. consequent; adv.phr. **par c.,** consequently, accordingly; adv. **-emment,** consequently.

conservateur, -trice [kɔ̃sɛrvatœ:r, -tris]. 1. s. (a) guardian, keeper, warden; **c. d'un musée,** curator of a museum; **c. de bibliothèque,** librarian; (b) Pol: conservative; (c) canner (of foodstuffs). 2. a. preserving (process).

conservatoire [kɔ̃sɛrvatwa:r], s.m. school, academy (of music, of drama).

conserve [kɔ̃sɛrv], s.f. preserve; preserved food; **conserves au vinaigre,** pickles; **bœuf de c.,** corned beef; **se nourrir de conserves,** to live on tinned, canned, foods.

conserv|er [kɔ̃sɛrve], v.tr. 1. (a) to preserve, to tin, to can (food); (b) to preserve (building); **c. le gibier,** to preserve game. 2. to keep, retain (rights); s.f. **-ation;** s.f. **-erie,** canning factory.

se conserver, (of goods) to keep.

considérable [kɔ̃siderabl], a. considerable. 1. eminent; well-to-do (person). 2. extensive (property); adv. **-ment.**

considération [kɔ̃siderasjɔ̃], s.f. consideration. 1. attention, thought. 2. reason, motive. 3. regard, esteem; (letter formula) **agréez l'assurance de ma haute c.,** I am yours very truly.

considérer [kɔ̃sidere], v.tr. (**je considère; je considérerai**) to consider. 1. **ce n'est pas à c.,** it is not to be thought of; **à tout c.,** all things considered. 2. to contemplate, gaze on. 3. to think highly of (s.o.).

consignataire [kɔ̃siɲatɛ:r], s.m. & f. Com: consignee.

consignateur [kɔ̃siɲatœ:r], s.m. Com: consignor.

consigne [kɔ̃siɲ], s.f. 1. (a) order(s), instructions; **manquer à la c.,** to disobey orders; **être de c.,** to be on duty; (b) password, countersign. 2. cloak-room; left-luggage office.

consign|er [kɔ̃siɲe], v.tr. 1. (a) to deposit (money); (b) Com: to consign (goods) (à, to). 2. to refuse admittance to (s.o.); **c. sa porte à qn,** to bar one's door to s.o.; s.f. **-ation,** consignment.

consist|ance [kɔ̃sistɑ̃:s], s.f. 1. (a) consistency; **étoffe sans c.,** flimsy material; (b) stability (of mind). 2. credit; **bruit sans c.,** unfounded rumour; a. **-ant,** firm.

consister [kɔ̃siste], v.i. **c. en qch.,** to consist of sth.

consol|er [kɔ̃sɔle], v.tr. to console, comfort; a. & s. **-ateur, -atrice,** (a) comforting; (b) comforter; s.f. **-ation.**

se consoler d'une perte, to get over a loss.

consolid|er [kɔ̃sɔlide], v.tr. 1. to consolidate, strengthen. 2. to fund (debt); **dette consolidée,** non consolidée, funded, floating, debt; s.f. **-ation.**

se consolider, to grow firm.

consommé [kɔ̃sɔme]. 1. a. consummate (skill, etc.). 2. s.m. Cu: beef-tea; clear soup.

consomm|er [kɔ̃sɔme], v.tr. 1. to consummate, accomplish. 2. to consume, use up (produce, etc.); abs. **il consommait dans un bar,** he was having a drink in a bar; **voiture qui consomme,** car heavy on petrol; s. **-ateur, -atrice,** (a) consumer; (b) customer (in café); s.f. **-ation,** consumption (of petrol, etc.); drink (in café).

consonne [kɔ̃sɔn], s.f. Ling: consonant.

consortium [kɔ̃sɔrsjɔm], Fin: Com:

consortium.

conspir|er [kɔ̃spire], *v.i.* to conspire, plot (**contre**, against); *s.* **-ateur, -atrice**, conspirator; *s.f.* **-ation**, conspiracy, plot.

conspuer [kɔ̃spɥe], *v.tr.* **1.** to decry, run down (s.o.). **2.** (*a*) to boo, hoot (play); (*b*) *Sp:* to barrack.

constance [kɔ̃stɑ̃:s], *s.f.* constancy; steadfastness.

const|ant [kɔ̃stɑ̃], *a.* **1.** (*a*) constant, steadfast; (*b*) firm, unshaken. **2.** constant, uniform; *adv.* **-amment.**

constat|er [kɔ̃state], *v.tr.* **1.** to establish (fact); **c. une erreur**, to find out a mistake. **2.** to state, record (sth.); *s.f.* **-ation**, verification, establishment (of fact).

constellation [kɔ̃stɛllasjɔ̃], *s.f.* constellation.

constern|er [kɔ̃stɛrne], *v.tr.* to dismay; *s.f.* **-ation**, consternation, dismay.

constip|er [kɔ̃stipe], *v.tr.* to constipate; *s.f.* **-ation.**

constitu|er [kɔ̃stitɥe], *v.tr.* to constitute. **1.** (*a*) to form, make (up); (*b*) to set up, institute (committee, etc.). **2.** (*a*) **c. qn son héritier**, to make s.o. one's heir; (*b*) **c. une rente à qn**, to settle an annuity on s.o.; *a.* **-ant**, constituent.

constitution [kɔ̃stitysjɔ̃], *s.f.* **1.** constituting, establishing; **c. de pension**, settling of an annuity. **2.** constitution. **3.** composition (of air, water, etc.); *a.* **-nel, -nelle**, constitutional.

construct|ion [kɔ̃stryksjɔ̃], *s.f.* construction. **1.** constructing. **2.** structure, building; *s.m.* **-eur**, constructor; *a.* **-if, -ive**, constructive.

construire [kɔ̃strɥi:r], *v.tr.* (*conj. like* CONDUIRE) to construct. **1.** to build; to make. **2.** to assemble (machine).

consul [kɔ̃syl], *s.m.* consul; *a.* **-aire**, consular; *s.m.* **-at**, consulate.

consult|er [kɔ̃sylte], *v.tr.* to consult; **ouvrage à c.**, work of reference; *a.* **-atif, -ative**, advisory (committee, opinion); *s.f.* **-ation.**

consumer [kɔ̃syme], *v.tr.* to consume. **1.** to wear away; **consumé par l'ambition**, eaten up with ambition. **2.** to use up (fortune).

se consumer, to waste away.

contact [kɔ̃takt], *s.m.* **1.** contact, touch; **garder le c.**, to keep touch; **prise de c.**, preliminary conversation. **2.** *El:* (*a*) connection, contact; **établir le c.**, to switch on; (*b*) switch. **3.** **verre de c.**, contact lens.

contacter [kɔ̃takte], *v.tr.* to contact (s.o.).

contagi|on [kɔ̃taʒjɔ̃], *s.f.* contagion; *a.* **-eux, -euse**, contagious, *F:* catching.

contamin|er [kɔ̃tamine], *v.tr.* (*a*) to contaminate; to pollute (water, etc.); (*b*) *Med:* to infect; *s.f.* **-ation.**

conte [kɔ̃:t], *s.m.* **1.** story, tale; **contes de bonne femme**, old wives'.tales. **2.** (tall) story, yarn; **c. à dormir debout**, cock-and-bull story.

contempl|er [kɔ̃tɑ̃ple], *v.tr.* **1.** to contemplate, to gaze at (sth.). **2.** to meditate on (sth.); *s.f.* **-ation.**

contemporain, -aine [kɔ̃tɑ̃pɔrɛ̃, -ɛn]. **1.** *a.* (*a*) contemporary; (*b*) contemporaneous (**de**, with). **2.** *s.* contemporary.

contenance [kɔ̃tnɑ̃:s], *s.f.* **1.** capacity (of bottle); **c. d'un champ**, area of a field. **2.** countenance, bearing; **faire bonne c.**, to put a good face on it.

contenir [kɔ̃tni:r], *v.tr.* (*conj. like* TENIR). **1.** to contain; **lettre contenant chèque**, letter enclosing cheque. **2.** to restrain; to control (temper, feelings).

se contenir, to keep one's temper.

content [kɔ̃tɑ̃], *a.* (*a*) content; (*b*) pleased (**de**, with); **être c. de soi**, to be pleased with oneself; (*c*) pleased; **je suis très c. de vous voir**, I am very pleased to see you; (*d*) glad; **comme elle était contente!** how glad she was!

content|er [kɔ̃tɑ̃te], *v.tr.* to content, satisfy (s.o.); to gratify (curiosity); *s.m.* **-ement.**

se contenter de qch., to be satisfied with sth.

contentieux, -euse [kɔ̃tɑ̃sjø, -ø:z]. **1.** *a.* contentious. **2.** *s.m. Adm:* legal department (of a bank, etc.).

contenu [kɔ̃tny]. **1.** *a.* restrained (style); pent-up (anger). **2.** *s.m.* contents (of parcel).

cont|er [kɔ̃te], *v.tr.* to tell, relate; **en c. (de belles à qn**, to take s.o. in; *s.* **-eur, -euse**, story teller.

conteste [kɔ̃tɛst], *s.f.* **sans c.**, indisputably.

contest|er [kɔ̃tɛste]. **1.** *v.tr.* to contest, dispute (point, right). **2.** *v.i.* to dispute, wrangle (**avec** with); *a.* **-able**, debatable; *s.f.* **-ation.**

contexte [kɔ̃tɛkst], *s.m.* context.

contigu, -uë [kɔ̃tigy], *a.* contiguous, adjoining. *Mth:* **angles contigus**, adjacent angles; *s.f.* **-ïté**, contiguity.

contin|ence [kɔ̃tinɑ̃:s], *s.f.* continence; *a.* **-ent**, chaste.

continent² [kɔ̃tinɑ̃], *s.m.* **1.** continent. **2.** land mass; *a.* **-al, pl. -aux**, continental.

contingent [kɔ̃tɛ̃ʒɑ̃]. **1.** *a.* contingent. **2.** *s.m.* (*a*) *Mil:* contingent; **le c. annuel**, the annual call up; (*b*) quota; ration.

contingent|er [kɔ̃tɛ̃ʒɑ̃te], *v.tr.* **1.** to fix quota for (imports, etc.). **2.** to distribute (films, etc.) according to quota; *s.m.* **-ement.**

contin|u [kɔ̃tiny], *a.* continuous, unceasing; *adv.* **-ûment.**

continu|er [kɔ̃tinɥe], *v.tr. & i.* to continue; to carry on (tradition); to go on (doing sth.); **c. sa route**, to proceed on one's way; **continuez!** go on! *s.f.* **-ation**; *a.* **-el, -elle**, continual, unceasing; *adv.* **-ellement**, continually; *s.f.* **-ïté**, continuity.

contorsion [kɔ̃tɔrsjɔ̃], *s.f.* contortion; *s.* **-niste**, contortionist.

contour [kɔ̃tuːr], *s.m.* **1.** outline. **2.** contour (-line).
contourn|er [kɔ̃turne], *v.tr.* **1.** to shape (design). **2.** to pass round, skirt (hill, wood); **c. la loi,** to get round the law. **3.** to twist, distort; *s.m.* **-ement.**
contract|er¹ [kɔ̃trakte], *v.tr.* **1.** (*a*) to contract (alliance); (*b*) to incur (debt); **c. une assurance,** to take out an insurance policy. **2.** to contract (habit); to catch (disease); *s.* **-uel, -uelle,** traffic warden.
contract|er², *v.tr.* to contract, to draw together; **traits contractés par la douleur,** features drawn with pain; *s.f.* **-ion,** contraction, shrinkage.
se contracter, to contract; to shrink.
contradic|tion [kɔ̃tradiksjɔ̃], *s.f.* **1.** contradiction; **esprit de c.,** contrariness. **2.** inconsistency; discrepancy; *a.* **-toire,** contradictory.
contraindre [kɔ̃trɛ̃ːdr], *v.tr.* (*conj. like* CRAINDRE) to constrain. **1.** to restrain. **2.** to compel; **je fus contraint d'obéir,** I was obliged to obey.
contraint [kɔ̃trɛ̃], *a.* constrained; forced (smile); stiff (manner).
contrainte [kɔ̃trɛ̃ːt], *s.f.* constraint. **1.** restraint. **2.** compulsion, coercion.
contraire [kɔ̃trɛːr], *a.* **1.** (*a*) contrary; opposite; **jusqu'à avis c.,** until further notice; (*b*) *s.m.* **au c.,** on the contrary. **2.** adverse; *s.m.* **aller au c. de qn,** to run counter to s.o.; *adv.* **-ment.**
contrari|er [kɔ̃trarje], *v.tr.* **1.** to thwart, oppose. **2.** to vex, annoy; *a.* **-ant,** annoying; *s.f.* **-été,** (*a*) contrariness; (*b*) annoyance.
contraste [kɔ̃trast], *s.m.* contrast; set-off.
contraster [kɔ̃traste], *v.i. & tr.* to contrast.
contrat [kɔ̃tra], *s.m.* contract, agreement; **c. de mariage,** marriage settlement; **c. d'assurance,** insurance policy.
contravention [kɔ̃travɑ̃sjɔ̃], *s.f.* infringement, breach (**au règlement,** of regulations); *Jur:* minor offence.
contre [kɔ̃ːtr]. **1.** *prep.* against; (*a*) **c. toute attente,** contrary to all expectation; (*b*) **s'assurer c. l'incendie,** to insure against fire; **s'abriter c. la pluie,** to shelter from the rain; (*c*) (in exchange) for; **livraison c. remboursement,** cash on delivery; (*d*) to; **parier à cinq c. un,** to bet five to one; (*e*) close to, by. **2.** *adv.* against; **parler pour et c.,** to speak for and against; **sa maison est tout c.,** his house is close by. **3.** *s.m.* (*a*) **par c.,** on the other hand; (*b*) *Bill:* kiss; (*c*) *Cards:* double.
NOTE: *In the hyphenated nouns and adjectives below,* **contre** *remains inv; for phonetics and irreg. pl. forms consult the second component.*
contre-amiral, *s.m.* rear-admiral.
contre-attaque, *s.f.* counter-attack.
contre-attaquer, *v.tr.* to counter-attack.
contrebalancer [kɔ̃trəbalɑ̃se], *v.tr.* (n. con-

trebalançons) to counterbalance, offset.
contreband|e [kɔ̃trəbɑ̃ːd], *s.f.* **1.** contraband, smuggling. **2.** contraband goods; *s.m.* **-ier,** smuggler.
contrebas (en) [ɑ̃kɔ̃trəba], *adv.phr.* **1.** (lower) down; below; **être en c. de qch.,** to be below the level of sth. **2.** downwards, down.
contrecarrer [kɔ̃trəkare], *v.tr.* to cross, thwart (s.o.).
contrecœur (à) [akɔ̃trəkœːr], *adv.phr.* unwillingly, reluctantly, grudgingly.
contrecoup [kɔ̃trəku], *s.m.* (*a*) rebound (of bullet); recoil; (*b*) jar (of blow); (*c*) repercussion; (*d*) after-effects (of action, shock, etc.).
contredire [kɔ̃trədiːr], *v.tr.* (*pr.ind.* **v. contredisez;** *otherwise like* DIRE) to contradict.
contredit [kɔ̃trədi], *adv.phr.* **sans c.,** assuredly, unquestionably.
contre-écrou, *s.m.* lock-nut.
contre-espionnage, *s.m.* counter-espionage.
contrefaçon [kɔ̃trəfasɔ̃], *s.f.* **1.** counterfeiting; infringement (of patent). **2.** counterfeit, forgery.
contrefaire [kɔ̃trəfɛːr], *v.tr.* (*conj. like* FAIRE). **1.** (*a*) to imitate; (*b*) **c. le mort,** to pretend to be dead. **2.** to counterfeit (coin); to pirate (book).
contrefait [kɔ̃trəfɛ], *a.* **1.** pretended (zeal); disguised (writing). **2.** counterfeit (coin); forged (signature). **3.** deformed (person).
contrefort [kɔ̃trəfɔːr], *s.m.* **1.** *Arch:* buttress. **2.** *Geog:* spur (of mountain); *pl.* foot-hills.
contre-jour (à), *adv.phr.* against the light; **assis à c.-j.,** sitting in one's own light.
contremaître, -tresse [kɔ̃trəmɛːtr, -trɛs], *s.* foreman, forewoman; overseer.
contremander [kɔ̃trəmɑ̃de], *v.tr.* to countermand, cancel, revoke (order); to call off (strike).
contre-ordre, *s.m.* counter-order; **sauf c.-o.,** unless I hear to the contrary.
contrepartie [kɔ̃trəparti], *s.f.* **1.** (*a*) opposite viewpoint; (*b*) other party (in transaction). **2.** (*a*) *Book-k:* contra; (*b*) duplicate (of document). **3.** *Sp:* return match.
contre-pied (à), *adv.phr.* **prendre une observation à c.-p.,** to misconstrue a remark; **à c.-p. de,** contrary to.
contre-plaqué, *a. & s.m.* laminated; (**bois**) **c.,** plywood; **c.-p. à trois épaisseurs,** three-ply.
contrepoids [kɔ̃trəpwa], *s.m.* counterbalance, counterweight; counterpoise.
contre-poil (à), *adv.phr. F:* **prendre qn à c.-p.,** to rub s.o. up the wrong way.
contrepoint [kɔ̃trəpwɛ̃], *s.m. Mus:* counterpoint.
contrepoison [kɔ̃trəpwazɔ̃], *s.m.* antidote.
contrer [kɔ̃tre]. **1.** *v.tr. Box:* to counter (blow). **2.** *v.i. Cards:* to double.

contre-saison (à), *adv.phr.* out of season.
contresens [kɔ̃trəsã:s], *s.m.* **1.** misinterpretation. **2.** wrong way (of material); **à c.**, in the wrong sense, direction. **3. à c. de**, in the contrary direction to.
contresigner [kɔ̃trəsiɲe], *v.tr.* to countersign.
contretemps [kɔ̃trətã], *s.m.* **1.** (*a*) mishap, hitch; (*b*) delay, inconvenience. **2.** *adv.phr.* **à c.**, unseasonably, inopportunely.
contrevenir [kɔ̃trəvni:r], *v.ind.tr.* (*conj. like* VENIR; *aux.* **avoir**) to contravene, infringe (**à un arrêté,** an order).
contrevent [kɔ̃trəvã], *s.m.* outside shutter.
contribuler [kɔ̃tribɥe], *v.i.* **1.** to contribute funds (**à qch.**, to sth.). **2.** to contribute, be conducive (**à**, to); *s.m. & f.* **-able,** taxpayer; *s.f.* **-tion,** tax; share.
contrit [kɔ̃tri], *a.* contrite, penitent.
contrition [kɔ̃trisjɔ̃], *s.f.* contrition, penitence.
contrôle [kɔ̃tro:l], *s.m.* **1.** (muster) roll; list. **2.** (*a*) testing, assaying (of gold); (*b*) hall-marking. **3.** (*a*) checking (of information, etc.); (*b*) *Adm:* inspection, supervision. **4. c. des naissances,** birth-control.
contrôler [kɔ̃trole], *v.tr.* **1.** to hall-mark (gold). **2.** to inspect (work); to check (tickets); to verify (a fact). **3.** to hold (s.o.) in check; *s.* **-eur, -euse,** inspector; ticket collector.
controverse [kɔ̃trɔvɛrs], *s.f.* controversy.
contumace [kɔ̃tymas], *s.f. Jur:* (*a*) non-appearance (in court); **condamné par c.,** sentenced in his absence; (*b*) contempt of court.
contusion [kɔ̃tyzjɔ̃], *s.f.* contusion, bruise.
contusionner [kɔ̃tyzjɔne], *v.tr.* to bruise.
convaincant [kɔ̃vɛ̃kã], *a.* convincing.
convaincre [kɔ̃vɛ̃:kr], *v.tr.* (*conj. like* VAINCRE). **1.** to convince (**de,** of). **2.** to convict; to prove (s.o.) guilty (**de,** of).
convalescence [kɔ̃valɛssã:s], *s.f.* convalescence; *a. & s.* **-cent, -cente.**
convenable [kɔ̃vnabl], *a.* **1.** suitable (**à,** for, to); becoming, proper. **2.** decent; seemly; *adv.* **-ment.**
convenance [kɔ̃vnã:s], *s.f.* **1.** suitability, fitness; **être à la c. de qn,** to meet s.o.'s fancy. **2.** propriety, decency; **manque de c.,** breach of (good) manners.
convenir [kɔ̃vni:r], *v.i.* (*conj. like* VENIR). **1.** (*conj. with* **avoir**) (*a*) to suit, fit; **sa figure me convient,** I like his face; **si cela vous convient,** if that is agreeable to you; (*b*) *impers.* **il convient de . . .,** it is advisable to. . . . **2.** (*conj. with* **avoir,** *and with* **être** *to denote a state of agreement*) (*a*) to agree; **c. de qch.,** to agree on, about, sth.; **ils sont convenus de le faire venir,** they are agreed to send for him; *impers.* **il fut convenu que . . .,** it was agreed that . . .; (*b*) **c. de qch.,** to admit sth.; **j'ai eu tort, j'en conviens,** I confess I was wrong.

convention [kɔ̃vãsjɔ̃], *s.f.* convention. **1.** covenant, agreement; **c. postale,** postal convention; **c. collective** = collective bargaining. **2.** **les conventions sociales,** the social conventions; *adj.phr.* **de c.,** conventional; *a.* **-nel, -nelle,** conventional.
convenu [kɔ̃vny], *a.* agreed (price); appointed (time); **c'est c.!** that's settled!
convergler [kɔ̃vɛrʒe], *v.i.* (**convergeant; ils convergeaient**) to converge; *s.f.* **-ence;** *a.* **-ent, -ente,** converging.
conversler [kɔ̃vɛrse], *v.i.* to converse, talk; *s.f.* **-ation,** conversation, talk.
conversion [kɔ̃vɛrsjɔ̃], *s.f.* **1.** conversion (to a faith). **2.** conversion, change (**en,** into).
converti, -ie [kɔ̃vɛrti], *s.* convert.
convertlir [kɔ̃vɛrti:r], *v.tr.* to convert. **1. c. qn à ses opinions,** to win s.o. over to one's opinions. **2. c. qch. en qch.,** to convert, turn, sth. into sth.; *a.* **-ible,** convertible (**en,** into); *s.m. El:* **-isseur,** transformer.
se convertir, to become converted.
convexe [kɔ̃vɛks], *a.* convex.
conviction [kɔ̃viksjɔ̃], *s.f.* **1.** conviction; firm belief. **2.** *Jur:* **pièce à c.,** exhibit.
convive [kɔ̃vi:v], *s.m. & f.* (*a*) guest (at table); (*b*) table-companion.
convocation [kɔ̃vɔkasjɔ̃], *s.f.* convocation, summons; convening (of assembly).
convoi [kɔ̃vwa], *s.m.* **1.** convoy. **2. c. funèbre,** funeral procession. **3.** train, convoy; *Rail:* **c. de marchandises,** goods train.
convoitler [kɔ̃vwate], *v.tr.* to covet, desire (sth.); *s.f.* **-ise,** covetousness.
convoquer [kɔ̃vɔke], *v.tr.* to summon, convoke (assembly); to convene (meeting).
convulsler [kɔ̃vylse], *v.tr.* to convulse; *a.* **-if, -ive,** convulsive; *adv.* **-ivement;** *s.f.* **-ion.**
convulsionner [kɔ̃vylsjɔne], *v.tr.* to convulse; **bruit qui convulsionne un pays,** rumour that throws a country into a state of upheaval.
coopérler [kɔɔpere], *v.i.* (**je coopère; je coopérerai**) to cooperate; to work together; *s.* **-ateur, -atrice,** fellow-worker; *a.* **-atif, -ative,** cooperative; *s.f.* **-ation,** cooperation; *s.f.* **-ative,** cooperative store.
coordination [kɔɔrdinasjɔ̃], *s.f.* coordination.
coordonner [kɔɔrdɔne], *v.tr.* to coordinate.
copain [kɔpɛ̃], *s.m. F:* friend, pal.
copeau, -eaux [kɔpo], *s.m.* shaving (of wood); chip.
Copenhague [kɔpenag]. *Pr.n.f.* Copenhagen.
copie [kɔpi], *s.f.* **1.** copy; *Adm:* **pour c. conforme,** certified true copy; *Typew:* carbon copy; *Sch:* (*a*) fair copy; (ii) (candidate's) paper. **2.** copy, reproduction (of picture); *Phot:* print.
copier [kɔpje], *v.tr.* **1.** to copy, transcribe; **c. qch. au propre,** to make a fair copy of sth. **2.**

to copy (picture); **c. qch. sur qch.**, to copy sth. from sth. **3.** to copy (s.o.).

copieu|x, -euse [kɔpjø, -øːz], *a.* copious; **repas c.**, hearty meal; *adv.* **-sement.**

copilote [kɔpilɔt], *s.m. Av:* second pilot.

copine [kɔpin], *s.f. F:* (girl) friend.

copiste [kɔpist], *s.m. & f.* copier. **1.** transcriber; **faute de c.**, clerical error. **2.** imitator.

copra(h) [kɔpra], *s.m. Com:* copra; **huile de c.**, coconut oil.

copropriété [kɔprɔpriete], *s.f.* joint ownership.

copulation [kɔpylasjɔ̃], *s.f.* copulation.

coq¹ [kɔk], *s.m.* (*a*) cock; **jeune c.**, cockerel; **au chant du c.**, at cock-crow; **vivre comme un c. en pâte**, to live like a fighting-cock; **c. du village**, cock of the walk; *Box:* **poids c.**, bantam-weight; (*b*) cock, male (of birds); **c. faisan**, cock-pheasant; **grand c. de bruyère**, capercaillie.

coq² *s.m. Nau:* (**maître-)c.**, (ship's) cook.

coque [kɔk], *s.f.* **1.** (*a*) shell (of egg); **un œuf à la c.**, a boiled egg; (*b*) shell, husk (of nut); *F:* **se renfermer dans sa c.**, to retire into one's shell. **2.** hull (of ship); **à double c.**, double-bottomed (ship); *s.m.* **-tier**, egg-cup.

coquelicot [kɔkliko], *s.m. Bot:* red poppy.

coqueluche [kɔklyʃ], *s.f.* (w)hooping cough; **être la c. des femmes**, to be the ladies' darling.

coqu|et, -ette [kɔkɛ, -ɛt]. **1.** *a.* (*a*) coquettish (woman, smile); (*b*) smart, dainty (garment); **elle est coquette**, (i) she likes pretty clothes; (ii) she likes to look attractive; **fortune assez coquette**, tidy fortune. **2.** *s.f.* **coquette**, flirt; *adv.* **-ettement**; *s.f.* **-etterie.**

coquillage [kɔkijaːʒ], *s.m.* **1.** shell-fish. **2.** (empty) shell (of shell-fish).

coquille [kɔkiːj], *s.f.* **1.** shell (of snail, oyster, etc.). **2.** **c. Saint-Jacques**, scallop. **3.** (*a*) shell (of nut); (*b*) **c. de beurre**, flake of butter; (*c*) *Typ:* misprint, literal.

coquin, -ine [kɔkɛ̃, -in]. **1.** *s.* rogue, rascal; **petite coquine!** little wretch! **2.** *a.* mischievous.

cor [kɔːr], *s.m.* **1.** tine (of antler). **2.** (*a*) **c. de chasse**, hunting-horn; (*b*) *Mus:* **c. d'harmonie**, French horn; **c. anglais**, cor anglais. **3.** corn (on the toe).

corail, *pl.* **-aux** [kɔraːj, -o], *s.m.* coral.

corbeau, -eaux [kɔrbo], *s.m.* **1.** *Orn:* crow; **grand c.**, raven. **2.** *Arch:* corbel, bracket.

corbeille [kɔrbɛːj], *s.f.* (open) basket; **c. à papier**, waste-paper basket; **c. à linge**, laundry basket.

corbillard [kɔrbijaːr], *s.m.* hearse.

cord|e [kɔrd], *s.f.* **1.** (*a*) rope, cord, line; **c. à linge**, clothes-line; **sauter à la c.**, to skip; (*b*) string; **c. de boyau**, catgut; **c. à piano**, piano wire; (*c*) halter, hangman's rope; gallows; **se mettre la c. au cou**, to put a halter round one's own neck; **supplice de la c.**, death by hanging;

(*d*) *Tex:* thread; **drap qui montre la c.**, threadbare cloth. **2.** *Mth:* chord. **3.** *Anat:* **cordes vocales**, vocal cords; *s.m.* **-age**, rope(s), gear.

cordeau, -eaux [kɔrdo], *s.m.* **1.** tracing-line, chalk-line; **tiré au c.**, perfectly straight. **2.** *Min:* slow-match, fuse.

cordée [kɔrde], *s.f. Mount:* roped (climbing) party.

cordial, *pl.* **-aux** [kɔrdjal, -o]. **1.** *s.m.* cordial; stimulant. **2.** *a.* cordial, hearty (welcome); *adv.* **-ement**; *s.f.* **-ité**, cordiality.

cordon [kɔrdɔ̃], *s.m.* **1.** (*a*) cord; **c. de la porte**, door-pull (*controlled by the* **concierge**); (*b*) **c. de soulier**, shoe-lace; (*c*) ribbon (of an order); (*d*) *El:* **c. souple**, flex. **2.** row, line; cordon (of police).

cordonn|ier [kɔrdɔnje], *s.m.* shoemaker, cobbler; *s.f.* **-erie**, (*a*) shoemaking; (*b*) cobbler's shop.

Corée (la) [lakɔre]. *Pr.n.* Korea.

coriace [kɔrjas], *a.* tough, leathery (meat, etc.).

Corinthe [kɔrɛ̃ːt]. *Pr.n.f. Geog:* Corinth; **raisins de C.**, currants.

corne [kɔrn], *s.f.* **1.** (*a*) horn (of cattle, sheep, etc.); (*b*) horn (of snail); (beetle's) antenna; **rentrer les cornes**, to draw in one's horns. **2.** **c. d'une page**, turned down corner, dog's-ear, of a page.

corneille [kɔrnɛːj], *s.f. Orn:* crow; rook; **c. des clochers**, jackdaw.

cornemuse [kɔrnəmyːz], *s.f. Mus:* bagpipes.

corn|er [kɔrne]. **1.** *v.i.* (*a*) to trumpet; (*b*) *Aut:* to sound the horn; to hoot. **2.** *v.tr.* **page cornée**, dog-eared page; *s.m.* **-ement.**

cornet [kɔrnɛ], *s.m.* **1.** *Mus:* **c. à pistons**, cornet. **2.** (*a*) **c. de glace**, ice-cream cornet; **c. de pâtisserie**, pastry horn; (*b*) **c. à dés**, dice-box; **c. de papier**, screw of paper; *s.m.* **-tiste**, cornet-player.

corniche [kɔrniʃ], *s.f.* **1.** cornice. **2.** ledge (of rock); (**route en) c.**, cliff road, corniche road.

cornichon [kɔrniʃɔ̃], *s.m. Hort:* gherkin.

Cornouailles [kɔrnwaːj]. *Pr.n.f. Geog:* Cornwall.

cornu [kɔrny], *a.* horned (animal).

cornue [kɔrny], *s.f. Ch:* retort.

corollaire [kɔrɔllɛːr], *s.m.* corollary.

corolle [kɔrɔl], *s.f. Bot:* corolla.

corporat|ion [kɔrpɔrasjɔ̃], *s.f.* corporation; *a.* **-if, -ive**, corporate.

corporel, -elle [kɔrpɔrɛl], *a.* corporeal (substance); corporal (punishment).

corps [kɔːr], *s.m.* **1.** body; *Jur:* **saisir qn au c.**, to arrest s.o.; **avoir le diable au c.**, to be full of devilment; **prendre c.**, to take, assume, shape; *Mil:* **les gardes du c.**, the bodyguards, the lifeguards; **saisir qn à bras-le-c.**, to grapple with s.o.; **lutter c. à c.**, to fight hand to hand. **2.** corpse. **3.** *Ch:* **c. simple**, element; **c.**

composé, compound. **4.** main part (of sth.); **faire c. avec qch.,** to be an integral part of sth.; *Nau:* **perdu c. et biens,** lost with all hands. **5. le c. diplomatique,** the diplomatic corps; **le c. enseignant, médical,** the teaching, the medical, profession; **c. d'armée,** army corps.

corps-de-garde [kɔːrdəgard], *s.m.inv. Mil:* guardroom.

corpul|ence [kɔrpylɑ̃:s], *s.f.* stoutness, corpulence; **de faible c.,** of slight build; *a.* **-ent, -ente,** stout, fat.

correct [kɔrɛkt], *a.* correct, proper (language, etc.); accurate (copy, etc.); *adv.* **-ement.**

correction [kɔrɛksjɔ̃], *s.f.* **1.** correction, correcting. **2.** reproof. **3.** correctness (of speech, dress); propriety (of speech, conduct); *a. Jur:* **tribunal correctionnel** = county court.

correspondance [kɔrɛspɔ̃dɑ̃:s], *s.f.* **1.** correspondence, agreement. **2.** (*a*) communication (between places); (*b*) *Rail:* connection (between trains); **billet de c.,** transfer ticket (on bus, etc.). **3.** (*a*) dealings (**avec,** with); (*b*) correspondence (by letter).

correspondant, -ante [kɔrɛspɔ̃dɑ̃, -ɑ̃:t]. **1.** *a.* (*a*) corresponding (**à,** to, with); (*b*) *Rail:* train c., connection. **2.** *s.* correspondent.

correspondre [kɔrɛspɔ̃:dr], *v.i.* **1.** to tally, agree (**à,** with); to correspond (**à,** to, with). **2.** to correspond (by letter)

corrida [kɔrida], *s.f.* bull-fight.

corridor [kɔridɔ:r], *s.m.* corridor, passage.

corrigé [kɔriʒe], *s.m. Sch:* **1.** fair copy (of work after correction). **2.** key; *F:* crib.

corriger [kɔriʒe], *v.tr.* (**n. corrigeons**). **1.** to correct; to rectify (mistake). **2.** to punish (child).

se corriger d'une habitude, to break oneself of a habit.

corrobor|er [kɔr(r)ɔbɔre], *v.tr.* to corroborate, confirm (statement); *s.f.* **-ation.**

corro|der [kɔrɔde], *v.tr.* to corrode, eat away; *a. & s.m.* **-sif, -sive;** *s.f.* **-sion.**

corrompre [kɔr(r)ɔ̃:pr], *v.tr.* to corrupt; to deprave; **homme corrompu,** corrupt, depraved, man.

se corrompre, (*a*) to become corrupt; (*b*) (*of meat, etc.*) to become tainted.

corrup|tion [kɔr(r)ypsjɔ̃], *s.f.* **1.** corruption; bribing (of witnesses). **2.** corruption, corruptness; *a. & s.* **-teur, -trice;** *a.* **-tible.**

corsage [kɔrsa:ʒ], *s.m.* bodice, blouse, *N.Am:* waist.

corse[1] [kɔrs], *a. & s.* Corsican.

Corse[2] (la). *Pr.n.* Corsica.

corset [kɔrsɛ], *s.m.* corset; *s.* **-ier, -ière.**

cortège [kɔrtɛ:ʒ], *s.m.* **1.** train, retinue. **2.** procession; **c. funèbre,** funeral procession.

corvée [kɔrve], *s.f.* boring, thankless, job; **quelle c.!** *F:* what a bind!

coryza [kɔriza], *s.m. Med:* cold in the head.

cosaque [kɔzak], *s.m.* Cossack.

cosmétique [kɔsmetik], *a. & s.m.* cosmetic.

cosmique [kɔsmik], *a.* cosmic.

cosmopolite [kɔsmɔpɔlit], *a. & s.m. & f.* cosmopolitan.

cosse [kɔs], *s.f.* pod, husk, hull.

cossu [kɔsy], *a. F:* well-to-do (person).

costaud [kɔsto], *a. & s.m. F:* hefty, tough (person).

costume [kɔstym], *s.m.* costume, dress; **c. de bain,** bathing costume.

cote [kɔt], *s.f.* **1.** (*a*) quota, share; (*b*) *Adm:* assessment. **2.** (*a*) *St. Exch: Com:* quotation; **c. des prix,** list of prices; (*b*) odds (on a horse).

côte [ko:t], *s.f.* **1.** rib; *Cu:* **c. de bœuf,** rib of beef; **c. première,** loin chop. **2.** (*a*) slope (of hill); (*b*) hill; **à mi-côte,** half-way up, down, the hill. **3.** coast, shore.

côté [kote], *s.m.* **1.** side; **assis à mes côtés,** sitting by my side; **appartement c. midi,** flat with southern aspect; **le vent vient du bon c.,** the wind is in the right quarter; **c'est son c. faible,** that is his weak spot; **prendre qch. du bon c.,** to take sth. well; **d'un c. . . .,** on the one hand **. . .;** **de tous (les) côtés,** on all sides; far and wide; **courir de c. et d'autre,** to run about in all directions; **de quel c. est l'hôtel?** whereabouts is the hotel? **se ranger d'un c.,** to take sides. **2.** *adv.phr.* (*a*) **de c.,** on one side; sideways; **mettre qch. de c.,** to put sth. aside; (*b*) **à c.,** on one side; near; **tirer à c.,** to miss (the mark); **à c. de,** by the side of; next to; beside.

coteau [kɔto], *s.m.* slope, hillside; *occ.* vineyard.

côtelette [kotlɛt, kɔ-], *s.f.* cutlet; chop.

coter [kɔte], *v.tr.* **1.** to assess; *Sch:* to mark (exercise, exam). **2. point coté,** spot height (on map). **3.** *Com:* to quote (share-prices, etc.); (*of racehorse*) **être très coté,** to be well-backed; (*of pers.*) **être bien coté,** to be appreciated, highly thought of.

coterie [kɔtri], *s.f.* (political, literary) set.

côtier, -ière [kotje, -jɛ:r]. **1.** *a.* coastal (trade, etc.); **fleuve c.,** short river; **chemin c.,** coast road. **2.** *s.m.* coaster; coasting vessel.

cotis|er [kɔtize], *v.tr.* to contribute, subscribe; *s.f.* **-ation;** *s.* **-ant, -ante,** subscriber.

coton [kɔtɔ̃], *s.m.* **1.** cotton; **fil de c.,** sewing cotton; **c. hydrophile,** cotton-wool; *s.m.* **-nier,** cotton plant.

côtoyer [kotwaje], *v.tr.* (**je côtoie**). **1.** to keep close to, hug (shore); to skirt (forest). **2.** to border on (river).

cou [ku], *s.m.* neck; **la peau du c.,** the scruff of the neck; **couper le c., serrer le c., à qn,** behead, to strangle, s.o.; **se jeter, sauter, au de qn,** to hug s.o.; **prendre ses jambes à son c.,** to take to one's heels.

couchage [kuʃa:ʒ], *s.m.* (**matériel de**) **c.,** bedding; **sac de c.,** sleeping bag.

couchant [kuʃɑ̃]. **1.** *a.* **soleil c.**, setting sun. **2.** *s.m.* (*a*) sunset; (*b*) **le c.**, the west.

couche [kuʃ], *s.f.* **1.** *usu. pl.* childbed, confinement, labour. **2.** (*a*) bed, layer; **c. (de bébé)**, (baby's) napkin, *F:* nappy, *N.Am:* diaper; **c. de fumier**, hotbed; **semer sur c.**, to sow in heat; (*b*) coat (of paint).

coucher [kuʃe]. I. *v.* **1.** *v.tr.* (*a*) to put (child) to bed; (*b*) to lay (sth. down, horizontally); **la pluie a couché les blés**, the rain has flattened the corn; **c. un fusil en joue**, to aim a gun. **2.** *v.i.* **c. à l'hôtel**, to sleep at the hotel.
II. **coucher**, *s.m.* **1.** **l'heure du c.**, bedtime. **2.** setting (of sun).
se coucher, (*a*) to go to bed; (*b*) to lie down; (*c*) (*of sun*) to set, go down.

couchette [kuʃet], *s.f.* **1.** (child's) cot, crib. **2.** berth, bunk (on ship), couchette (on train).

coucou [kuku], *s.m.* **1.** (*a*) *Orn:* cuckoo; (*b*) cuckoo-clock. **2.** *Bot:* cowslip.

coude [kud], *s.m.* **1.** elbow; **c. à c.**, side by side; **coup de c.**, nudge. **2.** (*a*) bend, elbow (of road); (*b*) bend, elbow (of pipe); **c. d'équerre**, right-angled bend; **c. en U**, U-bend.

coudées [kude], *s.f.pl.* **avoir ses c. franches**, (i) to have elbow-room; (ii) to have a free hand.

cou-de-pied [kudpje], *s.m.* instep; *pl. cous-de-pied.*

coudloyer [kudwaje], *v.tr.* (**je coudoie**) to elbow (s.o.); *s.m.* **-oiement.**

coudre [kudr], *v.tr.* (*pr.p.* **cousant**; *p.p.* **cousu**; *pr.ind.* **ils cousent**) to sew, stitch; **machine à c.**, sewing machine.

coudrier [kudrie], *s.m.* hazel(-tree).

couenne [kwan], *s.f.* (*a*) (thick) skin of pig; (*b*) bacon rind; pork crackling.

couiner [kwine], *v.i.* to squeak, to squeal; to whimper.

coulant [kulɑ̃]. **1.** *a.* running, flowing (liquid); **nœud c.**, slip-knot; noose. **2.** *s.m.* sliding ring; scarf-ring.

couler [kule]. **1.** *v.tr.* (*a*) to run, pour (liquid); **c. du plomb dans un joint**, to run lead into a joint; (*b*) **c. (à fond) un navire**, to sink a ship; (*c*) **c. une pièce dans la main de qn**, to slip a coin into s.o.'s hand. **2.** *v.i.* (*a*) (*of liquids*) to flow, run; (*b*) (*of ship*) **c. bas**, to founder. **couler**, to glide, slip; **se c. entre les draps**, to slip into bed.

couleur [kulœːr], *s.f.* colour. **1.** (*a*) tint, hue; *F:* **en avoir vu de toutes les couleurs**, to have had all sorts of experiences; (*b*) complexion; **être haut en c.**, to have a high colour; (*c*) *pl. Mil: Nau:* colours, flag. **2.** colour, paint; **boîte de couleurs**, box of paints. **3.** *Cards:* suit.

couleuvre [kulœːvr], *s.f.* (non-poisonous) snake; grass-snake; **paresseux comme une c.**, bone-idle; **avaler une c.**, to pocket an affront, *N.Am:* to eat crow.

coulisse [kulis], *s.f.* **1.** (*a*) groove, slot; **porte à c.**, sliding door; (*b*) slide; *Mus:* **trombone à c.**, slide-trombone. **2.** *Th:* **les coulisses**, the wings.

couloir [kulwaːr], *s.m.* **1.** corridor; *Rail:* **wagon à c.**, corridor carriage. **2.** channel, gully (for water); mountain gorge.

coup [ku], *s.m.* **1.** (*a*) knock, blow; rap (on the door); **c. de bec**, peck; **c. de couteau**, stab; **c. de baïonnette**, bayonet-thrust; **tenir le c.**, (i) to withstand the blow; (ii) *F:* to stick it; **en venir aux coups**, to come to blows; *prep.phr.* **à coups de**, with blows from (sth.); (*b*) **c. de feu**, shot; (*c*) **c. de vent**, gust of wind. **2.** stroke (*normal action of sth.*); (*a*) **c. d'aile**, stroke of the wing; **c. de dents**, bite; **boire qch. à petits coups**, to sip sth.; **c. de plume**, stroke of the pen; **sur le c. de midi**, on the stroke of twelve; (*b*) *Sp:* (i) stroke; (ii) *Fb:* kick; **c. d'envoi**, kick-off; (*c*) **c. de chance**, stroke of luck; (*d*) clap, peal (of thunder). **3.** influence; **agir sous le c. de la peur**, to act out of fear. **4.** (*a*) deed; **c. de tête**, impulsive act; **il médite un mauvais c.**, he's up to mischief; (*b*) **tout d'un c.**, **d'un seul c.**, at one go; **il fut tué sur le c.**, he was killed outright; **pour le c.**, for the moment; *El:* **c.**, after the event; **tout à c.**, suddenly; **c. sur c.**, in rapid succession.

coupable [kupabl]. **1.** *a.* (*a*) guilty (person); (*b*) culpable (act). **2.** *s.m. & f.* culprit; *adv.* **-ment.**

coupant [kupɑ̃]. **1.** *a.* cutting, sharp; **outils coupants**, edge-tools. **2.** *s.m.* (cutting) edge.

coupe¹ [kup], *s.f.* cup; (*a*) **c. à champagne**, champagne glass; (*b*) *Sp:* (winner's) cup.

coupe², *s.f.* **1.** (*a*) cutting (of hay); cutting out (of garment); **c. de cheveux**, hair-cut; (*b*) cut (of a coat); (*c*) section. **2.** *Cards:* cutting.

coupé [kupe]. **1.** *a.* cut up; broken (sleep); **vin c. d'eau**, wine and water. **2.** *s.m. Aut:* coupé.

coupe-gorge [kupgɔrʒ], *s.m.inv.* death-trap.

coupe-papier [kuppapje], *s.m.inv.* paper-knife.

couper [kupe], *v.tr.* to cut. **1.** **se c. le, au, doigt**, to cut one's finger; **c. la tête à qn**, to cut off s.o.'s head; *Cards:* **c. les cartes**, to cut. **2.** to cut across; **c. au plus court**, to take a short cut. **3.** to cut off, interrupt; (*a*) **c. la parole à qn**, to interrupt s.o.; **c. la respiration à qn**, to take s.o.'s breath away; (*b*) to turn off; *El:* **c. le courant**, to switch off the current; *P.T.T:* **c. la communication**, to ring off; (*c*) *Cards:* to trump; *s.m.* **-age.**

couperosé [kuproze], *a.* blotchy (complexion).

couple [kupl]. **1.** *s.m.* pair, (married) couple. **2.** *s.f.* (*a*) two, couple; (*b*) leash (for hounds).

coupler [kuple], *v.tr.* to couple; *El:* to connect.

couplet [kuple], *s.m.* verse (of song).

coupole [kupɔl], *s.f.* cupola.

coupon [kupɔ̃], *s.m.* **1.** cutting; **coupons d'étoffe**, remnants. **2.** *Fin:* coupon.

coupon-réponse [kupɔ̃repɔ̃ːs], *s.m. P.T.T:* **c.-r.**

international, international reply coupon; *pl.* *coupons-réponse.*

coupure [kupy:r], *s.f.* 1. cut (on finger). 2. (*a*) piece cut out; **c. de journal,** newspaper cutting; (*b*) **c. de courant,** power cut.

cour [ku:r], *s.f.* 1. court; (*a*) **à la c.,** at court; (*b*) **faire la c. à une jeune fille,** to court a girl. 2. **c. de justice,** court of justice. 3. court, yard; **c. de récréation,** school playground.

courage [kura:ʒ], *s.m.* courage; **du c.!** (i) cheer up! (ii) keep it up!

courageu|x, -euse [kuraʒø, -ø:z], *a.* courageous, brave; *adv.* **-sement.**

couramment [kuramã], *adv.* 1. easily, readily; fluently. 2. **c. employé,** in current use.

courant [kurã]. 1. *a.* (*a*) running; **chien c.,** hound; (*b*) flowing; **eau courante,** running water; (*c*) current; **le cinq c.,** the fifth inst.; **fin c.,** at the end of this month. 2. *s.m.* (*a*) current, stream; **c. d'air,** draught; (*b*) course; **dans le c. de l'année,** in the course of the year; **être au c. de l'affaire,** to know all about the matter; **mettre qn au c.,** to tell s.o. all about it.

courbature [kurbaty:r], *s.f.* stiffness, tiredness; **avoir une c.,** to be stiff all over.

courbe [kurb]. 1. *a.* curved. 2. *s.f.* (*a*) curve; sweep (of road); (*b*) curve, graph; **c. de niveau,** contour (line).

courber [kurbe]. 1. *v.tr.* to bend, curve; **c. le front,** to bow one's head. 2. *v.i.* to bend; to sag.

courg|e [kurʒ], *s.f. Bot:* gourd; vegetable marrow; *s.f. Cu:* **-ette,** (young) marrow, courgette.

cour|ir [kuri:r], *v.* (*pr.p.* **courant;** *p.p.* **couru;** *pr.ind.* **je cours;** *fu.* **je courrai;** *the aux. is* **avoir**). 1. *v.i.* to run; (*a*) **j'y cours,** I'm going directly; **arriver en courant,** to come running up; (*b*) *Sp:* to race; to run (in a race); (*c*) (*of ship*) to sail; **c. au large,** to stand out to sea; (*d*) to be current; **le bruit court que . . .,** rumour has it that . . .; **faire c. un bruit,** to spread a rumour; **par le temps qui court,** nowadays. 2. *v.tr.* (*a*) to hunt (animal); (*b*) **c. un risque,** to run a risk. 3. (*with cogn. acc.*) (*a*) **c. une course,** to run a race; (*b*) **c. le monde,** to roam the world over; *s.* **-eur, -euse,** runner; wanderer; gadabout.

couronne [kurɔn], *s.f.* 1. wreath (of flowers). 2. (king's) crown; (ducal) coronet.

couronn|er [kurɔne], *v.tr.* to crown (s.o. king); *s.m.* **-ement,** coronation.

courrier [kurje], *s.m.* 1. courier; messenger. 2. mail, post; **par retour du c.,** by return of post; **faire son c.,** to deal with one's correspondence.

courroie [kurwa], *s.f.* strap; (driving-)belt.

cours [ku:r], *s.m.* 1. (*a*) course; flow (of river); **c. d'eau,** stream; **donner libre c. à son imagination,** to give free rein to one's imagination; **année en c.,** current year; **travail en c.,** work

in progress; **en c. de route,** on the way; **au c. de l'hiver,** during the winter; (*b*) **voyage au long c.,** ocean voyage. 2. circulation, currency (of money); **avoir c.,** to be legal tender. 3. **c. du change,** rate of exchange. 4. (*a*) course (of lectures, of lessons); **finir ses c.,** to finish one's studies; (*b*) handbook, manual, textbook.

course [kurs], *s.f.* 1. run, running. 2. race, racing; **c. de vitesse,** sprint. 3. (*a*) excursion, outing; (*b*) journey; **payer (le prix de) sa c.,** to pay one's fare; **c'est une longue c. d'ici là,** it's a long way from here; (*c*) (business) errand; **faire des courses,** to go shopping. 4. path, course (of planet).

court¹ [ku:r]. 1. *a.* short; (*a*) **avoir l'esprit c.,** to be of limited intelligence; *s.m.* **se trouver à c.,** to find oneself short (of money); (*b*) (*in time*) **c. intervalle,** short interval; **de courte durée,** short-lived. 2. *adv.* short; **tourner c. à droite,** to turn sharp (to the) right; **tout c.,** simply.

court², *s.m.* (tennis) court.

courtaud, -aude [kurto, -o:d], *a. & s.* dumpy, squat (person).

court-circuit [kursirkɥi], *s.m. El:* short circuit; *pl.* **courts-circuits.**

courtier [kurtje], *s.m. Com:* broker; **c. en immeubles,** estate-agent; **c. de change,** bill-broker; jobber; **c. maritime,** ship-broker.

courtis|er [kurtize], *v.tr.* to court (s.o.); *s.m* **-an,** courtier; *s.f.* **-ane,** courtesan.

courtois [kurtwa], *a.* courteous; polite, urbane; *adv.* **-ement.**

courtoisie [kurtwazi], *s.f.* 1. courtesy politeness. 2. (act of) courtesy.

couru [kury], *a.* sought after; popular (actor event).

cousin¹, -ine [kuzɛ̃, -in], *s.* cousin.

cousin², *s.m. Ent:* gnat, midge.

coussin [kusɛ̃], *s.m.* cushion.

coussinet [kusinɛ], *s.m.* 1. small cushion; pad 2. *Mec.E:* bearing; **coussinets à billes,** ball bearings.

cousu [kuzy], *a.* sewn; **c. (à la) main,** hand stitched; *F:* **avoir la bouche cousue,** to kee one's mouth shut tight.

coût [ku], *s.m.* cost.

couteau, -eaux [kuto], *s.m.* knife; **c. de poch** pocket-knife; **c. à découper,** carving knife; **cou de c.,** stab; **ils sont à couteaux tirés,** they are a daggers drawn.

coutel|lerie [kutɛlri], *s.f.* 1. cutlery (trade c wares). 2. cutlery shop; *s.m.* **-ier,** cutler.

coût|er [kute], *v.i.* 1. to cost; **c. cher,** to b expensive; **coûte que coûte,** at all costs. 2. **ce me coûte à dire,** it pains me to have to say thi *a.* **-eux, -euse,** costly, expensive.

coutil [kuti], *s.m. Tex:* drill; (mattress) ticking

coutume [kutym], *s.f.* custom, habit; **avoir c. c faire qch,** to be in the habit of doing sth

comme de c., as usual.
coutum|ier, -ière [kutymjɛ, -jɛːr], *a.* customary; **droit c.,** common law; *adv.* **-ièrement.**
coutur|e [kutyːr], *s.f.* 1. sewing, needlework; **maison de haute c.,** fashion house. 2. seam (in dress); *s.* **-ier, -ière,** dressmaker.
couvée [kuve], *s.f.* 1. sitting, clutch (of eggs). 2. brood, hatch(ing) (of chicks).
couvent [kuvã], *s.m.* (*a*) convent, nunnery; (*b*) monastery.
couver [kuve]. 1. *v.tr.* (*of hen*) to sit on (eggs); *abs.* to brood, to sit; **c. le feu,** to brood over the fire; **couver qn des yeux,** to look fondly at s.o. 2. *v.i.* (*of fire*) to smoulder.
couvercle [kuvɛrkl], *s.m.* lid, cover.
couvert[1] [kuvɛːr], *a.* covered. 1. **allée couverte,** shady walk; **ciel c.,** overcast sky. 2. **rester c.,** to keep one's hat on. 3. **chaudement c.,** warmly dressed.
couvert[2], *s.m.* 1. cover(ing), shelter; **être à c.,** to be under cover; **se mettre à c.,** to take cover. 2. place (at table); **mettre, dresser, le c.,** to lay, set, the table; **ôter le c.,** to clear the table; **mettre trois couverts,** to lay for three.
couverture [kuvɛrtyːr], *s.f.* 1. covering, cover; blanket; **c. de lit,** bedspread; **c. en laine,** blanket; **c. en papier,** paper (book) jacket; **sous c. d'amitié,** under the cloak of friendship; *Av:* **c. aérienne,** air cover. 2. roofing. 3. *Com:* security, cover.
couveuse [kuvøːz], *s.f. Agr:* 1. sitting hen. 2. **c. artificielle,** incubator.
couvre-feu [kuvrəfø], *s.m.inv.* curfew.
couvre-lit [kuvrəli], *s.m.* bedspread, counterpane; *pl.* **couvre-lits.**
couvre-pied(s) [kuvrəpje], *s.m.* (*a*) coverlet; **c.-p. piqué,** (eider-down) quilt; (*b*) bedspread; *pl.* **couvre-pieds.**
couvrir [kuvriːr], *v.tr.* (*conj. like* OUVRIR) to cover (**de,** with). 1. **mur couvert de lierre,** wall overgrown with ivy; **c. ses desseins,** to conceal one's intentions; **c. le feu,** to bank (up) the fire; **c. une enchère,** to make a higher bid. 2. **c. une maison,** to roof a house; **maison couverte en chaume,** thatched house.
se couvrir. 1. (*a*) to clothe oneself (warmly); (*b*) to put on one's hat. 2. (*of weather*) to become overcast.
cowboy [kaubɔj], *s.m.* cowboy.
crabe [krab], *s.m.* crab.
craché [kraʃe], *a. F:* **c'est son père tout c.,** he's the dead spit of his father.
crach|er [kraʃe]. 1. *v.i.* (*a*) to spit; **il ne faut pas c. dessus,** it is not to be sneezed at; (*b*) (*of pen*) to splutter; (*c*) *El:* to spark. 2. *v.tr.* to spit (out); **c. des injures,** to hurl abuse; *s.m.* **-at,** spittle; *s.m.* **-ement,** spitting; *s.m.* **-eur;** *s.m.* **-in,** fine drizzle.

Cracovie [krakɔvi]. *Pr.n.f. Geog:* Cracow.
craie [krɛ], *s.f.* chalk.
craindre [krɛ̃ːdr], *v.tr.* (*pr.p.* **craignant;** *p.p.* **craint;** *pr.ind.* **je crains;** *p.h.* **je craignis**) (*a*) to fear, dread; to be afraid of (sth.); **je crains qu'il (ne) soit mort,** I fear he is dead; **il est à c. que . . .,** it is to be feared that . . .; **faire c. qch. à qn,** to put s.o. in fear of sth.; (*b*) *Com:* **craint l'humidité,** to be kept dry.
craint|e [krɛ̃ːt], *s.f.* fear, dread; awe; **de c. de tomber,** for fear of falling; **de c. que . . . (ne)** + *sub.,* lest . . .; *a.* **-if, -ive,** timid; *adv.* **-ivement,** timidly.
cramoisi [kramwazi], *a. & s.m.* crimson.
crampe [krãːp], *s.f. Med:* cramp.
crampon [krãpɔ̃], *s.m.* 1. cramp(-iron); clamp. 2. climbing-iron; stud (on boot); *Mount:* crampon. 3. *F:* (*of pers.*) bore.
cramponner (se) [səkrãpɔne], *v.pr.* **se c. à qch.,** to hold on to sth.; to clutch sth.
cran [krã], *s.m.* 1. notch; (*a*) cog (of wheel); **c. d'arrêt,** stop notch; catch (of knife); **au c. de sûreté,** at half-cock; (*b*) distance between holes (in strap); **descendre d'un c.,** to come down a peg. 2. *F:* **avoir du c.,** to have plenty of pluck, *F:* guts.
crâne [kraːn]. 1. *s.m.* skull; brain-pan. 2. *a. F:* (*a*) plucky (conduct); (*b*) jaunty (air); *adv.* **-ment.**
crân|er [krane], *v.i. F:* to swank, to swagger; *s.f.* **-erie,** (*a*) pluck; (*b*) swank; *s.* **-eur, -euse,** swank, swaggerer.
crapaud [krapo], *s.m.* 1. toad; *F:* **avaler un c.,** to pocket an insult. 2. *Fireworks:* jumping cracker. 3. tub easy-chair.
crapuleu|x, -euse [krapylø, -øːz], *a.* sordid, foul; *adv.* **-sement.**
craquer [krake], *v.i.* to crack; to crackle (*of hard snow*) to crunch (under the feet); (*of shoes*) to creak.
crass|e [kras]. 1. *a.f.* **ignorance c.,** crass ignorance. 2. *s.f.* (body) dirt; **né dans la c.,** born in squalor; *a.* **-eux, -euse,** filthy; squalid.
cratère [kratɛːr], *s.m.* crater.
cravache [kravaʃ], *s.f.* riding-whip; hunting-crop.
cravate [kravat], *s.f.* (neck-)tie; scarf.
crayeux, -euse [krejø, -øːz], *a.* chalky.
crayon [krejɔ̃], *s.m.* (*a*) pencil; **c. à bille,** ball-point pen; (*b*) pencil-drawing; **c. pastel,** crayon; -sketch.
créance [kreãːs], *s.f.* 1. belief, credit; **trouver c.,** to be believed. 2. trust; **lettre(s) de c.,** (i) credentials; (ii) letters of credit. 3. debt.
créancier, -ière [kreãsje, -jɛːr], *s.* creditor.
créa|tion [kreasjɔ̃], *s.f.* 1. (*a*) creation, creating; (*b*) founding (of institution); setting up (of a court, etc.). 2. **les merveilles de la c.,** the wonders of creation; *a. & s.* **-teur, -trice,** (i)

a. creative (power); (ii) *s.* creator; maker; inventor.

créature [kreaty:r], *s.f.* creature.

crécelle [kresɛl], *s.f.* (hand-)rattle; **voix de c.,** rasping voice.

crèche [krɛʃ], *s.f.* **1.** manger, crib. **2.** (public) day-nursery, crèche.

crédibilité [kredibilite], *s.f.* credibility.

crédit [kredi], *s.m.* **1.** credit, repute; prestige. **2.** credit; **vendre qch. à c.,** to sell sth. on credit; **faire c. à qn,** to give s.o. credit; **carte de c.,** credit card.

crédit|er [kredite], *v.tr.* **c.** qn du montant d'une **somme,** to credit s.o. with a sum; *s.* **-eur,** **-rice,** creditor.

credo [kredo], *s.m.inv.* creed.

crédul|e [kredyl], *a.* credulous; *s.f,* **-ité,** credulity.

créer [kree], *v.tr.* to create; **se c. une clientèle,** to build up a connection.

crémaillère [kremaje:r], *s.f.* **1.** pot-hanger; **pendre la c.,** to give a house-warming party. **2.** **chemin de fer à c.,** rack-railway.

créma|tion [kremasjɔ̃], *s.f.* cremation; *a. & s.m.* **-toire,** crematory; crematorium.

crème [krɛm], *s.f.* **1.** cream; (*a*) **c. fouettée,** whipped cream; **fromage à la c.,** cream-cheese; **c. (de gruyère, etc.),** processed cheese; **café c.,** white coffee; *a.inv.* **rubans c.,** cream(-coloured) ribbons; (*b*) *Cu:* custard, cream. **2.** **c. pour chaussures,** shoe cream, polish; **c. de beauté,** face cream; **c. à raser,** shaving cream.

crém|erie [kremri], *s.f.* creamery, dairy; milk-shop; *s.* **-ier, -ière,** dairyman, -woman.

crémeux, -euse [kremø, -ø:z], *a.* creamy.

crénaux [kreno], *s.m.pl.* battlements.

crénelé [krenle], *a.* **1.** battlemented (wall). **2.** toothed, notched.

créole [kreɔl], *a. & s. Ethn:* Creole.

créosote [kreɔzɔt], *s.f.* creosote.

créosoter [kreɔzɔte], *v.tr.* to creosote.

crêpe [krɛ:p]. **1.** *s.f.* pancake. **2.** *s.m.* (*a*) crape; **c. satin,** satin crêpe; (*b*) **c. de caoutchouc,** crêpe-rubber.

cré|pi [krepi], *a. & s.m.* rough-cast(ing).

crép|ir [krepi:r], *v.tr.* to rough-cast (wall); *s.m.* **-issage.**

crépit|er [krepite], *v.i.* to crackle; (*of rain*) to patter; (*of candle*) to sputter; *s.m.* **-ement.**

crépu [krepy], *a.* crisp, frizzy, fuzzy (hair).

crépuscul|e [krepyskyl], *s.m.* twilight; dusk; *a.* **-aire,** twilight.

cresson [kresɔ̃], *s.m. Bot:* cress; **c. de fontaine,** water-cress; *s.f.* **-nière,** watercress bed.

Crète [krɛ:t]. *Pr.n.f. Geog:* Crete.

crête [krɛ:t], *s.f.* **1.** comb, crest (of bird). **2.** (*a*) crest (of wave); (*b*) crest, ridge (of mountain); *El:* **puissance de c.,** peak power.

crétin [kretɛ̃], *s.m.* (*a*) cretin, idiot; (*b*) *F:* idiot.

creuser [krøze], *v.tr.* **1.** to hollow (out); to plough (a furrow); **front creusé de rides,** brow furrowed with wrinkles; **se c. le cerveau,** to rack one's brains. **2.** to excavate.

creuset [krøze], *s.m.* crucible, melting-pot.

creux, -euse [krø, -ø:z]. **1.** *a.* hollow; **chemin c.,** sunken road; **yeux c.,** deep-set eyes; **voix creuse,** deep voice; **avoir la tête creuse,** to be empty-headed; *adv.* **sonner c.,** to sound hollow. **2.** *s.m.* hollow (of the hand); hole (in the ground); trough (of wave); pit (of stomach).

crevasse [krəvas], *s.f.* crack (in skin); crevice (in wall); crevasse (in glacier); **avoir des crevasses aux mains,** to have chapped hands.

crev|er [krəve], *v.* (**je crève**). **1.** *v.i.* (*a*) to burst, split; **c. de rire,** to split (one's sides) with laughter; (*b*) (*of animals, P: of people*) to die; *F:* **c. de faim,** to be starving. **2.** *v.tr.* to burst (balloon, dam); to puncture (tyre); **c. un œil à qn,** to put out s.o.'s eye; *F:* **ça vous crève les yeux,** it's staring you in the face; *s.f.* **-aison,** puncture.

crevette [krəvɛt], *s.f.* **c. grise,** shrimp; **c. rouge,** prawn.

cri [kri], *s.m.* (*a*) cry (of animal, person); chirp (of bird, insect); **c. perçant,** shriek (of person); squeal (of animal); (*b*) shout, call; **pousser les hauts cris,** to make shrill protest; *F:* **le dernier c.,** the latest fashion.

criaill|er [kriaje], *v.i.* **1.** to cry out, bawl. **2.** to whine, complain, *F:* grouse; **c. après qn,** to nag, scold, s.o.; *s.f.* **-erie;** *s.* **-eur, -euse.**

criard [kria:r], *a.* (*a*) squalling, peevish; (*b*) **voix criarde,** shrill voice; **dettes criardes,** pressing debts; **couleur criarde,** loud colour.

crible [kribl], *s.m.* sieve, riddle; *Min:* **passer qch au c.,** to screen sth.

cribl|er [krible], *v.tr.* **1.** to sift, riddle. **2.** **c.** qn de **balles,** to riddle s.o. with bullets; **criblé de dettes,** up to one's eyes in debt; *s.m.* **-age.**

cric [krik], *s.m.* (lifting) jack.

criée [krie], *s.f.* auction; **vente à la c.,** sale by auction.

crier [krie]. **1.** *v.i.* (*a*) to cry; to call out, to shout; **c. après qn,** to carp at s.o.; **c. au secours,** to shout for help; (*b*) (*of mouse*) to squeak; (*of cricket*) to chirp; (*c*) (*of door*) to creak. **2.** *v.tr.* to cry, hawk (vegetables); **c. qch. sur les toits,** to cry sth. from the house-tops.

crim|e [krim], *s.m.* crime; *Jur:* felony; *a. &* **-inel, -inelle,** criminal.

Crimée (la) [lakrime]. *Pr.n.f. Geog:* the Crime[a]

crin [krɛ̃], *s.m.* horsehair; **les crins,** the man[e] and tail.

crinière [krinje:r], *s.f.* mane.

crique [krik], *s.f.* creek, cove.

crise [kri:z], *s.f.* **1.** crisis; (*a*) slump; (*b*) shorta[ge] (of housing, etc.). **2.** attack (of gout, etc.); **c.** **nerfs,** fit of hysterics; **avoir une c. de larmes,**

have a fit of crying.

crisp|er [krispe], v.tr. to contract, clench; **visage crispé par la douleur**, face contorted with pain; **cela me crispe,** it gets on my nerves.; a. F: -**ant**, aggravating; s.f. -**ation**, wincing; (nervous) twitching.

criss|er [krise], v.tr. & i. to grate; (of brakes) to squeak, squeal; s.m. -**ement**, grinding (of teeth); squeak(ing) (of brakes).

cristal, -aux [kristal, -o], s.m. 1. crystal. 2. crystal(-glass); **c. taillé,** cut glass.

cristall|iser [kristalize], v.tr. & i. to crystallize; a. -**in,** clear as crystal; s.f. -**isation.**

critique [kritik]. 1. a. critical; **examen c. d'un ouvrage,** critical examination of a work. 2. s.m. critic. 3. s.f. (a) criticism; (b) review; (c) censure.

critiqu|er [kritike], v.tr. (a) to criticize; (b) to censure; to find fault with (s.o., sth.); a. -**able,** open to criticism.

croass|er [krɔase], v.i. to caw; to croak; s.m. -**ement.**

croc [kro], s.m. 1. (a) hook; (b) pawl, catch. 2. canine tooth; fang (of wolf).

crochet [krɔʃɛ], s.m. hook. 1. croche hook; **dentelle au c.,** crochet-work. 2. **c. de serrurier,** skeleton key; **c. d'arrêt,** pawl, catch. 3. poison fang (of serpent); pl. talons (of eagle, etc.). 4. **faire un c.,** (of road) to take a sudden turn; (of pers.) to make a detour.

crochu [krɔʃy], a. hooked (nose); crooked (stick).

crocodile [krɔkɔdil], s.m. crocodile.

croire [krwa:r], v. (pr.p. **croyant;** p.p. **cru**). 1. v.tr. (a) **c. qch.,** to believe sth.; **il est à c. que** + ind., it is probable that . . .; **je ne crois pas que cela suffise,** I don't think that will be enough; **je (le) crois bien!** I should think so! **je crois que oui,** I believe so; **n'en croyez rien!** don't believe it! **à ce que je crois . . .,** to the best of my belief . . .; **il se croit tout permis,** he thinks he may do anything; (b) **c. qn,** to believe s.o.; **me croira qui voudra, mais . . .,** believe me or not, but . . .; F: **je te crois!** rather! of course! **croyez-m'en,** be advised by me; **je ne pouvais en c. mes yeux,** I couldn't believe my eyes. 2. v.i. (a) **c. à qch.,** to believe in (the existence of) sth.; **c'est à ne pas y c.,** it is beyond all belief; **c. au témoignage des sens,** to trust the evidence of one's senses; (b) **c. en qn,** to believe in, have faith in, s.o.

croisade [krwazad], s.f. Hist: crusade.

croisé [krwaze]. 1. a. crossed; **mots croisés,** crossword (puzzle); Agr: **race croisée,** crossbreed. 2. s.m. crusader.

croisée [krwaze], s.f. casement-window.

crois|er [krwaze]. 1. v.tr. (a) to cross; **rester les bras croisés,** (i) to stand with arms folded; (ii) to remain idle; **c. qn dans l'escalier,** to pass s.o.

on the stairs; **leurs regards se croisèrent,** their eyes met; (b) to interbreed, cross (animals, plants). 2. v.i. (of garment) to lap, fold over; Nau: to cruise; s.m. -**ement,** crossing.

croiseur [krwazœːr], s.m. Nau: cruiser.

croisière [krwazjɛːr], s.f. cruise.

croissance [krwasãːs], s.f. growth.

croissant [krwasã], s.m. 1. crescent (of moon). 2. Cu: croissant.

croître [krwaːtr], v.i. (pr.p. **croissant;** p.p. **crû,** f. **crue;** pr.ind. je **crois, il croît**) to grow, increase (in size, volume); **la rivière a crû,** the river has risen; **aller croissant,** to go on increasing.

croix [krwa], s.f. cross. 1. **la Sainte C.,** the Holy Rood; **la mise en C.,** the Crucifixion; **faire le signe de la c.,** to cross oneself; **la C. Rouge,** the Red Cross; Mil: **la C. de Guerre,** the Military Cross; **c. ou pile,** heads or tails. 2. Typ: dagger.

croquant [krɔkã], a. crisp (biscuit, etc.).

croque-mort [krɔkmɔːr], s.m. (undertaker's) mute; pl. croque-morts.

croquer [krɔke], v.tr. (a) to crunch, munch; **chocolat à c.,** eating chocolate; (b) to sketch; F: **elle est gentille à c.,** she's perfectly sweet.

croquette [krɔkɛt], s.f. Cu: rissole, croquette.

croquis [krɔki], s.m. sketch.

crosse [krɔs], s.f. 1. Sp: (hockey-)stick; (golf-)club. 2. (a) crook; (b) butt (of rifle).

crotale [krɔtal], s.m. rattlesnake.

crotte [krɔt], s.f. 1. dung. 2. mud, dirt.

crotter [krɔte], v.tr. to dirty, soil.

croul|er [krule], v.i. (of building) (a) to totter; (b) to collapse; Th: **faire c. la salle,** to bring the house down; a. & s.m. -**ant,** (i) ramshackle; (ii) s.m. F: back-number; **les croulants,** the (grand-)parents.

croupe [krup], s.f. 1. croup, rump (of horse); **monter en c.,** to ride pillion. 2. ridge (of hill).

croupier [krupje], s.m. croupier (at casino).

croupir [krupiːr], v.i. 1. to wallow (in filth, in sloth). 2. (of water) to stagnate.

croustillant [krustijã], a. crisp, crusty (pie).

croûte [krut], s.f. 1. crust (of bread); (cheese-) rind; **casser la c.,** to have a snack. 2. scab (on wound). 3. daub.

croy|ance [krwajãːs], s.f. belief (à, in); **c. en Dieu,** belief in God; a. & s. -**ant,** (i) believing; (ii) believer.

cru[1] [kry], a. 1. raw (meat); crude (colour). 2. adv.phr. **à c.,** next to the skin; adv. -**ûment,** crudely, roughly.

cru[2], s.m. locality in which wine is grown; **vin du c.,** local wine; **les grands crus,** the great wines; **sentir le c.,** to smack of the soil; **une histoire de son c.,** a story of his own invention.

cruauté [kryote], s.f. cruelty (envers, to).

cruche [kryʃ], s.f. pitcher, jug.

cruchon [kryʃɔ̃], s.m. small jug; carafe.

cruci|fier [krysifje], *v.tr.* to crucify; *s.m.* -fix, crucifix; *s.f.* -fixion; *a.* -forme, cruciform; cross-shaped.

crudité [krydite], *s.f.* indigestibility (of foods); hardness (of water); **manger des crudités,** to eat raw fruit and vegetables.

crue [kry], *s.f.* rising (of river); flood; **rivière en c.,** river in spate.

cru|el, -elle [kryɛl], *a.* cruel (**envers,** to); *adv.* -ellement, cruelly.

crustacés [krystase], *s.m.pl.* shellfish.

crypte [kript], *s.f.* crypt.

Cuba [kyba]. *Pr.n.f.* Cuba.

cub|e [kyb]. 1. *s.m.* cube. 2. *a.* **mètre c.,** cubic metre; *a.* -ique; *s.m.* -isme; *s.m. & f.* -iste.

cueill|ir [kœji:r], *v.tr.* (*pr.p.* **cueillant;** *pr.ind.* je **cueille;** *fu.* je **cueillerai**) to pick, pluck, gather (flowers, fruit); **c. des lauriers,** to win laurels; *F:* **c. qn au passage,** to buttonhole s.o.; *s.m.* -age, *s.f.* -aison, *s.f.* -ette, picking, gathering (of fruit, etc.).

cuiller, cuillère [kɥije:r], *s.f.* spoon.

cuillerée [kɥijre], *s.f.* spoonful.

cuir [kɥi:r], *s.m.* 1. hide. 2. leather; **c. vert,** raw hide; **c. verni,** patent leather.

cuirasse [kɥiras], *s.f.* 1. cuirass; **trouver le défaut dans la c. de qn,** to find s.o.'s weak spot. 2. armour (of warship, tank).

cuirassé [kɥirase]. 1. *a.* armoured; armour-plated. 2. *s.m.* armoured ship.

cuire [kɥi:r], *v.* (*conj. like* CONDUIRE). 1. *v.tr.* (*a*) to cook; **cuit à point,** done to a turn; (*b*) to bake (bricks). 2. *v.i.* (*a*) (*of food*) to cook; **c. à petit feu,** to cook slowly; to simmer; **faire c. un bifteck,** to cook a steak; (*b*) to burn, smart; **les yeux me cuisent,** my eyes are smarting; **il vous en cuira,** you'll regret it.

cuisant [kɥizɑ̃], *a.* smarting, burning (pain); biting (cold); bitter (disappointment).

cuisin|e [kɥizin], *s.f.* 1. kitchen; **batterie de c.,** cooking utensils. 2. (*a*) cookery; **faire la c.,** to do the cooking; (*b*) **les petites cuisines du métier,** the little tricks of the trade; *s.* -ier, -ière, cook; *s.f.* -ière, cooking-stove, cooker.

cuisse [kɥis], *s.f.* thigh; *Cu:* **c. de poulet,** chicken leg, *F:* drumstick.

cuivre [kɥi:vr], *s.m.* **c. rouge,** copper; **c. jaune,** brass; *Mus:* **les cuivres,** the brass.

cuivré [kɥivre], *a.* 1. copper-coloured; **teint c.,** bronzed complexion. 2. *Mus:* **sons cuivrés,** brassy tones.

cul [ky], *s.m.* (*a*) *P:* backside, bottom (of person); (*b*) rump (of animal).

culasse [kylas], *s.f.* 1. breech (of gun). 2. *Aut: etc:* (detachable) cylinder-head.

culbute [kylbyt], *s.f.* (*a*) somersault; **faire la c.,** to turn a somersault; (*b*) tumble; heavy fall.

culbut|er [kylbyte]. 1. *v.i.* to turn a somersault.

culbuteur [kylbytœ:r], *s.m.* 1. *El:* interrupteur à c., tumbler switch. 2. *Aut: etc:* moteur à c., overhead-valve engine. 3. tripper device; tipping device (for truck).

culinaire [kyline:r], *a.* culinary.

culminant [kylminɑ̃], *a.* **point c.,** highest point; height, climax.

culot [kylo], *s.m.* *F:* **avoir du c.,** to have plenty of cheek.

culotte [kylɔt], *s.f.* 1. *Cu:* rump (of beef). 2. **une c.,** a pair of breeches; (boy's) shorts; (woman's) panties.

culpabilité [kylpabilite], *s.f.* culpability, guilt.

culte [kylt], *s.m.* 1. worship; **avoir un c. pour qn,** to worship s.o. 2. form of worship; cult; **liberté du c.,** freedom of worship.

cultiv|er [kyltive], *v.tr.* 1. to cultivate, farm (land). 2. to cultivate (plants); *s.m.* -ateur, farmer.

cultur|e [kylty:r], *s.f.* 1. (*a*) cultivation, tilling (of the soil); (*b*) *pl.* land under cultivation. 2. culture (of the mind, etc.); **c. physique,** physical training; *a.* -el, -elle, cultural.

cupid|e [kypid], *a.* covetous, greedy, grasping; *s.f.* -ité, greed, cupidity.

curable [kyrabl], *a.* curable (disease).

curateur, -trice [kyratœ:r, -tris], *s.* *Jur:* trustee, administrator; guardian.

cure [ky:r], *s.f.* 1. care; *used only in* **personne n'en a c.,** nobody cares. 2. *Ecc:* obtenir une c., to be appointed to a parish. 3. *Med:* (course of) treatment; cure; **c. d'amaigrissement,** slimming cure.

curé [kyre], *s.m.* parish priest.

cure-dents [kyrdɑ̃], *s.m.inv.* tooth-pick.

cure-pipe [kyrpip], *s.m.* pipe-cleaner; *pl.* curepipes.

curer [kyre], *v.tr.* to pick (teeth); to clean (nails); to clean out, dredge (a drain, a river).

curieu|x, -euse [kyrjø, -ø:z], *a.* curious; (*a*) interested; **je serai c. de voir cela,** I shall be interested to see it; (*b*) inquisitive (**de,** about); (*c*) odd, peculiar; *adv.* -sement.

curiosité [kyrjozite], *s.f.* curiosity. 1. (*a*) interest; (*b*) inquisitiveness; (*c*) oddness, peculiarity. 2. curio.

cuv|e [ky:v], *s.f.* vat, tun; *s.f.* -ette, wash-basin (W.C.) pan.

cuver [kyve], *v.tr.* to ferment (wine); **c. son vin,** to sleep off one's drink.

cyanure [sjany:r], *s.m.* *Ch:* cyanide.

cyclable [siklabl], *a.* **piste c.,** cycle track.

cycl|e [sikl], *s.m.* 1. cycle (of events). 2. bicycle; *s.m.* -isme, cycling; *s.m. & f.* -iste.

cyclone [siklo:n], *s.m.* *Meteor:* cyclone.

cygne [siɲ], *s.m.* swan; **jeune c.,** cygnet.

cylind|re [silɛ̃:dr], *s.m.* cylinder; *a.* -rique cylindrical.

cymbale [sɛ̃bal], *s.f.* *Mus:* cymbal.

cynique [sinik]. **1.** *a.* shameless, cynical. **2.** *s.m.* cynic; *adv.* **-ment.**
cynisme [sinism], *s.m.* shamelessness, effrontery; cynicism.
cyprès [siprɛ], *s.m. Bot:* cypress.
cytise [sitiːz], *s.m. Bot:* laburnum.

D

D, d [de], *s.m.* (the letter) D, d.

dac, d'ac [dak], *int. F:* O.K.

dactylo [daktilo], *s.m. & f.* (*a*) typist; (*b*) *Fr.C:* typewriter (*machine*).

dada [dada], *s.m. F:* pet subject; **son dernier d.,** his latest craze.

dahlia [dalja], *s.m. Bot:* dahlia.

daigner [dɛɲe], *v.tr.* to deign, condescend; **elle n'a même pas daigné me voir,** she wouldn't even see me.

daim [dɛ̃], *s.m.* (*a*) (fallow) deer; buck; (*b*) buckskin; suede.

dall|e [dal], *s.f.* (*a*) flag(stone); (*b*) (stone) slab; *s.m.* **-age,** paving; tiled floor.

daltonisme [daltɔnism], *s.m.* colour-blindness.

Damas [damɑ(:s)]. **1.** *Pr.n.m. Geog:* Damascus. **2.** *s.m.* (*a*) *Tex:* damask; (*b*) *Bot:* damson.

dame¹ [dam], *s.f.* **1.** (*a*) lady; (*b*) married woman; *P:* **votre d.,** your missus. **2.** (*a*) **jeu de dames,** (game of) draughts, *N.Am:* checkers; (*b*) king (at draughts); queen (at cards and chess).

dame², *int.* **d. oui!** rather!

damier [damje], *s.m.* draught-board, *N.Am:* checker board; **tissu en damier,** check material.

damner [dɑne], *v.tr.* to damn.

dandin|er [dɑ̃dine], *v.tr.* to dandle (baby); *s.m.* **-ement.**

se dandiner, to waddle.

Danemark (le) [lədanmark]. *Pr.n.m.* Denmark.

danger [dɑ̃ʒe], *s.m.* danger, peril; **à l'abri du d.,** out of harm's way; **courir un d.,** to run a risk; **sans d.,** safe(ly); securely; *F:* **pas de d.!** not likely! no fear! *Med:* **hors de d.,** off the danger list; **il n'y a pas de d. qu'il vienne,** there is no fear of his coming.

dangereu|x, -euse [dɑ̃ʒrø, -ø:z], *a.* dangerous (**pour,** to); *adv.* **-sement.**

danois, -oise [danwa, -wa:z]. **1.** *a.* Danish; (**chien**) **d.,** great dane. **2.** *s.* Dane. **3.** *s.m. Ling:* Danish.

dans [dɑ̃], *prep.* **1.** (*of place*) (*a*) in; (*b*) within; **d. un rayon de dix kilomètres,** within a radius of ten kilometres; (*c*) into; **mettre qch. d. une boîte,** to put sth. into a box; **tomber d. l'oubli,** to sink into oblivion; (*d*) out of; **boire d. un verre,** to drink out of a glass; **copier qch. d. un livre,** to copy sth. out of a book; (*e*) **il a voyagé d. le monde,** he has travelled about the world. **2.** (*of time*) in, within; during; **d. le temps,** long

ago, formerly; **je serai prêt à partir d. cinq minutes,** I shall be ready to start in five minutes; **payer d. les dix jours,** to pay within ten days. **3.** (*a*) **être d. le commerce,** to be in trade; (*b*) **être d. la nécessité de . . .,** to be obliged to . . .; **d. cette occasion,** on this occasion; **d. ce but,** with this object (in view).

dansant [dɑ̃sɑ̃], *a.* **1.** dancing; springy (step, walk). **2. donner une soirée dansante,** to give a dance.

danse [dɑ̃:s], *s.f.* dance, dancing; **aimer la d.,** to be fond of dancing; **d. de Saint-Guy,** St. Vitus's dance.

dans|er [dɑ̃se], *v.i.* to dance; *s.* **-eur, -euse,** (*a*) dancer; (*b*) partner.

dard [da:r], *s.m.* (*a*) sting (of insect); forked tongue (of serpent); (*b*) tongue (of flame); (*c*) piercing ray (of sun).

darder [darde], *v.tr.* to shoot forth; **il darda sur moi un regard chargé de haine,** he shot a glance of hatred at me.

dare-dare [darda:r], *adv.* post-haste.

date [dat], *s.f.* date; **sans d.,** undated; (*of event*) **faire d.,** to mark an epoch; **être le premier en d.,** to come first; **je le connais de longue d.,** I've known for a long time; *Fin:* **emprunt à longue,** **à courte, d.,** long-dated, short-dated, loan.

dater [date]. **1.** *v.tr.* to date (letter). **2.** *v.i.* **à d. de ce jour,** from today; **qui date,** (i) *Hist:* epoch-making; (ii) *Cl:* old-fashioned.

datt|e [dat], *s.f. Bot:* date; *s.m.* **-ier,** date-palm.

dauphin [dofɛ̃], *s.m.* **1.** dolphin. **2.** dauphin.

davantage [davɑ̃ta:ʒ], *adv.* more; **il m'en faut d.,** I need still more; **je n'en dis pas d.,** I shall say no more.

de [də] (*before vowels and h 'mute'* d'. *De* + *def.art.* **le, les,** *are contracted into* **du, des**). **I.** *prep.* **1.** (*a*) from; **du matin au soir,** morning till night; **de vous à moi,** between ourselves; **de jour en jour,** from day to day; (*b*) (*time*) **il partit de nuit,** he left by night; (*c*) (*agent*) **accompagné de ses amis,** accompanied by his friends; **la statue est de Rodin,** the statue is by Rodin; **j'ai fait cela de ma propre main,** I did it all by myself; **vivre de sa plume,** to live by one's pen; (*d*) (*manner*) **répondre d'une voix douce,** to answer in a gentle voice; (*e*) (*cause*) **sauter de joie,** to jump for joy; (*f*) (*measure*) **je suis âgé de seize ans,** I am sixteen years old; **ma montre retarde de dix minutes,** my watch is ten minutes slow; (*g*) altéré de sang, thirsting for blood. **2.** (a) le livre de Pierre, Peter's book; le toit de la maison, the roof of the house; (b) (material) un pont de fer, an iron bridge; (c) (distinguishing mark) le professeur de français, the French master; le journal d'hier, yesterday's paper; (d) (partitive) un verre de vin, a glass of wine; quelque chose de bon, something good. **3.** (forming compound prepositions) près de la maison, near the house; autour du jardin, round the garden. **4.** (connecting vb. and object) manquer de courage, to lack courage; convenir d'une erreur, to admit an error. **II.** de, serving as a link word. **1.** le mieux était de rire, it was best to laugh; ils sont indignes de vivre, they are unfit to live. **2.** la ville de Paris, the town of Paris; un drôle de garçon, a funny chap; il y eut trois hommes de tués, three men were killed. **III.** de, partitive article, not prepositional, (used also as pl. of un, une) n'avez-vous pas des amis? have you got no friends? sans faire de fautes, without making any mistakes; donnez-nous de vos nouvelles, let us hear from you; vous êtes des lâches, you are cowards.

dé¹ [de], s.m. Gaming: die, pl. dice; dés pipés, loaded dice; coup de dé, cast of the die; le dé en est jeté, the die is cast.

dé², s.m. dé (à coudre), thimble.

débâcle [debɑ:kl], s.f. **1.** break(ing) up (of drift-ice). **2.** (a) downfall, collapse (of a business); (b) breakdown (in health).

déball|er [debale], v.tr. to unpack (goods); s.m. -age, unpacking.

débarbouiller (se) [sədebarbuje)], v.pr. to wash one's face.

débarcadère [debarkadɛːr], s.m. landing-stage, wharf.

débardeur [debardœːr], s.m. docker, stevedore.

débarqu|er [debarke]. **1.** v.tr. to unload (cargo); to disembark, land (passengers), to drop (pilot). **2.** v.i. to land, disembark (from boat); to alight (from train); s.m. -ement.

débarras [debara], s.m. riddance; (chambre de) d., lumber-room.

débarrass|er [debarase], v.tr. to disencumber; to clear (table); d. qn de qch., to relieve s.o. of sth.; d. le plancher, (i) to clear the floor; (ii) F: to clear out; s.m. -ement.

se débarrasser de qch., to get rid of sth.; to disentangle oneself from sth.

débat [deba], s.m. **1.** debate. **2.** dispute.

débattre [debatr], v.tr. (conj. like BATTRE) to debate, discuss; prix à d., price by arrangement.

se débattre, to struggle.

débauche [deboʃ], s.f. debauchery, dissolute living.

débauché, -ée [deboʃe]. **1.** a. debauched,

profligate. **2.** s. debauchee; s.m. rake.

débauch|er [deboʃe], v.tr. **1.** to lead (s.o.) astray; d. la jeunesse, to corrupt the young. **2.** Ind: to lay off (workers); to discharge (staff); s.m. -age, laying off (of workmen); s.m. -eur, (i) corrupter, seducer; (ii) (strike) picket.

débile [debil]. **1.** a. weakly (child); sickly (plant). **2.** s. un d. mental, a mental defective.

débill|iter [debilite], v.tr. to debilitate, weaken; s.f. -ité.

débit¹ [debi], s.m. (a) (retail) sale; (b) (retail) shop; esp. d. de tabac, tobacconist's; d. de boissons, public house.

débit², s.m. Com: debit.

débit|er¹ [debite], v.tr. **1.** to retail; to sell (goods) retail. **2.** to cut up (meat). **3.** d. des histoires, to spin yarns; s. -ant, -ante, retail dealer; retailer; s. -eur¹, -euse, usu. Pej: d. de calomnies, scandalmonger.

débit|er², v.tr. Com: to debit; s. -eur², -rice, debtor.

débl|ayer [debleje], v.tr. (je déblaye, je déblaie). **1.** to clear away (earth, etc.). **2.** d. un terrain, to clear a piece of ground; s.m. -aiement.

déblo|quer [debloke], v.tr. to free, to release; Fin: to unfreeze (funds); s.m. -cage.

déboire [debwaːr], s.m. disappointment.

débois|er [debwaze], v.tr. to deforest (land); s.m. -ement.

débonnaire [debɔnɛːr], a. good-natured, easy-going.

déborder [deborde]. **1.** v.i. to overflow, run over; elle déborde de vie, she's bubbling over with vitality; débordé de travail, snowed under with work. **2.** v.tr. to project, stick out, beyond (sth.); to overlap (sth.).

débouché [debuʃe], s.m. **1.** outlet (of passage). **2.** opening; chance of success; channel (for trade).

débouch|er¹ [debuʃe], v.tr. **1.** to clear (choked pipe). **2.** to uncork (bottle); s.m. -age; s.m. -ement.

déboucher², v.i. to emerge, issue (forth).

déboucler [debukle], v.tr. **1.** to unbuckle (belt). **2.** to take the curl out of (hair).

débours [debuːr], s.m. usu. pl. disbursement; out-of-pocket expenses.

débourser [deburse], v.tr. to spend (money).

debout [dəbu], adv. **1.** (a) (of thg) upright, on end; tenir d., to be kept upright; (of pers.) standing; se tenir d., to stand; places d. seulement, standing room only; F: ça ne tient pas d., that doesn't hold water; conte à dormir d., tall story; (b) (of pers.) être d., to be up; allons, d.! come on, get up! **2.** vent d., head wind.

déboutonner [debutɔne], v.tr. to unbutton.

débraillé [debraje], a. untidy, slovenly (person).

débray|er [debreje], v.i. (je débraye, je débraie). **1.** Aut: to declutch. **2.** Ind: F: (a) to go on strike; (*b*) to knock off; *s.m.* **-age**.

débris [debri], *s.m.pl.* remains, debris.

débrouillard, -arde [debruja:r, -ard], *a. & s.* resourceful (person).

débrouiller [debruje], *v.tr.* to unravel (thread); **d. une affaire**, to straighten out an affair.

se débrouiller, to extricate oneself (from difficulties); to manage; **qu'il se débrouille**, let him fend for himself; **débrouillez-vous!** that's your look-out!

début [deby], *s.m.* **1.** first appearance (of actor). **2.** beginning, start, outset; **appointements de d.**, starting salary.

débutant, -ante [debytã, -ã:t], *s.* beginner.

débuter [debyte], *v.i.* **1.** to make one's first appearance (on the stage). **2.** to begin, start.

décacheter [dekaʃte], *v.tr.* (*conj. like* CACHETER) to unseal, break open (letter).

décade [dekad], *s.f.* decade.

décadence [dekadã:s], *s.f.* decadence, decline, decay.

décadent [dekadã], *a.* decadent; in decay.

décaféinler [dekafeine], *v.tr.* to decaffeinize; **café décaféiné**, caffeine-free coffee; *s.f.* **-ation**.

décalaminler [dekalamine], *v.tr. Aut:* to decarbonize, *F:* decoke; *s.m.* **-age**.

décamper [dekãpe], *v.i. F:* to clear off, beat it.

décanter [dekãte], *v.tr.* to decant, pour off.

décapitler [dekapite], *v.tr.* to decapitate, behead; *s.f.* **-ation**.

décapotable [dekapɔtabl], *a. & s.m. Aut:* convertible.

décapsuller [dekapsyle], *v.tr.* to open (a bottle); *s.m.* **-ateur**, bottle opener.

décéder [desede], *v.i.* (*conj. like* CÉDER; *aux.* être) to die.

déceler [desle], *v.tr.* (**je décèle**) to disclose (fraud); to divulge, betray (secret).

décembre [desã:br], *s.m.* December; **au mois de d., en d.**, in the month of) December; **le premier, le sept, d.**, (on) the first, the seventh, of December.

décence [desã:s], *s.f.* (*a*) decency; (*b*) propriety; **choquer la d.**, to shock the proprieties.

déclent [desã], *a.* (*a*) decent; modest (dress, etc.); (*b*) proper, seemly (behaviour); *adv.* **-emment**, decently.

décentralisler [desãtralize], *v.tr.* to decentralize; *s.f.* **-ation**.

déception [desɛpsjõ], *s.f.* disappointment.

décerner [desɛrne], *v.tr.* to award, bestow (a prize, honour, etc.).

décès [desɛ], *s.m.* decease, death; **acte de d.**, death certificate.

décevloir [desəvwa:r], *v.tr.* (*conj. like* RECEVOIR). **1.** to deceive, delude. **2.** to disappoint; *a.* **-ant**, deceptive; disappointing.

déchaînler [deʃene], *v.tr.* to unchain, to let loose; *s.m.* **-ement**.

se déchaîner, to break out; **la tempête se déchaîna**, the storm broke.

décharge [deʃarʒ], *s.f.* **1.** (*a*) unloading (of cart); discharging (of cargo); (*b*) discharge (of firearm); (*c*) *El:* discharge. **2.** (*a*) relief, easing; (*b*) **obtenir une d. sur un impôt**, to obtain a rebate on a tax; (*c*) **témoin à d.**, witness for the defence; (*d*) release (of accused person). **3.** discharge, outlet; **tuyau de d.**, waste-pipe. **4.** (**lieu de**) **d. publique**, (town) rubbish dump.

déchargler [deʃarʒe], *v.tr.* (*n.* **déchargeons**). **1.** (*a*) to unload (cart); to discharge (cargo); (*b*) to unload (firearm); (*c*) **d. son cœur**, to unburden one's heart; (*d*) **d. son fusil sur qn**, to fire one's gun at s.o.; **d. sa colère sur qn**, to vent one's anger on s.o.; (*e*) to discharge (accumulator). **2.** (*a*) to lighten (ship); (*b*) **d. qn d'une accusation**, to acquit s.o. of a charge; **d. qn d'une dette**, to remit a debt; *s.m.* **-ement**.

se décharger. 1. (*a*) (*of gun*) to go off; (*b*) (*of anger*) to vent itself (**sur**, on). **2. se d. d'un fardeau**, to lay down a burden.

décharné [deʃarne], *a.* emaciated (limbs); gaunt (face); bony (fingers).

déchausser (se) [sədeʃose], *v.pr.* to take off one's shoes.

déchéance [deʃeã:s], *s.f.* **1.** downfall. **2.** lapse (of rights); expiration (of insurance policy).

déchet [deʃɛ], *s.m. usu. pl.* waste, refuse; **déchets radioactifs**, radioactive waste; **déchets de viande**, scraps.

déchiffrler [deʃifre], *v.tr.* to decipher, make out (inscription); to decode (message); *a.* **-able**, legible; *s.m.* **-ement**.

déchiqueté [deʃikte], *a.* jagged (edge).

déchiqueter [deʃikte], *v.tr.* (**je déchiquette**) to cut into strips, into shreds.

déchirler [deʃire], *v.tr.* to tear (garment); to tear up (paper); to tear open (envelope); **sons qui déchirent l'oreille**, ear-splitting sounds; **cris qui déchiraient le cœur**, heart-rending cries; *a.* **-ant**, heart-rending, harrowing; *s.m.* **-ement**, tearing.

déchu [deʃy], *a.* fallen; lapsed (policy).

décidé [deside], *a.* **1. chose décidée**, settled matter. **2.** resolute (person); determined (character). **3. être d. à faire qch.**, to be determined to do sth. **4. avoir une supériorité décidée sur qn**, to have decided superiority over s.o.; *adv.* **-ment**.

décider [deside], *v.tr.* **1.** (*a*) to decide, settle (question, dispute); **voilà qui décide tout!** that settles it! (*b*) **l'assemblée décida la guerre**, the assembly decided on war. **2. d. qn à faire qch.**, to persuade, induce, s.o. to do sth. **3.** *abs.* (*a*) **il faut que je décide**, I must make up my mind; (*b*) **d. de qch.**, to decide sth. **4. d. + *inf.*,** to decide (after deliberation) to (do sth.); **d. que + *ind.*,** to decide, settle, that . . . .

se décider. 1. to make up one's mind. **2. je ne puis pas me d. à le faire,** I cannot bring myself to do it. **3. se d. pour qn,** to decide in favour of s.o.

décimal, *pl.* **-aux** [desimal, -o], *a.* decimal.

décimale [desimal], *s.f.* decimal (fraction).

décim|er [desime], *v.tr.* to decimate; *s.f.* **-ation.**

décis|if, -ive [desizif, -i:v], *a.* **1.** decisive (battle); conclusive (evidence); critical, crucial (moment). **2.** peremptory (tone); *adv.* **-ivement.**

décision [desizjɔ̃], *s.f.* decision. **1.** (*a*) **forcer une d.,** to bring matters to a head; (*b*) *Jur:* ruling; award. **2.** resolution, determination.

déclam|er [deklame]. **1.** *v.tr.* to declaim (speech). **2.** *v.i.* to rant, spout; **d. contre qn,** to inveigh against s.o.; *s.f.* **-ation,** oratory; harangue; ranting; *a.* **-atoire,** declamatory.

déclar|er [deklare], *v.tr.* **1.** (*a*) to declare, make known (one's intentions); (*b*) *Cards:* **d. trèfle,** to call clubs. **2.** to declare, announce; (*a*) *pred.* **déclaré coupable,** found guilty; (*b*) to notify (birth); (*c*) **d. la guerre à qn,** to declare war on s.o.; (*d*) *Cust:* **avez-vous quelque chose à d.?** have you anything to declare? *s.f.* **-ation, d. sur serment,** affidavit.

se déclarer. 1. (*a*) **se d. pour qch.,** to declare for sth.; (*b*) to declare one's love. **2.** (*of fire, disease*) to break out.

déclench|er [deklɑ̃ʃe], *v.tr.* **1.** to unlatch (door). **2.** to release (mechanism). **3.** to set (machine) in motion; *s.m.* **-ement.**

déclic [deklik], *s.m.* **1.** pawl, catch; trigger. **2.** click.

déclin [deklɛ̃], *s.m.* decline, close (of day); waning (of moon); falling off; **au d. de sa vie,** in his declining years.

déclinaison [deklinɛzɔ̃], *s.f. Gram:* declension.

déclin|er [dekline]. **1.** *v.i.* (*of moon*) to wane. **2.** *v.tr.* to decline, refuse (offer). **3.** *v.tr. Gram:* to decline (noun).

déclivité [deklivite], *s.f.* declivity, slope, incline.

décocher [dekɔʃe], *v.tr. F:* **d. un coup à qn,** to hit out at s.o.; **d. un juron,** to rap out an oath.

décoiffer (se) [sədekwafe], *v.pr.* **1.** to take off one's hat. **2.** to get one's hair in a mess.

décolérer [dekɔlere], *v.i.* (**je décolère); je décolérerai**) *F:* to calm down; (*used esp. in the neg.*); **il ne décolérait pas,** he was still fuming.

décoll|er [dekɔle]. **1.** *v.tr.* to unstick, unglue. **2.** *v.i.* (*of aircraft*) to take off; *s.m.* **-age,** take-off.

décolleté [dekɔlte]. **1.** *a.* low-necked (dress). **2.** *s.m.* neck-line (of dress); **d. carré, en pointe,** square neck, V neck.

décoloration [dekɔlɔrasjɔ̃], *s.f.* discolouration.

décombres [dekɔ̃:br], *s.m.pl.* rubbish, debris (of building); ruins.

décommander [dekɔmɑ̃de], *v.tr.* to countermand; to cancel (meeting, etc.); **d. une grève,** to call off a strike.

décomposé [dekɔ̃poze], *a.* **visage d.,** drawn face; face distorted by grief or terror.

décompos|er [dekɔ̃poze], *v.tr.* **1.** to decompose (organic matter). **2.** to convulse, distort (face); *s.f.* **-ition.**

se décomposer. 1. (*of organic matter*) to rot, decay. **2.** (*of face*) to become convulsed.

déconcerté [dekɔ̃sɛrte], *a.* disconcerted, taken aback.

déconcerter [dekɔ̃sɛrte], *v.tr.* **1.** to upset (s.o.'s plans). **2.** to disconcert (s.o.).

se déconcerter, to lose one's assurance; **sans se d.,** unabashed.

déconseiller [dekɔ̃seje], *v.tr.* **d. qch. à qn,** to advise s.o. against sth.

décontenancer [dekɔ̃tnɑ̃se], *v.tr.* (**n. décontenançons**) to put (s.o.) out of countenance.

déconvenue [dekɔ̃vny], *s.f.* disappointment; mortification.

décor [dekɔ:r], *s.m.* **1.** decoration (of house, etc.). **2.** *Th:* scenery; *Aut: F:* **rentrer dans le d.,** to run off the road (into sth.); **peintre de décors,** scene-painter.

décor|er [dekɔre], *v.tr.* **1.** to decorate, ornament; *F:* to do up (house, etc.). **2.** to decorate (s.o.); *s.m.* **-ateur,** (house-)decorator; *a.* **-atif, -ative,** decorative; *s.f.* **-ation.**

décorum [dekɔrɔm], *s.m.* decorum.

découp|er [dekupe], *v.tr.* **1.** to cut up (paper); to carve (fowl); **couteau à d.,** carving-knife. **2.** to cut out (design); **d. un article dans un journal,** to cut out an article out of a newspaper; **scie à d.,** fret-saw; *s.f.* **-ure,** (i) cutting out; fretwork; (ii) (newspaper) cutting; (iii) indentation.

se découper, to stand out, show up (**sur,** against).

décourag|er [dekuraʒe], *v.tr.* (**n. décourageons). 1.** to discourage, dishearten. **2. d. un projet,** to discourage, *F:* pour cold water on, a scheme; *s.m.* **-ement.**

se décourager, to become disheartened, to lose heart.

décousu [dekuzy], *a.* (*a*) unsewn, unstitched (seam); (*b*) disconnected, disjointed (words, ideas); rambling (remarks); scrappy (conversation).

découvert [dekuvɛ:r]. **1.** *a.* (*a*) uncovered; **à visage d.,** openly, frankly; (*b*) open (country). **2. à d.,** uncovered, unprotected; *Fin:* overdrawn; **parler à d.,** to speak openly; **mettre qch. à d.,** to expose sth. to view.

découverte [dekuvɛrt], *s.f.* **1.** discovery (of land); **aller à la d.,** to explore, prospect. **2.** discovery, exposure (of plot).

découvrir [dekuvri:r], *v.tr.* (*conj. like* OUVRIR). **1.** (*a*) to uncover; (*b*) to lay bare; to unveil (statue); to disclose (secret); **d. ses dents,** to show one's teeth. **2.** to perceive, discern. **3.** *(a)* to discover (plot); to detect (criminal); *(b)* to discover (oxygen).

se découvrir. 1. to take off one's hat. **2.** *(of sky)* to clear up. **3.** to come to light.

décrass|er [dekrase], *v.tr.* to clean, cleanse, scour; to scale (boiler, etc.); *s.m.* -**age**; *s.m.* -**ement.**

décrépit [dekrepi], *a.* decrepit, senile; dilapidated.

décret [dekrɛ], *s.m.* decree; fiat, order.

décréter [dekrete], *v.tr.* (**je décrète; je décréterai**) to decree; to enact (law).

décrier [dekrie], *v.tr.* to disparage, decry (s.o.); to run (s.o., sth.) down.

décrire [dekriːr], *v.tr.* (*conj. like* ÉCRIRE). **1.** to describe (a sight). **2.** to describe (circle).

décroch|er [dekrɔʃe], *v.tr.* to take down (coat from peg); to disconnect (railway carriages); to take off, lift (telephone receiver); **d. le grand succès,** to make a big hit; *s.m.* -**age.**

décroissance [dekrwasãːs], *s.f.* decrease; diminution; wane (of the moon).

décroître [dekrwaːtr, -wɑ-], *v.i.* (*conj. like* CROÎTRE, *except p.p.* **décru**) to decrease, diminish; **aller (en) décroissant,** to decrease gradually.

décrotter [dekrɔte], *v.tr.* to clean (boots).

dédaigner [dedɛɲe], *v.tr.* to scorn, disdain; **cette offre n'est pas à d.,** this offer is not to be disdained.

dédaign|eux, -euse [dedɛɲø, -øːz], *a.* disdainful; scornful; *adv.* -**eusement.**

dédain [dedɛ̃], *s.m.* disdain, scorn; **avoir le d. de qch.,** to have a contempt for sth.

dedans [dədã]. **1.** *adv.* inside; within; in (it); *F:* **mettre qn d.,** to take s.o. in; **donner d.,** to fall into the trap; **en d.,** (on the) inside; within; **en d. de,** within. **2.** *s.m.* inside, interior (of house); **au d.,** (on the) inside; within; **au d. de,** inside, within.

dédicace [dedikas], *s.f.* dedication.

dédier [dedje], *v.tr.* to dedicate.

dédire (se) [sədediːr], *v.pr.* (*conj. like* DIRE, *except pr.ind.* **v.v. dédisez**) to retract (a statement); **se d. d'une promesse,** to go back on one's word.

dédit [dedi], *s.m.* **1.** retraction, withdrawal. **2.** breaking (of promise). **3.** penalty (for breaking contract, etc.).

dédommag|er [dedɔmaʒe], *v.tr.* (**n. dédommageons**) to compensate (s.o.); to make amends to (s.o.); **se faire d.,** to receive compensation; *s.m.* -**ement,** compensation, damages.

dédouan|er [dedwane], *v.tr.* to clear (goods) through the customs; *s.m.* -**ement.**

déduct|ion [dedyksjɔ̃], *s.f.* **1.** deduction, inference. **2.** *Com:* deduction, allowance; '**sans d.,**' 'terms net cash'; *a.* -**if, -ive,** deductive

(reasoning).

déduire [dedɥiːr], *v.tr.* (*conj. like* CONDUIRE). **1.** to deduce, infer. **2.** to deduct.

déesse [deɛs], *s.f.* goddess.

défaillance [defajãːs], *s.f.* *(a)* **la d. de ses forces,** the failing of his strength; **moment de d.,** weak moment; **d. de mémoire,** lapse of memory; *(b)* fainting fit; **tomber en d.,** to faint.

défaillir [defajiːr], *v.i. def.* (*pr.p.* **défaillant;** *pr.ind.* **je défaille;** *fu.* **je défaillirai**) *(a)* to become feeble; *(b)* to fail (in one's duty); **sans d.,** without flinching; *(c)* to faint.

défaire [defɛːr], *v.tr.* (*conj. like* FAIRE). **1.** to demolish; to destroy. **2.** *(a)* to undo; to untie; *(b)* **d. qn de qn,** to rid s.o. of s.o. **3.** to defeat (army).

se défaire. 1. to become undone. **2.** *(a)* **se d. de qn,** to get rid of s.o., *F:* to bump s.o. off; *(b)* **je ne veux pas m'en d.,** I don't want to part with it.

défait [defɛ], *a.* *(a)* drawn (features); *(b)* dishevelled (hair); *(c)* defeated; *(d)* undone (knot, screw).

défaite [defɛt], *s.f.* defeat; **essuyer une d.,** to suffer a defeat.

défaut [defo], *s.m.* **1.** absence, (total) lack (of sth.); **faire d.,** (i) to be absent; (ii) to fail, to give out; **le temps me fait d.,** I can't spare the time; **les provisions font d.,** there's a scarcity of provisions; **à d. de qch.,** for lack of, failing, sth. **2.** *(a)* fault, shortcoming; **c'est là son moindre d.,** that is the last thing one can reproach him with; *(b)* defect, flaw; **mettre qn en d.,** to put s.o. on the wrong track; to baffle s.o.; **prendre qn en d.,** to catch s.o. napping.

défaveur [defavœːr], *s.f.* disfavour, discredit.

défavorable [defavɔrabl], *a.* unfavourable (à, to); *adv.* -**ment.**

défavorisé [defavɔrize], *a. & s.* underprivileged (person).

défavoriser [defavɔrize], *v.tr.* to be unfair to (s.o.).

défectif, -ive [defɛktif; -iːv], *a.* defective (verb).

défection [defɛksjɔ̃], *s.f.* defection (from a cause); **faire d.,** to desert, *F:* to rat.

défectu|eux, -euse [defɛktɥø, -øːz], *a.* defective, faulty; *adv.* -**eusement.**

défectuosité [defɛktɥozite], *s.f.* defect, flaw.

défendable [defãdabl], *a.* defensible.

défendeur, -eresse [defãdœːr, -ərɛs], *s.* *Jur:* defendant; respondent.

défendre [defãːdr], *v.tr.* **1.** *(a)* to defend (cause); to uphold (right); *(b)* to protect (**contre,** against, from). **2.** to forbid, prohibit; **d. qch. à qn,** to forbid s.o. sth.

se défendre. 1. to defend oneself. **2.** **se d. de qch.,** to protect oneself from sth.; **il ne put se d. de sourire,** he could not refrain from smiling.

défense [defãːs], *s.f.* **1.** defence; **sans d.,** unprotected, defenceless. 2. tusk (of elephant). 3. prohibition; **d. d'entrer, de fumer,** no admittance, no smoking.

défenseur [defãsœːr], *s.m.* (*a*) protector, defender; (*b*) supporter, upholder (of a cause).

défens|if, -ive [defãsif, -iːv]. 1. *a.* defensive. 2. *s.f.* **se tenir sur la défensive,** to stand on the defensive; *adv.* **-ivement.**

déférence [deferãːs], *s.f.* deference, respect.

déférer [defere], *v.i.* (**je défère; je déférerai**) **d. à qn,** to defer to s.o.

déferler [defɛrle]. 1. *v.tr. Nau:* to unfurl (sail). 2. *v.i.* (*of waves*) to break.

défi [defi], *s.m.* (*a*) challenge; **relever un d.,** to take up a challenge; (*b*) defiance; **regard de d.,** defiant look.

défiance [defjãːs], *s.f.* 1. mistrust, distrust, suspicion. 2. **d. de soi-même,** diffidence.

défiant [defjã], *a.* mistrustful, distrustful.

déficient [defisjã]. 1. *a.* deficient; **enfant d.,** mentally deficient child. 2. *s.* **déficient, -ente,** mental defective.

déficit [defisit], *s.m.* deficit; shortage.

défier [defje], *v.tr.* (*a*) to challenge; (*b*) to defy, set at defiance; (*c*) to brave, to face (danger).

se défier de qn, to mistrust, distrust, s.o.

défigurer [defigyre], *v.tr.* to disfigure (s.o., sth.); to distort (the truth).

défilé [defile], *s.m.* 1. defile, gorge. 2. procession; *Mil:* march past; *Av:* fly-past; **d. de modes,** fashion show.

défiler [defile], *v.i.* (*a*) to march past; (*b*) to walk in procession.

défini [defini], *a.* definite.

définir [definiːr], *v.tr.* to define.

se définir, to become clear, distinct.

définit|if, -ive [definitif, -iːv], *a.* definitive; final; permanent; *adv.phr.* **en définitive,** finally; *adv.* **-ivement.**

définition [definisjɔ̃], *s.f.* definition; **par d.,** by that very fact; automatically.

déflation [deflasjɔ̃], *s.f.* deflation.

défoncé [defɔ̃se], *a.* 1. stove in; battered. 2. **chemin d.,** broken, bumpy, road.

défoncer [defɔ̃se], *v.tr.* (**n. défonçons**). 1. to stave in (boat); to smash in (box). 2. to break (sth.) up.

déformation [deformasjɔ̃], *s.f.* 1. (*a*) deformation; **d. professionnelle,** occupational bias; (*b*) *Phot:* distortion (of image). 2. warping.

déformer [deforme], *v.tr.* to deform; to put (hat, etc.) out of shape; *Phot:* **image déformée,** distorted image.

défraîchi [defrɛʃi], *a.* **articles défraîchis,** (shop-) soiled, faded, goods.

défrayer [defreje], *v.tr.* (**je défraie, je défraye**) **d. qn,** to pay s.o.'s expenses; **être défrayé de tout,** to have all expenses paid.

défrich|er [defriʃe], *v.tr.* to clear, reclaim (land

for cultivation); to break (new ground); *s.m.* **-age;** *s.m.* **-ement;** *s.* **-eur, -euse,** settler, pioneer.

défunt, -unte [defœ̃, -œ̃ːt], *a. & s.* defunct, deceased.

dégagé [degaʒe], *a.* (*a*) free, untrammelled (movements); **allure dégagée,** swinging stride; (*b*) free and easy (manner).

dégag|er [degaʒe], *v.tr.* (**n. dégageons**). 1. to redeem (pledge, mortgage). 2. (*a*) to disengage; to release; **d. une ville,** to relieve a town; (*b*) to clear (road, etc.); **dégagez, s'il vous plaît!** gangway, please! 3. to emit, give off (vapour, smell); *s.m.* **-ement.**

se dégager. 1. to free oneself, to get free. 2. (*of gas*) to be given off (**de,** by), to escape. 3. to emerge, come out.

dégarn|ir [degarniːr], *v.tr.* to take the trimming off (hat, dress); to strip (bed); *s.m.* **-issement.**

se dégarnir. 1. to become bald; (*of tree*) to lose its leaves. 2. (*of room*) to empty. 3. to run oneself short of money.

dégâts [degɑ], *s.m.pl.* damage.

dégel [deʒɛl], *s.m.* thaw.

dégeler [deʒle], *v.tr. & i., v.impers.* (**il dégèle**) to thaw.

dégénéré [deʒenere], *a. & s.* degenerate.

dégénér|er [deʒenere], *v.i.* (**je dégénère; je dégénérerai**) to degenerate (**de,** from; **en,** into); *s.f.* **-ation,** degeneracy; *s.f.* **-escence.**

dégivr|er [deʒivre], *v.tr. Aut: Av:* to de-ice; *H:* to defrost; *s.m.* **-age;** *s.m.* **-eur.**

dégonfl|er [degɔ̃fle], *v.tr.* 1. to deflate (tyre). 2. to reduce (swelling). 3. *P:* to debunk; *s.m.* **-ement,** deflation; debunking.

se dégonfler, (*of tyre*) to collapse, to go flat.

dégorger [degorʒe], *v.* (**n. dégorgeons**). 1. *v.tr.* to disgorge. 2. *v.i. & pr.* (*of stream*) to overflow.

dégourd|ir [degurdiːr], *v.tr.* to remove stiffness from (the limbs); to revive (by warmth, movement); *F:* to lick (s.o.) into shape.

se dégourdir, to lose one's numb, stiff, feeling; to stretch one's limbs; *F:* (*of pers.*) to improve (in manners).

dégoût [degu], *s.m.* disgust, distaste, dislike.

dégoûté [degute], *a.* 1. disgusted (**de,** with); sick (of). 2. squeamish.

dégoût|er [degute], *v.tr.* to disgust; **d. qn de qch.,** to disgust s.o. with sth.; *a.* **-ant,** disgusting, nasty.

se dégoûter de qch., to take a dislike to sth.

dégoutter [degute], *v.i.* 1. to drip, trickle; to fall drop by drop (**de,** from). 2. to be dripping (**de,** with).

dégrad|er [degrade], *v.tr.* 1. to degrade (s.o.) (from rank, etc.). 2. to deface, damage (sth.); *a.* **-ant,** degrading, lowering; *s.f.* **-ation.** 1. degradation. 2. wear and tear.

se dégrader, to lower oneself.

dégrafer [degrafe], *v.tr.* to unfasten, undo (dress).

degré [dəgre], *s.m.* **1.** (a) step (of stair); degree (of musical scale); (b) degree (of heat). **2.** degree (of relationship); **par degrés,** by degrees, gradually; *Mth:* **équation du second d.,** quadratic equation.

dégressif, -ive [degresif, -i:v], *a.* decreasing, graded (tax, tariff).

dégringol|er [degrɛ̃gɔle], *v.tr. & i. F:* (a) to tumble down; (b) to collapse; *s.f.* -**ade,** (a) tumble; (b) collapse.

dégriser (se) [sədegrize], *v.pr.* (a) to sober up; (b) *F:* to come to one's senses.

déguenillé [degnije], *a.* ragged, tattered.

déguerpir [degɛrpi:r], *v.i. F:* (a) (of tenant) to get out; (b) to clear out, decamp.

déguis|er [degize], *v.tr.* **1.** to disguise (s.o.) (en, as sth.). **2.** to disguise, conceal (truth); **parler sans rien d.,** to speak openly; *s.m.* -**ement.**

déguster [degyste], *v.tr.* to taste; to sip; to appreciate, enjoy (meal).

dehors [dəɔ:r]. **1.** *adv.* (a) out, outside; **coucher d.,** to sleep (i) out of doors, (ii) away from home; **'ne pas se pencher d.!'** 'do not lean out of the window!' (b) **en d.,** (on the) outside; outwards; **en d. du sujet,** beside the question. **2.** *s.m.* (a) outside, exterior; (b) *usu. in pl.* (outward) appearance.

déité [deite], *s.f.* deity.

déjà [deʒa], *adv.* **1.** already; **il est d. parti,** he has already left. **2.** before, previously; **je vous ai d. vu,** I have seen you before. **3.** yet; **faut-il d. partir?** need we, you, go yet?

déjeuner [deʒœne]. **I.** *v.i.* (a) to (have) breakfast; (b) to (have) lunch. **II. déjeuner,** *s.m.* **1.** lunch; **(petit) d.,** breakfast. **2.** breakfast cup and saucer.

delà [d(ə)la], *adv.* beyond. **1.** *prep.* **par d. les mers,** beyond the seas. **2.** *adv.* **au d.,** beyond; **n'allez pas au d. de 100 francs,** don't pay more than 100 francs; *s.m.* **l'au-d.,** the beyond.

délabré [delabre], *a.* tumble-down (house); impaired (health).

délabr|er [delabre], *v.tr.* to dilapidate; to wreck, ruin (house, fortune, health); *s.m.* -**ement. se délabrer,** (of house) to fall into decay; (of health) to become impaired.

délacer [delase], *v.tr.* (n. **délaçons**) to unlace.

délai [delɛ], *s.m.* **1.** delay. **2.** respite, time allowed; **à court d.,** at short notice; **dans le plus bref d.,** as soon as possible.

délaiss|er [delɛse], *v.tr.* to forsake, desert, abandon; *s.m.* -**ement,** desertion; loneliness.

délass|er [delase], *v.tr.* to rest, refresh (s.o.); *s.m.* -**ement,** relaxation. **se délasser,** to relax.

délayer [deleje], *v.tr.* (**je délaie, délaye**) to add water to (a powder); to water (liquid); *F:* **d. un**

discours, to pad a speech.

Delco [dɛlko], *s.m. Aut: R.t.m:* distributor.

délectable [delɛktabl], *a.* delightful, pleasant.

délégué, -ée [delege], *a. & s.* (a) delegate; (b) deputy.

délég|uer [delege], *v.tr.* (**je délègue; je déléguerai**). **1. d. qn pour faire qch.,** to delegate s.o. to do sth. **2.** to delegate (powers); *s.f.* -**ation.**

délibéré [delibere], *a.* deliberate; *adv.* -**ment.**

délibér|er [delibere], *v.* (**je délibère; je délibérerai**). **1.** *v.i.* (a) to deliberate; (b) to reflect, ponder. **2.** *v.tr.* to discuss (a matter); **c'est une affaire délibérée,** the matter is settled, decided; *s.f.* -**ation.**

délicat [delika], *a.* delicate. **1.** discerning (person); tactful (behaviour). **2.** sensitive; delicate (health). **3.** difficult, tricky (job). **4.** scrupulous; fussy (about one's food); *adv.* -**ement.**

délicatesse [delikates], *s.f.* delicacy. **1.** softness (of colouring). **2.** discernment; tactfulness; **avec d.,** tactfully. **3.** fragility; delicate state (of health). **4.** difficulty, awkwardness (of situation).

délici|eux, -euse [delisjø, -ø:z], *a.* delicious; delightful; *adv.* -**eusement.**

délier [delje], *v.tr.* to untie, undo; **le vin délie la langue,** wine loosens the tongue.

délimiter [delimite], *v.tr.* to delimit, demarcate (territory); to define (powers).

délinquance [delɛ̃kɑ̃:s], *s.f.* delinquency; **d. juvénile,** juvenile delinquency.

délinquant, -ante [delɛ̃kɑ̃, -ɑ̃:t], *s.* offender, delinquent.

délire [deli:r], *s.m.* delirium.

délirer [delire], *v.i.* to be delirious; to rave.

délit [deli], *s.m.* misdemeanour, offence.

délivr|er [delivre], *v.tr.* **1.** to deliver; to rescue (captive). **2.** to deliver, hand over (goods); *s.f.* -**ance.**

déloger [delɔʒe], *v.* (*conj. like* LOGER). **1.** *v.i.* to go off, move away. **2.** *v.tr.* to eject (tenant); to dislodge; to drive (s.o.) out.

déloyal, *pl.* -**aux** [delwajal, -o], *a.* disloyal, false (friend); dishonest, unfair (practice); *Sp:* **jeu d.,** foul play.

déloyauté [delwajote], *s.f.* disloyalty, perfidy.

delta [dɛlta], *s.m.* delta; *Av:* **aile en d.,** delta wing.

déluge [dely:ʒ], *s.m.* (a) deluge, flood; torrent (of abuse); **cela remonte au d.,** it's as old as the hills; (b) *F:* downpour (of rain).

demain [dəmɛ̃], *adv. & s.m.* tomorrow; **à d.!** see you tomorrow!

demande [d(ə)mɑ̃:d], *s.f.* **1.** (a) request, application; **faire la d. de qch.,** to ask for sth.; *F:* **il faut faire une d.,** you must fill in a form; (b) *Com:* demand; **l'offre et la d.,** supply and demand; (c) petition (for divorce). **2.** question, enquiry.

demander [d(ə)mᾶde], *v.tr.* **1.** to ask (for); **d. la paix,** to sue for peace; **on vous demande,** somebody wants to see you; **d. qch. à qn,** to ask s.o. for sth.; **on nous demanda nos passeports,** we were asked for our passports; **je demande à être entendu,** I ask to be heard. **2.** to desire, need, require. **3.** to ask, enquire; **d. à qn son avis,** to ask s.o.'s opinion; **je me demande pourquoi,** I wonder why.

démangler [demᾶʒe], *v.i.* (il démangea(it); *with dative of person*) to itch; **l'épaule me démange,** my shoulder is itching; *s.f.* **-eaison,** itching.

démaquiller (se) [sədemakije], *v.pr.* to take off one's make-up; *s.m.* **-ant,** cleansing cream, make-up remover.

démarcation [demarkasjɔ̃], *s.f.* demarcation; **ligne de d.,** dividing line.

démarche [demarʃ], *s.f.* **1.** gait, walk. **2.** step; **faire les démarches nécessaires,** to take the necessary steps.

démarrler [demare]. **1.** *v.tr.* to unmoor, cast off (boat); to start (car). **2.** *v.i.* (*of vehicle*) to start; (*of ship*) to get under way; (*of pers.*) to drive off; *s.m.* **-age;** *s.m.* **-eur,** *Aut:* self-starter.

démasquer [demaske], *v.tr.* to unmask; to expose.

démêler [demεle], *v.tr.* to disentangle (string); to comb out (hair); **d. un malentendu,** to clear up a misunderstanding.
se démêler, to extricate oneself.

déménagler [demenaʒe], *v.tr. & i.* (n. déménageons) to move (house); *F:* il déménage, he's taken leave of his senses; *F:* allez! déménagez! scram! *s.m.* **-ement,** removal; *s.m.* **-eur,** furniture remover.

démence [demᾶ:s], *s.f.* insanity, madness.

démener (se) [sədemne], *v.pr.* (*conj. like* MENER). **1.** to throw oneself about; to struggle. **2.** to be active; to make great efforts (**pour faire qch.,** to do sth.).

démenti [demᾶti], *s.m.* denial, contradiction.

démentir [demᾶti:r], *v.tr.* (*conj. like* MENTIR). **1.** to contradict (s.o.); to deny (fact). **2.** to belie.
se démentir, to contradict oneself; to go back on one's word.

démesuré [demøzyre], *a.* inordinate; beyond measure; unbounded; *adv.* **-ment.**

démettre (se) [sədemεtr], *v.pr.* (*conj. like* METTRE) **se d. de ses fonctions,** to resign one's post; to retire.

demeure [dəmœ:r], *s.f.* (place of) residence, dwelling place; abode.

demeurer [dəmœre], *v.i.* **1.** (*aux.* être) to remain; to stay (in a place); **demeurons-en là,** let's leave it at that; **ne pouvoir d. en place,** to be unable to keep still. **2.** (*aux.* avoir) to live, reside.

demi, -ie [dəmi]. **1.** *a.* (*a*) half; **deux heures et demie,** (i) two and a half hours; (ii) half-past two; (*b*) semi-; half-; **d.-litre,** half-litre; *Mus:* **d.-**ton, semitone; (*c*) **d.-cuit,** half-cooked. **2.** *s.m.* (*a*) **un d.,** a large glass of beer; (*b*) *Sp:* **les demis,** the half-backs; (*c*) *adv.phr.* **à d.,** half; **à d. mort,** half-dead; **faire les choses à d.,** to do things by halves. **3.** *s.f.* **demie,** half-hour; **il est la demie,** it is half-past.

NOTE: *In all the following compounds* DEMI *is inv; the second component takes the plural. For phonetics, consult the second component.*

demi-cercle, *s.m.* semicircle, half-circle.
demi-circulaire, *a.* semicircular.
demi-douzaine, *s.f.* half-dozen.
demi-finale, *s.f. Sp:* semi-final.
demi-frère, *s.m.* half-brother.
demi-heure, *s.f.* **une d.-h.,** half an hour.
demi-mot (à), *adv.phr.* **entendre (qn) à d.-m.,** to (know how to) take a hint.
demi-pension, *s.f.* half-board.
demi-place, *s.f.* half-fare (when travelling); half-price (at theatre).
demi-sec, *a. & s.m.* medium dry (wine).
demi-sel. **1.** *s.m.* slightly salted cream cheese. **2.** *a. inv.* **beurre d.-s.,** salt(ed) butter.
demi-sœur, *s.f.* half-sister.
démission [demisjɔ̃], *s.f.* resignation (from job).
demi-tarif, *s.m.* half-fare; half-price.
demi-tour, *s.m.* half-turn; **faire d.-t.,** to turn back.
demi-voix (à), *adv.phr.* in an undertone; under one's breath.
démobiliser [demɔbilize], *v.tr.* to demobilize; *s.f.* **-ation.**
démocrate [demɔkrat], *s.m. & f.* democrat.
démocratie [demɔkrasi], *s.f.* democracy.
démocratique [demɔkratik], *a.* democratic; *adv.* **-ment.**
démodé [demɔde], *a.* old-fashioned, obsolete, out of date.
démoder (se) [sədemɔde], *v.pr.* to go out of fashion.
demoiselle [dəmwazεl], *s.f.* **1.** (*a*) spinster; single woman; **son nom de d.,** her maiden name; (*b*) **d. d'honneur,** bridesmaid. **2.** young lady. **3.** dragon-fly.
démollir [demɔli:r], *v.tr.* to demolish, pull down (building); to ruin (reputation); *s.f.* **-ition.**
démon [demɔ̃], *s.m.* demon, devil, fiend.
démonstratlif, -ive [demɔ̃stratif, -i:v], *a.* demonstrative; *adv.* **-ivement.**
démonstration [demɔ̃strasjɔ̃], *s.f.* demonstration.
démonté [demɔ̃te], *a.* **1.** dismounted (cavalry). **2.** stormy (sea). **3.** (*of pers.*) flustered. **4.** (*of mechanism*) in pieces, dismantled.
démonte-pneu [demɔ̃tpnø], *s.m.* tyre-lever; *pl.* démonte-pneus.
démonter [demɔ̃te], *v.tr.* **1.** to unhorse, unseat (rider); **se laisser d.,** to get upset. **2.** to take down, dismantle; to remove (tyre).

se démonter, (a) (of mechanism) to come apart; (b) F: il ne se démonte pas pour si peu, he's not so easily put out.

démontr|er [demɔ̃tre], v.tr. 1. to demonstrate, to prove (the truth of sth.). 2. to indicate, show (sth.) clearly; a. -able, demonstrable.

démoralis|er [demɔralize], v.tr. to demoralize. 1. to corrupt, deprave. 2. to dishearten; s.f. -ation.

se démoraliser, to become demoralized.

démordre [demɔrdr], v.i. (usu. with neg.) ne pas d. de ses opinions, to stick to one's opinions.

démuni [demyni], a. unprovided (de, with); Com: être d. de (qch.), to be out of (an article).

démunir (se) [sədemyni:r], v.pr. se d. de qch., to part with sth.

dénaturé [denatyre], a. unnatural; hard-hearted; perverted (taste).

dénaturer [denatyre], v.tr. to misrepresent, distort (words); d. les faits, to garble the facts.

dénégation [denegasjɔ̃], s.f. denial.

dénich|er [deniʃe], v.tr. (a) to find, discover; comment m'avez-vous déniché? how did you ferret me out, discover my whereabouts? nous avons déniché un bon chauffeur, we have unearthed a good chauffeur; (b) to dislodge (bird); to rout out (animal); s.m. -ement.

dénier [denje], v.tr. to deny (crime).

dénigr|er [denigre], v.tr. to disparage; to run down; s.m. -ement.

dénombrement [denɔ̃brəmɑ̃], s.m. enumeration, counting; census.

dénombrer [denɔ̃bre], v.tr. to count; to take a census of.

dénominateur [denɔminatœ:r], s.m. denominator.

dénomination [denɔminasjɔ̃], s.f. denomination, name.

dénommer [denɔme], v.tr. to denominate, name; F: un dénommé Charles, a man named Charles.

dénonc|er [denɔ̃se], v.tr. (n. dénonçons) 1. to declare, proclaim. 2. (a) to denounce (s.o.); se d., to give oneself up; (b) to expose (vice); s.f. -iation.

dénonciateur, -trice [denɔ̃sjatœ:r, -tris]. 1. s. informer. 2. a. tell-tale (look).

dénoter [denɔte], v.tr. to denote, betoken.

dénouer [denwe], v.tr. 1. to unknot; to untie, undo; d. une intrigue, to unravel a plot. 2. to loosen (the tongue).

denrée [dɑ̃re], s.f. commodity; usu. pl. produce; denrées alimentaires, food(stuffs).

dense [dɑ̃:s], a. dense, crowded; close.

densité [dɑ̃site], s.f. denseness, density.

dent [dɑ̃], s.f. 1. tooth; avoir mal aux dents, to have toothache; se faire arracher une d., to have a tooth out; coup de d., bite; n'avoir rien à se mettre sous la d., to have nothing to eat;

jouer des dents, to munch away; rire à belles dents, to laugh heartily; manger du bout des dents, to pick at one's food; rire du bout des dents, to force a laugh; avoir les dents longues, (i) to be very hungry; (ii) to be grasping; garder une d. contre qn, to have a grudge against s.o.; être sur les dents, to be on edge. 2. tooth (of saw); cog (of wheel); prong (of fork).

denté [dɑ̃te], a. cogged, toothed (wheel).

dentelé [dɑ̃tle], a. notched, indented; serrated.

dentelle [dɑ̃tɛl], s.f. lace.

dentelure [dɑ̃tly:r], s.f. indentation; jagged outline (of coast).

dentier [dɑ̃tje], s.m. set of false teeth, denture.

dentifrice [dɑ̃tifris], s.m. tooth-paste, -powder; mouth-wash.

dentiste [dɑ̃tist], s.m. & f. dentist.

denture [dɑ̃ty:r], s.f. 1. set of (natural) teeth. 2. serrated edge. 3. Mec.E: cogs.

dénucléaris|er [denyklearize], v.tr. to free (zone) from nuclear weapons; s.f. -ation.

dénuder [denyde], v.tr. to denude, to lay bare, strip.

dénué [denɥe], a. without, short of; d. d'argent, without money; d. de raison, senseless; d. d'intelligence, devoid of intelligence.

dénu|er [denɥe], v.tr. to divest, strip (de, of); s.m. -ement, destitution, lack (of ideas, etc.).

dépann|er [depane], v.tr. to do emergency repairs to (car, etc.); to help (s.o.) out; s.m. -age, breakdown service; s.m. -eur, breakdown mechanic; s.f. -euse, breakdown lorry, N.Am: truck.

départ [depa:r], s.m. departure, starting; point de d., starting point; prix d. usine, price ex works.

département [departəmɑ̃], s.m. Adm: department.

dépassé [depase], a. out-of-date (state of knowledge, science, book, etc.).

dépasser [depase], v.tr. 1. (a) to pass beyond; d. le but, to overshoot the mark; d. les bornes, to overstep the bounds; (b) d. qn (à la course), to overtake, outstrip, s.o. 2. d. qn de la tête, to stand a head taller than s.o.; F: cela me dépasse, it's beyond me. 3. to exceed; d. la limite de vitesse, to exceed the speed-limit.

dépaysé [depeize], a. out of one's element; at a loss.

dép|ecer [depase], v.tr. (je dépèce) to cut up (carcass); to carve (meat); s.m. -ècement.

dépêche [depeʃ], s.f. (a) (official) despatch; (b) telegram.

dépêcher [depeʃe], v.tr. to dispatch.

se dépêcher, to hurry, to make haste; dépêchez vous! hurry up!

dépeigner [depeɲe], v.tr. to make (s.o.'s) hair untidy; personne dépeignée, unkempt person.

dépeindre [depɛ̃:dr], v.tr. (conj. like PEINDRE) to

depict, picture, describe (s.o., sth.).

dépendance [depãdã:s], *s.f.* **1.** dependence. **2.** (*a*) dependency (of a country); (*b*) *pl.* outbuildings. **3.** subjection; **être sous la d. de qn,** to be under s.o.'s domination.

dépend|re [depã:dr], *v.i.* to depend (**de,** on); **cela dépend,** that depends; we shall see; *a.* **-ant,** dependent (**de,** on).

dépens [depã], *s.m.pl. Com:* cost, expenses; **aux d. de qn,** at s.o.'s expense.

dépense [depã:s], *s.f.* expenditure, outlay (of money), expense.

dépenser [depãse], *v.tr.* **1.** to spend (money). **2.** to spend, consume (energy).

dépér|ir [deperi:r], *v.i.* to waste away; to wither; *s.m.* **-issement.**

dépeupl|er [depœple], *v.tr.* to depopulate; *s.m.* **-ement.**

dépist|er [depiste], *v.tr.* **1.** to track down. **2.** to outwit (s.o.); to put (s.o.) off the scent. **3.** to detect, to trace, to track (an epidemic, etc.); *s.m.* **-age.**

dépit [depi], *s.m.* spite, resentment; **par d.,** out of spite; **pleurer de d.,** to cry with vexation; **en d. de . . .,** in spite of. . . .

dépiter [depite], *v.tr.* to vex, to spite (s.o.).

se dépiter, to take offence; to be annoyed.

déplacé [deplase], *a.* out of place, ill-timed; *Pol:* **personnes déplacées,** displaced persons.

déplac|er [deplase], *v.tr.* (**n. déplaçons**) **1.** to displace; **d. un fonctionnaire,** to transfer a civil servant. **2.** to take the place of (s.o.); *s.m.* **-ement,** journey, movement(s).

se déplacer, (*a*) to move about, to travel; (*b*) to get out of place.

déplaire [deple:r], *v.ind.tr.* (*conj. like* PLAIRE) **d. à qn,** to displease s.o.; **ils se déplaisent,** they dislike each other.

se déplaire, to be displeased, dissatisfied; **se d. à Paris,** to dislike (living in) Paris.

déplaisant [deplezã], *a.* unpleasing, unpleasant.

dépliant [deplijã], *s.m.* folding map, etc; *Com:* folder.

déplier [deplie], *v.tr.* to unfold, spread out (newspaper, sheet, etc.).

déplor|er [deplɔre], *v.tr.* to deplore, lament; to regret; *a.* **-able,** deplorable, regrettable.

déployer [deplwaje], *v.tr.* (**je déploie**) **1.** to unfold, spread out; to unfurl (flag); *Mil:* to deploy (troops). **2.** to display (goods).

déplumer [deplyme], *v.tr.* to pluck (chicken).

se déplumer. 1. to moult. **2.** *F:* (*of pers.*) to become bald.

dépopulation [depɔpylasjɔ̃], *s.f.* depopulation.

déport|er [depɔrte], *v.tr.* to deport; *s.f.* **-ation.**

déposer [depoze], *v.tr.* **1.** (*a*) to deposit; to set (sth.) down; **ma voiture vous déposera à l'hôtel,** my car will drop you at the hotel; (*b*) (*of liquid*) to deposit (sediment). **2.** (*a*) **d. son**

argent à la banque, to deposit one's money at the bank; (*b*) *Com:* to register (trade-mark); (*c*) *Jur:* **d. une plainte,** to lodge a complaint; (*d*) *abs.* **d. (en justice),** to give evidence. **3.** to depose (king).

dépositaire [depozite:r], *s.m. & f.* **1.** depositary, trustee. **2.** (*a*) *Com:* sole agent; (*b*) **d. de journaux,** newsagent.

déposition [depozisjɔ̃], *s.f.* **1.** *Jur:* deposition; statement. **2.** deposing, deposition (of king).

dépôt [depo], *s.m.* **1.** (*a*) depositing; (*b*) deposit; **d. en banque,** bank deposit; **marchandises en d.,** (i) goods in bond; (ii) goods on sale or return. **2.** depository, depot; **d. de marchandises,** warehouse. **3.** deposit, sediment.

dépouille [depu:j], *s.f.* **1.** skin, hide (taken from animal); **d. mortelle,** mortal remains. **2.** *usu. pl.* spoils, booty.

dépouill|er [depuje], *v.tr.* **1.** to skin (eel). **2.** to deprive (**de,** of); to despoil; **d. un câble,** to strip a cable; *Art: etc:* **style dépouillé,** sober, severe, style. **3.** to analyse, to go through; **d. le scrutin,** to count the votes; **d. le courrier,** to open the mail; *s.m.* **-ement.**

se dépouiller, (*of reptile*) to cast its skin; (*of tree*) to shed its leaves.

dépourvu [depurvy], *a.* destitute, devoid (**de,** of); **pays d. d'arbres,** treeless country; **être pris au d.,** to be caught unawares.

dépravé [deprave], *a.* depraved.

dépréci|er [depresje], *v.tr.* **1.** to depreciate. **2.** (*a*) to underrate, undervalue; (*b*) to disparage; *a.* & *s.* **-ateur, -atrice,** (*a*) *a.* disparaging; (*b*) *s.* disparager; *s.f.* **-ation.**

se déprécier, to depreciate (in value).

dépression [depresjɔ̃], *s.f.* **1.** hollow, dip. **2.** **d. économique,** economic depression. **3.** *Meteor:* depression. **4.** depression; dejection.

déprimer [deprime], *v.tr.* to depress.

depuis [dǝpųi], *prep.* **1.** (*a*) (*of time*) since, for; **d. quand êtes-vous ici?** how long have you been here? **d. son enfance,** from childhood; (*b*) *adv.* since (then); afterwards, later; (*c*) **d. que** + *ind.,** since. . . . **2.** (*time, place*) from; **d. le matin jusqu'au soir,** from morning till night.

député [depyte], *s.m.* delegate; member of Parliament.

députer [depyte], *v.tr.* to depute (s.o.); to appoint (s.o.) as deputy; *s.f.* **-ation,** deputation, delegation.

déraciner [derasine], *v.tr.* **1.** to uproot; **se sentir déraciné,** to feel like a fish out of water. **2.** to eradicate (fault, abuse).

dérailler [derɑje], *v.i.* (*of train*) to become derailed; *F:* **il déraille,** he's talking nonsense.

déraisonn|er [derɛzɔne], *v.i.* to talk nonsense; *a.* **-able,** unreasonable; foolish.

dérang|er [derɑ̃ʒe], *v.tr.* (**n. dérangeons**) (*a*) to disarrange (papers); (*b*) to disturb, trouble; **si**

cela ne vous dérange pas, if it's no trouble to you; (c) to upset (plans); *s.m.* **-ement; en d.,** out of order.

se déranger, to move; **ne vous dérangez pas,** please don't move, don't trouble (yourself); **se d. pour obliger qn,** to go óut of one's way to oblige s.o.

déraper [derape], *v.i. Aut:* to skid.

déréglé [deregle], *a.* **1.** out of order. **2.** lawless; wild (life); immoderate (desires).

déréglement [dereɡləmɑ̃], *s.m.* **1.** disordered state; irregularity. **2.** dissoluteness, profligacy.

dérégler [deregle], *v.tr.* (**je dérègle; je déréglerai**) to upset, disarrange, disorder.

dérider [deride], *v.tr.* tò smoothe, to unwrinkle; *F:* to cheer (s.o.) up.

se dérider, to brighten up, to stop frowning.

dérision [derizjɔ̃], *s.f.* derision, mockery; **tourner qn en d.,** to hold s.o. up to ridicule.

dérisoire [derizwaːr], *a.* ridiculous, laughable (offer, etc.); absurdly low (price).

dérive [deriːv], *s.f.* leeway, drift; **aller en d.,** to drift; **à la d.,** adrift.

dériv|er[1] [derive]. **1.** *v.tr.* (a) to divert (stream); (b) *Ling:* to derive. **2.** *v.i.* to be derived (from a source); *s.f.* **-ation,** (i) diversion; (ii) derivation.

dériver[2], *v.i. Nau:* to drift.

dern|ier, -ière [dɛrnje, -jɛːr], *a. & s.* **1.** last, latest; (a) **faire un d. effort,** to make a final effort; **il arriva le d.,** he arrived last; **dans ces derniers temps,** latterly; **la dernière mode,** the latest fashion; (b) (*last of series*) **le mois d.,** last month; **le d. élève de la classe,** the bottom boy in the form; (c) **ce d. répondit . . .,** the latter answered. . . . **2.** (a) utmost, highest; **au d. degré,** to the highest degree; **entrer dans les derniers détails,** to enter into the minutest details; (b) lowest, worst; **le d. prix,** the lowest price; **le d. de mes soucis,** the least of my worries; **le d. des derniers,** the lowest of the low; *adv.* **-èrement.**

dérobé [derɔbe], *a.* hidden, concealed; **à la dérobée,** stealthily, secretly.

dérober [derɔbe], *v.tr.* **1.** (a) to steal, to make away with (sth.); (b) **d. qn au danger,** to save s.o. from danger. **2.** to hide, conceal.

se dérober. 1. to escape, steal away, slip away (à, from); **se d. aux coups,** to dodge the blows. **2. le sol se déroba,** the ground gave way.

dérouler [derule], *v.tr.* to unroll; to unwind.

se dérouler, to unfold; **le paysage se déroule devant nous,** the landscape spreads out before us; **les événements qui se déroulent,** the events which are taking place.

déroute [derut], *s.f.* rout; **être en (pleine) d.,** to be in (full) flight.

dérouter [derute], *v.tr.* **1.** (a) to lead (s.o.) astray; **d. les soupçons,** to throw s.o. off the scent; (b)

to divert (traffic). **2.** to confuse, baffle.

derrière [dɛrjɛːr]. **1.** *prep.* behind, at the back o (sth.); **laisser qn d. soi,** to leave s.o. behind. **2** *adv.* (a) behind, at the back, in the rear; **at taquer qn par d.,** to attack s.o. from behind **pattes de d.,** hind legs; (b) *Nau:* aft. **3.** *s.m.* (a back, rear (of building, etc.); (b) *F:* behind backside, bottom.

des [de, dɛ] = **de les;** *see* DE *and* LE.

dès [dɛ], *prep.* since, from; as early as; **d. s jeunesse . . .,** from childhood . . .; **d. l'abord** from the outset; **d. le matin,** first thing in th morning; **je commencerai d. aujourd'hui,** I wil begin this very day; *conj.phr.* **d. que** + *ind.* d **qu'il sera arrivé,** as soon as he arrives; *adv.phr* **d. lors,** ever since (then).

désabusé [dezabyze], *a. & s.* disillusioned, em bittered; **c'est un d.,** he's a disappointed man

désabuser [dezabyze], *v.tr.* to disabuse, un deceive (s.o.).

se désabuser (de qch.), to lose one's illusion (about sth.); to have one's eyes opened.

désaccord [dezakɔːr], *s.m.* **1.** (a) disagreemen dissension; (b) clash (of interests). **2.** *Mus:* dis cord; **en d.,** out of tune.

désagréable [dezagreabl], *a.* disagreeable, un pleasant; *adv.* **-ment.**

désagrég|er [dezagreʒe], *v.tr.* (**je désagrège, n désagrégeons; je désagrégerai**) to disintegrate *s.f.* **-ation.**

se désagréger, to break up.

désagrément [dezagremɑ̃], *s.m.* source of an noyance; nuisance.

désaltérant [dezalterɑ̃]. **1.** *a.* thirst-quenching **2.** *s.m.* thirst-quencher.

désaltérer (se) [sədezaltere], *v.pr.* (**je m désaltère; je me désaltérerai**) to quench one' thirst.

désappoint|er [dezapwɛ̃te], *v.tr.* to disappoint *s.m.* **-ement.**

désapprobateur, -trice [dezaprɔbatœːr, -tris] **1.** *s.* disapprover. **2.** *a.* disapproving censorious.

désapprobation [dezaprɔbasjɔ̃], *s.f.* disap proval, disapprobation.

désapprouver [dezapruve], *v.tr.* to disapprov of, object to (sth.).

désarmé [dezarme], *a.* **1.** disarmed. **2.** unarmec defenceless.

désarm|er [dezarme]. **1.** *v.tr.* (a) to disarr (criticism, etc.); (b) to unload (gun). **2.** *v.i.* t disarm; to disband (forces); *s.m.* **-ement.**

désastre [dezastr], *s.m.* disaster, calamity.

désastr|eux, -euse [dezastrø, -øːz], *a.* dis astrous, calamitous; *adv.* **-eusement.**

désavantage [dezavɑ̃taːʒ], *s.m.* disadvantage drawback.

désavantag|eux, -euse [dezavɑ̃taʒø, -øːz], *c* disadvantageous; *adv.* **-eusement.**

désaveu [dezavø], *s.m.* disavowal, denial; disclaimer.

désavouer [dezavwe], *v.tr.* to repudiate, deny; to disown.

se désavouer, to go back on one's word.

descendre [dɛsãːdr, de-]. **I.** *v.i.* (*aux.* être, *occ.* avoir) **1.** (*a*) to descend; to come, go, down; **d. d'un arbre**, to come down from a tree; **d. en glissant**, to slide down; **le baromètre descend**, the glass is falling; (*b*) to come, go, downstairs; **il n'est pas encore descendu**, he is not down yet. **2.** (*a*) to alight; **d. de cheval**, to dismount; **tout le monde descend!** all change! (*b*) **d. à un hôtel**, to put up at a hotel; **d. chez des parents**, to stay with relations. **3. la forêt descend jusqu'à la vallée**, the forest stretches down to the valley. **4.** (*of family*) to be descended (from). **II. descendre**, *v.tr.* (*aux.* avoir) **1. d. les marches, la rue**, to go down the steps, the street. **2.** (*a*) to take, bring, (sth.) down; **d. les bagages**, to bring down the luggage; (*b*) to lower, let down; (*c*) to shoot down, bring down (partridge, man); (*d*) to put down (passengers).

escente [dɛsãːt, de-], *s.f.* **1.** (*a*) descent (from height); (ski-)run; (*b*) **d. de police**, police raid; **d. sur les lieux**, visit to the scene (of a crime). **2.** letting down, lowering; **la D. de Croix**, the Descent from the Cross. **3.** (*a*) **d. dangereuse**, dangerous hill; (*b*) **d. de bain**, bathmat; **d. de lit**, (bed-side) rug.

escriptif, -ive [dɛskriptif, -iːv], *a.* descriptive.

escription [dɛskripsjõ], *s.f.* description.

éséquilibré [dezekilibre], *a.* unbalanced (mind, person).

éséquilibrer [dezekilibre], *v.tr.* to unbalance.

ésert [dezɛr]. **1.** *a.* deserted, uninhabited (place); lonely (spot); **île déserte**, desert island. **2.** *s.m.* desert.

ésertler [dezɛrte], *v.tr.* to desert; *s.m.* **-eur**, deserter; *s.f.* **-ion**, desertion.

ésespéré [dezɛspere]. **1.** *a.* desperate; hopeless; despairing. **2.** *s.* desperate person; *adv.* **-ment**.

ésespérler [dezɛspere]. (je **désespère**; je **désespérerai**) **1.** *v.i.* to despair; to lose hope. **2.** *v.tr.* to drive (s.o.) to despair; *a.* **-ant**, heartbreaking.

désespérer, to be in despair.

ésespoir [dezɛspwaːr], *s.m.* **1.** despair; **coup de d.**, act of despair. **2.** desperation; **en d. de cause**, in desperation; as a last resort.

éshabillé [dezabije], *s.m.* Cl: housecoat.

éshabiller [dezabije], *v.tr.* to undress (s.o.).

déshabiller, to undress.

éshabituer (se) [sədezabitɥe], *v.pr.* to break oneself of the habit (**de**, of).

éshériter [dezerite], *v.tr.* to disinherit (s.o.).

éshonneur [dezɔnœːr], *s.m.* dishonour, disgrace.

déshonorler [dezɔnɔre], *v.tr.* to dishonour, disgrace; *a.* **-able**; *a.* **-ant**, discreditable.

désignler [deziɲe], *v.tr.* **1.** to show, indicate. **2.** (*a*) to appoint, fix (day, date); (*b*) **d. qn à, pour, un poste**, to appoint s.o. to a post; *s.f.* **-ation**.

désillusion [dezillyzjõ], *s.f.* disillusion.

désillusionnler [dezillyzjɔne], *v.tr.* to disillusion; *s.m.* **-ement**.

désinfectler [dezɛ̃fɛkte], *v.tr.* to disinfect; *s.m.* **-ant**; *s.f.* **-ion**.

désintéressé [dezɛ̃terɛse], *a.* (*a*) disinterested; (*b*) unselfish.

désintéressler [dezɛ̃terɛse], *v.tr.* to buy out (partner); to pay off (creditor); *s.m.* **-ement**.

se désintéresser de qch., to take (i) no further interest, (ii) no part, in sth.; to let things slide.

désinvolte [dezɛ̃vɔlt], *a.* (*a*) easy, free (gait); (*b*) airy, detached (manner); (*c*) F: cheeky (answer).

désinvolture [dezɛ̃vɔltyːr], *s.f.* unselfconsciousness; free and easy manner; **avec d.**, airily, in an off-hand manner.

désir [deziːr], *s.m.* desire (**de**, for); wish.

désirler [dezire], *v.tr.* to desire, want; to wish for (sth.); **cela laisse à d.**, it leaves something to be desired, it's not quite up to the mark; *Com:* **madame désire?** what can I show you, madam? *a.* **-able, peu d.,** undesirable.

désister (se) [sədeziste], *v.pr.* to desist (from); *abs.* to withdraw (one's candidature), to stand down; **se d. d'une demande**, to waive a claim.

désobéir [dezɔbeiːr], *v.ind.tr.* **d. à qn**, to disobey s.o.

désobéisslance [dezɔbeisãːs], *s.f.* disobedience; *a.* **-ant**, disobedient.

désobligler [dezɔbliʒe], *v.tr.* (n. **désobligeons**) **1.** to disoblige (s.o.). **2.** to offend; *a.* **-eant**, disobliging; disagreeable, ungracious; *adv.* **-eamment**.

désœuvré [dezœvre], *a.* (*of pers.*) unoccupied, idle; at a loose end.

désœuvrement [dezœvrəmã], *s.m.* idleness; **par d.**, for want of something to do.

désolé [dezɔle], *a.* **1.** desolate (region). **2. je suis d. d'apprendre . . .**, I'm very sorry to hear. . . .

désoller [dezɔle], *v.tr.* **1.** to devastate (country). **2.** to distress (s.o.); *a.* **-ant**, distressing, sad; *s.f.* **-ation**.

se désoler, to grieve.

désordonné [dezɔrdɔne], *a.* **1.** disordered; ill-regulated (life); **maison désordonnée**, (i) untidy, (ii) badly run, house. **2.** disorderly, dissolute (person, life).

désordre [dezɔrdr], *s.m.* **1.** (*a*) disorder, confusion; **cheveux en d.**, untidy hair; (*b*) *Med:* **d. nerveux**, nervous disorder. **2.** disorderliness. **3.** *pl.* disturbances, riots.

désorganis|er [dezɔrganize], *v.tr.* to dis-
organize; *s.f.* -**ation.**

désorienté [dezɔrjɑ̃te], *a.* puzzled, at a loss; **je
suis tout d.**, I'm all at sea.

désormais [dezɔrmɛ], *adv.* from now on; in
future.

despot|e [dɛspɔt], *s.m.* despot; *a.* -**ique**,
despotic; *s.m.* -**isme**, despotism.

des|sécher [deseʃe], *v.tr.* (**je dessèche; je
dessécherai**). **1.** to dry (up). **2.** to season
(wood); to wither (plant); *s.m.* -**sèchement.**
se dessécher. 1. to dry up. **2.** to wither; to waste
away.

dessein [desɛ̃], *s.m.* **1.** design, plan. **2.** intention,
purpose; **dans ce d. . . .,** with this intention
. . .; **à d.,** on purpose.

desserrer [desere], *v.tr.* to loosen (screw); to
slacken (belt); **d. son étreinte,** to relax one's
hold.

dessert [desɛr], *s.m.* dessert.

desserv|ir¹ [desɛrviːr], *v.tr.* (*conj. like* SERVIR). **1.**
Ecc: to minister to (chapel, etc.). **2.** (*of railway,
etc.*) to serve (district); *s.m. Ecc:* -**ant**, priest-
in-charge.

desservir², *v.tr.* (*conj. like* SERVIR). **1.** to clear
(the table). **2.** to do (s.o.) a bad turn.

dessin [desɛ̃], *s.m.* **1.** (*a*) (art of) drawing,
sketching; (*b*) drawing, sketch; **d. animé,**
motion-picture cartoon. **2.** design, pattern. **3.**
draughtsmanship.

dessinateur, -trice [desinatœːr, -tris], *s.* **1.**
designer, dress-designer. **2.** draughtsman,
-woman.

dessiner [desine], *v.tr.* **1.** to draw, sketch; **d. qch.
d'après nature,** to draw sth. from nature. **2.** to
design; to lay out (garden). **3.** to show, outline
(s.o.'s figure); **visage bien dessiné,** finely
chiselled face.
se dessiner, to stand out, take shape.

dessous [dəsu]. **1.** *adv.* under(neath), below,
beneath; **marcher bras dessus bras d.,** to walk
arm in arm; **vêtements de d.,** underwear; **en d.,**
underneath; down(wards); **regarder qn en d.,**
to look at s.o. furtively. **2.** *s.m.* (*a*) lower part;
d. de plat, table-mat; **avoir le d.,** to get the
worst of it; *Cl:* **d. de robe,** (under-)slip; **les d. de
la politique,** the shady side of politics.

dessus [dəsy]. **1.** *adv.* above, over; (up)on; **mettre la main d.,** to lay hands on it, on them; **en
d.,** on top; above. **2.** *s.m.* (*a*) top, upper part; **d.
de lit,** bedspread; **d. de cheminée,** mantelpiece;
le d. du panier, the pick of the bunch; (*b*) **avoir
le d.,** to have the upper hand. **3. de d.,** from, off;
tomber de d. sa chaise, to fall off one's chair.

destin [dɛstɛ̃], *s.m.* fate, destiny.

destinataire [dɛstinatɛːr], *s.m. & f.* addressee
(of letter); consignee (of goods).

destination [dɛstinasjɔ̃], *s.f.* destination; **trains
à d. de Paris,** trains for Paris.

destinée [dɛstine], *s.f.* destiny.

destiner [dɛstine], *v.tr.* **1.** to destine. **2. d. qch. à
qn,** to intend sth. for s.o.

destitu|er [dɛstitɥe], *v.tr.* to dismiss, discharg
(s.o.); to remove (official) from office; *s.f.*
-**tion**, dismissal.

destructeur, -trice [dɛstryktœːr, -tris]. **1.** *a*
destroying (agent); destructive (child). **2.** *s*
destroyer.

destructif, -ive [dɛstryktif, -iːv], *a.* destructive

destruction [dɛstryksjɔ̃], *s.f.* destruction.

désuet, -ète [desɥe, -ɛt], *a.* obsolete (word); out-
of-date (custom).

désuétude [desɥetyd], *s.f.* disuse; **mot tombé e
d.,** obsolete word.

désunir [dezyniːr], *v.tr.* to disunite, divid
(people); to disconnect (parts).

détaché [detaʃe], *a.* **1.** (*a*) loose; **pièce
détachées,** spare parts; (*b*) isolated. **2**
detached, unconcerned (manner, etc.).

détach|er¹ [detaʃe], *v.tr.* to detach; (*a*) to ur
fasten; (*b*) to separate; to cut off; *s.m.* -**emen**
detachment; indifference (**de,** to).
se détacher. 1. to come undone. **2.** to break of
un bouton s'est détaché, a button has come of
3. se d. sur le fond, to stand out against th
background.

détach|er², *v.tr.* to remove stains from (sth.
s.m. -**age**; *s.m.* -**eur**, *s.m.* -**ant**, stain remove

détail [detaːj], *s.m.* **1.** *Com:* retail; **marchand a
d.,** retailer. **2.** detail; **donner tous les détails,** t
go into all the details.

détaill|er [detaje], *v.tr.* **1.** (*a*) to divide up; (*b*) t
retail. **2.** to relate (sth.) in detail; *s.* -**ant, -ant**
retailer.

détaler [detale], *v.i.* to decamp; *F:* to beat it,
scram.

détective [detɛktiːv], *s.m.* detective
private enquiry agent.

détendre [detɑ̃ːdr], *v.tr.* to slacken, relax;
l'esprit, to relax, to calm, the mind.
se détendre, to slacken, relax; **se d. pendant u
heure,** to relax, rest, for an hour; **la situation
détend,** the situation is easing.

détendu [detɑ̃dy], *a.* slack, relaxed; **jeunes ge
très détendus,** very (i) friendly, free-and-eas
(ii) unconventional, young men.

détenir [detniːr], *v.tr.* (*conj. like* TENIR). **1. d.
record,** to hold the record. **2.** (*a*) to deta
(s.o.); (*b*) to withhold, keep back.

détente [detɑ̃ːt], *s.f.* **1.** relaxation, slackenin
easing (of situation). **2.** trigger (of gun).

détention [detɑ̃sjɔ̃], *s.f.* detentio
imprisonment.

détenu, -e [detny], *s.* prisoner.

détergent [detɛrʒɑ̃], *s.m.* detergent.

détérior|er [deterjɔre], *v.tr.* to make worse; *s.*
-**ation.**
se détériorer, to deteriorate; to spoil.

déterminé [detɛrmine], *a.* **1.** determined, definite; **dans un sens d.,** in a given direction. **2.** determined, resolute.

déterminIer [detɛrmine], *v.tr.* **1.** to fix, to settle (meeting-place). **2.** to cause; to bring (sth.) about; *s.f.* **-ation.**

déterrer [detɛre], *v.tr.* to dig up, unearth; to exhume, disinter.

détestIer [detɛste], *v.tr.* to detest, hate; **se faire d. de tous, par tout le monde,** to get oneself disliked by everyone; *a.* **-able,** hateful.

détonIer [detɔne], *v.i.* to detonate, explode; *a. & s.m.* **-ant,** explosive; *s.m.* **-ateur,** detonator; *Rail:* fog signal; *s.f.* **-ation.**

étour [detu:r], *s.m.* detour, deviation; **sans détour(s),** plainly, frankly.

étourné [deturne], *a.* indirect, circuitous, roundabout (route); **chemin d.,** by-road.

étournIer [deturne], *v.tr.* **1.** (*a*) to divert (traffic, water-course); to turn (weapon) aside; **d. la conversation,** to change the conversation; (*b*) to turn away, avert (one's eyes). **2.** to misappropriate, embezzle (funds). **3. d. un avion,** to hijack a plane; *s.m.* **-ement,** (i) diversion; (ii) misappropriation; (iii) hijacking.

e détourner, to turn away, aside.

étraquIer [detrake], *v.tr.* to put (machine) out of order; **son intervention a tout détraqué,** his intervention has upset everything; **se d. l'estomac, les nerfs,** to wreck one's stomach, one's nerves; *s.m.* **-ement,** breakdown (of machine, health).

étremper [detrɑ̃pe], *v.tr.* to moisten, soak.

étresse [detrɛs], *s.f.* distress. **1.** grief, anguish. **2.** (*a*) (financial) straits; (*b*) *esp. Av: Nau:* **signal de d.,** distress signal; *F:* S O S.

étriment [detrimɑ̃], *s.m.* detriment, loss.

étritus [detrity:s], *s.m.* rubbish; refuse.

étroit [detrwa], *s.m. Geog:* strait(s).

étromper [detrɔ̃pe], *v.tr.* to undeceive.

étruire [detrɥi:r], *v.tr.* (*conj. like* CONDUIRE). **1.** to demolish. **2.** to destroy, ruin.

ette [dɛt], *s.f.* debt.

euil [dœj], *s.m.* **1.** (*a*) mourning, sorrow; (*b*) bereavement. **2.** (*a*) mourning (clothes); **grand d.,** deep mourning; **être en d. de qn,** to be in mourning for s.o.

ux [dø; *before a vowel sound in the same word group,* døz], *num.a.inv. & s.m.* two; **Charles D.,** Charles the Second; **d. fois,** twice; **tous (les) d.,** both; **tous les d. jours,** every other day; **entre d. âges,** middle-aged; *Ten:* **à d., deuce; à d. de jeu,** five (games) all.

uxième [døzjɛm], *num. a. & s.* second; **appartement au d.** (**étage**), flat on the second, *N.Am:* third, floor; *adv.* **-ment.**

ux-points [døpwɛ̃], *s.m. Typ:* colon.

valer [devale]. **1.** *v.i.* (*a*) to hurry down; (*b*) to slope down. **2.** *v.tr.* **d. la colline,** to hurry down

the hill.

dévaliser [devalize], *v.tr.* to rob (s.o.); to burgle (a house).

dévaluIer [devalɥe], *v.tr.* to devalue (currency); *s.f.* **-ation.**

devancIer [d(ə)vɑ̃se], *v.tr.* (*n.* **devançons**). **1.** to precede. **2.** to leave behind; to outstrip. **3.** to forestall; **d. les désirs de qn,** to anticipate s.o.'s wishes; *s.m.* **-ement;** *s.* **-ier, -ière,** predecessor.

devant [d(ə)vɑ̃]. **1.** *prep.* before, in front of; **marchez tout droit d. vous,** go straight ahead. **2.** *adv.* before, in front; **aller d.,** to go in front. **3.** *s.m.* front (part), fore-part; **d. de chemise,** shirt front; **d. de cheminée,** fire-screen; **prendre les devants,** to go on ahead; **gagner les devants,** to take the lead.

devanture [d(ə)vɑ̃ty:r], *s.f.* (*a*) front(age) (of building); (*b*) **d. de magasin,** shop-front.

dévastateur, -trice [devastatœ:r, -tris]. **1.** *s.* devastator, ravager. **2.** *a.* devastating, ravaging.

dévastation [devastasjɔ̃], *s.f.* devastation.

déveine [devɛn], *s.f. F:* (run of) ill-luck; **avoir la d., être dans la d.,** to be out of luck.

développIer [devlɔpe], *v.tr.* to develop (muscles); **d. ses dons naturels,** to improve one's natural gifts; **d. un projet,** to work out a plan; *s.m.* **-ement.**

devenir [dəvni:r], *v.pred.* (*conj. like* VENIR; *aux.* **être**) (*a*) to become; **qu'est-il devenu?** what has become of him? (*b*) to grow into; **d. homme,** to grow into a man; **d. vieux,** to grow old; **c'est à d. fou!** it is enough to drive one mad!

déversIer [devɛrse], *v.tr.* to pour (water); to dump (material); *s.m.* **-ement,** overflow; tipping (of lorry); dump.

se déverser, to flow, pour (**dans,** into).

dévêtir (se) [sədeveti:r], *v.pr.* (*conj. like* VÊTIR) to undress.

déviIer [devje], *v.i.* to deviate, swerve, diverge (**de,** from); **route déviée,** diversion; **faire d.** (**une balle**), to deflect (a bullet); *s.f.* **-ation,** curvature (of the spine); deviation; (road) diversion.

devinIer [d(ə)vine], *v.tr.* to guess; **cela se devine,** that's obvious; *s.f.* **-ette,** riddle.

dévisager [deviza3e], *v.tr.* (*n.* **dévisageons**) to stare at (s.o.), look (s.o.) full in the face.

devise [dəvi:z], *s.f.* **1.** (*a*) motto; (*b*) slogan. **2.** *Fin:* currency; **devises étrangères,** foreign currency; **d. forte,** hard currency.

dévoiler [devwale], *v.tr.* **1.** to unveil. **2.** to reveal, disclose (secret, etc.).

devoir [dəvwa:r]. **I.** *v.tr.* (*pr.p.* **devant;** *p.p.* **dû,** *f.* due; *pr.ind.* **je dois, ils doivent;** *p.h.* **je dus;** *fu.* **je devrai**). **1.** (*duty*) should, ought; (*a*) (*general precept*) **tu dois honorer tes parents,** you should honour your parents; (*b*) (*command*) vous **devez vous trouver à votre poste à trois heures**, you must be at your post at three o'clock; (*c*) **je ne savais pas ce que je devais faire**, I didn't know what I ought to do; **vous devriez lire ce livre**, you should read this book; **il aurait dû m'avertir**, he should have warned me. **2.** (*compulsion*) must, have to; **enfin j'ai dû céder**, at last I had to yield. **3.** (*futurity*) am to; **je dois partir demain**, I am to start tomorrow; **je devais venir, mais . . .,** I was to have come, but . . . . **4.** (*opinion expressed*) must; **vous devez avoir faim**, you must be hungry; **il ne doit pas avoir plus de 40 ans**, he can't be more than 40. **5. d. qch. à qn**, to owe s.o. sth.; **il doit de tous les côtés**, he owes money all round; **vous me devez cent francs**, you owe me a hundred francs; **la peine due à ces forfaits**, the penalties which these crimes deserve. **II. devoir**, *s.m.* **1.** (*a*) duty; **manquer à son d.**, to fail in one's duty; **il est de mon d. de . . .,** it is my duty to . . .; (*b*) *Sch:* exercise; homework, prep. **2.** *pl.* **mes devoirs à madame votre mère**, my respects to your mother; **rendre à qn les derniers devoirs**, to pay the last honours to s.o.

dévorer [devɔre], *v.tr.* to devour; **la soif me dévore**, I am consumed with thirst; **d. la route**, to eat up the miles.

dévot, -ote [devo, -ɔt]. **1.** *a.* devout, religious. **2.** *s.* devout person; *Pej:* bigot; **faux d.**, hypocrite; *adv.* **-ement**, devoutly.

dévotion [devosjɔ̃], *s.f.* devotion; piety.

dévoué [devwe], *a.* devoted, loyal; (*letter formulae*) **votre d. serviteur**, your obedient servant; **votre tout d.** = yours sincerely; *Com:* **toujours entièrement d. à vos ordres**, always at your service.

dévouement [devumɑ̃], *s.m.* self-sacrifice; devotion (to duty).

dévouer (se) [sədevwe]. **1.** to devote oneself (to a cause). **2. se d. pour qn**, to sacrifice oneself for s.o.

dextérité [dɛksterite], *s.f.* dexterity, skill (à, in).

diabète [djabɛt], *s.m. Med:* diabetes.

diable [djabl], *s.m.* devil; **tirer le d. par la queue**, to be hard up; **du d. si je le sais!** hanged if I know! **ce n'est pas le d.**, (i) it's not so very difficult; (ii) it's nothing to worry about; **bruit de tous les diables**, devil of a din; **pauvre d.!** poor beggar! **un grand d.**, a big, strapping, fellow; **c'est un bon d.**, he's not a bad fellow; **ce d. de parapluie**, that wretched umbrella.

diabolique [djabɔlik], *a.* diabolical, fiendish; *adv.* **-ment**.

diacre [djakr], *s.m. Ecc:* deacon.

diadème [djadɛm], *s.m.* diadem.

diagnostic [djagnɔstik], *s.m. Med:* diagnosis.

diagnostiquer [djagnɔstike], *v.tr. Med:* to diagnose.

diagonal, *pl* **-aux** [djagɔnal, -o]. **1.** *a.* diagonal. **2.** *s.f.* **diagonale**, diagonal (line); *adv.* **-ement**.

diagramme [djagram], *s.m.* diagram.

dialecte [djalɛkt], *s.m.* dialect.

dialogue [djalɔg], *s.m.* dialogue.

diamant [djamɑ̃], *s.m.* diamond.

diamétral, *pl.* **-aux** [djametral, -o], *a* diametrical; *adv.* **-ement**.

diamètre [djametr], *s.m.* diameter.

diapason [djapazɔ̃], *s.m. Mus:* **1.** diapason pitch. **2.** tuning-fork.

diaphane [djafan], *a.* diaphanous; translucent transparent.

diaphragme [djafragm], *s.m.* **1.** *Physiol* diaphragm, midriff. **2.** *Tchn:* diaphragm dividing plate.

diarrhée [djare], *s.f. Med:* diarrhoea.

dictateur [diktatœːr], *s.m.* dictator; *a.* **-orial** *pl.* **-aux**, dictatorial; *s.f.* **-ure**, dictatorship.

dictée [dikte], *s.f.* dictation.

dicter [dikte], *v.tr.* to dictate.

diction [diksjɔ̃], *s.f.* diction; **professeur de d.** teacher of elocution.

dictionnaire [diksjɔneːr], *s.m.* dictionary.

dicton [diktɔ̃], *s.m.* (common) saying.

dièse [djeːz], *s.m. Mus:* sharp.

diète [djɛt], *s.f.* diet.

diététicien, -ienne [djetetisjɛ̃, -jɛn], *s.* dietician

dieu, -ieux [djø]. **1.** *s.m.* (*a*) D., God; (*b*) (pagan god; **l'argent est son d.**, he worships money; (c **D. merci!** thank goodness! **D. sait que . .** heaven knows that. . . . **2.** *int. F:* **mon D.** good heavens!

diffamer [diffame], *v.tr.* to slander, libel (s.o.) *a.* **-ant**; slanderous, libellous; *s.* **-ateur** **-atrice**, slanderer, libeller; *s.f.* **-ation**, slander libel; *a.* **-atoire**, slanderous, libellous.

différence [diferɑ̃ːs], *s.f.* difference; **quelle d avec . . .!** what a difference from . . .! **à la d de . . .,** unlike. . . . **à la d. que . . .,** with thi difference that . . .; **d. d'âge**, disparity i years.

différencier [diferɑ̃sje], *v.tr.* (*a*) to differentiat (**de**, from); (*b*) to distinguish (**entre . . . e . . .,** between . . . and . . .); *s.f.* **-ation**.

différend [diferɑ̃], *s.m.* difference, dispute (**entr** between).

différent [diferɑ̃], *a.* different; **à différente reprises**, at various times; *adv.* **-emment**.

différer [difere], *v.* (**je diffère; je différerai**). **1.** *v.t* to defer; to put off (payment). **2.** *v.i.* to differ; **d'opinion**, to differ in opinion.

difficile [difisil], *a.* **1.** difficult; **les temps so difficiles**, times are hard. **2.** *F:* **il est d. à vivr** he is difficult to get on with; *s.* **faire le d.**, to b hard to please; *adv.* **-ment**, with difficulty.

difficulté [difikylte], *s.f.* difficulty.

difforme [difɔrm], *a.* deformed, misshapen.

difformité [difɔrmite], *s.f.* deformity.

diffusler [difyze], *v.tr.* **1.** to diffuse (light). **2.** *Rad:* to broadcast (news); *s.m.* -eur. **1.** *Mec.E:* mixer. **2.** *Rad:* loudspeaker; *s.f.* -ion.

digérer [diʒere], *v.tr.* (je **digère;** je **digérerai**) to digest.

digestlion [diʒestjɔ̃], *s.f.* digestion; *a.* -ible; *a.* -if, -ive, tube d., alimentary canal.

digital, *pl.* -aux [diʒital, -o]. **1.** *a.* **empreinte digitale,** finger-print. **2.** *s.f.* *Bot:* **digitale,** foxglove.

digne [diɲ], *a.* **1.** (*a*) deserving, worthy (**de,** of). **2.** dignified; *adv.* -ment.

dignitaire [diɲiteːr], *s.m.* dignitary.

dignité [diɲite], *s.f.* **1.** dignity; **air de d.,** dignified air. **2.** high position; dignity.

digression [digresjɔ̃], *s.f.* digression; **faire une d.,** to digress.

digue [dig], *s.f.* (*a*) dike, dam; embankment (of waterway); (*b*) breakwater; sea-wall.

dilapidler [dilapide], *v.tr.* **1.** to waste, squander (fortune). **2.** to misappropriate (funds); *s.f.* -ation.

dilatler [dilate], *v.tr.* to dilate, expand; *s.f.* -ation, dilation.

dilemme [dilɛm], *s.m.* dilemma.

diligence [diliʒãːs], *s.f.* **1.** (*a*) diligence, application; (*b*) haste, dispatch. **2.** (stage-)coach.

diliglent [diliʒã], *a.* diligent, industrious; *adv.* -emment.

diluler [dilɥe], *v.tr.* to dilute (**de,** with); *s.f.* -tion.

dimanche [dimãːʃ], *s.m.* Sunday; **venez d.,** come on Sunday; **il vient le d.,** he comes on Sundays.

dimension [dimãsjɔ̃], *s.f.* dimension, size.

diminué [diminɥe], *a.* **1.** *Mus:* diminished (interval). **2.** **bas d.,** fully-fashioned stocking. **3.** tapering (column). **4.** *s.m.* **un d. physique,** a physically handicapped person.

diminuler [diminɥe], *v.tr. & i.* to lessen; to diminish; to grow less; (*of prices*) to fall; *a.* -tif, -tive, diminutive; *s.m.* -tion, diminution.

dinde [dɛ̃ːd], *s.f.* turkey(-hen).

dindon [dɛ̃dɔ̃], *s.m.* turkey(-cock).

dindonneau, -eaux [dɛ̃dɔno], *s.m.* young turkey.

dîner [dine]. **I.** *v.i.* to dine, to have dinner. **II.** **dîner,** *s.m.* dinner; dinner party; *Fr.C:* lunch; *Fr.C:* **salle à d.,** dining-room.

dîneur, -euse [dinœːr, -øːz], *s.* diner.

diocèse [djɔsɛːz], *s.m.* *Ecc:* diocese.

diphtérie [difteri], *s.f.* *Med:* diphtheria.

diphtongue [diftɔ̃ːg], *s.f.* *Ling:* diphthong.

'iplomate [diplɔmat], *s.m.* diplomat(ist).

'iplomatie [diplɔmasi], *s.f.* **1.** diplomacy; **user de d.,** to use tact. **2.** **entrer dans la d.,** to enter the diplomatic service.

'iplomatique [diplɔmatik], *a.* diplomatic.

'iplôme [diploːm], *s.m.* diploma.

dire [diːr]. **I.** *v.tr.* (*pr.p.* **disant;** *p.p.* **dit;** *pr.ind.* **vous dites, ils disent**). **1.** to say, tell; (*a*) **d. qch. à qn,** to tell s.o. sth.; **envoyer d. à qn que . . .,** to send word to s.o. that . . .; **qu'en dira-t-on?** what will people say? **d. ce qu'on pense,** to speak one's mind; **je vous l'avais bien dit!** didn't I tell you so? **comme on dit,** as the saying goes; **cela ne se dit pas,** that is not said; *F:* **à qui le dites-vous?** don't I know it! **dites toujours!** go on! say it! **je ne sais comment d.,** I don't know how to put it; **à vrai d. . . .,** to tell the truth . . .; **pour ainsi d.,** so to speak; **vous l'avez dit,** exactly! *F:* you've said it! **cela va sans d.,** that goes without saying; **il n'y a pas à d.,** there is no denying it; **dites donc, I** say! (*b*) *Pred:* **on le dit mort,** he is reported (to be) dead; (*c*) **il ne se le fit pas d. deux fois,** he didn't wait to be told twice; (*d*) **faire d. qch. à qn,** (i) to make s.o. tell sth.; (ii) to send word of sth. to s.o. **2.** (*a*) **d. à qn de faire qch.,** to tell s.o. to do sth.; (*b*) **d. que** + *sub.* **dites qu'on le fasse entrer,** tell them to show him in. **3. d. des vers,** to recite poetry; **d. son chapelet,** to tell one's beads. **4.** (*a*) to express; **cela en dit beaucoup sur son courage,** it speaks volumes for his courage; (*b*) **cette musique ne me dit rien,** I don't care for this music; **ce nom ne me dit rien,** this name means nothing to me. **5.** (*a*) **vouloir d.,** to mean; (*b*) **qu'est-ce à d.?** what does this mean?

II. dire, *s.m.* statement; assertion.

direct [dirɛkt], *a.* direct, straight; *Rail:* **train d.,** through train; *T.V:* **émission en d.,** live broadcast; *adv.* -ement.

directeur, -trice [dirɛktœːr, -tris]. **1.** *s.* director, manager, manageress; headmaster, -mistress; editor (of paper); head (of firm); **d. général,** general manager; **d. gérant,** managing director. **2.** *a.* directing, controlling.

direction [dirɛksjɔ̃], *s.f.* **1.** (*a*) guidance; management (of firm); leadership (of party); (*b*) board of directors. **2.** direction, course; **train en d. de Bordeaux,** train for Bordeaux; *P.N:* **d. de la gare,** to the station. **3.** *pl.* directions, instructions.

dirigé [diriʒe], *a.* controlled; **économie dirigée,** planned economy.

dirigler [diriʒe], *v.tr.* (*n.* **dirigeons**). **1.** to direct, control; to conduct (orchestra). **2.** (*a*) to direct, guide; (*b*) **d. ses pas vers . . .,** to direct one's steps towards . . .; (*c*) to level, point (telescope, etc.) (**sur,** at); *a.* -eant, directing, guiding (power, principle); *s.m.* *Pol:* -isme, planning.

se diriger vers un endroit, to make one's way towards a place.

discernler [disɛrne], *v.tr.* to discern, distinguish (sth.); **d. qch. de qch.,** to discriminate between sth. and sth.; *a.* -able, discernible, visible; *s.m.*

-ement.

disciple [disipl], s.m. disciple, follower.

discipline [disiplin], s.f. discipline.

disciplin|er [disipline], v.tr. to discipline; -aire, (i) a. disciplinary; (ii) s.m. disciplinarian.

discontinu|er [diskɔ̃tinɥe], v.tr. & i. to discontinue; s.f. -ation.

discordant [diskɔrdɑ̃], a. discordant (sound); clashing (colours).

discorde [diskɔrd], s.f. discord, dissension, strife.

discothèque [diskɔtɛk], s.f. 1. record library. 2. disco(thèque).

discours [disku:r], s.m. 1. talk. 2. speech, address. 3. Gram: parties du d., parts of speech.

discourtois [diskurtwa], a. discourteous.

discrédit [diskredi], s.m. discredit; disrepute.

discréditer [diskredite], v.tr. to disparage; to run down; to discredit.

disc|ret, -ète [diskrɛ, -ɛt], a. (a) discreet; (b) quiet, unobtrusive; adv. -rètement.

discrétion [diskresjɔ̃], s.f. discretion.

discrimin|er [diskrimine], v.tr. to discriminate; s.f. -ation.

discussion [diskysjɔ̃], s.f. discussion, debate; la question en d., the question at issue; sans d. possible, indisputably.

discut|er [diskyte], v.tr. (a) to discuss, debate; discutons la chose, let us talk it over; (b) to question, dispute; a. -able, debatable.

disette [dizɛt], s.f. scarcity, dearth; famine.

disgrâce [disgrɑ̃:s], s.f. disfavour, disgrace.

disgracié [disgrasje], a. out of favour.

disgracier [disgrasje], v.tr. to dismiss from favour.

disgracieux, -euse [disgrasjø, -ø:z], a. 1. uncouth. 2. ungracious.

dislocation [dislɔkasjɔ̃], s.f. dislocation.

disloquer [dislɔke], v.tr. to dislocate; to put (machine) out of order.

disparaître [disparɛ:tr], v.i. (conj. like CONNAÎTRE; aux. avoir or être) to disappear; d. aux yeux de qn, to vanish before s.o.'s eyes.

disparate [disparat], a. (a) dissimilar; (b) ill-matched.

disparition [disparisjɔ̃], s.f. disappearance.

disparu [dispary], a. 1. missing. 2. extinct.

dispensaire [dispɑ̃sɛ:r], s.m. dispensary; out-patients' department.

dispense [dispɑ̃:s], s.f. (a) exemption; (b) Ecc: dispensation.

dispens|er [dispɑ̃se], v.tr. 1. to exempt; d. qn d'une tâche, to let s.o. off a task. 2. to dispense, distribute; s.f. -ation.

dispers|er [dispɛrse], v.tr. to disperse, scatter; s.f. -ion, dispersion; scattering.

disponibilité [dispɔnibilite], s.f. 1. availability (of seats). 2. pl. available time, funds.

disponible [dispɔnibl], a. available; at (s.o.'s)

disposal.

dispos [dispo], a.m. fit, well, in good form.

disposer [dispoze]. 1. v.tr. (a) to dispose arrange; (b) d. qn à faire qch., to dispose, incline, s.o. to do sth. 2. v.ind.tr. d. de qch., to dispose of sth.; disposez de moi, I am at you service; les moyens dont je dispose, the means at my disposal.

se disposer à faire qch., to get ready to do sth.

dispositif [dispozitif], s.m. apparatus, device; d de sûreté, safety device.

disposition [dispozisjɔ̃], s.f. disposition. 1 arrangement (of house); d. du terrain, lie of the land. 2. (a) state (of mind); (b) tendency; (c) p natural aptitude. 3. pl. (a) arrangements; pren dre toutes dispositions utiles, to take all usefu steps; (b) provisions (of will). 4. disposal; libr d. de soi-même, self-determination; fonds à m d., funds at my disposal.

disproportionné [disprɔpɔrsjɔne], a. dis proportionate; out of proportion.

disputable [dispytabl], a. disputable, debatable

dispute [dispyt], s.f. quarrel.

disput|er [dispyte], v.tr. (a) d. qch., to dispute contest, sth.; (b) d. un match, to play a match (c) F: d. qn, to tell s.o. off.

se disputer, to quarrel (pour, over, about).

disquaire [diskɛ:r], s.m. record dealer.

disqualifi|er [diskalifje], v.tr. Sp: to disqualify s.f. -cation.

disque [disk], s.m. 1. Sp: discus. 2. (a) disc (c moon, etc.); (b) d. d'embrayage, clutch plate (c) Rec: record, disc; d. microsillon, longu durée, microgroove, long-playing, record, I L.P.; (d) Anat: d. intervertébra (intervertebral) disc.

dissatisf|aire [disatisfɛ:r], v.tr. (conj. lik FAIRE) to dissatisfy; s.f. -action.

dissection [disɛksjɔ̃], s.f. dissection.

dissemblable [dis(s)ɑ̃blabl], a. dissimila unlike.

dissemblance [dis(s)ɑ̃blɑ̃:s], s.f. dissimilarity.

dissémin|er [dis(s)emine], v.tr. to scatte (seeds); to spread (germs, ideas); to di seminate (ideas); s.f. -ation.

dissension [dis(s)ɑ̃sjɔ̃], s.f. dissension, discorc

dissentiment [dis(s)ɑ̃timɑ̃], s.m. disagreement

disséquer [dis(s)eke], v.tr. (je dissèque; je di séquerai) to dissect.

dissertation [disɛrtasjɔ̃], s.f. (a) dissertation; (Sch: essay.

dissidence [dis(s)idɑ̃:s], s.f. dissidence; dissen

dissimil|aire [dis(s)imilɛ:r], a. dissimilar, u like; s.f. -arité.

dissimulé [dis(s)imyle], a. 1. hidden, secret. secretive, double-dealing (man).

dissimul|er [dis(s)imyle], v.tr. to dissemble, di simulate, conceal (feelings); abs. to dissembl s.f. -ation.

se dissimuler, to hide, to be hidden.
dissipation [disipasjɔ̃], s.f. 1. (a) dissipation, dispersion (of clouds); (b) wasting (of time), squandering (of money). 2. (a) dissipation, dissolute living; (b) Sch: inattention, fooling; frivolous conduct.
dissipé [disipe], a. (a) dissolute; gay (life); (b) Sch: inattentive (pupil).
dissiper [disipe], v.tr. (a) to dissipate, disperse, scatter (clouds); to clear up (misunderstanding); to dispel (fears); (b) to waste (time); to squander (money).
se dissiper, (of suspicions) to vanish; (of fog) to clear; (of storm) to blow over.
dissocier [dis(s)ɔsje], v.tr. to dissociate, separate; s.f. -ation.
dissolu [dis(s)ɔly], a. dissolute, profligate.
dissolution [dis(s)ɔlysjɔ̃], s.f. 1. disintegration, dissolution. 2. (a) dissolving; (b) solution. 3. dissolution (of parliament). 4. dissoluteness, profligacy.
dissolvant [dis(s)ɔlvɑ̃], a. & s.m. (dis)solvent; d. (pour ongles), (nail-varnish, N.Am: nail-polish) remover.
dissonance [dissɔnɑ̃ːs], s.f. 1. dissonance. 2. Mus: discord.
dissonant [dissɔnɑ̃], a. dissonant, discordant.
dissoudre [dis(s)udr], v.tr. (pr.p. dissolvant; p.p. dissous, f. dissoute; pr.ind. je dissous, il dissout) to dissolve. 1. to melt (substance) in a liquid. 2. (a) to disintegrate, decompose; (b) to dissolve (partnership).
se dissoudre. 1. se d. dans l'eau, to dissolve in water. 2. (of assembly) to break up.
dissuader [dis(s)ɥade], v.tr. d. qn de qch., de faire qch., to dissuade s.o. from (doing) sth.
dissuasion [dis(s)ɥazjɔ̃], s.f. dissuasion; Mil: arme de d., deterrent.
dissymétrie [dis(s)imetri], s.f. asymmetry.
distance [distɑ̃s], s.f. distance; suivre qn à d., to follow s.o. at a distance; de d. en d., at intervals.
distancer [distɑ̃se], v.tr. (n. distançons) to out-distance, outrun, outstrip.
distant [distɑ̃], a. distant.
distendre [distɑ̃ːdr], v.tr. to distend.
distension [distɑ̃sjɔ̃], s.f. distension.
distiller [distile], v.tr. Ind: to distil (spirits, water); to condense; s.f. -ation; s.f. -erie.
distinct [distɛ̃(ːkt)], a. 1. distinct, separate. 2. distinct, clear; adv. -ement.
distinctif, -ive [distɛ̃ktif, -iːv], a. distinctive, characteristic; adv. -ivement.
distinction [distɛ̃ksjɔ̃], s.f. distinction. 1. faire une d. entre deux choses, to make a distinction between two things; sans d., indiscriminately. 2. (a) distinction, honour; (b) decoration. 3. distinction, eminence.
distingué [distɛ̃ge], a. distinguished. 1. eminent,

noted (writer, etc.). 2. polished, refined (taste, etc.); avoir l'air d., to look distinguished.
distinguer [distɛ̃ge], v.tr. & i. to distinguish. 1. to mark, characterize. 2. to honour. 3. d. entre deux choses, to distinguish between two things; d. qch. de qch., to distinguish sth. from sth. 4. to discern; il fait trop noir pour bien d., it's too dark to see clearly.
se distinguer. 1. to distinguish oneself. 2. to be noticeable, conspicuous; to stand out.
distorsion [distɔrsjɔ̃], s.f. distortion.
distraction [distraksjɔ̃], s.f. 1. absent-mindedness. 2. diversion, amusement.
distraire [distrɛːr], v.tr. (conj. like ABSTRAIRE). 1. to distract, divert (s.o.'s attention). 2. to divert, amuse.
se distraire, to amuse oneself.
distrait [distrɛ], a. absent-minded; adv. -ement.
distribuer [distribɥe], v.tr. to distribute (provisions, letters, etc.); d. les cartes, to deal (out) the cards; Th: d. les rôles, to cast the parts (in a play).
distributeur, -trice [distribytœːr, -tris], s. 1. distributor. 2. s.m. (a) vending machine; d. d'essence, petrol pump; (b) Aut: distributor.
distribution [distribysjɔ̃], s.f. distribution; allotment (of duties); issue (of rations); Sch: d. de prix, speech-day; d. d'eau, water supply; El: tableau de d., switchboard.
dit [di], a. (a) settled, fixed; à l'heure dite, at the appointed time; (b) (so-)called; la zone dite tempérée, the so-called temperate zone.
divaguer [divage], v.i. (a) to digress; (b) to ramble (in delirium).
divan [divɑ̃], s.m. divan; couch.
diverger [divɛrʒe], v.i. (n. divergeons) to diverge (de, from); s.f. -ence, divergence; a. -ent, divergent.
divers, -verses [divɛːr, -vɛrs], a. pl. (a) diverse, varied; (frais) d., sundry expenses; Journ: faits d., news items; (b) indef.adj. (always preceding the sb.) various, sundry; en diverses occasions, on various occasions; adv. -ement.
diversifier [divɛrsifje], v.tr. to diversify, vary.
diversion [divɛrsjɔ̃], s.f. diversion; change.
diversité [divɛrsite], s.f. diversity.
divertir [divɛrtiːr], v.tr. to entertain, amuse; a. -issant; s.m. -issement.
se divertir, to amuse oneself.
dividende [dividɑ̃ːd], s.m. dividend.
divin [divɛ̃], a. divine; holy; sacred.
divinité [divinite], s.f. divinity.
diviser [divize], v.tr. to divide; s.m. Mth: -eur, divisor; a. -ible; s.f. -ion.
se diviser, to divide, to break up (en, into).
divorce [divɔrs], s.m. divorce.
divulguer [divylge], v.tr. to divulge, disclose, reveal.
dix [di, dis, diz], num.a. & s.m.inv. ten. 1. card. a.

(*at the end of the word-group* [dis]; *before sb. or adj. beginning with a vowel sound* [diz]; *before sb. or adj. beginning with a consonant* [di]) **il est dix heures** [dizœːr], it's ten o'clock; **j'en ai dix** [dis], I have ten; **le dix mai** [lədimɛ], the tenth of May. **2.** *s.m.inv.* (*always* [dis]) (*a*) **dix et demi,** ten and a half; (*b*) **Charles Dix,** Charles the Tenth.

dix-huit [dizɥit], *num.a. & s.m.inv.* **1.** eighteen. **2. le dix-huit mai,** the eighteenth of May.

dix-huitième [dizɥitjɛm], *num.a. & s.* eighteenth.

dixième [dizjɛm]. **1.** *num.a. & s.* tenth. **2.** *s.m.* tenth (part).

dix-neuf [diznœ(f)], *num.a. & s.m.inv.* **1.** nineteen. **2. le dix-neuf mai,** the nineteenth of May.

dix-neuvième [diznœvjɛm], *num.a. & s.* nineteenth.

dix-sept [dissɛt], *num.a. & s.m.inv.* **1.** seventeen. **2. le dix-sept mai,** the seventeenth of May.

dix-septième [dissɛtjɛm], *num.a. & s.* seventeenth.

dizaine [dizɛn], *s.f.* (about) ten; **une d. de personnes,** ten or a dozen people.

do [do], *s.m.inv. Mus:* (the note) C; **morceau en do,** piece in C.

docile [dɔsil], *a.* docile; *adv.* -**ment.**

docilité [dɔsilite], *s.f.* docility.

dock [dɔk], *s.m. Nau:* dock; dockyard.

docker [dɔkɛːr], *s.m.* docker.

docteur [dɔktœːr], *s.m.* **1. d. (en médecine),** doctor (of medicine), M.D.; **leur fille est d.,** their daughter is a doctor; **femme d.,** woman doctor. **2.** *Sch:* **d. en droit,** Doctor of Laws, LL.D.; **d. ès lettres,** Doctor of Literature, D.Litt.

doctrine [dɔktrin], *s.f.* doctrine, tenet.

document [dɔkymã], *s.m.* document.

documentaire [dɔkymãtɛːr]. **1.** *a.* documentary. **2.** *s.m.* documentary (film).

documenter [dɔkymãte], *v.tr.* **d. qn,** to provide s.o. with information, to brief s.o.

se documenter, to collect material (for book, etc.).

dogmatique [dɔgmatik], *a.* dogmatic.

dogme [dɔgm], *s.m.* dogma, tenet.

dogue [dɔg], *s.m.* mastiff.

doigt [dwa], *s.m.* finger; (*a*) **promener ses doigts sur qch.,** to finger, feel, sth.; **donner sur les doigts à qn,** to rap s.o. over the knuckles; **savoir qch. sur le bout du d.,** to have sth. at one's finger tips; **se mordre les doigts,** to bite one's nails with impatience; (*b*) **être à deux doigts de (la mort),** to be within an ace of (death); (*c*) **d. de pied,** toe.

domaine [dɔmɛn], *s.m.* **1.** domain; (real) estate, property; **d. public,** public property. **2.** field, scope (of a science, etc.).

dôme [dom], *s.m.* **1.** *Arch:* dome, cupola. **2. d. du**

palais, roof of the mouth.

domestique [dɔmɛstik]. **1.** *a.* domestic. **2.** *s.m. & f.* (domestic) servant.

domicile [dɔmisil], *s.m.* residence; *Jur:* domicile; **à d.,** at one's (private) house; **franco à d.,** carriage paid.

domicilié [dɔmisilje], *a.* resident, domiciled (à at).

dominer [dɔmine]. **1.** *v.i.* to rule. **2.** *v.tr.* to dominate; (*a*) to rule; to master, control; *Sp:* **d. la partie,** to have the best of the game; (*b*) to tower above (sth.); to overlook; *a.* **-ant,** dominating, dominant; *a.* **-ateur, -atrice,** domineering; *s.f.* **-ation.**

dominicain, -aine [dɔminikɛ̃, -ɛn], *a. & s.* **1.** *Ecc:* Dominican. **2.** *Geog:* **la République Dominicaine,** the Dominican Republic.

dominical, -aux [dɔminikal, -o], *a.* **l'oraison dominicale,** the Lord's prayer; **repos d.,** Sunday rest.

domino [dɔmino], *s.m.* domino.

dommage [dɔmaːʒ], *s.m.* **1.** (*a*) damage, injury (*b*) *F:* **quel d.!** what a pity! **2.** *pl.* (*a*) damage (to property); (*b*) *Jur:* **dommages-intérêts,** damages.

dompter [dõte], *v.tr.* to tame (animal); to break in (horse); to subdue, master; *a.* **-able;** *s.* **-eur, -euse,** tamer; horse-breaker.

don [dõ], *s.m.* **1.** giving. **2.** (*a*) gift, present; (*b*) gift, talent.

donation [dɔnasjõ], *s.f.* donation, gift.

donc. 1. *conj.* [dõːk], therefore, consequently. **2.** *adv.* [dõ] (*emphatic*) **mais taisez-vous d.!** for goodness sake be quiet! **allons d.!** (i) nonsense (ii) come on! **pensez d.!** just think!

donjon [dõʒõ], *s.m.* keep (of castle).

donnant [dɔnã], *a.* generous, open-handed; **peu d.,** close-fisted; *adv.phr.* **d.d.,** (i) give and take (ii) cash down.

données [dɔne], *s.f.pl.* data.

donner [dɔne], *v.tr.* to give. **1. d. des conseils,** to give advice; **d. à boire à qn,** to give s.o. something to drink; **je vous le donne en vingt,** I'll give you twenty guesses; *F:* **c'est donné,** it's dirt cheap; **s'en d. (à cœur joie),** to have a good time; **d. les cartes,** to deal (the cards). **2.** (*a*) to provide, furnish; (*of crops*) to yield; **cela donne à penser,** this gives food for thought; **d. un bon exemple,** to set a good example; **à un point donné,** at a given point; **étant donné qu'il est mineur,** inasmuch as he is not of age; (*b*) **d. faim à qn,** to make s.o. hungry. **3.** to attribute (sth. to s.o.); **elle se donne trente ans,** she claims to be thirty; **d. raison à qn,** to agree with s.o. **4.** (*a*) **fenêtre qui donne sur la cour,** window that looks out on the yard; (*b*) **d. de la tête contre qch.,** to knock one's head against sth.; **d. dans le piège,** to fall into the trap; *F:* **d. dedans,** to walk right into the trap; **il me donne**

sur les nerfs, he gets on my nerves; *F:* d. dans l'œil de, à, qn, to strike s.o.'s fancy; (*c*) le toit donne, the roof's giving way.

donneur, -euse [dɔnœːr, -øːz], *s.* (*a*) giver; *Med:* d. de sang, blood donor; d. de conseils, busybody, *N.Am: F:* wise guy; (*b*) *Cards:* dealer.

dont [dɔ̃], *rel.pron.* (= de qui, duquel, desquels, *etc.*) (*a*) from, by, with, whom or which; la famille d. je sors, the family from which I am descended; la femme d. il est amoureux, the woman with whom he is in love; (*b*) (of) whom, which; le livre d. j'ai besoin, the book (that) I want; voici ce d. il s'agit, this is what it is all about; (*c*) whose; la dame d. je connais le fils, the lady whose son I know; Mme Martin, d. le fils est médecin, Mrs Martin, whose son is a doctor.

dorénavant [dɔrenavɑ̃], *adv.* henceforth, from this time forward.

dorer [dɔre], *v.tr.* to gild.

dorloter [dɔrlɔte], *v.tr.* to fondle; to pamper.

dorm**i**r [dɔrmiːr], *v.i.* (*pr.p.* dormant; *pr.ind.* je dors). 1. to sleep; to be asleep; ne d. que d'un œil, to sleep with one eye open; d. sur les deux oreilles, (i) to sleep soundly; (ii) *F:* just to sit on one's behind (and do nothing); il dormait debout, he couldn't keep his eyes open. 2. to be dormant, inactive; eau qui dort, stagnant, still, water; *a.* -ant; *s.* -eur, -euse, sleeper.

dortoir [dɔrtwaːr], *s.m.* dormitory.

dorure [dɔryːr], *s.f.* 1. gilding. 2. gilt.

doryphore [dɔrifɔːr], *s.m. Ent:* Colorado beetle.

dos [do], *s.m.* back. 1. avoir le d. rond, to be round-shouldered; faire le gros d., (*of cat*) to arch its back; (*of pers.*) to put on airs; *F:* avoir qn sur le d., to be saddled with s.o.; *P:* j'en ai plein le d., I'm fed up with it. 2. back (of chair); voir au d., turn over.

dose [doːz], *s.f.* dose (of medicine).

dossier [dosje], *s.m.* 1. back (of seat). 2. (*a*) documents, file (relating to an affair); (*b*) record, dossier.

dot [dɔt], *s.f.* dowry.

doter [dɔte], *v.tr.* (*a*) to give a dowry to (bride); (*b*) to endow (hospital); (*c*) *Ind:* d. une usine de matériel neuf, to equip a works with new plant.

douairière [dwɛrjɛːr], *a. & s.f.* dowager.

douane [dwan], *s.f. Adm:* customs; visite de la d., customs examination; marchandises en d., bonded goods; (bureau de) d., customs-house.

douanier, -ière [dwanje, -jɛːr]. 1. *a.* tarif d., customs tariff; union douanière, customs union. 2. *s.m.* customs officer.

double [dubl]. 1. *a.* double, twofold; faire coup d., to kill two birds with one stone. 2. *adv.* voir d., to see double. 3. *s.m.* (*a*) double; bontés rendues au d., kindnesses returned twofold; (*b*)

duplicate, counterpart; facture en d., invoice in duplicate; *adv.* -ment.

doubler [duble]. 1. *v.tr.* (*a*) to double (the size, etc.); (*b*) to fold in two; to double; *Nau:* d. un cap, to round, weather, a cape; *Th:* d. un rôle, to understudy a part; *Aut:* défense de d., no overtaking, *N.Am:* no passing; (*c*) to line (coat); (*d*) *Cin:* to dub (film). 2. *v.i.* to double, to increase twofold.

doublure [dublyːr], *s.f.* 1. lining (of garment). 2. *Th:* understudy.

doucement [dusmɑ̃], *adv.* gently, softly; (to run, work) smoothly; allez-y d.! gently does it! allez-y d. pour l'électricité, go easy on the electricity.

douce**l**eux, -euse [dusrø, -øːz], *a.* 1. sweetish, sickly. 2. mealy-mouthed, smooth-tongued (person); *adv.* -eusement, insipidly.

douceur [dusœːr], *s.f.* 1. (*a*) sweetness (of honey, etc.); (*b*) *pl.* sweet things, sweets. 2. softness. 3. pleasantness. 4. gentleness; sweetness (of smile); mildness (of weather).

douche [duʃ], *s.f.* shower (bath).

doucher (se) [səduʃe], *v.pr.* to have, take, a shower.

doué [dwe], *a.* gifted.

douleur [dulœːr], *s.f.* suffering. 1. pain, ache. 2. sorrow, grief.

doulour**l**eux, -euse [dulurø, -øːz], *a.* painful. 1. aching; sore. 2. sad, distressing; *adv.* -eusement.

doute [dut], *s.m.* doubt, misgiving; avoir des doutes sur qch., to have misgivings about sth.; sans d., (i) doubtless; (ii) no doubt, probably; sans aucun d., without (any) doubt.

douter [dute], *v.i.* to doubt; d. de qn, to mistrust s.o.

se douter de qch., to suspect sth.; je ne me doutais pas qu'il fût là, I had no idea that he was there.

dout**l**eux, -euse [dutø, -øːz], *a.* doubtful, uncertain; *adv.* -eusement.

Douvres [duːvr]. *Pr.n.f. Geog:* Dover.

doux, *f.* douce [du, dus], *a.* (*a*) sweet; smooth, soft; eau douce, (i) fresh, (ii) soft, water; (*b*) pleasant, agreeable; (*c*) gentle; mild (weather); soft (light); (*d*) gentle; meek; (*e*) *adv.* tout d.! gently! *F:* filer d., to give in.

douzaine [duzɛn], *s.f.* dozen; une d. de personnes, about a dozen people; à la d., by the dozen.

douze [duːz], *num.a.inv. & s.m.inv.* twelve; le d. mai, the twelfth of May.

douzième [duzjɛm]. 1. *num.a. & s.* twelfth. 2. *s.m.* twelfth (part).

doyen, -enne [dwajɛ̃, -ɛn], *s.* 1. (*a*) *Ecc: Sch:* dean; (*b*) doyen (of the diplomatic corps). 2. être le d., la doyenne, de qn, to be s.o.'s senior.

dragée [draʒe], *s.f.* (*a*) sugar(ed) almond; (*b*)

Pharm: sugar-coated pill.
dragon [dragɔ̃], *s.m.* **1.** dragon. **2.** *Mil:* dragoon.
drague [drag], *s.f.* dredger.
drag|uer [drage], *v.tr.* **1.** to dredge. **2.** to drag (pond); to sweep (channel); *s.m.* -**age**; *s.m.* -**ueur**, dredger; mine-sweeper.
dramatique [dramatik], *a.* dramatic; **auteur d.**, playwright; *adv.* -**ment**, dramatically.
dramatiser [dramatize], *v.tr.* to dramatize.
dramaturge [dramatyrʒ], *s.m. & f.* dramatist, playwright.
drame [dram], *s.m.* **1.** (*a*) (*literary genre*) drama; (*b*) play. **2.** sensational affair; drama.
drap [dra], *s.m.* **1.** cloth. **2. d. (de lit)**, (bed-)sheet; **être dans de beaux draps**, to be in a fine mess, in a bad way.
drapeau, -eaux [drapo], *s.m.* flag; *Mil:* colour; **être sous les drapeaux**, to serve in the (armed) forces.
draper [drape], *v.tr.* to drape (article of furniture, curtains, etc.).
drap|erie [drapri], *s.f.* drapery; *s.* -**ier**, -**ière**, draper, clothier; cloth manufacturer.
Dresde [drɛzd]. *Pr.n.f. Geog:* Dresden.
dress|er [drɛse], *v.tr.* **1.** to erect, set up (monument, etc.); **d. la table**, to set, to lay, the table; **d. les oreilles**, to prick up one's ears. **2.** to draw up (plan, contract, list). **3.** to adjust. **4.** to train (animal); to break in (horse); to drill (recruit); *s.m.* -**age**; *s.* -**eur**, -**euse**, (animal) trainer; horse-breaker.
se dresser, (*a*) to stand up, rise; (*b*) to sit up, straighten up; to become all attention.
dressoir [drɛswaːr], *s.m.* sideboard, dresser.
dribbl|er [drible], *v.tr. Fb:* to dribble; *s.m.* -**eur**, dribbler.
drogue [drog], *s.f.* (*a*) drug; (*b*) chemical (as a commercial article); (*c*) narcotic.
drogué, -ée [droge], *s.* drug-addict.
droguer [droge], *v.tr.* (*a*) to dose; (*b*) to drug, dope (s.o.).
se droguer, to take drugs; to be a drug-addict.
droguerie [drogri], *s.f.* = hardware store.
droit¹, droite [drwa, drwat], *a.* **1.** straight, upright; **col d.**, stand-up collar; **angle d.**, right angle. **2.** (*a*) direct, straight; (*b*) **ligne droite**, *s.f.* **droite**, straight line; (*c*) *adv.* **allez tout d.**, keep straight on. **3.** straightforward, upright. **4.** (*a*) right (hand); (*b*) *s.f.* **droite**, right hand; *Aut:* **tenir la droite**, to drive on the right.
droit², s.m. 1. right; **droits civils**, civil rights; **avoir d. à qch.**, to have a right to sth.; **donner d. à qn**, to give a decision in favour of s.o.; **à bon d.**, with good reason. **2.** charge, fee, due; **droits d'auteur**, royalties. **3.** law; **faire son d.**, to study law.
droiture [drwatyːr], *s.f.* uprightness, rectitude.
drôle [droːl], *a.* funny, odd; **un d. de garçon**, a funny chap, *F:* a queer fish; **quelle d. d'idée!**

what a funny idea! *F:* **la d. de guerre**, the phon(e)y war (1939–40); *adv.* -**ment**.
dromadaire [drɔmadɛːr], *s.m. Z:* dromedary.
dru [dry]. **1.** *a.* thick, close-set. **2.** *adv.* **tomber d.**, to fall thick and fast.
du [dy] = **de le;** *see* DE *and* LE.
dû, f. due [dy]. **1.** *a.* due; (*a*) owing; **en port dû**, carriage forward; (*b*) proper; **en temps dû**, in due course. **2.** *s.m.* due; **à chacun son dû**, give the devil his due; *adv.* -**ment**, duly.
duc [dyk], *s.m.* **1.** duke. **2.** horned owl.
ducal, -aux [dykal, -o], *a.* ducal.
duché [dyʃe], *s.m.* duchy, dukedom.
duchesse [dyʃɛs], *s.f.* duchess.
duel [dɥɛl], *s.m.* duel, encounter; *s.m.* -**liste**, duellist.
dune [dyn], *s.f.* dune, sand-hill; down.
Dunkerque [dœ̃kɛrk]. *Pr.n.f. Geog:* Dunkirk.
duo [dɥo], *s.m. Mus:* duet.
dupe [dyp], *s.f.* dupe, *F:* sucker.
dup|er [dype], *v.tr.* to dupe, to swindle, to fool (s.o.); *s.f.* -**erie**, deception, hoax; *s.* -**eur**, -**euse**, swindler; hoaxer.
duplicateur [dyplikatœːr], *s.m.* duplicator.
duplication [dyplikasjɔ̃], *s.f.* duplication.
duplicité [dyplisite], *s.f.* duplicity, deceit.
dur [dyːr], *a.* **1.** hard; tough (meat, wood); **œufs durs**, hard-boiled eggs; *F:* **être d. à cuire**, (*of pers.*) to be a tough nut. **2.** hard, difficult; *adv.* **travailler d.**, to work hard. **3.** **avoir l'oreille dure**, to be hard of hearing. **4.** hard, harsh; **hiver d.**, hard winter. **5.** *s.m. P:* tough guy.
durabilité [dyrabilite], *s.f.* durability.
durable [dyrabl], *a.* durable, lasting; *adv.* -**ment**.
durant [dyrã], *prep.* during; **d. des siècles**, for centuries; **parler des heures d.**, to talk for hours on end.
durc|ir [dyrsiːr]. **1.** *v.tr.* to harden. **2.** *v.i. & pr.* to grow hard; *s.m.* **issement**.
durée [dyre], *s.f.* **1.** lasting quality; wear; life (of electric bulb); **essai de d.**, endurance test. **2.** duration.
durer [dyre], *v.i.* to last, endure.
dureté [dyrte], *s.f.* **1.** hardness; toughness. **2.** difficulty (of task). **3.** harshness, callousness.
durillon [dyrijɔ̃], *s.m.* callosity; corn (on sole of foot).
duvet [dyvɛ], *s.m.* **1.** (*a*) down (on chin, young bird, peach, etc.); under-fur (of animal); **d. du cygne**, swansdown. **2.** continental quilt, duvet **3.** *Tex:* nap.
dynamique [dinamik]. **1.** *a.* dynamic. **2.** *s.f.* dynamics.
dynamite [dinamit], *s.f.* dynamite.
dynamo [dinamo], *s.f. El.E:* dynamo.
dynastie [dinasti], *s.f.* dynasty.
dysenterie [disɑ̃tri], *s.f. Med:* dysentery.
dyspepsie [dispɛpsi], *s.f.* dyspepsia.

E

E, e [e], *s.m.* (the letter) E, e.

eau [o], *s.f.* water. **1. e. douce,** (i) fresh, (ii) soft, water; **ville d'e.,** watering-place; spa. **2.** (*a*) **cours d'e.,** water-course, stream; **jet d'e.,** fountain; **pièce d'e.,** lake, pond; **tomber à l'e.,** (i) to fall into the water; (ii) (*of plan*) to fall through; (*b*) **e. de pluie,** rainwater; **le temps est à l'e.,** it's wet weather; (*c*) **service des eaux,** water supply; **château d'e.,** water tower; **conduite d'e.,** water-main; **e. courante dans les chambres,** running water in the rooms. **3.** (*a*) **diamant de la première e.,** diamond of the first water; *F:* **cela lui fait venir l'e. à la bouche,** it makes his mouth water; **être tout en e.,** to be dripping with perspiration; (*b*) **e. de Cologne,** eau de cologne; **e. de toilette,** toilet water. **4.** *Atom.Ph:* **e. lourde,** heavy water.

eau-de-vie [odvi], *s.f.* spirits; brandy; *pl. eaux-de-vie.*

eau-forte [ofɔrt], *s.f.* **1.** *Ch:* nitric acid. **2.** etching; *pl. eaux-fortes.*

ébahlir [ebaiːr], *v.tr.* to astound, flabbergast; *s.m.* **-issement,** amazement.

ébauche [eboːʃ], *s.f.* rough sketch (of picture); outline (of a novel); **é. d'un sourire,** ghost of a smile.

ébauchler [eboʃe], *v.tr.* to sketch out (plan); **é. un sourire,** to give a faint smile; *s.m.* **-age;** *s.m.* **-eur.**

ébène [ebɛn], *s.f.* ebony.

ébéniste [ebenist], *s.m.* cabinet-maker.

ébloulir [ebluiːr], *v.tr.* to dazzle; *s.m.* **-issement,** dizziness.

éboulement [ebulmɑ̃], *s.m.* **1.** caving in (of wall). **2.** land-slide, landslip.

ébouler (s') [sebule], *v.pr.* to crumble, cave in.

éboulis [ebuli], *s.m.* **1.** mass of debris. **2.** scree.

ébouriffer [eburife], *v.tr.* to dishevel, ruffle (s.o.'s hair).

ébranller [ebrɑ̃le], *v.tr.* **1.** to shake. **2.** to set in motion; *s.m.* **-ement,** shock, agitation.

s'ébranler, to start moving, to get under way; (*of train*) to start; (*of bells*) to start ringing.

ébrécher [ebreʃe], *v.tr.* (**j'ébrèche; j'ébrécherai**) to notch; to make a notch in (sth.); to chip (a plate); to break (a tooth); **couteau ébréché,** jagged knife.

ébruiter (s') [sebruite], *v.tr.* (*of news, etc.*) to become known, to spread.

ébullition [ebylisjɔ̃], *s.f.* (*a*) ebullition, boiling; (*b*) turmoil.

écaille [ekɑːj], *s.f.* **1.** scale (of fish); splinter (of wood). **2.** shell (of oyster); **é. de tortue,** tortoiseshell.

écailller [ekɑje], *v.tr.* (*a*) to scale (fish); to open (oyster); (*b*) to flake off (paint).

écarlate [ekarlat], *s.f. & a.* scarlet.

écarquiller [ekarkije], *v.tr.* to open (the eyes) wide.

écart¹ [ekaːr], *s.m.* **1.** deviation; **faire un é.,** to step aside; (*of horse*) to shy. **2. à l'é.,** aside; **se tenir à l'é.,** to keep out of the way; to stand aside.

écart², *s.m. Cards:* discard.

écarté [ekarte], *a.* **1.** isolated, remote, lonely (house, spot). **2.** (far) apart; **se tenir les jambes écartées,** to stand with legs apart.

écartler [ekarte], *v.tr.* **1.** to separate, part. **2.** to move (s.o., sth.) aside; **é. un coup,** to ward off a blow. **3.** to divert (suspicion); *s.m.* **-ement,** separation; gap, space.

s'écarter. 1. to move aside. **2.** to move apart, diverge. **3.** to deviate, stray (**de,** from); **s'é. du sujet,** to wander from the subject.

ecclésiastique [ɛklezjastik]. **1.** *a.* ecclesiastical; clerical. **2.** *s.m.* ecclesiastic, clergyman.

écervelé [esɛrvəle], *a.* scatterbrained.

échafaud [eʃafo], *s.m.* **1.** scaffolding, staging. **2.** scaffold; *s.m.* **-age,** scaffolding.

échalote [eʃalɔt], *s.f. Bot:* shallot.

échancrure [eʃɑ̃kryːr], *s.f.* notch, nick (in wood); indentation (in coast-line).

échange [eʃɑ̃ːʒ], *s.m.* exchange.

échanger [eʃɑ̃ʒe], *v.tr.* (**n. échangeons**) to exchange.

échantillon [eʃɑ̃tijɔ̃], *s.m.* sample.

échappée [eʃape], *s.f.* space, interval; **é. (de vue),** vista (**sur,** over); **é. de soleil,** burst of sunshine.

échappement [eʃapmɑ̃], *s.m.* escape, leakage (of gas, water); *Aut:* exhaust(-pipe); **pot d'é.,** silencer.

échapper [eʃape], *v.i.* (*aux.* être *or* avoir) to escape; (*a*) **é. à qn,** to escape s.o.; **ce propos m'a échappé,** I failed to hear this remark; **il est vrai que ce propos m'est échappé,** it is true that I let slip this remark; **son nom m'échappe,** his name has slipped my memory; **é. à toute définition,** to defy definition; (*b*) (*aux.* avoir) *F:* **vous l'avez échappé belle,** you have had a narrow escape; (*c*) **laisser é. une larme,** to let fall a tear; **laisser é. l'occasion,** to miss the opportunity.

s'échapper, to escape; to break free.

écharpe [eʃarp], *s.f.* (*a*) sash; (*b*) scarf; (*c*) arm-sling.

échauder [eʃode], *v.tr.* to scald.

échauff'er [eʃofe], *v.tr.* (*a*) to (over)heat; (*b*) to warm; (*c*) to excite, inflame; *s.m.* **-ement**.

s'échauffer, (*a*) to become overheated; **ne vous échauffez pas**, don't get excited; (*b*) to warm (up); (*c*) (*of engine*) to run hot.

échéance [eʃeɑ̃:s], *s.f.* date (of payment); **venir à é.**, to fall due.

échec [eʃɛk], *s.m.* **1.** (*a*) check (at chess); **é. et mat**, checkmate; (*b*) check, failure. **2.** *pl.* (*a*) chess; (*b*) chessmen.

échelle [eʃɛl], *s.f.* **1.** (*a*) ladder; **é. à incendie, é. de sauvetage**, fire-escape; **faire la courte é. à qn**, to give s.o. (i) a leg up, (ii) a helping hand; **après cela il faut tirer l'é.**, we can never do better than that; (*b*) scale (of prices); (*c*) run, ladder (in stocking). **2.** scale (of map, plan, etc.).

échelon [eʃlɔ̃], *s.m.* rung (of ladder); **monter par échelons**, to rise by degrees. **2.** *Mil:* echelon (formation). **3.** grade, stage; **à l'é. ministériel**, at ministerial level.

échelonn'er [eʃlɔne], *v.tr.* to space out (objects); to spread out (payments); to stagger (holidays); *s.m.* **-ement**.

écheveau, -eaux [eʃvo], *s.m.* hank, skein (of yarn).

échevelé [eʃəvle], *a.* (*a*) dishevelled (hair); (*b*) wild, disorderly (dance, etc.).

échine [eʃin], *s.f.* spine, backbone; **avoir l'é. souple**, to be obsequious.

échiquier [eʃikje], *s.m.* **1.** chess-board; **en é.**, chequered. **2.** (*in Eng.*) **Chancelier de l'E.**, Chancellor of the Exchequer.

écho [eko], *s.m.* echo.

échoir [eʃwa:r], *v.i.* (*pr.p.* **échéant**; *p.p.* **échu**; *pr.ind.* **il échoit, ils échoient**; *p.d.* **il échoyait, il échéait**; *fu.* **il écherra**; *aux.usu.* **être**) **1.** **é. en partage à qn**, to fall to s.o.'s share; **le cas échéant**, in case of need. **2.** (*a*) (*of bill*) to fall due; (*b*) (*of tenancy*) to expire.

échouer [eʃwe], *v.i.* (*a*) *Nau:* to run aground, to ground; (*b*) to fail; **l'affaire échoua**, the business fell through.

éclabouss'er [eklabuse], *v.tr.* to splash, (be)spatter; *s.m.* **-ement**; *s.f.* **-ure**.

éclair [eklɛ:r], *s.m.* **1.** flash of lightning; *pl.* lightning. **2.** flash (of a gun). **3.** *Cu:* éclair.

éclairage [eklɛra:ʒ], *s.m.* lighting; illumination; **é. par projecteurs**, flood-lighting; **heure d'é.**, lighting-up time; **mauvais é.**, bad light(ing).

éclaircie [eklɛrsi], *s.f.* **1.** break, opening, rift (in clouds). **2.** clearing (in forest).

éclairc'ir [eklɛrsi:r], *v.tr.* **1.** to solve, explain (mystery). **2.** to thin (forest, sauce); to thin out (plants). **3.** to clarify (liquid); *s.m.* **-issement**.

s'éclaircir, (*a*) (*of the weather*) to clear (up); (*b*) **la situation s'éclaircit**, things are becoming clearer.

éclairé [eklɛre], *a.* (*a*) lit, illuminated; (*b*) enlightened; well-informed.

éclair'er [eklɛre]. **1.** *v.tr.* (*a*) to light, illuminate; **venez nous é.**, come and light the way; (*b*) to enlighten. **2.** *v.impers.* **il éclaire**, it's lightening; *s.m.* **-agiste**, lighting technician.

éclaireur, -euse [eklɛrœ:r, -ø:z], (*a*) *s.m. Mil:* scout; (*b*) *s.* (boy) scout; (girl) guide.

éclat [ekla], *s.m.* **1.** splinter; **voler en éclats**, to fly into pieces; **to be shattered. 2.** burst (of thunder); **rire aux éclats**, to laugh heartily; **faire (de l')é.**, to create a stir. **3.** (*a*) flash (of light); (*b*) glitter; brilliancy.

éclatant [eklatɑ̃], *a.* **1.** bursting. **2.** loud (sound). **3.** dazzling (light); vivid (colour); sparkling (jewels); brilliant (deed).

éclat'er [eklate]. **1.** *v.tr.* to split (branch, etc.); to burst (tyre, etc.). **2.** *v.i.* to burst, explode; (*of glass*) to fly (into pieces); **é. de rire**, to burst out laughing. **3.** *v.i.* (*of jewels*) to sparkle; *s.m.* **-ement**.

éclipse [eklips], *s.f.* eclipse.

éclipser [eklipse], *v.tr.* to eclipse.

s'éclipser, to disappear, vanish.

éclopé [eklɔpe], *a.* footsore; lame, crippled.

éclore [eklɔ:r], *v.i. def.* (*p.p.* **éclos**; *pr.ind.* **il éclôt, ils éclosent**; *p.d.* **il éclosait**; *no p.h.*; *aux. usu.* **être**, *occ.* **avoir**) **1.** (*of eggs*) to hatch (out). **2.** (*of flowers*) to open.

écluse [ekly:z], *s.f.* **1.** (*a*) (canal) lock; (*b*) sluice (-gate). **2.** *Geog:* **l'É.**, Sluys.

éclusier, -ière [eklyzje, -jɛ:r], *s.* lock-keeper.

écœur'er [ekœre], *v.tr.* **1.** to disgust, sicken, nauseate. **2.** to dishearten; *a.* **-ant**, disgusting; *s.m.* **-ement**, nausea; disgust.

école [ekɔl], *s.f.* school; (*a*) **é. maternelle**, kindergarten; **é. primaire**, primary school; **é. libre**, independent school; **é. mixte**, co-educational school; (*b*) **l'É. polytechnique** = the Military Academy (of Artillery and Engineering); **É. (supérieure) de Guerre** = Staff College; **é. militaire**, military academy; **é. d'équitation**, riding school.

écolier, -ière [ekɔlje, -jɛ:r], *s.* schoolboy, -girl.

éconduire [ekɔ̃dɥi:r], *v.tr.* (*conj. like* CONDUIRE) to show (s.o.) the door; to get rid of (s.o.) (politely).

économe [ekɔnɔm]. **1.** *s.m. & f.* bursar (of college); steward. **2.** *a.* economical, thrifty.

économie [ekɔnɔmi], *s.f.* **1.** economy; **é. politique**, political economy, economics. **2.** economy, thrift; **faire une é. de temps**, to save time. **3.** *pl.* savings; **faire des économies**, to save money.

économique [ekɔnɔmik], *a.* **1.** economic (doctrine); **sciences économiques**, economics. **2.** economical, inexpensive.

économiser [ekɔnɔmize], *v.tr.* to economize, save.

écorce [ekɔrs], *s.f.* bark (of tree); rind, peel; **l'é. terrestre,** the earth's crust.

écorch|er [ekɔrʃe], *v.tr.* **1.** to flay; to skin. **2.** to graze, rub off (the skin); *s.f.* **-ure,** graze.

écossais, -aise [ekɔsɛ, -ɛːz]. **1.** *a.* Scottish, Scots. **2.** *s.* Scot; Scotsman, -woman.

Écosse (l') [lekɔs]. *Pr.n.f. Geog:* Scotland.

écosser [ekɔse], *v.tr.* to shell (peas).

écot [eko], *s.m.* **1.** share, quota. **2.** score, bill, reckoning.

écoul|er (s') [ekule], *v.pr.* (*a*) to flow out, run out; (*b*) (*of time*) to pass, elapse, to slip away; *s.m.* **-ement,** outflow; plug-hole; waste-pipe.

écourter [ekurte], *v.tr.* to shorten.

écoute [ekut], *s.f.* **1.** *F:* **se tenir aux écoutes,** to keep one's ears open. **2.** *Rad:* reception, listening in; **station d'é.,** monitoring station; **ne quittez pas l'é.,** (i) don't switch off; (ii) *P.T.T:* hold the line, please.

écouter [ekute], *v.tr.* **1.** (*a*) to listen to (s.o., sth.); **é. de toutes ses oreilles,** to be all ears; **écoutez!** look here! (*b*) *Rad:* to listen in. **2.** to pay attention to (s.o.); **se faire é.,** to gain a hearing; *F:* **s'é. trop,** to coddle oneself.

écouteur, -euse [ekutœːr, -øːz], *s.* **1.** listener. **2.** *s.m.* (telephone) receiver; *Rad:* ear-phone.

écran [ekrɑ̃], *s.m.* screen; *Cin:* (film-)screen; *T.V: Phot:* filter; *T.V:* **le petit é.,** television.

écras|er [ekraze], *v.tr.* to crush; to squash; **se faire é.,** to get run over; **écrasé de travail,** overwhelmed with work; *s.m.* **-ement.**

s'écraser, to collapse, crumple up; (*of aircraft, person*) to crash (to earth).

écrevisse [ekrəvis], *s.f.* (fresh-water) crayfish.

écrier (s') [sekrie], *v.pr.* (*a*) to cry (out); (*b*) to exclaim.

écrin [ekrɛ̃], *s.m.* (jewel-)case.

écrire [ekriːr], *v.tr.* (*pr.p.* **écrivant;** *p.p.* **écrit;** *p.h.* **j'écrivis**) to write; (*a*) **machine à é.,** typewriter; **é. une lettre à la machine,** to type a letter; (*b*) to write (sth.) down; (*c*) to write (book).

écrit [ekri]. **1.** *a.* written (word). **2.** *s.m.* (*a*) writing; **coucher qch. par é.,** to set sth. down in writing; (*b*) written document; *pl.* works (of an author); (*c*) *Sch:* written examination.

écriteau, -eaux [ekrito], *s.m.* placard, bill, notice, sign.

écriture [ekrityːr], *s.f.* **1.** (hand-)writing; **é. à la machine,** typing. **2.** (*a*) *pl.* (legal, commercial) papers, documents; *Book-k:* entry, item; (*b*) **l'É. sainte,** Holy Scripture.

écrivain [ekrivɛ̃], *s.m.* author, writer.

écrou [ekru], *s.m.* (screw-)nut.

écroulement, *s.m.* collapse, downfall.

écroul|er (s') [sekrule], *v.pr.* to collapse, give way; (*of plans*) to fall through.

écueil [ekœːj], *s.m.* reef, (marine) shelf; snag; (*of ship*) **donner sur les écueils,** to strike the rocks.

écume [ekym], *s.f.* (*a*) froth; foam; lather; (*b*) scum.

écum|er [ekyme]. **1.** *v.tr.* to skim (soup, etc.); **é. les mers,** to scour the seas. **2.** *v.i.* to foam, froth; *s.m.* **-age.**

écumoire [ekymwaːr], *s.f.* skimmer, skimming ladle.

écureuil [ekyrœj], *s.m.* squirrel.

écurie [ekyri], *s.f.* stable.

écuyer, -ère [ekɥije, -ɛːr], *s.* **1.** *s.m.* equerry. **2.** *s.* rider, horseman, -woman.

eczéma [ɛgzema], *s.m.* eczema.

édifice [edifis], *s.m.* building, edifice.

édifi|er [edifje], *v.tr.* **1.** to erect, set up, build. **2.** (*a*) to edify; (*b*) to enlighten, instruct (s.o.); *s.f.* **-cation.**

Édimbourg [edɛ̃buːr]. *Pr.n.m. Geog:* Edinburgh.

édit [edi], *s.m.* edict.

éditer [edite], *v.tr.* **1.** to edit (text). **2.** to publish (book, etc.).

éditeur, -trice [editœːr, -tris], *s.* **1.** editor (of text). **2.** publisher.

édition [edisjɔ̃], *s.f.* **1.** edition. **2.** publishing.

éditorial, -aux [editɔrjal, -o]. **1.** *a.* editorial. **2.** *s.m.* leading article, leader.

éditorialiste [editɔrjalist], *s.m. & f.* (*a*) leader-writer; (*b*) *Rad:* programme editor.

Édouard [edwaːr]. *Pr.n.m.* Edward.

édredon [edrədɔ̃], *s.m.* eiderdown.

éducation [edykasjɔ̃], *s.f.* (*a*) education, upbringing; **é. physique,** physical training; (*b*) training (of animals); (*c*) upbringing, breeding; **personne sans é.,** ill-bred person; **il manque d'é.,** he has no manners.

effacement [efasmɑ̃], *s.m.* **1.** obliteration. **2.** retirement; self-effacement.

effacer [efase], *v.tr.* (**n. effaçons**) to efface, obliterate, delete, erase.

s'effacer. 1. to become obliterated; to wear away; **s'e. à l'eau,** to wash away. **2.** to stand aside.

effarant [efarɑ̃], *a.* bewildering, amazing.

effar|er [efare], *v.tr.* to frighten, scare, startle (s.o.); *s.m.* **-ement.**

s'effarer, to be frightened, scared, startled (**de, at, by**); to take fright (**de, at**).

effarouch|er [efaruʃe], *v.tr.* to startle, scare away; *s.m.* **-ement.**

s'effaroucher, to be startled (**de, at, by**); to take fright (**de, at**).

effectif, -ive [efɛktif, -iːv]. **1.** *a.* (*a*) effective, efficacious; (*b*) effective, actual; **valeur effective,** real value. **2.** *s.m. Mil:* effectives; complement; (total) staff; **crise d'effectifs,** shortage of manpower.

effectivement [efɛktivmɑ̃], *adv.* **1.** effectively. **2.** actually. **3.** (*as an answer*) that's so.

effectuer [efɛktɥe], *v.tr.* to effect, carry out.

efféminé [efemine], *a.* effeminate, unmanly.

effervescence [efɛrvɛssã:s], s.f. **1.** effervescence. **2.** être en e., to be seething with excitement.

effervescent [efɛrvɛssã], a. effervescent.

effet [efɛ], s.m. **1.** effect, result; **à cet e.**, to this end. **2.** (a) action, operation, working; **mettre un projet en e.**, to put a plan into action; **prendre e.**, to become operative; (b) **en e.**, as a matter of fact; indeed; **vous oubliez vos paquets!—en e.!** you are forgetting your parcels!—so I am! **3.** (a) impression; **cela fait bon e.**, it looks well; **manquer son e.**, to fall flat; (b) Art: **e. de lune**, moonlight effect or study. **4.** **effets à payer**, bills payable. **5.** pl. possessions, belongings; clothes, things; **effets mobiliers**, personal effects.

efficace [efikas], a. efficacious, effective, efficient.

efficacité [efikasite], s.f. effectiveness; efficiency.

effigie [efiʒi], s.f. effigy.

effilé [efile], a. **1.** Tex: frayed, fringed (material). **2.** slender, slim; tapering (fingers).

effiler [efile], v.tr. **1.** Tex: to unravel, to fray. **2.** to taper.

effleur|er [eflœre], v.tr. to touch lightly; to skim; to graze (surface); s.m. **-ement.**

effondr|er (s') [sefɔ̃dre], to fall in; to break down; to collapse; to subside; (of prices) to slump; s.m. **-ement.**

efforcer (s') [seforse], v.pr. **(n.n. efforçons) s'e. de faire qch.**, to make an effort to do sth.

effort [efo:r], s.m. **1.** effort, exertion; **faire un e. sur soi-même**, to try to control oneself. **2.** Mec: strain, stress.

effrayant [efrɛjã], a. **1.** frightful, terrifying, dreadful, appalling. **2.** F: tremendous, awful, ghastly.

effrayer [efrɛje], v.tr. **(j'effraie, j'effraye)** to frighten, scare, startle (s.o.). **s'effrayer**, to take fright; **s'e. de qch.**, to be frightened of sth.

effréné [efrene], a. unbridled; frantic.

effriter (s') [sefrite], to crumble (away).

effroi [efrwa], s.m. fright, terror, fear.

effronté [efrɔ̃te], a. shameless, bold; impudent; adv. **-ment.**

effronterie [efrɔ̃tri], s.f. effrontery, insolence, F: cheek.

effroyable [efrwajabl], a. frightful, dreadful; hideous; adv. **-ment.**

effusion [ef(f)yzjɔ̃], s.f. **1.** effusion, outpouring; **e. de sang**, bloodshed. **2.** effusiveness; **avec e.**, gushingly.

égal, -aux [egal, -o], a. **1.** (a) equal; **de force égale**, evenly matched; **à armes égales**, on equal terms; prep.phr. **à l'é. de**, equally with; (b) level, even. **2.** (all) the same; **cela m'est (bien) é.**, it's all the same to me; fair enough! **si**

cela vous est é., if you don't mind; adv. **-ement**, equally; also.

égaler [egale], v.tr. to equal, be equal to (sth.); **deux et deux égalent quatre**, two and two make four.

égaliser [egalize], v.tr. **1.** to equalize. **2.** to level.

égalité [egalite], s.f. **1.** equality; Ten: deuce. **2.** evenness, regularity (of surface, breathing, etc.).

égard [ega:r], s.m. consideration, respect; (a) **avoir é. à qch.**, to allow for sth.; to give full consideration to sth.; **eu é. à . . .**, in consideration of . . .; **à l'é. de**, with respect to; (b) **il est plein d'égards pour moi**, he can't do enough for me.

égaré [egare], a. **1.** stray, lost (sheep, etc.); out-of-the-way (village). **2.** distraught, distracted (face, mind).

égar|er [egare], v.tr. **1.** (a) to mislead (s.o.); (b) to mislay (sth.). **2.** to confuse (s.o.); s.m. **-ement.**

s'égarer. 1. to lose one's way; to get on the wrong track; **colis qui s'est égaré**, parcel that has gone astray. **2. son esprit s'égare**, his mind is wandering.

égayement [egɛjmã], s.m. enlivenment; amusement.

égayer [egɛje], v.tr. **(j'égaie, j'égaye)** to enliven; to cheer (s.o.) up; to brighten (up).

églant|ier [eglãtje], s.m. wild rose (bush); sweet briar (bush); s.f. **-ine**, wild rose (flower), dog-rose.

église [egli:z], s.f. church.

égoïsme [egoism], s.m. selfishness.

égoïste [egoist]. **1.** s.m. & f. selfish person; egoist. **2.** a. selfish; adv. **-ment.**

égorger [egorʒe], v.tr. **(n. égorgeons) 1.** to cut the throat of (s.o., an animal). **2.** to butcher, massacre, slaughter (persons).

égout [egu], s.m. sewer; drain.

égoutt|er [egute], v.tr. & i. to drain, strain off (cheese, water, etc.); s.m. **-age**, draining (off); s.m. **-ement**, drip, dripping (of water). **s'égoutter**, to drain, drip.

égratign|er [egratiɲe], v.tr. to scratch; s.f. **-ure**, scratch.

Égypte (l') [leʒipt]. Pr.n.f. Geog: Egypt.

égyptien, -ienne [eʒipsjɛ̃, -jɛn], a. & s. Egyptian.

eh [e], int. hey! **eh bien!** well! now then!

éjection [eʒɛksjɔ̃], s.f. ejection.

élabor|er [elabore], v.tr. to elaborate; to work out (plan); s.f. **-ation.**

élan¹ [elã], s.m. **1.** (a) spring, bound, dash; **prendre son é.**, to take off (for a jump); **saut sans é.**, standing jump; (b) impetus; **perdre son é.**, to lose (one's) momentum. **2.** burst, outburst (of feeling, etc.).

élan², s.m. Z: elk, moose.

élancé [elãse], a. tall and slim; slender.

élancer (s') [selãse]. **1. s'é. en avant,** to spring forward; **s'é. sur qn,** to rush at s.o.; **s'é. vers le ciel,** to soar skyward. **2.** to shoot up.

élarg|ir [elarʒiːr], *v.tr.* **1.** (*a*) to widen (road); to stretch (shoes); (*b*) to enlarge, extend (one's ideas, one's property). **2.** to set (prisoner) free; *s.m.* **-issement.**

s'élargir, (*a*) to widen out; (*b*) to grow, extend; (*c*) to become freer.

élasticité [elastisite], *s.f.* elasticity.

élastique [elastik], *a. & s.m.* elastic.

Elbe [ɛlb]. **1.** *Pr.n.f.* (the island of) Elba. **2.** *Pr.n.m.* l'E., the (river) Elbe.

électeur, -trice [elɛktœːr, -tris], *s.* elector, voter; **mes électeurs,** my constituents.

élection [elɛksjɔ̃], *s.f.* **1.** *Pol:* election. **2.** election, choice, preference; **mon pays d'é.,** the country of my choice.

électoral, -aux [elɛktɔral, -o], *a.* electoral; **faire une tournée électorale,** to canvass.

électorat [elɛktɔra], *s.m.* electorate.

électricien [elɛktrisjɛ̃], *s.m.* electrician; **ingénieur é.,** electrical engineer.

électricité [elɛktrisite], *s.f.* electricity.

électrifi|er [elɛktrifje], *v.tr.* to electrify; *s.f.* **-cation.**

électrique [elɛktrik], *a.* electric; electrical (unit, industry).

électris|er [elɛktrize], *v.tr.* to electrify (substance); to thrill (audience); *s.f.* **-ation.**

électrocution [elɛktrɔkysjɔ̃], *s.f.* electrocution.

électrode [elɛktrɔd], *s.m.* electrode.

électroménager [elɛktrɔmenaʒe], *a. & s.m.* (**appareils**) **électroménagers,** electric household appliances, *N.Am:* household electricals.

électron [elɛktrɔ̃], *s.m. Ph:* electron.

électronique [elɛktrɔnik]. **1.** *a.* electronic. **2.** *s.f.* electronics.

élégance [elegãːs], *s.f.* elegance; stylishness.

élég|ant [elegã], *a.* elegant, stylish, fashionable; *adv.* **-amment.**

élégie [eleʒi], *s.f.* elegy.

élément [elemã], *s.m.* **1.** element. **2.** (*a*) component unit; ingredient (of medicine); **mobilier par éléments,** unit furniture; (*b*) *El:* cell (of battery). **3.** *pl.* rudiments, first principles (of a science); data.

élémentaire [elemãtɛːr], *a.* elementary.

éléphant [elefã], *s.m.* elephant.

élevage [elva:ʒ], *s.m.* **1.** stock farming. **2.** stock farm; breeding establishment; ranch; (*in Austr.*) (sheep) station.

élévation [elevasjɔ̃], *s.f.* **1.** (*a*) elevation, lifting; *Ecc:* elevation; (*b*) erection, setting up (of statue, etc.). **2.** rise (in temperature, etc.). **3.** (*a*) altitude, height; (*b*) high ground, eminence. **4.** elevation, vertical section.

élève [elɛːv], *s.m. & f.* pupil; student.

élevé [elve], *a.* **1.** high, noble, lofty. **2. bien é.,**

well brought up, well-bred; **mal é.,** rude, ill-bred.

élev|er [elve], *v.tr.* (**j'élève**) **1.** to elevate, raise. **2.** (*a*) to erect, set up; (*b*) **é. une objection,** to raise an objection. **3.** to bring up, rear (child); to breed (horses); *s.* **-eur, -euse,** (stock)breeder.

s'élever. 1. to rise (up); **le compte s'élève à mille francs,** the bill comes, amounts, to a thousand francs. **2.** to raise oneself.

éligib|le [eliʒibl]. *a.* eligible; *s.f.* **-ilité.**

élimin|er [elimine], *v.tr.* to eliminate, get rid of; *s.f.* **-ation.**

élire [eliːr], *v.tr.* (*conj. like* LIRE) to elect, choose.

élite [elit], *s.f.* élite; flower, pick; **personnel d'é.,** picked personnel; **régiment d'é.,** crack regiment.

elle, elles [ɛl], *pers.pron.f.* **1.** (*subject*) she, it; they; **c'est elle,** it is she, *F:* it's her. **2.** (*object*) her, it; them; **chez elle,** with her, at her house.

elle-même, elles-mêmes [ɛlmɛːm], *pers.pron.f.* herself, itself; themselves.

élocution [elɔkysjɔ̃], *s.f.* elocution.

éloge [elɔ:ʒ], *s.m.* **1.** eulogy. **2.** praise; **faire l'é. de qn,** to speak highly of s.o.

éloigné [elwaɲe], *a.* far (away), distant, remote (place, time); **le plus é.,** farthest (off); **parent é.,** distant relative.

éloign|er [elwaɲe], *v.tr.* (*a*) to remove (sth.); to get (sth.) out of the way; to send (s.o.) away; **é. une pensée,** to dismiss a thought; (*b*) to postpone, put off (departure, payment); (*c*) **é. qn de qn,** to estrange s.o. from s.o.; *s.m.* **-ement.**

s'éloigner, to move off, withdraw.

éloquence [elɔkã:s], *s.f.* eloquence.

éloqu|ent [elɔkã], *a.* eloquent; *adv.* **-emment.**

élu [ely], *a.* chosen; successful (candidate); elected (member).

élucid|er [elyside], *v.tr.* to elucidate, clear up; *s.f.* **-ation.**

éluder [elyde], *v.tr.* to elude, evade, dodge (the law, a difficulty).

émaciation [emasjasjɔ̃], *s.f.* emaciation.

émacié [emasje], *a.* emaciated; wasted (face).

émail, émaux [ema:j, emo], *s.m.* enamel.

émailler [emaje], *v.tr.* **1.** to enamel. **2.** (*ceramics*) to glaze. **3.** (*of flowers*) to dot (the fields).

émancipé [emãsipe], *a.* uninhibited, unconventional.

émancip|er [emãsipe], *v.tr.* to emancipate; *s.f.* **-ation.**

s'émanciper, to free oneself from control.

emball|er [ãbale], *v.tr.* **1.** to pack (goods); to wrap up (parcel, etc.). **2.** *abs. Sp:* to spurt. **3.** to fire (s.o.) with enthusiasm; **il ne m'emballe pas,** I'm not (much) impressed by him; *s.m.* **-age,** packing; *s.m.* **-ement,** (i) racing (of engine); (ii) burst of enthusiasm; boom.

s'emballer, (*a*) (*of horse*) to bolt; (*b*) (*of engine*) to race; (*c*) to be carried away (by excitement);

ne vous emballez pas! keep cool!
embarcadère [ãbarkadɛːr], *s.m.* landing-stage; wharf, quay.
embarcation [ãbarkasjɔ̃], *s.f.* boat; *esp.* ship's boat.
embargo [ãbargo], *s.m.* embargo.
embarquۙer [ãbarke]. 1. *v.tr.* to embark (passengers); to ship (goods); to hoist in (boat); *Av:* to emplane; (*of bus*) to pick up (passengers). 2. *v.i. & pr.* to embark; *Av:* to emplane; to go on board (ship, plane, etc.); **embarquez!** all aboard! *s.m.* **-ement.**
embarras [ãbara], *s.m.* 1. obstruction, obstacle, encumbrance. 2. (*a*) difficulty, trouble; **se trouver dans l'e.**, to be in difficulties, *esp.* financial; (*b*) **faire des e.**, to make a fuss. 3. embarrassment; (*a*) perplexity; hesitation; **avoir l'e. du choix**, to have too much to choose from; (*b*) confusion.
embarrassant [ãbarasã], *a.* 1. cumbersome. 2. (*a*) perplexing; (*b*) embarrassing, awkward.
embarrasser [ãbarase], *v.tr.* to embarrass. 1. to encumber; to obstruct. 2. (*a*) to trouble, inconvenience; (*b*) to perplex; (*c*) to confuse (s.o.).
embaucher [ãboʃe], *v.tr.* to engage, take on, *N.Am:* to hire (workers); to hire (farm hands).
embaumer [ãbome], *v.tr.* 1. to embalm (corpse). 2. to perfume, scent; *abs.* **ces fleurs embaument**, these flowers have a delightful scent; (*with cognate accusative*) **sa chambre embaumait la violette**, her room was fragrant of violets.
embellۙir [ãbeliːr]. 1. *v.tr.* to embellish; to beautify. 2. *v.i.* to improve in looks; *s.m.* **-issement.**
embêtant [ãbɛtã], *a. F:* 1. annoying. 2. tiresome; **que c'est e.!** what a bore!
embêtۙer [ãbete], *v.tr.* 1. to annoy, plague (s.o.). 2. to bore (s.o.); *s.m.* **-ement**, annoyance; unpleasantness.
emblée (d') [dãble], *adv.phr.* directly; straight off.
emblématique [ãblematik], *a.* emblematic(al).
emblème [ãblɛm], *s.m.* 1. (*a*) emblem, device; (*b*) badge, crest. 2. symbol, sign.
emboîtۙer [ãbwate], *v.tr.* (*a*) to encase; (*b*) to pack in tins, boxes; (*c*) to fit (things) together; to joint, interlock; **e. le pas**, to fall into step (**à qn**, with s.o.); *s.m.* **-ement.**
embonpoint [ãbɔ̃pwɛ̃], *s.m.* stoutness; **prendre de l'e.**, to get fat.
embouchure [ãbuʃyːr], *s.f.* 1. mouthpiece. 2. (*a*) opening, mouth (of sack); (*b*) mouth (of river).
embourbۙer (s') [sãburbe], *v.pr.* to stick in the mud, to flounder; to get bogged down; *s.m.* **-ement.**
embouteillage [ãbuteja:ʒ], *s.m.* 1. bottling (of wine, etc.). 2. blocking, bottling up (of fleet in

harbour, etc.). 3. traffic jam.
embouteiller [ãbuteje], *v.tr.* 1. to bottle. 2. to block up, bottle up. 3. **circulation embouteillée**, congested traffic.
embranchement [ãbrãʃmã], *s.m.* 1. branching (off). 2. branch; (*a*) road junction; (*b*) *Rail:* branch-line.
embrasۙer [ãbraze], *v.tr.* to set fire to (sth.); to set (sth.) ablaze; *s.m.* **-ement**, conflagration.
s'embraser, to catch fire, to blaze up.
embrassۙer [ãbrase], *v.tr.* to embrace (s.o.). 1. (*a*) to hug (s.o.); (*b*) to kiss (s.o.); (*letter formula*) **'je vous embrasse de tout mon cœur,' 'with much love';** (*c*) to adopt (career). 2. to contain, include, cover (facts of a case); *s.f.* **-ade**, *s.m.* **-ement**, embrace.
embrasure [ãbrazyːr], *s.f.* embrasure; window-recess.
embrayۙer [ãbreje], *v.tr.* (**j'embraie, j'embraye**) *Mec:* to connect, couple, engage; *abs. Aut:* to let in the clutch; *s.m.* **-age**, clutch.
embrouillement [ãbrujmã], *s.m.* 1. entanglement. 2. confusion (of ideas).
embrouillۙer [ãbruje], *v.tr.* 1. to tangle (thread). 2. to confuse, muddle.
s'embrouiller, (*a*) to get muddled; (*b*) **l'affaire s'embrouille**, the affair is getting complicated.
embroussaillé [ãbrusaje], *a.* covered with bushes; *F:* tousled (hair).
embrumé [ãbryme], *a.* misty; clouded.
embrun [ãbrœ̃], *s.m.* spray, spindrift.
embryon [ãbrijɔ̃], *s.m. Biol:* embryo.
embuscade [ãbyskad], *s.f.* ambush.
embusqué [ãbyske], *s.m.* 1. man in ambush. 2. *F: Mil:* slacker, dodger, shirker (from active service).
embusquer (s') [sãbyske], *v.pr.* 1. to lie in ambush; to take cover. 2. *F:* (*in war*) to dodge active service.
émeraude [ɛmroːd]. 1. *s.f.* emerald. 2. *a.inv.* emerald green.
émerger [emɛrʒe], *v.i.* (**n. émergeons**) 1. to emerge. 2. to come into view.
émeri [ɛmri], *s.m.* emery; emery-powder.
émerveillۙer [emɛrveje], *v.tr.* to amaze; to fill (s.o.) with wonder, with admiration; *s.m.* **-ement.**
s'émerveiller, to marvel (**de**, at), to be filled with admiration (**de**, for).
émétique [emetik], *s.m.* emetic.
émetteur, -trice [emetœːr, -tris]. 1. *s.m. Rad:* transmitter. 2. *a. Rad:* **poste é.**, broadcasting station.
émettre [emɛtr], *v.tr.* (*conj. like* METTRE) 1. (*a*) to emit; to give off; (*b*) *Rad:* to broadcast. 2. to issue (bank-notes, tickets).
émeute [emøːt], *s.f.* riot; **faire é.**, to riot; **chef d'é.**, ringleader.
émiettۙer [emjete], *v.tr.* to crumble (bread); to

fritter away (a fortune); *s.m.* -**ement**.

émigrant, -ante [emigrã, -ã:t]. 1. *a.* emigrating; migratory (bird). 2. *s.* emigrant.

émigré, -ée [emigre], *s.* émigré.

émigr|er [emigre], *v.i.* 1. (*of birds*) to migrate. 2. (*of pers.*) to emigrate; *s.f.* -**ation**.

éminence [eminãs], *s.f.* eminence; (*a*) rising ground; (*b*) (moral, intellectual) superiority, prominence.

émin|ent [eminã], *a.* eminent; distinguished; *adv.* -**emment**.

émissaire [emisɛ:r], *s.m.* emissary; *a.* **bouc é.**, scapegoat.

mission [emisjɔ̃], *s.f.* 1. (*a*) emission; utterance (of sound); **d'une seule é. de voix**, in one breath; (*b*) *Rad:* broadcasting. 2. issue (of tickets, bank-notes, etc.).

mmagasin|er [ãmagazine], *v.tr.* 1. to store, warehouse. 2. to accumulate (energy); *s.m.* -**age**, storage; accumulation.

mmêler [ãmɛle], *v.tr.* (*a*) to tangle; (*b*) to mix up (facts); to muddle (story).

mménag|er [ãmenaʒe], *v.tr. & i.* (**j'emménageai(s)**) to move (s.o. into a house); to move in; *s.m.* -**ement**.

mmener [ãmne], *v.tr.* (**j'emmène**) to take (s.o.) away, out; **je vous emmène avec moi**, I am taking you with me.

mmitoufler (s') [sãmitufle], *v.pr.* to muffle (oneself) up.

moi [emwa], *s.m.* emotion, agitation; **toute la ville était en é.**, the whole town was agog with excitement.

motion [emosjɔ̃], *s.f.* emotion; excitement; thrill.

motionnant [emosjɔnã], *a.* exciting, thrilling.

motionner (s') [semosjɔne], *v.pr.* to become excited, agitated.

mousser [emuse], *v.tr.* (*a*) to blunt; to take the edge off; (*b*) to dull, deaden (senses); to take the edge off (appetite).

mouvant [emuvã], *a.* moving; (*a*) touching; (*b*) stirring, thrilling.

mouvoir [emuvwa:r], *v.tr.* (*p.p.* **ému;** *otherwise conj. like* MOUVOIR) to move; (*a*) to stir up, rouse; (*b*) to affect, touch; **facile à é.**, emotional.

mouvoir. 1. to get excited. 2. to be touched, moved; **sans s'é.**, calmly.

mpailler [ãpaje], *v.tr.* to stuff (animal).

mpaqueter [ãpakte], *v.tr.* (**j'empaquette**) to pack (sth.) up.

mparer (s') [sãpare], *v.pr.* **s'e. de qch.**, to take possession of sth; to get hold of sth.

mpêch|er [ãpeʃe], *v.tr.* to prevent, hinder, im-**ede;** *impers.* (**il**) **n'empêche que cela nous a coûté cher**, all the same, it has cost us a lot; *.m.* -**ement**, obstacle, hindrance.

mpêcher, (*always in the negative*) to refrain

(de, from); **je ne pus (pas) m'e. de rire**, I couldn't help laughing.

empereur [ãprœ:r], *s.m.* emperor.

empesé [ãpəze], *a.* starched (collar); *F:* stiff, starchy, formal (manner, style).

empeser [ãpəze], *v.tr.* (**j'empèse**) to starch (linen).

empester [ãpɛste], *v.tr.* to make (place) stink; **air empesté par le tabac**, air reeking of tobacco.

empêtr|er [ãpetre], *v.tr.* to entangle; *s.m.* -**ement**, entanglement.

emphase [ãfa:z], *s.f.* bombast; pomposity.

emphatique [ãfatik], *a.* bombastic; pompous; *adv.* -**ment**.

empl|iéter [ãpjete], (**j'empiète; j'empiéterai**) *v.i.* **e. sur le terrain de qn**, to encroach (up)on s.o.'s land; **e. sur les droits de qn**, to infringe s.o.'s rights; *s.m.* -**iètement**.

empiler [ãpile], *v.tr.* to stack, to pile (up).

empire [ãpi:r], *s.m.* 1. (*a*) dominion; sway; **sous l'e. d'un tyran**, under the rule of a tyrant; (*b*) influence, control; **e. sur soi-même**, self-control. 2. empire.

empirer [ãpire], *v.* to worsen. 1. *v.tr.* to make (sth.) worse. 2. *v.i.* to grow worse.

emplacement [ãplasmã], *s.m.* (*a*) site; (*b*) location; (*c*) place, spot.

emplâtre [ãplɑ:tr], *s.m.* 1. *Pharm:* plaster. 2. *F:* **c'est un e.**, he's completely spineless.

emplette [ãplɛt], *s.f.* purchase; **aller faire ses emplettes**, to go shopping.

emploi [ãplwa], *s.m.* 1. use, employment (of sth.); *Sch:* **e. du temps**, time-table (of work); **mode d'e.**, instructions for use. 2. employment, post; job.

employé, -ée [ãplwaje], *s.* employee; (shop-) assistant; **e. de banque**, bank clerk.

employer [ãplwaje], *v.tr.* (**j'emploie**) 1. to employ, use (sth.). 2. to employ (workmen).

s'employer, to occupy oneself; **il s'emploie à jardiner**, he spends his time gardening.

empocher [ãpoʃe], *v.tr. F:* to pocket (money); **e. un coup**, to be hit.

empoigner [ãpwaɲe], *v.tr.* 1. (*a*) to grasp, seize; (*b*) *F:* **ils se sont empoignés**, they had a set-to. 2. to arrest; to catch (criminal). 3. to thrill, grip (reader).

empoisonn|er [ãpwazɔne], *v.tr.* 1. to poison (s.o.); to infect (the air); *abs.* to stink. 2. *F:* to bore (s.o.) stiff; to pester (s.o.); *s.m.* -**ement;** *s.* -**eur, -euse**.

s'empoisonner, to take poison.

emporté [ãpɔrte], *a.* quick-tempered, hot-headed.

emport|er [ãpɔrte], *v.tr.* 1. to take away; **vin à e.**, wine for consumption off the premises. 2. (*a*) **le vent emporta son chapeau**, the wind blew off his hat; (*b*) **e. un fort**, to take a fort (by assault). 3. **se laisser e. par la colère**, to give way to anger. **4. l'e. sur qn,** to get the better of s.o.; *s.m.* **-ement,** fit of anger.

s'emporter, to lose one's temper.

empourprer (s') [sãpurpre], *v.pr.* **1.** (*of pers.*) to flush (up). **2.** (*of sky*) to turn crimson.

empreindre [ãprɛ̃:dr], *v.tr.* (*conj. like* PEINDRE) to impress, stamp; **souvenirs qui s'empreignent sur l'esprit,** memories that are stamped on the mind; **visage empreint de terreur,** face full of terror.

empreinte [ãprɛ̃:t], *s.f.* impression, (im)print; **e. des roues,** track of the wheels; **e. de pas,** footprint; **e. digitale,** fingerprint.

empressé, -ée [ãprese]. **1.** *a.* eager, zealous. **2.** *s.* busybody; **faire l'e. auprès de qn,** to fuss round s.o.

empressement [ãprɛsmã], *s.m.* eagerness, readiness, alacrity.

empresser (s') [sãprese], *v.pr.* **1.** to hurry, hasten (**de faire qch.,** to do sth.). **2. s'e. à faire qch.,** to show zeal in doing sth.; **s'e. auprès de qn,** to dance attendance on s.o.

emprisonn|er [ãprizɔne], *v.tr.* to imprison; *s.m.* **-ement.**

emprunt [ãprœ̃], *s.m.* borrowing; loan; **faire un e. à qn,** to borrow (money) from s.o.; **nom d'e.,** assumed name.

emprunt|er [ãprœ̃te], *v.tr.* to borrow (**à,** from); **e. un nom,** to assume a name; **le cortège emprunta la rue de Rivoli,** the procession went up the Rue de Rivoli; *s.* **-eur, -euse,** borrower.

ému [emy], *a.* moved, touched; upset.

émulation [emylasjõ], *s.f.* emulation, rivalry.

en¹ [ã], *prep.* **1.** (*a*) (*place*) **aller en ville,** to go (in)to town; **en ville,** in town; **venir en avion,** to come by air; (*with f. names of countries*) **être, aller, en France,** to be in, go to, France; (*b*) (*with pron.*) **un homme en qui j'ai confiance,** a man whom I trust; (*c*) **en l'honneur de qn,** in honour of s.o.; **regarder en l'air,** to look up at the sky. **2.** (*time*) **in; en été,** in summer; **né en 1945,** born in 1945; **d'aujourd'hui en huit,** today week. **3.** (*a*) (*state*) **être en deuil,** to be in mourning; **en réparation,** under repair; **en congé,** on leave; (*b*) (*material*) **montre en or,** gold watch; (*c*) (*manner*) **escalier en spirale,** spiral staircase; **docteur en médecine,** doctor of medicine; (*d*) into; **briser qch. en morceaux,** to break sth. into bits; **traduire une lettre en français,** to translate a letter into French; (*e*) **de mal en pis,** from bad to worse. **4. prendre la chose en philosophe,** to take the thing philosophically. **5. travailler en chantant,** to sing at one's work; **en attendant,** in the meantime; **elle sortit en dansant,** she danced out.

en², *unstressed adv. and pron.* **I. adv. 1.** from there; **vous avez été à Londres?—oui, j'en arrive,** you have been to London?—yes, I've just come from there. **2.** on that account; **s'en**

trouver mieux, to feel the better for it. **II. en,** *pron.inv.* **1.** (*a*) of him, her, it, them; **j'aime mieux n'en pas parler,** I would rather not speak about it; **les rues en sont pleines,** the streets are full of it, of them; **qu'en pensez-vous?** what do you think about it, them? (*b*) (*quantity*) **combien avez-vous de chevaux?—j'en ai trois,** how many horses have you got?—I have three; **combien en voulez-vous?** how many do you want? **prenez-en dix,** take ten; (*c*) (*replacing the possessive, when the possessor is inanimate*) **nous avons visité l'église et en avons admiré les vitraux,** we visited the church and admired its stained glass; (*d*) (*standing for a clause*) **vous remplacer, il n'en est pas capable,** he is not fit to take your place. **2.** some, any; **j'en ai,** I have some. **3.** (*indeterminate use*) **si le cœur vous en dit,** if you feel so inclined.

enamourer (s') [sãnamure], *v.pr.* to fall in love (**de,** with).

encadrement [ãkadrəmã], *s.m.* **1.** framing. **2.** framework; frame; setting.

encadrer [ãkadre], *v.tr.* to frame (picture); **jardin encadré de haies,** garden enclosed by hedges.

encaissé [ãkese], *a.* boxed in; deeply embanked (river); sunken (road).

encaiss|er [ãkese], *v.tr.* (*a*) to pack (goods) in cases; (*b*) to encash, collect (bill); *F:* **e. des coups,** to take (heavy) blows; *F:* **je ne peux pas l'e.,** I can't stand him; *s.m.* **-ement.**

encan [ãkã], *s.m.* (public) auction.

en-cas [ãka], *s.m.inv.* emergency supply, snack; **une somme en réserve comme en-c.,** a sum put by to fall back (up)on.

enceinte¹ [ãsɛ̃:t], *s.f.* **1.** surrounding wall. **2.** enclosure. **3.** loudspeaker enclosure.

enceinte², *a.f.* pregnant.

encens [ãsã], *s.m.* incense.

encercler [ãsɛrkle], *v.tr.* to encircle; to shut in.

enchaîn|er [ãʃene], *v.tr.* **1.** chain up. **2.** to link (up), connect (ideas); *s.m.* **-ement,** series; sequence.

enchanté [ãʃãte], *a.* **1.** enchanted. **2.** delighted (**de,** with); (*when introduced to s.o.*) **enchanté(e)! =** how do you do?

enchant|er [ãʃãte], *v.tr.* **1.** to enchant. **2.** to charm, delight; *s.m.* **-ement;** *s.* **-eur, -eresse,** enchanter, enchantress; charmer.

enchère [ãʃɛ:r], *s.f.* bid(ding); **mettre qch. au enchères,** to put sth. up for auction.

enchér|ir [ãʃeri:r], *v.i.* (*a*) to go up in price; (*b*) **sur qn,** to make a higher bid than s.o., to outbid s.o.; *s.* **-isseur, -isseuse,** bidder.

enchevêtr|er [ãʃvetre], *v.tr.* to mix up, confuse; tangle; *s.m.* **-ement,** tangle.

enclin [ãklɛ̃], *a.* inclined, disposed.

enclos [ãklo], *s.m.* enclosure; paddock.

enclume [ãklym], *s.f.* anvil; **être entre l'e. et le marteau,** to be between the devil and the deep blue sea.

encoignure [ãkɔɲyːr], *s.f.* corner, angle (of room).

encolure [ãkɔlyːr], *s.f.* **1.** *Rac:* **gagner par une e.,** to win by a neck. **2.** size in collars.

encombrant [ãkɔ̃brɑ̃], *a.* cumbersome; clumsy; (man) always in the way.

encombr|er [ãkɔ̃bre], *v.tr.* to encumber; to congest (the streets); **e. le marché,** to glut the market; **'n'encombrez pas le passavant,'** 'stand clear of the gangway'; *s.m.* **-ement.**

encontre (à l') [alãkɔ̃ːtr], *adv.phr.* **à l'e. de,** against; in opposition to; **aller à l'e. du danger,** to go out to meet danger.

encore [ãkɔːr], *adv.* **1.** *(a)* still; **hier e.,** only yesterday; *(b)* yet; **pas e.,** not yet; *(c)* more, again; **e. une tasse de café,** another cup of coffee; **quoi e.?** what else? **e. une fois,** once more. **2.** moreover, furthermore; **non seulement . . ., mais e. . . .,** not only . . ., but also . . .. **3.** *(restrictive)* *(a)* **e. si on pouvait lui parler,** if only one could speak to him; *(b)* *(with inversion)* **je n'ai qu'un ciseau, e. est-il émoussé,** I have only one chisel and even that is a blunt one; *(c) conj.phr.* **e. (bien) que** + *sub.,* (al)though; even though; **temps agréable e. qu'un peu froid,** pleasant weather if rather cold.

encourag|er [ãkuraʒe], *v.tr.* (**n. encourageons**) to encourage; *s.m.* **-ement.**

encourir [ãkuriːr], *v.tr. (conj. like* COURIR) to incur; **e. un risque,** to take a chance.

encrasser (s') [sãkrase], *v.pr.* to get dirty, greasy; to get clogged up; to soot up.

encre [ãːkr], *s.f.* ink; **e. de Chine,** Indian ink.

encrier [ãkrije], *s.m.* inkpot; inkstand; ink-well.

encyclopédie [ãsiklɔpedi], *s.f.* encyclopedia.

endémique [ãdemik], *a.* endemic (disease).

endetter (s') [sãdete], to get, run, into debt.

endiablé [ãdjable], *a.* *(a)* reckless, devil-may-care; *(b)* wild, frenzied (music).

endigu|er [ãdige], *v.tr.* **1.** to dam up (river). **2.** to (em)bank (river); *s.m.* **-ement.**

endimancher (s') [sãdimãʃe], *v.pr.* to dress (up) in one's Sunday best.

endolori [ãdɔlɔri], *a.* painful, sore; tender.

endommager [ãdɔmaʒe], *v.tr.* (**n. endommageons**) to damage, injure.

endormi [ãdɔrmi], *a.* **1.** *(a)* asleep, sleeping; *(b)* sleepy; *(c)* dormant. **2.** *(of limb)* numb.

endormir [ãdɔrmiːr], *v.tr. (conj. like* DORMIR) **1.** *(a)* to send (s.o.) to sleep; *(b)* *F:* to bore (s.o.). **2.** *(a)* to anaesthetize; *(b)* to benumb (limb). **3. e. les soupçons,** to allay suspicion.

s'endormir, to fall asleep.

endosser [ãdose], *v.tr.* **1.** to put on (clothes); **e. une responsabilité,** to shoulder, to take on, a

responsibility. **2.** to endorse (cheque).

endroit [ãdrwa], *s.m.* **1.** place, spot; **par endroits,** here and there. **2.** side, aspect; **prendre qn par son e. faible,** *F:* to get on the soft side of s.o. **3.** right side (of material).

enduire [ãdɥiːr], *v.tr. (conj. like* CONDUIRE) to smear, coat, plaster (over); **e. de peinture,** to paint over.

enduit [ãdɥi], *s.m.* **1.** coat, coating (of paint, tar, etc.). **2.** (water-)proofing. **3.** glaze.

endurc|ir [ãdyrsiːr], *v.tr.* **1.** to harden. **2.** to inure (à, to); *s.m.* **-issement.**

s'endurcir. 1. to become hardened; to become callous. **2.** to become fit, tough.

endur|er [ãdyre], *v.tr.* to endure, bear; *a.* **-able;** *s.f.* **-ance;** *a.* **-ant,** patient.

énergie [enerʒi], *s.f.* **1.** energy; force, vigour. **2.** (fuel and) power; **é. atomique,** atomic energy.

énergique [enerʒik], *a.* *(a)* energetic; *(b)* strong, drastic (measure); *adv.* **-ment.**

énerv|er [enerve], *v.tr.* **1.** to enervate, weaken (body, will). **2. é. qn,** to get on s.o.'s nerves; *a.* **-ant,** *F:* annoying, aggravating; *s.m.* **-ement,** nervous irritation.

enfance [ãfãːs], *s.f.* **1.** *(a)* childhood; **première e.,** infancy; *(b)* boyhood; girlhood. **2. retomber en e.,** to sink into one's second childhood, one's dotage.

enfant [ãfã], *s.m. & f.* child; boy; girl.

enfant|er [ãfãte], *v.tr.* to give birth to; *s.m.* **-ement,** childbirth.

enfantillage [ãfãtija:ʒ], *s.m.* childishness.

enfantin [ãfãtɛ̃], *a.* **1.** infantile. **2.** childish (voice, etc.).

enfer [ãfɛːr], *s.m.* hell, Hades; *F:* **aller un train d'e.,** to go hell for leather; **un bruit d'e.,** a hell of a noise.

enfermer [ãferme], *v.tr.* **1.** to shut (sth., s.o.) up; **tenir qn enfermé,** to keep s.o. shut, locked, up. **2.** to shut (sth.) in; to enclose.

enfiler [ãfile], *v.tr.* **1.** to thread (needle); to string (beads). **2.** to go along (a street). **3. e. ses vêtements,** to slip, to pull, on one's clothes.

enfin [ãfɛ̃]. **1.** *adv.* *(a)* finally, lastly; *(b)* in fact, in a word, in short; *(c)* at last. **2.** *int.* *(a)* at last! *(b)* **mais e., s'il acceptait!** but still, if he did accept! *(c)* **e.! ce qui est fait est fait,** well! what's done is done.

enflammé [ãflame], *a.* **1.** burning, blazing; fiery (sunset). **2.** glowing (cheeks). **3.** fiery (speech).

enflammer [ãflame], *v.tr.* **1.** to inflame. **1.** to ignite. **2.** to inflame (wound). **3.** to excite.

s'enflammer. 1. to catch fire. **2.** *(of pers.)* to flare up.

enfl|er [ãfle]. **1.** *v.tr.* to swell; **e. les joues,** to puff out one's cheeks. **2.** *v.i. & pr.* to swell; *s.m.* **-ement;** *s.f.* **-ure,** swelling.

enfoncé [ãfɔse], *a.* **1.** smashed (in), stove in. **2.** sunken, deep-set (eyes).

enfoncl er [ãfɔ̃se], *v.tr.* (n. **enfonçons**) (*a*) to drive (in) (nail); **e. la main dans sa poche**, to thrust one's hand into one's pocket; (*b*) to break open; **e. une porte**, to break down a door; *s.m.* -**ement**.

s'enfoncer, to penetrate, go deep (into sth.).

enfoul ir [ãfwi:r], *v.tr.* to hide (sth.) in the ground; to bury (dead animal, etc.); *s.m.* -**issement**.

enfourcher [ãfurʃe], *v.tr.* to mount (horse, bicycle).

enfourchure [ãfurʃy:r], *s.f.* fork, crotch.

enfreindre [ãfrɛ̃:dr], *v.tr.* (*conj. like* PEINDRE) to break (the law).

enfuir (s') [sãfɥi:r], *v.pr.* (*conj. like* FUIR) **1.** to flee, fly; to run away. **2.** (*of liquid*) to run out.

enfumé [ãfyme], *a.* (*a*) smoky (room, etc.); (*b*) smoke-blackened.

engagé [ãgaʒe], *a.* (*of writer, etc.*) committed.

engagl er [ãgaʒe], *v.tr.* (n. **engageons**) **1.** to pawn; **e. sa parole**, to pledge one's word. **2.** to engage (worker). **3.** (*a*) to catch, entangle (rope); to engage (gears); (*b*) **e. la clef dans la serrure**, to fit, insert, the key in the lock. **4.** to begin, start; to open (conversation). **5. e. qn à faire qch.**, to urge s.o. to do sth.; *a.* -**eant**, engaging, prepossessing; *s.m.* -**ement**.

s'engager. 1. s'e. à faire qch., to undertake to do sth.; **je suis trop engagé pour reculer**, I have gone too far to draw back. **2.** to enlist. **3.** (*a*) (*of rope*) to foul; (*b*) **l'armée s'engagea dans le défilé**, the army entered the pass; (*c*) (*of battle*) to begin.

engelure [ãʒly:r], *s.f.* chilblain.

engendrer [ãʒãdre], *v.tr.* **1.** to beget (child). **2.** to engender (strife, etc.); to generate (heat, etc.); to breed (disease).

engin [ãʒɛ̃], *s.m.* **1.** engine, machine; device; **engins de pêche**, fishing tackle. **2.** missile; **e. téléguidé**, guided missile.

engloutl ir [ãgluti:r], *v.tr.* **1.** to swallow. **2.** to engulf; to swallow up (ship, fortune); *s.m.* -**issement**, engulfment.

engorger [ãgɔrʒe], *v.tr.* (n. **engorgeons**) to choke (up), stop (up); to block, clog.

engouffrer [ãgufre], *v.tr.* to engulf, swallow up.

engourdi [ãgurdi], *a.* **1.** numb(ed); **j'ai le pied e.**, my foot has gone to sleep. **2.** dull, sluggish (mind).

engourdl ir (s') [sãgurdi:r]. **1.** (*of limb*) to grow numb; to go to sleep. **2.** (*of mind*) to become dull; *s.m.* -**issement**, numbness; sluggishness.

engrais [ãgrɛ], *s.m.* manure; **e. chimique**, fertilizer.

engraissl er [ãgrɛse]. **1.** *v.tr.* (*a*) to fatten; (*b*) to manure (land). **2.** *v.i.* to grow stout; *s.m.* -**ement**.

engrenage [ãgrəna:ʒ], *s.m.* **1.** *Mec.E:* gearing, set of gears; *Aut:* **e. de direction**, steering gear.

2. mesh (of circumstances); **être pris dans l'e.**, to get involved, caught up.

engueull er [ãgœle], *v.tr. P:* to abuse (s.o.); to tell (s.o.) where to get off; *s.f.* -**ade**, telling-off.

enhardir [ãardi:r], *v.tr.* to embolden.

s'enhardir, to pluck up courage.

énigmatique [enigmatik], *a.* enigmatic.

énigme [enigm], *s.f.* enigma, riddle.

enivrl er [ãnivre], *v.tr.* to intoxicate; to make (s.o.) drunk; *a.* -**ant**, heady; *s.m.* -**ement**, intoxication; ecstasy.

enjambée [ãʒãbe], *s.f.* stride.

enjamber [ãʒãbe], *v.tr.* (*a*) to bestride (horse); (*b*) to step over (obstacle); **trois ponts enjambent le fleuve**, three bridges span the river.

enjeu, -eux [ãʒø], *s.m. Gaming:* stake.

enjôll er [ãʒole], *v.tr.* to coax, wheedle; *a. & s.* -**eur, -euse**, coaxing; coaxer, wheedler.

enjoliver [ãʒɔlive], *v.tr.* to beautify, embellish.

enjoliveur [ãʒɔlivœ:r], *s.m. Aut:* wheel disc; hub cap.

enjoué [ãʒwe], *a.* playful, sprightly.

enjouement [ãʒumã], *s.m.* sprightliness.

enlacer [ãlase], *v.tr.* (n. **enlaçons**) (*a*) to entwine; (*b*) to clasp (s.o.) in one's arms; to hug (s.o.).

enlaidir [ãledi:r]. **1.** *v.tr.* to make (s.o.) ugly; to disfigure (s.o.). **2.** *v.i.* to grow ugly.

enlèvement [ãlɛvmã], *s.m.* **1.** removal. **2.** kidnapping; carrying off. **3.** *Mil:* storming (of position).

enlever [ãlve], *v.tr.* (**j'enlève**) **1.** (*a*) to remove; **e. le couvert**, to clear the table; **enlevé par la mer**, carried away by the sea; (*b*) **e. qch. à qn**, to take sth. from s.o. **2.** to carry off; to kidnap; **se faire e. par qn**, to elope with s.o. **3.** *Mil:* to storm (position). **4.** to raise; **e. le couvercle**, to lift the lid.

enliser (s') [sãlize], *v.pr.* to sink (into quicksand, bog); (*of car*) to get bogged down.

enneigement [ãnɛʒmã], *s.m.* snowfall; **bulletin d'e.**, snow report.

ennemi [ɛnmi]. **1.** *s.* enemy. **2.** *a.* hostile (**de**, to).

ennui [ãnɥi], *s.m.* **1.** worry, anxiety; **créer des ennuis à qn**, to make trouble for s.o.; **quel e.!** what a nuisance! **2.** boredom.

ennuyl er [ãnɥije], *v.tr.* (**j'ennuie**) **1.** (*a*) to annoy, worry (s.o.); (*b*) to bother (s.o.). **2.** to bore, weary (s.o.); *a.* -**ant**, annoying; *a.* -**euse**, boring.

s'ennuyer, (*a*) to be bored; (*b*) **s'e. de qn**, to miss s.o.

énoncl er [enɔ̃se], *v.tr.* (n. **énonçons**) **1.** to state (opinion). **2.** to articulate (word); *s.f.* -**iation**.

enorgueillir (s') [sãnɔrgœji:r], *v.pr.* **s'e. de qch.** to pride oneself on sth.

énorml e [enɔrm], *a.* enormous, huge; *a.* -**ément**.

énormité [enɔrmite], *s.f.* **1.** (*a*) enormity; outrageousness (of demand, etc.); (*b*) vastness hugeness. **2.** *F:* **commettre une é.**, to drop a clanger; **dire des énormités**, to say the most awful things.

enquérir (s') [sãkeri:r], *v.pr.* (*conj. like* ACQUÉRIR) to enquire, make enquiries (**de qn**, after s.o., **de qch.**, about sth.); **s'e. du prix**, to ask the price.

enquête [ãke:t], *s.f.* inquiry, investigation.

enraciné [ãrasine], *a.* deep-rooted; deep-seated.

enraciner (s') [sãrasine], *v.pr.* to take root; (*of habit*) to become established.

enragé [ãraʒe], *a.* (*a*) mad (dog); (*b*) enthusiastic, keen (fisherman, etc.), out-and-out (fanatic, etc.).

enrager [ãraʒe], *v.* (**n. enrageons**) **1.** *v.tr.* to enrage, to madden (s.o.). **2.** *v.i.* to fume; to be furious; **faire e. qn**, to make s.o. wild.

enregistr⎮er [ãr(ə)ʒistre], *v.tr.* **1.** to register, record (a birth, etc.); *Rail:* **e. ses bagages**, to register one's luggage. **2.** to record (music, etc.); **e. sur bande**, to tape, to record on tape; *s.m.* **-ement**.

enrhumer (s') [sãryme], *v.pr.* to catch cold.

enrichir [ãriʃi:r], *v.tr.* to enrich.

s'enrichir, to grow rich.

enrôl⎮er [ãrole], *v.tr.* to enrol; *s.m.* **-ement**.

enroué [ãrwe], *a.* hoarse, husky.

enrouement [ãrumã], *s.m.* hoarseness, huskiness.

enrouler [ãrule], *v.tr.* (*a*) to roll up (map); (*b*) to wrap (sth.) up (**dans**, in).

s'enrouler, to wind, coil (**autour de**, around).

ensanglanté [ãsãglãte], *a.* covered with blood; blood-stained.

enseigne [ãsɛɲ], *s.f.* (*a*) sign, index, token; (*b*) sign(-board).

enseignement [ãsɛɲmã], *s.m.* **1.** teaching; **entrer dans l'e.**, to go in for teaching; **il est dans l'e.**, he's a teacher, a schoolmaster. **2.** education, instruction.

enseigner [ãsɛɲe], *v.tr.* **1.** to show; to point out. **2.** (*a*) **e. les enfants**, to teach children; (*b*) **e. à qn à faire qch.**, to teach s.o. to do sth.; **e. l'anglais**, to teach English.

ensemble [ãsã:bl]. **1.** *adv.* together; **être bien e.**, to be good friends; **le tout e.**, (i) the general effect; (ii) the whole lot; **agir d'e.**, to act in concert. **2.** *s.m.* (*a*) whole, entirety; **vue d'e.**, general view; (*b*) cohesion, unity; **avec e.**, harmoniously; as one; (*c*) *H:* suite of furniture; *Cl:* ensemble.

ensevel⎮ir [ãsəvli:r], *v.tr.* to bury; *s.m.* **-issement**, burial.

ensoleillé [ãsɔleje], *a.* sunny.

ensorceler [ãsɔrsəle], *v.tr.* (**j'ensorcelle**) to bewitch; to captivate (s.o.).

ensuite [ãsɥit], *adv.* after(wards), then; **et e.?** what then?

ensuivre (s') [sãsɥi:vr], *v.pr.impers.* (*conj. like* SUIVRE; *used only in the third pers.*) to follow, ensue, result; **il s'ensuit que . . .**, it follows that **. . .; et tout ce qui s'ensuit**, *F:* and what not.

entaille [ãtɑ:j], *s.f.* (*a*) notch, nick; groove; (*b*) gash, slash; **à entailles**, slotted; notched.

entailler [ãtɑje], *v.tr.* (*a*) to notch, nick; (*b*) to gash, cut, slash.

entamer [ãtame], *v.tr.* **1.** to cut into (loaf); to open (bottle); **e. son capital**, to break into one's capital. **2.** to begin (conversation); **e. un sujet**, to broach a subject; *Cards:* **e. trèfles**, to open clubs.

entass⎮er, [ãtase], *v.tr.* (*a*) to accumulate; to heap (up); to stack (up) (cases); to amass (money); (*b*) to pack, crowd, cram (passengers, cattle) together; *s.m.* **-ement**.

s'entasser, (*a*) (*of thgs*) to accumulate; (*b*) to crowd together.

entendre [ãtã:dr], *v.tr.* **1.** to intend, mean; **e. faire qch.**, to intend, mean, to do sth.; **faites comme vous l'entendez**, do as you think best. **2.** (*a*) to hear; **e. parler de qch.**, to hear of sth.; **e. dire qch. à qn**, to hear s.o. say sth.; (*b*) to listen to (s.o., sth.); **veuillez m'e.**, give me a hearing; **à vous e. . . .**, according to you **. . . 3.** (*a*) **e. une langue**, to understand a language; **il n'entend pas la plaisanterie**, he can't take a joke; **c'est entendu**, agreed; **bien entendu!** of course! (*b*) to know all about (sth.); **je n'y entends rien**, I don't know the first thing about it.

s'entendre. 1. to agree; to understand one another. **2.** to be skilled (**à**, in); **s'e. en musique**, to know about music.

entente [ãtã:t], *s.f.* **1.** (*a*) understanding (**de**, of); (*b*) **mot à double e.**, word with a double meaning. **2.** agreement, understanding (**entre**, between); **e. cordiale**, friendly understanding.

entérite [ãterit], *s.f. Med:* enteritis.

enterr⎮er [ãtere], *v.tr.* to bury; *s.m.* **-ement**, burial; funeral.

en-tête [ãtɛt], *s.m.* (*a*) heading (of letter); **papier à en-t.**, headed notepaper; (*b*) *Typ:* headline (of page, column), *N.Am:* caption; *pl.* **en-têtes**.

entêté [ãtete], *a.* obstinate; pig-headed.

entêtement [ãtetmã], *s.m.* obstinacy, stubbornness.

entêter (s') [sãtete], *v.pr.* to be obstinate, stubborn.

enthousiasme [ãtuzjasm], *s.m.* enthusiasm.

enthousiasmer (s') [sãtuzjasme], *v.pr.* to be enthusiastic, to enthuse (**pour, de**, over).

enthousiaste [ãtuzjast]. **1.** *s.m. & f.* enthusiast. **2.** *a.* enthusiastic.

entier, -ière [ãtje, -je:r], *a.* **1.** entire, whole; **la France entière**, the whole of France; **lait e.**, full cream milk; **payer place entière**, to pay full fare. **2.** complete, full (authority, etc.). **3.** *adv.phr.* **en e.**, entirely, in full.

entièrement [ãtjɛrmã], *adv.* entirely, wholly.
entomolog|ie [ãtɔmɔlɔʒi], *s.f.* entomology; *a.*
-**ique**, entomological.
entonner [ãtɔne], *v.tr. Mus:* 1. to intone; **e. les**
louanges de qn, to sing s.o.'s praises. 2. to
strike up (a song).
entonnoir [ãtɔnwa:r], *s.m.* 1. funnel; **en (forme**
d')e., funnel-shaped. 2. (*a*) shell-hole, crater;
(*b*) corrie; *Geol:* sink-hole.
entorse [ãtɔrs], *s.f.* sprain, wrench.
entour [ãtu:r], *s.m.* **à l'e.,** around, round about; **à**
l'e. de, round (the town).
entourage [ãtura:ʒ], *s.m.* 1. surroundings. 2. set,
circle (of friends); environment.
entourer [ãture], *v.tr.* to surround (**de,** with).
entracte [ãtrakt], *s.m. Th:* 1. interval. 2.
interlude.
entraide [ãtrɛ(:)d], *s.f.* (*no pl.*) mutual aid.
entraider (s') [sãtrede], *v.pr.* to help one
another.
entrailles [ãtrɑ:j], *s.f.pl.* 1. entrails, bowels. 2.
heart; compassion; **être sans e.,** to be ruthless.
entr'aimer (s') [sãtreme], *v.pr.* to love one
another.
entrain [ãtrɛ̃], *s.m.* liveliness, briskness; spirit,
F: go; **faire qch. sans e.,** to do sth. in a half-
hearted manner.
entraîn|er [ãtrene], *v.tr.* 1. to carry along; to
carry away. 2. **se laisser e.,** to allow oneself to
be led astray, carried away. 3. to entail, involve. 4. *Sp:* to train (horse, athlete); to coach
(team); *s.m.* -**ement,** training.
entraver [ãtrave], *v.tr.* 1. to shackle; to hobble (a
horse). 2. to hinder, impede; **e. la circulation,**
to hold up the traffic.
entre [ã:tr], *prep.* 1. between; **femme e. deux**
âges, middle-aged woman; **e. les deux,** betwixt
and between. 2. (*a*) among(st); **ce jour e. tous,**
this day of all days; (*b*) **tomber e. les mains de**
l'ennemi, to fall into the enemy's hands; (*c*)
d'e., (from) among; **l'un d'e. eux,** one of them.
3. **ils s'accordent e. eux,** they agree among
themselves.
entrebâillé [ãtrəbaje], *a.* ajar, half-open (door).
entrechoquer (s') [sãtrəʃɔke], *v.pr.* (*a*) to
collide; (*b*) to knock against one another.
entrecôte [ãtrəko:t], *s.f. Cu:* steak (cut from
ribs), entrecote steak; **e. minute,** minute, thin
grilled, steak.
entrecouper [ãtrəkupe], *v.tr.* 1. to intersect. 2. to
interrupt.
entrée [ãtre], *s.f.* 1. entry, entering; **faire son e.,**
to make one's entrance. 2. admission, admit-
tance (to club); *P.N:* **e. interdite,** no admittance; **e. libre,** walk-around store. 3. way in;
entrance. 4. *Cu:* entrée.
entrefaite [ãtrəfɛt], *s.f.* **sur ces entrefaites,**
meanwhile, in the midst of all this.
entrelac|er [ãtrəlase], *v.tr.* (*conj. like* LACER) to

interlace; *s.m.* -**ement.**
entremêler (s') [sãtrəmele], *v.pr.* to (inter)mix,
(inter)mingle.
entremise [ãtrəmi:z], *s.f.* (*a*) intervention; (*b*)
mediation; **agir par l'e. de qn,** to act through
s.o.
entrepôt [ãtrəpo], *s.m.* warehouse, store.
entreprenant [ãtrəprənã], *a.* enterprising.
entreprendre [ãtrəprã:dr], *v.tr.* (*conj. like* PREN-
DRE) 1. to undertake; to take (sth.) in hand. 2.
to contract for (piece of work).
entrepreneur [ãtrəprənœ:r], *s.* contractor;
builder; **e. de transports,** forwarding agent; **e.**
de pompes funèbres, undertaker.
entreprise [ãtrəpri:z], *s.f.* 1. undertaking; venture; firm; **e. commerciale,** business concern.
2. **travail à l'e.,** work on, by, contract.
entrer [ãtre], *v.i.* (*aux. être*) 1. (*a*) to enter; to go
in, to come in; *P.N:* **défense d'e.,** no admittance; **e. en courant,** to run in; **e. en passant,** *F:*
to drop in (on s.o.); (*b*) **e. en fonction,** to take
up one's duties. 2. to enter into, take part in
(sth.); **vous n'entrez pour rien dans l'affaire,**
you are in no way concerned with the business.
entresol [ãtrəsɔl], *s.m.* entresol; mezzanine
(floor).
entretenir [ãtrətni:r], *v.tr.* (*conj. like* TENIR) 1. to
maintain; to keep up (correspondence, etc.); **e.**
une route, to keep a road in repair; **s'e. la main,**
to keep one's hand in. 2. (*a*) to maintain, support (family); (*b*) **e. des soupçons,** to entertain
suspicions. 3. **e. qn (de qch.),** to talk to s.o.
(about sth.).
s'entretenir. 1. to talk, converse (**avec,** with; **de,**
about). 2. *Sp:* to keep fit.
entretien [ãtrətjɛ̃], *s.m.* 1. upkeep, maintenance;
servicing (of car); **produits d'e.,** (household)
cleaning materials. 2. support (of family). 3.
conversation; interview.
entrevoir [ãtrəvwa:r], *v.tr.* (*conj. like* VOIR) to
catch sight, catch a glimpse, of; **laisser e. qch.**
à qn, to drop a hint of sth. to s.o.
entrevue [ãtrəvy], *s.f.* interview.
entrouvert [ãtruvɛ:r], *a.* half-open (window);
(door) ajar.
entrouvrir [ãtruvri:r], *v.tr.* (*conj. like* OUVRIR) to
half-open; to set (door) ajar.
énumér|er [enymere], *v.tr.* (**j'énumère;**
j'énumérerai) to enumerate; to count up; *s.*
-**ateur,** -**atrice,** enumerator; *s.f.* -**ation.**
envah|ir [ãvai:r], *v.tr.* 1. to invade, to overrun
(country, etc.); **envahi par l'eau,** flooded. 2. to
encroach upon (neighbour's land); *s.m.*
-**isseur,** invader; *s.m.* -**issement.**
enveloppe [ãvlɔp], *s.f.* 1. envelope, cover(-ing)
(of letter); wrapper. 2. sheathing, casing;
lagging (of boiler); outer cover (of tyre).
envelopp|er [ãvlɔpe], *v.tr.* to envelop; (*a*) to
wrap (sth.) up; **enveloppé de brume,** shrouded

in mist; (b) to cover; to lag (boiler); (c) to surround; **la nuit nous enveloppa,** darkness closed in upon us; *s.m.* -**ement.**

envenimer [ãvnime], *v.tr.* 1. to poison. 2. to aggravate, to embitter (quarrel).

envers[1] [ãvɛːr], *s.m.* wrong side, reverse, back (of material, etc.); **à l'e.,** (i) inside out; (ii) wrong way up.

envers[2], *prep.* towards; **mal agir e. qn,** to behave badly towards s.o.

envie [ãvi], *s.f.* 1. desire, longing; **avoir e. de qch.,** to want sth.; **avec e.,** longingly. 2. envy; **faire e. à qn,** to make s.o. envious; **porter e. à qn,** to envy s.o. 3. (a) hangnail; (b) birthmark.

envier [ãvje], *v.tr.* to envy. 1. to covet. 2. to be envious of (s.o.).

envieu|x, -euse [ãvjø, -øːz], *a.* envious (**de,** of); *adv.* -**sement.**

environ [ãvirɔ̃]. 1. *adv.* about. 2. *s.m.pl.* **environs,** surroundings, neighbourhood (of a place).

environn|er [ãvirɔne], *v.tr.* to surround; *s.m.* -**ement,** surroundings; environment.

envisager [ãvizaʒe], *v.tr.* (**n. envisageons**) to face, envisage; (a) to look (s.o.) in the face; (b) to consider (possibility); **e. l'avenir,** to look to the future; **cas non envisagé,** unforeseen case.

envoi [ãvwa], *s.m.* 1. sending, **e. de fonds,** remittance (of funds); *Fb:* **coup d'e.,** (i) kick-off; (ii) place-kick; free kick. 2. consignment, parcel.

envol [ãvɔl], *s.m.* 1. (a) (*of birds*) taking flight; (b) (*of aircraft*) taking off; **piste d'e.,** runway; **pont d'e.,** flight deck. 2. (a) flight; (b) take-off.

envoler (s') [sãvɔle], *v.pr.* (a) (*of bird*) to fly away; to take flight; (b) (*of aircraft*) to take off; (c) (*of hat*) to blow off.

envoyé [ãvwaje], *s.m.* messenger, *esp.* (Government) envoy; *Journ:* correspondent.

envoyer [ãvwaje], *v.tr.* (**j'envoie;** *fu.* **j'enverrai**) to send; **e. chercher qn,** to send for s.o.; *F:* **je ne le lui ai pas envoyé dire,** I told him straight; *F:* **e. promener qn,** to send s.o. packing.

épagneul, -eule [epaɲœl], *s.* spaniel.

épais, -aisse [epɛ, -ɛːs], *a.* thick (wall, etc.); **feuillage é.,** dense foliage; **avoir l'esprit é.,** to be dull-witted.

épaisseur [epɛsœːr], *s.f.* 1. thickness; depth. 2. density, thickness (of fog).

épaiss|ir [epɛsiːr]. 1. *v.tr.* to thicken. 2. *v.i. & pr.* to thicken, become thick; (*of pers.*) to become stout; (*of darkness*) to deepen; *s.m.* -**issement.**

épanch|er [epãʃe], *v.tr.* to pour out (liquid); to shed (blood); *s.m.* -**ement,** outpouring (of feeling); effusion (of blood).

s'épancher, to pour out one's heart.

épandre [epãːdr], *v.tr.* to spread; to shed (light).

s'épandre, (*of water, fire*) to spread.

épanoui [epanwi], *a.* (*of flower*) full-blown;

visage é., beaming face.

épanouir (s') [sepanwiːr], *v.pr.* 1. to open out, bloom. 2. (*of face*) to light up.

épanouissement [epanwismã], *s.m.* 1. (a) opening out (of flowers); (b) (*of the face*) beaming. 2. (full) bloom.

épargne [eparɲ], *s.f.* 1. saving, economy. 2. **vivre de ses épargnes,** to live on one's savings; **caisse d'é.,** savings bank; **bon d'e.** = national savings certificate.

épargner [eparɲe], *v.tr.* 1. to save (time, money); to economize; to be sparing, economical, with (sth.). 2. to spare (a prisoner's life).

éparpill|er [eparpije], *v.tr.* to disperse, scatter; *s.m.* -**ement.**

épatant [epatã], *a. F:* wonderful; fine; splendid; **c'est un type é.,** he's a great chap.

épater [epate], *v.tr. F:* to astound, flabbergast, amaze; to bowl (s.o.) over.

s'épater, *F:* **il ne s'épate de rien,** nothing surprises him.

épaule [epoːl], *s.f.* shoulder.

épaulette [epolɛt], *s.f. Cl:* (a) shoulder-strap; (b) *Mil:* epaulet(te).

épave [epaːv], *s.f. Nau:* wreck; derelict; *pl.* wreckage.

épée [epe], *s.f.* sword; rapier; **coup d'é.,** sword thrust; **coup d'é. dans l'eau,** wasted effort.

épeler [eple], *v.tr.* (**j'épelle**) to spell.

éperdu [eperdy], *c.* distracted, bewildered; **résistance éperdue,** desperate resistance; *adv.* -**ment.**

éperon [eprɔ̃], *s.m.* 1. *Equit:* spur. 2. spur (of mountain range).

éperonner [eprɔne], *v.tr.* to spur (horse); to urge (s.o.) on.

éphémère [efemɛːr]. 1. *a.* ephemeral, short-lived. 2. *s.m. Ent:* may-fly.

épi [epi], *s.m.* ear (of grain); spike (of flower).

épice [epis], *s.f.* spice; **pain d'é.,** gingerbread.

épicé [epise], *a.* highly spiced; hot (seasoning).

épicer [epise], *v.tr.* (**n. épiçons**) to spice.

épicerie [episri], *s.f.* (a) groceries; (b) grocer's shop.

épicier, -ière [episje, -jɛːr], *s.* grocer.

épidémie [epidemi], *s.f.* epidemic; outbreak (of disease).

épiderme [epidɛrm], *s.m.* epidermis, skin.

épier [epje], *v.tr.* 1. to watch; to spy (up)on (s.o.). 2. to be on the look-out for (opportunity).

épilepsie [epilɛpsi], *s.f.* epilepsy.

épileptique [epilɛptik], *a. & s.* epileptic.

épilogue [epilɔg], *s.m.* epilogue.

épinard [epina:r], *s.m. Bot: Cu:* (*usu.pl.*) spinach.

épine [epin], *s.f.* 1. thorn-bush. 2. thorn, prickle. 3. **é. dorsale,** spine, backbone.

épineux, -euse [epinø, -øːz], *a.* thorny, prickly; **affaire épineuse,** ticklish matter.

épingle [epɛ̃:gl], *s.f.* pin; **é. de sûreté, é. anglaise,** safety pin; **tiré à quatre épingles,** spick and span; **tirer son é. du jeu,** to get out of a venture without loss; **coups d'é.,** pin-pricks, petty annoyances.

épingler [epɛ̃gle], *v.tr.* to pin.

épique [epik], *a.* epic.

épisode [epizɔd], *s.m.* episode; instalment.

épitaphe [epitaf], *s.f.* epitaph.

épithète [epitɛt], *s.f.* epithet.

épître [epi:tr], *s.f.* epistle; *Ecc:* **côté de l'é.,** south side, epistle side (of the altar).

éploré [eplɔre], *a.* tearful, weeping.

épluch|er [eplyʃe], *v.tr.* **1.** to peel (potatoes, etc.). **2.** to examine (work) in detail; **é. une question,** to sift a question; *s.m.* **-age.**

épluchures [eplyʃy:r], *s.f.pl.* peelings, parings; refuse.

éponge [epɔ̃:ʒ], *s.f.* sponge; **passons l'é. là-dessus,** let's say no more about it.

épong|er [epɔ̃ʒe], *v.tr.* (n. **épongeons**) to sponge up, mop up (liquid); **s'é. le front,** to mop one's brow; *s.m.* **-eage.**

époque [epɔk], *s.f.* **1.** epoch, era, age; **faire é.,** to mark an epoch; **meubles d'é.,** antique furniture. **2. à l'é. de sa naissance,** at the time of his birth.

épouser [epuze], *v.tr.* **1.** to marry, wed. **2.** to take up, adopt, espouse (cause).

époussetier [epuste], *v.tr.* (**j'époussette**) to dust (furniture); *s.m.* **-age.**

épouvantable [epuvɑ̃tabl], *a.* dreadful, frightful; appalling; *adv.* **-ment.**

épouvantail, -ails [epuvɑ̃ta:j], *s.m.* scarecrow.

épouvante [epuvɑ̃:t], *s.f.* terror, fright; **film d'é.,** horror film.

épouvanter [epuvɑ̃te], *v.tr.* to terrify.

s'épouvanter, to take fright.

époux, -ouse [epu, -u:z], *s.* husband, *f.* wife.

éprendre (s') [seprɑ̃:dr], *v.pr.* (*conj. like* PRENDRE) to fall in love (**de qn,** with s.o.); to take a fancy (**de qch.,** to sth.).

épreuve [eprœ:v], *s.f.* **1.** (*a*) proof, test, trial; **amitié à l'é.,** staunch friendship; **à l'é. de qch.,** proof against sth.; (*b*) *Sch:* (examination) paper; (*c*) *Sp:* event. **2.** trial, affliction, ordeal. **3.** (*a*) *Typ:* proof (of book); (*b*) *Phot:* print.

épris [epri], *a.* in love (**de,** with).

éprouvé [epruve], *a.* **1.** experienced; **remède é.,** well-tried remedy. **2.** sorely tried; impaired (health); **région éprouvée,** stricken area.

éprouver [epruve], *v.tr.* **1.** to test, try. **2.** to feel, experience (sensation).

éprouvette [epruvɛt], *s.f.* test-tube.

épuisé [epɥize], *a.* (i) exhausted, tired, worn-out; (ii) out of print.

épuis|er [epɥize], *v.tr.* to exhaust. **1.** to use up, consume; to drain, empty (well). **2.** to wear, tire, (s.o.) out; *s.m.* **-ement.**

s'épuiser, to become exhausted.

équateur [ekwatœ:r]. **1.** *s.m.* equator; **sous l'é.,** at the equator. **2.** *Pr.n.m. Geog:* Ecuador.

équation [ekwasjɔ̃], *s.f. Mth:* equation.

équatorial, -aux [ekwatɔrjal, -o], *a.* equatorial.

équestre [ekɛstr], *a.* equestrian (statue).

équilibre [ekilibr], *s.m.* balance, stability.

équilibrer [ekilibre], *v.tr.* to balance.

équinoxe [ekinɔks], *s.m.* equinox.

équipage [ekipa:ʒ], *s.m.* **1.** *Nau:* crew; ship's company; *Av:* aircrew; **é. d'un camion,** crew of a lorry. **2.** pack of hounds, hunt; **maître d'é.,** master of hounds. **3.** (*general sense of "requisites"*) **é. d'atelier,** workshop equipment; **é. de pompe,** pump gear.

équipe [ekip], *s.f.* **1.** gang (of workmen); *Mil:* working party; **travailler par équipes,** to work in shifts; **chef d'é.,** foreman. **2.** *Sp:* team; side.

équip|er [ekipe], *v.tr.* to equip; to fit out; *s.m.* **-ement,** equipment; outfit.

équitable [ekitabl], *a.* (*a*) equitable, fair; (*b*) fair-minded; *adv.* **-ment.**

équitation [ekitasjɔ̃], *s.f.* horsemanship; **école d'é.,** riding school.

équité [ekite], *s.f.* equity, fairness.

équivalent [ekivalɑ̃], *a. & s.m.* equivalent.

équivaloir [ekivalwa:r], *v.i.* (*conj. like* VALOIR) to be equivalent, equal in value (**à,** to).

équivoque [ekivɔk]. **1.** *a.* (*a*) equivocal, ambiguous; (*b*) questionable, dubious (conduct). **2.** *s.f.* ambiguity (of expression).

érable [erabl], *s.m. Bot:* maple(-tree, -wood).

érafl|er [erafle], *v.tr.* to scratch, graze; *s.f.* **-ure.**

éraillé [eraje], *a.* scratched (surface); raucous (voice).

ère [ɛ:r], *s.f.* era; epoch; **en l'an 66 de notre è.,** in A.D. 66.

éreintant [erɛ̃tɑ̃], *a.* back-breaking (work).

éreinté [erɛ̃te], *a. F:* dead-beat, all-in.

éreint|er [erɛ̃te], *v.tr.* **1.** to exhaust (s.o.); to tire (s.o.) out. **2.** to criticize (author, etc.) unmercifully; *s.m.* **-ement.**

Érié [erje]. *Pr.n.m. Geog:* **le lac É.,** Lake Erie.

ériger [eriʒe], *v.tr.* (n. **érigeons**) **1.** to erect, set up, raise (a statue). **2.** to establish, set up (tribunal, etc.).

ermitage [ɛrmita:ʒ], *s.m.* hermitage.

ermite [ɛrmit], *s.m.* hermit.

éroder [erɔde], *v.tr.* to erode; to eat away (metal, coast, etc.).

érosion [erozjɔ̃], *s.f.* erosion; wearing away.

érotique [erɔtik], *a.* erotic; amatory (poem).

érotisme [erɔtism], *s.m.* eroticism.

errer [ɛr(r)e, ere], *v.i.* to roam, wander (about); **laisser e. ses pensées,** to let one's thoughts stray, run on.

erreur [ɛrœ:r], *s.f.* error. **1.** mistake, blunder, slip; **sauf e.,** if I am not mistaken. **2.** false belief, delusion.

:rroné [ɛrɔne], *a.* erroneous, wrong, mistaken.

:rudit, -ite [erydi, -it]. **1.** *a.* erudite, scholarly. **2.** *s.* scholar.

:rudition [erydisjɔ̃], *s.f.* erudition, scholarship.

:ruption [erypsjɔ̃], *s.f.* eruption.

:s [ɛs] = **en les; licencié ès lettres** = B.A.; M.A.

scabeau, -eaux [ɛskabo], *s.m.* (small) step-ladder.

scadre [ɛskadr], *s.f. Nau:* squadron; *Av:* wing; **chef d'e.,** *Nau:* Commodore; Squadron Commander; *Av:* Wing Commander.

scadrille [ɛskadri:j], *s.f. Nau:* flotilla; *Av:* flight.

scadron [ɛskadrɔ̃], *s.m. Mil:* squadron; *Av:* squadron; group.

scalade [ɛskalad], *s.f.* **1.** scaling, climbing; *Jur:* housebreaking. **2.** *Pol:* escalation.

scalader [ɛskalade], *v.tr.* to scale, climb (wall, etc.).

scale [ɛskal], *s.f. Nau:* port of call; *Av:* intermediate landing; **faire e. à,** to put in, touch down, at; **vol sans e.,** non-stop flight.

scalier [ɛskalje], *s.m.* staircase; (flight of) stairs; **e. roulant,** escalator.

scalope [ɛskalɔp], *s.f.* fillet, escalope (of veal).

scamotable [ɛskamɔtabl], *a.* folding (table); *Av:* retractable (undercarriage).

scamoter [ɛskamɔte], *v.tr.* **1.** (*of conjuror, etc.*) to conjure (sth.) away; to make (sth.) vanish; to skip, to scamp (job); *Av:* to retract (undercarriage). **2.** *F:* to steal, *F:* pinch; *s.m.* **-age.**

scamoteur [ɛskamɔtœ:r], *s.m.* **1.** conjuror. **2.** sneak thief.

scapade [ɛskapad], *s.f.* escapade; prank.

scargot [ɛskargo], *s.m.* snail.

scarpé [ɛskarpe], *a.* steep, precipitous, abrupt (slope); sheer (cliff).

scarpement [ɛskarpmɑ̃], *s.m.* steep slope; escarpment; descent.

scaut (l') [lɛsko]. *Pr.n.m. Geog:* the (river) Scheldt.

sclaffer (s') [sɛsklafe], *v.pr. F:* to burst out laughing; to roar with laughter.

sclavage [ɛsklava:ʒ] *s.m.* slavery.

sclave [ɛskla:v], *s.m. & f.* slave.

scompte [ɛskɔ̃:t], *s.m. Com:* discount, rebate; *Fin:* **le taux d'e.,** bank rate of discount, the bank rate.

scompter [ɛskɔ̃te], *v.tr.* **1.** *Com:* to discount (bill). **2. e. un succès,** to anticipate success.

scorte [ɛskɔrt], *s.f.* escort; convoy.

scorter [ɛskɔrte], *v.tr.* to escort; to convoy.

scouade [ɛskwad], *s.f.* squad, gang (of workmen).

scrime [ɛskrim], *s.f.* fencing, swordsmanship.

scrimeur [ɛskrimœ:r], *s.m.* fencer, swordsman.

scroc [ɛskro], *s.m.* swindler, sharper; crook.

scroquer [ɛskrɔke], *v.tr.* **1. e. qch. à qn,** to cheat s.o. of sth. **2. e. qn,** to swindle s.o.; *s.f.*

-erie, swindling; fraud.

espace [ɛspas], *s.m.* space. **1.** (*a*) distance, interval (between two objects); (*b*) interval (of time); **dans l'e. d'un an,** within the space of a year. **2.** void, infinity; **e. cosmique,** outer space; **la conquête de l'e.,** the conquest of space.

espacé [ɛspase], *a.* far between, far apart; at wide intervals.

espacer [ɛspase], *v.tr.* (*n.* **espaçons**) to space (out).

espadrille [ɛspadri:j], *s.f.* (rope-soled) sandal.

Espagne (l') [lɛspaɲ]. *Pr.n.f.* Spain.

espagnol, -ole [ɛspaɲɔl]. **1.** *a.* Spanish. **2.** *s.* Spaniard. **3.** *s.m. Ling:* Spanish.

espèce [ɛspɛs], *s.f.* (*a*) kind, sort; *Biol:* species; *P:* (**e. de . . .** *takes the gender and number of the following noun*) **cet e. d'idiot, cette e. d'idiote,** that silly fool; (*b*) *pl. Fin:* **espèces (monnayées),** specie, cash, coin.

espérer [ɛspere], *v.tr.* (**j'espère; j'espérerai**) to hope; **e. qch.,** to hope for sth.; **e. en qn,** to trust in s.o.; *s.f.* **-ance,** hope.

espiègle [ɛspjɛgl], *a. & s.* mischievous, roguish (child, etc.).

espion, -onne [ɛspjɔ̃, -ɔn], *s.* spy.

espionner [ɛspjɔne], *v.tr.* to spy (up)on; *abs.* to spy; *s.m.* **-age,** espionage.

espoir [ɛspwa:r], *s.m.* hope; **avoir bon e.,** to be full of hope.

esprit [ɛspri], *s.m.* **1.** spirit; (*a*) **le Saint-E.,** the Holy Ghost; **rendre l'e.,** to give up the ghost; **l'E. malin,** the Evil One; (*b*) ghost, phantom; (*c*) sprite. **2.** (*a*) **recueillir ses esprits,** to pull oneself together; **reprendre ses esprits,** to regain consciousness; to come to; (*b*) *Ch:* (volatile) spirit; **e. de vin,** spirit(s) of wine. **3.** (*a*) mind; **avoir l'e. tranquille,** to have a quiet mind; **elle avait l'e. ailleurs,** her thoughts were elsewhere; **avoir l'e. des affaires,** to have a turn for business; **perdre l'e.,** to go out of one's mind; **d'e. lent, vif,** slow-, quick-witted; (*b*) wit; **il fait de l'e.,** he is trying to be funny. **4.** spirit, feeling.

Esquimau, -aude, -aux [ɛskimo, -o:d, -o], *s. & a.* **1.** Eskimo. **2.** *s.m. F:* choc-ice.

esquinter [ɛskɛ̃te], *v.tr. F:* **1.** to exhaust, to tire (s.o.) out. **2.** to smash (sth.); to spoil, damage (sth.); **e. la voiture,** to ruin the car; **e. sa santé,** to ruin one's health.

esquisse [ɛskis], *s.f.* sketch; draft; outline.

esquisser [ɛskise], *v.tr.* to sketch, outline; **e. un sourire,** to give the ghost of a smile.

esquiver [ɛskive], *v.tr.* to avoid, dodge, evade (blow, etc.); *abs. Sp:* **e. de la tête,** to duck.

s'esquiver, to slip away; *F:* to make oneself scarce.

essai [esɛ], *s.m.* **1.** (*a*) trial, test(ing); **prendre qch. à l'e.,** to take sth. on approval; *Av:* **pilote**

d'e., test pilot; **e. de vitesse,** speed-trial; *(b) Metall:* assay(ing) (of ore). **2.** *(a)* attempt(ing), try; **coup d'e.,** first attempt; *(b) Lit:* essay; *Sp:* try (at rugby).

essaim [esɛ̃], *s.m.* swarm (of bees).

essaimer [esɛme], *v.i.* *(of bees)* to swarm.

essayer [eseje], *v.tr.* (**j'essaie, j'essaye**) **1.** *(a)* to test, try; *(b)* to try on (garment); *(c) Metall:* to assay; *(d)* **e. de qch.,** to try, taste, sth. **2. e. de faire qch.,** to try to do sth.

essence [esɑ̃s], *s.f.* **1.** *(a)* petrol, *N.Am:* gasoline, *F:* gas; *(b)* essence, extract. **2.** nature, spirit, natural quality; **l'e. de l'affaire,** the gist of the matter.

essentil|el, -elle [esɑ̃sjɛl]. **1.** *a.* essential. **2.** *s.m.* **l'e.,** the great thing, the main point; *adv.* **-ellement.**

essieu, -ieux [esjø], *s.m.* axle.

essor [esɔːr], *s.m.* (soaring) flight (of bird); **prendre son e.,** (i) to take wing, to soar; (ii) to spring into (vigorous) action; **e. d'une industrie,** rapid development of an industry.

essorl|er [esɔre], *v.tr.* to wring (washing) dry, to spin (washing) dry; *s.m.* **-age;** *s.f. H:* **-euse,** spin-drier.

essoufflé [esufle], *a.* out of breath, *F:* puffed.

essouffl|er [esufle], *v.tr.* to wind (horse, man); *s.m.* **-ement,** breathlessness.

s'essouffler, to get out of breath.

essuie-glace [esɥiglas], *s.m.* *Aut:* windscreen, *N.Am:* windshield, wiper; *pl.* **essuie-glaces.**

essuie-main(s) [esɥimɛ̃], *s.m.inv.* towel.

essuyer [esɥije], *v.tr.* (**j'essuie**) **1.** to wipe; to wipe up. **2.** to suffer, endure (defeat); **e. un refus,** to meet with a refusal.

est [ɛst]. **1.** *s.m. no pl.* east. **2.** *a.inv.* **les régions e. de la France,** the easterly parts of France.

estaminet [ɛstaminɛ], *s.m.* public house (in the N. of France); *F:* pub.

estampe [ɛstɑ̃ːp], *s.f.* print, engraving.

esthéticien, -ienne [ɛstetisjɛ̃, -jɛn], *s.* **1.** aesthetician. **2.** beauty-specialist, *N.Am:* beautician.

esthétique [ɛstetik]. **1.** *a.* aesthetic. **2.** *s.f.* aesthetics; *adv.* **-ment.**

estime [ɛstim], *s.f.* **1.** guesswork; *Nau:* reckoning; *adv.phr.* **à l'e.,** by guesswork. **2.** *(a)* estimation, opinion; *(b)* esteem, regard; **témoigner de l'e. pour qn,** to show regard for s.o.

estim|er [ɛstime], *v.tr.* **1.** *(a)* to estimate; to value; *(b)* to calculate (distance). **2.** *(a)* to consider; *(b)* to have a high opinion of (s.o.); *a.* **-able,** estimable; *s.* **-ateur, -atrice,** valuer; *s.f.* **-ation,** estimate, valuation.

estivant, -ante [ɛstivɑ̃, -ɑ̃ːt], *s.* summer visitor, holiday-maker.

estomac [ɛstɔma], *s.m.* stomach.

estrade [ɛstrad], *s.f.* platform, stage.

estropier [ɛstrɔpje], *v.tr.* to cripple, maim.

estuaire [ɛstɥɛːr], *s.m.* estuary.

esturgeon [ɛstyrʒɔ̃], *s.m.* *Ich:* sturgeon.

et [e], *conj.* and; **et son frère et sa sœur,** both hi brother and his sister; **j'aime le café; et vous?** like coffee; do you? (NOTE: *there is no 'liaison* with **et: j'ai écrit et écrit** [ʒeekrieekri]).

étable [etabl], *s.f.* cow-shed; cattle-shed.

établi [etabli], *s.m.* (work-)bench.

établ|ir [etabliːr], *v.tr.* **1.** *(a)* to establis (business, etc.); to fix (one's place of abode); **un camp,** to pitch a camp; to instal (machinery); *(b)* to establish, prove (fact). **2.** t draw up (plan); *Com:* **é. un compte, un devis** to make up an account, an estimate. **3.** to in stitute, create (tribunal); to lay down (rule); t found (colony). **4.** to set (s.o.) up in business *s.m.* **-issement.**

s'établir. 1. to settle (in a place). **2. s'é. épicier,** t set up as a grocer. **3.** *(of custom)* to becom established.

étage [etaːʒ], *s.m.* **1.** stor(e)y, floor (of building) **à deux étages,** two-storeyed. **2.** *(a)* tier, step **menton à deux étages,** double chin; *(b)* degree rank; **bistro de bas é.,** low, third-rate, pub.

étagère [etaʒɛːr], *s.f.* rack; shelf; (set of shelves.

étain [etɛ̃], *s.m.* **1.** tin. **2.** pewter.

étal|er [etale], *v.tr.* *(a) Com:* to display (goods) *(b)* to spread out (linen to dry); *(c)* to flaunt show off (one's wealth); *(d)* to stagge (payments); *s.m.* **-age,** display; window dressing; *s.m. & f.* **-agiste,** window-dresser.

étalon[1], *s.m.* stallion; stud-horse.

étalon[2], *s.m.* standard (of weights); **l'é. or,** th gold standard.

étamine [etamin], *s.f.* *Bot:* stamen.

étampe [etɑ̃ːp], *s.f.* **1.** stamp, die. **2.** *Tls:* punch

étanche [etɑ̃ːʃ], *a.* tight, impervious; **é. à l'eau,** **l'air,** watertight, airtight.

étanchl|er [etɑ̃ʃe], *v.tr.* **1.** *(a)* to sta(u)nc (blood); to stop (a leak); *(b)* to quench (one' thirst). **2.** to make (container) airtight, water tight; *s.f.* **-éité,** airtightness, watertightness.

étang [etɑ̃], *s.m.* pond, pool, mere.

étape [etap], *s.f.* stage (of journey); (i) halting place; **faire é.,** to stop; (ii) distance betwee two halting-places; **à, par, petites étapes, b** easy stages.

état [eta], *s.m.* **1.** state, condition; **mettre s affaires en é.,** to put one's affairs in order; **e bon, mauvais, é.,** in good, bad, repair; **hor d'é.,** out of order; *F:* **être dans tous ses états, t** be upset. **2.** *(a)* statement, return; **é. néant, n** return; **é. des dépenses,** statement of expenses *(b)* **faire é. de qch.,** to take sth. into account **faire grand é. de qn,** to think highly of s.o.; *(c Adm:* **é. civil,** civil status. **3.** profession, trade **il est épicier de son é.,** he is a grocer by trade. **4**

nation; state; government (in power); **homme d'é.**, statesman.

tatisé [etatize], *a.* state-controlled.

tatisme [etatism], *s.m.* state-control; state socialism.

tat-major [etamaʒɔ:r], *s.m.* (*a*) (general) staff; **officier d'é.-m.**, staff-officer; **carte d'é.-m.**, ordnance (survey) map; (*b*) headquarters; *pl.* *états-majors.*

tats-Unis (les) [lezetazyni]. *Pr.n.m.pl.* the United States (of America).

tau, -aux [eto], *s.m. Tls:* vice.

tayer [eteje], *v.tr.* (**j'étaie, j'étaye**) to shore up, prop (up).

té [ete], *s.m.* summer; **en é.**, in summer.

teindre [etɛ̃dr], *v.tr.* (*conj. like* PEINDRE) **1.** to extinguish, put out (fire); to turn off (gas); to switch off (light). **2.** to pay off (a debt).

'éteindre, (*a*) (*of fire*) to die out, to go out; (*b*) (*of colour*) to fade; (*of sound*) to die away.

teint [etɛ̃], *a.* (*a*) extinguished; **le feu est é.**, the fire is out; (*b*) extinct (race, volcano); (*c*) dull (colour); **voix éteinte**, faint voice.

tendard [etɑ̃da:r], *s.m.* colours, standard.

tendre [etɑ̃:dr], *v.tr.* **1.** to spread, stretch; to hang out (washing); **é. le bras**, to stretch out one's arm. **2. é. ses connaissances**, to extend one's knowledge.

'étendre. 1. (*a*) to lie down (at full length); (*b*) **s'é. sur un sujet**, to dwell at length on a subject. **2.** (*a*) to extend, stretch; (*b*) to spread.

tendu, -ue [etɑ̃dy]. **1.** *a.* (*a*) extensive (knowledge); far-reaching (influence); wide (plain); (*b*) outstretched (hands). **2.** *s.f.* **étendue**, extent; stretch (of water); expanse (of country); **é. d'une voix**, compass of a voice.

ternlel, -elle [etɛrnɛl], *a.* eternal; everlasting, endless; **soucis éternels**, never-ending worries; *adv.* **-ellement.**

ternité [eternite], *s.f.* eternity.

ternuler [etɛrnɥe], *v.i.* to sneeze; *s.m.* **-ement**, sneezing; sneeze.

ther [etɛ:r], *s.m. Ch: Med:* ether.

thiopie (l') [letjɔpi]. *Pr.n.f.* Ethiopia.

thique [etik]. **1.** *a.* ethical. **2.** *s.f.* ethics.

thnique [ɛtnik], *a.* ethnological, ethnic(al); racial (groups, etc.).

thnologlie [ɛtnɔlɔʒi], *s.f.* ethnology; *a.* **-ique**, ethnological; *adv.* **-iquement**, from the ethnological point of view.

tienne [etjɛn]. *Pr.n.m.* Stephen.

tinceller [etɛ̃sle], *v.i.* (**il étincelle**) **1.** to throw out sparks. **2.** (*of diamond*) to sparkle, flash; *s.m.* **-lement.**

tincelle [etɛ̃sɛl], *s.f.* spark.

tiqueter [etikte], *v.tr.* (**j'étiquète**) to label (luggage); to ticket (goods).

tiquette [etikɛt], *s.f.* **1.** label, ticket. **2.** etiquette.

tirer [etire], *v.tr.* to stretch; to draw out; **é. le fil**,

to draw wire.

s'étirer, to stretch oneself, one's limbs.

étoffe [etɔf], *s.f.* material; fabric; **avoir de l'é.**, to have plenty of grit; **il a l'é. d'un bon chef**, he has the makings of a good leader.

étoile [etwal], *s.f.* star. **1. coucher à la belle é.**, to sleep in the open. **2.** (*a*) star (of a decoration); (*b*) *Typ:* asterisk, star; *Com:* **cognac trois étoiles**, three star brandy. **3.** *Th: Cin:* star.

étoilé [etwale], *a.* starry, starlit (sky); **la Bannière étoilée**, the Star-spangled Banner.

étole [etɔl], *s.f. Ecc:* stole.

étonnlant [etɔnɑ̃], *a.* astonishing, surprising; *adv.* **-amment.**

étonnler [etɔne], *v.tr.* to astonish, amaze, surprise; **cela m'étonne que** + *sub.*, I am astonished that . . .; *s.m.* **-ement.**

s'étonner, to be astonished, surprised, to wonder (**de**, at).

étouffant [etufɑ̃], *a.* stifling, suffocating, stuffy (atmosphere); sultry (weather).

étouffée [etufe], *s.f. Cu: cuire (qch.) à l'é.**, to braise (meat, etc.).

étouffler [etufe]. **1.** *v.tr.* (*a*) to suffocate, smother (s.o.); (*b*) to stifle (cry); to suppress (revolt); **é. une affaire**, to hush up a matter. **2.** *v.i. & pr.* (*a*) to suffocate, choke; (*b*) **on étouffe ici**, it's stifling here; *s.m.* **-ement**, suffocation; choking sensation.

étourderie [eturd(ə)ri], *s.f.* **1.** thoughtlessness. **2.** thoughtless action; careless mistake.

étourdi [eturdi]. **1.** *a.* thoughtless; foolish. **2.** *s.* scatterbrain; *adv.* **-ment.**

étourdlir [eturdi:r], *v.tr.* **1.** to stun, daze; to make (s.o.) dizzy. **2.** to deaden (pain); *a.* **-issant**, deafening (noise); staggering (news); *s.m.* **-issement**, giddiness, dizziness.

étourneau, -eaux [eturno], *s.m. Orn:* starling.

étrange [etrɑ̃ʒ], *a.* strange, peculiar, queer; *adv.* **-ment.**

étranger, -ère [etrɑ̃ʒe, -ɛ:r]. **1.** (*a*) *a.* foreign; (*b*) *s.* foreigner, alien; (*c*) *s.m.* **vivre à l'é.**, to live abroad. **2.** (*a*) *a.* strange, unknown; (*b*) *s.* stranger. **3.** *a.* extraneous, foreign; not belonging (to sth.); irrelevant (**à**, to); **c'est é. à la question**, it's beside the point.

étrangeté [etrɑ̃ʒte], *s.f.* strangeness, oddness (of conduct, style).

étrangller [etrɑ̃gle], *v.tr.* **1.** (*a*) to strangle, throttle; (*b*) *v.i.* **é. de colère**, to choke with rage. **2.** to constrict, compress; *s.m.* **-ement.**

être [ɛ:tr]. **I.** *v.i. & pred.* (*pr.p.* **étant**; *p.p.* **été**; *pr.ind.* **je suis, tu es, il est, n. sommes, v. êtes, ils sont**; *pr. sub.* **je sois, n. soyons, ils soient**; *imp.* **sois, soyons**; *p.h.* **je fus**; *fu.* **je serai**) **1.** to be, to exist; **cela étant**, that being the case; **eh bien, soit!** well, so be it! **ainsi soit-il**, so be it; *Ecc:* amen. **2.** (*a*) **il est chef de gare**, he is a stationmaster; **c'est le chef de gare**, he's the stationmaster; (b) **l'homme est mortel**, man is mortal; **nous étions trois**, there were three of us; (c) **nous sommes le dix**, today is the tenth; **il est midi**, it is twelve o'clock; (d) **où en sommes-nous?** how far have we got? **c'en est trop!** this is too much! **il n'en est rien!** nothing of the kind! 3. (a) ê. à qn, to belong to s.o.; (b) **c'est à vous de jouer**, it's your turn to play. 4. (aux. use) **il est arrivé**, he has arrived. 5. (passive aux.) **il fut puni par son père**, he was punished by his father. 6. (= ALLER) **j'avais été à Paris**, I had been to Paris. II. **être**, s.m. 1. being, existence. 2. being, individual; **ê. humain**, human being.

étrein|dre [etrɛ̃:dr], v.tr. (conj. like ATTEINDRE) to embrace; to hug (s.o.); **é. qch. dans la main**, to grip, to grasp, sth.; **é. la main de qn**, to wring s.o.'s hand; s.f. **-te**.

étrenne [etrɛn], s.f. (usu. pl.) New-Year's gift.

étrenner [etrɛne], v.tr. to christen (an object), to use, wear, (sth.) for the first time; **é. une robe**, to christen a new dress, to wear a dress for the first time.

étrier [etrie], s.m. stirrup; **vider les étriers**, to fall off.

étroit [etrwa], a. 1. narrow; confined (space). 2. tight; tight(-fitting). 3. **être à l'é.**, (i) to be cramped for room; (ii) to be hard up; adv. **-ement**.

étude [etyd], s.f. 1. (a) study; **faire ses études à . . .**, to be educated at . . .; Sch: **l'é. du soir**, evening prep.; (b) research. 2. (a) office (of solicitor, etc.); (b) (lawyer's) practice.

étudiant, -ante [etydjã, -ã:t], s. student; undergraduate; **é. en médecine**, medical student; **é. de première année**, freshman; **é. de deuxième année**, N.Am: sophomore.

étudier [etydje], v.tr. (a) to study; (b) to investigate, go into (a question).

étui [etɥi], s.m. case, box; **é. à lunettes**, spectacle-case.

étymologie [etimɔlɔʒi], s.f. etymology.

eucalyptus [økalipty:s], s.m. eucalyptus.

Eucharistie (l') [løkaristi], s.f. Ecc: the eucharist.

euphém|isme [øfemism], s.m. euphemism; a. **-ique**, euphemistic.

Euratom [øratɔm]. Pr.n.f. Euratom.

Europe (l') [lørɔp]. Pr.n.f. Geog: Europe.

européen, -enne [ørɔpeɛ̃, -ɛn], a. & s. European.

Eurovision [ørɔvizjɔ̃]. Pr.n.f. T.V: Eurovision.

euthanasie [øtanazi], s.f. euthanasia.

eux [ø], pers. pron. m.pl. (a) they; (b) them.

eux-mêmes [ømɛːm], pers. pron. m.pl. themselves.

évacu|er [evakɥe], v.tr. to evacuate, withdraw; s.f. **-ation**.

évader (s') [sevade], v.pr. to escape; to run away.

évalu|er [evalɥe], v.tr. to value, appraise; to estimate; s.f. **-ation**.

évangélique [evãʒelik], a. evangelical.

évangile [evãʒil], s.m. gospel.

évanouir (s') [sevanwi:r], v.pr. 1. to vanish, disappear. 2. to faint.

évanouissement [evanwismã], s.m. 1. vanishing, disappearance. 2. faint(ing fit).

évaporation [evapɔrasjɔ̃], s.f. evaporation.

évaporé, -ée [evapɔre], a. F: feather-brained, irresponsible; s.f. **c'est une petite évaporée**, she's a bit flighty.

évaporer (s') [sevapɔre], v.pr. to evaporate.

évas|if, -ive [evazif, -i:v], a. evasive; adv. **-ivement**.

évasion [evazjɔ̃], s.f. 1. escape (from prison). 2. quibble, evasion. 3. Psy: escapism.

Ève [ɛ:v]. Pr.n.f. Eve, Eva; B.Lit: Eve.

évêché [eveʃe], s.m. 1. bishopric, diocese, see. 2. bishop's palace.

éveil [evɛ:j], s.m. 1. (a) awakening; (b) **être en é.**, to be wide-awake; **tenir qn en é.**, to keep s.o. on the alert. 2. warning; **donner l'é.**, to raise the alarm.

éveillé [eveje], a. 1. awake. 2. wide-awake; alert.

éveiller [eveje], v.tr. to wake (s.o.) up.

s'éveiller, to wake (up).

événement [evɛnmã], s.m. 1. event. 2. occurrence, incident; **faire é.**, to cause quite a stir.

éventail, -ails [evãta:j], s.m. fan.

éventrer [evãtre], v.tr. to disembowel; to rip open.

éventualité [evãtɥalite], s.f. possibility, eventuality.

éventuel, -elle [evãtɥel], 1. a. possible, contingent. 2. s.m. eventuality, contingency; adv. **-lement**, if necessary, possibly, should the occasion arise.

évêque [evɛ:k], s.m. bishop.

évertuer (s') [severtɥe], v.pr. to do one's utmost, to exert oneself.

éviction [eviksjɔ̃], s.f. eviction.

évidence [evidã:s], s.f. (a) obviousness, clearness (of fact); **se rendre à l'é.**, to bow to the facts; **il est de toute é. que . . .**, it is obvious that . . .; (b) conspicuousness; **être en é.**, to be (clearly) visible.

évid|ent [evidã], a. evident, obvious, plain; **c'est é.**, it stands to reason; adv. **-emment**.

évier [evje], s.m. (kitchen) sink.

évincer [evɛ̃se], v.tr. (n. évinçons) 1. to evict. 2. to oust, supplant.

évitement [evitmã]. 1. shunning, avoiding. Rail: shunting (of train); **gare d'é.**, siding; **route d'é.**, bypass. 3. passing-place; loop.

évit|er [evite], v.tr. (a) to avoid, shun; **é. un coup**, to dodge a blow; **é. de faire qch.**, to avoid doing sth.; **évitez qu'on ne vous voie,** avoid being seen; (*b*) **é. une peine à qn,** to spare s.o. trouble; *a.* **-able.**

volu|er [evɔlɥe], *v.i.* to evolve, develop; *Biol: etc:* to advance, to make progress; *s.f.* **-tion,** evolution.

voquer [evɔke], *v.tr.* (*a*) to evoke; (*b*) to call to mind.

xact [ɛgzakt], *a.* exact; (*a*) accurate, correct; **c'est e.,** it's quite true; (*b*) strict; rigorous; (*c*) punctual; *adv.* **-ement.**

xaction [ɛgzaksjɔ̃], *s.f.* exaction; extortion.

xactitude [ɛgzaktityd], *s.f.* (*a*) exactness, accuracy, exactitude; (*b*) punctuality.

xagér|er [ɛgzaʒere], *v.tr.* (**j'exagère; j'exagérerai**) to exaggerate, magnify (danger); to overstate (truth); to over-estimate, overrate (qualities); *s.f.* **-ation.**

xalté, -ée [ɛgzalte]. **1.** *a.* (*a*) impassioned; (*b*) hot-headed; (*c*) uplifted. **2.** *s.* fanatic.

xalt|er [ɛgzalte], *v.tr.* **1.** to exalt, glorify. **2.** to excite, inflame. **3.** to exalt, dignify; *s.f.* **-ation.** **'exalter,** to grow enthusiastic; *F:* to enthuse.

xamen [ɛgzamɛ̃], *s.m.* examination; (*a*) investigation;(*b*) *Sch:*exam(ination); **e. pour permis de conduire,** driving test; **le jury d'e.,** the examiners.

xamin|er [ɛgzamine], *v.tr.* to examine; to investigate; to inspect; to overhaul (machine); *s.* **-ateur, -atrice,** examiner; *Ind:* inspector.

xaspér|er [ɛgzaspere], *v.t.* (**j'exaspère; j'exaspérerai**) **1.** to exacerbate (pain). **2.** to exasperate, irritate; *s.f.* **-ation.**

exaspérer, (*of pers.*) to lose all patience.

xauc|er [ɛgzose], *v.tr.* (**n. exauçons**) to fulfil (wish); *s.m.* **-ement.**

xcavation [ɛkskavasjɔ̃], *s.f.* **1.** excavation, digging (out). **2.** excavation, hollow, pit.

xcédant, -ante [ɛksedɑ̃, -ɑ̃:t], *a.* **1.** surplus (money); excess (luggage). **2.** (*of pers.*) tiresome, exasperating.

xcédent [ɛksedɑ̃], *s.m.* excess, surplus.

xcéder [ɛksede], *v.tr.* (**j'excède; j'excéderai**) **1.** to exceed, go beyond. **2.** (*a*) to tire (s.o.) out; **excédé de fatigue,** worn out; (*b*) to overtax (s.o.'s) patience.

:cellence [ɛksɛlɑ̃:s], *s.f.* **1.** excellence, pre-eminence; **par e.,** pre-eminently. **2. votre E.,** your Excellency.

:cell|ent [ɛksɛlɑ̃], *a.* excellent; *adv.* **-emment.**

:celler [ɛksele], *v.i.* to excel (**à faire qch.,** in doing sth.).

:centricité [ɛksɑ̃trisite], *s.f.* eccentricity, oddity.

:centrique [ɛksɑ̃trik], *a.* eccentric, odd (person).

:cepté [ɛksɛpte], *prep.* except(ing).

:cept|er [ɛksɛpte], *v.tr.* to except, exclude.

:ception [ɛksɛpsjɔ̃], *s.f.* exception; **faire e. à**

une règle, to be an exception to a rule; **sauf e.,** with certain exceptions.

exceptionn|el, -elle [ɛksɛpsjɔnɛl], *a.* exceptional; out of the ordinary; *adv.* **-ellement.**

excès [ɛksɛ], *s.m.* (*a*) excess; **scrupuleux à l'e.,** scrupulous to a fault; over-scrupulous; (*b*) *pl.* **commettre des e.,** to commit excesses.

excess|if, -ive [ɛksɛsif, -i:v], *a.* excessive; extreme; undue; *adv.* **-ivement.**

excitation [ɛksitasjɔ̃], *s.f.* **1.** excitation (of the senses); **e. à la révolte,** incitement to rebellion. **2.** (state of) excitement.

excit|er [ɛksite], *v.tr.* to excite; (*a*) to arouse, stir up; (*b*) to inflame; to incite; (*c*) to stimulate (thirst, etc); *a.* **-ant,** exciting; *s.m.* **-ant,** stimulant; *s.f.* **-abilité;** *a.* **-able.**

exclamation [ɛksklamasjɔ̃], *s.f.* exclamation.

exclamer (s') [sɛksklame], *v.pr.* (*a*) to exclaim; (*b*) to protest loudly.

exclu|re [ɛkskly:r], *v.tr.* (*p.h.* **j'exclus**) to exclude, shut out, leave out; *s.f.* **-sion.**

exclus|if, -ive [ɛksklyzif, -i:v], *a.* exclusive, sole; *adv.* **-ivement.**

excommuni|er [ɛkskɔmynje], *v.tr.* to excommunicate; *s.f.* **-cation.**

excrément [ɛkskremɑ̃], *s.m. Physiol:* excrement.

excrétion [ɛkskresjɔ̃], *s.f. Physiol:* excretion.

excroissance [ɛkskrwasɑ̃:s], *s.f.* excrescence.

excursion [ɛkskyrsjɔ̃], *s.f.* excursion; (i) tour, trip; (ii) outing; **e. à pied,** walking tour; *F:* hike; *s.m. & f.* **-niste,** tourist; tripper.

excusable [ɛkskyzabl], *a.* excusable, pardonable; *adv.* **-ment.**

excuse [ɛksky:z], *s.f.* **1.** excuse. **2.** *pl.* apology; **faire ses excuses à qn,** to apologize to s.o.

excuser [ɛkskyze], *v.tr.* **1.** to make excuses, to apologize, for (s.o.). **2.** to excuse, pardon (s.o.); **se faire e.,** to decline, *F:* to cry off.

s'excuser, to excuse oneself; to apologize.

exécrable [egzekrabl], *a.* execrable; abominable; *adv.* **-ment.**

exécr|er [egzekre], *v.tr.* (**j'exècre; j'exécrerai**) to loathe, detest; *s.f.* **-ation.**

exécutant, -ante [egzekytɑ̃, -ɑ̃:t], *s. Mus:* performer.

exécut|er [egzekyte], *v.tr.* **1.** to execute; to carry out (plan); to perform. **2.** (*a*) to execute; to put to death; (*b*) *Jur:* to distrain upon (debtor); *s.* **-eur, -rice,** executor, executrix (of will); *a.* **-if, -ive,** executive.

s'exécuter. 1. to comply. **2.** to pay up.

exécution [egzekysjɔ̃], *s.f.* **1.** execution, performance; **mettre une idée à e.,** to carry an idea into effect. **2.** (*a*) **e. capitale,** execution; **ordre d'e.,** death-warrant; (*b*) *Jur:* distraint.

exemplaire[1] [egzɑ̃ple:r], *a.* exemplary.

exemplaire[2], *s.m.* (*a*) specimen (of work); (*b*) copy (of book).

exemple [ɛgzãːpl], *s.m.* 1. example; **donner l'e.,** to set an example; **joindre l'e. au précepte,** to suit the action to the word. 2. lesson, warning. 3. instance, precedent; **par e.,** for instance; *int.* **par e.!** the idea! **ah non, par e.!** no indeed!

exempt [ɛgzã], *a.* exempt, free; **e. de soucis,** carefree; **e. de droits,** duty free.

exempter [ɛgzãte], *v.tr.* **e. qn (de qch.),** to exempt, excuse, s.o. (from sth.).

exemption [ɛgzãpsjɔ̃], *s.f.* exemption; immunity (from tax, etc.); freedom (from anxiety).

exercé [ɛgzɛrse], *a.* practised (**à, in**).

exercer [ɛgzɛrse], *v.tr.* (**n. exerçons**) to exercise. 1. **e. son oreille,** to train one's ear. 2. to exert, make use of (force, etc.). 3. to practise (profession).

s'exercer à qch., to practise sth.

exercice [ɛgzɛrsis], *s.m.* exercise. 1. (*a*) **prendre de l'e.,** to take exercise; (*b*) *Mil:* drill. 2. (*a*) practice; use (of power); **avocat en e.,** practising barrister; **entrer en e.,** to take up one's duties; (*b*) **l'e. du culte,** public worship. 3. *Com:* (*a*) financial year; year's trading; (*b*) balance sheet.

exhaller [ɛgzale], *v.tr.* to exhale, emit; *s.f.* **-aison.**

exhaustif, -ive [ɛgzostif, -iːv], *a.* exhaustive.

exhiber [ɛgzibe], *v.tr.* to present, show, produce (passport, etc.); *Pej:* to show off (knowledge, etc.).

s'exhiber, *Pej:* to make an exhibition of oneself.

exhorter [ɛgzɔrte], *v.tr.* to exhort, urge; *s.f.* **-ation.**

exhumer [ɛgzyme], *v.tr.* (*a*) to exhume, disinter; (*b*) to unearth, bring to light.

exigeant [ɛgziʒã], *a.* exacting; hard to please.

exiger [ɛgziʒe], *v.tr.* (**n. exigeons**) 1. to exact; to insist upon. 2. to require, call for; *s.f.* **-ence,** requirement(s).

exigu, -uë [ɛgzigy], *a.* exiguous, tiny (flat, etc.); scanty (resources); slender (income); *s.f.* **-ïté.**

exil [ɛgzil], *s.m.* exile, banishment.

exilé, -ée [ɛgzile], *s.* exile.

exiler [ɛgzile], *v.tr.* to exile, banish.

exister [ɛgziste]. *v.i.* to exist, be; to live; *a.* **-ant,** existing; extant; *s.f.* **-ence.**

exode [ɛgzɔd], *s.m.* exodus; **e. rural,** rural depopulation.

exonérer [ɛgzɔnere], *v.tr.* (**j'exonère; j'exonérerai**) to exonerate; *s.f.* **-ation.**

exorbitant [ɛgzɔrbitã], *a.* exorbitant.

exotique [ɛgzɔtik], *a.* exotic.

expansif, -ive [ɛkspãsif, -iːv], *a.* expansive.

expansion [ɛkspãsjɔ̃], *s.f.* 1. expansion. 2. expansiveness; **avec e.,** effusively.

expatrier [ɛkspatrie], *v.tr.* to expatriate; *s.f.* **-ation.**

s'expatrier, to leave one's own country.

expectorer [ɛkspɛktɔre], *v.tr.* to expectorate;

to spit; *s.f.* **-ation.**

expédient [ɛkspedjã]. 1. *a.* expedient. 2. *s.m* expedient, device, shift; **vivre d'expédients, t** live by one's wits.

expédier [ɛkspedje], *v.tr.* to dispatch. 1. to ge rid of, dispose of (s.o.). 2. to expedite, hurr along (business). 3. to forward, send o (letter); to ship (goods); **e. par la poste,** to pos to mail; *s.* **-teur, -trice,** sender; *s.f.* **-tion** consignment; expedition.

expérience [ɛksperjãːs], *s.f.* 1. experience; **avo l'e. de qch.,** to have experience of, in, sth. experiment, test; **procéder à une e.,** to carr out an experiment.

expérimenté [ɛksperimãte], *a.* experience skilled (artisan).

expérimenter [ɛksperimãte], *v.tr.* to test, tr (remedy); *abs.* to make an experiment; *a.* **-a -aux,** experimental.

expert, -erte [ɛkspɛːr, -ɛrt]. 1. *a.* expert, skille (**en, dans,** in). 2. *s.m.* expert; connoisseu *Com:* valuer, appraiser; *adv.* **-ement.**

expert-comptable [ɛkspɛrkɔ̃tabl], *s.n* = chartered accountant; *pl.* **experts comptables.**

expertise [ɛkspɛrtiːz], *s.f.* 1. *Com:* expert a praisement; valuation. 2. expert's report.

expier [ɛkspje], *v.tr.* to expiate, atone for (si etc.); *s.f.* **-ation,** atonement.

expirer [ɛkspire], *v.* to expire. 1. *v.tr.* to breat out (air). 2. *v.i.* (*a*) to die; (*b*) to come to an en *s.f.* **-ation.**

explétif, -ive [ɛkspletif, -iːv], *a. & s.m.* expletiv

explicable [ɛksplikabl], *a.* explicabl explainable.

explicatif, -ive [ɛksplikatif, -iːv], explanatory.

explication [ɛksplikasjɔ̃], *s.f.* explanatio **demander une e. à qn,** to call s.o. to accoun

explicite [ɛksplisit], *a.* explicit, clear, plain; *aa* **-ment.**

expliquer [ɛksplike], *v.tr.* (*a*) to explain, mal clear; (*b*) to explain, account for; **je r m'explique pas pourquoi . . .,** I can't unde stand why . . ..

s'expliquer, to explain oneself; **s'e. avec qn, ** have it out with s.o.

exploit [ɛksplwa], *s.m.* exploit; fea achievement.

exploiter [ɛksplwate], *v.tr.* to exploit; *s.* **-ation.**

explorer [ɛksplore], *v.tr.* to explore; *s.* **-ateu -atrice,** explorer; *s.f.* **-ation.**

exploser [ɛksploze], *v.i.* to explode; *a. & s.r* **-if, -ive,** explosive; *s.f.* **-ion.**

exporter [ɛkspɔrte], *v.tr.* to export; *s.* **-ateu -atrice,** exporter; *s.f.* **-ation,** export.

exposé [ɛkspoze]. 1. *a.* (*a*) in an expos position; (*b*) liable (**à,** to). 2. *s.m.* statement (

facts, etc.).

exposer [εkspoze], *v.tr.* **1.** (*a*) to exhibit, show (pictures, etc.); (*b*) to set out (plans); **je leur ai exposé ma situation,** I explained to them how I was placed. **2.** to expose; to lay open; **e. sa vie,** to imperil one's life. **3.** to expose, lay bare (roots, etc.).

exposition [εkspozisjɔ̃], *s.f.* **1.** (*a*) exhibition, show; **e. internationale,** international exhibition; (*b*) exposure (to danger); (*c*) exposition, statement. **2.** aspect, exposure (of house).

exprès¹, -esse [εksprε, -εs]. **1.** *a.* express, explicit (order); **'défense expresse de fumer,'** 'smoking strictly prohibited'. **2.** [εksprεs], *a.inv. & s.m.* express (letter, etc.); *adv.* **-essément.**

exprès² [εksprε], *adv.* designedly, intentionally; **je ne l'ai pas fait e.,** I didn't do it on purpose.

express [εksprεs], *a. & s.m.* **1.** fast (train). **2.** *F:* (**café) e.,** espresso coffee.

expressif, -ive [εksprεsif, -iːv], *a.* expressive (face, smile); *adv.* **-ivement.**

expression [εksprεsjɔ̃], *s.f.* expression. **1.** squeezing out (of juice). **2.** utterance, voicing; show, manifestation. **3.** term, phrase.

expresso [εksprεso], *a. & s.m.* (**café) e.,** espresso coffee.

exprimer [εksprime], *v.tr.* to express. **1.** to squeeze out (juice). **2.** (*a*) to voice; (*b*) (*of looks, gestures, etc.*) to show, express (joy, anger); *a.* **-able,** expressible.

exproprier [εksprɔprie], *v.tr.* to expropriate; *s.f.* **-iation.**

expulser [εkspylse], *v.tr.* to expel; to eject; to turn (s.o.) out; to deport (alien); *s.f.* **-ion,** expulsion; deportation.

exquis [εkski], *a.* exquisite.

extase [εkstaːz], *s.f.* ecstasy; trance.

extasier (s') [sεkstazje], *v.pr.* to go into ecstasies.

extatique [εkstatik], *a.* ecstatic.

extensible [εkstɑ̃sibl], *a.* extending; expanding (bracelet, etc.).

extension [εkstɑ̃sjɔ̃], *s.f.* **1.** extension; (*a*) stretching; (*b*) spreading, enlargement. **2.** extent.

exténuer [εkstenɥe], *v.tr.* to exhaust; **être exténué,** to be tired out; *s.f.* **-ation,** exhaustion.

s'exténuer, to work oneself to death.

extérieur [εksterjœːr]. **1.** *a.* (*a*) exterior, outer, external; (*b*) foreign (trade). **2.** *s.m.* exterior, outside; *adv.* **-ement.**

exterminer [εkstεrmine], *v.tr.* to exterminate, destroy; *s.f.* **-ation.**

externat [εkstεrna], *s.m.* **1.** day-school. **2.** *Med:* non-resident medical studentship.

externe [εkstεrn]. **1.** *a.* (*a*) external, outer; **angle e.,** exterior angle; *Pharm:* **pour l'usage e.,** for external use; (*b*) **malade e.,** out-patient (at hospital). **2.** *s.* day-pupil.

extincteur [εkstɛ̃ktœːr], *s.m.* fire-extinguisher.

extinction [εkstɛ̃ksjɔ̃], *s.f.* extinction. **1.** (*a*) extinguishing, putting out; (*b*) abolition; paying off (of debt). **2.** (*a*) dying out (of species); (*b*) loss (of voice).

extirper [εkstirpe], *v.tr.* to eradicate, to root out; *s.f.* **-ation,** eradication.

extorquer [εkstɔrke], *v.tr.* to extort (money, etc.); to wring (promise) (**à qn,** from s.o.).

extorsion [εkstɔrsjɔ̃], *s.f.* extortion.

extra [εkstra]. **1.** *s.m.* (*usu. inv.*) extra; **payer les extra(s),** to pay for the extras. **2.** *a.inv.* extra-special (wine, etc.); outstanding, *F:* slap-up (entertainment). **3.** *adv.* extra(-fine, -strong, etc.).

extraction [εkstraksjɔ̃], *s.f.* extraction. **1.** extracting. **2.** descent, lineage.

extrader [εkstrade], *v.tr.* *Jur:* to extradite; *s.f.* **-ition.**

extra-fin [εkstrafɛ̃], *a.* superfine.

extraire [εkstrεːr], *v.tr.* (*conj. like* TRAIRE) to extract, draw out, take out (tooth, coal, etc.); **s'e. d'une situation difficile,** to get out of an awkward situation.

extrait [εkstrε], *s.m.* **1.** extract, essence; **e. de viande,** meat extract. **2.** extract, excerpt (from book); abstract (from deed, account); **e. de naissance** = birth certificate.

extraordinaire [εkstr(a)ɔrdinεːr], *a.* extraordinary; **par e.,** (i) for a wonder; (ii) for once in a while; *adv.* **-ment.**

extra-scolaire [εkstraskɔlεːr], *a.* **activités extra-scolaires,** out-of-school activities.

extravagance [εkstravagɑ̃ːs], *s.f.* extravagance; absurdity; exorbitance (of price).

extravagant [εkstravagɑ̃], *a.* extravagant; absurd; exorbitant (demand, price).

extrême [εkstrεm]. **1.** *a.* extreme; (*a*) farthest, utmost (point, etc.); (*b*) intense, excessive (cold, etc.); (*c*) drastic, severe (measure). **2.** *s.m.* extreme limit; **pousser les choses à l'e.,** to carry matters to extremes; *adv.* **-ment.**

extrême-onction [εkstrεmɔ̃ksjɔ̃], *s.f. Ecc:* extreme unction.

Extrême-Orient (l') [lεkstrεmɔrjɑ̃]. *Pr.n.m.* the Far East.

extrémiste [εkstremist], *s.m. & f.* extremist.

extrémité [εkstremite], *s.f.* (*a*) extremity, end; tip, point; (*b*) extremity, extreme (of misery); **pousser qch. à l'e.,** to carry sth. to extremes.

exubérance [εgzyberɑ̃ːs], *s.f.* exuberance.

exubérant [εgzyberɑ̃], *a.* exuberant.

exulter [εgzylte], *v.i.* to exult, rejoice; *s.f.* **-ation.**

ex-voto [εksvɔto], *s.m.inv.* ex-voto; votive offering.

F

F, f [ɛf], *s.m. & f.* (the letter) F, f.
fa [fɑ], *s.m.inv. Mus:* (the note) F; **morceau en fa,** piece in F.
fable [fɑ:bl], *s.f.* (*a*) fable; (*b*) story, tale.
fabricant, -ante [fabrikã, -ã:t], *s.* maker, manufacturer.
fabrique [fabrik], *s.f.* **1. prix de f.,** manufacturer's price; **marque de f.,** trade-mark. **2.** factory, works.
fabri|quer [fabrike], *v.tr.* to manufacture; **qu'est-ce que vous fabriquez?** (i) what are you making? (ii) *F:* what are you up to? *s.f.* **-cation.**
fabuleu|x, -euse [fabylø, -ø:z], *a.* **1.** fabulous. **2.** incredible; prodigious; **une somme fabuleuse,** a mint of money.
façade [fasad], *s.f.* façade, front(age).
face [fas], *s.f.* face. **1. sauver, perdre, la f.,** to save, lose, face. **2.** (*a*) face (of sth.); **f. avant, arrière,** front, back; (*b*) head side (of coin); **pile ou f.,** heads or tails; (*c*) side (of record). **3.** (*a*) **faire f. à des difficultés, à qn,** to cope with difficulties, with s.o.; (*b*) **portrait de f.,** full-face portrait; **vue de f.,** front-view; **la maison (d')en f.,** the house opposite; **regarder qn (bien) en f.,** to look s.o. full in the face. **4.** *prep.phr.* **f. à,** facing; **en f. de,** opposite; over against (sth., s.o.).
facétie [fasesi], *s.f.* joke; **dire des facéties,** to crack jokes.
facétieu|x, -euse [fasesjø, -ø:z], *a.* facetious; *adv.* **-sement.**
fâché [faʃe], *a.* **1.** sorry; **être f. de qch., pour qn,** to be sorry about sth., for s.o. **2.** angry; **être f. contre qn,** to be annoyed with s.o. **3. être f. avec qn,** to have fallen out with s.o.
fâcher [faʃe], *v.tr.* **1.** to grieve. **2.** to anger; to make (s.o.) angry; **soit dit sans vous f.,** if I may say so without offence, with all due deference.
se fâcher, to get angry; to lose one's temper; to take offence.
fâcheu|x, -euse [faʃø, -ø:z], *a.* troublesome, tiresome, annoying; **position fâcheuse,** awkward position; *adv.* **-sement.**
facile [fasil], *a.* **1.** easy; (*a*) **c'est f. à dire,** it's more easily said than done; (*b*) (i) **homme f. à vivre,** man easy to get on with; (ii) pliable, weak. **2.** facile, ready, quick; **je n'ai pas la parole f.,** I'm not a ready speaker; *adv.* **-ment.**
facilité [fasilite], *s.f.* **1.** (*a*) easiness (of task); **avec f.,** with ease; (*b*) **avoir la f. de faire qch.,** to enjoy facilities for doing sth.; *Com:* **facilités de**

paiement, easy terms. **2.** aptitude, talent, faci ty. **3.** pliancy.
faciliter [fasilite], *v.tr.* to facilitate; to ma (sth.) easier, easy.
façon [fasɔ̃], *s.f.* **1.** (*a*) (i) making, fashioning; (make; workmanship; **f. d'un habit,** cut of coat; **tailleur à f.,** bespoke tailor; **on prend à** customers' own materials made up; (*b*) **cuir porc,** imitation pigskin. **2.** (*a*) manner, moc way; **je le ferai à ma f.,** I shall do it (in) my ov way; **je lui dis, f. de rire, que . . .,** I said to hii by way of a joke, that . . .; **de la bonne** properly; **arranger qn de (la) belle f.,** to gi s.o. a good dressing down; (*b*) **il entra sa façon(s),** he entered unceremoniously; sa **plus de façons,** without any more ado; (*c*) **cette f.,** thus, in this way; **de toute f. j'ii** anyhow, I shall go; **en aucune f.!** by no mear **3.** *conj.phr.* **de f. à,** so as to.
façonner [fasɔne], *v.tr.* to work, shape; to ma (up) (dress).
fac-similé [faksimile], *s.m.* facsimile; ex copy; *pl. fac-similés.*
facteur, -trice [faktœ:r, -tris], *s.* **1.** musical strument maker. **2.** (*a*) carrier; (*b*) car-m (delivering parcels); transport agent; (*c*) po man. **2.** *Com:* agent, middleman. **3.** *s.m. M* factor; **le f. humain,** the human factor.
factice [faktis], *a.* artificial, imitation; dum (parcel).
faction [faksjɔ̃], *s.f.* **1.** sentry-duty, guard. faction; factious party; *s.m.* **-naire,** (i) sent (ii) picket.
facture [faktyːr], *s.f. Com:* invoice; bill (of sal
facturer [faktyre], *v.tr.* to invoice.
facultatif, -ive [fakyltatif, -iːv], *a.* optior **arrêt f.,** request stop.
faculté [fakylte], *s.f.* **1.** (*a*) option, right; faculty, ability; **facultés de l'esprit,** intellect powers; **l'aimant a la f. d'attirer le fer,** magnet has the property of attracting iron; *pl.* resources, means. **2.** faculty (of l medicine); **les différentes facultés (d'** université), the different schools.
fade [fad], *a.* insipid, flavourless (dish); point (joke).
fadeur [fadœːr], *s.f.* insipidity; sickliness taste, smell).
fading [fediŋ], *s.m. Rad:* fading, fade-out.
fagot [fago], *s.m.* faggot; bundle of firewo **sentir le f.,** to savour of heresy.
faible [fɛbl]. **1.** *a.* (*a*) feeble, weak; (*b*) **brise**

light breeze; **f. son,** faint sound; **faibles ressources,** scanty means. **2.** (*a*) *s.m.* weakness, failing; **avoir un f. pour qch., pour qn,** to have a weakness, *F:* soft spot, for sth, s.o.; (*b*) *s.m. & f. pl.* the weak; **les économiquement faibles,** the underprivileged; *adv.* **-ment.**

faiblesse [fɛblɛs], *s.f.* **1.** (*a*) feebleness, weakness; (*b*) **la f. humaine,** human frailty; (*c*) smallness (of sum). **2. f. chez qn,** failing in s.o.

faiblir [fɛbliːr], *v.i.* to weaken; to grow weak(er); **ma vue faiblit,** my sight is failing.

faïence [fajɑ̃ːs], *s.f.* crockery; earthenware.

failli, -ie [faji], *s.* (adjudicated) bankrupt.

faillible [fajibl], *a.* fallible.

faillir [fajiːr], *v.i.* (*pr.p.* **faillant;** *p.p.* **failli;** *p.h.* **je faillis**) (*rarely used in other tenses*). **1.** to fail; **f. à une promesse,** to fail to keep a promise; **sans f.,** without fail. **2. faillir +** *inf.* (*only in past hist. and compound tenses*) **j'ai failli manquer le train,** I nearly missed the train.

faillite [fajit], *s.f. Com:* failure, bankruptcy, insolvency; **faire f.,** to go bankrupt, to fail.

faim [fɛ̃], *s.f.* hunger; **avoir f.,** to be hungry; **manger à sa f.,** to eat one's fill.

fainéant, -ante [fɛneɑ̃, -ɑ̃ːt]. **1.** *a.* idle, lazy, slothful. **2.** *s.* idler, lazy-bones.

faire [fɛːr], *v.tr.* (*pr.p.* **faisant** [fəzɑ̃]; *p.p.* **fait** [fɛ]; *pr.ind. v.* **faites, ils font;** *pr.sub.* **je fasse;** *p.h.* **je fis;** *fu.* **je ferai**) I. to make. **1.** (*a*) **statue faite en, de, marbre,** statue made of marble; **vêtements tout faits,** ready-made clothes; **f. un chèque,** to write a cheque; (*b*) **f. la guerre,** to wage war; **le mariage ne se fera pas,** the marriage will not take place. **2.** (*a*) **f. sa fortune,** to make one's fortune; **se f. des amis,** to make friends; (*b*) **f. des provisions,** to lay in provisions; (*c*) *P:* **on vous a fait,** you've been had; **tu es fait, mon vieux,** you've had it, chum!

II. to do. **1.** (*a*) **que f.?** what's to be done? what can I, we, do? **faites vite!** look sharp! **f. de l'hypertension,** to have high blood pressure; **vous allez avoir de quoi f.,** you have your work cut out; **c'est bien fait!** (i) it's well done; (ii) it serves you right! (*b*) (= to say) **'vous partez demain!' fit-il,** 'you leave tomorrow!' he said. **2. f. la ronde,** to go one's rounds; **f. son devoir,** to do one's duty; **voilà qui est fait,** that's done, settled; **toute réflexion faite,** all things considered; **f. du sport,** to go in for sport; **il fait son droit,** he's reading law. **3. f. une promenade,** to go for (i) a walk, (ii) a drive. **4. combien cela fait-il?** how much does that come to? **5.** to be, constitute; **cela fera mon affaire,** that will suit me. **6.** to matter; **qu'est-ce que ça fait?** what does it matter? **si cela ne vous fait rien,** if you don't mind; **cela ne fait rien,** never mind, it doesn't matter.

III. **1.** to form; **ce professeur fait de bons élèves,** this master turns out good pupils;

démarche faite pour m'étonner, step calculated to astonish me. **2.** to arrange; **f. la chambre,** to clean, do, the bedroom; **f. sa malle,** to pack one's trunk; *Cards:* **à qui de f.?** whose deal is it? **3. qu'allez-vous f. de votre fils?** what are you going to make of your son? **il ne fait pas quarante ans,** he doesn't look forty. **4. f. le malade,** to sham illness, to pretend to be ill; **f. l'imbécile,** to play the fool.

IV. **1. en faire;** (*a*) **n'en faites rien,** do no such thing; (*b*) **c'en est fait de lui,** it's all up with him. **2. y faire; rien n'y fit,** nothing availed; **qu'y f.?** how can it be helped? **3.** *F:* **la faire; on ne me la fait pas!** nothing doing!

V. *impers.* **1. quel temps fait-il?** what is the weather like? **par le froid qu'il fait,** in this cold weather. **2. il fait mauvais voyager par ces routes,** it is hard travelling on these roads.

VI. (*syntactical constructions*) **1. je n'ai fait que le toucher,** I only touched it. **2. je ne fais que d'arriver,** I have only just arrived. **3. vous n'aviez que f. de parler,** you had no business to speak.

VII. *with inf.* = *causative verb.* **1.** (*the noun or pron. object is the subject of the inf.*) (*a*) **je le fis chanter,** I made him sing; **faites-le entrer,** show him in; (*b*) **faire +** *v.pr.* (i) (*reflexive pron. omitted*) **f. asseoir qn,** to make s.o. sit down; (ii) (*reflexive pron. retained*) **je le fis s'arrêter,** I made him stop. **2.** (*the noun or pron. is the object of the inf.*) (*a*) **f. f. deux exemplaires,** to have two copies made; (*b*) **se f. +** *inf.*; **un bruit se fit entendre,** a noise was heard. **3. f. f. qch. à qn,** to cause, get, s.o. to do sth.; **faites-lui lire cette lettre,** get him to read this letter.

se faire. 1. (*a*) to develop, mature; **son style se fait,** his style is forming; **ce fromage se fera,** this cheese will ripen; (*b*) to become; **se f. soldat,** to become a soldier, to enlist; (*c*) to adapt oneself; **se f. à qch.,** to get used to sth. **2.** *impers.* (*a*) **il se fait tard,** it is getting late; (*b*) **il se fit un long silence,** a long silence followed; **comment se fait-il que vous soyez en retard?** how is it that you are late?

faire-part [fɛrpaːr], *s.m.inv.* **f.-p. de naissance, décès,** announcement of birth, death; **f.-p. de mariage** = wedding invitation.

faisan [fəzɑ̃], *s.m.* (**coq**) **f.,** (cock-)pheasant.

faisceau, -eaux [fɛso], *s.m.* **1.** bundle (of sticks). **2.** beam, searchlight; **f. hertzien,** radio beam; *T.V:* **f. cathodique explorateur,** scanning electron beam; **f. électronique,** electron beam; **f. de lumière,** pencil of rays; **f. d'ampoules électriques,** cluster of electric light bulbs.

fait¹ [fɛ], *a.* fully developed; **homme f.,** (i) grown man; (ii) experienced man; **fromage f.,** ripe cheese.

fait², *s.m.* (*a*) act, deed; **prendre qn sur le f.,** to catch s.o. in the act; (*b*) fact; **être au f. de la question,** to know how things stand, to be *au fait* with the matter; **mettre qn au f., F:** to put s.o. in the picture; *adv.phr.* **au f., que venez-vous faire ici?** what have you come here for, anyway? **en f.,** as a matter of fact; *prep.phr.* **en f. de,** as regards; (*c*) occurrence, happening.

fait-divers [fɛdivɛːr], *s.m. Journ:* news item; **faits-divers,** news in brief.

faîte [fɛːt], *s.m.* **1.** *Const:* ridge (of roof). **2.** top, summit (of tree, house).

falaise [falɛːz], *s.f.* cliff.

fallacieu|x, -euse [falasjø, -øːz], *a.* fallacious, deceptive, misleading; *adv.* **-sement.**

falloir [falwaːr], *v. impers. def.* (*no pr.p; p.p.* **fallu;** *pr.ind.* **il faut;** *pr.sub.* **il faille;** *p.d.* **il fallait;** *fu.* **il faudra**) **1.** to be wanting, lacking, necessary; **il lui faut un nouveau pardessus,** he needs a new overcoat; **il m'a fallu trois jours pour le faire,** it took me three days to do it; **s'en f.,** to be lacking, wanting; **je ne suis pas satisfait, tant s'en faut,** I am not satisfied, far from it; **peu s'en faut,** very nearly; **comme il faut,** proper(ly). **2.** (*a*) **falloir** + *inf.,* **falloir que** + *sub.,* to be necessary, **il nous faut le voir, il faut que nous le voyions,** we must see him; **il fallait voir ça!** you ought to have seen it! **il fallait le dire!** why didn't you say so! *F:* **c'est ce qu'il faudra voir!** we must see about that! (*b*) (*with* **le** = *noun-clause*) **il viendra s'il le faut,** he will come if necessary.

falsifi|er [falsifje], *v.tr.* to falsify; to tamper with (document); *F:* to doctor, fake, cook; **f. le lait,** to adulterate milk; *s.f.* **-cation.**

fameu|x, -euse [famø, -øːz], *a.* **1.** famous. **2.** *F:* first-rate; **fameuse idée,** splendid idea; **vous êtes un f. menteur!** you're a heck of a liar! **ce n'est pas f.,** it isn't up to much; *adv.* **-sement.**

familial, *pl.* **-aux** [familjal, -o], *a.* **1.** family (life); *Com:* **pot f.,** family-size jar; *Adm:* **allocation familiale,** family allowance. **2.** *Aut: s.f.* **familiale,** seven-seater saloon; estate car.

familiariser (se) [səfamiljarize], *v.pr.* **se f. avec qch., avec qn,** to make oneself familiar with sth.; to get to know sth., s.o.

familiarité [familjarite], *s.f.* familiarity.

famili|er, -ère [familje, -ɛːr], *a.* **1.** domestic. **2.** familiar; **expression familière,** colloquialism; *s.* **un des familiers de la maison,** a friend of the family; *adv.* **-èrement.**

famille [famiːj], *s.f.* family; household; **chef de f.,** householder; **en f.,** as a family party; **dîner en f.,** to dine at home (informally); **cela tient de f.,** it runs in the family; **j'ai de la f. à Paris,** I have relatives in Paris; **esprit de f.,** clannishness.

famine [famin], *s.f.* famine, starvation.

fanatique [fanatik]. **1.** *a.* fanatic(al). **2.** *s.* fanatic.

fanatisme [fanatism], *s.m.* fanaticism.

faner (se) [səfane], *v.pr.* to wither, fade.

fanfare [fɑ̃faːr], *s.f.* **1.** (*a*) flourish (of trumpets) (*b*) fanfare. **2.** brass band.

fanfaronnade [fɑ̃faronad], *s.f.* boasting.

fange [fɑ̃ːʒ], *s.f.* mud, mire, filth.

fantaisie [fɑ̃tezi], *s.f.* **1.** (*a*) imagination, fancy de f., imaginary; (*b*) *Mus:* fantasia. **2.** fancy whim.

fantaisiste [fɑ̃tezist], *a. & s.* whimsical, freakish (person).

fantasque [fɑ̃task], *a.* odd, whimsical (person idea).

fantastique [fɑ̃tastik], *a.* fantastic; fanciful weird, eerie; *adv.* **-ment.**

fantoche [fɑ̃tɔʃ], *s.m.* marionette, puppe **gouvernement f.,** puppet government.

fantôme [fɑ̃toːm], *s.m.* phantom, ghos **gouvernement f.,** shadow cabinet.

faon [fɑ̃], *s.m. Z:* fawn.

farce [fars], *s.f.* (*a*) *Th:* farce; (*b*) practical joke

farceur, -euse [farsœːr, -øːz], *s.* **1.** practic: joker. **2.** joker, humorist.

farcir [farsiːr], *v.tr. Cu:* to stuff (poultry).

fard [faːr], *s.m.* make-up.

fardeau, -eaux [fardo], *s.m.* burden, load.

farder (se) [səfarde], *v.pr.* to make up (one face).

farfouill|er [farfuje], *v.tr. & i.* to rummag (about in, among); *s.m.* **-ement;** *s.* **-eu -euse.**

farine [farin], *s.f.* flour, meal; **fleur de f., pu** wheaten flour; **f. de maïs,** cornflour; **d'avoine,** oatmeal; **f. de riz,** ground rice.

farouche [faruʃ], *a.* **1.** fierce, wild, savage. **2.** (: shy, timid; (*b*) unsociable.

fart [faːr], *s.m.* wax (for skis).

fart|er [farte], *v.tr.* to wax (skis); *s.m.* **-age.**

fascicule [fasikyl], *s.m.* instalment, part (publication).

fascin|er [fas(s)ine], *v.tr.* to fascinate; *s.* **-ation.**

fascisme [fas(s)ism, faʃ-], *s.m. Pol:* fascism.

fasciste [fas(s)ist, faʃ-], *s.m. &f. Pol:* fascist.

faste [fast], *s.m.* ostentation, display.

fastidieu|x, -euse [fastidjø, -øːz], *a.* du tedious, wearisome, irksome; **besogn fastidieuses,** drudgery; **orateur f., pro** speaker; *adv.* **-sement.**

fastueu|x, -euse [fastɥø, -øːz], *a.* ostentatiou showy; sumptuous; *adv.* **-sement.**

fatal, *pl.* **-als** [fatal], *a.* **1.** fatal; **coup f., fa** blow. **2.** fated, inevitable; **c'était f.,** it w bound to happen; *adv.* **-ement.**

fatalisme [fatalism], *s.m.* fatalism.

fataliste [fatalist]. **1.** *s.* fatalist. **2.** *a.* fatalistic

fatalité [fatalite], *s.f.* **1.** fate, fatality. **2.** m chance, calamity. **3.** death, casualty.

fatigant [fatigɑ̃], *a.* **1.** tiring, fatiguing.

tiresome, tedious.

fatigue [fatig], *s.f.* (*a*) fatigue, weariness; (*b*) (metal) fatigue.

fatiguer [fatige]. 1. *v.tr.* (*a*) to tire (s.o.); (*b*) to overdrive (machine). 2. *v.i.* (*of engine, etc.*) to labour.

se fatiguer, to tire; to get tired.

fatuité [fatɥite], *s.f.* self-conceit, self-satisfaction, self-complacency.

faubourg [fobuːr], *s.m.* suburb.

faubourien, -ienne [foburjɛ̃, -jɛn]. 1. *a.* suburban (accent, etc.). 2. *s.* suburbanite.

faucher [foʃe], *v.tr.* 1. to mow, cut, reap (field); *Fb:* **f. son homme**, to bring down one's man. 2. *P:* to steal, pinch (sth.).

faucheur, -euse [foʃœːr, -øːz], *s.* 1. (*pers.*) mower, reaper. 2. *s.f.* **faucheuse**, mowing-machine.

faucille [fosiːj], *s.f.* sickle; reaping-hook.

faucon [fokɔ̃], *s.m. Orn:* falcon, hawk.

faufiler [fofile], *v.tr.* to tack, baste (seam); *s.m.* **-age.**

se faufiler, to thread, pick, one's way; **se f. le long du mur**, to creep along the wall; **se f. adroitement parmi les voitures**, to nip in and out of the traffic.

faune [foːn], *s.f.* fauna, animal life.

fausser [fose], *v.tr.* to falsify; to alter (facts); **f. les idées de qn**, to warp s.o.'s ideas; **f. compagnie à qn**, to give s.o. the slip; *s.m. & f.* **-aire**, forger.

fausseté [foste], *s.f.* 1. falseness, falsity. 2. falsehood, untruth. 3. duplicity.

faute [foːt], *s.f.* 1. lack, need, want; **faire f.**, to be lacking; **sans f.**, without fail; **f. de**, for want of; **f. de quoi . . .**, failing which . . .. 2. (*a*) fault, mistake; **f. d'orthographe**, spelling mistake; **f. d'impression**, misprint; (*b*) transgression, offence; (*c*) *Sp:* foul; *Ten:* fault; **f. de pied**, foot-fault.

fauteuil [fotœːj], *s.m.* 1. arm-chair, easy-chair; *Th:* **f. d'orchestre**, orchestra stall; **f. de balcon**, dress-circle seat; *Jur:* **f. électrique**, electric chair. 2. chair (at meeting); **occuper le f.**, to be in the chair.

fauteur, -trice [fotœːr, -tris], *s.* abettor (**de**, of); instigator (of rising); **f. de troubles**, (political) agitator; trouble-maker.

fautif, -ive [fotif, -iːv], *a.* 1. faulty, incorrect; **calcul f.**, miscalculation. 2. offending, at fault; *adv.* **-ivement.**

fauve [foːv]. 1. *a.* fawn-coloured, tawny. 2. *s.m.* (*a*) fawn (colour); (*b*) **les (grands) fauves**, big game.

fauvette [fovɛt], *s.f. Orn:* warbler.

faux¹, fausse [fo, foːs]. I. *a.* false. 1. untrue. 2. not genuine; (*a*) **fausse monnaie**, counterfeit coin(age); **fausse clef**, skeleton key; **fausses côtes**, floating ribs; *adv.* **rire qui sonne f.**, laugh

that has a false ring; (*b*) treacherous; *F:* **f. bonhomme**, shifty customer. 3. wrong, mistaken; **fausse date**, wrong date; **présenter la conduite de qn sous un f. jour**, to place s.o.'s conduct in a false light; **faire un f. pas**, to blunder; **faire fausse route**, *F:* to be on the wrong track; *adv.* **chanter f.**, to sing out of tune; *adv.phr.* **à f.**, wrongly; (*of wheel*) **tourner à f.**, to run out of true; *adv.* **-ssement.**

II. *s.m.* 1. **le f.**, the false; **bijouterie en f.**, imitation jewellery. 2. *Jur:* forgery.

faux², *s.f.* scythe.

faux-filet [fofilɛ], *s.m. Cu:* sirloin; *pl. faux-filets.*

faux-monnayeur [fomɔnɛjœːr], *s.m.* coiner; counterfeiter; *pl. faux-monnayeurs.*

faveur [favœːr], *s.f.* favour; (*a*) *Com:* **prix de f.**, preferential price; **billet de f.**, complimentary ticket; **à la f. de**, by the help of; (*b*) **faire une f. à qn**, to do s.o. a kindness.

favorable [favɔrabl], *a.* favourable; *adv.* **-ment.**

favori, -ite [favɔri, -it]. 1. *a. &. s.* favourite. 2. *s.m.pl.* (side-)whiskers.

favoriser [favɔrize], *v.tr.* to favour, to be partial to (s.o., sth.); **f. un dessein**, to further an object.

fébrile [febril], *a.* feverish (preparations).

fécond [fekɔ̃], *a.* prolific, fruitful, fertile.

fécondité [fekɔ̃dite], *s.f.* fecundity. 1. fruitfulness. 2. fertility.

fédéral, -aux [federal, -o], *a.* federal.

fédéraliser [federalize], *v.tr.* to federalize; *s.m.* **-isme**; *a. & s.* **-iste.**

fédération [federasjɔ̃], *s.f.* federation.

fée [fe], *s.f.* fairy; **conte de fées**, fairy-tale.

feeder [fidœːr], *s.m.* (gas) pipeline.

féerie [fe(ə)ri], *s.f.* 1. enchantment. 2. fairyland. 3. *Th:* fairy play; *a.* **-ique**, fairy-like, enchanting.

feindre [fɛ̃ːdr], *v.tr. & i.* (*conj. like* ATTEINDRE) to feign, simulate, sham; **f. de faire qch.**, to pretend to do sth.; **f. la maladie**, to malinger, to pretend to be ill.

feinte [fɛ̃t], *s.f.* pretence; *Sp:* feint.

fêler [fele], *v.tr.* to crack (glass, china, etc.).

félicité [felisite], *s.f.* felicity, bliss(fulness); happiness, joy.

féliciter [felisite], *v.tr.* **f. qn de qch.**, to congratulate s.o. on sth.; *s.f. usu. pl.* **-ation(s)**, congratulations.

se féliciter de qch., to be pleased with sth.; *abs. F:* to pat oneself on the back.

félin, -ine [felɛ̃, -in], *a.* feline; (*a*) *Z:* cat (family); *s.* **les grands félins**, the big cats; (*b*) *F:* catlike.

fêlure [fɛlyːr, fel-], *s.f.* crack (in china); split (in wood).

femelle [fəmɛl], *s.f. & a.* female (animal); she-(animal); cow-(elephant); hen-(bird).

féminin [feminɛ̃]. 1. *a.* feminine; **le sexe f.**, the female sex. 2. *s.m. Gram:* feminine (gender).

femme [fam], *s.f.* 1. woman. 2. wife. 3. **f. de**

F : 5

fémur

feu

chambre, housemaid; *Nau:* stewardess; **f. de ménage,** daily help, charwoman, *F:* daily, char.

fémur [femyːr], *s.m. Anat:* femur, thigh-bone.

fenaison [fənɛzɔ̃], *s.f.* 1. haymaking; hay-harvest. 2. haymaking-time.

fendre [fɑ̃ːdr], *v.tr.* to split; **f. l'air,** to rend the air; **f. la foule,** to force one's way through the crowd; **il gèle à pierre f.,** it is freezing hard.

fenêtre [f(ə)nɛːtr], *s.f.* window; **regarder par la f.,** to look out of the window; **mettre la tête à la f.,** to thrust one's head out of the window.

fente [fɑ̃ːt], *s.f.* (a) crack, crevice, chink; (b) slot.

féodal, -aux [feɔdal, -o], *a.* feudal.

fer [fɛːr], *s.m.* 1. iron; **f. forgé,** wrought iron. 2. (a) **f. de lance,** spearhead; (b) sword; **croiser le f. avec qn,** to cross swords with s.o. 3. *Tls:* **f. à souder,** soldering-iron; **marquer au f. chaud,** to brand; **f. à repasser** (laundry) iron. 4. *pl.* irons, chains, fetters; **être aux fers,** to be in irons. 5. **f. à cheval,** horseshoe; *F:* **tomber les quatre fers en l'air,** to go sprawling.

fer-blanc [fɛrblɑ̃], *s.m.* tinplate; **boîte en f.-b.,** tin, (tin) can; *pl. fers-blancs.*

férié [ferje], *a.* **jour f.,** (public) holiday.

ferme[1] [fɛrm]. 1. *a.* firm, steady; **terre f.,** (i) firm ground; (ii) mainland, terra firma; **attendre qn de pied f.,** to wait resolutely for s.o. 2. *adv.* firmly; **frapper f.,** to hit hard; **tenir f.,** to stand fast; **j'y travaille f.,** I am hard at it; *adv.* -**ment,** firmly, steadily, steadfastly.

ferme[2], *s.f.* farm.

fermé [fɛrme], *a.* 1. closed (door, window). 2. **visage f.,** inscrutable face; **monde f.,** exclusive society.

ferment [fɛrmɑ̃], *s.m.* ferment.

ferment|**er** [fɛrmɑ̃te], *v.i.* to ferment, *F:* to work; (*of dough*) to rise; *s.f.* -**ation.**

fermer [fɛrme]. 1. *v.tr.* (a) to close, shut; **f. sa porte à qn,** to close one's door against s.o.; **f. à clef,** to lock (a door); **f. les rideaux,** to draw the curtains; **f. boutique,** to shut up shop; **on ferme!** closing time! **f. l'électricité,** to switch off the light; **f. un robinet,** to turn off a tap; *P:* **ferme-la!** shut up! (b) **f. la marche,** to bring up the rear. 2. *v.i.* (*of door*) to close, shut.

se fermer, to close, shut.

fermeté [fɛrməte], *s.f.* firmness; steadfastness.

fermeture [fɛrmətyːr], *s.f.* 1. closing, shutting; **f. de la pêche,** close of the fishing season; **heure de f.,** (i) closing time; (ii) knocking-off time. 2. closing apparatus; *R.t.m:* **f. éclair,** zip fastener; shutter (of shop, etc.).

fermier, -ière [fɛrmje, -jɛːr], *s.* farmer; *f.* (woman) farmer; farmer's wife.

fermoir [fɛrmwaːr], *s.m.* clasp, catch, fastener.

féroce [ferɔs], *a.* ferocious, savage, wild, fierce; *adv.* -**ment.**

férocité [ferɔsite], *s.f.* ferocity, ferociousness.

ferraille [fɛraːj], *s.f.* old iron, scrap-iron.

ferré [fɛre], *a.* iron-shod; **souliers ferrés,** hob-nailed shoes; *Rail:* **voie ferrée,** permanent way; railway line.

ferrer [fɛre], *v.tr.* to fit, mount, (sth.) with iron; **f. un cheval,** to shoe a horse.

ferroviaire [fɛrɔvjɛːr], *a.* **trafic f.,** rail(way); *N.Am:* railroad, traffic.

ferrugineux, -euse [fɛrryʒinø, -øːz], *a* ferruginous.

ferry-boat [fɛribot], *s.m.* train ferry, car ferry; *pl. ferry-boats.*

fertile [fɛrtil], *a.* fertile, fruitful.

fertilis|**er** [fɛrtilize], *v.tr.* to fertilize; to make fruitful; *s.f.* -**ation.**

fertilité [fɛrtilite], *s.f.* fertility; fruitfulness.

fervent, -ente [fɛrvɑ̃, -ɑ̃ːt]. 1. *a.* fervent enthusiastic. 2. *s.* enthusiast, *F:* fan.

ferveur [fɛrvœːr], *s.f.* fervour; ardour.

fesse [fɛs], *s.f.* buttock.

fesser [fɛse], *v.tr. F:* to spank (s.o.).

festin [fɛstɛ̃], *s.m.* feast, banquet.

fête [fɛːt], *s.f.* 1. feast, festival; **f. légale,** publi holiday; **jour de f.,** holiday; **f. (de qn),** (s.o.'s name-day, saint's day; **souhaiter la f. à qn,** to wish s.o. many happy returns; **ce n'est pa tous les jours f.,** we'll make this an occasion; **fête mobile,** movable feast. 2. fête, fair; **f. d'avia tion,** air display, show. 3. festivity; **le villag était en f.,** the village was on holiday; **air de f festive air; **troubler la f.,** to spoil the party.

fête-Dieu [fɛtdjø], *s.f. Ecc:* Corpus Christi.

fêter [fɛte], *v.tr.* 1. **f. la naissance de qn,** celebrate s.o.'s birthday. 2. **f. qn,** to enterta s.o.

fétiche [fetiʃ], *s.m.* fetish.

fétide [fetid], *a.* fetid, stinking.

feu[1], **feux** [fø], *s.m.* 1. (a) fire; light (f cigarette); **visage en f.,** flushed face; **ustensil qui vont au f.,** fire-proof utensils; **prendre f.,** to catch fire; (ii) to fly into a rage; (b) heat, dour; **plein de f.,** full of drive. 2. (a) **faire du** to light a fire; **f. d'artifice,** fireworks; **f. de j bonfire; (b) **j'en mettrais la main au f.,** I wou swear to it; **faire mourir qn à petit f.,** (i) to k s.o. by inches; (ii) to keep s.o. tenterhooks. 3. **armes à f.,** firearms; **faire f.,** fire; **faire long f.,** to hang fire; **tué au f.,** killed action. 4. light; *Av:* **f. de balisage,** bounda light; *Av:* **feux de bord,** *Nau:* **feux de rou navigation lights; **tous feux éteints,** witho lights; *Aut:* **feux de position, de stationneme** side, parking, lights; **f. arrière,** rear light; **fe de circulation,** *F:* **f. rouge,** traffic lights; **donner le f. vert à qn,** to give s.o. the gre light, the go-ahead; **f. clignotant,** winking wa ing light (at cross-roads).

feu[2], *a.* late, deceased. 1. (*between article and s and variable*) **la feue reine,** the late queen.

(preceding the article and inv.) **feu la reine,** the late queen.

euillage [fœja:ʒ], *s.m.* foliage.

euille [fœ:j], *s.f.* 1. leaf (of plant). 2. **f. de métal,** sheet of metal. 3. **f. de papier,** sheet of paper; **f. de route,** *Mil:* travel warrant; **f. quotidienne,** daily (news-)paper; *Adm:* **f. d'impôt,** (i) tax-return sheet; (ii) notice of assessment; **f. de paie,** pay slip.

euilleter [fœjte], *v.tr.* (**je feuillette**) (*a*) to turn over, flip through, the pages of (book); (*b*) *Cu:* **pâte feuilletée,** flaky pastry.

eutre [fø:tr], *s.m.* 1. felt. 2. felt hat.

ève [fɛ:v], *s.f.* broad bean.

évrier [fevrie], *s.m.* February; **au mois de f., en f.,** in (the month of) February; **le premier, le sept, f.,** (on) the first, the seventh, of February.

iançailles [f(i)jāsa:j], *s.f.pl.* engagement (**avec,** to).

iancé, -ée [fjāse], *s.* fiancé(e).

iancer (se) [səfjāse], *v.pr.* to become engaged (**à, avec,** to).

iasco [fjasko], *s.m.inv.* fiasco.

ibre [fibr], *s.f.* fibre.

ibreux, -euse [fibrø, -ø:z], *a.* fibrous, stringy.

iceller [fisle], *v.tr.* (**je ficelle**) to tie up, do up (with string); *s.m.* **-age.**

icelle [fisɛl], *s.f.* string, twine.

iche [fiʃ], *s.f.* (*a*) slip (of paper); (hotel) registration form; *Ind:* **f. de contrôle,** docket; (*b*) card, ticket (of membership); (*c*) index card; **mise sur fiches,** card-indexing.

icher [fiʃe], *v.tr.* 1. to drive in (stake, etc.); **f. une épingle dans qch.,** to stick a pin into sth. 2. *P:* (*p.p.* **fichu;** *the inf. is usu.* **fiche**) (*a*) **fichez-moi la paix!** shut up! (*b*) **fichez(-moi) le camp!** out you go! hop it! (*c*) **f. qn. à la porte,** to throw s.o. out.

e fiche(r), *P:* (*a*) **se f. par terre,** to fall; (*b*) **se f. dedans,** to make a mistake; to put one's foot in it; (*c*) **se f. de qn,** to make fun of s.o.; (*d*) **je m'en fiche (pas mal)!** I couldn't care less.

ichier [fiʃje], *s.m.* card-index; card-index cabinet.

ichu [fiʃy], *a. P:* 1. rotten (weather). 2. **il est f.,** it's all up with him, he's had it.

ictif, -ive [fiktif, -i:v], *a.* fictitious, imaginary.

iction [fiksjɔ̃], *s.f.* fiction, invention.

idèle [fidɛl], *a.* faithful, loyal, staunch; **copie f.,** exact copy; *s. Ecc:* **les fidèles,** (i) the faithful; (ii) the congregation; *adv.* **-ment.**

idélité [fidelite], *s.f.* fidelity, faithfulness; **serment de f.,** oath of allegiance.

ier¹, -ère [fje:r], *a.* 1. proud. 2. haughty; *F:* stuck-up. 3. *F:* **tu m'as fait une fière peur,** a fine fright you gave me; *adv.* **-èrement.**

ier² (se) [səfje], to trust; **se f. à qn,** to trust s.o.; **fiez-vous à moi,** leave it to me.

ierté [fjerte], *s.f.* 1. pride, self-respect. 2. pride,

haughtiness.

fièvre [fjɛ:vr], *s.f.* fever; **avoir la f.,** to have a temperature.

fiévreux, -euse [fjevrø, -ø:z], *a.* feverish; *adv.* **-eusement.**

figer [fiʒe], *v.tr.* (**figeant**) to coagulate, congeal. **se figer,** to coagulate; (*of blood*) to clot; **sourire figé,** set smile.

figue [fig], *s.f.* 1. fig. 2. **f. de Barbarie,** prickly pear.

figuier [figje], *s.m.* 1. fig-tree. 2. **f. de Barbarie,** prickly pear.

figuratif, -ive [figyratif, -i:v], *a.* figurative, emblematic; *adv.* **-ivement.**

figure [figy:r], *s.f.* 1. figure, form, shape; **prendre f.,** to take shape; **figures de cire,** waxworks. 2. (*a*) face, countenance; *Cards:* **les figures,** the court-cards; (*b*) appearance.

figuré [figyre], *a.* figurative; *adv.phr.* **au f.,** in the figurative sense; figuratively.

figurer [figyre]. 1. *v.tr.* to represent. 2. *v.i.* to appear, figure; *Th:* **f. sur la scène,** to walk on.

se figurer qch., to imagine sth.; **figurez-vous la situation,** picture the situation to yourself.

fil [fil], *s.m.* 1. (*a*) thread; **f. à coudre,** sewing-cotton; **brouiller les fils,** to muddle things up; (*b*) **f. métallique, f. de fer,** wire; *P.T.T:* **donner, F: passer, un coup de f. à qn,** to ring s.o. up, *N.Am:* to call s.o.; **être au bout du f.,** to be on the phone, on the line. 2. grain (of wood). 3. **f. de l'eau,** current; **au f. de l'eau,** with the stream; **au f. des jours et des ans,** day after day, year after year. 4. (cutting) edge (of a razor, etc.).

filament [filamã], *s.m.* filament; fibre (of plant); thread (of silk, etc.).

file [fil], *s.f.* file (of soldiers); **en, à la, f. indienne,** in single file; **deux heures à la f.,** two hours on end; **prendre la f.,** to queue up.

filer [file]. I. *v.tr.* 1. to spin (flax, etc.). 2. *Nau:* to pay out (cable); **f. doux,** to sing small. 3. (*of detective*) to shadow.

II. *v.i.* to slip by; **le temps file,** time flies; **les autos filaient sur la route,** cars were speeding along the road; *F:* **f. (en vitesse),** to cut and run; **il a filé,** he's bolted; **f. à l'anglaise,** to take French leave.

filet¹ [file], *s.m.* 1. fine thread; **f. de lumière,** thin streak of light; **f. d'eau,** thin trickle of water; **ajoutez un f. de citron,** add a dash of lemon. 2. *Cu:* fillet (of beef, fish, etc.).

filet², *s.m.* net(ting); **f. de pêche,** fishing net; **f. (à provisions),** string bag; **f. (à cheveux),** hairnet; *Rail:* **f. à bagages,** luggage rack.

filial, -aux [filjal, -o]. 1. *a.* filial. 2. *s.f.* **filiale,** (*a*) *Com:* subsidiary company; (*b*) provincial branch (of association); *adv.* **-ement.**

filigrane [filigran], *s.m.* 1. filigree (work). 2. watermark (of bank-notes).

fille [fiːj], *s.f.* **1.** daughter. **2.** girl; **jeune f.,** girl; **nom de jeune f.,** maiden name; **vieille f.,** old maid, spinster; **rester f.,** to remain single. **3.** f. **de cuisine,** kitchen maid; **f. de salle,** waitress.

fille-mère [fiːjmɛːr], *s.f.* unmarried mother; *pl. filles-mères.*

fillette [fijɛt], *s.f.* little girl.

filleul, -eule [fijœl], *s.* godchild; godson, goddaughter.

film [film], *s.m.* film; *Cin:* film, *N.Am:* movie; **tourner un f.,** to make, shoot, a film; **f. d'actualité(s),** news film, news reel; **f. fixe (d'enseignement),** film-strip.

filmer [filme], *v.tr. Cin:* to film (scene).

filmothèque [filmɔtɛk], *s.f.* film library.

filon [filɔ̃], *s.m. Min:* vein, seam, lode (of mineral).

filou, -ous [filu], *s.m.* pickpocket, thief, swindler.

filouter [filute], *v.tr.* **f. qn,** to swindle, cheat, s.o.; *s.m.* **-age.**

fils [fis], *s.m.* son; **c'est bien le f. de son père,** he's a chip of, off, the old block; **être le f. de ses œuvres,** to be a self-made man; **M. Duval f.,** Mr. Duval junior; **le f. Duval,** young Duval.

filtre [filtr], *s.m.* filter, percolator; *a.* **bout f.,** filter tip (of cigarette); **papier f.,** filter paper.

filtrer [filtre]. **1.** *v.tr.* to filter, strain. **2.** *v.i. & pr.* to filter, percolate; *s.m.* **-age.**

fin[1] [fɛ̃], *s.f.* **1.** end, close, termination; expiration (of contract); **f. prématurée,** untimely death; **f. de semaine,** weekend; *F:* **tu es stupide à la f.!** you really are very stupid! **2.** end, aim, purpose; **à quelle f.?** for what purpose? **à deux fins,** serving a double purpose.

fin[2]**, fine** [fɛ̃, fin], *a.* (*a*) **au f. fond de la campagne,** in the depths of the country; (*b*) fine, first class; **vins fins,** choice wines; *s.f.* **une fine,** a liqueur brandy; (*c*) subtle, shrewd; **avoir l'oreille fine,** to be quick of hearing; **f. comme l'ambre,** sharp as a needle; *s.m.* **jouer au plus f.,** to have a battle of wits; (*d*) fine, small, slender; **traits fins,** delicate features; *adv.* **café moulu f.,** finely ground coffee; *adv.* **-ement.**

final, -als [final]. **1.** *a.* final. **2.** *s.f. Sp:* **finale,** final.

finaliste [finalist], *s.m. & f. Sp:* finalist.

finance [finɑ̃ːs], *s.f.* **1.** finance. **2.** *pl.* finances, resources; **ministre des Finances** = Chancellor of the Exchequer; **le Ministère des Finances** = the Treasury, the Exchequer.

financer [finɑ̃se], *v.tr.* (**n. finançons**) to finance, back (undertaking); *s.m.* **-ement.**

financier [finɑ̃sje]. **1.** *a.* financial. **2.** *s.m.* financier.

finesse [finɛs], *s.f.* fineness. **1.** good quality (of material); delicacy (of execution). **2.** (*a*) subtlety, shrewdness; **f. d'ouïe,** quickness of hearing; **f. d'esprit,** shrewdness of mind; (*b*) cunning, guile; (*c*) piece of cunning. **3.** fineness (of dust,

etc.).

fini [fini], *a.* **1.** finished, ended; *F:* **il est f.,** he's done for. **2.** (*a*) accomplished (actor, etc.); (*b*) *s.m.* finish. **3.** finite (space, tense).

finir [finiːr]. **1.** *v.tr.* to finish, end. **2.** *v.i.* to come to an end, finish; **il finira mal,** he'll come to a bad end; **en f. avec qch.,** to have done with sth.; **cela n'en finit pas,** there is no end to it; **pour en f.,** to cut the matter short.

finish [finiʃ], *s.m. Sp:* finish.

finlandais, -aise [fɛ̃lɑ̃dɛ, -ɛːz]. **1.** *a.* Finnish. **2.** *s.* Finn.

Finlande (la) [lafɛ̃lɑ̃ːd]. *Pr.n.f. Geog:* Finland.

finnois, -oise [finwa, -waːz]. **1.** *a.* Finnish. **2.** (*a*) *s.* Finn; (*b*) *s.m.Ling:* Finnish.

firmament [firmamɑ̃], *s.m.* firmament, sky.

fisc (le) [ləfisk], *s.m.* (*a*) the Treasury, the Exchequer; (*b*) the Inland Revenue.

fiscal, -aux [fiskal, -o], *a.* fiscal.

fission [fisjɔ̃], *s.f.* splitting, fission; **f. de l'atome,** nuclear fission.

fissure [fis(s)yːr], *s.f.* fissure, cleft.

fiston [fistɔ̃], *s.m. F:* son; **viens, f.,** come along, sonny.

fixe [fiks], *a.* **1.** fixed, firm; **regard f.,** intent gaze. **2.** fixed, regular, settled; **beau (temps) f.,** set fair; *P.N:* **arrêt f.,** all buses stop here; *adv.* **-ement;** *s.f.* **-ité.**

fixer [fikse], *v.tr.* **1.** to fix; to make (sth.) firm, fast; **f. l'attention de qn,** to hold s.o.'s attention; **f. qn,** to stare at s.o. **2.** to fix, determine; **le jour et l'heure,** to decide (up)on, to appoint the day and the time.

flacon [flakɔ̃], *s.m.* bottle; flask.

flagrant [flagrɑ̃], *a.* flagrant, glaring; **pris en délit,** caught in the act.

flair [flɛːr], *s.m.* (*a*) (*of dogs*) scent, (sense of smell; (*b*) (*of pers.*) flair.

flairer [flɛre], *v.tr.* (*a*) (*of dog*) to scent, to nose out (game); **f. le danger,** to smell danger; (*b*) smell (flower).

flamand, -ande [flamɑ̃, -ɑ̃ːd]. **1.** *a.* Flemish. **2.** Fleming. **3.** *s.m. Ling:* Flemish.

flamant [flamɑ̃], *s.m. Orn:* flamingo.

flambant [flɑ̃bɑ̃], *a.* blazing, flaming; *adv.* **ha(tout) f. neuf,** brand-new coat.

flambeau, -eaux [flɑ̃bo], *s.m.* torch; **retraite a flambeaux,** torchlight tattoo.

flamber [flɑ̃be]. **1.** *v.i.* to flame, blaze. **2.** *v.tr.* singe (fowl, hair, etc.).

flamboyant [flɑ̃bwajɑ̃], *a.* **1.** flaming (fire); fie(eyes); *Arch:* **gothique f.,** late Gothic. **2.** flamboyant.

flamboyer [flɑ̃bwaje], *v.i.* (**il flamboie**) to bla

flamme [flɑːm], *s.f.* **1.** flame; **tout en flamme,** ablaze; **par le fer et la f.,** with fire and sword. **2.** pennant, streamer.

flan [flɑ̃], *s.m. Cu:* baked egg custard.

flanc [flɑ̃], *s.m.* flank, side; **f. de coteau,** hillside

battre du f., to heave, pant; **prêter le f. à la critique,** to lay oneself open to criticism.

Flandre (la) [flãːdr]. *Pr.n.f. Geog:* Flanders.

flanelle [flanɛl], *s.f.* flannel; **f. de coton,** flannelette.

flân|er [flane], *v.i.* to loaf about; to stroll; *F:* to hang about; to dawdle; to saunter; *s.f.* **-erie,** dawdling; idling; *s.* **-eur, -euse,** idler; loafer.

flanquer [flãke], *v.tr. F:* to throw, chuck; **f. un coup de pied à qn,** to land s.o. a kick; **f. qn à la porte,** to throw s.o. out.

flaque [flak], *s.f.* puddle, pool.

flash [flaʃ], *s.m.* **1.** *Phot:* flash. **2.** news flash; *pl. flashes.*

flasque [flask], *a.* flaccid (flesh); flabby (hand); **se sentir f.,** to feel limp.

flatt|er [flate], *v.tr.* **1.** to stroke, caress (an animal). **2.** to delight; **spectacle qui flatte les yeux,** sight that delights the eyes; **f. les caprices de qn,** to humour s.o.'s fancies. **3.** to flatter; *s.f.* **-erie;** *a. & s.* **-eur, -euse.**

se flatter, to flatter oneself, delude oneself.

flatulence [flatylãːs], *s.f. Med:* flatulence, *F:* wind.

fléau, -aux [fleo], *s.m.* **1.** (*a*) scourge; calamity; plague; (*b*) boring person. **2.** beam, arm (of balance).

flèche [flɛʃ], *s.f.* **1.** (*a*) arrow; (*b*) direction sign, arrow. **2.** spire (of church).

fléch|ir [fleʃiːr]. **1.** *v.tr.* (*a*) to bend; (*b*) to move to pity. **2.** *v.i.* to give way; *s.m.* **-issement.**

flegmatique [flɛgmatik], *a.* phlegmatic, imperturbable, stolid; *adv.* **-ment.**

flegme [flɛgm], *s.m.* phlegm; imperturbability, impassivity.

Flessingue [flesɛ̃ːg]. *Pr.n. Geog:* Flushing.

flétan [fletã], *s.m. Fish:* halibut.

flétrir¹ [fletriːr], *v.tr.* to blight (hopes).

se flétrir, (*of colours*) to fade; (*of flowers*) to wither.

flétrir², *v.tr.* **f. la réputation de qn,** to cast a slur on s.o.'s character.

fleur [flœːr], *s.f.* **1.** flower; (*a*) blossom, bloom; (*b*) **être dans la f. de l'âge,** to be in the prime of life; (*c*) bloom (on peach). **2.** (= SURFACE) **à f. d'eau,** at water-level; **voler à f. d'eau,** to skim the water; **yeux à f. de tête,** prominent eyes; *s.m. & f.* **-iste,** florist.

fleuri [flœri], *a.* **1.** in bloom, in flower. **2.** flowery (path); florid (complexion, style).

fleurir [flœriːr], *v.i.* **1.** (*a*) (*of plants*) to flower, bloom; (*b*) (*pr.p.* **florissant**) to flourish, prosper. **2.** *v.tr.* to decorate (table, etc.) with flowers.

fleuve [flœːv], *s.m.* (large) river.

flexib|le [flɛksibl], *a.* flexible, pliable; *s.f.* **-ilité.**

flic [flik], *s.m. P:* policeman, cop; **f. de la route,** speed-cop.

flirt [flœrt], *s.m. F:* **1.** flirtation, flirting. **2.** mon f.,

my boyfriend, my girlfriend.

flirter [flœrte], *v.i.* to flirt.

flocon [flɔkɔ̃], *s.m.* flake; **f. de neige,** snow-flake; **céréales en flocons,** breakfast foods, cereals.

floconneux, -euse [flɔkɔnø, -øːz], *a.* fleecy, fluffy (clouds, wool, etc.).

floral, -aux [flɔral, -o], *a.* floral.

flore [flɔːr], *s.f. Bot:* flora.

florissant [flɔrisã], *a.* flourishing, prosperous.

flot [flo], *s.m.* **1.** (*a*) wave; (*b*) **flots de larmes,** floods of tears; **couler à flots,** to gush forth. **2.** floating; (*of ship*) **à f.,** afloat; *F:* **remettre qn à f.,** to restore s.o.'s fortunes.

flottant [flɔtã], *a.* (*of ship, debt*) floating; **robe flottante,** flowing robe; wavering, undecided (mind).

flotte [flɔt], *s.f.* fleet.

flotter [flɔte]. **1.** *v.i.* (*a*) to float; (*b*) to wave (in the wind); (*c*) to waver. **2.** *v.tr.* **f. du bois,** to float timber.

flottille [flɔtiːj], *s.f. Nau:* flotilla.

flou [flu], *a.* woolly (outline); hazy (horizon); **cheveux flous,** fluffy hair.

fluctu|er [flyktɥe], *v.i.* to fluctuate; *s.f.* **-ation.**

fluet, -ette [flyɛ, -ɛt], *a.* thin, slender.

fluide [flɥid], *a. & s.m.* fluid.

fluorescence [flyɔrɛs(s)ãːs], *s.f.* fluorescence.

fluorescent [flyɔrɛs(s)ã], *a.* fluorescent; **éclairage f.,** strip lighting.

flûte [flyt], *s.f.* **1.** flute; **petite f.,** piccolo. **2.** long thin loaf (of bread).

fluvial, -aux [flyvjal, -o], *a.* fluvial; river (police); **voie fluviale,** waterway.

flux [fly], *s.m.* flow; flood.

fluxion [flyksjɔ̃], *s.f. Med:* inflammation.

foi [fwa], *s.f.* faith. **1.** **manque de f.,** breach of faith; **ma f., oui!** indeed, yes! **2.** belief, trust; **avoir f. en qn,** to have faith in s.o. **3.** (religious) faith, belief.

foie [fwa], *s.m.* liver.

foin [fwɛ̃], *s.m.* hay; **faire les foins,** to make hay; **tas de f.,** haycock; **rhume des foins,** hay fever.

foire [fwaːr], *s.f.* fair; **champ de f.,** fair-ground.

fois [fwa], *s.f.* time, occasion; **une f.,** once; **deux f.,** twice; **encore une f.,** once more; **une (bonne) f. pour toutes,** once (and) for all; **à la f.,** at one and the same time.

foison [fwazɔ̃], *s.f.* abundance; **à f.,** plentifully; in abundance.

foisonner [fwazɔne], *v.i.* to abound (**de,** in, with).

folâtre [fɔlaːtr], *a.* playful, frisky, frolicsome; *adv.* **-ment.**

folie [fɔli], *s.f.* **1.** madness; **être pris de f.,** to go mad. **2.** folly; piece of folly; **dire des folies,** to talk wildly; **faire des folies,** (i) to act foolishly; (ii) to be extravagant.

follement [fɔlmã], *adv.* madly. **1.** foolishly, unwisely. **2.** extravagantly.

fomenter [fɔmãte], *v.tr.* to foment; to stir up (trouble).

foncé [fɔ̃se], *a.* dark (colour); **des rubans bleu f.,** dark blue ribbons.

foncer [fɔ̃se], *v.* (**n. fonçons**) 1. *v.tr.* to deepen, darken (the colour of sth.). 2. *v.i.* **f. sur qn,** (*a*) to rush, swoop (down), upon s.o.; (*b*) (*of bull, footballer*) to charge s.o.

foncier, -ière [fɔ̃sje, -jɛ:r], *a.* 1. of the land; **propriété foncière,** landed property; **impôt f.,** land tax. 2. fundamental; **bon sens f.,** innate common sense; *adv.* **-èrement,** fundamentally.

fonction [fɔ̃ksjɔ̃], *s.f.* function, office; (*a*) **entrer en fonctions,** to take up one's duties; **faire f. de . . .,** to act as . . .; (*b*) **fonctions de l'estomac, du cœur,** functions of the stomach, of the heart.

fonctionnaire [fɔ̃ksjɔnɛ:r], *s.m.* civil servant; official.

fonctionner [fɔ̃ksjɔne], *v.i.* 1. to function. 2. to act, work; **les trains ne fonctionnent plus,** the trains are no longer running; *s.m.* **-ement.**

fond [fɔ̃], *s.m.* 1. (*a*) bottom (of well, etc.); seat (of trousers, chair); **au fin f. de . . .,** at the very bottom of . . .; (*b*) bottom, bed (of the sea); **grands fonds,** ocean deeps; **hauts, petits, fonds,** shallows; *adv.phr.* **à f.,** thoroughly; **visser une pièce à f.,** to screw a piece home; **connaître un sujet à f.,** to be an expert in a subject. 2. foundation; **rebâtir une maison de f. en comble,** to rebuild a house from top to bottom; **faire f. sur qch.,** to rely on sth.; **cheval qui a du f.,** horse with staying power; *Journ:* **article de f.,** leading article; **au f.,** basically, fundamentally, at bottom; **f. de teint,** (make-up) foundation. 3. back, far end; **f. d'un tableau,** background of a picture; **fonds de boutique,** oddments; old stock; **bruits de f.,** background noises.

fondamental, -aux [fɔ̃damãtal, -o], *a.* fundamental; basic; **couleurs fondamentales,** primary colours.

fondé [fɔ̃de], *a.* 1. founded, justified; **nous ne sommes pas fondés à leur refuser ce droit,** we are not entitled to refuse them this right. 2. *s.m.* **f. de pouvoir,** proxy.

fonder [fɔ̃de], *v.tr.* to found, set up, start (a business); to lay the foundations of (a building); to base, build (one's hopes) (**sur, on**); *s.* **-ateur, -atrice,** founder; *s.f.* **-ation,** (endowed) institution; *s.m.* **-ement,** foundation, base.

se fonder sur qch., to place one's reliance on sth.; **je me fonde sur ce que vous venez de me dire,** I'm basing myself on what you've just said.

fondre [fɔ̃:dr]. 1. *v.tr.* (*a*) to smelt (ore); (*b*) to melt (snow); (*c*) to cast (bell); (*d*) to dissolve,

melt (sugar, etc.); (*e*) to blend (colours). 2. *v.* to melt, dissolve; **f. en larmes,** to dissolve in(to tears. 3. *v.i.* to swoop down (upon the prey).

fondrière [fɔ̃drie:r], *s.f.* (*a*) bog, quagmire; (*b* muddy hole (in road); *Fr.C:* **f. de mousse** muskeg.

fonds [fɔ̃], *s.m.* 1. (*a*) **f. de commerce,** business (*b*) stock(-in-trade). 2. (*a*) funds; ready money **rentrer dans ses f.,** to get one's money back; (*b* means, resources; **placer son argent à f. perdu** to purchase a life annuity; *Fin:* stocks securities.

fontaine [fɔ̃tɛn], *s.f.* 1. spring, source, well. 2 fountain.

fonte [fɔ̃:t], *s.f.* 1. (*a*) melting; thawing (of snow (*b*) smelting (of ore); (*c*) casting, founding. 2 cast iron.

fonts [fɔ̃], *s.m.pl. Ecc:* font.

football [futbɔl], *s.m.* (association) football, *f* soccer; *s.m.* **-eur.**

footing [futiŋ], *s.m. Sp:* walking (for trainin purposes).

forage [fɔra:ʒ], *s.m.* 1. drilling, boring; sinkin (of well). 2. bore-hole; sink-hole.

forain [fɔrɛ̃], *a. & s.* **spectacle f.,** travelling shov (**marchand**) **f.,** stall-keeper (at fair); **fê foraine,** fun fair.

forçat [fɔrsa], *s.m.* convict.

force [fɔrs], *s.f.* 1. strength, force, vigour; (*a* **mourir dans la f. de l'âge,** to die in the prime (life; **être à bout de forces,** to be exhausted; **to** **de f.,** feat (of strength or skill); (*b*) forc violence, compulsion; **f. majeure,** ci cumstances outside one's control; **f. lui fe d'obéir,** he had no alternative but to obey; **o gré ou de f.,** willy-nilly; **à toute f.,** at all costs. 2 (*a*) force, power; **f. motrice,** motive power; (* **les forces armées,** the armed forces. 3. *a.inv.* **gens,** many people. 4. **à f. de,** by dint of, b means of.

forcément [fɔrsemã], *adv.* inevitably.

forcené, -ée [fɔrsəne]. 1. *a.* frantic, mad, fre zied. 2. *s.* madman, madwoman.

forcer [fɔrse], *v.tr.* (**n. forçons**) to force. 1. compel. 2. (*a*) to break open (door, etc.), force (lock); **f. la caisse,** to break into the till; **sa prison,** to break jail; **f. la consigne,** to for one's way in; (*b*) to strain (heart, etc.); to for (plants). 3. *v.i.* **f. de vitesse,** to increase spee

forer [fɔre], *v.tr.* to drill, bore; to sink (a we *s.m.* (*pers.*) **-eur,** driller; *s.f.* **-euse,** drill(i machine).

forestier, -ière [fɔrɛstje, -jɛ:r], *a.* pertaining tc forest; **exploitation forestière,** lumbering.

foret [fɔre], *s.m. Tls:* drill.

forêt [fɔre], *s.f.* forest.

forfait¹ [fɔrfe], *s.m.* crime, outrage.

forfait², *s.m.* contract; **travail à f.,** (i) contra work; (ii) job work; **acheter qch. à f.,** to b sth. outright.

forfait³, *s.m. Sp: etc:* **déclarer f.**, to scratch (a horse from a race), to withdraw from a competition.

forfaitaire [fɔrfɛtɛːr], *a.* contractual; **marché f.**, (transaction by) contract, outright purchase; **paiement f.**, lump sum; **prix f.**, contract price.

forge [fɔrʒ], *s.f.* **1.** smithy, forge. **2.** *usu. pl.* ironworks.

forger [fɔrʒe], *v.tr.* (n. forgeons) to forge. **1. fer forgé**, wrought iron. **2.** to forge (document); to make up (excuse).

forgeron [fɔrʒərɔ̃], *s.m.* (black)smith.

formaliser (se) [səfɔrmalize], *v.pr.* to take offence (**de**, at).

formaliste [fɔrmalist], *a.* formal, stiff (mind, etc.).

formalité [fɔrmalite], *s.f.* **1.** formality; **sans autre f.**, without further ado. **2. sans formalité(s)**, without ceremony.

format [fɔrma], *s.m.* format (of book); **f. de poche**, pocket size.

forme [fɔrm], *s.f.* **1.** form, shape; **formes athlétiques**, athletic build; **sans f.**, shapeless. **2.** form; method of procedure; **faire qch. dans les formes**, to do sth. with due decorum; **pour la f.**, for form's sake.

formel, **-elle** [fɔrmɛl], *a.* formal, strict, categorical (order); explicit (declaration); flat (denial), absolute (veto); *adv.* **-lement**.

form|er [fɔrme], *v.tr.* to form. **1.** to make, create; to draw up (plan). **2.** to shape, fashion; to train (child); to school (horse); to mould (s.o.'s character); *s.f.* **-ation**.

formidable [fɔrmidabl], *a.* (*a*) fearsome, formidable; (*b*) *F:* tremendous, wonderful, terrific; **elle est f.!** she's (i) fantastic! (ii) smashing!

formule [fɔrmyl], *s.f.* **1.** (*a*) formula; (*b*) (set) form of words. **2.** *Adm: etc:* (printed) form.

formuler [fɔrmyle], *v.tr.* to formulate; to draw up (document); to give expression to (a wish).

fort [fɔːr]. **I.** *a.* **1.** (*a*) strong; **trouver plus f. que soi**, to meet one's match; **c'est une forte tête**, he is pig-headed, very stubborn; **forte mer**, heavy sea; **d'une voix forte**, in a loud voice; **c'est plus f. que moi!** I can't help it! **c'est trop f.!** it's too bad! **ce qu'il y a de plus f., c'est que . . .**, the best part of it is that . . .; (*b*) **ville forte**, fortified town. **2.** large; **femme forte**, stout woman; *adv.* **-ement**.
II. *adv.* **1.** strongly; **frapper f.**, to strike hard; *F:* **y aller f.**, to exaggerate. **2.** very, extremely; **j'ai f. à faire**, I have a great deal to do.
III. *s.m.* **1.** strong part; **au f. de l'hiver**, in the depths of winter; **au (plus) f. du combat**, in the thick of the fight. **2.** fort, stronghold; *s.f.* **-eresse**, fortress.

fortifi|er [fɔrtifje], *v.tr.* to strengthen; to fortify

(town); to confirm (suspicions); *s.m.* **-ant**, tonic; *s.f.* **-cation**.

fortuit [fɔrtɥi], *a.* fortuitous; (by) chance; **rencontre fortuite**, casual meeting; **cas f.**, accident; *adv.* **-ement**.

fortune [fɔrtyn], *s.f.* **1.** fortune, chance, luck; **dispositif de f.**, makeshift. **2.** piece of (good, bad) luck. **3.** fortune, riches; **avoir de la f.**, to be well off.

fosse [foːs], *s.f.* **1.** pit, hole; *Aut:* inspection pit. **2.** grave.

fossé [fose], *s.m.* ditch, trench.

fossette [fosɛt, fo-], *s.f.* dimple.

fossile [fosil], *a. & s.m.* fossil.

fossoyeur [foswajœːr], *s.m.* grave-digger.

fou, **fol**, **folle** [fu, fɔl] (*the form* **fol**, *used in the m. before a vowel within the word-group, is confined to sense* 1 (*b*).) **1.** *a.* (*a*) mad, insane; **f. à lier**, raving mad; **f. de joie**, beside oneself with joy; **être f. de qn**, to be madly in love with s.o.; (*b*) foolish, silly; **un fol espoir**, a mad hope; (*c*) prodigious; **succès f.**, tremendous success; **il gagne un argent f.**, he makes no end of money; **à une allure folle**, at breakneck speed; (*d*) not under control, out of control; **herbes folles**, rank weeds. **2.** *s.* (*never* **fol**) (*a*) madman, madwoman; lunatic; (*b*) fool; **plus on est de fous plus on rit**, the more the merrier. **3.** *s.m. Chess:* bishop.

foudre [fudr], *s.f.* thunderbolt, lightning; **coup de f.**, (i) thunderbolt; (ii) unexpected disaster; (iii) love at first sight.

foudro|yer [fudrwaje]. **1.** *v.tr.* (**je foudroie**) to strike down; to blast; to crush, to overwhelm; **arbre foudroyé**, blasted tree; **cette nouvelle m'a foudroyé**, I was thunderstruck at the news; **elle le foudroya d'un regard**, she gave him a withering look. **2.** *v.i.* to thunder; *s.m.* **-iement**, blasting.

fouet [fwɛ], *s.m.* whip, lash; **coup de f.**, (i) cut (of whip); (ii) stimulus; **collision de plein f.**, head-on collision.

fouetter [fwɛte], *v.tr.* to whip, flog, lash; to beat; **avoir d'autres chiens, d'autres chats, à f.**, to have other fish to fry.

fougère [fuʒɛːr], *s.f. Bot:* fern; bracken.

fougue [fug], *s.f.* fire, ardour, spirit; **équipe pleine de f.**, team full of dash.

fougueu|x, **-euse** [fugø, -øːz], *a.* fiery, ardent, spirited; impetuous; *adv.* **-sement**.

fouille [fuːj], *s.f.* **1.** *usu. pl.* excavation; *Archeol:* dig. **2.** search(ing) (of a suspect).

fouiller [fuje]. **1.** *v.tr.* (*a*) to dig, excavate; (*b*) to search (luggage); to frisk (passenger); **f. un tiroir**, to ransack a drawer. **2.** *v.i.* **f. dans une armoire**, to rummage in a cupboard.

fouine [fwin], *s.f. Z:* (stone-)marten; **à figure de f.**, weasel-faced; **des yeux de f.**, ferrety eyes.

foulard [fulaːr], *s.m.* **1.** *Tex:* foulard. **2.** (*a*) silk handkerchief; (b) silk scarf.

foule [ful], s.f. crowd; throng.

fouler [fule], v.tr. 1. to press; to trample (down) (grass); to crush (grapes). 2. to sprain, strain, wrench (wrist, etc.); F: **ne pas se f. la rate,** P: **ne pas se la f.,** to take it easy; s.f. **-ure,** sprain.

four [fuːr], s.m. 1. (a) oven; (b) Cu: **petits fours,** fancy biscuits, petits fours. 2. kiln, furnace. 3. Th: **faire f.,** to be a flop.

fourbe [furb], a. rascally, knavish.

fourberie [furbəri], s.f. 1. deceit, cheating. 2. swindle.

fourche [furʃ], s.f. (pitch)fork; (garden) fork.

fourcher [furʃe], v.i. to fork, branch, divide.

fourchette [furʃet], s.f. (table) fork.

fourchu [furʃy], a. forked; **pied f.,** cloven hoof.

fourgon [furgɔ̃], s.m. van, wag(g)on; s.f. Aut: **-nette,** light van.

fourmi [furmi], s.f. Ent: ant; **avoir des fourmis,** to have pins and needles.

fourmilière [furmiljeːr], s.f. ant-hill, ant's nest.

fourmiller [furmije], v.i. 1. to swarm; to teem. 2. **le pied me fourmille,** I've got pins and needles in my foot; s.m. **-ement.**

fourneau, -eaux [furno], s.m. (a) furnace (of boiler, etc.); bowl (of pipe); (b) **f. à gaz,** gas-stove, -cooker; (c) **haut f.,** blast furnace.

fournée [furne], s.f. batch (of loaves, etc.).

fournir [furniːr], v.tr. to supply, furnish, provide; **magasin bien fourni,** well-stocked shop; v.ind.tr. **f. aux besoins de qn,** to supply s.o.'s wants; s. **-isseur, -isseuse,** supplier.

fourniture [furnityːr], s.f. 1. supplying, providing. 2. pl. supplies; **fournitures de bureau,** office requisites.

fourré [fure], s.m. thicket.

fourreau, -eaux [furo], s.m. sheath, cover, case; Mec. E: sleeve.

fourrer [fure], v.tr. 1. to cover, line, with fur. 2. F: to stuff, cram; **f. son nez partout,** to poke one's nose into everything; s.m. **-eur,** furrier.

fourrure [furyːr], s.f. 1. fur, skin; hair, coat (of animal). 2. Aut: **f. de frein,** brake lining.

fourvoyer [furvwaje], v.tr. (**je fourvoie**) to mislead (s.o.).

se fourvoyer, to lose one's way, to go astray.

fox [fɔks], s.m. F: fox-terrier.

foyer [fwaje], s.m. 1. fire(-place), hearth, grate. 2. source (of heat); focus (of infection). 3. (a) hearth, home; **f. d'étudiants,** students' union, club; (b) Th: **f. du public,** foyer; **foyer des artistes,** green-room. 4. focus (of lens); **verres à double f.,** bifocal lenses.

fracas [fraka], s.m. din; (sound of a) crash.

fracasser [frakase], v.tr. to smash (sth.) to pieces; to shatter (sth.).

fraction [fraksjɔ̃], s.f. fraction.

fracture [fraktyːr], s.f. 1. breaking open, forcing (of door, lock). 2. fracture (of bone).

fracturer [fraktyre], v.tr. 1. to force (lock); to break open (door). 2. to fracture (bone).

fragile [fraʒil], a. 1. fragile; brittle. 2. frail; s.f. **-ité,** brittleness; frailty.

fragment [fragmã], s.m. fragment.

fraîchement [freʃmã], adv. 1. coolly. 2. freshly, recently.

fraîcheur [freʃøːr], s.f. 1. coolness, chilliness. 2. freshness.

frais¹, fraîche [fre, freʃ]. 1. a. fresh; (a) cool; (b) new, recent; **œufs f.,** new-laid eggs; **peinture fraîche,** wet paint; (c) **teint f.,** fresh complexion. 2. (a) s.m. **prendre le f.,** to take the air; **à mettre au f.,** to be kept in a cool place; **peint de f.,** freshly painted; (b) s.f. **la fraîche,** the cool of the evening.

frais², s.m.pl. expenses, cost; **menus f.,** petty expenses; **rentrer dans ses f.,** to get one's money back; **faire les f. de la conversation,** (i) to contribute a large share of the talk; (ii) to be the subject of the conversation; **j'en suis pour mes f.,** I've had all my trouble for nothing.

fraise [freːz], s.f. strawberry; s.m. **-ier,** strawberry-plant.

framboise [frãbwaːz], s.f. raspberry; s.m. **-sier,** raspberry-cane.

franc¹ [frã], s.m. franc.

franc², franche [frã, frãːʃ], a. 1. free; **f. de port,** post-free; carriage paid; Fb: **coup f.,** free kick. 2. (a) frank; open, candid; **avoir son f. parler,** to speak one's mind; **y aller de f. jeu,** to be quite straightforward about it; (b) real, true; downright; adv. **-chement.**

français, -aise [frãse, -eːz]. 1. a. French. 2. s. Frenchman, -woman; **les F.,** the French. 3. s.m. French (language).

France (la) [lafrãːs]. Pr.n.f. Geog: France; **en F.** in France; **les vins de F.,** French wines.

franchir [frãʃiːr], v.tr. (a) to clear (obstacle); to jump (over); to get over; (b) to pass through; to cross; **f. le mur du son,** to break the sound barrier; s.m. **-issement.**

franchise [frãʃiːz], s.f. 1. freedom (of a city). 2. exemption; **importer qch. en f.,** to import sth. free of duty, duty free; **en f. = O.H.M.S.** 3. frankness, candour.

franc-maçon [frãmasɔ̃], s.m. freemason; pl. francs-maçons.

franc-maçonnerie [frãmasɔnri], s.f. freemasonry.

franco [frãko], adv. free, carriage-free.

François [frãswa]. Pr.n.m., **Françoise** [-waːz] Pr.n.f. Francis, Frank; f. Frances.

franc-parler [frãparle], s.m. bluntness of speech; plain speaking.

frange [frãːʒ], s.f. fringe.

frappant [frapã], a. striking (likeness, etc.).

frapper [frape], v.tr. 1. (a) to strike, hit; **f. un coup,** to strike a blow; **f. des marchandises**

d'un droit, to impose a duty on goods; f. à la porte, to knock at the door; on frappe, there's a knock; f. du pied, to stamp (one's foot); (b) to strike (coin). 2. to chill (wine); servir frappé, serve chilled; whisky frappé, whisky on the rocks.

fraternel, -elle [fraternɛl], a. fraternal, brotherly; adv. -lement.

fraternisler [fraternize], v.i. to fraternize; s.f. -ation.

fraternité [fraternite], s.f. fraternity, brotherhood.

fraude [froːd], s.f. 1. fraud, deception; smuggling. 2. fraudulence, deceit; par f., under false pretences.

fraudler [frode]. 1. v.tr. to defraud, cheat. 2. v.i. to cheat; s. -eur, -euse.

frauduleulx, -euse [frodylø, -øːz], a. fraudulent; adv. -sement.

frayer [freje], v.tr. (je fraye, je fraie) se f. un passage, to clear a way (for oneself).

frayeur [frejœːr], s.f. fright; fear, dread.

fredonner [frədɔne], v.tr. to hum (tune).

frégate [fregat], s.f. frigate; capitaine de f., commander.

frein [frɛ̃], s.m. 1. (horse's) bit; (in wider sense) bridle; mettre un f. aux désirs de qn, to curb s.o.'s desires; curiosité sans f., unbridled curiosity. 2. brake; f. à disque, disc brake; mettre le f., to put on the brake; to brake.

freiner [frene], v.tr. 1. abs. to put on the brakes. 2. f. la production, to check production.

frêle [frɛːl], a. frail, weak.

frelon [frəlɔ̃], s.m. Ent: hornet.

frémlir [fremiːr], v.i. 1. to quiver; (of leaves) to rustle. 2. to tremble, shake, shudder; s.m. -issement.

frêne [frɛːn], s.m. ash (tree or timber).

frénésie [frenezi], s.f. frenzy, madness; applaudir avec f., to applaud frantically.

frénétique [frenetik], a. frantic, frenzied; adv. -ment.

fréquence [frekɑ̃ːs], s.f. frequency; Med: f. du pouls, pulse rate; El: Rad: etc: courant à haute, basse, f., high-, low-frequency, current; modulation de f., frequency modulation.

fréqulent [frekɑ̃], a. frequent; adv. -emment.

fréquentler [frekɑ̃te]. 1. v.tr. (a) to frequent; to visit (place) frequently; to attend (school, church); (b) f. qn, to associate with s.o.; quels gens fréquente-t-il? what company does he keep? 2. v.i. f. chez qn, to be on visiting terms with s.o.; s.f. -ation; mauvaise fréquentation, bad company.

frère [frɛːr], s.m. brother.

fresque [frɛsk], s.f. Art: fresco.

fret [frɛ], s.m. freight. 1. freightage. 2. chartering. 3. load, cargo; freight.

fréter [frete], v.tr. (je frète) 1. to freight (ship). 2. to charter (ship, plane).

friable [friabl], a. friable, crumbly.

friand, -ande [friɑ̃, -ɑ̃ːd], a. fond of delicacies; être f. de sucreries, to have a sweet tooth; s.f. -ise, delicacy, titbit.

fric [frik], s.m. P: dough, lolly.

friche [friʃ], s.f. waste land; fallow land.

fricot [friko], s.m. F: made-up dish; stew; faire le f., to do the cooking.

fricoter [frikɔte], v.tr. & i. F: 1. to stew; to cook; elle fricote bien, she's a good cook. 2. to cook up (sth. underhand).

friction [friksjɔ̃], s.f. friction.

frileulx, -euse [frilø, -øːz], a. sensitive to the cold; chilly (person); adv. -sement.

frimas [frima], s.m. (hoar-)frost; rime.

friplerie [fripri], s.f. (a) secondhand goods; (b) rubbish, frippery; s. -ier, -ière, secondhand clothes dealer.

frire [friːr], v.tr. & i.def. (p.p. frit; for the v.tr. the defective parts are supplied by faire f.) to fry; je fais f. des pommes de terre, I'm frying potatoes.

frise [friːz], s.f. Arch: frieze.

frisé [frize], a. curly (hair); laitue frisée, curly lettuce.

friser [frize]. 1. (a) v.tr. to curl, wave; (b) v.i. (of hair) to curl. 2. v.tr. to touch, skim; f. la prison, narrowly to avoid prison; f. la soixantaine, to be close to sixty, to be nearly sixty.

frisson [frisɔ̃], s.m. (a) shiver (from cold); (b) shudder, thrill; j'en ai le f., it gives me the shudders; (c) thrill (of pleasure).

frissonnler [frisɔne], v.i. (a) to shiver, shudder; (b) to be thrilled (with delight); (c) to quiver (with impatience); s.m. -ement.

frit [fri], a. fried; pommes de terre frites, s.f. frites, French fried potatoes; chips.

frivolle [frivɔl], a. frivolous, shallow; s.f. -ité.

froid [frwa]. I. a. 1. cold; il fait f., it is cold; j'ai f. aux mains, my hands are cold; chambre froide, (i) cold room; (ii) chilling chamber (for meat). 2. cold (person); chilly (manner); sourire f., frigid smile; garder la tête froide, to keep cool (and collected).

II. s.m. 1. cold; conservation par le f., cold storage; il fait un f. de loup, it's bitterly cold. 2. coldness; il y a du f. entre eux, there is a coolness between them; vivre en f. avec qn, to get on badly with s.o.; adv. -ement; s.f. -eur, coldness (of temperament, manner, style).

froissler [frwase], v.tr. 1. to crumple, to rumple (sth.) (up). 2. f. qn, to give offence to s.o.; s.m. -ement.

se froisser, to take offence.

frôller [frole], v.tr. to touch lightly; to brush; to rub (past, against, s.o., sth.); s.m. -ement.

fromage [frɔmaːʒ], s.m. cheese.

froment [frɔmɑ̃], s.m. wheat.

froncier [frɔ̃se], *v.tr.* (n. **fronçons**) 1. **f. les sourcils**, to knit one's brows; to frown. 2. (*needlework*) to gather; *s.m.* **-ement**.

fronde [frɔ̃:d], *s.f.* (*a*) sling; (*b*) (toy) catapult.

front [frɔ̃], *s.m.* 1. forehead, brow; **et vous avez le f. de me dire cela!** you have the face, the impudence, to tell me that! 2. face, front (of building, etc.); **f. de bataille**, battle front; **faire f. à qch.**, to face sth. 3. **de f.**, abreast.

frontière [frɔ̃tjɛ:r], *s.f.* frontier(-line); border (-line).

frontispice [frɔ̃tispis], *s.m.* frontispiece.

frottier [frɔte], *v.tr.* to rub; **se f. les mains**, to rub one's hands; **f. le parquet**, to rub up, polish, the floor; **f. une allumette**, to strike a match; *s.m.* **-ement**.

froussie [frus], *s.f. P:* funk, fear; **avoir la f.**, to have the wind up; *s. P:* **-ard, -arde**, (*of pers.*) funk, coward.

fructifier [fryktifje], *v.i.* to fructify, to bear fruit; *Fin:* to bear interest.

fructuleux, -euse [fryktɥø, -ø:z], *a.* fruitful; profitable; *adv.* **-eusement**.

frugal, -aux [frygal, -o], *a.* frugal; *adv.* **-ement**; *s.f.* **-ité**.

fruit [frɥi], *s.m.* fruit.

fruitier, -ière [frɥitje, -jɛ:r]. 1. *a.* **arbre f.**, fruit-tree. 2. *s.* fruiterer, greengrocer.

fruste [fryst], *a.* worn (coin); rough (style, manners).

frustrier [frystre], *v.tr.* 1. to frustrate, disappoint. 2. to defraud (s.o.) (**de qch.**, of sth.); *s.f.* **-ation**.

fuel(-oil) [fjul(ɔjl)], *s.m.* fuel oil; domestic fuel (oil).

fugitif, -ive [fyʒitif, -i:v]. 1. *s.* fugitive. 2. *a.* fleeting, transitory; passing (desire).

fuir [fɥi:r], *v.* (*pr.p.* **fuyant**) 1. *v.i.* (*a*) to flee, run away; (*b*) (*of horizon*) to recede; (*c*) (*of tap*) to leak. 2. *v.tr.* to shun, avoid (s.o.).

fuite [fɥit], *s.f.* 1. flight, running away. 2. leak; leakage; **la f. des cerveaux**, the brain drain.

fume-cigarette [fymsigarɛt], *s.m.inv.* cigarette-holder.

fumée [fyme], *s.f.* (*a*) smoke; **charbon sans f.**, smokeless coal; (*b*) steam (of soup); **les fumées du vin**, the fumes of wine.

fumier [fyme]. 1. *v.i.* (*a*) to smoke; (*b*) (*of soup*) to steam; **f. de colère**, to fume, to rage. 2. *v.tr.* **f. une pipe**, to smoke a pipe; **défense de f.**, no smoking; *s.* **-eur, -euse**, smoker; *a.* **-eux, -euse**, smoky; heady (wine).

fumier [fymje], *s.m.* 1. manure, dung. 2. dunghill; manure heap.

fumiste [fymist], *s.m.* (i) practical joker; (ii) humbug.

funèbre [fynɛbr], *a.* 1. funeral (ceremony); **marche f.**, dead-march. 2. funereal, gloomy.

funérailles [fynera:j], *s.f.pl.* funeral.

funéraire [fynerɛ:r], *a.* funerary; **pierre f.,** tombstone.

funeste [fynɛst], *a.* deadly, fatal; **influence f.**, disastrous influence.

funiculaire [fynikylɛ:r], *s.m.* funicular railway.

fur [fy:r], *s.m. now only used in the adv.phr.* **au f. et à mesure**, (in proportion) as, progressively; **fournir des articles au f. et à mesure des besoins**, to supply articles as they are wanted.

furet [fyrɛ], *s.m.* (*a*) *Z:* ferret; **jeu du f.**, hunt-the-slipper; (*b*) inquisitive person, Nosy Parker.

furetier [fyrte], *v.i.* (**je furette**) (*a*) to ferret, go ferreting; (*b*) **f. dans les armoires**, to ferret, pry about, rummage, in the cupboards; *a. & s.* **-eur, -euse**, (i) prying; (ii) Nosy Parker.

fureur [fyrœ:r], *s.f.* 1. fury, rage, wrath. 2. fury, passion; **avoir la f. de bâtir**, to have a craze for building, to be building mad; **chanson qui fait f.**, song that is all the rage, hit.

furibond [fyribɔ̃], *a.* furious; full of fury.

furie [fyri], *s.f.* 1. **c'est une f.**, she's a fury. 2. fury, rage; **en f.**, infuriated.

furieulx, -euse [fyrjø, -ø:z], *a.* furious; in a passion; *adv.* **-sement**.

furoncle [fyrɔ̃:kl], *s.m. Med:* boil.

furtilf, -ive [fyrtif, -i:v], *a.* furtive, stealthy; *adv.* **-vement**.

fuseau, -eaux [fyzo], *s.m.* 1. *Tex:* spindle. 2. **f. horaire**, time zone. 3. taper; *pl. Cl:* (i) ski trousers; (ii) drainpipe trousers.

fusée [fyze], *s.f.* (*a*) rocket; **f. éclairante**, flare; **f. porte-amarre**, rocket apparatus; **avion (à) f.**, rocket-propelled aircraft; **f. mère**, first-stage rocket; (*b*) fuse.

fuselage [fyzla:ʒ], *s.m. Av:* fuselage.

fuselé [fyzle], *a. Aut:* streamlined; **doigts fuselés**, tapering fingers.

fusible [fyzibl], *s.m. El:* fuse.

fusil [fyzi], *s.m.* gun; rifle; **à une portée de f. d'ici**, within gunshot distance from here; **coup de f.**, gunshot, rifle-shot; report (of a gun).

fusillade [fyzijad], *s.f.* fusillade, rifle-fire.

fusiller [fyzije], *v.tr.* (*a*) to shoot (down) (men); (*b*) to execute (by shooting); to shoot (spy).

fusion [fyzjɔ̃], *s.f.* 1. fusion, melting; dissolving. 2. coalescing (of ideas, etc.). 3. *Com:* merger, amalgamation.

fût [fy], *s.m.* 1. stock (of rifle). 2. (*a*) shaft (of column); (*b*) bole (of tree). 3. cask, barrel.

futaie [fyte], *s.f.* wood, forest; **arbre de haute f.,** timber-tree.

futile [fytil], *a.* futile, trifling; idle (pretext); *adv.* **-ment**.

futilité [fytilite], *s.f.* futility.

futur [fyty:r], *a.* future (time, tense, etc.).

fuyant [fɥijɑ̃], *a.* 1. fleeing (animal); fleeting (moment). 2. receding (forehead). 3. **regard f.**, shifty expression.

fuyard, -arde [fɥija:r, -ard], *s.* (panic-stricken) fugitive, runaway.

G

G, g [ʒe], s.m. (the letter) G, g.

garbardine [gabardin], s.f. **1.** Tex: gabardine. **2.** (gabardine) raincoat.

Gabon (le) [ləgabɔ̃]. Pr.n.m. Geog: Gabon.

gâcher [gaʃe], v.tr. to spoil (sheet of paper); to bungle (job); **g. sa vie**, to make a mess of one's life.

gâchette [gaʃɛt], s.f. trigger; F: **avoir la g. facile**, to be trigger-happy.

gâchis [gaʃi], s.m. F: **quel g.!** what a mess!

gaffe [gaf], s.f. **1.** (a) boat-hook; (b) Fish: gaff. **2.** F: **faire une g.**, to put one's foot in it; to make a blunder.

gage [ga:ʒ], s.m. **1.** pledge, security; **mettre qch. en g.**, to pawn sth.; **prêteur sur gages**, pawnbroker. **2.** token, sign. **3.** forfeit. **4.** pl. wages, pay.

gager [gaʒe], v.tr. (n. gageons) **1.** to wager, bet (avec, contre, with, against); (to bet at races, etc., is PARIER). **2.** Fin: to guarantee, secure (a loan); s.f. -eure, wager, bet.

gagnant, -ante [gaɲɑ̃, -ɑ̃:t]. **1.** a. winning (ticket). **2.** s. winner.

gagne-pain [gaɲpɛ̃], s.m.inv. **1.** (means of) living, livelihood. **2.** bread-winner.

gagner [gaɲe], v.tr. **1.** (a) to earn; **g. sa vie**, to earn, make, one's living; (b) to gain; **c'est autant de gagné**, it is so much to the good; **j'y gagnerai**, I shall gain by it. **2.** (a) to win, gain (a victory); (b) **g. la partie**, to win the game; (c) **g. tous les cœurs**, to win all hearts. **3.** to reach, arrive at (a place). **4.** to gain (up)on, overtake; **gagné par le sommeil**, overcome by sleep. **5.** v.i. Med: (of disease) to spread.

gai [ge, gɛ], a. gay; (a) merry, lively; (b) bright, cheerful; adv. **-ement**.

gaieté [gete], s.f. gaiety, mirth, cheerfulness; **faire qch. de g. de cœur**, to do sth. of one's own free will.

gaillard [gaja:r]. **1.** a. (a) strong, vigorous; (b) merry, cheery. **2.** s.m. **grand g.**, (great) strapping fellow. **3.** s.m. Nau: **g. d'avant**, forecastle; **g. d'arrière**, poop.

gain [gɛ̃], s.m. **1.** (a) gain, profit; (b) earnings. **2.** (a) winning (of contest); **avoir g. de cause**, to win one's case; (b) winnings.

gaine [gɛːn], s.f. sheath, casing; Cl: girdle, roll-on.

galant [galɑ̃]. **1.** a. (a) gay, elegant; (b) attentive to women; gallant; (c) **g. homme**, man of honour, gentleman. **2.** s.m. ladies' man; adv. **-amment**; s.f. usu. pl. **-anterie**, (i) (love)

affair; (ii) compliment, pretty speech.

galaxie [galaksi], s.f. galaxy; the Milky Way.

gale [gal], s.f. Med: scabies; Vet: mange.

galère [galɛːr], s.f. Nau: galley; **mais que diable allait-il faire dans cette g.?** but what the hell was he doing there?

galerie [galri], s.f. **1.** (a) gallery; **g. de portraits**, portrait gallery; (b) Fr.C: porch (of house); **g. marchande**, shopping centre. **2.** Th: balcony, gallery; **première g.**, dress circle; **seconde g.**, upper circle; **troisième g.**, gallery; **jouer pour la g.**, to play to the gallery. **3.** Min: gallery. **4.** Aut: roof rack.

galet [galɛ], s.m. (a) pebble; **gros g.**, boulder; (b) pl. shingle; **plage de galets**, shingle beach.

galette [galɛt], s.f. girdle-cake; **g. des Rois**, Twelfth-night cake.

galeux, -euse [galø, -øːz], a. mangy; **brebis galeuse**, black sheep.

galimatias [galimatja], s.m. gibberish.

Galles [gal]. Pr.n.f. **le pays de G.**, Wales.

gallicisme [galisism], s.m. Ling: gallicism.

gallois, -oise [galwa, -waːz]. **1.** a. Welsh. **2.** s. Welshman, -woman; **les G.**, the Welsh. **3.** s.m. Ling: Welsh.

gallo-romain [galɔrɔmɛ̃], a. Gallo-Roman.

galoche [galɔʃ], s.f. (a) clog; (b) overshoe.

galon [galɔ̃], s.m. **1.** braid. **2.** pl. (N.C.O.'s) stripes; (officer's) gold braid.

galop [galo], s.m. gallop; **au petit g.**, at a canter.

galoper [galɔpe], v.i. & tr. to gallop.

galopin [galɔpɛ̃], s.m. urchin; young scamp.

galvaniser [galvanize], v.tr. **1.** to galvanize; to give new life to (undertaking). **2.** Metall: to galvanize.

gambade [gɑ̃bad], s.f. leap, gambol.

gambader [gɑ̃bade], v.i. to leap; to gambol.

gamelle [gamɛl], s.f. small metal bowl; mess-tin, -kettle.

gamin, -ine [gamɛ̃, -in], s. child, youngster.

gamme [gam], s.f. **1.** Mus: scale, gamut. **2.** range, series (of colours, etc.).

Gand [gɑ̃]. Pr.n.m. Geog: Ghent.

gang [gɑ̃ːg], s.m. F: (a) gang; (b) racket.

gangrène [gɑ̃grɛn], s.f. gangrene.

gangster [gɑ̃gstɛːr], s.m. F: gangster; hooligan.

gant [gɑ̃], s.m. glove; **souple comme un g.**, easy-going; **g. de toilette** = (face-)flannel.

ganter [gɑ̃te], v.tr. to glove; (a) to put on, wear, gloves; (b) to fit (s.o.) with gloves; **g. du sept**, to take sevens in gloves.

se ganter, to put on one's gloves.

garage [gara:ʒ], s.m. **1.** Rail: shunting; **voie de g.**, siding. **2.** (a) garage; **g. de canots**, boathouse; **g. d'autobus**, bus depot; **g. d'avions**, hangar; (b) passing place (on narrow road).

garagiste [garaʒist], s.m. Aut: (a) garage proprietor, manager; (b) garage mechanic.

garant, -ante [garɑ̃, -ɑ̃:t], s. (a) guarantor, surety, bail; **se porter g. pour qn**, (i) to answer for s.o.; (ii) to go, stand, bail for s.o.; (b) s.m. authority, guarantee.

garantie [garɑ̃ti], s.f. guarantee; **donner une g. pour qn**, to stand security for s.o.

garantir [garɑ̃ti:r], v.tr. **1.** to warrant, guarantee; **g. un fait**, to vouch for a fact. **2.** to shelter, protect.

garçon [garsɔ̃], s.m. **1.** (a) boy, lad; (b) son. **2.** young man; **g. d'honneur**, best man; F: **brave g., bon g.**, decent chap; **beau g.**, good-looking fellow. **3.** bachelor. **4.** waiter; steward; s.f. **-nière**, bachelor's flat.

garde¹ [gard], s.m. & f. **1.** (a) keeper; (b) watchman; **g. champêtre**, rural policeman; **g. forestier**, ranger. **2.** Mil: guardsman.

garde², s.f. **1.** (a) guardianship, care, custody; **chien de g.**, watch-dog; **être sous bonne g.**, to be in safe custody; **avoir qch. en g.**, to have charge of sth.; (b) guarding, protection; (c) keeping. **2.** (a) watch(ing); (b) care, guard; **être sur ses gardes**, to be on one's guard; **g. à toi!** look out! Mil: **'g.-à-vous!'** 'attention!' **3.** prendre g. (a) **prendre g. à qch.**, (i) to beware of sth.; (ii) to notice, to pay attention to, sth.; (b) **faire qch. sans y prendre g.**, to do sth. without meaning it, inadvertently; (c) **prendre g. à, de, faire qch.**, to be careful not to do sth., to avoid doing sth.; **prenez g. de tomber**, mind you don't fall. **4.** guard; (a) **être de g.**, to be on guard; (b) **la g.**, the Guards.

NOTE: Consult the second component of garde- compounds for phonetics.

garde-barrière, s.m. & f. gate-keeper (at level-crossing); pl. **gardes-barrière(s)**.

garde-bébé, s.m. & f. baby-sitter; pl. **garde-bébés**.

garde-boue, s.m.inv. mudguard.

garde-chasse, s.m. gamekeeper; pl. **gardes-chasse(s)**.

garde-côte, s.m. **1.** coast-guard; pl. **gardes-côtes**. **2.** (a) coast-guard vessel; (b) coast-defence ship; pl. **garde-côtes**.

garde-feu, s.m.inv. (a) fender; (b) fireguard; For: **tranchée g.-f.**, fire line.

garde-fou, s.m. **1.** parapet. **2.** railing, handrail (of bridge); pl. **garde-fous**.

garde-malade. **1.** s.m. male nurse. **2.** s.f. nurse; pl. **gardes-malade(s)**.

garde-manger, s.m.inv. larder, pantry; (meat) safe.

garder [garde], v.tr. to keep. **1.** to guard, protect; **g. les enfants, la boutique**, to mind the children, the shop; **g. qn à vue**, to keep a close watch on s.o. **2.** (a) to retain; **g. un vêtement**, (i) to keep a garment; (ii) to keep a garment on; (b) to preserve; **g. une poire pour la soif**, to put something by for a rainy day; **g. les apparences**, to keep up appearances. **3.** to remain in (a place); **g. le lit, la chambre**, to be laid up, to stay in bed, in one's room. **4.** to observe, respect; **g. un secret, sa parole**, to keep a secret, one's word.

se garder. **1.** to protect oneself; **garde-toi!** look out (for yourself)! **2.** (a) **se g. de qch.**, to beware of sth.; (b) **se g. de faire qch.**, to take care not to do sth.

garde-robe, s.f. wardrobe (= (i) piece of furniture; (ii) clothes); pl. **garde-robes**.

gardien, -ienne [gardjɛ̃, -jɛn], s. guardian, keeper; caretaker; (museum) attendant; (prison) warder; **g. de la paix**, policeman; Sp: **g. de but**, goalkeeper.

gare¹ [ga:r], int. look out! mind yourself! **g. à lui si . . .**, woe betide him if . . .

gare², s.f. (railway) station; **g. maritime**, harbour station; **g. de marchandises**, goods station N.Am: freight depot; **g. routière**, coach station; **g. aérienne**, air terminal.

garenne [garɛn], s.f. (rabbit-)warren.

garer [gare], v.tr. **1.** to shunt (train). **2.** (a) to garage (car); (b) to park (car).

gargouille [gargu:j], s.f. (a) (water-)spout (of roof-gutter); (b) Arch: gargoyle.

garnement [garnəmɑ̃], s.m. (mauvais) g. scapegrace, scamp, rogue.

garni [garni], a. **1. bourse bien garnie**, well-lined purse; Cu: **plat g.**, meat with vegetables. **2** usu. Pej: **chambres garnies**, furnished apartments.

garnir [garni:r], v.tr. **1.** to furnish, provide (with). **2.** to trim (dress, hat). **3.** to lag (boiler); to pack (piston); to line (brake).

garnison [garnizɔ̃], s.f. garrison.

garniture [garnity:r], s.f. **1.** fittings. **2.** trimming(s); lagging (of boiler); ring (of piston); (brake) lining.

garrotter [garɔte], v.tr. **1.** to tie up (prisoner). **2** to strangle (s.o.).

gars [gɑ], s.m. F: boy; (young) man; **allons-y, les g.!** come on, boys!

Gascogne (la) [lagaskɔɲ]. Pr.n.f. Geog: Gascony; **le Golfe de G.**, the Bay of Biscay.

gascon, -onne [gaskɔ̃, -ɔn], a. & s. Ethn: Gascon.

gas-oil [gazwal, -ɔjl], s.m. Diesel oil.

gaspiller [gaspije], v.tr. to squander; to waste, spoil; s.m. **-age**, wastefulness; s. **-eur, -euse** waster, wasteful person.

gastrique [gastrik], *a.* gastric.

gastrite [gastrit], *s.f. Med:* gastritis.

gastronomi|e [gastronomi], *s.f.* gastronomy; *a.* -**que.**

gâté [gate], *a.* spoilt; tainted (meat); rotten, decayed (fruit, teeth); **enfant g.,** spoilt child.

gâteau, -eaux [gato], *s.m.* cake; (open) tart; **g. sec,** (sweet) biscuit; *F: a.* **papa g.,** (i) indulgent father; (ii) sugar daddy.

gâter [gate], *v.tr.* to spoil. 1. **cela ne gâte rien,** that won't do any harm. 2. to pamper, spoil (child).

se gâter, to spoil, deteriorate; **les affaires se gâtent,** things are going wrong; **le temps se gâte,** the weather's breaking up.

gauch|e [goːʃ], *a.* 1. awkward, clumsy. 2. left; (*a*) **main g.,** left hand; (*b*) *s.f.* **assis à ma g.,** seated on my left; (*c*) *Pol:* **la g.,** the Left. 3. *adv.phr.* **à gauche,** on the left, to the left; *adv.* -**ement,** awkwardly; *a. & s. Pol:* -**iste,** left-wing; (*pers.*) left-winger.

gaucherie [goʃri], *s.f.* 1. left-handedness. 2. awkwardness, clumsiness.

gaufre [goːfr], *s.f.* 1. **g. de miel,** honeycomb. 2. *Cu:* waffle.

gaufrette [gofrɛt], *s.f. Cu:* wafer biscuit.

gaullisme [golism], *s.m. Hist: Pol:* Gaullism.

gaulliste [golist]. *Pol:* (*a*) *s.m. & f.* Gaullist, follower of General de Gaulle; (*b*) *a.* Gaullist.

gaulois, -oise [golwa, -waːz]. 1. *a.* Gallic; **esprit g.,** (broad) Gallic humour. 2. *s.* **les G.,** the Gauls; *s.f. R.t.m:* **Gauloise,** brand of cigarettes.

Gautier [gotje]. *Pr.n.m.* Walter.

gaver [gave], *v.tr.* to cram (poultry); **se g. de nourriture,** to gorge.

gaz [gaːz], *s.m.* gas.

gaze [gaːz], *s.f.* gauze; **g. métallique,** wire gauze.

gazelle [gazɛl], *s.f. Z:* gazelle.

gazeu|x, -euse [gazø, -øːz], *a.* 1. gaseous. 2. aerated (water); fizzy (drink).

gazoduc [gazodyk], *s.m.* gas pipeline.

gazon [gazõ], *s.m.* (*a*) (short) grass; turf; (*b*) lawn.

gazouill|er [gazuje], *v.i.* (*of bird*) to twitter; (*of child*) to babble; to prattle; *s.m.* -**ement;** *s.m.* -**is,** twittering; babbling.

geai [ʒɛ], *s.m. Orn:* jay.

géant, -ante [ʒeã, -ãːt]. 1. *s.* giant, *f.* giantess. 2. *a.* gigantic; *Com:* giant (size).

geindre [ʒɛ̃ːdr], *v.i.* (*conj. like* ATTEINDRE) to whine, whimper.

gel [ʒɛl], *s.m.* frost, freezing.

gélatine [ʒelatin], *s.f.* gelatine.

gélatineux, -euse [ʒelatinø, -øːz], *a.* gelatinous.

gelé [ʒ(ə)le], *a.* 1. frozen. 2. frost-bitten.

gelée [ʒ(ə)le], *s.f.* 1. frost. 2. jelly.

geler [ʒ(ə)le], *v.* (**je gèle**) 1. *v.tr.* to freeze. 2. *v.i.* (*a*) to become frozen; to freeze; (*b*) *impers.* **il gèle à pierre fendre,** it is freezing hard.

geler, to freeze, solidify.

gelure [ʒəlyːr], *s.f. Med:* frostbite.

Gémeaux [ʒemo], *s.pl. Astr:* Gemini.

gém|ir [ʒemiːr], *v.i.* to groan, moan; to wail; *s.m.* -**issement.**

gemme [ʒɛm], 1. (*a*) *s.f.* gem; precious stone; (*b*) *a.* **sel g.,** rock-salt. 2. *s.f.* pine resin.

gênant [ʒenã], *a.* 1. cumbersome; in the way. 2. embarrassing, awkward.

gencive [ʒãsiːv], *s.f. Anat:* gum.

gendarme [ʒãdarm], *s.m.* gendarme, policeman.

gendarmerie [ʒãdarməri], *s.f.* 1. (*a*) (*in Fr.*) the state police force; (*b*) **la G. royale du Canada,** the Royal Canadian Mounted Police. 2. = police headquarters.

gendre [ʒãːdr], *s.m.* son-in-law.

gène [ʒɛn], *s.m. Biol:* gene.

gêne [ʒɛ(ː)n], *s.f.* 1. discomfort, embarrassment; **sans g.,** free and easy. 2. want; **être dans la g.,** to be hard up.

gêné [ʒene], *a.* embarrassed; ill at ease.

généalogie [ʒenealɔʒi], *s.f.* genealogy; pedigree.

généalogique [ʒenealɔʒik], *a.* genealogical; **arbre g.,** family-tree; pedigree.

gêner [ʒene], *v.tr.* 1. to constrict, cramp; **mes souliers me gênent,** my shoes pinch. 2. to hinder, impede; to be in (s.o.'s) way. 3. to inconvenience, embarrass.

se gêner, to put oneself out; **je ne me suis pas gêné pour le lui dire,** I made no bones about telling him so.

général, -aux [ʒeneral, -o]. 1. *a.* general; **en règle générale,** as a general rule; *Th:* **répétition générale,** *s.f.* **générale,** dress-rehearsal. 2. *s.m. Mil:* general. 3. *s.f.* **générale;** (*a*) the general's wife; (*b*) alarm call; *adv.* -**ement.**

généralis|er [ʒeneralize], *v.tr.* to generalize; *s.f.* -**ation.**

généralité [ʒeneralite], *s.f.* generality; **dans la g. des cas,** in most cases.

générateur, -trice [ʒeneratœːr, -tris]. 1. *a.* generating. 2. *s.m. El:* generator.

génér|er [ʒenere], *v.tr.* (**je génère; je générerai**) to generate; *s.f.* -**ation.**

généreu|x, -euse [ʒenerø, -øːz], *a.* 1. noble, generous (soul). 2. liberal, generous; *adv.* -**sement.**

générosité [ʒenerozite], *s.f.* generosity; munificence.

Gênes [ʒɛ(ː)n]. *Pr.n.f. Geog:* Genoa.

genèse [ʒɔnɛːz], *s.f.* genesis, origin; *B:* **la G.,** (the Book of) Genesis.

genêt [ʒ(ə)nɛ], *s.m. Bot:* broom.

génétique [ʒenetik], *s.f.* genetics.

gêneur, -euse [ʒɛnœːr, -øːz], *s. F:* spoil-sport; intruder.

Genève [ʒ(ə)nɛːv]. *Pr.n.f. Geog:* Geneva.

genévrier [ʒ(ə)nevrie], *s.m. Bot:* juniper(-tree).

génial, -aux [ʒenjal, -o], *a.* full of genius; inspired; **idée géniale,** brilliant idea.

génie [ʒeni], *s.m.* **1.** (*a*) (guardian) spirit; (presiding) genius; (*b*) genie, jinn. **2. homme de g.,** man of genius. **3.** (*pers.*) genius. **4.** (*a*) **le g. civil,** (civil) engineering; (*b*) *Mil:* **le G.** = the Royal Engineers, *U.S:* the Engineer Corps.

genièvre [ʒənjɛ:vr], *s.m.* **1.** *Bot:* juniper-berry; juniper-tree. **2.** gin.

génisse [ʒenis], *s.f.* heifer.

génital, -aux [ʒenital, -o], *a.* genital; **les organes génitaux,** the genitals.

génois, -oise [ʒenwa, -wa:z], *a. & s.* Genoese.

genou, -oux [ʒ(ə)nu], *s.m.* knee; **à genou(x)!** down on your knee(s)! kneel down! **être à genoux,** to be kneeling.

genre [ʒɑ̃:r], *s.m.* **1.** genus, kind; **le g. humain,** the human race, mankind. **2.** kind, manner; **c'est plus dans son g.,** that's more in his line. **3.** (artistic) style, manner. **4.** *Gram:* gender.

gens [ʒɑ̃], *s.m.pl.* (*most attributive adjectives preceding* **gens** *take the feminine form, but the word-group is felt as masculine;* **ces bonnes gens sont venus me trouver; quels sont ces gens? quels** *or* **quelles sont ces bonnes gens?** *tout varies according to the attributive adjective has a distinctive feminine ending or not:* **toutes ces bonnes gens,** *but* **tous ces pauvres gens.**) **1.** people, folk. **2.** (*a*) **jeunes gens,** (i) young people; (ii) young men; (*b*) **g. du monde,** society people; **g. de bien,** honest folk; **g. de robe,** lawyers; **les g. du pays,** *F:* the locals; (*c*) **g. de maison,** servants.

gentil, -ille [ʒɑ̃ti, -i:j], *a.* (*a*) pleasing, nice; **c'est g. à vous de m'écrire,** it is very kind of you to write to me; (*b*) **sois gentil(le),** be a good boy, a good girl; (*to adult*) *F:* be an angel, be a dear.

gentilhomme [ʒɑ̃tijɔm], *s.m.* man of gentle birth; gentleman; *pl. gentilshommes* [ʒɑ̃tizɔm].

gentillesse [ʒɑ̃tijɛs], *s.f.* **1.** (*a*) prettiness, engaging manner; (*b*) **auriez-vous la g. de . . .,** would you be so very kind as to . . .. **2.** *pl.* **dire des gentillesses,** to say nice things.

gentiment [ʒɑ̃timɑ̃], *adv.* nicely; prettily.

Geoffroi [ʒɔfrwa]. *Pr.n.m.* Godfrey, Geoffrey.

géographlie [ʒeɔgrafi], *s.f.* geography; *a.* **-ique,** geographic(al).

géologlie [ʒeɔlɔʒi], *s.f.* geology; **-ique,** geological.

géologue [ʒeɔlɔg], *s.* geologist.

géométrlie [ʒeɔmetri], *s.f.* geometry; **g. plane,** plane geometry; **g. dans l'espace,** solid geometry; *a.* **-ique,** geometric(al).

Georges [ʒɔrʒ]. *Pr.n.m.* George.

géranium [ʒeranjɔm], *s.m. Bot:* geranium.

gérant, -ante [ʒerɑ̃, -ɑ̃:t], *s.* manager, director; *f.* manageress; **g. d'immeuble,** landlord's agent; *Journ:* **rédacteur g.,** managing editor.

gerbe [ʒɛrb], *s.f.* sheaf (of corn, of flowers); **g. d'étincelles,** shower of sparks; **g. d'eau,** spray of water.

gerçure [ʒɛrsy:r], *s.f.* crack, cleft; chap (in skin).

gérer [ʒere], *v.tr.* (**je gère;** *fu.* **je gérerai**) to manage (business, hotel).

germain, -aine [ʒɛrmɛ̃, -ɛn], *a.* **frère g.,** own brother, full brother; **cousin g.,** first cousin.

germe [ʒɛrm], *s.m. Biol:* germ.

germler [ʒɛrme], *v.i.* to germinate; to shoot; *s.f.* **-ination.**

gésier [ʒezje], *s.m.* gizzard.

gésir [ʒezi:r], *v.i. def.* (*pr.p.* **gisant;** *pr.ind.* **il gît,** *n.* **gisons**) to lie; (*on gravestone*) **ci-gît, ci-gisent,** here lies, here lie.

geste [ʒɛst], *s.m.* gesture, motion, movement; **d'un g. de la main,** with a wave of the hand; **faire un g.,** to make a gesture.

gesticuller [ʒɛstikyle], *v.i.* to gesticulate; *s.f.* **-ation.**

gestion [ʒɛstjɔ̃], *s.f.* (*a*) management (of factory, etc.); administration; **mauvaise g.,** maladministration; (*b*) administratorship.

geyser [ʒezɛ:r], *s.m. Geol:* geyser.

Ghana (le) [ləgana]. *Pr.n.m. Geog:* Ghana.

gibecière [ʒibsjɛ:r], *s.f.* game-bag.

gibet [ʒibɛ], *s.m.* gibbet, gallows.

gibier [ʒibje], *s.m.* game (= *wild animals*); **gros g.,** big game; **g. d'eau,** wildfowl.

giboulée [ʒibule], *s.f.* sudden shower (*usu. with snow or hail*).

giboyeux, -euse [ʒibwajø, -ø:z], *a.* well stocked with game; **pays g.,** good game country.

gicler [ʒikle], *v.i.* to squirt out; (*of blood*) to spurt (out).

gicleur [ʒiklœ:r], *s.m. Aut: Mec:* (spray) nozzle: jet.

gifle [ʒifl], *s.f.* slap in the face; box on the ear.

gifler [ʒifle], *v.tr.* to slap, smack (s.o.'s) face; t box (s.o.'s) ears.

gigantesque [ʒigɑ̃tɛsk], *a.* gigantic; huge.

gigot [ʒigo], *s.m.* leg of mutton.

gilet [ʒilɛ], *s.m.* waistcoat, vest; **g. de corps** (man's) singlet, (under)vest.

Gilles [ʒil]. *Pr.n.m.* Giles.

gin [dʒin, ʒin], *s.m.* gin.

gingembre [ʒɛ̃ʒɑ̃:br], *s.m.* ginger.

girafe [ʒiraf], *s.f. Z:* giraffe.

giration [ʒirasjɔ̃], *s.f.* gyration.

giratoire [ʒiratwa:r], *a.* gyratory; **sens g** roundabout.

girl [gœrl], *s.f.* chorus girl.

girofle [ʒirɔfl], *s.m. Bot:* clove; **clou de g.,** clove

giroflée [ʒirɔfle], *s.f. Bot:* **g. des jardins,** stocl **g. des murailles,** wallflower.

girouette [ʒirwɛt], *s.f.* weathercock; vane.

gisement [ʒizmɑ̃], *s.m.* (*a*) *Geol:* layer, bed; **pétrolifère,** oil-field; (*b*) *Min:* lode, vein.

gîte [ʒit], *s.m.* **1.** (*a*) resting-place; **n'avoir pas g.,** to have nowhere to lay one's head, to homeless; (*b*) form (**of hare**). **2.** stratur deposit (of ore). **3.** leg of beef; **g. à la noix,** silverside.

givre [ʒiːvr], *s.m.* hoar-frost, rime.

glace [glas], *s.f.* **1.** ice; **retenu, pris, par les glaces,** ice-bound. **2.** (*a*) (plate-)glass; (*b*) (looking-)glass, mirror; **g. à main,** hand mirror; (*c*) *Rail:* window. **3.** *Cu:* ice(-cream).

glacé [glase], *a.* **1.** (*a*) frozen (river, etc.); (*b*) chilled, icy, cold; **j'ai les pieds glacés,** my feet are frozen; (*c*) iced (coffee, etc.). **2.** glazed, glossy; **cerises glacées,** glacé cherries.

glacer [glase], *v.tr.* (**n. glaçons**) **1.** (*a*) to freeze; (*b*) to ice (water); (*c*) to ice (cake). **2.** to glaze (pastry); *Phot:* **g. une épreuve,** to glaze a print.

glaciaire [glasjɛːr], *a.* *Geol:* glacial (erosion); **période g.,** ice-age.

glacial, -als, *or* **-aux** [glasjal, -o], (*pl. rare*) *a.* icy; frosty; **la zone glaciale,** the arctic region; **politesse glaciale,** icy politeness; *adv.* **-ement.**

glacier [glasje], *s.m.* *Geol:* glacier.

glaçon [glasɔ̃], *s.m.* (*a*) block of ice; floe; (*b*) icicle; (*c*) ice cube.

glaïeul [glajœl], *s.m.* *Bot:* gladiolus.

gland [glɑ̃], *s.m.* **1.** acorn. **2.** tassel.

glande [glɑ̃ːd], *s.f.* gland.

glaner [glane], *v.tr.* to glean; *s.* **-eur, -euse,** gleaner.

glapir [glapiːr], *v.i.* to yelp, yap; (*of fox*) to bark; *s.m.* **-issement.**

glas [glɑ], *s.m.* knell.

glissade [glisad], *s.f.* **1.** slip; *Av:* **g. sur l'aile, sur la queue,** side-slip, tail dive. **2.** sliding; **faire une g.,** to slide. **3.** slide (on ice).

glisser [glise]. **I.** *v.i.* **1.** to slip. **2.** to slide (on ice, etc.). **3.** to glide (over the water, etc.). **II.** *v.tr.* **g. qch. dans la poche de qn,** to slip sth. into s.o.'s pocket; *s.m.* **-ement;** *s.f.* **-ière,** groove, slide.

glisser, to creep, steal (**dans,** into).

global, -aux [glɔbal, -o], *a.* total, aggregate, inclusive (sum); lump (payment).

globe [glɔb], *s.m.* **1.** globe, sphere; **g. électrique,** electric light globe. **2. g. de l'œil,** eyeball.

globulaire [glɔbylɛːr], *a.* globular.

globule [glɔbyl], *s.m.* globule.

globuleux, -euse [glɔbylø, -øːz], *a.* globular.

gloire [glwaːr], *s.f.* **1.** glory; **travailler pour la g.,** to work for nothing. **2.** boast, pride; **se faire g. de qch.,** to glory in sth. **3.** glory, halo, nimbus.

glorieux, -euse [glɔrjø, -øːz], *a.* **1.** glorious. **2.** proud; **g. de qch.,** vain of, conceited about, sth. **3.** *s.m.* boaster; **faire le g.,** to brag, to swagger; *adv.* **-sement.**

glorifier [glɔrifje], *v.tr.* to praise, glorify.

glorifier, to boast.

glossaire [glɔsɛːr], *s.m.* glossary.

glousser [gluse], *v.i.* (*of hen*) to cluck; (*of turkey*) to gobble; (*of pers.*) to chuckle; *s.m.* **-ement.**

glouton, -onne [glutɔ̃, -ɔn]. **1.** *a.* greedy, gluttonous. **2.** *s.* (*a*) glutton; (*b*) *s.m.* *Z:* wolverine; *adv.* **-nement;** *s.f.* **-nerie,** gluttony.

gluant [glɥɑ̃], *a.* sticky, gummy.

glucose [glykoːz], *s.m.* glucose; **g. sanguin,** blood sugar.

glutineux, -euse [glytinø, -øːz], *a.* glutinous.

glycérine [gliserin], *s.f.* glycerin(e).

glycine [glisin], *s.f.* *Bot:* wistaria.

go [go], *used in the adv.phr. F:* **tout de go.** **1.** easily, without a hitch. **2.** all of a sudden.

goal [goːl], *s.m.* *Fb:* goalkeeper.

gobelet [gɔblɛ], *s.m.* goblet, cup.

gober [gɔbe], *v.tr.* to swallow, gulp down; *F:* **g. des mouches,** to stand gaping.

goéland [gɔelɑ̃], *s.m.* *Orn:* (sea-)gull.

goélette [gɔelɛt], *s.f.* schooner.

goémon [gɔemɔ̃], *s.m.* seaweed.

goguenard, -arde [gɔgnaːr, -ard]. **1.** *a.* bantering, jeering, sarcastic. **2.** *s.* joker; facetious, sarcastic, person.

goitre [gwaːtr], *s.m.* goitre.

golf [gɔlf], *s.m.* golf; **terrain de g.,** golf links, golf course.

golfe [gɔlf], *s.m.* gulf, bay; **le Courant du G.,** the Gulf-Stream, the North Atlantic Drift.

gomme [gɔm], *s.f.* **1.** gum; **g. arabique,** gum arabic; **g. laque,** shellac; *Comest:* **g. à mâcher,** chewing gum. **2. g. élastique, à effacer,** (india-) rubber, eraser.

gommer [gɔme], *v.tr.* **1.** to gum, to stick (sth.). **2.** to erase, to rub out. **3.** *Mec.E:* to stick, jam; **piston gommé,** gummed piston; *a.* **-eux, -euse,** sticky.

gond [gɔ̃], *s.m.* hinge-pin (of door); *F:* **sortir de ses gonds,** to lose one's temper; **mettre qn hors de ses gonds,** to make s.o. lose his temper.

gondole [gɔ̃dɔl], *s.f.* gondola.

gonfler [gɔ̃fle]. **1.** *v.tr.* (*a*) to inflate, distend; to pump up (tyre); to puff out (one's cheeks); (*b*) to swell; (*c*) *F:* to hot up, soup up (car engine). **2.** *v.i. & pr.* to become inflated; *s.m.* *Aut:* **-age,** inflation (of tyres); *s.m.* **-ement,** inflating, inflation.

gorge [gɔrʒ], *s.f.* **1.** (*a*) throat, neck; (*b*) bosom, bust (of woman). **2.** throat, gullet; **avoir la g. serrée,** to have a lump in one's throat; **crier à pleine g.,** to shout at the top of one's voice; **rire à g. déployée,** to laugh heartily. **3.** *F:* **faire des gorges chaudes de qch.,** to laugh unpleasantly, gloat, over sth. **4.** *Geog:* gorge.

gorgée [gɔrʒe], *s.f.* mouthful, draught; **boire à petites gorgées,** to sip.

gorger [gɔrʒe], *v.tr.* (**n. gorgeons**) to stuff, gorge. **se gorger (de qch.),** to stuff oneself (full of sth.).

gorille [gɔriːj], *s.m.* (*a*) *Z:* gorilla; (*b*) *F:* (personal) bodyguard.

gosier [gozje], *s.m.* throat; gullet.

gosse [gɔs], *s.m. & f. F:* youngster, kid.

gothique [gɔtik], *a.* Gothic.
gouaillerie [gwajri], *s.f.* banter, chaff, joking.
goudron [gudrɔ̃], *s.m.* tar.
goudronn|er [gudrɔne], *v.tr.* to tar; *s.m.* -age, tarring.
gouffre [gufr], *s.m.* gulf, pit, abyss; *Geol:* swallow hole.
goulet [gulɛ], *s.m.* narrow part, neck (of object); gully (in mountains).
goulot [gulo], *s.m.* neck (of bottle).
goul|u, -ue [guly], *a.* greedy; *adv.* -ûment.
goupille [gupiːj], *s.f.* (linch)pin.
goupillon [gupijɔ̃], *s.m.* **1.** sprinkler (for holy water). **2.** brush (for gum, bottle).
gourde [gurd], *s.f.* **1.** *Bot:* gourd. **2.** water-bottle, flask. **3.** *F:* idiot, dimwit, dope.
gourmand, -ande [gurmɑ̃, -ɑ̃:d]. **1.** *a.* greedy. **2.** *s.* gourmand, glutton.
gourmandise [gurmɑ̃di:z], *s.f.* **1.** greediness, gluttony. **2.** *pl.* sweetmeats, dainties.
gourmet [gurmɛ], *s.m.* gourmet, epicure.
gousse [gus], *s.f.* pod, shell, husk (of peas, etc.); **g. d'ail,** clove of garlic.
gousset [gusɛ], *s.m.* (*a*) gusset; (*b*) waistcoat pocket.
goût [gu], *s.m.* **1.** (sense of) taste. **2.** flavour, taste; bouquet (of wine); **g. du terroir,** local flavour, native tang. **3.** liking, preference, taste; **le g. du jour,** the fashion of the day; **chacun (à) son g., à chacun son g.,** everyone to his taste; **une maison à mon g.,** a house to my liking; **prendre g. à qch.,** to develop a taste for sth. **4. avoir du g.,** to have good taste; **mauvais g.,** (i) bad taste; (ii) lack of taste.
goûter [gute]. I. *v.tr.* **1.** to taste (food). **2.** to enjoy, appreciate. **3. g. à qch.,** to take a little of sth, to taste sth.
II. *s.m.* = (afternoon) tea.
goutte [gut], *s.f.* **1.** drop (of liquid). **2.** spot, splash (of colour); speck; fleck. **3.** *F:* small quantity; **une g. de bouillon,** a sip, a mouthful, of soup; **g. de cognac,** dash, nip, spot, of brandy. **4.** (*thus used only with* **comprendre, entendre, voir**) **je n'y vois g.,** (i) I can't see a thing; (ii) I can make nothing of it; **on n'y voyait g.,** it was pitch-dark. **5.** *Med:* gout.
goutteux, -euse [gutø, -ø:z], *a. & s. Med:* gouty (person).
gouttière [gutjɛ:r], *s.f.* **1.** *Const:* gutter, guttering. **2.** spout, rain-pipe.
gouvernail [guvɛrna:j], *s.m. Nau:* rudder, helm.
gouvernante [guvɛrnɑ̃:t], *s.f.* housekeeper.
gouvernement [guvɛrnəmɑ̃], *s.m.* **1.** (*a*) government, management; (*b*) governorship; (*c*) steering, management (of boat, aircraft). **2.** (the) government; *a.* **-al, -aux,** governmental.
gouvern|er [guvɛrne], *v.tr.* **1.** *Nau:* to steer (ship). **2.** to govern, rule. **3.** (*a*) to manage, administer; (*b*) to govern (country); *s.m.* **-eur,**

governor.
grâce [grɑ:s], *s.f.* **1.** grace, charm; **les grâces de la femme,** feminine charm; **de bonne g.,** willingly. **2.** favour; **rentrer en g., to** reingratiate oneself (**auprès de,** with); **de g.!** for pity's sake! **3.** (act of) grace; **coup de g.,** finishing stroke, final blow; **demander une g. à qn,** to ask a favour of s.o. **4.** (*a*) *Jur:* free pardon; **je vous fais g. cette fois-ci,** I'll let you off this time; (*b*) **demander g.,** to cry for mercy; **je vous fais g. du reste,** you needn't do any more **5.** thanks; (*a*) *pl.* **action de grâces** thanksgiving; (*b*) *prep.phr.* **g. à,** thanks to owing to.
gracier [grasje], *v.tr.* to pardon.
gracieu|x, -euse [grasjø, -ø:z], *a.* **1.** graceful. **2** (*a*) gracious; (*b*) **à titre g.,** as a favour; gratis **exemplaire envoyé à titre g.,** complimentary copy; *adv.* **-sement.**
grade [grad], *s.m.* **1.** rank; dignity; grade. **2** (university) degree. **3.** *Mil:* rank; **monter en g.** to be promoted.
gradé [grade], *s.m. Mil:* non-commissioned officer, N.C.O.; **tous les gradés,** all rank (commissioned and non-commissioned).
gradin [gradɛ̃], *s.m.* step, tier.
graduation [graduasjɔ̃], *s.f.* **1.** graduation. **2** scale.
gradué, -elle [graduel], *a.* (*a*) graduated; **verre g** measuring glass; graduated measure; (*b* graded, progressive (exercises, etc.).
graduel, -elle [graduel], *a.* gradual, progressive *adv.* **-lement.**
grain[1] [grɛ̃], *s.m.* **1.** (*a*) grain; grain of corn; (*b* corn. **2.** berry, bean (of coffee); **g. de raisin** grape; **g. de beauté,** beauty spot; mole. **3.** particle, atom; grain (of salt). **4.** bead. **5.** grain texture (of wood, leather, etc.).
grain[2], *s.m.* squall; gust of wind.
graine [grɛn], *s.f.* seed (of plants); **g. de li** linseed; **monter en g.,** to run to seed.
graisse [grɛs], *s.f.* grease, fat; **g. de rôt** dripping.
graiss|er [grɛse], *v.tr.* to grease, lubricate, oil; **la patte à qn,** to grease s.o.'s palm; *s.m.* **-ag** *a.* **-eux, -euse,** greasy; fatty.
grammaire [gram(m)ɛ:r], *s.f.* grammar.
grammairien, -ienne [gram(m)ɛrjɛ̃, -jɛn], grammarian.
grammatical, -aux [gram(m)atikal, -o], grammatical; *adv.* **-ement.**
gramme [gram], *s.m. Meas:* gram(me).
grand, grande [grɑ̃, grɑ̃:d], *a.* **1.** (*a*) tall (stature); large, big (in size); **homme g., t** man; **grands bras,** long arms; **grands pieds, b** feet; (*b*) chief, main; **g. chemin,** main roa *Nau:* **le g. mât,** the mainmast; **g. resso** mainspring; (*c*) **quand tu seras g.,** when y are grown up; **les grandes personnes, t**

grown-ups; *Sch:* **les grandes classes,** the upper forms; (*d*) *adv.* **porte(s) grande(s) ouverte(s),** wide-open door(s); *adv.phr.* **en g.,** (i) on a large scale; (ii) full size. **2.** large; **le g. public,** the general public; **en grande partie,** to a great extent. **3. les grands hommes,** great men; **le g. monde,** (high) society; **grands vins,** high-class wines. **4. grandes pensées,** great, noble, thoughts. **5. il fait g. jour,** it is broad daylight; **il est g. temps de partir,** it is high time we were off. **6.** *s.m.* **les grands de la terre,** the great ones of the earth.

NOTE: *In the following compounds* **grand** *is invariable, unless otherwise indicated, and the second part of the compound takes the plural. For phonetics consult the second component.*

grand-chose, *indef.pron.m.inv.* (*usu.* coupled with **pas** *or* **sans**) much; **il ne fait pas g.-c.,** he doesn't do much.

Grande-Bretagne (la). *Pr.n.f.* Great Britain.

grandeur [grãdœ:r], *s.f.* **1.** (*a*) size; height (of tree, etc.); **de g. naturelle, g. nature,** full-size(d); (*b*) extent; scale. **2.** greatness; (*a*) importance; grandeur; (*b*) majesty, splendour; (*c*) nobility.

grandiose [grãdjo:z], *a.* grand, imposing.

grandir [grãdi:r]. **1.** *v.i.* (i) to grow tall; (ii) to grow up. **2.** *v.tr.* (*a*) to make (sth.) greater; to increase; (*b*) to magnify, to exaggerate (an incident); *s.m.* **-issement,** growth, increase.

grand(-)livre, *s.m.* ledger; *pl.* **grands-livres.**

grand-maman, *s.f.* F: grandma, granny.

grand-mère, *s.f.* grandmother.

grand-messe, *s.f.* Ecc: high mass.

grand-oncle, *s.m.* great-uncle; *pl.* **grands-oncles.**

grand-papa, *s.m.* F: grandpa, grandad; *pl.* **grands-papas.**

grand-peine (à), *adv.phr.* with great difficulty.

grand-père, *s.m.* grandfather; *pl.* **grands-pères.**

grand-route, *s.f.* highway, high road.

grand-rue, *s.f.* high street, main street.

grands-parents, *s.m.pl.* grandparents.

grand-tante, *s.f.* great-aunt.

grange [grã:3], *s.f.* barn.

granit [grani(t)], *s.m.* granite.

granuler [granyle], *v.tr.* **1.** to granulate. **2.** *Art:* to stipple; *a.* **-aire,** granular; *a.* **-eux, -euse,** granulous.

graphique [grafik]. **1.** *a.* graphic (sign, method). **2.** *s.m.* diagram, graph; *adv.* **-ment.**

graphite [grafit], *s.m.* graphite, plumbago.

grappe [grap], *s.f.* cluster, bunch (of grapes).

gras, grasse [gra, gra:s], *a.* **1.** (*a*) fat; fatty; *Cu:* **matières grasses,** fats; (*b*) rich (food); **régime g.,** meat diet; **faire g.,** to eat meat; (*c*) *s.m.* fat (of meat). **2.** fat, stout. **3.** greasy, oily. **4.** thick;

boue grasse, thick, slimy, mud; **toux grasse,** loose cough.

gratification [gratifikasjõ], *s.f.* (*a*) gratuity; tip; (*b*) bonus.

gratis [gratis], *adv.* gratis; free of charge.

gratitude [gratityd], *s.f.* gratitude, gratefulness.

gratte [grat], *s.f.* F: pickings, perks, rake-off.

gratte-ciel [gratsjɛl], *s.m.inv.* skyscraper.

gratter [grate], *v.tr.* **1.** to scrape, scratch; **plume qui gratte,** scratchy pen. **2.** to erase (a word); *s.m.* **-ement,** scratching; *s.m.* **-oir,** scraper.

gratuit [gratɥi], *a.* gratuitous; (*a*) free; (*b*) **insulte gratuite,** gratuitous, wanton, insult; *adv.* **-ement.**

grave [gra:v], *a.* **1.** (*a*) grave; solemn; sober; (*b*) important (business), severe, serious (illness). **2. voix g.,** deep voice. **3.** *Gram:* **accent g.,** grave accent; *adv.* **-ment.**

graver [grave], *v.tr.* to cut, engrave, carve; **g. à l'eau forte,** to etch; *Rec:* to record (music, etc.); *s.m.* **-eur,** engraver; etcher; *s.f.* **-ure,** engraving, etching; (book) illustration; recording.

gravier [gravje], *s.m.* gravel, grit.

gravillon [gravijõ], *s.m.* fine gravel; *P.N:* **gravillons,** loose chippings.

gravir [gravi:r], *v.tr.* to climb; to ascend (ladder, mountain).

gravité [gravite], *s.f.* **1.** *Ph:* gravity. **2.** gravity, seriousness.

graviter [gravite], *v.i.* **1.** to gravitate. **2.** to revolve.

gré [gre], *s.m.* **1.** liking, taste; **au g. de mes désirs,** just as I could wish. **2.** will, pleasure; **de mon plein g.,** of my own accord; **bon g. mal g.,** whether we like it or not; willy-nilly; **au g. des flots,** at the mercy of the waves. **3. savoir (bon) g. à qn de qch.,** to be grateful to s.o. for sth.

grec, grecque [grɛk]. **1.** *a.* Greek, Grecian. **2.** *s.* Greek. **3.** *s.m.* **le g.,** (the) Greek (language).

Grèce (la) [lagrɛs]. *Pr.n.f.* Geog: Greece.

greffe [grɛf], *s.f.* **1.** Hort: graft, slip. **2.** grafting. **3.** *Surg:* **g. du cœur,** heart transplant.

greffer [grɛfe], *v.tr.* Hort: Surg: to graft; *s.m.* **-age;** *s.m.* **-eur.**

greffier [grɛfje], *s.m.* **1.** clerk (of the court). **2.** registrar.

grégaire [gregɛ:r], *a.* gregarious.

grêle¹ [grɛ(:)l], *a.* slender, thin (leg); high-pitched (voice).

grêle², *s.f.* (*a*) hail; (*b*) **g. de coups,** shower of blows.

grêler [grɛle]. **1.** *v.impers.* **il grêle,** it's hailing. **2.** *v.tr.* to damage (crops) by hail.

grêlon [grɛlõ], *s.m.* hailstone.

grelot [grəlo], *s.m.* (small round) bell; sleigh bell.

grelotter [grəlote], *v.i.* to tremble, shake, shiver (with cold, fear).

grenade [grənad], *s.f.* **1.** *Bot:* pomegranate. **2.**

Mil: etc: (*a*) grenade; (*b*) **g. sous-marine,** depth-charge.

grenat [grəna]. **1.** *s.m.* garnet. **2.** *a.inv.* garnet-red.

grenier [grənje], *s.m.* **1.** granary, storehouse; **g. à foin,** hay loft. **2.** attic, garret.

grenouille [grənu:j], *s.f.* **1.** frog. **2.** *P:* mess funds, club money; funds (of a society); **manger la g.,** to make off with the cash.

grès [grɛ], *s.m.* **1.** sandstone. **2. poterie de g.,** stoneware; **g. flambé,** glazed earthenware.

grésil [grezi(l)], *s.m.* sleet; frozen rain.

grésill|er [grezije], *v.i.* (*a*) to crackle; (*of frying-pan*) to sizzle; (*b*) (*of crickets*) to chirp; *s.m.* -ement.

grève [grɛːv], *s.f.* **1.** strand; (sea-)shore; (sandy) beach. **2.** strike (of workmen); **se mettre en g.,** to go on strike; **g. de la faim,** hunger strike; **g. sauvage,** wild-cat strike; **g. du zèle,** working to rule.

gréviste [grevist], *s.m. & f.* striker; **g. de la faim,** hunger-striker.

grief [gri(j)ɛf], *s.m.* grievance.

grièvement [gri(j)ɛvmã], *adv.* severely, grievously (wounded, etc.).

griffe [grif], *s.f.* claw; talon; **coup de g.,** scratch.

griffonn|er [grifɔne], *v.tr.* to scrawl, scribble (off) (letter, etc.); *abs.* to scrawl, to scribble; to doodle; *s.m.* -age.

grignot|er [griɲɔte], *v.tr.* to nibble (sth.); to pick at (food); *s.m.* -ement.

gril [gri(l)], *s.m. Cu:* grid(iron), grill.

grillade [grijad], *s.f.* grill, grilled steak.

grillage [grija:ʒ], *s.m.* (metal) grating; wire-netting.

grille [griːj], *s.f.* (*a*) (iron) bars; (*b*) iron gate; (*c*) railings; (*d*) fire-grate.

grille-pain [grijpɛ̃], *s.m.inv.* toaster.

griller [grije], *v.tr.* **1.** to grill (meat); to toast (bread). **2.** (*a*) to burn, scorch; (*b*) *El:* to burn out (bulb); *Aut:* **g. un feu rouge,** to jump the lights.

grillon [grijɔ̃], *s.m. Ent:* cricket.

grimace [grimas], *s.f.* grimace, wry face; **faire des grimaces,** (i) to pull faces; (ii) to put on airs.

grimac|er [grimase], *v.i.* (**n. grimaçons**) to grimace; to make faces; *F:* to simper; *s.f.pl.* -eries, grimacing; affectation.

grimp|er [grɛ̃pe], *v.i.* to climb (up); **g. à une corde,** to swarm up a rope; *v.tr.* **g. une montagne,** to climb a mountain; *s.* -eur, -euse, climber.

grinc|er [grɛ̃se], *v.i.* (**n. grinçons**) to grate; to grind; to creak; **g. des dents,** to grind, grit, one's teeth; *s.m.* -ement.

grincheux, -euse [grɛ̃ʃø, -øːz]. **1.** *a.* grumpy, bad-tempered; whining. **2.** *s.* grumbler, grouser.

grippe [grip], *s.f.* **1.** dislike, aversion; **prendre qn en g.,** to take a dislike to s.o. **2.** *Med:* influenza, *F:* flu.

gris [gri]. **1.** *a.* (*a*) grey; (*b*) grey-haired; **barbe grise,** grey beard; (*c*) **temps g.,** dull weather; **faire grise mine,** to look anything but pleased; (*d*) *F:* (slightly) tipsy, fuddled; **un peu g.,** a bit high. **2.** *s.m.* (*a*) grey (colour); (*b*) (= **tabac g.**) **un paquet de g.** = a packet of shag.

grisâtre [grizɑːtr], *a.* greyish.

griser [grize], *v.tr. F:* to make (s.o.) tipsy; **grisé par le succès,** intoxicated with success.

se griser, to get tipsy, fuddled.

griserie [grizri], *s.f.* **1.** tipsiness. **2.** intoxication; exhilaration.

grive [griːv], *s.f. Orn:* thrush.

Groenland (le)[ləgrɔɛnlɑ̃(ːd)]. *Pr.n.m* Greenland.

grog [grɔg], *s.m.* toddy; grog.

grogn|er [grɔɲe], *v.i.* **1.** (*a*) to grunt; (*b*) to growl. **2.** to grumble; to grouse; *s.m.* -ement.

grognon [grɔɲɔ̃]. **1.** *s.m. or f.* grumbler, grouser. **2.** *a.* (*f.* -on *or* -onne), grumbling, peevish.

groin [grwɛ̃], *s.m.* snout (of pig).

grommeler [grɔmle], *v.i.* (**je grommelle**) to grumble, mutter.

grond|er [grɔ̃de]. **1.** *v.i.* (*a*) to growl, snarl; (*b*) to rumble; to boom; **le tonnerre gronde,** there's rumble of thunder; (*c*) **g. contre qn,** to grumble at s.o. **2.** *v.tr.* to scold; *s.m.* -ement; *s.f.* -erie scolding.

gros, grosse [gro, groːs]. **1.** *a.* (*a*) big, bulky stout; **g. bout,** thick end (of stick); **g. se** coarse salt; **grosse voix,** gruff voice; big voice **g. mot,** coarse expression; **jouer g. (jeu),** play for high stakes; **g. temps,** heavy, ba weather; *F:* **les g. bonnets,** the bigwigs; **avoir** **cœur g.,** to be sad at heart; (*b*) **grosse de tro** **mois,** three months pregnant; **action grosse d** **conséquences,** action big with consequence: (*c*) *adv.* **gagner g.,** to earn a great deal. **2.** *s.n* (*a*) bulk, chief part; **le plus g. est fait,** tl hardest part (of the job) is done; **g. de l'é** height of summer; (*b*) **en g.,** (i) roughl broadly; on the whole; (ii) **acheter en g.,** to bu in bulk; (*c*) *Com:* wholesale (trade). **3.** *s* **grosse,** *Com:* gross; twelve dozen.

groseill|e [grozɛːj], *s.f.* **1.** (red, white) currant. **g. à maquereau,** gooseberry; *s.m.* -ie currant-bush.

grossesse [grosɛs], *s.f.* pregnancy.

grosseur [grosœːr], *s.f.* size, bulk, volum *Med:* swelling, growth.

grossi|er, -ière [grosje, -jeːr], *a.* (*a*) coar rough; (*b*) **ignorance grossière,** crass i norance; **faute grossière,** glaring blunder; rude, unmannerly (**envers,** to); vulgar, coars *adv.* -èrement.

grossièreté [grosjɛrte], *s.f.* (*a*) coarsene roughness (of object); (*b*) rudeness, coarsene (of manner, etc.); (c) grossness, glaring nature (of mistake).

grossIir [grosiːr]. **1.** v.tr. to enlarge, to swell, to magnify; **torrent grossi par les pluies,** torrent swollen by the rain. **2.** v.i. to increase, swell; a. **-issant;** s.m. **-issement.**

grossiste [grosist], s.m. wholesaler.

grotesque [grotɛsk], a. (a) grotesque; (b) ludicrous, absurd.

grotte [grot], s.f. grotto.

grouillIer [gruje], v.i. to crawl, swarm (**de,** with); s.m. **-ement.**

se grouiller, P: to hurry; **grouille-toi!** get a move on!

groupe [grup], s.m. group (of people); clump (of trees); party (of people).

groupIer [grupe], v.tr. to group, to arrange (in groups); s.m. **-ement.**

se grouper, to gather; to bunch (together).

grue [gry], s.f. **1.** Orn: crane; **faire le pied de g.,** to cool one's heels. **2.** F: (a) **grande g.,** great gawk of a woman; (b) prostitute, tart. **3.** (hoisting) crane.

gruyère [gryjɛːr], s.m. Gruyere (cheese).

gué [ge], s.m. ford; a. **-able,** fordable.

guenille [gənij], s.f. tattered garment, old rag; **en guenilles,** in rags.

guenon [gənɔ̃], s.f. she-monkey.

guêpe [gɛ(ː)p], s.f. Ent: wasp.

guêpier [gepje], s.m. **1.** wasps' nest; **tomber dans un g.,** to bring a hornets' nest about one's ears. **2.** Orn: bee-eater.

guère [gɛːr], adv. (always with neg. expressed or understood) hardly; not much, not many; **je ne l'aime g.,** I don't care much for him; **il n'y a g. plus de six ans,** hardly more than six years ago; **il ne tardera g. à venir,** he will not be long in coming; **il ne s'en faut (de) g.,** it's not far short.

guéridon [geridɔ̃], s.m. pedestal table.

guérilla [gerija], s.f. band of guerrillas; **guerre de guérillas,** guerrilla warfare.

guérir [geriːr]. **1.** v.tr. to cure, heal. **2.** v.i. (a) to be cured; to recover; (b) (of wound) to heal.

guérison [gerizɔ̃], s.f. **1.** recovery. **2.** (a) cure (of disease); (b) healing (of wound).

guérisseur, -euse [gerisœːr, -øːz], s. (a) healer; (b) quack (doctor); (c) faith healer.

guérite [gerit], s.f. **1.** sentry-box. **2.** cabin, shelter (for watchman).

Guernesey [gɛrnəzɛ]. Pr.n.m. Geog: Guernsey.

guerre [gɛːr], s.f. **1.** war, warfare; **g. sur mer,** naval warfare; **g. froide,** cold war; **g. chaude,** shooting war. **2.** strife, feud; adv.phr. **de g. lasse,** for the sake of peace.

guerrier, -ière [gɛrje, -jɛːr]. **1.** a. warlike. **2.** s.m. warrior.

guet [gɛ], s.m. watch(ing); look-out; **avoir l'œil au g.,** to keep a sharp look-out.

guet-apens [gɛtapɑ̃], s.m. ambush, snare; pl. **guets-apens.**

guetter [gete], v.tr. to lie in wait for, to be on the look-out for (s.o.).

gueule [gœl], s.f. **1.** mouth (of carnivorous animal, of dog); P: face, F: mug; **ta g.!** shut up! F: **avoir la g. de bois,** to have a hangover. **2.** mouth (of tunnel); muzzle (of gun).

gueule-de-lion [gœldəljɔ̃], s.f., **gueule-de-loup** [gœldəlu], s.f. Bot: antirrhinum, snapdragon; pl. **gueules-de-lion(-loup).**

gueuler [gœle], v.tr. & i. P: to bawl, shout; to bawl out (song, etc.).

gueuleton [gœltɔ̃], s.m. P: blow-out, tuck-in; **un g. à tout casser,** a hell of a blow-out.

gueux, -euse [gø, -øːz], s. beggar; tramp.

gui [gi], s.m. Bot: mistletoe.

guichet [giʃɛ], s.m. **1.** (a) wicket(-gate); (b) spy hole, judas, grating (in door). **2.** turnstile; Rail: (platform) barrier. **3.** booking-office; Th: box office; (bank, post-office) position.

guide[1] [gid], s.m. **1.** (a) guide; conductor; (b) s.f. (girl) guide. **2.** guide(-book).

guide[2], s.f. rein.

guider [gide], v.tr. to guide, direct, lead.

guidon [gidɔ̃], s.m. handle-bar (of bicycle).

guigne [giɲ], s.f. F: bad luck.

guignol [giɲol], s.m. (a) = Punch; (b) = Punch and Judy show.

Guillaume [gijoːm]. Pr.n.m. William.

guillemets [gijmɛ], s.m.pl. Typ: inverted commas, quotation marks.

guillotine [gijotin], s.f. **1.** guillotine. **2.** **fenêtre à g.,** sash-window.

guillotiner [gijotine], v.tr. to guillotine.

guindé [gɛ̃de], a. stiff, stilted; starchy (person).

Guinée (la) [lagine]. Pr.n.f. Geog: Guinea.

guinguette [gɛ̃gɛt], s.f. (suburban) café (with music and dancing, usu. in the open).

guirlande [girlɑ̃ːd], s.f. garland, wreath.

guise [giːz], s.f. manner, way, fashion; **faire à sa g.,** to do as one pleases; **en g. de,** (i) by way of; (ii) instead of.

guitare [gitaːr], s.f. Mus: guitar.

guttural, -aux [gytyral, -o]. **1.** a. guttural; throaty. **2.** s.f. Ling: **gutturale,** guttural.

Guyane (la) [lagɥijan]. Pr.n.f. Geog: Guyana; **la G. française,** French Guiana.

gymkhana [ʒimkana], s.m. gymkhana.

gymnase [ʒimnaːz], s.m. gymnasium.

gymnaste [ʒimnast], s.m. gymnast.

gymnastique [ʒimnastik]. **1.** a. gymnastic. **2.** s.f. gymnastics.

gynécologie [ʒinekolɔʒi], s.f. gynaecology.

gynécologue [ʒinekolog], s. gynaecologist.

gyroscope [ʒiroskop], s.m. gyroscope.

gyrostabilisateur [ʒirostabilizatœːr], s.m. Av: gyrostabilizer.

gyrostat [ʒirosta], s.m. gyrostat.

H

Words beginning with an "aspirate" h are shown by an asterisk.

H, h [aʃ], *s.m. & f.* (the letter) H, h.
habile [abil], *a.* clever, skilful, cunning, artful; **mains habiles,** skilled hands; **être h. à la vente,** to be smart at selling things; *adv.* **-ment.**
habileté [abilte], *s.f.* (*a*) ability, skill, skilfulness; (*b*) cleverness, smartness.
habillement [abijmã], *s.m.* 1. clothing, dressing. 2. clothes, dress.
habiller [abije], *v.tr.* (*a*) to dress (s.o.); (*b*) to clothe, to provide (s.o.) with clothes.
s'habiller, to dress.
habit [abi], *s.m.* 1. dress, costume; *pl.* clothes. 2. (*a*) coat; (*b*) **être en h.,** to be in evening dress, in tails. 3. (monk's, nun's) habit.
habitable [abitabl], *a.* habitable, fit for habitation.
habitant, -ante [abitã, -ã:t], *s.* (*a*) inhabitant; resident, dweller; (*b*) occupier (of flat, etc.); (*c*) inmate (of house, institution).
habitat [abita], *s.m.* habitat (of animal, plant).
habitation [abitasjɔ̃], *s.f.* 1. habitation; dwelling; **le problème de l'h.,** the housing problem. 2. dwelling(-place), residence; **immeuble d'h.,** residential building; **h. à loyer modéré (HLM)** = council house, council flat.
habiter [abite]. 1. *v.tr.* (*a*) to inhabit, to live in (a place); (*b*) to occupy (house). 2. *v.i.* to live, reside.
habitude [abityd], *s.f.* (*a*) habit, custom; **se faire une h. de . . .,** to make it one's practice to . . .; **d'h.,** usually, ordinarily; **comme d'h.,** as usual; (*b*) knack; **je n'en ai plus l'h.,** I'm out of practice.
habitué, -ée [abitye], *s.* regular attendant, regular customer; habitué; frequent visitor.
habituel, -elle [abityɛl], *a.* usual, customary; habitual; *adv.* **-lement.**
habituer [abitye], *v.tr.* to accustom (qn à qch., s.o. to sth.).
s'habituer, to get used, to get accustomed (à, to).
***hache** [aʃ], *s.f.* axe.
***haché** [aʃe], *a.* 1. jerky (style). 2. **mer hachée,** choppy sea.
***hache-légumes** [aʃlegym], *s.m.inv. Cu:* vegetable-cutter, -mincer.
***hacher** [aʃe] *v.tr.* (*a*) to chop (up); **h. menu,** to mince; (*b*) to hack (up), mangle.

***hachette** [aʃɛt], *s.f.* hatchet.
***hache-viande** [aʃvjã:d], *s.m.inv. Cu:* mincer.
***hachis** [aʃi], *s.m. Cu:* mince.
***haddock** [adɔk], *s.m.* smoked haddock.
***hagard** [agaːr], *a.* haggard, wild(-looking).
***haie** [ɛ], *s.f.* (*a*) hedge; **h. vive,** quickset hedge; (*b*) line, row (of troops).
***haillon** [ajɔ̃], *s.m.* rag (of clothing).
***haine** [ɛːn], *s.f.* hatred; detestation.
***haineux, -euse** [ɛnø, -øːz], *a.* full of hatred.
***haïr** [aiːr], *v.tr.* (**je hais, n. haïssons;** *imp.* **hais**) to hate, detest.
***haïssable** [aisabl], *a.* hateful, detestable.
***halage** [alaːʒ], *s.m.* towing; **chemin de h.,** towpath.
***hâle** [ɑːl], *s.m.* tan; sunburn.
haleine [alɛn], *s.f.* breath; **perdre h.,** to get out of breath; **hors d'h.,** out of breath; **travail de longue h.,** long and exacting task; **politique de longue h.,** long-term policy.
***haler** [ale], *v.tr.* to tow; to haul.
***hâler** [ɑle], *v.tr.* (*of sun*) to tan (s.o.).
se hâler, to get sunburnt, tanned.
***haletant** [altã], *a.* panting, breathless, out of breath; gasping (for breath).
***haleter** [alte], *v.i.* (**je halète**) to pant; to gasp (for breath); *s.m.* **-ètement.**
***hall** [ɔl], *s.m.* 1. (palatial) entrance hall; (hotel) lounge. 2. *Ind:* bay, shop, room; **h. de montage,** assembly shop.
***halle** [al], *s.f.* (covered) market.
***hallier** [alje], *s.m.* thicket, copse, brake.
hallucination [al(l)ysinasjɔ̃], *s.f.* hallucination, delusion.
***halo** [alo], *s.m.* 1. *Meteor:* halo. 2. *Phot:* halation.
***halte** [alt], *s.f.* 1. stop, halt; **faire h.,** (*of train*) to stop, to call (at station). 2. stopping-place, resting-place.
***hamac** [amak], *s.m.* hammock.
***Hambourg** [ãbuːr]. *Pr.n.m.* Hamburg.
***hambourgeois, -oise** [ãburʒwa, -waːz]. 1. *a.* of Hamburg. 2. *s.* native, inhabitant, of Hamburg; Hamburger.
***hameau, -eaux** [amo], *s.m.* hamlet.
hameçon [amsɔ̃], *s.m.* (fish-)hook; **mordre à l'h.,** to nibble at the bait.
***hampe** [ã:p], *s.f. Cu:* thin flank (of beef); breast (of venison); spiced breast-bacon (of pork).

*hamster [amstɛːr], s.m. Z: hamster.

*hanche [ɑ̃ːʃ], s.f. 1. hip; les (deux) poings sur les hanches, with arms akimbo. 2. haunch (of horse); pl. hind-quarters.

*handicap [ɑ̃dikap], s.m. handicap.

*handicapler [ɑ̃dikape], v.tr. to handicap; s.m. -age; s.m. -eur.

*hangar [ɑ̃gaːr], s.m. 1. (open) shed; shelter; h. à bateaux, boat-house. 2. Av: hangar.

*hanneton [antɔ̃], s.m. Ent: cockchafer, maybug.

*hanter [ɑ̃te], v.tr. (of ghost) to haunt; être hanté par une idée, to be obsessed by an idea.

*hantise [ɑ̃tiːz], s.f. haunting memory; obsession.

*happer [ape], v.tr. (of birds, etc.) to snap up, seize (insects); F: être happé par les flics, to be nicked by the fuzz.

*harangue [arɑ̃ːg], s.f. harangue; speech.

*haranguer [arɑ̃ge], v.tr. to harangue; F: to lecture (s.o.).

*haras [ara], s.m. 1. stud-farm. 2. stud.

*harassler [arase], v.tr. (a) to tire (out), exhaust; (b) to harass, worry; s.m. -ement.

*harceler [arsəle], v.tr. (je harcèle) to harass, torment; to harry; Av: to buzz (aircraft); h. qn de questions, to pester s.o. with questions.

*hardes [ard], s.f.pl. (worn) clothes.

*hardi [ardi], a. bold, audacious; (a) daring, fearless; (b) rash; (c) impudent; adv. -ment.

*hardiesse [ardjɛs], s.f. 1. boldness; (a) daring; (b) impudence, effrontery; il a eu la h. de m'écrire, he had the audacity, the cheek, to write to me. 2. bold, daring, act.

*harem [arɛm], s.m. harem.

*hareng [arɑ̃], s.m. herring; h. bouffi, bloater; h. saur, red herring; h. fumé, kipper; serrés comme des harengs, packed like sardines.

*hargneulx, -euse [arɲø, -øːz], a. snarling; peevish, cantankerous (person); nagging (woman); adv. -sement.

*haricot [ariko], s.m. h. (blanc), haricot bean; haricots verts, French beans; haricots d'Espagne, scarlet runners; P: c'est la fin des haricots, it's the bloody limit.

harmonie [armɔni], s.f. 1. (a) harmony; agreement; en h. avec . . ., in keeping with . . .; (b) harmoniousness. 2. Mus: harmony.

harmonieulx, -euse [armɔnjø, -øːz], a. (a) harmonious, tuneful (sound); (b) harmonious (family); adv. -sement.

harmoniser [armɔnize], v.tr. to harmonize; to match (colours).

s'harmoniser, to harmonize, agree (avec, with), (of colours) to tone in (avec, with), to match.

*harnachler [arnaʃe], v.tr. to harness; s.m. -ement, harness; saddlery.

*harnais [arnɛ], s.m. (a) harness; (b) saddlery.

*harple [arp], s.f. Mus: harp; s. -iste, harpist.

*harpon [arpɔ̃], s.m. harpoon; pêche au h., spear fishing.

*harponner [arpɔne], v.tr. to harpoon; to anchor (aerial).

*hasard [azaːr], s.m. (a) chance, luck, accident; coup de h., stroke of luck; fluke; au h., at a guess, at random; par h., by accident, by chance; (b) risk, danger; à tout h., (i) at all costs; (ii) on the off chance; (iii) just in case.

*hasarder [azarde], v.tr. to risk, venture.

se hasarder, to take risks; se h. à faire qch., to venture to do sth.

*hasardeux, -euse [azardø, -øːz], a. hazardous, perilous.

*hâte [ɑːt], s.f. haste, hurry; avoir h. de faire qch., to be in a hurry to do sth.; à la h., in haste, hastily; en toute h., with all possible speed.

*hâter [ɑte], v.tr. to hasten; to hurry (sth.) on; h. le pas, to quicken one's pace.

se hâter, to hasten, hurry.

*hâtilf, -ive [ɑtif, -iːv], a. (a) forward, early (spring, fruit); premature (decision); precocious (fruit, plant); (b) hasty, hurried, ill-considered (plan); adv. -vement.

*hausse [oːs], s.f. rise, rising (of temperature, etc.); Com: Fin: h. des prix, rise in prices; les affaires sont à la h., business is looking up.

*haussler [ose]. 1. v.tr. to raise, lift; h. un mur, to heighten a wall; h. les prix, to raise prices; h. les épaules, to shrug (one's shoulders). 2. v.i. to rise; s.m. -ement.

*haut [o], I. a. 1. high; (a) tall (grass, etc.); lofty (building); homme de haute taille, tall man; haute mer, high seas, open sea; à mer haute, at high tide; (b) important, great; h. fonctionnaire, important official; la haute finance, high finance; (c) raised; marcher la tête haute, to carry one's head high; lire à haute voix, to read aloud; (d) (to a high degree) être h. en couleur, to have a high colour; haute trahison, high treason. 2. upper, higher; le plus h. étage, the top floor.

II. adv. 1. high (up), above, up; h. les mains! hands up! parler h., to speak loudly; parlez plus h.! speak up! 2. back; comme il est dit plus h., as aforesaid.

III. s.m. 1. height; avoir deux mètres de h., to be six feet tall. 2. top; upper part; le h. de la table, the head of the table; les hauts et les bas, the ups and downs (of life). 3. regarder qn de h. en bas, to look at s.o. contemptuously; to look down on s.o.; du h. en bas, (i) downwards; (ii) from top to bottom; en h., (i) above; (ii) upstairs; adv. -ement.

*hautain [otɛ̃], a. haughty.

*hautbois [obwɑ], s.m. Mus: oboe.

*haut-de-forme [odfɔrm], s.m. top hat; pl. hauts-de-forme.

*hauteur [otœːr], s.f. 1. (a) height, elevation;

altitude; *Av:* **prendre de la h.**, to climb; **à la h. de qch.**, abreast of, level with, sth.; **se montrer à la h. de la situation**, to prove equal to the occasion; *F:* **être à la h.**, to be up to the mark, up to it; (*b*) *Mus:* pitch (of note); (*c*) loftiness (of ideas). **2.** haughtiness. **3.** high place; hilltop.

*__haut-fond__ [ofɔ̃], *s.m.* shoal, shallow; *pl. hautsfonds.*

*__haut-fourneau__ [ofurno], *s.m. Ind:* blast furnace; *pl. hauts-fourneaux.*

*__haut-le-corps__ [olkɔːr], *s.m.inv.* sudden start, jump.

*__haut-parleur__ [oparlœːr], *s.m. Rad:* loudspeaker; amplifier; *pl. haut-parleurs.*

*__Havane__ [avan]. **1.** *Pr.n.f.* **la H.**, Havana. **2.** *s.m.* Havana (cigar).

*__hâve__ [ɑːv], *a.* haggard, gaunt; sunken (cheeks).

*__havre__ [ɑːvr], *s.m.* harbour, haven, port.

*__havresac__ [avrəsak], *s.m.* haversack; (workman's) tool bag.

Hawaï [awaj(i)]. *Pr.n. Geog:* Hawaii; **les îles H.**, the Hawaiian Islands.

hawaïen, -ïenne [awajɛ̃, -jɛn], *a. & s. Geog:* Hawaiian.

*__Haye (la)__ [laɛ]. *Pr.n.f. Geog:* the Hague.

hebdomadaire [ɛbdɔmadɛːr], *a. & s.m.* weekly (paper, magazine).

héberger [ebɛrʒe], *v.tr.* (**n. hébergeons**) to harbour; to lodge, shelter; to put (s.o.) up.

hébété [ebete], *a.* dazed, vacant, bewildered.

hébéter [ebete], *v.tr.* (**j'hébète; j'hébéterai**) to dull, stupefy; to daze; *s.m.* **-ement**, stupefaction; dazed condition.

hébraïque [ebraik], *a.* Hebraic, Hebrew.

hébreu, -eux [ebrø], *a. & s.m.* Hebrew (person or language) (**hébraïque** *is used for the f.*).

hécatombe [ekatɔ̃ːb], *s.f.* (*a*) hecatomb; (*b*) great slaughter; **les hécatombes de la route,** the toll of road accidents.

*__hein__ [ɛ̃], *int.* (*a*) (*expressing surprise*) eh? what? (*b*) **il fait beau aujourd'hui, h.?** fine day, isn't it?

hélas [elɑːs], *int.* alas!

Hélène [elɛn]. *Pr.n.f.* Helen.

*__héler__ [ele], *v.tr.* (**je hèle; je hélerai**) to hail, call (a taxi); to hail (a ship).

hélice [elis], *s.f. Nau: Av:* propeller, screw.

hélicoptère [elikɔptɛːr], *s.m.* helicopter.

héligare [eligaːr], *s.f.* helicopter station.

héliport [elipɔːr], *s.m.* heliport.

helvétique [ɛlvetik], *a.* Swiss; **la Confédération H.**, Switzerland.

*__hem__ [ɛm], *int.* (a)hem! hm!

hématite [ematit], *s.f. Miner:* haematite.

hémicycle [emisikl], *s.m. Arch:* hemicycle; **l'h. de la Chambre,** the floor of the Chamber (of Deputies).

hémisphère [emisfɛːr], *s.m.* hemisphere; **l'h. nord, sud,** the northern, southern, hemisphere.

hémisphérique [emisferik], *a.* hemispheric(al).

hémoglobine [emɔɡlɔbin], *s.f.* haemoglobin.

hémophilie [emɔfili], *s.f. Med:* haemophilia.

hémorragie [emɔraʒi], *s.f. Med:* haemorrhage; bleeding.

hémorroïdes [emɔrɔid], *s.f.pl. Med:* haemorrhoids, *F:* piles.

*__henn__|**ir** [ɛniːr], *v.i.* to whinny; to neigh; *s.m.* **-issement.**

Henri [ɑ̃ri]. *Pr.n.m.* Henry.

Henriette [ɑ̃rjɛt]. *Pr.n.f.* Henrietta, Harriet.

héraldique [eraldik]. **1.** *a.* heraldic. **2.** *s.f.* heraldry.

*__héraut__ [ero], *s.m.* herald.

herbacé [ɛrbase], *a. Bot:* herbaceous.

herbage [ɛrbaːʒ], *s.m.* **1.** grassland; pasture. **2.** grass, herbage.

herbe [ɛrb], *s.f.* **1.** herb, plant; **fines herbes,** herbs (for seasoning); **omelette aux fines herbes,** savoury omelet; **mauvaise h.,** weed. **2.** grass; **couper l'h. sous le pied à qn,** to cut the ground from under s.o.'s feet. **3. en h.,** (i) unripe (corn, etc.); (ii) budding (poet), (diplomat) in the making.

herbeux, -euse [ɛrbø, -øːz], *a.* grassy.

herbivore [ɛrbivɔːr], *Z:* **1.** *a.* herbivorous, grass-eating. **2.** *s.m.* herbivore.

herborist|**e** [ɛrbɔrist], *s.m. & f.* herbalist; *s.f.* **-erie,** herbalist's shop.

herculéen, -enne [ɛrkyleɛ̃, -ɛn], *a.* Herculean (strength, task).

héréditaire [ereditɛːr], *a.* hereditary.

hérédité [eredite], *s.f.* **1.** *Biol:* heredity. **2.** *Jur:* right of inheritance.

hérésie [erezi], *s.f.* heresy.

hérétique [eretik]. **1.** *a.* heretical. **2.** *s.* heretic.

*__hérissé__ [erise], *a.* **1.** bristling (**de,** with). **2.** spiky; bristly; prickly.

*__hériss__|**er** [erise], *v.tr.* (*a*) to bristle (up); (*of bird*) to ruffle (feathers); (*b*) to make (sth.) bristle; to cover with spikes; *s.m.* **-ement.**

se hérisser, to bristle (up); (*of hair*) to stand on end.

*__hérisson__ [erisɔ̃], *s.m. Z:* hedgehog.

héritage [eritaːʒ], *s.m.* inheritance, heritage.

hériter [erite]. **1.** *v.i.* **h. d'une fortune,** to inherit a fortune. **2.** *v.tr.* **h. qch. de qn,** to inherit sth. from s.o.

héritier, -ière [eritje, -jɛːr], *s.* heir, *f.* heiress.

hermétique [ɛrmetik], *a.* tight(-closed), hermetically sealed; *adv.* **-ment.**

hermine [ɛrmin], *s.f.* **1.** *Z:* stoat, ermine. **2.** *Com:* ermine (fur).

*__hernie__ [ɛrni], *s.f.* hernia, rupture; **h. discale,** slipped disc. **2.** *Aut:* bulge, swelling (in tyre).

héroïne[1] [erɔin], *s.f.* heroine.

héroïne[2], *s.f. Ch:* heroin.

héroïque [erɔik], *a.* heroic; *adv.* **-ment.**

héroïsme [erɔism], *s.m.* heroism.

*héron [erɔ̃], *s.m. Orn:* heron.

*héros [ero], *s.m.* hero.

*hersler [erse], *v.tr. Agr:* to harrow; *s.m.* -age, harrowing.

hertzien, -ienne [ɛrtsjɛ̃, -jɛn], *a. El:* hertzian.

hésitler [ezite], *v.i.* 1. to hesitate, waver. 2. to falter; *a.* -ant; *s.f.* -ation.

hétérogène [eterɔʒɛn], *a.* (*a*) heterogeneous, dissimilar; (*b*) incongruous (collection); mixed (society).

*hêtre [e(:)tr], *s.m.* beech (tree or timber).

heure [œːr], *s.f.* hour. 1. (*a*) heures de pointe, rush hours; heures creuses, off-peak hours; *Journ:* la dernière h., stop-press news; *Ind:* heures supplémentaires, overtime; (*b*) (*time of day*) quelle h. est-il? what time is it? cinq heures moins dix, ten (minutes) to five; (*c*) (*appointed hour*) *Aut:* h. d'éclairage, lighting-up time; à l'h. dite, at the appointed time; être à l'h., to be punctual, on time; *Fr.C:* h. avancée, summer time; (*d*) (*present time*) pour l'h., for the present; à l'h. qu'il est, (i) by this time; (ii) nowadays, just now; (*e*) time, period; cette mode a eu son h., this fashion has had its day; j'attends mon h., I'm biding my time. 2. *adv.phrs.* de bonne h., early; de meilleure h., earlier; faire qch. sur l'h., to do sth. right away; tout à l'h., (i) just now, a few minutes ago; (ii) presently, directly; à tout à l'h.! so long! see you later! 3. *int.* à la bonne h.! well done!

heureulx, -euse [œrø, -øːz], *a.* 1. happy. 2. (*a*) successful; l'issue heureuse des négociations, the happy outcome of the negotiations; (*b*) lucky; h. au jeu, lucky at cards. 3. (*a*) favourable, lucky, fortunate; grâce à un h. hasard, by a fortunate coincidence; (*b*) début h., auspicious beginning. 4. felicitous, happy, apt (phrase); *adv.* -sement.

heurt [œːr], *s.m.* shock, knock, bump; tout s'est fait sans h., everything went smoothly.

heurter [œrte], *v.tr. & i.* 1. to knock (against), run into; h. du pied contre une pierre, to stub one's toe against a stone. 2. to shock, offend (s.o.'s feelings).

se heurter. 1. se h. à une difficulté, to come up against a difficulty. 2. to collide.

exagone [ɛgzagɔn]. 1. *a.* hexagonal. 2. *s.m.* hexagon.

hiberner [iberne], *v.i.* to hibernate.

hibou, -oux [ibu], *s.m. Orn:* owl; jeune h., owlet.

hideulx, -euse [idø, -øːz], *a.* hideous; *adv.* -sement.

ier [ieːr, jeːr], *adv.* yesterday; h. soir, last night.

hiérarchie [jerarʃi], *s.f.* hierarchy; h. de commandement, chain of command.

hiérarchique [jerarʃik], *a.* hierarchical; par voie h., through the official channels; *adv.* -ment.

hiéroglyphe [jerɔglif], *s.m.* (*a*) hieroglyph; (*b*) *pl.* hieroglyphics.

hi-fi [ifi], *a. Rad: etc: F:* hi-fi, high-fidelity.

hilarité [ilarite], *s.f.* hilarity, mirth, laughter; provoquer l'h. générale, to raise a general laugh.

Himalaya (l') [limalaja]. *Pr.n.m. Geog:* Himalaya; les monts H., the Himalayas.

hindou, -e [ɛ̃du], *a. & s. Ethn:* Hindu.

*hippie [ip(p)i], *a. & s. F:* hippie.

hippique [ip(p)ik], *a.* relating to horses; equine; concours h., (i) horse-show; (ii) race meeting.

hippopotame [ip(p)ɔpɔtam], *s.m. Z:* hippopotamus.

hirondelle [irɔ̃dɛl], *s.f. Orn:* swallow; h. de fenêtre, house-martin; h. de cheminée, swallow, *N.Am:* barn swallow.

hirsute [irsyt], *a.* hairy, shaggy.

*hisser [ise], *v.tr.* to hoist (up), pull up.

se hisser le long du mur, to climb up the wall; se h. sur la pointe des pieds, to stand on tiptoe.

histoire [istwaːr], *s.f.* 1. (*a*) history; (*b*) h. naturelle, natural history. 2. story, tale; livre d'histoires, story-book; c'est toujours la même h., it's the old, old story; *F:* c'est stupide, cette h.-là, the whole thing's silly; *F:* il est sorti, h. de prendre l'air, he went out just to get some air; *F:* en voilà une h.! what a lot of fuss! 3. *F:* fib, story; tout ça c'est des histoires, that's all bunkum. 4. faire des histoires, to make a fuss; il faut éviter d'avoir des histoires, we must keep out of trouble.

historien, -ienne [istɔrjɛ̃, -jɛn], *s.* historian.

historique [istɔrik]. 1. *a.* historic(al); *F:* c'est h., it actually happened. 2. *s.m.* historical record; faire l'h. des événements du mois dernier, to give a chronological account of last month's events; *adv.* -ment.

histrionique [istriɔnik], *a.* histrionic; theatrical, stagy.

hiver [iveːr], *s.m.* winter; en h., in winter; temps d'h., wintry weather; vêtements, sports, d'h., winter clothing, sports.

hivernage [ivernaːʒ], *s.m.* 1. wintering (of cattle, etc.). 2. winter season.

hivernal, -aux [ivernal, -o], *a.* winter (cold); wintry (weather).

hiverner [iverne], *v.i.* to winter.

*hochler [ɔʃe], *v.tr. & i.* h. (de) la tête, (i) to shake one's head; (ii) to nod; (iii) to toss the head; *s.m.* -ement.

*hockey [ɔkɛ], *s.m. Sp:* hockey; *Fr.C:* (ice) hockey; h. sur glace, ice hockey.

*holà [ola], *int.* 1. hallo! 2. stop! not so fast!

*holding [ɔldiŋ], *s.m. Fin:* holding company.

*hollandais, -aise [ɔlɑ̃dɛ, -ɛːz]. 1. *a.* Dutch. 2. *s.* Dutchman, -woman; les H., the Dutch. 3. *s.m. Ling:* le h., Dutch.

*Hollande [ɔlɑ̃ːd]. 1. *Pr.n.f.* Holland. 2. *s.m.*

(fromage de) H., Dutch cheese.

*homard [ɔmaːr], s.m. lobster.

homélie [ɔmeli], s.f. homily.

homéopathie [ɔmeɔpati], s.f. hom(o)eopathy; a. -ique, hom(o)eopathic.

homérique [ɔmerik], a. homeric (poem, laughter).

homicide¹ [ɔmisid]. 1. s.m. & f. homicide. 2. a. homicidal.

homicide², s.m. homicide (as a crime); h. involontaire, manslaughter.

hommage [ɔmaːʒ], s.m. 1. homage. 2. pl. respects, compliments; mes hommages à Mme X, my compliments to Mrs. X. 3. tribute, token; h. de l'éditeur, exemplaire en h., presentation copy.

homme [ɔm], s.m. man; (a) mankind; de mémoire d'h., within living memory; (b) (individual) il n'est pas mon h., he is not the man for me; trouver son h., to meet one's match; (c) l'abominable h. des neiges, the abominable snowman.

homme-grenouille [ɔmgrənuj], s.m. Nau: frogman; pl. hommes-grenouilles.

homme-sandwich [ɔmsɑ̃dwitʃ], s.m. sandwichman; pl. hommes-sandwichs.

homogène [ɔmɔʒɛn], a. homogeneous.

homologue [ɔmɔlɔg]. 1. a. homologous. 2. s.m. homologue; opposite number.

homologuer [ɔmɔlɔge], v.tr. 1. (a) Jur: to confirm, ratify; to grant probate of (will); (b) prix homologués, authorized charges. 2. to confirm; Sp: to ratify (sporting records); record homologué, official record.

homonyme [ɔmɔnim]. 1. a. homonymous. 2. s.m. (a) homonym; (b) F: namesake.

homosexuel, -elle [ɔmɔsɛksɥɛl], a. homosexual; s.f. -alité.

*Hongrie (la) [laɔ̃gri]. Pr.n.f. Hungary.

*hongrois, -oise [ɔ̃grwa, -waːz], a. & s. Geog: Hungarian.

honnête [ɔnɛ(ː)t], a. 1. honest, honourable, upright. 2. courteous, well-bred; civil (envers, to). 3. reasonable, fair; adv. -ment.

honnêteté [ɔnɛtte], s.f. 1. honesty, uprightness. 2. courtesy, civility. 3. fairness.

honneur [ɔnœːr], s.m. 1. honour; se faire h. de qch., to be proud of sth.; se piquer d'h., to make it a point of honour; cour d'h. (d'un lycée), main quadrangle. 2. faire h. au dîner, to do justice to the dinner; j'ai l'h. de vous faire savoir que . . ., I beg to inform you that . . .; jouer pour l'h., to play for love. 3. pl. (marks of esteem) rendre les derniers honneurs à qn, to pay the last tribute to s.o.; faire (à qn) les honneurs de la maison, to do the honours of the house (to s.o.). 4. faire h. à sa signature, to honour one's signature. 5. Cards: les honneurs, honours.

honorable [ɔnɔrabl], a. (a) honourable; vieillesse h., respected old age; (b) respectable; reputable; s.f. -ilité, respectability; adv. -lement.

honoraire [ɔnɔrɛːr]. 1. a. honorary. 2. s.m. usu.pl. fee(s) (of professional man); honorarium; (lawyer's) retainer.

honorer [ɔnɔre], v.tr. 1. (a) to honour; to respect; Com: votre honorée du . . ., your favour of the . . .; mon honoré confrère, my respected colleague; (b) to do honour to (s.o.); (c) Com: to honour, meet (one's obligations). 2. to do credit to (s.o.).

honorifique [ɔnɔrifik], a. honorary (title, rank, etc.).

*honte [ɔ̃ːt], s.f. 1. (a) (sense of) shame; avoir h. to be ashamed; faire h. à qn, to put s.o. to shame; (b) fausse h., bashfulness, self-consciousness. 2. (cause of) shame, disgrace; couvrir qn de h., to bring shame on s.o., to disgrace s.o.

*honteux, -euse [ɔ̃tø, -øːz], a. 1. ashamed. 2. bashful, shamefaced. 3. shameful, disgraceful; adv. -sement.

hôpital, -aux [ɔpital, -o], s.m. hospital, infirmary; salle d'h., ward.

*hoquet [ɔkɛ], s.m. 1. hiccup. 2. gasp (of surprise, terror).

horaire [ɔrɛːr]. 1. a. signal h., time-signal. 2. s.m time-table.

*horde [ɔrd], s.f. horde.

horizon [ɔrizɔ̃], s.m. horizon, sky-line.

horizontal, -aux [ɔrizɔ̃tal, -o]. 1. a. horizontal 2. s.f. horizontale, horizontal line; adv -ement.

horloge [ɔrlɔːʒ], s.f. clock; il est deux heures à l'h., it's two by the clock.

horloger [ɔrlɔʒe], s.m. clock and watch maker.

horlogerie [ɔrlɔʒri], s.f. 1. clock-making mouvement d'h., clockwork. 2. watchmaker's clockmaker's, shop.

hormone [ɔrmɔn], s.f. hormone.

hormonothérapie [ɔrmɔnɔterapi], s.f. hor monotherapy, hormone treatment.

horoscope [ɔrɔskɔp], s.m. horoscope.

horreur [ɔr(r)œːr], s.f. horror. 1. frappé d'h. horror-stricken. 2. repugnance, disgust; avoi qch. en h., to have a horror of sth. 3. (quality of) horror, awfulness. 4. quelle h. d'enfant what a horrid child! les horreurs de la guerre the horrors, atrocities, of war.

horrible [ɔr(r)ibl], a. horrible, awful; adv -ment.

horrifier [ɔr(r)ifje], v.tr. (p.d. & pr. sub. n horrifiions, v. horrifiiez) to horrify; a. -ique horrific, hair-raising.

horripilant [ɔr(r)ipilɑ̃], a. F: exasperating maddening.

*hors [ɔr], prep. (liaison with r: hors elle [ɔrɛl]

1. (*a*) out of, outside; **longueur h. tout,** overall length; (*b*) except; **tous h. un seul,** all but one. 2. *prep.phr.* **h. de,** out of, outside (of); **h. d'ici!** get out! **être h. d'affaire,** to have got through one's difficulties; (*of sick pers.*) to be out of danger; **être h. de soi,** to be beside oneself.

hors-bord [ɔrbɔːr], *s.m.inv.* outboard motor (boat).

hors-concours [ɔrkɔ̃kuːr], *a.,* *adv.* & *s.m.inv.* not competing, hors concours, ineligible for competition (because of superiority).

hors-d'œuvre [ɔrdœːvr], *s.m.inv. Cu:* hors-d'œuvre.

hors-jeu [ɔrʒø], *a.* & *s.m.inv. Sp:* off-side.

hors-la-loi [ɔrlalwa], *s.m.inv.* outlaw.

hors-texte [ɔrtɛkst], *s.m.inv.* (inset) plate (in book).

ortensia [ɔrtɑ̃sja], *s.m.* hydrangea.

orticole [ɔrtikɔl], *a.* horticultural.

orticulture [ɔrtikylty:r], *s.f.* horticulture; gardening.

ospice [ɔspis], *s.m.* 1. hospice. 2. (*a*) old people's home; (*b*) children's home.

ospitalier, -ière [ɔspitalje, -jɛːr], *a.* hospitable.

ospitalis|er [ɔspitalize], *v.tr.* to send (s.o.) to hospital; *s.f.* **-ation.**

ospitalité [ɔspitalite], *s.f.* hospitality.

ostie [ɔsti], *s.f.* (eucharistic) host.

ostile [ɔstil], *a.* hostile; unfriendly.

ostilité [ɔstilite], *s.f.* 1. hostility (**contre,** to); enmity, ill-will. 2. *pl.* hostilities.

ôte, hôtesse [oːt, oːtɛs], *s.* 1. host, *f.* hostess; landlord, landlady; **hôtesse de l'air,** air hostess. 2. (*f.* **hôte**) guest, visitor; **un(e) h. payant(e),** a paying guest.

ôtel [otɛl], *s.m.* 1. public building; **h. de ville,** town-hall; **l'h. des Monnaies** = the Mint. 2. (*a*) hotel; (*b*) **h. meublé, garni,** residential hotel (providing lodging but not board).

ôtelier, -ière [otəlje, -jɛːr], (*a*) *s.* innkeeper; hotel-keeper; (*b*) *a.* **l'industrie hôtelière,** the hotel trade.

ôtellerie [otɛlri], *s.f.* hostelry, inn; **l'h.,** the hotel trade.

houblon [ublɔ̃], *s.m. Bot:* hop(s).

houe [u], *s.f. Tls:* hoe.

houer [ue], *v.tr.* to hoe.

houille [uːj], *s.f.* 1. (pit-)coal. 2. **h. blanche,** hydro-electric power.

houiller, -ère [uje, -ɛːr]. 1. *a.* coal-bearing. 2. *s.f.* **houillère,** coal-mine; colliery.

houle [ul], *s.f.* swell, surge (of sea); **grosse h.,** heavy swell.

houleux, -euse [ulø, -øːz], *a.* heavy, angry (sea); **réunion houleuse,** stormy meeting.

houppe [up], *s.f.* (*a*) tuft; pompon; powder-puff; (*b*) tassel.

hourra [ura], *int.* & *s.m.* hurrah(!).

houspiller [uspije], *v.tr.* to hustle (s.o.); to jostle; to handle roughly; to bully (s.o.).

*****housse** [us], *s.f.* (*a*) loose cover; (*b*) dust sheet.

*****houx** [u], *s.m. Bot:* holly.

*****hublot** [yblo], *s.m. Nau:* scuttle, port-hole.

*****huche** [yʃ], *s.f.* (*a*) bin; **la h. au pain,** the bread-bin; (*b*) hopper (of flour-mill).

*****huée** [ye, ɥe], *s.f.* 1. shouting, whoop(ing). 2. *pl.* booing; jeering, jeers.

*****huer** [ye, ɥe]. 1. *v.i.* (*a*) to shout, whoop; (*b*) (*of owl*) to hoot. 2. *v.tr.* to boo (actor).

*****Hugues** [yg]. *Pr.n.m.* Hugh.

huile [ɥil], *s.f.* oil; **h. comestible,** edible oil; **h. de lin,** linseed oil; **h. minérale,** mineral oil; **peinture à l'h.,** oil-painting; *F:* **les huiles,** the big shots.

huiler [ɥile], *v.tr.* to oil; to lubricate, grease.

huileux, -euse [ɥilø, -øːz], *a.* oily, greasy.

huis [ɥi], *s.m. Jur:* **à h. clos,** in camera.

huissier [ɥisje], *s.m. Jur:* (*a*) process-server; bailiff; (*b*) **h. audiencier,** court usher.

*****huit** [ɥit], *num.a.inv.* & *s.m.inv.* (*as card. adj. before a noun or adj. beginning with a consonant sound* [ɥi]) eight; **h. jours,** a week; **d'aujourd'hui en h.,** today week.

*****huitaine** [ɥitɛn], *s.f.* 1. (about) eight. 2. week; **dans la h.,** in the course of the week.

*****huitante** [ɥitɑ̃ːt], *num.a.inv.* (*Swiss and Belgian usage*) eighty.

*****huitantième** [ɥitɑ̃tjɛm], *num.a.* (*Swiss and Belgian usage*) eightieth.

*****huitième** [ɥitjɛm]. 1. *num.a.* & *s.* eighth. 2. *s.m.* eighth (part).

huître [ɥiːtr], *s.f.* oyster.

humain [ymɛ̃], *a.* 1. human; **le genre h.,** mankind. 2. humane; *adv.* **-ement.**

humaniser [ymanize], *v.tr.* to humanize; to make (s.o.) more humane, gentler; to civilize.

humanitaire [ymanitɛːr], *a.* & *s.* humanitarian.

humanité [ymanite], *s.f.* humanity; (*a*) human nature; (*b*) mankind; (*c*) humaneness, kindness.

humble [œ̃:bl], *a.* humble; *adv.* **-ement.**

humecter [ymɛkte], *v.tr.* to damp, moisten.

*****humer** [yme], *v.tr.* **h. le parfum d'une fleur,** to smell a flower; **h. l'air frais,** to breathe in the fresh air.

humérus [ymerys], *s.m. Anat:* humerus.

humeur [ymœːr], *s.f.* (*a*) humour, mood; **de méchante h.,** in a bad temper; **être en h. de faire qch.,** to be in the mood to do sth.; (*b*) temper; **avoir l'h. vive,** to be quick-tempered; **avec h.,** irritably.

humide [ymid], *a.* damp, moist, humid; **temps h. et chaud,** muggy weather; **temps h. et froid,** raw weather.

humidificateur [ymidifikatœːr], *s.m. H:* humidifier.

humidité [ymidite], *s.f.* humidity, damp(ness); moisture; '**craint l'h.,**' 'to be kept dry.'

humilier [ymilije], *v.tr.* to humiliate, humble (s.o.); *a.* -ant, humiliating; *s.f.* -ation. s'humilier jusqu'à faire qch., to stoop to doing sth.
humilité [ymilite], *s.f.* humility, humbleness.
humoriste [ymɔrist], *s.* humorist.
humoristique [ymɔristik], *a.* humorous.
humour [ymuːr], *s.m.* humour.
humus [ymys], *s.m. Hort:* humus, leaf-mould.
***hurler** [yrle]. 1. *v.i.* to howl; to roar. 2. *v.tr.* to bawl out (song); *s.m.* -ement; *a. & s.* -eur, -euse, (i) howling; (ii) howler, yeller.
***hutte** [yt], *s.f.* hut, shed, shanty.
hybrider [ibride], *v.tr. Biol:* to hybridize, to cross; *s.m.* -isme.
hydrate [idrat], *s.m. Ch:* hydrate, hydroxide.
hydraulique [idrolik]. 1. *a.* hydraulic; énergie h., hydro-electric power. 2. *s.f.* (*a*) hydraulics; (*b*) hydraulic engineering.
hydravion [idravjɔ̃], *s.m.* sea-plane.
hydroélectrique [idrɔelɛktrik], *a.* hydro-electric.
hydrogène [idrɔʒɛn], *s.m. Ch:* hydrogen.
hydrophile [idrɔfil], *a.* absorbent (cotton-wool).
hydropisie [idrɔpizi], *s.f. Med:* dropsy.
hyène [jɛn], *s.f. Z:* hyena.
hygiène [iʒjɛn], *s.f.* hygiene; h. publique, public health.

hygiénique [iʒjenik], *a.* hygienic; sanitary papier h., toilet paper; serviette h., sanitary towel.
hymne [imn]. 1. *s.m.* patriotic song; h. national national anthem. 2. *s.f. Ecc:* hymn.
hypercritique [iperkritik], *a.* hypercritical over-critical.
hyperfréquence [iperfrekɑ̃ːs], *s.f.* very high frequency; *pl.* microwaves.
hypergol [ipergɔl], *s.m. Rockets:* hypergol.
hypermétropie [ipermetrɔpi], *s.f.* hypermetropia, long-sightedness.
hypertension [ipertɑ̃sjɔ̃], *s.f.* hypertension, high blood pressure.
hypnotiser [ipnɔtize], *v.tr.* to hypnotize; *a.* -ique; *s.m.* -isme; *s.m. & f.* -iste.
hypocrisie [ipɔkrizi], *s.f.* hypocrisy; cant.
hypocrite [ipɔkrit]. 1. *a.* hypocritical. 2. *s.m. & f.* hypocrite; *adv.* -ment.
hypothécaire [ipɔtekɛːr], *s.m. & f.* mortgagee.
hypothèque [ipɔtɛk], *s.f.* mortgage.
hypothéquer [ipɔteke], *v.tr.* (j'hypothèque; j'hypothéquerai) to mortgage.
hypothèse [ipɔtɛːz], *s.f.* hypothesis assumption.
hypothétique [ipɔtetik], *a.* hypothetical.
hystérie [isteri], *s.f. Med:* hysteria; *a.* -ique, hysteric(al).

I

I, i [i], s.m. **1.** (the letter) I, i. **2. i grec,** (the letter) Y, y.

Ibérique [iberik], a. Geog: Iberian; **la péninsule i.,** the Iberian peninsula.

iceberg [isbɛrg, ajsbɛrg], s.m. iceberg.

ici [isi], adv. **1.** here; **i.-bas,** here below, on earth; **passez par i.,** step this way; P.T.T: **i. Dupont,** Dupont speaking. **2.** now; **jusqu'i.,** up to now; hitherto; **d'i.** (à) **lundi,** by Monday; **d'i. peu,** before long.

idéal [ideal]. **1.** a. (pl. **idéaux**) [ideo], ideal; **un monde i.,** an ideal world; **le beau i.,** the ideal of beauty. **2.** s.m. (pl. **idéals, idéaux**) ideal; adv. **-ement;** s.m. **-isme;** a. & s.m. & f. **-iste.**

idée [ide], s.f. **1.** idea; (a) notion; **on n'a pas i. de cela,** you can't imagine it; **quelle i.!** the idea! **i. de génie,** i. **lumineuse,** brainwave; **i. fixe,** obsession; (b) view, opinion; (en) **faire à son i.,** to do just what one likes; (c) whim, fancy; **comme l'i. m'en prend,** just as the fancy takes me; **se marier à son i.,** to marry according to one's fancy. **2.** mind; **j'ai dans l'i. que . . .,** I have a notion that . . .; **cela m'est sorti de l'i.,** it's gone clean out of my head.

identif|ier [idɑ̃tifje], v.tr. to identify; s.f. **-cation.**

s'identifier à une cause, to become identified with, to identify oneself with, a cause.

identique [idɑ̃tik], a. identical (à, with); adv. **-ment.**

identité [idɑ̃tite], s.f. identity.

idéolog|ie [ideɔlɔʒi], s.f. **1.** ideology. **2.** Pej: vague theorizing; a. **-ique,** ideological.

idiomatique [idjɔmatik], a. idiomatic; **expression i.,** idiom.

idiome [idjo:m], s.m. (a) idiom, dialect; (b) language.

idiot, -ote [idjo, -ɔt]. **1.** a. (a) Med: idiot (child, etc.); (b) idiotic; senseless. **2.** s. (a) Med: idiot, imbecile; (b) idiot, fool; adv. **-ement.**

idiotie [idjosi], s.f. **1.** (a) idiocy, imbecility; (b). mental deficiency. **2.** (rank) stupidity; **faire une i.,** to do sth. stupid.

idiotisme [idjɔtism], s.m. idiom, idiomatic expression.

idol|e [idɔl], s.f. (a) idol, image; **faire une i. de qn,** to idolize s.o.; (b) idol (of the public); a. **-âtre,** idolatrous; s.f. **-âtrie.**

idyll|e [idil], s.f. idyll; romance; a. **-ique.**

if [if], s.m. yew(-tree).

ignare [iɲa:r]. **1.** a. ignorant. **2.** s. ignoramus.

ignifuge [ignify:ʒ]. **1.** a. fire-proof. **2.** s.m. fire-proof(ing) material.

ignifuger [ignifyʒe], v.tr. (**j'ignifugeai(s); n. ignifugeons**) to fire-proof.

ignoble [iɲɔbl], a. (a) base; disgraceful; (b) wretched, sordid (dwelling).

ignominie [iɲɔmini], s.f. ignominy, shame; disgrace.

ignominieu|x, -euse [iɲɔminjø, -ø:z], a. ignominious, shameful, disgraceful; adv. **-sement.**

ignorance [iɲɔrɑ̃:s], s.f. **1.** ignorance. **2.** pl. errors, mistakes, blunders.

ignor|ant, -ante [iɲɔrɑ̃, -ɑ̃:t]. **1.** a. ignorant, uninstructed. **2.** s. ignoramus, dunce; adv. **-amment.**

ignoré [iɲɔre], a. unknown.

ignorer [iɲɔre], v.tr. not to know; to be ignorant, unaware, of (sth.).

il, ils [il]. **1.** pers.pron.nom.m. (of pers.) he, they; (of thg) it, they. **2.** il inv. it, there; (a) **il est vrai que j'étais là,** it is true that I was there; **il est six heures,** it's six o'clock; (b) (with impers. vbs) **il faut partir,** we must start; **il y a quelqu'un à la porte,** there is someone at the door.

île [i:l], s.f. **1.** island, isle; **habiter dans une î.,** to live on an island. **2.** Petroleum Ind: **î. de forage,** offshore drilling rig.

illégal, -aux [il(l)egal, -o], a. illegal, unlawful; adv. **-ement.**

illégalité [il(l)egalite], s.f. illegality.

illégitime [il(l)eʒitim], a. illegitimate; unlawful; adv. **-ment.**

illégitimité [il(l)eʒitimite], s.f. illegitimacy (of child); unlawfulness (of marriage); spuriousness (of title).

illettré [il(l)etre], a. illiterate, uneducated.

illicite [il(l)isit], a. illicit, unlawful; Sp: **coup i.,** foul; adv. **-ment.**

illimité [il(l)imite], a. unlimited, boundless.

illisible [il(l)izibl], a. illegible, unreadable; adv. **-ment.**

illogique [il(l)ɔʒik], a. illogical; inconsequent; inconsistent; adv. **-ment.**

illumin|er [il(l)ymine], v.tr. **1.** (a) to illuminate; (b) to light up. **2.** to enlighten; s.f. **-ation.**

illus|ion [il(l)yzjɔ̃], s.f. **1.** illusion; **se faire i. à soi-même,** to deceive oneself. **2.** delusion; **se faire i.,** to labour under a delusion; s.m. & f. **-ionniste,** conjurer; a. **-oire,** illusory.

illustre [il(l)ystr], a. illustrious, famous,

I:1

renowned.

illustré [il(l)ystre]. **1.** *a.* illustrated. **2.** *s.m.* illustrated magazine.

illustr|er [il(l)ystre], *v.tr.* to illustrate (book, etc.); *s.m.* **-ateur,** (book) illustrator; *s.f.* **-ation.**

s'illustrer, to become famous (**par,** for, through); to win fame, renown.

îlot [ilo], *s.m.* **1.** islet, small island. **2.** block (of houses).

image [ima:ʒ], *s.f.* image. **1.** reflection. **2.** likeness, representation; (*a*) **à l'i. de qn,** in the likeness of s.o.; (*b*) picture, figure; **livre d'images,** picture-book. **3.** mental picture, impression. **4.** simile, metaphor.

imagé [imaʒe], *a.* (*of style, etc.*) vivid; full of imagery.

imagin|er [imaʒine], *v.tr.* to imagine. **1.** to invent, devise; **i. un projet,** to think out a plan. **2.** to fancy, picture; **tout ce qu'on peut i. de plus beau,** the finest thing imaginable; *a.* **-able;** *a.* **-aire,** imaginary; *a.* **-atif, -ive,** imaginative (person, plan); *s.f.* **-ation.**

imbattable [ɛ̃batabl], *a.* unbeatable (prices, record).

imbécile [ɛ̃besil]. **1.** *a.* (*a*) imbecile, half-witted; (*b*) silly, idiotic. **2.** *s.m. & f.* (*a*) imbecile; (*b*) idiot, fool.

imbécillité [ɛ̃besilite], *s.f.* **1.** (*a*) imbecility; (*b*) silliness, stupidity. **2.** stupid action, speech.

imberbe [ɛ̃berb], *a.* beardless; callow (youth).

imbiber [ɛ̃bibe], *v.tr.* **1. i. qch. de qch.,** to soak sth. in sth. **2.** (*of liquid*) to permeate, soak. **3.** to soak up, imbibe.

s'imbiber. 1. to become saturated (**de,** with); to absorb. **2.** to become absorbed; to sink in.

imbu [ɛ̃by], *a.* imbued, soaked; **i. de préjugés,** steeped in prejudice.

imbuvable [ɛ̃byvabl], *a.* undrinkable, not fit to drink.

imit|er [imite], *v.tr.* to imitate; (*a*) to copy; (*b*) to mimic; to take (s.o.) off; to impersonate (s.o.); (*c*) to forge (signature, etc.); *s.* **-ateur, -atrice;** *a.* **-atif, -ative;** *s.f.* **-ation.**

immaculé [im(m)akyle], *a.* immaculate; undefiled.

immangeable [ɛ̃mɑ̃ʒabl], *a.* uneatable.

immanquable [ɛ̃mɑ̃kabl], *a.* certain, inevitable; *adv.* **-ment.**

immatérialité [im(m)aterialite], *s.f.* immateriality.

immatériel, -ielle [im(m)aterjɛl], *a.* **1.** immaterial, unsubstantial. **2.** intangible (assets, etc.).

immatri|culer [im(m)atrikyle], *v.tr.* to register, enrol (s.o., car, document); **voiture immatriculée 809 HC 64,** car with number (plate) 809 HC 64; **il y a deux millions d'immatriculés,** there are two million (households,

etc.) on the registers; *s.f.* **-culation** registration.

immaturité [im(m)atyrite], *s.f.* immaturity.

immédiat [im(m)edja(t)], *a.* immediate. **1.** (*a* direct (cause); (*b*) close at hand; near; (*c* urgent. **2.** without delay; *adv.* **-ement.**

immen|se [im(m)ɑ̃:s], *a.* **1.** immeasurable boundless. **2.** immense, vast, huge; *adv* **-sément;** *s.f.* **-sité,** immensity.

immensurable [im(m)ɑ̃syrabl], *a* immeasurable.

immer|ger [im(m)ɛrʒe], *v.tr.* (n. **immergeons** (*a*) to immerse, plunge, dip; to lay (a sub marine cable); (*b*) to bury (s.o.) at sea; to com mit (a body) to the deep; *s.f.* **-sion,** immer sion; submergence.

immérité [im(m)erite], *a.* unmerited undeserved.

immeuble [im(m)œbl], *s.m.* (*a*) real estate landed property; (*b*) block of flats; (business premises.

immigré, -ée [im(m)igre], *s.* immigrant.

immigr|er [im(m)igre], *v.i.* to immigrate; *a. &* **-ant, -ante;** *s.f.* **-ation.**

immin|ence [im(m)inɑ̃:s], *s.f.* imminence; (**-ent, -ente,** imminent, impending.

immiscer (s') [sim(m)ise], *v.pr.* (n.n. **immisçon** **s'i. dans une affaire,** to interfere in a matter.

immobile [im(m)ɔbil], *a.* **1.** motionless, still, ur moved; **visage i.,** set face. **2.** immovable; firn

immobilier, -ière [im(m)ɔbilje, -jɛ:r], *a.* **bien immobiliers,** *s.m.* **immobilier,** real estat société immobilière,** building society; **agenc immobilière,** estate agency; **agent i.,** esta agent.

immobilis|er [im(m)ɔbilize], *v.tr.* to immobiliz **Com:** to lock up, tie up (capital); *s.f.* **-ation** **immobilité** [im(m)ɔbilite], *s.f.* immobility fixity; **i. politique,** ultra-conservatism.

immodéré [im(m)ɔdere], *a.* immoderat excessive, inordinate; *adv.* **-ment.**

immonde [im(m)ɔ̃:d], *a.* filthy; vile.

immondices [im(m)ɔ̃dis], *s.f.pl.* dirt, refus dépôt d'i.,** rubbish tip.

immoral, -aux [im(m)ɔral, -o], *a.* immoral; co rupt; *adv.* **-ement.**

immoralité [im(m)ɔralite], *s.f.* immoralit licentiousness.

immortaliser [im(m)ɔrtalize], *v.tr.* t immortalize.

immort|el, -elle [im(m)ɔrtɛl]. **1.** *a.* immorta undying. **2.** *s.m.pl.* **les immortels,** the immo tals, *esp.* the members of the **Académ Française. 3.** *s.f.* **immortelle,** everlastin (flower); *s.f.* **-alité.**

immuable [im(m)ɥabl], *a.* immutable, u alterable; fixed, unchanging; *adv.* **-ment.**

immun|iser [im(m)ynize], *v.tr. Med:* to in munize (s.o.) (**contre,** against); *s.m.* **-isan**

protective serum; *s.f.* -**isation.**
i**mmutabilité** [im(m)ytabilite], *s.f.*
immutability.
i**mpact** [ɛ̃pakt], *s.m.* impact, shock; collision.
i**mpair** [ɛ̃pɛːr], *a.* odd, uneven (number); *s.m. F:*
commettre un i., to drop a brick.
i**mpalpable** [ɛ̃palpabl], *a.* impalpable,
intangible.
i**mpardonnable** [ɛ̃pardɔnabl], *a.* unpardonable.
i**mparfait** [ɛ̃parfɛ], *a.* 1. unfinished, uncompleted. 2. imperfect, defective. 3. *a. & s.m.*
Gram: imperfect (tense); *adv.* -**ement.**
i**mpartial**, -**aux** [ɛ̃parsjal, -o], *a.* impartial, un-
biassed, fair-minded, unprejudiced; *adv.*
-**ement.**
i**mpartialité** [ɛ̃parsjalite], *s.f.* impartiality.
i**mpassable** [ɛ̃pɑsabl], *a.* impassable (barrier);
unfordable (river).
i**mpasse** [ɛ̃pɑːs], *s.f.* 1. blind alley, dead-end;
cul-de-sac; *P.N:* **i.**, no through road. 2.
deadlock; **se trouver dans une i.**, to find oneself
in a dilemma, *F:* in a fix.
i**mpassibilité** [ɛ̃pasibilite], *s.f.* impassiveness.
i**mpassible** [ɛ̃pasibl], *a.* impassive. 1. unmoved,
unperturbed; calm. 2. unimpressionable;
callous; *adv.* -**ment.**
i**mpatienter** [ɛ̃pasjɑ̃te], *v.tr.* to annoy, to
irritate (s.o.); *s.f.* -**ence;** *a.* -**ent;** *adv.* -**emment** [ɛ̃pasjamɑ̃], impatiently.
'**impatienter**, to lose patience.
i**mpayable** [ɛ̃pɛjabl], *a.* priceless; *F:* killingly
funny.
i**mpeccabilité** [ɛ̃pekabilite], *s.f.* impeccability.
i**mpeccable** [ɛ̃pekabl], *a.* impeccable; *adv.*
-**ment.**
i**mpénétrabilité** [ɛ̃penetrabilite], *s.f.* 1. im-
penetrability. 2. inscrutability; *a.* -**able;** *adv.*
-**ablement.**
i**mpénitent** [ɛ̃penitɑ̃], *a.* impenitent,
unrepentant.
i**mpensable** [ɛ̃pɑ̃sabl], *a.* unthinkable.
i**mper** [ɛ̃pɛːr], *s.m. Cl: F:* mac.
i**mpératif**, -**ive** [ɛ̃peratif, -iːv]. 1. *a.* imperious,
peremptory (tone, etc.). 2. *s.m. Gram:* imperative (mood); **à l'i.**, in the imperative; *adv.*
-**ivement.**
i**mpératrice** [ɛ̃peratris], *s.f.* empress.
i**mperceptible** [ɛ̃perseptibl], *a.* imperceptible;
adv. -**ment.**
i**mperfection** [ɛ̃perfeksjɔ̃], *s.f.* imperfection;
defect, flaw.
i**mpérial**, -**aux** [ɛ̃perjal, -o]. 1. *a.* imperial. 2. *s.f.*
impériale, top (deck) (of bus); **autobus à i.**,
double-decker (bus).
i**mpérieux**, -**euse** [ɛ̃perjø, -øːz], *a.* 1. imperious, haughty. 2. imperative, pressing; *adv.*
-**sement.**
i**mpérissable** [ɛ̃perisabl], *a.* imperishable,
undying.

i**mperméabiliser** [ɛ̃permeabilize], *v.tr.* to
(water)proof (cloth, etc.); *s.f.* -**bilité.**
i**mperméable** [ɛ̃permeabl]. 1. *a.* impervious; **i. à
l'eau,** waterproof, watertight. 2. *s.m. Cl:*
waterproof; raincoat.
i**mpersonnel**, -**elle** [ɛ̃persɔnɛl], *a.* impersonal
(style, verb); *adv.* -**ellement.**
i**mpertinence** [ɛ̃pertinɑ̃ːs], *s.f.* impertinence,
pertness, rudeness; *a.* -**ent;** *adv.* -**emment**
[ɛ̃pertinamɑ̃], impertinently.
i**mperturbabilité** [ɛ̃perturbabilite], *s.f.* imperturbability; *a.* -**able;** *adv.* -**ablement.**
i**mpétueux**, -**euse** [ɛ̃petɥø, -øːz], *a.* impetuous;
impulsive; *adv.* -**sement.**
i**mpétuosité** [ɛ̃petɥozite], *s.f.* impetuosity;
impulsiveness.
i**mpie** [ɛ̃pi], *a.* impious; blasphemous.
i**mpiété** [ɛ̃pjete], *s.f.* impiety, godlessness.
i**mpitoyable** [ɛ̃pitwajabl], *a.* (*a*) pitiless (**à,
envers,** towards); ruthless; (*b*) relentless; *adv.*
-**ment.**
i**mplacabilité** [ɛ̃plakabilite], *s.f.* implacability;
a. -**able;** *adv.* -**ablement.**
i**mplanter** [ɛ̃plɑ̃te], *v.tr.* to plant; to implant.
s'**implanter**, to take root; *F:* **s'i. chez qn,** to foist
oneself on s.o.
i**mplicite** [ɛ̃plisit], *a.* implicit; (*a*) implied (intention); (*b*) absolute (faith); *adv.* -**ment.**
i**mpliquer** [ɛ̃plike], *v.tr.* to implicate, involve.
i**mplorer** [ɛ̃plɔre], *v.tr.* to implore, beseech (s.o.).
i**mpoli** [ɛ̃pɔli], *a.* impolite, rude (**envers, avec,**
to); *adv.* -**ment.**
i**mpolitesse** [ɛ̃pɔlitɛs], *s.f.* 1. impoliteness; (*a*)
discourtesy; (*b*) rudeness. 2. act of
discourtesy.
i**mpolitique** [ɛ̃pɔlitik], *a.* impolitic, ill-advised;
adv. -**ment,** ill-advisedly.
i**mpopularité** [ɛ̃pɔpylarite], *s.f.* unpopularity;
a. -**aire,** unpopular.
i**mportance** [ɛ̃pɔrtɑ̃ːs], *s.f.* importance; (*a*)
consequence, moment; **affaire d'i.,** important
matter; *Rail:* **i. du retard,** number of minutes
(train is) late; **i. du dommage,** extent of the
damage; (*b*) social importance, position; (*c*)
Pej: self-importance; **faire l'homme d'i.,** to
talk, act, big; *a.* -**tant,** important.
i**mporter**¹ [ɛ̃pɔrte], *v.tr.* to import (goods); *a. &
s.* -**ateur, -atrice,** (i) importing (firm); (ii) importer; *s.f.* -**ation.**
i**mporter**², *v.i.* (*mainly used in the third pers.*) to
be of importance; to matter. 1. **les choses qui
importent,** the things that matter. 2. *impers.*
n'importe, no matter, never mind; **n'importe
qui, quoi,** anyone, anything; **venez n'importe
quel jour,** come any day.
i**mportun**, -**une** [ɛ̃pɔrtœ̃, -yn]. 1. *a.* impor-
tunate; tiresome; unwelcome; **je crains de
vous être i.,** I'm afraid I'm disturbing you. 2. *s.*
nuisance.

importunément [ɛ̃pɔrtynemɑ̃], *adv.* importunately.

importun|er [ɛ̃pɔrtyne], *v.tr.* to importune; (*a*) to bother, pester; (*b*) to annoy; *s.f.* -**ité**.

imposé, -ée [ɛ̃poze]. **1.** *a.* prescribed, set (task, etc.); *Com:* **prix i.,** fixed price. **2.** *s.* tax-payer.

impos|er [ɛ̃poze]. **I.** *v.tr.* **1.** to impose, prescribe; to set (task); to dictate (terms); **i. une règle,** to lay down a rule; **i. (le) silence à qn,** to enjoin silence on s.o.; **i. le respect,** to command respect. **2.** *Adm:* (*a*) **i. des droits sur qch.,** to tax sth.; (*b*) **i. qn,** to tax s.o. **II.** *v.i.* **1.** (**en**) **i.,** to inspire respect. **2.** (**en**) **i. à qn,** (i) to impose on s.o.; (ii) to impress s.o.; *a.* -**ant,** imposing, commanding (figure, etc.); *a.* -**able,** taxable; *s.f.* -**ition,** imposition; tax(ation).

s'imposer. 1. to assert oneself. **2. s'i. à qn,** to thrust, foist, oneself upon s.o. **3.** to be indispensable; **une visite au Louvre s'impose,** we, you, simply must visit the Louvre.

imposs|ibilité [ɛ̃pɔsibilite], *s.f.* impossibility; *a.* -**ible.**

imposteur [ɛ̃pɔstœːr], *s.m.* impostor.

imposture [ɛ̃pɔstyːr], *s.f.* imposture. **1.** deception, trickery. **2.** swindle.

impôt [ɛ̃po], *s.m.* tax, duty.

impotence [ɛ̃pɔtɑ̃ːs], *s.f.* helplessness, infirmity.

impotent, -ente [ɛ̃pɔtɑ̃, -ɑ̃ːt]. **1.** *a.* helpless, bedridden, crippled. **2.** *s.* helpless invalid; cripple.

impraticable [ɛ̃pratikabl], *a.* **1.** impracticable, unworkable. **2. chemin i.,** road unfit for traffic; *Sp:* (*of ground*) unfit for play.

imprécation [ɛ̃prekasjɔ̃], *s.f.* imprecation, curse.

imprécis [ɛ̃presi], *a.* vague, indefinite.

imprégn|er [ɛ̃preɲe], *v.tr.* (**j'imprègne; j'imprégnerai**) to impregnate (**de,** with); *s.f.* -**ation.**

s'imprégner de qch., to become soaked with sth.; to soak up, to soak in, sth.

imprenable [ɛ̃prənabl], *a.* impregnable; **vue i.,** view that cannot be spoiled.

impression [ɛ̃prɛsjɔ̃], *s.f.* **1.** *Typ:* printing; **faute d'i.,** misprint; **i. en couleurs,** colour print. **2.** impression; **i. de pas,** footprints. **3.** (mental) impression.

impressionn|er [ɛ̃prɛsjɔne], *v.tr.* to impress, affect; to make an impression (up)on (s.o.); *a.* -**able;** *a.* -**ant,** impressive.

imprévisible [ɛ̃previzibl], *a.* unforeseeable.

imprévoy|ance [ɛ̃prevwajɑ̃ːs], *s.f.* (*a*) lack of foresight; (*b*) improvidence; *a.* -**ant,** improvident.

imprévu [ɛ̃prevy]. **1.** *a.* unforeseen, unexpected (event). **2.** *s.m.* (*a*) unexpected character (of event); (*b*) unforeseen events; **sauf i.,** barring accidents; **en cas d'i.,** in case of an emergency; **imprévus,** unforeseen expenses.

imprimé [ɛ̃prime], *s.m.* printed paper; book (official) form; *P.T.T:* **imprimés,** printe matter.

imprim|er [ɛ̃prime], *v.tr. Typ:* to print; *s.* -**erie,** printing works; press; *s.m.* -**eu** printer.

improb|abilité [ɛ̃prɔbabilite], *s.f.* im probability; *a.* -**able.**

product|if, -ive [ɛ̃prɔdyktif, -iːv], *a.* u productive; *adv.* -**ivement.**

impromptu [ɛ̃prɔ̃pty]. **1.** *adv.* withou preparation; impromptu. **2.** *a. often inv.* u premeditated; impromptu; extempore, off th cuff (speech, etc.).

impropre [ɛ̃prɔpr], *a.* (*a*) incorrect, wrong; (*b*) à qch., unfit for sth.; *adv.* -**ment.**

impropriété [ɛ̃prɔpriete], *s.f.* impropriety; i correctness; incorrect use (of word, etc.).

improvis|er [ɛ̃prɔvize], *v.tr.* **1.** to improvise; di cours improvisé, impromptu speech. **2.** *abs.* speak extempore; *s.f.* -**ation,** improvisation

improviste (à l') [alɛ̃prɔvist], *adv.phr.* u expectedly; **prendre qn à l'i.,** to take s. unawares.

imprudence [ɛ̃prydɑ̃ːs], *s.f.* imprudenc rashness.

imprud|ent [ɛ̃prydɑ̃], *a.* imprudent, rash; u wise, incautious (action); *adv.* -**emmen** [ɛ̃prydamɑ̃].

impud|ence [ɛ̃pydɑ̃ːs], *s.f.* impudence; cheek; (*a*) effrontery; (*b*) shamelessness; -**ent,** impudent; *F:* cheeky.

impuiss|ance [ɛ̃pɥisɑ̃ːs], *s.f.* impotenc powerlessness, helplessness; *a.* -**ant,** imp tent, helpless.

impulsif, -ive [ɛ̃pylsif, -iːv], *a.* impulsive.

impulsion [ɛ̃pylsjɔ̃], *s.f.* **1.** (*a*) *El:* impulse; **i.** courant, current impulse, surge; **radar à i** pulsions, pulse radar; (*b*) impetus, stimulus. sous l'i. du moment, on the spur of th moment.

impun|i [ɛ̃pyni], *a.* unpunished; *adv.* -**émen** with impunity.

impunité [ɛ̃pynite], *s.f.* impunity.

impur [ɛ̃pyːr], *a.* impure.

impureté [ɛ̃pyrte], *s.f.* impurity.

imput|er [ɛ̃pyte], *v.tr.* to impute, attribute; *Con* i. des frais à, sur, un compte, to charl expenses to an account; *a.* -**able,** attributab (à, to); *s.f.* -**ation,** charge.

inabordable [inabɔrdabl], *a.* unapproachabl inaccessible; prohibitive (price).

inacceptable [inaksɛptabl], *a.* unacceptable.

inaccessib|le [inaksesibl], *a.* inaccessible, una proachable; *F:* un-get-at-able (place, etc.); **i.** la pitié, incapable of, proof against, pity; *s* -**ilité.**

inaccoutumé [inakutyme], *a.* unaccustomed. unused (à, to). **2.** unusual.

inachevé [inaʃve], a. unfinished, uncompleted.
inact|if, -ive [inaktif, -i:v], a. inactive; idle; adv.
-ivement.
inac|tion [inaksjɔ̃], s.f. inaction, idleness; s.f.
-tivité, inactivity.
inadmiss|ible [inadmisibl], a. inadmissible
(request, etc.); s.f. -ibilité.
inadvertance [inadvɛrtɑ̃:s], s.f. 1. inadverten-
cy; par i., inadvertently. 2. oversight, mistake;
carelessness.
inaliénable [inaljenabl], a. Jur: untransferable
(property); indefeasible (right); rendre un legs
i., to tie up a succession; adv. -ment.
inaltérable [inalterabl], a. 1. that does not
deteriorate; i. à l'air, unaffected by air. 2. (a)
unalterable; (b) unfailing, unvarying (good
humour).
inamovible [inamɔvibl], a. irremovable; untransferable (employee); (post) held for life.
inanimé [inanime], a. 1. inanimate, lifeless. 2.
senseless, unconscious.
inanité [inanite], s.f. 1. inanity, futility. 2. inane
remark.
inapaisable [inapɛzabl], a. inappeasable.
inapaisé [inapɛze], a. unappeased.
inaperçu [inapɛrsy], a. (a) unseen, unperceived,
unobserved; (b) unnoticed, unremarked;
passer i., to escape notice; to escape detection.
inapplicable [inaplikabl], a. inapplicable.
inappréciable [inapresjabl], a. 1. inappreciable.
2. inestimable, invaluable.
inapprécié [inapresje], a. unappreciated.
inapte [inapt]. 1. a. inapt; unfit (à, for); unsuited
(à, to). 2. s.m. les inaptes, the unemployable.
inaptitude [inaptityd], s.f. inaptitude; unfitness
(à, for).
inarticulé [inartikyle], a. (a) inarticulate (sound,
etc.); (b) Z: inarticulate(d), not jointed.
inassouv|i [inasuvi], a. unappeased (hunger);
unquenched (thirst); a. -issable, insatiable.
inattaquable [inatakabl], a. unassailable (position, etc.); unquestionable (right); i. par les
acides, aux acides, acid-proof.
inattendu [inatɑ̃dy], a. unexpected, unforeseen.
inatten|tion [inatɑ̃sjɔ̃], s.f. inattention (à, to),
carelessness; faute d'i., careless mistake; a.
-tif, -tive; adv. -tivement.
inaudible [inodibl], a. inaudible.
inaugur|er [inogyre], v.tr. to inaugurate; a. -al,
pl. -aux, inaugural (speech, etc.); s.f. -ation.
incalculable [ɛ̃kalkylabl], a. incalculable.
incandes|cence [ɛ̃kɑ̃dɛs(s)ɑ̃:s], s.f. in-
candescence; a. -cent, incandescent.
incapable [ɛ̃kapabl], a. 1. incapable, unfit; inefficient. 2. i. de faire qch., unable to do sth.;
Jur: i. de tester, not competent to make a will.
3. s.m. or f. les (majeurs) incapables, the legal-
ly incapacitated; F: c'est un i., he's useless.
incapacité [ɛ̃kapasite], s.f. 1. incapacity, un-

fitness, inefficiency. 2. Adm: i. permanente,
permanent disablement; i. de travail, industrial
disablement.
incarcér|er [ɛ̃karsere], v.tr. (j'incarcère; j'in-
carcérerai) to imprison (s.o.); s.f. -ation,
imprisonment.
incarné [ɛ̃karne], a. Rel: le Verbe i., the Word
Incarnate; c'est le diable i., he's the devil
incarnate.
incendiaire [ɛ̃sɑ̃djɛ:r]. 1. a. incendiary; inflam-
matory. 2. s. (a) incendiary; (b) fire-brand.
incendie [ɛ̃sɑ̃di], s.m. (outbreak of) fire; poste
d'i., fire station; pompe à i., fire-engine; i.
volontaire, arson.
incendi|er [ɛ̃sɑ̃dje], v.tr. (p.d. & pr. sub. n. in-
cendiions) to set (house, forest, etc.) on fire; to
set fire to (sth.); to burn (sth.) down.
incertain [ɛ̃sɛrtɛ̃], a. (a) uncertain, doubtful; (b)
unreliable.
incertitude [ɛ̃sɛrtityd], s.f. (a) uncertainty, incertitude, doubt; (b) indecision.
incessamment [ɛ̃sɛsamɑ̃], adv. immediately,
forthwith, without delay, as soon as possible;
j'arriverai i., I shall get there any moment.
incessant [ɛ̃sɛsɑ̃], a. unceasing, ceaseless;
never-ending (quarrels).
incidemment [ɛ̃sidamɑ̃], adv. incidentally.
incident [ɛ̃sidɑ̃], s.m. incident; (a) occurrence,
happening; arriver sans i., to arrive without
mishap; (b) difficulty, hitch; i. technique,
technical hitch.
incinér|er [ɛ̃sinere], v.tr. (j'incinère; j'in-
cinérerai) (a) to burn to ashes; (b) to cremate;
s.m. -ateur, incinerator; s.f. -ation.
incis|if, -ive [ɛ̃sizif, -i:v]. 1. a. incisive, sharp, cut-
ting (remark, etc.). 2. s.f. incisive, incisor; adv.
-ivement.
incision [ɛ̃sizjɔ̃], s.f. incision. 1. cutting; Surg:
lancing (of a boil, etc.). 2. cut; i. chirurgicale,
operation wound.
incit|er [ɛ̃site], v.tr. to incite; to urge (on); s.f.
-ation, incitement (à, to).
incivil [ɛ̃sivil], a. uncivil, rude, discourteous;
adv. -ement.
incivilisé [ɛ̃sivilize], a. uncivilized.
incivilité [ɛ̃sivilite], s.f. incivility, rudeness.
inclinaison [ɛ̃klinɛzɔ̃], s.f. incline, slope; slant;
tilt; pitch (of roof); comble à forte, à faible, i.,
high-pitched, low-pitched, roof; Av: angle d'i.,
angle of bank, of roll.
inclination [ɛ̃klinasjɔ̃], s.f. inclination. 1. bending, bow(ing) (of body); nod (of head). 2. (a)
bent, propensity; avoir de l'i. à faire qch., to
feel inclined to do sth.; (b) attachment, love;
mariage d'i., marriage for love.
incliner [ɛ̃kline]. 1. v.tr. to incline; (a) to slant,
slope; (b) to tip up; to tilt; (c) to bend, bow (the
head); (d) i. qn à faire qch., to influence,
predispose, s.o. in favour of doing sth. 2. v.i.

(a) (of wall, etc.) to lean, slope; (b) **i. à la pitié,** to incline, be disposed, to pity.

s'incliner. 1. to slant, slope; *Nau:* to list; *Av:* to bank. 2. **s'i. devant qn,** to yield to s.o.; **j'ai dû m'i.,** I had to give in.

inclus [ɛ̃kly], *a.* (a) enclosed (in letter); (b) included; **jusqu'à la page 5 incluse,** up to and including page 5.

inclus|if, -ive [ɛ̃klyzif, -i:v], *a.* inclusive; *adv.* -**ivement.**

inclusion [ɛ̃klyzjɔ̃], *s.f.* (a) enclosing (of document in a letter); (b) inclusion.

incohér|ence [ɛ̃kɔerɑ̃:s], *s.f.* incoherence; disjointedness (of speech); *a.* -**ent.**

incolore [ɛ̃kɔlɔ:r], *a.* colourless.

incomber [ɛ̃kɔ̃be], *v.i.* (*used only in the third pers.*) **i. à qn,** to be incumbent on, to devolve upon, s.o.; *impers.* **il nous incombe de . . .,** we must, should . . ..

incombustible [ɛ̃kɔ̃bystibl], *a.* incombustible; fireproof.

incommod|e [ɛ̃kɔmɔd], *a.* inconvenient; uncomfortable; awkward; *adv.* -**ément.**

incommoder [ɛ̃kɔmɔde], *v.tr.* to inconvenience, incommode, disturb, s.o.; **la fumée ne vous incommode pas?** you don't mind my smoking? (*of food, etc.*) to upset (s.o.).

incomparable [ɛ̃kɔ̃parabl], *a.* incomparable, unrivalled, matchless; *adv.* -**ment.**

incompat|ibilité [ɛ̃kɔ̃patibilite], *s.f.* incompatibility (of duties, etc.; of temperament); *a.* -**ible;** *adv.* -**iblement.**

incompét|ence [ɛ̃kɔ̃petɑ̃:s], *s.f.* incompetence; *a.* -**ent,** inefficient; not qualified.

incompl|et, -ète [ɛ̃kɔ̃plɛ, -ɛt], *a.* incomplete; *adv.* -**ètement.**

incompréhensible [ɛ̃kɔ̃preɑ̃sibl], *a.* incomprehensible; *adv.* -**ment.**

incompréhen|sion [ɛ̃kɔ̃preɑ̃sjɔ̃], *s.f.* incomprehension, lack of understanding; obtuseness; *a.* -**sif, -sive,** uncomprehending; obtuse (mind).

incompris [ɛ̃kɔ̃pri], *a.* (*of pers.*) misunderstood; unappreciated.

inconcevable [ɛ̃kɔ̃s(ə)vabl], *a.* inconceivable, unthinkable, unimaginable; *adv.* -**ment.**

inconciliable [ɛ̃kɔ̃siljabl], *a.* irreconcilable, incompatible (**avec,** with).

inconditionnel, -elle [ɛ̃kɔ̃disjɔnɛl], *a.* unconditional (consent, support); *adv.* -**lement.**

inconduite [ɛ̃kɔ̃dɥit], *s.f.* loose living; *Jur:* misconduct.

inconfort [ɛ̃kɔ̃fɔr], *s.m.* discomfort; *a.* -**able,** uncomfortable; *adv.* -**ablement.**

incongru [ɛ̃kɔ̃gry], *a.* 1. incongruous, foolish. 2. improper.

incongruité [ɛ̃kɔ̃grɥite], *s.f.* (a) incongruity, absurdity; (b) impropriety, tactlessness (of behaviour); (c) foolish, tactless, remark,

action.

inconnu, -ue [ɛ̃kɔny]. 1. *a.* unknown. 2. *s.* (a) unknown person; (i) stranger; (ii) (mere) nobody; (c) *s.m.* **l'i.,** the unknown. 3. *s.f. Mth:* **inconnue,** unknown quantity.

inconsci|ence [ɛ̃kɔ̃sjɑ̃:s], *s.f.* unconsciousness (**de,** of); *a.* -**ent,** unconscious (act); thoughtless (person); *adv.* -**emment** [ɛ̃kɔ̃sjamɑ̃], unconsciously, unknowingly.

inconséqu|ence [ɛ̃kɔ̃sekɑ̃:s], *s.f.* inconsistency, inconsequence, irrelevance; *a.* -**ent.**

inconsist|ance [ɛ̃kɔ̃sistɑ̃:s], *s.f.* 1. insubstantiality, lack of firmness; looseness, softness (of soil). 2. inconsistency.

inconsolable [ɛ̃kɔ̃sɔlabl], *a.* unconsolable, inconsolable; disconsolate.

inconstance [ɛ̃kɔ̃stɑ̃:s], *s.f.* 1. inconstancy fickleness. 2. changeableness; *Biol:* instability

inconstant [ɛ̃kɔ̃stɑ̃], *a.* 1. inconstant; *Sp:* joueu **i.,** erratic player. 2. changeable; *Biol:* variabl (type).

inconstitutionnel, -elle [ɛ̃kɔ̃stitysjɔnɛl], *a.* un constitutional; *adv.* -**lement.**

incontestable [ɛ̃kɔ̃tɛstabl], *a.* undeniable beyond all question; *adv.* -**ment.**

inconvenance [ɛ̃kɔ̃vnɑ̃:s], *s.f.* (a) impropriety unseemliness; (b) breach of (good) manners **dire des inconvenances,** to make indiscree remarks.

inconvenant [ɛ̃kɔ̃vnɑ̃], *a.* improper, unseemly ill-bred, indiscreet (remarks).

inconvénient [ɛ̃kɔ̃venjɑ̃], *s.m.* disadvantage drawback; **il n'y a pas d'i.,** there's n objection.

incorpor|er [ɛ̃kɔrpɔre], *v.tr.* to incorporate; *s.,* -**ation.**

incorrect [ɛ̃kɔrɛkt], *a.* incorrect; (a) inaccurat wrong; (b) untrue; (c) **tenue incorrecte,** (i slovenly dress; (ii) unsuitable clothes (for th occasion); (d) (*of pers.*) impolite, rude; *adv* -**ement.**

incorrigible [ɛ̃kɔriʒibl], *a.* incorrigible; *F* hopeless; *adv.* -**ment.**

incorruptible [ɛ̃kɔr(r)yptibl], *a.* incorruptible (a) proof against decay; (b) unbribable; *adv* -**ment.**

incrédibilité [ɛ̃kredibilite], *s.f.* incredibility.

incrédule [ɛ̃kredyl]. 1. *a.* incredulous (**à l'égar de,** of). 2. *s.* unbeliever.

incrédulité [ɛ̃kredylite], *s.f.* incredulity.

increvable [ɛ̃krəvabl], *a.* puncture-proof (tyre *P:* tireless (person).

incrimin|er [ɛ̃krimine], *v.tr. Jur:* to incriminat accuse, indict (s.o.); *s.f.* -**ation.**

incroyable [ɛ̃krwajabl], *a.* incredible, un believable; *adv.* -**ment.**

incruster [ɛ̃kryste], *v.tr.* to encrust; *Tchn:* to i lay (**de,** with).

s'incruster. 1. (*of boiler, etc.*) to become furre

up. **2.** *F:* to dig oneself in; **il s'incruste,** he stays too long.

incuba|tion [ɛ̃kybasjɔ̃], *s.f.* incubation, hatching period; *s.m.* **-teur,** incubator.

inculp|er [ɛ̃kylpe], *v.tr.* to indict, charge; *s.f.* **-ation,** indictment, charge.

inculquer [ɛ̃kylke], *v.tr.* to inculcate (à, in), to instil (à, into).

inculte [ɛ̃kylt], *a.* uncultivated, wild; waste (land); untutored (mind).

incurable [ɛ̃kyrabl], *a. & s.* incurable.

incursion [ɛ̃kyrsjɔ̃], *s.f.* inroad, incursion.

Inde [ɛ̃:d]. *Pr.n.f. Geog:* (*a*) **l'I.,** India; (*b*) **les Indes,** the Indies.

indéc|ence [ɛ̃desɑ̃:s], *s.f.* indecency; *a.* **-ent;** *adv.* **-emment** [ɛ̃desamɑ̃].

indéchiffrable [ɛ̃deʃifrabl], *a.* unintelligible; illegible; indecipherable.

indécis [ɛ̃desi], *a.* **1.** unsettled, open (question); doubtful; vague. **2.** (*of pers.*) (*a*) undecided, in two minds; (*b*) irresolute; *a.* **-if, -ive,** indecisive; *adv.* **-ivement,** indecisively.

indéfendable [ɛ̃defɑ̃dabl], *a.* indefensible.

indéfini [ɛ̃defini], *a.* **1.** indefinite; *Gram:* **pronom, article, i.,** indefinite pronoun, article. **2.** undefined; *adv.* **-ment,** indefinitely; *a.* **-ssable,** undefinable.

indéfrichable [ɛ̃defriʃabl], *a.* (land) unfit for cultivation; waste (land).

indélicat [ɛ̃delika], *a.* coarse; tactless; unscrupulous; *adv.* **-ement.**

indélicatesse [ɛ̃delikatɛs], *s.f.* **1.** (*a*) tactlessness; (*b*) unscrupulousness. **2.** unscrupulous, dishonest, action.

indémaillable [ɛ̃demajabl], *a.* ladder-proof (stocking).

indemne [ɛ̃dɛmn], *a.* (*a*) without loss; (*b*) undamaged; (*c*) uninjured.

indemnis|er [ɛ̃demnize], *v.tr.* to indemnify, compensate; *s.f.* **-ation,** compensation.

indemnité [ɛ̃demnite], *s.f.* (*a*) indemnity, compensation; (*b*) penalty (for delay); (*c*) allowance, grant; **i. de chômage,** unemployment benefit; **i. parlementaire** = M.P.'s salary.

indéniable [ɛ̃denjabl], *a.* undeniable; *adv.* **-ment.**

indépend|ance [ɛ̃depɑ̃dɑ̃:s], *s.f.* independence; *a.* **-ant,** independent; *adv.* **-amment** [ɛ̃depɑ̃damɑ̃], independently.

indescriptible [ɛ̃deskriptibl], *a.* indescribable; beyond description; *adv.* **-ment.**

indésirable [ɛ̃dezirabl], *a. & s.* undesirable.

indestructible [ɛ̃destryktibl], *a.* indestructible; *adv.* **-ment.**

indéterminé [ɛ̃detɛrmine], *a.* undetermined, indefinite.

index [ɛ̃dɛks], *s.m.inv.* **1.** (*a*) forefinger; (*b*) pointer (of balance); indicator. **2.** index (of book); **i. du coût de la vie,** cost of living index.

index|er [ɛ̃dɛkse], *v.tr.* **1.** to index. **2.** to peg (prices); *s.f.* **-ation,** (i) (card-)indexing; (ii) price-pegging.

indicateur, -trice [ɛ̃dikatœ:r, -tris]. **1.** *a.* indicatory; **poteau i.,** sign-post; **lampe indicatrice,** tell-tale lamp. **2.** *s.m.* (*a*) (railway) time-table; (street) directory; (*b*) indicator, gauge.

indicatif, -ive [ɛ̃dikatif, -i:v]. **1.** *a.* indicative (**de, of**). **2.** *a. & s.m. Gram:* indicative (mood). **3.** *s.m. Rad: P.T.T:* etc: **i. d'appel,** call number; **i. du poste,** station signal; **i. (musical),** signature tune.

indication [ɛ̃dikasjɔ̃], *s.f.* indication. **1.** (*a*) (piece of) information; (*b*) sign, token; clue. **2.** *esp.pl.* instruction(s); **indications de mode d'emploi,** directions for use.

indice [ɛ̃dis], *s.m.* **1.** indication, sign; mark, token. **2.** index; **i. du coût de la vie,** cost of living index.

indicible [ɛ̃disibl], *a.* (*a*) inexpressible, unutterable; unspeakable; (*b*) indescribable; *adv.* **-ment.**

indien, -ienne [ɛ̃djɛ̃, -jɛn]. **1.** *a & s.* Indian. **2.** *s.f. Tex:* **indienne,** chintz.

indiffér|ence [ɛ̃diferɑ̃:s], *s.f.* indifference; unconcern; apathy; heartlessness; *a.* **-ent;** *adv.* **-emment** [ɛ̃diferamɑ̃].

indig|ence [ɛ̃diʒɑ̃:s], *s.f.* poverty, want; *a.* **-ent,** poor, needy.

indigène [ɛ̃diʒɛn], *a. & s.* native.

indigeste [ɛ̃diʒɛst], *a.* **1.** indigestible; stodgy (food). **2.** undigested, ill-arranged (work); heavy (book).

indigestion [ɛ̃diʒɛstjɔ̃], *s.f.* indigestion.

indigne [ɛ̃diɲ], *a.* unworthy. **1.** undeserving. **2.** shameful (action, conduct); *adv.* **-ment.**

indign|er [ɛ̃diɲe], *v.tr.* to make (s.o.) indignant; *s.f.* **-ation.**

s'indigner, to become, to be, indignant.

indignité [ɛ̃diɲite], *s.f.* **1.** (*a*) unworthiness; (*b*) baseness (of an action). **2. souffrir des indignités,** to suffer indignities, humiliations.

indigo [ɛ̃digo], *s.m.* indigo; *a.inv.* **des rubans indigo,** indigo-blue ribbons.

indiquer [ɛ̃dike], *v.tr.* to indicate; (*a*) to point out; **i. qch. du doigt,** to point to sth.; (*b*) to show; (*c*) to appoint, name (a day, etc.); **c'était indiqué,** it was the obvious thing to do.

indirect [ɛ̃dirɛkt], *a.* (*a*) indirect; **éclairage i.,** concealed lighting; (*b*) circumstantial (evidence); (*c*) underhand (methods); (*d*) **contributions indirectes,** excise revenue; *adv.* **-ement.**

indiscipliné [ɛ̃disipline], *a.* undisciplined, unruly.

indiscr|et, -ète [ɛ̃diskrɛ, -ɛt]. **1.** *a.* indiscreet; (*a*) (over-)curious, *F:* nosy (person); (*b*) tactless; (*c*) (person) who gives away secrets. **2.** *s.* (*a*) tactless, meddlesome, person; *F:* Nosy Parker; (*b*) teller of secrets; eavesdropper; *adv.* -ètement.

indiscrétion [ēdiskresjō], *s.f.* indiscretion.

indiscutable [ēdiskytabl], *a.* indisputable, unquestionable; obvious; *adv.* -ment.

indispensable [ēdispãsabl], *a.* indispensable. 1. obligatory. 2. essential (à, to); *adv.* -ment.

indisposé [ēdispoze], *a.* 1. indisposed, unwell; off colour. 2. i. **contre qn**, unfriendly, illdisposed, towards s.o.

indisposer [ēdispoze], *v.tr.* 1. (*of food*) to upset (s.o.). 2. to antagonize (s.o.); *s.f.* -**ition**.

indisputable [ēdispytabl], *a.* indisputable, unquestionable; *adv.* -ment.

indissoluble [ēdis(s)olybl], *a.* 1. insoluble (salt, etc.). 2. indissoluble (bond, friendship).

indistinct [ēdistē(:kt)], *a.* indistinct; hazy, blurred; faint (noises); dim (light); *adv.* -ement.

individu [ēdividy], *s.m.* 1. individual. 2. *F: Pej:* person; **quel est cet i.?** who's that fellow? **un i. louche**, a shady customer.

individualité [ēdividɥalite], *s.f.* individuality.

individuel, -elle [ēdividɥɛl], *a.* individual; personal (liberty, etc.); private (fortune); *adv.* -lement.

indivisible [ēdivizibl], *a.* indivisible.

indo-européen, -enne [ēdoørɔpeē, -ɛn], *a. & s. Ethn: Ling:* Indo-European; *pl. indoeuropéens, -ennes.*

indolence [ēdɔlã:s], *s.f.* indolence; *a.* -ent; *adv.* -emment [ēdɔlamã].

indomptable [ēdɔtabl], *a.* unconquerable; untam(e)able; unmanageable.

indompté [ēdɔte], *a.* unconquered; untamed.

Indonésie (l') [lēdɔnezi]. *Pr.n.f. Geog:* Indonesia.

indu [ēdy], *a.* undue; unwarranted; *adv.* -ûment, unduly, improperly; *Adm:* without permission.

indubitable [ēdybitabl], *a.* beyond doubt, indubitable, unquestionable; *adv.* -ment.

induction [ēdyksjō], *s.f. El:* **courant d'i.**, induced current; **bobine d'i.**, induction coil.

induire [ēdɥi:r], *v.tr.* (*pr.* **j'induis, n. induisons**; *p.h.* **j'induisis**; *p.p.* **induit**) 1. *usu. Pej:* to induce, tempt (s.o. to do sth.). 2. to infer, induce (conclusion).

indulgence [ēdylʒã:s], *s.f.* indulgence, leniency; *a.* -ent.

industrialiser [ēdystrialize], *v.tr.* to industrialize; *s.f.* -**ation**, industrialization.

industrie [ēdystri], *s.f.* 1. activity; industry. 2. industry, trade, manufacture.

industrie-clef [ēdystriklɛf], *s.f.* key industry; *pl. industries-clefs.*

industriel, -elle [ēdystriɛl]. 1. *a.* industrial. 2. *s.m.* manufacturer, industrialist.

industrieux, -euse [ēdystriø, -ø:z], *a.* busy, industrious; *adv.* -sement.

inébranlable [inebrãlabl], *a.* unshak(e)able; (*a*) immovable, firm; (*b*) resolute, steadfast.

inédit [inedi], *a.* 1. unpublished (book). 2. new, original (plan).

ineffable [inefabl], *a.* ineffable, unutterable.

ineffaçable [inefasabl], *a.* ineffaceable (memory); indelible (stain).

inefficace [inefikas], *a.* ineffectual; inefficacious; useless (remedy).

inégal, -aux [inegal, -o], *a.* 1. unequal. 2. (*a*) un even, rough; (*b*) irregular; *adv.* -ement.

inégalé [inegale], *a.* unequalled.

inégalité [inegalite], *s.f.* 1. inequality, disparity 2. unevenness.

inélégant [inelegã], *a.* inelegant; *adv.* -amment [inelegamã], inelegantly.

inéligible [ineliʒibl], *a.* ineligible.

inepte [inɛpt], *a.* inept, foolish, idiotic; *adv.* -ment.

ineptie [inɛpsi], *s.f.* ineptitude, stupid remark.

inépuisable [inepɥizabl], *a.* inexhaustible; un failing (patience, etc.).

inéquitable [inekitabl], *a.* inequitable, unfair; *adv.* -ment.

inerte [inɛrt], *a.* inert; sluggish; dull.

inertie [inɛrsi], *s.f.* 1. inertia. 2. sluggishness.

inespéré [inɛspere], *a.* unhoped-for, unexpecte

inestimable [inɛstimabl], *a.* inestimable invaluable.

inévitable [inevitabl], *a.* 1. unavoidable. 2. in evitable; *adv.* -ment.

inexact [inɛgzakt], *a.* 1. inexact, inaccurate, i correct; wrong. 2. unpunctual; slack, lax; *ad* -ement.

inexactitude [inɛgzaktityd], *s.f.* 1. inaccurac inexactitude; mistake. 2. unpunctualit slackness.

inexcusable [inɛkskyzabl], *a.* inexcusable; *a* -ment.

inexistant [inɛgzistã], *a.* non-existent.

inexorable [inɛgzɔrabl], *a.* inexorable, unrele ting; *adv.* -ment.

inexpérience [inɛkspɛrjã:s], *s.f.* inexperience

inexpérimenté [inɛkspɛrimãte], *a.* 1. i experienced; unskilled. 2. untested (process)

inexplicable [inɛksplikabl], *a.* inexplicable, u accountable; *adv.* -ment.

inexploitable [inɛksplwatabl], *a.* unworkal (mine), uncultivable (land).

inexploité [inɛksplwate], *a.* unexploited; u tapped (resources).

inexploré [inɛksplɔre], *a.* unexplored.

inexprimable [inɛksprimabl], *a.* inexpressib *adv.* -ment.

inextinguible [inɛkstēg(ɥ)ibl], *a.* i extinguishable, unquenchable (fire, thirst).

inextricable [inɛkstrikabl], *a.* inextricable; a

-ment.

infaillibilité [ɛ̃fajibilite], *s.f.* infallibility.

infaillible [ɛ̃fajibl], *a.* infallible. 1. unerring. 2. certain, sure, unfailing (remedy, etc.); *adv.* -ment.

infaisable [ɛ̃fəzabl], *a.* unfeasible; **c'est i.**, it can't be done.

infâme [ɛ̃fɑ:m], *a.* infamous; unspeakable.

infamie [ɛ̃fami], *s.f.* 1. infamy, dishonour. 2. foul deed; shabby trick.

infanterie [ɛ̃fɑ̃tri], *s.f.* infantry; **i. aéroportée**, airborne infantry.

infantile [ɛ̃fɑ̃til], *a.* infantile (disease); **psychiatrie i.**, child psychiatry.

infantilisme [ɛ̃fɑ̃tilism], *s.m.* retarded development.

infarctus [ɛ̃farkty:s], *s.m. Med:* **i. du myocarde**, coronary thrombosis.

infatigable [ɛ̃fatigabl], *a.* indefatigable, untiring, tireless; *adv.* -ment.

infatuation [ɛ̃fatɥasjɔ̃], *s.f.* self-conceit.

infect [ɛ̃fɛkt], *a.* stinking; foul; **odeur infecte**, stench; *F:* **temps i.**, filthy weather.

infect|**er** [ɛ̃fɛkte], *v.tr.* 1. to infect (**de**, with). 2. to pollute, taint; *a.* -ieux, -ieuse, infectious; *s.f.* -ion.

inférer [ɛ̃fere], *v.tr.* (**j'infère;** *fu.* **j'inférerai**) to infer (**de**, from).

inférieur, -eure [ɛ̃ferjœːr], *a.* inferior. 1. (*a*) (*in place or amount*) lower; (*b*) (*in quality*) poor (goods); (*c*) (*in position*) **d'un rang i.**, of a lower rank. 2. **i. à**, inferior to; below. 3. *s.* inferior.

infériorité [ɛ̃ferjorite], *s.f.* inferiority; *Psy:* **complexe d'i.**, inferiority complex.

infernal, -aux [ɛ̃fɛrnal, -o], *a.* infernal; *adv.* -ment.

infertile [ɛ̃fɛrtil], *a.* infertile, unfruitful, barren.

infester [ɛ̃fɛste], *v.tr.* to infest, overrun.

infidèle [ɛ̃fidɛl]. 1. *a.* unfaithful; disloyal; false; misleading; **mémoire i.**, untrustworthy memory. 2. *s.* infidel.

infidélité [ɛ̃fidelite], *s.f.* infidelity (**envers**, to); (*a*) unfaithfulness; (*b*) inaccuracy (of translation, etc.); (*c*) (religious) unbelief.

infiltr|**er (s')** [sɛ̃filtre], *v.pr.* 1. to percolate, seep (**dans**, into); to filter, soak in. 2. to infiltrate; *s.f.* -ation.

infime [ɛ̃fim], *a.* 1. lowly, mean (rank, etc.). 2. *F:* tiny, minute.

infini [ɛ̃fini]. 1. *a.* infinite; boundless, immeasurable (space); innumerable. 2. *s.m.* **l'i.**, the infinite; *adv.phr.* **à l'i.**, to infinity, boundlessly; *adv.* -ment, infinitely; **je regrette infiniment**, I'm terribly sorry.

infinité [ɛ̃finite], *s.f.* (*a*) *Mth: etc:* infinity; (*b*) **l'i. de l'espace**, the boundlessness of space; **une i. de raisons**, endless reasons.

infinitésimal, -aux [ɛ̃finitezimal, -o], *a.* infinitesimal.

infinitif, -ive [ɛ̃finitif, -iːv], *a.* & *s.m. Gram:* infinitive (mood).

infirme [ɛ̃firm]. 1. *a.* (*a*) infirm; (*b*) disabled, crippled; (*c*) weak, feeble, frail. 2. *s.* (*a*) invalid; (*b*) cripple.

infirm|**erie** [ɛ̃firməri], *s.f.* hospital, infirmary; sick bay; *s.* -ier, -ière, nurse.

infirmité [ɛ̃firmite], *s.f.* (*a*) infirmity (of body or mind); (*b*) physical disability.

inflamm|**ation** [ɛ̃flamasjɔ̃], *s.f.* 1. ignition, firing (of explosives). 2. *Med:* inflammation; *a.* -able, inflammable, *N.Am:* flammable.

inflation [ɛ̃flasjɔ̃], *s.f. Pol.Ec:* inflation; *s.m.* -nisme, inflationism; *a.* -niste.

inflexibilité [ɛ̃flɛksibilite], *s.f.* inflexibility.

inflexible [ɛ̃flɛksibl], *a.* inflexible, unbending; unyielding (will); rigid (attitude); **i. à toutes les prières**, unmoved by all entreaties; *adv.* -ment.

infliger [ɛ̃fliʒe], *v.tr.* (**n. infligeons**) to inflict.

influ|**encer** [ɛ̃flyɑ̃se], *v.tr.* (**n. influençons**) to influence; to put pressure (up)on (s.o.); *s.f.* -ence; *a.* -ent, influential.

information [ɛ̃fɔrmasjɔ̃], *s.f.* (*a*) inquiry; *Jur:* **ouvrir une i.**, to begin legal proceedings; **prendre des informations (sur qn)**, to make inquiries (about s.o.); **service d'informations**, information service; **Ministère de l'I.**, Ministry of Information; *Rad: T.V:* pl. news (bulletin); (*b*) **je vous envoie, pour votre i. . . .**, I am sending you for your information . . .; (*c*) (*computers, radar*) (**éléments d')i.**, data (for computer processing); **traitement de l'i.**, data processing.

informatique [ɛ̃fɔrmatik]. 1. *s.f.* **l'i.**, data processing (industry); **le monde de l'i.**, the computer world. 2. *a.* **réseau i.**, information network.

informe [ɛ̃fɔrm], *a.* (*a*) formless, shapeless; (*b*) ill-formed; mis-shapen.

inform|**er** [ɛ̃fɔrme]. 1. *v.tr.* **i. qn de qch.**, to inform s.o. of sth.; **mal informé**, misinformed. 2. *v.i. Jur:* **i. sur un crime, contre qn**, to investigate a crime, s.o.; **i. contre qn**, to inform against s.o.; *s.* -ateur, -atrice, informant; *a.* -atif, -ative.

s'informer, to make inquiries.

infortune [ɛ̃fɔrtyn], *s.f.* misfortune, bad luck.

infortuné [ɛ̃fɔrtyne], *a.* unfortunate, unlucky.

infraction [ɛ̃fraksjɔ̃], *s.f.* infraction. 1. infringement. 2. breach (of law, etc.).

infranchissable [ɛ̃frɑ̃ʃisabl], *a.* impassable, insuperable (difficulty).

infrasonore [ɛ̃frasɔnɔːr], *a.* infrasonic.

infréquent [ɛ̃frekɑ̃], *a.* infrequent, rare.

infroissable [ɛ̃frwasabl], *a. Cl: etc:* crease-resisting; uncrushable.

infructueu|**x, -euse** [ɛ̃fryktɥø, -øːz], *a.* (*a*) unfruitful, barren; (*b*) fruitless, unavailing; (*c*) un-

profitable; *adv.* -**sement.**
infuser [ɛ̃fyze], *v.tr.* to infuse. **1.** to instil (à, into).
2. to steep, macerate.
s'infuser, to infuse; (*of tea*) to draw.
infusion [ɛ̃fyzjɔ̃], *s.f.* infusion; decoction; **i. de
tilleul**, lime-blossom tea.
ingénier (s') [sɛ̃ʒenje], *v.pr.* **s'i. à faire qch.**, to
exercise one's wits to do sth.
ingénieur [ɛ̃ʒenjœːr], *s.m.* (graduate) engineer; **i.
conseil**, consulting engineer; **i. des travaux
publics**, civil engineer.
ingénieu|x, -**euse** [ɛ̃ʒenjø, -øːz], *a.* ingenious,
clever; *adv.* -**sement.**
ingéniosité [ɛ̃ʒenjɔzite], *s.f.* ingenuity;
cleverness.
ingénu [ɛ̃ʒeny], *a.* ingenuous, artless, naive, unsophisticated; **faire l'i.**, to affect simplicity;
adv. -**ment.**
ingénuité [ɛ̃ʒenɥite], *s.f.* ingenuousness,
artlessness; simplicity.
ingérer (s') [sɛ̃ʒere], *v.pr.* **(je m'ingère, n.n. in-
gérons) s'i. dans une affaire**, to interfere in,
meddle with, a matter.
ingouvernable [ɛ̃guvɛrnabl], *a.* ungovernable.
ingrat [ɛ̃gra], *a.* **1.** ungrateful **(envers, to,
towards). 2.** unprofitable; thankless (soil,
task). **3.** (*a*) unpleasing, repellent; (*b*) **l'âge i.,**
the awkward age. **4.** *s.* ungrateful, heartless,
person.
ingratitude [ɛ̃gratityd], *s.f.* **1.** ingratitude, un-
gratefulness. **2.** thanklessness (of task).
ingrédient [ɛ̃gredjã], *s.m.* ingredient,
constituent.
inguérissable [ɛ̃gerisabl], *a.* (*a*) incurable; (*b*)
inconsolable (grief).
inhabile [inabil], *a.* (*a*) unfitted (à, to); **i. à voter,**
not qualified to vote; (*b*) clumsy; incompetent
(workman, etc.); *adv.* -**ment,** awkwardly.
inhabitable [inabitabl], *a.* uninhabitable.
inhabité [inabite], *a.* uninhabited.
inhabitué [inabitɥe], *a.* unaccustomed (à, to).
inhaler [inale], *v.tr.* to inhale.
inhérent [inerã], *a.* inherent (à, in).
inhospitalier, -**ière** [inɔspitalje, -jɛːr], *a.*
inhospitable.
inhumain [inymɛ̃], *a.* inhuman; unfeeling.
inhumanité [inymanite], *s.f.* inhumanity.
inimaginable [inimaʒinabl], *a.* unimaginable;
unthinkable.
inimitable [inimitabl], *a.* inimitable; matchless;
adv. -**ment.**
inimité [inimite], *a.* never yet imitated.
inimitié [inimitje], *s.f.* enmity, hostility, ill-
feeling.
inintellig|ent [inɛ̃tɛl(l)iʒã], *a.* unintelligent; ob-
tuse; *adv.* -**emment.**
inintelligible [inɛ̃tɛl(l)iʒibl], *a.* unintelligible;
adv. -**ment.**
ininterrompu [inɛ̃tɛrɔ̃py], *a.* uninterrupted;

unbroken.
inique [inik], *a.* iniquitous; *adv.* -**ment.**
iniquité [inikite], *s.f.* iniquity.
initial, -**aux** [inisjal, -o]. **1.** *a.* initial (letter, price
etc.); starting. **2.** *s.f.* **initiale,** initial (letter); *adv*
-**ement.**
initia|tion [inisjasjɔ̃], *s.f.* initiation (à, into); *a.* **&**
s. -**teur**, -**trice,** (i) initiatory; (ii) initiator.
initiative [inisjatiːv], *s.f.* initiative; **syndicat d'i.**
tourist bureau.
initier [inisje], *v.tr.* to initiate (s.o.) (à, in); **êtr**
initié, *F:* to be in the know.
s'initier, to learn; **s'i. aux détails d'un com**
merce, to get the hang of a business.
injecter [ɛ̃ʒɛkte], *v.tr.* to inject.
s'injecter, (*of eyes*) to become bloodshot.
injection [ɛ̃ʒɛksjɔ̃], *s.f.* injection; (*a*) *E:* **moteu**
à i. (directe), (direct) injection engine; (*b*) **i. in**
traveineuse, intravenous injection; (*c*) *Const*
grouting.
injonction [ɛ̃ʒɔ̃ksjɔ̃], *s.f. Jur:* injunction.
injudicieu|x, -**euse** [ɛ̃ʒydisjø, -øːz], *a.* in
judicious; *adv.* -**sement.**
injure [ɛ̃ʒyːr], *s.f.* **1.** wrong, injury. **2.** insult; *p*
abuse.
injuri|er [ɛ̃ʒyrje], *v.tr.* to abuse (s.o.); to cal
(s.o.) names; *a.* -**eux,** -**euse,** abusive, in
sulting; *adv.* -**eusement.**
injuste [ɛ̃ʒyst], *a.* unjust, unfair; *adv.* -**ment.**
injustice [ɛ̃ʒystis], *s.f.* injustice, unfairnes
(envers, towards).
injustifiable [ɛ̃ʒystifjabl], *a.* unjustifiable
unwarrantable.
injustifié [ɛ̃ʒystifje], *a.* unjustified, unwarrante
inlassable [ɛ̃lasabl], *a.* untiring, unwearyin
(efforts); tireless (man); *adv.* -**ment.**
inné [in(n)e], *a.* innate, inborn.
innoc|ence [inɔsãːs], *s.f.* innocence; (*a*
guiltlessness; (*b*) simplicity; naïveté; (*a*
harmlessness; *a.* **&** *s.* -**ent,** -**ente; a** d
-**emment.**
innombrable [in(n)ɔ̃brabl], *a.* innumerabl
numberless, countless.
innova|tion [in(n)ɔvasjɔ̃], *s.f.* innovation; *a.*
s. -**teur**, -**trice,** (i) innovative; (ii) innovator.
inoccupé [inɔkype], *a.* unoccupied. **1.** idle.
vacant; uninhabited (house).
inocul|er [inɔkyle], *v.tr.* to inoculate; *s.*
-**ation.**
inodore [inɔdɔːr], *a.* odourless; scentless.
inoffens|if, -**ive** [inɔfãsif, -iːv], *a.* inoffensiv
harmless; *adv.* -**ivement.**
inond|er [inɔ̃de], *v.tr.* to inundate, flood (field
etc.); to glut (market); *s.f.* -**ation,** flood.
inopérable [inɔperabl], *a. Med:* inoperab
(tumour, patient).
inopiné [inɔpine], *a.* sudden, unexpected; *a*
-**ment.**
inopport|un, -**une** [inɔpɔrtœ̃, -yːn], *a.* **1.** ino

portune. 2. unseasonable, ill-timed; *adv.*
-unément.

inorganique [inɔrganik], *a.* inorganic.

inoubliable [inubliabl], *a.* unforgettable.

inouï [inui, inwi], *a.* unheard of; (*a*) unparalleled,
extraordinary (behaviour); (*b*) *F:* **il est i.,** he's
incredible, he's outrageous.

inox [inɔks], *a. & s.m. F:* (acier) i., stainless
(steel).

inoxydable [inɔksidabl], *a.* rustproof; **acier i.,**
s.m. inoxydable, stainless steel.

inqualifiable [ɛ̃kalifjabl], *a.* beyond words; unspeakable (behaviour).

inquiet, -ète [ɛ̃kjɛ, -ɛt], *a.* (*a*) restless, fidgety;
(*b*) anxious, uneasy.

inquiét|er [ɛ̃kjete], *v.tr.* (**j'inquiète; j'inquiéterai**)
to worry (s.o.); *s.f.* -**ude,** anxiety.

s'inquiéter, to worry.

insaisissable [ɛ̃sɛzisabl], *a.* (*a*) elusive; (*b*)
imperceptible.

insatiable [ɛ̃sasjabl], *a.* insatiable; *adv.* -**ment.**

inscription [ɛ̃skripsjɔ̃], *s.f.* **1.** (*a*) entering,
recording (in diary, etc.); (*b*) registration,
enrolment; **feuille d'i.,** entry form. **2.** (*a*) inscription (on tomb); entry (in account book);
(*b*) directions (on signpost); notice.

inscrire [ɛ̃skriːr], *v.tr.* (*pr.p.* **inscrivant;** *p.p.* **inscrit;** *p.h.* **j'inscrivis**) **1.** (*a*) to inscribe, write
down; (*b*) to register; to enter (s.o.'s) name; (*c*)
Ind: **i.** (**un employé**) **à l'arrivée, à la sortie,** to
clock (an employee) in, out. **2.** to inscribe,
engrave (epitaph).

s'inscrire, to put down one's name.

inscrutable [ɛ̃skrytabl], *a.* inscrutable; *adv.*
-**ment.**

insect|e [ɛ̃sɛkt], *s.m.* insect; *s.m.* -**icide,**
insecticide.

insécurité [ɛ̃sekyrite], *s.f.* insecurity.

insensé, -ée [ɛ̃sɑ̃se], *a.* (*a*) mad, insane; *s.* madman, -woman; (*b*) senseless, foolish; (*c*) rash,
extravagant, wild (scheme, etc.).

insensibilis|er [ɛ̃sɑ̃sibilize], *v.tr. Med:* to
anaesthetize; *s.f.* -**ation.**

insens|ibilité [ɛ̃sɑ̃sibilite], *s.f.* (*a*) insen-
sitiveness; (*b*) indifference, callousness
(**envers,** to); *a.* -**ible,** insensitive; indifferent;
imperceptible; *adv.* -**iblement.**

inséparable [ɛ̃separabl], *a.* **1.** inseparable. **2.**
s.m.pl. Orn: love-birds.

insérer [ɛ̃sere], *v.tr.* (**j'insère; j'insérerai**) to insert; *s.f.* **insertion.**

insidieu|x, -euse [ɛ̃sidjø, -øːz], *a.* insidious; *adv.*
-**sement.**

insigne¹ [ɛ̃siɲ], *a.* **1.** distinguished, remarkable
(**par,** for); **faveur i.,** signal favour. **2.** *Pej:*
notorious, arrant, out and out (liar, etc.).

insigne², *s.m.* distinguishing mark; badge.

insignifi|ance [ɛ̃siɲifjɑ̃s], *s.f.* insignificance,
unimportance; *a.* -**ant,** insignificant.

insinu|er [ɛ̃sinɥe], *v.tr.* to insinuate. **1.** to insert
(gently); **i. le doigt dans une plaie,** to probe a
wound with one's finger. **2.** to hint at (sth.); **que
voulez-vous i.?** what are you hinting, *F:* getting, at? *a.* -**ant,** insinuating; *s.f.* -**ation.**

s'insinuer, to penetrate; to creep (in); to worm
one's way (through, into).

insipide [ɛ̃sipid], *a.* insipid; (*a*) tasteless; (*b*) dull,
vapid, flat; tame (story).

insist|er [ɛ̃siste], *v.i.* to insist; **i. sur un fait,** to
dwell, lay stress, (up)on a fact; *s.f.* -**ance,**
insistence.

insociable [ɛ̃sɔsjabl], *a.* unsociable.

insolation [ɛ̃sɔlasjɔ̃], *s.f.* (*a*) sunstroke; (*b*) a
touch of the sun.

insol|ence [ɛ̃sɔlɑ̃ːs], *s.f.* insolence, imper-
tinence; *a.* -**ent;** *adv.* -**emment** [ɛ̃sɔlamɑ̃].

insolite [ɛ̃sɔlit], *a.* unusual; strange, odd,
peculiar (noises, words).

insoluble [ɛ̃sɔlybl], *a.* insoluble (substance,
problem); **situation i.,** deadlock.

insolvable [ɛ̃sɔlvabl], *a. Com:* insolvent.

insomniaque [ɛ̃sɔmnjak]. **1.** *a.* suffering from
insomnia. **2.** *s.m. & f.* insomniac.

insomnie [ɛ̃sɔmni], *s.f.* insomnia, sleeplessness;
nuit d'i., sleepless night.

insondable [ɛ̃sɔ̃dabl], *a.* unfathomable.

insonore [ɛ̃sɔnɔːr], *a.* sound-proof, insulating
(material, etc.).

insonoris|er [ɛ̃sɔnɔrize], *v.tr. Cin: Rad: etc:* to
sound-proof; *s.f.* -**ation,** sound-proofing.

insouci|ance [ɛ̃susjɑ̃ːs], *s.f.* (*a*) unconcern; (*b*)
thoughtlessness, casualness; *a.* -**ant;** *adv.*
-**amment** [ɛ̃susjamɑ̃], *a.* -**eux, -euse,**
heedless, casual; *adv.* -**eusement.**

insoupçonné [ɛ̃supsɔne], *a.* unsuspected (**de,**
by, of).

insoutenable [ɛ̃sutnabl], *a.* **1.** untenable; indefensible. **2.** unbearable.

inspec|ter [ɛ̃spɛkte], *v.tr.* to inspect; *s.f.* -**tion,**
inspection.

inspecteur, -trice [ɛ̃spɛktœːr, -tris], *s.* inspector
(of schools, police); overseer (of works); shopwalker; surveyor (of mines, etc.).

inspir|er [ɛ̃spire], *v.tr.* to inspire. **1. i. le respect,**
to inspire respect. **2.** to inhale, to breathe in; *a.*
-**ateur, -atrice,** inspiring (thought, etc.); *s.f.*
-**ation,** inspiration.

instabilité [ɛ̃stabilite], *s.f.* instability.

instable [ɛ̃stabl], *a.* unstable; shaky; unsteady;
unreliable.

install|er [ɛ̃stale], *v.tr.* (*a*) to install; (*b*) to set up;
to fit up, equip; *s.f.* -**ation,** equipment; installation; plant.

s'installer, to settle (down); to make oneself at
home; **s'i. comme médecin,** to set up as a
doctor.

instance [ɛ̃stɑ̃ːs], *s.f.* (*a*) *pl.* requests, entreaties;
(*b*) *Jur:* action, suit; **tribunal d'i.**

= magistrate's court.

inst|ant¹ [ɛ̃stɑ̃], *a.* pressing, urgent; *adv.* -**am-ment** [ɛ̃stamɑ̃].

instant², *s.m.* moment, instant; **par instants**, off and on; **un i.!** wait a moment!

instantané [ɛ̃stɑ̃tane]. 1. *a.* instantaneous. 2. *s.m. Phot:* snapshot; *adv.* -**ment**.

instaur|er [ɛ̃stɔre], *v.tr.* to found, to set up; *s.* -**ateur**, -**atrice**, founder; *s.f.* -**ation**, founding (of republic, etc.).

instiga|tion [ɛ̃stigasjɔ̃], *s.f.* instigation, incitement; *s.* -**teur**, -**trice**, instigator.

instinct [ɛ̃stɛ̃], *s.m.* instinct; **d'i.**, instinctively; *a.* -**if**, -**ive**, instinctive; *adv.* -**ivement**.

institu|er [ɛ̃stitɥe], *v.tr.* to institute; (*a*) to establish, to set up, to found (an institution, etc.); **i. une enquête**, to institute an inquiry; (*b*) to appoint (official); *s.f.* -**tion**.

institut [ɛ̃stity], *s.m.* institute, institution; **l'I. (de France)**, the Institute (composed of five Academies).

instituteur, -trice [ɛ̃stitytœ:r, -tris], *s.* (primary school) teacher.

instruc|tion [ɛ̃stryksjɔ̃], *s.f.* instruction. 1. *pl.* instructions, directions, orders. 2. education; **avoir de l'i.**, to be well educated. 3. *Jur:* preliminary investigation (of case); **juge d'i.**, examining magistrate; *s.m.* -**teur**; *a.* -**tif**, -**tive**.

instruire [ɛ̃strɥi:r], *v.tr.* (*pr.p.* **instruisant; p.p. instruit; p.h. j'instruisis**) 1. **i. qn de qch.**, to inform s.o. of sth. 2. to teach, instruct.

instruit [ɛ̃strɥi], *a.* educated; well-read.

instrument [ɛ̃strymɑ̃], *s.m.* (*a*) instrument, implement; (*b*) (musical) instrument; (*c*) (legal) instrument (deed, contract, writ, etc.).

instrument|er [ɛ̃strymɑ̃te]. 1. *v.i. Jur:* to order (legal) instrument (**contre qn**, against s.o.). 2. *v.tr. Mus:* to score, orchestrate (opera, etc.); *a.* -**al**, -**aux**, instrumental; *s.f.* -**ation**, scoring; *s.m. & f.* -**iste**, instrumentalist.

insu [ɛ̃sy], *s.m.* **à l'i. de qn**, without s.o.'s knowledge, without s.o. knowing.

insubor|dination [ɛ̃sybɔrdinasjɔ̃], *s.f.* insubordination; *a.* -**donné**, insubordinate.

insuccès [ɛ̃syksɛ], *s.m.* failure; miscarriage (of plan).

insuffis|ance [ɛ̃syfizɑ̃:s], *s.f.* 1. insufficiency; inadequacy. 2. incapacity, incompetence, inefficiency (of staff); *a.* -**ant**; *adv.* -**amment**.

insulaire [ɛ̃sylɛ:r]. 1. *a.* insular. 2. *s.* islander.

insuline [ɛ̃sylin], *s.f.* insulin.

insulte [ɛ̃sylt], *s.f.* insult.

insult|er [ɛ̃sylte], *v.tr.* to insult, affront (s.o.); *a.* -**ant**, offensive.

insupportable [ɛ̃sypɔrtabl], *a.* unbearable, unendurable; intolerable (pain, conduct); **il est i.!** he's the limit!

insurgé, -ée [ɛ̃syrʒe], *s.* insurgent, rebel.

insurger (s') [sɛ̃syrʒe], *v.pr.* (**n. n. insurgeons**) to rise (in rebellion); to revolt.

insurmontable [ɛ̃syrmɔ̃tabl], *a.* insurmountable, insuperable (obstacle); unconquerable (aversion).

insurrection [ɛ̃syr(r)ɛksjɔ̃], *s.f.* insurrection, rising.

intact [ɛ̃takt], *a.* intact; (*a*) untouched; (*b*) unsullied, unblemished (reputation, etc.).

intangible [ɛ̃tɑ̃ʒibl], *a.* intangible.

intarissable [ɛ̃tarisabl], *a.* inexhaustible, unfailing (well, spring, imagination); endless (chatter).

intégral, -aux [ɛ̃tegral, -o], *a.* integral, entire whole; **paiement i.**, payment in full; *adv.* -**ement**, wholly, in full.

intégrant [ɛ̃tegrɑ̃], *a.* integral (part, etc.); **faire partie intégrante de . . .**, to be part and parcel of . . ..

intégrité [ɛ̃tegrite], *s.f.* integrity; uprightness honesty.

intellect [ɛ̃tɛl(l)ɛkt], *s.m.* intellect, understanding; *a. & s.* -**uel**, -**uelle**, intellectual; *adv.* -**uellement**.

intellig|ence [ɛ̃teliʒɑ̃:s], *s.f.* 1. understanding comprehension. 2. intelligence, intellect. 3 **vivre en bonne i. avec qn**, to live on good term with s.o.; **être d'i. avec qn**, to have an understanding with s.o., to be in collusion wit s.o.; *a.* -**ent**, intelligent; clever; *adv.* -**emmen** [ɛ̃teliʒamɑ̃].

intelligible [ɛ̃teliʒibl], *a.* (*a*) intelligible, un derstandable; (*b*) clear, distinct; *adv.* -**ment**.

intempér|ance [ɛ̃tɑ̃perɑ̃:s], *s.f.* intemperance *a.* -**ant**, intemperate.

intempérie [ɛ̃tɑ̃peri], *s.f. usu. pl.* bad weather **imperméable aux intempéries**, weather-proof

intempestif, -ive [ɛ̃tɑ̃pɛstif, -i:v], *a.* untimel (remark); inopportune (arrival).

intenable [ɛ̃tnabl], *a.* untenable.

intendant [ɛ̃tɑ̃dɑ̃], *s.m.* (*a*) steward, bailiff; (*b* manager; (*c*) bursar.

intense [ɛ̃tɑ̃:s], *a.* intense (cold); severe (pain deep (colour); intensive (propaganda).

intensifier [ɛ̃tɑ̃sifje], *v.tr.* (*p.d. & pr.sub.* **n. inte sifiions**) to intensify.

intensité [ɛ̃tɑ̃site], *s.f.* intensity; force (of wind depth (of colour); strength (of current).

intention [ɛ̃tɑ̃sjɔ̃], *s.f.* intention; (*a*) purpos design; (*b*) will, wish; **à l'i. de**, for (the sake of

intentionné [ɛ̃tɑ̃sjɔne], *a.* (*used only in:*) **bien mal i.**, well-, ill-, disposed (**envers qn**, towar s.o.).

intentionnel, -elle [ɛ̃tɑ̃sjɔnɛl], *a.* intentiona deliberate; *adv.* -**lement**.

inter [ɛ̃tɛ:r], *s.m.* 1. *P. T. T: F:* trunks; **appeler l'** to make a trunk call, a long distance call. 2. *S F:* **i. gauche**, inside left.

interaction [ɛ̃tɛraksjɔ̃], *s.f.* reciprocal action.

interarmes [ɛ̃terarm], *a.inv. Mil:* combined (staff, operations).
interastral, -aux [ɛ̃terastral, -o], *a.* interstellar (space).
intercéder [ɛ̃tersede], *v.i.* (**j'intercède**) to intercede (**auprès de,** with).
intercepter [ɛ̃tersɛpte], *v.tr.* to intercept; to cut off (steam); to shut out (light).
interception [ɛ̃tersɛpsjɔ̃], *s.f.* interception; *Rad:* **i. des émissions,** monitoring; *Av:* **raid d'i.,** intruder raid.
interconnecter [ɛ̃tɛrkɔnɛkte], *v.tr. El:* to connect up (circuits).
intercontinental, -aux [ɛ̃tɛrkɔ̃tinɑ̃tal, -o], *a.* intercontinental; **engin i.,** intercontinental ballistic missile.
interdiction [ɛ̃terdiksjɔ̃], *s.f.* prohibition.
interdire [ɛ̃terdiːr], *v.tr. (conj. like* DIRE, *except pr.ind. and imp.* **interdisez**) **1.** to forbid, prohibit; *P.N:* '**entrée interdite (au public),**' 'no admittance'; '**passage interdit,**' 'no thoroughfare'; **i. à qn de faire qch.,** to forbid s.o. to do sth.; *Av:* **i. (un avion) de vol,** to ground (an aircraft). **2.** to disconcert, bewilder.
interdit [ɛ̃terdi], *a.* disconcerted; taken aback.
intéressant [ɛ̃teresɑ̃], *a.* interesting; **prix intéressants,** attractive prices.
intéressé [ɛ̃teresе], *a.* **1.** interested; concerned; **le premier i.,** (the person) most directly affected. **2.** selfish.
intéresser [ɛ̃terese], *v.tr.* to interest; *(a)* to give (s.o.) a financial interest; *(b)* to affect, concern; *(c)* to be interesting to; *(d)* **i. qn à une cause,** to interest s.o. in a cause.
s'intéresser, to become interested (à, in), to put money (**dans,** into); to take an interest (**à qn, qch.,** in s.o., sth.).
intérêt [ɛ̃terɛ], *s.m.* interest. **1.** share, stake (in business). **2.** advantage, benefit; **il y a i. à . . .,** it is desirable to . . .; *Rail:* **ligne d'i. local,** branch-line. **3.** (feeling of) interest; **porter i. à qn,** to take an interest in s.o. **4.** *Fin:* **i. composé,** compound interest.
intérieur [ɛ̃terjœːr]. **1.** *a. (a)* interior; inner (room); internal (part, etc.); *(b)* inward (feelings); *(c)* domestic (administration). **2.** *s.m. (a)* interior, inside; **à l'i.,** inside, on the inside; *(b)* home, house; **vie d'i.,** home life; **femme d'i.,** domesticated woman; *(c) Adm:* **le Ministère de l'I.** = the Home Office; *(d) Sp:* **i. gauche,** inside left; *adv.* **-ement.**
intérim [ɛ̃terim], *s.m.* interim; **faire l'i. (de qn),** to deputize (for s.o.); **assurer l'i.,** to carry on (during s.o.'s absence); to act as locum (tenens).
interjection [ɛ̃terʒɛksjɔ̃], *s.f.* interjection.
interlocuteur, -trice [ɛ̃terlɔkytœːr, -tris], *s.* speaker (in a conversation); **mon i.,** the person with whom I was speaking, *F:* the person I was speaking to.
interloquer [ɛ̃terlɔke], *v.tr.* to disconcert (s.o.).
intermède [ɛ̃termɛd], *s.m.* **1.** interruption, interval. **2.** *Th:* interlude.
intermédiaire [ɛ̃termedjɛːr]. **1.** *a.* intermediate, intervening (state, time). **2.** *s.m.* agent, intermediary; *Com:* middleman. **3.** *s.m.* intermediary, agency.
interminable [ɛ̃terminabl], *a.* interminable; endless; *adv.* **-ment.**
intermittent [ɛ̃termitɑ̃], *a.* intermittent; irregular (pulse); casual (worker).
internat [ɛ̃terna], *s.m.* **1.** living-in (system, period); resident medical studentship. **2.** boarding school.
international, -aux [ɛ̃ternasjɔnal, -o], *a.* international.
interne [ɛ̃tern]. **1.** *a.* internal. **2.** *s. (a) Sch:* boarder; *(b) =* house surgeon, *N.Am:* intern.
intern|er [ɛ̃terne], *v.tr.* to intern; *s.m.* **-ement,** internment.
interpeller [ɛ̃terpele], *v.tr.* to call out to (s.o.); *(of sentry)* to challenge (s.o.); *Pol:* to heckle; *Jur:* to call on (s.o.) to answer.
interphone [ɛ̃terfɔn], *s.m.* house telephone; intercom.
interplanétaire [ɛ̃terplanetɛːr], *a.* interplanetary; **fusée i.,** space rocket.
interpoler [ɛ̃terpɔle], *v.tr.* to interpolate.
interposer [ɛ̃terpoze], *v.tr.* to interpose.
s'interposer, to intervene.
interprète [ɛ̃terprɛt], *s.m. & f.* interpreter.
interprét|er [ɛ̃terprete], *v.tr.* (**j'interprète; j'interpréterai**) to interpret; *s.f.* **-ation.**
interroga|tion [ɛ̃terɔgasjɔ̃], *s.f.* interrogation. **1.** questioning; **point d'i.,** question-mark. **2.** question, query, enquiry; *Sch:* oral test, *F:* oral; **i. écrite,** (written) paper; *a. & s.* **-teur, -trice,** (i) interrogatory; (ii) questioner; *a.* **-tif, -tive;** *s.m.* **-toire,** (cross-)examination.
interroger [ɛ̃terɔʒe], *v.tr.* (**n. interrogeons**) to examine (candidate), interrogate (witness).
interrompre [ɛ̃terɔ̃pr], *v.tr. (conj. like* ROMPRE) *(a)* to interrupt; *(b)* to intercept; *(c)* to stop, suspend (traffic); to break (journey).
s'interrompre, to break off.
interrompu [ɛ̃terɔ̃py], *a.* **sommeil i.,** broken sleep.
interrup|tion [ɛ̃terypsjɔ̃], *s.f. (a)* interruption; *(b)* stoppage; break(ing off); *El:* disconnection; *s.m. El:* **-teur,** switch.
intersection [ɛ̃tersɛksjɔ̃], *s.f. (a)* intersection; *(b)* crossing (of roads).
interstice [ɛ̃terstis], *s.m.* interstice; chink.
interurbain [ɛ̃teryrbɛ̃], *s.m. P.T.T:* **appeler l'i.,** to make a trunk call, a long distance call.
intervalle [ɛ̃terval], *s.m.* interval. **1.** distance, gap, space (**entre,** between). **2.** period (of time); **dans l'i.,** in the meantime.

intervenir [ɛ̃tɛrvəni:r], *v.i.* (*conj. like* TENIR; *aux.* être) 1. to intervene; (*a*) to interpose, to step in, *F:* to butt in; (*b*) to interfere. 2. *impers.* to happen, occur; **un changement est intervenu**, a change has taken place.

intervention [ɛ̃tɛrvɑ̃sjɔ̃], *s.f.* 1. intervening, intervention; *Med:* **i. chirurgicale,** operation; **offre d'i.,** offer of mediation. 2. interference.

interviewer[1] [ɛ̃tɛrvju(v)e], *v.tr.* to interview (s.o.).

interviewer[2] [ɛ̃tɛrvju(v)œ:r], *s.m.* interviewer.

intestin [ɛ̃tɛstɛ̃], *s.m. Anat:* intestine, bowel, gut; **les intestins,** the bowels.

intime [ɛ̃tim], *a.* intimate. 1. inward; deep-seated (thoughts, fears). 2. close (friend); cosy (room); *s.* **un, une, i.,** an intimate friend; *adv.* **-ment.**

intimider [ɛ̃timide], *v.tr.* to intimidate; to make (s.o.) shy, self-conscious; **nullement intimidé,** nothing daunted; *a.* **-ant,** intimidating; awe-inspiring; *s.f.* **-ation.**

intimité [ɛ̃timite], *s.f.* intimacy; (*a*) closeness (of friendship); (*b*) privacy; **dans l'i.,** in private (life).

intituler [ɛ̃tityle], *v.tr.* to call, to give a title to; **livre intitulé** *Concise Dictionary,* book entitled *Concise Dictionary.*

s'intituler, (*a*) to be called, entitled; **ce livre s'intitule** *Concise Dictionary,* this book is entitled *Concise Dictionary;* (*b*) *often Pej:* to call oneself; **s'i. baron,** to call oneself a baron.

intolérable [ɛ̃tɔlerabl], *a.* intolerable, unbearable; *adv.* **-ment.**

intolérance [ɛ̃tɔlerɑ̃:s], *s.f.* intolerance; *a.* **-ant.**

intoxication [ɛ̃tɔksikasjɔ̃], *s.f.* poisoning; **i. alimentaire,** food poisoning.

intoxiquer [ɛ̃tɔksike], *v.tr. Med:* to poison; to give (s.o.) food poisoning.

intraitable [ɛ̃trɛtabl], *a.* (*a*) intractable, unmanageable; (*b*) obstinate.

intramusculaire [ɛ̃tramyskylɛ:r], *a. Med:* intramuscular (injection).

intransigeant [ɛ̃trɑ̃ziʒɑ̃], *a.* uncompromising, strict (moral code); intransigent (in politics); **sur ce point il est i.,** on this point he's adamant.

intransitif, -ive [ɛ̃trɑ̃sitif, -i:v], *a. & s.m. Gram:* intransitive.

intraveineux, -euse [ɛ̃travenø, -ø:z], *a. Med:* intravenous (injection).

intrépide [ɛ̃trepid], *a.* intrepid, dauntless, fearless; *adv.* **-ment.**

intrépidité [ɛ̃trepidite], *s.f.* fearlessness.

intrigant [ɛ̃trigɑ̃]. 1. *a.* intriguing, scheming. 2. *s.* schemer, wire-puller.

intrigue [ɛ̃trig], *s.f.* intrigue. 1. (*a*) plot, scheme; (*b*) (love-)affair. 2. plot (of play).

intriguer [ɛ̃trige]. 1. *v.tr.* to puzzle, intrigue. 2. *v.i.* to scheme, plot, intrigue.

introduction [ɛ̃trɔdyksjɔ̃], *s.f.* introduction; *a.* **-toire,** introductory.

introduire [ɛ̃trɔdɥi:r], *v.tr.* (*pr.p.* **introduisant;** *p.p.* **introduit;** *p.h.* **j'introduisis**) to introduce; (*a*) to insert (key in lock, etc.); (*b*) to bring in; to admit, to usher (s.o.) in.

s'introduire, to get in, enter.

introuvable [ɛ̃truvabl], *a.* (*a*) undiscoverable; not to be found; (*b*) matchless, incomparable.

intrus, -use [ɛ̃try, -y:z]. 1. *a.* intruding. 2. *s.* intruder, *F:* gate-crasher.

intrusion [ɛ̃tryzjɔ̃], intrusion.

intuition [ɛ̃tɥisjɔ̃], *s.f.* intuition; *a.* **-tif, -tive,** intuitive.

inusable [inyzabl], *a.* hard-wearing; everlasting.

inusité [inyzite], *a.* (*a*) unusual; (*b*) not in common use.

inutile [inytil], *a.* (*a*) useless, unavailing; vain; (*b*) needless, unnecessary; *adv.* **-ment.**

invaincu [ɛ̃vɛ̃ky], *a.* unconquered, unbeaten.

invalide [ɛ̃valid]. 1. *a.* (*a*) infirm; disabled; (*b*) *Jur:* invalid (document). 2. *s.* (*a*) invalid; (*b*) *s.m.* disabled soldier, pensioner.

invalider [ɛ̃valide], *v.tr. Jur:* to invalidate (will, election); to quash (election); *Med:* to cripple.

invariable [ɛ̃varjabl], *a.* invariable, unvarying; *adv.* **-ment.**

invasion [ɛ̃vazjɔ̃], *s.f.* invasion.

invective [ɛ̃vɛkti:v], *s.f.* (*a*) invective; (*b*) *pl.* abuse.

invectiver [ɛ̃vɛktive]. 1. *v.i.* **i. contre qn,** to inveigh against s.o. 2. *v.tr.* to abuse, to hurl abuse at (s.o.).

invendable [ɛ̃vɑ̃dabl], *a.* unsaleable.

inventaire [ɛ̃vɑ̃tɛ:r], *s.m.* inventory; *Com:* stock list; **faire, dresser, l'i.,** (i) to draw up an inventory; (ii) to take stock.

inventer [ɛ̃vɑ̃te], *v.tr.* to invent; (*a*) to find out discover; **il n'a pas inventé la poudre,** he'll never set the Thames on fire; (*b*) to devise; to make up, *F:* to dream up (story); *s.m.* **-eur, -**ventor; *a.* **-if, -ive,** inventive.

invention [ɛ̃vɑ̃sjɔ̃], *s.f.* 1. (*a*) invention, inventing; **l'i. du téléphone,** the invention of th telephone; (*b*) imagination, inventiveness. 2 (*a*) (*thing invented*) invention, device; (*b* fabrication, lie.

inverse [ɛ̃vɛrs]. 1. *a.* inverse, opposite. 2. *s.m* opposite, reverse; *adv.* **-ment,** conversely.

inverser [ɛ̃vɛrse], *v.tr.* to reverse (current, image, result); *s.m. El:* **-eur,** current reverse *s.f.* **-ion,** inversion, reversal.

invertébré [ɛ̃vɛrtebre], *a. & s.m.* invertebrate.

investigation [ɛ̃vɛstigasjɔ̃], *s.f.* investigatio *a. & s.* **-gateur, -gatrice,** (i) investigating; (i investigator.

investir [ɛ̃vɛsti:r], *v.tr.* to invest (money); *s.m* **-issement,** investment (of capital); *s.m* **-isseur,** *Fin:* investor.

invétéré [ɛ̃vetere], *a.* inveterate.

invincible [ɛ̃vɛ̃sibl], *a.* invincible, unconquerable; *adv.* -ment.

inviolable [ɛ̃vjɔlabl], *a.* inviolable; sacred; *adv.* -ment.

invisibilité [ɛ̃vizibilite], *s.f.* invisibility.

invisible [ɛ̃vizibl], *a.* invisible; *adv.* -ment.

invite [ɛ̃vit], *s.f.* 1. invitation, inducement (à, to). 2. *Cards:* lead; call for a suit; i. d'atouts, call for trumps.

invit|er [ɛ̃vite], *v.tr.* to invite. 1. i. qn à entrer, to invite s.o. in. 2. (*a*) i. le désastre, to court disaster; (*b*) i. qn à faire qch., to request s.o. to do sth.; *s.f.* -ation.

invocation [ɛ̃vɔkasjɔ̃], *s.f.* invocation.

involontaire [ɛ̃vɔlɔ̃tɛːr], *a.* involuntary, unintentional; *adv.* -ment.

invoquer [ɛ̃vɔke], *v.tr.* 1. to call upon, to invoke (the aid of) (the Deity, etc.); i. l'aide de la justice, to appeal to the law. 2. i. une raison, to put forward a reason.

invraisembl|ance [ɛ̃vrɛsɑ̃blɑ̃ːs], *s.f.* unlikeliness, improbability; *a.* -able, improbable; histoire i., tall story; chapeau i., incredible hat.

invulnérabilité [ɛ̃vylnerabilite], *s.f.* invulnerability.

invulnérable [ɛ̃vylnerabl], *a.* invulnerable; *adv.* -ment.

iode [jɔd], *s.m.* iodine.

iodure [jɔdyːr], *s.m. Ch:* iodide.

ion [jɔ̃], *s.m. Ph: Ch:* ion.

ionique [jɔnik], *a. Atom. Ph:* thermionic (valve); moteur-fusée i., ion rocket.

Irak (l') [lirak]. *Pr.n.m. Geog:* Irak, Iraq.

irakien, -ienne [irakjɛ̃, -jɛn], *a. & s,* Iraqi.

Iran (l') [lirɑ̃]. *Pr.n.m. Geog:* Iran.

iranien, -ienne [iranjɛ̃, -jɛn], *a. & s. Geog:* Iranian.

Iraq (l') [lirak]. *Pr.n.m. Geog:* Iraq.

iraquien, -ienne [irakjɛ̃, -jɛn], *a. & s.* Iraqi.

irascibilité [iras(s)ibilite], *s.f.* irascibility; hot temper.

irascible [iras(s)ibl], *a.* irascible; *F:* peppery.

iris [iris], *s.m.* 1. iris (of eye). 2. *Bot:* iris, flag.

irlandais, -aise [irlɑ̃dɛ, -ɛːz]. 1. *a.* Irish. 2. *s.* Irishman; Irishwoman. 3. *s.m. Ling:* Irish, Erse.

Irlande (l') [lirlɑ̃ːd]. *Pr.n.f. Geog:* Ireland; l'I. du Nord, Northern Ireland.

iron|ie [irɔni], *s.f.* irony; *a.* -ique, ironic(al); *adv.* -iquement.

irradier [ir(r)adje], *v.i.* to (ir)radiate; (*of pain*) to spread.

irrationnel, -elle [ir(r)asjɔnɛl], *a.* irrational; *adv.* -lement.

irréalisable [ir(r)ealizabl], *a.* unrealizable.

irréconciliable [ir(r)ekɔ̃siljabl], *a.* irreconcilable; *adv.* -ment.

irrécouvrable [ir(r)ekuvrabl], *a.* irrecoverable.

irrécupérable [ir(r)ekyperabl], *a.* irreparable (loss, etc.); non-recoverable.

irréel, -elle [ir(r)eɛl], *a.* unreal.

irréfléchi [ir(r)efleʃi], *a.* 1. unconsidered, thoughtless. 2. hasty, rash.

irréflexion [ir(r)eflɛksjɔ̃], *s.f.* thoughtlessness.

irréfutable [ir(r)efytabl], *a.* irrefutable; *adv.* -ment.

irrégul|arité [ir(r)egylarite], *s.f.* 1. irregularity. 2. unpunctuality; *a.* -ier, -ière, irregular; *adv.* -ièrement.

irrémédiable [ir(r)emedjabl], *a.* irremediable; *adv.* -ment.

irremplaçable [ir(r)ɑ̃plasabl], *a.* irreplaceable.

irréparable [ir(r)eparabl], *a.* irreparable; *adv.* -ment.

irréprochable [ir(r)eprɔʃabl], *a.* irreproachable; *adv.* -ment.

irrésistible [ir(r)ezistibl], *a.* irresistible; *adv.* -ment.

irrésolu [ir(r)ezɔly], *a.* 1. irresolute, wavering (nature); faltering (steps). 2. unsolved (problem); *adv.* -ment.

irrespectueu|x, -euse [ir(r)ɛspɛktɥø, -øːz], *a.* disrespectful; *adv.* -sement.

irrespon|sabilité [ir(r)ɛspɔ̃sabilite], *s.f.* irresponsibility; *a.* -sable, irresponsible.

irrévérenc|e [ir(r)everɑ̃ːs], *s.f.* irreverence; *a.* -ieux, -ieuse, irreverent; *adv.* -ieusement.

irrévocable [ir(r)evɔkabl], *a.* irrevocable; *adv.* -ment.

irrigation [ir(r)igasjɔ̃], *s.f.* 1. *Agr:* irrigation. 2. *Med:* spraying, douching; i. du côlon, colonic irrigation.

irriguer [ir(r)ige], *v.tr. Agr:* to irrigate. 2. *Med:* to spray, to douche.

irrit|er [ir(r)ite], *v.tr.* to irritate; *s.f.* -abilité; *a.* -able; *adv.* -ablement; *s.f.* -ation.

s'irriter. 1. to grow angry (contre, with). 2. (*of sore*) to become inflamed.

irruption [ir(r)ypsjɔ̃], *s.f.* irruption; faire i. dans une salle, to burst into a room.

islandais, -aise [islɑ̃dɛ, -ɛːz], *Geog:* 1. *a.* Icelandic. 2. *s.* Icelander. 3. *s.m. Ling:* l'i., Icelandic.

Islande (l') [lislɑ̃ːd]. *Pr.n.f. Geog:* Iceland.

isolant [izɔlɑ̃]. 1. *a.* (*a*) isolating; (*b*) insulating; bouteille isolante, vacuum flask; (*c*) soundproof. 2. *s.m.* insulator.

isolateur, -trice [izɔlatœːr, -tris], *El:* 1. *a.* insulating. 2. *s.m.* insulator.

isolement [izɔlmɑ̃], *s.m.* 1. isolation, loneliness. 2. *El:* insulation.

isolément [izɔlemɑ̃], *adv.* separately; singly; vivre i., to live alone.

isoler [izɔle], *v.tr.* 1. isolate. 2. *El:* to insulate.

s'isoler, to live apart (from society).

isoloir [izɔlwaːr], *s.m. Adm:* polling-booth.

Isorel [izɔrɛl], *s.m. R.t.m:* hardboard.
Israël [israɛl]. *Pr.n.m. Geog:* Israel.
israélien, -ienne [israeljɛ̃, -jɛn], *a. & s.m. & f. Geog:* Israeli.
issue [isy], *s.f.* **1.** exit, way out; outlet; **i. de secours,** emergency exit; **voie sans i.,** dead end. **2.** issue, conclusion, outcome. **3.** *pl. Ind:* by-products.
isthme [ism], *s.m. Geog:* isthmus.
Italie (l') [litali]. *Pr.n.f. Geog:* Italy.
italien, -ienne [italjɛ̃, -jɛn]. **1.** *a. & s.* Italian. **2.** *s.m. Ling:* l'i., Italian.
italique [italik], *a. & s.m. Typ:* italic (type); italics.

itinéraire [itinerɛːr], *s.m.* itinerary; (*a*) route, way; (*b*) roadbook, (road) guide book.
itinérant [itinerã], *a.* itinerant.
ivoire [ivwaːr], *s.m.* ivory; *Geog:* **la Côte d'I.,** the Ivory Coast.
ivoirien, -ienne [ivwarjɛ̃, -jɛn]. *Geog:* **1.** *a.* of the Ivory Coast Republic. **2.** *s.* inhabitant of the Ivory Coast.
ivre [iːvr], *a.* drunk, intoxicated; **i. de joie.** mad with joy.
ivresse [ivrɛs], *s.f.* (*a*) intoxication, drunkenness; (*b*) rapture.
ivrogne [ivrɔŋ], *s.m.* drunkard.

J

J, j [ʒi], *s.m.* (the letter) J, j; *Mil: etc:* **le jour J,** D-day.

jabot [ʒabo], *s.m.* **1.** crop (of bird). **2.** *Cost:* frill, ruffle.

jacasser [ʒakase], *v.i. F:* to chatter, jabber.

jacinthe [ʒasɛ̃ːt], *s.f. Bot:* hyacinth; **j. des bois,** bluebell.

Jacqueline [ʒaklin]. *Pr.n.f.* Jacqueline.

Jacques [ʒɑːk]. *Pr.n.m.* James.

Jacquot [ʒako]. **1.** *Pr.n.m. F:* Jim, Jimmy. **2.** *s.m.* West African grey parrot, *F:* Poll (-parrot), Polly.

jade [ʒad], *s.m.* jade(-stone).

jadis [ʒadis], *adv.* formerly, once; **au temps j.,** in the olden days.

jaguar [ʒagwaːr], *s.m.* jaguar.

jaillir [ʒajiːr], *v.i.* to spring (up); to shoot forth; to gush (forth); (*of sparks*) to fly; *s.m.* -**issement.**

jais [ʒɛ], *s.m. Miner:* jet.

jalonner [ʒalɔne], *v.tr.* to stake out; to blaze (a trail); *s.m.* -**age**; *s.m.* -**ement.**

jalouser [ʒaluze], *v.tr.* to envy (s.o.); to be jealous of (s.o.).

jalousie [ʒaluzi], *s.f.* **1.** jealousy. **2.** Venetian blind.

jaloux, -ouse [ʒalu, uːz], *a.* (*a*) jealous; (*b*) careful; **j. de sa réputation,** careful of one's reputation.

Jamaïque (la) [laʒamaik]. *Pr.n.f.* Jamaica.

jamaïquain, -aine [ʒamaikɛ̃, -ɛn], *a. & s.* Jamaican.

jamais [ʒamɛ]. **1.** *adv.* ever; **à tout j.,** for ever and ever. **2.** *adv.* (*with neg. expressed or understood*) never; **c'est le cas ou j.,** now or never; **j. de la vie!** never! out of the question! **3.** *s.m.* **au grand j.!** never, never!

jambe [ʒɑ̃ːb], *s.f.* **1.** leg; *F:* **prendre ses jambes à son cou,** to take to one's heels; **avoir les jambes rompues,** to be worn out; **n'avoir plus de jambes,** to be tired out. **2. j. de force,** strut, prop, brace.

jambon [ʒɑ̃bɔ̃], *s.m.* ham.

jante [ʒɑ̃ːt], *s.f.* rim (of wheel).

janvier [ʒɑ̃vje], *s.m.* January; **au mois de j., en j.,** in (the month of) January; **le premier, le sept, j.,** (on) the first, the seventh, of January.

Japon (le) [ləʒapɔ̃]. *Pr.n.m. Geog:* Japan; **au J.,** in, to, Japan.

japonais, -aise [ʒaponɛ, -ɛːz], *a. & s.* Japanese.

japper [ʒape], *v.i.* (*of dog, fox*) to yelp, yap; *s.m.* -**ement.**

jaquette [ʒakɛt], *s.f.* (*a*) (*man's*) morning coat; (*b*) (*woman's*) jacket; (*c*) *Fr.C:* nightdress; (*d*) dust-jacket (of book).

jardin [ʒardɛ̃], *s.m.* garden; **j. potager,** kitchen garden, vegetable garden; **j. des plantes,** botanical garden; *Sch:* **j. d'enfants,** kindergarten.

jardiner [ʒardine], *v.i.* to garden; *s.m.* -**age**, gardening; *s.m.* -**et**, small garden.

jardinier, -ière [ʒardinje, -jɛːr]. **1.** *a.* **plantes jardinières,** garden plants. **2.** *s.* gardener. **3.** *s.f.* **jardinière,** flower-stand, window-box; *Cu:* **jardinière de légumes,** macédoine of vegetables; *Sch:* **jardinière d'enfants,** kindergarten mistress.

jargon [ʒargɔ̃], *s.m.* (*a*) jargon; (*b*) slang.

jarret [ʒarɛ], *s.m.* **1.** bend of the knee; hock (of cow, horse); **avoir le j. solide,** to be strong on one's legs. **2.** *Cu:* knuckle (of veal); shin (of beef).

jarretelle [ʒartɛl], *s.f.* (stocking or sock) suspender; *N.Am:* garter.

jarretière [ʒartjɛːr], *s.f.* garter; **Ordre de la J.,** Order of the Garter.

jaser [ʒaze], *v.i.* (*a*) to chatter (**de,** about); to gossip; **j. comme une pie (borgne),** to talk nineteen to the dozen; (*b*) to blab; to tell tales; *a. & s.* -**eur, -euse.**

jasmin [ʒasmɛ̃], *s.m. Bot:* jasmine.

jauge [ʒoːʒ], *s.f.* **1.** (*a*) gauge; capacity (of cask); (*b*) *Nau:* tonnage (of ship). **2.** *Mec.E:* gauge; *Aut:* dipstick.

jauger [ʒoʒe], *v.tr.* (**n. jaugeons**) to gauge; *s.m.* -**eage**, gauging, measuring.

jaune [ʒoːn]. **1.** *a.* yellow; *Aut:* **feu j.,** amber light; *adv.* **rire j.,** to give a sickly smile; **voir j.,** to see everything with a jaundiced eye. **2.** *s.m.* (*a*) yellow (colour); **ocre j.,** yellow ochre; (*b*) **j. d'œuf,** yolk (of egg); (*c*) *Ind:* blackleg, scab; *a.* -**âtre**, yellowish; sallow (complexion); *s.f.* -**isse**, jaundice.

jaunir [ʒoniːr]. **1.** *v.tr.* to colour (sth.) yellow. **2.** *v.i.* to grow, turn, yellow; to fade.

Javel [ʒavɛl], *s.m.* **eau de J.,** (potassium-chloride) disinfectant; bleach.

javelliser [ʒavelize], *v.tr.* to chlorinate (water); *s.f.* -**ation.**

jazz [dʒaːz], *s.m.* jazz.

je, *before vowel* **j'** [ʒ(ə)], *pers.pron.nom.* I.

Jean [ʒɑ̃]. *Pr.n.m.* John; **la Saint-J.,** Midsummer Day.

Jeann|e [ʒan]. *Pr.n.f.* Jane, Joan, Jean; *Pr.n.f.* -**ette**, Jenny, Janet.

Jeannot [ʒano]. *Pr.n.m. F:* Johnny, Jack.

jeep [(d)ʒip], *s.f. Aut:* jeep.

jerrycan [ʒerikan], *s.m.* jerrycan.

jésuit|e [ʒezųit], *s.m. Ecc:* Jesuit; *a.* -**ique**, jesuitic(al); *Pej:* plausible.

Jésus [ʒezy]. *Pr.n.m.* Jesus; **J.-Christ**, Jesus Christ; **l'an 44 avant J.-C.**, the year 44 B.C.

jet [ʒɛ], *s.m.* **1.** (*a*) throw, cast; (*b*) *Metall:* cast, casting; **faire qch. d'un seul j.**, to do sth. at one go. **2.** (*a*) jet, gush (of liquid); flash (of light); **j. d'eau**, fountain; (*b*) young shoot (of tree). **3.** spout.

jetée [ʒəte], *s.f.* jetty, pier; breakwater.

jeter [ʒəte], *v.tr.* (**je jette**) to throw, fling; to throw away; **j. qch. de côté**, to toss, throw, sth. aside; **j. un cri**, to utter a cry; **j. un regard (sur qn)**, to cast a glance (at s.o.); **j. les fondements d'un édifice**, to lay the foundations of a building; *Nau:* **j. la sonde**, to heave the lead.

se jeter à bas de son lit, to jump out of bed; **se j. sur qn**, to attack s.o.; **se j. à l'eau**, (i) to jump into the water; (ii) to take the plunge; (iii) to drown oneself; **se j. au cou de qn**, to fall on s.o.'s neck.

jeton [ʒətɔ̃], *s.m. Cards: etc:* counter; chip; (telephone) token, *N.Am:* slug.

jeu, jeux [ʒø], *s.m.* **1.** (*a*) play; **j. de mots**, play on words; pun; **j. d'esprit**, witticism; **les forces en j.**, the forces at work; **se faire (un) j. de qch.**, to make light of sth.; (*b*) (manner of) playing; **j. muet**, dumb show. **2.** (*a*) **ce n'est pas de j.**, that's not fair; **jouer beau j.**, to play fair; (*b*) (*place*) **terrain de jeux**, sports ground; **j. de tennis**, (lawn-)tennis courts; **j. de boules**, bowling-green, -alley. **3.** **j. d'échecs**, chess set, set of chessmen; **j. de cartes**, pack, *N.Am:* deck, of cards; **j. d'outils**, set of tools. **4.** gaming, gambling, play; **jouer gros j.**, to play for high stakes; **faites vos jeux!** put down your stakes! place your bets! **5.** *Mec:* play; **trop de j.**, too much play; **prendre du j.**, to work loose.

jeudi [ʒødi], *s.m.* Thursday; **j. saint**, Maundy Thursday.

jeun (à) [aʒœ̃], *adj.phr.* fasting.

jeune [ʒœn], *a.* (*a*) young; youthful; **j. homme**, youth; **j. fille**, girl; **jeunes gens**, young people; (*b*) younger; **M. Dupont J.**, Mr Dupont junior.

jeûne [ʒø:n], *s.m.* fast(ing).

jeûner [ʒøne], *v.i.* to fast.

jeunesse [ʒœnɛs], *s.f.* (*a*) youth; boyhood; girlhood; **organismes de j.**, youth organizations; (*b*) youthfulness (of appearance).

joaill|erie [ʒɔajri], *s.f.* **1.** jeweller's trade. **2.** jewellery; *s.* -**ier**, -**ière**, jeweller.

joie [ʒwa], *s.f.* **1.** joy; delight; gladness; **feu de j.**,

bonfire; *adv.phr.* **à cœur j.**, to one's heart's content. **2.** mirth, merriment.

joindre [ʒwɛ̃:dr], *v.tr.* (*pr.p.* **joignant**; *p.p.* **joint**; *pr.ind.* **je joins, il joint**; *p.h.* **je joignis**) **1.** to join; (*a*) to bring together; **j. les deux bouts**, to make (both) ends meet; (*b*) to add; **j. le geste à la parole**, to suit the action to the word; **j. l'utile à l'agréable**, to combine business with pleasure; (*c*) **j. son régiment**, to join one's regiment; **comment puis-je vous j.?** how can I get in touch with you? **2.** (*a*) (*of houses, etc.*) to adjoin; (*b*) *v.i.* (*of windows, etc.*) to fit, to meet.

se joindre, to join, unite.

joint [ʒwɛ̃]. **1.** *a.* joined, united; **pieds joints**, feet close together; *Com:* **pièces jointes**, enclosures. **2.** *s.m.* joint, join; *s.f. Anat: Tchn:* -**ure**, joint.

joli [ʒɔli]. **1.** *a.* pretty; nice; **jolie à croquer**, pretty as a picture. **2.** *s.m.* **voilà du j.!** here's a nice mess! *adv.* -**ment**.

jonc [ʒɔ̃], *s.m.* (*a*) *Bot:* rush; (*b*) **canne de j.**, Malacca cane.

joncher [ʒɔ̃ʃe], *v.tr.* **j. la terre de fleurs**, to strew the ground with flowers.

jonction [ʒɔ̃ksjɔ̃], *s.f.* junction, joining.

jongl|er [ʒɔ̃gle], *v.i.* to juggle; *s.f.* -**erie**; *s.m* -**eur**.

jonquille [ʒɔ̃ki:j], *s.f. Bot:* (*a*) jonquil; (*b* daffodil.

Jordanie (la) [laʒɔrdani]. *Pr.n.f. Geog:* Jordan.

jordanien, -ienne [ʒɔrdanjɛ̃, -jɛn], *a. & s* Jordanian.

joue [ʒu], *s.f.* cheek; **coucher, mettre, qn en j.,** aim (a gun) at s.o.

jouer [ʒwe], *v.* to play. **I.** *v.i.* **1.** (*a*) **j. avec qn**, t play with s.o.; (*b*) **j. aux cartes, au tennis**, t play cards, tennis; (*c*) **j. du piano**, to play th piano; **j. des coudes**, to elbow one's way; **j. de dents**, to munch away. **2.** to gamble. **3.** **faire** (**qch.**), to bring (sth.) into action; **faire j. ressort**, to release a spring.

II. *v.tr.* **1.** to stake; **j. gros jeu**, to play fo high stakes. **2.** (*a*) to play (card); (*b*) to act, pe form (a play); **j. la surprise**, to feign surprise. . to trick, fool (s.o.).

se jouer. 1. faire qch. en se jouant, to do st easily. **2. se j. de qn**, to trifle with, to mal fun of, s.o.

jouet [ʒwe], *s.m.* toy.

joueur, -euse [ʒwœːr, -øːz], *s.* **1.** (*a*) player (game); **être beau j.**, to be a good loser; (*b*) pe former, player (on an instrument). **2.** gambl speculator.

joufflu [ʒufly], *a.* chubby(-cheeked).

joug [ʒu(g)], *s.m.* yoke.

jou|ir [ʒwiːr], *v.i.* **j. de**, to enjoy; (*a*) **j. de la vie**, enjoy life; (*b*) **j. d'une bonne réputation**, have a good reputation; *s.f.* -**issance**, enjoyment; (*b*) possession.

joujou, -oux [ʒuʒu], *s.m.* (*child's word*) toy.
jour [ʒuːr], *s.m.* day. 1. (day)light; (*a*) le petit j.,
the morning twilight; il fait j., it is light; il fait
grand j., it is broad daylight; (*b*) mettre qch. au
j., to bring sth. to light; to publish (fact);
attenter aux jours de qn, to make an attempt
on s.o.'s life; (*c*) lighting; j. d'atelier, studio
lighting; voir qch. sous son vrai j., to see sth. in
its true light. 2. aperture, opening; j. de
l'escalier, well (of staircase); à jour(s), open-
work (stockings), hemstitched (hem). 3. (*in
restaurant*) plat du j., 'today's special'; être de
j., to be on duty for the day; de nos jours,
nowadays; vivre au j. le j., to live from hand to
mouth; du j. au lendemain, at a moment's
notice; à un de ces jours! *F:* so long! mettre à
j., to bring up to date.
journal, -aux [ʒurnal, -o], *s.m.* 1. journal, diary,
record; *Nau:* j. de bord, log-book. 2.
newspaper; les journaux, the press; *Rad: T.V:
etc:* j. parlé, télévisé, the news; *s.m.* -isme,
journalism; *s.m. & f.* -iste; *a.* -istique.
journalier, -ière [ʒurnalje, -jɛːr]. 1. *a.* daily
(task, etc.); everyday (occurrence). 2. *s.m.*
day-labourer; *Aut: etc:* (totalisateur) j., trip
recorder.
journée [ʒurne], *s.f.* 1. day(time); dans la j., in
the course of the day. 2. (*a*) day's work;
travailler à la j., to work by the day; femme de
j., charwoman, daily help; *F:* daily; aller en j.,
to go out charring; (*b*) day's wages; (*c*) day's
march; voyager à petites journées, to travel by
easy stages; (*d*) day (of battle); gagner la j., to
win the day.
journellement [ʒurnɛlmɑ̃], *adv.* daily; every
day.
jovial, -aux [ʒɔvjal, -o], *a.* jovial, jolly, merry;
adv. -ement; *s.f.* -ité.
joyau, -aux [ʒwajo], *s.m.* jewel; les joyaux de la
Couronne, the regalia, the Crown jewels.
joyeux, -euse [ʒwajø, -øːz], *a.* merry, joyous; j.
Noël! merry Christmas! *adv.* -isement,
joyfully.
jubilé [ʒybile], *s.m.* jubilee.
jubiler [ʒybile], *v.i.* to exult; *s.f.* -ation.
jucher [ʒyʃe], *v.i.* (*of birds*) to roost; to perch;
s.m. -oir, perch; hen-roost.
judiciaire [ʒydisjɛːr], *a.* judicial, legal (inquiry,
error); *adv.* -ment.
judicieux, -euse [ʒydisjø, -øːz], *a.* judicious,
discerning; peu j., injudicious; *adv.* -sement.
juge [ʒyːʒ], *s.m.* judge; j. d'instruction
= examining magistrate; j. d'instance
= police-court magistrate; je vous en fais j., I
appeal to you; *Sp: Games:* umpire; referee;
Rac: judge.
jugement [ʒyʒmɑ̃], *s.m.* judg(e)ment. 1. *Jur:* (*a*)
trial (of case); mettre, faire passer, qn en j., to
bring s.o. to trial; le j. dernier, doomsday; (*b*)

decision, award; sentence. 2. opinion, estimation. 3. discernment, discrimination; montrer
du j., to show good sense; erreur de j., error in,
of, judgment.
juger [ʒyʒe]. I. *v.tr.* (n. jugeons) 1. (*a*) to judge;
to try (cases, prisoner); to pass sentence on;
(*b*) to pass judgment on; to criticize. 2. (*a*) to
think, believe, consider; on le jugeait fou, people thought he was mad; (*b*) jugez de ma surprise, imagine my surprise; à en juger par . . .,
judging by. . . .
II. juger, jugé, *s.m.* faire qch. au jugé, au
juger, to do sth. by guesswork.
jugulaire [ʒygylɛːr]. 1. *a. & s.f.* jugular (vein). 2.
s.f. chin-strap.
juif, juive [ʒɥif, ʒɥiːv]. 1. *a.* Jewish. 2. *s.* Jew, *f.*
Jewess; *F:* le petit j., the funny-bone.
juillet [ʒɥijɛ], *s.m.* July; au mois de j., en j., in
(the month of) July; le premier, le sept, j., (on)
the first, the seventh, of July.
juin [ʒɥɛ̃], *s.m.* June; au mois de j., in (the month
of) June; le premier, le sept, j., (on) the first, the
seventh, of June.
jumeau, -elle, *pl.* -eaux [ʒymo, -ɛl]. I. *a. & s.*
twin; trois jumeaux, triplets; maisons jumelles,
semi-detached houses; lits jumeaux, twin beds.
II. *s.f.pl.* binoculars; jumelles de théâtre,
opera-glasses.
jumeller [ʒymle], *v.tr.* (je jumelle, n. jumelons)
(*a*) to arrange in pairs; *Aut:* pneus jumelés,
dual tyres; textes jumelés, bilingual texts; (*b*)
to twin (towns); *s.m.* -age, twinning.
jument [ʒymɑ̃], *s.f.* mare; j. poulinière, brood
mare.
jumping [ʒœmpiŋ], *s.m. Equit:* show-jumping.
jungle [ʒœ̃ːgl], *s.f.* jungle.
jupe [ʒyp], *s.f.* (woman's) skirt.
jupon [ʒypɔ̃], *s.m.* (*a*) petticoat, underskirt; waist
slip; (*b*) *P:* girl, woman, *P:* skirt; courir le j., to
chase the girls.
juré, -ée [ʒyre], *s.* juryman, -woman, juror; les
jurés, the jury.
jurer [ʒyre], *v.tr.* to swear. 1. j. sa foi, to pledge
one's word. 2. (*to promise*) faire j. le secret à
qn, to swear s.o. to secrecy. 3. (*to assert*) j'en
jurerais, I would swear to it. 4. abs. (*a*) to
swear (profanely); to curse; (*b*) (*of colours*) to
clash.
juridiction [ʒyridiksjɔ̃], *s.f.* jurisdiction; *a.* -nel,
-nelle.
juridique [ʒyridik], *a.* judicial; legal; conseiller
j., legal adviser; frais juridiques, legal charges;
adv. -ment.
juron [ʒyrɔ̃], *s.m.* (profane) oath; *F:* swear-
word.
jury [ʒyri], *s.m.* 1. *Jur:* jury; chef, membre, du j.,
foreman, member, of the jury. 2. selection
committee; board (of examiners).
jus [ʒy], *s.m.* 1. juice. 2. gravy. 3. *P:* (*a*) water; (*b*)

petrol, *N.Am:* gas; (*c*) electric current. 4. *Art:* (*a*) (preliminary colour-wash); (*b*) glaze (on oil-painting).

jusant [ʒyzɑ̃], *s.m.* ebb(-tide).

jusque [ʒysk(ə)], *prep.* **1.** as far as; up to; **jusqu'ici,** so far; **jusque-là,** thus far; **depuis Londres jusqu'à Paris,** all the way from London to Paris; **jusqu'à chez lui,** right up to his door; **ils furent tués jusqu'au dernier,** they were killed to a man. **2.** till, until; **jusqu'à présent,** till now. **3.** (*intensive*) **il sait jusqu'à nos pensées,** he knows our very thoughts. **4.** *conj. phr.* **jusqu'à ce que,** *usu.* + *sub.,* till, until.

juste [ʒyst], *a.* **1.** just, right, fair; (*a*) **rien de plus j.,** nothing could be fairer; (*b*) **magistrat j.,** upright judge. **2.** right, exact, accurate; (*a*) **le mot j.,** the exact word, the right word; **c'est j.,** that is so! that's right! **rien de plus j.,** you are perfectly right; (*b*) **bottines trop justes,** tight boots; **ration bien j.,** very scanty, bare, ration; **vêtement bien j.,** skimpy garment; **c'est tout j. s'il sait lire,** he can barely read. **3.** *adv.* (*a*) rightly; **frapper j.,** to strike home; **chanter j.,** to sing in tune; (*b*) exactly, precisely; (*c*) barely; **échapper tout j.,** to escape by the skin of one's

teeth. **4.** *adv.phr.* **je ne sais pas au juste si . . .,** I do not exactly know whether . . .; **comme de j.,** as is only fair; *adv.* **-ment,** justly, rightly, deservedly; precisely, exactly.

justesse [ʒystɛs], *s.f.* **1.** exactness, accuracy; **raisonner avec j.,** to argue soundly. **2. arriver de j.,** to arrive just in time.

justice [ʒystis], *s.f.* **1.** justice; **c'est j. que** + *sub.,* it is only right that . . .; **en toute j.,** by rights; **se faire j.,** (*of criminal*) to commit suicide; **demander j. à qn,** to seek redress from s.o. **2.** law, legal proceedings; **citer qn en j.,** to go to law with s.o.; **Palais de J.,** Law Courts; **gens de j.,** (i) officers of the Court; (ii) lawyers.

justifi|er [ʒystifje], *v.tr.* **1.** to justify, vindicate (s.o.'s conduct, etc.); to warrant (action, expenditure). **2.** to prove, make good (assertion); *a.* **-able;** *adv.* **-ablement;** *s.f.* **-cation.**

se justifier, to clear oneself; to justify oneself.

jute [ʒyt], *s.m. Tex:* jute; **toile de j.,** hessian.

juteux, -euse [ʒytø, -øːz], *a.* juicy.

juvénile [ʒyvenil], *a.* juvenile; youthful; *Jur:* **délinquence j.,** juvenile delinquency.

juxtapos|er [ʒykstapoze], *v.tr.* to place side by side, to juxtapose; *s.f.* **-ition.**

K

K, k [kɑ], *s.m.* (the letter) K, k.
kaki¹ [kaki], *s.m. & a.inv.* khaki.
kaki², *s.m. Bot:* persimmon.
kangourou [kãguru], *s.m. Z:* kangaroo.
kaolin [kaɔlɛ̃], *s.m.* kaolin, china clay.
kapok [kapɔk], *s.m.* kapok.
Kenya (le) [ləkenja]. *Pr.n.m. Geog:* Kenya.
képi [kepi], *s.m.* kepi; peaked cap.
kermesse [kɛrmɛs], *s.f.* (*a*) (Flemish) village
fair; (*b*) charity fête.
kérosène [kerɔzɛn], *s.m.* paraffin (oil), kerosene.
kidnappler [kidnape], *v.tr.* to kidnap; *s.* -eur,
-euse, kidnapper.
kilo(gramme) [kilo, kilɔgram], *s.m.* kilo-
gram(me).
kilomètre [kilɔmɛtr], *s.m.* kilometre.

kilométrique [kilɔmetrik], *a.* borne k.
=milestone.
kilowatt [kilɔwat], *s.m.* kilowatt.
kiosque [kjɔsk], *s.m.* 1. (*a*) kiosk; k. à musique,
bandstand; k. de jardin, summer-house; (*b*)
newspaper-stall; flower-stall. 2. *Nau:* conning-
tower (of submarine).
klaxon [klaksɔ̃], *s.m. Aut: R.t.m:* hooter, horn.
klaxonner [klaksɔne], *v.i. Aut:* to hoot, sound the
horn.
kleptomane [klɛptɔman], *a. & s.* kleptomaniac.
kleptomanie [klɛptɔmani], *s.f.* kleptomania.
knock-out [knɔkut, nɔkaut], *a.inv. Sp:* mettre
(qn) k.-o., to knock (s.o.) out.
krach [krak], *s.m.* (financial) crash; failure (of a
bank, etc.).
kyste [kist], *s.m. Med:* cyst.

L

L, l [εl], s.m. or f. (the letter) L, l; l mouillé(e), liquid l.

la¹ [la], def. art. & pron.f. See LE¹,².

la², s.m.inv. Mus: (the note) A; concerto en la, concerto in A.

là [la], adv. 1. (of place) there; (a) les choses en sont là, this is the state of things at the moment; F: ôtez-vous de là! get out of there! passez par là, go that way; (b) (emphatic use) c'est là la question, that's the question; que dites-vous là? what is that you are saying? ce, cette, etc.... -là, see CE¹ 1, CE² 2; celui-là, celle-là, see CELUI. 2. (of time) then; d'ici là, between now and then. 3. (= CELA) qu'entendez-vous par là? what do you mean by that? 4. int. (a) là! voilà qui est fait, there now! that's done; (b) oh là là! oh dear! Good Lord!

là-bas [laba], adv. (over) there.

labeur [labœːr], s.m. labour, toil, hard work; terre en l., ploughed land.

labo [labo], s.m. F: lab.

laborantin, -ine [labɔrãtɛ̃, -in], s. laboratory, F: lab, assistant.

laboratoire [labɔratwaːr], s.m. laboratory, F: lab.

laborieu|x, -euse [labɔrjø, -øːz], a. 1. arduous, hard (work, etc.); laboured (style). 2. laborious, hard-working (people); les classes laborieuses, the working classes; adv. -sement.

labour [labuːr], s.m. tilling; ploughing; terres de l., les labours, ploughed land.

labour|er [labure], v.tr. to till; to plough; l. à la bêche, to dig; a. -able, arable (land); s.m. -eur, farm-hand, esp. ploughman.

lac [lak], s.m. lake.

lacer [lase], v.tr. (n. laçons) to lace (up).

lacér|er [lasere], v.tr. (je lacère; je lacérerai) to tear, lacerate; s.f. -ation.

lacet [lasɛ], s.m. 1. lace (of shoe). 2. hairpin bend; sentier en lacets, zigzag path. 3. noose, snare (for rabbits, etc.).

lâche [lɑːʃ], a. 1. loose, slack; lax. 2. cowardly; s.m. un l., a coward; adv. -ment, (i) slackly; (ii) in a cowardly manner.

lâch|er [lɑʃe]. 1. v.tr. to release; (a) to slacken; l. un coup de fusil, to fire a shot; Aut: l. le frein, to release the brake; (b) to let go; to release (bomb); to drop (parachutist); F: l. qn, to drop s.o.; l. pied, to give ground; lâchez-moi, let me

go; (c) to set free; l. un chien, to let loose a dog; l. un juron, to let out an oath. 2. v.i. mes nerfs lâchèrent, my nerve went; s. -eur, -euse, F: quitter.

lâcheté [lɑʃte], s.f. 1. (a) cowardice; (b) act of cowardice. 2. (a) despicableness; baseness; (b) low, base, action; encore une l.! another piece of treachery!

laconique [lakɔnik], a. laconic; (man) of few words; adv. -ment.

là-contre [lakɔ̃ːtr], adv. to the contrary.

lacrymogène [lakrimɔʒɛn], a. gaz l., tear gas.

lacté [lakte], a. milky; régime l., milk diet; Astr: la Voie lactée, the Milky Way.

lacune [lakyn], s.f. lacuna, gap; blank (in memory).

là-dedans [lad(ə)dã], adv. in there; inside.

là-dehors [ladəɔːr], adv. outside.

là-dessous [latsu], adv. under there; underneath.

là-dessus [latsy], adv. on that; thereupon.

lagune [lagyn], s.f. lagoon.

là-haut [lao], adv. up there; il y a quelqu'un là-h. is there anyone upstairs?

laï|ciser [laisize], v.tr. to secularize (school etc.); s.f. -cisation; s.m. -cisme; s.f. -cité.

laid [lɛ], a. (a) ugly; unsightly; (of face) plain; (b mean, shabby (action).

laideur [lɛdœːr], s.f. 1. ugliness; plainness. 2 meanness.

lain|e [lɛn], s.f. wool; s.m. -age, woollen article pl. woollen goods; a. -eux, -euse, fleec woolly.

laïque [laik]. 1. a. secular (education); la (dress); école l. =state school. 2. s. les laïque the laity.

laisse [lɛs], s.f. leash, lead.

laisser [lɛse], v.tr. 1. to let, allow; je les ai laissé dire, I let them talk away; l. voir qch., to reve sth.; se l. aller, to let oneself go; se aller dans un fauteuil, to sink into an arm chair; laissez-le faire! leave it to him! il ‹ laissa faire, he offered no resistance. 2. (a) leave (sth., s.o., somewhere); l. sa valise à consigne, to leave one's case at the left-lugga office; l. là qn, to leave s.o. in the lurch; (b) (i vous laisse libre d'agir, I leave you free to ac (ii) to leave (sth.) alone; l. les détails, to pass ov the details; laissez donc! don't bother! do worry! (iii) vous pouvez nous l., you may lea us; (c) laissez-moi vos clefs, leave me your key

je vous le laisserai à bon compte, I will let you have it cheap; **cela laisse (beaucoup) à désirer,** it leaves much to be desired; (d) **ne pas l. de faire qch.,** not to fail to do sth.; **cela ne laisse pas de m'inquiéter,** I feel anxious all the same.

laisser-aller [leseale], s.m.inv. carelessness, slovenliness.

laisser-faire [lesefe:r], s.m. non-interference; laissez-faire.

laissez-passer [lesepase], s.m.inv. pass, permit.

lait [le], s.m. milk. 1. **l. entier,** whole, full cream, milk; **l. écrémé,** skim(med) milk; **l. cru certifié** =tuberculin-tested, T.T., milk; **petit l.,** whey; **l. concentré sucré,** condensed milk; **l. concentré non sucré,** evaporated milk; **l. en poudre,** dried milk; **au l.,** with milk; **café au l.,** white coffee; **l. de poule,** egg-nog; **vache à l.,** milch cow. 2. **l. de coco,** coconut milk; **l. de chaux,** lime-wash; **l. de ciment,** grout.

laitage [leta:ʒ], s.m. dairy produce.

laitance [letã:s], s.f. Ich: milt; Cu: soft roe.

laiterie [letri], s.f. 1. dairy. 2. (a) dairy-work; (b) dairy-farming.

laiteux, -euse [letø, -ø:z], a. milk-like, milky.

laitier, -ière [letje, -je:r]. 1. a. **l'industrie laitière,** the milk industry; **produits laitiers,** dairy produce. 2. s. (a) milkman; milkwoman, milkmaid; (b) dairyman; dairymaid.

laiton [letõ], s.m. brass.

laitue [lety], s.f. lettuce; **l. pommée,** cabbage lettuce; **l. romaine,** cos lettuce.

lambeau, -eaux [lãbo], s.m. scrap, bit, shred (of cloth, etc.); **vêtements en lambeaux,** clothes in tatters.

lambris [lãbri], s.m. panelling, wainscoting; s.m. **-sage,** panelling, lining (of room).

lame [lam], s.f. 1. (a) lamina, thin plate, strip (of metal); leaf (of spring); **l. de jalousie,** slat of a Venetian blind; (b) blade (of sword, razor); **visage en l. de couteau,** hatchet-face. 2. wave; **l. de fond,** ground-swell; **l. de houle,** roller.

lamentable [lamãtabl], a. 1. lamentable, deplorable (accident, etc.); mournful (voice). 2. (of result) feeble; shockingly bad; **il s'est montré l.,** he put up a poor show; adv. **-ment.**

lamenter (se) [səlamãte], v.pr. to lament; to wail; **se l. sur son sort,** to bewail one's lot; s.f. **-ation.**

lamifié [lamifje], a. & s.m. laminated (plastic, glass, etc.).

laminer [lamine], v.tr. to roll, to flat(ten), to laminate (metal, plastic, etc.); to calender, plate-glaze (paper); s.m. **-age;** s.m. **-eur;** s.m. **-oir,** rolling mill.

lampadaire [lãpade:r], s.m. Furn: 1. standard lamp. 2. candelabrum.

lampe [lã:p], s.f. 1. lamp. 2. (a) **l. de poche,** (electric) torch; flash-light; (b) Rad: valve.

lampée [lãpe], s.f. draught, gulp (of wine, etc.).

lamper [lãpe], v.tr. to swig, toss off (drink).

lampion [lãpjõ], s.m. (a) fairy light (for illuminations); (b) Chinese lantern; (c) Fr.C: Ecc: votive light, candle.

lance [lã:s], s.f. 1. (a) spear; (b) lance; (c) harpoon. 2. **l. à eau,** water-hose nozzle.

lance-bombes [lãsbõ:b], s.m.inv. 1. Artil: trench mortar. 2. Av: bomb rack.

lance-fusées [lãsfyze], s.m. inv. Mil: etc: rocket launcher.

lancer [lãse], v.tr. (n. lançons) 1. to throw, fling, hurl; F: to shy, to chuck (a stone); Sp: to pitch; to toss; Fish: to cast; **l. un coup d'œil à qn,** to dart a glance at s.o. 2. to start, set going; (a) **l. un cheval,** to start a horse off at full gallop; **l. un chien contre qn,** to set a dog on s.o.; (b) to launch (ship, rocket); to release (bomb); to float (company); s.m. **-ement.** **se lancer en avant,** to rush forward; **se l. dans les affaires,** to launch out into business.

lanciner [lãsine]. 1. v.i. (of pain) to shoot; to throb. 2. v.tr. **ce problème me lancine,** this problem is getting me down.

landau [lãdo], s.m. baby carriage, pram.

lande [lã:d], s.f. sandy moor; heath; waste; N.Am: barren.

langage [lãga:ʒ], s.m. language; speech (of the individual); **tenir un l. aimable, grossier, à qn,** to speak amiably, rudely, to s.o.; **changer de l.,** to change one's tune; **l. courant,** everyday speech; **en voilà un l.!** that's no way to talk! **troubles du l.,** defective speech.

langage-machine [lãgaʒmaʃin], s.m. computer language; pl. **langages-machine.**

langouste [lãgust], s.f. spiny lobster; crayfish; s.f. **-ine,** Dublin Bay prawn; pl. Com: scampi.

langue [lã:g], s.f. 1. tongue; **tirer la l.,** (i) to put out one's tongue; (ii) (of dog) to hang out its tongue; (with reference to riddle) **donner sa l. au chat,** to give up; **mauvaise l.,** backbiter. 2. tongue (of flame); spit (of land). 3. language, speech, tongue (of a people); **professeur de langues vivantes,** modern-language master, mistress; F: **l. verte,** slang.

languette [lãget], s.f. small tongue (of wood); strip (of tin-foil); tongue (of shoe).

languir [lãgi:r], v.i. to languish; to mope; to be listless; (of business) to be slack; (of conversation) to flag; **ne nous faites pas l.,** don't keep us on tenterhooks; Th: **l'action languit,** the action drags; s.f. **-eur,** listlessness; a. **-issant,** listless.

lanière [lanje:r], s.f. thin strap; thong.

lanterne [lãtern], s.f. lantern.

laper [lape], v.tr. & i. (of dog, etc.) to lap (up) (water, milk, etc.).

lapin, -ine [lapẽ, -in], s. rabbit, f. doe; **l. mâle,** buck rabbit; **l. de garenne,** wild rabbit; **l. de clapier,** tame rabbit.

lapon, -one [lapõ, -ɔn]. **1.** *a.* Lapp, Lappish. **2.** *s.* Lapp, Laplander.

Laponie (la) [lalapɔni]. *Pr.n.f.* Lapland.

laps [laps], *s.m.* un l. de temps, a space of time.

laque [lak]. **1.** *s.f.* *(a)* lac; l. **en écailles,** shellac; *(b) Paint:* (crimson) lake; *(c) Toil:* lacquer; hairspray; *(d) Aut:* cellulose lacquer, *F:* dope. **2.** *s.m.* lacquer; l. **de Chine,** japan.

laquer [lake], *v.tr.* to lacquer; to japan.

larcin [larsɛ̃], *s.m. Jur:* larceny; petty theft.

lard [la:r], *s.m.* *(a)* fat (*esp.* of pork); *(b)* bacon.

larg|e [larʒ]. **1.** *a.* *(a)* broad, wide; l. **d'épaules,** broad-shouldered; **d'un geste l.,** with a sweeping gesture; *(b)* large, big, ample. **2.** *s.m.* *(a) Nau:* open sea; **brise du l.,** sea-breeze; **prendre le l.,** to put to sea; **au l. de Cherbourg,** off Cherbourg; *(b)* breadth; **se promener de long en l.,** to walk up and down; *adv.* **-ement;** *s.f.* **-esse,** liberality; *s.f.* **-eur,** width.

larme [larm], *s.f.* tear.

larm|oyer [larmwaje], *v.i.* (**je larmoie**) **1.** (*of the eyes*) to water. **2.** *Pej:* to snivel; *a.* **-oyant,** tearful; maudlin; *s.m.* **-oiement,** weeping.

larve [larv], *s.f.* larva; grub (of insect).

laryngite [larɛ̃ʒit], *s.f. Med:* laryngitis.

larynx [larɛ̃ks], *s.m. Anat:* larynx.

las, lasse [lɑ, lɑ:s], *a.* tired, weary.

laser [lazɛr], *s.m. Ph:* laser.

lass|er [lase], *v.tr.* to tire, weary; to exhaust (s.o.'s patience); *s.f.* **-itude.**

se lasser, to grow weary; to tire.

lasso [laso], *s.m.* lasso.

latent [latɑ̃], *a.* latent (disease, etc.); hidden, concealed.

latéral, -aux [lateral, -o], *a.* lateral; **rue latérale,** side-street; *adv.* **-ement.**

latin, -ine [latɛ̃, -in]. **1.** *a. & s.m.* Latin; **le Quartier l.,** the Latin Quarter; **l'Amérique latine,** Latin America; **les Latins,** the Latin races. **2.** *s.m. Ling:* Latin; *F:* l. **de cuisine,** dog-Latin; **être au bout de son l.,** to be at one's wits' end; **j'y perds mon l.,** I can't make head or tail of it.

latitude [latityd], *s.f.* **1.** latitude, scope, freedom. **2.** *Geog:* latitude.

latte [lat], *s.f.* lath, batten, slat.

lauréat, -ate [lɔrea, -at], *s.* laureate; l. **du prix Nobel,** Nobel prizewinner.

laurier [lɔrje], *s.m.* *(a) Bot:* laurel; *(b) Cu:* **feuille de l.,** bay leaf; *(c)* l.**-rose,** oleander.

lavabo [lavabo], *s.m.* **1.** wash-hand basin. **2.** (*place for washing*) lavatory.

lavande [lavɑ̃:d], *s.f. Bot:* lavender.

lavandière [lavɑ̃djɛr], *s.f.* **1.** washerwoman; laundress. **2.** *Orn:* wagtail.

lave [la:v], *s.f. Geol:* lava.

lave-glace [lavglas], *s.m. Aut:* windscreen-, *N.Am:* windshield-, washer; *pl.* lave-glaces.

lav|er [lave], *v.tr.* to wash; **se l. les mains,** to wash one's hands; l. **la vaisselle,** to wash up,

N.Am: to wash the dishes; **se l. la tête,** to wash one's hair; l. **la tête à qn,** to haul s.o. over the coals; *a.* **-able,** washable; *s.m.* **-oir,** wash-house.

se laver, to wash (oneself).

lavette [lavɛt], *s.f.* *(a)* (dish-)mop; l. **métallique,** pot-scourer; *(b)* dish cloth.

lave-vaisselle [lavvɛsɛl], *s.m.inv.* dish-washer; washing-up machine.

laxatif, -ive [laksatif, -i:v], *a. & s.m. Med:* laxative, aperient.

le¹, la, les [lə, la, lɛ], *def.art.* (**le** and **la** are elided to **l'** before a vowel or h 'mute'; **le** and **les** contract with **à, de,** into **au, aux; du, des**) the. **1.** (*particularizing*) *(a)* **j'apprends le français,** I am learning French; **l'un . . . l'autre,** (the) one . . . the other; **il est arrivé le lundi 12,** he arrived on Monday the 12th; *(b)* **la France,** France; *(c)* **le colonel Chabot,** Colonel Chabot; *(d)* **le Dante,** Dante; **le Caire,** Cairo; *(e)* (*with most feast-days*) **à la Noël,** at Christmas; *(f)* (*often with parts of the body*) **hausser les épaules,** to shrug one's shoulders; **elle ferma les yeux,** she closed her eyes. **2.** (*forming superlatives*) **mon ami le plus intime,** my most intimate friend; **c'est elle qui travaille le mieux,** she works best. **3.** (*generalizing*) **je préfère le café au thé,** I prefer coffee to tea. **4.** (*distributive*) **cinq francs la livre,** five francs a pound. **5.** (*rendered by indef. art in Eng.*) *(a)* **donner l'exemple,** to set an example; *(b)* **il n'a pas le sou,** he hasn't a penny.

le², la, les, *pers.pron.* **1.** (*replacing sb.*) him, her, it, them; *(a)* **je ne le lui ai pas donné,** I did not give it to him; **les voilà!** there they are! *(b)* (*following the vb.*) **donnez-le-lui,** give it to him. **2.** *neut.pron.* **le** *(a)* (*replacing an adj. or a s. used as an adj.*) **êtes-vous mère?—je le suis,** are you a mother?—I am; *(b)* (*replacing clause*) (i) so; **il me l'a dit,** he told me so; (ii) **vous le devriez,** you ought to (do so).

lécher [leʃe], *v.tr.* (**je lèche; je lécherai**) to lick (up); **se l. les doigts,** to lick one's fingers; *F:* **s'en léchait les doigts,** he smacked his lips over it; **l. les bottes de qn,** *F:* to suck up to s.o.; *F:* **les vitrines,** to go window-shopping.

leçon [ləsõ], *s.f.* lesson.

lecteur, -trice [lɛktœ:r, -tris], *s.* *(a)* reader; foreign language assistant (at university).

lecture [lɛkty:r], *s.f.* reading.

ledit, ladite, *pl.* **lesdits, lesdites** [lədi, ladi, ledi, ledit] (*contracted with à and de to* **auxdit(e)s, dudit, desdit(e)s**) *a.* the aforesaid.

légal, -aux [legal, -o], *a.* legal; statutory; **légale,** statutory holiday; *adv.* **-ement.**

légal|iser [legalize], *v.tr.* **1.** to legalize. **2.** attest, certify (signature, etc.); *s.f.* **-ité,** legality, lawfulness.

légataire [legatɛr], *s.m. & f. Jur:* legatee, he

légation [legasjɔ̃], *s.f.* legation.

légend|**e** [leʒɑ̃:d], *s.f.* 1. legend. 2. (*a*) inscription (on coin); (*b*) caption (of illustration); (*c*) key, *N.Am:* legend (to diagram, etc.); list of conventional signs (on map, etc.); *a.* -**aire**, legendary.

lég|**er**, -**ère** [leʒe, -ɛ:r]. 1. *a.* (*a*) light; **avoir le sommeil l.**, to be a light sleeper; **avoir la main légère**, to be quick with one's hands; (*b*) slight (pain); gentle (breeze); faint (sound). 2. *adv.phr.* **à la légère**, lightly; **conclure à la légère**, to jump to conclusions; *adv.* -**èrement**; *s.f.* -**èreté**, lightness.

légion [leʒjɔ̃], *s.f.* legion; **la L. étrangère**, the Foreign Legion; **L. d'honneur**, Legion of Honour; *s.m.* -**naire**, legionary; soldier of the Foreign Legion; member of the Legion of Honour.

législa|**tion** [leʒislasjɔ̃], *s.f.* legislation; *s.* -**teur**, -**trice**, legislator, law-giver; *a.* -**tif**, -**tive**, legislative; *s.f.* -**ture**.

légiste [leʒist], *s.m*, jurist; **médecin l.**, forensic pathologist; **expert l.**, forensic scientist.

légitime [leʒitim], *a.* 1. legitimate, lawful. 2. justifiable; well-founded (fears, etc.); *Jur:* **l. défense**, self-defence; *adv.* -**ment**.

légitim|**er** [leʒitime], *v.tr.* 1. to legitimate, legitimatize (child). 2. to justify (action, claim). 3. to recognize (title); *s.f.* -**ation**; *s.f.* -**ité**, legitimacy.

legs [lɛ, lɛg], *s.m.* legacy, bequest.

léguer [lege], *v.tr.* (**je lègue; je léguerai**) to bequeath.

légume [legym], *s.m.* 1. vegetable; **légumes verts**, greens; **légumes secs**, dried vegetables. 2. *F:* **gros l.**, *s.f.* **grosse l.**, big shot.

Léman [lemɑ̃]. *Pr.n.m.* **le lac L.**, the Lake of Geneva.

lendemain [lɑ̃dmɛ̃], *s.m.* next day; **le l. matin**, the next morning, the morning after; **songer au l.**, to think of the morrow, of the future; **du jour au l. il devint célèbre**, he became famous overnight; **des succès sans l.**, short-lived successes.

l|**ent, lente** [lɑ̃, lɑ̃:t], *a.* slow; *adc.* -**ement**; *s.f.* -**eur**, slowness; *pl.* delays.

lentille [lɑ̃ti:j], *s.f.* 1. *Cu:* lentil. 2. *Opt:* lens (for telescope, spectacles, etc.); **l. cornéenne**, contact lens.

léopard [leopa:r], *s.m.* leopard.

lèpre [lɛpr], *s.f.* leprosy.

lépreux, -euse [leprø, -ø:z]. 1. *a.* leprous. 2. *s.* leper.

lequel, laquelle, lesquels, lesquelles [ləkɛl, lakɛl, lekɛl], *pron.* (*contracted with* **à** *and* **de** *to* **auquel, auxquel(le)s; duquel, desquel(le)s**) 1. *rel.pron.* who, whom; which; (*a*) (*of thgs after prep.*) **décision par laquelle . . .**, decision whereby . . .; (*b*) (*of pers.*) **la dame avec laquelle elle était sortie**, the lady with whom

she had gone out; (*c*) (*to avoid ambiguity*) **le père de cette jeune fille, lequel est très riche,** the girl's father, who is very rich; (*d*) (*adjectival*) **il écrira peut-être, auquel cas . . .**, perhaps he will write, in which case . . .. 2. *interr.pron.* **lequel d'entre nous?** which one of us?

lesbien, -ienne [lɛzbjɛ̃, -jɛn], *a. & s.f.* lesbian.

lèse-majesté [lɛzmaʒɛste], *s.f.* high treason, lese-majesty.

léser [leze], *v.tr.* (**je lèse, n. lésons**) (*a*) to wrong (s.o.); to injure (s.o.); (*b*) (*of action*) to prove injurious to (s.o., sth.).

lésin|**er** [lezine], *v.i.* to be stingy, close-fisted; to haggle (**sur**, over); *s.* -**eur**, -**euse**, haggler.

lessive [lesi:v], *s.f.* 1. detergent. 2. (household) washing; (*a*) **faire la l.**, to do the washing; (*b*) articles washed; **étendre la l.**, to hang out the washing.

lessiver [lesive], *v.tr.* 1. to wash (linen, etc.). 2. *P:* **être lessivé**, to be cleaned out.

leste [lɛst], *a.* light; nimble, agile; **maman avait la main l.**, mother was always ready to give one a spanking; **plaisanterie un peu l.**, rather a naughty joke; *adv.* -**ment**.

létharg|**ie** [letarʒi], *s.f.* lethargy, inactivity; *a.* -**ique**, lethargic.

lettre [lɛtr], *s.f.* letter. 1. **écrire qch. en toutes lettres**, to write sth. out in full. 2. **au pied de la l.**, literally. 3. (*a*) *P.T.T:* letter; (*b*) **l. recommandée**, registered letter; (*b*) **l. de change**, bill of exchange. 4. *pl.* literature; **homme de lettres**, man of letters.

lettré [letre]. 1. *a.* well-read. 2. *s.* scholar; well-read man.

leucém|**ie** [løsemi], *s.f. Med:* leukaemia; *a. & s.m. & f.* -**ique**, (i) leukaemic; (ii) leukaemia sufferer.

leur[1] [lœ:r]. 1. *poss.a.* their; **leurs père et mère,** their father and mother. 2. **le leur, la leur, les leurs,** (*a*) *poss.pron.* theirs; (*b*) *s.m.* (i) their own; **ils n'y mettent pas du leur,** they don't pull their weight; (ii) *pl.* their own (friends); **je m'intéresse à eux et aux leurs,** I am interested in them and in theirs; (iii) **ils continuent à faire des leurs,** they go on playing their old tricks.

leur[2], *pers.pron. see* **LUI**[1].

leurrer [lœre], *v.tr.* to lure; to entice.

levain [ləvɛ̃], *s.m.* leaven.

levant [ləvɑ̃]. 1. *a.m.* **soleil l.**, rising sun. 2. *s.m.* (*a*) **le l.**, the east; (*b*) *Geog:* **le L.**, the Levant.

levé [ləve]. 1. *a.* (*a*) raised; **dessin à main levée,** freehand drawing; **voter à main levée,** to vote by a show of hands; (*b*) (*of pers.*) up; out of bed. 2. *s.m.* **l. d'un terrain,** plan, survey, of a piece of land.

levée [ləve], *s.f.* 1. (*a*) raising, lifting; (*b*) gathering (of crops, etc.); *P.T.T:* collection (of letters); **la l. est faite,** the box has been cleared. 2. (*a*) embankment, sea-wall; (*b*) *Mec:* up-

stroke (of piston); lift (of cam); (c) *Cards:* **faire une l.,** to take a trick.
lever [ləve]. **I.** *v.tr.* (**je lève**) **1.** (*a*) to raise, to lift (up); **l. les yeux,** to look up; **l. l'ancre,** to weigh anchor; (*b*) to raise (siege); to close (meeting); (*c*) **l. une difficulté,** to remove a difficulty. **2.** to lift (root crops); to levy (a tax); to collect (letters), to gather (crops). **3. l. un plan,** to draw, get out, a plan. **4.** *v.i.* (*of dough*) to rise; (*of plants*) to shoot. **II.** *s.m.* **1.** (*a*) rising; getting up (from bed); (*b*) levee; (*c*) **l. du soleil,** sunrise. **2.** *Th:* **un l. de rideau en un acte,** a one-act curtain-raiser.
se lever. (*a*) to stand up; **se l. de table,** to leave the table; (*b*) to get up (from bed); to rise; *F:* **se l. du pied gauche,** to get out of bed on the wrong side; (*c*) **le vent se lève,** the wind is rising, is getting up.
levier [ləvje], *s.m.* **1.** lever; **force de l.,** leverage; *Aut:* **l. de changement (de vitesse),** gear lever. **2.** crowbar.
levraut [ləvro], *s.m.* leveret; young hare.
lèvre [lɛːvr], *s.f.* **1.** lip; **rire du bout des lèvres,** to laugh in a forced manner; **pincer les lèvres,** to purse one's lips. **2.** rim (of crater).
lévrier [levrije], *s.m.* greyhound.
levure [ləvyːr], *s.f.* yeast.
lézard [lezaːr], *s.m.* lizard.
lézardé [lezarde], *a.* (*of wall*) cracked, full of cracks.
liaison [ljɛzɔ̃], *s.f.* **1.** (*a*) joining, binding; bonding (of bricks, etc.); (*b*) *Ling:* liaison; (*c*) *Cu:* thickening (of sauce). **2.** intimacy; close relationship; **l. d'affaires,** business connection.
liasse [ljas], *s.f.* bundle (of letters); wad (of banknotes); file (of papers).
Liban (le) [ləbɑ̃]. *Pr.n.m. Geog:* Lebanon.
libanais, -aise [libanɛ, -ɛːz], *a. & s.* Lebanese.
libellule [libellyl], *s.f. Ent:* dragon-fly.
libéral, -aux [liberal, -o], *a.* liberal; *adv.* **-ement;** *s.f.* **-ité,** liberality.
libérl er [libere], *v.tr.* (**je libère; je libérerai**) to liberate, release; to set (s.o.) free; *s.* **-ateur, -atrice;** *s.f.* **-ation.**
liberté [libɛrte], *s.f.* **1.** liberty, freedom; *Jur:* (**mise en) l. provisoire, sous caution,** bail; **parler en toute l.,** to speak freely; **mon jour de l.,** my day off. **2. prendre des libertés avec qn,** to take liberties with s.o.
librairl e [librɛːr], *s.m. & f.* bookseller; *s.f.* **-ie,** bookselling, the book trade; bookshop.
libre [libr], *a.* free. **1.** (*a*) **quand je suis l.,** when I'm off duty; **je suis l. de mon temps,** my time's my own; (*b*) **l. de soucis,** carefree; (*c*) **conversation l.,** free, broad, conversation. **2.** clear, open (space); vacant (seat); *P.T.T:* **'pas l.,'** 'line engaged'; (*taxi sign*) **'l.,'** 'for hire'; *adv.* **-ment.**
libre-échangl e [librefɑ̃ːʒ], *s.m.* free trade; *s.m.*

-iste, free-trader.
libre-service [librəsɛrvis], *s.m.* self-service (shop, restaurant); *pl.* **libres-services.**
Libye (la) [labi]. *Pr.n.f. Geog:* Libya.
libyen, -enne [libjɛ̃, -jɛn], *a. & s. Geog:* Libyan.
licence [lisɑ̃ːs], *s.f.* licence. **1.** (*a*) leave, permission; *Adm:* **l. d'importation,** import licence; (*b*) *Sch:* **passer sa l.,** to take one's degree. **2.** (*a*) abuse of liberty; (*b*) licentiousness.
licencié, -iée [lisɑ̃sje], *s. Sch:* graduate.
licencil er [lisɑ̃sje], *v.tr.* (*pr. sub. & p.d.* n. **licenciions**) to disband (troops); to lay off (workmen); *s.m.* **-ement.**
licite [lisit], *a.* licit, lawful, permissible; *adv.* **-ment.**
lie [li], *s.f.* lees, dregs (of wine, etc.).
lie-de-vin [lidvɛ̃], *a. & s.m.inv.* wine-colour(ed).
liège [ljɛːʒ], *s.m.* **1.** *Bot:* cork-oak. **2.** cork.
lien [ljɛ̃], *s.m.* tie, bond.
lil er [lje], *v.tr.* (*pr. sub. & p.d.* n. **liions**) **1.** (*a*) to bind, tie, tie up; **l'intérêt nous lie,** we have common interests; **l. des idées,** to link ideas; (*b*) *Cu:* **l. une sauce,** to thicken a sauce. **2. l. conversation avec qn,** to enter into conversation with s.o.; *s.m.* **-age.**
se lier. 1. se l. (d'amitié) avec qn, to form a friendship with s.o. **2.** to bind oneself (by contract). **3.** *Cu:* (*of sauces*) to thicken; (*of gravel*) to bind.
lierre [ljɛːr], *s.m.* ivy.
lieu, -eux [ljø], *s.m.* **1.** place; (*a*) locality, spot; **le l. du sinistre,** the scene of the disaster; **en tout l.,** everywhere; **je tiens ce renseignement de bon l.,** I have this information from a good source; **en (tout) premier l.,** in the first place, first of all; **en dernier l.,** finally; (*b*) *pl.* premises. **2.** (*a*) **avoir l.,** to take place; (*b*) ground(s), cause; **il y a (tout) l. de supposer que + ind.,** there is (every) reason for supposing that . . .; (*c*) **tenir l. de qch.,** to take the place of sth.; **au l. de,** instead of; **au l. que + ind.,** whereas. **3. lieux communs,** commonplaces, platitudes.
lieutenant [ljøtnɑ̃], *s.m.* (*a*) *Mil: Nau:* lieutenant; *Av:* flying officer; (*b*) *Merchant Navy:* mate.
lieutenant-colonel [ljøtnɑ̃kɔlɔnɛl], *s.m. Mil:* lieutenant-colonel; *Av:* wing-commander; *pl.* **lieutenants-colonels.**
lièvre [ljɛːvr], *s.m. Z:* hare; **mémoire de l.,** memory like a sieve.
liftier, -ière [liftje, -jɛːr], *s.* lift-attendant, *N.Am* elevator operator.
ligne [liɲ], *s.f.* line. **1.** (*a*) cord; **l. de pêche,** fishing-line; (*b*) **l. droite,** straight line; *Fb:* **l. de touche,** touch line; *Tennis:* **l. de fond,** base line; (*c*) (out)line; **voiture qui a de la l.,** car with clean lines; **grandes lignes d'une œuvre,** broad outline of a work; **soigner sa l.,** to watch one's

figure; (d) l. de flottaison, water-line (of ship); *Artil:* l. de tir, line of fire; **descendre en l. directe de . . .**, to be lineally descended from . . .; (e) l. de maisons, row of houses; **question qui vient en première l.**, question of primary importance; **hors l.**, out of the ordinary; (f) écris-moi deux lignes, drop me a line. 2. (a) l. (de chemin de fer), (railway) line; l. aérienne, maritime, air, steamship, line, l. d'autobus, bus service; (b) l. téléphonique, telephone line; l. partagée, party line.

lignée [liɲe], *s.f.* issue; (line of) descendants.

ligoter [ligɔte], *v.tr.* to bind (s.o.) hand and foot; to lash (thgs) together.

ligue [lig], *s.f.* league, confederacy.

lilas [lila]. 1. *s.m. Bot:* lilac. 2. *a.inv.* lilac.

limace [limas], *s.f.* slug.

limaçon [limasɔ̃], *s.m.* snail; **escalier en l.**, spiral staircase.

limande [limɑ̃:d], *s.f. Ich:* dab.

lime [lim], *s.f. Tls:* file; l. à ongles, nail-file.

limer [lime], *v.tr.* to file; to file down.

limier [limje], *s.m.* bloodhound.

limite [limit], *s.f.* 1. boundary; limit; l. d'âge, age limit; *Sp:* limites du jeu, boundary-lines. 2. cas l., borderline case; vitesse l., maximum speed; date l., deadline.

limiter [limite], *v.tr.* 1. to bound, to mark the bounds of (countries, property). 2. to limit; to restrict; *s.f.* -ation; *a.* -rophe, adjacent (de, to).

limon¹ [limɔ̃], *s.m.* mud, silt.

limon², *s.m. Bot:* sour lime.

limonade [limɔnad], *s.f.* (fizzy) lemonade.

limpide [lɛ̃pid], *a.* limpid, clear; *s.f.* -ité, limpidity.

lin [lɛ̃], *s.m.* 1. flax; graine de l., linseed; huile de l., linseed oil. 2. (tissu de) l., linen.

linéaire [lineɛ:r], *a.* linear; mesures linéaires, measures of length; dessin l., geometrical, machine, drawing.

linge [lɛ̃:ʒ], *s.m.* 1. (made-up) linen; l. de table, table-linen; l. (de corps), underwear. 2. piece of linen; essuyer qch. avec un l., to wipe sth. with a cloth.

lingerie [lɛ̃ʒri], *s.f.* underwear; lingerie.

lingot [lɛ̃go], *s.m. Metall:* ingot; or, argent, en lingots, bullion.

linguiste [lɛ̃gɥist], *s.m. & f.* linguist; -ique, (i) *a.* linguistic; (ii) *s.f.* linguistics.

lino [lino]. *F:* (a) *s.m. H:* lino; (b) *s.m. Art:* linocut; (c) *s.f. Typ:* linotype.

linoléum [linɔleɔm], *s.m.* linoleum.

linotte [linɔt], *s.f. Orn:* linnet; *F:* tête de l., feather-brained person.

linotype [linɔtip], *s.f. R.t.m:* Linotype (machine); *s.f.* -typie, Linotype setting; *s.m. & f.* -typiste, Linotype operator.

linteau, -eaux [lɛ̃to], *s.m.* lintel.

lion, -onne [ljɔ̃, -ɔn], *s.* 1. lion, *f.* lioness. 2. *Astr:* le L., Leo; *s.m.* -ceau, -eaux, lion cub.

lippe [lip], *s.f.* thick (lower) lip; *a.* -u, thick-lipped.

liquéfier [likefje], *v.tr.* to liquefy; *a.* -fiable; *s.f.* -faction.

liqueur [likœ:r], *s.f.* 1. liqueur; vin de l., dessert wine. 2. *Ch:* liquid, solution; l. titrée, standard solution; *Atom.Ph:* feed.

liquide [likid]. 1. *a.* liquid; argent l., ready money. 2. *s.m.* (a) liquid, fluid; *Com:* liquides, wet goods; l. antigel, antifreeze; l. antigivrant, anti-icing fluid; (b) *F:* drink.

liquider [likide], *v.tr.* 1. to liquidate; (a) to wind up (a business); (b) to settle (account); *F:* to liquidate (s.o.). 2. to realize (one's fortune); to sell off; *Com:* l. des marchandises, to clear out goods; *s.f.* -ation. 1. liquidation. 2. selling off; clearance sale.

lire [li:r], *v.tr.* (*pr.p.* lisant; *p.p.* lu) 1. to read; l. à haute voix, to read aloud; l. dans la pensée de qn, to read s.o.'s thoughts; dans l'attente de vous l., hoping to hear from you. 2. l. une communication, to read out a notice.

lis [lis], *s.m.* lily.

Lisbonne [lizbɔn]. *Pr.n.f. Geog:* Lisbon.

liseron [lizrɔ̃], *s.m.* bindweed, convolvulus.

liseur, -euse [lizœ:r, -ø:z]. 1. *a.* given to, fond of, reading; le public l., the reading public. 2. *s.m. & f.* a (great) reader. 3. *s.f.* (a) book wrapper, jacket; (b) bed-jacket.

lisible [lizibl], *a.* 1. legible (writing). 2. readable (book); *adv.* -lement, legibly; *s.f.* -ilité.

lisière [lizjɛ:r], *s.f.* 1. selvedge (of cloth). 2. edge, border (of field, forest, etc.).

lisse [lis], *a.* smooth, glossy, polished; sleek.

lisser [lise], *v.tr.* to smooth, gloss, polish; (of bird) se l. les plumes, to preen its feathers.

liste [list], *s.f.* list, roll, register; *Mil: etc:* roster; grossir la l., to swell the numbers; *Pol:* venir en tête de l., to head the poll.

lit [li], *s.m.* 1. bed; bedstead; l. d'ami, spare bed; prendre le l., to take to one's bed; garder le l., to be laid up; cloué au l., bed-ridden; l. de mort, deathbed; enfant du second l., child of the second marriage. 2. (a) bed, layer (of soil, sand); (b) bed (of river). 3. set (of the tide); être dans le l. de la marée, to be in the tideway; dans le l. du vent, in the wind's eye; *s.f.* -erie, bedding.

litanie [litani], *s.f.* litany; réciter toujours la même l., to keep harping on the same thing.

litière [litjɛ:r], *s.f.* (stable-)litter; faire la l. d'un cheval, to bed down a horse.

litige [liti:ʒ], *s.m. Jur:* litigation; lawsuit; cas en l., case at-issue, in dispute.

litre [litr], *s.m. Meas:* litre (about 1¾-pints); vin au l., wine on draught; *Aut:* dix litres aux cent (kilomètres) = thirty miles to the gallon.

littéraire [literɛ:r], *a.* literary.

littéral, -aux [literal, -ɔ], *a.* literal; *adv.* **-ement.**

littérateur [literatœːr], *s.m.* literary man; man of letters.

littérature [literatyːr], *s.f.* literature.

littoral, -aux [litɔral, -ɔ]. **1.** *a.* littoral, coastal (region, etc.). **2.** *s.m.* coastline; littoral; **le l. de la Mer Rouge,** the shores of the Red Sea.

liturgile [lityrʒi], *s.f.* liturgy; *a.* **-que,** liturgical.

livide [livid], *a.* livid; ghastly (pale).

Livourne [livurn]. *Pr.n. Geog:* Leghorn.

livraison [livrɛzɔ̃], *s.f.* delivery (of goods); **l. franco,** delivered free; **payable à l.,** cash on delivery, payable on delivery; **prendre l. de qch.,** to take delivery of sth.; *P.N: Com:* **l. à domicile,** we deliver.

livre[1] [liːvr], *s.f.* pound. **1.** (*weight*) **vendre qch. à la l.,** to sell sth. by the pound. **2.** (*money*) **l. sterling,** pound sterling.

livre[2], *s.m.* book; **l. de classe,** school book; **l. de poche,** paperback; *Book-k:* **tenue des livres,** book-keeping.

livrler [livre], *v.tr.* **1.** (*a*) to deliver; to give up; **livré à soi-même,** left to oneself; **l. un secret,** to betray a secret; **l. ses secrets à qn,** to confide one's secrets to s.o.; (*b*) **l. bataille,** to join battle (à, with). **2.** to deliver (goods); *s.* **-eur, -euse,** delivery man, girl.

se livrer, to give oneself up (to justice, to drink, to despair).

livret [livrɛ], *s.m.* **1.** (savings bank, etc.) book. **2.** *Mus:* libretto.

local, -aux [lɔkal, -ɔ]. **1.** *a.* local (authority, etc.); *Rail:* **ligne d'intérêt l.,** branch line. **2.** *s.m.* (*a*) premises, building; **l. d'habitation,** residential unit; **locaux commerciaux,** business premises; (*b*) *Fb:* **les locaux,** the home side; *adv.* **-ement;** *s.f.* **-ité,** locality, district.

localtion [lɔkasjɔ̃], *s.f.* (*a*) (i) hiring; (ii) letting out on hire; (*b*) (i) renting, tenancy; (ii) letting (of house, etc.); **agent de l.,** house agent; **prix de l.,** rent; (*c*) *Th:* **bureau de l.,** box-office; *s.m. & f.* **-taire,** tenant.

lock-out [lɔk(a)ut], *s.m.inv. Ind:* lockout.

lock-outer [lɔk(a)ute], *v.tr. Ind:* to lock out (the personnel).

locomotive [lɔkɔmɔtiːv], *s.f. Rail:* locomotive, engine.

locution [lɔkysjɔ̃], *s.f.* expression, phrase.

logarithme [lɔgaritm], *s.m.* logarithm; **table de logarithmes,** *F:* log table.

loge [lɔːʒ], *s.f.* **1.** hut, cabin; (porter's, etc.) lodge. **2.** *Th:* box.

logement [lɔʒmɑ̃], *s.m.* **1.** lodging, housing; billeting (of troops); **la crise du l.,** the housing shortage. **2.** (*a*) accommodation; lodgings; *F:* digs; **l. garni, meublé,** furnished rooms; **le l. et la nourriture,** board and lodging; (*b*) *Mil:* quarters; billet.

loger [lɔʒe], *v.* (**n. logeons**) **1.** *v.i.* to lodge, live; to

be billeted; **l. en garni,** to live in digs. **2.** *v.tr.* (*a*) to lodge; to put (s.o.) up; (*b*) to place, put; **je ne sais où l. mes livres,** I don't know where to put my books.

se loger. 1. (*a*) to go into lodgings; (*b*) to build, to find, a house. **2.** (*of ball, etc.*) to get stuck (in a tree, on the roof).

logique [lɔʒik]. **1.** *a.* logical; reasoned. **2.** *s.f.* logic; *adv.* **-ment.**

logis [lɔʒi], *s.m.* home, house, dwelling; **garder le l.,** to stay in; **corps de l.,** main building.

loi [lwa], *s.f.* **1.** (*a*) law; **homme de l.,** lawyer; **faire la l. à qn,** to lay down the law to s.o.; **mettre (qn) hors la l.,** to outlaw (s.o.); (*b*) act (of Parliament); law, statute; **projet de l.,** bill. **2.** law (of nature, etc.); **les lois de la pesanteur,** the laws of gravity; **les lois du jeu,** the rules of the game.

loin [lwɛ̃], *adv.* far; **plus l.,** farther (on); further; **moins l.,** less far. **1.** (*a*) (*of place*) **la poste est l.,** the post office is a long way off; **il ira l.,** he'll go far; **l. derrière lui,** far behind him; **de l.,** (i) by far; (ii) from afar; (*b*) *s.m.* **au l.,** in the (far) distance. **2.** (*of time*) distant; **ce jour est encore l.,** that day is yet far off; **de l. en l.,** at long intervals.

lointain [lwɛ̃tɛ̃]. **1.** *a.* distant, remote (country, period). **2.** *s.m.* **dans le l.,** in the distance, in the background.

loir [lwar], *s.m. Z:* dormouse.

loisible [lwazibl], *a.* permissible, optional; **il lui est l. de refuser,** it is open to him to refuse.

loisir [lwaziːr], *s.m.* leisure; **avoir des loisirs,** to have some spare time; **à l.,** at leisure, at your (his, etc.) convenience.

londonien, -ienne [lɔ̃dɔnjɛ̃, -jɛn]. **1.** *a.* of London. **2.** *s.* Londoner.

Londres [lɔ̃dr]. *Pr.n. usu. f. Geog:* London.

long, longue [lɔ̃, lɔ̃ːg]. **1.** *a.* long; (*a*) (*of space*) **ruban l. de cinq mètres,** ribbon five metres long; **vue longue,** long sight; (*b*) (*of time*) **l. soupir,** long-drawn sigh; **elle fut longue à s'en remettre,** she was a long time getting over it; à **la longue,** in the long run. **2.** *s.m.* **lengt** ; (*a*) (*of space*) **table qui a six pieds de l.,** table six foot long; **en l.,** lengthwise; **de l. en large,** up and down, to and fro; **étendu de tout son l.,** stretched at full length; **s'amarrer le l. d'un navire,** to moor alongside a ship; **se faufiler le l. du mur,** to creep along the wall; (*b*) (*of time*) **tout le l. du jour,** all day long; (*c*) (*of amount*) **inutile d'en dire plus l.,** I need say no more **regard qui en dit l.,** look which speaks volumes; *adv.* **-uement,** (i) for a long time; (ii) slowly, deliberately.

long-courrier [lɔ̃kurje], *a. & s.m. Nau: Av:* **1.** ocean-going (ship); liner; long-range (aircraft); airliner. **2.** captain (of a liner); *pl.* **long-courriers.**

onge [lõːӡ], *s.f. Cu:* loin (of veal).

onger [lõӡe], *v.tr.* (n. **longeons**) to keep to the edge of (wood, etc.), to skirt; to hug (the coast, the wall).

ongévité [lõӡevite], *s.f.* longevity, long life.

ongitud‚e [lõӡityd], *s.f.* longitude; *a.* -inal, -inaux, longitudinal.

ongtemps [lõtã]. 1. *adv.* long; a long time. 2. *s.m.* il y a l., long ago; depuis l., for a long time; avant l., before long.

ongueur [lõgœːr], *s.f.* length. 1. couper qch. en l., to cut sth. lengthwise; tirer un discours en l., to spin out, drag out, a speech. 2. *Rac:* gagner par une, d'une, l., to win by a length.

ongue-vue [lõgvy], *s.f.* telescope; *pl.* longues-vues.

opin [lɔpɛ̃], *s.m.* l. de terre, patch, plot (of ground).

oquace [lɔkas], *a.* loquacious, talkative; garrulous.

oquacité [lɔkasite], *s.f.* loquacity, talkativeness; garrulity, garrulousness.

oque [lɔk], *s.f.* rag; *F:* (*of pers.*) être comme une l., to feel like a wet rag.

oquet [lɔkɛ], *s.m.* latch (of door).

ors [lɔːr], *adv.* (*a*) depuis l., ever since then; *F:* pour l. . . ., so . . ., then . . .; (*b*) l. . . . que, when; l. de sa naissance, when he was born.

orsque [lɔrsk(ə)], *conj.* (*becomes* lorsqu' *before a vowel*) when; l. j'entrai, when I entered; lorsqu'il sera parti, when he's gone.

ot [lo], *s.m.* 1. (*a*) share; portion, lot; (*b*) prize (in a lottery); gros l., first prize. 2. lot, parcel (of goods); batch (of goods, people).

oterie [lɔtri], *s.f.* (*a*) lottery; (*b*) raffle, draw.

otion [losjõ], *s.f. Pharm: etc:* lotion.

otir [lɔtiːr], *v.tr.* 1. to divide (sth.) into lots; to parcel out (estate into building lots). 2. être bien loti, to be well provided for; to be well off; mal loti, badly off.

otissement [lɔtismã], *s.m.* 1. (*a*) parcelling out; allotment, dividing up; (*b*) development (of building land). 2. (*a*) building plots; (*b*) housing development.

ouable [lwabl], *a.* laudable, praiseworthy; commendable (de, for); *adv.* -ment.

ouage [lwaːӡ], *s.m.* hiring, hire; voiture, avion, de l., hired car, charter aircraft.

ouange [lwãːӡ], *s.f.* praise; chanter ses propres louanges, to blow one's own trumpet.

ouche¹ [luʃ], *a.* 1. squint-eyed. 2. (*a*) ambiguous; (*b*) shady, suspicious; *s.m.* il y a du l., there's something fishy.

ouche², *s.f.* (soup) ladle.

ouch‚er [luʃe], *v.i.* to squint; l. de l'œil gauche, to have a cast in the left eye; *s.* -eur, -euse, squinter, cross-eyed person.

ouer¹ [lue, lwe], *v.tr.* 1. to hire out, let (out);

maison à l., house to let. 2. to hire; to rent (à, from); l. une place d'avance, to book a seat.

louer², *v.tr.* to praise, commend; l. qn de, pour, qch., to praise s.o. for sth.

se louer de qch., to be pleased with sth.

loufoque [lufɔk], (*a*) *a. F:* cracked, bats, crazy; (*b*) *s. F:* crank, crackpot, *N.Am:* screwball.

Louis [lwi, lui]. *Pr.n.m.* Lewis; Louis.

Louise [lwiːz]. *Pr.n.f.* Louisa, Louise.

loup [lu], *s.m.* wolf; marcher à pas de l., to walk stealthily; il fait un froid de l., it's bitterly cold.

loupe [lup], *s.f.* magnifying-glass.

lourd [luːr], *a.* (*a*) heavy; ungainly; ponderous; *Aut:* poids l., heavy lorry, *F:* juggernaut; terrain l., heavy ground; j'ai la tête lourde, I feel headachy: *adv.* peser l., to weigh heavy; (*b*) clumsy; dull; dull-witted; (*c*) incident l. de conséquences, incident heavy with consequences; lourde bévue, gross blunder, *F:* clanger; (*d*) close, sultry (weather); *adv.* -ement; *s.f.* -eur, heaviness.

lourdaud [lurdo]. 1. *a.* (*a*) loutish; lumpish, clumsy (fellow); (*b*) dull-witted (person). 2. *s.* (*a*) lout; (*b*) blockhead, *F:* dimwit.

loutre [lutr], *s.f. Z:* otter; *Com:* l. d'Amérique, nutria.

louve [luːv], *s.f. Z:* she-wolf; *s.m.* -teau, -teaux, wolf-cub; *Scouting:* (wolf-)cub.

louvoyer [luvwaje], *v.i.* (je louvoie) (*a*) *Nau:* to tack; (*b*) to scheme, manœuvre.

loyal, -aux [lwajal, -o], *a.* 1. honest, fair; jeu l., fair play. 2. loyal, faithful; true (friend); *adv.* -ement; *s.m.* -isme, (political, etc.) loyalty.

loyauté [lwajote], *s.f.* 1. honesty, uprightness; manque de l., dishonesty, unfairness. 2. loyalty, fidelity (envers, towards).

loyer [lwaje], *s.m.* rent(al).

lubie [lybi], *s.f.* whim, fad; encore une de ses lubies! another of his (her) little ideas!

lubrifi‚er [lybrifje], *v.tr.* to lubricate; to grease, oil; *a. & s.m.* -ant, lubricant; *s.f.* -cation, greasing.

Luc [lyk]. *Pr.n.m.* Luke.

lucarne [lykarn], *s.f.* (*a*) dormer-window, attic window; (*b*) skylight.

lucide [lysid], *a.* lucid, clear (mind); clear-headed (person); *adv.* -ment.

lucidité [lysidite], *s.f.* lucidity, clearness.

lucrat‚if, -ive [lykratif, -iːv], *a.* lucrative, profitable; *adv.* -ivement, lucratively, profitably.

lueur [lyœːr], *s.f.* 1. gleam, glimmer; à la l. des étoiles, by starlight. 2. l. momentanée, flash of light.

luge [lyːӡ], *s.f.* luge; toboggan.

lugubre [lygyːbr], *a.* lugubrious, dismal, gloomy, mournful; *adv.* -ment.

lui¹, *pl.* **leur** [lɥi, lœ(ː)r], *pers.pron.m. & f.* (to) him, her, it, them; (*a*) (*unstressed*) je le lui

donne, I give it (to) him, (to) her; **donnez-lui-en**, give him some; **cette maison leur appartient**, this house belongs to them; (*b*) (*stressed in imp.*) **montrez-le-leur**, show it to them.
lui², *pl.* **eux** [lɥi, ø], *stressed pers.pron.m.* (*a*) he, it, they; **c'est lui**, it is he, *F:* it's him; **ce sont eux**, *F:* **c'est eux**, it is they, *F:* it's them; **lui et sa femme**, he and his wife; (*b*) him, it, them; **lui je le connais**, I know *him*; **j'accuse son frère et lui**, I accuse him and his brother; **ce livre est à eux**, this book is theirs; (*c*) (*refl.*) him(self), it(self), them(selves); **ils ne pensent qu'à eux**, they think of nobody but themselves.
luire [lɥiːr], *v.i.* (*pr.p.* **luisant**; *p.p.* **lui** (*no f.*); *p.h.* **il luisit** *is rare*) to shine; **le jour luit**, day is breaking.
luisant, -ante [lɥizɑ̃, -ɑ̃ːt]. 1. *a.* shining, bright; shiny, glossy; gleaming. 2. *s.m.* gloss, sheen.
lumière [lymjɛːr], *s.f.* light; **l. du jour, du soleil, l. électrique**, daylight, sunlight, electric light; **mettre en l. les défauts de . . .**, to bring out the faults of . . .; **faire la l. sur une affaire**, to clear up a matter.
luminaire [lyminɛːr], *s.m.* (*a*) luminary, light; star, sun; (*b*) *coll.* lights, lighting.
lumineu|x, -euse [lyminø, -øːz], *a.* luminous; *adv.* **-sement**.
lunaire [lynɛːr], *a.* (*a*) lunar; **paysage l., moonscape; fusée l.**, moon rocket; **piéton l., moonwalker; secousse l.**, moonquake; (*b*) **avoir l'esprit l.**, to be a dreamer.
lunch [lœ̃ːʃ], *s.m.* (*a*) snack; (*b*) buffet meal; *pl.* **lunch(e)s.**
lundi [lœ̃di], *s.m.* Monday.
lune [lyn], *s.f.* 1. moon; **se poser sur la l.**, to land on the moon; **l. de miel**, honeymoon; **être dans la l.**, to be wool-gathering. 2. **en forme de l.**, crescent-shaped. 3. **pierre de l.**, moonstone.
lunette [lynɛt], *s.f.* 1. **l. d'approche**, telescope; field-glass. 2. *pl.* **lunettes**, spectacles. 3. *Cu:*

merrythought, wishbone (of fowl). 4. *Arch:* *Fort:* lunette; *Aut:* **l. arrière**, rear window; **l. panoramique**, wrap-round rear window.
lustre [lystr], *s.m.* 1. lustre, polish, gloss. 2. chandelier; **l. électrique**, (electric) chandelier.
lustrer [lystre], *v.tr.* to glaze, polish (up); **le poil lustré du chat**, the cat's glossy coat.
lutrin [lytrɛ̃], *s.m.* *Ecc:* lectern; *Fr.C:* music stand.
lutte [lyt], *s.f.* 1. wrestling; **l. libre**, freestyle wrestling. 2. (*a*) contest, struggle, tussle; **l. à mort**, life-and-death struggle; **l. contre la maladie**, disease prevention; (*b*) strife; **la l. des classes**, class warfare.
lutt|er [lyte], *v.i.* 1. to wrestle. 2. to struggle, fight, compete; to battle (with s.o.); **l. de vitesse avec qn**, to race s.o.; *s.* **-eur, -euse**, wrestler; fighter.
luxation [lyksasjɔ̃], *s.f.* *Med:* dislocation (of joint).
luxe [lyks], *s.m.* luxury; **gros l.**, ostentation; **train de l.** = Pullman train.
Luxembourg (le) [lələyksɑ̃buːr]. *Pr.n.m.* Luxemburg.
luxueu|x, -euse [lyksɥø, -øːz], *a.* luxurious, rich; sumptuous; *adv.* **-sement**.
luzerne [lyzɛrn], *s.f.* lucern(e); *N.Am:* alfalfa.
lycée [lise], *s.m.* = grammar, high, school; technique, technical college.
lycéen, -enne [liseɛ̃, -ɛn], *s.* pupil at a *lycée* grammar school boy, girl.
lymph|e [lɛ̃ːf], *s.f.* lymph; *a.* **-atique** lymphatic.
lynx [lɛ̃ːks], *s.m.* lynx.
Lyon [ljɔ̃]. *Pr.n.* *Geog:* Lyons.
lyonnais, -aise [ljɔnɛ, -ɛːz], *a. & s.* *Geog:* (native) of Lyons.
lyre [liːr], *s.f.* *Mus:* lyre.
lyrique [lirik], *a.* lyric(al) (poem, etc.); **poète l.**, lyric poet; *s.m.* **lyrisme**, lyricism.

M

M, m [ɛm], s.m. or f. (the letter) M, m.

m'. see ME.

ma [ma], poss.a.f. see MON.

macabre [makɑːbr], a. macabre; gruesome (discovery); grim (humour, etc.).

macaron [makarɔ̃], s.m. Cu: macaroon.

macédoine [masedwan], s.f. (a) m. de fruits, fruit salad; (b) medley.

macérler [masere], v.tr. (je macère; je macérerai) to macerate; to steep, soak; s.f. -ation, steeping, soaking.

Mach [mak], s.m. Av: (nombre de) M., Mach number; voler à M. deux, to fly at Mach two.

mâchefer [maʃfɛːr], s.m. clinker, slag.

mâcher [maʃe], v.tr. to chew, masticate; m. le mors, le frein, to champ at the bit, to be impatient; je ne vais pas lui m. les mots, I shan't mince words with him.

machin [maʃɛ̃], s.m. F: 1. thingamy, thingummy; Mme M., Mrs What's her name. 2. gadget; passe-moi le m., pass me the what's-it.

machinal, -aux [maʃinal, -o], a. mechanical, unconscious (action); geste m., involuntary gesture; adv. -ement.

machine [maʃin], s.f. 1. machine; coll: machinery; (a) H: m. à coudre, sewing machine; m. à laver, washing machine; m. à laver la vaisselle, dishwasher; (b) Com: etc: m. à écrire, typewriter; écriture à la m., typing; m. à calculer, calculating machine; m. à calculer électronique, computer; (c) motorcycle; (d) Ind: les grosses machines, the heavy plant; machines agricoles, agricultural machinery. 2. engine; (a) m. à vapeur, steam-engine; m. à pétrole, à gaz, oil, gas, engine; (b) Rail: locomotive; (c) Nau: la m., the engine room.

machine-outil [maʃinuti], s.f. machine-tool; pl. machines-outils.

machinler [maʃine], v.tr. to scheme, plot; affaire machinée d'avance, put-up job; s.f. -ation, plot.

mâchoire [maʃwaːr], s.f. 1. (a) jaw; (b) jawbone. 2. mâchoires d'un étau, jaws of a vice.

mâchonnler [maʃone], v.tr. 1. to chew; to munch. 2. to mumble; s.m. -ement.

maçon [masɔ̃], s.m. (a) mason; m. en briques, bricklayer; (b) (free)mason; s.m. -nage, mason's work; s.f. -nerie, masonry; (free)masonry.

maculler [makyle], v.tr. to stain, spot; s.m. -age.

madame, pl. mesdames [madam, medam, mɛ-], s.f. 1. (a) Madame, Mme, Dupont, Mrs Dupont; Mesdames, Mmes, Dupont, the Mrs Dupont; (not rendered in Eng.) M. la marquise de . . ., the Marchioness of . . .; m. la directrice, the manageress, the headmistress; comment va m. votre mère? how is your mother? (b) (used alone) (pl. ces dames) voici le chapeau de m., here is Mrs X's hat; ces dames n'y sont pas, the ladies are not at home. 2. (a) (in address, more extensively used than in Eng.) Madam; entrez, mesdames, please come in; (b) (in letter writing) Madame (always written in full), Dear Madam; (implying previous acquaintance) Chère Madame, Dear Mrs X.

Madeleine [madlɛn]. 1. Pr.n.f. (a) Magdalen(e); (b) Madel(e)ine. 2. s.f. Cu: madeleine.

mademoiselle, pl. mesdemoiselles [madmwazɛl, medmwazɛl, mɛ-], s.f. 1. Miss: Mademoiselle, Mlle, Smith, Miss Smith; Mesdemoiselles Smith, the Misses Smith; voici le chapeau de m. here's Miss X's hat; (not rendered in Eng.) comment va m. votre cousine? how is your cousin? voici m. la directrice, here's the manageress, the headmistress. 2. (a) (in address) merci, m., thank you, Miss X; (b) (pl. ces demoiselles) que prendront ces demoiselles? what can I offer you, ladies? (c) (in letter writing) Mademoiselle (always written in full), Dear Madam; (implying previous acquaintance) Chère Mademoiselle, Dear Miss X.

Madère [madɛːr]. 1. Pr.n.f. Geog: Madeira. 2. s.m. Madeira (wine).

madone [madɔn], s.f. madonna.

madrier [madrije], s.m. (piece of) timber; beam; thick board, plank.

magasin [magazɛ̃], s.m. 1. (a) shop, store; grand m., department store; m. à libre service, self-service store; employé(e) de m., shop assistant; courir, F: faire, les magasins, to do, go, the round of the shops; (b) store, warehouse. 2. magazine (of rifle, camera, Cin: of projector); s.m. -age, warehousing; s.m. -ier, warehouseman, storekeeper.

magazine [magazin], s.m. (illustrated) magazine.

magicien, -ienne [maʒisjɛ̃, -jɛn], s. magician, wizard; sorcerer, f. sorceress.

maglie [maʒi], s.f. magic; a. -ique, magical; adv. -iquement.

magis|trat [maʒistra], *s.m.* magistrate; judge; **il est m.**, he sits on the Bench; *a.* **-tral, -traux**, masterful (manner); masterly (work); *adv.* **-tralement;** *s.f.* **-trature**, magistrature.

magnanime [maɲanim], *a.* magnanimous; *adv.* **-ment**.

magn|ésie [maɲezi], *s.f. Ch: Pharm:* 1. magnesia. 2. **sulfate de m.**, Epsom salts; *s.m.* **-ésium**, magnesium.

magné|tiser [maɲetize], *v.tr.* to magnetize; *a.* **-tique**, magnetic; *s.m.* **-tisme**, magnetism.

magnéto [maɲeto], *s.f. Aut:* magneto.

magnétophone [maɲetɔfɔn], *s.m.* tape recorder.

magnifi|er [maɲifje, maɲ-], *v.tr.* (*p.d. & pr.sub. n.* **magnifiions**) to magnify, glorify; to idealize; *s.f.* **-cence**, magnificence; *a.* **-que**, magnificent; *adv.* **-quement**.

mai [mɛ], *s.m.* 1. May; **au mois de m., en m.,** in (the month of) May; **le premier m.,** (on) the first of May, (on) May day; **le sept m.,** (on) the seventh of May. 2. maypole.

maigre [mɛːgr]. 1. *a.* (*a*) thin, skinny, lean; **homme grand et m.,** tall thin man; (*b*) lean (meat); scanty (vegetation); poor (land); **m. repas,** frugal meal; **jour m.,** day of abstinence. 2. *s.m.* lean (part of meat); *adv.* **-ment**, meagrely, scantily.

maigreur [mɛgrœːr], *s.f.* 1. thinness, leanness. 2. poorness, meagreness.

maigrir [mɛgriːr]. 1. *v.i.* to grow thin, lean; to lose weight; **j'ai maigri de dix kilos,** I have lost ten kilos. 2. *v.tr.* (*a*) (*of illness*) to make (s.o.) thin(ner); (*b*) (*of dress*) to make (s.o.) look thin(ner).

mail [maːj], *s.m.* 1. avenue, promenade. 2. sledge-hammer.

maille [maːj], *s.f.* 1. (*a*) stitch (in knitting); (*b*) link (of chain). 2. mesh (of net).

maillet [majɛ], *s.m. Tls:* mallet; maul; beetle.

maillon [majɔ̃], *s.m.* link (of a chain).

maillot [majo], *s.m. Cl:* (*a*) **m. de corps,** vest; (*b*) **m. de bain,** swimsuit; (*c*) *Sp:* jersey; singlet.

main [mɛ̃], *s.f.* 1. hand; (*a*) **serrer la m. à (qn),** to shake hands with (s.o.); **donner un coup de m. à (qn),** to lend (s.o.) a (helping) hand; **en venir aux mains,** to come to blows; **je n'en mettrais pas la m. au feu,** I shouldn't like to swear to it; **haut les mains! hands up! à bas les mains! hands off! faire m. basse sur qch.,** to lay hands on, to help oneself to, sth.; **affaire conclue sous la m.,** hole-and-corner deal; (*b*) (*hand used for gripping sth.*) **prendre qch. à deux mains,** to take, grasp, sth. with both hands; **avoir sans cesse l'argent à la m.,** to be constantly paying out money; **tenir le succès entre ses mains,** to have success within one's grasp; **mettre la m. sur qch.,** to lay hands on sth.; (*c*) **faire qch. en un tour de m.,** to do sth. in a twinkling; **se faire la m.,** to get one's hand in; **il a perdu la m.,** he is

out of practice; **avoir le coup de m.,** to have the knack; *Com:* **fait (à la) m.,** hand-made; (*d*) *Equit:* **rendre la m. à son cheval,** to give one's horse its head; *Aut:* **avoir sa voiture en m.,** to have the feel of one's car; **être sous la m. de qn,** to be under s.o.'s thumb; **avoir la haute m. sur . . .,** to have supreme control over . . .; **gagner haut la m.,** to win hands down; (*e*) *adv.phr.* **de longue m.,** for a long time (past) (friend) of long standing. 2. hand (writing). 3. *Cards:* hand. 4. **m. de papier,** quire. 5. **m. courante,** hand-rail.

main-d'œuvre [mɛ̃dœːvr], *s.f.* 1. labour; man power; **m.-d'œ. spécialisée,** semi-skilled labour; **m.-d'œ. qualifiée,** skilled labour; **embaucher de la m.-d'œ.,** to take on hands. 2. cost of labour. 3. workmanship; *pl.* **mains-d'œuvre**.

maintenant [mɛ̃tnɑ̃], *adv.* now.

maintenir [mɛ̃tniːr], *v.tr.* (*conj. like* TENIR) to maintain; (*a*) to keep, hold, (sth.) in position; (*b*) **m. sa famille par son travail,** to support one's family by one's work; (*c*) to uphold, keep (the law).

se maintenir. 1. to last well. 2. to hold on; **les prix se maintiennent,** prices are keeping up. 3. to be maintained, to continue; **le temps se maintient,** the weather's holding.

maintien [mɛ̃tjɛ̃], *s.m.* 1. maintenance, upholding, keeping (of law, order). 2. bearing, carriage; **il n'a pas de m.,** he's awkward; **perdre son m.,** to lose countenance.

maire [mɛːr], *s.m.* mayor.

mairie [mɛri], *s.f.* 1. office of mayor; term of office of mayor. 2. local government, local administration. 3. town-hall; municipal buildings.

mais [mɛ], 1. *adv.* (*emphatic*) **m. oui!** why, certainly! **m. non!** not at all! **m. qu'avez-vous donc?** why, what's the matter? 2. *conj.* but.

maïs [mais], *s.m.* maize, *N.Am:* corn; **farine de m.,** cornflour, *N.Am:* cornstarch.

maison [mɛzɔ̃], *s.f.* 1. house; (*a*) **m. de ville, de banlieue, de campagne,** town, suburban, country, house; **m. de plaisance,** holiday home; **m. de rapport,** (block of) flats, apartment house; **m. garnie,** furnished house (for letting); (*b*) **m. de commerce,** business house, firm; (*c*) home; **à la m.,** at home; **tenir la m.,** to keep house. 2. family; (*a*) **être de la m.,** to be one of the family; **le fils de la m.,** the son of the house; (*b*) dynasty; (*c*) household, staff; **gens de m.,** domestic staff; (*d*) **m. de santé,** (i) nursing home; (ii) mental hospital; **m. de repos,** rest home, convalescent home; **m. de retraite,** old people's home; **m. de la jeunesse,** youth centre, club.

maître, -esse [mɛːtr, mɛtrɛs], *s.* 1. (*a*) master, mistress; **devenir m. de qch.,** to become the owner of sth.; (*b*) **m., maîtresse, d'école**

primary school teacher; **m. de chapelle,** choir-master; (c) skilled craftsman; **m. charpentier,** master carpenter; **c'est fait de main de m.,** it is a masterpiece; **coup de m.,** master stroke; (d) works owner; (e) employee in charge; **m. d'œuvre,** foreman; *Jur:* **m. clerc,** (lawyer's) managing clerk; *Nau:* **m. d'équipage,** boatswain; **m. d'hôtel,** (i) butler; (ii) head waiter; (iii) *Nau:* chief steward; (f) (*title applied to notaries and advocates*) Maître. 2. *attrib.* (a) **maîtresse femme,** capable woman; **m. filou,** arrant scoundrel; (b) chief, principal; **maîtresse poutre,** main girder. 3. *s.f.* **maîtresse,** mistress.

maîtrise [mɛtriːz], *s.f.* 1. *Sch:* (a) mastership; **m. ès lettres** = Master of Arts degree; (b) choir school (attached to a cathedral). 2. mastery; **m. de soi,** self-control.

maîtriser [mɛtrize], *v.tr.* to master; to subdue; to control.

majesté [maʒɛste], *s.f.* 1. **sa M.,** His, Her, Majesty. 2. (a) stateliness; (b) grandeur.

majestueu|x, -euse [maʒɛstɥø, -øːz], *a.* majestic; *adv.* -**sement.**

majeur [maʒœːr], *a.* (a) major, greater; **en majeure partie,** for the most part; *Geog:* **le lac M.,** Lake Maggiore; (b) **être absent pour raison majeure,** to be unavoidably absent; **affaire majeure,** important business; **cas de force majeure,** case of absolute necessity; (c) **devenir m.,** to come of age.

major|er [maʒɔre], *v.tr.* 1. to make an additional charge on (bill); **m. une facture de 10%,** to put 10% on an invoice. 2. to raise the price of (sth.); *s.f.* -**ation,** increase (in price).

major|ité [maʒɔrite], *s.f.* 1. majority. 2. *Jur:* **atteindre sa m.,** to come of age; *a.* -**itaire: vote m.,** majority vote.

Majorque [maʒɔrk]. *Pr.n.f. Geog:* Majorca.

majuscule [maʒyskyl], *a. & s.f.* capital (letter).

mal¹, maux [mal, mo], *s.m.* 1. evil; (a) hurt, harm; **faire du m.,** to do harm; **vouloir du m. à qn,** to wish s.o. evil; **il n'y a pas grand m.!** there's no great harm done! (b) **prendre qch. en m.,** to take sth. amiss; **tourner qch. en m.,** to put the worst interpretation on sth.; (c) wrong(doing); **le bien et le m.,** right and wrong, good and evil; **il ne songe pas à m.,** he doesn't mean any harm. 2. (a) ailment; pain; **vous allez prendre (du) m.,** you will catch your death of cold; **m. de tête,** headache; **m. de mer,** seasickness; **m. de gorge,** sore throat; **vous me faites (du) m.,** you are hurting me; **avoir le m. du pays,** to be homesick; (b) **se donner du m. pour faire qch.,** to take pains to do sth.

mal², adv. 1. (a) badly, ill; **faire qch. tant bien que m.,** to do sth. after a fashion; **s'y m. prendre,** to go the wrong way about it; **m. à l'aise,** ill at ease; **vous ne feriez pas m. de . . .,** it wouldn't

be a bad plan to . . .; (b) **aller, se porter, m.,** to be ill; **être au plus m.,** to be dangerously ill; (c) *F:* **pas m. (de qch.),** a fair amount (of sth.); **pas m. de gens,** a good many people; **j'ai pas m. envie de rester,** I've a good mind to stay. 2. (*with adj. function*) (a) not right; (b) uncomfortable; badly off; **nous ne sommes pas m. ici,** we are quite comfortable here; (c) **ils sont m. ensemble,** they are on bad terms; (d) **se trouver m.,** to faint; (e) *F:* **pas m.,** of good appearance, quality; **il n'est pas m.,** he's (i) quite good-looking, (ii) quite presentable.

malade [malad], 1. *a.* ill, sick, unwell; **tomber m.,** to fall ill; **dent m.,** aching tooth; **jambe m.,** bad leg; **esprit m.,** disordered mind. 2. *s.* sick person; invalid; *Med:* patient.

malad|ie [maladi], *s.f.* illness, sickness; disease; complaint; **faire une m.,** to be ill; *F:* **il en fait une m.,** he's very upset about it; **m. par carence,** deficiency disease; **m. de foie, de cœur,** liver, heart, complaint; *Vet:* **m. des chiens, de Carré,** distemper; *a.* -**if, -ive,** sickly.

maladresse [maladrɛs], *s.f.* 1. clumsiness, awkwardness; tactlessness. 2. blunder.

maladroit, -oite [maladrwa, -wat]. 1. *a.* (a) unskilled, clumsy, awkward; (b) blundering. 2. *s.* blunderer; *adv.* -**ement.**

malai, -aie, malais, -aise¹ [malɛ, -eːz], *a. & s.* Malay(an); Malaysian; **la péninsule malaise,** the Malay peninsula.

malaise² [malɛːz], *s.m.* 1. uneasiness, discomfort. 2. indisposition.

malaisé [malɛze], *a.* difficult; *adv.* -**ment,** with difficulty.

Malaisie (la) [malɛzi]. *Pr.n.f.* 1. the Malay Archipelago. 2. Malaysia.

malappris, -ise [malapri, -iz]. 1. *a.* uncouth, ill-bred. 2. *s.* lout; **c'est un m.,** he has no manners.

malavisé [malavize], *a.* ill-advised; injudicious; tactless.

Malawi (le) [ləmalawi]. *Pr.n.m. Geog:* Malawi.

Malaysia (la) [malɛzja]. *Pr.n.f. Geog:* Malaysia.

malchanc|e [malʃɑ̃s], *s.f.* bad luck; **par m.,** as ill luck would have it; *a.* -**eux, -euse,** unlucky.

malcommode [malkɔmɔd], *a.* inconvenient; *F:* (*of pers.*) difficult; **il est bien m.,** he's very awkward.

mâle [maːl], *a. & s.m.* 1. male; cock (bird); dog (fox); bull (elephant); (*of animals*) he-; **un ours m.,** a he-bear. 2. **courage m.,** manly courage; **style m.,** virile style.

malédiction [malediksjɔ̃], *s.f.* curse.

malencontreu|x, -euse [malɑ̃kɔ̃trø, -øːz], ill-timed, awkward, unlucky (day, remark); unlucky (person); tiresome (person); *adv.* -**sement.**

malentendu [malɑ̃tɑ̃dy], *s.m.* misunderstanding.

malfaisant [malfəzɑ̃], *a.* evil-minded; harmful; evil.

malfaiteur, -trice [malfɛtœːr, -tris], *s.* criminal; offender.

malgache [malgaʃ], *a. & s.* Malagasy, Madagascan; **la République M.**, the Malagasy Republic.

malgré [malgre], *prep.* in spite of; notwithstanding; **m. tout**, for all that.

malhabile [malabil], *a.* unskilful; clumsy, awkward; *adv.* **-ment**.

malheur [malœːr], *s.m.* **1.** misfortune; (*a*) calamity, accident; *F:* **faire un m.**, (i) to do something desperate; (ii) to commit murder; (*b*) misfortune, unhappiness. **2.** bad luck, ill luck; **quel m.!** what a pity! **par m.**, unfortunately; **jouer de m.**, to be unlucky.

malheureu|x, -euse [malœrø, -øːz], *a.* (*a*) (*of pers.*) unfortunate, unhappy; badly off; **le m.!** poor man! **m.!** wretch! (*b*) unlucky; **candidat m.**, unsuccessful candidate; **c'est bien m. pour vous!** it is hard luck on you! **le voilà enfin, ce n'est pas m.!** here he comes at last, and a good job too! (*c*) paltry, wretched; **une malheureuse pièce de cinq francs**, a miserable five-franc piece; *adv.* **-sement**, unfortunately, unluckily.

malhonnête [malɔnɛt], *a.* (*a*) dishonest; **un m. homme**, a dishonest man; (*b*) rude, impolite; **un homme m.**, a rude, uncivil, man.

Mali (le) [ləmali]. *Pr.n.m. Geog:* Mali.

malice [malis], *s.f.* **1.** (*a*) malice, maliciousness, spitefulness; **ne pas voir m. à qch.**, to see no harm in sth.; (*b*) mischievousness, naughtiness. **2.** (*a*) smart remark; **dire des malices**, to tease; (*b*) trick; **faire une m.**, to play a trick.

malicieu|x, -ieuse [malisjø, -jøːz], *a.* (*a*) mischievous, naughty; (*b*) ironic, mocking (smile); joking, bantering (remark); *adv.* **-sement**.

maligne, *see* MALIN.

malignité [maliɲite], *s.f.* (*a*) malignity, malignancy; (*b*) spite(fulness).

malin, -igne [malɛ̃, -iɲ], *a.* **1.** malignant; (*a*) evil, wicked; *s.m.* **le M.**, the Devil; (*b*) malicious; (*c*) **tumeur maligne**, malignant tumour. **2.** shrewd, cunning; *s.* **c'est un m.**, *F:* he knows a thing or two.

malingre [malɛ̃ːgr], *a.* sickly, puny.

malintentionné [malɛ̃tɑ̃sjɔne], *a. & s.* ill-intentioned, spiteful (person).

malle [mal], *s.f.* trunk, box; *Aut:* boot, *N.Am:* trunk; **faire sa m.**, to pack; *s.f.* **-ette**, (small) (suit)case.

malmener [malməne], *v.tr.* (**je malmène**) (*a*) to ill-treat; (*b*) to abuse (s.o.).

malodorant [malɔdɔrɑ̃], *a.* evil-smelling, smelly, stinking.

malpeigné [malpeɲe]. **1.** *a.* unkempt (person), tousled (hair). **2.** *s.* sloven; (*of woman*) slut, slattern.

malprop|re [malprɔpr], *a.* (*a*) dirty, grubby, slovenly, untidy; (*b*) dirty, unsavoury (business, conduct); *s.f.* **-reté**, dirtiness; dirt, indecency; *adv.* **-rement**.

malsain, -aine [malsɛ̃, -ɛːn], *a.* **1.** unhealthy, unwholesome.

malséant [malseɑ̃], *a.* unseemly; unbecoming (conduct, etc.).

maltais, -aise [maltɛ, -ɛːz], *a. & s.* Maltese.

Malte [malt]. *Pr.n.f. Geog:* Malta.

maltrait|er [maltrɛte, -tre-], *v.tr.* to ill-treat, ill-use (s.o., by word or deed); to manhandle (s.o.); *s.m.* **-ement**, ill-treatment.

malveill|ant [malvɛjɑ̃], *a.* (*a*) malevolent, malicious; (*b*) spiteful; *s.f.* **-ance**, spitefulness; foul play.

maman [mamɑ̃, mɔmɑ̃], *s.f. F:* mummy, mum.

mamelle [mamɛl], *s.f.* breast; *Z:* udder.

mamelon [mamlɔ̃], *s.m.* **1.** *Anat:* (*a*) nipple, teat; (*b*) dug (of animal). **2.** rounded hillock; knoll. **3.** *Mec:* boss; gudgeon; lubrication nipple.

mammifère [mammifɛːr], *s.m.* mammal.

manche[1] [mɑ̃ːʃ], *s.f.* **1.** (*a*) sleeve; *F:* **ça, c'est une autre paire de manches!** that's quite another matter; (*b*) **m. d'incendie**, fire-hose; **m. à air**, air-shaft. **2.** (*a*) *Cards:* hand (played in a single game; **nous sommes m. à m.**, we are a game all); (*b*) *Sp:* heat; (*c*) *Ten:* set. **3.** *Geog:* **la M.**, the (English) Channel.

manche[2], *s.m.* handle; **m. à balai**, broomstick.

manchette [mɑ̃ʃɛt], *s.f.* **1.** cuff. **2.** (newspaper) headline.

manchon [mɑ̃ʃɔ̃], *s.m.* (*a*) *Mec: E:* casing, sleeve; muff; **m. d'accouplement**, coupling sleeve, bush(ing) (of bearing); *Aut:* **m. d'embrayage**, coupling, clutch; (*b*) gas-mantle.

manchot, -ote [mɑ̃ʃo, -ɔt]. **1.** *a. & s.* one-armed, one-handed (person). **2.** *s.m. Orn:* penguin.

mandarine [mɑ̃darin], *s.f.* tangerine (orange).

mandat [mɑ̃da], *s.m.* **1.** (*a*) mandate; commission; **territoire sous m.**, mandated territory; (*b*) *Jur:* proxy. **2.** *Jur:* warrant; **m. d'arrêt**, warrant for arrest. **3.** order (to pay); money order; draft; *P.T.T:* **m. postal** = postal order.

mandataire [mɑ̃datɛːr], *s.m. & f.* **1.** mandatory (of electors, etc.). **2.** (*pers.*) proxy; representative. **3.** *Jur:* authorized agent; attorney; trustee.

mandat-poste [mɑ̃dapɔst], *s.m.* = postal order, money order; *pl.* **mandats-poste**.

mander [mɑ̃de], *v.tr.* **1.** *Journ:* **on mande . . .**, it is reported from . . . **2.** *Jur:* to summon (witness, accused) to appear; **m. d'urgence**, to send for s.o. urgently.

manège [manɛːʒ], *s.m.* **1.** (*a*) riding-school

equitation; (b) (salle de) m., riding-school; manege; (c) m. de chevaux de bois, merry-go-round; roundabout. 2. stratagem, trick; j'observais leur m., I was watching their little game.

nanette [manɛt], s.f. handle, hand-lever.

nangler [mãʒe]. I. v.tr. (n. mangeons) 1. to eat; salle à m., dining-room; donner à m. à qn, aux poules, to feed s.o., the hens; m. à sa faim, to eat one's fill. 2. m. son argent, to squander one's money; a. -eable, edible; s.f. -eaille, F: grub; s.f. -eoire, manger, trough; s. -eur, -euse, eater.
II. s.m. food.

nange(-)tout [mãʒtu], s.m.inv. 1. Hort: (a) sugar-pea; (b) French bean, N.Am: string-bean. 2. F: spendthrift.

naniable [manjabl], a. manageable; easy to handle; handy (tool).

naniaque [manjak], a. & s. 1. maniac; raving mad(man, -woman). 2. finicky, faddy (person); s. fusspot, crank.

nanie [mani], s.f. (a) Med: mania, obsession; m. de la persécution, persécution mania; (b) mania, craze; avoir la m. des tableaux, to be mad on pictures; il a ses petites manies, he has his little fads.

nanier [manje], v.tr. (p.d. & pr.sub. n. maniions) 1. to feel (cloth); to handle (tool). 2. to handle (affair); to manage, control (horse, business); m. les avirons, to ply the oars; a. -able, manageable, handy (tool); s.m. -ement.

nanlière [manjɛːr], s.f. 1. manner, way; laissez-moi faire à ma m., let me do it my own way; de cette m., thus; in this way; de m. ou d'autre, somehow or other; en quelque m., in a way; de (telle) m. que, so that. 2. pl. manners; F: faire des manières, to affect reluctance; s.m. -iérisme, mannerism.

naniéré [manjere], a. affected (person, behaviour).

nanifeste¹ [manifɛst], a. obvious, evident; adv. -ment.

nanifeste², s.m. manifesto, proclamation; (ship's) manifest.

nanifestler [manifɛste], v.tr. 1. to manifest; to reveal; to evince (opinion); to show, express (joy, grief). 2. abs. to demonstrate (politically, etc.); s. -ant, -ante, Pol: demonstrator; s.f. -ation, demonstration.

e manifester, to appear; to show itself; il ne s'est pas encore manifesté, he hasn't got in touch with me yet.

nanigance [manigãːs], s.f. F: (a) intrigue; (b) pl. underhand practices; wire-pulling.

nanigancer [manigãse], v.tr. (n. manigançons) F: to scheme, to plot; qu'est-ce qu'ils manigancent? what are they up to?

nanipuller [manipyle], v.tr. 1. to manipulate; to

handle, operate (apparatus). 2. to manipulate, F: rig (accounts, election, etc.); s. -ateur, -atrice, manipulator; s.f. -ation.

manivelle [manivɛl], s.f. crank, Aut: (starting-) handle.

mannequin [mankɛ̃], s.m. 1. (a) Art: lay figure; (b) Dressm: dummy. 2. mannequin, model.

manœuvre [manœːvr]. 1. s.f. (a) working, driving (of machine); (b) Nau: handling (of ship); maître de m., boatswain; (c) Mil: drill, exercise; tactical exercise; (army) manœuvre; (d) Rail: shunting; (e) F: scheme, manœuvre, intrigue. 2. s.m. (unskilled) workman.

manœuvrer [manœvre]. 1. v.tr. (a) to work, operate; (b) to handle (ship); (c) Rail: to shunt. 2. v.i. to scheme, manœuvre.

manque [mãːk], s.m. lack, want; deficiency; shortage; m. de parole, breach of faith.

manqué [mãke], a. missed (opportunity); unsuccessful (attempt); coup m., miss, failure; garçon m., tomboy.

manquler [mãke]. I. v.i. 1. (a) to lack, be short of, sth.; m. de courage, to lack courage; (b) il a manqué (de) tomber, he nearly fell; (c) impers. il s'en manque de beaucoup, far from it. 2. to fail; (a) to be wanting, deficient; les mots me manquent, words fail me; les vivres commencent à m., provisions are running short; il ne manquait plus que cela! that's the last straw! (b) to give way; le cœur lui manqua, his heart failed him; (c) to be absent, missing; m. à qn, to be missed by s.o.; ça me manque, I miss it; (d) to fall short; m. à sa parole, to break one's word; m. à une règle, to violate a rule; abs. le coup a manqué, the attempt miscarried; (e) ne manquez pas de nous écrire, be sure to write to us; s.m. -ement, failure, omission.
II. v.tr. 1. to miss (target, train); il l'a manqué belle, he had a narrow escape. 2. m. sa vie, to wreck, F: mess up, one's life.

mansarde [mãsard], s.f. Arch: 1. (fenêtre en) m., dormer-window. 2. attic, garret.

manteau, -eaux [mãto], s.m. 1. coat; m. de neige, mantle of snow; m. de la nuit, cover of night. 2. m. de cheminée, mantelpiece.

manucure [manykyːr], s.m. & f. manicurist, manicure; trousse de m., manicure set.

manuel, -elle [manɥɛl]. 1. a. manual (work). 2. s.m. manual, handbook.

manufacture [manyfaktyːr], s.f. factory; works.

manufacturler [manyfaktyre], v.tr. to manufacture; a. -ier, -ière, manufacturing (town, etc.).

manuscrit [manyskri], a. & s.m. manuscript.

manutention [manytãsjɔ̃], s.f. handling (of stores, materials, etc., for storage, transport or sale); s.m. & f. Ind: etc: -naire, warehouseman, handler, packer.

mappemonde [mapmɔ̃ːd], *s.f.* map of the world in two hemispheres; **m. céleste**, planisphere.

maquereau, -eaux [makro], *s.m. Ich:* mackerel.

maquet|te [maket], *s.f.* miniature, scale model; demonstration model; *s.m. & f.* **-tiste**, model maker.

maquill|er [makije], *v.tr. Th:* to make up (s.o.'s face); *s.m.* **-age**, make-up.

se maquiller, to make up (one's face).

maquis [maki], *s.m.* (i) (Mediterranean) scrub, bush; (ii) underground forces; **prendre le m.**, to go underground, to take to the maquis.

maquisard [makizaːr], *s.m.* man of the maquis, maquisard.

maraîch|er, -ère [mareʃe, -ɛːr]. (*a*) *a.* **jardin m.**, market garden; (*b*) *s.* market-gardener, *N.Am:* truck farmer; *s.m.* **-age**, market gardening.

marais [marɛ], *s.m.* marsh(land); bog, fen.

maraud|er [marode], *v.i.* (*a*) to maraud, to thieve; (*b*) *F:* (*of taxi*) to cruise (in search of fares); *s.* **-eur, -euse**, petty thief.

marbre [marbr], *s.m.* (*a*) marble; (*b*) marble (statue).

marbré [marbre], *a.* marbled; mottled; veined.

marc [maːr], *s.m.* 1. marc (of grapes, etc.); (**eau de vie de**) **m.**, marc (brandy). 2. (used) tea-leaves; coffee-grounds.

marchand, -ande [marʃɑ̃, -ɑ̃ːd]. 1. *s.* dealer, merchant; shopkeeper; tradesman; **m. en gros, en détail**, wholesaler, retailer; **m. de poisson**, fishmonger; **m. de tabac**, tobacconist; **m. des quatre saisons**, costermonger; hawker (of fruit and vegetables). 2. *a.* (*a*) saleable, marketable (article); (*b*) trading; **quartier m.**, shopping centre; **navire m.**, merchant ship.

marchand|er [marʃɑ̃de], *v.tr.* (*a*) to haggle, to bargain, over (sth.); (*b*) **il ne marchande pas sa peine**, he spares no pains; *s.m.* **-age**, bargaining; *s.* **-eur, -euse**, haggler; *s.f.* **-ise**, merchandise, *pl.* goods.

marche [marʃ], *s.f.* 1. step, stair. 2. (*a*) walking; **aimer la m.**, to be fond of walking; **ralentir sa m.**, to slacken one's pace; **se mettre en m.**, to set out, start off; (*b*) march; (i) **ouvrir la m.**, to lead the way; (ii) *Mus:* **m. funèbre**, dead march. 3. (*a*) running (of trains); sailing (of ships); **mettre en m. un service**, to start, run, a service; (*b*) **entrer dans le garage en m. arrière**, to back into the garage. 4. (*a*) running, going, working (of machine); (*of machine*) **être en m.**, to be running, working; (*b*) course (of events); march (of time).

marché [marʃe], *s.m.* 1. (*a*) deal, bargain; **c'est m. fait**, it's a bargain; *F:* done! **par-dessus le m.**, into the bargain; (*b*) **bon m.**, cheap(ness); **à meilleur m.**, cheaper; **articles bon m.**, low-priced goods, bargains; (*c*) **m. noir**, black

market. 2. market; **le M. commun**, the Com‖ mon Market.

marchepied [marʃəpje], *s.m.* (*a*) steps (of alta‖ throne, etc.); (*b*) *Veh:* footboard; running‖ board.

marcher [marʃe], *v.i.* 1. to tread. 2. (*a*) to wal‖ go; **deux choses qui marchent toujours ensen‖ ble**, two things that always go together; **faço‖ de m.**, gait; (*b*) to obey orders; **faire m. qn, ‖** to order s.o. about; (ii) to pull s.o.'s leg;‖ **marchera**, he'll do it; (**je ne**) **marche pa‖** nothing doing! (*c*) to march; **en avant, march‖** quick march! 3. (*a*) (*of trains*) to move, trave‖ go; (*of ships*) to sail; **le temps marche**, tin‖ goes on; **les affaires marchent**, business ‖ brisk; **est-ce que ça marche?** are you gettir‖ on all right? (*b*) (*of machine*) to work, run, g‖ **ma montre ne marche plus**, my watch wor‖ go.

marcheur, -euse [marʃœːr, -øːz]. 1. *s.* walke‖ **bon m.**, (i) good walker; (ii) (*of horse*) go‖ goer; *Pej:* **vieux m.**, old rake. 2. *a.* walki‖ (animal); **navire bon m.**, fast ship.

mardi [mardi], *s.m.* Tuesday; **m. gras**, Shro‖ Tuesday.

mare [maːr], *s.f.* (stagnant) pool; pond.

marécag|e [mareka:ʒ], *s.m.* bog, swamp;‖ **-eux, -euse**, boggy, swampy.

maréchal, -aux [mareʃal, -o], *s.m.* 1. **m.-ferra‖** shoeing-smith; farrier. 2. marshal (of roy‖ household, etc.). 3. *Mil:* (*a*) **m. (de France‖** field-marshal; (*b*) **m. des logis**, (caval‖ sergeant.

marée [mare], *s.f.* 1. tide; **m. haute, basse, hi‖** low, water, high, low, tide; **port de m.**, tid‖ harbour. 2. fresh (seawater) fish; **train de ‖** fish train; **arriver comme m. en carême**, ‖ arrive in the nick of time.

margarine [margarin], *s.f.* margarine.

marge [marʒ], *s.f.* (*a*) border, edge (of ditc‖ road, etc.); (*b*) margin (of book); **note en ‖** marginal note.

Margot [margo]. *Pr.n.f.* Margot, Maggie.

Marguerite [margərit]. 1. *Pr.n.f.* Margaret.‖ *s.f. Bot:* (**petite**) **m.**, daisy; **m. des champs**, ‖ eye daisy.

mari [mari], *s.m.* husband.

mariage [marja:ʒ], *s.m.* marriage; ‖ matrimony; **leur m. est en ruine**, their marria‖ is on the rocks; **m. d'amour**, love match;‖ wedding; **m. religieux**, wedding (in church);‖ civil, civil marriage (before the may‖ = marriage before the registrar); **acte de ‖** marriage certificate.

Marie [mari]. *Pr.n.f.* Mary; **la Vierge M., ‖** Virgin Mary.

marié, -ée [marje], *a. & s.* 1. married (perso‖ **nouveau m., nouvelle mariée**, bridegro‖ bride; **nouveaux mariés**, newly-weds; vi‖

mariés, old couple. 2. *s.* **le, la, marié(e)**, the bridegroom, the bride.

marier [marje], *v.tr.* (*p.d. & pr. sub.* **n. mar ions**) 1. to marry; (*a*) (*of priest*) to join (two people) in marriage, to marry (a couple); (*b*) to give (one's daughter) in marriage; **fille à m.**, marriageable daughter. 2. to join, unite; **m. des couleurs**, to blend colours.

se marier, (*a*) to marry, to get married; **se m. avec qn**, to marry s.o.; (*b*) (*of colour*) **se m. avec qch.**, to go with sth.

marin, -ine¹ [marɛ̃, -in]. 1. *a.* marine (plant, engine); **carte marine**, chart; **mille m.**, nautical mile; **avoir le pied m.**, to be a good sailor. 2. *s.m.* sailor, seaman; **se faire m.**, to go to sea.

marine² [marin], *s.f.* 1. **terme de m.**, nautical term. 2. the sea service; **la m. marchande**, the merchant navy, the mercantile marine; **la m. de guerre**, the Navy. 3. *a.inv.* navy-blue; **un costume m.**, a navy(-blue) suit.

marin er [marine], *v.tr.* (*a*) to pickle; to salt; (*b*) *Cu:* to marinate, to souse; *s.f.* -**ade**, marinade; *s.m.* -**age**.

marital, -aux [marital, -o], *a.* marital; *Jur:* **autorisation maritale**, husband's authority; *adv.* -**ement**, maritally; **vivre m.**, to cohabit.

maritime [maritim], *a.* maritime; **ville m.**, seaside town; **commerce m.**, sea-borne trade; **mouvement m.**, movement of shipping; *Journ:* shipping intelligence; **assurance m.**, marine insurance; **agent m.**, shipping agent; **arsenal m.**, naval dockyard; *Rail:* **gare m.**, harbour station.

marmaille [marmɑːj], *s.f. coll. F:* children; kids, brats.

marmelade [marməlad], *s.f.* (*a*) compote (of fruit); **m. de pommes**, stewed apples; (*b*) *F:* **mettre qn en m.**, to pound s.o. to a jelly.

marmite [marmit], *s.f.* (*a*) (cooking-)pot; pan; **m. à conserves**, preserving pan; **m. à pression, m. autoclave**, pressure cooker; (*b*) *Mil:* dixie, camp-kettle.

marmott er [marmɔte], *v.tr.* to mumble, mutter; *s.m.* -**age**, -**ement**, mumbling; *s.* -**eur**, -**euse**, mumbler.

Maroc (le) [ləmarɔk]. *Pr.n.m.* Morocco; **au M.**, in, to, Morocco.

marocain, -aine [marɔkɛ̃, -ɛn], *a. & s.* Moroccan; *Tex:* **crêpe m.**, marocain.

maroquin [marɔkɛ̃], *s.m.* morocco(-leather).

maroquinerie [marɔkinri], *s.f. Com:* fancy leather work; morocco-leather goods; (fancy) leather shop.

marquant [markɑ̃], *a.* prominent, outstanding (incident, personality, etc.).

marque [mark], *s.f.* mark; (*a*) **m. de fabrique**, trade mark; brand; **m. déposée**, registered trade mark; **produits de m.**, branded goods; (*b*) **personnages de m.**, distinguished people;

porter la m. du génie, to bear the stamp of genius; **marques d'amitié**, tokens of friendship.

marqu er [marke]. 1. *v.tr.* to mark; (*a*) to put a mark on (sth.); (*b*) to record, note; *Games:* **m. les points**, to keep the score; (*c*) to indicate, show; **la pendule marque dix heures**, the clock says ten o'clock; **m. le pas**, to mark time. 2. *v.i.* to stand out, make a mark; **notre famille n'a jamais marqué**, our family has never been remarkable; *s.* -**eur**, -**euse**, marker; scorer.

marquis [marki], *s.m.* marquis, marquess.

marquise [markiːz], *s.f.* 1. marchioness. 2. (*a*) awning; (*b*) glass porch.

marraine [marɛn], *s.f.* godmother; sponsor (at baptism).

marrant [marɑ̃], *a. P:* (*a*) (screamingly) funny; **ce n'est pas m.**, it's no joke; (*b*) funny, odd, queer; **vous êtes m., vous, alors!** you're the limit! **il n'est pas m.**, he's wet.

marre [maːr], *adv. P:* **avoir m. de qch., de qn**, to be fed up with sth., s.o.; **j'en ai m.**, I've had enough.

marrer (se) [səmare], *v.pr. P:* to die (of laughing); to have a good time; **tu me fais m.**, you make me laugh.

marron [marɔ̃]. 1. *s.m.* (*a*) (edible) chestnut; (*b*) **m. d'Inde**, horse-chestnut. 2. *a.inv. & s.m.* chestnut(-colour); maroon; **chaussures m.**, tan shoes; *s.m.* -**nier**, chestnut tree; **m. d'Inde**, horse-chestnut tree.

mars [mars], *s.m.* **au mois de m., en m.**, in (the month of) March; **le premier m.**, (on) the first of March; **le sept m.**, (on) the seventh of March; **blé de m.**, spring wheat.

marseillais, -aise [marseje, -ɛːz], *a. & s. Geog:* Marseillais; **la Marseillaise**, the Marseillaise.

Marseille [marsɛːj]. *Pr.n. Geog:* Marseilles.

marsouin [marswɛ̃], *s.m. Z:* porpoise.

marteau, -eaux [marto], *s.m.* (*a*) hammer; (*b*) (door) knocker.

marteler [martəle], *v.tr.* (**je martèle**) to hammer; *Metalw:* to hammer out; **cuivre martelé**, hand-wrought copper; **m. à froid**, to cold-hammer.

martial, -aux [marsjal, -o], *a.* martial; warlike; soldierly (bearing, etc.); **loi martiale**, martial law; **cour martiale**, court martial; *adv.* -**ement**, (i) in a warlike, (ii) in a soldierly, manner.

martien, -ienne [marsjɛ̃, -jɛn]. *a. & s. Astr:* Martian.

Martin [martɛ̃]. 1. *Pr.n.m.* Martin; (*name given to a donkey*) = Neddy; **ours M.**, Bruin; Teddy-Bear.

martinet [martinɛ], *s.m. Orn:* swift.

martin-pêcheur [martɛ̃pɛʃœːr], *s.m. Orn:* kingfisher; *pl.* **martins-pêcheurs.**

martre [martr], *s.f. Z:* marten; **m. zibeline**, sable; **m. du Canada**, mink.

martyr, -yre¹ [martiːr], *s.* martyr.

martyre² [marti:r], *s.m.* martyrdom.

martyriser [martirize], *v.tr.* to make a martyr of; to torture.

marx|isme [marksism], *s.m. Pol:* Marxism; *a. & s.* -iste, Marxist.

mascarade [maskarad], *s.f.* masquerade.

mascaret [maskarɛ], *s.m.* bore, tidal wave (in estuary).

mascotte [maskɔt], *s.f.* mascot; charm.

masculin [maskylɛ̃], *a.* 1. male. 2. masculine.

masque [mask], *s.m.* 1. mask; (protective) mask; **m. à gaz**, gas mask, respirator; **m. de chirurgien**, (surgeon's) operating mask; **m. sous-marin**, (skin-diver's) mask; **m. (antirides, facial)**, face-pack; **m. mortuaire**, death mask. 2. (*a*) *Th:* masque; (*b*) masquerader, mummer.

masquer [maske], *v.tr.* to mask; (*a*) **se m.**, to put on a mask; (*b*) to hide, screen; *Mil:* **m. une batterie**, to conceal a battery; *Aut:* **virage masqué**, blind corner.

massacrante [masakrɑ̃:t], *a.f.* (*used in the phr.*) **être d'une humeur m.**, to be in a vile temper.

massacre [masakr], *s.m.* (*a*) massacre, slaughter; *F:* butchery; (*b*) (*at a fair*) **jeu de m.** = Aunt Sally.

massacr|er [masakre], *v.tr.* 1. to massacre, slaughter. 2. *F:* to bungle, spoil (work); to murder (music); to ruin (clothes); *s.* -eur, -euse, bungler.

massage [masa:ʒ], *s.m.* massage.

masse [mas], *s.f.* mass. 1. (*a*) **tomber comme une m.**, to fall like a log; (*b*) **m. de gens**, crowd; **psychologie des masses**, mass psychology; *F:* **il n'y en a pas des masses**, there aren't an awful lot; **en m.**, in a body. 2. *El:* **mettre le courant à la m.**, to earth the current; *Atom.Ph:* **m. critique**, critical mass.

massepain [maspɛ̃], *s.m.* marzipan.

masser¹ [mase], *v.tr.* to mass (crowds, etc.). **se masser**, to form a crowd.

mass|er², *v.tr.* to massage; *s.* -eur, -euse, masseur, masseuse.

mass|if, -ive [masif, -i:v]. 1. *a.* (*a*) massive, bulky; (*b*) **argent m.**, solid silver; (*c*) **bombardement m.**, heavy raid. 2. *s.m.* (*a*) clump (of shrubs); (*b*) *Geog:* mountain mass; massif; *adv.* -ivement.

massue [masy], *s.f.* club, bludgeon; **coup de m.**, staggering blow.

mastic [mastik], *s.m.* 1. mastic (resin). 2. **m. à vitres**, (glazier's) putty.

masti|quer [mastike], *v.tr.* to masticate, chew; *s.f.* -cation, chewing.

masure [mazy:r], *s.f.* tumbledown cottage; hovel, shanty.

mat¹ [mat], *a.* mat(t), unpolished, dull; **son m.**, dull sound; thud.

mat², *s.m. Chess:* (check)mate.

mât [mɑ], *s.m.* mast, pole.

match [matʃ], *s.m. Sp:* match; **m. de football, de rugby**, football, rugby, match; **m. prévu** fixture; **faire m. nul**, to tie; *pl. matchs, matche* [matʃ].

matelas [matlɑ], *s.m.* mattress; **m. pneumatique** inflatable mattress; **m. de mousse, foan** rubber, plastic foam, mattress.

matelass|ier [matlase], *v.tr.* to pad, cushion stuff (chair, etc.); *s.* -ier, -ière, mattress maker.

matelot [matlo], *s.m.* sailor, seaman.

mater [mate], *v.tr.* (*a*) *Chess:* to (check)mate; (*b* F:* **m. qn**, to master s.o.

matérialiser [materjalize], *v.tr.* **m. un projet, t** realize a plan.

se matérialiser, to materialize.

matérial|isme [materjalism], *s.m.* materialism *a. & s.* -iste, (i) materialistic; (ii) materialist.

matériau [materjo], *s.m. Civ.E:* buildin material.

matériaux [materjo], *s.m.pl.* materials.

matériel, -elle [materjel]. 1. *a.* (*a*) materia physical (body); (*b*) materialistic, sensu (pleasures, mind); (*c*) **besoins matériels**, bodi' needs. 2. *s.m.* plant; implements; material(s *Rail:* **m. roulant**, rolling-stock; **m. de campin** camping equipment; **m. scolaire**, education equipment; *Ind:* **m. lourd**, heavy plant; *ac* -lement.

maternel, -elle [maternel], *a.* maternal. motherly (care, etc.); **école maternelle**, *s.f.* maternelle, nursery school. 2. (*a*) **aïeul n** maternal grandfather; (*b*) **langue maternel** mother tongue; *adv.* -lement.

maternité [maternite], *s.f.* 1. maternit motherhood. 2. maternity hospital.

math(s) [mat], *s.f.pl. Sch: F:* maths; **fort en n** good at maths.

mathématicien, -ienne [matematisjɛ̃, -jɛn], *s* mathematician.

mathématique [matematik]. 1. mathematical. 2. *s.f.* (*usu. pl.*) mathematics

matheux, -euse [matø, -ø:z], *s. F:* maths fie

matière [matjɛ:r], *s.f.* 1. material; **matiè** premières, raw materials. 2. matter, sv stance; **m. grasse**, fat; **m. plastique**, plastic. subject; topic, theme; **table des matières, ta** of contents; **entrer en m.**, to broach the sv ject; **il n'y a pas m. à rire**, it's no laugh matter.

matin [matɛ̃]. 1. *s.m.* morning; **de grand m.**, e ly in the morning; **rentrer au petit m.**, to cc home with the milk; **un de ces (quatre) mat** one of these (fine) days. 2. *adv.* **se lever très** to get up very early.

matinal, -aux [matinal, -o], *a.* 1. morn (breeze, etc.); **à cette heure matinale**, at early hour. 2. **comme tu es m.!** you are up v early! *adv.* -ement.

matinée [matine], s.f. 1. morning, forenoon; dans la m., in the course of the morning; faire (la) grasse m., to sleep late, F: to have a lie in. 2. Th: etc: matinée.

matois, -oise [matwa, -waːz]. 1. a. sly, cunning, crafty. 2. s. sly person; c'est un fin m., he's a cunning type.

matou [matu], s.m. tom cat; F: un vilain m., a nasty customer.

matraque [matrak], s.f. bludgeon; F: coup de m., barefaced overcharging (in a restaurant).

matri|culer [matrikyle], v.tr. 1. to enter (s.o.'s) name on a register, to enrol (s.o.). 2. to give a registration number to (car, etc.); s.m. -cule, registration number.

matrimonial, -aux [matrimɔnjal, -o], a. matrimonial.

matrone [matrɔn], s.f. 1. stout elderly woman; matron. 2. Pej: vieille m., old hag.

Matthieu [matjø]. Pr.n.m. Matthew.

nâture [matyːr], s.f. masts; masts and spars.

naturité [matyrite], s.f. maturity; ripeness.

naudire [modiːr], v.tr. (pr.p. maudissant; p.p. maudit; pr.sub. je maudisse; p.h. je maudis) to curse.

naudit [modi], a. (a) (ac)cursed; (b) quel m. temps! what damnable weather!

naugréer [mogree], v.i. to curse, fume; to grumble (contre, at).

1aurice [mɔris]. Pr.n.m. Maurice; Geog: l'île M., Mauritius.

1ausolée [mozɔle], s.m. mausoleum.

1aussade [mosad], a. (a) surly, sullen; grumpy, disgruntled; peevish; (b) temps m., dull, gloomy, weather; adv. -ment.

1auvais [mɔvε], a. (a) evil, ill; bad; wicked (person); de plus en plus m., worse and worse; le plus m., the worst; c'est un m. sujet, F: he's a bad lot; (b) ill-natured; c'est une mauvaise langue, she has a vicious tongue; (c) nasty, unpleasant; m. pas, dangerous situation; mer mauvaise, rough sea; trouver qch. m., to dislike sth.; prendre qch. en mauvaise part, to take offence at sth.; adv: sentir m., to smell bad; il fait m., the weather is bad; (d) m. pour la santé, bad for the health; assez m., plutôt m., none too good; rather bad; (e) mauvaise santé, poor health; faire de mauvaises affaires, to be doing badly (in business); (f) wrong (due to a mistake); c'est la mauvaise clef, it's the wrong key; rire au m. endroit, to laugh in the wrong place.

1auve [moːv], a. & s.m. mauve.

aximum [maksimɔm], a. & s.m. maximum; au m., to the highest degree; pl. maximums, (esp. for scientific terms) maxima.

azout [mazut], s.m. fuel oil; chauffage central au m., oil-fired central heating.

e [m(ə)], before a vowel sound m', pers.pron.

(a) (acc.) me; me voici, here I am; (b) (dat.) (to) me; donnez-m'en, give me some; (c) (with pr. vbs.) myself; je me lave, I wash myself; je me suis dit que . . ., I said to myself that . . ..

méandre [meɑ̃ːdr], s.m. meander (of river); winding (of road).

mécanicien, -ienne [mekanisjɛ̃, -jɛn]. 1. s.m. (a) mechanic; m. auto, motor mechanic; m. radio, (de) radar, radio, radar, mechanic; (b) Nau: chef m., chief engineer; Rail: engine-driver; Av: m. d'avion, air(craft) mechanic; m. de bord, m. navigant, flight mechanic, operational engineer. 2. s.f. mécanicienne, machinist; sewing-woman (in factory).

mécanique [mekanik]. 1. a. mechanical. 2. s.f. (a) mechanics; (b) piece of machinery; adv. -ment.

mécanis|er [mekanize], v.tr. to mechanize; s.f. -ation, mechanization.

mécanisme [mekanism], s.m. 1. mechanism, machinery; works. 2. working; technique.

méchanceté [meʃɑ̃ste], s.f. 1. (a) wickedness, mischievousness; (b) unkindness, spitefulness; faire qch. par m., to do sth. out of spite. 2. spiteful act, word; quelle m.! F: what a horrid thing to do, to say!

méch|ant, -ante [meʃɑ̃, -ɑ̃ːt], a. (a) unpleasant, disagreeable; être de méchante humeur, to be in a (bad) temper; une méchante affaire, a nasty business; (b) spiteful, cruel, unkind (person); (c) naughty, mischievous (child); s. oh, le m.! oh, the naughty boy! (d) spiteful; vicious; s. ne faites donc pas le m., don't be nasty; adv. -amment.

mèche [meʃ], s.f. 1. (a) wick; (b) fuse (of mine); F: vendre la m., to give the show away. 2. lock (of hair). 3. Tls: bit, drill.

mécompte [mekɔ̃ːt], s.m. 1. miscalculation, error in reckoning. 2. mistaken judgment; disappointment; il a eu un grand m., he's been badly let down.

mécon|naître [mekɔnɛːtr], v.tr. (conj. like CONNAÎTRE) to fail to recognize; not to appreciate (s.o.'s talent); to disregard; m. les faits, to ignore the facts; a. -naissable, hardly recognizable, unrecognizable.

méconnu [mekɔny], a. unrecognized, misappreciated, unappreciated; misunderstood.

mécontent, -ente [mekɔ̃tɑ̃, -ɑ̃ːt]. 1. a. discontented, dissatisfied (de, with); il est m. de ce que vous avez dit, he's annoyed, displeased, with what you said. 2. s. malcontent.

mécontent|er [mekɔ̃tɑ̃te], v.tr. to dissatisfy, displease, annoy (s.o.); s.m. -ement, dissatisfaction (de, with); displeasure (de, at).

Mecque (la) [lamεk]. Pr.n.f. Geog: Mecca.

médaill|e [medaːj], s.f. 1. medal; le revers de la m., the other side of the picture. 2. (porter's) badge. 3. Arch: medallion; s.m. -on, medallion; locket.

médecin [metsɛ̃, medsɛ̃], *s.m.* doctor, physician; **femme m.,** woman doctor; **m. consultant,** consultant; **m. du travail,** works doctor; **m. conventionné,** contract doctor.

médecine [metsin, medsin], *s.f.* (*a*) (art of) medicine; **m. générale,** general practice; **m. légale,** forensic medicine; **m. du travail,** industrial medicine; **m. vétérinaire,** veterinary medicine; (*b*) the medical profession.

média|tion [medjasjɔ̃], *s.f.* mediation; *s.* -**teur,** -**trice,** mediator; intermediary.

médical, -**aux** [medikal, -o], *a.* medical.

médicament [medikamɑ̃], *s.m.* medicine.

médicinal, -**aux** [medisinal,~o], *a.* medicinal.

médiéval, -**aux** [medjeval, -o], *a.* medi(a)eval.

médiocre [medjɔkr], *a.* mediocre; second-rate, moderate (ability, etc.); **vin m.,** poor wine; *adv.* -**ment.**

médiocrité [medjɔkrite], *s.f.* mediocrity.

mé|dire [medi:r], *v.i.* (*conj. like* DIRE, *except pr.ind. and imp.* **médisez**) **m. de qn,** to speak ill of s.o.; to slander s.o.; to run s.o. down; *s.f.* -**disance,** slander; scandalmongering; *a. & s.* -**disant,** -**ante,** (i) *a.* backbiting, slanderous; (ii) *s.* slanderer.

médit|er [medite]. **1.** *v.i.* to meditate, to muse. **2.** *v.tr.* to contemplate (a journey); to have (an idea) in mind; *a.* -**atif,** -**ative,** meditative; *s.f.* -**ation.**

Méditerranée (la mer) [lameːrmediterane]. *Pr.n. f. Geog:* the Mediterranean (Sea).

méditerranéen, -**enne** [mediteraneɛ̃, -ɛn], *a.* Mediterranean (climate, etc.).

médium [medjɔm], *s.m. Psychics:* medium.

médoc [medɔk], *s.m.* (*also* **vin de M.**) Medoc (claret).

méduse [medy:z], *s.f.* jellyfish.

méduser [medyze], *v.tr. F:* to petrify; to paralyse with fear, astonishment.

meeting [mitiŋ], *s.m. Pol: Sp:* meeting, rally; **m. d'aviation,** air display.

méfait [mefɛ], *s.m.* misdeed; **méfaits d'un orage,** damage caused by a storm.

méfi|ance [mefjɑ̃:s], *s.f.* distrust; *a.* -**ant,** distrustful, suspicious.

méfier (se) [səmefje], *v.pr.* **se m. de qn,** to distrust s.o.; **méfiez-vous des voleurs,** beware of pickpockets; *abs.* to be on one's guard.

mégarde (par) [parmegard], *adv.phr.* inadvertently; through carelessness; accidentally.

mégère [meʒɛːr], *s.f.* shrew, termagant; bad-tempered woman.

mégot [mego], *s.m. F:* fag-end (of cigarette); butt (of cigar).

meilleur [mejœːr], *a.* **1.** (*comp. of* BON) better; **un m. emploi,** a better job; **de meilleure heure,** earlier; **m. marché,** cheaper; *adv.* **il fait m.,** the

weather is better. **2.** (*sup. of* BON) **le meilleur,** (i) the better (of two); (ii) the best; *s.* **c'est celui-là le m.,** it's the best, he's the best.

mélancol|ie [melɑ̃kɔli], *s.f.* melancholy, dejection, gloom; *a.* -**ique,** melancholy, gloomy; *adv.* -**iquement.**

mélange [melɑ̃:ʒ], *s.m.* **1.** mixing; blending (of tea, etc.); crossing (of breeds); *Cards:* shuffling. **2.** mixture; blend; miscellany; mix (of cement); **sans m.,** unmixed, unadulterated. **3. m. de toutes sortes de gens,** medley of all kinds of people.

mélanger [melɑ̃ʒe], *v.tr.* (n. mélangeons) to mix to mingle; to blend (teas); **m. tous les dossiers,** to mix up all the files.

mélasse [melas], *s.f.* molasses, treacle; m raffinée, golden syrup.

mêlée [mele], *s.f.* (*a*) conflict, mêlée; (*b*) F scuffle, free fight; (*c*) *Rugby Fb:* scrum.

mêler [mele], *v.tr.* to mix, mingle, blend; (*a*) **il es mêlé à tout,** he has a finger in every pie; (*b*) t put out of order, to muddle (papers); to tangl (hair); to confuse; **m. les cartes,** to shuffle th cards; **vous avez bien mêlé les cartes!** a nic mess you've made of it!
se mêler, to mix, mingle, blend; **se m. à la foule** to lose oneself in the crowd; **se m. à la convez sation,** to join in the conversation, *F:* to chi in; **se m. de politique,** to dabble in politics.

mélèze [meleːz], *s.m.* larch(-tree, -wood).

mélod|ie [melɔdi], *s.f.* melody, tune; *a.* -**ieu** -**ieuse,** melodious, tuneful; *adv.* -**ieusement**

mélodram|e [melɔdram], *s.m.* melodrama; -**atique.**

méloman|ie [melɔman], *s.* music-lover; **être m** to be music-mad; *s.f.* -**ie,** melomania, passio for music.

melon [məlɔ̃], *s.m.* **1.** *Bot:* melon. **2.** (**chapea m.,** bowler (hat).

membrane [mɑ̃bran], *s.f.* **1.** *Anat:* membrane. *Rec:* diaphragm.

membre [mɑ̃:br], *s.m.* member. **1.** (*a*) limb; (member (of a club, a society, a family); **m. c Parlement,** member of Parliament. **2.** co stituent part; **les membres de la phrase,** t members of the sentence.

membrure [mɑ̃bryːr], *s.f.* (*a*) *coll.* limt **homme à forte m.,** powerfully built man; (frame(work) (of building, etc.).

même [meːm]. **1.** *a.* (*a*) same; **être du m. âge,** be of the same age; **en m. temps,** at the sar time; at once; *pron.neut.* **cela revient au m.,** comes to the same thing; (*b*) (*following t noun*); very; **c'est cela m.,** that's the very thin (*c*) self; **elle est la bonté m.,** she is kindne itself; **moi-m.,** myself; **vous-m.,** yourself; **vo mêmes,** yourselves; **eux-mêmes,** themselves. *adv.* even; **m. si je le savais,** even if I knew. *adv.phr.* **de m.,** in the same way; likewise;

m. que, (just) as, like; tout de m., all the same; for all that; boire à m. la bouteille, to drink straight out of the bottle; des maisons bâties à m. le trottoir, houses built flush with the pavement; escalier taillé à m. la pierre, steps cut out of the solid rock; être à m. de faire qch., to be able to do sth.; to be in a position to do sth.

mémé [meme], s.f. F: grandma, granny.

mémo [memo], s.m. F: memo.

mémoire[1] [memwaːr], s.f. memory; (a) si j'ai bonne m., if I remember rightly; (b) recollection, remembrance; garder la m. de qch., to keep sth. in mind; j'ai eu un trou de m., my mind went blank.

mémoire[2], s.m. 1. (a) memorial; (written) statement; report; (b) memoir, thesis. 2. (contractor's) account; bill (of costs). 3. pl. (autobiographical) memoirs.

mémorable [memɔrabl], a. memorable; eventful (year, etc.); adv. -ment.

mémorandum [memɔrɑ̃dɔm], s.m. 1. memorandum, note. 2. note-book.

menace [mənas], s.f. threat, menace.

menacer [mənase], v.tr. (n. menaçons) to threaten, menace; m. qn du poing, to shake one's fist at s.o.; m. de faire qch., to threaten to do sth.; a. -çant, threatening (look, sky).

ménage [menaːʒ], s.m. 1. (a) housekeeping; (b) faire le m., to do the housework; faire des ménages, to go out charring; femme de m., charwoman, daily (help). 2. household equipment; se monter en m., to furnish one's house. 3. household, family; (a) jeune m., young married couple; se mettre en m., to set up house; (b) faire bon, mauvais, m. (ensemble), to live happily, unhappily, together.

ménagement [menaʒmɑ̃], s.m. caution, care; consideration; parler sans ménagement(s), to speak bluntly, tactlessly.

ménager[1] [menaʒe], v.tr. (n. ménageons) 1. (a) to save; to be sparing of (sth.); m. sa santé, to take care of one's health; m. qn, to deal tactfully with s.o.; ne le ménagez pas, don't spare him; (b) sans m. ses paroles, without mincing one's words. 2. to contrive, arrange; m. une surprise à qn, to prepare a surprise for s.o.; bien m. un terrain, to make the most of a piece of ground; m. une sortie, to provide an exit.

ménager[2], -ère [menaʒe, -ɛːr]. 1. a. (a) connected with the house; travaux ménagers, housework; enseignement m., domestic science; Salon des Arts ménagers = Ideal Home Exhibition; (b) housewifely (virtues, etc.); (c) thrifty, sparing; s. être m. de ses éloges, to be sparing of praise. 2. s.f. (a) (i) housewife; (ii) housekeeper; (b) canteen of cutlery.

ménagerie [menaʒri], s.f. menagerie.

mendlier [mɑ̃dje], v.i. & tr. (p.d. & pr.sub. n. mendiions) to beg; s. -iant, -iante, beggar; s.f. -icité, begging.

menée [məne], s.f. intrigue; pl. (political) scheming; déjouer les menées de qn, to outwit s.o.

menler [m(ə)ne], v.tr. (je mène) 1. to lead; (a) m. qn à sa chambre, to take s.o. to his room; (b) to be, go, ahead (of); m. le deuil, to be chief mourner; Games: m. par huit points, to lead by eight points; (c) cela nous mène à croire que . . ., that leads us to believe that . . .; (d) to control, manage (children, etc.); mari mené par sa femme, henpecked husband. 2. to drive (horse); to steer (boat). 3. to manage, conduct (business); m. une campagne, to conduct a campaign (contre, against); m. une vie tranquille, to lead a quiet life; s. -eur, -euse, leader; ring-leader, agitator.

menhir [meniːr], s.m. menhir; standing stone.

méningite [menɛ̃ʒit], s.f. Med: meningitis.

menottes [mənɔt], s.f. pl. handcuffs.

mensongle [mɑ̃sɔ̃ːʒ], s.m. lie, falsehood; petit m., fib; gros m., out-and-out lie; whopper; a. -er, -ère, lying; deceitful.

menstruation [mɑ̃stryasjɔ̃], s.f. menstruation.

mensualité [mɑ̃syalite], s.f. monthly payment, instalment.

mensuel, -elle [mɑ̃syɛl], a. monthly (publication, payment, etc.); adv. -lement.

mensuration [mɑ̃syrasjɔ̃], s.f. measurement; pl. (of a man) measurements, (of a girl) F: vital statistics.

mental, -aux [mɑ̃tal, -o], a. mental; adv. -ement.

mentalité [mɑ̃talite], s.f. mentality.

menteur, -euse [mɑ̃tœːr, -øːz]. 1. a. (a) lying (person); given to lying; (b) false, deceptive (appearance, etc.). 2. s. liar.

menthe [mɑ̃ːt], s.f. Bot: mint; m. verte, spearmint, garden mint; m. anglaise, poivrée, peppermint; pastilles de m., peppermints.

mention [mɑ̃sjɔ̃], s.f. (a) mention; faire m. de qn, to refer to, to mention, s.o.; Sch: reçu avec m., passed with distinction; (b) P.T.T: endorsement; m. "inconnu," endorsed 'not known'; (c) reference (at head of letter).

mentionner [mɑ̃sjɔne], v.tr. to mention.

mentir [mɑ̃tiːr], v.i. (pr.p. mentant; pr.ind. je mens) to lie; to tell lies; sans m.! on my honour!

menton [mɑ̃tɔ̃], s.m. chin.

menu [məny]. 1. a. small; (a) fine (gravel); slender, slight (figure); tiny; menue monnaie, small change; (b) trifling; petty; menus détails, minor details; menus frais, petty expenses. 2. adv. small, fine; hacher m., to chop up small; to mince. 3. s.m. (a) raconter qch. par le m., to

relate sth. in detail; (*b*) (*in restaurant*) menu.
menuis|erie [mənцizri], *s.f.* **1.** joinery, woodwork, carpentry. **2.** joiner's shop; *s.m.* **-ier**, joiner, carpenter.
méprendre (se) [səməprã:dr], *v.pr.* (*conj. like* PRENDRE) to be mistaken, to make a mistake (sur, quant à, about); **il n'y a pas à s'y m.**, there can be no mistake about it.
mépris [mepri], *s.m.* contempt, scorn.
méprise [mepri:z], *s.f.* mistake.
mépris|er [meprize], *v.tr.* to despise, scorn; to hold (s.o., sth.) in contempt; *a.* **-able**, contemptible, despicable; *a.* **-ant**, scornful.
mer [mɛ:r], *s.f.* sea; (*a*) **la haute m.**, the open sea; **au bord de la m.**, at the seaside; **partir à la m.**, to go to, leave for, the seaside; **partir en m.**, to go to sea; **mal de m.**, seasickness; **grosse m.**, heavy sea; **m. dure, mauvaise,** rough sea; **sur m.**, afloat; **prendre la m.**, to put (out) to sea; **mettre une embarcation à la m.**, to lower a boat; (*b*) **basse m.**, low water; **m. haute**, high tide.
mercantile [mɛrkãtil], *a.* mercantile; commercial.
mercenaire [mɛrsənɛ:r]. **1.** *a.* mercenary, venal. **2.** *s.m. Mil:* mercenary.
merc|erie [mɛrsəri], *s.f.* haberdashery, drapery; *s.* **-ier, -ière,** haberdasher, (small-scale) draper.
merci [mɛrsi]. **1.** *adv.* (*a*) thank you; (*b*) no, thank you; **prenez-vous du thé?—m.!** will you have some tea?—no, thank you. **2.** *s.m.* **adresser un cordial m. à qn,** to thank s.o. heartily; *usu. iron:* **grand m.!** many thanks! **3.** *s.f.* mercy; **à la m. de qn,** at s.o.'s mercy.
mercredi [mɛrkrədi], *s.m.* Wednesday.
mercure [mɛrky:r], *s.m. Ch:* mercury, quicksilver.
mère [mɛ:r], *s.f.* **1.** mother; *F:* **la m. Dupont,** old Mrs Dupont; *Ecc:* **M. supérieure,** Mother Superior. **2.** *attrib.* (*a*) **la reine m.**, the Queen Mother; (*b*) *Com:* **maison m.**, parent establishment.
mère-patrie [mɛrpatri], *s.f.* mother country; *pl.* **mères-patries.**
méridional, -aux [meridjɔnal, -o]. **1.** *a.* south(ern). **2.** *s.* southerner; southern Frenchman.
mérinos [merino:s], *s.m.* merino (sheep, cloth).
meris|e [məri:z], *s.f.* wild cherry; *s.m.* **-ier,** wild cherry(-tree); **pipe en m.**, cherry-wood pipe.
mérite [merit], *s.m.* merit; (*a*) worth; **chose de peu de m.**, thing of little worth, value; (*b*) excellence, talent; **homme de m.**, man of talent, of ability.
mérit|er [merite], *v.tr.* **1.** to deserve, merit; **cela mérite d'être vu,** it is worth seeing. **2.** to earn (a reward, a favour); *a.* **-oire**, meritorious, deserving.

merian [mɛrid], *s.m. Ich:* whiting.
merle [mɛrl], *s.m. Orn:* blackbird; **jaser comme un m.**, to chatter like a magpie.
merlu(s) [mɛrly], *s.m. Ich:* hake.
merluche [mɛrlyʃ], *s.f.* **1.** *Ich:* hake. **2.** dried (unsalted) cod.
merveille [mɛrvɛ:j], *s.f.* marvel, wonder; **crier m.**, to exclaim in admiration; **à m.**, excellently; **se porter à m.**, to be in excellent health.
merveilleu|x, -euse [mɛrvɛjø, -ø:z], *a.* marvellous, wonderful; *adv.* **-sement.**
mes. *see* MON.
mésalliance [mezaljã:s], *s.f.* misalliance; **faire une m.**, to marry beneath one.
mésaventure [mezavãty:r], *s.f.* misadventure, mishap.
mesdames, -demoiselles. *see* MADAME, MADEMOISELLE.
mésentente [mezãtã:t], *s.f.* misunderstanding, disagreement.
mésestim|er [mezɛstime], *v.tr.* **1.** to underestimate, undervalue, underrate. **2.** to have a poor opinion of (s.o.); *s.f.* **-ation,** underestimation, underrating.
mésinterprét|er [mezɛ̃tɛrprete], *v.tr.* (*conj. like* INTERPRÉTER) to misinterpret, misconstrue; *s.f.* **-ation,** misinterpretation.
méson [mezɔ̃], *s.m. Atom.Ph:* meson.
mesquin [mɛskɛ̃], *a.* (*a*) mean, shabby (appearance); paltry, petty (excuse); (*b*) mean, stingy (person); *adv.* **-ement.**
mesquinerie [mɛskinri], *s.f.* **1.** meanness; (*a*) pettiness; (*b*) niggardliness. **2.** shabby, mean action.
mess [mɛs], *s.m. Mil:* (officers', N.C.O.s') mess.
message [mɛsa:ʒ], *s.m.* message.
messag|er, -ère [mɛsaʒe, -ɛ:r], *s.* **1.** messenger. **2.** *s.m.* carrier; *s.f.* **-erie,** carrying trade (esp. by sea or rail).
messe [mɛs], *s.f. Ecc:* mass.
messeigneurs. *see* MONSEIGNEUR.
Messie [mesi, mɛ-]. *Pr.n.m.* Messiah.
messieurs. *see* MONSIEUR.
mesure [məzy:r], *s.f.* measure. **1.** (*a*) **prendre m. de qn,** (i) to take s.o.'s measurements; (ii) to size s.o. up; **dans une certaine m.**, to a certain degree; *adv.phr.* **à m.**, in proportion, successively; one by one; **à m. que,** (in proportion) as; **à m. que je reculais il s'avançait,** (fast as) I retired he advanced; (*b*) **prendre ses mesures,** to take action; **prendre ses mesures** to make one's arrangements. **2.** (*a*) gauge, standard; **poids et mesures,** weights and measures; (*b*) (*quantity measured*) **une m. de vin,** a measure of wine. **3.** required size, amount; **garder la m.**, to keep within bounds; **être en m. de faire qch.**, to be in a position to do sth. **4.** *Mus:* (*a*) bar; (*b*) time; **battre la m.**, to beat time.

mesuré [məzyre], *a.* measured (tread, etc.); temperate, restrained, moderate (language, etc.).

mesur|er [məzyre], *v.tr.* 1. (*a*) to measure (dimensions, quantity); (*of tailor*) **m. un client,** to take a customer's measurements; (*b*) **colonne qui mesure dix mètres (de hauteur),** column ten metres high; (*c*) **m. la nourriture à qn,** to grudge s.o. his food, to ration s.o.'s food. 2. to calculate; to weigh (one's words); *s.m.* **-age,** measuring, measurement.

se mesurer avec, contre, qn, to measure one's strength against s.o.; to pit oneself against s.o.

métairie [meteri, -tɛ-], *s.f.* farm (held on a share-cropping agreement).

métal, -aux [metal, -o], *s.m.* metal; *a.* **-lique,** metallic; *s.f.* **-lurgie,** metallurgy; *a.* **-lurgique,** metallurgic(al); *s.m.* **-lurgiste.**

métamor|phoser [metamɔrfoze], *v.tr.* to metamorphose, transform; *s.f.* **-phose,** metamorphosis, transformation.

se métamorphoser, to change completely.

métaphor|e [metafɔːr], *s.f.* metaphor; figure of speech; *a.* **-ique,** metaphorical; *adv.* **-iquement.**

métayage [meteja:ʒ], *s.m. Agr:* share-cropping (system).

métayer, -ère [meteje, -ɛːr], *s.* share-cropper.

météo [meteo], *F:* 1. *s.f.* (*a*) weather report; (*b*) the meteorological office. 2. *s.m.* (*pers.*) meteorologist, *F:* weather man.

météor|e [meteɔːr], *s.m.* meteor; *a.* **-ique,** meteoric.

météorite [meteɔrit], *s.m. or f.* meteorite.

météoro|logie [meteɔrɔlɔʒi], *s.f.* meteorology; *s.m. & f.* **-logiste, -logue,** meteorologist.

météorologique [meteɔrɔlɔʒik], *a.* meteorological; **bulletin m.,** weather report, forecast; **station, navire, m.,** weather station, ship.

méthod|e [metɔd], *s.f.* method, system; *a.* **-ique,** methodical; *adv.* **-iquement.**

méticuleu|x [metikylø, -ø:z], *a.* meticulous, punctilious; scrupulously careful (person); *adv.* **-sement.**

métier [metje], *s.m.* 1. trade, profession, craft, occupation, business; **quel est votre m.?** what do you do (for a living)? what's your job? **m. manuel,** handicraft; **gens de m.,** professionals, experts; **tours de m.,** tricks of the trade; **parler m.,** to talk shop; **terme de m.,** technical term; **risques de m.,** occupational hazards; *F:* **quel m.!** what a life! 2. *Tex:* **m. à tisser,** loom.

métis, -isse [metis]. 1. *a.* half-bred; cross-bred; mongrel (dog, etc.); hybrid (plant); *Tex:* **toile métisse,** cotton-linen mixture. 2. *s.* half-breed; half-caste; mongrel; (*of plant*) hybrid.

mètre¹ [metr], *s.m. Lit:* metre.

mètre², *s.m.* 1. *Meas:* metre. 2. (metre) rule; **m. à ruban,** tape-measure.

métr|er [metre], *v.tr.* (**je mètre**) 1. to measure (by the metre). 2. *Const:* to survey (for quantities); *s.m.* **-age,** (i) measuring, quantity surveying; (ii) (metric) length; *s.m.* **-eur,** quantity surveyor; **-ique,** *a.* metric (system, etc.).

Métro (le) [ləmetro], *s.m.* the underground (railway); *N.Am:* subway.

métropole [metrɔpɔl], *s.f.* (*a*) capital city; (*b*) parent state; (*c*) (archbishop's) see.

mets [mɛ], *s.m.* (article of prepared) food; dish (of food).

mettable [mɛtabl], *a.* (*of clothes, etc.*) wearable, fit to wear.

metteur [mɛtœːr], *s.m.* **m. en scène,** (i) *Th:* producer; (ii) *Cin:* director; *Rad:* **m. en ondes,** producer.

mettre [mɛtr], *v.tr.* (*p.p.* **mis;** *pr.ind.* **je mets, il met;** *p.h.* **je mis**) 1. (*a*) to put, lay, place, set; **m. la table,** to lay the table; **m. un enjeu,** to lay a stake; **m. le feu à qch.,** to set sth. on fire; **m. qn à la porte,** to turn s.o. out; **j'y mettrai tous mes soins,** I will give the matter every care; **m. du temps à faire qch.,** to take time over sth.; (*b*) to put (clothes) on; **qu'est-ce que je vais m.?** what shall I wear? **ne plus m.,** to leave off (a garment); **m. ses gants,** to put on one's gloves. 2. to set, put (in a condition); **m. une machine en mouvement,** to set a machine going; **m. la télé plus fort,** to turn up the telly; **m. en vente une maison,** to put a house up for sale; **m. une terre en blé,** to put a field under corn. 3. (*a*) to admit, grant; **mettons que vous ayez raison,** suppose you are right; **mettons cent francs,** let's say a hundred francs; (*b*) **mettez que je n'ai rien dit,** consider that unsaid.

se mettre. 1. (*a*) to go, get; **se m. au lit,** to go to bed; (*b*) **se m. à l'œuvre, au travail,** to set to work; **je ne peux pas m'y m.,** I can't start on it; (*c*) **se m. à faire qch.,** to begin to do sth.; **se m. à rire,** to start laughing; *impers.* **il se mit à pleuvoir,** it began to rain. 2. to dress; **se m. en smoking,** to put on a dinner-jacket; **être bien mis,** to be well dressed. 3. **se m. en route,** to start on one's way. 4. **le temps se met au beau, à la pluie,** the weather is turning fine, wet.

meuble [mœbl], *s.m.* piece of furniture; **être dans ses meubles,** to have a home of one's own; **m. de famille,** heirloom; **meubles de salon, de salle à manger,** drawing-room, dining-room, suite.

meublé [mœble]. 1. *a.* furnished (room, etc.); **non m.,** unfurnished; **cave bien meublée,** well-stocked cellar. 2. *s.m.* furnished apartment(s); **vivre en m.,** to live in lodgings, *F:* in digs.

meubler [mœble], *v.tr.* to furnish; to stock (farm, cellar) (**de,** with); **rideaux qui meublent bien,** curtains that furnish a room well; **m. ses loisirs,** to occupy, fill up, one's free time.

meugl|er [møgle], *v.i.* (*of cow*) to low, to moo;

s.m. -ement, mooing, lowing.

meule [mø:l], *s.f.* 1. (*a*) millstone; (*b*) m. à aiguiser, à affûter, grindstone; (*c*) m. de fromage, round cheese. 2. stack, rick (of hay).

meun|ier [mønje], *s.m.* miller; *s.f.* -erie, milling (trade).

meurtre [mœrtr], *s.m. Jur:* murder; au m.! murder!

meurtrier, -ère [mœrtrije, -ɛːr]. 1.*a.* murderous; deadly (weapon). 2. *s.* murderer,*f.* murderess. 3. *s.f. Fort:* meurtrière, loophole.

meurtr|ir [mœrtriːr], *v.tr.* to bruise; *s.f.* -issure, bruise.

meute [mø:t], *s.f.* (*a*) pack (of hounds); (*b*) *F:* mob (of pursuers); (*c*) *Scouting:* (cub) pack.

mexicain, -aine [mɛksikɛ̃, -ɛn], *a. & s. Geog:* Mexican.

Mexico [mɛksiko]. *Pr.n. Geog:* Mexico City.

Mexique (le) [ləmɛksik]. *Pr.n.m. Geog:* Mexico (state).

mi¹ [mi], *adv.* half, mid-, semi-; la mi-avril, mid-April; à mi-hauteur, halfway up, down.

mi², *s.m.inv. Mus:* (the note) E; morceau en mi, piece in E.

miaou [mjau], *s.m.* miaow, mew (of cat).

mi-août [miu], *s.f.inv.* mid-August.

miaul|er [mjole], *v.i.* to mew, to miaow; to caterwaul; *s.m.* -ement.

mica [mika], *s.m.* mica.

mi-carême [mikarɛm], *s.f.* mid-Lent; *pl. mi-carêmes.*

miche [miʃ], *s.f.* round loaf.

Michel [miʃɛl]. *Pr.n.m.* Michael; la Saint-M., Michaelmas.

micheline [miʃlin], *s.f.* rail-car.

mi-chemin (à) [amiʃmɛ̃], *adv.phr.* halfway.

mi-clos [miklo], *adj.* half-closed, half-shut (eyes, shutters, etc.); *pl. mi-clos*(es).

mi-corps (à) [amikɔːr], *adv.phr.* to the waist; saisi à mi-c., caught round the waist; portrait à mi-c., half-length portrait.

mi-côte (à) [amikoːt], *adv.phr.* halfway up, down, the hill.

micro [mikro], *s.m. F:* mike.

microbe [mikrɔb], *s.m.* microbe, germ.

microfilm [mikrɔfilm], *s.m. Phot:* microfilm.

microfilm|er [mikrɔfilme], *v.tr.* to microfilm; *s.m.* -age.

microphone [mikrɔfɔn], *s.m.* microphone; (*a*) mouthpiece (of telephone); (*b*) *Rad: etc: F:* mike; m. espion, m. caché, detectophone, *F:* bug.

microphotograph|ie [mikrɔfɔtɔgrafi], *s.f.* 1. microphotography. 2. microphotograph; *a.* -ique.

microscope [mikrɔskɔp], *s.m.* microscope.

microscop|ie [mikrɔskɔpi], *s.f.* microscopy; *a.* -ique.

microsillon [mikrɔsijɔ̃], *s.m. Rec:* 1.

microgroove. 2. (disque) m., long-playing record, *F:* L.P.

midi [midi]. *s.m. no pl.* 1. midday, noon, twelve o'clock; arriver sur le m., *F:* sur les m., to arrive about noon; sur le coup de m., *F:* à m. pile, on the stroke of twelve; avant m., a.m.; après m., p.m.; m. et demi, half-past twelve; chercher m. à quatorze heures, to look for difficulties where there aren't any. 2. (*a*) south; chambre au m., room facing south; (*b*) le M. (de la France), the South of France.

mi-distance (à) [amidistâːs], *adv.phr.* halfway, midway.

mie [mi], *s.f.* crumb (of loaf, as opposed to crust).

miel [mjɛl], *s.m.* honey; paroles de m., honeyed words; lune de m., honeymoon.

mielleu|x, -euse [mjɛlø, -øːz], *a.* 1. goût m. taste of honey. 2. *usu. Pej:* honeyed, sugary soft-spoken (person); *adv.* -sement, blandly with honeyed words.

mien, mienne [mjɛ̃, mjɛn], (*a*) *poss.pron.* le m. la mienne, les miens, les miennes, mine; un de vos amis et des miens, a friend of yours and mine; (*b*) *s.m.* (i) my own (property); mine; I m. et le tien, mine and yours; (ii) *s.m.pl.* j'ai été renié par les miens, I have been disowned by my own people; (*c*) *s.f.pl.* on dit que j'ai encor fait des miennes, they say I've been up to m old tricks again.

miette [mjɛt], *s.f.* (*a*) crumb (of broken bread (*b*) morsel, scrap; mettre un vase en miettes, t smash a vase to smithereens.

mieux [mjø], *adv.* 1. *comp.* better; (*a*) ça va m things are improving; pour m. dire . . ., to b more exact . . .; *adv.phr.* faire qch. à qui m m., to vie with one another in doing sth.; (*b*) (with adj. function) (i) c'est on ne peut m., couldn't be better; (ii) vous serez m. dans fauteuil, you will be more comfortable in th armchair; (*c*) *s.m.* le m. est l'ennemi du bie leave well alone; faute de m., for want something better; elle ressemble à sa mèr mais en m., she's like her mother, but bette looking; je ne demande pas m., I shall b delighted. 2. *sup.* le m., (the) best; (*a*) la fem le m. habillée de Paris, the best-dressed woma in Paris; (*b*) (with adj. function) (i) c'est tout qu'il y a de m., there is absolutely nothi better; (ii) être le m. du monde avec qn, to on the best of terms with s.o.; (*c*) *s.m.* faire son m., to do one's best.

mièvre [mjɛːvr], *a.* finicky, affected (sty manner).

mignon, -onne [miɲɔ̃, -ɔn]. 1. *a.* dainty, tin adorable. 2. *s.* pet, darling.

migraine [migrɛn], *s.f.* migraine.

migr|ation [migrasjɔ̃], *s.f.* migration; *a.* -ate -atrice, migrating; migrant; *a.* -atoi migratory (movement, etc.).

mijaurée [miʒɔre], *s.f.* conceited, affected, *F:* stuck-up, woman.

mijoter [miʒɔte], *v.tr. Cu:* to stew (sth.) slowly, to let (sth.) simmer; **m. un projet**, to turn a scheme over in one's mind.

mil [mil], *a.* (*used only in writing out dates* A.D.) thousand; **l'an mil neuf cent trente**, the year 1930.

milieu, -eux [miljø], *s.m.* 1. middle, midst; **au m. de**, amid(st); **au beau m. de la rue**, right in the middle of the street. 2. (*a*) *Ph:* medium; (*b*) surroundings, environment; (social) sphere; **les gens de mon m.**, people in my set; **dans les milieux autorisés**, in responsible quarters; (*c*) **le m., les gens du m.**, the underworld. 3. middle course; mean; **le juste m.**, the happy medium.

militaire [militɛːr]. 1. *a.* military; **service m.**, military service; **camion m.**, army lorry, *N.Am:* truck. 2. *s.m.* (*a*) soldier; **les militaires**, the armed forces; (*b*) army life; the army (as a profession); **passer du civil au m.**, to leave civilian life for the army.

militant, -ante [militã, -ãːt]. 1. *a.* militant (church, policy). 2. *s.* militant; **les militants d'un parti**, the fighting wing of a party.

militar|iser [militarize], *v.tr.* to militarize (a nation, a zone); *s.f.* **-isation**; *s.m.* **-isme**; *a. & s.m. & f.* **-iste**.

militer [milite], *v.i.* to militate (**pour**, in favour of; **contre**, against); **cela milite en sa faveur**, that tells in his favour.

millage [milaːʒ], *s.m. Fr.C:* mileage.

mille[1] [mil], *num.a.inv. & s.m.inv.* thousand; **m. hommes**, a thousand men; **m. un**, a thousand and one; **il a des m. et des cents**, he has tons of money.

mille[2], *s.m.* mile.

millésime [mil(l)ezim], *s.m.* (*a*) date (on coin); (*b*) *Ind:* year of manufacture; (*of wine*) year, vintage.

millet [mijɛ], *s.m. Bot:* millet; (**grains de**) **m.**, canary-seed.

milliard [miljaːr], *s.m.* milliard, *N.Am:* billion.

milliardaire [miljardɛːr], *a. & s.m. & f.* multimillionaire.

millième [miljɛm], 1. *num.a & s.* thousandth. 2. *s.m.* (one-)thousandth (part).

millier [milje], *s.m.* (about a) thousand; a thousand or so; **des milliers**, thousands.

million [miljõ], *s.m.* million.

millionnaire [miljɔnɛːr], *a. & s.* millionaire.

mim|e [mim], *s.m.* 1. *Th:* mime. 2. *s.m. & f.* (*pers.*) (*a*) mime; (*b*) mimic.

mimer [mime], *v.tr.* 1. *Th:* to mime (a scene). 2. to mimic, to ape (s.o.).

minable [minabl], *a. F:* seedy-looking (person); shabby (appearance); **un salaire m.**, a mere pittance.

minaud|er [minode], *v.i.* to simper, smirk; *s.f.* **-erie**, simpering, smirking; **faire des minauderies**, to have a simpering manner.

mince [mɛ̃ːs]. 1. *a.* thin; slender, slim (person); scanty (income). 2. *int. P:* **m. alors!** well! good heavens!

minceur [mɛ̃sœːr], *s.f.* thinness; slenderness, slimness; scantiness (of income, knowledge).

mine[1] [min], *s.f.* 1. mine; (*a*) **m. de houille**, coalmine; **m. à ciel ouvert**, opencast mine; (*b*) *Mil: etc:* **m. flottante**, floating mine; **champ de mines**, minefield. 2. **m. de plomb**, graphite, black-lead; **m. (de crayon)**, (pencil) lead.

mine[2], *s.f.* 1. (*general appearance*) **juger les gens sur la m.**, to judge people by appearances; **il ne paie pas de m.**, his appearance is against him, he doesn't look up to much. 2. (*facial expression*) (*a*) (*of health*) **avoir bonne, mauvaise, m.**, to look well, ill; **il a une sale m.**, he *does* look ill; (*b*) **faire la m.**, to look sulky; **faire grise m. à qn**, to greet s.o. coldly.

miner [mine], *v.tr.* to mine, undermine; *P.N: danger!* terrain miné, danger! beware of mines; **miné par l'envie**, consumed with envy.

minerai [minrɛ], *s.m.* ore.

minéral, -aux [mineral, -o]. 1. *a.* mineral; **source minérale**, spa. 2. *s.m.* mineral.

minéralogique [mineralɔʒik], *a.* 1. mineralogical. 2. *Adm:* **numéro m.**, registration number (of car); **plaque m.**, number plate (of car).

minéralog|iste [mineralɔʒist], *s.m. & f.* mineralogist; *s.f.* **-ie**, mineralogy.

mineur[1] [minœːr], *s.m.* (*a*) miner; **m. de houille**, coal miner, collier; **m. de fond**, underground worker; (*b*) *Mil:* sapper.

mineur[2], **-eure**. 1. *a.* (*a*) minor, lesser; (*b*) *Jur:* under age. 2. *s.* minor.

mini [mini], *s.f.* 1. *Aut: R.t.m:* mini. 2. *Cost: F:* mini (skirt).

miniatur|e [minjatyːr], *s.f.* miniature; *adv.phr.* **en m.**, on a small scale; *s.m. & f.* **-iste**, miniaturist.

minier, -ière [minje, -jɛːr]. 1. *a.* mining (industry, district). 2. *s.f.* **minière**, surface, opencast, mine.

minime [minim], *a.* small; trivial; trifling.

minimum [minimɔm], minimum. 1. *s.m.* **m. de vitesse**, minimum speed; **m. vital**, minimum living wage; **thermomètre à minima**, minimum thermometer; *pl. minima, minimums.* 2. *a.* **la largeur, les largeurs, minimum, les largeurs minima**, the minimum width(s).

ministère [ministɛːr], *s.m.* 1. (*a*) agency; (*b*) *Ecc:* **le saint m.**, the ministry. 2. *Adm:* ministry; (*a*) office; **entrer au m.**, to take office; (*b*) **former un m.**, to form a ministry, a government; (*c*) government department; **M. des Affaires étrangères** = Foreign Office, *U.S:* State

Department.

ministériel, -elle [ministerjel], *a.* ministerial; **crise ministérielle,** cabinet crisis.

ministre [ministr], *s.m.* minister; Secretary of State; **Premier M.,** Prime Minister; **M. des Affaires étrangères,** Foreign Secretary, *U.S:* Secretary of State.

minor│ité [minɔrite], *s.f.* **1.** *Jur:* infancy. **2. être en m.,** to be in the minority; **les minorités ont leurs droits,** minorities have their rights; *a.* **-itaire,** minority.

Minorque [minɔrk]. *Pr.n. Geog:* Minorca.

minorquin, -ine [minɔrkɛ̃, -in], *a. & s. Geog:* Minorcan.

minoterie [minɔtri], *s.f.* **1.** (large) flour-mill. **2.** flour-milling.

minuit [minɥi], *s.m.* midnight; **m. et demi,** half-past twelve at night.

minuscule [minyskyl], *a.* (*a*) small, minute, tiny; (*b*) **lettre m.,** *s.f.* **m.,** small letter.

minute [minyt], *s.f.* **1.** minute (of hour, degree); **réparations à la m.,** repairs while you wait. **2.** *Adm:* minute, draft; record (of deed).

minuterie [minytri], *s.f.* (*a*) **m. d'enregistrement,** counting mechanism (of meter); (*b*) automatic time-switch (on staircase); timer (on cooker).

minutie [minysi], *s.f.* minute detail; trifle.

minutieu│x, -ieuse [minysjø, -jøːz], *a.* scrupulously careful (person); minute, detailed (inspection, work); *adv.* **-sement.**

mioche [mjɔʃ], *s.m. &f. F:* small child; urchin.

mi-pente (à) [amipɑ̃:t], *adv.phr.* halfway up, down, the hill.

miracle [mira:kl], *s.m.* miracle; **faire un m.,** to perform, work, a miracle; **fait à m.,** marvellously well done.

miraculeu│x, -euse [mirakylø, -øːz], *a.* miraculous; *F:* marvellous; **remède m.,** wonder drug; *adv.* **-sement.**

mirage [mira:ʒ], *s.m.* mirage.

miroir [mirwa:r], *s.m.* mirror, looking-glass.

miroit│er [mirwate], *v.i.* to flash; to glisten; (*of water*) to shimmer; (*of jewel, lights*) to sparkle; *s.m.* **-ement,** flashing; glisten(ing); sheen; *s.f.* **-erie,** mirror-factory, -trade, -shop; *s.* **-ier, -ière,** mirror-maker, -manufacturer; mirror-dealer.

misanthrop│e [mizɑ̃trɔp]. **1.** *s.m.* misanthrope. **2.** *a.* misanthropic(al); *s.f.* **-ie,** misanthropy; *a.* **-ique,** misanthropic(al).

mise [mi:z], *s.f.* **1.** (*a*) (*putting of sth. in a place*) placing; putting; **m. à l'eau,** launching (of ship); **m. en bouteilles,** bottling (of wine, etc.); **m. en plis,** setting (of hair); (*b*) setting; **m. en liberté,** release; **m. en retraite,** pensioning (off); **m. en garde,** warning, caution; **m. en marche,** starting (of engine); *Rad:* **m. en ondes,** production. **2.** dress, way of dressing; **soigner sa m.,** to dress with care. **3.** (*a*) *Gaming:* stake; (*b*) bid

(at auction); (*c*) **m. (de fonds),** investment (of capital).

misérable [mizerabl]. **1.** *a.* miserable; (*a*) unhappy, unfortunate; wretched; (*after s.*) poor; **quartier m.,** poverty-stricken district; (*b*) despicable, mean. **2.** *s.* (*a*) poor wretch; (*b*) scoundrel, wretch; *adv.* **-ment.**

misère [mizeːr], *s.f.* **1.** (*a*) misery; (*b*) trouble; **misères domestiques,** domestic worries. **2.** extreme poverty; destitution; **crier m.,** to plead poverty. **3.** *F:* trifle; **cent francs? une m.!** a hundred francs? a mere nothing!

miséreux, -euse [mizerø, -øːz], *a. & s.* **1.** poverty-stricken (person). **2.** shabby-genteel, seedy-looking (person).

miséricord│e [mizerikɔrd], *s.f.* mercy, mercifulness; **crier m.,** to beg for mercy; *a.* **-ieux, -ieuse,** merciful.

miss [mis], *s.f. F:* beauty queen; **Miss France,** Miss France.

missile [misil], *s.m. Mil: etc:* (guided) missile.

mission [misjɔ̃], *s.f.* mission; *Mil:* mission, com mission; **en m.,** on detached service; *Ecc:* **mis sions étrangères,** foreign missions; *s.m* **-naire,** missionary.

mistral [mistral], *s.m. Meteor:* (in *S.E. France* mistral.

mite [mit], *s.f.* **1.** mite; **m. du fromage,** chees mite. **2.** clothes-moth.

mité [mite], *a.* moth-eaten.

mi-temps [mitɑ̃], *s.f.inv.* **1.** *Sp:* **la mi-t.,** hal time. **2.** *adv.phr.* **emploi à mi-t.,** part-time job.

miteux, -euse [mitø, -øːz], *a. F:* shabb (clothes); tatty (furniture); **hôtel m.,** third-rat hotel; *s.* **un m., une miteuse,** a shabby ma woman.

miti│ger [mitiʒe], *v.tr.* (**n. mitigeons**) **1.** t mitigate (penalty). **2.** to relax (rule); *s* **-gation,** mitigation.

mitrail│ler [mitraje], *v.tr.* to machine-gun; t rake (enemy's troops, etc.) with machine-gu fire; *s.f.* **-ette,** sub-machine-gun; **m. sten,** ste gun; *s.f.* **-euse,** machine-gun.

mi-vitesse (à) [amivites], *adv.phr.* at halfspee

mi-voix (à) [amivwa], *adv.phr.* in an underton under one's breath, in a subdued voice.

mixage [miksa:ʒ], *s.m. Cin: etc:* mixing (sounds).

mixe(u)r [miksœ:r], *s.m. H:* **1.** mixer. liquidizer.

mixte [mikst], *a.* **1.** mixed (race, bathing, etc **commission m.,** joint commission; **école n** co-educational school; *s.m. Ten:* **double n** mixed doubles. **2.** serving a double purpos **train m.,** composite train (goods a passengers); **billet m.,** combined rail and ro ticket.

mobi│le [mɔbil]. **1.** *a.* (*a*) mobile, movable; ■ unstable, changeable, fickle (nature); ■

detachable; **objectif m.**, screw-on lens; (*d*) moving (target); changing (expression); **escalier m.**, moving staircase, escalator. **2.** *s.m.* (*a*) body in motion; *Art:* mobile; (*b*) driving power; (i) **premier m. dans un complot**, prime mover in a plot; (ii) **m. d'un crime**, motive of a crime; *s.f.* **-ité**, mobility, movableness; changeableness.

mobilier, -ière [mɔbilje, -jɛːr]. **1.** *a. Jur:* movable, personal; **héritier m.**, heir to personal estate; *Fin:* **valeurs mobilières**, stocks and shares. **2.** *s.m.* (*a*) furniture; (*b*) suite of furniture; **m. de salon**, drawing-room suite.

mobilis∣er [mɔbilize], *v.tr.* to mobilize (troops, etc.); to liberate (capital); **m. ses amis**, to round up one's friends; *a.* **-able**; *s.f.* **-ation.**

mocassin [mɔkasɛ̃], *s.m.* mocassin; *pl.* casual shoes, casuals, *N.Am:* loafers.

moche [mɔʃ], *a. F:* rotten (conduct, etc.); poor, shoddy (work); dowdy (person); **elle est m. à pleurer**, she's as ugly as sin.

mode¹ [mɔd], *s.f.* **1.** fashion; **être de m., à la m.**, to be in fashion, in vogue; **à la m. de . . .**, after the style of . . .; **passé de m.**, out of fashion, out of date; **jupe très m.**, stylish, fashionable, skirt; **la haute m.**, the fashion trade. **2.** *pl. Com:* (*a*) ladies' dresses, fashions; (*b*) **(articles de) modes**, millinery.

mode², *s.m.* **1.** *Gram:* mood. **2.** method, mode; "**m. d'emploi**," 'directions for use'.

modèle [mɔdɛl]. **1.** *s.m.* (*a*) model, pattern; **m. déposé**, registered pattern; **m. réduit**, scale model; (*b*) *Cost:* model dress, hat. **2.** *s.m.* (artist's) model. **3.** *a.* **un époux m.**, a model, exemplary, husband.

model∣er [mɔdle], *v.tr.* (**je modèle**) to model; to mould; *s.m.* **-age**, modelling; *s.m.* **-eur.**

nodérateur, -trice [mɔderatœːr, -tris]. **1.** *a.* moderating, restraining. **2.** *s.* moderator. **3.** *s.m.* regulator.

∣no∣dérer [mɔdere], *v.tr.* (**je modère; je modérerai**) **1.** to moderate, restrain; to slacken (speed); **m. son impatience**, to curb one's impatience. **2.** to reduce (price, etc.); *s.f.* **-dération;** *a.* **-déré**, moderate, temperate; *adv.* **-dérément.**

∣e modérer. **1.** to control oneself, to keep calm. **2.** (*of wind, weather*) to abate.

noderne [mɔdɛrn], *a.* modern.

∣odern∣iser [mɔdɛrnize], *v.tr.* to modernize; *s.f.* **-isation;** *s.m.* **-isme;** *s.f.* **-ité**, up-to-dateness.

nodest∣e [mɔdɛst], *a.* modest; unassuming; quiet (dress); *adv.* **-ement;** *s.f.* **-ie**, modesty.

∣odifi∣er [mɔdifje], *v.tr.* to modify (statement, penalty); to alter, change (plan); *a.* **-cateur, -catrice**, modifying; *s.f.* **-cation**, modification, alteration.

∣odique [mɔdik], *a.* moderate, reasonable

(cost); slender (income).

modiste [mɔdist], *s.f., occ. m.* milliner, modiste.

modul∣er [mɔdyle], *v.tr. El: Mus:* to modulate; *s.f.* **-ation;** *Rad:* **m. de fréquence**, frequency modulation.

moelle [mwal], *s.f.* **1.** marrow (of bone); **corrompu jusqu'à la m.**, rotten to the core. **2.** *Bot:* pith.

moelleu∣x, -euse [mwalø, -øːz], *a.* **1.** (*a*) marrowy (bone); (*b*) *Bot:* pithy. **2.** (*a*) soft, velvety (to touch); mellow (wine, voice, light); **tapis m.**, springy carpet; **couleur moelleuse**, soft colour; (*b*) *s.m.* softness; mellowness (of voice, etc.); *adv.* **-sement.**

mœurs [mœrs], *s.f.pl.* (i) morals; (ii) manners (of people); customs (of country); habits (of animals); **avoir de bonnes m.**, to be of good moral character; **gens sans m.**, unprincipled people; *Adm:* **la brigade**, *F:* **la police, des m.**, the vice squad.

moi [mwa]. **1.** *stressed pers.pron.* (*a*) (*subject*) I; **c'est m.**, it is I, *F:* it's me; **elle est invitée et m. aussi**, she is invited and so am I; **m., je veux bien**, for my part, I'm willing; (*b*) (*object*) me; **à m.!** help! **de vous à m.**, between you and me; **ce livre est à m.**, this book is mine; **un ami à m.**, a friend of mine; (*c*) (*after imp.*) (i) (*object*) **laissez-m. tranquille**, leave me alone; (ii) (*indirect object*) **donnez-le-m.**, give it (to) me. **2.** *s.m.* ego, self; **le culte du m.**, egoism.

moignon [mwaɲɔ̃], *s.m.* stump (of amputated limb, sawn-off branch).

moindre [mwɛ̃ːdr], *a.* **1.** *comp:* less(er); **m. prix**, lower price; **quantité m.**, smaller quantity. **2.** *sup.* **le, la, m.**, the least; **le m. d'entre nous**, the least of us.

moine [mwan], *s.m.* monk, friar.

moineau, -eaux [mwano], *s.m. Orn:* sparrow.

moins [mwɛ̃]. **1.** *adv.* (*a*) *comp:* less; **m. encore**, still more, even less; **m. d'argent**, less money; **m. de dix francs**, less than ten francs; **en m. de dix minutes**, within, under, in less than, ten minutes; **dix francs de m.**, (i) ten francs less; (ii) ten francs short; *prep.phr.* **à moins de**, unless, barring; **à m. d'avis contraire**, unless I hear to the contrary; **à moins que** + *sub.*, unless; **à m. que vous (ne) l'ordonniez**, unless you order it; **rien m. que**, (*ambiguous*) (i) anything but; (ii) nothing less than; **non m. que**, as well as; quite as much as; (*b*) *sup.* **le m.**, least; **les élèves les m. appliqués**, the least industrious pupils; **pas le m. du monde**, not in the least (degree); by no means; *s.* **c'est bien le m. (qu'il puisse faire)**, it is the least he can do; *adv.phr.* **du m.**, at least, that is to say, at all events; **au m.**, at least (= not less than); **vous compterez cela en m.**, you may deduct that. **2.** (*a*) *prep.* minus, less; **six m. quatre égale deux**, six minus four, take away four, equals two; **une heure m. cinq**, five (minutes) to one; (*b*) *s.m. Mth:* minus sign.

moiré [mware], *a. Tex:* watered, moiré (silk).

mois [mwa], *s.m.* month; **le m. en cours**, the current month; **le onze du m. prochain, du m. dernier**, the eleventh of next, last, month; *Com:* the 11th proximo, ultimo; **de ce m.**, of this month, *Com:* instant.

Moïse [mɔiːz]. **1.** *Pr.n.m. B.Hist:* Moses. **2.** *s.m.* wicker cradle; **m. de toile**, carry-cot.

moisi [mwazi]. **1.** *a.* mouldy, mildewy; musty. **2.** *s.m.* mould, mildew; **sentir le m.**, to smell musty.

moislir [mwaziːr], *v.i. & pr.* to mildew; to go mouldy; **m. dans un bureau**, to moulder in an office; *s.f.* **-issure**, mildew, mould(iness); mustiness.

moisson [mwasɔ̃], *s.f.* **1.** (*a*) harvest(ing) (of cereals); **faire la m.**, to harvest; (*b*) harvest-time. **2.** (cereal) crop; **rentrer la m.**, to gather in the crops.

moissonnler [mwasɔne], *v.tr.* to reap; to harvest, gather (crops); to win (glory); *s.* **-eur**, **-euse**, (*pers.*) harvester; *s.f.* reaping machine, reaper.

moissonneuse-batteuse [mwasɔnøz-batøːz], *s.f.* combine-harvester; *pl. moissonneuses-batteuses.*

moite [mwat], *a.* moist (brow); (**froid et) m.**, clammy; **chaleur m.**, muggy heat.

moitié [mwatje]. **1.** *s.f.* half; **couper qch. par (la) m.**, to cut sth. in half; **une bonne m.**, a good half; **m. plus**, half as much again; **être de m. avec qn**, to share and share alike; *adv.phr.* **à m.**, half; **à m. mort**, half-dead; **à m. cuit**, half-cooked. **2.** *adv.* **m. l'un, m. l'autre**, half and half.

molaire [mɔlɛːr], *a. & s.f.* molar (tooth).

môle [moːl], *s.m.* mole; (harbour) breakwater.

moléculle [mɔlekyl], *s.f.* molecule; *a.* **-aire**, molecular.

molester [mɔlɛste], *v.tr.* to molest.

mollement [mɔlmɑ̃], *adv.* (*a*) softly (cushioned chair); (*b*) slackly, feebly; **travailler m.**, to work indolently.

mollesse [mɔlɛs], *s.f.* (*a*) softness (of cushion); flabbiness; (*b*) slackness, lifelessness; (*c*) indolence.

mollet [mɔlɛ], *s.m.* calf (of leg).

mollir [mɔliːr], *v.i.* (*a*) to soften; to become soft; (*b*) (*of rope, effort*) to slacken; (*of wind*) to die down, to abate; **mes jambes mollissent**, my legs are giving way.

moment [mɔmɑ̃], *s.m.* moment; **le m. venu . . .**, when the time had come . . .; **j'ai répondu sur le m.**, I answered on the spur of the moment; **arriver au bon m.**, to arrive in the nick of time; **passer un bon m.**, to enjoy oneself; **par moments**, at times, now and again; **à tout m.**, **à tous moments**, constantly; **dans mes moments perdus**, in my spare time; **au m. donné**, at the appointed time; *conj.phr.* **du m. que . . .**, (i) from the moment when . . .; (ii) seeing that . . .; *a.* **-ané**, momentary (effort); temporary (absence); *adv.* **-anément**, momentarily.

momie [mɔmi], *s.f.* (*Egyptian, etc.*) mummy.

mon, ma, mes [mɔ̃, ma, mɛ], *poss.a.* (**mon** *is used instead of* **ma** *before f. words beginning with vowel or h 'mute'.*) my; **mon ami, mon amie**, my friend; **un de mes amis**, a friend of mine; **oui, mon oncle**, yes, Uncle; **non, mon colonel**, no, sir.

monarlchie [mɔnarʃi], *s.f.* monarchy; *a.* **-chique**, monarchic(al); *a. & s.* **-chiste**, monarchist.

monarque [mɔnark], *s.m.* monarch.

monastère [mɔnastɛːr], *s.m.* monastery; convent.

monastique [mɔnastik], *a.* monastic.

monceau, -eaux [mɔ̃so], *s.m.* heap, pile (o' stones, etc.).

mondain, -aine [mɔ̃dɛ̃, -ɛn], *a.* **1.** mundane worldly (pleasures, etc.); worldly-minded (per son). **2.** (*of society*) fashionable (resort, etc.) **réunion mondaine**, society gathering; *s.* u **mondain**, a man about town; **une mondaine**, society woman.

monde [mɔ̃ːd], *s.m.* **1.** world; (*a*) **le m. entier**, th whole world; *Geog:* **l'ancien, le nouveau, M** the Old, the New, World; **le tiers m.**, the thir world; **mettre un enfant au m.**, to give birth a child; **venir au m.**, to be born; **il est encore d ce m.**, he's still alive; **pour rien au m.**, not f the world, not on any account; **être le mieux d m. avec qn**, to be on the best of terms with s.c **vieux comme le m.**, (as) old as the hills; (society; **le beau m.**, (fashionable) society; **grand m.**, high society; **le m. savant**, the wo of science; **homme du m.**, man of the world. people; **avoir du m. à dîner**, to have people dinner; **il connaît son m.**, he knows the peop he has to deal with; **tout le m.**, everybody.

mondial, -aux [mɔ̃djal, -o], *a.* world-wic **guerre mondiale**, global warfare; **la premiè deuxième, guerre mondiale**, World War O Two, the First, Second, World War.

monégasque [mɔnegask], *a. & s.* (native) Monaco.

monétaire [mɔnetɛːr], *a.* monetary; **unité d'un pays**, currency of a country.

moniteur, -trice [mɔnitœːr, -tris], *s.* instruct *f.* instructress; *Sp:* coach; *Aut:* driving instr tor; assistant (in holiday camp).

monnaie [mɔnɛ], *s.f.* **1.** money; **pièce de** coin; **m. légale**, legal tender; (**hôtel de) la** the Mint; *F:* **payer qn en m. de singe**, to let whistle for his money. **2.** change; **petite** small change, petty cash; *F:* **rendre à qn la de sa pièce**, to pay s.o. (back) in his own c

monnay|er [mɔnɛje], *v.tr.* (je monnaie, je monnaye) to coin, mint; *s.m.* -**age**, minting, coining; *s.m.* -**eur**, minter; **faux m.**, counterfeiter.

monocoque [mɔnɔkɔk], *a. & s.f. Av:* monocoque; *Aut:* monoshell; **carrosserie m.**, monopiece body.

monogramme [mɔnɔgram], *s.m.* monogram.

monographie [mɔnɔgrafi], *s.f.* monograph.

monolo|guer [mɔnɔlɔge], *v.i.* to soliloquize; *s.m.* -**gue**, monologue, soliloquy; *s.m.* -**gueur**, soliloquizer.

monomanie [mɔnɔmani], *s.f.* monomania, obsession.

monopole [mɔnɔpɔl], *s.m.* monopoly; **m. d'État**, State monopoly; *Com: Fin:* **m. des prix**, price ring.

monopolis|er [mɔnɔpɔlize], *v.tr.* to monopolize; *s.f.* -**ation**, monopolization.

monorail [mɔnɔraːj], *a. & s.m.* monorail.

monosyllа|be [mɔnɔsil(l)ab]. **1.** *a.* monosyllabic. **2.** *s.m.* monosyllable; *a.* -**bique**, monosyllabic.

mono|tonie [mɔnɔtɔni], *s.f.* monotony; *a.* -**tone**, dull, monotonous (life).

monseigneur [mɔ̃sɛɲœːr], *s.m.* **1.** (*a*) (*title of dignity*) His Royal Highness; his Eminence; his Grace; his Lordship; *pl. nosseigneurs*; (*b*) your Royal Highness; your Eminence; your Grace; your Lordship; *pl. messeigneurs*. **2.** *F:* **pince(-)m.**, (burglar's) jemmy; *pl. pinces(-)monseigneurs, pinces(-)monseigneur.*

monsieur, *pl.* **messieurs** [m(ə)sjø, mɛsjø], *s.m.* **1.** (*a*) **Monsieur, M., Jules Durand**, Mr Jules Durand; **Messieurs, MM., Durand et Cie**, Messrs Durand and Co.; **m. le duc**, (i) the Duke (of); (ii) his, your, Grace; **comment va m. votre oncle?** how is your uncle? (*b*) **m. Jean**, (*of adult*) Mr John, (*of small boy*) Master John; (*c*) (*used alone*) **voici le chapeau de m.**, here is Mr X's hat; **m. n'y est pas**, Mr X is not at home. **2.** (*a*) (*in address*) sir; **bonsoir, messieurs**, good evening, gentlemen; **m. a sonné?** did you ring, sir? **que prendront ces messieurs?** what will you have, gentlemen? (*b*) (*in letter writing*) (i) (*to stranger*) **Monsieur** (*always written in full*), Dear Sir; (ii) (*implying previous acquaintance*) **Cher Monsieur**, Dear Mr X. **3.** (gentle)man; **le m. qui vient de sortir**, the (gentle)man who has just gone out.

monst|re [mɔ̃ːstr]. **1.** *s.m.* (*a*) monster, monstrosity; (*b*) monster; **les monstres marins**, the monsters of the deep. **2.** *a.* huge; colossal; monster; *a.* -**rueux, -rueuse**, monstrous; unnatural; colossal; shocking; *adv.* -**rueusement**.

mont [mɔ̃], *s.m.* mount, mountain; **promettre monts et merveilles à qn**, to promise s.o. the earth.

mont|agne [mɔ̃taɲ], *s.f.* (*a*) mountain; **montagnes russes**, switchback, roller-coaster, scenic railway; (*b*) mountain region; (*c*) **m. de glace**, iceberg; *s.* -**agnard, -agnarde**, (*a*) *s.* mountain dweller; highlander; (*b*) *a.* mountain, highland (people, etc.); *a.* -**agneux, -agneuse**, mountainous (country).

montant [mɔ̃tɑ̃]. **1.** *a.* rising, ascending; **chemin m.**, uphill road; **marée montante**, rising tide; **robe montante**, high-necked dress; *Rail:* **train m.**, up train. **2.** *s.m.* (*a*) upright (of ladder); post, pillar; *Fb:* **les montants**, the goal-posts; (*b*) total amount (of debt, account).

monté [mɔ̃te], *a.* **1.** mounted (man); **cavalier bien m.**, well mounted rider. **2.** *F:* **il était m.**, il avait la tête montée, his blood was up, he was worked up, excited; **coup m.**, put-up job.

monte-charge [mɔ̃tʃarʒ], *s.m.inv.* hoist, goods lift, *N.Am:* elevator.

montée [mɔ̃te], *s.f.* **1.** (*a*) rise, rising; **tuyau de m.**, uptake pipe; (*b*) uphill pull, climb; *Aut:* **essai de m.**, climbing test; **vitesse en m.**, climbing speed. **2.** gradient, slope (up).

monte-pente [mɔ̃tpɑ̃ːt], *s.m.* ski-lift; *pl. monte-pentes*.

monte-plats [mɔ̃tpla], *s.m.inv.* service lift; plate hoist.

monter [mɔ̃te]. **I.** *v.i.* (aux. usu. être, occ. avoir) **1.** (*a*) to climb (up), mount, ascend; to go upstairs; **m. se coucher**, to go (up) to bed; (*b*) to climb on, into (sth.); **m. à cheval**, (i) to mount; (ii) to ride; **m. à bord**, to go on board (a ship). **2.** (*a*) to rise, to go up; **frais montant à mille francs**, expenses amounting to one thousand francs; **faire m. les prix**, to raise the prices; to send prices up; **le sang lui monte à la tête**, the blood rushes to his head; *F:* **m. comme une soupe au lait**, to flare up, *F:* to go off the deep end (easily); (*b*) (*of road*) to ascend, to climb; (*c*) (*of pers.*) **m. dans l'estime de qn**, to rise in s.o.'s estimation.
II. *v.tr.* **1.** to mount; (*a*) to climb (up), go up, ascend; (*b*) *Mil:* **m. la garde**, to mount guard; (*c*) to ride (horse); *Rac:* **Jones monte Comet**, Jones is riding Comet. **2.** *Nau:* to man (boat). **3.** (*a*) to raise, take up; **m. du vin de la cave**, to bring up, fetch up, wine from the cellar; (*b*) *F:* **se m. la tête**, to get excited. **4.** to set (jewel); to fit on (tyre); to erect (apparatus); to equip; **m. un magasin**, to open a shop; **m. un complot**, to hatch a plot.

se monter. 1. to amount, to add up (à, to). **2.** to equip oneself (en, with); to lay in a stock of (sth.).

montre [mɔ̃tr], *s.f.* **1.** (*a*) show, display; (*b*) shop-window; show-case. **2.** watch; **m.(-bracelet)**, (wrist-)watch.

montrer [mɔ̃tre], *v.tr.* to show; (*a*) to display, exhibit; (*b*) to point out; (*c*) **m. à qn à faire qch.**, to show s.o. how to do sth.; **montrez-moi comment faire,** show me how to do it.

se montrer. (*a*) **se m. au bon moment,** to appear at the right moment; (*of sum*) to come out; (*b*) **il se montra prudent,** he showed prudence.

monture [mɔ̃tyːr], *s.f.* **1.** mount (horse, camel, etc.); (saddle) horse. **2.** setting (of jewel); mount(ing) (of picture); frame (of spectacles); **lunettes sans m.,** rimless glasses.

monument [mɔnymɑ̃], *s.m.* **1.** monument, memorial; **m. aux morts,** War Memorial. **2.** public or historic building; **m. historique,** classified historical monument; *a.* **-al, -aux,** monumental.

moquer (se) [səmɔke], *v.pr.* **se m. de qn,** to make fun of s.o.; **vous vous moquez,** you're joking; **c'est se m. du monde!** it is the height of impertinence!

moqu|erie [mɔkri], *s.f.* mockery; derision; *a. & s.* **-eur, -euse,** (i) *a.* mocking; (ii) *s.* scoffer.

moral, -aux [mɔral, -o]. **1.** *a.* (*a*) moral; ethical; (*b*) mental, intellectual; **courage m.,** moral courage. **2.** *s.m.* (state of) mind; morale; **relever le m. de, à, qn,** to raise s.o.'s spirits.

morale [mɔral], *s.f.* **1.** (*a*) morals; **contraire à la m.,** immoral; (*b*) ethics; moral science; **faire de la m. à qn,** to lecture s.o. **2.** moral (of a story); *adv.* **-ment.**

mora|liser [mɔralize]. **1.** *v.i.* to moralize. **2.** *v.tr.* to lecture, sermonize (s.o.); *s.m. & f.* **-liste.**

moralité [mɔralite], *s.f.* **1.** (*a*) morality; (good) moral conduct; (*b*) morals; honesty; **personne de m. douteuse,** person of doubtful honesty. **2.** moral (of a story).

morbid|e [mɔrbid], *a.* morbid; *adv.* **-ement;** *s.f.* **-ité,** morbidity, morbidness.

morceau, -eaux [mɔrso], *s.m.* **1.** morsel, piece (of food); **aimer les bons morceaux,** to like good things (to eat); *F:* **manger un m.,** to have a snack; *F:* **gober le m.,** to swallow the bait. **2.** piece (of soap, cloth; poetry, music; land, etc.); bit, scrap; lump (of sugar).

morc|eler [mɔrsəle], *v.tr.* (**je morcelle**) to cut up (sth.) into small pieces; **m. une propriété,** to break up, to parcel out, an estate; *s.m.* **-ellement.**

mordant [mɔrdɑ̃]. **1.** *a.* (*a*) eating away; corrosive; **lime mordante,** file that has plenty of bite; (*b*) mordant, biting, caustic. **2.** *s.m.* (*a*) corrosiveness; bite (of file); (*b*) mordancy, pungency.

mordoré [mɔrdɔre], *a. & s.m.* bronze (colour).

mordre [mɔrdr], *v.tr. & ind.tr.* to bite; (*a*) *F:* **quel chien l'a mordu?** what's bitten him? **il s'en mord les pouces,** he bitterly regrets it; **se m. les poings d'impatience,** to gnaw one's fingers with impatience; (*b*) **m. à, dans, une pomme,** to take a bite out of an apple; *Fish:* **ça mord,** I've got a bite; (*c*) (*of cog-wheels*) to catch, engage.

mordu, -e [mɔrdy], *a. F:* mad; **m. du cinéma,** mad on films; *s.* **les mordus du football,** football fans.

morfondre (se) [səmɔrfɔ̃:dr], to be bored to death.

morgue [mɔrg], *s.f.* **1.** pride, arrogance. **2.** mortuary, morgue.

moribond [mɔribɔ̃], *a.* moribund, dying, at death's door.

morne [mɔrn], *a.* dejected; gloomy; dull (weather); dreary.

morose [mɔroːz], *a.* morose, moody; gloomy.

morphin|e [mɔrfin], *s.f.* morphia; morphine; *s.m. & f.* **-omane,** morphia addict.

mors [mɔːr], *s.m.* **1.** *Tls:* jaw (of vice). **2.** *Equit:* bit (of bridle); **ronger son m.,** (i) (*of horse*) to champ the bit; (ii) *F:* (*of pers.*) to fret.

morsure [mɔrsyːr], *s.f.* **1.** bite. **2.** *Engr:* biting, etching.

mort¹, morte [mɔːr, mɔrt]. **1.** *a.* (*a*) dead (pers. language); **m. et enterré,** dead and buried; (*of a place*) **un petit trou à moitié m.,** a dead(-and) alive little hole; (*b*) **temps m.,** time wasted; *Mec:* **point m.,** (i) neutral position (of lever); (ii) *Aut:* neutral gear; (*c*) **eau morte,** stagnant water; *Art:* **nature morte,** still life. **2.** *s.* dead person; **le morts,** the departed; *Ecc:* **jour, fête, des morts,** All Soul's day; **l'office des morts,** the funera[l] service; **tête de m.,** skull; **faire le m.,** (i) to pr[e]tend to be dead; (ii) to lie low; *Aut: F:* **la place d[u] m.,** the front passenger seat. **3.** *s.m. Cards:* dummy.

mort², *s.f.* 1. death; *Jur:* **arrêt de m.,** deat[h] sentence; **m. civile,** civil death; **se donner [la] m.,** to take one's own life; **mourir de sa bell[e] m.,** to die a natural death; **il avait la m. dan[s] l'âme,** he was sick at heart. **2. m. aux rat[s],** rat-poison.

mortalité [mɔrtalite], *s.f.* mortality; death rat[e]; **m. infantile,** infant mortality.

mortel, -elle [mɔrtɛl], *a.* mortal; (*a*) destined [to] die; *s.* **un m., une mortelle,** a mortal; (*b*) fat[al] (wound); (*c*) *F:* deadly dull; **je l'ai attendu de[ux] mortelles heures,** I waited two mortal hou[rs] for him; (*d*) deadly; **ennemi m.,** mortal enem[y]; *adv.* **-lement.**

mortier [mɔrtje], *s.m.* mortar. **1.** (*a*) **pilon et m[ortier],** pestle and mortar; (*b*) *Artil:* **m. de tranché[e],** trench-mortar. **2.** *Const:* **m. ordinaire,** lim[e] mortar; **bâti à chaux et à m.,** built to last f[or] ever.

mortifi|er [mɔrtifje], *v.tr.* (*p.d. & pr. sub.* **n. m[e] tifions**) (*a*) to mortify (one's passions); (*b*) [to] mortify (s.o.); to hurt (s.o.'s) feelings; *a.* **-a[nt],** mortifying; *s.f.* **-cation,** humiliation.

mort-né, -née [mɔrne], *a.* (*a*) still-born; **projet m.-né,** abortive plan; *pl.* **mort-nés, -né[es]**

mortuaire [mɔrtɥɛːr], *a.* mortuary; **drap [m.],** pall; **acte, extrait, m.,** death certificate; **cha[pelle]**

bre m., death-chamber.

morue [mɔry], *s.f. Ich:* cod.

mosaïque [mɔzaik], *s.f. Art:* mosaic.

Moscou [mɔsku]. *Pr.n. Geog:* Moscow.

moscovite [mɔskɔvit], *a. & s. Geog:* Muscovite.

mosquée [mɔske], *s.f.* mosque.

mot [mo], *s.m.* word; **prendre qn au m.,** to take s.o. at his word; **faire du m. à m.** [motamo], to translate word for word; **dire deux mots à qn,** to have a word with s.o.; **le dernier m. du confort,** the last word in comfort; **ignorer le premier m. de la chimie,** not to know the first thing about chemistry; **en quelques mots,** briefly, in a nutshell; **au bas m.,** at the lowest estimate; **gros m.,** coarse expression; **le m. de l'énigme,** the key to the enigma; **voilà le fin m. de l'affaire!** so that's what's at the bottom of it! **faire comprendre qch. à qn à mots couverts,** to give s.o. a hint of sth.; **écrire un m. à qn,** to drop s.o. a line; **tranchons le m., vous refusez,** to put it bluntly, you refuse; **bon m.,** witty remark, *F:* wisecrack; **avoir le m. pour rire,** to be fond of a joke; **mots croisés,** crossword (puzzle); (*computers*) **m. de commande,** control word.

motard [mɔtaːr], *s.m. F:* m. (**de la route**) = speed cop; **m. d'escorte,** motor-cycle outrider.

motel [mɔtɛl], *s.m.* motel.

moteur, -trice [mɔtœːr, -tris]. 1. *a.* motive, propulsive, driving (power); **roue motrice,** driving wheel; **voiture à roues avant motrices,** car with front-wheel drive; **unité motrice,** power unit; **force motrice,** driving force. 2. *s.m.* motor, engine; **m. à essence,** petrol engine; **m. à deux, à quatre, temps,** two-stroke, four-stroke, engine; **m. d'avion,** aero-engine.

motif [mɔtif]. 1. *a.* motive. 2. *s.m.* (*a*) motive, incentive; reason; **soupçons sans m.,** groundless suspicions; (*b*) *Art:* motif; design; ornament; *Mus:* theme.

motion [mɔsjõ], *s.f.* motion, proposal.

motiver [mɔtive], *v.tr.* 1. to state the reason for; **m. une décision sur qch.,** to base a decision on sth. 2. to justify, warrant; **refus motivé,** justifiable refusal.

moto [mɔto], *s.f. F:* motorbike.

motoculture [mɔtokyltyːr], *s.f.* mechanized farming; *s.m.* **-teur,** (power-driven) cultivator.

motocyclette [mɔtosiklɛt], *s.f.* motor cycle, *F:* motorbike; *s.m.* **-iste,** motor cyclist.

motofaucheuse [mɔtofoʃøːz], *s.f.* motor-scythe.

motonautisme [mɔtonotism], *s.m.* motor-boating; *a.* **-ique; sport m.,** motorboating.

motoriser [mɔtorize], *v.tr.* to motorize, to mechanize; *s.f.* **-ation,** mechanization.

motte [mɔt], *s.f.* 1. mound. 2. clod, lump (of earth); **m. de gazon,** sod, turf.

mou, mol, *f.* **molle** [mu, mɔl]. 1. *a.* (*the masc. form* **mol** *is used before vowel or h 'mute'*) soft; slack; weak, flabby. 2. *s.m.* slack (of rope).

mouchard [muʃaːr], *s.m. F:* (*a*) informer; police spy; (*b*) (mechanical) speed-check (on vehicles); (*c*) watchman's clock; (*d*) *Av:* observation plane, snooper.

mouche [muʃ], *s.f.* 1. fly; **m. commune,** housefly; **m. bleue,** bluebottle; **prendre la m.,** to take offence; **quelle m. vous pique?** what is the matter with you? *F:* **c'est une fine m.,** he's a cunning, crafty, chap; *Box:* **poids m.,** flyweight. 2. (*a*) spot, speck; (*b*) bull's-eye (of target); **faire m.,** to score a bull.

moucher [muʃe], *v.tr.* (*a*) to wipe (child's) nose; (*b*) *F:* to snub (s.o.), to tell (s.o.) off.

se moucher, to wipe, blow, one's nose.

moucheron [muʃrõ], *s.m.* midge; gnat.

moucheter [muʃte], *v.tr.* (**je mouchette**) to spot, speckle; **mer mouchetée d'écume,** foam-flecked sea.

mouchoir [muʃwaːr], *s.m.* **m.** (**de poche**), (pocket) handkerchief; **m. de tête,** head scarf.

moudre [mudr], *v.tr.* (*pr.p.* **moulant;** *p.p.* **moulu**) to grind (corn, coffee, etc.).

moue [mu], *s.f.* pout; **faire la m.,** to purse one's lips, to pout, to look sulky.

mouette [mwet], *s.f. Orn:* gull.

mouillé [muje], *a.* 1. moist, damp, wet; **m. jusqu'aux os,** wet through; *F:* (*pers.*) **poule mouillée,** wet, drip. 2. (*of ship*) at anchor, moored.

mouiller [muje], *v.tr.* 1. to wet, moisten, damp. 2. *Nau:* (*a*) **m. l'ancre,** to drop anchor; **m. un navire,** to bring a ship to anchor; (*b*) to lay (mine). 3. to palatalize (consonant); *s.m.* **-age,** *Nau:* (*a*) anchoring; (*b*) anchorage.

se mouiller, to get wet; (*of eyes*) to fill with tears.

moule¹ [mul], *s.m.* mould; matrix.

moule², *s.f.* mussel; *P:* (*pers.*) drip, wet; fool.

mouler [mule], *v.tr.* (*a*) to cast (statue); (*b*) to mould; **se m. sur qn,** to model oneself on s.o.; **robe qui moule,** dress that clings (to the figure); *s.m.* **-age,** casting, moulding.

moulin [mulɛ̃], *s.m.* mill; (*a*) **m. à vent,** windmill; *F:* **faire venir l'eau au m.,** to bring grist to the mill; (*b*) **m. à légumes,** vegetable mill; **m. à poivre, à café,** pepper, coffee, mill.

moulu [muly], *a.* (*a*) ground, powdered; (*b*) dead-beat, fagged out; aching all over.

moulure [mulyːr], *s.f.* (ornamental) moulding.

mourant, -ante [murã, -ã:t]. 1. *a.* dying; **d'une voix mourante,** in a faint voice, faintly. 2. *s.* dying man, woman.

mourir [muriːr], *v.i.* (*pr.p.* **mourant;** *p.p.* **mort;** *pr.ind.* **je meurs, ils meurent;** *pr.sub.* **je meure, nous mourions;** *p.h.* **il mourut;** *fu.* **je mourrai;** *aux.* **être**) to die; **il est mort hier,** he died yesterday; **m. de faim,** (i) to die of starvation; (ii) *F:* to be starving; **faire m. qn,** to put s.o. to death; *F:* **il me fera m.,** he will be the death of me; **m. d'envie de faire qch.,** to be dying to do sth.; **m. de peur,** to be scared to death; **s'ennuyer à m.,** to be bored to death; **je mourais de rire,** I nearly died laughing; **c'est à m. de rire,** it's simply killing.

mousse[1] [mus], *s.f.* **1.** moss; **couvert de m.,** moss-grown. **2.** froth, foam (of beer, sea, etc.); lather (of soap); *Cu:* **m. au chocolat,** chocolate mousse. **3.** *Ind:* **m. de plastique, de caoutchouc,** foam plastic, foam rubber. **4.** *Knitting:* **point m.,** moss stitch.

mousse[2], *s.m.* ship's boy.

mousseline [muslin], *s.f. Tex:* muslin; **m. de soie,** chiffon; *Cu:* **gâteau m.,** sponge cake; **pommes (de terre) m.,** creamed potatoes.

mousser [muse], *v.i.* to froth, foam; to lather; (*of wine*) to sparkle, *F:* to fizz; *a.* **-eux, -euse,** (*a*) mossy; (*b*) foaming; sparkling (wine).

moustache [mustaʃ], *s.f.* (*a*) moustache; (*b*) whiskers (of cat).

mousti|que [mustik], *s.m. Ent:* (*a*) mosquito; (*b*) gnat; *s.f.* **-quaire,** mosquito net.

moutard [muta:r], *s.m. P:* urchin; brat.

moutard|e [mutard], *s.f.* (*a*) mustard; (*b*) *attrib.* **jaune m.,** mustard yellow; *s.m.* **-ier,** mustard pot.

mouton [mutɔ̃], *s.m.* **1.** sheep; **élevage de moutons,** sheep breeding; *Equit:* **saut de m.,** bucking (of horse). **2.** *Cu:* mutton; **ragoût de m.,** mutton stew; *Com:* sheepskin. **3.** *Civ.E:* ram. **4.** *pl.* white horses (on sea).

moutonn|er [mutɔne], *v.i.* (*of sea*) to break into white horses; to froth; *s.m.* **-ement;** *a.* **-eux, -euse,** foam-flecked; fleecy (clouds).

se moutonner, (*of sky*) to become covered with fleecy clouds.

mouvant [muvɑ̃], *a.* (*a*) mobile; (*b*) unstable, changeable; **sables mouvants,** quicksand(s).

mouvement [muvmɑ̃], *s.m.* movement. **1.** motion; **faire un m.,** to move; **se mettre en m.,** to start off; **le m. d'une grande ville,** the bustle of a large town; **ville sans m.,** lifeless, dull, town; *Mec:* **pièces en m.,** moving parts (of a machine); **m. perpétuel,** perpetual motion; *Mus:* (i) movement (of symphony, etc.); (ii) **presser le m.,** to quicken the time. **2.** (*a*) change, modification; **m. de terrain,** undulation in the ground; **être dans le m.,** to be in the swim, up to date; **m. de personnel,** staff changes; (*b*) **m. d'humeur,** outburst, fit, of temper; (*c*) agitation, emotion; **m. populaire,** rising of the people. **3.** traffic; *Rail:* **mouvements des trains,** train arrivals and departures; *Journ:* **mouvements des navires,** shipping intelligence. **4.** works, action, movement; **m. d'horlogerie,** clockwork.

mouvementé [muvmɑ̃te], *a.* **1.** animated, lively; full of incident. **2.** **terrain m.,** undulating ground.

mouvoir [muvwa:r], *v.tr.* (*pr.p.* **mouvant;** *p.p.* **mû, mue;** *pr.ind.* **je meus, ils meuvent;** *pr.sub.* **je meuve,** n. **mouvions, ils meuvent**) to drive (machinery, etc.); to propel (ship, etc.); **mû par turbine,** turbine-driven; **mû par la colère,** moved by anger.

se mouvoir, to move, stir; **faire m. qch.,** to set sth. going, in motion.

moyen[1], **-enne** [mwajɛ̃. -ɛn]. **1.** *a.* (*a*) middle; **les classes moyennes,** the middle classes; **le m. âge** [mwajɛnɑ:ʒ], the Middle Ages; (*b*) average, mean (speed, level, price, etc.); **le Français m.,** the average Frenchman; = the man in the street; (*c*) medium; **de taille moyenne,** medium-sized, middle-sized. **2.** *s.f.* **moyenne,** average; **en moyenne,** on an average.

moyen[2], *s.m.* means; (*a*) **m. de transport,** means of transport; *Ind:* **moyens de production,** capital goods; **employer les grands moyens,** to take extreme measures; **y a-t-il m. de le faire?** is it possible to do it? **il n'y a pas m.,** it can't be done; **dans la (pleine) mesure de mes moyens,** to the utmost of my ability; **enfant qui a des moyens,** talented child; **homme sans moyens,** man of no resource; **enlever les moyens à qn** to cramp s.o.'s style; (*b*) **vivre au delà de ses moyens,** to live beyond one's means; **je n'en ai pas les moyens,** I can't afford it.

moyennant [mwajɛnɑ̃], *prep.* on (a certain) condition; **faire qch. m. finance,** to do sth. for a consideration; **m. un prix convenu,** for an agreed price; **m. quoi,** in consideration of which.

moyeu, -eux [mwajø], *s.m.* hub.

mue [my], *s.f.* **1.** (*a*) moulting (of birds); shedding of the antlers; changing of skin; (*b*) moulting-time; (*c*) feathers moulted; antlers etc., shed. **2.** breaking of the voice (at puberty).

muer [mɥe], *v.i.* (*of bird*) to moult; (*of reptile*) to shed, slough, the skin; (*of stag*) to shed the antlers; (*b*) (*of voice*) to break (at puberty).

muet, -ette [mɥe, -ɛt]. **1.** *a.* dumb, mute; (*a*) unable to speak; **m. de colère,** speechless with anger; (*b*) unwilling to speak; **rester m.,** to remain silent; (*c*) without word or sound; **douleur muette,** silent sorrow; *Th:* **rôle m.,** silent part; *Gram:* **lettre muette,** silent letter; **'h' m.,** mute 'h'. **2.** *s.* dumb person.

muf|le [myfl], *s.m.* **1.** muzzle (of ox, etc.). **2.** face, mug; **il a une vraie tête de m.,** he has really coarse face; *s.f.* **-erie,** boorishness.

muflier [myflije], *s.m. Bot:* antirrhinum, snapdragon.

mug|ir [myʒi:r], *v.i.* (*a*) (*of cow*) to low; bellow; (*b*) (*of sea, wind*) to roar; to boom; *s.m.* **-issement.**

muguet [mygε], *s.m. Bot:* lily of the valley.
mulâtre [mylɑːtr], *a. & s.* mulatto, half-caste.
mule[1] [myl], *s.f.* (she-)mule.
mule[2], *s.f.* bedroom slipper; mule.
mule|**t**[1] [mylε], *s.m.* (he-)mule; *s.m.* **-tier**, mule-driver.
mulet[2], *s.m. Ich:* grey mullet.
mulot [mylo], *s.m.* field-mouse.
multicolore [myltikɔlɔːr], *a.* multi-coloured.
multiple [myltipl]. **1.** *a.* multiple, manifold; multifarious (duties, etc.); **maison à succursales multiples**, chain store. **2.** *s.m. Mth:* multiple.
multipli|**er** [myltiplije], *v.tr. & i.* to multiply (**par**, by); *s.f.* **-cation**; *s.f.* **-cité**, multiplicity.
se multiplier, (*a*) to multiply; **les crimes se multiplient**, crime is on the increase; (*b*) to be here, there, and everywhere.
multitude [myltityd], *s.f.* multitude (**de**, of); crowd; multiplicity.
municipal, **-aux** [mynisipal, -o], *a.* municipal; **conseil m.**, local council.
municipalité [mynisipalite], *s.f.* municipality; (*a*) local administrative area; (*b*) local council; (*c*) town hall.
munir [myniːr], *v.tr.* to furnish, equip, provide (**de**, with); **se m. de provisions**, to provide oneself with food; **se m. de patience**, to possess one's soul in patience.
munitions [mynisjɔ̃], *s.f.pl.* stores, supplies; ammunition.
mur [myːr], *s.m.* wall; **mettre qn au pied du m.**, to drive s.o. into a corner; **donner de la tête contre un m.**, to run one's head against a brick wall; *Av:* **m. du son**, sound barrier; *s.f.* **-aille**, high wall.
mûr [myːr], *a.* ripe (fruit, etc.); mellow (wine); mature (mind, age); *adv.* **-ement**, with mature consideration.
mural, **-aux** [myral, -o], *a.* mural; **peintures murales**, wall paintings, murals; **carte murale**, wall map; **pendule murale**, wall clock.
mûr|**e** [myːr], *s.f.* **1.** mulberry. **2. m.** (**de ronce**), blackberry; *s.m.* **-ier**, mulberry (tree); **m. sauvage**, blackberry bush.
murer [myre], *v.tr.* to wall in; to wall up, brick up (doorway, etc.).
mûrir [myriːr], *v.tr. & i.* to ripen, mature.
murmure [myrmyːr], *s.m.* murmur, murmuring.
murmurer [myrmyre], *v.tr. & i.* (*a*) to murmur; (*b*) to grumble; **m. entre ses dents**, to mutter; (*c*) to whisper (a secret); to breathe (a prayer); **vent qui murmure dans le feuillage**, wind sighing among the leaves.
muscad|**e** [myskad], *s.f.* (**noix**) **m.**, nutmeg; *s.m.* **-ier**, nutmeg tree.
muscat [myska], *a. & s.m. Vit:* (**raisin**) **m.**, muscat grape; (**vin**) **m.**, muscatel.
mus|**cle** [myskl], *s.m.* muscle; *a.* **-clé**, muscular; brawny; *a.* **-culaire**; **système m.**, muscular

system; *a.* **-culeux**, **-culeuse**, muscular, *F:* beefy (person).
museau, **-eaux** [myzo], *s.m.* (*a*) muzzle, snout (of animal); (*b*) *F:* **joli petit m.**, nice little face; **vilain m.**, ugly mug.
musée [myze], *s.m.* (*a*) museum; (*b*) **m. de peinture**, picture gallery, art gallery.
mus|**eler** [myzle], *v.tr.* (**je muselle**) to muzzle (dog, *F:* the press, etc.); *F:* **m. qn**, to make s.o. hold his tongue; *s.m.* **-ellement**; *s.f.* **-elière**, (dog) muzzle.
muséum [myzeɔm], *s.m.* natural history museum.
musical, **-aux** [myzikal, -o], *a.* musical; *adv.* **-ement**.
music-hall [myzikoːl], *s.m.* music hall; **numéros de m.-h.**, variety turns; *pl. music-halls.*
musicien, **-ienne** [myzisjɛ̃, -jen], *a. & s.* **1.** musician; **elle est bonne musicienne**, (i) she is very musical; (ii) she's a good player; **oreille musicienne**, good ear for music. **2.** bandsman; performer; **orchestre de deux musiciens**, two-piece band.
musique [myzik], *s.f.* **1.** music; **mettre des paroles en m.**, to set words to music; **m. de chambre**, chamber music; **m. d'orchestre**, orchestral music; **m. d'ambiance**, background music; **travail en m.**, music while you work; *F:* **m. de chats**, caterwauling; **faire une m. enragée**, to make an awful din; **ses parents ont fait une m. énorme**, his (her) parents made a terrible fuss (about it); **ça, c'est une autre m.!** that's another problem! **2.** band; **m. de la ville**, municipal band; **chef de m.**, bandmaster.
musulman, **-ane** [myzylmã, -an], *a. & s.* Moslem.
mut|**ation** [mytasjɔ̃], *s.f.* change, alteration; *Biol: Mus:* mutation; *s.f.* **-abilité**; *a.* **-able**; *a. & s. Biol:* **-ant**, **-ante**, mutant.
mutil|**er** [mytile], *v.tr.* (*a*) to mutilate, maim; *s.m.* **mutilé de guerre**, disabled ex-serviceman; (*b*) to deface; *s.f.* **-ation**.
mutiner (se) [səmytine], *v.pr.* to rise in revolt; to mutiny, to rebel.
mutisme [mytism], *s.m.* dumbness, muteness; **se renfermer dans le m.**, to maintain a stubborn silence.
mutualité [mytɥalite], *s.f.* **1.** reciprocity. **2.** mutual insurance; **société de m.**, friendly society.
mutuel, **-elle** [mytɥεl], *a.* mutual; **société de secours mutuels**, friendly society; *adv.* **-lement**.
my|**ope** [mjɔp], *a. & s.* short-sighted (person); *s.f.* **-opie**, short-sightedness.
myosotis [mjɔzɔtis], *s.m. Bot:* forget-me-not.
myriade [mirjad], *s.f.* myriad.
myrte [mirt], *s.m. Bot:* myrtle.
myrtille [mirtiːj], *s.f. Bot:* bilberry.

mystère [mistɛːr], *s.m.* mystery.
mystérieu|x, -euse [misterjø, -øːz], *a.*
mysterious; uncanny; *s.m.* **le m. séduit
toujours les hommes,** men are always attracted by the mysterious; *adv.* **-sement.**
mysticisme [mistisism], *s.m.* mysticism.
mystifi|er [mistifje], *v.tr.* (*p.d. & pr.sub.* n.
mystifiions) (*a*) to mystify; (*b*) to hoax; to pull
(s.o.'s) leg; *a. & s.* **-cateur, -catrice,** (i) *a.*

mystifying; (ii) *s.* hoaxer, practical joker; *s.f.*
-cation, hoax.
mystique [mistik]. **1.** *a.* mystic(al). **2.** *s.* mystic.
myth|e [mit], *s.m.* myth, legend; *a.* **-ique,**
mythical; *a. & s.* **-omane,** mythomaniac.
mytholo|gie [mitɔlɔʒi], *s.f.* mythology; *a.*
-gique, mythological.
myxomatose [miksɔmatoːz], *s.f. Vet:*
myxomatosis.

N

N, n [ɛn], *s.m. or f.* (the letter) N, n.

acelle [nasɛl], *s.f.* **1.** skiff, wherry, dinghy. **2.** (*a*) *Av:* (*on jet planes*) (engine) pod; (*b*) body (of pram).

acre [nakr], *s.f.* mother of pearl.

acré [nakre], *a.* pearly (lustre).

age [naːʒ], *s.f.* **1.** rowing, sculling; **chef de n.,** stroke (oarsman). **2.** (*a*) swimming; **traverser une rivière à la n.,** to swim across a river; *F:* **être en n.,** to be bathed in perspiration; (*b*) stroke (in swimming); **n. libre,** freestyle.

ageoire [naʒwaːr], *s.f.* fin (of fish); flipper.

ager [naʒe], *v.i.* (n. nageons) **1.** *Nau:* to row; to scull. **2.** to swim; (*a*) **n. la brasse,** to swim, do, the breast-stroke; **n. entre deux eaux,** (i) to swim under water; (ii) to trim, to run with the hare and hunt with the hounds; (*b*) to float (on liquid), be submerged (in liquid); **le bois nage sur l'eau,** wood floats on water; *F:* **je nage complètement,** I'm all at sea; **n. dans l'abondance,** to be rolling in money; *s.* **-eur, -euse,** (*a*) swimmer; (*b*) oarsman.

aguère [nagɛːr], *adv.* not long since, a short time ago.

aïf, -ïve [naif, -iːv], *a.* **1.** ingenuous, naive. **2.** simple-minded, credulous, *F:* green; *adv.* **-vement;** *s.f.* **-veté,** simplicity, naïvety.

ain, naine [nɛ̃, nɛn]. **1.** *s.* dwarf; *F:* midget. **2.** *a.* dwarf(ish) (person, plant, etc.).

aissance [nɛsãːs], *s.f.* birth; (*a*) **anniversaire de n.,** birthday; **lieu de n.,** birthplace; **donner n. à un enfant,** to give birth to a child; **contrôle, limitation, des naissances,** birth control; *Adm:* **extrait de n.,** birth certificate; (*b*) descent, extraction; **de haute n.,** high-born; **être français de n.,** to be French by birth; (*c*) **la n. du jour,** dawn; (*d*) source (of river); **point de n.,** point of origin; **donner n. à une rumeur,** to give rise to a rumour.

aissant [nɛsã], *a.* new-born; budding; dawning (day).

aître [nɛːtr], *v.i.* (pr.p. naissant; p.p. né; pr.ind. je nais, ils naissent; p.h. je naquis; aux. être) (*a*) to be born; **il est né en 1880,** he was born in 1880; *F:* **je ne suis pas né d'hier,** I was not born yesterday; *impers.* **il naît cent enfants par mois,** a hundred children are born every month; (*b*) (*of hopes, fears*) to be born, to spring up; **faire n. un sourire,** to provoke a smile; (*c*) (*of vegetation*) to spring up, come up;

(*d*) (*of plan, of river*) to originate, rise, arise; **faire n.,** to awaken, arouse (suspicion, etc.).

napalm [napalm], *s.m.* napalm; **bombe au n.,** napalm bomb.

naphte [naft], *s.m.* naphtha; mineral oil.

nappe [nap], *s.f.* **1.** (*a*) table-)cloth; **mettre, ôter, la n.,** to lay, to remove, the cloth; (*b*) cloth, cover; **n. d'autel,** altar cloth. **2.** sheet (of ice, water, fire, petroleum); **n. de mazout,** oil slick.

narcisse [narsis], *s.m. Bot:* narcissus.

narcotique [narkɔtik], *a. & s.m. Med:* narcotic.

narguer [narge], *v.tr.* to flout, *F:* to cheek (s.o.); to defy (s.o.); to snap one's fingers at (s.o.).

narine [narin], *s.f.* nostril.

narquois, -oise [narkwa, -waːz], *a.* quizzing, bantering (tone, smile); *adv.* **-oisement.**

narration [nar(r)asjɔ̃], *s.f.* **1.** narrating, narration. **2.** narrative; *s.* **-teur, -trice,** narrator, (story-)teller; *a.* **-tif, -tive.**

nasal, -aux [nazal, -o]. **1.** *a.* nasal. **2.** *s.f. Ling:* **nasale,** nasal; *adv.* **-ement.**

naseau, -eaux [nazo], *s.m.* nostril (of horse, ox).

nasiller [nazije], *v.i.* to speak through the nose; *a.* **-ard,** nasal (tone).

natal, -als [natal], *a.* (*rarely used in the pl.*) native (land); **ville natale,** birthplace; **mon pays n.,** my native land.

natalité [natalite], *s.f.* birth-rate; **réglementation de la n.,** birth control.

natation [natasjɔ̃], *s.f.* swimming.

natif, -ive [natif, -iːv]. **1.** *a.* native; (*a*) **je suis n. de Londres,** I am London born; (*b*) natural, in-born; **bon sens n.,** mother wit. **2.** *s.m. & f.* native.

nation [nasjɔ̃], *s.f.* nation; **les Nations Unies,** the United Nations.

national, -aux [nasjɔnal, -o]. **1.** *a.* national. **2.** *s.m.pl.* **nationaux,** nationals (of a country). **3.** *s.f.* **nationale,** main road, = "A" road.

nationaliser [nasjɔnalize], *v.tr.* to nationalize; *s.f.* **-isation;** *s.m.* **-isme;** *a. & s.m. & f.* **-iste;** *s.f.* **-ité,** nationality.

natte [nat], *s.f.* **1.** mat, matting (of straw). **2.** plait, braid (of hair).

naturaliser [natyralize], *v.tr.* **1.** *Adm: etc:* to naturalize; **se faire n. (britannique),** to take out (British) naturalization papers, to take (British) nationality. **2.** (*a*) to mount, stuff, (animal, etc.); (*b*) to acclimatize (plant, animal); *s.f.* **-isation;** *s.m. & f.* **-iste,** (*a*) naturalist; (b) taxidermist.

nature [naty:r], s.f. nature. **1. plus grand que n.,** larger than life; **n. morte,** still-life (painting). **2.** (a) kind, character; **n. du sol,** nature of the soil; (b) character, disposition, temperament; **il est timide de n.,** he is naturally shy; F: **c'est une petite n.,** he's a weakly sort of person. **3.** kind; **payer en n.,** to pay in kind. **4.** a.inv. Cu: **pommes n.,** plain boiled potatoes; **café n.,** black coffee.

naturel, -elle [natyrɛl]. **1.** a. natural; (a) **histoire naturelle,** natural history; **enfant n.,** illegitimate child; **de grandeur naturelle,** life-size; **mais c'est tout n.,** (but) it was a pleasure, N.Am: you're welcome; (b) **don n.,** natural gift; (c) natural, unaffected (person). **2.** s.m. nature, character, disposition; **avoir un heureux n.,** to have a happy disposition; adv. **-lement.**

naufrage [nofra:ʒ], s.m. (ship)wreck.

naufragé, -ée [nofraʒe]. **1.** a. (ship)wrecked. **2.** s. castaway.

nauséle [noze], s.f. (a) nausea; **avoir des nausées,** to feel squeamish, sick; **odeur qui donne la n.,** nauseating smell; (b) disgust; **son air protecteur me donne la n.,** his patronizing manner makes me sick; a. **-abond,** nauseating, foul (smell, etc.).

nautique [notik], a. nautical; **sports nautiques,** aquatic sports; **ski n.,** water skiing; **club n.,** sailing club, boat club; **carte n.,** (sea) chart.

naval, -als [naval], a. naval, nautical (terms, station, etc.); **chantier de construction navale,** ship(-building) yard; **l'École navale,** the Naval College.

navarin [navarɛ̃], s.m. mutton stew; haricot mutton.

navet [navɛ], s.m. turnip.

navette [navɛt], s.f. shuttle; (of vehicle) **faire la n.,** to ply (to and fro); **véhicule qui fait n.,** vehicle running a shuttle service.

naviglabilité [navigabilite], s.f. **1.** navigability (of river, etc.). **2.** seaworthiness; airworthiness; a. **-able.**

navigant [navigã], a. **personnel n.,** s.m.pl. **les navigants,** (i) Nau: sea-going personnel; (ii) Av: flying personnel; aircrew.

naviguer [navige]. **1.** v.i. to sail, navigate. **2.** v.tr. to navigate (ship, aircraft); s.m. **-ateur,** navigator; s.f. **-ation,** navigation.

navire [navi:r], s.m. ship, vessel.

navire-citerne [navirsitɛrn], s.m. Nau: tanker; pl. **navires-citernes.**

navlrer [navre], v.tr. to grieve (s.o.) deeply; to cut (s.o.) to the heart, to break (s.o.'s) heart; a. **-rant,** heart-rendering; a. **-ré,** heartbroken.

nazli, -ie [nazi], a. & s. Pol: Nazi; s.m. **-isme.**

ne, n' [n(ə)], neg.adv. not. **1.** used alone (i.e. with omission of **pas**) with **cesser, oser, pouvoir,**

savoir, importer; je ne saurais vous le dire, I can't tell you; always used without **pas** in the phr. **n'importe,** never mind, it doesn't matter. **2.** in the following constructions: (a) **que ne ferait-il pour vous?** what would he not do for you? (b) **si je ne me trompe . . .,** unless I am mistaken . . .; **voilà six mois que je ne l'ai vu,** it is now six months since I saw him; **qu'à cela ne tienne!** by all means! **je n'ai que faire de votre aide,** I don't need your help. **3.** used with a vague negative connotation; (a) (expressions of fear) **je crains qu'il (ne) prenne froid,** I am afraid he may catch cold; (b) **évitez, prenez garde, qu'on (ne) vous voie,** avoid being seen; take care not to be seen; **à moins qu'on (ne) vous appelle,** unless they call you; (c) (comparison) **il est plus vigoureux qu'il (ne) paraît,** he is stronger than he looks.

néanmoins [neɑ̃mwɛ̃], adv. nevertheless, none the less; for all that; yet; still.

néant [neɑ̃], s.m. (a) nothingness; **réduire qch. à n.,** to annihilate sth., to wipe sth. out; (b) (when filling in form) none; nil.

nébuleulx, -euse [nebylø, -ø:z], a. nebulous; (a) cloudy, hazy (sky, view); (b) unintelligible, obscure; adv. **-sement,** nebulously, obscurely; unintelligibly.

nécessaire [nesɛsɛ:r]. **1.** a. necessary, needful; **choses qu'il est n. de savoir,** things one should know; **se rendre n. à qn,** to make oneself indispensable to s.o. **2.** s.m. (a) necessaries; **je ferai le n.,** I'll see to it; (b) outfit; kit (of some sort); **n. à ouvrage,** (i) work basket; (ii) housewife; **n. de toilette,** dressing-case; **n. de nettoyage,** cleaning kit; adv. **-ment.**

nécessité [nesesite], s.f. necessity; **il est de toute n. de (faire qch.),** it is essential to (do sth.); **denrées de première n.,** essential foodstuff; **selon les nécessités,** as circumstances may require; **être dans la n.,** to be in want.

nécessitler [nesesite], v.tr. to necessitate, require, entail (sth.); a. **-eux, -euse,** needy; need, in want.

nécrologie [nekrolɔʒi], s.f. obituary notice; Journ: deaths.

néerlandais, -aise [neɛrlɑ̃dɛ, -ɛ:z]. **1.** a. Dutch. **2.** s. Netherlander, Dutchman, Dutchwoman.

nef [nɛf], s.f. nave (of church); **n. latérale,** aisle.

néfaste [nefast], a. luckless, ill-omened; baneful; **influence n.,** pernicious influence.

négatlif, -ive [negatif, -i:v]. **1.** a. negative (answer, quantity, etc.); **dessin n.,** blueprint; s.m. Phot: negative. **2.** s.f. **négative,** negative; **soutenir la négative,** to speak against the motion; to take the other side; adv. **-ivement,** negatively.

négation [negasjɔ̃], s.f. **1.** negation, denial. Gram: negative.

négligé [negliʒe]. **1.** a. (a) neglected (opportuty, etc.); (*b*) careless, slovenly (dress, appearance); **intérieur n.**, badly-kept house. **2.** *s.m.* (*a*) slovenliness (in one's appearance); (*b*) *Cost:* négligé(e).

néglig|**er** [negliʒe], *v.tr.* (n. **négligeons**) **1.** to neglect (one's health, one's duty); to be careless of (sth.); **se n.**, to neglect oneself. **2.** (*a*) to disregard (advice, etc.); (*b*) **n. de faire qch.**, to leave sth. undone; *a.* -**able**, negligible; *s.f.* -**ence**, carelessness; *a.* -**ent**; *adv.* -**emment**.

négoc|**e** [negɔs], *s.m.* trade, business; *s.m.* -**iant**, (wholesale) merchant, dealer.

négoci|**er** [negɔsje], *v.tr.* to negotiate; *s.f.* -**abilité**; *a.* -**able**; *s.* -**ateur**, -**atrice**, negotiator; *s.f.* -**ation**, negotiation.

nègre, négresse [nɛːgr, negrɛs]. **1.** *s.* (*a*) negro, *f.* negress; (*b*) *F:* ghost-writer. **2.** *a.* (*f.* **nègre**) **la race nègre,** the negro race.

neige [nɛːʒ], *s.f.* snow; **n. fondue,** sleet, slush; **boule de n.,** snowball; **train de n.,** winter sports train; *Ind:* **n. carbonique,** dry ice; *Cu:* **blancs d'œufs battus en n.,** white of eggs beaten stiff.

neig|**er** [neʒe], *v.impers.* (**il neigeait**) to snow; *a.* -**eux**, -**euse**, snowy, snow-covered.

nénuphar [nenyfaːr], *s.m. Bot:* water-lily.

Néo-gallois, -oise [neogalwa, -waːz], *s.* New South Welshman, -woman; *pl. Néo-gallois, -oises.*

néolithique [neɔlitik], *a.* neolithic.

néon [neɔ̃], *s.m. Ch:* neon; **tube au n.,** neon tube.

néophyte [neɔfit], *s.m.* (*a*) neophyte; (*b*) beginner, tyro.

néo-zélandais, -aise [neozelɑ̃dɛ, -ɛːz]. **1.** *a.* New Zealand (Government, butter). **2.** *s.* New Zealander; *pl. néo-zélandais, -aises.*

nerf [nɛːr, nɛrf, *pl. always* nɛːr], *s.m.* **1.** *Anat:* nerve; **maladie des nerfs,** nervous complaint; **attaque de nerfs,** (fit of) hysterics; **porter sur les nerfs à qn,** to get on s.o.'s nerves; *F:* **avoir les nerfs en boule, à fleur de peau,** to be on edge, to be jumpy. **2.** *F:* sinew, tendon, ligament; **mets-y du n.!** [nɛrf], put some guts into it! **manquer de n.,** to lack energy, stamina, *F:* pep.

nerveu|**x, -euse** [nɛrvø, -øːz], *a.* **1.** nervous (system, illness). **2.** sinewy, wiry; vigorous; **moteur n.,** responsive engine. **3.** highly-strung, *F:* nervy (person); *adv.* -**sement**.

nervosité [nɛrvozite], *s.f.* irritability, state of nerves, edginess.

nervure [nɛrvyːr], *s.f.* (*a*) nervure, rib, vein (of leaf); (*b*) branch (of mountain-group); (*c*) flange, rib; grill (of radiator, etc.).

n'est-ce pas [nɛspɑ], *adv.phr.* (*inviting assent*) **vous venez, n'est-ce pas?** you are coming, aren't you? **vous ne venez pas, n'est-ce pas?** you are not coming, are you? **il fait chaud, n'est-ce pas?** it's hot, isn't it? **il ne comprend pas, n'est-ce pas?** he doesn't understand, does

he? **non, n'est-ce pas?** I shouldn't think so!

net, nette [nɛt], *a.* **1.** clean, spotless; *F:* **j'ai les mains nettes,** my hands are clean; I had nothing to do with it; **n. d'impôt,** tax free; **maison nette comme un sou neuf,** house as clean as a new pin. **2.** (*a*) clear; distinct; plain; **contours nets,** sharp outlines; *Phot: etc:* **image nette,** clear, sharp, picture; (*b*) **poids n.,** net weight. **3.** *adv.* (*a*) plainly, flatly, outright; **refuser n.,** to refuse point-blank; **s'arrêter n.,** to stop dead; (*b*) **voir n.,** to see distinctly; *adv.* -**tement**.

netteté [nɛt(ə)te], *s.f.* **1.** cleanness; cleanliness. **2.** (*a*) clearness; distinctness; sharpness (of image); (*b*) flatness (of refusal).

nettoy|**er** [nɛtwaje], *v.tr.* (**je nettoie**) to clean; to scour; **n. à sec,** to dry-clean; *s.m.* -**age**, cleaning; *s.* -**eur**, -**euse**, cleaner (*pers. or machine*).

neuf[1] [nœf, nœv], *num. a. inv. & s.m. inv.* nine. **1.** *card. a.* (*at the end of the word-group* [nœf]; *before* **ans** *and* **heures** [nœv]; *otherwise before vowel sounds* [nœf]; *before a noun or adj. beginning with a consonant usu.* [nœ], *often* [nœf]) **n. francs** [nœfrɑ̃], nine francs; **il a n. ans** [nœvɑ̃], he's nine years old. **2.** *ordinal uses, etc.* (*always* [nœf]) **le n. mai,** the ninth of May; **Louis N.,** Louis the Ninth.

neuf[2], **neuve** [nœf, nœːv]. **1.** *a.* (*a*) new; **à l'état (de) n.,** in new condition, as new; (*b*) **pays n.,** new country; (*c*) *F:* **qu'est-ce qu'il y a de n.?** what's the news? **2.** *s.m.* **habillé de n.,** dressed in new clothes; **meublé de n.,** newly furnished; **il y a du n.,** I have news for you; *adv.phr.* **à n.,** anew; **remettre qch. à n.,** to renovate sth., to do sth. up.

neurasthén|**ie** [nørasteni], *s.f.* neurasthenia; *a.* -**ique**, neurasthenic.

neuro|**logie** [nørɔlɔʒi], *s.f. Med:* neurology; *s.m.* -**logue**, neurologist.

neutralis|**er** [nøtralize], *v.tr.* to neutralize; *s.f.* -**ation**.

neutralité [nøtralite], *s.f.* neutrality; **n. armée,** armed neutrality; **sortir de la n.,** to take sides.

neutre [nøːtr], *a.* **1.** neuter. **2.** neutral; *s.m.* **droits des neutres,** rights of neutrals.

neutron [nøtrɔ̃], *s.m. El:* neutron.

neuvième [nœvjɛm]. **1.** *num. a. & s.* ninth. **2.** *s.m.* ninth (part); *adv.* -**ment**.

neveu, -eux [nəvø], *s.m.* nephew.

névral|**gie** [nevralʒi], *s.f.* neuralgia; *a.* -**gique**.

névrite [nevrit], *s.f.* neuritis.

névrosé, -ée [nevroze], *a. & s. Med:* neurotic (patient).

nez [ne], *s.m.* **1.** nose; (*a*) **parler, chanter, du n.,** to speak, sing, through one's nose; **faire un pied de n. à qn,** to cock a snook at s.o.; (*b*) sense of smell; (*of dogs*) scent; **avoir bon n.,** to be shrewd, far-seeing; (*c*) *F:* **n. à n.,** face to face; **fermer la porte au n. de qn,** to shut the door in s.o.'s face; **regarder qn sous le n.,** to look defiantly at s.o.; **rire au n. de qn,** to laugh in s.o.'s face. 2. bow, nose, head (of ship, aircraft).

ni [ni], *conj.* (**ne** *is either expressed or implied*) nor, or; (*a*) **ni moi (non plus),** neither do I; **sans argent ni bagages,** without money or luggage; (*b*) **il ne mange ni ne boit,** he neither eats nor drinks; (*c*) **ni . . . ni,** neither . . . nor; **ni l'un ni l'autre,** neither (of them).

niais, -aise [njɛ, -ɛːz]. 1. *a.* simple, foolish (person); inane (smile). 2. *s.* fool, idiot; **petite niaise!** you little silly! *adv.* **-ement.**

niaiserie [njɛzri], *s.f.* 1. silliness, foolishness. 2. **dire des niaiseries,** to talk nonsense.

niche¹ [niʃ], *s.f.* 1. niche, nook, recess (in wall, etc.). 2. **n. à chien,** (dog-)kennel.

niche², *s.f. F:* trick, prank; practical joke.

nichée [niʃe], *s.f.* nest(ful) (of birds); brood; litter (of puppies).

nicher [niʃe]. 1. *v.i.* (*of bird*) to build a nest; to nest; *F:* to live, dwell; **où nichez-vous?** *F:* where do you hang out? 2. *v.tr.* to put, lodge (sth. in a niche).

nickel [nikɛl], *s.m.* nickel; *s.m.* **-age,** nickel-plating.

niçois, -oise [niswa, -waːz], *a. & s.* (native) of Nice.

Nicolas [nikɔla]. *Pr.n.m.* Nicholas.

nicotine [nikɔtin], *s.f.* nicotine.

nid [ni], *s.m.* 1. nest; **faire un n.,** to build a nest; **trouver le n. vide,** to find the bird flown; **n. à poussière,** dust-trap. 2. (*a*) *Nau:* (submarine) pen; **n. de mitrailleuses,** nest of machine-guns; (*b*) **n. de poule,** pot-hole (in a road).

nièce [njɛs], *s.f.* niece.

nier [nje], *v.tr.* to deny (fact); *abs.* **l'accusé nie,** the accused pleads not guilty; **il n'y a pas à le n.,** there's no denying it.

nigaud, -aude [nigo, -oːd], (*a*) *s.* simpleton, booby; fool; *F:* clot; **quel n.!** what an ass! (*b*) *a.* silly; *F:* clottish; **elle est un peu nigaude,** she is rather simple.

Niger (le) [ləniʒɛːr]. *Pr.n.m. Geog:* the (river) Niger; **la République du N.,** the Niger Republic.

Nigéria (le) [ləniʒerja]. *Pr.n.m. Geog:* Nigeria.

Nil (le) [lənil]. (*a*) *Pr.n.m.* the (river) Nile; (*b*) *adj.phr.inv.* **bleu de N.,** Nile-blue; (**vert de**) **N.,** eau-de-nil.

nimbe [nɛ̃ːb], *s.m.* nimbus, halo.

nimbus [nɛ̃bys], *s.m.* nimbus; rain-cloud.

nippe [nip], *s.f.usu.pl.* rig-out; **je n'ai plus une n. à me mettre,** I haven't a rag to my back.

nitrate [nitrat], *s.m. Ch:* nitrate.

nitre [nitr], *s.m.* nitre, saltpetre.

niveau, -eaux [nivo], *s.m.* level. 1. (*instruments*) **n. à bulle d'air,** spirit-level; **n. à lunette,** sur-

veyor's level; *Mec: etc:* **n. d'huile,** oil gauge; *Aut:* **n. d'essence,** petrol gauge; *Rail:* **passage à n.,** level-crossing. 2. (*a*) **n. (intensité) sonore,** sound level; **baisse, hausse, de n.,** drop, rise, of level; (*b*) **le n. de la mer,** sea level; **n. des basses, des hautes, eaux,** low-water, high-water, mark; (*c*) **n. de vie,** standard of living; **être au n. de qch.,** to be on a par with sth.

niveller [nivle], *v.tr.* (**je nivelle**) to level, to even up, down; *s.m.* **-lement,** levelling.

noble [nɔbl]. 1. *a.* noble. 2. *s.* noble(man), noblewoman; **les nobles,** the nobility; *adv.* **-ment.**

noblesse [nɔblɛs], *s.f.* nobility.

nocle [nɔs], *s.f.* 1. (*a*) wedding; wedding reception; (*b*) wedding-party; **voyage de noces,** honeymoon (trip); (*c*) **épouser qn en secondes noces,** to marry for the second time. 2. *F:* **faire la n.,** to go on the spree, on a binge; *s.* **-eur, -euse,** *F:* reveller; fast liver.

nocif, -ive [nɔsif, -iːv], *a.* injurious, harmful, hurtful, noxious (à, to).

noctambulle [nɔktɑ̃byl], *s. F:* fly-by-night, night-bird; *s.m.* **-isme,** *F:* going out on the tiles.

nocturne [nɔktyrn]. 1. *a.* nocturnal; *Bot:* night-flowering; **attaque n.,** night attack. 2. *s.m. Mus:* nocturne.

Noël [nɔɛl], *s.m.* 1. Christmas; **à N.,** at Christmas; **la nuit de N.,** Christmas Eve; **le Père N.,** Father Christmas, Santa Claus. 2. **un n.,** (*a*) a Christmas carol; (*b*) a Christmas present.

nœud [nø], *s.m.* 1. (*a*) knot; **faire un n.,** to make, tie, a knot; *F:* **les nœuds de l'amitié,** the ties of friendship; (*b*) **le n. de la question,** the crux of the matter; (*c*) *Cost:* bow; **faire un n.,** to tie a bow. 2. (*a*) knot (in timber); (*b*) node, joint (in stem of grass). 3. **n. de voies ferrées,** railway junction. 4. *Nau.Meas:* knot.

noir [nwaːr]. 1. *a.* black; (*a*) **race noire,** negro race; (*b*) dark, swarthy; (*c*) dark; gloomy; **il fait déjà n.,** it's dark already; **ma bête noire,** my pet aversion; **misère noire,** dire poverty; (*d*) dirty, grimy (hands); (*e*) base (ingratitude). 2. *s.* black man, woman; negro, negress. 3. **n.** (*a*) **voir tout en n.,** to look at the dark side of everything; **broyer du n.,** to have a fit of the blues; **être en n., porter le n.,** to wear black, to be in mourning; (*b*) bull's-eye (of target); *F:* **mettre dans le n.,** to hit the mark; (*c*) **avoir des noirs,** to have bruises; (*d*) **n. de fumée,** lampblack; **avoir peur du n.,** to be afraid of the dark. 4. *s.f.* **noire;** (*a*) (*at roulette*) black; (*b*) (*in balloting*) black ball; (*c*) *Mus:* crochet; *a.* **-âtre,** blackish, darkish; *a. & s.* **-aud, -aude,** swarthy (person).

noirclir [nwarsiːr]. 1. *v.i.* to become, turn, black; to darken. 2. *v.tr.* (*a*) to blacken; **n. du papier,** to scribble; (*b*) to sully (sth.); **n. la réputation**

de qn, to blacken s.o.'s character; *s.f.* **-eur,** blackness; gloominess; baseness; *s.m.* **-issement,** blackening.

noiset|te [nwazɛt]. 1. *s.f.* hazel-nut. 2. *a.inv.* nut-brown (colour); *s.m.* **-ier,** hazel tree.

noix [nwa], *s.f.* 1. walnut. 2. nut; **n. de coco,** coconut; **n. d'acajou,** cashew nut.

nom [nɔ̃], *s.m.* 1. name; **n. de famille,** surname; **n. de guerre,** assumed name; pen-name; **n. de théâtre,** stage name; **faux n.,** alias; **n. et prénoms,** full name; **ça n'a pas de n.!** it is unspeakable! **n. de n.!** good Heavens! for Heaven's sake! **fait en mon n.,** done on my behalf, by my authority. 2. *Gram:* noun, substantive; **n. commun,** common noun; **n. propre,** proper noun.

nomade [nɔmad]. 1. *a.* nomadic; wandering (tribe); migratory (game); roving (instinct). 2. *s.m.pl.* **nomades,** nomads; *P.N:* **stationnement interdit aux nomades,** no gypsies.

nombre [nɔ̃:br], *s.m.* number. 1. *(a)* **n. atomique,** atomic number; *(b)* **n. de . . .,** a good many . . .; **ils ont vaincu par le n.,** they conquered by force of numbers; **ils sont au n. de huit,** there are eight of them; **mettre qn au n. de ses intimes,** to number s.o. among one's friends. 2. *Gram:* number.

nombr|er [nɔ̃bre], *v.tr.* to number, reckon, count (up); *a.* **-eux, -euse,** numerous.

nombril [nɔ̃bri], *s.m.* navel.

nominal, -aux [nɔminal, -o], *a.* nominal; **appel n.,** roll-call; **valeur nominale,** face value; *adv.* **-ement.**

nomina|tion [nɔminasjɔ̃], *s.f.* 1. nomination (for a post). 2. appointment; **recevoir sa n.,** to be appointed; *a. & s.m.* **-tif, -tive,** (i) état n., list of names; (ii) *Gram:* nominative (case).

nommer [nɔme], *v.tr.* 1. to name; **on le nomma Paul,** they called him Paul; *Jur:* **le nommé Dupont,** the man Dupont. 2. *(a)* to mention by name; *(b)* **n. un jour,** to appoint a day. 3. to appoint (to a post); **être nommé au grade de . . .,** to be promoted to the rank of . . .. **se nommer.** 1. to state one's name. 2. to be called, named.

non [nɔ̃], *adv. (no liaison with the following word except in compounds)* no; not. 1. **fumezvous?—n.,** do you smoke?—no (, I don't); **mais n.!** no indeed! **n. pas!** not at all! **je pense que n.,** I think not; **faire signe que n.,** to shake one's head; **n. (pas) que je le craigne,** not that I fear him; *s.m.inv.* **les n. l'emportent,** the noes have it. 2. **n. loin de la ville,** not far from the town. 3. *(in compound words)* **pacte de n.agression,** non-aggression pact.

nonagénaire [nɔnaʒenɛ:r], *a. & s.* nonagenarian.

non-alcoolisé [nɔnalkɔlize, nɔ̃-], *a.* nonalcoholic, *F:* soft (drink); *pl.* **non-alcoolisé(e)s.**

non-aligné [nɔnaliɲe, nɔ̃-], *a. Pol:* non-aligned, non-committed (countries); *pl.* **non-aligné(e)s.**

non-belligérance [nɔ̃bɛl(l)iʒerɑ̃:s], *s.f.* nonbelligerency.

nonce [nɔ̃:s], *s.m.* **n. du Pape,** Papal Nuncio.

nonchal|ance [nɔ̃ʃalɑ̃:s], *s.f.* nonchalance, unconcern; indolence; *a.* **-ant;** *adv.* **-amment.**

non-combattant [nɔ̃kɔ̃batɑ̃], *a. & s.m.* noncombatant; *pl.* **non-combattants.**

non-existant [nɔnegzistɑ̃, nɔ̃-], *a.* non-existent; *pl.* **non-existants.**

non-livraison [nɔ̃livrɛzɔ̃], *s.f. Com:* nondelivery.

non-négociable [nɔ̃negɔsjabl], *a. Com:* unnegotiable (cheque, etc.); *pl.* **non-négociables.**

non-respect [nɔ̃rɛspɛ], *s.m.* failure to observe (road sign, etc.).

non-sens [nɔ̃sɑ̃:s], *s.m.inv.* meaningless sentence, action.

non-valable [nɔ̃valabl], *a.* 1. *Jur:* invalid (clause). 2. *(of ticket, passport)* not valid; *pl.* **non-valables.**

non-valeur [nɔ̃valœ:r], *s.f.* 1. object of no value; *Com:* bad debt; worthless security. 2. inefficient employee; *F:* passenger; *pl.* **nonvaleurs.**

nord [nɔ:r]. 1. *s.m. no pl.* north; **le grand N.,** the frozen North; **le grand N. Canadien,** the Canadian Far North; **la mer du N.,** the North Sea; **l'Amérique du N.,** North America; *F:* **perdre le n.,** to lose one's bearings. 2. *a.inv.* north, northern (side, latitude, etc.); **le pôle n.,** the North Pole.

nord-africain, -aine [nɔrafrikɛ̃, -ɛn], *a. & s.* North African; *pl.* **nord-africain(e)s.**

nord-américain, -aine [nɔramerikɛ̃, -ɛn], *a. & s.* North American; *pl.* **nord-américain(e)s.**

nord-est [nɔr(d)ɛst], *s.m.* north-east; *(wind)* north-easter.

nord-ouest [nɔr(d)wɛst], *s.m.* north-west; *(wind)* north-wester.

normal, -aux [nɔrmal, -o]. 1. *a. (a)* normal; **école normale** = college of education; *(b)* **poids n.,** standard weight. 2. *s.f.* **normale,** normal (temperature, etc.); *(a) Geom:* perpendicular; *(b)* **au-dessus de la normale,** above (the) normal; *adv.* **-ement;** *s.f.* **-ité,** normality, *N.Am:* normalcy.

normalien, -ienne [nɔrmaljɛ̃, -jɛn], *s.* student, former student, at a college of education.

normand, -ande [nɔrmɑ̃, -ɑ̃:d], *a. & s.* Norman; of Normandy; *F:* **réponse normande,** noncommittal answer.

Normandie (la) [lanɔrmɑ̃di]. *Pr.n.f. Geog:* Normandy.

norme [nɔrm], *s.f.* norm, standard; *Ind: Com:* **normes françaises (N.F.)** = British Standards.

Norvège (la) [lanɔrvɛ:ʒ]. *Pr.n.f. Geog:* Norway.

norvégien, -ienne [nɔrveʒjɛ̃, -jɛn]. 1. *a. & s.*

Norwegian. 2. *s.m. Ling:* Norwegian.

nostalg|ie [nɔstalʒi], *s.f.* nostalgia; home-sickness; *a.* **-ique**, nostalgic, homesick.

not|abilité [nɔtabilite], *s.f.* 1. notability. 2. person of distinction; *a. & s.m.* **-able**, notable; distinguished person; *adv.* **-ablement**.

notaire [nɔtɛːr], *s.m.* lawyer; *N.Am:* notary; *Scot:* notary public; **le n. y est passé**, it's a legal agreement.

notamment [nɔtamɑ̃], *adv.* (*a*) more particularly; especially; (*b*) among others . . ..

note [nɔt], *s.f.* 1. note, memorandum, memo, minute; **n. d'avis**, advice note. 2. annotation; **n. en bas de page**, footnote. 3. *Sch:* mark; **bonne n.**, good mark. 4. *Mus:* note; *F:* **changer de n.**, to change one's tune. 5. (*repute*) **un homme de n.**, a man of note. 6. bill, account; **régler, payer, la n.**, to settle (the bill, account), *F:* to foot the bill.

noter [nɔte], *v.tr.* 1. to note; to take notice of; **chose à n.**, thing worthy of notice; *F:* **notez bien!** mind you! 2. to put down, jot down.

notice [nɔtis], *s.f.* 1. notice, account. 2. review (of book). 3. instructions, directions; **n. d'emploi**, directions for use; **n. de fonctionnement**, operating manual.

notifi|er [nɔtifje], *v.tr.* (*p.d. & pr.sub.* **n. notifiions**) to notify; to intimate (sth. to s.o.); **n. son consentement**, to signify one's consent; *s.f.* **-cation**.

notion [nɔsjɔ̃], *s.f.* notion, idea; **perdre la n. du temps**, to lose count of time; **avoir quelques notions de chimie**, to have a smattering of chemistry.

notoire [nɔtwaːr], *a.* well-known (fact); of common knowledge; manifest (injustice); *adv.* **-ment**.

notoriété [nɔtɔrjete], *s.f.* notoriety (of fact); reputation (of pers.); **avoir de la n.**, to be well-known, to have a (good or bad) reputation.

notre, *pl.* **nos** [nɔtr, no], *poss.a.* our; **nos père et mère**, our father and mother.

nôtre [notr]. 1. *poss.pron.* ours; our own. 2. *s.m.* (i) our own (property, friends); **il préfère vos tableaux aux nôtres**, he prefers your pictures to ours; (ii) *pl.* **est-il des nôtres?** is he one of us?

nou|er [nwe, nue], *v.tr.* 1. to tie, knot. 2. **l'âge lui a noué les membres**, age has stiffened his joints. 3. **n. conversation avec qn**, to enter into conversation with s.o.; *a.* **-eux, -euse**, knotty, gnarled.

nouille [nuːj]. 1. *s.f. normally used in the pl. Cu:* noodles. 2. (*in sg.*) *s.f. P:* **c'est une n.**, he's, she's, a bit wet; **quelle n.!** what a drip!

nourri [nuri], *a.* 1. nourished, fed; **bien n.**, well-fed; **mal n.**, underfed. 2. rich, copious (style); thick-laid (paint); **acclamations nourries**, hearty, sustained, applause.

nourrice [nuris], *s.f.* 1. (wet-)nurse; **conte de n.**, nursery tale. 2. **mettre un enfant en n.**, to put out a child to nurse.

nourr|ir [nuriːr], *v.tr.* to nourish. 1. (*a*) to nurse (infant); (*b*) to bring up (children). 2. to feed (people, animals); to maintain (one's family); to board (pupils, employees). 3. to harbour (thoughts); to cherish (hope); *a.* **-issant**, nourishing (food, etc.); *s.m.* **-isson**, infant; *s.f.* **-iture**, food.

se nourrir. 1. se n. de lait, to live on milk. 2. to keep oneself.

nous [nu], *pers.pron.* 1. (*a*) (*subject*) we; (*b*) (*object*) us; to us; **lisez-le-n.**, read it to us; (*c*) (*reflexive*) **n. n. chauffons**, we are warming ourselves; (*d*) (*reciprocal*) **n. n. connaissons**, we know each other. 2. **n. autres Anglais**, we English; **n. l'avons fait n.-mêmes**, we did it ourselves; **ce livre est à n.**, that book is ours, belongs to us.

nouveau, -el, -elle¹, -eaux [nuvo, -ɛl], *a.* (*the form* **nouvel** *is used before m.sing. nouns beginning with a vowel or* h '*mute*'; *also occ. before* et) 1. new; **il n'y a rien de n.**, there is no news; *Sch:* **les nouveaux (élèves)**, the new boys; *s.m.* **j'ai appris du n.**, I have some news; **c'est du n.**, that's news to me. 2. (*a*) new, recent, fresh; (*b*) (*with adv. function*) newly, recently; **le nouvel arrivé, le n. venu**, the new-comer; **n. riche**, upstart. 3. another, fresh, further; **un nouvel époux**, another husband; **la nouvelle génération**, the rising generation; **jusqu'à nouvel ordre**, till further notice, orders; **le nouvel an**, the new year. 4. **de n.**, again; **à n.**, afresh, (all over) again; **étudier une question à n.**, to re-examine a question.

nouveau-né, -née [nuvone], *a. & s.* new-born (child); *pl.* **nouveau-nés, -nées**.

nouveauté [nuvote], *s.f.* 1. newness, novelty; **costume de haute n.**, costume in the latest style. 2. change, innovation. 3. new invention, new publication, etc. 4. *pl. Com:* fancy goods; **marchand de nouveautés**, draper.

nouvelle², *s.f.* 1. *usu. in pl.* (*a*) (piece of) news; *Journ:* **dernières nouvelles**, latest intelligence; (*b*) *pl.* tidings, news; **envoyez-moi de vos nouvelles**, let me hear from you; *F:* **vous m'en direz des nouvelles**, you will be delighted with it. 2. *Lit:* short story.

Nouvelle-Calédonie (la) [lanuvɛlkaledɔni] *Pr.n.f. Geog:* New Caledonia.

Nouvelle-Écosse (la) [lanuvɛlekɔs]. *Pr.n.f. Geog:* Nova Scotia.

Nouvelle-Galles du Sud (la [lanuvɛlgaldysyd]. *Pr.n.f. Geog:* New South Wales.

Nouvelle-Guinée (la) [lanuvɛlgine]. *Pr.n.f. Geog:* New Guinea.

nouvellement [nuvɛlmɑ̃], *adv.* newly, lately.

recently.

Nouvelle-Orléans (la) [lanuvɛlɔrleã]. *Pr.n.f.*
Geog: New Orleans.

Nouvelle-Zélande (la) [lanuvɛlzelã:d]. *Pr.n.f.*
Geog: New Zealand.

novembre [nɔvã:br], *s.m.* November; **au mois
de n.,** in (the month of) November; **le premier,
le sept, n.,** (on) the first, the seventh, of
November.

novice [nɔvis], *s.m. & f.* novice (in convent);
probationer; tyro; **il est encore n.,** he's still
raw.

noyade [nwajad], *s.f.* drowning (fatality).

noyau, -aux [nwajo], *s.m.* **1.** stone (of fruit);
kernel. **2.** *Ph: Biol:* nucleus (of cell, etc.); *Pol:*
n. communiste, communist cell.

noyer¹ [nwaje], *s.m. Bot:* walnut(-tree, -wood);
n. (blanc) **d'Amérique,** hickory.

noyer², *v.tr.* (je noie) to drown; to swamp,
deluge; **yeux noyés de larmes,** eyes filled with
tears.

se noyer, (a) to drown oneself; (b) to be
drowned; **un homme qui se noie,** a drowning
man.

nu [ny]. **1.** *a.* (a) unclothed; naked; bare; *Art:*
nude; **nu comme un ver,** stark naked. NOTE:
nu *before the noun it qualifies is invariable and
is hyphened to it, e.g.* **aller les pieds nus, aller
nu-pieds,** to go bare-footed; (b) uncovered,
plain, undisguised; **la vérité nue,** the naked
truth; (c) bare (room). **2.** *s.m.* **mettre qch. à nu,**
to lay bare, expose, sth.

nuage [nɥa:ʒ], *s.m.* (a) cloud; **nuages
pommelés,** mackerel sky; **nuages
nuages,** overcast sky; (b) haze, mist (before the
eyes); (c) gloom, shadow; **être dans les nuages,**
to be day-dreaming; *a.* **-eux, -euse,** cloudy,
overcast (sky).

nuance [nɥã:s], *s.f.* shade (of colour); hue,
nuance; **une n. de regret,** a touch of regret; **il y
a une n.,** there is a slight difference of meaning.

nucléaire [nyklɛɛːr], *a.* nuclear; **réaction, fission, n.,** nuclear reaction, nuclear fission.

nucléon [nykleɔ̃], *s.m. Atom.Ph:* nucleon.

nudisme [nydism], *s.m.* nudism; *a. & s.m. & f.*
-iste, nudist.

nudité [nydite], *s.f.* (a) nudity, nakedness; (b)
bareness (of rock, wall, etc.).

nues [ny], *s.f.pl.* skies; **porter qn (jusqu')aux
n.,** to praise s.o. to the skies; **tomber des n.,**
(i) to arrive unexpectedly; (ii) to be thunderstruck.

nuire [nɥiːr], *v.ind.tr.* (*p.p.* **nui,** *otherwise conj.*

like CONDUIRE) **n. à qn,** to be hurtful, harmful,
to s.o.; **cela ne nuira en rien,** that will do no
harm; **n. aux intérêts de qn,** to prejudice s.o.'s
interests.

nuisible [nɥizibl], *a.* hurtful, harmful, noxious,
detrimental (à, to); **n. à la santé,** detrimental to
health; *s.m.pl.* **les nuisibles,** vermin; *adv.*
-ment.

nuit [nɥi], *s.f.* night; (a) **cette n.,** (i) tonight; (ii)
last night; **partir de n.,** to depart by night; **je
n'ai pas dormi de la n.,** I didn't sleep a wink
all night; (b) darkness; **il se fait n.,** night is
falling; it is growing dark; **à la n. tombante,** at
nightfall; **à (la) n. close,** after dark.

nul, nulle [nyl]. **1.** (with ne *expressed or understood*) (a) *indef. a.* no; not one; **n. espoir,**
no hope; **sans nulle vanité,** without any conceit; (b) *indef.pron.* no one; nobody; **n. ne le
sait,** no one knows. **2.** *a.* (a) worthless; **homme
n.,** nonentity; (b) *Jur:* **n. et de n. effet,** null and
void; *Sp:* **partie nulle,** drawn game; draw; *Sp:*
course nulle, (i) dead heat; (ii) no race; *adv.*
-lement, (with ne, *expressed or understood*)
not at all.

nullifier [nyl(l)ifje], *v.tr.* (*p.d. & pr.sub.* **n.
nullifiions**) to nullify, neutralize (effort, etc.).

nullité [nyl(l)ite], *s.f.* **1.** nullity, invalidity. **2.** (a)
nothingness; non-existence; **n. des affaires,**
standstill in trade; (b) (of pers.) incompetence;
incapacity. **3.** nonentity; **ce sera toujours une
n.,** he'll never be any good.

numéral, -aux [nymeral, -o], *a. & s.m.* numeral.

numérique [nymerik], *a.* numerical; *adv.*
-ment.

numéro [nymero], *s.m.* (a) number; **la chambre
n. 20,** room number 20; **le dernier n. du
programme,** the last item on the programme;
F: **il aime faire son petit n.,** he likes doing his
little act; (b) size (of stock sizes).

numéroter [nymerɔte], *v.tr.* to number (street);
to page (book).

nuptial, -aux [nypsjal, -o], *a.* nuptial, bridal;
messe nuptiale, nuptial mass; **marche nuptiale,**
wedding-march.

nuque [nyk], *s.f.* nape of the neck.

nutrition [nytrisjɔ̃], *s.f.* nutrition; *a.* **-tif, -tive,**
nourishing; **valeur nutritive,** food value; *s.m. &
f.* **-tionniste,** dietitian.

nylon [nilɔ̃], *s.m. R.t.m: Tex:* nylon; **des nylons,**
nylons; **des bas, collants, n.,** nylon stockings,
tights.

nymphe [nɛ̃:f], *s.f.* **1.** nymph. **2.** *Biol:* pupa,
chrysalis.

O

O, o [o], *s.m.* (the letter) O, o.

oasis [oazis], *s.f.* oasis.

obél ir [ɔbeiːr], *v.ind.tr.* to obey; **o. à qn,** to obey s.o.; **se faire o.,** to compel, enforce, obedience; **o. à un ordre,** to comply with an order; **o. à la force,** to yield to force; *s.f.* **-issance,** obedience; *a.* **-issant,** obedient.

obélisque [ɔbelisk], *s.m. Archeol:* obelisk.

obèse [ɔbɛːz], *a.* obese, fat (person).

obésité [ɔbezite], *s.f.* obesity, corpulence.

objecl ter [ɔbʒɛkte], *v.tr.* to raise (sth.) as an objection; **on a objecté que . . .,** the objection has been raised that . . .; **on peut lui o. son âge,** his age is against him; *s.f.* **-tion,** objection.

objectif, -ive [ɔbʒɛktif, -iːv]. **1.** *a.* objective; **il est très o.,** he is unbias(s)ed. **2.** *s.m.* aim, object(ive), end. **3.** *s.m. Phot:* lens.

objet [ɔbʒɛ], *s.m.* **1.** (*a*) object, thing; **o. de luxe,** luxury article; (*b*) *Gram:* object, complement; **o. direct,** direct object. **2.** subject, (subject) matter; **l'o. de la conversation,** the subject of the conversation. **3.** object, aim, purpose (of action); **remplir son o.,** to attain one's end; **sans o.,** aimless.

obligation [ɔbligasjɔ̃], *s.f.* **1.** (*a*) (moral) obligation; duty; (*b*) **o. du service militaire,** liability to military service. **2.** *Jur:* recognizance, bond. **3.** *Com: Fin:* bond, debenture. **4.** obligation, favour.

obligatoire [ɔbligatwaːr], *a.* obligatory; compulsory, binding; **arrêt o. (de l'autobus),** compulsory bus stop; *adv.* **-ment.**

obligé [ɔbliʒe], *a.* (*a*) obliged, compelled (de faire qch., to do sth.); (*b*) inevitable, sure to happen; *F:* **c'est o. qu'il rate son examen,** he's bound to fail his exam; (*c*) obliged, grateful; **bien o.!** many thanks!

obligl er [ɔbliʒe], *v.tr.* (n. **obligeons**) **1.** to oblige, compel; **être obligé de faire qch.,** to be obliged to do sth. **2.** **o. qn,** to oblige s.o., to do s.o. a favour; *s.f.* **-eance,** kindness; *a.* **-eant,** obliging, kind; *adv.* **-eamment,** kindly.

s'obliger à faire qch., to make a point of doing sth.; to undertake to do sth.

oblique [ɔblik], *a.* oblique (line); slanting (stitch); devious (behaviour); **regard o.,** sideglance; *adv.* **-ment.**

oblitérl er [ɔblitere], *v.tr.* (**j'oblitère; j'oblitérerai**) **1.** to obliterate. **2.** to cancel (stamp); *s.f.* **-ation.**

oblong, -ongue [ɔblɔ̃, -ɔ̃ːg], *a.* oblong.

obscène [ɔpsɛn], *a.* obscene; lewd.

obscénité [ɔpsenite], *s.f.* obscenity; lewdness.

obscur [ɔpskyːr], *a.* **1.** dark; gloomy. **2.** obscure: (*a*) difficult to understand; **un écrivain o.,** an abstruse writer; (*b*) indistinct, dim (horizon etc.); (*c*) unknown, obscure, humble; **un o. écrivain,** an unknown writer; *adv.* **-ément;** *s.f.* **-ité,** obscurity; darkness.

obscurl cir [ɔpskyrsiːr], *v.tr.* to obscure; (*a*) to darken, cloud; (*b*) to dim (the sight); *s.m.* **-cissement,** darkening.

s'obscurcir, to grow dark; to become dim.

obsédant [ɔpsedɑ̃], *a.* haunting; obsessing (memory, thoughts).

obsédé, -ée [ɔpsede], *s.* sufferer from an obsession; **o. sexuel,** sex maniac.

obséder [ɔpsede], *v.tr.* (**j'obsède; j'obséderai**) (*a*) to beset; (*b*) to obsess; **obsédé par une idée** obsessed by an idea.

obsèques [ɔpsɛk], *s.f.pl.* funeral.

obséquieul x, -euse [ɔpsekjø, -øːz], *a* obsequious; *adv.* **-sement.**

observateur, -trice [ɔpsɛrvatœːr, -tris]. **1.** observer; *Mil: Av:* spotter; **o. des Nation Unies,** United Nations observer. **2.** *a.* observant, observing.

observl er [ɔpsɛrve], *v.tr.* to observe; (*a*) to keep (to), to comply with (rules, laws); (*b*) to watch **on nous observe,** we are being watched; (*c*) t note, notice; **faire o. qch. à qn,** to draw s.o.' attention to sth.; *s.f.* **-ance,** observance (o rule, law); *s.f.* **-ation,** observation; remark *s.m.* **-atoire,** observatory.

s'observer, to be careful, wary; to be on one' guard.

obsession [ɔpsɛsjɔ̃], *s.f.* obsession.

obstacle [ɔpstakl], *s.m.* obstacle (à, to); imped ment, hindrance; *Sp:* hurdle, jump; **faire o.** qch., to stand in the way of sth.

obstination [ɔpstinasjɔ̃], *s.f.* obstinacy, stub bornness; *F:* pig-headedness.

obstiné [ɔpstine], *a.* stubborn, obstinate; *F:* pig headed (person); *adv.* **-ment.**

s'obstiner [ɔpstine], *v.pr.* to show obstinacy **s'o. à qch.,** to persist in sth.

obstrucl tion [ɔpstryksjɔ̃], *s.f.* obstructior blockage; choking; clogging (of drains, etc. *a.* **-tif, -tive,** obstructive.

obstruer [ɔpstrye], *v.tr.* to obstruct, to bloc (street, the view); to choke (outlet); **tuya**

obstrué, choked pipe.

obtenir [ɔptəni:r], *v.tr.* (*conj. like* TENIR) to obtain, get; to gain, procure; **où cela s'obtient-il?** where can you get it?

obturateur [ɔptyratœ:r], *s.m.* obturator; closing device; *Mec. E:* stop-valve; throttle; *Phot:* shutter; **o. de joint**, gasket; **o. à neutrons**, neutron shutter.

obturler [ɔptyre], *v.tr.* to seal (aperture); to fill, stop (tooth); *s.f.* **-ation**, filling (in tooth).

obtus, -use [ɔpty, -y:z], *a.* **1.** blunt(ed) (point). **2.** dull, obtuse (person). **3.** *Geom:* obtuse (angle).

obus [ɔby], *s.m. Artil:* shell.

occasion [ɔkazjõ], *s.f.* **1.** (*a*) opportunity, occasion, chance; **saisir une o.**, to take, seize, an opportunity; **suivant l'o.**, as occasion arises; **à l'o.**, (i) when the opportunity presents itself; (ii) if, as, necessary; (*b*) bargain; **voiture d'o.**, secondhand, used, car; **c'est une véritable o.**, it's a real bargain. **2.** occasion, juncture; **pour l'o.**, for the occasion; in this particular case; **à l'o.**, in case of need. **3.** motive, reason, occasion; **o. d'une dispute**, cause of a quarrel; **dîner à votre o.**, dinner in your honour; *a.* **-nel, -nelle**, occasional; *adv.* **-nellement.**

occasionner [ɔkazjone], *v.tr.* to occasion, cause (sth., *usu. unpleasant*); **o. une dispute**, to cause a quarrel.

occident [ɔksidã], *s.m.* west, occident; *Pol:* **l'O.,** the West; *a.* **-al, -aux**, western.

occulte [ɔkylt], *a.* occult (science); hidden (cause).

occupé [ɔkype], *a.* busy; engaged; *P.T.T:* **ligne occupée**, line engaged, busy; **cette place est occupée**, this seat is taken.

occupler [ɔkype], *v.tr.* to occupy. **1.** (*a*) to live in (a house); (*b*) *Mil:* to hold (a fort); (*c*) to fill, take up (time, space, etc.); (*d*) **o. un poste important**, to hold, to fill, an important post. **2.** to give occupation to (s.o.); **o. qn**, to give s.o. something to do; *s.* **-ant, -ante**, occupier, occupant; *s.f.* **-ation**, occupation, business, employment; profession.

'occuper. 1. to keep oneself busy. **2. s'o. de qch.**, (i) to go in for (music, etc.); (ii) to attend to sth.; **je m'en occuperai**, I shall see to it; **qui s'occupe de ce qu'il dit?** who cares what he says? **occupe-toi de ce qui te regarde!** mind your own business!

occurrence [ɔkyr(r)ã:s], *s.f.* occurrence, event; **en l'o.**, in the circumstances.

océan [ɔseã], *s.m.* ocean; *a.* **-ique**, oceanic.

Océanie (l') [lɔseani]. *Pr.n.f. Geog:* the South Sea Islands.

ocre [ɔkr], *s.f.* ochre.

octane [ɔktan], *s.m. Ch:* octane; **indice d'o.**, octane number.

octave [ɔkta:v], *s.f. Mus: etc:* octave.

octobre [ɔktɔbr], *s.m.* October; **au mois d'o.**, en

o., in (the month of) October; **le premier, le sept, o.**, (on) the first, the seventh, of October.

octogénaire [ɔktɔʒenɛ:r], *a. & s.m. & f.* octogenarian.

octogonle [ɔktɔgɔn], *s.m. Geom:* octagon; *a.* **-al, -aux**, eight-sided, octagonal.

octroyer [ɔktrwaje], *v.tr.* (**j'octroie**) to grant, concede (à, to).

oculaire [ɔkylɛ:r]. **1.** *a.* ocular (demonstration, etc.); **témoin o.**, eyewitness. **2.** *s.m. Opt:* eyepiece; *Cin:* viewfinder (of camera).

oculiste [ɔkylist], *s.m.* oculist.

ode [ɔd], *s.f. Lit:* ode.

odeur [ɔdœ:r], *s.f.* odour, smell, scent (of tobacco, etc.); **bonne o.**, pleasant smell; fragrance; **mauvaise o.**, bad smell, stench; **sans o.**, scentless.

odieulx, -euse [ɔdjø, -ø:z]. **1.** *a.* odious; hateful (person, vice). **2.** *s.m.* odiousness, hatefulness (of an action); *adv.* **-sement.**

odorant [ɔdɔrã], *a.* sweet-smelling.

odorat [ɔdɔra], *s.m.* (sense of) smell; **avoir l'o. fin**, to have a good nose.

œil, *pl.* **yeux** [œ:j, jø], *s.m.* **1.** eye; **il a les yeux** [lezjø] **bleus**, he has blue eyes; **je n'ai pas fermé l'o. de la nuit**, I didn't sleep a wink all night; **fermer les yeux sur qch.**, to connive at sth.; **risquer un o.**, to take a peep; **ouvrir de grands yeux**, to open one's eyes wide; **ouvrir les yeux à qn**, to open s.o.'s eyes; **il avait les yeux hors de la tête**, his eyes were popping out of his head; **regarder qn droit dans les yeux**, to look s.o. (full) in the face; **il ne travaille pour les beaux yeux de personne**, he doesn't do anything for love; **cela saute aux yeux**, it's obvious; **coûter les yeux de la tête**, to cost the earth. **2.** sight, look, eye; **cela charme les yeux**, it delights the eye; **chercher qn des yeux**, to look about for s.o.; **mesurer qch. à l'o.**, to measure sth. by eye; **avoir l'o.**, to be observant, sharp-eyed; **se consulter de l'o.**, to exchange glances; **à vue d'o.**, visibly; **coup d'o.**, (i) view; (ii) glance; **regarder qn d'un bon o.**, to look favourably upon s.o.; **vur du même o. que qn**, to see eye to eye with s.o.; **être très sur l'o.**, to be very strict. **3.** (*pl.* **œils**) (*a*) eye (of needle, etc.); (*b*) *Rad:* **o. cathodique**, magic eye. **4.** *Nau:* **l'o. du vent**, the wind's eye.

œillade [œjad], *s.f.* glance, ogle, leer; **lancer des œillades à qn**, to make eyes at s.o.

œillet [œjɛ], *s.m.* **1.** eyelet(-hole). **2.** *Bot:* pink; **o. des fleuristes**, carnation; **o. de(s) poète(s)**, sweet william; **o. d'Inde**, French marigold.

œuf [œf], *pl.* **œufs** [ø], *s.m.* (*a*) egg; *Cu:* **o. à la coque**, boiled egg; **o. mollet**, soft-boiled egg; **o. sur le plat**, fried egg; **œufs brouillés**, scrambled eggs; **en o.**, egg-shaped; **marcher sur des œufs**, to tread on thin ice; **il tondrait un o.**, he'd skin a flint; **tuer qch. dans l'o.**, to nip sth. in the bud;

(b) pl. eggs (of insect); spawn (of fish, etc.); (hard) roe (of fish).

œuvre [œːvr]. **1.** s.f. (a) work, working; **faire o. d'ami,** to behave like a friend; **mettre qn à l'o.,** to set s.o. to work; **se mettre à l'o.,** to get down to work; **il est fils de ses œuvres,** he's a self-made man; (b) **o. de bienfaisance,** charitable institution. **2.** s.f. (finished) work, production; **œuvres d'un écrivain,** works of a writer. **3.** s.m. (in sg.) **l'o. de Molière,** the works of Molière (as a whole).

offensant [ɔfɑ̃sɑ̃], a. offensive, insulting.

offense [ɔfɑːs], s.f. **1.** offence. **2.** sin, trespass; Ecc: **pardonne-nous nos offenses,** forgive us our trespasses. **3.** Jur: **o. à la Cour,** contempt of Court.

offenser [ɔfɑ̃se], v.tr. **1.** to offend, to give offence to (s.o.). **2.** (a) to be detrimental to, to injure (eyesight, lungs, etc.); (b) to offend; to shock (s.o.'s feelings).

s'offenser, to take offence (**de,** at).

offenslif, -ive [ɔfɑ̃sif, -iːv]. **1.** a. offensive (war, weapon). **2.** s.f. Mil: **l'offensive,** the offensive; **offensive de paix,** peace offensive; **offensive diplomatique,** diplomatic offensive; **offensive du froid,** cold snap; adv. **-ivement.**

offertoire [ɔfɛrtwaːr], s.m. Ecc: offertory.

office [ɔfis]. **1.** s.m. (a) office, functions, duty; **faire o. de secrétaire,** to act as secretary; adv.phr. **d'o.,** (i) officially; **avocat nommé d'o.,** barrister appointed by the Court; (ii) as a matter of course, automatically; (b) service, (good) turn; (c) Divine Service; (d) bureau, office; **o. de la main-d'œuvre,** employment exchange. **2.** s.f. (butler's) pantry.

officilel, -elle [ɔfisjɛl], a. official (statement); formal (call); adv. **-ellement.**

officier¹ [ɔfisje], v.i. (p.d. & pr.sub. n. **officiions**) to officiate; Ecc: to celebrate Mass.

officier², s.m. officer.

officieulx, -euse [ɔfisjø, -øːz]. **1.** a. (a) over-obliging; (b) unofficial; semi-official; (c) kindly-meant (advice, etc.). **2.** s. busybody; adv. **-sement,** unofficially.

offrande [ɔfrɑ̃ːd], s.f. Ecc: offering.

offrant [ɔfrɑ̃], s.m. **le plus o. (et dernier enchérisseur),** the highest bidder.

offre [ɔfr], s.f. offer, proposal; tender (for contract); **l'o. et la demande,** supply and demand.

offrir [ɔfriːr], v.tr. (conj. like COUVRIR) to offer; to give; **c'est pour o.,** it's for a present; **o. un cocktail,** to give a cocktail party; Com: **o. dix francs (d'un objet),** to offer, to bid, ten francs (for an object).

s'offrir. 1. (of pers.) to offer oneself; to volunteer (to do sth.). **2.** (of thg) to present itself; **le spectacle qui s'offrit à mes yeux,** the sight that met my eyes.

offusquer [ɔfyske], v.tr. to offend, shock (s.o.).

s'offusquer, to take offence (**de,** at).

ogivle [ɔʒiːv], s.f. **1.** Arch: ogive; pointed arch; **voûtes d'ogives,** ribbed vault. **2.** nose cone (of rocket); a. **-al, -aux,** pointed, ogival.

ogre, ogresse [ɔgr, ɔgrɛs], s. ogre, f. ogress; **manger comme un o.,** to eat like a horse.

ohé [ɔe], int. hi! hullo!

oie [wa], s.f. goose.

oignon [ɔɲɔ̃], s.m. **1.** (a) onion; **petits oignons,** (i) spring onions; (ii) pickling onions; P: **mêle-toi de tes oignons,** it's none of your business; (b) bulb (of tulip, etc.). **2.** bunion.

oiseau, -eaux [wazo], s.m. **1.** bird; **oiseaux de basse-cour,** poultry; **drôle d'o.,** queer customer. **2.** (bricklayer's) hod.

oiseau-mouche [wazomuʃ], s.m. Orn: humming bird; pl. oiseaux-mouches.

oiseau-tempête [wazotɑ̃pɛt], s.m. Orn: storm(y) petrel; pl. oiseaux-tempête.

oiselleur [wazlœːr], s.m. fowler, bird-catcher; s.m. **-ier,** bird-fancier; s.f. **-lerie,** bird shop; aviary.

oiseulx, -euse [wazø, -øːz], a. unnecessary; trifling (question); **dispute oiseuse,** pointless quarrel; adv. **-sement,** idly, unnecessarily.

oislif, -ive [wazif, -iːv]. **1.** a. idle; lazy. **2.** s. idler; adv. **-ivement,** idly, lazily; s.f. **-iveté,** idleness; leisure.

oisillon [wazijɔ̃], s.m. fledgling.

oison [wazɔ̃], s.m. gosling.

oléagineux, -euse [ɔleaʒinø, -øːz], a. **1.** oleaginous; oily. **2.** oil-producing (seeds, nuts).

olivâtre [ɔlivaːtr], a. olive-hued; sallow (complexion).

olivle [ɔliːv], s.f. (a) olive; **huile d'o.,** olive oil; (b) a.inv. olive-green; s.m. **-ier,** olive-tree; s.f. **-aie, -eraie,** olive grove.

olympiade [ɔlɛ̃pjad], s.f. Sp: Olympiad.

olympique [ɔlɛ̃pik], a. olympic; **les jeux olympiques,** the Olympic Games.

ombrage [ɔ̃braʒ], s.m. shade (of trees, etc.).

ombragé [ɔ̃braʒe], a. shaded, shady (path, spot).

ombrager [ɔ̃braʒe], v.tr. (il ombrageait) to shade; to protect (sth.) from the sun.

ombrageulx, -euse [ɔ̃braʒø, -øːz], a. **1.** nervous, skittish (horse). **2.** (of pers.) easily offended; touchy; (over-)sensitive; adv. **-sement.**

ombre¹ [ɔ̃ːbr], s.f. **1.** shadow. **2.** shade; **se reposer à l'o.,** to rest in the shade; **jeter une o. sur la fête,** to cast a gloom over the festivities. **3.** darkness; **à l'o. de la nuit,** under cover of darkness. **4.** (a) ghost, shade, shadowy figure; **n'être plus que l'o. de soi-même,** to be merely the shadow of one's former self; (b) **vous n'avez pas l'o. d'une chance,** you haven't the ghost of a chance. **5.** Art: **l'o. et la lumière,** light and shade; **il y a une o. au tableau,** there's a fly in the ointment.

ombre², *s.f.* terre d'o., umber.

ombrelle [ɔ̃brɛl], *s.f.* parasol, sunshade; *Av:* o. de protection aérienne, aerial umbrella.

omelette [ɔmlɛt], *s.f. Cu:* omelet(te); o. aux fines herbes, savoury omelet.

omettre [ɔmɛtr], *v.tr. (conj.* like METTRE) to omit; to leave out; o. de faire qch., to fail to do sth.

omission [ɔmisjɔ̃], *s.f.* omission; oversight; *Typ:* signe d'o., caret.

omnibus [ɔmnibys]. 1. *s.m.* horse (omni)bus. 2. *a.inv.* train o., slow train; des règles o., blanket rules.

omnipotence [ɔmnipɔtɑ̃:s], *s.f.* omnipotence; *a.* -ent, omnipotent.

omnipraticien, -ienne [ɔmnipratisjɛ̃, -jɛn], *s. Med:* general practitioner, *F:* G.P.

omnivore [ɔmnivɔːr], *a.* omnivorous.

omoplate [ɔmɔplat], *s.f.* shoulder-blade.

on [ɔ̃], *indef.pron. always subject of the vb.; occ.* becomes l'on, *esp. after a vowel sound.* one, people, they, we, etc.; on ne sait jamais, one never can tell; on dit, it is said; on frappe, there is a knock at the door; on demande une bonne cuisinière, wanted, a good cook. NOTE: *a pred. noun or adj. following on is fem. or pl. as the sense requires:* ici on est égaux, here we are all equal.

oncle [ɔ̃:kl], *s.m.* uncle.

onction [ɔ̃ksjɔ̃], *s.f. Ecc:* unction; l'extrême o., extreme unction.

onctueux, -euse [ɔ̃ktɥø, -ø:z], *a. (a)* unctuous; *(b) Pej:* oily, greasy (to the touch, in manner); *adv.* -sement.

onde [ɔ̃:d], *s.f.* 1. wave. 2. *(a)* wavy line; *(b)* corrugation. 3. *Ph:* etc: wave; o. sonore, sound wave; *Rad:* longueur d'o., wavelength; grandes, petites, ondes, long, medium, waves; ondes courtes, short waves.

ondée [ɔ̃de], *s.f.* heavy shower.

on-dit [ɔ̃di], *s.m.inv.* rumour, hearsay; idle talk.

ondoyant [ɔ̃dwajɑ̃], *a.* undulating, wavy; swaying (crowd); blé o., waving corn.

ondoyer [ɔ̃dwaje], *v.i.* (j'ondoie) to undulate, wave, ripple; to float on the breeze; *s.m.* -oiement, undulation.

ondulé [ɔ̃dyle], *a.* undulating, rolling (country); corrugated (iron, cardboard); wavy (hair).

onduller [ɔ̃dyle]. 1. *v.i.* to undulate, ripple. 2. *v.tr.* to wave (the hair); to corrugate (iron, cardboard); *a.* -ant, undulating; waving (corn); flowing (mane); *s.f.* -ation, undulation; (hair-)wave; *a.* -eux, -euse, wavy, sinuous (line, movement).

néreux, -euse [ɔnerø, -ø:z], *a.* onerous; burdensome (tax); heavy (expense); à titre o., subject to payment; *adv.* -sement, onerously.

ongle [ɔ̃:gl], *s.m.* (finger)nail; claw; ongles des pieds, des orteils, toenails; coup d'o., scratch;

se faire les ongles, to cut one's nails; se faire faire les ongles, to have a manicure; se ronger les ongles, (i) to bite one's nails; (ii) to be impatient; français jusqu'au bout des ongles, French to the finger-tips.

onze [ɔ̃:z], *num.a.inv. & s.m.inv.* NOTES: *the e of* le, de, *is not, as a rule, elided before* onze *and its derivatives, but there are exceptions:* le o. [ləɔ̃:z] avril, *but* entre o. [ɑ̃trɔ̃:z] heures et midi, *and occ.* le train d'o. heures; *except in* il est o. heures [ilɛ(t)ɔ̃zœ:r], *there is no liaison between* onze *and a preceding word:* eleven; *(a)* le o. avril, the eleventh of April; Louis O., Louis the Eleventh; *(b) Fb:* le o. de France, the French eleven, team.

onzième [ɔ̃zjɛm]. 1. *num.a. & s.* eleventh. 2. *s.m.* eleventh (part).

opacité [ɔpasite], *s.f.* opacity; cloudiness (of liquid); denseness (of the intellect).

opale [ɔpal], *s.f.* opal; la côte d'O., the Pas-de-Calais coast; *s.f.* -escence; *a.* -escent; *a.* -in, -ine, opaline.

opaque [ɔpak], *a.* opaque.

opéra [ɔpera], *s.m.* 1. opera. 2. opera-house.

opérateur, -trice [ɔperatœ:r, -tris], *s.* operator; machine-operator; *Cin:* camera man.

opératif, -ive [ɔperatif, -i:v], *a.* operative.

opération [ɔperasjɔ̃], *s.f.* 1. operation; working (of nature); process. 2. opérations militaires, military operations; *Av:* centre d'opérations, operational centre; o. chirurgicale, (surgical) operation. 3. transaction; deal.

opérer [ɔpere], *v.tr.* (j'opère; j'opérerai) to operate. 1. to bring about, to effect; o. un miracle, to work a miracle. 2. *(a)* to carry out, perform; *(b)* o. un malade, un abcès, to operate on a patient, an abscess; se faire o., to undergo an operation. 3. *abs. (of remedy)* to work, act. s'opérer, to take place, to come about.

opérette [ɔperɛt], *s.f.* operetta; musical comedy.

ophtalmologie [ɔftalmɔlɔʒi], *s.f.* ophthalmology; *a.* -gique, ophthalmologic(al); *s.m. &f.* -giste, oculist.

opiniâtre [ɔpinjɑtr], *a.* obstinate; *(a)* self-opinionated; *(b)* self-willed; stubborn; *(c)* persistent; résistance o., dogged resistance; *adv.* -ment; *s.f.* -té, obstinacy.

opinion [ɔpinjɔ̃], *s.f.* opinion (de, of; sur, about); view; donner bonne o. de sa capacité, to make a good impression.

opium [ɔpjɔm], *s.m.* opium.

opportun, -une [ɔpɔrtœ̃, -yn], *a. (a)* opportune, timely, well-timed; attendre l'heure opportune, to wait for the right moment; *(b)* expedient, advisable (measure, decision); *adv.* -ément, opportunely, seasonably.

opportunité [ɔpɔrtynite], *s.f.* 1. *(a)* opportuneness, timeliness, seasonableness; *(b)* expediency, advisability. 2. favourable occasion; opportunity; *s.m.* **-isme,** opportunism; time-serving; *s.m. & f.* **-iste,** opportunist; time-server.

opposé [ɔpoze]. **1.** opposed, opposing (armies); opposite (side, shore); **tons opposés,** contrasting colours. **2.** *s.m.* the contrary, reverse, opposite (of sth.).

opposer [ɔpoze], *v.tr.* **1.** to oppose; **o. une vigoureuse résistance,** to offer a vigorous resistance; **o. une équipe à une autre,** to match one team against another. **2.** to compare, to contrast (à, with).

s'opposer à qch., to oppose sth.; to be opposed to sth.

opposition [ɔpozisjɔ̃], *s.f.* **1.** opposition; *Pol:* **le parti de l'o.,** the opposition; *Com:* **frapper d'o.,** to stop payment of (cheque, etc.). **2.** contrast; **par o. à qch.,** as opposed to sth.

oppres|ser [ɔprɛse], *v.tr.* to oppress; (*a*) to weigh down; to lie heavy on (the chest, conscience); to impede (breathing); (*b*) to deject, depress; **souvenir qui oppresse,** depressing, saddening, memory; *s.m.* **-seur,** oppressor; *a.* **-sif, -sive,** oppressive; *s.f.* **-sion;** *adv.* **-sivement.**

opprim|er [ɔprime], *v.tr.* to oppress, crush (a people) (down); **peuple opprimé,** oppressed, crushed, nation; *a.* **-ant,** oppressive (tyrant).

opter [ɔpte], *v.i.* **o. pour qch.,** to decide in favour of sth., to choose sth.

opticien [ɔptisjɛ̃], *s.m.* optician.

optim|isme [ɔptimism], *s.m.* optimism; *a. & s.* **-iste,** (i) *a.* optimistic; (ii) *s.* optimist.

option [ɔpsjɔ̃], *s.f.* option, choice (**entre,** between); **demander une o.,** to ask for an option.

optique [ɔptik]. **1.** *a.* optic (nerve); optical. **2.** *s.f.* optics.

opul|ence [ɔpylɑ̃:s], *s.f.* opulence, affluence, wealth; *a.* **-ent,** rich.

opuscule [ɔpyskyl], *s.m.* pamphlet, tract.

or[1] [ɔ:r], *s.m.* **1.** gold; **or en barres,** bullion; *F:* **c'est en or,** it's a piece of cake; **affaire d'or,** excellent bargain. **2.** gold (colour); **chevelure d'or,** golden hair.

or[2], *conj.* now; **or donc,** well then.

oracle [ɔrakl], *s.m.* oracle.

orage [ɔra:ʒ], *s.m.* (thunder-)storm.

orageu|x, -euse [ɔraʒø, -ø:z], *a.* **1.** stormy; **discussion orageuse,** stormy discussion. **2.** threatening, thundery (weather, sky); *adv.* **-sement.**

oraison [ɔrɛzɔ̃], *s.f.* **1.** *now only used in* **o. funèbre,** funeral oration. **2.** prayer; **o. dominicale,** the Lord's Prayer.

oral, -aux [ɔral, -o]. **1.** *a.* oral (examination); verbal (deposition). **2.** *s.m.* oral examination, viva; *F:* **rater l'o.,** to fail in the viva; *adv.* **-ement,** orally, by word of mouth.

oran|ge [ɔrɑ̃:ʒ]. **1.** *s.f.* orange; **o. amère,** Seville orange; **o. sanguine,** blood orange; **o. navel,** navel orange. **2.** *s.m.* orange (colour); *a. inv.* orange(-coloured); *s.f.* **-geade,** orangeade; *s.m.* **-ger,** orange-tree; *s.f.* **-geraie,** orange grove; *s.f.* **-gerie,** orangery.

orateur [ɔratœ:r], *s.m.* orator, speaker.

oratoire [ɔratwa:r]. **1.** *a.* oratorical; **l'art o.,** the art of public speaking. **2.** *s.m.* chapel (for private worship); **les Pères de l'O.,** the Oratorians.

oratorio [ɔratɔrjo], *s.m. Mus:* oratorio.

orbite [ɔrbit], *s.f.* **1.** (*a*) orbit (of planet, etc.); **mettre un satellite en o.,** to put a satellite into orbit; (*b*) orbit, sphere of influence; **l'o. de la Russie, des U.S.A.,** the Russian, American, sphere of influence.

Orcades (les) [lezɔrkad]. *Pr.n.f.pl.* the Orkneys.

orches|tre [ɔrkɛstr], *s.m.* orchestra; **chef d'o.,** (i) conductor; (ii) bandmaster; **grand o.,** full orchestra; *Th:* **fauteuil d'o.,** orchestra stall; *a.* **-tral, -traux,** orchestral; *s.f.* **-tration.**

orchidée [ɔrkide], *s.f.* orchid.

orchis [ɔrkis], *s.m. Bot:* orchis; wild orchid.

ordinaire [ɔrdine:r]. **1.** *a.* ordinary, usual, normal; average; **vin o.,** table wine; **sa maladresse o.,** his usual clumsiness; **peu o.,** unusual, uncommon; *Fin:* **actions ordinaires,** ordinary shares; **de taille o.,** of average (i) height, (ii) size. **2.** *s.m.* (*a*) custom, usual practice; **d'o.,** usually, as a rule; **comme d'o.,** as usual; (*b*) **cela sort de l'o.,** it's out of the ordinary, it's unusual; **au-dessus de l'o.,** above the common run; (*c*) everyday meal; daily menu; **auberge où l'o. est excellent,** pub where the food is excellent; *adv.* **-ment,** usually, as a rule.

ordinal, -aux [ɔrdinal, -o], *a.* ordinal.

ordinateur [ɔrdinatœ:r], *s.m.* computer.

ordonnance [ɔrdɔnɑ̃:s], *s.f.* **1.** order, (general) arrangement. **2.** statute, order; **o. de police,** police regulation. **3.** **officier d'o.,** aide-de-camp; *Navy:* flag-lieutenant. **4.** *Mil:* (*a*) orderly; (*b*) *occ.m.* officer's servant. **5.** *Med:* prescription.

ordonné [ɔrdɔne], *a.* orderly (life, mind); tidy (person).

ordonner [ɔrdɔne], *v.tr.* **1.** to arrange (sth.). **2.** to order, command; **o. à qn de faire qch.,** to order s.o. to do sth.; *Med:* **o. un remède à qn,** to prescribe a remedy for s.o. **3.** to ordain (priest).

ordre [ɔrdr], *s.m.* order. **1.** **numéro d'o.,** serial number; **avec o.,** methodically; **avoir de l'o.,** to be (a) tidy (person); **sans o.,** untidy, untidily; **homme d'o.,** orderly, methodical, man; **mettre de l'o. dans qch.,** (i) to put sth. right; (ii) to tidy up (a room, etc.). **2.** *Jur:* **o. public,** law and order; **le service d'o.** = the police (on duty); **délit contre l'o. public,** breach of the peace. **o. du jour,** (i) agenda (of meeting); (ii) *Mil:*

order of the day; *Mil:* cité à l'o. (du jour) =mentioned in despatches. **4.** (*a*) order (of architecture, plants, animals, etc.); class, division, category; **de premier o.**, first-rate (firm, workman, actor); **renseignements d'o.** privé, enquiries of a private nature; **de l'o. de . . .,** in the order of . . .; in the region of . . .; (*b*) **o. religieux,** monastic order; (*c*) *pl. Ecc:* Holy Orders; **recevoir les ordres,** to be ordained; (*d*) decoration; **l'O. de la Jarretière,** the Order of the Garter. **5.** (*a*) command; warrant; **o. d'exécution,** death-warrant; **donner o. à qn de faire qch.,** to order s.o. to do sth.; **je reçus l'o. de revenir,** I was ordered back; **jusqu'à nouvel o.,** until further notice; (*b*) *Com:* **billet à o.,** promissory note.

ordur|e [ɔrdy:r], *s.f.* **1.** (*a*) dirt, filth; (*b*) excrement, dung; (*c*) filthiness; **dire des ordures,** to use filthy language. **2.** *pl.* sweepings, refuse; **ordures ménagères,** rubbish, garbage; *P.N:* **défense de déposer des ordures,** shoot no rubbish; *a.* **-ier, -ière,** filthy (book, language).

oreill|e [ɔrɛːj], *s.f.* ear. **1. avoir mal aux oreilles,** to have earache; **aux oreilles courtes, longues,** short-, long-eared; **baisser l'o.,** to be crestfallen; *F:* **il s'est fait tirer l'o.,** he took a lot of coaxing; **montrer le bout de l'o.,** to show the cloven hoof. **2. n'écouter que d'une o.,** to listen with half an ear; **souffler qch. à l'o. de qn,** to whisper sth. to s.o.; **dresser l'o.,** to prick up one's ears; **faire la sourde o.,** to turn a deaf ear; *s.m.* **-er,** pillow; *s.m.pl.* **-ons,** mumps.

orfèvre [ɔrfɛːvr], *s.m.* goldsmith, gold and silver smith; *s.f.* **-rie,** goldsmith's trade, shop; (gold, silver) plate.

organe [ɔrgan], *s.m.* **1.** organ (of sight, etc.); **les organes d'une machine,** the parts of a machine. **2.** (*a*) mouthpiece, spokesman; *Pol:* **l'o. d'un parti,** a party newspaper; **o. de publicité,** advertising medium; (*b*) agent, means, medium; **l'o. officiel,** the official record; **par un nouvel o.,** through another agency.

organique [ɔrganik], *a.* organic (disease, chemistry); *adv.* **-ment.**

organis|er [ɔrganize], *v.tr.* to organize; to arrange (a reception, a journey); *s.* **-ateur, -atrice,** organizer; *s.f.* **-ation,** organization. **'organiser,** to get into working order; to get settled.

organisme [ɔrganism], *s.m.* organism. **1.** *Anat:* system; **un o. de fer,** an iron constitution. **2. un o. comme l'O.N.U.,** a body such as U.N.O.

organiste [ɔrganist], *s.m. & f. Mus:* organist.

orge [ɔrʒ]. **1.** *s.f.* barley. **2.** *s.m.* **o. perlé,** pearl-barley.

orgelet [ɔrʒəlɛ], *s.m.* stye (on the eye).

orgue [ɔrg], *s.m.* **1.** (*also Ecc: s.f.pl.* **orgues**) *Mus:* organ. **2. o. de salon,** harmonium; **o. de**

cinéma, theatre organ; **o. de Barbarie,** barrel-organ.

orgueil [ɔrgœ:j], *s.m.* pride, arrogance; *a.* **-leux, -leuse,** arrogant, proud; *adv.* **-leusement.**

orient [ɔrjɑ̃], *s.m.* orient, east; *Pol:* **le proche, le moyen, l'extrême, O.,** the Near, Middle, Far, East; *a.* **-al, -aux,** eastern, oriental.

orientation [ɔrjɑ̃tasjɔ̃], *s.f.* **1.** orientation; **table d'o.,** panoramic table; **perdre le sens de l'o.,** to lose one's bearings, one's sense of direction; *Sch:* **o. professionnelle,** vocational guidance; *Rad:* positioning (of aerial). **2. o. d'une maison,** aspect of a house.

orienter [ɔrjɑ̃te], *v.tr.* **1.** to orient, orientate (building); (*a*) **terrasse orientée au sud,** terrace facing south; (*b*) *Rad:* **antenne orientée,** directional aerial; (*c*) to direct, guide (s.o.). **2.** *Surv:* to take the bearings of (spot). **s'orienter,** to take one's bearings; **s'o. vers la carrière diplomatique,** to prepare for (a career in) the diplomatic service; **s'o. vers le communisme,** to move towards communism.

orifice [ɔrifis], *s.m.* aperture, opening, orifice.

originaire [ɔriʒinɛ:r], *a.* originating (**de,** from, in); native (**de,** of); *adv.* **-ment,** originally.

original, -aux [ɔriʒinal, -o], *a. & s.* **1.** original (text); (*in typing*) top copy. **2.** (*a*) original; novel, fresh; (*b*) odd, queer; **c'est un o.,** he's a character; *adv.* **-ement.**

originalité [ɔriʒinalite], *s.f.* (*a*) originality; (*b*) eccentricity, oddity.

origine [ɔriʒin], *s.f.* origin. **1.** beginning. **2.** (*a*) extraction (of person); (*b*) nationality. **3.** source, derivation; **mots de même o.,** cognate words; *Post:* **bureau d'o.,** (postal) office of dispatch; *Com:* **champagne d'o.,** vintage champagne; **emballage d'o.,** original packing.

origin|el, -elle [ɔriʒinɛl], *a.* primordial, original; *adv.* **-ellement.**

orm|e [ɔrm], *s.m.* elm(-tree, -wood); **o. de montagne,** wych-elm; *s.m.* **-eau,** young elm.

orné [ɔrne], *a.* ornate; decorated; illuminated (letter); florid (style).

ornement [ɔrnəmɑ̃], *s.m.* ornament, adornment, embellishment; **sans o.,** unadorned, plain.

ornement|er [ɔrnəmɑ̃te], *v.tr.* to ornament, to decorate; *a.* **-al, -aux,** ornamental, decorative; *s.f.* **-ation.**

orner [ɔrne], *v.tr.* to ornament, adorn, decorate; **orné de rubis,** set with rubies; **hommes qui ornent leur siècle,** men who are the glory of their age.

ornière [ɔrnjɛ:r], *s.f.* rut.

ornitholo|gie [ɔrnitɔlɔʒi], *s.f.* ornithology; *a.* **-gique,** ornithological; *s.m. & f.* **-giste.**

orphelin, -ine [ɔrfəlɛ̃, -in], *s.* orphan; *a.* orphan(ed); **o. de père, de mère,** fatherless, motherless (boy); *s.m.* **-at** [-ina], orphanage.

orteil [ɔrtɛ:j], *s.m.* toe; **gros o.,** big toe.

orthodox|e [ɔrtɔdɔks], *a.* orthodox; *s.f.* -ie, orthodoxy.

orthographe [ɔrtɔgraf], *s.f.* spelling.

orthographier [ɔrtɔgrafje], *v.tr.* to spell.

orthopéd|ie [ɔrtɔpedi], *s.f.* orthopaedics; *a.* -ique; *s.m. & f.* -iste.

ortie [ɔrti], *s.f.* nettle; **o. brûlante,** stinging nettle.

os [ɔs; *pl.* o], *s.m.* bone; **trempé jusqu'aux os,** wet through; **il y laissera ses os,** he'll die there.

oscill|er [ɔsil(l)e], *v.i.* to oscillate. **1.** (*of pendulum*) to swing; to sway; to rock. **2.** to waver; (*of market*) to fluctuate; *a.* -ant; *s.f.* -ation; *a.* -atoire, oscillatory.

osé [oze], *a.* bold, daring (person, book, proposal); risqué (joke); **être trop o.,** to go too far.

oseille [ozɛ:j], *s.f. Bot:* sorrel.

oser [oze], *v.tr.* to dare, venture; **je n'ose pas le faire,** I daren't do it; **si j'ose m'exprimer ainsi,** if you don't mind my saying so.

osier [ozje], *s.m.* osier, water-willow; **panier d'o.,** wicker-basket.

ossature [ɔsaty:r], *s.f.* **1.** *Anat:* frame, skeleton. **2.** frame(-work), carcass (of building, etc.); **l'o. de la langue française,** the structure of the French language.

ossements [ɔsmã], *s.m.pl.* bones, remains (of dead men, animals).

osseux, -euse [ɔsø, -ø:z], *a.* bony (body, hand); **greffe osseuse,** bone graft.

ostensible [ɔstãsibl], *a.* open, patent to all; above board, visible, apparent; *adv.* -ment.

ostentation [ɔstãtasjõ], *s.f.* ostentation, show; display.

otage [ota:ʒ], *s.m.* hostage (de, for); surety.

otarie [ɔtari], *s.f.* sea-lion.

ôter [ote], *v.tr.* to remove; to take away; (*a*) ô. le couvert, to clear the table; ô. son pardessus, to take off one's overcoat; (*b*) ô. la vie à qn, to kill s.o.; (*c*) trois ôté de cinq égale deux, three from five leaves two; **il me l'a ôté des mains,** he snatched it away from me, out of my hands.

ou [u], *conj.* or. **1. voulez-vous du bœuf ou du jambon?** would you like beef or ham? **tôt ou tard,** sooner or later; **entrez ou sortez,** either come in or go out. **2. ou lui ou moi,** either him or me.

où [u], *adv.* **1.** *interrog.* where? **où en êtes-vous?** how far have you got with it? **d'où?** whence? where from? **d'où vient que . . .?** how does it happen that . . .? **jusqu'où?** how far? **déposez-le n'importe où,** put it down anywhere. **2.** *rel.* (*a*) where; **partout où il va,** wherever he goes; **vous trouverez ma pipe là où je l'ai laissée,** you'll find my pipe where I left it; (*b*) when; **du temps où il était jeune,** (in the days) when he was young; (*c*) in which, at which; **la maison où il demeure,** the house he

lives in. **3.** (*concessive*) **où que vous soyez** wherever you may be.

ouate [wat], *s.f.* (*usu.* la ouate, *occ.* l'ouate) (*a* wadding; (*b*) cotton wool; **o. hydrophile,** (ab sorbent) cotton wool.

ouaté [wate], *a.* **1.** padded; **robe de chambr ouatée,** quilted dressing-gown. **2.** fleec (clouds); soft (footsteps).

ouater [wate], *v.tr.* to pad; to quilt.

oubli [ubli], *s.m.* **1.** (*a*) forgetting, neglect (c duty, etc.); forgetfulness; (*b*) **tomber dans l'o** to sink into oblivion, to be forgotten. **2.** omi sion, oversight.

oublier [ublije], *v.tr.* to forget; (*a*) **j'ai oublié so nom,** his name has slipped my memory; **fai o. son passé,** to live down one's past; on n **nous le laissera pas o.,** we shall never hear th last of it; (*b*) to overlook, neglect.

s'oublier. 1. il ne s'oublie pas, he can look afte himself. **2.** to forget one's manners.

oublieux, -euse [ublijø, -ø:z], *a.* forgetful (d of); **o. de son devoir,** neglectful of his duty.

Ouessant [wɛsã]. *Pr.n.m. Geog:* Ushant.

ouest [wɛst]. **1.** *s.m. no pl.* west. **2.** *a.inv.* côté o western, west, side.

oui [wi], yes. **1.** *adv.* **je crois que o.,** I think s **faire signe que o.,** to nod assent, to nod one head in agreement. **2.** *s.m.inv.* (*in voting*) det cents oui, two hundred ayes.

ouï-dire [widi:r], *s.m.inv.* hearsay.

ouïe [wi], *s.f.* **1.** (sense of) hearing; **avoir l'o. fin** to be sharp of hearing. **2.** *pl.* gills (of fish).

ouragan [uragã], *s.m.* hurricane; **entrer en o.,** burst in (to a room).

ourler [urle], *v.tr.* **1.** *Needlew:* to hem; **o. à jou** to hemstitch. **2.** *Metalw:* to lap-joint (met edges).

ourlet [urlɛ], *s.m.* **1.** hem. **2.** edge (of crater); ri (of ear). **3.** lap-joint (in metal).

ours, -e [urs], *s.* **1.** *Z:* bear, *f.* she bear; **o. m léché,** boorish person. **2.** *Astr:* **la Gran Ourse,** the Great Bear; *s.m.* -on, bear cub.

oursin [ursɛ̃], *s.m.* sea-urchin; **o. violet,** edib sea-urchin.

outil [uti], *s.m.* tool, implement; **o. à main,** ha tool; **o. à moteur,** power tool.

outill|er [utije], *v.tr.* to equip, supply, (man) w tools, (factory) with plant; *s.m.* -age, set tools, kit; gear, plant; heavy equipment.

outrage [utra:ʒ], *s.m.* outrage; flagrant insu *Jur:* **o. à magistrat,** contempt of court.

outrag|er [utraʒe], *v.tr.* (**n. outrageons**) **1.** to : sult. **2.** to outrage (nature, the law); *a.* -ea insulting, outrageous; *a.* -eux, -euse, : sulting, outrageous; *adv.* -eusement.

outrance [utrã:s], *s.f.* à o., to the bitter e **guerre à o.,** war to the death.

outre [utr]. **1.** *prep.* (*a*) (*used only in a few phrases*) beyond; **o. mesure,** inordinately, ▪

duly, over-; **se fatiguer o. mesure,** to overtire oneself; (*b*) in addition to; **o. cela . . .,** besides that . . ., moreover . . .. **2.** *adv.* (*a*) **passer o.,** to go on, proceed further; **passer o. à la loi,** to defy, override, the law; (*b*) **en o.,** besides, moreover; over and above; (*c*) *conj.phr.* **o. que** + *ind.,* apart from the fact that . . ..

outré [utre], *a.* (*a*) exaggerated, extravagant (praise); far-fetched (idea); **d'une activité outrée,** hyperactive; (*b*) **o. de colère,** beside oneself with rage.

outre-Atlantique [utratlɑ̃tik], *adv.phr.* on the other side of the Atlantic.

outre-Manche [utrəmɑ̃:ʃ], *adv.phr.* on the other side of, across, the Channel.

outremer [utrəmɛ:r], *s.m.* (**bleu d')o.,** ultramarine (blue).

outre-mer [utrəmɛ:r], *adv.* overseas.

outrepasser [utrəpɑse], *v.tr.* to go beyond (a limit, one's rights); to exceed (given orders).

outrer [utre], *v.tr.* **1.** to carry (sth.) to excess; to overdo (sth.). **2.** to provoke (s.o.) beyond measure.

ouvert [uvɛr], *a.* open; (*a*) **porte grande ouverte,** wide-open door; **le gaz est o.,** the gas is on; **plaie ouverte,** gaping wound; *Surg:* **à cœur o.,** open-heart (surgery); **fleur ouverte,** flower in bloom; (*b*) **ville ouverte,** open town; **bateau o.,** open boat; (*c*) **o. la nuit,** open all night; (*d*) **caractère o.,** frank, open, nature; **avoir l'esprit o.,** to be open-minded; **parler à cœur o.,** to speak freely; *adv.* **-ement.**

ouverture [uvɛrty:r], *s.f.* **1.** (*a*) opening (of door, etc.); **o. d'hostilités,** outbreak of hostilities; (*b*) **faire des ouvertures à qn,** to make overtures to s.o.; (*c*) *Mus:* overture; (*d*) **heures d'o.,** business hours (of shop); visiting hours (of museum, etc.). **2.** (*a*) opening, aperture; gap, break (in wall, hedge); **les ouvertures (d'une maison),** the doors and windows; (*b*) span (of arch); *El:* **o. d'induit,** armature gap. **3.** (parachute) opening; **o. retardée,** delayed opening. **4. o. d'esprit,** broadmindedness.

ouvrable [uvrabl], *a.* **jour o.,** working day.

ouvrage [uvra:ʒ], *s.m.* work. **1.** (*a*) **se mettre à l'o.,** to set to work; (*b*) workmanship. **2.** piece of work; product; **ouvrages d'un écrivain,** works of a writer; *Civ.E:* **ouvrages d'art,** construction works (bridges, tunnels, etc.); **ouvrages de dames,** needlework, embroidery; **boîte à o.,** work-box.

ouvre-boîtes [uvrəbwat], *s.m.inv.* tin-opener; can-opener.

ouvre-bouteille(s) [uvrəbutɛ:j], *s.m.* bottle-opener; *pl.* **ouvre-bouteilles.**

ouvreuse [uvrø:z], *s.f.* usherette.

ouvrier, -ière [uvrije, -jɛ:r]. **1.** *s.* (*a*) worker; workman, craftsman; mechanic; operative; **o. agricole,** farm hand; **o. d'usine,** factory worker; (*b*) **première ouvrière,** forewoman; **être l'o. de sa fortune,** to be a self-made man. **2.** *a.* **les classes ouvrières,** the working classes; **conflits ouvriers,** industrial disputes; **syndicat o.,** trade union.

ouvrir [uvri:r], *v.* (*pr.p.* **ouvrant;** *p.p.* **ouvert;** *pr.ind.* **j'ouvre**) **1.** *v.tr.* to open; (*a*) to turn on (a tap, the gas); to switch on (electricity); **o. à qn,** to let s.o. in; (*b*) to cut through, open up (canal, wall, mine); **s'o. un chemin à travers la foule,** to push one's way through the crowd; (*c*) to begin; **o. un débat,** to open a debate; **o. une liste,** to head a list; **o. boutique,** to set up shop. **2.** *v.i.* **la scène ouvre par un chœur,** the scene opens with a chorus.

s'ouvrir, to open; **s'o. à qn,** to unburden oneself to s.o.

ovaire [ovɛ:r], *s.m. Anat: Bot:* ovary.

ovale [oval]. **1.** *a.* oval, egg-shaped; *Sp: F:* **ballon o.,** rugger ball. **2.** *s.m.* oval.

ovation [ovasjɔ̃], *s.f.* ovation.

ovoïde [ovoid], *a.* ovoid, egg-shaped.

oxydation [ɔksidasjɔ̃], *s.f. Ch:* oxidation; (*in engines, boilers, etc.*) corrosion; scale.

oxyde [ɔksid], *s.m. Ch:* oxide.

oxyder [ɔkside], *v.tr. Ch:* to oxidize.

s'oxyder, to rust, to become corroded.

oxygène [ɔksiʒɛn], *s.m. Ch:* oxygen.

oxygéné [ɔksiʒene], *a.* **eau oxygénée,** peroxide of hydrogen.

ozone [ozon], *s.m. Ch:* ozone.

P

P, p [pe], s.m. (the letter) P, p.
pacage [paka:ʒ], s.m. Agr: 1. pasture (land),
pasturage. 2. pasturing, grazing.
pacemaker [peismeikɛːr], s.m. Sp: Med:
pacemaker.
pacifi|er [pasifje], v.tr. (p.d. & pr.sub. n.
pacifiions) to pacify (country); to appease, to
calm (crowd, the mind); a. & s. -cateur,
-catrice, (i) a. peace-making; (ii) s.
peacemaker; s.f. -cation.
se pacifier, to calm down.
pacifique [pasifik], a. (a) peaceable (person,
agreement); (b) peaceful, quiet; coexistence p.,
peaceful coexistence; adv. -ment.
paci|fisme [pasifism], s.m. Pol: pacifism; s.m. &
f. -fiste.
pacte [pakt], s.m. pact, agreement.
pactiser [paktize], v.i. p. avec l'ennemi, avec sa
conscience, to treat with the enemy, to compromise with one's conscience.
pagaie [pagɛ], s.f. paddle (for canoe).
pagaïe [paga:j], pagaille [paga:j], s.f. disorder,
muddle, clutter; quelle p.! what a mess!
pagailleur, -euse [pagajœːr, -øːz], s. muddler.
paganisme [paganism], s.m. paganism.
pagay|er [pageje], v.tr. & i. (je pagaie) to paddle
(a canoe); s. -eur, -euse, paddler.
page [pa:ʒ], s.f. page (of book); F: être à la p., to
be up to date, in the know.
paie [pɛ], s.f. 1. pay, wages. 2. payment; jour de
p., pay day.
paiement [pɛmã], s.m. payment.
païen, -ïenne [pajɛ̃, -jɛn], a. & s. pagan,
heathen.
paill|e [pɑ:j], s.f. 1. straw; (a) botte de p., truss
of straw; chaise de p., straw-bottomed chair;
feu de p., flash in the pan; être sur la p., to be
down and out; tirer à la courte p., to draw lots;
(b) a.inv. straw-coloured. 2. menue p., chaff. 3.
p. de fer, steel wool; s.f. -asse, straw mattress;
s.m. -asson, (door-)mat.
pailleté [pajte], a. spangled (de, with).
paillette [pajɛt], s.f. (a) spangle; (b) (savon en)
paillettes, (soap) flakes.
pain [pɛ̃], s.m. 1. bread; p. frais, p. rassis, fresh,
stale, bread; p. grillé, toast; F: acheter qch.
pour une bouchée de p., to buy sth. for a song;
il ne vaut pas le p. qu'il mange, he is not worth
his salt. 2. loaf; (a) petit p., roll; ça se vend
comme des petits pains, it's selling like hot
cakes; (b) p. de savon, cake of soap.

pair [pɛːr]. 1. a. (a) equal; de p. (avec), on a pa
(with); marcher de p. avec qn, to keep pac
with s.o.; (b) Mth: nombres pairs, eve
numbers; P.N: stationnement jours pairs
parking on even dates (only). 2. s.m. (a) equal
(b) les pairs du royaume, the peers of th
realm. 3. s.m. (state of) equality; par; Fin: l
change est au p., the exchange is at par
adv.phr. au p.; étudiante au p., au pair studen
F: au pair (girl); s.f. -esse, peeress; s.f. -ie
peerage.
paire [pɛːr], s.f. pair (of gloves); brace (of birds
yoke (of oxen).
paisible [pɛzibl], a. peaceful, peaceable, quie
adv. -ment.
paître [pɛːtr], v. (pr.p. paissant; pr.ind. je pais)
v.tr. to feed upon; to crop (grass, etc.). 2. v.i.
feed; to graze, browse; to pasture.
paix [pɛ], s.f. peace; laissez-moi en p., leave m
alone; dormir en p., to sleep peacefully.
Pakistan (le) [ləpakistã]. Pr.n.m. Geo
Pakistan.
palace [palas], s.m. de luxe hotel.
palais¹ [palɛ], s.m. 1. palace. 2. p. de justice, la
courts; gens du p., lawyers, the legal fraternit
palais², s.m. palate; (a) roof of the mouth; (
(sense of) taste.
pâle [pɑl], a. pale (face, etc.); un sourire p., a wa
smile; faint (light).
palefrenier [palfrənje], s.m. groom, stablemar
paletot [palto], s.m. overcoat.
palette [palɛt], s.f. 1. (table-tennis) bat. 2. roue
palettes, blade-wheel. 3. (painter's) palette.
pâleur [palœːr], s.f. pallor, paleness.
palier [palje], s.m. 1. (a) landing (of stairs); (
stage, degree; taxes imposées par palier
graduated taxation. 2. Aut: level stretc
vitesse en p., speed on the flat.
pâlir [pɑliːr], v.i. to become pale; to grow dim;
fade.
palissad|e [palisad], s.f. fence, paling; (stre
hoarding; v.tr. -er, to fence in; to enclose.
palli|er [palje], v.tr. (p.d. & pr.sub. n. palliio
to palliate (offence, pain); to mitigate; a. & s.
-atif, -ative, palliative.
palmarès [palmarɛːs], s.m. Sch: prize-li
honours list.
palme [palm], s.f. 1. palm(-branch); rempor
la p., to bear the palm; to win the victor
recevoir les palmes (académiques), to
decorated by the Minister of Education;

decoration) **avec p.** = with bar. **2.** *Sp: etc:* fin, flipper (of a frogman).

palmé [palme], *a.* **1.** *Bot:* palmate (leaf). **2.** *Orn:* web-footed; **pied p.**, webbed foot; *P:* **les avoir palmées,** to be workshy.

palm|ier [palmje], *s.m.* palm-tree; **huile de p.**, palm-oil; *s.f.* **-eraie,** palm-grove; *s.m.* **-iste,** palmetto.

palombe [palɔ:b], *s.f.* ring-dove, wood-pigeon.

pâlot, -otte [palo, -ɔt], *a.* palish, peaky (look).

palourde [palurd], *s.f.* clam.

palpable [palpabl], *a.* palpable. **1.** tangible. **2.** obvious (error), plain (truth); *adv.* **-ment.**

palper [palpe], *v.tr.* to feel; to finger (sth.).

palpit|er [palpite], *v.i.* to palpitate; (*a*) to flutter; to quiver; (*b*) (*of heart*) to throb; (*c*) to thrill (with pleasure, fear, etc.); *a.* **-ant,** *F:* thrilling (film, novel); *s.f.* **-ation.**

paludisme [palydism], *s.m. Med:* malaria.

pamplemousse [pɑ̃pləmus], *s.m.* grapefruit.

pan [pɑ̃], *s.m.* **1.** skirt, flap (of garment); tail (of coat). **2. p. de mur,** bare wall, piece of wall; **maison à pans de bois,** half-timbered house; **p. de ciel,** patch of sky. **3.** face, side (of angular building); **tour à huit pans,** octagonal tower.

panacée [panase], *s.f.* panacea, universal remedy.

panache [panaʃ], *s.m.* (*a*) plume; **p. de fumée,** wreath, trail, of smoke; (*b*) **faire p.,** (i) to take a header (off horse, cycle); (ii) (*of car*) to overturn; (*c*) **il a du p.,** he has an air about him; **il aime le p.,** he likes to cut a dash.

panaché [panaʃe], *a.* parti-coloured, variegated (in colour); **foule panachée,** motley crowd; *Cu:* **salade panachée,** mixed salad; **glace panachée,** mixed ice; **bière panachée,** *s.m.* **panaché,** shandy.

panais [panɛ], *s.m.* parsnip.

panama (le) [ləpanama]. **1.** *Pr.n.m.* Panama. **2.** *s.m.* Panama hat.

pancarte [pɑ̃kart], *s.f.* placard, bill; (price)card.

paner [pane], *v.tr. Cu:* to breadcrumb; to cover (meat, fish) with breadcrumbs; to fry (chop, etc.) in breadcrumbs.

panier [panje], *s.m.* basket; **p. à papier,** waste paper basket; **jeter qch. au p.,** to throw sth. away; **p. à friture,** basket for deep frying; **p. à provisions,** shopping basket; **p. à salade,** (i) salad shaker; (ii) *F:* Black Maria; *F:* **c'est un p. percé,** he's a spendthrift; **le dessus du p.,** the pick of the basket; **le fond du p.,** the scrapings of the barrel.

panique [panik]. **1.** *a.* panic. **2.** *s.f.* panic, scare; stampede; **pris de p.,** panic-stricken; **sujet à la p.,** easily scared, *F:* panicky; *F:* **-quard,** scaremonger, alarmist.

panne [pan], *s.f.* (*a*) (mechanical) breakdown; (electrical) failure, *N.Am:* outage; **en p.,** out of order; **être en p. sèche,** to be out of petrol;

---

tomber en p., to break down; (*b*) (*of pers.*) **rester en p. devant une difficulté,** to stick at a difficulty; **laisser qn en p.,** to let s.o. down.

panneau, -eaux [pano], *s.m.* **1.** (door, wall, etc.) panel, panelling. **2. p. à affiches,** advertisement hoarding; *Aut:* **p. indicateur,** road sign; **p. de signalisation (routière),** traffic sign; *El: etc:* **p. de commande,** control board.

panoram|a [panɔrama], *s.m.* panorama; *a.* **-ique.**

pans|er [pɑ̃se], *v.tr.* **1.** to groom (horse). **2.** to dress (wound); to bandage (a casualty); *s.m.* **-age,** grooming (of horse); *s.m.* **-ement,** (i) dressing (of wound); (ii) (surgical) dressing.

pantalon [pɑ̃talɔ̃], *s.m.* (pair of) trousers; slacks.

panthéon [pɑ̃teɔ̃], *s.m.* pantheon; **le P.,** the Pantheon (in Paris); **son nom restera au p. de l'histoire,** his name will be famous in history.

panthère [pɑ̃tɛ:r], *s.f. Z:* panther.

pantin [pɑ̃tɛ̃], *s.m. Th:* puppet; *F:* **p. politique,** political stooge.

pantomime [pɑ̃tɔmim], *s.f.* pantomime; mime.

pantoufl|e [pɑ̃tufl], *s.f.* slipper; *s.m. F:* **-ard,** home-bird.

paon [pɑ̃], *s.m.* peacock.

papa [papa], *s.m. F:* dad(dy); *esp. N.Am:* pa; *Aut:* **marcher à la p.,** to potter along.

papal, -aux [papal, -o], *a.* papal.

papauté [papote], *s.f.* papacy.

pape [pap], *s.m. Ecc:* Pope.

pape|rasse [papras], *s.f. Pej. usu. pl.* official papers; old records, old papers; *F:* bumf; *s.f.* **-rasserie,** (accumulation of) old papers; red tape.

papet|erie [pap(ə)tri], *s.f.* **1.** stationer's shop, trade. **2.** stationery; *s.* **-ier, -ière.**

papier [papje], *s.m.* paper. **1.** (*a*) **p. gris,** brown paper; **p. journal,** newsprint; **p. beurre,** greaseproof paper; **p. à cigarettes,** cigarette paper; *Phot:* **p. sensible,** sensitized paper; **p. autovireur,** self-toning paper; **p. calque,** tracing paper; **p. à lettres,** notepaper; **p. machine,** typing paper; **p. brouillon,** rough paper; **p. démaquillant,** face tissue; **p. hygiénique,** toilet, lavatory, paper, *F:* loo paper; (*b*) **figure de p. mâché,** washed out face. **2.** (*a*) document, paper; **papiers domestiques,** family papers; *Adm:* **papiers (d'identité),** (identity) papers; (*b*) **être bien dans les papiers de qn,** to be in s.o.'s good books; (*c*) **p. timbré,** stamped paper; (*d*) *Com:* bill(s); (*e*) *pl. Nau:* **papiers de bord,** ship's papers. **3. p. d'alu(minium),** aluminium foil.

papillon [papijɔ̃], *s.m.* **1.** butterfly; **p. de nuit,** moth; *Sp:* **(nage) p.,** butterfly (stroke). **2.** inset (in book); *Tchn:* wing-nut.

papillot|er [papijɔte], *v.i.* (*of eyes*) to blink; (*of light*) to twinkle; *Cin:* to flicker; *s.m.* **-ement,** dazzle; flicker.

paquebot [pakbo], *s.m. Nau:* passenger steamer; liner.

pâquerette [pɑkrɛt], *s.f. Bot:* daisy.

Pâques [pɑːk]. **1.** *s.f.pl.* Easter; **joyeuses P.**, happy Easter; **faire ses P.**, to take the Sacrament at Easter; **P. fleuries**, Palm Sunday. **2.** *s.m.* (*contraction of* **jour de Pâques**, *used without article*) **à P. prochain**, next Easter.

paquet [pakɛ], *s.m.* parcel, packet; package; bundle; **p. de gens**, group of people; **p. de lettres**, bundle of letters; **faire un p.**, to do up a parcel; **p. de lessive**, packet of washing powder; **recevoir son p.**, to get a ticking-off; **donner son p. à qn**, to give s.o. the sack; **p. de sottises**, pack of nonsense; *Nau:* **p. de mer**, heavy sea.

par [par], *prep.* **1.** (*a*) (*of place*) by; through; **regarder p. la fenêtre**, to look out of the window; **p. mer et p. terre**, by land and sea; **il court p. les rues**, he runs about the streets; **p. tout le pays**, all over the country; **venez p. ici**, come this way; (*b*) (*of time*) on; in; **p. le passé**, in the past; **p. un jour d'hiver**, on a winter's day; **p. le froid qu'il fait**, in this cold weather. **2.** (*a*) (*showing the agent*) **il a été puni p. son père**, he was punished by his father; **faire qch. p. soi-même**, to do sth. unaided; **je l'ai appris p. les Martin**, I heard of it through, from, the Martins; (*b*) (*showing the means, instrument*) **réussir p. l'intrigue**, to succeed through intrigue; **envoyer qch. p. la poste**, to send sth. by post; **remarquable p. sa beauté**, remarkable for her beauty; (*c*) (*emphasis*) **vous êtes p. trop aimable**, you are far too kind. **3.** (*motive*) **j'ai fait cela p. amitié**, I did it out of friendship; **p. pitié!** for pity's sake! **4.** (*distributive*) **p. ordre alphabétique**, in alphabetical order; **trois fois p. jour**, three times a day. **5. p. + *inf.* commencer p. faire qch.**, to begin by doing sth. **6.** *adv.phr.* **p.-ci, p.-là**, (i) hither and thither; (ii) now and then, at odd times. **7.** *prep.phr.* **de p. le monde**, (i) somewhere in the world; (ii) throughout the world.

para [para], *s.m. F: Mil:* paratrooper.

parabol|e [parabɔl], *s.f.* **1.** parable; **parler en paraboles**, to speak in parables. **2.** *Geom:* parabola; *a. Geom:* **-ique**, parabolic; **radiateur p.**, parabolic reflector; (*of spacecraft*) **vitesse p.**, escape velocity.

parach|ever [paraʃve], *v.tr.* (**je parachève, n. parachevons**) to finish off (a job); to perfect; *s.m.* **-èvement**, finishing; perfecting.

parachute [paraʃyt], *s.m.* parachute.

parachut|er [paraʃyte]. (*a*) *v.tr. & i.* to parachute, to drop by parachute; (*b*) *v.tr.* to pitchfork (s.o. into a job, a situation); *s.m.* **-age**, parachuting; *s.m.* **-iste**, paratrooper.

parade [parad], *s.f.* **1.** *Mil:* parade. **2.** parade, show; **faire p. de ses bijoux**, to show off one's jewels.

parader [parade], *v.i.* **1.** *Mil:* to parade. **2.** to make a display.

paradis [paradi], *s.m.* paradise; *Orn:* **oiseau de p.**, bird of paradise.

paradox|e [paradɔks], *s.m.* paradox; *a.* **-al**, **-aux**, paradoxical; *adv.* **-alement**.

parafer [parafe], *v.tr.* to initial (document).

paraffine [parafin], *s.f. Ch:* paraffin; *Com:* paraffin wax; *Med:* **huile de p.**, liquid paraffin.

parages [paraːʒ], *s.m.pl.* (*a*) *Nau:* sea area; **les p. du Cap Horn**, the waters off Cape Horn; (*b*) **dans les p. de . . .**, near . . .; **que faites-vous dans ces p.?** what are you doing (around) here hereabouts?

paragraphe [paragraf], *s.m.* paragraph.

Paraguay [ləparagwɛ]. *Pr.n.m.* Paraguay (river or republic).

paraître [parɛtr], *v.i.* (*conj. like* CONNAÎTRE) to appear. **1.** (*a*) to make one's appearance; to come in sight; (*b*) (*of book*) to be published **"vient de p.,"** "just published." **2.** (*a*) to be visible, apparent; **cette tache paraît à peine**, the stain hardly shows; **laisser p. ses sentiments**, to show one's feelings; (*b*) **chercher à p.**, to show off, to make a display; *impers.* **il y paraît**, that's easy to see, that's quite apparent; **je suis très mal.—Il n'y paraît pas**, I'm very ill.—you don't look it. **3.** to seem, to look; (*a*) **il paraît triste**, he looks sad; (*b*) *impers.* **il paraît qu'elle fait des vers**, it seems she writes poetry; **à ce qu'il paraît**, (i) apparently; (ii) it would seem so; **il paraît que si, que oui**, so it appears; **paraît que non**, it seems not.

parallèle [paral(l)ɛl]. **1.** *a. & s.f. Geom:* paralle. **2.** *s.m.* (*a*) parallel, comparison; (*b*) *Geo:* parallel (of latitude); *adv.* **-ment**, in a parall. direction; concurrently.

paraly|ser [paralize], *v.tr.* (*a*) to paralyse; (*b*) to incapacitate, to cripple; *a.* **-sateur, -satric** paralysing (agent, etc.); *s.f.* **-sie**, paralysis; *& s. Med:* **-tique**, paralytic.

paraneige [paranɛʒ], *s.m.* snow-shield (ov mountain road, railway).

parapet [parapɛ], *s.m.* parapet.

paraphraser [parafraze], *v.tr.* (*a*) to paraphrase; (*b*) to expand, amplify, add (story, speech).

parapluie [paraplɥi], *s.m.* umbrella; **ouvrir s p.**, (i) to put up one's umbrella; (ii) to dod one's responsibilities; *Mil.Av:* **p. aérien**, aer umbrella.

parasit|e [parazit], *s.m.* **1.** (*a*) *Biol:* parasite; (*b* hanger-on, sponger; (*c*) *T.V: Rad: etc:* noi *pl.* **parasites**, interference, atmospheric statics. **2.** *a.* parasitic; *Rad:* **bruits parasit** interference; *s.m. Rad:* **-age**, interference; **-aire**, parasitic (disease); *a.* **-ique**, parasitic (habits, etc.).

parasol [parasɔl], *s.m.* sunshade; beach umbrella.

paratonnerre [paratɔnɛːr], *s.m.* lightning-conductor.

paravent [paravã], *s.m.* (draught-)screen.

parc [park], *s.m.* 1. park. 2. **p. à voitures,** car park, *N.Am:* parking lot; **p. d'attractions,** funfair; **p. pour enfants,** playpen; **p. à moutons,** sheepfold; **p. à huîtres,** oyster-bed. 3. fleet (of buses, etc.); *s.m.* **-age,** parking (of cars).

parcelle [parsɛl], *s.f.* small fragment; particle (of gold); plot, patch (of land).

parceller [parsɛle], *v.tr.* to divide into lots; to portion out (inheritance); **terrain parcellé,** land divided into (building, etc.) lots.

parce que [pars(ə)kə], *conj.phr.* because.

parchemin [parʃəmɛ̃], *s.m.* parchment; vellum; **papier p.** parchment paper.

parcimon|ie [parsimɔni], *s.f.* stinginess; *a.* **-ieux, -ieuse,** stingy, niggardly; *adv.* **-ieusement,** in a mean, niggardly, way.

par-ci par-là [parsiparla], *adv.* here and there.

parcmètre [parkmɛtr] *s.m.* parking meter.

parcourir [parkuriːr], *v.tr.* (*conj. like* COURIR) 1. to travel through, go over, wander over (country); **p. plusieurs kilomètres,** to cover several kilometres; **p. les mers,** to sail the seas. 2. to examine (cursorily); **p. un livre,** to glance through a book; **son regard parcourut l'horizon,** his eyes swept the horizon.

parcours [parkuːr], *s.m.* 1. (*a*) distance covered; (*b*) route (of bus); course (of river). 2. run, trip.

par-dessous [pardəsu], *prep. & adv.* under, beneath, underneath.

par-dessus [pardəsy], *prep. & adv.* over (the top of); **par-d. le marché,** into the bargain.

pardessus [pardəsy], *s.m.* 1. overcoat. 2. *Fr.C: pl.* overshoes.

pardon [pardɔ̃], *s.m.* pardon; (*a*) forgiveness (of an offence); **je vous demande p.,** I beg your pardon (de, for); **p. de vous avoir retenu,** I'm sorry to have kept you; **p.?** I beg your pardon? what did you say? (*b*) *Jur:* remission of a sentence; (*c*) *Ecc:* (*in Brittany*) (local processional) pilgrimage.

pardonn|er [pardɔne], *v.tr.* to pardon, forgive; (*a*) **pardonnez la liberté que je prends,** excuse the liberty I'm taking; (*b*) **p. à qn,** to pardon s.o.; **pardonnez-moi,** excuse me; *a.* **-able,** forgivable.

pare-boue [parbu], *s.m.inv.* mudguard.

pare-brise [parbriːz], *s.m.inv. Aut: Av: etc:* windscreen, *N.Am:* windshield.

pare-chocs [parʃɔk], *s.m.inv. Aut: N.Am:* bumper, fender.

pareil, -eille [parɛj]. 1. *a.* (*a*) like, alike; similar; (*b*) same, identical; **l'an dernier à p. jour,** this day last year; (*c*) such; like that; **en p. cas,** in such cases. 2. *s.* (*a*) **lui et ses pareils,** he and his

like; (*b*) equal, fellow, match; **il n'a pas son p.,** there's no one like him. 3. *s.f.* **la pareille,** the like; **rendre la pareille à qn,** to give s.o. tit for tat; *adv.* **-lement,** in a similar manner; also, likewise; **à vous p.!** the same to you!

pare-lumière [parlymjɛːr], *s.m.inv. Aut:* anti-dazzle shield.

parent, -ente [parã, -ãːt], *s.* 1. *s.m.pl.* parents; father and mother; **sans parents,** orphaned. 2. (blood) relation, relative; **être p. avec qn,** to be related to s.o.; **c'est une de mes parentes,** she's a relative of mine; **être parents par alliance,** to be connected, related, by marriage; *s.f.* **-aille,** *F: Pej:* **toute la p.,** the whole blessed family.

parenté [parãte], *s.f.* 1. relationship; **il n'y a pas de p. entre eux,** they're not related. 2. *coll.* family; relations.

parenthèse [parãtɛːz], *s.f. Typ:* bracket; **entre parenthèses,** in brackets; **soit dit par p.,** incidentally, by the way.

parer¹ [pare], *v.tr.* 1. to prepare; to dress, trim (meat, leather, timber). 2. to embellish, to decorate (**de,** with).

se parer, to dress oneself up.

parer². 1. *v.tr.* (*a*) to avoid, ward off (a collision, etc.); *Nau:* **p. un cap,** to clear, double, a headland; (*b*) *Box:* to parry, ward off (a blow). 2. *v.ind.tr.* **p. à qch.,** to provide, guard, against sth.; **on ne peut pas p. à tout,** accidents will happen; **p. au plus pressé,** to attend to the most urgent things first, to deal with first things first.

pare-soleil [parsɔlɛj], *s.m.inv. Aut:* sun-visor (on windscreen).

paresse [parɛs], *s.f.* (*a*) laziness, idleness; **par pure p.,** out of sheer laziness; (*b*) sluggishness (of mind, of the liver).

paresseu|x, -euse [parɛsø, -øːz]. 1. *a.* (*a*) lazy, idle; (*b*) sluggish; slow-acting. 2. *s.* lazy person, *F:* lazybones; *adv.* **-sement,** lazily.

parfait [parfɛ]. 1. *a.* perfect; (*a*) faultless; flawless; **en ordre p.,** in perfect order; **(c'est) p.!** excellent! (*b*) complete, thorough. 2. *s.m. Gram:* perfect (tense); *adv.* **-ement,** (i) perfectly; (ii) completely; (iii) quite so, exactly.

parfois [parfwa], *adv.* sometimes, at times.

parfum [parfœ̃], *s.m.* 1. perfume, fragrance, scent (of flower); bouquet (of wine). 2. *Toil:* scent, perfume. 3. flavour (of ice-cream, etc.).

parfum|er [parfyme], *v.tr.* (*a*) to scent (one's handkerchief); **elle se parfume trop,** she uses too much scent; (*b*) **l'air parfumé du soir,** the balmy evening air; (*c*) *Cu:* to flavour (**avec, à,** with); *s.f.* **-erie,** perfumery (and cosmetics) (trade, shop); *s.* **-eur, -euse,** perfumer.

pari [pari], *s.m.* 1. bet, wager. 2. betting; **le p. mutuel** = the Tote.

parier [parje], *v.tr.* (*p.d. & pr.sub. n.* **pariions**) to bet, to wager; **p. le double contre le simple,** to lay two to one; **p. pour, sur, un cheval,** to back a horse; **p. gros,** to bet heavily; **il y a gros à p. que . . .,** *F:* it's a dead cert that . . ..

Paris [pari]. *Pr.n.m. Geog:* Paris; **articles de P.,** fancy goods.

parisien, -ienne [parizjɛ̃, -jɛn], *a. & s.* Parisian; **l'agglomération parisienne,** Greater Paris.

parité [parite], *s.f.* parity; equality (of rank, condition, value); *Fin:* **échange à la p.,** exchange at par; *Atom.Ph:* parity.

parjure [parʒyːr]. **1.** *s.m.* perjury. **2.** *s.* perjurer.

parjurer (se) [səparʒyre], *v.pr.* to perjure oneself; to commit perjury.

parking [parkiŋ], *s.m.* car park, *N.Am:* parking lot.

parlant [parlɑ̃], *a.* speaking; talking; **cinéma p.,** talking cinema; *P.T.T:* **horloge parlante** = "Tim."

parlement [parləmɑ̃], *s.m.* parliament; legislative assembly; *a.* **-aire,** parliamentary.

parlementer [parləmɑ̃te], *v.i.* to parley; to negotiate; to discuss terms (**avec,** with).

parler [parle]. **I.** *v.i.* to speak, talk. **1.** (*a*) **p. haut,** to speak loudly; **p. bas,** to speak (i) in a low voice, (ii) in a whisper; **s'enrouer à force de p.,** to talk oneself hoarse; (*b*) **parlez-vous sérieusement?** are you serious? do you really mean it? **p. pour p.,** to talk for talking's sake; **parlons peu et parlons bien,** let us be brief and to the point; **p. pour ne rien dire,** (i) to make small talk; (ii) to talk drivel; **pour p. franchement . . .,** to put it bluntly . . .; **faire p. qn,** to loosen s.o.'s tongue; **façon de p.,** way of speaking; manner of speech; **c'est une façon de p.,** you can put it like that; **voilà ce qui s'appelle p.!** now you're talking! *P:* **tu parles!** you're telling me! you bet! not half! (*c*) **p. à qn,** to talk to s.o.; **elle a trouvé à qui p.,** she has met her match; (*d*) **il n'en parle jamais,** he never refers to it; **est-ce de moi que vous parlez?** do you mean me? **cela ne vaut pas la peine d'en p.,** it isn't worth mentioning; **entendre p. de qch.,** to hear of sth.; **faire p. de soi,** to get talked about; **on ne parle que de cela,** it's the talk of the town. **2. p. français,** to speak French; **l'anglais se parle partout,** English is spoken everywhere; **p. boutique,** to talk shop. **II. parler,** *s.m.* (way of) speaking; speech, language; **notre p. régional,** our local accent, dialect.

parleur, -euse [parlœːr, -øːz], *s.* talker, speaker.

parmi [parmi], *prep.* among(st), amid(st).

parodier [parɔdje], *v.tr.* (*p.d. & pr. sub. n.* **parodiions**) to parody; to take (s.o.) off; *s.f.* **-die,** parody; skit (**de,** on).

paroi [parwa], *s.f.* **1.** (*a*) (partition-)wall (between rooms); (*b*) wall (of rock); (rock) face; **la p. nord du pic,** the north face of the mountain; *Biol:* **p. d'une cellule,** cell wall. **2.** lining (of tunnel, stomach, etc.).

paroisse [parwas], *s.f.* parish; *a.* **-ial, -iaux** parochial, parish (hall); *s.* **-ien, -ienne** parishioner; *s.m.* **paroissien,** prayer-book.

parole [parɔl], *s.f.* **1.** (spoken) word; remark; **perdre le temps en paroles,** to waste time talking; **cette p. le piqua,** this remark went home. **2.** promise, word; **croire qn sur p.,** to take s.o.'s word; **manquer à sa p.,** to break one's word. **3.** speech, speaking; (*a*) delivery; **avoir la p. facile,** to be an easy speaker; **perdre la p.,** to lose the power of speech; (*b*) **adresser la p. à qn,** to speak to s.o.; **prendre la p.,** (to begin) to speak; **demander la p.,** to request leave to speak.

paroxysme [parɔksism], *s.m.* paroxysm (of anger, laughter, etc.); **être au p. de la colère,** to be in a towering rage.

parpaing [parpɛ̃], *s.m.* parpen; bonder; bond stone; breeze-block.

parquer [parke], *v.tr.* to pen (cattle); to fold (sheep); to park (artillery, cars).

parquet [parke], *s.m.* **1.** *Jur:* (*a*) well of the court; (*b*) public prosecutor's department; **déposer une plainte au p.,** to lodge a complaint in court. **2.** *Const:* (parquet) floor; **p. de chêne,** oak parquet; **p. ciré,** waxed, polished, floor.

parrain [parɛ̃], *s.m.* godfather; sponsor; *s.m.* **-age** [parɛnaːʒ], sponsorship.

parsemer [parsəme], *v.tr.* (**je parsème, parsemons**) to strew, sprinkle; **ciel parsemé d'étoiles,** sky studded with stars.

part [paːr], *s.f.* **1.** share, portion; (*a*) **diviser qch. en plusieurs parts,** to divide sth. into portions; to share sth. out; **avoir la meilleure p.,** to have the best of the bargain; (*b*) **pour ma p.,** as for me, personally (speaking); (*c*) **prendre qch. en bonne, en mauvaise, p.,** to take sth. in good, bad, part. **2.** share, participation; **prendre p. à qch.,** to take part in, to share in, sth.; **avoir p. à qch.,** to have a hand in sth.; **faire p. de qch. à qn,** to inform s.o. of sth.; **faire la p. de qch.,** take sth. into consideration. **3.** (*place where*) *adv.phrs.* **nulle p.,** nowhere; **autre p.,** somewhere else, *N.Am:* some place else; **faire des concessions de p. et d'autre,** to make concessions on both sides; **de p. en p.,** through and through, right through; **d'une p.,** on the one hand; **d'autre p.,** on the other hand; **dites-lui de ma p.,** tell him from me; *P.T.T:* **c'est de la p. de qui?** who's speaking? **4.** *adv.phrs.* **à p.,** apart, separately; **prendre qn à p.,** to take s.o. aside; **mettre de l'argent à p.,** to put money by; **plaisanterie à p.,** joking apart; **à p. quelques exceptions,** with a few exceptions.

partage [partaʒ], *s.m.* **1.** division; (*a*) sharing, division; (*b*) **il y a p. d'opinions,** opinions are divided; **p. d'un pays,** partition of a country; *Geog:* **ligne de p. des eaux,** watershed, *N.Am:* divide. **2.** share, portion, lot; **avoir qch. en**

to receive sth. as one's share.

partag|er [partaʒe], *v.tr.* (**n. partageons**) **1.** to divide; (*a*) to share out; (*b*) **les avis sont partagés**, opinions are divided; **p. le différend**, to split the difference. **2. ils se partagent les bénéfices**, they share the profits between them; **p. les idées de qn**, to agree with s.o.'s views. **3. être bien partagé**, to be well provided for; **c'est vous le mieux partagé**, you have the best of it; *a.* **-eable**, divisible. **se partager**, to divide; (*of river*) to branch; (*of road*) to fork.

partance [partɑ̃:s], *s.f. Nau:* departure; **pavillon de p.**, Blue Peter; **en p. pour**, bound for; *Av:* **avion en p. pour Toulouse**, plane taking off for Toulouse; *Rail:* **prendre le premier train en p.**, to take the first train out.

partant [partɑ̃]. **1.** *a.* departing. **2.** *s.m.* departing guest, traveller, etc.; *Sp: Rac:* starter; **il n'est pas p.**, he's a non-starter.

partenaire [partənɛ:r], *s.m. Games:* partner.

parterre [partɛ:r], *s.m.* **1.** flower-bed. **2.** *Th:* pit.

parti [parti], *s.m.* **1.** (political, etc.) party; **prendre p. pour, contre, qn**, to side with, against, s.o. **2.** (*marriageable person*) **un bon p.**, a good match. **3.** decision, choice; **prendre p.**, to make up one's mind; **prendre le p. de faire qch.**, to decide to do sth.; **en prendre son p.**, to make the best of it; **p. pris**, (i) set purpose; (ii) prejudice. **4.** advantage, profit; **tirer p. de qch.**, to turn sth. to account.

partial, -aux [parsjal, -o], *a.* partial; bias(s)ed; unfair (critic); one-sided; *adv.* **-ement**, with partiality.

partialité [parsjalite], *s.f.* partiality (**envers**, for, to); bias; unfairness.

participe [partisip], *s.m. Gram:* participle.

particip|er [partisipe], *v.i.* **1. p. à qch.**, (*a*) to participate, have a share, in sth.; (*b*) to take a hand in sth. **2. p. de**, to partake of, have some of the characteristics of (sth.); *s.* **-ant, -ante**, participator; *s.f.* **-ation**.

particular|iser [partikylarize], *v.tr.* **1.** to particularize (a case). **2.** to specify (details); to give particulars of (sth.); *s.f.* **-ité**, detail; peculiarity. **se particulariser**, to distinguish oneself from others (**par**, through); *Pej:* to make oneself conspicuous.

particule [partikyl], *s.f.* **1.** particle, *F:* atom; **une p. de sable**, a grain of sand. **2.** *Gram:* particle; **la p. = de** (before surname).

particul|ier, -ière [partikylje, -jɛ:r]. **1.** *a.* (*a*) particular, special; (*b*) peculiar, characteristic; (*c*) unusual, uncommon; (*d*) private (room, lesson); personal (account, secretary). **2.** *s.* private person; **simple p.**, private individual. **3.** *adv.phr.* **en p.**, particularly, in particular; **recevoir qn en p.**, to receive s.o. privately; *adv.*

-ièrement, particularly, specially.

partie [parti], *s.f.* **1.** part (of a whole); *Gram:* pl. parts (of speech); **les parties du corps**, the parts of the body; **en grande p.**, to a great extent; **vendre qch. par parties**, to sell sth. in lots; **tenue des livres en p. double**, double entry book-keeping. **2.** (*a*) party; **voulez-vous être de la p.?** will you join us? (*b*) game, match, contest; *F:* **vous avez la p. belle**, now's your chance! **3.** *Jur:* party (to dispute); **avoir affaire à forte p.**, to have a powerful opponent to deal with; **prendre qn à p.**, to take s.o. to task.

partiel, -elle [parsjɛl], *a.* partial, incomplete; *adv.* **-lement**, partially, in part.

partir [parti:r], *v.i.* (*conj. like* MENTIR. *Aux.* être) **1.** (*a*) to depart, leave, start; to set out; to go away; **je pars d'ici**, I'm leaving here; **p. pour, à, Paris**, to leave for, to set out for, Paris; **p. pour les vacances**, to go away for the holidays; *Sp:* **partez!** go! **p. au galop**, to set off at a gallop; **nous voilà partis!** now we're off! (*b*) to part, to give way; to break; (*of button, etc.*) to come off; **la corde part!** the rope's breaking! (*of gun*) to go off; **p. d'un éclat de rire**, to burst out laughing; (*c*) to emanate, spring (from); **il est parti de rien**, he started from nothing; (*d*) *adv.phr.* **à p. de**, (i) à **p. d'aujourd'hui**, from today (onward); (ii) à **p. du 15**, on and after the 15th; (iii) à **p. de trois heures**, after three o'clock. **2. faire p.**, to send off, dispatch (troops, etc.); to fire (gun); to let off (fireworks); to start (engine); **faire p. qn**, to send s.o. away; to turn s.o. out.

partisan, -ane [partizɑ̃, -an]. **1.** *s.* partisan, follower; *Pol:* backer. **2.** *s.m. Mil:* guer(r)illa (soldier), partisan.

partition [partisjɔ̃], *s.f.* **1.** partition, division. **2.** *Mus:* score.

partout [partu], *adv.* (*a*) everywhere; on all sides; in every direction; **un peu p.**, all over the place; almost everywhere; (*b*) all; all together; *Ten:* **quatre jeux p.**, four all.

parure [pary:r], *s.f.* **1.** (action of) ornamenting, adorning. **2.** (*a*) dress, finery; (*b*) ornament; set of jewellery, of collar and cuffs, etc.

parvenir [parvəni:r], *v.i.* (*conj. like* VENIR. *Aux.* être) **1.** to arrive; **p. à un endroit**, to reach a place; **votre lettre m'est parvenue**, your letter has reached me; **faire p. qch. à qn**, to forward sth. to s.o. **2.** (*a*) to reach (a great age); **p. à un accord**, to reach an agreement; **p. à faire qch.**, to manage to do sth.; (*b*) to succeed in life.

parvenu [parvəny], *s.* parvenu, upstart; **les parvenus**, the newly rich.

parvis [parvi], *s.m.* square (in front of a church).

pas¹ [pɑ], *s.m.* **1.** step, pace, stride; (*a*) **mesurer une distance au p.**, to pace off a distance; **allonger le p.**, to step out; **j'y vais de ce p.**, I am going at once; **marcher à grands p.**, to stride along; **faux p.,** (i) slip, stumble; (ii) (social) blunder; **avoir le p. sur qn,** to have precedence over s.o.; (b) **au p.,** at a walking pace; **avancer au p. gymnastique,** to advance at the double; **marquer le p.,** to mark time. **2.** footprint, footmarks, tracks. **3.** step (of stair); threshold; **le p. de la porte,** the door-step; *Com:* **p. de porte,** goodwill. **4.** passage; (mountain) pass; strait; **le P. de Calais,** the Straits of Dover; **mauvais p.,** tight corner; **sauter le p.,** to take the plunge. **5.** *Tchn:* **p. de vis,** thread of screw.

pas², *neg.adv.* **1.** not; **je ne sais p.,** I don't know; **p. moi,** not I; **nous marchons peu ou p.,** we walk little or not at all; *F:* **p. vrai?** really? **p. du tout,** not at all; (strengthening non) **non p. qu'il soit beau,** not that he's handsome; **non p.!** not at all! **2. p. un,** (a) **p. un mot ne fut dit,** not a word was spoken; (b) **il connaît Paris mieux que p. un,** he knows Paris better than anyone.

passable [pɑsabl], *a.* passable, tolerable; so so; *adv.* **-ment.**

passage [pɑsaːʒ], *s.m.* passage. **1.** crossing (of sth.); passing over; going past (a place); (a) **guetter le p. de qn,** to lie in wait for s.o.; **livrer p. à qn,** to allow s.o. to pass; **p. d'un train,** passing of a train; **j'attends le p. du facteur,** I'm waiting for the postman to pass; **droit de p.,** right of way; *P.N:* **p. interdit au public,** no thoroughfare; **être de p. dans une ville,** to be only passing through a town; (b) *Nau:* **payer son p.,** to pay for one's passage; (c) **p. du jour à la nuit,** transition from day to night; *Meteor:* **p. pluvieux,** rainy interval. **2.** (a) way, way through; **p. souterrain,** subway; **p. clouté,** pedestrian crossing; *Nau:* channel; (b) arcade; (c) *Rail:* **p. à niveau,** level crossing. **3.** passage (in book).

passag|er, -ère [pɑsaʒe, -ɛːr]. **1.** *a.* (a) **oiseau p.,** bird of passage; migratory bird; (b) fleeting, transitory (beauty, etc.); (c) **rue passagère,** busy thoroughfare. **2.** *s.* passenger; *adv.* **-ère-ment,** for a short time; momentarily.

passant, -ante [pɑsɑ̃, -ɑ̃ːt], *s.* passer-by.

passe [pɑs], *s.f.* **1.** (a) *Fb: etc:* pass; **p. en avant, en arrière,** forward, back, pass; *Ten:* **p. de jeu,** rally; *Fenc:* pass, thrust; (b) **p. d'armes,** passage of arms; (c) **mot de p.,** password. **2.** *Nau:* fairway; navigable channel. **3.** **être en mauvaise p.,** to be in a tight corner; **être en bonne p.,** to be in a strong position; **race en p. de disparaître,** race threatened with extinction.

passé, -ée [pɑse]. **1.** *a.* (a) past (time, event); **la semaine passée,** last week; **il est quatre heures passées,** it's after four; (b) over; **l'orage est p.,** the storm's over; (c) faded (colour, material). **2.** *s.m.* **le p.,** the past, former times; *Gram:* past (tense). **3.** *prep.* **p. cette date,** after this date.

passe-partout [pɑspartu], *s.m.inv.* **1.** master-key. **2.** crosscut saw.

passe-passe [pɑspɑs], *s.m. no pl.* **tour de p.-p.,** conjuring trick.

passe-plat [pɑspla], *s.m.* serving hatch; *pl.* **passe-plats.**

passeport [pɑspɔːr], *s.m.* passport.

passer [pɑse]. **I.** *v.i.* **1.** (aux. avoir or être) to pass; to go past; to proceed; **p. sur un pont,** to cross a bridge; **faire p. le plat,** to hand the dish round; **par où est-il, a-t-il, passé?** which way did he go? **je ne peux pas p.,** I can't get by; **se ranger pour laisser p. qn,** to stand aside to make room for s.o.; **laissez p.,** admit bearer; *adv.phr.* **en passant,** by the way; **dire qch. en passant,** to mention sth. casually; **p. son chemin,** to go one's way; **(faire) p. le café,** to filter the coffee. **2.** (aux. être) **p. chez qn,** to call on s.o.; **est-ce que le facteur est passé?** has the postman been? **3.** (aux. avoir) to undergo, pass through (sorrow, sickness); **j'ai passé par là,** I've been through it; **tout le monde y passe,** it happens to us all. **4.** (aux. avoir) to pass away; (a) to disappear, to cease; **la douleur a passé,** the pain has passed off, gone; **p. de mode,** to go out of fashion; **couleurs qui passent,** colours that fade; (b) to elapse, to go by; **comme le temps passe (vite)!** how (quickly) time flies! **faire p. le temps,** to pass the time. **5.** (aux. avoir or être) to die. **6.** *pred.* (a) (aux. avoir or être) to become; **p. capitaine,** to be promoted captain; (b) (aux. avoir) **p. pour,** to be considered, to pass for; **se faire p. pour,** to pass oneself off as. **7.** (aux. avoir) to be accepted, to pass muster; **qu'il revienne demain, passe encore,** if he returns tomorrow well and good; **cela ne passe pas,** that won't do; **enfin, passe pour lui!** well, that's all right as far as he is concerned. **II. passer,** *v.tr.* **1.** to pass, cross (a bridge, the sea); **p. la frontière,** to cross the frontier. **2.** (a) to carry across; to ferry (goods) over; **passer des marchandises en fraude,** to smuggle in goods; (b) **p. qch. à qn,** to hand sth. to s.o.; **je vous passe sa secrétaire,** I'll put you through to his secretary; *Cin:* to show (film); (c) **p. sa tête par la fenêtre,** to put one's head in at the window; **p. une chemise,** to slip on a shirt. **3.** to pass, spend (time). **4.** to exceed, go beyond; **cela passe ma capacité,** that's beyond my powers; **cela passe la mesure,** that's going too far. **5.** to pass over; (a) to excuse (fault); **je vous passe cela,** I grant you that; (b) to omit, leave out; **p. qch. sous silence,** to pass over sth. in silence. **6.** (a) **p. une loi,** to pass a law; (b) **p. un examen,** to sit for an examination. **7.** to strain (liquid); to sift (flour); **p. le café,** to percolate the coffee.

se passer. 1. to happen; to take place; **que se passe-t-il?** what's happening? *F:* what's up? (a) to pass away, to cease; (of fashion) not last; **mon mal de tête se passe,** my headache is passing off, is going; **cela ne se passera pas ainsi,** I shall not let it rest at that; (*b*) (*of flowers, colours, beauty*) to fade. **3. se p. de qch.,** to do without sth.

passerelle [pɑsrɛl], *s.f.* 1. footbridge. 2. *Nau:* bridge; **p. de débarquement, d'embarquement,** gangway; *Av:* (passenger) steps.

passe-temps [pɑstɑ̃], *s.m.inv.* pastime, diversion; hobby.

passe-thé [pɑste], *s.m.inv.* tea-strainer.

passeur, -euse [pɑsœːr, -øːz], *s.* 1. (*a*) ferryman, ferrywoman; (*b*) *Pol:* **p. (de frontière),** frontier runner, escape agent.

passible [pɑsibl], *a.* liable (**de,** to, for).

pass|if, -ive [pasif, -iːv]. 1. *a.* (*a*) passive (obedience); *Gram:* **voix passive,** passive voice; (*b*) *Com:* **dettes passives,** liabilities. 2. *s.m.* (*a*) *Gram:* passive; (*b*) *Com:* debt; *adv.* **-ivement.**

passion [pɑsjɔ̃], *s.f.* 1. **la P.,** the Passion (of Christ). 2. **p. pour la musique,** passion for music; **éprouver une grande p. pour qn,** to be passionately in love with s.o.; **parler avec, sans, p.,** to speak passionately, dispassionately.

passionnant [pɑsjɔnɑ̃], *a.* entrancing, thrilling; exciting (story, episode).

passionné, -ée [pɑsjɔne], *a.* passionate (love; prejudice for, against, s.o., sth.); *s.* enthusiast, *F:* fan; *adv.* **-ment.**

passionnel, -elle [pɑsjɔnɛl], *a.* pertaining to the passions; **crime p.,** crime due to jealousy, crime passionnel.

passionner [pɑsjɔne], *v.tr.* to impassion; to excite (s.o.) with passion; to interest passionately, to intrigue; **le sport le passionne,** he's passionately keen on sport; **livre qui passionne,** thrilling book.

se passionner de, pour, qch., to become enthusiastic about sth.

passoire [pɑswɑːr], *s.f. Cu:* strainer; **p. à légumes,** colander; (flour, sugar) sifter.

pastel [pastɛl], *s.m. Art:* pastel.

pastèque [pastɛk], *s.f.* water-melon.

pasteur [pastœːr], *s.m.* 1. shepherd. 2. *Ecc:* (Protestant) minister.

pasteuris|er [pastœrize], *v.tr.* to pasteurize (milk, etc.); *s.f.* **-ation.**

pastille [pɑstiːj], *s.f.* lozenge; **p. de chocolat,** chocolate drop.

pastoral, -aux [pastɔral, -o], *a.* pastoral (life; poetry; *Ecc:* letter).

pataug|er [patoʒe], *v.i.* (**n. pataugeons**) (*a*) to flounder (in the mud); (*b*) to paddle (in sea); *s.m.* **-eage,** floundering (in mud, in a speech); *s.* **-eur, -euse,** flounderer; paddler.

pâte [pɑːt], *s.f.* 1. (*a*) *Cu:* paste; pastry; **p. à pain,** dough; **p. brisée,** short pastry; *pl.* **pâtes** (**alimentaires**), pasta, noodles; **mettre la main à la p.,** to lend a hand; (*b*) (paper) pulp; (*c*) **p. dentifrice,** tooth-paste.

pâté [pɑte], *s.m.* 1. (*a*) *Cu:* **p. en croûte,** (meat) pie; (*b*) pâté; **p. en terrine,** potted meat; **p. de foie,** liver pâté. 2. block (of houses). 3. blot, blob (of ink).

patelin [patlɛ̃], *s.m. F:* village, small place; **c'est mon p.,** that's my village, my birthplace; **quel sale p.!** what a dump!

patente [patɑ̃ːt], *s.f.* licence (to exercise a trade).

patère [patɛːr], *s.f.* hat-peg, coat-peg.

paternel, -elle [patɛrnɛl], *a.* paternal; **du côté p.,** on the father's side; *adv.* **-lement.**

paternité [patɛrnite], *s.f.* paternity, fatherhood.

pâteux, -euse [pɑtø, -øːz], *a.* (*a*) pasty, clammy; **pain p.,** doughy bread; **bouche pâteuse,** dry mouth; (*b*) thick (voice); muddy (ink).

pathétique [patetik]. 1. *a.* pathetic, moving, touching (story, situation). 2. *s.m.* pathos, the pathetic; *adv.* **-ment.**

patholo|gie [patɔlɔʒi], *s.f.* pathology; *a.* **-gique,** pathological; *s.m. & f.* **-giste.**

patibulaire [patibylɛːr], *a.* relating to the gallows; **une mine p.,** a hangdog look.

patience [pasjɑ̃ːs], *s.f.* patience, long-suffering; **être à bout de p.,** to be out of patience; **jeu de p.,** puzzle, *esp.* jig-saw puzzle.

pati|ent, -ente [pasjɑ̃, -ɑ̃ːt]. 1. *a.* patient; (*a*) long-suffering; forbearing; (*b*) enduring, patient (under suffering). 2. *s.* (surgical) patient; *adv.* **-emment.**

patienter [pasjɑ̃te], *v.i.* to exercise patience; to wait patiently.

patin [patɛ̃], *s.m.* (*a*) skate; **patins à roulettes,** roller skates; (*b*) runner (of sledge); brake shoe, brake block; (*c*) *H:* felt sole (for polishing floors).

patine [patin], *s.f.* patina (on bronze, etc.).

patin|er [patine], *v.i.* 1. to skate; to roller-skate. 2. (*of wheel*) to skid; (*of belt, clutch*) to slip; *Aut:* **p. sur place,** to spin; *s.m.* **-age,** skating; *s.* **-eur, -euse,** skater; *s.f.* **-oire,** skating, ice, rink.

patinette [patinɛt], *s.f.* (child's) scooter.

pâtiss|erie [pɑtisri], *s.f.* 1. pastry; fancy cake. 2. pastry-, cake-, making. 3. teashop; confectioner's (trade, shop); *s.* **-ier, -ière,** pastry cook; confectioner.

patois [patwa], *s.m.* (*a*) patois; provincial dialect; (*b*) jargon.

patraque [patrak], *a. F:* **se sentir p.,** to feel seedy, out of sorts, off colour.

patriar|che [patriarʃ], *s.m.* patriarch; *a.* **-cal, -caux;** *adv.* **-calement.**

patrie [patri], *s.f.* fatherland; native land; **mère p.,** mother country.

patrimoine [patrimwan], *s.m.* heritage.

patriot|e [patriɔt]. 1. *a.* patriotic. 2. *s.* patriot; **il**

est mauvais p., he's unpatriotic; *a.* -**ique**; *adv.* -**iquement**; *s.m.* -**isme.**

patron, -onne [patrɔ̃, -ɔn], *s.* **1.** patron (saint). **2.** (*a*) master, mistress (of house); employer; head (of firm); proprietor; owner, *F:* boss; (*b*) *Nau:* skipper. **3.** *s.m.* pattern (for dress); model; (**taille**) **p.,** stock size; *s.m.* -**age,** patronage, support.

patrouill|e [patru:j], *s.f.* patrol; *v.i.* -**er,** to patrol; *s.m.* -**eur,** patrol boat, ship, aircraft.

patte [pat], *s.f.* **1.** paw; foot (of bird); leg (of insect); **marcher à quatre pattes,** to go on all fours; **animaux à quatre pattes,** four-footed animals; **pattes de devant, de derrière,** forelegs, hind legs; **faire p. de velours,** (i) (*of cat*) to draw in its claws; (ii) to show the velvet glove; **tomber sous la p. de qn,** to fall into s.o.'s clutches. **2.** flap (of pocket); tab, strap (on garment).

patte-d'oie [patdwa], *s.f.* **1.** cross-roads; fork; Y-junction. **2.** crow's-foot (wrinkle); *pl. pattes-d'oie.*

pâture [paty:r], *s.f.* **1.** food, feed, fodder (of animals). **2.** pasture.

pâtur|er [patyre], *v.i.* (*of cattle, etc.*) to graze, to feed; *s.m.* -**age,** (i) grazing; (ii) pasture.

paume [po:m], *s.f.* **1.** palm (of hand). **2.** (**jeu de**) **p.,** (i) (real) tennis; (ii) (real) tennis-court.

paupér|iser [poperize], *v.tr.* to reduce (s.o., a class of people) to destitution; *s.f.* -**isation;** *s.m.* -**isme.**

paupière [popjɛ:r], *s.f.* eyelid.

pause [po:z], *s.f.* pause. **1.** *Ind: etc:* meal-break; **p.-café,** coffee break, (=) tea break; **faire une p.,** to pause. **2.** *Mus:* rest.

pauvre [po:vr]. **1.** *a.* poor; (*a*) needy, in want; **un homme p.,** a poor man; (*b*) unfortunate; **le p. homme!** poor fellow! **p. de moi!** poor me! (*c*) wretched; shabby; **un p. dîner,** a wretched dinner; **assis auprès d'un p. feu,** seated by a miserable little fire; *F:* **p. idiot!** silly fool! **2.** *s.* poor man, poor woman; pauper; *adv.* -**ment,** poorly, wretchedly; **p. vêtu,** shabbily dressed; *s.f.* -**té,** poverty, want.

pavaner (se) [səpavane], *v.pr.* to strut (about); to show off.

pavé [pave], *s.m.* **1.** paving-stone, -block. **2.** pavement; **p. en briques, en béton,** brick, concrete, pavement; the streets; **battre le p.,** (i) to loaf about the streets; (ii) to tramp the streets (looking for work); **mettre qn sur le p.,** to turn s.o. out of his job.

pav|er [pave], *v.tr.* to pave; *F:* **les rues en sont pavées,** it's, they're, as common as dirt; *s.m.* -**age,** paving; **carreau de p.,** flagstone, paving flag.

pavillon [pavijɔ̃], *s.m.* **1.** detached house; **p. de banlieue,** suburban house; **p. de jardin,** summer-house; **p. de chasse,** shooting-lodge.

2. *Nau:* flag, colours; **p. de poupe,** ensign; **p. de départ,** Blue Peter; **hisser son p.,** to hoist one's colours; **saluer du p.,** to dip the flag.

pavois|er [pavwaze], *v.tr.* to deck (ship, streets, etc.) with flags, with bunting; **rues pavoisées,** streets gay with bunting; *s.m.* -**ement.**

pavot [pavo], *s.m. Bot:* poppy.

paye [pɛ:j], *s.f.* **1.** pay; wages. **2.** payment; **jour de p.,** payday.

payer [peje], *v.tr.* (je paye, je paie) (*a*) **p. qn,** to pay s.o.; **se faire p.,** to collect one's money; **trop payé, trop peu payé,** overpaid, underpaid; **p. qn de paroles,** to put s.o. off with fine words; **p. de sa personne,** (i) to risk one's own skin; (ii) to do one's bit; **p. d'audace,** to take the risk; **p. d'effronterie,** to put a bold face on it; (*b*) to pay, settle (debt); (*c*) to pay for (sth.); **p. qch. à qn,** to pay s.o. for sth.; **p. un dîner à qn,** to stand s.o. a dinner; **je me suis payé une glace,** I treated myself to an icecream; **se p. la tête de qn,** to make fun of s.o.; **cela ne se paie pas,** money cannot buy it; **vous me le paierez!** I'll make you pay for, be sorry for, this! **port payé,** carriage paid, postage paid.

pays [pe(j)i], *s.m.* country; (*a*) land; **un p. étranger,** a foreign country; **les p. chauds,** the tropics; **voir du p.,** to travel a great deal, to see the world; (*b*) region, district, locality; **p. perdu,** out-of-the-way place; **être en p. de connaissance,** to be among friends; **vin du p.,** local wine; (*c*) **p. de montagne(s),** hill country; *pl.* **p. bas,** lowlands; **p. côtier,** seaboard, coastal country; (*d*) native land; home; **avoir le mal du p.,** to be homesick.

paysag|e [peiza:ʒ], *s.m.* **1.** landscape; scenery. **2.** *Art:* landscape (painting); *s.m.* -**iste** landscape painter, -gardener.

paysan, -anne [peizɑ̃, -an]. **1.** *s.* countryman -woman; farmer; farm labourer. **2.** *a.* country rustic.

Pays-Bas (les) [lepeiba]. *Pr.n.m.* the Netherlands.

péag|e [pea:ʒ], *s.m.* **1.** toll; **pont, autoroute, à p.** toll bridge, motorway. **2.** toll-house; *s.* -**er** -**ère,** toll collector.

peau, -eaux [po], *s.f.* **1.** skin; **à même la p.,** next to the skin; **à fleur de p.,** skin-deep; **prendre qn par la p. du cou,** to take s.o. by the scruff of th neck; **sauver sa p.,** to save one's bacon; *F* **avoir qn dans la p.,** to be crazy about s.o. **2** pelt, fur; hide, leather. **3.** peel, skin (of fruit). **4** coating; film, skin (of boiled milk, etc.).

pêch|e¹ [pɛ:ʃ], *s.f.* peach; *s.m.* -**er¹,** peach tree

pêche², *s.f.* **1.** fishing; **p. à la ligne,** angling; **p. à l mouche,** fly-fishing. **2.** catch (of fish). **3** fishery; **grande p.,** deep-sea fishing; **p. côtièr** inshore fishing; **p. au chalut,** trawling.

péché [peʃe], *s.m.* sin; transgression; **les péché capitaux,** the deadly sins; **son p. mignon,** h besetting sin; **péchés de jeunesse,** indiscretions of youth.

pécher [peʃe], *v.i.* (je **pèche;** je **pécherai**) to sin; to err; to offend against (conventions, etc.).

pêcher² [peʃe], *v.tr.* **1.** to fish for (trout, etc.); **p. à la ligne,** to angle; **p. la baleine,** to hunt whales. **2. p. une truite,** to catch a trout; *F:* **où avez-vous pêché cela?** where did you get hold of that?

pécheur, pécheresse [peʃœːr, peʃrɛs], *s.* sinner, offender, transgressor; **vieux p.,** hardened old sinner.

pêcheur, -euse [peʃœːr, -øːz]. **1.** *s.* fisher; fisherman, -woman; **p. à la ligne,** angler; **p. de perles, de corail,** pearl, coral, diver. **2.** *s.m.* fishing boat.

pécule [pekyl], *s.m.* savings; nest-egg; **perdre son p.,** to lose all one's savings; *Mil: etc:* gratuity (on discharge).

pédale [pedal], *s.f.* pedal; treadle (of lathe, etc.); **frein à p.,** footbrake; **p. d'embrayage,** clutch pedal; *Mus:* **petite, grande, p.,** soft, loud, pedal.

pédaller [pedale], *v.i.* to pedal; to cycle; *s.* **-eur, -euse,** pedal(l)er; cyclist.

pédalo [pedalo], *s.m.* pedal craft; water bicycle.

pédant, -ante [pedã, -ãːt]. **1.** *s.* pedant. **2.** *a.* pedantic; *a.* **-esque,** pedantic; *s.m.* **-isme,** pedantry.

pédialtrie [pedjatri], *s.f. Med:* pediatrics; *s.m. & f.* **-tre,** pediatrician.

pédicure [pedikyːr], *s.m. & f.* chiropodist.

peigne [pɛɲ], *s.m.* comb.

peignler [peɲe], *v.tr.* to comb (out); **mal peigné,** slatternly (person); tousled (hair); *s.m.* **-oir,** dressing-gown.

se peigner, to comb one's hair.

peindre [pɛ̃ːdr], *v.tr.* (*pr.p.* **peignant;** *p.p.* **peint;** *pr.ind.* **je peins;** *p.h.* **je peignis**) **1.** to paint; **p. qch. en vert,** to paint sth. green; **p. au pistolet,** to paint with a spray-gun; **p. une carte,** to colour a map; **papier peint,** wallpaper. **2. p. un coucher de soleil,** to paint a sunset; **p. à l'huile, à l'aquarelle,** to paint in oils, in water colours; **cette action le peint bien,** that action is typical of him.

peine [pɛn], *s.f.* **1.** punishment, penalty; **p. capitale,** capital punishment; **sous p. de mort,** on pain of death. **2.** (*a*) sorrow, affliction; **faire de la p. à qn,** to grieve, distress, s.o.; **cela fait p. à voir,** it is painful to see; **être en p. de qn,** to worry about s.o.; (*b*) **être dans la p.,** to be in distress, in trouble. **3.** pains, trouble; **prendre, se donner, de la p. pour faire qch.,** to take trouble over doing sth.; **donnez-vous la p. de vous asseoir,** please take a seat; **c'est p. perdue,** it's a waste of effort, of time; **c'était bien la p. de venir!** we might as well have stayed at home! **homme de p.,** odd-job man. **4.** difficulty; *adv.phr.* **à**

grand-p., with great difficulty. **5.** *adv.phr.* **à p.,** hardly, barely, scarcely.

peiner [pene]. **1.** *v.tr.* to pain, distress, upset (s.o.). **2.** *v.i.* to toil, labour; **il est toujours à p.,** he's always hard at it; *Aut:* **le moteur peine,** the engine's labouring.

peintre [pɛ̃ːtr], *s.m.* painter. **1.** (**artiste**) **p.,** artist; **une femme p.,** a woman artist, painter. **2. p. en bâtiment(s),** house-painter.

peinture [pɛ̃tyːr], *s.f.* **1.** painting; **faire de la p.,** to paint. **2.** picture, painting. **3.** paint, colour; **"attention à la p.!"** "wet paint."

Pékin [pekɛ̃]. *Pr.n.m. Geog:* Peking.

pékinois, -oise [pekinwa, -waːz], (*a*) *a. & s.* Pekin(g)ese, of Peking; (*b*) *s.m.* (*dog*) pekin(g)ese, *F:* peke.

pelage [pəlaːʒ], *s.m.* coat, wool, fur (of animal).

pelé [pəle], *a.* bald; bare, hairless (skin); **campagne pelée,** bare countryside.

pêle-mêle [pɛlmɛl]. **1.** *adv.* pell-mell, higgledy-piggledy. **2.** *s.m.inv.* jumble; medley; confusion; muddle.

peler [pə(ə)le], (je **pèle**) **1.** *v.tr.* to peel, skin (fruit, etc.). **2.** *v.i.* (*of skin, etc.*) to peel.

pèlerin, *f.* (*rare*) **-ine** [pɛlrɛ̃, -in], *s.* pilgrim; *s.m.* **-age,** pilgrimage.

pelle [pɛl], *s.f.* **1.** shovel, scoop; dustpan; (child's) spade; *Civ.E:* **p. automatique,** grab; power shovel; *F:* **ramasser une p.,** to come a cropper. **2.** blade (of oar); *s.f.* **-tée,** spadeful, shovelful.

pellelterie [pɛltri], *s.f.* **1.** *coll.* fur-skins, pelts. **2.** fur-trade; *s.* **-tier, -tière,** furrier.

pellicule [pel(l)ikyl], *s.f.* **1.** (*a*) thin skin; film (of ice, oil); (*b*) *Phot:* film. **2.** *pl.* scurf, dandruff.

pelote [pə(ə)lɔt], *s.f.* **1.** ball (of wool); **avoir les nerfs en p.,** to be nervy, on edge; *F:* **faire sa (petite) p.,** to make one's pile; to feather one's nest. **2.** *Sp:* **p. basque,** pelota.

peloton [pə(ə)lɔtɔ̃], *s.m.* **1.** group (of people); *Sp:* **le p.,** the ruck (of runners in a race). **2.** *Mil:* squad, party.

pelouse [pə(ə)luːz], *s.f.* lawn; grass-plot; green (sward); *Golf:* **p. d'arrivée,** (putting-)green.

peluche [pə(ə)lyʃ], *s.f. Tex:* plush; **ours en p.,** teddy-bear.

pelure [pə(ə)lyːr], *s.f.* peel, skin; paring; rind; **p. d'oignon,** dark rosé wine; *Com:* **papier p.,** (i) copying paper; (ii) onion skin paper.

pénal, -aux [penal, -o], *a.* penal (code).

pénaliser [penalize], *v.tr. Sp: Games:* to penalize (a competitor, a player); *s.f.* **-ation.**

pénalité [penalite], *s.f. Jur: Sp:* penalty.

penaud [pəno], *a.* crestfallen; **d'un air p.,** shamefacedly, sheepishly.

penchant [pãʃã]. **1.** *a.* sloping, inclined, leaning (wall, tower). **2.** *s.m.* (*a*) slope; (*b*) **p. à, pour, vers, qch.,** tendency to, leaning towards, sth.

pencher [pãʃe], *v.* to incline, bend, lean. **1.** *v.tr.* **p.**

la tête en avant, to lean forward. 2. *v.i.* to lean (over); to incline; **faire p. la balance,** to turn the scale.
se pencher, to bend, stoop, lean; (*a*) **se p.** (**en, au**) **dehors,** to lean out; (*b*) **se p. sur** (**un sujet**), to study (a subject); **se p. sur les malheurs de qn,** to feel for s.o.'s misfortunes.
pendant [pɑ̃dɑ̃]. **I.** *a.* **1.** hanging, pendent; **joues pendantes,** flabby cheeks. **2.** pending (lawsuit); **la question reste pendante,** the question remains in abeyance, in suspense. **II. pendant,** *s.m.* **1.** pendant; **p. d'oreille,** drop earring. **2.** match, fellow; **ces deux tableaux** (**se**) **font p.,** these two pictures make a pair. **III. pendant,** *prep.* during; **je lis p. le repas,** I read during my meal; **p. l'été,** in summer; **p. trois jours,** for three days; *conj.phr.* **p. que,** while, whilst.
penderie [pɑ̃dri], *s.f.* hanging cupboard, wardrobe.
pendre [pɑ̃:dr]. **1.** *v.tr.* (*a*) to hang (sth.) up; **p. le linge,** to hang out the washing; (*b*) to hang (on the gallows). **2.** *v.i.* to hang (down), to sag.
pendu [pɑ̃dy]. **1.** *a.* hanged, hung; hanging (lamp, etc.); **avoir la langue bien pendue,** to be a great talker. **2.** *s.* person who has been hanged.
pendule [pɑ̃dyl]. **1.** *s.m.* pendulum. **2.** *s.f.* clock.
pénétr|er [penetre], *v.* (**je pénètre; je pénétrerai**) to penetrate. **1.** *v.i.* to enter; **l'eau avait pénétré partout,** the water had got in everywhere. **2.** *v.tr.* to penetrate, to pierce, to fathom; (*a*) **p. la pensée de qn,** to see through s.o.; **p. un secret,** to fathom a secret; (*b*) **votre lettre m'a pénétré de douleur,** your letter has filled me with grief; *s.f.* **-abilité;** *a.* **-able;** *a.* **-ant,** penetrating, sharp (wind, glance); *s.f.* **-ation,** penetration; insight, acuteness (of mind); shrewdness.
pénible [penibl], *a.* **1.** laborious, arduous, hard (task, etc.). **2.** painful, distressing (sight, news); sad (life, event); *adv.* **-ment.**
péniche [peniʃ], *s.f.* barge; canal-boat; lighter; *Mil:* **p. de débarquement,** landing craft.
pénicilline [penisilin], *s.f. Med:* penicillin.
péninsul|e [penɛ̃syl], *s.f.* peninsula; *a.* **-aire,** peninsular.
pénit|ence [penitɑ̃:s], *s.f.* **1.** penitence, repentance. **2.** penance; **mettre un enfant en p.,** to punish a child; **il est en p.,** he's in disgrace; *s.m.* **-encier,** reformatory (prison); *a. & s.* **-ent, -ente,** penitent.
Pennsylvanie (**la**) [lapɑ̃silvani, -pɛ̃-]. *Pr.n.f. Geog:* Pennsylvania.
pénombre [penɔ̃:br], *s.f.* half-light, semi-darkness.
pensée[1] [pɑ̃se], *s.f. Bot:* pansy.
pensée[2], *s.f.* thought; **perdu dans ses pensées,** lost in thought; **saisir la p. de qn,** to grasp s.o.'s

meaning; **libre p.,** free thinking.
pens|er [pɑ̃se], *v.* to think. **1.** *v.ind.tr.* **p. à qn, à qch.,** to think of s.o., sth.; **je l'ai fait sans y p.,** I did it without thinking; (**y**) **pensez-vous!** what an idea! **vous n'y pensez pas!** you don't mean it! **ah, j'y pense!** by the way! **rien que d'y p.,** the mere thought (of it); **faire p. qn à qch.,** to remind s.o. of sth. **2.** *v.i.* **manière de p.,** attitude of mind; **pensez donc!** *F:* just fancy! **3.** *v.tr.* (*a*) **je le pensais bien,** I thought as much; (*b*) **je le pense fou,** I think he's mad; (*c*) **p. du bien de qn,** to think well of s.o.; (*d*) **je pense le voir demain,** I expect to see him tomorrow; **j'ai pensé mourir de rire,** I nearly died with laughter, laughing; *a.* **-ant,** thinking (man, woman); **bien pensant,** orthodox, right-thinking; *s.* **-eur, -euse,** thinker; *a.* **-if, -ive,** thoughtful; *adv.* **-ivement.**
pension [pɑ̃sjɔ̃], *s.f.* **1.** pension, allowance; **p. de retraite,** (retirement) pension; **p. viagère,** life annuity; **p. alimentaire,** (i) allowance for board; (ii) *Jur:* alimony. **2.** (*a*) payment for board (and lodging); **être en p. chez qn,** to board with s.o.; (*b*) **p. de famille,** residential hotel; boarding-house. **3.** (*a*) boarding-school fees; (*b*) (private) boarding-school; *s.m. & f.* **-naire,** (*a*) pensioner; (*b*) boarder; *s.m.* **-nat** (*a*) boarding school; (*b*) boarding establishment (attached to school).
pensionner [pɑ̃sjɔne], *v.tr.* to pension (s.o.); to grant a pension to (s.o.).
pente [pɑ̃:t], *s.f.* (*a*) slope, incline, gradient; **p. ascendante, descendante,** uphill, downhill slope; *P.N: Aut:* **p. 10%,** hill 1 in 10; **p. d'un toit,** pitch of a roof; **p. transversale** (**d'une route**), camber; (*b*) bent, inclination; **suivre sa p.,** to follow one's inclinations.
Pentecôte [pɑ̃tko:t], *s.f.* Whitsun(tide); **dimanche de la P.,** Whit-Sunday.
pénurie [penyri], *s.f.* (*a*) scarcity, shortage (of money, goods, staff); lack (of words); (*b*) poverty.
pépé [pepe], *s.m. F:* grand-dad, grandpa.
pépi|er [pepje], *v.i.* (*of birds*) to cheep, chirp; *s.m.* **-ement.**
pépin[1] [pepɛ̃], *s.m.* **1.** pip (of apple, grape, etc). **2.** *F:* hitch; **avoir un p.,** to be in difficulties.
pépin[2], *s.m. F:* umbrella, *F:* brolly.
pépin|ière [pepinjɛ:r], *s.f. Hort:* seed-bed, nursery (garden); *s.m.* **-iériste,** nurseryman, gardener.
perçant [pɛrsɑ̃], *a.* piercing, penetrating (eye, shriek); keen, sharp (wits); shrill (voice, whistle); biting (wind).
percée [pɛrse], *s.f.* (*a*) glade, vista, clearing (in forest); (*b*) break, opening (in hedge, wall); (*of sun, etc.*) **faire une p.,** to break through.
perce-neige [pɛrs(ə)nɛ:ʒ], *s.m. or f.inv. Bot:* snowdrop.

perce-oreille [pɛrsɔrɛːj], *s.m. Ent:* earwig; *pl. perce-oreilles.*

perceptible [pɛrsɛptibl], *a.* 1. perceptible (à, by, to); discernible. 2. collectable (tax); *adv.* -ment.

perceptif, -ive [pɛrsɛptif, -iːv], *a.* perceptive (person).

percep|tion [pɛrsɛpsjɔ̃], *s.f.* 1. perception (through the senses). 2. collection, receipt (of taxes, duties, rent); *s.m.* -teur, tax-collector.

per|cer [pɛrse], *v.* (n. perçons) 1. *v.tr.* (*a*) to pierce, to go through; **p. un abcès,** to lance an abscess; **p. un secret,** to penetrate a secret; **p. l'avenir,** to foresee the future; (*b*) to perforate; to make a hole, an opening, in (sth.); **p. une porte dans un mur,** to make a door in a wall; (*c*) **p. un trou,** to bore a hole. 2. *v.i.* to pierce; to come through; **ses dents percent,** he's cutting his teeth; *s.m.* -çage, piercing, boring, drilling; tapping (of cask); *s.m.* -cement, perforation, piercing; tunnelling; sinking (of well); *s.f.* -ceuse, drill, drilling machine.

percevoir [pɛrsəvwaːr], *v.tr.* (*conj. like* RECEVOIR) 1. to perceive, discern (with the senses, intellect). 2. to collect (taxes).

perche [pɛrʃ], *s.f.* (thin) pole; *Sp:* **saut à la p.,** pole-vaulting.

percher [pɛrʃe], *v.i.* (*of birds*) to perch, roost.

se percher, (*of bird*) **se p. sur une branche,** to alight, perch, on a branch.

perclus, *f.* -use, *F:* -ue [pɛrkly, -yːz], *a.* stiff-jointed; **p. de rhumatismes,** crippled with rheumatism.

percolateur [pɛrkɔlatœːr], *s.m.* (coffee) percolator.

percussion [pɛrkysjɔ̃], *s.f.* percussion, impact; *Mus:* **instruments à p.,** percussion instruments; *s.m. & f.* -niste, percussion player.

percut|er [pɛrkyte], *v.tr. & i.* to strike (sth.); **la voiture percuta (contre) un arbre,** the car hit a tree; *a.* -ant, percussive, percussion; *Artil:* **tir p.,** percussion fire; *s.m.* -eur, striker (of gun, fuse).

perdant, -ante [pɛrdɑ̃, -ɑ̃ːt]. 1. *a.* losing; **billet p.,** blank (ticket, at lottery). 2. *s.* loser.

perdre [pɛrdr], *v.tr.* 1. to ruin, destroy; **le jeu le perdra,** gambling will be the ruin of him. 2. to lose; **p. sa vie, un procès,** to lose one's life, a law-suit; **p. la partie,** to lose the game; **vous ne perdrez rien pour attendre,** you will lose nothing by waiting; **p. son temps,** to waste (one's) time. 3. *abs.* (*a*) **le fût perd,** the cask is leaking; **vous n'y perdrez pas,** you won't lose by it; (*b*) **p. (sur ses concurrents),** to fall behind (one's competitors).

perdre. 1. to be lost; **se p. dans la foule,** to vanish, disappear, lose oneself, in the crowd. 2. to lose one's way; *F:* **je m'y perds,** I can't make head or tail of it.

perdr|ix [pɛrdri], *s.f.* partridge; **p. grise,** common partridge; *s.m.* -eau, -eaux, partridge poult, young partridge.

perdu [pɛrdy], *a.* 1. ruined; done for; **âme perdue,** lost soul. 2. lost; **heures perdues,** (i) spare time; (ii) wasted time; *Com:* **emballage p.,** non-returnable packing. 3. **à corps p.,** recklessly; **tirer à coup p.,** to fire at random.

père [pɛːr], *s.m.* 1. father; **de p. en fils,** from father to son; **M. Dupont p.,** Mr Dupont senior; *F:* **le p. Dupont,** old (Mr) Dupont; **p. de famille,** family man; **valeurs de p. de famille,** gilt-edged securities; **nos pères,** our forefathers. 2. *Ecc:* **le Saint P.,** the Holy Father, the Pope; **le (révérend) P. Martin,** Father Martin.

péremptoire [perɑ̃ptwaːr], *a.* (*a*) peremptory (tone); (*b*) unanswerable, decisive (argument); *adv.* -ment, peremptorily.

perfection [pɛrfɛksjɔ̃], *s.f.* perfection; **à la p.,** to perfection, perfectly; **la p. même,** perfection itself.

perfectionn|er [pɛrfɛksjɔne], *v.tr.* 1. to perfect. 2. to improve (a machine, a method); *s.m.* -ement, perfecting; improving; **cours de p.,** refresher course.

se perfectionner dans, en, qch., to improve one's knowledge of (science, etc.); **se p. en allemand,** to improve one's German.

perfide [pɛrfid], *a.* treacherous; perfidious; false (friend, etc.); *adv.* -ment.

perfor|er [pɛrfɔre], *v.tr.* to perforate; to bore (through), to drill; to punch; **carte perforée,** punch card; *s.* -ateur, -atrice, punch, drill; *s.f.* -ation; *s.* -eur, -euse, (*a*) card punch operator (man or girl); (*b*) *f.* perforating machine.

périclitant [periklitɑ̃], *a.* unsound, shaky (business).

péricliter [periklite], *v.i.* (*of undertaking*) to be in danger; **ses affaires périclitent,** his business is in a bad way.

péril [peril], *s.m.* peril, danger; risk.

périlleu|x, -euse [perijø, -øːz], *a.* perilous, dangerous; **saut p.,** somersault; *adv.* -sement.

périmé [perime], *a.* out-of-date; expired (bill); (ticket) no longer valid; lapsed (passport).

périmètre [perimɛtr], *s.m.* perimeter.

périod|e [perjɔd], *s.f.* (*a*) period; cycle; (*b*) period of time; age, era; (*c*) *Gram:* period; complete sentence; *a. & s.m.* -ique; *a.* periodical, recurrent, intermittent; *s.m.* un p., a periodical (publication); *adv.* -iquement.

péripétie [peripesi], *s.f.* 1. sudden change of fortune (in novel, in life). 2. *pl.* vicissitudes; ups and downs (of life); adventures.

périphérie [periferi], *s.f.* 1. periphery; circumference. 2. outskirts (of town); *a.* -ique: **boulevard p.,** ring road.

pér|ir [peri:r], *v.i.* to perish; to be destroyed; to die; *a.* **-issable**, perishable.

périscope [periskɔp], *s.m.* periscope.

péritonite [peritɔnit], *s.f. Med:* peritonitis.

perle [pɛrl], *s.f.* 1. pearl. 2. bead (of glass, metal, etc.).

permanence [pɛrmanɑ̃:s], *s.f.* 1. permanence; **assemblée en p.**, permanent assembly. 2. (office, etc.) always open to the public; **il y a (une) p.**, there's always s.o. on duty; **p. de trois employés**, staff of three always on duty; **p. de police**, police station open night and day.

permanent [pɛrmanɑ̃]. 1. *a.* permanent (court, committee); **armée permanente**, standing army; *Cin:* **spectacle p.**, *s.m.* **p.**, continuous performance. 2. *s.f. Hairdr:* **permanente**, permanent wave, *F:* perm.

permettre [pɛrmɛtr], *v.tr. (conj. like* METTRE*)* to permit, allow; **p. qch. à qn**, to allow s.o. sth.; **p. à qn de faire qch.**, to let s.o. do sth., to allow s.o. to do sth.; **permis à vous de ne pas me croire**, you are at liberty to believe me or not; **permettez! excuse me! allow me! vous permettez? may I? se p. de faire qch.**, to venture to do sth.; **se p. un verre de vin**, to indulge in a glass of wine.

permis [pɛrmi]. 1. *a.* allowed, permitted, lawful, permissible. 2. *s.m. Adm:* permit, licence; **p. de chasse**, game licence; *Aut:* **p. de conduire**, driving licence; *(for foreigners)* **p. de séjour** = certificate of registration; **p. de construire**, building licence.

permission [pɛrmisjɔ̃], *s.f. (a)* permission, leave; *(b) Mil: etc:* leave of absence; pass; *s.m.* **-naire**, soldier on leave; *Navy:* liberty man.

pernicieu|x, -ieuse [pɛrnisjø, -jø:z], *a.* pernicious, injurious, harmful; *adv.* **-sement**.

péror|er [perɔre], *v.i.* to hold forth; to speechify, to spout; *s.f.* **-aison**, peroration.

Pérou (le) [ləperu]. *Pr.n.m. Geog:* Peru; *F:* **ce n'est pas le P.**, it is not highly paid, it's no great catch; **gagner le P.**, to make a fortune.

perpendiculaire [pɛrpɑ̃dikylɛ:r], *a. & s.f.* perpendicular; *adv.* **-ment**.

perpétr|er [pɛrpetre], *v.tr.* **(je perpètre; je perpétrerai)** to perpetrate (a crime, etc.); *s.f.* **-ation**.

perpét|uer [pɛrpetɥe], *v.tr.* to perpetuate; to carry on (a name); to keep up, alive (a tradition, a memory); *s.f.* **-uation**; *a.* **-uel, -uelle**, perpetual, everlasting, never-ending; (sentence) for life; *adv.* **-uellement**.

se perpétuer, to remain, to survive, to become established.

perpétuité [pɛrpetɥite], *s.f.* perpetuity, endlessness; **à p.**, in perpetuity; (penal servitude) for life.

perplexe [pɛrplɛks], *a.* perplexed, puzzled.

perplexité [pɛrplɛksite], *s.f.* perplexity.

perquisition [pɛrkizisjɔ̃], *s.f.* thorough search or inquiry; **mandat de p.**, search-warrant.

perquisition|ner [pɛrkizisjɔne], *v.i. Jur:* to make a search (of premises, etc.); *s.m.* **-neur**, searcher (holding a warrant).

perron [pɛrɔ̃], *s.m.* (flight of) steps (leading to building).

perroquet [pɛrɔkɛ], *s.m. Orn:* parrot.

perruche [pɛryʃ], *s.f. Orn:* (a) parakeet; (b) hen parrot; (c) **p. ondulée**, budgerigar.

perru|que [pɛryk], *s.f.* wig; *s.* **-quier, -quière**, wig maker.

persécu|ter [pɛrsekyte], *v.tr.* (a) to persecute; (b) to pester (s.o.); *s.* **-teur, -trice**, persecutor; *s.f.* **-tion**.

persévér|er [pɛrsevere], *v.i.* **(je persévère; je persévérerai)** to persevere **(dans,** in); *s.f.* **-ance**; *a.* **-ant**, persevering.

persiflage [pɛrsifla:ʒ], *s.m.* (ill-natured) banter.

persil [pɛrsi], *s.m. Bot:* parsley.

persique [pɛrsik], *a.* (ancient) Persian; *Geog:* le **Golfe P.**, the Persian Gulf.

persist|er [pɛrsiste], *v.i.* to persist; *s.f.* **-ance**, persistence; **avec p.**, doggedly; *a.* **-ant**, persistent; lasting, enduring.

personnage [pɛrsɔna:ʒ], *s.m. (a)* personage; **être un p.**, to be somebody, *F:* a big shot; **un triste p.**, a poor specimen; *(b)* character (in play, novel).

personnalité [pɛrsɔnalite], *s.f.* personality. 1 individuality; **il a de la p.**, he's a real person. 2 personage; **c'est une p.**, he's an important man. 3. *pl.* **faire des personnalités**, to make personal, offensive, remarks.

personne [pɛrsɔn]. 1. *s.f.* person; *(a)* individual; **les grandes personnes**, grown-ups; **une tierce p.**, a third party; **3 francs par p.**, 3 francs a head; *(b)* **en p.**, in person; personally; **il est bonté en p.**, he is kindness itself; *(c) (the human body)* **elle est bien de sa p.**, she's very attractive, good-looking; **exposer sa p.**, to risk death; *(d) Gram:* **écrire à la troisième p.**, to write in the third person. 2. *pron.indef.m.inv.* **p.**, anyone, anybody *(with vaguely implied negation)*; **il s'y connaît comme p.**, nobody better at it than he is; **il travaille plus fort que p.**, he works harder than anyone; *(b) (with not expressed or understood)* no one; nobody; **qui est là?—p.**, who's there?—no one; **il n'y a p. de blessé**, nobody's been hurt; **je n'ai vu p.**, didn't see anyone; **sans nommer p.**, without mentioning any names, naming no names.

personnel, -elle [pɛrsɔnɛl]. 1. *a.* person (letter, business, *Gram:* pronoun); **stricteme p.**, not transferable. 2. *s.m. (a)* personnel, sta *(factory, farm)* hands; **p. ouvrier**, workmen; **p. technique**, technical staff; **p. d'administratio de bureau**, administrative, clerical, staff; (*Mil: etc:* manpower; *adv.* **-lement**.

personnifi|er [pɛrsɔnifje], *v.tr.* (*p.d. & pr.sub.* **n. personnifiions**) (*a*) to personify; (*b*) to typify; *s.f.* **-cation.**

perspectif, -ive [pɛrspɛktif, -iːv]. **1.** *a.* perspective (plan, etc.). **2.** *s.f.* **perspective,** (*a*) *Art:* perspective; (*b*) outlook, view, prospect; **avoir qch. en perspective,** to have sth. in view; (*c*) **une longue perspective de hêtres,** a long vista of beech trees.

perspi|cacité [pɛrspikasite], *s.f.* perspicacity, shrewdness; *a.* **-cace,** shrewd.

persuadé [pɛrsɥade], *a.* persuaded, convinced, sure (**de,** of; **que,** that).

persuader [pɛrsɥade], *v.tr.* **p. qn,** to persuade, convince, s.o.; **p. qn de faire qch.,** to persuade s.o. to do sth.; **p. à qn de faire qch.,** to induce s.o. to do sth.; **il s'est persuadé que . . .,** he's convinced that . . .

persuas|ion [pɛrsɥazjɔ̃], *s.f.* **1.** persuasion. **2.** conviction, belief; *a.* **-if, -ive,** persuasive (tone, manner).

perte [pɛrt], *s.f.* **1.** ruin, destruction; **il court à sa p.,** he's heading for disaster. **2.** loss; **vendre à p.,** to sell at a loss; **p. de temps,** waste of time; **parler en pure p.,** to waste one's breath. **3.** loss, leakage (of heat, pressure, voltage, etc.).

pertinence [pɛrtinãːs], *s.f.* pertinence, relevance; **avec p.,** competently.

pertin|ent [pɛrtinã], *a.* pertinent; relevant (**à,** to); **non p.,** irrelevant; *adv.* **-emment.**

perturbation [pɛrtyrbasjɔ̃], *s.f.* (*a*) agitation (of mind); (*b*) **perturbations atmosphériques,** atmospheric disturbances; *Meteor:* depression; *Rad: F:* atmospherics.

perturb|er [pɛrtyrbe], *v.tr.* to distress (s.o.'s mind); to disturb (the peace); *a. & s.* **-ateur, -atrice,** (*a*) *a.* disturbing, upsetting; (*b*) *s.* upsetter, disturber (of the peace, etc.).

pervers, -erse [pɛrvɛːr, -ɛrs]. **1.** *a.* perverse, depraved. **2.** *s.* depraved, immoral, person; **p. sexuel,** sexual pervert; *adv.* **-ement.**

pervers|ion [pɛrvɛrsjɔ̃], *s.f.* perversion (of morals, etc.); warping (of the mind); *s.f.* **-ité.**

pervertir [pɛrvɛrtiːr], *v.tr.* to pervert, to corrupt.

se pervertir, to become depraved.

pesage [pəzaːʒ], *s.m.* **1.** weighing; **bascule de p.,** weighing machine; **bureau de p.,** weigh-house. **2.** *Rac:* (*a*) weighing in; (*b*) weighing-in room; (*c*) paddock; the enclosure.

pes|ant [pəzã], *a.* heavy, weighty; ponderous, clumsy (style, writer); sluggish (mind); *adv.* **-amment.**

pesanteur [pəzãtœːr], *s.f.* **1.** weight; *Ph:* gravity. **2.** (*a*) heaviness; (*b*) dullness (of mind).

pèse-bébé [pɛzbebe], *s.m.* baby scales; *pl.* **pèse-bébés.**

pèse-lettre(s) [pɛzlɛtr], *s.m.* letter-balance, letter-scales; *pl.* **pèse-lettres.**

pèse-personne [pɛzpɛrsɔn], *s.m.* bathroom scales; *pl.* **pèse-personnes.**

peser [pəze], *v.* (**je pèse**) **1.** *v.tr.* to weigh (a parcel; one's words); to ponder (advice). **2.** *v.i.* (*a*) to weigh; to be heavy; **le temps lui pèse,** time hangs heavily on his hands; (*b*) **p. sur un mot,** to lay stress on a word.

pessim|isme [pɛsimism], *s.m.* pessimism; *a. & s.* **-iste,** (*a*) *a.* pessimistic; (*b*) *s.* pessimist.

peste [pɛst], *s.f.* plague, pestilence; *F:* (*of child*) nuisance; **petite p.,** little devil.

pester [pɛste], *v.i.* **p. contre le mauvais temps,** to curse the (bad) weather; *abs.* **il pestait,** he was grumbling, cursing.

pestilentiel, -elle [pɛstilãsjɛl], *a.* pestilential; stinking, fetid; **odeur pestilentielle,** stench.

pétale [petal], *s.m. Bot:* petal.

pétan|que [petãːk], *s.f.* (game resembling) bowls (in S. of France); *s.m.* **-queur,** *pétanque*-player.

pétard [petaːr], *s.m.* (*a*) *Rail:* fog-signal; (*b*) (firework) cracker.

pétill|er [petije], *v.i.* (*of burning wood*) to crackle; (*of drink*) to sparkle, fizz, bubble; (*of eyes*) to sparkle; **pétillant d'esprit,** sparkling with wit; *s.m.* **-ement.**

petit, -ite [pəti, -it], *a. & s.* **1.** *a.* (*a*) small; little; **un p. homme,** a little man; **c'est un homme p.,** he's short; **une toute petite maison,** a tiny little house; **petite brise,** light breeze; **faire une petite visite,** to pay a short visit, a short call; **en p.,** on a small scale, in miniature; **p. à p.,** little by little, gradually; *F:* **le p. coin,** the lavatory, *F:* the loo; (*b*) (*indicating appreciation or disapproval*) *F:* **un p. coup de rouge,** a nice drop of red wine; **sa petite santé,** his, her, precious health; (*c*) lesser, minor; **petite industrie,** small-scale industry; *Com:* **petite caisse,** petty cash; **petits pois,** (garden) peas. **2.** insignificant, petty; **p. négociant,** small tradesman; **petite propriété,** smallholding. **3.** mean, ungenerous; **petites âmes,** small-minded people. **4.** (*a*) **p. enfant,** little child; **les petits Anglais,** English children; **les petites Martin,** the little Martin girls; **p. chien, chat,** puppy, kitten; (*b*) *s.* **le p., la petite,** the baby; **pauvre petit(e),** poor little thing. **5.** *s.m.* young (of animals); **faire des petits,** to have young.

petite-fille [p(ə)titfiːj], *s.f.* grand-daughter; *pl.* **petites-filles.**

petitesse [pətitɛs], *s.f.* (*a*) smallness, diminutiveness (of an object); slenderness; (*b*) meanness, pettiness; **faire des petitesses,** to do shabby, mean, things.

petit-fils [p(ə)tifis], *s.m.* grandson; *pl.* **petits-fils.**

pétition [petisjɔ̃], *s.f.* petition.

pétition|ner [petisjɔne], *v.i.* to petition; *s.m. & f.* **-aire,** petitioner.

petit-neveu [p(ə)tinvø], *s.m.* great nephew; *pl.* **petits-neveux.**

petits-enfants [p(ə)tizɑ̃fɑ̃], *s.m.pl.* grand-children.

pétri|fier [petrifje], *v.tr.* to petrify; **pétrifié de peur**, paralysed with fear; *s.f.* **-fication**.

pétrin [petrɛ̃], *s.m.* kneading-trough; *F:* **être dans le p.**, to be in the soup.

pétr|ir [petriːr], *v.tr.* to knead (dough); to mould, shape (s.o.'s character); *s.m.* **-issage**, kneading, moulding; *s.* **-isseur, -isseuse**, kneader.

pétrole [petrɔl], *s.m.* petroleum; **p. brut**, crude oil; **p. lampant**, paraffin oil, *N.Am:* kerosene.

pétrolier, -ière [petrɔlje, -jɛːr]. 1. *a.* **l'industrie pétrolière**, the (mineral-)oil industry. 2. *s.m.* (oil) tanker.

pétrolifère [petrɔlifɛːr], *a.* oil-bearing; **gisement p.**, oil-field.

peu [pø]. 1. *adv.* (*a*) little; **p. ou point**, little or none; **manger p. (ou point)**, to eat little (or nothing); **quelque p. surpris**, somewhat surprised; **p. de chose**, little; not much; **pour si p. de chose**, for so small a matter; (*b*) few; **p. de gens**, few people; **p. d'entre eux**, few of them; **p. de jours après**, not long after; (*c*) not very; **un-; non-; p. utile**, not very useful; **p. intelligent**, unintelligent; **p. honnête**, dishonest; **p. abondant**, scarce. 2. *s.m.* (*a*) little, bit; **son p. d'éducation**, his lack of education; **un p. de vin**, a little wine; **encore un p.?** a little more? *F:* **ça, c'est un p. fort!** that's really a bit much! **pour un p. on eût crié**, we very nearly shouted; **écoutez un p.**, just listen; (*b*) **p. après**, shortly after; **sous p.**, before long; **depuis p.**, lately.

peuple [pœpl], *s.m.* people. 1. nation; **le p. français**, the French people. 2. **le p.**, the masses; **les gens du p.**, the lower classes; the people.

peupl|er [pœple], *v.tr.* to people, populate (a country); to stock (poultry yard, fish-pond); to plant (a forest); **rues peuplées de gens**, streets thronged with people; **pays très peuplé**, densely populated country; *s.m.* **-ement**, population, peopling (of a region); stocking (of river, game reserve); plantation (of trees); *Bot:* vegetation (of a region).

peuplier [pœplije], *s.m.* poplar.

peur [pœːr], *s.f.* fear, fright, dread; **avoir p.**, to be afraid; **n'ayez pas p.!** don't be afraid; **j'ai p. qu'il (ne) soit en retard**, I fear he may be late; **prendre p.**, to take fright; *F:* **avoir une p. bleue**, to be in a blue funk; **laid à faire p.**, frightfully ugly.

peureu|x, -euse [pœrø, -øːz], *a.* timorous; easily frightened; nervous, timid (nature); *adv.* **-sement**.

peut-être [pøtɛtr], *adv.* perhaps, maybe, possibly; **p.-ê. que oui**, perhaps so; **p.-ê. bien qu'il viendra**, it is very likely he will come.

phare [faːr], *s.m.* 1. lighthouse; *Av:* **p. (d'aéro-**port), (airport) beacon; **p. d'atterrissage**, landing light. 2. *Aut:* headlight; **p. en code**, dipped headlight.

pharis|ien, -ienne [farizjɛ̃, -jɛn], *s.* pharisee; hypocrite; *a.* **-aïque**, pharisaic(al); hypocritical.

pharmac|ie [farmasi], *s.f.* 1. (*a*) pharmacy, dispensing; (*b*) chemist's shop, *N.Am:* drug store; (*c*) medicine-chest; *a. & s.f.* **-eutique**, (*a*) *a.* pharmaceutic(al); (*b*) *s.f.* pharmaceutics; *s.* **-ien, -ienne**, chemist, pharmacist.

phénol [fenɔl], *s.m. Com:* carbolic acid.

phéno|mène [fenɔmɛn], *s.m.* (*a*) phenomenon (of nature, etc.); (*b*) (*pers.*) marvel, *F:* freak; **jeune p.**, infant prodigy; *a.* **-ménal, -ménaux**, phenomenal; *adv.* **-ménalement**.

philanthrop|e [filɑ̃trɔp], *s.m. & f.* philanthropist; *s.f.* **-ie**, philanthropy; *a.* **-ique**, philanthropic.

philatél|ie [filateli], *s.f.* stamp collecting, philately; *a.* **-ique**, philatelic; *s.m. & f.* **-iste**, philatelist, stamp collector.

Philippe [filip]. *Pr.n.m.* Philip.

philosoph|e [filɔzɔf]. 1. *s.m. &f.* philosopher. 2. *a.* philosophical; *a.* **-ique**, philosophic(al); *adv.* **-iquement**.

phobie [fɔbi], *s.f.* phobia, morbid fear; **avoir une p. du téléphone**, to have a horror of the telephone.

phonétique [fonetik]. 1. *a.* phonetic. 2. *s.f.* phonetics; *adv.* **-ment**.

phonique [fɔnik], *a.* acoustic; *P.T.T:* **appel p.**, buzzer; **isolation p.**, sound-proofing.

phono [fɔno], *s.m. F:* gramophone; record-player.

phonograph|e [fɔnɔgraf], *s.m.* gramophone, record-player; *s.f.* **-ie**, sound-recording.

phonothèque [fɔnɔtɛk], *s.f.* tape and record library.

phoque [fɔk], *s.m. Z:* seal.

phosphate [fɔsfat], *s.m. Ch:* phosphate; **p. de chaux**, calcium phosphate.

photo [foto], *s.f. F:* photo; **faire de la p.**, to go in for photography; *Sp:* **décision par p.**, *s.f.in* **p.-finish**, photo-finish; *s.m.* **photo-robot**, identikit picture; *pl.* **photos-robots**.

photocop|ier [fotokɔpje], *v.tr.* to photostat; *s.f.* **-ie**, photocopy, photostat.

photograph|e [fotograf], *s.m. & f.* photographer; *s.f.* **-ie**, (i) photography; (ii) photograph; *v.tr.* **-ier**, to photograph; *a.* **-ique**, photographic; *adv.* **-iquement**.

phrase [fraːz], *s.f.* 1. sentence; **faire des phrases**, to speak in flowery language; **parler sans p.**, to speak straight out. 2. *Mus:* phrase.

physicien, -ienne [fizisjɛ̃, -jɛn], *s.* physicist.

physiolog|ie [fizjɔlɔʒi], *s.f.* physiology; **végétale**, plant physiology; *a.* **-iqu**(e), physiological; *adv.* **-iquement**; *s.m. & f.* **-ist**(e), physiologist.

physionomie [fizjɔnɔmi], *s.f.* physiognomy; face; (*of thg*) appearance, aspect, specific character; **p. repoussante**, repulsive face; **il manque de p.**, his face lacks character; **la p. paisible des rues**, the peaceful aspect of the streets.

physiothéra|pie [fizjɔterapi], *s.f. Med:* physiotherapy; *a.* **-pique**, physiotherapeutic; *s.m. &f.* **-piste**, physiotherapist.

physique [fizik]. 1. *a.* physical; **douleur p.**, bodily pain; **culture p.**, physical culture; **force p.**, strength. 2. *s.f.* physics. 3. *s.m.* physique (of person); *adv.* **-ment**, physically.

piailler [pjaje], *v.i.* (*of small birds*) to cheep; (*of children*) to squall, squeal.

pianiste [pjanist], *s.m. &f.* pianist.

piano [pjano], *s.m.* piano; **p. à queue**, grand piano; **p. droit**, upright piano.

pic¹ [pik], *s.m.* 1. pick, pickaxe; **p. pneumatique**, pneumatic drill. 2. (mountain-)peak; *adv.phr.* **à p.**, perpendicular(ly), sheer; **sentier à p.**, precipitous path; **arriver, tomber, à p.**, to come in the nick of time.

pic², *s.m. Orn:* woodpecker; **p. épeiche**, great spotted woodpecker; **pic vert**, [pivɛːr], green woodpecker.

picorer [pikɔre]. *v.i.* (*of bird*) to forage; to pick, scratch about (for food).

picot|er [pikɔte]. 1. *v.tr.* (*a*) (*of bird*) to peck (at) (food, etc.); (*b*) **fumée qui picote les yeux**, smoke that makes the eyes smart. 2. *v.i.* to smart, tingle; *s.m.* **-ement**, tingling, smarting (sensation).

pie [pi]. 1. *s.f. Orn:* magpie. 2. *a.inv.* piebald (horse, cow); **vache p. rouge**, red and white cow.

pièce [pjɛs], *s.f.* 1. piece; (*a*) **p. de gibier**, head of game; **p. de musée**, museum piece; **vin en p.**, wine in the cask; **p. de blé**, corn-field; **p. d'eau**, sheet of water, ornamental lake; **ils coûtent mille francs p.**, they cost a thousand francs apiece; **p. de monnaie**, coin; **grosse p.**, ten-franc piece; **donner la p. à qn**, to give s.o. a tip; **travail à la p.**, aux pièces, piece-work; (*b*) *Jur:* **pièces d'un procès**, documents in a case; (*c*) **p. de théâtre**, play. 2. piece, part; (*a*) **p. de bœuf**, joint of beef; **pièces d'une machine**, parts of a machine; **pièces détachées**, (i) spare parts; (ii) component parts; **pièces de voiture, d'avion**, car, aircraft, parts; (*b*) *Games:* (chess-)piece; (draughts)man; (*c*) room (in house); **un (appartement de) trois pièces**, a three-roomed flat; (*d*) patch; **mettre une p. à un vêtement**, to patch a garment. 3. fragment, bit.

pied [pje], *s.m.* 1. (*a*) foot; **frapper du p.**, to stamp one's foot; **mettre p. à terre**, to alight; to dismount; to step ashore; **marcher sur les pieds de qn**, to tread on s.o.'s toes; *F:* **être bête comme ses pieds**, to be unbelievably stupid; (*to dog*) **au p.!** heel! **avoir bon p. bon œil**, to be hale and hearty; **faire qch. au p. levé**, to do sth. off-hand, at a moment's notice; **se lever du p. gauche**, to get out of bed on the wrong side; **coup de p.**, kick; **à p.**, on foot, walking; **aller à p.**, to walk; **récolte sur p.**, standing crop; **remettre qn sur p.**, (i) to restore s.o. to health; (ii) to set s.o. on his feet again; *F:* **ça lui fera les pieds!** that'll serve him right! *P:* **il me casse les pieds**, he bores me stiff; (*b*) footing, foothold; **perdre p.**, to lose one's foothold; to get out of one's depth; **le p. me manqua**, I lost my footing; **tenir p.**, to stand firm; **payer qn sur le p. de . . .**, to pay s.o. at the rate of . . . . 2. (*a*) foot (of stocking, bed); base (of wall); **au p. de la montagne**, at the foot of the mountain; (*b*) leg (of chair); stem, foot (of glass); (*c*) **p. de céleri**, head of celery; (*d*) stand, rest. 3. *Meas:* foot. 4. *Lit:* (metrical) foot.

pied-à-terre [pjetatɛːr], *s.m.inv.* pied-à-terre; (*in town*) small flat (for occasional use).

pied-d'alouette [pjedalwɛt], *s.m.* larkspur, delphinium; *pl. pieds-d'alouette.*

pied-de-poule [pjedpul], *s.m. Tex:* broken check, houndstooth (material); *pl. pieds-de-poule.*

piédestal, -aux [pjedestal, -o], *s.m.* pedestal.

pied-noir [pjenwaːr], *s.m. &f. F:* Algerian-born Frenchman, -woman; *pl. pieds-noirs.*

piège [pjɛːʒ], *s.m.* trap, snare; **p. à loups**, mantrap; **tendre un p.**, to set a trap (**à**, for).

pierr|e¹ [pjɛːr], *s.f.* stone; (*a*) **p. de taille**, ashlar, freestone; **poser la première p.**, to lay the foundation stone; **p. à aiguiser, à affûter**, grindstone; **p. à huile**, hone; **p. précieuse**, gem; (*b*) *Med:* calculus; *s.f.* **-aille**, ballast, road metal, rubble; *s.f.pl.* **-eries**, precious stones; *a.* **-eux, -euse**, stony.

Pierre². *Pr.n.m.* Peter.

Pierrot [pjero]. *s.m.* 1. *Pr.n.m. F:* little Peter. 2. *s.m. Th:* Pierrot, clown; *F:* **c'est un drôle de p.**, he's a queer fish.

piété [pjete], *s.f.* piety.

piétin|er [pjetine]. 1. *v.tr.* to trample, stamp, on (sth.); to tread under foot. 2. *v.i.* **p. de rage**, to dance with rage; **p. sur place**, to mark time; **cette affaire piétine**, this business is hanging fire; *s.m.* **-ement**, stamping, trampling (with the feet).

piéton [pjetɔ̃], *s.m.* pedestrian; **passage pour piétons**, pedestrian crossing.

piètre [pjɛtr], *a.* wretched, poor (meal, etc.); lame (excuse).

pieu, *pl.* **-eux** [pjø], *s.m.* stake, post; *Civ.E:* pile.

pieu|x, -euse [pjø, -øːz], *a.* pious, devout; *adv.* **-sement**.

pigeon, -onne [piʒɔ̃, -ɔn], *s.* 1. pigeon; **p. voyageur**, carrier-pigeon. 2. *F:* (*pers.*) sucker;

plumer un p., to fleece a mug.

pignon [piɲ3], s.m. 1. gable, gable-end. 2. *Mec:* pinion; gear.

pile[1] [pil], s.f. 1. pile; heap. 2. pier (of bridge). 3. *El:* battery; **p. de rechange,** spare battery, refill (for torch); *Atom.Ph:* **p. atomique,** atomic pile; **p. couveuse,** breeder reactor.

pile[2]. 1. s.f. reverse (of coin); **p. ou face,** heads or tails. 2. adv. *F:* **s'arrêter p.,** to stop dead; **ça tombe p.,** that comes in the nick of time; **à six heures p.,** on the dot of six.

piller [pile], v.tr. to pound; to crush; to grind; s.m. **-age,** pounding; crushing; grinding.

pilier [pilje], s.m. pillar, column, post.

piller [pije], v.tr. to pillage, loot, ransack; **p. un auteur,** to plagiarize, steal from, an author; s.m. **-age,** pillage, looting; a. & s. **-ard, -arde,** (a) a. pilfering; (b) s. looter.

pilonner [pilɔne], v.tr. to pound; to ram (concrete, earth); *Mil:* to flatten (with bombs, shell fire); s.m. **-age.**

pilotage [pilɔta:ʒ], s.m. *Nau: Av:* pilotage, piloting; *Av:* **p. sans visibilité,** blind flying; **école de p.,** flying school.

pilote [pilɔt], s.m. 1. (a) *Nau:* (i) helmsman; (ii) pilot; **p. de mer,** sea pilot; **p. de port, p. fluvial,** harbour, river, pilot. 2. *Av:* pilot; **p. de ligne,** airline pilot; **p. d'essai,** test pilot; **p. commandant de bord,** pilot in command; **p. breveté,** licensed pilot.

piloter [pilɔte], v.tr. to pilot (ship, aircraft); to drive (racing car); **p. qn dans Londres,** to show s.o. round London.

pilule [pilyl], s.f. *Pharm:* pill; **prendre la p.,** to be on the pill; **avaler la p.,** to submit to humiliation; to swallow sth. hook, line and sinker.

piment [pimã], s.m. pimento; *Cu:* red pepper; **donner du p. à une histoire,** to add spice to a story.

pimpant [pɛ̃pã], a. smart, spruce.

pin [pɛ̃], s.m. pine(-tree); **p. d'Ecosse,** Scots fir, Scotch fir; **pomme de p.,** pine cone; fir cone.

pinard [pina:r], s.m. *P:* wine; plonk.

pince [pɛ̃:s], s.f. 1. (a) pincers, pliers; *Surg:* forceps; **p. à sucre,** sugar-tongs; (b) clip; **p. à linge,** clothes-peg; **p.-monseigneur,** (burglar's) jemmy; pl. pinces-monseigneur. 2. claw (of lobster, etc.). 3. *Cl:* pleat; dart.

pincé [pɛ̃se], a. affected, supercilious; **sourire p.,** wry smile.

pinceau, -eaux [pɛ̃so], s.m. (artist's) paintbrush.

pincée [pɛ̃se], s.f. pinch (of salt, etc.).

pincer [pɛ̃se], v.tr. (n. pinçons) 1. to pinch, nip. 2. to grip, hold fast; *F:* **se faire p.,** to get caught, pinched; s.m. **-ement,** (i) pinching, nipping; (ii) pang, twinge (of pain, regret).

pince-sans-rire [pɛ̃ssãri:r], s.m.inv. *F:* man of dry (and ironical) humour.

pincettes [pɛ̃sɛt], s.f.pl. (a) tweezers; ((fire-)tongs; pair of tongs; **il n'est pas à prend** **avec des p.,** I wouldn't touch him with a bar pole.

pinède [pinɛd], s.f. (in S. of France) pine plant tion, forest.

pingre [pɛ̃:gr], F: 1. a. mean, stingy. 2. s.m. & miser, skinflint.

pinson [pɛ̃s3], s.m. *Orn:* finch; **p. des arbr** chaffinch.

pintade [pɛ̃tad], s.f. guinea-fowl.

pioche [pjɔʃ], s.f. pickaxe, pick, mattock.

piocher [pjɔʃe], v.tr. (a) to dig (with a pick); v.tr. & i. *Sch: F:* to grind, swot, at (sth.); **p. s** anglais, to swot up one's English; **il faut tou** temps p., it's a constant grind.

piolet [pjɔlɛ], s.m. ice-axe.

pion [pj3], s.m. 1. *Sch: F: Pej:* master on duty, charge of prep. 2. (a) *Chess:* pawn; *Draughts:* piece, man.

pionnier [pjɔnje], s.m. pioneer.

pipe [pip], s.f. pipe. 1. tube (for liquid, gas). (tobacco-)pipe; **p. de bruyère,** briar (pipe).

piquant, -ante [pikã, -ã:t]. 1. a. pungent (smel hot (mustard); tart, biting (flavour); piqua (story). 2. s.m. point (of story); pungency. s.m. prickle, thorn; quill (of porcupine); spik

pique[1] [pik], s.m. *Cards:* spade(s).

pique[2], s.f. pique, ill-feeling; **par p.,** out of spi

piqué [pike], a. 1. quilted, padded (garment); p **la machine,** machine-stitched. 2. worm-eat (book); damp-spotted (mirror); **p. d** **mouches,** fly-blown; *P:* **être p.,** to be m nuts. 3. sour (wine). 4. *Av:* descente piqu s.m. **p.,** nose-dive; **attaquer en p.,** to di bomb.

pique-nique [piknik], s.m. picnic; pl. piq niques.

piquer [pike], v.tr. 1. (a) to prick, sting; (of gr etc.) to bite; *F:* **quelle mouche vous piqu** what's biting you? **la fumée pique les ye** smoke makes the eyes smart; (b) to net pique (s.o.); **p. la jalousie de qn,** to arouse s.c jealousy. 2. to prick, puncture (sth.). 3. stick, insert (sth. into sth.); **p. une fleur dans** boutonnière, to stick a flower in one's b tonhole. 4. **p. une tête,** to take a header, to di

se piquer. 1. to prick oneself. 2. to take offen 3. **se p. de qch., de faire qch.,** to pride one on sth., on doing sth.

piquet [pikɛ], s.m. 1. peg, stake, post. 2. M picket; **p. d'incendie,** fire picket; **p. de grè** strike picket.

piquette [pikɛt], s.f. acid, vinegary, poor qu ty, wine.

piqûre [piky:r], s.f. 1. (a) prick; sting; bite (of sect); (b) (hypodermic) injection. 2. punctu small hole; pit (in metal, etc.); (a) **p. de v** wormhole (in wood, etc.); moth-hole (in g ment); (b) (machine-)stitching; quilting; **point de p.,** lockstitch.

pirate [pirat], s.m. (a) pirate; (b) plagiarist.

pire [piːr]. **1.** comp.a. worse; **cent fois p.,** a hundred times worse; **le remède est p. que le mal,** the cure is worse than the disease. **2.** sup. (a) a. **le p., la p., les pires,** the worst; **le p. des malheurs,** the worst of all misfortunes; (b) s. **s'attendre au p.,** to expect the worst.

pis¹ [pi], s.m. udder, dug (of cow, etc.).

pis², adv. (chiefly in certain set phrases; usu. form is **plus mal**) **1.** comp: worse; **aller de mal en p.,** to go from bad to worse; **tant p.!** never mind! **pour ne pas dire p.,** to say no more. **2.** sup. **le p.,** (the) worst; s.m. **mettre les choses au p.,** to suppose the worst.

pis(-)aller [pizale], s.m.inv. last resort, resource; makeshift.

piscine [pisin], s.f. swimming pool; **p. olympique,** olympic swimming pool; **p. couverte, de plein air,** indoor, open-air, swimming pool.

pissenlit [pisãli], s.m. Bot: dandelion.

pistache [pistaʃ], s.f. pistachio(-nut).

piste [pist], s.f. **1.** (a) running-track; race-track; **courses de p.,** track-racing; **tour de p.,** lap; **être en p.,** to be in the running; (b) Av: runway; **p. d'envol,** take-off strip; **p. d'atterrissage,** landing strip; Adm: **route à double p.,** dual carriageway, N.Am: two-lane highway; **p. cyclable,** cycle track; Cin: **p. sonore,** soundtrack. **2.** track, trail, scent; **faire fausse p.,** to be on the wrong track.

pistolet [pistɔlɛ], s.m. pistol.

piston [pistɔ̃], s.m. **1.** Mch: piston (of machine, pump, etc.); F: **avoir du p.,** to have friends in high places. **2.** Mus: **cornet à pistons,** cornet.

piteux, -euse [pitø, -øːz], a. piteous, pitiable, miserable; adv. -**sement.**

pitié [pitje], s.f. pity, compassion; **sans p.,** pitiless(ly); **regarder qn d'un œil de p.,** to look compassionately at s.o.; **faire p.,** to arouse pity.

pitoyable [pitwajabl], a. (a) pitiable, pitiful; (b) paltry, despicable (excuse, etc.); adv. -**ment.**

pittoresque [pitɔrɛsk]. **1.** a. picturesque, graphic (description, style). **2.** s.m. picturesqueness, vividness (of style, etc.).

pivert [pivɛːr], s.m. Orn: green woodpecker.

pivoine [pivwan], s.f. Bot: peony.

pivot [pivo], s.m. pivot, pin, axis; swivel.

pivoter [pivɔte], v.i. to pivot; to swivel, revolve; to turn, hinge (**sur,** on, upon); Aut: to slew round; s.m. -**ement.**

placard [plakaːr], s.m. **1.** (wall-)cupboard. **2.** poster, bill, placard.

placarder [plakarde], v.tr. to post up (a bill) on a wall.

place [plas], s.f. place. **1.** (a) position; **changer sa chaise de p.,** to shift one's chair; **tout remettre**

en p., to tidy up; **rester sur p.,** F: to stay put; **il ne peut pas rester en p.,** he can't keep still; (b) stead; **à votre p.,** if I were you; (c) **faire p. à qn,** to make room, make way, for s.o.; **occuper beaucoup de p.,** to take up a great deal of room; **p. aux dames!** ladies first! **2.** (a) seat; Aut: etc: **voiture à deux, à quatre, places,** two-seater, four-seater; **prix des places,** (i) fares; (ii) prices of admission; (b) situation, office, job; **perdre sa p.,** to lose one's job. **3.** locality, spot; **p. (publique),** (public) square, market-place; **sur p.,** on the spot.

placement [plasmã], s.m. **1.** (a) bureau de p., (i) employment bureau, agency; (ii) Employment Exchange; (b) sale, disposal; **trouver un p. rapide pour un article,** to find a quick sale for an article. **2.** investment; **faire des placements,** to invest money.

placer [plase], v.tr. (n. **plaçons**) to place. **1.** (a) to put, set (in a certain place); to find a place for (a guest, a spectator); (b) to find a situation, a job, for (s.o.); **p. des ouvriers,** to find jobs for workmen; **gens bien placés,** people of good position; (c) to invest (money). **2.** to sell, dispose of (goods); s. -**ier, -ière,** (i) s.m. Com: door-to-door salesman; (ii) s. clerk (at Employment Exchange).

se placer. 1. to take one's seat, one's place. **2.** to obtain a situation, to find a job.

placide [plasid], a. placid; calm; unruffled (temper); adv. -**ment.**

plafond [plafɔ̃], s.m. **1.** ceiling (in house). **2.** (maximum attainable or permissible) Av: ceiling, maximum flying height; Aut: maximum speed; Com: **prix p.,** maximum price; **fixer un p. à un budget,** to fix a ceiling to a budget; **il a atteint son p.,** he's hit his ceiling; **crever le p.,** to exceed the limit.

plafonner [plafɔne]. **1.** v.tr. to ceil (room). **2.** v.i. Av: to fly at the ceiling; Aut: to go flat out; Pol.Ec: **les prix plafonnent à . . .,** prices have reached the ceiling of . . .; **la production plafonne,** output has reached its ceiling; s.m. -**nage,** ceiling work; s.m. -**neur,** ceiling plasterer; s.m. -**nier,** ceiling light; Aut: roof light.

plage [plaːʒ], s.f. (a) beach, shore; (b) seaside resort.

plagiat [plaʒja], s.m. plagiarism; a. & s.m. -**aire,** plagiarist.

plaider [plɛde], v.tr. to plead (a cause); **p. coupable,** to plead guilty; abs. **il faudra p.,** we shall have to go to court; s. -**eur, -euse,** litigant, suitor; s.f. -**oirie,** counsel's speech.

plaie [plɛ], s.f. (a) wound, sore; (b) **p. sociale,** social evil; (c) F: (of pers.) **quelle p.!** what a pest!

plaignant, -ante [plɛɲã, -ãːt], a. & s. Jur: plaintiff.

plaindre [plɛ̃:dr], *v.tr.* (*conj. like* ATTEINDRE) to pity.
se plaindre, to complain.
plaine [plɛn], *s.f.* plain; flat open country.
plain-pied [plɛ̃pje], *s.m.* **1.** suite of rooms on one floor. **2.** *adv.phr.* **de p.-p.,** on one floor, on a level (**avec,** with).
plaint|e [plɛ̃:t], *s.f.* **1.** moan, groan. **2.** (*a*) complaint; (*b*) *Jur:* indictment, complaint; **porter p. contre qn,** to lodge a complaint against s.o.; *a.* **-if, -ive,** plaintive (tone); querulous (person, tone); *adv.* **-ivement.**
plaire [plɛ:r], *v.ind.tr.* (*pr.p.* **plaisant;** *p.p.* **plu;** *pr.ind.* **il plaît**) **p. à qn,** to please s.o.; **cet homme me plaît,** I like this man; **vous lui plaisez beaucoup,** he's greatly taken with you, attracted to you; **ses chansons plaisent,** his, her, songs go down well; *impers.* **s'il vous plaît,** (if you) please; **plaît-il?** I beg your pardon? **comme il vous plaira,** as you like.
se plaire, to be pleased, be happy; **je me plais beaucoup à Paris,** I enjoy, I love, being in Paris; **la vigne se plaît sur les coteaux,** the vine thrives, does well, on hillsides.
plaisanc|e [plɛza̅:s], *s.f.* **bateau de p.,** yacht, pleasure-boat; **maison de p.,** house in the country; **port de p.,** marina; **navigation de p.,** yachting, sailing; *s.m.* **-ier,** yachtsman, sailing enthusiast.
plais|ant [plɛzã]. **1.** *a.* (*a*) pleasant, agreeable; **un homme p.,** a pleasant, *F:* nice, man; (*b*) funny, amusing; **ton moitié p.,** half joking tone; **un homme p.,** an amusing man; (*c*) (*always before the noun*) ridiculous, absurd. **2.** *s.m.* **un mauvais p.,** a practical joker; **faire le p.,** to act the fool; *adv.* **-amment.**
plaisant|er [plɛzãte]. **1.** *v.i.* to joke, jest; **je ne plaisante pas,** I'm serious; **dire qch. en plaisantant,** *F:* **histoire de p.,** to say sth. for a joke, for fun; **vous plaisantez!** you don't mean it! **2.** *v.tr.* to tease, poke fun at (s.o.); *s.f.* **-erie,** joke, joking; *s.m.* **-in,** malicious, practical, joker.
plaisir [plɛzi:r], *s.m.* pleasure. **1.** delight; **cela fait p. à voir,** it is pleasant to see; **au p. de vous revoir,** good-bye; I hope we shall meet again; **à votre bon p.,** at your convenience; **à p.,** ad lib. **2.** (*a*) amusement, enjoyment; **partie de p.,** picnic, outing; (*b*) **vie de plaisirs,** gay life; **lieu de p.,** place of amusement; night haunt.
plan¹ [plã]. **1.** *a.* even, level, flat (surface). **2.** *s.m.* (*a*) plane; **p. d'eau** (broad) stretch of water; (*b*) **premier p.,** (i) *Art:* foreground; (ii) *Th:* downstage; (iii) *Cin:* close shot; **gros p.,** close-up; **passer au second p.,** (i) (*of project*) to be put aside; (ii) (*of pers.*) to take a back seat; **sur le p. national,** on a national, nation-wide, scale.
plan², *s.m.* plan; (*a*) drawing; draft; **lever les plans d'une région,** to survey a district; **p.**

cadastral, survey map; **p. urbain,** town plan; (*b*) scheme, project, design.
planche [plã:ʃ], *s.f.* **1.** (*a*) board, plank; **p. de parquet,** floor board; **p. à dessin,** drawing board; **p. à pain,** bread board; *Aut:* **p. de bord,** instrument panel; (*b*) shelf (of cupboard). **2.** *Art:* (printed) plate, engraving.
plancher [plãʃe], *s.m.* (boarded) floor; **p. en ciment,** cement floor; *Adm:* **prix p.,** (rock-)bottom price.
plan|er [plane], *v.i.* (*a*) (*of bird*) to soar; to hover; (*b*) *Av:* to glide; **vol plané,** glide, volplane; *s.m. Av:* **-eur,** glider.
planète [planɛt], *s.f. Astr:* planet.
planifi|er [planifje], *v.i. Adm:* to plan; *s.f.* **-cation,** planning.
plant [plã], *s.m.* seedling.
plantation [plãtasjɔ̃], *s.f.* **1.** planting (of trees seeds). **2.** (tea, coffee, etc.) plantation; **p. d'oranges,** orange grove.
plante¹ [plã:t], *s.f.* sole (of the foot).
plante², *s.f.* plant; **p. potagère,** vegetable; herb **p. à fleurs,** flowering plant; **p. d'appartement.** house plant; **p. de serre,** hothouse, greenhouse plant.
plant|er [plãte], *v.tr.* **1.** to plant, set (seeds). **2.** to fix, set (up); **p. un pieu,** to drive a stake; **p. une tente,** to pitch a tent; **p. un drapeau,** to raise a flag; *F:* **p. là qn,** to leave s.o. in the lurch; *s.m.* **-eur,** planter.
se planter, to stand, take one's stand; **se p. su ses jambes,** to take a firm stand.
planton [plãtɔ̃], *s.m. Mil:* orderly.
plantureu|x, -euse [plãtyrø, -ø:z], *a.* **1.** copious, abundant; lavish (meal). **2.** rich, fer tile (countryside); luxuriant (vegetation); *adv* **-sement.**
plaque [plak], *s.f.* **1.** (*a*) plate, sheet (of metal) slab (of marble, chocolate, etc.); patch (o snow); (*b*) **p. tournante,** turn-table; pivot; (*c*) **photographique,** photographic plate. **2.** (o namental) plaque; **p. de porte,** door plat name plate; **p. commémorative,** (votive) table **3.** badge; **p. d'identité,** identity disc; *Aut:* **d'immatriculation,** number plate.
plaqué [plake], *a. & s.m.* **1.** (**métal**) **p.,** plate metal, plated goods; electroplate; *F:* **c'est d p.,** it's sham, cheap, stuff. **2.** (**bois**) **p.,** veneere wood.
plaquer [plake], *v.tr.* **1.** to veneer (wood); plate (metal); **plaqué de sang, de boue,** cake with blood, with mud; *Rugby Fb:* to tackle (o ponent). **2.** *Mus:* to strike (and hold) a chor **3.** *F:* to abandon, desert, *F:* ditch, chuck (s.o **pourquoi l'avez-vous plaqué?** why did yo throw him over? **tout p.,** to chuck everythir up.
se plaquer. 1. to flatten oneself (**contre,** agains (ground, wall); **se p. contre le sol,** to lie flat.

Av: to pancake.
plastic [plastik], *s.m.* plastic (explosive jelly); *s.m.* **-age**, plastic bomb attack.
plastique [plastik]. **1.** *a.* plastic; *Com:* **matière p.**, plastic; **bois p.**, plastic wood. **2.** *s.f.* (*a*) art of modelling; (*b*) physique (of dancer, etc.). **3.** *s.m. Ind:* plastic; **p. mousse**, foam plastic; **p. stratifié**, laminated plastic.
plat [pla]. **1.** *a.* (*a*) flat, level; **mer plate**, smooth sea; **calme p.**, dead calm; (*b*) dull, insipid, tame; **style p.**, commonplace style; **vin p.**, dull, flat, wine; *Aut:* **moteur p.**, unresponsive engine; (*c*) *adv.phr.* **à p.**, flat; **tomber à p.**, to fall flat (on one's face); **pneu à p.**, flat tyre; **être à p.**, to be exhausted, *F:* all in. **2.** *s.m.* (*a*) flat (part); blade (of oar); *Sp:* **le p.**, flat racing; (*b*) *Cu:* dish (container or contents); *F:* **mettre les petits plats dans les grands**, to make a great spread; **mettre les pieds dans le p.**, to put one's foot in it; (*c*) *Cu:* course (at dinner); **p. de résistance**, main course, main dish.
platane [platan], *s.m. Bot:* plane-tree.
plateau, -eaux [plato], *s.m.* **1.** (*a*) tray; (*b*) pan, scale (of balance). **2.** *Geog:* plateau, table-land. **3.** platform; *Th:* floor (of the stage); *Cin:* set; **p. tournant**, revolving stage. **4.** *Tchn:* disc, plate; *Aut:* **p. d'embrayage**, clutch plate; **p. d'un tourne-disque**, (gramophone) turn-table.
plate-bande [platbɑ̃:d], *s.f.* flower-bed; *F:* **ne marchez pas dans mes plates-bandes**, mind your own business; *pl. plates-bandes.*
plate-forme [platfɔrm], *s.f.* **1.** platform (of bus); flat roof (of house); foot-plate (of locomotive). **2.** *Av: etc:* **p.-f. de lancement**, launching platform (for aircraft); launching pad (for rocket); *pl. plates-formes.*
platine[1] [platin], *s.m.* platinum.
platine[2], *s.f. Rec:* playing deck.
platitude [platityd], *s.f.* **1.** flatness, dullness (of character, style). **2.** commonplace remark, platitude.
plâtre [plɑːtr], *s.m.* (*a*) plaster; **p. de moulage**, plaster of Paris; (*b*) *Med:* cast; **mettre une jambe dans le p.**, to put a leg in plaster.
plâtrer [plɑtre], *v.tr.* to plaster (wall, ceiling); to plaster up (hole, crack); *Med:* to put (leg, etc.) in plaster; *Med:* **appareil plâtré**, cast; *s.m.* **-as**, (plaster) débris, rubble; *s.m.* **-ier**, plasterer.
plausible [plozibl], *a.* plausible (statement, theory); *adv.* **-ment**.
plébiscite [plebisit], *s.m.* plebiscite.
plein [plɛ̃]. **1.** *a.* full; (*a*) filled, replete (**de**, with); **p. de vie**, full of life; **bouteille pleine**, full bottle; **pleine bouteille**, bottleful (**de**, of); *Th:* **salle pleine à craquer**, house crammed to bursting point; (*b*) complete, entire, whole; **pleine lune**, full moon; **p. pouvoir**, full power; **p. sud**, due south; **pleine mer**, (i) high tide; (ii) the high seas; **de p. gré**, of one's own free will; (*c*) solid

(tyre, etc.); **trait p.**, continuous line; **table en acajou p.**, solid mahogany table; (*d*) **en p. visage**, full in the face; **en p. hiver**, in the depth of winter; **en p. air**, in the open; **en p. jour**, in broad daylight; (*e*) **respirer à pleins poumons**, to breathe deep; (*f*) *adv.* **il avait des larmes p. les yeux**, his eyes were full of tears. **2.** *s.m.* (*a*) fully occupied space; *Aut:* **faire le p.** (d'essence), to fill up with petrol; (*b*) full (extent); **la lune est dans son p.**, the moon is at the full; **la saison bat son p.**, the season is in full swing; (*c*) **en p. dans le centre**, right in the middle; *adv.* **-ement**, fully, entirely, quite.
plein-emploi [plɛ̃ɑ̃plwa], *s.m.inv. Pol: Ind:* full employment.
plein-temps [plɛ̃tɑ̃], *a.inv.* **ouvrier p.-t.**, full-time workman.
plénipotentiaire [plenipɔtɑ̃sjɛːr], (*a*) *a. & s.m.* plenipotentiary; (*b*) *s.m.* authorized agent (with full powers to act).
pleurer [plœre]. **1.** *v.tr.* to weep, mourn, for (s.o.). **2.** *v.i.* (*a*) to weep, to shed tears, to cry (**sur**, over; **pour**, for); **p. de joie**, to weep for joy; (*b*) (*of eyes*) to water, to run.
pleurnicher [plœrniʃe], *v.i.* to whimper, whine, snivel, grizzle; *s.* **-ard, -arde**; *s.* **-eur, -euse**, whiner, sniveller; *a.* **-eur, -euse**, tearful, whining.
pleuvoir [plœvwaːr], *v.* (*p.p.* **plu**; *pr.ind.* **il pleut, ils pleuvent**; *fu.* **il pleuvra**) to rain. **1.** *v.impers.* **il pleut à petites gouttes**, it's drizzling; **il pleut à verse**, it's pouring (with rain). **2.** **les invitations lui pleuvent de tous les côtés**, invitations are pouring in on him from all sides.
pleuvoter [plœvɔte], *v.i. F:* to drizzle.
pli [pli], *s.m.* **1.** (*a*) *Cl:* fold, pleat; tuck; *Hairdr:* **mise en plis**, set; (*b*) wrinkle, pucker; *Geol:* fold; (*c*) crease (in trousers, etc.); **faux p.**, (unintentional) crease. **2.** bend (of the arm). **3.** cover, envelope (of letter); **nous vous envoyons sous ce p.** . ., we send you herewith . ., please find enclosed . . .; **sous p. séparé**, under separate cover.
plie [pli], *s.f. Ich:* plaice.
plier [plije]. **1.** *v.tr.* (*p.d. &pr.sub. n.* **pliions**) (*a*) to fold (up); to strike (tent); (*b*) to bend (metal bar, etc.); **p. qn à la discipline**, to bring s.o. under discipline. **2.** *v.i.* (*a*) to bend; (*b*) to submit, yield; *a.* **-able**, flexible; *a. & s.m.* **-ant**, (*a*) *a.* folding; (*b*) *s.m.* folding chair.
se plier aux circonstances, to yield, to bow to circumstances.
plisser [plise]. **1.** *v.tr.* (*a*) to pleat (skirt); (*b*) to crease, crumple; **p. les yeux**, to screw up one's eyes. **2.** *v.i. & pr.* to crease, crumple, pucker; *s.m.* **-age**, pleating (of skirt, kilt); crinkling (of paper); *s.m.* **-ement**, (*a*) pleating (of material); corrugation (of sheet metal); (*b*) crumpling, puckering (of material, paper, skin); (*c*) *Geol:*

fold.

ploiement [plwamɑ̃], *s.m.* folding, bending (of material, paper, etc.).

plomb [plɔ̃], *s.m.* **1.** lead. **2.** shot; **petit p.,** birdshot; **gros p.,** buckshot. **3. fil à p.,** plumbline; **à p.,** upright, vertical(ly). **4.** *El:* **p.** (de sûreté), fuse, cut-out; **faire sauter les plombs,** to blow the fuses.

plomb|er [plɔ̃be], *v.tr.* (*a*) to cover, sheathe, sth. with lead; (*b*) to weight with lead; (*c*) **p. une dent,** to fill a tooth; (*d*) *Cust:* to seal (goods); *s.m.* **-age,** filling (of tooth); *s.f.* **-erie,** (*a*) leadwork, plumbing; (*b*) plumber's trade, shop; *s.m.* **-ier,** plumber.

plonge [plɔ̃:ʒ], *s.f.* washing up (in restaurant); **faire la p.,** to wash up.

plongée [plɔ̃ʒe], *s.f.* (*a*) plunge, dive; (*b*) submersion (of submarine).

plong|er [plɔ̃ʒe], *v.* (*n.* **plongeons**) **1.** *v.i.* to plunge; (*a*) to dive; to take a header; (*b*) (*of submarine*) to submerge. **2.** *v.tr.* to plunge, immerse (s.o., sth., in liquid); **p. la main dans sa poche,** to thrust one's hand into one's pocket; *s.m.* **-eoir,** diving-board; *s.m.* **-eon,** plunge, dive; *a. & s.* **-eur, -euse,** (*a*) *a.* diving (bird, etc.); (*b*) *s.* diver; washer-up.

se plonger, to immerse oneself (**dans,** in) (study, a book).

ploy|er [plwaje], *v.* (**je ploie**) **1.** *v.tr.* to bend (the knee). **2.** *v.i.* to bow (under burden); *a.* **-able,** pliable, flexible.

pluie [plɥi], *s.f.* rain; (*a*) **p. battante,** pouring rain, downpour; **p. d'orage,** thunder shower; **p. fine,** drizzle; **temps de p.,** wet weather; **le temps est à la p.,** it looks like rain; **"craint la p.,"** "to be kept dry"; **parler de la p. et du beau temps,** to talk about the weather, of nothing in particular; *F:* **faire la p. et le beau temps,** to be the boss, the big noise, to rule the roost; (*b*) **p. de balles,** spatter of bullets; **p. de sable,** sandstorm.

plum|e [plym], *s.f.* **1.** feather; **gibier à plumes,** game birds; **oiseau sans plumes,** unfledged bird. **2.** (pen) nib; **stylo à p. ou stylo à bille?** fountain pen or ball-point? **trait de p.,** stroke of the pen; **dessin à la p.,** pen and ink drawing; *s.m.* **-age,** plumage; *s.m.* **-eau, -eaux,** featherduster.

plumer [plyme], *v.tr.* to pluck (poultry); *F:* to fleece (s.o.).

plupart (la) [laplypa:r], *s.f.* (the) most; the greater, greatest, part; **la p. des hommes,** the majority of men, most men; **la p. d'entre eux,** most of them; **la p. du temps,** most of the time; in most cases; generally; **pour la p.,** mostly.

pluriel, -elle [plyrjɛl], *a. & s.m. Gram:* plural.

plus [ply], *often* |plys| *at the end of a word-group, or before a vowel:* **plus on est de fous, plus on rit** [plyzɔ̃nɛdfuplyzɔ̃ri]. **1.** *adv.* (*a*) more; **il est p. grand que moi,** he is taller than I; **deux fois p. grand,** twice as large; **p. de dix hommes,** more than ten men; **p. loin,** farther on; **p. tôt,** sooner; **pour ne pas dire p.** [*often* plys], to say the least; **il y en a tant et p.,** there is any amount of it; (*b*) **(le) p.,** most; **la p. longue rue, la rue la p. longue, de la ville,** the longest street in the town; **une ascension des p. hasardeuses,** a most perilous ascent; **c'est tout ce qu'il y a de p. simple,** nothing could be simpler; (*c*) (*with negative expressed or understood*) **ne . . . p.,** no more, no longer; **p. de doute,** there is no longer any doubt about it; **p. rien,** nothing more; **p. que dix minutes!** only ten minutes left! (*d*) *adv. phr.* **non p.,** (not) either; **ni moi non p.,** neither do I, did I, am I, shall I, etc.; (*e*) (*often* [plys]) plus, also, besides, in addition; **cent francs d'amende, p. les frais,** a hundred francs fine and costs; (*f*) *adv. phr.* **de p.,** more; **rien de p., merci,** nothing else, thank you; **de p. en p.,** more and more; **en p.,** in addition, (i) into the bargain; (ii) extra; **le vin est en p.,** wine is extra. **2.** *s.m.* (*a*) more; **sans p.,** (just that and) nothing more; (*b*) most; **(tout) au p.,** at (the very) most; (*c*) *Mth:* plus (sign).

plusieurs [plyzjœ:r], *a. & pron.pl.* several.

plus-value [plyvaly], *s.f.* increase in value; appreciation (of land-value, etc.); excess yield, surplus; *pl.* **plus-values.**

plutôt [plyto], *adv.* (*a*) rather, sooner; **ne pleurez pas, riez p.,** don't cry, laugh instead; (*b*) rather on the whole; **il faisait p. froid,** the weather was cold if anything.

pluvieux, -ieuse [plyvjø, -jø:z], *a.* rainy (season); wet (weather).

pneu, *pl.* **pneus** [pnø], *s.m.* (pneumatic) tyre, *N.Am:* tire.

pneumatique [pnømatik], *a.* pneumatic; air-(pump, etc.); **outil p.,** compressed-air tool; **canot p.,** rubber dinghy; **matelas p.,** rubber, inflatable, mattress.

pneumonie [pnømɔni], *s.f.* pneumonia, congestion of the lungs.

poche [pɔʃ], *s.f.* **1.** pocket; **couteau de p.,** pocket knife; **livre de p.,** paperback, *N.Am:* pocketbook; **mettre la main à la p.,** to pay up; **j'y suis de ma p.,** I am out of pocket by it; *F:* **mettez ça dans votre p. (et votre mouchoir dessus),** put that in your pipe and smoke it; **connaître qch comme le fond de sa p.,** to know sth. like the back of one's hand; **il n'a pas la langue dans sa p.,** he has plenty to say for himself; **mettre sa langue dans sa p.,** to hold one's tongue. **2.** (*a*) bag, pouch; paper, plastic, bag; **p. d'air,** (i) *Av:* air-pocket; (ii) airlock; (*b*) *Biol:* sac. **3.** *pl.* bags, pouches (under the eyes).

pocher [pɔʃe]. **1.** *v.tr. Cu:* to poach (eggs); *F:* **œil poché,** black eye. **2.** *v.i.* (*of clothes*) to get baggy.

pochette [pɔʃɛt], *s.f.* (*a*) small pocket; pouch

handbag, *esp.* clutch-bag; (*b*) pocket-case (of instruments); (*c*) **p. d'allumettes**, book of matches; **p. de papeterie**, compendium (of notepaper).

poêle¹ [pwal, pwɑːl], *s.f.* frying-pan.

poêle², *s.m.* stove; **p. à feu continu**, slow-combustion stove; **p. à gaz**, gas stove; **p. de cuisine**, cooker.

poème [pɔɛm], *s.m.* poem; *F:* **c'est un p.**, it's priceless.

poésie [pɔezi], *s.f.* 1. poetry. 2. poem; piece of poetry.

poète [pɔɛt]. 1. *s.m.* poet; **Mme X. est un p. distingué**, Mrs X. is a distinguished poet(ess). 2. *a.* **femme p.**, woman poet; poetess.

poétique [pɔetik], *a.* (*a*) poetic (inspiration, licence); (*b*) poetical (works); *adv.* **-ment**.

poids [pwɑ], *s.m.* weight. 1. (*a*) heaviness; **perdre, reprendre, du p.**, to lose weight; to put on weight again; **vendre au p.**, to sell by weight; **le p. n'y est pas**, this is short weight; (*b*) importance; **son opinion a du p.**, his opinion carries weight; **gens de p.**, people of consequence. 2. (*a*) **p. de dix kilos**, ten-kilo weight; (*b*) **les p. d'une horloge**, the weights of a clock; (*c*) *Sp:* **lancer le p.**, to put the weight. 3. load, burden; *Av: etc:* **p. utile**, pay-load; **p. mort,** dead weight; *Aut:* **p. lourd**, heavy lorry, *F:* juggernaut.

poignant [pwaɲɑ̃], *a.* poignant; **spectacle p.**, (i) agonizing, (ii) thrilling, sight.

poignard [pwaɲaːr], *s.m.* dagger; **coup de p.**, stab; **la nouvelle lui fut un coup de p.**, the news cut him to the quick, was a severe blow to him.

poignarder [pwaɲarde], *v.tr.* to stab (s.o.).

poigne [pwaɲ], *s.f. F:* grip, grasp; **montrer de la p.**, to show energy; **il manque de p.**, he lacks grip.

poignée [pwaɲe], *s.f.* 1. (*a*) handful; **à poignées**, in handfuls; by the handful; **une p. d'hommes**, a handful, small number, of men; (*b*) **p. de main**, handshake. 2. handle (of door, cycle); hilt (of sword); haft, handhold (of tool); *Aut: etc:* **p. à condamnation**, handle with locking device, with safety-catch.

poignet [pwaɲɛ], *s.m.* 1. wrist; **faire qch. à la force du p.**, to do sth. (i) by sheer strength, (ii) by sheer hard work. 2. wristband; cuff (of garment).

poil [pwal], *s.m.* 1. (*a*) (*of animal*) hair, fur; **à p. long**, long-haired, shaggy; **monter à p.**, to ride bareback; (*b*) coat (of animals); **cheval d'un beau p.**, sleek horse; **chien au p. rude, à p. dur**, wire-haired, rough-haired, dog; (*c*) nap (of cloth); pile (of velvet); (*d*) **poils d'une brosse**, bristles of a brush. 2. (*of pers.*) hair (on the body); *P:* **à p.**, naked; **se mettre à p.**, to strip naked; *F:* **il a du p.**, he's got guts; **avoir un p. (dans la main)**, to be workshy.

poilu [pwaly]. 1. *a.* hairy, shaggy. 2. *s.m. F:* French soldier (1914–18).

poinçon [pwɛ̃sɔ̃], *s.m.* 1. bradawl. 2. (*a*) (perforating) punch; (*b*) **p. de contrôle**, hall-mark.

poinçonner [pwɛ̃sɔne], *v.tr.* 1. (*a*) to prick, bore; (*b*) to punch. 2. (*a*) to punch, clip (ticket); (*b*) to stamp, hall-mark (silver, etc.); *s.m.* **-age**; *s.m.* **-eur**, (*a*) puncher; (*b*) ticket collector; *s.f.* **-euse**, ticket-punch.

poindre [pwɛ̃ːdr], *v.i.* (*defective; 3rd. pers. sing. only;* il point; il poignait; il poindra; used esp. in *inf.*) (*of daylight*) to dawn, break; (*of plants*) to sprout.

poing [pwɛ̃], *s.m.* fist; **serrer les poings**, to clench one's fists; **montrer le p. (à qn)**, to shake one's fist (at s.o.); **coup de p.**, punch; **dormir à poings fermés**, to sleep soundly.

point¹ [pwɛ̃], *s.m.* 1. hole (in strap). 2. (*a*) *Needlew: Knitting:* stitch; (*b*) (*acute pain*) **p. au dos**, stabbing pain in one's back; **p. de côté**, stitch in one's side. 3. point; (*a*) (*in time*) **le p. du jour**, daybreak; **arriver à p. nommé**, to arrive in the nick of time; (*b*) (*in space*) **p. de départ, d'arrivée**, starting, arrival, point; **p. de vue**, (i) (*panorama*) view(point); (ii) point of view, standpoint; *Mec.E:* **p. d'appui**, fulcrum (of lever); purchase; **mettre (qch.) au p.**, to focus, adjust (sth.); to tune (engine); to perfect (invention); *F:* **c'est au p.**, it's just right. 4. (*a*) point, dot; full stop, *N.Am:* period; **deux points**, colon; **p. d'exclamation**, exclamation mark; (*b*) *Sp:* point, score; **marquer les points**, to keep the score; (*c*) *Sch:* mark; (*d*) speck, spot, dot. 5. (*a*) point, stage, degree; **à ce p. que**, so much so that; **au dernier p.**, to the last degree; **faire le p. d'(une question)**, to take stock of (a question); (*b*) **en bon p.**, in good condition; (*c*) **à point**, in the right condition; **viande cuite à p.**, meat done to a turn. 6. point, particular; **p. capital**, main point; **p. de droit**, point of law; *s.m.* **point-virgule**, semi-colon; *pl.* **points-virgules**.

point², *negative adv.* (*used only in a few expressions*) **peu ou p.**, little or not at all; **je n'en ai p.**, I've none at all.

pointe [pwɛ̃t], *s.f.* 1. (*a*) point (of pin); head (of arrow); toe (of shoe); **coup de p.**, thrust; **en p.**, tapering; pointed; **sur la p. des pieds**, on tiptoe; *Ind:* **heures de p.**, rush hours; peak period; (*b*) **p. du jour**, daybreak; **p. d'ironie**, touch of irony; *Cu:* **p. d'ail**, touch of garlic; *Sp:* **p. de vitesse**, spurt, sprint. 2. *Geog:* **p. de terre**, spit, tongue (of land).

pointer¹ [pwɛ̃te], *v.tr.* 1. to check, tick off (names on list); *Ind:* **p. à l'arrivée, à la sortie**, to clock in, out. 2. to point, level (telescope); to aim, point (gun). *s.m.* **-age**, checking; *Ind:* **pendule de p.**, attendance clock; *s.m. Ind:* **-eur**, checker, time-keeper.

pointer². **1.** *v.tr.* to thrust, prick, stab. **2.** *v.i.* to appear; (*of plant*) to sprout; (*of steeple*) to soar upwards.

pointillé [pwɛ̃tije]. **1.** *a.* dotted (line); stippled (engraving); spotted (pattern). **2.** *s.m.* (*a*) **détacher suivant le p.**, tear along the dotted line; (*b*) stippling; **dessin au p.**, stippled design.

pointilleu|x, -euse [pwɛ̃tijø, -ø:z], *a.* **1.** touchy (person). **2.** (*a*) particular; fastidious; (*b*) finicky (person).

pointu [pwɛ̃ty], *a.* sharp-pointed; (*of dog*) **oreilles pointues**, prick ears; **aux oreilles pointues**, prick-eared.

pointure [pwɛ̃ty:r], *s.f.* size (in shoes, gloves, etc.).

poir|e [pwa:r], *s.f.* **1.** pear; **couper la p. en deux**, to split the difference. **2.** *El:* pear-switch. **3.** *P:* (*a*) face, mug; (*b*) mug, sucker; **quelle p.!** what a fool! *s.m.* **-ier**, pear-tree.

poireau, -eaux [pwaro], *s.m.* leek; **planté comme un p.**, rooted to the spot.

pois [pwa], *s.m.* **1.** pea; **p. de senteur**, sweet pea. **2.** *Cu:* **petits p.**, green peas. **3.** **tissu à p.**, spotted, polka dot, material.

poison [pwazɔ̃], *s.m.* poison.

poisseux, -euse [pwasø, -ø:z], *a.* sticky.

poisson [pwasɔ̃], *s.m.* fish; **p. d'eau douce, p. de mer**, freshwater fish, sea fish; **p. d'avril**, April fool; **être comme un p. dans l'eau**, to be in one's element; *Astr:* **les Poissons**, Pisces.

poitrine [pwatrin], *s.f.* (*a*) breast, chest; **rhume de p.**, cold on the chest; **tour de p.**, chest measurement; (*b*) *Cu:* brisket (of beef).

poivre [pwavr], *s.m.* pepper; **grain de p.**, peppercorn.

poivré [pwavre], *a.* peppery (food); pungent (smell); **récit p.**, spicy tale; **prix p.**, stiff price.

poivr|er [pwavre], *v.tr.* to pepper (food); **p. l'addition**, to stick it on (the bill); *s.m.* **-ier**, pepper-pot; *s.m.* **-on**, sweet pepper.

polaire [pɔlɛ:r], *a.* polar; **l'étoile p.**, *s.* **la p.**, the pole star; *Geog:* **cercle p.**, polar circle; *El:* **champ p.**, polar field.

pôle [po:l], *s.m. Geog: El:* pole.

poli [pɔli]. **1.** *a.* (*a*) polished; bright (metal); glossy, sleek (horse's coat); (*b*) polished, elegant (style, manners); courteous (person); (*c*) polite, well-mannered; (*to child*) **sois p.!** mind your manners! **2.** *s.m.* polish, gloss; **ce bois prend un beau p.**, this wood takes a high polish; *adv.* **-ment**, politely.

police¹ [pɔlis], *s.f.* **1.** policing; **faire la p.**, to keep order; **plaque de p. d'un véhicule**, registration number of a vehicle. **2.** police (force); **p. de la route**, traffic police; **p. judiciaire (P.J.)** = CID; **p. des mœurs** = vice squad; **appeler p. secours**, to call the police, to dial 999; **agent de p.**, police constable, policeman; **remettre qn entre les mains de la p.**, to give s.o. in charge.

police², *s.f.* (insurance) policy.

policier, -ière [pɔlisje, -jɛ:r]. **1.** *a.* **chien p.**, police dog; **roman p.**, detective novel. **2.** *s.m.* (*a*) police officer; detective; (*b*) detective novel.

poliomyélite [pɔljɔmjelit], *s.f.*, *F:* **polio** [pɔljo], *s.f. Med:* poliomyelitis, *F:* polio.

pol|ir [pɔli:r], *v.tr.* **1.** to polish (metal, stone, wood, etc.); to burnish. **2.** to polish, refine (one's style, manners); *s.m.* **-issage;** *s.* **-isseur, -isseuse,** (*a*) (*pers.*) polisher; (*b*) *s.f.* **-isseuse,** polishing machine, polisher; *s.f.* **-issoire,** (shoe-)polishing brush.

polisson, -onne [pɔlisɔ̃, -ɔn], *s.* naughty child; scamp; *s.f.* **-nerie**, mischievousness.

politesse [pɔlitɛs], *s.f.* politeness; good manners; courtesy; **se confondre en politesses,** to fall over oneself to be polite.

politicien, -ienne [pɔlitisjɛ̃, -jɛn], *s. usu. Pej:* politician.

politique [pɔlitik]. **1.** *a.* (*a*) political (party, rights); **homme p.**, politician; **économie p.**, economics; (*b*) politic, prudent (person, behaviour); diplomatic (answer). **2.** *s.f.* (*a*) policy; (*b*) politics; *adv.* **-ment.**

pollu|er [pɔl(l)ɥe], *v.tr.* to pollute (the atmosphere, the environment); *s.f.* **-tion.**

polo [pɔlo], *s.m.* **1.** *Sp:* polo. **2.** *Cl:* sweat shirt, T-shirt.

Pologne (la) [lapɔlɔɲ]. *Pr.n.f. Geog:* Poland.

polonais, -aise [pɔlɔnɛ, -ɛ:z]. **1.** (*a*) *a.* Polish; (*b*) *s.* Pole. **2.** *s.m. Ling:* Polish. **3.** *s.f. Danc: Mus:* **polonaise**, polonaise.

poltron, -onne [pɔltrɔ̃, -ɔn]. **1.** *a.* easily frightened; timid; cowardly; *F:* funky. **2.** *s.* coward; *F:* funk; *s.f.* **-nerie**, cowardice; timidity.

polyarthrite [pɔliartrit], *s.f. Med:* **p. chronique évolutive**, rheumatoid arthritis.

poly|copier [pɔlikɔpje], *v.tr.* to stencil; to duplicate; *s.f.* **-copie,** (duplicated) copy.

polyculture [pɔlikylty:r], *s.f.* mixed farming.

polyéthylène [pɔlietilɛn], *s.m.* polythene.

polyglotte [pɔliglɔt], *a. & s.* polyglot.

Polynésie (la) [lapɔlinezi]. *Pr.n.f. Geog:* Polynesia.

polynésien, -ienne [pɔlinezjɛ̃, -jɛn], *a. & s.* Polynesian.

polysyllab|le [pɔlisil(l)ab], *s.m.* polysyllable; *a.* **-ique**, polysyllabic.

polytechnique [pɔliteknik], *a.* polytechnic.

pommade [pɔmad], *s.f.* pomade; ointment.

pomm|e [pɔm], *s.f.* **1.** (*a*) apple; **p. à couteau**, eating apple; **p. à cidre**, cider apple; **p. sauvage**, crab-apple; (*b*) **p. de terre**, potato; **bifteck aux pommes (frites)**, steak and chips; **purée de pommes (de terre)**, mashed potatoes; **pommes chips**, potato crisps; (*c*) **p. de pin**, fir cone, pine cone. **2.** knob (of bedstead, walking-stick); head (of cabbage); **p.**

d'arrosoir, rose of a watering-can; *s.f.* -**eraie**, apple-orchard; *s.f.* -**ette**, cheek-bone; *s.m.* -**ier**, apple tree.

pommelé [pɔmle], *a.* dappled, mottled; **jument gris p.**, dapple-grey mare; **ciel p.**, mackerel sky.

pompe¹ [pɔ̃:p], *s.f.* pomp, ceremony, display; **entrepreneur de pompes funèbres**, undertaker, *N.Am: esp. U.S:* mortician.

pompe², *s.f.* pump; **p. à incendie**, fire-engine; *Aut:* **p. à air, à essence**, air-pump, petrol-pump; **p. à graissage**, grease gun.

pomper [pɔ̃pe], *v.tr.* to pump; *s.m.* -**ier**, fireman.

pompeux, -euse [pɔ̃pø, -ø:z], *a.* pompous; *adv.* -**sement**.

pompiste [pɔ̃pist], *s.m. & f. Aut:* petrol-pump attendant.

pompon [pɔ̃pɔ̃], *s.m.* pompon; (ornamental) tuft (esp. on French sailors' caps); *F:* **à lui le p.**, he's easily first.

ponce [pɔ̃:s], *s.f.* **(pierre) p.**, pumice-stone.

ponctualité [pɔ̃ktɥalite], *s.f.* punctuality.

ponctuel, -elle [pɔ̃ktɥɛl], *a.* punctual **(dans, en, in)**; **p. à remplir ses devoirs**, punctual in the execution of his duties; *adv.* -**lement**.

ponctuer [pɔ̃ktɥe], *v.tr.* to punctuate; *s.f.* -**ation**.

pondre [pɔ̃:dr], *v.tr.* to lay (eggs); *abs.* to lay; *s.f.* -**euse**, laying bird, layer.

poney [pɔnɛ], *s.m.* pony.

pont [pɔ̃], *s.m.* **1.** (a) bridge; **p. tournant**, swing-bridge; *Av:* **p. aérien**, air-lift; **p. à bascule**, weighbridge; *Adm:* **les ponts et chaussées**, the Highways Department, department of civil engineering; (b) *Ind:* platform, stage, bridge; **p. de chargement**, loading bridge; *Ind:* **p. roulant**, overhead crane. **2.** deck (of ship).

pontife [pɔ̃tif], *s.m.* pontiff; **le souverain P.**, the Pope; *a.* -**ical, -icaux**, pontifical, papal; *adv.* -**icalement**.

pont-levis [pɔ̃l(ə)vi], *s.m.* drawbridge; lift-bridge (of canal); *pl.* **ponts-levis**.

popote [pɔpɔt]. **1.** *s.f. F:* **faire p. ensemble**, to mess together; **faire la p.**, to do the cooking. **2.** *a.inv.* stay-at-home (person); **elle est terriblement p.**, she's never out of the kitchen; she's always fussing round the house.

populace [pɔpylas], *s.f. Pej:* populace, rabble, riff-raff.

populaire [pɔpylɛːr], *a.* popular; (a) *Pol:* of, for, the people; **démocratie p.**, people's democracy; **manifestation p.**, mass demonstration; (b) **expression p.**, (i) un-educated, (ii) slangy, expression; **chanson p.**, (i) folk-song; (ii) popular song; (c) **se rendre p.**, to make oneself popular; *adv.* -**ment**.

populariser [pɔpylarize], *v.tr.* to popularize (an idea); to make (s.o.) popular; *s.f.* -**isation**; *s.f.* -**ité**.

population [pɔpylasjɔ̃], *s.f.* population; *a.* -**eux, -euse**, populous, densely populated.

porc [pɔːr], *s.m.* **1.** pig, *N.Am:* hog. **2.** *Cu:* pork.

porcelaine [pɔrsəlɛn], *s.f.* porcelain, china(ware).

porcelet [pɔrsəlɛ], *s.m.* young pig; piglet.

porche [pɔrʃ], *s.m.* porch.

porcherie [pɔrʃəri], *s.f.* piggery; pigsty.

porcin [pɔrsɛ̃], *a.* porcine; **élevage p.**, pig-breeding; pig-farm.

pore [pɔːr], *s.m.* pore; *a.* -**eux, -euse**, porous; *s.f.* -**osité**, porosity, porousness.

port¹ [pɔːr], *s.m.* harbour, haven, port; **arriver à bon p.**, to arrive safely; **capitaine de p.**, harbour-master; **droits de p.**, harbour dues; **p. maritime**, seaport; **p. fluvial**, river port; **p. militaire**, naval base; **p. de pêche**, fishing port; **p. d'escale**, port of call.

port², *s.m.* **1.** (a) (act of) carrying (arms, etc.); (b) wearing (of uniform). **2.** cost of transport; postage; **en p. dû**, carriage forward. **3.** bearing, gait, carriage (of person); *a.* -**able**, portable; wearable; *s.m.* -**age**, conveyance, transport (of goods).

portail, -ails [pɔrtaːj], *s.m.* (main) gate, gateway; main door (of church); great west door (of cathedral).

portant [pɔrtɑ̃]. **1.** *a.* **être bien p.**, to be in good health; to be fit. **2.** *s.m. Tchn:* supporter, stay, strut.

portatif, -ive [pɔrtatif, -iːv], *a.* portable; easily carried; **machine à écrire portative**, portable typewriter, *F:* portable; **poste (de radio) p.**, portable radio; *Com:* **glaces portatives**, ices to take away.

porte [pɔrt], *s.f.* **1.** gate(way), doorway, entrance; **p. cochère**, carriage entrance; *Ski:* gate; pair of flags; *Tchn:* **p. de visite**, inspection-door, manhole; *Nau: Av:* hatch. **2.** door; **p. d'entrée**, front door; **p. de service**, back door; **p. tournante**, revolving door; **p. coulissante**, sliding door; **trouver p. close**, to find nobody at home; **demander la p.**, to call to the concierge to open the door; **écouter aux portes**, to eavesdrop; *s.m. Com:* **(p.-)à(-)p.**, door-to-door canvassing, selling. **3.** eye (of hook and eye).

porte-affiches [pɔrtafiʃ], *s.m.inv.* notice-board.

porte-avions [pɔrtavjɔ̃], *s.m.inv.* aircraft carrier.

porte-bagages [pɔrt(ə)bagaːʒ], *s.m.inv.* (a) luggage-rack; (b) *Aut:* roof-rack; (c) *Rail:* trolley.

porte-bébé [pɔrt(ə)bebe], *s.m.inv.* **1.** baby-carrier (on bicycle). **2.** carry-cot.

porte-billets [pɔrt(ə)bijɛ], *s.m.inv.* notecase, *N.Am:* billfold.

porte-bonheur [pɔrt(ə)bɔnœːr], *s.m.inv.* lucky charm, mascot.

porte-clefs [pɔrt(ə)kle], s.m.inv. key-ring.

porte-couteau [pɔrt(ə)kuto], s.m. knife-rest; pl. porte-couteaux.

portée [pɔrte], s.f. 1. (a) litter, brood (of animals, birds); (b) Mus: stave; **au-dessus de la p.,** in alt. 2. (a) reach (of one's arm); range, scope; **à p. de la main,** within reach; **à p. de voix,** within call; **hors de p. de la voix humaine,** out of range of the human voice; (b) bearing, full significance; **la p. d'une affirmation,** the full significance of a statement; **affirmation d'une grande p.,** weighty statement.

porte-fenêtre [pɔrt(ə)fənɛːtr], s.f. French window; pl. portes-fenêtres.

portefeuille [pɔrt(ə)fœːj], s.m. 1. portfolio; Pol: **ministre sans p.,** minister without portfolio; **accepter un p.,** to accept office. 2. wallet, notecase, N.Am: billfold; **avoir un p. bien garni,** to be rich; Fin: **(effets en) p.,** investments, securities; **p. d'assurances,** portfolio (of insurance broker); **jupe en p.,** wrap-over skirt; F: **lit en p.,** apple-pie bed.

portemanteau, -eaux [pɔrt(ə)mãto], s.m. coat(-and-hat)-rack, -stand.

porte(-)mine [pɔrt(ə)min], s.m. propelling pencil; pl. porte-mine(s).

porte-monnaie [pɔrt(ə)mɔnɛ], s.m.inv. purse.

porte-parole [pɔrt(ə)parɔl], s.m.inv. spokesman.

porter [pɔrte]. 1. v.tr. to carry; (a) to bear, support (a burden); (b) to wear (clothes); **p. un nom illustre,** to bear an illustrious name; **p. du noir, une bague,** to wear black, a ring; **p. la soutane, les armes,** to be a priest, a soldier; (c) to carry, convey, take (sth. somewhere); **il porta le verre à ses lèvres,** he lifted the glass to his lips; (d) **p. un coup à qn,** to strike s.o.; **p. ses regards sur qn,** to look at s.o.; **p. une accusation contre qn,** to bring a charge against s.o.; (e) to inscribe, enter; **portez cela à mon compte,** put that down to me; **p. un nom sur une liste,** to enter a name on a list; (f) to induce, incline, prompt; **tout me porte à croire que . . .,** everything leads me to believe that . . .; (g) to produce, bring forth; **argent qui porte intérêt,** money that bears interest; **p. des fruits,** to bear fruit; (h) **p. témoignage,** to bear witness. 2. v.i. (a) to rest, bear; **la perte porte sur nous,** we have to stand the loss; (b) to hit, reach; **aucun des coups de feu ne porta,** none of the shots took effect; **sa voix porte bien,** his voice carries well.

se porter. 1. to go, proceed (to a place); **se p. au secours de qn,** to go to s.o.'s help. 2. **se p. bien, mal, à merveille,** to be well, unwell, to be in the best of health. 3. **se p. caution, candidat,** to stand as surety, as candidate.

porte-serviettes [pɔrt(ə)sɛrvjɛt], s.m.inv. towel-rail; **rouleau p.-s.,** roller (for roller-

towel).

porteur, -euse [pɔrtœːr, -øːz], s. (a) porter carrier; bearer (of news, etc.); Fin: **p. d'u chèque,** payee of a cheque; **p. d'actions** shareholder; **titre au p.,** bearer bond; (b) Aut **gros p.,** heavy (petrol) tanker; Av: **avion gros moyen, p.,** large, medium, transport aircraft.

porte-voix [pɔrt(ə)vwa], s.m.inv. loudhailer megaphone.

portier, -ière[1] [pɔrtje, -jɛːr], s. (a) porter, door keeper, N.Am: janitor (of a block of flats); (b (of hotel, etc.) commissionaire; (c) Fb: etc goalkeeper.

portière[2], s.f. 1. door (of carriage, car, railwa carriage). 2. door curtain.

portion [pɔrsjɔ̃], s.f. portion, share, par helping (of food).

portique [pɔrtik], s.m. 1. portico, porch. 2 Sp: **p. du but,** goal mouth; (gymnastic) ga lows. 3. Mec: **p. roulant,** travelling-gantr crane.

Porto [pɔrto]. 1. Pr.n.m. Geog: Oporto. 2. s.m (vin de) **p.,** port (wine); **p. rouge, blanc,** rub white, port.

portrait [pɔrtrɛ], s.m. portrait, likeness; s.m -iste, portrait-painter.

portugais, -aise [pɔrtygɛ, -ɛːz]. 1. a. & s. Po tuguese. 2. s.m. Ling: Portuguese.

Portugal (le) [ləpɔrtygal]. Pr.n.m. Geog Portugal.

pose [poːz], s.f. 1. fitting, fixing; installatio laying, placing; **p. d'un tapis,** laying of carpet; **p. de câbles sous-marins,** cable-layin 2. (a) pose, attitude, posture; Golf: **p. d'u balle,** lie of a ball; (b) posing, affectation; sa p.,** unaffectedly. 3. Phot: (time of) exposure

posé [poze], a. staid, grave, calm, sedate (pe son); steady (bearing, person); **voix posé** even, steady, voice; calm voice.

poser [poze]. 1. v.i. (a) to rest, lie (on sth. **poutre qui pose sur un mur,** beam that rests o a wall; (b) to pose (as artist's model); to sit (f one's portrait; (c) to pose; to show off. 2. v.t (a) to place, put (sth. somewhere); **p. so chapeau,** to put down one's hat; **p. un avion,** land an aircraft; **p. une question à qn,** to put question to s.o.; to ask s.o. a question; (b) put up, fix (up) (curtain, etc.).

se poser, (of bird) to settle, alight; (of aircraft) land.

poseur, -euse [pozœːr, -øːz]. 1. s. Tchn: lay (of pipes, cables, etc.); Rail: **p. de voie,** pla layer; Navy: **p. de mines,** minelayer. 2. a. & (person) who poses; **il est un peu p.,** he's rath affected.

posit|if, -ive [pozitif, -iːv], a. (a) positive, actu: **c'est p.,** that's so; (b) practical (mind); matte of-fact (person); adv. -**ivement.**

position [pozisjɔ̃], s.f. position. 1. (a) situatio

site (of house, town); position (of ship, aircraft, etc.); (b) posture, attitude; *Golf:* stance; (c) tactical position; (d) condition, circumstances; **p. gênante,** embarrassing situation; **p. sociale,** social status. 2. post, situation, job.

osologie [pozɔlɔʒi], *s.f. Med: etc:* dosage.

ossédé, -ée [pɔsede]. 1. *a.* possessed (**de,** by, of); infatuated, dominated (by passion, idea, etc.). 2. *s.* person possessed; madman, -woman, maniac.

osséder [pɔsede], *v.tr.* (**je possède; je posséderai**) 1. to be in possession of (sth.); (a) to possess, own; **p. un titre,** to hold a title; (b) to be master of (subject); (c) to curb, control (one's tongue); (d) **quel démon le possède?** what devil possesses him? 2. *F:* **je me suis fait p.,** I've been had.

e posséder, to contain oneself, one's temper, one's emotions; **il ne se possède plus,** he is no longer able to control himself.

ossession [pɔsesjɔ̃], *s.f.* 1. possession; **être en p. de qch.,** to own sth. 2. property; *in pl.* **possessions;** *s.m.* **-eur,** owner, occupier; *a.* **-if, -ive,** possessive.

ossible [pɔsibl]. 1. *a.* possible; **c'est bien p.,** it's quite likely; **pas p.!** you can't mean it! not really! 2. *s.m.* **dans la mesure du p.,** as far as possible; **faire tout son p. pour . . .,** to try one's hardest to . . .; **il s'est montré aimable au p.,** he couldn't have been nicer; *s.f.* **-ilité,** possibility.

oste¹ [pɔst], *s.f.* (a) post; **les Postes et Télécommunications,** the postal services; = the Post Office; **par p. aérienne,** by airmail; **mettre une lettre à la p.,** to post a letter; (b) **(bureau de) p.,** post office; **receveur, -euse, des postes,** postmaster, postmistress; *a.* **-al, -aux,** postal (service).

oste², *s.m.* 1. (a) post, station; **être en p. à . . .,** to be stationed at . . .; (b) **p. d'incendie,** fire station; **p. de police,** police station; **conduire qn au p.,** to run s.o. in; (c) **p. (de radio, de T.S.F.),** radio, wireless, set; **p. de télévision,** television set; **p. récepteur,** receiving set; *P.T.T:* **p. (téléphonique) public,** (public) call box; **p. 35,** extension 35. 2. post, appointment, job.

oster [pɔste], *v.tr.* to post, mail (letter).

oster (se) [səpɔste], *v.pr.* to take up a position; to take one's stand.

ostérieur [pɔsterjœr]. 1. *a.* posterior; (a) (of time) subsequent (**à,** to), later; (b) (of place) hinder, hind, back; **partie postérieure de la tête,** back part of the head. 2. *s.m. F:* posterior, buttocks, bottom, backside, behind; *adv.* **-ement.**

ostérité [pɔsterite], *s.f.* posterity, descendants.

osthume [pɔstym], *a.* posthumous (child, fame).

postiche [pɔstiʃ]. 1. *a.* false (hair); **cils postiches,** artificial eyelashes. 2. *s.m.* wig, hair-piece.

postopératoire [pɔstoperatwaːr], *a. Med:* post-operative (care, etc.).

postscolaire [pɔstskɔleːr], *a. Sch:* continuation (classes); **enseignement p.,** further education.

postsynchroniser [pɔstsɛ̃krɔnize], *v.tr. Cin:* to postsynchronize, to dub (soundtrack to film); *s.f.* **-ation,** dubbing.

posture [pɔstyːr], *s.f.* 1. attitude, position (of the body). 2. position, footing (in society, business); **être en bonne, en mauvaise, p. pour . . .,** to be well, badly, placed to . . ..

pot [po], *s.m.* 1. pot, jug, can, jar; **p. à fleurs,** flower-pot; **pot(s) à eau** [pɔtao, poao], water jug(s); **p. à lait** [poalɛ], **p. au lait** [pɔtolɛ], milk jug, can; *F:* **payer les pots cassés,** to carry the can; **dîner à la fortune du p.,** to take pot-luck. 2. *Aut:* **p. d'échappement,** silencer, *N.Am:* muffler.

potable [pɔtabl], *a.* drinkable; fit to drink; **eau p.,** drinking water.

potage [pɔtaːʒ], *s.m.* soup.

potager, -ère [pɔtaʒe, -ɛːr], *a. Cu:* **herbes potagères,** pot-herbs; **plante potagère,** vegetable; **jardin p.,** kitchen-garden.

pot-au-feu [potofø], *s.m.inv.* 1. soup-pot, stock-pot. 2. boiled beef with vegetables. 3. *a.inv.* plain, homely, commonplace (matter, person).

pot-de-vin [podvɛ̃], *s.m. F:* 1. tip. 2. bribe; *pl.* **pots-de-vin.**

poteau, -eaux [poto], *s.m.* post, pole, stake; *Fb:* goalpost; **p. indicateur,** signpost; **p. télégraphique,** telegraph pole; *Sp:* **p. de départ, d'arrivée,** starting-, winning-, post; *Rac: (of horse)* **rester au p.,** to be left at the post.

potelé [pɔtle], *a.* plump and dimpled; chubby (child).

potence [pɔtãːs], *s.f.* 1. gallows, gibbet. 2. support, arm, cross-piece, bracket.

potentiel, -elle [pɔtãsjɛl]. 1. *a.* potential. 2. *s.m.* (a) potentialities (of a country, etc.); (b) *El:* potential; *adv.* **-ellement.**

poterie [pɔtri], *s.f.* 1. pottery (works). 2. pottery; **p. de terre, de grès,** earthenware, stoneware.

potiche [pɔtiʃ], *s.f.* (large) vase (*esp.* Chinese or Japanese porcelain).

potier [pɔtje], *s.m.* potter; **terre de p.,** potter's clay.

potin [pɔtɛ̃], *s.m. F:* (a) piece of gossip; (b) *pl.* gossip, tittle-tattle.

potiron [pɔtirɔ̃], *s.m.* pumpkin.

pou, *pl.* **poux** [pu], *s.m.* louse; *pl.* lice.

poubelle [pubɛl], *s.f.* dustbin, *N.Am:* garbage can, trash can.

pouce [puːs], *s.m.* 1. thumb; *F:* **donner un coup de p. à qn, qch.,** to shove s.o., sth., on; **manger sur le p.,** to have a snack; *Fr.C:* **faire du p.,** to hitch-hike. 2. *Meas:* inch.

poudre [pu:dr], *s.f.* 1. powder; (*a*) **p. d'or,** gold-dust; **p. abrasive,** grinding powder; **savon en p.,** soap powder; **sucre en p.,** caster sugar; **café en p.,** instant coffee; (*b*) face powder. 2. (*general term for*) explosives; **p. à canon,** gunpowder; **la nouvelle se répandit comme une trainée de p.,** the news spread like wildfire.

poudr|er [pudre], *v.tr.* to powder; to sprinkle with powder; to dust on (flour, etc.); **se p.,** to powder (one's face, etc.); *s.f.* **-erie,** (gun)powder factory; *a.* **-eux, -euse,** (*a*) dusty (clothes, road); (*b*) powdery (snow); *s.m.* **-ier,** (powder) compact; *s.f.* **-ière,** powder magazine.

pouf [puf]. 1. *int.* (*a*) (*of s.o., sth., falling*) plop! (*b*) (*denoting heat, relief*) phew! 2. *s.m. H:* pouf; humpty.

pouff|er [pufe], *v.i.* **p. (de rire),** to burst out laughing, to guffaw; *s.m.* **-ement,** guffawing.

poulain [pulɛ̃], *s.m.* colt, foal; *Sp:* trainee.

poul|e [pul], *s.f.* 1. (*a*) hen; fowl; **p. au pot,** boiled fowl; **ma (petite) p.!** my dear! **lait de p.,** egg-flip, egg-nog; **chair de p.,** goose flesh; (*b*) **p. d'eau,** moorhen; **p. faisane,** hen pheasant; (*c*) *P:* fast young woman; bird. 2. (*a*) (*at games*) pool; (*b*) sweepstake; *s.f.* **-arde,** fattened pullet; *s.m.* **-et,** chicken; **p. de chair,** broiler; *s.m.* **-ailler,** (*a*) hen-house; (*b*) *Th:* gallery, *F:* the gods.

pouliche [puliʃ], *s.f.* filly.

poulie [puli], *s.f.* 1. pulley ((i) sheave; (ii) block). 2. (belt-)pulley; driving wheel.

pouls [pu], *s.m. Med:* pulse.

poumon [pumɔ̃], *s.m.* lung; **p. d'acier,** iron lung; **respirer à pleins poumons,** to draw a deep breath.

poupe [pup], *s.f. Nau:* stern, poop; **avoir le vent en p.,** (i) to have the wind aft; (ii) *F:* to be doing well.

poupée [pupe], *s.f.* doll.

poupon, -onne [pupɔ̃, -ɔn], *s.* baby; *s.f.* **-nière,** day-nursery.

pour [pu:r]. I. *prep.* for. 1. (*a*) instead of; **allez-y p. moi,** go in my place, instead of me; **agir p. qn,** to act on s.o.'s behalf; (*b*) **laisser qn p. mort,** to leave s.o. for dead; *F:* **c'est p. de bon,** I mean it, I'm serious; (*c*) (*direction*) **je pars p. la France,** I am starting for France; **le train p. Paris,** the Paris train; (*d*) (*time*) (i) **p. toujours,** for ever; **il sera ici p. quatre heures,** he will be here by four o'clock; (ii) **j'en ai p. huit jours,** it will take me a week; **p. quinze jours,** for a fortnight; (*e*) (*purpose*) **je suis ici p. affaires,** I'm here on business; (*f*) because of; **p. moi,** on my account, for me; **p. la forme,** for form's sake; (*g*) **parler p. qn,** to speak in favour of s.o.; *adv.* **moi, je suis p.,** I'm in favour of it; (*h*) with regard to; **p. moi,** for my part; (*i*) **dix p. cent,**

ten per cent. 2. **pour** + *inf.* (*a*) (in order) to; **il faut manger p. vivre,** one must eat to live; **p. ainsi dire,** so to speak; (*b*) although; **p. être petit il n'en est pas moins brave,** though small he is none the less brave; **nous ne perdrons rien p. attendre,** we shall lose nothing by waiting; (*c*) because of; **je le sais p. l'avoir vu,** I know it because I saw it, him; (*d*) of a nature to; **cela n'est pas p. me surprendre,** that does not come as a surprise to me. 3. (*a*) **p. que** + *sub.,* in order that; **il est trop tard p. qu'elle sorte,** it is too late for her to go out; (*b*) **p.** (+ *adj. or sb.*) **que** + *sub.,* however, although; **cette situation p. terrible qu'elle soit,** this situation, terrible though it may be; (*c*) **p. peu que** + *sub.,* if only if ever; **p. peu que vous hésitiez, vous êtes fichu,** if you hesitate at all, you're lost. II. **pour,** *s.m.* **peser le p. et le contre,** to weigh the pros and cons.

pourboire [purbwa:r], *s.m.* tip, gratuity.

pourcentage [pursɑ̃ta:ʒ], *s.m.* percentage; rate (of interest); commission.

pourchasser [purʃase], *v.tr.* to pursue (obstinately); **p. un débiteur,** to dun a debtor.

pourparler(s) [purparle], *s.m.usu.pl* negotiations (**avec,** with).

pourpre [purpr]. 1. *s.f.* (*a*) purple (dye) (of the ancients); (*b*) royal, imperial, dignity; **né dans la p.,** born in the purple. 2. *s.m.* crimson; rich red. 3. *a.* **manteau p.,** crimson cloak.

pourquoi [purkwa], *adv. & conj.* why; **p. faire** what for? **p. cela?** why so? **mais p. donc?** what on earth for? **voilà p.,** that's why; **p. pas? p. non?** why not?

pourr|ir [puri:r]. 1. *v.i.* to rot, decay; to go bad. 2. *v.tr.* to rot; *s.m.* **-issement,** decay; *s.f.* **-iture,** rot(tenness).

se pourrir, (*of fruit*) to go bad; (*of egg*) to addle.

poursuite [pursɥit], *s.f.* 1. pursuit; chase. 2. *usu.pl. Jur:* lawsuit, action; prosecution.

poursuivant, -ante [pursɥivɑ̃, -ɑ̃:t], *s. Jur:* plaintiff; prosecutor.

poursuivre [pursɥi:vr], *v.tr.* (*conj. like* SUIVRE) 1. to pursue; to chase; **poursuivi par la guigne,** dogged by bad luck. 2. **p. qn en justice,** to prosecute s.o. 3. to pursue, continue, go on with (work, a story); **il faut p. la chose,** we must go through with it; **p. un avantage,** to follow up an advantage; *abs.* **poursuivez,** go on; continue (your story).

pourtant [purtɑ̃], *adv.* nevertheless, however, still, (and) yet.

pourtour [purtu:r], *s.m.* periphery, circumference (of building, space); **p. d'une cathédrale,** precincts of a cathedral; **mur de p.,** enclosure wall.

pourvoir [purvwa:r], *v.* (*pr.p.* **pourvoyant;** *p.p.* **pourvu;** *pr.ind.* **je pourvois;** *pr.sub.* **je pourvoie**) to provide. 1. *v.ind.tr.* **p. aux frais,**

defray the cost. **2.** *v.tr.* (*a*) **p. qn de qch.,** to supply s.o. with sth.; **se p. d'argent,** to provide oneself with money; (*b*) to equip, fit **(de,** with); **la voiture est pourvue d'un poste,** the car is equipped with, fitted with, a radio.

pourvu que [purvykə], *conj.phr.* provided (that); so long as; **p. qu'il ne fasse pas de gaffes!** I only hope he doesn't put his foot in it!

pousse [pus], *s.f.* **1.** growth (of hair, leaves, feathers). **2.** young shoot, sprout.

poussée [puse], *s.f.* **1.** *Mec: etc:* thrust; **centre de p.,** pressure centre; **force de p.,** upward thrust; *Av: Meteor:* **p. du vent,** wind pressure. **2.** pushing, pressure (of crowd). **3.** push, shove; *Fb:* **p. irrégulière,** foul. **4.** growth (of hair, pimples, teeth); rising (of sap, temperature); upsurge.

pousser [puse]. **1.** *v.tr.* (*a*) to push, shove, thrust; **p. qn du coude,** to nudge s.o.; **p. le verrou,** to shoot the bolt; **p. la porte,** (i) to push the door to; (ii) to push the door open; (*b*) to drive, impel; **p. qn à faire qch.,** to push s.o. into doing sth.; (*c*) to push on; **p. un cheval,** to urge on a horse; *Com:* **p. la vente,** to push sales; (*d*) to put forth, shoot out (leaves); (*e*) to utter (cry). **2.** *v.i.* (*a*) to push; **p. à la roue,** to put one's shoulder to the wheel; (*b*) to push on, make one's way (to a place); (*c*) (*of plants*) to grow; **les enfants poussent,** the children are shooting up; **laisser p. sa barbe,** to grow a beard; *s.f.* **-ette,** (child's) push-chair.

se pousser, to push oneself forward; to shove, elbow, one's way to the front; **elle sait se p. dans le monde,** she's very pushing; *F:* **pousse-toi,** shove up.

poussière [pusjɛːr], *s.f.* **1.** (*a*) dust; **nuage de p.,** cloud of dust; (*b*) speck of dust; (*c*) *F:* **mille francs et des poussières,** a thousand francs plus (a little bit). **2.** **p. d'eau,** (fine) spray; spindrift; *a.* **-iéreux, -iéreuse,** dusty.

poussif, -ive [pusif, -iːv], *a.* broken-winded (horse); wheezy, short-winded (person).

poussin [pusɛ̃], *s.m.* (*a*) chick; (*b*) *Cu:* spring chicken.

poutre [puːtr], *s.f.* **1.** (wooden) beam; balk. **2.** girder.

poutrelle [putrɛl], *s.f.* small beam; girder; joist.

pouvoir [puvwaːr]. **I.** *v.tr.* (*pr.p.* **pouvant;** *p.p.* **pu,** *pr.ind.* **je puis** or **je peux** (*always* **puis-je),** **tu peux, il peut, ils peuvent;** *pr.sub.* **je puisse;** *fu.* **je pourrai**) **1.** to be able; **je ne peux (pas) le faire,** I can't do it; **cela ne peut (pas) se faire,** it can't be done; **comment a-t-il pu dire cela?** how could he say that? **il aurait pu le faire s'il avait voulu,** he could have done it if he had wanted to; **on n'y peut rien,** it can't be helped; **il travaille on ne peut mieux,** he could not work better; **n'en plus p.,** to be tired out, exhausted; *v.pr.* **si cela se peut,** if possible. **2.**

"may"; (*a*) to be allowed; **vous pouvez partir,** you may go; **puis-je entrer?** may, can, I come in? (*b*) **puissiez-vous dire vrai!** may what you say be true! **3.** to be possible, probable; **cela se peut (bien),** it may be (so); **il pouvait avoir dix ans,** he may, might, have been ten; **advienne que pourra,** come what may; *v.pr.* **il se peut que + sub.,** it may be that . . ..

II. pouvoir, *s.m.* power. **1.** force, means; **en dehors de mon p.,** beyond my power. **2.** influence, power; **être au p. de qn,** to be in s.o.'s power. **3.** (*a*) **p. paternel,** paternal authority; (*b*) competence, warrant, power; **en dehors de mes pouvoirs,** not within my competence; (*c*) *Pol:* **le parti au p.,** the party in power. **4.** *Jur:* power of attorney; procuration; **avoir plein(s) pouvoir(s) pour agir,** to have full powers to act.

prairie [prɛri], *s.f.* (*a*) meadow; (*b*) grassland, *N.Am:* prairie; *Geog:* **la P.,** the Prairies.

praticable [pratikabl], *a.* practicable; (*a*) feasible (plan, idea, etc.); (*b*) passable, negotiable (road, ford, etc.); *s.f.* **-ilité.**

praticien [pratisjɛ̃], *s.m.* (legal, medical) practitioner.

pratique¹ [pratik], *a.* practical, useful (method, article); handy (gadget); convenient (time, bus); *adv.* **-ment,** in actual fact.

pratique², *s.f.* **1.** practice; application (of theory); **c'est de p. courante,** it's the usual practice; it's quite commonly done. **2.** (*a*) practice, experience; **perdre la p. de qch.,** to lose the knack of sth., to get out of practice; (*b*) *Jur:* practice (of the law); **terme de p.,** legal term; (*c*) dealings; **avoir des pratiques avec l'ennemi,** to have dealings with the enemy. **3.** **pratiques religieuses,** religious observances.

pratiquer [pratike], *v.tr.* **1.** to practise (virtue, religion); to employ, use; **il pratique le football,** he plays football; **p. une méthode,** to employ a method; **p. la médecine,** to practise medicine; *abs.* **il ne pratique pas,** he doesn't practise (his religion); *Com:* **les cours pratiqués,** the ruling prices. **2.** **p. une ouverture dans un mur,** to make an opening in a wall; **p. un sentier,** to make a path.

pré [pre], *s.m.* meadow; **prés salés,** salt meadows.

préalable [prealabl]. **1.** *a.* (*a*) previous (à, to); (*b*) preliminary (agreement, etc.). **2.** *s.m.* **au p.,** as a preliminary.

précaire [prekɛːr], *a.* precarious (tenure, authority); delicate (health); *adv.* **-ment.**

précaution [prekosjɔ̃], *s.f.* **1.** precaution; **mesures de p.,** precautionary measures. **2.** caution, wariness; care; **avec p.,** cautiously; carefully.

précédence [presedɑ̃ːs], *s.f.* precedence (de, of); priority (de, over).

précéd|ent [presedã]. **1.** *a.* preceding, previous, former; **à la page précédente,** on the page before. **2.** *s.m.* precedent; **créer un p.,** to set, create, a precedent; *adv.* **-emment,** previously, already, earlier.

précéder [presede], *v.tr.* (**je précède, n. précédons; je précéderai**) **1.** to precede; to go before (s.o., sth.). **2. p. qn,** to have precedence over s.o.

précepteur, -trice [preseptœ:r, -tris], *s.* tutor; (private) teacher; *f.* governess; **il est mon p. en politique,** he's my political mentor, guide.

prêcher [preʃe], *v.tr.* **1.** to preach; **p. l'économie,** to preach economy; *abs.* **il prêche mal,** he's a poor preacher; **p. d'exemple,** to practise what one preaches. **2.** to preach to (s.o.); to lecture (s.o.).

précieu|x, -euse [presjø, -ø:z], *a.* (*a*) precious; (*b*) valuable; (*c*) affected (manner, style); *adv.* **-sement.**

précipice [presipis], *s.m.* precipice.

précipit|er [presipite], *v.tr.* **1.** (*a*) to precipitate; to hurl, throw, down; **p. un peuple dans la guerre,** to plunge a nation into war; (*b*) *Ch:* to precipitate (a substance). **2.** to hurry, hasten; to rush, precipitate; **p. son départ,** to hasten one's departure; **il ne faut rien p.,** don't (let's) rush anything; *s.f.* **-ation,** (*a*) *Ch:* precipitation; (*b*) violent hurry; *adv.* **-amment.**

se précipiter, to dash, to rush (headlong).

précis [presi]. **1.** *a.* precise, exact, definite; **à deux heures précises,** at two o'clock precisely; **en termes p.,** in distinct terms. **2.** *s.m.* abstract, summary; précis (of document, etc.); *adv.* **-ément,** exactly.

préciser [presize], *v.tr.* (*a*) to specify; to state precisely; **sans rien p.,** without going into details; **p. les détails,** to go into further detail; (*b*) *abs.* to be precise, explicit.

se préciser, (*of ideas*) to become clear; (*of danger*) to take shape.

précision [presizjõ], *s.f.* **1.** precision, exactness, accuracy; **instruments de p.,** precision instruments. **2.** *pl.* precise details; **demander des précisions sur qn,** to ask for full particulars (about s.o.).

précoce [prekɔs], *a.* precocious (talent, child); early, forward (season, fruit).

précombustion [prekõbystjõ], *s.f.* **moteur diesel à chambre de p.,** precombustion engine.

préconditionné [prekõdisjɔne], *a. Com:* packaged.

préconiser [prekɔnize], *v.tr.* to (re)commend (s.o., sth.); to advocate (course of action).

précontraint [prekõtrɛ̃], *a.* **béton p.,** prestressed concrete.

précurseur [prekyrsœ:r]. **1.** *s.m.* precursor, forerunner. **2.** *a.m.* precursory, premonitory

(sign).

prédécesseur [predesɛsœ:r], *s.m.* predecessor.

prédicateur [predikatœ:r], *s.m.* preacher.

prédilection [predilɛksjõ], *s.f.* predilection partiality.

pré|dire [predi:r], *v.tr.* (*conj. like* DIRE *excep pr.ind. & imp.* **v. prédisez**) to predict, foretell *s.f.* **-diction,** prediction, forecast.

prédispos|er [predispoze], *v.tr.* to predispose (à to); to prejudice (s.o., in favour of, agains s.o., sth.); *s.f.* **-ition.**

prédomin|er [predɔmine], *v.i.* to predominate to have the upper hand (**sur,** over); *s.f.* **-ance** *a.* **-ant.**

préémin|ence [preeminã:s], *s.f.* pre-eminenc (**sur,** over); *a.* **-ent.**

préfabriqué [prefabrike]. **1.** *a.* prefabricated. *s.m.* **le p.,** prefabricated units; *F:* (*hous* prefab.

préface [prefas], *s.f.* preface, foreword.

préfect|ure [prefɛkty:r], *s.f.* **1.** *Fr.Adm:* prefe ture. **2. la P. de police,** the headquarters of th (Paris) police; *a.* **-oral, -oraux,** prefector(i) (administration, staff).

préférable [preferabl], *a.* preferable (**à,** to better; *adv.* **-ment.**

préfér|er [prefere], *v.tr.* (**je préfère; je préférer** to prefer; to like (s.o., sth.) better; *a.* **-é, -é** favourite; *s.f.* **-ence;** *a.* **-entiel, -entiel** preferential.

préfet [prefɛ], *s.m.* **1.** *Fr.Adm:* prefect. **2. le p. police,** the prefect of police.

préfixe [prefiks], *s.m.* prefix; **code lett** number.

préhist|oire [preistwa:r], *s.f.* prehistory; **-orien, -ienne,** prehistorian; *a.* **-oriqu** prehistoric.

préjudice [preʒydis], *s.m.* prejudice, detrime (moral) injury; wrong; *Jur:* tort; **à mon p.,** my detriment; **porter p. à qn,** to inflict inju loss, on s.o.

préjudic|ier [preʒydisje], *v.i.* (*p.d. & pr.sub.* **préjudiciions**) to be detrimental (**à,** to); **-iable,** prejudicial, harmful, injurious.

préjugé [preʒyʒe], *s.m.* prejudice, bi preconceived idea; **avoir un p. contre** **étrangers,** to have a prejudice, to prejudiced, against foreigners; **sans préjug** unprejudiced.

préjuger [preʒyʒe], *v.tr.* (*conj. like* MANGER) prejudge.

prélasser (se) [səprelase], *v.pr.* **se p. dans** **fauteuil,** to loll in an armchair; **le chat** **prélassait au soleil,** the cat was basking in sun.

prélèvement [prelɛvmã], *s.m.* **1.** deduction advance; setting apart (of a share, of a who **2.** (*a*) sample; **faire un p. de lait,** to take a sa ple of milk; (*b*) amount, sum, deducted; *Ba*

= standing order (for payment of regular accounts).

▶**rélever** [prelve], *v.tr.* (*conj. like* LEVER) to deduct, set apart, in advance.

▶**réliminaire** [prelimine:r]. **1.** *a.* preliminary. **2.** *s.m.pl.* preliminaries.

▶**rélude** [prelyd], *s.m.* prelude (**de, à,** to).

▶**rématuré** [prematyre], *a.* premature, untimely; *adv.* -**ment.**

▶**rémédit**|**er** [premedite], *v.tr.* to premeditate, to plan (sth.) ahead; **de dessein prémédité,** of set purpose; **insulte préméditée,** deliberate insult; *s.f.* -**ation.**

▶**rem**|**ier, -ière** [prɔmje, -jɛ:r], *a. & s.* first. **1.** (*a*) **le p. janvier,** the first of January; **le p. de l'an,** New Year's day; **dans les premiers temps,** at first; **en p.** (**lieu**), in the first place; firstly; **du p. coup,** at the first attempt; **le p. venu vous dira cela,** anyone will tell you that; *Nau:* **p. voyage,** maiden voyage (of ship); *Aut:* **première (vitesse),** bottom, first (gear); (*b*) **sens p. d'un mot,** original meaning of a word; *Ind: Com:* **matières premières,** raw materials. **2.** (*place*) **demeurer au p.,** to live on the first floor; **p. plan,** foreground. **3.** (*rank*) **le tout p.,** the foremost; **p. ministre,** Prime Minister, Premier; *Rail:* **voyager en première,** to travel first (class); *Mth:* **nombres premiers,** prime numbers; *Th:* **p. rôle,** lead; **jeune p.,** juvenile lead. **4.** *Sch:* (**classe de**) **première** = sixth form. **5.** *s.f.* **première,** (*a*) forewoman; (*b*) *Th:* first night; *adv.* -**ièrement.**

▶**remier-né, première-née** [prɔmjene, prɔmjerne], *a. & s.* first-born; *pl. premiers-nés, premières-nées.*

▶**émonition** [premɔnisjɔ̃], *s.f.* premonition.

▶**émunir** (**se**) [səpremyni:r], *v.pr.* to provide (**contre,** against); to be prepared (**contre,** for); to be on one's guard (**contre,** against).

endre [prɑ̃:dr], *v.* (*pr.p.* **prenant;** *p.p.* **pris;** *pr.ind.* **ils prennent;** *pr.sub.* **je prenne;** *p.h.* **je pris**). **I.** *v.tr.* to take. **1.** to take (up), to take hold of (sth.); (*a*) **aller p. son pardessus,** to fetch, get, one's overcoat; **je sais comment le p.,** I know how to manage him; **p. qch. sur la table, dans un tiroir,** to take sth. from the table, out of a drawer; **où avez-vous pris cela?** (i) where did you get that, take that from? (ii) where did you get that idea? (*b*) **p. des pensionnaires,** to take (in) boarders; **p. qn, qch., au sérieux,** to take s.o., sth., seriously; **vous avez mal pris mes paroles,** you have misunderstood what I said; (*c*) **p. qch. à qn,** to take sth. from s.o.; (*d*) **c'est à p. ou à laisser,** take it or leave it; **à tout p.,** on the whole; everything considered; **à bien p. les choses,** rightly speaking; *F:* **en p. à son aise,** to take it easy; to slack; **le p. de haut,** to put on airs; to be scornful about it. **2.** to take, capture; (*a*) **p. un poisson,** to catch a fish; **p. qn**

à mentir, to catch s.o. (out) in a lie; **que je vous y prenne!** let me catch you at it! **on ne m'y prendra pas!** I know better! (*b*) **l'envie lui prend de partir,** he is seized with a desire to go away; **qu'est-ce qui lui prend?** what's up with him now? **bien lui en prit,** it was lucky for him that he did. **3.** (*a*) **je passerai vous p. à votre hôtel,** I shall call for you at your hotel; **p. des voyageurs,** to take, pick, up passengers; (*b*) **p. une chambre,** to take, rent, a room; **p. un ouvrier,** to engage a workman; (*c*) **p. qn pour exemple,** to take s.o. as an example; (*d*) **p. une personne pour une autre,** to take one person for another; (*e*) **p. un bain,** to take a bath; (*f*) **p. une maladie,** to catch an illness; (*g*) **p. un air innocent,** to put on an innocent air; **p. du poids,** to put on weight; (*h*) **p. de l'âge,** to be getting on in years. **4. p. le train,** to take the train; **p. à travers champs,** to strike across the fields; *abs.* **"p. à gauche,"** "bear left"; *Nau:* **p. le large,** to take to the open sea.

II. prendre, *v.i.* **1.** (*a*) (*of cement, etc.*) to set; (*of fat*) to congeal; (*b*) to freeze; (*c*) to seize up, to jam; (*d*) *Cu:* to catch, to stick (in the pan). **2. le feu a pris,** the fire has caught; **le vaccin a pris,** the vaccine has taken; **ça ne prend pas!** it won't wash!

se prendre. 1. (*a*) to catch, to be caught; **son manteau se prit à un clou,** her coat (got) caught on a nail; (*b*) **se p. d'amitié pour qn,** to take a liking to s.o. **2. se p. à rire, à pleurer,** to begin to laugh, to cry. **3. s'en p. à qn,** to lay the blame on s.o. **4. il sait comment s'y p.,** he knows how to set about it.

preneur, -euse [prənœ:r, -ø:z], *s.* taker; *Fin: Com:* buyer, purchaser; *Jur:* lessee, leaseholder.

prénom [prenɔ̃], *s.m.* Christian name; first name, *N.Am:* given name.

préoccup|**er** [preɔkype], *v.tr.* to preoccupy, engross (s.o.); **il y a quelque chose qui la préoccupe,** she has something on her mind; **sa santé me préoccupe,** I'm anxious about his, her, health; *a.* -**ant,** disquieting, worrying; *s.f.* -**ation.**

préparateur, -trice [preparatœ:r, -tris], *s.* **1.** laboratory assistant; demonstrator; **p. en pharmacie,** chemist's assistant. **2. p. d'une révolution,** s.o. who paves the way for a revolution.

prépar|**er** [prepare], *v.tr.* **1.** to prepare; to get ready (meal, speech, lesson, etc.); **p. du thé,** to brew tea; **p. un devis,** to get out an estimate. **2. p. qn à qch.,** to train, fit, s.o. for sth.; **préparé aux fonctions publiques,** trained for public office. **3. p. un examen,** to read for an examination; *s.m.pl.* -**atifs,** preparations; *s.f.* -**ation,** preparation, preparing; *a.* -**atoire,** preparatory.

se préparer. 1. il se prépare quelque chose, there's something afoot. 2. se p. à partir, to get ready to leave, to go.

prépondér|ance [prepɔ̃derɑ̃:s], *s.f.* preponderance (sur, over); *a.* -ant.

préposé, -ée [prepoze], *s. Adm:* (*usu.* minor) official; traffic warden; p. (des postes), postman; p. des douanes, customs officer; p. au vestiaire, cloakroom attendant.

préposition [prepozisjɔ̃], *s.f. Gram:* preposition.

près [prɛ]. 1. *adv.* near. 2. *adv.phr.* (*a*) à . . . p.; à cela p., with that exception; à cela p. que, except that; à peu p., nearly, about; il était à peu p. certain, it was fairly certain; le mieux équipé à beaucoup p., by far the best equipped; au plus p., to the nearest point; (*b*) de p., close, near; from close to; tirer de p., to fire at close range; rasé de p., close-shaven; il n'y regarde pas de si p., he is not so particular as all that. 3. *prep.phr.* p. de qn, near, close to, s.o.; assis tout p. du feu, seated close by the fire; p. de partir, about to start.

présage [preza:ʒ], *s.m.* presage, portent, foreboding; mauvais p., bad omen.

présager [prezaʒe], *v.tr.* (n. présageons) to presage. 1. to portend, betoken (misfortune). 2. to predict; to augur.

presbyte [prezbit], *a.* long-sighted (person).

presbytère [prezbite:r], *s.m. R.C.Ch:* priest's house, presbytery.

prescience [presjɑ̃:s, prɛss-], *s.f.* prescience, foreknowledge (de, of).

prescr|ire [preskri:r], *v.tr.* (*conj. like* ÉCRIRE) to prescribe, lay down; to stipulate for (quality, etc.); to prescribe (remedy) (à, to); *s.f.* -iption.

présélection [preseleksjɔ̃], *s.f.* 1. preliminary aptitude tests. 2. short-listing (for job). 3. *Aut: etc:* boîte de vitesse à p., preselector gear-box.

présence [prezɑ̃:s], *s.f.* presence, attendance; (*a*) *Sch:* régularité de p., regular attendance; faire acte de p., to put in an appearance, *F:* to show up; *Ind:* feuille de p., time sheet; en p., face to face; (*b*) p. d'esprit, presence of mind.

présent [prezɑ̃], *a.* present; (*a*) les personnes présentes, those present; (*b*) le temps p., *s.m.* le p., the present (time); à p., just now; jusqu'à p., until now, as yet; dès à p., from now on, henceforth; à p. que . . ., now that . . .; *Gram:* verbe au p., verb in the present tense; (*c*) esprit p., alert mind; ready wit.

présent|er [prezɑ̃te]. 1. *v.tr.* to present, offer; *Cl:* to model (a dress); p. une excuse à qn, to offer an apology to s.o.; p. ses hommages à qn, to pay one's respects to s.o.; p. ses pièces d'identité, son passeport, to submit proofs of identity, to show one's passport; *Sch: F:* p. un examen, to sit for an exam; *Pol:* p. un projet de loi, to in-

troduce a bill. 2. *v.tr.* p. qn à qn, to introduce s.o. to s.o.; p. qn comme candidat, to put s.o. up a candidate. 3. *v.i.* il présente bien, he's (a man) o good appearance; *a.* -able; *s.f.* -ation, (i presentation; (ii) (formal) introduction (à qn, t s.o.); *s.m.* -oir, *Com:* display unit.

se présenter. 1. une occasion se présente, an op portunity occurs, presents itself; si le cas s présente, if the case arises; attendre que qch. s présente, to wait for sth. to turn up; la chos se présente bien, the matter looks promisin; 2. to present oneself; se p. aux élections, t stand at the elections; se p. à qn, to introduc oneself to s.o.; se p. à un examen, to sit a examination.

préserv|er [prezɛrve], *v.tr.* to preserve, t protect (de, from); *a. & s.m.* -atif, -ative; *s.* -ation.

présid|er [prezide], *v.tr. & i.* (*a*) p. un conseil, ♦ preside over a council; (*b*) to preside, to be ♦ the chair; *s.f.* -ence, presidency; chai manship; *s.* -ent, -ente; *a.* -entiel, -entiell presidential (chair, etc.).

présomp|tion [prezɔ̃psjɔ̃], *s.f.* presumption; (♦ presumptive evidence; (*b*) presumptuousnes rabattre la p. de qn, to put s.o. in his place; -tif, -tive, (heir) presumptive; *a.* -tueu -tueuse, presumptuous, brash; *ad* -tueusement.

presque [prɛsk], *adv.* 1. almost, nearly. 2. (*wi negative*) scarcely, hardly; p. jamais, har ever; p. rien, next to nothing.

presqu'île [prɛskil], *s.f.* peninsula.

pressant [presɑ̃], *a.* pressing, urgent (nee request, danger).

presse [prɛs], *s.f.* 1. press, pressing-machine; à imprimer, printing press; livre sous p., bo in the press. 2. press, newspapers.

pressé [prese], *a.* 1. crowded, compresse citron p., (i) squeezed lemon; (ii) fresh lemo juice. 2. être p., to be in a hurry; je suis très I'm in a great hurry; ce n'est pas p., it's r urgent.

presse-citron [pressitrɔ̃], *s.m.inv.* lemo squeezer.

presse-fruits [presfrɥi], *s.m.inv.* juice extract

pressent|ir [presɑ̃ti:r], *v.tr.* (*conj. like* MENT 1. to have a presentiment, a foreboding, (sth.); faire p. qch. à qn, to give s.o. an inkl of sth. 2. p. qn (sur qch.), to sound s.o. out ♦ sth.); *s.m.* -iment, foreboding.

presse-papiers [prespapje], *s.m.inv.* pap weight.

presse-purée [prespyre], *s.m.inv.* potat vegetable-, masher.

press|er [prese], *v.tr.* to press. 1. to sque (lemon, etc.). 2. to press (upon); to be pressé par ses créanciers, dunned by creditors; p. qn de questions, to ply s.o. v questions. **3.** to hurry, push, (s.o.) on; **p. le pas,** to quicken one's steps; **qu'est-ce qui vous presse?** why are you in such a hurry? *abs.* **l'affaire presse,** the matter is urgent; **il n'y a rien qui presse,** there's no hurry; *s.m.* **-oir,** (wine-, oil-, cider-) press.

e presser. 1. to crowd, to throng. **2.** to hurry, make haste.

ressing [prɛsiŋ], *s.m.* *Com: F:* (i) dry-cleaner's; (ii) dry-cleaning.

ression [prɛsjɔ̃], *s.f.* **1.** pressure; (*a*) **p. atmosphérique,** atmospheric pressure; *Med:* **p. artérielle,** blood pressure; **bière (à la) p.,** beer on draught; *Aut: etc:* **contrôleur de p.,** pressure gauge (for tyres); *Mec:* **graissage sous p.,** pressure greasing; *Av:* **cabine sous p.,** pressurized cabin; (*b*) *El:* tension; (*c*) **exercer une p. sur qn,** to bring pressure to bear on s.o. **2. un bouton (à) p.,** un, une, **p.,** a press stud, snap fastener, *F:* popper.

reste [prɛst], *a* quick, nimble; alert (in action, speech); **avoir la main p.,** (i) to be quick, skilful, with one's hands; (ii) to be quick to slap (a child); *adv.* **-ment.**

restidigita|tion [prɛstidiʒitasjɔ̃], *s.f.* conjuring; *s.m.* **-teur,** conjurer.

restig|e [prɛsti:ʒ], *s.m.* prestige; high reputation; **sans p.,** undistinguished; **publicité de p.,** prestige advertising; *a.* **-ieux, -ieuse,** marvellous.

ésumer [prezyme], *v.tr.* to presume. **1. p. qn innocent,** to assume s.o. to be innocent; **le voleur présumé,** the alleged thief; **il est à p. que . . .,** the presumption is that . . .. **2.** (*a*) **p. de faire qch.,** to presume to do sth.; (*b*) **trop p. de soi,** to presume too much; **trop p. de ses forces,** to overestimate one's strength.

ésupposer [presypoze], *v.tr.* to presuppose; to take (sth.) for granted; to imply.

êt¹ [prɛ], *a.* ready, prepared.

êt², *s.m.* **1.** loan (of money, books, etc.); (*of library book*) **exclu du p.,** not to be taken away; **caisse de prêts,** loan bank; **p. hypothécaire,** mortgage loan. **2.** advance (on wages).

êt-à-porter [prɛtaporte], *s.m.* *coll.* ready-made clothing.

êtendant, -ante [prɛtɑ̃dɑ̃, -ɑ̃:t], *s.* **1.** applicant, candidate; claimant. **2.** *s.m.* suitor.

êtendre [prɛtɑ̃:dr], *v.tr.* **1.** to claim (as a right); to maintain, assert; to require (sth.). **2.** to claim; **je prétends que c'est faux,** I maintain that) it's a lie; **à ce qu'on prétend,** as people claim, assert. **3.** *v.ind.tr.* **p. à qch.,** to lay claim to sth.; **p. aux honneurs,** to aspire to honours.

êtendu [prɛtɑ̃dy], *a.* alleged, would-be; self-tyled.

êten|tion [prɛtɑ̃sjɔ̃], *s.f.* (*a*) pretension, claim à, to); (*b*) **homme sans prétentions,** un-

assuming man; *a.* **-tieux, -tieuse,** pretentious, *F:* showy; *adv.* **-tieusement.**

prêt|er [prɛte], *v.tr.* **1.** to lend; (*a*) **p. qch. à qn,** to lend sth. to s.o.; **p. de l'argent à un ami,** to lend a friend some money; **p. sur gage(s),** to lend against security; (*b*) **p. attention,** to pay attention; **p. l'oreille,** to listen; **p. la main (à qn),** to lend (s.o.) a hand; **p. serment,** to take the oath; to be sworn. **2.** to attribute, ascribe; **l'esprit qu'on lui prête,** the wit attributed to him; **p. de généreux sentiments à qn,** to credit s.o. with generous feelings. **3.** *v.ind.tr.* **privilège qui prête aux abus,** privilege that lends itself to abuses; *s.* **-eur, -euse,** lender.

se prêter, to lend oneself, to be a party (à, to); (to) fall in (à, with); **si le temps s'y prête,** weather permitting.

prétexte [pretɛkst], *s.m.* pretext, excuse; **ce n'était qu'un p.,** it was only a blind; **sous aucun p.,** on no account, not on any account.

prétexter [pretɛkste], *v.tr.* to pretext; **p. la fatigue,** to plead fatigue.

prêtr|e [prɛtr], *s.m.* priest; *s.f.* **-esse,** priestess; *s.f.* **-ise,** priesthood.

preuve [prœ:v], *s.f.* proof, evidence; **faire p. d'intelligence,** to show intelligence; **faire ses preuves,** to prove oneself; to show one's mettle.

prévaloir [prevalwa:r], *v.i.* (*conj. like* VALOIR, *except pr.sub.* je prévale) to prevail; to have the upper hand; **faire p. son droit,** to make good one's right.

préven|ance [prɛv(ə)nɑ̃:s], *s.f.* (kind) attention; kindness; **manquer de p.,** to be inconsiderate; *a.* **-ant,** kind, attentive, obliging (**envers,** to).

prévenir [prɛv(ə)ni:r], *v.tr.* (*conj. like* TENIR) **1.** (*a*) to forestall, anticipate (s.o.'s wishes); (*b*) to prevent, ward off (illness, danger). **2.** to predispose, to bias (s.o. in favour of s.o.); **p. qn contre qn,** to prejudice s.o. against s.o. **3.** to inform, forewarn (s.o. of sth.); **p. qn de qch.,** to give s.o. notice of sth.

préventif, -ive [prevɑ̃tif, -i:v], *a.* **1.** preventive (medicine, etc.); **à titre p.,** as a preventive. **2.** *Jur:* **détention préventive,** detention on suspicion; detention awaiting trial.

prévention [prevɑ̃sjɔ̃], *s.f.* **1.** predisposition (**en faveur de,** in favour of); prejudice, bias (**contre,** against); **observateur sans p.,** unbias(s)ed observer. **2.** *Jur:* imprisonment on suspicion. **3. p. contre la maladie,** disease control; *Adm:* **la p. routière,** road safety (i) measures, (ii) squad; **p. contre la pollution,** pollution control.

prévenu, -ue [prevny]. **1.** *a.* prejudiced; biassed. **2.** *s. Jur:* the accused.

prévis|ion [previzjɔ̃], *s.f.* (*a*) anticipation; **en p. de qch.,** in the expectation of sth.; **selon toute p.,** in all likelihood; (*b*) *Meteor:* (weather) forecast; (*c*) *Fin:* **p. budgétaire,** (budget) estimates; *a.* -**ible**, foreseeable.

prévoir [prevwaːr], *v.tr.* (*conj. like* VOIR *except fu. and condit.* **je prévoirai, je prévoirais**) **1.** to foresee, forecast (events, etc.). **2.** to make provision for; to provide for (sth.); **chiffre prévu pour les dépenses**, estimate of expenditure; **c'est prévu dans le projet**, it's catered for, provided for, in the plan; *Av: Aut: etc:* **vitesse prévue**, designed speed.

prévoy|ance [prevwajãːs], *s.f.* foresight, precaution; **société de p.**, provident society; *a.* -**ant**, provident; far-sighted (administration, etc.).

prier [prije], *v.tr.* **1.** to pray. **2.** to ask, beg, beseech; **je vous en prie!** do, please! please, do! **je vous prie . . .,** please . . .; **se faire p.**, to require much pressing; **faire qch. sans se faire p.**, to do sth. without having to be asked twice.

prière [prijeːr], *s.f.* **1.** prayer. **2.** request; **p. de ne pas fumer**, please do not smoke, no smoking please.

primaire [primεːr], *a.* primary (school, education); *El:* **courant p.**, inducing current.

prime [prim], *s.f.* **1.** *Fin: Ins:* premium; **faire p.**, to be at a premium. **2.** *Com: Adm:* (*a*) subsidy, grant; (*b*) bonus.

primer [prime], *v.tr.* to award a prize to (s.o., sth.); **taureau primé**, prize bull; **roman primé**, prize-winning novel.

primesautier, -ière [primsotje, -jεːr], *a.* impulsive, spontaneous; **avoir l'esprit p.**, (i) to be impulsive; (ii) to be quick-witted.

primeur [primœːr], *s.f.* **1.** newness, freshness; **avoir la p. d'une nouvelle**, to be the first to hear a piece of news. **2.** *usu.pl.* **cultiver des primeurs**, to grow early vegetables, fruit.

primevère [primvεːr], *s.f. Bot:* primula; **p. à grandes fleurs**, primrose; **p. commune**, cowslip.

primit|if, -ive [primitif, -iːv], *a.* (*a*) primitive, primeval, original, earliest (times, etc.); *Opt:* **couleurs primitives**, primary colours; (*b*) first, original; **la question primitive**, the original question; (*c*) primitive, crude (customs); *adv.* -**ivement**, originally.

prince [prɛ̃ːs], *s.m.* prince.

princesse [prɛ̃ses], *s.f.* princess; *F:* **aux frais de la p.**, at the expense of the State, the firm, *F:* on the house.

prince|lier, -ière [prɛ̃sje, -jεːr], *a.* princely; **habitation princière**, palatial house; **honoraires princiers**, princely fees; *adv.* -**ièrement**, like a prince; in princely fashion.

principal, -aux [prɛ̃sipal, -o]. **1.** *a.* principal, chief, leading; **associé p.**, senior partner. **2.** *s.m.* (*a*) principal, chief; headmaster; **principaux d'une ville**, leading citizens (of a town); (*b*) principal thing, main point; **c'est le p.**, that's the main thing; *F:* that's it; (*c*) *Com:* principal; capital sum.

principauté [prɛ̃sipote], *s.f.* principality.

principe [prɛ̃sip], *s.m.* principle; (*a*) primary cause; (*b*) fundamental truth; (*c*) rule of conduct; **en p.**, as a rule, usually; in theory.

printanier, -ière [prɛ̃tanje, -jεːr], *a.* spring (flowers); spring-like (weather).

printemps [prɛ̃tɑ̃], *s.m.* spring, springtime; **au p.**, in (the) spring.

priorit|é [priɔrite], *s.f.* priority; **actions de p.**, preference shares; *Aut:* **p.** (**de passage**), right of way; *P.N:* **p. à droite** = give way; **route à p.**, major road; *a.* -**aire**, priority.

pris [pri], *a.* **1.** (*a*) (*of seat, etc.*) engaged, occupied; taken; (*b*) (*of pers.*) busy, occupied. **2.** **p. de peur**, panic-stricken; **p. de colère**, in rage; **avoir le nez p.**, to have a cold (in the head), to have a blocked nose.

prise [priːz], *s.f.* **1.** hold, grasp, grip; (*a*) **trouver p. à qch.**, to get a grip of sth.; **avoir p. sur qn**, to have a hold over s.o.; **lâcher p.**, to let go; (*b*) **être aux prises avec qn**, to be at grips with s.o.; **mettre les gens aux prises,** to set people by the ears; (*c*) *Mec: Aut:* engagement, mesh(ing) (of gears); **en p.** (**directe**), in top (gear). **3.** (*a*) taking, capture; **la p. de la Bastille,** the fall of the Bastille; (*b*) **p. de vues,** filming, shooting; *Ci:* **p. de son,** recording. **4.** (*thing taken*) **p. de poisson,** catch of fish; **p. de minerai,** ore sample; *Med:* **p. de sang,** blood sample; *El:* (**de courant**), (wall-)plug, point; **p. de terre,** earth connection.

priser [prize], *v.tr.* (*a*) to appraise, value (goods); (*b*) to set a (high) value on (sth.); to prize, treasure (sth.).

prism|e [prism], *s.m.* prism; *a.* -**atique,** prismatic.

prison [prizɔ̃], *s.f.* **1.** prison, jail; **aller en p.**, go to prison, to jail. **2.** imprisonment; **faire la p.**, to serve a prison sentence; *s.* -**nier, -nière,** prisoner.

privé [prive]. **1.** *a.* private (person, life, enterprise); *P.N:* **propriété privée,** private property. **2.** *s.m.* private life; private (*as opposed to* nationalized) industry; **dans le p.**, (i) in private life; (ii) in a private firm; (iii) in private, privately.

priv|er [prive], *v.tr.* to deprive (s.o. of sth.); **je vous en prive pas?** I'm not depriving you? can you spare it? *s.f.* -**ation,** privation, hardship; **se priver de qch.**, to deny oneself sth.

privilège [privilεːʒ], *s.m.* (*a*) privilege; prerogative; (*b*) licence, grant; **p. d'une banque,** bank charter; **accorder un p. à qn,** to license s.o.

privilégié [privileʒje], *a.* (*a*) privileged; licensed; *Fin:* **banque privilégiée,** chartered bank; **créance privilégiée,** preferential debt

action **privilégiée**, preference share.
privilégier [privileʒje], *v.tr.* (*pr.sub. & p.d.* n.
privilégiions) to privilege, to license; to grant a
charter to (a bank, etc.).
prix [pri], *s.m.* **1.** (*a*) value, worth, cost; **à tout p.,**
at all costs; **faire qch. à p. d'argent,** to do sth.
for money; **se vendre à p. d'or,** (i) to fetch huge
prices; (ii) to sell oneself for gold; **à aucun p.,**
not at any price; (*b*) price; **p. courant,** market
price; **p. de revient,** cost price; **au dernier p.,** at
rock-bottom price; **un p. d'ami,** special terms;
blocage des p., price freezing, price pegging;
(**repas à**) **p. fixe,** table d'hôte (meal); **articles de
p.,** expensive goods; **c'est hors de p.,** the price
is prohibitive; **n'avoir pas de p.,** to be priceless;
(*c*) charge; **p. du voyage,** fare. **2.** reward, prize.
probab|le [prɔbabl], *a.* probable, likely; *s.f.*
-ilité, probability; *adv.* **-lement.**
probité [prɔbite], *s.f.* probity, integrity, honesty.
prob|lème [prɔblɛm], *s.m.* problem; **p. de
mathématiques,** mathematical problem;
problèmes politiques, political problems; **cela
pose des problèmes!** that's a problem! **c'est un
constant p.,** *F:* it's a continual headache; *a.*
-lématique, problematical.
rocédé [prɔsede], *s.m.* **1.** proceeding, dealing,
conduct; **je ne sais quel p. employer,** I don't
know what line of action to take; **procédés
honnêtes,** (i) courteous behaviour; (ii) square
dealing. **2.** process; method (of working); **p.
chimique,** chemical process.
rocéd|er [prɔsede], *v.i.* (**je procède,** n.
procédons) **1.** (*a*) to proceed; to originate (**de,**
in); **p. à une enquête,** to initiate an inquiry; (*b*)
Jur: to take proceedings (**contre qn,** against
s.o.); (*c*) to act. **2.** to proceed (**de,** from); *s.f.*
-ure, procedure; proceedings.
rocès [prɔsɛ], *s.m.* **p. civil,** lawsuit; **p. criminel,**
(criminal) trial; **intenter un p. à qn,** to
prosecute s.o.
rocession [prɔsɛsjɔ̃], *s.f.* procession.
rocès-verbal [prɔsɛvɛrbal], *s.m.* **1.** (official)
report; minute(s) (of meeting); record (of
evidence). **2.** policeman's report (against s.o.);
F: **j'ai attrapé un p.-v.,** I've been had up; *F:* **on
m'a collé un p.-v.,** I've got a ticket; *pl. procès-
verbaux.*
rochain [prɔʃɛ̃]. **1.** *a.* (*a*) nearest; **le village p.,**
the nearest village; **cause prochaine,** imme-
diate cause; (*b*) next; **dimanche p.,** next
Sunday; *Com:* **fin p.,** at the end of next month;
(*c*) near at hand; **dans un avenir p.,** in the near
future, before long. **2.** *s.m.* neighbour, fellow-
creature; *adv.* **-ement,** soon, shortly.
roche [prɔʃ]. **1.** *adv.* near; **tout p.,** close at
hand; **de p. en p.,** by degrees, step by step; **p.
de mourir,** near death. **2.** *a.* near,
neighbouring; **mon plus p. voisin,** my nearest
neighbour; **ses proches (parents),** his near

relations; his next of kin.
Proche-Orient (**le**) [ləprɔʃɔrjɑ̃]. *Pr.n.m. Geog:*
the Near East.
proclam|er [prɔklame], *v.tr.* to proclaim,
declare, publish; **p. le résultat du scrutin,** to
declare the poll; *s.f.* **-ation.**
procuration [prɔkyrasjɔ̃], *s.f. Com: Fin: Jur:*
procuration, proxy, power of attorney.
procur|er [prɔkyre], *v.tr.* **p. qch. à qn,** to
procure, obtain, get, sth. for s.o.; **se p. de
l'argent,** to raise, obtain, find, money; **se p. une
clientèle,** to work up a connection; **impossible
à se p.,** unobtainable; *a.* **-able,** obtainable.
procureur, procuratrice [prɔkyrœːr,
prɔkyratris], *s.* **1.** *Jur:* proxy. **2.** *s.m.* **p. de la
République** = public prosecutor, *N.Am:* dis-
trict attorney; **p. général** = Attorney General.
prodige [prɔdiːʒ], *s.m.* prodigy, wonder, marvel;
faire des prodiges, to work wonders; **un p. de
cruauté,** a monster of cruelty; *a.* **enfant p.,** infant prodigy.
prodigieu|x, -euse [prɔdiʒjø, -øːz], *a.*
prodigious, extraordinary, amazing; *adv.*
-sement.
prodigue [prɔdig]. **1.** *a.* prodigal, lavish,
wasteful (**de,** of). **2.** *s.* spendthrift.
prodig|uer [prɔdige], *v.tr.* **1.** to be prodigal,
lavish, of (sth.). **2.** to waste, squander; *adv.*
-alement; *s.f.* **-alité,** extravagance.
se prodiguer. 1. to take pains to please. **2. se p.
en éloges,** to be lavish of praise.
product|eur, -trice [prɔdyktœːr, -tris]. **1.** *a.*
productive (**de,** of); producing. **2.** *s.* producer;
a. **-if, -ive;** *s.f.* **-ivité.**
production [prɔdyksjɔ̃], *s.f.* **1.** production;
exhibiting; **p. d'une carte d'identité,** showing of
an identity card. **2.** (*a*) producing, production;
generation (of electricity, etc.); **p. de la voix,**
voice production; (*b*) *Pol.Ec: Ind: etc:* production, output; **capacité de p.,** output capacity;
augmenter la p., to increase production; **p. en
série,** mass production; **p. nationale,** national
product; *Cin: T.V:* film, etc., production.
produire [prɔdɥiːr], *v.tr.* (*conj. like* CONDUIRE)
1. to produce, bring forward. **2.** to produce,
yield. **3.** to produce, bring about.
se produire, to occur, happen; to take place.
produit [prɔdɥi], *s.m.* (*a*) product; **produits
agricoles,** farm produce; **produits chimiques,**
chemicals; **produits de beauté,** cosmetics; (*b*)
proceeds, yield; takings; **p. d'une vente,**
proceeds of a sale; **p. net,** net earnings.
profane [prɔfan]. **1.** *a.* profane; (*a*) secular
(history, music); (*b*) unhallowed, sacrilegious.
2. *s.* uninitiated person; layman; *F:* outsider.
profan|er [prɔfane], *v.tr.* **1.** to profane; to
desecrate (church, etc.); to violate (a grave). **2.**
to misuse, degrade (talent, genius); *s.* **-ateur,
-atrice,** desecrator; *s.f.* **-ation,** desecration.

proférer [prɔfere], *v.tr.* (je **profère**; je proférerai) to utter (a word, an oath, an accusation).

profes|ser [prɔfese], *v.tr.* 1. to profess (opinion, religion). 2. to teach, to be a professor of, a lecturer in (a subject); to exercise (a calling); *s.f.* -**sion**; *a.* -**sionnel**, -**sionnelle**, professional; *adv.* -**sionnellement**.

professeur [prɔfesœːr], *s.m.* professor; schoolmaster, -mistress.

professionnalisme [prɔfesjɔnalism], *s.m. Sp:* professionalism.

professorat [prɔfesɔra], *s.m.* 1. professorship; lectureship. 2. *coll:* the teaching profession.

profil [prɔfil], *s.m.* 1. profile, side-face. 2. *Ind:* contour, outline; section; **p. en long, en travers**, longitudinal, cross-, section.

profiler [prɔfile], *v.tr.* 1. to profile; to draw (sth.) in section. 2. to shape (a piece); to cut (a piece) to shape, to pattern.

se profiler, to be outlined, silhouetted (**sur**, on, **contre**, against).

profit [prɔfi], *s.m.* profit, benefit; **mettre qch. à p.**, to turn sth. to account.

profit|er [prɔfite], *v.i.* 1. (*a*) **p. de qch.**, to take advantage of sth.; to turn sth. to account; **p. de l'occasion**, to seize the opportunity; (*b*) **p. sur une vente**, to make a profit on a sale. 2. **p. à qn**, to benefit s.o. 3. (*of child, animal*) to thrive, grow; *a.* -**able**; *adv.* -**ablement**; *s.* -**eur**, -**euse**, profiteer.

profond [prɔfɔ̃]. 1. *a.* (*a*) deep (well, lake; voice); (*b*) deep-seated, underlying (cause, etc.); (*c*) profound; deep (sleep). 2. *adv.* **creuser p.**, to dig deep. 3. *s.m.* **au plus p. de mon cœur**, in the depths of my heart; **au plus p. de la nuit**, at dead of night; *adv.* -**ément**; *s.f.* -**eur**, depth.

profus [prɔfy], *a.* profuse; *adv.* -**sément**.

profusion [prɔfyzjɔ̃], *s.f.* profusion, profuseness; abundance; lavishness.

progéniture [prɔʒenityːr], *s.f.* offspring.

program|mation [prɔgramasjɔ̃], *s.f.* (*of computers*) programming; *s.* -**mateur**, -**matrice**, (computer) programmer.

programme [prɔgram], *s.m.* programme; *Pol:* platform (of party); *Sch:* syllabus; **p. d'études**, curriculum.

progrès [prɔgrɛ], *s.m.* progress.

progress|er [prɔgrese], *v.i.* (*a*) to progress, advance; to make headway; (*b*) to improve; *a.* -**if**, -**ive**, progressive; gradual (growth, etc.); *adv.* -**ivement**.

prohib|er [prɔibe], *v.tr.* to prohibit, forbid; *a.* -**itif**, -**itive**, prohibitory (law); prohibitive (price); *s.f.* -**ition**.

proie [prwa], *s.f.* prey; *Ven:* quarry; **oiseau, bête, de p.**, bird, beast, of prey; **la ville fut la p. des flammes**, the town was destroyed by fire.

projecteur [prɔʒɛktœːr], *s.m.* (*a*) searchlight; (*b*) floodlight; (*c*) *Cin: etc:* projector; spotlight.

projectile [prɔʒɛktil], *s.m.* projectile; missile.

projection [prɔʒɛksjɔ̃], *s.f.* 1. (*a*) projection; throwing (forward, up, out); *Ind:* **p. de sable,** sand blasting; (*b*) *Cin: etc:* **appareil de p.**, projector; **conférence avec projections**, lecture with films, slides; (*c*) beam of light; searchlight, spotlight. 2. *Mth: Arch:* plan; **p. horizontale,** ground plan; (*map making*) **p. de Mercator,** Mercator's projection; -**niste**, *s.m. & f. Cin:* projectionist.

projet [prɔʒɛ], *s.m.* (*a*) project, plan; scheme; (*b*) plan (of building).

projeter [prɔʒ(ə)te], *v.tr.* (je **projette**, n projetons) to project. 1. to throw; to cas (stone, shadow). 2. to plan, contemplate (; journey).

se projeter, to project, stand out.

prolét|ariser [prɔletarize], *v.tr.* t proletarianize; *s.m. coll.* -**ariat**, th proletariat; *a. & s.m. & f.* -**aire**, *a.* -**arien -arienne**, proletarian.

prolifique [prɔlifik], *a.* prolific.

prologue [prɔlɔg], *s.m.* prologue (**de**, to).

prolongation [prɔlɔ̃gasjɔ̃], *s.f.* prolongation (; time); lengthening (of stay, holiday); **p. d'u billet**, extension of a (railway) ticket; **p. de l scolarité**, raising of the school-leaving age; S; **jouer les prolongations**, to play extra time.

prolong|er [prɔlɔ̃ʒe], *v.tr.* (**n. prolongeons**) prolong; to protract, extend, to spin o (speech, etc.); **visite très prolongée**, protract visit; *Mth:* **p. une droite**, to produce a line; *s.* -**ement**, extension.

se prolonger, to be prolonged; to continu extend.

promenade [prɔmnad], *s.f.* 1. (*a*) walking (exercise); (*b*) stroll, outing; **faire une p.** pied), to go for a walk; **faire une p. à cheval,** go for a ride, to go riding; **p. en vélo**, cycle rid **p. en bateau**, row, sail, boat trip; **faire une p. voiture**, to go for a drive, to go out in the car. promenade, (public) walk, avenue.

promen|er [prɔmne], *v.tr.* (je **promène**) 1. (*a*) take (s.o.) for a walk, a drive, etc.; (*b*) to tal lead, (s.o.) about; **p. le chien**, to exercise t dog. 2. **p. sa main sur qch.**, to pass, run, on hand over sth.; **p. son regard sur qch.**, to r one's eye over sth.; *s.* -**eur**, -**euse**, walk hiker, pedestrian; stroller.

se promener, to walk; to go for a walk, fo drive, etc.; **se p. dans les rues**, to stroll abo the streets; *F:* **envoyer p. qn**, to send s packing; **va te p.!** get out! *P:* scram!

promesse [prɔmɛs], *s.f.* promise.

promett|re [prɔmɛtr], *v.tr.* (*conj. like* METT to promise. 1. (*a*) **p. qch. à qn**, to promise sth.; **p. à qn de faire qch.**, to promise s.o. to sth.; *F:* **je vous promets qu'on s'est amusé** I'll say we had a good time! (*b*) **se p. qch.**

promise oneself sth.; **je me promets (de boire) une bière,** I'm looking forward to (having) a beer. **2. le temps promet de la chaleur,** it promises to be warm; *abs. F:* **ça promet!** that looks good! *a.* **-eur, -euse,** promising, attractive (invitation); full of promise.

romontoire [prɔmɔ̃twaːr], *s.m. Geog:* promontory; headland, cape.

romoteur, -trice [prɔmɔtœːr, -tris], *s.* (*a*) promoter, originator (**de,** of); (*b*) *Sp:* promoter, organizer; *Com:* **p. de ventes,** sales promoter; (*c*) **p.**(**-constructeur**), property developer.

romotion [prɔmosjɔ̃], *s.f.* **1.** (*a*) promotion; **p. à l'ancienneté, au choix,** promotion by seniority, by selection; (*b*) list of appointments; (*c*) **p. sociale,** rise in the social scale. **2.** *Sch:* (*of students*) year; class.

rompt [prɔ̃], *a.* prompt, quick, ready; *adv.* **-ement** [prɔ̃t(ə)mã]; *s.f.* **-itude,** promptitude, quickness.

romu [prɔmy], *a.* promoted, raised (**à,** to).

ronom [prɔnɔ̃], *s.m. Gram:* pronoun.

ronominal, -aux [prɔnɔminal, -o], *a. Gram:* pronominal.

rononcé [prɔnɔ̃se], *a.* pronounced, decided (taste, feature, etc.); **nez p.,** large nose; **accent p.,** marked, strong accent; **peu p.,** faint.

rononcier [prɔnɔ̃se], *v.tr.* (**n. prononçons**) to pronounce. **1.** (*a*) **j'ai entendu p. mon nom,** I heard my name (mentioned); (*b*) **sans p. un mot,** without a word; (*c*) **p. un discours,** to deliver a speech. **2.** to articulate; **mot difficile à p.,** word hard to pronounce; *s.f.* **-iation,** pronunciation.

prononcer, to express one's opinion; to make a decision.

ronostic [prɔnɔstik], *s.m.* forecast; **p. des courses,** racing forecast; **p. du temps,** weather forecast.

ronostiquer [prɔnɔstike], *v.tr.* **1.** to forecast. **2.** *Med:* to make a prognosis.

opagande [prɔpagãːd], *s.f.* propaganda; publicity; *Com:* **faire de la p.,** to advertise.

opalger [prɔpaʒe], *v.tr.* (**n. propageons**) to propagate; to spread (abroad); *s.f.* **-gation;** *s.* **-gateur, -gatrice,** spreader (of news, disease).

propager. 1. (*of disease*) to spread. **2.** (*of living creatures*) to propagate, reproduce.

opane [prɔpan], *s.m.* propane (gas).

opension [prɔpãsjɔ̃], *s.f.* propensity, tendency, inclination (**à,** to).

opergol [prɔpɛrgɔl], *s.m.* (rocket) propellant.

ophète, prophétesse [prɔfɛːt, prɔfetɛs], *s.* prophet, seer; *f.* prophetess.

ophéltiser [prɔfetize], *v.tr.* (*a*) to prophesy; (*b*) to foretell; *s.f.* **-tie** [-si], prophecy; *a.* **-tique,** prophetic; *adv.* **-tiquement,** prophetically.

propice [prɔpis], *a.* propitious; auspicious; favourable (**à,** to s.o.; to, for, sth.).

proportion [prɔpɔrsjɔ̃], *s.f.* **1.** proportion, ratio; **toute(s) proportion(s) gardée(s),** making all due allowance. **2.** *pl.* size; **salle de vastes proportions,** enormous room; *a.* **-nel, -nelle,** proportional (**à,** to); *adv.* **-nellement.**

proportionné [prɔpɔrsjɔne], *a.* **1. bien p.,** well-proportioned (body, etc.); fully-fashioned (stockings, etc.). **2.** proportionate, suited (**à,** to).

propos [prɔpo], *s.m.* **1.** purpose, resolution. **2.** subject, matter; **à ce p.,** in connection with this; **à tout p.,** at every turn; **dire qch. à p.,** to say sth. to the point; **arriver fort à p.,** to arrive in the nick of time; **à p., avez-vous lu ce livre?** by the way, have you read this book? **3.** utterance, remark; *pl.* talk, gossip; **changer de p.,** to change the subject.

proposier [prɔpoze], *v.tr.* to propose (plan); to propound (theory, idea); **p. de l'argent à qn,** to offer s.o. money; **il m'a proposé des tapis,** he tried to sell me some carpets; **p. un candidat,** to suggest, put forward, a candidate; *s.f.* **-ition,** proposal, proposition.

se proposer. 1. to offer oneself, to come forward. **2. se p. qch.,** to have sth. in view.

propre [prɔpr]. **1.** *a.* (*a*) proper (meaning, etc.); *Gram:* **nom p.,** proper noun; (*b*) peculiar (**à,** to); **symptôme p. à une maladie,** symptom peculiar to a disease; **une façon de marcher à lui propre,** his own special way of walking; (*c*) own; **de mes propres yeux,** with my own eyes; **ses idées lui sont propres,** his ideas are his own; (*d*) appropriate, proper; **p. à tout,** fit for anything; **p. à rien,** good for nothing; **le mot p.,** the right word; (*e*) neat, clean; **linge p.,** clean linen; *F:* **nous voilà propres!** we're in a nice mess! **ça, c'est du p.!** what a mess! **2.** *s.m.* (*a*) property, attribute, nature; **le p. des poissons est de nager,** swimming is natural to, in the nature of, fish(es); (*b*) **en p.,** in one's own right; *adv.* **-ment.**

propreté [prɔprəte], *s.f.* cleanliness; neatness.

propriélté [prɔpriete], *s.f.* **1.** (*a*) ownership; **p. littéraire,** copyright; **p. industrielle,** patent rights; (*b*) property, estate; **p. immobilière,** real estate. **2.** property, characteristic; **les propriétés du cuivre,** the properties of copper. **3.** propriety, correctness (of terms, language); *s.m. & f.* **-taire,** owner; landlord, landlady.

propulsier [prɔpylse], *v.tr. Av: Nau:* to propel; *a.* **-if, -ive,** propelling (power, screw, etc.); *s.f.* **-ion,** propulsion.

propulseur [prɔpylsœːr], *s.m.* propeller; **p. à hélice,** screw propeller; **avion à p. atomique,** nuclear aircraft.

proroger [prɔrɔʒe], *v.tr.* (**n. prorogeons**) **1.** to prorogue (Parliament). **2.** to extend (time-limit).

prosaïque [prɔzaik], *a.* prosaic, commonplace, matter-of-fact; *adv.* -**ment**, in a matter-of-fact manner.

pros∣crire [prɔskriːr], *v.tr.* (*conj. like* ÉCRIRE) (*a*) to proscribe, outlaw, banish (s.o.); (*b*) *F:* to taboo (a practice); *s.f.* -**cription**, outlawry; *F:* tabooing; *a. & s.* -**crit**, (i) *a.* banned; (ii) *s.* outlaw.

prose [proːz], *s.f.* prose.

prospect∣er [prɔspɛkte], *v.tr.* **1.** *Min:* to prospect. **2.** *Com:* to canvass for (customers); *s.m.* -**eur**, prospector: canvasser.

prospectif, -ive [prɔspɛktif, -iːv], *a.* prospective, future (visit); probable, expected (event).

prospection [prɔspɛksjɔ̃], *s.f.* **1.** *Min:* prospecting, prospection; **p. pétrolière**, oil prospecting. **2.** *Com:* canvassing.

prospectus [prɔspɛktys], *s.m.* **1.** prospectus. **2.** handbill; leaflet.

prospère [prɔspɛːr], *a.* **1.** favourable. **2.** prosperous, thriving, flourishing (person, business).

prospér∣er [prɔspere], *v.i.* (**je prospère; je prospérerai**) to prosper, thrive; *s.f.* -**ité**, prosperity.

prosterner (se) [səprɔstɛrne], *v.pr.* (*a*) to prostrate oneself; to bow down (**devant**, before); (*b*) to grovel.

prostituée [prɔstitɥe], *s.f.* prostitute.

prostitu∣er [prɔstitɥe], *v.tr.* to prostitute (person, talent); *s.f.* -**tion**, prostitution.

prostration [prɔstrasjɔ̃], *s.f.* prostration. **1.** lying prone. **2.** *Med:* (nervous) exhaustion.

protec∣teur, -trice [prɔtɛktœːr, -tris]. **1.** *s.* (*a*) protector, protectress; (*b*) patron, patroness. **2.** *a.* (*a*) protecting, protective; (*b*) patronizing (tone); *s.f.* -**tion**, protection, patronage; *s.m.* -**torat**, protectorate.

protég∣er [prɔteʒe], *v.tr.* (**je protège, n. protégeons; je protégerai**) **1.** to protect (s.o., an industry). **2.** to shelter, guard (**contre**, against). **3.** to patronize, to be a patron of (the arts, etc.); *s.* -**é**, -**ée**, protégé(e).

protestant, -ante [prɔtɛstɑ̃, -ɑ̃ːt], *a. & s.* protestant; *s.m.* -**isme**.

protest∣er [prɔtɛste]. **1.** *v.tr.* (*a*) to protest, solemnly to declare; (*b*) *Com:* to protest (a bill). **2.** *v.i.* (*a*) **p. de son innocence**, to protest one's innocence; (*b*) **p. contre qch.**, to protest against sth., *N.Am:* to protest sth.; to challenge (a statement); *s.f.* -**ation**, protest; **réunion de p.**, protest meeting.

prothèse [prɔtɛːz], *s.f.* artificial limb; **p. dentaire**, false teeth, denture, etc.

protocole [prɔtɔkɔl], *s.m.* protocol; correct procedure, formalities.

proton [prɔtɔ̃], *s.m. Atom.Ph:* proton.

protoplasme [prɔtɔplasm], *s.m. Biol:* protoplasm.

prototype [prɔtɔtip], *s.m.* prototype.

protubér∣ance [prɔtyberɑ̃ːs], *s.f.* protuberance knob (on stick, etc.); **couvert d** **protubérances**, knobbly; *a.* -**ant**.

prouesse [pruɛs], *s.f.* **1.** valour. **2. p.** (**sportive** etc.), achievement (in sport, etc.); exploit.

prouver [pruve], *v.tr.* **1.** to prove (a fact). **2. p. s** **capacité**, to give proof of (one's) capacity.

provenance [prɔvnɑ̃ːs], *s.f.* source, origin; **trai** **en p. de Lille**, train from Lille.

provençal, -aux [prɔvɑ̃sal, -o], *a. &* **s** Provençal; of Provence.

provenir [prɔvniːr], *v.i.* (*conj. like* TENIR) **t** proceed, result, come (**de**, from); to **origina** (**de**, in, from); **d'où proviennent ces difficultés** what do these difficulties arise from?

proverb∣e [prɔvɛrb], *s.m.* proverb; *a.* -**ia** -**iaux**, proverbial; *adv.* -**ialemen** proverbially.

providen∣ce [prɔvidɑ̃ːs], *s.f.* providence; **é** -**tiel**, -**tielle**, providential, fortunate; *ad* -**tiellement**, providentially.

provinc∣e [prɔvɛ̃ːs], *s.f.* **1.** province. **2.** (*in o* *position to the capital*) **vivre en p.**, to live in **tl** country; **manières de p.**, countrified ways; **é** -**ial**, -**iaux**, provincial; country; *Pe* countrified.

proviseur [prɔvizœːr], *s.m. Sch:* headmaster (**é** a lycée).

provision [prɔvizjɔ̃], *s.f.* **1.** provision, stor supply; **aller aux provisions, faire s∣** **provisions**, to go shopping. **2.** *Com:* fund reserve; **chèque sans p.**, dishonoured, *F:* du bouncing, cheque.

provisoire [prɔvizwaːr]. **1.** *a.* provisional; **a** ting; temporary (manager, etc.); **dividende** interim dividend. **2.** *s.m.* what is temporar **parfois le p. dure longtemps**, the provision sometimes lasts a long time; *adv.* -**ment**.

provo∣quer [prɔvɔke], *v.tr.* **1.** to provoke (s.o **2.** to induce, instigate; **p. qn au crime**, to inc s.o. to crime; **p. la révolte**, to instigate a revo **p. qn à boire**, to egg s.o. on to drink. **3.** cause, bring about (an explosion); **p. un ac∣** **dent**, to cause, to be the cause of, an accider **p. la curiosité**, to arouse curiosity; **p. des co** **mentaires**, to give rise to comments; *a.* -**car** provocative; aggressive; tantalizing; *a. &* -**cateur, -catrice**, (*a*) *a.* provocative; (*b*) instigator; *s.f.* -**cation**.

proximité [prɔksimite], *s.f.* proximit nearness; **à p.**, near at hand, close by; **p. é** **sang**, near relationship.

prud∣e [pryd]. **1.** *a.* prudish. **2.** *s.f.* prude; **s** -**erie**), prudery, prudishness.

prud∣ence [prydɑ̃ːs], *s.f.* prudence; carefulne *a.* -**ent**, prudent; discreet; *adv.* -**emment**.

prun|e [pryn], *s.f.* plum; **p. de damas,** damson; *a.inv.* plum-coloured; *s.m.* **-ier,** plum-tree.

pruneau, -eaux [pryno], *s.m.* prune.

prunel|le [prynɛl], *s.f.* **1.** *Bot:* sloe. **2.** pupil (of the eye); *s.m.* **-lier,** blackthorn.

Prusse (la) [laprys]. *Pr.n.f. Geog: Hist:* Prussia; **bleu de P.,** Prussian blue.

prussien, -ienne [prysjɛ̃, -jɛn], *a.* & *s.* Prussian.

psalmodier [psalmɔdje], *v.i.* (*pr. sub.* & *p.d.* **n. psalmodiions**) to intone, to chant.

psau|me [psoːm], *s.m.* psalm; *s.m.* **-tier,** psalter, psalm-book.

pseudonyme [psødɔnim]. **1.** *a.* pseudonymous. **2.** *s.m.* pseudonym; nom de plume.

psychana|lyser [psikanalize], *v.tr.* to psychoanalyse; *s.f.* **-lyse,** psychoanalysis; *s.m.* & *f.* **-lyste,** psychoanalyst; *a.* **-lytique,** psychoanalytic.

psycholo|gie [psikɔlɔʒi], *s.f.* psychology; *a.* **-gique,** psychological; *adv.* **-giquement;** *s.* **-gue,** psychologist.

puant [pɥɑ̃], *a.* stinking, foul-smelling.

puanteur [pɥɑ̃tœːr], *s.f.* stench; foul smell, stink.

publ|ic, -ique [pyblik]. **1.** *a.* public (life, meeting, monument, etc.); **la chose publique,** the public service; **questions d'intérêt p.,** public matters; **les hommes publics,** men in public life; *Adm:* **le ministère p.,** the public prosecutor. **2.** *s.m.* **le p.,** the public, the people; **le grand p.,** the general public, *F:* the man in the street; *adv.* **-iquement,** publicly, openly.

publ|ier [pyblije], *v.tr.* (*pr.sub.* & *p.d.* **n. publiions**) (*a*) to publish; to make public; to proclaim; **p. un ordre,** to issue an order; (*b*) to publish (book, etc.); *s.f.* **-ication;** *s.f.* **-icité,** publicity, advertising; advertisement; **faire de la p.,** to advertise; *a.* **-icitaire,** advertising (campaign, etc.).

puc|e [pys], *s.f.* flea; **marché aux puces,** flea market, junk market; *F:* **avoir la p. à l'oreille,** to be suspicious; *s.m.* **-eron,** green-fly.

pudeur [pydœːr], *s.f.* (*a*) modesty; sense of decency; (*b*) (sense of) discretion; **une sorte de p. l'empêchait d'en parler,** a kind of reticence prevented him from talking about it; **rougir de p.,** to blush for shame.

pudibond [pydibɔ̃], *a.* easily shocked; prudish.

pudique [pydik], *a.* modest; chaste; *adv.* **-ment.**

puer [pɥe], *v.i.* to stink, to smell; **p. l'ail,** to smell of garlic.

puéricul|ture [pɥerikyltyːr], *s.f.* child welfare; **p. prénatale,** ante-natal care; **suivre un cours de p.,** to take a course in infant welfare; *s.f.* **-trice,** nursery nurse.

puéril [pɥeril], *a.* puerile, childish; *adv.* **-ement;** *s.f.* **-ité,** childishness.

pugil|at [pyʒila], *s.m. Sp:* pugilism; boxing; *s.m. Sp:* **-isme,** boxing; *s.m.* **-iste,** pugilist, boxer.

puîné, -ée [pɥine], *a.* & *s.* younger (brother or sister).

puis [pɥi], *adv.* (*a*) then, afterwards, next; (*b*) besides; **et p. après?** (i) what then? (ii) what about it? *F:* so what?

puiser [pɥize], *v.tr.* to draw (water) (**à, dans,** from); **p. une idée chez un auteur,** to take, get, derive, an idea from a writer.

puisque [pɥisk(ə)], *conj.* (**puisqu'** *before an initial vowel*) since, as; **p. je te dis que je l'ai vu!** but I tell you I saw it!

puiss|ance [pɥisɑ̃ːs], *s.f.* power. **1.** force (of habit); strength (of the wind); power (of an engine); **p. en chevaux,** horse-power; **moteur à grande p.,** heavy duty engine; *Av:* **p. au décollage,** take-off power; **maximum de p.,** maximum output, *El:* power; *Mth:* **p. d'un nombre,** power of a number. **2.** sway, authority; **avoir qn en sa p.,** to have s.o. in one's power; **p. paternelle, maternelle,** parental authority. **3. les puissances européennes,** the European powers; **p. mondiale,** world power; *a.* **-ant,** powerful, strong; mighty.

puits [pɥi], *s.m.* **1.** well, hole. **2.** shaft, pit (of mine).

pull(-over) [pul(ɔvœːr, -ɔvɛːr)], *s.m. Cl:* pullover.

pullul|er [pylyle], *v.i.* (*a*) to multiply rapidly; (*b*) to be found in profusion; to swarm; *s.f.* **-ation;** *s.m.* **-ement,** swarming.

pulmonaire [pylmɔnɛːr]. **1.** *a.* pulmonary (artery, etc.); **congestion p.,** congestion of the lungs. **2.** *s.m.* & *f.* consumptive.

pulpe [pylp], *s.f.* pulp; *a.* **-eux, -euse,** pulpy.

pulsation [pylsasjɔ̃], *s.f.* pulsation. **1.** throbbing; beating. **2.** throb; (heart-)beat.

pulvéris|er [pylverize], *v.tr.* (*a*) to pulverize; to grind (sth.) to powder; (*b*) to spray (liquid); *s.m.* **-ateur,** (*a*) pulverizer; (*b*) spray(er); *s.f.* **-ation,** (*a*) crushing; (*b*) spraying.

punaise [pynɛːz], *s.f.* **1.** *Ent:* bug. **2.** drawing-pin.

pun|ir [pyniːr], *v.tr.* to punish; *a.* **-issable,** punishable; *a.* **-itif, -itive,** punitive; *s.f.* **-ition,** punishment.

pupille¹ [pypil], *s.m.* & *f. Jur:* ward; **pupilles de la Nation,** war orphans.

pupille², *s.f.* pupil (of the eye).

pupitre [pypitr], *s.m.* **1.** desk; **p. à musique,** music-stand; *P.T.T: etc:* **p. de distribution,** switch desk; (*computers*) **p. (de commande),** control desk, console. **2.** *Mus:* group (of instruments); **chef de p.,** leader (of a group).

pur [pyːr], *a.,* pure. **1. or p.,** pure gold; **la pure vérité,** the plain truth; **p. hasard,** mere chance. **2. ciel p.,** clear sky; *adv.* **-ement.**

purée [pyre], *s.f. Cu:* (*a*) **p. (de pommes de terre),** mashed potatoes; (*b*) purée.

pureté [pyrte], *s.f.* purity; pureness (of liquid, air, morals, style, etc.); clearness (of the sky).

purgatif, -ive [pyrgatif, -iːv], *a. & s.m. Med:* purgative.

purgatoire [pyrgatwaːr], *s.m. Theol:* purgatory.

purge [pyrʒ], *s.f.* 1. (*a*) *Med:* purge; (*b*) *Pol:* purge. 2. *Mch:* draining; **robinet de p.**, drain cock. 3. *Jur:* paying off, redemption (of mortgage).

purger [pyrʒe], *v.tr.* (**n. purgeons**) (*a*) to purge, cleanse, clear (out); (*b*) **p. une hypothèque,** to redeem, pay off (a mortgage); to clear (oneself) (of debt, etc.); (*c*) *Mec.E:* to drain (cylinder); to bleed (pipe).

purifiler [pyrifje], *v.tr.* (*pr.sub. & p.d.* **n. purifiions**) to purify, cleanse, sweeten (air, water, etc.); to refine (metal); *s.* **-cateur, -catrice,** cleanser; *s.f.* **-cation,** purification.

puritain, -aine [pyritɛ̃, -ɛn]. **1.** *s.* puritan. **2.** *a.* puritanical.

pur-sang [pyrsɑ̃], *s.m.inv.* thoroughbred.

putatlif, -ive [pytatif, -iːv], *a.* supposed presumed, reputed; **père p.,** putative, sup posed, father; *adv.* **-ivement,** reputedly.

putréIfier [pytrefje], *v.tr.* to putrefy, to rot; t decompose (sth.); *s.f.* **-faction,** decomposi tion, decay.

se putréfier, to become putrid, *F:* to go bad.

pyjama [piʒama], *s.m.* pyjamas, *N.Am* pajamas; **un p.,** a pair of pyjamas; **dormir e p.,** to sleep in pyjamas.

pylône [piloːn], *s.m.* pylon; *P.T.T: etc:* lattic mast.

pyramidle [piramid], *s.f.* pyramid; *a.* **-al, -aux** pyramidal.

Pyrénéles (les) [lepirene]. *Pr.n.f.pl. Geog:* th Pyrenees; *a.* **-en, -enne,** Pyrenean.

python [pitɔ̃], *s.m.* python.

Q

Q, q [ky], *s.m.* (the letter) Q, q.

qu'= **que** *before a vowel or* **h** *mute.*

quadragénaire [kwadraʒenɛːr], *a. & s.* quadragenarian, forty-year-old (man, woman).

Quadragésime [kwadraʒezim], *s.f. Ecc:* Quadragesima (Sunday).

quadrangulaire [kwadrɑ̃gylɛːr], *a.* quadrangular, four-cornered (building, etc.).

quadratique [kwadratik], *a. Mth:* quadratic.

quadrilat|ère [k(w)adrilatɛːr], *s.m.* quadrilateral; *a.* **-éral, -éraux,** quadrilateral, four-sided.

quadrillé [kadrije], *a.* squared, cross-ruled; chequered; **carte quadrillée,** grid map.

quadrimoteur, -trice [k(w)adrimɔtœːr, -tris], *a. & s.m. Av:* four-engined (aircraft).

quadriréacteur [kwadrireaktœːr], *s.m. Av:* four-engined jet aircraft.

quadrisyllabique [kwadrisil(l)abik], *a.* four-syllabled (word).

quadrupède [k(w)adrypɛd]. **1.** *a.* four-footed (animal). **2.** *s.m.* quadruped.

quadruple [k(w)adrypl], *a. & s.m.* quadruple, fourfold; **payer le q. du prix,** to pay four times the price.

quadruplés, -ées [k(w)adryple], *s.pl.* quadruplets, *F:* quads.

quai [ke], *s.m.* (*a*) quay, wharf; pier; **propriétaire, gardien, de q.,** wharfinger; **à q.,** alongside the quay; (*b*) (river) embankment; (*c*) *Rail:* platform; **le train est à q.,** the train's in; *P.N:* **accès aux quais,** to the trains.

qualificatif, -ive [kalifikatif, -iːv], *a.* qualifying.

qualifié [kalifje], *a.* qualified (to do sth.); **ouvrier q., non-q.,** skilled, unskilled, worker.

qualifi|er [kalifje], *v.tr.* (*pr.sub. & p.d.* n. **qualifiions**) **1.** to style, term, qualify; **acte qualifié de crime,** action termed a crime; *F:* **q. qn de menteur,** to call s.o. a liar. **2.** *Gram:* to qualify. **3.** *Sp: etc:* to qualify (for an athletic, etc., event); *s.f.* **-cation.**

se qualifier. 1. se q. colonel, to call, style, oneself colonel. **2. se q. pour une fonction,** to qualify for an office.

qualité [kalite], *s.f.* **1.** quality; **de bonne q.,** of good quality. **2.** characteristics, property (of sth.); **qualités curatives d'une drogue,** curative properties of a drug. **3.** qualification, capacity; profession, occupation; *Adm:* **nom, prénom et q.,** name, Christian name and occupation or

description; **agir en sa q. d'avocat,** to act (in his capacity) as a barrister; **avoir les qualités requises pour un poste,** to have the necessary qualifications for a job; **avoir q. d'électeur,** to be qualified to vote; **avoir q. pour agir,** to be authorized, qualified, to act.

quand [kɑ̃], when. **1.** *conj.* (*a*) **je le lui en parlerai q. je le verrai,** I'll mention it to him when I see him; *F:* **q. je vous le disais!** didn't I tell you so! (*b*) **q. (même),** (i) even if, even though, although; (ii) **je le ferai q. même,** I'll do it all the same. **2.** *adv.* **q. viendra-t-il?** when will he come? **à q. la noce?** when is the wedding to be? **depuis q. êtes-vous à Paris?** how long, since when, have you been in Paris?

quant à [kɑ̃ta], *adv.phr.* **q. à moi,** as for me; **q. à cela,** as far as that goes; **q. à l'avenir,** as regards the future.

quantité [kɑ̃tite], *s.f.* quantity; **q. de gens,** a lot of people; **en q.,** in bulk; **en grande q.,** *F:* **en q. industrielle,** in large quantities; **par petites quantités,** in small amounts.

quarantaine [karɑ̃tɛn], *s.f.* **1.** (about) forty, some forty (years, pages, etc.); **approcher de la q.,** to be getting on for forty. **2.** quarantine; **mettre un navire, des voyageurs, en q.,** to quarantine a ship, passengers.

quarante [karɑ̃t], *num.a.inv. & s.m.inv.* forty; *F:* **je m'en fiche comme de l'an q.,** I don't care a damn.

quart [kaːr], *s.m.* **1.** quarter, fourth part; *Com:* **remise du q.,** 25% discount; **dans un petit q. d'heure,** in a few minutes; **passer un mauvais q. d'heure,** to have a trying moment, a bad time of it; **il est deux heures et q.,** it's a quarter past two; **trois quarts,** three quarters; **cinq heures trois quarts,** a quarter to six; **q. de cercle,** quadrant. **2.** *Nau:* **q. de vent,** point of the compass (= 11° 15'). **3.** *Nau:* watch; **être de q.,** to be on watch. **4.** *esp. Mil:* (quarter-litre) mug; **un q. de beurre,** 250 grammes of butter.

quartier [kartje], *s.m.* **1.** quarter, fourth part; **q. de la lune,** quarter of the moon; *Cu:* **q. d'agneau,** quarter of lamb. **2.** part, portion; **mettre qch. en quartiers,** to tear sth. to pieces. **3.** (*a*) district, neighbourhood (of town); **q. des spectacles,** theatreland; **q. des affaires,** business district, *N.Am:* downtown; **je ne suis pas du q.,** I don't live round here; (*b*) *Nau:* **de quel q. vient le vent?** what quarter is the wind in? (*c*) *Mil:* **rentrer au q.,** to return to quarters, barracks; **q. général,** headquarters. **4.** quarter, mercy; **demander q.,** to ask for quarter.

quartz [kwarts], *s.m.* quartz, rock-crystal.

quasi [kazi], *adv.* quasi, almost; **q. aveugle,** all but blind; **j'en ai la q.-certitude,** I'm almost, all but, sure of it.

quatorze [katɔrz], *num.a.inv.* fourteen; **page q.,** page fourteen; **Louis Q.,** Louis the Fourteenth; **le q. juillet,** the fourteenth of July.

quatorzième [katɔrzjɛm], *num.a. & s.* fourteenth; *adv.* **-ment.**

quatre [katr], *num.a.inv. & s.m.inv.* four; **les q. saisons,** the four seasons; **Henri Q.,** Henry the Fourth; **demeurer au (numéro) q.,** to live at number four; **un de ces q. matins,** one of these (fine) days, some time soon; **à q. pas d'ici,** close by; **il se mettrait en q. pour vous,** he would do anything for you.

Quatre-Cantons [katr(ə)kɑ̃tɔ̃]. *Pr.n.m.pl. Geog:* **le lac des Q.-C.,** the Lake of Lucerne.

quatre-vingt-dix [katrəvɛ̃dis], *num.a. & s.m.* ninety.

quatre-vingt-dixième [katrəvɛ̃dizjɛm], *num.a. & s.* ninetieth.

quatre-vingtième [katrəvɛ̃tjɛm], *num.a. & s.* eightieth.

quatre-vingts [katrəvɛ̃], *num.a. & s.m.* (*omits the final* s *when followed by a num.a. or when used as an ordinal*) eighty; **quatre-vingt-un,** eighty-one; **quatre-vingt-onze,** ninety-one.

quatrième [katriɛm]. **1.** *num.a. & s.* fourth. **2.** *s.m.* **habiter au q.,** to live on the fourth floor.

quatuor [kwatyɔːr], *s.m. Mus:* quartet.

que[1] [k(ə)], *rel.pron.* that; whom; which; what. **1. advienne que pourra,** come what may. **2. menteur que tu es!** you liar! **couvert qu'il était de poussière,** covered with dust as he was; **purs mensonges que tout cela!** that's all a pack of lies! **c'est une belle maison que la vôtre,** yours is a fine house. **3. les livres que vous avez achetés,** the books you have bought. **4. les jours qu'il fait chaud,** on (the) days when it is warm.

que[2], *interr.pron.neut.* what? **1. que voulez-vous?** what do you want? **que dire?** what could I say? **2.** (*a*) **qu'est-il arrivé?** what has happened? (*b*) **que devenir?** what's to become of us? **3.** (*a*) (= POURQUOI) **que ne le disiez-vous?** why didn't you say so? (*b*) (= COMME) **qu'il est beau!** how handsome he is! (*c*) (= COMBIEN) **que de gens!** what a !ot of people!

que[3], *conj.* that; but (that); lest. **1. je désire qu'il vienne,** I want him to come; **je pense que non,** I think not. **2.** (*a*) **qu'elle entre!** let her come in! **que je vous y reprenne!** let me catch you at it again! (*b*) (i) **qu'il pleuve ou qu'il fasse du vent,** whether it rains or blows; (ii) **que tu le veuilles ou non,** whether you wish it or not. **3. il**

l'affirmerait que je ne le croirais pas, even if he said it was true, I would not believe it. **4. approchez qu'on vous entende,** come nearer so that we can hear you; **il y a trois jours que je ne l'ai vu,** it is three days since I saw him. **5. quand il entrera et qu'il vous trouvera ici,** when he comes in and finds you here. **6. à ce que, de ce que; je ne m'attendais pas à ce qu'on entrât,** I did not expect anyone to come in; **on s'alarmait de ce qu'il ne reparaissait pas,** alarm was felt at his failure to appear again. **7.** (*in comparisons*) **aussi grand, plus grand, moins grand, que moi,** as tall as, taller than, less tall than, I (am). **8.** (*a*) **ne . . . que,** only; **il n'a qu'une jambe,** he has only one leg; **je n'ai que 100 francs,** I have only a hundred francs; (*b*) **sans . . . que; j'étais sans ami que mon chien,** I had no friend but my dog; (*c*) **ne . . . pas que,** not only; **il n'y a pas que lui qui le sache,** he's not the only one who knows it; (*d*) **il ne me reste plus que vingt francs,** I have only twenty francs left; **plus que dix minutes!** only ten minutes left! (*e*) **à peine était-il rentré que le téléphone sonna,** he had scarcely come in when the telephone rang. **9.** *F:* **que non!** surely not! **que si!** surely yes! **que non pas!** not at all!

Québec [kebɛk]. *Pr.n.m.* Quebec.

quel, quelle [kɛl], *a. & pron.* what, which. **1. q. que soit le résultat, je le ferai,** whatever the result may be, I will do it; **quels que soient ces hommes,** whoever these men may be. **2.** (*interrogative*) **quelle heure est-il?** what's the time? **q. livre lisez-vous?** which book are you reading? **quels sont ces messieurs?** who are these gentlemen? **3.** (*exclamatory*) **q. homme!** what a man!

quelconque [kɛlkɔ̃k], *a.* **1.** any (whatever). **2 répondre d'une façon q.,** to make some sort of reply. **3. c'est un homme très q.,** he's a very ordinary kind of man; *F:* **son travail est q.,** his work isn't up to much.

quelque [kɛlk(ə)]. **1.** *a.* (*a*) some, any; **adressez vous à q. autre,** apply to someone else; (*b*) some, a few; **il y a quelques jours,** a few days ago; **cent et quelques mètres,** a hundred odd metres; (*c*) **q. . . . qui, que,** whatever, what soever; **q. chose qu'il vous ait dite,** whatever (thing) he said to you. **2.** *adv.* (*a*) some, about; **q. dix ans,** some ten years; (*b*) **q. . . . que** however; **q. grandes que soient ses fautes** however great his faults may be.

quelque chose [kɛlkəʃoːz], *indef.pron.m.inv* something, anything; **q. c. de nouveau,** sth new; **il y a q. c.,** there's sth. up, sth. the matter

quelquefois [kɛlkəfwa], *adv.* sometimes; now and then.

quelque part [kɛlkəpaːr], *adv.* somewhere; **doit se cacher q. p.,** he must be hidin somewhere.

quelqu'un, quelqu'une [kɛlkœ̃, kɛlkyn]; *pl.*
quelques-uns, -unes [kɛlkəzœ̃, -yn], *in-def.pron.* **1.** *m. & f.* one (or other); **vous le
trouverez dans q. des autres magasins,** you'll
find it in one of the other shops; **quelques-
un(e)s d'entre nous,** a few of us. **2.** *m.* someone,
somebody; anyone, anybody; **q. me l'a dit,**
someone told me so; **est-il venu q.?** has
anybody come? **q. d'autre,** someone else; **q. de
trop,** one too many.
querelle [kərɛl], *s.f.* quarrel, dispute; **querelles
de famille,** family squabbles; family feuds.
querell|er [kərɛle], *v.tr.* **q. qn,** to quarrel with
s.o.; *a.* **-eur, -euse,** quarrelsome; **une
(femme) querelleuse,** a shrew, a nagger.
se quereller, to quarrel, wrangle.
qu'est-ce que [kɛskə], *interr.pron.* what? (*a*)
(*object*) **qu'est-ce que vous voulez?** what do
you want? (*b*) **qu'est-ce que c'est que ça?**
what's that?
qu'est-ce qui [kɛski], *interr.pron.* (*subject*)
what? **qu'est-ce qui est arrivé?** what's
happened?
question [kɛstjɔ̃], *s.f.* (*a*) question, query; **poser
une q. à qn,** to ask s.o. a question; **son adhésion ne fait pas q.,** there is no doubt, no question, of his adherence; **mettre qch. en q.,** to
question sth.; to challenge (a statement, etc.);
(*b*) question, matter, point, issue; **questions
d'actualité,** topics of the day; **sortir de la q.,** to
wander from the point.
question|ner [kɛstjɔne], *v.tr.* to question (s.o.);
to ask (s.o.) questions; *s.m.* **-naire,**
questionnaire.
quête [kɛt], *s.f.* **1.** quest, search; **se mettre en q.
de qch.,** to go in search of sth.; **gens en q. de
plaisir,** pleasure-seekers. **2.** *Ecc: etc:* collection; **faire la q.,** to take up the collection; to
pass the hat round.
quêter [kɛte], *v.tr.* to collect (alms).
queue [kø], *s.f.* **1.** (animal's) tail; **q. de renard,**
fox's brush; **finir en q. de poisson,** to fizzle out.
2. tail (of comet); handle (of pan); pin (of
brooch); pigtail; **habit à q.,** (swallow-)tail coat.
3. (tail-)end, fag-end; **venir en q.,** to bring up
the rear; **être à la q. de la classe,** to be at the
bottom of the class. **4.** queue; **faire (la) q.,** to
queue up. **5.** (billiard) cue.
qui¹ [ki], *rel.pron.* **1.** **un livre qui traite de ces
questions,** a book which deals with, dealing
with, these questions; **je le vois qui vient,** I see
him coming. **2.** (*object*) whom; which; (*a*) **voilà
l'homme à qui je pensais, de qui je parlais,**
there is the man of whom I was thinking,
speaking; **adressez-vous à qui vous voudrez,**
apply to whoever you please, to anyone you
like; (*b*) **on se dispersa qui d'un côté, qui d'un
autre,** we scattered, some going one way, some
the other. **3.** (*a*) **qui que,** who(so)ever;

whom(so)ever; (*b*) **qui que ce soit,** anyone
(whatever).
qui², *interr.pron.m.sg.* who? whom? (*a*) **qui a dit
cela?** who said that? **qui désirez-vous voir?**
whom do you wish to see? **à qui est ce canif?**
whose is this knife? **qui d'autre?** who(m) else?
elle épouse je ne sais plus qui, she's marrying I
forget who(m); **c'était à qui l'aiderait,** they
vied with each other in helping him; *F:* **il est
là—qui ça? qui donc?** he's there—who? (*b*)
qui des deux a raison? which of the two is
right?
quiconque [kikɔ̃:k], *indef.pron.m.sg.* **1.**
who(so)ever; anyone who; **q. désobéira sera
puni,** whoever disobeys, anyone who disobeys, shall be punished. **2. pas un mot de cela
à q.,** not a word of that to anybody.
qui est-ce que [kiɛskə], *interr.pron.* whom? **qui
est-ce que vous désirez voir?** whom do you
wish to see?
qui est-ce qui [kiɛski], *interr.pron.* who? (*a*) **qui
est-ce qui vous l'a dit?** who told you so? (*b*) (*in
indirect questions*) *F:* **je ne sais pas qui est-ce
qui vous a dit ça,** I don't know who told you
that.
quille¹ [ki:j], *s.f.* ninepin, skittle; **jeu de quilles,** (i)
set of ninepins, of skittles; (ii) skittle-alley;
Bill: **partie de quilles,** pin pool.
quille², *s.f. Nau:* keel (of ship).
quincaill|erie [kɛ̃kajri], *s.f.* **1.** hardware, iron-
mongery. **2.** hardware (i) business, (ii) shop;
s.m. **-ier,** ironmonger.
quinine [kinin], *s.f.* quinine.
quinquina [kɛ̃kina], *s.m.* (*a*) *Pharm:* cinchona;
Peruvian bark; (*b*) **vin de q.,** tonic wine.
quinte [kɛ̃:t], *s.f.* **1.** *Mus:* fifth, quint; **q.
diminuée, augmentée,** diminished, augmented,
fifth. **2. q. de toux,** fit of coughing.
quintuplés, -ées [kɛ̃typle], *s.pl.* quintuplets, *F:*
quins.
quinzaine [kɛ̃zɛn], *s.f.* **1.** (about) fifteen, some
fifteen; **une q. de francs,** fifteen francs or so. **2.**
fortnight, two weeks; **dans la q.,** within a
fortnight.
quinze [kɛ̃:z], *num.a.inv. & s.m.inv.* **1.** fifteen;
Louis Q., Louis the Fifteenth; **le q. mai,** (on)
the fifteenth of May; **demeurer au (numéro) q.,**
to live at number fifteen; **Ten: q. à, partout,**
fifteen all; *Rugby Fb:* **le q. de France,** the
French fifteen. **2. q. jours,** a fortnight, two
weeks; **aujourd'hui en q.,** today fortnight;
tous les q. jours, once a fortnight, once every
two weeks.
quinzième [kɛ̃zjɛm], *num.a. & s.* fifteenth.
quiproquo [kiprɔko], *s.m.* mistake (taking of
one thing for another); misunderstanding.
quittance [kitɑ̃:s], *s.f.* receipt, discharge.
quitte [kit], *a.* **1.** free, quit; **être q. de dettes,** to
be out of debt; **nous sommes quittes,** I'm quits

with you; **il en a été q. pour la peur,** he got off with a fright. **2.** *inv. in adv. use;* **je le ferai q. à être grondé,** I'll do it even if I am told off.

quitter [kite], *v.tr.* **1. q. la partie,** to throw up the sponge, to cry off. **2.** to leave (place, person); **q. ses habits,** to take off one's clothes.

qui-vive [kivi:v], *s.m.inv. Mil:* sentry's challenge; **être sur le q.-v.,** to be on the alert.

quoi¹ [kwa], *rel.pron.* what. **1.** (*a*) **c'est en q. vous vous trompez,** that is where you are wrong; (*b*) **il a bien autre chose à q. penser!** he has something else to think about! **2. de q.; il a de q. vivre,** he has enough to live on; **il y a de q. vous faire enrager,** it's enough to drive you mad; **il n'y a pas de q.,** no thanks, no apologies, are needed; don't mention it. **3. sans q.,** otherwise. **4. q. qui, q. que;** (*a*) **q. qui survienne,** whatever comes of it; **q. qu'il en soit,** be that as it may; (*b*) **q. que ce soit,** anything (whatever).

quoi², *interr.pron.* what? (*a*) **q. de nouveau? what news? eh bien! q.?** well, what about it? (*b*) **vous désirez q.?** what is it you want? **un je-ne-sais-q.,** an indescribable something; (*c*) **à q. bon?** what's the use?

quoique [kwak(ə)], *conj. usu.* + *sub.* (al)though; **quoiqu'il soit pauvre,** although he's poor; **je suis heureux q. garçon,** I'm happy though (I'm) a bachelor.

quote-part [kɔtpa:r], *s.f.* share, quota, portion; *pl.* **quotes-parts.**

quotidien, -ienne [kɔtidjɛ̃, -jɛn]. **1.** *a.* daily, everyday; **la vie quotidienne,** everyday life. **2.** *s.m.* (*a*) **les quotidiens,** the daily papers; (*b*) **le q.,** everyday life; *adv.* **-nement,** daily, every day.

quotient [kɔsjɑ̃], *s.m.* **1.** *Mth:* quotient. **2. q. intellectuel,** intelligence quotient, I.Q.

R

R, r [ɛːr], *s.m.* (the letter) R, r.

rabâch|er [rabɑʃe], *v.tr.* **ils rabâchent toujours la même chose,** they are for ever harping on the same string; *s.m.* **-age,** (tedious, boring) harping, repetition.

rabais [rabɛ], *s.m.* rebate, discount; **vendre qch. au r.,** to sell sth. at a reduced price.

rabaisser [rabɛse], *v.tr.* **1.** to lower (sth., one's voice); *Com:* to reduce (price). **2.** (*a*) to disparage, belittle (s.o., sth.); (*b*) to humble (s.o., s.o.'s pride).

rabatt|re [rabatr], *v.tr.* (*conj. like* BATTRE) **1.** to fold back; to bring down; to stitch down, to fell (a seam); to flatten (a metal edge); **porte rabattue contre le mur,** door folded back to the wall; **le vent rabat la fumée,** the wind beats down the smoke. **2.** to reduce, lessen; (*a*) *Com:* **r. tant du prix,** to take so much off the price; **r. les centimes,** to knock off the centimes; (*b*) **r. l'orgueil de qn,** to take down s.o.'s pride. **3. r. les flammes,** to beat back the flames; **r. le gibier,** to beat up the game; *a.* **-able; siège r.,** folding, fold-back, seat; *s.m.* **-age,** (i) lowering (of prices); (ii) cutting back (of roses, etc.); (iii) beating (for game); heading off (of fugitives).

rabbin [rabɛ̃], *s.m. Rel:* rabbi.

rabot [rabo], *s.m. Tls:* plane.

raboter [rabɔte], *v.tr.* to plane (wood).

rabougri [rabugri], *a.* stunted, dwarfed (person, plant).

rabrouer [rabrue], *v.tr.* to snub (s.o.); to treat (s.o.) brusquely; *F:* to jump down (s.o.'s) throat.

raccommod|er [rakɔmɔde], *v.tr.* **1.** to mend, repair; to darn (sock). **2.** to reconcile (two persons); *a.* **-able,** mendable, repairable (watch, garment); *s.m.* **-age,** mending, repairing; darning; *s.m.* **-ement,** reconciliation; making up (of quarrel).

accorder [rakɔrde], *v.tr. Mec.E: El: etc:* to join, connect, to link up.

accourci [rakursi]. **1.** *a.* shortened (skirt, etc.); short, squat; abridged. **2.** (*a*) **en r.,** (i) briefly; (ii) on a small scale; **l'histoire en r.,** the story in brief; **la société en r.,** society in miniature; (*b*) *Art:* foreshortening; (*c*) **prendre (par) un r.,** to take a short cut.

ccourc|ir [rakursiːr]. **1.** *v.tr.* (*a*) to shorten; **r. le pas,** to shorten step; (*b*) to abridge, curtail; to cut short. **2.** *v.i. & pr.* to grow shorter; to shrink; *s.m.* **-issement. 1.** shortening; abridgement; curtailment. **2.** growing shorter; shrinking.

raccrocher [rakrɔʃe], *v.tr.* to hang (sth.) up again; *P.T.T:* to ring off.

race [ras], *s.f.* race. **1.** descent, strain; **de r. noble,** of noble blood. **2.** stock, breed; **chien de r.,** pedigree dog; **de r. croisée,** crossbred; (*of pers.*) **avoir de la r.,** to be distinguished, aristocratic.

rachat [raʃa], *s.m. Com: Fin:* repurchase, buying back; **offre de r.,** takeover bid.

racheter [raʃte], *v.tr.* (*conj. like* ACHETER) (*a*) to repurchase; to buy back; to take over; (*b*) to redeem (a debt, a pledge); (*c*) to ransom (prisoner).

racine [rasin], *s.f.* (*a*) root; (*b*) *Mth:* **r. carrée,** square root.

rac|isme [rasism], *s.m.* racialism; *a. & s.* **-iste,** racialist.

racler [rakle], *v.tr.* to scrape; **se r. la gorge,** to clear one's throat.

racontar [rakɔ̃taːr], *s.m. F:* piece of (ill-natured) gossip.

racont|er [rakɔ̃te], *v.tr.* to tell, relate, narrate (tale, fact, adventures); **il vous en raconte,** he's telling you a tall story; *a.* **-able,** tellable; that can be told; *s.* **-eur, -euse,** (story)teller, narrator.

radar [radar], *s.m.* radar.

rade [rad], *s.f. Nau:* roadstead, roads.

radeau, -eaux [rado], *s.m.* raft.

radiateur [radjatœːr], *s.m.* radiator; (*a*) **r. de chauffage central,** central-heating radiator; **r. électrique,** electric fire; **r. à convection,** convector heater; **r. soufflant,** fan heater; (*b*) *Aut: etc:* (car) radiator.

radiation [radjasjɔ̃], *s.f. Ph: El: Atom.Ph:* radiation.

radical, -aux [radikal, -o], *a. & s.m. Mth: Bot: Pol:* radical; *adv.* **-ement,** radically.

radieux, -euse [radjø, -øːz], *a.* radiant; beaming; **ciel r.** dazzling sky; **elle entra radieuse,** she came in beaming (with joy).

radio [radjo], *F:* **1.** *s.m.* (*a*) radiogram; (*b*) radio operator. **2.** *s.f.* (*a*) radio, wireless; **à la r.,** on the radio; **il a passé à la r. hier soir,** he was on the air last night; (*b*) radiotelegraphy; (*c*) radio (set); (*d*) X-ray photograph; **passer une r.,** to be X-rayed, to have an X-ray.

radio(-)act|if, -ive [radjoaktif, -iːv], *a.* radioactive; *s.f.* **-ivité.**

radiobalise R:2 **raisin**

radiobalise [radjɔbaliːz], s.f. radio beacon; marker beacon.

radiobalis|er [radjɔbalize], v.tr. to equip (a route) with a radio-navigation system; s.m. -**age**, radio-beacon navigation.

radiodiffus|er [radjɔdifyze], v.tr. to broadcast; s.f. -**ion**, broadcasting.

radioélectricien, -ienne [radjɔelɛktrisjɛ̃, -jɛn], **radioélectronicien, -ienne** [radjɔelɛktrɔnisjɛ̃, -jɛn], s. radio and television engineer; electronics engineer.

radioémission [radjɔemisjɔ̃], s.f. 1. broadcasting. 2. broadcast.

radiogénique [radjɔʒenik], a. **voix r.**, good broadcasting voice.

radiogramme [radjɔgram], s.m. radiogram, radio telegram.

radiographie [radjɔgrafi], s.f. (a) radiography; X-ray photography; (b) X-ray photograph.

radioguidage [radjɔgidaːʒ], s.m. Av: Nau: radio direction, radio control.

radiolo|gie [radjɔlɔʒi], s.f. radiology; s. -**gue**, radiologist.

radionavigation [radjɔnavigasjɔ̃], s.f. radio navigation.

radioreportage [radjɔrəpɔrtaːʒ], s.m. (radio, television) news reporting, commentary; running commentary.

radioscopie [radjɔskɔpi], s.f. radioscopy; X-ray examination.

radiosond|e [radjɔsɔ̃ːd], s.f. Meteor: radiosonde; s.m. -**age**.

radiothérapie [radjɔterapi], s.f. Med: radiotherapy, X-ray treatment.

radis [radi], s.m. radish.

radium [radjɔm], s.m. radium.

radot|er [radɔte], v.i. to (talk) drivel; to ramble on; s.m. -**age**, drivel; **tomber dans le r.**, to fall into one's dotage; s. -**eur, -euse**, dotard.

radouc|ir [radusiːr], v.tr. to calm, soften; to smooth (s.o.) down; to mollify (s.o.); s.m. -**issement**, softening (of character, etc.); calming down (of temper); (of weather) change for the better.

se radoucir. 1. to grow calmer. 2. (of weather) to grow milder.

rafale [rafal], s.f. (a) squall; strong gust, blast (of wind); (b) burst of gun-fire.

raffin|er [rafine], v.tr. (a) to refine (sugar, etc.); (b) to polish (style, manners, etc.); s.m. -**ement**, (over-)refinement; affectation (of style, taste, etc.); s.m. -**age**, (sugar, oil, etc.) refining.

se raffiner, to become refined.

raffinerie [rafinri], s.f. refinery.

raffol|er [rafɔle], v.i. **r. de qch.**, to be excessively fond of, F: to adore, sth.; s.m. -**ement**, F: infatuation (**de**, for).

rafistoler [rafistɔle], v.tr. F: to patch (sth.) up; to

get (sth.) going again.

rafraîch|ir [rafreʃiːr], v.tr. 1. to cool, refresh; **la pluie a rafraîchi l'air**, the rain has cooled the air; to air (a room). 2. (a) to freshen up (a colour, a painting); to do up, renovate; to revive; (b) **r. la mémoire à qn**, to refresh s.o.'s memory; a. -**issant**, refreshing, cooling; s.m. -**issement.** 1. cooling (of liquid); freshening up, reviving (of colour). 2. usu. pl. refreshments; cold drinks.

se rafraîchir. 1. (of weather) to grow cooler. 2. to refresh oneself; to have a (cool) drink.

ragaillardir [ragajardiːr], v.tr. to make (s.o.) feel better; F: to cheer (s.o.) up.

rage [raːʒ], s.f. 1. rabies. 2. rage, fury; **la tempête fait r.**, the storm is raging; F: **cela fait r.**, it is all the rage; **r. d'écrire**, mania for writing.

rag|er [raʒe], v.i. (n. rageons) F: to rage; to be in a rage; to fume; to be furious; **ça me fait r. de voir ça!** it makes me wild, mad, infuriated, to see it! a. -**eant**, F: maddening, infuriating; a. -**eur, -euse**, violent-tempered (person); infuriated (tone, reply); adv. -**eusement**, furiously; in a violent temper.

ragoût [ragu], s.m. Cu: stew, ragout.

raid [rɛd], s.m. 1. Mil: raid. 2. Sp: long-distance rally, endurance test.

raide [rɛd]. 1. a. (a) stiff (limb, joints, drapery etc.); tight, taut; **cheveux raides**, straight and wiry hair; (b) stiff, starchy (manner, etc.); inflexible, unbending (character); (c) steep, abrupt (hill, path); (d) F: **ça, c'est un peu r.**, that's a bit thick! **il en a vu de raides**, he's had some queer experiences. 2. adv. (a) **frapper r.**, to strike hard; (b) **tomber r. mort**, to drop dead.

raideur [rɛdœːr], s.f. 1. stiffness; starchiness; inflexibility. 2. steepness, abruptness (of slope, etc.).

raidir [rɛdiːr], v.tr. to stiffen; to tighten.

se raidir. 1. to stiffen, to grow stiff. 2. **se r. contre le malheur**, to steel oneself, brace oneself against misfortune.

raie[1] [rɛ], s.f. 1. line, stroke. 2. streak (in marble etc.); stripe (on animal, material). 3. parting (of the hair).

raie[2], s.f. Ich: ray, skate.

raifort [rɛfɔːr], s.m. horse-radish.

rail [raːj], s.m. Rail: rail; **poser des rails**, to lay rails; (of train) **sortir des rails**, to jump the rails; to derail; **remettre l'économie sur les rails**, to put the economy on its feet again.

raill|er [rɑje], v.tr. to laugh at, to make fun of (s.o.); s.f. -**erie**, joking, mocking; a. & s. -**eur, -euse**, (i) a. mocking, joking; (ii) s. scoffer, joker.

rainure [rɛnyːr], s.f. groove, channel, furrow.

raisin [rɛzɛ̃], s.m. **le r., du r.**, grapes; **grappe de raisin**, bunch of grapes; **grain de r.**, grape; **rais**

secs, raisins; **raisins de Corinthe,** (dried) currants; **raisins de Smyrne,** sultanas.
raison [rɛzɔ̃], s.f. **1.** reason, motive, ground **(de, for); pas tant de raisons!** don't argue so much! **r. de plus,** all the more reason; **r. d'être,** reason, object, justification (for sth.). **2.** reason; **perdre sa r., n'avoir plus sa r.,** to be unhinged, out of one's mind; **ramener qn à la r.,** to bring s.o. to his senses; **parler r.,** to talk sense. **3.** reason, justification; **avoir r.,** to be right; **se faire une r.,** to accept the inevitable, make the best of a bad job; **comme de r.,** as one might expect. **4.** satisfaction, reparation; **se faire r. à soi-même,** to take the law into one's own hands; **avoir r. de qn,** to get the better of s.o. **5.** *Com:* **r. sociale,** name, style (of a firm). **6.** *Mth:* **r. géométrique,** geometrical ratio; **à r. de,** at the rate of.
raisonnable [rɛzɔnabl], *a.* reasonable; *adv.* **-ment.**
raisonné [rɛzɔne], *a.* reasoned, rational (analysis, argument); *Com:* **catalogue r.,** descriptive catalogue.
raisonn∣er [rɛzɔne]. **1.** *v.i.* to reason; to argue; **r. juste,** to argue correctly. **2.** *v.tr.* **r. qn,** to reason with s.o.; **il faut vous r.,** you must try to be reasonable; *s.m.* **-ement,** reasoning; *a. & s.* **-eur, -euse,** (*a*) *a.* reasoning, rational; argumentative; (*b*) *s.* reasoner; arguer.
∣ajeun∣ir [raʒœni:r]. **1.** *v.tr.* to rejuvenate (s.o.). **2.** *v.i.* to grow young again; **vous avez rajeuni,** you look years younger; *s.m.* **-issement,** rejuvenation (of s.o.).
∣ajust∣er [raʒyste], *v.tr.* to readjust (sth.); to put (sth.) straight; **r. sa cravate,** to (re)adjust one's tie; *s.m.* **-ement,** readjustment.
∣âle [rɑ:l], *s.m.* rattle (in the throat); death-rattle.
∣alenti [ralãti]. **1.** *a.* slow(er); **au trot r.,** at a slow trot. **2.** *s.m.* slow motion; **scène au r.,** scene in slow motion; *Ind:* **tourner au r.,** to slow down production; **moteur au r.,** idling engine.
∣alent∣ir [ralãti:r], *v.tr. & i.* to slacken, slow down; *P.N:* **ralentir!** drive slowly!, slow! *s.m.* **-issement,** slowing down.
∣∣er [rale], *v.i.* **1.** (*a*) to be at one's last gasp; (*b*) to be in agony. **2.** *F:* to be in a foul temper; to be hopping mad.
∣alli∣er [ralje], *v.tr. (pr.sub. & p.d.* **n. ralliions) 1.** (*a*) to rally, assemble (troops, etc.); (*b*) to rejoin (ship). **2.** to rally, to win (s.o.) over; *s.m.* **-ement,** rally(ing); assembly.
∣llonge [ralɔ̃:ʒ], *s.f.* (*a*) extension(-piece); (*b*) extra leaf (of table).
∣llonger [ralɔ̃ʒe], (**n. rallongeons**) (*a*) *v.tr.* to lengthen, to make longer (a skirt, a table, etc.); (*b*) *v.i.* **les jours rallongent,** the days are drawing out.
∣lumer [ralyme], *v.tr.* to relight; to rekindle (fire, etc.).

rallye [rali], *s.m. Sp: Aut:* (*a*) race meeting; (*b*) (car) rally.
ramassage [ramasa:ʒ], *s.m.* gathering, collecting, picking up; **r. à la pelle,** shovelling up; **r. scolaire,** school bus service.
ramasser [ramase], *v.tr.* **1.** to gather (sth.) together (in a mass, a pile); **village ramassé autour de son église,** village clustering round its church. **2.** to collect, gather. **3. r. son mouchoir,** to pick up one's handkerchief; *F:* **r. une bûche,** to come a cropper.
se ramasser. 1. to collect, gather (into a crowd). **2.** to gather oneself (for an effort); (*of tiger, etc.*) to crouch (for a spring). **3.** to pick oneself up (after a fall).
rame[1] [ram], *s.f.* oar, scull.
rame[2], *s.f.* **1.** ream (of paper). **2.** (*a*) string (of barges); (*b*) string (of railway carriages, trucks); (*c*) made-up train; **la r. directe pour Tours,** the through coach(es) for Tours; **r. de Métro,** underground train.
rameau, -eaux [ramo], *s.m.* **1.** (*a*)(small) branch, bough, twig; (*b*) **le dimanche des Rameaux,** Palm Sunday. **2.** branch, ramification (of family, language, etc.).
ramener [ramne], *v.tr.* (*conj. like* MENER) to bring (s.o., sth.) back (again); **r. qn en voiture,** to drive s.o. home; **r. ses pensées en arrière,** to cast one's thoughts back.
ramer [rame], *v.i.* to row.
ramier [ramje], *a.m. & s.m. Orn:* (**pigeon**) **r.,** wood-pigeon.
ramifi∣er (se) [səramifje], *v.tr. & pr.* to ramify, branch out, divide; *s.f.* **-cation.**
ramoll∣ir [ramɔli:r], *v.tr.* **1.** to soften (wax, etc.). **2.** to weaken (s.o.'s courage, etc.); *s.m.* **-issement,** softening.
ramon∣er [ramɔne], *v.tr.* to sweep (chimney); *s.m.* **-eur,** sweep.
rampe [rã:p], *s.f.* **1.** (*a*) slope, rise, incline; (*b*) *Civ. E:* gradient, upgrade. **2.** banisters, hand-rail. **3.** *Th:* footlights.
ramp∣er [rãpe], *v.i.* to creep, crawl; (*of plant*) to creep, trail; **r. devant les grands,** to cringe to, fawn upon, the great; **r. dans la misère,** to live in abject poverty; *a. & s.m.* **-ant,** (*a*) *a.* creeping, crawling (pers., plant); grovelling, cringing; (*b*) *s.m.pl. Av: F:* **les rampants,** the ground staff.
ramure [ramy:r], *s.f.* branches, boughs, foliage.
rancart [rãka:r], *s.m.* **mettre qch., qn, au r.,** to cast sth. aside, to retire (official); to shelve (sth.).
rance [rã:s], *a.* rancid, rank.
rancœur [rãkœ:r], *s.f.* rancour; bitterness (of mind); resentment.
rançon [rãsɔ̃], *s.f.* ransom.
rançonn∣er [rãsɔne], *v.tr.* to hold (s.o.) to ransom; to ransom (s.o.); *s.m.* **-ement,** holding

(of s.o.) to ransom; extortion.

rancun|e [rɑ̃kyn], *s.f.* rancour, spite, malice; **garder r. à qn**, to bear s.o. a grudge; *a. & s.* **-ier, -ière**, vindictive, spiteful (person).

randonnée [rɑ̃dɔne], *s.f.* outing, run, trip, excursion; **randonnées de week-end**, weekend excursions.

rang [rɑ̃], *s.m.* **1.** (*a*) row, line; **remettre un livre à son r.**, to put a book back in its place; **r. de tricot, d'oignons**, row of knitting, of onions; **r. de perles**, string of pearls; (*b*) *Mil:* **former les rangs**, to fall in; **rompre les rangs**, to dismiss; **sortir du r.**, to rise from the ranks. **2.** (*a*) rank; station; **arriver au premier r.**, to come to the front; **par r. d'âge**, according to age; (*b*) **r. social**, social status.

rangé [rɑ̃ʒe], *a.* **1.** orderly, tidy, well-ordered (room, desk). **2.** steady (person); **homme rangé dans ses habitudes**, man of regular habits.

rangée [rɑ̃ʒe], *s.f.* row, line; tier (of seats); **r. de chiffres**, array of figures.

ranger [rɑ̃ʒe], *v.tr.* (**n. rangeons**) **1.** to arrange; to draw up (troops). **2.** (*a*) to put away; (*b*) **r. la foule**, to keep the crowd back; **r. la voiture**, to pull (the car) in to the side. **3.** (*a*) to arrange, tidy; **r. une chambre**, to tidy a room; (*b*) **le mariage l'a rangé**, marriage has steadied him down.

se ranger. **1.** to draw up, line up. **2. se r. du côté de qn**, to side with s.o. **3. se r. (de côté)**, to get out of the way. **4. il s'est rangé**, he has settled down.

ranimer [ranime], *v.tr.* to revive, to put new life into (s.o., sth.); **on l'a ranimé avec un verre d'eau-de-vie**, they brought him round with a glass of spirits; **r. la colère de qn**, to reawaken s.o.'s anger; **r. l'assemblée**, to put fresh life into the meeting.

se ranimer, to revive; to cheer up; (*of fire*) to burn up.

rapace [rapas], *a.* **1.** rapacious; **bêtes rapaces**, predatory animals; *s.m.pl. Orn:* **les rapaces**, birds of prey. **2.** rapacious, grasping (person).

rapacité [rapasite], *s.f.* rapacity.

rapatrié, -iée [rapatrije]. **1.** *a.* repatriated; **soldats rapatriés**, home-coming soldiers. **2.** *s.* repatriate.

rapatri|er [rapatrije], *v.tr.* (*pr.sub. & p.d.* **n. rapatriions**) to repatriate; to send s.o. home (from abroad); *s.m.* **-ement**, repatriation.

râpe [rɑːp], *s.f.* rasp; (cheese-, nutmeg-) grater.

râpé [rɑpe]. **1.** *a.* (*a*) grated (cheese); (*b*) threadbare (garment). **2.** *s.m.* grated cheese.

râper [rɑpe], *v.tr.* to rasp; to grate.

rapetiss|er [raptise]. **1.** *v.tr.* to make (sth.) smaller; to reduce; to shorten (garment); to shrink (cloth). **2.** *v.i. & pr.* to shorten; to become shorter, smaller; (*of material*) to shrink.

rapide [rapid]. **1.** *a.* (*a*) rapid, swift, fast; (*b*) steep (slope). **2.** *s.m.* (*a*) rapid (in river); (*b*) express (train); *adv.* **-ment**.

rapidité [rapidite], *s.f.* (*a*) rapidity, swiftness; (*b*) steepness.

rapié|cer [rapjese], *v.tr.* (**je rapièce; je rapiécerai**) to patch (garment); *s.m.* **-çage**, patching (of garment).

rappel [rapɛl], *s.m.* **1.** (*a*) recall (of ambassador, etc.); (*b*) **r. à l'ordre**, call(ing) to order. **2.** *Mil:* **r. sous les drapeaux**, recall to the colours (of reservists); *Th:* curtain call. **3.** reminder (of speed limit in built-up areas); **lettre de r.**, (letter of) reminder. **4.** *Adm:* repeal (of decree). **5.** *Mec:* readjustment; **vis de r.**, adjusting screw; *Typew:* **r. arrière**, back spacer. **6.** *Med:* piqûre de r., booster injection.

rappeler [raple]. (*conj. like* APPELER) **1.** *v.tr.* (*a*) to recall; *P.T.T:* to call back; (*b*) **r. qn à l'ordre**, to call s.o. to order. **2.** *v.tr.* to call back to mind; **vous me rappelez mon oncle**, you remind me of my uncle; **rappelez-moi à son bon souvenir**, remember me (kindly) to him. **3.** *v.i. Mount:* to rope down.

se rappeler qch., to recall, remember, sth.; to call sth. to mind.

rapport [rapɔːr], *s.m.* **I. 1.** return, yield; **maison de r.**, block of flats (for letting). **2.** (*a*) (official) report; (*b*) report, account. **II. 1.** relation, connection (**avec**, with); **en r. avec qch.**, in keeping with sth.; **par r. à qch.**, in comparison with sth. **sous tous les rapports**, in every respect. **2.** *Mth:* ratio, proportion. **3.** relations, intercourse; **avoir des rapports avec qn**, to be in touch with s.o.

rapporter [rapɔrte], *v.tr.* **1.** to bring back. **2.** to bring in, yield; **cela ne rapporte rien**, it doesn't pay. **3.** (*a*) **r. un fait**, to report, relate, a fact; (*b*) *F:* to tell tales. **4.** to ascribe, attribute; **r. qch. à une cause**, to ascribe sth. to a cause. **5.** to revoke (decree); to cancel (an order); **r. un ordre de grève**, to call off a strike.

se rapporter. **1.** to agree, tally (**avec**, with). **2.** to refer, relate (**à**, to). **3. s'en r. à qn**, to rely on s.o.; **je m'en rapporte à vous**, (i) I take your word for it; (ii) I leave it to you.

rapporteur, -euse [rapɔrtœːr, -øːz], *s.* **1.** talebearer, sneak. **2.** *s.m.* reporter, recorder; *Pol:* **r. d'une commission**, chairman of a commission. **3.** *s.m. Mth:* protractor.

rapproché [raprɔʃe], *a.* near (in space or time) (**de**, to); **maisons très rapprochées**, houses very close together; **yeux rapprochés**, close-set eyes.

rapproch|er [raprɔʃe], *v.tr.* **1.** (*a*) to bring (objects) closer together; **r. une chaise du feu**, to draw up a chair to the fire; (*b*) to bring (persons) together; **un intérêt commun les rapproche**, a common interest brings, draw

them together; (c) to reconcile (two persons). **2. r. des faits,** to compare facts; s.m. **-ement.**
se rapprocher de qch., to draw near(er) to sth.

apt [rapt], s.m. Jur: abduction (of a minor); kidnapping.

aquette [rakɛt], s.f. **1.** Games: racket, racquet. **2.** snow-shoe.

arle [raːr], a. **1.** (a) rare, uncommon, exceptional (merit, beauty, talent); (b) unusual (occurrence). **2.** thin, sparse, scanty (hair, grass); adv. **-ement;** s.f. **-eté,** rarity; scarcity; infrequency.

as, rase [ra, raz]. **1.** a. (a) close-cropped (hair); **à poil r.,** short-haired (dog); (b) bare, blank; **en rase campagne,** in the open country; **faire table rase,** to make a clean sweep; **sa mémoire est une table rase,** his memory is a complete blank; (c) **cuillerée rase,** level spoonful. **2.** s.m. short-nap cloth. **3. au r. de,** (on a) level with, flush with; **voler au r. du sol,** to fly close to the ground.

asade [razad], s.f. brim-full glass; bumper.

ase-mottes [razmɔt], s.m. Av: **vol en r.-m.,** hedge-hopping; **faire du r.-m.,** to skim the ground.

asler [raze], v.tr. **1.** (a) to shave; (b) F: to bore (s.o.). **2.** to raze to the ground. **3.** (a) to graze, brush, skim (over); (b) **r. la côte, le mur,** to hug the shore, the wall; a. **-ant,** F: boring; s. **-eur, -euse,** F: bore.
raser, (a) to shave; (b) F: to be bored.

soir [razwaːr], s.m. razor; F: (of pers.) **quel r.!** what a bore!

assasiler [rasazje], v.tr. (pr.sub. & p.d. n. **rassasiions) 1.** to satisfy (hunger). **2.** to sate, satiate, surfeit, cloy (**de, with); s.m. **-ement,** satisfying (of hunger, etc.); full meal; surfeit.
rassasier, to eat one's fill.

ssembler [rasãble], v.tr. to assemble; to gather together; **r. toutes ses forces,** to summon up all one's strength; s.m. **-ement,** assembling, collecting; Mil: fall in; parade; assemblage, crowd; **lieu de r.,** rallying point.
rassembler, to assemble, to come together; Mil: to fall in.

sseoir [raswaːr], v.tr. (conj. like ASSEOIR) **1.** to reseat (s.o.); to replace (a statue, etc.) on its base. **2.** to settle, compose (one's ideas).
rasseoir, to sit down again.

sséréner (se) [səraserene], v.pr. (je me **rassérène; je me rassérénerai)** (of weather) to clear (up); (of pers.) to brighten up.

sis [rasi], a. (a) calm, staid, sedate (disposition, mind); (b) **pain r.,** stale bread.

surer [rasyre], v.tr. to reassure, cheer.
rassurer, to feel reassured; **rassurez-vous,** set your mind at rest, F: don't worry.

[ra], s.m. rat; **mort aux rats, rat-poison.

atiner [ratatine], v.tr. & pr. to shrivel (up); to

shrink; to dry up; **petit vieux ratatiné,** wizened little old man.

rate [rat], s.f. Anat: spleen; F: **se dilater la r.,** to have a good laugh; **ne pas se fouler la r.,** to take things easy.

raté, -ée [rate]. **1.** a. miscarried, ineffectual; **coup r.,** (i) misfire; (ii) fluffed shot; Av: **atterrissage r.,** bad landing; **ce fut une vie ratée,** his life was a failure. **2.** s. (of pers.) failure, F: washout. **3.** s.m. misfire; Aut: **le moteur avait des ratés,** the engine was misfiring.

râteau, -eaux [rato], s.m. Tls: rake.

râtelier [ratəlje], s.m. **1.** rack (in a stable). **2. r. à pipes, à outils,** pipe-rack, tool-rack. **3.** (a) row of teeth; (b) F: set of false teeth, denture.

rater [rate]. **1.** v.i. (a) (of gun) to miss fire, misfire; (b) (of enterprise, etc.) to fail; to miscarry. **2.** v.tr. (a) **r. son coup,** to miss the mark; (b) F: **r. une affaire,** to fail in an affair; **r. son train,** to miss one's train; **r. un examen,** to fail an exam.; **j'ai raté l'occasion,** I missed the chance.

ratière [ratjɛːr], s.f. rat-trap.

ratifiler [ratifje], v.tr. (pr.sub. & p.d. n. **ratifiions)** to ratify (treaty); to confirm (decision); s.f. **-cation,** ratification.

ration [rasjɔ̃], s.f. ration(s), allowance; **mettre qn à la r.,** to put s.o. on short rations.

rationnel, -elle [rasjonɛl], a. rational; adv. **-lement,** rationally.

rationnler [rasjone], v.tr. to ration; s.m. **-ement,** rationing.

ratisser [ratise], v.tr. to rake (path, etc.); F: **la police les a ratissés,** the police nabbed the lot; **r. le quartier,** to comb the district.

rattacher [ratafe], v.tr. **1.** to refasten, retie (sth.); **r. le chien,** to tie the dog up again. **2.** (a) to bind (s.o. to a party, his family); (b) to link up, connect (ideas, problems).
se rattacher à qch. 1. to be fastened to sth. **2.** to be connected with sth.

rattraper [ratrape], v.tr. **1.** to recapture; to catch (s.o., sth.) again; **je vous rattraperai!** I'll get my own back on you! **2.** to overtake; to catch up on (s.o.). **3.** to recover (one's money, lost time).
se rattraper de ses pertes, to make good one's losses; to recoup oneself.

raturer [ratyre], v.tr. to erase, scratch out; to cross out (a word).

rauque [roːk], a. hoarse, raucous, harsh (voice).

ravage(s) [ravaːʒ], s.m.usu.pl. havoc, devastation, ravages.

ravager [ravaʒe], v.tr. (n. **ravageons)** to ravage, devastate (the country); to play havoc with (sth.).

ravaudler [ravode], v.tr. (a) to mend, patch (old clothes); to darn (stockings); (b) to botch, bungle (work); s.m. **-age,** mending, darning.

ravi [ravi], *a.* **1.** entranced, enraptured. **2.** delighted (**de,** with); overjoyed (**de,** at); **je suis r. de vous voir,** I'm delighted to see you.

ravin [ravɛ̃], *s.m.* ravine, gully.

ravir [raviːr], *v.tr.* to delight (s.o.); **elle chante à ravir,** she sings delightfully; **cela lui va à r.,** she looks charming in it.

raviser (se) [sǝravize], *v.pr.* to change one's mind.

ravissant [ravisɑ̃], *a.* entrancing, bewitching; delightful, lovely.

ravissement [ravismɑ̃], *s.m.* rapture, ecstasy, delight; **être dans le r.,** to be in raptures.

ravisseur [ravisœːr], *s.m.* abductor, kidnapper.

ravitaill|er [ravitaje], *v.tr. Adm: Mil: Ind: etc:* to supply, provision, replenish (**en,** with); **r. par air (des unités encerclées, etc.),** to drop supplies to (encircled units, etc.); **r. un navire en mer,** to replenish, refuel, a ship at sea; **r. un avion en vol,** to refuel an aircraft in flight; **r. une ville en viande,** to supply a town with meat; *s.m.* **-ement,** replenishment (**en,** with); supply.

raviver [ravive], *v.tr.* **1.** to revive (fire, hope, memory). **2.** to brighten up (colour); **r. une plaie,** to re-open an old sore.

rayer [reje], *v.tr.* (**je raie, je raye**) **1.** (*a*) to scratch; to score; (*b*) to rule, line (paper); (*c*) to stripe (fabric, etc.). **2.** to strike out (word).

rayon[1] [rɛjɔ̃], *s.m.* **1.** ray; beam (of light); **r. de lune,** moonbeam. **2.** radius (of circle). **3.** spoke (of wheel).

rayon[2], *s.m.* **1. r. de miel,** honeycomb. **2.** (*a*) shelf (of cupboard); *pl.* set of shelves; (*b*) *Com:* (*in shop*) (i) department; (ii) counter; **magasin à rayons multiples,** department store; **r. des soldes,** bargain counter; **ce n'est pas mon r.,** that's not in my line.

rayonne [rɛjɔn], *s.f. Tex:* rayon.

rayonn|er [rɛjɔne], *v.i.* (*a*) *Ph:* to radiate; (*b*) to beam, shine; **il rayonnait de joie,** he was radiant, beaming, with joy; (*c*) **six avenues rayonnent autour de la place,** six avenues radiate from the square; *s.m.* **-ement,** (i) *Ph:* radiation; (ii) radiance.

rayure [rɛjyːr], *s.f.* **1.** (*a*) stripe, streak; (*b*) scratch; (*c*) groove. **2.** striking out, scoring out (of word).

raz [ra], *s.m.* strong current; race; **r. de marée,** tidal wave.

réacteur [reaktœːr], *s.m.* **1.** *El:* reactor, *F:* choke. **2.** *Av: Mec:* jet engine; **r. inversé,** retro rocket; **r. de propulsion,** propulsion-jet engine; jet aircraft. **3.** *s.m.* **r. atomique,** nuclear reactor; atomic pile.

réaction [reaksjɔ̃], *s.f.* reaction; **avion à r.,** jet aircraft.

réactionnaire [reaksjɔnɛːr], *a. & s.* reactionary.

réadaptation [readaptasjɔ̃], *s.f.* **1.** rehabilita-

tion. **2.** readjustment.

réagir [reaʒiːr], *v.i.* to react.

réalis|er [realize], *v.tr.* to realize. **1.** to carry out (plan); to create (a work of art); *Cin: T.V: etc* to produce (a programme). **2.** to realize (one's assets); to sell out (shares); *Com:* to clear (out stock; *a.* **-able,** realizable; workable; s **-ateur, -atrice,** author, creator (of work o art); *Cin: T.V:* producer; *s.f.* **-ation,** carrying out (of plan); selling out (of shares, etc.); *Cin T.V:* production.

réalité [realite], *s.f.* reality.

réapparition [reaparisjɔ̃], *s.f.* reappearance.

réarm|er [rearme], *v.tr.* **1.** *Mil:* to rearm. **2.** *Nau* to refit, recommission; *s.m.* **-ement.**

rébarbatif, -ive [rebarbatif, -iːv], *a.* grim, fo bidding (face); **style r.,** unpleasing style; **suj r.,** dull subject.

rebâtir [rǝbɑtiːr], *v.tr.* to rebuild.

rebattre [rǝbatr], *v.tr.* (*conj. like* BATTRE) **1.** (*c* to beat (sth.) again; (*b*) to reshuffle (cards). *F:* **r. les oreilles à qn de qch.,** to din sth. int s.o.'s ears; **j'en ai les oreilles rebattues,** I'm sic (and tired) of hearing (about) it.

rebelle [rǝbɛl]. **1.** *a.* rebellious; stubbor obstinate; **minerai r.,** refractory ore. **2.** *s.* rebe

rebeller (se) [sǝrǝbele], *v.pr.* to rebel, to rise, revolt (**contre,** against).

rébellion [rebeljɔ̃], *s.f.* rebellion, rising, revolt

rebondi [rǝbɔ̃di], *a.* rounded, chubby (cheeks plump (body); **petite femme rebondie,** plum buxom, little woman; **ventre r.,** corporation

rebond|ir [rǝbɔ̃diːr], *v.i.* to rebound; to bounc *s.m.* **-issement,** rebound(ing), resilience.

rebord [rǝbɔːr], *s.m.* **1.** edge, border, rim; **d'une fenêtre,** window sill. **2.** flange (of she metal, pipe, etc.).

rebouch|er [rǝbuʃe], *v.tr.* to stop, block, pl (sth.) up again; to recork (bottle); *s.m.* **-ag**

rebours [rǝbuːr], *s.m.* wrong way (of the grai contrary, reverse; *adv.phr.* **à r.,** against t grain, the wrong way; **à, au, r. de,** contrary

reboutonner [rǝbutɔne], *v.tr.* to rebutton, button (a garment) up again.

rebrousse-poil (à) [arǝbruspwal], *adv.p* **brosser un chapeau à r.-p.,** to brush a hat wrong way, against the nap; **prendre qn à r.** to rub s.o. up the wrong way.

rebrousser [rǝbruse], *v.tr.* **r. chemin,** to t back; to retrace one's steps.

rebuffade [rǝbyfad], *s.f.* rebuff; snub.

rebut [rǝby], *s.m.* (**article de**) **r.,** reject, rejec article; rubbish; **papier de r.,** waste pap **marchandises de r.,** trash; *Ind:* **pièces de r.** **rebuts,** rejects; **mettre qch. au r.,** to throw away; *P.T.T:* **bureau des rebuts,** dead-le office; *Pej:* **le r. de la population,** the dreg the population.

rebuter [rǝbyte], *v.tr.* **1.** to rebuff, snub (s.o.

to reject, discard (sth.); to throw (sth.) aside. **3.** to dishearten, discourage (s.o.). **4.** to shock, disgust (s.o.); **sa vulgarité me rebute,** his vulgarity revolts me.

se rebuter. 1. to become disheartened. **2.** to feel disgusted.

écalcitrant [rekalsitrã], *a.* recalcitrant, refractory, obstinate, rebellious (person).

ecalé, -ée [rəkale], *a. & s. Sch: F:* failed (candidate); **les recalés,** the failures.

ecaler [rəkale], *v.tr. F:* to fail (s.o. in an exam.).

écapituller [rekapityle], *v.tr.* to recapitulate; to sum up; *s.f.* **-ation.**

ecel [rəsɛl], *s.m.* receiving (of stolen goods).

eceler, recéler [rəs(ə)le, rəsele], *v.tr.* **(je recèle; je recélerai)** *Jur:* **1.** to receive (stolen goods). **2.** to conceal.

eceleur, -euse [rəslœːr, -øːz], *s. Jur:* receiver, *F:* fence.

ecensement [rəsãsmã], *s.m.* (a) *Adm:* census; (b) counting (of votes).

éclent [resã], *a.* recent (event, etc.); **j'en ai la mémoire récente,** it's fresh in my mind; *adv.* **-emment,** recently, lately, of late.

écépissé [resepise], *s.m.* (acknowledgment of) receipt.

écepteur, -trice [resɛptœːr, -tris]. **1.** *a.* receiving (apparatus, etc.); *Rad: etc:* **poste r.,** receiving (i) station, (ii) set. **2.** *s.m. P.T.T:* **r. (téléphonique),** (telephone) receiver; **décrocher le r.,** to lift the receiver.

éception [resɛpsjõ], *s.f.* **1.** (a) receipt (of letter); (b) taking delivery (of goods); acceptance, taking over (of equipment, etc., from manufacturers). **2.** (a) welcome; **faire une bonne r. à qn,** to welcome s.o. warmly; (b) (official, court) reception; (c) party. **3.** *Rad: etc:* **appareil, poste, de r.,** receiving set. **4.** (hotel) reception desk, office; *Com:* enquiry office.

ecette [rəsɛt], *s.f.* **1.** receipts, returns. **2.** receiving; receipt (of stores). **3.** *Cu:* recipe.

eceveur, -euse [rəsəvœːr, -øːz], *s.* **1.** receiver. **2.** (a) **r. des postes,** postmaster, postmistress; (b) conductor, conductress (of bus).

evoir [rəsəvwaːr], *v.tr.* (*pr.p.* **recevant;** *p.p.* **reçu;** *pr.ind.* **je reçois, ils reçoivent;** *pr.sub.* **je reçoive;** *fu.* **je recevrai) 1.** to receive (letter); to incur (blame); **r. un prix,** to get, win, a prize; *Com:* **nous avons bien reçu votre lettre,** we are in receipt of your letter. **2.** (a) to receive, welcome (s.o.); (b) to entertain (friends, etc.); **lle sait r.,** she knows how to give a good party; (c) **elle reçoit des pensionnaires,** she takes in boarders; (d) **être reçu à un examen,** to pass an examination; **être reçu médecin,** to qualify as a) doctor.

hange [rəʃãːʒ], *s.m.* replacement; **vêtements, nge, de r.,** change of clothes, underwear; *Mec: Aut: etc:* **pièces de r.,** spare parts, spares.

réchappé, -ée [reʃape], *s.* survivor (of disaster, etc.).

réchapper [reʃape], *v.i.* (*aux.* **avoir** *or* **être**) to escape (**de,** from) (disaster, accident, wreck, dangerous illness, etc.).

recharge [rəʃarʒ], *s.f.* refill (for ball-point pen, etc.); recharging, recharge (of battery); *Aut: etc:* **mettre l'accu en r.,** to put the battery on charge.

rechargler [rəʃarʒe], *v.tr.* (*conj. like* MANGER) (a) to recharge (battery); (b) to reload (lorry, ship); (c) to refill (pen, etc.); *a.* **-eable,** that takes a refill; that can be recharged; *s.m.* **-ement,** recharging, reloading, refilling.

réchaud [reʃo], *s.m.* (a) small portable cooker; (b) hot-plate.

réchauffé [reʃofe], *s.m.* (a) warmed-up food; (b) rehash; stale news, joke; **c'est du r.,** I've heard that one before.

réchauffer [reʃofe], *v.tr.* **1.** to reheat; to warm (sth.) up again; **voilà qui vous réchauffera,** that will warm you up. **2. r. le zèle de qn,** to rekindle s.o.'s zeal; **r. le cœur à qn,** to comfort s.o.

se réchauffer, to warm oneself (up).

rêche [rɛʃ], *a.* harsh, rough (surface, wine, humour).

recherche [rəʃɛrʃ], *s.f.* **1.** (a) search, pursuit; **aller, partir, à la r. de qn,** to go off, set out, to look for s.o.; **courir à la r. d'un médecin,** to run for a doctor; (b) **r. scientifique, médicale,** scientific, medical, research. **2.** studied refinement, elegance; **mis avec r.,** dressed with meticulous care; **style sans r.,** unaffected style.

recherché [rəʃɛrʃe], *a.* **1. article r.,** article in demand. **2.** choice, elaborate (jewels, dress, etc.); **d'un travail r.,** of exquisite workmanship. **3.** strained, laboured (style, expression, etc.).

rechercher [rəʃɛrʃe], *v.tr.* (a) to search for, inquire into (causes, etc.); (b) to seek (after), to try to obtain.

rechute [rəʃyt], *s.f.* relapse, setback.

récidivler [residive], *v.i.* **1.** to repeat an offence; to relapse into crime. **2.** (*of disease*) to recur; *s.m. & f.* **-iste,** habitual criminal, *F:* old lag.

récif [resif], *s.m.* reef.

récipient [resipjã], *s.m.* container, receptacle; (storage) bin, tank.

réciprocité [resiprɔsite], *s.f.* reciprocity.

réciproque [resiprɔk]. **1.** *a.* reciprocal, mutual (duties, benefits); *Mth: etc:* convertible (terms); inverse (ratio). **2.** *s.f.* **rendre la r. à qn,** to get even with s.o.; *adv.* **-ment.**

récit [resi], *s.m.* narrative; account; **faire le r. de sa vie,** to tell the story of one's life.

récitler [resite], *v.tr.* to recite (poem, etc.); *s.m.* **-al, -als,** (musical) recital; *s.f.* **-ation.**

réclame [reklam], *s.f.* (a) advertising; publicity; **faire de la r.,** to advertise; **article (en) r.,** special offer; (b) advertisement; **r. lumineuse,**

illuminated sign.

réclam|er [reklame]. **1.** *v.i.* to complain; to lodge a complaint; **r. contre qch.**, to protest against, object to, sth. **2.** *v.tr.* (*a*) to claim (sth.); (*b*) to claim (sth.) back (**à,** from (s.o.)); (*c*) to beg for; (*d*) to call for; **r. qch. à grands cris,** to clamour for sth.; **plante qui réclame beaucoup de soins,** plant that demands constant care; *s.f.* **-ation,** (i) complaint, protest; (ii) claim, demand.

reclass|er [rəklase], *v.tr.* to reclassify, rearrange, redistribute; *s.m.* **-ement.**

reclus, -use [rəkly, -y:z], *s.* recluse.

recoin [rəkwɛ̃], *s.m.* nook, recess; **coins et recoins,** nooks and crannies.

récolte [rekɔlt], *s.f.* **1.** (*a*) harvesting (of grain), vintaging (of grapes); (*b*) collecting, gathering (of documents, etc.). **2.** harvest, crop(s); vintage; **r. sur pied,** standing crop.

récolter [rekɔlte], *v.tr.* **1.** to harvest; to gather in. **2.** to collect, gather.

recommand|er [rəkɔmɑ̃de], *v.tr.* **1. r. qn à ses amis,** to recommend s.o. to one's friends. **2. r. la prudence à qn,** to advise s.o. to be careful; **je vous recommande de . . .,** I strongly advise you to . . .. **3.** to register (letter); *s.f.* **-able,** to be recommended; respectable (hotel, etc.); advisable; *s.f.* **-ation,** (i) recommendation; testimonial; (ii) advice; (iii) *P.T.T:* registration.

recommenc|er [rəkɔmɑ̃se], *v.* (**n. recommençons**) **1.** *v.tr.* to begin (sth.) (over) again; **r. sa vie,** to start life afresh. **2.** *v.i.* to do it again; to start afresh; **le voilà qui recommence!** he's at it again! *s.m.* **-ement,** beginning again.

récompense [rekɔ̃pɑ̃:s], *s.f.* recompense, reward, prize.

récompenser [rekɔ̃pɑ̃se], *v.tr.* to reward, recompense (**qn de qch.,** s.o. for sth.).

réconcili|er [rekɔ̃silje], *v.tr.* (*pr.sub. & p.d.* **n. réconciliions**) to reconcile (persons, inconsistencies); to make it up between (two persons); *a.* **-able,** reconcilable; *s.f.* **-ation.**

se réconcilier avec qn, to make it up with s.o.

reconduire [rəkɔ̃dɥi:r], *v.tr.* (*conj. like* CONDUIRE) (*a*) to see (s.o.) home; to take (s.o.) back (to a place); (*b*) to accompany (s.o.) to the door; to show (s.o.) out.

réconfort [rekɔ̃fɔ:r], *s.m.* (*a*) consolation, comfort; (*b*) stimulant.

réconfort|er [rekɔ̃fɔrte], *v.tr.* **1.** to strengthen, refresh (s.o.); to stimulate (s.o.); **il est l'heure de se r.,** it's time for a little refreshment; *a. & s.m.* **-ant,** (*a*) *a.* strengthening; comforting; (*b*) *s.m.* tonic, stimulant.

reconnaissable [rəkɔnɛsabl], *a.* recognizable (**à,** by, from, through).

reconnaissance [rəkɔnɛsɑ̃:s], *s.f.* **1.** recognition (of s.o., sth.). **2.** (*a*) recognition, acknowledgment; (*b*) **donner une r. à qn,** to

give s.o. an I.O.U. **3.** reconnoitring, reconnaissance; **r. du littoral,** charting of the coast. **4.** gratitude.

reconnaissant [rəkɔnɛsɑ̃], *a.* (*a*) grateful (**envers,** to; **de,** for) ; (*b*) thankful (**de,** for).

reconnaître [rəkɔnɛtr], *v.tr.* (*conj. like* CONNAÎTRE) **1.** to recognize; to know (s.o.) again; **r. qn à sa démarche,** to know, tell, s.o. by his walk; **se r. dans ses enfants,** to see oneself in one's children; **je vous reconnais bien là!** that's just like you! **2.** (*a*) to recognize, acknowledge (truth); to admit (a mistake); **reconnu pour incorrect,** admittedly incorrect; (*b*) to own, acknowledge; **r. sa signature,** to acknowledge one's signature. **3.** to reconnoitre, explore. **4. r. une faveur,** to be grateful for a favour.

se reconnaître. 1. se r. vaincu, to admit to being beaten. **2.** (*a*) to collect oneself; (*b*) to get one's bearings; **je ne m'y reconnais plus,** I am quite at sea.

reconquérir [rəkɔ̃keri:r], *v.tr.* (*conj. like* ACQUÉRIR) to regain, recover (one's self-esteem); to win back (territory).

reconstitu|er [rəkɔ̃stitɥe], *v.tr.* to reconstitute; to reconstruct (a crime); to restore (s.o.'s health); *s.f.* **-tion.**

reconstruction [rəkɔ̃stryksjɔ̃], *s.f.* reconstruction.

reconstruire [rəkɔ̃strɥi:r], *v.tr.* (*conj. like* CONSTRUIRE) to reconstruct, rebuild.

record [rəkɔ:r], *s.m.* **1.** *Sp:* record; **r. mondial,** world record. **2.** *attrib.* **dans un temps r.,** record time; *Ind:* peak (output, etc.); **chiffre record** figure.

recourbé [rəkurbe], *a.* bent, curved.

recourir [rəkuri:r], *v.i.* (*conj. like* COURIR) **1.** to run (a race, etc.) again. **2. r. à qn, à l'aide de qn,** to have recourse to s.o., to call on s.o. for help; **r. à la justice,** to take legal proceedings; **r. à la violence,** to resort to violence.

recours [rəku:r], *s.m.* recourse, resort, resource; **r. à l'arbitrage,** appeal to arbitration; **en dernier r.,** as a last resort.

recouvr|er [rəkuvre], *v.tr.* **1.** to recover, to get back (one's property); to regain (health, strength). **2.** to recover, collect (debts); *s.m.* **-ement**[1], recovery, collection.

recouvr|ir [rəkuvri:r], *v.tr.* (*conj. like* COUVRIR) **1.** to re-cover. **2.** (*a*) to cover (sth.) (over); **fauteuil recouvert de velours,** armchair covered in velvet; (*b*) to cover (up), hide (faults). **3.** to overlap; *s.m.* **-ement**[2]. **1.** covering. **2.** (*a*) covering; (*b*) overlapping.

se recouvrir, (*of sky*) to cloud over.

récréation [rekreasjɔ̃], *s.f.* recreation, amusement, relaxation.

récrier (se) [sərekrije], *v.pr.* **1. se r. d'admiration,** to exclaim, cry out, in admiration. **2. se r. contre qch.,** to expostulate, protest, against sth.

récrimin|er [rekrimine], *v.i.* to recriminate; *s.f.* -ation.

récrire [rekriːr], *v.tr.* (*conj. like* ÉCRIRE) to rewrite; to write (sth.) over again; to make a fresh copy of (sth.).

recroquevillé [rəkrɔkvije], *a.* shrivelled, curled up; (fingers) knotted (by arthritis).

recrue [rəkry], *s.f.* recruit; new member (of party, etc.).

recrut|er [rəkryte], *v.tr.* to recruit (men, supporters); *s.m.* -ement, recruiting.

rectang|le [rɛktɑ̃ːgl]. 1. *a.* right-angled. 2. *s.m.* rectangle; *a.* -ulaire, rectangular.

rectifi|er [rɛktifje], *v.tr.* (*pr.sub. & p.d.* n. rectifiions) to rectify, correct (calculation, mistake); to amend (text); *s.f.* -cation, correction, amendment.

rectiligne [rɛktiliɲ], *a.* rectilinear.

rectitude [rɛktityd], *s.f.* 1. straightness (of line). 2. rectitude, uprightness, integrity (of character).

reçu [rəsy]. 1. *a.* received, accepted, recognized, prevailing (opinion, custom, etc.). 2. *s.m. Com:* receipt (for money, goods).

recueil [rəkœːj], *s.m.* collection, compilation (of poems, etc.); miscellany; anthology; **r. des lois,** compendium of laws.

recueillement [rəkœjmɑ̃], *s.m.* self-communion, meditation, contemplation.

recueillir [rəkœjiːr], *v.tr.* (*conj. like* CUEILLIR) 1. to collect, gather (anecdotes, curios); to set down (s.o.'s words); to catch (rainwater); to pick up (news). 2. to gather, get in (crops); **r. un héritage,** to inherit; **r. les suffrages,** to win the election. 3. to take in, to shelter (s.o. in need); **r. un orphelin,** to give an orphan a home.

se recueillir, to collect oneself, one's thoughts; to commune with oneself; to meditate.

recul [rəkyl], *s.m.* 1. backward movement; recession; *Aut:* **phare de r.,** reversing light. 2. kick (of rifle). 3. room to move back; *Ten:* **cinq mètres de r.,** five yards runback; **prendre du r.,** (*a*) to step back(wards); (*b*) to adopt a detached attitude.

recul|er [rəkyle]. 1. *v.i.* to move back, recede; to retreat; to recoil; (*of rifle*) to kick; **il n'y a plus moyen de r.,** there's no going back; **ne r. devant rien,** to shrink from nothing. 2. *v.tr.* (*a*) to move back; **r. un cheval,** to rein back, to back, a horse; (*b*) to postpone, put off (doing sth.); *s.m.* -ement.

se reculer, to draw back; to move back; to stand back.

reculons (à) [arəkylɔ̃], *adv.phr.* backwards.

récupér|er [rekypere], *v.tr.* (je récupère; je récupérerai) 1. to recover; to get (sth.) back; *F:* **je l'ai récupéré au bar,** I retrieved him from, fished him out of, the bar. 2. to recover,

salvage (waste material). 3. to recoup (a loss); **la journée chômée sera récupérée,** the lost day will be made up; *s.f.* -ation.

rédacteur, -trice [redaktœːr, -tris], *s.* 1. writer, drafter (of document). 2. member of the staff (of a newspaper); **r. sportif,** sports editor; **r. politique,** political correspondent; *T.V: etc:* **r. des informations,** newscaster; **r. en chef,** editor.

rédaction [redaksjɔ̃], *s.f.* 1. (*a*) drafting (of document); (*b*) editing. 2. *coll.* editorial staff. 3. *Sch:* essay.

rédemption [redɑ̃psjɔ̃], *s.f.* redemption, redeeming (of loan).

redevable [rəd(ə)vabl], *a.* être r. de qch. à qn, to be indebted to s.o. for sth.; to owe (one's life, etc.) to s.o.; to be accountable to s.o. for sth.

redevance [rəd(ə)vɑ̃ːs], *s.f.* (*a*) dues; (*b*) royalties; (*c*) (television, etc.) fee.

redevenir [rədəvniːr], *v.i.* (*conj. like* TENIR) **r. jeune,** to grow young again.

rédiger [rediʒe], *v.tr.* (n. rédigeons) 1. to draw up, draft (agreement); to write (article). 2. to edit.

redire [rediːr], *v.tr.* (*conj. like* DIRE) 1. to tell, say, (sth.) again; to repeat. 2. **trouver à r. à qch.,** to take exception to sth.; to find fault with sth.

redoubl|er [rəduble], *v.tr. & v.i.* to redouble, increase (a dose, one's efforts); **r. ses cris,** to shout louder than ever; *Sch:* **r. une classe,** to stay down; **la pluie redoubla,** the rain came on worse than ever; *s.m.* -ement.

redout|er [rədute], *v.tr.* to dread, fear (s.o., sth.); *a.* -able, redoubtable, formidable.

redress|er [rədrese], *v.tr.* 1. (*a*) to set (sth.) upright again; (*b*) to right (boat). 2. (*a*) to straighten (sth.) (out); (*b*) **r. la tête,** to hold up one's head; to look up; (*c*) to redress, to right (a wrong, grievance); to rectify (mistake); *s.m.* -ement.

se redresser. 1. (*a*) **se r. sur son séant,** to sit up again; (*b*) (*of boat*) to right. 2. to draw oneself up.

réduction [redyksjɔ̃], *s.f.* 1. (*a*) reduction; cutting down (of expenditure, etc.); (*b*) *Surg:* **d'une fracture, etc.,** setting of a fracture, etc.; (*c*) *Mec:* gearing down; gear ratio; *El:* **r. de tension,** stepping down of voltage. 2. **réductions de salaires,** wage-cuts; **supprimer les réductions,** to restore the cuts; **r. des prix,** price-reduction; **r. sur la quantité,** discount for quantity; **r. du taux de l'escompte,** lowering of the minimum lending rate.

réduire [reduiːr], *v.tr.* (*conj. like* CONDUIRE) 1. to reduce (pressure, speed, prices, etc.). 2. (*a*) **r. qn à la misère,** to reduce s.o. to poverty; (*b*) *Surg:* to reduce, set (a fracture, etc.).

se réduire. 1. **se r. au strict nécessaire,** to confine oneself to what is strictly necessary. 2. **les frais**

se réduisent à peu de chose, in fact the expenses come to very little; **se r. en poussière,** to crumble into dust; *Cu:* **la sauce s'est réduite,** the sauce has boiled down.

réduit[1] [redɥi], *a.* reduced; **prix r.,** cut price; **modèle r.,** scaled-down model; **édition réduite,** abridged edition; **vitesse réduite,** reduced speed; *Com:* **débouchés réduits,** restricted market.

réduit[2], *s.m.usu. Pej:* **un misérable r.,** a wretched hovel; **r. servant de placard,** alcove used as a cupboard.

réel, -elle [reɛl], *a.* real, actual; **un fait r.,** a true fact; **salaire r.,** net earnings; *Com:* **offre réelle,** cash offer; *adv.* **-lement,** in reality.

réélire [reeliːr], *v.tr. (conj. like* LIRE) to re-elect.

réévalu|er [reevalɥe], *v.tr.* to revalue; to estimate again; *Fin:* **r. le franc,** to revalue the franc; *s.f.* **-ation.**

refaire [rəfɛːr], *v.tr. (conj. like* FAIRE) **1.** to remake; to do (sth.) again; **c'est à r.,** it will have to be done (over) again. **2.** to repair, to do up (house); to do over (a dress); to recover (one's health). **3.** *F:* to dupe; to take (s.o.) in; **on vous a refait,** you've been had.

se refaire. 1. to recuperate; to recover one's health. **2.** to retrieve one's losses.

réfectoire [refɛktwaːr], *s.m.* refectory, dining-hall.

référence [referɑ̃ːs], *s.f. (a)* reference, referring; **livre, ouvrage, de r.,** reference book, work of reference; *(b) Corr:* reference (on letter, etc.); *(c) pl.* (employer's) reference, testimonial.

referendum, référendum [referɛ̃dɔm], *s.m.* referendum.

référer [refere], *v.* (**je réfère; je référerai**) *v.tr.* to refer, ascribe (sth. to sth.); to refer, attribute (sth. to s.o.).

se référer. 1. se r. à qch., to refer to sth. **2. se r. à qn,** to ask s.o.'s opinion; **s'en r. à qn,** to refer the matter to s.o.

refermer [rəfɛrme], *v.tr.* to reclose; to shut (door) again.

se refermer, (*of door*) to close again; (*of wound*) to heal.

réfléchi [refleʃi], *a.* reflective, thoughtful (person); deliberate, considered (opinion); **réponse réfléchie,** careful answer.

réfléchir [refleʃiːr]. **1.** *v.tr.* to reflect (light). **2.** *v.i.* **r. sur, à, qch.,** to reflect, to ponder, on sth.; **réfléchissez donc!** think again! think it over! **donner à r. à qn,** to give s.o. food for thought; **parler sans r.,** to speak without thinking, hastily.

se réfléchir, (*of light, heat*) to be reflected; (*of sound*) to reverberate.

réflecteur, -trice [reflɛktœːr, -tris]. **1.** *a.* reflecting (mirror, panel, etc.); *Atom.Ph:* **substance réflectrice,** tamper material. **2.** *s.m.* reflector.

reflet [rəflɛ], *s.m.* reflection; reflected light; **r. des eaux,** gleam on the waters; **chevelure à reflets d'or,** hair with glints of gold; **il n'est qu'un pâle r. de son père,** he's only a pale reflection of his father.

refléter [rəflete], *v.tr.* (**il reflète; il reflétera**) to reflect (light).

refleurir [rəflœriːr], *v.i.* **1.** to flower, blossom, again. **2.** (*of art, etc.*) to flourish anew. **3.** *v.tr.* **r. une tombe,** to put fresh flowers on a grave.

réflexe [reflɛks]. **1.** *a. Ph: Physiol:* reflex (light, action). **2.** *s.m. Physiol:* reflex; **avoir des réflexes,** to react quickly.

réflexion [reflɛksjɔ̃], *s.f.* **1.** reflection, reflexion (of light). **2.** reflection, thought; (**toute**) **r. faite,** everything considered. **3.** remark; **une r. désobligeante,** an unpleasant remark.

refluer [rəflɥe], *v.i.* to flow back; (*of tide*) to ebb.

reflux [rəfly], *s.m.* ebb tide; **le flux et le r.,** the ebb and flow.

réforme [refɔrm], *s.f.* **1.** reformation, reform (of abuses, etc.). **2.** *(a) Mil:* discharge on medical grounds; invaliding out of the service; *(b) Ind:* **r. du matériel,** scrapping of the plant.

réformé, -ée [reforme], *s. (a)* Protestant; member of one of the reformed Churches; *(b) s.m. Mil:* man invalided out of the service; **réformés de guerre avec invalidité,** disabled ex-servicemen.

réform|er [reforme], *v.tr.* **1.** to reform, amend. **2.** *(a) Mil:* to invalid (officer, soldier) out of the army; (*of recruit*) **réformé pour myopie,** rejected on account of short-sight(edness); *(b) Ind:* to scrap (the plant); *s.* **-ateur, -atrice,** (religious, social) reformer; *s.f.* **-ation,** reform; *Rel:* **la R.,** the Reformation.

refoul|er [rəfule], *v.tr.* to drive back, force back; to compress (water, steam); to hurl back (the enemy); to suppress (feelings, instincts); *Psy:* to repress (an instinct, a desire); *s.m.* **-ement,** *Psy:* suppression (of desires).

réfractaire [refraktɛːr], *(a) a.* refractory, insubordinate (person); *(b) a.* fire(proof) (clay, brick); **r. aux acides,** acid-proof; **r. au poison,** proof against poison; *(c) s.* rebel; conscientious objector.

réfraction [refraksjɔ̃], *s.f. Ph:* refraction (of rays, etc.); *Cin:* **film à r.,** three-D film.

refrain [rəfrɛ̃], *s.m.* **1.** refrain, burden (of a song); **toujours le même r.,** always the same old story. **2. r. en chœur,** chorus.

refréner [rəfrene], *v.tr.* (**je refrène; je refrénerai**) to curb, bridle, restrain; to control (passions, etc.).

réfrigér|er [refriʒere], *v.tr.* (**je réfrigère; je réfrigérerai**) to refrigerate; **viande réfrigérée,** chilled meat; *s.m.* **-ateur,** refrigerator, *F:* fridge; *s.f.* **-ation,** refrigeration, chilling (of meat, etc.).

refroid|ir [rəfrwadi:r]. **1.** *v.tr.* (*a*) to cool, chill (air, water); (*b*) **laisser r. la soupe,** to let the soup cool down; *Ind:* **refroidi par (l')air, par (l')eau,** air-, water-cooled (engine); (*c*) to damp (sympathy, enthusiasm); to cool (off) (s.o.'s sympathy). **2.** *v.i. & pr.* to grow cold; to cool down; **le temps s'est refroidi,** it's grown, turned, colder; *Med:* **se r.,** to catch a chill; *s.m.* **-issement,** cooling (down); *Med:* a chill; *s.m.* **-isseur,** cooling agent; cooling system; *Ind:* cooler.

refuge [rəfy:ʒ], *s.m.* refuge; shelter; (climber's) hut; (*on road*) lay-by.

réfugié, -ée [refyʒje], *s.* refugee.

réfugier (se) [sərefyʒje], *v.pr.* to take refuge.

refus [rəfy], *s.m.* refusal; **essuyer un r.,** to meet with a refusal; **ce n'est pas de r.,** I can't say no to that.

refuser [rəfyze], *v.tr.* **1.** (*a*) to refuse, decline; **r. tout talent à qn,** to deny that s.o. has any talent; **r. la porte à qn,** to deny s.o. admittance; (*b*) (*of horse*) to refuse, to ba(u)lk. **2.** to reject; *Sch:* **r. un candidat,** to fail a candidate; **être refusé,** to fail.
se refuser à qch., to object to, set one's face against, sth.; **se r. à l'évidence,** to shut one's eyes to the evidence.

réfut|er [refyte], *v.tr.* to refute (a theory); to disprove (a theory, a statement); *s.f.* **-ation,** refutation, rebuttal, disproof (**de,** of).

regagner [rəgɑɲe], *v.tr.* **1.** to regain, recover, win back (s.o.'s confidence, etc.); **r. le temps perdu,** to make up for lost time. **2.** to get back to (a place); to regain; **r. son foyer, son domicile,** to go home.

régal, -als [regal], *s.m.* (*a*) feast; (*b*) treat; **pour nous, le gibier est un r.,** for us, game is a treat.

régaler [regale], *v.tr. F:* to entertain, feast (s.o.); **c'est moi qui régale,** I'm standing treat.
se régaler, *F:* to feast; to treat oneself; **on s'est bien régalé,** we did ourselves well.

regard [rəga:r], *s.m.* look, glance, gaze; **yeux sans r.,** lack-lustre eyes; **chercher qn du r.,** to look round for s.o.; **détourner le r.,** to look away; **r. appuyé,** stare; **attirer le(s) regard(s),** to attract attention.

regarder [rəgarde], *v.tr.* **1.** (*a*) to regard, consider; (*b*) **ne r. que ses intérêts,** to consider only one's own interests; (*c*) *v.ind.tr.* **r. à qch.,** to pay attention to sth.; **je n'y regarde pas de si près,** I am not as particular, as fussy, as (all) that; (*d*) to concern (s.o.); **cela me regarde,** that's my business; **cela ne vous regarde pas,** that's no concern of yours; **en ce qui me regarde,** as far as I'm concerned. **2.** to look at; **puis-je r.?** may I have a look? **r. qn fixement,** to stare at s.o.; **se faire r.,** to attract attention; **r. à la fenêtre,** to look in at the window; **r. par la fenêtre,** to look out of the window. **3.** to look

on to; to face (sth.); **la maison regarde le midi,** the house faces south.

régate [regat], *s.f.* regatta; **r. à voiles,** yacht races.

régence [reʒɑ̃:s], *s.f.* regency.

régénér|er [reʒenere], *v.tr.* (**je régénère; je régénérerai**) to regenerate; to reactivate; *a. & s.* **-ateur, -atrice,** (*a*) *a.* regenerating; *Atom.Ph:* **pile régénératrice,** breeder reactor; (*b*) *s.m. Ind:* regenerator, regenerating plant; *s.f.* **-ation.**

régent [reʒɑ̃], *s.m.* regent.

régie [reʒi], *s.f.* **1.** *Jur:* administration, stewardship; management, control; **en r.,** (i) in the hands of trustees; (ii) under state supervision. **2. r. des impôts indirects,** excise (administration); **r. française des tabacs,** French State tobacco company.

régime [reʒim], *s.m.* **1.** regime; form of administration; **le r. du travail,** the organization of labour; **le r. actuel,** the present order of things. **2.** *Med:* diet; **se mettre au r.,** to diet. **3.** *Gram:* object; **cas r.,** objective case. **4.** bunch, cluster (of bananas, dates).

régiment [reʒimɑ̃], *s.m.* regiment; *a.* **-aire,** regimental.

région [reʒjɔ̃], *s.f.* region, territory, area; *a.* **-al, -aux,** regional, local.

régl|ir [reʒi:r], *v.tr.* to govern, rule; to manage (estate); **les lois qui nous régissent,** the laws that govern us; *s.m.* **-isseur,** steward, manager, agent; (farm) bailiff.

registre [rəʒistr], *s.m.* **1.** register; record; account-book; minute-book; *Adm:* **les registres de l'état civil,** the registers of births, marriages and deaths. **2.** *Mus:* register; (i) compass; (ii) tone quality. **3. r. de cheminée,** register, damper (of chimney).

réglable [reglabl], *a.* adjustable.

réglage [regla:ʒ], *s.m.* (*a*) regulating, adjusting, adjustment (of apparatus, watch); (*b*) *Rad: T.V: etc:* tuning; **changer de r.,** to switch over to another station.

règle [regl], *s.f.* **1.** rule, ruler; **r. à calcul,** sliderule. **2.** rule (of conduct, art, grammar, etc.); **tout est en r.,** everything is in order; *Av:* **règles de vol à vue,** visual flight rules; *Ind:* **règles d'exploitation,** operating rules; **règles du jeu,** rules of the game; *F:* **bataille en r.,** stand-up fight. **3. prendre qn pour r.,** to take s.o. as an example. **4.** *pl. Med: F:* menses, (monthly) period.

réglé [regle], *a.* ruled (paper); **papier non r.,** plain paper. **2.** (*a*) regular; steady; **vie réglée,** well-ordered life; *F:* **c'est r. (comme du papier à musique),** it's inevitable; (*b*) **l'affaire est réglée,** the business is settled.

règlement [regləmɑ̃], *s.m.* **1.** settlement, adjustment (of difficulty, account, etc.); *Com:* payment. 2. regulation(s); statutes (of university, etc.); **r. d'instruction,** training manual.

réglement|er [reglǝmɑ̃te], *v.tr.* to regulate; to make rules for (sth.); to bring (sth.) under regulation; *a.* **-aire,** regular, statutory; **tenue r.,** regulation uniform; *s.f.* **-ation,** making of rules; regulating, regulation; *coll.* regulations.

régler, *v.tr.* (**je règle; je réglerai**) 1. to rule (paper). 2. (*a*) to regulate, order; (*b*) to regulate, adjust; **r. sa montre,** to set one's watch right. 3. (*a*) to settle (account); (*b*) **r. ses affaires,** to set one's affairs in order. **se régler sur qn,** to take s.o. as an example.

réglisse [reglis], *s.f.* liquorice.

règne [rɛɲ], *s.m.* 1. (animal, vegetable, mineral) kingdom. 2. reign (of a king, truth, reason, etc.).

régner [reɲe], *v.i.* (**je règne; je régnerai**) (*of monarch*) to reign, rule; to be prevalent; **le calme règne,** calm prevails.

regorger [rǝgɔrʒe], *v.i.* (**n. regorgeons**) (*a*) to overflow, run over; (*b*) to abound; to be glutted; **les trains regorgent de gens,** the trains are packed with people.

régression [regresjɔ̃], *s.f.* 1. regression; retreat, recession. 2. *Biol:* throw-back; regression; *Psy:* regression. 3. decline (in business); drop (in sales, etc.).

regret [rǝgrɛ], *s.m.* regret (**de,** of, for); **faire qch. à r.,** to do sth. reluctantly.

regrett|er [rǝgrɛte], *v.tr.* 1. to regret (s.o., sth.); **je regrette de vous avoir fait attendre,** I'm sorry I kept you waiting; **je regrette!** (I'm) sorry! 2. **r. un absent,** to miss an absent friend; *a.* **-able,** regrettable, unfortunate (mistake); *adv.* **-ablement.**

régularis|er [regylarize], *v.tr.* to regularize (sth.); to put (document, etc.) into proper form; to put (sth.) in order; to equalize; to straighten out (irregular business); *s.f.* **-ation.**

régularité [regylarite], *s.f.* (*a*) regularity; (*b*) steadiness, evenness; (*c*) equability; (*d*) punctuality.

régul|ier, -ière [regylje, -jɛːr]. 1. *a.* (*a*) regular; (*b*) steady; even; orderly; **vie régulière,** ordered life; (*c*) **humeur régulière,** equable temper. 2. *a. & s.m.* regular (soldier, priest); *adv.* **-ièrement.**

réhabilit|er [reabilite], *v.tr.* 1. to rehabilitate (s.o.'s good name); to discharge (bankrupt); to reinstate (s.o. in his rights). 2. to clean and renovate (buildings); *s.f.* **-ation.**

rehauss|er [rǝose], *v.tr.* 1. to raise; to make (a house, etc.) higher; **r. le prix du pain,** to raise the price of bread. 2. to heighten (colour); to accentuate (a detail).

réimprimer [reɛ̃prime], *v.tr.* to reprint.

Reims [rɛ̃s]. *Pr.n.m. Geog:* Rheims.

rein [rɛ̃], *s.m.* 1. *Anat:* kidney. 2. *pl.* loins, back;

se casser les reins, to break one's back; **la chute des reins,** the small of the back; **il a les reins solides,** (i) he's a sturdy fellow; (ii) *F:* he's a man of substance.

reine [rɛn], *s.f.* (*a*) queen; **la R. mère,** the Queen Mother; (*b*) **r. (des abeilles),** queen-bee.

reine-claude [rɛnkloːd], *s.f.* greengage; *pl. reines-claudes.*

réintégr|er [reɛ̃tegre], *v.tr.* (**je réintègre; je réintégrerai**) 1. **r. qn (dans ses fonctions),** to reinstate s.o. (in his position, his job). 2. **r. son domicile,** to return to one's home; *s.f.* **-ation,** reinstatement.

réitér|er [reitere], *v.tr.* (**je réitère; je réitérerai**) to reiterate, repeat; **demandes réitérées,** repeated requests; *s.f.* **-ation.**

rejet [rǝʒɛ], *s.m.* 1. (*a*) throwing out, up; (*b*) material thrown out; spoil (earth); *pl.* (volcanic) ejectamenta. 2. rejection (of proposal, etc.); *Med:* rejection (of transplant); *Jur:* dismissal of an appeal.

rejeter [rǝʒ(ǝ)te], *v.tr.* (*conj. like* JETER) 1. (*a*) to throw, fling, (sth.) back; to return; (*b*) to throw up. 2. to transfer; **r. la faute sur d'autres,** to lay the blame on others. 3. to reject; **r. un projet de loi,** to throw out a bill. **se rejeter.** 1. to fall back (**sur,** on); **se r. sur les circonstances,** to lay the blame on circumstances. 2. **se r. en arrière,** to leap, dart, spring, back(wards).

rejeton [rǝʒtɔ̃], *s.m.* 1. shoot, sucker (of plant). 2. descendant, offspring.

rejoindre [rǝʒwɛ̃ːdr], *v.tr.* (*conj. like* ATTEINDRE) 1. to rejoin, reunite, to join (together) again; **petites rues qui vont r. les grandes voies,** side streets which connect with the main arteries. 2. to rejoin, overtake, catch up (with) (s.o.) (again). **se rejoindre.** 1. to meet. 2. to meet again.

réjoui [reʒwi], *a.* jolly, cheerful (person); **air r.,** happy expression.

réjou|ir [reʒwiːr], *v.tr.* (*a*) to delight, gladden (s.o.); (*b*) **r. la compagnie,** to amuse the company; *s.f.* **-issance,** rejoicing; *pl.* festivities. **se réjouir.** 1. to rejoice (**de,** at, in); to be glad (**de,** of); **se r. de qch.,** to be delighted at sth. 2. to enjoy oneself.

relâche [rǝlɑːʃ]. 1. *s.m.* (*a*) slackening; (*b*) relaxation, respite; rest (from regular work); breathing space; **travailler sans r.,** to work without stopping; (*c*) *Th: P.N:* **r.,** closed. 2. *s.f. Nau:* (*a*) call; putting in; **faire une r.,** to call at a port; (*b*) port of call.

relâch|er [rǝlɑʃe]. 1. *v.tr.* (*a*) to loosen, slacken (cords, spring, etc.); *Mch:* **r. la pression,** to slack off pressure; (*b*) to relax (discipline); (*c*) *Cu:* to thin (down) (sauce, etc.). 2. to let (a bird, etc.) go; **r. un prisonnier,** to release a prisoner. 3. *v.i. Nau:* to put into port; *s.m.*

-**ement**, slackening, relaxation.
·elais [rǝlɛ], s.m. **1.** (a) relay; Ind: shift; Sp: course de r., relay race; prendre le r., to take over; (b) stage (in race); r. gastronomique, restaurant with a reputation for good food; Aut: r. routier, service station with restaurant, etc.; Aut: r. (d'essence), filling station. **2.** Tchn: relay; P.T.T: r. téléphonique, telephone relay; El: Rad: etc: station r., relay station; r. de radiodiffusion, relay broadcasting station.
·lanⅼcer [rǝlãse], v.tr. (conj. like COMMENCER) **1.** to throw (sth.) back; Ten: to return (the ball). **2.** (a) r. une industrie, to give a new impetus to, F: to boost, an industry; (b) Aut: r. le moteur, to restart the engine; s.m. -cement.
·later [rǝlate], v.tr. to relate, state (facts).
·latⅼif, -ive [rǝlatif, -iːv], a. (a) relative (position, value); (b) questions relatives à un sujet, questions relating to a matter; adv. -ivement.
·lation [rǝlasjõ], s.f. relation. **1.** les relations humaines, human relations; être en r. avec qn, to be in touch with s.o.; en relations d'amitié (avec qn), on friendly terms (with s.o.); relations tendues, strained relations; P.T.T: être mis en r. avec qn, to be put through to s.o.; r. étroite entre deux faits, close connection between two facts. **2.** account, narrative.
·lativité [rǝlativite], s.f. relativity; théorie de la r., theory of relativity.
·lax [rǝlaks], a. & s.m. (fauteuil) r., reclining chair.
·laxⅼer (se) [sǝrǝlakse], v.pr. to relax; s.f. -ation.
·layer [rǝleje], v.tr. (je relaie, je relaye) (a) to relay, relieve (s.o.), take turns with (s.o.); (b) Sp: (in relay race) to take over from (s.o.); (c) El: P.T.T: Rad: etc: to relay (message, broadcast, etc.).
·léguer [rǝlege], v.tr. (je relègue, n. reléguons) to relegate; r. qch. au grenier, to banish sth. to the attic.
·lent [rǝlã], s.m. musty smell, taste.
·levé [rǝlve]. **1.** a. (a) raised, erect (head, etc.); turned up, stand-up (collar); (b) exalted (position); noble (sentiment); (c) highly-spiced (dish, anecdote). **2.** s.m. summary; r. de consommation, (gas, electricity) meter reading; r. officiel, official return; Com: r. de compte(s), statement (of account).
ⅼlever [rǝlve], v. (conj. like LEVER) **I.** v.tr. **1.** (a) to raise, lift, set, (sth.) up again; (b) to pick up (sth. from the ground); (c) to raise (sth. higher); to turn up (a collar, a skirt); r. la tête, to look up; r. les salaires, to raise wages. **2.** (a) to call attention to (sth.); r. les fautes d'un ouvrage, to point out, criticize, the defects of a work; (b) r. qn, to take s.o. up sharply. **3.** (a) to bring into relief; to enhance, heighten (effect, colour, etc.); (b) Cu: to season (a sauce, etc.).

4. to relieve (s.o.); to take (s.o.'s) place. **5.** r. qn de ses fonctions, to relieve s.o. of his office. **6.** to record (temperature, etc.); Com: to make out (account); to read (meter). **7.** Nau: to take the bearing(s) of (land); Surv: r. un terrain, to survey, plot, a piece of land. **II.** reⅼlever, v.i. **1.** r. de maladie, to have just recovered from an illness. **2.** r. de qn, to be dependent on, responsible to, s.o.; s.m. -èvement.
se relever. 1. to rise to one's feet (again), to get up (again); to pick oneself up. **2.** les affaires se relèvent, business is looking up. **3.** (a) to rise again; (b) se r. de qch., to recover from sth.; il ne s'en relèvera pas, he'll never get over it.
relief [rǝljɛf], s.m. Sculp: etc: relief; Geog: carte en r., raised relief map, 3-dimensional map; la Bretagne a moins de r. que le Massif central, Brittany is less mountainous than the Massif Central.
relier [rǝlje], v.tr. (a) to connect, join; (b) to bind (book).
relieur [rǝljœːr], s.m. **1.** (book)binder. **2.** springback binder.
religieuⅼx, -euse [rǝliʒjø, -øːz]. **1.** a. religious; sacred (music, etc.). **2.** s.m. monk; s.f. religieuse, nun. **3.** s.f. Cu: (type of) éclair; adv. -sement.
religion [rǝliʒjõ], s.f. (a) religion; (b) se faire une r. de qch., to make sth. a point of conscience.
reliquaire [rǝlikɛːr], s.m. reliquary, shrine.
relique [rǝlik], s.f. relic (of saint).
relire [rǝliːr], v.tr. (conj. like LIRE) to re-read; to read (over) again.
reliure [rǝljyːr], s.f. **1.** bookbinding; atelier de r., bindery. **2.** binding (of book).
reluiⅼre [rǝlɥiːr], v.i. (conj. like CONDUIRE) to shine; to glitter, glisten, gleam; faire r. qch., to polish sth. up; a. -sant, shining, glittering.
remaniⅼer [rǝmanje], v.tr. (pr.sub. & p.d. n. remaniions) (a) to rehandle (material); (b) to recast, alter, adapt (a play, etc.); s.m. -ement, alteration, modification.
remarier (se) [sǝrǝmarje], v.pr. to remarry; to marry again.
remarquable [rǝmarkabl], a. (a) remarkable, noteworthy (par, for); distinguished (par, by); (b) strange, astonishing; il est r. qu'il n'ait rien entendu, it's a wonder that he heard nothing; adv. -ment.
remarque [rǝmark], s.f. remark; faire une r., to make a (critical) remark.
remarquer [rǝmarke], v.tr. (a) to remark, notice, observe; faire r. qch. à qn, to point sth. out to s.o.; (b) se faire r., to attract attention; (c) remark, observe, say.
remballⅼer [rãbale], v.tr. to repack; to pack, to bale, (goods) again; s.m. -age, repacking.
rembarquⅼer [rãbarke]. **1.** v.tr. to re-embark

(passengers). **2.** *v.i. & pr.* to re-embark, to go on board again; *s.m.* -**ément.**

remblai [rãblɛ], *s.m.* embankment, bank; **route en r.,** embanked road.

remblayer [rãbleje], *v.tr.* (**je remblaie, je remblaye**) to embank, to bank (up) (road, railway line, snow).

rembourr|er [rãbure], *v.tr.* to stuff, upholster, pad (armchair, etc.); *s.m.* -**age,** stuffing, padding, upholstering.

rembours|er [rãburse], *v.tr.* **1.** to repay, refund (expenses, etc.); **r. un emprunt,** to return, repay, a loan. **2. r. qn de qch.,** to reimburse s.o. for sth.; **on m'a remboursé,** I got my money back; *a.* -**able,** (*of loan, etc.*) repayable; refundable; redeemable (annuity, etc.); *s.m.* -**ement,** repayment; redemption (of annuity, etc.).

rembrunir [rãbryniːr], *v.tr.* **1.** to make (sth.) dark(er). **2.** to cast a gloom over (the company).

se rembrunir, (*of sky*) to cloud over, to grow dark; (*of pers.*) to become gloomy.

remède [rəmɛd], *s.m.* remedy, cure; **c'est sans r.,** it can't be helped.

remédi|er [rəmedje], *v.ind.tr.* (*pr.sub. & p.d.* **n. remédiions**) **r. à qch.,** to cure sth., to put sth. right; *a.* -**able,** remediable.

remembr|er [rəmãbre], *v.tr. Adm: Agr:* to reallocate, regroup (land); *s.m.* -**ement,** reallocation, regrouping, of land.

remerci|er [rəmersje], *v.tr.* (*pr.sub. & p.d.* **n. remerciions**) **1.** (*a*) **r. qn de qch.,** to thank s.o. for sth.; (*b*) to decline; **du café?—je vous remercie,** (will you) have some coffee?—no, thank you. **2.** to dismiss (employee); *s.m.* -**ement,** thanks, acknowledgment.

remettre [rəmɛtr], *v.tr.* (*conj. like* METTRE) **1.** to put (sth.) back (again); (*a*) **r. son chapeau,** to put one's hat on again; **r. un os,** to set a bone; **r. en état,** to repair (sth.); (*b*) **r. l'esprit de qn,** to calm, compose, s.o.'s mind; (*c*) (**se**) **r. qn,** to recall s.o. **2.** (*a*) **r. une dépêche à qn,** to hand a telegram to s.o.; (*b*) **r. une charge,** to hand over one's duties. **3.** (*a*) to pardon, forgive (an offence); **r. une peine,** to remit a penalty; (*b*) *Com:* to allow (discount). **4.** to postpone; **r. une affaire au lendemain,** to put off a matter till the next day.

se remettre. 1. (*a*) **se r. au lit,** to go back to bed; **le temps se remet au beau,** *abs.* **le temps se remet,** the weather is clearing up again; (*b*) **se r. au travail,** to start work again. **2. se r. d'une maladie,** to recover from an illness; **remettez-vous!** pull yourself together! **3. s'en r. à qn,** to leave it to s.o.

réminiscence [reminissãːs], *s.f.* **1.** reminiscence. **2.** vague recollection.

remise [rəmiːz], *s.f.* **1.** (*a*) putting back (of sth. in

its place); (*b*) **r. en état,** repairing. **2.** (*a* delivery (of letter); (*b*) remission (of penalty debt, tax). **3.** *Com:* (*a*) remittance (of a sum o money); (*b*) discount, allowance. **4.** shed outhouse.

rémission [remisjõ], *s.f.* remission (of sin, o debt); **travailler sans r.,** to work without break.

remontée [rəmõte], *s.f.* climb (of road, after run ning downhill); *Av:* climbing (after a dive) *Sp:* good recovery (after a bad start); **mécanique,** ski-lift.

remonte-pente [rəmõtpãːt], *s.m.* ski-lift; *p remonte-pentes.*

remonter [rəmõte]. **1.** *v.i.* (*aux. usu.* **être,** occ **avoir**) (*a*) to go up (again); **r. à cheval,** t remount one's horse; (*b*) to go back; **r. plu haut,** to go further back; **tout cela remont loin,** all that goes back a long way, a long time **2.** *v.tr.* (*a*) to go, climb, up again; **r. la rue,** to g up the street; (*b*) **r. ses chaussettes,** to pull u one's socks; (*c*) to wind (up) (clock); **r. courage de qn,** *F:* **r. qn,** to revive s.o. courage, *F:* to buck s.o. up; **un verre de vi vous remontera,** a glass of wine will put yo right; (*d*) **r. sa garde-robe,** to replenish one wardrobe.

remontrance [rəmõtrãːs], *s.f.* remonstrance.

remontrer [rəmõtre], *v.tr.* (*a*) to show demonstrate, (sth.) again; (*b*) (**en**) **r. à qn,** t give advice to s.o., to remonstrate with s.o.

remords [rəmɔːr], *s.m.* remorse, self-reproach **un r.,** a twinge of remorse; **pris de r** conscience-stricken.

remorque [rəmɔrk], *s.f.* **1.** towing. **2.** tow-line. (*a*) tow; vessel towed; (*b*) *Aut:* trailer; **r. (d camping,** caravan, *U.S:* camping trailer; (*Rail:* **rame r.,** slip portion (of train).

remorqu|er [rəmɔrke], *v.tr.* to tow; to haul; *s.n* -**eur,** tug(-boat).

remous [rəmu], *s.m.* eddy; wash (of ship); swi (of the tide); backwash; *Av: Aut: etc:* **r. d'ai** (i) slip-stream; (ii) eddy; **il y a eu un r. dans foule,** there was a movement in the crowd; **livre va provoquer des r.,** this book will cause stir.

rempart [rãpaːr], *s.m.* rampart.

remplaçable [rãplasabl], *a.* replaceable.

remplaçant, -ante [rãplasã, -ãːt], *s.* substitut locum (tenens).

remplac|er [rãplase], *v.tr.* (**n. remplaçons**) **1.** take the place of (s.o., sth.); to deputize fc (s.o.). **2.** (*a*) to replace; **r. qch. par qch.,** replace sth. by sth.; (*b*) to supersede (s.o.); *s.n* -**ement,** replacement, substitution; **pneu de r** spare tyre; **pile de r.,** (torch) refill.

rempl|ir [rãpliːr], *v.tr.* **1.** to fill up, to refill (glas etc.) (**de,** with); to occupy, take up (time). **2.** **l'air de ses cris,** to fill the air with one's cries.

to fill up, fill in (a form). **4.** to fulfil (a promise, an order); *Th:* **r. un rôle,** to play a part; *s.m.* **-issage,** filling up.

emporter [rãpɔrte], *v.tr.* **1.** to take (sth.) back, away. **2.** to carry off (prize); to achieve (success); to win (victory).

emue-ménage [rəmymena:ʒ], *s.m.inv.* stir, bustle; confusion, upset.

emuer [rəmɥe]. **1.** *v.tr.* to move; to shift; to stir (coffee, etc.); to turn over (the ground); **r. les masses,** to stir up the masses. **2.** *v.i.* to move, stir, *F:* budge; *(to child)* **ne remue pas!** don't fidget!

e remuer, to move, stir; to bustle about; **remuez-vous un peu!** get a move on!

émunér|er [remynere], *v.tr.* **(je rémunère; je rémunérerai)** *(a)* to reward (s.o.); *(b)* to pay for (services); **collaborateurs rémunérés,** paid helpers; *a.* **-ateur, -atrice,** paying, profitable (work, etc.); *s.f.* **-ation,** payment.

enâcl|er [rənakle], *v.i.* *(a)* to snort, to sniff (à qch., at sth.); *(b)* to show reluctance; to hang back; to jib (at a job); *s.m.* **-eur,** *(a)* shirker; *(b)* grumbler.

enaissance [rənɛsã:s], *s.f.* *(a)* rebirth; *(b)* **r. des lettres,** revival of letters; *(c)* *Hist:* **la R.,** the Renaissance.

enaître [rənɛ:tr], *v.i.* *(conj. like* NAÎTRE) **1.** to be born again; **r. à la vie,** to take on a new lease of life. **2.** to reappear; *(of plants, etc.)* to grow, spring up, again; *(of hope, etc.)* to revive.

enard, -arde [rəna:r, -ard], *s.* fox, *f.* vixen.

enardeau, -eaux [rənardo], *s.m.* fox-cub.

enchér|ir [rãʃeri:r], *v.i.* *(of goods)* *(a)* to get dearer; to increase in price; **tout renchérit,** everything's going up; *(b)* **r. sur qn,** (i) to out-bid s.o.; (ii) to go one better than s.o.; *s.m.* **-issement,** rise in price.

encontre [rãkõ:tr], *s.f.* **1.** *(a)* meeting, en-counter; **aller à la r. de qn,** to go to meet s.o.; **connaissance de r.,** chance acquaintance; *(b)* **r. de deux automobiles,** collision of two cars. **2.** encounter, skirmish; *Sp:* match; *Box:* fight.

ncontrer [rãkõtre], *v.tr.* to meet, to fall in with (s.o.); **r. l'ennemi,** to encounter the enemy; **r. les yeux de qn,** to catch s.o.'s glance; **r. un obstacle,** to encounter a difficulty; **le tramway a rencontré un autobus,** the tram ran into a bus.

rencontrer. 1. *(a)* to meet; *(b)* to collide; *(c)* to occur; **comme cela se rencontre!** how lucky! how things do happen! **2.** *(of ideas)* to agree.

endement [rãdmã], *s.m.* *(a)* produce, yield; return, profit; *(b)* *Ind:* output (of worker); out-put, production (of mine, etc.); *(c)* efficiency, performance (of machine, etc.).

endez-vous [rãdevu], *s.m.inv.* rendezvous. **1.** appointment. **2.** meeting-place; regular haunt (of friends, club members, etc.).

rendormir [rãdɔrmi:r], *v.tr.* *(conj. like* MENTIR) to send, lull, (s.o.) to sleep again.

se rendormir, to go to sleep again.

rendre [rã:dr], *v.tr.* **1.** *(a)* to give back, return, restore (sth.); to repay (money); **je le lui rendrai!** I'll be even with him! *(b)* to render, give; **r. la justice,** to administer justice; **r. compte de qch.,** to account for sth.; *(c)* to yield; to give, produce; **placement qui rend 10%,** investment that brings in 10%; **terre qui ne rend rien,** un-productive land; *Mch:* **le moteur rend bien,** the engine runs well. **2.** to convey, deliver (goods); **prix rendu,** delivery price. **3.** *(a)* to bring up, throw up (food); **r. l'âme,** to give up the ghost, to die; *(b)* *Jur:* **r. un jugement,** to deliver a judgment. **4.** to give up, surrender (a fort, etc.). **5.** to reproduce, render, express; **elle rend très bien Chopin,** she plays Chopin very well. **6.** **il se rend ridicule,** he is making himself ridiculous.

se rendre. 1. se r. dans un lieu, to go to, make one's way to, a place; **se rendre chez qn,** to call on s.o. **2.** *(a)* to surrender; to give in; **rendez-vous!** hands up! *(b)* **se r. à la raison,** to yield to reason.

rendu [rãdy], *a.* **r. (de fatigue),** exhausted.

rêne [rɛn], *s.f. usu. pl.* rein.

renégat, -ate [rənega, -at], *s.* renegade, turncoat.

renfermé [rãfɛrme]. **1.** *a.* uncommunicative (person). **2.** *s.m.* **sentir le r.,** to smell stuffy, fusty.

renfermer [rãfɛrme], *v.tr.* **1.** to shut (sth.) up again. **2.** *(a)* to shut, lock, (sth., s.o.) up; *(b)* to restrict; **se r. dans ses instructions,** to confine oneself to one's instructions. **3.** to contain, comprise, enclose; **livre qui renferme des idées modernes,** book that contains new ideas.

renfl|er [rãfle], *v.tr. & i.* to swell (out); to bulge; *s.m.* **-ement,** swelling, bulge.

renfloul|er [rãflue], *v.tr.* to refloat (stranded ship); *Com:* to set (business) on its feet again; *s.m.* **-age,** refloating (of ship).

renforcé [rãfɔrse], *a.* stout, strengthened; rein-forced (nylon).

renforc|er [rãfɔrse], *v.tr.* **(n. renforçons)** *(a)* to reinforce; *(b)* to strengthen; *(c)* to intensify; *s.m.* **-ement,** strengthening, reinforcement; intensification.

se renforcer, to gather strength.

renfort [rãfɔ:r], *s.m.* **1.** reinforcement(s); **en r.,** in support; *El:* **batterie de r.,** booster battery. **2.** strengthening piece; backing.

renfrogné [rãfrɔɲe], *a.* frowning (face); sullen (person); glum (look).

renfrogner (se) [sərãfrɔɲe], *v.pr.* to frown, scowl.

renier [rənje], *v.tr.* **(pr.sub. & p.d. n. reniions) 1.** to disown (friend, opinion); to repudiate (opinion); to betray (friend). **2.** (*a*) to disavow (action); (*b*) to abjure (one's faith); *s.m.* -**ement.**

renifl|er [rənifle]**1.** *v.i.* (*a*) to sniff, snort; **r. sur qch.,** to turn up one's nose at sth.; (*b*) to snivel. **2.** *v.tr.* (*a*) to sniff (up) (sth.); **il sait r. une bonne affaire,** he's got a (good) nose for a bargain; (*b*) to sniff, smell (a flower, etc.); *s.m.* -**ement.**

renne [rɛn], *s.m.* **Z:** reindeer.

renom [rənɔ̃], *s.m.,* **renommée** [rənɔme], *s.f.* renown, fame; good name; reputation.

renommé [rənɔme], *a.* renowned, famous, celebrated; **pays r. pour ses vins,** country well-known for its wines.

renonc|er [rənɔ̃se], *v.ind.tr.* (**n.** renonçons) (*a*) **r. à qch.,** to renounce, give up, sth.; **r. à faire qch.,** (i) to give up doing sth.; (ii) to drop the idea of doing sth., to give sth. up as a bad job; **y renoncer,** to give it up; **r. à la lutte,** to give up the struggle, *F:* to throw up the sponge, to quit; (*b*) (*at cards*) to revoke; *s.m.* -**ement,** renouncement (à, of); self-denial; *s.f.* -**iation,** renunciation, abnegation.

renouer [rənwe], *v.tr.* (*a*) to tie (up), knot, (sth.) again; to join (thgs) again; (*b*) to renew, resume (correspondence, etc.); **r. (amitié) avec qn,** to renew one's friendship with s.o.

renouvel|er [rənuvle], *v.tr.* (**je renouvelle**) **1.** (*a*) to renew, to renovate; **r. ses pneus,** to get a new set of tyres; (*b*) **r. son personnel,** to renew one's staff; (*c*) **r. la face du pays,** to transform the country. **2.** to renew (promise, treaty, etc.); to revive (custom); *Com:* **r. une commande,** to repeat an order; *a.* -**able;** *s.m.* -**lement,** renovation; renewal.

se renouveler. 1. to be renewed. **2.** to recur; to happen again.

rénovateur, -trice [renɔvatœːr, -tris]. **1.** *a.* renovating. **2.** *s.* renovator, restorer. **3.** *s.m.* **Dom.Ec:** (paint, surface) restorer.

rénovation [renɔvasjɔ̃], *s.f.* **1.** renovation, restoration. **2.** renewing, renewal (of promise, treaty).

renseignement [rɑ̃sɛɲmɑ̃], *s.m.* (piece of) information; **donner des renseignements sur qch.,** to give information about sth.; **prendre des renseignements sur qn,** to enquire about s.o.; **bureau de renseignements,** information bureau; *P.N:* **renseignements,** enquiries.

renseigner [rɑ̃sɛɲe], *v.tr.* **r. qn sur qch.,** to give s.o. information about sth.; **on vous a mal renseigné,** you have been misinformed.

se renseigner sur qch., to make enquiries, find out, about sth.

rente [rɑ̃t], *s.f.* **1.** annuity, pension, allowance; **r. viagère,** life annuity. **2.** *usu. pl.* (unearned) income; **vivre de ses rentes,** to live on one's private means. **3.** **rente(s) (sur l'état),** (government) stock(s).

rentier, -ière [rɑ̃tje, -jɛːr], *s.* **1.** (*a*) *Fin.* stockholder, fundholder; (*b*) annuitant. **2.** person of independent means.

rentrant, -ante [rɑ̃trɑ̃, -ɑ̃ːt]. **1.** *a.* (*a*) *Mth:* re entrant (curve, angle); **angle r.,** reflex angle; (*b Av:* retractable (undercarriage). **2.** *s.* *Sp:* new player.

rentrée [rɑ̃tre], *s.f.* **1.** (*a*) return, home-coming; **sa r. en France,** on his return to France; (o spacecraft*) **r. atmosphérique,** re-entry into th atmosphere; (*b*) re-opening (of schools); nev session (of Parliament); *Sch:* **la r. (des classes** the beginning of term. **2.** (*a*) receipt (o money); collection (of taxes); (*b*) bringing i (of crops); harvest-home.

rentrer [rɑ̃tre]. **I.** *v.i.* (*aux.* être) **1.** (*a*) to re-enter to come, to go, in again; **r. dans ses droits, t** recover one's rights; *Th:* **Macbeth rentre,** enter Macbeth; (*b*) to return home; **il es l'heure de r.,** it's time to go home; (*c*) (*o schools, law-courts*) to re-open, to resume; (*o Parliament*) to reassemble; (*d*) **faire r. se fonds,** to call in one's money. **2.** (*a*) to enter, g in; **r. en soi-même,** to retire within oneself; (*b F:* **les jambes me rentrent dans le corps,** I'r too tired to stand any longer; I'm whacked; (*c cela ne rentre pas dans mes fonctions,** that' not part of my job.

II. rentrer, *v.tr.* to take in, bring in; **r. l récolte,** to gather in the harvest; **qui a rentré le chaises?** who brought the chairs in? *Av:* t retract (the undercarriage); **r. sa chemise, l** tuck in one's shirt.

renverse [rɑ̃vɛrs], *s.f.* **tomber à la r.,** (i) to fa (over) backwards; (ii) to be bowled over (by piece of news, etc.).

renvers|er [rɑ̃vɛrse], *v.tr.* (*a*) to reverse, inver **r. les rôles,** to turn the tables (on s.o.); (*b*) t turn (sth.) upside down; *Com:* **ne pas r.,** th side up; **tout r.,** to turn everything topsy-turv (*c*) to knock (sth.) over; to overturn, upset; t spill (liquid); **il a été renversé par une voitur** he was knocked down by a car; (*d*) t overthrow (government); (*e*) *F:* to astonis **cette histoire m'a renversé,** that busine staggered me; *s.m.* -**ement,** reversal, inve sion; overthrow.

se renverser, to fall over; to upset; to overtur to capsize; **se r. sur sa chaise,** to lean back one's chair.

renvoi [rɑ̃vwa], *s.m.* **1.** return(ing), sending bac (of goods). **2.** dismissal (of servant, etc.). putting off, postponement. **4.** referrin reference (of a matter to an authority); *Ju* transfer (of case to another court); (cros reference.

renvoyer [rɑ̃vwaje], *v.tr.* (*conj. like* ENVOYER) to send back; to return; to re-echo, reverbera (sound); to reflect (heat, light). **2.** (*a*) to ser (s.o.) away; (b) to dismiss, *F:* sack (an employee). **3.** to put off, postpone (a meeting, etc.). **4.** to refer (a question to a higher authority).

éorganis|er [reɔrganize], *v.tr.* to reorganize; *s.f.* -**ation.**

éouverture [reuvɛrtyːr], *s.f.* re-opening (of theatre, etc.).

:paire [rəpɛːr], *s.m.* den; lair; haunt (of wild animals, of criminals).

:pandre [repɑ̃ːdr], *v.tr.* **1.** to pour out; to spill (salt, wine); to shed (blood). **2.** to spread, scatter (light, etc.); to give off, to give out (heat, scent); **r. des nouvelles,** to spread news; **r. des fleurs sur le passage de qn,** to strew flowers in s.o.'s path.

: répandre. 1. (*of pers.*) (*a*) **il se répand beaucoup,** he goes out a great deal; (*b*) **se r. en éloges sur qn,** to be full of praise for s.o.; **se r. sur un sujet,** to spread oneself on a subject. **2.** (*a*) (*of liquid*) to spill; to run over; (*b*) to spread; **l'odeur s'en est répandue partout,** the smell of it spread everywhere; (*of news*) **une nouvelle, un bruit, se répand vite,** a piece of news, a rumour, spreads quickly.

:pandu [repɑ̃dy], *a.* widespread, prevalent.

paraître [rəparɛːtr], *v.i.* (*conj. like* CON-NAÎTRE; *aux.usu.* avoir) to reappear; (*of disease*) to recur.

parateur, -trice [reparatœːr, -tris]. **1.** *a.* repairing, restoring. **2.** *s.* repairer, mender.

paration [reparasjɔ̃], *s.f.* **1.** repairing; **être en r.,** to be under repair. **2.** atonement, amends.

parer [repare], *v.tr.* **1.** to repair, mend (shoe, bridge, machine, etc.); **r. ses pertes,** to make good one's losses. **2.** to make amends for (misdeed); to put (mistake) right; **r. les dégâts, :o make good the damage.**

parler [rəparle], *v.i.* to speak again; **nous en reparlerons,** we'll talk about it later.

partir [rəpartiːr], *v.i.* (*conj. like* MENTIR) **1.** (*aux.* être) to set out again; **je repars pour 'aris,** I'm off to Paris again. **2.** (*aux.* avoir) to retort, reply.

part|ir [repartiːr], *v.tr.* (*conj. like* FINIR) **1.** to distribute, divide, share out. **2.** to apportion; to assess; **r. des impôts,** to assess taxes; *Fin:* **r. les actions,** to allot shares; *s.f.* -**ition.**

as [rəpɑ], *s.m.* meal; **r. de noce** = wedding breakfast; **faire un r.,** to have a meal.

asser [rəpase]. **1.** *v.i.* (*aux.usu.* être) to pass by again, go by again; **r. chez qn,** to call on s.o. again. **2.** *v.tr.* (*a*) to pass over again; to cross (over) again; **r. la mer,** to cross the sea again; '*b*) **r. qch. dans son esprit,** to go over sth. in one's mind; (*c*) **repassez-moi du pain,** pass me some (more) bread; **repassez-moi cette lettre, :t me see that letter again;** (*d*) to sharpen, grind (knife, tool, etc.); (*e*) to iron (clothes); **fer**

à r., iron; **planche à r.,** ironing-board.

repatri|er [rəpatrije], *v.tr.* (*pr.sub. & p.d.* **n. repatriions**) to repatriate (s.o.); *s.m.* -**ement,** repatriation.

repêch|er [rəpeʃe], *v.tr.* (*a*) to fish (sth.) up (again), out (again); (*b*) to rescue; *F:* to fish out (drowning man); (*c*) *Sch:* **r. un candidat,** to give a candidate a second chance (at an oral exam); *F:* **les collés en juin peuvent se r. en octobre,** the June failures can have a second chance in October; **r. un ami dans l'embarras,** to rescue a friend in difficulties; *s.m.* -**age.**

repenser [rəpɑ̃se]. **1.** *v.i.* to think again (à, about) (sth.); **j'y repenserai,** I'll think it over; **je n'y ai pas repensé,** I didn't give it another thought. **2.** *v.tr.* **r. un problème,** to reconsider a question.

repentir (se) [sərəpɑ̃tiːr]. **I.** *v.pr.* (*conj. like* MEN-TIR) to repent; **se r. de qch.,** to be sorry for sth. **II. repentir,** *s.m.* repentance; remorse.

répercussion [repɛrkysjɔ̃], *s.f.* repercussion; reverberation.

répercuter [repɛrkyte], *v.tr.* **1.** to reverberate, reflect back (sound); to reflect (light, heat). **2.** **la taxe se répercutera sur les consommateurs,** the tax will be passed on to the consumers.

repère [rəpɛːr], *s.m.* **point de r.,** guide mark; landmark.

repér|er [repere], *v.tr.* (**je repère; je repérerai**) to locate (fault, etc.); *Av:* to identify (aircraft); *Mil:* to locate (target); *F:* to spot (gun, aircraft, etc.); to spot, pick out; **r. qn dans la foule,** to pick s.o. out in the crowd; *Rac:* **r. les gagnants,** to pick the winners; *s.m.* -**age.**

répertoire [repɛrtwaːr], *s.m.* **1.** list, catalogue; **r. d'adresses,** (i) directory; (ii) address-book. **2.** repertory, repository; **c'est un vrai r. d'anec-dotes,** he's a perfect mine of stories. **3.** *Th:* repertoire.

répét|er [repete], *v.tr.* (**je répète; je répéterai**) (*a*) to repeat; to say, do, (sth.) (over) again; (*b*) *Th:* to rehearse.

se répéter. 1. (*of pers.*) to repeat oneself. **2.** (*of event*) to recur, to happen again; **cela ne se répétera pas,** it won't happen again.

répétition [repetisjɔ̃], *s.f.* **1.** (*a*) repetition (of word, action, etc.); **fusil à r.,** repeating rifle; **montre à r.,** repeater (watch); (*b*) reproduction, replica. **2.** *Th:* rehearsal (of play); (band, choral) practice.

repeupl|er [rəpœple], *v.tr.* to repeople, to repopulate (country); to restock (river, pond); to replant (forest); **la ville se repeuple,** the town's population is on the increase again; *s.m.* -**ement.**

repiqu|er [rəpike], *v.tr.* to prick, pierce (sth.) again; to (machine-)stitch (sth.) again; *Hort:* to plant out, prick out (seedlings); **plant à r.,** bedding-plant; *s.m.* -**age,** *Hort:* pricking out, planting out (of seedlings).

répit [repi], *s.m.* respite; breathing space.

replac|er [rǝplase], *v.tr.* (n. **replaçons**) **1.** to replace; to put (sth.) back in its place; to re-invest (money). **2. r. qn,** to find a new job for s.o.; (*of employee*) **se r.,** to find a new job; *s.m.* **-ement.**

replet, -ète [rǝplɛ, -ɛt], *a.* stoutish, *F:* podgy.

repli [rǝpli], *s.m.* **1.** fold, crease. **2.** winding, bend, meander; coil (of rope, serpent, river). **3.** (*a*) *Mil:* withdrawal; (*b*) *Fin:* recession; drop (in share prices).

replier [rǝplije], *v.tr.* **1.** to fold up (again); to coil (sth.) up; to tuck in (edge); **r. un parapluie,** to close an umbrella. **2.** to withdraw (troops, outposts).

se replier. 1. (*a*) (*of object*) to fold up, turn back, coil up; (*b*) (*of stream, path*) to wind, turn, bend. **2. se r. sur soi-même,** to retire within oneself. **3.** *Mil:* to withdraw.

réplique [replik], *s.f.* **1.** retort, rejoinder; **avoir la r. prompte,** to be ready with an answer. **2.** *Th:* cue. **3.** *Art:* replica.

répliquer [replike], *v.i.* to retort; to answer back.

répondant [repɔ̃dɑ̃], *s.m.* **1.** *Ecc:* server (at mass). **2.** *Jur:* surety, guarantor.

répondre [repɔ̃:dr]. **1.** *v.tr.* to answer; *Ecc:* **r. la messe,** to make the responses (at mass). **2.** *v.ind.tr.* **r. à une question,** to answer, to reply to, a question; **r. à une demande,** to comply with a request; **r. à un besoin,** to answer a purpose, to meet a need; **ne pas r. à l'attente,** to fall short of expectation. **3.** *v.i.* **r. de qn,** to answer for s.o.; *F:* **je vous en réponds!** you bet! rather!

répons [repɔ̃], *s.m. Ecc:* response.

réponse [repɔ̃:s], *s.f.* (*a*) answer, reply; (*b*) response (to an appeal); (*c*) responsiveness, response (to stimulus).

reportage [rǝpɔrta:ʒ], *s.m. Journ:* (newspaper) report(ing); *Rad:* running commentary (on match, public event); (press, radio, television) report.

reporter[1] [rǝpɔrte], *v.tr.* **1.** to take back; **r. un livre à qn,** to take a book back to s.o. **2.** (*a*) **r. qch. à plus tard,** to postpone sth. until later; (*b*) *Com:* to carry forward (total).

se reporter à qch., to refer to sth.

reporter[2] [rǝpɔrtɛ:r], *s.m.* (press, etc.) reporter.

repos [rǝpo], *s.m.* **1.** (*a*) rest, repose; **en r.,** at rest; (*b*) pause, rest. **2.** peace, tranquillity (*esp.* of mind); **valeur de tout r.,** gilt-edged security.

repos|er [rǝpoze]. **1.** *v.tr.* to put (sth.) back; to replace (sth.). **2.** *v.tr.* **r. ses regards sur qch.,** to let one's glance rest on sth.; **r. sa tête sur un coussin,** to rest one's head on a cushion; **r. l'esprit,** to rest the mind. **3.** *v.i.* to lie, to rest; **le commerce repose sur le crédit,** trade is based on credit; **bruit qui ne repose sur rien,** groundless report; *a.* **-ant,** restful (holiday); refreshing (sleep).

se reposer. 1. to alight, settle, again; **l'oiseau se reposa sur la branche,** the bird settled on the bough again. **2.** (*a*) to rest; **travailler sans se r.** to work without resting; (*b*) **se r. sur qn,** to rely (up)on s.o.

repouss|er [rǝpuse]. **1.** *v.tr.* (*a*) to push back, thrust aside, repulse; **r. les volets,** to push back the shutters; **r. une accusation,** to deny a charge; **r. une mesure,** to reject a measure; (*b* to be repellent to (s.o.); to repel. **2.** (*a*) *v.tr.* (*o tree, plant, etc.*) to throw out (branches shoots) again; (*b*) *v.i.* (*of tree, plant, etc.*) t shoot (up) again; *a.* **-ant,** repulsive, repellen loathsome; **être d'une laideur repoussante, t** be repulsively ugly.

répréhensible [repreɑ̃sibl], *a.* reprehensibl *adv.* **-ment.**

reprendre [rǝprɑ̃:dr], *v.* (*conj. like* PRENDRE) *v.tr.* (*a*) to take again, retake, recapture (tow prisoner); (*b*) **r. sa place,** to resume one's sea **r. du pain,** to take, have, some more bread; **vous reprendrai en passant,** I'll pick you u again as I go by; **r. froid,** to catch cold agai (*c*) to take back (a gift); *Com:* **r. des invendu** to take back unsold articles, copies; **nos a ticles ne sont ni repris ni échangés,** our goo cannot be returned or exchanged; (*d*) resume, take up again; **r. le travail,** to resum work, go back to work; **r. des forces,** to rega strength; *abs.* **oui madame, reprit-il,** ye madam, he replied; (*e*) to reprove, admonis to find fault with (s.o., sth.). **2.** *v.i.* (*a*) recommence, return; **le froid a repris,** the co weather has set in again; **les affaires repre nent,** business is improving; *Aut:* (*of engine*) (**vivement**), to pick up (smartly); (*b*) (*of liqui* to freeze, set, again.

se reprendre. 1. to recover oneself, to p oneself together. **2.** to correct oneself speaking. **3. s'y r. à plusieurs fois,** to ma several attempts, to have several goes (at st at doing sth.).

représailles [rǝpreza:j], *s.f.pl.* reprisa retaliation; **user de r.,** to retaliate (**envers, o**

représent|er [rǝprezɑ̃te], *v.tr.* **1.** to present (st again; to re-introduce (s.o.). **2.** to represent; symbolize; (*a*) to depict, portray; **table représentant un moulin,** picture of a m **représentez-vous mon étonnement,** imagi picture, my astonishment; (*b*) to represe stand for, act for (s.o.); *Com: etc:* n **représentons la maison X et Cie,** we are age for, we represent, Messrs. X & Co.; *Jur:* lawyer) to appear for (s.o.). **3.** *Th:* (*a*) to p form, act (a play); (*b*) to act, to take (a part) **r. qch. à qn,** to represent, point out, sth. to s. *s.* **-ant, -ante,** representative, official; *C* agent; representative; (commercial) travell *a.* **-atif, -ative,** representative (body, et *s.f.* -ation, (*a*) (i) representation; (ii) *Com:* agency; (*b*) *Th:* performance; (*c*) protest.

e représenter. 1. (*of pers.*) to offer oneself again as a candidate; to reappear, to turn up again; (*of occasion*) to recur. 2. se r. comme officier, to represent oneself as an officer.

pressif, -ive [represif, -i:v], *a.* repressive (law, etc.).

pression [represjɔ̃], *s.f.* repression.

primande [reprimɑ̃:d], *s.f.* reprimand, reproof.

primandler [reprimɑ̃de], *v.tr.* to reprimand, reprove; *a.* -able, blameworthy.

primer [reprime], *v.tr.* to repress.

pris [rəpri]. 1. *s.m.* r. de justice, habitual offender, *F:* old lag. 2. *a. Com:* emballage non r., non-returnable packing.

prise [rəpri:z], *s.f.* 1. retaking, recapture. 2. (*a*) resumption, renewal; r. de travail, return to work; r. du froid, renewal of the cold spell; (*b*) à plusieurs reprises, on several occasions. 3. darn; point de r., darning stitch. 4. *Aut:* (car, etc., taken in) part exchange, *F:* trade-in.

priser [rəprize], *v.tr.* to mend, darn.

probateur, -trice [reprɔbatœ:r, -tris], *a.* reproachful; reproving; regard r., reproachful look.

probation [reprɔbasjɔ̃], *s.f.* reprobation, (severe) disapproval.

proche [rəprɔʃ], *s.m.* reproach; vie sans r., blameless life.

procher [rəprɔʃe], *v.tr.* 1. to reproach; je n'ai rien à me r., I have nothing to blame myself for. 2. r. un plaisir à qn, to grudge s.o. a pleasure.

producteur, -trice [rəprɔdyktœ:r, -tris]. 1. *a.* reproductive (organ). 2. *s.m.* animal kept for breeding purposes; breeder; r. d'élite, pedigree sire.

production [rəprɔdyksjɔ̃], *s.f.* 1. (*a*) reproduction; animaux de r., breeding stock; (*b*) reproduction, duplication (of documents, etc.). 2. copy, reproduction.

produire [rəprɔdɥi:r], *v.tr.* (*conj. like* CON-DUIRE) to reproduce; to duplicate, copy.

reproduire. 1. to recur; to happen again. 2. to reproduce, breed, multiply.

tile [reptil], *s.m.* reptile.

u [rəpy], *a.* satiated, full.

publicain, -aine [repyblikɛ̃, -ɛn], *a. & s.* republican.

publique [repyblik], *s.f.* (*a*) republic; la R. française, the French Republic; (*b*) community; la r. des lettres, the world of letters.

udiler [repydje], *v.tr.* (*pr.sub. & p.d.* n. épudiions) 1. to repudiate (wife, opinion). 2. to renounce (succession); *s.f.* -ation.

ugnance [repyɲɑ̃:s], *s.f.* 1. repugnance; (*a*) dislike (pour, à, to, of, for); aversion; (*b*) loathing (pour, à, of, for). 2. r. à faire qch., reluctance to do sth.

répugnler [repyɲe], *v.i.* 1. (*of pers.*) r. à qch., to feel repugnance to sth.; r. à faire qch., to feel reluctant to do sth. 2. r. à qn, to be repugnant to s.o.; *impers.* il me répugne de le faire, I am reluctant to do it, I shrink from doing it; *a.* -ant, repugnant, loathsome; disgusting.

répulsion [repylsjɔ̃], *s.f.* repulsion.

réputation [repytasjɔ̃], *s.f.* reputation, repute; jouir d'une bonne r., to have a good reputation; se faire une r., to make a name for oneself; perdre qn de r., to ruin s.o.'s character, s.o.'s good name.

réputé [repyte], *a.* well-known, famous; of high reputation.

requête [rəkɛt], *s.f.* request, petition; je viens à la r. de . . ., I have come at the request of . . ..

requiem [rəkɥi(j)ɛm], *s.m. Ecc:* prayer for the dead; (messe de) r., requiem (mass).

requin [rəkɛ̃], *s.m.* 1. *Ich:* shark; peau de r., shagreen. 2. *F:* shark, swindler.

requis [rəki], *a.* required, necessary; les qualités requises pour ce poste, the requisite qualities for this post; avec tout le soin r., with all due care.

réquisition [rekizisjɔ̃], *s.f.* (*a*) requisitioning, commandeering; (*b*) requisition.

réquisitionIner [rekizisjɔne], *v.tr.* to requisition; to commandeer (provisions, stores); *s.m.* -nement, requisitioning.

rescapé, -ée [rɛskape], *a. & s.* (person) rescued; survivor (of disaster).

réseau, -eaux [rezo], *s.m.* (*a*) network, system (of roads, etc.); r. fluvial, river system; (*b*) r. (électrique) national, national grid system; r. de distribution, distribution network; r. d'éclairage, d'énergie, lighting, power-supply, system; (*c*) *P.T.T:* r. télégraphique, téléphonique, telegraph, telephone, system; r. automatique, automatic, dial, (telephone) system; (*d*) r. d'espionnage, spy ring.

réserve [rezɛrv], *s.f.* 1. reserve, reservation; en r., in reserve; sous toutes réserves, without committing oneself. 2. (*a*) sous (la) r. de qch., subject to sth.; (*b*) reserve, caution (in speech, conduct, etc.). 3. (*a*) reserve (of provisions, water, energy); *pl.* reserves (of ore, petroleum, etc.); (*b*) *Mil:* officier de r., reserve officer; r. stratégique, strategic reserve; (*c*) *Fin:* réserves bancaires, bank reserves; mettre de l'argent en r., to put money by. 4. *Z: Biol:* r. naturelle, nature reserve; r. zoologique, wild life sanctuary.

réservler [rezɛrve], *v.tr.* (*a*) to reserve; to save up; to keep back; r. une place à qn, to reserve, keep, a seat for s.o.; tous droits réservés, all rights reserved; *P.N:* pêche réservée, private fishing; (*b*) to set apart, earmark, (money for a purpose); *s.f.* -**ation**; *s.m.* -**iste**, *Mil:* reservist.

se réserver pour qch., to reserve oneself, save oneself, hold back, wait, for sth.; **je me réserve,** I shall wait and see.

réservoir [rezɛrvwaːr], *s.m.* 1. reservoir. 2. tank, cistern.

résidence [rezidãːs], *s.f.* (*a*) residence; **lieu de r.,** place of residence; **en r. surveillée,** under house arrest; (*b*) home; **r. secondaire,** weekend cottage; holiday home.

résid|er [rezide], *v.i.* 1. to reside, dwell, live (**à, dans,** at, in). 2. **la difficulté réside en ceci,** the difficulty lies in this; **la souveraineté réside dans le peuple,** sovereign power resides in the people; *s.* -**ent,** -**ente,** resident; *a.* -**entiel, -entielle,** residential; **quartier r.,** residential district.

résidu [rezidy], *s.m.* residue; **résidus urbains,** town refuse.

résigné [reziɲe], *a.* resigned (**à,** to); meek, uncomplaining.

résign|er [reziɲe], *v.tr.* to resign, to give (sth.) up; **r. sa charge,** to relinquish one's appointment; to resign; **r. le pouvoir,** to lay down office; *s.f.* -**ation.**

se résigner à qch., to resign oneself to sth.

résine [rezin], *s.f.* resin.

résineux, -euse [rezinø, -øːz]. 1. *a.* resinous. 2. *s.m.pl.* **les r.,** conifers.

résistance [rezistãːs], *s.f.* 1. (*a*) resistance, opposition; (*b*) *Hist:* **la R.,** the Resistance (movement). 2. (*a*) strength, toughness; (*b*) staying power, stamina, endurance; **pièce de r.,** principal feature (of entertainment, etc.); *Cu:* **plat de r.,** main course.

résist|er [reziste], *v.ind.tr.* to resist; (*a*) **r. à qn,** to resist s.o., to offer resistance to s.o.; (*b*) **r. à qch.,** to withstand sth.; to hold out against (attack; temptation; pain); *a.* -**ant,** resistant, strong, tough; fast (colour); immune to infection); hard-wearing.

résolu [rezɔly], *a.* resolute, determined (person); *adv.* -**ment.**

résolution [rezɔlysjõ], *s.f.* 1. (*a*) solution (of problem); (*b*) termination (of agreement). 2. resolution, determination; (*a*) resolve; **prendre la r. de faire qch.,** to resolve, determine, to do sth.; (*b*) resoluteness; **manquer de r.,** to lack determination; (*c*) **adopter une r.,** to adopt a resolution.

résonance [rezɔnãːs], *s.f.* resonance.

résonner [rezɔne], *v.i.* to resound.

résoudre [rezudr], *v.tr.* (*pr.p.* **résolvant;** *p.p.* (i) **résolu,** (ii) *Ph:* **résous, -oute;** *pr.ind.* **je résous**) 1. (*a*) **r. qch. en qch.,** to resolve, dissolve, break up, sth. into sth.; (*b*) *Jur:* to annul, terminate (contract, etc.). 2. to resolve, clear up (difficulty); to solve; to settle (problem,

question). 3. **r. qn à faire qch.,** to persuade s.o to do sth.; **r. de partir,** to decide to go.

se résoudre à faire qch., to make up one's min to do sth.

respect [rɛspɛ], *s.m.* respect, regard; **r. de so** self-respect; **tenir qn en r.,** to keep s.o. at arm length, to hold s.o. in check; **sauf votre r.,** wit all due deference (to you); **veuillez bie présenter mes respects à Madame,** please giv my regards to your wife.

respect|er [rɛspɛkte], *v.tr.* to respect, hav regard for (s.o., sth.); **r. la loi, un contrat,** ↑ comply with the law, a contract; *s.f.* -**abilit** respectability; *a.* -**able,** respectable, worthy respect; fairly large, reasonably large (roon sum of money); *adv.* -**ablement.**

respect|if, -ive [rɛspɛktif, -iːv], *a.* respectiv **nos demeures respectives,** our respecti homes; *adv.* -**ivement.**

respectueu|x, -euse [rɛspɛktɥø, -øːz], respectful; dutiful (feelings, conduct); *Cor* **veuillez agréer mes sentiments r.,** you sincerely; *adv.* -**sement.**

respir|er [rɛspire]. 1. *v.i.* to breathe; **r. long ment,** to draw a deep breath; **laissez-moi** give me time to breathe. 2. *v.tr.* (*a*) to breat (in); to inhale; **aller r. un peu d'air,** to go out a breather; (*b*) **r. la vengeance,** to breathe (o vengeance); *s.m.* -**ateur,** *Mil: Med:* respirat mask; *s.f.* -**ation,** respiration, breathing; -**atoire,** respiratory (organ, etc.); **masque** oxygen mask.

resplendissant [rɛsplãdisã], *a.* resplende shining; glittering; **visage r. de santé,** f glowing with health.

respons|able [rɛspõsabl], *a.* responsi answerable, accountable (**envers,** to; **dev** before); **rendre qn r. de qch.,** to blame s.o. sth.; *s.f.* -**abilité,** responsibility.

ressac [rəsak], *s.m.* *Nau:* 1. undertow. 2. sur breakers.

ressaisir [rəseziːr], *v.tr.* to seize again; recapture.

se ressaisir, to regain one's self-control; to ↑ oneself together.

ressembl|er [rəsãble], *v.ind.tr.* **r. à qn,** to res ble, to be like, s.o.; **cela ne vous ressemble du tout,** it isn't a bit like you; *s.f.* -**a** resemblance, likeness; *a.* -**ant, -ante,** ↑ alike.

se ressembler, to be (a)like; **ils se ressemb comme deux gouttes d'eau,** they're as lik two peas.

ressent|ir [rəsãtiːr], *v.tr.* (*conj. like* MENTIR to feel (pain, joy, etc.); (*b*) to feel, experie (shock, etc.); *s.m.* -**iment,** res ment.

se ressentir d'un accident, d'une maladie, to the effects of an accident, an illness.

resserr|er [rəsere], *v.tr.* **1.** to contract, confine, shrink; to close up. **2.** to tie (up) again; to tighten; **r. les liens de l'amitié,** to draw the bonds of friendship closer; *s.m.* **-ement,** contraction, constriction; narrowness (of mind); heaviness (of heart).
se resserrer, to contract, shrink; (*of knot*) to become tighter.
ressort [rəsɔːr], *s.m.* **1.** (*a*) elasticity, springiness; (*b*) spring; **grand r.,** mainspring; **l'intérêt est un puissant r.,** self-interest is a powerful motive. **2.** *Jur:* (*a*) province, scope, competence; (*b*) **en dernier r.,** in the last resort.
ressort|ir [rəsɔrtiːr], *v.i.* (*conj. like* MENTIR, *except in* 3) **1.** (*a*) (*aux.* **être**) to come, go, out again; (*b*) *v.tr.* to bring out again. **2.** (*aux.* **être**) (*a*) to stand out, to be evident; **faire r. un fait,** to emphasize a fact; (*b*) to result, follow (**de, from**); **de ces faits il ressort que . . .,** from these facts it emerges that . . . .. **3.** (*aux.* **avoir**) (*pr.p.* **ressortissant;** *pr.ind.* **il ressortit;** *p.d.* **il ressortissait**) **r. à qn, à qch.,** to be under the jurisdiction of, to be amenable to a (country); *s.m.* **-issant,** national of a country.
ressource [rəsurs], *s.f.* **1.** (*a*) resource, resourcefulness; (*b*) **être ruiné sans r.,** to be irretrievably ruined. **2.** expedient, shift; **avoir mille ressources,** to be very resourceful; **en dernière r.,** in the last resort. **3.** *pl.* resources, means. **4.** *Av:* flattening out (from dive).
ressusciter [resysite]. **1.** *v.tr.* (*a*) to resuscitate (s.o.); to restore (s.o.) to life; (*b*) to revive (s.o.). **2.** *v.i.* to resuscitate, revive.
restant, -ante [rɛstɑ̃, ɑ̃ːt]. **1.** *a.* (*a*) remaining, left; (*b*) **poste restante,** poste restante. **2.** *s.m.* remainder, rest.
restaurant [rɛstɔrɑ̃], *s.m.* restaurant.
restaur|er [rɛstɔre], *v.tr.* (*a*) to restore (a building, finances, one's health, etc.); to re-establish (discipline, etc.); (*b*) to refresh (s.o.); **nourriture qui restaure,** satisfying food; *s.m.* **-ateur,** (i) restorer (of buildings, pictures, etc.); (ii) restaurant proprietor, manager; *s.f.* **-ation,** restoration, restoring (of building, statue, etc.; of dynasty; of finances, etc.); *Hist:* **la R.,** the Restoration.
restaurer, to take refreshment, to have sth. to eat.
reste [rɛst], *s.m.* **1.** rest, remainder, remains; **le r. de la vie,** the rest of one's life; **être en r.,** to be behindhand; to lag behind (in payments, etc.); **et le r.,** and so on; *adj.phr.* **de r.,** (to) spare, over and above; *adv.phr.* **au r., du r.,** besides, moreover. **2.** *pl.* (*a*) remnants, remains, leavings, scraps, left-overs (of a meal, etc.); (*b*) **restes mortels,** mortal remains.
rester [rɛste], *v.i.* (*aux.* **être**) **1.** to remain, to be left; **il me reste cinq francs,** I have five francs left; (**il**) **reste à savoir,** it remains to be seen. **2.**
(*a*) to stay, remain (behind); **r. au lit,** to stay in bed; **r. à travailler,** to stay (behind) to work; **en r. là,** to stop at that point; (*b*) **r. tranquille,** to keep still. **3.** to stay (in hotel, etc.); **où restez-vous?** where are you staying? **r. à Paris,** to stay in Paris (for a time).
restitu|er [rɛstitɥe], *v.tr.* **1.** (*a*) to restore (building, text); (*b*) *Jur:* to reinstate, rehabilitate (s.o.). **2.** to restore; to return, to hand (sth.) back; to make restitution of (sth.); *s.f.* **-tion,** restoration; restitution.
restreindre [rɛstrɛ̃ːdr], *v.tr.* (*conj. like* ATTEINDRE) to restrict; to curtail (expenses); **r. la production,** to cut down production.
se restreindre. 1. to cut down expenses; to retrench. **2.** to limit oneself (to essentials).
restreint [rɛstrɛ̃], *a.* restricted, limited (meaning, edition); confined (space).
restrictif, -ive [rɛstriktif, -iːv], *a.* restrictive (clause).
restriction [rɛstriksjɔ̃], *s.f.* restriction, limitation; **r. mentale,** mental reservation; **sans r.,** unreservedly.
résul|ter [rezylte], *v.i.* (*used only in the third pers. & pr.p.; aux. usu.* **être**) to result, follow; **il en est résulté beaucoup de mal,** much harm resulted, came, from this; *a.* **-tant,** resultant; consequent (**de,** upon); *s.m.* **-tat,** result, outcome.
résumé [rezyme], *s.m.* summary, résumé; abridged version; *adv.phr.* **en r.,** in short; to sum up.
résumer [rezyme], *v.tr.* to summarize; to sum up.
résurrection [rezyrɛksjɔ̃], *s.f.* **1.** resurrection (of the dead). **2.** revival, resurrection (of the arts, etc.).
rétabl|ir [retabliːr], *v.tr.* to re-establish, restore; **r. l'ordre,** to restore (public) order; **r. sa fortune,** to retrieve one's fortune; *s.m.* **-issement,** re-establishment; restoration (of order, of peace; of health, fortune).
se rétablir. 1. (*a*) to recover; to get well again; (*b*) **l'ordre se rétablit,** order is being restored. **2.** to re-establish oneself in s.o.'s favour.
retard [rətaːr], *s.m.* delay, slowness; backwardness (of child, harvest); **le train a du r.,** the train is late; **en r.,** late, behindhand; **votre montre a dix minutes de r.,** your watch is ten minutes slow.
retard|er [rətarde]. **1.** *v.tr.* (*a*) to retard, delay, to hold (s.o.) up; to make (s.o.) late; (*b*) to delay, put off (an event); (*c*) **r. la pendule,** to put back the clock. **2.** *v.i.* to be late, slow, behindhand; **ma montre retarde,** my watch is slow; **il retarde sur son siècle,** he's behind the times; *s.* **-ataire,** late-comer; laggard, *F:* slowcoach; *s.m.* **-ement,** retardment, retarding; delay, putting off; **bombe à r.,** time-bomb.

retenir [rətniːr], *v.tr.* (*conj. like* TENIR) **1.** (*a*) to hold (s.o., sth.) back; to detain; **r. l'attention,** to hold the attention; **r. qn à dîner,** to keep s.o. to dinner; **r. qn en otage,** to hold s.o. as hostage; *Nau:* **retenu par la marée,** tidebound; (*b*) to hold (sth.) in position; to secure (sth.). **2.** to retain; (*a*) **r. une somme sur le salaire de qn;** to keep so much back from s.o.'s wages; **r. qch. par cœur,** to remember sth. by heart; *Com:* **r. l'escompte,** to deduct the discount; (*b*) to engage (a servant); **r. des chambres (à un hôtel),** to book rooms (at a hotel), make (hotel) reservations. **3.** to restrain, check (anger, etc.); **r. un cri,** to stifle a cry; **r. son souffle,** to hold one's breath.
se retenir. 1. se r. à qch., to cling to sth. **2.** to restrain, control, oneself; to hold oneself in; **se r. de faire qch.,** to refrain from doing sth.
retentir [rətɑ̃tiːr], *v.i.* to (re)sound, echo, ring, reverberate; **un klaxon retentit,** a hooter sounded; *a.* **-issant,** resounding (voice), loud (noise); *s.m.* **-issement,** repercussions (of an event); **avoir peu de r.,** to pass almost unnoticed.
retenue [rət(ə)ny], *s.f.* **1.** (*a*) deduction, stoppage, docking (of pay, etc.); (*b*) sum kept back, stoppage. **2.** *Sch:* detention. **3.** reserve, discretion (of conduct).
réticence [retisɑ̃ːs], *s.f.* reticence, reserve.
rétif, -ive [retif, -iːv], *a.* restive, stubborn.
retiré [rətire], *a.* solitary, remote (place); **vivre r.,** to live in seclusion.
retirer [rətire], *v.tr.* **1.** (*a*) to pull out; to withdraw (sth.); **r. la clef de la serrure,** to take the key out of the lock; **r. ses bagages de la consigne,** to check out one's luggage from the cloakroom; **r. ses chaussures,** to take off one's shoes; (*b*) **r. un profit de qch.,** to derive a profit from sth. **2.** **r. qch. à qn,** to withdraw sth. from s.o.; to take sth. back from s.o.; **r. sa main,** to draw one's hand away; **r. le permis de conduire à qn,** to disqualify s.o. from driving; **r. sa parole,** to take back one's word, *F:* to back out.
se retirer. 1. to retire, withdraw. **2.** (*of waters*) to subside; (*of sea*) to recede.
retomber [rətɔ̃be], *v.i.* (*aux. usu.* être) **1.** to fall (down) again; **r. sur ses pieds,** to land on one's feet (again); **r. dans le chaos,** to fall back into chaos; **r. malade,** to fall ill again. **2.** to fall (back); **r. sur sa chaise,** to sink back into one's chair; **faire r. la faute sur qn,** to lay the blame on s.o. **3.** to hang down; **ses cheveux lui retombent dans le dos,** her hair hangs down her back.
retouche [rətuʃ], *s.f.* slight alteration (à, in, to) (dress, etc.); retouching, touching up (of picture, photograph, etc.).
retoucher [rətuʃe], *v.tr.* to retouch, touch up (picture, photograph); to alter (dress); **n'y**

retouchez pas, don't alter it, leave it alone.
retour [rətuːr], *s.m.* **1.** (*a*) twisting, winding; **tours et retours,** twists and turns; (*b*) turn, vicissitude, reversal (of fortune, opinion, etc.); **r. de conscience,** qualms of conscience; (*c*) recurrence (of attack, of illness). **2.** return; **dès mon r.,** as soon as I'm back; **voyage de r.,** return journey; **être de r.,** to be back (home); **par r. du courrier,** by return of post; **être sur le r.,** to be past middle age; **être perdu sans r.,** to be irretrievably lost; *Cin:* **r. en arrière,** flashback; *Aut:* **avoir des retours,** to backfire. **3.** return (for a kindness, service); **payer qch. qn, de r.,** to requite sth., s.o.
retourner [rəturne]. **1.** *v.tr.* (*a*) to turn (sth.) in side out; (*b*) to turn (sth.) over; **r. une carte,** to turn up a card; *F:* **cela m'a retourné les sangs,** it gave me quite a turn; (*c*) to turn (sth.) round; **r. la tête,** to turn one's head; **r. une situation,** to reverse a situation. **2.** *v.tr.* **r. qch. à qn,** to return sth. to s.o. **3.** *v.i.* (*aux.* être) (*a*) to return; to go back; (*b*) (*of mistake, crime, etc.*) **r. sur qn,** to recoil upon s.o. **4.** *impers.* **de quoi retourne-t-il?** *F:* what's it all about?
se retourner, (*a*) to turn (round); to turn over; **je sentais mon estomac se r.,** I felt my stomach heave; *F:* **avoir le temps de se r.,** to have time to look round; (*b*) to look round, to look back; **se r. sur qn,** to turn round and stare at s.o.; (*c*) **ils se retournèrent tous deux contre moi,** they both rounded on me; (*d*) *F:* **s'en retourner,** to return, go back.
rétracter [retrakte], *v.tr.* **1.** to retract, to draw in (claws). **2.** to withdraw; to go back on (one word, opinion).
se rétracter. 1. (*of materials*) to shrink. **2.** (*a*) to retract; (*b*) to withdraw a charge.
retrait [rətrɛ], *s.m.* **1.** shrinkage, shrinking, contraction (of wood, metal, cement, etc.). **2.** (*a*) withdrawal (of order); cancelling (of licence); (*b*) redemption, repurchase (of estate, etc.); recess (in wall); *adv.phr.* **en r.,** recess (shelves, etc.); **maison en r.,** house set back (from the road).
retraite [rətrɛt], *s.f.* **1.** *Mil:* retreat, retirement. **2.** *Mil:* tattoo; **battre la r.,** to beat, sound, the tattoo; **r. aux flambeaux,** torchlight tattoo. (*a*) retirement; **caisse de r.,** pension fund; **r. vieillesse,** old-age pension; **prendre sa r.,** retire (on a pension); (*b*) **vivre dans la r.,** to live in retirement; **maison de r.** = old people's home. **4.** (*a*) retreat; place of retirement; shelter; refuge; lair.
retraité, -ée [rətrete], *s.* pensioner; pers. retired on a pension.
retraiter [rətrete], *v.tr.* to pension (s.o.) (off); retire (s.o.); to place (officer) on the retired list.
retrancher [rətrɑ̃ʃe], *v.tr.* (*a*) **r. qch. de qch.,** cut off sth. from sth.; **r. un passage d'un livre,**

to strike a passage out of a book; (b) **se r. tout luxe,** to cut out all luxuries; *s.m.* **-ement.**

rétréc|ir [retresi:r], *v.i. & pr.* to contract; to grow narrow; (*of garment*) to shrink; *s.m.* **-issement,** narrowing; contracting; contraction; shrinking.

rétribuer [retribɥe], *v.tr.* to pay (employee, for a service); **travail rétribué,** paid work.

rétribution [retribysjɔ̃], *s.f.* remuneration; salary.

rétroactif, -ive [retrɔaktif, -i:v], *a.* retrospective; backdated.

rétrograde [retrɔgrad], *a.* retrograde, backward, reversed (motion).

rétrograder [retrɔgrade]. 1. *v.i.* to retrogress; to go back; *Mil:* to retreat; *Aut: etc:* to change down, *N.Am:* to shift down. 2. *v.tr.* to reduce to a lower rank.

rétrospect|if, -ive [retrɔspɛktif, -i:v], *a.* retrospective; **vue rétrospective,** *s.f.* **rétrospective,** retrospect; *Art:* *s.f.* **retrospective,** retrospective (exhibition); *adv.* **-ivement.**

retrousser [rətruse], *v.tr.* to turn up, roll up (sleeves, trousers); to tuck up (skirt); to twist up (moustache); **nez retroussé,** tip-tilted, snub, nose.

retrouver [rətruve], *v.tr.* (a) to find (s.o., sth.) (again); to meet (with) (s.o., sth.) again; **r. sa santé, ses forces,** to recover one's health, strength; (b) **aller r. qn,** to go and join s.o.; to go and see s.o.

se retrouver. 1. **se r. dans la même position,** to find oneself, to be, in the same position again; **quand je me retrouve à Paris . . .,** when I'm back in Paris . . .. 2. to find one's bearings; **je ne puis m'y r.!** I can't make it out! 3. to recover oneself; *F:* **s'y r.,** to cover expenses, to break even. 4. to meet again.

rétroviseur [retrɔvizœ:r], *s.m. Aut:* driving mirror, rear-view mirror, *N.Am:* rear-vision mirror.

réunion [reynjɔ̃], *s.f.* reunion. 1. bringing together, reuniting. 2. (a) coming together; **salle de r.,** assembly room; (b) assembly, gathering, meeting; **r. publique,** public meeting; (c) social gathering, party.

réunir [reyni:r], *v.tr.* to (re)unite; to join together; **r. le comité,** to call a committee meeting.

se réunir, (a) to meet; to gather together; (b) to join together; *Com:* to amalgamate; to unite.

réussi [reysi], *a.* successful, well performed, well done; **mal r.,** unsuccessful, spoilt (photograph, etc.).

réussir [reysi:r], 1. *v.i.* (a) to turn out (well, badly); **cela lui a mal réussi,** it turned out badly for him; (b) **r. dans qch.,** to succeed in sth.; (c) **la pièce a réussi,** the play is a success. 2. *v.tr.* to

make a success of (sth.); **X a réussi un but magnifique,** X scored a fine goal.

réussite [reysit], *s.f.* 1. issue, result, upshot; **bonne, mauvaise, r.,** successful, unfortunate, outcome. 2. success; **c'est une r.,** it's a success. 3. *Cards:* patience.

revaloir [rəvalwa:r], *v.tr.* (*conj. like* VALOIR, *used chiefly in the fu.*) to return, pay back, in kind; **je vous revaudrai cela!** (i) I'll get even with you! (ii) I'll pay you back!

revaloris|er [rəvalɔrize], *v.tr.* 1. (a) *Fin:* to revalue, revalorize (a currency); (b) to give a new value to (an idea, a theory). 2. to stabilize (prices) at a higher level; *s.f.* **-ation.**

revanche [rəvɑ̃:ʃ], *s.f.* 1. revenge; **prendre sa r. sur qn,** to get even with s.o.; **jouer la r.,** to play the return game. 2. requital; return service; **en r.,** (i) in return, in compensation; (ii) on the other hand.

rêvass|er [rɛvase], *v.i.* to muse; to day-dream; *s.f.* **-erie,** day-dreaming; daydream.

rêve [rɛ:v], *s.m.* 1. dream; **faire un r.,** to (have a) dream. 2. day-dream; **caresser un r.,** to cherish a dream; **c'est le r.!** it's ideal!

revêche [rəvɛʃ], *a.* 1. harsh, rough (cloth, wine). 2. bad-tempered, cantankerous (person); sour (face).

réveil [revɛ:j], *s.m.* 1. (a) waking, awakening; (b) *Mil:* **sonner le r.,** to sound reveille. 2. alarm (clock).

réveille-matin [revɛjmatɛ̃], *s.m.inv.* alarm (clock).

réveiller [reveje], *v.tr.* 1. to awake (s.o.); to wake (s.o.) up; to rouse (s.o.). 2. to awaken, stir up, rouse (feelings, memories).

se réveiller. 1. (*of pers.*) to wake (up). 2. (*of feelings*) to be awakened, roused, stirred up.

réveillon [revɛjɔ̃], *s.m.* midnight supper (*esp.* after midnight mass on Christmas Eve and New Year's Eve).

réveillonner [revɛjɔne], *v.i.* to see Christmas, the New Year, in.

révél|er [revele], *v.tr.* (**je révèle; je révélerai**) (a) to reveal, disclose; *F:* to let out (a fact, a secret); (b) to show; to reveal (kindness, good humour); to betray, reveal (faults, neglect); *a. & s.m.* **-ateur, -atrice,** (a) *a.* revealing, telltale; (b) *s.m. Phot:* developer; *s.f.* **-ation,** revelation; disclosure.

se révéler. 1. to reveal oneself. 2. (*of facts, etc.*) to be revealed; to come to light.

revenant [rəvnɑ̃], *s.m.* ghost.

revendi|quer [rəvɑ̃dike], *v.tr.* to claim, demand; **r. ses droits,** to assert one's rights; *a.* **-catif, -cative,** demanding, claiming; **journée revendicative,** day of protest; *s.f.* **-cation,** claim, demand.

revendre [rəvɑ̃:dr], *v.tr.* to resell; to sell (sth.) again.

revenir [rəvniːr], *v.i.* (*conj. like* TENIR; *aux.* être) 1. to return; to come back; **r. sur ses pas,** to retrace one's steps; **r. sur une promesse,** to go back on a promise. 2. **r. à qn,** (*a*) to return, come back, to s.o.; **à chacun ce qui lui revient,** to each one his due; (*b*) **son visage me revient,** I'm beginning to recall his face; (*c*) **son visage ne me revient pas,** I don't like his looks. 3. to recover; **r. d'une maladie,** to get over an illness; **r. d'une erreur,** to realize one's mistake; **je n'en reviens pas!** I can't get over it! **en r. d'une belle,** to have had a narrow escape; **r. de loin,** to have been at death's door; **r. à soi,** to recover consciousness. 4. **en r. à qch.,** **y r.,** to revert to sth.; **on en revient aux jupes longues,** we're going back to long skirts. 5. (*a*) to cost; **cela me revient à 50 francs,** it's costing me 50 francs; (*b*) **cela revient au même,** it comes to the same thing.

revenu [rəvny], *s.m.* income (of pers.); (State) revenue; *Com:* (i) yield (of investment); (ii) *pl.* incomings.

rêver [rɛve]. 1. *v.i.* to dream; (*a*) **r. de qch.,** to dream about sth.; (*b*) **r. à qch.,** to ponder over sth.; (*c*) **r. tout éveillé,** to be full of impossible schemes. 2. *v.tr.* to dream of (sth.); **vous l'avez rêvé!** you must have dreamt it!

réverbération [revɛrberasjɔ̃], *s.f.* reverberation, reflection (of light, heat); re-echoing (of sound).

réverbère [revɛrbɛːr], *s.m.* street-lamp.

réverbérer [revɛrbere], *v.tr.* (**il réverbère; il réverbérera**) to reverberate; (*of light, heat*) to reflect, to throw back; (*of sound*) to re-echo.

révérence [reveraːs], *s.f.* 1. reverence (**envers, pour,** for). 2. bow; curtsey.

révérend, -ende [reverɑ̃, -ɑ̃ːd], *a. Ecc:* reverend; **le r. père Martin,** (the) Reverend Father Martin; **la révérende Mère supérieure,** the reverend Mother Superior.

révérer [revere], *v.tr.* (**je révère, je révérerai**) to revere; to reverence.

rêverie [rɛvri], *s.f.* reverie; (day-)dreaming.

revers [rəvɛːr], *s.m.* 1. (*a*) reverse (of coin); wrong side (of material, etc.); other side (of page); *Ten: etc:* (**coup de**) **r.,** backhand stroke; (*b*) facing, lapel (of coat). 2. reverse (of fortune); **essuyer un r.,** to suffer a setback.

réversible [reversibl], *a.* reversible.

réversion [reversjɔ̃], *s.f. Jur:* reversion (**à,** to); *Biol:* reversion (to type).

revêtir [rəvetiːr], *v.tr.* (*conj. like* VÊTIR) 1. to clothe (s.o.) again; to reclothe. 2. (*a*) to clothe, dress; **revêtu d'une cape,** dressed in, wearing, a cloak; **r. qn d'une dignité,** to invest s.o. with a dignity; **pièce revêtue de votre signature,** document bearing your signature; (*b*) *Const:* to face (with stone), to coat (with paint), to case (with panelling, etc.). 3. **r. un habit,** to put on a coat;

r. la forme humaine, to assume human shape; *s.m.* **-ement,** facing, coating.

se revêtir. 1. to put on one's clothes again. 2. **se r. de qch.,** to put on sth.; to assume (a dignity, etc.).

rêveur, -euse [revœːr, -øːz]. 1. *a.* dreamy. 2. *s.* dreamer; *adv.* **-sement,** dreamily.

revient [rəvjɛ̃], *s.m.* (**prix de**) **r.,** cost price.

revirement [rəvirmɑ̃], *s.m.* sudden change (of fortune); revulsion (of feeling); **revirements d'opinion,** veerings of opinion.

réviser [revize], *v.tr.* 1. to revise (text, proof, etc.); to audit (accounts). 2. to examine (again); to overhaul (car, etc.); **moteur révisé,** reconditioned engine; *s.m.* **-eur,** reviser; auditor; proof-reader; *s.f.* **-ion,** inspection, testing; overhaul(ing).

revivre [rəviːvr], *v.i.* (*conj. like* VIVRE) to live again; to come to life again.

révocation [revɔkasjɔ̃], *s.f.* 1. revocation, repeal (of order, edict). 2. removal, dismissal (of official).

revoici [rəvwasi], *prep. F:* **me r.!** here I am again! **me r. riche,** I'm rich once more.

revoilà [rəvwala], *prep. F:* **le r.!** there he is again.

revoir [rəvwaːr], *v.tr.* (*conj. like* VOIR) 1. to see again; *s.m.inv.* **au r.,** goodbye. 2. to revise, re-examine.

révolte [revɔlt], *s.f.* revolt, rebellion; *Mil:* etc: mutiny.

révolté, -ée [revɔlte], *s.* rebel, insurgent; *Mil: etc:* mutineer.

révolter [revɔlte], *v.tr.* to revolt, disgust, sicken, shock (s.o.); *a.* **-ant,** revolting, shocking (sight); outrageous (behaviour).

se révolter, to revolt, rebel (**contre,** against).

révolu, *a.* (*of time*) completed; **avoir quarante ans révolus,** to have completed one's fortieth year.

révolution [revɔlysjɔ̃], *s.f.* (*a*) revolution (of wheel, etc.); (*b*) *Pol:* revolution; upheaval; **R.,** the (French) Revolution.

révolutionnaire [revɔlysjɔnɛːr], (*a*) *a.* & revolutionary; (*b*) *s.* revolutionist.

révolutionner [revɔlysjɔne], *v.tr.* (*a*) revolutionize (manners, customs); **r. la face du monde,** to change the face of the world; **r. l'industrie,** to revolutionize industry; (*b*) to upset (s.o.'s) calm(ness of mind).

revolver [revɔlvɛːr], *s.m.* revolver.

révoquer [revɔke], *v.tr.* 1. to revoke, cancel (decree, etc.); to countermand; **r. un ordre de grève,** to call off a strike. 2. to dismiss (official).

revue [rəvy], *s.f.* 1. *Mil:* review; inspection. (*a*) *Pub:* review, magazine; **r. scientifique,** scientific journal; (*b*) *Th:* revue.

rez-de-chaussée [redʃose], *s.m.inv.* (*a*) ground level; street level; (*b*) ground-floor, *N.Am:* first floor.

habiller (se) [sərabije], *v.pr.* (*a*) to dress (oneself) again; (*b*) to buy a new outfit.

héostat [reɔsta], *s.m. El:* rheostat; variable resistance.

hésus [rezys], *s.m.* **1.** *Z:* (**macaque**) **r.**, rhesus (monkey). **2.** *Physiol:* **facteur r.**, Rh, rhesus, factor; **r. positif, négatif, Rh** positive, negative.

hin (le) [lərɛ̃]. *Pr.n.m. Geog:* the Rhine.

hinocéros [rinɔserɔs], *s.m.* rhinoceros.

hodésie (la) [larɔdezi]. *Pr.n.f. Geog:* Rhodesia.

hodésien, -ienne [rɔdezjɛ̃, -jɛn], *a. & s. Geog:* Rhodesian.

hododendron [rɔdɔdɛ̃drɔ̃], *s.m. Bot:* rhododendron.

hubarbe [rybarb], *s.f. Bot:* rhubarb.

hum [rɔm], *s.m.* rum.

humatisant, -ante [rymatizɑ̃, -ɑ̃:t], *a. & s. Med:* rheumatic (subject).

humatisme [rymatism], *s.m.* rheumatism.

humato I logie [rymatɔlɔʒi], *s.f. Med:* rheumatology; *s.m. & f.* **-logue**, rheumatologist.

hume [rym], *s.m. Med:* cold.

iant [rijɑ̃], *a.* **1.** smiling (face, person). **2.** cheerful, pleasant (thought, countryside).

can I er [rikane], *v.i.* to laugh unpleasantly, derisively; *s.m.* **-ement**, sneering, derisive, laugh; *a.* **-eur, -euse**, derisive (air, etc.).

che [riʃ], *a.* **1.** rich, wealthy, well-off. **2.** valuable; handsome (gift); *adv.* **-ment**, richly.

chesse [riʃɛs], *s.f.* **1.** wealth; riches. **2.** richness; fertility.

cin [risɛ̃], *s.m.* **huile de r.**, castor oil.

cocher [rikɔʃe], *v.i.* (*a*) to rebound; to glance off; (*b*) (*of bullet*) to ricochet.

cochet [rikɔʃɛ], *s.m.* (*a*) rebound; (*b*) ricochet.

de [rid], *s.f.* **1.** wrinkle. **2.** ripple (on water).

deau, -eaux [rido], *s.m.* **1.** screen, curtain (of trees, etc.). **2.** (*a*) curtain, *N.Am:* drape; (*b*) *Th:* (drop-)curtain; (*c*) *Pol:* **le r. de fer**, the iron curtain.

der [ride], *v.tr.* **1.** (*a*) to wrinkle, line (the forehead); to shrivel (skin); (*b*) to corrugate (metal). **2.** to ripple (the water).

rider. 1. to wrinkle; to become lined. **2.** (*of water*) to ripple.

dicule [ridikyl]. **1.** *a.* ridiculous, laughable, ludicrous. **2.** *s.m.* (*a*) ridiculousness, absurdity; (*b*) ridicule.

diculiser [ridikylize], *v.tr.* to ridicule; to make (s.o., sth.) ridiculous; **se r.**, to make a fool of oneself.

en [rjɛ̃]. **I.** *pron.indef.m.* **1.** anything; (*in questions* **rien** *is preferred to* **quelque chose** *when a negative answer is expected*) **y a-t-il r. de plus triste?** is there anything more depressing? **2.** nothing, not anything; (*a*) **il n'y a r. à faire**, there is nothing to be done; **il ne**

vous faut r. d'autre? do you require anything else? **cela ne fait r.**, that doesn't matter; **comme si de r. n'était**, as if nothing had happened; **il n'en est r.!** nothing of the kind! **n'être pour r. dans une affaire**, to have no hand in a matter; (*b*) **que faites-vous?—r.**, what do you do?—nothing; **parler pour r.**, to waste one's breath; **merci, madame—de r.**, **monsieur**, thank you, madam—please don't mention it; **en moins de r.**, in less than no time; (*c*) **r. que**, nothing but, only, merely; **il tremblait r. qu'en le racontant**, only to tell of it made him tremble; (*d*) **on ne peut pas vivre de r.**, you can't live on nothing; **ce n'est pas r.!** that's something! **ce n'est pas pour r. que . . .**, it is not without good reason that . . ..
II. rien, *s.m.* **1.** trifle; mere nothing; **il le fera en un r. de temps**, he'll do it in no time. **2.** just a little; **ajouter un r. d'ail**, to add a touch of garlic.

rieur, -euse [rijœ:r, -ø:z]. **1.** *a.* laughing; fond of laughter. **2.** *s.* laugher; **avoir les rieurs de son côté**, to have the laugh on one's side.

rigide [riʒid], *a.* rigid; tense; fixed; *adv.* **-ment**.

rigidité [riʒidite], *s.f.* rigidity; stiffness; tenseness.

rigole [rigɔl], *s.f.* drain, gutter, channel.

rigol I er [rigɔle], *v.i. F:* (*a*) to laugh; **tu rigoles!** you're joking! (*b*) to have some fun, to enjoy oneself; *s.f. F:* **-ade**, fun, lark, spree; *a.* **-o, -ote**, *F:* comic, funny; queer, odd.

rigoureu I x, -euse [rigurø, -ø:z], *a.* rigorous (discipline, etc.). **1.** severe, harsh (sentence); climate). **2.** strict (orders, neutrality); **au sens r. du mot**, in the strict sense of the word; *adv.* **-sement**.

rigueur [rigœ:r], *s.f.* **1.** rigour, harshness, severity. **2.** strictness; *adv.phr.* **être de r.**, to be compulsory; **à la r.**, if need be.

rime [rim], *s.f.* rhyme.

rimer [rime]. **1.** *v.tr.* to versify; to put into rhyme. **2.** *v.i.* (*a*) to rhyme (**avec**, with); *F:* **cela ne rime à rien**, there's no sense in it; (*b*) to write verse.

rin I cer [rɛ̃se], *v.tr.* (n. **rinçons**) to rinse (clothes, etc.); to rinse out (a glass); *s.m.* **-çage**, rinsing; *Hairdr:* (colour) rinse.

riposte [ripɔst], *s.f.* riposte. **1.** *Box:* counter, return. **2.** (*a*) retort; (*b*) counterstroke.

riposter [ripɔste], *v.i.* **1.** *Box:* to counter. **2.** to retort.

rire [ri:r]. **I.** *v.i.* (*p.p.* **ri**) **1.** to laugh; **se tenir les côtes de r.**, to be convulsed, to shake, with laughter; **r. bruyamment**, to guffaw; **il n'y a pas de quoi r.**, it is no laughing matter; **r. de qn**, to laugh at s.o. **2.** to jest, joke; **vous voulez r.!** you're joking! **prendre qch. en riant**, to laugh sth. off; **pour r.**, for fun; *F:* **je l'ai fait, histoire de r.**, I did it for a joke.
II. rire, *s.m.* (*a*) laughter, laughing; **avoir un**

accès de fou r., to be overcome with uncontrollable laughter; (b) un r., a laugh; un gros r., a horse laugh, a guffaw; un r. bête, a silly laugh; a giggle, a titter.

ris¹ [ri], s.m. Nau: reef (in sail).

ris², s.m. Cu: r. de veau, sweetbread.

risée [rize], s.f. (a) mockery, derision; s'exposer à la r. publique, to expose oneself to public scorn; (b) laughing-stock, butt.

risible [rizibl], a. ludicrous, laughable (mistake).

risque [risk], s.m. risk; à tout r., at all hazards; à vos risques et périls, at your own risk; Ins: police tous risques, comprehensive, all-risks, policy; r. d'incendie, fire risk; r. du recours de tiers, third-party risk.

risqué [riske], a. risky, hazardous (business); chanson risquée, risky, risqué, song.

risquer [riske], v.tr. to risk, venture, chance; r. sa vie, to risk one's life; r. le coup, to chance it; je ne veux rien r., I'm not taking any chances; la grève risque de durer longtemps, the strike may (well) go on for a long time.

se risquer, to take a risk; se r. à faire qch., to venture to do sth.

ristourne [risturn], s.f. refund, rebate; Com: discount.

rite [rit], s.m. rite; Ecc: les rites catholiques, the Catholic rites; les rites de la vie quotidienne, the ritual of everyday life.

rituel, -elle [rituɛl]. 1. a. ritual. 2. s.m. ritual; ceremonial.

rivage [riva:ʒ], s.m. bank (of river); shore; beach.

rival, -aux [rival, -o], a. & s. rival.

rivaliser [rivalize], v.i. r. avec qn, (i) to rival s.o.; (ii) to compete, vie, with s.o.

rivalité [rivalite], s.f. rivalry, competition.

rive [ri:v], s.f. bank; shore.

river [rive], v.tr. (a) to rivet; (b) to clinch (nail); F: r. son clou à qn, to score off s.o.; to give s.o. a piece of one's mind.

riverain, -aine [rivrɛ̃, -ɛn]. 1. a. (a) riverside (property, etc.); (b) bordering on (a road, wood, etc.); wayside (property, etc.). 2. s. riverside resident; resident living along (road, etc.).

rivet [rivɛ], s.m. rivet.

riveter [rivte], v.tr. (je rivette) to rivet; s.m. -age, riveting.

rivière [rivjɛ:r], s.f. river, stream; (of volcano) r. de feu, river, stream, of fire.

rixe [riks], s.f. brawl, scuffle.

riz [ri], s.m. rice.

rizière [rizjɛ:r], s.f. rice-plantation; paddy field(s).

robe [rɔb], s.f. 1. (a) (woman's) dress; Com: gown; (child's) frock; (b) r. de chambre, dressing-gown; Cu: pommes de terre en r. de chambre, jacket potatoes; (c) (of lawyer, professor) robe, gown; les gens de r., the leg: profession. 2. (a) skin (of sausage); (b) coat (of horse, dog, etc.).

robinet [rɔbinɛ], s.m. (stop-)cock; tap, spigo: fermer le r., to turn off the tap.

robot [rɔbo], s.m. robot; Av: pilotless plan Adm: portrait r., identikit picture.

robust|e [rɔbyst], a. robust, strong, sturdy; aa -ement; s.f. -esse, robustness, sturdiness.

roc [rɔk], s.m. rock.

rocailleux, -euse [rɔkɑjø, -ø:z], a. rocky, ston

roche [rɔʃ], s.f. rock, boulder; r. de fond, be rock; eau de r., clear spring water.

rocher [rɔʃe], s.m. rock; crag.

rocheux, -euse [rɔʃø, -ø:z], a. rocky, stony; l (montagnes) Rocheuses, the Rock Mountains.

rod|er [rɔde], v.tr. (a) to grind; to polish (met part, gem); to grind in (a piston); (b) Aut: run in (a car); (c) to put (system) through trial period; s.m. -age, grinding; Aut: en running in.

rôd|er [rɔde], v.i. to prowl; to loiter (with evil i tent); a. & s. -eur, -euse, (a) a. prowling; (b) prowler.

rognon [rɔɲɔ̃], s.m. Cu: kidney.

roi [rwa], s.m. king; fête des Rois, Twelfth-nigl

roitelet [rwatlɛ], s.m. Orn: wren; r. hup goldcrest.

rôle [ro:l], s.m. 1. roll; list; register; roster; à to de r., by turns. 2. Th: part, rôle; distributi des rôles, cast (of the play); sortir de son r., exceed one's brief.

romain, -aine [rɔmɛ̃, -ɛn]. 1. a. & s. Rom: l'Empire r., the Roman Empire; chiff romains, Roman numerals. 2. s.f. romai cos lettuce.

roman¹ [rɔmɑ̃], s.m. (a) novel; r. policier, det tive novel; r. noir, thriller; r. de mœurs, so novel; (b) le r., (prose) fiction; il ne fait que r., he only writes fiction; (c) l'histoire de sa est tout un r., the story of his life is quit romance.

roman², -ane [rɔmɑ̃, -an], a. & s.m. 1. Li Romance. 2. Arch: romanesque; (in En Norman.

romance [rɔmɑ̃:s], s.f. Mus: (sentimental) so

romancier, -ière [rɔmɑ̃sje, -jɛ:r], s. novelist.

romand [rɔmɑ̃], a. Geog: la Suisse roman French(-speaking) Switzerland.

romanesque [rɔmanɛsk], a. romantic.

romanichel, -elle [rɔmaniʃɛl], s. gipsy, roma Pej: vagrant.

romant|ique [rɔmɑ̃tik], a. romantic; être pe to be prosaic, unimaginative; Lit.H Romantic (movement); s.m. -isme, Lit.H Romanticism.

romarin [rɔmarɛ̃], s.m. Bot: rosemary.

rompre [rɔ̃:pr], v. (pr.ind. il rompt) 1. v.tr break; (a) to break in two; (b) (of stream) r.

digues, to burst its banks; *F:* **r. la tête, les oreilles, à qn**, to drive s.o. crazy (with noise, questions); to deafen s.o.; **se r. la tête**, to rack one's brains; *Mil:* **rompez!** dismiss! (*c*) **r. le silence**, to break the silence; (*d*) **r. un choc**, to deaden a shock; (*e*) **r. un mariage**, to break off an engagement; **r. les relations diplomatiques**, to break off diplomatic relations; (*f*) **r. l'équilibre**, to upset the balance; (*g*) **r. un cheval**, to break in a horse; **r. qn aux affaires**, to train, to accustom, s.o. to business; **r. qn à la fatigue**, to inure s.o. to fatigue. **2.** *v.i.* **r. avec qn**, to break with s.o.; **r. avec une habitude**, to break (oneself of) a habit.

se rompre, to break; to snap, break off.

rompu [rɔ̃py], *a.* (*a*) broken; **r. de fatigue**, worn out; (*b*) broken in; **r. au travail**, used, inured, to work.

romsteck [rɔmstɛk], *s.m. Cu:* rump-steak.

ronce [rɔ̃:s], *s.f.* **1.** *Bot:* bramble; blackberry-bush. **2.** *F:* thorns.

ronchonn|er [rɔ̃ʃɔne], *v.i. F:* to grumble, grouse; *s.m.* **-ement**, grumbling; *s.* **-eur**, **-euse**, grumbler, grouser.

rond, ronde [rɔ̃, rɔ̃:d]. **1.** *a.* (*a*) round (ball, table); rounded; plump (figure); (*b*) **voix ronde**, full voice; **en chiffres ronds**, in round figures; **compte r.**, round sum. **2.** *adv.phr.* **tourner r.**, (i) to run true; (ii) to run smoothly; *F:* **ça ne tourne pas r.**, it's not, things aren't, working properly. **3.** *s.m.* (*a*) round, ring, circle; **le chat se met en r.**, the cat curls up; **tourner en r.**, (i) to go round in a circle; (ii) to get nowhere; (*b*) disc; *E:* washer; **r. de beurre**, pat of butter; *P:* **il n'a pas un r.**, he hasn't a penny; he's broke. **4.** *s.f.* **ronde**, (*a*) round, rondo; (*b*) round(s); (*of policeman*) beat; **faire la ronde**, to go the rounds; (*c*) **à la ronde**, around; **à trente kilomètres à la ronde**, for thirty kilometres round; *adv.* **-ement**, briskly; bluntly.

rondelet, -ette [rɔ̃dlɛ, -ɛt], *a.* roundish, plump-ish (person); **somme rondelette**, tidy sum (of money).

rondelle [rɔ̃dɛl], *s.f.* **1.** disc; slice (of sausage). **2.** (*a*) ring; (*b*) washer; (*c*) *Fr.C:* (ice-hockey) puck.

rondeur [rɔ̃dœ:r], *s.f.* **1.** roundness, rotundity; *pl.* rounded forms. **2.** outspokenness.

rond-point [rɔ̃pwɛ̃], *s.m.* (*a*) circus (where several roads meet); (*b*) **r.-p. (à sens giratoire)**, roundabout, *N.Am:* rotary, traffic circle; *pl.* **ronds-points**.

ronfl|er [rɔ̃fle], *v.i.* **1.** to snore. **2.** (*of wind, fire, etc.*) to roar; (*of organ*) to boom; *s.m.* **-ement**, (i) snoring, snore; (ii) roaring booming, humming (of machinery, etc.); *s.* **-eur**, **-euse**, (*a*) snorer; (*b*) *s.m. El:* buzzer.

rong|er [rɔ̃ʒe], *v.tr.* (*n.* **rongeons**) **1.** to gnaw; **les vers rongent le fruit**, worms eat into fruit; **se r. le cœur**, to fret one's heart out. **2.** (*of acid, rust*) to corrode; to eat away; *a. & s.* **-eur**, **-euse**, (*a*) *a.* rodent, gnawing (animal); (*b*) *s.m. Z:* rodent.

ronronn|er [rɔ̃rɔne], *v.i.* (*a*) to purr; (*b*) *Mec: El:* to hum; *s.m.* **-ement**.

rosace [rozas], *s.f.* rose(-window).

rosaire [rozɛ:r], *s.m. Ecc:* rosary.

rosâtre [roza:tr], *a.* pinkish.

rosbif [rɔzbif], *s.m.* roast beef.

rose [ro:z]. **1.** *s.f. Bot:* rose; (*a*) **r. sauvage**, dog rose; **sentimentalité à l'eau de r.**, sugary sentiment; *F:* **cela ne sent pas la r.**, it doesn't smell very nice; **essence de roses**, attar of roses; **découvrir le pot aux roses**, to find out the secret; (*b*) **r. trémière**, hollyhock. **2.** (*a*) *a.* pink; rosy; (*inv. in compounds*) **des rubans r. pivoine**, peony-red ribbons; *F:* **elle n'avait pas la vie bien r.**, she didn't have an easy time of it; (*b*) *s.m.* rose (colour); pink. **3.** *s.f.* (*a*) *Arch:* rose(-window); (*b*) *Nau:* **r. des vents**, compass-card, dial; (*c*) *Jewel:* rose (diamond), rose-cut diamond.

rosé [roze], *a.* rosy, pale pink; **vin r.**, *s.m. F:* **rosé**, rosé wine.

roseau, -eaux [rozo], *s.m. Bot:* reed.

rosée [roze], *s.f.* dew.

rosette [rozɛt], *s.f.* (*a*) bow (of ribbon); (*b*) rosette (*esp.* the rosette of the **Légion d'honneur**); (*c*) *Archeol:* **la pierre de R.**, the Rosetta stone.

rosier [rozje], *s.m.* rose-tree, rose-bush.

rosiériste [rozjerist], *s.m. & f.* rose-grower, rosarian.

rosse [rɔs]. **1.** *s.f.* (*a*) *F:* (horse) nag, screw; (*b*) *P:* **le patron est une r.**, the boss is a swine, a skunk. **2.** *a. P:* ill-natured, nasty (person); low-down (trick); **professeur r.**, beast of a master.

rosser [rɔse], *v.tr. F:* to give (s.o.) a beating, a thrashing, a hiding.

rossignol [rɔsiɲɔl], *s.m.* **1.** *Orn:* nightingale; *F:* **j'ai des rossignols**, there are funny noises in the car. **2.** skeleton key.

rotatif, -ive [rɔtatif, -i:v], *a.* rotary.

rotation [rɔtasjɔ̃], *s.f.* rotation.

roter [rɔte], *v.i. F:* to belch.

rôti [roti], *s.m.* roast (meat).

rôtie [roti], *s.f.* round of toast.

rotin [rɔtɛ̃], *s.m. Bot:* rattan; **meubles en r.**, cane furniture.

rôt|ir [roti:r]. **1.** *v.tr.* to roast; to toast; **pain rôti**, toast. **2.** *v.i.* to roast, to scorch; *s.m.* **-issage**, roasting; *s.f.* **-isserie**, grill room.

rotondité [rɔtɔ̃dite], *s.f.* rotundity.

rotule [rɔtyl], *s.f.* knee-cap.

rouage [rwa:ʒ], *s.m.* **1.** wheels; works (of a watch). **2.** (toothed) wheel; gear wheel, cog wheel.

roublard, -arde [rubla:r, -ard], *a. & F:* crafty, foxy, wily (person).

roucoul|er [rukule], *v.i.* to coo; *s.m.* **-ement**.

roue [ru], *s.f.* wheel; **r. avant, r. arrière**, front, back, wheel; **r. de secours,** spare wheel; **pousser à la r.,** to put one's shoulder to the wheel; **faire la r.,** to turn cartwheels.

rouer [rwe], *v.tr.* **r. qn de coups,** to beat s.o. black and blue.

rouge [ruːʒ]. **1.** *a.* red; (*a*) **fer r.,** red-hot iron; **devenir r. comme une pivoine, une tomate, un homard,** to turn as red as a beetroot; **r. de colère,** crimson with rage; *adv.* **se fâcher tout r.,** to lose one's temper completely; (*b*) (*inv. in compounds*) **r. sang,** blood red; **des rubans r. cerise,** cherry-red ribbons. **2.** *s.m.* (*a*) red; (*b*) rouge; **bâton de r., r. à lèvres,** lipstick; (*c*) red wine; *F:* **boire un coup de r.,** drink a glass of red wine.

rougeâtre [ruʒɑːtr], *a.* reddish.

rougeaud, -eaude [ruʒo, -oːd], *a. & s.* red-faced (person).

rouge-gorge [ruʒgɔrʒ], *s.m. Orn:* robin (redbreast); *pl.* **rouges-gorges.**

rougeole [ruʒɔl], *s.f. Med:* measles.

rougeoyer [ruʒwaje], *v.i.* (**il rougeoie**) (*of thgs*) (*a*) to turn red; (*b*) to glow (red).

rougeur [ruʒœːr], *s.f.* **1.** redness. **2.** blush, flush. **3.** red spot, blotch (on the skin).

rougir [ruʒiːr]. **1.** *v.tr.* (*a*) to redden; to turn (sth.) red; (*b*) to bring (metal) to a red heat; **fer rougi au feu,** iron heated red-hot; **r. le fer au blanc,** to heat iron white-hot; (*c*) to flush (the face). **2.** *v.i.* (*a*) to redden, to turn red; (*b*) to turn red; to blush; to flush (up); **r. de qch.,** to be ashamed of sth.

rouille [ruːj], *s.f.* **1.** rust. **2.** *Agr:* rust, mildew, blight.

rouiller [ruje], *v.tr.* to rust; to make (iron, etc.) rusty; **mon latin est un peu rouillé,** my Latin's a bit rusty; **avoir les jambes rouillées,** to be stiff in the joints (of the hips, knees).

se rouiller, to rust (up); to get rusty.

roulant [rulɑ̃], *a.* rolling; sliding (door); **escalier r.,** moving staircase, escalator; *Rail:* **matériel r.,** rolling stock; **personnel r.,** (train, lorry, etc.) crews.

rouleau, -eaux [rulo], *s.m.* **1.** roller; **r. compresseur,** road roller, steam roller. **2.** (*a*) roll (of paper); spool (of film); coil (of rope); **je suis au bout de mon r.,** I'm at the end of my tether; (*b*) *Cu:* **r. à pâtisserie,** rolling pin; **r. à peinture,** paint roller.

roulement [rulmɑ̃], *s.m.* **1.** rolling; *Aut:* **bande de r.,** tread (of tyre). **2.** rumbling (of thunder); roll(ing) (of drum). **3.** *Mec.E:* bearing; **r. à billes,** ball-bearing. **4.** (*a*) *Com:* **r. de fonds,** circulation of capital; (*b*) rotation-roll; **par r.,** (*of duties, etc.*) in rotation.

rouler [rule]. **1.** *v.tr.* (*a*) to roll (along); *Golf:* **coup roulé,** putt; (*b*) *F:* **r. qn,** to take s.o. in, to diddle s.o.; (*c*) to roll (the lawn); (*d*) to roll, wrap (up). **2.** *v.i.* (*a*) to roll; **r. (en voiture),** to drive; **r. sur l'autoroute,** to drive, travel, along

the motorway, *N.Am:* freeway; **voiture qui très peu roulé,** car with a very low mileage; *A* **r. sur le sol,** to taxi; *F:* **ça roule, les affaire** business is good; **la conversation roulait sur** sport, we were talking about sport; **tout rou** sur lui, everything turns upon him; **r. par** monde, to knock about the world; (*b*) to ro rumble; (*c*) **auto qui roule bien,** car that ru well; (*d*) *Nau:* (*of ship*) to roll.

se rouler, (*a*) to roll (over and over); (*b*) to roll (into a ball).

roulette [rulɛt], *s.f.* **1.** caster; roller; small whee **patins à roulettes,** roller-skates; *F:* **ça marc comme sur des roulettes,** things are going li clockwork. **2.** (game of) roulette.

roulis [ruli], *s.m. Nau:* rolling (of ship); **coup r.,** lurch; (*of pers.*) **marcher avec un r.,** to wa with a rolling gait.

roulotte [rulɔt], *s.f.* (gypsies') caravan; **r.** **camping),** (touring) caravan, *N.Am:* trailer.

roumain, -aine [rumɛ̃, -ɛn], *a. & s.* Rumania

Roumanie (la) [larumani]. *Pr.n.f. Geo* Rumania.

roupill|er [rupije], *v.i. F:* to snooze, to take nap; to doze; *s. F:* **-eur, -euse,** snoozer; *s.* **-on,** nap; snooze.

rouquin, -ine [rukɛ̃, -in], *a. & s. F:* red-, ginge carroty-haired (person); *s.* redhead.

rouspét|er [ruspete], *v.i.* (**je rouspète**) *F:* grumble, grouse, bellyache, protest; to sh fight; **il n'a pas rouspété,** he went like a lam *a. & s.* **-eur, -euse,** (*a*) quarrelsom grumbling; (*b*) *s.* quarrelsome perso grumbler; grouser.

roussâtre [rusɑːtr], *a.* reddish.

rousse [rus], *see* ROUX.

rousseur [rusœːr], *s.f.* redness; **tache de** freckle.

roussir [rusiːr]. **1.** *v.tr.* (*a*) to redden; *Cu:* brown; **viande roussie,** meat done brown; to scorch, singe. **2.** *v.i.* (*a*) to turn brown; redden; (*b*) to singe; to get scorched.

route [rut], *s.f.* **1.** road; **r. nationale, r. de gran communication, grande r.** = A road, first cl road, main road, major road, *N.Am:* highw **r. départementale,** secondary road, B road route; way; **se mettre en r.,** to set out; **frais r.,** travelling expenses; **en r.!** let's go! **fair avec qn,** to travel with s.o.; **mettre des trava en r.,** to start operations; **mettre en r. moteur,** to start (up) the engine.

routier, -ière [rutje, -jɛːr], *a. & s.* **1.** *a.* ca **routière,** road-map; **réseau r.,** road netwo **police routière,** traffic police; **transpo routiers,** road transport; **gare routière,** (i) b coach, station; (ii) road haulage depot. **2.** *s* **gros r.,** heavy (goods) lorry, *N.Am:* hea truck; **r.,** long-distance lorry driver, *N.A* truck driver, trucker; **restaurant routiers** = transport café.

routine [rutin], *s.f.* routine.

routinier, -ière [rutinje, -jɛːr], *a.* routine (duties).

rouvrir [ruvriːr], *v.tr. & i. (conj. like* COUVRIR) to reopen, to open again.

se rouvrir, to open again; to reopen.

roux, rousse [ru, rus]. **1.** (*a*) *a.* (russet-)red, (reddish-)brown; (*of hair*) red; (*inv. in compounds*) **chevelure blond r.,** sandy hair; (*b*) *s.* red-haired person. **2.** *s.m.* (*a*) russet, reddish-brown (colour); (*b*) *Cu:* roux.

royal, -aux [rwajal, -o], *a.* royal, regal, kingly; *adv.* **-ement,** royally; **s'amuser r.,** to enjoy oneself enormously.

royaliste [rwajalist], *a. & s.* royalist.

royaume [rwajoːm], *s.m.* kingdom, realm.

Royaume-Uni (le) [lərwajomyni]. *Pr.n.m.* the United Kingdom.

royauté [rwajote], *s.f.* royalty; kingship.

ruban [rybã], *s.m.* **1.** (*a*) ribbon, band; **r. de chapeau,** hatband; **rubans de décorations,** medal ribbons; (*b*) **r. de coton,** tape; **mètre à r.,** measuring-tape; **r. adhésif, autocollant,** self-adhesive, *F:* sticky, tape; **r. magnétique,** magnetic, recording, tape. **2.** metal strip; **r. d'acier,** steel band. **3.** *Ind:* **r. transporteur,** belt conveyor.

rubéole [rybeɔl], *s.f. Med:* German measles.

rubis [rybi], *s.m.* ruby; **montée sur r.,** jewelled (watch).

rubrique [rybrik], *s.f.* (*a*) rubric; (*b*) *Journ: etc:* heading; item.

ruche [ryʃ], *s.f.* (bee-)hive.

rucher [ryʃe], *s.m.* apiary.

rude [ryd], *a.* **1.** (*a*) uncouth, unpolished; (*b*) rough; stiff, hard; harsh; rugged. **2.** (*a*) hard, arduous; **r. épreuve,** severe trial; (*b*) gruff, ungracious, brusque. **3.** **r. appétit,** hearty appetite; **r. adversaire,** tough opponent; *adv.* **-ment,** roughly, severely; **être r. fatigué,** to be awfully tired.

rudesse [rydɛs], *s.f.* **1.** uncouthness. **2.** roughness, ruggedness (of a surface, a material). **3.** (*a*) severity (of winter, of a task); (*b*) abruptness, bluntness (of manner).

rudiment [rydimã], *s.m.* **1.** *Biol:* rudiment (of a tail, etc.). **2.** *pl.* rudiments, smattering (of knowledge, etc.); **bien posséder les rudiments d'une matière,** to be well grounded in a subject; *a.* **-aire,** rudimentary (organ; civilization).

rudoiement [rydwamã], *s.m.* browbeating; bullying.

rudoyer [rydwaje], *v.tr.* (**je rudoie**) to treat roughly; to browbeat, to bully (s.o.); to knock (s.o.) about; to ill-treat (an animal).

rue [ry], *s.f.* street, thoroughfare; **la grande r.,** the high street; **r. à sens unique,** one-way street; **il demeure r. de Tournoi,** he lives in the Rue de Tournoi; **courir les rues,** (i) to run about the streets; (ii) to be common talk.

ruée [rɥe], *s.f.* rush, onrush; **la r. vers l'or,** the gold rush.

ruelle [rɥɛl], *s.f.* lane; alley.

ruer [rɥe], *v.i.* to kick, to lash out.

se ruer sur qn, to hurl, fling, oneself at s.o.; **se r. à la fenêtre,** to rush to the window.

rugby [rygbi], *s.m.* Rugby (football); **r. à quinze,** Rugby Union; **r. à treize,** Rugby League.

rugir [ryʒiːr], *v.i.* to roar; to howl; *s.m.* **-issement.**

rugosité [rygozite], *s.f.* **1.** rugosity, ruggedness, roughness. **2.** wrinkle, corrugation.

rugueux, -euse [rygø, -øːz], *a.* (*a*) rugged, rough; gnarled (tree); (*b*) wrinkled, corrugated.

ruine [rɥin], *s.f.* ruin. **1.** downfall; decay (of building, etc.). **2.** (*usu. in pl.*) ruins.

ruiner [rɥine], *v.tr.* to ruin, destroy; *a.* **-eux, -euse,** ruinous.

ruisseau, -eaux [rɥiso], *s.m.* **1.** brook; (small) stream. **2.** (street) gutter.

ruisseler [rɥisle], *v.i.* (**il ruisselle**) **1.** (*of water*) to stream (down), run (down). **2.** (*of surface*) to run, to drip; *s.m.* **-lement,** streaming, running (of water, etc.).

rumeur [rymœːr], *s.f.* **1.** (*a*) distant murmur, hum (of traffic); (*b*) din, clamour; **tout est en r.,** everything's in an uproar. **2.** rumour.

ruminer [rymine], *v.tr.* **1.** *abs.* (*of cattle, etc.*) to ruminate; to chew the cud. **2.** **r. une idée,** to ruminate on, over, about, an idea; *a. & s.* *Z:* **-ant, -ante,** ruminant; *s.f.* **-ation.**

rupestre [rypɛstr], *a.* **art r.,** cave art; **peintures rupestres,** rock, cave, paintings.

rupture [ryptyːr], *s.f.* breaking, rupture; (*a*) breaking down; bursting (of dam, etc.); (*b*) breaking (in two); rupture; fracture; (*c*) breaking up; (*d*) breaking off; discontinuance; **r. de contrat,** breach of contract.

rural, -aux [ryral, -o]. **1.** *a.* rural; **vie rurale,** country life; **facteur r.,** country postman. **2.** *s.m.* **les ruraux,** country people.

ruse [ryːz], *s.f.* ruse, trick, wile, dodge.

rusé [ryze], *a. & s.* artful, crafty, sly; astute (person).

russe [rys], *a. & s.* Russian.

Russie (la) [larysi]. *Pr.n.f. Geog:* Russia.

rustaud, -aude [rysto, -oːd].· **1.** *a.* boorish, uncouth (appearance, person). **2.** *s.m.* boor; bumpkin, *N.Am:* hick.

rustique [rystik], *a.* (*a*) rustic; (*b*) hardy (plant).

rustre [rystr]. **1.** *a.* boorish. **2.** *s.m.* boor, lout, clodhopper, *N.Am:* hick.

rythme [ritm], *s.m.* rhythm.

rythmique [ritmik], *a.* rhythmic.

S

S, s [εs], *s.m. & f.* (the letter) S, s.

sa [sa], *poss.a.f. see* SON¹.

sabbat [saba], *s.m.* **1.** (Jewish) Sabbath. **2.** (witches') sabbath, midnight revels; *F:* **faire un s. de tous les diables,** to make a frightful row.

sabl|e [sɑbl], *s.m.* **1.** sand; **sables mouvants,** quicksands; *s.f.* **-ière,** sandpit; *a.* **-onneux, -onneuse,** sandy (shore); gravelly (path).

sabl|er [sɑble], *v.tr.* **1.** to sand, gravel (path, etc.). **2.** *F:* **s. le champagne,** to celebrate with champagne; *s.m.* **-age,** sanding (of path, icy road, etc.).

sabord [sabɔr], *s.m. Nau:* port(-hole); **s. d'aération,** air port; **s. de charge,** cargo door.

sabord|er [sabɔrde], *v.tr.* **1.** to scuttle (ship). **2.** to ruin, destroy (sth.); *s.m.* **-age,** *s.m.* **-ement,** scuttling (of ship).

sabot [sabo], *s.m.* **1.** clog, sabot; **(baignoire) s.,** slipper-bath. **2.** (horse's) hoof. **3. s. de frein,** brake shoe.

sabot|er [sabɔte], *v.tr.* to botch (a job); to do wilful damage to (machinery, etc.); to sabotage; *s.m.* **-age,** (i) botching, scamping (of work); (ii) sabotage (of machinery, tools, etc.); *s.* **-eur, -euse,** (i) bungler, botcher; (ii) saboteur.

sabre [sɑːbr], *s.m.* sabre; sword.

sac¹ [sak], *s.m.* sack, bag; **s. à main,** handbag; **s. à ouvrage,** workbag; **s. à outils,** toolbag; **s. de nuit,** travel-bag, overnight bag; **s. de couchage,** sleeping-bag; *F:* **s. percé,** spendthrift; **s. à vin,** boozer; **vider son s.,** to get it off one's chest, to come clean; **l'affaire est dans le s.,** it's as good as settled, it's in the bag.

sac², *s.m.* sacking, pillage.

saccade [sakad], *s.f.* jerk, start, jolt.

saccadé [sakade], *a.* jerky, abrupt (movement, style).

saccager [sakaʒe], *v.tr.* **(n. saccageons)** to sack, pillage (town); to ransack (house).

saccharine [sakarin], *s.f.* saccharin(e).

sachet [saʃɛ], *s.m.* sachet.

sacoche [sakɔʃ], *s.f.* satchel, wallet; toolbag; (cyclist's) saddlebag.

sacquer [sake], *v.tr.* = SAQUER.

sacre [sakr], *s.m.* anointing, coronation (of king); consecration (of bishop).

sacré [sakre], *a.* **1.** holy (scripture); sacred (place, etc.). **2.** *P:* **s. imbécile,** bloody fool; **il a une sacrée chance,** he's damn lucky.

sacrement [sakrəmã], *s.m. Ecc:* (a) sacrament; **fréquenter les sacrements,** to be a regular com-

municant; (b) *F:* the marriage tie.

sacrer [sakre]. **1.** *v.tr.* to anoint, crown (king); to consecrate (bishop). **2.** *v.i. F:* to curse and swear.

sacrifice [sakrifis], *s.m.* sacrifice.

sacrifier [sakrifje], *v.tr.* (*pr.sub. & p.d.* **n. sacrifiions**) (a) to sacrifice; to offer in sacrifice; (b) to sacrifice, give up (one's life, fortune) (**à qn, qch.,** to s.o., sth.).

sacrilège [sakrilɛːʒ]. **1.** *s.m.* sacrilege. **2.** *a.* sacrilegious (thought, person).

sacristain [sakristɛ̃], *s.m.* sacristan; sexton.

sacristie [sakristi], *s.f. Ecc:* sacristy, vestry.

sacro-saint [sakrosɛ̃], *a.* sacrosanct.

sad|isme [sadism], *s.m.* sadism; *a.* **-ique,** sadistic; *s.m. & f.* **-iste,** sadist.

safran [safrã]. **1.** *s.m. Bot:* saffron, crocus; **s. cultivé,** autumn crocus. **2.** *a.inv.* saffron-coloured.

sagac|e [sagas], *a.* sagacious, shrewd; *adv.* **-ement;** *s.f.* **-ité,** shrewdness.

sage [saːʒ], *a.* **1.** wise; learned ['lɔːnid]. **2.** judicious, discreet. **3.** well-behaved; good (child); **s. comme une image,** as good as gold; *adv.* **-ment.**

sage-femme [saʒfam], *s.f.* midwife; *pl.* **sages-femmes.**

sagesse [saʒɛs], *s.f.* **1.** (a) wisdom; (b) prudence discretion; **agir avec s.,** to act wisely. **2.** steadiness, good behaviour.

Sagittaire [saʒitɛːr]. *Pr.n.m. Astr:* Sagittarius.

saignant [sɛɲã], *a.* **1.** bleeding, raw (wound etc.). **2.** *Cu:* underdone, red, rare (meat).

saigner [sɛɲe]. **1.** *v.i.* (*of wound, etc.*) to bleed. **2** *v.tr.* to bleed; (i) *Med:* to draw blood from (s.o.); (ii) to bleed, to extort money from (s.o.) **s. qn à blanc,** *F:* to clean s.o. out.

saillant [sajã]. **1.** *a.* (a) projecting (roof balcony); **pommettes saillantes,** high cheek bones; **muscles saillants,** bulging muscles; (b) salient, striking, outstanding (feature, fact). **2** *s.m. Mil:* salient.

saillie [saji], *s.f.* **1.** (a) spurt, spring, bounc **avancer par (bonds et) saillies,** to advance b leaps and bounds; (b) sally, flash of wit. **2** projection.

sain, saine [sɛ̃, sɛn], *a.* (a) healthy, hale (per son); sound (judgment, doctrine); wholesom (food); sane; **s. d'esprit,** of sound mind; **s. sauf,** safe and sound; (b) *Nau:* clear, sa (anchorage); *adv.* **-ement.**

saindoux [sɛ̃du], *s.m.* lard.

saint, sainte [sɛ̃, sɛ̃:t]. **1.** *a.* holy; (*a*) **la Sainte Église,** the Holy Church; **les Saintes Écritures,** Holy Writ; **le Vendredi S.,** Good Friday; **le S.-Siège,** the Holy See; (*b*) saintly, godly (person); (*c*) hallowed, consecrated; **lieu s.,** holy place. **2.** *s.* saint; **la S.-Michel,** Michaelmas; **la S.-Jean,** Midsummer Day; **la S.-Sylvestre,** New Year's Eve.

saint-bernard [sɛ̃bɛrna:r], *s.m.inv.* St Bernard (dog).

Sainte-Hélène [sɛ̃telɛn]. *Pr.n. Geog:* Saint Helena.

Saint-Esprit (le) [ləsɛ̃tɛspri]. *Pr.n.m.,* the Holy Ghost, Spirit.

sainteté [sɛ̃təte], *s.f.* holiness, saintliness; sanctity; *Ecc:* **Sa Sainteté,** His Holiness (the Pope).

Saint-Laurent (le) [ləsɛ̃lɔrɑ̃]. *Pr.n.m. Geog:* the Saint Lawrence (river).

Saint-Père (le) [ləsɛ̃pɛ:r], *s.m.* the Holy Father.

saisir [sezi:r], *v.tr.* to seize; (*a*) to grasp; to take hold of (sth.); **être saisi (d'étonnement),** to be startled; (*b*) to perceive, apprehend; **je ne saisis pas,** I don't quite get the idea; **je n'ai pas saisi son nom,** I didn't get, catch, his name; *a.* **-issant,** piercing (cold); striking (likeness); thrilling (sight); *s.m.* **-issement,** thrill; shock; surprise.

se saisir de qch., to lay hands on sth.

saison [sɛzɔ̃], *s.f.* season; **en cette s.,** at this time of year; **en toute(s) saison(s),** all the year round; **de s.,** in season; **(propos) hors de s.,** illtimed (remarks); *a. & s.* **-nier, -nière,** (*a*) *a.* seasonal (employment, etc.); (*b*) *s.* seasonal worker.

salade [salad], *s.f.* (*a*) salad; **faire la s.,** to mix the salad; **quelle s.!** what a mess! (*b*) *Hort: Cu:* lettuce; endive, curly lettuce.

salaison [salɛzɔ̃], *s.f.* salting (of fish); curing (of bacon).

salarié, -ée [salarje]. **1.** *a.* (*a*) wage-earning; (*b*) paid (work). **2.** *s.* wage-earner.

salaud [salo], *s. P:* (*a*) filthy beast; (*b*) (dirty) bastard, swine; son of a bitch; **ça c'est un tour de s.,** that's a dirty trick.

sale [sal], *a.* dirty. **1.** (*a*) unclean, filthy; soiled (linen); (*b*) offensive, nasty. **2.** *F:* (*always before the noun*) **s. type,** rotten bastard; **s. coup,** dirty trick; **s. temps,** beastly weather.

saler [sale], *v.tr.* to salt. **1.** (*a*) to season with salt; (*b*) *F:* to sting, to fleece (the customers); **s. la note,** to stick it on (the bill). **2.** to salt, pickle; to cure (bacon).

saleté [salte], *s.f.* **1.** (*a*) dirtiness, filthiness (of pers., street, etc.); (*b*) dirt, filth; **ôtez cette s.!** take away that filth! (*c*) bit of dirt; **enlever les saletés du perroquet,** to clear up the parrot's mess. **2.** (*a*) nastiness, obscenity; (*b*) nasty, coarse, remark; **dire des saletés,** to talk smut.

salière [saljɛ:r], *s.f.* salt-cellar.

salir [sali:r], *v.tr.* to dirty, soil; **s. sa réputation,** to tarnish one's reputation.

se salir. 1. to get dirty; **tissu qui se salit facilement,** material that soils easily. **2.** to dirty one's clothes.

salive [sali:v], *s.f.* saliva, spittle; **perdre sa s.,** to waste one's breath.

salle [sal], *s.f.* **1.** hall; (large) room; **s. de séjour,** living room; **s. à manger,** (i) dining room; (ii) dining room suite. **2.** *Th:* auditorium, house; **toute la s. applaudit,** the whole house applauded.

salon [salɔ̃], *s.m.* (*a*) drawing-room; **jeux de s.,** parlour games; (*b*) saloon, cabin (in ship); (*c*) **s. de thé,** tea-room(s); **s. de coiffure,** hairdresser's (shop); (*d*) **s. de peinture,** art exhibition; **le S. de l'automobile,** the (French) Motor Show.

salubre [saly:br], *a.* healthy; wholesome; *s.f.* **-ité,** healthiness, wholesomeness; **s. publique,** public health.

saluer [salɥe], *v.tr.* (*a*) to salute; **s. qn de la main,** to wave to s.o.; (*b*) to greet, to hail (s.o.); **saluez-le de ma part,** give him my kind regards.

salut [saly], *s.m.* **1.** (*a*) safety; **le s. public,** public welfare; **port de s.,** haven of refuge; (*b*) salvation; **l'Armée du S.,** the Salvation Army. **2.** (*a*) bow, greeting; (*b*) *Mil:* salute.

salutaire [salytɛ:r], *a.* salutary, wholesome, beneficial; **exercer une influence s.,** to be a power for good.

salutation [salytasjɔ̃], *s.f.* salutation, greeting; **"salutations à votre famille,"** "kind regards to your family."

salvatrice [salvatris], *s.f. see* SAUVEUR.

salve [salv], *s.f. Artil:* **1.** **tirer une s.,** to fire a salvo. **2.** **tirer une s. (d'honneur),** to fire a salute.

samedi [samdi], *s.m.* Saturday.

sanatorium [sanatɔrjɔm], *s.m.* sanatorium.

sanctifier [sɑ̃ktifje], *v.tr.* (*pr.sub. & p.d.* n. **sanctifiions**) to make holy, to hallow; **s. le dimanche,** to observe the Sabbath; *s.f.* **-cation.**

sanction [sɑ̃ksjɔ̃], *s.f.* sanction. **1.** approbation; **s. royale,** royal assent; **s. de l'usage,** authority of custom. **2.** (*a*) **s. (pénale),** penalty; (*b*) *Pol:* **prendre des sanctions contre un pays,** to impose sanctions on a country.

sanctionner [sɑ̃ksjɔne], *v.tr.* to sanction. **1.** to approve, ratify. **2.** to penalize.

sanctuaire [sɑ̃ktɥɛ:r], *s.m.* (*a*) *Ecc.Arch:* sanctuary; (*b*) sanctuary, holy place; (*c*) (wild life, etc.) sanctuary.

sandale [sɑ̃dal], *s.f.* sandal.

sandwich [sɑ̃dwitʃ], *s.m.* **1.** sandwich; *attrib.* **verre s.,** laminated glass. **2.** *Geog:* **les îles S.,** the Sandwich Islands.

sang [sɑ̃], *s.m.* **1.** blood; **coup de s.,** stroke; **se faire du mauvais s.,** to worry; **mon s. n'a fait qu'un tour,** my heart leapt into my mouth. **2.** (*a*) blood, race, lineage; **cheval pur s.,**

thoroughbred (horse); (*b*) blood, kinship; **son propre s.**, one's own flesh and blood.

sang-froid [sɑ̃frwa], *s.m. no pl.* coolness, composure; *adv.phr.* **de s.-f.**, deliberately; in cold blood.

sanglant [sɑ̃glɑ̃], *a.* **1.** bloody (wound, battle); blood-stained (handkerchief). **2.** (*a*) cutting; cruel, bitter (reproach, etc.); **larmes sanglantes**, bitter tears; (*b*) deadly, unforgivable (insult).

sangle [sɑ̃:gl], *s.f.* strap, band, webbing; **s. de selle** (saddle) girth; **lit de s.**, camp-bed.

sanglier [sɑ̃gli(j)e], *s.m.* wild boar.

sanglot [sɑ̃glo], *s.m.* sob; **pousser des sanglots**, to sob.

sangloter [sɑ̃glɔte], *v.i.* to sob.

sanguin, -ine [sɑ̃gɛ̃, -in]. **I.** *a.* **1.** *Anat:* **groupe s.**, blood group; **transfusion sanguine**, blood transfusion; **vaisseaux sanguins**, blood vessels. **2.** full-blooded (person); sanguine (temperament). **II. sanguine**, *s.f.* **1.** red chalk drawing, sanguine. **2.** blood orange.

sanguinaire [sɑ̃ginɛ:r], *a.* bloodthirsty (person); bloody (fight).

sanitaire [sanitɛ:r]. **1.** *a.* (*a*) medical; **personnel, matériel, s.**, medical staff, stores; (*b*) *Plumb:* sanitary; **technique s.**, sanitary engineering; **matériel s.**, sanitary ware. **2.** *s.m.* (*a*) **le s.**, *F:* **les sanitaires**, sanitary ware, installations, *F:* (the) plumbing; (*b*) *F:* **le s.**, the plumber.

sans [sɑ̃], *prep.* **1.** (*a*) without; **il est revenu s. le sou**, he came back without a penny; **s. faute**, without fail; **il est bon ouvrier, s. plus**, he's a good workman, (but) nothing more; **vous n'êtes pas s. le connaître**, you must know him; **non s. difficulté**, not without difficulty; *conj. phr.* **s. que nous le sachions**, without our knowing it; (*b*) -less, -lessly; **agir s. peur**, to act fearlessly; **jour s. pluie**, rainless day; **être s. le sou**, to be penniless; (*c*) un-; **plaintes s. fin**, unending complaints. **2.** but for; **s. vous, je serais ruiné**, but for you, I should be ruined; **s. cela, s. quoi**, otherwise, else.

sans-façon [sɑ̃fasɔ̃]. **1.** *s.m.* (*a*) straightforwardness, bluntness (of speech, etc.); (*b*) unceremoniousness; (*c*) offhandedness. **2.** *a. & s. inv.* (*a*) homely, informal (person); (*b*) offhand (person).

sans-gêne [sɑ̃ʒɛn]. **1.** *s.m.* (offensive) offhandedness; over-familiarity. **2.** *a.inv.* unceremonious.

sans-souci [sɑ̃susi], *s.inv.* **1.** *s.m. & f.* easygoing, carefree, person. **2.** *s.m.* carefree manner; unconcern.

santé [sɑ̃te], *s.f.* health; well-being; **être en bonne, en parfaite, s.**, to be in good, in the best of, health; **avoir une s. fragile**, *F:* **une petite s.**, to be delicate; **respirer la s.**, to look the picture of health; **boire à la s. de qn**, to drink s.o.'s

health; **à votre s.!** your health! *F:* cheers! *Mil:* **le service de (la) s.**, the medical service.

saper [sape], *v.tr.* to sap, undermine (foundations, etc.); *s.m.* **-eur**, *Mil:* sapper; **s. du génie**, engineer sapper.

sapeur-pompier [sapœrpɔ̃pje], *s.m.* fireman; **les sapeurs-pompiers**, the fire-brigade.

sapin [sapɛ̃], *s.m.* **1.** (*a*) fir(-tree); (*b*) (**bois de) s.**, deal. **2.** *F:* coffin; **toux qui sent le s.**, churchyard cough.

sapinière [sapinjɛ:r], *s.f.* fir-plantation.

saquer [sake], *v.tr. P:* to sack (s.o.); to fire (s.o.); **être saqué**, to get the sack; to be fired.

sarcasme [sarkasm], *s.m.* (piece of) sarcasm; sarcastic remark.

sarcastique [sarkastik], *a.* sarcastic.

sarcler [sarkle], *v.tr.* to clean (field); to weed (garden); to hoe (turnips, vine).

sarcophage [sarkɔfa:ʒ], *s.m.* sarcophagus.

Sardaigne (la) [lasardɛɲ]. *Pr.n.f. Geog:* Sardinia.

sarde [sard], *a. & s. Geog:* Sardinian.

sardine [sardin], *s.f.* (*a*) *Ich:* sardine; (young) pilchard; (*b*) *Com:* sardine; **sardines à l'huile**, tinned sardines.

sarment [sarmɑ̃], *s.m.* vine-shoot.

Satan [satɑ̃]. *Pr.n.m.* Satan.

satané [satane], *a. F:* (intensive, always before the noun) devilish, confounded; **s. temps**, beastly weather! **c'est un s. menteur**, he's the devil of a liar.

satanique [satanik], *a.* satanic; fiendish (cruelty idea); *adv.* **-ment**.

satellite [satɛllit], *s.m.* satellite; **s. artificiel**, artificial satellite; **s. habité (par l'homme)**, manned satellite; **s. terrestre, lunaire**, earth orbiting, moon-orbiting, satellite; **s. de télécommunications**, (tele)communication satellite; **s. météorologique**, weather satellite, *a. & s.m. Pol:* (**pays) s.**, satellite (state).

satiété [sasjete], *s.f.* satiety; surfeit.

satin [satɛ̃], *s.m. Tex:* satin.

satir|e [sati:r], *s.f.* satire; *a.* **-ique**, satirical; *ad* **-iquement**.

satisfaction [satisfaksjɔ̃], *s.f.* **1.** satisfaction; contentment; gratification (of appetite desires). **2.** reparation, amends (**pour, de, for**).

satisfaire [satisfɛ:r], *v.* (*conj. like* FAIRE) satisfy. **1.** *v.tr.* (*a*) to content; to give satisfaction to (s.o.); **s. l'attente de qn**, to come up s.o.'s expectations; (*b*) to make amends (s.o.). **2.** *v.ind.tr.* **s. à qch.**, to satisfy, me (demands); to answer, meet (condition); carry out (undertaking, duty); to comply wi (the regulations).

satisfaisant [satisfəzɑ̃], *a.* satisfying, satisfa tory; **peu s.**, unsatisfactory.

satur|er [satyre], *v.tr.* to saturate (**de, with**); s **-ation**.

sauc|e [so:s], *s.f.* sauce; *s.f.* **-ière**, sauce-boa

saucisse [sosis], *s.f.* (fresh) sausage (requiring cooking).

saucisson [sosisɔ̃], *s.m.* (a) (large, dry) sausage; **s. à l'ail,** garlic sausage; (b) *P:* fool, nit(wit).

sauf[1], **sauve** [sof, so:v], *a.* safe, unhurt; **s'en tirer la vie sauve,** to get off with one's life; **sain et s.,** safe and sound.

sauf[2], *prep.* save, but, except (for); **il n'a rien s. ses gages,** he has nothing except, beyond, his wages; **s. correction,** subject to correction; **s. de rares exceptions,** with very few exceptions; **s. accidents, s. imprévu,** barring accidents, the unforeseen; **s. erreur ou omission,** errors and omissions excepted; **s. s'il pleut,** unless it rains; *conj.phr.* **s. que** + *ind.,* except that.

sauf-conduit [sofkɔ̃dɥi], *s.m.* safe-conduct; pass; *pl.* **sauf-conduits.**

sauge [so:ʒ], *s.f. Bot: Cu:* sage.

saugrenu [sogrəny], *a.* absurd, preposterous (question, idea).

saule [so:l], *s.m. Bot:* willow; **s. pleureur,** weeping willow.

saumâtre [somɑ:tr], *a.* brackish, briny.

saumon [somɔ̃], *s.m.* **1.** salmon; *a.inv.* **rubans saumon,** salmon-pink ribbons. **2.** *Metall:* ingot (of tin, etc.); pig (of lead, cast iron).

saumoné [somɔne], *a.* **truite saumonée,** salmon-trout.

saumure [somy:r], *s.f.* (pickling) brine; pickle.

aupoudr|er [sopudre], *v.tr.* to sprinkle; powder; *s.m.* **-age,** powdering, sprinkling; *s.m.* **-oir** [-wa:r], (flour) dredger; sugar sifter.

aur [sɔ:r], *a.m.* **hareng s.,** red herring.

aut [so], *s.m.* **1.** (a) leap, jump, vault; *Sp:* **s. en longueur, en hauteur,** long jump, high jump; **s. à la perche,** pole vault; **s. de haie,** hurdling; **au s. du lit,** on getting out of bed; **s. périlleux,** somersault; **faire un s. en ville,** to pop into town; **il n'y a qu'un s. d'ici là,** it's only a stone's throw (away); (b) **s. de température,** sudden rise, jump, in temperature. **2.** waterfall.

aut-de-lit [sodli], *s.m.* (light) dressing gown; *pl.* **sauts-de-lit.**

aute [so:t], *s.f.* jump (in price, temperature, etc.); *esp. Nau:* **s. de vent,** shift, change, of wind; **s. d'humeur,** (sudden) change of mood; *El:* **s. de tension,** surge.

auté [sote], *a. & s.m. Cu:* sauté; **pommes (de terre) sautées,** sauté potatoes.

aute-mouton [sotmutɔ̃], *s.m.inv. Games:* leapfrog.

auter [sote]. **1.** *v.i.* (*aux. avoir*) (a) to jump, leap, skip; **s. de joie,** to jump for joy; **s. à la perche,** to pole-vault; **s. du lit,** to leap out of bed; **s. à terre,** to jump down; **s. en parachute,** to jump, to bale out; **s. à la gorge de qn,** to fly at s.o.'s throat; **s. au cou de qn,** to fling one's arms round s.o.'s neck; *F:* **et que ça saute!** and make it snappy! (b) (*of mine, etc.*) to explode; to

blow up; (*of bank, etc.*) to go smash; (*of button, etc.*) to come off, fly off; (c) *Nau:* (*of wind*) to change, shift. **2.** *v.tr.* to jump (over), leap over, clear (ditch, etc.).

sauterelle [sotrɛl], *s.f.* grasshopper; **grande s. d'Orient,** locust.

sautiller [sotije], *v.i.* to hop; to skip, jump (about); **s'en aller en sautillant,** to skip off.

sauvage [sova:ʒ]. **1.** *a.* (a) primitive, uncivilized (people); wild, untamed (animal); barbarous (custom); (b) unsociable; shy; retiring; uncouth; (c) unauthorized; **grève s.,** wildcat strike; (d) **soldes sauvages,** slashed prices. **2.** *s.* (*f.occ.* **sauvagesse**) (a) savage; *Fr.C:* (American) Indian, *f.* **sauvagesse,** squaw; (b) unsociable person; *adv.* **-ment,** savagely; *s.f.* **-rie,** unsociability.

sauvegarde [sovgard], *s.f.* safeguard, safe keeping.

sauvegarder [sovgarde], *v.tr.* to safeguard, protect (s.o.'s honour, interests, etc.).

sauve-qui-peut [sovkipø], *s.m.inv.* stampede, panic flight.

sauver [sove], *v.tr.* (a) to save, rescue (s.o.); (b) to salve, salvage (ship, goods, etc.).

se sauver. 1. se s. d'un péril, to escape from a danger. **2.** to run away, to be off, *F:* to clear out.

sauvetage [sovta:ʒ], *s.m.* (a) life-saving; rescue; **s. aérien en mer,** air-sea rescue; **canot de s.,** lifeboat; **échelle de s.,** fire-escape; (b) salvage, salving; **remorqueur de s.,** salvage tug; **droits de s.,** salvage dues.

sauveur [sovœ:r], *s.m.,f.* **salvatrice** [salvatris], saver, preserver, deliverer; *Ecc:* **le S.,** the Saviour.

sav|ant, -ante [savɑ̃, -ɑ̃:t]. **1.** *a.* (a) learned ['lə:nid], scholarly (**en, in**); (b) skilful; **il a la main savante,** he has a skilful hand; **chien s.,** performing dog. **2.** *s.* scientist; scholar; *adv.* **-amment.**

saveur [savœ:r], *s.f.* **1.** savour, taste, flavour; **plein de s.,** full-flavoured; **sans s.,** insipid. **2.** pungency (of style).

Savoie (la) [lasavwa]. *Pr.n.f. Geog:* Savoy; *Cu:* **biscuit de S.** = sponge cake.

savoir [savwa:r]. **I.** *v.tr.* (*pr.p.* **sachant;** *p.p.* **su;** *pr.ind.* **je sais, n. savons, ils savent;** *p.d.* **je savais;** *fu.* **je saurai**) to know. **1.** (*to know through having learnt*) **s. une langue,** to know a language; **s. le chemin,** to know the way, the road. **2.** to be aware of (sth.); (a) **je ne savais pas cela,** I didn't know, wasn't aware of, that; **elle est jolie, et elle le sait bien,** she's pretty, and well she knows it! **il ne sait rien de rien,** he knows nothing at all about it; **vous en savez plus long que moi,** you know more (about it) than I do; **sans le s.,** unconsciously; **pas que je sache,** not that I'm aware of; (b) **je la sais in-**

telligente, I know her to be intelligent; **je vous savais à Paris,** I knew you were in Paris; (*c*) **je lui savais une grande fortune,** I knew him to be wealthy; (*d*) **ne s. que faire,** to be at a loss what to do. **3.** (*a*) **il n'en a rien su,** he never knew of it; **c'est à s.,** that remains to be seen; (*b*) **faire s. qch. à qn,** to inform s.o. of sth.; (*c*) (**à**) **savoir,** namely, that is to say. **4.** to know how, to be able; **savez-vous nager?** can you swim? **elle ne sait rien faire,** she's quite untrained. **5.** *pron.phrs.* (**un**) **je ne sais qui m'a écrit,** somebody or other wrote to me; **un je ne sais quoi de déplaisant,** something vaguely unpleasant; **un je sais tout,** a know-all; *excl.phrs.* **des robes, des chapeaux, que sais-je!** dresses, hats, and goodness knows what else! **Dieu sait!** Heaven knows!
II. savoir, *s.m.* knowledge, learning, scholarship.

savoir-faire [savwarfɛːr], *s.m.inv.* savoir-faire; ability; know-how.

savoir-vivre [savwarvivr], *s.m.inv.* savoir-vivre; good manners; good breeding; tact.

savon [savɔ̃], *s.m.* (*a*) soap; **pain de s.,** cake of soap; **s. de Marseille** = household soap; (*b*) *F:* **passer un s. à qn,** to give s.o. a good telling off; **recevoir un s.,** to catch it; *s.f.* **-nette,** cake of (toilet) soap; *a.* **-neux, -neuse,** soapy.

savonner [savɔne], *v.tr.* to soap; to wash (sth.) with soap; **se s. le menton,** to lather one's chin.

savour|er [savure], *v.tr.* to relish, enjoy (food, flattery, etc.); **s. une plaisanterie, sa vengeance,** to enjoy, gloat over, a joke, one's revenge; *a.* **-eux, -euse,** savoury, tasty; enjoyable, amusing.

Saxe (la) [lasaks]. *Pr.n.f.* Saxony; **porcelaine de S.,** Dresden china.

scabreu|x, -euse [skabrø, -øːz], *a.* **1.** difficult, risky, ticklish (work); *Mus:* **un passage s.,** a tricky passage. **2.** indelicate, embarrassing (question); improper (story).

scandale [skɑ̃dal], *s.m.* scandal; (cause of) shame; **c'est un s.,** it's disgraceful.

scandaleu|x, -euse [skɑ̃dalø, -øːz], *a.* scandalous, shameful, disgraceful; *adv.* **-sement.**

scandaliser [skɑ̃dalize], *v.tr.* to scandalize (s.o.); to shock (s.o.).
se scandaliser, to be scandalized, shocked (**de, at**).

scandinave [skɑ̃dinaːv], *a. & s.* Scandinavian.

Scandinavie (la) [laskɑ̃dinavi]. *Pr.n.f. Geog:* Scandinavia.

scaphandr|e [skafɑ̃ːdr], *s.m.* (*a*) diving-suit; (*b*) **s. (d'un cosmonaute),** space suit; *s.m.* **-ier,** diver (in diving-suit).

scarabée [skarabe], *s.m.* **1.** beetle. **2.** scarab.

scarlatine [skarlatin], *s.f. Med:* scarlet fever, scarlatina.

sceau, sceaux [so], *s.m.* seal; **s. de l'État,** State

seal; *Adm:* **les Sceaux** = the Great Seal; **apposer son s. à un document,** to set one's seal to a document; **sous le s. du secret,** under the seal of secrecy.

scélérat, -ate [selera, -at], *s.* scoundrel; villain.

scellé [sele]. **1.** *a.* sealed; under seal. **2.** *s.m. Jur:* (*imprint of official*) seal (on door, etc.); **lever les scellés,** to remove the seals.

sceller [sele], *v.tr.* **1.** (*a*) to seal; to seal up; *Jur:* **signé et scellé par moi,** given under my hand and seal; (*b*) *F:* to ratify, confirm; to seal. **2.** *Const:* to fix, fasten (a post, iron bar).

scénar|io [senarjo], *s.m. Th:* scenario; *Cin:* film script; *s.* **-iste,** scenario writer; script writer.

scène [sɛn], *s.f.* **1.** (*a*) stage; **entrer en s.,** to appear, come on; **mettre en s.,** to stage, produce (play, etc.); **metteur en s.,** producer; **mise en s.,** production; (*b*) the theatre; **les chefs-d'œuvre de la s.,** (the) masterpieces of the theatre. **2.** (*a*) *Th:* scene; (*b*) scene of action; (*c*) **c'était une s. pénible,** it was a painful scene; (*d*) *F:* angry discussion; **s. de ménage,** family scene, row.

scénique [senik], *a.* scenic; theatrical; **indications scéniques,** stage directions.

scepticisme [sɛptisism], *s.m.* scepticism, *N.Am:* skepticism.

sceptique [sɛptik]. **1.** *a.* sceptical, *N.Am:* skeptical. **2.** *s.* sceptic, *N.Am:* skeptic; *adv.* **-ment.**

sceptre [sɛptr], *s.m.* sceptre.

schéma [ʃema], *s.m.* (*a*) diagram; (sketch) plan; *El:* wiring diagram; *Mec:* **s. de graissage,** lubrication chart; (*b*) project, plan (for a book etc.); scheme, arrangement; *Ind:* plan.

schism|e [ʃism], *s.m.* schism; *a. & s.* **-atique,** schismatic.

sciatique [sjatik]. **1.** *a.* sciatic (nerve, etc.). **2.** *s.* Med: sciatica.

scie [si], *s.f.* **1.** saw; *Tls:* **s. à découper,** fret-saw, jigsaw; **s. égoïne,** (small) handsaw; **en dents de s.,** serrate(d). **2.** *F:* (*a*) bore, nuisance; (*b*) catchword, gag.

sciemment [sjamɑ̃], *adv.* knowingly, wittingly

science [sjɑ̃ːs], *s.f.* **1.** knowledge, learning, skill. **2.** science.

science-fiction [sjɑ̃sfiksjɔ̃], *s.f.* science fiction.

scientifique [sjɑ̃tifik]. **1.** *a.* scientific; **recherche s.,** scientific research. **2.** *s.* scientist; *a.* **-ment.**

sci|er [sje], *v.tr.* (*pr.sub. & p.d. n.* **sciions**) **1.** saw (wood, stone); *F:* **s. le dos à qn,** to bore s.o. stiff. **2.** to saw off (branch, etc.); *s.f.* **-erie,** sawmill; *s.m.* **-eur,** sawyer.

scintill|er [sɛ̃tije], *v.i.* to scintillate; to sparkle (*of star*) to twinkle; *T.V: Cin:* to flicker; *s.* **-ation,** scintillation; twinkling; flickering.

scission [sisjɔ̃], *s.f.* (*a*) scission, cleavage, split (in political party, etc.); (*b*) *Atom.Ph:* fission.

sciure [sjyːr], *s.f.* **s. de bois,** sawdust.

scolaire [skɔlɛːr], *a.* scholastic; **l'année s.,** the academic year; **livres scolaires,** school books, text books; **groupe s.** school block, school buildings; **vie s.,** school life.

scolaris|er [skɔlarize], *v.tr.* to provide education for (children); to equip (an area) with schools, etc.; *s.f.* **-ation,** (i) school attendance; (ii) schooling, education.

scolarité [skɔlarite], *s.f. Sch:* (*a*) **s. obligatoire,** compulsory school attendance; **prolongation de la s.,** raising of the school-leaving age; (*b*) **payer les scolarités,** to pay the school fees.

scorpion [skɔrpjɔ̃], *s.m.* scorpion; *Astr:* **le S.,** Scorpio.

scrupule [skrypyl], *s.m.* scruple, (conscientious) doubt (**sur,** about); **homme sans scrupules,** unscrupulous man; **ne s'embarrasser d'aucun s.,** to stick at nothing.

scrupuleu|x, -euse [skrypylø, -øːz], *a.* scrupulous (**sur,** about, over, as to); **peu s.,** unscrupulous; *adv.* **-sement.**

scrut|er [skryte], *v.tr.* to scrutinize; to scan; to examine closely; **s. qn du regard,** to give s.o. a searching look; *a.* **-ateur, -atrice,** searching (mind, look); **regarder qn d'un œil s.,** to look searchingly at s.o.

scrutin [skrytɛ̃], *s.m.* **1.** poll; **dépouiller le s.,** to count votes. **2. tour de s.,** ballot; **voter au s.,** to ballot. **3.** voting; (parliamentary) division; **procéder au s.,** to take the vote; (*in Eng. Parliament*) to divide; **projet adopté sans s.,** bill passed without a division.

sculpt|er [skylte], *v.tr.* to sculpture, to sculpt; to carve; **un amour sculpté,** a sculptured cupid; **bois sculpté,** carved wood; *s.m.* **-eur,** sculptor; **s. sur bois,** woodcarver.

sculpture [skyltyːr], *s.f.* sculpture; **s. sur bois,** wood-carving.

se [sə], *before a vowel sound* **s',** *pers.pron.acc. & dat.* **1.** (*a*) (*reflexive*) oneself; himself, herself, itself, themselves; **se flatter,** to flatter oneself; **elle s'est coupée au doigt, s'est coupé le doigt,** she has cut her finger; (*b*) (*reciprocal*) each other, one another; **il est dur de se quitter,** it is hard to part. **2.** (*giving passive meaning to active verbs*) **la clef s'est retrouvée,** the key has been found; **cet article se vend partout,** this article is sold everywhere; **la porte s'est ouverte,** the door opened, came open. **3.** (*in purely pronom. conjugation*) *see* S'EN ALLER, SE DÉPÊCHER, *etc. Note: se is often omitted before an infinitive dependent on* **faire, laisser, mener, envoyer, voir;** *e.g.* **faire taire les enfants; nous avons vu lever le soleil.**

séance [seɑ̃ːs], *s.f.* **1.** sitting, session, meeting; **déclarer la s. ouverte,** to open the meeting; **lever la s.,** to dissolve the meeting; **s. d'information,** briefing. **2.** (cinema, etc.) performance; **s. de spiritisme,** seance. **3.** (*a*) sitting (for one's portrait); (*b*) period, session (of work, training).

séant [seɑ̃]. **1.** (*a*) *a.* sitting; in session; **assemblée séante à Paris,** assembly sitting in Paris; (*b*) *s.m.* **se dresser sur son s.,** to sit up (in bed). **2.** *a.* becoming; fitting, seemly (dress, behaviour).

seau, seaux [so], *s.m.* pail, bucket; **s. à charbon,** coal-scuttle; **s. de ménage,** slop pail.

sec, sèche [sɛk, sɛʃ], *a.* **1.** (*a*) dry (weather, ground); **avoir la gorge sèche,** to be thirsty; (*b*) dried (fish, fruit); seasoned (wood); dry (wine); (*c*) **perte sèche,** dead loss. **2.** (*a*) spare, gaunt (man); lean (figure); **s. et nerveux,** wiry; (*b*) sharp, dry, curt (remark); incisive (tone); **donner un coup s. à qch.,** to give sth. a sharp blow, tap; **un merci tout s.,** a bare thank you; (*c*) unsympathetic, unfeeling (heart); *adv.* **rire s.,** to give a harsh, dry, laugh; (*d*) barren; dry, bald (narrative); (*e*) *F:* **faire qch. en cinq s.,** to do sth. in a jiffy. **3.** *adv.phr.* **à s.,** (i) dry; (ii) dried up; (iii) *F:* hard-up; **mettre une mare à s.,** to drain a pond; **navire à s.,** ship aground, high and dry.

sécession [sesɛsjɔ̃], *s.f.* secession; **faire s.,** to secede (**de,** from).

sèche-cheveux [sɛʃʃəvø], *s.m.inv.* hair drier.

sèche-linge [sɛʃlɛ̃ːʒ], *a.inv. H:* **armoire s.-l.,** drying cupboard.

sèchement [sɛʃmɑ̃], *adv.* curtly, tartly.

séch|er [seʃe], *v.* (**je sèche; je sécherai**) **1.** *v.tr.* to dry (clothes, one's tears); **la chaleur a séché le ruisseau,** the heat has dried up the stream. **2.** *v.i.* to dry; to become dry; **faire s. le linge,** to dry the linen; (*of plant, pers.*) **s. sur pied,** to wilt; *s.m.* **-age,** drying (of hay, clothes); seasoning (of wood); *Ind:* **s. par le vide,** vacuum drying.

sécheresse [seʃrɛs], *s.f.* **1.** (*a*) dryness (of the air, throat, etc.); (*b*) drought. **2.** (*a*) leanness, spareness (of figure); (*b*) curtness (of manner); (*c*) coldness, unfeelingness.

séchoir [seʃwaːr], *s.m.* **1.** drying place, room, ground. **2.** drier, drying apparatus; clothes-horse; towel-rail.

second, -onde [səgɔ̃, -ɔ̃ːd]. **1.** *a.* second; **habiter au s.** (**étage**), to live on the second, *N.Am:* third, floor. **2.** *s.m.* principal assistant; second (in command); *Nau:* first mate, first officer; *Navy:* **s. maître,** petty officer. **3.** *s.f.* **seconde,** (*a*) *Rail:* **voyager en seconde,** to travel second (class); (*b*) second (of time); **attendez une seconde! une seconde!** just a second!

secondaire [səgɔ̃dɛːr], *a.* **1.** secondary; **enseignement s.,** secondary education; **centre d'études secondaires** = comprehensive school. **2.** subordinate; of minor importance; **question d'importance s.,** minor question; side issue;

résidence s. = weekend cottage.

seconder [səgɔ̃de], *v.tr.* **1.** to second, back (s.o.) up. **2.** to forward, promote (s.o.'s plans).

secouer [səkwe], *v.tr.* **1.** (*a*) to shake (tree, one's head); (*b*) to shake up, rouse (s.o.); *F:* **secouez-vous! get a move on! snap out of it!** *F:* **s. (les puces à) qn,** (i) to tell s.o. off; (ii) to rouse s.o. to action. **2.** (*a*) to shake down (fruit); (*b*) **s. le joug,** to shake off the yoke; **s. la poussière de qch.,** to shake the dust off sth. **se secouer,** (*a*) to shake oneself; (*b*) to get a move on.

secourlir [səkuriːr], *v.tr.* (*conj. like* COURIR) to help, aid; *a.* **-able,** helpful, willing to help; **une main s.,** a helping hand; *s.m.* **-isme,** *Med:* first aid; *s.* **-iste,** first aid worker; relief worker.

secours [səkuːr], *s.m.* help, relief, aid; **au s.! help!** *Med:* **premiers s.,** first aid; *Adm:* **s. à domicile,** outdoor relief; **le s. aux enfants,** child-welfare work; **société de s. mutuels,** friendly society; **sortie de s.,** emergency exit; *Rail:* **convoi de s.,** break-down train; *Aut:* **roue de s.,** spare wheel.

secousse [səkus], *s.f.* shake, shaking; jolt, jerk; shock; **s. sismique,** earth tremor; **se dégager d'une s.,** to jerk oneself free; **s. politique,** political upheaval; **se remettre d'une s.,** to get over a shock.

secrlet, -ète [səkrɛ, -ɛt]. **1.** *a.* secret, hidden. **2.** *s.m.* (*a*) secret; **garder un s.,** to keep a secret; **être du s., dans le s.,** to be in the secret, *F:* in the know; (*b*) secrecy; privacy; **abuser du s. professionnel.** to commit a breach of confidence; *Ecc:* **le s. de la confession,** the seal of confession; *adv.* **-ètement.**

secrétaire [səkretɛːr]. **1.** *s.m. & f.* secretary; **s. particulier,** private secretary; **s. de mairie** = town clerk. **2.** *s.m. Orn:* secretary-bird.

secrétariat [səkretarja], *s.m.* **1.** secretaryship. **2.** secretary's office; secretariat.

secte [sɛkt]. *s.f.* sect.

secteur [sɛktœːr], *s.m.* **1.** sector; *Mth:* **s. circulaire,** sector of a circle. **2.** (*a*) area, district; *Com:* **s. de vente,** sales area; (*b*) *El:* mains; *Rad:* **poste s.,** mains set. **3.** field (of activity); **s. économique,** economic sector; **le s. privé,** private enterprise; **le s. public,** state enterprise.

section [sɛksjɔ̃], *s.f.* **1.** section, cutting. **2.** section; branch. **3.** *Mth:* (i) section; (ii) intersection. **4.** stage (on bus, etc., route).

séculaire [sekylɛːr], *a.* **1.** occurring once in a hundred years; secular. **2.** century-old; time-honoured (custom).

séculier, -ière [sekylje, -jɛːr]. **1.** *a.* (*a*) secular; (*b*) laic; lay. **2.** *s.m.* layman.

sécurité [sekyrite], *s.f.* **1.** security; freedom from fear; **s. de l'emploi,** guaranteed employment; *Adm:* **S. sociale** = National Health (Service). **2.** safety; **s. de la route,** road

safety; **compagnies républicaines de s.,** (C.R.S.), riot police.

sédatif, -ive [sedatif, -iːv], *a. & s.m. Med:* sedative.

sédentaire [sedɑ̃tɛːr], *a.* sedentary (way of life).

sédiment [sedimɑ̃], *s.m.* sediment, deposit; *a.* **-aire,** sedimentary.

séditieulx, -euse [sedisjø, -øːz], *a.* (*a*) seditious; (*b*) mutinous; **tenir des propos s.,** to talk treason; *adv.* **-sement.**

sédition [sedisjɔ̃], *s.f.* sedition; mutiny.

séducteur, -trice [sedyktœːr, -tris]. **1.** *s.* (*a*) tempter, *f.* temptress; (*b*) *s.m.* seducer. **2.** *a.* tempting (word, look); seductive (charm).

séduction [sedyksjɔ̃], *s.f.* **1.** seduction; enticement. **2.** charm, seductiveness.

sédulire [sedɥiːr], *v.tr.* (*conj. like* CONDUIRE) **1.** to seduce; to lead astray; to suborn (a witness). **2.** to fascinate, captivate, charm; to attract (s.o.); *a.* **-isant.**

segment [sɛgmɑ̃], *s.m. Geom: Mec: El: etc:* segment.

ségrégation [segregasjɔ̃], *s.f.* segregation; isolation; **s. raciale,** colour bar; apartheid; *s.m.* **-isme,** *Pol:* (policy of) racial segregation; *a. &* **s. -iste,** segregationist.

seiche [sɛʃ], *s.f. Moll:* cuttlefish.

seigle [sɛgl], *s.m.* rye; **pain de s.,** rye bread.

seigneur [sɛɲœːr], *s.m.* **1.** lord; nobleman. **2.** **le S.,** God; the Lord; **Notre-S.,** Our Lord; **le jour du S.,** the Lord's day, Sunday.

sein [sɛ̃], *s.m.* breast, bosom; **au s. de la famille,** in the bosom of the family; **au s. de la commission,** within, among the members of, the committee.

seize [sɛːz], *num.a.inv.* sixteen; **Louis S.,** Louis the Sixteenth; **le s. mai,** (on) the sixteenth of May; **demeurer au numéro s.,** to live at number sixteen.

seizième [sɛzjɛm], *num.a. & s.* sixteenth.

séjour [seʒuːr], *s.m.* **1.** (*a*) stay (in a place); (*b*) living room. **2.** (place of) abode; residence.

séjourner [seʒurne], *v.i.* to stay, stop (in place).

sel [sɛl], *s.m.* **1.** salt; **régime sans s.,** salt-free diet; **mettre son grain de s. dans tout,** to meddle; chip in. **2.** *F:* piquancy, wit.

sélection [selɛksjɔ̃], *s.f.* selection, choice; **professionnelle,** professional aptitude test; *S.* **match de s.,** trial game; *Biol:* **s. naturelle,** natural selection.

sélectionnler [selɛksjɔne], *v.tr.* to choose, select; to pick; *s.* **-eur, -euse,** selector.

sélectivité [selɛktivite], *s.f.* selectivity.

self-service [sɛlfsɛrvis], *s.m.* self-service store; **manger au s.-s.,** to eat in the cafeteria; *pl. self services.*

selle [sɛl], *s.f.* **1.** saddle; **être bien en s.,** to firmly established. **2.** *Cu:* **s. de mouton,** saddle of mutton; **s. de bœuf**, baron of beef.

ell|er [sele], *v.tr.* to saddle (horse); *s.f.* **-erie**, saddlery; harness room; *s.m.* **-ier**, saddler.

elon [s(ə)lɔ̃], *prep.* according to; **s. moi**, in my opinion; **c'est s.**, that's as may be; it all depends.

eltz [sɛls], *s.m.* **eau de s.**, soda-water.

emaine [səmɛn], *s.f.* (*a*) week; **deux fois par s.**, twice weekly; **fin de s.**, weekend; (*b*) working week; week's work; (*c*) week's pay.

emblable [sãblabl]. **1.** *a.* (*a*) alike; similar (**à**, to); like; **votre cas est s. au mien**, your case is similar to, like, mine; **en s. occasion**, on such an occasion; (*b*) such; **je n'ai rien dit de s.**, I said no such thing. **2.** *s.* fellow; (*a*) like, equal, counterpart; **vous ne trouverez pas son s.**, you will not find his like; (*b*) **nos semblables**, our fellow-men; *adv.* **-ment**.

mblant [sãblɑ̃], *s.m.* semblance, appearance; (outward) show; **faux s.**, pretence; **faire s. de faire qch.**, to pretend to be doing sth.; **sans faire s. de rien**, (i) surreptitiously; (ii) as if nothing had happened.

mbler [sãble], *v.i.* (*aux.* **avoir**) (*a*) to seem, to appear; **elle semblait malade**, she seemed ill; (*b*) *impers.* **à ce qu'il me semble**, as it strikes me; I think; **faites comme bon vous semble(ra)**, do as you think fit; **que vous en semble?** what do you think of it?

melle [səmɛl], *s.f.* **1.** sole (of shoe); **ne pas reculer d'une s.**, not to give way an inch; **battre la s.**, to be on the tramp. **2.** *Aut: etc:* tread (of tyre).

nence [səmɑ̃:s], *s.f.* **1.** seed. **2.** (*a*) **s. de perles**, seed pearls; (*b*) **s.** (**de tapissier**), (tin)tacks.

n|er [səme], *v.tr.* (**je sème**) **1.** to sow (seeds); **s. un champ**, to sow a field. **2.** to spread, strew, scatter (flowers, etc.); to spread abroad (news, rumours); **ciel semé d'étoiles**, star-spangled sky; **s. la terreur**, to spread terror. **3.** *F:* to shake off, shed (an unwanted person); **s. une connaissance**, to drop an acquaintance; **eur, -euse**, sower; spreader (of news, disease).

nestr|e [səmɛstr], *s.m.* **1.** half-year. **2.** six months' income. **3.** *Sch:* semester, term (of six months); *a.* **-iel, -ielle**, half-yearly.

i-circulaire [səmisirkylɛ:r], *a.* semicircular.

inaire [seminɛ:r], *s.m.* (*a*) seminary; (*b*) *Sch:* eminar; (*c*) training centre.

is [səmi], *s.m.* **1.** sowing. **2.** seedlings.

itique [semitik], *a.* Semitic.

nonce [səmɔ̃:s], *s.f.* reprimand, scolding, lling-off; **verte s.**, good talking-to; **s. con-gale**, (wifely) nagging.

oule [səmul], *s.f.* semolina.

at [sena], *s.m.* **1.** senate. **2.** senate-house.

at|eur [senatœ:r], *s.m.* senator; *a.* **-orial**, **riaux**, senatorial.

Sénégal (le) [ləsenegal]. *Pr.n.m. Geog:* Senegal; *a.* & *s.* **-ais**, **-aise**, Senegalese.

sénil|e [senil], *a.* (*a*) *Med:* senile; **dégénérescence s.**, senile degeneration; (*b*) senile, of an elderly person; **il parlait d'une voix s.**, he spoke like an old man; **il n'est pas du tout s.**, *F:* he's not at all gaga; *s.f.* **-ité**.

sens [sɑ̃:s], *s.m.* **1.** sense (of touch, sight, etc.); **les cinq s.**, the five senses; **s. moral**, conscience. **2.** sense, judgment, intelligence; **s. commun, bon s.**, common sense, good sense; **s. pratique**, practical sense; **à mon s.**, in my opinion. **3.** sense, meaning (of a word); **s'exprimer dans le même s.**, to express oneself to the same effect. **4.** direction, way; **retourner qch. dans tous les s.**, to turn sth. over and over; **rue à s. unique**, one-way street; **s. interdit**, no entry; **s. dessus dessous**, topsy-turvy.

sensation [sɑ̃sasjɔ̃], *s.f.* sensation. **1.** feeling; **s. de froid**, feeling of cold; **s. agréable de chaleur**, pleasant sense of warmth. **2.** excitement; **roman à s.**, sensational novel, *F:* thriller; **faire s.**, to make a sensation; **la pièce a fait s.**, the play was a hit; *a.* **-nel, -nelle**, sensational.

sensé [sɑ̃se], *a.* sensible, judicious (person, answer).

sensib|le [sãsibl], *a.* **1.** (*a*) sensitive, susceptible; **être peu s.**, to be insensitive, to have a thick skin; **être s. au froid**, to feel the cold; **toucher la corde s.**, to appeal to the emotions; (*b*) sympathetic; **cœur s.**, tender heart; (*c*) sensitive (balance, thermometer, etc.); *Phot:* **papier s.**, sensitized paper; (*d*) sensitive, tender (tooth, sore place); **l'endroit s.**, the sore point. **2.** sensible; perceptible; **le monde s.**, the tangible world; **un vide s.**, a noticeable gap; *s.f.* **-ilité**, sensibility; sensitiveness; *adv.* **-lement**, appreciably, perceptibly; *s.f.* **-lerie**, sentimentality, mawkishness, *F:* sob-stuff.

sensitif, -ive [sãsitif, -i:v], *a.* sensitive; having the faculty of feeling.

sensual|ité [sãsɥalite], *s.f.* sensuality; *a.* & *s.* **-iste**, (i) *a.* sensual; (ii) *s.* sensualist.

sensuel, -élle [sãsɥel], *a.* sensual.

sentence [sãtã:s], *s.f.* (*a*) sentence, judgment; (*b*) **rendre une s.** (**arbitrale**), to make an award.

sentencieu|x, -ieuse [sãtãsjø, -jø:z], *a.* sententious (style, writer); *adv.* **-sement**.

senteur [sãtœ:r], *s.f.* scent, perfume; *Bot:* **pois de s.**, sweet pea.

sentier [sãtje], *s.m.* (foot)path.

sentiment [sãtimã], *s.m.* **1.** (*a*) sensation, feeling (of joy, hunger, etc.); (*b*) sense, consciousness; **s. très vif de l'humour**, keen sense of humour; (*c*) **ses sentiments vis-à-vis de moi**, his feelings towards me. **2.** opinion; *a.* **-al, -aux**; *s.f.* **-alité**.

sentinelle [sãtinɛl], *s.f. Mil:* sentry; **faire (la) s.**, (i) to mount guard; (ii) to be on the watch.

sentir [sãti:r], v. (conj. like MENTIR) **1.** v.tr. (a) to feel; **s. quelque chose pour qn**, to feel drawn to s.o.; (b) to be conscious, sensible, of; **s. un danger**, to be conscious of danger; **l'effet se fera s.**, the effect will be felt; (c) to smell (odour, flower); F: **je ne peux pas le s.**, I can't stand him. **2.** v.i. (a) to taste of, smell of (sth.); **vin qui sent le bouchon**, corked wine; **la pièce sent l'humidité**, the room smells damp; (b) **s. bon**, to smell good; (c) to smell, to stink. **se sentir. 1. je me sens fatigué(e)**, I feel tired. **2. il ne se sent pas de joie**, he is beside himself with joy. **3.** (of pers.) to be conscious of one's own strength, one's capabilities, etc.; **l'artiste commence à se s.**, the artist is beginning to find his feet.

sépale [sepal], s.m. Bot: sepal.

séparé [separe], a. **1.** separate, different, distinct. **2.** separated, apart; **vivre s. de sa femme**, to live apart from one's wife.

séparer [separe], v.tr. **1.** to separate (**de**, from); to disunite, part; **s. les bons d'avec les mauvais**, to separate, set apart, the good from the bad. **2.** to divide, keep apart; **mur qui sépare deux champs**, wall dividing two fields; **une table le séparait de la porte**, a table was between him and the door; a. **-able**; s.f. **-ation**; adv. **-ément**, separately, individually. **se séparer. 1.** to separate, part (**de**, from); to part company; **se s. de sa femme**, to separate from one's wife; **se s. du monde**, to detach oneself from the world. **2.** (of river, road, etc.) to divide, branch off. **3.** (of crowd, assembly, etc.) to break up, disperse.

sépia [sepja], s.f. sepia (colour); (**dessin à la) s.**, sepia drawing.

sept [set], num.a.inv. & s.m.inv. seven; **le s. mai**, (on) the seventh of May; **Édouard S.**, Edward the Seventh.

septembre [septã:br], s.m. September; **en s.**, in September; **le premier, le sept, s.**, (on) the first, the seventh, of September.

septième [setjem]. **1.** num.a. & s. seventh; **demeurer au s.** (**étage**), to live on the seventh, NAm: eighth, floor. **2.** s.m. seventh (part); adv. **-ment.**

septique [septik], a. Med: septic; Hyg: **fosse s.**, septic tank.

septuagénaire [septɥaʒenɛ:r], a. & s. septuagenarian.

sépulcre [sepylkr], s.m. sepulchre; a. **-al**, **-aux**, sepulchral.

sépulture [sepylty:r], s.f. **1.** burial, interment; **refuser la s. à qn**, to refuse Christian burial to s.o. **2.** burial-place, tomb.

séquence [sekã:s], s.f. sequence.

séquestrer [sekestre], v.tr. to sequestrate (property); to lay an embargo on (ship); to isolate; to confine (s.o.) illegally; s.f. **-ation.**

séraphin [serafɛ̃], s.m. seraph; a. **-ique** seraphic, angelic (smile, etc.).

Sercq [serk]. Pr.n.m. Geog: (the island of) Sark

serein [sǝrɛ̃], a. (of weather, pers.) serene, calm

sérénade [serenad], s.f. serenade.

sérénité [serenite], s.f. serenity, calmness.

serf, serve [serf, serv], s. Hist: serf.

serge [serʒ], s.m. Tex: (woollen) serge.

sergent [serʒã], s.m. Mil: sergeant (in infantry air force); **s. fourrier**, **s. comptable** quartermaster-sergeant; **s. major** = senic quartermaster-sergeant; **s. instructeur**, dri sergeant.

série [seri], s.f. (a) series; succession; T.V: etc: (**d'émissions**), series; Med: **une s. de piqûres**, course of injections; **faire une s. de visites**, go on a round of visits; **s. noire**, chapter of a cidents, run of bad luck; (b) Bill: break; run (cannons); (c) Ind: **fabrication en s.**, ma production; Aut: **voiture de s.**, standa model; (**modèle) hors s.**, custom-built (mode Com: range, line (of goods); **fins de s.**, re nants, (of books) remainders.

sérieux, -euse [serjø, -ø:z]. **1.** a. (a) serio grave, sober; **s. comme un pape**, as solemn a judge; (b) serious-minded (person); earnest, genuine; **êtes-vous s.?** do you mean **homme s.**, responsible, reliable, man; **peu** irresponsible (person); **acheteur s.**, genui purchaser; (d) grave, weighty, importa (matter, etc.); **maladie sérieuse**, serious illne Com: **client s.**, good customer; **mais sérieuse**, reliable firm. **2.** s.m. seriousne gravity; **garder son s.**, to keep a straight fa adv. **-sement.**

serin [s(ǝ)rɛ̃], s.m. (a) Orn: canary; (b) a.inv. **gants jaune s.**, canary-yellow gloves.

seringue [s(ǝ)rɛ̃:g], s.f. syringe, squirt.

seringuer [s(ǝ)rɛ̃ge], v.tr. (a) to syringe; (b) squirt (liquid).

serment [sermã], s.m. (solemn) oath; **prêter** to take an oath; **déclaration sous s.**, sw statement; **faire un faux s.**, to commit perju

sermon [sermɔ̃], s.m. (a) sermon; (b) F: talki to, lecture.

sermonner [sermɔne], F: **1.** v.i. to sermonize v.tr. to lecture; to give a talking-to to (s.o.)

serpe [serp], s.f. bill-hook, hedging-bill.

serpent [serpã], s.m. serpent, snake.

serpenter [serpãte], v.i. (of river, road, etc. wind, meander, to curve; s.m. **-ement**, ding, curving, meandering (of road, river); **-in** [-ɛ̃], coil; (paper) streamer.

serpillière [serpijɛ:r], s.f. (a) packing cl sacking; (b) H: floor cloth.

serpolet [serpɔle], s.m. Bot: wild thyme.

serre [sɛ:r], s.f. **1.** greenhouse, conservat glass-house; **serre chaude**, hothouse. **2.** grip; **avoir la s. bonne**, to have a strong g

(b) pl. claws, talons (of bird of prey).

erré [sere], a. (a) tight (boots, knot, etc.); compact, serried (ranks); **les dents serrées,** with clenched teeth; **avoir le cœur s.,** to be sad at heart, to have a heavy heart; **surveillance serrée,** close supervision; (b) adv. **jouer s.,** to play a cautious game.

errler [sere], v.tr. 1. to put away, stow away (sth., in drawer, cupboard, etc.); **s. qch. sous clef,** to lock sth. up. 2. to press, squeeze, clasp; **s. la main à qn,** to shake s.o.'s hand; **s. le cou à qn,** to strangle s.o.; **cela me serre le cœur,** it wrings my heart. 3. to tighten; to screw up (nut, etc.); **s. les freins,** to put on the brakes; **s. qch. dans un étau,** to grip sth. in a vice; **s. les dents,** to clench one's teeth. 4. to close, close up; to press close together; Mil: **s. les rangs,** to close the ranks. 5. to keep close to; **s. la muraille,** to hug, skirt, the wall; Aut: P.N: **serrez à droite!** = keep to nearside (lane)! s.m. **-ement,** squeezing, pressure.

serrer. 1. to stand, sit, close together; to crowd; **se s. les uns contre les autres,** to huddle together. 2. to tighten; **ses lèvres se serrèrent,** his lips tightened; **mon cœur s'est serré,** my heart sank.

rurle [sery:r], s.f. lock; **s. de sûreté,** safety lock; **trou de la s.,** key-hole; s.m. **-ier,** (i) locksmith; (ii) ironsmith; **s. d'art,** art metal worker.

vant, -ante [servã, -ã:t]. 1. a. serving. 2. s.m. a) Artil: **les servants,** the gun crew; (b) Ten: erver; (c) Ecc: **s. (de messe),** server, altar boy.

. s.f. **servante,** (a) (maid-)servant, servant(-girl); (b) dinner waggon; dumb-waiter.

veur, -euse [servœ:r, -ø:z]. 1. barman, barmaid; waiter, waitress. 2. Cards: dealer; Ten: erver.

viable [servjabl], a. obliging; willing to help; dv. **-ment.**

vice [servis], s.m. 1. (a) service; **porte de s.,** radesmen's entrance; **escalier de s.,** ackstairs; (b) attendance, service (in hotel, tc.); **s. compris,** service included; **libre s.,** self-ervice (in shop, restaurant, etc.); (c) epartment; administrative authority; **chef de** , departmental head; **entreprise de s. public,** ublic utility undertaking; Com: **s. après** ente, after-sales service; Adm: **s. contractuel,** ontract service; (d) **s. militaire (obligatoire),** ompulsory military service; **être apte au s.,** be fit for service; **faire son s.,** to do one's ational service. 2. (a) duty; **officier de s.** derly officer; **s. courant,** routine duties; **s. de** ur, de nuit, day, night, duty; **tableau de s.,** ty roster; (b) Adm: **s. du personnel,** per-nnel department; **s. de renseignements,** quiry office; **s. des eaux,** water supply; **s.** stal, mail, postal, service; (c) Med: etc: les

services sociaux, the social services; **s. de (la) santé,** (national) health service. 3. (service rendered) **rendre un bon, un mauvais, s. à qn,** to do s.o. a good, a bad, turn; **à votre s.,** at your service. 4. (a) course (of a meal); (b) Rail: etc: **premier s.,** first service, sitting, for lunch, dinner. 5. set (of utensils); **s. de table,** dinner service.

serviette [servjet], s.f. 1. (a) (table-)napkin; (b) **s. de toilette,** towel; **s. hygiénique,** sanitary towel. 2. briefcase.

serville [servil], a. (of pers.) servile, cringing; s.f. **-ité,** servility.

servlir [servi:r], v. (conj. like MENTIR) to serve. 1. v.i. (a) to be useful (à qn, to s.o.); to be in use; **la machine peut s. encore,** the machine is still fit for use; **livres qui ont beaucoup servi,** much-used books; (b) **s. à qch.,** to be useful for sth.; **cela ne sert à rien de pleurer,** it's no good crying; (c) **s. de,** to serve as, be used as (sth.); **s. de prétexte,** to serve as a pretext. 2. v.tr. (a) to be a servant to (s.o.); to serve (s.o.); (b) abs. to serve (in army, etc.); (c) to serve, wait on; **Madame est servie,** dinner is served, madam; (d) to serve up, dish up (a meal); **servez-vous,** help yourself; (e) to help, be of service to (s.o.); (f) **s. la messe,** to serve at mass; (g) Ten: to serve; s.m. **-iteur,** servant; s.f. **-itude.**

se servir. 1. **se s. chez qn,** to buy one's provisions at a (particular) shop. 2. **se s. de qch.,** to use sth., to make use of sth.

servofrein [servofrẽ], s.m. Aut: etc: servo-brake.

servomoteur [servomotœ:r], s.m. Mec: servo-motor, auxiliary motor.

ses [se, se], poss.a. see SON¹.

session [sesjõ], s.f. session, sitting.

seuil [sœ:j], s.m. threshold; door-step; **au s. de l'hiver,** on the edge of winter; **s. de rentabilité,** break-even point.

seul [sœl], a. 1. (preceding the noun) (a) only, sole, single; **avancer comme un s. homme,** to advance as one man; **son s. souci,** his one, only, care; **pas un s.,** not a single one; (b) **la seule pensée m'effraie,** the bare thought frightens me. 2. (following the noun or used predicatively) **un homme s.,** a man by himself; **parler s. à s. à qn,** to speak to s.o. alone; **je l'ai fait tout s.,** I did it (by) myself. 3. **s. un homme pourrait l'entreprendre,** only a man could undertake it; **s. un expert pourrait nous conseiller,** only an expert could advise us; adv. **-ement,** only; solely, merely; even.

sève [se:v], s.f. (a) sap (of plant); (b) vigour, go; **la s. de la jeunesse,** the vigour of youth.

sévère [seve:r], a. severe. 1. stern, harsh; **climat s.,** hard climate. 2. strict, rigid; **mœurs sévères,** strict morals; adv. **-ment.**

sévérité [severite], s.f. severity; sternness; harshness.

sexagénaire [sɛgzaʒenɛ:r], *a. & s.* sexagenarian.

sex-appeal [sɛksapil], *s.m. F:* sex appeal.

sex|e [sɛks], *s.m.* sex; *a.* -**uel**, -**uelle**, sexual; *s.m.* -**ualisme**; *s.f.* -**ualité**.

sextuor [sɛkstɥɔ:r], *s.m. Mus:* sextet(te).

seyant [sɛjã], *a.* becoming (dress, colour); **coiffure seyante**, becoming hair style.

shampooing [ʃɑ̃pwɛ̃], *s.m.* shampoo; **faire un s. à qn**, to shampoo s.o.'s hair; **s. et mise en plis**, shampoo and set; **se faire un s.**, to wash one's hair.

shoot [ʃut], *s.m. Fb:* shot; **s. au but**, shot at goal.

short [ʃɔrt], *s.m. Cl:* (pair of) shorts.

si [si]. **I.** *conj.* (*by elision* **s'** *before* **il, ils**) **1.** if; (*a*) **si j'avais su**, had I but known, if I'd known; **si ce n'était mon rhumatisme**, if it weren't for my rheumatism; **si je ne me trompe**, if I'm not mistaken; **si seulement . . .**, if only . . .; (*b*) **s'il fut sévère, il fut juste**, if severe, he was just. **2.** whether, if; **je me demande si c'est vrai**, I wonder whether it's true; *F:* **vous connaissez Paris?—si je connais Paris!** you know Paris?— of course I know Paris! **3.** how; how much; **vous savez si je vous aime**, you know how I love you. **4.** what if; suppose; **et si elle l'apprend?** and what if she hears of it? **II.** *adv.* **1.** so; so much; (*a*) **un si bon dîner**, such a good dinner; (*b*) **il n'est pas si beau que vous**, he is not as handsome as you; (*c*) **si bien que**, with the result that. **2.** **si peu que ce soit**, however little it may be. **3.** (*in answer to a neg. question*) yes; **si fait**, yes indeed; **il n'est pas parti?—si**, he hasn't gone?—yes (, he has); **il ne s'en remettra pas—que si!** he won't get over it—yes he will!

siamois, -oise [sjamwa, -wa:z], *a. & s.* Siamese; **frères s., sœurs siamoises**, Siamese twins.

Sibérie (la) [lasiberi]. *Pr.n.f. Geog:* Siberia.

sibérien, -ienne [siberjɛ̃, -jɛn], *a. & s.* Siberian.

sibilant [sibilã], *a.* sibilant, hissing (sound).

Sicile (la) [lasisil]. *Pr.n.f. Geog:* Sicily.

sicilien, -ienne [sisiljɛ̃, -jɛn], *a. & s.* Sicilian.

sidéré [sidere], *a. F:* struck dumb (with astonishment, etc.), thunderstruck, flabbergasted, staggered.

sidérurg|ie [sideryrʒi], *s.f.* iron and steel processing, metallurgy of iron and steel; *a.* -**ique**; **industrie s.**, iron and steel industry.

siècle [sjɛkl], *s.m.* **1.** century. **2.** age, period (of time); **notre s.**, the age we live in; *F:* **il y a un s. que je ne vous ai vu**, I haven't seen you for ages.

siège [sjɛ:ʒ], *s.m.* **1.** seat, centre (of learning, activity, etc.); **s. social**, registered offices (of a company). **2.** *Mil:* siege. **3.** seat, chair; **s. au parlement**, seat in parliament; **le s. du juge**, the judge's bench. **4.** (*a*) seat (of chair); *Av:* **s. éjectable**, ejection seat; (*b*) seating (of valve, etc.).

siéger [sjeʒe], *v.i.* (**je siège**, n. **siégeons**; je

siégerai) **1.** (*of company*) to have its hea office; *Med:* **c'est là que siège le mal**, there the seat of the trouble. **2.** (*of assembly*) to si **3. s. à la Chambre**, to sit in the Chamber o Deputies; *Jur:* **s. au tribunal**, to be on th bench.

sien, sienne [sjɛ̃, sjɛn], his, hers, its, one's. *poss.a.* **mes intérêts sont siens**, my interests a his. **2. le s., la sienne, les siens, les siennes**, (*a poss.pron.* **ma sœur est plus jolie que la sienn** my sister is prettier than his, hers; (*b*) *s.m.* (i) **chacun le s.**, to each (one) his own; **y mettre d s.**, to contribute to an undertaking; (ii) *pl.* h own, her own, one's own (friends, family); (ii *F:* **il a encore fait des siennes**, he's been up t his tricks again.

sieste [sjɛst], *s.f.* siesta, nap; **faire une courte s** *F:* to have forty winks.

siffl|er [sifle]. **1.** *v.i.* (*a*) to whistle; (*of snak* goose, *etc.*) to hiss; (*of missile, bullet*) to whiz (*b*) to blow a whistle. **2.** *v.tr.* (*a*) to whistle (tune); (*b*) *Sp:* **s. une faute, la mi-temps,** whistle for a foul, for half-time; (*c*) to whist for (a dog); *Aut:* **se faire s. (par la police)**, to b pulled up (by the police); (*d*) *Th:* to hiss; *s.m* -**ement**, whistling; hissing; *s.m.* -**et**, ((*instrument*) whistle; (ii) (*sound*) whistle; -**eur**, -**euse**, whistler.

siffloter [sifl͜ote], *v.i.* to whistle to oneself, un one's breath; to whistle in snatches.

signal, -aux [siɲal, -o], *s.m.* (*a*) signal; **faire s., des signaux**, to signal; (*b*) *Adm:* A **signaux routiers**, road signs; **signa lumineux**, traffic lights; **s. clignotant**, fl signal.

signal|er [siɲale], *v.tr.* **1.** (*a*) to make (sth.) c spicuous; (*b*) to point out; **s. qch. à l'attenti de qn**, to draw s.o.'s attention to sth.; **s. un li à qn**, to recommend a book to s.o.; (*c*) report; to notify; **rien à s.**, nothing to report to signal; *s.m.* -**ement**, (physical) descript (of pers., article); particulars (of a car); *s Rail:* -**eur**, signaller, signalman.

se signaler, to distinguish oneself (**par,** by).

signalisation [siɲalizasjɔ̃], *s.f.* **1.** signalling **optique**, visual signalling. **2.** (road, etc.) sig **s. routière internationale**, internatio (system of) road signs; **panneau de s.,** dir tion indicator; **poteau de s.,** signpost; **feux s.**, traffic lights; *Av:* beaconing (of lan ground).

signature [siɲaty:r], *s.f.* **1.** signing. **2.** signat

signe [siɲ], *s.m.* sign. **1.** indication; mark, to (of friendship). **2.** symbol, mark. **3.** gest motion; **s. de tête**, nod; **faire signe à qn**, to bec to s.o.

signer [siɲe], *v.tr.* to sign (a document, a che one's name); *F:* **c'est signé**, it's easy to see v did that!

se signer, to cross oneself.

signifi|er [siɲfje], *v.tr.* (*pr.sub. & p.d.* **n. signifiions**) **1.** to mean, signify; **que signifie ce mot?** what does this word mean? **cela ne signifie rien,** (i) it doesn't mean anything; (ii) it's of no importance; (*denoting indignation*) **qu'est-ce que cela signifie?** what's the meaning of this? **2.** to intimate (sth.) clearly; **s. ses intentions à qn,** to notify s.o. of one's intentions; *a.* **-catif, -cative,** significant; *adv.* **-cativement;** *s.f.* **-cation,** meaning, sense; significance.

silence [silɑ̃ːs], *s.m.* **1.** silence; **faire s.,** to stop talking; **passer qch. sous s.,** to pass over sth. in silence; **rompre le s.,** to break (the) silence. **2.** *Mus:* rest.

silencieu|x, -euse [silɑ̃sjø, -øːz], **1.** *a.* silent; (*a*) taciturn; (*b*) noiseless; (*c*) still, peaceful. **2.** *s.m. Aut: etc:* silencer, *N.Am:* muffler; *adv.* **-sement.**

silex [silɛks], *s.m.* flint.

silhouette [silwɛt], *s.f.* (*a*) silhouette; (*b*) outline, form (of person, building, etc.); profile.

sillage [sija:ʒ], *s.m.* (*a*) wake, wash (of ship); (*b*) *Av:* slipstream.

sillon [sijɔ̃], *s.m.* (*a*) *Agr:* furrow; (*b*) line (on the forehead), wrinkle; (*c*) track (of wheel); wake (of ship); **s. de lumière,** streak of light; **éclairs en sillons,** forked lightning.

sillonner [sijone], *v.tr.* (*a*) to furrow; to plough (the seas); **montagne sillonnée par les torrents,** mountain scored by torrents; (*b*) to streak (the sky with light, etc.).

silo [silo], *s.m.* (*a*) *Agr:* silo; clamp; (*b*) silo, elevator; **s. à blé,** grain elevator.

similaire [similɛːr], *a.* similar (**à,** to); like; (persons, things) of the same kind; *adv.* **-ment.**

similarité [similarite], *s.f.* similarity, likeness.

simili [simili], *s.m. F:* imitation; **bijoux en s.,** costume jewellery.

similitude [similityd], *s.f.* similitude; resemblance, likeness (of two people, things); similarity (of ideas).

simple [sɛ̃ːpl], *a.* simple. **1.** (*a*) single (flower, ticket, etc.); *Ten:* **s. messieurs, dames,** men's, ladies', singles; *Mec:* **à s. effet,** single-acting; (*b*) (*not compound*) **avoir une chance s.,** to have an even chance; *Ch:* **corps s.,** element. **2.** (*a*) ordinary, common; **un s. particulier,** a private citizen; **s. soldat,** private (soldier); (*b*) **la vérité pure et s.,** the plain truth; **de la folie pure et s.,** sheer madness; **croire qn sur sa s. parole,** to believe s.o. on his word alone; (*c*) **gens simples,** plain people; (*d*) easy; **méthode s.,** easy method; **s. comme bonjour,** as easy as A.B.C. **3.** (*a*) simple-minded; half-witted; (*b*) ingenuous; credulous; *F:* green; *adv.* **-ment.**

simplicité [sɛ̃plisite], *s.f.* **1.** simplicity (of dress, manners); plainness. **2.** artlessness, simpleness; simple-mindedness.

simplifi|er [sɛ̃plifje], *v.tr.* (*pr.sub. & p.d.* **n. simplifiions**) to simplify; *a. & s.m.* **-cateur, -catrice,** (*a*) *a.* simplifying; (*b*) *s.* simplifier; *s.f.* **-cation.**

simulé [simyle], *a.* feigned, sham (illness, fight); fictitious, bogus (sale).

simul|er [simyle], *v.tr.* to simulate; to feign, sham; **s. une maladie,** to pretend to be ill; to malinger; *s.f.* **-ation,** simulation; pretence.

simultané [simyltane], *a.* simultaneous; *adv.* **-ment.**

sincère [sɛ̃sɛːr], *a.* sincere. **1.** frank, candid (person); **homme s.,** plain-spoken man. **2.** (*a*) genuine, honest (person); (*b*) genuine, sincere (feelings); (*letter ending*) **agréez mes sincères salutations,** yours sincerely; *adv.* **-ment.**

sincérité [sɛ̃serite], *s.f.* (*a*) sincerity, frankness, candour; **en toute s. . . .,** honestly (speaking) . . .; (*b*) genuineness.

sinécure [sineky:r], *s.f.* sinecure.

Singapour [sɛ̃gapu:r]. *Pr.n.m. Geog:* Singapore.

singe [sɛ̃ːʒ], *s.m.* (*a*) monkey, ape; **laid comme un s.,** as ugly as sin; (*b*) *F:* ape, imitator; (*c*) *F:* ugly person; fright.

sing|er [sɛ̃ʒe], *v.tr.* (**n. singeons**) to ape, mimic (s.o.); *s.f.* **-erie,** grimace; monkey trick.

singular|iser (se) [səsɛ̃gylarize], *v.pr.* to attract attention, to make oneself conspicuous; *s.f.* **-ité,** peculiarity; oddness.

singul|ier, -ière [sɛ̃gylje, -jɛːr], *a.* singular. **1.** peculiar (**à,** to). **2.** peculiar, remarkable (merit, virtue). **3.** (*a*) odd, curious (person, custom, fact); (*b*) conspicuous. **4.** *Gram:* **au s.,** in the singular; *adv.* **-ièrement.**

sinistre [sinistr]. **1.** *a.* sinister, ominous; **de s. mémoire,** of evil memory. **2.** *s.m.* (*a*) disaster, catastrophe (*esp.* fire, earthquake, shipwreck); (*b*) loss (through disaster); **évaluer le s.,** to estimate the damage.

sinistré, -ée [sinistre]. **1.** *a.* (person, place) that has suffered a disaster; **zone sinistrée,** disaster area. **2.** *s.* victim (of a disaster).

sinon [sinɔ̃], *conj.* **1.** otherwise, (or) else, if not. **2.** except; **il ne fait rien s. dormir,** he does nothing except, but, sleep.

sinueux, -euse [sinɥø, -øːz], *a.* sinuous; winding (path); meandering (stream).

sinuosité [sinɥozite], *s.f.* (*a*) sinuosity, winding; (*b*) bend (of river).

siphon [sifɔ̃], *s.m.* siphon.

sirène [sirɛn], *s.f.* **1.** siren, mermaid. **2.** (*a*) siren, hooter; (*b*) fog-horn.

sirop [siro], *s.m.* syrup; **s. de groseille(s), de cassis,** red-, black-, currant syrup.

siroter [sirɔte], *v.tr.* (*a*) *F:* to sip; (*b*) *abs.* to tipple.

sitôt [sito], *adv.* (*a*) (= AUSSITÔT) **s. que,** as soon as; (*b*) **vous ne le reverrez pas de s.,** it will be a long time before you see him again.

situation [sitɥasjɔ̃], *s.f.* situation. **1.** position, site (of town, etc.). **2.** state, condition; **exposer la s.,** to explain the state of affairs; **s. sociale,** station in life; **s. difficile,** predicament. **3. il a une belle s.,** he has a good job.

situer [sitɥe], *v.tr.* to place situate, locate (a house, etc.); *F:* **s. qn,** to size s.o. up.

six, *num.a.inv.* & *s.m.* (*before noun beginning with consonant* [si]; *before noun beginning with a vowel sound* [siz]; *otherwise* [sis]) six. **1.** *card.a.* **s. hommes** [sizɔm], six men; **s. petits enfants** [siptizɑ̃fɑ̃], six little children; **à s. heures** [asizœːr], at six o'clock; **j'en ai s.** [sis], I have six. **2.** (*ordinal use*) **le s. mai,** (on) the sixth of May; **Charles S.,** Charles the Sixth.

sixième [sizjɛm]. **1.** *num.a.* & *s.* sixth; **demeurer au s.** (**étage**), to live on the sixth, *N.Am:* seventh, floor. **2.** *s.m.* sixth (part). **3.** *Sch:* (**classe de**) **s.,** (*approx.* =) first form (of secondary school).

ski [ski], *s.m.* **1.** ski. **2.** skiing; **s. nautique,** water skiing.

slave [slaːv]. **1.** *a.* Slav, Slavonic. **2.** *s.* Slav.

slip [slip], *s.m.* **1.** *Cl:* (*for men*) slip; **s. de bain,** bathing slip; (*for women*) briefs. **2.** *Nau:* slipway (for launching).

smoking [smɔkiŋ], *s.m.* dinner-jacket, *N.Am:* tuxedo.

snob [snɔb], *s.m.* (*a*) pretentious person; snob; (*b*) follower of fashion; **ça fait très s.,** that's very smart.

snober [snɔbe], *v.tr. Pej:* to snub, to cold-shoulder (s.o.).

sobrie [sɔbr], *a.* temperate, abstemious (person); sober, quiet (style); *adv.* **-ement; s.f. -iété,** sobriety; moderation.

sobriquet [sɔbrikɛ], *s.m.* nickname.

sociab⎮le [sɔsjabl], *a.* sociable, companionable; **peu s.,** unsociable; *s.f.* **-ilité.**

social, -aux [sɔsjal, -o], *a.* social; (*a*) **l'ordre s.,** the social order; **œuvres sociales,** welfare activities; **guerre sociale,** class war; (*b*) *Com:* **raison sociale,** name, style, of the firm; **siège s.,** head office; **capital s.,** registered capital.

social⎮isme [sɔsjalism], *s.m.* socialism; *a.* & *s.* **-iste,** (*a*) *a.* socialistic; socialist; (*b*) *s.* socialist.

société [sɔsjete], *s.f.* **1.** (*a*) society; community; **devoirs envers la s.,** duty to society; (*b*) company; **aimer la s.,** to like company. **2.** (*a*) association, fellowship; club; (*b*) *Com:* company, firm; partnership; **s. filiale,** subsidiary company, branch; **s. anonyme,** public company; **s. à responsabilité limitée** = limited (liability) company; **s. d'exploitation,** development company.**3.** (*a*) companionship (of one's fellows); (*b*) (fashionable) society; **fréquenter la bonne s.,** to move in good society.

sociolo⎮gie [sɔsjɔlɔʒi], *s.f.* sociology; *a.* **-gique,** sociological.

sociologue [sɔsjɔlɔg], *s.* sociologist.

socle [sɔkl], *s.m.* base, pedestal, plinth; stand; socket.

sœur [sœːr], *s.f.* **1.** sister. **2.** *Ecc:* sister, nun.

soi [swa], *pers.pron.* (*often followed by* -**même**) oneself; himself, herself, itself, etc.; **chacun pour s.,** everyone for himself; **petits services qu'on se rend entre s.,** small mutual services; **être chez s.,** to be at home.

soi-disant [swadizɑ̃]. **1.** *a.inv.* (*a*) self-styled; **une s.-d. baronne,** a would-be baroness; (*b*) so-called; **les arts s.-d. libéraux,** the so-called liberal arts. **2.** *adv.* supposedly, ostensibly; **il est parti s.-d. pour revenir,** he went away, supposedly with the intention of returning.

soie [swa], *s.f.* **1.** bristle (of pig, etc.). **2.** silk; **robe de s.,** silk dress; **papier de s.,** tissue paper; *s.f.* **-rie,** silks, silk goods; silk trade.

soif [swaf], *s.f.* thirst; **avoir s.,** to be thirsty; **boire à sa s.,** to drink one's fill; **la s. du pouvoir,** the craving for power.

soigné [swaɲe], *a.* well-finished, carefully done; **repas s.,** carefully cooked meal; **air s.,** well-groomed, spruce, appearance; **peu s.** (**dans sa mise**), slovenly (in his, her, dress).

soigner [swaɲe], *v.tr.* to look after, take care of (s.o., sth.); to attend to (sth.); *Med:* to nurse (an invalid); to treat (a disease); to cure (an illness); **s. son travail,** to do one's work carefully; **s. son public,** to nurse one's public, one's admirers, *Pol: etc:* one's followers; **s. sa ligne,** to watch one's waistline.

soigneu⎮x, -euse [swaɲø, -øːz], *a.* careful; painstaking; tidy (pers.); *adv.* **-sement.**

soi-même [swamɛm], *pers.pron.* oneself; **faire qch. de s.-m.,** to do sth. of one's own accord.

soin [swɛ̃], *s.m.* care; (*a*) **le s. des enfants,** the care of children; **prendre s. de qn, qch.,** to look after s.o., sth.; (*on letters*) "**aux** (**bons**) **soins de . . .,**" "care of . . ."; (*b*) attention, trouble; **avoir s.,** to take care; (*c*) **avec s.,** carefully; with care; **manque de s.,** carelessness; (*d*) *pl.* attentions, solicitude; **soins médicaux, prénataux,** medical, prenatal, care; **recevoir des soins à l'hôpital,** to be treated in hospital; **soins à domicile,** home nursing; **être aux petits soins pour qn,** to wait on s.o. hand and foot.

soir [swaːr], *s.m.* evening; **à dix heures du s.,** at ten (o'clock) p.m.; **hier, demain,** (**au**) **s.,** yesterday evening, tomorrow evening; last night, tomorrow night.

soirée [sware], *s.f.* **1.** (duration of) evening. **2.** (*a*) (evening) party; **donner une s. dansante,** to give a dance; **tenue de s.,** evening dress; **habit de s.,** dress-suit; (*b*) *Th:* **représentation de s.,** evening performance.

soit [swa, *before a vowel or as interjection:* swat⎮ (*third pers. sing. of pr.sub. of* être) **1.** (*a*) *int:* **s.!** all right! O.K.! agreed! (*b*) (*retaining* *sub. value*) suppose; if, for instance; **s. ABC un triangle,** given a triangle ABC; (*c*) (*conj. of coordination*) **trois objets à dix francs, s. trente francs,** three articles at ten francs, that's thirty francs. 2. (*a*) *conj.* **s. l'un s. l'autre,** either one or the other; (*b*) **s. qu'il vienne ou qu'il ne vienne pas,** whether he comes or not.

soixantaine [swasɑ̃tɛn], *s.f.* about sixty; **il a passé la s.,** he's in his sixties.

soixante [swasɑ̃:t], *num.a.inv. & s.m.inv.* sixty; **page s.,** page sixty; **s. et un,** sixty-one; **s. et onze,** seventy-one.

soixante-dix [swasɑ̃tdis], *num.a.inv. & s.m.inv.* seventy.

soixante-dixième [swasɑ̃tdizjɛm], *num.a & s.* seventieth.

soixantième [swasɑ̃tjɛm], *num. a. & s.* sixtieth.

soja [sɔʒa], *s.m. Bot:* soya bean, soy.

sol [sɔl], *s.m.* (*a*) ground, earth; **rester cloué au s.,** (i) *Av:* to be grounded; (ii) to stand rooted to the spot; (*b*) *Agr:* soil.

sol-air [sɔlɛ:r], *a.inv. Mil:* **missile s.-a.,** ground-to-air missile.

solaire [sɔlɛ:r], *a.* solar (system, etc.).

soldat, -ate [sɔlda, -at], *s.* soldier; serviceman,*f.* servicewoman; **simple s.,** private; **s. de première classe,** lance-corporal; **se faire s.,** to join the army.

solde[1] [sɔld], *s.f. Mil: etc:* pay; **demi-s.,** half-pay; **s. de retraite,** pension.

solde[2], *s.m. Com:* 1. balance; **s. débiteur, créditeur,** debit, credit, balance; **"pour s.," "in settlement."** 2. (*a*) surplus stock, job lot; (*b*) **vente de soldes,** (i) clearance sale; (ii) bargain counter.

sole [sɔl], *s.f. Ich:* sole.

solécisme [sɔlesism], *s.m.* (*a*) *Gram:* solecism; (*b*) **s. (de conduite),** blunder, gaffe.

soleil [sɔlɛ:j], *s.m.* 1. sun. 2. sunshine; **il fait du s.,** the sun's shining; **avoir du bien au s.,** to own landed property; **coup de s.,** (i) sunburn; (ii) touch of sunstroke; **prendre un bain de s.,** to sunbathe. 3. *Bot:* sunflower. 4. *Fireworks:* catherine wheel.

solennel, -elle [sɔlanɛl], *a.* (*a*) solemn; (*b*) official; **distribution solennelle des prix,** formal prize-giving; **silence s.,** impressive silence; *adv.* **-lement.**

solennité [sɔlanite], *s.f.* (*a*) solemnity; (*b*) solemn ceremony; **les solennités de Pâques,** the Easter celebrations; (*c*) **parler avec s.,** to speak solemnly.

solidaire [sɔlidɛ:r], *a.* 1. *Jur:* jointly responsible; **être s. des actes de qn,** to be responsible for s.o.'s acts; **il n'est s. de personne,** he's answerable to no one. 2. interdependent; **nos intérêts sont solidaires,** our interests are bound up together; **être s. d'un mouvement,** to associate oneself with a movement; *adv.*

-ment.

solidarité [sɔlidarite], *s.f.* 1. joint responsibility. 2. (*a*) interdependence; (*b*) fellowship, solidarity; **grève de s.,** sympathetic strike; *F:* **débrayer par s. (avec),** to come out (on strike) in sympathy (with).

solid|**e** [sɔlid]. 1. *a.* (*a*) solid (food, etc.); (*b*) solid, strong; *Com:* sound, solvent. 2. *s.m.* solid (body); *adv.* **-ement;** *s.f.* **-ité,** solidity, strength.

solidifi|**er** [sɔlidifje], *v.tr.* (*pr.sub. & p.d.* **n.**

soliste [sɔlist], *s.m. &f.* soloist; *a.* **violon s.,** solo violin.

solitaire [sɔlitɛ:r]. 1. *a.* solitary, lonely, lonesome (person, life); **lieu s.,** deserted spot. 2. *s.m.* (*a*) recluse; (*b*) solitaire (game); (*c*) solitaire (diamond).

solitude [sɔlityd], *s.f.* 1. solitude, loneliness; **vivre dans la s.,** to live in seclusion. 2. (*usu. in pl.*) lonely spot; wilderness; solitude.

solive [sɔli:v], *s.f. Const:* joist, beam, rafter.

sollicit|**er** [sɔllisite], *v.tr.* to solicit (s.o., sth.); to beg for (favour, interview); **s. des voix,** to canvass for votes; *s.f.* **-ation;** *s.* **-eur,** petitioner, applicant; canvasser; *s.f.* **-ude,** (tender) care; concern.

solo [sɔlo], *s.m. Mus:* solo.

sol-sol [sɔlsɔl], *a.inv. Mil:* **missile s.-s.,** ground-to-ground missile.

solstice [sɔlstis], *s.m.* solstice.

solub|**le** [sɔlybl], *a.* soluble (substance); **café s.,** instant coffee; *s.f.* **-ilité.**

solution [sɔlysjɔ̃], *s.f.* 1. **s. de continuité,** gap; break; *El:* fault. 2. solution (of solid in liquid); **s. normale, concentrée,** standard, concentrated, solution. 3. solution (of, to, question, problem); answer; **s. de remplacement,** alternative solution; **s. de facilité,** easy way out.

solvab|**le** [sɔlvabl], *a.* (financially) solvent; *s.f.* **-ilité,** solvency.

somali, -ie [sɔmali], *a. & s. Geog:* Somali; **la Côte des Somalis,** French Somali Coast.

Somalie (la) [lasɔmali]. *Pr.n.f. Geog:* **la République de S.,** Somalia, the Somali Republic.

sombre [sɔ̃:br], *a.* dark, sombre, gloomy; *adv.* **-ment.**

sombrer [sɔ̃bre], *v.i.* (*of ship*) to founder; to sink; **sa raison sombra complètement,** his mind gave way completely.

sommaire [sɔmmɛ:r]. 1. *a.* (*a*) summary, succinct, concise; (*b*) summary, hasty; improvised. 2. *s.m.* summary, abstract, synopsis; *adv.* **-ment,** summarily, hastily; **vêtu s.,** scantily dressed.

somme[1] [sɔm], *s.f.* **bête de s.,** beast of burden.

somme[2], *s.f.* sum, amount; sum of money; **s. toute,** when all's said and done; **en s.,** on the whole, in short.

somme[3], *s.m.* nap; short sleep.

sommeil [sɔmɛːj], *s.m.* **1.** sleep, slumber; **avoir le s. dur**, to be hard to wake. **2.** drowsiness, sleepiness; **avoir s.**, to be sleepy.

sommeiller [sɔmeje], *v.tr.* to doze, nod; to sleep lightly; to take a nap; **s. dans son fauteuil**, to drop off, doze off, to take forty winks, in one's armchair.

sommelier [sɔməlje], *s.m.* (*in restaurant*) wine-waiter.

sommet [sɔmɛ], *s.m.* top, summit (of hill); apex (of angle, curve); *Pol:* **conférence au s.**, summit meeting.

sommier [sɔmje], *s.m.* **s. à ressorts**, box mattress; **s. métallique**, wire mattress; **s. en mousse**, foam rubber mattress.

somnambule [sɔmnɑ̃byl], *s.* somnambulist; sleepwalker.

somnol|er [sɔmnɔle], *v.i.* to drowse, doze; *s.f.* **-ence**, sleepiness, drowsiness; *a.* **-ent**, sleepy, drowsy.

somptueu|x, -euse [sɔ̃ptɥø, -øːz], *a.* sumptuous, magnificent (present, meal); **mener un train de vie s.**, to live extravagantly, lavishly; *adv.* **-sement**.

son[1], **sa, ses** [sɔ̃, sa, sɛ], *poss.a.* (**son** *is used instead of* **sa** *before fem. nouns beginning with a vowel or* h *"mute"*) his, her, its, one's; **un de ses amis**, a friend of his, of hers; **ses père et mère**, his, her, father and mother.

son[2], *s.m.* sound (of voice, instrument, etc.); **s. d'une cloche**, ringing of a bell; **s. du tambour, de la trompette**, beat of the drum, blare of the trumpet; *Mus: etc:* **s. aigu, grave**, high-, low-, pitched sound, tone; *Av:* **mur du s.**, sound barrier; *Cin: Rec:* **enregistrement du s.**, sound recording; **prise de s.**, sound pick-up.

son[3], *s.m.* bran; **tache de s.**, freckle.

sonate [sɔnat], *s.f. Mus:* sonata.

sondage [sɔ̃daːʒ], *s.m.* (*a*) *Nau: Av: etc:* sounding; **faire des sondages**, to take soundings; *Min:* boring; **faire des sondages**, to make borings; (*b*) *Med:* probing (of wound); (*c*) **s. d'opinion**, (public) opinion poll; **enquête par s.**, sample survey.

sonde [sɔ̃ːd], *s.f.* **1.** *Nau:* (*a*) sounding-line, plummet; **jeter la s.**, to heave the lead; (*b*) (*of whale*) **faire la s.**, to sound. **2.** *Meteor: Av: Surg:* probe. **3.** *Min:* borer; drill.

sonder [sɔ̃de], *v.tr.* **1.** (*a*) *Nau:* to sound; **on n'a jamais sondé ce mystère**, this mystery has never been fathomed; (*b*) *v.i.* (*of whale*) to sound. **2.** to probe, examine; investigate, test; *Med: Meteor:* to probe, to sound; **s. le terrain**, to see how the land lies.

songe [sɔ̃ːʒ], *s.m.* dream; **faire un s.**, to have a dream.

song|er [sɔ̃ʒe], *v.i.* (*n.* **songeons**) **1.** (*a*) to dream

(*de*, of); (*b*) to day-dream; **je songeais en moi-même que . . .**, I thought to myself that . . . . **2.** (*a*) **s. à qch.**, to think of sth.; **il ne faut pas y s.**, that's quite out of the question; (*b*) to imagine; **songez donc!** just think! just imagine! (*c*) to remember; **songez à ne pas être en retard**, mind you're not late; *s.f.* **-erie**, (day-)dreaming; *a.* **-eur, -euse**, dreamy; pensive.

sonique [sɔnik], *a.* sonic; **mur s.**, sound barrier; **détonation s.**, supersonic bang.

sonnant [sɔnɑ̃], *a.* **1.** striking; **à dix heures sonnantes**, on the stroke of ten. **2.** resounding; **monnaie sonnante**, hard cash.

sonné [sɔne], *a.* **il est dix heures sonnées**, it's past ten, it's gone ten; **elle a quarante ans sonnés**, she's on the wrong side of forty.

sonn|er [sɔne]. **1.** *v.i.* to sound; (*of clocks*) to strike; (*of bells*) to ring; to toll; **sa réponse sonne faux**, his reply does not ring true; **une adresse qui sonne bien**, a good address. **2.** *v.tr.* (*a*) to sound; **s. la cloche**, to ring the bell; *abs.* **on sonne**, there is a ring at the door; (*b*) to ring for (s.o.); *s.f.* **-erie**, (i) ringing (of bells); (ii) bell; (iii) trumpet-, bugle-, call; *s.f.* **-ette**, small bell; door-bell; **serpent à sonnettes**, rattlesnake.

sonore [sɔnɔːr], *a.* (*a*) resonant; echoing (cave, vault); (*b*) sonorous; deep-toned; ringing (voice); clear-toned (bell); resounding (laughter); **intensité s.**, sound intensity; (*c*) acoustic(al); *Ph:* **onde sonore**, sound-wave; *Cin:* **film s.**, sound film; **bande, piste, s.**, sound track.

soporifique [sɔpɔrifik], *a. & s.m.* (*a*) soporific; sleep-inducing (drug); (*b*) **discours s.**, tedious, boring, speech; *s.m.* **ce livre est un vrai s.**, this book sends you to sleep.

soprano [sɔprano], *s.m. & f.* soprano.

sorbet [sɔrbɛ], *s.m.* sorbet; water-ice.

sorbetière [sɔrbətjɛːr], *s.f.* ice-cream freezer.

sorc|ier, -ière [sɔrsje, -jɛːr], *s.* sorcerer, *f.* sorceress; wizard, *f.* witch; **vieille sorcière**, old hag; *s.f.* **-ellerie**, sorcery, witchcraft.

sordide [sɔrdid], *a.* **1.** sordid, squalid; filthy, dirty; **une pièce s.**, a squalid room. **2.** mean; vile.

Sorlingues (les) [lesɔrlɛ̃ːg]. *Pr.n.f.pl. Geog:* the Scilly Isles.

sornettes [sɔrnɛt], *s.f.pl.* nonsense; idle talk.

sort [sɔːr], *s.m.* **1.** lot, condition in life. **2.** destiny, fate; **ironie du s.**, irony of fate. **3.** chance, fortune, lot; **tirer au s.**, (i) to draw lots; (ii) *Fb: etc:* to toss, to spin the coin; **le s. en est jeté**, the die is cast. **4.** spell, charm.

sorte [sɔrt], *s.f.* **1.** manner, way; **ne parlez pas de la s.**, don't talk like that; *adv.phr.* **en quelque s.**, as it were, in a way; **parlez de s. qu'on vous comprenne**, speak so as to be understood; **en s. que** + *sub.*, so that, in such a manner that. **2.** sort, kind; **toute(s) sorte(s) de choses**, all kinds of things; **un homme de la s.,** a man of that sort; **je n'ai rien dit de la s.,** I said no such thing, nothing of the kind.

ortie [sɔrti], *s.f.* **1.** (*a*) going out; coming out; departure; exit; **faire une s. pour prendre l'air,** to go out for a breath of air; **à la s. des classes,** when the children come, came, out of school; (*b*) leaving (for good); retirement (of official); **à ma s. d'école,** when I left school; (*c*) outflow (of liquid); **s. d'eau,** water discharge; (*d*) *Com:* export (of goods, etc.); **droit de s.,** export duty; **sorties de fonds,** expenses, outgoings. **2.** trip, excursion; **faire une s. le dimanche,** to go for an outing on Sundays. **3.** *Mil:* sally, sortie; *Fb:* run out (by goalkeeper). **4.** exit, way out; **s. de secours,** emergency exit.

ortilège [sɔrtilɛːʒ], *s.m.* spell, charm.

ortir [sɔrtiːr], *v.* (*conj. like* MENTIR) **I.** *v.i.* (*aux.* être) **1.** (*a*) to go, come, out; **ne le laissez pas s.,** don't let him out; *Th:* **Macbeth sort,** exit Macbeth; **s. d'un emploi,** to leave a job; *abs.* **il sort à six heures,** he finishes work at six o'clock; (*b*) to go out (on foot); to drive out; to sail out; (*c*) **s. en courant,** to run out; (*d*) to have just come out; **je sors de table,** I have just got up from table; (*e*) **s. de son sujet,** to wander from one's subject. **2.** to go out, leave the house; **Madame est sortie,** Mrs X is out; **elle ne sort pas beaucoup,** she doesn't go out much. **3.** to get out, extricate oneself (from difficulty, danger); **il sortit vainqueur,** he came off victorious; *F:* **j'ai trop à faire, je n'en sors pas,** I've too much to do, I can't get through it. **4.** to spring, descend, come (from); **sorti du peuple,** sprung from the people; **officier sorti des rangs,** officer who has risen from the ranks. **5.** to stand out, stick out, project; **yeux qui sortent de la tête,** protruding eyes; **il finira par s. de l'obscurité,** he'll end by emerging from obscurity, *F:* making a breakthrough. **II.** *v.tr.* (*aux.* avoir) to take out, bring out; **s. la voiture,** to get the car out; **un enfant,** to take a child out; **le malade s'en sortira,** the patient will pull through; **s. un livre,** to publish a book. **III.** *s.m.* **au s. du théâtre,** on coming out of the theatre; **au s. de l'hiver,** at the end of winter.

osie [sɔzi, so-], *s.m.* (s.o.'s) double.

ot, sotte [so, sɔt]. **1.** *a.* (*a*) silly, stupid, foolish; (*b*) embarrassed, disconcerted; **rester tout s.,** to look, feel, foolish. **2.** *s.* fool, idiot, ass; *adv.* **-tement;** *s.f.* **-tise,** stupidity, foolishness.

ou [su], *s.m. A:* sou (= five centimes); (*still in F: use, although the coin has disappeared*) = penny; **être sans le s.,** to be penniless, *F:* broke; **être près de ses sous,** to be mean, *F:* stingy; **affaire de quatre sous,** twopenny halfpenny business; **pas ambitieux pour un s.,** not in the least ambitious; **il n'a pas pour deux sous de courage,** he hasn't a scrap of courage.

soubresaut [subrəso], *s.m.* (*a*) sudden start; bound; jolt; (*b*) sudden emotion; gasp.

souche [suʃ], *s.f.* **1.** stump (of tree); root stock (of iris, etc.); vine stock. **2. faire s.,** to found a family; **une famille de vieille s.,** an old family. **3.** *Com:* counterfoil stub (of cheque, receipt, etc.).

souci[1] [susi], *s.m. Bot:* marigold.

souci[2], *s.m.* care. **1.** solicitude; preoccupation; **mon s. de votre bien-être,** my concern for your welfare; **s. de la vérité,** regard for truth. **2.** anxiety, worry; **se faire du s.,** to worry; **donner des soucis à qn,** to cause s.o. anxiety; **soucis d'argent,** money troubles.

soucier (se) [susje], *v.pr.* (*pr.sub. & p.d.* **n.n. souciions**) to be concerned (**de qn, qch.,** about s.o., sth.); to care, to mind (about s.o., sth.); **se s. des autres,** to worry about other people; **ne se s. de rien,** not to bother about anything.

soucieu|x, -euse [susjø, -øːz], *a.* (*a*) anxious, concerned (**de,** about); (*b*) full of care; worried; *adv:* **-sement,** (i) anxiously; (ii) carefully.

soucoupe [sukup], *s.f.* saucer; **s. volante,** flying saucer.

Soudan (le) [ləsudɑ̃]. *Pr.n.m. Geog:* the Sudan.

soude [sud], *s.f. Ch: Ind:* soda; **cristaux de s.,** washing soda; **bicarbonate de s.,** bicarbonate of soda.

souder [sude], *v.tr.* (*a*) to solder; (*b*) to weld. **se souder. 1.** to weld. **2.** (*of bone*) to knit.

souffle [sufl], *s.m.* breath. **1.** (*a*) puff, blast (of air, wind); (*b*) *Av:* slipstream. **2.** respiration, breathing; **retenir son s.,** to hold one's breath; **couper le s. à qn,** to take s.o.'s breath away, to flabbergast s.o.; **être à son dernier s.,** to be at one's last gasp; **être à bout de s.,** to be out of breath; *Sp:* **équipe bien en s.,** team in good training.

soufflé [sufle]. **1.** *a.* (*a*) puffed up, puffy (face); **soufflé** (omelette); **cours soufflés,** inflated prices; *F:* **réputation soufflée,** exaggerated reputation; (*b*) *F:* **être s.,** to be flabbergasted, taken aback. **2.** *s.m. Cu:* soufflé.

souffl|er [sufle]. **1.** *v.i.* (*a*) to blow; (*b*) to recover one's breath; **laissez-moi le temps de s.,** give me time to get my breath back; (*c*) to pant; to puff; (*d*) **le vent souffle en tempête,** it's blowing a gale. **2.** *v.tr.* (*a*) to blow up (the fire); to blow out (a candle); (*b*) to breathe, utter (a word, sound); **ne pas s. mot de qch.,** not to breathe a word about sth.; **s. qch. à l'oreille de qn,** to whisper sth. to s.o.; (*c*) to prompt (an actor); (*d*) (*of explosion*) to blast (building, etc.); *F:* (*of event, etc.*) to take (s.o.) aback; **son culot nous a soufflés,** his cheek knocked us flat; **s. -eur, -euse,** *Th:* prompter.

soufflet [suflɛ], *s.m.* **1.** (pair of) bellows; *Ind:* fan. **2.** (*a*) box on the ear, slap in the face; (*b*) affront, snub.

souffrance [sufrɑ̃:s], s.f. 1. **en s.**, in suspense, in abeyance; **colis en s.**, parcels (i) awaiting delivery, (ii) to be called for. 2. suffering, pain.

souffrant [sufrɑ̃], a. (a) suffering; in pain; (b) unwell, poorly, ailing; **il a l'air s.**, he doesn't look well.

souffrir [sufri:r], v. (conj. like COUVRIR) to suffer. 1. v.tr. (a) to endure, undergo, put up with (pain, fatigue, loss, etc.); F: **je ne peux pas le s.**, I can't bear (the sight of) him; (b) to permit, allow; **souffrez que je vous dise la vérité**, allow me to tell you the truth. 2. v.i. (a) to feel pain; **souffre-t-il?** is he in pain? **mon bras me fait s.**, my arm hurts; **je souffre de le voir si changé**, it pains, grieves, me to see him so changed; (b) to suffer injury; (of thgs) to be injured, damaged (by sth.); **les vignes ont souffert de la gelée**, the vines have suffered from the frost; (c) (of trade, etc.) to be in a bad way.

soufre [sufr], s.m. sulphur; a.inv. **gants s.**, yellow gloves.

souhait [swɛ], s.m. wish, desire; **présenter ses souhaits à qn**, to offer s.o. one's good wishes; adv.phr. **à s.**, to one's liking; **réussir à s.**, to succeed to perfection.

souhaiter [swɛte], v.tr. to wish; (a) **s. les richesses**, to wish for wealth; to want to be rich; **je vous souhaite de réussir**, I hope you'll succeed; (b) **je vous souhaite une bonne année**, I wish you a happy new year; **s. bon voyage à qn**, to wish s.o. a good journey; a. **-able**, desirable.

souiller [suje], v.tr. 1. to soil, dirty (clothes, etc.) (de, with); **souillé de boue, de sang**, mud-, blood-, stained. 2. to pollute. 3. to tarnish, sully (one's name, honour); s.f. **-ure** [(suj)y:r], spot, stain; blot, blemish.

soûl [su]. 1. a. F: drunk, tipsy. 2. s.m. **manger, boire, rire, chanter, tout son s.**, to eat, drink, laugh, sing, to one's heart's content.

soulager [sulaʒe], v.tr. (n. **soulageons**) to ease (pressure); to relieve, alleviate (pain, grief); to soothe, comfort (s.o.'s mind, etc.); s.m. **-ement**, relief, alleviation.

se soulager. 1. to ease up, to work less. 2. to relieve one's feelings, one's mind. 3. F: to relieve nature.

soulever [sulve], v.tr. (**je soulève**) 1. (a) to raise (usu. with effort); to lift (up) (a weight); (b) to raise slightly; **s. le rideau**, to peep out under the curtain; (c) **s. une objection**, to raise an objection. 2. to rouse, stir up (people, a revolt); s.m. **-èvement**; **s. de cœur**, nausea; **s. d'un peuple**, uprising, revolt, of a people.

se soulever. 1. (a) to rise; **la mer se soulève**, the sea is rising, heaving, getting rougher; (b) (of the stomach) to heave, to turn. 2. (a) to raise oneself (with one's hands, etc.); (b) to revolt; to rise (in rebellion).

soulier [sulje], s.m. shoe.

souligner [suliɲe], v.tr. (a) to underline (a word etc.); (b) to emphasize, lay stress on (word fact); s.m. **-ement**.

soumettre [sumɛtr], v.tr. (conj. like METTRE) 1 to subdue (a people, province). 2. to submit refer, put (a question) (**à qn**, to s.o.). 3. **s. qch. à un examen**, to subject sth. to an examination **s. les enfants à la discipline**, to keep the children in order; **être soumis à des règles**, to be bound by rules.

se soumettre, to submit, yield, give in.

soumis [sumi], a. 1. submissive, obedient. 2 subject, amenable (to law, authority influence).

soumission [sumisjɔ̃], s.f. 1. (a) submission faire (sa) **s.**, to surrender, yield; (b) obedience submissiveness (**à**, to). 2. Com: tender (fo public works, etc.); **faire une s. pour un travail** to tender for a piece of work.

soupape [supap], s.f. Tchn: valve; **s. de sûreté** safety valve.

soupçon [supsɔ̃], s.m. suspicion. 1. **j'en avais** **s.!** I suspected as much! 2. surmise, conjec ture; **ne pas avoir le moindre s.**, not to have th slightest hint, inkling (of sth.). 3. F: sligh flavour, small quantity, dash (of vinegar, ga lic); touch (of fever, irony).

soupçonner [supsɔne], v.tr. 1. to suspect. 2. t surmise, conjecture.

soupçonneux, -euse [supsɔnø, -ø:z], a suspicious, distrustful; adv. **-sement**.

soupe [sup], s.f. soup; **il monte comme une s. a lait**, he flares up very easily; **venez manger la** **avec nous**, come and take pot-luck with us.

soupente [supɑ̃t], s.f. loft, garret.

souper [supe]. I. v.i. to have supper; F: **j'en** **soupé**, I've had enough of it.
II. **souper**, s.m. supper.

soupeser [supəze], v.tr. (**je soupèse**) to feel, tr the weight of (sth.) (in the hand); N.Am: to he (sth.); **s. les données d'un problème**, to weig up the data of a problem.

soupière [supjɛ:r], s.f. soup tureen.

soupir [supi:r], s.m. sigh; **pousser un s.**, to (hea a) sigh; **rendre le dernier s.**, to breathe one last.

soupirer [supire], v.i. (a) to sigh; (b) **s. apr qch.**, to long for sth.

souple [supl], a. (a) supple, pliant; flexible, lith **esprit s.**, versatile mind; Aut: **moteur s.**, flexib engine; (b) docile (person); adv. **-ement**; s. **-esse**, suppleness, flexibility; versatility.

source [surs], s.f. 1. spring; source (of river); ea **de s.**, spring water; **s. minérale, thermal** mineral, hot, spring. 2. origin (of evil, wealt news, etc.); **aller à la s. du mal**, to get to th root of the evil; **je le tiens de bonne s.**, I have on good authority.

ourcil [sursi], *s.m.* eyebrow.

ourciller [sursije], *v.i.* 1. to knit one's brows, to frown. 2. to wince, to flinch; **sans s.,** without turning a hair.

ourd, -e [suːr, surd]. 1. *a.* (*a*) deaf; (*b*) dull, muffled (sound); **tomber avec un bruit s.,** to fall with a thump; **hostilité sourde,** veiled hostility; **bâtiment s.,** soundproof building. 2. *s.* deaf person; **faire le s.,** (i) to sham deafness; (ii) to refuse to listen; *adv.* **-ement,** with a dull, hollow, sound; **agir s.,** to act in an underhand way.

ourd-muet, sourde-muette [surmɥɛ, surdmɥɛt]. 1. *a.* deaf-and-dumb. 2. *s.* deaf-mute; *pl. sourd(e)s-muet(te)s.*

ouricière [surisjɛːr], *s.f.* (*a*) mouse-trap; (*b*) trap, snare, *esp.* police trap; **tendre une s.,** to set a trap (**à,** for).

ourilre [suriːr]. **I.** *v.i.* (*conj. like* RIRE) 1. to smile (**à qn,** to, at, s.o.). 2. (*of thgs*) to please; to prove attractive (to s.o.); **l'idée me souriait assez,** I was rather taken with the idea. **II. sourire,** *s.m.* smile; **s. affecté,** smirk, simper; **garder le s.,** to keep smiling.

ouris [suri], *s.f.* mouse.

ournois, -oise [surnwa, -waːz], *a.* artful, sly, crafty (person); underhand (person, dealings); *adv.* **-ement.**

ous [su]. 1. *prep.* under(neath), beneath, below; **s. un arbre,** under a tree; **s. les flots,** beneath the waves; **avoir qch. s. la main,** to have sth. within (easy) reach; **s. clef,** under lock and key; **s. les tropiques,** in the tropics. 2. **sous-,** *pref.* sub-, under-.
NOTE: *Compound nouns and adjectives of which the first element is the prefix* **sous** *add a final* **s** *in the plural unless otherwise indicated.*

ous-alimentler [suzalimɑ̃te], *v.tr.* to underfeed, undernourish; *s.f.* **-ation.**

ous-bois [subwa], *s.m.inv.* 1. underwood, undergrowth. 2. *Art:* woodland scene.

ous-chef [suʃɛf], *s.m.* 1. deputy chief clerk. 2. assistant manager; **s.-c. de gare,** deputy stationmaster.

ous-comité [sukɔmite], *s.m.* sub-committee.

ous-couche [sukuʃ], *s.f.* substratum; underlying layer; (*of paint*) primer.

ouscripltion [suskripsjɔ̃], *s.f.* 1. (*a*) execution, signing (of deed); (*b*) subscription, signature. 2. *Fin:* subscription, application (**à des actions,** for shares). 3. subscription, contribution (of sum of money); *s.m.* **-teur,** subscriber.

ouscrire [suskriːr], *v.tr.* (*conj. like* ÉCRIRE) 1. to sign, execute (deed). 2. **s. un abonnement,** to take out a subscription; **s. mille francs,** to subscribe a thousand francs. 3. *abs.* **s. à une opinion,** to subscribe to an opinion.

ous-développé [sudevlɔpe], *a.* underdeveloped; **pays s.-d., industrie s.-développée,**
underdeveloped country, industry; underequipped industry.

sous-entendre [suzɑ̃tɑ̃ːdr], *v.tr.* to understand; not to express; to imply.

sous-entendu [suzɑ̃tɑ̃dy], *s.m.* thing understood; implication; **suggérer qch. par sousentendus,** to hint at sth.

sous-entrepreneur [suzɑ̃trəprənœːr], *s.m.* subcontractor.

sous-estimer [suzɛstime], *v.tr.* to underestimate, undervalue, underrate.

sous-exposer [suzɛkspoze], *v.tr. Phot:* to under-expose.

sous-gérant, -ante [suʒerɑ̃, -ɑ̃ːt], *s.* assistant manager, manageress.

sous-inspecteur, -trice [suzɛ̃spɛktœːr, -tris], *s.* assistant inspector, inspectress.

sous-lieutenant [suljøtnɑ̃], *s.m. Mil:* second-lieutenant; *Navy:* sub-lieutenant; *Av:* pilot officer.

sous-locataire [sulɔkatɛːr], *s.m. & f.* subtenant.

sous-location [sulɔkasjɔ̃], *s.f.* 1. sub-letting. 2. under-tenancy, sub-lease.

sous-louer [sulwe], *v.tr.* to sub-let, sub-lease.

sous-main [sumɛ̃], *s.m.inv.* blotting-pad, writing-pad.

sous-marin [sumarɛ̃]. 1. *a.* submarine (volcano, etc.); submerged (reef). 2. *s.m.* submarine; **s.-m. nucléaire,** nuclear-powered submarine; **s.-m. chasseur,** hunter-killer submarine.

sous-off [suzɔf], *s.m. Mil: F:* N.C.O., non-com.

sous-officier [suzɔfisje], *s.m.* 1. non-commissioned officer. 2. *Navy:* petty officer.

sous-préfecture [suprefɛktyːr], *s.f.* sub-prefecture (district, functions or residence).

sous-préfet [suprefɛ], *s.m. Fr.Adm:* sub-prefect.

sous-production [suprɔdyksjɔ̃], *s.f. Ind:* under-production.

sous-produit [suprɔdɥi], *s.m. Ind:* by-product.

sous-secrétaire [susəkretɛːr], *s.m. & f.* under-secretary; **s.-s. d'État,** Under-Secretary of State.

sous-seing [susɛ̃], *s.m.* private contract.

soussigné [susiɲe], *a. & s.* undersigned.

sous-sol [susɔl], *s.m.* 1. *Geol:* subsoil; *Min:* **travailleurs du s.-s.,** underground workers. 2. *Const:* basement; basement-flat; **garage en s.-s.,** (i) basement garage; (ii) underground car park.

sous-titre [sutitr], *s.m. Cin:* subtitle; caption.

soustrlaire [sustrɛːr], *v.tr.* (*conj. like* ABSTRAIRE) 1. to take away, abstract, purloin (document, etc.). 2. to screen, shield (**qn à qch.,** s.o. from sth.). 3. *Mth:* to subtract (**de,** from); *s.f.* **-action,** (*a*) removal, abstraction; (*b*) subtraction.

se soustraire à qch., to avoid, escape, get out of, sth.; **se s. aux regards,** to retire from sight.

sous-vêtement [suvɛtmɑ̃], *s.m.* undergarment;

pl. underclothes, underwear.

soutane [sutan], *s.f.* cassock; **prendre la s.,** to become a priest.

soute [sut], *s.f. Nau:* store-room; **s. à charbon,** coal-bunker; **soutes à mazout,** oil(-fuel) tanks; **s. à munitions,** magazine; **s. aux bagages,** (i) luggage room; (ii) *Av: etc:* luggage compartment.

souten|ir [sutni:r], *v.tr.* (*conj. like* TENIR) **1.** (*a*) to support; to hold, prop, (s.o., sth.) up; (*b*) to keep, maintain (family); (*c*) to back (up) (cause, person); to stand up for (s.o.); (*d*) to maintain, uphold (opinion); **il soutient que . . .,** he asserts that . . .; (*e*) to keep up, sustain, maintain (conversation, speed). **2.** (*a*) to bear, stand, endure (injury, reproach); (*b*) to sustain, withstand, hold out against (attack); **s. une dépense,** to afford, meet, an expense; *a.* -**able**; *a.* -**ant,** sustaining.

se soutenir. 1. to support, maintain, oneself; **je ne me soutiens plus,** I'm ready to drop. **2.** to last, continue; **l'intérêt se soutient,** the interest is kept up; **femme qui se soutient bien,** woman who wears well.

soutenu [sutny], *a.* sustained (attention, effort); unflagging, constant (interest); **marché s.,** steady market.

souterrain [sutɛrɛ̃]. **1.** *a.* underground, subterranean; **passage s.,** subway. **2.** *s.m.* (*a*) (large) cave; (*b*) underground workings; tunnel; (*c*) underground passage; subway.

soutien [sutjɛ̃], *s.m.* (*a*) support, prop; **il est sans s.,** he has nobody behind him; (*b*) supporter, upholder; **s. de famille,** breadwinner.

soutien-gorge [sutjɛ̃gɔrʒ], *s.m. Cl:* brassière, *F:* bra; *pl.* **soutiens-gorge.**

soutirer [sutire], *v.tr.* to draw off, to rack (wine); to tap (electric supply); **s. de l'argent à qn,** to get, squeeze, money out of s.o.

souvenir [suvni:r]. **I.** *v.impers.* (*conj. like* VENIR; *aux.* **être**) to occur to the mind; **autant qu'il m'en souvienne,** to the best of my recollection. **II.** *s.m.* **1.** remembrance, recollection, memory; **j'en ai un vague s.,** I have a dim memory of it; **veuillez me rappeler à son bon s.,** please remember me kindly to him. **2.** (*a*) memorial, memento; (*b*) (*token of remembrance*) keepsake, souvenir.

se souvenir de qch., to remember, to recall, sth.; **je me souviendrai,** I shall not forget; **faire s. qn de qch.,** to remind s.o. of sth.

souvent [suvã], *adv.* often; **le plus s.,** usually; more often than not.

souverain, -aine [suvrɛ̃, -ɛn]. **1.** *a.* sovereign (power, prince, etc.); **s. bonheur,** supreme happiness. **2.** *s.* sovereign; *s.f.* -**eté,** sovereignty.

sovi|et [sɔvjet], *s.m.* Soviet; *a.* -**étique,** Soviet.

soya [sɔja], *s.m. Bot:* soya bean, soy.

soyeux, -euse [swajø, -ø:z], *a.* silky.

spacieu|x, -euse [spasjø, -ø:z], *a.* spacious, roomy (flat, car); *adv.* -**sement,** spaciously, with plenty of room.

sparadrap [sparadra], *s.m.* adhesive plaster, sticking plaster.

spasme [spasm], *s.m.* spasm.

spastique [spastik], *a. & s.* (*a*) *a.* spastic (patient); (*b*) **un, une, s.,** a spastic.

spatule [spatyl], *s.f.* **1.** (*a*) spatula; **doigts en s.,** spatulate fingers; (*b*) spoon(-shaped) tool; (*c*) ski tip. **2.** *Orn:* spoonbill.

speaker, *f.* **speakerine** [spikœ:r, spik(ə)rin], *s. Rad: T.V:* announcer; (woman) announcer.

spécial, -aux [spesjal, -o], *a.* special, especial; **une affaire spéciale,** a particular piece of business; *Journ:* **notre envoyé s.,** our special correspondent; *adv.* -**ement.**

spécial|iser [spesjalize], *v.tr.* to specialize; **se s. dans qch.,** to specialize, to be a specialist, in sth.; *s.f.* -**isation**; *s.m. & f.* -**iste,** expert; *s.f.* -**ité,** speciality, special feature.

spécieu|x, -euse [spesjø, -ø:z], *a.* specious, plausible; *adv.* -**sement.**

spécif|ier [spesifje], *v.tr.* (*pr.sub. & p.d.* n. **spécifiions**) to specify; **s. des fonctions,** to lay down duties; *s.f.* -**ication**; *a.* -**ique,** specific; *adv.* -**iquement.**

spécimen [spesimɛn], *s.m.* specimen; *Pub:* free copy, inspection copy; *Pej:* **un drôle de s.,** an odd chap.

spectacle [spɛktakl], *s.m.* **1.** spectacle, sight; **se donner en s.,** to make an exhibition of oneself. **2.** *Th:* play, entertainment; *F:* **aller au s.,** to go to a show; **salle de s.,** (concert, etc.) hall, theatre; **s. payant,** sideshow (at bazaar, etc.). **3.** show, display; *Cin:* **film à grand s.,** epic.

spectateur, -trice [spɛktatœ:r, -tris], *s.* spectator, onlooker, bystander.

spectral, -aux [spɛktral, -o], *a.* spectral. **1.** ghostly, ghostlike. **2.** *Opt:* **couleurs spectrales,** colours of the spectrum.

spectre [spɛktr], *s.m.* **1.** spectre, ghost, apparition. **2.** *Opt:* spectrum.

spécul|er [spekyle], *v.i.* **1.** to speculate, cogitate (sur, on, about); to ponder (sur, over). **2.** *Fin:* to speculate; *s.* -**ateur, -atrice,** speculator; *a.* -**atif, -ative,** speculative; *s.f.* -**ation.**

spéléolo|gie [speleɔlɔʒi], *s.f.* speleology, potholing; *s.* -**gue.**

sperme [spɛrm], *s.m.* sperm, semen.

sphère [sfɛ:r], *s.f.* **1.** sphere; globe; **s. terrestre,** globe, the earth. **2. s. d'activité, d'influence, d'action,** sphere of activity, influence, field of action; **être hors de sa s.,** to be out of one's element.

sphérique [sferik], *a.* spherical.

sphinx [sfɛ̃:ks], *s.m.inv.* sphinx.

spinal, -aux [spinal, -o], *a. Anat:* spinal.

spiral, -aux [spiral, -o]. **1.** *a.* spiral; **ressort s.**

spiral spring. 2. *s.m.* hairspring (of watch). 3. *s.f.* spirale, spiral; en spirale, (i) *adv.* spirally; (ii) *a.* spiral.

spiritisme [spiritism], *s.m.* spiritualism.

spirituel, -elle [spirituɛl], *a.* 1. spiritual (power, life, etc.); concert s., concert of sacred music. 2. witty (person, answer, etc.); humorous, lively (expression, personality); *adv.* -lement.

spiritueux, -euse [spirituø, -ø:z]. 1. *a.* spirituous, alcoholic (drink). 2. *s.m. Adm:* spirituous liquor; les s., spirits.

splendeur [splɑ̃dœ:r], *s.f.* splendour; (*a*) brilliance, brightness (of the sun, etc.); (*b*) magnificence, glory (of a régime, a nation).

splendide [splɑ̃did], *a.* splendid.

spolier [spɔlje], *v.tr.* (*pr.sub. & p.d.* n. spoliions) to despoil, rob (s.o.) (de, of); to plunder, rifle (a house, etc.); *s.* -ateur, -atrice; *s.f.* -ation.

spongieux, -euse [spɔ̃ʒjø, -jø:z], *a.* spongy.

spontané [spɔ̃tane], *a.* spontaneous; *s.f.* -ité, spontaneity; *adv.* -ment.

sporadique [spɔradik], *a.* sporadic (disease); *adv.* -ment.

pore [spɔ:r], *s.f. Biol:* spore.

sport [spɔ:r]. 1. *s.m.* sport (excluding hunting, fishing and horse-racing); games; sports d'équipe, team games; sports d'hiver, winter sports. 2. *a.inv.* costume s., casual clothes; (*of pers.*) être très s., to be a sporty type; *a. & s.* -if, -ive, (*a*) *a.* sporting; les quotidiens sportifs, the sporting dailies; (*b*) *s.* sportsman, sportswoman; games-player; athlete; keen games-watcher.

square [skwa:r], *s.m.* (public) square (with garden).

squelette [skɔlɛt], *s.m.* (*a*) *Anat:* skeleton; (*b*) carcass, skeleton, framework (of ship, etc.); (*c*) skeleton, outline (of novel, etc.).

stabiliser [stabilize], *v.tr.* to stabilize; to steady; *s.f.* -ation; *s.m.* -ateur, stabilizer.

se stabiliser, to become stable, steady.

stable [stabl], *a.* stable. 1. firm, steady; caractère s., steady, balanced, character. 2. durable; lasting; paix s., lasting peace; *s.f.* -ilité, stability.

stade [stad], *s.m.* stadium, sports ground.

stage [sta:ʒ], *s.m.* training; course (of instruction); s. préparatoire, induction course; *s.m. & f.* -iaire, trainee.

stagnant [stagnɑ̃], *a.* stagnant (water, business); standing (water).

stagnation [stagnasjɔ̃], *s.f.* stagnation (of water, trade); (*of trade, etc.*) en s., at a standstill.

stalactite [stalaktit], *s.f. Geol:* stalactite.

stalagmite [stalagmit], *s.f. Geol:* stalagmite.

stalle [stal], *s.f.* 1. stall (in cathedral); (numbered) seat (in theatre); stalles d'orchestre, orchestra stalls. 2. stall, box (in stable).

stand [stɑ̃:d], *s.m.* 1. stand (on racecourse); stand, stall (at exhibition, show, etc.); stall (at fête). 2. (*a*) shooting-gallery; (*b*) rifle-range.

standard [stɑ̃da:r], *s.m.* 1. *P.T.T:* (house, office) switchboard. 2. s. de vie, standard of living. 3. *attrib.* standard (model, etc.); *s.* -iste, switchboard operator.

standardiser [stɑ̃dardize], *v.tr. Ind:* to standardize; *s.f.* -ation.

standing [stɑ̃diŋ], *s.m.* standing; appartement de grand s., luxury flat.

star [sta:r], *s.f. Cin: F:* star.

station [stasjɔ̃], *s.f.* 1. (*a*) (action of) standing; en s. derrière un arbre, standing, stationed, behind a tree; (*b*) position; s. debout, standing, upright, position. 2. break (in journey); (short) stop. 3. (*a*) *Rail:* halt; (small) station; s. de métro, underground station; s. d'autobus, bus stop; s. de taxis, taxi rank; (*b*) s. d'été, summer resort; s. de ski, ski resort; s. thermale, spa; s. balnéaire, seaside resort; (*c*) post, station; s. radio, de télévision, broadcasting station; *El:* s. centrale, power station.

stationner [stasjɔne], *v.i.* 1. to stop; to take up one's position; to halt. 2. (*of car, etc.*) to park; *P.N:* défense de s., no parking; no waiting; *a.* -naire, stationary; *s.m.* -nement, stopping; *P.N:* s. interdit, no parking.

station-service [stasjɔ̃sɛrvis], *s.f. Aut:* service station; *pl.* stations-service.

statique [statik]. 1. *a.* static (electricity). 2. *s.f.* statics.

statisticien, -ienne [statistisjɛ̃, -jɛn], *s.* statistician.

statistique [statistik]. 1. *a.* statistical. 2. *s.f.* statistics.

statue [staty], *s.f.* statue.

statuer [statɥe], *v.tr.* 1. to decree, enact, ordain. 2. *abs.* s. sur un litige, to settle a dispute.

stature [staty:r], *s.f.* stature, height (*esp.* of person).

statut [staty], *s.m.* statute, ordinance; regulation.

statutaire [statytɛ:r], *a.* statutory.

stellaire [stelɛ:r], *a.* stellar (light, etc.).

sténo [steno], *s. F:* 1. *s.m. & f.* shorthand typist. 2. *s.f.* shorthand typing.

sténodactylo [stenɔdaktilo], *s.* 1. *s.m. & f.* shorthand typist. 2. *s.f.* shorthand typing.

sténographie [stenɔgrafi], *s.f.* shorthand.

sténographier [stenɔgrafje], *v.tr.* (*pr.sub. & p.d.* n. sténographiions) to take down in shorthand.

sténotypie [stenɔtipi], *s.f.* stenotypy; *s.* -iste, stenotypist.

stère [stɛ:r], *s.m. Meas:* stere, cubic metre (of firewood).

stéréoscope [stereɔskɔp], *s.m. Opt:* stereoscope; *a.* -ique, stereoscopic.

stéréotyper [stereɔtipe], *v.tr. Typ:* to stereotype; **expression stéréotypée,** hackneyed phrase.

stérile [steril], *a.* sterile, unfruitful; barren (female, land); unprofitable (work).

stériliser [sterilize], *v.tr.* to sterilize; *s.f.* **-ation.**

stéthoscope [stetɔskɔp], *s.m. Med:* stethoscope.

stigmate [stigmat], *s.m. F:* stigma, brand of infamy, stain (on character).

stigmatiser [stigmatize], *v.tr.* to stigmatize **(de,** with); to brand (s.o.) with infamy.

stimulant [stimylɑ̃]. **1.** *a.* stimulating, stimulative. **2.** *s.m.* (a) *Med:* stimulant; (b) stimulus, incentive.

stimuler [stimyle], *v.tr.* to stimulate. **1.** to incite; to spur (s.o.) on. **2.** to stimulate; to whet (the appetite); **s. les affaires,** to give a fillip to business; *a. & s.* **-ateur, -atrice,** (a) *a.* stimulative; (b) *s.m. Surg:* **s. électrique du cœur,** pacemaker; *s.f.* **-ation.**

stipuler [stipyle], *v.tr.* to stipulate; to lay down (that . . .); *s.f.* **-ation.**

stock [stɔk], *s.m. Com:* stock (of goods); **s. en magasin,** stock in hand; *s.m.* **-age,** stocking, storage (of goods).

stoïcisme [stɔisism], *s.m.* stoicism; impassive courage.

stoïque [stɔik]. **1.** *a.* stoic, stoical. **2.** *s.* stoic; *adv.* **-ment.**

stop [stɔp]. **1.** *int. Nau: Aut: etc:* stop! **2.** *s.m. Aut:* (a) stoplight; (b) **brûler un s.,** to jump the (traffic) lights. **3.** *s.m. F:* **faire du s.,** to hitchhike.

stopper[1] [stɔpe]. **1.** *v.i.* (*of ship, etc.*) to stop; to come to a stop. **2.** *v.tr.* to stop (train); to check (cable); to stop (payment of a cheque).

stopper[2], *v.tr.* to mend (garment) invisibly; *s.m.* **-age,** invisible mending.

store [stɔːr], *s.m.* (inside or outside window-)blind; **s. vénitien,** Venetian blind.

strabisme [strabism], *s.m.* squinting.

strapontin [strapɔ̃tɛ̃], *s.m. Aut: Th:* flap-seat, folding seat.

stratagème [strataʒɛm], *s.m.* stratagem.

stratégie [strateʒi], *s.f.* strategy; generalship.

stratégique [strateʒik], *a.* strategic(al); *adv.* **-ment.**

stratégiste [strateʒist], *s.m.* strategist.

strict [strikt], *a.* strict; (a) **le s. nécessaire,** the bare essentials; (b) severe, exact (person); **s. en affaires,** exact in business matters; (c) plain, severe (suit, hair style); *adv.* **-ement.**

strident [stridɑ̃], *a.* strident, harsh (noise, voice).

striduler [stridyle], *v.i.* (*of cricket, grasshopper*) to chirr, to stridulate.

strié [strije], *a.* **1.** scored; scratched. **2.** fluted, grooved (column); ribbed (glass); corrugated (sheet iron).

strier [strije], *v.tr.* (*pr.sub. & p.d.* **n. striions**) **1.** to score, scratch. **2.** (a) to flute, groove; (b) to

streak.

structure [stryktyːr], *s.f.* structure; *a.* **-a** **-aux,** structural.

strychnine [striknin], *s.f.* strychnine.

studieux, -ieuse [stydjø, -jøːz], *a.* studiou *adv.* **-sement.**

studio [stydjo], *s.m.* **1.** studio; *Cin:* film studi *Rad:* **s. d'émission,** broadcasting studio.

stupéfier [stypefje], *v.tr.* (*pr. sub. & p.d.* **stupéfiions**) (a) *Med:* to stupefy; (b) t astound, amaze, dumbfound (s.o.); *s.f.* **-fa tion,** stupefaction, amazement; *a.* **-fai** stupefied; amazed, dumbfounded; *a. & s.n* **-fiant,** (a) *a.* (i) *Med:* stupefying (drug); (amazing; (b) *s.m. Med:* narcotic, drug.

stupeur [stypœːr], *s.f.* stupor. **1.** dazed state. amazement; **muet de s.,** dumbfounded.

stupide [stypid]. **1.** *a.* stupid; silly; foolish. *s.* stupid person; blockhead, *F:* idiot; a **-ement;** *s.f.* **-ité,** stupidity, foolishness.

style [stil], *s.m. Lit:* style; **un s. peu original,** unoriginal style; **dans le s. de Rubens,** after t Rubens manner; **robe, meubles, de s.,** peri dress, furniture.

stylo [stilo], *s.m. F:* fountain pen; **s. à bil** ballpoint pen.

su [sy], *s.m.* knowledge; *used in the phr.* **au su . . .,** to the knowledge of . . .; **à mon vu et s** to my certain knowledge.

suaire [sɥɛːr], *s.m.* winding-sheet; shroud.

suave [sɥaːv], *a.* (a) sweet, pleasant (mus scent); mild (cigar); (b) suave, bland (to manner); *adv.* **-ement;** *s.f.* **-ité,** sweetne suavity; blandness.

subalterne [sybaltɛrn]. **1.** *a.* subordinate, min (official, position). **2.** *s.m.* (a) underling; *Mil:* subaltern.

subdiviser [sybdivize], *v.tr.* to subdivide, split up; *s.f.* **-ion.**

subir [sybiːr], *v.tr.* to undergo, go through (pa etc.); to suffer, sustain (defeat, loss); to sub to (punishment, one's fate).

subit [sybi], *a.* sudden, unexpected (death, et *adv.* **-ement.**

subjonctif, -ive [sybʒɔ̃ktif, -iːv], *a. & s Gram:* subjunctive (mood); **verbe au s.,** vert the subjunctive.

subjuguer [sybʒyge], *v.tr.* to subjugate, s due; *s.f.* **-ation.**

sublime [syblim], *a.* sublime; lofty, exalted.

submerger [sybmɛrʒe], *v.tr.* (**n. submergeons** to submerge; (a) to flood (village, field); (b) swamp (boat); (c) to plunge (sth.) into water to overwhelm; **être submergé de travail,** to snowed under with work.

submersion [sybmɛrsjɔ̃], *s.f.* submersion. **1.** mersion; **mort par s.,** death by drowning flooding (of vineyards, meadows).

subordination [sybɔrdinasjɔ̃], *s*

subordination.

ubordonner [sybɔrdɔne], *v.tr.* to subordinate (à, to).

ubreptice [sybreptis], *a.* surreptitious; clandestine; *adv.* -**ment**.

ubséqulent [sypsekã], *a.* subsequent; ensuing; later (will, etc.); *adv.* -**emment** [-amã], subsequently.

ubside [sypsid], *s.m.* subsidy.

ubsidence [sypsidã:s], *s.f.* subsidence.

ubsidiaire [sypsidjɛːr], *a.* subsidiary, auxiliary, additional, accessory (à, to).

ubsistler [sybziste], *v.i.* **1.** to subsist; to (continue to) exist; **traité qui subsiste toujours**, treaty that still holds good. **2.** to live (**de**, on); **s. d'aumônes**, to live on charity; *s.f.* -**ance**, sustenance, maintenance, (one's) keep; provisions, supplies.

ubstance [sypstã:s], *s.f.* **1.** substance. **2.** matter, material, stuff; **s. étrangère**, extraneous substance; *El:* **s. isolante**, insulating material.

ıbstantiel, -elle [sypstãsjel], *a.* substantial; *adv.* -**lement**.

ıbstantif, -ive [sypstãtif, -iːv]. **1.** *a.* substantive. **2.** *s.m. Gram:* substantive, noun.

ıbstitluer [sypstitɥe], *v.tr.* **1.** to substitute (à, for). **2.** *Jur:* to entail (an estate); *s.f.* -**ution**. **substituer à qn**, to take the place of s.o.; **se s. à la justice**, to take the law into one's own hands.

ıbstitut [sypstity], *s.m.* assistant; deputy (to official); locum (tenens) (of doctor).

ıbterfuge [sypterfy:ʒ], *s.m.* subterfuge; **user de s.**, to evade the issue, to quibble.

ıbtil [syptil], *a.* subtle. **1.** (*a*) tenuous, thin; rarefied (air); (*b*) pervasive (scent). **2.** (*a*) acute; discerning, shrewd (mind); (*b*) delicate, fine (distinction); (*c*) *Pej:* crafty, cunning (mind, etc.); *adv.* -**ement**; *s.f.* -**ité**, subtlety; acuteness, shrewdness.

ıburbain [sybyrbɛ̃], *a.* suburban.

ıbvenir [sybvəniːr], *v.ind.tr.* (*conj. like* TENIR; *aux. avoir*) **s. aux besoins de qn**, to provide for the needs of s.o.

ıbvention [sybvãsjɔ̃], *s.f.* subsidy, subvention, grant (of money); *a.* -**nel**, -**nelle**, subventionary (payment).

ıbventionner [sybvãsjone], *v.tr.* to subsidize; to grant financial aid to (institution, etc.).

ıbverlsif, -ive [sybversif, -iːv], *a.* subversive (de, of); *s.f.* -**sion**.

ıc [syk], *s.m.* juice; *Bot:* sap.

ıccéder [syksede], *v.ind.tr.* (**je succède**; **je succéderai**) **s. à qn**, to succeed, follow after, s.o.; **s. à une fortune**, to inherit a fortune; **les années se succèdent**, the years follow one another.

ıccès [syksɛ], *s.m.* success; favourable result; *Com: etc:* **avoir du s.**, (i) to turn out a success;

(ii) *F:* to catch on; **livre à s.**, best-seller; **un s. fou**, a great success, *Th:* a smash hit; **pièce à s.**, hit.

successlion [syksesjɔ̃], *s.f.* succession. **1.** (*a*) series, sequence (of ideas, days); (*b*) **s. à la couronne**, succession to the crown. **2.** *Jur:* inheritance; (*a*) inheriting, coming into (property); **droits de s.**, death duties; (*b*) estate; *s.m.* -**eur**, successor; *a.* -**if**, -**ive**, successive; *adv.* -**ivement**.

succinct, -incte [syksɛ̃, syksɛ̃t], *a.* succinct, brief, concise (statement, etc.); *adv.* -**ement**.

succomber [sykɔ̃be], *v.i.* to succumb. **1.** to sink (under the burden of sth.); **je succombe au sommeil**, I can't stay awake. **2.** (*a*) to be overpowered, defeated; (*b*) to yield (to grief, etc.); **s. à l'émotion**, to be overcome by emotion; (*c*) to die.

succullent [sykylã], *a.* succulent, juicy; tasty; *s.f.* -**ence**, succulence; juiciness.

succursale [sykyrsal], *s.f.* branch (of firm, bank, store).

sucer [syse], *v.tr.* (**n. suçons**) to suck (milk, orange, bone, etc.).

sucre [sykr], *s.m.* sugar; **s. en poudre**, caster sugar; **s. cristallisé**, granulated sugar; **s. en morceaux**, lump sugar; **s. d'érable**, maple sugar.

sucré [sykre], *a.* **1.** sugared, sweetened (tea, etc.); sweet (cakes); **thé trop s.**, oversweet tea. **2.** sugary (words, manner); **elle fait la sucrée**, butter wouldn't melt in her mouth.

sucrer [sykre], *v.tr.* to sugar; to sweeten.

sucrerie [sykrəri], *s.f.* **1.** sugar refinery; sugar mill. **2.** *pl.* sweets, confectionery.

sucrier [sykrije], *s.m.* sugar basin.

sud [syd]. **1.** *s.m. no pl.* south; **maison exposée au s.**, house facing south. **2.** *a.inv.* south, southerly, southern.

sud-africain, -aine [sydafrikɛ̃, -ɛn], *a. & s. Geog:* South(-)African; **la République sud-africaine**, the Republic of South Africa.

sud-est [sydɛst]. **1.** *s.m. no pl.* south-east. **2.** *a.inv.* south-easterly; south-eastern.

sud-ouest [sydwɛst]. **1.** *s.m. no pl.* south-west. **2.** *a.inv.* south-westerly; south-western.

Suède (la) [lasɥɛd]. *Pr.n.f. Geog:* Sweden; **gants de s.**, suède gloves.

suédois, -oise [sɥedwa, -waːz]. **1.** *a.* Swedish. **2.** *s.* Swede. **3.** *s.m. Ling:* Swedish.

suer [sɥe], *v.i.* to sweat. **1.** (*a*) to perspire; *F:* **tu me fais s.!** you make me sick! (*b*) (*of walls*) to ooze, weep; (*c*) to labour, to drudge. **2.** (*with cogn. acc.*) (*a*) to exude (poison); (*b*) **s. du sang**, to sweat blood.

sueur [sɥœːr], *s.f.* sweat, perspiration; **être en s.**, to be sweating.

suffire [syfiːr], *v.i.* (*pr.p.* **suffisant**; *p.p.* **suffi**) (*a*) to suffice; to be sufficient; **cela ne me suffit pas**,

that won't do for me; *F:* **ça suffit,** that'll do! stop it! (*b*) **s. à qch.,** to be equal to sth., to doing sth.; **il ne peut pas s. à tout,** he cannot cope with everything.
suffis|ant [syfizɑ̃], *a.* **1.** sufficient, adequate, enough; **c'est s. pour le voyage,** that's enough for the journey. **2.** self-satisfied, self-important, bumptious, conceited (air, tone); *s.m.* conceited person, prig; **faire le s.,** to give oneself airs; *s.f.* **-ance,** (i) sufficiency, adequacy; (ii) self-conceit; self-complacency; *adv.* **-amment** [-amɑ̃], sufficiently, enough.
suffixe [syfiks], *s.m. Gram:* suffix.
suffo|quer [syfɔke]. **1.** *v.tr. (of smell, etc.)* to suffocate, stifle; **sans-gêne qui vous suffoque,** rudeness that takes one's breath away. **2.** *v.i.* **s. de colère,** to choke with anger; *s.f.* **-cation,** suffocation, choking.
suffrage [syfraʒ], *s.m.* suffrage, vote; **s. universel,** universal franchise.
suggérer [syɡʒere], *v.tr.* (**je suggère; je suggérerai**) to suggest.
suggest|if, -ive [syɡʒɛstif, -iːv], *a.* (*a*) suggestive; (*b*) evocative; *s.f.* **-ion.**
suicide [sɥisid], *s.m.* suicide.
suicid|er (se) [səsɥiside], *v.pr.* to commit suicide; **s. -é, -ée,** (*pers.*) suicide.
suie [sɥi], *s.f.* soot.
suif [sɥif], *s.m.* tallow, candle-grease.
suinter [sɥɛ̃te], *v.i.* (*of water, wall, rock*) to ooze, seep, sweat.
Suisse¹ (la) [lasɥis]. *Pr.n.f. Geog:* Switzerland; **la S. romande,** French(-speaking) Switzerland.
suisse². 1. *a.* Swiss; **femme s.,** Swiss woman. **2.** *s.m.* (*a*) **un S.,** a Swiss (man); (*b*) *Ecc:* verger; (*c*) **petit s.,** small cream cheese; **petit suisse;** (*d*) *Fr.C: Z:* chipmunk.
Suissesse [sɥisɛs], *s.f. often Pej:* Swiss (woman).
suite [sɥit], *s.f.* **1.** (*a*) continuation; **donner s. à une décision,** to give effect to, to follow up, a decision; **à la s. les uns des autres,** one after another; **à la s. de la décision prise . . .,** following the decision taken . . .; **dix voitures de s.,** ten cars in line; **dix jours de s.,** ten days running; **et ainsi de s.,** and so on; *adv.phr.* **tout de s.,** *F:* **de s.,** at once, immediately; **dans la s.,** subsequently, in process of time; **par la s.,** later on, afterwards; (*b*) sequel; **s. au prochain numéro,** to be continued in our next issue; (*c*) coherence, consistency (in reasoning); **propos sans s.,** desultory remarks; **avoir de la s. dans les idées,** to have a logical mind. **2.** suite, retinue, train. **3.** (*a*) series, sequence, succession; (*b*) *Mus:* **s. d'orchestre,** orchestral suite. **4.** consequence, result; **par s. de,** in consequence of (events, illness, etc.).
suivant [sɥivɑ̃]. **1.** *prep.* according to, in accordance with (one's taste, etc.). **2.** *a.* next,

following (page, day, etc.); **au s.!** next (person), please!
suivi [sɥivi], *a.* **1.** connected (speech); sustaine coherent (reasoning); close (busines relations); steadfast (policy). **2.** well-attende popular (lectures, classes, sermons).
suivre [sɥiːvr], *v.tr.* (*p.p.* **suivi;** *pr.ind.* **je suis, suit**) to follow. **1.** (*a*) to go behind, after (s.c sth.); **prière de faire s.,** please forward; **à s.,** be continued; (*b*) to understand; **je ne vous su pas,** I don't see your point; *F:* I'm not wi you; (*c*) to pursue (animal, enemy); (*d*) to pi heed to, to be attentive to (sth.); **suivez attentiv ment,** pay great attention; (*e*) to watch (over observe; (*f*) **s. une piste,** to follow up a clue. to succeed; to come after; **la peine suit crime,** punishment follows crime. **3.** (*a*) to g proceed, along (road, etc.); **s. son chemin,** go on one's way; (*b*) to obey, conform to; act upon; **s. un dessin,** to follow, copy, a pla **4.** (*a*) **s. des conférences,** to attend lectures; **un cours de français,** to take a course French; (*b*) to practise, exercise (professic calling).
sujet¹, -ette [syʒɛ, -ɛt], *a.* subject; liable, pror exposed (à, to); **s. à la mort,** mortal; **s. l'erreur,** liable to error; **s. à oublier,** apt forget.
sujet², *s.m.* **1.** subject; (*a*) cause, reason, grou (of complaint, anxiety, etc.); (*b*) subje matter; topic; **un beau s. de roman,** a fine si ject for a novel; (*c*) *Gram:* subject. **2.** dividual, fellow; **mauvais s.,** bad lot.
sulfate [sylfat], *s.m. Ch:* sulphate.
sulfure [sylfyːr], *s.m. Ch:* sulphide.
sulfurique [sylfyrik], *a. Ch:* sulphuric.
sultan [syltɑ̃], *s.m.* sultan.
super [sypɛːr]. **1.** *a. F:* super. **2.** *s.m. (occ.s.f.* *Aut:* (*petrol*) super. **3.** *s.m. Rec:* **un s. 33 tou** *F:* an L.P.
superbe [sypɛrb], *a.* (*a*) superb; stat (building); (*b*) magnificent (horse, weathe splendid, first-rate (business; display); *a* **-ment.**
supercarburant [sypɛrkarbyrɑ̃], *s.m.* hi grade petrol, *F:* super.
supercherie [sypɛrʃəri], *s.f.* deceit; fra swindle.
supérette [sypɛrɛt], *s.f. Com: F:* sm supermarket.
superficie [sypɛrfisi], *s.f.* (*a*) surface (of earth, etc.); (*b*) area (of a triangle, a field).
superficiel, -elle [sypɛrfisjɛl], *a.* superfic skin-deep (wound); shallow (mind); c **naissances superficielles,** sketchy knowlec *Ph:* **tension superficielle,** surface tension; c **-lement.**
superflu [sypɛrfly]. **1.** *a.* (*a*) superfluous, necessary; (*b*) **regrets superflus,** vain, usel

regrets. **2.** *s.m.* **avoir du s. en main-d'œuvre,** to be overstaffed; *s.f.* **-ité,** superfluity, superabundance.

supérieur, -eure [syperjœːr]. **1.** *a.* (*a*) upper (storey, etc.); (*b*) superior (**à,** to); **s. à la moyenne,** above, better than, average; **se montrer s. aux événements,** to rise above events; (*c*) higher, upper; **classes supérieures,** (i) upper classes (of society); (ii) *Sch:* upper forms; **enseignement s.,** higher, university, education; (*d*) *Com:* (articles) of superior quality. **2.** *s.* superior; (*a*) one's better; **il est votre s.,** (i) he's your superior (in rank, etc.); (ii) he's a better man than you; (*b*) head (of convent, monastery, seminary); **la Mère supérieure,** the Mother Superior; *adv.* **-ement,** superlatively well.

supériorité [syperjɔrite], *s.f.* superiority; **s. d'âge,** seniority; **air de s.,** superior air.

superlatif, -ive [syperlatif, -iːv], *a.* superlative.

supermarché [sypɛrmarʃe], *s.m. Com:* supermarket.

superposer [sypɛrpoze], *v.tr.* to superpose (**à,** on); to superimpose (colours, etc.); *a.* **-able,** superimposable.

superproduction [sypɛrprɔdyksjɔ̃], *s.f. Cin:* spectacular.

supersonique [sypɛrsɔnik], *a.* supersonic; **avion s.,** supersonic aircraft.

superstition [sypɛrstisjɔ̃], *s.f.* superstition; *a.* **-ieux, -ieuse,** superstitious; *adv.* **-ieusement,** superstitiously.

supplanter [syplɑ̃te], *v.tr.* to supplant; to supersede; to displace.

suppléant, -ante [sypleɑ̃, -ɑ̃ːt]. **1.** *s.* substitute (**de,** for); supply teacher; deputy; *Th:* understudy. **2.** *a.* acting, temporary (official, etc.); *s.f.* **-ance,** substitution; deputyship; supply (post).

suppléer [syplee]. **1.** *v.tr.* to take the place of, to deputize for, supply for (s.o.); **se faire s.,** to find a substitute. **2.** *v.i.* **s. à qch.,** to make up for, to compensate for, sth.; **s. à une vacance,** to fill a vacant post, a vacancy.

supplément [syplemɑ̃], *s.m.* (*a*) supplement, addition; (*b*) extra payment; *Rail:* excess fare; (*c*) supplement (to book); *a.* **-aire,** supplementary; **heures supplémentaires,** overtime.

suppliant, -ante [sypliɑ̃, -ɑ̃ːt]. **1.** *a.* supplicating, imploring, pleading (look, etc.). **2.** *s.* suppliant, supplicant.

supplice [syplis], *s.m.* (*a*) (severe corporal) punishment; torture; **le dernier s.,** capital punishment; (*b*) torment, anguish, agony; **être au s.,** to be on the rack.

supplier [syplije], *v.tr.* (*pr.sub. & p.d.* n. **suppliions**) to beseech, implore (s.o. for sth.); *s.f.* **-cation.**

support [sypɔːr], *s.m.* **1.** support, prop, stay. **2.** rest (for tools); stand (for lamp, etc.).

supporter [sypɔrte], *v.tr.* to support. **1.** to prop, hold up (building, etc.); to support, back up (person, theory). **2.** (*a*) to endure, suffer, bear (pain, misfortune); (*b*) to tolerate, put up with (rudeness, etc.); **s. l'humeur de qn,** to bear with s.o.'s temper; **je ne peux pas le s.,** I can't stand him; *a.* **-able.**

supposé [sypoze], *a.* supposed, alleged (thief, etc.); assumed, false (name, etc.).

supposer [sypoze], *v.tr.* **1.** to suppose, assume, imagine; **on le supposait riche,** he was thought to be wealthy; **supposez-vous à Paris,** imagine yourself in Paris. **2.** to presuppose, imply; **cela lui suppose du courage,** it implies courage on his part; *s.f.* **-ition.**

supprimer [syprime], *v.tr.* **1.** to suppress (newspaper, etc.); to abolish (law, tax); to omit, cut out (word); to remove (difficulty); to quell (revolt); *F:* **s. qn,** to do away with s.o. **2. s. qch. à qn,** to deprive s.o. of sth; *s.f.* **-ession.**

suprématie [sypremasi], *s.f.* supremacy.

suprême [syprɛːm], *a.* (*a*) supreme; highest (degree); paramount (importance); (*b*) last (honours); **l'heure s.,** the hour of death; *adv.* **-ment.**

sur¹ [syr], *prep.* **1.** (*a*) on, upon; **assis s. une chaise,** sitting on a chair; **s. toute la ligne,** all along the line; *P.N:* **virages s. 2 kilomètres,** bends for 2 kilometres; *F:* **la clef est s. la porte,** the key's in the door; (*b*) towards; **avancer s. qn,** to advance on, against, s.o.; **tirer s. l'âge,** to be growing old; **le train s. Orléans,** the train for Orléans; (*c*) over, above; **être s. un travail,** to be engaged in, on, a piece of work; **s. toute(s) chose(s),** above all (things); (*d*) about, concerning; **interroger qn s. ses motifs,** to question s.o. about, as to, his motives. **2.** (*of time*) (*a*) about, towards; **s. le soir,** towards evening; (*b*) **s. quoi,** whereupon; **s. ce, je vous quitte,** and now I must leave you. **3.** out of; (*a*) **un jour s. quatre,** one day out of four; (*b*) **vous vous payerez s. le surplus,** you will pay yourself out of what remains over. **4.** (*in measurements*) by; **huit mètres s. six,** eight metres by six.

sur² [syːr], *a.* sour (fruit); tart.

sûr [syːr], *a.* sure. **1.** (*a*) safe, secure; **plage sûre,** safe bathing; **peu s.,** insecure, unsafe; **jouer au plus s.,** to play for safety; **pour le plus s.,** to be on the safe side; (*b*) trustworthy, reliable (memory); trusty (friend); **temps s.,** settled weather; **avoir le coup d'œil s.,** to have an accurate eye; **goût s.,** discerning taste; **avoir la main sûre, le pied s.,** to have a steady hand, to be sure-footed; *Com:* **maison sûre,** firm of good standing. **2.** certain; **remède s.,** infallible remedy; *adv.phr.* **à coup s.,** for certain; without fail; *F:* **bien s.!** to be sure! of course;

bien s.? really? do you mean it? **bien s. que non!** of course not! *adv.* -**ement.**

surabond|ance [syrabɔ̃dɑ̃:s], *s.f.* superabundance; *a.* -**ant,** superabundant.

suranné [syrane], *a.* antiquated, old-fashioned; out-of-date.

surcharge [syrʃarʒ], *s.f.* 1. overloading. 2. (*a*) overload; additional burden; (*b*) excess weight (of luggage). 3. additional charge (on account rendered).

surcharger [syrʃarʒe], *v.tr.* (**n. surchargeons**)(*a*) to overburden, overload; (*b*) to overtax, overcharge.

surchauffer [syrʃofe], *v.tr.* to overheat.

surchoix [syrʃwa], *s.m.* finest quality; *attrib.* **viande s.,** prime quality meat.

surcompresseur [syrkɔ̃presœ:r], *s.m. Aut:* supercharger.

surcongélation [syrkɔ̃ʒelasjɔ̃], *s.f.* deep-freezing, *N.Am:* quick-freezing.

surcroît [syrkrwa], *s.m.* addition, increase; **par s.,** into the bargain, besides; **pour s. de malheur,** to make matters worse.

surdité [syrdite], *s.f.* deafness.

sureau, -eaux [syro], *s.m.* elder(-tree).

surestim|er [syrestime], *v.tr.* to overestimate, over-value (price, cost); **s. qn,** to overestimate s.o.; *s.f.* -**ation,** overestimate, overvaluation.

sûreté [syrte], *s.f.* 1. safety, security; (*police*) **agent de la S.,** detective; **la S.,** the Criminal Investigation Department, = New Scotland Yard. 2. sureness (of hand, foot); unerringness, soundness (of taste, judgment). 3. *Com:* surety, security.

surface [syrfas], *s.f.* surface; (*a*) outside; **s. unie,** smooth surface; **tout en s.,** superficial; (*b*) area; **s. utile,** working surface; **s. corrigée,** real floor space; *Com:* **les grandes surfaces,** the hypermarkets, supermarkets, etc.

surfaire [syrfɛ:r], *v.tr.* (*conj. like* FAIRE) to overestimate, overrate; **s. un auteur,** to overpraise an author.

surfin [syrfɛ̃], *a. Com:* superfine.

surgelé [syrʒəle], *a. & s.m.* deep-frozen; (**produits**) **surgelés,** deep-frozen foods, *N.Am:* quick-frozen food.

surgir [syrʒi:r], *v.i.* (*aux. avoir, occ. être*) to rise; to come into view; to loom (up); **des difficultés ont surgi,** difficulties have cropped up.

surhomme [syrɔm], *s.m.* superman.

surhumain [syrymɛ̃], *a.* superhuman.

surimpos|er [syrɛ̃poze], *v.tr.* 1. to superimpose. 2. (*a*) to increase the tax on (sth.); (*b*) to overtax; *s.f.* -**ition,** over-taxation.

sur-le-champ [syrləʃɑ̃], *adv.* at once; on the spot; there and then.

surlendemain [syrlɑ̃dmɛ̃], *s.m.* **le s.,** the next day but one; two days later.

surmen|er [syrməne], *v.tr.* (**je surmène**) to overwork (s.o., one's staff); *s.m.* -**age,** overwork, over-exertion; **s. intellectuel,** mental strain.

se surmener, to overwork; to over-exert oneself; to work too hard; *F:* to overdo it.

surmonter [syrmɔ̃te], *v.tr.* 1. to surmount; to (over-)top; to rise higher than (sth.). 2. to overcome, surmount (obstacle, emotion); to get over (difficulty).

surnager [syrnaʒe], *v.i.* (**n. surnageons**) (*a*) to float on the surface; (*b*) to remain afloat.

surnaturel, -elle [syrnatyrɛl], *a.* (*a*) supernatural; *s.m.* **le s.,** the supernatural; (*b*) extraordinary, inexplicable; uncanny.

surnom [syrnɔ̃], *s.m.* nickname.

surnommer [syrnɔme], *v.tr.* to nickname (s.o., sth.).

surnuméraire [syrnymerɛ:r], *a. & s.m.* supernumerary.

surpasser [syrpase], *v.tr.* to surpass. 1. to be higher than (s.o., sth.); to overtop (sth.). 2. to go beyond, to exceed; to outdo; *F:* **cela me surpasse,** that beats me.

surpeuplé [syrpœple], *a.* overpopulated overcrowded.

surplis [syrpli], *s.m. Ecc:* surplice.

surplomb|er [syrplɔ̃be]. 1. *v.i.* (*of wall, rock* etc.) to overhang; to jut out. 2. *v.tr.* t overhang, hang over; *s.m.* -**ement,** ove hang.

surplus [syrply], *s.m.* surplus, excess; **payer le s.** to pay the difference; **au s.,** besides, what' more; moreover.

surpoids [syrpwa], *s.m.* overweight; exces weight.

surprenant [syrprənɑ̃], *a.* surprising astonishing.

surprendre [syrprɑ̃:dr], *v.tr.* (*conj. like* PRE DRE) to surprise. 1. (*a*) to come upon (s.o.) u expectedly; to catch (s.o.) unawares; **la nu nous surprit,** night overtook us; (*b*) to interce (glance); to overhear. 2. to astonish; **ce ne me surprend pas,** I'm not surprised that.

surpris [syrpri], *a.* surprised.

surprise [syrpri:z], *s.f.* surprise; **à sa grande** much to his surprise; **quelle bonne s.!** what pleasant surprise!

sursaut [syrso], *s.m.* (involuntary) start, jum **se réveiller en s.,** to wake up with a start.

sursauter [syrsote], *v.i.* to start (involuntaril to give a jump; **faire s. qn,** to startle s.o.

sursis [syrsi], *s.m. Jur:* delay; respite; repriev **condamné à un an de prison avec s.,** given suspended prison sentence of one year.

surtout [syrtu], *adv.* particularly, especial principally, above all; **s. n'oubliez pas ma l tre!** don't forget my letter, whatever you do

surveill|er [syrveje], *v.tr.* to supervise, oversee, superintend; to watch (over), observe; to look after, keep an eye on (children); *Sch:* to invigilate (an exam); *s.f.* -**ance**, supervision; *s.* -**ant**, -**ante**, supervisor, superintendent, overseer; inspector; *Sch:* invigilator.

survenir [syrvəni:r], *v.i.* (*conj. like* TENIR; *aux.* être) (*of events*) to supervene, happen; (*of difficulty*) to arise; (*of pers.*) to arrive unexpectedly, *F:* to turn up out of the blue.

surviv|re [syrvi:vr], *v.ind.tr.* (*conj. like* VIVRE; *aux.* avoir) to survive, outlive (à qn, à qch., s.o., sth.); s. à la tempête, to weather the storm; *s.f.* -**ance**, survival; *a. & s.* -**ant**, -**ante**, (i) *a.* surviving; (ii) *s.* survivor.

survoler [syrvɔle], *v.tr. Av:* to fly over (the sea, a country); s. une question, to get a general view of a question.

suscept|ible [syseptibl], *a.* susceptible. **1. s. d'être prouvé**, susceptible of proof; **s. d'amélioration**, open to improvement; **les documents susceptibles de vous intéresser**, the documents likely to interest you. **2.** (*a*) sensitive, delicate (organ, substance); (*b*) (*of pers.*) touchy, easily offended; *s.f.* -**ibilité**.

suciter [sys(s)ite], *v.tr.* **1.** to create (enemies); to give rise to (difficulties); s. de l'étonnement, to cause astonishment; s. des ennuis à qn, to create petty annoyances for s.o. **2.** to (a)rouse (envy); to instigate, stir up (revolt, etc.).

suspect [syspɛ(kt)]. **1.** *a.* suspicious, doubtful, suspect; **devenir s.**, to arouse suspicion; **être s. à qn de qch.**, to be suspected by s.o. of sth.; **cela m'est s.**, I don't like the look of it. **2.** *s.m.* suspect.

suspecter [syspɛkte], *v.tr.* to suspect (s.o.); to doubt (sth.).

suspendre [syspã:dr], *v.tr.* to suspend. **1.** to hang up. **2.** (*a*) to defer, stay (judgment, revenge); to stop (payment); *Aut:* **s. un permis de conduire**, to suspend a driving licence; (*b*) **s. un fonctionnaire**, to suspend an official.

suspendu [syspãdy], *a.* suspended; hanging; **pont s.**, suspension bridge; **voiture bien suspendue**, well-sprung car.

suspens (en) [ãsyspã], *adv.phr.* in suspense; (i) in uncertainty; (ii) in abeyance.

suspension [syspãsjɔ̃], *s.f.* suspension. **1.** hanging (up). **2.** (*a*) (temporary) discontinuance, interruption; *Gram:* **points de s.**, points of suspension; dots; (*b*) **s. d'un fonctionnaire**, suspension of an official. **3.** (*a*) hanging lamp; ceiling light; (*b*) *H: Aut: etc:* springs, springing; *Aut:* suspension.

suspicion [syspisjɔ̃], *s.f.* suspicion; **être en s.**, to be suspected.

svelt|e [svɛlt], *a.* slender, slim; *s.f.* -**esse**, slimness.

sybaritique [sibaritik], *a.* sybaritic, self-indulgent.

sycomore [sikɔmɔ:r], *s.m. Bot:* sycamore.

syllab|e [sil(l)ab], *s.f.* syllable; *a.* -**ique**.

sylphe [silf], *s.m.*, **sylphide** [silfid], *s.f.* sylph; **taille de sylphide**, sylphlike waist.

sylvestre [silvɛstr], *a.* woodland (creatures); sylvan (landscape, flora).

sylviculture [silvikylty:r], *s.f.* forestry.

symbol|e [sɛ̃bɔl], *s.m.* **1.** symbol; conventional sign. **2.** *Ecc:* creed; **le s. des Apôtres**, the Apostles' Creed; *a.* -**ique**; *adv.* -**iquement**.

symbol|iser [sɛ̃bɔlize], *v.tr.* to symbolize; *s.m.* -**isme**.

symétrie [simetri], *s.f.* symmetry.

symétrique [simetrik], *a.* symmetrical; *adv.* -**ment**.

sympa [sɛ̃pa], *a. F:* likeable, attractive.

sympathie [sɛ̃pati], *s.f.* sympathy; (*a*) instinctive attraction; **se prendre de s. pour qn**, to take a liking to s.o.; (*b*) **idées qui ne sont pas en s.**, conflicting ideas.

sympathique [sɛ̃patik], *a.* **1.** sympathetic; **être s. aux idées de qn**, to be in sympathy with s.o.'s ideas. **2.** likeable, attractive (personality); **il m'était tout de suite s.**, I took to him at once; **entourage s.**, congenial surroundings; *adv.* -**ment**.

sympathiser [sɛ̃patize], *v.i.* to sympathize (avec, with); (*of two persons*) to be friendly; **deux femmes qui ne sympathisent pas**, two women who don't get on.

symphoni|e [sɛ̃fɔni], *s.f. Mus:* symphony; *a.* -**que**.

symptôme [sɛ̃pto:m], *s.m.* symptom; sign, indication.

synchronisé [sɛ̃krɔnize], *a.* synchronized; **feux synchronisés**, linked traffic lights.

synchronis|er [sɛ̃krɔnize], *v.tr.* to synchronize (qch. avec qch., sth. with sth.); *s.f.* -**ation**.

syncope [sɛ̃kɔp], *s.f.* **1.** *Med:* syncope; faint, fainting fit; **s. mortelle**, heart-failure. **2.** *Mus:* (*a*) syncopation; (*b*) syncopated note.

syndic|at [sɛ̃dika], *s.m.* syndicate; **s. professionnel**, trade association; **s. patronal**, employers' federation; **s. d'initiative**, tourist bureau; **s. (ouvrier)**, trade union; *a.* -**al**, -**aux**, syndical (chamber); **mouvement s.**, trade union movement; *s.m.* -**alisme**, trade unionism; *s.* -**aliste**, trade unionist.

synode [sinɔd], *s.m. Ecc:* synod.

synonyme [sinɔnim]. **1.** *a.* synonymous (de, with). **2.** *s.m.* synonym.

synthétique [sɛ̃tetik], *a.* synthetic; *Tex:* **fibre s.**, synthetic fibre; *adv.* -**ment**, synthetically.

Syrie (1a) [lasiri]. *Pr.n.f. Geog:* Syria.
syrien, -ienne [sirjɛ̃, -jɛn], *a. & s.* Syrian.
systématique [sistematik], *a.* systematic; *F:* hide-bound (opinion, person); *Med:* routine (examination, etc.); *adv.* **-ment.**
système [sistɛm], *s.m.* system; (*a*) method, plan; un nouveau s., a new device; *Mth:* s. **décimal, métrique,** decimal, metric, system; (*b*) *Tchn:* s. **de commandes,** control system; s. **d'éclairage,** lighting system; *F:* le s. D, wangling; *Med:* s. **nerveux,** nervous system; *F:* il me tape sur le s., he gets on my nerves.

T

, t [te], *s.m.* (the letter) T, t; **t euphonique** *forms a link between verbal endings in* **-a, -e** *and the pronouns* **il, elle, on; va-t-il? ira-t-elle? donne-t-on?**

t [ta], *poss.a.f. see* TON¹.

tabac¹ [taba]. *s.m.* **1.** *Bot:* tobacco(-plant). **2.** tobacco; **t. à priser,** snuff; **débit, bureau, de t.,** tobacconist's (shop); **débitant de t.,** tobacconist; **prendre du t.,** to take snuff.

tabac², *s.m. F:* (*esp. of police*) **passer qn à t.,** to beat s.o. up, to give s.o. the third degree.

tabasser [tabase], *v.tr. F:* to beat (s.o.) up.

tabatière [tabatjɛːr], *s.f.* snuff-box.

table [tabl], *s.f.* **1.** table; **t. pliante,** folding table; **t. (à thé) roulante,** tea trolley; **t. à repasser,** ironing table; *Pol: etc:* **t. ronde,** round-table conference. **2.** **mettre, dresser, la t.,** to lay the table; **la t. est bonne,** the food's good; **se mettre à t.,** to sit down to table; **sortir de t.,** to leave the table. **3.** (*flat surface*) *H:* hotplate (of cooker); **t. de travail,** working surface, top. **4.** list, catalogue; **t. alphabétique,** alphabetical index; **t. de multiplication,** multiplication table.

tableau, -eaux [tablo], *s.m.* **1.** (*a*) board; *Sch:* **t. noir,** blackboard; **t. d'annonces,** notice board; *Aut:* **t. de bord,** dashboard; *El:* **t. de distribution,** switchboard; (*b*) (*in hotel*) key-rack. **2.** picture, painting. **3.** (*a*) list, table; **t. de service,** duty roster; *Aut:* **t. de graissage,** lubrication chart; (*b*) **être rayé du t.,** to be struck off the rolls.

tablette [tablɛt], *s.f.* **1.** (*a*) shelf (of bookcase, etc.); (*b*) flat slab; **t. de cheminée,** mantelpiece. **2.** bar, slab (of chocolate); *Pharm:* tablet, lozenge.

tablier [tablije], *s.m.* **1.** apron; **t. d'enfant,** pinafore; *F:* (*of servant*) **rendre son t.,** to give notice. **2.** *Aut:* dashboard.

tabou [tabu]. **1.** *s.m.* taboo. **2.** *a.* (*often inv.*) taboo(ed).

tabouret [taburɛ], *s.m.* (*a*) high stool; (*b*) footstool.

tache [taʃ], *s.f.* stain, spot; blob (of colour); blemish, bruise (on fruit); **t. d'encre,** blot; **t. de rousseur, de son,** freckle.

tâche [taːʃ], *s.f.* task; **travail, ouvrier, à la t.,** piecework, piece worker; **prendre à t. de faire qch.,** to make it one's duty, to undertake, to do sth.

tacher [taʃe], *v.tr.* to stain, spot (garment, etc.); to sully (s.o.'s reputation).

tâcher [taʃe], *v.i.* to try, endeavour (**de,** to).

tacheté [taʃte], *a.* spotted, speckled; freckled; **chat t.,** tabby cat.

tacite [tasit], *a.* tacit; implied, understood; *adv.* **-ment.**

taciturne [tasityrn], *a.* taciturn, uncommunicative; (man) of few words; *s.f.* **-ité,** taciturnity.

tacot [tako], *s.m. Aut: F:* old crock (of a car), *N.Am:* jalopy.

tact [takt], *s.m.* tact; **avoir du t.,** to be tactful; **manque de t.,** tactlessness.

tactique [taktik]. **1.** *a.* tactical; **appui t.,** close support. **2.** *s.f.* tactics; *s.m.* **-icien** [-isjɛ̃], tactician.

taffetas [tafta], *s.m. Tex:* taffeta.

Tage (le) [lətaːʒ]. *Pr.n.m. Geog:* the (river) Tagus.

Tahiti [taiti]. *Pr.n. Geog:* Tahiti.

taie [tɛ], *s.f.* **t. d'oreiller,** pillowcase, -slip.

taillader [tajade], *v.tr.* to slash, gash; *Cl:* **jupe tailladée,** slashed skirt; *F:* **t. un article,** to make cuts in a (newspaper, etc.) article.

taille [taːj, taːj], *s.f.* **1.** cutting (of diamonds, etc.); *Hort:* pruning, trimming; **t. de cheveux,** hair-cutting. **2.** method of cutting; cut (of garment). **3.** edge of knife, etc.); **coup de t.,** cut, slash. **4.** (*a*) stature, height (of pers.); dimensions (of monument, etc.); **t. debout,** full height (of s.o.); **être de grande t., de t. moyenne, de petite t.,** to be very tall, of medium height, small, short; *Com:* **quelle est votre t.?** what size do you take? *F:* **il est de t. à se défendre,** he is big enough to look after himself; (*b*) figure, waist; **tour de t.,** waist measurement; **être bien pris de t.,** to have an elegant, good figure.

taille-crayons [tajkrɛjɔ̃], *s.m.inv.* pencil-sharpener.

taille-légumes [tajlegym], *s.m.inv.* vegetable slicer.

taille-pain [tajpɛ̃], *s.m.inv.* bread-slicer.

tailler [taje, taje], *v.tr.* (*a*) to cut (diamond, grass, hair); to hew (stone); to prune (tree); to trim, clip (hedge, beard); to dress (vine); **t. un crayon,** to sharpen a pencil; (*b*) to cut out (a garment); **complet bien taillé,** well-cut suit; **il est taillé pour commander,** he's cut out to be a leader.

tailleur, -euse [tajœːr, -øːz], *s.* **1.** (*a*) cutter; hewer; (*b*) tailor, tailoress. **2.** *s.m.* (**costume**) **t.,**

(woman's) tailored suit.

taillis [tɑji], *s.m.* copse, coppice; *a.* **bois t.**, brushwood.

tain [tɛ̃], *s.m.* silvering (for mirrors); **glace sans t.**, plate-glass.

taire [tɛːr], *v.tr.* (*pr.p.* **taisant;** *p.p.* **tu**) to say nothing about (sth.); **t. le nom de qn,** to keep s.o.'s name secret.

se taire, to hold one's tongue, to be silent; **faire t. qn,** to silence s.o., *F:* to shut s.o. up; **tais-toi!** be quiet! *F:* shut up! dry up!

talc [talk], *s.m.* talc; French chalk; *Toil:* **(poudre de) t.,** talcum powder.

talent [talɑ̃], *s.m.* talent, aptitude, faculty, gift.

taloche [talɔʃ], *s.f. F:* cuff (on the head); *F:* **flanquer une t. à qn,** to clout s.o., to box s.o.'s ears.

talon [talɔ̃], *s.m.* **1.** heel. **2.** (*a*) (*at cards*) stock (not yet dealt out); reserve; (*b*) fag-end, remnant; heel (of loaf); (*c*) **t. de souche,** counterfoil, stub (of cheque, etc.).

talonn|er [talɔne], *v.tr.* (*a*) to follow closely; (*b*) to spur on, urge (horse); (*c*) *Rugby Fb:* to heel (out); *s.m.* **-ement;** *s.m. Rugby Fb:* **-eur,** hooker.

talus [taly], *s.m.* **1.** slope; **en t.,** sloping. **2.** bank, embankment, ramp; **t. gazonné,** turfed bank.

tambour [tɑ̃buːr], *s.m.* **1.** drum; **bruit de t.,** drumming (sound); **t. de basque,** tambourine; **sans t. ni trompette,** quietly, without fuss. **2.** drummer; **t. de ville,** town-crier. **3.** (*a*) barrel, cylinder, drum (of oil); *El:* (cable) drum; *E:* **t. de frein,** brake drum; (*b*) revolving door.

tambouriner [tɑ̃burine], *v.i.* (*a*) to beat a drum; (*b*) to drum (with the fingers).

tambour-major [tɑ̃burmaʒɔːr], *s.m. Mil:* drummajor; *pl.* **tambours-majors.**

tamis [tami], *s.m.* sieve, sifter; strainer.

Tamise (la) [latamiːz]. *Pr.n.f.* the (river) Thames.

tamiser [tamize], *v.tr.* to pass (sth.) through a sieve; to sift, screen; to strain; **rideaux qui tamisent la lumière,** curtains that soften, subdue, the light.

tampon [tɑ̃pɔ̃], *s.m.* **1.** plug, stopper; waste plug (of bath, etc.). **2.** (*a*) (inking-)pad; (*b*) rubber stamp. **3.** *Surg:* wad, pad; tampon. **4.** **t. (de choc),** buffer.

tamponner [tɑ̃pɔne], *v.tr.* **1.** to plug (a wound, etc.). **2.** to dab; **se t. le front,** to mop one's brow. **3.** *Aut: Rail: etc:* (*of car, train*) to run into, collide with (another car, train).

tancer [tɑ̃se], *v.tr.* (*n.* **tançons**) to scold (s.o.); **t. qn vertement,** to haul s.o. over the coals; to give s.o. a good telling-off.

tandis que [tɑ̃di(s)kə], *conj.phr.* (*a*) whereas; (*b*) while, whilst.

tangente [tɑ̃ʒɑ̃ːt], *s.f. Geom:* tangent; *F:* **s'échapper par la t.,** to fly off at a tangent; t⟨ dodge the question.

Tanger [tɑ̃ʒe]. *Pr.n. Geog:* Tangier(s).

tangible [tɑ̃ʒibl], *a.* tangible.

tango [tɑ̃go], *s.m.* tango.

tang|uer [tɑ̃ge], *v.i.* (*of ship*) to pitch; *s.m.* **-age** pitching.

tanière [tanjɛːr], *s.f.* den, lair; (fox's) earth.

tanker [tɑ̃kɛːr], *s.m. Nau:* (oil) tanker.

tann|er [tane], *v.tr.* **1.** to tan (leather). **2.** *P:* (*a* to bore, pester (s.o.); (*b*) **t. (le cuir à) qn,** ⟨ thrash s.o.; *s.f.* **-erie,** tannery; *s.m.* **-eu** tanner.

tant [tɑ̃], *adv.* **1.** (*a*) so much; **t. de bonté,** s⟨ much kindness; **pour, à, t. faire,** *F:* **t. qu'à fair** j'aimerais autant . . .,** while I'm about it, if comes to that, I'd just as soon . . .; **il a t.** ⟨ **plus d'argent,** he has any amount of money **faire t. et si bien que . . .,** to work to such goo purpose that . . .; **t. s'en faut,** far from it; **soit peu,** a little, somewhat; (*b*) so many; ⟨ many; **t. d'amis,** so many friends; **tous t. qu** **vous êtes,** the whole lot of you; (*c*) so; to such degree; **en t. que,** in so far as; (*d*) **t. aimab** **qu'il soit,** however pleasant he may be; (*e*⟩ **mieux,** so much the better; I'm very gla⟨ good! **t. pis!** so much the worse; it can't ⟨ helped! what a pity! **2.** (*a*) as much, as w⟨ (as); **j'ai couru t. que j'ai pu,** I ran as hard a⟨ could; **t. aux Indes qu'ailleurs,** both in Ind⟨ and elsewhere; **t. bien que mal,** somehow ⟨ other, after a fashion; (*b*) **t. que,** as long, as f⟨ (as); **t. que je vivrai,** as long as I live; **t. que vue s'étend,** as far as the eye can see; **t. q** **vous y êtes,** while you're at it.

tante [tɑ̃ːt], *s.f.* aunt; **t. par alliance,** aunt marriage; **t. à la mode de Bretagne,** very ⟨ tant relative.

tantième [tɑ̃tjɛm], *s.m. Com:* percentage, sha⟨ quota (of profits, etc.).

tantôt [tɑ̃to], *adv.* **1.** soon, presently; **je revi⟨ t.,** I'll be back (i) soon, later, presently, (ii) t⟨ afternoon; **à t.,** goodbye for now; see y⟨ again soon! **2.** just now; a little while ago. **3** **triste, t. gai,** now sad, now gay.

taon [tɑ̃], *s.m.* horse-fly, cleg.

tapag|e [tapaːʒ], *s.m.* din, uproar; *F:* rack⟨ row; **faire du t.,** to kick up a row; *a. & s.* **-e** **-euse,** noisy, rowdy (person); a⟨ **-eusement.**

tape [tap], *s.f.* tap, rap, pat, slap; **t. sur l'épa⟨ sur la joue,** slap on the shoulder, pat on ⟨ cheek.

tape-à-l'œil [tapalœːj]. **1.** *a.inv.* loud, flashy *s.m.inv.* flashy goods.

tap|er [tape], *v.tr. F:* to tap, strike, hit; **t. la po⟨ to slam the door; **t. une lettre,** to type a let⟨ *abs.* **savoir t.,** to know how to type; **t. un air** ⟨

piano), to thump out a tune (on the piano); **t. sur les nerfs de qn,** to get on s.o.'s nerves; **le soleil tape,** *F:* **ça tape,** it's pretty hot; *F:* **t. qn de dix francs,** to touch s.o. for ten francs; *s.f.* **-ette,** (*a*) carpet beater; (*b*) fly swatter; *s.* **-eur, -euse,** cadger.

apioca [tapjɔka], *s.m.* tapioca.

apis [tapi], *s.m.* **1.** cloth, cover; **t. de table,** table-cloth; **t. vert,** gaming table; **mettre qch. sur le t.,** to bring sth. up for discussion. **2.** carpet. **3.** *Ind:* **t. roulant,** conveyor belt.

apiss|er [tapise], *v.tr.* to paper (room); **murs tapissés d'affiches,** walls covered with posters; **t. une boîte de papier,** to line a box with paper; *s.f.* **-erie,** tapestry; wallpaper; *s.m.* **-ier,** upholsterer.

apoter [tapɔte], *v.tr. F:* to pat (child's cheek, etc.); **t. un air,** to strum a tune.

quin, -ine [takɛ̃, -in]. **1.** *a.* (given to) teasing. **2.** *s.* tease.

quin|er [takine], *v.tr.* to tease; to worry; *s.f.* **-erie,** teasing.

rd [taːr], *adv.* late; **plus t.,** later (on); **pas plus t. qu'hier,** only yesterday; *s.m.* **sur le t.,** (i) late in the day; (ii) late in life.

rd|er [tarde], *v.i.* **1.** to delay; **sans t.,** without delay; **t. en chemin,** to loiter on the way; **t. à faire qch.,** to be slow in, to put off, doing sth. **2.** *impers.* **il lui tarde de partir,** he is longing to get away; *a.* **-if, -ive,** belated (regrets); late (hour, fruit); backward (crop); *adv.* **-ivement,** belatedly.

re [taːr], *s.f.* **1.** (*a*) *Com:* depreciation, loss in value (due to damage, waste); (*b*) (physical, moral) defect, blemish; taint. **2.** tare; **t. réelle,** actual tare; **t. par épreuve,** average tare.

rif [tarif], *s.m.* (*a*) tariff, price-list; (*b*) scale of charges; *P.T.T:* **tarifs postaux,** postal rates; *Rail:* **billet à demi-t.,** **à plein t.,** half-fare ticket; full-fare ticket; *a.* **-aire,** tariff (laws).

r|ir [tariːr]. **1.** *v.tr.* (*a*) to dry up (spring, tears); (*b*) to exhaust. **2.** *v.i.* (*of water, etc.*) to dry up, run dry; *a.* **-issable,** liable to run dry; *s.m.* **-issement,** drying up, exhaustion (of waters, resources).

tare [tartaːr], *a. & s.* Ta(r)tar; *Cu:* **sauce t., tartare** sauce; (steak) **t.,** steak tartare.

te [tart], *s.f. Cu:* (open) tart; flan.

telette [tartəlɛt], *s.f. Cu:* tartlet.

tine [tartin], *s.f.* slice of bread and butter, bread and jam, etc.

[ta], *s.m.* (*a*) heap, pile (of stones, wood, etc.); **t. de foin,** haycock; **t. de blé,** stook, shock, of corn; **piquer dans le t.,** to help oneself; (*b*) large quantity (of people, things); **un t. de mensonges,** a pack of lies; **il y en a des t.** (et des t.), here are heaps of them; (*c*) *F: Pej:* **quel t. de gens!** what a gang! **t. d'imbéciles!** bunch of fools!

tasse [tɑːs], *s.f.* cup; **t. à café,** coffee cup; **t. de café,** cup of coffee; **boire dans une t.,** to drink out of a cup.

tass|er [tase], *v.tr.* to compress; to squeeze, (objects) together; to ram, pack, tamp (earth, etc.); *s.m.* **-ement,** cramming, squeezing, (together), compressing.

se tasser. 1. (*of earth, foundations*) (*a*) to settle, set; (*b*) to sink, subside. **2.** to crowd (up) together; to huddle together; **tassez-vous un peu,** squeeze up a bit.

tâter [tate], *v.tr.* to feel, touch; to finger, handle (sth.); **t. le terrain,** to explore the ground; **avancer en tâtant,** to grope one's way forward.

tatillon, -onne [tatijɔ̃, -ɔn]. **1.** *a.* meddlesome; niggling, finicky. **2.** *s.* busybody; niggler.

tâtonn|er [tatɔne], *v.i.* **1.** to grope (in the dark); to feel one's way. **2.** to proceed cautiously, tentatively; *s.m.* **-ement.**

tâtons (à) [atatɔ̃], *adv.phr.* gropingly; **chercher qch. à t.,** to grope, feel, for sth.

tatou|er [tatwe], *v.tr.* to tattoo (the body); *s.m.* **-age,** (*a*) tattooing; (*b*) tattoo.

taudis [todi], *s.m.* miserable room; hovel; slum.

taule [toːl], *s.f. P:* prison, jug.

taup|e [toːp], *s.f. Z:* mole; *s.f.* **-inière,** mole-hill.

taur|eau, -eaux [tɔro], *s.m.* bull; **course de taureaux,** bullfight; *Astr:* **le T.,** Taurus; *s.f.* **-omachie,** (art of) bullfighting.

taux [to], *s.m.* rate (of wages, of discount); (established) price; **t. de pension,** pension scale; **t. du change, d'intérêt,** rate of exchange, of interest.

taxe [taks], *s.f.* **1.** (*a*) fixed price; fixed rate; (*b*) charge; rate; **t. postale,** postage; **t. supplémentaire,** surcharge. **2.** tax, duty.

tax|er [takse], *v.tr.* **1.** to regulate the price of (bread, etc.), the rate of (wages, postage); **t. une lettre,** to surcharge (a letter). **2.** to tax, impose a tax on (luxuries, etc.). **3.** to accuse (s.o. of cowardice, etc.); *s.f.* **-ation;** *a.* **-able.**

taxi [taksi], *s.m.* taxi(-cab).

taxiderm|ie [taksidɛrmi], *s.f.* taxidermy; *s.m.* **-iste,** taxidermist.

taxiphone [taksifɔn], *s.m. P.T.T:* public call-box.

Tchad [tʃad], *Pr.n.m. Geog:* **1.** Lake Chad. **2.** **la République du T.,** the Republic of Chad.

tchécoslovaque [tʃekɔslɔvak], *a. & s. Geog:* Czech, Czechoslovak(ian).

Tchécoslovaquie (la) [latʃekɔslɔvaki]. *Pr.n.f. Geog:* Czechoslovakia.

tchèque [tʃɛk], *a. & s.* Czech.

te, *before a vowel* **t'** [t(ə)], *pers.pron.sg., unstressed;* (*a*) (*acc.*) you; (*b*) (*dat.*) (to) you; (*c*) (*with pronom. vbs.*) **tu te fatigues,** you are tiring yourself.

technic|ien, -ienne [tɛknisjɛ̃, -jɛn], *s.* technician; *s.f.* **-ité,** technicality.

technique [tɛknik]. **1.** *a.* technical (terms, reasons, details). **2.** *s.f.* (*a*) technics; **t. de la construction,** structural engineering; **t. du froid,** refrigerating engineering; (*b*) technique (of artist, specialist, etc.); **t. opérationnelle,** know-how; *adv.* **-ment.**

techno‖logie [tɛknɔlɔʒi], *s.f.* technology; *a.* **-logique,** technological; *s.m.* & *f.* **-logue,** technologist.

teindre [tɛ̃:dr], *v.tr.* (*conj. like* ATTEINDRE) **1.** to dye. **2.** to stain, tinge, colour.

teint [tɛ̃], *s.m.* **1.** dye, colour; **bon t., grand t.,** fast dye. **2.** complexion, colour; **au t. frais, jaune,** fresh-, sallow-, complexioned.

teinte [tɛ̃:t], *s.f.* (*a*) tint, shade; (*b*) **t. de malice, d'ironie,** touch, tinge, of malice, of irony.

teinter [tɛ̃te], *v.tr.* to tint; **verres teintés,** tinted glasses; **eau teintée de vin,** water tinged with wine.

teintur‖e [tɛ̃ty:r], *s.f.* **1.** dyeing. **2.** (*a*) dye; (*b*) colour, tinge. **3.** *Pharm:* tincture; **t. d'iode,** tincture of iodine; *s.f.* **-erie,** dyeing and cleaning business; *s.* **-ier, -ière,** dyer and cleaner.

tel, telle [tɛl], *a.* **1.** such; (*a*) **un t. homme,** such a man; **de telles choses,** such things; (*b*) **en t. lieu,** in such and such a place; **je sais telle maison où . . .,** I could mention a house where . . .; (*c*) **à t. point,** to such, to so great, an extent. **2.** (*a*) like; as; **t. père, t. fils,** like father, like son; (*b*) **t. que,** such as, like; **un homme t. que lui,** a man like him; **voir les choses telles qu'elles sont,** to look facts in the face; (*c*) **t. quel; je vous achète la maison telle quelle,** I'll buy the house from you just as it stands. **3.** *pron.* such a one; **t. l'en blâmait, t. l'en excusait,** one would blame him, another would excuse him; **t. qui,** he who, many a one who; *s.* **un t., une telle,** so-and-so; **nous dînons chez les un t.,** we dine at the so-and-so's; *adv.* **-lement,** to such a degree; **c'est t. facile,** it's so easy.

télé [tele], *s.f. F:* telly.

télécommande [telekɔmɑ̃:d], *s.f.* remote control; **dispositif de t.,** telecontrol system, unit.

télécommander [telekɔmɑ̃de], *v.tr.* to operate by remote control.

télécommunication [telekɔmynikasjɔ̃], *s.f.* telecommunication.

télégramme [telegram], *s.m.* telegram.

télégraphe [telegraf], *s.m.* telegraph.

télégraph‖ier [telegrafje], *v.tr. & i.* to wire; to cable; *s.f.* **-ie,** telegraphy; *a.* **-ique,** telegraphic; *s.* **-iste,** telegraphist.

téléguid‖er [telegide], *v.tr.* to radio-control (aircraft, etc.); **missile téléguidé,** guided missile; *s.m.* **-age,** remote control.

téléimprimeur [teleɛ̃primœ:r], *s.m.* teleprinter.

télépath‖ie [telepati], *s.f.* telepathy; *a.* **-ique,** telepathic.

téléphone [telefɔn], *s.m.* telephone, *F:* phone; **automatique,** dial phone; **t. intérieur,** hous phone, intercom; *Pol:* **t. rouge,** hot line (U.S.⁄ to Kremlin); **t. vert,** hot line (Élysée t Kremlin); **coup de t.,** phone call; *F:* **t. arab‹** grapevine.

téléphon‖er [telefɔne], *v.tr. & i.* to telephone; ‖ phone, ring, (s.o.); *N.Am:* to call (s.o.); to gi‹ (s.o.) a ring; *s.f.* **-ie,** telephony; *a.* **-iqu‹ cabine t.,** phone box; **appel t.,** phone call; *s.r* & *f.* **-iste,** (telephone) operator.

télescope [telɛskɔp], *s.m.* telescope.

télescop‖er [telɛskɔpe], *v.i., tr. & pr.* ‹ telescope; (*of railway coaches in crash*) ‹ crumple up; to concertina; *a.* **-iqu‹** telescopic.

téléski [teleski], *s.m.* ski-lift.

téléspectateur, -trice [telespɛktatœ:r, -tris], (tele)viewer.

télévision [televizjɔ̃], *s.f.* television.

téméraire [temerɛ:r], *a.* rash, reckless; a‹ **-ment.**

témérité [temerite], *s.f.* **1.** temerity, rashne‹ recklessness, foolhardiness. **2.** rash deed.

témoign‖er [temwaɲe]. **1.** *v.i.* to testify; to be witness; to give evidence. **2.** *v.tr. or ind.tr.* **(de)** qch., to testify to sth.; **t. sa bonne volon** to give proof of (one's) good will; *s.m.* **-ag** testimony; evidence.

témoin [temwɛ̃], *s.m.* **1.** witness; (*a*) **être t. d'‹ accident,** to witness an accident; (*b*) **appeler ‹ à t.,** to call s.o. to witness; (*c*) second (in du‹ **2.** (*a*) boundary mark; (*b*) *Ind: etc:* **échantill‹ t.,** check sample; **lampe t.,** telltale lamp; a **partement t.,** show flat.

tempe [tɑ̃:p], *s.f. Anat:* temple.

tempérament [tɑ̃peramɑ̃], *s.m.* **1.** (*a*) (physic‹ constitution, temperament; **paresseux par** constitutionally lazy, lazy by nature; (moral) temperament; **t. placide, viole** placid, violent, temper. **2.** *Com:* **à t.,** by stalments; **vente à t.,** hire purchase.

tempér‖ance [tɑ̃perɑ̃:s], *s.f.* (*a*) temperan‹ moderation; (*b*) teetotalism; *a.* **-a‹** temperate, moderate (person).

température [tɑ̃peraty:r], *s.f.* temperature **d'ébullition,** boiling point; **t. ambiante,** ro‹ temperature.

tempérer [tɑ̃pere], *v.tr.* (**je tempère; tempérerai**) to temper, moderate (heat, an‹ etc.).

tempête [tɑ̃pɛt], *s.f.* storm; tempest; **t. de nei** blizzard, snowstorm; **le vent souffle en t.,** blowing a hurricane.

tempétueu‖x, -euse [tɑ̃petɥø, -ø:z], tempestuous; stormy (weather, se‹ boisterous (wind, welcome); violent (per‹ *adv.* **-sement.**

temple [tɑ̃:pl], *s.m.* **1.** temple. **2.** (Protest‹

church; chapel.
temporaire [tãpɔrɛ:r], *a.* temporary; provisional; *adv.* **-ment.**
temporis|er [tãpɔrize], *v.i.* to temporize; to play for time; *s.* **-ateur, -atrice,** temporizer, procrastinator; *s.m.* **El:** (automatic) time switch; *s.f.* **-ation,** procrastination; calculated delay.
temps [tã], *s.m.* **1.** time; (*a*) **vous avez bien le t.,** (**tout**) **le t. voulu,** you have plenty of time, all the time you need; **de t. en t.,** from time to time; **à plein t., à mi-t.,** full-, part-time (employment); (*b*) (i) while, period; **il y a peu de t.,** a little while ago; **entre t.,** meanwhile; **t. d'arrêt,** pause, halt; **marquer un t.,** to pause; (ii) term (of service); (*c*) age, days, time(s); **le bon vieux t.,** the good old days; **au t. jadis,** in times past; **dans la suite des t.,** in the course of time; **par le t. qui court,** nowadays; **être de son t.,** to be up to date; (*d*) hour, time; **en t. voulu,** in due time; **il serait t.!** it's about time! **il n'est plus t.,** it's too late. **2.** weather; **par tous les t.,** in all weathers; **prévision du t.,** weather forecast. **3.** *Gram:* tense. **4.** *Mus:* beat; time.
tenable [tənabl], *a.* (*usu. with neg.*) tenable, defensible; bearable; **par cette chaleur, le bureau n'est pas t.,** the office is unbearable in this heat.
tenace [tənas], *a.* tenacious; clinging; tough; dogged; retentive.
ténacité [tenasite], *s.f.* tenacity, toughness.
tenaille [tənɑ:j], *s.f.* pincers; tongs.
tenant, -ante [tənã, -ã:t]. **1.** *a. used in expr.* **séance tenante,** then and there. **2.** *s.* defender (of an opinion); supporter (of a government); *Sp:* holder (of a title). **3.** *s.m.* (*of landed property*) **d'un seul t.,** all in one block.
tendance [tãdã:s], *s.f.* tendency, inclination, propensity, trend; **tendances vers le communisme,** communist leanings.
tendon [tãdɔ̃], *s.m.* tendon, sinew.
tendre[1] [tã:dr], *a.* tender; (*a*) soft; delicate (colour, shade); early (age); (*b*) fond, affectionate.
tendre[2]. **1.** *v.tr.* (*a*) to stretch, tighten (cord, belt); **t. un ressort,** to set a spring; (*b*) to pitch (tent); to spread (sail); to lay (carpet); to hang (wallpaper); (*c*) to stretch out, hold out; **t. la main,** to hold out one's hand; (*d*) to (over)strain, to stretch; **rapports tendus,** strained relations. **2.** *v.i.* to tend, lead, conduce (**à,** to); **où tendent ces questions?** what's the aim, F: the idea, of these questions?
se tendre, to become taut; to become strained.
tendresse [tãdrɛs], *s.f.* tenderness; fondness; love; **avec t.,** lovingly.
tendu [tãdy], *a.* tense, taut, tight; **avoir les nerfs tendus,** to be tense, on edge; **ventre t.,** distended stomach; **situation tendue,** tense

situation.
ténèbres [tenɛbr], *s.f.pl.* darkness, gloom.
ténébreu|x, -euse [tenebrø, -ø:z], *a.* **1.** gloomy, dark, sombre (wood, prison). **2.** mysterious, sinister; **une ténébreuse affaire,** a dark, mysterious, affair; *adv.* **-sement.**
teneur [tənœ:r], *s.f.* **1.** tenor, purport (of document). **2.** *Tchn:* amount, content, percentage; **t. en eau,** degree of humidity, moisture content; **t. en or,** gold content.
tenir [təni:r], *v.* (*pr.p.* **tenant;** *p.p.* **tenu;** *pr.ind.* **je tiens, ils tiennent;** *pr.sub.* **je tienne;** *p.h.* **je tins;** *fu.* **je tiendrai**) I. *v.tr.* **1.** to hold; (*a*) **t. qch. à la main,** to hold sth. in one's hand; **t. serré qch.,** to hold sth. tight; **je tiens mon homme,** I've got my man; **voiture qui tient bien la route,** car that holds the road well; **tiens! tenez!** (look) here! (*b*) to contain; **tonneau qui tient vingt litres,** cask that holds twenty litres; *v.i.* **tout ça tient en deux mots,** all that can be said in a couple of words; (*c*) to retain; **baril qui tient l'eau,** barrel that holds water; (*d*) **t. de,** to have, get, derive, (sth.) from; **il tient sa timidité de sa mère,** he gets his shyness from his mother; (*e*) to keep, stock (groceries, etc.). **2. t. un magasin, une école,** to keep a shop, to run a school; **t. la caisse,** to have charge of the cash; **Mlle X tenait le piano,** Miss X was at the piano. **3.** (*a*) to hold, maintain (opinion, line of conduct); to keep (one's word); (*b*) **t. de grands discours,** to hold forth at great length; (*c*) **t. son rang,** to keep up one's position; (*d*) **t. qn en grand respect,** to hold s.o. in great respect. **4.** to hold back, restrain (s.o.). **5.** (*a*) to hold, keep (sth. in a certain state, position); **t. qch. en état,** to keep sth. in good order; **tenez votre gauche,** keep to the left; (*b*) **t. la chambre,** to be confined to one's room (through illness). **6.** to occupy, take up (space); **vous tenez trop de place,** you're taking up too much room. **7. t. qn captif,** to keep s.o. prisoner; **tenez-vous-le pour dit,** I shan't tell you again; take that as final.
II. **tenir,** *v.i.* **1.** (*a*) to hold; to adhere; to hold on firmly; **clou qui tient bien,** nail that holds well; **la porte tient,** the door's stuck; (*b*) **sa terre tient à la mienne,** his estate borders on mine; (*c*) to remain; **ne pas t. en place,** to be restless; **il ne tient plus sur ses jambes,** he's ready to drop. **2.** (*a*) **t.** (**bon**), to hold out, to stand fast; **je n'y tiens plus,** I can't stand it any longer; (*b*) to last, endure; **couleur qui tient bien,** fast colour; **le vent va t.,** the wind will last, continue, go on. **3. t. pour,** to hold for, be in favour of (s.o., sth.). **4. t. à qch.,** (*a*) to value, prize, sth.; **t. à faire qch.,** to be bent on doing sth.; **il tient à vous voir,** he insists on seeing you; (*b*) to depend on, result from, sth.; **à quoi cela tient-il?** what's the reason for it? *impers.* **il ne tient**

qu'à vous de le faire, it rests entirely with you to do it; **qu'à cela ne tienne,** never mind that. **5. t. de qn,** to take after s.o.; **cela tient du miracle,** it sounds like a miracle; **cela tient de (la) famille,** it runs in the family.
se tenir. 1. (*a*) to keep, be, remain; to stand, sit; **se t. chez soi,** to stay at home; **tenez-vous là!** stay where you are! **se t. tranquille,** to keep quiet; **tiens-toi droit,** sit up, stand up, straight; (*b*) **se t. à qch.,** to hold on to sth. **2.** to contain oneself; **je ne pouvais me t. de rire,** I couldn't help laughing. **3. se t. à qch.,** to keep to sth.; to abide by sth.; **s'en t. à qch.,** to confine oneself to sth.; to be satisfied, content, with sth.; **je ne sais pas à quoi m'en t.,** I don't know what to believe, what to think about it, where I stand.
tennis [tenis], *s.m.* **1.** (lawn) tennis; **t. de table,** table tennis. **2.** (lawn-)tennis court. **3.** *pl.* tennis shoes.
ténor [tenɔːr], *s.m.* (*a*) *Mus:* tenor; (*b*) *F: Pol: etc:* star performer.
tension [tɑ̃sjɔ̃], *s.f.* **1.** (*a*) tension; stretching; tightening; (*b*) strain, stress; *Tchn:* **t. de rupture,** breaking strain. **2.** tightness (of rope, etc.); tenseness (of relations, etc.). **3.** pressure; (*a*) *Med:* **t. artérielle,** blood pressure; *F:* **faire de la t.,** to suffer from high blood pressure; (*b*) *El:* voltage; **haute t.,** high voltage, tension.
tente [tɑ̃ːt], *s.f.* (*a*) tent; (*b*) booth (at fair, market); (*c*) awning.
tent|er [tɑ̃te], *v.tr.* **1.** to tempt (s.o.); **se laisser t.,** to yield to temptation; **t. la chance,** to try one's luck. **2.** to attempt, try; **t. une expérience,** to try an experiment; **t. de, faire qch.,** to try to do sth.; *a.* **-ant,** tempting, alluring, enticing (opportunity, etc.); *a. & s.* **-ateur, -atrice,** (*a*) *a.* tempting; (*b*) *s.* tempter, temptress; *s.f.* **-ation,** temptation; *s.f.* **-ative,** attempt.
tenture [tɑ̃tyːr], *s.f.* (*a*) hangings; *Fr.C:* curtain, *N.Am:* drape; (*b*) **(papier-)t.,** wallpaper.
tenu [tǝny], *a.* (*a*) **bien t.,** well-kept; tidy (house); neat (garden); **mal t.,** ill-kept, neglected (child, garden); untidy (house); (*b*) **être t. de, à, faire qch.,** to be obliged to do sth.; **être t. au secret professionnel,** to be bound by professional secrecy.
ténu [teny], *a.* tenuous, thin; slender, fine; subtle (distinction).
tenue [tǝny], *s.f.* **1.** (*a*) holding, session (of assizes, etc.); (*b*) keeping, managing, running (of shop, house, etc.); **t. des livres,** book-keeping. **2.** bearing, behaviour; **avoir de la t.,** to have good manners; *Aut:* **t. de route,** road-holding qualities. **3.** dress; **en grande t.,** in full dress; **t. de ville,** town clothes; **t. de tous les jours,** casuals.
térébenthine [terebɑ̃tin], *s.f.* turpentine; **essence de t.,** (oil of) turpentine, *F:* turps.

tergal [tɛrgal], *s.m. R.t.m:* terylene.
tergivers|er [tɛrʒivɛrse], *v.i.* to equivocate; to beat about the bush; to dodge the issue; *s.f.* **-ation.**
terme[1] [tɛrm], *s.m.* **1.** term, end, limit (of life, journey, etc.); **mener qch. à bon t.,** to carry sth. through. **2.** (appointed) time; **accouchement avant t.,** premature childbirth; *Ind: etc:* **prévisions à court t., à long t.,** short-range, long-range, forecasts. **3.** (*a*) quarter (of rent); term; (*b*) quarter's rent; (*c*) quarter day.
terme[2], *s.m.* **1.** term, expression; **t. de métier,** technical term; **en d'autres termes,** in other words; **il m'a dit en termes propres,** he told me in so many words. **2.** *pl.* wording; terms, conditions. **3.** *pl.* terms, footing; **être en bons termes avec qn,** to be on good terms with s.o.
termin|er [tɛrmine], *v.tr.* to terminate. **1.** to limit (estate, etc.). **2.** to end, finish; to conclude (bargain, etc.); to complete (job, contract); **t. ses jours en paix,** to end one's days in peace; **en avoir terminé avec qch.,** to have finished with sth.; *s.f.* **-aison,** termination, ending.
se terminer, to end; to come to an end.
terminus [tɛrminys], *s.m.* (railway, coach, etc.) terminus; (air) terminal.
terne [tɛrn], *a.* dull, lustreless; **voix t.,** flat voice; **yeux ternes,** lack-lustre eyes; **vie t.,** drab life.
ternir [tɛrniːr], *v.tr.* to tarnish, dull, dim.
se ternir, to tarnish; to grow dull.
terrain [tɛrɛ̃], *s.m.* ground; (*a*) piece of ground, plot of land; **t. à bâtir,** building site; **t. vague,** waste ground; (*b*) country, ground; **t. accidenté,** hilly country; **t. vallonné,** undulating ground; (*c*) ground, soil; **t. gras,** rich soil; **t. mou,** soft soil; (*d*) *Sp: etc:* (football, etc.) field ground; (golf) course, links; *Av:* **t. d'atterrissage,** landing strip, airstrip; (*e*) *Mil:* **gagner, céder, du t.,** to gain, lose, ground; **être sur son t.,** to be on familiar ground, in one's element.
terrasse [tɛras], *s.f.* (*a*) terrace; bank; **culture e t.,** terrace cultivation; (*b*) pavement (in front o a café); *Const:* balcony, verandah, terrace *N.Am:* porch; **toit en t.,** flat roof.
terrass|er [tɛrase], *v.tr.* **1.** to embank; to di (foundations, etc.). **2.** (*a*) to lay (s.o.) low; **t. u adversaire,** to throw, to floor an opponent; (*l* (*of grief, illness*) to overwhelm, crush (s.o.) *s.m.* **-ement,** embankment; *s.m.* **-ier,** navvy.
terr|e [tɛːr], *s.f.* **1.** earth; (*a*) the world; **jusqu'a bout de la t.,** to the world's end; (*b*) groun land; **tremblement de t.,** earthquake; **tombe par t.,** to fall down (from standing position **tomber à t.,** to fall down (from height); (*c ship*) **être à t.,** to be aground; **descendre à t.,** t land, disembark; *adj.phr.* (*of pers.*) **être t. à t** to be matter-of-fact, commonplace. **2.** so land; **t. grasse,** rich land. **3.** (*a*) estate, prope

ty; (*b*) **terres étrangères,** foreign lands; *Geog:* **la T. de Feu,** Tierra del Fuego. **4.** loam, clay; **sol en t. battue,** mud floor; **t. cuite,** terra cotta; *s.m. Hort:* **-eau, -eaux,** compost; *a.* **-estre,** terrestrial; worldly.

Terre-Neuve [tɛrnœːv]. **1.** *Pr.n.f. Geog:* Newfoundland. **2.** *s.m.inv.* Newfoundland dog.

terre-neuvien, -ienne [tɛrnœvjɛ̃, -jɛn], (*a*) *a.* (of) Newfoundland; (*b*) *s.* Newfoundlander.

terre-plein [tɛrplɛ̃], *s.m.* (*a*) earth platform; terrace; (*b*) (*on road*) **t.-p. de stationnement,** lay-by; **t.-p. circulaire,** central island (of roundabout); *pl.* **terre-pleins.**

terreur [tɛrœːr], *s.f.* terror; dread; **fou de t.,** wild with fear.

terreux, -euse [tɛrø, -øːz], *a.* (*a*) earthy (taste, smell); (*b*) grubby, dirty (hands); muddy (colour); unhealthy, ashen (complexion).

terrible [tɛribl], *a.* terrible, dreadful; *adv.* **-ment.**

terrier[1] [tɛrje], *s.m.* burrow, hole (of rabbit); earth (of fox); set (of badger).

terrier[2], *a.m. & s.m.* (**chien) t.,** terrier.

terrif|ier [ter(r)ifje], *v.tr.* (*pr.sub. & p.d.* **n. terrifiions**) to terrify (s.o.); *a.* **-iant; roman t.,** thriller.

terrine [tɛrin], *s.f.* **1.** (earthenware) pot; terrine (for baking pâtés, etc.). **2. t. de pâté de campagne, de canard,** baked farmhouse pâté, duck pâté.

erri|toire [tɛritwaːr], *s.m.* territory; *a.* **-torial, -toriaux,** territorial.

erroir [tɛrwaːr], *s.m. Agr:* soil; **sentir le t.,** to smack of the soil; **mots du t.,** local words, sayings.

error|iser [tɛrɔrize], *v.tr.* (*a*) to terrorize; (*b*) to terrify; *s.m.* **-isme;** *s.m. & f.* **-iste.**

ertre [tɛrtr], *s.m.* hillock, mound, knoll.

es [te, tɛ], *poss. a. see* TON[1].

est [tɛst], *s.m.* test, trial; *Psy:* **t. de capacité intellectuelle,** intelligence test; **t. d'intelligence pratique,** aptitude test; **t. professionnel,** vocational, trade, test.

esta|ment[1] [tɛstamã], *s.m.* will, testament; *a.* **-mentaire,** testamentary; *s.* **-teur, -trice,** testator,*f.* testatrix.

estament[2], *s.m. B:* **l'ancien, le nouveau, T.,** the Old, the New, Testament.

tard [tɛtaːr], *s.m.* tadpole.

te [tɛt], *s.f.* head. **1.** (*a*) **tenir t. à qn,** to stand up to s.o.; **j'en ai par-dessus la t.,** I can't stand it any longer; **ne (pas) savoir où donner de la t.,** not to know which way to turn; **dîner t. à t.,** to dine alone together; **avoir mal à la t.,** to have a headache; **se laver la t.,** to wash one's hair; **signe de t.,** nod; (*b*) face, appearance; *F:* **faire la t.,** to be sulky; **il a une bonne t.,** he looks a decent fellow; **avoir une sale t.,** to be a nasty-looking customer. **2.** headpiece, brains, mind; **c'est une femme de t.,** she is a capable woman;

mauvaise t., unruly person; **en faire à sa t.,** to have one's way, to please oneself. **3.** (*a*) leader; (*b*) summit, crown, top (of volcano, etc.); **t. de chapitre,** chapter heading; (*c*) head (of nail, screw, pin, etc.); (*d*) front place; *Rail:* **voiture de t.,** front carriage; *Rac:* **prendre la t.,** to take the lead; **t. de ligne,** (i) *Rail:* terminus; (ii) head of taxi-rank; **être à la t. de la classe,** to be top of the form.

tête-à-tête [tɛtatɛt], *s.m.inv.* private interview; **tête-à-tête.**

têtu [tety, tɛ-], *a.* stubborn, obstinate; mulish.

texte [tɛkst], *s.m.* (*a*) text (of author, book, etc.); *Bookb:* **gravure hors t.,** plate; full-page engraving; (*b*) letterpress (to illustration).

textile [tɛkstil], *a. & s.m.* textile; **textiles artificiels,** synthetic textiles; **le t.,** the textile industries.

Thaïlande (la) [lataïlãːd]. *Pr.n. Geog:* Thailand.

thé [te], *s.m.* **1.** tea. **2.** tea-party; *s.f.* **-ière,** teapot.

théâtr|e [teaːtr], *s.m.* **1.** theatre, playhouse. **2.** stage; **mettre une pièce au t.,** to stage, put on, a play; **se retirer du t.,** to give up the stage. **3.** (*a*) dramatic art; **pièce de t.,** play; **faire du t.,** to be on the stage, to be an actor; **coup de t.,** dramatic turn (to events); (*b*) plays, dramatic works (of s.o.); **le t. anglais,** English drama; *a.* **-al, -aux,** theatrical, *Pej:* stagy; *adv.* **-alement.**

thème [tɛm], *s.m.* (*a*) theme, topic; subject; **t. d'actualité,** topic of the day; **thèmes littéraires,** literary subjects; (*b*) *Sch:* prose; **t. latin,** Latin prose; (**élève) fort en t.,** hardworking (not necessarily brilliant) (pupil).

théolog|ie [teɔlɔʒi], *s.f.* theology; **docteur en t.,** doctor of divinity; D.D.; *s.* **-ien, -ienne,** (i) theological student; (ii) theologist, theologian; *a.* **-ique,** theological.

théorème [teɔrɛm], *s.m.* theorem.

théor|ie [teɔri], *s.f.* theory; *a.* **-ique,** theoretic(al); *adv.* **-iquement.**

théor|iser [teɔrize], (*a*) *v.i.* to theorize; (*b*) *v.tr.* to theorize about (sth.); *s.m. & f.* **-iste,** theorist, theorizer.

théosophie [teɔzɔfi], *s.f.* theosophy.

thérap|ie [terapi], *s.f. Med:* therapy; **t. rééducative,** occupational therapy.

thermal, -aux [tɛrmal, -o], *a.* thermal; **eaux thermales,** hot springs; **station thermale,** spa.

thermomètre [tɛrmɔmɛtr], *s.m.* thermometer.

thermonucléaire [tɛrmɔnykleɛːr], *a. Atom.Ph:* thermonuclear.

thermostat [tɛrmɔsta], *s.m.* thermostat.

thermostatique [tɛrmɔstatik]. **1.** *a.* thermostatic (control, etc.). **2.** *s.f.* thermostatics.

thermothérapie [tɛrmɔterapi], *s.f. Med: Vet:* thermotherapy; heat treatment.

thèse [tɛːz], *s.f.* **1.** thesis, proposition, argument;

pièce à t., problem play; **en t. générale,** generally speaking. **2.** *Sch:* thesis; **soutenir, défendre, sa t.,** to uphold, defend, one's thesis (before a jury).

thon [tɔ̃], *s.m. Ich:* tunny(-fish).

thorax [tɔraks], *s.m. Anat:* thorax, chest.

thym [tɛ̃], *s.m. Bot:* thyme.

thyroïde [tirɔid], *a. Anat:* thyroid (gland).

tibia [tibja], *s.m. Anat:* tibia, shin-bone; **s'érafler le t.,** to bark one's shin.

Tibre (le) [lətibr]. *Pr.n.m.* the (river) Tiber.

tic [tik], *s.m.* (*a*) *Med:* tic; nervous twitch(ing); (*b*) *F:* (unconscious) habit; mannerism.

ticket [tikɛ], *s.m.* numbered slip, check; **t. de réservation,** reserved-seat ticket; **t. de quai,** platform ticket.

tiède [tjɛd], *a.* tepid; lukewarm (bath, friendship); (*of air*) mild; *adv.* **-ment,** in a lukewarm manner; halfheartedly.

tiédeur [tjedœ:r], *s.f.* tepidity, lukewarmness; **agir avec t.,** to act halfheartedly.

tien, tienne [tjɛ̃, tjɛn]. **1.** *poss.a.* yours; **mes intérêts sont tiens,** my interests are yours. **2. le t., la tienne, les tiens, les tiennes;** (*a*) *poss.pron.* **ma sœur se promène avec la tienne,** my sister is out walking with yours; (*b*) *s.m.* (i) your own (property, etc.); yours; **si tu veux du mien, donne-moi du t.,** if you want some of mine, give me some of yours; **il faut y mettre du t.,** you must contribute your share; you must make concessions; (ii) *pl.* **les tiens,** your own (people); (iii) *F:* **tu as encore fait des tiennes,** you have been up to your old tricks again.

tiens [tjɛ̃], *int.* **1.** hullo! **2. t., c'est Philippe!** look, it's Philip! **3. t., t.!** indeed? well, well!

tiercé [tjɛrse], *s.m. Rac:* **le t., pari t.,** forecast of the first three horses.

tiers, *f.* **tierce** [tjɛːr, tjɛrs], *s.* (*a*) third (part); **remise d'un t. (du prix),** discount of a third; *F:* a third off; **payer le t. provisionnel,** to pay the provisional one-third (of French income tax); (*b*) third person, third party; **assurance au t.,** third party insurance.

tige [tiːʒ], *s.f.* **1.** (*a*) stem, stalk (of plant); (*b*) trunk, bole (of tree). **2.** (*a*) shaft (of column); shank (of key); (*b*) rod; *Mch:* **t. du piston,** piston-rod.

tignasse [tiɲas], *s.f.* shock, mop (of hair).

tigre, tigresse [tigr, tigrɛs], *s. Z:* tiger, *f.* tigress.

tigré [tigre], *a.* striped; **chat t.,** tabby cat; **lis t.,** tiger-lily.

tilleul [tijœl], *s.m. Bot:* lime tree; **(infusion de) t.,** lime-blossom tea.

timbale [tɛ̃bal], *s.f.* **1.** *Mus:* kettledrum. **2.** metal drinking-cup. **3.** *Cu:* (*a*) timbale mould; (*b*) **t. de langouste,** lobster timbale.

timbre [tɛ̃ːbr], *s.m.* **1.** (*a*) **t. électrique,** electric bell; *F:* **avoir le t. fêlé,** to have a screw loose; (*b*) timbre, quality in tone (of voice, in-

strument). **2.** (*a*) stamp (on document); **t. de la poste,** postmark; (*b*) **t.(-poste);** (postage) stamp.

timbré [tɛ̃bre], *a.* **1.** sonorous (voice). **2.** *F:* crack-brained (pers.); dotty, off his head.

timbre-poste [tɛ̃br(ə)pɔst], *s.m.* (postage) stamp; *pl.* **timbres-poste.**

timbre-quittance [tɛ̃br(ə)kitɑ̃ːs], *s.m.* receipt stamp; *pl.* **timbres-quittance.**

timbr|er [tɛ̃bre], *v.tr.* to stamp (passport, letter); *s.m.* **-age.**

timide [timid], *a.* timid; (*a*) timorous, apprehensive; (*b*) shy, bashful; diffident (**envers,** with); *adv.* **-ment.**

timidité [timidite], *s.f.* timidity; (*a*) timorousness; (*b*) shyness, bashfulness.

timoré [timɔre], *a.* timorous, easily scared.

tintamarre [tɛ̃tamaːr], *s.m. F:* din, racket, noise.

tint|er [tɛ̃te]. **1.** *v.tr.* to ring, toll (bell). **2.** *v.i.* (*a*) (*of bell*) to ring, toll; (*of small bells*) to tinkle; (*of coins, metal*) to jingle; **faire t. les verres,** to clink glasses; (*b*) (*of the ears*) to buzz, tingle; **les oreilles ont dû vous t. hier soir,** your ears must have been burning last night (*i.e.* you were being talked about); *s.m.* **-ement** ringing; tinkling; buzzing.

tique [tik], *s.f. Arach:* tick, cattle-tick; **t. du chien,** dog-tick; **fièvre à tiques,** tick fever.

tiquer [tike], *v.i.* (*a*) *F:* (*of face*) to twitch; (*b*) to wince; to show signs of emotion, annoyance; **n'a pas tiqué,** he didn't turn a hair.

tir [tiːr], *s.m.* **1.** shooting; gunnery. **2.** fire, firing; **à t. rapide,** quick-firing. **3.** rifle-range; shooting gallery.

tirade [tirad], *s.f.* (*a*) *Th:* declamatory speech; (*b*) tirade; vituperative speech; **t. d'injures,** string of insults.

tiraill|er [tirɑje], *v.tr.* **1.** to pull (s.o., sth.) about; *F:* **tiraillé entre deux émotions,** torn between opposing emotions. **2.** *abs.* to shoot aimlessly; *s.m.* **-ement,** (i) tugging; (ii) **t. d'estomac,** pang(s) of hunger; (iii) wrangling, friction; *s.m.* **-eur,** skirmisher; sharp-shooter.

se tirailler, *Fr.C:* to scuffle.

tirant [tirɑ̃], *s.m.* **t. d'eau,** (ship's) draught.

tire [tiːr], *s.f.* **voleur à la t.,** pickpocket.

tiré, -ée [tire]. **1.** *a.* (*a*) drawn, tired, haggard, peaky (features); (*b*) **aux cheveux tirés,** with scraped back hair; (*c*) **tiré par les cheveux,** far-fetched. **2.** *s. Com:* drawee. **3.** *s.f.* **tirée,** long distance, long haul.

tire-bouchon [tirbuʃɔ̃], *s.m.* corkscrew; *pl.* **tire-bouchons.**

tire-ligne [tirliɲ], *s.m.* drawing-pen; *pl.* **tire-lignes.**

tire(-)lire [tirliːr], *s.f.* money-box; piggy bank.

tir|er [tire]. **I.** *v.tr.* **1.** to pull out; to stretch; **t. ses chaussettes,** to pull up one's socks; *Agr:* **t. lait,** to milk (the cows). **2.** to pull, tug, draw;

la jambe, to limp; **t. les rideaux,** to draw the curtains (to or apart); **t. la porte,** to pull the door to, to close the door; *F:* **être tiré à quatre,** to be worried on every side. **3.** (*a*) to pull off (gloves, shoes); (*b*) **t. son chapeau à qn,** to raise one's hat to s.o.; **là-dessus il nous-a tiré le chapeau,** thereupon he (raised his hat and) departed. **4.** to pull out, take out, extract; **t. un journal de sa poche,** to pull a paper out of one's pocket; **t. une dent à qn,** to pull out, draw, s.o.'s tooth; **t. du vin,** to draw wine (from the cask); **t. de l'eau,** to draw water; **t. plaisir de qch.,** to derive pleasure from sth. **5.** (*a*) to draw (a line); (*b*) to print (off) (proofs, copies, photos); (*c*) *Com:* to draw (bill of exchange). **6.** (*a*) to shoot, fire; **t. un lièvre,** to shoot (at) a hare; **t. à blanc,** to fire blank (cartridge); (*b*) **t. (des armes),** to fence. **7.** *Nau:* (*of ship*) to draw (twenty feet of water). **II. tirer,** *v.i.* **1.** to pull (on cable, etc.). **2.** (*a*) to incline (to); to verge (on); **bleu tirant sur le vert,** blue tending to green; **le jour tire à sa fin,** the day is drawing to its close; (*b*) **t. sur la gauche,** to incline to the left. **3.** (*of chimney, etc.*) to draw; *s.m.* **-age,** (i) pulling, hauling; (ii) draught (of flue); (iii) drawing (of lottery, bonds); (iv) *Typ: Phot: etc:* (*a*) printing (off); (*b*) (print) run, edition (of book); (v) drawing (of cheque); *s.* **-eur, -euse,** marksman, -woman.

ꞓe tirer d'affaire, (i) to get out of trouble; (ii) to tide over a difficulty; to manage.

ꞓiret [tirɛ], *s.m. Typ:* (*a*) hyphen; (*b*) dash; (*c*) **ligne de tirets,** broken line.

ꞓiroir [tirwaːr], *s.m.* drawer.

ꞓiroir-caisse [tirwarkɛs], *s.m. Com:* till; *pl. tiroirs-caisses.*

ꞓisane [tizan], *s.f.* infusion (of herbs).

ꞓisonner [tizɔne], *v.tr.* to poke, stir (the fire); **t. une querelle,** to fan a quarrel; *s.m.* **-ier,** poker.

ꞓisser [tise], *v.tr.* to weave; **métier à t.,** (weaving) loom; *s.m.* **-age,** (i) weaving; (ii) cloth mill; *s.* **-erand, -erande,** *s.* **-eur, -euse,** weaver.

ꞓissu [tisy], *s.m.* (*a*) texture; **vêtement d'un t. serré,** closely woven garment; (*b*) fabric, tissue, textile; cloth; material; **t. pour pantalon,** trousering; **t. métallique,** wire mesh; **t. de mensonges,** string of lies.

ꞓre [tiːtr], *s.m.* **1.** (*a*) (official) title; form of address; (*b*) *adj.phr.* **en t.,** titular; on the regular staff. **2.** (*a*) diploma, certificate; (*b*) title-deed; (*c*) *Fin:* warrant, bond, certificate; *pl.* stocks and shares, securities. **3.** title, claim, right; **à t. de. . .,** (i) by right of . . .; (ii) by way of . . .; **à t. d'essai,** (i) experimentally; (ii) *Com:* on approval; **à quel t.?** by what right? **4.** (*a*) title (of book); (*b*) heading (of chapter); **les gros titres,** big headlines. **5.** grade (of ore); fineness (of coinage); *Ch:* strength (of solution).

titré [titre], *a.* **1.** titled (person). **2.** qualified (teacher). **3.** *Ch:* standard (solution).

titrer [titre], *v.tr.* **1.** to give a title to (s.o., sth.). **2.** *Tchn:* to standardize (solution); to assay (ore); *s.m.* **-age.**

tituber [titybe], *v.i.* to reel (about); to lurch; to stagger.

titulaire [titylɛːr]. **1.** *a.* titular (bishop, professor, etc.); **membre t.,** regular member. **2.** *s.* holder (of right, title, certificate, etc.); bearer (of passport).

toast [tost], *s.m.* **1.** toast; **porter un t.,** to propose a toast, the health of s.o. **2. t. beurré,** piece of buttered toast.

toboggan [tɔbɔgɑ̃], *s.m.* toboggan; chute (in swimming bath, etc.).

toc [tɔk]. **1.** (*a*) *int.* **t. t.!** tap, tap! (*b*) *s.m.* tap, rap (on door, etc.). **2.** *s.m. F:* **bijoux en t.,** imitation jewellery.

tocsin [tɔksɛ̃], *s.m.* tocsin; alarm-bell.

Togo (**le**) [lɔtogo]. *Pr.n.m. Geog:* Togo(land); **République du T.,** Republic of Togo.

togolais, -aise [tɔgɔlɛ, -ɛːz], *a. & s. Geog:* Togolese.

toi [twa], *stressed pers. pron.* (*subject or object*) you; **c'est t.,** it's you; **ce livre est à t.,** this book is yours; **tais-t.,** be quiet! *F:* shut up!

toile [twal], *s.f.* **1.** (*a*) linen, linen cloth; **t. à chemises,** shirting; **t. à matelas,** ticking; (*b*) cloth; **t. cirée,** (i) oilcloth; (ii) *Nau:* oilskin; (*c*) canvas; (*d*) **t. métallique,** wire gauze; (*e*) **t. d'araignée,** cobweb; spider's web. **2.** oil painting; canvas. **3.** *Nau:* sail.

toilette [twalɛt], *s.f.* **1.** dressing-table. **2. faire sa t.,** to wash and dress; to dress; **faire un bout de t.,** to have a wash and brush up; to tidy oneself; **cabinet de t.,** dressing-room (with wash-basin). **3.** lavatory; (*in restaurant*) cloakroom; ladies' room. **4.** (woman's) dress, costume; **aimer la t.,** to be fond of dress.

toi-même [twamɛːm], *pers.pron.* yourself; **tu me l'as dit t.-m.,** you told me yourself.

toison [twazɔ̃], *s.f.* **1.** fleece. **2.** *F:* mop, shock (of hair).

toit [twa], *s.m.* **1.** roof; **crier qch. sur les toits,** to proclaim sth. from the housetops; *Aut:* **t. ouvrant,** sliding, sunshine, roof. **2. le t. paternel,** the home, the paternal roof.

toiture [twatyːr], *s.f.* roofing, roof.

tôle [toːl], *s.f.* sheet-metal; **t. ondulée,** corrugated iron; *s.f.* **-erie,** (*a*) rolling mills; (*b*) sheet iron and steel plate goods; (*c*) *Aut: etc:* steelwork; *s.m.* **-ier,** sheet-iron worker, merchant; *Aut:* panel beater.

tolérable [tɔlerabl], *a.* bearable, tolerable; *adv.* **-ment.**

tolérer [tɔlere], *v.tr.* (**je tolère; je tolérerai**) (*a*) to tolerate (opinion, a person); (*b*) to allow tacitly, wink at (abuses); (*c*) *Med:* to tolerate

(drug); *s.f.* **-ance;** *a.* **-ant.**
tomate [tɔmat], *s.f.* tomato; **sauce t.,** tomato sauce.
tombe [tɔ̃:b], *s.f.* (*a*) tomb, grave; (*b*) tombstone.
tombeau, -eaux [tɔ̃bo], *s.m.* tomb; monument; **t. de famille,** family vault.
tombée [tɔ̃be], *s.f.* fall (of rain, snow, etc.); **à la t. de la nuit,** at nightfall.
tomber [tɔ̃be], *v.i.* (*aux.usu.* être) **1.** to fall, fall down, drop down; (*of aircraft*) to crash; *impers.* **il tombe de la neige,** it's snowing; *F:* **t. dans les pommes,** to pass out, to faint; **faire t. qch.,** to knock sth. over; **laisser t. qch.,** to drop sth.; **fruits tombés,** windfalls; *Journ:* **le journal est tombé,** the paper has gone to bed. **2.** (*of wind, anger, fever, etc.*) to drop, abate, subside, die down; (*of conversation*) to flag; **le feu tombe,** the fire is dying down. **3. t. en disgrâce,** to fall into disgrace; **t. dans un piège,** to fall into a trap; **t. dans la misère,** to fall into poverty. **4. t. sur l'ennemi,** to attack, fall on, the enemy. **5. t. sur qn, qch.,** to fall in with s.o., come across sth.; **t. juste,** to come, to happen, at the right moment. **6.** to fail; *Th:* **la pièce est tombée (à plat),** the play flopped. **7.** to fall, hang down; **les cheveux lui tombent dans le dos,** her hair hangs down her back; **jupe qui tombe bien,** skirt that hangs well. **8. t. amoureux de qn,** to fall in love with s.o.; **t. malade, mort,** to fall ill, dead.
tombereau, -eaux [tɔ̃bro], *s.m.* tip-cart.
tome [to:m, tɔm], *s.m.* (heavy) volume; tome.
ton¹, ta, tes [tɔ̃, ta, te], *poss.a.* (**ton** *is used instead of* **ta** *before fem. words beginning with a vowel or h "mute"; for use of* **ton,** *as opposed to* **votre,** *see* TU) your; **un de tes amis,** a friend of yours; **ton ami(e),** your friend; **tes père et mère,** your father and mother.
ton², s.m. 1. (*a*) tone, intonation; **hausser le t.,** to raise (the tone of) one's voice; **parler d'un t. dur,** to speak harshly; **faire baisser le t. à qn,** to take s.o. down a peg (or two); **elle te prend sur ce t.?** is that how she speaks to you? (*b*) tone, manners, breeding; **c'est de mauvais t.,** it's bad form, bad manners, vulgar. **2.** *Mus:* (*a*) (**hauteur du**) **t.,** pitch; (*b*) key. **3.** tone, tint, colour.
tondeur, -euse [tɔ̃dœ:r, -ø:z]. **1.** *s.* shearer (of cloth, sheep), clipper. **2.** *s.f.* **tondeuse,** (*a*) *Agr:* shearing machine; (hair) clippers; (*b*) lawnmower.
tondre [tɔ̃:dr], *v.tr.* to shear (cloth, sheep); to clip (hair, horse, hedge); **t. le gazon,** to mow the lawn.
tonifi|er [tɔnifje], *v.tr.* (*pr.sub. & p.d.* n. **tonifiions**) to brace, to tone up (the nervous system, etc.); to invigorate; *s.f.* **-cation.**
tonique [tɔnik], *a.* **1.** *Med:* (*a*) **médicament t.,** *s.m.* **tonique,** tonic; (*b*) stimulating, revivifying.

2. *Ling:* tonic (accent); accented, stressed (syllable). **3.** *Mus:* **note t.,** *s.f.* **tonique,** key-note.
tonnage [tɔna:ʒ], *s.m. Nau:* tonnage, burthen (of ship); tonnage, capacity (of a port); **droit de t.,** (duty based on) tonnage.
tonne [tɔn], *s.f.* **1.** tun; (large) cask. **2.** *Meas:* metric ton (= 1000 kilograms).
tonneau, -eaux [tɔno], *s.m.* **1.** cask, barrel; **bière au t.,** draught beer. **2.** *Nau:* ton.
tonner [tɔne], *v.i.* to thunder; *impers.* **il tonne,** it's thundering.
tonnerre [tɔnɛ:r], *s.m.* thunder.
tonte [tɔ̃:t], *s.f.* **1.** (*a*) sheep-shearing; clipping; (*b*) clip; (*c*) shearing-time. **2.** *Hort:* mowing (of lawn); clipping (of hedge, etc.).
top [tɔp], *s.m. Rad: T.V:* time signal; **les tops,** the pips.
topaze [tɔpa:z], *s.f.* topaz.
toper [tɔpe], *v.i. F:* to agree, consent (*usu.* to a bargain); to shake hands on it; **tope là!** done! agreed!
topinambour [tɔpinãbu:r], *s.m. Bot:* Jerusalem artichoke.
topograph|ie [tɔpɔgrafi], *s.f.* topography; *a.* **-ique,** topographical; **le service t.** = the Ordnance Survey.
toqué [tɔke], *a. F:* (*a*) crazy, cracked; (*b*) **être t. de qn,** to be infatuated with s.o., to be madly in love with s.o.; **il est t. de la télé,** he's got the telly on the brain.
torche [tɔrʃ], *s.f.* torch; **t. électrique,** electric torch; (*of parachute*) **se mettre en t.,** to snake.
torchis [tɔrʃi], *s.m.* **mur en t.,** cob, mud, wall.
torchon [tɔrʃɔ̃], *s.m.* floor-cloth; dish-cloth duster; **le t. brûle chez eux,** they're always bickering.
tordant [tɔrdã], *a. F:* screamingly funny.
tordre [tɔrdr], *v.tr.* to twist; to wring (clothes, one's hands); **t. la bouche,** to pull a wry face.
se tordre, to writhe, twist; *F:* **se t. (de rire),** to split one's sides laughing; **il y a de quoi se t.,** it's enough to make a cat laugh.
tordu, -ue [tɔrdy], *a.* **1.** twisted; buckled; (chassis, etc.); **nerfs tordus,** nerves on edge; **traits tordus,** distorted features. **2.** (*a*) **esprit t.,** warped mind; (*b*) *F:* **être (complètement) t.,** to be mad; *s.* **c'est un t., une tordue,** he's, she's quite mad!
toréador [tɔreadɔ:r], *s.m.* bullfighter.
tornade [tɔrnad], *s.f.* tornado.
torpeur [tɔrpœ:r], *s.f.* torpor.
torpille [tɔrpi:j], *s.f.* torpedo.
torpill|er [tɔrpije], *v.tr.* **1.** to torpedo (ship, etc). **2.** to mine (harbour); **zone torpillée,** mined area; *s.m.* **-age,** torpedoing; *s.m. Navy:* **-eur** (i) torpedo expert; (ii) (small) destroyer.
torrent [tɔr(r)ã], *s.m.* torrent, mountain stream; **il pleut à torrents,** it's raining in sheets; **t.**

larmes, flood of tears.
torrentiel, -elle [tɔr(r)ɑ̃sjɛl], *a.* torrential; **pluie torrentielle,** torrential rain; *adv.* **-lement.**
torride [tɔrid], *a.* torrid (zone); scorching (heat).
torse [tɔrs], *s.m.* torso (of statue, of pers.); **travailler le t. nu,** to work stripped to the waist; *F:* **bomber le t.,** to stick out one's chest.
torsion [tɔrsjɔ̃], *s.f.* torsion; twisting (of rope, wire, etc.); *Aut:* **barre de t.,** torsion bar (spring).
tort [tɔːr], *s.m.* wrong. 1. error, fault; **être dans son t.,** to be in the wrong; **donner t. à qn,** to decide against, to lay the blame on, s.o.; **à t. ou à raison,** rightly or wrongly; **à t. et à travers,** at random. 2. injury, harm, damage; **la grêle a fait beaucoup de t. dans la région,** the hail has done a great deal of damage, has played havoc, in the district; **faire (du) t. à qn,** (i) to wrong s.o.; to do s.o. an injustice; (ii) to damage s.o.'s cause, business, reputation.
torticolis [tɔrtikɔli], *s.m.* crick in the neck; stiff neck.
tortill|er [tɔrtije]. 1. *v.tr.* to twist (up), to twirl, to twiddle (one's moustache). 2. *v.i.* (a) **t. des hanches,** to swing the hips (in walking); (b) to prevaricate, quibble; **il n'y a pas à t.,** it's no use shilly-shallying; **dites-le-lui sans t.,** tell him straight (out); *s.m.* **-ement,** wriggling.
se tortiller, to wriggle, twist; to writhe, squirm.
tortue [tɔrty], *s.f.* tortoise; **t. de mer,** turtle.
tortueu|x, -euse [tɔrtɥø, -øːz], *a.* tortuous, winding (road); twisted (tree); crooked, underhand (conduct); *adv.* **-sement.**
torture [tɔrtyːr], *s.f.* torture.
torturer [tɔrtyre], *v.tr.* to torture (prisoner); to cause (s.o.) intense suffering; **la jalousie le torturait,** he was tortured by jealousy; **se t. la cervelle,** to rack one's brains.
tôt [to], *adv.* (a) soon; **t. ou tard,** sooner or later; **pas de si t.,** not as soon as (all) that; **revenez au plus t.,** come back as soon as possible; (b) **se lever t.,** to rise early; **venez t.,** come early; *P:* **c'est pas trop t.!** and about time too!
total, -aux [tɔtal, -o]. 1. *a.* total, complete, entire, whole. 2. *s.m.* whole, total; *adv.* **-ement.**
totalisateur, -trice [tɔtalizatœːr, -tris]. 1. *a.* adding (machine, etc.). 2. *s.m.* adding machine; *Rac:* totalizator, *F:* tote.
totalitaire [tɔtalitɛːr], *a.* totalitarian.
totalitarisme [tɔtalitarism], *s.m.* totalitarianism.
totalité [tɔtalite], *s.f.* totality, whole; **pris dans sa t.,** taken as a whole; in the aggregate.
toubib [tubib], *s.m.* *F:* doctor, quack, medico; *Mil:* M.O.
touchant [tuʃɑ̃]. 1. *a.* touching, moving, affecting (speech, book). 2. *prep.* touching, concerning, about (a subject, a person).
touche [tuʃ], *s.f.* 1. touch, touching; *Fb:* throw-

in; **pierre de t.,** touchstone, test; *Sp:* **ligne de t.,** touch line. 2. key (of typewriter, piano, computer, etc.).
toucher [tuʃe]. I. *v.* to touch. 1. *v.tr.* (a) **t. le but,** to hit the mark; **t. un chèque,** to cash a cheque; **t. son salaire,** to get one's pay, *abs.* **t.,** to be paid; *Mil:* **t. des rations,** to draw rations; (b) to move, affect (s.o.); **t. qn jusqu'aux larmes,** to move s.o. to tears; (c) to concern, affect (s.o.); **en ce qui vous touche,** as far as you are concerned; (d) *Nau:* **t. à un port,** to call at a port; **t. (le fond),** to touch bottom; to go aground; (e) **t. qn par lettre, au téléphone,** to reach, contact, s.o. by letter, by phone; **je n'ai pas pu le t.,** I couldn't get hold of him. 2. (a) *v.tr.* to touch on, deal with; to allude to (a subject); (b) *v.ind. tr.* to meddle, interfere (à, with); **ne pas t. à un plat,** to leave a dish untasted; **sans avoir l'air d'y t.,** in a detached manner. 3. *v.i.* (a) **t. à qch.,** to be in touch, in contact, with sth.; to be near to sth.; to border on sth.; (b) **cela touche de très près à mes intérêts,** it closely affects my interests.
II. **toucher,** *s.m.* touch, feel (of sth.).
se toucher, to touch, adjoin.
touff|e [tuf], *s.f.* tuft; wisp (of hair, straw); clump, cluster (of trees); *a.* **-u,** bushy; thick.
toujours [tuʒuːr], *adv.* 1. always, ever; **un ami de t.,** a lifelong friend. 2. still; **cherchez t.,** go on looking. 3. nevertheless, all the same; **je peux t. essayer,** anyhow I can try.
toupet [tupɛ], *s.m.* 1. (a) tuft of hair, quiff; (b) forelock. 2. *F:* cheek, impudence, sauce; nerve.
toupie [tupi], *s.f.* top; peg-top, spinning-top; **ronfler comme une t.,** to snore like a pig; **vieille t.,** old frump.
tour¹ [tuːr], *s.f.* 1. tower; *Av:* **t. de contrôle,** control tower. 2. *Chess:* castle, rook.
tour², *s.m.* 1. (a) (turning-)lathe; (b) **t. de potier,** potter's wheel. 2. (a) circumference, circuit; **faire le t. du monde,** to go round the world; *Sp:* **t. de piste,** lap; circuit; **t. de poitrine,** chest measurement; (b) **t. de lit,** bed-valance; *Cl:* **t. de cou,** (fur) necklet; (c) **tours et retours d'un chemin,** twists and turns of a road; (d) turn (of phrase); shape, contour (of face); course, direction (of business affair); **l'affaire prend un mauvais t.,** the matter is taking a bad turn; (e) **t. de reins,** twist, strain, (w)rick, in the back. 3. (a) round, revolution, turn (of a wheel, etc.); **frapper à t. de bras,** to strike with all one's might; **donner un t. de clef,** to turn the key in, to lock, the door; **son sang n'a fait qu'un t.,** it gave him a dreadful shock; (b) stroll; (c) trip, tour. 4. rotation, turn; **chacun (à) son t.,** each one in his turn; **t. à t.,** in turn; **à t. de rôle,** in turn. 5. trick, feat; **t. de main,** knack, trick of the trade; **t. d'adresse,** (i) piece of sleight of

hand; (ii) feat of acrobatics; **t. de force**, feat of strength.

tourb|e [turb], *s.f.* peat, turf; *a.* -**eux**, -**euse**, peaty, boggy; *s.* -**ier**, -**ière**, (i) *s.m.* peat worker; (ii) *s.f.* peat bog.

tourbillon [turbijɔ̃], *s.m.* **1.** whirlwind; swirl (of dust); **t. de neige**, flurry of snow. **2.** (*a*) whirlpool; (*b*) eddy (of water, wind); (*c*) whirl, bustle (of life, business, etc.).

tourbillonn|er [turbijɔne], *v.i.* to whirl (round); to eddy, swirl; *s.m.* -**ement**.

tourelle [turɛl], *s.f.* turret; *Mil: etc:* (gun, etc.) turret.

tour|isme [turism], *s.m.* tourist trade; **agence, bureau, de t.**, travel agency; *Aut:* **voiture de t.**, private car; *s.m.* -**iste**; *a.* -**istique**; **guide t.**, tourist guide.

tourment [turmɑ̃], *s.m.* (*a*) torment, torture; (*b*) anguish, pain; (*c*) (*of pers.*) **il est le t. de ma vie**, he's the bane of my life.

tourmente [turmɑ̃:t], *s.f.* gale, storm, tempest; **t. de neige**, blizzard; **la t. politique**, the political turmoil, upheaval.

tourmenté [turmɑ̃te], *a.* (*a*) contorted; jagged, broken (coastline); (*b*) tormented, tortured (conscience, expression); (*c*) agitated, turbulent (sea, life).

tourmenter [turmɑ̃te], *v.tr.* **1.** to torture, torment. **2.** (*a*) to harass, worry; (*b*) to plague, pester (s.o.).

se tourmenter, to fret, worry; to be anxious.

tournant [turnɑ̃]. **1.** *a.* (*a*) turning; revolving; **fauteuil t.**, swivel chair; **pont t.**, swing-bridge; (*b*) winding (road); spiral (staircase). **2.** *s.m.* (*a*) turning, bend; street corner; *Aut:* **t. brusque**, dangerous corner; (*b*) turning point (in history, in one's life).

tourne-disque(s) [turnədisk], *s.m. Rec:* record player; *pl.* **tourne-disques**.

tournedos [turnədo], *s.m. Cu:* tournedos; fillet steak.

tournée [turne], *s.f.* **1.** round, tour (of official); (doctor's) round of visits; (judge's) circuit; **la t. du facteur**, the postman's round. **2.** *F:* **payer une t.**, to stand a round (of drinks); **c'est la t. du patron**, it's on the house.

tourner [turne], *v.* to turn. **1.** *v.tr.* (*a*) to fashion, shape, on a lathe; (*b*) to revolve, turn round, rotate; **t. la tête**, to turn one's head; **t. le dos à qn**, to turn one's back on s.o.; *Cin:* **t. un film**, to shoot a film; *Cu:* **t. une crème**, to stir a custard; *Fb:* **t. la mêlée**, to wheel the scrum; (*c*) to change, convert; **t. qn en ridicule**, to hold s.o. up to ridicule; (*d*) to turn over (the page); (*e*) to get round; to evade (a difficulty, the law). **2.** *v.i.* (*a*) to revolve; to go round; **t. autour du pot**, to beat about the bush; **le pied lui a tourné**, he twisted his ankle; (*b*) to change direction; **tournez à gauche**, turn to the left; **t. court**, (i) to

turn short; (ii) to end suddenly; (*c*) to turn out, result; (*of pers.*) **mal t.**, to go to the bad; (*d*) *Cin:* **t. dans un film**, to act in a film; (*e*) *abs.* (*of fruit*) to colour, ripen; **lait qui tourne**, milk that is curdling, turning, going bad.

se tourner, (*a*) **se t. vers qn**, to turn towards s.o.; (*b*) to turn round.

tournesol [turnəsɔl], *s.m.* **1.** *Bot:* sunflower. **2.** **papier (de) t.**, litmus paper.

tournevis [turnəvis], *s.m. Tls:* screwdriver.

tourniquet [turnikɛ], *s.m.* **1.** **t.(-compteur)**, turnstile. **2.** (*a*) *Fireworks:* catherine-wheel; (*b*) garden sprinkler. **3.** *Surg:* tourniquet.

tournoi [turnwa], *s.m. Sp: etc:* (tennis, etc.) tournament; (whist) drive; (bridge) tournament.

tourn|oyer [turnwaje], *v.i.* (**je tournoie**) to turn round and round; (*of birds*) to wheel; to whirl; to spin; (*of water*) to eddy, swirl; *s.m.* -**oiement**, (i) twirling, whirling; spinning; wheeling; eddying, swirling; (ii) giddiness, dizziness.

tournure [turny:r], *s.f.* **1.** turn, course (of events); **les affaires prennent une mauvaise t.**, things are shaping badly, are looking black. **2.** shape, form, figure; **t. d'esprit**, turn of mind.

tourte [turt], *s.f.* raised pie; (covered) tart.

tourtereau, -eaux [turtəro], *s.m.* young turtledove; *F:* **faire les tourtereaux**, to bill and coo.

tourterelle [turtərɛl], *s.f.* turtle-dove.

Toussaint (la) [latusɛ̃]. *Pr.n.f.* All Saints' day; All-Hallows; **la veille de la T.**, Hallowe'en.

touss|er [tuse], *v.i.* to cough; *s.* -**eur**, -**euse**, cougher.

toussot|er [tusɔte], *v.i.* (*a*) to clear one's throat; to cough slightly; (*b*) to have a slight cough; *s.m.* -**ement**, slight cough; *s.f.* -**erie**, *F:* constant slight coughing.

tout, toute, *pl.* **tous, toutes** [tu, tut, tu, tut] (*when* **tous** *is a pron. it is pronounced* [tu:s]) all. **I.** *a.* **1.** (*noun undetermined*) any, every; all; **t. autre que vous**, anybody but you; **j'ai toute raison de croire que . . .**, I have ever reason to believe that . . .; **repas à tout heure**, meals served at any time. **2.** (*intensive*) **de toute force il nous faut . . .**, we absolutel must . . .; **à la toute dernière minute**, at th very last moment; **à toute vitesse**, at full speed **t. à vous**, entirely yours. **3.** the whole; all; **t. monde**, everybody; **toute la journée**, the who day; **pendant t. l'hiver**, throughout the winte **4.** all, every; **tous les jours**, every day; **tous l invités**, all the guests. **5.** **tous (les) deux**, bot **tous les deux jours**, every other day. **6.** **c'e toute une histoire**, it's a long story. **II.** *pron.* **1.** *sg.neut.* all, everything; **mange de t.**, he eats anything (and everything **c'est t. ce qu'il y a de plus beau**, it is mo beautiful; **c'est t. dire**, I needn't say more; **drôle comme t.**, awfully funny. **2.** *pl.* **tous** [tu:

à la fois, all together.
III. tout, *s.m.* **le t.,** the whole; the lot; *adv.phr.*. **du t. au t.,** entirely; **pas du t.,** *F:* **du t.,** not at all. **IV. tout,** *adv.* (*intensive*) (*before a fem. adj. beginning with a consonant or h "aspirate"* **tout** *becomes* **toute**) **1.** quite, entirely; **t. nouveau**(x), **toute**(s) **nouvelle**(s), quite new; **t. de noir vêtue, toute vêtue de noir,** dressed all in black; **des lutteurs de t. premier ordre,** wrestlers of the very first order; **t. fait,** ready-made; **t. au bout,** right at the end; **c'est t. comme chez nous!** it's just like home! **t. à fait,** quite, entirely; **t. au plus,** at the very most; **t. à vous,** yours ever; **elle est toute petite,** she's quite small. **2. t. en parlant,** while speaking. **3. t. ignorant qu'il est, qu'il soit,** ignorant though he may be. **4. être t. oreilles,** to be all ears.

out-à-l'arrière [tutalarjɛːr], *a.inv. Aut:* rear-engined.

out-à-l'avant [tutalavã], *a.inv. Aut:* front-wheel drive.

ut-à-l'égout [tutalegu], *s.m.inv.* main drainage.

utefois [tutfwa], *adv.* yet, nevertheless, however.

utou, -tous [tutu], *s.m.* (*child's word*) doggie.

ux [tu], *s.f.* cough.

xicolo|gie [tɔksikɔlɔʒi], *s.f.* toxicology; *a.* **-gique,** toxicological; *s.m. & f.* **-gue,** toxicologist.

xico|mane [tɔksikɔman], *s.m. & f.* drug addict; *s.f.* **-manie,** drug addiction.

xique [tɔksik]. **1.** *a.* toxic; **gaz t.,** poison gas. **2.** *s.m.* poison.

c [trak], *s.m. F:* funk; (stage-)fright; **avoir le t.,** o have the wind up.

cas [traka], *s.m.* worry, trouble, bother.

cass|er [trakase], *v.tr.* to worry, bother (s.o.); *s.m.* **-ement,** worrying, bothering; *s.f.* **-erie,** vorry, fuss; interference; *a.* **-ier, -ière,** (i) annoying, tiresome; (ii) pestering, interfering person); fussy (person).

racasser, to worry.

ce [tras], *s.f.* trace; (*a*) trail, track, spoor; *ootprint(s)* (of person); (*b*) weal, scar, mark of wound, etc.); (*c*) (slight) trace (of poison, tc.).

cer [trase], *v.tr.* (**n. traçons**) to trace; to plot curve); to lay out (road); to map out (route); *t* draw (a line); to outline (plan).

t [trakt], *s.m.* tract; leaflet.

teur [traktœːr], *s.m.* tractor.

tion [traksjɔ̃], *s.f.* (*a*) traction; pulling; (*b*) action; draught; *Aut:* **t. avant,** front-wheel rive.

toriste [traktɔrist], *s.m.* tractor driver.

lition [tradisjɔ̃], *s.f.* (*a*) tradition; (*b*) lklore; *a.* **-nel, -nelle,** traditional, usual,

habitual; **matériel t.,** conventional equipment; *adv.* **-nellement.**

traduc|tion [tradyksjɔ̃], *s.f.* **1.** translating. **2.** translation; *s.* **-teur, -trice,** translator.

traduire [tradɥiːr], *v.tr.* (*conj. like* CONDUIRE) (*a*) to translate; (*b*) to decode (a cable); (*c*) *Computers:* **t. une carte,** to interpret a card; to interpret, explain, express (feeling, idea, etc.).

trafic [trafik], *s.m.* traffic. **1.** trading, trade; (*a*) **le t. des vins,** the wine trade; (*b*) *Pej:* traffic, illicit trading; **t. des stupéfiants,** drug traffic. **2. t. ferroviaire,** rail(way) traffic; **t. routier, aérien,** road, air, traffic.

trafi|quer [trafike], *v.i. usu. Pej:* to traffic, deal, trade; **t. de, en, qch.,** to traffic in sth.; **t. de sa conscience,** to sell one's conscience; *s.* **-quant, -quante,** *Pej:* (drug, etc.) trafficker; *F:* dope peddler; **t. du marché noir,** black marketeer.

tragéd|ie [traʒedi], *s.f.* tragedy; *s.* **-ien, -ienne,** tragedian.

tragique [traʒik], (*a*) *a.* tragic (writer, play, event); (*b*) *s.m.* **cela tourne au t.,** the thing is becoming tragic; *adv.* **-ment.**

trah|ir [traiːr], *v.tr.* to betray. **1.** to reveal, disclose, give away (secret). **2. t. qn,** to deceive s.o.; *F:* to let s.o. down; **ne me trahissez pas,** don't give me away; *F:* don't split on me; *s.f.* **-ison,** treason; treachery; betrayal, betraying (de, of).

train [trɛ̃], *s.m.* **1.** (*a*) train, string, line (of vehicles, etc.); series; set (of wheels); *Aut:* **t. avant, arrière,** front, back, axle (assembly); **t. de pneus,** set of tyres; (*b*) *Rail:* train; **t. de voyageurs, de marchandises,** passenger, goods, train; **t. de luxe,** Pullman (express); **t. omnibus,** stopping train; **t. auto-couchettes,** car-sleeper; (*c*) *Mil:* train (of transport); (*d*) suite, attendants; (*e*) quarters (of horse); **t. de derrière, de devant,** hindquarters, forequarters; (*f*) *Av:* **t. d'atterrissage,** undercarriage. **2.** movement; (*a*) pace, rate; **à fond de t.,** at top speed; (*b*) **mettre qch. en t.,** to set sth. going; **en t. de faire qch.,** (busy) doing sth.; **il est en t. de travailler,** he is working; **les choses vont leur t.,** things are going on as usual; (*c*) **mener grand t.,** to live on a grand scale. **3.** mood; **être en t.,** to be in good form.

traînée [trɛne, trene], *s.f.* trail (of smoke, etc.); train (of gunpowder); *Av:* **t. (de condensation),** vapour trail.

traîn|er [trɛne, trene]. **1.** *v.tr.* to drag, pull, draw, (sth.) along; to spin out (a speech); to drawl; **t. la jambe,** to be lame; **t. le pied,** to lag behind. **2.** *v.i.* (*a*) to lag behind; to straggle; (*b*) to linger; to dawdle; (*c*) to lie about; **laisser t. ses affaires,** to leave one's belongings lying about; (*d*) to flag, droop, languish; **il traîne depuis longtemps,** he's been in poor health for a long time; **l'affaire traîne,** the matter is hanging fire; **t. en longueur,** to drag (on); *s.* **-ard, -arde,** straggler; *s.m.* **-eau, -eaux,** sledge.

se traîner. 1. to crawl (along). **2.** to trail along.

train-train [trɛ̃trɛ̃], *s.m. F:* routine, daily round; **le t.-t. de la vie,** the daily grind.

traire [trɛːr], *v.tr.* (*pr.p.* **trayant;** *p.p.* **trait;** *pr.ind.* **ils traient;** *no p.h.*) to milk (a cow); **machine à t.,** milking machine, milker.

trait [trɛ], *s.m.* **1.** pulling; **tout d'un t.,** at one stretch; **cheval de t.,** draught-horse, carthorse. **2.** (*a*) **armes de t.,** missile weapons; (*b*) arrow, dart; **partir comme un t.,** to be off like a shot; **t. de satire,** gibe; (*c*) beam (of light); (*d*) **t. d'esprit,** flash of wit. **3.** draught, gulp; **d'un (seul) t.,** at one gulp. **4.** (*a*) stroke, line, dash; (*b*) **t. d'union,** hyphen. **5.** (*a*) feature (of face); **traits fins,** delicate features; (*b*) trait (of character). **6.** act, deed (of courage, kindness); **t. de génie,** stroke of genius.

traite [trɛt], *s.f.* **1.** stretch (of road); stage (of journey); **(tout) d'une t.,** at a stretch, without interruption. **2.** transport (of goods); trading; **la t. des blanches,** white slavery. **3.** *Com:* (banker's) draft; bill (of exchange). **4.** milking.

traité [trete], *s.m.* **1.** treatise. **2.** *Pol:* treaty.

traitement [trɛtmɑ̃], *s.m.* **1.** treatment; (*a*) **mauvais t.,** ill-usage, maltreatment; **t. brutal,** rough treatment; *Med:* **premier t.,** first-aid; (*b*) processing (of raw material). **2.** salary; (officer's) pay; **augmenter les traitements des enseignants,** to raise teachers' salaries.

trait|er [trete], *v.* to treat. **1.** *v.tr.* (*a*) **t. qn bien, mal,** to treat s.o. well, badly; (*b*) **t. qn de lâche,** to call s.o. a coward; (*c*) **t. un malade,** to treat a patient; (*d*) *Ind:* to process (raw material); (*e*) to entertain. **2.** *v.tr.* (*a*) to negotiate; (*b*) to discuss, deal with (a subject). **3.** *v.i.* (*a*) **t. de la paix,** to treat for peace; (*b*) **t. d'un sujet,** to deal with a subject; *s.* **-able,** manageable, docile (person); tractable, malleable (material); *s.m.* **-eur,** caterer.

traît|re, traîtresse [trɛːtr, trɛtrɛs]. **1.** *a.* treacherous, traitorous, perfidious (person); vicious (animal). **2.** *s.* traitor, traitress; **en t.,** treacherously; *adv.* **-reusement,** treacherously; *s.f.* **-rise,** treachery.

trajectoire [traʒɛktwaːr], *s.f. Astr: Space: Artil: etc:* trajectory, path (of comet, satellite, projectile, missile, etc.).

trajet [traʒɛ], *s.m.* (*a*) journey (by rail, etc.); passage; **j'ai fait une partie du t. en avion,** I flew part of the way; (*b*) path (of projectile).

trame [tram], *s.f.* **1.** *Tex:* woof, weft; **la t. de la vie,** the web, thread, of life. **2.** plot, conspiracy. **3.** *T.V:* raster; frame.

tram(way) [tram(wɛ)], *s.m.* tram(car), *N.Am:* streetcar.

tranchant [trɑ̃ʃɑ̃]. **1.** *a.* (*a*) cutting, sharp (tool, knife); keen (edge); (*b*) trenchant (words, opinion); peremptory. **2.** *s.m.* (cutting) edge (of knife).

tranche [trɑ̃ʃ], *s.f.* **1.** (*a*) slice (of bread, meat), rasher (of bacon); (*b*) block, portion (of share issue, lottery prizes). **2.** slab. **3.** edge (of coin); **livre doré sur t.,** gilt-edged book.

tranchée [trɑ̃ʃe], *s.f.* trench; *Agr:* drain; cuttin (through forest); **t. garde-feu,** fire break.

trancher [trɑ̃ʃe]. **1.** *v.tr.* (*a*) to slice (bread, etc. to cut; (*b*) to cut short (discussion); to sett (question) out of hand; **t. le mot,** to spea plainly; (*c*) to decide, settle (difficulty). **2.** *v (of colours, characteristics)* to contra strongly; **t. sur le ciel,** to stand out against th sky.

tranquille [trɑ̃kil], *a.* tranquil; (*a*) calm, sti quiet; (*b*) quiet, peaceful; (*c*) undisturbe **laissez-moi t.,** leave me alone; *adv.* **-ment.**

tranquill|iser [trɑ̃kilize], *v.tr.* to tranquillize; reassure (s.o.) **(sur,** on, about); to set at rest, soothe (s.o.'s mind); *s.m. Med:* **-isa** tranquillizer; *s.f.* **-ité,** quiet, peace.

se tranquilliser. 1. (*of sea, storm*) to ca down. **2.** to set one's mind at rest, to ma oneself easy (about sth.).

transaction [trɑ̃zaksjɔ̃], *s.f.* (*a*) *Com:* transa tion; *pl.* dealings, deals; (*b*) *pl.* **transactio d'une société,** proceedings of a society.

transat [trɑ̃zat], *s.m.* deck chair.

transatlantique [trɑ̃zatlɑ̃tik]. **1.** *a.* transatla tic. **2.** *s.m.* (Atlantic) liner.

transbord|er [trɑ̃sbɔrde, trɑ̃z-], *v.tr.* **1.** (*a*) tranship; (*b*) *Rail: Av:* to transfer (passenge goods). **2.** to convey, ferry, (passengers, e across (river); *s.m.* **-ement,** transhipment; *s* **-eur; pont t., bac t.,** transporter bridge, tr ferry.

transcr|ire [trɑ̃skriːr], *v.tr.* (*conj. like* ÉCRIRE to transcribe, write out (notes, etc.); *Book* to post up (ledger). **2.** *Mus:* to transcribe piece for the piano); *s.m.* **-ipteur,** transcrit *s.f.* **-iption,** (i) transcription; (ii) copy.

transe [trɑ̃s], *s.f.* **1.** *usu. pl.* fright, fear; **é dans des transes,** to be shivering in or shoes. **2.** (hypnotic) trance.

transfér|er [trɑ̃sfere], *v.tr.* (**je transfère; transférerai**) (*a*) to transfer; to remove (s sth.) from one place to another; (*b*) *Jur:* **t. propriété,** to convey an estate; *a.* **-able.**

transfigur|er [trɑ̃sfigyre], *v.tr.* to transfigu *s.f.* **-ation.**

se transfigurer, to be, become, transfigured

transform|er [trɑ̃sfɔrme], *v.tr.* to transfo change (**en,** into); to reshape (a dre *Rugby Fb:* to convert (a try); *a.* **-able; : -ateur,** *esp. El:* transformer; *s.f.* **-ation** transformation (**en,** into); (ii) conversion.

se transformer, to change, turn (**en**, into).

ransgress|er [trãsgrese], *v.tr.* to transgress, infringe (the law); *s.m.* **-eur**; *s.f.* **-ion**.

ransi [trãsi, -zi], *a.* chilled; perished with cold; paralysed with fear.

ransiger [trãziʒe], *v.i.* (*n.* **transigeons**) to compromise; **ne pas t.**, to be adamant.

ransistor [trãzistɔ:r], *s.m. Rad:* transistor (set).

ransit [trãzit], *s.m.* **1. maison de t.**, forwarding agency. **2.** *Rail:* through traffic; *a.* **-aire**, relating to transit of goods.

ransiter [trãzite]. **1.** *v.tr.* to forward (goods). **2.** *v.i.* (*of goods*) to be in transit.

ransitif, -ive [trãzitif, -i:v], *a. Gram:* transitive (verb).

ans|ition [trãzisjɔ̃], *s.f.* transition; **sans t.**, abruptly; *a.* **-itoire**, transitory, transient; **mesure t.**, temporary measure; *adv.* **-itoirement.**

anslucide [trãslysid], *a.* translucent.

ansmett|re [trãsmɛtr], *v.tr.* (*conj. like* MET-TRE) **1.** to transmit; to pass on, convey (light, heat, message); *Rad: T.V:* to broadcast (programme). **2.** *Jur:* to transfer, convey (property); *s.m.* **-eur**, *El: Rad: etc:* transmitter.

ansmission [trãsmisjɔ̃], *s.f.* **1.** transmission; passing on (of order); sending (of message); *Rad: T.V:* **t. en direct**, live broadcast; **t. en différé**, recorded broadcast. **2.** *E:* **la t.**, the transmission (gear); **arbre de t.**, driving shaft. **3.** *Adm:* **t. des pouvoirs**, handing over; *Jur:* conveyance, transfer(ence) (of property).

anspercer [trãsperse], *v.tr.* (*n.* **transperçons**) to (trans)pierce; to transfix; to stab, to pierce (s.o., sth.) through.

anspir|er [trãspire], *v.i.* **1.** (*aux.* **avoir**) to perspire. **2.** (*aux.* **avoir** *or* **être**) to transpire; (*of news*) to leak out; *s.f.* **-ation**, perspiration, sweat.

ansplanter [trãsplãte], *v.tr.* to transplant.

ansport [trãspɔ:r], *s.m.* **1.** transport, carriage of goods, passengers); **les transports en commun**, public transport; **frais de t.**, freight charges. **2.** troopship; transport aircraft. **3.** ransport, rapture; outburst of feeling.

ansporter [trãspɔrte], *v.tr.* **1.** to transport, onvey, transfer (goods, etc.). **2.** to transport, o enrapture; **cette bonne nouvelle l'a ransporté**, he was overjoyed by the good ews.

anspos|er [trãspoze], *v.tr.* to transpose; *s.f.* **ition.**

ansversal, -aux [trãsversal, -o], *a.* transverse, ransversal; cross (section, gallery); *adv.* **ement**, transversely, crosswise.

ap|e [trap], *s.f.* **1.** trap, pitfall. **2.** (*a*) trapoor; (*b*) flap door; (*c*) hatch; *s.m.* **-eur**, apper (of wild animals).

trapu [trapy], *a.* thick-set, squat, stocky (man, horse).

traqu|er [trake], *v.tr.* **1.** to hunt down, run to earth (hunted animal, criminal). **2.** *v.i. F:* to get stage fright; *s.m.* **-eur**, tracker.

travail, -aux [trava:j, -o], *s.m.* work. **1.** (*a*) labour, toil; **instruments de t.**, (i) tools; (ii) reference books; **se mettre au t.**, to start, get down to, work; **cesser le t.**, (i) to stop work; (ii) to knock off (for the day); (iii) to down tools; **t. de tête**, brainwork; **t. manuel**, manual labour; **t. en série**, mass production; (*b*) working, operation; **t. de la digestion**, working of the digestion; **t. du vin**, fermenting of wine; (*c*) occupation, employment; **trouver du t.**, to find a job; *Adm:* **travaux publics**, public works. **2.** (*a*) piece of work; **quel beau t.!** what a fine piece of work! (*b*) (literary) work; **un t. sur les métaux**, a work, a book, on metals. **3. d'un beau t.**, of fine workmanship.

travaill|er [travaje]. **1.** *v.tr.* (*a*) to torment, obsess; **quelque chose le travaille**, something's worrying him; **se t. l'esprit**, to worry; (*b*) to work (up)on (s.o.); to bring pressure to bear (up)on (s.o.); (*c*) to work, fashion, shape (wood, metal, etc.); **t. la pâte**, to knead the dough; **t. son style**, to polish one's style. **2.** *v.i.* to work, labour, toil; **t. ferme**, to work hard; *a. & s.* **-eur, -euse**, (*a*) *a.* industrious; (*b*) *s.* worker; *s.m.* **-iste**, Labour Party member.

travelling [travəliŋ], *s.m. Cin:* dolly, travelling platform (for the camera).

travers [trave:r], *s.m.* **1.** breadth; *adv.phr.:* **en t.**, across, crosswise; *prep.phr.* **en t. de**, across; **à t. qch., au t. de qch.**, through sth. **2. de t.**, askew, crooked, the wrong way; **tout est allé de t.**, everything went wrong; **regarder qn de t.**, to look askance, to scowl, at s.o.

traverse [travers], *s.f.* **1.** (**chemin de) t.**, crossroad, short cut. **2.** (**barre de) t.**, cross-bar, cross-piece; *Rail:* sleeper.

traversée [traverse], *s.f.* **1.** (*a*) passage, (sea) crossing; **avoir, faire, une belle, mauvaise, t.**, to have a calm, rough, crossing; (*b*) **faire la t. d'une ville**, to cross, pass through, a town. **2. t. de voie**, (railway) crossing.

traverser [traverse], *v.tr.* to traverse; to cross; to go through (town, crisis); **t. qch. de part en part**, to go clean through sth.

traversin [traversɛ̃], *s.m.* bolster (of bed).

travest|ir [travesti:r], *v.tr.* **1.** to disguise; **t. un homme en femme**, to disguise a man as a woman; **bal travesti**, fancy-dress ball, costume ball. **2.** to travesty, parody, burlesque (poem, play); **t. la pensée de qn**, to misrepresent, distort, s.o.'s thoughts; *s.m.* **-issement**, (i) disguise; (ii) travesty (of truth, etc.).

trébucher [trebyʃe], *v.i.* to stumble; **faire t. qn**, to trip s.o. up.

trèfle [trɛfl], *s.m.* 1. *Bot:* trefoil, clover. 2. *Arch:* trefoil; *Civ.E:* **croisement en t.,** clover-leaf intersection. 3. *Cards:* clubs.

treille [trɛːj], *s.f.* vine-arbour; *s.m.* **-age,** *s.m.* **-is,** (i) trellis(-work), lattice; **t. métallique,** wire netting; (ii) *s.m.pl.* **-is,** *Cl:* dungarees, denims.

treize [trɛːz], *num.a.inv.* & *s.m.inv.* thirteen; **Louis T.,** Louis the Thirteenth; **le t. mai,** (on) the thirteenth of May.

treizième [trɛzjɛm], *num.a.* & *s.* thirteenth; *adv.* **-ment.**

tréma [tremɑ], *s.m.* diaeresis.

tremble [trãːbl], *s.m. Bot:* aspen.

trembller [trãble], *v.i.* (*a*) to tremble, shake; to quake; (*of light*) to quiver, flicker; (*of voice*) to quaver; **t. de froid, de colère, de fièvre,** to shiver with cold, to shake with anger, to shiver, shake, with fever; **la terre a tremblé,** there was an earth tremor; (*b*) to tremble, quake, with fear; *s.m.* **-ement,** trembling, shaking; **t. de terre,** earth tremor; earthquake.

tremblotler [trãblɔte], *v.i.* to tremble slightly; to quiver; (*of voice*) to quaver; (*of light*) to flicker; *s.m.* **-ement.**

trempe [trãːp], *s.f.* 1. (*a*) steeping, dipping, soaking; (*b*) *Metall:* tempering, hardening (of steel). 2. (*a*) temper (of steel); (*b*) quality; **les hommes de sa t.,** men of his stamp, men like him.

tremper [trãpe]. 1. *v.tr.* (*a*) to mix, dilute, with water; (*b*) to soak, steep; to drench; **trempé comme une soupe,** soaked to the skin; (*c*) *Metall:* to temper, harden (steel). 2. *v.i.* (*of dirty linen, etc.*) to soak, to steep.

tremplin [trãplɛ̃], *s.m.* springboard; diving-board; ski-jump.

trentaine [trãtɛn], *s.f.* (about) thirty, some thirty; **une t. de francs,** about thirty francs; **avoir passé la t.,** to be in the thirties.

trente [trãːt], *num.a.inv.* & *s.m.inv.* thirty.

trentième [trãtjɛm]. 1. *num.a.* & *s.* thirtieth. 2. *s.m.* thirtieth (part).

trépidler [trepide], *v.i.* 1. (*of machines, etc.*) to vibrate. 2. to be in a nervous, tremulous, state; *s.f.* **-ation,** tremor, vibration; trepidation.

trépied [trepje], *s.m.* (*a*) tripod; (*b*) *Cu:* trivet.

trépignler [trepiɲe]. 1. *v.i.* **t. de colère, de joie,** to dance with rage, to jump for joy. 2. *v.tr.* to trample down (earth, etc.); *s.m.* **-ement.**

très [trɛ], *adv.* very, most; (very) much.

trésor [trezɔːr], *s.m.* 1. treasure; *F:* **mon t.,** darling. 2. *pl.* **entasser des trésors,** to accumulate riches; **les trésors de la terre,** the treasures, wealth, of the earth. 3. **le T. (public),** the (French) Treasury; *s.f.* **-erie,** (i) treasury; the Exchequer; (ii) treasurership; office of treasurer; *s.* **-ier, -ière,** treasurer, paymaster, -mistress.

tressailllir [tresajiːr], *v.i.* (*conj. like* CUEILLIR) to start; to give a start; to quiver; **t. de douleur,** to wince with pain; to shudder (from fear); **faire t. qn,** to startle s.o.; *s.m.* **-ement.**

tressauter [tresote], *v.i.* to start, jump (with fear, surprise, etc.); (*of thgs*) to jolt, to be jolted.

tresse [trɛs], *s.f.* plait (of hair).

tresser [trese], *v.tr.* to plait (hair, straw); to weave (basket).

tréteau, -eaux [treto], *s.m.* trestle, support, stand; *Th:* **monter sur les tréteaux,** to go on the stage.

treuil [trœːj], *s.m.* winch, windlass; winding drum.

trève [trɛːv], *s.f.* (*a*) truce; (*b*) respite, intermission; **t. de plaisanteries!** that's enough joking!

tri [tri], *s.m.* sorting (out); classifying; *Rail:* **et bureau de t.,** sorting office; *a.* **-able,** sortable, that can be sorted; *s.m.* **-age,** sorting; **t. à main,** hand-picking.

triangle [triãːgl], *s.m.* triangle; *a.* **-ulaire.**

tribord [tribɔːr], *s.m. Nau:* starboard (side).

tribu [triby], *s.f.* tribe.

tribulation [tribylasjɔ̃], *s.f.* tribulation; trouble, trial.

tribunal, -aux [tribynal, -o], *s.m.* tribunal; *Jur:* the Bench; (*b*) (law-)court.

tribune [tribyn], *s.f.* 1. (speaker's) platform. (*a*) gallery; (*in Parliament*) **la t. publique,** strangers' gallery; (*b*) grandstand; (*c*) **t. d'orgues,** organ-loft; (*d*) (*literary, political, etc.*) cussion) forum.

tributaire [tribytɛːr], *a.* & *s.m. Geog:* tributary (river).

trichler [triʃe], *v.i.* & *tr.* to cheat; to trick (s.o.); *s.f.* **-erie,** cheating; trickery; *s.* **-eur, -euse,** cheat.

tricolore [trikɔlɔːr], *a.* tricolour(ed); **le drapeau t.,** the French flag; *Adm:* **feux tricolores,** traffic lights; *s.m.pl. Sp: F:* **les Tricolores,** the French team.

tricot [triko], *s.m.* 1. knitting; knitted wear, jersey-fabric; *Com:* knitwear. 2. (*a*) (knitted) jersey; jumper; *F:* woolly; (*b*) (under)vest.

tricotler [trikɔte], *v.tr.* to knit; *s.* **-eur, -euse,** knitter, (*a*) *s.m.* knitting frame; (*b*) *s.f.* (*pe*) knitter; knitting machine.

triler [trije], *v.tr.* (*p.d.* & *pr.sub.* **n. triions**) (*a*) sort; (*b*) to pick out, sort out (the best); *s.* **-eur, -euse,** sorter.

trigonométrlie [trigɔnɔmetri], *s.f.* trigonometry; *a.* **-ique,** trigonometric(al).

trimer [trime], *v.i.* to work hard, slave away (at sth.).

trimestlre [trimɛstr], *s.m.* 1. quarter; three months; *Sch:* term; **par t.,** quarterly; every term. 2. quarter's salary; quarter's rent; three term's fees; *a.* **-riel, -rielle,** quarterly.

tringle [trɛ̃gl], *s.f.* rod; **t. de rideau,** curtain-

Trinité [trinite], *s.f.* 1. *Theol:* Trinity; (fête de) la T., Trinity Sunday. 2. *Geog:* (île de) la T., Trinidad.

trinquer [trɛ̃ke], *v.i.* (*a*) to clink glasses (before drinking); t. à qn, qch., to drink to sth., s.o.; (*b*) *F:* to drink (heavily), to booze; t. avec qn, to have a drink (or two) with s.o.

triomph|e [triɔ̃:f], *s.m.* triumph; porter (qn) en t., to carry (s.o.) shoulder high; to chair (s.o.); arc de t., triumphal arch; *a.* -al, -aux, triumphal; *adv.* -alement, triumphantly.

triompher [triɔ̃fe], *v.i.* 1. to triumph; t. d'une difficulté, to overcome a difficulty; t. dans un art, to excel in an art. 2. to exult, glory (in sth.); t. du malheur de qn, to gloat over s.o.'s misfortune.

trip|e [trip], *s.f. usu. pl.* (*a*) *F:* entrails (of animal); (*b*) *Cu:* tripe; *s.f.* -erie, offal shop, trade; tripe shop; *s.* -ier, -ière, tripe, offal, dealer; tripe butcher.

triple [tripl], *a. & s.m.* treble, threefold, triple.

tripler [triple], *v.tr. & i.* to treble, triple; to increase threefold.

tripot|er [tripote]. 1. *v.i.* (*a*) to fiddle about, mess about; t. dans l'eau, to dabble in the water; (*b*) to engage in shady business; t. dans la caisse, to tamper with the cash. 2. *v.tr.* (*a*) to finger, handle (s.o., sth.); to paw (s.o.); to meddle with (sth.); (*b*) to deal dishonestly with (money); (*c*) *impers.* il se tripote quelquechose, there's something up, something afoot, *F:* something cooking; *s.m.* -age; *s.* -eur, -euse, mischiefmaker, schemer.

triste [trist], *a.* sad. 1. (*a*) sorrowful, miserable (person); melancholy (face, news); (*b*) dreary, dismal (life, weather, room); faire t. figure, to pull a long face. 2. unfortunate, painful (duty); c'est une t. affaire, it's a bad job. 3. poor, sorry, wretched (meal, excuse); *adv.* -ment.

tristesse [tristɛs], *s.f.* (*a*) sadness; melancholy, gloom; (*b*) dullness, dreariness.

trivial, -iaux [trivjal, -jo], *a.* vulgar, low, coarse (expression); *adv.* -ement; *s.f.* -ité, vulgarism, coarse expression.

troc [trɔk], *s.m.* exchange (in kind); barter; faire du t., *F:* to swop.

troène [trɔɛn], *s.m. Bot:* privet.

trognon [trɔɲɔ̃], *s.m.* core (of apple); stump (of cabbage, etc.).

trois [trwa], *before a vowel sound in the same word group* [trwa:z], *num.a.inv. & s.m.* three; t. enfants [trwazɑ̃fɑ̃], three children; t. hommes [trwazɔm], three men; les t. quarts du temps, most of the time; Henri T., Henry the Third; le t. mai, (on) the third of May; *num.a. & s.* -ième, third; personnes du t. âge, retired people.

trombe [trɔ̃:b], *s.f.* 1. waterspout. 2. t. de vent, whirlwind; t. d'eau, cloudburst; entrer, sortir,

en t., to burst in, out.

trombone [trɔ̃bɔn], *s.m.* 1. *Mus:* trombone (instrument or player). 2. *F:* (wire) paper clip.

trompe [trɔ̃:p] *s.f.* 1. (*a*) horn; t. de chasse, hunting horn; (*b*) hooter. 2. proboscis (of insect); trunk (of elephant).

trompe-l'œil [trɔ̃plœ:j], *s.m.inv.usu. Pej:* deceptive appearance; illusion; eye-wash; piece of bluff, of camouflage.

tromp|er [trɔ̃pe], *v.tr.* to deceive. 1. (*a*) to cheat; to impose upon (s.o.); (*b*) to betray, be unfaithful to (wife, husband). 2. (*a*) to mislead; t. les espérances de qn, to disappoint s.o.'s hopes; (*b*) to outwit, baffle, elude (s.o.); (*c*) to find relief for (grief, boredom); to while away (time); t. la faim, to stave off hunger; *s.f.* -erie, fraud, cheating; illusion; *a. & s.* -eur, -euse, (*a*) *a.* deceitful, deceptive; (*b*) *s.* deceiver; *adv.* -eusement.

se tromper, to be mistaken; to be wrong; il n'y a pas à s'y t., there is no doubt about it.

trompette [trɔ̃pɛt]. 1. *s.f.* trumpet. 2. *s.m. Mil:* trumpeter.

tronc [trɔ̃], *s.m.* 1. (*a*) trunk (of tree, of body); bole, stem (of tree); (*b*) parent stock (of family). 2. collecting-box (in church). 3. *Mth:* frustrum (of cone).

tronçon [trɔ̃sɔ̃], *s.m.* (broken) piece, end, stump.

tronçonn|er [trɔ̃sɔne], *v.tr.* to cut (wood, etc.) into lengths; to cut up; *s.m.* -age, *s.m.* -ement, cutting (of wood, etc.) into pieces; *s.f.* -euse, chain saw.

trône [tro:n], *s.m.* throne.

tronquer [trɔ̃ke], *v.tr.* (*a*) to truncate; to mutilate (statue); (*b*) to curtail, cut down.

trop [tro]. 1. *adv.* too; (*a*) (*with adj.*) too, over-; t. fatigué, over-tired; (*b*) (*with vb.*) too much, unduly, over-; t. travailler, to over-work, to work too hard; je ne sais t. que dire, I hardly know what to say. 2. *s.m.* too much, too many; être de t., to be in the way, unwelcome; *adv.phr.* par t., (altogether) too (much).

trophée [trofe], *s.m.* trophy.

tropicalis|er [trɔpikalize], *v.tr. Com:* to tropicalize (transistor, electrical equipment, etc.); *s.f.* -ation.

tropi|que [trɔpik], *s.m. Geog:* tropic (of Cancer, Capricorn); *pl.* les tropiques, the tropics; *a.* -cal, -caux.

trop-plein [troplɛ̃], *s.m.* overflow (of bath, dam); *pl.* trop-pleins.

troquer [trɔke], *v.tr.* to exchange, barter, *F:* swop (qch. contre qch., sth. for sth.).

trot [tro], *s.m.* trot; t. assis, bumping trot; t. enlevé, rising, *N.Am:* posting, trot.

trotte [trɔt], *s.f.* distance, run; il y a une bonne t. d'ici là, it's a good step from here.

trott|er [trɔte], *v.i.* (*of horse or rider*) to trot; (*of mice*) to scamper; *F:* elle est toujours à t.,

she's always on the go; **air qui vous trotte par
la tête**, haunting tune; *s.* **-eur, -euse,** (i)
trotter; trotting horse, mare; (ii) *s.f.* seconds
hand (of watch); *s.f.* **-inette,** (child's) scooter;
s.m. **-oir,** pavement, *N.Am:* sidewalk.
trou [tru], *s.m.* hole; **percer un t.,** to bore a hole
(**dans,** in); **boucher un t.,** (i) to stop a hole; (ii)
to pay a debt; *F:* **boire comme un t.,** to drink
like a fish; **t. de mémoire,** lapse of memory,
blank; *Av:* **t. d'air,** air-pocket.
troublant [trublɑ̃], *a.* disturbing. **1.** disquieting,
disconcerting. **2.** perturbing.
trouble [trubl]. **I.** *a.* **1.** turbid, cloudy; dim;
murky; **avoir la vue t.,** to be dim-sighted. **2.**
confused.
II. *s.m.* (*a*) confusion, disorder; (*b*) agitation,
perturbation; (*c*) *pl.* public disturbances.
troubler [truble], *v.tr.* **1.** to make (liquid, etc.)
cloudy, thick, muddy. **2.** to disturb (silence, the
peace); **t. le repos,** to make a disturbance. **3.** to
perturb; (*a*) to confuse, upset, discompose
(s.o.); (*b*) to agitate, excite, stir.
se troubler. 1. (*of sky*) to become overcast, to
cloud over; (*of vision*) to become blurred; to
grow dim. **2.** to falter; to get confused;
l'orateur se troubla, the speaker got flustered;
sans se t., unconcerned, unruffled.
trouée [true], *s.f.* gap, opening, breach (in hedge,
etc.).
trouer [true], *v.tr.* to make a hole, holes, in (a
wall, etc.); to perforate; **troué aux coudes,** out
at the elbows.
trouill|e [tru:j], *s.f. P:* **avoir la t.,** to be in a funk;
flanquer la t. à qn, to put the wind up s.o.; *s. P:*
-ard, -arde, funk.
troupe [trup], *s.f.* **1.** (*a*) troop, band (of people);
gang (of thieves); (*b*) *Th:* troupe; (*c*) herd;
flock (of cows, sheep). **2.** *Mil:* (*a*) troop;
officier de t., regimental officer; (*b*) *pl.* troops,
forces.
troupeau, -eaux [trupo], *s.m.* herd, drove;
flock; *P.N:* **(passage de) troupeaux,** cattle
crossing.
trousse [trus], *s.f.* **1.** bundle, package. **2.** case,
kit (of instruments). **3. être aux trousses de qn,**
to be after s.o., on s.o.'s heels.
trousseau, -eaux [truso], *s.m.* **1. t. de clefs,**
bunch of keys. **2.** (*a*) outfit (of clothing); (*b*)
(bride's) trousseau.
trouvaille [truva:j], *s.f.* (lucky) find, windfall.
trouver [truve], *v.tr.* to find (sth. sought). **1.**(*a*)**je
lui trouve d'excellentes qualités,** I think he has
excellent qualities; **je lui trouve mauvaise
mine,** I think he looks unwell; **aller t. qn,** to go
and (i) find, (ii) see, s.o.; (*b*) to discover, invent
(a process, etc.). **2. t. par hasard,** to discover,
hit upon, come across (sth.); **c'est bien trouvé!**
happy thought! **3.** to think, consider; **vous
trouvez?** you think so?

se trouver. 1. (*a*) to be; **je me trouvais alors à
Paris,** I was then in Paris; (*b*) to feel; **se t. bien
de qch.,** to feel all the better for sth.; **se t.
mieux,** to feel better. **2.** to happen; to turn out;
cela se trouve bien, this is most opportune; *impers.* **il se trouve que . . .,** it happens that . . ..
truc [tryk], *s.m. F:* **1.** (*a*) knack; **trouver le t.,** to
find, learn, the knack; (*b*) trick, dodge; **les
trucs du métier,** the tricks of the trade. **2.** contraption, gadget.
trucage [tryka:ʒ], *s.m.* **1.** faking (of antiques,
etc.); *F:* cooking (of accounts); cheating. **2.**
fake; *Cin:* *pl.* special effects.
truelle [tryɛl], *s.f.* **1.** trowel. **2. t. à poisson,** fish-
slice.
truffe [tryf], *s.f.* (*a*) truffle; (*b*) dog's nose.
truffé [tryfe], *a.* stuffed (with mistakes).
truie [trɥi], *s.f.* sow; **peau de t.,** pigskin.
truite [trɥit], *s.f. Ich:* trout.
truqu|er [tryke], *v.tr.* **1.** to fake (antiques,
balance-sheet, etc.); *F:* to cook (accounts); to
rig (an election). **2.** *abs.* to cheat; *s.m.* **-age** =
TRUCAGE; *s.* **-eur, -euse,** humbug, fraud,
trickster; faker.
tu [ty], *pers.pron.nom.* (*familiar form of address
to relations, close friends, children, animals*)
you; **qui es-tu, toi?** and who are *you*? *F:* **être à
tu et à toi avec qn,** to be on familiar terms with
s.o.
tub|e [tyb], *s.m.* **1.** tube, pipe. **2.** (*container*) **t. de
dentifrice, de peinture,** tube of toothpaste, of
paint; *a.* **-ulaire,** tubular.
tubercule [tybɛrkyl], *s.m.* **1.** *Bot:* tuber. **2.** *Med:*
tubercle.
tubercul|ose [tybɛrkylo:z], *s.f.* tuberculosis; *a.*
-eux, -euse, tubercular.
tu|er [tɥe], *v.tr.* to kill. **1.** to slaughter, butcher
(animals). **2.** to kill (s.o.); **t. qn raide,** (i) to kill
s.o. on the spot; (ii) to shoot s.o. dead; **se faire
t.,** to get killed; **tué à l'ennemi,** killed in action;
a. **-ant,** killing (work); boring, exasperating
(pers.); *s.f.* **-erie,** slaughter, carnage; *s.m.*
-eur, killer, murderer; **t. à gages,** hired
assassin.
se tuer. 1. (*a*) to kill oneself, commit suicide; (*b*)
to get killed. **2. je me tue à vous le dire,** I'm sick
and tired of telling you.
tue-tête (à) [atytɛt], *adv.phr.* at the top of one's
voice; **crier à t.-t.,** to bawl, yell.
tuile [tɥil], *s.f.* **1.** (roofing) tile. **2.** *F:* (piece of)
bad luck; **quelle t.!** what a blow!
tulipe [tylip], *s.f. Bot:* tulip.
tumeur [tymœ:r], *s.f. Med:* tumour.
tumulte [tymylt], *s.m.* tumult, hubbub, uproar.
tumultueu|x, -euse [tymyltɥø, -ø:z], *a.*
tumultuous, noisy, riotous (gathering, etc.);
adv. **-sement.**
tunique [tynik], *s.f. Cl:* tunic.
Tunisie (la) [latynizi]. *Pr.n.f. Geog:* Tunisia.

tunnel [tynɛl], *s.m.* tunnel; **percer un t.**, to drive a tunnel; **t. routier**, road tunnel; **t. de chemin de fer**, rail(way) tunnel; **le t. sous la Manche**, the Channel Tunnel.

turbid|e [tyrbid], *a.* (*esp of liquid*) turbid, muddy, cloudy; *s.f.* **-ité**, muddiness, cloudiness.

turbine [tyrbin], *s.f.* turbine.

turboréacteur [tyrbɔreaktœːr], *s.m.* turbojet.

turbot [tyrbo], *s.m. Ich:* turbot.

turbotrain [tyrbɔtrɛ̃], *s.m. Rail:* turbotrain.

turbul|ence [tyrbylɑ̃ːs], *s.f.* turbulence; *a.* **-ent**, turbulent, restless, unruly.

turc, *f.* **turque** [tyrk]. **1.** *a.* Turkish. **2.** *s.* (*a*) Turk; (*b*) *s.m. Ling:* Turkish.

turf [tyrf], *s.m.* **1.** race-course. **2. le t.**, racing; the turf; *s.m.* **-iste**, race-goer.

Turquie (la) [latyrki]. *Pr.n.f. Geog:* Turkey.

turquoise [tyrkwaːz]. **1.** *s.f.* turquoise. **2.** *a.inv.* & *s.m.inv.* turquoise (blue).

tutelle [tytɛl], *s.f.* **1.** *Jur:* tutelage, guardianship. **2.** (*a*) *Pol:* trusteeship; (*b*) protection.

tuteur, -trice [tytœːr, -tris]. **1.** *s.* (*a*) guardian; (*b*) *F:* protector. **2.** *s.m. Hort:* prop, stake.

tut|oyer [tytwaje], *v.tr.* (**je tutoie**) to address (s.o.) as **tu** and **toi**; to be on familiar terms with (s.o.); *s.m.* **-oiement**.

tuyau, -aux [tɥijo], *s.m.* **1.** (*a*) pipe, tube; **t. d'eau, de gaz**, water, gas, pipe; **t. flexible**, rubber, plastic, tubing; **t. d'incendie**, fire-hose; **t. d'arrosage**, garden-hose; **t. de cheminée**, chimney-flue; **t. d'orgue**, organ-pipe; *Aut:* **t. d'échappement**, exhaust pipe; (*b*) stem (of pipe). **2.** *F:* (*horse-racing*) tip; **avoir des tuyaux**, to be in the know.

tympan [tɛ̃pɑ̃], *s.m.* drum (of ear); **bruit à briser le t.**, ear-splitting noise.

type [tip], *s.m.* **1.** type; *Com:* pattern, sample; model. **2.** *F:* character; **drôle de t.**, queer chap; **c'est un pauvre t.**, he's a poor sort of chap; **un chic t.**, a good sort. **3.** *Typ:* type.

typhoïde [tifɔid], *a.* **fièvre t.**, *s.f.* **t.**, typhoid (fever); enteric fever.

typhon [tifɔ̃], *s.m. Meteor:* typhoon.

typhus [tifys], *s.m. Med:* typhus (fever).

typique [tipik], *a.* typical. **1.** symbolical. **2.** true to type, representative; **le Français t.**, the typical, ordinary, Frenchman; *adv.* **-ment**.

typographe [tipɔgraf], *s.m., F:* **typo** [tipo], *s.m.* typographer, printer.

typograph|ie [tipɔgrafi], *s.f.* **1.** typography; printing. **2.** printing works; *a.* **-ique**, typographic(al); **erreur t.**, misprint.

tyran [tirɑ̃], *s.m.* tyrant.

tyran|niser [tiranize], *v.tr.* to tyrannize over (s.o.); *s.f.* **-nie**, tyranny; *a.* **-nique**, tyrannical; *adv.* **-niquement**.

Tyrol (le) [lɔtirɔl]. *Pr.n.m. Geog:* (the) Tyrol; *a.* & *s.* **-ien, -ienne**, Tyrolese, Tyrolean.

U

U, u [y], *s.m.* (the letter) U, u.

ulcère [ylsɛːr], *s.m.* ulcer; sore.

ulcér|er [ylsere], *v.tr.* (**il ulcère; il ulcérera**) (*a*) *Med:* to ulcerate; (*b*) to wound, embitter (s.o.); *s.f.* **-ation,** (i) ulceration; (ii) embitterment (of feelings); *a.* **-eux, -euse,** ulcerous, ulcerated (wound, feelings); covered with ulcers.

ultérieur [ylterjœːr], *a.* **1.** ulterior. **2.** subsequent (**à,** to); later (date, meeting); *Com:* further (orders, etc.); *adv.* **-ement.**

ultimatum [yltimatɔm], *s.m.* ultimatum; *pl.* **ultimatums.**

ultime [yltim], *a.* ultimate, final, last.

ultra-rapide [yltrarapid], *a.* high-speed; split-second; *pl.* **ultra-rapides.**

ultra-secret, -ète [yltrasəkrɛ, -ɛt], *a.* top secret; *pl.* **ultra-secrets, -ètes.**

ultra(-)son [yltrasɔ̃], *s.m.* *Ph:* ultra-, super-, sound; **science des u.**(-)**sons,** ultrasonics.

ultrasonique [yltrasɔnik], *a.* supersonic.

ultrasonore [yltrasɔnɔːr], *a.* *Ph:* supersonic; super-audible (frequency, etc.).

ultra-terrestre [yltraterɛstr], *a.* ultra-terrestrial; *pl.* **ultra-terrestres.**

ultra(-)violet, -ette [yltravjɔlɛ, -ɛt], *a.* ultra-violet (lamp, rays).

un, une [œ̃, yn]. **1.** *num.a. & s.* (*a*) one; **chambre à un lit,** single bedroom; **un à un,** one by one; **une heure,** one o'clock; **page un,** page one; *Th:* **le un,** the first act; *Journ:* **la une,** front page (of a newspaper); *F:* **en savoir plus d'une,** to know a thing or two; *F:* **il était moins une,** that was a close shave; **une, deux, trois, partez!** one, two, three, go! (*b*) one (and indivisible); **c'est tout un,** it's all one, all the same. **2.** *indef.pron.* one; (**l'**)**un d'entre nous,** one of us; **les uns disent que . . .,** some say that . . .. **3.** *indef.art.* (*pl.* **des**) a, an (*pl.* some); (*a*) **venez me voir un lundi,** come and see me some Monday; **pour une raison ou pour une autre,** for some reason or other; (*b*) (*intensive*) **tu m'as fait une peur!** you gave me such a fright!

unanim|e [ynanim], *a.* unanimous; of one mind; *adv.* **-ement;** *s.f.* **-ité,** unanimity; **à l'u.,** unanimously.

Unesco [ynɛsko]. *Pr.n.f.* Unesco.

uni [yni], *a.* **1.** (*a*) united (family, etc.); (*b*) **le Royaume-Uni,** the United Kingdom; **les États-Unis,** the United States. **2.** smooth, level, even (ground, etc.). **3.** plain (colour); **chat argenté u.,** self-silver (Persian) cat; *s.m.* **ne**

porter que de l'u., to dress in a plain style.

unième [ynjɛm], *num.a.* (*used only in compounds*) first; **trente et u.,** thirty-first.

unifier [ynifje], *v.tr.* (*pr.sub. & p.d.* **n. unifiions**) to unify (ideas); to consolidate (debt); to standardize.

uniform|e [ynifɔrm]. **1.** *a.* uniform, unvarying; **vie u.,** regular life. **2.** *s.m. Mil: etc:* uniform; **endosser l'u.,** to enlist; **quitter l'u.,** to leave the service; *adv.* **-ément;** *s.f.* **-ité,** uniformity.

unilatéral, -aux [ynilateral, -o], *a.* unilateral; one-sided; *P.N:* **stationnement u.,** parking on one side only.

union [ynjɔ̃], *s.f.* union. **1.** junction, coalition, combination. **2.** society, association. **3.** marriage. **4.** unity, agreement.

unique [ynik], *a.* **1.** sole, only, single (specimen, etc.); *Adm:* (**rue à**) **sens u.,** one-way street; **voie u.,** single-track (railway); **ma seule et u. crainte,** my one and only fear. **2.** unique, un-rivalled (talent, etc.); *F:* **il est u.,** he's priceless; *adv.* **-ment.**

unir [yniːr], *v.tr.* **1.** to unite, join; **u. les plaisirs aux affaires,** to combine business with pleasure; **u. le geste à la parole,** to suit the action to the word. **2.** to smooth, level; **u. une pelouse,** to level a lawn.

s'unir, to unite, join; **s'u. à qn,** (i) to join forces with s.o.; (ii) to marry s.o.

unisson [ynisɔ̃], *s.m. Mus:* unison; **à l'u.,** (i) in unison; (ii) in keeping.

unité [ynite], *s.f.* **1.** (*a*) unit (of measure); (*b*) *Mth:* unity, one; *Com:* **prix de l'u.,** unit price. **2.** unity; (*a*) oneness (of God, etc.); (*b*) uniformity (of action, etc.).

univer|s [yniveːr], *s.m.* universe; **la théorie de l'expansion de l'u.,** the theory of the expanding universe; **par tout l'u.,** all over the world; *a.* **-sel, -selle,** universal; *adv.* **-sellement.**

universitaire [yniversiteːr]. **1.** *a.* university (studies, town, etc.); **cité u.** = (students') hall(s) of residence. **2.** *s.m. & f.* member of the teaching profession; **c'est un u.,** he's an academic.

université [yniversite], *s.f.* university.

uranium [yranjɔm], *s.m. Ch:* uranium.

urbain [yrbɛ̃], *a.* urban (population); town (house).

urban|isme [yrbanism], *s.m.* town planning; *a. & s.m. & f.* **-iste,** (*a*) *a.* **urban;** (*b*) *s.* town planner.

ɪrbanité [yrbanite], *s.f.* urbanity.

ɪrgＩence [yrʒɑ̃:s], *s.f.* urgency; emergency; **en cas d'u.,** in case of emergency; *Med:* **salle d'u.,** emergency ward; *a.* **-ent,** urgent, pressing (matter, need, etc.); *adv.* **-emment** [-amɑ̃], urgently.

rinＩe [yrin], *s.f.* urine; *s.m.* **-oir,** (public) urinal.

ɪrne [yrn], *s.f.* (*a*) urn; (*b*) **u. de scrutin,** ballot-box; **aller aux urnes,** to go to the polls.

ɪrticaire [yrtikɛ:r], *s.f. Med:* urticaria, nettle-rash, *F:* hives.

s a g e [yza:ʒ], *s.m.* **1.** (*a*) use, using, employment; **mettre un article en u.,** to put an article into use; **faire u. de qch.,** to use, to make use of, sth.; *Pharm:* **pour l'u. externe,** for external application; **article à mon u.,** article for my personal use; **article d'u.,** article for everyday use; (*b*) wear, service (of garments, etc.); **garanti à l'u.,** guaranteed to wear well. **2.** (*a*) usage; custom; **phrases d'u.,** conversational commonplaces; **comme d'u.,** as usual; (*b*) practice, experience; **l'u. du monde,** good breeding; **c'est l'u.,** it's the done thing.

ɪsagé [yzaʒe], *a.* worn, used (article); secondhand (car); **plaisanterie usagée,** well-worn joke.

ɪsager, -ère [yzaʒe, -ɛ:r], *s.* user (of sth.); **les usagers de la route,** road users.

ɪsé [yze], *a.* worn (out); shabby (garment); **u. par le chagrin,** careworn; **c'est u.!** that's an old one! **eaux usées,** waste water; industrial discharge.

ɪser [yze]. **1.** *v.i.* **u. de qch.,** to use sth., make use of sth.; **en bien u. avec qn,** to treat s.o. well. **2.** *v.tr.* (*a*) to use (up), consume; (*b*) to wear (out, away, down).

ɪuser, to wear (away); **mon habit s'use,** my coat's wearing out.

usine [yzin], *s.f.* works, factory, mill, plant.

usité [yzite], *a.* used; in use; current; **le mot n'est plus u.,** the word is no longer in current use.

ustensile [ystɑ̃sil], *s.m.* utensil, implement; **u. de cuisine,** kitchen utensil; **u. de jardinage,** gardening tool.

usuel, -elle [yzɥɛl], *a.* usual, customary, habitual, common, ordinary; **connaissances usuelles,** knowledge of everyday things; **le français u.,** everyday French; *adv.* **-lement.**

usurＩe¹ [yzy:r], *s.f.* usury; **pratiquer l'u.,** to practise usury; **rendre un bienfait avec u.,** to repay a service with interest; *a. & s.* **-ier, -ière,** (*a*) *a.* usurious (moneylender); (*b*) *s.* usurer.

usure², *s.f.* wear (and tear) (of furniture, machinery, etc.); *Aut:* (*of tyres*) **u. de roulement,** tread wear; *Mil:* **guerre d'u.,** war of attrition.

usurpＩer [yzyrpe]. **1.** *v.tr.* to usurp (throne, etc.). **2.** *v.i.* **u. sur les droits de qn,** to encroach on s.o.'s rights; *s.* **-ateur, -atrice,** usurper; *s.f.* **-ation.**

utＩile [ytil], (*a*) *a.* useful, serviceable; **puis-je être u. en rien?** can I be of any use? **en temps u.,** in (good) time; **je vous répondrai en temps u.,** I'll answer you in due course; (*b*) *s.m.* **joindre l'u. à l'agréable,** to combine business with pleasure; *adv.* **-ment.**

utiliser [ytilize], *v.tr.* to utilize; to make use of; to turn (sth.) to account.

utilitaire [ytilitɛ:r], *a. & s.m. & f.* utilitarian; *Aut:* **véhicules utilitaires,** commercial vehicles.

utilité [ytilite], *s.f.* utility, use(fulness); service; **n'être d'aucune u.,** to be of no earthly use.

utopie [ytɔpi], *s.f.* utopia.

V

V, v [ve], *s.m.* (the letter) V, v.

vacanc|e [vakɑ̃:s], *s.f.* **1.** vacancy; vacant post. **2.** *pl.* vacation, holidays; (*of Parliament*) recess; *Sch:* **les grandes vacances,** the summer holidays; the long vacation; **vacances de neige,** winter, skiing, holiday; **être en vacance(s),** to be on holiday; *s.* **-ier, -ière,** holiday-maker.

vacant [vakɑ̃], *a.* vacant, unoccupied (house, job).

vacarme [vakarm], *s.m.* uproar, din, hubbub.

vaccin [vaksɛ̃], *s.m. Med:* vaccine, lymph.

vaccin|er [vaksine], *v.tr. Med:* to vaccinate; to immunize; to inoculate (s.o., **contre,** against); **se faire v.,** to get vaccinated, inoculated; *s.f.* **-ation.**

vach|e [vaʃ], *s.f.* cow; **vaches laitières,** dairy cattle; *P:* **v. à lait,** mug, sucker; *F:* **le plancher des vaches,** terra firma; **parler français comme une v. espagnole,** to murder the French language; **manger de la v. enragée,** to have a rough time of it; *s.m.* **-er,** cowhand, cowman.

vacill|er [vasije], *v.i.* **1.** (*a*) to be unsteady; **entrer en vacillant,** to stagger, to lurch, in; **v. sur ses jambes,** to be shaky, groggy, uncertain, on one's legs; (*b*) (*of light*) to flicker. **2.** to vacillate, waver; to shilly-shally; *s.f.* **-ation.**

vadrouille [vadru:j], *s.f.* (floor-) mop.

va-et-vient [vaevjɛ̃], *s.m.inv.* (*a*) movement to and fro; (i) backward and forward motion; (ii) see-saw motion; *a.inv.* **porte v.-et-v.,** swing door; *El:* two-way (wiring, switch); (*b*) coming and going (of people).

vagabond, -onde [vagabɔ̃, -ɔ̃:d]. **1.** *a.* vagabond, vagrant, roving (life). **2.** *s.* vagabond; tramp.

vagabond|er [vagabɔ̃de], *v.i.* to be a vagabond, to rove; to be, to go, on the tramp; to play truant; *s.m.* **-age,** vagrancy.

vagissement [vaʒismɑ̃], *s.m.* cry, wail(ing) (of new-born infant).

vague¹ [vag], *s.f.* wave; **grosse v.,** billow, sea; **v. de fond,** tidal wave.

vague². **1.** *a.* vague, indefinite; dim (recollection); sketchy (notions). **2.** *s.m.* vagueness, indefiniteness; *adv.* **-ment.**

vague³. **1.** *a.* **regard v.,** vacant stare; **terrain v.,** (piece of) waste land; vacant site, *N.Am:* vacant lot. **2.** *s.m.* empty space; **regard perdu dans le v.,** abstracted look.

vaillance [vajɑ̃:s], *s.f.* valour, bravery, courage, gallantry.

vaill|ant [vajɑ̃]. **1.** *a.* (*a*) valiant, brave, courageous; stout (heart); (*b*) *F:* in good fettle, **être v.,** to be in good health; to be well and strong; **je ne suis pas v.,** I'm not up to the mark. **2.** *adv.* **n'avoir pas un sou v.,** to be penniless; *adv.* **-amment** [-amɑ̃].

vain [vɛ̃], *a.* **1.** vain; (*a*) sham, unreal, empty, **vaines promesses,** hollow promises; (*b*) ineffectual, useless. **2.** vain, conceited; *adv.* **-ement,** vainly, to no purpose.

vaincre [vɛ̃:kr], *v.tr.* (*pr.p.* **vainquant;** *pr.ind.* **vaincs;** *p.h.* **je vainquis**) **1.** (*a*) to vanquish, defeat (an enemy); (*b*) *Sp:* to beat (a rival). **2.** to overcome, conquer (disease, difficulties, etc.).

vainqueur [vɛ̃kœ:r]. **1.** *s.m.* (*a*) victor, conqueror; (*b*) *Sp:* winner. **2.** *a.m.* conquering, victorious (hero, etc.).

vaisseau, -eaux [veso], *s.m.* **1.** **v. spatial,** spacecraft; **v. spatial habité,** manned spacecraft. **2.** *Anat:* vessel, canal, duct; **v. sanguin,** blood vessel.

vaissel|le [vesɛl], *s.f.* plates and dishes, crockery; **laver la v.,** to wash up; **eau de v.,** dishwater; *s.m. Furn:* **-ier,** dresser.

val [val], *s.m.* valley, vale; *Geog:* **V. de Loire,** the Loire Valley (between Gien and Tours); *the pl. is usu.* **vals,** *except in the phr.* **par monts et par vaux** [vo], up hill and down dale.

valable [valabl], *a.* valid; **billet v. pour un mois,** ticket valid, good, for a month; **interlocuteur v.,** authorized representative; *F:* **un roman v.** (quite) a good novel.

valet [valɛ], *s.m.* **1.** *Cards:* knave, jack. **2.** **v. de chambre,** valet, manservant; **v. de ferme,** farm-hand.

valeur [valœ:r], *s.f.* **1.** (*a*) (relative) value, worth, **attacher de la v. à qch.,** to set a value on sth.; **mettre une terre en v.,** to develop land; **objet de v.,** valeurs, valuables; (*b*) import, weight, value; **mettre un mot en v.,** to emphasize a word; **renseignements sans v.,** worthless information. **2.** *Fin:* (*a*) asset; (*b*) *pl.* bills, shares, securities.

valeureu|x, -euse [valœrø, -ø:z], *a.* valorous, brave, gallant (in battle); *adv.* **-sement.**

valid|e [valid], *a.* **1.** valid (contract, reason). *Mil: etc:* fit for service; able-bodied; *s.f.* **-ité,** validity.

valise [vali:z], *s.f.* (*a*) suitcase; (*b*) **la** ...

diplomatique, the diplomatic bag.

vallée [vale], *s.f.* valley.

vallon [valɔ̃], *s.m.* small valley; glen.

vallonné [valɔne], *a.* undulating (country).

valoir [valwaːr], *v.tr. & i.* (*pr.p.* **valant;** *p.p.* **valu;** *pr.ind.* je **vaux,** il **vaut;** *pr.sub.* je **vaille;** *fu.* je **vaudrai**) **1.** (*a*) to be worth (in money or quality); **ce tissu vaut dix-sept francs le mètre,** this material is worth seventeen francs a metre; **à v. sur (une somme),** on account of (a sum); **ne pas v. grand-chose,** not to be worth much; **cela ne vaut rien,** that's no good; **ce n'est rien qui vaille,** it is not worth having; (*b*) to be equivalent to; **c'est une façon qui en vaut une autre,** it is as good a way as any other; (*c*) *impers.* **il vaut mieux qu'il en soit ainsi,** (it is) better that it should be so; **il vaudrait mieux partir,** it would be better to leave; **autant vaut rester ici,** we may as well stay here; (*d*) **faire v. qch.,** to make the most of sth.; **faire v. ses droits,** to assert one's claims; **se faire v.,** (i) to make the most of oneself; (ii) to push oneself forward. **2.** to be worth, to deserve, merit (sth.).

valse [vals], *s.f.* waltz.

valser [valse], *v.i.* to waltz; **faire v. qn,** (i) to waltz with s.o.; (ii) *F:* to lead s.o. a dance; to keep s.o. on the hop.

valve [valv], *s.f.* valve.

vandale [vɑ̃dal], *s.m.* vandal; *s.m.* **-isme,** vandalism.

vanille [vaniːj], *s.f. Cu:* vanilla; **gousse de v.,** vanilla bean, pod; **glace à la v.,** vanilla icecream.

vanité [vanite], *s.f.* **1.** vanity. **2.** conceit, self-sufficiency; egotism; **sans v.,** with all due modesty.

vaniteux, -euse [vanitø, -øːz], *a.* vain, conceited, egotistical; *adv.* **-sement,** conceitedly.

vanne [van], *s.f.* sluice(-gate), water-gate.

vanneau, -eaux [vano], *s.m. Orn:* lapwing, peewit, plover.

vanner [vane], *v.tr.* to winnow; *P:* **être vanné,** to be dead beat; *s.f.* **-erie,** (i) basket-making; (ii) wickerwork; *s.* **-eur, -euse,** winnower; *s.m.* **-ier,** basket-maker.

vanter [vɑ̃te], *v.tr.* to praise (s.o., sth.); to speak highly of (sth.); *a. & s.* **-ard, -arde,** (*a*) *a.* boasting, bragging (person); (*b*) *s.* boaster; *s.f.* **-ardise,** boastfulness.

se vanter, to boast, brag; **se v. d'être . . .,** to pride oneself on being . . ..

va-nu-pieds [vanypje], *s.m. & f.inv.* (barefoot) tramp; beggar.

vapeur¹ [vapœːr], *s.f.* vapour; haze; fumes; **v. (d'eau),** steam; **bateau à v.,** steamer, steamship.

vapeur², *s.m.* steamer, steamship.

vaporiser [vapɔrize], *v.tr.* to atomize, spray

(liquid); to spray (sth.) with scent; *s.m.* **-ateur,** atomizer, spray(er); scent spray.

vaquer [vake], *v.i.* **v. à qch.,** to attend to sth.; to concern oneself with sth.; **v. au ménage,** to see to, cope with, the housework; **le matin je vaque à mes affaires,** in the morning I get on with my work.

varech [varɛk], *s.m.* wrack, seaweed, kelp.

vareuse [varøːz], *s.f. Nau:* (*a*) (sailor's) jersey; (*b*) pilot-coat.

varicelle [varisɛl], *s.f. Med:* chicken pox.

varié [varje], *a.* varied; varying; diversified (types); variegated (colours).

varier [varje], *v.* (*pr.sub. & p.d.* n. **variions**) **1.** *v.tr.* to vary; to diversify. **2.** *v.i.* (*of wind, opinion, etc.*) to vary, change; (*of market, etc.*) to fluctuate; *a.* **-able;** *s.f.* **-ation.**

variété [varjete], *s.f.* **1.** variety (**de,** of); diversity (of opinions, etc.). **2.** *Biol:* variety (of plant, etc.).

variole [varjɔl], *s.f. Med:* smallpox.

Varsovie [varsɔvi]. *Pr.n.f. Geog:* Warsaw.

vase¹ [vaːz], *s.m.* vase, vessel, receptacle; **v. à fleurs,** flower vase; *Ch:* **v. gradué,** graduated vessel; **v. clos,** retort.

vase², *s.f.* mud, silt, slime, ooze.

vaseline [vazlin], *s.f. R.t.m:* vaseline.

vaseux, -euse [vazø, -øːz], *a.* **1.** muddy, slimy (river, pond). **2.** *P:* seedy, out-of-sorts; **il a l'air v.,** he looks a bit washed-out; **excuse vaseuse,** lame excuse; **idées vaseuses,** woolly ideas.

vasistas [vazistaːs], *s.m.* fanlight (over door); ventilator (in window-pane).

vaste [vast], *a.* vast, immense, spacious.

vau (à) [avo], *adv.phr.* **à v.-l'eau,** with the stream; **tout va à v.-l'eau,** everything is going to rack and ruin.

vaurien, -ienne [vorjɛ̃, -jɛn], *s.* (*a*) waster, rotter, bad lot; loafer, good-for-nothing; (*b*) *F:* **petit v.!** you little rascal!

vautour [votuːr], *s.m. Orn:* vulture.

vautrer (se) [səvotre], *v.pr.* (*a*) (*of pig, etc.*) to wallow (in mud); **se v. dans la débauche,** to wallow in debauchery; (*b*) *F:* to sprawl (on the grass, a sofa).

veau, veaux [vo], *s.m.* **1.** (*a*) calf; *F:* **pleurer comme un v.,** to weep noisily, to blubber; (*b*) **v. marin,** seal. **2.** *Cu:* veal; **côtelette de v.,** veal chop. **3.** calf(-leather); calfskin.

vécu [veky], *a.* **1.** **choses vécues,** actual experiences. **2.** (play, novel, etc.) true to life, founded on fact.

vedette [vədɛt], *s.f.* **1.** (*a*) *Navy:* picket-boat; **v. lance-torpilles,** motor torpedo-boat; (*b*) motor-launch. **2.** (*a*) **mots en v.,** words displayed in bold type; **mettre en v.,** to highlight; (*b*) *Th: Cin:* star.

végéter [veʒete], *v.i.* (je **végète;** je **végéterai**) **1.** (*of plant*) to grow. **2.** to lead a dull life, to vegetate; *a. & s.* -al, -aux, (*a*) *a.* plant (life), vegetable (kingdom); (*b*) *s.m.* plant; *a. & s.* -arien, -arienne, vegetarian; *s.m.* -arisme, vegetarianism; *s.f.* -ation, vegetation; *Med:* végétations adénoïdes, adenoids.

véhém|ent [veemã], *a.* vehement, violent (speech, etc.); *s.f.* -ence, vehemence; *adv.* -entement.

véhicule [veikyl], *s.m.* vehicle.

veille [vɛ:j], *s.f.* 1. (*a*) sitting up, staying up (at night); watching (by night); (*b*) vigil; (*c*) *Mil:* (night) watch; *Nau:* look-out; (*d*) wakefulness; entre la v. et le sommeil, between waking and sleeping. 2. (*a*) eve; preceding day; la v. de Noël, Christmas Eve; la v. au soir, the night before; (*b*) être à la v. de la ruine, to be on the brink, the verge, of ruin.

veillée [veje], *s.f.* 1. night-nursing (of the sick); vigil. 2. evening (spent with friends, over the fire, *esp.* in winter); faire la v. chez des voisins, to spend the evening with neighbours.

veill|er [veje]. 1. *v.i.* (*a*) to sit up, keep awake; (*b*) to watch, be on the look-out; (*c*) v. sur qn, qch., to look after s.o., sth.; (*d*) v. à qch., to see to sth.; v. au grain, to look out for squalls. 2. *v.tr.* to sit up with, watch over (sick person, etc.); *s.* -eur, -euse, (i) watcher (by night); (ii) *s.f.* night-light; pilot (burner, light); en veilleuse, (light, gas) turned low, dimmed.

vein|e [vɛn], *s.f.* 1. *Anat: Bot:* vein. 2. (*a*) *Geol:* vein; lode (of ore); seam (of coal); (*b*) vein, humour, inspiration; être en v. de faire qch., to be in the mood to do sth.; (*c*) *F:* luck; porter v. à qn, to bring s.o. good luck; coup de v., (i) stroke of luck; (ii) fluke; pas de v., rotten luck; *a. & s. F:* -ard, -arde, (*a*) *a.* lucky (person); (*b*) *s.* lucky person, lucky dog; (sacré) v.! you lucky devil!

vélin [velɛ̃], *s.m.* (*a*) vellum (parchment); (*b*) (papier) v., wove paper.

vélo [velo], *s.m. F:* (push-)bike; aller à, en, v., to cycle; faire du v., to go in for cycling; *s.m.* -drome, cycle(-racing) track.

vélocité [velɔsite], *s.f.* speed, velocity, swiftness.

velours [v(ə)lu:r], *s.m.* velvet.

velouté [v(ə)lute]. 1. *a.* velvety; soft as velvet; downy; vin v., mellow wine. 2. *s.m.* softness (of material); bloom (on fruit).

velu [vəly], *a.* hairy.

venaison [vənɛzɔ̃], *s.f. Cu:* venison.

vénal, -als, -aux [venal, -o], *a.* 1. venal, purchasable (office, privilege, etc.); *Com:* valeur vénale, market value. 2. *Pej:* venal, mercenary, corrupt (person, press); *adv.* -ement, venally; in a mercenary, corrupt, manner; *s.f.* -ité, venality.

venant [vənã]. 1. *a.* (*of child, plant, etc.*) thriving. 2. *s.m.* à tout v., à tous venants, to all comers.

vendable [vãdabl], *a.* saleable, marketable.

vendange [vãdã:ʒ], *s.* ˙ 1. (*often in pl.*) vintage (season). 2. (*a*) vintaging; grape-gathering grape harvest; (*b*) the grapes.

vendang|er [vãdãʒe], *v.tr. & i.* (n. vendangeons) to vintage; to gather (the grapes); *s.* -eur -euse, vintager, grape harvester, grape picker.

vendetta [vãdɛta, -eta], *s.f.* vendetta.

vend|re [vã:dr], *v.tr.* 1. to sell; v. qch. à qn, to sel sth. to s.o.; v. à terme, to sell on credit; v. à crédit, to sell on hire purchase; v. comptant, t sell for cash; v. un objet trois francs, to sell a object for three francs; maison à v., house fo sale; l'art de v., salesmanship; articles qui s vendent bien, mal, ready sellers, slow sellers. 2 v. qn, to betray s.o.; *s.* -eur, -euse, seller salesman, -woman; *Jur:* (*f.* venderesse vendor.

vendredi [vãdrədi], *s.m.* Friday; le v. saint Good Friday.

vénéneux, -euse [venenø, -ø:z], *a.* poisonou (plant).

vénér|er [venere], *v.tr.* (je vénère; je vénérerai to venerate, reverence, revere; to worship (saint); *a.* -able; *s.f.* -ation.

vénerie [venri], *s.f.* venery; (science of) hunting termes de v., hunting terms.

vénérien, -ienne [venerjɛ̃, -jɛn], *a.* Mea venereal (disease).

vengeance [vãʒã:s], *s.f.* 1. revenge; par v., ou of revenge, revengefully. 2. vengeanc retribution.

veng|er [vãʒe], *v.tr.* (nous vengeons) to aveng *a. & s.* -eur, -eresse, (*a*) *a.* avengin revengeful; (*b*) *s.* avenger, revenger.

se venger, to be revenged; to have one's reveng

véniel, -elle [venjɛl], *a.* venial (sin).

venimeux, -euse [vənimø, -ø:z], *a.* venomou (*a*) poisonous (snake); (*b*) spiteful (criti tongue).

venin [vənɛ̃], *s.m.* venom; (*a*) poison (of snak etc.); (*b*) spite, malice.

venir [v(ə)ni:r], *v.i.* (*pr.p.* venant; *p.p.* ven *pr.ind.* je viens; ils viennent; *pr.sub.* je vienn *p.h.* je vins; *fu.* je viendrai; *aux.* être) to com 1. (*a*) je viens! I'm coming! ne faire qu'aller v., to be always on the go; je ne ferai qu'aller v., I shall come straight back; mais ven donc, do come along; il est venu vers moi, came up to me; v. au monde, to be born; fai v. qn, to send for, fetch, s.o.; voir v. qn, to s s.o. coming; *F:* je vous vois v.! I can see wh you are getting at; être bien venu, to welcome; *impers.* il vient ici toutes sortes gens, all sorts of people call here; est-il ve qn? has anyone called? (*b*) venez me trouver quatre heures, come and see me at fo o'clock; (*c*) v. de faire qch. (*pr. & p.d. only*), have (only) just done sth.; il vient de sortir, has just gone out. **2.** (*denoting origin*) (*a*) **il vient d'Amérique,** he comes from America; **mot qui vient du latin,** word derived from Latin; **tout cela vient de ce que . . .,** all this is the result of. . .; (*b*) *impers.* **d'où vient(-il) que . . .?** how is it that . . .? **3.** (*a*) to occur, to come; **le premier exemple venu,** the first example that comes to mind; **l'idée me vient que . . .,** it occurs to me that . . .; (*b*) **v. à faire qch.,** to happen to do sth. **4.** (*a*) to attain, reach; **l'eau leur venait aux genoux,** the water was up to their knees; (*b*) **v. à bien,** to succeed; (*c*) **en v. aux mains,** to come to blows; **les choses en sont-elles venues là?** have things come to such a pass? **5.** (*of plants, teeth, children, etc.*) to grow, grow up; **bien v.,** to thrive; **arbre mal venu,** stunted tree.

'enise [vəniːz]. *Pr.n.f.* Venice.

énitien, -ienne [venisjɛ̃, -jɛn], *a. & s.* Venetian; **store v.,** Venetian blind.

nt [vɑ̃], *s.m.* **1.** (*a*) wind; **v. frais,** strong breeze; **coup de v.,** gust of wind, squall; *Nau:* gale; **entrer, sortir, en coup de v.,** to dash in, out; **il fait du v.,** it's windy (weather); *Sailing:* **aller v. arrière,** to run before the wind; **sous le v.,** to leeward; **au v. de . . .,** to windward of . . .; **côté du v.,** weather-side; **côté sous le v.,** lee-side; (*b*) **aire de v.,** point of the compass; (*c*) air; **en plein v.,** in the open air; **mettre qch. au v.,** to hang out. in. out to air; (*d*) blast (of gun); *Av:* **v. de l'hélice,** slipstream; (*e*) wind, breath; *Med:* wind, flatulence. **2.** *Ven:* scent; **avoir v. de qch.,** to get wind of sth.

nte [vɑ̃ːt], *s.f.* sale; **salle des ventes,** auction-room.

ntiller [vɑ̃tile], *v.tr.* to ventilate, air (room, a difficult question); *s.m.* **-ateur,** ventilator; (electric) fan; *s.f.* **-ation.**

ntre [vɑ̃ːtr], *s.m.* **1.** (*a*) abdomen, belly; **tomber à plat v.,** to fall flat (on one's face); *Av:* **atterrissage sur le v.,** belly landing; (*b*) stomach; **n'avoir rien dans le v.,** to be starving; (*c*) **prendre du v.,** to put on weight. **2.** *Tchn:* bulge, swell; belly.

ntriloque [vɑ̃trilɔk], *s.* ventriloquist.

ntru, -ue[1] [vɑ̃try], *a.* corpulent, fat; *F:* pot-bellied.

nu, -ue[1] [v(ə)ny]. **1.** *a.* (*with adv., esp.* **bien, mal**) **bien v.,** healthy, thriving; **mal v.,** sickly, stunted (child). **2.** *s.* **premier, dernier, nouveau, v.,** first, last, to arrive, new-comer; **le premier v. vous dira cela,** anybody will tell you that; **le dernier v.,** (i) the latest arrival; (ii) *Pej:* a mere nobody.

nue[2] [v(ə)ny], *s.f.* coming, arrival (of s.o., sth.); **des allées et venues,** comings and goings.

pres [vɛpr], *s.f.pl. Ecc.* vespers; evensong.

r [vɛːr], *s.m.* **1.** worm; *Med:* **v. solitaire,** tapeworm. **2.** (*a*) grub, larva, maggot; **tirer les vers du nez à qn,** to pump s.o.; (*b*) **v. luisant,**

glow-worm; (*c*) **v. à soie,** silk-worm.

véracité [verasite], *s.f.* veracity; truthfulness; truth (of a statement).

véranda [verɑ̃da], *s.f.* veranda(h), *N.Am:* porch.

verbal, -aux [vɛrbal, -o], *a.* verbal; *adv.* **-ement.**

verbe [vɛrb], *s.m. Gram:* verb.

verbeux, -euse [vɛrbø, -øːz], *a.* verbose, long-winded; prosy; *adv.* **-eusement;** *s.f.* **-osité,** verbosity, wordiness.

verdâtre [vɛrdɑːtr], *a.* greenish.

verdeur [vɛrdœːr], *s.f.* **1.** greenness (of immaturity, of wood). **2.** tartness, acidity (of wine, fruit). **3.** vigour; vitality (of old age).

verdict [vɛrdikt], *s.m. Jur:* finding of the jury; verdict.

verdir [vɛrdiːr]. **1.** *v.tr.* to make (sth.) green; to paint (sth.) green. **2.** *v.i.* to become, turn, green.

verdoyant [vɛrdwajɑ̃], *a.* verdant, green (meadow, etc.).

verdure [vɛrdyːr], *s.f.* **1.** (*a*) greenness; (*b*) verdure, greenery; **théâtre de v.,** open-air theatre. **2.** *Cu:* salad vegetables; pot herbs.

véreux, -euse [verø, -øːz], *a.* **1.** maggoty (fruit). **2.** of dubious character; *F:* fishy; **financier v.,** shady financier; **dettes véreuses,** bad debts.

verge [vɛrʒ], *s.f.* (*a*) rod, wand, switch; (*b*) rod (of pendulum); beam (of balance); (*c*) *Bot:* **v. d'or,** golden rod; (*d*) *Anat:* penis.

verger [vɛrʒe], *s.m.* orchard.

verglacé [vɛrglase], *a.* **route verglacée,** icy road.

verglas [vɛrgla], *s.m.* glazed frost; (*on roads, etc.*) black ice; **plaque de v.,** icy patch (on the road).

vergogne [vɛrgɔɲ], *s.f.* **sans v.,** shameless(ly).

vergue [vɛrg], *s.f. Nau:* yard; **bout de v.,** yard-arm.

véridique [veridik], *a.* true, truthful, authentic; *adv.* **-ment.**

vérifier [verifje], *v.tr.* (*pr.sub. & p.d.* n. **vérifiions**) **1.** to verify; to check; to audit (accounts). **2.** to verify, confirm; *s.* **-cateur, -catrice,** (i) (*pers.*) inspector; checker; tester; (ii) testing machine, device; (iii) *s.f. Computers:* verifier; *s.f.* **-cation.**

vérin [verɛ̃], *s.m. Tchn:* jack.

véritable [veritabl], *a.* **1.** true. **2.** real, genuine; *adv.* **-ment.**

vérité [verite], *s.f.* **1.** truth; *adv.phr.* **en v.,** really, actually. **2.** fact, truth; **les vérités scientifiques,** scientific truth, facts; **c'est la v.,** it's a fact; *F:* **c'est la vraie,** it's the honest truth; **dire à qn ses quatre vérités,** to tell s.o. a few home truths. **3.** sincerity; **parler avec un air de v.,** to speak with a show of sincerity.

vermeil, -eille [vɛrmɛːj]. **1.** *a.* vermilion; bright red; ruby (lips); rosy (cheeks). **2.** *s.m.* silvergilt.

vermicelle [vɛrmisɛl], *s.m. Cu:* vermicelli.

vermillon [vɛrmijɔ̃], *s.m.* vermilion; bright red.

vermine [vɛrmin], *s.f.* vermin.

vermoulu [vɛrmuly], *a.* (*a*) worm-eaten; (*b*) decrepit.

vermout(h) [vɛrmut], *s.m.* vermouth.

verni [vɛrni], *a.* varnished; **cuir v.**, patent leather; *s.m.pl.* (**souliers**) **vernis**, patent (leather) shoes.

vernir [vɛrniːr], *v.tr.* to varnish; to (French-)polish; to japan (iron, leather).

vernis [vɛrni], *s.m.* varnish, polish, glaze, gloss; *attrib.* **peinture v.**, gloss paint; **v. au tampon,** French polish; **v. à ongles,** nail varnish.

vernissage [vɛrnisaːʒ], *s.m.* (*a*) varnishing, glazing; **v. au tampon,** French-polishing; (*b*) private view (at an exhibition).

vérole [vɛrɔl], *s.f. Med:* **petite v.,** smallpox.

verre [vɛːr], *s.m.* **1.** glass; **v. de couleur,** stained glass; **v. dépoli,** frosted glass; **papier de v.,** sand-paper. **2.** (*object made of glass*) **il porte des verres,** he wears glasses; **v. de contact,** contact lens; **v. de montre,** watch glass; **v. grossissant,** magnifying glass. **3.** (*a*) **v. à boire,** (drinking-)glass; **v. à vin,** wineglass, stemmed glass; **v. à Bordeaux,** claret glass; (*b*) **glass(ful); boire un petit v.,** to have a drop of spirits; **prendre un v. de trop,** to have one too many; **tempête dans un v. d'eau,** storm in a tea-cup. **4. v. soluble,** water-glass.

verrerie [vɛr(ə)ri], *s.f.* (*a*) glassmaking; (*b*) glassware; **magasin de v. et porcelaine,** glass and china shop; **v. allant au four,** oven(-proof) glass(ware).

verrou [vɛru], *s.m.* bolt, bar; **pousser le v.,** to bolt the door, to shoot the bolt; **tirer le v.,** to un-bolt (a door); **être sous les verrous,** to be in jail.

verrouill|er [vɛruje], *v.tr.* to bolt (a door); *s.m.* **-age,** bolting, locking; locking device, mechanism.

verrue [vɛry], *s.f.* wart.

vers[1] [vɛːr], *s.m.* verse, line (of poetry).

vers[2], *prep.* **1.** (*of place*) toward(s), to. **2.** (*of time*) (*a*) toward(s); **v. la fin du siècle,** towards the end of the century; (*b*) about; **venez v. (les) trois heures,** come about three.

versant [vɛrsã], *s.m.* slope, side (of mountain); **v. de colline,** hillside.

versatil|e [vɛrsatil], *a.* changeable, inconstant, fickle; *s.f.* **-ité,** inconstancy, fickleness.

verse [vɛrs], *adv.phr.* **à v.,** in torrents; **il pleut à v.,** it's pouring (down).

versé [vɛrse], *a.* versed, experienced, practised, well up (**dans, en,** in) (the arts, etc.).

Verseau [vɛrso]. *Pr.n.m. Astr:* **le V.,** Aquarius.

vers|er [vɛrse], *v.tr.* (*a*) to overturn, upset (sth.); (*b*) to pour (out) (a drink); (*c*) to shed (tears); (*d*) to pay (in), to deposit (money); *s.m.* **-ement,** (i) pouring out; (ii) *Fin:* payment, paying in, deposit; **en plusieurs versements,** by instalments; **premier v.,** down payment.

version [vɛrsjõ], *s.f.* **1.** *Sch:* translation, unseer **2.** version, account (of event, etc.).

verso [vɛrso], *s.m.* verso, back (of sheet c paper); **voir au v.,** see overleaf.

vert [vɛːr]. **1.** *a.* (*a*) green; *Aut:* **feu v.,** green light **légumes verts,** greens; (*b*) **bois v.,** green wood **plantes vertes,** evergreens; **haricots verts** French beans; **fruits verts,** unripe fruit; (*c* **verte vieillesse,** green old age; (*d*) shar (reprimand); (*e*) spicy, blue (story, etc. **langue verte,** slang. **2.** *s.m.* (*a*) (the colou green; **des rubans v. bouteille,** bottle-green rib bons; (*b*) **mettre un cheval au v.,** to turn horse out to grass; *adv.* **-ement,** sharpl rudely.

vert-de-gris [vɛrdəgri], *s.m.inv.* verdigris.

vertébral, -aux [vertebral, -o], *a.* vertebra **colonne vertébrale,** spine.

vertébré [vertebre], *a. & s.m. Z:* vertebrate *s.m.pl.* **vertébrés,** vertebrates.

vertical, -aux [vertikal, -o], *a.* vertical; perpe dicular; upright; *adv.* **-ement.**

vertige [vertiːʒ], *s.m.* dizziness, giddiness; **avo le v.,** to feel dizzy; **avoir des vertiges,** to ha dizzy spells; **avoir facilement le v.,** to have bad head for heights.

vertigineu|x, -euse [vertiʒinø, -øːz], *a.* ve tiginous; dizzy, giddy (height); breaknec breathtaking (speed); staggering (rise prices); *Med:* **accès v.,** fit of vertigo; *aa* **-sement.**

vertu [vɛrty], *s.f.* **1.** virtue. **2.** chastity. **3.** qualit property (of remedy, etc.); *prep.phr.* **en v. d** by virtue of; under (the terms of) (a treaty, e arrangement); *a.* **-eux, -euse,** (i) virtuous; (chaste.

verve [vɛrv], *s.f.* animation, zest, verve; **être** **v.,** to be in the best of form; **plein de v.,** livel spirited.

vésicule [vezikyl], *s.f. Anat:* **v. biliaire,** ga bladder.

vessie [vesi], *s.f.* bladder.

veste [vɛst], *s.f. Cl:* (short) jacket.

vestiaire [vɛstjɛːr], *s.m.* (*a*) cloakroom; lock room (of school, factory, etc.); *F:* **mon v.,** s **vous plaît,** my things, my coat, please; (*b*) h and coat rack.

vestibule [vɛstibyl], *s.m.* (entrance-)hall.

vestige [vɛstiːʒ], *s.m.* trace, remains (prehistoric man, etc.); **vestiges du passé,** reli of the past.

veston [vɛstõ], *s.m.* (man's) jacket; **complet** lounge suit.

vêtement [vɛtmã], *s.m.* garment; *pl.* **cloth** clothing; **industrie du v.,** clothing trad **vêtements de sport, de plage,** sportswe **vêtements de dessous,** underwe underclothing.

vétéran [veterã], *s.m.* veteran; old campaigne

étérinaire [veterinɛːr]. 1. a. veterinary (medicine, etc.). 2. s.m. veterinary surgeon, F: vet.

étille [vetiːj], s.f. trifle; mere nothing; s'arrêter à des vétilles, to make a fuss about trifles.

êtir [vetiːr], v.tr. (pr.p. vêtant; p.p. vêtu; pr.ind. je vêts) to clothe; to dress; chaudement vêtu, warmly clad.

e vêtir, to dress; to put on one's clothes.

eto [veto], s.m. veto; mettre son v. à qch., to veto sth.; droit de v., right of veto.

étusté [vetyste], s.f. decay, decrepitude.

euf, veuve [vœf, vœːv]. 1. a. widowed (man, woman). 2. s. widower, f. widow.

euvage [vœvaːʒ], s.m. widowhood; widowerhood.

exⁱer [vɛkse], v.tr. to annoy, offend, hurt (s.o.); v. qn par une réflexion, to upset s.o. by a remark; a. -ant, vexing, annoying; s.f. -ation, infliction; mortification.

abilité [viabilite], s.f. 1. practicability, traffic condition (of a road). 2. development (of site ready for building).

aduc [vjadyk], s.m. viaduct.

ager, -ère [vjaʒe, -ɛːr], a. for life; rente viagère, life annuity; life interest; acheter, vendre, une maison en v., to buy, sell, a house on an instalment system to provide the seller with a life annuity.

ande [vjãːd], s.f. meat; flesh; v. de boucherie, butcher's meat; v. frigorifiée, frozen, chilled, meat; v. surgelée, deep-frozen meat; v. fraîche, fresh meat; v. rouge, blanche, red, white, meat.

brant [vibrã], a. 1. vibrating, vibrant. 2. (a) ringing (voice); (b) stirring (speech).

brⁱer [vibre], v.i. to vibrate; faire v. le cœur de qn, to stir, to thrill, s.o.; s.f. -ation; a. -atoire, vibratory, vibrating.

caire [vikeːr], s.m. Ecc: curate (of parish); assistant priest.

ce [vis], s.m. 1. (a) vice, depravity; (b) vice; moral failing. 2. fault, defect, blemish; v. de construction, faulty construction; v. caché, latent defect; v. propre, inherent defect (in goods).

e-amiral [visamiral], s.m. vice-admiral; pl. vice-amiraux.

e-chancelier [visʃãsəlje], s.m. vice-chancellor; pl. vice-chanceliers.

e-président [visprezidã], s.m. (a) vice-president; (b) vice-chairman; pl. vice-présidents.

ié [visje], a. vitiated, corrupt; polluted, ainted.

ⁱier [visje], v.tr. (pr.sub. & p.d. n. viciions) to vitiate, corrupt, spoil; v. l'air, to taint, pollute, he air; a. -iateur, -iatrice, vitiating, contaminating; s.f. -iation.

ieuⁱx, -ieuse [visjø, -jøːz], a. vicious. 1.

depraved (person). 2. defective, faulty, imperfect; cercle v., vicious circle; locution vicieuse, incorrect expression. 3. tricky, restive, bad-tempered (horse); adv. -sement, faultily; imperfectly; parler v., to speak incorrectly.

vicinal, -aux [visinal, -o], a. chemin v., local road.

vicomte [vikɔ̃ːt], s.m. viscount.

vicomtesse [vikɔ̃tɛs], s.f. viscountess.

victime [viktim], s.f. victim, sufferer; être la v. d'une illusion, to labour under a delusion.

victoire [viktwaːr], s.f. victory; chanter, crier, v., to crow, to triumph.

victorieuⁱx, -ieuse [viktɔrjø, -jøːz], a. victorious; adv. -sement.

victuailles [viktɥaːj], s.f.pl., food.

vidange [vidãːʒ], s.f. (a) draining, emptying (of cesspools, ditches); Aut: oil change; faire la v., to change the oil; (b) pl. sediment, sludge.

vide [vid]. 1. a. empty (room); blank (space); unoccupied (seat); v. de sens, devoid of meaning. 2. s.m. (a) empty space; void; blank; combler les vides, to fill up the gaps; (b) Ph: vacuum; nettoyage par le v., vacuum cleaning; (c) emptiness; regarder dans le v., to stare into space; adv.phr. à v., empty; camion revenant à v., lorry returning empty; (of car engine) tourner à v., to run in neutral.

vide-ordures [vidɔrdyːr], s.m.inv. (domestic) rubbish chute.

vider [vide], v.tr. 1. to empty; to clear out (room, drawer); videz vos verres! drink up! v. les lieux, to vacate the premises; F: to clear out. 2. to clean (fish); to draw (fowl). 3. to settle (question).

se vider, to empty; to become empty.

vie [vi], s.f. life. 1. être en v., to be alive; avoir la v. dure, to be hard to kill; to die hard; donner la v. à un enfant, to give birth to a child; il y va de la v., it's a case of life and death; musique pleine de v., lively, animated, music. 2. lifetime; entre eux c'est à la v. à la mort, they are sworn friends; nommé à v., appointed for life. 3. existence, mode of life; c'est la v.! such is life! changer de v., to mend one's ways; mauvaise v., loose living. 4. living, livelihood; niveau de v., standard of living; le coût de la v., the cost of living; gagner sa v., to earn one's living.

vieillard [vjejaːr], s.m. (f. usu. vieille) old man; les vieillards, old people; the elderly.

vieillesse [vjejɛs], s.f. (a) (old) age; dans leur v., in their old age; (b) age (of building, custom).

vieillir [vjejiːr]. 1. v.i. (a) to grow old; (b) to age (in appearance); (c) to become obsolete, out of date; ce mot a vieilli, this word is obsolescent; (d) (of wine, cheese, etc.) to mature. 2. v.tr. to age; to make (s.o.) look older; ce chapeau la

vieillit, that hat ages her.

vieillissement [vjejismɑ̃], *s.m.* ageing, growing old.

vierge [vjɛrʒ]. **1.** *s.f.* (*a*) virgin, maid(en); **la (Sainte) V.,** the Blessed Virgin (Mary); (*b*) *Astr:* **la V.,** Virgo. **2.** *a.* virgin, virginal; **fille v., homme v.,** virgin; **terre, forêt, v.,** virgin soil, forest; **page v.,** blank page; **réputation v.,** untarnished reputation.

Viêt-nam (le) [ləvjɛtnam]. *Pr.n.m. Geog:* Vietnam.

vietnamien, -ienne [vjɛtnamjɛ̃, -jɛn], *a. & s.* Vietnamese.

vieux, vieil, *f.* **vieille** [vjø, vjɛ(:)j], *a.* (*the form* **vieil** *is used before masc. nouns beginning with a vowel or h "mute," but* **vieux** *also occurs in this position*) **1.** old; (*a*) **se faire v.,** to be getting on (in years); *s.* **un v., une vieille,** an old man, an old woman; **un v. du volant,** a veteran motorist; *F:* (*with no sense of old age*) **eh bien, mon v.!** well, old chap! **mes v.,** my (old) people, my parents; (*b*) of long standing; **un vieil ami,** an old friend; **une vieille fille,** an old maid; **un v. garçon,** a (confirmed) bachelor; **il est v. dans ce métier,** he's an old hand at this job; *s. F:* **un v. de la vieille,** a veteran. **2.** (*a*) old, ancient; worn, shabby; stale (news); **v. papiers,** waste paper; *adj.phr.inv.* **v. jeu,** old-fashioned; **doctrines v. jeu,** antiquated doctrines; (*b*) *inv.* **des rubans vieil or,** old-gold ribbons.

vif, vive [vif, vi:v]. **1.** *a.* (*a*) alive, living; **de vive force,** by main force; **de vive voix,** by word of mouth; **eau vive,** spring water; **vives eaux** [viv-zo], spring tide; (*b*) lively, animated; fast; **vive allure,** rapid gait, brisk pace; (*c*) sharp (wind, retort); **vive arête,** sharp edge; *adv.* **il gèle v.,** it's freezing hard; (*d*) keen, quick (wit); vivid (imagination); (*e*) **couleurs vives,** bright colours. **2.** *s.m. Jur:* living person. **3.** *s.m.* living flesh; quick; **blessé au v.,** stung to the quick.

vigilance [viʒilɑ̃:s], *s.f.* vigilance; watchfulness; *a.* **-ant,** watchful, alert.

vigne [viɲ], *s.f.* **1.** *Vit:* (*a*) vine; (*b*) vineyard. **2.** *Bot:* **v. vierge,** Virginia creeper.

vigneron, -onne [viɲrɔ̃, -ɔn], *s.* vine-grower; viticulturist.

vignette [viɲɛt], *s.f.* vignette; (*a*) *Typ:* text illustration; head-, tail-, piece; ornamental border; (*b*) *Adm: Aut:* vignette; special tax label.

vignoble [viɲɔbl], *s.m.* vineyard.

vigoureux, -euse [vigurø, -ø:z], *a.* vigorous, strong, sturdy; *adv.* **-sement.**

vigueur [vigœ:r], *s.f.* **1.** vigour, strength; **reprendre (de la) v.,** to regain strength; **se sentir sans v.,** to feel exhausted; **s'exprimer avec v.,** to express oneself forcibly. **2.** (*of decree*) **en v.,** in force; **entrer en v.,** to come into effect.

vil [vil], *a.* cheap, low-priced; **vendre qch. à v.**

prix, to sell sth. dirt cheap.

vilain, -aine [vilɛ̃, -ɛn]. **1.** *s.* (*a*) *F:* **oh, le v.! vilaine!** you naughty boy! you naughty gir (*b*) *F:* trouble; **il y aura du v.,** there's going be trouble. **2.** *a.* (*a*) nasty, bad, unpleasa (person, thoughts, weather); **c'est un v. mon sieur,** *P:* **un v. coco,** he's a nasty piece of wor **un v. tour,** a mean, dirty, trick; (*b*) ugly; nas (wound); **un v. mot,** an ugly word; **il fait v.,** it filthy weather; (*c*) shabby (hat); sordi wretched (street).

vilebrequin [vilbr(ə)kɛ̃], *s.m.* (*a*) *Tls:* brace a bit; (*b*) *Mec:* (**arbre à**) **v.,** crankshaft.

villa [vil(l)a], *s.f.* house (in a residential are **petite v. de banlieue,** little house in the subur

village [vila:ʒ], *s.m.* village; **il est bien de son** he's very countrified, awkward (in manner)

villageois, -oise [vilaʒwa, -wa:z]. **1.** *s.* villag **2.** *a.* rustic, country.

ville [vil], *s.f.* town, city; **v. d'eaux,** spa; **être v.,** to be in town; **en v.,** (*on letters*) loc **toilette de v.,** (woman's) town clothes; **tenue v.,** (man's) lounge suit; **hôtel de v.,** town-h city hall.

villégiature [vil(l)eʒaty:r], *s.f.* (*a*) stay in country; (*b*) **en v.,** on holiday; *s.m. & f.* -is holidaymaker.

vin [vɛ̃], *s.m.* wine; **les grands vins,** vint wines; **v. ordinaire, v. de table,** dinner wine **de Bordeaux,** claret; **v. de Bourgogne,** Burg dy; **v. du Rhin,** hock; **offrir un v. d'honneu qn,** to hold a reception in honour of s.o.

vinaigre [vinɛ:gr], *s.m.* vinegar; *s.f.* **-et** French dressing; *s.m.* **-ier,** (i) vine manufacturer, merchant; (ii) vinegar cruet.

vindicatif, -ive [vɛ̃dikatif, -i:v], *a.* vindicti spiteful, (re)vengeful; *adv.* **-ivement.**

vineux, -euse [vinø, -ø:z], *a.* **1.** (*of wine*) f bodied. **2.** vinous (flavour). **3.** **année vine** good vintage year.

vingt [vɛ̃], *num.a.inv. & s.m.inv.* twenty; **v. et** [vɛ̃teœ], twenty-one; **v.-deux** [vɛ̃tdœ], twer two; **le v. juin** [ləvɛ̃ʒɥɛl], (on) the twentiet June; **les années v.,** the twenties (1920–29); **moins de v. ans,** the teenagers.

vingtaine [vɛ̃tɛn], *s.f.* (about) twenty; a sc **une v. de gens,** some twenty people.

vingtième [vɛ̃tjɛm]. **1.** *num.a. & s.* twentieth *s.m.* twentieth (part).

vinicole [vinikɔl], *a.* wine(-growing), viticult (district).

Vintimille [vɛ̃timi:j], *Pr.n. Geog:* Ventimigl

viol [vjɔl], *s.m.* **1.** *Jur:* rape. **2.** **v. du se professionnel,** violation of professio secrecy.

violacé [vjɔlase], *a.* purplish-blue (colour).

violation [vjɔlasjɔ̃], *s.f.* violation, infringem breach (of treaty, law, etc.).

violâtre [vjɔlɑ:tr], *a.* purplish.

violence [vjɔlɑ̃:s], *s.f.* violence, force; **se faire v.,** to keep one's feelings under control.

viol|ent [vjɔlɑ̃], *a.* violent (person, wind, pain, death, etc.); fierce (encounter); *adv.* -**emment** [-amɑ̃].

violenter [vjɔlɑ̃te], *v.tr.* **1.** to do violence to (s.o.); **v. qn pour lui faire faire qch.,** to force s.o. to do sth.

violer [vjɔle], *v.tr.* **1.** to violate; to transgress (law); to break (treaty, faith). **2.** to rape (a woman).

violet, -ette [vjɔlɛ, -ɛt]. **1.** *a.* violet, purple; *s.m.* (the colour) violet. **2.** *s.m. Z: F:* sea squirt. **3.** *s.f. Bot:* **violette**, violet.

violon [vjɔlɔ̃], *s.m.* **1.** (*a*) violin; **c'est son v. d'Ingres,** it's his hobby; *F:* **accordez vos violons,** make sure you all tell the same story; (*b*) violin (player); *F:* **payer les violons,** to pay the piper. **2.** *P:* **le v.,** the cells, the lock-up. **3.** *Nau:* **violons de mer,** fiddles (for the tables); *s.m. & f.* -**iste**, violinist.

violoncell|e [vjɔlɔ̃sɛl], *s.m. Mus:* (*a*) violoncello, cello; (*b*) cello (player); cellist; *s.m. & f.* -**iste**, violoncellist, cellist.

vipère [vipɛːr], *s.f.* viper, adder; *F:* (*of pers.*) snake; **langue de v.,** spiteful, venomous, tongue.

virage [vira:ʒ], *s.m.* **1.** turning, cornering (of car, plane, etc.); *Nau:* tacking, going about; *Av:* **v. sur l'aile,** bank(ing); *Ski:* turn. **2.** *Aut:* (sharp) turn, corner, bend.

vir|er [vire]. **1.** *v.i.* to turn; to sweep round; (*a*) *Aut:* to take a bend, a corner; to corner; **v. court,** to corner sharply; (*b*) to slew round, swing about; (*c*) *Nau:* **v. de bord,** to tack; *Av:* to bank. **2.** *v.tr.* (*a*) to turn (sth.) over; **v. une crêpe,** to toss a pancake; (*b*) *Bank:* to transfer (money to an account); *Phot:* to tone (a print); *s.m.* -**ement**, turning; sweeping round; **v. de bord,** tacking; transfer (of money); **banque de v.,** clearing bank.

irginité [virʒinite], *s.f.* virginity.

irgule [virgyl], *s.f.* (*a*) *Gram:* comma; (*b*) *Mth:* = decimal point; **trois v. cinq (3,5)** = three point five (3·5).

iril [viril], *a.* virile; (*a*) male; (*b*) manly; **l'âge v.,** manhood; *adv.* -**ement**, like a man; *s.f.* -**ité**.

irtuel, -elle [virtɥɛl], *a.* virtual; *adv.* -**lement**.

irtuos|e [virtɥoːz], *s.m. & f. Mus:* virtuoso; **un v. du ski,** a brilliant skier; *s.f.* -**ité**, virtuosity.

irul|ent [virylɑ̃], *a.* virulent (disease); violent, virulent (poison, satire, etc.); *s.f.* -**ence.**

irus [virys], *s.m. Med:* virus; **maladie à v.,** virus disease.

⸱s [vis], *s.f.* screw; **v. à droite, à gauche,** right-handed, left-handed, screw or thread; *F:* **serrer la v. à qn,** to put the screw on s.o.; **escalier à v.,** spiral staircase.

⸱sa [viza], *s.m.* visa.

visage [viza:ʒ], *s.m.* face, countenance; **homme au v. agréable,** pleasant-faced man; **faire son v.,** to make (one's face) up; **à deux visages,** double-faced; **avoir bon v.,** to look well; **faire bon v. à qn,** to smile on s.o., to be friendly to s.o.; **voir les choses sous leur vrai v.,** to see things as they are.

visagiste [vizaʒist], *s.m. or f. R.t.m:* beautician; face specialist.

vis-à-vis [vizavi]. **1.** *adv.phr.* opposite; **assis v.-à-v.,** sitting face to face. **2.** *prep.phr.* **v.-à-v. de,** (*a*) opposite, facing; (*b*) towards, with respect to, with regard to (s.o., sth.). **3.** *s.m.* person opposite; *Cards:* partner.

visée [vize], *s.f.* **1.** aim; sighting; **ligne de v.,** line of sight. **2.** *usu.pl.* aims; plans; ambitions.

vis|er¹ [vize]. **1.** *v.i.* to aim (**à,** at); **v. à faire qch.,** to aim at doing sth. **2.** *v.tr.* (*a*) to aim, take aim, at (s.o., sth.); *Golf:* **v. la balle,** to address the ball; (*b*) *Surv:* to sight; to take a sight on (sth.); (*c*) to have (sth.) in view; (*d*) to allude to (s.o., sth.); *s.* -**eur**, -**euse**, aimer; *s.m. Phot:* viewfinder; sighting-piece; *Av:* **v. de lancement,** bomb sights.

viser², *v.tr. Adm:* to visa; to countersign.

visib|le [vizibl], *a.* **1.** (*a*) visible, perceptible; (*b*) obvious, manifest, evident (sign, falsehood, etc.); **très v.,** conspicuous. **2.** (*a*) ready to receive visitors; **je ne suis v. à personne,** I'm not at home to anyone; (*b*) disengaged; **je ne serai pas v. avant midi,** I shall be engaged until midday; (*c*) (*of exhibition, etc.*) open to the public; *s.f.* -**ilité**, visibility; *Av:* **pilotage sans v.,** blind flying; *adv.* -**lement.**

visière [vizjɛːr], *s.f.* (*a*) vizor (of helmet); (*b*) peak (of cap); (*c*) eye-shade.

vision [vizjɔ̃], *s.f.* vision. **1.** (*a*) eyesight; (*b*) sight, view; **v. momentanée (de qch.),** glimpse (of sth.). **2.** (mental) vision; imagination; **les visions d'un poète,** a poet's visions; *a. & s.* -**naire**, visionary; dreamer.

visionneuse [vizjɔnøːz], *s.f. Cin: Phot:* viewer.

visite [vizit], *s.f.* visit. **1.** (*a*) (social) call; **faire une petite v. à qn,** to drop in on s.o.; **carte de v.,** visiting-card; (*b*) caller, visitor. **2.** visit, call (of doctor). **3.** (*a*) inspection; overhauling; survey; **v. médicale,** medical examination; **v. de la douane,** customs examination; (*b*) **v. dirigée,** conducted tour (of museum, etc.).

visit|er [vizite], *v.tr.* **1.** to visit (s.o.); to call on (a friend, a client). **2.** (*a*) to examine, inspect (building, machinery, etc.); (*b*) to visit, search (house, etc.); *Cust:* **v. les valises,** to examine suitcases; (*c*) **on nous a fait v. l'usine,** we were shown over the factory; *a.* -**able**, worth visiting; *s.* -**eur**, -**euse**, visitor; inspector.

vison [vizɔ̃], *s.m. Z:* mink; *Com:* mink coat.

visqueux, -euse [viskø, -øːz], *a.* viscous, sticky, gluey; tacky (glue); thick (oil); slimy (secretion).

visser [vise], *v.tr.* to screw, screw on, screw down, screw up (sth.).

visuel, -elle [vizɥel], *a.* visual; **champ v.,** field of vision.

vital, -aux [vital, -o], *a.* 1. vital; **force vitale,** vital force. 2. vital (**pour,** to); **question vitale,** vital question; *s.f.* -**ité,** vitality.

vitamine [vitamin], *s.f. Bio-Ch:* vitamin.

vite [vit], *adv.* quickly, fast, rapidly, speedily; **faites v.!** make haste! hurry up! **allons, et plus v. que cela!** now then, be quick about it! **au plus v.,** as quickly as possible.

vitesse [vitɛs], *s.f.* speed, rapidity; velocity; rate; **en v.,** quickly, speedily; **partir en v.,** to rush off; **gagner qn de v.,** to outstrip s.o.; **prendre de la v.,** to gather pace; *Av:* **perte de v.,** stall; *Aut:* **faire de la v.,** to speed; **indicateur de v.,** speedometer; **v. acquise,** impetus; *Aut:* **boîte de vitesses,** gear-box; **première v.,** bottom gear; **filer en quatrième v.,** (i) to drive in top (gear); (ii) *F:* to disappear at top speed.

viticole [vitikɔl], *a.* viticultural; wine-growing (district); wine (industry).

viticult|ure [vitikyltyːr], *s.f.* vine-growing; *s.m.* -**eur,** wine-grower.

vitrail, -aux [vitraːj, -o], *s.m.* leaded glass window; *esp.* stained glass (church) window.

vitre [vitr], *s.f.* pane; window-pane.

vitr|er [vitre], *v.tr.* to glaze; *a.* -**eux, -euse,** vitreous (mass); glassy (appearance); *s.m.* -**ier,** glazier.

vitrine [vitrin], *s.f.* 1. shop-window; **faire une v.,** to dress a window; **regarder, lécher, les vitrines,** to go window-shopping. 2. glass case, glass cabinet; *Com:* showcase.

vitriol [vitri(j)ɔl], *s.m.* vitriol.

vitupér|er [vitypere], *v.i.* (**je vitupère, n. vitupérons**) to vituperate, protest, storm (**contre qn, qch.,** against s.o., sth.); *s.f.* -**ation.**

vivace [vivas], *a.* (*a*) long-lived; (*b*) *Bot:* hardy; (*c*) *Bot:* perennial; (*d*) **haine v.,** undying, inveterate, hatred.

vivacité [vivasite], *s.f.* 1. **v. à agir,** promptness to act. 2. hastiness (of temper); petulance; **avec v.,** hastily, sharply. 3. (*a*) acuteness (of feeling); heat (of a discussion); intensity (of a passion); (*b*) vividness, brilliancy (of colour, light). 4. vivacity, vivaciousness, animation, liveliness.

vivant [vivɑ̃]. 1. *a.* (*a*) alive, living; **il est encore v.,** he's still alive; **être le portrait v. de qn,** to be the very image of s.o.; **langue vivante,** modern language; (*b*) lively, animated (scene, etc.); (*c*) vivid, live (narrative, picture). 2. *s.m.* (*a*) living being; (*b*) **bon v.,** man who enjoys (the pleasures of) life. 3. *s.m.* **de son v.,** during his lifetime, in his day.

vivement [vivmɑ̃], *adv.* 1. (*a*) briskly, sharply,

smartly; (*b*) **répondre v.,** to answer sharply. 2. (*a*) keenly, deeply; **regretter qch. v.,** to be extremely sorry about sth.; (*b*) **remercier qn v.,** to thank s.o. warmly; (*c*) **v. recommandé,** highly recommended.

vivier [vivje], *s.m.* fish preserve, fish tank.

vivifier [vivifje], *v.tr.* (*pr.sub. & p.d.* **n. vivifiions**); to vivify; to vitalize; to endue with life; to invigorate; **v. une entreprise,** to give fresh life to an undertaking.

vivre [viːvr]. I. *v.i.* (*p.p.* vécu; *pr.ind.* je vis) to live. 1. to be alive; **vive le roi!** long live the King! *Mil:* **qui vive?** who goes there? **ne rencontrer âme qui vive,** to meet no one; *Prov:* **qui vivra verra,** time will tell. 2. to spend one's life; **il a beaucoup vécu,** he has seen life; **savoir v.,** to know how to behave. 3. to subsist; **il faut que tout le monde vive,** everyone must live; **avoir de quoi v.,** to have enough to live on. II. **vivres,** *s.m.pl.* provisions, supplies, victuals.

vocabulaire [vɔkabyleːr], *s.m.* vocabulary.

vocal, -aux [vɔkal, -o], *a.* vocal (promise, music prayer; *Anat:* cords); *adv.* -**ement.**

vocation [vɔkasjɔ̃], *s.f.* 1. vocation; (divine) call 2. vocation; calling, bent, inclination.

vocifér|er [vɔsifere], *v.i.* (**je vocifère, je vociférerai**) to vociferate (**contre,** against); to shout, bawl, yell (insults); *s.f.* -**ation** vociferation; *pl.* shouts, yells.

vœu, vœux [vø], *s.m.* 1. vow. 2. wish; **tous me vœux!** all good wishes!

vogue [vɔg], *s.f.* fashion, vogue; **être en v.,** to b popular, in fashion.

voici [vwasi], *prep.* 1. here is, are; **la v. qui vien** here she comes; **v. ce dont il s'agit,** this is wha it's all about; **mon ami que v. vous le dira, m** friend here will tell you; **la petite histoire qu v.,** the following little story. 2. (= IL Y A) **je l'a vu v. trois ans,** I saw him three years ago.

voie [vwa], *s.f.* 1. (*a*) way, road, route, trac *Adm: Aut:* traffic lane; **v. de communicatio** road, thoroughfare; *P.N:* **v. sans issue, n** through road; **par v. de terre,** by lan overland; **par v. de mer,** by sea; **v. aérienne, a** route; (*b*) *Ven:* (*often pl.*) tracks (of game **mettre qn sur la v.,** to give s.o. a clue, to put s. on the right track; (*c*) *Rail:* **v. ferrée,** railwa track; railway line; **v. de garage,** siding; (* *Nau:* **v. d'eau,** leak; (*e*) *Anat:* passage, duct; **voies respiratoires,** the respiratory tract(s). way; **voies et moyens,** ways and means; **par diplomatique,** through (normal) diploma channels; **affaire en bonne v.,** affair going we *Jur:* **voies de fait,** acts of violence; **en venir a voies de fait,** to come to blows.

voilà [vwala], *prep.* 1. (*a*) there is, are; **la pend que v.,** that clock (over there); **en v. asse** that's enough (of it)! that will do! **en v. u idée!** what an idea! **v. tout,** that's all; **v. qui**

curieux! that's odd! le v. qui entre, there he is coming in; (in restaurant) v., monsieur! coming, sir! (b) (= VOICI) me v.! here I am! 2. (= IL Y A) v. dix ans que je le connais, I've known him ten years.

voile [vwal]. I. s.f. sail; grande v., mainsail; toutes voiles dehors, all sails set. II. s.m. (a) veil; (of nun) prendre le v., to take the veil; sous le v. de la religion, under the cloak of religion; (b) Tex: voile.

voiler [vwale], v.tr. (a) to veil (face); (b) to veil, obscure, dim; to muffle; (c) Phot: to fog (print). se voiler, (of sky, etc.) to become overcast, to cloud over.

voilier [vwalje], s.m. 1. sailing-ship, -boat; windjammer. 2. sail-maker.

voilure [vwaly:r], s.f. (a) sails (of ship); (b) Av: wing(s), flying surface, aerofoil; (c) Ph: aerodynamic surface.

voir [vwa:r], v.tr. (pr.p. voyant; p.p. vu; pr.ind. ils voient; pr.sub. je voie; p.h. je vis; fu. je verrai) 1. (a) to see; to set eyes (up)on (s.o., sth.); to sight (ship); à le v., to judge by his looks; monument qui se voit de loin, monument that can be seen from afar; v. trouble, to see things through a mist; to be dim-sighted; voyez vous-même! see for yourself! Iron: voyez un peu! just look at him, it! faire v. qch. à qn, to show sth. to s.o.; faites v.! let me see it! 2. v. + inf. (a) v. venir qn, to see s.o. coming; F: je vous vois venir! I can see what you're getting at; (b) v. faire qch. à qn, to see s.o. do sth. 3. (a) to visit; aller v. qn, to go and see s.o.; v. du pays, to travel; (b) il ne voit personne, he receives no one. 4. (a) to understand; ne pas v. le sens d'un mot, not to understand the meaning of a word; F: ni vu, ni connu, nobody's any the wiser for it; (b) to perceive, observe; cela se voit, that's obvious; vous voyez ça d'ici, you can imagine what it's like. 5. (a) to examine, to look into, to see about (sth.); v. une affaire à fond, to look into a matter thoroughly; c'est ce que nous verrons! that remains to be seen; il n'a rien à v. là-dedans, it has nothing to do with him; (b) il va v. à nous loger, he'll see that we have somewhere to stay; (c) int. voyons! (i) let's see; (ii) come, now! 6. être bien vu de tous, to be highly esteemed by all; mal vu, poorly considered; disliked; F: je ne peux pas le v., I can't bear the sight of him.

voire [vwa:r], adv. indeed; v. (même), and even; j'en suis ahuri, v. révolté, I am astounded, indeed, disgusted.

voirie [vwari], s.f. 1. system of roads; la grande v., the high roads; le service de v., the highways department. 2. refuse dump; jeter les ordures à la v., to dump the refuse.

voisin, -ine [vwazɛ̃, -in]. 1. a. neighbouring,

adjoining; la chambre voisine, the next room; le village le plus v., the nearest village; v. de la mort, at death's door. 2. s. neighbour.

voisiner [vwazine], v.i. 1. to visit one's neighbours; nous voisinons, we're neighbourly, we're friendly. 2. (of thgs) to be placed side by side; to adjoin; s.m. -age, proximity, nearness; neighbourhood.

voiture [vwaty:r], s.f. (a) (horse-drawn) carriage; aller en v., to drive; (b) car, N.Am: automobile; (c) Rail: v. (de chemin de fer), (railway) coach, carriage, N.Am: car; en v.! take your seats; (d) v. d'enfant, perambulator, F: pram.

voix [vwa], s.f. 1. voice; parler à v. haute, à v. basse, to speak loudly, in a loud voice, in a subdued voice, in an undertone; (of dogs) donner de la v., to bark, to bay. 2. demeurer sans v., to remain speechless; d'une commune v., by common consent; mettre une question aux v., to put a question to the vote; la Chambre alla aux v., the House divided; avoir v. au chapitre, to have a say in the matter.

vol¹ [vɔl], s.m. 1. (a) flying, flight; prendre son v., to take wing; au v., on the wing; à v. d'oiseau, as the crow flies; vue à v. d'oiseau, bird's-eye view; (b) Av: v. numéro 450 pour Bruxelles, flight number 450 for Brussels; heures de v., flying hours; v. à voile, gliding. 2. flock, flight (of birds).

vol², s.m. theft; stealing; v. avec effraction, housebreaking; v. à l'étalage, shop-lifting; v. à l'américaine, confidence trick.

volage [vɔlaʒ], a. fickle, inconstant, flighty.

volaille [vɔlɑːj], s.f. poultry, fowls; marchand de v., poulterer; foies de v., chicken livers.

volant [vɔlɑ̃]. I. a. 1. flying; fluttering. 2. loose; movable; feuille volante, loose leaf. II. s.m. 1. Games: shuttlecock; v. au filet, badminton. 2. fly-wheel. 3. hand-wheel; Aut: steering-wheel. 4. Dressm: flounce.

volatil [vɔlatil], a. Ch: etc: volatile.

volatile [vɔlatil], s.m. winged creature; bird, esp. farmyard bird.

volatiliser [vɔlatilize], v.tr. (a) Ch: to volatilize; (b) P: on lui avait volatilisé sa montre, s.o. had pinched his watch; s.f. -ation. se volatiliser, (of ideas, etc.) to vanish into thin air.

vol-au-vent [vɔlɔvɑ̃], s.m.inv. Cu: vol-au-vent.

volcan [vɔlkɑ̃], s.m. volcano.

volcanique [vɔlkanik], a. volcanic.

volée [vɔle], s.f. 1. flight (of bird, projectile, etc.); prendre sa v., to take wing; lancer qch. à toute v., to hurl sth.; Fb: coup de v., punt; Ten: volley. 2. flock, flight (of birds); rank, standing; scientifique de première v., top-ranking scientist. 3. (a) volley (of missiles); (b) shower (of blows); une bonne v., a sound thrashing; (c)

v. de cloches, full peal of bells; sonner à toute v., to set all the bells ringing.

voler[1] [vɔle], v.i. to fly; (a) v. de ses propres ailes, to fend for oneself; on aurait entendu v. une mouche, you could have heard a pin drop; (b) Av: to fly; (c) to travel fast; to move with speed; le temps vole, time flies.

voler[2], v.tr. 1. to steal (sth.); F: il ne l'a pas volé, he richly deserves it. 2. (a) to rob (s.o.); (b) to swindle, cheat (s.o.); s. -eur, -euse, thief, robber; burglar; au v.! stop thief!

volet [vɔle], s.m. 1. sorting board (for seeds, etc.); trié sur le v., hand-picked. 2. shutter; Phot: shutter.

voleter [vɔlte], v.i. (il volette) (of bird) to flutter; to flit.

volière [vɔljɛːr], s.f. aviary.

volontaire [vɔlɔ̃tɛːr], a. 1. voluntary; spontaneous (act); Mil: engagé v., s.m. volontaire, volunteer. 2. self-willed, headstrong, obstinate; menton v., firm chin; adv. -ment.

volonté [vɔlɔ̃te], s.f. 1. will; (a) v. de fer, iron will; manque de v., spinelessness; ne pas avoir de v., to have no will of one's own; (b) faire qch. de bonne v., to do sth. of one's own free will, willingly, spontaneously, with good grace; (c) suivre sa v., to have one's own way; adv.phr. à v., at will, at pleasure, ad lib. 2. pl. (a) les dernières volontés (de qn), (s.o.'s) last will and testament; (b) whims, caprices; elle fait ses quatre volontés, she does just what she pleases.

volontiers [vɔlɔ̃tje], adv. (a) willingly, gladly, with pleasure; très v., I'd love to; il cause v., he's fond of talking; (b) readily, easily.

volt [vɔlt], s.m. El.Meas: volt.

voltage [vɔltaːʒ], s.m. El: voltage.

volte-face [vɔltafas], s.f.inv. turning round; volte-face; wheel round; face-about; faire v.-f., to reverse one's opinions, one's policy; to change sides.

voltiger [vɔltiʒe], v.i. (n. voltigeons) (of bird, insect) to fly about; to flit; to flutter, flap; s.m. -ement, fluttering; flitting.

volubilis [vɔlybilis], s.m. Bot: convolvulus.

volubilité [vɔlybilite], s.f. volubility.

volume [vɔlym], s.m. 1. volume, tome. 2. (a) volume, bulk, mass; (b) volume (of sound).

volumineux, -euse [vɔlyminø, -øːz], a. 1. voluminous, bulky, large. 2. voluminous (writer).

volupté [vɔlypte], s.f. (sensual) pleasure.

voluptueux, -euse [vɔlyptɥø, -øːz]. 1. a. voluptuous. 2. s. voluptuary, sensualist; adv. -sement.

volute [vɔlyt], s.f. Arch: etc: volute, helix; scroll; ressort en v., helical spring; v. de fumée, wreath of smoke.

vomir [vɔmiːr], v.tr. (a) to vomit; abs. to be sick,

to throw up; (b) to belch forth (smoke); s.m. -issement, vomit(ing).

voracle [vɔras], a. voracious (animal, appetite, reader); ravenous (animal, pers.); adv. -ement; s.f. -ité, voraciousness.

vote [vɔt], s.m. 1. (a) vote; (b) voting, ballot(ing), poll; droit de v., franchise. 2. loi en cours de v., bill before the House; v. d'une loi, passing of a bill; v. de confiance, vote of confidence.

voter [vɔte]. 1. v.i. to vote; (in Parliament) to divide; v. à main levée, to vote by (a) show of hands. 2. v.tr. (a) to pass, carry (a bill); (b) to vote (money); s. -ant, -ante, voter.

votif, -ive [vɔtif, -iːv], a. votive (offering).

votre, pl. vos [vɔtr, vo], poss.a. your; v. fils et v. fille, your son and (your) daughter; un de vos amis, one of your friends; vos père et mère, your father and mother.

vôtre [voːtr], le vôtre, la vôtre, les vôtres; (a) poss.pron. yours; your own; F: à la v.! here's to you! cheers! (b) s.m. (i) il faut y mettre du v., you must do your share; (ii) pl. your own (friends, family, etc.); je suis des vôtres, I'm on your side; (iii) F: vous avez encore fait des vôtres, you've been up to (some of) your tricks again.

vouer [vwe], v.tr. to vow, dedicate, consecrate; v. sa vie à l'étude, to devote one's life to study.

vouloir [vulwaːr]. I. v.tr. (pr.p. voulant; p. voulu; pr.ind. je veux, il veut, ils veulent; pr.sub. je veuille, ils veuillent; imp. in 1. only voulez, otherwise veuille, veuillez; fu. je voudrai) 1. to will; to be determined on; Dieu le veuille! please God! il ne faut que v., the will is everything; vous l'avez voulu! you have only yourself to blame! 2. (a) to want, to wish (for), to desire; faites comme vous voudrez, as you please; qu'il le veuille ou non, whether he chooses or not; je ne veux pas! I will not have it! que voulez-vous! well, what do, did you expect? ils ne veulent pas de moi, they won't have me; adv.phr. en veux-tu, en voilà, take as much as you like; (b) pred. je te veux heureuse, I want you to be happy; (c) en v. à qn, to bear s.o. a grudge; ne m'en veuillez pas, don't be angry with me; à qui en voulez-vous, what's the trouble now? s'en v., to be angry with oneself. 3. v. + inf., v. que + sub. (a) will, to require, to demand; le mauvais sort voulut qu'il arrivât trop tard, as ill-luck would have it he arrived too late; je veux être obéi, intend, mean, to be obeyed; v. absolument faire qch., to insist (up)on doing sth.; (b) want, wish; il voulait me frapper, he wanted to hit me; que voulez-vous que je fasse? what do you expect me to do? rentrons, voulez-vous, let us go in, shall we? (c) to try to (do sth.) voulut arrêter le coup, he tried to stop the blow; (d) to mean, intend; je voulais écrire livre sur ce sujet, I meant to write a book on this subject; **faire qch. sans le v.,** to do sth. unintentionally; (*e*) **v. bien faire qch.,** to consent, be willing, to do sth.; **je veux bien que vous veniez,** I'd like you to come; **veuillez (bien) vous asseoir,** do (please) sit down; won't you sit down? (*f*) (*with* **bien** *used as an intensive*) **voulez-vous bien vous taire!** *will* you be quiet! *F:* do shut up! **4.** to be convinced, to insist; **il veut absolument que je me sois trompé,** he insists, he will have it, that I was mistaken. **5.** to require, need, demand; **la vigne veut un terrain crayeux,** vines require a chalky soil. **II. vouloir,** *s.m.* will; **bon, mauvais, v.,** goodwill, ill will (**pour, envers,** towards).

voulu [vuly], *a.* **1.** required, requisite (formalities, etc.); **la longueur voulue,** the required length; **j'agirai en temps v.,** I shall take action at the proper moment. **2.** deliberate, intentional; **impertinence voulue,** studied impertinence.

vous [vu], *pers.pron.sg. & pl.* **1.** (*a*) (*subject*) you; (*b*) (*object*) you, to you; (*c*) (*refl.*) **v. v. êtes donné bien de la peine,** you have given yourself much trouble; (*d*) (*reciprocal*) **v. v. connaissez,** you know one another. **2.** (*stressed*) (*a*) (*subject*) you; **v. et votre femme,** you and your wife; **v. autres Anglais,** you English; (*b*) (*object*) **c'est à v. de jouer,** it is your turn to play.

vous-même(s) [vumɛm], *pers.pron.* yourself; yourselves; **faites-le v.-m.,** do it yourself, yourselves.

voûte [vut], *s.f.* vault, arch.

voûté [vute], *a.* (*a*) vaulted, arched (roof, etc.); (*b*) stooping, bent (person); **dos v.,** bent back, round shoulders.

voûter [vute], *v.tr.* to arch, vault (over) (a roof). **se voûter,** to become bent, bowed, round-shouldered.

voyage [vwaja:ʒ], *s.m.* journey, voyage; **aimer les voyages,** to be fond of travel; **v. d'affaires,** business trip; **v. touristique accompagné,** conducted tour; **v. de noces,** honeymoon; **il est en v.,** he is travelling, he's away; **compagnon de v.,** (i) travelling companion; (ii) fellow passenger; **bon v.!** pleasant journey! have a good trip!

voyager [vwajaʒe], *v.i.* (*n.* **voyageons**) (*a*) to travel; to make a journey; (*b*) *Com:* to travel, to be on the road; **v. pour les vins,** to travel in wine; *s.* **-eur, -euse,** traveller; passenger; **v. de commerce,** commercial traveller.

voyant, -ante [vwajɑ̃, -ɑ̃:t]. **1.** *s.* clairvoyant. **2.** *a.* gaudy, loud (colour); showy, conspicuous.

3. *s.m.* pilot light, indicator light; warning light.

voyelle [vwajɛl], *s.f.* vowel.

voyou [vwaju], *s.m. F:* (young) loafer, layabout; hooligan.

vrac [vrak], *s.m.* (*now used in*) **en v.,** loose, in bulk; **marchandises en v.,** loose goods (not packed); **acheter des livres en v.,** to buy a job lot of books; **faire le v.,** to transport goods in bulk.

vrai [vrɛ]. **1.** *a.* (*a*) true, truthful; **c'est (bien) v.!** true! *F:* **pour de v.,** really, seriously; (*b*) true, real, genuine; (*c*) downright, regular (liar, etc.); **c'est une vraie attrape,** it's a proper swindle. **2.** *adv.* truly, really, indeed; **à v. dire,** as a matter of fact; *F:* **vous m'écrirez, pas v.?** you *will* write to me, won't you? **3.** *s.m.* truth; **il y a du v. dans ce bruit,** there's some truth in the rumour.

vraiment [vrɛmɑ̃], *adv.* really, truly, in truth; **v.?** indeed? is that so?

vraisemblable [vrɛsɑ̃blabl]. **1.** *a.* probable, likely. **2.** *s.m.* what is probable, likely; **au delà du v.,** beyond the bounds of probability; *adv.* **-ment.**

vraisemblance [vrɛsɑ̃blɑ̃:s], *s.f.* probability, likelihood.

vrille [vri:j], *s.f.* **1.** *Bot:* tendril. **2.** *Tls:* gimlet. **3.** *Av:* spin; **descente en v.,** spinning dive.

vrombir [vrɔ̃bi:r], *v.i.* to buzz; to hum; to throb; *s.m.* **-issement.**

vu, vue¹ [vy]. **1.** *s.* **être le bien vu, la bien vue, de qn,** to be s.o.'s favourite; **au vu de tous,** openly, publicly. **2.** *prep.* considering, seeing; **vu la chaleur, je voyagerai de nuit,** in view of the heat I'll travel by night.

vue² [vy], *s.f.* **1.** sight; **avoir bonne v.,** to have good (eye)sight; **perdre qn de v.,** to lose (i) sight of, (ii) touch with, s.o.; **personnes les plus en v.,** people most in the public eye. **2.** (*a*) view; **échange de vues,** exchange of views; (*b*) view, inspection; **la v. n'en coûte rien,** looking costs nothing. **3.** view; outlook; **hôtel avec v. sur la mer,** hotel with a sea view; **v. plongeante,** view from above.

vulgaire [vylgɛ:r]. **1.** *a.* vulgar; (*a*) common, everyday; (*b*) low, coarse. **2.** *s.m.* **le v.,** the common people.

vulgariser [vylgarize], *v.tr.* **1.** to popularize (knowledge). **2.** to coarsen, vulgarize; *s.f.* **-ation,** popularization (of knowledge). **se vulgariser,** to grow vulgar.

vulgarité [vylgarite], *s.f.* vulgarity.

vulnérable [vylnerabl], *a.* vulnerable; *s.f.* **-ilité,** vulnerability.

W

W, w [dublǝve], *s.m.* (the letter) W, w.

wagon [vagɔ̃], *s.m. Rail:* (passenger) carriage, coach, *N.Am:* car; (goods) wagon, truck; **w. détaché**, slip coach; **monter en w.**, to get into the train.

wagon-citerne [vagɔ̃sitɛrn], *s.m.* tank car; *pl. wagons-citernes.*

wagon-lit [vagɔ̃li], *s.m.* sleeping-car, *F:* sleeper; *pl. wagons-lits.*

wagon-restaurant [vagɔ̃rɛstɔrɑ̃], *s.m.* restaurant-car; dining-car; *pl. wagons-restaurants.*

walkie-talkie [wɔkitɔki, walkitalki], *s.m. Rad:* walkie-talkie; *pl. walkies-talkies.*

wallon, -onne [valɔ̃, -ɔːn; wa-]. **1.** *a. & s. Geog:* Walloon. **2.** *s.m. Ling:* Walloon.

water [watɛːr], *s.m.usu.pl. F:* lavatory, toilet; *F:* loo, *N.Am:* john.

watt [wat], *s.m. El.Meas:* watt, ampère-volt.

W.-C. [dublǝvese, vese], *s.m.usu.pl.* lavatory, *F:* loo, *N.Am:* john.

week-end [wikɛnd], *s.m.* weekend; **partir e** **w.-e.**, to go away for the weekend.

whisky [wiski], *s.m.* whisky; *pl. whiskys.*

wolfram [vɔlfram], *s.m. Miner:* wolfram tungsten.

X

X, x [iks], *s.m.* (the letter) X, x; *Jur:* = person or persons unknown; *Med:* **rayons X,** X rays; **je vous l'ai dit x fois,** I've told you a thousand times.

xénophobie [ksenɔfɔb], (*a*) *a.* xenophobic; (*b*) *s.m. & f.* xenophobe; *s.f.* **-ie,** xenophobia.

Xérès [kseres, gzeres]. **1.** *Pr.n. Geog:* Jerez. **2.** *s.m.* (*also* **vin de X.**) sherry.

xylophone [ksilɔfɔn], *s.m. Mus:* xylophone.

Y

*an asterisk (*) before a noun indicates that the def.art. is **le** or **la**, not **l'***

Y, y¹ [igrɛk], *s.m.* (the letter) Y, y.

y² [i], *unstressed adv. & pron.* **1.** *adv.* there; here; **j'y suis, j'y reste!** here I am and here I stay! **Madame y est-elle?** is Mrs X at home? *F:* **ah, j'y suis!** ah, now I understand! **pendant que vous y êtes,** while you are at it. **2.** *pron.inv.* (*a*) (*standing for thgs*) **j'y gagnerai,** I shall gain by it; **je m'y attendais,** I expected as much; (*b*) **je n'y manquerai pas,** I shall not fail to do so; (*c*) (*standing for pers. just mentioned*) **pensez-vous à lui?—oui, j'y pense,** are you thinking of him?—yes, I am. **3.** (*indeterminate uses*) **je vous y prends!** I have caught you (in the act)! **ça y est!** [sajɛ], (i) that's done! (ii) that's done it! I knew it! (iii) all right! **il y est pour quelque chose,** he's got a hand in it; he's got a finger in the pie. **4. vas-y** [vazi], (i) go there; (ii) get on

with it!

*yacht [jɔt, jat], *s.m. Nau:* yacht; *s.m.* -**ing** yachting.

*yaourt [jaurt], *s.m. Comest:* yogurt, yoghurt yaourt.

yeux [jø], *s.m.pl. see* ŒIL.

*yé-yé [jeje]. **1.** *a.inv.* pop; **chanson yé-yé,** po song; **chanteur, -euse, yé-yé,** pop singer. **2.** (*a s.m.* pop music; (*b*) *s.* pop-mad teenager.

*yole [jɔl], *s.f. Nau:* gig, yawl; **y. d'amira** galley.

*yougoslave [jugɔslaːv], *a. & s. Geog* Yugoslav.

*Yougoslavie (la) [lajugɔslavi]. *Pr.n.f. Geog* Yugoslavia.

*youyou [juju], *s.m. Nau:* dinghy.

Z

Z, z [zɛd], *s.m.* (the letter) Z, z.
Zaïre (le) [zazaiːr]. *Pr.n.m.* Zaire.
Zambèze (le) [lɔzãbɛːz]. *Pr.n.m. Geog:* the Zambezi (river).
Zambie (la) [lazãbi]. *Pr.n.f. Geog:* Zambia.
zèbre [zɛbr], *s.m.* **1.** zebra. **2.** *F:* individual, type; **qui sont-ils, ces zèbres-là?** who are those types?
zébré [zebre], *a.* striped (**de**, with); stripy.
zébrure [zebryːr], *s.f.* **1.** stripe. **2.** (series of) stripes; zebra markings.
zèle [zɛːl], *s.m.* zeal, enthusiasm (**pour**, for); **il y met du z.**, he puts his heart and soul into it; *Ind:* **grève du z.**, work to rule (strike); **pas de z.!** don't overdo it!
zélé, -ée [zele], *a. & s.* zealous (person); **trop z.**, over-zealous; **peu z.**, slack, remiss.
zénith [zenit], *s.m.* zenith.
zéro [zero], *s.m.* **1.** nought; *in telephone numbers* O [ou]; *Biol:* **groupe z.**, (blood) group O; *Ten:* **z. partout**, love all; **quinze à z.**, fifteen love. **2.** starting point, zero (of various scales); **partir de z.**, to start from scratch.
zeste [zest], *s.m. Cu:* lemon, orange, peel, zest; **z. confit**, candied peel.
zézayer [zezeje], *v.i. & tr.* (**je zézaie, je zézaye**) to lisp; *s.m.* **-iement**, lisping, lisp.
zibeline [ziblin], *s.f.* **1.** *Z:* (**martre**) **z.**, sable. **2.** *Cl:* sable (fur).
zigzag [zigzag], *s.m.* zigzag; **éclair en z.**, forked lightning.
zigzaguer [zigzage], *v.i.* to zigzag; (*of bat, etc.*) to flit about; *Aut:* to drive erratically.
zinc [zɛ̃ːg], *s.m.* **1.** zinc; *Com:* spelter. **2.** *F:* (zinc) counter, bar (in café).
zingueur [zɛ̃gœːr], *s.m.* zinc worker; zinc roofer; *s.f.* **-erie**, zinc trade; zincware.
zodiaque [zɔdjak], *s.m.* zodiac.
zona [zɔna], *s.m. Med:* shingles.
zone [zoːn], *s.f.* zone; sphere (of influence); (*a*) *Geog:* **z. tempérée**, temperate zone; **z. des alizés**, trade-wind belt; *Geol:* **z. houillère**, coal belt; **z. gazéifère**, natural gas(-producing) area; (*b*) *Adm:* **z. verte**, green belt; *Aut;* **z. bleue** = pink zone; parking-meter zone; **z. quadrillée**, box junction; **z. postale**, postal area; (*c*) *Pol.Ec:* **z. de libre-échange**, free-trade area; (*d*) *Rad: etc:* **z. de silence radio**, skip zone; **z. de brouillage**, interference area.
zoo [zo, zoo], *s.m. F:* zoo.
zoologie [zɔɔlɔʒi], *s.f.* zoology; *a.* **-gique**, zoological; *s.m. & f.* **-giste**, zoologist.
zouave [zwaːv], *s.m. Mil:* zouave; *F:* **faire le z.**, to act the goat.
zoulou, -ous [zulu], *a. & s.* Zulu.
zut [zyt], *int. F:* (*a*) (*expressing anger*) damn! blast it! (*b*) (*contempt*) shut up! **z. pour vous!** go to hell! (*c*) I can't be bothered.

Common Abbreviations

Abbreviations read as initials unless the phonetic spelling is shown.

Abréviations courantes

Les abréviations se lisent comme lettres initiales à moins que la prononciation phonétique ne soit donnée.

A. 1. *association,* association, ass(oc)., fellowship. **2.** *Ph: masse atomique,* atomic mass.

a., *Meas: are,* 100 square metres.

ac., *Com: acompte,* payment on account.

A.D., *anno Domini,* A.D.

ADN, *acide désoxyribonucléique,* desoxyribonucleic acid, DNA

ad(r)., *adresse,* address.

A. & M., *Arts et Métiers.*

A.F., *allocations familiales* = family allowance.

AFP, *Agence France-Presse.*

agr., *agriculture,* agriculture, agr(ic)., ag.

AITA, *Association internationale des transports aériens,* International Air Transport Association, IATA.

AJ, *Auberge de jeunesse,* Youth Hostel.

a.m., *ante meridiem,* a.m.

A.M., *Arts et Métiers.*

A.-M., *Alpes-Maritimes.*

amp., *El: ampère,* ampere, amp.

anc., *ancien,* old.

AOC, *appellation d'origine contrôlée.*

appt, *appartement,* flat, *N.Am:* apartment.

ap(r). J.-C., *après Jésus-Christ,* anno Domini, A.D.

arr., *Adm: arrondissement,* district, dist.

a.s., *assurances sociales.*

auj., *aujourd'hui,* today.

av., *Book-k: avoir,* credit, cr.

av., *avenue,* Avenue, Av.

avdp., *Meas: avoirdupois,* avoirdupois, avoir., avdp.

av. J.-C., *avant Jésus-Christ,* before Christ, B.C.

B.-A., *Basses-Alpes.*

BAA, *Sch: Brevet d'apprentissage agricole.*

bacc., *Sch: baccalauréat.*

BCG, *(vaccin) bacille (de) Calmette et Guérin,* BCG (vaccine).

bd, *boulevard,* Boulevard, Boul.

B.-du-R., *Bouches-du-Rhône.*

beau, *Com: bordereau,* memorandum, invoice.

BEPC, *Sch: Brevet d'études du premier cycle du second degré.*

B.F. 1. *Banque de France,* Bank of France. **2.** *basse fréquence,* low frequency, L.F.

BIT, *Bureau international du travail,* International Labour Office, ILO.

bld, *boulevard,* Boulevard, Boul.

BN, *Bibliothèque Nationale.*

BNP, *Banque nationale de Paris.*

B.O., *Bulletin Officiel.*

boul., *boulevard,* Boulevard, Boul.

B.-P., *Basses-Pyrénées.*

B.-Rh., *Bas-Rhin.*

bté, *breveté,* patent.

Bx-A., *Beaux-Arts.*

C. 1. *Ph: Celsius,* Celsius, C. **2.** *El: coulomb,* coulomb, C.

c. 1. *cent,* hundred, c., ct., cent. **2.** *Num: centime,* centime, c. **3.** *Ph: centigrade,* centigrade, C. **4.** *Jur: contre,* versus, v.

c.a., *El: courant alternatif,* alternating current, A.C.

c.-à-d., *c'est-à-dire,* that is to say, i.e.

CAF, *Com: coût, assurance, fret,* cost, insurance, and freight, CIF.

Cap., *Mil: capitaine,* captain, Capt.

cap. 1. *Fin: capital,* capital, cap. **2.** *Geog: capitale,* capital, cap.

CAP, *Sch: (a) Certificat d'aptitude pédagogique (enseignement primaire)* = Teacher's

diploma; (b) *Certificat d'aptitude professionnelle.*
CAPES [kapɛs], *Certificat d'aptitude au
professorat de l'enseignement secondaire*
= Diploma of Education, Dip.Ed.
CAPET [kapɛt], *Certificat d'aptitude au
professorat de l'enseignement technique.*
cc., *centimètre(s) cube(s),* cubic centimetre(s),
cc., c.c.
c.c., *El: courant continu,* direct current, D.C.
CC, *Corps Consulaire.*
CCI, *Chambre de Commerce internationale,*
International Chamber of Commerce.
CCP, *compte courant postal, compte chèque
postal,* Giro account.
CD, *Corps diplomatique.*
c. de f., *chemin de fer,* railway, rly, *N.Am:*
railroad.
C.-du-N., *Côtes-du-Nord.*
CECA |seka|, *Communauté européenne du
charbon et de l'acier,* European Coal and Steel
Community, ECSC
CED, *Communauté européenne de défense,*
European Defence Community, EDC.
CEE, *Communauté économique européenne,*
European Economic Community, EEC.
CEEA, *Communauté européenne de l'énergie
atomique,* Euratom.
CEG, *Sch: collège d'enseignement général.*
cent., *centime,* centime, c.
CEP, *Sch: Certificat d'études primaires.*
CERN [sɛrn], *Centre européen pour la
recherche nucléaire.*
certif., *Sch: certificat,* certificate, cert.
CES, *Sch: collège d'enseignement secondaire.*
CET, *Sch: collège d'enseignement technique.*
cf., *confer.* cf.
CFDT, *Confédération française démocratique
du travail.*
CFTC, *Confédération française des travailleurs
chrétiens.*
cg., *Meas: centigramme,* centigramme, cg.
CGT, *Confédération Générale du Travail,*
General Confederation of Labour.
CGT-FO, *Confédération Générale du Travail-
force ouvrière.*
ch., *Mec: cheval,* horse-power, h.p.
ch. de f., *chemin de fer,* railway, rly, *N.Am:*
railroad.
ch.-l., *chef-lieu* = country town.
Cie, *Com: Compagnie,* Company, Co.
CIO, *Comité international olympique,* International Olympic Committee, IOC.
cl., *Meas: centilitre,* centilitre, cl.
cm., *Meas: centimètre,* centimetre, cm.; cm^2,
centimètre(s) carré(s), square centimetre(s),
cm^2; **cm^3,** *centimètre(s) cube(s),* cubic cen-
timetre(s); **cm/s.,** *Rec: centimètres par
seconde* = inches per second, i.p.s.

CM, *Sch: cours moyen.*
CNRS, *Centre national de la recherche
scientifique.*
Co., *Com: Compagnie,* Company, Co.
Col., *Mil: colonel,* Colonel, Col.
com., *Com: commission,* commission, com(m).
coul., *El: coulomb,* coulomb, C.
cpte, *Com: compte,* account, acc.
CQFD, *Geom: ce qu'il fallait démontrer,* quod
erat demonstrandum, QED.
cr., *Book-k: crédit,* credit, cr.
CREDIF [krɛdif], *Centre de recherche et
d'étude pour la diffusion du français.*
CRF, *Croix-Rouge française,* French Red
Cross.
CRS, *Compagnies républicaines de sécurité,* (in
France) State security police, riot police; **un
CRS,** a member of the CRS.
ct, *Corr: courant,* instant, inst.
CV, *curriculum vitae.*
c.v., *Mec: cheval-vapeur,* horse-power, h.p.

D, *(route) départementale* = B road.
dB., *décibel,* decibel, db, dB.
D.C., *Mus: da capo,* D.C.
DCA, *Mil: défense contre avions,* anti-aircraft
defence.
DDT, *Ch: dichloro-diphényl-trichloréthane*
DDT.
déb., *Book-k: débit,* debit, d(eb).
déc., *décembre,* December, Dec.
dem., *demain,* tomorrow.
dép., *Adm: département.*
DES, *diplôme d'études supérieures.*
div. 1. *St.Exch: dividende,* dividend, div. **2.** *Mil:
division,* division, div.
dm., *dimanche,* Sunday, Sun.
dne, *douane,* customs.
do, d°, *dito,* ditto, do.
dol(l)., *dollar,* dollar, dol., $.
douz., *douzaine,* dozen, doz.
Dr, *docteur,* Doctor, Dr.
DST, *Direction de la surveillance du territoire*
= Home Security Branch.
dz., *Com: douzaine,* dozen, doz.

E. 1. *est,* east, E. **2.** *Excellence,* Excellency.
ECG, *électrocardiogramme,* electrocardiogram,
ECG.
éd., *édition,* edition, ed(it).
EDF [ødeef, edeef], *Électricité de France.*
EEG, *électroencéphalogramme,* electro-
encephalogram, EEG.
E.-et-L., *Eure-et-Loir.*
EGF, *Électricité et Gaz de France.*
ELO, *École des Langues Orientales,* School
Oriental Languages.
E.-M., *Mil: état-major,* headquarters, HQ.
E.N., *Sch: École normale.*

ENA, *École nationale d'administration.*
E.-N.-E., *est-nord-est,* east-north-east, ENE.
ENS, *École normale supérieure.*
env., *environ,* about.
e.o.o.e., e. & o.e., *Com: erreur ou omission exceptée,* errors and omissions excepted, E. & O.E.
E.-S.-E., *est-sud-est,* east-south-east, ESE.
&, *et commercial,* ampersand.
établ., établt, *établissement,* establishment, est.
etc., *et caetera,* etcetera, etc.
Ets., *établissements,* establishments.
E.-U., *États-Unis,* United States, US.
Euratom [œratɔm], *Communauté européenne de l'énergie atomique,* Euratom.
ex. 1. *exemple,* example, ex. **2.** *Book-k: exercice,* year's trading.
Exc., *Excellence,* Excellency, Exc.

F. 1. *Fahrenheit,* Fahrenheit, F. **2.** *franc(s),* franc(s).
f. 1. *franc(s),* franc(s). **2.** *féminin,* feminine, fem.
f. à b., *Com: franco à bord,* free on board, f.o.b.
fasc., *Publ: fascicule,* number.
faub., *faubourg,* suburb, sub.
FB, *franc belge,* Belgian franc.
FC, *football club.*
f.c(t)., *Corr: fin courant,* at the end of this month.
fco, *Com: franco,* free of charge, f.o.c., carriage paid, C.P.
fév., *février,* February, Feb.
FF, *francs français.*
FG, *Fin: frais généraux,* overheads.
FIDES [fides], *Fonds d'investissements pour le développement économique et social.*
fg. 1. *figure,* illustration, figure, fig. **2.** *figuré,* figurative, fig.
FISE, *Fonds international de secours à l'enfance,* United Nations International Children's Emergency Fund, UNICEF.
fl. 1. *florin,* florin, fl. **2.** *fleuve,* river, riv.
FMI, *Fonds monétaire international,* International Monetary Fund, IMF
FO, *Pol: Force ouvrière.*
f.p., *Corr: fin prochain,* at the end of next month.
F. 1. *Ecc: Frère,* Brother, Br. **2.** *Geog: France,* France.
fr(s)., *franc(s),* franc(s).
FS, 1. *franc suisse,* Swiss franc. **2.** *Post: faire suivre,* please forward.

g. 1. *gauche,* left, 1. **2.** *Meas: gramme(s),* gramme(s), gr. **3.** *Ph: gravité,* gravity, gr.
Gal, *Mil: Général,* General, Gen.
gal, *général,* general, gen.
Gar., *Garonne.*
G.-B., *Grande-Bretagne,* Great Britain, GB.
GDF, *Gaz de France.*

gend., *Mil: gendarmerie.*
Gir., *Gironde.*
GQG, *Mil: Grand quartier général,* General Headquarters, GHQ.
gr., *Meas: gramme(s),* gramme(s), gr.

h., *heure,* hour, h.
ha., *Meas: hectare,* hectare.
H.-A., *Hautes-Alpes.*
HC, 1. *hors concours,* not competing. **2.** *Mil: hors cadre,* not on the strength. **3.** *hors classe,* unclassified.
HEC, *(école des) hautes études commerciales.*
HF, *haute fréquence,* high frequency, HF.
hg., *Meas: hectogramme,* hectogramme, hectog.
H.-G., *Haute-Garonne.*
hl., *Meas: hectolitre,* hectolitre, hect.
H.-L., *Haute-Loire.*
HLM, *habitation à loyer modéré.*
H.-M., *Haute-Marne.*
H.-P., *Hautes-Pyrénées.*
H.-Rh., *Haut-Rhin.*
H.-Sav., *Haute-Savoie.*
HT, 1. *El: haute tension,* high voltage, HV. **2.** *hors taxe.*
H.-V., *Haute-Vienne.*
Hz, *El.E: hertz,* cycles per second, c.p.s.

ibid., *ibidem,* ibidem, ibid.
id., *idem,* idem.
I.-et-L., *Indre-et-Loire.*
I.-et-V., *Ille-et-Vilaine.*
IFOP [ifɔp], *Institut français d'opinion publique.*
IGAME [igam], *Inspecteur général de l'administration en mission extraordinaire.*
IIP, *Institut international de la presse,* International Press Institute.
ind., *industrie,* industry, ind.
inéd., *inédit,* unpublished, unpub.
inf., *Mil: infanterie,* infantry, inf.
ing(én)., *ingénieur,* engineer, eng(r).
INSEE, *Institut national des statistiques et des études économiques.*
Insp. gén., *inspecteur général,* Inspector General.

J., j. 1. *Mil: jour* = zero day. **2.** *El: joule,* joule, j.
JAC [ʒak], *jeunesse agricole catholique.*
janv., *janvier,* January, Jan.
J.-B., *Jean-Baptiste.*
J.-C., *Jésus-Christ,* Jesus Christ, J.C.
JEC [ʒek], *jeunesse étudiante catholique.*
JIC [ʒik], *jeunesse indépendante chrétienne.*
J.-J., *Jean-Jacques.*
JO, 1. *Journal Officiel.* **2.** *Jeux Olympiques,* Olympic Games.
JOC [ʒɔk], *jeunesse ouvrière catholique.*

jr, *jour,* day, d.
juil., *juillet,* July, Jul.

k., *kilo,* kilo, k.
kc., *El: kilocycle,* kilocycle, kc.
kg(r)., *Meas: kilogramme,* kilogramme, kilo, kg.
kHz, *El: kilohertz,* kilocycle, kc.
kilo, *Meas: kilogramme,* kilogramme, kilo, kg.
km., *Meas: kilomètre(s),* kilometre(s), km; **km/h.,** *kilomètres (à l')heure,* kilometres per hour, km.p.h.
k.o., *Box: knock-out,* knockout, K.O.; *il a été mis k.o.,* he was knocked out, he was K.O.'d.
kVA, *El: kilovoltampère,* kilovolt-ampere(s), kva.
kW., *El: kilowatt,* kilowatt, kw.
kWh., *El: kilowatt(s)-heure,* kilowatt-hour(s), kwhr.

L, *livre sterling,* pound sterling, £.
l., *Meas: litre,* litre, l.
lat., *Geog: latitude,* latitude, lat.
lb., *Meas: livre,* pound, lb.
L.-et-C., *Loir-et-Cher.*
L.-et-G., *Lot-et-Garonne.*
Lieut, *Mil: lieutenant,* Lieutenant, Lt, Lieut.
Lieut-Col., *Mil: lieutenant-colonel,* Lieutenant-Colonel, Lieut.-Col.
loc.cit., *loco citato,* at the place cited, loc.cit.
log., *Mth: logarithme,* logarithm, log.
long., *Geog: longitude,* longitude, long.
LSD, *Pharm: lysergique synthétique diéthylamine,* lysergic acid diethylamide, LSD.
Lt, *Mil: lieutenant,* Lieutenant, Lt.
Ltée., *Fr.C: limitée,* Limited (Company), Ltd.

M. 1. *Monsieur,* Mr. 2. *mardi,* Tuesday, Tu. 3. *mercredi,* Wednesday, Wed.
m. 1. *mort,* died, deceased, d. 2. *mon,* my. 3. *masculin,* masculine, masc., m. 4. *Meas: mètre,* metre, m.; **m²,** *mètre carré,* square metre, m²; **m³,** *mètre cube,* cubic metre, m³.
max., *maximum,* maximum, max.
Me., *mercredi,* Wednesday, Wed.
Mᵉ, *Jur: Maître.*
M.-et-L., *Maine-et-Loire.*
M.-et-M., *Meurthe-et-Moselle.*
mg., *Meas: milligramme,* milligramme, mg.
Mgr., *Ecc: Monseigneur,* Monsignor, Mgr.
Min., *Adm: Ministre,* Minister.
min., *minimum,* minimum, min.
Mlle, *mademoiselle,* Miss.
Mlles, *mesdemoiselles,* the Misses.
MM., *Messieurs,* Messrs.
mm., *Meas: millimètre(s),* millimetre(s), mm.; **mm²,** *millimètre(s) carré(s),* square millimetre(s), mm²; **mm³,** *millimètre(s) cube(s),* cubic millimetre(s), mm³.

Mme, *Madame,* Mrs.
Mmes, *Mesdames,* Mesdames.
MRP, *Pol: Mouvement républicain populaire.*
MS, *manuscrit,* manuscript, MS; **MSS,** *manuscrits,* manuscripts, MSS.

N. 1. *nord,* north, N. 2. *(route) nationale* = A Road.
N.-D., *Notre-Dame,* Our Lady.
NDE, *note de l'éditeur.*
NDLR, *note de la rédaction,* editor's note.
N.-E., *nord-est,* north-east, NE, N.E.
nég., *Fin: négociable,* negotiable.
nég(t)., *négociant,* wholesaler.
N.-N.-E., *nord-nord-est,* north-north-east, NNE.
N.-N.-O., *nord-nord-ouest,* north-north-west, NNW.
No, Nᵒ, nᵒ, *numéro,* number, No., no.
N.-O., *nord-ouest,* north-west, NW.
nov., *novembre,* November, Nov.
NRF, *Nouvelle Revue française.*
N.-S. (J.-C.), *Ecc: Notre-Seigneur (Jésus Christ),* our Lord (and Saviour) (Jesu. Christ).
NT, *Nouveau Testament,* New Testament, NT.
N.-W., *nord-ouest,* north-west, NW.

O., *ouest,* west, W.
OCDE, *Organisation de coopération et* développement économique, Organization fc Economic Co-operation and Developmen OECD.
oct., *octobre,* October, Oct.
OEA, *Organisation des États américain* Organization of American States, OAS.
OECE, *Organisation européenne de coopér* tion économique, Organization for Europea Economic Co-operation, OEEC.
OIPC, *Organisation internationale de poli* criminelle, Interpol.
OIT, *Organisation internationale du trava* International Labour Organization, ILO.
OMS, *Organisation mondiale de la san* World Health Organization, WHO.
O.-N.-O., *ouest-nord-ouest,* west-north-we WNW.
ONU [ony], *Organisation des Nations Uni* United Nations Organization, UNO.
op., *Mus: opus,* opus, op.
op.cit., *opere citato,* in the work quoted, op.c
ord., *ordinaire,* ordinary, ord.
ORL, *Med: oto-rhino-laryngologie.*
O.-S.-O., *ouest-sud-ouest,* west-south-we WSW, W.S.W.
OTAN [ɔtᾶ, ɔtan], *Organisation du traité* l'Atlantique nord, North Atlantic Tre. Organization, NATO.
OTASE [ɔtaz], *Organisation du traité de l'A*

du sud-est, South-East Asia Treaty Organization, SEATO.

OVNI [ovni, ɔvni], *objet volant non identifié*, unidentified flying object, UFO.

P., *Ecc: Père*, Father.

P1, P2, P3, . . . *(ouvrier) professionnel (de) premier, deuxième, troisième, échelon*, skilled worker grade 1, 2, 3 . . ..

p. 1. *page*, page, p. **2.** *par*, per, p. **3.** *pour*, per; **p. %**, *pour cent*, per cent.

P.-B., *Pays-Bas*, Netherlands.

PC, *Pol: parti communiste*.

PCF, *Pol: parti communiste français*.

P.-de-C., *Pas-de-Calais*.

P.-de-D., *Puy-de-Dôme*.

PDG, *président directeur général*, chairman.

P. et C., *Adm: Civ.E: ponts et chaussées*, highway department.

P. et T. [peete], *Postes et Télécommunications* = the Post Office, *F:* the G.P.O.

p. ex., *par exemple*, for example, e.g.

p.g.c.d., *Mth: plus grand commun diviseur*, highest common factor, H.C.F.

PJ, 1. *police judiciaire* = Criminal Investigation Department, CID. **2.** *pièces jointes*, enclosures, encl.

p.m., *post meridiem*, p.m.

PMU, *pari mutuel urbain*.

PNB, *produit national brut*, gross national product, GNP.

P.-O., *Pyrénées-Orientales*.

p.p., *port payé*, carriage paid, C.P.

PPC, *pour prendre congé*, to take leave.

Pr., **Prof.**, *professeur*, Professor, Prof.

PS, 1. *post scriptum*, postscript, P.S. **2.** *Pol: parti socialiste*.

PTT, *postes, télégraphes et téléphones* = the Post Office, *F:* the GPO.

PV, *procès-verbal*.

QG, *Mil: quartier général*, headquarters, HQ.

QI, *quotient d'intelligence, intellectuel*, intelligence quotient, IQ.

qn, *quelqu'un*, someone, s.o.

q., *quelques*, some.

qqf., *quelquefois*, sometimes.

q.v., *quod vide*, which see, q.v.

r., *rue*, road, Rd.

RATP, *Régie autonome des transports parisiens*, Paris transport authority.

R., *Ecc: Révérend*, Reverend, Rev.

RD, *route départementale* = B road.

RDA, *République démocratique allemande*, German Democratic Republic, GDR.

réf., *référence*, reference, ref.

Rgt., *Mil: régiment*, regiment, Rgt.

RER, *Rail: réseau express régional*.

RF, *République française*, (the) French Republic.

RFA, *République fédérale allemande*, Federal Republic of Germany.

Rh., *Med: rhésus*, rhesus, Rh.

RN, *route nationale* = A road.

ro, *recto*, recto, ro.

roy., *royaume*, kingdom.

RP, *Révérend Père*, Reverend Father.

RSFSR, *République soviétique fédérative socialiste de Russie*, Russian Socialist Federated Soviet Republic, RSFSR.

RSVP, *réponse s'il vous plaît*, the favour of an answer is requested, RSVP.

S. 1. *sud*, south, S. **2.** *Ecc: Saint*, Saint, St.

SA, *Com: société anonyme*, limited company.

SABENA [sabena], *Société anonyme belge d'exploitation de la navigation aérienne*.

SARL, *société à responsabilité limitée* = limited liability company.

Sciences po., *Institut d'études politiques de Paris*.

SDECE, *Service de documentation étrangère et de contre-espionnage*, French Intelligence and counter-Intelligence Branch.

S.-E., *sud-est*, south-east, SE.

sec., *seconde*, second (of time), sec.

SECAM [sekam], *T.V: séquentiel à mémoire*.

s.e. & o., **s.e. ou o.**, *Com: sauf erreur ou omission*, errors and omissions excepted, E. & O.E.

SEITA [seita, sɛ:ta], *Service et exploitation industrielle des tabacs et allumettes*.

sept., *septembre*, September, Sept.

S.-et-L., *Saône-et-Loire*.

S.-et-M., *Seine-et-Marne*.

S.-et-O., *Seine-et-Oise*.

SHAPE [ʃep], Supreme Headquarters Allied Powers (Europe).

SI, *syndicat d'initiative*, tourist office.

SIMCA [simka], *Société industrielle de mécanique et carrosserie automobiles*.

SJ, *Ecc: Societatis Jesu*, of the Society of Jesus, S.J.

s.l.n.d., *sans lieu ni date*, of no address and no date.

SMIC, *salaire minimum interprofessionnel de croissance*.

SMIG [smig], *salaire minimum interprofessionnel garanti* = guaranteed minimum wage.

SNCF, *Société nationale des chemins de fer français*.

S.-O., *sud-ouest*, south-west, SW.

SOFRES, *Société française d'enquêtes pour sondage d'opinion*.

SOS, *W.Tel: Nau:* SOS.

SP, *sapeurs-pompiers*, fire brigade.

S.-P., *Ecc: Saint-Père*, Holy Father, H.F.

SPA, *Société protectrice des animaux* = Royal Society for the Prevention of Cruelty to Animals, RSPCA.

s.-pref., *sous-préfecture,* sub-prefecture.

SS, 1. *Sa Sainteté,* His Holiness, H.H. **2.** *Adm: Sécurité Sociale,* National Health Service, NHS.

S.-S.-E., *sud-sud-est,* south-south-east, SSE.

S.-S.-O., *sud-sud-ouest,* south-south-west, SSW.

St, *Saint,* Saint, St.

Ste, *Sainte,* Saint, St.

Sté, *Com: Société,* Company, Co.

succ. 1. *successeur,* successor, succ. **2.** *succursale,* branch, br.

succle, *succursale,* branch, br.

suiv., *suivant,* following, fol.

SVP, *s'il vous plait,* (if you) please.

S.-W., *sud-ouest,* SW.

T. 1. *Meas:* (a) *tesla,* tesla, T.; (b) *téra-,* tera-. **2.** *Com: tare,* tare, t.

t., 1. *tour,* turn, revolution, rev.; **t/mn.,** *tours par minute,* revolutions per minute, r.p.m., rpm. **2.** *tome,* volume, vol. **3.** *Meas: tonne,* metric ton.

TA, *Med: tension artérielle,* blood pressure.

tel. 1. *télégraphique,* telegraphic. **2.** *téléphone,* telephone, tel.

TEP, *Théâtre de l'Est parisien.*

T.-et-G., *Tarn-et-Garonne.*

THT, *El: très haute tension,* very high voltage.

TNP, *Théâtre national populaire.*

TNT, *Exp: trinitrotoluène,* trinitrotoluene, TNT.

tom., *tome,* volume, vol.

TP, *travaux publics,* public works.

t.-p., *timbre-poste,* stamp.

t.p.m., *Mec.E: tours par minute,* revolutions per minute, rpm, r.p.m.

trav. pub., *travaux publics,* public works.

TSF, *téléphonie sans fil; F: la TSF,* the radio; *F: une TSF,* a radio set.

TSVP, *tournez s'il vous plaît,* please turn over, PTO.

t.t.c., *toutes taxes comprises,* tax inclusive.

TV, *télévision,* television, TV.

TVA, *taxe à, sûr, la valeur ajoutée,* value added tax, VAT.

UNEF [ynɛf], *Union nationale des étudiants de France.*

UNESCO [ynɛsko], *Organisation des Nations Unies pour l'éducation, la science et la culture,* United Nations Educational, Scientific and Cultural Organization, UNESCO.

UNICEF, United Nations International Children's Emergency Fund.

UNR, *Pol:* **1.** *Union nationale de la résistance.* **2.** *Union pour la nouvelle république.*

UNRRA [ynra, unra], *Administration des Nations Unies pour la reconstruction et l'assistance,* the United Nations Relief and Rehabilitation Administration, UNRRA.

UP, *Union postale,* Postal Union.

UPU, *Union postale universelle,* Universal Postal Union, UPU.

URSS [yrs], *Union des républiques socialistes soviétiques,* Union of Socialist Soviet Republics, USSR.

USA, (*les*) *États-Unis,* (the) United States, USA, US.

V., *El: volt,* volt, v.

v. 1. *voyez, voir,* see. **2.** *votre,* your, yr.

VDQS, *vin délimité de qualité supérieure.*

Ve, *veuve,* widow.

vend., *vendredi,* Friday, Fri.

vo, *verso,* verso, vo.

vol., *volume,* volume, vol.

W., *El: watt,* watt, w.

WC, w.c. [vese], *water-closet,* water-closet WC.

wh., *El: watt(s)-heure,* watt-hour(s), wh.

Xbre, *décembre,* December, Dec.

%, *pour cent,* per cent, %.

‰, *pour mille,* per thousand, ‰.

PART II

ENGLISH–FRENCH

ANGLAIS–FRANÇAIS

PRONONCIATION

Un tableau des signes phonétiques employés pour les mots anglais est donné ci-dessous; nous attirons toutefois l'attention de l'usager sur les points suivants:

    (a) L'accent tonique est indiqué par un accent précédant la syllabe accentuée, *p. ex.* **sugar** [ˈʃugər], **impossible** [imˈpɔsibl]. Il est à noter que certains mots, surtout des composés, peuvent avoir deux accents toniques.

    (b) Les caractères mis entre parenthèses, *p. ex.* **nation** [ˈneiʃ(ə)n], signifient que le mot peut se prononcer aussi bien avec que sans le son correspondant à cette lettre.

    (c) Le son [r] ne s'entend généralement pas devant une consonne ou devant une pause; on emploie le caractère italique [*r*] à la fin des mots tels que **better, four, here,** pour indiquer que le son [r] peut se faire entendre dans ces mots dans le cas, et uniquement dans le cas, où le mot suivant dans la phrase commence par une voyelle sans qu'il y ait de pause, *p. ex.* **here and now** [ˈhiərənd ˈnau].

    (d) Les mots tels que **which, why, what** ont été écrits avec l'[h] entre parenthèses, à savoir [(h)witʃ], [(h)wai], [(h)wɔt]; l'[h] peut se faire entendre, mais on prononce souvent ces mots sans [h], surtout en parlant vite.

Les consonnes suivantes ont été omises du tableau, parce que le signe phonétique correspond à la lettre utilisée dans le mot écrit:

b, d, h, l, m, n, p, t, v.

TABLEAU DES SIGNES PHONÉTIQUES
VOYELLES

[i:]	bee, fever, sea, police	[ɔi]	boil, toy, oyster, loyal
[iə]	beer, appear, real	[ou]	low, soap, rope, no, diploma
[i]	bit, added, physics	[u]	put, wool, would, full
[e]	bet, menace, leopard, said, bury	[u:]	shoe, prove, too, true, truth
[ei]	date, day, nail	[uə]	surely, tourist
[ɛə]	bear, bareness, heir, airy, there-	[ʌ]	cut, sun, son, some, cover, rough
	fore	[ə:]	burn, learn, herb, whirl
[æ]	bat, add	[ə]	china, annoy, treachery, photo-
[ai]	aisle, height, life, fly, type		graph
[ɑ:]	art, cart, ask	[(ə)]	nation, ocean, reason, sudden
[au]	fowl, house, bough	[jə]	opinion, pillion
[ɔ]	lot, wasp, what	[ju]	huge, duke, beauty
[ɔ:]	all, haul, short, saw		

CONSONNES

[f]	fat, laugh, ruffle, rough, elephant	[ks]	except, exercise, expect, axe,
[s]	sat, scene, mouse, psychology		accident
[θ]	thatch, ether, faith, breath	[kʃ]	action, eviction
[z]	zinc, buzz, houses, fuse	[g]	go, ghost, guard, again, egg, peg,
[ð]	that, the, mother, breathe		rogue
[ʃ]	sham, dish, pressure, ocean,	[gz]	exist, exact
	nation, machine	[χ]	loch
[tʃ]	chat, search, church, thatch, rich	[ŋ]	bang, sing, link, anchor
[ʒ]	pleasure, vision	[ŋg]	anger, finger, English
[dʒ]	rage, edge, pigeon, jet, digit,	[r]	rat, arise, barring
	spinach, judge	[*r*]	sailor, martyr, finger, here
[k]	act, cat, ache, kitten, technique	[j]	yacht, yet

A

A, a¹ [ei], s. **1.** (la lettre) A, a m; A1, de première qualité; (*house number*) 51a, 51 bis. **2.** *Mus:* la m. **3.** A bomb, bombe ƒ A.

a², *before a vowel* an [*stressed* ei, æn, *unstressed* ə, ən], *indef. art.* **1.** un, une; a man, un homme; an apple, une pomme; an M.P. [ən'em'piː] = un député. **2.** (*def. art. in Fr.*) (*a*) to have a red nose, avoir le nez rouge; (*b*) to have a taste for sth., avoir le goût de qch.; (*c*) (*generalizing use*) a woman takes life too seriously, les femmes prennent la vie trop au sérieux. **3.** (*distributive use*) five pence a pound, cinq pence la livre; five francs a head, cinq francs par tête; three times a week, trois fois par semaine. **4.** it gives me an appetite, cela me donne de l'appétit. **5.** (*a*) (= *a certain, a particular*) I know a Doctor Smith, je connais un certain docteur Smith; in a sense, dans un certain sens; (*b*) (= *the same; with at, of*) to eat two at a time, en manger deux à la fois; to come in two at a time, entrer deux par deux; to be of a size, être de la même grandeur, de (la) même taille; (*c*) (= *a single*) I haven't understood a word, je n'ai pas compris un seul mot; not a penny, pas un sou. **6.** (*art. omitted in Fr.*) (*a*) he's a doctor, il est médecin; (*b*) (*before nouns in apposition*) Caen, a town in Normandy, Caen, ville de Normandie; (*c*) (*in many verb-phrases*) to make a fortune, faire fortune; to have a right to sth., avoir droit à qch.; (*d*) what a man! quel homme! what a pity! quel dommage! (*e*) in a taxi, en taxi; to live like a prince, vivre en prince; to sell at a loss, vendre à perte.

aback [ə'bæk], *adv.* to be taken a., être déconcerté, interdit; se déconcerter.

abandon [ə'bændən], *v.tr.* abandonner; délaisser (sa famille); renoncer à (un projet); to a. oneself to despair, s'abandonner, se laisser aller, au désespoir.

abase [ə'beis], *v.tr.* abaisser, humilier (qn); to a. oneself, s'abaisser, s'humilier; a'basement, s. abaissement m, humiliation ƒ; humilité ƒ.

abash [ə'bæʃ], *v.tr.* décontenancer, déconcerter, interdire; to be abashed at sth., être confus, interdit, de qch.

abate [ə'beit], *v.i.* (*of storm, pain, fear*) se calmer, s'apaiser; (*of flood*) baisser; (*of wind*) se modérer, tomber.

abbess, *pl.* -es ['æbes, *pl.* -iz], s. abbesse ƒ.

abbey ['æbi], s. **1.** abbaye ƒ. **2.** a. (church), (église) abbatiale (ƒ).

abbot ['æbət], s. abbé m (d'un monastère).

abbreviate [ə'briːvieit], *v.tr.* abréger (un nom, un livre); **abbrevi'ation**, s. abréviation ƒ.

abdicate ['æbdikeit], *v.tr. & i.* abdiquer (un trône); renoncer à (un droit); **abdi'cation**, s. abdication ƒ; renonciation ƒ.

abdomen ['æbdəmen], s. *Anat: Ent:* abdomen m; bas-ventre m; **ab'dominal**, a. abdominal, -aux.

abduct [æb'dʌkt], *v.tr.* enlever, kidnapper (qn); **ab'duction**, s. enlèvement m, kidnapping m.

aberration [æbə'reiʃ(ə)n], s. **1.** aberration ƒ, déviation ƒ. **2.** mental a., égarement m de l'esprit; confusion mentale; folie ƒ.

abet [ə'bet], *v.tr.* (**abetted**) to a. s.o. in a crime, encourager qn à un crime; to aid and a. s.o., être le complice de qn; **a'betting**, s. (**aiding and**) a., complicité ƒ.

abeyance [ə'beiəns], s. suspension ƒ (d'une loi); the matter is still in a., la question est toujours en suspens.

abhor [əb'hɔːr], *v.tr.* détester; avoir (qn, qch.) en horreur; **ab'horrent**, a. to be a. to s.o., répugner à qn.

abide [ə'baid]. **1.** *v.i.* to a. by a promise, tenir sa promesse. **2.** *v.tr.* I can't a. him, je ne peux pas le sentir.

ability [ə'biliti], s. **1.** capacité ƒ, pouvoir m (de faire qch.). **2.** habileté ƒ, capacité ƒ; intelligence ƒ; to do sth. to the best of one's a., faire qch. de son mieux; a man of great a., un homme très doué.

abject ['æbdʒekt], a. **1.** abject; misérable. **2.** (*a*) bas, vil; (*b*) servile; -ly, *adv.* misérablement.

ablaze [ə'bleiz], *adv. & a.* en feu, en flammes; to be a., flamber; a. with anger, fou de colère.

able ['eibl], a. **1.** (*a*) capable, compétent, habile; *Nau:* a. seaman, matelot m de deuxième classe; (*b*) to be a. to do sth., (i) savoir, être capable de, faire qch.; (ii) (*as infinitive to the vb.* CAN) pouvoir, être à même de, être en état de, faire qch.; a. to pay, en mesure de payer. **2.** a. piece of work, (i) œuvre ƒ de talent; (ii) travail bien fait; **'able-'bodied**, a. (homme) fort, robuste; **'ably**, *adv.* habilement; avec talent.

ablutions [ə'bluːʃənz], *s.pl.* ablutions ƒ.

abnormal [æb'nɔːməl, əb-], a. anormal, -aux; -ally, *adv.* anormalement; **abnor'mality**, s. (i) anomalie ƒ; (ii) difformité ƒ; bizarrerie ƒ.

aboard [ə'bɔːd]. **1.** *adv.* à bord; to go a., monter à bord; s'embarquer. **2.** *prep.* a. (*a*) ship, à bord

A:1

d'un navire.

abode [ə'boud], *s. Lit. & Hum:* maison *f; Jur:* **of no fixed a.,** sans domicile fixe.

abolish [ə'bɔliʃ], *v.tr.* abolir, supprimer (un droit, un abus); abroger (une loi); **abo'lition,** *s.* abolition *f;* suppression *f.*

abominable [ə'bɔminəbl], *a.* abominable; odieux; **-ably,** *adv.* abominablement.

abominate [ə'bɔmineit], *v.tr.* abominer; avoir (qch.) en horreur; **abomi'nation,** *s.* abomination *f.*

aborigine [æbə'ridʒini:], *s.* aborigène *mf;* **abo'riginal,** *a.* aborigène.

abortion [ə'bɔ:ʃ(ə)n], *s.* 1. avortement *m.* 2. *F:* œuvre mal venue, manquée; **a'bort,** *v.tr.* faire avorter (un projet); **a'bortive,** *a.* avorté, manqué.

abound [ə'baund], *v.i.* abonder (**in, with,** en), affluer; foisonner.

about [ə'baut], *adv. & prep.* 1. (*a*) autour (de); (*b*) de côté et d'autre; **don't leave those papers lying a.,** ne laissez pas traîner ces papiers; **there's a great deal of flu a.,** il y a beaucoup de grippe actuellement; (*c*) **there's sth. unusual a. him,** il y a chez lui quelque chose d'inhabituel; (*d*) **to do sth. turn (and turn) a.,** faire qch. à tour de rôle. 2. *Nau:* **ready a.!** pare à virer! *Mil:* **a. turn!** demi-tour! 3. environ, presque; **there are a. thirty,** il y en a une trentaine; **that's a. right,** c'est à peu près cela; **it's a. time,** (i) il est presque temps; (ii) *Iron:* il est grand temps! **he came a. three o'clock,** il est venu vers trois heures. 4. au sujet de; **to enquire a. sth.,** se renseigner sur qch.; **to quarrel a. nothing,** se disputer à propos de rien; **what's it all a.?** de quoi s'agit-il? **to speak a. sth.,** parler de qch.; **what a. my bath?** et mon bain? 5. (*a*) **to be a. to do sth.,** être sur le point de faire qch.; (*b*) **this is how I go a. it,** voici comment je m'y prends; **you haven't been long a. it,** il ne vous a pas fallu longtemps (pour le faire); **while you are a. it,** pendant que vous y êtes.

above [ə'bʌv], *adv. & prep.* 1. au-dessus (de); (*a*) **the water reached a. their knees,** l'eau leur montait jusqu'au-dessus des genoux; (*b*) **to hover a. the town,** planer au-dessus de la ville; **a voice from a.,** une voix d'en haut; **view from a.,** vue plongeante; (*c*) **his voice was heard a. the din,** on entendait sa voix par-dessus le tumulte; **the Seine a. Paris,** la Seine en amont de Paris; (*d*) **he is a. me in rank,** il est mon supérieur hiérarchique; **you must show yourself a. prejudice,** il faut être au-dessus des préjugés; **to live a. one's means,** vivre au-delà de ses moyens; **a. all . . .,** surtout . . ., pardessus tout . . .. 2. (*in book*) **see paragraph a.,** voir le paragraphe ci-dessus; **as a.,** comme ci-dessus. 3. (*of pers.*) **to be a. (all) suspicion,** être au-dessus de tout soupçon; **a'bove-'board,**

a. loyal, franc; **his conduct was a.-b.,** sa conduite a été franche et ouverte; **a'bove-'mentioned, a'bove-'named,** *a.* susmentionné, susnommé, susdit.

abrasion [ə'breiʒ(ə)n], *s.* (*a*) (usure *f* par le) frottement; (*b*) *Med:* éraflure *f* (de la peau); **a'brasive,** *a.* abrasif, -ive.

abreast [ə'brest], *adv.* (*a*) de front; sur la même ligne; (*b*) (*of pers.*) **to walk a.,** marcher côte à côte; **to be a. of the times,** être de son temps; **to keep wages a. of the cost of living,** maintenir les salaires au niveau du coût de la vie.

abridge [ə'bridʒ], *v.tr.* abréger (un ouvrage); raccourcir (un chapitre); **abridged edition,** édition réduite; **a'bridg(e)ment,** *s.* raccourcissement *m;* abrégé *m.*

abroad [ə'brɔ:d], *adv.* 1. à l'étranger; **to live a.,** vivre à l'étranger; **to return from a.,** revenir de l'étranger. 2. au loin; **scattered a.,** éparpillé de tous côtés; **the news got a.,** la nouvelle s'est répandue.

abrupt [ə'brʌpt], *a.* (départ, caractère) brusque; (départ) brusqué, précipité; (ton) cassant; (style) heurté, saccadé; **-ly,** *adv.* brusquement; **a'bruptness,** *s.* brusquerie *f;* précipitation *f* (d'un départ).

abscess ['æbses, -iz], *s.* abcès *m.*

abscond [əb'skɔnd], *v.i.* se soustraire à la justice; s'enfuir, s'évader (**from,** de) décamper, déguerpir. *F:* filer.

absence ['æbs(ə)ns], *s.* 1. absence *f; Jur:* **sentenced in (his, her) a.,** condamné(e) par contumace. 2. **in the a. of information,** faute de, à défaut de, renseignements. 3. **a. of mind,** distraction *f.*

absent. 1. *a.* ['æbs(ə)nt], (*a*) absent; (*b*) manquant. II. *v.pr.* [æb'sent], **to a. oneself,** s'absenter; **absen'tee,** *s.* absent; -ente manquant, -ante (à l'appel); **absen'teeism,** *s.* absentéisme *m;* **'absent-'minded,** *a.* distrait; **-ly,** *adv.* distraitement; d'un air distrait. **'absent-'mindedness,** *s.* distraction *f.*

absolute ['æbsəl(j)u:t], *a.* (*a*) absolu; **a. power,** pouvoir absolu, illimité; **a. majority,** majorité absolue; (*b*) *F:* **he's an a. idiot,** c'est un parfait imbécile; **it's an a. scandal,** c'est un véritable scandale; **-ly,** *adv.* absolument; **you're a. right!** vous avez complètement raison!

absolution [æbsə'l(j)u:ʃ(ə)n], *s. Ecc:* absolution *f.*

absolve [əb'zɔlv], *v.tr.* 1. absoudre (**s.o. of a sin,** qn d'un péché). 2. affranchir (**s.o. from a vow,** qn d'un vœu).

absorb [əb'sɔ:b], *v.tr.* 1. (*a*) absorber (un liquide); (*b*) **to a. a shock,** amortir un choc. 2. **he was absorbed in his business,** ses affaires l'absorbaient; **ab'sorbent,** *a. & s.* absorbant (*m*); **ab'sorber,** *s. Aut:* **shock a.,** amortisseur *m.*

absorption [əb'sɔ:pʃ(ə)n, əb'zɔ:-], *s.* 1. absorption *f* (de chaleur). 2. **a. (of sounds, of shocks)**, amortissement *m* (de sons, de chocs).

abstain [əb'stein], *v.i.* s'abstenir (**from sth.**, de qch.).

abstemious [əb'sti:miəs], *a.* sobre, tempérant; **-ly**, *adv.* sobrement; frugalement; **ab'stemiousness**, *s.* sobriété *f*, tempérance *f*; abstinence *f*.

abstention [əb'stenʃ(ə)n], *s.* abstention *f*, abstinence *f* (**from**, de).

abstinence ['æbstinəns], *s.* abstinence *f* (**from**, de).

abstract. I. *a. & s.* ['æbstrækt], abstrait (*m*); **a. painting**, peinture abstraite. **II.** *s.* ['æbstrækt], résumé *m*; abrégé *m*, précis *m*; **the a. of an account**, le relevé d'un compte. **III.** *v.tr.* [æb'strækt]. 1. soustraire, dérober, voler (**sth. from s.o.**, qch. à qn); détourner (de l'argent); soustraire (des documents). 2. *Ch: Ind:* extraire (par distillation); **ab'stracted**, *a.* distrait; rêveur, -euse; **-ly**, *adv.* distraitement; **ab'straction**, *s.* 1. soustraction *f.* 2. idée abstraite; abstraction *f*.

abstruse [æb'stru:s], *a.* abstrus.

absurd [əb'sɔ:d], *a.* absurde; déraisonnable; **it's a.!** *F:* c'est idiot! **-ly**, *adv.* absurdement; **ab'surdity**, *s.* absurdité *f*.

abundant [ə'bʌndənt], *a.* abondant; copieux; **-ly**, *adv.* abondamment; copieusement; en abondance; **a'bundance**, *s.* abondance *f*, affluence *f*.

abuse. I. *s.* [ə'bju:s]. 1. (*a*) abus *m*; (*b*) **to remedy an a.**, redresser un abus; (*c*) emploi abusif (d'un terme). 2. insultes *fpl*, injures *fpl*. **II.** *v.tr.* [ə'bju:z]. 1. abuser de (son autorité, la confiance de qn). 2. (*a*) médire de (qn); dénigrer (qn); (*b*) injurier (qn); dire des injures à (qn); **a'busive**, *a.* 1. (emploi) abusif d'un mot). 2. (propos) injurieux; (homme) grossier; **-ly**, *adv.* 1. abusivement. 2. injurieusement; grossièrement.

abysmal [ə'bizm(ə)l], *a.* sans fond; insondable; **a. ignorance**, ignorance profonde.

abyss, *pl.* **-es** [ə'bis, -iz], *s.* abîme *m*; gouffre *m*.

Abyssinia [æbi'siniə]. *Pr.n. Geog:* l'Ethiopie *f*; l'Abyssinie *f*; **Aby'ssinian**, *a. & s.* éthiopien, -ienne, abyssinien, -ienne.

acacia [ə'keiʃə], *s. Bot:* acacia *m*.

academic [ækə'demik], *a.* académique; (*a*) **a. discussion**, discussion abstraite; **the question is a.**, cela n'a aucun intérêt pratique; **out of purely a. interest**, par simple curiosité; (*b*) **a. career**, carrière *f* universitaire; **-ally**, *adv.* académiquement.

academy [ə'kædəmi], *s.* académie *f*; *esp. Scot: Sch:* = lycée *m*; **the Royal A. (of Arts)**, l'Académie royale des Beaux-Arts (de Londres), = le Salon; **a. of music**, conservatoire *m*;

military a., école *f* militaire; **fencing a.**, salle *f* d'escrime; **acade'mician**, *s.* académicien, -ienne.

accede [æk'si:d], *v.i.* 1. **to a. to the throne**, monter sur le trône. 2. **to a. to a request**, accueillir une demande.

accelerate [æk'seləreit]. 1. *v.tr.* accélérer (la marche, un travail); précipiter (les événements); activer (un travail). 2. *v.i. Aut:* accélérer; (*of motion*) s'accélérer; **accele'ration**, *s.* accélération *f*; **ac'celerator**, *s.* accélérateur *m*.

accent. I. *s.* ['æksənt], accent *m*. 1. **to have a German a.**, avoir l'accent allemand. 2. (*a*) *Gram:* accent; (*b*) **fashion with the a. on youth**, mode qui met l'accent sur la jeunesse. **II.** *v.tr.* [æk'sent], accentuer (une syllabe, une voyelle); appuyer sur (une syllabe); **he accented his speech with taps on the table**, il accentuait son discours en tapant sur la table.

accentuate [æk'sentjueit], *v.tr.* accentuer, appuyer sur (un détail); **accentu'ation**, *s.* accentuation *f*.

accept [ək'sept], *v.tr. & ind.tr.* accepter (un cadeau); agréer (les prières de qn); admettre (les excuses de qn); **the accepted custom**, l'usage admis; **accepted opinion**, idées reçues, l'opinion courante; **ac'ceptable**, *a.* acceptable, agréable (**to**, à); **ac'ceptance**, *s.* acceptation *f*; accueil *m* favorable (à qch.); réception *f* (d'un article commandé); **accep'tation**, *s.* acception *f*, signification *f* (d'un mot).

access ['ækses], *s.* 1. accès *m*, abord *m*; **difficult of a.**, d'un accès difficile; **easy of a.**, abordable; **a. road**, route *f* d'accès; **to have a. to s.o.**, avoir accès auprès de qn; avoir ses entrées chez qn. 2. **a. of fever, of rage**, accès de fièvre, de colère; **ac'cessible**, *a.* (endroit) accessible; (*of pers.*) abordable, accueillant.

accession [ək'seʃ(ə)n, æk-], *s.* **a. to power**, accession *f* au pouvoir; **a. to the throne**, avènement *m* au trône; (*in library*) **accessions**, additions *f* (à la bibliothèque).

accessory [æk'sesəri]. 1. *a.* accessoire, subsidiaire (**to**, à). 2. *s.* accessoire *m* (d'une machine); article *m* d'équipement. 3. *s. & a.* **a. to a crime**, complice *mf* d'un crime.

accident ['æksid(ə)nt], *s.* (*a*) accident *m*; **by a.**, accidentellement; **by a pure a.**, par pur hasard; (*b*) **serious a.**, accident grave; **fatal a.**, accident mortel; fatalité *f*; **the victims of an a.**, les accidentés *m*; **a. insurance**, assurance-accident *f*; **acci'dental**, (*a*) *a.* accidentel, fortuit; **a. meeting**, rencontre *f* de hasard; (*b*) *s. Mus:* accident *m*; **-ally**, *adv.* accidentellement; par hasard.

acclaim [ə'kleim], *v.tr.* acclamer; **accla'mation**, *s.* acclamation *f*.

acclimatize [ə'klaimətaiz], *v.tr.* acclimater; **to**

become acclimatized, s'acclimater; acclimati'zation, s. acclimatation f.

accommodate [ə'kɔmədeit], v.tr. 1. (a) accommoder; to a. oneself to circumstances, s'accommoder, se conformer, s'adapter, aux circonstances; (b) ajuster, adapter (qch. à qch.). 2. to a. s.o., accommoder, servir, obliger, qn. 3. loger, recevoir (tant de personnes); a'ccommodating, a. (of pers.) complaisant, serviable, accommodant; peu difficile (with regard to, sur); Pej: (of morals) facile; accommo'dation, s. (a) accommodement m, adaptation f (to, à); règlement m (d'une dispute); to come to an a., arriver à un compromis; s'arranger (à l'amiable); (b) logement m; we have no sleeping a., nous n'avons pas de chambres; N.Am: did you have good accommodations in France? étiez-vous bien logés en France?

accompany [ə'kʌmp(ə)ni], v.tr. 1. accompagner; to be accompanied by s.o., être accompagné de qn. 2. Mus: to a. s.o. on the piano, accompagner qn au piano; a'ccompaniment, s. accompagnement m; a'ccompanist, s. Mus: accompagnateur, -trice.

accomplice [ə'kʌmplis, -'kɔm-], s. complice mf.

accomplish [ə'kʌmpliʃ, -'kɔm-], v.tr. accomplir, exécuter, venir à bout de (qch.); to a. one's object, atteindre son but; a'ccomplished, a. (a) (musicien) accompli, achevé; a. fact, fait accompli; (b) he's very a., il est très doué; a'ccomplishment, s. 1. accomplissement m (d'une tâche). 2. usu.pl. talents m d'agrément.

accord [ə'kɔːd], s. 1. accord m, consentement m; with one a., d'un commun accord. 2. to do sth. of one's own a., faire qch. de son plein gré; a'ccordance, s. accord m; in a. with your instructions, conformément à vos ordres; in a. with truth, conforme à la vérité; a'ccording, adv. 1. conj.phr. a. as, selon que, suivant que, + ind. 2. prep.phr. (a) a. to the orders, selon les ordres; a. to age, par rang d'âge; (b) a. to him, d'après lui; à l'en croire; a. to that, d'après cela; -ly, adv. 1. to act a., agir en conséquence. 2. en conséquence, donc; a. I wrote to him, je lui ai donc écrit.

accordion [ə'kɔːdiən], s. accordéon m.

accost [ə'kɔst], v.tr. accoster, aborder (qn, un navire).

account [ə'kaunt]. I. s. 1. (a) compte m, note f; current a., compte courant; my bank a., mon compte en banque; the accounts (of a firm), la comptabilite (d'une entreprise); to keep the accounts, tenir les livres, les comptes; to pay a sum on a., payer un acompte, verser des arrhes; to have an a., N.Am: a charge a., with s.o., avoir un compte chez qn; expense a., indemnité f pour frais professionnels; (b) exposé m; a. of expenses, note de frais; (c) to turn sth. to a., tirer

parti de qch.; profiter de qch.; (d) to call s.o. to a., demander une explication à qn; he gave a good a. of himself, il s'en est bien tiré. 2. (a) (person) of some a., (personne) qui compte; to be of some a., être (tenu) en grande estime; to take sth. into a., tenir compte de qch.; (b) on a. of s.o., à cause de qn; I was nervous on his a., j'avais peur pour lui; on a. of sth., à cause de qch.; on every a., sous tous les rapports; on no a., not on any a., dans aucun cas, pour rien au monde; (c) to act on one's own a., agir de sa propre initiative. 3. to give an a. of sth., faire le récit de qch.; by all accounts, au dire de tout le monde. II. v.tr. & ind.tr. 1. to a. oneself lucky, s'estimer heureux. 2. (a) to a. for sth., rendre raison de (sa conduite); expliquer (une circonstance); (b) I can't a. for it, je n'y comprends rien; there's no accounting for tastes, chacun son goût; a'ccountable, a. responsable (for, de, to, envers); (être) redevable (d'une somme); a'ccountancy, s. (a) comptabilité f; (b) profession f de comptable; tenue f des livres; a'ccountant, s. comptable m; chartered a. = expert-comptable m; a'ccounting, s. comptabilité f.

accredit [ə'kredit], v.tr. accréditer (qn, qch.); to a. an ambassador (to a government), accréditer un ambassadeur (auprès d'un gouvernement); a'ccredited, a. (of pers.) autorisé.

accumulate [ə'kjuːmjuleit]. 1. v.tr. accumuler, amasser (une fortune, etc.). 2. v.i. s'accumuler, s'amonceler, s'entasser; accumu'lation, s. accumulation f, amoncellement m; amas m, monceau m, tas m; a'ccumulator, s. El: accumulateur m, F: accu m.

accurate ['ækjurit], a. exact, juste, précis; to take a. aim, viser juste; (traduction, dessin) fidèle; -ly, adv. exactement, avec précision; 'accuracy, s. exactitude f; précision f.

accuse [ə'kjuːz], v.tr. accuser (s.o. of sth., qn de qch.); accu'sation, s. accusation f; a'ccusative, a. & s. Gram: accusatif (m); a'ccused, s. Jur: the a., le, la, prévenu(e); a'ccuser, s. accusateur; -trice; -ly, adv. d'une manière accusatrice.

accustom [ə'kʌstəm], v.tr. accoutumer habituer (s.o. to sth., qn à qch.); to a. oneself to discipline, se faire à la discipline; a'ccustomed, a. 1. to be a. to sth., to doing sth., être accoutumé à qch., être habitué à faire qch.; to get a. to sth., to doing sth., s'accoutumer à qch., se faire à qch.; s'habituer à faire qch. 2. habituel, coutumier; d'usage; the long-a. journey, le voyage familier.

ace [eis], s. 1. (of cards, etc.) as m. 2. Sp: etc: a driver, as du volant.

acerbity [ə'səːbiti], s. acerbité f.

acetate ['æsiteit], s. Ch: acétate m; Ind

cellulose a., acétocellulose *f.*

acetic [ə'si:tik], *a. Ch:* acétique; **a. acid,** acide *m* acétique.

acetylene [ə'setili:n], *s. Ch:* acétylène *m;* **a. welding,** soudure *f* autogène.

ache [eik]. I. *s.* mal *m,* douleur *f;* **stomach a.,** mal de ventre; **I have a stomach a.,** j'ai mal au ventre. II. *v.i.* **my head, back, aches,** j'ai mal à la tête, au dos; **it makes my heart a.,** cela me serre le cœur; **'aching,** *a.* douloureux, endolori; **an a. tooth,** une dent malade.

achieve [ə'tʃi:v], *v.tr.* 1. accomplir (un exploit); réaliser (une entreprise). 2. acquérir (de l'honneur). 3. atteindre (un but); **to a. victory,** remporter la victoire; **he'll never a. anything,** il n'arrivera jamais à rien; **a'chievement,** *s.* 1. accomplissement *m,* réalisation *f* (d'un projet, d'une ambition). 2. exploit *m,* chose *f* accomplie.

acid ['æsid]. 1. *a.* (*a*) acide; **a. drops,** bonbons acidulés; (*b*) (*of character, expression*) revêche, aigre. 2. *s.* acide *m;* **a'cidity,** *s.* acidité *f;* aigreur *f* (d'une réponse).

acknowledge [ək'nɔlidʒ], *v.tr.* 1. reconnaître, avouer (qch.); reconnaître (qn); **to a. a debt,** reconnaître une dette; **he refused to a. his son,** il a refusé de reconnaître son fils; **to a. oneself beaten,** s'avouer vaincu. 2. répondre à (un salut); **to a. (receipt of) a letter,** accuser réception d'une lettre; **ack'nowledg(e)ment,** *s.* reconnaissance *f* (d'un bienfait); aveu *m* (d'une faute); reçu *m* (d'un paiement); **a. of receipt,** accusé *m* de réception (d'une lettre).

acne ['ækni], *s. Med:* acné *f.*

acorn ['eikɔ:n], *s. Bot:* gland *m* (du chêne).

acoustic [ə'ku:stik]. 1. *a.* acoustique. 2. *s.pl.* **acoustics,** acoustique *f.*

acquaint [ə'kweint], *v.tr.* 1. **to a. s.o. with sth.,** informer qn de qch.; faire savoir qch. à qn; **to a. s.o. with the facts,** mettre qn au courant. 2. (*a*) **to be acquainted with s.o.,** connaître qn; (*b*) **to become acquainted with s.o.,** faire connaissance avec qn; **a'quaintance,** *s.* 1. connaissance (**with,** de); **to make the a. of s.o.,** faire connaissance avec qn. 2. (*pers.*) connaissance; **to have a wide circle of acquaintances,** avoir des relations étendues.

acquiesce [ækwi'es], *v.i.* acquiescer (à une demande); donner son assentiment (**in,** à); **acqui'escence,** *s.* assentiment *m;* **acqui'escent,** *a.* consentant.

acquire [ə'kwaiər], *v.tr.* acquérir (qch.); **to a. a habit,** prendre une habitude.

acquisition [ækwi'ziʃ(ə)n], *s.* acquisition *f;* **a'quisitive,** *a.* âpre au gain.

acquit [ə'kwit], *v.tr.* (**acquitted**) 1. acquitter (un accusé); **to a. s.o. of sth.,** absoudre qn de qch. 2. **to a. oneself of a duty,** s'acquit-

ter d'un devoir; **he acquitted himself well,** il s'en est bien tiré; **a'quittal,** *s.* 1. acquittement *m* (d'un accusé). 2. exécution *f* (d'un devoir).

acre ['eikər], *s. Meas:* acre *f;* **'acreage,** *s.* superficie *f* (en mesures agraires).

acrid ['ækrid], *a.* 1. (goût *m,* fumée *f*) âcre. 2. (style) mordant; (critique) acerbe; **-ly,** *adv.* avec âcreté; avec acerbité; **a'cridity,** *s.* âcreté *f.*

acrimonious [ækri'mouniəs], *a.* acrimonieux, (*esp. of women*) acariâtre; **the discussion became a.,** la discussion s'est envenimée; **-ly,** *adv.* avec acrimonie; **'acrimony,** *s.* acrimonie *f;* aigreur *f.*

acrobat ['ækrəbæt], *s.* acrobate *mf;* **acro'batic,** *a.* acrobatique.

across [ə'krɔs], *adv. & prep.* en travers (de). 1. (*a*) **to walk a. (a street),** traverser (une rue); **to run a.,** traverser en courant; **to go a. a bridge,** franchir, passer (sur), un pont; (*b*) **to lay sth. a. (sth.),** mettre qch. en travers (de qch.); (*c*) **to come, run, a. s.o.,** rencontrer qn (par hasard). 2. (*a*) **the distance a.,** la distance en largeur; **the river is a kilometre a.,** le fleuve a un kilomètre de large; (*b*) **he lives a. the street (from us),** il demeure de l'autre côté de la rue, en face.

act [ækt]. I. *s.* 1. acte *m;* (*a*) **a. of kindness,** acte de bonté; (*b*) **A. of Parliament,** loi *f,* décret *m.* 2. action *f;* **an a. of folly,** une folie; **to catch s.o. in the a.,** prendre qn sur le fait. 3. *Th:* acte (d'une pièce); numéro *m* (dans un cirque). II. *v.* 1. *v.tr.* (*a*) *Th:* jouer (une pièce); **to a. a part,** tenir un rôle; **to a. the fool,** faire l'imbécile; (*b*) **was only acting,** il faisait semblant; (*c*) **to a. the part of an honest man,** agir en honnête homme. 2. *v.i.* agir; (*a*) **I acted for the best,** j'ai fait pour le mieux; **to a. for, on behalf of, s.o.,** agir au nom de qn; représenter qn; **to a. as secretary to s.o.,** servir de secrétaire à qn; **to a. upon advice,** suivre un conseil; (*b*) **the pump is not acting well,** la pompe ne marche pas bien; **the engine acts as a brake,** le moteur fait fonction de frein; (*c*) *Th: Cin:* jouer; **'acting. I.** *a.* suppléant; intérimaire, provisoire. II. *s.* 1. action *f.* 2. (*a*) jeu *m* (d'un acteur); production *f* (d'une pièce de théâtre); (*b*) **to go in for a.,** faire du théâtre; (*c*) **it's only a.,** c'est de la comédie.

action ['ækʃ(ə)n], *s.* 1. action *f* (d'une personne); **to take a.,** agir; **to suit the a. to the word,** joindre le geste à la parole; **to come into a.,** entrer en action, en jeu; **out of a.,** hors de service, détraqué, en panne. 2. (*deed*) action, acte *m,* fait *m.* 3. *Th:* action (d'une pièce). 4. (*a*) action, gestes *mpl* (d'un joueur); (*b*) mécanisme *m* (d'une montre). 5. *Jur:* **a. at law,** procès *m;* **to bring an a. against s.o.,** intenter une action à, contre, qn. 6. action, engagement *m;* **to go into**

a., engager le combat; **killed in a.,** mort au champ d'honneur; **'actionable,** a. *Jur:* poursuivable; (action) qui expose (qn) à des poursuites judiciaires.

active |'æktiv|, a. **1.** actif; agile, alerte; **a. volcano,** volcan *m* en activité; **a. brain,** cerveau éveillé; **a. imagination,** imagination vive. **2. to take an a. part in sth.,** prendre une part active à qch.; *Mil:* **to be on the a. list,** être en activité; **on a. service,** en campagne; **'activate,** *v.tr.* activer; **ac'tivity,** *s.* activité *f*; **the a. of the street,** le mouvement de la rue.

actor |'æktər|, *s.* acteur *m,* comédien *m,* artiste *m.*

actress |'æktris|, *s.* actrice *f,* comédienne *f.*

actual |'æktju(ə)l|, *a.* réel, véritable; **it's an a. fact, an a. case,** c'est un fait positif, un cas concret; **-ally,** *adv.* (*a*) réellement, véritablement, effectivement; **he a. said . . .,** il est allé (même) jusqu'à dire . . .; **actu'ality,** *s.* réalité *f.*

actuate |'æktjueit|, *v.tr.* **1.** mettre en action, actionner (une machine). **2.** animer, faire agir (qn); **actuated by jealousy,** poussé par la jalousie.

acute |ə'kju:t|, *a.* **1.** (angle, accent) aigu. **2.** (douleur) aiguë, intense. **3.** (*a*) **a. ear,** oreille fine, ouïe fine; **a. sight,** vue perçante; (*b*) (esprit) fin, pénétrant; **-ly,** *adv.* vivement; intensément; avec finesse; **a'cute-'angled,** *a.* (triangle *m*) acutangle; **a'cuteness,** *s.* intensité *f* (d'une douleur); finesse *f* (de l'ouïe); acuité *f* (de la vision); perspicacité *f* (de l'esprit).

ad |æd|, *s. F:* (*in newspaper*) annonce *f.*

adamant |'ædəmənt|, *a.* **to be a.,** être inflexible, intransigeant.

adapt |ə'dæpt|, *v.tr.* adapter, ajuster, approprier, accommoder (**sth. to sth.,** qch. à qch.); remanier (une œuvre); **adapta'bility,** *s.* faculté *f* d'adaptation; **a'daptable,** *a.* adaptable, ajustable; **he's very a.,** il s'arrange de tout; **a. mind,** esprit *m* souple; **adap'tation,** *s.* adaptation *f*; **a'dapter, a'daptor,** *s.* **1.** adaptateur *m.* **2.** *El:* raccord *m* (de lampe); *Rec:* centreur *m* (de tourne-disque).

add |æd|. **1.** *v.tr.* (*a*) ajouter, joindre (**to,** à); **added to which . . .,** ajoutez que . . .; (*b*) (*say besides*) ajouter; **he added that . . .,** il ajouta que . . .. **2.** *v.i.* **to a. to s.o.'s difficulties,** ajouter aux embarras de qn; **to a. to a house,** faire une addition à une maison. **3.** *v.tr. Mth:* **to a. (together) ten numbers,** additionner, totaliser, dix chiffres; **'adding machine,** *s.* machine *f* à calculer; **'add 'up,** *v.tr. & i.* additionner (des chiffres); *F:* **it doesn't a. up,** cela n'a ni sens ni raison.

adder |'ædər|, *s.* vipère *f.*

addict |'ædikt|, *s.* **drug a.,** toxicomane *mf*; *Sp: etc: F:* fanatique *mf*; **a'ddicted,** *a.* **a. to drink,**

adonné à la boisson; **a'ddiction,** *s.* manie *f* (pathologique); **drug a.,** toxicomanie *f.*

addition |ə'diʃ(ə)n|, *s.* **1.** addition *f*; **additions to the staff,** adjonction *f*, additions, au personnel; **in a.,** en outre, de plus, par surcroît. **2.** *Mth:* addition; **a'dditional,** *a.* supplémentaire, additionnel; **an a. reason,** une raison de plus; **'additive,** *s.* additif *m*; *Aut: etc:* **anti-carbon a.,** décalaminant *m.*

address |ə'dres|. **I.** *s.* **1.** adresse *f* (d'une lettre); **a. book,** carnet *m,* répertoire *m,* d'adresses. **2.** discours *m,* allocution *f,* conférence *f.* **3. forms of a.,** titres *m* de politesse. **II.** *v.tr.* **1.** (*a*) **to a. a letter to s.o.,** adresser une lettre à qn; (*b*) **to a. a letter,** mettre, écrire, l'adresse sur une lettre. **2. to a. s.o.,** (i) aborder qn; (ii) adresser la parole à qn, à une réunion; **to a. the crowd,** haranguer la foule. **3.** *Golf:* viser (la balle); **addre'ssee,** *s.* destinataire *mf.*

adduce |ə'dju:s|, *v.tr.* alléguer, apporter (des preuves); citer (une autorité).

adenoids |'ædənɔidz|, *s.pl. Med:* végétations *f* (adénoïdes).

adept |'ædept|. **1.** *a.* **to be a. at doing sth.,** être expert, habile, à qch. **2.** *s.* adepte *mf*; expert *m* (**in,** en).

adequate |'ædikwət|, *a.* **1.** suffisant; **a. reward,** juste récompense; **a. help,** aide efficace. **2. he is a. to the task,** il est à la hauteur de la tâche; **-ly** *adv.* suffisamment.

adhere |əd'hiər|, *v.i.* **1.** (*of thg*) adhérer, se coller. **2.** (*of pers.*) (*a*) **to a. to a proposal, to a party** adhérer à une proposition, à un parti; (*b*) **to a. to one's decision,** persister dans sa décision; **to a. to a promise,** tenir une promesse; **ad'herence,** *s.* **1.** (*of thg*) adhérence *f,* adhésion *f* (**to,** à). **2.** (*of pers.*) attachement *m* (**to,** à); **ad'herent,** *a. & s.* adhérent, -ente.

adhesion |əd'hi:ʒ(ə)n|, *s.* **1.** adhésion *f* (**to,** à) accession *f* (à un parti). **2.** *Med:* adhérence *f* *Aut:* **road a.,** adhérence au sol (des pneus) **ad'hesive** [-'hi:z-]. **1.** *a.* adhésif, collant; **a. tape,** ruban adhésif. **2.** *a.* adhérent; *Med:* **a. plaster,** sparadrap *m.* **3.** *s.* adhésif *m,* colle *f.*

adipose |'ædipous|, *a.* adipeux; **a. tissue,** graisse animale.

adjacent |ə'dʒeis(ə)nt|, *a.* (angle, terrain adjacent; attenant; (terrain) avoisinant.

adjective |'ædʒiktiv|, *s. Gram:* adjectif *m* **adjec'tival,** *a.* adjectif; *adv.* **-ally,** adjectivement.

adjoin |ə'dʒɔin|. **1.** *v.tr.* avoisiner (un lieu toucher à, attenir à (qch.). **2.** *v.i.* **the two houses a.,** les deux maisons se touchent **a'djoining,** *a.* (*a*) contigu, -uë; avoisinan (*b*) **the a. room,** la pièce voisine.

adjourn |ə'dʒə:n|. **1.** *v.tr.* ajourner, renvoyer un autre jour. **2.** *v.i.* (*of meeting*) (i) s'ajourne (**until,** à); (ii) lever la séance; **a'djournmen**

s. (a) ajournement m, suspension f (d'une affaire); (b) renvoi m, remise f (d'une séance, etc.).

adjudicate [ə'dʒu:dikeit], v.tr. & i. juger, décider (une affaire); rendre un arrêt; décerner (un prix); **adjudi'cation**, s. jugement m, décision f, arrêt m; a**'djudicator**, s. arbitre m; (in competitions, etc.) membre m du jury.

adjunct ['ædʒʌŋkt], s. accessoire m (of, de); addition f (to, à) (qch.).

adjust [ə'dʒʌst], v.tr. 1. arranger (une affaire); régler (un différend). 2. (a) ajuster (qch. à qch.); **to a. oneself to new conditions,** s'adapter à de nouvelles conditions; (b) régler (une montre); monter (un appareil); (c) ajuster, arranger (son chapeau, etc.); a**'djustable**, a. ajustable; réglable; a**'djustment**, s. ajustement m (d'un différend); réglage m (d'un mécanisme); mise f au point (d'un instrument).

administer [əd'ministər], v.tr. administrer, régir (un pays); gérer (des biens, une affaire); **to a. justice,** dispenser, rendre, la justice; **to a. an oath to s.o.,** assermenter qn; **adminis'tration**, s. (a) administration f, gestion f (d'une affaire, etc.); (b) administration (de la justice, des sacrements); coll. l'administration, les pouvoirs publics; (c) U.S: gouvernement m, ministère m. **ad'ministrative**, a. administratif; **ad'ministrator**, s. administrateur m gestionnaire m.

admiral ['ædm(ə)rəl], s. amiral m, pl. aux; **'Admiralty (the)**, Pr.n. l'Amirauté f, = le Ministère de la Marine.

admire [əd'maiər], v.tr. admirer; **'admirable**, a. admirable; adv. **-ably**, admirablement; **admi'ration**, s. admiration f; **ad'mirer**, s. admirateur, -trice; **ad'miring**, a. (regard) admiratif; **-ly**, adv. avec admiration.

admission [əd'miʃ(ə)n], s. 1. admission f, accès m (à un emploi, une école, etc.); **a. free**, entrée libre. 2. (a) admission, acceptation f (d'une preuve); (b) confession f (d'un crime); aveu m; **ad'missible**, a. (idée f, projet m) admissible; Jur: recevable.

admit [əd'mit], v. (admitted) 1. v.tr. (a) admettre (qn à qch.); laisser entrer (qn); **a. bearer,** laissez passer; (b) admettre (des excuses); reconnaître (sa faute); **to a. one's guilt,** s'avouer coupable. 2. v.ind.tr. **it admits of no doubt,** cela ne permet aucun doute; **ad'mittance,** s. entrée f (to, dans); accès m (to, à, auprès de); **no a.,** entrée interdite· **ad'mitted,** a. a. custom, usage admis; **-ly,** adv. de l'aveu général; **a. incorrect,** reconnu (pour) incorrect.

admonish [əd'mɔniʃ], v.tr. faire une remontrance à (qn); **ad'monishment,** s. **admo'nition,** s. réprimande f, remontrance f.

ado [ə'du:], s. agitation f; bruit m; still used in: **without (any) more a.,** sans plus de façons;

much a. about nothing, beaucoup de bruit pour rien.

adolescence [ædə'les(ə)ns], s. adolescence f; **ado'lescent,** a. & s. adolescent, -ente.

adopt [ə'dɔpt], v.tr. 1. adopter (un enfant). 2. adopter (une ligne de conduite); choisir, embrasser (une carrière); **to a. a patronizing tone,** prendre un ton protecteur; a**'dopted,** a. **a. son,** fils adoptif; a**'doption,** s. adoption f; a**'doptive,** a. (père, enfant) adoptif.

adore [ə'dɔːr], v.tr. adorer (qn, qch.); a**'dorable,** a. adorable; **-ably,** adv. adorablement, à ravir; **ado'ration,** s. adoration f; a**'dorer,** s. adorateur, -trice.

adorn [ə'dɔːn], v.tr. orner, parer (with, de); a**'dornment,** s. ornement m, parure f.

adrenalin [ə'drenəlin], s. adrénaline f.

Adriatic (Sea) (the) [ðiːeidri'ætik('siː)], a. & s. (la mer) Adriatique.

adrift [ə'drift], adv. Nau: à la dérive; **to cast s.o. a.,** (i) abandonner, (ii) renvoyer, qn; mettre qn sur le pavé; **to cut oneself a. from s.o.,** rompre avec qn.

adroit [ə'drɔit], a. adroit; habile; **-ly,** adv. adroitement, habilement; a**'droitness,** s. adresse f, dextérité f.

adulation [ædju'leiʃ(ə)n], s. adulation f.

adult [ə'dʌlt, a. occ. 'ædəlt], a. & s. adulte (mf).

adulterate [ə'dʌltəreit], v.tr. adultérer (une substance, des aliments); frelater (du vin); **adulte'ration,** s. adultération f; frelatage m.

adulterer, f. **-eress** [ə'dʌltərər, -ərəs], s. adultère mf; a**'dultery,** s. adultère m.

advance [əd'vaːns]. I. s. 1. (a) marche f en avant; mouvement m en avant; **to make an a.,** avancer; Mil: **a. guard,** avant-garde f; (b) **to arrive in a.,** arriver en avance; **to pay in a.,** payer d'avance; **to book in a.,** retenir (une place) à l'avance. 2. avancement m, progrès m (des sciences). 3. **to make advances to s.o.,** faire des avances f à qn, des démarches f auprès de qn; (of a woman) provoquer, F: aguicher (un homme). 4. Com: (a) avance de fonds; **a. on securities,** prêt m sur titres; (b) augmentation f (de prix); hausse f; (c) (at auction sale) **any a.?** qui dit mieux? II. v. 1. v.tr. (a) avancer (le pied); (b) avancer (l'heure d'un paiement, etc.); (c) avancer (une opinion); (d) faire avancer, progresser (les sciences); (e) augmenter, hausser (les prix); **to a. s.o. money,** avancer de l'argent à qn. 2. v.i. s'avancer **(towards,** vers); (a) **the work is advancing,** le travail avance, fait des progrès; (of civil servants, etc.) recevoir de l'avancement; **ad'vanced,** a. (a) (poste) avancé; (opinions) avancées; (b) **a. mathematics,** mathématiques supérieures; (c) **the season is (well) a.,** c'est la fin de la saison; **ad'vancement,** s. avancement m (d'une carrière); progrès m (de la science).

advantage [əd'vɑ:ntidʒ], s. avantage m; **to take a. of sth., s.o.,** profiter de qch.; exploiter qn; **to turn sth. to a.,** tirer parti de qch.; **to show sth. off. to a.,** faire valoir qch.; **advan'tageous,** a. avantageux (**to,** pour); profitable; utile; **-ly,** adv. avantageusement; utilement.

advent ['ædvənt], s. 1. Ecc: avent m. 2. arrivée f; venue f.

adventure [əd'ventʃər], s. aventure f; entreprise hasardeuse; **ad'venturer,** s. (in all senses) aventurier m; **ad'venturous,** a. aventureux, audacieux; (homme) téméraire, hardi; **an a. life,** une vie aventureuse; **an a. plan,** un projet hasardeux, risqué.

adverb ['ædvə:b], s. Gram: adverbe m.

adversary ['ædvəs(ə)ri], s. adversaire mf.

adverse ['ædvə:s], a. adverse; (a) contraire, opposé (à une politique, etc.); **a. wind,** vent contraire; (b) ennemi (**to,** de); hostile (**to,** à, envers); (c) défavorable; **-ly,** adv. **to influence s.o. a.,** exercer une influence défavorable sur qn; **ad'versity,** s. adversité f, infortune f; (période f de) mauvaise fortune.

advert ['ædvə:t], s. F: (in newspaper) annonce f.

advertise ['ædvətaiz], v.tr. & i. faire de la réclame, de la publicité, pour (un produit, un événement, etc.); F: **you needn't a. the fact,** vous n'avez pas besoin de le crier sur les toits; **ad'vertisement,** s. publicité f; annonce f; affiche f; **'advertiser,** s. auteur m d'une annonce, annonceur m; **'advertising,** s. (i) (métier m de la) publicité; (ii) réclame f; **a. agency,** agence f de publicité.

advice [əd'vais], s. (no pl.) (a) conseil(s) m(pl), avis m; **piece of a.,** conseil; **to ask for a.,** demander conseil; (b) Com: avis.

advise [əd'vaiz], v.tr. (a) **to a. s.o.,** conseiller qn; **to a. s.o. to do sth.,** conseiller à qn de faire qch.; (b) **to a. sth.,** recommander qch. (à qn); (c) **to a. against sth.,** déconseiller qch.; **ad'visable,** a. (démarche f) recommandable, à conseiller; **it might be a. to . . .,** peut-être conviendrait-il de . . .; **ad'visedly,** adv. à dessein; en connaissance de cause; **ad'viser,** s. conseiller, -ère; **ad'visory,** a. consultatif.

advocacy ['ædvəkəsi], s. **a. of a cause,** appui donné à une cause.

advocate. I. s. ['ædvəkət], avocat m; défenseur m (d'une cause). II. v.tr. ['ædvəkeit], préconiser, recommander; plaider en faveur de (qch.).

Aegean [i(:)'dʒi:ən], a. & s. Geog: (la mer) Égée.

aegis ['i:dʒis], s. **under the a. of,** sous l'égide de.

aerial ['ɛəriəl]. 1. a. aérien. 2. s. Rad: antenne f.

aero- ['ɛərou-]. pref. aérien, de l'air; used in **'aerodrome,** s. aérodrome m; **'aerody'namics,** s.pl. aérodynamique f; **'aeronaut,** s. aéronaute m; **'aero'nautics,** s.pl.

aéronautique f; **'aeroplane,** s. avion m; **'aerosol,** s. aérosol m.

aesthetic [i:s'θetik], a. esthétique.

afar [ə'fɑ:r], adv. **from a.,** de loin.

affable ['æfəbl], a. affable, courtois (**to,** envers); **-ably,** adv. avec affabilité; **affa'bility,** s. affabilité f, courtoisie f.

affair [ə'fɛər], s. affaire f; **that is my a.,** ça, c'est mon affaire; **his affairs are in disorder,** ses affaires sont en désordre; (love-)**a.,** intrigue (amoureuse, galante); **in the present state of affairs,** du train où vont les choses; F: **what a terrible a.!** en voilà du propre!

affect[1] [ə'fekt], v.tr. (a) affecter (une manière); **to a. generosity,** faire parade de générosité; (b) simuler (la piété); **to a. stupidity,** faire l'idiot; **a'ffected**[1], a. (a) affecté, maniéré; (b) simulé; **-ly,** adv. avec affectation; **affec'tation,** s. **a'ffectedness,** s. affectation f.

affect[2], v.tr. 1. atteindre, toucher; attaquer (qn); affecter (un organe); influer sur (qch.); **the climate has affected his health,** le climat a altéré sa santé; **it affects me personally,** cela me touche personnellement. 2. affecter, affliger, toucher (qn); **nothing affects him,** rien ne le touche, ne l'émeut. 3. toucher, concerner (qn, qch.); **that does not a. the matter,** cela ne fait rien à l'affaire; **a'ffected**[2], a. (a) atteint (d'une maladie); (b) ému, touché; **a'ffecting,** a. touchant, attendrissant; **a'ffection,** s. (a) affection f, attachement m; tendresse f; amitié f; (b) Med: affection, maladie f (du cœur, du foie); **a'ffectionate,** a. affectueux; **-ly,** adv. affectueusement.

affidavit [æfi'deivit], s. Jur: déclaration f par écrit et sous serment.

affiliate [ə'filieit], v.tr. affilier (un membre à une société); s'affilier (à une société); **affiliate company,** filiale f; **affili'ation,** s. affiliation (à une société); **political affiliations,** attaches politiques.

affinity [ə'finiti], s. (a) affinité f; (b) conformité de caractère.

affirm [ə'fə:m], v.tr. 1. affirmer, soutenir (that que). 2. Jur: confirmer, homologuer (un jugement); **affir'mation,** s. affirmation f; Jur: confirmation f (d'un jugement); **a'ffirmative** 1. a. affirmatif. 2. s. **the answer is in the a.,** la réponse est oui; **-ly,** adv. affirmativement.

afflict [ə'flikt], v.tr. affliger; désoler; tourmenter (qn); **a'ffliction,** s. affliction f; calamité f.

affluence ['æfluəns], s. abondance f, richesse f; **'affluent,** a. opulent; riche; **in a. circumstances,** très à l'aise.

afford [ə'fɔ:d], v.tr. (usu. with can) (a) avoir les moyens (de faire qch.); être en mesure (de faire qch.); **I can't a. it,** mes moyens ne me permettent pas; c'est trop cher pour moi; **I can a. to wait,** je peux attendre.

afforestation [əfɔris'teiʃ(ə)n], s. (a) boisement m, afforestation f; (b) reboisement m.

affront [ə'frʌnt], s. affront m, offense f.

Afghanistan [æfgænis'tɑ:n]. Pr.n. Geog: l'Afghanistan m.

afield [ə'fiːld], adv. to go far a., aller très loin.

afloat [ə'flout], adv. & a. à flot; sur l'eau; to keep a ship a., maintenir un navire à flot; (of pers.) to keep a., surnager.

afoot [ə'fut], adv. a plan is a. to . . ., on envisage un projet pour . . .; there's something a., il se prépare quelque chose.

afraid [ə'freid], a. effrayé; to be a., avoir peur (of sth., de qch.); craindre (qch.); don't be a., n'ayez pas peur; to make s.o. a., faire peur à qn; effrayer qn; I was a. of offending him, j'avais peur de l'offenser; I am a. he will die, je crains qu'il ne meure; I'm a. it's so! j'en ai (bien) peur! I'm a. he's out, je regrette, mais il est sorti; I'm a. it's true, je crains bien que ce ne soit que trop vrai.

afresh [ə'freʃ], adv. de nouveau, à nouveau.

Africa ['æfrikə]. Pr.n. Geog: l'Afrique f.

African ['æfrikən], a. & s. africain, -aine.

aft [ɑ:ft], adv. Nau: sur, à, vers, l'arrière (d'un navire).

after ['ɑ:ftər]. I. adv. après. 1. (place, order) to come a., venir après, venir à la suite (de qn, qch.); you speak first, I'll speak a., parlez d'abord, je parlerai ensuite. 2. (time) I never spoke to him a., je ne lui ai plus jamais parlé; I heard of it a., je l'ai appris plus tard; the week a., la semaine d'après; the day a., le lendemain. II. prep. après. 1. (place) (a) to walk a. s.o., marcher après qn; (b) to run a. s.o., courir après qn; the police are a. you, la police est à vos trousses; what's he a.? (i) qu'est-ce qu'il a en tête? (ii) qu'est-ce qu'il cherche? I see what you're a., je vois où vous voulez en venir. 2. (time) on and a. the 15th, à partir du quinze; a. hours, après le travail, la fermeture; the day a. tomorrow, après-demain; a. all, après tout, enfin; it is a. five (o'clock), il est cinq heures passées; N.Am: half a. five, cinq heures et demie; he read page a. page, il lut page sur page. 3. (order) a. you, sir, après vous, monsieur. 4. (manner) a. a pattern, d'après, suivant, un modèle. III. conj. après que + ind.; I come a. he goes, je viens après qu'il est parti; 'after(-)care, s. surveillance f (i) des convalescents; (ii) de délinquants juvéniles; 'after-effect(s), s.(pl.), suites fpl, contrecoup m, répercussion f (d'un évènement); séquelles fpl (d'une maladie); 'aftermath, s. 1. Agr: regain m. 2. suites fpl, répercussion f (d'un événement); 'after'noon, s. après-midi m inv; good a.! bonjour! 'afters, s.pl. Cu: F: dessert m; 'afterthought, s. réflexion f après coup; 'afterwards, adv. après, plus tard, ensuite.

again [ə'gein, -'gen], adv., often rendered by a vb. with the pref. re-: to begin a., recommencer; to do (sth.) a., refaire (qch.); to come down, up, a., redescendre, remonter. 1. (a) de nouveau, encore; once a., encore une fois; here we are a.! F: nous revoilà! don't do it a.! ne recommencez pas! a. and a., à plusieurs reprises; now and a., de temps en temps; as large a., deux fois aussi grand; (b) (back) to send sth. back a., renvoyer qch.; to come a., revenir; F: come a.? pardon? 2. (a) de plus, d'ailleurs, en outre; (b) (then) a., (and) a., d'autre part.

against [ə'geinst, -'gen-], prep. contre. 1. I have nothing to say a. that, je n'ai rien à redire à cela; I did it a. my will, je l'ai fait à contrecœur; a. the rules, contraire aux règlements; warned a. s.o., mis en garde contre qn; F: to run up a. s.o., rencontrer qn par hasard; leaning a. the wall, appuyé contre le mur; to go a. nature, aller à l'encontre de la nature. 2. (a) my rights (as) a. the Government, mes droits vis-à-vis du Gouvernement; (b) over a. the school, en face de l'école. 3. to show up a. a background, se détacher sur un fond.

agate ['ægət], s. agate f.

age [eidʒ]. I. s. 1. âge m; (a) middle a., âge mûr; to be past middle a., être sur le retour; what a. are you? quel âge avez-vous? to be under a., être mineur; to come of a., atteindre sa majorité; to be of an a. to marry, être en âge de se marier; (b) (old) a., vieillesse f: retirement a., l'âge de la retraite; a. limit, limite f d'âge; to come into the 15–20 a. group, faire partie du groupe des 15 à 20 ans. 2. (a) âge, époque f, siècle m; Hist: the Middle Ages, le moyen âge; the atomic a., l'ère f atomique; (b) F: it's ages since I saw him, I haven't seen him for ages, il y a une éternité que je ne l'ai vu. II. v. 1. v.i. vieillir; prendre de l'âge. 2. v.tr. vieillir; rendre (qn) vieux; aged, a. 1. ['eidʒid], âgé, vieux. 2. [eidʒd], (a) a. twenty years, âgé de vingt ans; (b) I found him greatly a., je l'ai trouvé bien vieilli; 'ageing, a. & s. 1. a. vieillissant. 2. s. vieillissement m.

agency ['eidʒənsi], s. 1. (a) action f, opération f; through the a. of water, par l'action de l'eau; (b) agent m; natural agencies, agents naturels; (c) entremise f. 2. Com: agence f, bureau m; travel a., agence de voyage.

agenda [ə'dʒendə], s. ordre m du jour; programme m (d'une réunion).

agent ['eidʒənt], s. (a) agent m; to be a free a., avoir son libre arbitre; (b) Com: agent; représentant m; (c) secret a., agent secret.

agglomeration [əgləmə'reiʃ(ə)n], s. agglomération f.

aggravate ['ægrəveit], v.tr. 1. (a) aggraver (une faute); envenimer (une querelle); (b) augmenter (l'indignation, la douleur). 2. *F:* agacer, exaspérer (qn); **'aggravating**, *a.* (*a*) **a. circumstances**, circonstances aggravantes; (*b*) *F:* exaspérant, agaçant; **aggra'vation**, *s.* (*a*) aggravation *f*; envenimement *m* (d'une querelle); (*b*) *F:* agacement *m*, exaspération *f*.

aggregate ['ægrigət]. 1. *a. Ind:* **a. output**, rendement global. 2. *s.* ensemble *m*, total *m*; **in the a.**, en somme, dans l'ensemble.

aggression [ə'greʃ(ə)n], *s.* agression *f*; **a'ggressive**, *a.* agressif; **-ly**, *adv.* d'une manière agressive, d'un ton agressif; **a'ggressor**, *s.* agresseur *m*.

aggrieved [ə'gri:vd], *a.* chagriné; blessé; **to be a.**, to feel (oneself) a., se sentir lésé.

aghast [ə'gɑ:st], *a.* consterné (**at, de**); sidéré.

agile ['ædʒail], *a.* agile, leste; **a'gility** [-'dʒil-], *s.* agilité *f*.

agitate ['ædʒiteit], *v.tr.* 1. agiter, remuer (qch.). 2. agiter, troubler (qn). 3. *abs.* **to a. for, against, sth.**, ameuter l'opinion pour, contre, qch.; **'agitated**, *a.* agité; ému; troublé; **agi'tation**, *s.* 1. agitation *f*; mouvement *m*. 2. émotion *f*; trouble *m*. 3. **political a.**, agitation politique; **'agitator**, *s.* agitateur *m*.

agnostic [æg'nɔstik], *a. & s.* agnostique (*mf*).

ago [ə'gou], *adv.* **ten years a.**, il y a dix ans; **a little while a.**, tout à l'heure; tantôt; **long a.**, il y a longtemps; **no longer a. than last week**, pas plus tard que la semaine dernière.

agog [ə'gɔg], *adv. & a.* **to be (all) a. to do sth.**, être impatient de faire qch.; **the whole town was a.**, toute la ville était en émoi.

agonized ['ægənaizd], *a.* (cri) d'angoisse.

agonizing ['ægənaiziŋ], *a.* (*of pain*) atroce; (*of spectacle*) navrant, angoissant; **a. cry**, cri déchirant.

agony ['ægəni], *s.* 1. angoisse *f*; **to suffer agonies**, être au supplice; *Journ: F:* **a. column**, annonces personnelles. 2. **to be in the death a.**, être à l'agonie.

agrarian [ə'grɛəriən], *a.* (mesure, loi) agraire.

agree [ə'gri:], *v.i. & tr.* 1. consentir (**to, à**); **I a. that he was mistaken**, j'admets qu'il s'est trompé; **to a. with s.o. about the price**, convenir du prix avec qn; **unless otherwise agreed**, sauf arrangement contraire. 2. (*of pers.*) (*a*) être d'accord; tomber d'accord; (*b*) **to a. with s.o. on, in, a matter**, (i) être du même avis que qn, (ii) être d'accord avec qn, sur une question; **I don't a. with this theory**, je n'accepte pas cette théorie. 3. (*of thgs*) (*a*) s'accorder (ensemble); (*b*) *Gram:* s'accorder; (*c*) convenir (**with, à**); **the climate does not a. with him**, le climat ne lui convient pas, *F:* ne lui va pas; **the treatment didn't a. with him**, le traitement ne lui a pas réussi; **a'greeable**, *a.* agréable (**to, à**); (*of pers.*) aimable; **-ably**,

adv. agréablement; **a'greement**, *s.* 1. convention *f*, contrat *m*. 2. **to be in a. with s.o.**, être d'accord avec qn; **by mutual a.**, de gré à gré; à l'amiable. 3. *Gram:* accord *m* (**with**, avec).

agriculture ['ægrikʌltʃər], *s.* agriculture *f*; **agri'cultural**, *a.* agricole; **agri'culturalist**, agriculteur *m*; exploitant *m* agricole.

aground [ə'graund], *adv. Nau:* échoué; **to run a.**, échouer, s'échouer.

ahead [ə'hed], *adv.* **the ship was straight a.**, l navire était droit devant; **to draw a. of s.o.**, dépasser qn; **to go a.**, avancer, faire de progrès; **to go on a.**, prendre les devants; **a. of s.o.**, en avant de qn; **to be two hours a. of s.o.**, avoir deux heures d'avance sur qn; **to look a.**, penser à l'avenir; *Nau:* **full speed a.!** en avan toute!

aid [eid]. I. *v.tr.* aider, assister (qn); venir à l'aid de (qn). II. *s.* (*a*) aide *f*, assistance *f*; appui *n* **in a. of**, au profit de; **collection in a. of . .**, quête *f* en faveur de . . .; *F:* **what's this in a of?** c'est en l'honneur de quoi? (*b*) **hearing a** appareil auditif; **audio-visual aids**, aide audiovisuelles.

ailment ['eilmənt], *s.* mal *m*, *pl.* maux; malad (légère); **'ailing**, *a.* souffrant; mal portan **he's always a.**, il a une petite santé.

aim [eim]. I. *v.* 1. *v.tr.* (*a*) **to a. a stone, a blow, s.o.**, lancer une pierre, porter un coup, à qn; (viser; **to a. a gun at s.o.**, viser qn; (*c*) **measu aimed against our industry**, mesure dirig contre notre industrie. 2. *v.ind.tr.* (*a*) **to a. s.o. (with a gun)**, coucher qn en joue; (*b*) **wh are you aiming at?** quel but poursuivez-vou **to a. at becoming Prime Minister**, aspirer devenir premier ministre. II. *s.* 1. **to miss one a.**, manquer son but; **to take a. at**, viser. 2. b objet *m*; **aimless**, *a.* sans but, sans obj **-ly**, *adv.* (vivre, errer) sans but.

air ['ɛər]. I. *v.tr.* 1. aérer (une pièce); **to a. t laundry**, chauffer le linge (propre); mettre linge à l'air; **to a. one's grievances**, exposer s griefs. 2. **to a. one's opinions, one's knowledg** faire parade de ses opinions, de son savo **'airing**, ventilation *f* (d'une pièce); aération *f*; **a. c board**, armoire *f* sèche-linge.

II. *s.* 1. (*a*) air *m*; **fresh, foul, a.**, air frais, vic **breath of a.**, souffle *m* (d'air); **to walk on** être au comble du bonheur; être aux ang **there's sth. in the a.**, il se prépare qch.; **to tra by a.**, voyager par avion; (*b*) *attrib.* **a. raid**, taque aérienne; **the Fleet A. A** = l'Aéronavale *f*; **the Royal A. For** = l'Armée de l'air; (*c*) *Rad: etc:* **to be on a.**, parler à la radio; être radiodiffusé. 2. *M* air. 3. air, apparence *f*; **an a. of comfort**, un de confort; **to put on airs**, faire l'importa

'airbase, s. base f d'aviation; 'airbed, s. matelas m pneumatique; 'airborne, a. aéroporté; 'air brake, s. frein m à air comprimé; 'air-con'ditioned, a. climatisé; 'aircon'ditioner, s. climatiseur m; 'aircon'ditioning, s. climatisation f, conditionnement m (de l'air); 'air-cooled, a. refroidi par l'air; (moteur) à refroidissement par l'air; 'aircraft, s. (inv. in pl.) avion m; 'aircraftman, -men, s. soldat m (de l'Armée de l'air); 'aircrew, s. équipage m d'avion; 'airdrome, s. N.Am: aérodrome m; 'airfield, s. champ m d'aviation; 'air-hostess, s. Av: hôtesse f de l'air; 'airless, a. 1. (of room) renfermé. 2. (of weather) sans vent; 'air letter, s. aérogramme m; 'airlift, s. pont aérien; 'airline, s. service m de transports aériens; 'airliner, s. avion m de ligne; 'airmail, s. service postal aérien; by a., par avion; 'airman, -men, s. aviateur m; 'Air 'Marshal, s. Général m de corps d'armée aérien; 'air-mattress, s. matelas m pneumatique; 'air me'chanic, s. mécanicien m d'avion; 'airplane, s. avion m; 'air pocket, s. Av: trou m d'air; 'airport, s. aéroport m; 'air raid, s. raid aérien; 'airship, s. dirigeable m; 'air-sickness, s. mal m de l'air, d'avion; 'airstrip, s. Av: terrain m d'atterrissage; 'air terminal, s. aérogare f; 'airtight, a. étanche (à l'air); 'air-to-'air, a. (missile) air-air; 'air-to-'ground, a. (missile) air-sol; 'air traffic con'trol, s. contrôle m de la circulation aérienne; 'air traffic con'troller, s. contrôleur m de la circulation aérienne; 'airway, s. route, ligne, aérienne; 'airwoman, -women, s. aviatrice f; 'airworthiness, s. certificate of a., certificat m de navigabilité; 'airworthy, a. muni d'un certificat de navigabilité; 'airy, a. 1. bien aéré; ouvert à l'air. 2. léger: (of promise) vain; (of conduct) insouciant, désinvolte; 'airily, adv. légèrement; avec désinvolture; 'airy-'fairy, a. a.-f. plan, projet m impraticable, infaisable.

'sle [ail], s. nef latérale (d'une église); passage m (entre bancs); couloir central (d'autobus, etc.).

tch [eitʃ], s. to drop one's aitches, ne pas aspirer les h.

ar [ə'dʒa:r], adv. & a. (of door) entrebâillé; entrouvert.

kimbo [ə'kimbou], adv. with arms a., les (deux) poings sur les hanches.

kin [ə'kin], adv. feeling a. to fear, sentiment qui approche de l'effroi, ressemblant à l'effroi.

abaster [æla'ba:stər], s. albâtre m.

acrity [ə'lækriti], s. empressement m; entrain m.

arm [ə'la:m]. I. v.tr. 1. (a) donner l'alarme à (qn); (b) alerter (qn). 2. (frighten) effrayer; to be alarmed at sth., s'effrayer, s'émouvoir, de

qch. II. s. 1. alarme f, alerte f; to give the a., donner l'alarme; false a., fausse alerte. 2. avertisseur m; a. (clock), réveille-matin m inv, réveil m; a'larming, a. alarmant; inquiétant; a'larmist, s. alarmiste mf.

alas [ə'læs, -la:s], int. hélas!

Albania [æl'beiniə]. Pr.n. Geog: l'Albanie f.

albatross, pl. -es ['ælbətrɔs, -iz], s. albatros m.

albino, pl. -os [æl'bi:nou], s. albinos mf.

album ['ælbəm], s. album m.

alcohol ['ælkəhɔl], s. alcool m; alco'holic. 1. a. alcoolique. 2. s. (pers.) alcoolique mf; 'alcoholism, s. alcoolisme m.

alcove ['ælkouv], s. 1. alcôve f (de chambre). 2. niche f, enfoncement m (dans un mur).

alder ['ɔ:ldər], s. Bot: aune m.

alderman, -men ['ɔ:ldəmən], s. = conseiller municipal (d'une grande ville).

Alderney ['ɔ:ldəni]. Pr.n. Geog: Aurigny m.

ale [eil], s. bière (légère) anglaise; pale a., bière blonde.

Alec(k) ['ælik]. Pr.n.m. Alexandre, F: Alex; F: a smart A., un combinard.

alert [ə'lə:t]. 1. a. (a) alerte, vigilant; (b) actif, vif. 2. s. alerte f; to be on the a., être sur le qui-vive; -ly, adv. d'une manière alerte; a'lertness, s. 1. vigilance f; promptitude f (in doing sth., à faire qch.). 2. vivacité f; promptitude, agilité f.

Alexander [ælig'za:ndər]. Pr.n. Alexandre m.

alfresco [æl'freskou], a. & adv. en plein air; a. meal, (i) repas m sur l'herbe; pique-nique m; (ii) repas sous la tonnelle.

algebra ['ældʒibrə], s. algèbre f; alge'braic, a. algébrique; -ally, adv. algébriquement.

Algeria [æl'dʒiəriə]. Pr.n. Geog: l'Algérie f; Al'gerian, a. & s. algérien, ienne; Al'giers, Pr.n. Geog: Alger m.

alias ['eiliəs]. 1. adv. autrement dit; Jones, a. Hardy, l'homme Jones, dit Hardy. 2. s. (pl. aliases ['eiliəsiz]) nom m d'emprunt; faux nom; to have several aliases, avoir plusieurs noms de rechange.

alibi ['ælibai], s. alibi m; to establish an a., prouver son alibi.

alien ['eiliən]. 1. a. & s. étranger, -ère. 2. a. a. to sth., contraire, opposé, à qch.

alienate ['eiliəneit], v.tr. 1. Jur: aliéner (des biens, etc.). 2. détacher, éloigner, (s')aliéner (qn); alie'nation, s. aliénation f.

alight¹ [ə'lait], v.i. 1. descendre; mettre pied à terre; to a. from the train, etc., descendre du train, etc. 2. (of birds, planes) se poser; Av: atterrir, (on the sea) amerrir.

alight², a. allumé; en feu; to set sth. a., mettre le feu à qch.; to catch a., s'allumer, prendre feu.

align [ə'lain]. 1. v.tr. aligner; mettre (des objets) en ligne. 2. v.i. s'aligner; se mettre en ligne; a'lignment, s. alignement m.

alike [ə'laik]. **1.** *a.* semblable, pareil, ressemblant; **you are all a.!** vous vous ressemblez tous! **all things are a.** to him, tout lui est égal. **2.** *adv.* pareillement; de même; **dressed a.,** habillés de même; **winter and summer a.,** été comme hiver.

alimentary [æli'mentəri], *a.* alimentaire; *Anat:* **a. canal,** tube digestif; **alimen'tation,** *s.* alimentation *f.*

alimony ['æliməni], *s. Jur:* pension *f* alimentaire.

alive [ə'laiv], *a.* **1.** (*a*) vivant, en vie; **to be burnt a.,** être brûlé vif; **it's good to be a.!** il fait bon vivre! **dead or a.,** mort ou vif; (*b*) **to keep the conversation a.,** entretenir la conversation. **2. to be a. to the danger,** se rendre compte du danger. **3. he's very much a.,** (i) il est très remuant; (ii) il a l'esprit très éveillé. **4. the street was a. with people,** la rue fourmillait de monde.

alkali ['ælkəlai], *s. Ch:* alcali *m;* **'alkaline,** *a.* alcalin.

all [ɔːl]. **I.** *a., pron., & adv.* **1.** tout; (*a*) **a. day,** (pendant) toute la journée; **a. men,** tous les hommes; **a. the others,** tous les autres; **a. his life,** toute sa vie; **a. the way,** tout le long du chemin; **is that a. the luggage you're taking?** c'est tout ce que vous emportez de bagages? **for a. his wealth . . .,** en dépit de, malgré, sa fortune. . .; **with a. speed,** au plus vite, à toute vitesse; **at a. hours,** à toute heure; **you are not as ill as a. that,** vous n'êtes pas malade à ce point-là; (*b*) **a. of us,** nous tous; **a. together,** tous, toutes, à la fois, ensemble; (*c*) **we a. love him,** nous l'aimons tous; **take it a.,** prenez le tout; *Sp:* **five a.,** cinq à cinq; *Ten:* **fifteen a.,** quinze A; (*d*) *neut.* **almost a.,** presque tout; **for a. he may say,** quoi qu'il en dise; **a. that I did,** tout ce que j'ai fait; **that's a.,** c'est tout, voilà tout; **is that a.?** (i) est-ce tout? (ii) *Iron:* la belle affaire! **2.** (*a*) **once for a.,** une fois pour toutes; **for a. I know,** autant que je sache; (*b*) **most of a.,** surtout; (*c*) **not at a.,** pas du tout; **if you hesitate at a.,** pour peu que vous hésitiez; (*d*) **a. but impossible,** presque impossible; **I a. but fell,** j'ai failli tomber; (*e*) **taking it a. in a.,** à tout prendre; **they were a. in a. to each other,** ils étaient dévoués l'un à l'autre; **he thinks he's a. in a. to the business,** il s'imagine indispensable. **3.** *adv.* tout; **to be (dressed) a. in black,** être habillé tout de noir; **she is a. ears,** elle est tout oreilles; **a. the better,** tant mieux; **you will be a. the better for it,** vous vous en trouverez mieux; **the hour came a. too soon,** l'heure n'est arrivée que trop tôt; **a. at once,** (i) (*suddenly*) tout à coup; (ii) (*at one time*) tout d'un coup; *F:* **he's not a. there,** il est un peu simple d'esprit. **II.** *s.* tout *m,* totalité *f;* **to stake one's a.,** risquer le tout pour le tout; **to lose one's a.,** perdre tout

son avoir; **'all(-)clear,** *s.* (signal *m* de) fin d'alerte; **'All(-)'Hallows,** *s.* la Toussaint **'all-'in,** *a.* (*of person*) épuisé; *Ins:* **a.-in policy** police *f* tous risques; **a.-in price,** prix tout compris; *Sp:* **a.-in wrestling,** catch *m;* **'all(-)'night** *a.* **a.(-)n. service,** permanence *f* de nuit; **'all 'out,** *a.* **a.-o. effort,** effort *m* maximum; **'all 'rounder,** *s. F:* homme universel; **'all 'star,** *a. Th: Cin:* **a.(-)s. performance** pièce, film joué exclusivement par des vedettes; **'all-time,** *a.* **a.-t. high,** record plus élevé.

Allah ['ælə]. *Pr.n.* Allah *m.*

allegation [æli'geiʃ(ə)n], *s.* allégation *f.*

allege [ə'ledʒ], *v.tr.* alléguer, prétendre (**that,** que + *ind.*); **to a. an urgent appointment,** prétexter un rendez-vous urgent; **a'lleged,** *a.* **a. information,** prétendu renseignement; **the a. thief,** le voleur présumé.

allegiance [ə'liːdʒ(ə)ns], *s.* fidélité *f* (**to,** à).

allergy ['ælədʒi], *s. Med:* allergie *f;* **a'llergic** *a.* **I'm a. to fish,** le poisson ne me réussit pas.

alleviate [ə'liːvieit], *v.tr.* alléger, soulager (la douleur); adoucir (le chagrin); **allevi'ation** *s.* soulagement *m,* adoucissement *m;* allègement *m.*

alley ['æli], *s.* (*in garden*) allée *f;* (*in town*) ruelle *f,* passage *m.*

alliance [ə'laiəns], *s.* **1.** alliance *f;* **to enter into an a.,** s'allier (**with,** avec). **2. a. by marriage,** alliance.

allied ['ælaid], *a.* **1.** allié (**to, with,** avec); **the powers,** les puissances alliées. **2.** de la même famille, de la même nature; **a. industries,** industries *f* connexes.

alligator ['æligeitər], *s. Rept:* alligator *m.*

allocate ['æləkeit], *v.tr.* allouer, assigner (qch. à qn); **to a. a sum to sth.,** affecter une somme à qch.; attribuer (des fonctions); **allo'cation** **1.** allocation *f;* attribution *f* (de fonctions). part, somme, assignée.

allot [ə'lɔt], *v.tr.* (**allotted**) **1. to a. sth. to s.o.,** attribuer, assigner, qch. à qn. **2.** répartir, attribuer; **a'llotment,** *s.* **1.** (*a*) attribution *f* (qch. à qn); (*b*) partage *m,* répartition *f;* attribution *f.* **2.** (*a*) portion *f,* part *f,* lot *m;* allotments, jardins ouvriers.

allow [ə'lau], *v.tr.* **1. to a. a claim,** admettre une requête. **2.** (*a*) (*permit*) permettre, souffrir; **a. s.o. to do sth.,** permettre à qn de faire qch.; **a. me!** permettez(-moi)! (*b*) **to a. oneself to be deceived,** se laisser tromper. **3.** (*a*) **to a debtor time to pay,** accorder un délai à un débiteur; (*b*) *Com:* **to a. s.o. a discount,** consentir une remise à qn; (*c*) *v.ind.tr.* **to a. for s.** tenir compte de qch.; **after allowing for .** déduction faite de . . .; **a'llowable,** *a.* missible; légitime; **-ably,** *adv.* d'une man

admissible; légitimement; **a'llowance**, s. **1.**
pension ƒ alimentaire; rente ƒ; *Adm:* **family
allowances**, allocations familiales; (*of food,
etc.*) ration ƒ. **2.** *Com:* remise ƒ, rabais *m.* **3.** to
make a. for sth., tenir compte de qch.

alloy ['ælɔi], *s.* alliage *m.*

allude [ə'l(j)uːd], *v.ind.tr.* **to a. to sth.,** (*of pers.*)
faire allusion à qch.; (*of phrase*) se rapporter à
qch.

allure [ə'l(j)uər], *v.tr.* attirer, séduire; **a'lluring**,
a. attrayant, séduisant.

llusion [ə'l(j)uːʒ(ə)n], *s.* allusion ƒ.

lluvial [ə'luːviəl], *a. Geol:* (terrain) alluvial.

lly. **I.** *v.tr.* [ə'lai], **to a. oneself,** s'allier (to, with,
à, avec). **II.** *s.* **ally,** *pl.* **allies** ['ælai, -z], allié,
-iée.

lmanac ['ɔːlmənæk], *s.* almanach *m.*

lmighty [ɔːl'maiti]. **1.** *a.* tout-puissant; *F:* **an a.
din,** un bruit de tous les diables. **2.** *s.* **the A.,** le
Tout-Puissant.

lmond ['ɑːmənd], *s.* **1.** amande ƒ; *a.* **paste,
icing,** pâte ƒ d'amandes; **ground almonds,**
amandes pilées. **2.** a.(**-tree**), amandier
m.

lmost ['ɔːlmoust], *adv.* presque; à peu près; **it's
a. noon,** il est bientôt, près de, midi; **he a. fell,** il
a failli tomber.

ms [ɑːmz], *s. pl.* aumône ƒ; **to give a. to s.o.,**
faire l'aumône à qn.

oft [ə'lɔft], *adv.* en haut; en l'air.

one [ə'loun], *a.* **1.** seul; **I did it a.,** je l'ai fait à
moi seul; **I want to speak to you a.,** je voudrais
vous parler seul à seul. **2. to leave s.o., sth., a.,**
(i) laisser qn, qch., tranquille; (ii) laisser qn
faire; (iii) ne pas se mêler de qch.

ong [ə'lɔŋ]. **1.** *prep.* le long de; **to go a. a street,**
suivre une rue; **to walk a. the riverside,** longer
la rivière; **trees a. the river,** arbres qui bordent
la rivière. **2.** *adv.* (*a*) **to move a.,** avancer; **come
a.!** venez donc! **he'll be a. in ten minutes,** il va
s'amener dans dix minutes; (*b*) **I knew that all
a.,** je le savais dès le commencement; (*c*) **a.
with,** avec; **I can't get a. with him,** on ne s'ac-
corde pas ensemble; **a'long'side,** *adv. & prep.*
le long de (la rivière, etc.); *Nau:* **to come a.,** accoster, aborder à quai.

oof [ə'luːf], *adv. & a.* **to keep a.,** se tenir à
l'écart, éloigné; **he kept very much a.,** il s'est
montré très distant; **a'loofness,** *s.* réserve ƒ.

oud [ə'laud], *adv.* à haute voix; (tout) haut.

e [ælp], *s.* alpe ƒ; pâturage *m* de montagne;
Geog: **the Alps,** les Alpes.

phabet ['ælfəbet], *s.* alphabet *m*;
alpha'betical, *a.* alphabétique; **-ally,** *adv.*
alphabétiquement.

ine ['ælpain], *a.* (club) alpin; (paysage)
alpestre; (plantes) alpins.

eady [ɔːl'redi], *adv.* déjà.

satian [æl'seiʃ(ə)n]. **1.** *a. & s. Geog:* alsacien,

-ienne. **2.** (*dog*) chien-loup *m*; berger
allemand.

also ['ɔːlsou], *adv.* aussi; **he saw it a.,** il l'a vu
également; lui aussi l'a vu.

altar ['ɔːltər], *s.* autel *m.*

alter ['ɔːltər]. **1.** *v.tr.* (*a*) retoucher (un dessin);
modifier (qch.); changer de (plans); **that alters
matters,** voilà qui change tout; (*b*) fausser (les
faits). **2.** *v.i.* **he has greatly altered,** il a bien
changé; **alte'ration,** *s.* changement *m,*
modification ƒ; remaniement *m*; retouche ƒ.

alternate. **I.** *a.* [ɔːl'təːnit], alternatif; alterné; **to
come on a. days,** venir tous les deux jours;
-ly, *adv.* alternativement; tour à tour. **II.** *v.*
[ɔːl'təːneit]. **1.** *v.tr.* faire alterner (deux choses).
2. *v.i.* alterner (**with,** avec); se succéder (tour à
tour); **'alternating,** *a.* alternant, alterné; *El:*
(courant) alternatif; *Mec:* (mouvement) alternatif, de va-et-vient; **alter'nation,** *s.* alter-
nance ƒ.

alternative [ɔːl'təːnətiv]. **1.** *a.* alternatif; **an a.
proposal,** une contre-proposition. **2.** *s.* alternative ƒ; **to have no a.,** n'avoir pas le choix;
-ly, *adv.* avec l'alternative de; **a. you could
walk,** ou bien vous pourriez marcher.

although [ɔːl'ðou], *conj.* quoique, bien que
(+ *sub*).

altitude ['æltitjuːd], *s.* **1.** altitude ƒ, élévation ƒ. **2.**
usu.pl. hauteur(s) ƒ.

alto, *pl.* **-os** ['æltou, -ouz], *s. Mus:* **1.** alto *m.* **2.** (*a*)
(*male*) haute-contre ƒ; (*b*) (*female*) contralto
m.

altogether [ɔːltə'geðər], *adv.* (*a*) (*wholly*) entièrement, tout à fait; (*b*) (*on the whole*) somme
toute; **taking things a.,** à tout prendre; (*c*) **how
much a.?** combien en tout?

aluminium [ælju'miniəm], *s. N.Am:* **aluminum**
[ə'luːminəm], *s.* aluminium *m, F:* alu *m.*

alumnus, *pl.* **-ni** [ə'lʌmnəs, -nai], *s. N.Am:* ancien élève, étudiant.

always ['ɔːlweiz], *adv.* toujours.

a.m. ['ei'em], *abbr. for* **ante meridiem,** avant
midi; **nine a.m.,** neuf heures du matin.

amalgam [ə'mælgəm], *s.* amalgame *m.*

amalgamate [ə'mælgəmeit]. **1.** *v.tr.* amalgamer
(des idées); fusionner (des sociétés). **2.** *v.i.* (*of
metals*) s'amalgamer; (*of companies*)
fusionner; **amalga'mation,** *s.* **1.** amalgamation ƒ. **2.** fusion ƒ.

amass [ə'mæs], *v.tr.* amasser, accumuler (une
fortune).

amateur ['æmətəːr], *s.* amateur *m*; *attrib. a.*
painter, peintre *m* amateur; **a. work,** travail *m*
d'amateur; **ama'teurish,** *a.* (travail, etc.)
d'amateur; **-ly,** *adv.* en amateur.

amaze [ə'meiz], *v.tr.* confondre, stupéfier,
frapper de stupeur; **a'mazed,** *a.* confondu,
stupéfait; **a'mazement,** *s.* stupéfaction ƒ;
stupeur ƒ; **a'mazing,** *a.* stupéfiant; **-ly,** *adv.*

étonnamment; (réussir) à merveille.

Amazon [ˈæməz(ə)n]. *Pr.n.* **the (river) A.,** l'Amazone *f.*

ambassador [æmˈbæsədər], *s.* ambassadeur *m*; **(woman) ambassador,** ambassadrice *f.*

ambassadress, *pl.* **-es** [æmˈbæsədris, -iz], *s.* **1.** (*ambassador's wife*) ambassadrice *f.* **2.** (*woman ambassador*) ambassadrice *f.*

amber [ˈæmbər], *s.* ambre *m*; *a.* **light,** feu jaune.

ambiguous [æmˈbigjuəs], *a.* **1.** ambigu, *f.* -uë; équivoque. **2.** incertain; (style) obscur, confus; **-ly,** *adv.* avec ambiguïté; d'une manière équivoque; **ambi′guity,** *s.* ambiguïté *f*; équivoque *f.*

ambition [æmˈbiʃ(ə)n], *s.* ambition *f*; **am′bitious,** *a.* ambitieux; **-ly,** *adv.* ambitieusement.

ambivalent [æmˈbivələnt], *a.* ambivalent.

amble [ˈæmbl], *v.i.* **to a. (along),** marcher d'un pas tranquille.

ambulance [ˈæmbjuləns], *s.* ambulance *f.*

ambush [ˈæmbuʃ]. **I.** *v.tr.* **to a. (s.o.),** attirer (qn) dans un piège, un traquenard. **II.** *s.* embuscade *f*; guet-apens *m*; piège *m*, traquenard *m*; **to lie in a.,** être à l'affût.

ameliorate [əˈmiːliəreit]. **1.** *v.tr.* améliorer. **2.** *v.i.* s'améliorer, s'amender; **amelio′ration,** *s.* amélioration *f.*

amen [ˈɑːˈmen], *int.* amen.

amenable [əˈmiːnəbl], *a.* soumis (à la discipline); docile (aux conseils); **a. to reason,** raisonnable.

amend [əˈmend]. **1.** *v.tr.* (*a*) amender, modifier (un projet de loi); corriger (un texte); (*b*) réformer (sa vie). **2.** *v.i.* s'amender, se corriger; **a′mendment,** *s.* (*a*) modification *f*; rectification *f*; (*b*) *Pol:* amendement *m*; **a′mends,** *s.pl.* réparation *f*, compensation *f*; **to make a. for an injury,** réparer un tort.

amenity [əˈmiːniti], *s.* **1.** aménité *f*, charme *m* (d'un lieu). **2.** *pl.* **the amenities of life,** les commodités *f* de l'existence; **the amenities of the house,** les agréments *m*, les commodités, de la maison.

America [əˈmerikə]. *Pr.n.* l'Amérique *f*; **North, South, A.,** l'Amérique du Nord, du Sud.

American [əˈmerikən], *a. & s.* américain, -aine; **A. Indian,** Amérindien, -ienne.

amethyst [ˈæmiθist], *s.* améthyste *f.*

amiable [ˈeimiəbl], *a.* aimable **(to,** envers); **-ably,** *adv.* aimablement; **amia′bility,** *s.* amabilité *f* **(to,** envers); **after a few amiabilities,** après quelques paroles aimables.

amicable [ˈæmikəbl], *a.* (*of manner*) amical; (*of pers.*) bien disposé; **-ably,** *adv.* (i) amicalement; (ii) (arranger qch.) à l'amiable.

amid(st) [əˈmid(st)], *prep.* au milieu de; parmi.

amiss [əˈmis], *adv. & a.* **1. to take sth. a.,** prendre qch. en mauvaise part. **2. that doesn't come a.,**

cela n'arrive pas mal à propos; **something's a.,** il y a quelque chose qui cloche.

ammonia [əˈmouniə], *s. Ch:* ammoniaque *f.*

ammunition [æmjuˈniʃ(ə)n], *s.* munitions *f pl* (de guerre).

amnesia [æmˈniːziə], *s. Med:* amnésie *f.*

amnesty [ˈæmnisti], *s.* amnistie *f.*

among(st) [əˈmʌŋ(st)], *prep.* parmi; entre; (*a*) **sitting a. her children,** assise au milieu de ses enfants; (*b*) **we are a. friends,** nous sommes entre amis; (*c*) **to count s.o. a. one's friends,** compter qn au nombre de ses amis; (*d*) **do it a. you,** faites-le entre vous.

amoral [eiˈmɔrəl], *a.* amoral, -aux.

amorous [ˈæmərəs], *a.* amoureux; **a. verse,** poésie *f* érotique; **-ly,** *adv.* amoureusement, avec amour.

amortize [ˈæmɔːtaiz], *v.tr. Com:* amortir (une dette).

amount [əˈmaunt]. **I.** *s.* **1.** *Com:* somme *f*, montant *m*, total *m*; **have you the right a.?** avez vous votre compte? **a. of expenses,** montant de la dépense. **2.** quantité *f*; *F:* **to spend any a. of money,** dépenser énormément d'argent. **II.** *v.i.* **1.** (*of money*) s'élever, (se) monter (**to,** à); **I don't know what my debts a. to,** j'ignore le montant de mes dettes. **2. that amounts to the same thing,** cela revient au même. **3. he'll never a. to much,** il ne fera jamais grand-chose.

ampere [ˈæmpɛər], *s. Meas:* ampere *m.*

amphibian [æmˈfibiən], *a. & s.* **1.** *Z:* amphibie (*m*). **2.** *Mil:* (véhicule *m*) amphibie; **am′phibious,** *a.* amphibie.

amphitheatre [ˈæmfiθiətər], *s. Arch:* amphithéâtre *m*; **a. of mountains,** cirque *m* de montagnes.

ample [ˈæmpl], *a.* ample. **1. a. resources,** grosses ressources. **2. to make a. apology,** faire d'amples excuses; **you have a. time,** vous avez largement, grandement, le temps; **′amply,** *adv.* amplement, grandement.

amplify [ˈæmplifai], *v.tr.* amplifier (une idée, le courant, le son); **′amplifier,** *s. El: Rad:* amplificateur *m.*

amputate [ˈæmpjuteit], *v.tr.* amputer; **his leg was amputated,** il fut amputé de la jambe; **ampu′tation,** *s.* amputation *f.*

amuse [əˈmjuːz], *v.tr.* amuser, divertir; faire rire (qn); **to a. oneself,** s'amuser, se divertir (**doing sth.,** à faire qch.); **to be amused by sth.,** s'amuser de qch.; **a′musement,** *s.* amusement *m*, divertissement *m*; **a. park,** parc *m* d'attractions; **a′musing,** *a.* amusant, divertissant; **highly a.,** désopilant, *F:* tordant; **the a. thing about it is . . .,** le plus beau de l'affaire c'est que . . .; **-ly,** *adv.* d'une manière amusante.

an, *see* **a².**

anachronism [əˈnækrənizm], *s.* anachronisme *m*; **anachro′nistic,** *a.* anachronique.

anaemia [ə'ni:miə], *s.* anémie *f*; **a'naemic,** *a.* anémique.

anaesthetic [ænis'θetik], *a. & s.* anesthésique (*m*); **a'naesthetist** [ə'ni:sθətist], *s.* anesthésiste *mf.*

analogous [ə'næləgəs], *a.* analogue (to, with, à).

analogy [ə'nælədʒi], *s.* analogie *f* (to, with, avec); **ana'logical,** *a.* analogique; **-ally,** *adv.* analogiquement; par analogie.

analyse ['ænəlai:z], *v.tr.* analyser; faire l'analyse de (qch); **a'nalysis,** *pl.* **-es** [ə'nælisis, -i:z], *s.* analyse *f*; **'analyst,** *s.* analyste *mf*; **ana'lytic(al),** *a.* analytique.

anarchy ['ænəki], *s.* anarchie *f*; **'anarchist,** *s.* anarchiste *mf.*

anathema [ə'næθəmə], *s.* anathème *m.*

anatomy [ə'nætəmi], *s.* anatomie *f*; **ana'tomical,** *a.* anatomique.

ancestor ['ænsestər], *s.* ancêtre *m*; aïeul *m, pl.* aïeux; **an'cestral,** *a.* héréditaire; **his a. home,** la maison de ses ancêtres; **'ancestry,** *s.* 1. race *f*; lignée *f*; ascendance *f.* 2. *coll.* ancêtres *mpl*; aïeux *mpl.*

anchor ['æŋkər]. I. *s.* ancre *f.* II. *v.* 1. *v.tr.* ancrer (un navire). 2. *v.i.* jeter l'ancre; mouiller; **to a. off Dover,** mouiller au large de Douvres; **'anchorage,** *s.* (*a*) ancrage *m,* mouillage *m*; (*b*) droits *mpl* d'ancrage; **'anchoring,** *s.* (*a*) action *f* d'ancrer (un navire); (*b*) ancrage *m,* mouillage *m*; **a.-place, -berth,** ancrage, mouillage.

anchovy ['æntʃəvi, æn'tʃouvi], *s.* anchois *m.*

ancient ['einʃ(ə)nt], *a.* ancien; (*a*) de vieille date; (*b*) **the a. world,** le monde antique; *s.* **the ancients,** les anciens.

ancillary [æn'siləri], *a.* subordonné, accessoire (to, à).

and [ænd, ənd], *conj. et.* 1. (*a*) **a knife a. fork,** un couteau et une fourchette; (*b*) (*with numerals*) **two hundred a. two,** deux cent deux; **four a. a half,** quatre et demi; **four a. three quarters,** quatre trois quarts; **an hour a. twenty minutes,** une heure vingt minutes; (*c*) **to walk two a. two,** marcher deux par deux; **now a. then,** de temps en temps; (*d*) (*intensive repetition*) **better a. better,** de mieux en mieux. 2. (*connecting clauses*) (*a*) **he sang a. danced,** il chantait et dansait; (*b*) **wait a. see,** attendez voir; **try a. help me,** tâchez de m'aider.

Andes ['ændi:z]. *Pr.n. Geog:* **the A.,** les Andes *f.*

Andorra [æn'dɔ:rə]. *Pr.n. Geog:* (la République d')Andorre *f.*

Andrew ['ændru:]. *Pr.n.* André *m.*

anecdote ['ænikdout], *s.* anecdote *f.*

anemone [ə'nemən], *s. Bot:* anémone *f.*

angel ['eindʒəl], *s.* ange *m*; *F:* **you're an a.!** tu es chic! tu es un amour! **be an a.,** sois chic; **angelic,** [æn'dʒelik], *a.* angélique.

anger ['æŋgər], *s.* colère *f*; emportement *m*; **fit of a.,** accès *m* de colère; **to act in a.,** agir sous le coup de la colère.

angle[1] ['æŋgl], *s.* (*a*) angle *m*; **at an a. of . . .,** sous un angle de . . .; **at an a.,** en biais; (*b*) (*corner*) coin *m*; (*c*) point *m* de vue.

angle[2], *v.i.* pêcher à la ligne; **to a. for compliments,** quêter des compliments; **'angler,** *s.* pêcheur *m* à la ligne; **'angling,** *s.* pêche *f* à la ligne.

Anglican ['æŋglikən], *a. & s. Ecc:* anglican, -ane; **the A. Church,** l'Église anglicane.

anglicism ['æŋglisizm], *s.* anglicisme *m.*

Anglo-Saxon ['æŋglou'sæks(ə)n]. 1. *a. & s.* anglo-saxon, -onne. 2. *s. Ling:* l'anglo-saxon *m.*

angora [æŋ'gɔ:rə], *a. & s.* **a. goat, cat, rabbit,** chèvre *f*, chat *m*, lapin *m*, angora; angora *m*; *Tex:* (tissu *m*) angora (*m*).

angry ['æŋgri], *a.* fâché, irrité (**with s.o. about sth.,** contre qn de qch.); **to get a. with s.o.,** se fâcher contre qn; **to make s.o. a.,** fâcher, exaspérer, qn; mettre qn en colère; **a. voices,** voix irritées; **a. sky,** ciel à l'orage; **'angrily,** *adv.* en colère, avec colère.

anguish ['æŋgwiʃ], *s.* angoisse *f*; douleur *f*; **to be in a.,** être au supplice.

angular ['æŋgulər], *a.* (rocher) anguleux; (*of pers.*) décharné.

animal ['ænim(ə)l], *a. & s.* animal, -aux (*m*); **a. life,** la vie animale; **a. painter,** animalier *m.*

animate ['ænimeit], *v.tr.* (*a*) animer; (*b*) encourager, stimuler; **'animated,** *a.* animé; *Cin:* **a. cartoons,** dessins animés; **ani'mation,** *s.* animation *f*; vivacité *f*; entrain *m*; **'animator,** *s.* animateur, -trice (d'un groupe, d'un club); dessinateur, -trice de dessins animés.

animosity ['æni'mositi], *s.* animosité *f.*

aniseed ['ænisi:d], *s.* (graine *f* d')anis *m.*

ankle ['æŋkl], *s.* cheville *f*; **a. socks,** socquettes *fpl.*

Ann(e) [æn]. *Pr.n.* Anne *f.*

annex [æ'neks, ə'n-], *v.tr.* (*a*) annexer (**sth. to sth.,** qch. à qch.); (*b*) ajouter, joindre (une pièce à un document); **annex'ation,** *s.* annexion *f* (**of,** de); **'annex(e),** *s.* annexe *f* (d'un hôtel).

annihilate [ə'naiəleit], *v.tr.* anéantir; supprimer (qch., *F:* qn); **annihi'lation,** *s.* anéantissement *m.*

anniversary [æni'və:s(ə)ri], *s.* anniversaire *m*; **wedding a.,** anniversaire de mariage; **hundredth a.,** centenaire *m.*

annotate ['ænəteit], *v.tr.* annoter; **anno'tation,** *s.* annotation *f.*

announce [ə'nauns], *v.tr.* annoncer (qn, qch.); **he announced his intentions to me,** il m'a fait part de ses intentions; **a'nnouncement,** *s.* annonce *f*, avis *m*; (*of birth, marriage, etc.*) faire-part *m*; **a'nnouncer,** *s. Rad: T.V:* speaker *m*, speakerine *f.*

annoy [ə'nɔi], *v.tr.* **1.** (*vex*) contrarier (qn). **2.** (*inconvenience*) gêner, ennuyer, importuner; **a'nnoyance**, *s.* **1.** chagrin *m*; **a look of a.**, un air de contrariété *f.* **2.** désagrément *m*, ennui *m*; **a'nnoyed**, *a.* contrarié, ennuyé; **a'nnoying**, *a.* contrariant, ennuyeux; **how a.!** quel ennui!

annual ['ænju(ə)l]. **1.** *a.* annuel. **2.** *s.* (*a*) *Bot:* plante annuelle; (*b*) (*book, etc.*) annuaire *m*; **-ally**, *adv.* annuellement; tous les ans.

annuity [ə'nju:iti], *s.* rente (annuelle); **life a.**, rente viagere.

annul [ə'nʌl], *v.tr.* (**annulled**) annuler; abroger (une loi); dissoudre (un mariage); **a'nnulment**, *s.* annulation *f*; dissolution *f* (d'un mariage).

anode ['ænoud], *s. El:* anode *f.*

anomaly [ə'nɔməli], *s.* anomalie *f*; **a'nomalous**, *a.* anormal, -aux; **-ly**, *adv.* irrégulièrement.

anonymous [ə'nɔniməs], *a.* anonyme; **-ly**, *adv.* anonymement; **ano'nymity**, *s.* anonymat *m*.

anorak ['ænəræk], *s. Cl:* anorak *m.*

another [ə'nʌðər], *a. & pron.* **1.** (*an additional*) encore (un(e)); **a. cup of tea**, encore une tasse de thé; **in a. ten years**, dans dix ans d'ici; **without a. word**, sans un mot de plus. **2.** (*a similar*) un(e) autre, un(e) second(e); **such a.**, un autre du même genre; **there's not such a. man**, il n'a pas son pareil, *F:* il n'y en a pas deux comme lui. **3.** (*a different*) un(e) autre; **that is (quite) a. matter**, c'est tout autre chose; **a. dress**, (i) une autre robe; (ii) une nouvelle robe; **we'll do it a. time**, on le fera une autre fois; *F:* **tell me a.!** va conter ça ailleurs! **4.** (*a*) **science is one thing, art is a.**, la science est une chose, l'art en est une autre; **one way or a.**, d'une façon ou d'une autre; (**taking**) **one year with a.**, bon an mal an; **taking one (thing) with a.**, l'un dans l'autre; (*b*) (*reciprocal pron.*) **one a.**, l'un l'autre, les uns les autres; **near one a.**, près l'un de l'autre, l'un près de l'autre; **love one a.**, aimez-vous les uns les autres; **to help one a.**, s'entr'aider.

answer ['ɑ:nsər]. **I.** *s.* **1.** réponse *f* (à une question); réplique *f* (à une critique); **he has an a. to everything**, il a réponse à tout; **I could find no a.**, je n'ai rien trouvé à répondre; *Com:* **an a. will oblige**, réponse, s'il vous plaît. **2.** solution *f* (d'un problème). **II.** *v.tr. & i.* répondre (à qn, à une lettre); **to a. for s.o.**, (i) (= *instead of*) répondre pour qn; (ii) se porter garant de qn; **to a. back**, répliquer; **don't a. back!** pas de répliques! **to a. the door**, aller ouvrir (la porte); **to a. (to) a description**, répondre à un signalement; **to a. the purpose**, faire l'affaire; **he has a lot to a. for**, il est responsable de bien des choses; **'answerable**, *a.* **the Company is not a. for . . .**, la Compagnie ne répond pas de . . .; **to be a. to an authority**, relever d'une autorité; **he's a. to nobody**, il ne doit de comptes à personne; **'answering**, *a.* **an a. cry**, un cri jeté en réponse.

ant [ænt], *s.* fourmi *f*; **white a.**, fourmi blanche; termite *m*; **'ant-hill**, *s.* fourmilière *f.*

antagonize [æn'tægənaiz], *v.tr.* éveiller l'antagonisme *m*, l'hostilité *f*, de (qn); éloigner (qn); **an'tagonism**, *s.* antagonisme *m*, opposition *f*; **antago'nistic**, *a.* opposé, hostile (**to**, à).

antarctic [ænt'ɑ:ktik], *a. & s.* (l')antarctique (*m*).

antecedent [ænti'si:d(ə)nt]. **1.** *a.* antécédent antérieur (**to**, à). **2.** *s.* antécédent *m*; his **antecedents**, son passé.

antedate ['ænti'deit], *v.tr.* antidater (un document); précéder (un événement).

antediluvian [æntidi'lu:viən], *a.* antédiluvien.

antelope ['æntiloup], *s. Z:* antilope *f.*

antenatal ['ænti'neitl], *a.* prénatal, -als.

antenna, *pl.* **-ae** [æn'tenə, -i:], *s. Ent:* antenne *f Rad: T.V:* antenne.

anteroom ['æntiru:m], *s.* antichambre *f.*

anthem ['ænθəm], *s.* **1.** *Ecc.Mus:* motet *m*. **national a.**, hymne national.

anthology [æn'θɔlədʒi], *s.* anthologie *f.*

Anthony ['æntəni]. *Pr.n.* Antoine *m.*

anthracite ['ænθrəsait], *s. Min:* anthracite *m.*

anthropology [ænθrə'pɔlədʒi], *s.* anthropolog *f*; **anthropo'logical**, *a.* anthropologiqu **anthro'pologist**, *s.* anthropologue *m* anthropologiste *mf.*

anti- ['ænti-], *pref.* anti-, contre-; **'an 'aircraft**, *a.* anti-aérien; **a.-a. gun**, canon an aérien; **'antibi'otic**, *a. & s.* antibiotique (*n* **'antibody**, *s.* anticorps *m*; **'anti'climax**, retour *m* à l'ordinaire, au terre à terre; **'a ti'clockwise**, *a. & adv.* dans le sens inver des aiguilles d'une montre; **'a ticonsti'tutional**, *a.* anticonstitionn **'anti'cyclone**, *s.* anticyclone *m*; **'antidote** antidote *m*, contre-poison *m*; **'anti-freeze** *Aut:* anti-gel *m inv*; **'anti-'icer**, *s. Av:* a tigivrant *m*; **'anti-'knock**, *s. Aut: etc:* pro antidétonant; **'anti-'nuclear**, *a.* a tinucléaire, antiatomique; **anti'septic**, *a. &* antiseptique (*m*); **'anti-'skid**, *a.* antidérapa **'anti'social**, *a.* antisocial; **'anti-'tank**, *Mil:* **a.-t. weapon**, engin *m* anti-chars; **'** ti'theft, *a.* (dispositif) antivol *inv.*

anticipate [æn'tisipeit], *v.tr.* **1.** (*a*) **to a. eve** anticiper sur les événements; savourer plaisir) d'avance; (*b*) escompter (un résult **2. to a. s.o.**, prévenir, devancer, qn; **to a. s. wishes**, aller au-devant des désirs de qn. **3.** ticiper, avancer (un paiement). **4.** prévoir, visager (une difficulté); **antici'pation**, *s.* ticipation *f.*

antics ['æntiks], *s.pl.* bouffonneries *fpl*; g

bades *fpl*; cabrioles *fpl*.

Antilles (the) [ðiːænˈtiliːz]. *Pr.n. Geog:* les Antilles *f*.

antipathy [ænˈtipəθi], *s*. antipathie *f* (to, pour); **antipa'thetic**, *a*. antipathique (to, à).

antipodes (the) [ðiːænˈtipədiːz], *s.pl.* les antipodes *m*.

antiquary [ˈæntikwəri], *s*. amateur *m*, marchand *m*, d'antiquités; antiquaire *mf*; **anti'quarian. 1.** *a*. d'antiquaire. **2.** *s*. antiquaire *mf*; **a. bookseller**, libraire *m* spécialiste en vieilles éditions.

antique [ænˈtiːk]. **1.** *a*. antique; **a. furniture**, meubles *mpl* d'époque. **2.** *s*. objet *m* antique; **a. dealer**, antiquaire *mf*; **a. shop**, magasin *m* d'antiquités; **'antiquated** [-kweitid], *a*. vieilli; démodé; **an'tiquity** [-kwiti], *s*. l'antiquité (grecque, etc.).

antirrhinum [æntiˈrainəm], *s. Bot:* muflier *m*, gueule-de-loup *f*.

ntithesis, *pl.* -es [ænˈtiθisis, -iːz], *s*. **1.** antithèse *f* (to, of, de). **2.** opposé *m*, contraire *m* (de); **anti'thetic(al)**, *a*. antithétique; **-ally**, *adv*. par antithèse.

antler [ˈæntlər], *s*. andouiller *m*; **the antlers**, les bois *m*.

ntwerp [ˈæntwəːp]. *Pr.n. Geog:* Anvers *m*.

nus [ˈeinəs], *s. Anat:* anus *m*.

nvil [ˈænvil], *s. Metalw:* enclume *f*.

nxiety [ænˈzaiəti], *s*. (*a*) inquiétude *f*; **deep a.**, angoisse *f*, anxiété *f*; (*b*) **a. for s.o.'s safety**, sollicitude *f* pour la sécurité de qn.

nxious [ˈæŋ(k)ʃəs], *a*. **1.** (*a*) inquiet, soucieux (**about**, sur, de, au sujet de); (*b*) inquiétant; **an a. moment**, un moment d'anxiété. **2.** désireux; **to be a. for sth., to do sth.**, désirer vivement qch., faire qch.; **not very a. to see her**, peu soucieux de la voir; **to be a. to meet s.o.**, tenir beaucoup à voir qn; **-ly**, *adv*. **1.** (*a*) avec inquiétude; (*b*) anxieusement. **2.** avec sollicitude. **3.** avec impatience.

ny [ˈeni]. **I.** *a. & pron.* (*replaces 'some' in interr. or neg. sentences*) **1. have you a. milk?** avez-vous du lait? **have you a.?** en avez-vous? **if a. of them should see him**, si aucun d'entre eux le voyait; **there are few if a.**, il y en a peu ou pas (du tout); **he knows English if a. man does**, il sait l'anglais comme pas un. **2.** (*a*) **not a.**, ne . . . aucun, nul; **I can't find a.**, je n'en trouve pas; **he hasn't a. money**, il n'a pas d'argent; **he hasn't a. reason to complain**, il n'a aucune raison de se plaindre; (*b*) (*with implied negation*) **the impossibility of giving him a. education**, l'impossibilité de lui donner aucune éducation. **3.** (*a*) (*no matter which*) n'importe le)quel; **come a. day** (**you like**), venez n'importe quel jour; **a. doctor will tell you that**, n'importe quel médecin vous le dira; **that may happen a. day**, cela peut arriver d'un jour à

l'autre; **draw a. two cards**, tirez deux cartes quelconques; (*b*) (*any and every*) **at a. hour of the day**, à toute heure de la journée. **II.** *adv*. **I cannot go a. further**, je ne peux aller plus loin; **will you have a. more tea?** voulez-vous encore du thé?

anybody [ˈenibɔdi], **anyone** [ˈeniwʌn], *s. & pron.* **1.** quelqu'un; (*with implied negation*) personne; **do you see a. over there?** voyez-vous quelqu'un là-bas? **does a. dare to say so?** y a-t-il personne qui ose le dire? **2. not a.**, ne . . . personne; **there was hardly a.**, il n'y avait presque personne. **3.** (*no matter who*) n'importe qui; tout le monde; **a. will tell you so**, le premier venu vous le dira; **a. would think him mad**, on le croirait fou; **a. who had seen him at that time**, quiconque l'aurait vu alors; **a. but me**, tout autre que moi; **I haven't met a. else**, je n'ai rencontré personne d'autre.

anyhow [ˈenihau]. **1.** *adv*. **to do sth. a.**, faire qch. n'importe comment. **2.** *conj*. en tout cas, de toute façon; **a. you can try**, vous pouvez toujours essayer.

anything [ˈeniθiŋ], *pron. & s*. quelque chose; (*with implied negation*) rien; **can I do a. for you?** puis-je vous être utile à quelque chose? **is there a. more pleasant than . . .?** est-il rien de plus agréable que . . .? **if a. should happen to him**, s'il lui arrivait quelque malheur. **2. not a.**, ne . . . rien; **hardly a.**, presque rien. **3.** (*no matter what*) n'importe quoi; tout; **he eats a.**, il mange de tout; **a. you like**, tout ce que vous voudrez; **he is a. but mad**, il n'est rien moins que fou. **4.** *adv.phr.* (*intensive*) *F:* **to work like a.**, travailler avec acharnement; **it's raining like a.**, il pleut tant qu'il peut; **it's as easy as a.**, c'est simple comme tout, *F:* comme bonjour.

anyway [ˈeniwei], *adv. & conj.* en tout cas, de toute façon; **a. you can try**, vous pouvez toujours essayer.

anywhere [ˈeniwɛər], *adv*. **1.** n'importe où; **can you see it a.?** peux-tu le voir quelque part? **a. else**, partout ailleurs. **2. not . . . a.**, nulle part; en aucun endroit.

aorta [eiˈɔːtə], *s. Anat:* aorte *f*.

apart [əˈpaːt], *adv*. à part. **1.** (*aside*) de côté; **to live a. from the world**, vivre éloigné du monde. **2.** (*separate*) **to get two things a.**, séparer deux choses; **to come a.**, se détacher, se défaire; **to take a machine a.**, démonter une machine; **you can't tell them a.**, on ne peut pas les distinguer l'un de l'autre. **3.** (*a*) (*distant*) **they are a mile a.**, ils sont à un mille l'un de l'autre; **lines ten centimetres a.**, lignes espacées de dix centimètres; (*b*) **a. from the fact that . . .**, hormis que . . ., outre que . . .; **joking a.**, plaisanterie à part; *F:* sans blague!

apartheid [əˈpaːteit], *s*. (*in S. Africa*) ségrégation *f* (raciale).

apartment [əˈpaːtmənt], *s*. (*a*) salle *f*; pièce *f*; (*b*) (*usu. pl.*) logement *m*; appartement *m*; **to let furnished apartments**, louer en meublé; (*c*) *N.Am:* appartement; **a. block**, immeuble (divisé en appartements).

apathy ['æpəθi], *s.* apathie *f*, nonchalance *f*, indifférence *f*; **apa'thetic**, *a.* apathique, indifférent; **-ally**, *adv.* avec indifférence; nonchalamment, avec nonchalance.

ape [eip]. **I.** *s. Z:* (grand) singe (sans queue). **II.** *v.tr.* singer; imiter; mimer (qn); contrefaire.

aperient [ə'piəriənt], *a. & s. Med:* laxatif (*m*).

aperitif [ə'peritif], *s.* apéritif *m*.

aperture ['æpətjuər], *s.* ouverture *f*, orifice *m*.

apex, *pl.* **-es, apices** ['eipeks, -iz, 'eipisi:z], *s.* sommet *m* (d'un triangle); point culminant (d'une carrière).

aphis, *pl.* **-ides** ['eifis, -idi:z], *s. Ent:* aphidé *m*; puceron *m*.

apiary ['eipiəri], *s.* rucher *m*.

apiculture ['eipikʌltʃər], *s.* apiculture *f*; **api'culturist**, *s.* apiculteur, -trice.

apiece [ə'pi:s], *adv.* chacun; **to cost five francs a.**, coûter cinq francs (la) pièce; **to receive a present a.**, recevoir chacun un cadeau.

apologetic [əpɔlə'dʒetik], *a.* (ton) d'excuse; **to be very a. (for, about)**, se confondre en excuses (de, pour); **he was quite a. about it**, il s'en est excusé vivement; **-ally**, *adv.* en manière d'excuse; en s'excusant.

apologize [ə'pɔlədʒaiz], *v.i.* **to a. to s.o. for sth.**, s'excuser de qch. auprès de qn; **a'pology**, *s.* excuses *fpl.*

apostle [ə'pɔsl], *s.* apôtre *m*; **the A.'s Creed**, le Symbole des Apôtres.

apostrophe [ə'pɔstrəfi], *s.* apostrophe *f*.

appal [ə'pɔ:l], *v.tr.* (**appalled**) consterner; épouvanter (qn); **we are appalled at the idea**, nous sommes glacés d'horreur à cette pensée; **a'ppalling**, *a.* épouvantable, effroyable; **-ly**, *adv.* épouvantablement, effroyablement.

apparatus [æpə'reitəs], *s.* appareil *m*; dispositif *m*.

apparent [ə'pærənt], *a.* apparent, manifeste, évident; **-ly**, *adv.* **1.** évidemment, manifestement. **2.** apparemment; **this is a. true**, il paraît que c'est vrai.

apparition [æpə'riʃ(ə)n], *s.* **1.** apparition *f*. **2.** fantôme *m*, revenant *m*.

appeal [ə'pi:l]. **I.** *s.* **1.** appel *m*; *Jur:* **Court of A.**, cour *f* d'appel; **to lodge an a.**, se pourvoir en appel. **2. to make an a. to s.o.'s generosity**, faire appel à la générosité de qn; **an a. for calm**, un appel au calme; **she has great a.**, elle a beaucoup de charme. **3.** prière *f*, supplication *f*. **II.** *v.i.* faire appel (à qn); **to a. for help**, demander secours (à qn); (*of thing*) **to a. to s.o.**, attirer, séduire, qn; **if it appeals to you**, si le cœur vous en dit; **that doesn't a. to me**, cela ne me dit rien; **a'ppealing**, *a.* (regard) suppliant;

(ton) émouvant; (personnalité) sympathique; **-ly**, *adv.* d'un ton, d'un regard, suppliant.

appear [ə'piər], *v.i.* **1.** (*become visible*) paraître, apparaître; se montrer. **2.** (*present oneself publicly*) (*a*) se présenter; *Jur:* **to a. before a court**, comparaître devant un tribunal; **to a. for s.o.**, représenter qn; (*b*) **to a. on the stage**, entrer en scène; (*c*) (*of book*) paraître. **3.** (*a*) (*seem*) **to a. sad**, paraître triste; **so it appears**, il paraît que oui; **it appears that you are wrong**, il paraît que vous avez tort; (*b*) (*be manifest*) **as will presently a.**, comme on le verra bientôt; **a'ppearance**, *s.* **1.** (*a*) apparition *f*; entrée *f*; **to put in an a.**, paraître, se montrer, se présenter; **to make one's first a.**, débuter; faire ses débuts; (*b*) comparution *f* (devant un tribunal). **2.** (*a*) (*look, aspect*) apparence *f*, air *m*, mine *f*; **to have a good a.**, se présenter bien; **at first a.**, première vue; au premier abord; (*b*) (*semblance*) apparence; **by all appearance(s)**, selon toute apparence; **for the sake of appearances**, pour sauver les apparences; pour la forme.

appease [ə'pi:z], *v.tr.* apaiser; **a'ppeasement**, *s.* apaisement *m*; **policy of a.**, politique d'apaisement, de conciliation.

append [ə'pend], *v.tr.* attacher, joindre (qch.); **to a. a signature to a document**, apposer une signature sur un document; **to a. marginal notes**, ajouter des notes en marge; **a'ppendage**, *s.* accessoire *m*.

appendix, *pl.* **-es, -ices** [ə'pendiks, -i -isi:z], *s.* appendice *m*; **appendi'citis** [-'saitis], *s.* appendicite *f*.

appetite ['æpitait], *s.* appétit *m*; **to have a good a.**, avoir bon appétit; **'appetizer**, *s.* (*a*) apéritif *m*; (*b*) amuse-gueule *m inv*; **'appetizing**, appétissant, alléchant.

applaud [ə'plɔ:d], *v.tr.* applaudir (qn); **a'pplause**, *s.* applaudissements *mpl.*

apple ['æpl], *s.* pomme *f*; **a. core**, trognon *m* pomme; **eating a.**, pomme à couteau; **stewed apples**, compote *f* de pommes; **a. pie, tart**, tourte *f*, tarte *f*, aux pommes; **in a. pie order**, en ordre parfait; **a. pie bed**, lit *m* portefeuille; **a. tree**, pommier *m*; **a. green**, pomme *inv*.

appliance [ə'plaiəns], *s.* (*a*) appareil *m*, instrument *m*, dispositif *m*; engin *m*; (*b*) accessoires *m*; attirail *m*.

apply [ə'plai], *v.tr. & i.* **1.** (*a*) appliquer (**sth. sth.**, qch. sur qch.); faire l'application de (qch. à qch.); **to a. the brakes**, serrer le frein, freiner; **applied mathematics**, mathématiques appliquées; (*b*) **this applies to my case**, ceci s'applique à mon propre cas; (*c*) **to a. one's mind to sth.**, s'appliquer à qch. **2. to a. to s.o.**, s'adresser, recourir, à qn (pour avoir qch.); **a. for a job**, solliciter, poser sa candidature un emploi; **a'pplicable,** *a.* applicable (**to,** à); approprié (**to,** à); **'applicant,** *s.* 1. candidat *m* (à un emploi, etc.). 2. *Jur:* demandeur, -eresse; **appli'cation,** *s.* 1. (*a*) application *f* (de qch. à, sur, qch.); *Pharm:* **for external a.,** pour usage *m* externe; (*b*) (*thing applied*) application, enduit *m*. 2. assiduité *f,* application; **he lacks a.,** il manque de suite *f,* de concentration *f.* 3. demande *f,* requête *f;* **a. for a job, for help,** demande d'emploi, de secours; **to make a. to s.o. for sth.,** s'adresser à qn pour avoir qch.; **samples on a.,** échantillons sur demande.

appoint [ə'pɔint], *v.tr.* 1. nommer; (*a*) **to a. s.o. ambassador,** nommer qn ambassadeur; (*b*) **to a. s.o. to sth.,** nommer qn à qch. 2. fixer (l'heure, un endroit); arrêter (un jour); **a'ppointed,** *a.* 1. désigné; nommé; **at the a. time,** à l'heure dite. 2. équipé, monté; **well a. house,** maison bien installée; **a'ppointment,** *s.* 1. rendez-vous *m inv*; *Adm:* convocation *f.* 2. (*a*) nomination *f* (à un emploi); (*b*) emploi *m.*

appraise [ə'preiz], *v.tr.* priser, évaluer (qch.) (**at so much,** à tant); faire l'expertise de (dégâts, etc.); **a'ppraisal,** *s.* évaluation *f,* estimation *f;* **official a.,** expertise *f;* **a'ppraiser,** *s.* **official a.,** (commissaire-)priseur *m;* expert *m.*

appreciate [ə'priːʃieit], 1. *v.tr.* apprécier; faire cas de (qch.); se rendre compte de (qch.); **songs greatly appreciated,** chansons très goûtées. 2. *v.tr. & i.* (*a*) *Fin:* hausser (la valeur de qch.); (*b*) (*of goods, etc.*) augmenter de valeur; hausser de prix; **a'ppreciable,** *a.* appréciable; sensible; **-ably,** *adv.* sensiblement; **appreci'ation,** *s.* 1. appréciation *f,* (i) *Fin:* hausse *f;* (ii) estimation *f,* évaluation *f.* 2. critique *f* (d'un livre, etc.); **a'ppreciative,** *a.* (jugement) élogieux; (*of pers.*) reconnaissant; **to be a. of music, etc.,** apprécier, être sensible à, la musique, etc.; **-ly,** *adv.* favorablement; avec satisfaction; avec reconnaissance.

apprehend [æpri'hend], *v.tr.* 1. arrêter (qn). 2. appréhender, redouter (l'avenir); **appre'hension,** *s.* appréhension *f,* crainte *f;* **appre'hensive,** *a.* timide, craintif.

apprentice [ə'prentis], *s.* apprenti, -ie; **a'pprenticeship,** *s.* apprentissage *m.*

approach [ə'prəutʃ]. I. *s.* 1. approche *f;* abord *m*; **his a. to the problem,** sa façon d'aborder le problème; **to make approaches to s.o.,** faire des avances à qn. 2. voie *f* d'accès; approches (d'une ville). II. *v.* 1. *v.i.* (s')approcher. 2. *v.tr.* (*a*) **we are approaching London,** nous approchons de Londres; **to a. perfection,** approcher de la perfection; (*b*) s'approcher de (qn, qch.); aborder, approcher (qn); **to be easy to a.,** avoir l'abord facile; (*c*) **to a. a question,** aborder, s'attaquer à, une question; **a'pproachable,** *a.* accessible; (*of pers.*) abor-

dable; **a'pproaching,** *a.* approchant; **his a. death,** sa mort prochaine; **the a. car,** la voiture venant en sens inverse.

approbation [æprə'beiʃ(ə)n], *s.* 1. approbation *f;* assentiment *m.* 2. jugement *m* favorable; **smile of a.,** sourire approbateur; **a'probatory,** *a.* approbateur, -trice.

appropriate. I. *v.tr.* [ə'prouprieit], s'approprier (qch.); s'emparer de (qch.). II. *a.* [ə'proupriət]. 1. approprié; **style a. to the subject,** style qui convient au sujet. 2. propre, convenable (**to, for,** à); **an a. comment,** une observation juste, à propos; **a'ppropriateness,** *s.* convenance *f,* justesse *f,* à-propos *m* (d'une action, d'une remarque).

appropriation [əproupri'eiʃ(ə)n], *s.* 1. appropriation *f,* prise *f* de possession (**of,** de). 2. (*a*) affectation *f* (de qch. à un usage); (*b*) affectation de fonds. 3. *Adm:* crédit *m* (budgétaire).

approve [ə'pruːv]. 1. *v.tr.* approuver, sanctionner (une action); **read and approved,** lu et approuvé; **approved school** = centre *m* d'éducation surveillée. 2. *v.ind.tr.* **to a. of sth.,** approuver qch.; **I don't a. of your friends,** vos amis ne me plaisent pas; **a'pproval,** *s.* approbation *f;* **to nod a.,** approuver de la tête; *Com:* **on a.,** à l'essai; **a'pproving,** *a.* approbateur, -trice; **-ly,** *adv.* d'un air approbateur.

approximate [ə'prɔksimət], *a.* (calcul) approximatif; **-ly,** *adv.* approximativement; **approxi'mation,** *s.* approximation *f;* chiffre approximatif.

apricot ['eiprikɔt], *s.* 1. abricot *m.* 2. **a.**(**tree**) abricotier *m.*

April ['eipril], *s.* avril *m*; **A. fool's day,** le premier avril; **to make an A. fool of s.o.,** faire un poisson d'avril à qn.

apron ['eiprən], *s.* tablier *m*; *Av:* aire *f* de manœuvre, de stationnement; **to be tied to one's mother's apron-strings,** être pendu(e) aux jupons de sa mère.

apse [æps], *s. Arch:* abside *f.*

apt [æpt], *a.* 1. (mot) juste, (expression) heureuse. 2. **a. to do sth.,** (*a*) (*of pers.*) enclin, porté, à faire qch.; **we are a. to believe that . . .,** on croit facilement que . . .; (*b*) (*of thg*) (**gadget**) **a. to go wrong,** (dispositif) sujet à, susceptible de, se détraquer. 3. (élève) intelligent; **to be a. at sth.,** être doué pour qch.; **-ly,** *adv.* 1. avec justesse; avec à-propos. 2. adroitement; **'aptitude,** *s.* aptitude *f* (**for,** à, pour); **'aptness,** *s.* (*a*) justesse *f* (d'une observation); (*b*) tendance *f* (à faire qch.).

aqualung ['ækwəlʌŋ], *s.* scaphandre *m* autonome.

aquamarine [ækwəmə'riːn], *s.* aigue-marine *f.*

aquarium, *pl.* **-iums, -ia** [ə'kwɛəriəm, -iəmz, -iə], *s.* aquarium *m.*

Aquarius [ə'kwɛəriəs]. *Pr.n. Astr:* le Verseau.
aquatic [ə'kwætik], *a.* (plante, etc.) aquatique.
aqueduct ['ækwidʌkt], *s.* aqueduc *m.*
aquiline ['ækwilain], *a.* aquilin.
Arab ['ærəb], *a. & s.* (*pers. or horse*) arabe (*mf*).
Arabian [ə'reibiən], *a.* arabe, d'Arabie; **the A. Nights,** les Mille et une Nuits.
Arabic ['ærəbik]. **1.** *a.* (gomme) arabique; (langue) arabe; **A. numerals,** chiffres *m* arabes. **2.** *s. Ling:* l'arabe *m.*
arable ['ærəbl], *a.* (terre) arable, labourable.
arbitrate ['a:bitreit]. **1.** *v.tr.* arbitrer, juger (un différend). **2.** *v.i.* arbitrer; **'arbitrary,** *a.* arbitraire; **-ily,** *adv.* arbitrairement; **arbi'tration,** *s.* arbitrage *m;* **'arbitrator,** *s.* arbitre *m.*
arc [a:k], *s. Mth: El:* arc *m;* **'arc-lamp,** *s.* lampe *f* à arc.
arcade [a:'keid], *s.* (*a*) arcade(s) *f* (en bord de rue); (*b*) passage *m* (à boutiques).
arch [a:tʃ]. **I.** *v.* **1.** *v.tr,* (*a*) voûter (un passage, une porte); (*b*) arquer, cambrer (le dos); (*of cat*) **to a. its back,** faire le gros dos. **2.** *v.i.* se voûter, former voûte. **II.** *s.* **1.** voûte *f,* arc *m;* cintre *m;* **centre a.,** voûte maîtresse; **a. of a vault,** arceau *m;* arche *f* (d'un pont). **2.** *Anat:* **a. of the eyebrows,** l'arc des sourcils; **a.** (**of the foot**), cambrure *f* (du pied); **to suffer from fallen arches,** avoir le pied plat; **'archway,** *s.* passage voûté; portail *m* (d'une église).
arch- [a:tʃ], *pref.* **a.-enemy,** grand adversaire.
archaeology [a:ki'ɔlədʒi], *s.* archéologie *f;* **archaeo'logical,** *a.* archéologique; **archae'ologist,** *s.* archéologue *mf.*
archaic [a:'keiik], *a.* archaïque.
archangel ['a:keindʒ(ə)l], *s.* archange *m.*
archbishop ['a:tʃ'biʃəp], *s.* archevêque *m;* **arch'bishopric,** *s.* archevêché *m.*
archery ['a:tʃəri], *s.* tir *m* à l'arc; **'archer,** *s.* archer *m.*
archipelago, *pl.* **-s, -es** [a:ki'peləgou, -z], *s.* archipel *m.*
architect ['a:kitekt], *s.* architecte *m;* **'architecture,** *s.* architecture *f.*
archives ['a:kaivz], *s.pl.* archives *f;* **'archivist** ['a:kivist], *s.* archiviste *mf.*
archpriest ['a:tʃ'pri:st], *s.* archiprêtre *m.*
arctic ['a:ktik], *a.* arctique; **a. weather,** temps glacial; *s.* **the A.,** l'Arctique *m;* **A. circle,** cercle *m* arctique.
ardent ['a:dənt], *a.* ardent; **-ly,** *adv.* ardemment; avec ardeur.
ardour ['a:dər], *s.* ardeur *f.*
arduous ['a:djuəs], *a.* (travail) ardu, pénible, difficile; (chemin) escarpé; (calcul) laborieux; **-ly,** *adv.* péniblement; **'arduousness,** *s.* difficulté *f* (d'une tâche, etc.).
area ['ɛəriə], *s.* **1.** aire *f,* superficie *f;* surface *f.* **2.** région *f;* **postal a.,** zone postale; **sterling a.,** zone sterling; **the London a.,** l'agglomération

londonienne; **an a. of agreement,** un terrain d'entente.
arena [ə'ri:nə], *s.* arène *f.*
Argentina [a:dʒ(ə)n'ti:nə]. *Pr.n. Geog:* la République Argentine.
Argentine ['a:dʒəntain], *a. Geog:* **the A.** (**Republic**), la République Argentine.
argue ['a:gju:], *v.* (**arguing; argued**). **1.** *v.tr.* discuter, débattre (une question). **2.** *v.i.* (*a*) argumenter (**about, against, sth.,** sur, contre, qch.); **to a. from sth.,** tirer argument de qch.; (*b*) discuter, (se) disputer, raisonner (**with s.o. about sth.,** avec qn sur qch.); plaider (**for, against, sth.,** pour, contre, qch.); **'arguable,** *a.* (opinion) discutable, soutenable; **'argument,** *s.* **1.** argument *m* (**for, against,** en faveur de, contre); **to follow s.o.'s** (**line of**) **a.,** suivre le raisonnement de qn; **for the sake of a.,** à titre d'exemple. **2.** discussion *f,* dispute *f*; **argu'mentative,** *a.* (*of* *pers.*) raisonneur -euse; **argu'mentativeness,** *s.* esprit raisonneur.
aria ['a:riə], *s. Mus:* aria *f.*
arid ['ærid], *a.* aride; **a'ridity,** *s.* aridité *f.*
Aries ['ɛəriz]. *Pr.n. Astr:* le Bélier.
arise [ə'raiz], *v.i.* (**arose; arisen**) **1.** (*of pers.*) **leader arose,** un chef a surgi. **2.** (*a*) (*of the*) s'élever, survenir, se présenter; **a storm aros** une tempête est survenue; (*of difficulty*) présenter; **should the occasion a.,** le ca échéant; (*b*) émaner, provenir, résulter (**from** de); **problems that a. from . . .,** problèmes q résultent de . . ..
aristocrat ['æristəkræt], *s.* aristocrate *m;* **aris'tocracy,** *s.* aristocratie *f;* **aristo'crati** *a.* aristocratique.
arithmetic [ə'riθmətik], *s.* arithmétique *f,* calc *m.*
ark [a:k], *s.* arche *f;* **Noah's A.,** l'arche de No
arm¹ [a:m], *s.* **1.** bras *m;* **a.-in-a.,** bras dessu bras dessous; **she took my a.,** elle me prit bras; **to put one's a. round s.o.,** prendre qn p la taille; **to keep s.o. at a.'s length,** tenir qn distance; **to welcome s.o. with open arn** recevoir qn à bras ouverts. **2.** bras, accoud *m* (de fauteuil); fléau *m* (de balance); bras (mer);**'armband,** *s.* brassard *m;***'armchair** fauteuil *m;* **'armful,** *s.* brassée *f;* **in armfu by the a.,** à pleins bras, plein les bra **'armhole,** *s. Cl:* emmanchure *f;* **'armlet,** brassard *m;* **'armpit,** *s.* aisselle *f.*
arm². **I.** *v.* **1.** *v.tr.* armer (qn). **2.** *v.i.* s'armer (**against s.o.,** contre qn); prendre les armes. *s.* **1.** *usu. pl.* arme(s) *f* (*pl*); **to be up in arn** (**against s.o.**), s'insurger (contre qn); se ge darmer (contre qn); **the arms race,** la cou aux armements. **2.** (**coat of**) **arms,** armoir *fpl;* **'armaments,** *s.pl.* armements *m* matériel *m* de guerre; **armed,** *a.* armé (**wi**

de); **the a. forces,** les forces armées; **'armour,** *s.* armure *f*; **'armoured,** *a.* cuirassé; blindé; **a. car,** (i) voiture blindée; (ii) fourgon *m* bancaire; **'armoury,** *s.* armurerie *f*; **'army,** *s.* armée *f*; **the Salvation A.,** l'Armée du Salut.

armistice ['ɑːmistis], *s.* armistice *m*.

aroma [ə'roumə], *s.* arome *m*; bouquet *m* (d'un vin); **aro'matic.** 1. *a.* aromatique; (parfum) balsamique. 2. *s.* aromate *m*.

around [ə'raund]. 1. *adv.* autour, à l'entour; **all a.,** tout autour, de tous côtés; **the woods a.,** les bois d'alentour. 2. *prep.* autour de; **the country a. the town,** les environs *m*, la périphérie, de la ville; **it cost a. five pounds,** cela a coûté environ cinq livres.

arouse [ə'rauz], *v.tr.* 1. (*a*) réveiller, éveiller (qn); (*b*) secouer (qn) (de sa paresse); stimuler (qn). 2. exciter, susciter (un sentiment, une émotion).

arrange [ə'rein(d)ʒ], *v.tr.* arranger, aménager. 1. (*a*) (*set in order*) disposer, ranger (des livres); (*b*) adapter, arranger (pour piano). 2. (*plan beforehand*) arranger; **to a. to do sth.,** s'arranger pour faire qch.; **to a. a time,** fixer une heure; **it was arranged that . . .,** il a été convenu que . . .; **to a. for sth. to be done,** prendre des dispositions pour que qch. se fasse. 3. (*settle*) ajuster, arranger (une dispute); **a'rrangement,** *s.* 1. arrangement *m*, disposition *f* (de qch.); aménagement *m* (d'une maison). 2. accord *m*, entente *f* (avec qn); **price by a.,** prix *m* à débattre.

array [ə'rei], *s.* étalage *m* (**of tools,** d'outils).

arrears [ə'riəz], *s.pl.* arriéré *m*; **rent in a.,** loyer arriéré; **to get into a.,** se mettre en retard; s'arriérer.

arrest [ə'rest]. I. *s.* 1. arrestation *f*; **under a.,** en état d'arrestation. 2. arrêt *m*, suspension *f* (d'un mouvement); *Med:* **cardiac a.,** arrêt de cœur, insuffisance *f* cardiaque. II. *v.tr.* arrêter (un mouvement, un malfaiteur); fixer (l'attention de qn); **a'rresting,** *a.* **an a. sight,** un spectacle frappant, impressionnant.

arrive [ə'raiv], *v.i.* 1. arriver (**at, in,** à, dans); **we arrived at three o'clock,** nous sommes arrivés à trois heures; **to a. unexpectedly,** survenir. 2. **to a. at a conclusion,** arriver, aboutir, à une conclusion; **to a. at a price,** fixer un prix; **a'rrival,** *s.* arrivée *f*; arrivage *m* (de marchandises); **a new a.,** un nouveau venu.

arrogant ['ærəgənt], *a.* arrogant; **a. tone,** ton *m* rogue; **-ly,** *adv.* avec arrogance; **'arrogance,** *s.* arrogance *f*; morgue *f*.

arrow ['ærou], *s.* flèche *f*; **to shoot, let fly, an a.,** lancer, décocher, une flèche.

arsenal ['ɑːsənl], *s.* arsenal *m*, -aux.

arsenic ['ɑːsnik], *s.* arsenic *m*.

arson ['ɑːsn], *s.* incendie *m* volontaire.

[ɑːt], *s.* 1. art *m*; **work of a.,** œuvre *f* d'art; **the**

(fine) **arts,** les beaux-arts; **arts and crafts,** arts et métiers; **a. exhibition, show,** exposition *f* (d'œuvres) d'art. 2. adresse *f*, habileté *f*; **to use every a.,** user de tous les artifices; **'artful.** *a.* (*often Pej.*) (*a*) ingénieux; (*b*) rusé; **'artfully,** *adv.* astucieusement; **'artfulness,** *s.* astuce *f*; **'art-school,** *s.* école *f* des beaux-arts.

arteriosclerosis [ɑː'tiəriousklə'rousis], *s. Med:* artériosclérose *f*.

artery ['ɑːtəri], *s.* 1. *Anat:* artère *f*. 2. artère, grande route; **ar'terial,** *a.* 1. *Anat:* artériel. 2. **a. road,** grande voie de communication; grande route.

artesian [ɑː'tiːziən, -'tiːʒən], *a.* **a. well,** puits *m* artésien.

arthritis [ɑː'θraitis], *s. Med:* arthrite *f*; **rheumatoid a.,** rhumatisme *m* articulaire; **ar'thritic,** *a.* arthritique.

artichoke ['ɑːtitʃouk], *s.* 1. **(globe) a.,** artichaut *m*. 2. **Jerusalem a.,** topinambour *m*.

article ['ɑːtikl], *s.* 1. (*a*) *Adm: Jur: Com:* article *m*, clause *f* (d'un contrat); **articles of association,** contrat *m* de société; (*b*) **a. of faith,** article de foi. 2. article (de journal). 3. (*a*) article, objet *m*; (*b*) **a. of clothing,** vêtement *m*. 4. *Gram:* article (défini, indéfini).

articulate. I. [ɑː'tikjuleit], *v.tr. & i.* articuler (un mot); **articulated lorry,** semi-remorque *f*. II. [ɑː'tikjulət], *a.* (langage) articulé, net, distinct.

artificial [ɑːti'fiʃ(ə)l], *a.* 1. artificiel. 2. factice, simulé; **-ally,** *adv.* artificiellement.

artillery [ɑː'tiləri], *s.* artillerie *f*; **ar'tilleryman,** *pl.* **-men,** *s.* artilleur *m*.

artisan [ɑːti'zæn], *s.* artisan *m*, ouvrier qualifié.

artist ['ɑːtist], *s.* artiste *mf*, *esp.* artiste peintre *mf*; **he's an a.,** il est peintre; **ar'tistic,** *a.* artistique; **-ally,** *adv.* artistiquement; avec art; **'artistry,** *s.* art *m*.

artiste [ɑː'tiːst], *s. Th:* artiste *mf*,

artless ['ɑːtlis], *a.* 1. naturel; sans artifice. 2. naïf, ingénu; **-ly,** *adv.* 1. naturellement. 2. naïvement; **'artlessness,** *s.* 1. naturel *m*. 2. naïveté *f*.

arty ['ɑːti], *a. F:* qui affiche des goûts artistiques.

as [æz], (*unstressed*) [əz]. I. *adv.* 1. (*in principal clause*) aussi, si; **you're as tall as I am,** *F:* **me,** vous êtes aussi grand que moi. 2. **I worked as hard as I could,** j'ai travaillé tant que j'ai pu. 3. **as from the 15th,** à partir du 15; **as to that,** quant à cela; **to question s.o. as to his motives,** interroger qn sur ses motifs; **as for you . . .,** quant à vous . . .

II. **as,** *conj. & rel. adv.* (*in subordinate clause*) 1. (*degree*) (*a*) que; **you are as tall as he is,** *F:* **as him,** vous êtes aussi grand que lui; (*b*) comme; **as pale as death,** pâle comme la mort; **by day as well as by night,** le jour comme la nuit. 2. (*concessive*) **ignorant as he is,** tout ignorant qu'il est; **be that as it may,** quoi qu'il en soit. **3.** (*manner*) (*a*) comme; **do as you like,** faites comme vous voudrez; **leave it as it is,** laissez-le tel qu'il est; **as it is,** les choses étant ainsi; (*b*) **to consider s.o. as a friend,** considérer qn comme un ami; **to act as a father,** agir en père; **to treat s.o. as a stranger,** traiter qn en étranger; **he was often ill as a child,** enfant, il était souvent malade. **4.** (*time*) (*a*) **one day as I was sitting . . .,** un jour que j'étais assis . . .; (*b*) **he grew more charitable as he grew older,** il devenait plus charitable en vieillissant. **5.** (*reason*) **as you're not ready we can't go,** comme, puisque, vous n'êtes pas prêt, nous ne pouvons pas partir. **6.** (*result*) **he's not so foolish as to believe it,** il n'est pas assez bête pour le croire. **III. as,** *rel. pron.* **beasts of prey, such as the lion,** les fauves, tels que, comme, le lion.

asbestos [æz′bestɔs, əs-], *s.* amiante *m.*

ascend [ə′send]. **1.** *v.i.* monter. **2.** *v.tr.* monter sur (le trône); gravir (une colline); remonter (un fleuve); **a′scendancy, -ency,** *s.* influence *f* (**over s.o.,** sur qn); **a′scendant, -ent,** *s.* **to be in the a.,** avoir le dessus; **A′scension,** (*a*) *s. Ecc:* **A.-day,** (fête *f* de) l'Ascension *f*; (*b*) *Pr.n. Geog:* **A. Island,** (Ile *f* de) l'Ascension; **a′scent,** *s.* (*a*) ascension (d'une montagne); montée *f*; (*b*) pente *f.*

ascertain [æsə′tein], *v.tr.* constater, s'assurer, s'informer, de (la vérité de qch.).

ascetic [ə′setik]. **1.** *a.* ascétique. **2.** *s.* ascète *mf*; **a′sceticism,** *s.* ascétisme *m.*

ascribe [ə′skraib], *v.tr.* attribuer, imputer (**to,** à); **a′scribable,** *a.* attribuable, imputable (**to,** à).

asdic [′æzdik], *s. Nau:* asdic *m.*

aseptic [ei′septik], *a. Med:* aseptique.

ash[1] [æʃ], *s. Bot:* frêne *m.*

ash[2], *s.* (*a*) cendre(s) *f(pl)*; **cigar a.,** cendre de cigare; **to reduce to ashes,** réduire en cendres; ′**ash(-)bin,** *N.Am:* ′**ashcan,** *s.* boîte *f* à ordures, aux ordures; poubelle *f*; ′**ashen,** *a.* blême; ′**ashpan,** *s.* cendrier *m* (de poêle); ′**ashtray,** *s.* cendrier *m* (de fumeur); ′**Ash ′Wednesday,** le mercredi des Cendres; ′**ashy,** *a.* **1.** couvert de cendres. **2. his face went a.,** il est devenu blême.

ashamed [ə′ʃimd], *a.* honteux, confus; **to be a. of s.o., sth.,** avoir honte de qn, qch.; **I'm a. of you,** vous me faites honte; **you ought to be a. of yourself,** vous devriez avoir honte.

ashore [ə′ʃɔ:r], *adv. Nau:* **1.** à terre; **to put (passengers) a.,** débarquer (des passagers). **2.** échoué; (*of ship*) **to run a.,** s'échouer.

Asia [′eiʃə]. *Pr.n. Geog:* l'Asie *f*; **A. Minor,** l'Asie Mineure; ′**Asian. 1.** *a.* asiatique; **A. flu,** grippe *f* asiatique. **2.** *s.* asiate *mf*; **Asi′atic,** *a. & s.* asiatique *mf.*

aside [ə′said]. **1.** *adv.* de côté; à l'écart; à part; **to put sth. a.,** écarter qch.; mettre qch. de côté; **to**

stand a., (i) se tenir à l'écart; (ii) se ranger; **putting that a. . . .,** à part cela . . .; **I took him a.,** je l'ai pris à part; *Th:* (**words spoken**) **a.** (paroles dites) en aparté. **2.** *s. Th:* aparté *m*; **in an a.,** en aparté.

asinine [′æsinain], *a.* stupide, sot, *f.* sotte.

ask [ɑ:sk], *v.tr. & i.* (**asked** [ɑ:skt]) demander. **1.** (*inquire*) **to a. s.o. a question,** poser une question à qn; **a. a policeman,** adressez-vous à un agent (de police); *F:* **a. me another!** je n'ai pas la moindre idée; **if you a. me . . .,** à mon avis . . .. **2.** (*a*) **to a. s.o. a favour,** demander un faveur à qn; (*b*) **to a. six francs for sth.,** demander six francs pour qch., de qch. **3.** (*a*) **t a. to do sth.,** demander à faire qch.; (*b*) **to a s.o. to do sth.,** demander à qn de faire qch. (*a*) **to a. about sth.,** se renseigner sur qch.; **to a s.o. about sth.,** interroger qn sur qch.; (*b*) **to a after s.o.,** demander des nouvelles de qn. **5.** (*a*) **to a. for s.o.,** demander à voir qn; (*b*) **to a. fo sth.,** demander qch.; solliciter qch.; **to a. fo sth. back,** redemander un objet prêté. **6.** **t a. s.o. to lunch,** inviter qn à déjeuner; **to a. s.o back,** inviter qn pour lui rendre la politesse ′**asking,** *s.* **it's yours for the a.,** il n'y a qu'à demander.

askance [əs′kæns, -′kɑ:ns], *adv.* **to look a. a s.o.,** regarder qn de travers, avec méfiance.

askew [ə′skju:], *adv.* de biais, de côté.

asleep [ə′sli:p], *adv. & a.* endormi. **1. to be a** dormir; **to fall a.,** s'endormir. **2. my foot's a.,** j'ai le pied engourdi.

asparagus [ə′spærəgəs], *s. coll.* asperges *fpl.*

aspect [′æspekt], *s.* **1.** exposition *f*, orientation **house with a south(ern) a.,** maison qui orientée vers, donne sur, le midi. **2.** aspect **to examine all the aspects of a question** examiner tous les aspects d'une question; **see sth. in its true a.,** voir qch. sous son vrai jour.

aspen [′æspən], *s. Bot:* tremble *m.*

asperity [æs′periti], *s.* (*a*) âpreté *f* (du reproche); (*b*) rigueur *f* (du climat).

aspersion [ə′spə:ʃ(ə)n], *s.* calomnie *f*; **to ca aspersions upon s.o.,** dénigrer qn.

asphalt [′æsfælt], *s.* asphalte *m.*

asphyxiate [æs′fiksieit], *v.tr.* asphyxie **as′phyxia,** *s.* asphyxie *f*; **asphyxi′ation,** *s* asphyxie *f.*

aspirate [′æsp(ə)rət], *a. & s. Ling:* **1.** *a.* aspiré *s.* (*a*) lettre aspirée; (*b*) (la lettre) h.

aspire [ə′spaiər], *v.i.* aspirer; **to a. to sth.,** aspirer à qch.; ambitionner qch.; **aspi′ration** [æspə′reiʃ(ə)n], *s.* aspiration *f*; **a′spiring,** *a.* ambitieux.

aspirin [′æspirin], *s. Pharm:* aspirine *f*; **take a.,** prenez un comprimé d'aspirine.

ass [æs], *s.* **1.** âne, *f.* ânesse. **2.** *F:* sot, *f.* ânesse; âne; **to make an a. of oneself,** agir d manière idiote; se donner en spectacle.

assailant [ə'seilənt], s. assaillant, -ante.

assassinate [ə'sæsineit], v.tr. assassiner (qn); **a'ssassin**, s. assassin m; **assassi'nation**, s. assassinat m.

assault [ə'sɔːlt]. **I.** v.tr. **1.** attaquer, donner l'assaut à (une ville). **2.** attaquer (qn); **to be assaulted**, être victime d'une agression. **II.** s. (a) Mil: assaut m; (b) attaque f; Jur: **unprovoked a.**, agression f; **a. and battery**, coups mpl et blessures fpl.

assemble [ə'sembl]. **1.** v.tr. (a) assembler (des personnes, le parlement); (b) monter (une machine). **2.** v.i. s'assembler; se rassembler; **a'ssembly**, s. **1.** assemblée f; **in open a.**, en séance publique. **2.** assemblement m, réunion f. **3.** assemblage m, montage m (d'une machine); Ind: **a. line**, chaîne f de montage; **a. shop**, atelier m de montage.

assent [ə'sent]. **I.** v.i. acquiescer (**to**, à), donner son assentiment (**to**, à). **II.** s. assentiment m, consentement m, acquiescement m.

assert [ə'sɔːt], v.tr. (a) **to a. one's rights**, revendiquer ses droits; **to a. oneself**, s'imposer; **you must a. your authority**, il vous faut imposer votre autorité; (b) **to a. that . . .**, affirmer que . . .; **a'ssertion**, s. revendication f (de ses droits); affirmation f; **a'ssertive**, a. autoritaire.

assess [ə'ses], v.tr. (a) répartir, établir (un impôt); (b) estimer, évaluer (qch.); imposer, taxer (qn); **to a. s.o. at so much**, imposer qn à tant; **a'ssessment**, s. **1.** (a) évaluation f (de dégâts); (b) imposition f (d'un contribuable, d'un immeuble); cotisation f (du contribuable); **a. of damages**, fixation f de dommages-intérêts. **2.** (amount) cote f; **a'ssessor**, s. Adm: **a. of taxes**, contrôleur m (des contributions directes).

asset ['æset], s. **1.** possession f; avoir m; **he's one of our assets**, c'est une de nos valeurs. **2.** pl. Fin: actif m, avoir m; Jur: **personal assets**, biens m meubles; **real assets**, biens immobiliers.

assiduous [ə'sidjuəs], a. assidu; **-ly**, adv. assidûment; **assi'duity**, s. assiduité f, diligence f (**in doing sth.**, à faire qch.).

assign [ə'sain], v.tr. **1.** assigner (qch. à qn). **2.** céder, transférer (qch. à qn); **assignation** [æsig'nei ʃ(ə)n], s. distribution f (de biens); transfert m (de biens, d'actions, de brevet, etc.); rendez-vous (galant); **a'ssignment**, s. **1.** allocation f, attribution f (de qch. à qn); transfert m (de biens). **2.** tâche assignée.

assimilate [ə'simileit], v.tr. **1.** assimiler (**to**, à). **. to a. food**, assimiler des aliments; **assimi'lation**, s. **1.** assimilation f (**to**, **with**, à). **2.** assimilation f (des aliments).

assist [ə'sist], v.tr. (a) aider (qn); (b) **to a. s.o. in**

misfortune, secourir qn dans le malheur; **a'ssistance**, s. aide f, secours m; **cán I be of any a.?** puis-je vous aider? **a'ssistant. 1.** a. adjoint, auxiliaire, sous-; **a. manager**, sousdirecteur, -trice; sous-gérant, -ante; Sch: **a. master, mistress**, professeur m suppléant (de lycée). **2.** s. aide mf; Com: vendeur, -euse; (in office, etc.) employé, -ée; collaborateur, -trice; **laboratory a.**, laborantin, -tine.

assizes [ə'saiziz], s.pl. Jur: assises f.

associate. I. [ə'souʃieit], v.tr. & i. (s')associer (**with s.o., sth.**, avec, à, qn, qch.). **II.** [ə'souʃiət], s. associé, -ée; adjoint, -e; camarade mf; **associ'ation**, s. association f; **a. football**, football m.

assorted [ə'sɔːtid], a. (**well-**)a., (bien) assorti; **ill-a. couple**, ménage mal assorti; **a'ssortment**, s. assortiment m.

assume [ə'sjuːm], v.tr. **1.** (a) prendre sur soi, assumer (une responsabilité); se charger d'(un devoir); (b) **to a. power**, prendre possession du pouvoir; s'attribuer, s'approprier (un droit); **to a. a name**, adopter un nom. **2.** présumer, supposer (qch.); tenir (qch.) comme établi; **assuming (that) the story is true**, en supposant que l'histoire soit vraie; **a'ssumed**, a. supposé, feint, faux; **a. piety**, fausse dévotion; **a. name**, pseudonyme m; **a'ssumption**, s. **1.** Ecc: **the A.**, l'Assomption f (de la Vierge). **2. a. of office**, entrée f en fonctions. **3.** supposition f, hypothèse f.

assure [ə'ʃuər], v.tr. (a) (make safe) **to a. s.o. against sth.**, assurer qn contre qch.; **to a. s.o.'s life**, assurer la vie de qn; (b) (make certain) **to a. s.o.'s peace**, assurer la paix de qn; (c) (affirm) **to a. s.o. of sth.**, assurer qn de qch.; **he will do it, I a. you!** il le fera, je vous en réponds! **be assured that . . .**, soyez certain que . . .; **a'ssurance**, s. **1.** (a) (certainty) assurance f; (b) promesse (formelle); affirmation f. **2. life a.**, assurance sur la vie. **3.** assurance; aplomb m; **a'ssured. 1.** a. **a. success**, succès assuré. **2.** a. & s. a. (**person**), assuré(e); **-ly** [ə'ʃuəridli], adv. assurément, à coup sûr.

aster ['æstər], s. Bot: aster m.

asterisk ['æstərisk], s. astérisque m.

astern [ə'stəːn], adv. Nau: (a) à l'arrière, sur l'arrière; (b) **to go a.**, faire marche arrière; **full speed a.!** en arrière toute! (c) **to have the wind a.**, avoir le vent (en) arrière, en poupe f.

asteroid ['æstərɔid], s. astéroïde m.

asthma ['æsmə], s. asthme m; **asth'matic**, a. & s. asthmatique (mf).

astigmatism [æ'stigmətizm], s. Opt: Med: astigmatisme m; **astig'matic**, a. Opt: Med: astigmate.

astonish [ə'stɔniʃ], v.tr. étonner, surprendre; **to be astonished at seeing sth.**, s'étonner de voir qch.; **to look astonished**, avoir l'air étonné, surpris; **a'stonishing,** *a.* étonnant, surprenant; **-ly,** *adv.* étonnamment; **a'stonishment,** *s.* étonnement *m,* surprise *f*; **a look of blank a.,** un regard ébahi.

astound [ə'staund], *v.tr.* confondre; stupéfier; **a'stounding,** *a.* abasourdissant.

astray [ə'strei], *a. & adv.* égaré; **to go a.,** s'égarer; **to lead s.o. a.,** débaucher qn, entrainer qn dans l'inconduite.

astride [ə'straid], *adv. & prep.* à califourchon; **to get a. a horse,** enfourcher un cheval; **to sit a. a chair,** s'asseoir à cheval sur une chaise.

astrology [ə'strɔlədʒi], *s.* astrologie *f*; **a'strologer,** *s.* astrologue *m.*

astronaut ['æstrənɔ:t], *s.* astronaute *mf*; **astro'nautics,** *s.* (*usually with sing. const.*) astronautique *f.*

astronomy [ə'strɔnəmi], *s.* astronomie *f*; **a'stronomer,** *s.* astronome *m;* **astro'nomic(al),** *a.* astronomique; **sales reach a. figures,** les ventes atteignent des chiffres astronomiques.

astrophysics ['æstrou'fiziks], *s.* (*usually with sing. const.*) astrophysique *f.*

astute [ə'stju:t], *a.* fin, avisé, pénétrant; **-ly,** *adv.* 1. avec finesse. 2. astucieusement; **a'stuteness,** *s.* finesse *f,* pénétration *f.*

asylum [ə'sailəm], *s.* 1. asile *m,* (lieu *m* de) refuge *m.* 2. hospice *m.*

at [æt], *prep.* à. 1. (*a*) **at table, at school,** à table, à l'école; **at hand,** sous la main; **at sea,** en mer; (*b*) **at home,** à la maison, chez soi; **at the tailor's,** chez le tailleur; (*c*) **to sit at the window,** se tenir près de la fenêtre; **the rain came in at the window,** la pluie est entrée par la fenêtre. 2. **at six o'clock,** à six heures; **at present,** à présent; **two at a time,** deux à la fois; **at night,** la nuit. 3. **at two francs a kilo,** à deux francs le kilo; **at five kilometres per hour,** à cinq kilomètres à l'heure. 4. **at my request,** sur ma demande; **at all events,** en tout cas; **he did not like it at all,** il ne l'a pas aimé du tout. 5. **good at games,** sportif, -ive. 6. (*a*) **to look at sth.,** regarder qch.; **to be surprised at sth.,** être étonné de qch.; **to catch at sth.,** s'accrocher à qch.; (*b*) **to laugh at s.o.,** se moquer de qn; (*c*) **to be at work,** être au travail; **she's at it again!** voilà qu'elle recommence! **while we are at it,** pendant que nous y sommes.

atheism ['eiθiizm], *s.* athéisme *m;* **'atheist,** *s.* athée *mf.*

Athens ['æθənz]. *Pr.n.* Athènes *f;* **A'thenian** [ə'θi:njən], *a. & s.* athénien, -ienne; d'Athènes.

athlete ['æθli:t], *s.* athlète *mf;* **ath'letic,** *a.* athlétique; **he looks a.,** il a l'air sportif; **ath'letics,** *s.pl.* sports *m* (athlétiques); culture *f* physique.

Atlantic [ət'læntik], *a. & s.* **the A. (Ocean),** l'océan *m* Atlantique, l'Atlantique *m.*

atlas ['ætləs], *s.* atlas *m.*

atmosphere ['ætməsfiər], *s.* atmosphère *f* (terrestre, planétaire); **a happy a.,** une ambiance joyeuse; **atmos'pheric.** 1. *a.* atmosphérique. 2. *s.pl. Rad:* **atmospherics,** parasites *mpl.*

atoll ['ætɔl], *s.* atoll *m.*

atom ['ætəm], *s.* atome *m;* **a. bomb,** bombe *f* atomique; **smashed to atoms,** réduit en miettes; **a'tomic,** *a.* atomique; **a. age,** âge *m* atomique; **a. energy,** énergie *f* atomique; **a. pile,** pile *f* atomique, réacteur *m* nucléaire; **a. physicist,** atomiste *mf; Mil:* **a. warfare,** guerre *f* atomique.

atomize ['ætəmaiz], *v.tr.* atomiser, pulvériser vaporiser (un liquide); **'atomizer,** *s* atomiseur *m,* pulvérisateur *m,* vaporisateur *m*

atone [ə'toun], *v.ind.tr.* **to a. for,** expier (un faute); **a'tonement,** *s.* expiation *f,* réparation *f* **(for a fault,** d'une faute).

atrocious [ə'trouʃəs], *a.* (crime) atroce (plaisanterie *f,* goût *m*) exécrable; **-ly,** *adv* atrocement, exécrablement; **a'trocity,** *:* atrocité *f.*

attach [ə'tætʃ]. 1. *v.tr.* attacher, lier, fixer **(sth. t** sth., qch. à qch.); annexer (un document). *v.i.* s'attacher; **a'ttaché,** *s.* attaché, -ée (d'an bassade); **a'ttachment,** *s.* 1. (*affection*) a' tachement *m* **(of s.o. for s.o.,** de qn pour qn affection *f* **(for,** pour). 2. accessoire *m* (d'un machine).

attack [ə'tæk]. I. *v.tr.* attaquer; **to a. s.o.,** a taquer qn; **to a. a problem,** s'attaquer à u problème. II. *s.* 1. attaque *f*; assaut *m;* **to ma an a. (up)on,** attaquer (qn); s'attaquer à (u problème). 2. *Med:* attaque; crise *f* (de nerfs accès *m* (de fièvre); **a'ttacker,** *s.* attaquant agresseur *m.*

attain [ə'tein]. 1. *v.tr.* atteindre, arriver parvenir à (un grand âge); **to a. knowledg** acquérir des connaissances. 2. *v.ind.tr.* **to a. perfection,** atteindre à la perfection; **a'tainable,** *a.* accessible; à la portée **(by s.o.,** qn); **a'ttainment,** *s.* 1. réalisation *f* **(of an a bition,** etc., d'une ambition, etc.). 2. *usu.* connaissance(s) *f(pl)*; **man of remarkable tainments,** homme d'un savoir formidable.

attempt [ə'tem(p)t]. I. *v.tr.* (*a*) **to a. to do sth.,** sayer, tenter, tâcher, de faire qch.; (*b*) **to a. i possibilities,** tenter l'impossible; **attempt murder,** tentative *f* d'assassinat. II. *s.* tentati *f,* essai *m,* effort *m;* **first a.,** coup *m* d'essai **succeed at the first a.,** réussir du premier co **to give up the a.,** y renoncer.

attend [ə'tend]. 1. *v.ind.tr.* (*a*) **to a. to sth., fa** attention à qch., s'occuper de qch.; (*b*) **ser** (un client). 2. *v.tr.* (*a*) soigner (un malade); **to a. school,** aller à l'école; **to a. a meeti** assister à une réunion; **to a. (a course of) l**

tures, suivre un cours; **a′ttendance,** s. **1.** (of doctor) **a. on** s.o., visites fpl à qn. **2.** présence f (à une réunion, à un cours); **regular a.,** assiduité f, régularité f de présence; **there was a good a.,** l'assistance était nombreuse; **school a.,** fréquentation f scolaire; **a′ttendant,** s. surveillant, -ante; (in museum, etc.) gardien, -ienne; Th: ouvreuse f.

attention [ə′tenʃ(ə)n]. **1.** s. (a) attention f (**to,** à); **to turn one's a. to sth.,** porter son attention sur qch.; **to pay a. to** s.o., prêter (son) attention à qn; **pay a.!** faites attention! **to attract a.,** se faire remarquer; (b) soins mpl, entretien m. **2.** int. Mil: **a.!** garde à vous!

attentive [ə′tentiv], a. **1.** attentif (**to,** à); soigneux, soucieux (**to,** de). **2. a. to** s.o., assidu, empressé, auprès de qn; prévenant pour qn; **-ly,** adv. attentivement.

attenuate [ə′tenjueit], v.tr. atténuer.

attic [′ætik], s. mansarde f; grenier m.

attire [ə′taiər], s. vêtement(s) m(pl); costume m.

attitude [′ætitjuːd], s. (a) attitude f, pose f, port m (de tête); (b) **a. of mind,** disposition f d'esprit; (c) **to maintain a firm a.,** rester ferme.

attorney [ə′təːni], s. **1.** N.Am: = avoué m; **District A.** = Procureur m de la République. **2. A. General,** Avocat m du Gouvernement et chef du barreau. **3.** fondé m de pouvoir(s). **4. power of a.,** procuration f.

attract [ə′trækt], v.tr. **1.** attirer (**to,** à, vers). **2.** séduire, attirer (qn); **a′ttraction,** s. **1.** attraction f (**to, towards,** vers). **2.** usu. pl. séduction f; attractions, attraits mpl; **the chief a. at a party,** le clou de la fête; **a′ttractive,** a. attrayant, séduisant; **-ly,** adv. d'une manière attrayante; **a′ttractiveness,** s. attrait m, charme m.

attribute. I. v.tr. [ə′tribjuːt], attribuer, imputer (**to** s.o., **sth.,** à qn, qch.). **II.** s. [′ætribjuːt]. **1.** attribut m, qualité f. **2.** symbole m, attribut; **a′t-tributable,** a. attribuable, imputable (**to,** à); **attri′bution,** s. attribution f (**to,** à).

attrition [ə′triʃ(ə)n], s. attrition f; usure f par le frottement; **war of a.,** guerre f d'usure.

aubergine [′oubədʒiːn], s. aubergine f.

auburn [′oːbən], a. **a. hair,** cheveux mpl châtain roux.

auction [′oːkʃ(ə)n]. **I.** v.tr. vendre (qch.) aux enchères; vendre (des denrées) à la criée. **II.** s. vente f aux enchères, à la criée; **to put sth. up to, for, a.,** mettre qch. aux enchères; **auc-tion′eer,** s. commissaire-priseur m; **′auction room,** s. salle f des ventes.

audacious [oː′deiʃəs], a. **1.** audacieux, hardi, intrépide. **2.** Pej: effronté; **-ly,** adv. **1.** avec audace. **2.** Pej: effrontément.

audacity [oː′dæsiti], s. **1.** audace f; intrépidité f. **2.** Pej: effronterie f.

audible [′oːdibl], a. perceptible (à l'oreille); dis-

tinct, audible; **he was scarcely a.,** on l'entendait à peine; **-ibly,** adv. distinctement; **audi′bility,** s. audibilité f.

audience [′oːdjəns], s. **1.** audience f; **to grant** s.o. **an a.,** accorder une audience à qn. **2.** assistance f, auditoire m, public m.

audio(-)visual [′oːdiou′vizju(ə)l], a. audio-visuel, -elle.

audit [′oːdit]. **I.** v.tr. vérifier (des comptes). **II.** s. vérification f (de comptes); **′auditor,** s. expert-comptable m.

audition [oː′diʃən], s. audition f, séance f, d'essai.

auditorium [oːdi′toːriəm], s. salle f (de théâtre, de concerts).

augment [oːg′ment]. **1.** v.tr. augmenter, accroître (qch.) (**with, by,** de). **2.** v.i. augmenter, s'accroître; **augmen′tation,** s. augmentation f, accroissement m.

August [′oːgəst], s. août m; **in A.,** au mois d'août; **the fifth of A.,** le cinq août.

aunt [ɑːnt], s. tante f; **′auntie, ′aunty,** s. F: (children's speech) tata f, tantine f.

au pair [′ou′pɛər], a. & s. **an au p. girl, an au p.,** une étudiante au pair.

aurora [oː′roːrə], s. **a. borealis,** aurore boréale.

auspices [′oːspisiz], s.pl. auspices m; **under favourable a.,** sous d'heureux auspices; **aus′picious,** a. favorable, propice; de bon augure; **-ly,** adv. favorablement; **aus′piciousness,** s. aspect m favorable (d'une entreprise, d'un événement).

austere [oːs′tiər], a. austère; (maison) sans luxe, dépouillée, d'un goût sévère; **-ly,** adv. austèrement; **aus′terity,** s. austérité f; absence f de luxe; sévérité f de goût; **time(s) of a.,** période f de restrictions.

Australia [ɔs′treiliə]. Pr.n. l'Australie f; **Aus′tralian,** a. & s. australien, -ienne.

Austria [′ɔstriə]. Pr.n. l'Autriche f; **′Austrian,** a. & s. autrichien, -ienne.

authentic [oː′θentik], a. authentique; digne de foi; **-ally,** adv. authentiquement; **au′then-ticate,** v.tr. **1.** certifier. **2.** vérifier; **authen-ti′cation,** s. certification f (d'une signature, etc.); validation f; **authen′ticity** [-′tisiti], s. authenticité f.

author [′oːθər], s. auteur m; **′authorship,** s. **1.** profession f d'auteur. **2. to establish the a. of a book,** identifier l'auteur d'un livre.

authorize [′oːθəraiz], v.tr. autoriser (qch.); **to a.** s.o. **to do sth.,** autoriser qn à faire qch.; **authori′tarian,** a. autoritaire; **au′thoritative,** a. **1.** (caractère) autoritaire; (ton) péremptoire. **2.** (document) qui fait autorité; (renseignement) de bonne source; **-ly,** adv. **1.** autoritairement. **2.** avec autorité; **au′thority,** s. **1.** autorité f; **to have a. over** s.o., avoir autorité sur qn; **who's in a. here?** qui

commande ici? **2.** autorisation ƒ (de faire qch.).
3. on good a., de bonne source. **4. the
authorities,** l'administration ƒ; **authori′za-
tion,** s. autorisation ƒ; **′authorized,** a.
autorisé; **a. by custom,** sanctionné par l'usage;
the A. Version (of the Bible), la traduction
anglaise de la Bible de 1611; **a. prices,** prix
homologués.
auto- [′ɔːtou, ′ɔːtə], pref. auto-; **auto-
bio′graphical,** a. autobiographique; **auto-
bi′ography,** s. autobiographie ƒ; **au′to-
cracy,** s. autocratie ƒ; **′autocrat,** s. autocrate
m; **auto′cratic,** a. autocratique; **′auto-
graph. I.** s. autographe m. **II.** v.tr. écrire son
autographe dans (un livre), signer, dédicacer
(un livre); **′automat,** s. restaurant m à dis-
tributeurs automatiques; **auto′matic,** a.
automatique; **a. pistol,** automatique m; **a.
(telephone),** l'automatique m; Computers: **a.
programming,** programmation ƒ automatique;
auto′matics, s. pl. l'automatique ƒ; **auto′ma-
tion,** s. automatisation ƒ, automation ƒ;
au′tomatize, v.tr. automatiser; **au′tomaton,**
s. automate m; **′automobile,** s. N.Am:
auto(mobile) ƒ, voiture ƒ; **au′tonomous,** a.
autonome; **au′tonomy,** s. autonomie ƒ;
′autopsy, s. autopsie ƒ; **′auto(-)su′ggestion,**
s. autosuggestion ƒ.
autumn [′ɔːtəm], s. automne m; **au′tumnal**
[ɔ′tʌmnəl], a. automnal; d'automne.
auxiliary [ɔːg′ziliəri], a. & s. auxiliaire (mf).
avail [ə′veil]. **I.** v.tr. & i. **to a. oneself of sth.,** se
servir de qch.; user de qch.; profiter de qch.; **to
a. oneself of an opportunity,** saisir une occasion. **II.** s. **it's of no a.,** c'est inutile; cela ne sert
à rien; **availa′bility,** s. disponibilité ƒ (de
matériaux); **a′vailable,** a. (a) disponible; Fin:
a. funds, fonds liquides, disponibles; (b)
accessible.
avalanche [′ævəlɑːn(t)ʃ], s. avalanche ƒ.
avarice [′ævəris], s. avarice ƒ; **ava′ricious,** a.
avare.
avenge [ə′ven(d)ʒ], v.tr. venger (qn); **a′venger,**
s. vengeur, -eresse; **a′venging,** a. vengeur, ƒ.
-eresse.
avenue [′ævənjuː], s. (a) avenue ƒ; (b) esp.
N.Am: boulevard m; (c) chemin m d'accès; (d)
promenade plantée d'arbres.
average [′ævəridʒ]. **I. 1.** s. moyenne ƒ; **on an a.,**
en moyenne; **above the a.,** au-dessus du commun. **2.** a. **the a. Englishman,** l'Anglais moyen;
a. specimen, échantillon normal. **II.** v.tr. & i.
établir, faire, la moyenne (des chiffres, etc.); **he
averages eight hours' work a day,** il travaille en
moyenne huit heures par jour.
averse [ə′vəːs], a. **to be a. to sth.,** répugner à
qch.; être opposé à qch.; **he's not a. to a glass
of beer,** il prend volontiers un verre de bière;
a′version, s. **1.** aversion ƒ, répugnance ƒ; **to**

take an a. to s.o., prendre qn en grippe. **2.** obje
m d'aversion; **my pet a.,** ma bête noire.
avert [ə′vəːt], v.tr. détourner (les yeux, un coup
(from, de); écarter, prévenir (un danger).
aviary [′eiviəri], s. volière ƒ.
aviation [eivi′eiʃ(ə)n], s. aviation ƒ; **′aviator,** s
aviateur, -trice; **avi′onics,** s.pl. l'avionique ƒ
avid [′ævid], a. avide **(of, for,** de); **-ly,** ad
avidement, avec avidité; **a′vidity,** s. avidité ƒ
avocado [ævə′kɑːdou], s. **a. (pear),** (poire
d')avocat m.
avoid [ə′vɔid], v.tr. **1.** éviter (qn, qch.); **to a
doing sth.,** éviter de faire qch. **2.** se soustraire
(qch.); **to a. notice,** se dérober aux regard
a′voidable, a. évitable; **a′voidance,** s
action ƒ d'éviter; **her a. of me,** son soin
m'éviter.
avoirdupois [ævədə′pɔiz], s. (a) poids m d
commerce; (b) F: embonpoint m.
avowal [ə′vauəl], s. aveu m.
avowed [ə′vaud], a. (ennemi, etc.) avér
notoire; déclaré; **a′vowedly** [-idli], a
ouvertement, franchement; **he's a.
revolutionary,** il est franchemen
révolutionnaire.
await [ə′weit], v.tr. (a) attendre (qch., qn); Co
awaiting your orders, dans l'attente de vos
dres; (b) **parcels awaiting delivery,** colis m
souffrance.
awake [ə′weik]. **I.** v. (awoke, awoken) **1.** v.i.
s'éveiller, se réveiller; (b) **to a. to the dang
prendre conscience du danger. 2.** v.tr. éveill
réveiller (qn). **II.** a. éveillé; **I was a.,** je ne d
mais pas; **wide a.,** bien éveillé.
awaken [ə′weikən], v.tr. & i. **1.** éveiller
curiosité, les soupçons m). **2.** (a) réveiller (q
(b) se réveiller; **a′wakening,** s. (a) réveil m;
a rude a., une amère désillusion.
award [ə′wɔːd]. **I.** v.tr. adjuger, décerner
prix, etc.). **II.** s. prix m, récompense ƒ; **a′war
ing,** s. décernement m (d'un prix).
aware [ə′wɛər], a. avisé, informé, instruit
sth., de qch.); **to be a. of sth.,** savoir, ne
ignorer; **not that I'm a. of,** pas que
sache; **to become a. of sth.,** apprendre qch
away [ə′wei], adv. loin; au loin. **1.** (a) **to go
partir, s'en aller; the ball rolled a.,** la ball
roulé plus loin; (b) **to run a.,** s'enfuir; **to t
s.o. a.,** emmener qn; **to carry a.,** emporter;
a.! allez-vous-en! F: fichez le camp! **take it
emportez-le! 2.** (expressing continuousn
sing a.! continuez à chanter! **to do sth. righ
faire qch. tout de suite. 3.** (a) **far a.,** dan
lointain; au loin; **five paces a.,** à cinq pas d
(b) **when he is a.,** quand il n'est pas là; **wh
have to be a.,** lorsque je dois m'absenter
(from work) absent; Sp: **a. match,** matc
l'extérieur. **4.** (time) **I knew him a. bac
1950,** je l'ai connu dès 1950.

awe [ɔː], s. crainte f, terreur f; respect m; **to stand in a. of s.o.**, (i) craindre, redouter, qn; (ii) être intimidé par qn; **'awe-inspiring**, a. terrifiant, imposant; **a.-i. sight**, spectacle grandiose; **'awe-struck**, a. 1. frappé d'une terreur mystérieuse. 2. intimidé; **'awful**, a. 1. terrible, terrifiant. 2. (*intensive*) *F:* terrible; affreux; **what a. weather!** quel temps de chien! **an a. din**, un bruit terrible; **'awfully**, adv. *F:* (*intensive*) **I'm a. sorry**, je regrette infiniment; **a. funny**, drôle comme tout.

while [ə'wail], adv. pendant quelque temps; un moment; **wait a.**, attendez un peu.

wkward ['ɔːkwəd], a. 1. (*clumsy*) gauche, maladroit; **the a. age**, l'âge ingrat. 2. (*ill at ease*) embarrassé, gêné. 3. fâcheux, gênant; **an a. situation**, une situation délicate. 4. incommode, peu commode; **a. corner**, virage difficile; **he's an a. customer**, c'est un homme difficile; il n'est pas commode; **-ly**, adv. 1. gauchement, maladroitement. 2. d'une manière embarrassée; **'awkwardness**, s. 1. (a) gaucherie f; maladresse f; (b) manque m de grâce. 2. embarras m. 3. (*of situation*)

délicatesse f.

awl [ɔːl], s. *Tls:* alène f, poinçon m, perçoir m.

awning ['ɔːniŋ], s. tente f, vélum m; auvent m (de tente, de caravane camping).

awry [ə'rai], adv. & a. de travers; de guingois; (*of plans, etc.*) **to go all a.**, aller tout de travers; avorter.

axe [æks]. **I.** s. hache f; cognée f (de bûcheron); **to have an a. to grind**, agir dans un but intéressé. **II.** v.tr. *Adm:* réduire (les dépenses); **to a. a number of officers**, mettre à pied un nombre d'officiers.

axiom ['æksiəm], s. axiome m; **axio'matic**, a. axiomatique; **it's a.**, c'est évident.

axis, pl. **axes** ['æksis, 'æksi:z], s. axe m.

axle ['æksl], s. 1. a.(-tree), essieu m; *Aut:* **rear a.**, pont m (arrière). 2. arbre m, axe m (d'une roue); **'axle-arm**, s. fusée f (de l'essieu); **'axle-box**, s. boîte f à graisse; **'axle-pin**, s. clavette f d'essieu.

azalea [ə'zeiliə], s. *Bot:* azalée f.

Azores (the) [ðiə'zɔːz]. *Pr.n.pl.* les Açores f.

azure ['æʒər]. 1. s. azur m. 2. a. **an a. sky**, un ciel d'azur.

B

B, b [biː], s. **1.** (la lettre) B, b m. **2.** Mus: si m.

babble ['bæbl]. **I.** s. **1.** babillage m. **2.** bavardage m. **3.** murmure m (d'un ruisseau). **II.** v.i. (a) babiller; (b) bavarder, jaser; (c) (of stream) murmurer; **'babbler,** s. bavard, -arde; jaseur, -euse.

babel ['beib(ə)l], s. **it was an absolute b.,** c'était un vacarme à ne pas s'entendre; **b. of talk,** brouhaha m de conversation.

baboon [bə'buːn], s. Z: babouin m.

baby ['beibi], s. **1.** bébé m; **I've known him since he was a b.,** je l'ai vu naître; **the b. of the family,** le benjamin, la benjamine; F: **to be left holding the b.,** avoir l'affaire sur les bras, payer les pots cassés; F: **that's your b.,** débrouille-toi! **2.** attrib. (a) d'enfant, de bébé; F: **b. face,** visage poupard; (b) de petites dimensions, esp. **b. grand,** piano m (à) demi-queue; crapaud m; (c) (young animal) **b. elephant,** bébé éléphant; **'baby-carriage,** s. voiture f d'enfant; poussette f; **'baby-carrier,** s. moïse m; **'baby-clothes,** s.pl. layette f; **'babyhood,** s. première enfance; **'babyish,** a. **b. (character, etc.),** (caractère, etc.) puéril; **'baby-scales,** s.pl. pèse-bébé m, pl. pèse-bébés; **'baby-sit,** v.i. **(baby-sat),** garder les bébés; **'baby-sitter,** s. gardienne f.

bachelor ['bætʃələr], s. **1.** célibataire m, garçon m; **old b.,** vieux garçon; **b. girl,** jeune fille indépendante. **2.** Sch: bachelier, -ière; **B. of Arts, of Science,** approx. = licencié(e) ès lettres, ès sciences.

bacillus, pl. **-i** [bə'siləs, -ai], s. Biol: bacille m.

back [bæk]. **I.** s. **1.** (a) dos m; **to fall on one's b.,** tomber à la renverse; **to do sth. behind s.o.'s b.,** faire qch. à l'insu de qn; **to be glad to see the b. of s.o.,** être content de voir partir qn; **to put s.o.'s b. up,** mettre qn en colère; **b. to b.,** dos à dos; adossés; **b. to front,** sens devant derrière; **with one's b. to the wall,** acculé; aux abois; F: **to put one's b. into sth.,** s'appliquer à qch.; (b) les reins m; **to break one's b.,** se casser les reins, s'éreinter; **to break the b. of the work,** faire le plus gros du travail. **2.** (a) dos (d'un livre); verso m (d'une page); dossier m (d'une chaise); (b) **the b. of the hand,** le revers de la main; **he knows London like the b. of his hand,** il connaît Londres comme (le fond de) sa poche; (c) derrière m (de la tête); arrière m (d'une maison, d'une voiture); **let's go round to the b. (of the house),** allons à l'arrière; **the dress fastens at the b.,** la robe se ferme dans le dos; **idea at the b. of one's mind,** idée f d[e] derrière la tête; arrière-pensée f. **3.** (a) Fb[.] arrière m; **the backs,** l'arrière-défense f; (b) Th: fond m (d'une salle); **the b. of the stage,** l'arrière-scène f.

II. a. (a) arrière, de derrière; **b. door,** porte f de service; F: **to get in by the b. door,** entrer par l[a] petite porte; **b. room,** pièce f sur le derrière, su[r] la cour; F: **b. room boy,** savant m (qui travaill[e] à l'arrière-plan); **the b. streets of a town,** les bas quartiers d'une ville; **b. seat,** siège [m] arrière; **to take a b. seat,** (i) s'asseoir sur u[n] banc à l'arrière; (ii) s'effacer; passer au secon[d] plan; Aut: **b. axle,** pont m arrière; **b. whe[el,]** roue arrière; (b) **b. rent,** arriéré(s) m(pl) [de] loyer; **b. pay,** rappel m de traitement.

III. adv. **1.** (place) (a) en arrière; **stand b[.,]** rangez-vous! **house standing b. from the roa[d,]** maison f en retrait; (b) dans le sens contrai[re;] **to hit b.,** rendre coup pour coup; **to call s.o. [back,]** rappeler qn; **to come b.,** revenir; **to put sth. [back,]** remettre qch. à sa place; (c) **as soon as I get [back,]** dès mon retour. **2.** (time) **some few years b.,** i[l] a quelques années; **as far b. as 1939,** déjà [en] 1939; dès 1939.

IV. v.tr. & i. **1.** v.i. reculer; Aut: faire marc[he] arrière; **to b. into a lane,** entrer en marc[he] arrière dans un chemin. **2.** v.tr. soutenir (q[n,] financer (qn, Th: une pièce); parier, miser, s[ur] (un cheval); jouer (un cheval); mettre (u[ne] voiture) en marche arrière; **'backache[,** s.] douleurs fpl de reins; **'back'bencher,** s. P[.] député m sans portefeuille; **'backbite,** v.tr. [&] médire (de qn); **'backbiter,** s. mauvais[e] langue; **'backbone,** s. colonne vertébra[le;] échine f; F: **he's got no b.,** c'est un emplât[re;] **'back-breaking,** a. (travail, etc.) éreinta[nt;] **'backcloth,** s. Th: toile f de fond; **'back'd[own,]** v.tr. antidater; **'back'down,** v.i. rabattre de [ses] prétentions; se dédire; **'backer,** s. partis[an,] -ane; Com: Fin: commanditaire m; R[a:] parieur, -euse; **'back'fire. 1.** v.i. A[ut:] pétarader; **the plan backfired,** le projet leur [est] retombé sur le dos. **2.** s. Aut: contre-allum[age] m; pétarade f; **'background,** s. fond [m;] arrière-plan m; **he keeps in the b.,** il s'effac[e,] se tient dans l'ombre; **'backhand,** a. [&] Ten: etc: **b. (stroke),** coup m de reve[rs;] **'back'handed,** a. **b. compliment,** complim[ent] m à rebours; **'back'hander,** s. coup m revers de la main; *F:* riposte inattendue, attaque déloyale; '**backing**, *s.* **1.** renforcement *m* (d'un mur). **2.** *Sp:* paris *mpl* (sur un cheval). **3.** *Aut:* marche *f* arrière; '**backlash**, *s.* effet *m* de boumerang, contre-courant politique; '**backless**, *a.* (robe) sans dos; (banc) sans dossier; '**backlog**, *s.* arriéré *m* (de travail); '**backnumber**, *s.* (*a*) vieux numéro (d'un journal); (*b*) *F:* (*of pers.*) to be a b., être vieux jeu; être un croulant, une croulante; '**back'out**, *v.i. Aut:* sortir en marche arrière; *F:* retirer sa promesse; se dédire; '**back-'pedal**, *v.i.* (-**pedalled**), faire marche arrière; '**backside**, *s. Anat: F:* derrière *m*; '**back'stage**, *adv.* derrière la scène, dans les coulisses; '**back'stairs**, *s.* escalier *m* de service; b. **influence**, protections en haut lieu; b. **gossip**, propos *m* d'antichambre; '**back 'up**. **1.** *v.tr.* soutenir (qn, qch.); prêter son appui à (qn). **2.** *v.i. Aut: N.Am:* faire marche arrière; '**backward**, *a.* (mouvement *m*) en arrière; (enfant) retardé; to be b. in doing sth., être (i) lent; (ii) peu empressé, à faire qch.; '**backwardness**, *s.* lenteur *f* d'esprit; hésitation *f*, lenteur, à faire qch.; '**backwards**, *adv.* en arrière; to fall b., tomber à la renverse; to walk b., marcher à reculons; to walk b. and forwards, marcher, se promener, de long en large; '**backwater**, *s.* eau arrêtée (par un bief); bras *m* de décharge (d'une rivière); to live in a b., vivre (i) dans un bled; (ii) dans un coin paisible; '**backwoods**, *s.pl.* forêts *f* vierges (de l'Amérique du Nord); to live in the b., vivre au bout du monde; '**back'yard**, *s.* (*a*) arrière-cour *f*; (*b*) *N.Am:* jardin *m* derrière.

bacon ['beik(ə)n], *s.* lard *m*; bacon *m*; **streaky b.**, petit lard; *F:* to save one's b., sauver sa peau; se tirer d'affaire; *F:* to bring home the b., revenir triomphant, *F:* décrocher la timbale.

bacteria [bæk'tiəriə], *s.pl. Biol:* bactéries *fpl*; **bac'tericide**, *s.* bactéricide *m*; **bacterio'logical**, *a.* bactériologique; **bacteri'ologist**, *s.* bactériologiste *mf*, bactériologue *mf*.

bad [bæd]. **I.** *a.* mauvais. **1.** (*a*) (*inferior*) b. **air**, air vicié; b. **meat**, viande avariée; b. **coin**, pièce fausse; (*of food*) to go b., se gâter, s'avarier; (*b*) (*incorrect*) b. **translation**, mauvaise traduction; b. **shot**, coup mal visé; to be b. at (lying, etc.), ne pas savoir (mentir, etc.); *F:* it isn't half b., ce n'est pas mal du tout; (*c*) (*unfortunate*) to be in a b. way, être en mauvais état; he'll come to a b. end, il finira mal; it wouldn't be a b. thing to . . ., on ne ferait pas mal de . . . ; from b. to worse, de mal en pis. **2.** (*a*) (*wicked*) b. man, méchant homme; b. book, mauvais livre; he's a b. lot, c'est un vaurien, une fripouille; (*b*) (*unpleasant*) b. news, mauvaise nouvelle; b. smell, mauvaise odeur; to have a

b. cold, avoir un gros rhume; to be in a b. temper, être de mauvaise humeur; to be on b. terms with s.o., être mal, en mauvais termes, avec qn; that's too b.! c'est le bouquet! it's too b. you can't come, c'est dommage que vous ne puissiez pas venir; he's not b.-looking, il n'est pas mal; *F:* il n'est pas mal fichu; (*c*) b. accident, grave accident; b. mistake, faute *f* grave; lourde méprise; to be b. for s.o., sth., ne rien valoir pour qn, qch.; it's b. for your health, c'est mauvais pour la santé; (*d*) *F:* (*ill*) she's very b. today, elle est très mal aujourd'hui; she has a b. finger, elle a mal au doigt; my b. leg, ma jambe malade; -**ly**, *adv.* **1.** mal; to do b., mal réussir; things are going b., les choses vont mal; to be doing b., faire de mauvaises affaires. **2.** b. wounded, gravement, grièvement, blessé; the b. disabled, les grands mutilés. **3.** to want sth. b., (i) avoir grand besoin; (ii) avoir grande envie, de qch. **II.** *s.* (*a*) to take the b. with the good, accepter la mauvaise fortune aussi bien que la bonne; (*b*) (*of pers.*) to go to the b., mal tourner; (*c*) I'm 500 francs to the b., je perds 500 francs; '**badness**, *s.* **1.** mauvaise qualité; mauvais état. **2.** (*of pers.*) méchanceté *f*.

badge [bædʒ], *s.* **1.** insigne *m*; plaque *f*; médaille *f*. **2.** symbole *m*; signe distinctif.

badger[1] ['bædʒər], *s. Z:* blaireau *m*.

badger[2], *v.tr.* harceler, tourmenter, tracasser, importuner (qn).

badminton ['bædmintən], *s.* badminton *m*.

baffle ['bæfl], *v.tr.* (*a*) confondre, déconcerter (qn); (*b*) déjouer; frustrer (un complot); dérouter (les soupçons).

bag [bæg]. **I.** *s.* **1.** sac *m*; (diplomatic) b., valise *f* (diplomatique); paper b., poche *f*, sac *m*, en papier; shopping b., cabas *m*; *P:* there's bags of it, il y en a des tas, il y en a à gogo; travelling b., sac de voyage. **2.** *Anat:* sac, poche; (cow's) b., pis *m*, mamelle *f* (de vache); bags under the eyes, poches sous les yeux. **3.** *Ven:* the b., le tableau (de chasse): to get a good b., faire bonne chasse; *F:* in the b., sûr et certain; dans le sac. **4.** *pl. F:* pantalon *m*. **II.** *v.* (bagged) **1.** *v.i.* (*of garment*) bouffer. **2.** *v.tr.* tuer (du gibier) Ou: empocher, s'emparer de (qch.); mettre la main sur (qch.); '**bagging**, *s.* (i) mise *f* en sac; (ii) toile *f* à sac; '**baggy**, *a.* (vêtement) trop ample; (pantalon) flottant, bouffant.

bagatelle [bægə'tel], *s.* **1.** bagatelle *f*. **2.** billard anglais.

baggage ['bægidʒ], *s.* **1.** *Mil:* bagage *m*. **2.** bagages *mpl*; *Rail: N.Am:* b. car, fourgon *m* à bagages; b. check, bulletin *m* de bagages.

bagpipes ['bægpaips], *s.pl.* cornemuse *f*.

Bahamas (the) [ðəbə'haːməz]. *Pr.n. Geog:* les Lucayes *f*; les Bahamas *f*.

bail[1] [beil]. **I.** *s. Jur:* (*a*) cautionnement *m*; (*b*) (*pers.*) caution *f*, garant *m*; to go b. for s.o., se porter garant de qn. **II.** *v.tr. Jur:* **to b. s.o. out,** se porter caution pour obtenir l'élargissement provisoire de qn.

bail², *v.tr.* **to b. out the water, a boat,** écoper l'eau d'une embarcation; vider un canot.

bailiff ['beilif], *s.* **1.** agent *m* de poursuites; huissier *m.* **2.** régisseur *m,* intendant *m* (d'un domaine).

bait [beit]. **I.** *s.* (*a*) *Fish:* amorce *f*; (*b*) appât *m,* leurre *m.* **II.** *v.tr.* **1.** harceler (un animal). **2.** amorcer (un hameçon).

bake [beik]. **1.** *v.tr.* cuire, faire cuire (qch.) (au four). **2.** *v.i.* (*of bread, etc.*) cuire (au four); **'bakehouse,** *s.* fournil *m,* boulangerie *f*; **'baker,** *s.* boulanger *m*; **the b.'s wife,** la boulangère; **the b.'s shop,** la boulangerie; **'bakery,** *s.* boulangerie *f*; **'baking.** (*a*) *s.* cuisson *f* (du pain, etc.); (*b*) *adv.* **b. hot,** excessivement chaud; **'baking-dish,** *s.* plat *m* allant au four; **'baking-powder,** *s.* levure artificielle.

balance ['bæləns]. **I.** *s.* **1.** balance *f*; **to hang in the b.,** rester en balance. **2.** équilibre *m*; aplomb *m*; **to keep one's b.,** se tenir en équilibre; **to lose one's b.,** perdre l'équilibre; **b. of power,** la balance des pouvoirs. **3.** *Com:* (*a*) **b. in hand,** solde créditeur; **b. due,** solde débiteur; *Fin:* **b. of payments,** balance des paiements; **b. of trade,** balance commerciale; (*b*) **to strike a b.,** dresser le bilan; **b. sheet,** bilan; **on b.,** à tout prendre. **II.** *v.* **1.** *v.tr.* (*a*) balancer, peser (les conséquences); (*b*) mettre, maintenir, (un objet) en équilibre; équilibrer (des forces); faire contrepoids à (qch.); (*c*) *Fin: Com:* balancer, solder (un compte); **to b. the budget,** équilibrer le budget. **2.** *v.i.* (*a*) (*of accounts*) se solder; (*b*) osciller, balancer; **'balanced,** *a.* équilibré; compensé; **'balancing. I.** *a.* **1.** (mouvement *m*) de bascule. **2.** (*of spring, etc.*) (ressort) compensateur. **II.** *s.* **1.** balancement *m*; hésitation *f*. **2.** (*a*) mise *f* en équilibre; équilibrage *m*; (*b*) solde *m* (des comptes). **3.** ajustement *m,* compensation *f*.

balcony ['bælkəni], *s.* balcon *m.*

bald [bɔːld], *a.* **1.** chauve; **to go b.,** *F:* se déplumer. **2.** (*of style*) plat, sec; **-ly,** *adv.* platement, sèchement; **'bald-'headed,** *a.* (à la tête) chauve; **to go at it b.-h.,** y aller tête baissée; **'baldness,** *s.* calvitie *f*; alopécie *f*; **b. of style,** platitude *f,* sécheresse *f*.

bale¹ [beil], *s. Com:* balle *f,* ballot *m* (de marchandises, etc.).

bale², *v.i. Av:* **to b. out,** sauter en parachute.

Balearic [bæli'ærik], *a. Geog:* **the B. Islands,** les îles *f* Baléares.

balk [bɔːk]. **1.** *v.tr.* contrarier (qn); (*a*) **to b. s.o.'s plans,** frustrer les desseins de qn; (*b*) entraver (qn). **2.** *v.i.* (*of horse*) refuser (l'obstacle); (*of pers.*) **to b. at sth.,** reculer devant qch.

Balkan ['bɔːlkən], *a. Geog:* balkanique; **the B. States,** *s.* **the Balkans,** les Etats *m* balkaniques.

ball¹ [bɔːl], *s.* **1.** boule *f* (de neige); balle *f* (de tennis); ballon *m* (de football); bille *f* (de billard); pelote *f* (de laine); *E:* **b. bearing(s),** roulement *m* à billes; **to keep the b. rolling,** soutenir la conversation, le jeu; **to start the b. rolling,** mettre le bal en train; **to be on the b.,** connaître son affaire; **to play b.,** coopérer; jouer le jeu. **2.** globe *m* (de l'œil); **'ball(-)cock,** *s.* robinet *m,* soupape *f,* à flotteur; **'ballpoint,** *s.* **b. (pen),** stylo *m* (à) bille.

ball², *s.* bal *m, pl.* bals; **'ballroom,** *s.* salle *f* de bal.

ballad ['bæləd], *s.* **1.** *Mus:* romance *f*. **2.** *Lit:* ballade *f*.

ballast ['bæləst], *s.* **1.** *Nau:* lest *m*. **2.** *Rail:* ballast *m,* empierrement *m*.

ballet ['bælei], *s.* ballet *m*; **b. dancer,** danseur, -euse, de ballet; *f.* ballerine; **balle'rina** [bælə'riːnə], *s.* ballerine *f*.

ballistics [bə'listiks], *s.pl.* (*usu. with sing. const.*) balistique *f*.

balloon [bə'luːn], *s.* ballon *m*.

ballot ['bælət]. **I.** *s.* (*a*) tour *m* de scrutin; **to vote by b.,** voter au scrutin; (*b*) scrutin *m,* vote *m*; **b. paper,** bulletin *m* de vote; **b. box,** urne *f* (de scrutin). **II.** *v.i.* voter au scrutin.

balmy ['bɑːmi], *a.* (air, temps) embaumé, par fumé; d'une douceur délicieuse.

balsa ['bɔlsə], *s.* balsa *m*.

Baltic ['bɔːltik], *a. & s.* **1.** **the B. (Sea),** la (mer Baltique. **2.** **B. port,** port *m* balte.

balustrade [bæləs'treid], *s.* (*a*) balustrade *f*; (*b* accoudoir *m,* appui *m* (de fenêtre, etc.).

bamboo [bæm'buː], *s.* bambou *m*.

bamboozle [bæm'buːzl], *v.tr.* mystifier, enjôle embobeliner (qn); **to b. s.o. out of sth.,** soutire qch. à qn.

ban [bæn]. **I.** *s.* (*a*) ban *m,* proscription *f*; (*b*) *Ecc* interdit *m.* **II.** *v.tr.* (**banned**) interdire (q qch.); mettre (un livre) à l'index.

banal [bə'nɑːl, bæ'nɑːl, 'beinl], *a.* banal, -au ordinaire; **ba'nality,** *s.* banalité *f*.

banana [bə'nɑːnə], *s.* banane *f*; **b. (tree** bananier *m*.

band¹ [bænd], *s.* **1.** (*a*) lien *m*; cercle *m*; ruban (d'un chapeau); **elastic, rubber, b.,** élastique *n Rad:* **frequency b.,** bande *f* de fréquence; (*b* bande *f*; **paper b.,** bande de papier. **2.** *F* bande, courroie *f* (de transmission); **b. sav** scie *f* à ruban.

band². **I.** *s.* **1.** (*a*) bande *f,* troupe *f*; (*b*) com pagnie *f*. **2.** *Mus:* (*a*) orchestre *m*; (*b*) M musique *f*; **brass b.,** fanfare *f*. **II.** *v.i.* **to together,** (i) se réunir en bande; (ii) s'ameute **'bandmaster,** *s.* chef *m* de musiqu **'bandsman,** *s.* musicien *m*; **'bandstand,** kiosque *m* à musique; **'band-wagon,** *s.*

jump on the b.-w., se mettre dans le mouvement; se ranger du bon côté.
bandage ['bændidʒ]. **I.** s. *Med:* bandage m; bande f; **crêpe b.,** bande Velpeau; pansement m. **II.** *v.tr.* bander (une plaie); mettre un pansement sur (une blessure).
bandit ['bændit], s. bandit m, brigand m.
bandy¹ ['bændi], *v.tr.* (se) renvoyer (des paroles); échanger (des plaisanteries).
bandy², a. **b. legs,** jambes bancales; **'bandy-legged,** a. bancal, -als.
bane [bein], s. fléau m, peste f; *F:* **it's the b. of my life,** cela m'empoisonne l'existence.
bang [bæŋ]. **I.** s. coup (violent); détonation f; claquement m (de porte); **supersonic b.,** double bang m; **to go off with a b.,** détoner. **II.** v. **1.** *v.i.* (a) **to b. at, on, the door,** frapper avec bruit à la porte; (b) (*of door*) claquer. **2.** *v.tr.* frapper (violemment); (faire) claquer (la porte). **III.** *int.* boum! **b. in the middle,** en plein milieu; **'banging,** s. coups violents; claquement m; détonations fpl.
bangle [bæŋgl], s. bracelet m.
banish ['bæniʃ], *v.tr.* bannir, exiler (qn); **'banishment,** s. bannissement m, exil m.
banisters ['bænistəz], s.pl. rampe f (d'escalier).
banjo, pl. **-oes,** *N.Am:* **-os** ['bændʒou, -ouz], s. *Mus:* banjo m.
bank¹ [bæŋk]. **I.** s. **1.** (a) talus m; *Civ.E:* remblai m; *Rail:* rampe f; (b) banc m (de sable); (c) digue f. **2.** berge f; rive f (d'une rivière). **3.** *Av:* virage m sur l'aile. **II.** v. **1.** *v.tr.* **to b. (up),** endiguer (une rivière); surhausser (un virage); couvrir (un feu); remblayer, terrasser (de la terre). **2.** *v.i.* (*of clouds, etc.*) s'entasser, s'amonceler; *Av:* s'incliner, virer (sur l'aile).
bank². **I.** s. (a) banque f; **merchant b.,** banque d'affaires; **b. account,** compte m en banque; **b. clerk,** employé(e) de banque; **b. holiday,** jour férié; **b. book,** livret m de banque; (b) bureau m de banque; **branch b.,** succursale f. **II.** *v.tr. & i.* **1.** mettre, déposer, de l'argent en banque. **2. to b. on sth.,** compter sur qch.; **'banker,** s. banquier m; **'banking,** s. **1.** opérations fpl de banque. **2.** (*profession*) la banque; **'banknote,** s. billet m de banque.) **'bankrupt,** a. & s. (commerçant, etc.) failli (m); **to go b.,** faire faillite; **'bankruptcy,** s. faillite f.
bank³, s. clavier m (d'un orgue); rangs mpl (d'une machine à écrire); *Cin:* **b. of projectors,** rampe f de projecteurs.
banner ['bænər], s. bannière f, étendard m.
banns [bænz], s.pl. bans m (de mariage).
banquet ['bæŋkwit], s. banquet m; dîner m de gala; **to give a b.,** offrir un banquet.
bantam ['bæntəm], s. coq m, poule f, (de) Bantam; coq (de combat) nain; **b.-weight (boxer),** (boxeur m) poids m coq.
banter ['bæntər], s. raillerie f, persiflage m.

baptize [bæp'taiz], *v.tr.* baptiser; **'baptism,** s. baptême m; **'Baptist,** s. baptiste mf.
bar [bɑːr]. **I.** s. **1.** (a) barre f (de fer); tablette f (de chocolat); barre (de savon); lingot m (d'or); (b) pl. barreaux m (d'une cage); **to be behind bars,** être sous les verrous; (c) (**harbour**) **b.,** barre (de sable). **2.** empêchement m, obstacle m; **colour b.,** ségrégation raciale. **3.** *Jur:* (a) barre (des accusés); **the prisoner at the b.,** l'accusé(e); (b) barreau (des avocats); **to be called to the b.,** être reçu avocat. **4.** bar m; buvette f; comptoir m (dans un bar). **5.** (a) ligne f, trait m; (b) *Mus:* mesure f. **II.** *v.tr.* (**barred**) **1.** barrer (la route). **2.** défendre, interdire (une action); désapprouver (une personne, une habitude). **3.** rayer (de lignes); barrer. **III.** *prep.* (*also* **'barring**) excepté, sauf; à l'exception de (qn, qch.); **bar(ring) accidents,** sauf accident.
barb [bɑːb]. **I.** s. barbillon m. **II.** *v.tr.* garnir (qch.) de barbillons; **barbed,** a. **b. wire,** fil (de fer) barbelé.
Barbados [bɑː'beidouz]. *Pr.n. Geog:* la Barbade.
barbarian [bɑː'bɛəriən], s. barbare mf; **bar'baric** [-'bærik], a. barbare; **bar'barity,** s. barbarie f, cruauté f; **'barbarous,** a. barbare; cruel, inhumain; **-ly,** adv. cruellement.
barbecue ['bɑːbikjuː], s. barbecue m.
barber ['bɑːbər], s. coiffeur m pour hommes; (*in Eng.*) **b.'s pole,** enseigne f de barbier; **b.'s,** *N.Am:* **b., shop,** salon m de coiffure pour hommes.
bare ['bɛər]. **I.** a. **1.** nu; dénudé; **b. legs,** jambes nues; **b. countryside,** pays nu, dénudé, pelé; **the trees are already b.,** les arbres sont déjà dépouillés; **to lay (sth.) b.,** mettre à nu, exposer (qch.); *El:* **bare wire,** fil dénudé. **2. to earn a b. living,** gagner tout juste de quoi vivre; **b. necessities,** juste ce qu'il faut pour vivre; **b. majority,** faible majorité; **-ly,** adv. à peine, tout juste. **II.** *v.tr.* mettre (qch.) à nu; dénuder (qch.); **'bareback,** adv. **to ride b.,** monter (un cheval) à nu, à cru, à poil; **'barefaced,** a. (mensonge) éhonté, cynique; **'barefoot,** adv. nu-pieds; (à) pieds nus; **'bare'headed,** a. & adv. nu-tête, tête nue; **'bareness,** s. nudité f; dénuement m; sécheresse f (de style).
bargain ['bɑːgin]. **I.** s. **1.** (a) marché m, affaire f; (b) **a real b.,** une véritable occasion; **into the b.,** par-dessus le marché; **it's a b.!** c'est entendu! **2. b. sale,** vente f de soldes. **II.** *v.i.* (a) négocier (**with s.o.,** avec qn); **I didn't b. for that!** je ne m'attendais pas à cela! (b) **to b. with s.o.,** marchander avec qn; **to b. over sth.,** marchander qch.; **'bargain counter,** s. *Com:* rayon m des soldes; **'bargaining,** s. marchandage m; **collective b.,** convention collective.
barge¹ [bɑːdʒ], s. chaland m, péniche f; **bar'gee,** s. marinier m.

barge², *v.i.* *F:* **to b. into sth.**, venir se heurter contre qch.; **to b. in**, intervenir mal à propos.

baritone ['bæritoun], *a.* & *s.* *Mus:* **b. (voice)**, (voix *f* de) baryton *m.*

bark¹ [ba:k]. **I.** *s.* écorce *f* (d'arbre). **II.** *v.tr.* écorcer (un arbre); **to b. one's shins**, s'érafler les tibias.

bark². **I.** *s.* (*a*) (*of dog*) aboiement *m*; **his b. is worse than his bite**, il fait plus de bruit que de mal; (*b*) (*of fox*) glapissement *m.* **II.** *v.i.* (*a*) (*of dog*) aboyer (**at**, après, contre); **to b. up the wrong tree**, suivre une fausse piste; (*b*) (*of fox*) glapir; **'barking. 1.** *a.* (chien) aboyeur. **2.** *s.* aboiement *m.*

barley ['ba:li], *s.* orge *f*; **b. sugar**, sucre *m* d'orge.

barmaid ['ba:meid], *s.f.* serveuse *f* de café.

barman, *pl.* **-men** ['ba:mən], *s.* garçon *m* de café; barman *m*, *pl.* -men.

barn [ba:n], *s.* grange *f*; **'barnyard**, *s.* basse-cour *f.*

barnacle ['ba:nəkl], *s.* **1.** *Crust:* bernacle *f*, bernache *f.* **2.** *Orn:* **b. goose**, bernache, bernacle nonnette.

barometer [bə'rɔmitər], *s.* baromètre *m.*

baron ['bærən], *s.* baron *m*; **'baroness**, *s.* baronne *f*; **'baronet**, *s.* baronnet *m.*

barrack ['bærək]. **I.** *s.* **1.** *Mil:* (*usu. pl.*) caserne *f*; (*of cavalry*) quartier *m*; **confined to barracks**, consigné (au quartier); **b. room**, chambrée *f*; **b. room language, jokes**, propos *mpl*, plaisanteries *fpl*, de caserne, de chambrée. **2.** *Pej:* **great b. of a place**, grand bâtiment (laid). **II.** *v.tr.* chahuter; huer (une équipe, etc.).

barrage ['bæra:ʒ], *s.* **1.** barrage *m* (d'un lac, d'un fleuve). **2.** *Mil:* tir *m* de barrage; **b. of questions**, feu roulant de questions.

barrel ['bærəl], *s.* **1.** tonneau *m*, barrique *f*, fût *m* (de vin); **herring b.**, caque *f.* **2.** cylindre *m*; canon *m* (de fusil). **3.** **b. organ**, orgue *m* de Barbarie.

barren ['bærən], *a.* stérile, improductif; (terre *f*) aride; **'barrenness**, *s.* stérilité *f.*

barricade [bæri'keid]. **I.** *s.* barricade *f.* **II.** *v.tr.* barricader.

barrier ['bæriər], *s.* (*a*) barrière *f*; (*b*) obstacle *m* (au progrès, etc.).

barrister ['bæristər], *s.* avocat *m.*

barrow ['bærou], *s.* **1.** (**wheel-)b.**, brouette *f.* **2.** **hawker's b.**, baladeuse *f*; voiture *f* à bras; **b. boy**, marchand *m* des quatre saisons; **'barrowful**, *s.* brouettée *f.*

barter ['ba:tər]. **I.** *s.* échange *m*; troc *m.* **II.** *v.tr.* **to b. sth. for sth.**, échanger, troquer, qch. contre qch.; faire le troc; **'barter a'way**, *v.tr. Pej:* vendre (sa liberté, ses droits); trafiquer (son honneur).

base [beis]. **I.** *s.* **1.** base *f*; **aviation b.**, base d'aviation; **submarine b.**, nid *m* de sous-marins; **rocket b.**, base de lancement de fusées. **2.** (*a*) partie inférieure; fondement *m*; base; (*of apparatus*) socle *m*, pied *m.* **II.** *v.tr.* fonder (**on**, sur); **to b. oneself on sth.**, se baser, se fonder, sur qch. **III.** *a.* bas, vil; (motif *m*) indigne; (métal) vil; **-ly**, *adv.* bassement, vilement; **'baseless**, *a.* sans base, sans fondement; **'basement**, *s.* sous-sol *m*; **'baseness**, *s.* bassesse *f.*

baseball ['beisbɔ:l], *s. Sp:* base-ball *m.*

bash [bæʃ]. **I.** *s.* *F:* (*a*) coup *m*, enfoncement *m*; **your hat has had a b.**, votre chapeau est cabossé; **to have a b. at sth.**, s'attaquer à, s'essayer à, qch.; *F:* tenter le coup; (*b*) coup (de poing) violent; *P:* gnon *m.* **II.** *v.tr.* *F:* cogner (qn, qch.); **to b. sth. in**, défoncer qch.; **to b. s.o. about**, assommer, houspiller, qn; **'basher**, *s.* *F:* cogneur *m.*

bashful ['bæʃfəl], *a.* (*a*) timide; (*b*) modeste, pudique; **-fully**, *adv.* (*a*) timidement; (*b*) pudiquement; **'bashfulness**, *s.* timidité *f*, fausse honte.

basic ['beisik], *a.* (principe, etc.) fondamental; **b. vocabulary**, vocabulaire *m* de base; **b. pay**, salaire *m* de base; **-ally**, *adv.* fondamentalement.

basin ['beisn], *s.* **1.** *H:* (*a*) bassin *m*; écuelle *f*, bol *m*; **large b.**, bassine *f*; (*b*) (**wash-)b.**, cuvette *f*, lavabo *m.* **2.** *Geog:* bassin (d'un fleuve).

basis, *pl.* **bases** ['beisis, 'beisi:z], *s.* base *f*, fondement *m.*

bask [ba:sk], *v.i.* se chauffer (au soleil); prendre le soleil.

basket ['ba:skit], *s.* corbeille *f*; panier *m*; **waste paper b.**, corbeille à papier(s); **shopping b.**, panier *m* à provisions; **the pick of the b.**, le dessus du panier; **'basketball**, *s. Sp:* basket (-ball) *m*; **'basketchair**, *s.* chaise *f*, fauteuil *m* en rotin; **'basket-maker**, *s.* vannier *m*; **'basket-work**, *s.* vannerie *f.*

Basle [ba:l]. *Pr.n. Geog:* Bâle *f.*

Basque [bæsk, ba:sk], *a.* & *s. Ethn:* basque (*mf*); *a.* basquais, -aise.

bass [beis], *a.* & *s. Mus:* basse *f*; **b. voice**, voix de basse.

bassoon [bə'su:n], *s. Mus:* basson *m.*

bastard ['ba:stəd, 'bæ-], *a.* & *s.* (*a*) bâtard, -e; (*b*) *s. P:* salaud *m*; **'bastardize**, *v.tr.* abâtardir.

baste [beist], *v.tr. Cu:* arroser (un rôti); **'basting**, *s.* arrosage *m* (d'un rôti).

bat¹ [bæt], *s. Z:* chauve-souris *f*, *pl.* chauve-souris.

bat². **I.** *s.* **1.** batte *f* (de cricket); **to do sth. off one's own b.**, faire qch. de son (propre) chef. palette *f*, raquette *f* (de ping-pong). **II.** (**batte 1.** *v.i.* (*cricket, etc.*) manier la batte; être guichet. **2.** *v.tr.* *F:* **he never batted an eyelid**, n'a pas sourcillé, bronché; **'batsman**, **-men**, *s.* (*at cricket*) batteur *m.*

batch [bætʃ], *s.* fournée *f* (de pain); paquet *m*

lettres); lot *m* (de marchandises).

bate [beit], *v.tr.* (*only used in*) **to speak with bated breath,** parler en baissant la voix.

bath, *pl.* **baths** [bɑ:θ, bɑ:ðz]. I. *s.* 1. bain *m*; **to take, have, a b.,** prendre un bain. 2. baignoire *f*. II. *v.* 1. *v.tr.* baigner (un enfant). 2. *v.i.* prendre un bain; **'bath mat,** *s.* descente *f* de bain; **'bathroom,** *s.* salle *f* de bain(s); **bath(-)salts,** *s.pl.* sels *m* pour le bain; **'bath(-)towel,** *s.* serviette *f* de bain; **'bath(-)tub,** *s.* baignoire *f*.

bathe [beið]. I. *v.tr. & i.* baigner; se baigner; laver, lotionner (une plaie). II. *s.* bain *m* (de mer, de rivière); baignade *f*; **'bather,** *s.* baigneur, -euse; **'bathing,** *s.* (*a*) bains *mpl* (de mer, de rivière); baignades *fpl*; **b. costume, suit,** maillot *m* (de bain); **b. trunks,** slip *m* (de bain); (*b*) lotion *f* (d'une plaie).

baton ['bæt(ə)n, -tɔ̃], *s.* bâton *m* (de maréchal, de chef d'orchestre, d'agent de police).

battalion [bə'tæljən], *s. Mil:* bataillon *m*.

batten ['bætn], *s.* latte *f*.

batter[1] ['bætər], *s. Cu:* pâte *f* lisse; pâte à frire.

batter[2]. 1. *v.tr.* battre, bosseler (du cuivre, de l'argent). 2. *v.i.* **to b. at the door,** frapper avec violence à la porte; **'battered,** *a.* délabré; (visage) meurtri; abîmé; (enfant) maltraité; **old b. hat,** vieux chapeau cabossé.

battery ['bæt(ə)ri], *s.* 1. *Artil:* batterie *f*. 2. (*a*) *El:* pile *f*, batterie; (*b*) *El:* **(storage-)b.,** accumulateur *m, F:* accu *m*; (*c*) *Agr:* éleveuse *f* (à poulets), batterie. 3. *Jur:* **assault and b.,** coups *mpl* et blessures *fpl*.

battle ['bætl]. I. *s.* bataille *f*, combat *m*; **b. axe,** (i) hache *f* d'armes; (ii) *F:* (*of woman*) (*old*) **b. axe,** virago *f*; *Mil:* **b. dress,** tenue *f* de campagne; **to give b.,** livrer bataille; **that's half the b.,** c'est bataille à moitié gagnée; **to fight s.o.'s battles,** prendre le parti de qn; **b. royal,** bataille en règle. II. *v.i.* se battre, lutter (**with s.o. for sth.,** avec qn pour qch.); **to b. against the wind,** lutter contre le vent; **'battlefield,** *s.* champ *m* de bataille; **'battlements,** *s.pl.* créneaux *mpl*; **'battleship,** *s.* cuirassé *m*.

bauxite ['bɔ:ksait], *s. Miner:* bauxite *f*.

Bavaria [bə'vɛəriə]. *Pr.n.* la Bavière.

Bavarian [bə'vɛəriən], *a. & s.* bavarois, -e.

bawl [bɔ:l], *v.tr. & i.* brailler; crier à tue-tête; **to b. out abuse,** hurler des injures.

bay[1] [bei], *s. Bot:* laurier *m*; **b.-tree,** laurier; *Cu:* **b. leaf,** feuille *f* de laurier.

bay[2], *s. Geog:* baie *f*.

bay[3], *s.* 1. (*of bridge*) travée *f*. 2. enfoncement *m*; baie *f*; *Aut:* **parking b.,** place *f* de stationnement; *Com:* **loading b.,** quai *m* de chargement; *Nau: etc:* **sick b.,** infirmerie *f*; **'bay-'window,** *s.* fenêtre *f* en saillie.

bay[4]. I. *v.i.* aboyer; donner de la voix. II. *s.* (*also* **'baying**) aboiement *m* (d'un chien de chasse);

to be at bay, être aux abois.

bay[5], *a. & s.* (cheval) bai (*m*).

bayonet ['beiənit], *s. Mil:* baïonnette *f*.

bazaar [bə'zɑ:r], *s.* 1. bazar (oriental). 2. vente *f* de charité; kermesse *f*.

be [stressed bi: *unstressed* bi], *v.i.* (**was,** *pl.* **were; been**) être. 1. (*a*) **Mary is pretty, Mary's pretty,** Marie est jolie; **seeing is believing,** voir c'est croire; **isn't he lucky!** il en a de la chance! (*b*) **he is, he's, an Englishman,** il est Anglais, c'est un Anglais; **if I were you . . .,** à votre place . . .; (*c*) **three and two are five,** trois et deux font cinq. 2. (*a*) **don't be long,** ne tardez pas (à revenir); **to be in danger,** se trouver en danger; **I was at the meeting,** j'ai assisté à la réunion; **I don't know where I am,** (i) je ne sais pas où je suis; (ii) je ne sais pas où j'en suis; **here I am,** me voici; (*b*) **how are you?** comment allez-vous? (*c*) **how much is that?** combien cela coûte-t-il? **how far is it to London?** combien y a-t-il d'ici à Londres? (*d*) **when is the concert?** quand le concert aura-t-il lieu? **Christmas is on a Sunday this year,** Noël tombe un dimanche cette année; **tomorrow is Friday,** c'est demain vendredi. 3. (*a*) **to be** (= *feel*) **cold, afraid, etc.,** avoir froid, peur, etc.; (*b*) **to be twenty (years old),** avoir vingt ans. 4. (*a*) **that may be,** cela se peut; **well, so be it!** eh bien, soit! **everything must remain just as it is,** tout doit rester tel quel; **however that may be,** quoi qu'il en soit; (*b*) *impers.* **there is, there are,** il y a; **what is there to see?** qu'est-ce qu'il y a à voir? **there will be dancing,** on dansera; **there were a dozen of us,** nous étions une douzaine. 5. **he had been and inspected the land,** il était allé inspecter le terrain; **I have been into every room,** j'ai visité toutes les pièces; **where have you been?** d'où venez-vous? **has anyone been?** est-il venu quelqu'un? 6. *impers.* (*a*) **it is late,** il est tard; **it is a fortnight since I saw him,** il y a quinze jours que je ne l'ai vu; (*b*) **it's fine,** il fait beau (temps); (*c*) **it is said,** on dit; **it's for you to decide,** c'est à vous de décider; **what is it?** (i) que voulez-vous? (ii) qu'est-ce qu'il y a? **as it were,** pour ainsi dire. 7. (*auxiliary uses*) (*a*) **I am, was, doing sth.,** je fais, faisais, qch.; **they are always laughing,** ils sont toujours à rire; **I've (just) been writing,** je viens d'écrire; **I've been waiting for a long time,** j'attends depuis longtemps; (*b*) (*passive*) (i) **he was killed,** il fut tué; **he is allowed to smoke,** on lui permet de fumer; (ii) **he is to be pitied,** il est à plaindre; **what's to be done?** que faire? (*c*) (*expressing futurity*) **I'm to see him tomorrow,** je dois le voir demain. 8. **the bride to be,** la fiancée, la future. 9. **are you happy?—I am,** êtes-vous heureux?—oui, je le suis; **he's back—is he?** il est de retour—vraiment? **so you're back, are you?** alors vous voilà de retour? **'being.** I. *a.*

for the time b., pour le moment. II. *s.* 1.
existence *f*; **to bring a plan into b.**, réaliser un
projet. 2. être *m*; (*a*) **all my b.**, tout mon être;
(*b*) **a human b.**, un être humain.

beach [bi:tʃ], *s.* plage *f*, grève *f*, rivage *m*; **b. hut**,
cabine *f* (de plage); **'beachhead,** *s.* Mil: tête *f*
de pont; **'beachwear,** *s. coll.* vêtements *mpl*
de plage.

beacon ['bi:k(ə)n], *s. Av:* balise *f*; *Nau:* **b. (light)**,
fanal *m*, phare *m*; *Aut:* **Belisha b.**, sphère *f*
orange indiquant un passage clouté.

bead [bi:d], *s.* 1. (*for prayers*) (**string of**) **beads,**
chapelet *m*; **to tell one's beads**, dire son
chapelet. 2. perle *f*; (**string of**) **beads**, collier
m.

beagle ['bi:gl], *s.* (chien courant) beagle (*m*), F:
bigle *m*.

beak [bi:k], *s.* (*a*) bec *m* (d'oiseau); *F:* nez
crochu; (*b*) *P:* magistrat *m*.

beaker ['bi:kər], *s.* gobelet *m*; coupe *f*.

beam [bi:m]. I. *s.* 1. (*a*) poutre *f* solive *f*; (*b*) fléau
m (d'une balance). 2. *Nau:* (*of ship*) **to be on
her b. ends**, être engagé; (*of pers.*) **to be on
one's b. ends**, être à bout de ressources. 3. (*a*)
rayon *m* (de lumière); **b. of delight,** large
sourire *m*; (*b*) **b. navigation,** navigation *f*
radiogoniométrique; **wireless b.,** faisceau *m*
hertzien; *T.V:* **electron b.,** faisceau électronique; *F:* **to be off b.,** dérailler; *Rad:* **b.
system,** émission *f* aux ondes dirigées. II. *v.i.*
(*of the sun, of pers.*) rayonner; *Rad:* émettre;
(**to be) beamed in on . . .,** (être) dirigé vers
. . .; **'beaming,** *a.* rayonnant; (soleil, visage)
radieux.

bean [bi:n], *s.* (*a*) **broad b.,** fève *f*; **runner beans,**
haricots d'Espagne; **French beans,** *N.Am:*
string beans, haricots verts; *F:* **to be full of
beans,** être plein d'entrain; **he hasn't a b.,** il n'a
pas le sou, un radis; (*b*) **coffee b.,** grain *m* de
café.

bear[1] ['bɛər], *s.* 1. (*a*) ours *m*; **she-b.,** ourse *f*; **b.
cub,** ourson *m*; **polar b.,** ours blanc; (*b*) *Astr:*
the Great B., la Grande Ourse. 2. *St.Exch:*
baissier *m*; **'bear-garden,** *s.* **to turn the place
into a b.-g.,** mettre le désordre partout;
'bearish, *a.* (*of pers.*) bourru.

bear[2], *v.tr. & i.* (**bore** [bɔ:r]; **borne** [bɔ:n]) (*a*)
porter (un fardeau, un nom, une date); **the
letter bears my signature,** la lettre porte ma
signature; (*b*) supporter (la douleur); soutenir
(un poids); **he could b. it no longer,** il n'en
pouvait plus; **I can't b. the sight of him,** je ne
peux pas le sentir; **I can't b. to see it,** je ne peux
pas en supporter la vue; **to b. with s.o.,** être indulgent pour qn; (*c*) *Aut: etc:* **b. to the right,**
obliquez à droite, prenez à droite; (*d*) **to bring
all one's strength to b. on . . .,** peser (de toutes
ses forces) sur . . .; **to bring one's mind to b. on
sth.,** porter son attention sur qch.; **to bring a**

telescope, a gun, **to b. on sth.,** braquer une
lunette, un fusil, sur qch.; (*e*) **to b. a child,**
donner naissance à un enfant; *Fin:* **to b. interest,** porter intérêt; **'bearable,** *a.* supportable; **'bear 'down,** *v.i.* **to b. d. (up)on s.o.,**
foncer sur qn; **'bearer,** *s.* (*pers.*) porteur,
-euse (d'un chèque, de bonnes nouvelles);
titulaire *mf* (d'un passeport); *Fin:* **b. bond,** titre
m au porteur; **'bearing,** *s.* (*a*) *E:* (i) palier *m*,
roulement *m*; (ii) coussinet *m*; (*b*) (*usu. pl.*)
orientation *f*; **to take a ship's bearings,** faire le
point; **to take one's bearings,** s'orienter; **to lose
one's bearings,** perdre le nord; **'bear 'out,** *v.tr.*
confirmer, justifier (une assertion); **'bear 'up.**
1. *v.tr.* soutenir (qn, qch.). 2. *v.i.* **to b. up under
misfortune,** faire face au malheur; **how are
you?—bearing up,** comment ça va?—je me
défends.

beard ['bi:əd], *s.* barbe *f*; **'bearded,** *a.* barbu
'beardless, *a.* imberbe; sans barbe.

beast [bi:st], *s.* 1. bête *f*; **wild b.,** (i) bête sauvage
(ii) bête féroce. 2. *pl. Agr:* bétail *m*, bestiaux
mpl. 3. (*of pers.*) *F:* **what a b.!** quel animal
quel abruti! **that b. of a foreman!** ce chameau
de contremaître! **'beastliness,** *s.* 1. bestialité
f; brutalité *f*. 2. saleté *f* (d'esprit); **'beastly.** 1
a. F: sale, dégoûtant, infect; **what b. weather
quel sale temps!** 2. *adv. F:* (*intensive*) terrible
ment, bigrement.

beat [bi:t]. I. *v.tr. & i.* (**beat; beaten**) battre (qn
qch.). 1. **to b. on the door,** frapper à la porte;
b. a drum, battre du tambour; **to b. a retreat,** s
retirer; **to b. time,** battre la mesure; **to b. about
the bush,** tourner autour du pot. 2. (*a*) **to b. th
enemy,** battre l'ennemi; **that beats everything**
ça c'est le comble! (*b*) devancer (qn); *Sp:* etc
to b. the record, battre le record. II. *s.* 1. (*a*
battement *m* (du cœur); (*b*) *Mus:* mesure
temps *m*. 2. ronde *f* (d'un agent de police
'beat 'back, *v.tr.* repousser (qn); rabattre (le
flammes); **'beat 'down.** 1. *v.tr.* (*a*) **to b. st
down,** (r)abattre qch.; (*b*) **to b. s.o. down**
marchander avec qn. 2. *v.i.* **the sun beats dow
upon our heads,** le soleil donne sur nos tête
'beaten, *a.* 1. **the b. track,** les sentiers battu
house off the b. track, maison écartée. 2. (fe
battu, martelé; **'beating,** *s.* 1. battement *m* (d
cœur). 2. (*a*) coups *mpl*; rossée *f*; (*b*) défaite
'beat 'off, *v.tr.* repousser (une attaque); **'bea
'up,** *v.tr.* 1. battre (des œufs, de la crème).
rosser (qn).

beautiful ['bju:tifəl], *a.* beau, belle; magnifiqu
-fully, *adv.* admirablement, parfaitemen
'beautify, *v.tr.* embellir (qn, qch.); **'beauty,**
beauté *f*; **b. treatment,** soins *mpl* de beauté;
specialist, esthéticienne *f*; **b. parlour,** institut
de beauté; **'beauty(-)spot,** *s.* coin *m*, site *r*
pittoresque.

beaver ['bi:vər], *s. Z:* castor *m*.

because [bi'kɔz]. 1. *conj.* parce que. 2. *prep. phr.* **b. of** sth., à cause de qch.

beck [bek], *s.* **to be at** s.o.'s **b. and call**, obéir à qn au doigt et à l'œil.

beckon ['bek(ə)n], *v.tr. & i.* faire signe (**to** s.o., à qn); appeler (qn) de la main, d'un geste.

become [bi'kʌm], *v.* (**became** [bi'keim]; **become**) *v.i.* devenir; se faire; (*a*) **to b. old,** vieillir; **to b. a priest,** se faire prêtre; **to b. accustomed to** sth., s'accoutumer à qch.; (*b*) **what's b. of him?** qu'est-il devenu? **be'coming,** *a.* **her dress is very b.,** sa robe lui va très bien.

bed [bed]. I. *s.* lit *m.* 1. **twin beds,** lits jumeaux; **double b.,** grand lit; **spare b.,** lit d'ami; **to go to b.,** se coucher; (*illness*) **to take to one's b.,** s'aliter; garder le lit; **to get into b.,** se mettre au lit; **to get out of b.,** se lever; **to put a child to b.,** coucher un enfant; **to make the beds,** faire les lits. 2. (*a*) lit (d'une rivière); banc *m* (d'huîtres); (**flower**) **b.,** parterre *m*; (*b*) *Miner:* gisement *m.* II. *v.tr.* (**bedded**) (*a*) **to b.** (**down**) **the horses, cows,** faire la litière aux chevaux, aux vaches; (*b*) **to b.** (**out**) **plants,** dépoter des plantes; **'bedclothes,** *s.pl.* couvertures *f* (de lit); literie *f*; **'bedcover,** *s.* dessus *m* de lit; **'bedding,** *s.* 1. literie *f.* 2. (*of plants*) **b.** (**out**), dépotage *m*; **'bed-jacket,** *s.* liseuse *f*; **'bedridden,** *a.* cloué au lit; **'bed-rock,** *s. Geol:* roche *f* de fond; **to get down to b.-r.,** descendre au fond des choses; **b.-r. price,** dernier prix; **'bedroom,** *s.* chambre *f* à coucher; **'bedside,** *s.* chevet *m*; bord *m* du lit; **b. rug,** descente *f* de lit; **b. lamp,** lampe *f* de chevet; **b. manner,** comportement *m* (d'un médecin) au chevet du malade; **'bed-'sitting-room,** *F:* **'bed-'sitter, 'bed-'sit,** *s.* (appartement-)studio *m*; chambre meublée; **'bedspread,** *s.* couvre-lit *m*; **'bedtime,** *s.* heure *f* du coucher.

bedlam ['bedləm], *s.* chahut *m* à tout casser.

Bedouin ['beduin], *a. & s.* bédouin.

bedraggled [bi'drægld], *a.* trempé d'eau.

bee [bi:], *s.* abeille *f*; **'beehive,** *s.* ruche *f*; **'bee(-)keeper,** *s.* apiculteur, -trice; **'bee(-)keeping,** *s.* apiculture *f*; **'beeline,** *s.* ligne droite; **to make a b. for** sth., aller droit vers qch.; **'beeswax,** *s.* cire *f* d'abeilles.

beech [bi:tʃ], *s.* hêtre *m*; **copper b.,** hêtre rouge; **b. nut,** faîne *f*.

beef [bi:f], *s. Cu:* bœuf *m*; **roast b.,** rôti *m* de bœuf; rosbif *m*; **corned b.,** corned-beef *m*; **b. tea,** bouillon *m*; **'beef-steak,** *s. Cu:* bifteck *m*; **'beefy,** *a. F:* costaud.

beer ['bi:ər], *s.* bière *f*; **b. glass,** bock *m*; **to order a b.,** demander une bière, un demi.

beet [bi:t], *s.* betterave *f*; **sugar b.,** betterave à sucre.

beetle ['bi:tl], *s. Ent:* coléoptère *m*; scarabée *m*.

beetroot ['bi:tru:t], *s.* betterave *f*.

before [bi'fɔr]. 1. *adv.* (*a*) (*place*) en avant;

devant; **this page and the one b.,** cette page et la précédente; (*b*) (*time*) auparavant, avant; **the day b.,** le jour précédent, la veille; **the year b.,** l'année d'avant, un an auparavant; **I have seen him b.,** je l'ai déjà vu. 2. *prep.* (*a*) (*place*) devant; **to stand b.** s.o., se tenir devant qn; **b. my eyes,** sous mes yeux; (*b*) (*time*) avant; **b. long,** avant longtemps; **it ought to have been done b. now,** ce devrait être déjà fait; **we are b. our time,** nous sommes en avance; **b. answering,** avant de répondre; (*c*) **b. everything else,** avant tout. 3. *conj.* **come and see me b. you leave,** venez me voir avant que vous (ne) partiez, avant de partir, avant votre départ; **be'forehand,** *adv.* préalablement, au préalable; **to pay b.,** payer d'avance.

befriend [bi'frend], *v.tr.* secourir (qn); venir en aide à (qn); se montrer l'ami de (qn).

beg [beg], *v.tr. & i.* (**begged**) 1. mendier. 2. **to b. a favour of** s.o., solliciter une faveur de qn; **to b.** s.o. **to do** sth., supplier qn de faire qch.; **I b.** (**of**) **you!** je vous en prie! **'begging,** *s.* mendicité *f*.

beggar ['begər], *s.* 1. mendiant, -ante. 2. individu *m*; **poor b.!** pauvre diable! **lucky b.!** veinard! **'beggarly,** *a.* minable, misérable; **b. wage,** salaire dérisoire.

begin [bi'gin], *v.tr. & i.* (**began** [bi'gæn]; **begun** [bi'gʌn]) commencer; **to b. to do** sth., commencer à, de, faire qch.; **to b. to laugh,** se mettre à rire; **to b. with,** (tout) d'abord; pour commencer; **to b. again,** recommencer; **be'ginner,** *s.* débutant, -ante; novice *mf*; **be'ginning,** *s.* commencement *m*; début *m* (d'une carrière); origine *f*; **at the b.,** au commencement, au début; **to make a b.,** commencer, débuter.

behalf [bi'hɑ:f], *s.* 1. **on b. of** s.o., au nom de qn; **I come on b. of Mr X,** je viens de la part de M. X. 2. **to plead on** s.o.'s **b.,** plaider en faveur de qn. 3. **don't worry on my b.,** ne vous inquiétez pas à mon sujet.

behave [bi'heiv], *v.i.* **to b. well,** se conduire, se comporter, bien; **to b. well, badly, towards** s.o., bien, mal, agir envers qn; **to know how to b.,** savoir vivre; (*to child*) **b. yourself!** sois sage! **be'haved,** *a. used with adv. prefixed:* **well(-)b.,** sage, poli; qui se conduit bien; **badly(-)b.,** sans tenue, qui se conduit mal; **be-'haviour,** *s.* tenue *f*, maintien *m*; conduite *f* (**to, towards,** s.o., avec, envers, qn).

behead [bi'hed], *v.tr.* décapiter (qn); **he was beheaded,** on lui coupa la tête.

behind [bi'haind]. 1. *adv.* derrière; par derrière; (*a*) **to come b.,** venir derrière; suivre; **to stay, remain, b.,** rester en arrière; (*b*) **to be b. with one's work,** être en retard dans son travail. 2. *prep.* (*a*) derrière; **look b. you,** regardez derrière vous; **what's b. all this?** qu'y a-t-il derrière tout cela? **to be b.** (= *to support*) **s.o.**, soutenir qn; (*b*) en arrière de, en retard sur (qch.); **country b. its neighbours**, pays en arrière de ses voisins. **3.** *s. F:* derrière *m*; **to sit on one's b.**, ne rien faire; **to kick s.o.'s b.**, botter le derrière de, à, qn; **be'hindhand**, *adv. & a.* en arrière; en retard; attardé.

beige [bei3], *a.* (couleur *f*) beige.

belated [bi'leitid], *a.* **1.** (voyageur) attardé. **2.** (repentir) tardif; (invité) en retard; **-ly**, *adv.* un peu tard, tardivement; sur le tard; trop tard.

belch [bel(t)ʃ]. **I.** *v.* **1.** *v.i.* éructer. **2.** *v.tr.* **to b. (forth) flames**, vomir des flammes. **II.** *s.* éructation *f*; **'belching**, *s.* **1.** éructations *fpl.* **2.** vomissement *m* de flammes.

belfry ['belfri], *s.* beffroi *m*, clocher *m*.

Belgian ['beld3ən], *a. & s.* belge (*mf*); de Belgique.

Belgium ['beld3əm]. *Pr.n.* la Belgique.

believe [bi'li:v]. **1.** *v.tr.* (*a*) croire; ajouter foi à (un bruit); **I b. (that) I'm right**, je crois avoir raison; **I b. not**, je crois que non; **I b. so**, je crois que oui; **to make s.o. b. that . . .**, faire accroire à qn que . . .; (*b*) **to b. s.o.**, croire qn; **if he's to be believed**, à l'en croire. **2.** *v.i.* (*a*) **to b. in God**, croire en Dieu; (*b*) **to b. in s.o.'s word**, croire à la parole de qn. **3.** **to make b. to do sth.**, faire semblant de faire qch.; **be'lief**, *s.* croyance *f*; conviction *f*; foi *f*; **be'lievable**, *a.* croyable; **be'liever**, *s.* croyant, -ante.

belittle [bi'litl], *v.tr.* rabaisser, déprécier, amoindrir (qn, le mérite de qn).

bell [bel], *s.* **(clapper-)b.**, cloche *f*; (*smaller*) clochette *f*; (*in house*) sonnette *f*; (*fixed bell*) timbre *m*; **sleigh-b.**, grelot *m*; **electric b.**, sonnerie *f* (électrique); **chime of bells**, carillon *m*; **to ring the b.**, sonner; *F:* **that rings a b.**, cela me rappelle, me dit, quelque chose; **'bellboy**, *s., esp. N.Am:* groom *m* (d'hôtel); chasseur *m*; **'bellpush**, *s.* bouton *m* (de sonnerie); **'bell-ringer**, *s.* carillonneur *m*; **'bell-tower**, *s.* clocher *m*.

belligerent [be'lid3ərənt], *a. & s.* belligérant (*m*).

bellow ['belou]. **I.** *v.i.* beugler, mugir; hurler. **II.** *s.* beuglement *m*, mugissement *m*; hurlement *m* (de colère, de douleur).

bellows ['belouz], *s.pl.* **1.** soufflet *m* (pour le feu); **a pair of b.**, un soufflet. **2.** soufflerie *f* (d'une forge, d'un orgue).

belly ['beli], *s.* ventre *m*; **'belly-ache. I.** *s. F:* mal *m* de ventre; colique *f.* **II.** *v.i. P:* ronchonner, rouspéter, bougonner; **'belly(-)flop**, *s. F: Swim:* **to do a b.(-)f.**, faire un plat; **'belly-'landing**, *s. Av:* atterrissage *m* sur le ventre; **'bellyful**, *s.* plein ventre; *F:* **to have had a b.**, en avoir plein le dos.

belong [bi'lɔŋ], *v.i.* **1.** appartenir (**to**, à); **that book belongs to me**, ce livre m'appartient, ce livre est à moi; (*of land*) **to b. to the Crown**,

dépendre de la Couronne. **2.** (*be appropriate*) être propre (à qch.). **3. to b. to a society**, être membre d'une société; **put it back where it belongs**, remettez-le à sa place; **I b. here**, je suis d'ici; **be'longings**, *s.pl.* affaires *f*, effets *m*; **personal belongings**, objets personnels.

beloved. 1. [bi'lʌvd], *a.* **b. by all**, aimé de tous. **2.** [bi'lʌvid], *s.* bien-aimé(e).

below [bi'lou]. **1.** *adv.* (*a*) en bas, (au-)dessous; **here b. (on earth)**, ici-bas; (*b*) **the passage quoted b.**, le passage cité (i) ci-dessous, (ii) ci-après. **2.** *prep.* au-dessous de; (*a*) **b. the knee**, au-dessous du genou; (*b*) **b. the average**, au dessous de la moyenne; (*c*) **b. the surface**, sous la surface; (*d*) **b. the bridge**, en aval du pont.

belt [belt]. **I.** *s.* **1.** ceinture *f*; (**woman's suspender**) **b.**, gaine *f*; *Av: Aut:* **seat b.**, ceinture de sécurité; *Box:* **to hit s.o. below the b.**, donner à qn un coup déloyal. **2.** *E:* courroie *f* (de transmission). **3.** *Adm:* **green b.**, zone verte; **standard(-)time b.**, fuseau horaire. **II.** *v.i* **1.** *F:* **to b. along**, courir, aller, à toute vitesse. **2.** *P:* **b. up!** boucle-la!

bench [ben(t)ʃ], *s.* **1.** (*a*) banc *m*; banquette *f*; (*b*) *Jur:* **the B.**, (i) la magistrature; (ii) (*the Judges*) la Cour. **2.** (*a*) établi *m* (de menuisier); (*b*) *E:* **testing-b.**, banc d'essai.

bend [bend]. **I.** *v.tr. & i.* (**bent**) **1.** courber, plier (le bras); fléchir (le genou); baisser (la tête); arquer (le dos); **to b. beneath a burden**, plier, fléchir, se courber, sous un fardeau; **to b. the elbow**, s'adonner à la boisson. **2.** *v.tr.* **to b. sth. out of shape**, forcer, fausser, qch. **II.** *S:* **1.** courbure *f*, courbe *f*; (*of pipe*) coude *m*; (*of road*) virage *m*; *P.N:* **bends for 3 miles**, virage sur 5 kilomètres; *P:* **to be round the b.**, être fou, cinglé, dingue. **2.** *Med: F:* **the bends**, mal *m* de caissons; **'bend 'down**, *v.i.* se courber, se baisser; **'bend 'forward**, *v.i.* se pencher en avant.

beneath [bi'ni:θ]. **1.** *adv.* dessous, au-dessous, en bas. **2.** *prep.* au-dessous de; sous; **it's b. him**, c'est indigne de lui.

benedictine. 1. [beni'diktin], *a. & s. Ecc:* bénédictin, -e. **2.** [beni'dikti:n], *s.* (*liqueur*) bénédictine *f*.

benediction [beni'dikʃ(ə)n], *s.* bénédiction *f*.

benefactor ['benifæktər], *s.* bienfaiteur *m*; **'benefactress**, *s.* bienfaitrice *f*.

beneficent [bi'nefisənt], *a.* **1.** bienfaisant. **2.** salutaire.

beneficial [beni'fiʃ(ə)l], *a.* salutaire; profitable, avantageux; **-ally**, *adv.* avantageusement.

beneficiary [beni'fiʃəri], *a. & s.* bénéficiaire (*mf*).

benefit ['benifit]. **I.** *s.* **1.** avantage *m*, profit *m*. **2.** *Adm:* indemnité *f*, allocation *f*; **unemployment b.**, indemnité de chômage; prestation *f* medical b., prestation médicale; **national insurance benefits**, prestations sociales; **maternity b.**, allocation de maternité. II. *v.* 1. *v.i.* **to b. by, from, sth.**, profiter de qch. 2. *v.tr.* **to b. s.o.** profiter à qn.

benevolence [bi'nevələns], *s.* bienveillance *f*, bonté *f*; **be'nevolent**, *a.* bienveillant (**to**, envers); **b. society**, association *f* de bienfaisance; **-ly**, *adv.* avec bienveillance.

benign [bi'nain], *a.* (*a*) (*of pers.*) bénin, *f.* bénigne; doux, *f.* douce; (*b*) *Med:* **b. tumour**, tumeur bénigne.

bent [bent]. I. *a.* 1. (*a*) courbé, plié; **b. back**, dos voûté; (*b*) faussé, fléchi; (*c*) *P:* malhonnête. 2. **b. on doing sth.**, déterminé, résolu, à faire qch. II. *s.* penchant *m*, inclination *f*, disposition *f* (**for**, pour).

bequeath [bi'kwi:ð], *v.tr.* léguer (**to**, à); **be'quest**, *s.* legs *m*; (*in museum*) fonds *m*.

bereave [bi'ri:v], *v.tr.* (*p.p.* **bereft** or **bereaved**) priver (**s.o. of sth.**, qn de qch.); *s.pl.* **the bereaved**, la famille du mort; **be'reavement**, *s.* perte *f* (d'un parent); deuil *m*.

beret ['berei], *s.* béret *m*.

Bermuda [bə(:)'mju:də]. *Pr.n. Geog:* les Bermudes *f.*

berry ['beri], *s. Bot:* baie *f.*

berth [bə:θ], *s.* 1. *Nau: etc:* (*a*) **to give a ship, s.o., a wide b.**, éviter un navire, qn; (*b*) (**anchoring**) **b.**, poste *m* de mouillage, d'amarrage. 2. *Nau: Rail:* couchette *f.* 3. place *f*, emploi *m*.

beseech [bi'si:tʃ], *v.tr.* (**besought** [bi'sɔ:t]) supplier, adjurer, conjurer (**s.o. to do sth.**, qn de faire qch.).

beside [bi'said], *prep.* 1. à côté, auprès, de (qn, qch.). 2. (*a*) **b. the point**, en dehors du sujet; (*b*) **to be b. oneself**, être hors de soi; (*with joy*) être transporté de joie.

besides [bi'saidz]. 1. *adv.* (*a*) en outre, en plus; **nothing b.**, rien de plus; (*b*) **it's too late; b., I'm tired**, il est trop tard; d'ailleurs je suis fatigué. 2. *prep.* sans compter (qn, qch.); **others b. him**, d'autres que lui.

besiege [bi'si:dʒ], *v.tr.* assiéger.

bespatter [bi'spætər], *v.tr.* éclabousser (**s.o., sth., with mud, etc.**, qn, qch., de boue, etc.).

bespoke [bi'spouk], *a.* **b.** (**garment**), (vêtement) (fait) sur commande, sur mesure; **b. tailor, shoemaker**, tailleur *m*, cordonnier *m*, à façon.

best [best]. 1. *a. & s.* (*a*) (le) meilleur, (la) meilleure; le mieux; **b. man (at a wedding)**, garçon *m* d'honneur; (**dressed**) **in one's b.** (**clothes**), endimanché; **the b. of it is that . . .**, le plus beau de l'affaire, c'est que . . .; **to know what is b. for s.o.**, savoir ce qui convient le mieux à qn; **it would be b. to . . .**, le mieux serait de . . .; **to do one's b.**, faire de son mieux, faire (tout) son possible; **he did his b. to smile**, il s'est efforcé de sourire; **to be at one's**

b., être en train, en forme; **to get, have, the b. of it, of the bargain**, l'emporter; avoir le dessus; **the b. part of an hour**, une heure ou peu s'en faut; **all the b.!** bonne chance! **to make the b. of a bad bargain**, faire bonne mine à mauvais jeu; (*b*) *adv.phr.* **at (the) b.**, pour (en) dire le mieux; **to act for the b.**, agir pour le mieux; **to the b. of my belief, knowledge**, à ce que je crois; autant que je sache. 2. *adv.* (*a*) **he does it b.**, c'est lui qui le fait le mieux; **I comforted her as b. I could**, je l'ai consolée de mon mieux; **do as you think b.**, faites comme bon vous semble(ra); (*b*) **the b. dressed man**, l'homme le mieux habillé; **'best-'seller**, *s.* (*a*) livre *m* à succès, best-seller *m*, *pl.* best-sellers; article *m* de grosse vente; (*b*) auteur *m* à gros tirages.

bestial ['bestjəl], *a.* bestial.

bet [bet]. I. *s.* pari *m*, gageure *f*; **to make, lay, a b.**, faire un pari. II. *v.tr.* (**bet; betting**) parier; **'better**, *s.* parieur *m*; **'betting**, *s.* les paris *mpl*; **b. shop** = bureau *m* du pari mutuel.

betray [bi'trei], *v.tr.* 1. trahir (qn, sa patrie); vendre (qn). 2. révéler, montrer, laisser voir (son ignorance, etc.); livrer (un secret); **be'trayal**, *s.* trahison *f*; **be'trayer**, *s.* traître, -esse.

better ['betər]. I. *a., s., & adv.* 1. *a.* meilleur; **b. days**, des jours meilleurs; **he's a b. man than you**, il vaut plus que vous; (*at games*) **you are b. than I**, vous êtes plus fort que moi; **I had hoped for b. things**, j'avais espéré mieux; **the b. part of the day**, la plus grande partie du jour. 2. *a. & s.* mieux; **that's b.**, voilà qui est mieux; **so much the b.**, tant mieux; **to get b.**, (i) (*of thgs*) s'améliorer; (ii) (*of pers.*) guérir, se remettre; **the weather is b.**, il fait meilleur; **to be b. (in health)**, aller mieux; **to get the b. of s.o.**, l'emporter sur qn. 3. *adv.* (*a*) mieux; **b. and b.**, de mieux en mieux; **to think b. of it**, se raviser; **b. still**, mieux encore; **you'd b. stay**, vous feriez bien de rester; **we'd b. be going**, il est temps de rentrer; (*b*) **b. known**, plus connu; **he's b. off where he is**, il est bien mieux où il est. II. *v.tr.* (*a*) améliorer; rendre meilleur; **to b. oneself**, améliorer sa position; (*b*) surpasser (un exploit).

between [bi'twi:n], *prep.* entre; (*a*) **no one can come b. us**, personne ne peut nous séparer; (*b*) **b. now and Monday**, d'ici (à) lundi; (*c*) **b. twenty and thirty**, de vingt à trente; (*c*) **b. ourselves**, entre nous; **b. you and me and the gatepost**, soit dit entre nous.

bevel ['bevəl]. I. *s.* angle *m* oblique; biseau *m*. II. *v.tr.* biseauter; tailler (un bord) en biseau.

beverage ['bevəridʒ], *s.* boisson *f.*

bevy ['bevi], *s.* bande *f*, troupe *f* (*esp.* **of girls**, de jeunes filles).

beware [bi'wɛər], *v.ind.tr.* (*used only in the inf. and imp.*) se méfier de (qn, qch.); **b.!** prenez garde! *P.N:* **b. of the dog!** chien méchant!

bewilder [bi'wildər], *v.tr.* désorienter, égarer (qn); ahurir (qn); **be'wildered**, *a.* désorienté; ahuri; **I'm bewildered,** j'y perds la tête; **be'wildering**, *a.* déroutant; **be'wilderment**, *s.* désorientation *f*; ahurissement *m*.

bewitch [bi'witʃ], *v.tr.* (a) ensorceler, jeter un sort à (qn); (b) charmer, enchanter (qn); **be'witching**, *a.* ravissant.

beyond [bi'jɔnd]. **1.** *adv.* au delà, par delà, plus loin. **2.** *prep.* au delà de, par delà; **b. all praise,** au-dessus de tout éloge; **it's b. me,** cela me dépasse; **b. doubt,** hors de doute; **b. belief,** incroyable(ment); **that's b. a joke,** cela dépasse les bornes de la plaisanterie. **3.** *s. F:* **he lives at the back of b.,** il habite un trou perdu, en plein bled.

bias ['baiəs], *s.* **1. material cut on the b.,** tissu coupé en biais *m*. **2.** parti pris; penchant *m* (pour qch.); **vocational b.,** déformation professionnelle; **'bias(s)ed,** *a.* partial, -aux; **to be b. against s.o.,** avoir de la prévention contre qn.

bib [bib], *s.* bavette *f* (d'enfant).

Bible ['baibl], *s.* Bible *f*; **biblical** ['biblikl], *a.* biblique.

bibliography [bibli'ɔgrəfi], *s.* bibliographie *f*; **bibli'ographer,** *s.* bibliographe *m*.

bibliophile ['biblioufail], *s.* bibliophile *m*.

bicarbonate [bai'kɑ:bənit], *s.* bicarbonate *m* (**of soda, etc.,** de soude, etc.).

bicentenary ['baisen'ti:nəri], *s.* bicentenaire *m*.

biceps ['baiseps], *s. Anat:* biceps *m*.

bicker ['bikər], *v.i.* se quereller, se chamailler.

bicycle ['baisikl]. **I.** *s.* bicyclette *f*, vélo *m*. **II.** *v.i.* faire du vélo.

bid [bid]. **I.** *v.tr. & i.* **1.** (**bade; bidden**) **to b. s.o. welcome,** souhaiter la bienvenue à qn. **2.** (**bid; bidden**) (a) (*at auction sale*) faire une offre (pour qch.); (b) (*at cards*) demander, appeler (trois carreaux, etc.). **II.** *s.* (a) (*at auction sale*) enchère *f*, offre *f*; **to make a b. for power,** tenter un coup d'état; **escape b.,** tentative *f* d'évasion; (b) (*at cards*) appel *m*, demande *f*; **no b.!** parole! **'bidder,** *s.* enchérisseur *m*; **'bidding,** *s.* **1.** ordre *m*; **to do s.o.'s b.,** exécuter les ordres de qn. **2.** enchères *fpl*, mises *fpl*; (*cards*) **the b. is closed,** l'enchère est faite.

bide [baid], *v.tr. only used in* **to b. one's time,** attendre son heure, attendre le bon moment.

biennial [bai'enjəl], *a. & s. Bot:* **b. (plant),** plante bisannuelle.

bier ['bi:ər], *s.* (a) civière *f*; (b) (= *hearse*) corbillard *m*.

bifocal [bai'fouk(ə)l], *a.* bifocal, -aux; **b. glasses,** *s.* **bifocals,** verres *mpl* à double foyer.

bifurcate ['baifə:keit], *v.i.* (*of road*) bifurquer; **bifur'cation,** *s.* bifurcation *f*.

big [big]. (**bigger; biggest**) **1.** *a.* (a) (*large*) grand; (*bulky*) gros; **b. hotel,** grand hôtel; **b. man,** (i) homme de grande taille; (ii) gros homme; (iii) homme marquant; **b. fortune,** grosse fortune; *F:* **to earn b. money,** gagner gros; **b. drop in prices,** forte baisse de prix; **to have b. ideas,** voir grand; *F:* **b. noise, b. shot,** gros bonnet; **b. game,** les grands fauves; **b. business,** les grosses affaires; **b. brother,** frère aîné; **to grow big(ger),** (i) grandir; (ii) grossir; (b) **b. with consequences,** lourd de conséquences. **2.** *adv.* **to talk b.,** faire l'important.

bigamy ['bigəmi], *s.* bigamie *f*; **'bigamist,** *s.* bigame *mf*; **'bigamous,** *a.* bigame.

bigot ['bigət], *s.* fanatique *mf*; sectaire *mf*; **'bigoted,** *a.* fanatique; au zèle, à l'esprit, étroit; **'bigotry,** *s.* bigoterie *f*; fanatisme *m*; étroitesse *f* d'esprit.

bigwig ['bigwig], *s. F:* gros bonnet, grosse légume.

bike [baik], *s. F:* (= BICYCLE) vélo *m*, bécane *f*.

bikini [bi'ki:ni], *s.* bikini *m*.

bilateral [bai'læt(ə)rəl], *a.* bilatéral.

bilberry ['bilbəri], *s. Bot:* airelle *f*; myrtille *f*.

bile [bail], *s.* bile *f*.

bilge [bildʒ], *s. Nau:* **b.(-water),** eau *f* de cale; *P:* **to talk b.,** dire des bêtises *f*.

bilingual [bai'liŋgwəl], *a.* bilingue.

bilious ['biliəs], *a.* bilieux; (tempérament *m*) colérique; **b. attack,** accès *m* de bile; **to feel b.,** avoir l'estomac barbouillé; **'biliousness,** *s.* crise *f* du foie.

bill¹ [bil], *s.* bec *m* (d'oiseau).

bill², *s.* **1.** *Com:* note *f*, facture *f*, mémoire *m*; (*in restaurant*) addition *f*. **2.** (a) *N.Am:* billet *m* de banque; (b) *Fin:* **b. of exchange,** lettre *f* de change; traite *f*. **3.** affiche *f*, placard *m*, écriteau *m*; **stick no bills!** défense d'afficher! **that will fill the b.,** cela fera l'affaire. **4.** (a) **b. of fare,** carte *f* du jour; menu *m*; (b) *Nau:* **b. of lading,** connaissement *m*; **clean b. of health,** patente *f* de santé nette; (c) **b. of sale,** acte *m* de vente; facture. **5.** projet *m* de loi; **'billboard,** *s.* panneau *m* d'affichage; **'billfold,** *s. N.Am:* portefeuille *m*.

Bill³. *Pr.n.m.* (*diminutive of* **William**) Guillaume.

billet ['bilit]. **I.** *v.tr. Mil:* loger (des troupes chez qn). **II.** *s. Mil:* logement *m* (chez l'habitant).

billiard ['biljəd], *s.* **1.** *pl.* **billiards,** (jeu *m* de) billard *m*. **2. b. ball,** bille *f* (de billard); **b. room** (salle *f* de) billard; **b. table,** billard; **b. cue,** queue *f* de billard.

billion ['biljən], *s.* billion *m*, *N.Am:* milliard *m*.

billygoat ['biligout], *s.* bouc *m*.

bin [bin], *s.* coffre *m*, huche *f*; **bread b.,** huche à pain; **wine b.,** casier *m* à bouteilles.

bind [baind], *v.tr.* (**bound** [baund]) attacher, lier **1.** (a) **bound hand and foot,** pieds et poings liés; (b) **to b. sth. (down) to sth.,** attacher, fixer qch. à qch. **2. to b. (up) a wound,** bander une blessure. **3.** relier (un livre); **paper bound**

broché; **bound in boards**, cartonné. **4.** lier, engager (qn); **to b.** oneself to do sth., s'engager à faire qch. **5.** *v.i. F:* ronchonner; **'binding. I.** *a.* **1.** obligatoire **(upon s.o.,** pour qn); (promesse *f*, contrat *m*) qui lie (qn). **2.** (agent) agglomérant. **II.** *s.* **1.** agglutination *f*; fixation *f*. **2.** reliure *f* (d'un livre).

binge [bin(d)ʒ], *s. F:* **to go on a b.,** faire la bombe.

bingo ['biŋgou], *s.* loto *m* (joué collectivement).

binoculars [bi'nɔkjuləz], *s.pl.,* jumelle(s) *f.*

biochemistry ['baiou'kemistri], *s.* biochimie *f*; **'bio'chemical,** *a.* biochimique; **'bio'chemist,** *s.* biochimiste *m.*

biography [bai'ɔgrəfi], *s.* biographie *f*; **bi'ographer,** *s.* biographe *mf*; **bio'graphical,** *a.* biographique.

biology [bai'ɔlədʒi], *s.* biologie *f*; **bio'logical,** *a.* biologique; **bi'ologist,** *s.* biologiste *mf.*

biophysics ['baiou'fiziks], *s.pl.* (*usu. with sg. const.*) biophysique *f*; **'bio'physical,** *a.* biophysique; **'bio'physicist** [-sist], *s.* biophysicien, -ienne.

biped ['baiped], *a. & s.* bipède (*m*).

birch [bə:tʃ], *s.* **1.** *Bot:* bouleau *m.* **2. b.(-rod),** verge *f*, poignée *f* de verges (pour fouetter).

bird [bə:d], *s.* **1.** oiseau *m*; *F:* **to give s.o. the b.,** (i) envoyer promener qn; (ii) *Th:* siffler qn. **2.** *P:* (*a*) individu *m*, type *m*; (*b*) jeune fille *f* (volage); poule *f*; **'bird's-eye. 1.** *s. Bot:* véronique *f.* **2.** *a.* **b.'s-e. view,** vue *f* à vol d'oiseau; **'bird watcher,** *s.* ornithologue *mf*; observateur, -trice, des mœurs des oiseaux.

birth [bə:θ], *s.* **1.** naissance *f*; **French by b.,** Français de naissance; **b. certificate,** acte *m*, extrait *m*, de naissance; **b. control,** limitation *f*, contrôle *m*, des naissances; **b. rate,** natalité *f.* **2. to give b. to a child,** donner naissance, donner le jour, à un enfant; (*of animal*) **to give b.,** mettre bas; **'birthday,** *s.* anniversaire *m* (de naissance); *F:* **to be in one's b. suit,** être à poil; **'birthmark,** *s.* envie *f*; tache *f* de naissance; **'birthplace,** *s.* lieu *m* de naissance; maison natale.

Biscay ['biskei]. *Pr.n. Geog:* **the Bay of B.,** le golfe de Gascogne.

biscuit ['biskit], *s.* biscuit *m*; **fancy biscuits,** gâteaux secs; **b. factory, trade,** biscuiterie *f.*

bisect [bai'sekt], *v.tr.* couper, diviser (en deux parties égales).

bishop ['biʃəp], *s.* **1.** *Ecc:* évêque *m.* **2.** *Chess:* fou *m*; **'bishopric,** *s.* évêché *m.*

bismuth ['bizməθ], *s. Miner:* bismuth *m.*

bit[1] [bit], *s.* **1.** mors *m* (d'une bride); **to take the b. between one's teeth,** prendre le mors aux dents, s'emballer. **2.** *Tls:* mèche *f* (de vilebrequin).

bit[2], *s.* **1.** (*a*) morceau *m*; (*b*) bout *m*, brin *m*; **b. of paper,** bout de papier; **b. of straw,** brin de

paille; **to come to bits,** tomber en morceaux; **to do one's b.,** y mettre du sien. **2.** (*a*) **a b.** (**of**), un peu (de); **he's a b. jealous,** il est un peu jaloux; **he's a b. of a liar,** il est tant soit peu menteur; **wait a b.!** attendez un peu! **a good b. older,** sensiblement plus âgé; **b. by b.,** peu à peu; **not a b. (of it)!** n'en croyez rien! **it's not a b. of use,** cela ne sert absolument à rien; (*b*) **a b. of news,** une nouvelle; **a b. of luck,** une chance.

bitch [bitʃ]. **I.** *s.* **1.** chienne *f.* **2.** *P:* (*of woman*) garce *f.* **II.** *v.tr. P:* **to b.** (sth.) **up,** gâcher, saboter (une affaire, l'ouvrage).

bite [bait]. **I.** *v.tr.* (**bit; bitten**) mordre. **1.** donner un coup de dent à (qch.); (*of insect*) piquer; **to b. one's nails,** se ronger les ongles; **to get bitten,** se faire mordre; **to be bitten with a desire to do sth.,** brûler de faire qch. **2. the acid bites the metal,** l'acide attaque le métal; **to b. off more than one can chew,** tenter qch. au-dessus de ses forces; *F:* **to b. s.o.'s head off,** rembarrer qn. **II.** *s.* **1.** (*a*) coup *m* de dent; (*b*) *Fish:* touche *f.* **2.** piqûre *f*, morsure *f*; **'biting,** *a.* mordant; (vent) piquant, cinglant; (froid) perçant.

bitter ['bitər]. **1.** *a.* (goût) amer; (vent) mordant, cinglant; (ennemi) implacable; (ton) âpre; **b. remorse,** remords cuisants; **b. experience,** expérience cruelle; **b. enemies,** ennemis acharnés, à mort; **b. hatred,** haine acharnée; **to the b. end,** à outrance, jusqu'au bout. **2.** *s.* (*a*) bière blonde (anglaise) sous pression; (*b*) *pl.* **bitters,** bitter(s) *m*, amer(s) *m*; **-ly,** *adv.* amèrement, avec amertume; **it was b. cold,** il faisait un froid de loup; **'bitterness,** *s.* (*a*) amertume *f*; (*b*) rancune *f*, rancœur *f.*

bitumen ['bitjumin], *s.* bitume *m*; **bi'tuminous,** *a.* bitumineux.

bivouac ['bivuæk]. **I.** *s. Mil:* bivouac *m.* **II.** *v.i.* (**bivouacked**) bivouaquer.

bi-weekly ['baiwi:kli]. **1.** (*a*) *a.* de tous les quinze jours; (*b*) *adv.* tous les quinze jours. **2.** (*a*) *a.* bihebdomadaire; (*b*) *adv.* deux fois par semaine.

bizarre [bi'za:r], *a.* bizarre.

black [blæk]. **I.** *a.* noir; (*of pers.*) **to look b.,** faire une vilaine figure; avoir l'air furieux; **to beat s.o. b. and blue,** rosser qn (de coups); **b. eye,** œil poché; **b. market,** marché noir; **b. pudding,** boudin *m*; **b. magic,** magie noire, sorcellerie *f*; **b. despair,** sombre désespoir. **II.** *s.* (*a*) noir *m*; **she always wears b.,** elle ne porte que du noir; **b. and white photograph,** photographie *f* en noir et blanc; **to set sth. down in b. and white,** coucher qch. par écrit; (*b*) (*pers.*) noir, noire. **III.** *v.tr.* noircir (qch.); **to b. sth. out,** effacer, rayer, qch.; **to b. shoes,** cirer des chaussures; **'black'beetle,** *s.* blatte *f*, cafard *m*; **'blackberry,** *s.* mûre *f* de ronce; **b. bush,** ronce *f*; **'blackbird,** *s. Orn:* merle *m*;

'blackboard, s. tableau noir; 'black-currant, s. cassis m; 'blacken, v.tr. noircir; obscurcir (une pièce); 'blackguard ['blægɑ:d], s. canaille f; 'blackleg, s. Ind: F: renard m, jaune m; 'blacklist. 1. s. liste noire (des suspects, des indésirables). 2. v.tr. to b. s.o., mettre le nom de qn sur la liste noire; 'blackmail. I. s. chantage m. II. v.tr. soumettre (qn) à un chantage; F: faire chanter (qn); 'blackmailer, s. maitre-chanteur m; 'blackness, s. noirceur f; obscurité f; 'black 'out. 1. v.tr. to b.o. a house, masquer les lumières, faire le black-out, dans une maison. 2. v.i. perdre connaissance; 'blacksmith, s. forgeron m, maréchal-ferrant m.

bladder ['blædər], s. vessie f.

blade [bleid], s. 1. brin m (d'herbe). 2. lame f (de couteau, de rasoir). 3. pelle f, pale f (d'aviron); aile f, pale (d'hélice)..

blame [bleim]. I. s. 1. reproches mpl; condamnation f. 2. faute f; responsabilité f; **to put the b. on s.o.**, rejeter le blâme sur qn. II. v.tr. blâmer, condamner (qn); **to b. s.o. for doing sth.**, reprocher à qn de faire, d'avoir fait, qch.; **he's to b.**, il y a de sa faute; **he's entirely to b.**, il a tous les torts; **you've only yourself to b.**, vous l'avez voulu; **I'm in no way to b.**, (i) je n'ai rien à me reprocher; (ii) on ne peut rien me reprocher; 'blameless, a. innocent, irréprochable; -ly, adv. irréprochablement.

blanch [blɑ:n(t)ʃ]. 1. v.tr. blanchir (des légumes); monder (des amandes). 2. v.i. (of pers.) blêmir, pâlir.

blancmange [blə'mɔnʒ], s. Cu: = blanc-manger m.

bland [blænd], a. doux, suave.

blandishment ['blændiʃmənt], s. (usu. pl.) flatterie f; cajoleries fpl.

blank [blæŋk]. I. a. 1. (papier) blanc; **b. page,** page blanche; **b. cheque,** chèque en blanc; **b. verse,** vers blancs, non rimés. 2. **b. look,** regard sans expression; **to look b.,** avoir l'air ahuri, déconcerté; **b. despair,** profond découragement; -ly, adv. **to look b. at s.o.,** regarder qn (i) d'un air ahuri, (ii) sans expression. II. s. 1. (a) N.Am: formulaire m, formule f; **telegraph b.,** imprimé à télégramme; **to fill out a b.,** remplir une formule, une feuille; (b) (in document) blanc m, vide m; (in one's memory) trou m, lacune f, vide m; **to leave blanks,** laisser des blancs; **my mind's a b.,** j'ai la tête vide. 2. (in lottery) billet blanc; **to draw a b.,** échouer.

blanket ['blæŋkit], s. 1. couverture f (de lit); **electric b.,** couverture chauffante. 2. attrib. Adm: général; **b. order,** ordre m d'une portée générale.

blare ['blɛər]. 1. v.i. (of trumpet) sonner; **the radio is blaring away,** la radio fonctionne à

tue-tête. 2. s. son m (éclatant).

blasé ['blɑ:zei], a. blasé.

blaspheme [blæs'fi:m], v.i. & tr. blasphémer; **blas'phemer,** s. blasphémateur, -trice; 'blasphemous [-fəməs], a. (of words) blasphématoire, impie; -ly, adv. avec impiété; 'blasphemy [-fəmi], s. blasphème m.

blast [blɑ:st]. I. s. 1. coup m de vent; rafale f. 2. **b. on the whistle, on the siren,** coup de sifflet, de sirène. 3. Metall: air m, vent m (de la soufflerie); **to be going full b.,** être en pleine activité. 4. (a) (of explosion) souffle m; (b) Min: (i) coup de mine; (ii) charge f d'explosif. II. v.tr. (a) Min: faire sauter (à la dynamite, etc.); (b) ruiner, briser, détruire (les espérances, l'avenir de qn); (c) (of lightning) foudroyer (un arbre); (d) int. F: **b.! diable! zut!** 'blasted, a. F: sacré; 'blast-furnace, s. haut fourneau m; 'blasting, s. (a) Min: travail m aux explosifs; P.N: **beware of b.!** attention aux coups de mine! 'blast-off, s. mise f à feu (d'une fusée); 'blast-screen, s. Av: déflecteur m de souffle.

blatant ['bleitənt], a. 1. d'une vulgarité criarde. 2. (mensonge) flagrant; (injustice) criante.

blaze [bleiz]. I. s. 1. flamme(s) f(pl), flambée f; **in a b.,** en feu, en flammes. 2. flamboiement m (du soleil); éclat m (des couleurs). 3. pl. F: **to work like blazes,** travailler furieusement; **go to blazes!** allez au diable! II. v.i. (of fire) flamber; (of sun) flamboyer; (of jewels, etc.) étinceler; 'blazing, a. en feu; enflammé; (soleil) flambant.

blazer ['bleizər], s. Cl: blazer m.

bleach [bli:tʃ]. I. v.tr. & i. blanchir; Ch: etc: (se) décolorer; **to b. (one's) hair,** décolorer, oxygéner, blondir, les cheveux. II. s décolorant m; lessive f.

bleak [bli:k], a. 1. (terrain) exposé au vent. 2. (temps) triste et froid; (vent) glacial. 3. **b. prospects,** avenir m morne; **b. smile,** sourire pâle, glacé.

bleary ['bli:əri], a. 1. (of eyes) troubles, larmoyants, chassieux. 2. (of outline) vague, imprécis; 'bleary-eyed, a. aux yeux troubles, larmoyants.

bleat [bli:t], v.i. bêler; F: **what's he bleating about?** de quoi se plaint-il? 'bleating, (also bleat), s. bêlement m.

bleed [bli:d], v. (bled) 1. v.tr. saigner; **to b. s.o. white,** saigner qn à blanc. 2. v.i. saigner; perdre du sang; **his nose is bleeding,** il saigne du nez; 'bleeding. I. a. saignant; **with a b. heart,** le cœur fendu. II. s. écoulement m de sang; saignement m (de nez, etc.).

bleep [bli:p]. 1. v.i. faire bip-bip. 2. s. bip-bip m

blemish ['blemiʃ]. I. s. 1. défaut m; imperfection f. 2. souillure f, tache f, tare f. II. v.tr. tacher, souiller.

blend [blend]. **I.** v. **1.** v.tr. mélanger (qch. à, avec, qch.); couper (des vins); allier, marier (deux couleurs); mélanger (des thés, des cafés). **2.** v.i. se mêler, se mélanger, se confondre (**into**, en); (of colours) s'allier, se marier; (of parties) fusionner. **II.** s. mélange m (de cafés, de thés, etc.); '**blending**, s. mélange m; coupage m (de vins); alliance f (de deux qualités); fusion f (d'idées, de races).

bless [bles], v.tr. (**blessed** [blest], occ. **blest**) bénir; **God b. you!** que (le bon) Dieu vous bénisse! **to be blessed with good health, many children**, jouir d'une bonne santé, d'une nombreuse famille; int. (expressing surprise) **b. my soul!** tiens, tiens, tiens! **well, I'm blest!** par exemple! (when s.o. sneezes) **b. you!** à vos, tes, souhaits!

blessed ['blesid], a. (a) Ecc: **the B. Virgin**, la Sainte Vierge; **the B. Martyrs**, les bienheureux martyrs; (b) F: (intensive) **the whole b. day**, toute la sainte journée; **what a b. nuisance!** quel fichu contretemps! **that b. boy!** ce sacré garçon! '**blessing**, s. (a) bénédiction f; (b) usu. pl. **the blessings of civilization**, les avantages m, les bienfaits m, de la civilisation.

blight [blait]. **I.** s. **1.** (a) rouille f, brûlure f; (on cereals) charbon m; (on potatoes) brunissure f; (b) (insect) puceron m. **2.** influence f néfaste, fléau m. **II.** v.tr. rouiller (le blé, etc.); flétrir (les espérances); '**blighter**, s. P: canaille f; **you b.!** espèce f d'animal! **lucky b.**, veinard, -arde.

blind[1] [blaind]. **I.** a. **1.** aveugle; (a) **b. in one eye**, borgne; **b. from birth**, aveugle-né(e); **struck b.**, frappé de cécité f; **to turn a b. eye to sth.**, fermer les yeux sur qch.; (b) **to be b. to s.o.'s faults**, ne pas voir les défauts de qn; (c) adv. Av: **to fly b.**, voler sans visibilité f; voler en P.S.V. **2. b. alley**, impasse f; **-ly**, adv. aveuglément; en aveugle; à l'aveuglette. **II.** v.tr. **1.** aveugler (qn). **2.** éblouir (qn); '**blindfold**. **I.** v.tr. bander les yeux de, à (qn). **II.** a. & adv. les yeux bandés; '**blindness**, s. **1.** cécité f. **2.** (= ignorance) aveuglement m.

blind[2], s. **1.** (outside sun-)**b.**, store m; roller **b.**, store sur rouleau; **Venetian b.**, store vénitien. **2.** masque m, feinte f.

blink [bliŋk], v.i. (a) battre des paupières; cligner des yeux; clignoter; (b) v.tr. **to b. the facts**, fermer les yeux sur la vérité; '**blinkers**, s.pl. œillères fpl (de cheval); '**blinking**, s. (a) clignotement m (des yeux); (b) refus m de faire face à, d'envisager, un fait.

bliss [blis], s. béatitude f, félicité f; '**blissful**, a. (bien)heureux; **b. days**, jours sereins.

blister ['blistər]. **I.** s. (a) ampoule f, bulle f; (b) (in paint) cloque f, boursouflure f. **II.** v. **1.** v.tr. couvrir d'ampoules. **2.** v.i. se couvrir d'ampoules; (of paint) (se) cloquer.

blithering ['bliðəriŋ], a. F: sacré.

blitz [blits]. **I.** s. F: bombardement m aérien. **II.** v.tr. **the house was blitzed**, la maison a été (i) endommagée, (ii) détruite (par un bombardement).

blizzard ['blizəd], s. tempête f de neige.

bloated ['bloutid], a. boursouflé, gonflé, bouffi; **b. face**, visage congestionné.

bloater ['bloutər], s. hareng bouffi; craquelot m.

blob [blob], s. (of paint) tache f; (of ink) pâté m.

bloc [blok], s. Pol: bloc m.

block [blok]. **I.** s. **1.** (a) bloc m (de marbre); bille f, tronçon m (de bois); Aut: **engine b.**, bloc moteur; (b) P: tête f, caboche f. **2.** (a) pâté m, ilot m (de maisons); **b. of flats**, immeuble m; **school b.**, groupe m scolaire; N.Am: **he lives two blocks from us**, il habite à deux rues de nous; (b) in Austr: lot m (de terrains); (c) Fin: tranche f (d'actions). **3. traffic b.**, encombrement m, embouteillage m. **4. b. capitals, letters**, majuscules f d'imprimerie. **II.** v.tr. bloquer, obstruer; **to b. the traffic**, gêner la circulation; P.N: **road blocked**, rue barrée; **block'ade**. **I.** s. blocus m. **II.** v.tr. bloquer (un port, etc.); '**blockage**, s. obstruction f (d'un tuyau); embouteillage m (dans une rue); '**blockhead**, s. F: idiot m, sot m; '**block 'up**, v.tr. boucher, bloquer (un trou); condamner (une porte); obstruer (un tuyau).

blond, f. **blonde** [blond], a. & s. blond, -e; '**blondness**, s. blondeur f.

blood [blʌd], s. sang m; (a) **without shedding b.**, sans effusion de sang; **to draw b.**, faire saigner qn; **it makes my b. boil**, cela m'indigne; **his b. ran cold**, son sang se glaça, se figea (dans ses veines); **in cold b.**, de sang-froid; **there is bad b. between them**, il y a de vieilles rancunes entre eux; **the committee needs new b.**, le comité a besoin d'être rajeuni; Med: **b. pressure**, tension artérielle; **to have high b. pressure**, faire de l'hypertension f; **b. vessel**, vaisseau sanguin; **b. transfusion**, transfusion f de sang; **b. poisoning**, septicémie f; **b. donor**, donneur, -euse, de sang; **b. group**, groupe sanguin; (b) **it runs in the b.**, c'est dans le sang; **blue b.**, sang royal, aristocratique; **b. horse**, (cheval) pur-sang (m); **b. orange**, (orange) sanguine (f); '**bloodbath**, s. carnage m, massacre m; '**bloodcurdling**, a. qui vous fige le sang; '**bloodhound**, s. limier m; '**bloodless**, a. **1.** exsangue, anémié. **2.** (victoire, etc.) sans effusion de sang; '**bloodshed**, s. carnage m; '**bloodshot**, a. **b. eye**, œil injecté de sang; (of eye) **to become b.**, s'injecter; '**bloodstain**, s. tache f de sang; '**blood-stained**, a. taché, souillé, de sang; '**blood-test**, s. Med: prise f de sang; '**bloodthirsty**, a. sanguinaire; assoiffé de sang; '**bloody**, a. **1.** sanglant, taché de sang; (combat) sanglant; (tyran) sanguinaire. **2.** P: (a) (intensive) sacré; **a b.**

liar, un sacré menteur; (b) adv. **it's b. hot,** il fait bigrement chaud; **it's a b. nuisance!** c'est bigrement embêtant! **'bloody-'minded,** a. P: pas commode; **a b.-m. fellow,** un mauvais coucheur.

bloom [blu:m]. **I.** s. **1.** (i) fleur f; (ii) floraison f, épanouissement m; **in full b.,** épanoui; en pleine fleur; **in the b. of youth,** dans la fleur de l'âge. **2.** velouté m, duvet m (d'un fruit). **II.** v.i. fleurir, être en fleur; **'blooming,** a. (a) en fleur; (b) florissant; (c) F: fichu, sacré.

blossom ['blɔsəm]. **I.** s. fleur f (des arbres); **orange b.,** fleur d'oranger. **II.** v.i. fleurir; **to b. out,** s'épanouir.

blot [blɔt]. **I.** s. tache f; (of ink) pâté m. **II.** v.tr. (blotted) **1.** tacher, souiller; (of ink) faire des pâtés sur (qch.). **2.** sécher (l'encre d'une lettre); **'blotter,** s. (bloc) buvard (m); **'blotting paper,** s. (papier) buvard (m).

blotchy ['blɔtʃi], a. (teint) brouillé, couperosé.

blouse [blauz]. s. Cl: chemisier m; blouse f.

blow[1] [blou], v.tr. & i. **(blew** [blu:]; **blown)** souffler; (of wind) **it's blowing hard,** il fait grand vent; **it's blowing a gale,** le vent souffle en tempête; **to b. the dust off,** souffler la poussière; **to b. on one's fingers,** souffler dans ses doigts; **to b. the organ,** souffler l'orgue; **to b. one's nose,** se moucher; **to b. one's own trumpet,** chanter ses propres louanges; El: **to b. a fuse,** faire sauter le plomb; P: **b. the expense!** je me moque de la dépense! **'blow a'way,** v.tr. **the wind is blowing the clouds away,** le vent chasse les nuages; **'blow 'down,** v.tr. (of wind) abattre, renverser (un arbre); **'blowfly,** s. mouche f à viande; **'blow 'in.** 1. v.tr. (of wind) enfoncer (une vitre). 2. v.i. F: (of pers.) entrer en passant; **'blowlamp,** s. lampe f à souder; chalumeau m; **'blow 'off.** 1. v.tr. (of wind) emporter (un chapeau, etc.) (of machine) **to b. o. steam,** lâcher de la vapeur. 2. v.i. (of hat) s'envoler; **'blow 'out.** 1. v.tr. souffler, éteindre (une bougie); **to b. o. one's cheeks,** gonfler ses joues. 2. v.i. (of candle) s'éteindre; (of paper) s'envoler (par la fenêtre); **'blow-out,** s. P: gueuleton m; **'blow 'over,** v.i. & tr. (se) renverser; (of storm) se calmer; (of scandal) rentrer dans l'oubli, **'blow 'up.** 1. v.i. (of mine, etc.) éclater, sauter, exploser. 2. v.tr. faire sauter, (faire) exploser (une mine, etc.); gonfler (un pneu); agrandir (une photo).

blow[2], s. **1.** coup m; (with fist) coup de poing; (with stick) coup de bâton; **to come to blows,** en venir aux mains; Sp: **knock-out b.,** knock-out m, F: K.-O.; **b. to s.o.'s prestige,** atteinte f au crédit de qn. **2.** coup (du sort).

blubber[1] ['blʌbər], s. graisse f de baleine.

blubber[2]. F: v.i. (a) pleurer bruyamment; (b) pleurnicher.

bludgeon ['blʌdʒən]. **I.** s. gourdin m, matraque f. **II.** v.tr. matraquer (qn).

blue [blu:]. **I.** a. (a) bleu; **dark b.,** bleu foncé; **light b.,** bleu clair; Med: **b. baby,** enfant bleu; (b) (of pers.) **to feel b.,** avoir le cafard; broyer du noir; (c) F: **you can talk till you're b. in the face,** tu as beau parler; (d) F: **b. film,** film m porno. **II.** s. **1.** bleu m; **dark b., Oxford b.,** bleu foncé inv; **light b., Cambridge b.,** bleu clair inv; **navy b.,** bleu marine inv; **out of the b.,** soudain, soudainement; (événement) imprévu. **2.** **(washing-)b.,** bleu de lessive. **III.** v.tr. **1.** teindre, colorer, qch. en bleu. **2.** F: **to b. one's money,** gaspiller son argent; **'bluebell,** s. jacinthe f des prés, des bois; **'bluebottle,** s. mouche f à viande; **'blue-eyed,** a. (a) aux yeux bleus; (b) F: innocent; **mother's b.-e. boy,** le petit chou-chou de maman; **'blue-'pencil.** v.tr. (-pencilled) marquer au crayon bleu; censurer (une lettre, un article); **'blueprint,** s. plan détaillé; **'blue stocking,** s.f. bas-bleu m.

bluff[1] [blʌf]. **I.** a. (a) (of cliff) escarpé, à pic; (b) (of pers.) brusque; un peu bourru. **II.** s. Geog: cap m à pic; à-pic m; **'bluffness,** s. brusquerie (amicale); franc-parler m.

bluff[2]. **I.** s. bluff m; **to call s.o.'s b.,** relever un défi. **II.** v.tr. & i. bluffer (qn); faire du bluff.

blunder ['blʌndər]. **I.** s. bévue f, maladresse f; F: gaffe f, impair m. **II.** v.i. **1.** faire une bévue, une gaffe, une maladresse. **2.** **to b. into s.o.,** heurter qn, se heurter contre qn; **to b. through,** s'en tirer tant bien que mal; **'blunderer,** s. maladroit, -e; gaffeur, -euse; **'blundering,** a. maladroit.

blunt [blʌnt]. **I.** a. **1.** émoussé; (instrument) épointé. **2.** (of pers.) brusque, carré; **the b. fact** le fait brutal; -ly, adv. brusquement, carrément, brutalement; **to speak b.,** parler net. **II** v.tr. émousser (un couteau); épointer (un crayon); **'bluntness,** s. **1.** manque m de tranchant. **2.** brusquerie f; franchise f; **b. of speech,** franc-parler m.

blur [blə:r], v.tr. (blurred) **1.** brouiller, troubler; **eyes blurred with tears,** yeux voilés de larmes. **2.** Typ: maculer.

blurb [blə:b], s. Pub: annonce (avantageuse) publicitaire.

blurt [blə:t], v.tr. **to b. out a secret,** laisser échapper un secret.

blush [blʌʃ]. **I.** s. (a) rougeur f (de timidité, de honte); (b) incarnat m (des roses); **the first b. of dawn,** les premières rougeurs de l'aube; **at first b.,** au premier abord. **II.** v.i. rougir; **'blushing,** a. rougissant, timide.

bluster ['blʌstər]. **I.** s. (a) fureur f, fracas m (de l'orage); (b) air m bravache, fanfaronnade f. **II.** v.i. (a) (of wind) souffler en rafales; (b) (of pers.) parler haut; faire le fanfaron; **'blusterer,** s. fanfaron, -onne; **'blustery,** a (vent) violent.

boar [bɔːr], *s. Z:* verrat *m*; **wild b.**, sanglier *m*.

board [bɔːd]. **I.** *s.* **1.** planche *f*, madrier *m*; **bread b.**, planche à pain; **ironing b.**, planche à repasser; *Aut: Av:* **fascia b.**, tableau *m* de bord. **2.** nourriture *f*, pension *f*; **b. and lodging**, chambre(s) *f(pl)* et pension; **(job) with b. and lodging**, (emploi) logé et nourri. **3.** **b. of inquiry**, commission *f* d'enquête; **b. of examiners**, jury *m* (d'examen); *Com:* **b. of directors**, conseil *m* d'administration *f*; **b. meeting**, réunion *f* du conseil. **4.** *Nau: Av:* **to go on b.**, monter à bord; s'embarquer. **II.** *v.* **1.** *v.i.* être en pension; **to b. with a family**, prendre pension dans une famille. **2.** *v.tr.* monter à bord d'(un navire, un avion); monter dans (un train, un autobus); **'boarder,** *s.* pensionnaire *mf*; *Sch:* interne *mf*; **'boarding card,** *s.* carte *f* d'accès à bord; **'boarding house,** *s.* pension *f* de famille; **'boarding school,** *s.* pensionnat *m*, internat *m*.

boast [boust]. **I.** *v.* **1.** *v.i.* se vanter; **to b. that one can do sth.**, se vanter de pouvoir faire qch.; **that's nothing to b. of**, il n'y a pas là de quoi être fier; **without wishing to b. . . .**, sans vanité . . . **2.** *v.tr.* **the school boasts a fine library**, l'école possède une belle bibliothèque. **II.** *s.* vantardise *f*; **'boaster,** *s.* vantard *m*; **'boastful,** *a.* vantard; **'boastfulness,** *s.*, **'boasting,** *s.* vantardise *f*.

boat [bout], *s.* bateau *m*; (i) canot *m*; barque *f* (de pêcheur); embarcation *f*; (ii) navire *m*; **ship's b.**, embarcation de bord; **to go by b.**, prendre le bateau; **to be all in the same b.**, être tous dans le même panier; *attrib.* **b. builder**, constructeur *m* de canots, de bateaux; **b. race**, course *f* de bateaux, *esp.* match *m* d'aviron, régate(s) *f(pl)*; **b. train**, train *m* du bateau; **'boathouse,** *s.* hangar *m*, garage *m*, pour canots; **'boating,** *s.* canotage *m*; **b. club**, cercle *m*, club *m*, d'aviron.

boatswain ['bousn], *s. Nau:* maître *m* d'équipage.

bob[1] [bɔb], *s.* **1.** coiffure *f* à la Jeanne d'Arc. **2.** (*a*) *N.Am:* patin *m* (de traîneau); (*b*) **b.(-sleigh)**, bob(-sleigh) *m*.

bob[2], *v.i.* **(bobbed)** (*a*) se mouvoir de haut en bas et de bas en haut; s'agiter; (*of boat, bather*) **to b. up and down in the water**, danser sur l'eau; (*b*) **to b. up**, surgir brusquement; **to b. up again**, revenir à la surface.

bob[3]. *Pr.n.* Robert *m*, Bob *m*.

bobbin ['bɔbin], *s.* bobine *f*.

bobby ['bɔbi]. **1.** *Pr.n.m. diminutive of* **Robert**. **2.** *F:* agent *m* de police, *F:* flic *m*; **'bobby-pin,** *s. N.Am:* pince *f* à cheveux; **'bobby-socks,** *s.pl. N.Am:* socquettes *f*.

bodice ['bɔdis], *s.* corsage *m* (d'une robe).

body ['bɔdi], *s.* **1.** (*a*) corps *m*; **(dead) b.**, cadavre *m*; **over my dead b.!** à mon corps défendant! (*b*) sève *f*, générosité *f* (d'un vin); (*c*) consistance *f*. **2.** **legislative b.**, corps législatif; **public b.**, corporation *f*; **large b. of people**, foule nombreuse; **to come in a b.**, venir en masse. **3.** (*main part*) corps (de document); nef *f* (d'église); *Aut:* carrosserie *f*; **'bodiless,** *a.* sans corps; **'bodily. 1.** *a.* corporel, physique; **to supply one's b. needs**, pourvoir à ses besoins matériels; **b. pain**, douleur *f* physique. **2.** *adv.* (*a*) corporellement; (*b*) **they resigned b.**, ils ont démissionné en corps; **'bodyguard,** *s.* (*a*) garde *f* du corps; (*b*) (*pers.*) garde *m* du corps; **'bodywork,** *s. Aut:* carrosserie *f*.

bog [bɔg]. **I.** *s.* fondrière *f*; marécage *m*. **II.** *v.tr.* **(bogged)** *usu. in the passive,* **to get bogged down**, s'embourber, s'enliser; **'boggy,** *a.* marécageux.

bogey ['bougi], *s.* **1.** épouvantail *m*; spectre *m*. **2.** *Golf:* la normale du parcours.

boggle [bɔgl], *v.i.* rechigner, reculer (**at sth.**, devant qch.; **at doing sth.**, à faire qch.); **the mind boggles**, cela confond l'imagination.

bogus ['bougǝs], *a.* faux, *f.* fausse; feint, simulé.

boil[1] [bɔil], *s. Med:* furoncle *m*.

boil[2]. **I.** *v.* **1.** *v.i.* bouillir; **to begin to b.**, entrer en ébullition; **to b. fast, gently**, bouillir à gros, à petits, bouillons; *Cu:* **allow to b. slowly**, faites mijoter; **to keep the pot boiling**, maintenir l'entrain (dans une réunion). **2.** *v.tr.* faire bouillir; *Cu:* cuire, faire cuire, à l'eau; **boiled egg**, œuf à la coque. **II.** *s.* (*of water*) **to come to, go off, the b.**, commencer à bouillir, cesser de bouillir; **the kettle is on the b.**, l'eau bout; **'boil a'way,** *v.i.* (*of liquid*) se réduire; **'boil 'down. 1.** *v.tr.* réduire, faire réduire (une sauce); résumer, condenser (un article, un livre). **2.** *v.i.* se réduire; se borner, se résumer (**to**, à); **'boiler,** *s.* chaudière *f*; **b. suit**, bleu(s) *m(pl)* de chauffe; **'boiling. I.** *s.* ébullition *f*; **b. point**, point *m* d'ébullition. **II.** *a.* bouillant; *adv.* **b. hot**, tout bouillant; **'boil 'over,** *v.i.* (*of milk, etc.*) se sauver, s'en aller.

boisterous ['bɔist(ǝ)rǝs], *a.* bruyant, turbulent; tapageur; (*of wind*) violent; (*of sea*) agité; **-ly,** *adv.* (*a*) bruyamment; (*b*) tempétueusement; **'boisterousness,** *s.* turbulence *f*; violence *f* (du vent); agitation *f* (de la mer).

bold [bould], *a.* **1.** hardi; audacieux; (regard) assuré, confiant; **b. stroke**, coup d'audace. **2.** impudent, effronté. **3.** **b. cliff**, falaise escarpée; **-ly,** *adv.* **1.** hardiment; audacieusement; **to assert sth. b.**, affirmer qch. avec confiance. **2.** effrontément; **'boldness,** *s.* **1.** hardiesse *f*; audace *f*. **2.** effronterie *f*. **3.** escarpement *m* (d'une falaise).

Bolshevik ['bɔlʃǝvik], *a. & s.* bolcheviste (*mf*); **'Bolshevism,** *s.* bolchevisme *m*.

bolster ['boulstər]. **I.** *s.* traversin *m*. **II.** *v.tr.* **to b. s.o. up,** soutenir, appuyer, qn (qui a tort).
bolt [boult]. **I.** *s.* **1. (thunder) b.,** coup *m* de foudre; **b. from the blue,** événement *m* imprévu. **2. (sliding) b.,** verrou *m*; **(rifle) b.,** culasse *f* mobile. **3.** *E:* boulon *m*; cheville *f*; **nuts and bolts,** boulonnerie *f*. **4.** fuite *f*; **to make a b. (for it),** déguerpir, filer. **II.** *v.* **1.** *v.i.* (*of pers.*) décamper; (*of horse*) s'emballer. **2.** *v.tr.* gober; avaler à grandes bouchées; *F:* bouffer (son dîner). **3.** *v.tr.* (*a*) verrouiller (une porte); (*b*) boulonner, cheviller. **III.** *adv.* **b. upright,** tout droit; droit comme un piquet.
bomb [bom]. **I.** *s.* bombe *f*; **atom b.,** bombe atomique; **plastic b.,** (bombe au) plastic *m*; **to release a b.,** lâcher, larguer, une bombe; *Av:* **b. rack,** râtelier *m* à bombes; **b. disposal,** (i) désobusage *m*; (ii) déminage *m*; **b. disposal squad,** équipe *f* de déminage; *F:* **it's going like a b.,** ça marche à merveille. **II.** *v.tr.* bombarder (une ville); **bom'bard,** *v.tr.* bombarder; **bom'bardment,** *s.* bombardement *m*; **'bomber,** *s.* bombardier *m*; **'bombing,** *s.* bombardement *m*; **dive b.,** bombardement en piqué; **'bombshell,** *s.* **this was a b. to us all,** cette nouvelle nous a consternés; **it came like a b.,** il est tombé des nues.
bombastic [bom'bæstik], *a.* (style) grandiloquent, ampoulé; emphatique; **-ally,** *adv.* d'un style ampoulé, enflé; emphatiquement; avec emphase.
bona fide ['bounə'faidi], *a. & adv.* de bonne foi; **b. f. offer,** offre sérieuse.
bonanza [bə'nænzə], *s.* bonanza *m*, filon *m* riche.
bond [bond], *s.* **1.** lien *m*; attache *f*; **bonds of friendship,** liens d'amitié. **2.** (*a*) engagement *m*, contrat *m*; obligation *f*; (*b*) *Fin:* bon *m*; **bearer b.,** titre *m* au porteur; **premium bonds,** bons à lots; (*c*) *Jur:* caution *f*. **3.** *Com:* (*of goods*) **to be in b.,** être à l'entrepôt; **'bondage,** *s.* esclavage *m*, servitude *f*.
bone [boun]. **I.** *s.* **1.** os *m*; **(fish-)b.,** arête *f*; **b.(-)china,** demi-porcelaine *f*; **b. dry,** absolument sec; **b. idle, b. lazy,** paresseux comme une couleuvre; **I feel it in my bones,** j'en ai le pressentiment; **to make no bones about doing sth.,** ne pas se gêner pour faire qch. **2.** *pl.* (*of the dead*) ossements *m*. **II.** *v.tr.* désosser (la viande); ôter les arêtes d'(un poisson); **'bonehead,** *s. F:* nigaud *m*, tête *f* de bois; **'boneless,** *a.* désossé; sans os; sans arêtes; (*of pers.*) mou; **'bony,** *a.* **1.** osseux. **2.** (*of pers., animal*) décharné. **3.** (*of meat*) plein d'os; (*of fish*) plein d'arêtes.
bonfire ['bonfaiər], *s.* feu *m* de joie; feu de jardin.
bonnet ['bonit], *s.* **1.** *Cl:* bonnet *m*, béret *m* (écossais); béguin *m* (d'enfant). **2.** *Aut:* capot *m*.

bonus, *pl.* **-uses** ['bounəs, -əsiz], *s.* surpaye *f*, boni *m*; prime *f*; **b. on shares,** bonification *f* sur les actions; **cost-of-living b.,** indemnité *f* de vie chère; *Ins:* **no-claim b.,** bonification pour non-sinistre.
boo [bu:]. **I.** *int.* hou! **II.** *v.tr. & i.* huer, conspuer (qn).
booby ['bu:bi], *s.* nigaud *m*; **'booby prize,** *s.* prix (décerné par plaisanterie) au dernier; **'booby-trap,** *s.* piège *m*.
book [buk]. **I.** *s.* **1.** (*a*) livre *m*; *F:* bouquin *m*; **b. club,** club *m* du livre; **b. post,** service *m* (postal) des imprimés; **b. knowledge,** connaissances livresques; **school b., text b.,** livre de classe note b., carnet *m*; **exercise b.,** cahier *m*; (*b*) livret *m* (d'un opéra). **2.** (*a*) registre *m*; **account b.,** livre de comptes; **cheque b.,** carnet de chèques; **bank b.,** livret de banque; **to be in s.o.'s bad books,** être mal vu de qn; **to bring s.o. to b. for sth.,** forcer qn à rendre compte de qch.; (*b*) **b. of tickets,** carnet de billets; (*c*) **telephone b.,** annuaire *m* du téléphone; (*d*) *Rac:* **betting b.,** livre de paris; **to make a b.,** faire un livre; *F:* **that suits my b.,** ça fait mon affaire; (*e*) **b. of matches,** allumettes *fpl* en pochette. **II.** *v.tr.* **1.** inscrire, enregistrer (une commande); *Com:* **shall I b. it for you?** dois-je le charger à votre compte? **2.** retenir, réserver (une chambre, une place); *Rail: etc: abs.* **to book** prendre son billet; *Aut: F:* **I was booked for speeding** = j'ai eu une contravention, *F:* un P.V., pour excès de vitesse; **'bookable,** *a.* qui peut être retenu, réservé; **'bookbinder,** relieur *m*; **'bookbinding,** *s.* reliure *f*; **'bookcase,** *s.* bibliothèque *f*; **'bookie,** *s. F:* book(maker) *m*; **'booking,** *s.* (*a*) enregistrement *m*, inscription *f*; (*b*) *Th: etc:* réservation (des places); (*c*) (*of artist*) engagement *m*; (*a*) **b. clerk,** employé, -e, du guichet; **b. office,** guichet *m*; **'bookish,** *a.* (*of pers.*) studieux (connaissance *f*) livresque; **'book-keeper,** comptable *m*; **'book-keeping,** *s.* comptabilité *f*; **'booklet,** *s.* (*a*) livret *m*; (*b*) opuscule *m*; **'booklover,** *s.* bibliophile *mf*; **'bookmaker** *s.* bookmaker *m, F:* book *m*; **'bookmark(er)** *s.* signet *m*; **'bookmobile,** *s. N.Am:* bibliobus *m*; **'bookseller,** *s.* libraire *mf*; **second-hand b.,** bouquiniste *m*; **'bookshelf,** *s.* rayon *m*, étagère *f* (de bibliothèque); **'bookshop,** librairie *f*; **'bookstall,** *s.*, **'bookstand,** *s.* étalage *m* de livres. **2.** bibliothèque *f* (de gare, de rue); **'book trade,** *s.* (*a*) industrie *f* du livre (*b*) (commerce *m* de) librairie *f*; **'bookworm,** *s.* liseur acharné; bouquineur *m*.
boom[1] [bu:m], *s.* **1.** barrage *m* (à l'entrée d'une rade); chaîne *f* (de fermeture); barre *f*. **2.** *Na:* bout-dehors *m*; *Cin:* perche *f* (de microphone).
boom[2]. **I.** *s.* **1.** grondement *m* (du canon); mugissement *m* (du vent); bang *m* (supe...

sonique). 2. *Com:* (*a*) hausse *f* rapide, boom *m*; (*b*) vague *f* de prospérité; (période *f* de) vogue *f*. **II.** *v.i.* **1.** gronder, mugir; (*of organ*) ronfler. **2.** *Com:* être en hausse; **business is booming**, le commerce va très fort.

boomerang ['buːməræŋ]. **1.** *s.* boomerang *m*. **2.** *v.i.* **his policy boomeranged**, sa politique s'est retournée contre lui.

boon [buːn], *s.* bienfait *m*, avantage *m*.

boor ['buər], *s.* rustre *m*, rustaud *m*; **what a b.!** quel ours! **'boorish**, *a.* rustre, grossier; **'boorishness**, *s.* grossièreté *f*; manque *m* de savoir-vivre.

boost [buːst]. **I.** *v.tr.* **1.** soulever (qn) par derrière; faire de la réclame pour (qn, qch.). **2.** *El:* survolter. **II.** *s.* **to give (s.o., sth.) a b.**, (i) soulever (qn) par derrière; (ii) faire de la réclame pour (qn, qch.); **'booster**, *s.* **1.** *El:* survolteur *m*. **2.** (*a*) *Med:* **b. dose**, dose *f* de rappel; (*b*) **b. (rocket)**, fusée *f* de relancement; **'boosting**, *s.* **1.** *F:* réclame *f*. **2.** *El:* survoltage *m*.

boot [buːt]. **I.** *s.* **1.** chaussure *f*; bottine *f*; **high b.**, botte *f*; **ankle b.**, bottillon *m*; **b. and shoe manufacturer**, fabricant *m* de chaussures; **to put on one's boots**, se chausser; **to take off one's boots**, se déchausser; **the b. is on the other foot**, c'est tout (juste) le contraire; *F:* **to get the (order of the) b.**, être congédié; **b. polish**, crème *f* à chaussures; **b. lace**, lacet *m* (de chaussure). **2.** *Aut:* coffre *m*. **II.** *v.tr.* *F:* flanquer des coups de pied à (qn); **to b. s.o. out**, mettre, flanquer, qn à la porte; **boo'tee**, *s.* chausson *m* (de bébé); **'bootmaker**, *s.* bottier *m*; cordonnier *m*; **boots**, *s.* (*in hotel*) garçon d'étage.

booty ['buːti], *s.* butin *m*.

booze [buːz]. **I.** *s.* *P:* boisson (alcoolisée). **II.** *v.i.* *P:* boire (beaucoup); faire la noce, la bombe; **'boozer**, *s.* *P:* **1.** ivrogne *m*. **2.** bistrot *m*.

boracic [bə'ræsik], *a.* *Ch:* borique; **b. ointment**, pommade *f* à l'acide borique; **b. powder**, poudre boriquée.

borax ['bɔːræks], *s.* *Ch:* borax *m*.

border ['bɔːdər]. **I.** *s.* **1.** bord *m* (d'un lac); lisière *f*, bordure *f* (d'un bois); marge *f* (d'un chemin); frontière *f* (d'un pays). **2.** (*a*) (= *edging*) bordure; encadrement *m*; (*b*) **grass b.**, cordon *m* de gazon. **II.** *v.i.* **to b. on (sth.)**, toucher à (qch.); être limitrophe d'(un autre pays); friser (la folie, la catastrophe); **'bordering**, *a.* contigu, *f.* -uë; voisin (**on**, de); **statement b. on falsehood**, déclaration *f* qui frise le mensonge; **'borderline**, *s.* ligne *f* de séparation, limites *fpl*, bornes *fpl* (d'une catégorie); **b. case**, cas *m* limite.

bore¹ [bɔːr]. **I.** *v.tr. & i.* creuser; forer (un puits); **to b. through (sth.)**, percer, perforer (qch.); **to b. for water, minerals**, sonder, faire un sondage, pour trouver de l'eau, des minerais. **II.** *s.*

calibre *m* (d'une arme à feu, d'un tuyau, etc.); **'borehole**, *s.* *Min:* trou *m* de sonde, de mine.

bore². **I.** *v.tr.* ennuyer, *F:* raser, assommer, enquiquiner (qn); **to be bored stiff, bored to tears**, s'ennuyer à mourir; avoir le cafard. **II.** *s.* (*of pers.*) raseur, -euse; (*of thg*) ennui *m*, corvée *f*; **'boredom**, *s.* ennui *m*; **'boring**, *a.* ennuyeux; *F:* rasant, rasoir (*inv.*), assommant, barbant.

bore³, *s.* (*in river*) mascaret *m*.

born [bɔːn]. **1.** *p.p.* (*of v.* **to bear**, *passive use*) **to be b.**, naître; venir au monde; **he was b. in 1950**, il est né en 1950; **b. in London**, né(e) à Londres. **2.** *a.* **a Londoner b. and bred**, un vrai Londonien de Londres; **a b. poet**, un poète-né; **a b. gentleman**, un gentleman de naissance; *F:* **a b. fool**, un parfait idiot. **3.** *s.* **her latest b.**, son dernier né, sa dernière née.

borough ['bʌrə], *s.* ville *f*.

borrow ['bɔrou], *v.tr.* emprunter (**from**, à); **to b. at interest**, emprunter à intérêt; **'borrower**, *s.* emprunteur, -euse; **'borrowing**, emprunts *mpl*.

bosom ['buzəm], *s.* sein *m*; poitrine *f*.

boss¹ [bɔs]. **I.** *s.* *F:* (*a*) **the b.**, le patron, le chef; (*b*) *Ind:* contremaître *m*. **II.** *v.tr.* *F:* mener, diriger; **to b. the show**, diriger toute l'affaire; régenter tout le monde; **'bossy**, *a.* autoritaire.

boss², *a. & s.* *P:* **to make a b. (shot) of, at, sth.**, louper qch.; **'boss-eyed**, *a.* *F:* qui louche.

bosun ['bousn], *s.* *Nau:* maître *m* d'équipage.

botany ['bɔtəni], *s.* botanique *f*; **bo'tanical**, *a.* botanique; **'botanist**, *s.* botaniste *mf*.

botch [bɔtʃ], *v.tr.* *F:* **1.** bousiller, saboter (un travail, etc.). **2.** **to b. up**, réparer grossièrement, rafistoler (un appareil, des souliers, etc.).

both [bouθ]. **1.** *a. & pron.* tous (les) deux, toutes (les) deux; l'un(e) et l'autre; **to hold sth. in b. hands**, tenir qch. à deux mains; **on b. sides**, des deux côtés; **b. alike**, l'un comme l'autre. **2.** *adv.* **b. you and I**, (et) vous et moi; **she b. attracts and repels me**, elle m'attire et me repousse à la fois; **I'm fond of music b. ancient and modern**, j'aime la musique tant ancienne que moderne.

bother ['bɔðər]. **I.** *v.tr.* gêner, ennuyer, tracasser, tourmenter (qn); **don't b. me!** laissez-moi tranquille! *F:* **I can't be bothered**, ça m'embête; **b. (it)!** zut! **I can't be bothered to do it**, j'ai la flemme de le faire; **don't b. to bring a mac**, ce n'est pas la peine de prendre un imper. **2.** *v.i.* **he doesn't b. about anything**, il ne s'inquiète de rien. **II.** *s.* ennui *m*; embêtement *m*; tracas *m*; **'bothered**, *a.* inquiet; embarrassé.

bottle ['bɔtl]. **I.** *s.* **1.** bouteille *f*; (*small*) flacon *m*; (*wide-mouthed*) bocal *m*; **b. opener**, ouvre-bouteilles *m*; décapsuleur *m*; **wine b.**, bouteille à vin; **b. of wine**, bouteille de vin; **b. party**, réunion *f* intime où chacun apporte à boire; **b.**

rack, casier *m* à bouteilles. 2. **feeding b.,** biberon *m*. 3. **hot water b.,** bouillotte *f*. II. *v.tr.* mettre (du vin) en bouteilles; mettre (des fruits) en bocal; **'bottled,** *a*. (*a*) en bouteille; (*b*) *F:* ivre; **'bottle-fed,** *a*. nourri au biberon; **'bottle-feeding,** *s*. allaitement artificiel; **'bottleneck,** *s*. 1. goulot *m* (de bouteille). 2. *Aut: Adm:* embouteillage *m* (de la circulation); **'bottle 'up,** *v.tr.* 1. embouteiller (la circulation). 2. **to b. up one's feelings, one's anger,** étouffer ses sentiments, ravaler sa colère; **'bottling,** *s*. mise *f* en bouteille(s), en bocal.

bottom ['bɔtəm], *s*. 1. (*a*) bas *m* (d'une colline, d'un escalier, d'une page); (*b*) fond *m*; **at the b. of the garden,** au fond du jardin; (*of ship*) **to go to the b.,** couler; **prices have touched rock b.,** les prix sont au plus bas; **at b., he's not a bad fellow,** au fond, ce n'est pas un mauvais garçon; (*of pers.*) **to be at the b. of sth.,** être l'instigateur, -trice, de qch. 2. bas-fond *m* (de terrain). 3. **to knock the b. out of an argument,** démolir un argument; **the b. has fallen out of the market,** le marché s'est effondré. 4. *Anat: F:* derrière *m*, postérieur *m*; **'bottomless,** *a*. sans fond; insondable.

bough [bau], *s*. branche *f*, rameau *m*.

boulder ['bouldər], *s*. grosse pierre (roulée).

bounce [bauns]. I. *v*. 1. *v.i.* & *tr.* (*a*) (*of ball*) rebondir; (*b*) (*of pers.*) **to b. in,** entrer en coup de vent; (*c*) *F:* faire l'important; (*d*) **I hope this cheque won't b.,** j'espère que ce n'est pas un chèque sans provision. 2. *v.tr.* (*a*) faire rebondir (une balle); (*b*) **to b. s.o. into doing sth.,** pousser qn à faire qch. (sans lui laisser le temps de réfléchir); (*c*) *N.Am: F:* flanquer (qn) à la porte. II. *s*. 1. (*of ball*) rebondissement *m*, bond *m*. 2. (*of pers.*) vantardise *f*, épate *f*; **'bouncer,** *s*. *F:* 1. vantard *m*. 2. expulseur *m*, videur *m*. 3. chèque sans provision; **'bouncing,** *a*. rebondissant; **b. baby,** bébé resplendissant (de vie et de santé); **b. cheque,** chèque sans provision.

bound[1] [baund]. I. *s*. (*usu. pl.*) limite(s) *f*, bornes *fpl*; *Sch:* **out of bounds,** (endroit) défendu aux élèves; **to go beyond all bounds,** dépasser toutes les bornes; **to keep within bounds,** rester dans la juste mesure. II. *a*. **b. for,** en partance pour; en route pour, allant à.

bound[2]. I. *s*. bond *m*, saut *m*; **at a b.,** d'un seul bond. II. *v.i.* bondir, sauter.

bound[3], *a*. 1. lié. 2. (*a*) **to be b. to do sth.,** être obligé, tenu, de faire qch.; **to be in honour b. to do sth.,** être engagé d'honneur à faire qch.; **to be b. by rules,** être soumis à des règles; (*b*) **it's b. to happen,** c'est fatal; **we're b. to be successful,** nous réussirons à coup sûr.

boundary ['baund(ə)ri], *s*. limite *f*, bornes *fpl*; frontière *f*.

bounty ['baunti], *s*. (*a*) don *m*, gratification *f* (à un employé, etc.); (*b*) *Adm:* indemnité *f*; prime *f*; subvention *f*; **'bountiful,** *a*. bienfaisant, généreux.

bouquet ['bukei, bu'kei], *s*. bouquet *m*.

bourbon ['buəbən], *s*. *N.Am:* whisky *m* de maïs.

bout [baut], *s*. 1. *Sp:* tour *m*, reprise *f*; **wrestling b.,** assaut *m* de lutte. 2. accès *m* (de fièvre), at taque *f* (de grippe).

boutique [bu:'ti:k], *s*. (*a*) petit magasin d modes; boutique *f*; (*b*) (*in store*) **teenage b** rayon *m* des jeunes.

bow[1] [bou], *s*. 1. arc *m*; **to have two strings t one's b.,** avoir deux cordes à son arc. 2. *Mus* archet *m* (de violon). 3. nœud *m* (de ruban); **b. tie,** nœud papillon. 4. **b. window,** fenêtre *f* e saillie (courbe); bow-window *m*; **'bow legged,** *a*. bancal, *pl.* -als.

bow[2] [bau]. I. *s*. salut *m*; inclination *f* de têt **with a b.,** en saluant, en s'inclinant. II. *v*. 1. *v.* s'incliner; baisser la tête. 2. *v.tr.* incline baisser (la tête); fléchir (le genou); courbe voûter (le dos); **to become bowed,** se voûter

bow[3] [bau], *s*. (*a*) *Nau:* (*often in pl.*) avant *r* étrave *f*; **to cross the bows of a ship,** couper route d'un navire; (*b*) *Av:* nez *m*.

bowels ['bauəlz], *s.pl. Anat:* intestins *m*, e trailles *f*; (*esp. of animals*) *F:* boyaux *m*; **bow complaint,** affection intestinale; **the b. of t earth,** les entrailles de la terre.

bowl[1] [boul], *s*. bol *m*; coupe *f* (de crista (= *basin*) cuvette *f*, bassin *m*; **washing-up** bassine *f*.

bowl[2]. I. *v.tr.* (*a*) rouler, faire courir (un cercea (*b*) *Bowls:* lancer, rouler (la boule); (*c*) *Crick* (i) servir (la balle); (ii) renverser le guiche (qn). II. *s*. boule *f*; (**game of**) **bowls,** (i) (jeu boules; pétanque *f*; (ii) *N.Am:* (jeu de) quil *f*; **'bowler**[1], *s*. 1. joueur, -euse, de boules, pétanque. 2. (*at cricket*) serveur *m*, lanceur **'bowling,** *s*. 1. (*a*) jeu *m* de boules, pétanque; **b. green,** (terrain pour) jeu boules; (*b*) **b. alley,** bowling *m*; **'bowl 'ov** *v.tr.* (*a*) renverser (les quilles avec la boule); déconcerter (qn); *F:* **his cheek bowled me ov** son toupet m'a épaté.

bowler[2] ['boulər], *s*. **b. (hat),** (chapeau *m*) me (*m*).

box[1] [bɔks], *s*. *Bot:* buis *m*; **'boxwood,** *s*. (t *m* de buis).

box[2], *s*. 1. boîte *f*; (*small*) coffret *m*; (*la wooden*) caisse *f*; (*of cardboard*) carton **letter b., post b.,** boîte aux lettres; (**postal number,** numéro *m* de boîte postale. 2. (*a*) loge *f*; (*b*) (*in stable*) box *m*, *pl.* boxes; **witness b.** = barre *f* des témoins; **'boxful** pleine boîte, pleine caisse; **'Boxing Day,** lendemain de Noël; **'box-office,** *s*. *Th:* bur *m* de location; guichet *m*; **'boxroom**

(chambre f de) débarras m; 'box-spanner, s. Tls: clef f à tube.
box³. I. s. b. on the ear, gifle f, claque f. II. v. 1. v.tr. to b. s.o.'s ears, gifler qn. 2. v.i. boxer, faire de la boxe; 'boxer¹, s. boxeur m, pugiliste m; 'boxing, s. la boxe; b. gloves, gants m de boxe; b. match, match m de boxe.
boxer² ['bɔksər], s. (chien m) boxer m.
boy [bɔi], s. (a) garçon m; F: gamin m, gosse m; an English b., un jeune Anglais; when I was a b., quand j'étais petit; F: my dear b.! mon cher (ami)! old b.! mon vieux! the old b., (i) le paternel; (ii) le patron; (b) Sch: élève m; an old b., un ancien élève; (c) fils m; this is my b., voici mon garçon; (d) domestique m, ouvrier m, indigène; (e) the grocer's b., le garçon épicier; 'boyfriend, s. flirt m, ami m, amoureux m; 'boyhood, s. enfance f, adolescence f (d'un garçon); 'boyish, a. puéril, enfantin, d'enfant; 'boylike, a. de gamin; en vrai garçon.
boycott ['bɔikɔt]. I. v.tr. boycotter. II. s. mise f en interdit; boycottage m; 'boycotting, s. boycottage m.
bra [brɑ:], s. soutien-gorge m inv.
brace [breis]. I. s. 1. Const: etc: attache f, lien m; croisillon m; jambe f de force; (dental) b., rectificateur m dentaire. 2. s.pl. Cl: bretelles f. 3. inv. couple f (de perdrix, etc.). 4. Tls: b. (and bit), vilebrequin m. II. v.tr. 1. ancrer, amarrer; armer (une poutre). 2. fortifier (le corps); to b. s.o. up, remonter qn; to b. oneself to do sth., se raidir pour faire qch.; 'bracing, a. (air, climat) fortifiant, tonifiant.
bracelet ['breislit], s. bracelet m.
bracken ['bræk(ə)n], s. fougère f.
bracket ['brækit]. I. s. (a) support m; console f; Arch: corbeau m; (b) (electric wall-)b., applique f; (c) Typ: etc: round b., parenthèse f; square b., crochet m; accolade f; (d) Adm: the middle-income b., la tranche des salariés moyens. II. v.tr. (bracketed) (a) mettre (des mots, des chiffres) entre parenthèses, entre crochets; (b) réunir (des mots) par une accolade; (c) faire un rapport, une association, entre (des personnes, des idées).
brackish ['brækiʃ], a. (of water) saumâtre.
bradawl ['brædɔ:l], s. Tls: alêne plate; poinçon m.
brag [bræg], v.i. (bragged) se vanter; 'bragging. 1. a. vantard. 2. s. vantardise f.
braid [breid], s. galon m, ganse f; gold b. (on uniforms, etc.), galon (sur des uniformes d'officier, etc.).
braille [breil], s. Braille m; b. type, caractères mpl Braille.
brain [brein]. I. s. 1. cerveau m; electronic b., cerveau électronique; F: to turn s.o.'s b., tourner la tête à qn; to have an idea on the b., être obsédé par une idée; I've got that tune on

the b., j'ai cet air dans la tête. 2. pl. cervelle f; matière cérébrale; Cu: calves' brains, cervelle de veau; to blow s.o.'s brains out, brûler la cervelle à qn; to rack one's brains, se creuser la cervelle; he has brains, il est intelligent; b. drain, fuite f des cerveaux. II. v.tr. to b. s.o., (i) défoncer le crâne à qn; (ii) assommer qn; 'brainchild, s. idée, conception, originale; 'braininess, s. F: intelligence f; 'brainless, a. stupide; 'brainwash, v.tr. faire un lavage de crâne, de cerveau à (qn); 'brainwashing, s. lavage m de crâne, de cerveau; 'brainwave, s. inspiration f, F: trouvaille f; 'brainwork, s. travail intellectuel; 'brainy, a. F: intelligent, débrouillard.
braise [breiz], v.tr. Cu: braiser; cuire (qch.) à l'étouffée; braised beef, bœuf m en daube.
brake [breik]. I. s. frein m; hand b., frein à main; disc b., frein à disque; b. fluid, liquide m pour freins, F: Lockheed m (R.t.m.); b. lining, garniture f de frein; to put on, apply, the brakes, serrer le frein; to release the b., lâcher le frein. II. v.tr. & i. mettre le frein; freiner; 'braking, s. freinage m; b. distance, distance f d'arrêt.
bramble ['bræmbl], s. ronce f.
bran [bræn], s. son m.
branch [brɑ:n(t)ʃ]. I. s. 1. branche f, rameau m (d'un arbre). 2. (a) branche, bras m (d'un fleuve); Rail: etc: embranchement m; b. line, ligne f d'intérêt local; (b) branche (d'une famille); (c) Com: succursale f, filiale f. II. v. 1. v.i. to b. out, se ramifier; (of pers.) to b. out into . . ., étendre ses activités à . . .; (of road, etc.) to b. (off, away), bifurquer. 2. v.tr. El: brancher (un circuit); dériver (le courant).
brand [brænd]. I. s. 1. brandon m, tison m. 2. (a) fer chaud; (b) marque (faite avec un fer chaud). 3. Com: (a) marque (de fabrique); (b) sorte f, qualité f (d'une marchandise). II. v.tr. 1. marquer (au fer chaud). 2. to b. s.o. as a liar, noter, stigmatiser, qn comme menteur; 'branded, a. (a) marqué à chaud; (b) b. goods, produits m de marque; b. image, image m de marque; 'branding, s. impression f au fer chaud; b. iron, fer m à marquer; 'brand new, a. tout (flambant) neuf.
brandish ['brændiʃ], v.tr. brandir.
brandy ['brændi], s. eau-de-vie f, cognac m; liqueur b., fine champagne f; b. and soda, fine f à l'eau.
brass [brɑ:s], s. 1. cuivre m jaune; laiton m; b. plate, plaque f de cuivre; F: b. hat, officier m d'état-major; F: the top b., les grosses légumes, les gros bonnets. 2. (a) H: les cuivres, les robinets m, etc.; (b) Mus: the b., les cuivres; b. band, fanfare f; (c) (in churches) brasses, plaques f mortuaires en cuivre. 3. P: argent m, fric m. 4. P: (= cheek) toupet m, culot m. 5. attrib. F: to get down to b. tacks, en venir aux

faits; **'brassy,** *a.* (*a*) qui ressemble au cuivre;
(*b*) (son) cuivré, claironnant; (*c*) (*of pers.*)
effronté.

brassière ['bræsiər], *s.* soutien-gorge *m inv*;
strapless b., bustier *m.*

brat [bræt], *s.* marmot *m*, mioche *mf.*

bravado [brə'vɑːdou], *s.* bravade *f.*

brave [breiv]. I. *a.* courageux, brave; **-ly,** *adv.*
courageusement. II. *v.tr.* braver, défier (qn);
affronter (un danger); **'bravery,** *s.* courage *m.*

bravo [brɑː'vou], *int.* bravo!

brawl [brɔːl]. I. *s.* rixe *f,* bagarre *f.* II. *v.i.* se
bagarrer, se chamailler; **'brawler,** *s.*
bagarreur, -euse.

brawn [brɔːn], *s.* **1.** muscles *mpl.* **2.** *Cu:* fromage
m de tête, de hure; **'brawny,** *a.* (*of pers.*)
musclé, *F:* costaud.

bray [brei], *v.i.* braire.

brazen ['breizn]. I. *a.* **1.** d'airain. **2. b.**(-faced),
effronté, impudent; **b. lie,** mensonge *m*
cynique. II. *v.tr.* **to b. it out,** payer d'effronterie,
crâner.

Brazil [brə'zil]. *Pr.n. Geog:* le Brésil.

Brazilian [brə'ziljən], *a.* & *s.* brésilien, -ienne.

breach [briːtʃ], *s.* **1.** infraction *f;* **b. of the law,**
violation *f* de la loi; **b. of faith,** manque *m* de
parole; **b. of trust,** abus *m* de confiance; **b. of
the peace,** attentat *m* contre l'ordre public; **b.
of promise,** violation de promesse de mariage.
2. brouille *f,* rupture *f* (entre amis, etc.). **3.**
brèche *f* (dans un mur).

bread [bred], *s.* (*a*) pain *m*; **wholemeal b.,** pain
complet; **French b.,** flûte *f,* baguette *f*; **a loaf of
b.,** un pain; **b. and butter,** pain beurré; **to earn
one's b. and butter,** gagner sa croûte; **slice of
b.,** tranche *f* de pain; **slice of b. and butter,** tartine *f*; **b. and butter letter,** lettre *f* de digestion;
he knows which side his b. is buttered, il sait où
est son avantage; **b. and milk,** pain au lait; (*b*)
attrib. **b. basket,** (i) corbeille *f* à pain; (ii) *P:* estomac *m*; **b. bin,** huche *f* à pain; **b. sauce,** sauce
f à la mie de pain; **'breadcrumbs,** *s.pl. Cu:*
chapelure *f*; **'breadline,** *s.* **on the b.,** indigent;
sans ressources; **'bread(-)winner,** *s.* gagne-
pain *m inv*; soutien *m* de famille.

breadth [bredθ], *s.* **1.** largeur *f*; **the table is three
feet in b.,** la table a trois pieds de large. **2.**
largeur (de pensée, de vues).

break [breik]. I. *s.* **1.** rupture *f*; (*a*) brisure *f,*
cassure *f,* fracture *f*; brèche *f*; ouverture *f*;
éclaircie *f* (à travers les nuages); lacune *f* (dans
une succession); **b. in the voice,** (i) altération *f*
de la voix; (ii) mue *f* (à la puberté); **b. (in a
journey),** arrêt *m*; **to work without a b.,**
travailler sans relâche; **b. in continuity,** solution *f* de continuité; *T.V: etc:* **b. in transmission,** incident *m* technique; (*b*) **b. in the
weather,** changement *m* de temps; (*c*)
(= *quarrel*), rupture, brouille *f*; (*d*) **to have a**

lucky b., avoir de la veine. **2.** (*a*) (moment *m*
de) repos *m*, répit *m*; **the coffee b.,** la pause-
café; (*b*) *Sch:* intervalle *m*; récréation *f.* **3. b. of
day,** point *m* du jour. II. *v.* (**broke; broken**) **1.**
v.tr. (*a*) casser, briser, rompre; **to b. one's arm,**
se casser le bras; **to b. (the) silence,** rompre le
silence; **to b. one's journey,** interrompre son
voyage; **to b. the sound barrier,** franchir le mur
du son; *abs.* **to b. even,** joindre les deux bouts;
(*b*) **to b. gaol,** s'évader de prison; *Mil:* **to b.
bounds,** violer la consigne; (*c*) **to b. s.o.'s heart,**
briser, crever, le cœur de qn; (*d*) **to b. a fall,**
amortir une chute; (*e*) (*of money losses*) ruiner
(qn); (*of grief*) briser (qn); **to b. the bank,** faire
sauter la banque; *Mil:* casser (un officier); (*f*)
to b. the peace, troubler l'ordre public; **to b. the
law,** enfreindre la loi; **to b. one's word,**
manquer de parole. **2.** *v.i.* (*a*) (se) casser, se
rompre, se briser; (*of wave*) déferler; (*b*) (*of
heart*) se briser; se fendre, crever; (*of weather*)
changer; (*c*) **to b. with s.o.,** rompre avec qn; (*of
day*) poindre; (*d*) (*of voice*) (i) (*at puberty*)
muer; (ii) (*with emotion*) s'altérer; (*e*) (*of
storm*) éclater; **to b. into a laugh,** éclater de
rire; **'breakable,** *a.* fragile; **'breakables,** *s.p.*
objets *m* fragiles; **'breakage,** *s.* rupture *f*; bris
m (de verre, etc.); casse *f*; **to pay for
breakages,** payer la casse; **'break a'way.** **1.**
v.tr. détacher (**from,** de). **2.** *v.i.* se détache
(**from,** de); s'échapper, s'évader; **'break
'down. 1.** *v.tr.* abattre, démolir, renverser; **t
b. d. all opposition,** vaincre toute opposi-
tion. **2.** *v.i.* (*a*) (*of health*) s'altérer; (*of plan*)
échouer; (*of bridge*) s'effondrer; (*b*) (*of pers.*)
(i) éclater en sanglots; (ii) tomber malade; (
(*of car*) rester en panne; **'breakdown,** *s.* **1.** (
rupture *f* (de négociations); arrêt compl
(dans un service); (*b*) répartition *f* (de la p
pulation par âge, etc.); (*c*) *Med:* **nervous b
dépression nerveuse. 2.** *Aut: etc:* panne *f*; **
lorry,** dépanneuse *f*; camion-grue *n*
'breaker, *s.* brisant *m*, vague déferlant
'break 'in. 1. *v.tr.* (*a*) enfoncer; défoncer (u
porte, etc.); (*b*) *Equit:* **to b. in a horse,** dress
un cheval; **to b. oneself in to a new job, etc.,**
plier à un nouvel emploi, etc. **2.** *v.i.* (*a*) **to b.
on s.o.,** interrompre qn; *abs.* **to b. in,**
tervenir; (*b*) s'introduire par effraction; **'bre
'loose,** *v.i.* **1.** se dégager de ses liens; s'évad
s'échapper; s'affranchir (**from,** de). **2.**
anger, etc.) se déchaîner; **'breakneck,** *a.* **at
speed,** à une vitesse folle; **'break 'off. 1.** *v
(*a*) casser, rompre; (*b*) interrompre, aba
donner; **the engagement is broken off,**
fiançailles sont rompues. **2.** *v.i.* (*a*) se détach
se dégager (**from sth.,** de qch.); (*b*) disc
tinuer; **'break 'open,** *v.tr.* enfoncer, forcer (
coffre-fort; **'break 'out,** *v.i.* **1.** (*of war, e*
éclater. **2.** s'échapper, s'évader; **'bre**

'**through,** v.tr. percer; enfoncer; **to b. t. a barrier,** abs. **to b. t.,** enfoncer une barrière; se frayer un passage; **the sun breaks through (the clouds),** le soleil perce les nuages; '**breakthrough,** s. percée f (technologique); solution soudaine (à un problème); '**break'up,** 1. v.tr. mettre (qch.) en morceaux; démolir; disperser (la foule); rompre (une conférence). 2. v.i. (a) (of empire, ship) se démembrer; (of crowd) se disperser; **he's beginning to b. up,** il commence à décliner; (b) se séparer; (c) Sch: entrer en vacances; (d) (of weather) se gâter, se brouiller; '**breakwater,** s. briselames m inv; môle m.

reakfast ['brekfəst]. I. s. (petit) déjeuner; **continental b.,** café complet; **wedding b.,** repas m de noce; **to have b.,** prendre son petit déjeuner; **b. cup and saucer,** déjeuner m. II. v.i. prendre son petit déjeuner.

'**reast** [brest], s. 1. sein m. 2. poitrine f; poitrail m (de cheval); Cu: blanc m (de volaille); **to press s.o. to one's b.,** serrer qn sur son cœur; **to make a clean b. of it,** tout avouer. 3. Cl: **b. pocket,** poche f (de) poitrine; Swimming: **b. stroke,** brasse f; '**breast-feeding,** s. allaitement naturel.

'**reath** [breθ], s. haleine f, souffle m, respiration f; **to draw b.,** respirer; **to take a deep b.,** respirer profondément; **all in the same b.,** tout d'une haleine, sans souffler; **to hold one's b.,** retenir son souffle; **to gasp for b.,** haleter; **he caught his b.,** il eut un sursaut; **to lose one's b.,** perdre haleine; **to get one's b. back,** reprendre haleine; **to waste one's b.,** perdre ses paroles; **out of b.,** à bout de souffle; essoufflé; **to take s.o.'s b. away,** couper la respiration à qn; suffoquer, interloquer, qn; **to speak under one's b.,** parler à voix basse; '**breathalyser (test),** s. Adm: alcootest m; '**breathless,** a. hors d'haleine; essoufflé; **-ly,** adv. en haletant.

'**reathe** [bri:ð]. 1. v.i. respirer, souffler. 2. v.tr. respirer; **to b. the air in, out,** aspirer, exhaler, l'air; **to b. a sigh,** laisser échapper un soupir; **to b. one's last,** rendre le dernier soupir; **don't b. a word of it!** n'en soufflez pas un mot! '**breather,** s. F: moment m de repos; **give me a b.!** laisse-moi souffler! **to go out for a b.,** sortir prendre l'air; '**breathing,** s. respiration f; souffle m; **b. apparatus,** appareil m respiratoire; **b. space,** le temps de souffler; répit m.

'**eeches** ['britʃiz], s.pl. **(pair of) b.,** culotte f, pantalon m.

'**eed** [bri:d]. I. v. **(bred)** 1. v.tr. (a) produire, engendrer (le crime, etc.); (b) élever (du bétail); abs. faire de l'élevage. 2. v.i. multiplier, se reproduire; (of ideas) se propager. II. s. race f; lignée f; **bred,** a. (used in compounds)

country-b., élevé(e) à la campagne; **well-b.,** bien élevé; '**breeder,** s. 1. Agr: éleveur m. 2. Atom. Ph: **b. reactor,** réacteur (auto)générateur m; '**breeding,** s. 1. (a) reproduction f; (b) élevage m; **he goes in for b.,** il fait de l'élevage. 2. éducation f; **(good) b.,** savoir-vivre m.

breeze [bri:z]. I. s. vent assez fort; brise f; **stiff b.,** vent frais. II. v.i. F: **to b. in, out,** entrer, sortir, en coup de vent; '**breeziness,** s. cordialité bruyante, jovialité f; verve f (d'un discours); '**breezy,** a. 1. venteux. 2. (of pers.) jovial, désinvolte; **b.** welcome, accueil m cordial (et bruyant); **-ily,** adv. avec jovialité.

breeze-block ['bri:zblɔk], s. Const: parpaing m.

Bremen ['breimən]. Pr.n. Geog: Brême f.

Breton [bretən]. 1. a. & s. breton, -onne. 2. s. Ling: le breton.

breviary ['bri:viəri], s. Ecc: bréviaire m.

brevity ['breviti], s. brièveté f, concision f; courte durée (d'un séjour).

brew [bru:]. 1. v.tr. brasser (la bière); abs. brasser; faire de la bière. 2. v.i. (a) s'infuser; (b) **there's a storm brewing,** un orage couve, se prépare; **there's something brewing,** il se trame quelque chose; '**brewer,** s. brasseur m; '**brewery,** s. brasserie f.

briars ['braiəz], s.pl. ronces f.

bribe [braib]. I. s. paiement m illicite; pot-de-vin m; **to accept a b.,** se laisser corrompre. II. v.tr. corrompre, acheter, soudoyer (qn); suborner (un témoin); '**bribery,** s. corruption f.

brick [brik], s. (a) brique f; **to drop a b.,** faire une gaffe, une bourde; F: **he came down on me like a ton of bricks,** il m'est tombé dessus; (b) **box of bricks,** boîte f de constructions; '**brickfield,** s. briqueterie f; '**bricklayer,** s. maçon m; '**brick-'red,** a. rouge brique inv.

bride [braid], s.f., **bridegroom** ['braidgru:m], s.m. (a) fiancée f, fiancé m (sur le point de se marier); (b) nouvelle mariée, nouveau marié; **the b. and (bride)groom,** les nouveaux mariés; '**bridal,** a. nuptial, -aux; de noces; **b. veil,** voile m de mariée; '**bridesmaid,** s.f. demoiselle d'honneur.

bridge[1] [bridʒ]. I. s. 1. pont m. 2. Nau: passerelle f (de commandement). 3. dos m, arête f (du nez). II. v.tr. jeter un pont sur (un fleuve); **to b. a gap,** combler une lacune; **bridging loan,** crédit m provisoire; '**bridgehead,** s. Mil: tête f de pont.

bridge[2], s. Cards: bridge m; **to play b.,** jouer au bridge, bridger.

bridle ['braidl]. I. s. (a) bride f; **to give a horse the b.,** rendre la bride à un cheval; **b. path,** piste f cavalière; (b) frein m. II. v. 1. v.tr. brider (un cheval); **to b. one's tongue,** mettre un frein à sa langue. 2. v.i. se rengorger; prendre la mouche.

brief [bri:f]. I. a. bref, f. brève; court; **in b.,** bref;

en deux mots; **-ly,** *adv.* brièvement; en peu de mots. **II.** *s.* **1.** *Jur: etc:* dossier *m*; *F:* **I don't hold much b. for him,** je n'ai guère confiance en lui. **2.** *pl.* **briefs,** *Cl:* slip *m.* **III.** *v.tr.* **1.** confier une cause à (un avocat). **2.** munir (qn) d'instructions, donner des directives à (qn); *Av:* briefer; **'briefcase,** *s.* serviette *f*; **'briefing,** *s.* **1.** constitution *f* du dossier (d'une affaire). **2.** instructions *fpl*, directives *fpl*; *Av:* briefing *m*; **'briefness,** *s.* brièveté *f*, concision *f*.

brigade [bri'geid], *s. Mil:* brigade *f*; **briga'dier,** *s.* général *m* de brigade.

brigand ['brigənd], *s.* brigand *m*, bandit *m*.

bright [brait], *a.* **1.** *(a)* lumineux; **b. light,** lumière vive; **b. eyes,** yeux brillants, lumineux; *(b)* *(of weather)* clair; *(c)* *(of colour)* vif, éclatant; **b. red,** rouge vif; *(d)* **to look on the b. side of things,** prendre les choses par le bon côté. **2.** *(a)* *(of pers.)* vif, animé; *(b)* *F:* **b. lad,** garçon éveillé; **he's not very b.,** il n'est pas très intelligent; **a. b. idea,** une idée lumineuse; **-ly,** *adv.* brillamment; avec éclat; **'brighten,** *v.* **1.** *v.tr.* faire briller (qch.); égayer (qn). **2.** *v.i.* **to b. (up),** *(of face, weather)* s'éclaircir; *(of pers.)* s'animer; **'brightness,** *s.* éclat *m*; clarté *f*; *(of pers.)* vivacité *f*; intelligence *f* (d'un enfant).

brilliant ['briljənt]. **I.** *a.* *(a)* brillant, éclatant; *(b)* *(of pers.)* très intelligent, très doué; brillant; **b. idea,** idée lumineuse; **-ly,** *adv.* brillamment; avec éclat. **II.** *s.* *(diamond)* brillant *m*; **'brilliance,** *s.* éclat *m*, brillant *m*.

brim [brim]. **I.** *s.* bord *m.* **II.** *v.* **(brimmed)** *v.i.* **to b. over,** déborder; **'brim'ful,** *a.* plein jusqu'au bord; débordant.

brine [brain], *s.* eau salée; saumure *f*.

bring [briŋ], *v.tr.* **(brought** [brɔːt]) *(a)* amener (qn); apporter (qch.); *(b)* **to b. tears (in)to s.o.'s eyes,** faire venir les larmes aux yeux de qn; **to b. s.o. luck,** porter bonheur à qn; *(c)* **to b. an action against s.o.,** intenter un procès à qn; *(d)* **to b. sth. into question,** mettre qch. en question; *(e)* **to b. sth. to perfection,** porter qch. à la perfection; *(f)* **to b. oneself to do sth.,** se résoudre à faire qch.; **'bring a'bout,** *v.tr.* *(a)* *(= cause)* amener, causer, déterminer, occasionner; **to b. a. an accident,** provoquer un accident; *(b)* effectuer, accomplir, opérer; **to b. a. a change,** opérer un changement; **'bring a'long,** *v.tr.* amener (qn); apporter (qch.); **'bring a'way,** *v.tr.* emmener (qn); emporter (qch.); **'bring 'back,** *v.tr.* rapporter (qch.); ramener (qn); **'bring 'down,** *v.tr.* **1.** abattre (un arbre); faire tomber (les fruits d'un arbre); faire crouler (une maison); terrasser (un adversaire); *Th:* **to b. d. the house, to b. the house d.,** faire crouler la salle. **2.** *(a)* faire descendre (qn); *(b)* descendre (une valise). **3.** abaisser, faire baisser (le prix); **'bring 'forward,** *v.tr.*

faire avancer (une chaise); avancer; *Com:* reporter (une somme); **'bring 'in,** *v.tr.* **1.** *(a[)* introduire, faire entrer (qn); **b. him in,** faites-l[e] entrer; *(b)* servir (le dîner). **2.** *Fin:* **to b. in in[-]terest,** rapporter. **3.** *(a)* déposer, présenter (u[n] projet de loi); *(b)* **to b. in a verdict,** rendre u[n] verdict; **'bring 'off,** *v.tr.* réussir, conduire [à] bien (une affaire); *F:* **to b. it o.,** réussir le coup[;] **'bring 'on,** *v.tr.* **1.** produire, occasionner (un[e] maladie, etc.). **2. the sun is bringing on th[e] plants,** le soleil fait pousser les plantes. **3.** *Th[:]* **an elephant is brought on to the stage,** on fa[it] entrer un éléphant en scène; **'bring 'out,** *v.t[r.]* **1.** sortir (qn, qch.). **2.** faire ressortir, mettre e[n] relief; faire valoir (une couleur). **3.** publie[r,] faire paraître (un livre); **'bring 'over,** *v.tr.* [1.] transporter, amener **(from,** de). **2. to b. s.[o.] o. to a cause,** gagner, rallier, qn à une cause[;] **'bring 'round,** *v.tr.* **1.** *(a)* rappeler (qn) à [la] vie; *(b)* remettre (qn) de bonne humeur; *(c)* convertir (qn à une opinion). **2.** (r)amener (l[a] conversation sur un sujet); **'bring to'gethe[r,]** *v.tr.* réunir; mettre (des personnes) en contac[t;] **'bring 'up,** *v.tr.* **1.** *(a)* monter (du vin de [la] cave); faire monter (qn); *(b)* **to b. up (one[']s] food),** vomir; rendre (son repas). **2. b. up yo[ur] chair to the fire,** approchez votre chaise du fe[u.] **3.** élever (des enfants). **4. to b. s.o. up befor[e] the court,** citer qn en justice. **5. to b. up a su[b-]ject,** mettre une question sur le tapi[s;] **'bringing 'up,** *s.* éducation *f* (des enfants).

brink [briŋk], *s.* bord *m*; **on the b. of ruin,** à de[ux] doigts de la ruine; **to be on the b. of tears,** êt[re] au bord des larmes.

brisk [brisk], *a.* vif, actif, alerte; **at a b. pace,** [à] vive allure; **b. trade,** commerce actif; **-ly,** *ad[v.]* vivement; avec entrain; **'briskness,** *s.* vivac[ité] *f*, animation *f*, entrain *m*; fraîcheur *f* (de l'ai[r).]

bristle [brisl]. **I.** *s.* soie *f.* **II.** *v.i.* **to b. (up),** [(of] *animal)* se hérisser; *(of pers.)* se rebiffer[,] hérisser; **'bristly,** *a.* couvert de poils raide[s.]

Britain ['britən]. *Pr.n. Geog:* **Great B.,** Grande-Bretagne.

British ['britiʃ], *a.* britannique; de la Gran[de] Bretagne; anglais, d'Angleterre; **the B. Isl[es,]** les îles *f* britanniques; *s.pl.* **the British,** [les] Anglais *m*; **'Britisher,** *s.* *U.S: Austr:* Angl[a]-aise; **'Briton,** *s.* **1. (ancient)** B., Breton, -o[nne] (de la Grande-Bretagne). **2.** Anglais, -aise.

Brittany ['britəni]. *Pr.n.* la Bretagne.

brittle [britl], *a.* fragile, cassant; **'brittlene[ss,]** *s.* fragilité *f*.

broach [brəutʃ], *v.tr.* **1.** percer, entamer (un fû[t).] **2.** entamer, aborder (une question).

broad [brɔːd], *a.* large; **b. grin,** sourire épano[ui;] **in b. daylight,** en plein jour; **it's as b. as [it's] long,** cela revient au même; **b. views,** id[ées] larges; **b. humour,** grosse gaieté; **-ly,** *a[dv.]* largement; **b. speaking,** généralement parla[nt,] '**broad-'brimmed**, (chapeau) à larges bords; '**broadcast. I.** *v.tr.* (**broadcast**) **1.** semer (le grain) à la volée; diffuser, répandre (une nouvelle). **2.** *Rad: T.V:* radiodiffuser. **II.** *s.* (radio-)émission *f.* **III. 1.** *adv.* (semer, répandre) à tout vent, à la volée. **2.** *a.* radiodiffusé; **b. announcement**, annonce *f* par radio, radiodiffusée; '**broadcaster**, *s.* radiodiffuseur *m*; speaker, -ine; '**broadcasting**, *s.* radiodiffusion *f*; '**broaden**, *v.tr. & i.* (s')élargir; '**broad-'minded**, *a.* to be b.-m., avoir l'esprit large; '**broad-'mindedness**, *s.* tolérance *f*, largeur *f* d'esprit; '**broad-'shouldered**, *a.* large d'épaules.

brocade [brə'keid], *s. Tex:* brocart *m*.

broccoli ['brɔkəli], *s. Hort:* brocoli *m*.

brochure ['brouʃər], *s.* brochure *f*, dépliant *m*.

brogue[1] [broug], *s.* soulier *m* de golf.

brogue[2], *s.* accent irlandais.

broil [brɔil], *v.tr. & i.* griller; '**broiler**, *s.* poulet *m* (à rôtir); '**broiling**, *a.* (*of the sun*) ardent, brûlant; **b. weather**, chaleur torride.

broke [brouk], *a. F:* **to be (stony-)b., dead b., flat b.**, être sans le sou, dans la purée, fauché (comme les blés).

broken ['brouk(ə)n], *a.* (*a*) cassé, brisé, rompu; (*b*) (terrain) accidenté; (sommeil) interrompu; (temps) variable; (*c*) **in a b. voice**, d'une voix entrecoupée; **in b. French**, en mauvais français; (*d*) **b. down**, cassé; (voiture) en panne; (moteur) détraqué; '**broken-'hearted**, *a.* au cœur brisé.

broker ['broukər], *s.* (*a*) courtier *m* (de commerce); (*b*) (**stock-**)**b.**, agent *m* de change; '**brokerage**, *s.* (frais *mpl* de) courtage *m*.

bromide ['broumaid], *s.* **1.** *Ch:* bromure *m*. **2.** *esp. N.Am:* (*a*) individu ennuyeux, raseur; (*b*) banalité *f*; lieu commun.

bronchial ['brɔŋkiəl], *a. Anat:* bronchial; **b. tubes**, les bronches *f*.

bronchitis [brɔŋ'kaitis], *s. Med:* bronchite *f*.

bronze [brɔnz]. **I. 1.** *s.* bronze *m*. **2.** *attrib.* **b. statue**, statue de, en, bronze. **II.** *v.* **1.** *v.tr.* bronzer (le fer, etc.). **2.** *v.i.* se bronzer (au soleil).

brooch [broutʃ], *s.* broche *f*.

brood [bru:d]. **I.** *s.* couvée *f* (de poussins); *F:* enfants *mpl*; *F:* marmaille *f*. **II.** *v.i.* **1.** (*of hen*) couver. **2.** broyer du noir; **to b. over, on (an idea, a plan)**, couver (une idée, un projet); **to b. over the fire**, couver le feu; '**broody**, *a.* (*a*) (poule) couveuse; (*b*) (*of pers.*) distrait, rêveur.

brook [bruk], *s.* ruisseau *m*.

broom [bru:m, brum], *s.* **1.** *Bot:* genêt *m*. **2.** *H:* balai *m*; '**broomstick**, *s.* manche *m* à balai.

broth [brɔθ], *s.* bouillon *m*, potage *m*.

brothel ['brɔθəl], *s.* bordel *m*.

brother ['brʌðər], *s.* **1.** frère *m*; **older, younger, b.**, frère aîné, cadet. **2.** confrère *m* (d'un corps de métier). **3.** *Ecc:* frère; '**brotherhood**, *s.* confraternité *f*; fraternité *f*; *Ecc:* confrérie *f*; '**brother-in-law**, *s.* beau-frère *m*, *pl.* beaux-frères; '**brotherly**, *a.* fraternel, de frères.

brow [brau], *s.* (*a*) *Anat:* front *m*; (*b*) *Anat:* sourcil *m*; (*c*) front, croupe *f* (de colline); '**browbeat**, *v.tr.* (**-beat; -beaten**) intimider, rudoyer, rabrouer (qn).

brown [braun]. **I.** *a.* (*a*) brun; marron; **b. bread**, pain *m* bis; **b. paper**, papier *m* d'emballage; **b. sugar**, cassonade *f*; **b. hair**, cheveux châtains; (*b*) bruni (par le soleil), bronzé. **II.** *s.* brun *m*; marron *m*. **III.** *v.* **1.** *v.tr.* brunir; *Cu:* rissoler (la viande); faire dorer (le poisson, etc.); faire roussir (une sauce). **2.** *v.i.* se brunir; *Cu:* roussir; '**brownish**, *a.* brunâtre; '**brown'off**, *v.tr. F:* décourager (qn); **to be browned off**, avoir le cafard, broyer du noir.

brownie ['brauni], *s.* (*a*) (*Guide Movement*) Jeannette *f*; (*b*) *Cu: N.Am:* petit gâteau au chocolat.

browse [brauz], *v.tr. & i.* (*a*) (*of animals*) brouter; (*b*) (*of pers.*) feuilleter des livres, inspecter des antiquités (dans un magasin).

bruise [bru:z]. **I.** *s.* meurtrissure *f*; contusion *f*; bleu *m*. **II.** *v.tr.* meurtrir, contusionner; **to b. one's arm**, se meurtrir le bras.

brunch [brʌn(t)ʃ], *s. F:* repas *m* tenant lieu de *breakfast* et de *lunch*.

brunette [bru(:)'net], *a. & s.* (*of woman*) brune (*f*), brunette (*f*).

brunt [brʌnt], *s.* choc *m*; **the b. of the battle**, le plus fort de la bataille; **to bear the b. of s.o.'s anger**, soutenir le poids de la colère de qn; **to bear the b. of the expense**, faire tous les frais.

brush [brʌʃ]. **I.** *s.* **1.** broussailles *fpl*. **2.** (*a*) brosse *f*; (*b*) (**paint-**)**b.**, pinceau *m*; **flat b.**, queue-de-morue *f*; (*c*) queue *f* (de renard). **3.** coup *m* de brosse (à des vêtements, etc.). **4.** rencontre *f*, échauffourée *f* (avec l'ennemi). **II.** *v.* **1.** *v.tr.* brosser (son costume); se brosser (les cheveux); frôler (une surface). **2.** *v.i.* **to b. past, against, s.o., sth.**, frôler qn, qch., en passant; '**brush a'side**, *v.tr.* écarter (qn, qch.); '**brush a'way**, *v.tr.* enlever (qn); d'un coup de brosse; écarter (une difficulté); '**brush 'down**, *v.tr.* donner un coup de brosse à (qn, qch.); '**brush 'off**, *v.tr.* to b. the dust o., enlever la poussière (à la brosse); '**brushoff**, *s. F:* to give s.o. the b., envoyer promener qn; '**brush 'up**, *v.tr.* to b. up one's French, dérouiller son français; '**brushwood**, *s.* broussailles *fpl*.

brusque [bru(:)sk], *a.* brusque; (ton) rude, bourru; **-ly**, *adv.* avec brusquerie; '**brusqueness**, *s.* brusquerie *f*, rudesse *f*.

Brussels ['brʌslz]. *Pr.n. Geog:* Bruxelles *f*; **B. sprouts**, choux *mpl* de Bruxelles.

brute [bru:t], *s.* brute *f*; **you b.!** espèce *f* d'animal! *F:* **a b. of a job**, un métier, un travail,

F: un boulot, de chien; b. **force**, force brutale;
'brutal, a. brutal; **-ally,** adv. brutalement;
bru'tality, s. brutalité f; **'brutalize,** v.tr.
brutaliser (qn).
bubble ['bʌbl]. I. s. **1.** bulle f (d'air, de savon);
bouillon m (de liquide bouillant). **2.** projet m
chimérique; **b. scheme,** entreprise véreuse. II.
v.i. bouillonner; (of wine) pétiller; **to b. over,**
déborder; **'bubbly. 1.** a. (of wine, etc.)
pétillant. **2.** s. F: (vin m de) champagne m.
buck [bʌk]. I. s. **1.** (a) daim m; chevreuil m; (b)
mâle m (du lapin, lièvre, etc.). **2.** Equit: (of
horse) b. (**-jump**), saut m de mouton. **3.** N.Am:
F: dollar m. II. v.i. (of horse) faire un saut de
mouton; **to b. s.o. off,** désarçonner qn; **'buck
'up. 1.** v.tr. **to b. s.o. up,** remonter (le courage
de) qn; stimuler, ragaillardir, qn. **2.** v.i. (i)
reprendre courage; (ii) se hâter; **b. up!** (i)
courage! (ii) dépêche-toi!
bucket ['bʌkit], s. seau m; **'bucketful,** s. plein
seau.
buckle ['bʌkl]. I. s. boucle f (de ceinture, etc.). II.
v. **1.** v.tr. boucler (une ceinture). **2.** v.i. (of metal,
etc.) **to b. (up),** se déformer, (se) gondoler,
gauchir; F: **to b. (down) to a task,** s'atteler à un
travail.
buckram ['bʌkrəm], s. Tex: bougran m.
buckwheat ['bʌkwi:t], s. sarrasin m; blé noir; **b.
cakes,** galettes de blé noir.
bud [bʌd]. I. s. **1.** bourgeon m; **to come into b.,**
bourgeonner. **2.** bouton m (de fleur). **3.** Anat:
taste b., papille f gustative. II. v.i. (**budded**)
bourgeonner; (of flower) boutonner; **'budding,** a. (a) qui bourgeonne, bourgeonnant; **a
b. rose,** un bouton de rose; (b) **b. artist,** artiste
mf en herbe.
Buddhism ['budiz(ə)m], s. le bouddhisme;
'Buddhist. 1. s. bouddhiste. **2.** a. bouddhique.
buddy ['bʌdi], s. esp. N.Am: F: ami m, copain m.
budge [bʌdʒ], v.i. bouger, céder; reculer;
remuer.
budget ['bʌdʒit]. I. s. budget m. II. v.i.
budgétiser; **to b. for sth.,** inscrire qch. au
budget.
buff [bʌf], a. & s. jaune clair inv; F: **in the b.,** tout
nu, à poil.
buffalo, pl. **-oes** ['bʌfəlou, -ouz], s. Z: buffle m.
buffer ['bʌfər], s. appareil m de choc; amortisseur m; Rail: butoir m; Pol: **b. state,** état m
tampon.
buffet ['bʌfei, 'bu-], s. buffet m; (on menu) **cold b.,**
viandes froides; assiette anglaise.
buffeted ['bʌfitid], a. battu, secoué; **b. by the
waves, the wind,** ballotté, battu, par les vagues,
(fortement) secoué par le vent.
buffoon [bʌ'fu:n], s. bouffon m; **to act the b.,**
faire le bouffon; **bu'ffoonery,** s. bouffonneries
fpl.
bug [bʌg]. I. s. (a) punaise f; (b) N.Am: F: petite

bestiole, insecte m; (c) F: microbe m
(quelconque); **the flu b.,** l'infection grippale, la
grippe; (d) F: micro clandestin. II. v.tr.
(**bugged**) F: installer un micro clandestin dans
(une maison).
bugbear ['bʌgbɛər], s. bête noire.
bugle ['bju:gl], s. clairon m; **'bugler,** s. clairon
m.
build [bild]. I. v.tr. (**built**) bâtir (une maison);
construire (un navire, une route, etc.); **to b.
(up)on a piece of land,** bâtir un terrain. II. s.
carrure f; taille f; **'builder,** s. entrepreneur m
(en bâtiments); constructeur m (de navires,
d'avions, etc.); **'build 'in,** v.i. **built-in cupboards,** placards incorporés; **'building,** s. **1.**
construction f; **b. land,** terrain m à bâtir; **b. estate,** lotissement m. **2.** bâtiment m; immeuble
m; **public b.,** édifice public; **b. society,** société f
immobilière; **'build 'up.** (a) v.tr. (faire) bâtir
(un lotissement); (se) créer (une réputation);
built-up area, agglomération f (urbaine); (b)
v.i. **traffic is building up,** la circulation devien
très dense; **pressure is building up,** la pression
s'accumule.
bulb [bʌlb], s. **1.** Bot: bulbe m, oignon m. **2.** El:
ampoule f; lampe f.
Bulgaria [bʌl'gɛəriə]. Pr.n. la Bulgarie
Bul'garian, a. & s. bulgare (mf).
bulge [bʌldʒ]. I. s. bombement m, ventre m
renflement m. II. v.i. **to b. (out),** bomber
ballonner; faire ventre; faire saillie; **ba
bulging with fruit,** sac bourré de fruits; **bulgin
stomach,** ventre ballonnant.
bulk [bʌlk], s. **1.** Com: **in b.,** en blo
globalement; en gros; **b. buying,** achat m e
gros. **2.** grandeur f, grosseur f, volume m.
the (great) b. (of mankind), la masse, la plupa
(des hommes); **'bulky,** a. volumineux, encor
brant; gros.
bull [bul], s. **1.** (a) taureau m; (b) **b. elephan
éléphant** m mâle. **2.** St.Exch: haussier r
spéculateur m à la hausse; **'bull-dog,**
bouledogue m; **'bulldozer,** s. bulldozer r
'bullfight, s. corrida f; course f de taureau
'bullfighter, s. toréador m; **'bullfinch,** s.
Orn: bouvreuil m. **2.** Equit: haie f avec foss
bullfinch m; **'bullfrog,** s. grenouille-taure
f; Fr.C: ouaouaron m; **'bullock,** s. bœ
m; **'bullring,** s. arène f (pour les cours
de taureaux); **'bull's-eye,** s. noir m, mouc
f (d'une cible).
bullet ['bulit], s. balle f (de carabine,
revolver); **'bullet-headed,** a. à tête ronc
'bullet-proof, a. à l'épreuve des balles.
bulletin ['bulitin], s. bulletin m, communiqué
news b., bulletin d'actualités; T.V: etc: infc
mations fpl.
bullion ['buliən], s. or m, argent m, en lingots
bully ['buli]. I. s. brute f; persécuteur m. II. v.

intimider; malmener, brutaliser (qn); **'bullying. I.** *a.* brutal. **II.** *s.* intimidation *f*; brutalité *f*.

bum [bʌm]. **I.** *s.* **1.** *Anat: F:* derrière *m*. **2.** *esp. N.Am:* clochard *m*; fainéant *m*; vagabond *m*. **II.** *v.i.* (**bummed**) **to b. off s.o.,** vivre aux crochets de qn; **to b. a dinner off s.o.,** se faire payer à dîner par qn.

bumble-bee ['bʌmblbi:], *s. Ent:* bourdon *m*.

bumf [bʌmf], *s.* **1.** *P:* papier *m* hygiénique. **2.** *Adm: coll. F:* paperasserie *f*.

bump [bʌmp]. **I.** *s.* **1.** choc (sourd); secousse *f*, heurt *m*; cahot *m*. **2.** bosse *f*. **II.** *v.* **1.** *v.tr.* cogner, frapper. **2.** *v.i.* se cogner, se heurter, buter (**into, against,** contre); **to b. into s.o.,** rencontrer qn par hasard; **'bump 'off,** *v.tr. P:* assassiner, supprimer (qn); **'bumpy,** *a.* (chemin, etc.) cahoteux; défoncé.

bumper ['bʌmpər], *s.* **1. b. crop,** récolte magnifique. **2.** *Aut:* pare-chocs *m inv.*

bumptious ['bʌm(p)ʃəs], *a.* présomptueux, suffisant; **-ly,** *adv.* d'un air suffisant; **'bumptiousness,** *s.* suffisance *f*.

bun [bʌn], *s.* **1.** *Cu:* petit pain au lait. **2.** (cheveux enroulés en) chignon *m*.

bunch [bʌntʃ], *s.* (*a*) botte *f* (de radis); bouquet *m* (de fleurs); grappe *f* (de raisin); trousseau *m* (de clefs); (*b*) **he's the best of the b.,** c'est lui le meilleur (de la bande).

bundle ['bʌndl]. **I.** *s.* paquet *m* (de linge); ballot *m* (de marchandises); liasse *f* (de papiers); fagot *m* (de bois). **II.** *v.tr.* (*a*) **to b. sth. up,** empaqueter qch.; ramasser, mettre, qch. en paquet; **to b. everything into a drawer,** fourrer tout en pagaille dans un tiroir; (*b*) **to b. s.o. out of the house,** flanquer qn à la porte.

bung [bʌŋ]. **I.** *s.* bonde *f*; tampon *m*. **II.** *v.tr.* **to b. up,** bondonner (un fût); boucher (un trou); *F:* **my nose is all bunged up,** j'ai le nez bouché; *F:* **b. it in a drawer,** fourre-le dans un tiroir.

bungalow ['bʌŋgəlou], *s.* bungalow *m*; maison *f* sans étage.

bungle ['bʌŋgl], *v.tr.* bousiller, gâcher; rater (une affaire); **'bungler,** *s.* bousilleur, -euse; gâcheur, -euse; maladroit, -oite; **'bungling. I.** *a.* maladroit. **II.** *s.* bousillage *m*, gâchis *m*; maladresse *f*.

bunk[1] [bʌŋk], *s.* couchette *f*; **b. beds, bunks,** lits superposés.

bunk[2], *s. & v.i. F:* **to do a b., to b.,** filer, décamper.

bunker ['bʌŋkər], *s.* **1.** soute *f* (à charbon, à mazout). **2.** *Golf:* bunker *m*. **3.** *Mil:* blockhaus *m*, abri bétonné.

bunkum ['bʌŋkəm], *s. F:* blague *f*, bêtises *fpl*.

bunny ['bʌni], *s. F:* **b. rabbit,** Jeannot lapin *m*.

bunting ['bʌntiŋ], *s. coll.* drapeaux *mpl*, pavillons *mpl*.

buoy [bɔi]. **I.** *s. Nau:* bouée *f*; balise flottante. **II.** *v.tr.* **1. to b. (s.o., sth.) up,** soutenir (qn, qch.).

2. to b. a channel, *Av:* **a runway,** baliser un chenal, une piste; **'buoyancy,** *s.* **1.** flottabilité *f*. **2.** (*of pers.*) entrain *m*; ressort *m*; **'buoyant,** *a.* **1.** flottable, léger. **2.** (*of pers.*) plein d'entrain; **b. step,** pas *m* élastique; *Com:* **b. market,** marché soutenu.

burden ['bəːdn]. **I.** *s.* fardeau *m*, charge *f*; **to be a b. to s.o.,** être à charge à qn; **to make s.o.'s life a b.,** rendre la vie dure à qn; **beast of b.,** bête de somme. **II.** *v.tr.* charger, alourdir (**s.o. with sth.,** qn de qch.); **to b. people with taxes,** accabler les gens d'impôts.

bureau, *pl.* **-eaux** ['bjuərou, -ouz], *s.* **1.** *Furn:* bureau *m*; secrétaire *m*. **2.** (*a*) (*office*) bureau; **information b.,** bureau de renseignements; (*b*) service *m* (du gouvernement).

bureaucracy [bjuə'rɔkrəsi], *s.* bureaucratie *f*; **bureaucrat** ['bjuərəkræt], *s.* bureaucrate *m*; **bureau'cratic,** *a.* bureaucratique.

burglar ['bəːglər], *s.* cambrioleur *m*; **b. alarm,** signalisateur *m* anti-vol; **'burglarize,** *v.tr. N.Am:* cambrioler; **'burglar(-)proof,** *a.* (coffre-fort, etc.) incrochetable, inviolable; **'burglary,** *s.* vol *m* avec effraction; cambriolage *m*; **'burgle,** *v.tr.* cambrioler.

Burgundy ['bəːgəndi]. **1.** *Pr.n.* la Bourgogne. **2.** *s.* (*pl.* **-ies**) (vin *m* de) bourgogne *m*; **Bur'gundian,** *a. & s.* bourguignon, -onne.

burial ['beriəl], *s.* enterrement *m*; **'burial-ground,** *s.* cimetière *m*; **'burial-service,** *s.* office *m* des morts.

burlesque [bəː'lesk]. **I.** *a. & s.* burlesque (*m*). **II.** *v.tr.* travestir, parodier.

burly ['bəːli], *a.* (*of pers.*) solidement bâti; de forte carrure.

Burma ['bəːmə]. *Pr.n. Geog:* la Birmanie.

Burmese [bəː'miːz], *a. & s.* birman, -e.

burn [bəːn]. **I.** *v.tr. & i.* (**burnt, burned**) brûler; **to b. sth. to ashes,** réduire qch. en cendres; **to b. one's fingers,** se brûler les doigts; **to be burnt to death,** être carbonisé; **all the lights were burning,** toutes les lumières étaient allumées. **II.** *s.* brûlure *f*; **'burner,** *s.* (*of gas cooker*) brûleur *m*; **Bunsen b.,** bec *m* Bunsen; **'burn 'down,** *v.tr.* brûler, incendier (une ville, etc.); détruire (une maison) par le feu; **'burn 'out,** *v.tr.* (*a*) **their house was burnt out,** le feu a complètement détruit l'intérieur de leur maison; **the fire has burned out,** le feu s'est éteint, est mort; (*b*) *El:* brûler (une bobine); griller (une lampe); **burnt,** *a.* brûlé, carbonisé; **b. taste,** goût de brûlé; **'burn'up. 1.** *v.tr.* brûler, consumer. **2.** *v.i.* (*of fire*) se ranimer, flamber.

burp [bəːp], *v.i. F:* éructer.

burrow ['bʌrou]. **I.** *s.* terrier *m* (de lapin, etc.). **II.** *v.i.* (*of rabbits, etc.*) (i) fouir la terre; (ii) se terrer.

bursar ['bəːsər], *s. Sch:* économe *m*; **'bursary,** *s. Sch:* **1.** économat *m*. **2.** bourse *f* (d'études).

burst [bəːst]. **I.** *v.* (**burst**) **1.** *v.i.* (*a*) éclater, faire explosion; (*of boiler*) sauter; (*of tyre*) crever; (*of bud*) éclore; **to b. in pieces,** voler en éclats; (*b*) **to b. with laughter,** crever de rire; (*c*) **a cry b. from his lips,** un cri s'échappa de ses lèvres; (*d*) **to b. into bloom,** fleurir, s'épanouir; **to b. into tears,** fondre en larmes; (*e*) **to b. into a room,** entrer dans une pièce en coup de vent; **I was bursting to tell him,** je mourais d'envie de le lui dire. **2.** *v.tr.* faire éclater; crever (un ballon); rompre (ses liens). **II.** *s.* éclatement *m,* explosion *f*; jet *m,* jaillissement *m* (de flamme); coup *m* (de tonnerre); éclat *m* (de rire); salve *f* (d'applaudissements); poussée *f* (d'activité); **'burst 'in,** *v.i.* faire irruption; entrer en coup de vent; **'burst 'open. 1.** *v.tr.* enfoncer (une porte). **2.** *v.i.* (*of door*) s'ouvrir tout d'un coup; **'burst 'out,** *v.i.* (*of pers.*) s'écrier, s'exclamer; **to b. out laughing,** éclater de rire.

bury ['beri], *v.tr.* (**buried**) enterrer, inhumer, ensevelir (un mort); enfouir (un trésor); **to b. oneself in the country,** s'enterrer dans la campagne; **'burying,** *s.* **1.** enterrement *m*; ensevelissement *m.* **2.** enfouissement *m.*

bus, *pl.* **buses** [bʌs, 'bʌsiz], *s.* autobus *m, F:* bus *m*; (*country bus*) car *m*; **double decker b.,** autobus à impériale; **to miss the b.,** (i) manquer, rater, le bus; (ii) laisser échapper l'occasion; **b. station,** gare routière; **b. route,** ligne *f* d'autobus; **b. stop,** arrêt *m* d'autobus; *P.N:* **all buses stop here,** arrêt obligatoire; **to drive the school b.,** faire le ramassage scolaire; **'busman,** *pl.* **-men,** *s.* (i) conducteur *m,* (ii) receveur *m,* d'autobus; **to take a b.'s holiday,** faire du métier en guise de congé.

bush [buʃ], *s.* **1.** (*a*) buisson *m*; (*b*) fourré *m,* taillis *m.* **2.** (*Africa, Austr.*) **the b.,** la brousse; **'bushy,** *a.* (*of hair*) touffu; (*of ground, eyebrows*) broussailleux.

business ['biznis], *s.* **1.** affaire *f,* besogne *f,* occupation *f*; **to have b. with s.o.,** avoir affaire avec qn; **it's my b. to . . .,** c'est à moi de . . .; **it's none of your b.,** cela ne vous regarde pas; **to send s.o. about his b.,** envoyer promener qn. **2.** (*a*) les affaires; **b. is b.,** les affaires sont les affaires; **to go into b.,** entrer dans les affaires; **to do b. with s.o.,** faire des affaires avec qn; **to mean b.,** avoir des intentions sérieuses; *attrib.* **b. hours,** heures d'ouverture; **b. house,** maison de commerce; (*b*) fonds *m* de commerce; **'businesslike,** *a.* **1.** (*of pers.*) capable; pratique. **2.** (*of manner*) sérieux; **'businessman,** *pl.* **-men,** *s.* homme *m* d'affaires.

bust[1] [bʌst], *s.* **1.** *Sculp:* buste *m.* **2.** poitrine *f.*

bust[2], *a. P:* **to go b.,** faire faillite.

bust[3], *v.tr.* (**bust**) *F:* casser (un jouet, etc.).

bustle ['bʌsl]. **I.** *v.i.* **to b.** (**about**), se remuer, s'activer, s'affairer. **II.** *s.* remue-ménage *m*;

'bustling, *a.* affairé; empressé; agissant.

busy ['bizi]. *a.* affairé, occupé; actif; **b. day,** jour chargé; **b. street,** rue mouvementée, passante; **to be b. doing sth.,** s'occuper à faire qch.; **to keep oneself b.,** s'activer, s'occuper; **'busily,** *adv.* avec empressement; d'un air affairé; **'busybody,** *s.* officieux, -euse.

but [bʌt]. **1.** *conj.* mais; **b. I tell you I saw it!** (mais) puisque je vous dis que je l'ai vu! **b. yet, b. all the same,** néanmoins. **2.** *adv.* ne . . . que; seulement; **he is nothing b. a student,** ce n'est qu'un étudiant; **one can b. try,** on peut toujours essayer; **had I b. known!** si j'avais su! **3.** *conj. or prep.* (= *except*) (*a*) **all b. he, b. him,** tous sauf lui, excepté lui; **anything b. that,** tout plutôt que cela; **he's anything b. a hero,** il n'est rien moins qu'un héros; **there's nothing for it b.** **to obey,** il n'y a qu'à obéir; (*b*) **b. for,** sans; **b. for that,** à part cela.

butane ['bjutein], *s. Ch:* butane *m.*

butcher ['butʃər]. **I.** *s.* boucher *m*; **b.'s shop,** boucherie *f.* **II.** *v.tr.* **1.** abattre (des bêtes de boucherie). **2.** égorger, massacrer; **'butchery** *s.* **1.** boucherie *f.* **2.** massacre *m,* boucherie.

butler ['bʌtlər], *s.* maître *m* d'hôtel (d'une maison privée).

butt[1] [bʌt], *s.* barrique *f,* futaille *f*; gros tonneau; **water b.,** tonneau (pour l'eau de pluie).

butt[2], *s.* **1.** bout *m*; souche *f* (d'arbre, de chèque); *F:* mégot *m* (de cigarette, de cigare). **2.** gro bout, talon *m* (de canne à pêche). **3.** crosse (de fusil); **'butt-'end,** *s.* extrémité inférieure gros bout.

butt[3], *s.* **1.** *pl. Mil:* **the butts,** le champ de tir **2.** but *m,* cible *f*; (*of pers.*) souffre-douleu *m inv.*

butt[4]. **I.** *s.* coup *m* de tête; coup de corne. **II.** *v.* *v.tr.* donner un coup de corne à (qn). **2.** *v.i.* **to b in, to b. into the conversation,** intervenir sa façon dans la conversation, interrompre.

butter ['bʌtər]. **I.** *s.* beurre *m*; **b. bean,** haricot beurre; **b. dish,** beurrier *m*; **b. knife,** couteau à beurre. **II.** *v.tr.* beurrer (du pain); **to b. s.o. up,** flatter, flagorner, qn; **'buttercup,** *s. B* bouton *m* d'or; **'butter-fingers,** *s.* maladroi **'butterscotch,** *s.* caramel *m* au beurre.

butterfly ['bʌtəflai], *s.* **1.** *Ent:* papillon *m. Swimming:* **b. (stroke),** brasse *f* papillon.

buttock ['bʌtək], *s.* **1.** fesse *f*; *pl.* **buttocks,** l fesses, le derrière. **2.** *pl.* croupe *f* (de cheval, bœuf).

button ['bʌtn]. **I.** *s.* bouton *m.* **II.** *v.tr.* **to b. s up,** boutonner qch.; **'buttonhole,** *s.* bouto nière *f*; **to wear a b.,** porter une fleur à boutonnière.

buttress ['bʌtris]. **I.** *s. Const:* contrefort *flying b.,* arc-boutant *m.* **II.** *v.tr.* arc-bout étayer.

buy [bai], *v.tr.* (**bought**) acheter (**sth. from s.**

qch. à qn); 'buy 'back, *v.tr.* racheter; 'buyer, *s.* acheteur, -euse; *Com:* chef *m* de rayon; 'buy 'out, *v.tr.* désintéresser (un associé); 'buy 'over, *v.tr.* corrompre, acheter (qn); 'buy 'up, *v.tr.* rafler, accaparer (des denrées, etc.).

buzz [bʌz]. **I.** *s.* bourdonnement *m* (d'un insecte); brouhaha *m* (de conversations); *Rad: etc: F:* (bruits *m* de) friture *f*. **II.** *v.* **1.** *v.i.* bourdonner; vrombir. **2.** *v.tr. Av: F:* harceler (un avion); 'buzzer, *s. Ind:* sirène *f*; *El: etc:* vibreur *m*, vibrateur *m*; 'buzzing, *s.* bourdonnement *m*; **b. in the ears,** tintement *m* d'oreilles; 'buzz 'off, *v.i. P:* décamper, filer.

buzzard ['bʌzəd], *s. Orn:* buse *f*.

by [bai]. **I.** *prep.* **1.** (*near*) (au)près de, à côté de; **by the sea,** au bord de la mer; **by oneself,** seul; à l'écart; **I have no money by me,** je n'ai pas d'argent (i) sous la main, (ii) disponible. **2.** (*a*) par; **by land and sea,** par terre et par mer; **to be punished by s.o.,** être puni par qn; **made by hand,** fait (à la) main; **known by the name of X,** connu sous le nom d'X; **by force,** de force; **by mistake,** par (suite d'une) erreur; **three metres by two,** trois mètres sur deux; **I'll come by car, by train,** je viendrai en auto, en train; **by the 6 o'clock train,** par le train de six heures; (*b*) **by doing that you will offend him,** en faisant cela vous l'offenserez; **we shall lose nothing by waiting,** nous ne perdrons rien pour attendre; **what do you gain by doing that?** que gagnez-vous à faire cela? **3. by right,** de droit; **by rights,** de toute justice; **to judge by appearances,** juger sur l'apparence; **three o'clock by my watch,** trois heures d'après ma montre; **to sell sth. by the kilo,** vendre qch. au kilo. **4. by degrees,** par degrés; **by turn(s),** tour à tour; **one by one,** un à un. **5. by day,** de jour, le jour; **by Monday,** d'ici lundi; **by three o'clock,** avant trois heures; **he ought to be here by now,** il devrait être déjà ici. **6. I know him by sight,** je le connais de vue; **he's a grocer by trade,** il est épicier de son métier. **II.** *adv.* **1.** près; **close by,** tout près; **taking it by and large,** à tout prendre. **2. to put sth. by,** mettre qch. de côté. **3. to pass by,** passer. **4.** *adv.phr.* **by and by,** tout à l'heure, bientôt; **by the way,** à propos. **III.** *a. & pref.* secondaire; *Pol:* **by-election,** élection partielle; 'by(-)law, *s.* arrêté *m* municipal; 'bypass. **I.** *s.* route *f* de contournement, d'évitement; déviation *f*. **II.** *v.tr.* contourner, éviter (une ville); 'by(-)path, *s.* sentier écarté; 'by-product, *s. Ind:* sous-produit *m*; dérivé *m*; 'by-road, *s.* chemin détourné; chemin vicinal; 'bystander, *s.* assistant, -ante; spectateur, -trice.

bye [bai], *s.* **1.** *Sp:* (*of player*) **to have a b.,** être exempt (d'un match). **2.** (*at cricket*) point *m* obtenu par une balle passée.

bye(-bye) ['bai('bai)], *int. F:* au revoir!

C

C, c. [si:], *s.* **1.** (la lettre) C, c *m.* **2.** *Mus:* ut *m*, do *m.*
cab [kæb], *s.* taxi *m*; ' **cab-driver,** *s.* chauffeur *m* de taxi; ' **cab-rank,** *s.* station *f* de taxis.
cabbage ['kæbidʒ], *s.* chou *m*, *pl.* choux; **c. lettuce,** laitue pommée; **c. white (butterfly),** piéride *f*, papillon *m* blanc, du chou.
cabin ['kæbin], *s.* **1.** cabane *f*, case *f.* **2.** (*a*) *Rail:* poste *m* de conduite; (*b*) *Nau:* cabine *f*; **c. cruiser,** yacht *m* de plaisance; (*c*) *Av:* carlingue *f.*
cabinet [kæbinit], *s.* **1.** (*a*) meuble *m* à tiroirs; (*b*) **glass c.,** vitrine *f*; **c. maker,** ébéniste *m*; **c. making, c. work,** ébénisterie *f.* **2.** *Pol:* **the C.,** le gouvernement; le cabinet, le conseil des ministres; **to form a c.,** former un cabinet; **shadow c.,** conseil des ministres fantôme; **c. minister,** ministre *m* d'état; **c. crisis,** crise ministérielle.
cable ['keibl]. **I.** *s.* **1.** câble *m.* **2.** *P.T.T:* câble; **to lay a c.,** poser un câble (sous-marin). **3.** (*also* **cablegram**) câblogramme *m*, câble. **II.** *v.tr. & i.* câbler.
caboodle [kə'bu:dl], *s.* *P.* **the whole c.,** tout le bataclan.
cache [kæʃ]. **I.** *s.* cache *f*, cachette *f.* **II.** *v.tr.* cacher (qch.).
cackle ['kækl]. **I.** *s.* **1.** (*of hen, F: of pers.*) caquet *m*; **cut your c.!** en voilà assez! *P:* la ferme! **2.** (*a*) ricanement *m*; (*b*) **a c. of laughter,** un rire saccadé. **II.** *v.i.* **1.** caqueter. **2.** ricaner.
cactus, *pl.* **-ti** ['kæktəs, -ti], *s.* *Bot:* cactus *m*; plante grasse.
cad [kæd], *s.* **1.** goujat *m.* **2.** canaille *f*; salaud *m*; ' **caddish,** *a.* **a c. sort of chap,** un type plutôt canaille; ' **caddishness,** *s.* goujaterie *f*; canaillerie *f.*
cadaverous [kə'dævərəs], *a.* cadavéreux.
caddie ['kædi], *s.* *Golf:* caddie *m.*
caddy, *pl.* **-ies** ['kædi, -iz], *s.* **(tea-)c.,** boîte *f* à thé.
cadence ['keid(ə)ns], *s.* **1.** cadence *f*, rythme *m*, battement *m.* **2.** *Mus:* cadence.
cadet [kə'det], *s.* élève *m* (i) d'une école militaire, (ii) de la préparation militaire.
cadge [kædʒ], *v.tr. & i.* écornifler; chiner; quémander; ' **cadger,** *s.* écornifleur, -euse; chineur, -euse; quémandeur, -euse.
Caesarian [si:'zɛəriən], *a. & s.* *Med:* **C. (operation, section),** opération césarienne.
café ['kæfei], *s.* café-restaurant *m*; **cafeteria** [kæfi'tiəriə], *s.* cafétéria *f.*

cage [keidʒ], *s.* **1.** cage *f.* **2.** cabine *f* (d'ascenseur); **cage-bird,** *s.* oiseau *m* d'appartement.
cagey ['keidʒi], *a.* *F:* prudent, défiant, précautionneux; **to be c. about one's age,** cacher astucieusement son âge.
Cairo ['kaiərou]. *Pr.n. Geog:* le Caire.
cajole [kə'dʒoul], *v.tr.* cajoler; enjôler; **ca'jolery,** *s.* cajolerie(s) *f*(*pl*); enjôlement *m.*
cake [keik]. **I.** *s.* **1.** gâteau *m*; **c. shop,** pâtisserie *f*; *F:* **that takes the c.!** c'est la fin des haricots! *F:* **it's a piece of c.,** c'est donné. **2.** pain *m* (de savon); tablette *f* (de chocolat); *Cu:* **fish cakes,** croquettes *f* de poisson; **cattle c.,** tourteau *m.* **II.** *v.i.* former une croûte; faire croûte; s'agglutiner; (*of blood, etc.*) se cailler; **caked with mud,** plaqué de boue.
calamity [kə'læmiti], *s.* **1.** calamité *f*, infortune *f*, malheur *m.* **2.** désastre *m*; sinistre *m*; **ca'lamitous,** *a.* (événement) calamiteux, désastreux.
calcium ['kælsiəm], *s.* calcium *m.*
calculate ['kælkjuleit], *v.tr. & i.* calculer; évaluer; estimer (une distance); faire un calcul; compter; ' **calculated,** *a.* (*a*) **c. insolence,** insolence délibérée, calculée; (*b*) **words c. to reassure us,** paroles propres à nous rassurer; ' **calculating.** **1.** *a.* calculateur. **2.** (*also* **calcu'lation**) *s.* calcul *m*; estimation *f*; ' **calculator,** *s.* machine *f* à calculer calculatrice *f.*
calendar ['kælindər], *s.* calendrier *m*; **tear-off c.** calendrier bloc, à effeuiller.
calf¹, *pl.* **calves** [kɑ:f, kɑ:vz], *s.* **1.** (*a*) veau *m* **cow in c.,** vache pleine; (*b*) *Leath:* veau vachette *f.* **2.** petit *m* (de certains animaux) **elephant c.,** éléphanteau *m.*
calf², *pl.* **calves,** *s.* mollet *m* (de la jambe).
calibre ['kælibər], *s.* (*a*) calibre *m* (d'un canon d'un tube); (*b*) **a man of his c.,** un homme d son calibre, de son envergure *f.*
call [kɔ:l]. **I.** *s.* **1.** (*a*) (*shout*) appel *m*, cri (d'appel); (*b*) cri (d'un oiseau). **2.** (*summons* (*a*) appel; **to come at s.o.'s c.,** venir à l'appel d qn; **to be within c.,** être à portée de voix; **to giv s.o. a c.,** appeler qn; (*b*) **telephone c.,** app téléphonique; coup *m* de téléphone, *F:* coup d fil; **local c.,** communication locale; **personal c** appel avec préavis; (*c*) *Th:* **curtain c.,** rappel (d'un acteur). **3.** visite *f*; **to pay a c. on s.** faire une visite à qn; *F:* **to pay a c.,** aller fai pipi; *Nau:* **port of c.,** port *m* d'escale,

relâche. **4.** demande *f* (d'argent); *Fin:* appel de fonds. **II.** *v.* **1.** *v.tr.* (*a*) appeler (qn); crier (qch.); (*b*) (*summon*) héler (un taxi); téléphoner à (qn); faire venir, appeler (un docteur); (*c*) **c. me at six o'clock,** réveillez-moi à six heures; (*d*) **he's called Martin,** il s'appelle Martin; **to c. s.o. names,** injurier qn; **to c. s.o. a liar,** traiter qn de menteur. **2.** *v.i.* (*a*) **to c. at s.o.'s house,** (i) faire une visite chez qn; (ii) passer chez qn; **has anyone called?** est-il venu qn? (*b*) *Nau:* faire escale (à un port); (*of train*) **to c. at every station,** s'arrêter à toutes les gares; **'call 'back. 1.** *v.tr.* rappeler (qn); (*on telephone*) **please c. me b. later,** veuillez me rappeler plus tard. **2.** *v.i.* **I shall c. b. for it,** je repasserai le prendre; **'call box,** *s.* cabine *f* (téléphonique); **'call-boy,** *s.* **1.** *Th:* avertisseur *m*. **2.** *N.Am:* chasseur *m* (d'hôtel); **'caller,** *s.* visiteur, -euse; *P.T.T:* demandeur, -euse (au téléphone); **'call for,** *v.ind.tr.* (*a*) **to c. f. help,** crier au secours; (*b*) venir prendre, venir chercher (qn); (*c*) **to c. f. an explanation,** demander une explication; **'call-girl,** *s.* prostituée *f* (sur rendez-vous téléphonique); **'call 'in,** *v.tr.* **1.** faire entrer (qn); faire rentrer (les enfants). **2.** retirer (une monnaie) de la circulation. **3. to c. in a specialist,** faire appel à un spécialiste; **'calling,** *s.* vocation *f*; état *m*; métier *m*; **'call 'off,** *v.tr.* **to c. off a dinner, a strike,** décommander un dîner, une grève; **'call on,** *v.tr.* **1.** faire une visite chez (qn). **2.** faire appel à (qn); **'call 'out,** *v.i.* appeler; appeler au secours; **'call 'up,** *v.tr.* **1.** évoquer (des souvenirs). **2.** appeler (qn) au téléphone. **3.** *Mil:* mobiliser (un réserviste); **'call-up,** *s.* mobilisation *f*.

callous ['kæləs], *a.* (*of pers.*) insensible, endurci; **-ly,** *adv.* sans pitié, sans cœur.

calm [kɑ:m]. **I.** *a.* calme, tranquille; **-ly,** *adv.* avec calme; tranquillement. **II.** *s.* (*also* **'calmness**) calme *m*; tranquillité *f*; **'calm 'down.** *v.tr.* calmer, apaiser; **to c. s.o. down,** pacifier qn. **2.** *v.i.* (*of storm, grief*) **to c. down,** se calmer, s'apaiser.

calorie ['kæləri], *s.* calorie *f*.

calumny ['kæləmni], *s.* calomnie *f*; **ca'lumniate,** *v.tr.* calomnier (qn); **ca'lumniator,** *s.* calomniateur, -trice.

calve [kɑ:v], *v.i.* vêler; **'calving,** *s.* vêlage *m*.

cam [kæm], *s.* *Mec:* came *f*; excentrique *f*; **'camshaft,** *s.* *Mec:* arbre *m* à came(s), à excentrique.

camber ['kæmbər]. **I.** *s.* courbure *f* (d'une poutre); bombement *m* (d'une route). **II.** *v.tr.* bomber (une chaussée); cambrer (une poutre); **'cambered,** *a.* arqué, courbé.

Cambodia [kæm'boudiə]. *Pr.n. Geog:* le Cambodge.

camel ['kæm(ə)l], *s.* chameau *m*; **she-c.,** chamelle *f*; **'camel-driver,** *s.* chamelier *m*.

camellia [kə'mi:liə], *s. Bot:* camélia *m*.

camera ['kæm(ə)rə], *s.* appareil *m* (photographique); *Cin:* **cine c.,** caméra *f*; **'cameraman,** *pl.* **-men,** *s.m.* photographe de la presse; *Cin:* cameraman *m*, *pl.* -men ((i) opérateur *m*; (ii) cinéaste *m*).

Cameroon [kæmə'ru:n]. *Pr.n. Geog:* **the C. Republic,** le Cameroun.

camouflage ['kæmuflɑ:ʒ]. **I.** *s.* camouflage *m*. **II.** *v.tr.* camoufler.

camp [kæmp]. **I.** *s.* camp *m*; campement *m*; **to pitch a c.,** établir un camp; **to strike c.,** lever le camp; **holiday c.,** (*for adults*) camp *m* de vacances; (*for children*) colonie *f* de vacances; **c. bed,** lit *m* de camp; **c. chair,** pliant *m*. **II.** *v.i.* camper; faire du camping; **to c. out,** vivre sous la tente; **'camper,** *s.* campeur, -euse; **'camping,** *s.* camping *m*; **c. equipment,** matériel *m* de camping; **c. site,** terrain *m* de camping, camping *m*.

campaign [kæm'pein]. **I.** *s.* campagne *f* (militaire); **political, electoral, c.,** campagne politique, électorale; **sales c.,** campagne de vente. **II.** *v.i.* faire (une) campagne, des campagnes.

camphor ['kæmfər], *s.* camphre *m*; **'camphorated,** *a.* **c. oil,** huile camphrée.

campus, -puses ['kæmpəs, -pəsiz], *s.* (**university**) **c.,** campus *m* (universitaire).

can¹ [kæn]. **I.** *s.* **1.** bidon *m* (d'huile); broc *m* (d'eau). **2.** boîte *f* (de conserves, de bière). **II.** *v.tr.* (**canned**) mettre (des aliments) en boîte, conserver; **canned,** *a.* **1.** (*of food*) en conserve; (*of drink*) en boîte. **2.** *P:* ivre.

can², *modal aux. v.* (*pres.* **can,** *neg.* **cannot, can't;** *pret:* **could,** *neg.* **could not, couldn't**). **1.** pouvoir; **I c. do it,** je peux, je puis, le faire; **I cannot allow that,** je ne saurais permettre cela; **as soon as I c.,** aussitôt que je pourrai; **that cannot be,** cela ne se peut pas; **what c. it be?** qu'est-ce que cela peut être? **Mr X? what c. he want?** M. X? qu'est-ce qu'il peut bien me vouloir? **she's as pleased as c. be,** elle est on ne peut plus contente. **2.** savoir; **I c. swim,** je sais nager. **3.** (*permission,* = **may**) **when c. I move in?** quand pourrai-je emménager? **4.** (*not translated*) **I c. see nothing,** je ne vois rien. **5.** **you c. but try,** vous pouvez toujours essayer.

Canada ['kænədə]. *Pr.n. Geog:* le Canada; **in C.,** au Canada.

Canadian [kə'neidjən], *a. & s.* canadien, -ienne.

canal [kə'næl], *s.* canal, -aux *m*; **the Suez C.,** le Canal de Suez; **branch c.,** canal de dérivation; *Anat:* **the alimentary c.,** le canal alimentaire.

Canary [kə'nɛəri]. **1.** *Pr.n. Geog:* **the C. Islands, the Canaries,** les îles Canaries. **2.** *s. Orn:* serin *m*.

cancel ['kæns(ə)l], *v.tr.* (**cancelled**) annuler; résilier; biffer (un mot); supprimer (un train);

oblitérer (un timbre); *Mth:* éliminer; **cance'llation**, *s.* annulation *f.*

cancer ['kænsər], *s.* **1.** cancer *m*; **c. patient,** cancéreux, -euse; **c. specialist,** cancérologue *m.* **2.** *Astr:* le Cancer; **Tropic of C.,** le tropique du Cancer; **'cancerous,** *a.* cancéreux.

candid ['kændid], *a.* franc, *f.* franche; sincère; **-ly,** *adv.* franchement, sincèrement.

candidate ['kændidət], *s.* candidat, -e, aspirant, -e, prétendant, -e **(for sth.,** à qch.).

candle ['kændl], *s.* **wax c.,** bougie *f*; **tallow c.,** chandelle *f*; **church c.,** cierge *m*; **to burn the c. at both ends,** brûler la chandelle par les deux bouts; **he can't hold a c. to you,** il ne vous arrive pas à la cheville; **'candlelight,** *s.* lumière *f* de chandelle; **by c.,** à la chandelle, aux chandelles; **'Candlemas,** *s.* *Ecc:* la Chandeleur; **'candlestick,** *s.* chandelier *m*; bougeoir *m.*

candour ['kændər], *s.* franchise *f*, bonne foi, sincérité *f.*

candy, *pl.* **-ies** ['kændi, -iz], *s. esp. N.Am:* bonbon *m*; **c. store,** confiserie *f*; **'candy-striped,** *a.* pékiné.

cane [kein]. **I.** *s.* **1.** canne *f*, jonc *m*; rotin *m*; *(walking-stick)* canne; **Malacca c.,** (canne de) jonc; *(for punishment)* canne; **c. furniture,** meubles *mpl* en rotin. **2.** **raspberry c.,** framboisier *m*; **sugar c.,** canne à sucre; **c. sugar,** sucre *m* de canne. **II.** *v.tr.* **1.** battre, frapper (qn) (à coups de canne). **2.** canner (une chaise); **'caning,** *s. Sch:* correction *f.*

canine ['kænain, 'kei-], *a.* canin; de chien; **c. tooth,** canine *f.*

canister ['kænistər], *s.* boîte *f* (en fer blanc).

canker ['kæŋkər]. **I.** *s.* **1.** chancre *m.* **2.** influence corruptrice; plaie *f*; fléau *m.* **II.** *v.tr.* ronger; corrompre (qn, une âme).

cannibal ['kænibəl], *s. & a.* cannibale *(mf)*; anthropophage *(mf)*; **'cannibalism,** *s.* cannibalisme *m*; **'cannibalize,** *v.tr. Mec: F: (of cars, etc.)* cannibaliser; **to c. an engine,** démonter un moteur (pour utiliser les pièces détachées).

cannon ['kænən]. **I.** *s.* **1.** *Mil:* canon *m*; pièce *f* d'artillerie. **2.** *Bill:* carambolage *m.* **II.** *v.i. Bill:* caramboler; **to c. into s.o.,** heurter qn violemment.

canoe [kə'nu:], *s.* **1.** *Sp:* **(Canadian) c.,** canoë *m*; *Fr.C:* canot *m*; périssoire *f.* **2.** pirogue *f*; **ca'noeist,** *s.* canoëiste *mf.*

canon¹ ['kænən], *s.* **1.** *(a)* canon *m* (de la messe); *(b)* **c. law,** droit *m* canon; *(c)* règle *f*, critère *m.* **2.** *Mus:* canon.

canon², *s. Ecc:* chanoine *m.*

canopy, *pl.* **-ies** ['kænəpi, -iz], *s.* dais *m*; baldaquin *m* (de lit); *(over doorway)* auvent *m*, marquise *f.*

cant [kænt]. **1.** *s.* *(a)* jargon *m*; argot *m*; *(b)*

langage *m* hypocrite. **2.** *a.* **c. phrase,** cliché *m*; **'canting,** *a.* hypocrite.

cantankerous [kæn'tæŋk(ə)rəs], *a.* revêche, acariâtre; d'humeur hargneuse; **can'tankerousness,** humeur *f* revêche, acariâtre.

cantata [kæn'tɑːtə], *s. Mus:* cantate *f.*

canteen [kæn'tiːn], *s.* **1.** cantine *f.* **2.** **c. of cutlery,** ménagère *f.*

canter ['kæntər]. **I.** *s.* *Equit:* petit galop; *Rac:* **to win in a c.,** arriver bon premier. **II.** *v.i.* aller au petit galop.

Canterbury ['kæntəb(ə)ri]. *Pr.n.* Cantorbéry *m*; *Bot:* **C. bell,** campanule *f* à grosses fleurs.

canvas ['kænvəs], *s.* **1.** *Tex:* (grosse) toile; toile à voiles; **under c.,** sous la tente. **2.** *Art:* **a fine c.,** une belle toile.

canvass ['kænvəs], *v.tr.* solliciter (des suffrages, *Com:* des commandes); *abs.* **to c.,** faire une tournée électorale; *Com:* faire la place; **'canvasser,** *s.* solliciteur, -euse; *Com:* démarcheur, -euse; *Pol:* agent électoral; **'canvassing,** *s.* prospection *f*; sollicitation *f* (de suffrages); *Com:* démarchage *m.*

canyon ['kænjən], *s.* cañon *m.*

cap [kæp]. **I.** *s.* **1.** *(with peak)* casquette *f*; toque (de magistrat, de chef, de jockey); képi *m* (de militaire); *Sch:* **c. and gown,** costume *m* académique. **2.** *Tchn:* chapeau *m* (de protection); capuchon *m* (de stylo). **3.** **percussion c.,** amorce *f*; **bottle c.,** capsule *f.* **II.** *v.tr.* **(capped) 1.** coiffer, couronner (qch. de qch.); capsuler (une bouteille). **2.** *(outdo)* surpasser; **that caps it all!** ça c'est le bouquet!

capable ['keipəbl], *a.* capable, compétent; **-ably,** *adv.* avec compétence; **capa'bility,** capacité *f* **(of doing sth.,** pour faire qch. faculté *f* **(to do sth.,** de faire qch.).

capacity [kə'pæsiti], *s.* **1.** *(a)* contenance *f* (d'un tonneau); *(b)* rendement *m* (d'une locomotive); **seating c.,** nombre *m* de places assises; *T* **house filled to c.,** salle *f* comble. **2.** capacité *f* **(for,** pour); **c. for doing sth.,** aptitude *f* à faire qch.; **ca'pacious,** *a.* vaste, spacieux; ample

cape¹ [keip], *s. Cl:* pèlerine *f*, cape *f.*

cape², *s.* cap *m*, promontoire *m*; **Cape Tow** *Pr.n. Geog:* le Cap.

caper¹ ['keipər], *s. Cu:* câpre *f.*

caper². **I.** *s.* cabriole *f*, gambade *f.* **II.** *v.i.* **to (about),** faire des cabrioles; gambader.

capillary [kə'piləri], *a. & s.* capillaire *(m).*

capital¹ ['kæpitl], *s. Arch:* chapiteau *m.*

capital². **I.** *a.* **1.** capital, -aux; **c. letter,** *s.* **c.,** (lettre) majuscule *(f)*; **c. city,** *s.* **c.,** (ville) capital *(f).* **2.** *Jur:* **c. punishment,** peine capitale. **3.** **of c. importance,** c'est de la plus haute importance. **4.** **c.! excellent! fameux!** **-ally,** *adv.* admirablement. **II.** *s.* *Fin:* capital *m*, capitaux *mpl*, fonds *mpl*; **working c.,** fonds roulement; **to make c. out of sth.,** profiter de qch.; **'capitalism,** s. capitalisme m; **'capitalist,** s. capitaliste mf; **capitali'zation,** s. capitalisation f (des fonds); **'capitalize. 1.** v.tr. capitaliser. **2.** v.i. **to c. on sth.,** tourner qch. à son avantage.

capitulate [kə'pitjuleit], v.i. capituler; **capitu'lation,** s. capitulation f.

capon ['keipən], s. Cu: chapon m, poulet m.

caprice [kə'priːs], s. **1.** caprice m, lubie f. **2.** Mus: caprice.

capricious [kə'priʃəs], a. capricieux; **-ly,** adv. capricieusement; **ca'priciousness,** s. humeur capricieuse, inégale.

Capricorn ['kæprikɔːn], s. Astr: le Capricorne; **Tropic of C.,** le tropique du Capricorne.

capsize [kæp'saiz]. **1.** v.i. (of boat) chavirer. **2.** v.tr. faire chavirer.

capstan ['kæpstən], s. cabestan m.

capsule ['kæpsjuːl], s. capsule f (de fleur, de bouteille, pharmaceutique, etc.).

captain ['kæptin]. **I.** s. (a) chef m, capitaine m; (b) Sp: chef d'équipe; (c) Mil: Nau: (rank) capitaine; Mil: Av: **group c.,** colonel m; Civil Av: (pilote) commandant m de bord, (as title) commandant. **II.** v.tr. commander (une compagnie); conduire (une expédition); Sp: diriger, mener (une équipe); **'captaincy,** s. (a) grade m de capitaine; **to obtain one's c.,** passer capitaine; (b) conduite f, commandement m (d'une équipe, etc.).

aption ['kæpʃən], s. (in newspaper) en-tête m; (under illustration) légende f.

aptivate ['kæptiveit], v.tr. charmer, captiver, séduire (qn).

aptive ['kæptiv]. **1.** a. captif. **2.** s. captif, -ive, prisonnier, -ière; **cap'tivity,** s. captivité f.

apture ['kæptʃər]. **I.** s. (action, pers. or thg) capture f, prise f. **II.** v.tr. capturer (une ville); prendre (sth. from s.o., qch. à qn); Com: **to c. the market,** accaparer la vente; Rad: etc: capter (un programme); **'captor,** s. capteur m.

ar [kaːr], s. auto(mobile) f, voiture f; Rail: N.Am: voiture, wagon m; Rail: **dining c.,** wagon-restaurant m; **sleeping c.,** wagon-lit m; **freight c.,** wagon de marchandise(s); **c. ferry,** ferry-boat m; **c. licence** = carte grise; permis m de circulation; **c. sleeper,** train m autocouchette(s); **'car park,** s. parking m; stationnement autorisé; **underground c. p.,** parking souterrain.

rafe [kə'raːf, -æf], s. carafe f.

ramel ['kærəmel], s. **1.** Cu: caramel m; **c. custard,** crème f caramel. **2.** bonbon m au caramel.

rat ['kærət], s. Meas: carat m; **eighteen-c. gold,** or m au titre 750, à dix-huit carats.

ravan ['kærəvæn], s. Aut: (touring) c.,

caravane f; remorque f; F: camping m; **gipsy c.,** roulotte f.

caraway ['kærəwei], s. Cu: carvi m, cumin m (des prés).

carbohydrate ['kaːbou'haidreit], s. Ch: hydrate m de carbone.

carbolic [kaː'bɔlik], a. Ch: phénique; Com: **c. acid,** phénol m.

carbon ['kaːbən], s. **1.** Ch: carbone m. **2.** Typew: **c. (paper),** papier m carbone; **c. (copy),** copie f, double m.

carbonate ['kaːbənət], s. Ch: carbonate m.

carbonic [kaː'bɔnik], a. Ch: carbonique; **c. acid gas,** anhydride m carbonique.

carboniferous [kaːbə'nifərəs]. **1.** a. Geol: Min: carbonifère; (bassin) houiller. **2.** s. **the C. (period),** l'âge m carbonifère.

carbonize ['kaːbənaiz], v.tr. carboniser.

carboy ['kaːbɔi], s. bonbonne f.

carbuncle ['kaːbʌŋkl], s. **1.** escarboucle f. **2.** Med: anthrax m; bouton m (au visage).

carburettor, -er [kaːbju'retər], s. Aut: etc: carburateur m.

carcase, -cass ['kaːkəs], s. F: (i) cadavre m; (ii) corps m; **to save one's c.,** sauver sa peau.

card [kaːd], s. **1.** (playing-)c., carte f (à jouer); **a game of cards,** une partie de cartes; **c. table,** table f de jeu; **to play one's cards well,** bien jouer son jeu; **to lay one's cards on the table,** mettre cartes sur table; **to have a c. up one's sleeve,** avoir encore une ressource; **it's quite on the cards,** il est bien possible; **he's a c.,** c'est un original. **2.** (a) (visiting) **c.,** carte (de visite); **identity c.,** carte d'identité; Adm: **passport control c.,** fiche f de voyageur; (b) **admission c.,** carte, billet m, d'entrée; **'cardboard,** s. carton m; **'card-'index. 1.** s. (a) fichier m, classeur m; (b) catalogue m sur fiches. **2.** v.tr. mettre sur fiches; **'card-sharper,** s. tricheur m.

cardigan ['kaːdigən], s. tricot m; cardigan m.

cardinal ['kaːdinl]. **I.** a. cardinal, -aux; **the c. numbers,** les nombres cardinaux. **II.** s. **1.** Ecc: cardinal m. **2.** Orn: **c. bird,** cardinal.

cardiogram ['kaːdiougræm], s. cardiogramme m; **'cardiograph,** s. cardiographe m; **cardi'ographer,** s. cardiographe mf.

cardiology [kaːdi'ɔlədʒi], s. cardiologie f; **cardi'ologist,** s. cardiologue m.

care ['kɛər]. **I.** s. **1.** souci m, inquiétude f. **2.** soin(s) m(pl), attention f, ménagement m; **to take c. in doing sth.,** apporter du soin à faire qch.; **to take c.! not to do sth.,** se garder de faire qch.; **take c.!** faites attention! prenez garde! **to take c. of one's health,** ménager sa santé; **that matter will take c. of itself,** cela s'arrangera tout seul. **3.** soin(s), charge f, tenue f; (on letter) **c. of, c/o, Mrs X,** aux bons soins de Mme X. **4. cares of State,** responsabilités f d'état. **II.** v.i. **1.** se soucier, s'inquiéter, se

préoccuper (**for, about,** de); **I don't c.!** I
couldn't c. less! ça m'est égal! peu m'importe!
F: je m'en fiche! **2. to c. for s.o.,** (i) aimer qn;
(ii) soigner qn; **'carefree,** *a.* insouciant; sans
souci; **'careful,** *a.* **1.** soigneux (**of,** de); attentif; **be c.!** prenez garde! faites attention! **2.** prudent, circonspect; **c. housewife,** ménagère
regardante; **-fully,** *adv.* **1.** soigneusement. **2.**
prudemment; **'carefulness,** *s.* **1.** soin *m*,
attention *f.* **2.** prudence *f*; **'careless,** *a.* **1.** insouciant; **c. mistake,** faute *f* d'inattention. **2.**
négligent; **-ly,** *adv.* avec insouciance;
négligemment; sans soin; **'carelessness,** *s.* **1.**
insouciance *f*; inattention *f.* **2.** négligence *f*;
'caretaker, *s.* concierge *mf* (de maison); gardien *m* (d'immeuble, de musée).

career [kə'riər]. **I.** *s.* **1.** course (précipitée); **to**
stop in mid c., rester en (beau) chemin. **2.**
carrière *f*; *Sch:* **careers master, mistress,**
orienteur, -euse, professionnel(le). **II.** *v.i.*
courir rapidement, follement; **to c. along,** aller
à toute vitesse.

caress [kə'res]. **I.** *s.* caresse *f.* **II.** *v.tr.* caresser.

cargo, *pl.* **-oes** ['ka:gou, -ouz], *s. Nau:*
cargaison *f*, chargement *m*; **c. boat,** cargo *m.*

Caribbean [kæri'bi(:)ən], *a.* **the C. (Sea),** la mer
des Antilles, des Caraïbes; **C. Islands,** les Antilles *f.*

caricature. I. *s.* ['kærikətjuər], caricature *f.* **II.**
v.tr. caricaturer (qn, un rôle); **carica'turist,** *s.*
caricaturiste *mf.*

carmine ['ka:main, -min]. **1.** *s.* carmin *m..* **2.** *a.*
carminé; carmin *inv.*

carnage ['ka:nid3], *s.* carnage *m.*

carnal ['ka:nl], *a.* charnel, -elle ((i) sensuel, -elle
(ii) sexuel, -elle); **c. sins,** péchés *m* de la chair.

carnation [ka:'neiʃ(ə)n], *s. Bot:* œillet *m.*

carnival ['ka:niv(ə)l], *s.* carnaval *m, pl.* -als.

carnivore ['ka:nivɔ:r], *s. Z:* carnassier *m*;
car'nivorous, *a.* (*a*) (*of animal*) carnassier;
(*b*) *Bot:* carnivore.

carol ['kærəl], *s.* chant *m*; **Christmas c.,** noël *m.*

carp[1] [ka:p], *s. inv. Ich:* carpe *f.*

carp[2], *v.i.* **to c. at sth.,** trouver à redire à qch.

Carpathians (the) [ðəka:'peiθiənz]. *Pr.n.*
Geog: les Carpates *mpl.*

carpenter ['ka:pintər], *s.* charpentier *m*;
menuisier *m* (en bâtiments); **'carpentry,** *s.*
charpenterie *f*; (grosse) menuiserie.

carpet ['ka:pit]. **I.** *s.* tapis *m*; **Brussels c.,**
moquette *f* de Bruxelles; **c. sweeper,** balai *m*
mécanique; *F:* (*of pers.*) **to be on the c.,** être sur
la sellette. **II.** *v.tr.* recouvrir d'un tapis, d'une
moquette.

carriage ['kærid3], *s.* **1.** port *m*, transport *m*;
Com: **c. free,** franco; **c. paid,** port payé; **c.**
forward, (en) port dû. **2.** port, maintien *m*; **easy**
c., allure dégagée. **3.** (*a*) (**horse and**) **c.,** voiture
f; équipage *m*; **c. and pair,** voiture à deux

chevaux; (*b*) *Rail:* voiture, wagon *m.* **4.** chariot
m (d'une machine à écrire); **'carriage-**
builder, *s.* carrossier *m*; **'carriage-building,**
s. (*trade*) carrosserie *f*; **'carriageway,** *s. Aut:*
dual c., route *f* à double voie.

carrier ['kæriər], *s.* **1.** (*a*) porteur, -euse; (*b*)
Com: transporteur *m*; routier *m*; camionneur
m; (*c*) **c. pigeon,** pigeon *m* voyageur. **2. support**
m; **c. bag,** (grand) sac en papier. **3.** *Av: Navy:*
(*aircraft*) **c.,** porte-avions *m inv.*

carrion ['kæriən], *s.* charogne *f.*

carrot ['kærət], *s. Hort:* carotte *f*; **'carroty,** *a.*
(homme) roux, (jeune fille) rousse.

carry ['kæri], *v.tr.* (**carried**) **1.** porter (un
paquet); transporter (des marchandises). **2. to**
c. sth. into effect, mettre qch. à exécution. **3.**
Mil: emporter (une position) d'assaut; **to c. all**
before one, vaincre toutes les résistances; **to c.**
one's hearers with one, entraîner son
auditoire; **to c. one's point,** imposer sa manière
de voir. **4.** (i) adopter, (ii) faire adopter (une
proposition). **5.** *abs.* **his voice carries well,** sa
voix porte bien; **'carry a'long,** *v.tr.* emporter,
entraîner; **'carry a'way,** *v.tr.* **1.** emporter;
emmener; enlever. **2.** transporter (qn) (de joie);
carried away by his feelings, entraîné par ses
émotions; **'carry-cot,** *s.* porte-bébé *m inv*;
'carry 'forward, *v.tr. Book-k:* reporter (une
somme); **'carry 'off,** *v.tr.* **1.** emporter (qch.);
emmener, enlever (qn). **2. to c. off the prize,**
remporter le prix; **'carry 'on. 1.** *v.tr.* poursuivre; continuer; exercer (un métier); entretenir (une correspondance); soutenir (une
conversation). **2.** *v.i.* (*a*) *Adm:* assurer l'intérim;
c. on! continuez! (*b*) persévérer, persister; (*c*) *F:*
se comporter; **don't c. on like that!** ne vous emballez pas comme ça! **she carried on dreadfully,**
elle nous a fait une scène terrible; **'carry 'out,**
v.tr. mettre à exécution, effectuer; **'carry**
'through, *v.tr.* mener à bonne fin.

cart [ka:t]. **I.** *s.* charrette *f*; **to put the c. befor**
the horse, mettre la charrue devant les bœuf
F: **to be in the c.,** être dans de beaux draps. **I**
v.tr. charrier; *F:* **to c. (s.o., sth.) about,** trim
baler (qn, qch.); **'carthorse,** *s.* cheval *m* d
trait; **a fine c.,** un superbe gros trai
'cartload, *s.* charretée *f*; **'cartwheel,** *s.* (
roue *f* de charrette; (*b*) **to turn cartwheels,** fai
la roue.

cartographer [ka:'tɔgrəfər], *s.* cartographe *m*
carton ['ka:tən], *s.* (*a*) carton *m*; (*b*) (boîte *f* d
carton; (*c*) *Com:* cartouche *f* (de cigarettes)

cartoon [ka:'tu:n], *s.* (*a*) *Art:* carton *m*;
Journ: dessin *m* humoristique; caricature
(politique); (*c*) *Cin:* dessin animé; **car'tooni**
s. dessinateur *m* (humoristique); caricaturi
m.

cartridge ['ka:trid3], *s.* cartouche *f*; **blank c**
cartouche à blanc; **c. paper,** papier fort.

carve [kɑːv], *v.tr.* **1.** sculpter, graver, ciseler (du marbre, du bois). **2.** découper (la viande); '**carving,** *s.* **1.** *Art:* sculpture *f*; gravure *f*, ciselure *f*. **2.** découpage *m* de la viande; **c. knife, fork,** couteau *m*, fourchette *f*, à découper.

cascade [kæs'keid]. **I.** *s.* chute *f* d'eau; cascade *f*. **II.** *v.i.* tomber en cascade; cascader.

case[1] [keis], *s.* **1.** cas *m*; cas d'espèce; **if that's the c.,** s'il en est ainsi; **that's often the c.,** cela arrive souvent; **it's a c. for the doctor,** c'est affaire au médecin; **in any c.,** en tout cas; **just in c.,** à tout hasard; **in most cases,** en général. **2.** *Med:* cas; malade *mf*; blessé, -e; **the serious cases,** les grands malades; **a patient's c. history,** le dossier (médical) d'un malade. **3.** *Jur:* cause *f*, affaire *f*; **famous cases,** causes célèbres; **the c. for the Crown,** l'accusation *f*. **4.** *Gram:* cas.

case[2], *s.* **1.** caisse *f*, colis *m* (de marchandises). **2.** (a) étui *m* (à lunettes, à cigarettes); écrin *m* (pour bijoux); (b) **(display) c.,** vitrine *f*; (c) **(suit)case,** mallette *f*, valise *f*. **3.** **pillow c.,** taie *f* d'oreiller.

casement ['keismənt], *s.* châssis *m* de fenêtre à deux battants; '**casement-window,** *s.* croisée *f*.

cash [kæʃ]. **I.** *s.no pl.* espèces *fpl*; argent comptant; **to be out of c.,** ne pas être en fonds; *F:* être à sec; **hard c.,** espèces sonnantes; **c. down,** argent (au) comptant; **to pay c. (down),** payer comptant, *F:* payer cash; **c. price,** prix *m* au comptant; **c. with order,** payable à la commande; **c. on delivery (C.O.D.),** contre remboursement; **c. box,** caisse *f*; cassette *f*; **c. desk, caisse; c. register,** caisse enregistreuse. **II.** *v.tr.* **to c. a cheque,** toucher un chèque; **to c. in on sth.,** tirer profit de qch.; **ca'shier**[1], *s.* caissier, -ière.

cashew [kæ'ʃuː], *s. Bot:* acajou *m* à pommes; **c. nut,** noix *f* d'acajou.

cashier[2] [kæ'ʃiər], *v.tr.* casser (un officier).

casino, *pl.* **-os** [kə'siːnou, -ouz], *s.* casino *m*.

cask [kɑːsk], *s.* barrique *f*, fût *m*, tonneau *m*.

casket ['kɑːskit], *s.* **1.** coffret *m*, cassette *f*. **2.** *N.Am:* (coffin) cercueil *m*.

Caspian ['kæspiən], *a. Geog:* **the C. Sea,** la mer Caspienne.

casserole ['kæsəroul], *s.* **1.** cocotte *f* (en terre). **2.** ragoût *m* en cocotte.

cassette [kæ'set], *s.* **1.** *Phot:* chargeur *m*. **2.** (for tape recorder) cassette *f*.

cassock ['kæsək], *s. Ecc:* soutane *f*.

cast [kɑːst]. **I.** *s.* **1.** (a) jet *m* (d'une pierre); coup *m* (de dés); lancer *m* (du filet); (b) *Fish:* bas *m* de ligne. **2.** **plaster c.,** (moulage *m* au) plâtre. **3. c. of mind,** tournure *f* d'esprit; **c. of features,** physionomie *f*. **4. to have a c. in one's eye,** avoir une tendance à loucher. **5.** *Th:* distribu-

tion *f* (des rôles); la troupe; **with the following c. . . .,** avec le concours de . . .. **II.** *v.tr.* (**cast; cast**) **1.** jeter, lancer (une pierre); projeter (une ombre); **to c. a glance at s.o., sth.,** jeter un regard sur qn, un coup d'œil sur qch. **2.** *Fish:* **to c. the line,** lancer la ligne. **3.** donner (un suffrage). **4. to c. (up) figures,** additionner des chiffres. **5.** fondre (du métal); mouler (un cylindre); couler (une statue). **6.** *Th:* **to c. a play,** distribuer les rôles d'une pièce. **III.** *a.* (métal) coulé; **c.-iron,** fonte *f*; **c.-iron excuse,** excuse *f* irréfutable; '**cast a'way,** *v.tr.* (a) jeter au loin; rejeter; (b) **to be c. a.,** faire naufrage; '**castaway,** *s.* naufragé, -ée; '**cast 'down,** *v.tr.* (a) jeter bas; (b) **to be c. d.,** être abattu, déprimé; '**casting. I.** *a.* **to give the c. vote,** départager les voix. **II.** *s.* (a) *Ind:* moulage *m*, fonte *f*; (b) pièce *f* de fonte, pièce coulée; (c) *Th:* distribution *f* des rôles; '**cast 'off,** *v.tr.* (a) rejeter, renier (qn); **c.-o. clothing,** vêtements *mpl* de rebut; (b) *Nau:* larguer (les amarres); (c) *Knitting:* **to c. o.,** arrêter les mailles; '**cast 'on,** *v.tr. Knitting:* monter (des mailles).

castanets [kæstə'nets], *s.pl.* castagnettes *f*.

caste [kɑːst], *s.* caste *f*; **to lose c.,** déroger (à son rang).

castigate ['kæstigeit], *v.tr.* châtier, corriger (qn).

Castile [kæs'tiːl]. *Pr.n. Geog:* la Castille; *Com:* **C. soap,** savon blanc.

castle ['kɑːsl], *s.* **1.** château (fort). **2.** *Chess:* tour *f*. **II.** *v.tr. & abs. Chess:* roquer.

castor, -er ['kɑːstər], *s.* **1.** saupoudroir *m; c.* **sugar,** sucre *m* en poudre. **2.** roulette *f* (de fauteuil).

castor oil ['kɑːstər'ɔil], *s.* huile *f* de ricin.

casual ['kæʒju(ə)l, 'kæʒ-], *a.* (a) fortuit, accidentel, -elle; **c. labour,** main-d'œuvre *f* temporaire; (b) insouciant; **to give a c. answer,** répondre d'un air désinvolte; *Cl:* **c. clothes,** costume *m* sport; **-ally,** *adv.* (a) par hasard, en passant; (b) négligemment; avec désinvolture; '**casualness,** *s.* indifférence *f*; insouciance *f*.

casualty, *pl.* **-ies** ['kæʒjuəlti, 'kæʒ-, -iz], *s.* **1.** accident *m* (de personne); **c. ward,** salle *f* des accidentés. **2.** mort, -e; blessé, -e.

cat [kæt], *s.* **1.** (a) chat, *f.* chatte; **tom c.,** matou *m*; **to be like a c. on hot bricks,** être sur des épines; **to let the c. out of the bag,** vendre la mèche; **they quarrel like c. and dog,** ils s'entendent comme chien et chat; **it's not big enough to swing a c. in,** c'est grand comme un mouchoir de poche; (b) *F:* (of pers.) **an old c.,** une vieille chipie. **2.** *Z:* **the (great) cats,** les grands félins. **3.** *attrib.* **c. burglar,** monte-en-l'air *m inv*; **c. nap,** sieste *f*; somme *m*; '**catcall,** *s.* sifflet *m*; '**cat's-eye,** *s.* (on roads) cataphote *m* (R.t.m.); catadioptre *m*; '**catwalk,** *s.* passerelle *f* de visite.

cataclysm ['kætəklizm], *s.* cataclysme *m*.

catacombs ['kætəku:mz], *s.pl.* catacombes *f*.

catalogue ['kætələg]. **I.** *s.* catalogue *m*, liste *f*; **subject c.**, catalogue raisonné. **II.** *v.tr.* cataloguer.

catamaran ['kætəməræn], *s. Nau:* catamaran *m*.

catapult ['kætəpʌlt]. **I.** *s.* **1.** fronde *f*. **2.** *Av: Rockets:* catapulte *f* (de lancement). **II.** *v.tr. Av: etc:* lancer (un avion, une fusée).

cataract ['kætərækt], *s.* cataracte *f* (d'un fleuve, de l'œil).

catarrh [kə'tɑ:r], *s. Med:* catarrhe *m*.

catastrophe [kə'tæstrəfi], *s.* catastrophe *f*; désastre *m*; **cata'strophic**, *a.* désastreux; catastrophique.

catch [kætʃ]. **I.** *v.* (**caught** [kɔ:t]; **caught**) **1.** *v.tr.* (*a*) attraper, prendre; saisir (une allusion); prendre, avoir, ne pas manquer (le train); *Fish: etc:* **to c. nothing**, ne rien attraper; revenir bredouille; (*b*) *F:* **c. me (doing such a thing)!** il n'y a pas de danger! (*c*) **we were caught in the storm**, l'orage nous a surpris; (*d*) rencontrer (le regard de qn); saisir (des sons); **I didn't c. what you said**, je n'ai pas entendu ce que vous disiez; (*e*) accrocher; **the car caught him as it passed**, la voiture l'a happé au passage; (*f*) attraper (une maladie). **2.** *v.i.* (*a*) **to c. at sth.**, s'accrocher à qch.; (*b*) (*of cogwheel*) mordre; (*of door-bolt*) s'engager; (*c*) (*of fire*) prendre; (*d*) *Cu:* **to c. in the pan**, attacher. **II.** *s.* **1.** prise *f*. **2.** *Fish:* **a good c.**, une bonne pêche. **3.** (*on door*) loquet *m*. **4.** (*deception*) attrape *f*; **there's a c. in it**, c'est une attrape; **c. question**, colle *f*; question insidieuse. **5.** *Mus:* chant *m* à reprises; canon *m*; **'catching**, *a.* (*of illness*) contagieux, infectieux; (*of tune*) entraînant; **'catch 'on**, *v.i. F:* (*a*) (*of fashion, etc.*) prendre; (*b*) comprendre, *F:* piger; **'catch 'out**, *v.tr. F:* prendre (qn) sur le fait; **'catch 'up**, *v.tr.* rattraper (qn); *v.i.* **to c. up with s.o.**, rattraper qn; **'catchword**, *s.* scie *f*, rengaine *f*; **'catchy**, *a.* **c. tune**, air entraînant.

catechize ['kætikaiz], *v.tr.* **1.** catéchiser. **2.** questionner, interroger (qn); **'catechism**, *s.* catéchisme *m*; **'catechist**, *s.* catéchiste *m*.

categorical [kætə'gɔrik(ə)l], *a.* catégorique; **-ally**, *adv.* catégoriquement.

category ['kætig(ə)ri], *s.* catégorie *f*.

cater ['keitər], *v.i.* **to c. for s.o.**, approvisionner qn; **to c. for all tastes**, pourvoir à tous les goûts; **'caterer**, *s.* approvisionneur *m*; pourvoyeur *m*; traiteur *m*; **'catering**, *s.* approvisionnement *m*.

caterpillar ['kætəpilər], *s. Ent:* chenille *f*; **c.-tractor**, autochenille *f*.

caterwaul ['kætəwɔ:l], *v.i.* miauler, crier (comme les chats la nuit).

cathedral [kə'θi:drəl], *s.* cathédrale *f*; **c. city**, ville épiscopale, évêché *m*.

Catherine ['kæθ(ə)rin]. *Pr.n.* Catherine *f*; *Fireworks:* **C. wheel**, soleil *m*; roue *f* à feu.

cathode ['kæθoud], *s. El: T.V:* cathode *f*; **c. rays**, rayons *m* cathodiques; **ca'thodic**, *a.* **c. beam**, faisceau *m* cathodique.

catholic ['kæθ(ə)lik]. **1.** *a.* (*a*) universel, -elle; (*b*) tolérant; **c. mind**, esprit *m* large; **c. taste**, goûts éclectiques. **2.** *a. & s. Ecc:* catholique (*mf*); **ca'tholicism** [-isizm], *s.* catholicisme *m*.

catkin ['kætkin], *s. Bot:* chaton *m*.

cattle ['kætl], *s. coll. inv.* bétail *m*; bestiaux *mpl*; **c. shed**, étable *f*; **c. breeding**, élevage *m* du bétail; *P.N:* **c. crossing**, passage *m* de troupeaux; **c. show**, comices *m* agricoles.

catty ['kæti], *a.*, **cattish** ['kætiʃ], *a. F:* (*esp. of woman*) méchant(e); rosse; **c. answer**, réponse aigre-douce; **'cattiness**, *s.*, **'cattishness**, *s. F:* méchanceté *f*, rosserie *f*.

caucus ['kɔ:kəs], *s. Pol:* comité électoral.

cauldron ['kɔ:ldrən], *s.* chaudron *m*.

cauliflower ['kɔliflauər], *s.* chou-fleur *m*, pl. choux-fleurs.

cause [kɔ:z]. **I.** *s.* **1.** cause *f*. **2.** raison *f*, motif *m*; sujet *m*; **to have good c. for doing sth.**, fair qch. à bon droit; **and with good c.**, et pou cause; **to show c.**, exposer ses raisons. **3.** (*a Jur:* cause; procès *m*; (*b*) **to work for a good c** travailler pour une bonne cause; **to take u s.o.'s c.**, épouser la querelle de qn. **II.** *v.tr.* causer, occasionner (un malheur); provoque (un incendie). **2. to c. s.o. to do sth.**, faire fai qch. à qn.

causeway ['kɔ:zwei], *s.* (*a*) chaussée *f*; (*b*) lev *f*, digue *f*.

caustic ['kɔstik]. **1.** *a.* caustique; **c. wit**, esp mordant. **2.** *s. Pharm:* caustique *m*; **-ally**, *aa* d'un ton mordant.

cauterize ['kɔ:təraiz], *v.tr.* cautérise **cauteri'zation**, *s.* cautérisation *f*.

caution ['kɔ:ʃ(ə)n]. **I.** *s.* **1.** précaution prévoyance *f*, prudence *f*. **2.** (*a*) avis *m*, ave tissement *m*; **c.!** attention! (*b*) réprimande *f*. *v.tr.* **1.** avertir (qn); mettre (qn) sur ses gard **2.** menacer (qn) de poursuites à la procha occasion; **'cautious**, *a.* circonspect, prude **to play a c. game**, jouer serré; **-ly**, *a* prudemment; **'cautiousness**, *s.* prudence *f*

cavalcade [kæv(ə)'keid], *s.* cavalcade *f*.

cavalry ['kæv(ə)lri], *s.* cavalerie *f*.

cave [keiv]. **I.** *s.* caverne *f*, antre *m*, grotte *f*; *trib.* **c. art**, art *m* rupestre; **c. bear**, ours *m F* cavernes. **II.** *v.i.* **to c. in**, s'effondrer; (*F pers.*) céder; **'caveman**, *pl.* **-men**, *s.* l'hom *m* des cavernes.

cavern ['kævən], *s.* caverne *f*; souterrain **yawning c.**, grotte béante.

caviar(e) ['kævia:r], *s.* caviar *m*.

cavil ['kævil], *v.i.* (**cavilled**) chicaner, ergoter

c. at sth., pointiller sur qch.; **he's always cavilling,** il trouve à redire sur tout.

cavity ['kæviti], *s.* cavité *f*; creux *m*; trou *m*; (*in tooth*) carie *f* (dentaire).

caw [kɔ:], *v.i.* croasser.

cease [si:s], *v.tr. & i.* **1.** cesser ((**from**) **doing sth.,** de faire qch.). **2. to c. work,** cesser le travail; **without ceasing,** sans arrêt; **'cease-'fire,** *s. Mil:* cessez-le-feu *m inv*; **'ceaseless,** *a.* incessant; sans arrêt; **-ly,** *adv.* sans cesse; sans arrêt.

cedar ['si:dər], *s. Bot:* cèdre *m*.

cede [si:d], *v.tr.* céder (une propriété, une terre).

cedilla [si'dilə], *s.* cédille *f*.

ceiling ['si:liŋ], *s.* (*a*) plafond *m*; (*b*) *Meteor:* **cloud c.,** plafond nuageux; (*c*) **to fix a c. to a budget,** fixer un plafond à un budget; **output has reached its c.,** la production plafonne.

celebrate ['selibreit], *v.tr.* célébrer (la mémoire de qn); commémorer, *F:* fêter (un événement); **'celebrated,** *a.* célèbre (**for,** par); renommé (**for,** pour); **cele'bration,** *s.* célébration *f*, commémoration *f* (d'un événement, etc.); *F:* **this calls for a c.,** il faut arroser ça; **ce'lebrity,** *s.* (*a*) célébrité *f*, renommée *f*; (*b*) (*of pers.*) **he's, she's, a c.,** c'est une célébrité.

celery ['seləri], *s. Hort:* céleri *m*; **head of c.,** pied *m* de céleri.

celestial [si'lestiəl], *a.* céleste; *Av:* **c. navigation,** navigation *f* par visée astronomique.

celibate ['selibət], *a. & s.* célibataire (*mf*); **'celibacy,** *s.* célibat *m*.

cell [sel], *s.* **1.** cellule *f*. **2.** *El:* élément *m* (de pile); **dry c.,** pile sèche. **3.** *Biol:* cellule. **4.** *Pol:* **communist c.,** noyau *m* communiste; **'cellular,** *a.* cellulaire.

cellar ['selər], *s.* cave *f*; **'cellarman,** *pl.* **-men,** *s.* sommelier *m*.

cello, *pl.* **-os** ['tʃelou, -ouz], *s.* violoncelle *m*; **'cellist,** *s.* violoncelliste *mf*.

cellophane ['seləfein], *s. R.t.m:* Cellophane *f*.

cellulose ['seljulous], *s.* cellulose *f*.

Celt [kelt], *s. Ethn:* celte *mf*; **'Celtic,** *a.* celtique; celte.

cement [si'ment]. **I.** *s.* ciment *m*. **II.** *v.tr.* cimenter; **ce'ment-mixer,** *s.* bétonnière *f*.

cemetery ['semətri], *s.* cimetière *m*.

cenotaph ['senəta:f], *s.* cénotaphe *m*.

censer ['sensər], *s. Ecc:* encensoir *m*.

censor ['sensər]. **I.** *s. Adm:* censeur *m*; **banned by the c.,** interdit par la censure. **II.** *v.tr.* interdire (une pièce de théâtre, etc.); passer (une lettre) par le contrôle; **'censorship,** *s.* censure *f*.

censure ['senʃər]. **I.** *s.* censure *f*, blâme *m*; *Pol:* **vote of c. (on the Government),** motion *f* de censure (contre le gouvernement). **II.** *v.tr.* censurer; (i) blâmer, condamner; (ii) critiquer.

census ['sensəs], *s.* recensement *m*.

cent [sent], *s.* **1.** (*coin*) cent *m* [sɛnt]; **I haven't got a c.,** je n'ai pas le sou. **2. per c.,** pour cent [sɑ̃].

centenary [sen'ti:nəri], *a. & s.* (anniversaire *m*) centenaire (*m*); **cente'narian,** *s.* centenaire *mf*.

centigrade ['sentigreid], *a.* centigrade.

centimetre ['sentimi:tər], *s. Meas:* centimètre *m*.

centipede ['sentipi:d], *s.* centipède *m*, mille-pattes *m inv*.

central ['sentrəl], *a.* central; **c. heating,** chauffage central; **-ally,** *adv.* centralement, au centre; **'centralize,** *v.tr.* centraliser.

Central African Republic (the) [ðə'sentrəl'æfrikənri'pʌblik]. *Pr.n. Geog:* la République Centrafricaine.

centre ['sentər]. **I.** *s.* **1.** centre *m*; milieu *m*, (d'une table); foyer *m* (d'érudition, d'infection); **in the c.,** au centre; **infant welfare c.,** consultation *f* de nourrissons; *Ph:* **c. of gravity,** centre de gravité; **out of c.,** décentré. **2.** *attrib.* central; **the c. arch,** l'arche centrale, du centre; *Pol:* **c. party,** parti *m* du centre. **II. 1.** *v.tr.* placer (qch.) au centre; **to c. one's affections on s.o.,** concentrer toute son affection sur qn; *Fb:* centrer (le ballon), *abs.* centrer. **2.** *v.i.* **to c. in, on, round, s.o., sth.,** se concentrer dans, sur, autour, qn, qch.; **'centre 'forward,** *s. Fb:* avant-centre *m*; **'centre 'half,** *s. Fb:* demi-centre *m*.

centrifugal [sen'trifjug(ə)l, sentri'fju:g(ə)l], *a.* centrifuge; **c. force,** force *f* centrifuge; **c. machine,** centrifugeur *m*, centrifugeuse *f*.

centuple ['sentju:pl], *v.tr.* centupler.

century ['sentʃəri], *s.* **1.** siècle *m*; **in the twentieth c.,** au vingtième siècle. **2.** (*at cricket*) centaine *f*.

ceramics [sə'ræmiks], *s.pl.* (*usu. with sing. const.*) la céramique.

cereal ['siəriəl], *a. & s.* (*usu. pl.*) céréale (*f*); (**breakfast**) **cereals,** céréales (en flocons).

ceremony ['serimə̃ni], *s.* cérémonie *f*; **with c.,** solennellement; **without c.,** sans cérémonie; sans façon; **to attend a c.,** assister à une cérémonie; **to stand on c.,** faire des cérémonies, des façons; **cere'monial,** **1.** *a. de* cérémonie. **2.** *s.* cérémonial *m*; **-ally,** *adv.* en grande cérémonie; **cere'monious,** *a.* cérémonieux; **-ly,** *adv.* avec cérémonie.

cert [sə:t], *s. F:* **a dead c.,** une certitude (absolue); une affaire sûre; **it's a c.,** c'est couru (d'avance).

certain ['sə:t(ə)n], *a.* certain. **1. to be c. of sth.,** être certain, sûr, de qch.; **I'm almost c. of it,** j'en ai la presque certitude; **to know sth. for c.,** être bien sûr de qch.; **to make c. of sth.,** (i) s'assurer de qch.; (ii) s'assurer qch. **2. there are c. things,** il y a certaines choses; **c. people,** (de) certaines gens, certains *mpl*; **-ly,** *adv.* (*a*) cer-

tainement; assurément; à coup sûr; (b) (assent) assurément; parfaitement; **'certainty**, s. certitude f; chose certaine; certitude (morale), conviction f; **to bet on a c.**, parier à coup sûr.
certificate [sə'tifikit], s. **1.** certificat m, attestation f; Fin: titre m (d'actions). **2. c. (of competency)**, certificat; diplôme m, brevet m. **3.** acte m; **birth c.**, acte de naissance; **death c.**, acte de décès. **4. savings c.**, bon m d'épargne.
certify ['sə:tifai], v.tr. **1.** (a) certifier, déclarer, attester; **to c. a death**, constater un décès; (b) authentiquer, homologuer, légaliser (un document); (c) diplômer, breveter (qn). **2.** v.ind.tr. **to c. to sth.**, attester qch.; **certi'fiable**, a. F: **he's c.!** il est fou à lier! **'certified**, a. **c. lunatic**, aliéné(e) interdit(e).
certitude ['sə:titju:d], s. certitude f.
cessation [se'seiʃ(ə)n], s. cessation f, arrêt m.
cession ['seʃ(ə)n], s. cession f; abandon m (de marchandises, de droits, etc.).
cesspool ['sespu:l], s. fosse f d'aisance.
Ceylon [si'lɔn]. Pr.n. Geog: Ceylan m.
Chad [tʃæd]. Pr.n. Geog: (i) **Lake C.**, le lac Tchad; (ii) **the Republic of C.**, le Tchad.
chafe [tʃeif]. **1.** v.tr. user, échauffer (qch.) (par le frottement); écorcher (la peau). **2.** v.i. (a) s'user (par le frottement); (of rope) s'érailler, raguer; (b) **to c. at sth.**, s'énerver de qch.
chaff [tʃɑ:f]. **I.** s. **1.** Agr: paille hachée. **2.** raillerie f; persiflage m. **II.** v.tr. railler, taquiner; persifler.
chaffinch ['tʃæfin(t)ʃ], s. Orn: pinson m.
chagrin [si'lɔn], s. chagrin m, dépit m.
chain [tʃein]. **I.** s. (a) chaîne f; **to pull the c.**, tirer la chasse d'eau; (b) chaîne (de montagnes); (c) **c. store**, magasin m à succursales multiples; (d) **c. reaction**, réaction f en chaîne. **II.** v.tr. attacher, retenir, (qch.) par une chaîne; **the dog's chained up**, le chien est attaché, est à la chaîne; **'chain-smoker**, s. fumeur, -euse, de cigarettes à la file.
chair ['tʃeər], s. (a) chaise f, siège m; **to take a c.**, s'asseoir; (b) Sch: chaire f (de professeur de Faculté); (c) **to be in the c.**, occuper le fauteuil (présidentiel); présider; **to take the c.**, prendre la présidence; **'chairman**, pl. **-men**, s. président, -ente; **Mr C., Madam C.**, M. le Président, Mme la Présidente; **'chairmanship**, s. présidence f.
chalet ['ʃælei], s. chalet m.
chalice ['tʃælis], s. Ecc: calice m.
chalk [tʃɔ:k]. **I.** s. **1.** craie f; Art: pastel m; **French c.**, talc m, stéatite f. **2.** F: **not by a long c.**, tant s'en faut. **II.** v.tr. **1.** (a) (i) marquer, (ii) blanchir, (qch.) à la craie; (b) talquer, saupoudrer (de talc. **2. to c. (up) sth. on a board**, écrire qch. à la craie sur un tableau; F: **c. it up (to me)**, mettez-le à mon compte;

'chalky, a. **1.** crayeux. **2.** (teint) pâle.
challenge ['tʃælin(d)ʒ]. **I.** s. **1.** (a) défi m; provocation f; (b) interpellation f. **2.** Jur: récusation f (du jury). **3.** Sp: challenge m. **II.** v.tr. **1.** (a) défier; provoquer (qn au combat); (b) interpeller (qn). **2.** disputer, mettre en question (la parole de qn); Jur: récuser (un juré); **'challenger**, s. provocateur, -trice; Sp: challengeur m; **'challenging**, a. (of remark look) provocateur, -trice; (air) de défi.
chamber ['tʃeimbər], s. (a) **audience c.**, salle d'audience; **council c.**, salle du conseil; (b) **music**, musique f de chambre; (b) H: **c. (pot)** vase m de nuit; (c) Adm: **C. of Commerce** chambre f de commerce; (d) pl. **chambers** cabinet m, étude f (d'un avocat); Jur: **to hear** **case in chambers**, juger une cause en référé **'chambermaid**, s. femme f de chambre.
chammy-leather ['ʃæmileðər], s. (peau f de chamois m.
chamois ['ʃæmwa:], s. chamois m; **'chamois leather**, ['ʃæmi-], s. (peau f de) chamois.
Champagne [ʃæm'pein]. **1.** Pr.n. Geog: Champagne. **2.** s. (vin m de) champagne m.
champion ['tʃæmpjən]. **I.** s. champion, -onne. v.tr. soutenir, défendre (une cause, une per sonne); **'championing**, s. défense f (d'un cause); **'championship**, s. (a) défense f (d'un cause); (b) Sp: championnat m.
chance [tʃɑ:ns]. **I.** s. **1.** (a) chance f, hasard sort m; **by c.**, par hasard; **the chances are th** . . ., il y a fort à parier que . . .; **to do sth. the off c.**, faire qch. à tout hasard; **I'm n** **taking any chances**, je ne veux rien laisser hasard; (b) **to have an eye to the main c.**, veil à ses propres intérêts, s'attacher au solide. occasion f; **to stand a c.**, avoir des chances succès. **3. to take a c.**, encourir un risque. **4.** trib. fortuit, accidentel; **c. discover** découverte accidentelle; **a c. acquaintan** une connaissance de rencontre; **c. comer**, s venant, -ante. **II.** v. **1.** v.i. **to c. to do sth.**, fa qch. par hasard; **if I c. to find it**, si je viens à trouver. **2.** v.tr. **to c. it**, risquer le coup; **to** **one's luck**, F: **to c. one's arm**, tenter sa chan **'chancy**, a. incertain; hasardeux, risqué.
chancel ['tʃɑ:nsəl], s. Ecc.Arch: **1.** sanctuaire **2.** chœur m.
chancellor ['tʃɑ:nsələr], s. chancelier m; **C.** **the Exchequer** = Ministre m des Finances.
chandelier [ʃændə'li:ər], s. lustre m.
change ['tʃein(d)ʒ]. **I.** s. **1.** changement m; ret m (de la marée); revirement m (d'opinion) **for the better, the worse**, changement mieux, en mal; **to make a c.**, effectuer changement (**in, à**); **for a c.**, comme distract f; pour changer; **c. of front**, volte-face f Aut: **gear c.**, changement de vitesse. **2. c.** **clothes**, vêtements mpl de rechange. **3. m**

naie f; **small c.,** petite monnaie; *F:* **he won't get much c. out of me,** il perdra ses peines avec moi. **4. to ring the changes on a subject,** ressasser, rabâcher, un sujet. **II.** *v.* **1.** *v.tr.* changer; (*a*) modifier (ses plans); **to c. one's tune,** changer de ton; **to c. the subject,** changer de sujet; (*b*) **to c. one's clothes,** *abs.* **to c.,** changer de vêtements; se changer; (*c*) *Rail:* **to c. trains,** *abs.* **to c.,** changer de train; **all c.!** tout le monde descend! (*d*) échanger (**sth. for sth.,** qch. contre qch.); (*e*) **to c. a banknote,** (i) changer un billet (de banque); (ii) donner la monnaie d'un billet (de banque); **to c. travellers' cheques,** changer des chèques de voyage. **2.** *v.i.* (se) changer (**into,** en); se modifier; **to c. for the better,** changer en mieux; **the weather's changing,** (i) le temps tourne au beau; (ii) le temps se gâte; **'changeable,** *a.* (*of pers.*) changeant; (*of weather*) variable, inconstant; **'changeless,** *a.* immuable; **'changing.** **I.** *a.* changeant. **II.** *s.* changement *m*; *Mil:* relève f (de la garde); *Sp:* *attrib.* **c. room,** vestiaire *m.*

channel ['tʃænl], *s.* **1.** lit *m* (d'une rivière). **2.** (*a*) passe f, chenal *m* (d'un port); (*b*) *Geog:* détroit *m*, canal *m*; **the (English) C.,** la Manche; **the C. Islands, Isles,** les îles Anglo-Normandes. **3.** canal, conduit *m*. **4.** voie f; *Adm:* **the official channels,** la voie hiérarchique; **channels of communication (of a country),** artères f (d'un pays). **5.** *Rad: T.V:* chaîne f.

chant [tʃɑːnt]. **I.** *s. Mus:* chant *m*; *Ecc:* (i) plain-chant *m*; (ii) psalmodie f; **Gregorian c.,** chant grégorien. **II.** *v.tr. & i. Ecc:* (*a*) psalmodier; (*b*) **to c. slogans,** scander, entonner, des slogans.

chaos ['keiɔs], *s.* chaos *m*; **cha'otic,** *a.* chaotique; désorganisé; **-ally,** *adv.* sans ordre.

chap[1] [tʃæp]. **I.** *s.* gerçure f, crevasse f. **II.** *v.i.* (**chapped**) se gercer, se crevasser.

chap[2], *s.* garçon *m*, type *m*, individu *m*; **old c.,** mon vieux; **a queer c.,** un drôle de gars.

chapel ['tʃæpl], *s.* (*a*) chapelle f; oratoire (particulier; royal; d'un collège); (*b*) (*in Eng.*) temple *m* non-conformiste; **'chapel-goer,** *s.* non-conformiste mf.

chaperon ['ʃæpəroun]. **I.** *s.* chaperon *m*. **II.** *v.tr.* (**chaperoned**) chaperonner (une jeune fille).

chaplain ['tʃæplin], *s. Ecc:* aumônier *m*; chapelain *m*.

chapter ['tʃæptər], *s.* **1.** chapitre *m*; **to give c. and verse,** citer ses autorités; **a c. of accidents,** une suite de malheurs. **2.** *Ecc:* chapitre *m*; **c. house,** salle f du chapitre, salle capitulaire.

char[1] [tʃɑːr], *v.* (**charred**) **1.** *v.tr.* carboniser. **2.** *v.i.* se carboniser.

char[2], *F:* **I.** *s.* femme f de ménage. **II.** *v.i.* **to go out charring,** faire des ménages.

char[3], *s. F:* thé *m*; **a cup of c.,** une tasse de thé.

character ['kæriktər], *s.* **1.** *Typ:* caractère *m*, let-

tre f. **2.** caractère; marque distinctive; **books of that c.,** livres de ce genre; **to be in c. with sth.,** s'harmoniser avec qch.; **work that lacks c.,** œuvre f qui manque de cachet. **3.** **man of (strong) c.,** homme de caractère, de volonté. **4.** (*a*) **of bad c.,** de mauvaise réputation; mal famé; (*b*) **to give s.o. a good, bad, c.,** dire du bien, du mal, de qn. **5.** (*a*) personnage *m* (de roman, etc.); (*b*) **a public c.,** une personnalité; **a bad c.,** un mauvais sujet; **he's a c.,** c'est un original, *F:* un numéro; **characte'ristic. 1.** *a.* caractéristique. **2.** *s.* trait *m*, particularité f; **-ally,** *adv.* d'une manière caractéristique; **'characterize,** *v.tr.* caractériser (qn, qch.); **'characterless,** *a.* sans caractère.

charcoal ['tʃɑːkoul], *s.* **1.** charbon *m* (de bois). **2.** *Art:* fusain *m*; **c. drawing,** (dessin *m* au) fusain; **'charcoal 'grey,** *a.* (gris) anthracite *inv.*

charge ['tʃɑːdʒ]. **I.** *s.* **1.** (*a*) charge f (d'une cartouche, etc.); (*b*) *El:* charge. **2.** (*a*) frais *mpl*, prix *m*; **list of charges,** tarif *m*; **c. for admittance,** prix des places; **no c. for admission,** entrée gratuite; *Com:* **free of c.,** (i) gratis, franco; (ii) à titre gratuit, à titre gracieux; **c. account,** compte crédit d'achats; (*b*) **to be a c. on s.o.,** être à la charge de qn. **3.** charge; emploi *m*; fonction f. **4.** garde f, soin *m*; **to take c. of s.o., sth.,** se charger, avoir soin, de qn, de qch.; **person in c.,** préposé, -ée; *Jur:* **to give s.o. in c.,** faire arrêter qn. **5.** *Jur:* charge; chef *m* d'accusation; **to bring a c. against s.o.,** porter une accusation contre qn. **II.** *v.tr.* **1.** charger (un fusil, un accumulateur) (**with,** de). **2.** *Jur: etc:* **to c. s.o. with a crime,** imputer un crime à qn. **3.** *Com: etc:* charger, imputer; débiter (les frais au client); **c. it on the bill,** portez-le sur la note; **to c. fifty francs a metre,** demander cinquante francs le mètre; **'charger,** *s.* chargeur *m* (d'accumulateur).

charisma [kæ'rizmə], *s.* charisme *m*; **charis'matic,** *a.* charismatique.

charity ['tʃæriti], *s.* **1.** charité f; **out of c.,** par charité. **2.** (*a*) acte *m* de charité; (*b*) charité, aumônes *fpl*; bienfaisance f. **3.** œuvre f de bienfaisance, de charité; fondation pieuse; *pl.* **charities,** bonnes œuvres; **'charitable,** *a.* (personne) charitable; (œuvre) de bienfaisance; **c. work,** bonnes œuvres; **-ably,** *adv.* charitablement.

Charles [tʃɑːlz]. *Pr.n.m.* Charles.

charm [tʃɑːm]. **I.** *s.* **1.** charme *m* (**against,** contre); sortilège *m*, sort *m*; **it works like a c.,** ça marche à merveille. **2.** (*a*) amulette f, fétiche *m*; (*b*) porte-bonheur *m inv.* **3.** charme, agrément *m*; **the c. of an alpine landscape,** le charme d'un paysage alpestre; **he lacks c.,** il manque de charme. **II.** *v.tr.* charmer, enchanter; **'charming,** *a.* charmant; **a c. woman, dress,** une femme, une robe, ravissante; **-ly,** *adv.* d'une façon charmante; **c. dressed,** habillée à ravir.

chart [tʃɑːt]. **I.** *s.* **1.** *Nau:* carte (marine). **2.** (*a*) (*of statistics*) graphique *m*, diagramme *m*; (*b*) **organisation c.,** organigramme *m*. **II.** *v.tr. Nau:* dresser la carte d'(une côte, etc.); porter (une série de relèvements) sur un graphique.

charter ['tʃɑːtər]. **I.** *s.* **1.** charte *f* (d'une ville); statuts *m* (d'une société); **bank c.,** privilège *m* (d'une banque); *Pol:* **the Atlantic C.,** la Charte de l'Atlantique. **2.** affrètement *m* (d'un navire, d'un avion); **c. plane,** (i) avion-taxi *m*; (ii) charter *m*; **c. flight,** vol *m* charter. **II.** *v.tr.* **1.** instituer (une compagnie) par charte; **chartered accountant** = expert *m* comptable. **2.** affréter (un navire, un avion).

charwoman, *pl.* **-women** ['tʃɑːwumən, -wimin], *s.* femme *f* de ménage.

chary ['tʃɛəri], *a.* prudent, circonspect; **to be c. of, in, doing sth.,** hésiter à faire qch.; **c. of praise,** avare de louanges.

chase [tʃeis]. **I.** *v.tr.* poursuivre; donner la chasse à (qn); **to c. away a dog,** chasser un chien. **II.** *s.* poursuite *f*; **to give c. to s.o.,** donner la chasse à qn, poursuivre, pourchasser, qn; **wild goose c.,** poursuite vaine.

chasm ['kæz(ə)m], *s.* gouffre béant; vide *m* énorme.

chassis ['ʃæsi], *s. Aut:* châssis *m*.

chaste [tʃeist], *a.* (*of pers.*) chaste, pudique; (*of style*) pur; châtié; **'chastity,** *s.* **1.** chasteté *f*. **2.** *Art: Lit:* pureté *f*; simplicité *f* (de style).

chasten ['tʃeisn], *v.tr.* (*a*) châtier, éprouver; (*b*) rabattre l'orgueil de (qn); **'chastened,** *a.* assagi; radouci.

chastise [tʃæs'taiz], *v.tr.* châtier; infliger une correction à (qn); corriger (un enfant); **'chastisement,** *s.* châtiment *m*; punition *f*.

chat [tʃæt]. **I.** *v.* (chatted) **1.** *v.i.* causer, bavarder. **2.** *v.tr. F:* **to c. up (a girl),** baratiner (une fille). **II.** *s.* causerie *f*, causette *f*.

chatter ['tʃætər]. **I.** *v.i.* **1.** (*of birds*) caqueter; jacasser; (*of pers.*) bavarder, papoter; **to c. like a magpie,** jaser comme une pie (borgne). **2.** (*of teeth*) claquer. **II.** *s.* **1.** papotage *m*; bavardage *m*. **2.** claquement *m* (des dents); **'chatterbox,** *s.* grand(e) bavard(e); **to be a great c.,** avoir la langue bien pendue.

chauffeur ['ʃoufər, ʃou'fəːr], *s.* chauffeur *m*.

chauvinism ['ʃouvinizm], *s.* chauvinisme *m*.

cheap [tʃiːp]. **1.** *a.* (*a*) (à) bon marché; **cheaper,** (à) meilleur marché, moins cher; **dirt c.,** à vil prix; pour rien; **it's c. and nasty,** c'est de la camelote; **to do sth. on the c.,** faire qch. à peu de frais; (*b*) de peu de valeur. **2.** *adv.* (à) bon marché; **-ly,** *adv.* (à) bon marché; à peu de frais; **he got off cheap(ly),** il en est quitte à bon compte; **'cheapen,** *v.tr.* diminuer la valeur de (qch.); **'cheapness,** *s.* bon marché; médiocrité *f* (de qch.).

cheat [tʃiːt]. **I.** *v.* **1.** *v.tr.* tromper; frauder (qn), voler (qn). **2.** *v.tr. & i.* (*at games*) tricher. **II.** *s.* (*a*) trompeur, -euse; escroc *m*; imposteur *m*; (*b*) (*at games*) tricheur, -euse; **'cheating,** *s.* **1.** tromperie *f*; fourberie *f*. **2.** (*at games*) tricherie *f*.

check¹ [tʃek]. **I.** *v.* **1.** *v.tr.* (*a*) *Chess:* mettre (le roi) en échec; (*b*) faire échec à (qn, qch.); arrêter (une attaque); (*c*) refouler, retenir (ses larmes, sa colère); réprimer, refréner (une passion); (*d*) réprimander (un enfant); (*e*) vérifier (un compte); **to c. (off),** pointer (des noms sur une liste); **to c. (up) information,** contrôler des renseignements. **2.** *v.i.* hésiter, s'arrêter (**at sth.,** devant qch.). **II.** *s.* **1.** (*a*) *Chess:* échec *m*; (*b*) revers *m*, échec. **2.** contrôle *m*; vérification *f* (d'un compte, etc.); **c. sample,** échantillon *m* témoin; (*b*) ticket *m*; bulletin *m* (de bagages); *N.Am:* **c. room,** consigne *f*; (*c*) *esp. N.Am:* addition *f*, note *f*; (*d*) *P: N.Am:* **to hand in one's checks,** mourir, *P:* poser sa chique. **3.** *N.Am:* chèque *m*; **'check 'in,** *v.i. esp. N.Am:* **1.** s'inscrire à l'hôtel. **2.** *Ind:* signer à l'arrivée, pointer. **3.** *v.tr.* mettre (ses bagages) à la consigne; **'checking,** *s.* **1.** répression *f*. **2.** contrôle *m*; vérification *f*; **'checklist,** *s.* liste *f* de contrôle; **'checkmate. 1.** *s.* échec *m* et mat *m*. **II.** *v.tr.* faire échec et mat à (qn); contrecarrer, déjouer (les projets de qn); **'check 'out,** *v. esp. N.Am:* **1.** *v.i.* (régler sa note et) quitter l'hôtel. **2.** *v.tr.* retirer (ses bagages) (de la consigne); **'check-out,** *s.* caisse *f* (dans un supermarché); **'check 'over,** *v.tr.* vérifier; contrôler; **'check(-)up,** *s. Med:* examen médical complet; inspection médicale.

check², *s. Tex:* carreau *m*; (tissu) à carreaux; **broken c.,** pied-de-poule *m*; **'checked,** *a.* (tissu, etc.) à carreaux; quadrillé; **'checkers,** *s. N.Am:* jeu *m* de dames.

cheek [tʃiːk]. **I.** *s.* **1.** joue *f*; **c. bone,** pommette *f*; **c. by jowl with s.o.,** côte à côte avec qn. **2.** *F:* toupet *m*, effronterie *f*, impudence *f*; **what damned c.!** quel culot! c'est se ficher du monde! **II.** *v.tr.* faire l'insolent avec (qn); *F:* se payer la tête de (qn); **'cheeky,** *a.* insolent *F:* effronté; **-ily,** *adv.* d'un air, d'un ton effronté.

cheer ['tʃiər]. **I.** *s.* hourra *m*; *pl.* **cheers,** acclamations *f*, bravos *m*; applaudissement *m*; *F:* **cheers!** à la vôtre! **II.** *v.* **1.** *v.tr.* (*a*) **c. s.o. (up),** égayer, ragaillardir qn; relever l(e) moral de qn; (*b*) applaudir (qn, qch.). **2.** *v.i.* (*a*) **c. up,** reprendre sa gaieté; se ragaillardir; (*b*) applaudir; **'cheerful,** *a.* (*of pers.*) gai; de bonn(e) humeur; **-fully,** *adv.* allègrement; de bon cœur; **'cheerfulness,** *s.* (*of pers.*) gaieté *f*; bonn(e) humeur; contentement *m*; **'cheering,** *s.* acclamation *f*; applaudissements *mpl*; **'chee[r] leader,** *s.* meneur, -euse, de ban; **'cheerless,** *a.*

morne, triste, sombre; '**cheery**, a. joyeux, gai, guilleret; -**ily**, adv. gaiement.

cheese [tʃiːz]. **I.** s. fromage m; **c. biscuit**, biscuit non sucré; **c. straws**, allumettes f au fromage. **II.** v.tr. P: **c. it!** en voilà assez! la ferme! **to be cheesed off**, avoir le cafard; '**cheesecake**, s. tarte f au fromage blanc; '**cheesecloth**, s. gaze f; '**cheesemonger**, s. fromager, -ière; marchand(e) de fromage; '**cheeseparing**. **1.** s. parcimonie f, lésine f. **2.** a. **c. economy**, économies fpl de bouts de chandelle.

chef [ʃef], s. chef m de cuisine.

chemical ['kemik(ə)l]. **1.** a. chimique. **2.** s.pl. **chemicals**, produits m chimiques.

chemist ['kemist], s. **1.** pharmacien, -ienne; **c.'s shop**, pharmacie f. **2.** chimiste m; **analytical c.**, chimiste analyste, chimiste expert.

chemistry ['kemistri], s. chimie f; **inorganic c.**, chimie minérale; **organic c.**, chimie organique; **applied c.**, chimie appliquée; **c. of metals**, métallochimie f.

cheque [tʃek], s. chèque m; **c. book**, carnet m de chèques; **crossed c.**, chèque barré; **to pay by c.**, payer par chèque.

chequer ['tʃekər], v.tr. **1.** quadriller (un tissu, etc.). **2.** diaprer, bigarrer. **3.** diversifier, varier; '**chequered**, a. quadrillé, à carreaux, en damier; **c. career**, vie mouvementée; '**chequering**, s. quadrillage m.

cherish ['tʃeriʃ], v.tr. **1.** chérir (qn, qch.). **2.** bercer, caresser (un espoir); nourrir (une idée, des illusions).

cherry ['tʃeri], s. **1.** s. cerise f; **black-heart c.**, guigne noire; **white-heart c.**, bigarreau m; **wild c.**, merise f. **2.** s. **c. tree**, cerisier m; **c. orchard**, cerisaie f. **3.** a. **c.(-red)**, cerise inv; '**cherry 'pie**, s. (i) tourte f aux cerises; (ii) Bot: héliotrope m; '**cherry-stone**, s. noyau m de cerise.

cherub, pl. **cherubs**, **cherubim** ['tʃerəb, -z, -əbim], s. chérubin m; **che'rubic**, a. chérubique; (air m) de chérubin.

chess [tʃes], s. jeu m d'échecs; **to play c.**, jouer aux échecs; '**chessboard**, s. échiquier m; '**chessmen**, s.pl. pièces f (du jeu d'échecs).

chest [tʃest], s. **1.** coffre m, caisse f; **c. of drawers**, commode f. **2.** Anat: poitrine f; **cold on the c.**, rhume m de poitrine; **to have a weak c.**, avoir les bronches délicates; F: **to get it off one's c.**, dire ce qu'on a sur le cœur.

chestnut ['tʃesnʌt]. **1.** s. (a) châtaigne f; marron m; (b) **c. (tree)**, châtaignier m; marronnier m; (c) F: plaisanterie usée. **2.** attrib. (colour) châtain; (cheval) alezan.

chew [tʃuː], v.tr. mâcher, mastiquer; F: **to c. sth. over**, méditer, ruminer, qch., une idée; P: **to c. the rag**, bavarder; '**chewing gum**, s. chewing-gum m.

chic [ʃiːk], a. élégant, chic.

chick [tʃik], s. poussin m.

chicken ['tʃikin], s. poulet m; Cu: poulet m; **spring c.**, poussin m; coll. volaille f; F: **she's no c.**, elle n'est plus toute jeune; **c. farm**, élevage m de volaille; '**chickenfeed**, s. F: petite monnaie; '**chicken-'hearted**, a. poltron; '**chicken-pox**, s. Med: varicelle f.

chicory ['tʃikəri], s. Bot: **1.** chicorée f; Com: **(ground) c.**, (poudre f de) chicorée; **coffee with c.**, café m à la chicorée. **2.** endive f.

chief [tʃiːf]. **1.** s. (a) chef m; F: **the c.**, le patron; (b) **in c.**, en chef; **commander-in-c.**, commandant m en chef. **2.** a. principal, -aux; premier, -ière; (en) chef; **c. guest**, hôte m d'honneur; **c. engineer**, ingénieur m en chef; -**ly**, adv. **1.** surtout, avant tout. **2.** principalement; '**chieftain**, s. chef m de clan.

chiffon ['ʃifɔn], s. Tex: mousseline f de soie.

chilblain ['tʃilblein], s. engelure f.

child, pl. **children** [tʃaild, 'tʃildrən], s. enfant mf; **take the c. with you**, emmenez le petit, la petite; **from a c.**, dès son enfance; **that's c.'s play**, ça, c'est facile! **problem c.**, enfant difficile; **c. welfare centre**, centre m de protection infantile; '**childbirth**, s. couches fpl; accouchement m; '**childhood**, s. enfance f; '**childish**, a. enfantin, d'enfant; **to grow c.**, retomber en enfance; -**ly**, adv. comme un enfant, puérilement; '**childishness**, s. Pej: enfantillage m, puérilité f; '**childless**, a. sans enfant(s); '**childlike**, a. enfantin; naïf, -ïve.

Chile ['tʃili]. Pr.n. Geog: le Chili.

chill [tʃil]. **I.** s. **1.** (a) Med: **to catch a c.**, prendre froid; (b) **c. of fear**, frisson m de crainte. **2.** (a) **to take the c. off**, dégourdir (l'eau), chambrer (le vin); (b) **to cast a c. over the party**, jeter un froid sur l'assemblée. **II.** v.tr. (a) refroidir, glacer (qch.); réfrigérer (la viande); **chilled meat**, viande frigorifiée; (b) faire frissonner (qn); (of pers.) **chilled to the bone**, morfondu; transi (de froid); '**chilliness**, s. froid m, fraîcheur f (du temps); froideur f (d'un accueil); '**chilly**, a. **1.** (a) (of pers.) frileux; **to feel c.**, avoir froid; (b) (of weather) frais. **2.** (of pers., manner) froid; **c. politeness**, politesse glaciale.

chime [tʃaim]. **I.** s. carillon m. **II.** v.i. & tr. carillonner; **chiming clock**, pendule f à carillon.

chimney ['tʃimni], s. (a) cheminée f (de maison, d'usine); (b) (funnel) cheminée f; (c) Mount: cheminée f; '**chimney-pot**, s. pot m de cheminée; '**chimney-stack**, s. (a) souche f (de cheminée); (b) cheminée f d'usine; '**chimney-piece**, s. (manteau m de) cheminée f; '**chimney-sweep(er)**, s. ramoneur m.

chimpanzee [tʃimpæn'ziː], s. chimpanzé m.

chin [tʃin], s. menton m.

China ['tʃainə]. **1.** Pr.n. Geog: la Chine; **Communist C.**, la République populaire de Chine.

2. *s.* **china,** (i) porcelaine *f*; faïence fine; (ii) vaisselle *f* de porcelaine.

Chinese [tʃai'ni:z], **1.** *a.* & *s.* chinois, -e; **the C. People's Republic,** la République populaire de Chine. **2.** *s. Ling:* le chinois.

chink¹ [tʃiŋk], *s.* fente *f*, crevasse *f* (dans un mur); entre-bâillement *m* (de la porte).

chink². **I.** *s.* tintement *m* (du métal, du verre, de la monnaie). **II.** *v.* **1.** *v.tr.* faire sonner (son argent); faire tinter (des verres). **2.** *v.i.* sonner (sec).

chintz [tʃints], *s. Tex:* perse *f*, indienne *f*.

chip [tʃip]. **I.** *s.* **1.** éclat *m*, copeau *m* (de bois); écaille *f*, éclat (de marbre); **to have a c. on one's shoulder,** en vouloir à tout le monde; **he's a c. of(f) the old block,** c'est bien le fils de son père. **2.** brisure *f*, écornure *f* (d'assiette). **3.** *Cu:* **chips,** (pommes de terre) frites *fpl*; *N.Am:* **(potato) chips,** (pommes *fpl*) chips *mpl*. **4.** (*at cards, etc.*) jeton *m*. **II.** *v.tr.* (**chipped**) **1.** tailler par éclats. **2.** ébrécher (une tasse); écorner (un meuble); **to c. a piece off sth.,** enlever un morceau à qch.; **'chipboard,** *s.* carton gris; **'chip 'in,** *v.i.* intervenir; placer son mot; **'chip 'off,** *v.i.* (*of paint, etc.*) s'écailler; **'chippings,** *s.pl.* éclats *m*, copeaux *m*; *P.N:* **loose c.,** gravillons *m*.

chipmunk ['tʃipmʌŋk], *s. Z:* tamia *m* rayé; *Fr.C:* suisse *m*.

chiropodist [ki'rɔpədist], *s.* pédicure *mf*; **chi'ropody,** *s.* chirurgie *f* pédicure.

chirp [tʃə:p], *v.i.* (*of birds*) pépier, gazouiller; (*of grasshoppers, crickets*) crier; *F:* faire cri-cri *m*; **'chirpy,** *a.* d'humeur gaie.

chisel [tʃizl]. **I.** *s.* ciseau *m*. **II.** *v.tr.* (**chiselled**) (*a*) ciseler; buriner (le métal); (*b*) *P:* rouler, carotter (qn).

chit [tʃit], *s.* (*a*) lettre *f*; petit mot; (*b*) note *f*.

chit-chat ['tʃittʃæt], *s. F:* bavardages *mpl*, commérages *mpl.*

chivalrous ['ʃivəlrəs], *a.* chevaleresque; courtois; **'chivalry,** *s.* conduite *f* chevaleresque; courtoisie *f.*

chives [tʃaivz], *s.pl. Bot:* ciboulette *f.*

chlorate ['klɔ:reit], *s. Ch:* chlorate *m.*

chloride ['klɔ:raid], *s. Ch:* chlorure *m.*

chlorine ['klɔ:ri:n], *s. Ch:* chlore *m*; **'chlorinate,** *v.tr.* chlorurer (de l'eau).

chloroform ['klɔrəfɔ:m], *s. Med:* chloroforme *m.*

chlorophyll ['klɔrəfil], *s. Ch:* chlorophylle *f.*

choc-ice ['tʃɔkais], *s. F:* esquimau *m.*

chock [tʃɔk], *s.* cale *f*; coin *m*; **'chock-a-'block, 'chock-'full,** *a.* plein comme un œuf; (salle *f*) comble.

chocolate ['tʃɔklət]. **1.** *s.* chocolat *m*; **slab of c.,** tablette *f* de chocolat; **plain c.,** chocolat à croquer; **milk c.,** chocolat au lait; **a c.,** une crotte de chocolat; **a cup of c.,** une tasse de

chocolat. **2.** *a.* (de couleur) chocolat *inv.*

choice [tʃɔis]. **I.** *s.* **1.** choix *m*; (*a*) préférence *f*; **for c.,** de préférence; (*b*) alternative *f*; **you have no c. in the matter,** vous n'avez pas le choix. **2.** assortiment *m*, choix; **to have a wide c.,** avoir largement de quoi choisir. **II.** *a.* (article, mot) bien choisi; (article) de choix.

choir ['kwaiər], *s.* chœur *m*; **'choirboy,** *s.* jeune choriste *m*; **'choir-master,** *s.* maître *m* de chapelle.

choke [tʃouk]. **I.** *v.* **1.** *v.tr.* étouffer, suffoquer (qn); **to c. (up) a pipe,** obstruer, boucher, un tuyau (**with,** de). **2.** *v.i.* (*a*) étouffer, étrangler (**with,** de); **to c. with laughter,** suffoquer de rire; (*b*) s'engorger, s'obstruer (**with,** de). **II.** *s.* **1.** *Aut:* starter *m.* **2.** étranglement *m* de voix. **3.** *Bot:* foin *m* (d'un artichaut); **'choke 'back,** *v.tr.* refouler (ses larmes, ses paroles); **'choke 'off,** *v.tr. F:* (*a*) to c. s.o. o. (from) doing sth., dissuader qn de faire qch.; (*b*) se débarrasser de (qn); **'choking,** *s.* étouffement *m*, suffocation *f*, étranglement *m*; **'choky,** *a.* étouffant, suffocant.

cholera ['kɔlərə], *s. Med:* choléra *m.*

cholesterol [kɔ'lestərɔl], *s. Med:* cholestérol *m.*

choose [tʃu:z], *v.tr.* (**chose** [tʃouz], **chosen** [tʃouzn]). **1.** choisir; faire choix de (qch.); **to c. a method,** adopter une méthode; **there's nothing to c. between them,** l'un vaut l'autre. **2.** **I don't c. to do so,** il ne me plaît pas de le faire; **when I c.,** quand je voudrai; **I do as I c.,** je fais comme il me plaît, comme je l'entends; **'choosing,** *s.* choix *m*; **the difficulty of c.,** l'embarras du choix; **'choosy,** *a. F:* a c. customer, un client, une personne, difficile; **'chosen,** *a.* choisi; *s.pl.* les élus.

chop¹ [tʃɔp], *s.* **1.** coup *m* de hache, de couperet. **2.** *Cu:* côtelette *f.*

chop², *v.tr.* (**chopped**) couper, fendre; **to c. sth.** hacher qch.; **'chop 'down,** *v.tr.* abattre (un arbre); **'chop 'off,** *v.tr.* trancher (qch.); **'chop 'up,** *v.tr.* couper (qch.) en morceaux; **'chopper,** *s.* couperet *m*; hachoir *m*; **'choppy** *a.* c. sea, mer agitée, houleuse.

chopsticks ['tʃɔpstiks], *s.pl.* baguettes *f.*

choral ['kɔ:rəl], *a. Mus:* **1. c. society,** (société chorale (*f*). **2.** chanté en chœur.

chord [kɔ:d], *s. Mus:* accord *m.*

chore [tʃɔ:r], *s.* corvée *f*; **to do the chores,** faire l ménage.

choreography [kɔri'ɔgrəfi], *s.* chorégraphie *f*; **chore'ographer,** *s.* chorégraphe *m.*

chorister ['kɔristər], *s.* choriste *m*; *Ecc:* chantr *m.*

chorus, *pl.* **-uses** ['kɔ:rəs, -əsiz], *s.* **1.** chœur *n* **c. of praise,** concert *m* de louanges. **2.** refrai *m* (d'une chanson); **to join in the c.,** fair chœur, reprendre en chœur; **'chorus(-)girl,** *Th:* girl *f.*

Christ [kraist]. *Pr.n.* le Christ; Jésus-Christ *m.*

christen ['krisn], *v.tr.* baptiser (un enfant, un navire); to c. a new dress, étrenner une robe neuve; 'christening, *s.* baptême *m.*

Christian ['kristiən], *a. & s.* chrétien, -ienne; C. name, nom *m* de baptême; Christi'anity, *s.* christianisme *m.*

Christmas ['krisməs], *s.* Noël *m*; at C., à Noël, à la Noël; merry C.! joyeux Noël! C. card, carte *f* de Noël; C. carol, noël *m*; C. Day, le jour de Noël; C. Eve, *s.* la veille de Noël; C. tree, arbre *m* de Noël; Father C., le père Noël.

chrome [kroum], *s.* (*a*) c. leather, cuir chromé; (*b*) c. steel, acier chromé; (*c*) c. yellow, jaune de chrome.

chromium ['kroumiəm], *s. Ch:* chrome *m*; c. plating, chromage *m*; to polish the c., faire briller les chromes.

chromosome ['kroumɔsoum], *s. Biol:* chromosome *m.*

chronic ['krɔnik], *a.* (*a*) *Med:* chronique; c. ill-health, invalidité *f*; (*b*) *F:* constant, continuel.

chronicle ['krɔnikl]. I. *s.* chronique *f.* II. *v.tr.* to c. events, faire la chronique des événements; raconter les faits; 'chronicler, *s.* chroniqueur, -euse.

chronological [krɔnə'lɔdʒik(ə)l], *a.* chronologique; in c. order, par ordre de dates; -ally, *adv.* chronologiquement, par ordre chronologique.

chronometer [krə'nɔmitər], *s.* chronomètre *m.*

chrysalis, *pl.* -ises ['krisəlis, -isiz], *s. Ent:* chrysalide *f.*

chrysanthemum [kri'sænθiməm], *s.* chrysanthème *m.*

chubby ['tʃʌbi], *a.* boulot, -otte; (*of face*) joufflu.

chuck [tʃʌk], *v.tr. F:* (*a*) jeter, lancer (une pierre, etc.); (*b*) lâcher, plaquer (qn); (*c*) c. it! en voilà assez! (*d*) to c. one's weight about, faire l'important; (*e*) to c. s.o. out, flanquer qn à la porte; (*f*) to c. up one's job, démissionner; 'chucker-'out, *s. F:* videur *m.*

chuckle ['tʃʌkl]. I. *v.i.* rire tout bas, glousser, rire sous cape (at, over, sth., de qch.). II. *s.* rire étouffé; gloussement *m* (de rire).

chum [tʃʌm], *s. F:* copain *m*, copine *f.*

chump [tʃʌmp], *s.* 1. *Cu:* chop, côtelette *f* de gigot. 2. *F:* (silly) c., nigaud *m*, cruche *f.*

chunk [tʃʌŋk], *s.* gros morceau (de bois, etc.); quignon *m* (de pain).

church [tʃəːtʃ], *s.* 1. église *f*; temple (protestant). 2. to go into, enter, the C., entrer dans les ordres; to go to c., aller à l'office, à la messe; c. hall, salle paroissiale; to be a c. goer, être pratiquant, -ante; 'church'warden, *s.* marguillier *m*; 'churchyard, *s.* cimetière *m.*

churlish ['tʃəːliʃ], *a.* (*a*) mal élevé; grossier; (*b*) hargneux, grincheux; -ly, *adv.* avec mauvaise grâce; 'churlishness, *s.* (*a*) grossièreté *f*; (*b*)

tempérament hargneux.

churn [tʃəːn]. I. *s.* 1. baratte *f.* 2. bidon *m* à lait. II. *v.tr.* battre (le beurre), ruminer (une pensée); 'churn 'out, produire à la chaîne.

chute [ʃuːt], *s.* chute *f* d'eau.

chutney ['tʃʌtni], *s. Cu:* chutney *m.*

cider ['saidər], *s.* cidre *m.*

cigar [si'gɑːr], *s.* cigare *m.*

cigarette [sigə'ret], *s.* cigarette *f*; ciga'rette-case, *s.* étui *m* à cigarettes, porte-cigarettes *m* *inv*; ciga'rette end, *s.* mégot *m*; ciga'rette-holder, *s.* fume-cigarette *m.*

cinder ['sindər], *s.* 1. cendre *f.* 2. *pl.* (*partly burnt coal*) escarbilles *fpl*; 'cinder-track, *s.* piste *f* (en) cendrée.

cine-camera ['sini'kæm(ə)rə], *s. Cin:* caméra *f.*

cinema ['sinimə], *s.* (*a*) le cinéma, le ciné; (*b*) (salle *f* de) cinéma.

cinnamon ['sinəmən], *s.* cannelle *f.*

cipher ['saifər], *s.* 1. *Mth:* zéro *m*; he's a mere c., c'est une nullité. 2. (*a*) chiffre *m*; to send a message in c., transmettre une dépêche en chiffre; (*b*) message chiffré. 3. (*monogram*) chiffre.

circle ['səːkl]. I. *s.* 1. cercle *m*; *N.Am:* traffic c., rond-point *m*; to run round in circles, tourner en rond. 2. révolution *f*, orbite *f* (d'une planète); to come full c., revenir à son point de départ. 3. *Th:* dress c., (premier) balcon; upper c., seconde galerie. 4. milieu *m*, coterie *f*; in theatrical circles, dans le monde du théâtre; the inner c., le cercle intime (d'amis); *Pol:* le groupe dirigeant. II. *v.* 1. *v.tr.* to c. sth., faire le tour de qch. 2. *v.i.* to c. round (sth.), tournoyer autour de (qch.); circuit ['səːkit], *s.* 1. pourtour *m* (d'une ville). 2. (*a*) révolution *f* (du soleil); (*b*) to make a c. of the town, faire le tour de la ville; (*c*) tournée *f*, circuit *m*; *Jur:* to go on c., aller en tournée. 3. *El:* circuit; short c., court-circuit *m*; closed c. television, télévision à circuit fermé; cir'cuitous [sə'kjuːitəs], *a.* (chemin) détourné; by c. means, par des moyens indirects; 'circular, *a. & s.* circulaire; c. (letter), (lettre *f*) circulaire *f.*

circulate ['səːkjuleit], *v.tr. & i.* (*a*) (faire) circuler; (*b*) (faire) distribuer, mettre en circulation (de l'argent); faire circuler (un bruit); cir-cu'lation, *s.* circulation *f* (du sang, de l'argent); tirage *m* (d'un journal); *Fin:* c. of capital, roulement *m* de fonds.

circumference [sə'kʌmf(ə)rəns], *s.* circonférence *f*; on the c., à la circonférence.

circumflex ['səːkəmfleks], *a. & s.* (accent), accent *m* circonflexe.

circumscribe ['səːkəmskraib], *v.tr.* 1. circonscrire. 2. limiter (des pouvoirs); circum'scription, *s.* (*a*) restriction *f*; (*b*) région délimitée; (*c*) région, circonscription (administrative).

circumstances ['səːkəmstənsiz], *s.pl.* circonstances *fpl* ; **in, under, the c.**, dans ces circonstances; puisqu'il en est ainsi; **under no c.**, en aucun cas; sous aucun prétexte; d'aucune manière; **under any c.**, en tout état de cause; **under similar c.**, en pareille occasion; **that depends on c.**, c'est selon; **if his c. allow**, si ses moyens le permettent; **in easy c.**, dans l'aisance; **circum'stantial**, *a.* circonstanciel; **c. evidence**, preuves indirectes.

circus, *pl.* **-uses** ['səːkəs, -əsiz], *s.* cirque *m*; **travelling c.**, cirque forain.

cirrhosis [si'rousis], *s. Med:* cirrhose *f.*

Cistercian [sis'təːʃ(ə)n], *a. & s. Ecc:* cistercien, -ienne; **the C. Order**, l'ordre *m* de Cîteaux.

cistern ['sistən], *s.* réservoir *m* à eau (sous les combles); (*underground*) citerne *f*; *H:* (réservoir de) chasse *f* d'eau.

citadel ['sitədel], *s.* citadelle *f.*

cite [sait], *v.tr.* **1.** *Jur:* citer (qn devant un tribunal); assigner (un témoin). **2.** citer (un auteur). **3.** *Mil:* citer (un militaire pour son courage); **ci'tation**, *s.* **1.** *Jur:* citation *f* (à comparaître); mandat *m*, sommation *f* (à, de, comparaître). **2.** citation (d'un auteur). **3.** *Mil:* citation (pour une décoration).

citizen ['sitizən], *s.* citoyen, -enne; **c. of Europe, of the world**, Européen, -enne; cosmopolite *mf* ; **'citizenship**, *s.* **1.** droit *m* de cité; nationalité *f.* **2. good c.**, civisme *m.* **3. to have French c.**, jouir de la citoyenneté française.

citric ['sitrik], *a. Ch:* (acide) citrique.

citrus ['sitrəs], *a.* **c. fruit**, agrumes *mpl.*

city ['siti], *s.* (*a*) grande ville; **the C.**, la Cité de Londres; **he's in the C.**, il est dans la finance; (*b*) ville épiscopale; **c. hall**, hôtel *m* de ville.

civic ['sivik]. **1.** *a.* civique; **the c. authorities**, les autorités municipales; **c. centre**, centre civique, social. **2.** *s.pl.* (*with sing. const.*) *Sch:* **civics**, instruction *f* civique.

civil ['siv(i)l], *a.* **1.** civil; **c. rights**, droits civiques; **c. war**, guerre civile; **c. defence**, défense passive; *Adm:* **c. servant**, fonctionnaire *mf* ; **in c. life**, dans le civil. **2.** poli, courtois; **-illy**, *adv.* courtoisement, poliment; **ci'vilian**, *a. & s.* civil (*m*); **in c. life**, dans le civil; **ci'vility**, *s.* courtoisie *f*, politesse *f.*

civilize ['sivilaiz], *v.tr.* civiliser; **civili'zation**, *s.* civilisation *f*; **'civilized**, *a.* civilisé; (homme) cultivé.

claim [kleim]. **I.** *s.* **1.** demande *f*; revendication *f*; réclamation *f.* **2.** droit *m*, titre *m*, prétention *f* (**to sth.**, à qch.); **to lay c. to sth.**, s'attribuer qch.; **to put in a c.**, faire valoir ses droits. **3.** (*debt*) créance *f.* **4.** *Jur:* réclamation; **to put in a c. for damages**, réclamer des dommages-intérêts *m*; *Adm:* **disputed claims office**, le contentieux. **5.** concession (minière). **II.** *v.tr.* (*a*) réclamer, revendiquer (un droit); demander (de l'attention); (*b*) **to c. that . . .**, prétendre,

affirmer, soutenir, que . . .; **to c. kinship with s.o.**, se prétendre parent de qn; (*c*) **to c. one's luggage**, reprendre ses bagages (à la consigne); **'claimant**, *s.* prétendant, -ante; revendicateur, -trice; *Jur:* demandeur, -eresse; **rightful c.**, ayant droit *m.*

clairvoyant [klɛə'vɔiənt], *s. Psychics:* clairvoyant, -ante; voyant, -ante; spirite *mf* ; **clair'voyance**, *s.* clairvoyance *f*; spiritisme *m.*

clamber ['klæmbər], *v.i.* grimper (des pieds et des mains); **to c. over a wall**, escalader un mur.

clammy ['klæmi], *a.* (*of skin*) (froid et) moite; (*of weather*) (froid et) humide; **'clamminess**, *s.* moiteur froide.

clamour ['klæmər]. **I.** *s.* clameur *f*; cris *mpl.* **II.** *v.i.* vociférer; pousser des cris; **to c. for sth.**, réclamer qch. à grands cris; **'clamorous**, *a.* bruyant; **a c. crowd**, une foule vociférante.

clamp [klæmp]. **I.** *s. Tchn:* crampon *m*; agrafe *f* serre-joint *m.* **II.** *v.* **1.** *v.tr.* agrafer; brider. **2.** *v.* **to c. down** (i) **on s.o.**, visser qn, (ii) **on an abuse** supprimer un abus; **'clamp-down**, *s.* **c.-d.** o**r credit**, resserrement *m* du crédit.

clan [klæn], *s.* **1.** clan *m*; **the head of the c.,** chef de clan. **2.** (*a*) tribu *f*; (*b*) coterie *f*, cliqu**e** *f*; **'clannish**, *a.* dévoué aux intérêts du clan de la coterie; **'clannishness**, *s.* esprit *m* d**e** corps (d'un clan, d'une famille, d'une coterie); **'clansman**, *pl.* **-men**, *s.* membre *m* d'un clan

clandestine [klæn'destin, -ain], *a.* clandestin subreptice.

clang [klæŋ]. **I.** *s.* son *m* métallique; bruit reten tissant. **II.** *v.i.* retentir, résonner; **'clanger**, *s.* *F:* **to drop a c.**, faire une boulette.

clank [klæŋk]. **I.** *s.* bruit métallique; cliquetis *n* **II.** *v.* **1.** *v.i.* rendre un bruit métallique. **2.** *v.t* faire sonner (le métal).

clap [klæp]. **I.** *s.* **1.** (*a*) battement *m* (de mains **to give s.o. a c.**, applaudir qn; (*b*) tape *f* (de l main); **a friendly c. on the shoulder**, un pet coup amical sur l'épaule. **2. c. of thunder**, cou de tonnerre. **II.** *v.* (**clapped**) **1.** *v.tr.* (*a*) **to one's hands**, battre des mains; **to c. s.o. on th back**, donner à qn une tape dans le dos; **to c. s.o. in prison**, fourrer qn en prison; **to c. a gun s.o.'s head**, appuyer brusquement un revolv à la tête de qn; **the first time I clapped eyes him**, la première fois que je l'ai aperçu. **2.** v applaudir; **'clapping**, *s.* battement *m* d mains; applaudissements *mpl.*

claptrap ['klæptræp], *s.* boniment *m*; phrase vides.

claret ['klærət], *s.* vin *m* de Bordeaux (roug bordeaux *m.*

clarify ['klærifai]. **1.** *v.tr.* clarifier (le beurr éclaircir (l'esprit); **to c. a questio** débroussailler une question. **2.** *v.i.* se clarifie s'éclaircir; **clarifi′cation**, *s.* clarification *f*, mise *f* au point.

clarinet [klæri′net], *s.* clarinette *f*.

clarity [′klæriti], *s.* clarté *f*.

clash [klæʃ]. **I.** *s.* **1.** fracas *m*; résonnement *m* (de cloches); choc *m* (de verres). **2.** (*a*) conflit *m* (d'opinions); (*between mobs*) échauffourée *f*; (*b*) disparate *f* (de couleurs). **II.** *v.i.* (*of opinions*) s'opposer; (*of interests*) se heurter; (*of colours*) détonner, jurer; **the dates c.**, les deux rendez-vous (etc.) tombent le même jour.

lasp [klɑːsp]. **I.** *s.* fermeture *f* (de manteau); fermoir *m* (de porte-monnaie, de collier). **II.** *v.tr.* **1.** agrafer, fermer (un bracelet, un collier). **2.** (*a*) serrer, étreindre (qn); **to c. s.o.'s hand**, serrer la main à qn; **′claspknife**, *s.* couteau pliant, couteau de poche.

lass [klɑːs], *s.* classe *f*. **1.** **the middle c.**, la bourgeoisie; **the classes**, les classes moyennes; **the working c.**, les classes ouvrières, la classe ouvrière; **c. struggle**, lutte *f* des classes. **2.** *Sch:* **the French c.**, la classe de français; **evening classes**, cours *m* du soir. **3.** catégorie *f*, sorte *f*, genre *m*; **c. of ships**, type *m* de navires; *Sch:* (*at university*) = mention obtenue; **classifi′cation** [klæ-], *s.* classification *f*; **′classify** [′klæ-], *v.tr.* classer; **′classroom**, *s.* (salle *f* de) classe *f*; **′classy**, *a.* *F:* *often Iron:* bon genre; **that looks c.**, ça fait chic.

lassic [′klæsik], *a.* & *s.* classique (*m*); **′classical**, *a.* classique.

latter [′klætər]. **I.** *s.* **1.** bruit *m* (de vaisselle, de ferraille), vacarme *m*. **2.** brouhaha *m* (de conversation). **II.** *v.i.* faire du fracas; se choquer avec bruit; **to c. downstairs**, descendre bruyamment l'escalier.

lause [klɔːz], *s.* **1.** clause *f*, article *m*. **2.** *Gram:* membre *m* de phrase; **main c.**, proposition principale; **subordinate c.**, proposition subordonnée.

laustrophobia [klɔːstrə′foubiə], *s.* *Med:* claustrophobie *f*.

law [klɔː]. **I.** *s.* griffe *f* (de félin); serre *f* (d'oiseau de proie); pince *f* (d'un homard); (*of cat*) **to sharpen its claws**, faire ses griffes; **to draw in its claws**, faire patte *f* de velours. **II.** *v.tr.* **1.** griffer, égratigner (qn, qch.). **2.** *v.i.* **to c. at sth.**, s'accrocher à qch.; **′claw-hammer**, *s.* marteau *m* à panne fendue.

lay [klei], *s.* argile *f*; (terre-)glaise *f*.

lean [kliːn]. **I.** *a.* propre, net; **to keep sth. c.**, tenir qch. propre; **keep the conversation c.!** pas de grossièretés *f*! **c. break**, cassure nette, franche; **the doctor gave me a c. bill of health**, le docteur m'a trouvé en pleine forme; **c. hands**, (i) mains *f* propres; (ii) (*clean from crime*) mains nettes; **to come c.**, (i) (*of laundry*) se blanchir, se nettoyer; (ii) (*of pers.*)

avouer, en faire cœur net; **-ly**, *adv.* proprement, nettement. **II.** *adv.* tout à fait; **I c. forgot**, j'ai complètement oublié; **they got c. away**, ils ont décampé sans laisser de traces. **III.** *v.tr.* nettoyer (qch.); récurer (les casseroles); faire (une chambre); vider (un poisson); **to c. one's teeth, one's nails**, se brosser les dents, se curer les ongles; **to c. up**, (tout) nettoyer; faire le nettoyage; **′cleaner**, *s.* **1.** (*pers.*) nettoyeur, -euse; femme *f* de ménage; **dry c.**, nettoyeur à sec. **2.** **vacuum c.**, aspirateur *m*; **′cleaning**, *s.* nettoyage *m*; **dry c.**, nettoyage à sec, dégraissage *m*; **c. up of the kitchen**, nettoyage de la cuisine; **c. up of a gang**, nettoyage d'un gang; **cleanliness** [′klenlinəs], **′cleanness**, *s.* propreté *f*; netteté *f*; **′clean-′shaven**, *a.* sans barbe (ni moustache); (visage *m*) glabre.

cleanse [klenz], *v.tr.* **1.** curer (un égout). **2.** purifier (le sang); **′cleansing. 1.** *a.* assainissant, purifiant; **c. cream**, démaquillant *m*. **2.** *s.* curage *m* (d'un égout); purification *f* (du sang).

cleanser [′klenzər], *s.* pâte *f*, poudre *f*, liquide *m*, à nettoyer.

clear [′kliər]. **I.** *a.* **1.** (*a*) clair, limpide; net, *f.* nette; **on a c. day**, par temps clair; **as c. as day**, clair comme le jour; (*b*) **c. conscience**, conscience nette. **2.** **c. indication**, signe certain, évident; **c. case of bribery**, cas de corruption manifeste. **3.** **to make one's meaning c.**, se faire comprendre; **c. thinker**, esprit lucide. **4.** **to be c. about sth.**, être convaincu de qch. **5.** **c. profit**, bénéfice clair et net; **c. loss**, perte sèche; **c. majority**, majorité absolue; **three c. days**, trois jours francs. **6.** libre, dégagé (of, de); *Mil:* **'all c.!'** "fin d'alerte"; **the coast is c.**, le champ est libre; **-ly**, *adv.* clairement, nettement; évidemment. **II.** *a. or adv.* **to steer, to keep, c. of s.o., sth.**, éviter qn, qch.; se garer (pour éviter un danger); **stand c.!** gare! garez-vous! **stand c. of the door!** dégagez la porte! **III.** *v.* **1.** *v.tr.* (*a*) éclaircir; **to c. the air**, (i) rafraîchir l'air; (ii) mettre les choses au point; (*b*) **to c. s.o. (of a charge)**, innocenter qn (d'une accusation); **to c. oneself**, se disculper; (*c*) dégager (une route); désencombrer (une salle); déblayer (un terrain); défricher (une lande); **to c. the table**, desservir; enlever le couvert; (*d*) **to c. the decks**, ranger des affaires qui traînent; **to c. the letter box**, lever les lettres; faire la levée; **to c. one's plate**, faire assiette nette; **to c. one's throat**, s'éclaircir le gosier, tousser un coup; *Com:* **to c. goods**, solder des marchandises; *P.N.:* **to c.**, en solde; (*e*) **to c. a barrier**, franchir une barrière; (*of ship*) **to c. the harbour**, quitter le port; (*f*) acquitter (une dette); affranchir (une propriété); solder, liquider (un compte); virer (un chèque). **2.** *v.i.* (*of the weather*) **to c. (up)**, s'éclaircir; se lever; se mettre au beau; (*of mist*) **to c. (away)**, se dissiper; **′clearance**, *s.*

1. (*at customs*) dédouanement *m.* 2. **slum** c., suppression *f* des taudis. 3. *Com:* c. **sale** (vente *f* de) soldes *fpl*; '**clear a**'**way**, *v.tr.* enlever, ôter; écarter (qch.); *abs.* (*of table*) desservir; '**clear-cut**, *a.* net,*f.* nette; '**clear-**'**headed**, *a.* qui voit juste; perspicace; '**clearing**, *s.* 1. *Jur:* désinculpation *f* (de qn). 2. enlèvement *m* (de débris); dégagement *m* (d'une voie). 3. (*in forest*) clairière *f*; c. **bank**, banque de virement; '**clearness**, *s.* clarté *f*; netteté *f* (d'une image); '**clear** '**off**, *v.tr. & i.* s'acquitter de (ses dettes); *F:* filer, décamper; '**clear** '**out**, *v.tr. & i.* nettoyer (une pièce); *F:* filer, décamper; '**clear-out**, *s.* nettoiement *m*, évacuation *f*; '**clear** '**up**, *v.tr. & i.* éclaircir, élucider (un problème); (*of weather*) s'éclaircir, se lever; remettre de l'ordre dans (une pièce); '**clearway**, *s.* route *f* à stationnement interdit.

clef [klef], *s. Mus:* clef *f*; **the bass, the treble, c.**, la clef de fa, de sol.

cleft [kleft]. I. *s.* fente *f*, fissure *f*, crevasse *f.* 2. *a. Med:* c. **palate**, palais *m* fendu.

clematis [klə'meitis], *s. Bot:* clématite *f.*

clement ['klemənt], *a.* 1. clément, indulgent (**to**, envers, pour). 2. (*of weather*) doux,*f.* douce; '**clemency**, *s.* 1. clémence *f* (**to s.o.**, envers, pour, qn). 2. douceur *f* (du temps).

clench [klen(t)ʃ], *v.tr.* serrer (les dents, le poing); **with clenched hands**, les mains crispées; **with clenched fists**, le poing serré.

clergy ['klə:dʒi], *s.* 1. *coll.* clergé *m.* 2. membres *mpl* du clergé; '**clergyman**, *pl.* -**men**, *s. Ecc:* pasteur *m* (protestant).

clerical ['klerik(ə)l], *a.* 1. clérical, -aux; du clergé. 2. *Adm:* c. **work**, travail *m* de bureau; c. **error**, faute *f* de copiste.

clerk [klɑːk, *N.Am:* klə:k], *s.* 1. employé, -ée, de bureau; clerc *m* (de notaire); **bank** c., employé, -ée, de banque; **chief** c., **head** c., chef *m* de bureau. 2. *N.Am:* vendeur, -euse.

clever ['klevər], *a.* 1. habile, adroit; **to be c. with one's hands**, être adroit de ses mains; **that's not very c.**, ça, c'est pas malin. 2. (*a*) **to be c.**, être intelligent; **he's c. at maths**, il est fort en math(s); (*b*) *F:* (*smart*) **he was too c. for us**, il nous a roulés; (*c*) c. **device**, dispositif ingénieux; -**ly**, *adv.* habilement, adroitement; avec intelligence; '**cleverness**, *s.* 1. habileté *f.* 2. intelligence *f*; ingéniosité *f.*

cliché ['kliːʃei], *s.* cliché *m.*

click [klik]. I. *s.* 1. bruit sec; clic *m*; cliquetis *m* (de verre, de métal). 2. *Tchn:* cliquet *m*; déclic *m.* II. *v.* 1. *v.tr. & i.* (*a*) cliqueter; claquer; (*b*) cliqueter; faire tic-tac; **to c. one's heels**, (faire) claquer les talons. 2. *v.i. F: that clicks!* ça me rappelle quelque chose; **it suddenly clicked**, tout à coup il a compris.

client ['klaiənt], *s.* client, -ente.

clientele [klaiən'tel, kli:ã'tel], *s.* clientèle *f.*

cliff [klif], *s.* falaise *f.*

climate ['klaimət], *s.* climat *m.*

climax ['klaimæks], *s.* comble *m*, apogée *m*, plu[ ] haut point; **this brought matters to a c.**, ce fu[ ] le comble.

climb [klaim]. I. *s.* 1. ascension *f*; *Aut: Sp:* **hill** c[ ] course *f* de côte; *Av:* **rate of c.**, vitesse *f* ascen[ ] sionnelle. 2. montée *f*; côte *f*; **stiff c.**, grimpée *[ ]* II. *v.tr. & i.* 1. (*a*) monter, gravir; grimper à (u[ ] arbre); monter à (l'échelle); escalader (un[ ] falaise); **to c. a mountain**, faire l'ascension[ ] d'une montagne; **to c. over the wall**, franchir l[ ] mur; (*b*) **the road climbs**, la route va en mon[ ] tant. 2. **to c. to power**, s'élever au pouvoir. 3[ ] *Av:* monter; prendre de l'altitude; '**clim**[ ] '**down**, *v.i.* 1. descendre. 2. *F:* en rabattre[ ] '**climber**, *s.* 1. alpiniste *mf.* 2. arriviste *m[ ]* '**climbing**, *s.* escalade *f*; montée *f*; (**moun**[ ] **tain**) c., alpinisme *m.*

clinch [klin(t)ʃ]. I. *v.* 1. *v.tr.* (*a*) river; (*b*) conclu[ ] (un marché). 2. *v.i. Box:* se prendre corps-[ ] corps. II. *s.* corps-à-corps *m*; clinch *m*; a[ ] crochage *m*; *Box:* **to get into a c.**, se prend[ ] corps-à-corps.

cling [kliŋ], *v.i.* (**clung** [klʌŋ]) (*a*) s'attacher, s'a[ ] crocher, se cramponner (**to**, à); **to c. close t**[ ] **s.o.**, se serrer contre qn; **to c. together**, (i) rest[ ] étroitement unis; (ii) se tenir étroitemen[ ] enlacés; (*b*) adhérer (**to**, à).

clinic ['klinik], *s. Med:* clinique *f*; '**clinica**[ ] *a.* clinique; c. **thermometer**, thermomè[ ] médical.

clink[1] [kliŋk]. I. *s.* tintement *m*, choc *m* ([ ] verres). II. *v.* 1. *v.i.* tinter. 2. *v.tr.* faire tinte[ ] faire résonner; **to c. glasses (with s.o.)**, trinqu[ ] (avec qn).

clink[2], *s. P:* prison *f*, taule *f.*

clip[1] [klip]. I. *s.* pince *f*, attache *f*; (**wire**) **paper** [ ] trombone *m.* II. *v.tr.* (**clipped**) pincer, serre[ ] agrafer (des papiers).

clip[2]. I. *s.* 1. tonte *f* (de moutons). 2. *P:* taloche [ ] 3. *F:* **to go at a good c.**, marcher à gran[ ] vitesse. II. *v.tr.* (**clipped**) 1. tondre ([ ] mouton); tailler (une haie). 2. poinçonner ([ ] billet); '**clipping**, *s.* coupure *f* (de journal).

clique [kliːk], *s.* coterie *f*, clique *f*; pet[ ] chapelle.

cloak [klouk]. I. *s.* manteau *m*; **under the c.** [ ] **darkness**, sous le voile de la nuit. II. *v.* [ ] masquer (ses projets); '**cloakroom**, *s.* [ ] vestiaire *m.* 2. (*in hotel, etc.*) toilette *f.* 3. *R*[ ] consigne *f.*

cloche [klɔʃ]. I. *s. Hort:* cloche *f.* II. *v.tr.* cloch[ ] mettre sous cloche.

clock [klɔk]. I. *s.* (*a*) (*large*) horloge *f*; (*smalle*[ ] pendule *f*; **grandfather** c., horloge comtoise,[ ] parquet; *P.T.T:* **the speaking** c., l'horlo[ ] parlante; **it's two o'clock**, il est deux heures;

·ork round the c., (i) *Ind:* faire les trois-huits
·; (ii) travailler vingt-quatre heures sur vingt-
uatre; (*b*) compteur *m* kilométrique (d'une
·oiture, d'un taxi); *F:* compteur (d'électricité,
·e gaz, etc.). **II.** *v.* **1.** *v.tr.* chronométrer (une
·ourse, etc.). **2.** *v.i. Ind:* **to c. in, out, to c. on,
ff,** pointer à l'arrivée, au départ; **'clock-
golf,** *s.* jeu *m* de clock-golf; **'clockwise,** *a. &
dv.* dans le sens des aiguilles d'une montre;
:lockwork, *s.* mouvement *m* d'horlogerie; **to
·o like c.**, aller, marcher, comme sur des
·oulettes.

g [klɔg]. **I.** *v.tr.* **(clogged)** (*a*) boucher,
·bstruer (un tuyau); (*b*) **to c. the wheels of
·overnment**, entraver la marche du
·ouvernement. **II.** *s.* galoche *f,* sabot *m.*
·**ster** ['klɔistər], *s.* cloître *m.*
·e¹ [klous]. **I.** *a.* **1.** (*a*) bien fermé; clos; (*b*) **the
·oom smells c.**, ça sent le renfermé ici; **c.
·reather**, temps lourd; (*c*) **c. secret**, secret im-
·énétrable; (*d*) **c. season**, chasse fermée. **2. c.
·onnection**, rapport étroit; **c. friend**, ami(e) in-
·me; **c. resemblance**, ressemblance exacte; **c.
·ranslation**, traduction *f* fidèle; **to keep a c.
·ratch on s.o.**, surveiller qn de près; **to cut hair
·.**, couper les cheveux ras; (*of contest*) à forces,
chances, égales; **c. election**, élection vive-
·1ent contestée; *Rac:* **c. finish**, arrivée serrée.
·. peu communicatif; **to be c. about sth.**, être
·éservé à l'égard de qch.; **to play a c. game,
·0uer serré. 4.** avare, regardant; **-ly,** *adv.* **1.** (*a*)
·troitement; (*b*) (interroger qn) à fond. **2. c.
·acked in a box**, serrés dans une boîte. **II.** *adv.*
·**. c. shut**, étroitement fermé. **2.** près, de près,
·uprès; **to follow c. behind s.o.**, suivre qn de
·rès; **to stand c. together**, se tenir serrés. **3.** (*a*)
·**. at hand, c. by**, tout près, tout proche; (*b*) **to
·e c. on fifty**, friser la cinquantaine; **'close-
·cropped**, *a.* (*of hair*) coupé ras; (*of grass*)
·ondu de près; **'close-'fisted**, *a.* ladre; *F:*
·ingre; **'close-'fitting**, *a.* (vêtement) ajusté,
·ollant; **'closeness**, *s.* **1.** proximité *f,* rap-
·rochement *m.* **2.** exactitude *f* (d'une
·essemblance, etc.). **3.** manque *m* d'air;
·ourdeur *f* (du temps). **4.** réserve *f* (de qn);
·aractère peu communicatif (de qn). **5.** ladrerie
·*F:* pingrerie *f;* **'close-up**, *s. Cin:* gros
·lan.
·e² [klous], *s.* **1.** *Jur:* clôture *f.* **2.** (*a*) clos *m,*
·nclos *m;* (*b*) enceinte *f* (de cathédrale).
·e³ [klouz]. **I.** *v.* **1.** *v.tr.* (*a*) fermer; barrer (une
·ue); *Book-k:* **to c. the books**, régler les livres;
·5) conclure, terminer; fermer (un débat); (*c*) **to
·. the ranks**, serrer les rangs. **2.** *v.i.* (*a*) (se)
·ermer; se refermer; (*b*) finir; se terminer; (*c*) **to
·. round s.o.**, encercler qn; (*d*) **to c. with s.o.**,
·) conclure le marché avec qn; (ii) se pren-
·re corps à corps avec qn. **II.** *s.* fin *f;* conclu-
·on *f;* bout *m* (de l'année); **to draw to a c.**,

prendre fin; **closed**, *a.* **1.** fermé; **behind c. doors**,
à huis clos; *P.N:* **road c.**, route barrée. **2.** *Ind:* **c.
shop**, entreprise fermée aux travailleurs non-
syndiqués; **c. circuit television**, télévision *f* à circuit fermé; **'close 'down**, *v.tr. & i.* fermer (le
magasin, l'usine); *Rad:* *T.V:* terminer
l'émission; **'close 'in**, *v.i.* (*a*) **the days are
closing in**, les jours (se) raccourcissent; (*b*) **to c.
in on s.o.**, cerner qn de près; **'closing. I.** *a.* qui
se ferme; dernier, final; **the c. bid**, la dernière
enchère; *Fin:* **c. prices**, derniers cours. **II.** *s.* **1.**
fermeture *f* (d'une usine); **early c. day**, jour *m*
où les magasins sont fermés l'après-midi.
2. clôture *f* (d'un compte); **'close 'up.** **1.**
v.tr. boucher; barrer; fermer (complètement).
2. *v.i.* (*a*) (*of aperture*) s'obturer, se renfermer;
(*b*) se serrer, se tasser; **'closure**, *s.* fermeture
f.
clot [klɔt]. **I.** *s.* **1.** *Med:* caillot *m* (de sang); **c. on
the brain**, embolie *f* cérébrale. **2.** *F:* idiot, -ote,
imbécile *mf.* **II.** *v.* **(clotted)** **1.** *v.tr.* coaguler. **2.**
v.i. (*of cream*) se cailler; (*of blood*) se figer.
cloth, *pl.* **cloths** [klɔθ, klɔθs], *s.* **1.** *Tex:* (*a*) tissu
m de laine; drap *m;* (*b*) (*linen, cotton*) toile *f;*
Bookb: **c. binding**, reliure *f* toile. **2.** (*a*) linge *m;*
(**dish-**)**c.**, torchon *m;* (*b*) (**table-**)**c.**, (i) (*of linen*)
nappe *f;* (ii) tapis *m* (de table); **to lay the c.**,
mettre la nappe.
clothe [klouð], *v.tr.* **(clothed** [klouðd], *rarely*
clad [klæd]) vêtir, revêtir, habiller (**in, with,**
de); **warmly clothed**, chaudement vêtu;
clothes [klouðz], *s.pl.* vêtements *mpl;* **suit of
c.**, complet *m;* costume *m;* **to put on, take off,
one's c.**, s'habiller; se déshabiller; **c. brush**,
brosse *f* à habits; **c. drier**, séchoir; **c. horse**,
séchoir *m;* **c. line**, corde *f* à (étendre le) linge; **c. peg,
c. pin**, pince *f* à linge; **'clothing**, *s.* **1.** vêtements *mpl.* **2.** **the c. trade**, l'industrie *f* du
vêtement.
cloud [klaud]. **I.** *s.* **1.** nuage *m;* **to drop from the
clouds**, tomber des nues; **to be under a c.**, être
l'objet de soupçons. **2.** nuage, voile *m* (de
fumée, de poussière, etc.). **II.** *v.* **1.** *v.tr.* couvrir,
voiler, obscurcir (le ciel); couvrir (une vitre) de
buée *f.* **2.** *v.i.* (*of sky*) **to c. over**, se couvrir, se
voiler (de nuages); s'assombrir; **'cloudburst**,
s. trombe *f* d'eau; rafale *f* de pluie; **'cloud-
capped**, *a.* couronné de nuages; **'cloudiness**,
s. aspect nuageux (du ciel); **'cloudless**, *a.* (ciel
m) sans nuages; **'cloudy**, *a.* (temps) couvert;
(ciel) nuageux, assombri.
clout [klaut]. **I.** *s. F:* claque *f,* taloche *f.* **II.** *v.tr. F:*
to c. s.o., flanquer une taloche à qn.
clove [klouv], *s.* **1.** clou *m* de girofle. **2.** *Hort:* **c.
of garlic**, gousse *f* d'ail.
cloven ['klouv(ə)n], *a.* **c.-hoofed**, au pied
fourchu, au sabot fendu.
clover ['klouvər], *s. Bot:* trèfle *m;* *F:* **to be in c.**,
être comme un coq en pâte; **c. leaf**, feuille *f* de

trèfle; *Civ. E:* **c. leaf intersection,** croisement *m* en trèfle.

clown [klaun]. **I.** *s.* bouffon *m*; clown *m* (de cirque). **II.** *v.i.* faire le clown; **'clowning,** *s.* bouffonnerie *f.*

cloy [klɔi], *v.i.* (*of food, sweets*) rassasier; écœurer; **'cloying,** *a.* rassasiant, écœurant.

club [klʌb]. **I.** *s.* **1.** (*a*) massue *f*, gourdin *m*; (*b*) *Golf:* crosse *f.* **2.** *Cards:* trèfle *m.* **3.** (*a*) club, cercle *m*; **literary c.,** cercle littéraire; (*b*) association *f*, société *f*; **youth c.,** foyer *m* des jeunes; **tennis, golf, c.,** club de tennis, de golf. **II.** *v.* (**clubbed**) **1.** *v.tr.* frapper (qn) avec une massue; matraquer qn. **2.** *v.i.* **to c. together,** (*a*) mettre ses ressources *f* en commun; (*b*) se cotiser; **'club-foot,** *s.* pied-bot *m*; **'clubhouse,** *s. Sp:* pavillon *m.*

cluck [klʌk], *v.i.* (*of hen*) glousser; **'clucking,** *s.* gloussement *m.*

clue [kluː], *s.* indication *f*, indice *m*; **to find the c. to sth.,** trouver la clef de qch.; **to give s.o. a c.,** mettre qn sur la voie, sur la piste; **the clues of a crossword puzzle,** les définitions *f*; *F:* **I haven't a c.,** je n'en sais rien, je n'ai pas la moindre idée; **'clueless,** *a. F:* **he's quite c.,** il ne sait jamais rien.

clump [klʌmp], *s.* groupe *m*, bouquet *m* (d'arbres); massif (d'arbustes, de fleurs).

clumsy ['klʌmzi], *a.* **1.** maladroit, gauche. **2.** (*of shape*) lourd, informe; **-ily,** *adv.* maladroitement, gauchement; **'clumsiness,** *s.* maladresse *f*, gaucherie *f.*

cluster ['klʌstər]. **I.** *s.* grappe *f* (de raisins); groupe *m*, bosquet *m* (d'arbres); nœud *m* (de diamants); amas *m* (d'étoiles). **II.** *v.i.* **to c. round (s.o., sth.),** se grouper, se rassembler, autour de (qn, qch.).

clutch[1] [klʌtʃ]. **I.** *s.* **1.** (*a*) **to be in, to fall into, s.o.'s clutches,** être, tomber, dans les griffes *f*, sous la patte, de qn; (*b*) **to make a c. at sth.,** tâcher de saisir qch. **2.** *Aut:* embrayage *m*; **to let in the c.,** embrayer; **to let out the c.,** débrayer; **automatic c.,** autodébrayage *m.* **II.** *v.tr. & ind. tr.* **to c. (at) sth.,** saisir qch.; s'agripper à qch.

clutch[2], *s.* couvée *f* (d'œufs).

clutter ['klʌtər]. **I.** *s.* encombrement *m*, pagaille *f*, confusion *f.* **II.** *v.tr.* **to c. (up) (a room),** encombrer (une pièce) (**with,** de).

coach [koutʃ]. **I.** *s.* **1.** (auto)car *m*; **to go on a c. tour,** faire une excursion en car; *Rail:* voiture *f*, wagon *m.* **2.** (*a*) professeur *m* qui donne des leçons particulières; (*b*) *Sp:* entraîneur *m.* **II.** *v.tr.* (*a*) donner des leçons particulières à (qn); (*b*) *Sp:* entraîner (qn).

coagulate [kou'ægjuleit], *v.tr. & i.* (*of blood*) (se) coaguler, (se) figer; (*of milk*) (se) cailler; **coagu'lation,** *s.* coagulation *f.*

coal [koul], *s.* charbon *m*; houille *f*; **live coals,** braise *f*; charbons ardents; **to haul s.o. ove the coals,** réprimander, semoncer, qn; **c merchant,** marchand *m* de charbon **'coalfield,** *s.* bassin *m* houiller; **'coalman, p -men,** *s.* livreur *m* de charbon; **'coal-mine, s** mine *f* de houille, de charbon; houillère *f* **'coal-miner,** *s.* (ouvrier *m*) mineur *m*; **'coal mining,** *s.* exploitation *f* houillère; **'coal scuttle,** *s.* seau *m* à charbon.

coalesce [kouə'les], *v.i.* s'unir; se fondr (ensemble); *Ch:* se combiner; *Pol: Ind:* (*of pa ties, firms*) (se) fusionner, (s')amalgamer.

coalition [kouə'liʃ(ə)n], *s.* coalition *f.*

coarse [kɔːs], *a.* **1.** grossier, vulgaire, rêche; **laugh,** gros rire; **c. words,** mots grossier grossièretés *f.* **2.** (*of material*) gros, grossie rude; **to have a c. skin,** avoir la peau rude; **-l** *adv.* grossièrement; **'coarseness,** *s.* grossièreté *f* (de manières, etc.); grosseur *m* fil (d'un tissu).

coast [koust]. **I.** *s.* côte *f*, rivage *m*, littoral *r* **from c. to c.,** d'une mer à l'autre. **II.** *v.i. & tr. Nau:* suivre la côte; côtoyer le rivage. **2. to down (a hill),** (i) (*on bicycle*) descendre en ro libre; (ii) *Aut:* descendre (une côte) le mote débrayé; **'coastal,** *a.* côtier; **c. navigatio** navigation côtière; cabotage *m*; **'coaster, 1.** *Nau:* caboteur *m.* **2.** *H:* dessous *m* bouteille, de verre; **'coastguard,** *s.* garde-cô *m*, *pl.* gardes-côte; **'coastline,** *s.* littoral *m.*

coat [kout]. **I.** *s.* **1.** (*a*) (*for men*) veste *f*; vest *m*; (*b*) (*for women*) manteau *m*; (*c*) **c. of arn** armoiries *fpl.* **2.** robe *f* (d'un chien, d' cheval); pelage *m* (d'un fauve). **3.** couche *f* peinture). **II.** *v.tr.* enduire (qch.) (**with,** de); revêtir, armer (un câble); *Cu:* **to c. sth. (w chocolate, etc.),** enrober, napper, qch. **'coat(-)hanger,** *s.* cintre porte-vêtements *m inv*; **'coat-hook,** *s.* patèr

coax [kouks], *v.tr.* cajoler, enjôler, câlin **'coaxing. 1.** *a.* câlin, cajoleur. **2.** *s.* cajoleri enjôlement *m.*

cobalt ['koubɔːlt], *s. Ch:* cobalt *m.*

cobber ['kɔbər], *s. F: Austr:* copain *m.*

cobble [kɔbl], *s.* **c.(-stone),** galet *m*, pavé caillou *m* (de chaussée).

cobbler ['kɔblər], *s.* cordonnier *m.*

cobra ['koubrə, 'kɔbrə], *s. Rept:* cobra *m.*

cobweb ['kɔbweb], *s.* toile *f* d'araignée.

cocaine [kou'kein], *s. Pharm:* cocaïne *f*; **c. dict,** cocaïnomane *mf.*

cock [kɔk]. **I.** *s.* **1.** (*a*) coq *m*; *P:* **old c.,** r vieux; *F:* **c. and bull story,** histoire *f* à do debout; (*b*) oiseau *m* mâle. **2.** (*a*) robinet *m Sm.a:* chien *m* (de fusil); **to go off at hal** mal démarrer. **II.** *v.tr.* **1.** **to c. one's ears,** (i *animal*) dresser les oreilles; (ii) (*of pe* dresser l'oreille; **to c. an eye at s.o.,** lancer œillade à qn. **2.** armer (un fusil); **'cock**

doodle'-doo! *int.* cocorico! '**cock-a-'hoop,**
a. to be c.-a-h., être triomphant, jubilant;
'**cock-crow,** *s.* at c.-c., au (premier) chant du
coq; à l'aube *f*; **cocked,** *a.* c. **hat,** chapeau *m* à
cornes; '**cock-'sure,** *F:* '**cocky,** *a.* sûr de soi;
suffisant.

cockade [kɔ'keid], *s.* cocarde *f*.

cockatoo [kɔkə'tu:], *s. Orn:* cacatoès *m.*

cockchafer ['kɔktʃeifər], *s. Ent:* hanneton *m.*

cockerel ['kɔk(ə)rəl], *s.* jeune coq *m.*

cock-eyed ['kɔkaid], *a. F:* 1. (qn) qui louche. 2.
de travers, de guingois.

cockle[1] ['kɔkl], *s. Moll:* bucarde *f,* clovisse *f,*
coque *f.*

cockle[2], *v.i.* se recroqueviller; (*of paper*) gondoler; (*of cloth*) goder.

cockney ['kɔkni], *a. & s.* cockney *mf,* londonien,
-ienne; c. **accent,** accent *m* populaire de
Londres.

cockpit ['kɔkpit], *s. Av:* habitacle *m*; poste *m* de
pilotage.

cockroach ['kɔkroutʃ], *s. Ent:* blatte *f*; cafard
m.

cocktail ['kɔkteil], *s.* cocktail *m*; c. **lounge,** bar
m; c. **party,** cocktail; c. **snack,** amuse-gueule
m.

cocoa ['koukou], *s.* cacao *m.*

coconut ['koukənʌt], *s.* 1. noix *f* de coco *m*; c.
shy, jeu *m* de massacre. 2. c. **palm,** cocotier *m*;
c. **matting,** (i) tapis végétal; (ii) (*doormat*)
tapis-brosse *m, pl.* tapis-brosses.

cocoon [kə'ku:n], *s. Ent:* cocon *m.*

cod [kɔd], *s. inv.* c. (**fish**), morue *f*; **salt** c., morue
salée; **dried, smoked,** c., morue sèche, fumée;
merluche *f*; (**fresh**) c., cabillaud *m*; '**cod-
fisher,** *s.* morutier *m*; '**cod-fishing,** *s.* pêche *f*
à la morue; '**cod-liver oil,** *s. Pharm:* huile *f* de
foie de morue.

coddle ['kɔdl], *v.tr.* gâter, choyer (qn); **to** c.
oneself, se dorloter.

code [koud]. I. *s.* 1. code *m*; c. **of honour,**
règles *fpl,* de l'honneur; **the Highway C.,** le
code de la route. 2. (*a*) c. **word,** mot convenu,
de passe; (*b*) (*secret*) chiffre *m*; **to write a
message in** c., chiffrer un message. II. *v.tr.*
(*a*) coder (une dépêche); (*b*) chiffrer (un
message).

codicil ['kɔdisil], *s.* codicille *m* (d'un testament).

co-director [koudai'rektər, -di-], *s.* codirecteur,
-trice; coadministrateur *m.*

co-ed ['kou'ed], *F:* 1. *a. & s.* (école *f*) mixte. 2.
s. N.Am: élève *f* d'une école mixte.

co-education ['kouedju'keiʃ(ə)n], *s.* coéduca-
tion *f*; '**co-edu'cational,** *a.* co-e. **school,** école
mixte.

coefficient [koui'fiʃənt], *s.* coefficient *m*; *Ind:* c.
of safety, facteur *m* de sécurité.

coerce [kou'ə:s], *v.tr.* forcer, contraindre (**s.o.
into doing sth.,** qn à faire qch.); **co'ercion,** *s.*

contrainte *f*.

coexist ['kouig'zist], *v.i.* coexister (**with,** avec).

coexistence ['kouig'zistəns], *s.* coexistence *f*
(**with,** avec); concomitance *f*.

coffee ['kɔfi], *s.* café *m*; c. **bar,** café; **black** c.,
café noir; (*in Switzerland*) café nature; **white**
c., café au lait, café crème; **instant** c., café
soluble; **ground** c., café moulu; c. **grounds,**
marc *m* de café; c. **cup,** tasse *f* à café; c. **mill,**
moulin *m* à café; c. **pot,** cafetière *f*.

coffin ['kɔfin], *s.* cercueil *m.*

cog [kɔg], *s. Mec:* dent *f* (d'une roue dentée);
'**cogwheel,** *s. Mec:* roue dentée.

cogent ['koudʒənt], *a.* (argument) irrésistible;
(motif) puissant; (raison) valable.

cohere [kou'hiər], *v.i.* (*a*) (*of whole, of parts*) se
tenir ensemble; adhérer; (*b*) s'agglomérer; (*c*)
(*of argument*) être conséquent; se tenir; se
suivre (logiquement); **co'herence,** *s.* 1. cohésion *f*; adhésion *f*. 2. (*of ideas, style*) suite *f*
(logique), cohésion *f*; **co'herent,** *a.* cohérent;
(*of thinker*) qui a de la suite dans les idées; -**ly,**
adv. avec cohérence.

cohesion [kou'hi:ʒ(ə)n], *s.* cohésion *f*;
adhérence *f*; **co'hesive** [-'hi:siv], *a.* cohésif.

coil [kɔil]. I. *s.* 1. rouleau *m* (de corde). 2. (*a*) pli
m, repli *m* (d'un cordage); anneau *m* (d'un
serpent); (*b*) **coils of smoke,** tourbillons *m* de
fumée. 3. *El:* enroulement *m*, bobine *f*. II. *v.* 1.
v.tr. (en)rouler (un cordage); **to** c. (**itself**) **up,** (*of
snake*) s'enrouler; (*of cat*) se mettre en rond; (*of
pers.*) se pelotonner; **coiled spring,** ressort *m* à
boudin. 2. *v.i.* serpenter.

coin [kɔin]. I. *s.* 1. pièce *f* de monnaie. 2. *coll.*
monnaie(s) *f(pl)*, espèces *fpl.* II. *v.tr.* 1. **to** c.
money, (i) frapper de la monnaie; (ii) faire des
affaires d'or. 2. inventer, forger (un mot
nouveau); '**coinage,** *s.* (*a*) système *m*
monétaire; (*b*) monnaie(s) *f(pl)*.

coincide [kouin'said], *v.i.* 1. coïncider (**with,**
avec). 2. s'accorder, être d'accord (**with,** avec);
co'incidence, *s.* coïncidence *f*; **coinci'dental,** *a.* (effet *m*) de coïncidence.

coke [kouk], *s.* coke *m.*

colander ['kʌləndər], *s. Cu:* passoire *f.*

cold [kould]. I. *a.* froid. 1. (*a*) **it's** c., il fait froid;
to grow c., se refroidir; c. **front,** front froid; c.
meat, viandes froides, assiette anglaise; *Ind:
Com:* c. **storage,** conservation *f* par le froid; c.
store, entrepôt *m* frigorifique; (*b*) **to be** c., **to
feel** c., avoir froid; **my feet are as** c. **as ice,** j'ai
les pieds glacés; *F:* **to have** c. **feet,** *P:* avoir la
frousse. 2. **a** c. **reception,** un accueil froid; **to
give s.o. the** c. **shoulder,** se montrer, être, froid
avec, envers, qn; c. **war,** guerre froide; **that
leaves me** c., cela ne me fait ni chaud ni froid;
-**ly,** *adv.* froidement. II. *s.* 1. froid *m*; **heat and**
c., le chaud et le froid; c. **wave,** vague *f* de
froid; **to leave s.o. out in the** c., laisser qn à

l'écart. **2.** *Med:* rhume *m*; **to have a c.,** être
enrhumé; **c. in the head,** rhume de cerveau; **to
catch (a) c.,** s'enrhumer; prendre froid; **they
all had colds,** ils étaient tous enrhumés; **'cold-
'blooded,** *a.* **1.** (animal) à sang froid. **2.** (*of
pers.*) froid; insensible; à sang-froid; (*of action*) prémédité; délibéré; **'cold-'hearted,** *a.*
au cœur froid, sec; **'coldness,** *s.* froideur *f*,
froidure *f* (du climat, etc.); froideur (de
caractère, d'un accueil).

collaborate [kə'læbəreit], *v.i.* collaborer (**with,**
avec); **collabo'ration,** *s.* collaboration *f*;
Hist: Pej: collaborationnisme *m*;
co'llaborator, *s.* collaborateur, -trice.

collapse [kə'læps]. **I.** *s.* **1.** écroulement *m*, effondrement *m*; débâcle *f* (d'un pays). **2.** *Med:*
affaissement subit. **II.** *v.i.* s'affaisser;
s'écrouler; s'effondrer; **co'llapsible,** *a.* pliant;
démontable; escamotable; rabattable.

collar ['kɔlər]. **I.** *s.* **1.** (*a*) col *m* (de robe); collet *m*
(de manteau); **to seize s.o. by the c.,** saisir qn
au collet; (*b*) (**attached**) **shirt c.,** col de
chemise; (**detachable**) **c.,** faux col; **size in
collars,** encolure *f*; **white-c. worker,** employé
m (de bureau); **blue-c. worker,** ouvrier manuel.
2. collier *m* (de chien). **3.** *E:* anneau *m*, collier,
collet. **II.** *v.tr. F:* pincer, mettre la main sur (qn,
qch.); **'collar-bone,** *s.* clavicule *f*.

collate [kɔ'leit], *v.tr.* collationner, comparer,
conférer (des textes); **co'llator,** *s.* celui qui
collationne des textes.

collateral [kə'læt(ə)rəl], *a. & s.* **1.** collatéral,
-aux. **2.** concomitant, additionnel; **c. security,**
garantie accessoire; **-ally,** *adv.* parallèlement.

colleague ['kɔli:g], *s.* collègue *mf*; confrère
m.

collect [kə'lekt]. **1.** *v.tr.* (*a*) rassembler (la foule);
assembler (des matériaux); **to c. the letters,**
lever les lettres; (*b*) collectionner (des timbres);
(*c*) percevoir, lever (des impôts); toucher (une
traite); **to c. a debt,** faire rentrer une créance;
abs. **to c.** (**for charity**) faire la quête (pour une
œuvre de bienfaisance); (*d*) recueillir,
rassembler (ses idées); ramasser (ses forces);
to c. oneself, se reprendre; **to c. one's thoughts,**
se recueillir; (*e*) aller chercher (ses bagages,
etc.). **2.** *v.i.* (*of people*) s'assembler, se
rassembler; (*of thgs*) s'amasser; **co'llected,** *a.*
(*a*) recueilli; (*b*) (plein) de sang-froid; **-ly,** *adv.*
(*a*) avec recueillement; (*b*) avec calme, avec
sang-froid; **co'llection,** *s.* **1.** rassemblement
m (de gens); recouvrement *m* (d'une somme);
perception *f* (des impôts); levée *f* (des lettres).
2. *Ecc: etc:* quête *f*, collecte *f*. **3.** amas *m*,
assemblage *m*. **4.** collection *f* (de timbres, etc.);
recueil *m* (de proverbes, de chansons);
co'llective, *a.* collectif; **c. farm,** ferme collective; **c. bargaining** = convention collective;
co'llector, *s.* (*a*) collectionneur, -euse

(d'objets d'art, etc.); (*b*) (**tax**) **c.,** percepteur *r*
(des contributions directes); receveur *m* (de
contributions indirectes); **ticket c.,** contrôleu
m.

college ['kɔlidʒ], *s.* collège *m*; *Sch:* = l'Unive
sité *f*; **when I was at c.,** quand j'étais à l
Faculté; **military c.,** école *f* militaire; **c.** o
education = école normale; **c.** (of secondar
education) = lycée *m*; **technical c.** = lycé
technique; **agricultural c.** = institut *i*
agronomique.

collide [kə'laid], *v.i.* se rencontrer, se heurter; **t**
c. with sth., heurter qch.; entrer en collisio
avec qch., percuter qch.

collie ['kɔli], *s.* chien *m* de berger écossais, colle
m.

colliery ['kɔljəri], *s.* houillère *f.*

collision [kə'liʒ(ə)n], *s.* collision *f*; tamponn
ment *m* (de trains); abordage *m* (de navires
head-on c., choc *m* de plein fouet.

colloquial [kə'loukwiəl], *a.* familier; de (la) co
versation; **c. French,** le français parlé; **-all**
adv. familièrement; **co'lloquialism,**
expression, tournure, familière.

collusion [kə'lu:ʒ(ə)n], *s.* collusion *f*; **to act in**
with s.o., agir de complicité avec qn.

Colombia [kə'lɔmbiə]. *Pr.n. Geog:* la Colomb
colon ['koulən], *s.* **1.** deux-points *m*. **2.** *Ana*
côlon *m*.

colonel ['kə:nl], *s.* colonel *m*; **c.'s wife,** colone
f; **Queen Elizabeth, c.-in-chief of the Lond**
Scottish, la reine Elizabeth, colone
d'honneur des London Scottish.

colonnade [kɔlə'neid], *s.* colonnade *f.*

colony ['kɔləni], *s.* colonie *f*; **co'lonial,** *a. &*
colonial, -aux; **co'lonialism** *s. P*
colonialisme *m*; **co'lonialist,** *s.* colon
colonialiste (*mf*); **'colonist,** *s.* colon *i*
coloni'zation, *s.* colonisation *f*; **'coloniz**
v.tr. coloniser.

Colorado [kɔlə'rɑ:dou]. *Pr.n. Geog:* **1.**
Colorado. **2.** *Ent:* **C. beetle,** doryphore *m*.

colossal [kə'lɔs(ə)l], *a.* colossal; démesu
-ally, *adv.* colossalement, démesurément.

colour ['kʌlər]. **I.** *s.* **1.** couleur *f*; **the c. proble**
le (problème du) racisme; **c. bar,** ségrégati
raciale; **local c.,** couleur locale. **2.** mati
colorante; pigment *m*; **water c.,** aquarelle *f*
c., couleur à l'huile, à l'essence (
térébenthine). **3.** teint *m*, couleurs; **c. sche**
l'arrangement, la disposition, des coloris;
change c., changer de visage, de couleur; pâl
high c., vivacité *f* de teint; *F:* **to be off c.,** n'ê
pas dans son assiette. **4.** *usu. pl.* couleurs (d'
parti); *Nau:* pavillon *m*; (**regimental**) **colou**
drapeau *m*; **to pass (an examination) w**
flying colours, passer haut la main; **to stick**
one's colours, rester fidèle à ses principes
show oneself in one's true colours, jeter

masque. **II.** *v.* **1.** *v.tr.* colorer, colorier. **2.** *v.i.*
rougir; **'colour-blind**, *a.* daltonien; **'colour-
blindness**, *s.* daltonisme *m*; **'coloured**, *a.* (*a*)
coloré; colorié; (*b*) (personne) de couleur;
'colourful, *a.* coloré; (style) pittoresque; **c.
landscape**, paysage éclatant; **what a c.
character!** quel type original! **'colourless**, *a.*
incolore; terne; pâle.

colt [koult], *s.* **1.** poulain *m*. **2.** *Sp:* débutant *m*,
novice *m*.

Columbia (British) ['britiʃkə'lʌmbiə]. *Pr.n.
Geog:* la Colombie britannique.

column ['kɔləm], *s.* **1.** *Arch:* colonne *f*; *Anat:*
spinal c., colonne vertébrale. **2.** *Mec: Av:* **control c.**, levier *m* de commande; **steering c.**,
colonne de direction; *Pol:* **fifth c.**, cinquième
colonne. **3.** *Journ:* **the theatrical c.**, la rubrique
des théâtres; **'columnist**, *s.* journaliste *mf*.

coma ['koumə], *s. Med:* coma *m*; **to fall into a c.**,
perdre connaissance; **'comatose**, *a.*
comateux.

omb [koum]. **I.** *s.* **1.** peigne *m*. **2.** crête *f* (de
coq). **II.** *v.tr.* peigner; **to c. one's hair**, se
peigner; **'comb 'out**, *v.tr.* (i) démêler (les
cheveux); (ii) (*of police*) ratisser (un quartier); **to
c. o. a department**, éliminer les incapables d'un
service.

ombat ['kɔmbæt]. **I.** *s.* combat *m*; **unarmed c.**,
conflit sans armes. **II.** *v.* (**combated**) **1.** *v.i.*
combattre (**with, against,** contre). **2.** *v.tr.* lutter
contre, combattre (une épidémie); **'comba-
tant**, *a. & s.* combattant, -ante; **'combative**,
a. combatif; agressif; batailleur.

ombine. I. [kəm'bain], *v.* **1.** *v.tr.* combiner;
allier (**with**, à); **to c. business with pleasure**,
joindre l'utile à l'agréable. **2.** *v.i.* (*a*) (*of people*)
s'unir, s'associer (**against,** contre); (*b*) (*of parties, firms*) (se) fusionner; (*c*) *Ch:* se combiner.
II. ['kɔmbain], *s.* **1.** *Fin:* cartel *m*, trust *m*; *Agr:*
c. harvester, moissoneuse-batteuse *f*; **com-
bi'nation**, *s.* **1.** association *f*. **2.** combinaison
f; concours *m* (de circonstances). **3.** chiffre *m*
(de la serrure d'un coffre-fort). **4.** (**motorcycle**)
c., moto(cyclette) *f* à side-car; **com'bined**, *a.*
c. efforts, efforts réunis, conjugués; *Mil: etc:* **c.
exercises**, (i) opération *f* interarmes; (ii) opération amphibie.

ombustion [kəm'bʌstʃ(ə)n], *s.* combustion *f*;
spontaneous c., inflammation spontanée; **slow
c. stove**, poêle *m* à combustion continue; **combustible. 1.** *a.* combustible. **2.** *s.* (*a*) matière *f*
nflammable; (*b*) (*fuel*) combustible *m*.

me [kʌm], *v.i.* **1.** (*p.t.* **came** [keim], *p.p.* **come**)
. venir, arriver; **he comes this way every
week**, il passe par ici tous les huit jours; **here he
omes!** le voilà qui arrive! **coming!** voilà! on y
a! j'y vais! **to c. for sth.**, venir chercher qch.;
. and see me soon, venez me voir bientôt; *F:*
e had it coming to him, ça lui pendait au nez;

F: **to c. to** (**one's senses**), (i) reprendre connaissance; (ii) recouvrer sa raison; (iii) se
ressaisir; *F:* **what are things coming to?** où
allons-nous? **c. now!** allons! voyons! **2. that
comes on page 20**, cela se trouve à la page 20;
how does the door c. to be open? comment se
fait-il que la porte soit ouverte? **3.** (*a*) **what will
c. of it?** qu'en adviendra-t-il? **that's what
comes of doing . . .**, voilà ce qui arrive quand
. . .; (*b*) **to c. of a good family**, être d'une
bonne famille. **4.** (*in shop*) **how much does it c.
to?** combien cela fait-il? **he'll never c. to much**,
il ne fera jamais grand-chose; **it comes to this**,
cela revient à ceci; **c. to that, why are you
here?** mais à propos, que fais-tu ici? **it must c.
to that**, il faudra bien en arriver là; **that doesn't
c. within my duties**, cela ne rentre pas dans
mes fonctions. **5. that comes easy to him**, cela
lui est facile; **to c. expensive**, coûter cher. **6. I
have c. to believe that . . .**, j'en suis venu à
croire que . . . . **7. the time to c.**, l'avenir *m*; **for
three months to c.**, pendant trois mois encore;
to c. undone, se défaire; **'come a'cross. 1.**
v.tr. trouver, rencontrer, (qn, qch.) sur son
chemin. **2.** *v.i. F:* se faire comprendre; faire une
impression; **'come 'after**, *v.i.* **1.** (*a*) suivre (qn,
qch.); (*b*) succéder à (qn). **2.** suivre; venir plus
tard; **'come a'long**, *v.i.* arriver, venir; **'come
'back**, *v.i.* revenir; **'come-back**, *s.* retour *m*
(en vogue, au pouvoir); **'come 'by**, *v.i.* **1.**
passer. **2.** obtenir (de l'argent); acquérir
(un objet); **'come 'clean**, *v.i. F:* avouer;
'come 'down, *v.i.* descendre; (*of rain, etc.*)
tomber; (*of prices*) baisser; **to c. d.** (**in the
world**), déchoir; **to c. d. on s.o.**, (i) semoncer
vertement qn; (ii) blâmer sévèrement qn; *F:* **to
c. d. handsomely**, se montrer généreux; **'come-
down**, *s. F:* humiliation *f*; déchéance *f*; **'come
'forward**, *v.i.* **1.** s'avancer. **2. to c. f. as a candidate**, se présenter comme candidat; **'come
'in**, *v.i.* **1.** entrer. **2.** (*of tide*) monter; (*of fashion*)
entrer en vogue. **3.** (*of funds*) rentrer. **4.** (*a*) **to c.
in handy for s.o., for sth.**, servir à qn à qch.; (*b*)
Sp: **to c. in first**, arriver premier. **5. to c. in for
sth.**, recevoir qch.; *F:* **and where do I c. in?** et
moi, quand est-ce que j'entre en jeu? **'come'into**, *v.i.* **1.** (*of ideas*) **to c. i. s.o.'s mind**, se
présenter à l'esprit de qn. **2. to c. i. a property,**
entrer en possession d'une propriété; **'come
'off**, *v.i.* **1. to c. o. a horse**, tomber de cheval; **to
c. o. the gold standard**, abandonner l'étalon or;
F: **c. o. it!** en voilà assez! allons donc! allez
raconter ça ailleurs! **2.** (*a*) (*of button, etc.*)
découdre; se détacher; sauter; (*b*) (*of event*)
avoir lieu; (*of attempt*) réussir, aboutir; (*c*) **to c.
o. badly**, s'en mal tirer; **he came off victorious**, il
en sortit vainqueur; **'come 'on**, *v.i.* (*a*)
s'avancer; (*b*) faire des progrès; (*c*) (*of winter*)
venir, arriver; (*of night*) tomber; **the rain came**

on, il s'est mis à pleuvoir; **I've got a cold coming
on,** je sens que je suis en train d'attraper un
rhume; (*d*) (*of lawsuit*) **the case comes up
tomorrow,** le procès sera entendu demain; (*e*)
Th: (*of actor*) entrer en scène; **'come'out,** *v.i.*
1. to c. o. of a place, a room, sortir d'un lieu,
quitter une salle. **2.** (*a*) *Ind:* **to c. o. (on strike),** se
mettre en grève; (*b*) *Sch:* **to c. o. first,** être reçu
premier; (*c*) (*of stars*) paraître; (*of buds*) éclore;
(*d*) (*of stain*) s'enlever, s'effacer; (*e*) (*of book*)
paraître; (*f*) (*of problem*) se résoudre; (*g*) *Phot:*
you've c. o. well, vous êtes très réussi; **'come
'over,** *v.i.* **what has c. o. you?** qu'est-ce qui vous
prend? **to c. o. funny,** se sentir mal; **'comer,** *s.*
first c., premier venu, première venue; **'come
'round,** *v.i.* (*a*) *F:* **c. r. and see me some time,**
venez me voir un de ces jours; (*b*) reprendre
connaissance; revenir à soi; (*c*) **to c. r. to s.o.'s
way of thinking,** se ranger à l'avis de qn; **'come
'under,** *v.i.* **1. to c. u. s.o.'s influence,** tomber
sous, subir, l'influence de qn. **2. to c. u. a
heading,** être compris sous un article; **'come
'up,** *v.i.* (*a*) **c. up to my room,** montez chez moi;
(*b*) **to c. up to s.o.,** s'approcher de qn; (*c*) (*of
plants*) sortir de terre; pousser; (*d*) **to c. up (for
discussion),** venir sur le tapis; (*of lawsuit*) **the
case comes up tomorrow,** le procès sera entendu demain; (*e*) **to c. up to s.o.'s expectations,**
répondre à l'attente de qn; (*f*) **he doesn't c. up to
his brother,** il n'égale pas son frère; (*g*) **to c. up
against sth., s.o.,** (i) se heurter à, contre, qch.;
(ii) entrer en conflit avec qn; (*h*) *F:* **the table
comes up well,** la table revient bien (à
l'astiquage); (i) **to c. up to the surface again,**
remonter sur l'eau; **'coming. I.** *a.* **the c. year,**
l'année qui vient, l'année prochaine; **the c.
storm,** l'orage qui approche; **an up and c. man,**
un homme d'avenir. **II.** *s.* venue *f*; arrivée *f*; approche *f*; **a lot of c. and going,** beaucoup de va-
et-vient *m*.

comedy ['kɔmədi], *s.* **1.** comédie *f*; le genre comique; **musical c.,** opérette *f*; **co'median**
[kə'mi:diən], *s.* comédien, -ienne; comique
m.

comet ['kɔmit], *s.* comète *f*.

comfort ['kʌmfət]. **I.** *s.* **1.** consolation *f*;
soulagement *m*; **to take c.,** se consoler. **2.** bien-
être *m*; **I like c.,** j'aime mes aises. **3.** confort *m*;
aisance *f*; **every modern c.,** tout le confort
moderne; **to live in c.,** vivre dans l'aisance. **II.**
v.tr. **1.** consoler, soulager (qn). **2.** redonner du
courage à (qn); **comfortable** ['kʌmftəbl], *a.*
confortable; agréable; **make yourself c.,**
mettez-vous à l'aise; **it's so c. here,** il fait si bon
ici; **c. income,** revenu suffisant; **-ably,** *adv.*
confortablement, agréablement; **to be c. off,**
avoir de quoi (vivre), être à l'aise; **'comfor-
ting,** *a.* réconfortant; **'comfortless,** *a.*
dépourvu de confort; triste; **'comfy,** *a. F:*
confortable.

comic ['kɔmik]. **1.** *a.* comique, risible; **what
a c. idea!** quelle drôle d'idée! **the c. side of a
situation,** le côté drôle d'une situation. **2.** *s.*
(*a*) *Th:* comique *m*; (*b*) journal *m* de bandes
dessinées.

comma ['kɔmə], *s.* (*a*) virgule *f*; (*b*) **inverted
commas,** guillemets *m*.

command [kə'mɑ:nd]. **I.** *s.* **1.** ordre *m*, commandement *m*; **done at s.o.'s c.,** fait sur les ordres de qn; *Th:* **C. Performance,** représentation commandée par le Souverain. **2.** *Mil:* etc
under the c. of . . ., sous le commandement *m*
. . .; **second in c.,** commandant *m* en second
3. (*a*) connaissance *f*, maîtrise *f* (d'une langue
d'un métier); (*b*) **self-c., c. over oneself**
maîtrise de soi; (*c*) **the money at my c.,** le
fonds à ma disposition. **II.** *v.tr.* **1.** ordonne
commander (**s.o. to do sth.,** à qn de faire qch.
2. commander (un régiment). **3.** avoir (qch.)
sa disposition. **4. to c. attention,** forcer l'atte
tion; **to c. respect,** inspirer le respect; **to c.
high price,** se vendre à haut prix; **comma**
dant [kɔmən'dænt], *s.* commandant *m*
comman'deer, *v.tr.* réquisitionner (qch.
co'mmander, *s. Mil:* commandant *m*; *Na*
capitaine *m* de frégate; **co'mmanding,** *a.*
(officier) commandant. **2.** (ton) d'autorité, **c**
commandement; **co'mmandment,** *s.* com
mandement (divin); **co'mmando,** *s. Mil:* com
mando *m*.

commemorate [kə'meməreit], *v.tr.* co
mémorer (qn, qch., le souvenir de qn, qch.).

commence [kə'mens], *v.tr. & i.* commencer;
c. to do sth., commencer à, de, faire qch.; **to**
operations, entamer les opération
co'mmencement, *s.* **1.** commenceme
m, début *m*. **2.** *Sch: N.Am:* = jour *m*, cé
monie *f*, de collation de diplômes univ
sitaires.

commend [kə'mend], *v.tr.* **1.** recomman
confier (qch. à qn). **2.** louer (qn de **s**
courage); **to c. s.o. for doing sth.,** approu
qn d'avoir fait qch.; **co'mmendable,**
louable; **-ably,** *adv.* d'une manière loua
commen'dation, *s.* éloge *m*; approbation

commensurate [kə'menʃərət], *a.* proportio
(**to, with,** à); **-ly,** *adv.* proportionnellement
with, à).

comment ['kɔment]. **I.** *s.* commentaire *m*;
comments, please! pas de commentaires,
vous plaît! **to call for c.,** provoquer
critiques. **II.** *v.i.* **1. to c. on a text,** comme
un texte. **2. to c. on s.o.'s behaviour,** critiq
la conduite de qn; faire des observations
qn; **'commentary,** *s.* commentaire *m*; (
ning) c., radio-reportage *m*; reportage *n*
direct; **'commentator,** *s.* commentat
-trice; *T.V:* etc: radio-reporter *m*.

commerce ['kɔməːs], s. commerce m; les affaires f; co'mmercial. 1. a. commercial; c. vehicle, camionnette f. 2. s. T.V: émission f publicitaire; co'mmercialize, v.tr. commercialiser.

commissar [kɔmi'saːr], s. commissaire m (du peuple).

commission [kə'miʃ(ə)n]. I. s. commission f. 1. Royal C., commission d'enquête (ordonnée par décret parlementaire); Mil: to get one's c., être nommé officier; to resign one's c., démissionner. 2. ordre m, mandat m; to carry out a c., s'acquitter d'une commission. 3. Nau: to put a ship into c., armer un navire; aircraft in c., avion m en service; my car is out of c., ma voiture est en panne. 4. Com: commission; pourcentage m. 5. perpétration f (d'un crime). II. v.tr. 1. nommer (un officier) à un commandement; commander (un tableau, etc.). 2. armer (un navire); co'mmission 'agent, s. courtier m; commissio'naire, s. chasseur m (d'hôtel); coursier m; co'm-missioner, s. (a) c. for oaths, solicitor qui reçoit des déclarations sous serment; (b) c. of police = commissaire m de police; co'm-missioning, s. Nau: armement m (d'un navire).

ommit [kə'mit], v.tr. (committed) 1. commettre, confier (sth. to s.o.'s care, qch. aux soins de qn). 2. to c. s.o. (to prison), envoyer qn en prison; to c. for trial, écrouer; mettre en accusation. 3. to c. oneself, se compromettre; without committing myself, sous toutes réserves. 4. commettre (un crime); co'm-mitment, s. (usu. pl.) engagement(s) m(pl); co'mmittal, s. mise f en terre (d'un cadavre); Jur: internement; c. order, mandat m de dépôt.

ommittee [kə'miti], s. comité m, commission f, conseil m; c. of management, conseil d'administration; Ind: joint production c., comité d'entreprise.

mmodious [kə'moudiəs], a. spacieux; (of flat) confortable, convenable; co'm-modiousness, s. amples dimensions f, confort m (d'une maison, d'une pièce).

mmodity [kə'mɔditi], s. marchandise f; denrée f; article m; basic commodities, produits m de base.

mmodore ['kɔmədɔːr], s. (a) Nau: chef m de division; commodore m; (b) air-c., général m de brigade (aérienne); (c) capitaine m (d'un yacht-club).

mmon ['kɔmən]. I. a. 1. commun (to, à); c. wall, mur mitoyen; c. knowledge, connaissance générale, opinion courante; the C. Market, le Marché commun. 2. (a) ordinaire; c. occurrence, chose fréquente; c. honesty, la probité la plus élémentaire; in c. use, d'usage

courant; c. name (of a plant), nom m vulgaire (d'une plante); (b) de peu de valeur; the c. people, les gens du peuple; very c. cloth, tissu m très ordinaire. 3. vulgaire; trivial; -ly, adv. communément, ordinairement; d'habitude. II. s. 1. terrain, pré, communal. 2. to have sth. in c. (with s.o.), avoir qch. en commun (avec qn); out of the c., extraordinaire; 'commoner, s. homme m, femme f, du peuple; bourgeois, -oise; 'commonplace. 1. s. lieu commun; banalité f. 2. a. banal, -als; 'commons, s. 1. le peuple; the House of C., la Chambre des Communes. 2. to be on short c., faire maigre chère; 'com-mon'sense, s. le sens commun, le bon sens; 'Commonwealth (the), s. le Commonwealth (britannique).

commotion [kə'mouʃ(ə)n], s. 1. confusion f, agitation f, commotion f. 2. troubles mpl.

communal ['kɔmjun(ə)l], a. communal, communautaire.

commune¹ ['kɔmjuːn], s. commune f.

commune² [kə'mjuːn], v.i. converser, s'entretenir (with s.o., avec qn); to c. with oneself, rentrer en soi-même.

communicate [kə'mjuːnikeit]. 1. v.tr. & i. communiquer (avec qn; faire connaître (une nouvelle à qn); to c. by letter, communiquer par lettre. 2. v.i. Ecc: communier; recevoir la communion; co'mmunicable, a. Med: contagieux, transmissible; co'mmunicant, s. Ecc: communiant, -ante; communi'cation, s. 1. communication f; Rail: c. cord, corde f de signal, d'alarme. 2. to get into c. with s.o., entrer en relations f, en communication, avec qn; co'mmunicative, a. communicatif; expansif; co'mmunion, s. 1. relations fpl, rapports mpl (with s.o., avec qn). 2. Ecc: (Holy) C., la communion; co'mmuniqué, s. communiqué m.

communism ['kɔmjunizm], s. communisme m; 'communist, s. communiste mf.

community [kə'mjuːniti], s. 1. communauté f (de biens, d'intérêts). 2. communauté (religieuse). 3. (a) the c., l'État m; le public; (b) the (European) C., la Communauté (européenne), le Marché commun; (c) c. centre, centre civique, social, de loisirs (d'une ville); c. singing, chansons populaires reprises en chœur par l'assistance.

commute [kə'mjuːt]. (a) v.tr. Jur: commuer (une peine); (b) v.i. faire un (long) trajet journalier pour se rendre à son travail; co'mmuter, s. Rail: etc: abonné, -ée; personne qui fait un (long) trajet journalier.

compact¹ ['kɔmpækt], s. convention f, pacte m, accord m.

compact². I. a. [kəm'pækt]. compact; serré, tassé. II. s. ['kɔmpækt], (a) poudrier m (de sac à main); (b) N.Am: Aut: petite voiture.

companion [kəm'pænjən], s. 1. camarade *mf*; compagnon, *f.* compagne. 2. (*a*) manuel *m*; vade-mecum *m*; **com'panionable**, *a.* d'une société agréable; **-ably**, *adv.* sociablement; **com'panionship**, *s.* (*a*) compagnie *f*; (*b*) camaraderie *f.*

company ['kʌmpəni], *s.* 1. compagnie *f*; **to keep s.o. c.**, tenir compagnie à qn; **to part c.** (**with s.o.**), se séparer (de qn). 2. assemblée *f*, compagnie; bande *f.* 3. (*associates*) compagnie, société *f*; **he's very good c.**, il est fort amusant; **avoid bad c.**, prenez garde aux mauvaises fréquentations. 4. *Com: Ind:* (i) compagnie; (ii) société; **joint stock c.**, société par actions; **limited c.**, société à responsabilité limitée; **Smith and Company** (*usu.* **and Co.**), Smith et Cie. 5. (*a*) *Th:* troupe *f*; **touring c.**, troupe en tournée; (*b*) *Nau:* **the ship's c.**, l'équipage *m.* 6. *Mil:* compagnie.

compare [kəm'pɛər]. 1. *v.tr.* comparer (**to, with**, à, avec); (**as**) **compared with**, en comparaison de; **to c. a copy with the original**, confronter une copie avec l'original; **to c. notes**, échanger ses impressions avec qn. 2. *v.i.* **he can't c. with you**, il ne vous est pas comparable; **to c. favourably with sth.**, ne le céder en rien à qch.; **comparable** ['kɔmp(ə)rəbl], *a.* comparable (**with, to**, avec, à); **-ably**, *adv.* comparablement; **com'parative**, *a.* comparatif, relatif; **he's a c. stranger**, je ne le connais guère; **c. cost**, coût relatif; **-ly**, *adv.* comparativement, par comparaison (**to**, à); relativement; **com'parison**, *s.* comparaison *f*; **c. between**, comparaison entre; **there is no c. between them**, ils ne peuvent être comparés.

compartment [kəm'pɑːtmənt], *s.* 1. compartiment *m*; **water-, air-tight c.**, compartiment étanche à l'eau, à l'air; *Rail:* **first-class c.**, compartiment de première (classe); **smoking c.**, compartiment fumeurs. 2. case *f* (d'un tiroir, etc.).

compass ['kʌmpəs], *s.* 1. (**a pair of**) **compasses**, un compas. 2. boussole *f*; compas; **pocket c.**, boussole de poche; **mariner's c.**, compas (de mer); **the points of the c.**, les aires *f* de vent; **'compass-card**, *s. Nau:* rose *f* des vents.

compassion [kəm'pæʃ(ə)n], *s.* compassion *f*; **to have c. on s.o.**, avoir de la compassion pour qn; avoir pitié de qn; **com'passionate**, *a.* compatissant (**to, towards, s.o.**, pour qn); *Mil:* **c. leave**, permission exceptionnelle (pour raisons familiales); **-ly**, *adv.* avec compassion.

compatible [kəm'pætibl], *a.* compatible (**with**, avec); **compati'bility**, *s.* compatibilité *f.*

compatriot [kəm'pætriət], *s.* compatriote *mf.*

compel [kəm'pel], *v.tr.* (**compelled**) **to c. s.o. to do sth.**, contraindre, forcer, obliger, qn à faire qch.; **he compels respect**, il impose le respect;

com'pelling, *a.* **c. force**, force compulsive; **c. curiosity**, curiosité *f* irrésistible.

compensate ['kɔmpənseit]. 1. *v.tr.* (*a*) **to c. s.o. for sth.**, dédommager qn de qch.; (*b*) rémunérer (qn); (*c*) *Mec:* compenser (un pendule, etc.). 2. *v.i.* **to c. for sth.**, (i) remplacer, racheter, qch.; (ii) compenser qch.; **com'pen'sation**, *s.* compensation *f*; dédommagement *m*; indemnisation *f*; **Workmen's C. Act**, loi *f* sur les accidents du travail; **in c.**, en revanche *f.*

compère ['kɔmpɛər]. I. *s. Rad: Th:* compère *m.* II. *v.tr.* être le compère d'(un programme).

compete [kəm'piːt], *v.i.* 1. **to c. with s.o.**, faire concurrence à qn. 2. **to c. for a prize**, concourir pour un prix; **to c. with s.o. for a prize**, disputer un prix à qn.

competent ['kɔmpitənt], *a.* 1. capable. 2. compétent; **-ly**, *adv.* 1. avec compétence. 2. d'une manière suffisante; **'competence**, *s.* 1. compétence *f*; capacité *f.* 2. attributions *fpl* (d'un fonctionnaire); **it lies beyond my c.**, c'est en dehors de mes pouvoirs. 3. suffisance *f* de moyens de vivre; **to have a bare c.**, avoir tout juste de quoi vivre.

competition [kɔmpə'tiʃ(ə)n], *s.* 1. rivalité *f*, concurrence *f.* 2. concours *m.* 3. *Com:* concurrence; **unfair c.**, concurrence déloyale; **com'petitive**, *a.* **c. spirit**, esprit *m* de concurrence; **c. prices**, prix concurrentiels; **com'petitor**, *s.* concurrent, -ente.

compile [kəm'pail], *v.tr.* compiler; dresser (un catalogue); composer (un recueil); **compi'lation**, *s.* compilation *f*; **com'piler**, *s.* compilateur, -trice.

complacent [kəm'pleis(ə)nt], *a.* content de soi-même; **c. air**, air suffisant; **-ly**, *adv.* (*a*) avec satisfaction; (*b*) avec suffisance; **com'placency**, *s.* (*a*) satisfaction *f*; (*b*) contentement *m* de soi-même; suffisance *f.*

complain [kəm'plein], *v.i.* 1. se plaindre (**of**, de; **that**, que); **I have nothing to c. of**, je n'ai pas à me plaindre. 2. porter plainte (**against s.o.**, contre qn); **com'plainer**, *s.* réclamant, -ante; mécontent, -ente; **com'plaint**, *s.* 1. grief *m*; plainte *f*; **to lodge a c. against s.o.**, porter plainte contre qn. 2. maladie *f*; mal *m.*

complement ['kɔmplimənt]. I. *s.* 1. *Navy:* effectif *m*; **full c.**, effectif complet. 2. complément. II. *v.tr.* compléter; **comple'mentary**, *a.* complémentaire.

complete [kəm'pliːt]. I. *a.* 1. (*a*) complet; entier; **the staff is c.**, le personnel est au complet; (*b*) terminé. 2. parfait, achevé; **he's a c. idiot**, c'est un parfait idiot. II. *v.tr.* 1. compléter, achever, accomplir. 2. **to c. a form**, remplir une formule; **-ly**, *adv.* complètement; **com'pleteness**, *s.* état complet, plénitude *f* (d'un succès); **com'pletion**, *s.* achèvement *m*, terminaison

near c., près d'être achevé; (*of house*) **possession on c.** (*of contract*), prise *f* de possession dès la signature du contrat.

complex ['kɔmpleks]. **1.** *a.* complexe. **2.** *s.* (*a*) **an industrial c.,** un complexe industriel; (*b*) *Psy:* complexe *m*; **inferiority c.,** complexe d'infériorité; **com'plexity,** *s.* complexité *f.*

complexion [kəm'plekʃ(ə)n], *s.* teint *m.*

complicate ['kɔmplikeit], *v.tr.* compliquer; **compli'cation,** *s.* complication *f.*

complicity [kəm'plisiti], *s.* complicité *f* (**in,** à).

compliment ['kɔmplimənt]. **I.** *s.* compliment *m*; **to send one's compliments to s.o.,** se rappeler au bon souvenir de qn. **II.** *v.tr.* complimenter, féliciter (qn) (**on sth.,** de qch.); **compli'mentary,** *a.* flatteur; **c. copy,** exemplaire envoyé à titre gracieux; **c. ticket,** billet de faveur.

comply [kəm'plai], *v.i.* **to c. with** (**sth.**), se conformer à (qch.); observer (une règle); accéder à (une demande); **com'pliance,** *s.* acquiescement *m* (**with,** à); *Pej:* (**base**) **c.,** soumission *f* (abjecte); **com'pliant,** *a.* obligeant, accommodant; souple; servile.

component [kəm'pounənt]. **1.** *a.* **c. parts,** parties constituantes; *Ind:* pièces détachées. **2.** *s.* composant *m*; partie composante; *Ind:* pièce détachée.

compose [kəm'pouz], *v.tr.* **1.** composer; **to c. music, etc.,** composer de la musique, etc. **2.** arranger, accommoder (un différend). **3.** (*a*) **to c. one's features,** se composer le visage; (*b*) **c. yourself!** calmez-vous! **com'posed,** *a.* calme, tranquille; **-ly** [kəm'pouzidli], *adv.* tranquillement; avec calme; **com'poser,** *s.* *Mus:* compositeur, -trice; **compo'sition,** *s.* **1.** composition *f*, constitution *f* (de qch.). **2.** mélange *m*, composé *m*. **3.** (*a*) *Mus:* composition; (*b*) *Sch:* dissertation *f*, rédaction *f*; narration *f*; **com'positor** [-'pɔzitər], *s.* *Typ:* compositeur *m*, typographe *m*; **com'posure,** *s.* sang-froid, *m*; calme *m.*

compost ['kɔmpɔst], *s.* compost *m*; terreau *m.*

compound ['kɔmpaund]. **I.** *a.* (*a*) composé; *Fin:* **c. interest,** intérêts composés; *Med:* **c. fracture,** fracture compliquée; (*b*) complexe; **c. addition,** addition *f* de nombres complexes. **II.** *s.* (corps *m*) composé (*m*); *Gram:* mot composé. **III.** *v.tr.* [kəm'paund]. *Jur:* **to c. a felony,** pactiser avec un crime.

comprehend [kɔmpri'hend], *v.tr.* (*a*) (*understand*) comprendre; (*b*) (*embrace*) comprendre, englober.

comprehension [kɔmpri'henʃ(ə)n], *s.* compréhension *f*; **compre'hensible,** *a.* compréhensible, intelligible; **-ibly,** *adv.* d'une manière compréhensible, intelligible; **compre'hensive,** *a.* compréhensif; **c. knowledge,** connaissances étendues; **c. school** = centre *m*

d'études secondaires, C.E.S.; **-ly,** *adv.* dans un sens très étendu; largement; **compre'hensiveness,** *s.* étendue *f*, portée *f* (d'un mot, d'une offre).

compress. I. *v.tr.* [kəm'pres]. **1.** comprimer (un gaz, etc.). **2.** condenser (un discours); concentrer (son style). **II.** *s.* ['kɔmpres]. *Med:* compresse *f*; **com'pression,** *s.* compression *f*; concentration *f* (du style); **com'pressor,** *s.* compresseur *m* (de gaz, etc.); *Const:* **c. unit,** compresseur mobile.

comprise [kəm'praiz], *v.tr.* comprendre, comporter, renfermer.

compromise ['kɔmprəmaiz]. **I.** *s.* compromis *m*; **to agree to a c.,** transiger. **II.** *v.* **1.** *v.tr.* compromettre. **2.** *v.i.* compromettre, transiger; **'compromising,** *a.* compromettant.

compulsion [kəm'pʌlʃ(ə)n], *s.* contrainte *f*; **under c.,** par contrainte; **com'pulsive,** *a.* **c. thinking,** pensée obsédante; **c. smoker, gambler,** fumeur, -euse, joueur, -euse, chronique; **com'pulsory,** *a.* obligatoire; **-rily,** *adv.* obligatoirement.

compunction [kəm'pʌŋ(k)ʃ(ə)n], *s.* componction *f*; remords *m*; **without c.,** sans scrupule.

compute [kəm'pju:t], *v.tr.* computer, calculer, estimer; **compu'tation,** *s.* calcul *m*, estimation *f*; **beyond c.,** incalculable; **com'puter,** *s.* ordinateur *m.*

comrade ['kɔmreid], *s.* camarade *m*, compagnon *m*; **'comradeship,** *s.* camaraderie *f.*

con [kɔn]. *F:* **I.** *s.* déception *f*, duperie *f.* **II.** *v.tr.* escroquer; **I've been conned,** on m'a eu.

concave ['kɔnkeiv], *a.* concave.

conceal [kən'si:l], *v.tr.* cacher; dissimuler (la vérité, etc.); tenir secret (un projet); **to c. sth. from s.o.,** cacher qch. à qn; taire qch. à qn; **con'cealed,** *a.* caché, dissimulé; **c. turning,** virage masqué; **c. lighting,** éclairage indirect; **con'cealment,** *s.* dissimulation *f* (de la vérité); action *f* de cacher (qch.), de se cacher; **to keep s.o. in c.,** tenir qn caché.

concede [kən'si:d], *v.tr.* concéder; **to c. that one is wrong,** admettre que l'on a tort.

conceit [kən'si:t], *s.* vanité *f*, suffisance *f*; **con'ceited,** *a.* suffisant, vaniteux, **-ly,** *adv.* avec suffisance.

conceive [kən'si:v], *v.tr.* **1.** concevoir (un enfant, un projet). **2.** *v.i.* **to c. of sth.,** (s')imaginer, comprendre, qch.; **con'ceivable,** *a.* concevable, imaginable.

concentrate ['kɔnsəntreit]. **I.** *v.* **1.** *v.tr.* concentrer. **2.** *v.i.* (*a*) se concentrer; (*b*) **to c. on sth.,** concentrer son attention sur qch. **II.** *s.* concentré *m*; **tomato c.,** concentré de tomate; **concen'tration,** *s.* **1.** concentration *f*; **power of c.,** faculté *f* de concentration, d'application. **2.** *Mil:* concentration (de troupes, etc.); *Pol:* **c. camp,** camp *m* de concentration.

concentric |kɔn'sentrik|, *a.* concentrique.

concept |'kɔnsept|, *s.* concept *m*; idée générale; notion; **con'ception,** *s.* conception *f* (d'un enfant, d'une idée).

concern |kən'sɜːn|. **I.** *s.* **1.** intérêt *m* **(in,** dans); **it's no c. of mine,** cela ne me regarde pas, ce n'est pas mon affaire. **2.** souci *m*, anxiété *f*, inquiétude *f* **(about,** à l'égard de); **to show deep c. about sth., s.o.,** se montrer très inquiet de qch., au sujet de qn. **3.** *(a) Com:* entreprise *f*; fonds *m* de commerce; **his factory's a very big c.,** sa fabrique est une grosse affaire; *(b) F:* machin *m*, truc *m*. **II.** *v.tr.* **1.** *(a)* concerner, regarder, intéresser (qn, qch.); **that does not c. me,** cela ne me regarde pas; **it concerns him to know . . .,** il lui importe de savoir . . .; **as far as I'm concerned . . .,** en ce qui me concerne . . ., quant à moi . . .; *(b)* **to c. oneself with sth.,** s'intéresser à, s'occuper de, se mêler de, qch. **2.** *(a)* **his honour is concerned,** il s'agit de son honneur; **the persons concerned,** les intéressés; *(b)* **to be concerned about s.o., sth.,** s'inquiéter, être inquiet, de qn, de qch.; **he looked very much concerned,** il avait l'air très soucieux.

concert |'kɔnsət|, *s.* **1.** concert *m*, accord *m*; **to act in c. (with s.o.),** agir de concert (avec qn). **2.** *Mus:* concert; séance musicale; **con'certed,** *a.* **c. action,** action concertée; **'concert-hall,** *s.* salle *f* de concert.

concertina |kɔnsə'tiːnə|, *s. Mus:* accordéon hexagonal.

concerto, *pl.* **-os** |kən'tʃəːtou, -'tʃɛət, -ouz|, *s.* concerto *m*.

concession |kən'seʃ(ə)n|, *s.* concession *f* (de terrain, d'opinion); **mining c.,** concession minière; *Com:* réduction *f* (de prix).

conciliate |kən'silieit|, *v.tr.* concilier, réconcilier (des intérêts opposés); **concili'ation,** *s.* conciliation *f*; **c. board,** conseil *m* d'arbitrage; **con'ciliator,** *s.* conciliateur, -trice; **con-'ciliatory,** *a.* conciliant; conciliatoire.

concise |kən'sais|, *a.* concis; **-ly,** *adv.* avec concision; **con'ciseness,** *s.* concision *f*.

conclave |'kɔnkleiv|, *s. Ecc:* conclave *m*; assemblée *f*, réunion *f*.

conclude |kən'kluːd|, *v.tr. & i.* **1.** conclure; arranger, régler (une affaire). **2.** terminer, conclure, achever. **3. from this I c. that . . .,** de ceci je conclus que . . .; **con'cluding,** *a.* **c. (chapter, etc.),** (chapitre, etc.) final; **con'clusion,** *s.* **1.** conclusion *f* (d'un traité). **2.** fin *f*, conclusion (d'une lettre); **in c.,** pour conclure. **3. to come to the c. that . . .,** conclure que . . .; **it's a foregone c.,** c'est prévu; **con-'clusive,** *a.* concluant, décisif; *(of test)* probant; **-ly,** *adv.* d'une manière concluante, probante.

concoct |kən'kɔkt|, *v.tr.* **1.** composer; confec-

tionner (un plat). **2.** imaginer; combiner, machiner (un plan, un complot); **con'coction,** *s.* conception *f* (d'un plan); *F:* boisson *f*, plat *m* (de sa propre composition); **c. of lies,** tissu *m* de mensonges.

concord |'kɔnkɔːd|, *s.* concorde *f*, harmonie *f*, paix *f*, entente *f*.

concourse |'kɔnkɔːs|, *s.* *(a)* foule *f* (de personnes); *(b) N.Am:* hall *m* (degare).

concrete |'kɔnkriːt|. **I.** *a.* concret, -ète; **c. proposal,** proposition *f* pratique. **II.** *s.* béton *m*; **reinforced c.,** béton armé; **c. work,** bétonnage *m*; **'concrete(-)mixer,** *s.* bétonnière *f*.

concur |kən'kəːr|, *v.i.* **(concurred)** **1.** *(of events)* coïncider. **2.** être d'accord **(with s.o.,** avec qn) **concurrence** |kən'kʌrəns|, *s.* **1.** concours *m* (de circonstances); coopération *f* (de personnes). **2.** *(of pers.)* accord *m*; approbation *f*. **concurrent** |kən'kʌrənt|, *a.* concourant simultané; coexistant; **-ly,** *adv.* concurremment **(with,** avec); *Jur:* **the two sentences to run c.,** avec confusion des deux peines.

concussion |kən'kʌʃ(ə)n|, *s. Med:* commotion (cérébrale).

condemn |kən'dem|, *v.tr.* **1.** condamner; **to c. (c criminal) to death,** condamner (un criminel) à mort. **2. to c. stores,** réformer du matériel. **3** déclarer (qn) coupable. **4.** censurer, blâmer **condem'nation,** *s.* condamnation *f*; censure *f*, blâme *m*.

condense |kən'dens|. **1.** *v.tr.* condenser; serrer (son style); concentrer (un produit). **2.** *v.i.* condenser: **conden'sation,** *s.* condensation *f*; **con'densed,** *a.* condensé; **c. milk,** lait condensé, concentré; **con'denser,** *s.* **1.** *E:* condenseur *m*. **2.** *El:* condensateur *m*.

condescend |kɔndi'send|, *v.i.* condescendre faire qch.); **conde'scending,** *a.* condescendant; **to be c.,** se montrer condescendant (s.o.,** envers qn); **-ly,** *adv.* avec condescendance; **to treat s.o. c.,** traiter qn de haut en bas **conde'scension,** *s.* condescendance *f* (t envers, pour (qn)).

condiment |'kɔndimənt|, *s.* condiment *m* assaisonnement *m*.

condition |kən'diʃ(ə)n|. **I.** *s.* condition *f*. **1.** *on c. that,** à condition que, de; **on c. that we g home early,** à condition de rentrer tôt; à condition que nous rentrions de bonne heure. *(a)* état *m*, situation *f*; **to keep oneself in c.,** maintenir en forme; **to be in good c.,** être bonne forme; **factory working condition,** conditions de travail à l'usine; *(b)* état civil; *Meteor:* **weather conditions,** conditions atmosphériques. **II.** *v.tr.* conditionner (la soie laine, l'air, etc.); **con'ditional,** *a. & s.* conditionnel *(m)*; **-ally,** *adv.* conditionnellement sous certaines conditions; **con'ditioner,** **(air-)c.,** climatiseur *m*.

condole [kən'doul], *v.i.* **to c. with s.o.**, exprimer ses condoléances à qn; **con'dolence**, *s.* condoléances *fpl.*

condone [kən'doun], *v.tr.* trouver des excuses pour (qch.); pardonner (une action); racheter (des défaillances).

conduce [kən'dju:s], *v.i.* contribuer, tendre (**to,** à); **con'ducive**, *a.* favorable (**to,** à).

conduct. I. *s.* ['kɔndʌkt], conduite *f*; **c. of affairs**, conduite, gestion *f*, des affaires; manière *f* de se conduire. **II.** *v.tr.* [kən'dʌkt]. **1.** conduire; **conducted tours**, excursions accompagnées; vacances *f* en groupe. **2.** mener, gérer (des affaires); diriger (un orchestre). **3.** *Ph:* être conducteur de (la chaleur, etc.); **con'duction**, *s. Ph:* conduction *f*, transmission *f* (de la chaleur, etc.); **con'ductor**, *s.* **1.** (*a*) chef *m* d'orchestre; (*b*) (*f.* **conductress**) receveur, -euse (d'autobus); *Rail: N.Am:* chef *m* de train. **2.** *Ph:* conducteur (de la chaleur, de l'électricité).

:one [koun], *s.* **1.** cône *m*; **truncated c.**, tronc *m* de cône, cône tronqué; *Mil:* **nose c.** (**of rocket**), ogive *f* (de fusée); **ice-cream c.**, cornet *m* de crème glacée. **2.** *Bot:* pomme *f*, cône (de pin, de houblon); **'cone-bearing**, *a. Bot:* conifère; **'cone-shaped**, *a.* conique.

:onfab ['kɔnfæb], *s. F:* causerie *f*.

:onfectionery [kən'fekʃən(ə)ri], *s.* confiserie *f*; pâtisserie *f*; **con'fectioner**, *s.* confiseur *m*; **baker and c.**, boulanger-pâtissier *m*.

⸱onfederate. I. *v.* [kən'fedəreit] **1.** *v.tr.* confédérer (des États). **2.** *v.i.* (*a*) se confédérer (**with,** avec); (*b*) conspirer (**against,** contre). **II.** [kən'fedərət]. **1.** *a.* confédéré (**with,** avec). **2.** *s.* (*a*) confédéré *m*; (*b*) *Jur:* complice *mf*; **con'federacy**, *s.*, **confede'ration**, *s.* confédération *f*.

⸱onfer [kən'fə:r], *v.* (**conferred**) **1.** *v.tr.* conférer; **to c. a favour on s.o.**, accorder une faveur à qn. **2.** *v.i.* conférer, entrer en consultation; **'conference** ['kɔnfərəns], *s.* **1.** entretien *m*, consultation *f*; **press c.**, conférence *f* de presse. **2.** congrès *m*.

⸱onfess [kən'fes], *v.tr.* **1.** (*a*) confesser, avouer (une faute); (*b*) *abs.* faire des aveux; (*c*) *v.ind.tr.* **to c. to a crime**, avouer un crime. **2.** *Ecc:* (*a*) **to c.** (**oneself**), se confesser; (*b*) confesser (un pénitent); **con'fession**, *s.* **1.** confession *f*, aveu *m*. **2.** *Ecc:* **to go to c.**, aller à confesse *f*; **to make one's c.**, faire sa confession, se confesser; **con'fessional. 1.** *a.* confessionnel. **2.** *s. Ecc:* confessional *m*; **con'fessor**, *s.* confesseur *m*.

⸱onfetti [kən'feti(:)], *s.* confetti *m*.

⸱onfide [kən'faid]. **1.** *v.tr.* confier; **to c. sth. to s.o.'s care**, confier qch. à la garde de qn. **2.** *v.i.* **to c. in s.o.**, se confier à qn; **'confidence**, *s.* **1.** (*a*) confiance *f* (**in s.o.,** sth., en qn, qch.); (*b*)

assurance *f*, confiance, hardiesse *f*. **2.** confidence *f*; **in strict c.**, à titre essentiellement confidentiel. **3. c. trick**, *N.Am:* **c. game**, vol *m* à l'américaine; **'confident**, *a.* assuré; **c. of success**, sûr de réussir; **-ly,** *adv.* **1.** avec confiance. **2.** avec assurance; **confi'dential**, *a.* confidentiel; **c. clerk**, homme *m* de confiance; **c. secretary**, secrétaire particulier, -ière; **-ally,** *adv.* confidentiellement; à titre confidentiel; **con'fiding**, *a.* (*of pers.*) confiant; sans soupçons.

confine [kən'fain], *v.tr.* (*a*) (r)enfermer, emprisonner (qn); **to be confined to bed**, être alité; être obligé de garder le lit; (*b*) **to c. oneself to doing sth.**, se borner à faire qch.; **to c. oneself to facts**, s'en tenir aux faits; (*c*) **confined space**, espace resserré, restreint; **con'finement**, *s.* (*a*) emprisonnement *m*; réclusion *f*; **to be in solitary c.**, être au secret; (*b*) (*of woman*) couches *fpl*, accouchement *m*.

confirm [kən'fə:m], *v.tr.* **1.** (r)affermir (son pouvoir); fortifier (une résolution); confirmer (qn dans une opinion). **2.** confirmer (un traité); ratifier (un prix). **3.** confirmer, corroborer (une nouvelle); **confirming my letter**, en confirmation *f* de ma lettre. **4.** *Ecc:* confirmer; **to be confirmed**, recevoir la confirmation; **con'fir'mation**, *s.* **1.** (r)affermissement *m* (de l'autorité de qn); confirmation *f* (d'un traité, d'une nouvelle). **2.** *Ecc:* confirmation *f*; **con'firmed**, *a.* (fumeur) invétéré; (ivrogne *m*) incorrigible; (célibataire) endurci.

confiscate ['kɔnfiskeit], *v.tr.* confisquer; **con'fis'cation**, *s.* confiscation *f*.

conflagration [kɔnflə'greiʃ(ə)n], *s.* conflagration *f*.

conflict. I. *s.* ['kɔnflikt], conflit *m*, lutte *f*. **II.** *v.i.* [kən'flikt], être en conflit, en contradiction (**with s.o.**, avec qn); **con'flicting**, *a.* incompatible (**with,** à); opposé (**with,** à); **c. evidence**, témoignages discordants.

confluence ['kɔnfluəns], *s. Geog:* confluent *m*.

conform [kən'fɔ:m], *v.i.* se conformer (**to, with,** à); **to c. to fashion**, suivre la mode; **to c. to the law**, obéir aux lois; **con'formable**, *a.* conforme (**to,** à); **-ably,** *adv.* conformément (**to,** à); **con'formity**, *s.* conformité (**to, with,** à).

conformation [kɔnfə'meiʃ(ə)n, -fɔ:'m-], *s.* conformation *f*, structure *f*.

confound [kən'faund], *v.tr.* **1.** confondre, troubler, renverser. **2.** *F:* **c. you!** au diable! **c. it!** zut!

confront [kən'frʌnt], *v.tr.* **1.** affronter, faire face à (un danger, etc.). **2. to c. s.o. with witnesses**, confronter qn avec des témoins.

confrontation [kɔnfrʌn'teiʃ(ə)n], *s.* **1.** confrontation *f* (de témoins, etc.). **2.** affrontement *m*.

confuse [kən'fju:z], *v.tr.* **1.** mêler, brouiller. **2. to c. sth. with sth.**, confondre qch. avec qch. **3.** (*a*) embrouiller (qn); **to get confused,** s'embrouiller; (b) bouleverser, troubler (qn); **to get confused,** se troubler; **con'fused,** a. (a) embrouillé; (b) bouleversé; ahuri; (c) confus; **-ly** [-zidli], adv. confusément; d'un air confus; **con'fusing,** a. embrouillant; déroutant; **it is very c.,** on s'y perd; **con'fusion,** s. confusion f; désordre m.

congeal [kən'dʒi:l]. 1. v.tr. congeler, geler. 2. v.i. (a) se congeler; geler; (b) (of blood, oil) se figer.

congenial [kən'dʒi:niəl], a. (a) **we have c.** tastes, nous avons des goûts en commun; (b) **c. spirit,** esprit sympathique, aimable; **c. employment,** travail agréable; **-ally,** adv. agréablement.

congenital [kən'dʒenitl], a. congénital; **c. idiot,** (i) idiot, -ote, de naissance; (ii) F: parfait idiot.

conger ['kɔŋgər], s. Ich: **c.**(-eel), congre m.

congest [kən'dʒest]. 1. v.tr. (a) Med: congestionner; (b) encombrer, embouteiller (la circulation, les rues). 2. v.i. Med: se congestionner; **con'gested,** a. 1. Med: congestionné. 2. encombré, embouteillé; (of traffic) **to become c.,** s'embouteiller; **c. area,** région surpeuplée; **con'gestion,** s. 1. Med: congestion f. 2. encombrement m (de rue, de circulation); surpeuplement m.

conglomeration [kəngləmə'reiʃ(ə)n], s. conglomération f.

congratulate [kən'grætjuleit], v.tr. féliciter (qn de qch.); **congratu'lation,** s. (usu. pl.), félicitation(s) f(pl).

congregate ['kɔŋgrigeit], v.i. se rassembler, s'assembler; **the swallows are congregating,** les hirondelles se rassemblent; **congre'gation,** s. (in church) assistance f.

congress ['kɔŋgres], s. 1. réunion f (de travail). 2. congrès m; N.Am: session f du Congrès; Pol: **Trades Union C.** = Confédération Générale du Travail.

conical ['kɔnikl], a. conique.

conifer ['kɔnifər], s. Bot: conifère m; **coniferous** [kə'nifərəs], a. Bot: conifère.

conjectural [kən'dʒektʃərəl], a. conjectural.

conjecture [kən'dʒektʃər]. I. s. conjecture f, supposition f; présomption f; **to hazard a c.,** risquer une hypothèse. II. v.tr. conjecturer, supposer; soupçonner.

conjugate ['kɔn(d)ʒugeit], v.tr. conjuguer (un verbe); **conju'gation,** s. conjugaison f.

conjunction [kən'dʒʌŋ(k)ʃ(ə)n], s. conjonction f; **in c. with s.o.,** de concert avec qn.

conjunctivitis [kən(d)ʒʌŋ(k)ti'vaitis], s. Med: conjonctivite f.

conjuncture [kən'dʒʌŋ(k)tʃər], s. conjoncture f, circonstance f, occasion f.

conjure ['kʌndʒər], (a) v.tr. **to c. up,** évoquer (qch.); **a name to c. with,** un nom tout-puissant; (b) v.i. faire des tours de passe-passe; **'conjuring,** s. prestidigitation f; **'conjuror,**

s. prestidigitateur m.

conker ['kɔŋkər], s. F: marron m d'Inde.

connect [kə'nekt]. 1. v.tr. (a) (re)lier, (ré)unir, rattacher, joindre (**with, to,** à); **connected by telephone,** relié par téléphone; El: **connected to the mains,** branché sur le secteur; (b) associer (**sth. with sth.,** qch. avec, à, qch.); (c) **to be connected with a family,** être allié à, avec, une famille. 2. v.i. se lier, se relier, se joindre, se réunir; Rail: etc: **to c. with (a train),** faire correspondance avec (un train); **co'nnected,** a. 1. (a) **c. speech,** discours suivi; (b) **two closely c. trades,** deux métiers connexes. 2. **to be well connected,** être bien apparenté; **co'nnection,** s. 1. rapport m, liaison f (des choses); connexion f, suite f (des idées); **in c. with . . .,** à propos de . . .; **in this c.,** à ce propos; **in another c.,** d'autre part. 2. **to form a c. with s.o.,** établir des rapports, des relations f, avec qn. 3. parenté f; liens mpl de famille; **he's a c. of mine,** c'est un de mes parents. 4. Rail: correspondance f. 5. Mec.E: connexion f, assemblage m; P.T.T: **wrong c.,** fausse communication. 6. (a) raccord m; (b) El: contac[t] m; prise f de courant.

connive [kə'naiv], v.i. **to c. at an abuse,** tolérer fermer les yeux sur un abus; **co'nnivance,** s [.] connivence f; complicité f; **to do sth. wit[h]** s.o.'s c., faire qch. d'intelligence avec qn.

connoisseur [kɔnə'sə:r], s. connaisseur m, [f], occ. -euse.

conquer ['kɔŋkər], v.tr. conquérir; vaincre '**conquering,** a. conquérant; victorieux; th[e] **c. hero,** le héros triomphant; **'conqueror,** [s] conquérant m (d'un pays); vainqueur m.

conquest ['kɔŋkwest], s. conquête f.

conscience ['kɔnʃəns], s. conscience f; **to have [a]** clear, an easy, c., avoir la conscience nett[e] tranquille; **to be c.-stricken,** être pris d[e] remords; **for c. sake,** par acquit m de con[science]; **to have a guilty c.,** avoir mauvais[e] conscience; **consci'entious,** a. conscien[-]cieux; **c. objector,** objecteur m de conscienc[e] **-ly,** adv. consciencieusement; **consci'en[-]tiousness,** s. conscience f; droiture f.

conscious ['kɔnʃəs], a. 1. (a) **to be c. of st[h]** avoir conscience de qch.; **to become c. of st[h]** s'apercevoir de qch.; (b) **c. movement,** mouv[e-] ment conscient. 2. **to be c.,** avoir sa co[n-] naissance; **-ly,** adv. consciemmen[t] '**consciousness,** s. 1. conscience f, sentime[nt] m (**of,** de). 2. **to lose c.,** perdre connaissance, s'évanouir; **to regain c.,** revenir à soi.

conscript. I. v.tr. [kən'skript], enrôler, engag[e] II. s. ['kɔnskript], conscrit m; **con'scriptio[n]** s. conscription f.

consecrate ['kɔnsikreit], v.tr. consacrer; bé[n-] **to c. one's life to a work,** vouer sa vie, se vou[e] à un travail; **conse'cration,** s. 1. consécr[a-] tion *f*; sacre *m* (d'un roi). **2. the c. of a whole life,** le dévouement d'une vie entière.

consecutive [kən'sekjutiv], *a.* consécutif; **on three c. days,** trois jours de suite; **-ly,** *adv.* consécutivement.

consensus [kən'sensəs], *s.* **1.** consensus *m*, unanimité *f*, accord *m*.

consent [kən'sent]. **I.** *v.i.* consentir; **I c.,** j'y consens; je veux bien. **II.** *s.* consentement *m*; assentiment *m*; **by common c.,** d'une commune voix, d'un commun accord.

consequence ['kɔnsikwəns], *s.* **1.** conséquence *f*; suites *fpl*; **in c.,** par conséquent; **in c. of** . . ., par suite de . . .. **2.** importance *f*; conséquence; **it's of no c.,** cela ne fait rien; **'consequent,** *a.* **c. upon,** résultant de; **-ly,** *adv.* & *conj.* par conséquent; conséquemment; **conse'quential,** *a.* **1.** conséquent, consécutif **(to,** à). **2.** (*of pers.*) suffisant; plein d'importance.

conserve [kən'sə:v], *v.tr.* conserver, préserver; **conser'vation,** *s.* conservation *f*, protection *f*; **con'servative.** **1.** *a.* **at a c. estimate,** au bas mot. **2.** *a.* & *s. Pol:* conservateur, -trice; **con'servatory,** *s.* **1.** *Hort:* serre *f*. **2.** conservatoire *m* (de musique).

consider [kən'sidər], *v.tr.* **1.** (*a*) considérer (une question); envisager (une possibilité); **I will c. it,** j'y réfléchirai; **considered opinion,** opinion réfléchie; **all things considered,** (toute) réflexion faite; (*b*) prendre (une offre) en considération; étudier, examiner (une proposition). **2. to c. s.o.'s feelings,** ménager qn; **to c. the expense,** regarder à la dépense. **3. I c. him crazy,** je le considère comme fou; **c. it done,** tenez-le pour fait; **to c. oneself happy,** s'estimer heureux; **we c. that he ought to do it,** à notre avis il doit le faire; **con'siderable,** *a.* considérable; **-ably,** *adv.* considérablement; **con'siderate,** *a.* prévenant, plein d'égards **(towards s.o.,** pour, envers, qn); **-ly,** *adv.* avec égards, avec prévenance; **conside'ration,** *s.* **1.** considération *f*; **to take sth. into c.,** tenir compte de qch.; **question under c.,** question *f* à l'examen, à l'étude. **2.** importance *f*; **money is no c.,** l'argent n'entre pas en ligne de compte; **con'sidering,** *prep.* **c. his age,** étant donné son âge; **c. the circumstances,** vu les circonstances; *F:* **it's not so bad c.,** somme toute ce n'est pas si mal.

consignee [kɔnsai'ni:], *s.* consignataire *m*.

consignment [kən'sainmənt], *s.* **1.** envoi *m*, expédition *f* (de marchandises). **2.** (*goods sent*) envoi, arrivage *m* (de marchandises).

consist [kən'sist], *v.i.* **to c. of sth.,** consister en, dans, se composer de, qch.

consistent [kən'sistənt], *a.* **1.** (*of pers.*) conséquent; logique; **ideas that are not c.,** idées qui ne se tiennent pas. **2.** compatible, d'accord

(with, avec); **-ly,** *adv.* **1.** avec logique. **2.** conformément **(with,** à); **con'sistency,** *s.* **1.** consistance *f*. **2.** uniformité *f* (de conduite).

console [kən'soul], *v.tr.* consoler (**s.o. for a loss,** qn d'une perte); **conso'lation,** *s.* consolation *f*; **con'soling,** *a.* consolant; consolateur, -trice.

consolidate [kən'sɔlideit], *v.tr.* consolider, (r)affermir; **consoli'dation,** *s.* consolidation *f*, (r)affermissement *m*.

consonant ['kɔnsənənt], *s. Ling:* consonne *f*.

consort. I. *s.* ['kɔnsɔ:t] époux, -ouse; **prince c.,** prince consort. **II.** *v.i.* [kən'sɔ:t], frayer avec (qn); fréquenter (qn).

consortium [kən'sɔ:tjəm], *s. Fin: Com:* consortium *m*; groupe *m* d'entreprises.

conspicuous [kən'spikjuəs], *a.* **1.** manifeste; **in a c. position,** bien en évidence; **to be c.,** attirer les regards. **2.** frappant, marquant; **to make oneself c.,** se faire remarquer; **c. gallantry,** bravoure insigne; **-ly,** *adv.* manifestement; bien en évidence.

conspiracy [kən'spirəsi], *s.* conspiration *f*, conjuration *f*; **con'spirator,** *s.* conspirateur, -trice; conjure, -ée.

conspire [kən'spaiər]. **1.** *v.i.* conspirer **(against,** contre); **to c. to do sth.,** complater de faire qch. **2.** (*of events, etc.*) contribuer, concourir; **everything conspired to make him late,** tout a contribué à le mettre en retard.

constable ['kʌnstəbl], *s.* agent *m* de police; *approx.* = gendarme *m*; **constabulary** [kən'stæbjuləri], *s. coll.* la police.

constant ['kɔnstənt], *a.* (*a*) constant; stable; invariable; (*b*) (bruit) incessant, continuel; (*c*) (ami) loyal, fidèle; **-ly,** *adv.* constamment, continuellement; **'constancy,** constance *f*.

constellation [kɔnstə'leiʃ(ə)n], *s.* constellation *f*.

consternation [kɔnstə'neiʃ(ə)n], *s.* consternation *f*; atterrement *m*; **to look at each other in c.,** se regarder atterrés.

constipated ['kɔnstipeitid], *a. Med:* constipé; **consti'pation,** *s.* constipation *f*.

constituent [kən'stitjuənt]. **1.** *a.* constituant, constitutif. **2.** *s.* élément constitutif; composant *m*. **3.** *s.pl.* mandants *m* (d'un député); électeurs *m*; **con'stituency,** *s.* circonscription électorale.

constitute ['kɔnstitju:t], *v.tr.* constituer; **consti'tution,** *s.* **1.** constitution *f*, composition *f*. **2.** *Pol:* constitution (d'un État); **con'stitutional,** *a.* constitutionnel; **-ally,** *adv.* **1.** constitutionnellement. **2.** par tempérament.

constrained [kən'streind], *a.* (sourire) forcé; (air) gêné; **con'straint,** *s.* **1.** contrainte *f*; **to put s.o. under c.,** retenir qn de force. **2.** gêne *f*, contrainte; retenue *f*.

constrict [kən'strikt], *v.tr.* resserrer, étrangler; **con'striction,** *s.* resserrement *m*, étranglement *m*.

construct [kən'strʌkt], *v.tr.* construire; bâtir; **con'struction**, *s.* 1. construction *f*, édifice *m*, bâtiment *m*; **under c., in course of c.,** en construction. 2. *Gram:* construction (de la phrase); **to put a wrong c. on sth.,** mal interpréter qch.; interpréter, entendre, qch. de travers; interpréter, entendre, qch. de travers; **con'structive,** *a.* constructif; (esprit) créateur; **con'structor,** *s.* constructeur *m*.

consul ['kɔns(ə)l], *s.* consul *m*; **the French c.,** le consul de France; **'consular,** *a.* consulaire; **'consulate,** *s.* consulat *m*; **C. General,** consulat général; **the French C.,** le consulat de France.

consult [kən'sʌlt]. 1. *v.tr.* (*a*) consulter (qn sur qch.); (*b*) **to c. one's own interests,** consulter ses intérêts. 2. *v.i.* consulter (avec qn); **to c. together,** délibérer; se consulter; **con'sultant,** *s.* médecin consultant, chirurgien consultant; expert *m* conseil; **consul'tation,** *s.* consultation *f*; **con'sultative,** *a.* consultatif; **con'sulting,** *a.* **c. engineer,** ingénieur *m* conseil; **c. hours, c. room,** heures *f*, cabinet *m*, de consultation.

consume [kən'sju:m], *v.tr.* (*a*) (*of fire*) consumer, dévorer; (*b*) consommer (des vivres); **con'sumer,** *s.* consommateur, -trice; **c. goods,** biens *m* de consommation.

consummate¹ [kən'sʌmət], *a.* (artiste) consommé, achevé; **to be a c. master of a craft,** être passé maître d'un métier; **c. liar,** menteur achevé.

consummate² ['kɔnsəmeit], *v.tr.* consommer (un mariage, un sacrifice); **consu'mmation,** *s.* 1. consommation *f* (d'un mariage). 2. perfection *f* (d'un art). 3. fin *f*; but *m*; comble *f* (d'une belle vie).

consumption [kən'sʌm(p)ʃ(ə)n], *s.* 1. consommation *f*. 2. *Med:* phtisie *f*; tuberculose *f*.

contact ['kɔntækt]. I. *s.* contact *m*; **to be in c. with s.o.,** être en rapport avec qn; **c. lens,** verre *m*, lentille *f*, de contact. II. *v.tr.* contacter, se mettre en rapport avec (qn).

contagion [kən'teidʒ(ə)n], *s.* contagion *f*; **con'tagious,** *a.* contagieux.

contain [kən'tein], *v.tr.* 1. (*a*) contenir; (*b*) (*comprise, include*) contenir, renfermer; comprendre, comporter; **to c. the latest improvements,** comporter les derniers perfectionnements. 2. (*restrain*) contenir, maîtriser (son indignation); **con'tainer,** *s.* récipient *m*, contenant *m*; réservoir *m*; *El:* bac *m* (d'accumulateur); *Com:* boîte *f*; *Rail: etc:* containe(u)r *m*.

contaminate [kən'tæmineit], *v.tr.* contaminer; corrompre; souiller; **contami'nation,** *s.* contamination *f*; souillure *f*.

contemplate ['kɔntempleit]. 1. (*a*) *v.tr.* contempler; (*b*) *v.i.* se recueillir; méditer. 2. *v.tr.* (*a*)

prévoir, envisager; (*b*) **to c. doing sth.,** projeter, se proposer, de faire qch.; **contem'plation,** *s.* (*a*) contemplation *f*; (*b*) méditation *f*, recueillement *m*; (*c*) **in c. of an attack,** en prévision d'une attaque; **con'templative,** *a.* contemplatif.

contemporary [kən'temp(ə)rəri]. 1. *a.* contemporain (**with,** de); **c. events,** événements actuels. 2. *s.* **our contemporaries,** nos contemporains; **contempo'raneous,** *a.* contemporain (**with,** de); **-ly,** *adv.* **c. with . . .,** à la même époque que . . ..

contempt [kən'tem(p)t], *s.* 1. mépris *m*; dédain *m*; **beneath c.,** tout ce qu'il y a de plus méprisable. 2. *Jur:* **c. of court,** (i) outrage *m* au tribunal, offense *f* à la cour; (ii) refus *m* de comparaître; **con'temptible,** *a.* méprisable; **-ibly,** *adv.* d'une manière méprisable; **con'temptuous,** *a.* dédaigneux (**of,** de); méprisant; (geste *m*) de mépris; **-ly,** *adv.* avec mépris.

contend [kən'tend]. 1. *v.i.* combattre, lutter (**with, against,** contre); disputer, discuter (**with s.o. about sth.,** avec qn sur qch.); **to c. with s.o. for sth.,** disputer, contester, qch. à qn. 2. *v.tr.* **to c. that . . .,** prétendre, soutenir, affirmer, que + *ind.*

content¹ ['kɔntent], *s.* (*a*) contenu *m*, volume *m* (d'un solide); contenance *f*, capacité *f* (d'un vase); (*b*) *pl.* **contents,** contenu (d'une bouteille, d'une lettre); (*of book*) (**table of**) **contents,** table *f* des matières; (*c*) *Ch: Min:* teneur *f*, titre *m* (en or, etc.).

content² [kən'tent]. I. *v.tr.* 1. contenter, satisfaire (qn). 2. **to c. oneself with (doing) sth.,** se contenter de (faire) qch., se borner à faire qch. II. *a.* satisfait, content (**with,** de). III. *s.* contentement *m*, satisfaction *f*; **con'tented,** *a.* content, satisfait (**with,** de); **-ly,** *adv.* (vivre) content; **con'tentedness,** *s.,* **con'tentment,** *s.* contentement *m*.

contention [kən'tenʃ(ə)n], *s.* 1. dispute *f*, démêlé *m*, débat *m*; **to be a bone of c.,** être une pomme de discorde. 2. affirmation *f*, prétention *f*; **my c. is that . . .,** je soutiens que . . .; **con'tentious,** *a.* chicaneur, -euse; (*of issue*) contentieux.

contest. I. *v.tr.* [kən'test] (*a*) contester, débattre (une question); (*b*) *Pol:* **to c. a constituency,** disputer une circonscription; (*c*) *Jur:* attaquer (un testament); contester (une dette). **II.** *s.* ['kɔntest] (*a*) combat *m*, lutte *f* (**with,** avec, contre); (*b*) concours *m*; **con'testant,** *s.* 1. contestant, -ante. 2. compétiteur, -trice; con current, -ente.

context ['kɔntekst], *s.* contexte *m*.

continent ['kɔntinənt], *s.* *Geog:* continent *m*; **conti'nental,** *a.* *Geog:* continental; (pays *m*, habitant *m*) de l'Europe (continentale); **breakfast,** café complet.

contingent [kən'tindʒənt]. **1.** a. (a) éventuel, fortuit, accidentel; (b) **c. on sth.**, sous (la) réserve de qch.; (of event) **to be c. upon sth.**, dépendre de qch. **2.** s. Mil: contingent m; **con'tingency**, s. éventualité f; cas imprévu; pl. Com: contingencies, frais divers; **to provide for contingencies**, parer à l'imprévu.

continue [kən'tinju(:)]. **1.** v.tr. (a) continuer; poursuivre (son travail); reprendre (une conversation); **to be continued**, à suivre; (b) **to c. to do sth.**, continuer à, de, faire qch. **2.** v.i. (se) continuer; se prolonger; **con'tinual**, a. continuel; **-ally**, adv. continuellement; sans cesse, sans arrêt; **con'tinuance**, s. continuation f; persistance f, durée f; **continu'ation**, s. **1.** continuation f. **2.** prolongement (d'un mur); suite f (d'une histoire); **conti'nuity**, s. continuité f; Rad: Cin: script m (d'un programme, d'un film); **c. girl**, script-girl f, pl. -girls, F: script f; **con'tinuous**, a. continu; Cin: etc: **c. performance**, spectacle permanent; **-ly**, adv. sans interruption.

contort [kən'tɔːt], v.tr. tordre, contourner; **face contorted by pain**, visage tordu, crispé, par la douleur; **con'tortion**, s. contorsion f.

contour ['kɔntuər], s. contour m; profil m (du terrain); (on map) **c. (line)**, courbe f de niveau.

contraband ['kɔntrəbænd], s. contrebande f.

contraception [kɔntrə'sepʃ(ə)n], s. contraception f; **contra'ceptive**, a. & s. contraceptif (m), anticonceptionnel; **c. methods**, méthodes contraceptives, anticonceptionnelles.

contract. I. v. [kən'trækt]. **1.** v.tr. & i. (se) contracter, (se) crisper (les traits); (se) resserrer, (se) rétrécir. **2.** (a) v.tr. contracter (une obligation, etc.); (b) v.i. **to c. for work**, entreprendre des travaux par forfait. **II.** s. ['kɔntrækt]. **1.** pacte m; contrat m; acte m (de vente, etc.); **by private c.**, à l'amiable; de gré à gré. **2.** entreprise f; adjudication f; **to put work out to c.**, mettre un travail à l'entreprise; **con'traction**, s. contraction f; rétrécissement m; **con'tractor**, s. entrepreneur m.

contradict [kɔntrə'dikt], v.tr. contredire; démentir; **contra'diction**, s. contradiction f; démenti m; **contra'dictory**, a. contradictoire; opposé (to, à).

contralto, pl. -os [kən'træltou, -ouz], s. Mus: contralto m.

contraption [kən'træpʃ(ə)n], s. F: dispositif m, machin m, truc m.

contrary ['kɔntrəri]. **1.** a. (a) contraire (to, à); opposé (à), en opposition (avec); (b) [kən'trɛəri], indocile; (enfant) rebelle. **2.** s. contraire m; **on the c.**, au contraire; **unless you hear to the c.**, à moins d'avis contraire. **3.** adv. contrairement (to, à); en opposition (to, à,

avec); **contrariness** [kən'trɛərinis], s. esprit m de contradiction.

contrast. I. v.tr. & i. [kən'trɑːst], contraster, faire contraste (with, avec). **II.** s. ['kɔntrɑːst], contraste m (between, entre); **colours in c.**, couleurs fpl en opposition.

contravene [kɔntrə'viːn], v.tr. transgresser, enfreindre (la loi); **contra'vention**, s. **c. of a law**, contravention f, infraction f, à la loi.

contribute [kən'tribju(:)t], v.tr. & i. collaborer (à un journal); aider (au succès); **to c. to (sth.)**, contribuer à, F: cotiser pour (une œuvre, etc.); **to c. one's share**, payer sa part; **contri'bution**, s. **1.** contribution f; cotisation f. **2.** article m (écrit pour un journal); **con'tributor**, s. collaborateur, -trice; **con'tributory**, a. contribuant, contributif.

contrite ['kɔntrait], a. contrit, pénitent, repentant; **-ly**, adv. d'un air pénitent; **contrition** [kən'triʃ(ə)n], s. contrition f.

contrive [kən'traiv], v.tr. (a) inventer, combiner; (b) pratiquer, ménager; **to c. to do sth.**, trouver moyen de faire qch.; se débrouiller pour faire qch.; **con'trivance**, s. appareil m; dispositif m; engin m; F: truc m.

control [kən'troul]. **I.** s. (a) autorité f; **she has no c. over her children**, elle ne sait pas tenir ses enfants; (b) maîtrise f; **circumstances beyond our c.**, circonstances en dehors de notre action; **to lose c. of oneself**, ne plus se maîtriser; **self c.**, le contrôle de soi-même; **everything's under c.**, tout est (fin) prêt; **(foreign) exchange c.**, contrôle des changes; **birth c.**, contrôle, régulation f, limitation f, des naissances; (c) gouverne f, manœuvre f; **the controls**, les commandes; **at the controls**, aux commandes; (d) surveillance f; **under government c.**, assujetti au contrôle du gouvernement. **II.** v.tr. (controlled) **1.** diriger; régler; **to c. the traffic**, réglementer la circulation. **2.** maîtriser, gouverner; **to c. oneself**, se maîtriser, se dominer, se contrôler; **con'troller**, s. (a) (pers.) contrôleur, -euse; (b) Mec: commande f.

controversial [kɔntrə'vəːʃ(ə)l], a. controversable, discutable; (of pers.) enclin à la polémique; **very c. question**, question très controversée; **con'troversy**, s. controverse f, polémique f, discussion f.

contusion [kən'tjuːʒ(ə)n], s. contusion f; meurtrissure f.

conundrum [kə'nʌndrəm], s. **1.** devinette f. **2.** énigme f.

conurbation [kɔnəː'beiʃ(ə)n], s. conurbation f.

convalesce [kɔnvə'les], v.i. relever de maladie; être en convalescence (at, à); **conva'lescence**, s. convalescence f; **conva'lescent**, a. & s. convalescent, -ente.

convene [kən'viːn]. **1.** v.tr. convoquer, réunir

(une assemblée). 2. *v.i.* s'assembler, se réunir.

convenience [kən'vi:njəns], *s.* **1.** commodité *f*, convenance *f*; **at your c.**, à votre bon plaisir; **at your earliest c.**, le plus tôt (qu'il vous sera) possible; **to make a c. of s.o.**, abuser de la bonté de qn. **2.** (**public**) **c.**, W.C. public. **3.** *pl.* commodités, agréments *m*; **all modern conveniences**, tout le confort moderne; **con'venient**, *a.* commode, pratique; **if it's c. to you**, si cela vous convient, si cela ne vous dérange pas; **-ly**, *adv.* commodément; sans inconvénient.

convent ['kɔnvənt], *s.* couvent *m* (de femmes).

convention [kən'venʃən], *s.* **1.** (*a*) convention *f*; (*b*) accord *m*, contrat *m*. **2.** *usu. pl.* convenances *fpl*, bienséances *fpl*; **con'ventional**, *a.* **1.** conventionnel. **2.** (*a*) courant, normal; classique; **the c. type of car**, la voiture ordinaire, classique; *Mil: etc:* (*of arms,* = *not atomic*) **c. weapons**, les armes conventionnelles, classiques; (*b*) (*pers., style*) sans originalité; **-ally**, *adv.* conventionnellement; normalement.

converge [kən'və:dʒ], *v.tr. & v.i.* (faire) converger (**on**, sur); **con'vergence**, *s.* convergence *f*; **con'vergent**, *a.* convergent; **con'verging**, *a.* convergent, concourant.

conversant [kən'və:s(ə)nt], *a.* familier, intime (**with**, avec); **to be c. with a subject**, être versé dans, compétent en, au courant d'une matière.

converse [kən'və:s], *v.i.* causer; **conver'sation**, *s.* conversation *f*, entretien *m*; **preliminary c.**, prise *f* de contact.

conversion [kən'və:ʃ(ə)n], *s.* **1.** conversion *f* (de qn à qch.); **c. to Christianity**, conversion au christianisme. **2.** transformation *f*, conversion; **c. of water into steam**, conversion de l'eau en vapeur; **c. of funds to one's own use**, détournement *m* de fonds; *St.Exch:* **fraudulent c. of stocks**, lavage *m* des titres; **c. of a room to office use**, aménagement *m* d'une pièce en bureau.

convert. I. *v.tr.* [kən'və:t]. **1.** convertir (qn). **2.** transformer, changer, convertir (**sth. into sth.**, qch. en qch.); *Rugby Fb:* **converted goal**, but *m* de transformation; **to c. a room into an office**, aménager une pièce en bureau. **II.** *s.* ['kɔnvə:t], converti, -ie; **con'verter**, *s.* (appareil) convertisseur (*m*); *Rad:* adapteur *m*; **converti'bility**, *s.* convertibilité *f*; **con'vertible. 1.** *a.* convertible, convertissable (**into**, en). **2.** *s.* *Aut:* décapotable *f*.

convex ['kɔnveks], *a.* convexe.

convey [kən'vei], *v.tr.* transporter, porter, conduire (qn, qch.); transmettre (le son); **to c. one's meaning**, communiquer, faire comprendre, sa pensée; **con'veyance**, *s.* **1.** transport *m*; moyen *m* de transport; transmission *f*. **2.**

véhicule *m*; voiture *f*; *Adm:* **public c.**, véhicule de transport en commun; **con'veyor**, *s.* (*pers.*) porteur, -euse (d'une lettre); **c. belt**, tapis roulant.

convict. I. *v.tr.* [kən'vikt], **to c. s.o.** (**of a crime, an error**), convaincre qn (d'un crime, d'une erreur); **he was convicted**, il a été reconnu coupable. **II.** *s.* ['kɔnvikt]. *Jur:* détenu, -ue; forçat *m*; **con'viction**, *s.* **1.** condamnation *f*. **2.** (*belief*) conviction *f*; persuasion *f*.

convince [kən'vins], *v.tr.* convaincre, persuader (**s.o. of sth.**, qn de qch.); **con'vincing**, *a.* convaincant; **-ly**, *adv.* d'une façon convaincante.

convoke [kən'vouk], *v.tr.* convoquer (une assemblée); **convo'cation**, *s.* (*a*) convocation *f* (d'une assemblée); (*b*) *Ecc:* assemblée *f*, synode *m*.

convolvulus [kən'vɔlvjuləs], *s.* *Bot:* volubilis *m*, *F:* liseron *m*.

convoy ['kɔnvɔi]. **I.** *s.* convoi *m*. **II.** *v.tr.* *Mil: Navy:* convoyer, escorter.

convulse [kən'vʌls], *v.tr.* **1.** bouleverser (la vie de qn); ébranler (la terre). **2.** **to be convulsed with laughter**, se tordre de rire; **face convulsed with terror**, visage décomposé par la terreur; **con'vulsions**, *s.pl.* **1.** *Med:* convulsions *fpl*. **2.** **to be in c.** (**of laughter**), se tordre de rire; **con'vulsive**, *a.* convulsif; *Med:* **c. movements**, soubresauts *mpl*.

coo [ku:], *v.i.* roucouler; (*of baby*) gazouiller; **'cooing**, *s.* roucoulement *m*.

cook [kuk]. **I.** *v.* **1.** *v.tr.* (*a*) (faire) cuire; *abs.* faire la cuisine; cuisiner; (*b*) **to c. the accounts**, tripoter, truquer, les comptes. **2.** *v.i.* (*of food*) cuire. **II.** *s.* cuisinier, -ière; **she's a first-rate c.**, c'est un cordon-bleu; **'cookbook**, *s.* *N.Am* livre *m* de cuisine; **'cooker**, *s.* **1.** cuisinière *f*. **2.** pomme *f* à cuire; **'cookery**, *s.* (l'art de) la cuisine; **c. book**, livre *m* de cuisine; **'cookie**, *s.* *N.Am:* biscuit *m*, petit gâteau sec; **'cooking**, *s.* **1.** cuisson *f*; **c. apple**, pomme *f* à cuire. **2.** cuisine *f*; **c. utensils**, batterie *f* de cuisine.

cool [ku:l]. **I.** *a.* (*a*) frais, *f.* fraîche; **c. drink**, boisson rafraîchissante; **it's c.**, il fait frais; *P.N:* **to be kept in a c. place**, garder au frais; (*b*) (*of pers.*) **to keep c.**, garder son sang-froid; **keep c.!** du calme! (*c*) **to give s.o. a c. reception**, faire un accueil froid à qn; (*d*) *F:* **he's a c. customer**, il ne se laisse pas démonter; **-ly**, *adv.* **1.** fraîchement. **2.** de sang-froid. **3.** froidement. **II.** *s.* frais *m*; fraîcheur *f*; **to put the wine in the c.**, mettre le vin au frais; **in the c. of the evening**, à la fraîcheur du soir. **III.** *v.tr. & i.* (se) rafraîchir, (se) refroidir; **'cool 'down**, *v.i.* se rafraîchir; (*after anger*) s'apaiser, se calmer; **'cooler**, *s.* **1.** rafraîchisseur *m*; *Ind:* réfrigéra.. *m*; refroidisseur *m*. **2.** *F:* boisso. rafraîchissante. **3.** *P:* prison *f*, taule *f*.

'cooling. 1. *a.* rafraîchissant. 2. *s.*
rafraîchissement *m;* refroidissement *m;*
'coolness, *s.* 1. fraîcheur *f* (de l'air). 2. sang-
froid *m,* aplomb *m.* 3. froideur *f* (d'un accueil);
'cool 'off, *v.i.* (*of enthusiasm*) se refroidir.
coop [ku:p]. I. *s.* cage *f* à poules; mue *f.* II. *v.tr.*
enfermer (des poules) dans une mue; *F:* to c.
s.o. up, tenir qn enfermé.
co-operate [kou'ɔpəreit], *v.i.* coopérer (with s.o.
in sth., avec qn à qch.); agir en commun; co-
ope'ration, *s.* coopération *f;* co-'operative,
a. & s. 1. *a.* coopératif; c. stores, société
coopérative de consommation. 2. *s.* co-
operative, *F:* co-op, coopérative *f* (vinicole,
etc.).
co-opt [kou'ɔpt], *v.tr.* coopter (qn).
co-ordination [kouɔ:di'neiʃ(ə)n], *s.* coordination *f.*
cop [kɔp]. *P:* I. *s.* (= *policeman*) flic *m.* II. *v.tr.*
(copped) attraper, pincer (qn).
cope [koup], *v.i.* (*a*) to c. with s.o., tenir tête à qn;
(*b*) to c. with a situation, faire face à une
situation; I'll c., je me débrouillerai.
Copenhagen [koupən'heigən]. *Pr.n.*
Copenhague *f.*
copious ['koupjəs], *a.* copieux, abondant; -ly,
adv. copieusement.
copper ['kɔpər], *s.* 1. cuivre *m* (rouge). 2. *H:*
lessiveuse *f.* 3. *attrib.* de cuivre, en cuivre; c.
(coloured), cuivré. 4. (*a*) *P:* flic *m;* (*b*) *pl. F:*
coppers, sous *mpl.*
coppice ['kɔpis], *s.,* copse [kɔps], *s.* taillis
m.
copy ['kɔpi]. I. *v.tr.* 1. copier; imiter, reproduire
(un tableau, etc.); to c. s.o., se modeler sur qn.
2. to c. (out) a letter, copier, transcrire, une lettre. II. *s.* 1. copie *f;* reproduction *f.* 2. copie,
transcription *f;* rough c., brouillon *m; Typew:*
carbon c., double *m.* 2. exemplaire *m* (d'un
livre); numéro (d'un journal). 3. *Journ:* sujet *m*
d'article; 'copying, *s.* transcription *f;* imitation *f;* 'copyright. I. *s.* copyright *m.* II. *v.tr.*
déposer (un livre).
coquette [kɔ'ket], *s.* coquette *f;* co'quettish, *a.*
(sourire) provocant, *F:* aguichant.
coral ['kɔrəl], *a.* 1. corail *m, pl.* coraux.
cord [kɔ:d], *s.* (*a*) corde *f;* cordon *m;* ficelle *f;* (*b*)
Anat: the vocal cords, les cordes vocales; um-
bilical c., cordon ombilical; the spinal c., le
cordon médullaire.
cordial ['kɔ:djəl], *a.* cordial; (sentiments)
chaleureux; -ally, *adv.* cordialement; cor-
di'ality, *s.* cordialité *f.*
cordon ['kɔ:dən]. I. *s.* cordon *m.* II. *v.tr.* to c. off,
isoler, cerner; the road was cordoned off by
troops, on isola la rue par un cordon de
troupes.
Cordova ['kɔ:dəvə]. *Pr.n. Geog:* Cordoue
(Espagne); Cordoba (Argentine).

corduroy ['kɔ:dərɔi, -djurɔi], *s. Tex:* velours
côtelé, à côtes.
core [kɔ:r]. I. *s.* 1. centre *m,* cœur *m* (d'une
masse, d'un arbre, etc.); trognon *m* (d'une
pomme, etc.); *Min: etc:* noyau *m;* c. sample,
carotte *f.* II. *v.tr.* vider (une pomme).
cork [kɔ:k]. I. *s.* 1. liège *m;* c. oak, chêne-liège
m, pl. chênes-lièges. 2. bouchon *m;* to draw
the c. of a bottle, déboucher une bouteille.
II. *v.tr.* to c. a bottle, boucher une bouteille;
corked, *a.* (*of wine*) qui sent le bouchon;
'corkscrew, *s.* tire-bouchon *m, pl.* tire-
bouchons.
corn[1] [kɔ:n], *s. coll:* grains *mpl,* blé(s) *m(pl);*
céréales *fpl;* Indian c., *N.Am:* c., maïs *m, Fr.C:*
blé d'Inde; 'corn-cob, *s.* épi *m* de maïs;
'cornflour, *s.* fécule *m* de maïs; 'cornflower,
s. Bot: bluet *m;* 'cornstarch, *s. N.Am:* fécule *m*
de maïs.
corn[2], *s.* cor *m* (au pied); to tread on s.o.'s corns,
froisser qn.
cornea ['kɔ:niə], *s. Anat:* cornée *f* (de l'œil).
corned [kɔ:nd], *a.* c. beef, bœuf *m* de conserve;
corned-beef *m.*
corner ['kɔ:nər]. I. *s.* 1. coin *m,* angle *m* (de
maison, de rue, etc.); c. cupboard, encoignure
f. 2. tournant *m; Aut:* virage *m;* blind c., virage
sans visibilité. 3. *Com:* monopole *m.* II. *v.* 1.
v.tr. accaparer (le marché). 2. *v.i. Aut:* prendre
un virage; to c. sharply, virer court.
cornet ['kɔ:nit], *s.* 1. *Mus:* cornet *m* à pistons. 2.
ice-cream c., cornet de crème glacée.
cornice ['kɔ:nis], *s.* 1. corniche *f.* 2. (*overhang*)
snow, rock, c., corniche de neige, de rocher.
Cornwall ['kɔ:nwəl]. *Pr.n.* (le comté de) Cornouailles *f;* 'Cornish, *a.* cornouaillais.
coronary ['kɔrənəri], *a. Anat:* c. artery, artère *f*
coronaire; *Med:* c. thrombosis, infarctus *m* du
myocarde; *F:* a c., une thrombose.
coronation [kɔrə'neiʃ(ə)n], *s.* couronnement *m,*
sacre *m* (d'un roi).
coroner ['kɔrənər], *s. Jur:* officier civil chargé
d'instruire, assisté d'un jury, en cas de mort
violente ou subite.
coronet ['kɔrənit], *s.* (*a*) (petite) couronne; (*b*)
diadème *m.*
corporal[1] ['kɔ:p(ə)rəl], *s. Mil:* (*of infantry*)
caporal *m,* -aux; (*of cavalry*) brigadier *m.*
corporal[2], *a.* c. punishment, châtiment corporel.
corporate ['kɔ:p(ə)rət], *a.* 1. constitué (en
corps); formant (un) corps; *Jur:* body c., c.
body, corps constitué; corporation. 2. de corps;
c. feeling, esprit *m* de corps.
corps constitué. 2. *Com:* société enregistrée. 3.
municipal c., conseil municipal.
corps [kɔ:r], *s.inv.* corps *m;* Army c., corps
d'armée; the Diplomatic C., le corps
diplomatique.
corpse [kɔ:ps], *s.* cadavre *m.*

corpulent ['kɔːpjulənt], *a.* corpulent; '**corpulence,** *s.* corpulence *f.*

corpuscle ['kɔːpʌsl], *s.* corpuscule *m*; **blood corpuscles,** globules sanguins.

correct [kə'rekt]. **I.** *v.tr.* **1.** corriger (une faute). **2.** rectifier (une erreur), punir (qn). **II.** *a.* **1.** correct, exact; (réponse) juste. **2.** conforme à l'usage; **-ly,** *adv.* correctement, exactement; **co'rrection,** *s.* **1.** correction *f* (d'un devoir); rectification *f* (d'une erreur). **2.** punition *f*; **co'rrective,** *a.* correctif; **co'rrectness,** *s.* correction *f*, convenance *f* (de tenue); exactitude *f*, justesse *f.*

correlate ['kɔrəleit]. **I.** *s.* corrélatif *m*. **II.** **1.** *v.i.* correspondre, être corrélatif, rapporter (**with, to,** à). **2.** *v.tr.* mettre (qch.) en corrélation (**with,** avec); **corre'lation,** *s.* corrélation *f.*

correspond [kɔris'pɔnd], *v.i.* **1.** correspondre, être conforme (**with, to,** à). **2.** correspondre (**with s.o.,** avec qn); **they c.,** ils s'écrivent; **corres'pondence,** *s.* **1.** correspondance *f.* **2.** correspondance, courrier *m*; **c. course,** cours *m* par correspondance; **corres'pondent,** *s.* correspondant, -ante; *Journ:* **from our special c.,** de notre envoyé spécial; **corres'ponding,** *a.* correspondant; **-ly,** *adv.* également.

corridor ['kɔridɔːr], *s.* couloir *m*, corridor *m*; *Rail:* **c. carriage,** wagon *m* à couloir.

corroborate [kə'rɔbəreit], *v.tr.* corroborer, confirmer (une déclaration); **corrobo'ration,** *s.* corroboration *f.*

corrode [kə'roud], *v.tr. & i.* (se) corroder; **co'rrosion,** *s.* corrosion *f*; **co'rrosive,** *a. & s.* corrosif (*m*).

corrugated ['kɔrugeitid], *a.* **c. iron,** tôle ondulée.

corrupt [kə'rʌpt]. **I.** *v.tr.* corrompre (qn, un témoin); dépraver (la jeunesse). **II.** *a.* corrompu; **c. press,** presse vénale; **co'rruption,** *s.,* **co'rruptness,** *s.* corruption *f.*

corset ['kɔːsit], *s. Cl:* corset *m.*

Corsica ['kɔːsikə]. *Pr.n. Geog:* la Corse; '**Corsican,** *a. & s.* corse *mf.*

cortisone ['kɔːtizoun], *s. Bio-Ch: Med:* cortisone *f.*

cos [kɔs], *s.* **c. (lettuce),** (laitue *f*) romaine (*f*).

cosh [kɔʃ]. **I.** *s.* F: matraque *f*. **II.** *v.tr.* F: matraquer, assommer (qn).

cosmetic [kɔz'metik], *a. & s.* cosmétique (*m*).

cosmic ['kɔzmik], *a.* cosmique; **c. rays,** rayons *m* cosmiques.

cosmonaut ['kɔzmounɔːt], *s.* cosmonaute *mf.*

cosmopolitan [kɔzmə'pɔlit(ə)n], *a. & s.* cosmopolite (*mf*).

cost [kɔst]. **I.** *v.* (**cost; cost**) **1.** *v.i.* coûter; **it c. him 50 francs,** cela lui revient à 50 francs; **whatever it costs,** coûte que coûte. **2.** *v.tr. Ind: Com:* **to c. an article,** établir le prix de revient d'un article. **II.** *s.* **1.** coût *m*; frais *mpl*; **c. of living,** coût de la vie; **at the c. of one's life,** au prix de sa vie; **at all costs,** à tout prix; **whatever the c.,** coûte que coûte. **2.** *pl. Jur:* frais d'instance; '**costing,** *s.* établissement *m* du prix de revient; '**costliness,** *s.* haut prix; prix élevé; '**costly,** *a.* (*a*) de grand prix; de luxe; (*b*) coûteux.

coster(monger) ['kɔstə(mʌŋgər)], *s.* marchand *m* des quatre saisons.

costume ['kɔstjuːm], *s.* costume *m*; (**women's tailor-made**) **c.,** tailleur *m*; **bathing c.,** maillot *m* (de bain); **theatrical c.,** costume de théâtre.

cosy ['kouzi], *a.* chaud, confortable; (*of pers.*) bien au chaud; **it's c. here,** il fait bon ici; **-ly,** *adv.* confortablement; douillettement.

cot [kɔt], *s.* lit *m* d'enfant.

cottage ['kɔtidʒ], *s.* **1.** chaumière *f*. **2.** villa *f*; petite maison de campagne; cottage *m*.

cotton ['kɔtn], *s.* **1.** (*a*) coton *m*; (*b*) (**sewing-**)**c.,** fil *m* à coudre; **c. goods, cottons,** cotonnades *fpl*; **printed c.,** indienne *f*; **c. wool,** ouate *f*, coton hydrophile. **2. c. mill,** filature *f* de coton; **c. plantation,** cotonnerie *f.*

couch [kautʃ], *s.* canapé *m*, divan *m.*

cough [kɔf]. **I.** *s.* toux *f*; **to have a c.,** tousser; **c. lozenge,** pastille *f* contre la toux, pastille pectorale. **II.** (*a*) *v.i.* tousser; F: **to c. up,** payer. P: cracher; (*b*) *v.tr.* F: **to c. up money,** cracher de l'argent, du fric; '**coughing,** *s.* fit of c.,** quinte *f* de toux.

council ['kauns(i)l], *s.* **1.** conseil *m*; **to hold c.,** tenir conseil; **town c.,** conseil municipal; **county c.** = conseil général; **c. house, flat** = habitation *f* à loyer modéré (H.L.M.); **c. estate,** cité municipale. **2.** *Ecc:* concile *m*; '**councilchamber,** *s.* salle *f* du conseil; '**councillor,** *s.* conseiller municipal; **county c.** = conseiller général.

counsel ['kauns(ə)l], *s.* **1.** délibération *f*; consultation *f*; **to take c. (together),** se consulter se concerter. **2.** conseil *m*, avis *m*. **3.** dessein *m* intention *f*; **to keep one's (own) c.,** garder ses projets pour soi. **4.** *Jur:* avocat *m*; **c. i chambers,** avocat-conseil *m, pl.* avocats conseils; '**counsellor,** *s.* conseiller *m*; con seiller d'ambassade.

count[1] [kaunt]. **I.** *v.* *v.tr.* compter; calculer dénombrer (des troupeaux); **to c. the cos** compter, calculer, la dépense; **to c. the votes** dépouiller le scrutin; **counting from tomorrow** à compter de demain. **2.** *v.i.* **to c. on s.o.,** comp ter sur qn; **to c. on doing sth.,** compter fai qch. **3.** avoir de l'importance; **every minut counts,** il n'y a pas une minute à perdre; **he's man who counts,** c'est quelqu'un. **II.** *s.* comp *m*; calcul *m*; dépouillement *m* (du scrutin); ((*people*) dénombrement *m*; **to keep c. of . .** tenir le compte de . . .; **to lose c.,** perdre compte; **blood c.,** numération *f* globulair *Tchn:* **c. down,** compte à rebours: *Box:* ◄

take the c., être mis knock-out, *F:* k.-o.;
'**counting,** *s.* compte *m;* dépouillement *m* (du
scrutin); **c. house,** comptabilité *f;* '**countless,**
a. innombrable.
count², *s.* (*title*) comte *m.*
countenance ['kauntinəns]. I. *s.* visage *m;* figure
f; **to keep one's c.,** ne pas se laisser
décontenancer; **to lose c.,** se décontenancer;
perdre contenance. II. *v.tr.* autoriser, approuver (une action); encourager, appuyer
(qn).
counter¹ ['kauntər], *s.* 1. *E:* compteur *m;* **speed
c., revolution c.,** compteur de tours, compte-
tours *m inv.* 2. *Games:* fiche *f;* jeton *m.* 3. (*a*)
(*in bank*) guichet *m;* (*b*) (*in shop*) comptoir *m.*
counter². I. *a.* (*a*) contraire, opposé (**to,** à); (*b*) *in
compounds often translated by* contre-. II. *adv.*
en sens inverse; à contre-sens; **to run c. to
one's orders,** aller à l'encontre de ses instructions. III. *v.tr.* contrarier (qn, qch.); arrêter (un
mouvement); parer, bloquer (un coup);
'**counteract,** *v.tr.* neutraliser (une influence);
parer à (un résultat); '**counter-attack. I.** *s.*
contre-attaque *f.* II. *v.tr. & i.* contre-attaquer;
'**counter'balance,** *v.tr.* faire contrepoids à
(qch.); compenser (une force);
'**countercharge,** *s. Jur:* contre-accusation *f;*
'**counter-demon'stration,** *s.* contre-
manifestation *f;* '**counter-'espionage,** *s.*
contre-espionnage *m;* '**counterfeit**
['kauntəfit]. I. *a.* faux. II. *v.tr.* contrefaire (la
monnaie, etc.); '**counterfoil,** *s.* souche *f,* talon
m (de chèque, etc.); '**countermand,** *v.tr.* contremander; révoquer (un ordre); '**counterpane,** *s.* couvre-lit *m;* '**counterpart,** *s.* contrepartie *f;* '**counterpoise,** *s.* contrepoids *m;*
'**counter-revo'lution,** contre-révolution *f,*
counter-revolutionary, *a.* contre-
révolutionnaire; '**countersign,** *v.tr.* contresigner, viser (un document); '**countersink,**
v.tr. (-**sank; -sunk**), fraiser, encastrer.
countess ['kauntis], *s.* comtesse *f.*
country ['kʌntri], *s.* 1. (*a*) pays *m,* région *f;* **open
c.,** rase campagne; **broken c.,** pays accidenté;
Pol: **to go to the c.,** consulter le corps électoral;
(*b*) (*native country*) patrie *f.* 2. (*a*) (*as opposed
to the capital*) province *f;* (*b*) campagne *f;* **c.
life,** vie *f* à la campagne; **house in the c.,**
maison *f* à la campagne; **c. house,** manoir *m;*
gentilhommière *f;* château *m;* **countryman,**
pl. -**men,** *s.* **countrywoman,** *pl.* -**women,** *s.*
1. compatriote *mf.* 2. paysan, -anne; campagnard, -arde; '**countryside,** *s.* paysage *m,*
pays *m.*
county ['kaunti], *s.* comté *m* (= département *m*);
c. town, chef-lieu *m* de comté, *pl.* chefs-lieux.
coup [ku:], *s.* coup *m* d'état; **to bring off a c.,**
réussir un coup.
couple ['kʌpl]. I. *s.* (*a*) couple *m;* **to work in**

couples, se mettre à deux pour travailler; **in a
c. of minutes,** dans un instant; (*b*) couple
(d'époux); **the young c.,** les jeunes mariés. II.
v.tr. coupler, accoupler (deux idées); apparier (le mâle et la femelle); associer (deux
noms); '**couplet,** *s.* distique *m;* '**coupling,** *s.*
accouplement *m* (de deux choses); apparie-
ment *m* (des animaux); accolement *m* (de deux
noms).
coupon ['ku:pon], *s.* coupon *m; P.T.T:* **international reply c.,** coupon-réponse international; **petrol c.,** bon *m* d'essence; *Com:*
free-gift c., bon-prime *m, pl.* bons-primes.
courage ['kʌridʒ], *s.* courage *m;* **to have the c. of
one's convictions,** avoir le courage de ses
opinions; **to pluck up c.,** prendre son courage à
deux mains; **courageous** [kə'reidʒəs], *a.*
courageux; -**ly,** *adv.* courageusement.
courgette [kuə'ʒet], *s. Hort:* courgette *f.*
courier ['kuriər], *s.* courrier *m,* messager *m;* (*of
tourist party*) guide *m.*
course [kɔ:s], *s.* 1. (*a*) cours *m;* marche *f* (des
événements); **in c. of time,** avec le temps; à la
longue; **in the ordinary c. (of things),** normalement; **in c. of construction,** en cours de
construction; **in due c.,** en temps voulu, en
temps utile; **let things take their c.,** laissez
faire; (*b*) **of c.,** bien entendu; naturellement; **of
c. not!** bien sûr que non! (*c*) **as a matter of c.,**
comme de juste, comme de raison. 2. (*a*) *Sch:*
cours; **to take a c.,** suivre un cours; **to publish
a French c.,** publier une méthode de français;
(*b*) *Med:* traitement *m,* régime *m.* 3. (*a*) route *f,*
direction *f;* (*b*) **a c. of action,** une ligne de conduite; **to take one's own c.,** agir à sa guise. 4.
Cu: service *m,* plat *m.* 5. *Sp:* (*a*) champ *m,*
terrain *m* (de courses); (*b*) piste *f.*
court [kɔ:t]. I. *s.* 1. (*a*) cour (royale); **the C. of St
James's,** la cour de la Reine d'Angleterre; (*b*)
to pay c. to s.o., faire la cour à qn. 2. *Jur:* cour,
tribunal *m;* **c.-room,** salle *f* d'audience; **c. of
appeal,** cour d'appel; **assize c.,** (*building*)
palais *m* de justice. 3. **tennis c.,** court *m,* tennis
m. II. *v.tr.* 1. courtiser, faire la cour à (une
femme). 2. rechercher, solliciter (des
applaudissements, etc.); **to c. danger,** aller au-
devant du danger; **courteous** ['kə:tjəs], *a.*
courtois, poli (**to,** envers); -**ly,** *adv.* courtoisement, avec politesse; **courtesy** ['kə:-], *s.* courtoisie *f,* politesse *f;* **by c. of . . .,** avec le concours gracieux, la bienveillance, de . . .; **courtier** ['kɔ:-], *s.* courtisan *m;* '**court-'martial. I.**
s. conseil *m* de guerre, cour martiale. II. *v.tr.*
faire passer (qn) en conseil de guerre;
'**courtship,** *s.* cour (faite à une femme);
'**courtyard,** *s.* cour *f* (de maison).
cousin ['kʌzn], *s.* cousin, -ine; **first c.,** cousin(e)
germain(e).
cove [kouv], *s. Geog:* anse *f;* petite baie.

covenant ['kʌvənənt]. **I.** s. **1.** Jur: convention f, contrat m. **2.** Pol: pacte m, traité m. **II.** v. **1.** v.tr. promettre, accorder, (qch.) par contrat. **2.** v.i. **to c. with s.o. for sth.**, convenir (par contrat) de qch. avec qn.

cover ['kʌvər]. **I.** s. **1.** couverture f; tapis m (de table); (of chair) **loose c.**, housse f; **outer c. of tyre**, enveloppe f de pneu; **umbrella c.**, fourreau m de parapluie; **car c.**, bâche f. **2.** couvercle m (de marmite); Mec: carter m. **3.** couverture (d'un livre); **to read a book from c. to c.**, lire un livre d'un bout à l'autre. **4.** Corr: enveloppe f; **under separate c.**, sous pli séparé. **5.** abri m; **to take c.**, se mettre à l'abri. **6.** Fin: Com: couverture, provision f, marge f; Ins: **full c.**, garantie totale. **7.** attrib. (at restaurant) **c. charge**, couvert m. **II.** v.tr. **1.** couvrir (**with**, de); recouvrir, envelopper. **2.** franchir, parcourir (une distance). **3. to c. s.o. with a revolver**, braquer un revolver sur qn. **4.** comprendre, englober (les faits, etc.). **5.** Journ: couvrir (un événement); **'coverage**, s. Journ: **news c.**, informations fpl; **'covering. I.** a. **c. letter**, (a) lettre f d'explication; (b) lettre confirmative. **II.** s. couverture f; enveloppe f; **'cover 'up**, v.tr. couvrir (qch.) entièrement; dissimuler (la vérité).

coverlet ['kʌvəlit], s. couvre-lit m; couvre-pieds m inv.

covet ['kʌvit], v.tr. (**coveted**) convoiter; **'covetous**, a. avide (de gain, etc.); **-ly**, adv. avec convoitise, avidement.

cow [kau]. **I.** s. **1.** vache f; **milking c.**, vache laitière; **c. in calf**, vache pleine. **2.** (of elephant, seal, etc.) femelle f. **3.** Austr: P: **it's a fair c.**, c'est moche. **II.** v.tr. intimider, dompter (qn, un animal); **'cowboy**, s. cowboy m; **'cowhand**, s. **'cowman**, pl. **-men**, s. vacher m, bouvier m; **'cowhide**, s. (peau f de) vache f; **'cowshed**, s. étable f.

coward ['kauəd], s. lâche mf; **'cowardice**, s. lâcheté f; **'cowardly**, a. lâche.

cower ['kauər], v.i. se blottir, se tapir; **to c. before s.o.**, trembler devant qn.

cowl [kaul], s. **1.** capuchon m. **2.** capuchon, abat-vent m inv (de cheminée).

cowslip ['kauslip], s. Bot: (fleur f de) coucou m.

cox [kɔks], s., **coxswain** ['kɔksn], s. **1.** Nau: patron m (d'une chaloupe). **2.** Sp: (rowing) esp. cox, barreur m.

coy [kɔi], a. timide, farouche; **-ly**, adv. timidement; **'coyness**, s. timidité f.

crab¹ [kræb], s. Crust: crabe m, cancre m; (rowing) F: **to catch a c.**, engager un aviron.

crab², s. **c.(-apple)**, pomme f sauvage.

crack [kræk]. **I.** s. **1.** (a) claquement m (de fouet); détonation f, coup sec; (b) **c. on the head**, coup violent sur la tête. **2.** fente f, fissure f; (in wall) lézarde f; (in pottery) fêlure f. **3.** to

have a c. at s.o., faire une plaisanterie aux dépens de qn. **II.** a. d'élite; de première force; **c. player**, as m, crack m. **III.** v. **1.** v.tr. (a) faire claquer (un fouet); (b) fêler (un verre); fracturer (un os); F: **to c. a bottle (with s.o.)**, boire une bouteille (avec qn). **2.** v.i. (a) craquer; claquer; (b) se fêler; se fissurer, (of wall) se lézarder; (c) F: **to get cracking**, se grouiller; (d) F: **to c. down on s.o.**, laver la tête à qn; **cracked**, a. fêlé; fendu; F: (of pers.) timbré, toqué, loufoque; **'cracker**, s. **1.** (a) (firework) pétard m; (b) (Christmas cracker) diablotin m. **2.** N.Am: biscuit m (sec); **'crackers**, a. F: **he's c.**, il est cinglé; **'cracking**, s. cracking m, craquage m (du pétrole); **c. plant**, cracking m; **'crack 'up**, F: **1.** v.tr. vanter, prôner (qn, qch.). **2.** v.i. (of pers.) flancher, s'effondrer.

crackle ['krækl]. **I.** v.i. craqueter; (of fire) pétiller; grésiller. **II.** s. craquement m; crépitement m; grésillement m; **'crackling**, s. (of pork) couenne f.

cradle ['kreidl], s. berceau m; **'cradle-song**, s. berceuse f.

craft [krɑːft], s. **1.** ruse f; fourberie f. **2.** métier (manuel); profession f. **3.** inv. Nau: bateau m; embarcation f; **'craftiness**, s. ruse f, astuce f; **'craftsman**, pl. **-men**, s. **1.** artisan m; ouvrier qualifié; homme m de métier. **2.** artiste m dans son métier; **'crafty**, a. astucieux, rusé; **-ily**, adv. astucieusement.

crag [kræg], s. rocher escarpé, à pic.

cram [kræm], v. (**crammed**) **1.** v.tr. (a) fourrer (sth. into sth., qch. dans qch.); **to c. one's shopping into a bag**, fourrer ses achats dans un sac; Th: **the house was crammed**, la salle était bondée; (b) gaver (une volaille); (c) Sch: F: chauffer (un candidat). **2.** v.i. F: (a) s'entasser (into a car, etc.), dans une voiture, etc.); (b) se gorger de nourriture; (c) **to c. for an exam**, potasser un examen; **'cram-'full**, a. bondé, bourré; **'crammer**, s. Sch: bachoteur m.

cramp [kræmp]. **I.** s. **1.** Med: crampe f. **2.** Tls: etc: happe f, agrafe f, crampon m; serre-joint m. **II.** v.tr. **1.** gêner; **to c. s.o.'s style**, priver qn de ses moyens. **2.** (a) cramponner, agrafer (de pierres, etc.); (b) presser, serrer (à l'étau); **cramped**, a. à l'étroit; gêné; **c. style**, style contraint; **'crampon**, s. crampon m à glace.

cranberry ['krænbəri], s. Bot: canneberge f.

crane [krein]. **I.** s. Orn: Mec: grue f. **II.** v.tr. **to c. one's neck**, allonger le cou.

cranium ['kreiniəm], s. crâne m.

crank [kræŋk], s. Mec.E: manivelle f; **c. case**, carter m (du moteur). **2.** (pers.) maniaque m; original m; **'cranky**, a. (of pers.) d'humeur difficile; capricieux.

crash [kræʃ]. **I.** s. **1.** fracas m; **a c. of thunder**, coup de tonnerre m. **2.** catastrophe f; débâcle f; Fin: krach m. **3.** Aut: Av: accident m;

helmet, casque (protecteur). **II.** *v.i.* (*a*)
éclater, tomber, avec fracas; (*b*) *Aut:* **to c. into
a tree**, percuter un arbre; (*c*) *Av:* (*of plane*)
s'écraser sur le sol; **'crash-dive,** *s.* plongée *f*
raide (d'un sous-marin); **'crash-land,** *v.i. Av:*
atterrir brutalement, *F:* casser du bois; **'crash
programme,** *attrib.* programme choc,
accéléré, d'urgence; **'crash-proof,** *a.*
antichoc.
crate [kreit], *s.* caisse *f* à claire-voie; cageot *m*.
crater ['kreitər], *s.* cratère *m* (d'un volcan).
crave [kreiv], *v.i.* **to c. for sth.,** désirer ardemment qch.; **'craving,** *s.* désir ardent, obsédant.
crawl [krɔːl]. **I.** *v.i.* **1.** ramper; aller à quatre
pattes; *Aut: F:* faire du surplace. **2. to be
crawling with vermin,** grouiller de vermine. **3.**
Swimming: crawler; faire, nager, le crawl. **II.**
s. Swimming: crawl *m*; **'crawlers,** *s.pl. Cl:*
barboteuse *f*.
crayfish ['kreifiʃ], *s.* **1.** (**fresh-water**) c.,
écrevisse *f*. **2.** langouste *f*.
crayon ['kreiən, -ən], *s.* pastel *m*.
craze [kreiz], *s.* manie *f* (**for sth.,** de qch.); **camping is his latest c.,** le camping, c'est sa dernière
rage; **'craziness,** *s.* folie *f*, démence *f*; **'crazy,**
a. **1.** fou, *f.* folle; toqué; **c. with fear,** affolé (de
terreur); **to drive s.o. c.,** rendre qn fou. **2.
c. paving,** dallage irrégulier; **-ily,** *adv.*
follement.
creak [kriːk]. **I.** *v.i.* crier, grincer; (*of shoes*)
craquer. **II.** *s.* (*also* **'creaking**) cri *m*; grincement *m*; craquement *m*.
cream [kriːm]. **I.** *s.* **1.** (*a*) crème *f*; **c. cheese,**
fromage blanc; **ice c.,** glace *f*; (*b*) **the c. of the
joke,** le plus beau de l'histoire. **2.** crème (de
beauté); **cleansing c.,** démaquillant *m*. **3.** *attrib.*
c.(-coloured), crème *inv.* **II.** *v.tr.* (*a*) écrémer (le
lait); *Cu:* travailler (du beurre) en crème;
creamed potatoes, purée *f* de pommes de terre;
'creamery, *s.* **1.** crémerie *f*. **2.** laiterie (industrielle); coopérative laitière; **'creamy,** *a.*
crémeux.
crease [kriːs]. **I. 1.** *v.tr.* (*a*) plisser, faire des
(faux) plis à (qch.); **well-creased trousers,** pantalon *m* au pli impeccable; (*b*) chiffonner,
froisser (une robe). **2.** *v.i.* prendre un faux pli.
II. *s.* (faux) pli; **c.-resisting,** infroissable.
create [kriːˈeit], *v.tr.* (*a*) créer; produire (un objet,
un chef-d'œuvre, une impression); (*b*) *abs.*
P: rouspéter, faire une scène; **cre'ation,** *s.*
création *f*; **the latest c.,** la dernière mode;
cre'ative, *a.* créateur, -trice; **cre'ator,** *s.*
créateur, -trice.
creature ['kriːtʃər], *s.* **1.** créature *f*, être *m*. **2.**
animal *m*, bête *f*. **3. not a c. was to be seen,** on
ne voyait âme qui vive. **4. man is the c. of circumstances,** l'homme dépend des circonstances. **5.** *attrib.* **c. comforts,** l'aisance
matérielle; le confort.

crèche [kreiʃ], *s.* crèche *f*; pouponnière *f*.
credentials [kriˈdenʃ(ə)lz], *s.pl.* pièces
justificatives, d'identité.
credible ['kredibl], *a.* croyable; digne de foi;
-ibly, *adv.* **to be c. informed of sth.,** tenir qch.
de bonne source; **credi'bility,** *s.* crédibilité *f*;
c. gap, perte *f* de confiance, divergence *f*.
credit ['kredit]. **I.** *s.* **1.** croyance *f*, foi *f*; **to give c.
to a report,** ajouter foi à un bruit. **2.** crédit *m*,
influence *f*, réputation *f* (**with s.o.,** auprès de
qn). **3.** mérite *m*, honneur *m*; **I gave him c. for
more sense,** je lui croyais plus de jugement; **it
does him c.,** cela lui fait honneur. **4.** (*a*) *Com:*
crédit; **to give s.o. c.,** faire crédit à qn; **to sell on
c.,** vendre à crédit, à terme; *Bank:* **c. slip,**
bulletin *m* de versement; **c. balance,** solde *m*
créditeur; **c. card,** carte *f* de crédit; (*b*) *Book-k:*
c. side, avoir *m*; **c. note,** note *f*, facture *f*, de
crédit. **II.** *v.tr.* **1.** ajouter foi à, croire. **2.** attribuer, prêter (une qualité à qn); **I credited
you with more sense,** je vous croyais plus de
jugement; **to be credited with having done sth.,**
passer pour avoir fait qch. **3.** *Com:* créditer
(**with,** de); **to c. s.o. with a sum,** créditer qn
d'une somme; **'creditable,** *a.* (action) estimable, honorable, **-ably,** *adv.*
honorablement; **'creditor,** *s.* créancier, -ière.
credulous ['kredjuləs], *a.* crédule; **-ly,** *adv.*
crédulement; avec crédulité; **cre'dulity,** *s.*,
credulousness, *s.* crédulité *f*.
creed [kriːd], *s.* **1.** *Ecc:* credo; **the Apostles'
C.,** le symbole des Apôtres. **2.** *Pol: etc:* profession *f* de foi; credo.
creek [kriːk], *s.* crique *f*; ruisseau *m* (côtier); *F:*
to be up the c., cela lui fait honneur.
creep [kriːp]. **I.** *v.i.* (**crept**) **1.** ramper; (*of pers.*) se
traîner, se glisser; **to c. into bed,** se glisser dans
son lit. **2.** (*of plant, etc.*) grimper. **II.** *s.* **1.** *P:*
personnage déplaisant. **2.** *pl. F:* **it gives me
the creeps,** ça me donne la chair de poule;
'creeper, *s. Bot:* plante grimpante, ram-
pante; **Virginia c.,** vigne *f* vierge.
cremate [kriˈmeit], *v.tr.* incinérer (un mort);
cre'mation, *s.* incinération *f*, crémation *f* (des
morts); **crematorium** [kreməˈtɔːriəm], *s.*
(four *m*) crématoire (*m*); crématorium *m*.
creosote ['kriːəsout], *s.* créosote *f*.
crêpe [kreip], *s.* **1.** crêpe *m*; **c. paper,** papier *m*
crêpe; **c. nylon tights,** collants *mpl* mousse. **2.
c.(-rubber) soles,** semelles *f* (de) crêpe.
crescent ['kres(ə)nt], *s.* (*a*) croissant *m*; (*b*) rue *f*
en arc de cercle.
cress [kres], *s. Bot:* cresson *m*.
crest [krest], *s.* **1.** crête *f* (de coq). **2.** (*of hills, etc.*)
crête, sommet *m*, arête *f*. **3.** armoiries *fpl*;
'crestfallen, *a.* (*of pers.*) abattu, découragé.
Crete [kriːt]. *Pr.n. Geog:* la Crète; **'Cretan,** *a.* &
s. crétois, -oise.
crevasse [krəˈvæs], *s.* crevasse *f* (glaciaire).

crevice ['krevis], *s.* fente *f*; crevasse *f*, lézarde *f* (de mur); fissure *f* (de rocher).

crew [kruː], *s.* **1.** *Nau:* équipage *m*; (*of rowing boat*) équipe *f.* **2.** *Pej:* bande *f*, troupe *f.* **3. c. cut,** coupe *f* (de cheveux) en brosse.

crib [krib]. **I.** *s.* **1.** mangeoire *f*, râtelier *m.* **2.** lit *m* d'enfant; *Ecc:* crèche *f.* **3.** *Sch:* *F:* traduction *f* (d'auteur), corrigé *m* (de thèmes, etc.) (employés subrepticement). **II.** *v.tr.* (**cribbed**) *Sch:* *F:* copier (un devoir sur un camarade).

crick [krik]. **I.** *s.* **c. in the neck,** torticolis *m*; **c. in the back,** tour *m* de reins. **II.** *v.tr.* **to c. one's neck, one's back,** se donner le torticolis, un tour de reins.

cricket¹ [krikit], *s.* *Ent:* grillon *m*, cricri *m.*

cricket², *s.* *Games:* cricket *m*; **that's not c.,** cela n'est pas loyal; cela ne se fait pas; **'cricketer,** *s.* joueur *m* de cricket.

crime [kraim], *s.* (*a*) crime *m*; (*b*) délit *m*; **'criminal. 1.** *a.* criminel; **the C. Investigation Department** = la Police judiciaire. **2.** *s.* criminel, -elle; **habitual c.,** repris *m* de justice; récidiviste *mf*; **-ally,** *adv.* criminellement.

crimson ['krimz(ə)n], *a.* & *s.* cramoisi (*m*); pourpre (*m*).

cringe [krindʒ], *v.i.* (*a*) s'humilier, ramper (**to, before, s.o.,** devant qn); (*b*) se dérober (de crainte d'un coup); **'cringing,** *a.* **1.** craintif. **2.** servile, obséquieux.

crinkle ['kriŋkl]. **1.** *v.tr.* froisser, chiffonner (du papier); **crinkled paper,** papier ondulé, gaufré; papier crêpe. **2.** *v.i.* se froisser, se chiffonner.

cripple ['kripl]. **I.** *s.* estropié, -ée; boiteux, -euse; infirme *mf.* **II.** *v.tr.* (*a*) estropier (qn); **crippled with rheumatism,** perclus de rhumatismes; (*b*) disloquer (une machine); paralyser (l'industrie, la volonté de qn).

crisis, *pl.* **crises** ['kraisis, -iːz], *s.* crise *f.*

crisp [krisp]. **1.** *a.* (*a*) (biscuit) croquant, croustillant; (*b*) (style) nerveux; (ton) tranchant; (*c*) (air) vif. **2.** *s.* (potato) **crisps,** (pommes *fpl*) chips *mpl*; **'crispness,** *s.* **1.** qualité croustillante (d'un biscuit, etc.) **2.** netteté *f* (de style, *Mus:* d'exécution). **3.** froid vif (de l'air).

criterion, *pl.* **-ia** [krai'tiəriən, -iə], *s.* critère *m.*

critic ['kritik], *s.* (*a*) critique *m* (littéraire, etc.); **armchair c.,** critique en chambre; (*b*) censeur *m* (de la conduite d'autrui); (**carping**) **c.,** critiqueur, -euse; **'critical,** *a.* critique; **c. situation,** situation critique, dangereuse; **-ally,** *adv.* **1.** to look c. at sth., examiner qch. en critique. **2. to be c. ill,** être dangereusement malade; **'criticism,** *s.* critique *f*; **'criticize,** *v.tr.* **1.** critiquer (qch.). **2.** censurer, blâmer (qn).

croak [krouk]. **I.** *v.i.* **1.** (*of frog*) coasser; (*of raven*) croasser. **2.** *P:* mourir. **II.** *s.* coasse-ment *m* (de grenouille); croassement *m* (de corbeau); **'croaky,** *a.* (voix) enrouée, rauque.

crochet ['krouʃei, -ʃi]. **I.** *s.* (travail *m* au) crochet *m.* **II.** *v.* (**crocheted** ['krouʃeid]) (*a*) *v.tr.* faire (qch.) au crochet; (*b*) *v.i.* faire du crochet.

crock [krɔk]. **I.** *s.* **1.** (*a*) cruche *f*; (*b*) pot *m* de terre. **2.** *Aut:* *F:* tacot *m.* **3.** (*of pers.*) **he's an old c.,** c'est un homme fini, claqué. **II.** *v.i.* *F:* **to c. (up),** tomber malade; flancher; **'crockery,** *s.* faïence *f*, poterie *f.*

crocodile ['krɔkədail], *s.* crocodile *m.*

crocus, *pl.* **-uses** ['kroukəs, -əsiz], *s.* *Bot:* crocus *m.*

crony ['krouni], *s.* compère *m*, commère *f*; **old c.,** *F:* vieux copain.

crook [kruk]. **I.** *s.* **1.** houlette *f* (de berger); crosse *f* (d'évêque). **2.** angle *m*; courbure *f*; coude *m.* **3.** *F:* escroc *m.* **II.** *a.* *Austr:* *F:* malade, souffrant; **crooked** ['krukid], *a.* **1.** tordu; tortueux; de travers. **2.** malhonnête; **-ly,** *adv.* **1.** tortueusement. **2.** de travers; **'crookedness** [-idnis], *s.* **1.** sinuosité *f.* **2.** perversité *f*; malhonnêteté *f.*

croon [kruːn], *v.tr.* & *i.* chantonner; **'crooner,** *s.* chanteur, -euse, de charme.

crop [krɔp]. **I.** *s.* **1.** jabot *m* (d'un oiseau). **2.** récolte *f*, moisson *f*; **the crops,** la récolte. **II** *v.tr.* (**cropped**) (*a*) tondre, tailler, couper (une haie, etc.); (*b*) (*of animal*) brouter, paître (l'herbe); **'cropper,** *s.* *F:* **to come a c.,** (i) faire une chute; (ii) faire faillite; (iii) se heurter à un obstacle imprévu; **'crop up,** *v.i.* *F:* surgir.

croquet ['kroukei], *s.* (jeu *m* de) croquet *m.*

cross [krɔs]. **I.** *s.* **1.** croix *f*; **the Red C.,** la Croi rouge. **2.** croisement *m*; mélange *m* (de races (*b*) métis, -isse. **II.** *v.* *v.tr.* (*a*) croiser; (*b*) *Ecc* **to c. oneself,** se signer; (*c*) barrer (un chèque (*d*) traverser (la rue); passer (sur) (un pont franchir (le seuil d'une maison). **2.** *v.i.* (*a*) (roads, etc.*) se croiser; (*b*) passer (d'un lieu à u autre); **to c. from Calais to Dover,** faire traversée de Calais à Douvres. **III.** *a.* & *cor bined form.* **1.** (*a*) transversal; **c. sectio** coupe, section, transversale; tranche *f* (de population); (*b*) contraire, opposé; **they are c. purposes,** un malentendu, un désacco d'opinion, existe entre eux; **c. reference,** ren m (dans un livre). **2.** (*of pers.*) maussade, mauvaise humeur; fâché; **-ly,** *adv.* av mauvaise humeur; **'crossbar,** *s.* (barre *f* d traverse *f*; entretoise *f*; **'cross-breed,** *s.* ra croisée; **'cross-'check,** *v.tr.* contre-vérifi **'cross-exami'nation,** *s.* contr interrogatoire *m*; **'cross-ex'amine,** *v.* contre-interroger; **'cross-eyed,** *a.* qui louch **'cross-grained,** *a.* *F:* (*of pers.*) revê grincheux; **'crossing,** *s.* **1.** traversée *f* (de mer); **pedestrian c.,** passage *m* pour piétons croisement *m*; intersection *f*; **level c.,** pass à niveau. **3.** croisement de races; **'cross-'legged,** *a.* (s'asseoir) les jambes croisées; **'crossroads,** *s.pl.* carrefour *m*; **'crossword,** *s. c.* **(puzzle),** mots croisés.

crotch [krɔtʃ], *s.* (*a*) entrecuisse *m*; (*b*) fourche *f* (du pantalon).

crotchet ['krɔtʃit], *s.* **1.** *Mus:* noire *f.* **2.** *F:* (*a*) lubie *f*, caprice *m*; (*b*) idée *f* fixe; manie *f*; **'crotchety,** *a.* capricieux; d'humeur difficile.

crouch [krautʃ], *v.i.* se blottir, se tapir; s'accroupir.

croupier ['kru:piər], *s.* croupier *m.*

crow[1] [krou], *s.* **1.** *Orn:* corneille *f*; (*as a class*) **the crows,** les corbeaux; **as the c. flies,** à vol d'oiseau; *N.Am:* **to eat c.,** avaler des couleuvres; **'crowbar,** *s. Tls:* pince *f* à levier; **'crow's-feet,** *s.pl.* pattes-d'oie *f.*

crow[2], *v.i.* **1.** (*of cock*) chanter; **to c. over s.o.,** chanter victoire sur qn. **2.** (*of baby*) gazouiller; **'crowing,** *s.* **1.** chant *m* (du coq). **2.** gazouillement *m* (de bébé).

crowd [kraud]. **I.** *s.* **1.** foule *f*; (*often Pej:*) bande *f* (de gens); *Cin:* les figurants. **II.** *v.* **1.** *v.tr.* serrer, (en)tasser; **we're too crowded here,** on est gêné ici; **the hall is crowded (with people),** la salle est bondée; *Th:* **crowded house,** salle comble. **2.** *v.i.* **to c. (together),** se presser en foule.

crown [kraun]. **I.** *s.* **1.** (*a*) couronne *f* (d'or, de fleurs); **c. prince,** prince héritier; (*b*) *attrib.* **c. jewels,** joyaux *mpl* de la Couronne; **C. lawyer,** avocat *m* du Gouvernement, du Ministère public; **C. witness,** témoin *m* à charge. **2.** (*a*) sommet *m*, haut *m* (de la tête); (*b*) **c. of a hat,** calotte *f*, forme *f*, d'un chapeau; (*c*) cime *f* (d'un arbre, d'une montagne); bombement *m* (d'un pont); *Aut:* **to drive on the c. of the road,** conduire sur l'axe de la chaussée. **3. c. cork,** capsule *f* (métallique) de bouteille; **c. cork opener,** décapsuleur *m.* **II.** *v.tr.* **1.** couronner, sacrer (un roi). **2.** récompenser (les efforts de qn).

crucial ['kru:ʃəl], *a.* décisif, critique.

crucifix ['kru:sifiks], *s.* crucifix *m*; **roadside c.,** calvaire *m*; **cruci'fixion,** *s.* crucifixion *f*; **'crucify,** *v.tr.* crucifier.

crude [kru:d], *a.* (*a*) (à l'état) brut; (*b*) (*of colour*) cru; (*c*) (*of manners*) grossier; **-ly,** *adv.* crûment; grossièrement; **'crudeness,** *s.,* **'crudity,** *s.* crudité *f* (d'expression, de couleurs); grossièreté *f* (de manières).

cruel ['kruəl], *a.* cruel; **-ly,** *adv.* cruellement; **'cruelty,** *s.* cruauté *f* (**to,** envers); **society for the prevention of c. to animals,** société protectrice des animaux.

cruet ['kru:it], *s. H:* huilier *m.*

cruise [kru:z]. **I.** *s.* croisière *f.* **II.** *v.i.* **1.** *Nau:* croiser; *Aut: Av: Nau:* **cruising speed,** vitesse *f* de croisière, vitesse économique. **2.** (*of taxi*) faire la maraude; **'cruiser,** *s. Nau:* (*a*) croiseur *m*; (*b*) (**cabin**) **c.,** yacht *m* de plaisance.

crumb [krʌm], *s.* **1.** (*a*) miette *f*; **bread crumbs,** chapelure *f.* **2.** (*opposed to crust*) mie *f*; **'crumble,** *v.tr. & i.* (s')émietter; (s')effriter; *v.i.* (*of masonry*) s'écrouler.

crumpet ['krʌmpit], *s. Cu:* sorte de crêpe épaisse, sans sucre (servie rôtie et beurrée); *F:* **a nice bit of c.,** une jolie fille, une belle pépée.

crumple ['krʌmpl], *v.tr.* friper, froisser (qch.).

crunch [krʌn(t)ʃ]. **I.** *v.* **1.** *v.tr.* croquer; broyer. **2.** *v.i.* (*of snow, etc.*) crisser; craquer. **II.** *s.* **1.** coup *m* de dents. **2.** bruit *m* de broiement; craquement *m*, crissement *m.*

crusade [kru:'seid]. **I.** *s.* **1.** *Hist:* croisade *f.* **2.** campagne *f*, croisade (**for, against,** sth., pour, contre, qch.). **II.** *v.i.* **1.** *Hist:* aller en croisade. **2.** mener une campagne (**for, against,** sth., pour, contre, une cause, etc.); **cru'sader,** *s. Hist:* croisé *m.*

crush [krʌʃ]. **I.** *v.tr.* (*a*) écraser; **to c. sth. into a box,** fourrer qch. dans une boîte; (*b*) **crushed with grief,** accablé de douleur; (*c*) froisser (une robe); (*d*) *Min:* broyer, concasser. **II.** *s.* presse *f*, foule *f*; **'crushing,** *a.* écrasant; **-ly,** *adv.* d'un ton écrasant.

crust [krʌst], *s.* **1.** croûte *f.* **2.** écorce *f*, croûte; **'crusty,** *a.* (pain *m*) qui a une forte croûte; (biscuit) croustillant.

crustacean [krʌs'teiʃ(i)ən], *s.* crustacé *m.*

crutch [krʌtʃ], *s.* **1.** béquille *f.* **2.** (*a*) entrecuisse *m*; (*b*) fourche *f* (du pantalon).

crux [krʌks], *s.* nœud *m* (d'une difficulté, etc.); point capital (d'une discussion); **the c. of the matter,** le nœud de la question.

cry [krai]. **I.** *v.tr. & i.* (**cried**) **1.** crier; **to c. (out),** pousser un cri, des cris; **to c. for help,** crier au secours. **2.** (= **say**) s'écrier; **"that's not true!"** **he cried,** "c'est faux!" s'écria-t-il. **3.** pleurer; verser des larmes. **II.** *s.* **1.** cri *m* (de douleur); plainte *f.* **2.** action *f* de pleurer; pleurs *mpl*; **'cry 'down,** *v.tr.* décrier (qn); **'crying.** **1.** *a.* **c. injustice,** injustice criante; **c. evil,** abus scandaleux. **2.** *s.* cri(s) *m*(*pl*); clameur *f*; pleurs *mpl,* larmes *fpl*; **fit of c.,** crise *f* de larmes; **'cry 'off,** *v.i.* se dédire, se récuser.

crypt [kript], *s.* crypte *f.*

cryptic ['kriptik], *a.* secret, occulte; **c. silence,** silence *m* énigmatique; **-ally,** *adv.* (parler) à mots couverts.

crystal ['kristl], *s.* **1.** cristal *m*, **-aux.** **2.** **c.(-glass),** cristal; **'crystalline,** *a.* cristallin; **crystalli'zation,** *s.* cristallisation *f*; **'crystallize.** **1.** *v.tr.* cristalliser; **crystallized fruit,** fruits confits, fruits candis. **2.** *v.i.* (se) cristalliser; **crysta'llography,** *s.* cristallographie *f.*

cub [kʌb], *s.* petit *m* (d'un animal); **fox c.,** renardeau *m*; **bear c.,** ourson *m*; **lion c.,**

lionceau *m*; **wolf c.**, (*also in Scouting*) louveteau *m*.

cubby-hole ['kʌbihoul], *s.* 1. cachette *f.* 2. placard *m*.

cube [kju:b]. **I.** *s.* cube *m*; **c. root**, racine *f* cubique. **II.** *v.tr. Mth:* cuber; *'*cubic, *a.* cubique; **c. metre**, mètre cube; **c. capacity**, volume *m*; **c. equation**, équation *f* du troisième degré.

cubicle ['kju:bikl], *s.* alcôve *f* (d'un dortoir); cabine *f* (d'une piscine).

cubism ['kju:bizm], *s. Art:* cubisme *m*.

cuckoo ['kuku:]. 1. *s. Orn:* coucou *m*. 2. *a. F:* niais, -e; **he's c.**, il est cinglé; *'*cuckoo clock, *s.* (pendule *f* à) coucou *m*.

cucumber ['kju:kʌmbər], *s.* concombre *m*.

cud [kʌd], *s.* **to chew the c.**, ruminer.

cuddle ['kʌdl]. 1. *v.tr.* serrer (qn) doucement dans ses bras. 2. *v.i.* **to c. up to s.o.**, se pelotonner contre qn.

cue[1] [kju:], *s.* (*a*) *Th:* réplique *f*; **to take (up) one's c.**, donner la réplique; (*b*) avis *m*, mot *m*, indication *f*; **to take one's c. from s.o.**, s'ajuster, s'aligner, sur qn.

cue[2], *s.* queue *f* (de billard).

cuff[1] [kʌf], *s.* 1. poignet *m* (de chemise); (*starched*) manchette *f*. 2. (*of coat*) revers *m*; *N.Am:* **trouser cuffs**, revers de pantalon. 3. *F:* **to speak off the c.**, faire un discours impromptu; *'*cuff-links, *s.pl.* boutons *m* de manchettes (jumelés).

cuff[2]. **I.** *s.* taloche *f*, calotte *f*. **II.** *v.tr.* talocher, calotter (qn); flanquer une taloche à (qn).

cul-de-sac ['kʌldəsæk], *s.* impasse *f*.

culinary ['kʌlinəri], *a.* culinaire.

culminate ['kʌlmineit], *v.i.* **to c. in sth.**, se terminer en qch.; **culminating point**, point culminant; **culmi'nation**, *s.* aboutissement *m*; point culminant.

culpability [kʌlpə'biliti], *s.* culpabilité *f*; *'*culpable, *a.* coupable; -ably, *adv.* coupablement.

culprit ['kʌlprit], *s.* 1. *Jur:* accusé, -ée. 2. coupable *mf*.

cult [kʌlt], *s.* culte *m* (of, de).

cultivate ['kʌltiveit], *v.tr.* 1. cultiver, exploiter (la terre). 2. **to c. s.o.'s friendship**, cultiver l'amitié de qn; *'*cultivated, *a.* (esprit) cultivé; culti'vation, *s.* culture *f*; *'*cultivator, *s.* 1. (*pers.*) cultivateur, -trice. 2. (*machine*) motoculteur *m*.

culture ['kʌltʃər], *s.* culture *f* (des champs, de l'esprit, des bacilles etc.); *'*cultured, *a.* (esprit) cultivé, de grande culture; **c. pearl**, perle *f* de culture.

cumbersome ['kʌmbəsəm], *a.* encombrant, gênant, incommode.

cumulative ['kju:mjulətiv], *a.* cumulatif.

cunning ['kʌniŋ]. **I.** *s.* 1. (*a*) ruse *f*, finesse *f*; (*b*)

Pej: **low c.**, astuce *f*. 2. (*skill*) adresse *f*, habileté *f*. **II.** *a.* 1. rusé; malin, *f.* maligne; astucieux. 2. (*a*) **c. device**, dispositif ingénieux; (*b*) *N.Am:* *F:* gentil, coquet; -ly, *adv.* avec ruse; astucieusement.

cup [kʌp], *s.* 1. tasse *f*; **c. of tea**, tasse de thé; *F:* **that's not my c. of tea**, ce n'est pas mes oignons. 2. *Sp:* coupe *f*; **c. tie**, match *m* éliminatoire; **c. final**, finale *f* du championnat. 3. bonnet *m* (de soutien-gorge); *'*cupful, *s.* pleine tasse.

cupboard ['kʌbəd], *s.* armoire *f*; placard *m*; *F:* **c. love**, amour intéressé.

cupidity [kju(:)'piditi], *s.* cupidité *f*; convoitise *f*.

curate ['kjuərət], *s. Ecc:* vicaire *m*; *'*curacy, *s. Ecc:* vicariat *m*.

curator [kjuə'reitər], *s.* conservateur *m* (de musée).

curb [kə:b]. **I.** *s.* 1. mors *m* (d'un cheval); **c. chain**, gourmette *f*; **to put a c. on one's spending**, mettre un frein à ses dépenses. 2. **c.(-stone)**, bordure *f* (de trottoir); *Aut:* **to hit the c.**, heurter le trottoir. **II.** *v.tr.* réprimer, contenir (sa colère); modérer (son impatience).

curdle ['kə:dl], *v.i.* (*of milk*) se cailler; (*of blood*) se figer.

cure ['kjuər]. **I.** *v.tr.* 1. **to c. s.o. of an illness**, guérir qn d'une maladie. 2. (*a*) saler, fumer (la viande); saurer (des harengs); (*b*) saler (des peaux). **II.** *s.* 1. guérison *f*. 2. (*a*) cure *f*; **to take a c.**, suivre un traitement; (*b*) remède *m*; *'*curing, *s.* 1. guérison *f*. 2. salaison *f*.

curfew ['kə:fju:], *s.* couvre-feu *m*.

curio, *pl.* **-os** ['kjuəriou, -ouz], *s.* curiosité *f*; bibelot *m*.

curiosity [kjuəri'ɔsiti], *s.* 1. curiosité *f*. 2. obje curieux; rareté *f*; *'*curious, *a.* (*a*) curieux; (*Pej:* curieux, indiscret; (*c*) curieux, singulie -ly, *adv.* (*a*) curieusement; (*b*) singulièremen

curl [kə:l]. **I.** *s.* boucle *f* (de cheveux); (*of hair*) **i curls**, bouclé, frisé. **II.** *v.* 1. *v.tr.* & *i.* ondule boucler, friser (les cheveux). 2. *v.i.* (*of pape leaf*) se recroqueviller; (*of smoke*) s'élever e spirales; (*of waves*) déferler; *'*curler, *s.* Haird bigoudi *m*; *'*curl 'up, *v.i.* se mettre e boule; se pelotonner; *'*curly, *a.* bouclé, fris *Hort:* **c. lettuce**, (laitue *f*) frisée.

currant ['kʌrənt], *s.* 1. **red c.**, groseille *f* grappes); **black c.**, cassis *m*; **red-c. bus** groseiller *m*; **black-c. bush**, cassis. 2. (*dri fruit*) raisin *m* de Corinthe.

currency ['kʌrənsi], *s.* unité *f* monétaire (d' pays); monnaie *f*; **foreign c.**, devise (étrangères); **hard c.**, devises fortes.

current ['kʌrənt]. **I.** *s.* 1. (*a*) courant *m*; fil *m* l'eau; (*b*) *Meteor:* **air, atmospheric, c.**, coura (d'air); (*c*) **the c. of events**, le cours d événements. 2. **electric c.**, courant électriqu *F:* le courant. **II.** *a.* courant, en cours;

number (of a paper), dernier numéro (d'un journal); c. reports, bruits *m* qui courent; in c. use, d'usage courant; c. events, actualités *f*; -ly, *adv.* couramment; actuellement.

curriculum [kə'rikjuləm], *s.* programme *m* d'études; c. vitae, curriculum vitae *m*.

curry¹ ['kʌri], *s. Cu: (powder or dish)* cari *m*, curry *m*.

curry², *v.tr.* 1. étriller (un cheval). 2. corroyer (le cuir). 3. to c. favour with s.o., s'insinuer dans les bonnes grâces de qn; 'curry-comb, *s.* étrille *f*.

curse [kə:s]. I. *s.* 1. (*a*) malédiction *f*; (*b*) juron *m*; gros mot. 2. fléau *m*, calamité *f*. II. *v.* 1. *v.tr.* maudire (qn, qch.). 2. *v.i.* sacrer, jurer; 'cursed [-sid], *a.* maudit; *F:* what c. weather! quel fichu temps!

cursory ['kə:səri], *a.* (coup d'œil) rapide, superficiel; -ily, *adv.* rapidement; à la hâte.

curt [kə:t], *a.* brusque; sec; -ly, *adv.* brusquement, sèchement.

curtail [kə:'teil], *v.tr.* abréger; écourter (un article); diminuer (l'autorité de qn); restreindre (ses dépenses).

curtain ['kə:t(ə)n]. I. *s.* rideau *m*; *Pol:* iron c., rideau de fer; *Th: Cin:* rideau; safety c., rideau métallique. II. *v.tr.* garnir de rideaux; to c. off a room, masquer une pièce par un rideau; 'curtain-call, *s. Th:* rappel *m* (d'un acteur); 'curtain-rod, *s.* tringle *f*.

curve [kə:v]. I. *s.* (*a*) courbe *f*; flat c., courbe ouverte; c. of an arch, voussure *f* d'une voûte; (*b*) c. in the road, tournant *m*; *Aut:* virage *m*. II. *v.* 1. *v.tr.* courber. 2. *v.i.* décrire une courbe; curvature ['kə:vətʃər], *s.* courbure *f*; *Med:* c. of the spine, déviation *f* de la colonne vertébrale; curved, *a.* courbé, courbe.

cushion ['kuʃ(ə)n]. I. *s.* coussin *m*. II. *v.tr.* 1. garnir (un siège) de coussins. 2. amortir (un coup).

cushy ['kuʃi], *a. F:* (emploi) facile.

cussedness ['kʌsidnis], *s. F:* perversité *f*; out of pure c., rien que pour embêter le monde.

custard ['kʌstəd], *s. Cu:* crème *f* (au lait); œuf(s) *m* au lait; baked c., flan *m*; caramel c., crème caramel.

custody ['kʌstədi], *s.* 1. garde *f*; in safe c., en lieu sûr. 2. emprisonnement *m*; détention *f*; to take s.o. into c., arrêter qn; cus'todian, *s.* gardien, -ienne; conservateur *m* (de monument).

custom ['kʌstəm], *s.* 1. coutume *f*, usage *m*, habitude *f*. 2. *pl.* customs, *Adm:* (bureaux de la) douane; c. officer, douanier *m*. 3. *Com:* (*a*) (*of shop*) clientèle *f*; (*b*) patronage *m* (du client); (*c*) c. made, built, fait sur commande; *Ind:* hors série; (vêtement) fait sur mesure; c. tailor, tailleur *m* à façon; 'customary, *a.* habituel, d'usage; -ily, *adv.* habituellement; 'customer, *s.* client, -ente; *F:* a queer c., un drôle de type; ugly c., sale type.

cut [kʌt]. I. *v.tr. & i.* (cut; cut) 1. couper, tailler; to c. one's finger, se couper au doigt; to have one's hair c., se faire couper les cheveux; this remark c. him to the quick, cette parole le piqua au vif; that cuts both ways, c'est un argument à deux tranchants; *Com:* to c. prices, faire des prix de concurrence. 2. to c. a speech short, raccourcir un discours; to c. s.o. short, couper la parole à qn; *F:* c. it short! abrégez! 3. to c. into the conversation, intervenir dans la conversation. 4. couper (les cartes); to c. for deal, tirer pour la donne. 5. to c. s.o. (dead), faire semblant de ne pas voir qn; to c. an appointment, manquer exprès à un rendez-vous; *Sch:* to c. a lecture, sécher un cours. II. *s.* 1. coupe *f*; réduction *f* (des salaires); *El:* coupure *f* (du courant). 2. (*wound*) coupure; balafre *f*. 3. short c., raccourci *m*. 4. *Cu:* c. off the joint, tranche *f* de rôti; cheap cuts, bas morceaux. III. *a.* 1. (cristal) taillé; *Cl:* well c., de bonne coupe; c. and dried opinions, opinions toutes faites. 2. c. prices, prix de concurrence; 'cut'down, *v.tr.* abattre (un arbre); rogner (des dépenses); *Ind:* restreindre (la production); 'cut'in, *v.i.* 1. se mêler à la conversation. 2. *Aut:* (*after passing*) to c. in on s.o., couper la route à qn; 'cutlery, *s.* coutellerie *f*; 'cut'off, *v.tr.* (*a*) couper, détacher; (*b*) to c. o. s.o.'s retreat, couper la retraite à qn; (*c*) *El:* to c. o. the current, interrompre le courant; 'cut'out, *v.tr.* 1. (*a*) couper, enlever; exciser; (*b*) *F:* to c. s.o. o., supplanter qn. 2. découper (des images); to c. o. a garment, tailler un vêtement; to be c. o. for sth., avoir des dispositions pour qch. 3. supprimer; retrancher; 'cutter, *s.* 1. (*pers.*) coupeur *m*; tailleur *m* (de pierres). 2. *Tls:* coupoir *m*, lame *f*; rotary c., roue *f* à couteaux. 3. *Nau:* canot *m* (d'un navire de guerre); 'cut-throat, *s.* 1. (*pers.*) coupe-jarret *m*. 2. c.-t. competition, concurrence acharnée; 'cutting. I. *a.* 1. c. edge, tranchant *m* (d'un outil). 2. c. wind, vent cinglant. 3. (*of remark*) mordant. II. *s.* 1. coupure (prise dans un journal). 2. (*of plant*) bouture *f*. 3. *Rail: etc:* tranchée *f*; voie encaissée; 'cut'up, *v.tr.* (*a*) découper (une volaille); (*b*) *F:* to be c. up about sth., être affligé de qch. 2. *v.i. F:* to c. up rough, se fâcher.

cute [kju:t], *a.* gentil, coquet; 'cuteness, *s. F:* intelligence, finesse.

cutlet ['kʌtlit], *s.* (*a*) côtelette *f* (de mouton, de veau); (*b*) *Cu:* croquette *f* de viande.

cyanide ['saiənaid], *s. Ch:* cyanure *m*.

cycle ['saikl]. I. *s.* 1. cycle *m*; *Geol:* période *f*. 2. *F:* bicyclette *f*, *F:* vélo *m*; c. track, piste *f* cyclable; c.-racing track, vélodrome *m*. II. *v.i.* faire de la bicyclette; aller à bicyclette; *F:* faire du vélo; 'cycling, *s.* cyclisme *m*; 'cyclist, *s.* cycliste *mf*; racing c., coureur *m* cycliste.

cyclone ['saikloun], *s. Meteor:* cyclone *m.*

cygnet ['signit], *s. Orn:* jeune cygne *m.*

cylinder ['silindər], *s.* cylindre *m;* **cy'lindrical,** *a.* cylindrique.

cynic ['sinik], *s.* censeur *m* caustique; railleur *m;* sceptique *m;* **'cynical,** *a.* cynique; sceptique; désabusé; **-ally,** *adv.* d'un ton sceptique; caustiquement; **'cynicism,** *s.* **1.** scepticisme

railleur; désillusionnement *m.*

cypress ['saiprəs], *s. Bot:* cyprès *m.*

Cyprus ['saiprəs]. *Pr.n.* (l'île *f* de) Chypre *f;* **'Cypriot,** *a. & s.* cypriote (*mf*).

cyst [sist], *s. Med:* kyste *m.*

Czech [tʃek], *a. & s.* tchèque (*mf*).

Czechoslovakia ['tʃekouslə'vækiə]. *Pr.n.* la Tchécoslovaquie.

D

D, d [di:], s. 1. (la lettre) D, d, m. 2. Mus: ré m.

dab¹ [dæb]. I. s. 1. coup léger; tape f. 2. tache f (d'encre, de peinture); pl. F: empreintes digitales. 3. a. & s. F: to be a d., a d. hand, at sth., être calé, être un as, en qch. II. v.tr. (dabbed) 1. donner une tape à (qn). 2. tapoter; tamponner; **to d. one's eyes (with a handkerchief)**, se tamponner les yeux (avec un mouchoir).

dab², s. Ich: limande f, carrelet m.

dabble ['dæbl], v.i. (a) barboter (dans l'eau); (b) F: **to d. in law, in politics,** s'occuper un peu de droit; se mêler de politique.

dachshund ['dækshund], s. teckel m.

dad [dæd], **daddy** ['dædi], s. papa m; '**daddy-'long-legs,** s. tipule f. Ent:

daffodil ['dæfədil], s. Bot: narcisse m des bois; jonquille f.

daft [dɑ:ft], a. F: 1. écervelé. 2. toqué; **don't be d.,** ne fais pas l'imbécile.

dagger ['dægər], s. 1. poignard m, dague f; **to be at daggers drawn,** être à couteaux tirés (**with s.o.,** avec qn).

dahlia ['deilia], s. Bot: dahlia m.

daily ['deili]. 1. a. journalier, quotidien; **d. help,** s., F: **daily,** femme f de ménage; **d. (paper),** quotidien m. 2. adv. journellement, quotidiennement.

dainty ['deinti], a. 1. (of food) friand. 2. (of pers.) délicat, exquis; **-ily,** adv. délicatement; '**daintiness,** s. délicatesse f, raffinement m.

dairy ['dɛəri], s. 1. laiterie f; **d. produce,** produits laitiers. 2. (shop) crémerie f; '**dairy cattle,** s. coll. vaches laitières; '**dairy farming,** s. l'industrie f laitière; '**dairyman,** pl. **-men,** s. Com: laitier m; crémier m.

dais ['deiis], s. estrade f.

daisy ['deizi], s. Bot: marguerite f; **common d.,** pâquerette f.

dale [deil], s. vallée f, vallon m; esp. **in the Yorkshire Dales,** le pays vallonné du Yorkshire.

dam [dæm]. I. s. barrage m. II. v.tr. (dammed) **to d. (up),** contenir, endiguer (un cours d'eau, un lac).

damage ['dæmidʒ]. I. s. 1. dommage(s) m(pl), dégâts mpl; avarie(s) f(pl); **there's no great d. done,** il n'y a pas grand mal. 2. préjudice m, tort m. 3. pl. Jur: dommages-intérêts m. II. v.tr. 1. endommager; avarier; abîmer. 2. faire tort, nuire, à (qn); '**damaged,** a. avarié, en-

dommagé; '**damaging,** a. préjudiciable, nuisible.

Damascus [də'mæskəs]. Pr.n. Geog: Damas m.

damn [dæm]. I. 1. s. juron m; gros mot; F: **I don't care a d.,** je m'en fiche. 2. a. F: **he does d. all,** il ne fait, F: ne fiche, rien. 3. int. **d. it!** zut! II. v.tr. 1. (of critic) **to d. a book,** condamner un livre; perdre; ruiner (qn, un projet). 2. damner; (of God) réprouver. 3. **d. your impudence!** que le diable vous emporte! '**damnable** ['dæmnəbl], a. odieux; **-ably,** adv. odieusement, F: bigrement (mauvais); **dam'nation,** s. damnation (éternelle); **damned,** a. 1. damné, réprouvé. 2. F: (a) **what a d. nuisance!** quel empoisonnement! **he's a d. nuisance!** comme il est casse-pieds! il est enquiquinant! (b) adv. diablement; **it's d. hard,** c'est bigrement difficile; '**damning,** a. qui porte condamnation f; **d. evidence,** preuves accablantes.

damp [dæmp]. I. s. humidité f. II. v.tr. 1. mouiller (qch.); humecter (le linge). 2. **to d. down the fire,** étouffer le feu. 3. refroidir (le courage de qn); décourager (qn). III. a. humide; (of skin) moite; '**dampen,** v.i. (a) devenir humide; (b) (of ardour, courage) se refroidir; '**damper,** s. 1. F: événement déprimant; **to put a d. on the company,** jeter un froid sur la compagnie. 2. (in Austr.) pain m en galette, sans levain. 3. Tchn: registre m (de foyer); Mec: El: Aut: etc: amortisseur m; '**dampness,** s. humidité f; (of skin) moiteur f; '**damp-proof,** a. imperméable.

damson ['dæmz(ə)n], s. prune f de Damas.

dance [dɑ:ns]. I. s. 1. danse f. 2. bal m, pl. bals; soirée dansante. II. v. 1. v.i. (a) danser; **to d. with s.o.,** faire danser qn; (b) **to d. for joy,** danser de joie; **to d. with rage,** trépigner de colère. 2. v.tr. (a) danser (une valse, le twist, etc.); (b) **to d. attendance on s.o.,** faire l'empressé auprès de qn; '**danceband,** s. orchestre m de musique de danse; '**dance-hall,** s. bal m public; dancing m; '**dancing,** s. la danse; '**dancer,** s. danseur, -euse.

dandelion ['dændilaiən], s. Bot: pissenlit m.

dandruff ['dændrəf], s. pellicules fpl (du cuir chevelu).

Dane [dein], s. 1. Danois, -oise. 2. **(Great) Dane,** (chien) danois; '**Danish. 1.** a. danois. 2. Ling: le danois.

danger ['deindʒər], s. danger m, péril m; **to be in**

d., courir un danger; **out of d.,** *Med:* **off the d. list,** hors de danger; *P.N:* **d., road up,** attention aux travaux; **'dangerous,** *a.* dangereux, périlleux; **-ly,** *adv.* dangereusement.
dangle ['dæŋgl], *v.i.* pendiller, pendre; **with legs dangling,** les jambes ballantes.
dank [dæŋk], *a.* humide (et froid).
dapper ['dæpər], *a.* (*esp. of a man*) pimpant; élégant.
dare ['dɛər], *v.* **1.** modal aux. (**dared, dare**) oser; **how d. you!** vous osez! vous avez cette audace! **I d. say,** sans doute; peut-être bien. **2.** *v.tr.* (*a*) **to d. to do sth.,** oser faire qch.; (*b*) **to d. s.o. to do sth.,** défier qn de faire qch.; **'dare-devil,** *s.* casse-cou *m inv*; **'daring. I.** *a.* (i) audacieux, hardi; (ii) téméraire; **-ly,** *adv.* audacieusement, témérairement. **II.** *s.* (i) audace *f*, hardiesse *f*; (ii) témérité *f*.
dark [dɑ:k]. **I.** *a.* **1.** sombre, obscur, noir; **it's d.,** il fait nuit, il fait noir; **the sky grew d.,** le ciel s'assombrit. **2.** (*of colour*) foncé, sombre. **3.** (*of pers.*) brun; basané. **4.** sombre, triste; **to look on the d. side of things,** voir tout en noir. **5.** **to keep sth. d.,** tenir qch. secret; **-ly,** *adv.* obscurément. **II.** *s.* **1.** ténèbres *fpl*, obscurité *f*; **after d.,** à la nuit close. **2. to be (kept) in the d.,** être (laissé) dans l'ignorance; **'darken. 1.** *v.tr.* obscurcir; assombrir. **2.** *v.i.* s'obscurcir; (*of sky, etc.*) s'assombrir; **'darkening,** *s.* assombrissement *m*; **'darkness,** *s.* **1.** obscurité *f*, ténèbres *fpl*. **2.** (*of colour*) (teinte) foncée.
darling ['dɑ:liŋ], *s. & a.* bien-aimé, -ée; **my d.!** mon chéri! ma chérie! **what a d. (child, bird)!** quel amour (d'enfant, d'oiseau)! **he's mother's d.,** c'est un enfant gâté.
darn [dɑ:n]. **I.** *s.* reprise *f*. **II.** *v.tr.* repriser, ravauder (des bas); **'darning,** *s.* reprise *f*; **d. needle,** aiguille *f* à repriser.
dart [dɑ:t]. **I.** *s.* **1.** (*a*) dard *m*, trait *m*; (*b*) (**game of**) **darts,** (jeu *m* de) fléchettes *f*; (*c*) *Cl:* pince *f*. **2. to make a d. across the road,** foncer, se précipiter, à travers la rue. **II.** *v.* **1.** *v.tr.* (*of sun*) darder (ses rayons). **2.** *v.i.* se précipiter, s'élancer, foncer (**across the road,** à travers la rue); **to d. in, out,** entrer, sortir, en coup de vent.
dash [dæʃ]. **I.** *s.* **1.** *Cu: etc:* soupçon *m*, goutte *f* (de cognac dans la sauce); pointe *f* (de vanille). **2. d. of colour,** tache *f*, touche *f*, de couleur. **3.** trait *m*; *Typ:* tiret *m*. **4.** (i) attaque soudaine; (ii) course *f* à toute vitesse; élan *m*; ruée *f*; **to make a d. forward,** s'élancer; **to make a d. at sth.,** se précipiter sur qch. **5.** élan, impétuosité *f*, fougue *f*; *F:* **to cut a d.,** faire de l'effet *m*. **II.** *v.* **1.** *v.tr.* **to d. sth. to pieces,** fracasser qch.; **to d. s.o.'s hopes,** anéantir les espoirs de qn. **2.** *v.i.* (*a*) se heurter (contre qch.); (*b*) **to d. at s.o., sth.,** se précipiter sur qn, qch.; (*c*) **I have to d.**

(**off**), il faut que je me sauve; **'dash a'long,** *v.i.* filer à fond de train; **'dash a'way,** *v.i.* s'éloigner en coup de vent; **'dashboard,** *s.* tableau *m* de bord; **'dashing,** *a.* (*of pers.*) plein d'élan; (*of horse*) fringant.
data ['deitə], *s.pl.* données *f*; **d. processing,** l'informatique *f*.
date[1] [deit], *s.* datte *f*; **'date-palm,** *s.* dattier *m*.
date[2]. **I.** *s.* date *f*; (*a*) **what's the d. today?** quelle est la date aujourd'hui? **to be up to d.,** être à la page; **to be up to d. with one's work,** être à jour dans son travail; **to bring (sth.) up to d.,** remettre (qch.) au point; **out of d.,** démodé; (*b*) *Com:* **interest to d.,** intérêts *mpl* à ce jour; **d. of a bill,** échéance *f* d'un billet; **three months after d.,** trois mois de date; (*c*) *F:* **to have a d. with s.o.,** avoir rendez-vous avec qn. **II.** *v.* **1.** *v.tr.* (*a*) dater (une lettre); (*b*) prendre rendez-vous avec (qn); (*c*) assigner une date à (un tableau). **2.** *v.i.* (*a*) **to d. back,** remonter (au Xᵉ siècle etc.); (*b*) **his style is beginning to d.,** son style commence à dater; **'dateless,** *a.* sans date.
daub [dɔ:b]. **I.** *s.* **1.** barbouillage *m*. **2.** (*picture*) croûte *f*. **II.** *v.tr.* barbouiller, enduire (**with, de**).
daughter ['dɔ:tər], *s.* fille *f*; **'daughter-in-law** *s.* belle-fille *f*, *pl.* belles-filles; bru.
daunt [dɔ:nt], *v.tr.* intimider, décourager; (*esp. in phrase*) **nothing daunted,** aucunement intimidé; sans se laisser abattre; **'dauntless,** *a.* intrépide.
dawdle ['dɔ:dl]. *v.i.* flâner; **'dawdler,** *s.* flâneur -euse; traînard, -arde; **'dawdling,** *s.* flânerie *f*.
dawn [dɔ:n]. **I.** *s.* aube *f*, aurore *f*; **at d.,** au point du jour. **II.** *v.i.* (*of day*) poindre; se lever; **at last it dawned on me that . . .,** enfin il me vint l'esprit que . . ..
day [dei], *s.* **1.** (*a*) jour *m*; **it's a fine d.,** il fait beau aujourd'hui; (*working, etc., day*) journée *f*; **a d. (long),** toute la journée; **to work by the d.,** travailler à la journée; **twice a d.,** deux fois par jour; **this d. week,** (d')aujourd'hui en huit; **the d. before (sth.),** la veille (de qch.); **the d. after (sth.),** le lendemain (de qch.); **every other d.,** tous les deux jours; **d. after d.,** jour après jour; **d. by d.,** jour par jour; de jour en jour; **from d. to d.,** de jour en jour; (*b*) **d. labourer,** ouvrier; **d. nursery,** pouponnière *f*, garderie *f* (d'enfants); *Sch:* **d. school,** externat *m*; **d. boy, girl,** externe *mf*; **d. boarder,** demi-pensionnaire *mf*; *Ind:* **d. shift,** équipe *f* de jour. **2.** (*a*) **what d. of the month is it?** c'est le combien aujourd'hui? **he may arrive any d.,** il peut arriver d'un jour à l'autre; **d. off,** jour de congé; (*b*) fête *f*; **All Saints' D.,** la fête de la Toussaint; **Easter D.,** le jour de Pâques; **Michaelmas D.,** la Saint-Michel. **3. the good old days,** le bon vieux temps; **in days past,** autrefois; **in our own day,** de nos jours; **in my young days,** du temps de

ma jeunesse; **I was a student in those days,** j'étais étudiant à ce moment-là, à cette époque; **to this d.,** encore aujourd'hui; **in days to come,** dans un temps futur, à l'avenir; **to have had its d.,** avoir fait son temps; **'daybreak,** s. aube f; **'daydream. I.** s. rêverie f; rêvasserie f. **II.** v.i. rêver (creux); rêvasser; **'daylight,** s. (lumière f de) jour m; **by d.,** de jour; **in broad d.,** en plein jour.

aze [deiz]. **I.** s. (after a blow, etc.) étourdissement m; **(mental) d.,** stupéfaction f; **to be in a d.,** être hébété. **II.** v.tr. (of blow) étourdir (qn); (of drug, etc.) stupéfier, hébéter.

azzle ['dæzl], v.tr. éblouir, aveugler; **'dazzling,** a. éblouissant, aveuglant; **-ly,** adv. **d. beautiful,** d'une beauté éblouissante.

ad [ded]. **I.** a. **1.** (a) mort; **he's d.,** il est mort, décédé; **the d. man, woman,** le mort, la morte; **to kill s.o.** (stone) **d.,** tuer qn raide; **d. as a door-nail, as mutton,** mort et bien mort; (b) (of limb) **to go d.,** s'engourdir; **the line went d.,** on a coupé la communication. **2. d. season,** morte-saison; **d. period,** période f d'inactivité. **3. to come to a d. stop,** s'arrêter net, F: pile; **d. calm,** calme plat; **d. silence,** silence m de mort; **d. secret,** profond secret; **d. level,** niveau parfait; **d. loss,** perte sèche; **to be in d. earnest,** être tout à fait sérieux; **he's a d. shot,** il ne rate jamais son coup. **4.** El: **d. cell,** pile f à plat. **II.** s. **1.** pl. **the d.,** les morts m. **2. at d. of night,** au milieu de la nuit; **in the d. of winter,** au (plus) fort de l'hiver. **III.** adv. (a) absolument; **d. drunk,** ivre mort; **d. tired,** éreinté, F: claqué; **d. slow,** au grand ralenti; (b) **to stop d.,** s'arrêter net, F: pile; **to arrive d. on time,** F: arriver pile; (c) **to be d. against sth.,** être absolument opposé à qch.; **'dead(-and)-a'live,** a. (endroit) mort, triste; **'dead-'beat. 1.** a. épuisé, éreinté, fourbu. **2.** s. N.Am: P: (a) clochard m; (b) filou m; **'deaden,** v.tr. amortir (un coup); étouffer (un bruit); émousser (les sens); **'dead 'end,** s. impasse f; **'deadline,** s. date f limite; **'deadlock,** s. impasse f; situation f inextricable; **'deadly. 1.** a. mortel; **d. hatred, d. poison,** haine mortelle, implacable; poison mortel. **2.** adv. mortellement; **it was d. cold,** il faisait un froid de loup; **'dead 'march,** s. Mus: marche f funèbre; **'deadpan,** esp. N.Am: F: (a) a. (visage m) figé; (b) s. pince-sans-rire m inv; **'dead-'weight,** s. poids mort.

af [def], a. sourd; **d. and dumb,** sourd-muet; **to turn a d. ear (to s.o.),** faire la sourde oreille (à qn); **'deaf-aid,** s. aide-ouïe m inv; **'deafen,** v.tr. assourdir (qn); rendre (qn) sourd; **'deafening,** a. assourdissant; **'deaf-'mute,** s. sourd-muet, f. sourde-muette; **'deafness,** s. surdité f.

al¹ [di:l], s. **a good d.,** beaucoup (of, de); **that's saying a good d.,** ce n'est pas peu dire; adv. **he**

is a good **d. better,** il va beaucoup mieux.

deal². I. v. (dealt) **1.** v.tr. (a) **to d. out (gifts, etc.),** distribuer, répartir (des dons, etc.) **(to, among,** entre); (b) **to d. s.o. a blow,** donner, porter, un coup à qn; (c) donner (les cartes). **2.** v.i. (a) **to d. with (s.o., sth.),** avoir affaire à (qn); traiter de, s'occuper de (qch.); **to d. with a piece of business,** conclure une affaire; **to d. with a problem,** venir à bout d'un problème; Com: **to d. in timber,** faire le commerce du bois; (b) Cards: faire la donne, donner. **II.** s. **1.** Cards: la donne; **whose d. is it?** à qui de donner? **2.** Com: affaire f; marché m; **'dealer,** s. **1.** Cards: donneur m. **2.** Com: (a) négociant m **(in,** en); distributeur m **(in,** de); (b) marchand, -ande **(in,** de); **'dealing,** s. **1. d. (out),** distribution f. **2.** pl. **to have dealings with s.o.,** avoir des relations f avec qn; **fair dealings,** loyauté f, honnêteté f (en affaires).

dean [di:n], s. Ecc: Sch: doyen m.

dear ['diər]. **I.** a. (a) cher **(to,** à); **my d. fellow,** mon cher; (in letter) **D. Madam,** Madame, Mademoiselle; **D. Sir,** Monsieur; **D. Mr Smith,** cher Monsieur; (b) cher, coûteux; **-ly,** adv. **1.** cher, chèrement; **you'll pay d. for this,** cela vous coûtera cher. **2. d. loved,** tendrement, bien, aimé(e); **he d. loves his house,** il est très attaché à sa maison. **II.** s. cher, f. chère; **my d.,** cher ami, chère. **III.** adv. (vendre, payer) cher. **IV.** int. **d. me!** mon Dieu! **oh d.!** (i) diable! oh là là! (ii) F: mince (alors)!

dearth [dəːθ], s. disette f, pénurie f (de vivres, de livres, etc.).

death [deθ], s. **1.** mort f; **to die a violent d.,** mourir de mort violente; **till d.,** pour la vie; **he'll be the d. of me,** (i) il me fera mourir; (ii) il me fait mourir de rire; P: **to catch one's d.,** attraper la crève; **to be sick to d. of sth.,** en avoir plein le dos; en avoir ras le bol. **2.** Adm: décès m; **d. rate,** mortalité f; P.N: (in newspaper) **deaths,** nécrologie f; **d. duty,** droit m de succession. **3.** la mort; **to be at d.'s door,** être à l'article de la mort; **'deathbed,** s. lit m de mort; **'death-blow,** s. coup mortel, fatal; **'deathless,** a. (of fame, etc.) impérissable, immortel; **'deathly,** adv. **d. pale,** d'une pâleur mortelle; **'death-trap,** s. casse-cou m inv; Aut: virage, croisement, dangereux.

debar [di'bɑːr], v.tr. **(debarred) to d. s.o. from sth.,** exclure qn de qch.; **to d. s.o. from doing sth.,** défendre à qn de faire qch.

debase [di'beis], v.tr. avilir, dégrader (qn); altérer, déprécier (la monnaie); **de'basing,** a. avilissant; **de'basement,** s. dégradation f; altération f, dépréciation f (des monnaies).

debate [di'beit]. **I.** s. débat m, discussion f; **(public) d.,** conférence f contradictoire, conférence débat. **II.** v. **1.** v.tr. débattre, discuter, agiter (une question); **a much debated question,** une question fort controversée. **2.** *v.i.* discuter, disputer (**with s.o. on sth.,** avec qn sur qch.); **de′batable,** *a.* contestable, discutable.

debauch [di′bɔːtʃ], *v.tr.* débaucher, corrompre (qn); **de′bauched,** *a.* débauché, corrompu; **de′bauchery,** *s.* débauche *f*; dérèglement *m* de mœurs.

debility [di′biliti], *s. Med:* affaiblissement *m*.

debit [′debit]. **I.** *s. Book-k:* débit *m*, doit *m*; **d. balance,** solde débiteur. **II.** *v.tr.* **1.** débiter (un compte). **2.** **to d. s.o. with a sum,** porter une somme au débit de qn.

debris [′debriː], *s.* débris *mpl*; (*of buildings*) décombres *mpl*.

debt [det], *s.* dette *f*; créance *f*; **bad debts,** mauvaises créances; **to be in d.,** être endetté; avoir des dettes; **to be out of d.,** être quitte de dettes; **′debtor,** *s.* **1.** débiteur, -trice. **2.** *Book-k:* **d. side,** débit *m*, doit *m*.

debunk [diː′bʌŋk], *v.tr. F:* déboulonner (qn).

début [′deibjuː], *s. esp. Th:* début *m*.

decade [′dekeid], *s.* décennie *f*.

decadence [′dekədəns], *s.* décadence *f*; **′decadent,** *a.* décadent.

decamp [di′kæmp], *v.i.* décamper, filer.

decanter [di′kæntər], *s.* carafe *f*.

decapitate [di′kæpiteit], *v.tr.* décapiter (qn), couper la tête à (qn).

decarbonize [diː′kɑːbənaiz], *v.tr. Aut:* décarboniser, décalaminer (un cylindre); **decarboni′zation,** *s.* decalaminage *m*, décrassage *m*.

decay [di′kei]. **I.** *s.* **1.** décadence *f* (d′un pays, d′une famille); délabrement *m* (d′un bâtiment); **senile d.,** affaiblissement *m* sénile; (*of house*) **to fall into d.,** tomber en ruine. **2.** (*a*) pourriture *f*, corruption *f*; (*b*) carie *f* (des dents). **II.** *v.i.* tomber en décadence; (*of house*) tomber en ruine; se délabrer; pourrir; (*of teeth*) se carier.

decease [di′siːs], *s. Adm:* décès *m*; **de′ceased. 1.** *a.* décédé; **David Martin, d.,** (le) feu David Martin; **the d. Queen,** la feue reine; feu la reine. **2.** *s.* **the d.,** le défunt, la défunte.

deceit [di′siːt], *s.* tromperie *f*, duperie *f*; **de′ceitful,** *a.* trompeur, faux, *f.* fausse; **-fully,** *adv.* faussement, avec duplicité; **de′ceitfulness,** *s.* nature trompeuse; fausseté *f*.

deceive [di′siːv], *v.tr.* tromper, abuser (qn); en imposer à (qn).

December [di′sembər], *s.* décembre *m*.

decent [′diːsnt], *a.* **1.** (*a*) bienséant, convenable; (*b*) décent, honnête, modeste. **2.** passable; assez bon; **the food is quite d.,** la nourriture est convenable. **3. a very d. fellow,** un très bon garçon; **-ly,** *adv.* **1.** convenablement. **2.** assez bien; **′decency,** *s.* **1.** décence *f*, bienséance *f* (de costume, etc.). **2. the decencies, common d.,** les convenances (sociales); le respect hu-

main. **3.** (**sense of**) **d.,** pudeur *f*.

decentralize [diː′sentrəlaiz], *v.tr.* décentraliser; **decentrali′zation,** *s.* décentralisation *f*.

deception [di′sepʃ(ə)n], *s.* tromperie *f*, duperie *f*, fraude *f*; **de′ceptive,** *a.* trompeur; décevant; **-ly,** *adv.* trompeusement.

decide [di′said]. **1.** *v.tr.* (*a*) décider (une question); trancher (une question); statuer su... (une affaire); (*b*) décider de (qch.); **nothing ha... been decided yet,** il n′y a encore rien de décidé (*c*) **to d. to do sth.,** se décider à faire qch.; **have decided what I shall do,** mon parti e... pris. **2.** *v.i.* **to d. on sth.,** se décider à qch.; **to ... on a day,** fixer un jour; **to d. for, in favour o... s.o.,** se décider pour, en faveur de, qn **de′cided,** *a.* **1.** (*of opinion*) arrêté; (... *manner*) décidé; **in a d. tone,** d′un ton ne... résolu; **a d. refusal,** un refus catégorique. ... incontestable; **a d. difference,** une diff... rence marquée; **-ly,** *adv.* **1.** résolument, av... décision. **2.** incontestablement, décid... ment; **de′ciding,** *a.* décisif; **the d. game,** belle.

deciduous [di′sidjuəs], *a. Bot:* (arbre) à feuill... caduques.

decimal [′desiməl]. **1.** *a.* décimal; **d. poi...** = virgule *f*. **2.** *s.* décimale *f*; **recurring d.,** fra... tion *f* périodique.

decipher [di′saifər], *v.tr.* déchiffrer.

decision [di′siʒ(ə)n], *s.* **1.** (*a*) décision *f* (d′u... question); (*b*) décision, jugement *m*, arrêt *m*. décision, résolution *f*; **to come to a d.,** arriv... à, prendre, une décision. **3.** résolution (... caractère); fermeté *f*, décision; **de′cisi...** [di′saisiv], *a.* **1.** décisif; (*of experiment*) co... cluant. **2.** (ton) tranchant, net; **-l...** décisivement.

deck [dek], *s.* (*a*) *Nau:* pont *m*; (*b*) (*of bus*) **top...** impériale *f*; (*c*) *N.Am:* jeu *m* (de carte... **′deck-chair,** *s.* transatlantique *m, F:* trans... *m*.

declaim [di′kleim]. **1.** *v.i.* déclamer (**against s...** **sth.,** contre qn, qch.). **2.** *v.tr.* déclamer (... vers, etc.).

declare [di′kleər], *v.tr. & i.* (*a*) déclarer (**sth....** **s.o.,** qch. à qn); **to d. war,** déclarer la gue... (**on, against,** à); **have you anything to d.?** ave... vous quelque chose à déclarer? (*b*) *Jur:* **to ... s.o. guilty,** déclarer qn coupable; **to d. t... bargain off,** rompre le marché; (*c*) (*at cards*)... **d. trumps,** appeler l′atout; *abs.* **to d.,** annonc... son jeu; (*d*) **to d. oneself,** prendre parti; ◆ *epidemic*) se déclarer, éclater; **decla′rati...** [deklə′reiʃ(ə)n], *s.* déclaration *f*; **customs** déclaration en douane; (*at cards*) annonce...

decline [di′klain]. **I.** *s.* déclin *m* (du jour, d′... empire); baisse *f* (de prix); **to be on the ...** décliner; (*of pers.*) être sur le retour (d′âge)...

prices) être en baisse. **II.** *v.* **1.** *v.tr.* (*a*) refuser (poliment); décliner (un honneur); *abs.* s'excuser; (*b*) *Gram:* décliner (un nom). **2.** *v.i.* décliner; baisser; **de'clining,** *a.* **d. sun,** soleil couchant; **in one's d. years,** au déclin de la vie.

declutch ['di:'klʌtʃ], *v.i.* *Aut:* débrayer.

ecode ['di:'koud], *v.tr.* transcrire (une dépêche) en clair; **de'coding,** *s.* transcription *f* en clair.

ecolonize [di:'kɔlənaiz], *v.tr.* décoloniser; **decoloni'zation,** *s.* décolonisation *f.*

ecompose ['di:kəm'pouz], *v.i.* (*a*) décomposer; (*b*) pourrir; **'decompo'sition,** *s.* décomposition *f;* putréfaction *f.*

econtaminate ['di:kən'tæminèit], *v.tr.* **1.** désinfecter. **2.** décontaminer; **'decontami'nation,** *s.* **1.** désinfection *f.* **2.** décontamination *f.*

écor ['deikɔ:r], *s. Th:* décor *m.*

ecorate ['dekəreit], *v.tr.* **1.** décorer, orner (**with,** de); décorer (un appartement). **2.** décorer (un soldat, etc.); **deco'ration,** *s.* **1.** décoration *f.* **2.** décor *m* (d'un appartement). **3.** décoration, médaille *f;* **'decorative,** *a.* décoratif; **'decorator,** *s.* (**house**) **d.,** peintre décorateur (d'appartements); tapissier *m.*

ecoy [di'kɔi, 'di:kɔi]. **I.** *s.* leurre *m*, amorce *f.* **II.** *v.tr.* leurrer; **to d. s.o. into a trap,** attirer qn dans un piège; **'decoy-bird,** *s.* (oiseau *m* de) leurre; appeau *m.*

ecrease. I. *s.* ['di:kri:s]. diminution *f*, décroissance *f;* **on the d.,** en baisse, en décroissance; **d. in speed,** ralentissement *m.* **II.** *v.tr. & i.* [di:'kri:s], diminuer; décroître; s'amoindrir; **de'creasing,** *a.* décroissant; (tarif) dégressif; (taxe) dégressive; **-ly,** *adv.* en diminuant; en décroissant.

ecree [di'kri:]. **I.** *s.* **1.** *Adm:* décret *m*, édit *m*, arrêté *m.* **2.** *Jur:* décision *f*, arrêt *m*, jugement *m.* **II.** *v.tr.* décréter, ordonner.

ecrepit [di'krepit], *a.* **1.** (*of pers.*) décrépit; caduc, -uque. **2.** (*of thg*) vermoulu; (*of house, etc.*) qui tombe en ruine; **de'crepitude,** *s.* décrépitude *f;* caducité *f.*

ecry [di'krai], *v.tr.* dénigrer.

edicate ['dedikeit], *v.tr.* **1.** consacrer (une église); **to d. one's life to sth.,** se vouer à qch. **2.** dédier (un livre) (**to,** à); **dedi'cation,** *s.* **1.** consécration *f* (d'une église). **2.** dédicace *f* (d'un livre).

educe [di'dju:s], *v.tr.* déduire, conclure (**from,** de).

educt [di'dʌkt], *v.tr.* déduire, retrancher (**from,** de); rabattre (qch. sur le prix); **de'duction,** *s.* **1.** déduction *f;* (*of pay*) retenue *f.* **2.** déduction, conclusion *f* (**from a discussion,** tirée d'un débat).

eed [di:d], *s.* **1.** (*a*) action *f*, acte *m;* (*b*) **brave d.,** haut fait; **outstanding d.,** exploit *m;* (*c*) **to be**

ruler in d., if not in name, être chef *m* en fait, sinon en titre. **2.** *Jur:* acte notarié; **'deed-box,** *s.* coffret *m* à documents.

deep [di:p]. **I.** *a.* **1.** (*a*) profond; **to be ten feet d.,** avoir dix pieds de profondeur; être profond de dix pieds; *F:* **to go off the d. end,** (i) se mettre en colère; (ii) prendre les choses au tragique; **d. in study,** plongé dans l'étude; (*b*) **d. sigh,** profond soupir. **2.** (*a*) (*of colour*) foncé, sombre; (*b*) **in a d. voice,** d'une voix profonde, grave. **3.** rusé, malin, -igne, astucieux. **II.** *adv.* **1.** profondément. **2. d. into the night,** très avant dans la nuit. **III.** *s.* **the d.,** (*a*) les profondeurs *f*, l'abîme *m;* (*b*) l'océan *m;* **the ocean deeps,** la région abyssale; **'deepen,** *v.* **1.** *v.tr.* (*a*) approfondir, creuser; (*b*) rendre (un sentiment) plus intense; (*c*) foncer (une couleur). **2.** *v.i.* devenir plus profond; s'approfondir; **'deepening,** *s.* approfondissement *m;* **'deep 'freeze. I.** *s.* congélateur *m.* **II.** *v.tr.* surgeler; **'deep 'fry,** *v.tr. & i. Cu:* (faire) cuire en friteuse; **'deeply,** *adv.* profondément; **to go d. into sth.,** pénétrer fort avant dans qch., approfondir qch.; **'deepness,** *s.* **1.** profondeur *f;* gravité *f* (d'un son). **2.** astuce *f* (d'une personne); **'deep-'rooted,** *a.* profondément enraciné; **'deep-'seated,** *a.* profond; fermement établi; **d.-s. conviction,** conviction *f* intime; *Med:* **d.-s. cough,** toux bronchiale.

deer ['diər], *s.inv.* (**red**) **d.,** cerf *m;* **fallow d.,** daim *m;* **roe(-)d.,** chevreuil *m;* **'deerskin,** *s.* peau *f* de daim.

deface [di'feis], *v.tr.* défigurer; mutiler; **de'facement,** *s.* défiguration *f*, mutilation *f.*

defamatory [di'fæmətri], *a.* diffamatoire, diffamant; **defa'mation** [defə'meiʃ(ə)n], *s.* diffamation *f.*

default [di'fɔ:lt]. **I.** *s.* **1.** manquement *m* (à un engagement); défaut *m;* *Jur:* contumace *f.* **2.** *prep.phr.* **in d. of,** à défaut de; faute de. **II.** *v.i.* faire défaut; manquer à ses engagements; **de'faulter,** *s.* délinquant, -ante.

defeat [di'fi:t]. **I.** *s.* **1.** défaite *f.* **2.** renversement *m* (d'un projet); insuccès *m* (d'une entreprise). **II.** *v.tr.* **1.** battre, vaincre (une armée). **2.** renverser (un gouvernement); faire échouer (un projet); **to d. the ends of justice,** contrarier la justice.

defect. I. *s.* ['di:fekt], défaut *m*, imperfection *f;* vice *m* (de construction); **physical d.,** défaut; tare *f.* **II.** *v.i.* [di'fekt], déserter, passer à l'ennemi; **de'fection,** *s.* défection *f;* **de'fective,** *a.* défectueux, imparfait; **d. memory,** mémoire *f* infidèle; (**mentally**) **d. child,** enfant retardé, anormal; **d. brakes,** freins en mauvais état; freins mauvais.

defence [di'fens], *s.* **1.** (*a*) défense *f*, protection *f;* *Mil:* défenses. **2.** (*a*) défense, justification *f;* (*b*)

Jur: défense; **counsel for the d.,** défenseur *m*; **witness for the d.,** témoin *m* à décharge; **de'fenceless,** *a.* sans défense; **de'fensive. 1.** *a.* défensif. **2.** *s.* **to be on the d.,** se tenir sur la défensive.

defend [di'fend], *v.tr.* **1.** défendre, protéger (**from, against,** contre). **2.** défendre, justifier (une opinion). **3.** *Jur:* défendre (un accusé); **de'fendant,** *s. Jur:* défendeur, -eresse; accusé, -ée; **de'fender,** *s.* défenseur *m*.

defer [di'fə:r], *v.tr.* (**deferred**) ajourner; renvoyer, retarder (une affaire); reculer (un paiement); suspendre (un jugement); **de'ferment,** *s.* ajournement *m*.

deference ['def(ə)rəns], *s.* déférence *f*; respect *m*; **defe'rential,** *a.* (air *m*, ton *m*) de déférence.

defiance [di'faiəns], *s.* défi *m*; **de'fiant,** *a.* provocant; (air *m*) de défi; intraitable; **-ly,** *adv.* d'un air de défi.

deficiency [di'fiʃənsi], *s.* **1.** manque *m*, insuffisance *f*, défaut *m* (**of, de**). **2.** défaut, imperfection *f*. **3.** *Med:* carence *f* (**in, of,** de); **d. diseases,** maladies *f* de carence; **de'ficient,** *a.* insuffisant, incomplet; **to be d. in sth.,** manquer de qch.

deficit ['defisit], *s. Com: Fin:* déficit *m*.

defile[1] ['di:fail], *s. Geog:* défilé *m*.

defile[2] [di'fail], **1.** *v.i.* (*of troops*) défiler. **2.** *v.tr.* souiller, salir.

define [di'fain], *v.tr.* **1.** définir; **to d. one's position,** préciser son attitude. **2.** déterminer (l'étendue de qch.); formuler (ses pensées); délimiter (un territoire). **3. well-defined outlines,** contours nettement dessinés; **'definite** ['definit], *a.* **1.** défini; bien déterminé; **d. answer,** réponse *f* catégorique; *Com:* **d. order,** commande *f* ferme. **2.** *Gram:* **d. article,** article défini; **-ly,** *adv.* décidément; **defi'nition,** *s.* **1.** définition *f*. **2.** *Rad: etc:* netteté *f* (du son, etc.); **de'finitive,** *a.* définitif.

deflate [di'fleit], *v.tr.* dégonfler; **deflated tyre,** pneu dégonflé, à plat; **that's deflated him!** voilà qui l'a dégonflé! **de'flation,** *s.* **1.** dégonflement *m*. **2.** *Fin:* déflation *f*.

deflect [di'flekt]. **1.** *v.tr.* (faire) dévier; détourner. **2.** *v.i.* (se) dévier, se détourner.

deform [di'fɔ:m], *v.tr.* déformer; **de'formed,** *a.* (*of pers.*) contrefait, difforme; **de'formity,** *s.* difformité *f*.

defraud [di'frɔːd], *v.tr.* **1.** frauder (le fisc, etc.). **2.** **to d. s.o. of sth.,** escroquer qch. à qn.

defray [di'frei], *v.tr.* **to d. s.o.'s expenses,** défrayer qn; **to d. the cost of sth.,** couvrir les frais de qch.

defreeze ['di:'fri:z], *v.tr.* (**defroze** ['di:'frouz]; **defrozen** ['di:frouz(ə)n]) décongeler (des aliments, etc.); **de'freezing,** *s.* décongélation

f; **de'frost** [di:'frɔst], *v.tr.* dégivrer (u réfrigérateur); **de'froster,** *s.* dégivreur *m*.

deft [deft], *a.* adroit, habile; **-ly,** *adv* adroitement; **'deftness,** *s.* adresse *f*, habileté *f* dextérité *f*.

defunct [di'fʌŋkt]. **1.** *a.* défunt; décédé. **2.** *s.* th **d.,** le défunt, la défunte.

defy [di'fai], *v.tr.* défier (qn); mettre (qn) au défi **to d. description,** défier toute description; **to d danger, an attack,** résister au danger, à un attaque.

degenerate. I. *v.i.* [di'dʒenəreit], dégénére (**from,** de; **into,** en); (s')abâtardir. **II.** *a.* & [di'dʒenərət], dégénéré, -ée; *a.* abâtard **de'generacy,** *s.* **degene'ration,** *s.* dégénér tion *f*, dégénérescence *f*; abâtardissement *m*.

degrade [di'greid], *v.tr.* (*a*) dégrader, casser (u officier); (*b*) avilir, dégrader (qn); **degra'da tion** [degrə'deiʃ(ə)n], *s.* (*a*) dégradation *f*; (*b* avilissement *m*, abrutissement *n* **de'grading,** *a.* avilissant, dégradant.

degree [di'gri:], *s.* degré *m*. **1.** (*a*) **to some d.,** à u certain degré; **in the highest d.,** au plus ha degré; **in some d.,** dans une certaine mesure; **a d.,** au plus haut degré; **by slow degrees,** pe à petit, lentement; **d. of humidity,** teneur *f* e eau; *F:* **third d.,** passage *m* à tabac, cuisinag *m* (d'un prisonnier); (*b*) *Mth: Ph: etc:* deg (d'un cercle, de température). **2.** *Sch:* grade (universitaire); **he has a d.** =il a sa licence.

dehydrate ['di:haidreit], *v.tr. Ch: In* déshydrater; **dehy'dration,** *s.* déshydrat tion *f*.

de-ice ['di:'ais], *v.tr. Av: Aut:* dégivrer; **'d 'icing,** *s.* dégivrage *m*; **'de-'icer,** *s.* dégivre *m*.

deign [dein], *v.tr.* **1. to d. to do sth.,** daigner fai qch. **2.** *usu. neg.* **he did not d. to answer,** il n pas daigné répondre.

dejected [di'dʒektid], *a.* abattu, déprimé; **-l** *adv.* d'un air découragé; **de'jection,** découragement *m*.

delay [di'lei]. **I.** *s.* **1.** délai *m*, retard *m*; **witho further d.,** sans plus tarder. **2.** retardement **II.** *v.* **1.** *v.tr.* (*a*) retarder, remettre (une affair (*b*) retenir, arrêter, retarder (qn). **2.** *v.i.* s tarder (**in doing sth.,** à faire qch.); (*b*) s' tarder; **de'layed,** *a. Phot:* **d. action shutt** obturateur *m* à action différée; *Mil:* **d. acti bomb,** bombe *f* à retardement.

delegate. I. *s.* ['deligət]. délégué, -ée. **II.** *v* ['deligeit], déléguer; **dele'gation,** *s.* délé tion *f*.

delete [di'li:t], *v.tr.* effacer, rayer (un mot, et **de'letion,** *s.* **1.** rature *f*, suppression *f*. passage supprimé.

deliberate. I. *a.* [di'lib(ə)rət]. **1.** délibé prémédité, voulu; **d. insolence,** insole calculée. 2. (*of pers.*) (*a*) réfléchi, avisé; (*b*) lent; sans hâte; **d. tread,** pas mesuré; **-ly,** *adv.* 1. à dessein; exprès. 2. (agir) posément, sans hâte, délibérément. II. *v.tr. & i.* [di'libəreit], délibérer (on, de, sur); **to d. on a question,** délibérer d'une question; **delibe'ration,** *s.* 1. (*a*) délibération *f,* réflexion *f;* (*b*) *pl.* **the deliberations of an assembly,** les débats *m* d'une assemblée. 2. (*a*) **to act with d.,** agir posément, après réflexion; (*b*) sage lenteur *f.*

elicacy ['delikəsi], *s.* délicatesse *f.* 1. (*a*) finesse *f* (d'un dessin); sensibilité *f* (d'un instrument de précision); (*b*) faiblesse *f* (de santé); (*c*) **d.** (of feeling), pudeur *f;* '**delicate,** *a.* délicat; (*a*) **to have a d. touch,** avoir de la légèreté de doigté; **a d. wit,** l'esprit fin; (*b*) **d. feelings,** sentiments raffinés; (*c*) **d. situation,** situation délicate; (*d*) **d. health,** santé *f* fragile; **-ly,** *adv.* délicatement.

elicatessen ['delikə'tes(ə)n], *s.* plats cuisinés; charcuterie *f;* **d.** (shop), charcuterie.

elicious [di'liʃəs], *a.* délicieux, exquis; **-ly,** *adv.* délicieusement.

light [di'lait]. I. *s.* 1. délices *fpl,* délice *m.* 2. joie *f;* **much to the d. of the children,** à la grande joie des enfants. II. *v.* 1. *v.tr.* enchanter, ravir, réjouir (qn). 2. *v.i.* **to d. in doing sth.,** se délecter à faire qch.; **de'lighted,** *a.* enchanté, ravi (with, at, de); **to be d. to do sth.,** être enchanté de faire qch.; **I shall be d.,** je ne demande pas mieux; **de'lightful,** *a.* délicieux, ravissant; **-fully,** *adv.* délicieusement; (chanter, etc.) à ravir.

linquency [di'liŋkwənsi], *s.* 1. culpabilité *f;* **juvenile d.,** délinquance *f* juvénile. 2. délit *m,* faute *f;* écart *m* de conduite; **de'linquent,** *a.* & *s.* 1. délinquant, -ante, coupable (*mf*). 2. *N.Am:* **d. taxes,** impôts non payés.

lirious [di'liriəs], *a.* (malade) en délire; délirant; **d. with joy,** fou de joie; **de'lirium,** *s.* délire *m.*

liver [di'livər], *v.tr.* 1. délivrer (s.o. from sth., qn de qch.). 2. **to d. sth. to s.o.,** livrer, délivrer, qch. à qn; **to d. up,** restituer, rendre (to, à). 3. remettre, délivrer (un paquet); livrer (des marchandises); distribuer (des lettres); **to d. a message,** faire une commission; *Com:* **delivered free,** livraison franco. 4. porter, donner (un coup); lancer (une attaque). 5. faire, prononcer (un discours); prononcer, rendre (un jugement); **de'liverance,** *s.* délivrance *f* libération *f* (from, de); **de'liverer,** *s.* libérateur, -trice; sauveur *m;* **de'livery,** *s.* 1. (*ed:* accouchement *m.* 2. livraison *f* (d'un paquet); distribution *f* (des lettres); **d. note,** bulletin *m* de livraison; **d. man,** livreur *m;* **cash on d.,** payable à livraison.

delta ['deltə], *s.* 1. *Geog:* delta *m.* 2. *Ind:* **d. metal,** (métal *m*) delta; *Av:* **d. wing aircraft,** avion *m* aux ailes (en) delta.

delude [di'lju:d], *v.tr.* 1. abuser, tromper (qn); **to d. oneself,** s'abuser; se faire illusion. 2. duper (qn); en faire accroire à (qn); **de'lusion,** *s.* illusion *f;* erreur *f;* **to be under a d.,** se faire illusion; s'abuser; **de'lusive,** *a.* illusoire; trompeur; **-ly,** *adv.* illusoirement; trompeusement.

deluge ['delju:dʒ]. I. *s.* déluge *m.* II. *v.tr.* inonder (with, de).

demand [di'mɑ:nd]. I. *s.* 1. demande *f,* réclamation *f,* revendication *f.* 2. *Com:* **supply and d.,** l'offre *f* et la demande; **to be in d.,** être demandé. 3. *pl.* **to make many demands on s.o.'s time,** exiger beaucoup de qn. II. *v.tr.* demander, réclamer (qch. à qn); exiger (qch. de qn).

demeanour [di'mi:nər], *s.* air *m,* tenue *f,* maintien *m.*

demented [di'mentid], *a.* fou, *f.* folle.

demise [di'maiz], *s.* décès *m,* mort *f.*

demister [di:'mistər], *s.* *Aut:* dispositif *m* antibuée.

demobilize [di:'moubilaiz], *F:* **demob** [di:'mɔb], (**demobbed**) *v.tr.* *Mil:* démobiliser; '**demobili'zation,** *F:* **de'mob,** *s.* démobilisation *f.*

democracy [di'mɔkrəsi], *s.* démocratie *f;* **people's d.,** démocratie populaire; '**democrat,** *s.* démocrate *mf;* **demo'cratic,** *a.* démocratique; **-ally,** *adv.* démocratiquement.

demography [de'mɔgrəfi], *s.* démographie *f.*

demolish [di'mɔliʃ], *v.tr.* démolir; **demo'lition** [demə'liʃ(ə)n], *s.* démolition *f.*

demon ['di:mən], *s.* démon *m,* diable *m;* **demo'niacal** [dimə'naiəkl], *a.* démoniaque, diabolique.

demonstrate ['demənstreit]. 1. *v.tr.* (*a*) démontrer (une vérité); (*b*) décrire, expliquer (un système); *Com:* faire la démonstration d'(une voiture, un appareil, etc.). 2. *v.i.* *Pol:* manifester; **demon'stration,** *s.* 1. démonstration *f* (d'une vérité, d'un appareil). 2. témoignages *m* (d'affection). 3. *Pol:* manifestation *f,* *F:* manif *f;* **de'monstrative,** *a.* démonstratif; **-ly,** *adv.* 1. (prouver qch.) démonstrativement. 2. (accueillir qn) avec effusion *f;* '**demonstrator,** *s.* 1. démonstrateur *m.* 2. *Sch: Pharm:* préparateur *m.* 3. *Pol:* manifestant, -ante.

demoralize [di'mɔrəlaiz], *v.tr.* démoraliser (les troupes, etc.); **demorali'zation,** *s.* démoralisation *f.*

demur [di'mə:r], *v.i.* (**demurred**) faire des difficultés; soulever des objections (at, to, contre).

demure [di'mjuər], a. (jeune fille) posée, sérieuse.

den [den], s. tanière f, repaire m ((i) de fauves, (ii) de voleurs).

denial [di'naiəl], s. 1. refus m; **d. of justice,** déni m de justice. 2. démenti m; **a flat d.,** un démenti catégorique.

Denmark ['denmɑːk]. Pr.n. Geog: le Danemark.

denier ['deniə], s. **a 15 d. stocking,** un bas 15 deniers mpl.

denim ['denim], s. Tex: 1. tissu m de coton sergé. 2. pl. Cl: esp. Mil: **denims,** treillis mpl.

denomination [dinɔmi'neiʃ(ə)n], s. 1. dénomination f. 2. Ecc: culte m, secte f, confession f. 3. catégorie f; **coins of all denominations,** pièces de toutes valeurs; **denomi'national,** a. Ecc: confessionnel, sectaire; **de'nominator,** s. Mth: **common d.,** dénominateur commun.

denote [di'nout], v.tr. 1. dénoter. 2. signifier.

denounce [di'nauns], v.tr. 1. (a) dénoncer (qn à la justice); (b) démasquer (un imposteur). 2. s'élever contre (un abus).

dense [dens], a. 1. Ph: dense. 2. épais; **d. smoke,** fumée épaisse; **d. crowd,** foule compacte. 3. stupide, bête; -ly, adv. **d. wooded country,** pays fortement boisé; **d. populated,** très peuplé; **'denseness,** s. épaisseur f (du brouillard, etc.). 2. stupidité f; **'density,** s. 1. Ph: densité f. 2. compacité f (du sol); densité (de la population).

dent [dent]. I. s. marque f de coup; bosselure f; renfoncement m. II. v.tr. bosseler, bossuer.

dentist ['dentist], s. dentiste m; **'dental,** a. dentaire; **d. surgeon,** chirurgien dentiste; **'dentistry,** s. art m dentaire; **'denture,** s. dentier m, F: râtelier m.

denude [di'njuːd], v.tr. dénuder.

denunciation [dinʌnsi'eiʃ(ə)n], s. 1. dénonciation f. 2. (a) condamnation f; (b) accusation publique.

deny [di'nai], v.tr. 1. nier (un fait); démentir (une nouvelle); **I don't d. it,** je n'en disconviens pas; **there is no denying the fact,** c'est un fait indéniable. 2. **to d. s.o. sth.,** refuser qch. à qn. 3. **to d. oneself sth.,** se refuser qch.; se priver de qch.

deodorant [di:'oudərənt], **deodorizer** [di:'oudəraizər], s. désodorisant m, déodorant m.

depart [di'pɑːt], v.i. 1. s'en aller, partir. 2. **to d. from a rule,** s'écarter d'une règle; **de'parted,** a. 1. (of glory, etc.) passé, évanoui. 2. (of pers.) mort, défunt; **de'parture,** s. 1. départ m; **to take one's d.,** s'en aller. 2. **a new d.,** (i) une nouvelle tendance; (ii) un nouvel usage.

department [di'pɑːtmənt], s. 1. (a) Adm:

département m, service m, bureau m; **head ⟨…⟩ (a) d.,** chef m de service; (b) Com: rayon ⟨…⟩ comptoir m; **d. store,** grand magasin. ⟨…⟩ ministère m; U.S: **State D.** = Ministère d⟨…⟩ Affaires étrangères; **depart'mental,** ⟨…⟩ départemental.

depend [di'pend], v.i. 1. dépendre (on, de); th⟨…⟩ **depends entirely on you,** cela ne tient qu⟨…⟩ vous; **that depends, it all depends,** cela dépen⟨…⟩ F: c'est selon. 2. **to d. (up)on s.o.,** compter s⟨…⟩ qn; **d. (up)on it,** comptez là-dessus; **de'pe⟨…⟩ dable,** a. (of pers.) digne de confiance; ⟨…⟩ news) sûr, bien fondé; **de'pendants,** s.⟨…⟩ charges f de famille; **de'pendence,** s. d. ⟨…⟩ s.o., dépendance f de qn; confiance f en q⟨…⟩ **de'pendent,** a. (a) dépendant (on, de); **two ⟨…⟩ children,** deux enfants à charge; (b) Gram: **clause,** proposition subordonnée.

depilatory [di'pilətəri], a. & s. dépilatoire (m⟨…⟩

deplete [di'pliːt], v.tr. épuiser (des provisio⟨…⟩ etc.); **de'pletion,** s. épuisement m.

deplore [di'plɔːr], v.i. déplorer; regret⟨…⟩ vivement; **de'plorable,** a. déplorable, lame⟨…⟩ table; **-ably,** adv. lamentablement.

depopulate [di:'pɔpjuleit], v.tr. dépeupl⟨…⟩ **depopu'lation,** s. dépopulation f (d'un pay⟨…⟩ dépeuplement m (de la campagne, d'u⟨…⟩ forêt); **rural d.,** exode rural.

deport [di'pɔːt], v.tr. (a) expulser (un étran⟨…⟩ d'un pays); (b) déporter (un condamné politique); **deportation** [di:pɔː'teiʃ(ə)n], s. expulsion; (b) déportation f; **depor'tee,** déporté, -ée.

deportment [di'pɔːtmənt], s. (a) tenue f, m⟨…⟩ tien m; (b) conduite f; manière f d'agir.

depose [di'pouz], v.tr. 1. déposer (un roi). 2. J⟨…⟩ déposer, témoigner (that, que); **depo'siti⟨…⟩ s.** 1. déposition f (d'un roi). 2. Jur: dépositi⟨…⟩ témoignage m.

deposit [di'pɔzit]. I. s. 1. **bank d.,** dépôt m banque; **d. account,** compte m à terme. 2⟨…⟩ **pay a d.,** verser, donner, des arrhes fpl dépôt(s); sédiment m; Aut: etc: **carbon ⟨…⟩ calamine f; to form a d.,** se déposer. II. v.t⟨…⟩ déposer (qch. sur qch.). 2. **to d. money, ⟨…⟩** signer, déposer, de l'argent. 3. abs. (of liq⟨…⟩ déposer; **de'positor,** s. déposant, -ante ⟨…⟩ banque); **de'pository,** s. dépôt m, entrepô⟨…⟩

depot ['depou, N.Am: 'diːpou], s. (a) dépô⟨…⟩ entrepôt m; (b) **bus d.,** garage m d'auto⟨…⟩ **goods d.,** dépôt de marchandises; (c) N.⟨…⟩ Rail: gare f.

deprave [di'preiv], v.tr. dépraver, corrom⟨…⟩ pervertir (qn); **de'pravity** [-'præv-]⟨…⟩ dépravation f, perversité f.

deprecate ['deprəkeit], v.tr. désapprou⟨…⟩ déconseiller (une action); **'deprecating ⟨…⟩** désapprobateur; **depre'cation,** s. dé⟨…⟩

probation *f.*

epreciate [di'pri:ʃieit]. **1.** *v.tr.* (*a*) déprécier (la valeur, le prix, de qch.); (*b*) déprécier, dénigrer, qn. **2.** *v.i.* se déprécier; (*of shares*) baisser; **depreci'ation,** *s.* (*a*) dépréciation *f*; (*b*) **annual d.,** amortissement *m.*

epress [di'pres], *v.tr.* **1.** abaisser; baisser (qch.); appuyer sur (la pédale, etc.). **2.** décourager (qn, le commerce); attrister (qn); **de'pressed,** *a.* triste, abattu; **to feel d.,** *F:* avoir le cafard; **de'pressing,** *a.* attristant, déprimant; **de'pression,** *s.* **1.** abaissement *m* (de qch.). **2.** *Meteor:* dépression *f*, cyclone *m.* **3.** dénivellement *m* (de terrain). **4.** crise *f* (économique); marasme *m* (des affaires). **5.** découragement *m*; abattement *m.*

prive [di'praiv], *v.tr.* priver (qn de qch.); **to d. oneself,** s'infliger des privations; **depri'vation** [depri-], *s.* privation *f*; perte *f* (de droits).

pth [depθ], *s.* **1.** (*a*) profondeur *f*; (*b*) fond *m*, hauteur *f* (de l'eau); **to get out of one's d.,** (i) perdre pied; (ii) sortir de sa compétence; (*c*) épaisseur *f* (d'une couche). **2.** (*a*) gravité *f* (d'un son); (*b*) portée *f* (de l'intelligence); (*c*) intensité *f* (de coloris). **3.** fond (d'une forêt); milieu *m* (de la nuit); **in the d. of winter,** au plus fort de l'hiver. **4.** *pl.* **in the depths of despair,** dans le plus profond désespoir; **'depth-charge,** *s. Nau:* grenade sous-marine; **'depth-finder,** *s. Nau:* sonic d.-f., sondeur *m* sonore.

pute [di'pju:t], *v.tr.* **1.** déléguer (**powers to s.o.,** des pouvoirs à qn); **to d. s.o. to do sth.,** députer, déléguer, qn à faire qch.; **depu'tation,** *s.* députation *f*, délégation *f*; **'deputize,** *v.i.* **to d. for s.o.,** remplacer qn; faire l'intérim de qn; **'deputy,** *s.* fondé *m* de pouvoir; substitut *m* (d'un juge); délégué *m* (d'un fonctionnaire); *Fr.Pol:* député *mf*; **d. chairman,** vice-résident *m*; **d. mayor,** (maire *m*) adjoint *m.*

ail [di'reil], *v.tr.* faire dérailler (un train); **le'railment,** *s.* déraillement *m.*

ange [di'reindʒ], *v.tr.* (*a*) déranger (qn, la anté); désorganiser, bouleverser (les projets e qn); (*b*) déranger le cerveau de (qn); **his ind is deranged,** c'est un détraqué; **e'rangement,** *s.* dérangement *m* (de esprit); dérèglement *m* (d'un mécanisme).

elict ['derilikt]. **1.** *a.* abandonné, délaissé, à abandon. **2.** *s.* (*a*) objet abandonné; *esp.* avire abandonné; épave *f*; (*b*) épave umaine.

de [di'raid], *v.tr.* tourner en dérision; railler, e moquer de (qn); **de'rision** [di'riʒ(ə)n], *s.* érision *f*; **object of d.,** objet de risée *f*; **e'risive, de'risory,** *a.* moqueur; **-ively,** dv. d'un air moqueur.

ive [di'raiv], *v.tr. & i.* **1.** (*a*) tirer (son origine) **rom sth.,** de qch.); devoir (son bonheur)

(**from sth.,** à qch.); trouver (du plaisir) (**from sth.,** à qch.); **income derived from investment,** revenu provenant de placements; (*b*) **word derived from Latin,** mot qui vient du latin. **2. to be derived,** *v.i.* **to d.,** dériver, (pro)venir (**from,** de); **deri'vation** [deri-], *s.* dérivation *f*; **de'rivative** [di'ri-], *a. & s. Gram: Ch: Ind:* dérivé (*m*).

dermatitis [də:mə'taitis], *s. Med:* dermatite *f*; **derma'tologist,** *s.* dermatologiste *mf*, dermatologue *mf*; **derma'tology,** *s. Med:* dermatologie *f.*

derogatory [di'rɔgətəri], *a.* (remarque) qui abaisse (qn); **d. meaning,** sens péjoratif.

derrick ['derik], *s.* (*a*) (*crane*) chèvre *f*; (*b*) *Oil Ind:* derrick *m*; (*c*) *Nau:* mât *m* de charge.

derv [də:v], *s.* gas-oil *m.*

descend [di'send]. **1.** *v.i.* (*a*) descendre; (*of darkness*) tomber; (*b*) **to d. to s.o.'s level,** s'abaisser au niveau de qn; **to d. to lying,** descendre, s'abaisser, jusqu'au mensonge; (*c*) **to be descended from s.o.,** descendre de qn; (*of property*) **to d. from father to son,** passer de père en fils. **2.** *v.tr.* descendre, dévaler (une pente, un escalier); **de'scendant,** *s.* descendant, -ante; *pl. coll.* **descendants,** postérité *f*; **de'scent,** *s.* **1.** descente *f.* **2.** (*family, etc.*) descendance *f.*

describe [dis'kraib], *v.tr.* **1.** (*a*) décrire, dépeindre; (*b*) **to d. s.o. as . . .,** qualifier qn de . . .. **2.** décrire (une courbe); **des'cription,** *s.* **1.** (*a*) description *f*; (*b*) *Adm:* signalement *m*; désignation *f* (de marchandises). **2.** sorte *f*, espèce *f*, genre *m*; **people of this d.,** les gens de cette espèce; **des'criptive,** *a.* descriptif.

desert¹ [di'zə:t], *s.* (*usu.pl.*) mérite(s) *m*(*pl*); **to get one's deserts,** avoir ce que l'on mérite.

desert² ['dezət], *a. & s.* désert (*m*).

desert³ [di'zə:t], *v.tr.* (*a*) *Mil:* déserter; (*b*) abandonner, délaisser (qn); **de'serted,** *a.* (*of pers.*) abandonné; (*of place*) désert; **de'serter,** *s. Mil:* déserteur *m*; **de'sertion,** *s.* **1.** abandon *m*, délaissement *m.* **2.** *Mil:* désertion *f*; *Pol:* défection *f.*

deserve [di'zə:v], *v.tr.* mériter (qch.); **to d. praise,** être digne d'éloges; **he (richly) deserves it!** il ne l'a pas volé! **deservedly** [di'zə:vidli], *adv.* à juste titre; à bon droit; **de'serving,** *a.* (*of pers.*) méritant; (*of action*) méritoire.

desiccate ['desikeit], *v.tr.* dessécher; déshydrater.

design [di'zain]. **I.** *s.* **1.** dessein *m*, intention *f*, projet *m*; **by d.,** à dessein. **2.** (*decorative*) d., dessin *m* d'ornement. **3.** *Ind: etc:* dessin; étude *f*, avant-projet *m* (d'une machine, etc.); modèle *m*; **car of the latest d.,** voiture dernier modèle; **machine of faulty d.,** machine mal étudiée. **II.** *v.tr.* préparer (un projet); créer (une robe);

établir (un plan); étudier, calculer; **de′signing. I.** *a.* intrigant. **II.** *s.* dessin *m* (d'une machine); création *f* (d'une œuvre d'art); **designedly** [di′zainidli], *adv.* à dessein; **de′signer,** *s. Com:* dessinateur, -trice.

designate [′dezigneit], *v.tr.* **1.** désigner, nommer (qn à une fonction). **2.** (*of things*) indiquer (qch.); **desig′nation,** *s.* **1.** désignation *f* (à un emploi). **2.** désignation, nom *m*.

desire [di′zaiǝr]. **I.** *s.* **1.** désir *m*, souhait *m*; **I feel no d. to travel,** je n'éprouve aucune envie de voyager. **2. at s.o.'s d.,** à la demande de qn. **II.** *v.tr.* désirer (qch.); avoir envie de (qch.); **it leaves much to be desired,** cela laisse beaucoup à désirer; **de′sirable,** *a.* désirable; à désirer; souhaitable; **-ably,** *adv.* d'une manière désirable; **de′sirous,** *a.* **to be d. of doing sth.,** être désireux de faire qch.

desk [desk], *s.* **1.** *Sch:* pupitre *m*; (*office*) bureau *m.* **2.** *Com:* **pay at the d.!** payez à la caisse!

desolate. I. *a.* [′desǝlǝt], *a.* **1.** (lieu) désert. **2.** (*of pers.*) affligé. **II.** *v.tr.* [′desǝleit]. ravager (un pays); **deso′lation,** *s.* désolation *f*, dévastation *f* (d'un pays); chagrin *m*, affliction *f* (d'une personne).

despair [dis′pɛǝr]. **I.** *s.* désespoir *m*; **to be in d.,** être au désespoir; **to drive s.o. to d.,** désespérer qn. **II.** *v.i.* (*a*) désespérer (**of doing sth.,** de faire qch.); (*b*) perdre espoir, (se) désespérer; **des′pairing,** *a.* désespéré; **-ly,** *adv.* désespérément.

desperate [′desp(ǝ)rǝt], *a.* **1.** (*a*) (*of condition, illness*) désespéré; (*b*) **d. remedy,** remède héroïque. **2.** (*a*) **a d. man,** un désespéré; (*b*) **d. conflict,** combat acharné; **to do something d.,** faire un malheur; **-ly,** *adv.* (*a*) désespérément, avec acharnement; **d. ill,** gravement malade; **despe′ration,** *s.* **in d.,** au désespoir; **to drive s.o. to d.,** pousser qn à bout.

despicable [′despikǝbl, dis′pik-], *a.* méprisable; **-ably,** *adv.* bassement.

despise [dis′paiz], *v.tr.* (*a*) mépriser (qn); (*b*) dédaigner (qch.).

despite [dis′pait], *prep.* **d. (sth.),** en dépit de (qch.), malgré (qch.).

despondency [dis′pɔndǝnsi], *s.* découragement *m*, abattement *m*; **des′pondent,** *a.* découragé, abattu; **-ly,** *adv.* d'un air découragé, abattu.

despot [′despɔt], *s.* tyran *m*; **des′potic,** *a.* **1.** (pouvoir) despotique. **2.** (*of pers.*) arbitraire; tyrannique; **-ally,** *adv.* despotiquement, arbitrairement; **′despotism,** *s.* despotisme *m*.

dessert [di′zǝːt], *s.* dessert *m*; **d. spoon,** cuiller *f* à dessert.

destination [desti′neiʃ(ǝ)n], *s.* destination *f*.

destine [′destin], *v.tr.* destiner (**for,** à); **′destiny,**

s. destin *m*, destinée *f*; le sort.

destitute [′destitjuːt], *a.* **1.** dépourvu, dénué (o de). **2.** indigent; sans ressources; **to be utter′** **d.,** manquer de tout; **desti′tution,** *s.* i digence *f*; misère *f*.

destroy [dis′trɔi], *v.tr.* **1.** détruire; anéantir. tuer, abattre (une bête); **des′troyer,** *s.* destructeur, -trice. **2.** *Nau:* destroyer *r* **des′troying,** *a.* destructeur, -trice.

destruction [dis′trʌkʃ(ǝ)n], *s.* destruction *f*; t **d. caused by the fire,** les ravages *m* du fe drugs were his d., c'est la drogue qui l'a perd **des′tructive,** *a.* destructif; **a d. child,** brise-tout *inv*; **des′tructiveness,** *s.* **1.** pouv *m* destructeur (d'une bombe). **2.** (*of per* penchant *m* à détruire.

desultory [′desǝlt(ǝ)ri], *a.* décousu; sans su **d. conversation,** conversation à bâtons ro pus; **d. reading,** lectures *fpl* sans méthode.

detach [di′tætʃ], *v.tr.* détacher, séparer (fro de); **de′tached,** *a.* **1.** détaché; **d. hou** maison séparée. **2.** (*of pers.*) désintéressé; **manner,** air détaché, indifférent; **de′tachab** *a.* détachable, amovible; **de′tachment,** *s.* séparation *f* (**from,** de); décollement *m.* **2.** *pers.*) détachement *m*; indifférence *f*. **3.** *I* peloton *m*.

detail [′diːteil]. **I.** *s.* détail *m*, particularité *f* **every d.,** de point en point. **II.** *v.tr.* détaill raconter (qch.) en détail; énumérer (les fai **to d. s.o. for a duty,** affecter qn à un service

detain [di′tein], *v.tr.* **1.** détenir (qn en prison) retenir (qn); empêcher (qn) de par **detai′nee,** *s. Jur:* détenu, -ue.

detect [di′tekt], *v.tr.* **1.** découvrir (le coupab **2.** trouver; détecter; localiser (une fuite gaz); **de′tection,** *s.* **1.** découverte *f*; **to esc** **d.,** passer inaperçu; *Rad: etc:* détection **sound d.,** détection par le son; **de′tective** agent *m* de la Sûreté; **private d.,** détective m **story,** roman policier; **de′tector,** *s. Te* détecteur *m*; indicateur *m*; **mine d.,** détec de mines.

detention [di′tenʃ(ǝ)n], *s.* **1.** (*a*) détention *f* prison); (*b*) *Sch:* retenue *f*. **2.** retar (inévitable); arrêt *m*.

deter [di′tǝːr], *v.tr.* (**deterred**) détour décourager (**s.o. from doing sth.,** qn de qch.).

detergent [di′tǝːdʒǝnt], *a. & s.* détersif détergent (*m*); lessive *f*.

deteriorate [di′tiǝriǝreit], *v.i.* (*a*) (se) détérie (*b*) diminuer de valeur; (*c*) (*of race*) dégén **deterio′ration,** *s.* (*a*) détérioration *f* dégénération *f*.

determine [di′tǝːmin], *v.tr. & i.* **1.** (*a*) déterm fixer (une date, des conditions); (*b*) délir (une frontière); (*c*) constater (la natur qch.). **2.** décider (une question). **3. to d. to do sth.**, résoudre de faire qch. **4.** *v.tr. Jur:* résoudre (un contrat); **de′termined,** *a.* **1.** (*of pers.*) déterminé, résolu. **2. to be d. to do sth.**, être résolu de faire qch.; **-ly,** *adv.* résolument; **determi′nation,** *s.* **1.** détermination *f,* résolution *f;* **air of d.,** air résolu. **2.** *Jur:* résolution (d'un contrat, etc.); expiration *f* (d'un contrat).

deterrent [di′terənt], *s. Mil: Pol:* arme *f* de dissuasion; **to act as a d.,** exercer un effet préventif.

detest [di′test], *v.tr.* détester; **de′testable,** *a.* détestable; **-ably,** *adv.* détestablement; **detes′tation,** *s.* détestation *f* (**of,** de); **to hold sth. in d.,** détester qch.

dethrone [di′θroun], *v.tr.* détrôner (un roi).

detonate [′detəneit], *v.tr.* faire détoner, faire sauter (une mine); **deto′nation,** *s.* détonation *f,* explosion *f;* ′**detonator,** *s.* détonateur *m;* amorce *f.*

detour [′di:tuər], *s.* détour *m.*

detriment [′detrimənt], *s.* détriment *m,* dommage *m;* **to the d. of . . .,** au préjudice de . . .; **detri′mental,** *a.* nuisible (**to,** à); **-ally,** *adv.* nuisiblement.

deuce [dju:s], *s.* **1.** (*of dice, dominoes, cards*) deux *m.* **2.** *Ten:* à deux; égalité *f* (à quarante). **3.** *F:* le diable.

deuterium [djuː(:)′tiəriəm], *s. Atom.Ph:* deutérium *m.*

devalue [′di:′vælju:], *v.tr.* dévaluer, dévaloriser (une monnaie); **devalu′ation,** *s.* dévaluation *f.*

devastate [′devəsteit], *v.tr.* dévaster, ravager; ′**devastating,** *a.* **1.** (*of storm*) dévastateur, -trice. **2.** (charme) fatal; **that's a d. argument,** c'est un raisonnement accablant; **-ly,** *adv. F:* **d. funny,** d'un comique à se tordre; **deva′station,** *s.* dévastation *f.*

develop [di′veləp]. **1.** *v.tr.* (*a*) développer (les facultés); amplifier (une pensée); (*b*) **to d. a district,** exploiter, mettre en valeur, une région; (*c*) **to d. heat,** engendrer de la chaleur; (*d*) contracter (une maladie); (*e*) *Phot:* révéler, développer. **2.** *v.i.* (*a*) se développer; (*b*) se manifester; **de′veloping,** *s.* **1.** développement *m;* mise *f* en valeur, exploitation *f* (d'une région); **d. countries,** pays *mpl* en voie de développement. **2.** *Phot:* développement; **de′veloper,** *s. Phot:* révélateur *m;* **de′velopment,** *s.* **1.** développement *m* (des facultés); **retarded d.,** infantilisme *m.* **2.** exploitation *f* (d'une région). **3. a new d.,** un fait nouveau; **to await further developments,** attendre la suite des événements.

deviate [′di:vieit], *v.i.* dévier, s'écarter (**from,** de); **devi′ation,** *s.* déviation *f* (**from,** de); écart *m.*

device [di′vais], *s.* **1.** (*a*) expédient *m,* moyen *m;*

to leave s.o. to his own devices, livrer qn à lui-même; (*b*) stratagème *m,* ruse *f.* **2.** dispositif *m,* appareil *m; F:* truc *m,* gadget *m.* **3.** emblème *m,* devise *f.*

devil [′devl], *s.* (*a*) diable *m;* démon *m;* **the d. take him!** que le diable l'emporte! **to go to the d.,** se ruiner; (*b*) **what the d. are you doing?** que diable faites-vous là? **how the d. . . . .?** comment diable . . .? **to work like the d.,** travailler avec acharnement; **there'll be the d. to pay,** ça nous, vous, coûtera cher; ′**devilish,** *a.* (*a*) diabolique; (*b*) diaboliquement. **2.** *F:* bigrement; ′**devil-may-′care,** *a.* (esprit *m*) (i) téméraire, (ii) insouciant; ′**devilment,** *s.,* ′**devilry,** *s.* **1.** méchanceté *f;* **there's some d. afoot,** il se trame quelque chose. **2. to be full of d.,** avoir le diable au corps.

devious [′di:viəs], *a.* (*of aims, methods*) détourné, tortueux.

devise [di′vaiz], *v.tr.* combiner (un projet); inventer, imaginer (un appareil); tramer (un complot).

devoid [di′vɔid], *a.* dénué, dépourvu (**of,** de).

devolution [di:və′lu:ʃ(ə)n], *s. Pol:* décentralisation administrative.

devote [di′vout], *v.tr.* vouer, consacrer (du temps à qch.); **to d. oneself to sth., to study,** se vouer à qch., s'adonner à l'étude; **de′voted,** *a.* dévoué, attaché (**to,** à); **d. to work,** assidu au travail; **-ly,** *adv.* avec dévouement; **de′votion,** *s.* **1.** dévotion *f* (à Dieu). **2.** dévouement *m* (**to s.o.,** à qn); **d. to work,** assiduité *f* au travail.

devour [di′vauər], *v.tr.* dévorer; **de′vouring,** *a.* dévorant.

devout [di′vaut], *a.* **1.** dévot, pieux. **2.** (*of wish*) fervent, sincère; **-ly,** *adv.* **1.** dévotement. **2.** sincèrement.

dew [dju:], *s.* rosée *f;* ′**dewdrop,** *s.* goutte *f* de rosée.

dexterity [deks′teriti], *s.* dextérité *f;* habileté *f;* ′**dext(e)rous,** *a.* adroit, habile (**in doing sth.,** à faire qch.); **-ly,** *adv.* avec dextérité; habilement.

diabetes [daiə′bi:ti:z], *s. Med:* diabète *m;* **dia′betic** [-′betik], *a. & s.* diabétique (*mf*).

diabolical [daiə′bɔlik(ə)l], *a.* (cruauté) diabolique; (complot) infernal; **-ally,** *adv.* diaboliquement.

diagnose [′daiəgnouz], *v.tr.* diagnostiquer; **diag′nosis,** *pl.* **-oses,** *s. Med:* diagnostic *m.*

diagonal [dai′ægən(ə)l]. **1.** *a.* diagonal. **2.** *s.* diagonale *f;* **-ally,** *adv.* diagonalement, en diagonale.

diagram [′daiəgræm], *s.* **1.** diagramme *m,* tracé *m,* schéma *m.* **2.** graphique *m* (de température, etc.).

dial ['daiəl]. **I.** s. cadran m. **II.** v.tr. & i. (dialled) P.T.T: appeler (qn) à l'automatique; composer un numéro; **to d. 999,** appeler Police Secours; **'dialling,** s. composition f du numéro; **d. tone,** tonalité continue.

dialect ['daiəlekt], s. dialecte m; **provincial d.,** patois m.

dialogue ['daiələg], s. dialogue m.

diameter [dai'æmitər], s. diamètre m; **dia'metrical,** a. diamétral; **-ally,** adv. diamétralement.

diamond ['daiəmənd], s. **1.** diamant m; **d. merchant, d. cutter,** diamantaire m; Tls: **cutting d.,** diamant de vitrier. **2.** (a) (of shape) losange m; **d. panes,** vitres en forme de losange; (b) Cards: carreau m; Sp: U.S: terrain m de baseball; **d.-shaped,** en losange.

diaper ['daiəpər], s. N.Am: couche f (de bébé).

diaphragm ['daiəfræm], s. **1.** Anat: diaphragme m. **2.** Tchn: diaphragme.

diarrhoea [daiə'riːə], s. Med: diarrhée f; **verbal d.,** verbomanie f.

diary ['daiəri], s. **1.** journal m (intime). **2.** agenda m; **desk d.,** bloc m calendrier; **'diarist,** s. auteur m d'un journal (particulier).

dice [dais], s.pl. dés m (à jouer).

Dick [dik]. Pr.n.m. (dim. of **Richard**) Richard.

Dictaphone ['diktəfoun], s. R.t.m: Dictaphone m.

dictate [dik'teit]. **1.** v.tr. dicter (une lettre, etc.). **2.** v.i. faire la loi; **I won't be dictated to,** je n'ai pas d'ordres à recevoir; **dic'tation,** s. dictée f; **dic'tator,** s. Pol: dictateur m; **dicta'torial,** a. **1.** (pouvoir) dictatorial. **2.** (ton) impérieux; **-ally,** adv. impérieusement; autoritairement; **dic'tatorship,** s. dictature f.

dictionary ['dikʃ(ə)nri], s. dictionnaire m.

diddle ['didl], v.tr. **1.** P: rouler, carotter (qn). **2.** N.Am: **to d. (away)** (one's time, etc.), flâner.

die¹ [dai], s. **1.** Minting: coin m. **2.** Metalw: matrice f; **'die-casting,** s. moulage m mécanique.

die², v.i. (**died**) **1.** mourir; (of animals) crever; **to be dying,** être à l'agonie; **he died yesterday,** il est mort hier; (of pers.) **to d. hard,** vendre chèrement sa vie; **this superstition will d. hard,** cette superstition aura la vie dure. **2.** **to d. of laughing,** mourir de rire; **I'm dying of thirst,** je meurs de soif; **to be dying to do sth.,** mourir, brûler, d'envie de faire qch. **3.** **his secret died with him,** il emporta son secret dans le tombeau; **his fortune dies with him,** sa fortune s'éteindra avec lui; **'die a'way,** v.i. (of sound) s'affaiblir; s'éteindre; **'die 'down,** v.i. (of fire) baisser; (of wind) s'apaiser; (of excitement) se calmer; **'diehard,** s. réactionnaire m endurci; **'die 'out,** v.i. (of race) s'éteindre; (of custom) disparaître.

diesel ['diːz(ə)l], a. & s. **d.** (oil), gaz-oil m; **d.** (engine), (i) (locomotive f) diesel; (ii) (moteur m) diesel.

diet ['daiət]. **I.** s. **1.** nourriture f. **2.** régime m (alimentaire); **to be on a d.,** être au régime. **II.** v.i. se mettre, être, au régime; **die'tetics** s.pl. (usu. with sg. constr.) diététique f **die'tician,** s. diététicien, -ienne.

differ ['difər], v.i. **1.** différer (**from,** de); être différent (de). **2.** **to d. about sth.,** ne pas s'accorder sur qch.; **to agree to d.,** garder chacun son opinion.

difference ['dif(ə)rəns], s. **1.** différence f, écart m (between, entre); **I don't quite see the d.,** je ne saisis pas la nuance; **d. in age,** différence d'âge; **with only a slight d.,** à peu de chose près; **makes no d.,** cela ne fait rien; **that makes all the d.,** voilà qui change tout. **2.** **to split the d.,** partager le différend. **3.** dispute f, différend m; **settle your differences,** mettez-vous d'accord; **'different,** a. **1.** différent (**from,** de); **to do sth quite d.,** faire tout autre chose; **that's quite a matter,** ça, c'est une autre affaire. **2.** divers, différent; **d. people saw him,** différentes personnes l'ont vu; **at d. times,** à diverses reprises; **-ly,** adv. **1.** différemment; **he speaks d. from you,** il ne parle pas de la même manière que vous. **2.** diversement; (people) **d. dressed,** (de gens) diversement habillés, en costumes divers.

differential [difə'renʃəl]. **1.** a. différentiel. **2.** différentielle f.

differentiate [difə'renʃieit], v.tr. différencier (**sth. from sth.,** qch. de qch.); abs. **to between two things,** faire la différence entre deux choses.

difficult ['difikəlt], a. (a) difficile, malaisé; **it is to believe that . . .,** on a peine à croire que . . .; (b) (of pers.) difficile; peu commode; **d. get on with,** (personne) difficile à vivre; **'difficulty,** s. **1.** difficulté f; **the d. is to . . .,** difficile, c'est de . . .; **with great d.,** à grand peine. **2.** obstacle m; **I see no d. about it,** je vois pas d'inconvénient; **to make difficulties,** faire des difficultés. **3.** embarras m, ennui m; **be in a d.,** être dans l'embarras; **money difficulties,** soucis mpl d'argent; **to get out of one's difficulties,** se tirer d'affaire; débrouiller.

diffidence ['difidəns], s. manque m d'assurance, modestie excessive; **'diffident,** a. qui manque d'assurance; **I was d. about speaking to h,** j'hésitais à lui parler; **-ly,** adv. timidement; hésitant.

diffuse [di'fjuːz]. **1.** v.tr. répandre; diffuser. **2.** (of light) se diffuser; **di'ffusion,** s. (of r light, etc.) diffusion f; (of ideas, of rayonnement m.

dig [dig]. **I.** s. **1.** (a) **to give s.o. a d. in the**

pousser qn du coude; (*b*) **to have a d. at s.o.**, lancer un sarcasme à qn; **that's a d. at you**, c'est une pierre dans votre jardin. **2. a(n archaeological) d.**, une fouille (d'intérêt archéologique). **II.** *v.* (**digging; dug** [dʌg]) **1.** *v.tr.* (*a*) bêcher, retourner (la terre); (*b*) creuser (un trou). **2.** *v.tr.* enfoncer (**sth. into sth.**, qch. dans qch.). **3.** *v.i.* (*a*) *F:* loger en garni; (*b*) faire des fouilles (archéologiques); '**digger**, *s.* **1.** bêcheur *m*; terrassier *m*; fouilleur *m* (de monuments); *Austr: P:* Australien *m*. **2.** *Agr:* plantoir *m*; (**potato-)d.**, arracheuse *f*; '**digging**, *s.* (*a*) bêchage *m*; excavation *f*; (*b*) fouilles *fpl*; '**dig'in. 1.** *v.tr.* enterrer (le fumier); **to d. oneself in(to a place)**, s'incruster, s'ancrer. **2.** *v.i.* *F:* manger, bouffer; **digs**, *s.pl.* *F:* logement *m*; **to live in d.**, loger en garni; '**dig'up**, *v.tr.* déraciner (une plante); mettre à jour (un trésor); piocher (la terre); déterrer (un cadavre).

‖igest. I. *s.* ['daidʒest], sommaire *m*, abrégé *m*. **II.** *v.tr.* [dai'dʒest]. **1.** (*a*) mettre (des faits) en ordre; (*b*) résumer (un compte rendu). **2.** digérer (des aliments); **di'gestible**, *a.* digestible; **di'gestion**, *s.* digestion *f*; **sluggish d.**, digestion laborieuse; **to spoil one's d.**, s'abimer l'estomac; **di'gestive. 1.** *a.* digestif. **2.** *s.* digestif *m*.

‖igit ['didʒit], *s.* **1.** doigt *m*; doigt de pied. **2.** *Mth:* chiffre *m* (arabe).

‖ignify ['dignifai], *v.tr.* donner de la dignité à (qch.); **dignified**, *a.* plein de dignité; (air) digne; '**dignitary**, *s.* dignitaire *m*; '**dignity**, *s.* **1.** dignité *f*; **it's beneath your d. to accept**, vous ne pouvez pas vous abaisser (jusqu')à accepter. **2.** dignité; (haut) rang.

‖gress [dai'gres], *v.i.* faire une digression (**from**, de); s'écarter (du sujet); **di'gression**, *s.* digression *f*, écart *m*.

‖ke [daik], *s.* **1.** (*a*) digue *f*, levée *f*; (*b*) chaussée surélevée. **2.** fossé *m*.

‖apidate [di'læpideitid], *a.* délabré, décrépit; **dilapi'dation**, *s.* délabrement *m*, dégradation *f* (d'une maison).

‖ate [dai'leit], *v.i.* (*a*) (*of eyes, etc.*) se dilater; (*b*) **to d. (up)on a topic**, s'étendre sur un sujet; **di'lation**, *s.* dilatation *f*.

‖atory ['dilət(ə)ri], *a.* lent (à agir); (*of action*) tardif.

‖emma [di'lemə, dai-], *s.* embarras *m*; **to be in a d.**, être très embarrassé.

‖igence ['dilidʒ(ə)ns], *s.* assiduité *f*, diligence *f*; '**diligent**, *a.* assidu, diligent; **-ly**, *adv.* avec assiduité; diligemment.

‖y-dally ['dilidæli], *v.i.* *F:* traîner, *F:* rainasser; barguigner, baguenauder.

‖ute [dai'lju:t], *v.tr.* **1.** diluer, couper (le vin). **2.** atténuer (une doctrine). **3.** délaver, délayer (une couleur); **di'lution**, *s.* dilution *f*.

dim [dim]. **I.** *a.* (*of light*) faible; pâle; (*of memory*) incertain, vague; **to grow d.**, (*of light*) baisser; (*of sight*) se troubler; (*of recollection*) s'effacer; *F:* **to take a d. view of** (sth., s.o.), avoir une piètre opinion de (qch., qn); **he's a d. sort of chap**, c'est un mou; il est moche; **-ly**, *adv.* faiblement; vaguement, confusément. **II.** *v.* (**dimmed**) **1.** *v.tr.* (*a*) obscurcir; ternir (un miroir); (*b*) *Aut:* **to d. the headlights**, mettre (les phares) en code. **2.** *v.i.* (*of light*) baisser; (*of outlines*) s'effacer; '**dimness**, *s.* **1.** faiblesse *f* (d'éclairage); obscurité *f* (d'une salle). **2.** *F:* stupidité *f*; '**dimwit**, *s.* *F:* (espèce *f* d')idiot *m*, andouille *f*.

dime [daim], *s.* *U.S:* *F:* dime *f* (= dix cents).

dimension [di'menʃ(ə)n, dai-], *s.* dimension *f*; *Ind:* cote *f*; **di'mensional**, *a.* **two-, three-d.**, à deux, à trois, dimensions..

diminish [di'miniʃ]. **1.** *v.tr.* diminuer; amoindrir. **2.** *v.i.* diminuer, décroître; aller en diminuant; **dimi'nution**, *s.* diminution *f*; amoindrissement *m*; **di'minutive. 1.** *a.* & *s.* *Gram:* diminutif (*m*). **2.** *a.* tout petit; minuscule.

dimple ['dimpl], *s.* fossette *f*.

din [din], *s.* tapage *m*, vacarme *m*.

dine [dain], *v.i.* dîner; **to d. out**, dîner (i) en ville, (ii) chez des amis; '**diner**, *s.* **1.** (*pers.*) dîneur, -euse. **2.** *Rail:* (*also* **dining car**) wagon-restaurant *m*; '**dining-room**, *s.* salle *f* à manger.

dinghy [diŋ(g)i], *s.* *Nau:* canot *m*, youyou *m*; **rubber d.**, canot pneumatique.

dingy ['dindʒi], *a.* défraîchi; (*of colour*) terne; **d. white**, d'un blanc sale; '**dinginess**, *s.* propreté douteuse.

dinner ['dinər], *s.* dîner *m*; **public d.**, banquet *m*; **to be having d.**, être à table; **d. jacket**, smoking *m*; **d. party**, dîner (prié); **to give a d. party**, avoir, inviter, qn, du monde, à dîner; **d. service**, service *m* de table; **d. time**, l'heure *f* du dîner.

dinosaur ['dainəsɔ:r], *s.* dinosaure *m*.

dint [dint], *s.* *used in the phr.* **by d. of**, à force de.

diocese ['daiəsis], *s.* *Ecc:* diocèse *m*; **di'ocesan** [dai'ɔsisən], *a.* & *s.* diocésain (*m*).

dip [dip]. **I.** *s.* **1.** immersion *f* (de qch. dans un liquide). **2.** plongée *f* (du terrain). **3.** *F:* baignade *f*; **I'm going for a d.**, je vais me baigner. **II.** *v.* (**dipped**) **1.** *v.tr.* (*a*) plonger, tremper (qch. dans un liquide); immerger (un métal); *F:* **to d. one's hand into one's pocket**, débourser; (*b*) *Aut:* **to d. the headlights**, se mettre en code; (*c*) *Nau: Av:* **to d. (one's flag, one's wings)**, saluer. **2.** *v.i.* (*of road, etc.*) plonger; (*b*) (*of sun*) baisser; (*c*) **to d. into a book**, feuilleter un livre; (*d*) puiser (dans sa bourse); '**dipping**, *s.* immersion *f*, plongée *f*; *Ind:* décapage *m*; '**dipstick**, *s.* *Aut:* jauge *f* de carter.

diphtheria [dif'θiəriə], *s.* *Med:* diphtérie *f*.

diploma [di'ploumə], *s.* diplôme *m.*

diplomacy [di'plouməsi], *s.* diplomatie *f;* **'diplomat,** *s.,* **di'plomatist,** *s.* diplomate *m;* **diplo'matic,** *a.* 1. diplomatique; **the d. service,** la diplomatie, la Carrière. 2. adroit, prudent; **d. answer,** réponse *f* politique; **-ally,** *adv.* 1. diplomatiquement. 2. avec tact.

dipsomania [dipsou'meiniə], *s.* dipsomanie *f;* **dipso'maniac,** *F:* **dipso,** *a. & s.* dipsomane *(mf).*

dire ['daiər], *a.* désastreux, affreux; **d. necessity,** nécessité implacable; **d. poverty,** misère noire.

direct [dai'rekt, di-]. I. *v.tr.* 1. gérer, régir (une entreprise). 2. *(a)* **to d. s.o.'s attention to sth.,** attirer l'attention de qn sur qch.; *(b)* **to d. one's efforts to(wards) an end,** orienter ses efforts vers un but. 3. **could you d. me to the station?** pourriez-vous m'indiquer le chemin de la gare? 4. *(a)* **to d. s.o. to do sth.,** ordonner à qn de faire qch.; **as directed,** selon les instructions; *(b)* *(of judge)* **to d. the jury,** instruire le jury. II. 1. *a. (a)* direct; **d. cause,** cause immédiate; **d. taxation,** contributions directes; *Gram:* **d. object,** complément direct; *(b)* franc, *f.* franche; *(c)* absolu, formel; **d. answer,** réponse catégorique; *(d) El:* **d. current,** courant continu. 2. *adv.* (aller) directement, tout droit; **-ly.** 1. *adv. (a)* (aller) directement, tout droit; **to go d. to the point,** aller droit au fait; *(b)* absolument; **d. contrary,** diamétralement opposé (**to,** à); **d. opposite the church,** juste en face de l'église; *(c) (of time)* tout de suite, tout à l'heure. 2. *conj.* aussitôt que, dès, que; **di'rectness,** *s.* franchise *f* (d'une réponse).

direction [dai'rekʃ(ə)n, di-], *s.* 1. direction *f,* administrateur *m,* directeur *m* (d'une société); *m;* **in every d.,** en tous sens. 3. *(usu. pl.)* instruction(s) *f(pl);* **directions for use,** mode *m* d'emploi.

director [dai'rektər, di-], *s. (pers.)* administrateur *m,* directeur *m* (d'une société); gérant *m* (d'une entreprise); **Board of Directors,** conseil *m* d'administration; *Th: Cin:* metteur *m* en scène; **di'rectorate,** *s.* (conseil *m* d')administration; **di'rectory,** *s.* 1. *(a)* annuaire *m* (des téléphones); *(b)* **street and trade d.,** le Bottin *(R.t.m:).* 2. *N.Am:* conseil *m* d'administration.

dirge [də:dʒ], *s.* chant *m* funèbre.

dirt [də:t], *s.* saleté *f.* 1. boue *f,* crotte *f,* ordure *f;* **to throw d. at s.o.,** éclabousser la réputation de qn; **to talk d.,** parler grossièrement; **it's d. cheap,** c'est pour trois fois rien. 2. malpropreté *f;* **'dirt-farmer,** *s. N.Am:* exploitant *m* agricole; **'dirtiness,** *s.* 1. saleté *f,* malpropreté *f.* 2. *(of speech)* grossièreté *f;* *(of action)* bassesse *f;* **'dirt-track,** *s. Sp:* piste *f* en cendrée; **'dirty.** I.

a. 1. sale, malpropre, crasseux; crotté. 2. **d. weather,** mauvais temps, *Nau:* gros temps. 3. a **d. trick,** un vilain tour; *F:* **to do the d. on s.o.,** jouer un mauvais tour à qn, faire une sale coup à qn; **it's a d. business,** c'est une sale affaire; **-ily,** *adv.* salement. 1. malproprement. 2. bassement. II. *v.* 1. *v.tr.* salir, encrasser (qch.) 2. *v.i. (of material, etc.)* **to d. easily,** se salir facilement.

disability [disə'biliti], *s. (a)* **physical d.,** infirmité *f;* *(b) Adm:* invalidité *f.*

disable [dis'eibl], *v.tr.* mettre hors de combat estropier (qn); **disabled ex-servicemen,** mutilé *m* de guerre; **dis'ablement,** *s.* 1. mise *f* hors de combat. 2. invalidité *f;* incapacité *f* d travail.

disadvantage [disəd'va:ntidʒ], *s.* désavantag *m,* inconvénient *m;* **to take s.o. at a d.,** prendr qn au dépourvu; **disadvantageous** ['disæd va:n'teidʒəs], *a.* désavantageux, défavorab (**to,** à).

disagree [disə'gri:], *v.i.* 1. *(a)* être en désaccor ne pas être d'accord (**with,** avec); *(b)* **to d. wit s.o.,** donner tort à qn; **I d.,** je ne suis pas de c avis. 2. se brouiller (**with s.o.,** avec qn). 3. wi **disagrees with him,** le vin lui est contraire; t **climate disagrees with me,** le climat ne me co vient pas; **disa'greeable,** *a. (of pers., thin* désagréable; *(of incident)* fâcheux; **-ably,** *ad* désagréablement; fâcheusement; **di a'greeableness,** *s. (of pers.)* mauvai humeur; mauvais caractère; **disa'greemen** *s.* 1. différence *f* (**between,** entre). 2. désacco *m* (**with s.o. about sth.,** avec qn sur qch.); querelle *f,* brouille *f.*

disappear [disə'piər], *v.i.* disparaître; **he d appeared from view,** il disparut à nos yeu **disa'ppearance,** *s.* disparition *f.*

disappoint [disə'point], *v.tr. (a)* désappoin (qn); *(b)* décevoir, chagriner (qn); **to be dis pointed in love,** avoir des chagrins d'amo *(c)* décevoir (les espérances de qn); trom (l'attente de qn); **disa'ppointing,** décevant; **disa'ppointment,** *s.* déception déboire *m.*

disapprove [disə'pru:v], *v.i.* **to d. of sth.,** dés prouver qch.; **disa'pproval,** *s.* désappro tion *f* (**of s.o., sth.,** de qn, qch.); **look of** regard *m* désapprobateur; **disa'pproving** *adv.* avec désapprobation; d'un air, d'un t désapprobateur.

disarm [dis'a:m], *v.tr. & i.* désarmer; **dis' ming,** *a.* (franchise, etc.) qui vous désar **dis'armament,** *s. Pol:* désarmement *m.*

disarrange [disə'reindʒ], *v.tr.* déranger (q mettre (qch.) en désordre; **disa'rrangem** *s.* dérangement *m;* désordre *m.*

disaster [di'za:stər], *s.* désastre *m;* *(by*

flood, etc.) sinistre *m*; **di'sastrous,** *a.* désastreux; funeste; **-ly,** *adv.* désastreusement.

disband [dis'bænd], *v.tr.* licencier (des troupes, etc.).

disbelieve [disbi'li:v]. **1.** *v.tr.* ne pas croire (qn, qch.). **2.** *v.i.* **to d. in sth.,** ne pas croire à qch.; **disbe'lief,** *s.* incrédulité *f*; **disbe'liever,** *s.* incrédule *mf.*

disc [disk], *s.* (*a*) disque *m*; (*b*) (*of cardboard, etc.*) rondelle *f*; *Mus:* disque (pour tournedisque); *Rad:* **d. jockey,** présentateur *m* (de disques); *Med:* **slipped d.,** hernie discale; *Aut:* **wheel d.,** enjoliveur *m*; **d. brake,** frein *m* à disque; **d. clutch,** embrayage *m* à disques.

discard [dis'ka:d], *v.tr.* **1.** (*at bridge*) se défausser d'(une couleur). **2.** mettre (qch.) de côté; se défaire de (qch.); abandonner, renoncer à (un projet).

discern [di'sə:n], *v.tr.* distinguer, discerner; **di'scernible,** *a.* perceptible; **di'scerning,** *a.* (*of pers.*) judicieux; (*of intelligence*) pénétrant; (*of taste*) sûr; **di'scernment,** *s.* discernement *m.*

discharge. **I.** *s.* ['distʃa:dʒ]. **1.** déchargement *m* (d'un navire). **2.** décharge *f*, déversement *m* (d'eau); débit *m* (d'une pompe); **d. pipe,** tuyau *m* de vidange; (*b*) *El:* décharge. **3.** renvoi *m* (d'un employé). **4.** *Jur:* (*a*) mise *f* en liberté, élargissement *m* (d'un prisonnier); (*b*) acquittement *m* (d'un accusé). **5.** (*a*) paiement *m* (d'une dette); (*b*) quittance *f.* **II.** *v.* [dis'tʃa:dʒ]. **1.** *v.tr.* (*a*) décharger (un navire); (*b*) décharger (un fusil); (*c*) *El:* décharger; (*d*) congédier (un employé); (*e*) *Jur:* libérer; acquitter; (*f*) **to d. a patient,** renvoyer un malade guéri; **he was discharged from hospital yesterday,** il est sorti de l'hôpital hier; (*g*) régler, solder (une dette). **2.** *v.i.* se décharger; *Med:* (*of wound*) suppurer.

disciple [di'saipl], *s.* disciple *m.*

discipline ['disiplin]. **I.** *s.* discipline *f.* **II.** *v.tr.* **to d. (s.o.),** discipliner (qn); **discipli'narian,** *s.* disciplinaire *m*; **he's no d.,** il n'a pas de discipline *f.*

disclaim [dis'kleim], *v.tr.* désavouer; **to d. all responsibility,** dénier toute responsabilité.

disclose [dis'klouz], *v.tr.* révéler (qch.); divulguer (un secret); **dis'closure,** *s.* révélation *f* (de la pensée de qn); divulgation *f* (d'un secret).

disco ['diskou], *s.* *F:* discothèque *f.*

discolour [dis'kʌlər], *v.tr.* (*a*) décolorer; (*b*) ternir, délaver (un tissu); **discolo(u)'ration,** *s.* décoloration *f.*

discomfort [dis'kʌmfət], *s.* (*a*) manque *m* de confort; (*b*) malaise *m*, gêne *f.*

disconcert [diskən'sə:t], *v.tr.* déconcerter, interloquer (qn); **discon'certing,** *a.* déconcertant, troublant.

disconnect [diskə'nekt], *v.tr.* **1.** désunir, séparer, détacher, disjoindre (**sth. from sth.,** qch. de qch.); décrocher (des wagons). **2.** *El:* débrancher (une prise); (*of telephone*) couper (la communication); **disco'nnected,** *a.* **1.** (*a*) détaché, isolé; (*b*) *El:* débranché, coupé. **2.** (*of speech*) décousu; **-ly,** *adv.* (parler) sans suite, à bâtons rompus.

disconsolate [dis'kɔnsələt], *a.* tout triste; inconsolable; désolé; **-ly,** *adv.* tristement.

discontent [diskən'tent], *s.* mécontentement *m*; **discon'tented,** *a.* mécontent (**with,** de); peu satisfait (de son sort); **-ly,** *adv.* avec mécontentement.

discontinue [diskən'tinju:]. **1.** *v.tr.* discontinuer (qch.); **to d. one's visits,** cesser ses visites. **2.** *v.i.* cesser; **discon'tinuance,** *s.* cessation *f* (de fabrication, du travail); **discon'tinuous,** *a.* discontinu; **-ly,** *adv.* sans continuité; de façon intermittente.

discord ['diskɔ:d], *s.* **1.** discorde *f*, désunion *f.* **2.** *Mus:* (i) dissonance *f*; (ii) accord dissonant; **dis'cordant,** *a.* **1.** (*a*) (*of sound*) discordant; (*b*) *Mus:* dissonant. **2.** **d. opinions,** opinions opposées.

discotheque ['diskoutek], *s.* discothèque *f.*

discount. **I.** *s.* ['diskaunt]. **1.** *Com:* remise *f*, ristourne *f*; **to sell sth. at a d.,** vendre qch. au rabais. **2.** *Fin:* escompte *m.* **II.** *v.tr.* **1.** ['diskaunt]. *Com:* escompter (un effet). **2.** [dis'kaunt]. (*a*) ne pas tenir compte de (qch.); faire peu de cas de (l'avis de qn).

discourage [dis'kʌridʒ], *v.tr.* décourager (qn); **to become discouraged,** se décourager; **dis'couraging,** *a.* décourageant; **-ly,** *adv.* d'une manière décourageante; **dis'couragement,** *s.* découragement *m.*

discourteous [dis'kə:tiəs], *a.* impoli; **-ly,** *adv.* **to behave d. to s.o.,** faire une impolitesse à qn; **dis'courtesy,** *s.* impolitesse *f.*

discover [dis'kʌvər], *v.tr.* découvrir, trouver; (*a*) **to d. a new gas,** découvrir un gaz nouveau; (*b*) **I discovered too late that . . .,** je m'aperçus trop tard que . . .; **dis'coverer,** *s.* découvreur, -euse d'une terre inconnue, d'une loi naturelle); **dis'covery,** *s.* découverte *f*; **voyage of d.,** voyage *m* d'exploration; *F:* (*of a find*) trouvaille *f.*

discredit [dis'kredit]. **I.** *s.* **1.** doute *m.* **2.** discrédit *m* (de qn, de qch.); déconsidération *f* (de qn). **II.** *v.tr.* **1.** ne pas croire, mettre en doute (une rumeur). **2.** discréditer (une opinion); déconsidérer (qn); **dis'creditable,** *a.* peu digne; **-ably,** *adv.* de façon indigne, déshonorânte.

discreet [dis'kri:t], *a.* **1.** avisé, sage; **a d. smile,** un petit sourire contenu. **2.** discret, -ète; **-ly,**

adv. 1. avec réserve. 2. discrètement; **dis′cre-tion**, *s.* 1. discrétion *f*; **I shall use my d.**, je ferai comme bon me semblera. 2. sagesse *f*, jugement *m*, prudence *f*; **to reach years of d.**, atteindre l'âge de (la) raison; **to use d.**, agir avec discrétion. 3. silence judicieux.

discrepancy [dis′krepənsi], *s.* désaccord *m*; divergence *f* (de témoignage, etc.).

discriminate [dis′krimineit]. 1. *v.tr.* distinguer (**from, de, d'avec**). 2. *v.i.* (*a*) distinguer, établir une distinction (**between,** entre); (*b*) **to d. in favour of s.o.**, faire des distinctions en faveur de qn; **dis′criminating,** *a.* (*of pers.*) plein de discernement; judicieux; **d. purchaser,** acheteur avisé; *Adm:* **d. tariff,** tarif différentiel; **discrimi′nation,** *s.* 1. discernement *m.* 2. jugement *m*; **man of d.,** homme judicieux. 3. distinction *f*; **racial d.,** discrimination raciale; **d. in favour of . . .,** préférence donnée à . . ..

discus [′diskəs], *s. Sp:* disque *m.*

discuss [dis′kʌs], *v.tr.* discuter, débattre (un problème); agiter (une question); **d. the matter with him,** concertez-vous avec lui là-dessus; **dis′cussion,** *s.* discussion *f*; agitation *f* (d'une question); **question under d.,** question en discussion.

disdain [dis′dein]. I. *s.* dédain *m* (**of, de**). II. *v.tr.* dédaigner; **dis′dainful,** *a.* dédaigneux (**of, de**); **-fully,** *adv.* dédaigneusement.

disease [di′zi:z], *s.* maladie *f*; mal *m*; **di′seased,** *a.* 1. malade. 2. morbide; malsain.

disembark [disem′bɑ:k], *v.tr. & i.* débarquer; **disembar′kation,** *s.* débarquement *m.*

disenchantment [disin′tʃɑ:ntmənt], *s.* désenchantement *m*; désillusion *f.*

disengage [disin′geidʒ]. 1. *v.tr.* dégager (qch. de qch.). 2. *v.i.* se dégager; *Mec:* se déclencher; **disen′gaged,** *a.* libre, inoccupé.

disentangle [disin′tæŋgl], *v.tr.* démêler, désentortiller (une ficelle); débrouiller (une situation); **disen′tanglement,** *s.* dégagement *m*; démêlage *m* (**of a skein of wool,** d'un écheveau).

disfavour [dis′feivər], *s.* défaveur *f*; **to fall into d.,** tomber en disgrâce; **to incur s.o.'s d.,** déplaire à qn.

disfigure [dis′figər], *v.tr.* défigurer; enlaidir (le visage, un paysage); **dis′figurement,** *s.* défiguration *f*; enlaidissement *m.*

disgorge [dis′gɔ:dʒ], *v.tr.* dégorger; rendre (des objets volés).

disgrace [dis′greis]. I. *s.* 1. disgrâce *f*; (*of child*) **to be in d.,** être en pénitence *f.* 2. honte *f*, déshonneur *m*; **to be a d. to one's family,** être la honte de sa famille. II. *v.tr.* disgracier (un ministre); déshonorer (qn); **dis′graceful,** *a.* honteux, déshonorant; scandaleux; **-fully,**

adv. honteusement, d'une manière scandaleuse; **he behaved d.,** sa conduite a été indigne.

disgruntled [dis′grʌntld], *a.* contrarié, mécontent (**at, de**); **d. mood,** humeur *f* maussade.

disguise [dis′gaiz]. I. *s.* 1. déguisement *m*; travestissement *m*; **in d.,** déguisé. 2. feinte *f*; fausse apparence; **to throw off all d.,** laisser tomber le masque. II. *v.tr.* 1. déguiser, travestir (qn). 2. (*a*) déguiser (sa pensée); masquer (une odeur); (*b*) **there is no disguising the fact that . . .,** il faut avouer que . . .; (*c*) **to d. one's feelings,** dissimuler ses sentiments.

disgust [dis′gʌst]. I. *s.* 1. dégoût (profond) (**at, for,** pour). 2. profond mécontentement; **he resigned in d.,** écœuré, il a donné sa démission. II. *v.tr.* dégoûter; écœurer (qn); **dis′gusting,** *a.* dégoûtant; répugnant; écœurant.

dish [diʃ]. I. *v.tr.* **to d. up,** servir (le repas); **to d. out,** (i) servir (la viande); (ii) payer (de l'argent). II. *s.* 1. plat *m*; **vegetable d.,** légumier *m*; **earthenware d.,** terrine *f*; **to wash the dishes,** faire la vaisselle. 2. plat *m* (de viande etc.); mets *m*; **′dishcloth,** *s.* torchon *m*; **′dishwasher,** *s.* lave-vaisselle *m*; **′dishwater,** *s.* eau *f* de vaisselle; *F:* (*of thin soup*) lavasse *f.*

dishearten [dis′hɑ:tn], *v.tr.* décourager, abattre, démoraliser (qn); **dis′heartening,** *a.* décourageant; (travail) ingrat.

dishevelled [di′ʃev(ə)ld], *a.* 1. échevelé, dépeigné. 2. aux vêtements chiffonnés.

dishonest [dis′ɔnist], *a.* malhonnête; déloyal; **-ly,** *adv.* malhonnêtement; **dis′honesty,** *s.* malhonnêteté *f*; improbité *f*; **a piece of d.,** une malhonnêteté.

dishonour [dis′ɔnər]. I. *s.* 1. déshonneur *m.* chose déshonorante. II. *v.tr.* 1. déshonorer **to d. one's word,** manquer à sa parole. 2. *Com:* **dishonoured cheque,** chèque impayé; **dis′honourable,** *a.* 1. (*of pers.*) sans honneur. 2. (*of action*) honteux, indigne; **-ably,** *adv.* d'une façon peu honorable.

disillusion [disi′lju:ʒ(ə)n]. I. *s.* désillusion *f.* II. *v.tr.* désillusionner, désabuser, désenchanter (qn); **disi′llusionment,** *s.* désillusionnement *m*, désenchantement *m.*

disincentive [disin′sentiv], *s.* facteur de découragement, qui décourage (le travail, etc.).

disinclination [disinkli′neiʃ(ə)n], *s.* répugnance *f*, aversion *f* (**for, to,** pour).

disinclined [disin′klaind], *a.* **to be d. to do sth.,** être peu disposé à faire qch.

disinfect [disin′fekt], *v.tr.* désinfecter; **disin′fectant,** *a. & s.* désinfectant (*m*).

disingenuous [disin′dʒenjuəs], *a.* sans franchise; faux, *f.* fausse; **-ly,** *adv.* sans franchise; **disin′genuousness,** *s.* manque de franchise; mauvaise foi.

disinherit [disin'herit], *v.tr.* déshériter.
disintegrate [dis'intigreit]. 1. *v.tr.* désagréger; effriter (la pierre). 2. *v.i.* se désagréger; s'effriter; **disinte'gration,** *s.* désagrégation *f,* effritement *m.*
disinterested [dis'intristid], *a.* désintéressé; **-ly,** *adv.* avec désintéressement; **dis-'interestedness,** *s.* désintéressement *m.*
disjointed [dis'dʒɔintid], *a.* disjoint; (discours) sans suite; (style) décousu.
disk [disk], *s. see* DISC.
dislike [dis'laik]. I. *s.* aversion *f,* répugnance *f* (to, of, for, pour); **to take a d. to s.o.,** prendre qn en grippe. II. *v.tr.* ne pas aimer; détester (qn); **I don't d. him,** il ne me déplaît pas; **to be disliked by all,** être mal vu de tous.
dislocate ['disləkeit], *v.tr.* (*a*) disloquer (une machine); désorganiser (les affaires); (*b*) luxer, déboîter (un membre); **to d. one's jaw,** se décrocher la mâchoire; **dislo'cation,** *s.* (*a*) dislocation *f;* désorganisation *f;* (*b*) luxation *f,* déboîtement *m* (d'un membre).
dislodge [dis'lɔdʒ], *v.tr.* 1. déloger (qn). 2. détacher; **a stone had become dislodged,** une pierre s'était détachée.
disloyalty [dis'lɔialti], *s.* infidélité *f,* déloyauté *f;* **dis'loyal,** *a.* infidèle; déloyal; **-ally,** *adv.* infidèlement, déloyalement.
dismal ['dizməl], *a.* sombre, triste; lugubre; **-ally,** *adv.* lugubrement, tristement.
dismantle [dis'mæntl], *v.tr.* démonter (une machine).
dismay [dis'mei]. I. *s.* consternation *f.* II. *v.tr.* consterner, épouvanter.
dismiss [dis'mis], *v.tr.* 1. congédier (qn); donner congé à (qn); destituer (un fonctionnaire). 2. (*a*) congédier (qn) (aimablement); (*b*) dissoudre (une assemblée). 3. **to d. sth. from one's thoughts,** bannir, chasser, qch. de ses pensées. 4. **let's d. the subject,** n'en parlons plus; brisons là. 5. (*a*) écarter (une proposition); (*b*) **to d. the accused,** acquitter l'inculpé. 6. *Mil:* **dismiss!** rompez! **dis'missal,** *s.* 1. congédiement *m,* renvoi *m* (d'un employé); destitution *f* (d'un fonctionnaire). 2. acquittement *m* (d'un inculpé).
dismount [dis'maunt]. 1. *v.i.* descendre (de cheval, de vélo, etc.); mettre pied à terre. 2. *v.tr.* démonter (i) (un cavalier), (ii) (une machine).
disobey [disə'bei], *v.tr.* désobéir à (qn); **diso'bedience,** *s.* désobéissance *f* (**to s.o.,** à qn); **diso'bedient,** *a.* désobéissant.
disobliging [disə'blaidʒiŋ], *a.* désobligeant.
disorder [dis'ɔːdər]. I. *s.* 1. désordre *m,* confusion *f.* 2. **civil d.,** désordre, tumulte *m.* 3. *Med:* affection *f,* troubles *mpl* (de digestion, etc.); **nervous d.,** troubles nerveux; **mental d.,**

dérangement *m* d'esprit. II. *v.tr.* déranger; mettre le désordre dans (les affaires de qn); **dis'orderliness,** *s.* 1. désordre *m.* 2. turbulence *f;* **dis'orderly,** *a.* 1. désordonné; en désordre. 2. (*of mob*) turbulent. 3. (*of pers.*) désordonné, déréglé.
disorganize [dis'ɔːgənaiz], *v.tr.* désorganiser; **to become disorganized,** se désorganiser; **disorgani'zation,** *s.* désorganisation *f.*
disown [dis'oun], *v.tr.* désavouer (qn, qch.); renier (sa foi).
disparage [dis'pæridʒ], *v.tr.* déprécier, dénigrer (qn, qch.); discréditer (qn); **dis'paraging,** *a.* 1. (terme) de dénigrement; dépréciateur. 2. peu flatteur; **-ly,** *adv.* **to speak d. of s.o.,** parler de qn en termes peu flatteurs; **dis'paragement,** *s.* dénigrement *m.*
dispassionate [dis'pæʃənət], *a.* 1. sans passion; calme. 2. impartial; **-ly,** *adv.* 1. sans passion; avec calme. 2. sans parti pris.
dispatch [dis'pætʃ]. I. *v.tr.* 1. (*a*) expédier (des marchandises); envoyer (qn, qch.); (*b*) **to d. current business,** expédier les affaires courantes. 2. tuer, achever (une bête blessée). II. *s.* 1. expédition *f;* envoi *m* (de qn, qch.); *Com:* **d. note,** bulletin *m* d'expédition. 2. expédition (d'une affaire); promptitude *f,* diligence *f;* **with the utmost d.,** au plus vite; **d. box,** boîte *f* à documents; **d. case,** serviette *f* (en cuir); *Mil:* **d. rider,** estafette *f.*
dispel [dis'pel], *v.tr.* (**dispelled**) chasser, dissiper (la crainte, etc.).
dispense [dis'pens]. 1. *v.tr.* (*a*) dispenser, distribuer (des aumônes); (*b*) administrer (la justice); (*c*) *Pharm:* préparer (des médicaments); **to d. a prescription,** exécuter une ordonnance. 2. *v.i.* **to d. with sth.,** se passer de qch.; **dis'pensary,** *s.* (*a*) pharmacie *f;* (*b*) officine *f* de pharmacie; **dis'penser,** *s.* distributeur *m* automatique; **dis'pensing,** *s.* *Pharm:* préparation *f* (des ordonnances); **d. chemist,** pharmacien, -ienne, diplômé(e).
disperse [dis'pəːs]. 1. *v.tr.* disperser (les nuages). 2. *v.i.* se disperser; **dis'persal,** *s.,* **dis'persion,** *s.* dispersion *f;* diffusion *f* (de chaleur, etc.).
dispirited [di'spiritid], *a.* découragé, abattu; **-ly,** *adv.* d'un air découragé.
displace [dis'pleis], *v.tr.* 1. déplacer (qch.). 2. (*a*) déplacer, destituer; (*b*) remplacer (**by,** par); évincer (qn); **dis'placement,** *s.* déplacement *m;* changement *m* de place.
display [dis'plei]. I. *s.* 1. étalage *m* (de marchandises); manifestation *f* (de colère); **air d.,** fête *f* aéronautique; *Com:* **d. window,** vitrine *f;* **d. unit,** présentoir *m.* 2. étalage (de luxe); parade *f,* apparat *m;* affichage *m* (d'opinions). II. *v.tr.* 1. exhiber, étaler, exposer (des marchandises);

to **d. a notice,** afficher un avis. **2.** manifester. **3.** étaler, afficher (son luxe). **4.** révéler (son ignorance).

displease [dis'pli:z], *v.tr.* déplaire à (qn); contrarier, mécontenter (qn); **dis'pleasing,** *a.* déplaisant, désagréable (**to,** à); **dis'pleasure** [dis'pleʒər], *s.* déplaisir *m*, mécontentement *m*.

dispose [dis'pouz], *v.tr. & i.* **1.** (*a*) disposer, arranger (des objets); (*b*) **to d. of sth.,** se défaire de qch.; **to d. of a matter,** régler une affaire. **2.** *Com:* **to d. of goods,** écouler, placer, des marchandises; **to d. of a business,** céder son fonds; **to be disposed of,** à vendre; **dis'posable,** *a.* (serviettes, etc.) à jeter; **dis'posal,** *s.* **1. d. unit,** broyeur *m* à ordures. **2. to be at s.o.'s d.,** être à la disposition, au service, de qn. **3.** cession *f* (de biens); **for d.,** à vendre; **dis'posed,** *a.* **1. to be well, ill, d. (towards s.o.),** être bien, mal, intentionné (envers qn). **2. I am d. to help you,** je suis disposé à vous aider; **dispo'sition,** *s.* **1.** disposition *f.* **2.** caractère *m*, naturel *m* (de qn). **3.** penchant *m*, tendance *f* (**to,** à).

dispossess [dispə'zes], *v.tr.* déposséder (qn) (**of sth.,** de qch.).

disproportionate [disprə'pɔ:ʃənət], *a.* disproportionné (**to,** à); **-ly,** *adv.* d'une façon disproportionnée.

disprove [dis'pru:v], *v.tr.* réfuter (un dire); démontrer la fausseté d'(une déclaration).

dispute [dis'pju:t]. **I.** *s.* **1.** contestation *f*, débat *m*; **the matter in d.,** l'affaire dont il s'agit; **beyond d.,** incontestable. **2.** querelle *f*, dispute *f.* **II.** *v.* **1.** *v.i.* (*a*) **to d. with s.o. about sth.,** débattre qch. avec qn; (*b*) se disputer. **2.** *v.tr.* (*a*) débattre (une question); (*b*) contester (une affirmation).

disqualify [dis'kwɔlifai], *v.tr.* **1.** rendre incapable (**for sth.,** de faire qch.). **2. to d. s.o. from driving,** retirer le permis de conduire à qn. **3.** *Sp:* disqualifier (un joueur); **disqualifi'cation,** *s.* **1.** incapacité *f* (**to act,** à agir). **2.** cause *f* d'incapacité (**for,** à). **3.** *Sp:* disqualification *f.*

disregard [disri'gɑ:d]. **I.** *s.* indifférence *f*, insouciance *f* (**of, for,** à l'égard de); **d. of a rule,** désobéissance *f* à une règle. **II.** *v.tr.* ne tenir aucun compte de (qn, qch.); **to d. a rule,** désobéir à une règle.

disremember [disri'membər], *v.tr. N.Am: F:* oublier.

disrepair [disri'peər], *s.* délabrement *m*; **to fall into d.,** tomber en ruines; **in a state of d.,** délabré.

disrepute [disri'pju:t], *s.* **to bring sth. into d.,** discréditer qch.; **disreputable** [dis'repjutəbl], *a.* **1.** (*of action*) honteux. **2.** (*of pers.*) de mauvaise réputation; **d. house,** maison *f* louche. **3.** (*of clothes*) minable.

disrespect [disri'spekt], *s.* manque *m* d'égards, de respect (**for,** envers); **disre'spectful,** *a.* irrespectueux, irrévérencieux; **-fully,** *adv.* (parler) avec irrévérence.

disrupt [dis'rʌpt], *v.tr.* désorganiser (une administration); interrompre (une réunion); **dis'ruption,** *s.* interruption *f.*

dissatisfaction ['dissætis'fækʃ(ə)n], *s.* mécontentement *m* (**with, at,** de); **dis'satisfied,** *a.* mécontent (**with, at,** de).

dissect [di'sekt], *v.tr.* disséquer; **di'ssection,** *s.* **1.** dissection *f.* **2.** découpage *m.*

dissension [di'senʃ(ə)n], *s.* dissension *f.*

dissent [di'sent]. **I.** *s.* **1.** dissentiment *m*; avis *m* contraire. **2.** *Ecc:* dissidence *f.* **II.** *v.i.* différer (**from s.o. about sth.,** de qn sur qch.). **2.** *Ecc:* être dissident; **di'ssenter,** *s. Ecc:* dissident, -ente.

dissertation [disə'teiʃ(ə)n], *s.* dissertation *f.*

disservice ['dissə:vis], *s.* mauvais service rendu; **to do s.o. a d.,** rendre un mauvais service à qn.

dissimilar [di'similər], *a.* dissemblable (**to,** à; de); différent (**to,** de).

dissimulate [di'simjuleit], *v.tr.* dissimuler; cacher (un fait); **dissimu'lation,** *s.* dissimulation *f.*

dissipate ['disipeit]. **1.** *v.tr.* dissiper (une fortune). **2.** *v.i.* se dissiper; **'dissipated,** *a.* dissipé; **d. man,** débauché; **dissi'pation,** *s.* **1.** dissipation *f* (du brouillard); gaspillage *m* (d'une fortune). **2.** vie désordonnée.

dissociate [di'souʃieit], *v.tr.* désassocier (**from,** de); **to d. oneself from a question,** se désintéresser d'une affaire.

dissolute ['disəlju:t], *a.* dissolu, débauché; **to lead a d. life,** vivre dans la débauche.

dissolve [di'zɔlv]. **1.** *v.tr.* dissoudre, faire dissoudre (un sel, etc.). **2.** *v.i.* se dissoudre, fondre.

dissuade [di'sweid], *v.tr.* **to d. s.o. from doing sth.,** dissuader qn de faire qch.; **di'ssuasion,** *s.* dissuasion *f.*

distance ['distəns], *s.* **1.** (*a*) distance *f*, éloignement *m*; **within speaking d.,** à portée de voix; **seen from a d.,** vu de loin; (*b*) **in the d.,** dans le lointain, au loin. **2.** distance, intervalle *m*; **keep s.o. at a d.,** tenir qn à distance, *Sp:* **long race,** course *f* de fond; *P. T. T:* **long d. call,** appel interurbain; **'distant,** *a.* **1.** (*a*) (endroit) éloigné; (pays) lointain; **to have a d. view of sth.,** voir qch. de loin; **d. likeness,** faible ressemblance; (*b*) (*in time*) éloigné, reculé; **memory,** souvenir lointain. **2.** (*of pers.*) réservé, froid, distant; **-ly,** *adv.* **1.** de loin; **related,** d'une parenté éloignée. **2.** avec réserve; froidement.

distaste [dis'teist], *s.* dégoût *m* (**for,** de); ave

sion *f*, répugnance *f* (**for**, pour); **dis'tasteful**, *a.* désagréable (au goût); déplaisant, antipathique (**to s.o.**, à qn); **to be d. to s.o.**, répugner à qn.

distemper¹ [dis'tempər]. **I.** *s.* (*for walls*) détrempe *f*, badigeon *m*. **II.** *v.tr.* **to d.** (**a wall**), badigeonner (un mur); **dis'tempering**, *s.* badigeonnage *m*.

distemper², *s.* (*of dogs*) maladie *f* du jeune âge.

distend [dis'tend]. **1.** *v.tr.* dilater, gonfler (un ballon, etc.). **2.** *v.i.* (*a*) se dilater; (*b*) se distendre; **dis'tension**, *s.* dilatation *f*, distension *f*, gonflement *m*.

distil [dis'til], *v.tr.* (**distilled**) distiller (l'eau); raffiner (le pétrole); **dis'tiller**, *s. Ind:* (*pers.*) distillateur *m*; **dis'tillery**, *s. Ind:* distillerie *f*.

distinct [dis'tiŋ(k)t], *a.* **1.** distinct, différent (**from**, de); **to keep two things d.**, distinguer entre deux choses. **2.** distinct, net; **d. promise**, promesse formelle. **3.** caractérisé, marqué; **d. preference**, préférence marquée; **-ly**, *adv.* **1.** (*a*) distinctement, clairement; (*b*) **I told him d.**, je le lui ai dit expressément. **2.** indéniablement, décidément; **dis'tinction**, *s.* **1.** distinction *f* (**between**, entre). **2.** (*excellence*) distinction; **to gain d.**, se distinguer; **dis'tinctive**, *a.* distinctif; **dis'tinctness**, *s.* clarté *f*, netteté *f*; caractere nettement différent (de deux choses).

distinguish [dis'tiŋgwiʃ]. **1.** *v.tr.* (*a*) distinguer, discerner; (*b*) distinguer, différencier (**from**, de); (*c*) **to d. oneself by . . .**, se signaler, se faire remarquer, par . . .. **2.** *v.i.* faire une distinction (**between**, entre); **dis'tinguished**, *a.* (homme) distingué; **d. writer**, écrivain *m* de marque, de distinction; **d. people**, personnages *m* de marque.

distort [dis'tɔːt], *v.tr.* (*a*) tordre; (*of anger*) décomposer, convulser (le visage); (*b*) fausser, dénaturer (les faits, la vérité); **distorted ideas**, idées biscornues; *Rad: T.V:* **distorted sound, image**, son déformé, image déformée; **dis'tortion**, *s.* déformation *f*; distorsion *f*; décomposition *f* (des traits).

distract [dis'trækt], *v.tr.* **1.** (*a*) distraire (l'attention de qn); (*b*) brouiller (l'esprit). **2.** affoler (qn); **dis'tracted**, *a.* **1.** distrait, inattentif. **2.** affolé, éperdu; **like one d.**, comme un affolé; **-ly**, *adv.* comme un affolé; **dis'traction**, *s.* **1.** distraction *f.* **2.** confusion *f.* **3.** affolement *m.*

distress [dis'tres]. **I.** *s.* **1.** détresse *f*, angoisse *f.* **2.** misère *f*; gêne *f.* **3.** détresse, embarras *m*; **companions in d.**, compagnons d'infortune. **II.** *v.tr.* affliger, angoisser, chagriner (qn); **dis'tressed**, *a.* **1.** affligé, désolé. **2.** *Pol: etc:* conomiquement faible; **dis'tressing**, *a.* affligeant, angoissant; fâcheux.

distribute [dis'tribju(ː)t], *v.tr.* distribuer, répar-

tir; *Com:* être concessionnaire *mf* de, vendre (un produit); **distri'bution**, *s.* distribution *f*, répartition *f*; **dis'tributor**, *s.* **1.** (*a*) distributeur, -trice; (*b*) concessionnaire *mf* (d'un produit). **2.** *El:* distributeur de courant; *Aut:* distributeur d'allumage, *F:* Delco *m* (*R.t.m.*); **d. arm**, rotor *m* du Delco.

district ['distrikt], *s.* **1.** région *f*, territoire *m*, district *m.* **2.** (*a*) *Adm:* **electoral d.**, circonscription électorale; *Com:* **d. manager**, directeur *m* régional; (*b*) quartier *m* (d'une ville); **d. nurse**, (infirmière) visiteuse (*f*).

distrust [dis'trʌst]. **I.** *s.* méfiance *f*, défiance *f.* **II.** *v.tr.* se méfier, se défier de (qn, qch.); **dis'trustful**, *a.* méfiant, défiant (**of**, de); soupçonneux; **-fully**, *adv.* avec méfiance.

disturb [dis'təːb], *v.tr.* **1.** déranger (qn); troubler (le repos); agiter, remuer (une surface); **please don't d. yourself**, ne vous dérangez pas. **2.** inquiéter, troubler (qn); **dis'turbance**, *s.* **1.** dérangement *m*; *Meteor:* perturbation *f* (atmosphérique); *Rad: etc:* (bruit *m*) parasite (*m*). **2.** bruit *m*, tapage *m*; **to make, cause, create, a d.**, troubler l'ordre public. **3.** agitation *f*, trouble *m* (de l'esprit); **dis'turbing**, *a.* perturbateur; **d. news**, nouvelle fâcheuse.

disuse [dis'juːs], *s.* désuétude *f*; **to fall into d.**, tomber en désuétude.

disused [dis'juːzd], *a.* hors d'usage; (*of church, etc.*) désaffecté; (*of door, window*) condamné.

ditch [ditʃ]. **I.** *s.* fossé *m*. **II.** *v.tr. F:* **to d. s.o., sth.**, abandonner qn, qch.; **to d. one's car**, abandonner sa voiture (au bord de la route); *Av:* **to d. a plane**, faire un amerrissage forcé.

dither ['diðər]. **I.** *v.i.* être incapable de se décider. **II.** *s. F:* **to be all of a d.**, être tout agité.

ditto ['ditou], *s.* idem; de même.

divan [di'væn], *s.* divan *m*; **d.-bed**, lit-divan *m*, *pl.* lits-divans, divan-lit *m*, *pl.* divans-lits.

dive [daiv]. **I.** *s.* **1.** (*a*) plongeon *m*; (*b*) plongée *f* (d'un sous-marin); (*c*) *Av:* piqué *m*; **to d. bomb**, attaquer en piqué; **d.-bombing**, attaque *f* en piqué. **2.** *F:* gargote *f.* **II.** *v.i.* (*a*) plonger (**into**, dans); **to d. head first**, piquer une tête (**into**, dans); (*b*) *Av:* **to** (**nose-**)**d.**, piquer (du nez); (*c*) (*of submarine*) plonger; **'diver**, *s.* (*a*) plongeur *m*; (*b*) scaphandrier *m*; **'diving-board**, *s.* plongeoir *m*, tremplin *m*; **'diving-suit**, *s.* scaphandre *m*.

diverge [dai'vəːdʒ], *v.i.* diverger, s'écarter; **di'vergence**, *s.* divergence *f*; **di'vergent**, *a.*, **di'verging**, *a.* divergent.

diverse [dai'vəːs], *a.* **1.** divers, différent. **2.** divers, varié; **-ly**, *adv.* diversement; **di'versify**, *v.i.* diversifier; **di'versity**, *s.* diversité *f.*

diversion [dai'vəːʃ(ə)n], *s.* **1.** détournement *m*, déviation *f* (de la circulation, d'une route). **2.** (*a*) diversion *f* (de l'esprit); **to create a d.**, faire

diversion; (b) divertissement m, distraction f.
divert [dai'vəːt, di-], v.tr. **1.** détourner; écarter
(un coup); **to d. s.o.'s attention,** distraire
l'attention de qn. **2.** divertir, amuser.
divide [di'vaid]. **1.** v.tr. (a) diviser (qch. en parties); **divided between hatred and pity,** partagé
entre la haine et la pitié; (b) partager, répartir
(**among,** entre); **we d. the work among us,** nous
nous partageons le travail; (c) Mth: diviser; (d)
séparer (**from,** de); (e) désunir (une famille). **2.**
v.i. (a) se diviser, se partager (**into,** en); (of
road) (se) bifurquer; (b) Pol: aller aux voix;
dividend ['dividend], s. Fin: dividende m.
divine[1] [di'vain], a. (a) divin; (b) F: admirable;
what a d. place! quel lieu charmant! **-ly,** adv.
divinement; **di'vinity** [-'viniti], s. **1.** divinité f;
dieu m. **2.** Sch: théologie f.
divine[2], v.tr. deviner (l'avenir); prédire,
prophétiser; **di'viner,** s. devin, f. devineresse;
water d., sourcier m; **di'vining-rod,** s.
baguette f de sourcier.
division [di'viʒ(ə)n], s. **1.** division f, partage m
(**into,** en). **2.** répartition f, partage (de bénéfices).
3. division, désunion f. **4.** Mth: division. **5.** Pol:
(a) **parliamentary d.,** circonscription électorale; (b) vote m; **divisible** [di'vizibl], a.
divisible (**by,** par); **divisor** [di'vaizər], s. Mth:
diviseur m.
divorce [di'vɔːs]. **I.** s. divorce m. **II.** v.tr. (of husband, wife) divorcer d'avec (qn); **he wants to
get divorced,** il veut divorcer; **divor'cee**
[-'siː], s. divorcé, -ée.
divulge [di'vʌldʒ, dai-], v.tr. divulguer (un
secret).
dizziness ['dizinis], s. étourdissement m, vertige
m; **'dizzy,** a. **1. to feel d.,** avoir le vertige; **to
make s.o. d.,** étourdir qn; **my head is d.,** la tête
me tourne. **2.** (of height, speed) vertigineux;
-ily, adv. vertigineusement.
do [duː], v. (**did; done**) **I.** v.tr. **1.** (perform) faire
(son devoir); **what do you do (for a living)?**
quel est votre métier? **to do good,** faire le bien;
he did brilliantly at his exam., il a réussi
brillamment (son examen); **the car was doing
sixty,** la voiture faisait du soixante; **are you
doing anything tomorrow?** avez-vous quelque
chose en vue pour demain? **what are you
doing?** (i) qu'est-ce que vous faites? (ii) qu'est-
ce que vous êtes en train de faire? (iii) que
devenez-vous? **it isn't done,** cela ne se fait pas;
I shall do nothing of the sort, no such thing, je
n'en ferai rien; **what's to be done?** que faire?
what can I do for you? en quoi puis-je vous
être utile? **well done!** bravo! à la bonne heure!
F: **that's done it!** ça c'est le bouquet! F:
nothing doing! rien à faire! ça ne prend pas! **2.**
(a) faire (une chambre, les cheveux à qn); (b)
cuire, faire cuire (la viande, etc.); **done to a**

turn, cuit à point; (c) **to do a sum,** faire un
calcul; (d) F: visiter, faire (un musée); (e) F:
(cheat) escroquer (qn); mettre (qn) dedans; **to**
do s.o. out of sth., soutirer qch. à qn; (f) F:
they do you very well here, on mange très bien
ici; **to do oneself well,** faire bonne chère. **3.** (a)
F: **to be done in,** être éreinté, exténué; (b) (after
a bargain made) **done!** tope là! c'est marché
fait! **4. how do you do?** (i) comment allez-
vous? (ii) (on being introduced to s.o.)
enchanté (de faire votre connaissance); **to be**
doing well, faire de bonnes affaires; **he's a lad**
who will do well, c'est un garçon qui réussira.
5. (to serve, suffice) **that will do,** (i) c'est bien;
(ii) en voilà assez! **this room will do for the**
office, cette pièce ira bien pour le bureau; **that**
won't do, cela ne fera pas l'affaire; **I will make**
it do, je m'en arrangerai; **that will do me,** cela
fera mon affaire. **II.** verb substitute. **1. why act**
as you do? pourquoi agir comme vous le
faites? **he writes better than I do,** il écrit mieux
que moi. **2. may I open these letters?—please**
do, puis-je ouvrir ces lettres?—faites donc!
vous en prie! **did you see him?—I did,** l'avez-
vous vu?—oui (je l'ai vu); **I like coffee; do**
you? j'aime le café; et vous? **you like him,**
don't you? vous l'aimez, n'est-ce pas? **don't**
ne faites pas cela! finissez! **3. you like Paris? so**
do I, vous aimez Paris? moi aussi. **III.** v.aux.
(emphasis) **he 'did go,** il y est bien allé; **why**
don't you work?—I 'do work! pourquoi ne
travaillez-vous pas?—mais si, je travaille! **'do**
he indeed? non vraiment? **'do sit down,**
asseyez-vous donc! **'do shut up!** voulez-vous
bien vous taire! **2.** (usual form in questions and
negative statements) **do you see him?** le voyez-
vous? **we do not know,** nous ne le savons pas;
don't do it! n'en faites rien! **IV.** (with certain
prepositions) **1. to do well, badly, by s.o.,** bien,
mal, agir envers qn; **he has been hard done by,**
il a été traité durement. **2.** F: **do for; to do for**
s.o., (a) faire le ménage de qn; (b) tuer qn; faire
son affaire à qn; **I'm done for,** j'ai mon compte; je suis perdu; (c) détruire, ruiner (qn). **3.**
(a) **to have to do with s.o.,** avoir affaire à qn;
have to do with sth., être mêlé à qch.; (of thg)
avoir rapport à qch.; **to have nothing to do**
with a matter, n'être pour rien dans une affaire;
jealousy has a lot to do with it, la jalousie y est
pour beaucoup; (b) **what have I done with my**
bag? où ai-je mis mon sac? **I can't do with that**
noise, je ne peux pas supporter le bruit; (c) **how**
many can you do with? combien en désirez-
vous? **I could do with a cup of tea,** je prendrais
bien une tasse de thé. **4. to do without,** se
passer de (qch.). **V.** **do,** s. (pl. **do's**) F: (a) **it's a**
poor do! c'est plutôt minable! (b) F: réception
f; soirée f; **'do a'gain,** v.tr. **1.** refa-

recommencer (qch.). **2. I won't do it again,** je ne le ferai plus; **'do a'way,** *v.i.* **to d. away with,** abolir; supprimer (un usage); détruire (qch.);**'doing,** *s.* **1. that takes some d.,** ce n'est pas facile. **2.** (*usu. pl.*) (*a*) agissements *mpl*; (*b*) événements *mpl*, activités *fpl*; **'do 'out,** *v.tr.* faire, nettoyer (une pièce); **'do 'up,** *v.tr.* **1.** remettre (qch.) à neuf. **2.** faire, ficeler (un paquet); boutonner, agrafer (un vêtement). **3.** *F:* **to be done up,** être éreinté, fourbu; n'en pouvoir plus.

ocile ['dousail], *a.* docile; **-ly,** *adv.* docilement; **docility** [dou'siliti], *s.* docilité *f.*

ock[1] [dɔk], *v.tr.* diminuer, rogner (le salaire de qn).

ock[2]. **I.** *s.* *Nau:* (*a*) bassin *m* (d'un port); **the docks,** les docks *m*; (*b*) **dry d.,** cale sèche; **floating dock,** dock flottant; *Aut: Av:* **to be in d.,** être en réparation *f.* **II.** *v.* **1.** *v.tr.* faire entrer (un navire) au bassin. **2.** *v.i.* entrer au bassin; **'docker,** *s.* docker *m*;**'docking,** *s.* **1.** entrée *f* au bassin. **2.** arrimage *m* (d'engins spatiaux); **'dockyard,** *s.* chantier naval; **naval d.,** arsenal *m* maritime.

ck[3], *s.* *Jur:* banc *m* des prévenus.

ctor ['dɔktər]. **I.** *s.* **1.** *Sch:* docteur *m* (ès sciences, etc.). **2.** docteur, médecin *m*; **woman d.,** (femme) docteur; **she's a d.,** elle est médecin. **II.** *v.tr.* **1.** (*a*) soigner (un malade); (*b*) ...oper (un cheval); (*c*) châtrer (un chat, etc.). **3.** *F:* truquer (des comptes).

...trine ['dɔktrin], *s.* doctrine *f.*

...cument ['dɔkjumənt], *s.* document *m*; ...ocu'mentary. **1.** *a.* documentaire. **2.** *a. & s.* *Cin: T.V: etc:* (film *m*) documentaire (*m*).

...dderer ['dɔdərər], *s.* *F:* gâteux, -euse; **doddery,** *a.* *F:* tremblant, branlant.

...ge [dɔdʒ]. **I.** *s.* **1.** *Sp:* esquive *f.* **2.** (*a*) ruse *f,* ...rtifice *m*; (*b*) truc *m*, ficelle *f*; **an old d.,** un ...oup classique. **II.** *v.* **1.** *v.i.* (*a*) se jeter de côté; ...) *Sp:* esquiver; (*c*) biaiser. **2.** *v.tr.* esquiver (...un coup); éviter (qn); **'dodgy,** *a.* *F:* **d. situa-**...on, situation délicate.

[dou], *s.* *Z:* **1.** daine *f.* **2.** (*of tame rabbit*) ...pine *f*; (*of wild rabbit, hare*) hase *f*; ...oeskin, *s.* peau *f* de daim.

[dɔg]. **I.** *s.* **1.** chien, *f.* chienne; **sporting-d.,** ...ien de chasse; **house d.,** chien de garde; **d.** ...cing, *F:* **the dogs,** courses de lévriers; **you** ...cky d.! veinard! *P:* **dirty d.,** sale type *m.* **2.** *E:* ...ien, cliquet *m*, détente *f*; *H:* **fire-d.,** chenet . **II.** *v.tr.* (**dogged**) suivre (qn) à la piste; filer ...n); **to d. s.o.'s footsteps,** talonner qn; **'dog-**...ollar, *s.* **1.** collier *m* de chien. **2.** *F:* faux col *m* ...cclésiastique; **'dog-ear,** *v.tr.* **to d.-e. a** ...ok, corner, faire des cornes à, un livre; ...g-'tired, *a.* *F:* éreinté, vanné; **'dog-**...use, *s.* (*a*) *N.Am:* niche *f*; (*b*) **to be in the**

d.-h., être en défaveur (auprès de qn); **'dog paddle,** *s.* *Swimming:* nage *f* à la chien.

dogged ['dɔgid], *a.* obstiné; résolu, tenace; **-ly,** *adv.* avec ténacité; opiniâtrement; **'doggedness,** *s.* courage *m* tenace; persévérance *f.*

dogma ['dɔgmə], *s.* dogme *m*; **dogmatic** [dɔg'mætik], *a.* **1.** dogmatique. **2.** autoritaire, tranchant; **-ally,** *adv.* d'un ton autoritaire, tranchant.

dole [doul]. **I.** *s.* allocation *f* de chômage; **to go on the d.,** s'inscrire au chômage. **II.** *v.tr.* **to d. sth. out,** distribuer qch. (parcimonieusement).

doleful ['doulfəl], *a.* (mine) lugubre; (cri) douloureux; (*of pers.*) triste, larmoyant; **-fully,** *adv.* tristement, douloureusement.

doll [dɔl]. **I.** *s.* poupée *f.* **II.** *v.tr.* **to d. oneself up,** se pomponner; **'dolly,** *s.* *F:* poupée *f.*

dollar ['dɔlər], *s.* dollar *m.*

dollop ['dɔləp], *s.* *F:* morceau *m* (informe), portion *f* (de qch. de mou); **a d. of jam, of ice-cream,** une (bonne) cuillerée, portion, de confiture, de crème glacée.

dolphin ['dɔlfin], *s.* *Z:* dauphin *m.*

domain [də'mein], *s.* domaine *m*; terres *fpl* propriété *f.*

dome [doum], *s.* dôme *m.*

domestic [də'mestik], *a.* **1.** domestique; **d.** (**servant**), *s.* domestique *mf*, bonne *f*; **d. science,** (i) les arts ménagers; (ii) enseignement ménager. **2. d. animal,** animal *m* domestique. **3.** (*of pers.*) casanier; (femme) d'intérieur; **do'mesticate,** *v.tr.* apprivoiser (un animal); **do'mesticated,** *a.* (*of animal*) apprivoisé; (*of woman*) bonne ménagère.

domiciled ['dɔmisaild], *a.* domicilié, demeurant (**at,** à).

dominant ['dɔminənt]. **1.** *a.* dominant. **2.** *s.* *Mus:* dominante *f.*

dominate ['dɔmineit], *v.tr. & i.* **to d.** (**over**) **s.o.,** dominer qn; **the fort dominates the town,** la forteresse commande la ville;**'dominating,** *a.* dominant; **domi'nation,** *s.* domination *f.*

domineer [dɔmi'niər], *v.i.* **1.** se montrer autoritaire. **2. to d. over s.o.,** tyranniser qn; **domi'neering,** *a.* autoritaire; **a d. person,** un petit tyran.

dominion [də'minjən], *s.* **1.** domination *f,* autorité *f.* **2.** dominion *m*; **the D. of Canada,** le Dominion du Canada.

domino ['dɔminou], *s.* domino *m*; **to play dominos,** jouer aux dominos.

don [dɔn], *s.m.* = professeur (d'université); **'donnish,** *a.* (air, etc.) pédant.

donate [də'neit, dou-], *v.tr.* faire un don de (qch.); *Med:* **to d. blood,** donner du sang; **do'nation,** *s.* donation *f,* don *m.*

donkey ['dɔŋki], *s.* **1.** âne, *f.* ânesse; baudet *m*; **d.**

work, travail de routine; **to talk the hind-leg off a d.**, jaser comme une pie borgne; **I haven't seen him for donkey's years**, il y a une éternité que je ne l'ai vu. 2. *F:* imbécile *mf*, âne *m*.

donor ['dounər], *s.* 1. donateur, -trice. 2. *Med:* **blood d.**, donneur, -euse (de sang).

doodle [du:dl], *v.i.* griffonner, faire des dessins (en pensant à autre chose).

doom [du:m]. **L** *s.* 1. destin *m* (funeste); sort (malheureux). 2. perte *f*, ruine *f*. 3. **the day of d.**, le jugement dernier. **II.** *v.tr.* condamner (qn) (to, à); **doomed man**, homme perdu; **to be doomed to failure**, être voué à l'échec; **'doomsday,** *s.* le (jour du) jugement dernier; **till d.**, (i) jusqu'à la fin du monde; (ii) indéfiniment.

door [dɔ:r], *s.* 1. porte *f*; **folding d.**, porte à deux battants; **sliding d.**, porte à coulisse; **two doors away**, deux portes plus loin; **to show s.o. the d.**, éconduire qn; **to turn s.o. out of doors**, mettre qn à la porte; *Com:* **d.-to-d. selling**, porte à porte *m*; **he's a d.-to-d. salesman**, il fait du porte à porte. 2. portière *f* (de voiture); **'door-keeper,** *s.* portier *m*; concierge *mf*; **'door-knob,** *s.* bouton *m*; **'doorman,** *pl.* -men, *s.* portier *m*; **'door-mat,** *s.* paillasson *m*; **'door-step,** *s.* seuil *m*, pas *m* (de la porte); **'doorway,** *s.* (encadrement *m* de la) porte; **in the d.**, sur le pas de la porte.

dope [doup]. **I.** *s.* *F:* 1. stupéfiant *m*, narcotique *m*; **d. habit**, toxicomanie *f*. 2. **to get the d.**, se mettre au courant; se tuyauter. **II.** *v.tr.* administrer un narcotique à (qn); doper (un cheval); *F:* **to d. (oneself)**, prendre des stupéfiants; **'dop(e)y,** *a.* 1. (*a*) stupéfié, hébété (par un narcotique); (*b*) abruti (par la fatigue). 2. *F:* stupide; engourdi.

dormant ['dɔ:mənt], *a.* (*of passions, etc.*) assoupi, endormi; **to lie d.**, sommeiller, dormir; **d. volcano**, volcan *m* en repos, en sommeil.

dormitory ['dɔ:mətri], *s.* dortoir *m*; **d. town**, ville *f* dortoir.

dormouse, *pl.* -mice ['dɔ:maus, -mais], *s.* *Z:* loir *m*.

dose [dous]. **I.** *s.* dose *f* (de médicament). **II.** *v.tr.* administrer, donner, un médicament à (qn); **'dosage,** *s.* posologie *f* (d'un médicament).

dot [dɔt]. **I.** *s.* point *m*; **he arrived on the d.**, il est arrivé à l'heure, pile. **II.** *v.tr.* (**dotted**) 1. mettre un point sur (un i). 2. pointiller; **dotted line**, ligne *f* en pointillé; **hillside dotted with houses**, coteau parsemé de villas.

dote [dout], *v.i.* **to d. (up)on s.o.**, aimer qn à la folie; **'dotage,** *s.* seconde enfance; gâtisme *m*; **'doting,** *a.* 1. radoteur. 2. qui montre une tendresse ridicule.

dotty ['dɔti], *a.* *F:* toqué, piqué.

double [dʌbl]. **I.** *a.* 1. (*a*) double; **with a d.**

meaning, à deux sens, à double sens; **d.** bedroom, chambre à deux personnes, à deux lits; **to reach d. figures**, atteindre les deux chiffres; **to play a d. game**, jouer double jeu, ménager la chèvre et le chou; (*b*) de grandeur de force, double; **d. whisky**, double whisky *m*. 2. (*of pers.*) **bent d.**, courbé en deux. 3. **d. number**, le double; deux fois autant; **d. the length (of)**, deux fois plus long (que); **I'm d. your age**, je suis deux fois plus âgé que vous; -bly, *adv.* doublement. **II.** *adv.* **to see d.**, voir double. **III.** *s.* 1. double *m*; deux fois autant. 2. (*of pers.*) double; sosie *m*. 3. **at the d.**, au pas de course; au pas gymnastique. 4. *Ten:* men's **doubles**, double messieurs. **IV.** *v.* 1. *v.tr.* doubler (un chiffre); *Th:* **to d. parts**, jouer deux rôles; (*b*) *Nau:* **to d. a cape**, doubler un cap; (*at bridge*) contrer. 2. *v.i.* (se) doubler; **to d. (back)**, faire un brusque crochet; **'doubl-'barrelled,** *a.* (fusil) à deux coups; *F:* (nom) rallonge; **'double-'bass,** *s.* *Mus:* contrebasse *f*; **'double-'breasted,** *a.* (gilet, etc.) croisé; **'double-'cross,** *v.tr.* *F:* duper, tromper (qn); **'double-'decker,** *s.* 1. (autobus) à impériale. 2. (sandwich) double *m*; **'double-de'clutch,** *v.i.* *Aut:* faire un double débrayage; **'double-'edged,** *a.* (arme *f*, outil *m*, argument *m*) à deux tranchants; **'double-'parking,** *s.* *Aut:* stationnement *m* en double file; **'double-'quick,** *a.* & *adv.* **d.-q.**, **in d.-q. time**, (i) au pas gymnastique; (ii) en moins de rien; **'double-'up,** *v.i.* se (re)plier; **to d. up with laughter**, tordre de rire; *F:* **to d. up with s.o.**, partager une chambre avec qn.

doubt [daut]. **I.** *v.* 1. *v.tr.* douter (de la parole de qn); **I d. whether he will come**, je doute qu'il vienne. 2. *v.i.* **he doubted no longer**, il n'hésita plus. **II.** *s.* doute *m*; **to be in d.**, être dans le doute; **to have one's doubts about sth.**, avoir des doutes sur qch.; **beyond d.**, **without a doubt**, sans le moindre doute; **no d.**, sans doute; **'doubtful,** *a.* 1. (*of thg*) douteux; (*of pers.*) décis, incertain. 2. **d. society**, compagnie louche, équivoque; **in d. taste**, d'un goût douteux; -**fully**, *adv.* 1. d'un air de doute. 2. hésitant; **'doubtfulness,** *s.* 1. ambiguïté *f*, incertitude *f*. 3. indécision *f*; **'doubtless,** *adv.* sans doute; probablement.

dough [dou], *s.* 1. pâte *f* (à pain). 2. *F:* fric *m*; **'doughnut,** *s.* *Cu:* beignet *m*.

dove [dʌv], *s.* colombe *f*; **'dovecot,** *s.* colombier *m*; pigeonnier *m*.

Dover ['douvər]. *Pr.n. Geog:* Douvres; **Straits of D.**, le Pas de Calais.

dovetail ['dʌvteil]. **I.** *s.* *Carp:* queue-d'aronde *f*. **II.** *v.* 1. *v.tr.* assembler à queue-d'aronde. 2. se joindre, se raccorder.

dowdy ['daudi], *a.* (femme, toilette) sans

élégance; **'dowdiness,** *s.* manque *m* d'élégance.

down[1] [daun], *s.* duvet *m.*

down[2]. **I.** *adv.* **1.** (*direction*) vers le bas; (de haut) en bas; **to go d.,** descendre; **to fall d.,** tomber (i) (*from a height*) à terre, (ii) (*from a standing position*) par terre; **cash d.,** (argent *m*) comptant; **d. with the traitors!** à bas les traîtres! (*to a dog*) **d. !** à bas! couché! **2.** (*position*) **d. below,** en bas, en contrebas; **d. there,** là-bas; **d. here,** ici; **he isn't d.** yet, il n'est pas encore descendu; **to be d. with 'flu,** être grippé; *F:* **d. under,** aux antipodes; **the blinds were d.,** les stores étaient baissés; **face d.,** face en dessous; **head d.,** la tête en bas; **the sun is d.,** le soleil est couché; (*of price*) **bread is d.,** le pain a baissé; **your tyres are d.,** vos pneus sont dégonflés, à plat. **3. d. to recent times,** jusqu'à présent; **d. to here,** jusqu'ici. **4. to be d. on s.o.,** en vouloir à qn; **to be d. in the mouth,** être découragé, abattu; *F:* **to be d. and out,** être ruiné, *F:* fichu. **II.** *prep.* **her hair is hanging d. her back,** les cheveux lui pendent dans le dos; **to go d. the street,** descendre la rue; **d. (the) river,** en aval; **to fall d. the stairs,** tomber en bas de l'escalier; **d. town,** en ville. **III.** *a. Mus:* **d. beat,** temps fort; *Com:* **d. payment,** acompte *m.* **IV.** *s. F:* **to have a d. on s.o.,** en vouloir à qn, avoir une dent contre qn; **the ups and downs of life,** les péripéties de la vie. **V.** *v.tr.* **to d. tools,** (i) cesser de travailler; (ii) se mettre en grève; **'down-at-'heel,** *a.* (soulier) éculé; (*of pers.*) râpé; **'downcast,** *a.* abattu, déprimé; **'downfall,** *s.* chute *f;* écroulement *m* (d'un empire); **'downgrade. I.** **. on the d.,** sur le déclin. **II.** *v.tr.* réduire (qn, qch.) à une position inférieure; **'down-'hearted,** *a.* découragé; déprimé, abattu; **down'hill,** *adv.* **to go d.,** (i) (*of road*) aller en descendant; (*of car, etc.*) descendre (la côte); (ii) être sur le déclin; **'downpour,** *s.* grosse averse; **'downright. 1.** *adv.* (*a*) tout à fait, complètement; (*b*) nettement, carrément. **2.** *a.* (*a*) (*of pers., language*) direct, franc; (*b*) absolu, véritable; **d. lie,** mensonge éclatant; **down'stairs. 1.** *adv.* en bas, au rez de chaussée. **. *a.*** (pièces) d'en bas; **'downstream,** *adv.* en aval. **'downtown,** *a. & s. N.Am:* **d.** (sector), centre commercial (d'une ville); **'downward,** **. (mouvement) descendant, en bas; 'downwards,** *adv.* de haut en bas; en descendant; **face d.,** face en dessous.

downs [daunz], *s.pl.* collines crayeuses (du sud de l'Angleterre).

doze [douz]. **I.** *s.* petit somme. **II.** *v.i.* sommeiller; **to d. off,** s'assoupir.

dozen ['dʌzn], *s.* douzaine *f.* **1.** (*inv. in pl.*) **half a d.,** une demi-douzaine; **six d. bottles,** six douzaines de bouteilles; *F:* **to talk nineteen to**

the d., avoir la langue bien pendue. **2.** (*pl.* dozens) **dozens of people,** beaucoup de gens.

drab [dræb], *a.* gris; brun; beige; **d. existence,** existence terne; **d. clothes,** vêtements de couleur terne.

draft [drɑ:ft]. **I.** *s.* **1.** *Mil:* détachement *m*; *U.S:* conscription *f.* **2.** *Com:* traite *f;* lettre *f* de change. **3.** plan *m,* tracé *m*; ébauche *f.* **4.** brouillon *m* (de lettre). **II.** *v.tr.* **1.** détacher (des troupes); *U.S:* appeler (des conscrits) sous les drapeaux. **2.** désigner, affecter, qn à un poste. **3.** rédiger (un acte); faire le brouillon d'(une lettre); **'draftsman,** *s.,* **'draftsmanship,** *s. see* draughtsman, draughtsmanship.

drag [dræg], *v.* (**dragged**) **1.** *v.tr.* (*a*) trainer, tirer; entraîner (qn); **to d. sth. about, along,** traîner qch.; **to d. s.o. along,** entraîner qn; **to d. one's feet,** montrer peu d'empressement (à faire qch.); (*b*) draguer (un étang). **2.** *v.i.* (*a*) (*of pers.*) traîner, rester en arrière; (*of thg*) traîner à terre; (*of lawsuit, etc.*) traîner en longueur; (*of conversation*) languir; (*b*) offrir de la résistance; **'drag a'way,** *v.tr.* (*a*) entraîner, emmener, de force; (*b*) arracher (qn) (**from,** à, de); **'drag 'in,** *v.tr.* faire entrer de force; **'drag 'out,** *v.tr.* **to d. s.o. out of bed,** tirer qn de son lit; **to d. the truth out of s.o.,** arracher la vérité à qn.

dragon ['drægən], *s.* dragon *m*; **'dragon-fly,** *s.* libellule *f.*

dragoon [drə'gu:n], *v.tr.* **to d. s.o. into doing sth.,** contraindre qn à faire qch.

drain [drein]. **I.** *s.* **1.** canal *m,* -aux (de décharge); tranchée *f,* rigole *f.* **2.** égout *m.* **3.** **d.(-pipe),** tuyau *m,* canalisation *f,* d'écoulement. **4.** perte *f,* fuite *f* (d'énergie); **d. on the resources,** cause *f* d'épuisement des ressources. **II.** *v.* **1.** *v.tr.* (*a*) **to d. water (off, away),** évacuer, faire écouler, des eaux; faire égoutter l'eau; (*b*) vider (un verre, un fût); assécher, drainer (un terrain); vider (un étang); *Aut:* **to d. the sump,** vidanger le carter; (*c*) **to d. s.o. dry,** saigner qn à blanc. **2.** *v.i.* (*of water, etc.*) **to d. (away),** s'écouler; (*of thg*) s'égoutter; **'drainage,** *s.* système *m* d'égouts; **main d.,** tout-à-l'égout *m inv;* **'draining,** *s.* assèchement *m,* drainage *m* (d'un terrain); **d. board,** égouttoir *m.*

drake [dreik], *s.* canard *m* mâle.

drama ['drɑ:mə], *s.* **1.** drame *m.* **2. the d.,** l'art *m* dramatique; le théâtre; **dramatic** [drə'mætik], *a.* dramatique; **a d. effect,** un effet théâtral; **-ally,** *adv.* dramatiquement; **'dramatist,** *s.,* auteur *m* dramatique; **'dramatize,** *v.tr.* dramatiser; adapter (un roman) à la scène.

drape [dreip]. **I.** *v.tr.* draper, tendre (**with, in,** de). **II.** *s. pl. N.Am:* **drapes,** rideaux *mpl.*

draper ['dreipər], *s.* marchand *m* de tissus, de nouveautés; **'draper's (shop),** *s.,* **'drapery,**

s. magasin *m* de tissus, de nouveautés; mercerie *f.*

drastic ['dræstik], *a.* **to take d. measures,** prendre des mesures énergiques, rigoureuses; **-ally,** *adv.* énergiquement, rigoureusement.

draught [drɑːft], *s.* **1.** traction *f,* tirage *m*; **d. horse,** cheval *m* de trait. **2.** *Fish:* coup *m* de filet; pêche *f.* **3.** *(drinking)* trait *m,* coup (de vin); **at a d.,** d'un seul trait. **4.** *Nau:* tirant *m* d'eau (d'un navire). **5.** *pl.* **draughts,** (jeu *m* de) dames *fpl*; **d. board,** damier *m.* **6.** *(in a room)* courant *m* d'air; *(of chimney)* tirage *m.* **7. beer on d.,** bière *f* (à la) pression; **'draughty,** *a.* plein de courants d'air; (rue, etc.) exposée à tous les vents.

draughtsman, *pl.* **-men** ['drɑːftsmən], *s.* **1.** *Ind:* dessinateur *m.* **2.** pion *m* (du jeu de dames); **'draughtsmanship,** *s.* **1.** l'art *m* du dessin industriel; *Ind:* le dessin. **2.** talent *m* de dessinateur.

draw [drɔː]. **I.** *s.* **1.** tirage *m*; *F:* **to be quick on the d.,** avoir (i) la gâchette facile, (ii) la repartie prompte. **2.** *(a)* tirage au sort; *(b)* loterie *f*; *(c)* tombola *f.* **3.** attraction *f*; clou *m* (de la fête); *(of play)* **to be a d.,** faire recette. **4.** *Sp:* partie nulle; résultat nul. **II.** *v.* **1.** *v.tr.* **(drew; drawn)** *(a)* tirer (un verrou); (i) fermer, (ii) ouvrir (les rideaux); *(b)* tirer, remorquer (une caravane); *(c)* *(take in)* aspirer (de l'air); *(d)* *(attract)* attirer (une foule); *(e)* tirer, retirer, ôter **(sth. from sth.,** qch. de qch.); arracher (un clou, une dent); **to d. lots for sth.,** tirer qch. au sort; *(f)* **to d. water,** puiser, tirer de l'eau; *(g)* toucher (de l'argent); *(h)* vider (une volaille); *(i)* **to d. a blank,** *F:* revenir bredouille; *(j)* tracer (un plan); tirer (une ligne); dresser (une carte); dessiner (un paysage); *(k)* **to d. a cheque,** tirer un chèque; *(l)* *Sp:* **to d. (a game),** faire match nul. **2.** *v.i.* *(a)* **to d. near (to s.o.),** s'approcher (de qn); **to d. to one side,** se ranger; **to d. into a station,** entrer en gare; **to d. round (the table),** s'assembler (autour d'une table); *(b)* *(of day, etc.)* **to d. to an end,** toucher à sa fin; *(c)* *(of chimney)* tirer; *(of pump)* aspirer; *(d)* **to let the tea d.,** laisser infuser le thé; **'draw a'long,** *v.tr.* traîner, entraîner (qn, qch.); **'draw a'side. 1.** *v.tr.* *(a)* détourner, écarter (qch.); *(b)* prendre (qn) à l'écart. **2.** *v.i.* s'écarter; se ranger; **'draw 'back. 1.** *v.tr.* *(a)* tirer en arrière; retirer (la main); *(b)* tirer, ouvrir (les rideaux). **2.** *v.i.* (se) reculer; se retirer en arrière; **'drawback,** *s.* inconvénient *m,* désavantage *m*; **'draw 'down,** *v.tr.* faire descendre; baisser (les stores); **'drawer,** *s.* tiroir *m*; **chest of drawers,** commode *f*; **sth. for her bottom d.,** qch. pour son trousseau; **'draw 'in. 1.** *v.tr.* *(a)* *(of cat)* rentrer, rétracter (ses griffes); *(b)* aspirer (l'air). **2.** *v.i.* **the days are drawing in,** les jours

diminuent; **'drawing,** *s.* **1.** tirage *m,* puisage *m* (d'eau); extraction *f* (d'une dent). **2.** dessin *m*; **freehand d.,** dessin à main levée; **rough d.,** ébauche *f,* croquis *m*; **d.-board,** planche *f* à dessin; **d. paper,** papier *m* à dessin; **d. pin,** punaise *f*; **'drawing-room,** *s.* salon *m*; **drawn,** *a.* **1.** tiré; **d. features,** traits tirés, décomposés. **2.** *Sp:* **d. match,** match nul; **'draw 'off,** *v.tr.* *(a)* retirer, ôter (ses gants); *(b)* détourner (l'attention); *(c)* soutirer (un liquide); **'draw 'on,** *v.i.* **evening was drawing on,** la nuit, approchait; **'draw 'out,** *v.tr.* **1.** sortir, retirer (qch. de qch.); arracher (un clou). **2.** prolonger; tirer (une affaire) en longueur; **'draw 'up. 1.** *v.tr.* *(a)* lever (un store); relever (ses manches); **to d. oneself up,** se (re)dresser; *(b)* **to d. up a chair (to the table),** approcher une chaise (de la table); *(c)* dresser, rédiger (un document); établir (un compte). **2.** *v.i.* *(a)* **to d. up to the table,** s'approcher de la table; *(b)* s'arrêter; *(of car)* stopper.

drawl [drɔːl]. **I.** *s.* voix traînante. **II.** *v.i.* parler d'une voix traînante.

dread [dred]. **I.** *s.* crainte *f,* terreur *f,* épouvante *f*; **to stand, be, in d. of s.o.,** craindre, redouter qn. **II.** *v.tr.* redouter, craindre (qn, qch.); **'dreadful,** *a.* **1.** terrible, redoutable. **2.** atroce, épouvantable; **it's something d.,** c'est quelque chose d'affreux; **-fully,** *adv.* terriblement, affreusement; *F:* **I'm d. sorry,** je regrette infiniment.

dream [driːm]. **I.** *s.* rêve *m,* songe *m*; **to have a d.,** faire un rêve, un songe; **sweet dreams!** faites de beaux rêves! **day-d.,** rêverie *f,* rêvasserie *f.* **II.** *v.tr. & i.* **(dreamed, dreamt) 1.** rêver. **2.** rêvasser. **3. I shouldn't d. of doing it,** jamais je ne m'aviserais de faire cela; **'dreamer,** *s.* rêveur, -euse. **2.** songeur, -euse; **'dreaming,** *s.* rêves *mpl*; songes *mpl*; **'dreamy,** *a.* rêveur, songeur; **-ily,** *adv.* d'un air rêveur.

dreary ['driəri], *a.* triste, morne; **-ily,** *adv.* tristement, lugubrement; **'dreariness,** *s.* tristesse *f*; aspect *m* morne (de qch.).

dredge [dredʒ], *v.tr. & i.* draguer, dévaser (un chenal); **to d. for sth.,** draguer à la recherche de qch.; **'dredger,** *s.* drague *f*; **'dredging,** *s.* dragage *m.*

dregs [dregz], *s.pl.* lie *f* (de vin, etc.).

drench [dren(t)ʃ], *v.tr.* tremper, mouiller (qn, de); **drenched to the skin,** trempé jusqu'aux os; **'drenching,** *a.* **d. rain,** pluie battante.

Dresden ['drezdən]. *Pr.n. Geog:* Dresde *f*; **d. china,** porcelaine *f* de Saxe.

dress [dres]. **I.** *s.* **1.** *(a)* habillement *m*; habits *mpl*; vêtements *mpl*; **in full d.,** en grande tenue; **evening d.,** tenue de soirée; *(b)* *Th:* **d. circle,** (premier) balcon; **d. rehearsal,** (répétition) générale *(f).* **2.** robe *f,* toilette *f.* **II.** *v.tr.* **1.**

habiller, vêtir (qn); **well, badly, dressed,** bien, mal, habillé; bien, mal, mis; (*b*) *v.pr. & i.* **to d.** (**oneself**), s'habiller; faire sa toilette. **2.** orner, parer (**with**, de); *Com:* **to d. the window,** faire la vitrine, faire l'étalage *m.* **3.** *Mil:* (s')aligner. **4.** *Med:* panser (une blessure). **5.** (*a*) *Tchn:* apprêter (une surface); dresser, tailler (des pierres); (*b*) *Cu:* apprêter, accommoder (un mets); garnir (un plat); '**dress 'down,** *v.tr. F:* chapitrer, semoncer (qn); '**dresser,** *s.* **1.** (*pers.*) (*a*) *Th:* habilleur, -euse; (*b*) *Ind:* apprêteur, -euse, dresseur *m* (de pierres, etc.). **2.** (*a*) *H:* buffet *m* de cuisine; (*b*) *N.Am:* coiffeuse *f*; '**dressing,** *s.* **1.** habillement *m*, toilette *f.* **2.** *Cu:* (**salad-**)**d.,** assaisonnement *m* (pour la salade), genre sauce mayonnaise; **French d.,** vinaigrette *f.* **3.** *Med:* pansement *m.* **4.** *attrib.* **d. gown,** *s.* robe *f* de chambre; **d. room,** (i) cabinet *m* de toilette; (ii) *Th:* loge *f* (d'acteur); **d. station,** *Med:* poste *m* de secours; **d. table,** coiffeuse *f*; '**dressmaker,** *s.* couturier, -ière; '**dressmaking,** *s.* couture *f*; confection *f*; '**dress 'up,** *v.i.* se parer; *F:* s'attifer; se travestir; '**dressy,** *a.* (*often Pej:*) chic, élégant; (*of woman*) **too d.,** trop habillée, *F:* fagotée.

-ibble ['dribl]. **1.** *v.i.* baver. **2.** *v.tr. Fb:* dribbler (le ballon); '**dribbler,** *s.* **1.** baveur, -euse. **2.** *Fb:* dribbleur *m*; '**dribbling,** *s.* **1.** égouttement *m* (d'un liquide). **2.** *Fb:* dribbling *m.*

iblet ['driblit], *s.* petite quantité; **to pay in driblets,** payer petit à petit.

ied [draid], *a.* séché, desséché; **d. fruit,** fruits secs; **d. eggs,** œufs *m* en poudre.

ift [drift]. **I.** *s.* **1.** (*a*) mouvement *m*; (*b*) direction *f*, sens *m* (d'un courant); (*c*) cours *m*, marche *f* (des événements). **2.** *Nau:* dérive *f.* **3.** tendance *f*, portée *f* (de questions, etc.). **4.** amoncellement *m*, *Fr.C:* banc *m* (de neige); congère *f.* **II.** *v.i.* (*a*) flotter; *Nau:* dériver; *Av:* déporter; (*b*) **to let oneself d.,** se laisser aller; (*c*) (*of snow*) s'amonceler, s'amasser; (*d*) (*of events*) tendre (vers un but); '**driftwood,** *s.* bois flottant.

ill[1] [dril]. **I.** *s.* **1.** *Tls:* (*a*) foret *m*, mèche *f*; (*b*) vilebrequin *m*; (*electric*) perceuse *f.* **2.** (*a*) (*dentist's*) fraise *f*; (*b*) *Civ.E:* foreuse *f*; **pneumatic d.,** perforatrice *f* à air comprimé. **3.** *Mil: etc:* exercice(s) *m*(*pl*), manœuvre(s) *f*(*pl*); *F:* **what's the d.?** qu'est-ce qu'on fait? **II.** *v.* **1.** *v.tr. E:* forer; perforer; **to d. for oil,** forer pour rechercher du pétrole. **2.** *v.tr.* faire faire l'exercice à (des hommes); faire manœuvrer (des soldats). **3.** *v.i.* faire l'exercice; manœuvrer.

ill[2], *s. Tex:* coutil *m* (pour matelas); treillis *m.*

nk [driŋk]. **I.** *s.* **1.** (*a*) boire *m*; **food and d.,** le boire et le manger; (*b*) **to give s.o. a d.,** donner à boire à qn; faire boire qn; offrir à boire à qn; **to have a d.,** se désaltérer; boire quelque chose;

to have a d. of water, boire un verre d'eau; (*c*) consommation *f*; **to have a d.,** prendre quelque chose, prendre un verre; *F:* boire un coup. **2.** boisson *f*, breuvage *m*; **soft d.,** boisson sans alcool; **strong d.,** liqueurs fortes; spiritueux *mpl.* **3.** boisson; ivrognerie *f*; **the d. problem,** le problème de l'alcoolisme; **to take to d.,** s'adonner à la boisson; **to be the worse for d.,** avoir trop bu; être ivre. **II.** *v.tr.* (**drank; drunk**) boire. **1.** **will you have something to d.?** voulez-vous boire quelque chose? **to d. the waters,** prendre les eaux; **d. your soup,** mange ta soupe. **2.** *abs.* boire, s'adonner à la boisson; '**drinkable,** *a.* (*a*) (vin) buvable; (*b*) (eau) potable; '**drinker,** *s.* buveur, -euse; '**drinking,** *s.* ivrognerie *f*, alcoolisme *m*; **d. trough,** abreuvoir *m*, auge *f* (pour bétail); **d. water,** eau *f* potable; '**drink 'up,** *v.tr.* achever de boire; vider (un verre); **drunk. 1.** *a.* ivre; soûl; **to get d.,** s'enivrer, se soûler. **2.** *s.* **a d.,** un ivrogne.

drip [drip], *v.i.* (**dripped**) dégoutter, s'égoutter; tomber goutte à goutte; '**drip-'dry,** *a. Cl:* (tissu *m*) à ne pas repasser; '**dripping. I.** *a.* ruisselant; **d. tap,** robinet *m* qui fuit. **II.** *s.* **1.** égouttement *m.* **2.** *Cu:* graisse *f* de rôti.

drive [draiv]. **I.** *s.* **1.** promenade *f* en voiture. **2.** battue *f* (de gibier). **3.** *E:* (mouvement *m* de) propulsion *f*; transmission *f*; actionnement *m*; *Aut:* **left-hand d.,** conduite *f* à gauche; **direct d.,** prise directe; **front-wheel d.,** traction *f* avant. **4.** *Sp:* (*a*) *Golf:* coup *m* de départ; (*b*) *Ten:* drive *m.* **5.** (*of pers.*) **to have lots of d.,** être très dynamique. **6.** *Cards:* **bridge d.,** tournoi *m* de bridge. **II.** *v.* (**drove; driven**) **1.** *v.tr.* (*a*) chasser, pousser (devant soi); **to d. cattle,** conduire le bétail (aux champs); **to d. game,** rabattre le gibier; (*b*) faire marcher (une machine); conduire (un cheval, une auto); **to d. s.o. to the station,** conduire qn à la gare; **can you d.?** savez-vous conduire? (*c*) pousser (qn à une action); contraindre (qn à faire qch.); **he was driven to it,** on lui a forcé la main; **to d. s.o. out of his senses,** rendre qn fou; (*d*) surcharger (qn) de travail, exploiter (qn); (*e*) enfoncer (un clou); percer (un tunnel); (*f*) **to d. a bargain,** faire, conclure, un marché. **2.** *v.i.* (*a*) (*of clouds*) **to d. before the wind,** chasser devant le vent; (*b*) **to d. (along the road),** rouler (sur la route); **to d. to London,** se rendre en voiture à Londres; **to d. on the right,** circuler à droite; '**drive a'long. 1.** *v.tr.* chasser, pousser (qn, qch., devant soi). **2.** *v.i.* rouler (en voiture); '**drive at,** *v.tr.* **what are you driving at?** à quoi voulez-vous en venir? '**drive a'way. 1.** *v.tr.* chasser, eloigner, repousser (qn). **2.** *v.i. Aut:* s'en aller, démarrer; '**drive 'back. 1.** *v.tr.* (*a*) refouler, faire reculer (qn); (*b*) reconduire (qn) en voiture. 2. *v.i.* rentrer, revenir, en voiture; **'drive 'down,** *v.i.* se rendre en voiture (de la ville à la campagne, de Londres en province); **'drive 'in.** 1. *v.tr.* enfoncer (un clou); visser (une vis). 2. *v.i.* entrer (en voiture); **'drive-in,** *s.* (a) *Aut:* piste *f* de ravitaillement; (b) *N.Am:* cinéma *m* en plein air; (c) *N.Am:* restoroute *m* (*R.t.m.*); **'drive 'on,** *v.i. Aut:* continuer sa route; **'drive 'over,** *v.i.* se rendre (chez qn, à un endroit) en voiture; **'driver,** *s. Aut:* conducteur, -trice; chauffeur *m* (de taxi); **'drive 'through,** *v.tr.* traverser, passer par, (une ville) en voiture; **'driving.** I. *a.* 1. **d. force,** force motrice. 2. **d. rain,** pluie battante. II. *s.* conduite *f* (d'une voiture); **d. school,** auto-école *f*; **d. test,** examen *m* pour permis de conduire; **d. wheel,** (i) *E:* roue motrice; (ii) *Aut:* volant *m*.

drivel ['drivl], *s. F:* radotage *m*; balivernes *fpl*; **to talk d.,** radoter.

drizzle ['drizl]. I. *s.* bruine *f*, crachin *m*. II. *v.i.* bruiner, crachiner, pleuvoter; **'drizzly,** *a.* bruineux; **a d. day,** une journée bruineuse.

drone [droun], *s.* 1. (a) *Ent:* abeille *f* mâle; faux-bourdon *m*; (b) fainéant *m*. 2. (a) bourdonnement *m* (d'insectes, etc.); (b) ronronnement *m*, vrombissement *m* (d'un moteur).

droop [dru:p]. 1. *v.i.* (a) (*of head, etc.*) (se) pencher; s'abaisser; (b) (*of flower*) pencher, languir; (c) **to revive s.o.'s drooping spirits,** remonter le courage à qn. 2. *v.tr.* baisser, pencher (la tête); abaisser (les paupières); laisser pendre (les ailes).

drop [drɔp]. I. *s.* 1. (a) goutte *f*; **d. by d.,** goutte à goutte; **a d. of wine,** une goutte, un doigt, de vin; **he's had a d. too much,** il a bu un coup de trop; (b) peppermint **d.,** pastille *f* de menthe. 2. (a) chute *f*; **d. in prices,** chute, baisse *f*, de prix; *El:* **d. in voltage,** chute de tension; (b) *Mil.Av:* parachutage *m*. II. *v.* (**dropped**) 1. *v.i.* (a) tomber goutte à goutte, dégoutter (**from,** de); (b) (*of pers.*) tomber, se laisser tomber; **I'm ready to d.,** je tombe de fatigue; (c) (*of prices*) baisser; (*of wind*) se calmer, tomber; (*d*) **there the matter dropped,** l'affaire en resta là. 2. *v.tr.* (a) laisser tomber, lâcher (qch.); larguer, lancer (une bombe); *Knitting:* sauter, laisser tomber (une maille); (b) **to d. s.o. a line,** écrire un mot à qn; (c) perdre (de l'argent) (**over sth.,** sur qch.); (*d*) (*set down*) **I'll d. you at your door,** je vous déposerai chez vous en passant; (*e*) omettre, supprimer (une lettre, une syllabe); (*f*) baisser (les yeux, la voix); (*g*) abandonner (un travail, un projet); renoncer à (une idée); (*h*) *F:* **d. it!** en voilà assez! **'dropper,** *s. Med:* compte-gouttes *m.inv;* **'drop 'in,** *v.i.* entrer (chez qn) en passant; **'drop 'off,** *v.i.* tomber, se détacher; **'drop 'out.** 1. *v.tr.* omettre, supprimer. 2. *v.i.* **to d.o.** (**of a contest**), se retirer,

renoncer; **to d.o. of a class,** abandonner un cours; **'dropout,** *s.* (personne) (i) qui a abandonné ses études, (ii) qui refuse la société.

drought [draut], *s.* (période *f* de) sécheresse *f*; disette *f* d'eau.

drown [draun], *v.tr.* 1. noyer; **to d. oneself,** se noyer; se jeter à l'eau; **to be drowned,** *v.i.* **to d.** se noyer; **a drowning man,** un homme qui se noie. 2. inonder, submerger (une prairie). 3. étouffer, couvrir (un son); **drowned,** *a.* noyé; **a d. man,** un noyé.

drowse [drauz], *v.i.* somnoler, s'assoupir; **'drowsiness,** *s.* somnolence *f*; **'drowsy,** *a.* assoupi, somnolent; **to feel d.,** avoir sommeil; **-ily,** *adv.* d'un air, d'un ton, somnolent; à demi endormi.

drudge [drʌdʒ]. I. *s.* femme *f*, homme *m*, de peine. II. *v.i.* trimer, peiner; **'drudgery,** *s.* travail pénible, ingrat; métier *m* d'esclave.

drug [drʌg]. I. *s.* 1. produit *m* pharmaceutique, drogue *f*. 2. narcotique *m*, stupéfiant *m*, drogue *f*; **d. addict,** toxicomane *mf*; *F:* drogué, -ée; **d. addiction,** toxicomanie *f*. 3. *Com:* (*of article*) **to be a d. on the market,** être invendable. II. *v.tr.* (**drugged**) donner un narcotique à (qn); **d. oneself,** s'adonner aux stupéfiants; se droguer; **'druggist,** *s.* pharmacien *m*; **'drugstore,** *s. N.Am:* drug(-)store *m*; magasin *m* où l'on vend divers produits (alimentation, hygiène, pharmacie).

druid ['dru(:)id], *s.* druide *m*.

drum [drʌm]. I. *s.* 1. *Mus:* tambour *m*, caisse *f*; **big d.,** grosse caisse; *Mil:* **the drums,** batterie *f*; **with drums beating,** tambour(s) battant(s); **d. major,** tambour major *m*. 2. *Anat:* tympan *m*. 3. tonneau *m* (en fer); tonnelet *m*. II. *v.* (**drummed**) 1. *v.i.* battre du tambour, tambouriner. 2. *v.tr.* **to d. sth. into s.o.'s head,** enfoncer qch. dans la tête de qn; **'drummer,** *s.* tambour *m*; **'drumstick,** *s.* 1. baguette *f* de tambour. 2. *Cu:* pilon *m* (d'une volaille).

drunk [drʌŋk], *a.* (*compare* **drink**) (a) ivre, gris; **to get d.,** s'enivrer; (b) enivré, grisé (**with success,** par le succès); **'drunkard,** *s.* ivrogne *f*, ivrognesse; soûlard, -arde; **'drunken,** *a.* **d. state,** état *m* d'ivresse, d'ébriété; **-ly,** *adv.* comme un ivrogne; **'drunkenness,** *s.* 1. ivresse *f*. 2. (*habitual*) ivrognerie *f*.

dry [drai]. I. *a.* 1. (a) *a.* sec, *f.* sèche; (*of well*) à sec; (*of country*) aride; **d. land,** terre *f* ferme; **to run d.,** se dessécher; (b) **d. bread,** pain sec; **to be kept d.,** craint l'humidité; (c) (*of pers.*) **to feel d.,** avoir soif; **d. work,** travail qui donne soif; (*d*) (*of wine*) sec, brut; **medium d.,** demi-sec; (*e*) **d. state,** état où les boissons alcooliques sont prohibées. 2. aride; sans intérêt. 3. **d. humour,** esprit mordant; **a man of d. humour,** un pince-sans-rire; **drily, dryly,**

d'un ton sec; sèchement. **II.** *v.* **(dried) 1.** *v.tr.*
(faire) sécher (qch.); **to d. the dishes,** essuyer la
vaisselle; **to d. one's eyes,** s'essuyer les yeux. **2.**
v.i. sécher, se dessécher; **to put sth. out to d.,**
mettre qch. à sécher dehors; ' **dry-'clean,** *v.tr.*
nettoyer (des vêtements) à sec; ' **dry-**
' **cleaner's,** *s.* pressing *m*; ' **dry-'cleaning,** *s.*
nettoyage *m* à sec; ' **dryer,** ' **drier,** *s.* **1.** *Ind:*
séchoir *m*; *H:* **spin d.,** essoreuse *f*; **hair d.,**
séchoir (à cheveux); ' **drying,** *s.* séchage *m*;
dessèchement *m*; essuyage *m*; **spin d.,** es-
sorage *m*; ' **dryness,** *s.* **1.** sécheresse *f*, aridité *f*.
2. sévérité *f* (du ton); aridité (de l'esprit); ' **dry**
' **off,** *v.,* ' **dry ' out,** *v.* **1.** *v.tr.* faire sécher (qch.).
2. *v.i.* (*of moisture*) s'évaporer; ' **dry ' up,** *v.i.* **1.**
(*of well*) se dessécher, tarir. **2.** *F:* se taire; *P:* **d.**
up! la ferme! **3.** *F:* essuyer la vaisselle.

dual [' dju(:)əl], *a.* double; *Aut: etc:* **d. ignition,**
double allumage *m*; **d. wheels,** roues jumelées;
d. carriageway, route *f* à double
chaussée; *Psy:* **d. personality,** dédoublement *m*
de la personnalité.

dub [dʌb], *v.tr.* **(dubbed)** *Cin:* doubler (un film).
dubious [' dju(:)biəs], *a.* **1.** douteux; (*a*) incertain, vague; (*b*) équivoque, louche. **2.** hésitant,
d. expression, air de doute; -ly, *adv.* d'un air,
d'un ton, de doute; ' **dubiousness,** *s.* **1.** incertitude *f.* **2.** caractère douteux, équivoque *f.*

duchess [' dʌtʃis], *s.* duchesse *f.*
duchy [' dʌtʃi], *s.* duché *m.*

duck [dʌk]. **I.** *s.* **1.** *Orn:* (*a*) (*female of* **drake**)
cane *f*; (*b*) (*generic*) canard *m*; **wild d.,** canard
sauvage; *Cu:* **d. and green peas,** canard aux
petits pois; **a lame d.,** une entreprise qui
marche mal. **2.** *Cricket:* **to make a d.,** faire
chou blanc. **II.** *v.* **1.** *v.i.* se baisser (instinctivement). **2.** *v.tr.* (*a*) plonger (qn) dans l'eau;
(*b*) baisser (subitement) la tête; ' **ducking,** *s.*
bain forcé; **to give s.o. a d.,** *F:* faire boire une
tasse à qn; ' **duckling,** *s.* caneton *m.*

dud [dʌd], *a.* & *s.* *F:* incapable; **he's a d.,** (i) c'est
un zéro; (ii) c'est un raté; **d. cheque,** chèque *m*
sans provision; **the note was a d.,** le billet était
faux.

due [dju:]. **I.** **1.** *a.* (*a*) exigible; échéant, échu; **bill**
d. on 1st May, effet payable le premier mai; **the**
balance d. to us, le solde qui nous revient; (*of*
bill, etc.) **to fall d.,** venir à échéance; **when d.,** à
l'échéance; (*b*) dû, *f.* due; juste, mérité; **in d.**
form, dans les formes voulues en règle; dans
les règles; **after d. consideration,** après mûre
réflexion; (*c*) **what is it d. to?** à quoi cela tient-
il? (*d*) **the train is d. at two o'clock,** le train
arrive à deux heures. **2.** *adv.* **d. north,** droit vers
le nord. **II.** *s.* **1.** dû *m*; **to give everyone his d.,**
donner à chacun son dû; **to give s.o. his d.,** rendre justice à qn. **2.** *pl.* **dues,** droits *mpl,* frais
mpl.

duel [dju(:)əl], *s.* duel *m*; **to fight a d.,** se battre en
duel.
duet [dju(:)'et], *s. Mus:* duo *m*; (*for piano*)
morceau *m* à quatre mains.
duffel [' dʌfəl], *s.* **d. coat,** duffle-coat *m*; **d. bag,**
sac *m* de campeur, de marin.
duke [dju:k], *s.* duc *m*; ' **dukedom,** *s.* duché *m.*
dull [dʌl], *a.* **1.** lent, lourd; à l'esprit obtus, épais;
to be d. of sight, hearing, avoir la vue faible,
l'oreille dure; **a d. ache,** une douleur sourde.
2. (bruit) sourd, étouffé, mat. **3.** *Com:*
(marché) calme, inactif. **4.** triste, morne;
déprimé. **5.** triste, ennuyeux; **as d. as**
ditchwater, ennuyeux comme un jour de pluie;
a deadly d. task, une besogne abrutissante,
assommante. **6.** (*of colour*) terne; mat. **7.** (*of*
weather) triste, sombre. **8.** (*of tool*) émoussé;
' **dully,** *adv.* **1.** lourdement; ennuyeusement. **2.**
sourdement, faiblement; sans éclat;
' **dullness,** *s.* **1.** lenteur *f*, lourdeur *f*, de l'esprit.
2. matité *f* (d'un son). **3.** ennui *m*; tristesse *f.* **4.**
Com: stagnation *f* (du marché); marasme *m.*
duly [' dju:li], *adv.* **1.** dûment, justement; convenablement. **2.** en temps voulu.
dumb [dʌm], *a.* **1.** muet, *f.* muette; **d. animals,** les
bêtes; **to strike s.o. d.,** rendre qn muet. **2.** *F:*
sot, *f.* sotte; -ly, *adv.* sans mot dire; en silence;
' **dumbness,** *s.* **1.** mutisme *m*; silence *m.* **2.** *F:*
sottise *f*; niaiserie *f.*
dumbbell [' dʌmbel], *s.* haltère *m.*
dumbfound [dʌm'faund], *v.tr.* abasourdir,
stupéfier, ahurir (qn); **dumb'founded,** *a.*
abasourdi, ahuri; **I'm d.,** je n'en reviens pas.
dummy [' dʌmi], *s.* **1.** *Com:* homme *m* de paille.
2. (*a*) mannequin *m*; (*b*) chose *f* factice (pour
vitrine); (*c*) (**baby's**) **d.,** sucette *f.* **3.** *Cards:*
mort *m.* **4.** *attrib.* postiche; faux, *f.* fausse.
dump [dʌmp]. **I.** *s.* **1.** tas *m*, amas *m*; **rubbish d.,**
décharge publique. **2.** dépôt *m.* **3.** *F:* **what a**
d.! quel trou! **II.** *v.tr.* **1.** décharger (un camion
de matériau); déposer (qch.) (lourdement). **2.**
se défaire de (qch.); *Com:* **to d. goods,** faire du
dumping; ' **dumping,** *s.* dumping *m.*
dumpling [' dʌmpliŋ], *s. Cu:* boulette *f* (de pâte,
servie avec le bœuf bouilli, etc.); **apple d.,**
pomme enrobée.
dumps [dʌmps], *s.pl.* *F:* **to be (down) in the d.,**
avoir le cafard, broyer du noir; ' **dumpy,** *a.*
trapu; boulot; **a d. little man,** un courtaud.
dun [dʌn], *v.tr.* **(dunned)** harceler (un débiteur).
dunce [dʌns], *s.* ignorant, -ante; âne *m.*
dune [dju:n], *s.* (**sand-)d.,** dune *f.*
dung [dʌŋ], *s.* **1.** bouse *f* (de vache); crottin *m* (de
cheval). **2.** *Agr:* fumier *m*; ' **dunghill,** *s.* tas *m*
de fumier.
dungarees [dʌŋgə'ri:z], *s. pl. Cl:* combinaison *f*;
bleus *mpl* (de mécanicien); *F:* salopette *f.*
dungeon [' dʌn(d)ʒ(ə)n], *s.* cachot *m.*

Dunkirk [dʌn'kə:k]. *Pr.n. Geog:* Dunkerque *f.*
dupe [dju:p]. **I.** *s.* dupe *f.* **II.** *v.tr.* duper, tromper (qn).
duplex ['dju:pleks], *s. N.Am:* maison *f* pour deux familles.
duplicate. I. *a.* & *s.* ['dju:plikət], double (*m*); **d. parts**, pièces *f* de rechange; **in d.**, en double exemplaire. **II.** *v.tr.* ['dju:plikeit], reproduire (un document) en double exemplaire; faire le double de (qch.); **'duplicating,** *s.* (*a*) duplication *f*; (*b*) reproduction *f*; **dupli'cation,** *s.* (*a*) duplication *f*; reproduction *f*; **'duplicator,** *s.* duplicateur *m.*
duplicity [dju:'plisiti], *s.* duplicité *f*; mauvaise foi.
durable ['djuərəbl], *a.* durable; résistant; **dura'bility,** *s.* durabilité *f*; durée *f* (d'un tissu); *Adm:* stabilité *f*; *Ind:* résistance *f* (de matériaux, etc.).
duration [dju(ə)'reiʃ(ə)n], *s.* (*of time*) durée *f*; étendue *f* (de la vie).
during ['djuəriŋ], *prep.* pendant, durant; **d. the winter**, au cours de l'hiver.
dusk [dʌsk], *s.* crépuscule *m, Fr.C:* brunante *f*; **at d.**, à la brune, à la nuit tombante; **'dusky,** *a.* (*of complexion*) brun foncé; (*of pers.*) noiraud.
dust [dʌst]. **I.** *s.* poussière *f.* **II.** *v.tr.* **1.** saupoudrer (**a cake, etc., with sugar,** un gâteau, etc., de sucre). **2.** épousseter (un meuble); **'dustbin,** *s.* poubelle *f*; **'duster,** *s.* chiffon *m,* torchon *m*; **feather d.,** plumeau *m*; **'dusting,** *s.* **1.** saupoudrage *m.* **2.** époussetage *m*; **'dust-jacket,** *s.* (*for book*) jaquette *f*; **'dustman,** *pl.* **-men,** *s.* boueur *m,* boueux *m*; **'dustpan,** *s.* pelle *f* à main; **'dust-up,** *s. F:* querelle *f*; **'dusty,** *a.* poussiéreux.
Dutch [dʌtʃ]. **1.** *a.* hollandais; de Hollande. **2.** *s.* (*a*) **the Dutch,** les Hollandais; (*b*) *Ling:* le hollandais. **3.** *adv. F:* **to go d.,** payer chacun son écot (pour un repas, etc.); **'Dutchman,** *pl.*

-men, *s.* Hollandais *m.*
duty ['dju:ti], *s.* **1.** obéissance *f*, respect *m.* **2.** devoir *m* (**to,** envers); **to do one's d.,** faire son devoir; **from a sense of d.,** par devoir. **3.** fonction(s) *f* (*pl*); *Adm:* **to take up one's duties,** entrer en fonctions; **to do d. for s.o.,** remplacer qn. **4.** service *m*; **to be on d.,** être de service. **5.** droit *m*; **customs d.,** droit(s) de douane; **'dutiable,** *a.* soumis aux droits de douane; **'dutiful,** *a.* respectueux, soumis; **-fully,** *adv.* avec soumission; **'duty-'free,** *a.* exempt de droits (de douane).
dwarf [dwɔ:f]. **I.** *s.* & *a.* nain, *f.* naine. **II.** *v.tr.* rabougrir (une plante); rapetisser (qch.) (par contraste); **'dwarfish,** *a.* (de) nain, chétif.
dwindle ['dwindl], *v.i.* **to d. (away),** diminuer, dépérir; **'dwindling,** *a.* diminuant.
dye [dai]. **I.** *s.* **1.** teinture *f*, teint *m*; **fast d.,** grand teint. **2.** matière colorante; colorant *m.* **II.** *v.tr.* teindre; **to d. sth. black,** teindre qch. en noir; **to have a dress dyed,** faire teindre une robe; **'dyeing,** *s.* **1.** teinture *f* (d'un tissu). **2.** (*trade, shop*) teinturerie *f*; **'dyer,** *s.* teinturier *m;* **dyer's and cleaner's (shop, business),** pressing *m.*
dying ['daiiŋ]. **1.** *a.* mourant, agonisant; (son *m*) qui s'éteint. **2.** *s.* agonie *f*, mort *f.*
dyke [daik], *s.* digue *f*, levée *f.*
dynamic [dai'næmik], *a.* (*of pers.*) (caractère) dynamique, énergique.
dynamite ['dainəmait]. **I.** *s.* dynamite *f.* **II.** *v.* faire sauter (des roches) à la dynamite; dynamiter (un bâtiment).
dynamo, *pl.* **-os** ['dainəmou, -ouz], *s.* dynamo *f.*
dysentery ['disəntri], *s. Med:* dysenterie *f.*
dyslexia [dis'leksiə], *s. Med:* dyslexie *f.*
dyspepsia [dis'pepsiə], *s. Med:* dyspepsie *f.* **dys'peptic,** *a.* & *s.* dyspepsique (*mf*), dyspeptique (*mf*).

E

E, e [i:], s. 1. (la lettre) E, e m. 2. *Mus:* mi m; **key of E flat,** clef *f* de mi bémol.

each [i:tʃ]. 1. *a.* chaque; **e. day,** chaque jour; tous les jours; **e. one of us,** chacun, chacune, de nous. 2. *pron.* (*a*) chacun, -une; **e. of us,** chacun d'entre nous; (*b*) **we earn £10 e., we e. earn £10,** nous gagnons dix livres chacun; (*c*) **e. other,** l'un(e) l'autre, les un(e)s les autres; **to be afraid of e. other,** avoir peur l'un de l'autre; **separated from e. other,** séparés l'un de l'autre.

eager ['i:gər], *a.* (*a*) ardent, passionné; **to be e. to do sth.,** être impatient de faire qch.; (*b*) **e. pursuit,** âpre poursuite *f*; **e. desire,** vif désir; **-ly,** *adv.* ardemment, passionnément, avidement; **'eagerness,** s. ardeur *f*; impatience *f*; vif désir.

eagle [i:gl], s. *Orn:* aigle *mf*; **golden e.,** aigle royal; **'eagle-'eyed,** *a.* aux yeux d'aigle; au regard d'aigle; **'eaglet,** s. aiglon m.

ear¹ ['iər], s. oreille *f*; **your ears must have burned,** les oreilles ont dû vous tinter; *F:* **I am up to my ears in work,** je suis débordé de travail; **he went off with a flea in his e.,** il est parti l'oreille basse; **to have sharp ears,** avoir l'oreille, l'ouïe, fine; **to have an e. for music,** avoir l'oreille musicienne; **to keep one's ears open,** se tenir aux écoutes; **'ear-ache,** s. **to have e.-a.,** avoir mal m à l'oreille, aux oreilles; **'earmark,** v.tr. **to e. funds for a purpose,** affecter des fonds à un projet; **'earphone,** s. *Rad: etc:* écouteur m; **'earring,** s. boucle *f* d'oreille; **'earshot,** s. **within e.,** à portée de voix.

ear², s. épi m (de blé, etc.).

earl [ə:l], s. comte m (*f.* **countess,** *q.v.*); **'earldom,** s. comté m; titre m de comte.

early ['ə:li]. I. *a.* 1. (*a*) **in the e. morning,** de bon, de grand, matin; **in e. summer,** au commencement de l'été; **to be an e. riser,** se lever de bon matin, de bonne heure; se lever tôt; être matinal; **to keep e. hours,** se coucher (et se lever) tôt; (*b*) **e. youth,** première jeunesse; **e. age,** âge m tendre; **at an e. age,** dès l'enfance. 2. (*of fruit, flowers*) précoce, hâtif; **e. vegetables, fruit,** primeurs *fpl*; **e. death,** mort prématurée. 3. prochain, rapproché; **at an e. date,** prochainement, bientôt. II. *adv.* (*a*) de bonne heure; tôt; **earlier,** plus tôt; **too e.,** trop tôt; de trop bonne heure; **to arrive five minutes e.,** arriver avec cinq minutes d'avance; **e. in the morning,** le matin de bonne heure; **e. in the**

afternoon, au commencement, au début, de l'après-midi; **as e. as the tenth century,** dès le dixième siècle; **as e. as possible,** aussitôt que possible; (*b*) **to die e.,** (i) mourir jeune; (ii) mourir prématurément.

earn [ə:n], v.tr. 1. gagner (de l'argent). 2. mériter (des éloges); gagner, mériter (l'affection de qn); **'earnings,** s.pl. 1. salaire m, gages *mpl*. 2. profits *mpl*, bénéfices *mpl*.

earnest ['ə:nist]. 1. *a.* (*a*) sérieux; **e. worker,** ouvrier consciencieux; (*b*) **e. request,** demande pressante. 2. *s.* **in e.,** sérieusement; **to be in e.,** être sérieux; ne pas plaisanter; **it is raining in real e.,** il pleut pour de bon; **-ly,** *adv.* d'un ton sérieux; (travailler) de bon cœur, avec zèle; **'earnestness,** s. gravité *f*, sérieux m (de ton); caractère sérieux (d'une discussion); ferveur *f* (d'une prière).

earth [ə:θ], s. 1. terre *f*; (*a*) le monde; **on e.,** sur terre; **where on e. have you been?** où diable étiez-vous? (*b*) le sol; **down to e.,** terre à terre; réaliste. 2. terrier m, tanière *f* (d'un renard); (*of fox*) **to go to e.,** se terrer; **to run s.o. to e.,** dénicher qn. 3. *El:* **e. (cable),** câble m de terre; prise *f* de terre; **'earthen,** *a.* de terre; **'earthenware,** s. poterie *f* (de terre); **glazed e.,** faïence *f*; **'earthly,** *a.* 1. terrestre. 2. **there's no e. reason for . . .,** il n'y a pas la moindre raison (du monde) pour . . .; **he hasn't an e. (chance),** il n'a pas l'ombre d'une chance (de réussir); **'earthquake,** s. tremblement m de terre; séisme m; **'earthworks,** s.pl. travaux m en terre, de terrassement; **'earthworm,** s. ver m de terre; **'earthy** *a.* terreux; **e. taste,** goût terreux; (*of pers.*) matériel, grossier.

earwig ['iəwig], s. *Ent:* forficule *f*, perce-oreille m.

ease [i:z]. I. s. 1. (*a*) tranquillité *f*; repos m, bien-être m, aise *f*; **to be at one's e.,** être à son aise; **to set s.o.'s mind at e.,** tirer qn de son inquiétude; **to put s.o. at e.,** mettre qn à son aise; (*b*) **e. from pain,** soulagement m. 2. **to live a life of e.,** vivre (i) dans l'oisiveté *f*, (ii) une vie de loisirs. 3. (*a*) aisance *f* (de manières); (*b*) simplicité *f* (de réglage); facilité *f* (de manœuvre); **with e.,** facilement; aisément. II. v.tr. 1. (*a*) adoucir, calmer (la souffrance); soulager (un malade); (*b*) calmer, tranquilliser (l'esprit). 2. débarrasser, délivrer (qn de qch.). 3. détendre, relâcher, soulager (un cordage, un ressort); desserrer (une vis); **'ease 'off, 'up,**

v.i. (*a*) *F:* se relâcher; moins travailler; (*b*) diminuer la vitesse; ralentir; **'easiness,** *s.* **1.** bien-être *m*, commodité *f*. **2.** aisance *f*, grâce *f* (de manières, etc.). **3.** insouciance *f*. **4.** facilité *f* (d'un travail). **5.** (*a*) humeur *f* facile; (*b*) jeu *m* facile (d'une machine); douceur *f* (de roulement).

easel ['iːzl], *s.* chevalet *m* (de peintre).

east [iːst]. **1.** *s.* (*a*) est *m*, orient *m*, levant *m*; **to the e.,** à l'est (**of,** de); (*b*) **the E.,** l'Orient; **the Far, Middle, Near, E.,** l'extrême, moyen, proche, Orient. **2.** *adv.* à l'est, à l'orient. **3.** *a.* (vent) d'est, (pays) de l'est; **'easterly. 1.** *a.* **e. wind,** vent *m* d'est. **2.** *adv.* vers l'est; **'eastern,** *a.* est, de l'est; oriental; **'eastwards,** *adv.* à l'est, vers l'est.

Easter ['iːstər], *s.* Pâques *m*; **E. Day,** le jour de Pâques; **E. egg,** œuf *m* de Pâques.

easy ['iːzi]. **I.** *a.* **1.** (*a*) à l'aise; **to feel easier,** se sentir plus à son aise; se sentir mieux; (*b*) tranquille; sans inquiétude. **2.** (*a*) (*of manners, etc.*) aisé, libre; **e. style,** style facile; (*b*) **e. fit,** (i) *Cl:* coupe *f* ample; (ii) *Mec:* ajustage *m* lâche. **3.** (*a*) **e. task,** travail facile, aisé; *F:* **as e. as anything,** simple comme bonjour; **that's e. to see,** cela se voit; **within e. reach of** (sth.), à distance commode de (qch.); (*b*) (*of pers.*) facile, accommodant, complaisant; **e. to get on with,** d'un commerce facile; (*c*) **to travel by e. stages,** voyager par petites étapes; **to come in an e. first,** arriver bon premier; *Com:* **by e. payments,** avec facilités de paiement; **-ily,** *adv.* **1.** tranquillement, à son aise, paisiblement; **to take life e.,** se laisser vivre. **2.** (*a*) doucement, sans secousse; (*b*) avec confort. **3.** facilement, avec facilité; sans difficulté. **II.** *adv.* *F:* **to take things e.,** prendre les choses en douceur; **take it e.!** ne vous faites pas de bile! **to go e. with s.o., sth.,** ménager qn, qch.; **'easy-'chair,** *s.* fauteuil *m*; bergère *f*; **'easy-going,** *a.* (*a*) insouciant; (*b*) d'humeur facile; facile à vivre.

eat [iːt], *v.tr. & i.* (**ate** [et]; **eaten**) manger; **to ask for something to e.,** demander à manger; **to e. one's breakfast, dinner, supper,** déjeuner, dîner, souper; **fit to e.,** mangeable; bon à manger; **I thought he was going to e. me,** j'ai cru qu'il allait m'avaler; **to e. one's words,** se rétracter; **'eatable. 1.** *a.* bon à manger. **2.** *s.pl.* comestibles *m*; **'eat a'way,** *v.tr.* ronger, éroder; (*of acid*) mordre, attaquer (un métal); **'eating,** *s.* manger *m*; *attrib.* **e. apple,** pomme *f* à couteau; **eats,** *s.pl.* *F:* la boustifaille; **'eat 'up,** *v.tr.* **1.** achever de manger, dévorer; **e. up your bread!** finis ton pain! **to e. up the miles,** dévorer la route. **2.** consumer (qch.) sans profit; **car that eats up petrol,** voiture *f* qui consomme trop d'essence. **3.** *F:* **to be eaten up**

(with sth.), être dévoré (d'orgueil, d'ambition, etc.).

eaves [iːvz], *s.pl.* (*of house*) avance *f* (du toit); avant-toit *m*.

eavesdrop ['iːvzdrɔp], *v.i.* (**eavesdropped**) écouter aux portes; **'eavesdropper,** *s.* écouteur, -euse, aux portes.

ebb [eb]. **I.** *s.* **1.** reflux *m*, jusant *m*, baisse *f* (de la marée); **e. tide,** marée descendante. **2.** déclin *m* (de la fortune); **to be at a low e.,** être très bas. **II.** *v.i.* **1.** (*of tide*) baisser. **2.** (*of life, etc.*) décliner, baisser; **to e. away,** s'écouler.

ebony ['ebəni], *s.* ébène *f*; bois *m* d'ébène.

ebullient [i'bʌljənt], *a.* (*of pers.*) débordant, exubérant; plein de vie.

eccentric [ik'sentrik, ek-], *a. & s.* excentrique (*mf*); original, -ale, -aux; **eccen'tricity,** *s.* excentricité *f* de caractère; bizarrerie *f*, originalité *f*.

ecclesiastical [ikliːzi'æstik(ə)l], *a.* ecclésiastique.

echo[1] ['ekou]. **I.** *s.* (*pl.* **echoes**) écho *m*. **II.** *v.* **1.** *v.tr.* répéter. **2.** *v.i.* (*a*) faire écho; (*b*) retentir.

éclair [ei'klɛər], *s.* *Cu:* **chocolate é.,** éclair *m* au chocolat.

eclipse [i'klips]. **I.** *s.* éclipse *f* (de la lune, etc.). **II.** *v.tr.* **1.** éclipser. **2.** (*of pers.*) éclipser, surpasser (qn).

economy [i(ː)'kɔnəmi], *s.* **1.** économie *f*; **to practise e.,** économiser; *Aut:* **e. run,** concours *m* de consommation. **2.** **political e.,** économie politique; **controlled e.,** économie dirigée; **planned e.,** économie planifiée; **eco'nomic,** *a.* **e. problem,** problème *m* d'ordre économique; **e. rent,** loyer rentable, qui rapporte; **eco'nomical,** *a.* (*a*) (*of pers.*) économe; (*b*) (*methods, etc.*) économique; **-ally,** *adv.* économiquement; **to use sth. e.,** ménager qch.; **eco'nomics,** *s. pl.* **1.** l'économie *f* politique. **2.** rentabilité *f*, aspect financier (d'une affaire); **e'conomist,** *s.* économiste *mf* (politique); **e'conomize,** *v.tr.* économiser, ménager; *abs.* faire des économies.

ecstasy ['ekstəsi], *s.* **1.** transport *m* (de joie), ravissement *m*; **to go into ecstasies over sth.,** s'extasier devant qch. **2.** extase *f* (religieuse, etc.).

Ecuador ['ekwədɔːr]. *Pr.n. Geog:* (République de) l'Équateur *m*.

eddy ['edi]. **I.** *s.* (*of water, wind*) remous *m*; tourbillon *m*; tournoiement *m*. **II.** *v.i.* (*of water*) faire des remous; (*of wind*) tourbillonner, tournoyer.

edge [edʒ]. **I.** *s.* **1.** fil *m*, tranchant *m* (d'une lame, etc.); **to put an e. on a blade,** (re)donner du fil, affiler, une lame; **to take the e. off sth.,** émousser (un couteau, un plaisir, l'appétit). **2.** bord *m*, rebord *m*; tranche *f* (d'un livre);

pers.) **on e.**, énervé. **3.** lisière *f*, bordure *f* (d'un bois); bord, rive *f* (d'une rivière); liséré *m*, bord (d'un tissu). **II.** *v.tr. & i.* **1. to e. (a tool, etc.)**, aiguiser, affiler, affûter (un outil, etc.). **2. to e. (one's way) into a room**, se faufiler, se glisser, dans une pièce; **to e. away (from s.o., sth.)**, s'éloigner (tout) doucement (de qn, qch.); **'edgeways, 'edgewise**, *adv.* de côté; de chant; **I can't get a word in e.**, impossible de placer un mot; **'edgy**, *a. F:* (*of pers.*) nerveux; énervé.

edible ['edibl], *a.* comestible; bon à manger.

edifice ['edifis], *s.* édifice *m*; (grand) bâtiment.

Edinburgh ['edinb(ə)rə]. *Pr.n. Geog:* Édimbourg; **native of E.**, Édimbourgeois, -oise.

edit ['edit], *v.tr.* (*a*) annoter, éditer (un texte); (*b*) rédiger (un journal); **edited by . . .**, (série *f* de textes, journal, etc.) sous la direction de . . .; **'editing**, *s.* **1.** annotation *f* (d'un texte). **2.** rédaction *f* (d'un journal). **3.** *Cin:* montage *m*; **e'dition** [i'dif(ə)n], *s.* édition *f*; **limited e.**, édition à tirage limité; **'editor**, *s.* **1.** éditeur *m* (d'un texte). **2.** (*a*) directeur *m* (d'une série de textes); (*b*) rédacteur *m* en chef (d'un journal); (*c*) *Rad: T.V:* **programme e.**, éditorialiste *mf*; **edi'torial. 1.** *a.* éditorial; **the e. staff**, la rédaction. **2.** *s.* article *m* de fond, de tête; éditorial *m*.

educate ['edjukeit], *v.tr.* **1.** (*a*) donner de l'instruction à (qn), instruire (qn); **he was educated in France**, il a fait ses études en France; (*b*) faire faire ses études à (un enfant). **2.** former (qn, le goût de qn); **educated man**, homme cultivé; **edu'cation**, *s.* **1.** éducation *f*. **2.** enseignement *m*, instruction *f*; **he's had a good e.**, il a fait de bonnes études; **adult e.**, enseignement post-scolaire; **university e.**, éducation supérieure; **edu'cational**, *a.* (maison *f*, ouvrage *m*) d'éducation, d'enseignement; **e. method**, procédé *m* pédagogique; **e. film**, film éducatif.

Edward ['edwəd]. *Pr.n. m.* Édouard.

eel [i:l], *s.* anguille *f*.

eerie ['iəri], *a.* étrange, mystérieux.

efface [i'feis], *v.tr.* effacer; oblitérer (qch.).

effect[1] [i'fekt], *s.* **1.** (*a*) effet *m*, influence *f*; résultat *m*; conséquence *f*; **to have an e. on s.o.**, produire de l'effet sur qn; **to have no e.**, ne produire aucun effet; **nothing has any e. on it**, rien n'y a fait; **to take e.**, (i) faire (son) effet; (ii) (*of regulations*) entrer en vigueur; (iii) (*of drugs*) agir, opérer; **to no e.**, en vain; sans résultat; **to carry into e.**, mettre à exécution; (*b*) sens *m*, teneur *f* (d'un document); **words to that e.**, quelque chose d'approchant. **2.** *pl.* **personal effects**, biens *mpl*, effets (personnels); *Th:* **stage effects**, effets scéniques. **3.** en fait, en réalité; **e'ffective. 1.** *a.* (*a*) efficace; effectif; (*b*) (tableau, etc.) qui fait de l'effet. **2.**

s.pl. Mil: **effectives**, effectifs *m*; **-ly**, *adv.* **1.** avec effet, efficacement. **2.** effectivement; en réalité. **3.** d'une façon frappante.

effect[2], *v.tr.* effectuer, accomplir, réaliser (qch.).

effectual [i'fektjuəl], *a.* **1.** efficace. **2.** (contrat) valide; (règlement) en vigueur; **-ally**, *adv.* efficacement.

effeminate [i'feminət], *a. & s.* efféminé (*m*); **to grow e.**, s'amollir.

effervesce [efə'ves], *v.i.* être, entrer, en effervescence; (*of drinks*) mousser; **effer'vescence**, *s.* effervescence *f*.

efficacious [efi'keifəs], *a.* efficace; **-ily**, *adv.* efficacement; avec efficacité; **effi'caciousness**, *s.*, **'efficacy**, *s.* efficacité *f*.

efficiency [i'fif(ə)nsi], *s.* **1.** efficacité *f* (d'un remède). **2.** rendement *m* (d'une machine); bon fonctionnement (d'une administration, d'une entreprise). **3.** capacité *f*, compétence *f* (d'une personne); **e'fficient**, *a.* (*a*) (*of method, work*) efficace; (*b*) *Ind:* (*of machine, factory*) qui fonctionne bien; (*c*) (*of pers.*) capable, compétent; **-ly**, *adv.* d'une manière efficace, compétente.

effort ['efət], *s.* effort *m*; **to make an e. to do sth.**, s'efforcer de faire qch.; **he spares no e.**, il ne s'épargne pas; **'effortless**, *a.* (*a*) sans effort; (*b*) facile.

effusive [i'fju:siv], *a.* démonstratif, expansif; **to be e. in one's thanks**, se confondre en remerciements; **-ly**, *adv.* avec effusion, avec expansion; **e'ffusiveness**, *s.* effusion *f*; volubilité *f*.

egg[1] [eg], *s.* œuf *m*; **boiled e.**, œuf à la coque; **hard-boiled e.**, œuf dur; **fried e.**, œuf sur le plat; **scrambled eggs**, œufs brouillés; **a bad e.**, (i) un œuf pourri; (ii) *F:* un vaurien; **'egg-cup**, *s.* coquetier *m*; **'egg-plant**, *s.* aubergine *f*; **'egg-shaped**, *a.* ovoïde; **'eggshell**, *s.* coquille *f* d'œuf; **'egg-spoon**, *s.* cuiller *f* à œufs.

egg[2], *v.tr.* **to e. s.o. on (to do sth.)**, pousser, inciter, encourager, qn (à faire qch.).

egoism ['egouizm], *s.* égoïsme *m*; **'egoist**, *s.* égoïste *mf*; **ego'istic(al)**, *a.* égoïste.

egotism ['egoutizm], *s.* égotisme *m*; **'egotist**, *s.* égotiste *mf*; **ego'tistic(al)**, *a.* égotiste.

Egypt ['i:dʒipt]. *Pr.n. Geog:* l'Egypte *f*; **E'gyptian**, *a. & s.* égyptien, -ienne; **Egyp'tologist**, *s.* égyptologue *mf*; **Egyptology**, *s.* égyptologie *f*.

eiderdown ['aidədaun], *s.* édredon *m*.

eight [eit], *num.a. & s.* huit (*m*); **to be e. (years old)**, avoir huit ans; **page twenty-e.**, page vingt-huit; **it's e. o'clock**, il est huit heures; **eigh'teen**, *num.a. & s.* dix-huit (*m*); **eigh'teenth**, *num.a. & s.* (*a*) dix-huitième; (*b*) **(on) the e. (of May)**, le dix-huit (mai); **Louis the E.**, Louis Dix-huit; **eighth**, *num.a. & s.* (*a*) huitième; (*b*) **on the e. (of April)**, le huit (avril);

Henry the E., Henri Huit; (c) one-e., un huitième; **'eighty,** num.a. & s.m. quatre-vingts; e.-one, quatre-vingt-un.

Eire ['ɛərə]. Pr.n. Geog: l'Eire f.

either ['aiðər]. 1. a. & pron. (a) l'un(e) et l'autre; **on e. side,** de chaque côté; des deux côtés; (b) l'un(e) ou l'autre; **e. of them,** soit l'un(e), soit l'autre; n'importe lequel; **I don't believe e. of you,** je ne vous crois ni l'un ni l'autre. 2. conj. & adv. (a) e. ... or ..., ou ..., ou ...; soit ..., soit ...; **e. come in or go out,** entrez ou sortez; (b) **not ... e.,** ne ... non plus; **nor I,** F: me, e.! ni moi non plus.

ejaculate [i'dʒækjuleit], v.tr. 1. Physiol: éjaculer. 2. pousser, lancer (un cri, un juron); **ejacu'lation,** s. 1. Physiol: éjaculation f. 2. cri m, exclamation f.

eject [i'dʒekt], v.tr. 1. jeter, émettre (des flammes, etc.). 2. expulser, F: éjecter, sortir (un locataire); **e'jection,** s. éviction f, expulsion f; **e'jector,** s. Mec: éjecteur m; Av: **e. seat,** siège m éjectable.

eke [i:k], v.tr. **to e. out,** ménager, économiser, faire durer (ses revenus, les vivres); allonger (la sauce); **to e. out one's income by writing,** gagner un petit surplus en écrivant.

elaborate [i'læb(ə)rət], a. compliqué; (of style) travaillé; (of inspection) minutieux; -ly, adv. avec soin; minutieusement.

elapse [i'læps], v.i. (of time) s'écouler; (se) passer.

elastic [i'læstik], a. & s. élastique (m); **elas'ticity,** s. élasticité f; ressort m (de caractère); souplesse f (de corps).

elated [i'leitid], a. transporté; **to feel e.,** se sentir plein de joie.

elation [i'leiʃ(ə)n], s. 1. exaltation f. 2. joie f, gaieté f.

elbow ['elbou]. I. s. 1. coude m; **to rest one's e. on sth.,** s'accouder sur qch.; (of pers.) **to lift the e.,** être adonné à la boisson. 2. coude, genou m (d'un tuyau). II. v.tr. & i. coudoyer (qn); pousser (qn) du coude; **to e. s.o. aside,** écarter qn d'un coup de coude; **to e. (a way) through the crowd,** se frayer un passage à travers la foule; **'elbow-grease,** s. F: put some e.-g. into it! mettez-y un peu de nerf! **'elbow-room,** s. to have e.-r., avoir ses coudées franches; être au large.

elder ['eldər]. 1. a. aîné, plus âgé. 2. s. aîné, -ée; plus âgé, -ée; **to obey one's elders,** obéir à ses aînés; **'elderly.** 1. a. d'un certain âge. 2. s. coll. the e., les personnes âgées; **'eldest,** a. aîné.

elect [i'lekt], v.tr. 1. **to e. (to do sth.),** choisir (de faire qch.). 2. élire (qn député, etc.); **the Mayor e.,** le futur maire; **e'lection,** s. élection f; **general, parliamentary, e.,** élections législatives; **e'lector,** s. électeur, -trice, votant, -ante.

electricity [ilek'trisiti, elek-], s. électricité f; **e'lectric,** a., **e'lectrical,** a. électrique; **-ally,** adv. électriquement; **e. driven,** actionné par électricité, par électromoteur; **elec'trician,** s. Ind: électricien m; réparateur m d'appareils électriques; **electrifi'cation,** s. 1. électrisation f (d'un corps). 2. électrification f (d'un chemin de fer, etc.); **e'lectrify,** v.tr. 1. électriser (un corps, son auditoire). 2. électrifier (un chemin de fer); **e'lectro'cardiogram,** s. électrocardiogramme m; **e'lectrocute,** v.tr. électrocuter (qn); **e'lectrode,** s. électrode f; **elec'trolysis,** s. électrolyse f; **elec'tron,** s. électron m; **elec'tronic.** 1. a. électronique. 2. s.pl. **electronics,** (science f de) l'électronique f; **e. specialist,** électronicien, -ienne; **e'lectrotech'nology,** s. électrotechnique f; **e'lectro'therapy,** s. Med: électrothérapie f.

elegance ['eligəns], s. élégance f; **'elegant,** a. élégant; N.Am: F: excellent; de premier ordre; **-ly,** adv. élégamment.

element ['elimənt], s. élément m. 1. **to be in, out of, one's e.,** être dans, hors de, son élément; pl. **exposed to the elements,** exposé aux intempéries f. 2. (a) partie f (d'un tout); (b) **the human e.,** le facteur humain. 3. Ch: corps m simple. 4. pl. rudiments m (d'une science); **ele'mentary,** a. élémentaire.

elephant ['elifənt], s. **(bull) e.,** éléphant m (mâle) **cow e.,** éléphant femelle; **white e.,** objet inutile et encombrant; **ele'phantine,** a. 1. éléphantin; **e. wit,** esprit lourd. 2. (of size, proportions) éléphantesque.

elevate ['eliveit], v.tr. élever (l'hostie); relever (son style); **'elevated,** a. 1. élevé; **e. position,** position élevée. 2. (overhead) surélevé; **ele'vation,** s. 1. élévation f (de l'hostie; de qn en rang). 2. élévation (d'une montagne). 3. Ind: sectional e., coupe verticale; front e., façade f; **'elevator,** s. 1. Agr: grain e. élévateur m à grains. 2. N.Am: ascenseur m. 3. Av: gouvernail m d'altitude.

eleven [i'levn]. 1. num a. & s. onze (m); **there ar only e. of them,** ils ne sont que onze; **the o'clock train,** le train d'onze heures; **to be e. (years old),** avoir onze ans; **page e.,** page onze it's e. o'clock, il est onze heures. 2. s. Cricke équipe f de onze joueurs. 3. s.pl. F: **elevenses** casse-croûte m (à onze heures du matin) **e'leventh,** num.a. & s. onzième; **at the e. hou au dernier moment; (on) the e.,** le onze (d mois).

elicit [i'lisit], v.tr. **to e. the facts,** tirer les faits a clair; **to e. a reply from s.o.,** obtenir un réponse de qn.

eligible ['elidʒibl], a. (a) **to be e.,** avoir droit (fo sth., à qch.); (b) **e. for a job,** admissible à u

emploi; **eligi'bility,** s. éligibilité f.
eliminate [i'limineit], v.tr. éliminer; supprimer, écarter (une éventualité); **e'liminating,** a. éliminateur; Sp: **e. heats,** épreuves f éliminatoires; **elimi'nation,** s. élimination f.
élite [ei'li:t], s. élite f.
elk [elk], s. Z: élan m; **Canadian e.,** orignal m.
elm [elm], s. orme m.
elocution [elə'kju:ʃ(ə)n], s. élocution f, diction f; **elo'cutionist,** s. professeur m d'élocution, de diction.
elongate ['i:lɔŋgeit], v.tr. allonger, étendre.
elope [i'loup], v.i. (of girl) s'enfuir avec un amant; se faire enlever.
eloquence ['eləkwəns], s. éloquence f; **'eloquent,** a. éloquent; **e. look,** regard m qui en dit long; **-ly,** adv. éloquemment.
else [els]. 1. adv. autrement; **come in, or e. go out,** entrez ou bien sortez. 2. (a) a. or adv. **anyone e.,** (i) toute autre personne; tout autre, n'importe qui d'autre; (ii) interr: **did you see anybody e.?** avez-vous vu encore quelqu'un? **anything e.,** (i) n'importe quoi d'autre; (ii) **anything e., madam?** et avec cela, madame? **someone e.,** quelqu'un d'autre, un autre; **something e.,** autre chose m; **nothing e.,** rien m d'autre; **nothing e., thank you,** plus rien, merci; **what e. can I do?** que puis-je faire d'autre, de mieux? **everything e.,** tout le reste; (b) adv. **everywhere e.,** partout ailleurs; **somewhere e.,** autre part; ailleurs; **nowhere e.,** nulle part ailleurs; **'else'where,** adv. ailleurs, autre part.
elucidate [i'lu:sideit], v.tr. élucider, éclaircir (un problème); **eluci'dation,** s. élucidation f.
elude [i'lju:d], v.tr. éviter (une question); tourner (la loi); échapper à (la poursuite); se soustraire à (la justice).
elusive [i'lju:siv], a. insaisissable, intangible; **e. reply,** réponse évasive; **-ly,** adv. évasivement.
emaciated [i'meiʃieitid], a. amaigri, décharné; **emaci'ation,** s. amaigrissement m (extrême).
emancipate [i'mænsipeit], v.tr. émanciper (qn); affranchir (un esclave); **emanci'pation,** s. émancipation f; affranchissement m.
embalm [im'ba:m, em-], v.tr. 1. embaumer (un cadavre); conserver la mémoire de (qn). 2. embaumer, parfumer (l'air).
embankment [im'bæŋkmənt, em-], s. (a) digue f; levée f de terre; (b) talus m; remblai m; **river e.,** berge f, quai m, d'un fleuve.
embargo, pl. -oes [im'ba:gou, em-, -ouz], s. embargo m; (of ship, goods) **to be under an e.,** être séquestré.
embark [im'ba:k, em-]. 1. v.tr. embarquer (les passagers). 2. v.i. s'embarquer (à bord d'un navire, dans une affaire); **embar'kation,** s. embarquement m; **e. card,** carte f d'accès à bord.

embarrass [im'bærəs, em-], v.tr. embarrasser, gêner (qn); déconcerter (qn); **em'barrassed,** a. embarrassé; gêné; **em'barrassment,** s. embarras m, gêne f.
embassy ['embəsi], s. ambassade f.
embellish [im'beliʃ], v.tr. embellir, orner (qch.); enjoliver (un récit); **em'bellishment,** s. embellissement m, ornement m.
embers ['embəz], s.pl. braise f; cendres ardentes.
embezzle [im'bezl], v.tr. détourner (des fonds); **em'bezzlement,** s. détournement m de fonds; **em'bezzler,** s. (pers.) auteur m d'un détournement de fonds.
embitter [im'bitər], v.tr. aigrir (le caractère de qn); envenimer (une querelle); **em'bittered,** a. aigri; envenimé (by, par).
emblem ['embləm], s. emblème m, symbole m; insigne (sportif); **emble'matic,** a. emblématique.
embody [im'bɔdi, em-], v.tr. 1. incarner. 2. réaliser, concrétiser (une idée); personnifier (une qualité). 3. Jur: incorporer; **em'bodiment,** s. incarnation f; personnification f; incorporation f.
embrace [im'breis, em-]. I. s. étreinte f, embrassement m. II. v.tr. 1. embrasser, étreindre (qn). 2. embrasser, adopter (une cause).
embroider [im'brɔidər, em-], v.tr. Needlew: (a) broder; (b) broder, enjoliver (un récit); **em'broidery,** s. broderie f.
embryo, pl. -os ['embriou, -ouz], s. Biol: embryon m; **in e.,** (i) (à l'état) embryonnaire; (ii) **plans in e.,** projets m à l'état embryonnaire.
emend [i:'mend], v.tr. corriger (un texte).
emerald ['emərəld]. 1. s. émeraude f. 2. a. & s. **e.-green,** (vert) émeraude (m).
emerge [i'mə:dʒ], v.i. 1. émerger (from, de); surgir (de l'eau, etc.). 2. déboucher (from, de); sortir (d'un trou). 3. (of difficulty) se dresser; surgir; **from these facts it emerges that . . .,** de ces faits il ressort que . . .; **e'mergence,** s. apparition f (d'un nouvel état); **e'mergent,** a. **e. nations,** nations émergentes.
emergency [i'mə:dʒənsi], s. circonstance f critique; cas urgent, imprévu; Med: **an e.,** une urgence; **e. ward,** salle f d'urgence; **to provide for emergencies,** parer à l'imprévu; **in this e.,** en cette conjoncture; **in case of e.,** au besoin; en cas d'urgence; **state of e.,** état m d'urgence; **e. repairs,** réparations d'urgence; **e. exit,** sortie f de secours.
emery ['eməri], s. émeri m; **e. paper, e. cloth,** papier m, toile f, d'émeri.
emigrate ['emigreit], v.i. émigrer; **'emigrant,** a. & s. émigrant, -ante; **emi'gration,** s. émigration f.
eminence ['eminəns], s. éminence f. 1. élévation

f (de terrain); monticule *m*. **2.** grandeur *f*, distinction *f*. **3.** *Ecc:* **Your E.,** votre Éminence; **'eminent,** *a.* éminent; **-ly,** *adv.* éminemment; par excellence.

emit [i'mit], *v.tr.* **(emitted)** dégager, émettre (de la chaleur); exhaler, répandre (une odeur); lancer (des étincelles); rendre (un son); **e'mission,** *s.* émission *f*, dégagement *m* (de chaleur, etc.).

emotion [i'mouʃ(ə)n], *s.* émotion *f*; trouble *m*, attendrissement *m*; **to appeal to the emotions,** faire appel aux sentiments; **e'motional,** *a.* (*a*) émotif; émotionnel; (*b*) **e. voice,** voix émue; **to be e.,** s'attendrir facilement.

emperor ['empərər], *s.* empereur *m*.

emphasize ['emfəsaiz], *v.tr.* accentuer, appuyer sur, souligner (un fait); faire ressortir (une qualité); **'emphasis,** *s.* **1.** force *f*; (énergie d')accentuation *f*. **2. to ask with e.,** demander avec insistance; **to lay e. on a fact,** appuyer sur un fait. **3.** *Ling:* accent *m* d'insistance; **em'phatic,** *a.* (manière) énergique; (ton) autoritaire; (refus) net, positif; **-ally,** *adv.* énergiquement, positivement.

empire ['empaiər], *s.* empire *m*.

empiric(al) [im'pirik(əl), em-], *a.* empirique; **-ally,** *adv.* empiriquement.

employ [im'plɔi, em-], *v.tr.* employer (qn, son temps, etc.); faire usage de (la force); **to be employed in doing sth.,** s'occuper, être occupé, à faire qch.; **employ'ee,** *s.* employé, -ée; **the firm's employees,** le personnel de la maison; **em'ployer,** *s. Ind:* patron, -onne; maître, maîtresse; **the employers of labour,** les employeurs de main-d'œuvre; *coll.* **the employers,** le patronat; **employer's union,** syndicat patronal; **em'ployment,** *s.* emploi *m*, travail *m*; place *f*, situation *f*; **e. agency,** bureau *m* de placement; **to find e. for s.o.,** placer qn; **to be out of e.,** être en chômage.

empower [im'pauər], *v.tr.* **to e. s.o. to do sth.,** autoriser qn à faire qch.

empress ['empris], *s.* impératrice *f*.

empty ['em(p)ti]. **I.** *v.* **1.** vider; décharger (un wagon); vidanger (un carter). **2.** *v.i.* (*of river, etc.*) se décharger, se déverser (**into,** dans); (*of hall, etc.*) se dégarnir, se vider. **II.** **1.** *a.* vide (**of,** de); (*a*) (immeuble) inoccupé; (estomac) creux; (*b*) **e. words,** vaines paroles. **2.** *s.pl. Com:* **empties,** (i) caisses *f*, (ii) bouteilles *f*, vides; **'emptiness,** *s.* vide *m*; **'empty-'handed,** *a.* les mains vides; **to return e.-h.,** revenir bredouille.

emulate ['emjuleit], *v.tr.* rivaliser avec, imiter (qn); **emu'lation,** *s.* émulation *f*.

enable [i'neibl, e-], *v.tr.* **to e. s.o. to do sth.,** rendre qn capable, mettre qn à même, de faire qch.

enamel [i'næməl]. **I.** *s.* **1.** émail *m*, *pl.* émaux. **2.**

vernis *m*; laque *f*; **e. paint,** peinture laquée. **II.** *v.tr.* **(enamelled) 1.** émailler (la porcelaine). **2.** ripoliner; vernir, vernisser; laquer (des meubles, etc.); **enamelled kettle,** bouilloire *f* en fer émaillé.

encampment [in'kæmpmənt], *s.* campement *m*; camp *m*.

enchant [in'tʃɑ:nt], *v.tr.* **1.** enchanter, ensorceler. **2.** enchanter, charmer, ravir (qn); **en'chanting,** *a.* enchanteur; ravissant, charmant; **-ly,** *adv.* à ravir; **en'chanter,** *f.* **-tress,** *s.* enchanteur, enchanteresse; **en'chantment,** *s.* enchantement *m*; ensorcellement *m*; ravissement *m*.

encircle [in'sə:kl], *v.tr.* ceindre, encercler; entourer (une armée); **en'circlement,** *s.* **en'circling,** *s.* encerclement *m*.

enclose [in'klouz], *v.tr.* **1.** enclore, clôturer (un champ) (**with,** de). **2.** inclure, renfermer, joindre (**in,** dans); *Com:* **enclosed (herewith) please find ...,** veuillez trouver ci-inclus ...; **en'closure,** *s.* **1.** clôture *f*. **2.** (*a*) enclos *m*, clos *m*; (*b*) *Rac:* le pesage. **3.** *Com:* pièce annexée; document ci-joint.

encore ['ɔŋkɔ:r]. **I.** *s. & int.* bis *m*. **II.** *v.tr.* bisser (un acteur); *abs.* crier bis.

encounter [in'kauntər]. **I.** *s.* **1.** rencontre *f*. **2** combat *m*. **II.** *v.tr.* rencontrer (un obstacle); éprouver (des difficultés); affronter (l'ennemi)

encourage [in'kʌridʒ], *v.tr.* **1.** encourager enhardir (qn). **2.** encourager, inciter (qn à faire qch.). **3.** favoriser (la recherche); **en'courage ment,** *s.* encouragement *m*; **en'couraging,** *a* encourageant; **-ly,** *adv.* d'une manièr encourageante.

encroach [in'kroutʃ], *v.i.* **to e. on,** empiéter s (une terre); **to e. on s.o.'s time,** abuser d temps de qn; **en'croachment,** *s.* empiétemen *m* (**on,** sur); usurpation *f* (des droits de qn).

encumber [in'kʌmbər], *v.tr.* encombrer (**witl** de); embarrasser, gêner (qn, le mouvement **en'cumbrance,** *s.* embarras *m*, charge *f*; **to b an e. to s.o.,** être à charge à qn; **withou (family) encumbrances,** sans charges d famille.

encyclop(a)edia [insaiklə'pi:diə], *s.* e cyclopédie *f*; **encyclo'p(a)edic,** *a.* (savoir *n* encyclopédique.

end [end]. **I.** *s.* **1.** bout *m*, extrémité *f*; fin *f*; *F etc:* **to change ends,** changer de camp; **the house,** la dernière maison (de la rue); **to g hold of the wrong e. of the stick,** comprend de travers; *F:* **to keep one's e. up,** ne pas laisser démonter; ténir bon; *F:* **to be at a loo e.,** avoir du temps à perdre; *adv.phrs.* **e. to bout à bout; **from e. to e.,** d'un bout à l'autr **for two hours on e.,** (pendant) deux heures suite; *Aut:* **big e.,** tête *f* de bielle. **2.** limite borne *f*; **to the ends of the earth,** jusqu'au bout du monde. **3.** bout, fin (du mois); terme *m* (d'un procès); **we shall never hear the e. of it,** cela va être des histoires sans fin; **and there's an e. of it!** et voilà tout! **to make an e. of sth.,** en finir avec qch.; achever qch.; mettre fin à qch.; **to come to an e.,** prendre fin; **in the e.,** (i) à la longue; (ii) à la fin; enfin; *F:* **no e. of . . .,** une infinité de . . .; *F:* **it'll do you no e. of good,** ça vous fera énormément de bien; **to come to a bad e.,** mal finir. **4.** fin, but *m*, dessein *m*; **private ends,** intérêt(s) personnel(s); **with this e. in view,** dans cette intention; à cet effet. **II.** *v.* **1.** *v.tr.* finir, achever, terminer (un ouvrage); conclure (un discours). **2.** *v.i.* finir, se terminer; **'ending,** *s.* **1.** terminaison *f*, achèvement *m*. **2.** fin *f* (d'un ouvrage); **happy e.,** dénouement heureux; **'endless,** *a.* **1.** (*a*) (voyage *m*) sans fin; (*b*) (espace *m*) sans bornes; infini. **2.** (*in time*) éternel; **-ly,** *adv.* sans fin; éternellement; perpétuellement; **'endpaper,** *s. Bookb:* (page *f* de) garde *f*; **'endways,** *adv.* de chant, sur chant.

endanger [in'deindʒər], *v.tr.* mettre en danger; risquer (sa vie); compromettre (ses intérêts).

endear [in'diər], *v.tr.* rendre (qn, qch.) cher (**to,** à); **he endeared himself to everyone,** il s'est fait aimer de tout le monde; **en'dearing,** *a.* qui inspire l'affection. **2.** (mot, geste) tendre, affectueux; **-ly,** *adv.* tendrement, affectueusement; **en'dearments,** *s.pl.* caresses *f*; mots *m* tendres.

endeavour [in'devər]. **I.** *s.* effort *m*, tentative *f*. **II.** *v.i.* s'efforcer, essayer, tâcher (de faire qch.).

endorse [in'dɔːs], *v.tr.* **1.** endosser (un chèque); viser (un passeport); *Com:* avaliser (un effet). **2.** appuyer (l'opinion de qn); souscrire à (une décision); **en'dorsement,** *s.* **1.** endossement (d'un chèque); (*on passport*) mention *f* spéciale. **2.** approbation *f*; adhésion *f* (à une opinion).

endow [in'dau], *v.tr.* doter (qn) (**with,** de); fonder (une œuvre charitable); **endowed with great talents,** doué de grands talents; **en'dowment,** *s.* **1.** (*a*) dotation *f*; (*b*) fondation *f*. **2.** **e. insurance,** assurance *f* à terme fixe, à capital différé.

endure [in'djuər]. **1.** *v.tr.* supporter, endurer (le malheur). **2.** *v.i.* durer, rester; **en'durable,** *a.* supportable; **en'durance,** *s.* **1.** (*a*) endurance *f*, résistance *f* (à la fatigue, etc.); **beyond e.,** insupportable; (*b*) **e. test,** (i) *E:* essai *m* de durée; (ii) *Sp:* épreuve *f* d'endurance. **2.** patience *f*; **en'during,** *a.* durable, permanent; patient, endurant.

enemy ['enəmi], *s.* (*a*) ennemi, -ie; (*b*) *coll.* **the e.,** l'ennemi, l'adversaire *m*.

energy ['enədʒi], *s.* énergie *f*, force *f*; vigueur *f*;

atomic e., énergie atomique; **ener'getic,** *a.* énergique; **-ally,** *adv.* énergiquement; **'energize,** *v.tr.* donner de l'énergie à (qn); stimuler (qn); amorcer (une dynamo).

enervate ['enəveit], *v.tr.* affaiblir, amollir, énerver (le corps, la volonté).

enforce [in'fɔːs], *v.tr.* **1.** faire valoir (un argument); appuyer (une demande). **2.** mettre en vigueur, exécuter; **to e. one's rights,** faire valoir ses droits; **to e. the law,** appliquer la loi. **3. to e. a rule,** faire observer un règlement; **to e. obedience,** se faire obéir.

engage [in'geidʒ], *v.tr. & i.* **1.** engager (sa parole); **to e. to do sth.,** s'engager à faire qch. **2.** (*a*) embaucher (des ouvriers); (*b*) retenir, réserver (une chambre); louer (un taxi). **3. to e. s.o. in conversation,** lier conversation avec qn. **4.** *E:* (*a*) mettre en prise (un engrenage); (*b*) (*of cogwheel*) s'engrener (**with,** avec); **en'gaged,** *a.* **1. to become e.,** se fiancer. **2.** (*of seat, taxi*) occupé, pris; **en'gagement,** *s.* **1.** (*a*) promesse *f*, obligation *f*; (*b*) rendez-vous *m*. **2.** fiançailles *fpl*; **e. ring,** bague *f* de fiançailles. **3.** *E:* embrayage *m*; mise *f* en prise; **en'gaging,** *a.* (*of pers.*) attrayant, séduisant.

engine ['endʒin], *s.* **1.** machine *f*, appareil *m*. **2.** *Rail:* locomotive *f*; **electric e.,** locomotrice *f*. **3.** moteur *m*; **two-stroke e.,** moteur à deux temps; **'engine-driver,** *s.* mécanicien *m*; **engi'neer. I.** *s.* **1.** ingénieur *m*. **2.** *Nau:* mécanicien *m*. **3.** *Mil:* soldat *m* du génie; **the Engineers,** le génie. **II.** *v.tr.* **1.** construire (en qualité d'ingénieur). **2.** machiner (un coup); manigancer (une affaire); **engi'neering,** *s.* technique *f* de l'ingénieur; l'industrie *f* mécanique; **chemical e.,** la chimie industrielle; **electrical e.,** électrotechnique *f*; **nuclear e.,** génie *m* atomique; **electronic e.,** l'électronique *f*; **production e.,** technique de la production.

England ['iŋglənd]. *Pr.n. Geog:* l'Angleterre *f*; **in E.,** en Angleterre.

English ['iŋgliʃ]. **1.** *a. & s.* anglais, -aise; **the E.,** les Anglais. **2.** *s. Ling:* l'anglais *m*; la langue anglaise; **'Englishman,** *pl.* **-men,** *f.* **'Englishwoman,** *pl.* **-women,** *s.* Anglais, -aise.

engrave [in'greiv], *v.tr.* graver; **en'graver,** *s.* graveur *m*; **en'graving,** *s.* (*process or print*) gravure *f*; (*print*) estampe *f*.

engross [in'grous], *v.tr.* absorber, occuper (qn, l'attention de qn); **to become engrossed in sth.,** s'absorber dans qch.

engulf [in'gʌlf], *v.tr.* engloutir, engouffrer.

enhance [in'hɑːns], *v.tr.* rehausser (le mérite de qn, qch.); augmenter (le plaisir); relever (la beauté de qn).

enigma [i'nigmə], *s.* énigme *f*; **enig'matic,** *a.* énigmatique.

enjoy [in'dʒɔi], v.tr. 1. aimer, goûter; prendre plaisir à (qch.); **to e. one's dinner,** trouver le dîner bon; **to e. oneself,** s'amuser; **to e. doing sth.,** prendre plaisir à faire qch. 2. jouir de, posséder (la santé, la confiance de qn); **en'joyable,** a. agréable; (of food) savoureux; **an e. evening,** une excellente soirée; **-ably,** adv. agréablement; avec plaisir; **en'joyment,** s. 1. jouissance f (d'un droit, etc.). 2. plaisir m.

enlarge [in'lɑːdʒ]. 1. v.tr. (a) agrandir; augmenter (sa fortune); élargir (un trou); Phot: agrandir (un cliché); (b) développer; amplifier (une idée). 2. v.i. **to e. (up)on,** s'étendre sur (un sujet); **en'largement,** s. agrandissement m; **en'larger,** s. Phot: agrandisseur m.

enlighten [in'laitn], v.tr. éclairer (qn sur un sujet); **en'lightened,** a. éclairé; **en'lightenment,** s. éclaircissements mpl (on, sur).

enlist [in'list]. 1. v.tr. (a) enrôler (un soldat); **to e. the services of s.o.,** s'assurer le concours de qn. 2. v.i. s'engager, s'enrôler; **en'listed,** a. U.S: Mil: **e. man,** simple soldat, marin; **en'listment,** s. Mil: engagement m, enrôlement m.

enliven [in'laiv(ə)n], v.tr. (a) animer (qn, qch.); stimuler (les affaires); (b) égayer (une fête).

enmity ['enmiti], s. hostilité f; haine f (**towards, for, s.o.,** envers, pour, qn); **to be at e. with s.o.,** être en guerre ouverte avec qn.

enormous [i'nɔːməs], a. énorme; (succès) fou; **-ly,** adv. énormément.

enough [i'nʌf]. 1. a. & s. assez; **e. money,** assez d'argent; **I've had e. of it,** j'en ai assez; **that's e.,** (i) cela suffit; (ii) en voilà assez! **more than e.,** plus qu'il n'en faut; **have you e. to pay the bill?** avez-vous de quoi payer? **he has e. to live on,** il a de quoi vivre; **it was e. to drive one crazy,** c'était à vous rendre fou. 2. adv. (a) **good e.,** assez bon; (b) **you know well e. what I mean,** vous savez très bien ce que je veux dire; **curiously e., oddly e.,** chose curieuse; **she sings well e.,** elle ne chante pas mal.

enquire [in'kwaiər], v.i. s'informer, se renseigner (sur qch.); **to e. after s.o.,** demander des nouvelles de la santé de qn; **to e. into sth.,** faire des recherches sur qch.; **en'quiry,** s. 1. enquête f; **to hold an e.,** procéder à une enquête. 2. demande f de renseignements; **enquiries,** bureau m de renseignements.

enrage [in'reidʒ], v.tr. rendre (qn) furieux; faire (en)rager (qn).

enrapture [in'ræptʃər], v.tr. ravir, enchanter (un auditoire).

enrich [in'ritʃ], v.tr. enrichir; **en'richment,** s. enrichissement m.

enrol [in'roul], v.tr. (**enrolled**) enrôler, encadrer (des recrues); embaucher (des ouvriers); im-matriculer (des étudiants).

ensign ['ens(ə)n], s. Nau: 1. pavillon national; **red e.** = pavillon marchand. 2. U.S: enseigne m (de vaisseau de deuxième classe).

enslave [in'sleiv], v.tr. asservir; **en'slavement,** s. asservissement m.

ensue [in'sjuː], v.i. s'ensuivre; **a long silence ensued,** il se fit un long silence.

ensure [in'ʃuər], v.tr. 1. assurer (**against, from,** contre); garantir (de). 2. assurer (le succès).

entail [in'teil, en-], v.tr. amener, entraîner (des conséquences); occasionner (des dépenses); comporter (des difficultés).

entangle [in'tæŋgl], v.tr. 1. empêtrer; **to get entangled,** s'empêtrer; **to get entangled in a shady affair,** se trouver entraîné dans une affaire louche. 2. emmêler (du fil); embrouiller (les idées); (of thread) **to get entangled,** s'emmêler; **en'tanglement,** embrouillement m, enchevêtrement m.

entente [ɑ̃ː'tɑ̃ːt], s. entente f.

enter ['entər]. 1. v.i. entrer (**into, through,** dans, par); **to e. into relations with s.o.,** entrer en relations avec qn. 2. v.tr. (a) entrer, pénétrer, dans (une maison); monter dans (une voiture); s'engager dans (un défilé); s'engager sur (une route); (b) **to e. the Army,** entrer au service, se faire soldat; (c) **to e. a name on a list,** inscrire un nom sur une liste; **to e. a horse for a race,** engager un cheval dans une course; abs. **to e. (for a race),** se faire inscrire (pour une course).

enterprise ['entəpraiz], s. 1. entreprise f; Pol.Ec: **private e.,** secteur privé; **public e.,** secteur public. 2. esprit m d'entreprise, hardiesse f; **'enterprising,** a. entreprenant.

entertain [entə'tein], v.tr. 1. amuser, divertir (qn). 2. offrir un repas à (qn); abs. recevoir des amis. 3. admettre, accueillir (une proposition). 4. concevoir (une idée); éprouver (des craintes); nourrir, caresser (un espoir); **enter'taining,** a. amusant, divertissant; **enter'tainment,** s. 1. (a) divertissement m; **much to the e. of the crowd,** au grand amusement de la foule; (b) Th: etc: spectacle m. 2. hospitalité f; Adm: **e. allowance,** frais mpl de représentation.

enthusiasm [in'θjuːziæzm], s. enthousiasme m (**for, about,** pour); **en'thuse,** v.i. s'enthousiasmer, se passionner (**over, about, sth.,** de, pour, qch.); **en'thusiast,** s. enthousiaste mf; fervent(e), F: enragé(e) (du ski, etc.); **enthusi'astic,** a. enthousiaste; **to become e. over sth.,** s'enthousiasmer pour qch.; **-ally,** adv. avec enthousiasme.

entice [in'tais], v.tr. attirer, séduire (qn); attirer (un animal dans un piège).

entire [in'taiər], a. (a) entier, tout; **the e. population,** la population (tout) entière; (b) entier complet; **an e. success**, un vrai succès; **-ly**, *adv.* entièrement, tout à fait; **en'tirety**, *s.* intégralité *f*; **in its e.**, en entier, totalement, intégralement.

entitle [in'taitl], *v.tr.* **to e. s.o. to do sth.**, donner à qn le droit de faire qch.; **en'titled**, *a.* **to be e. to sth.**, avoir droit à qch.; **to be e. to do sth.**, être en droit, avoir le droit, de faire qch.; **en'titlement**, *s.* droit *m*, titre *m* (à qch., à avoir qch.); **e. to a pension**, droit à la retraite.

entity ['entiti], *s.* entité *f*.

entomology [entə'mɔlədʒi], *s.* entomologie *f*; **entomo'logical**, *a.* entomologique.

entrance[1] ['entrəns], *s.* **1.** (*a*) entrée *f*; *P.N:* **no e.**, défense d'entrer; **to make one's e.**, faire son entrée; **e. gate**, barrière *f*; grille *f* d'entrée; (*b*) admission *f*, accès *m*; **e. fee**, (i) prix *m* d'entrée; (ii) (*for club, etc.*) droit *m* d'inscription. **2.** **main e.**, entrée principale; **side e.**, porte *f* de service.

entrance[2] [in'trɑːns], *v.tr.* extasier, ravir (qn); **en'trancing**, *a.* enchanteur, ravissant.

entrap [in'træp], *v.tr.* (**entrapped**) prendre (qn) au piège.

entreat [in'triːt], *v.tr.* **to e. s.o. to do sth.**, prier, supplier, qn de faire qch.; **en'treating**, *a.* (ton, regard) suppliant; **-ly**, *adv.* d'un air, d'un ton, suppliant; **en'treaty**, *s.* prière *f*, supplication *f*.

entrench [in'trenʃ], *v.tr. Mil:* retrancher; **firmly entrenched**, solidement retranché.

entrepreneur [ɑ̃trəprə'nəːr], *s. Com:* entrepreneur *m*; **entrepre'neurial**, *a.* (décision) d'entrepreneur.

entrust [in'trʌst], *v.tr.* **to e. s.o. with (a task, etc.)**, charger qn d'(une tâche, etc.); **to e. (a secret, a child, to s.o.)**, confier (un secret, un enfant, à qn).

entry ['entri], *s.* **1.** (*a*) entrée *f*; *P.N:* **no e.**, (i) (*= one way street*) sens interdit; (ii) passage interdit (au public); (*b*) **to make one's e.**, faire son entrée; (*c*) début *m* (dans la politique, etc.). **2.** (*a*) enregistrement *m*; inscription *f*; (*b*) *Book-k:* **single, double, e.**, comptabilité *f* en partie simple, en partie double. **3.** *Sp:* inscription (d'un concurrent).

entwine [in'twain]. **1.** *v.tr.* (*a*) entrelacer; (*b*) enlacer (**with**, de). **2.** *v.i.* s'entrelacer.

enumerate [i'njuːməreit], *v.tr.* énumérer, détailler (des faits, des articles); **enume'ration**, *s.* énumération *f*.

enunciate [i'nʌnsieit], *v.tr.* **1.** énoncer, exprimer (une opinion). **2.** prononcer, articuler (distinctement).

envelop [in'veləp], *v.tr.* (**enveloped**) envelopper (**in**, dans, de); **envelope** ['envəloup, 'ɔn-], *s.* enveloppe *f*; **to put a letter in an e.**, mettre une lettre sous enveloppe.

environment [in'vaiərənmənt], *s.* milieu *m*, entourage *m*; ambiance *f*, environnement *m*; **the Department of the E.**, le Ministère de l'Environnement; **environ'mental**, *a.* (étude) qui a rapport à l'environnement.

envisage [in'vizidʒ], *v.tr.* envisager (une difficulté, un danger).

envoy ['envɔi], *s.* envoyé, -ée (diplomatique).

envy ['envi]. **I.** *s.* **1.** envie *f*; **to be green with e.**, être dévoré d'envie, *F:* en faire une jaunisse. **2.** objet *m* d'envie. **II.** *v.tr.* envier, porter envie à (qn); **to e. s.o. sth.**, envier qch. à qn; **'enviable**, *a.* enviable, digne d'envie; **'envious**, *a.* envieux; **-ly**, *adv.* avec envie.

ephemeral [i'femərəl], *a.* (beauté *f*, joie *f*) éphémère.

epic ['epik]. **1.** *a.* épique. **2.** *s.* poème *m* épique; épopée *f*.

epicure ['epikjuər], *s.* gourmet *m*, gastronome *m*; **epicu'rean**, *a.* épicurien.

epidemic [epi'demik]. **1.** *a.* épidémique. **2.** *s.* épidémie *f*.

epigram ['epigræm], *s.* épigramme *f*.

epilepsy ['epilepsi], *s.* épilepsie *f*; **epi'leptic**, *a.* & *s.* épileptique (*mf*).

epilogue ['epilɔg], *s.* épilogue *m*.

Epiphany [i'pifəni], *s. Ecc:* l'Épiphanie *f*; *F:* le jour, la fête, des Rois.

episcopal [i'piskəp(ə)l], *a.* épiscopal; **e. ring**, anneau pastoral; (*esp. U.S:* & *Scot:*) **the E. Church**, l'église épiscopale.

episode ['episoud], *s.* épisode *m*.

epitaph ['epitɑːf], *s.* épitaphe *f*.

epithet ['epiθet], *s.* épithète *f*.

epoch ['iːpɔk], *s.* époque *f*, âge *m*; **'epoch-making**, *a.* historique, mémorable, inoubliable.

equable ['ekwəbl], *a.* uniforme, régulier; **e. temperament**, humeur égale; **equa'bility**, *s.* uniformité *f* (de climat); égalité *f*, régularité *f* (d'humeur).

equal ['iːkwəl]. **I.** *v.tr.* (**equalled**) égaler (**in**, en). **II.** *a.* (*a*) égal (**to, with**, à); **to be on e. terms**, être sur un pied d'égalité (avec qn); **all things being e.**, toutes choses égales; **to get e. with s.o.**, se venger de qn; (*b*) **to be e. to the occasion**, être à la hauteur de la situation; **I don't feel e. to (doing) it**, je ne m'en sens pas le courage. **III.** *s.* égal, -ale; pair *m*; **your equals**, vos pareils; **to treat s.o. as an e.**, traiter qn d'égal à égal; **-ally**, *adv.* également, pareillement; **equality** [i'kwɔliti], *s.* égalité *f*; **'equalize.** **1.** *v.tr.* (*a*) égaliser; *Fb:* **to e. (the score)**, marquer égalité de points; (*b*) compenser, équilibrer (des forces, etc.). **2.** *v.i.* (*a*) s'égaliser; (*b*) s'équilibrer.

equanimity [ekwə'nimiti], *s.* égalité *f* d'âme, de caractère; tranquillité *f* d'esprit; équanimité *f*.

equation [i'kweiʒ(ə)n], *s. Mth:* équation *f*.

equator [i'kweitər], s. équateur m; **at the e.,** sous l'équateur; **equa'torial,** a. équatorial.

equestrian [i'kwestriən]. **1.** a. (statue) équestre. **2.** s. cavalier, -ière.

equilateral [i:kwi'lætərəl], a. *Mth:* équilatéral.

equilibrium [i:kwi'libriəm], s. équilibre m, aplomb m.

equine ['ekwain], a. équin; de cheval; **e. race,** race chevaline.

equinox ['ekwinɔks, 'i:k-], s. équinoxe m; **equi'noctial** [-'nɔkʃ(ə)l], a. équinoxial; **e. tides,** grandes marées; **e. gale,** vent m d'équinoxe.

equip [i:'kwip], v.tr. **(equipped) 1.** équiper, armer (un navire, etc.). **2.** meubler, monter (une maison); outiller, monter (une usine); **to e. s.o. with a weapon,** munir qn d'une arme; **well-equipped,** (laboratoire) bien installé; (ménage) bien monté; **e'quipment, s.** (a) équipement m; armement m (d'un navire); outillage m (d'une usine); installation f (d'un laboratoire); (b) **maintenance e.,** matériel m d'entretien; **sports e.,** équipement sportif; **camping e.,** matériel de camping.

equity ['ekwiti], s. équité f, justice f;'**equitable,** a. équitable, juste; **-ably,** adv. avec justice, équitablement.

equivalent [i'kwivələnt], a. & s. équivalent (m); **e'quivalence,** s. équivalence f; *Fin:* parité f (de change).

equivocate [i'kwivəkeit], v.i. user d'équivoque f; équivoquer; tergiverser; **e'quivocal,** a. (a) équivoque; ambigu, f. -uë; (b) incertain, douteux; louche; **-ally,** adv. d'une manière équivoque; **equivo'cation,** s. équivoque f; tergiversation f.

era ['iərə], s. ère f.

eradicate [i'rædikeit], v.tr. extirper (des préjugés); déraciner (des plantes).

erase [i'reiz], v.tr. effacer; raturer, gommer (un mot); **e'raser,** s. gomme f (à effacer); **e'rasure,** s. rature f.

erect [i'rekt]. **I.** a. (of pers.) droit, debout; **with tail e.,** la queue levée; **with head e.,** la tête haute. **II.** v.tr. **1.** dresser (un mât, un échafaudage). **2.** ériger, construire (un édifice); **e'rection,** s. **1.** (a) dressage m (d'un mât); (b) construction f (d'un édifice), érection f (d'une statue); montage m, installation f (d'une machine). **2.** bâtisse f, construction, édifice m.

erode [i'roud], v.tr. éroder; ronger; (of acid) corroder; **e'rosion,** s. érosion f; usure f; *Geog:* érosion, dénudation f.

erotic [i'rɔtik], a. érotique; **e'roticism,** s. érotisme m.

err [ə:r], v.i. (a) pécher; **to e. out of ignorance,** pécher par ignorance; (b) se tromper.

errand ['erənd], s. commission f, course f; **to run errands,** faire des courses.

erratic [i'rætik], a. **1.** irrégulier. **2.** (of pers.) excentrique, fantasque; **e. life,** vie désordonnée; **-ally,** adv. sans méthode, sans règle.

error ['erər], s. **1.** erreur f, faute f, méprise f; **printer's e.,** faute d'impression; **typing e.,** faute de frappe. **2. to be in e.,** être dans l'erreur; avoir tort; **erroneous** [i'rouniəs], a. erroné, faux; **-ly,** adv. à tort; par erreur.

erudite ['eru:dait], a. érudit, savant; **eru'dition,** s. érudition f.

erupt [i'rʌpt], v.i. (of volcano) entrer en éruption; faire éruption; **e'ruption,** s. (a) éruption f; (b) accès m (de colère, etc.).

escalate ['eskəleit], v.i. (of prices) monter (en flèche); (of conflict) s'intensifier (rapidement); **esca'lation,** s. escalade f (des prix, d'un conflit).

escalator ['eskəleitər], s. escalier roulant.

escape [is'keip, es-]. **I.** s. (a) fuite f, évasion f; **to make one's e.,** s'échapper, se sauver; **to have a narrow e.,** l'échapper belle; *Jur: Com:* **e. clause,** clause f échappatoire; (b) échappement m, fuite (de gaz, etc.); (c) (fire-)e., escalier m de secours. **II.** v. **1.** v.i. s'échapper **(from, out of,** de); prendre la fuite; s'évader (de prison); (of gases) se dégager, fuir. **2.** v.tr. (of pers.) (a) échapper à (un danger); (b) **to e. notice,** passer inaperçu; **that fact escaped me,** ce fait m'avait échappé; **'escapade,** s. escapade f, frasque f; **esca'pee,** s. évadé, -ée; **es'capism,** s. évasion f (de la réalité).

escort. I. s. ['eskɔ:t], escorte. f. **II.** v.tr. [is'kɔ:t, es-], escorter; **to e. s.o. home,** reconduire qn.

Eskimo ['eskimou], a. & s. esquimau, -aude.

esoteric [esou'terik], a. ésotérique.

especial [is'peʃ(ə)l], a. spécial, particulier; **-ally,** adv. surtout, particulièrement.

espionage ['espiɔnɑːʒ], s. espionnage m.

esplanade [esplə'neid], s. esplanade f.

espresso [es'presou], s. **e. (coffee),** café express.

esquire [is'kwaiər, es-], s. (abbr. **Esq.,** used in the written address on envelope) **J. Martin, Esq.** = Monsieur J. Martin.

essay ['esei], s. **1.** essai m, effort m; tentative f. **2.** (a) *Lit:* essai; (b) *Sch:* dissertation f; composition f (littéraire).

essence ['esəns], s. essence f; **the e. of the matter,** le fond de l'affaire; **meat e.,** extrait m de viande; **essential** [i'senʃəl]. **1.** a. (outil, produit) essentiel, indispensable. **2.** s. usu. pl. l'essentiel m; **-ally,** adv. essentiellement.

establish [is'tæbliʃ], v.tr. **1.** établir (un gouvernement); fonder (une maison de commerce); créer (une agence); se faire (une réputation); **to e. oneself (in business),** s'établir; **to e. oneself in a new house**

s'installer dans une maison neuve. 2. établir, constater (un fait); démontrer (l'identité de qn); **established reputation,** réputation *f* solide; **es′tablishment,** *s.* 1. (*a*) constatation *f* (d'un fait); (*b*) établissement *m* (d'une industrie); création *f* (d'un système); fondation *f* (d'une maison de commerce); **a business e.,** une maison de commerce. 2. personnel *m* (d'une maison). 3. **the E.,** l'ordre établi.

estate [is′teit, es-], *s.* 1. (*a*) domaine *m*; (*b*) succession *f* (d'un défunt). 2. (*a*) terre *f,* propriété *f*; (*b*) **housing e.,** (i) lotissement *m*; (ii) cité *f,* groupe *m* de HLM; (*c*) **e. agent,** agent immobilier; **e. agency,** agence immobilière; (*c*) *Aut:* **e. car,** break *m.*

esteem [is′ti:m]. I. *s.* estime *f,* considération *f*; **to hold s.o. in high, in low, e.,** avoir qn en haute estime; peu estimer qn. II. *v.tr.* 1. estimer (qn); priser (qch.). 2. estimer, considérer (**as, comme**); **estimable** [′estiməbl], *a.* estimable.

estimate. I. *s.* [′estimət]. 1. appréciation *f,* évaluation *f*; **to form a correct e. of sth.,** se faire une idée exacte de qch.; **at the lowest e.,** au bas mot. 2. (**building**) **e.,** devis *m* (de construction); **to put in an e.,** soumissionner; **e. of expenditure,** chiffre prévu pour les dépenses. II. *v.tr.* [′estimeit], estimer, évaluer (les frais); **estimated cost,** coût estimatif; **esti′mation,** *s.* jugement *m.*

estuary [′estju(ə)ri], *s.* estuaire *m.*

etch [etʃ], *v.tr.* graver à l'eau-forte; **′etcher,** *s.* aquafortiste *mf,* graveur *m* à l'eau-forte; **′etching,** *s.* eau-forte *f, pl.* eaux-fortes.

eternity [i(:)′tə:niti], *s.* éternité *f*; **e′ternal,** *a.* (*a*) éternel; (*b*) *F:* continuel; sans fin; **-ally,** *adv.* éternellement.

ether [′i:θər]. *s.* éther *m.*

ethics [′eθiks], *s.pl.* (*usu. with sg. const.*) éthique *f,* morale *f*; **′ethic(al),** *a.* moral.

Ethiopia [i:θi′oupjə]. *Pr.n. Geog:* l'Éthiopie *f.*

ethnology [eθ′nɔlədʒi], *s.* ethnologie *f*; **ethno′logical,** *a.* ethnologique; **eth′nologist,** *s.* ethnologue *mf.*

etiquette [′etiket], *s.* étiquette *f*; convenances *fpl*; cérémonial *m*; le protocole (diplomatique, etc.).

etymology [eti′mɔlədʒi], *s.* étymologie *f*; **etymo′logical,** *a.* étymologique; **-ally,** *adv.* étymologiquement; **ety′mologist,** *s.* étymologiste *mf.*

Eucharist (the) [ðə′ju:kərist], *s. Ecc:* l'eucharistie *f.*

eulogy [′ju:lədʒi], *s.* éloge *m,* panégyrique *m*; **′eulogize,** *v.tr.* faire l'éloge, le panégyrique, de (qn, qch.).

euphemism [′ju:fəmizm], *s.* euphémisme *m*; **euphe′mistic,** *a.* euphémique; **-ally,** *adv.* par euphémisme.

euphoria [ju:′fɔ:riə], *s.* euphorie *f.*

Europe [′juərəp]. *Pr.n. Geog:* l'Europe *f*; **Euro′pean,** *a. & s.* européen, -enne.

Eurovision [′juərəviʒ(ə)n]. *Pr.n.* Eurovision *f.*

euthanasia [ju:θə′neiziə], *s.* euthanasie *f.*

evacuate [i′vækjueit], *v.tr.* évacuer; **evacu′ation,** *s.* évacuation *f.*

evade [i′veid], *v.tr.* 1. éviter (un coup, un danger); se soustraire à (un châtiment); tourner (une question); déjouer (la vigilance de qn). 2. (*of things*) échapper à (l'intelligence).

evaluate [i′væljueit], *v.tr.* évaluer (les dommages); **evalu′ation,** *s.* évaluation *f* (des dommages).

evanescent [i:və′nesənt], *a.* évanescent; (gloire, etc.) éphémère.

evangelical [i:væn′dʒelikəl], *a.* qui appartient à la religion reformée.

evaporate [i′væpəreit]. 1. *v.tr.* faire évaporer (un liquide). 2. *v.i.* s'évaporer, se vaporiser; **evapo′ration,** *s.* évaporation *f.*

evasion [i′veiʒ(ə)n], *s.* 1. évitement *m*; dérobade *f.* 2. échappatoire *f*; **without e.,** sans détours; **evasive** [i′veisiv], *a.* évasif; **-ly,** *adv.* évasivement.

eve [i:v], *s.* veille *f*; **Christmas E.,** la veille de Noël.

even [′i:v(ə)n]. I. *a.* 1. (*a*) (*of surface*) uni; plan; égal; uniforme; (*b*) (*of spacing, weights, etc.*) égal. 2. (souffle) régulier; **e. pace,** allure uniforme; **e. temper,** humeur égale. 3. *Sp:* **to be e.,** être manche à manche, être à égalité; **to get e. with s.o.,** rendre la pareille à qn; *Fin:* **to break e.,** ne faire ni pertes ni profits. 4. (*a*) (nombre) pair; **odd or e.,** (pair ou impair); (*b*) **e. money,** compte rond. 5. *Com:* **of e. date,** de même date; **-ly,** *adv.* 1. (étendre qch.) uniment. 2. (*a*) (respirer) régulièrement; (diviser) également; (*b*) **e. matched,** de force égale. II. *v.tr.* 1. aplanir, niveler, égaliser (une surface). 2. rendre égal; **that will e. things up,** cela rétablira l'équilibre. III. *adv.* même; (*with comparative*) encore; (*with negative*) seulement, même; **e. the cleverest,** même les plus habiles; **e. the children knew,** même les enfants le savaient; **that would be e. worse,** ce serait encore pire; **without e. speaking,** sans seulement parler; **e. so,** mais cependant, quand même; encore; **e. now,** à l'instant même; **e. then,** même alors; **′evenness,** *s.* 1. égalité *f*; régularité *f* (de mouvement). 2. sérénité *f* (d'esprit); égalité (d'humeur).

evening [′i:vniŋ], *s.* soir *m*; soirée *f*; **this e.,** ce soir; **tomorrow e.,** demain (au) soir; **in the e.,** le soir, au soir; **at nine o'clock in the e.,** à neuf heures du soir; (**on**) **the previous e., the e. before,** la veille au soir; **on the e. of the next day, the next e.,** le lendemain (au) soir; **one fine**

summer e., (par) un beau soir d'été; **every e.,** tous les soirs; **all (the) e.,** toute la soirée; *Th:* **e. performance,** (représentation de) soirée; **'evening-'dress,** s. (*man*) tenue *f* de soirée; **to be in e.-d.,** être en smoking *m*; (*woman*) robe *f* du soir; toilette *f* de soirée.

event [i'vent], s. **1.** cas *m*; **in the e. of his refusing,** au cas, dans le cas, où il refuserait. **2.** événement *m*; (*a*) **in the course of events,** au cours des événements; (*b*) issue *f*, résultat *m*; **in either e.,** dans l'un ou l'autre cas; **in any e.,** quoi qu'il arrive; **at all events,** dans tous les cas; en tout cas. **3.** *Sp:* (*a*) réunion sportive; (*b*) (*athletics*) **field events,** épreuves *f* sur terrain; **track events,** courses *f* sur piste; **e'ventful,** *a.* plein d'événements; mouvementé; (jour) mémorable.

eventual [i'ventjuəl], *a.* **1.** (profit, etc.) éventuel. **2.** définitif; final; **his e. ruin,** sa ruine finale; **-ally,** *adv.* finalement, en fin de compte, par la suite, dans la suite; **eventu'ality,** s. éventualité *f.*

ever ['evər], *adv.* **1.** jamais; (*a*) **if e. I catch him,** si jamais je l'attrape; **nothing e. happens,** il n'arrive jamais rien; **he hardly e. smokes,** il ne fume presque jamais; **do you e. miss the train?** vous arrive-t-il jamais de manquer le train? **it started to rain harder than e.,** il se mit à pleuvoir de plus belle; **it's as warm as e.,** il fait toujours aussi chaud; (*b*) **e. since (then),** dès lors, depuis (lors); **they lived happily e. after,** depuis lors ils vécurent toujours heureux. **2.** (*a*) toujours; *Corr:* **yours e.,** bien (cordialement) à vous; (*b*) **for e.,** pour toujours; à jamais, à perpétuité; **gone for e.,** parti sans retour; **for e. and e.,** à tout jamais; **Scotland for e.!** vive l'Écosse! **he's for e. grumbling,** il grogne sans cesse. **3.** (*intensive*) (*a*) **as quick as e. you can,** du plus vite que vous pourrez; **e. so difficult,** difficile au possible; **e. so long ago,** il y a bien, bien longtemps; **I waited e. so long,** j'ai attendu un temps infini; **thank you e. so much,** merci infiniment; (*b*) **how e. did you manage?** comment diable avez-vous fait? **what e. shall we do?** qu'est-ce que nous allons bien faire? **what e.'s the matter with you?** mais qu'est-ce que vous avez donc? **why e. not?** mais pourquoi pas? **'evergreen. 1.** *a.* toujours vert; (arbre) à feuilles persistantes. **2.** *s.pl.* plantes vertes; **ever'lasting,** *a.* (*a*) éternel; (*b*) (*of object*) solide, durable; (*c*) perpétuel; (plaintes) sans fin.

every ['evri], *a.* (*a*) chaque; tout; tous; **e. day,** chaque jour, tous les jours; **e. other day,** tous les deux jours; **e. few minutes,** toutes les cinq minutes; **I expect him e. minute,** je l'attends d'un instant à l'autre; (*b*) (*intensive*) **I have e. reason to believe that . . .,** j'ai toute raison de

croire que . . .; (*c*) **e. 'one,** chacun, chacune; tout le monde; **'everybody, 'everyone,** *indef.pron.* chacun; tout le monde; tous; **as e. knows,** comme chacun sait; **e.'s here,** tout le monde est ici; **'every'day,** *a.* journalier, quotidien; **e. occurrence,** fait banal; **e. life,** la vie quotidienne; **e. clothes,** vêtements de tous les jours; **e. English,** l'anglais usuel; **in e. use,** d'usage courant; **'everything,** *indef. pron.* tout; **they sell e.,** on y vend de tout; **'everywhere,** *adv.* partout.

evict [i'vikt], *v.tr.* évincer, expulser (qn) (**from,** de); **e'viction,** s. éviction *f*, expulsion *f.*

evidence ['evid(ə)ns], s. **1.** évidence *f*; **a man much in e.,** un homme très en vue; **his sister was not in e.,** sa sœur n'était pas là. **2.** signe *m*, marque *f*; (*of pers.*) **to give e. of intelligence,** faire preuve d'intelligence. **3.** (*a*) preuve *f*; (*b*) *Jur:* témoignage *m*; **to give e.,** témoigner; (*c*) *Jur:* **the e. for the prosecution,** les témoins *m* à charge; **to turn Queen's e.,** *U.S:* **State's e.,** dénoncer ses complices (sous promesse de pardon); **'evident,** *a.* évident; **-ly,** *adv.* évidemment, manifestement.

evil ['i:v(ə)l]. **1.** *a.* mauvais; (*a*) **e.-minded,** mal intentionné, malveillant; (*b*) méchant; **e. influence,** influence néfaste. **2.** *s.* mal *m*, *pl.* maux; **a social e.,** une plaie sociale; **to speak e. of s.o.,** dire du mal de qn.

evoke [i'vouk], *v.tr.* évoquer, susciter (un sourire); **evo'cation** [ivə-], s. évocation *f*; **e'vocative** [i'vɔk-], *a.* évocateur.

evolve [i'vɔlv]. **1.** *v.tr.* dérouler; développer (des projets); élaborer (une méthode); développer, déduire (une théorie). **2.** *v.i.* (*a*) (*of events*) se dérouler; (*b*) (*of race, species*) se développer, évoluer; **evo'lution** [i:və-], s. évolution *f.*

ewe [ju:], s. brebis *f.*

ex- [eks], *pref.* ex-; **ex-minister,** ex-ministre *m* **ex-schoolmaster,** ancien professeur.

exacerbate [eg'zæsəbeit], *v.tr.* exacerber aggraver (une douleur, etc.).

exact[1] [ig'zækt, eg-], *a.* exact; (*a*) **e. details** détails précis; **e. copy,** copie textuelle (d'un document); (*b*) **the e. word,** le mot juste; **-ly** *adv.* exactement, précisément; tout juste justement; **e.!** parfaitement! **ex'actitude,** *s.* **ex'actness,** s. exactitude *f*, précision *f.*

exact[2], *v.tr.* (*a*) exiger (**from,** de); (*b*) extorque (une rançon); (*c*) réclamer (beaucoup d soins); **ex'acting,** *a.* (*of pers.*) exigeant; (*o work*) astreignant; **ex'action,** s. deman exorbitante (d'argent).

exaggerate [ig'zædʒəreit], *v.tr.* exagérer **exagge'ration,** s. exagération *f.*

examine [ig'zæmin, eg-], *v.tr.* examiner; in specter (une machine); *Cust:* visiter (le bagages); vérifier (des comptes); *Sch:* fair

passer un examen à (qn); **ex'am,** *Sch: F:*
examen; **competitive e.,** concours *m*;
exami'nation, *s.* examen *m*; vérification *f*;
visite (médicale); **exami'nee,** *s. Sch:* candidat, -ate; **ex'aminer,** *s.* 1. inspecteur, -trice.
2. *Sch:* examinateur, -trice; **the examiners,** le
jury (d'examen).
example [ig'zɑ:mpl], *s.* exemple *m.* 1. **to quote
sth. as an e.,** citer qch. en exemple; **for e.,** par
exemple. 2. précédent *m.* 3. **to set an e.,** donner
l'exemple; **to take s.o. as an e.,** prendre exemple sur qn.
exasperate [ig'zɑ:spəreit], *v.tr.* exaspérer, irriter (qn); **exaspe'ration,** *s.* exaspération *f*;
to drive s.o. to e., pousser qn à bout.
excavate ['ekskəveit], *v.tr.* creuser (un tunnel);
fouiller (la terre); *abs.* faire des fouilles;
exca'vation, *s.* excavation *f*; fouille *f*;
Archeol: usu. pl. fouilles; **'excavator,** *s.
Civ. E:* excavateur *m*, excavatrice *f.*
exceed [ik'si:d, ek-], *v.tr.* (*a*) excéder, dépasser
(ses droits); **to e. one's powers,** sortir de sa
compétence; *Aut:* **to e. the speed limit,**
dépasser la vitesse légale; (*b*) surpasser (**in,
en**); **ex'ceedingly,** *adv.* très, extrêmement,
excessivement.
excel [ik'sel, ek-], *v.* (**excelled**) 1. *v.i.* exceller (**in,
at, sth.,** à qch.). 2. *v.tr.* surpasser (qn); **to e.
oneself,** se surpasser; **'excellence,** *s.*
excellence *f*; perfection *f* (d'un ouvrage); mérite
m (de qn); **'excellency,** *s.* **Your E.,** (votre)
Excellence; **'excellent,** *a.* excellent, parfait;
-ly, *adv.* excellemment, parfaitement.
except [ik'sept, ek-]. I. *v.tr.* excepter, exclure
(**from,** de). II. *prep.* excepté; à l'exception de;
sauf; **he does nothing e. sleep,** il ne fait rien
sinon dormir; **nobody heard it e. myself,** il n'y
a que moi qui l'aie entendu; **e. by agreement
. . .,** sauf accord . . .; **e. that,** excepté que,
sauf que; **ex'ception,** *s.* 1. exception *f*; **with
the e. of,** à l'exception de, exception faite de;
with that e., we are agreed, à cela près, nous
sommes d'accord; **with certain exceptions,**
sauf exceptions. 2. objection *f*; **to take e. to
sth.,** (i) trouver à redire à qch.; (ii) s'offenser, se
froisser, de qch.; **ex'ceptionable,** *a.*
blâmable, répréhensible; **ex'ceptional,** *a.*
exceptionnel; **-ally,** *adv.* exceptionnellement.
excerpt ['eksəpt], *s.* extrait *m*, citation *f.*
excess. *s.* 1. [ik'ses], excès *m*; **in e., to e.,**
(jusqu')à l'excès. 2. (*a*) [ik'ses] excédent *m* (de
poids, etc.); (*b*) *a.* ['ekses]. *Rail: etc:* **e. fare,**
supplément *m*; **e. luggage,** bagages *mpl* en surpoids *m*; **ex'cessive,** *a.* excessif; immodéré;
extrême; **-ly,** *adv.* excessivement; (boire) à
l'excès.
exchange [iks'tʃeindʒ, eks-]. I. *s.* 1. échange *m*;
e. and barter, troc *m*; **in e. (for sth.),** en

échange (de qch.); (**car, etc., taken in) part e.,**
reprise *f.* 2. *Fin:* **foreign e.,** change (extérieur);
rate of e., taux *m* du change; **foreign e. counter,**
bureau *m* de change; **at the current rate of e.,**
au change du jour. 3. (*a*) bourse *f* (des valeurs);
(*b*) **telephone e.,** central *m* (téléphonique). II.
v.tr. échanger, troquer (qch. pour, contre,
qch.).
exchequer [iks'tʃekər, eks-], *s.* (*a*) **the E.,** (i) la
Trésorerie, le fisc; (ii) le Trésor public; (iii) = le
Ministère des Finances; (*b*) **the Chancellor of
the E.** = le Ministre des Finances.
excise ['eksaiz], *s.* contributions indirectes; **the
E. office,** la Régie; **e. officer,** employé de la
Régie.
excite [ik'sait], *v.tr.* 1. provoquer, exciter (un
sentiment); susciter (de l'intérêt); **to e. s.o.'s
curiosity,** piquer la curiosité de qn. 2. (*a*)
exciter, enflammer (une passion); (*b*) agiter,
émouvoir, surexciter (qn); **don't get excited!** ne
vous énervez pas! **excita'bility,** *s.* 1.
émotivité *f.* 2. *El:* excitabilité *f*; **ex'citable,** *a.*
(*of pers.*) émotionnable, surexcitable; **ex'citement,** *s.* agitation *f*, surexcitation *f*; **the thirst
for e.,** la soif des sensations fortes; **the e. of
departure,** l'émoi *m* du départ; **what's all the e.
about?** qu'est-ce qui se passe? **to cause great
e.,** faire sensation; **ex'citing,** *a.* passionnant,
émouvant, captivant; (roman) palpitant; *Sp:*
an e. game, une partie mouvementée.
exclaim [iks'kleim, eks-], *v.i.* s'écrier,
s'exclamer; **excla'mation,** *s.* exclamation *f*;
e. mark, point *m* d'exclamation.
exclude [iks'klu:d, eks-], *v.tr.* (*a*) exclure (**from,**
de); (*b*) écarter (le doute); **ex'cluding,** *prep.* à
l'exclusion de; **ex'clusion,** *s.* 1. exclusion *f*
(**from,** de). 2. refus *m* d'admission (**from,** à);
ex'clusive, *a.* 1. **e. rights,** droits exclusifs. 2. **a
very e. club,** un cercle très fermé. 3. *adv.* sans
compter les extras; **price of the dinner, e. of
wine,** prix du dîner, vin non compris; **-ly,** *adv.*
exclusivement.
excommunicate [ekskə'mju:nikeit], *v.tr.*
excommunier; **'excommuni'cation,** *s.*
excommunication *f.*
excrescence [iks'kresns, eks-], *s.* excroissance
f.
excrete [eks'kri:t], *v.tr.* excréter; **excrement**
['ekskrəmənt], *s.* excrément *m*; **ex'creta,** *s.pl.*
excrétions *f*; **ex'cretion,** *s.* excrétion *f.*
excruciating [iks'kru:ʃieitiŋ], *a.* (*of pain*)
atroce, affreux; **an e. joke,** une plaisanterie
atroce; **-ly,** *adv.* atrocement; **it's e. funny,** c'est
à se tordre (de rire).
excursion [iks'kə:ʃ(ə)n, eks-], *s.* excursion *f*;
voyage *m* d'agrément; partie *f* de plaisir; *Aut:
etc:* randonnée *f.*
excuse. I. *s.* [iks'kju:s, eks-]. excuse *f*, prétexte *m*;

to make excuses, s'excuser. II. *v.tr.* [iks'kju:z, eks-]. (*a*) excuser, pardonner (qn); **e. me!** (i) excusez-moi! (ii) pardon! (*b*) excuser, dispenser (qn de faire qch.); **ex'cusable,** [-'kju:zəbl], *a.* excusable, pardonnable.

execrate ['eksikreit], *v.tr.* exécrer, détester (qn); **'execrable,** *a.* exécrable, détestable; **-ably,** *adv.* détestablement; **exe'cration,** *s.* exécration *f*, détestation *f*.

execute ['eksikju:t], *v.tr.* 1. (*a*) exécuter (un travail); s'acquitter d'(une tâche); *Jur:* **to e. a deed,** souscrire un acte; (*b*) exécuter, jouer (un morceau de musique). 2. exécuter (un criminel); **exe'cution,** *s.* 1. (*a*) exécution *f* (d'un projet); **to put a plan into e.,** mettre un projet à exécution; (*b*) *Jur:* souscription *f*(d'un acte); (*c*) (i) exécution (d'un morceau de musique); (ii) jeu *m* (d'un musicien). 2. exécution (d'un criminel); **exe'cutioner,** *s.* bourreau *m*; **ex'ecutive.** 1. *a.* exécutif. 2. *s.* (pouvoir) exécutif (*m*); **executor,** *s., f.* -trix, [eg'zekjutər, -triks], exécuteur, -trice, testamentaire.

exemplary [ig'zempləri, eg-], *a.* exemplaire; **an e. pupil,** un élève modèle.

exempt [ig'zem(p)t, eg-]. I. *v.tr.* exempter, exonérer, dispenser (qn de qch.). II. *a.* exempt, dispensé; **e. from taxation,** franc d'impôts; **ex'emption,** *s.* exemption *f*, exonération *f*, dispense *f* (**from sth.,** de qch.).

exercise ['eksəsaiz]. I. *s.* 1. exercice *m* (de son intelligence, etc.); **physical e.,** exercice physique; **to take physical e.,** faire du sport. 2. (*a*) *Sch:* **written e.,** devoir *m*; **e. book,** cahier *m*; (*b*) *U.S:* cérémonies *f* (de distribution de prix, etc.). II. *v.tr.* 1. exercer (un droit); pratiquer (un métier); **to e. a right,** user d'un droit. 2. (*a*) **to e. oneself,** prendre de l'exercice; (*b*) *v.i.* s'entraîner. 3. **to e. s.o.'s patience,** mettre à l'épreuve la patience de qn.

exert [ig'zə:t, eg-], *v.tr.* 1. employer (la force); mettre en œuvre (la force, son talent); exercer (une influence). 2. **to e. oneself to do sth.,** se donner du mal, s'efforcer, à faire qch.; **ex'ertion,** *s.* effort(s) *m(pl)*.

exhaust [ig'zɔ:st]. I. *v.tr.* (*a*) épuiser, tarir (une source, ses ressources); (*b*) épuiser, éreinter, exténuer (qn); **I'm exhausted,** je n'en peux plus. II. *s.* E: (*a*) échappement *m* (de la vapeur, des gaz); (*b*) gaz *m* d'échappement; (*c*) *Aut:* **e. pipe,** tuyau *m* d'échappement; **ex'haustion,** *s.* épuisement *m* (du sol, de qn); **to be in a state of e.,** être à bout de forces; **ex'haustive,** *a.* **e. inquiry,** enquête approfondie; **-ly,** *adv.* **to treat a subject e.,** traiter un sujet à fond.

exhibit [ig'zibit, eg-]. I. *s.* 1. *Jur:* pièce *f* à conviction. 2. objet exposé (à une exposition). II. *v.tr.* 1. exhiber, montrer (un objet); exposer (des marchandises, des tableaux). 2. *Jur:* produire (une pièce à conviction); **exhibition** [eksi'biʃ(ə)n], *s.* exposition *f* (de tableaux, etc.); étalage *m* (de marchandises); démonstration *f* (d'un nouveau procédé); **to make an e. of oneself,** se donner en spectacle.

exhilarate [ig'ziləreit, eg-], *v.tr.* vivifier; mettre (à qn) la joie au cœur; **ex'hilarated,** *a.* ragaillardi; **ex'hilarating,** *a.* (*of air, climate*) vivifiant; **e. wine,** vin capiteux; **exhila'ration,** *s.* gaieté *f* de cœur; joie *f* de vivre.

exhume [eks'hju:m], *v.tr.* exhumer.

exile ['eksail]. I. *s.* exil *m*, bannissement *m*. II. *s.* exilé, -ée; banni, -ie. III. *v.tr.* exiler, bannir (qn) (**from,** de); **to e. oneself,** se dépayser, s'exiler.

exist [ig'zist, eg-], *v.i.* exister; **to continue to e.,** subsister; **we e. on very little,** nous vivons de très peu; **ex'istence,** *s.* existence *f*; vie *f*; **ex'isting,** *a.* actuel, présent; **in e. circumstances,** dans les circonstances actuelles.

exit ['eksit]. I. *s.* 1. *Th:* sortie *f*; **to make one's e.,** quitter la scène. 2. sortie; **emergency e.,** sortie de secours. II. *v.i. Th:* sortir.

exodus ['eksədəs], *s.* l'Exode *m* (des Hébreux); **there was a general e.,** il y eut une sortie générale.

exonerate [ig'zonəreit, eg-], *v.tr.* 1. exonérer, dispenser (**from,** de). 2. **to e. s.o. (from blame),** disculper qn; **exone'ration,** *s.* exonération *f*, disculpation *f*.

exorbitant [ig'zɔ:bitənt, eg-], *a.* exorbitant, extravagant; **e. price,** prix excessif, prix salé.

exotic [eg'zɔtik], *a.* exotique.

expand [iks'pænd, eks-]. 1. *v.tr.* (*a*) dilater (un gaz); développer (un abrégé); élargir (l'esprit); (*b*) déployer (les ailes). 2. *v.i.* se dilater; (*of chest*) se développer; **ex'panding,** *a.* 1. **the e. universe,** l'univers *m* en expansion. 2. **e. bracelet,** bracelet *m* extensible.

expanse [iks'pæns, eks-], *s.* étendue *f* (de pays); **ex'pansion,** *s.* dilatation *f* (d'un gaz, d'un métal); développement *m* (d'un abrégé, de la poitrine); **ex'pansive,** *a.* 1. (*of force*) expansif. 2. (*of pers.*) expansif, démonstratif. 3. (paysage) vaste, étendu.

expatiate [eks'peiʃieit], *v.i.* discourir (longuement), s'étendre (**on, upon, a subject,** sur un sujet).

expatriate. I. *v.tr.* [eks'pætrieit, -peit-], expatrier (qn). II. *a. & s.* [eks'pætriə, -peit-], expatrié, -ée; **expatri'ation,** *s.* expatriation *f*.

expect [iks'pekt, eks-], *v.tr.* 1. attendre (qn); s'attendre à (un événement); compter su (l'arrivée de qn); **I knew what to e.,** je savais quoi m'attendre; **I expected as much,** je m' attendais; **to e. to do sth.,** compter faire qch *abs. F:* **she's expecting,** elle attend un bébé. **to e. sth. from s.o.,** attendre, exiger, qch. de q what do you e. me to do? qu'attendez-vous de moi? I e. you to be punctual, je vous demanderai d'être à l'heure; how do you e. me to do it? comment voulez-vous que je le fasse? 3. I e. so, je pense que oui; ex′pectancy, s. attente f; expectative f; ex′pectant, a. qui attend; d'attente; e. mother, femme enceinte; Jur: e. heir, héritier m en expectative; -ly, adv. to gaze at s.o. e., regarder qn avec l'air d'attendre qch.; expec′tation, s. 1. attente f, espérance f. 2. usu. pl. expectative f d'héritage, espérances.

xpediency [iks′pi:diənsi, eks-], s. (a) convenance f, opportunité f (d'une mesure); (b) opportunisme m; ex′pedient. 1. a. convenable, opportun. 2. s. expédient m, moyen m; -ly, adv. convenablement.

xpedite [′ekspidait], v.tr. 1. activer (une mesure); accélérer, hâter (un processus). 2. expédier, dépêcher (une affaire); expe′dition, s. 1. (a) expédition f (au pôle sud, etc.); (b) excursion f. 2. célérité f, promptitude f; expe′ditious, a. (procédé) expéditif; (trajet) rapide; prompt; -ly, adv. avec célérité; promptement.

xpel [iks′pel, eks-], v.tr. (expelled) expulser (un locataire); bannir (qn d'une société); renvoyer (un élève).

xpenditure [iks′penditʃər, eks-], s. (a) dépense f (d'argent); consommation f (de gaz, de carburant); (b) (amount spent) the national e., les dépenses de l'État; ex′pendable, a. (matériel) non récupérable, non réutilisable; (troupes) sacrifiables.

xpense [iks′pens, eks-], s. 1. dépense f, frais mpl; Com: e. account, indemnité f pour frais professionnels; travelling expenses, frais de déplacement; to be a great e. to s.o., être une grande charge pour qn. 2. dépens mpl; a laugh at my e., un éclat de rire à mes dépens; ex′pensive, a. coûteux, cher; to be e., coûter cher inv; -ly, adv. to live e., vivre à grands frais; mener la vie large; ex′pensiveness, s. cherté f, prix élevé (d'un article).

xperience [iks′piəriəns, eks-]. I. s. expérience f; painful e., rude épreuve f; practical e., pratique f; he lacks e., il manque de pratique; facts within my e., faits à ma connaissance; have you had any previous e.? avez-vous déjà pratiqué ce métier? II. v.tr. éprouver; faire l'expérience de (qch.); ex′perienced, a. qui a de l'expérience, du métier; expérimenté.

xperiment [iks′perimənt, eks-]. I. s. expérience f; essai m; as an e., à titre d'essai. II. v.i. expérimenter, faire des expériences (on, with, ur avec); experi′mental, a. 1. expérimental. e. laboratory, laboratoire m d'expériences; nd: the e. department, le service des essais;

-ally, adv. expérimentalement.

expert [′ekspə:t]. I. a. habile, expert; -ly, adv. habilement, expertement. II. s. expert m; spécialiste mf; exper′tise, s. 1. expertise f. 2. compétence f; connaissances f techniques; ′expertness, s. adresse f; habileté f.

expire [iks′paiər, eks-], v.i. (a) expirer, mourir; (of hope) s'évanouir; (b) expirer, cesser, prendre fin; Com: expired bill, effet périmé; expired (insurance) policy, police expirée; expi′ration, s. expiration f; cessation f, terme m; échéance f; ex′piry, s. expiration f, terminaison f; terme m.

explain [iks′plein, eks-], v.tr. expliquer, éclaircir (qch.); to e. oneself, se justifier; to e. sth. away, donner une explication satisfaisante de (propos offensants); expla′nation [ekspla-], s. explication f; éclaircissement m; ex′planatory [eks′plæn-], a. explicatif.

explicable [iks′plikəbl, eks-], a. explicable.

explicit [iks′plisit, eks-], a. explicite; formel, catégorique; to be more e. in one's statements, préciser ses affirmations; -ly, adv. explicitement; catégoriquement.

explode [iks′ploud, eks-]. 1. v.tr. (a) discréditer (une théorie); (b) faire éclater (un obus); faire sauter (une mine). 2. v.i. faire explosion; éclater; sauter; to e. with laughter, éclater de rire.

exploit¹ [′eksploit], s. exploit m.

exploit² [iks′ploit, eks-], v.tr. exploiter (des minerais, la terre, la vigne, les talents de qn); exploi′tation, s. exploitation f (d'une mine, etc.).

explore [iks′plɔ:r, eks-], v.tr. explorer; explo′ration, s. exploration f; voyage of e., voyage m de découverte; ex′ploratory, a. (a) (voyage) de découverte; (b) (conversation) préliminaire; ex′plorer, s. explorateur, -trice.

explosion [iks′plouʒ(ə)n, eks-], s. 1. explosion f. 2. détonation f; ex′plosive [-′plouziv]. 1. a. (matière) explosible; (mélange) explosif. 2. explosif m, détonant m; atomic, nuclear, e., explosif atomique, nucléaire.

export. I. v.tr. [eks′pɔ:t], exporter. II. s. [′ekspɔ:t], (a) pl. exports, articles m d'exportation; exportations f; invisible exports, exportations invisibles; (b) e. trade, commerce m d'exportation; e. markets, marchés m pour les exportations; expor′tation, s. exportation f (de marchandises); ex′porter, s. exportateur, -trice.

expose [iks′pouz, eks-], v.tr. 1. exposer; to e. oneself to danger, s'exposer au danger. 2. (a) mettre (qch.) à découvert, à nu; to e. one's ignorance, afficher son ignorance; (b) to e. goods for sale, étaler des marchandises pour la vente. 3. démasquer (un escroc); dévoiler (un crime); ex′posed, a. (a) e. position, endroit exposé;

(*b*) (*laid bare*) à nu; **ex′posure,** *s.* **1.** (*a*) exposition *f* (à l'air); **to die of e.,** mourir de froid; (*b*) *Phot:* (temps *m* de) pose *f.* **2.** dévoilement *m* (d'un crime); **fear of e.,** crainte *f* d'un scandale. **3.** exposition, orientation *f* (d'un lieu, d'une maison).

expostulate [iks′pɔstjuleit, eks-], *v.i.* **to e. with s.o.,** faire des remontrances à qn; **expostu′lation,** *s.* (*often in pl.*) remontrance(s) *f(pl).*

express[1] [iks′pres, eks-]. **1.** *a.* (*of order*) exprès, -esse, formel; **for this e. purpose,** pour ce but même. **2.** *s. Rail:* **e. (train),** express *m*, rapide *m*; **-ly,** *adv.* **1.** expressément, formellement. **2.** **I did it e. to please you,** je l'ai fait à seule fin de vous plaire; **ex′pressway,** *s. U.S:* autoroute *f.*

express[2], *v.tr.* exprimer; **to e. a wish,** formuler un souhait; **to e. oneself in French,** s'exprimer en français; **ex′pression,** *s.* **1.** expression *f* (d'une pensée); **beyond e.,** inexprimable. **2.** expression, locution *f.* **3.** expression (du visage); **ex′pressive,** *a.* (visage, etc.) expressif; **-ly,** *adv.* avec expression.

expulsion [iks′pʌlʃ(ə)n, eks-], *s.* expulsion *f.*

expurgate [′ekspəːgeit], *v.tr.* expurger; **expur′gation,** *s.* expurgation *f.*

exquisite [eks′kwizit], *a.* (*a*) exquis; (*b*) (*of pleasure*) vif; (*c*) (*of workmanship*) exquis; (*of s.o.'s taste*) exquis, délicat; **-ly,** *adv.* d'une manière exquise.

ex-serviceman, *pl.* **-men** [′eks′səːvismən], *s.* ancien combattant.

extant [iks′tænt, eks-], *a.* existant; qui existe encore.

extempore [eks′tempəri]. **1.** *adv.* **to speak e.,** parler d'abondance, impromptu. **2.** *a.* improvisé, impromptu *inv*; **ex′temporize,** *v.tr. & i.* improviser.

extend [iks′tend, eks-]. **1.** *v.tr.* prolonger (une ligne, une période de temps); étendre, porter plus loin (les limites); accroître (un commerce); agrandir (son pouvoir); tendre (la main). **2.** *v.i.* s'étendre, s'allonger; se prolonger; continuer; **ex′tension,** *s.* **1.** extension *f*; prolongement *m*; agrandissement *m* (d'une usine). **2.** (r)allonge *f* (de table); annexe *f* (d'un bâtiment); *P.T.T:* **e. 35,** poste *m*, *Fr.C:* local *m*, 35; **e. ladder,** échelle *f* à coulisse. **3.** prolongation *f* (de congé); **ex′tensive,** *a.* étendu, vaste, ample; **e. knowledge,** connaissances étendues; **e. researches,** travaux approfondis; **-ly,** *adv.* **to use sth. e.,** se servir beaucoup de qch.

extent [iks′tent, eks-], *s.* étendue *f* (d'un terrain); importance *f* (des dégâts); **to a certain e.,** jusqu'à un certain point; dans une certaine mesure; **to a slight e.,** quelque peu.

extenuating [eks′tenjueitiŋ], *a.* **e. circumstance,**

circonstance atténuante.

exterior [eks′tiəriər]. **1.** *a.* extérieur **(to,** à); en dehors **(to,** de). **2.** *s.* extérieur *m*, dehors *mpl*: **on the e.,** à l'extérieur.

exterminate [eks′təːmineit], *v.tr.* exterminer; **extermi′nation,** *s.* extermination *f.*

external [eks′təːn(ə)l]. **1.** *a.* (*a*) externe; *Med:* **for e. application,** pour usage *m* externe; (*b*) extérieur; du dehors. **2.** *s.* (*usu. in pl.*) **to judge by externals,** juger les choses d'après les apparences; **-ally,** *adv.* extérieurement; à l'extérieur.

extinct [iks′tiŋ(k)t, eks-], *a.* (*a*) (*of volcano*) éteint; (*b*) (*of species*) disparu; **ex′tinction,** *s.* extinction *f* (d'un incendie, d'une race, d'une dette).

extinguish [iks′tiŋgwiʃ, eks-], *v.tr.* éteindre (un incendie); **ex′tinguisher,** *s.* (appareil) extincteur *m* (d'incendie).

extort [iks′tɔːt, eks-], *v.tr.* extorquer **(from s.o.,** qn); **to e. a promise from s.o.,** arracher une promesse à qn; **ex′tortion,** *s.* extorsion *f*; exaction *f* (d'impôts); arrachement *m* (d'une promesse); **ex′tortionate,** *a.* (prix) exorbitant.

extra [′ekstrə]. **1.** *a.* (*a*) en sus, de plus supplémentaire; **e. charge,** supplément *m* de prix; (*b*) de qualité supérieure; superfin, extra. **2.** *adv.* (*a*) plus que d'ordinaire; **strong,** extra-solide; **e. smart,** ultra-chic; (*b*) plus; **the wine is e.,** le vin est en plus. **3.** *s.* supplément *m* (de menu); édition spéciale (d'un journal); (*b*) *Cin:* figurant, -ante; (*c*) *pl.* **extras,** frais *m* supplémentaires.

extract. I. *s.* [′ekstrækt], extrait *m*; (*a*) **meat e.,** concentré *m* de viande; (*b*) *pl. Sch:* **extracts,** morceaux choisis. **II.** *v.tr.* [iks′trækt, eks-], extraire, tirer; arracher (une dent, un clou, etc.); **ex′traction,** *s.* **1.** extraction *f*, arrachement *m* (d'une dent, d'un clou). **2.** origine *f*; **be of French e.,** être d'origine française.

extradition [ekstrə′diʃ(ə)n], *s.* extradition *f.*

extraordinary [iks′trɔːd(i)nri, eks-], *a.* extraordinaire; (*a*) **a man of e. intelligence,** un homme d'une intelligence rare, remarquable; (*b*) **what an e. thing!** quelle affaire étrange, extraordinaire! (*c*) prodigieux, invraisemblable; **-ily,** *adv.* extraordinairement.

extravagance [iks′trævəgəns, eks-], *s.* extravagance *f.* **2.** prodigalités *fpl*, dépenses folles; **a piece of e.,** une dépense inutile, *F:* une folie; **ex′travagant,** *a.* **1.** extravagant; **praise,** éloges outrés. **2.** (*of pers.*) dépensier; (*of price*) exorbitant; **-ly,** *adv.* **1.** d'une façon extravagante; **to talk e.,** dire des folies. **2.** excessivement; à l'excès.

extreme [iks′triːm, eks-]. **1.** *a.* extrême; **e. age,** extrême vieillesse *f*; **e. youth,** gra jeunesse; **an e. case,** un cas exceptionnel; **to hold e. opinions,** avoir des opinions *f* extrémistes. **2.** *s.* **in the e.,** à l'excès; au dernier degré; **to drive s.o. to extremes,** pousser qn à bout; **-ly,** *adv.* extrêmement; au dernier point; **to be e. witty,** avoir énormément d'esprit.

extremity [iks'tremiti, eks-], *s.* **1.** extrémité *f*; point *m* extrême; bout *m* (d'une corde, etc.). **2.** *pl.* **the extremities,** les extrémités (du corps). **3.** **they are in great e.,** ils sont dans une grande gêne.

extricate ['ekstrikeit], *v.tr.* dégager; **to e. oneself from difficulties,** se débrouiller, se dépêtrer.

extrovert ['ekstrəvɔ:t], *a. & s.* extroverti.

exuberance [ig'z(j)u:b(ə)rəns, eg-], *s.* exubérance *f*; **ex'uberant,** *a.* exubérant; **-ly,** *adv.* avec exubérance.

exult [ig'zʌlt, eg-], *v.i.* **to e. over s.o.,** triompher de qn; **ex'ultant,** *a.* triomphant, exultant; **-ly,** *adv.* d'un air de triomphe.

eye [ai]. **I.** *s.* **1.** œil *m, pl.* yeux; (*a*) **to have blue eyes,** avoir les yeux bleus; **to open one's eyes wide,** ouvrir de grands yeux; **to do sth. with one's eyes open,** faire qch. en connaissance de cause; *F:* **to keep one's eyes skinned,** avoir l'œil (ouvert); **keep your eyes open!** ouvrez l'œil! ayez l'œil! **to open s.o.'s eyes,** éclairer, désabuser, qn; **to shut one's eyes to s.o.'s faults,** être aveugle sur les défauts de qn; **to shut one's eyes to the truth,** se refuser à l'évidence; **I'm up to my eyes in work,** j'ai du travail par-dessus la tête; **with tears in one's eyes,** les larmes aux yeux; (*b*) **to catch the e.,** frapper l'œil, attirer les regards; **to set, clap, eyes on sth.,** apercevoir, voir, qch.; (*c*) **to make eyes at s.o.,** faire de l'œil à qn; **to see e. to e. with s.o.,** voir les choses du même œil que qn; (*d*) **to keep an e. on s.o., sth.,** surveiller qn, qch.; **to keep a strict e. on s.o.,** surveiller qn de près; (*e*) **to have an e. for a horse,** s'y connaître en chevaux; (*f*) **to be very much in the public e.,** être très en vue; (*g*) **private e.,** détective privé. **2.** chas *m,* trou *m* (d'une aiguille). **II.** *v.tr.* **to e. s.o.,** regarder, observer, qn (avec attention); **'eyeball,** *s.* globe *m* oculaire; **'eyebrow,** *s.* sourcil *m*; **'eyelash,** *s.* cil *m*; **'eyelet,** *s.* œillet *m*; petit trou; **'eyelid,** *s.* paupière *f*; **'eye-opener,** *s.* révélation *f*; surprise *f*; **'eyepiece,** *s.* (*a*) oculaire *m* (de télescope); (*b*) viseur *m* (de théodolite); **'eyeshade,** *s.* visière *f*; **'eyesight,** *s.* vue *f*; **my e. is failing,** ma vue baisse; **'eyesore,** *s.* qch. qui blesse la vue; **that house is an e.,** cette maison est affreuse; **'eye-strain,** *s.* **to suffer from e.-s.,** avoir les yeux fatigués; **'eyewash,** *s.* **1.** *Med:* collyre *m*. **2.** *F:* **that's all e.,** tout ça, c'est du boniment; **'eye-witness,** *s.* témoin *m* oculaire.

F

F, f [ef], s. 1. (la lettre) F, f m or f. 2. Mus: fa m.
fable ['feibl], s. fable f, conte m; fabulous
['fæbjuləs], a. 1. fabuleux; légendaire. 2. F:
prodigieux; a f. price, un prix fou; -ly, adv.
fabuleusement; prodigieusement (riche, etc.).
fabric ['fæbrik], s. 1. édifice m; the f. of society,
l'édifice social. 2. Tex: tissu m; silk and
woollen fabrics, soieries f et lainages m. 3.
structure f, fabrique f (d'un édifice);
'fabricate, v.tr. inventer, fabriquer; fabri'cation, s. invention f; fabrication f; contrefaçon
f; a pure f., une pure invention.
façade [fæ'sɑːd], s. Arch: façade f.
face [feis]. I. s. 1. (a) figure f, visage m, face f; to
strike s.o. in the f., frapper qn au visage; I'll
never look him in the f. again, je me sentirai
toujours honteux devant lui; he won't show his
f. here again! il ne se risquera pas à remettre les
pieds ici! to bring the two parties f. to f., mettre
les deux parties en présence; in the f. of danger,
en présence du danger; I told him so to his f., je
ne le lui ai pas envoyé dire; (b) f. cream, crème
f de beauté; f. towel, serviette f de toilette; f.
cloth = gant m de toilette. 2. (a) mine f,
physionomie f; to make faces, faire des
grimaces; to keep a straight f., garder son
sérieux; to put a good f. on it, faire contre
mauvaise fortune bon cœur; (b) audace f, front
m; he had the f. to tell me so, il a eu l'aplomb m,
le toupet, de me le dire. 3. apparence f, aspect
m; on the f. of it, au premier aspect, à première
vue; Fin: f. value, valeur nominale; I took him
at his f. value, je l'ai jugé sur les apparences; to
save f., sauver les apparences. 4. (a) face
(d'une pièce de monnaie); f. down, face en
dessous; (b) devant m, façade f; face (d'une
falaise); (c) cadran m (de montre). II. v. 1. (a)
v.tr. affronter, faire face à; envisager (les faits);
let's f. it! voyons les choses comme elles sont!
to f. the music, tenir tête à l'orage; (b) v.i. to f.
up to a danger, affronter un danger. 2. (a) v.tr.
faire face à, se tenir devant; facing each other,
vis-à-vis l'un de l'autre; facing the street, qui
donne sur la rue; (b) v.i. house facing north,
maison exposée au nord; f. this way! tournez-
vous de ce côté! 'facial. 1. a. facial. 2. s. I'm
having a f., je me fais faire un traitement de
beauté; 'facing, s. 1. surfaçage m. 2. revers m
(d'un habit), parement m (d'un habit, d'un
mur); marble f., placage m de marbre.
facet ['fæsit], s. facette f (d'un diamant).

facetious [fə'siːʃəs], a. facétieux, plaisant
farceur; (style) bouffon; -ly, adv
facétieusement.
facility [fə'siliti], s. 1. facilité f; to speak with f.
parler avec facilité; to have facilities for doin,
sth., avoir la facilité de faire qch. 2. p
facilities, installations fpl; with cookin
facilities, avec la possibilité de faire la cuisine
we have no facilities for it, nous ne somme
pas équipés pour cela; fa'cilitate, v.t
faciliter.
facsimile [fæk'simili], s. fac-similé m.
fact [fækt], s. fait m; to look facts in the face, vo
les choses comme elles sont; to stick to fact
s'en tenir aux faits; it is a f. that . . ., il est de fa
que . . .; apart from the f. that . . ., hormis qı
. . .; to know for a f. that . . ., savoir pertinen
ment que . . .; the f. is, . . ., le fait est que . .
c'est que . . .; in f., de fait; in point of f., .
vérité, par le fait; as a matter of f., (i) à vr
dire; (ii) en effet.
faction ['fækʃ(ə)n], s. faction f, cabale f.
factor ['fæktər], s. 1. (pers.) Com: agent
(dépositaire). 2. (a) Mth: diviseur m, facte
m; prime f., diviseur premier; (b) safety
coefficient m, facteur, marge f, de sécurité.
facteur, considération f; the human f., l'
ment humain.
factory ['fæktəri], s. usine f, fabrique f; canni
f., conserverie f; f. inspector, inspecteur m
travail.
faculty ['fæk(ə)lti], s. faculté f.
fad [fæd], s. marotte f, manie f; 'faddy,
difficile (sur la nourriture, etc.).
fade [feid], v. I. v.i. 1. (of flowers) se faner,
flétrir; (of colour) passer; (of cloth) déteind
guaranteed not to f., garanti bon teint. 2. t
away, out, s'évanouir, s'affaiblir; to f. f
sight, se perdre de vue; she was fading av
elle dépérissait. II. v.tr. 1. faner; décolorer
Cin: to f. in, out, faire arriver, faire partir, (
scène) dans un fondu; 'fading, s.
flétrissure f; décoloration f; (b) Rad: fading
fag [fæg], s. F: 1. (a) fatigue f, peine f; what
quelle corvée! (b) brain f., surmenage m
cigarette f.
fail [feil]. I. adv.phr. without f., (i) sans faute
à coup sûr. II. v. 1. v.i. (a) manquer, faillir, f
défaut; to f. in one's duty, manquer, failli
son devoir; to f. to do sth., manquer, négli
de faire qch.; to f. s.o., manquer à

engagements envers qn; **his heart failed him,** le cœur lui manqua; (b) *Aut:* (*of brakes*) lâcher; (*of engine*) to f. to start, refuser de démarrer; (c) baisser; **the light is failing,** le jour baisse; **his memory is failing,** sa mémoire baisse; **he, his health, is failing,** sa santé baisse; (d) ne pas réussir; échouer; manquer son coup; *Sch:* être refusé (à un examen); **I f. to see why,** je ne vois pas pourquoi; (e) *Com:* faire faillite. 2. *v.tr. Sch:* refuser, recaler (un candidat); **'failing. I.** *s.* 1. (a) affaiblissement *m*, défaillance *f* (de forces); baisse *f* (de la vue); (b) non-réussite *f*; échec *m*. 2. faible *m*, faiblesse *f*; **with all his failings,** avec toutes ses faiblesses, tous ses défauts. II. *prep.* à défaut de; faute de (paiement); **f. advice to the contrary,** sauf avis contraire; **'failure,** *s.* 1. (a) manque *m*, manquement *m*, défaut *m*; (b) panne *f*; *El:* **power f.,** panne de courant; *Med:* **heart f.,** arrêt *m* de cœur. 2. (a) insuccès *m*, non-réussite *f*; avortement *m* (d'un projet); (b) *Com:* faillite *f*. 3. (a) (*pers.*) raté, -ée; (b) *Th:* **a dead f.,** un four noir.

faint [feint]. I. *a.* 1. (a) faible, affaibli; **f. hope,** faible espoir *m*; (b) (*of colour*) pâle; (*of sound*) léger; (*of idea*) vague; **not the faintest chance, idea,** pas la moindre chance, idée. 2. **to feel f.,** se sentir mal. II. *s.* évanouissement *m*, défaillance *f*. III. *v.i.* s'évanouir, défaillir; se trouver mal; **'fainting,** *s.* défaillance *f*, évanouissement *m*; **'faintly,** *adv.* 1. faiblement; (parler) d'une voix éteinte. 2. légèrement, un peu; **f. visible,** à peine visible; **'faintness,** *s.* (a) faiblesse *f*, légèreté *f*; (b) malaise *m*, faiblesse.

fair[1] ['fɛər], *s.* foire *f*; **fun f.** = fête *f* foraine; **'fairground,** *s.* champ *m* de foire.

fair[2]. I. *a.* 1. (*of pers., hair*) blond; (*of skin*) blanc; **f.-haired,** blond; aux cheveux blonds. 2. juste, équitable; **f. play,** (i) jeu loyal; (ii) traitement *m* juste; **it's not f.!** ce n'est pas juste! **as is only f.,** comme de juste; **f. enough!** ça va! **it's all f. and square,** c'est de bonne guerre; **by f. means or foul,** d'une manière ou d'une autre; de gré ou de force. 3. passable; assez bon; **he has a f. chance of success,** il a des chances de réussir; **the room's a f. size, it's a f.-sized room,** la pièce est assez grande. 4. **f. weather,** beau temps. II. *adv.* 1. (agir) loyalement, de bonne foi; **to play f.,** jouer beau jeu. 2. **to hit s.o. f. (and square) on the chin,** frapper qn en plein menton; **-ly,** *adv.* 1. impartialement, équitablement; **to treat s.o. f.,** traiter qn avec impartialité. 2. (agir) honnêtement, loyalement; **to come by sth. f.,** obtenir qch. à bon titre. 3. complètement, absolument; **it f. staggered me,** j'en étais renversé. 4. passablement; assez (riche); **f. certain,** à peu près certain; **'fairness,** *s.* 1. couleur blonde

(des cheveux); blancheur *f*, fraîcheur *f* (du teint). 2. équité *f*, honnêteté *f*, impartialité *f*; **in all f.,** en toute justice.

fairy ['fɛəri]. 1. *s.* fée *f*. 2. *a.* féerique; **f. godmother,** (i) marraine *f* fée; (ii) *F:* marraine gâteau; **f. queen,** reine *f* des fées; **f. story, tale,** (i) conte *m* de fées; (ii) conte invraisemblable; **'fairyland,** *s.* (a) le royaume des fées; (b) féerie *f*; **'fairylike,** *a.* féerique.

faith [feiθ], *s.* 1. (a) foi *f*, confiance *f*; **to have f. in s.o.,** avoir confiance en qn; (b) **the Christian f.,** la foi chrétienne. 2. (a) fidélité *f* à ses engagements; **to keep f. with s.o.,** tenir ses engagements envers qn; (b) **good f.,** bonne foi, loyauté *f*; **to do sth. in all good f.,** faire qch. en tout bien (et) tout honneur; **bad f.,** mauvaise foi, déloyauté *f*; **'faithful,** *a.* (a) (*of friend*) fidèle, loyal; (b) exact; **f. translation,** traduction *f* fidèle; **-fully,** *adv.* 1. fidèlement, loyalement; *Corr:* **we remain yours f.,** recevez l'expression de nos sentiments distingués. 2. exactement, fidèlement; **'faithfulness,** *s.* 1. fidélité *f*, loyauté *f* (**to,** envers). 2. fidélité, exactitude *f*.

fake [feik]. I. *s.* article faux, truqué; maquillage *m*. II. *v.tr.* truquer (des calculs); maquiller (un meuble); **to f. (up) a story,** inventer une histoire.

falcon ['fɔ:(l)kən], *s. Orn:* faucon *m*.

fall [fɔ:l]. I. *s.* 1. (a) chute *f* (d'un corps); descente *f* (d'un marteau); *Th:* chute, baisser *m* (du rideau); (b) **there has been a heavy f. of snow,** il est tombé beaucoup de neige. 2. *N.Am:* **the f.,** l'automne *m or f.* 3. (usu. pl.) chute (d'eau); cascade *f*, cataracte *f*. 4. baisse *f* (des prix); **f. in the value of money,** dépréciation de la monnaie. 5. perte *f*, ruine *f* (de qn). 6. renversement *m* (d'un gouvernement). 7. éboulement *m* (de terre). II. *v.i.* (**fell; fallen**) 1. (a) tomber (à terre, d'une échelle); **to f. into a trap,** donner dans un piège; **to f. into s.o.'s hands,** tomber entre les mains de qn; *F:* **to f. on one's feet,** avoir de la chance; **to let sth. f.,** laisser tomber qch.; **night is falling,** (i) la nuit tombe; (ii) le jour baisse; (b) **Christmas falls on a Thursday,** Noël tombe un jeudi. 2. (a) **to f. on one's knees,** tomber à genoux; (b) (*of building*) crouler, s'écrouler; **to f. to pieces,** tomber en morceaux. 3. (a) (*of barometer*) descendre, baisser; (*of wind*) tomber; (*of sea*) (se) calmer; (*of price*) baisser; (b) (*of ground*) aller en pente, descendre; **her eyes fell,** elle a baissé les yeux; **his face fell,** sa figure s'allongea; (c) déchoir (de sa position, dans l'estime de qn). 4. (a) **to f. on s.o.'s neck,** se jeter au cou de qn; (b) **suspicion fell on him,** les soupçons retombèrent sur lui; **the blame falls on me,** le blâme retombe sur moi. 5. (a) **to f. to s.o.'s share,** échoir (en partage) à qn; **it fell**

to me to do it, c'est moi qui ai dû le faire; (b) to f. **under suspicion**, devenir suspect; (c) to f. **into a habit**, contracter une habitude. **6.** (a) to f. **ill**, tomber malade; to f. **vacant**, se trouver vacant; (b) to f. **a victim to**, être victime de; **'fall 'back**, v.i. **1.** tomber en arrière, à la renverse. **2.** avoir recours (**on sth.**, à qch.); **'fall be'hind**, v.i. rester en arrière; **'fall 'down**, v.i. (a) tomber à terre, par terre; se prosterner (devant qn); (b) (of building) crouler, s'écrouler, s'effondrer; (c) F: **to f.d. on the job**, échouer dans une entreprise; **'fallen. 1.** a. f. **leaves**, feuilles tombées. **2.** s. **the f.**, les morts m (sur le champ de bataille); **'fall 'in**, v.i. **1.** (of roof, etc.) s'écrouler, s'effondrer. **2.** Mil: former les rangs; f. **in!** rassemblement! to f. **in with s.o.**, rencontrer qn par hasard. **3.** (of lease) expirer; **'fall 'off**, v.i. **1.** (of thg) tomber. **2.** (of followers) faire défection. **3.** (of profits) diminuer; **'fall 'out**, v.i. **1.** (a) tomber dehors; (b) (of hair) tomber; (c) Mil: rompre les rangs; f. **o.!** rompez! **2.** se brouiller, se fâcher (**with s.o.**, avec qn); **'fallout**, s. retombées radioactives); **'fall 'over. 1.** v.i. (of pers.) tomber (par terre); (of thg) se renverser, être renversé. **2.** v.tr. trébucher sur (un obstacle); **'fall 'through**, v.i. ne pas aboutir; **'fall 'to**, v.i. (a) entamer la lutte; (b) s'attaquer au repas.

fallacy ['fæləsi], s. (a) faux raisonnement; (b) erreur f; **fa'llacious**, a. fallacieux; trompeur.

fallow ['fælou], a. (of land) **to lie f.**, être en jachère, en friche.

false [fɔls], a. **1.** faux; f. **idea**, idée fausse; f. **report**, canard m; **to be in a f. position**, se trouver dans une position fausse. **2.** faux, perfide, infidèle; f. **accusation**, dénonciation calomnieuse; **to play s.o. f.**, trahir qn. **3.** (of hair, etc.) artificiel, postiche; (of coin) faux, contrefait; **-ly**, adv. faussement, à faux; **'falsehood**, s. mensonge m; **'falseness**, s. fausseté f; **'falsies**, s.pl. F: faux seins; **falsifi'cation**, s. falsification f; **'falsify**, v.tr. falsifier (un document); fausser (un bilan).

falter ['fɔltər], v.i. (a) (of voice) hésiter, trembler; (b) (of pers.) hésiter, vaciller; défaillir.

fame [feim], s. renom m, renommée f; **to win f.**, se faire un grand nom, se rendre célèbre.

familiar [fə'miliər], a. (a) familier, intime; **to be on f. terms with s.o.**, être familier avec qn; **he is too f.**, il se croit tout permis; (b) familier, bien connu; **in f. surroundings**, en pays de connaissance; **to be on f. ground**, être sur son terrain; (c) **to be f. with sth.**, être familier avec qch., bien connaître qch.; **-ly**, adv. familièrement; intimement; **famili'arity**, s. **1.** familiarité f, intimité f. **2.** f. **with sth.**, connaissance f de qch.; **fa'miliarize**, v.tr. **to f. s.o. with sth.**, habituer qn à qch.; **to f. oneself with**

sth., se familiariser avec qch.

family ['fæmili], s. famille f; **to be one of the f.**, être de la maison; f. **life**, vie familiale; f. **man**, (i) père m de famille; (ii) homme m d'intérieur; Com: **in a f.-size(d) jar**, en pot familial; A dm: f. **allowance**, allocation familiale; f. **planning**, limitation f des naissances, planning familial.

famine ['fæmin], s. (a) famine f; (b) disette f; **'famished**, a., **'famishing**, a. affamé; **I'm f.**, je meurs de faim.

famous ['feiməs], a. célèbre, renommé; **to become f. overnight**, devenir célèbre du jour au lendemain.

fan[1] [fæn]. **I.** s. **1.** éventail m. **2.** ventilateur (rotatif). **II.** v.tr. (**fanned**) éventer (qn); **to f. a quarrel**, envenimer une querelle; **'fanlight**, s. imposte f (au-dessus d'une porte).

fan[2], s. F: passionné, -ée; fan m, fana mf; **film f.**, cinéphile mf; **football f.**, fana de football; f. **club**, club m des fanas; **'fanmail**, s. F courrier m des admirateurs et admiratrice (d'une vedette).

fanatic [fə'nætik], s. fanatique mf; **fa'natical** a. fanatique; **-ally**, adv. fanatiquement **fa'naticism**, s. fanatisme m.

fancy ['fænsi]. **I.** s. **1.** (a) imagination f, fantaisie f; (b) idée f; **I have a f. that . . .**, j'ai idée que **. . . . 2.** (a) fantaisie, caprice m; **as the f. take me**, comme ça me chante; (b) fantaisie, goût m; **to take a f. to sth.**, prendre goût à qch.; te take a f. to s.o., (i) prendre qn en affection; (ii s'éprendre de qn. **II.** a. de fantaisie; f. **goods** nouveautés f; f. **dress**, travesti m; f.-**dress bal** bal travesti. **III.** v.tr. **1.** (a) s'imaginer, se figure (qch.); f. **that!** figurez-vous ça! (b) croir penser; I f. **I've seen him before**, j'ai l'impressio de l'avoir déjà vu. **2.** (a) **to f. sth.**, se sentir attir vers qch.; **I don't f. his offer**, son offre f ne me d rien; **let him eat anything he fancies**, il peu manger tout ce qui lui dit; Rac: **strongly fancie horse**, cheval très coté; (b) F: **to f. oneself**, gober; **'fanciful**, a. (a) (of pers.) capricieu fantasque; (b) (projet m) chimérique; (conte n imaginaire.

fang [fæŋ], s. (a) croc m (de loup); (b) crochet (de vipère).

fantasy ['fæntəsi, -zi], s. fantaisie f; **fan'tasti** a. fantastique; bizarre; invraisemblable; Co f. **reductions**, baisses phénoménales.

far [fɑːr]. **I.** adv. **1.** (a) (of place) loin; **to go** aller loin; **how f. is it from Paris to Bonn?** co bien y a-t-il de Paris à Bonn? **as f. as the e** **can reach**, à perte de vue; **to live f. away, f. o** demeurer au loin; f. **and wide**, de tous côt partout; (b) **to go so f. as to do sth.**, all jusqu'à faire qch.; **that's going too f.**, ce passe la mesure, les bornes; **as f. as I know**, a tant que je sache; **as f. as that goes**, pour ce q est de cela; **so f. so good,** c'est fort bien jusquelà; **in so f. as . . . ,** dans la mesure où . . . ; **to be f. from believing sth.,** être à cent lieues de croire qch.; **f. from it,** tant s'en faut; loin de là; **by f.,** de loin; **by f. the best,** de beaucoup le meilleur. **2.** (*of time*) **so f.,** jusqu'ici; **as f. as I can see,** autant que je puisse prévoir; **f. into the night,** bien avant dans la nuit; **as f. back as 1900,** déjà en 1900. **3.** (*for emphasis*) beaucoup, bien, fort; **it's f. better,** c'est beaucoup mieux; **f. more serious,** bien autrement sérieux; **f. advanced,** fort avancé; **f. and away the best,** de beaucoup le meilleur, bien préférable. **II.** *a.* **1.** lointain, éloigné. **2. at the f. end of the street,** à l'autre bout de la rue; **'faraway,** *a.* lointain, éloigné; **f. look,** regard perdu dans le vague; **'far-'fetched,** *a.* (*of argument, etc.*) forcé, outré; **'far-'reaching,** *a.* de grande envergure, d'une grande portée; **'far-'seeing, 'far-'sighted,** *a.* prévoyant; clairvoyant; perspicace; **far'sightedness,** *s.* prescience *f*; perspicacité *f*.

farce [fɑːs], *s.* *Th:* farce *f*; **'farcical,** *a.* risible, grotesque.

fare ['fɛər], *s.* **1.** (*a*) prix *m* du voyage, de la place; (*in taxi*) prix de la course; **single f.,** (prix du) billet simple; **return f.,** aller et retour *m*, aller-retour *m*; **fares, please!** les places, s'il vous plaît! (*b*) (*in taxi*) client, -ente; voyageur, -euse. **2.** chère *f*, manger *m*; **prison f.,** régime *m* de prison.

farewell [fɛə'wel], *int. & s.* adieu (*m*); **to bid s.o. f.,** dire adieu, faire ses adieux, à qn; **f. dinner,** dîner *m* d'adieu.

farm [fɑːm]. **I.** *s.* ferme *f*; **f. butter,** beurre *m* fermier; **f. labourer,** ouvrier *m* agricole. **II.** *v.* **1.** *v.tr.* cultiver (des terres). **2.** *v.i.* être cultivateur, agriculteur; **'farmer,** *s.* agriculteur *m*; cultivateur, -trice; exploitant, -ante, agricole; (**tenant**) **f.,** fermier, -ière; **stock f.,** éleveur, -euse; **'farmhouse,** *s.* (maison *f* de) ferme *f*; **'farming,** *s.* exploitation *f* agricole; agriculture *f*; **'farmyard,** *s.* cour *f* de ferme; basse-cour *f*.

farrier ['færiər], *s.* maréchal(-ferrant) *m*.

farther ['fɑːðər]. **1.** *adv.* plus loin (**than,** que); **f. off,** plus éloigné; **f. on,** plus en avant; plus loin; **f. back,** plus en arrière. **2.** *a.* plus lointain, plus éloigné; **'farthest. 1.** *a.* **f.** (**off**), le plus lointain, le plus éloigné. **2.** *adv.* le plus loin; **it was the f. that we went,** c'est le plus loin que nous ayons pénétré.

fascinate ['fæsineit], *v.tr.* fasciner, charmer, séduire; **to be fascinated by sth.,** être fasciné par qch.; **'fascinating,** *a.* enchanteur, séduisant; **f. book,** livre passionnant; **fasci'nation,** *s.* fascination *f*; charme *m*; attrait *m*.

fashion ['fæʃ(ə)n], *s.* **1.** manière *f* (de faire qch.); **in a peculiar f.,** d'une façon étrange; **after a f.,** tant bien que mal. **2.** mode *f*, vogue *f*; **in f.,** à la mode, de mode, en vogue; **out of f.,** passé de mode, démodé; **to become the f., come into f.,** devenir la mode; **f. house,** maison *f* de haute couture; **f. show,** présentation *f* de collections; **f. magazine,** journal *m* de modes; **'fashionable,** *a.* à la mode, élégant, en vogue; **a f. resort,** un endroit mondain; **-ably,** *adv.* élégamment, à la mode; **'fashioned,** *a.* (*of knitted goods*) **fully f.,** (entièrement) diminué, proportionné.

fast[1] [fɑːst]. **I.** *s.* jeûne *m*. **II.** *v.i.* jeûner; faire maigre.

fast[2]. **I.** *a.* **1.** (*a*) ferme, fixe, solide; **to hold s.o. f.,** tenir qn ferme; (*b*) *Nau:* amarré; (*c*) (*of colour*) solide, résistant; bon teint *inv.* **2.** (*a*) rapide; **f. train,** rapide *m*; (*b*) *F:* **he pulled a f. one on me,** il m'a joué un mauvais tour. **3.** (*of clock, etc.*) en avance; **my watch is five minutes f.,** ma montre avance de cinq minutes. **4.** *F:* (*of pers.*) dissipé; de mœurs légères; (trop) émancipé. **II.** *adv.* **1.** ferme, solidement; **to hold f.,** tenir ferme; tenir bon; **to stand f.,** tenir bon; **shut f.,** bien fermé; **to play f. and loose,** agir avec inconstance. **2.** vite, rapidement; **not so f.!** pas si vite! doucement! *F:* **he'll do it f. enough if you pay him,** il ne se fera pas prier si vous le payez.

fasten [fɑːsn]. **1.** *v.tr.* (*a*) attacher (qch. à qch.); **to f. the responsibility on s.o.,** mettre la responsabilité sur le dos de qn; (*b*) fixer, assurer; bien fermer (la porte); **to f.** (**up**) **one's dress,** agrafer, boutonner, sa robe. **2.** *v.i.* s'attacher, se fixer; **the door fastens with a bolt,** la porte se ferme au verrou; **'fastener,** *s.,* **'fastening,** *s.* attache *f*; (*of garment*) agrafe *f*; (*of window*) fermeture *f*.

fastidious [fæs'tidiəs], *a.* difficile (à contenter); délicat (**about sth.,** sur qch.); **-ly,** *adv.* d'un air de dégoût; avec une délicatesse exagérée; dédaigneusement.

fat [fæt]. **I.** *a.* (*a*) gros; gras; **to get f.,** engraisser; (*b*) *F:* **a f. lot you know about it!** comme si vous en saviez quelque chose! **II.** *s.* **1.** graisse *f*; **frying f.,** friture *f*; *F:* **the f.'s in the fire!** le feu est aux poudres! **2.** gras *m* (de viande); **to live on, off, the f. of the land,** vivre comme un coq en pâte; **'fathead,** *s.* *F:* imbécile *mf*; andouille *f*.

fate [feit], *s.* destin *m*, sort *m*; **to leave s.o. to his f.,** abandonner qn à son sort; **'fatal,** *a.* fatal; **f. blow,** coup fatal, mortel; **f. disease,** maladie mortelle; **f. mistake,** faute capitale; **'fatally,** *adv.* fatalement; mortellement (blessé); **fa'tality,** *s.* accident mortel; sinistre *m*; **there were no fatalities,** il n'y a pas eu de mort *f*; **'fated,** *a.* **1.**

fatal, inévitable. 2. destiné, condamné (**to do sth.**, à faire qch.); **'fateful**, *a.* (jour) décisif; (événement) de la première importance.

father ['fɑ:ðər], *s.* 1. père *m*; **yes, F.**, oui, (mon) père; oui, papa. 2. (*a*) **God the F.**, Dieu le Père; (*b*) **the Holy F.**, le Saint-Père; (*c*) **F. Martin**, (i) (*belonging to religious order*) le Père Martin; (ii) (*priest*) l'abbé Martin; **'father-in-law**, *s.* beau-père *m*; **'fatherless**, *a.* orphelin de père; **'fatherly**, *a.* paternel.

fathom ['fæðəm]. **I.** *s. Nau:* brasse *f.* **II.** *v.tr.* sonder (un mystère).

fatigue [fə'ti:g]. **I.** *s.* 1. fatigue *f.* 2. *Mil:* corvée *f.* **II.** *v.tr.* fatiguer, lasser (qn); **fa'tiguing**, *a.* fatigant, épuisant.

fatten ['fæt(ə)n]. 1. *v.tr.* **to f. (up)**, engraisser (des veaux). 2. *v.i.* engraisser; devenir gras; **'fatness**, *s.* embonpoint *m*, corpulence *f*; **'fattening**, 1. *a.* (*of food*) qui fait grossir. 2. *s.* engraissement *m*; **'fatty**, *a.* (*a*) graisseux, oléagineux; **f. foods**, aliments gras; (*b*) (*of tissue*) adipeux.

fatuous ['fætjuəs], *a.* sot, imbécile, idiot; **-ly**, *adv.* sottement; **fa'tuity**, *s.* sottise *f.*

faucet ['fɔ:sət], *s. N.Am:* robinet *m.*

fault [fɔlt], *s.* 1. (*a*) défaut *m* (de qn); imperfection *f*; **scrupulous to a f.**, scrupuleux à l'excès; **to find f. with s.o.**, trouver à redire contre qn; (*b*) *Tchn:* défaut; vice *m* (de construction). 2. faute *f*; **to be at f.**, être en défaut, être fautif; **whose f. is it?** à qui la faute? 3. *Ten:* faute. 4. *Geog:* faille *f*; **'faultfinder**, *s.* critiqueur, -euse; mécontent, -ente; **'faultfinding**, *s.* disposition *f* à critiquer; **'faultiness**, *s.* défectuosité *f*, imperfection *f*; **'faultless**, *a.* sans défaut, sans faute; impeccable, irréprochable; **-ly**, *adv.* parfaitement, d'une manière impeccable; **'faulty**, *a.* défectueux, imparfait; (*of reasoning*) erroné, inexact; (*of style*) incorrect.

fauna ['fɔ:nə], *s.* faune *f.*

favour ['feivər]. **I.** *s.* faveur *f*, approbation *f*, bonnes grâces; **to be in f. with s.o.**, être en faveur auprès de qn; jouir de la faveur de qn; **to be out of f.**, (i) être mal en cour; (ii) n'être plus en vogue. 2. grâce *f*; bonté *f*; faveur; **to do s.o. a f.**, faire une faveur à qn; obliger qn; **as a f.**, à titre gracieux; **to ask a f. of s.o.**, solliciter une grâce, une faveur, de qn. 3. partialité *f*, préférence *f*; **to show f. to s.o.**, favoriser qn. 4. **in f. of**, en faveur de; **to have everything in one's f.**, avoir tout pour soi; **to decide in s.o.'s f.**, donner gain de cause à qn; **to be in f. of sth.**, être partisan de qch.; tenir pour qch. **II.** *v.tr.* 1. favoriser, approuver, préférer; **to f. a scheme**, approuver un projet; **I don't f. the idea**, l'idée ne me plaît pas. 2. (*a*) avantager (qn); montrer de la partialité pour (qn); (*b*) faciliter (qch.); **circumstances that f. our interests**, cir-

constances favorables à nos intérêts; **'favourable**, *a.* favorable; (*of weather*) propice; (*of terms, circumstances*) bon, avantageux; **-ably**, *adv.* favorablement, avantageusement; **'favoured**, *a.* favorisé; **most f. nation**, nation la plus favorisée; **the f. few**, les élus *m*; **'favourite**, *a. & s.* favori, -ite; préféré -ée; **'favouritism**, *s.* favoritisme *m.*

fawn[1] [fɔ:n]. 1. *s. Z:* faon *m.* 2. *a. & s.* (*colour*) fauve (*m*).

fawn[2], *v.ind.tr.* **to f. on s.o.**, (i) (*of dog*) caresser qn; (ii) (*of pers.*) ramper devant qn; aduler qn; **'fawning**, *a.* (i) caressant; (ii) servile.

fear ['fiər]. **I.** *s.* crainte *f*, peur *f*; **deadly f.**, effroi *m*; **to stand in f. of s.o.**, redouter, craindre, qn; **to go in f. of one's life**, craindre pour sa vie; **for f. of making a mistake**, de crainte d'erreur; **no f.!** pas de danger! **II.** *v.tr.* 1. craindre, avoir peur de, redouter (qn, qch.). 2. (*a*) appréhender, craindre; **to f. for s.o.**, s'inquiéter au sujet de qn; **I f. it is too late**, je crains qu'il ne soit trop tard; (*b*) **I f. I'm late**, je crois bien être en retard; **'fearful**, *a.* 1. affreux, effrayant; **F. a f. mess**, un désordre effrayant. 2. peureux, craintif; **-fully**, *adv.* 1. affreusement, terriblement; **it's f. hot**, il fait terriblement chaud. 2. peureusement; **'fearless**, *a.* intrépide, courageux; **-ly**, *adv.* intrépidement, sans peur; **'fearlessness**, *s.* intrépidité *f*; **'fearsome**, *a.* redoutable, terrifiant.

feasible ['fi:zəbl], *a.* faisable, possible, praticable; **feasi'bility**, *s.* praticabilité *f*, faisabilité *f* (d'un projet).

feast [fi:st]. **I.** *s.* 1. (*jour m* de) fête *f.* 2. festin *m*, banquet *m.* **II.** *v.* 1. *v.i.* faire festin; se régaler (**on sth.**, de qch.). 2. *v.tr.* régaler, fêter (qn); **to f. one's eyes on sth.**, regarder qch. avec délices; **'feasting**, *s.* régal *m*; bonne chère.

feat [fi:t], *s.* 1. exploit *m*, haut fait. 2. tour *m* de force; **f. of engineering**, triomphe *m* de l'ingénieur.

feather ['feðər]. **I.** *s.* 1. plume *f*; **f. bed**, lit *m* de plume. 2. plumage *m*; **birds of a f. flock together**, qui se ressemble s'assemble. 3. **that's a f. in his cap**, c'est tout à son honneur. **II.** *v.tr. F:* **to f. one's nest**, faire sa pelote; **'feather-brained**, *a.* écervelé, étourdi.

feature ['fi:tʃər], *s.* 1. trait *m* (du visage); **the features**, la physionomie. 2. (*a*) trait caractéristique *f*, particularité *f*; **main feature**, grands traits; (*b*) spécialité *f*; (*c*) *Cin:* **f. (film)**, long métrage, *F:* grand film.

February ['februəri], *s.* février *m*; **in F.**, au mois de février.

federate ['fedəreit]. 1. *v.tr.* fédérer. 2. *v.i.* fédérer; **'federal**, *a.* fédéral; **fede'ration**, *s.* fédération *f.*

fee [fi:], *s.* (*a*) honoraires *mpl*; (*b*) **school fee**

frais *mpl* de scolarité; **examination f.**, droit *m* d'examen; **entrance f.**, droit d'entrée; *P.T.T:* **registration f.**, taxe *f* de recommandation.

feeble [fi:bl], *a.* (*a*) faible, infirme, débile; (*b*) *F:* (*of pers.*) mou, sans caractère; **-bly**, *adv.* faiblement; **'feeble-'minded**, *a.* d'esprit *m* faible; **'feebleness**, *s.* faiblesse *f,* débilité *f.*

feed [fi:d]. I. *s.* 1. (*a*) alimentation *f;* pâturage *m;* (*b*) nourriture *f,* pâture *f;* fourrage *m;* **to give the horse a f.**, donner à manger au cheval; *F:* **to be off one's f.**, bouder sur la nourriture; (*c*) *F:* repas *m,* festin *m;* **to have a good f.**, bien manger; faire bonne chère. 2. *Tchn:* alimentation (d'une machine); **gravity f.**, **pressure f.**, alimentation par gravité, sous pression. II. *v.* (**fed**) 1. *v.tr.* (*a*) nourrir; donner à manger à (qn); allaiter (un enfant); **to f. s.o. on sth.**, nourrir qn de qch.; (*b*) alimenter (une machine). 2. *v.i.* manger; (*of cattle*) paître, brouter; **to f. on sth.**, se nourrir de qch.;'**feeding**, *s.* alimentation *f;* **f. bottle**, biberon *m* (de bébé);'**feedpipe**, *s.* tuyau *m* d'alimentation;'**feed up**, *v.tr.* engraisser (un animal); suralimenter (qn); *F:* **I'm fed up**, j'en ai plein le dos, j'en ai marre.

feel [fi:l]. I. *s.* 1. toucher *m;* **rough to the f.**, rude au toucher. 2. (*a*) toucher, main *f* (du papier); **to recognize sth. by the f. of it**, reconnaître qch. au toucher; (*b*) sensation *f;* **the f. of a collar round my neck**, la sensation d'un faux-col autour de mon cou; (*c*) **he has the f. of his car**, il a sa voiture bien en main. II. *v.* (**felt**) 1. (*a*) *v.tr.* toucher, palper; tâter (le pouls); (*b*) *v.tr. & i.* **to f. about in the dark**, tâtonner dans l'obscurité; **to f. one's way**, (i) aller à tâtons; (ii) sonder le terrain; **to f. in one's pockets for sth.**, chercher qch. dans ses poches. 2. (*a*) *v.tr.* sentir; **to f. the floor trembling**, sentir trembler le plancher; (*b*) *v.tr. & i.* (res)sentir, éprouver; **to f. the cold**, être sensible au froid; être frileux; **to make one's authority felt**, affirmer son autorité; **to f. a kindly interest towards s.o.**, éprouver de la sympathie pour qn; **I f. for him**, il a toute ma sympathie; (*c*) *v.tr.* avoir conscience de (qch.); **I felt it necessary to intervene**, j'ai jugé nécessaire d'intervenir. 3. *v.i.* (*a*) **to f. cold**, avoir froid; **to f. ill**, se sentir malade; **to f. all the better for it**, s'en trouver mieux; **to f. certain that . . .**, être certain que . . .; (*b*) **I felt like crying**, j'avais envie de pleurer; **I don't f. like it**, ça ne me dit rien; **I f. like a cup of tea**, je prendrais bien une tasse de thé. 4. *v.i.* (*of thg*) **to f. hard**, être dur au toucher;'**feeler**, *s.* 1. *Ent: etc:* antenne *f,* palpe *f.* 2. **to put out a f.**, lancer un ballon d'essai; tâter le terrain; **peace feelers**, sondages *m* de paix;'**feeling**, *s.* 1. tâtage *m,* palpation *f* (de qch.). 2. (**sense of**) **f.**, toucher *m* ; **to have no f. in one's arm**, avoir le bras mort. 3. sensation

(douloureuse, etc.). 4. sentiment *m;* (*a*) **public f.**, le sentiment populaire; **no hard feelings!** sans rancune! (*b*) **I had a f. of danger**, j'avais le sentiment d'être en danger; (*c*) sensibilité *f,* émotion *f;* **have you no feelings!** vous n'avez donc pas d'âme!

feign [fein], *v.tr.* feindre, simuler; **to f. surprise**, affecter la surprise; **feigned**, *a.* feint, simulé; **feint.** I. *s. Mil:* fausse attaque; *Box:* feinte *f.* II. *v.i. Box:* feinter.

felicity [fə'lisiti], *s.* félicité *f,* bonheur *m.*

fell [fel], *v.tr.* abattre (un arbre).

fellow ['felou], *s.* 1. camarade *m,* compagnon *m,* confrère *m,* collègue *m;* **f. sufferer**, compagnon de misère; **f. feeling**, sympathie *f;* **f. creature**, semblable *mf;* **f. citizen**, concitoyen, -enne; **f. countryman**, **-woman**, compatriote *mf; Pol:* **f. traveller**, communisant, -ante. 2. (*of pers.*) semblable *m,* pareil *m;* (*of thg*) pendant *m.* 3. (*a*) (*at university*) professeur chargé de fonctions administratives; (*b*) membre *m,* associé, -ée (d'une société savante). 4. *F:* (*a*) homme *m,* garçon *m;* **a good f.**, un brave garçon, un bon type; **a queer f.**, un drôle de type; **the poor little f.**, le pauvre petit; (*b*) *Pej:* individu *m;* '**fellowship**, *s.* 1. communion *f,* communauté *f.* 2. association *f,* corporation *f,* (con)fraternité *f.*

felon ['felən], *s. Jur:* criminel, -elle; **fe'lonious** [-'louniəs], *a.* criminel;'**felony**, *s.* crime *m.*

felt [felt], *s.* feutre *m;* **f. pen**, crayon *m* feutre.

female ['fi:meil]. 1. *a.* (*a*) féminin; (de) femme; **f. child**, enfant du sexe féminin; (*b*) (*of animal*) femelle. 2. *s.f.* (*a*) femme; (*b*) femelle;'**feminine**, *a.* féminin.

fen [fen], *s.* marais *m,* marécage *m.*

fence [fens]. I. *s.* 1. clôture *f,* barrière *f,* palissade *f; F:* **to sit on the f.**, ménager la chèvre et le chou. 2. *F:* receleur, -euse. II. *v.* 1. *v.i.* faire de l'escrime. 2. *v.tr.* **to f. (in)**, clôturer (un terrain); '**fencing**, *s.* 1. escrime *f;* **f. master**, maître *m* d'escrime, d'armes. 2. **f. (in)**, clôture *f.* 3. clôture, barrière *f,* palissade *f;* **wire f.**, treillis *m* métallique. 4. *F:* recel *m.*

fend [fend]. 1. *v.tr.* **to f. off**, parer, détourner (un coup). 2. *v.i.* **to f. for oneself**, se débrouiller.

fender ['fendər], *s.* (*a*) *Furn:* garde-feu *m inv;* (*b*) *N.Am: Aut:* (i) garde-boue *m inv;* (ii) pare-choc(s) *m.*

ferment. I. *s.* ['fə:ment]. 1. ferment *m.* 2. (*a*) fermentation *f* (des liquides); (*b*) agitation *f* populaire; **the town is in a f.**, la ville est en effervescence. II. *v.i.* [fə'ment], fermenter; (*of wine*) travailler; **fermen'tation**, *s.* fermentation *f.*

fern [fə:n], *s. Bot:* fougère *f.*

ferocious [fə'rouʃəs], *a.* féroce; **-ly**, *adv.* avec

férocité; **fe′rocity** [-′rɔsiti], s. férocité f.
ferret [′ferit]. I. s. Z: furet m. II. v. 1. v.i. fureter;
chasser au furet; **to f. about,** fureter, fouiner,
partout. **2.** v.tr. **to f. out** sth., dénicher qch.;
′**ferreting,** s. furetage m; chasse f au furet.
ferry [′feri]. **1.** s. **1.** (endroit m de) passage m
(d′un cours d′eau en bac); bac m; **to cross the
f.,** passer le bac. **2. f. (boat),** bac; bachot m de
passeur; **train, car, f.,** ferry-boat m. II. v.tr. **to f.
the car across,** passer la voiture en bac;
′**ferryman,** pl. -**men,** s. passeur m.
fertile [′fɔːtail], a. (a) fertile, fécond; (b) (of egg)
fécondé; **fer′tility** [-′til-], s. fertilité f, fécondité
f; **fertili′zation,** s. fertilisation f; fécondation
f; ′**fertilize,** v.tr. fertiliser; féconder; ′**fertilizer,** s. engrais m.
fervour [′fɔːvər], s. passion f, ferveur f; ′**fervent,** a. ardent, fervent.
fester [′festər], v.i. suppurer; ′**festering,** a.
ulcéreux, suppurant.
festive [′festiv], a. joyeux; (air) de fête; **the f.
season,** Noël m; ′**festival,** s. fête f; **film f.,**
festival m du film; **fes′tivity,** s. fête f;
réjouissance f; festivité f.
festoon [fes′tuːn]. I. s. feston m, guirlande f. II.
v.tr. festonner (**with,** de).
fetch [fetʃ], v.tr. **1.** (a) aller chercher; **come and f.
me,** venez me chercher; **to f. water from the
river,** aller puiser de l′eau à la rivière; (b) apporter (qch.); amener (qch.). **2.** rapporter; **it
fetched a high price,** cela s′est vendu cher. **3.** F:
to f. s.o. a blow, flanquer un coup à qn; ′**fetch
′back,** v.tr. ramener; rapporter; ′**fetch
′down,** v.tr. faire descendre (qn); descendre
(qch.); ′**fetch ′in,** v.tr. rentrer (la lessive, etc.).
fête [feit]. I. s. fête f. II. v.tr. fêter; faire fête à (qn).
fetish [′fetiʃ], s. fétiche m.
fetter [′fetər]. I. v.tr. enchaîner (qn); charger de
fers; entraver (un cheval). II. s. usu. pl. **fetters,**
chaînes f, fers m; **in fetters,** enchaîné.
feud [fjuːd], s. **(blood) f.,** vendetta f; **family
feuds,** dissensions domestiques, familiales.
feudal [′fjuːdəl], a. féodal; ′**feudalism,** s. le
régime féodal; la féodalité.
fever [′fiːvər], s. fièvre f; **f. of excitement,** excitation f fébrile, fiévreuse; ′**fevered,** a. enfiévré,
fiévreux; ′**feverish,** a. fiévreux, fébrile; -**ly,**
adv. fiévreusement, fébrilement;
′**feverishness,** s. état fiévreux.
few [fjuː], a. **1.** (a) peu de; **he has f. friends,** il a
peu d′amis; **with f. exceptions,** à de rares
exceptions près; (b) **a f. (books, etc.),** quelques
(livres, etc.); **a f. more,** encore quelques-un(e)s;
in a f. minutes, dans quelques minutes; (c) peu
nombreux; **such occasions are f. (and far
between),** de telles occasions sont rares. **2.** (a)
peu (de gens); **f. of them,** peu d′entre eux; **there
are very f. of us,** nous sommes peu nombreux;

(b) quelques-uns, -unes; **I know a f. of them,**
j′en connais quelques-uns; **a f. thought
differently,** quelques-uns pensaient autrement;
there were a good f. of them, il y en avait pas
mal; ′**fewer,** a. **1.** moins (de); **20% f. visitors,**
20% de visiteurs en moins. **2.** plus rares;
moins nombreux; **the houses became f.,** les
maisons devenaient plus rares; ′**fewest,** a. **1.**
le moins (de). **2.** les plus rares, les moins
nombreux.
fiasco, pl. -os [fi′æskou, -ouz], s. fiasco m.
fibre [′faibər], s. (a) fibre f; filament m; (b) **glass
f.,** fibre de verre; **f. trunk,** malle f en fibre;
′**fibreboard,** s. panneau m de fibres
agglomérées; ′**fibreglass,** s. fibre f, laine f, de
verre; ′**fibrous,** a. fibreux; filamenteux.
fickle [fikl], a. inconstant, volage; ′**fickleness,**
s. inconstance f.
fiction [′fikʃ(ə)n], s. **1.** fiction f. **2. (works of) f.,**
romans m; ouvrages m d′imagination; **science
f.,** science-fiction f; **fic′titious,** a. fictif.
fiddle [fidl]. I. s. **1.** F: (instrument or player)
violon m; **to play second f.,** jouer un rôle
secondaire. **2.** F: combine f; **it′s just a f.,** ce
n′est que du tripotage. II. v. **1.** v.i. jouer du
violon. **2.** v.i. tripoter, bricoler, fignoler. **3.** v.tr.
to f. the expenses, ratiboiser sur les notes de
frais; **to f. the accounts,** maquiller la comptabilité; ′**fiddler,** s. F: **1.** joueur m de violon. **2.**
combinard m; ′**fiddling. 1.** a. futile, insignifiant. **2.** s. F: combines fpl.
fidelity [fi′deliti], s. fidélité f, loyauté f; Rec: **high
f.,** haute fidélité.
fidget [′fidʒit]. I. s. **1.** F: **to have the fidgets,** ne pa
tenir en place. **2. he′s a f.,** c′est un énervé. II
v.i. (a) ne pas tenir en place; (b) remuer
continuellement; **to f. (about),** remuer continuellement; s
trémousser; (b) s′impatienter; ′**fidgeting,** s
agitation nerveuse; nervosité; ′**fidgety,** a. (a
remuant, agité; (b) nerveux, impatient.
field [fiːld], s. **1.** (a) champ m; **in the fields,** au
champs; **f. glasses,** jumelles fpl; **f. sports,** (i
l′athlétisme m; la chasse et la pêche; (b) Mil: f
(of battle), champ de bataille; **to take the f.,** en
trer en campagne; **f. artillery,** artillerie f d
campagne; **f. officer,** officier supérieur; **f. day**
(i) Mil: jour m de grandes manœuvres; (ii
grande occasion; grand jour; (c) Fb: etc
terrain m; (d) Av: **landing f.,** terrai
d′atterrissage. **2.** (a) théâtre m, champ
domaine m (d′une science); **in the political f.**
sur le plan politique; (b) **f. study,** études f sur l
terrain. **3.** Rac: **the f.,** les coureurs m, les par
tants m; ′**field-′marshal,** s. Mil: maréchal m
′**fieldmouse,** s. Z: mulot m.
fiend [fiːnd], s. (a) démon m, diable m;
monstre m (de cruauté); ′**fiendish,**
diabolique, satanique; -**ly,** ad
diaboliquement.

fierce ['fiəs], a. féroce; (of battle) acharné; (of wind) furieux, violent; **f. brake,** frein brutal; **-ly,** adv. (a) férocement; (b) violemment; avec acharnement; **'fierceness,** s. violence f; férocité f (d'un animal); ardeur f (du feu); acharnement m (de la bataille).

fiery ['faiəri], a. **1.** ardent, brûlant, enflammé. **2.** (of pers.) (i) fougueux, emporté, impétueux; (ii) colérique.

fife [faif], s. Mus: fifre m.

fifteen [fif'ti:n], num.a. & s. quinze (m); **she is f.,** elle a quinze ans; Rugby Fb: **the French f.,** le quinze de France; **'fifteenth. 1.** num.a. & s. quinzième; **Louis the F.,** Louis Quinze; **the f. of August,** le quinze août. **2.** s. (fraction) quinzième m.

fifth [fifθ]. **1.** num.a. & s. cinquième; **Henry the F.,** Henri Cinq; Pol: **f. column,** cinquième colonne f. **2.** s. (fraction) cinquième m.

fifty ['fifti], num.a. & s. cinquante (m); **to go f.-f. with s.o.,** se mettre de moitié avec qn; **about f.,** une cinquantaine (de livres, etc.); **'fiftieth,** num.a. & s. cinquantième (m).

fig [fig], s. figue f; **green figs,** (i) figues blanches; (ii) figues fraîches; **f.(-tree),** figuier m; **'fig-leaf,** s. feuille f (i) de figuier, (ii) Art: de vigne.

fight [fait]. **I.** s. **1.** (a) combat m, bataille f; (b) assaut m; Box: match m; **hand to hand f.,** corps-à-corps m; **free f.,** (i) rixe f; (ii) mêlée générale; **f. to the death,** combat à outrance. **2.** (a) lutte f; (b) **to show f.,** résister; **there was no f. left in him,** il n'avait plus de cœur à se battre; il était à bout de forces. **II.** v. (**fought**) **1.** (a) v.i. se battre; combattre; lutter; **to f. against disease,** combattre la maladie; **dogs fighting over a bone,** chiens m qui se disputent un os; (b) v.tr. **to f. a battle,** livrer (une) bataille; **to f. one's way (out),** se frayer un passage (pour sortir); Jur: **to f. a case,** se défendre dans un procès. **2.** v.tr. se battre avec, contre (qn); combattre (qn, un incendie); lutter contre (qn); **'fighter,** s. **1.** combattant m. **2.** Av: chasseur m; **'fighting,** s. combat m; Sp: boxe f; **f. broke out in the crowd,** des rixes se sont produites dans la foule; Mil: **f. strength,** effectif m de combat, de guerre; **we've a f. chance,** ça vaut la peine de lutter.

figure ['figər]. **I.** s. **1.** figure f, forme extérieure; (of pers.) taille f, tournure f; **to keep one's f.,** garder sa ligne. **2.** (a) personne f; forme humaine; **a f. of fun,** une caricature; (b) personnage m, personnalité f; (in play, etc.) **the central f.,** le pivot de l'action; (c) figure, apparence f; **to cut a brilliant f.,** faire belle figure. **3.** Art: image f; **vase with Chinese figures,** vase m à personnages chinois; **f. of a cat,** image d'un chat. **4.** figure (géométrique); illustration f (dans un livre). **5.** Mth: etc: chiffre

m; **in round figures,** en chiffres ronds; **double figures,** dix ou plus; **a mistake in the figures,** une erreur de calcul; **to fetch a high f.,** se vendre cher; **the figures for 1975,** les statistiques f pour 1975. **6. f. of speech,** métaphore f; façon f de parler. **II.** v.i. **his name figures on the list,** son nom figure sur la liste; **'figurative,** a. figuré, métaphorique; **-ly,** adv. au figuré; **'figurehead,** s. (a) Nau: figure f de proue; (b) personnage purement décoratif.

filament ['filəmənt], s. filament m.

filbert ['filbət], s. noisette f.

filch [filtʃ], v.tr. chiper, barboter, chaparder (**sth. from s.o.,** qch. à qn).

file¹ [fail]. **I.** s. lime f. **II.** v.tr. limer; **'filing,** s. **1.** limage m. **2.** pl. **filings,** limaille f.

file². **I.** s. **1.** classeur m; **card-index f.,** fichier m; f. **card,** fiche f. **2.** liasse f (de papiers); dossier m; Publ: **f. copy,** exemplaire m d'archives. **II.** v.tr. **1.** classer (des fiches, etc.). **2.** Jur: **to f. a petition,** enregistrer une requête; **'filing,** s. classement m; f. **clerk,** archiviste mf; f. **cabinet,** classeur m, fichier m.

file³. **I.** s. file f; **in single, Indian, f.,** en file indienne, F: à la queue leu leu. **II.** v.i. **to f. past s.o.,** défiler devant qn; **to f. in, out,** entrer, sortir, à la file.

filial ['filiəl], a. filial.

filigree ['filigri:], s. filigrane m.

fill [fil]. **I.** s. **1.** suffisance f; **to eat, drink, one's f.,** manger à sa faim, boire à sa soif. **2.** (quantity) charge f, plein m. **II.** v. **1.** v.tr. (a) remplir, emplir (**with,** de); bourrer (sa pipe); charger (un wagon); **to be filled with admiration,** être rempli d'admiration; (b) combler (une brèche); obturer, plomber (une dent); **post to be filled,** emploi m à pourvoir; (c) occuper (un poste); **the thoughts that filled his mind,** les pensées qui occupaient son esprit; (d) Com: exécuter (une commande). **2.** v.i. (a) se remplir, s'emplir; **the hall is beginning to f.,** la salle commence à se garnir; (b) (of sail) s'enfler, porter; **'fill 'in,** v.tr. (a) combler, remplir (un trou); remblayer (un fossé); (b) remplir (un formulaire); insérer (la date); **'filling. I.** a. (of food) rassasiant. **II.** s. **1.** (r)emplissage m; chargement (d'un wagon); comblement (d'un trou); Dent: obturation f, plombage m; Aut: f. **station,** poste m d'essence, station-service f. **2.** (matière f de) remplissage; **cake with chocolate f.,** gâteau fourré au chocolat; **'fill 'out,** v. **1.** v.tr. N.Am: remplir (un formulaire). **2.** v.i. s'enfler, se gonfler; **'fill 'up. 1.** v.tr. (a) remplir (un verre) jusqu'au bord; combler (une mesure); Aut: **to f. up with petrol,** faire le plein d'essence; (b) boucher (un trou); (c) remplir (un formulaire). **2.** v.i. se remplir, s'emplir, se combler.

fillet ['filit]. **I.** *s.* filet *m* (de bœuf, de sole). **II.** *v.tr.* *Cu:* détacher, lever, des filets de (poisson).

filly ['fili], *s.* pouliche *f.*

film [film]. **I.** *s.* pellicule *f*, couche *f*, film *m* (de glace, d'huile); voile *m* (de brume). **2.** *Phot:* pellicule, film; **colour f.**, film (en) couleurs; **X-ray f.**, film radiographique. **3.** *Cin:* (*a*) film; **full-length f.**, (film de) long métrage; **to make a f.**, tourner un film; (*b*) **the films**, le cinéma; **f. library**, cinémathèque *f*; **f. club**, ciné-club *m*. **II.** *v.tr. Cin:* filmer, tourner (une scène); filmer (un roman); **to f. well**, être photogénique; **'filmstar,** *s.* vedette *f* (de l'écran); étoile *f* de cinéma; **'filmstrip,** *s.* film fixe (d'enseignement).

filter ['filtər]. **I.** *s.* (*a*) filtre *m*, épurateur *m*; **f. paper,** papier filtre; (*of cigarette*) **f. tip,** bout filtrant, bout filtre; (*b*) *Phot:* **colour f.,** filtre de couleur, écran coloré; (*c*) *T.V:* **tone f.,** filtre de tonalité. **II.** *v.* **1.** *v.tr.* filtrer (l'eau); épurer (l'air). **2.** *v.i.* (*a*) (*of water*) filtrer, s'infiltrer (**through**, à travers, par); (*b*) *Aut:* changer de file; **to f. to the right, to the left,** (se) glisser à droite, à gauche.

filth [filθ], *s.* **1.** (*a*) ordures *fpl*; immondices *mpl*; (*b*) saleté *f.* **2. to talk f.,** dire des obscénités *f*, des ordures; **'filthiness,** *s.* (*a*) saleté; obscénité *f*; **'filthy,** *a.* **1.** (*a*) sale, immonde, dégoûtant; **f. hovel,** taudis infect; **f. communist!** (*b*) **in a f. temper,** d'une humeur massacrante. **2.** (*of book, talk*) ordurier, crapuleux, obscène.

fin [fin], *s.* (*a*) (*of fish*) nageoire *f*; (*of shark*) aileron *m*; (*b*) (*of frogman*) palme *f.*

final ['fain(ə)l]. **1.** *a.* (*a*) final, dernier; **to put the f. touches to sth.,** mettre la dernière main à qch.; *Com:* **f. instalment,** dernier versement; (*b*) définitif, décisif; **am I to take that as f.?** c'est votre dernier mot? **2.** *s.pl. Sp:* **the finals,** les (épreuves) finales (*f*); *Sch:* **to take one's finals** = passer son dernier examen de licence; **-ally,** *adv.* finalement; **'finalist,** *s. Sp:* finaliste *mf*; **'finalize,** *v.tr.* mener (qch.) à bonne fin; mettre la dernière main à (qch.).

finale [fi'nɑːli], *s. Mus:* final(e) *m.*

finance [fai'næns, fi-]. **I.** *s.* finance *f*; **public f.,** finances publiques; **f. company,** société *f* de crédits. **II.** *v.tr.* financer, commanditer (une entreprise), **fi'nancial,** *a.* financier; **f. statement,** bilan *m*; *Adm:* **f. year,** exercice *m* (financier), année *f* budgétaire; **fi'nancier,** *s.* **1.** financier *m.* **2.** bailleur *m* de fonds; **fi'nancing,** *s.* financement *m.*

finch [finʃ], *s. Orn:* pinson *m.*

find [faind]. **I.** *s.* découverte *f* (de pétrole, etc.); trouvaille *f*; **it was an accidental f.,** je l'ai trouvé par accident. **II.** *v.tr.* (**found**) **1.** (*a*) trouver, rencontrer, découvrir; **you can f. them anywhere,** on les trouve partout; **to f. some difficulty in doing sth.,** éprouver quelque difficulté à faire qch.; (*b*) **I often f. myself smiling,** je me surprends souvent à sourire. **2.** (*by searching*) (*a*) **to f. a** (lost) **key,** retrouver une clef; **to try to f. sth.,** chercher qch.; **he's not to be found,** il est introuvable; **to f. a leak,** localiser une fuite; **I can't f. time,** je n'ai pas le temps (de faire qch.); (*b*) obtenir (une sûreté). **3.** (*a*) constater; **it has been found that . . .,** on a constaté que . . .; **you'll f. that I'm right,** vous verrez que j'ai raison; (*b*) **they will f. it easy,** cela leur sera facile; **we f. it very difficult,** nous avons beaucoup de peine (à faire qch.). **4.** *Jur:* **to f. s.o. guilty,** déclarer qn coupable. **5.** (*a*) **to f. the money for an undertaking,** fournir l'argent, procurer les capitaux, pour une entreprise; **I found him this job,** je lui ai procuré cet emploi; (*b*) **wages £20 all found,** gages £20 tout fourni; **'finding,** *s.* (*a*) *pl.* **findings,** découvertes *f*, résultats *m* (de ses recherches); (*b*) *Jur:* conclusion *f* (d'un tribunal, d'un jury); **'find 'out,** *v.* **1.** (*a*) *v.tr.* se rendre compte (des faits); **to f. out how to do sth.,** découvrir le moyen de faire qch.; (*b*) *v.i.* **to f. out about sth.,** se renseigner sur qch. **2.** *v.tr.* **to f. s.o. out,** (i) découvrir le vrai caractère de qn; (ii) trouver, prendre, qn en défaut.

fine¹ [fain]. **I.** *s. Jur:* amende *f.* **II.** *v.tr.* frapper (qn) d'une amende.

fine². **I.** *a.* **1.** (*a*) (*of metal, etc.*) fin, pur; (*b*) fin, subtil, raffiné; **f. distinction,** distinction *f* subtile. **2.** (*a*) beau; **a f. man, woman,** un bel homme, une belle femme; **the f. arts,** les beaux arts *m*; (*b*) **to appeal to s.o.'s finer feelings,** faire appel aux sentiments élevés de qn. **3.** (*a*) **of the finest quality,** de premier choix; **f. example,** bel exemple (de qch.); (*b*) excellent, magnifique; **a f. thing for him,** une excellente affaire pour lui; **we had a f. time,** nous nous sommes bien amusés; **that's f.!** voilà qui est parfait! (*c*) **that's all very f., but . . .,** tout ç c'est bien joli, mais . . .; **you're a f. one to talk,** c'est bien à vous de parler. **4.** **when the weather's f.,** quand il fait beau; **one of these days,** un de ces beaux jours. **5.** (*a*) fin, menu; **chop meat f.,** hacher fin, menu, la viande; (*b*) **edge,** tranchant affilé; **not to put too f. a point on it,** pour parler carrément; en termes crus; **nib,** plume pointue. **6. to cut it f.,** faire qch. tout juste, arriver de justesse. **II.** *int.* bon! entendu d'accord! **-ly,** *adv.* **1.** (*a*) finement, habilement (*b*) délicatement, subtilement; (*c*) **f. chopped** haché fin, menu. **2.** admirablement magnifiquement; **'fine-'looking,** *a.* bea **'fineness,** *s.* **1.** titre *m*, aloi *m* (de l'or); excellence *f.* **3.** finesse *f* (d'un tissu); délicatesse *f* (des sentiments); **'finery,** *s.* parure *f.*

finger ['fingər]. I. s. doigt m (de la main); **first f.**, index m; F: **don't you dare lay a f. on him**, je vous défends de le toucher; **you could count them on the fingers of one hand**, on pourrait les compter sur les doigts de la main; **he has a f. in every pie**, il est mêlé à tout; **f. tip**, bout m de doigt; **f.-tip control**, commande f au doigté; **he has the whole thing at his f. tips**, il est au courant de toute l'affaire. II. v.tr. manier, tâter, palper (qch.); **'fingering**, s. (a) maniement m; palpation f; (b) Mus: doigté m; **'fingernail**, s. ongle m (de la main); **'fingerprint**, s. empreinte digitale.

finicky ['finiki], a. méticuleux, vétilleux; (of pers.) fignoleur.

finish ['finiʃ]. I. s. 1. fin f; Sp: arrivée f (d'une course); **to fight to the f.**, aller jusqu'au bout; **that was the f. (of it)**, ce fut le coup de grâce; **to be in at the f.**, (i) assister à l'arrivée; (ii) voir la fin de l'aventure. 2. fini m, achevé m; finesse f de l'exécution; apprêt m (d'un drap). II. v. 1. v.tr. finir, terminer, achever; **to f. off a wounded animal**, achever une bête blessée. 2. v.i. (a) finir, cesser, se terminer; (b) **I've finished with it**, je n'en ai plus besoin; F: **I've finished with you**, tout est fini entre nous; **wait till I've finished with him!** attendez que je lui aie réglé son compte! (c) Rac: **to f. fourth**, arriver quatrième; **'finished** a. 1. (of article) fini, apprêté. 2. soigné, parfait; **a f. speaker**, un orateur accompli.

finite ['fainait], a. & s. Gram: fini (m).

Finland ['finlənd]. Pr.n. Geog: la Finlande; **Finn**, s. Finlandais, -aise; Finnois, -oise; **'Finnish**. 1.a. finlandais. 2. s. Ling: finnois m.

fir [fə:r], s. 1. Bot: f. (tree), sapin m; f. **plantation**, sapinière f; f. **cone**, pomme f de pin; pigne f. 2. (bois m de) sapin.

fire ['faiər]. I. s. 1. feu m; (a) **to light a f.**, faire du feu; **to sit over the f.**, garder le coin du feu; **electric, gas, f.**, radiateur m électrique, à gaz; f. **irons**, garniture f de foyer; f. **screen**, (i) devant m de cheminée; (ii) écran m ignifuge; (b) incendie m, sinistre m; **bush f.**, feu de brousse; f. **broke out, there was an outbreak of f.**, un incendie s'est déclaré; f.! au feu! **to catch f.**, prendre feu; **to set f. to sth.**, mettre (le) feu à qch.; **on f.**, en feu, en flammes; **the house is on f.**, la maison brûle; F: **to get on like a house on f.**, avancer à pas de géant; **to add fuel to the f.**, jeter de l'huile sur le feu; f. **alarm**, avertisseur m d'incendie; f. **brigade**, (corps m de) sapeurs-pompiers mpl; F: **the pompiers**; f. **engine**, pompe f à incendie; f. **escape**, (i) échelle f de sauvetage; (ii) escalier m de secours; f. **extinguisher**, extincteur m d'incendie; f. **insurance**, assurance-incendie f; U.S: f. **warden**, Can: f. **ranger**, guetteur m; (c) lumière f, éclat

m; feux (d'un diamant). 2. ardeur f, enthousiasme m. 3. Mil: feu, tir m, coups mpl de feu; **to cease f.**, cesser le feu; **to be under f.**, essuyer le feu; **we are under f.**, on tire sur nous; **close-range f.**, tir à courte distance; F: **a f. of questions**, un feu roulant de questions. II. v. 1. v.tr. (a) incendier (une maison); **to be fired with enthusiasm**, brûler d'enthousiasme; (b) cuire (de la poterie); (c) **oil fired (central) heating**, chauffage (central) à mazout; (d) **to f. a rocket**, lancer une fusée; **to f. a revolver at s.o.**, tirer un coup de revolver sur qn; **to f. a question at s.o.**, poser une question à qn à brûle-pourpoint; **without firing a shot**, sans tirer un coup; (e) renvoyer, congédier (un employé). 2. v.i. (a) **to f. at s.o.**, tirer sur qn; (b) **the revolver failed to f.**, le revolver a raté; (c) **the engine is firing badly**, le moteur tourne mal; **'firearm**, s. arme f à feu; **'fire a'way**, v.i. f. a.! allez-y! **'firebrand**, s. 1. tison m, brandon m. 2. (pers.) brandon de discorde; **'firebug**, s. 1. N.Am: Ent: luciole f. 2. incendiaire mf; **'firedog**, s. chenet m; **'fire-eater**, s. (a) avaleur m de feu; (b) batailleur m; **'firefly**, s. Ent: luciole f; **'fireguard**, s. 1. pare-étincelles m inv; garde-feu m inv. 2. (pers.) N.Am: guetteur m (d'incendies); **'firelight**, s. lumière f du feu; **'firelighter**, s. allume-feu m inv; **'fireman**, pl. -men, s. 1. chauffeur m; Rail: aide-conducteur m. 2. (sapeur-)pompier m; **'fireplace**, s. cheminée f, foyer m; **'fireproof**. 1. a. (a) incombustible, ignifuge; f. **door**, porte f coupe-feu; (b) Cer: réfractaire; f. **dish**, plat m allant au feu. 2. v.tr. ignifuger; **'fireside**, s. foyer m; coin m du feu; **'firetrap**, s. **this building's a real f.**, ce bâtiment est une véritable souricière (en cas d'incendie); **'firewater**, s. F: gnole f; **'firewood**, s. bois m de chauffage; bois à brûler; **'firework**, s. (a) pièce f d'artifice; (b) pl. **fireworks**, feu m d'artifice; **'firing**, s. 1. Cer: cuite f, cuisson f. 2. chauffage m, chauffe f; **oil f.**, chauffe au mazout. 3. Aut: allumage m (des cylindres). 4. Mil: tir m, feu m.

firm¹ [fə:m], s. maison f (de commerce); entreprise f; **a big f.**, une grosse entreprise; f. **of solicitors** = étude f de notaire.

firm². 1. a. ferme; (a) (of substance) consistant, compact; (of post) solide; (of touch) vigoureux, assuré; **as f. as a rock**, inébranlable; (b) (of friendship) constant; (of intention) résolu; **to be f.**, tenir bon; **a f. belief that . . .**, la ferme conviction que . . .; (c) Com: **article in f. demand**, article constamment demandé. 2. adv. **to stand f.**, tenir bon, tenir ferme; **-ly**, adv. 1. fermement, solidement; **I f. believe that . . .**, j'ai la ferme conviction que . . .. 2. d'un ton ferme; **'firmness**, s. fermeté f, solidité f, stabilité f.

first [fɜːst]. **I.** *a.* premier; (*a*) **the f. of April**, le premier avril; **at f. sight**, à première vue; **in the f. place**, d'abord; en premier lieu; **at the f. opportunity**, dès que possible; **I'll do it f. thing tomorrow**, je le ferai dès demain matin; **head f.**, (tomber) la tête la première; **on the f. floor**, (i) au premier étage; (ii) *N.Am:* au rez-de-chaussée; **Charles the F.**, Charles Premier; **f. aid**, premiers soins; secourisme *m*; *Med:* **f. aid post**, poste *m* de secours; *Publ:* **f. edition**, édition originale; *Th:* **f. night**, première *f*; *Aut:* **f. (gear)**, première (vitesse); (*b*) **to put f. things f.**, mettre en avant les choses essentielles; **of f. quality**, de premier choix; (*c*) **to have news at f. hand**, tenir une nouvelle de première main. **II.** *s.* **1.** (le) premier, (la) première; **to be the f. to do sth.**, être le premier à faire qch.; **to come in an easy f.**, arriver bon premier; **f. come, f. served**, les premiers vont devant. **2.** commencement *m*; **from f. to last**, depuis le début jusqu'à la fin; **from the f.**, dès le premier jour; **at f.**, au commencement; d'abord. **3. to travel f.**, voyager en première (classe); *Aut:* **to climb a hill in f.**, monter une côte en première (vitesse). **III.** *adv.* **1.** premièrement; au commencement, d'abord; **f. of all**, en premier lieu; **f. and last**, en tout et pour tout; **to say f. one thing and then another**, dire tantôt blanc, tantôt noir. **2. when I f. saw him**, quand je l'ai vu pour la première fois. **3.** plutôt; **I'd die f.**, plutôt mourir. **4. he arrived f.**, il arriva le premier; **you go f.!** passez devant! **ladies f.!** place aux dames! **-ly**, *adv.* premièrement, en premier lieu; **'first(-)'class. 1.** *a.* (wagon) de première classe; (marchandises) de première qualité, de premier choix; (hôtel) de premier ordre; **a f.-c. liar**, un menteur de premier ordre. **2.** *adv.* **to travel f. c.**, voyager en première; **to send a letter f. c.**, expédier une lettre en urgence; **'first(-)'rate. 1.** *a.* excellent, de premier ordre; *F:* **that's f.r.!** (i) ça c'est extra! (ii) bon! à la bonne heure! **2.** *adv.* *F:* **it's doing f.r.**, ça marche à merveille.

fish [fiʃ]. **I.** *s.* (*pl.* **fishes**, *coll.* **fish**) poisson *m*; **I caught six f.**, j'ai attrapé six poissons; **f. shop**, poissonnerie *f*; **fried f.**, poisson frit; **f. knife**, couteau *m* à poisson; **all's f. that comes to his net**, tout lui est bon; **I've other f. to fry**, j'ai d'autres chats à fouetter; *F:* **he's an odd f.**, c'est un drôle de type; **a poor f.**, un pauvre type. **II.** *v.* **1.** *v.i.* pêcher; **to go fishing**, aller à la pêche; **to f. for trout**, pêcher la truite; **to f. for compliments**, quêter des compliments *m*. **2.** *v.tr.* **to f. up a corpse**, (re)pêcher un cadavre; **to f. a pencil out of one's pocket**, tirer un crayon de sa poche; **'fishbone**, *s.* arête *f* (de poisson); **'fisherman**, *pl.* **-men**, *s.* pêcheur *m*; **'fishery**, *s.* pêche *f*; **whale f.**, pêche à la baleine; **deep-sea**

f., la grande pêche; **'fish-hook**, *s.* hameçon *m*; **'fishing**, *s.* la pêche; **underwater f.**, chasse, pêche, sous-marine; **f. boat**, bateau *m* de pêche; **f. line**, ligne *f* (de pêche); **f. net**, filet *m* de pêche; **f. rod**, canne *f* à pêche; **f. tackle**, articles *mpl*, attirail *m*, de pêche; **'fishmonger**, *s.* poissonnier *m*; marchand *m* de poisson; **the fishmonger's**, la poissonnerie; **'fishpond**, *s.* vivier *m*; étang (plein de poissons); **'fishy**, *a.* **1.** (odeur *f*) de poisson; *F:* **f. eyes**, yeux ternes, vitreux. **2.** *F:* louche; **it looks f. to me**, ça ne me dit rien qui vaille.

fission ['fiʃ(ə)n], *s.* *Ph:* fission *f*; **nuclear f.**, fission nucléaire; **f. products**, produits *m* de fission; **f. bomb**, bombe *f* à fission.

fissure ['fiʃər], *s.* fissure *f*, fente *f*, crevasse *f*.

fist [fist], *s.* poing *m*; **to clench one's fists**, serrer les poings.

fit[1] [fit], *s.* **1.** (*a*) accès *m*, attaque *f*; **f. of coughing**, quinte *f* de toux; (*b*) crise *f* épileptique; **fainting f.**, évanouissement *m*; *F:* **to throw a f.**, tomber en convulsions, piquer une crise; **he'll have a f. when he knows**, il en aura une congestion quand il le saura. **2. f. of crying**, crise de larmes; **to be in fits of laughter**, avoir le fou rire; **to work by fits and starts**, travailler par à-coups; **'fitful**, *a.* irrégulier, capricieux; **-fully**, *adv.* irrégulièrement, par à-coups.

fit[2]. **I.** *a.* **1.** bon, propre (**for sth.**, à qch.); **I've nothing f. to wear**, je n'ai rien à me mettre; **I'm not f. to be seen**, je ne suis pas présentable; **to think f. to do sth.**, juger convenable de faire qch.; **do as you think f.**, faites comme bon vous semble. **2.** capable; **f. for sth.**, en état de faire qch.; apte à qch.; **he's not f. for anything**, il n'est propre à rien; **that's all he's f. for**, il n'est bon qu'à cela; **I was f. to drop**, je tombais de fatigue. **3.** en bonne santé; **as f. as a fiddle**, en parfaite santé; **you don't look very f.**, vous n'avez pas bonne mine. **II.** *s.* ajustement *m*; adaptation *f*; **my dress is a tight f.**, ma robe est un peu serrée, un peu juste. **III.** *v.* **1.** *v.tr.* (*a*) (clothes, *etc.*) aller à (qn); être à la taille de (qn); **these shoes don't f. me very well**, ces souliers ne me vont pas très bien; (*b*) adapter, ajuster, accommoder (**sth. to sth.**, qch. à qch.); **to be fitted for a new dress**, faire l'essayage *m* d'une nouvelle robe; **to f. parts together**, monter, assembler, des pièces; (*c*) **to f. s.o. for doing sth.**, préparer qn à faire qch.; (*d*) **to f. sth. with sth.**, garnir, munir, pourvoir, qch. de qch. *v.i.* (*a*) **to f. (together)**, s'ajuster, s'adapter, se raccorder; (*b*) **your dress fits well**, votre robe vous va bien; **'fit 'in**, *v.i.* **to f. in with sth.**, être en harmonie avec qch.; **your plans don't f. in with mine**, vos projets ne s'accordent pas avec les miens; **'fitness**, *s.* **1.** (*of pers.*) aptitude

Aut: f. **to drive,** aptitude à conduire. **2.**
physical f., santé *f* physique; **'fit 'out,** *v.tr.*
équiper; **to f. s.o. out,** équiper qn (de
vêtements, etc.); **'fitted,** *a.* **1.** ajusté; **f. coat,**
manteau ajusté; **f. sheet,** drap *m* housse. **2.** (*of*
pers.) f. **for sth., for doing sth.,** fait pour qch.;
apte à faire qch.; **'fitter,** *s. Mec:* ajusteur *m*;
'fitting. 1. *a.* (*a*) convenable, approprié; **f.**
comment, observation *f* très juste; (*b*) **f. coat,**
manteau ajusté. **2.** *s.* (*a*) (i) ajustage *m*; **f. of**
sth. on sth., montage de qch. sur qch.; (ii) essayage *m* (de vêtements); (iii) *Com:* **made in**
three fittings, fabriqué en trois tailles, (*of*
shoes) en trois largeurs; (iv) **f. out,** équipement
m; **f. up,** aménagement *m* (d'un magasin, etc.);
(*b*) *pl.* **fittings,** installations *f*; accessoires *m*;
brass fittings, garnitures *f* en cuivre.
five [faiv], *num.a. & s.* cinq (*m*); **f. pence,**
(somme *f*, pièce *f*, de) cinq pence; **fivepenny**
['faifpəni], *a.* valant cinq pence; **f. stamp,** timbre *m* de cinq pence; **'fiver,** *s. F:* billet *m*,
somme *f*, de cinq livres, *U.S:* de cinq dollars.
fix [fiks]. **I.** *s.* **1.** embarras *m*, difficulté *f*; mauvais
pas; **to be in a f.,** être dans le pétrin. **2.** *P:*
piqûre *f* de drogue. **II.** *v.tr.* **1.** fixer, caler,
monter, attacher; **to f. one's attention on sth.,**
fixer son attention sur qch. **2.** *Phot: etc:* fixer.
3. fixer, établir (une limite); nommer (un jour);
there's nothing fixed yet, il n'y a encore rien de
décidé; **how are you fixed for money?** tu as de
l'argent? **to f. on sth.,** se décider pour qch. **4.**
(*a*) **I've fixed it with him,** je me suis arrangé
avec lui; (*b*) **I can f. your radio,** je peux réparer
votre radio; (*c*) préparer (un repas). **5.** *F:* (*a*)
I'll f. him! je lui ferai son affaire! (*b*) graisser la
patte à (qn); truquer (un match). **6.** *P:* faire une
piqûre de drogue à (qn); **to f. oneself,** se piquer;
fixed, *a.* (*a*) fixe; **of f. length,** de longueur con-
stante; **f. rule,** règle établie; **f. price,** prix *m* fixe;
f. smile, sourire figé; (*b*) *F:* (match, etc.)
truqué; **'fixing,** *s.* (*a*) fixation *f*, mise *f* en place;
Phot: fixage *m*; (*b*) **price f.,** fixation *f* des prix;
'fixture, *s.* **1.** appareil *m* fixe; *pl.* **fixtures,**
aménagements *m* (d'une maison); installations
f; **£1000 for fixtures and fittings,** £1000 de
reprise. **2.** *Sp:* rencontre (prévue), match
(prévu), engagement *m*; **f. list,** programme *m*
(des rencontres); **'fix 'up,** *v.tr.* **it's all fixed up,**
c'est une affaire réglée; **I can f. you up for the**
night, je puis vous héberger pour la nuit.
izz [fiz], *v.i.* (*of wine*) pétiller; **'fizzle 'out,** *v.i.*
(*of plan*) ne pas aboutir, avorter; **'fizzy,** *a.* (*of*
mineral water) gazeux; (*of wine*) mousseux.
abbergast ['flæbəgɑ:st], *v.tr.* abasourdir,
ahurir (qn); **I was flabbergasted,** j'en suis resté
éberlué.
abby ['flæbi], *a.* flasque; mou; (*of cheeks*) pendant; **he's a f. sort of person,** c'est un mou; il

est molasse; **'flabbiness,** *s.* flaccidité *f*;
mollesse *f* (de qn).
flag¹ [flæg], *s.* (**paving**) f., carreau *m* (en pierre);
dalle *f*; **'flagstone,** *s.* dalle *f*; **f. pavement,**
dallage *m* en pierre.
flag², *s.* **1.** drapeau *m*; *Nau:* pavillon *m*; **f. of**
truce, drapeau parlementaire; **f. signals,**
signalisation *f* par fanions; *Nau:* **f. of con-**
venience, pavillon de complaisance; **f. officer,**
officier général; **f. day,** jour de quête pour une
œuvre de bienfaisance. **2.** drapeau (de taximètre); **'flagpole,** *s.* mât *m* de drapeau;
'flagship, *s.* (navire *m*) amiral (*m*); **'flagstaff,**
s. mât (i) de drapeau, (ii) de pavillon; hampe *f*
de drapeau.
flag³, *v.i.* (**flagged**) s'alanguir; (*of conversation*)
traîner, languir; (*of zeal*) se relâcher.
flagrant ['fleigrənt], *a.* (*of offence*) flagrant,
énorme; **f. case,** cas *m* notoire; **f. injustice,** injustice flagrante, criante; **-ly,** *adv.*
scandaleusement.
flair ['flɛər], *s.* (*a*) flair *m*; (*b*) aptitude *f*; **a. f. for**
languages, le don des langues.
flake¹ [fleik]. **I.** *s.* (*a*) flocon *m* (de neige); (*b*)
écaille *f*, éclat *m* (de métal). **II.** *v.i.* **to f. (away,**
off), (*of metal*) s'écailler, (*of stone*) s'épaufrer;
paint that flakes off, peinture *f* qui s'écaille;
'flaky, *a.* **f. pastry,** pâte feuilletée.
flake², *v.i. P:* **to f. (out),** (i) s'évanouir; (ii) tomber
de fatigue; **to be flaked (out),** être vidé, crevé.
flamboyant [flæm'bɔiənt], *a.* flamboyant.
flame [fleim]. **I.** *s.* flamme *f*; **in flames,** en
flammes, en feu; **to burst into flame(s), go up in**
flames, s'enflammer brusquement; (*colour*)
rouge feu *inv.* **II.** *v.i.* flamber, jeter des
flammes; **'flameproof, 'flame-re'sistant,** *a.*
ignifuge, à l'épreuve des flammes;
'flamethrower, *s. Mil: Hort:* lance-flammes
m inv; **'flameware,** *s.* plats *mpl* allant au four,
au feu; **'flaming,** *a.* (*a*) (feu) flambant;
(maison) en flammes; (*b*) (soleil) ardent; **in a f.**
temper, d'une humeur massacrante; (*c*) *P:* **a f.**
idiot, un sacré imbécile.
flamingo, *pl.* **-o(e)s** [flə'miŋgou, -ouz], *Orn:* flamant *m* (rose).
flammable ['flæməbl], *a. N.Am:* inflammable.
flan [flæn], *s. Cu:* tarte *f* aux fruits.
Flanders ['flɑ:ndəz]. *Pr.n. Geog:* la Flandre.
flange [flændʒ], *s.* bride *f*, collerette *f*, collet *m*; **f.**
coupling, joint *m* à bride; **cooling f.,** ailette *f* à
refroidissement; **flanged,** *a. Aut:* (radiateur
m) à ailettes.
flank [flæŋk]. **I.** *s.* (*a*) flanc *m*; (*b*) *Cu:* flanchet *m*
(de bœuf). **II.** *v.tr.* être disposé à côté de (qch).
flannel ['flæn(ə)l], *s.* (*a*) flannelle *f*; **f. trousers,**
s. pl. **flannels,** un pantalon de flanelle; (*b*) (**floor**)
f., serpillière *f*; (**face**) **f.** = (i) gant *m* de toilette,
(ii) *Fr.C:* débarbouillette *f*.

flap [flæp]. **I.** s. **1.** battement m, coup m (d'aile); coup léger (de la main); F: **to get into a f.,** s'agiter, s'affoler; ne plus savoir où donner de la tête. **2.** (a) patte f (d'une enveloppe); (b) abattant m (de table); trappe f (de cave); (c) Av: (landing) f., volet m (d'atterrissage). **II.** v. (flapped) **1.** v.tr. battre (des ailes); agiter (les bras). **2.** v.i. (of sail, shutter) battre, claquer; F: (of pers.) s'affoler; **'flapping,** s. battement m, claquement m.

flare ['flɛər]. **I.** s. **1.** (a) flamboiement irrégulier; (b) feu m de signal; Av: **f. path,** piste éclairée; **ground f., landing f.,** fusée f, phare m, d'atterrissage. **2.** évasement m. **II.** v. **1.** v.i. flamboyer. **2.** v.tr. & i. (s')évaser; **'flare 'up,** v.i. (a) s'enflammer brusquement; lancer des flammes; (b) (of pers.) s'emporter; **he flares up at the least thing,** il monte comme une soupe au lait; **'flare-up,** s. (a) flambée soudaine; (b) F: altercation f, scène f.

flash [flæʃ]. **I.** s. (a) éclair m; éclat m (de flamme); lueur f (d'une arme à feu); **a f. of lightning,** un éclair; **f. of wit,** saillie f (d'esprit); **in a f.,** en un rien de temps; **a f. in the pan,** un feu de paille; (b) Atom.Ph: **f. burn,** brûlure f par irradiation; (c) Phot: flash m; **f. bulb,** ampoule f (de) flash; (d) (news) **f.,** flash. **II.** v. **1.** v.i. (a) jeter des éclairs; (of diamonds) étinceler; (b) **to f. past,** passer comme un éclair; **it flashed across my mind that . . .,** l'idée m'est venue tout d'un coup que . . .. **2.** v.tr. (a) faire étinceler (ses bijoux); (b) **to f. a light,** projeter un rayon de lumière; **'flashback,** s. **1.** retour m de flamme. **2.** Cin: retour en arrière; scène retrospective; **'flashily,** adv. **f. dressed,** à toilette tapageuse; **'flashing,** a. éclatant; **f. eyes,** yeux étincelants; **f. light,** feu, signal, clignotant, à éclats; **'flashy,** a. voyant, éclatant, tapageur.

flask [flɑːsk], s. flacon m; gourde f; **vacuum f.,** bouteille isolante.

flat [flæt]. **I.** a. **1.** (a) plat; horizontal; **f. roof,** toit plat; (b) plat, uni; **to beat sth. f.,** aplatir qch.; **a f. tyre,** N.Am: **a flat,** un pneu à plat; **as f. as a pancake,** plat comme une galette. **2.** net; **f. refusal,** refus net; **that's f.!** voilà qui est net! **3.** (a) monotone, ennuyeux; (of conversation) fade, insipide; **to feel f.,** se sentir à plat; (b) (of drink) éventé, plat; Aut: **the battery is f.,** la batterie est à plat; (c) **f. battery,** accumulateur à plat. **4.** uniforme; **f. rate,** taux m, tarif m, uniforme. **5.** (a) (son) sourd; (b) Mus: (i) bémol inv; (ii) **you're f.,** vous chantez en dessous du ton. **II.** adv. **1.** à plat; **to fall f. on one's face,** tomber à plat ventre; **the blow laid him f.,** le coup l'a terrassé. **2.** nettement, positivement; **he told me f. that . . .,** il m'a dit carrément que

. . .; **to be f. broke,** être à sec, être fauché; Aut: **to go f. out,** filer à toute allure. **3. to fall f.,** rater, manquer son effet. **4.** Mus: (chanter) en dessous du ton. **III.** s. **1.** (a) plat m; **with the f. of the hand,** avec la main plate; (b) N.Am: pneu m à plat. **2.** Rac: **the f.,** la saison du plat; **f. racing,** le plat. **3.** appartement m; **service f.,** appartement avec service; **block of flats,** immeuble m; **-ly,** adv. nettement, carrément; **to refuse f.,** refuser tout net; **'flatlet,** s. studio m; **'flatness,** s. (a) égalité f (d'une surface); (b) monotonie f (de l'existence); insipidité f (du style); (c) (of beer) évent m; **'flatten,** v.tr. & i. (s')aplatir; (s')aplanir; **to f. oneself against a wall,** se plaquer contre un mur; F: **to f. s.o.,** écraser, déconcerter, qn; Mus: **to f. a note,** bémoliser une note.

flatter ['flætər], v.tr. flatter (qn); **'flatterer,** s. flatteur, -euse; **'flattering,** a. flatteur; **-ly,** adv. flatteusement; **'flattery,** s. flatterie f, adulation f.

flaunt [flɔːnt], v.tr. étaler, afficher, faire étalage de (son luxe); s'afficher.

flavour ['fleivər]. **I.** s. saveur f; goût m; (of ice cream) parfum m. **II.** v.tr. assaisonner, parfumer; **to f. a sauce,** relever une sauce; **vanilla flavoured,** (parfumé) à la vanille; **'flavouring,** s. assaisonnement m; condiment m; **'flavourless,** a. sans saveur; insipide.

flaw [flɔː]. **I.** s. défaut m, défectuosité f, imperfection f; point m faible (d'un projet); (in glass) fêlure f. **II.** v.tr. endommager, défigurer; **'flawless,** a. sans défaut; parfait; (of technique) impeccable; **-ly,** adv. parfaitement, sans défaut.

flax [flæks], s. Bot: lin m; **'flaxen,** a. (of hair) blond (filasse); **f.-haired,** aux cheveux très blonds.

flay [flei], v.tr. écorcher (un animal); F: rosser (qn).

flea [fliː], s. Ent: puce f; **'fleabite,** s. **1.** morsure f, piqûre f, de puce. **2.** vétille f, bagatelle f, rien m; **'fleapit,** s. P: cinéma pouilleux.

fleck [flek]. **I.** s. petite tache, moucheture f. **II.** v.tr. tacheter, moucheter (with, de); **flecked with grey,** cheveux qui commencent à grisonner.

fledgling ['fledʒliŋ], s. Orn: oisillon m.

flee [fliː], v.i. (fled [fled]) fuir, s'enfuir, se sauver; **'fleeing,** a. en fuite.

fleece [fliːs]. **I.** s. **1.** toison f. **2.** Tex: **f.-lined,** doublé de molleton m. **II.** v.tr. F: tondre, écorcher, plumer (qn); **'fleecing,** s. écorcher f; **'fleecy,** a. (of wool) floconneux; (of cloud) moutonné.

fleet [fliːt], s. **1.** (a) flotte f; **the F. =** la Marine nationale; **the F. Air Arm =** l'Aéronavale; (b) **merchant f.,** flotte de commerce; **a fishi**

f., une flottille de pêche. 2. (a) **air f.,** flotte aérienne; (b) **a f. of coaches took the tourists to their hotel,** une caravane de cars a amené les touristes à leur hôtel.

fleeting ['fliːtiŋ], a. fugitif, fugace; **a f. visit,** une courte visite.

Fleming ['flemiŋ], s. *Geog:* Flamand, -ande; **'Flemish. 1.** a. flamand. **2.** s. *Ling:* flamand m.

flesh [fleʃ], s. **1.** (a) chair f; **to put on f.,** prendre de l'embonpoint; **to make s.o.'s f. creep,** donner la chair de poule à qn; **f. wound,** blessure f dans les chairs; (b) chair (d'une pêche, etc.); (c) **f. colour,** couleur f (de) chair. **2. in the f.,** en chair et en os; **his own f. and blood,** les siens; **it's more than f. and blood can bear,** c'est plus qu'on ne peut endurer; **'fleshy,** a. charnu.

flex [fleks]. **I.** v.tr. **to f. one's muscles,** faire jouer ses muscles. **II.** s. *El:* cordon m, câble m (souple); flexible m; **flexi'bility,** s. flexibilité f; souplesse f; **'flexible,** a. flexible, souple.

flick [flik]. **I.** s. petit coup (de fouet); (with finger) chiquenaude f; **at the f. of a switch,** juste en tournant, en appuyant sur, un bouton. **II.** v.tr. (with whip) effleurer (un cheval); (with finger) donner une chiquenaude à (qch.); **to f. sth. off with a duster,** faire envoler qch. d'un coup de torchon.

flicker ['flikər]. **I.** s. (a) tremblotement m; (of eyelid) battement m, clignement m; (b) **a f. of light,** une petite lueur tremblotante; (c) *Cin:* scintillement m; *T.V:* papillotement m. **II.** v.i. trembloter, vaciller, (of light) papilloter, clignoter; *Cin:* scintiller; **'flickering,** s. (a) tremblotement m, clignotement m; (b) *Cin:* scintillement m; *T.V:* papillotement m.

flight[1] [flait], s. **1.** vol m; (a) *Av:* **instrument f.,** vol aux instruments; (b) **f. of fancy,** élan m, essor m, de l'imagination. **2.** volée f, distance parcourue (par un oiseau); **time of f.,** durée f du trajet (d'un projectile); *Av:* **it's an hour's f. from London,** c'est à une heure de vol de Londres. **3.** *Av:* **f. A to Brussels,** vol A pour Bruxelles; *Space:* **earth-orbital f.,** vol en orbite terrestre. **4.** (a) bande f, vol (d'oiseaux); **in the top f.,** parmi les tout premiers; (b) *Av:* escadrille f. **5. f. of stairs,** volée f d'escalier; escalier m; **'flight-lieu'tenant,** s. *Av:* = capitaine m (d'aviation).

flight[2], s. fuite f; **to take (to) f.,** prendre la fuite; **the f. of capital,** l'exode m des capitaux.

flighty ['flaiti], a. frivole, écervelé, étourdi; **'flightiness,** s. instabilité f (de caractère); légèreté f, étourderie f.

flimsy ['flimzi]. **1.** a. sans solidité; (a) (tissu) léger, peu solide; (b) (of excuse) pauvre. **2.** s. papier m pelure; **'flimsiness,** s. manque m de solidité; légèreté f; futilité f (d'une excuse).

flinch [flintʃ], v.i. (a) reculer, fléchir; (b) tressaillir (de douleur); **without flinching,** sans broncher.

fling [fliŋ]. **I.** s. *F:* (a) **to have a f. at it,** tenter la chance; (b) **to have one's f.,** jeter sa gourme. **II.** v.tr. (**flung** [flʌŋ]) jeter (qch.); lancer (une balle); **to f. one's arms round s.o.'s neck,** se jeter au cou de qn; **to f. money about,** gaspiller son argent; **to f. sth. away,** se défaire de qch.; **to f. open the door,** ouvrir la porte d'un mouvement brusque; **to f. s.o. out,** flanquer qn à la porte; **to f. out one's arm,** étendre le bras d'un grand geste.

flint [flint], s. silex m; (for cigarette lighter) pierre f à briquet; *Archeol:* **f. implements,** outils m en pierre, silex taillés; *F:* **he'd skin a f.,** il tondrait un œuf.

flippant ['flipənt], a. léger, désinvolte; -**ly,** adv. légèrement; **'flippancy,** s. légèreté f, irrévérence f, désinvolture f.

flipper ['flipər], s. (of penguin) nageoire f, aile f; (of seal) (patte-)nageoire f; (of frogman) palme f.

flirt [fləːt]. **I.** s. coquette f. **II.** v.i. flirter; **flir'tation,** s. flirt m; **'flirting,** s. flirt m.

flit [flit], v.i. (**flitted**) (a) **to f. (away),** partir; **time was flitting away,** le temps passait rapidement; (b) **to f. by,** passer comme une ombre; **to f. about,** aller et venir sans bruit.

float [flout]. **I.** v. **1.** v.i. (a) flotter, nager (sur un liquide); surnager; (of boat) être à flot; (b) (of swimmer) faire la planche; (c) **clouds floating in the sky,** des nuages m qui flottent dans le ciel. **2.** v.tr. (a) **to f. timber downstream,** jeter du bois à flot perdu; (b) *Fin:* **to f. a loan,** émettre, lancer, un emprunt. **II.** s. *Fish: Tchn:* flotteur m; **'floating,** a. **1.** flottant, à flot. **2.** (a) libre, mobile; **f. population,** population flottante; (b) *Pol:* **f. voter,** voteur indécis; (c) **f. exchange rate,** taux m de change flottant.

flock [flɔk]. **I.** s. bande f, troupe f (d'animaux); troupeau m (de moutons). **II.** v.i. **to f. (together),** s'attrouper, s'assembler; **everyone is flocking to see the exhibition,** tout le monde se précipite pour voir l'exposition.

flog [flɔg], v.tr. (**flogged**) **1.** flageller (qn); fouetter, cravacher (un cheval); **to f. oneself (to death),** s'éreinter (à faire qch.). **2.** *F:* bazarder (qch.); **'flogging,** s. flagellation f.

flood [flʌd]. **I.** s. **1. f.** (tide), flot m, flux m. **2.** (a) inondation f; déluge m; *P.N:* **floods,** route inondée; (b) crue f (d'une rivière); (c) **a f. of tears,** un torrent de larmes. **II.** v. **1.** v.tr. inonder, submerger; *Aut:* **to f. the carburetter,** noyer le carburateur. **2.** v.i. (of river) déborder; être en crue; **'floodgate,** s. vanne f; **'flooding,** s. inondation f, submersion f; (of

river) débordement *m*; *P.N:* **road liable to f.**, chemin sujet aux inondations; **'floodlight.** **1.** *s.* projecteur *m.* **2.** *v.tr.* **(floodlighted** *or* **floodlit)** illuminer (un monument) par projecteurs.
floor [flɔːr]. **I.** *s.* **1.** plancher *m*, parquet *m*; **f. polish,** encaustique *f*; cire *f* à parquet. **2.** étage *m*; **ground f.,** rez-de-chaussée *m*; **first f.,** (i) premier étage; (ii) *N.Am:* rez-de-chaussée. **II.** *v.tr.* **1.** parqueter (une pièce). **2.** terrasser (un adversaire); *Sch:* coller (un candidat); **'floorboard,** *s.* planche *f* (du plancher); **'floorcloth,** *s.* serpillière *f*; **'floorshow,** *s.* spectacle *m* de cabaret.
flop [flɔp]. **I.** *s.* **1.** coup mat; bruit sourd. **2.** *F:* four *m*, fiasco *m.* **II.** *v.i.* **(flopped) 1. to f. (down),** se laisser tomber, s'affaler. **2.** *F:* échouer; *Th:* faire four.
florid ['flɔrid], *a.* (*of style*) fleuri; orné à l'excès; **to have a f. complexion,** être haut en couleur.
florist ['flɔrist], *s.* fleuriste *mf.*
flotilla [flə'tilə], *s.* flottille *f.*
flounce [flauns]. **I.** *s.* *Dressm:* volant *m.* **II.** *v.i.* **to f. in, out,** entrer, sortir, dans un mouvement d'indignation.
flounder ['flaundər], *v.i.* patauger, barboter; **to f. about in the water,** se débattre dans l'eau.
flour ['flauər], *s.* farine *f*; **f. mill,** minoterie *f*; moulin *m* à farine.
flourish ['flʌriʃ]. **I.** *s.* **1.** grand geste; brandissement *m* (d'épée). **2.** trait *m* de plume; (*after signature*) parafe *m.* **3.** *Mus:* fanfare *f* (de trompettes). **II.** *v.* **1.** *v.i.* (a) (*of plant*) bien venir; (b) (*of pers.*) être florissant, prospérer; (*of arts*) fleurir. **2.** *v.tr.* brandir (un bâton); **'flourishing,** *a.* florissant; prospère.
flout [flaut], *v.tr.* faire fi de (l'autorité de qn); se moquer d'(un ordre).
flow [flou]. **I.** *s.* **1.** (a) écoulement *m* (d'un liquide); (b) *El:* passage *m* (d'un courant); (c) flot *m*, flux *m* (de la marée). **2.** volume *m* (de liquide débité); débit *m* (d'un lac); **f. of traffic,** débit de la circulation. **3.** (a) courant *m*, cours *m* (d'eau); (b) flot, flux (de sang, de paroles); **what a f. of words!** quels flots d'éloquence! **II.** *v.i.* **1.** (a) couler, s'écouler; **to f. into the sea,** se jeter dans la mer; (b) (*of tide*) monter, remonter; (c) (*of blood, electric current*) circuler. **2.** (*of blood, tears*) se répandre; jaillir. **3.** dériver, découler (**from**, de); **'flow 'in,** *v.i.* (*of money, people*) affluer; **'flowing,** *a.* **1.** coulant; (*of tide*) montant. **2.** (*of draperies*) flottant.
flower ['flauər]. **I.** *s.* **1.** fleur *f*; **bunch of flowers,** bouquet *m* (de fleurs); **f. show,** exposition *f* horticole; **f. bed,** parterre *m*; **f. garden,** jardin *m* de fleurs, d'agrément; **at the f. shop,** chez le fleuriste; **f. vase,** vase *m* à fleurs. **2.** fine fleur, crème *f*, élite *f.* **3.** floraison *f*; **in f.,** en fleur; **in**

full f., en plein épanouissement; **to burst into f.,** fleurir. **II.** *v.i.* fleurir; **'flowering. 1.** *a.* **f. plant,** plante à fleurs. **2.** *s.* floraison *f*, fleuraison *f*; **'flowery,** *a.* fleuri.
flu [fluː], *s.* *F:* grippe *f.*
fluctuate ['flʌktjueit], *v.i.* fluctuer; **'fluctuating,** *a.* variable; **fluctu'ation,** *s.* fluctuation *f.*
flue [fluː], *s.* conduite *f*, tuyau *m*, de cheminée.
fluency ['fluːənsi], *s.* facilité *f* (de parole); **'fluent,** *a.* coulant, facile; **to be a f. speaker,** parler facilement; **-ly,** *adv.* couramment, avec facilité.
fluff [flʌf], *s.* **1.** duvet *m*, peluches *fpl*; (*under bed*) moutons *mpl.* **2.** fourrure douce (d'un jeune animal); **'fluffy,** *a.* (drap) pelucheux; (poussin) duveteux; **f. hair,** cheveux flous.
fluid ['fluːid], *a.* & *s.* fluide (*m*); liquide (*m*); **flu'idity,** *s.* fluidité *f.*
fluke [fluːk], *s.* coup *m* de veine, de hasard; chance *f.*
fluorescence [fluːə'res(ə)ns], *s.* fluorescence *f*; **fluo'rescent,** *a.* fluorescent.
fluorine ['fluːəriːn], *s.* *Ch:* fluor *m*; **'fluoride,** *s.* *Ch:* fluorure *f.*
flurry ['flʌri]. **I.** *s.* agitation *f*, bouleversement *m*, émoi *m*; **all in a f.,** tout en émoi. **II.** *v.tr.* agiter, effarer (qn); **to get flurried,** perdre la tête.
flush[1] [flʌʃ]. **I.** *s.* **1.** chasse *f* (d'eau). **2.** accès *m*, élan *m*; **in the first f. of victory,** dans l'ivresse de la victoire. **3.** (a) éclat *m*; **the first f. of youth,** le premier éclat de la jeunesse; (b) rougeur *f*, flot *m* de sang (au visage); **hot f.,** bouffée *f* de chaleur. **II.** *v.* **1.** *v.tr.* **to f. (out)** donner une chasse à (un égout). **2.** *v.i.* rougir; **he, his face, flushed,** il a rougi; le sang lui est monté au visage; **flushed,** *a.* rouge; enfiévré, empourpré; **f. with success,** ivre de succès.
flush[2], *a.* **1. to be f. (with money),** être en fonds. **2.** ras; de niveau; **to be f. with sth.,** être à fleur au ras, de qch.
Flushing ['flʌʃiŋ]. *Pr.n. Geog:* Flessingue *f.*
fluster ['flʌstər]. **I.** *s.* agitation *f*, trouble *m*; **in f.,** tout en émoi, tout déconcerté, bouleversé. **II.** *v.tr.* agiter, bouleverser; **to be flustered,** troubler; être démonté, bouleversé.
flute [fluːt], *s.* flûte *f*; **f. (player),** flûte; **'fluted,** à rainures *fpl*; à cannelures *fpl.*
flutter ['flʌtər]. **I.** *s.* **1.** volètement *m*, voltigement *m* (d'un oiseau); battement *m* (des ailes); palpitation *f* (du cœur); *T.V:* scintillation *f.* agitation *f*, trouble *m*, émoi *m*; **(all) in a f.,** tout en émoi. **3.** *F:* (petite) spéculation; quelque petits paris. **II.** *v.* **1.** *v.i.* voleter, battre des ailes; (*of flag*) flotter (au vent); (*of heart*) palpiter, battre. **2.** *v.tr.* (*of bird*) **to f. its wings,** battre des ailes.
fly[1] [flai], *s.* (a) *Ent:* mouche *f*; **a f. in the oin**

ment, un cheveu (dans la soupe); **there are no flies on him,** il n'est pas bête; **f. swatter,** chasse-mouches *m inv*; (*b*) *Fish:* mouche; **f. fishing,** pêche *f* à la mouche.

fly², *s.* 1. (*also* **flies**) braguette *f* (de pantalon). 2. *Th:* **the flies,** les cintres *m*, les dessus *m*; **'flyleaf,** *s.* (feuille *f* de) garde *f*; **'flywheel,** *s. Mec:* volant *m.*

fly³, *v.* (**flew** [flu:], **flown** [floun]) I. *v.i.* 1. (*a*) voler; **to f. high,** (i) voler haut; (ii) (*of pers.*) viser haut; **to find the birds flown,** trouver buisson creux; **as the crow flies,** à vol *m* d'oiseau; (*b*) *Av:* voler; **to f. to Paris,** se rendre à Paris en avion; **to f. over London,** survoler Londres. 2. (*of flag*) flotter. 3. (*a*) courir, aller à toute vitesse; (*of time*) fuir; **to f. (out) at s.o.,** (i) s'élancer sur qn; (ii) lancer des injures *f* à qn; **to f. into a rage,** s'emporter; **the door flew open,** la porte s'ouvrit en coup de vent; (*b*) (*of sparks*) jaillir; **to make the fur f.,** faire une scène; **to f. off the handle,** s'emporter; **to send s.o. flying,** envoyer rouler qn; (*c*) **to f. to pieces, to bits,** éclater, voler en éclats. 4. **to let f. at s.o.,** (i) tirer sur qn; (ii) flanquer un coup à qn. 5. fuir, s'enfuir; **to f. to s.o. (for protection),** se réfugier auprès de qn. II. *v.tr.* 1. battre (un pavillon). 2. lancer, faire voler (un cerf-volant). 3. *Av:* piloter (un avion); **to f. s.o. to Paris,** transporter qn à Paris par avion; **to f. the Channel,** survoler la Manche; **'fly a'way,** *v.i.* (*of bird*) s'envoler; **'fly 'back,** *v.i.* (*of steel rod*) faire ressort; **'flyer,** *s.,* **'flier,** *s.* aviateur, -trice; **'flying.** 1. *a.* (*a*) volant; **f. fish,** poisson volant; (*b*) *Mil:* **f. column,** colonne *f* mobile; **f. visit,** visite éclair; *Sp:* **f. start,** départ lancé; **to take a f. leap over a wall,** franchir un mur d'un saut. 2. *s.* vol *m*; aviation *f*; **f. club,** aéro-club *m, pl.* aéro-clubs; **f. hours,** heures *f* de vol; **'flyover,** *s. Civ.E:* saut-de-mouton *m, pl.* sauts-de-mouton; **'flypast,** *s.* défilé aérien.

▶al [foul], *s.* poulain *m.*

▶am [foum]. I. *s.* écume *f*; (*on beer*) mousse *f*; **f. rubber,** caoutchouc *m* mousse. II. *v.i.* (*of sea*) écumer, moutonner; (*of beer*) mousser; **to f. (at the mouth) (with rage),** écumer, être furieux.

▶b [fɔb], *v.tr.* (**fobbed**) **to f. s.o. off with sth., to f. sth. off on s.o.,** *F:* refiler qch. à qn.

▶cus, *pl.* **foci, focuses** ['foukəs, 'fousai, 'foukəsiz]. I. *s.* foyer *m*; **in f.,** au point. II. *v.* 1. *v.tr.* concentrer, faire converger (des rayons); focaliser (le faisceau électronique). 2. *v.i.* **all eyes focused on him,** il était le point de mire de tous les yeux; *Phot:* **to f. on an object,** mettre au point sur un objet; **'focal,** *a. Ph:* focal; **f. length,** longueur focale; **'focusing,** *s.* mise *f* au point.

▶dder ['fɔdər], *s.* fourrage *m.*

▶g [fɔg]. I. *s.* brouillard *m*; *Nau:* brume *f*; **I'm in**

a f., je ne sais plus où j'en suis; *Rail:* **f. signal,** pétard *m.* II. *v.* (**fogged**) 1. *v.tr.* brouiller (les idées); embrouiller (qn); *Phot:* voiler (un cliché). 2. *v.i. Phot:* se voiler; **'foggy,** *a.* 1. brumeux; **a f. day,** un jour de brouillard; **it's f.,** il fait du brouillard. 2. *Phot:* voilé; (esprit, etc.) confus; **I haven't the foggiest idea,** je n'en ai pas la moindre idée; **'foghorn,** *s. Nau:* sirène *f*; **'foglamp.** *s. Aut:* (phare *m*) antibrouillard *m.*

fog(e)y ['fougi], *s. F:* **old f.,** vieille baderne.

foible ['fɔibl], *s.* côté *m* faible, point *m* faible; faible *m* (de qn).

foil¹ [fɔil], *s.* 1. *Metalw:* feuille *f*, lame *f*; clinquant *m; Cu:* **household f., cooking f.,** feuille d'aluminium. 2. **to serve as a f. to** (s.o., sth.), servir de repoussoir *m* à (qn, qch.).

foil², *s. Fenc:* fleuret *m.*

foil³, *v.tr.* faire échouer, faire manquer; déjouer (un complot).

foist [fɔist], *v.tr.* refiler (**sth. on s.o.,** qch. à qn); **to have a difficult job foisted on one,** se trouver chargé d'une tâche difficile; **to f. oneself on s.o.,** s'implanter chez qn, s'imposer à qn.

fold¹ [fould], *s.* parc *m* à moutons; *F:* **to return to the f.,** revenir au bercail.

fold². 1. *s.* pli *m*, repli *m*; accident *m* (de terrain). II. *v.* 1. *v.tr.* (*a*) plier; **to f. back,** rabattre; (*b*) **to f. sth. in sth.,** envelopper qch. dans, de, qch.; **to f. s.o. in one's arms,** enlacer, serrer, qn dans ses bras; (*c*) **to f. one's arms,** (se) croiser les bras. 2. *v.i.* (*of shutters, screen*) se (re)plier; **'folding,** *a.* pliant; **f. chair,** chaise pliante; **f. ladder,** échelle brisée; **'fold 'up,** (*a*) *v.tr. & i.* (se) replier; (*b*) *v.i. F:* (*of business*) cesser les affaires; *Th:* **the play's folded up,** la pièce a été retirée.

foliage ['fouliidʒ], *s.* feuillage *m.*

folio, *pl.* **-os** ['fouliou, -ouz], *s.* 1. folio *m*, feuille *f*, feuillet *m* (de manuscrit). 2. (livre *m*) in-folio (*m inv*).

folk [fouk], *s.* (*a*) *pl.* (**folk,** *occ.* **folks**) gens *mf*, personnes *f*; **country f.,** campagnards; **my f.,** les miens; (*b*) **f. dance,** danse *f* folklorique; **f. song,** (i) chanson traditionnelle; (ii) (*modern*) folk-song *m*; **'folklore,** *s.* folklore *m.*

follow ['fɔlou]. I. *v.tr.* 1. suivre; (*a*) **to f. s.o. about,** suivre qn partout; **to f. one's nose,** aller tout droit devant soi; (*b*) **to f. a road,** suivre un chemin; (*c*) **night follows day,** la nuit succède au jour. 2. **to f. s.o.'s advice,** suivre le conseil de qn. 3. **I don't quite f. you,** je ne vous comprends pas très bien. II. *v.i.* 1. **to f. (after),** suivre; **as follows,** ainsi qu'il suit. 2. **to f. in s.o.'s footsteps,** marcher sur les traces de qn; **to f. close behind s.o.,** emboîter le pas à qn. 3. s'ensuivre, résulter (**from,** de); **'follower,** *s.* partisan *m*, disciple *m*; **'following.** 1. *a.* (*a*) suivant; **the f. day,** le jour suivant; (*b*) **the f. resolution,** la résolution que voici; (*c*) **two days**

f., deux jours de suite. **2.** s. *Pol:* parti *m*; *T.V:* **programme that has a wide f.**, programme très suivi; **'follow 'up,** *v.tr.* poursuivre (un avantage); exploiter (un succès).

folly ['fɔli], s. folie *f*, sottise *f*.

foment [fou'ment], *v.tr.* fomenter; **fomen'tation,** s. fomentation *f*.

fond [fɔnd], a. **1.** affectueux, tendre. **2. to be f. of s.o.**, aimer qn; **they are f. of each other**, ils s'aiment; **to be f. of music**, être amateur *m* de musique; **f. of sweets**, friand de sucreries; **-ly**, tendrement, affectueusement; **'fondness,** s. **1.** indulgence excessive. **2.** affection *f*, tendresse *f* **(for,** pour, envers). **3.** penchant *m*, prédilection *f*, goût *m*.

fondle ['fɔndl], *v.tr.* caresser, câliner.

font [fɔnt], s. fonts baptismaux.

food [fuːd], s. **1.** nourriture *f*; aliments *mpl*; vivres *mpl*; **f. counter, f. hall**, rayon *m* d'alimentation; **f. and clothing**, le vivre et le vêtement; **f. value**, valeur nutritive; **f. poisoning**, intoxication *f* alimentaire; **the f.-processing industry**, l'industrie *f* alimentaire; **to give s.o. f. for thought**, donner à penser à qn. **2.** manger *m*; **f. and drink**, le boire et le manger; **'foodstuffs,** s.pl. comestibles *m*.

fool [fuːl]. **I.** s. **1.** imbécile *mf*; idiot, -ote; sot, sotte; **to make a f. of oneself**, se rendre ridicule; **silly f.!** espèce d'idiot! **2.** dupe *f*; **to make a f. of s.o.**, berner qn, se payer la tête de qn. **II.** v. **1.** v.i. (a) faire la bête; **to f. around**, flâner; gâcher son temps; (b) **I was only fooling**, je n'étais pas sérieux. **2.** v.tr. duper (qn); se payer la tête de (qn); **'foolery,** s. (a) sottise *f*, bêtise *f*; (b) bouffonnerie *f*; **'foolhardy,** a. téméraire, imprudent; **'fooling,** s. (a) bouffonnerie *f*; (b) duperie *f* (de qn); **'foolish,** a. (a) fou, étourdi; **it's f. of him to . . .**, c'est fou de sa part de . . .; (b) sot, bête; **to do sth. f.**, faire une sottise, une bêtise; (c) absurde, ridicule; **to look f.**, avoir l'air penaud; **-ly,** adv. (a) follement, étourdiment; (b) sottement, bêtement; **'foolishness,** s. (a) folie *f*, étourderie *f*; (b) sottise *f*, bêtise *f*; **'foolproof,** a. (mécanisme *m*) indéréglable, indétraquable, à l'épreuve des fausses manœuvres.

foolscap ['fuːlskæp], s. papier *m* ministre.

foot [fut]. **I.** s. (pl. **feet** [fiːt]). **1.** pied *m*; (a) **to knock s.o. off his feet**, renverser qn; faire perdre l'équilibre à qn; **to keep on one's feet**, tenir pied, rester debout; **to find one's feet**, voler de ses propres ailes; se débrouiller; **to get on one's feet again**, (i) se relever; se remettre debout; (ii) se remettre (après une maladie); **to put one's f. down**, faire acte d'autorité; opposer qch. d'une façon catégorique; *Aut: F:* accélérer, appuyer sur le champignon; *F:* **to put one's f. in it**, mettre les pieds dans le plat; *F:* **to put one's feet up**,

se reposer; *F:* **to have cold feet**, avoir la frousse; **to put one's best f. forward**, (i) presser le pas; (ii) faire son meilleur effort; *F:* **he gets under your feet**, il se met dans vos jambes; *F:* **my f.!** mon œil! (b) marche *f*, allure *f*; **to have a light, a heavy, f.**, avoir le pied léger, lourd; (c) adv.phr. **on f.**, à pied; **to trample, tread, sth. under f.**, fouler qch. aux pieds. **2.** pied (d'animal à sabot); patte *f* (de chien, de chat, d'oiseau). **3.** (a) pied, semelle *f* (d'un bas); (b) bas bout (d'une table); pied (d'un lit); (c) base *f* (d'une colonne); patte *f* (d'un verre à vin). **4.** (a) *Lit:* (poetry) pied; (b) pied anglais (= 30 cm 48). **II.** v.tr. *F:* (a) **to f. it**, aller à pied; (b) **to f. the bill**, payer la note; **'foot-and-'mouth,** a. *Vet:* **f.-a.-m. disease**, fièvre *f* aphteuse; **'football,** s. **1.** ballon *m*. **2.** football *m*; **Rugby f.**, rugby *m*; **'footballer,** s. footballeur *m*; **'footbath,** s. bain *m* de pieds; **'footbrake,** s. frein *m* à pédale, au pied; **'footbridge,** s. passerelle *f*; **'footfall,** s. (bruit *m* de) pas *m*; **'foothills,** s.pl. contreforts *m* (d'un massif); **'foothold,** s. prise *f* pour le pied; **to get a f.**, prendre pied; **'footing,** s. (a) **to lose one's f.**, perdre pied; faire un faux mouvement; (b) **to gain a f.**, s'implanter; prendre pied; (c) **to be on a good f with s.o.**, être en bons termes avec qn; **'footlights,** s.pl. *Th:* rampe *f*; **'footman,** s. valet *m* de pied; laquais *m*; **'footmark,** s. empreinte *f* de pied; **'footnote,** s. note *f* au bas de la page; renvoi *m* en bas de page; **'footpath,** s. sentier *m*; (in street) trottoir *m*; **'footplate,** s. poste *m* de conduite (de locomotive); **'footplateman,** pl. -men, s. mécanicien *m* de locomotive; **'footprint,** s. **1.** empreinte *f* de pas. **2.** *Space:* aire *f* d'atterrissage (d'un module); **'footstep,** s. **1.** pas *m*. **2. to follow in s.o.'s footsteps**, marcher sur les traces de qn; **'footstool,** s. tabouret *m*; **'footwalk,** s. trottoir *m*; **'footwear,** s. chaussures *fpl*; **'footwork,** s. *Sp:* jeu *m* des pieds, des jambes.

for [fɔːr]. **I.** prep. pour. **1.** (a) (i) **member f. Liverpool**, député *m* pour Liverpool; (ii) **to act for s.o.**, agir pour qn; (b) **he wants her f. his wife,** la veut pour femme; (c) **to exchange one thing another**, échanger une chose contre une autre; **to sell sth. f. £100**, vendre qch. cent livres; (*N.Am:* *F:* **f. free**, gratis, pour rien. **2. he's (all) free trade**, il est pour le libre-échange; **cloth f. men**, vêtements *m* pour hommes. **3.** (a) **wh f.?** pourquoi (faire)? **what's that thing f.?** quoi sert ce truc-là? **f. sale**, à vendre; **f. exam ple**, par exemple; (b) **to marry s.o. f. his mone** épouser qn pour son argent; **to jump f. jo** sauter de joie. **4.** (a) **ship bound f. Americ** navire *m* en partance pour l'Amérique; **t train f. London**, le train allant à Londres; train de Londres; **change here f. York**, dir tion de York, changez de train; (*b*) **his feelings f. you,** ses sentiments envers vous. **5. we didn't see a house f. miles,** nous avons fait des kilomètres sans voir de maison; **bends f. 5 kilometres,** virages sur 5 kilomètres. **6.** (*a*) **I'm going away f. a fortnight,** je pars pour quinze jours; **he'll be away f. a year,** il sera absent pendant un an; **I'll come f. you tomorrow,** je viendrai vous prendre demain; (*b*) **he was away f. a fortnight,** il a été absent pendant quinze jours; (*c*) **I've been here f. three days,** je suis ici depuis trois jours. **7. this book is f. you,** ce livre est pour vous; **to make a name f. oneself,** se faire un nom; **to write f. the papers,** écrire dans les journaux. **8. to care f. s.o., sth.,** aimer qn, qch.; **fit f. nothing,** bon à rien; **ready f. dinner,** prêt à dîner; **too stupid f. words,** d'une bêtise incroyable; **oh f. a bit of peace!** que ne donnerais-je pour avoir de la paix! **now f. it!** allons-y! **9.** (*a*) **as f. him,** quant à lui; **see f. yourself!** voyez par vous-même! (*b*) **f. all that,** malgré tout; (*c*) **but f. her,** sans elle; (*d*) **translate word f. word,** traduisez mot à mot. **II.** *prep. introducing an infinitive clause.* **1. it's easy (enough) f. him to come,** il lui est facile de venir. **2. I've brought it f. you to see,** je l'ai apporté pour que vous le voyiez; **it's not f. me to decide,** ce n'est pas à moi de décider; **it's no good f. Mr X to talk,** M. X a beau parler. **3. he gave orders f. the trunks to be packed,** il a donné l'ordre de faire les malles; **it took an hour f. the taxi to get to the station,** le taxi a mis une heure pour aller à la gare; **to wait f. sth. to be done,** attendre que qch. se fasse. **4. it would be a disgrace f. you to back out now,** vous retirer maintenant serait honteux. **III.** *conj.* car.

orage ['fɔridʒ]. **I.** *s.* (*a*) fourrage(s) *m(pl)*; (*b*) *Mil:* **f. cap,** bonnet *m* de police. **II.** *v.i.* fourrager; **F: to f. about in a drawer,** fouiller dans un tiroir.

orbearance [fɔ:'bɛərəns], *s.* patience *f*; **for'bearing,** *a.* patient, endurant.

orbid [fə'bid], *v.tr.* (**forbade** [fə'bæd], **forbidden** [fə'bidn]) **1.** défendre, interdire; **smoking forbidden,** défense de fumer; **to f. s.o. to do sth.,** défendre à qn de faire qch.; **for'bidden,** *a.* défendu, interdit; **f. subjects,** sujets tabous; **for'bidding,** *a.* sinistre, rébarbatif; (temps) sombre; (ciel) menaçant.

orce [fɔ:s]. **I.** *s.* force *f*. **1.** (*a*) force, violence *f*; contrainte *f*; **the f. of circumstances,** la contrainte, la force, des circonstances; (*b*) influence *f*, autorité *f*; **f. of example,** influence de l'exemple. **2.** (*a*) force, énergie *f* (d'un coup); intensité *f* (du vent); (*b*) force, effort *m*; **f. of gravity,** force de la pesanteur; **nuclear f.,** force nucléaire. **3.** puissance *f*, force; **the (armed)**

forces, les forces armées; **the police f.,** la police; **in full f.,** en force. **4.** (*a*) vertu *f*, valeur *f* (d'un argument, etc.); (*b*) signification *f* (d'un mot). **5.** (*of law*) **to be in f.,** être en vigueur. **II.** *v.tr.* forcer. **1.** (*a*) **to f. s.o.'s hand,** forcer la main à qn; **to f. the pace,** forcer l'allure; **she forced a smile,** elle s'est forcée à sourire; (*b*) **to f. one's way,** se frayer un chemin; **to f. one's way into a house,** entrer, pénétrer, de force dans une maison. **2.** (*a*) contraindre, obliger; **to be forced to do sth.,** être forcé, obligé, de faire qch.; (*b*) **to f. sth. on s.o.,** forcer qn à accepter qch.; imposer qch. à qn; (*c*) **to f. a promise from s.o.,** extorquer, arracher, une promesse à qn; **'force 'back,** *v.tr.* **1.** repousser, faire reculer (l'ennemi, etc.). **2. to f. back one's tears,** refouler, avaler, ses larmes; **forced,** *a.* **1.** forcé, obligatoire; **f. sale,** vente forcée. **2.** forcé, contraint; **f. laugh,** rire forcé; **'forceful,** *a.* **1.** plein de force; énergique. **2.** (langage) énergique, vigoureux; **-fully,** *adv.* avec force; vigoureusement; **'forcible,** *a.* (entrée) de, par, force; **-ibly,** *adv.* **1.** par force, de force. **2.** énergiquement, vigoureusement.

forceps ['fɔ:seps], *s. inv. Surg:* **a (pair of) f.,** une pince.

ford [fɔ:d]. **I.** *s.* gué *m.* **II.** *v.tr.* guéer, traverser à gué.

fore [fɔ:r]. **I.** *a.* antérieur; de devant. **II.** *s.* (*a*) *Nau:* avant *m*; (*b*) **to the f.,** en vue, en évidence. **III.** *int. Golf:* attention! gare! devant! **'forearm,** *s.* avant-bras *m inv*; **'forecast. I.** *s.* prévision *f*; **weather f.,** prévision du temps, prévision météorologique. **II.** *v.tr.* calculer, prévoir; **forecastle** ['fouksl], *s. Nau:* poste *m* de l'équipage; **'forecourt,** *s.* avant-cour *f*, *pl.* avant-cours; **'forefather,** *s.* aïeul *m*, ancêtre *m*; **our forefathers,** nos aïeux; **'forefinger,** *s.* index *m*; **'foregoing,** *a.* précédent, antérieur; **the f.,** ce qui précède; **'foregone,** *a.* décidé d'avance; prévu; **it was a f. conclusion,** l'issue n'était pas douteuse; **'foreground,** *s.* premier plan; avant-plan *m*; **forehead** ['fɔrid], *s. Anat:* front *m*; **'foreland,** *s.* cap *m*, promontoire *m*; **'foreleg,** *s.* jambe *f* de devant; patte *f* de devant; **'forelock,** *s.* mèche *f* (de cheveux) sur le front; **to take time by the f.,** saisir l'occasion par les, aux, cheveux; **'foreman,** *s.* **1.** *Jur:* chef *m* du jury. **2.** *Ind:* contremaître; chef *m* d'équipe; **'foremast,** *s. Nau:* mât *m* de misaine; **'foremost. 1.** *a.* premier; le plus avancé. **2.** *adv.* **first and f.,** tout d'abord; d'abord et avant tout; **'forename,** *s.* prénom *m*; **'forerunner,** *s.* avant-coureur *m*, *pl.* avant-coureurs; **fore'see,** *v.tr.* (**foresaw** [-'sɔ], **forseen** [-'si:n]) prévoir, entrevoir; **fore'shadow,** *v.tr.* présager, annoncer; **'foresight,** *s.* (*a*) prévision *f* (de l'avenir); (*b*) prévoyance *f*; **he has plenty of f.**, il voit bien loin; **fore′stall**, *v.tr.* anticiper, devancer (qn, un événement); prendre les devants sur (un concurrent); **′foretaste**, *s.* avant-goût *m*, *pl.* avant-goûts; **fore′tell**, *v.tr.* (**foretold** [-′tould]) 1. prédire (l'avenir). 2. présager; **′forethought**, *s.* 1. préméditation *f.* 2. prévoyance *f*; **′forewoman**, *s. Ind:* contremaîtresse *f*; **′foreword**, *s.* préface *f*, avant-propos *m inv.*

foreign [′fɔrən], *a.* 1. étranger à, sans rapport avec (qch.); **feelings f. to his nature,** sentiments qui lui sont étrangers. 2. (*a*) **f. countries,** pays étrangers; **the F. Service,** le corps diplomatique; *Mil:* **f. service,** service *m* à l'étranger; **the F. Legion,** la Légion étrangère; (*b*) **f. trade,** commerce extérieur; **f. money order,** mandat international; **the F. Office** = le Ministère des Affaires étrangères; **′foreigner**, *s.* étranger, -ère.

forest [′fɔrist], *s.* forêt *f*; **deciduous f.,** forêt à feuilles caduques; **coniferous f.,** forêt de conifères; **f. guard, f. ranger,** garde forestier; **′forested**, *a.* couvert de forêts; **′forester**, *s.* garde forestier; **′forestry**, *s.* sylviculture *f*; **the F. Commission** = le service des Eaux et Forêts.

forfeit [′fɔːfit]. **I.** *s.* 1. amende *f.* 2. (*in game*) gage *m.* **II.** *v.tr.* perdre (ses droits, etc.); **to f. one's life,** payer de sa vie; **′forfeiture**, *s.* perte *f* (de ses droits, etc.).

forge[1] [fɔːdʒ]. **I.** *s.* forge *f.* **II.** *v.tr.* 1. forger (le fer). 2. (*a*) contrefaire (une signature); (*b*) *v.i.* commettre un faux; **forged**, *a.* 1. (fer) forgé. 2. (document, etc.) faux, contrefait; **′forger**, *s.* faussaire *mf*; **′forgery**, *s.* 1. contrefaçon *f* (d'une signature); falsification *f* (de documents). 2. faux *m*; **the signature was a f.,** la signature était contrefaite; **′forging**, *s.* 1. travail *m* de forge. 2. pièce forgée. 3. falsification *f.*

forge[2], *v.i.* **to f. ahead,** avancer à toute vitesse; gagner les devants.

forget [fɔ′get], *v.tr.* (**forgot** [-gɔt], **forgotten** [-′gɔtən]) 1. oublier (qch.); **I forgot all about those books,** j'ai complètement oublié ces livres; **to f. how to do sth.,** oublier comment faire qch.; ne plus savoir faire qch.; **f. about it!** n'y pensez plus! **and don't you f. it!** faites-y bien attention! **never to be forgotten,** inoubliable. 2. (*a*) omettre, oublier (de faire qch.); **don't f. to do it,** ne manquez pas de le faire; (*b*) oublier (son mouchoir, etc.); (*c*) négliger (son devoir); **for′getful**, *a.* 1. oublieux (of, de); **he's very f.,** il a très mauvaise mémoire. 2. négligent; **for′getfulness**, *s.* 1. (*a*) manque *m* de mémoire; (*b*) **a moment of f.,** un moment d'oubli. 2. négligence *f*; **for′get-me-not**, *s. Bot:* myosotis

m inv.

forgive [fə′giv], *v.tr.* (**forgave** [-geiv]; **forgiven** [-givn]) 1. pardonner (une injure, etc.). 2. **to f. s.o.,** pardonner à qn; **for′givable**, *a.* pardonnable; **for′giveness**, *s.* 1. pardon *m.* 2. indulgence *f*, clémence *f*; **for′giving**, *a.* indulgent; peu rancunier.

fork [fɔːk]. **I.** *s.* 1. *Agr:* fourche *f.* 2. fourchette *f* (de table). 3. branche fourchue (d'un arbre). 4. bifurcation *f* (de routes); **take the left f.,** prenez le chemin à gauche. 5. *Mus:* **tuning f.,** diapason *m.* **II.** *v.* 1. *v.i.* (*of road*) bifurquer; **f. right for York,** prenez à droite pour York. 2. *v.tr.* **to f. up, over,** fourcher, retourner (le sol); *F:* **to f. out,** *N.Am:* **to f. over, up, money,** allonger, abouler, de l'argent; *v.i.* **he had to f. out,** il a dû s'exécuter; **forked**, *a.* fourchu; **f. lightning,** éclair qui fait des zigzags.

forlorn [fə′lɔːn], *a.* (*a*) abandonné, délaissé; (*b*) **f. appearance,** mine *f* triste.

form [fɔːm]. **I.** *s.* 1. forme *f* (d'un objet); **in the f. of a dog,** sous la forme d'un chien; **statistics in tabular f.,** statistique *f* sous forme de tableau. 2. (*a*) forme, formalité *f*; **for form's sake,** pour la forme; **it's a mere matter of f.,** c'est une pure formalité; *F:* **you know the f.,** vous savez bien (i) ce qu'il faut faire, (ii) ce que ça veut dire; (*b*) **it's bad f.,** c'est de mauvais ton. 3. (*a*) formule *f*, forme; **it's only a f. of speech,** ce n'est qu'une façon de parler; (*b*) **to fill in,** *N.Am:* **to fill out, a f.,** remplir une formule, un formulaire. 4. *Sp:* forme; état *m*, condition *f*; **to be in (good) f.,** être en forme. 5. *Sch:* classe *f.* 6. banc *m*, banquette *f.* **II.** *v.* 1. *v.tr.* (*a*) former, faire; façonner; (*b*) former, organiser (une société, etc.); former, arrêter (un plan); (*c*) **to f. part of sth.,** faire partie de qch. 2. *v.i.* prendre forme, se former; **′format**, *s.* format *m* (d'un livre, etc.); **for′mation**, *s.* formation *f*; **′form room**, *s.* (salle *f* de) classe *f.*

formal [′fɔːm(ə)l], *a.* 1. formel, en règle; (*of order*) formel, positif. 2. cérémonieux, solennel; **f. dress,** *N.Am:* **s. formal,** tenue *f* (i) de cérémonie, (ii) de soirée. 3. (*a*) formaliste, cérémonieux; (*b*) (*of art, etc.*) conventionnel; (jardin) régulier, tiré au cordeau; **-ally**, *adv.* formellement. 2. cérémonieusement; **for′mality**, *s.* 1. formalité *f.* 2. cérémonie *f*, formalité(s).

former [′fɔːmər], *a.* 1. antérieur, précédent, ancien; **my f. pupils,** mes anciens élèves; **in times,** autrefois. 2. (*a*) **the f. alternative,** première alternative; (*b*) *pron.* **the f.,** celui-là, celle-là, ceux-là, celles-là; **-ly**, *adv.* autrefois.

formidable [′fɔːmidəbl], *a.* formidable, redoutable.

Formosa [fɔː′mousə]. *Pr.n. Geog:* la Formose.

formula [′fɔːmjulə], *s.* formule *f*; **′formulat**

v.tr. formuler.

forsake [fə'seik], *v.tr.* (**forsook** [fə'suk]; **for-saken** [fə'seikn]) 1. abandonner, délaisser (qn). 2. renoncer à, abandonner (qch.); **for'saken**, *a.* abandonné, délaissé.

forsythia [fɔ:'saiθiə], *s. Bot:* forsythia *m.*

fort [fɔ:t], *s. Mil:* fort *m.*

forth [fɔ:θ], *adv.* 1. **from this time f.**, dès maintenant; désormais. 2. **and so f.**, et ainsi de suite; **forth'coming**, *a.* 1. qui arrive; prochain, à venir. 2. (*pers.*) (*a*) sociable, expansif; (*b*) ouvert; franc, franche.

fortify ['fɔ:tifai], *v.tr.* fortifier; **fortifi'cation**, *s.* fortification *f.*

fortitude ['fɔ:titju:d], *s.* force *f* d'âme; courage *m.*

fortnight ['fɔ:tnait], *s.* quinzaine *f*; quinze jours *m*; **'fortnightly**. 1. *a.* bimensuel. 2. *adv.* tous les quinze jours.

fortress ['fɔ:tris], *s.* forteresse *f*; place forte.

fortuitous [fə'tju:itəs], *a.* fortuit, imprévu; **-ly**, *adv.* fortuitement; par hasard.

fortune ['fɔ:tʃən, -tju:n], *s.* fortune *f.* 1. (*a*) hasard *m*, chance *f*; **by good f.**, par bonheur; (*b*) destinée *f*, sort *m*; **to tell fortunes**, dire la bonne aventure; **f. teller**, diseur, -euse, de bonne aventure; **f. telling**, la bonne aventure. 2. (*a*) bonne chance; bonheur *m*; (*b*) richesses *fpl*, biens *mpl*; **to make a f.**, faire fortune; *F:* **to cost a small f.**, coûter un argent fou; **'fortunate**, *a.* 1. heureux, fortuné; **to be f.**, avoir de la chance. 2. propice, heureux; **how f.!** quelle chance! **-ly**, *adv.* 1. heureusement. 2. par bonheur.

forty ['fɔ:ti], *num.a. & s.* quarante (*m*); **about f. guests**, une quarantaine d'invités; **to have f. winks**, faire une courte sieste; **'fortieth**, *num. a. & s.* quarantième (*mf*).

forward ['fɔ:wəd]. I. *a.* 1. (mouvement) progressif, en avant. 2. avancé; précoce. II. *adv.* 1. **from that day f.**, à partir de ce jour-là; **to look f. to sth.**, attendre qch. avec plaisir. 2. (*a*) en avant; **to move f.**, avancer; **to go straight f.**, aller tout droit; **f.!** en avant! (*b*) à l'avant; (*c*) *Com:* **carried f.**, à reporter, report *m.* 3. **to come f.**, se proposer, s'offrir; **to thrust, push, oneself f.**, se mettre en évidence. III. *v.tr.* 1. avancer, favoriser (un projet). 2. expédier, envoyer; (*on letter*) **please f.**, prière de faire suivre; **'forwarding**, *s.* 1. avancement *m* (d'un projet). 2. expédition *f*, envoi *m* (des marchandises, etc.); **'forwardness**, *s.* 1. avancement *m.* 2. état avancé.

fossil ['fɔs(ə)l], *a. & s.* fossile (*m*); *F:* **an old f.**, un vieux fossile, une croûte.

foster ['fɔstər], *v.tr.* 1. élever, nourrir (un enfant). 2. entretenir, nourrir (une idée); **'foster-brother**, *s.* frère *m* de lait; **'foster-child**, *s.* nourrisson, -onne; **'foster-mother**, *s.* (mère)

nourricière; **'foster-sister**, *s.* sœur *f* de lait.

foul [faul]. I. *a.* 1. (*a*) infect, nauséabond; **f. air**, air vicié; (*b*) **f. crime**, crime *m* atroce, horrible; (*c*) *F:* **what f. weather!** quel sale temps! quel temps infect! 2. sale, malpropre, souillé. 3. **to fall f. of s.o.**, se brouiller avec qn. 4. (*a*) *Sp:* déloyal, -aux; **f. play**, jeu déloyal; (*b*) **f. play is not suspected**, on ne croit pas à un crime; **-ly**, *adv.* 1. salement. 2. abominablement; **f. murdered**, ignoblement assassiné. II. *s. Sp:* faute *f*; coup illicite, déloyal. III. *v.* 1. *v.tr.* (*a*) salir, souiller; (*b*) obstruer; engager (un cordage, etc.); *Nau:* surjaler, surpatter (l'ancre). 2. *v.i.* **to f. (up)**, (*of gun barrel, etc.*) s'encrasser; (*of pump*) s'engorger, prendre.

found [faund], *v.tr.* fonder, créer (une institution, etc.); **to f. a family**, fonder une famille; (*b*) baser, fonder (son opinion, etc.) (**on**, sur); (*of novel*) **founded on fact**, reposant sur des faits véridiques; **foun'dation**, *s.* 1. fondation *f* (d'une ville, d'une maison de commerce, etc.). 2. fondement *m*, fondation (d'un édifice); assise *f* (d'un mur); **the foundations of a building**, les fondements d'un bâtiment; **to lay the f. stone**, poser la première pierre. 3. (*a*) *Cl:* **f. (garment)**, gaine *f*; (*b*) (*makeup*) fond *m* de teint; **'founder¹**, *s.* fondateur *m* (d'une institution); souche *f* (d'une famille).

founder² ['faundər], *v.i. Nau:* sombrer.

foundling ['faundliŋ], *s.* enfant trouvé(e).

fount [faunt], *s. Typ:* fonte *f*; **wrong f.**, lettre *f* d'un autre œil.

fountain ['fauntin], *s.* fontaine *f*; **drinking f.**, borne-fontaine *f*; **f. pen**, stylo *m*; **'fountainhead**, *s.*; **to go to the f. for information**, prendre, puiser, son information à la source.

four [fɔ:r], *num.a. & s.* quatre (*m*); *Pol:* **the Big F.**, les Quatre Grands; **the f. corners of the earth**, les quatre coins du monde; **to go on all fours**, courir à quatre pattes; **f. at a time**, quatre à quatre; **'four-'engined**, *a.* quadrimoteur; **'fourfold**. 1. *a.* quadruple. 2. *adv.* quatre fois autant; au quadruple; **'four-'footed**, *a.* quadrupède; à quatre pattes; **'four-'part**, *a. Mus:* à quatre voix; **'four-'poster**, *s.* lit *m* à colonnes; **four'teen**, *num.a. & s.* quatorze (*m*); **four'teenth**, *num.a. & s.* quatorzième (*mf*); **Louis the F.**, Louis Quatorze; **fourth**. 1. *num.a. & s.* quatrième (*mf*); **on the f. of June**, le quatre juin. 2. *s.* (*a*) (*fraction*) quart *m*; (*b*) *Mus:* quarte *f*; **-ly**, *adv.* quatrièmement; en quatrième lieu.

fowl [faul], *s.* 1. *coll.* oiseaux *mpl*; **wild f.**, gibier *m* d'eau. 2. (*a*) poule *f*, coq *m*; volaille *f*; (*b*) *Cu:* **boiling f.**, poule; **'fowler**, *s.* oiseleur *m.*

fox [fɔks]. I. *s.* renard *m*; **she f.**, renarde *f*; **f. cub**, renardeau *m*; *Cl:* **f. fur**, (fourrure *f* de) renard. II. *v.tr.* (*a*) maculer, piquer (une gravure); (*b*)

F: mystifier, tromper (qn); **'foxglove,** *s. Bot:* digitale *f;* **'fox hole,** *s.* renardière *f;* **'foxhound,** *s.* chien courant; **'foxhunt(ing),** *s.* chasse *f* au renard; **'fox 'terrier,** *s.* fox *m;* **'foxy,** *a. F:* rusé.

foyer ['fɔiei], *s.* foyer *m* du public.

fraction ['frækʃ(ə)n], *s.* **1.** petite portion; fragment *m;* **to escape death by a f. of a second,** être à deux doigts de la mort. **2.** *Mth:* fraction *f;* **'fractional,** *a.* fractionnaire.

fractious ['frækʃəs], *a.* (a) difficile (de caractère); revêche; (b) pleurnicheur, -euse; **'fractiousness,** *s.* humeur hargneuse; (*of baby*) pleurnicherie *f.*

fracture ['fræktʃər]. **I.** *s.* fracture *f; Med:* **compound f.,** fracture compliquée. **II.** *v.tr.* casser, briser; *Med:* fracturer (un os).

fragile ['frædʒail], *a.* fragile; (*of pers.*) faible; *F:* **to feel f.,** avoir mal aux cheveux; **fragility** [frə'dʒiliti], *s.* fragilité *f.*

fragment ['frægmənt], *s.* fragment *m;* morceau *m;* **'fragmentary,** *a.* fragmentaire.

fragrance ['freigrəns], *s.* parfum *m;* odeur *f* agréable; **'fragrant,** *a.* parfumé, odorant.

frail [freil], *a.* **1.** fragile; frêle. **2.** (*of pers.*) faible, délicat; **'frailness,** *s.* faiblesse *f,* délicatesse *f* (de santé); **'frailty,** *s.* faiblesse morale; fragilité humaine.

frame [freim]. **I.** *s.* **1.** construction *f,* structure *f,* forme *f;* **f. of mind,** disposition *f* d'esprit. **2.** (a) ossature *f;* **man with a gigantic f.,** homme d'une taille colossale; (b) charpente *f* (d'un bâtiment); cadre *m* (d'une bicyclette); monture *f* (d'un parapluie); *N.Am:* **f. house,** maison *f* en bois. **3.** (a) cadre, encadrement *m* (d'un tableau); (b) chambranle *m,* châssis *m* (d'une fenêtre); (c) *Cin: T.V:* image *f.* **4.** *Hort:* châssis de couches. **II.** *v.tr.* **1.** former, régler (ses pensées). **2.** articuler (un mot); imaginer (une idée). **3.** encadrer (un tableau). **4.** *F:* **to f. s.o.,** inventer une fausse accusation contre qn; **'frame-up,** *s. F:* coup monté; **'framework,** *s.* **1.** charpente *f,* ossature *f,* carcasse *f.* **2.** cadre *m;* **within the f. of the United Nations,** dans le cadre des Nations Unies.

France [frɑːns]. *Pr.n. Geog:* la France.

Frances ['frɑːnsis]. *Pr.n.f.* Françoise.

franchise ['fræntʃaiz], *s.* droit *m* de vote.

Francis ['frɑːnsis]. *Pr.n.m.* François.

frank[1] [fræŋk], *a.* franc, *f.* franche; sincère; **-ly,** *adv.* franchement; ouvertement; **'frankness,** *s.* franchise *f,* sincérité *f.*

frank[2]. **I.** *s.* marque *f* d'affranchissement. **II.** *v.tr.* affranchir (une lettre).

frantic ['fræntik], *a.* frénétique; fou, *f.* folle (de joie, de douleur); **f. efforts,** efforts désespérés; *F:* **he drives me f.,** il me rend fou; **-ally,** *adv.* frénétiquement.

fraternal [frə'təːnl], *a.* fraternel; **fra'ternity,** *s.* fraternité *f.*

fraternize ['frætənaiz], *v.i.* fraterniser (**with,** avec).

fraud [frɔːd], *s.* **1.** (a) *Jur:* fraude *f;* (b) supercherie *f,* imposture *f.* **2.** *F:* imposteur *m;* **'fraudulence,** *s.* caractère frauduleux; **'fraudulent,** *a.* frauduleux; **-ly,** *adv.* frauduleusement.

fray[1] [frei], *s.* bagarre *f;* **ready for the f.,** prêt à se battre.

fray[2], *v.i.* (*of material*) s'érailler, s'effiler.

freak [friːk], *s.* **1.** caprice *m,* fantaisie *f,* lubie *f;* **f. of fortune,** jeu *m* de la fortune. **2.** **f.** (**of nature**), phénomène *m,* curiosité *f.* **3.** **f. weather,** temps inouï, extraordinaire; **'freakish,** *a.* bizarre.

freckle ['frekl]. **I.** *s.* tache *f* de rousseur, de son. **II.** *v.i.* se couvrir de taches de rousseur, de son; **'freckled,** *a.* couvert de taches de rousseur, de son.

free [friː]. **I.** *a. & adv.* **1.** (a) libre; (b) en liberté; **to set a prisoner f.,** libérer un prisonnier; **f. will,** libre arbitre *m;* **f. house,** débit *m* de boissons non lié à un fournisseur particulier. **2.** libre; is **this table f.?** est-ce que cette table est libre? *P.T.T:* **f. line,** ligne dégagée. **3.** (a) **to give s.o. a f. hand,** donner carte blanche à qn; **he is not f. to act,** il a les mains liées; (b) franc, *f.* franche, sans raideur; souple; (c) **to be f. from worry,** être sans souci; (d) **f. of duty, duty f.,** exempt de droits de douane; **f. trade,** libre-échange *m;* **you may bring in a bottle f.,** il y a tolérance d'une bouteille. **4.** (a) **f. offer,** offre spontanée; as **a f. gift,** en pur don; (b) libéral, -aux; **to be f. with one's money,** ne pas regarder à l'argent; (c) franc, ouvert, aisé; **f. and easy,** désinvolte; **to make f. with s.o.,** prendre des libertés *f* avec qn; **to make f. with sth.,** user librement de qch. **5.** gratuit; franco; **admission f.,** entrée gratuite; **post f.,** franco de port; **catalogue sent f. on request,** catalogue *m* franco sur demande; **-ly** *adv.* **1.** librement, volontairement. **2.** (parler) franchement, sans contrainte. **II.** *v.tr.* (a) affranchir (un peuple); libérer (qn); (b) débarrasser (**from,** de); dégager (un sentier); **'freedom,** *s.* **1.** liberté *f,* indépendance *f;* **f. of speech,** le franc-parler. **2.** franchise *f,* familiarité *f;* sans-gêne *m.* **3.** exemption *f,* immunité *f* (**from,** de); **f. of the city,** droit *m* de cité; **'freehand,** *a. & s.* (**drawing**), (dessin *m*) à main levée; **'free-handed,** *a.* généreux; **'freehold,** *a. Jur:* tenu en propriété perpétuelle et libre; **'freelance,** *a. & s. f.* (**journalist**), (journaliste) indépendant; **'freemason,** *s.* franc-maçon *m;* **'freemasonry,** *s.* franc-maçonnerie *f;* **'freestyle,** *s.* nage *f* libre; **'free'thinker,** libre penseur, *f.* libre penseuse.

freeze [fri:z]. **I.** *v.* (froze; frozen) **1.** *v.i.* (*a*) geler; **it's freezing,** il gèle; (*b*) se geler; se congeler; prendre; **the river is frozen,** la rivière est prise; **the smile froze on his lips,** le sourire s'est figé sur ses lèvres; (*c*) **to f. to death,** mourir de froid. **2.** *v.tr.* geler, congeler; **to deep f.,** surgeler; **to f. the blood (in one's veins),** glacer le sang, le cœur; **to f. wages,** bloquer les salaires. **II.** *s.* **1.** gelée *f*. **2. price f.,** blocage *m* des prix; **'freezer,** *s.* congélateur *m*; **'frozen,** *a.* (*a*) gelé; glacé; **I'm f. to death,** je meurs de froid; (*b*) (*of food*) congelé; surgelé; **f. peas,** petits pois surgelés.

freight [freit], *s.* **1.** fret *m* (d'un navire); (*b*) transport *m*; *N.Am:* **f. train,** train *m* de marchandises; **f. plane,** avion *m* de transport; **air f.,** transport par avion; **'freighter,** *s.* **1.** (*pers.*) affréteur *m.* **2.** (*vessel*) cargo *m*.

french [fren(t)ʃ]. **I.** *a.* **1.** (*a*) français; **F. Canadian,** canadien français; **F. Canada,** le Canada français; (*b*) **F. lesson,** leçon *f* de français; **F. master, mistress,** professeur *m* de français; (*c*) **F. dressing,** vinaigrette *f*; **F. window,** portefenêtre *f*, *pl.* portes-fenêtres; **to take f. leave,** filer à l'anglaise. **II.** *s.* **1.** *Ling:* le français, la langue française; **to speak F.,** parler français; **Canadian F.,** le français canadien, du Canada. **2.** (*a*) *pl.* **the F.,** les Français; (*b*) **F. Canadian,** Canadien français, Canadienne française; **'Frenchman,** *pl.* **-men,** *s.* Français *m*; **'French-'speaking,** *a.* francophone; **F.-s. Switzerland,** la Suisse romande; **'Frenchwoman,** *s.* Française *f*.

frenzy ['frenzi], *s.* frénésie *f*; transport *m* (de joie); **'frenzied,** *a.* affolé.

frequent. I. *a.* ['fri:kwənt]. **1.** répandu. **2.** fréquent; qui arrive souvent. **3.** (client, etc.) habituel; **-ly,** *adv.* fréquemment. **II.** *v.tr.* [fri'kwent], fréquenter; hanter (un endroit, une personne); **'frequency,** *s.* fréquence *f*; *W.Tel:* **very high f.,** très haute fréquence; **f. modulation,** modulation *f* de fréquence.

fresh [freʃ]. **I.** *a.* **1.** (*a*) nouveau, -el, -elle, -eaux; **to put f. courage into s.o.,** ranimer le courage de qn; (*b*) frais, *f.* fraîche; récent; **it is still f. in my memory,** j'en ai le souvenir tout frais. **2.** inexpérimenté, novice. **3.** (*a*) (beurre) frais; (légume) vert; (*b*) (air) frais, pur; **in the f. air,** en plein air; (*c*) **f. water,** (i) (*newly drawn*) eau fraîche; (ii) (*not salt*) eau douce. **4.** (*a*) (teint) frais, fleuri; **she's as f. as a daisy,** elle est fraîche comme une rose; (*b*) *F:* effronté; **-ly,** *adv.* nouvellement. **II.** *adv.* fraîchement, nouvellement, récemment; **'freshen. 1.** *v.i.* (*of temperature*) (se) rafraîchir; (*of wind*) fraîchir. **2.** *v.tr.* rafraîchir (l'air, etc.); **'freshman,** *pl.* **-men,** *s.* *Sch:* étudiant, -ante, de première année; **'freshness,** *s.* **1.** nouveauté *f* (d'un

événement). **2.** fraîcheur *f.* **3.** (*a*) vigueur *f*, vivacité *f*; (*b*) naïveté *f*, inexpérience *f*; (*c*) *F:* effronterie *f*, toupet *m*.

fret [fret], *v.* (fretted) **1.** *v.tr.* inquiéter, tracasser (qn). **2.** *v.pr. & i.* se tourmenter; se faire du mauvais sang; **the child was fretting for his mother,** l'enfant pleurnichait après sa mère; **stop fretting,** ne te fais pas de mauvais sang, de bile; **'fretful,** *a.* irritable; **f. baby,** bébé agité; **-fully,** *adv.* d'un air, d'un ton, chagrin, inquiet; avec irritation; **'fretfulness,** *s.* irritabilité *f.*

fretwork ['fretwə:k], *s.* travail ajouré (en bois); **'fretsaw,** *s.* scie *f* à découper.

friar ['fraiər], *s.* frère *m*, religieux *m*.

friction ['frikʃ(ə)n], *s.* **1.** friction *f.* **2.** frottement *m.* **3.** désaccord *m* (entre deux personnes).

Friday ['fraidi], *s.* vendredi *m*; **he's coming (on) F.,** il viendra vendredi; **he comes on Fridays,** il vient le vendredi; **Good F.,** le vendredi saint.

fridge [fridʒ], *s.* *F:* réfrigérateur *m*, frigo *m*.

friend [frend], *s.* **1.** ami, *f.* amie; **a f. of mine,** un(e) de mes ami(e)s; **to make friends with s.o.,** se lier d'amitié avec qn; **the Society of Friends,** les Quakers. **2.** connaissance *f*; **to have friends at court,** avoir des amis bien placés; avoir du piston; **'friendless,** *a.* délaissé; sans amis; **'friendliness,** *s.* bienveillance *f*, bonté *f* (**to, towards,** envers); dispositions amicales; **'friendly,** *a.* **1.** (sentiment) amical, sympathique; **to be on f. terms with s.o.,** être en bons rapports avec qn. **2.** (*of pers.*) bienveillant; bien disposé. **3. f. society,** mutuelle *f*; **'friendship,** *s.* amitié *f.*

frieze [fri:z], *s.* **1.** *Arch:* frise *f.* **2.** bordure *f.*

frigate ['frigət], *s.* *Navy:* frégate *f.*

fright [frait], *s.* **1.** peur *f*, effroi *m*; **to take f.,** s'effrayer, s'effarer (**at,** de); **to give s.o. a f.,** faire peur à qn. **2.** *F:* personne laide, grotesque; épouvantail *m*; **'frighten,** *v.tr.* effrayer; faire peur à (qn); **to be frightened,** avoir peur; **to be frightened to death,** mourir de peur; **to f. s.o. out of his wits,** faire une peur bleue à qn; **'frightened,** *a.* apeuré, épeuré; **easily f.,** peureux, poltron, *f.* -onne; **'frightening,** *a.* effrayant; **'frightful,** *a.* terrible, effroyable, affreux, épouvantable; **-fully,** *adv.* terriblement, effroyablement, affreusement; **'frightfulness,** *s.* horreur *f*, atrocité *f* (d'un crime, etc.).

frigid ['fridʒid], *a.* (*a*) glacial, -als; (très) froid; (*b*) **f. politeness,** politesse glaciale; (*c*) (*of woman*) frigide; **-ly,** *adv.* glacialement; très froidement; **fri'gidity,** *s.* (*a*) frigidité *f*; grande froideur; (*b*) frigidité (sexuelle).

frill [fril], *s.* (*a*) *Cost:* volant *m*, ruche *f*; *Cu:* papillote *f*; (*b*) **a plain meal without frills,** un repas simple sans présentation compliquée.

fringe [frindʒ], s. **1.** *Tex:* frange *f.* **2.** (*a*) bordure *f*, bord *m*; *T.V:* **f. area,** zone *f* limitrophe; **f. benefits,** compléments de salaire; avantages accessoires; (*b*) coiffure *f* à la chien.

frisk [frisk]. **1.** *v.i.* **to f.** (**about**), s'ébattre; faire des cabrioles. **2.** *v.tr. F:* fouiller (un suspect, un passager); **'friskiness,** *s.* folâtrerie *f*, vivacité *f*; **'frisky,** *a.* vif, folâtre; (cheval) fringant.

fritter[1] ['fritər], s. *Cu:* beignet *m.*

fritter[2], *v.tr.* **to f. away one's money,** gaspiller son argent.

frivolous ['frivələs], *a.* frivole; vain, futile; (*of pers.*) évaporé; **-ly,** *adv.* frivolement; **fri'volity** [-'vɔliti], *s.* frivolité *f.*

frizzle [frizl], *v.i.* grésiller.

frizzy ['frizi], *a.* frisotté; crêpelu.

frock [frɔk], *s. Cost:* **1.** robe *f.* **2.** froc *m* (de moine).

frog [frɔg], *s.* **1.** grenouille *f.* **2.** *F:* **to have a f. in one's throat,** avoir un chat dans la gorge; **'frogman,** *s.* homme-grenouille *m*; **'frogmarch,** *v.tr.* (*of police, etc.*) porter (qn) à quatre, le derrière en l'air.

frolic ['frɔlik]. **I.** *s.* (*a*) ébats *mpl*, gambades *fpl*; (*b*) fredaine *f*, divertissement *m.* **II.** *v.i.* (**frolicked**) se divertir, s'ébattre, folâtrer.

from [frɔm, frəm], *prep.* **1.** de; **f. flower to flower,** de fleur en fleur. **2.** depuis, dès, à partir de; **f. the beginning,** dès le commencement; **f. time to time,** de temps en temps; **f. his childhood,** depuis son enfance. **3.** (*a*) de, à; **he stole a pound f. her,** il lui a volé une livre; **to dissuade s.o. f. doing sth.,** dissuader qn de faire qch.; (*b*) **to shelter f. the rain,** s'abriter contre la pluie. **4.** (*a*) d'avec, de; **to distinguish good f. bad,** distinguer le bon d'avec le mauvais; (*b*) **to pick s.o. out f. the crowd,** distinguer qn parmi la foule; **to drink f. the brook,** boire au ruisseau. **5.** (*a*) **he comes f. Manchester,** (i) il est natif, originaire, de Manchester; (ii) il habite à Manchester; **a quotation f. Shakespeare,** une citation tirée de Shakespeare; **to write f. s.o.'s dictation,** écrire sous la dictée de qn; **f. your point of view,** à votre point de vue; (*b*) **tell him that f. me,** dites-lui cela de ma part; (*c*) **painted f. nature,** peint d'après nature. **6. to act f. conviction,** agir par conviction; **f. what I heard,** d'après ce que j'ai entendu dire; **f. what I can see,** à ce que je vois. **7. f. above,** d'en haut; **f. now on, f. today onwards,** à partir d'aujourd'hui.

frond [frɔnd], *s. Bot:* fronde *f* (de fougère).

front [frʌnt]. **I.** *s.* **1.** (*a*) front *m*, contenance *f*; **to put a bold f. on it,** faire bonne contenance; (*b*) **his profession is only a f.,** son métier n'est qu'une couverture. **2.** *Mil:* front. **3.** (*a*) devant *m*, partie antérieure; façade *f*, face *f* (d'un bâtiment); devant, plastron *m* (de chemise);

carriage in the f. of the train, voiture en tête du train; (*b*) esplanade *f.* **4. to come to the f.,** arriver au premier rang. **5.** *adv.phr.* **in f.,** devant, en avant; **in f. of,** (i) en face de; (ii) devant. **II.** *a.* antérieur, de devant, d'avant, de face; **f. seat,** siège au premier rang; **f. rank,** premier rang; **f. door,** porte *f* d'entrée, porte sur la rue; **f. room,** pièce *f* qui donne sur la rue. **III.** *v.tr. & i.* (*a*) **to f.** (**on**) **sth.,** faire face à qch., être tourné vers qch.; (*b*) **house fronted with stone,** maison *f* avec façade en pierre; **'frontage,** *s.* (longueur *f* de) façade *f* (d'une maison, etc.); **'frontal,** *a.* **1.** *Anat:* frontal -aux. **2.** *Mil:* (attaque, etc.) de front.

frontier ['frʌntiər], *s.* frontière *f.*

frontispiece ['frʌntispiːs], *s. Typ:* frontispice *m*

frost [frɔst]. **I.** *s.* gelée *f*, gel *m*; *F:* **Jack F.,** bonhomme Hiver; **ten degrees of f.,** dix degrés de froid. **II.** *v.tr.* **1.** geler (un arbre fruitier). (*a*) givrer (les vitres, etc.); (*b*) glacer (un gâteau); **'frostbite,** *s.* gelure *f*; **'frostbitten,** *a.* gelé; **'frosted,** *a.* **1.** givré. **2.** (*of glass*) dépoli; **'frosty,** *a.* **1.** gelé; glacial, -als; **f. day,** jour de gelée; **f. reception,** accueil glacial; **-ily,** *adv.* glacialement.

froth [frɔθ]. **I.** *s.* **1.** écume *f*; mousse *f* (de bière). **2.** *F:* futilités *fpl*; paroles creuses. **II.** *v.i.* écumer, mousser; **'frothy,** *a.* écumeux, écumant; mousseux.

frown [fraun]. **I.** *s.* froncement *m* des sourcils, regard sévère, désapprobateur. **II.** *v.i.* (*a*) froncer les sourcils; **to f. at s.o.,** regarder qn de travers, en fronçant les sourcils; **to f. upon a suggestion,** désapprouver une suggestion; (*b*) avoir l'air menaçant; **'frowning,** *s.* froncement *m* de sourcils.

frowsty ['frausti], *a. F:* qui sent le renfermé; **'frowstiness,** *s. F:* odeur *f* de renfermé.

frowzy ['frauzi], *a.* **1.** qui sent le renfermé; sale, mal tenu, peu soigné.

frugal ['fruːg(ə)l], *a.* **1.** (*of pers.*) frugal, -au; économe. **2.** (*of meal*) frugal, simple; **-ally,** *adv.* frugalement, sobrement; **fru'gality** [-'gæl-], *s.* frugalité *f.*

fruit [fruːt], *s.* fruit *m*; **dried f.,** fruits secs; **stewed f.,** compote *f* de fruits; **f. cake,** cake *m*; **f. tree,** arbre fruitier; **'fruiterer,** *s.* fruitier, -ière; **'fruitful,** *a.* (*of tree*) productif; (*of soil*) fertile, fécond; (*of work, etc.*) qui réussit; **fru'ition,** réalisation *f* (d'un projet); **to come to f.,** réussir; **'fruitless,** *a.* stérile, infructueux; efforts, vains efforts; **-ly,** *adv.* vainement.

frump [frʌmp], *s. F:* vieille caricature; **'frumpish,** *a. F:* (*of woman*) mal habillée; **f. hat,** chapeau informe.

frustrate [frʌs'treit], *v.tr.* (*a*) faire échouer (un projet); **to f. s.o.'s hopes,** frustrer l'espoir de qn; (*b*) contrecarrer (qn); **frus'tration,**

frustration *f.*

fry[1] [frai], *s. coll. Ich:* frai *m*, fretin *m*, alevin *m*; *F:* **the small f.**, les gens insignifiants.

fry[2]. **I.** *v.* **1.** *v.tr.* (faire) frire (la viande, etc.); **fried egg**, œuf *m* sur le plat. **2.** *v.i.* (*of food*) frire. **II.** *s.* friture *f*, nourriture frite; **French fries**, pommes (de terre) frites; **'frying**, *s.* friture *f*; **f.-pan**, poêle *f*; **to jump out of the f.-pan into the fire**, tomber d'un mal dans un pire.

fuddle ['fʌdl], *v.tr. F:* (*a*) soûler, griser; (*b*) brouiller les idées de (qn); **'fuddled**, *a. F:* **1.** soûl; gris. **2.** brouillé (dans ses idées).

fudge [fʌdʒ]. **I.** *s. Cu:* fondant (américain). **II.** *v.tr.* **to f.** the issue, escamoter la question.

fuel ['fjuəl]. **I.** *s.* combustible *m*; carburant *m*; **to add f. to the flames**, jeter de l'huile sur le feu. **II.** *v.tr.* (**fuelled**) (*a*) charger (un fourneau, etc.); (*b*) ravitailler (un navire, etc.) en combustibles; **'fuelling**, *s.* ravitaillement *m* en combustibles.

fug [fʌg], *s. F:* atmosphère étouffante et chaude, qui sent le renfermé; **'fuggy**, *a. F:* qui sent le renfermé.

fugitive [fju:dʒitiv]. **1.** *a.* fugitif. **2.** *s.* fugitif, -ive.

fulfil [ful'fil], *v.tr.* (*a*) répondre à, remplir (l'attente de qn); (*b*) satisfaire (un désir); exaucer (une prière); (*c*) accomplir (une tâche); **to f. a duty**, s'acquitter d'un devoir; **ful'filment**, *s.* (*a*) accomplissement *m*; (*b*) exaucement *m* (d'une prière); (*c*) exécution *f* (d'une condition).

full [ful]. **I.** *a.* **1.** plein, rempli, comble; **look f. of gratitude**, regard chargé de reconnaissance. **2.** plein, complet, -ète; **to be f. up**, avoir son plein; **f. up!** complet! *Th:* **f. house**, salle *f* comble. **3.** (*of facts, etc.*) ample, abondant, copieux; **f. particulars**, tous les détails. **4.** complet, entier; **f. pay**, paie entière; solde entière; **in f. flower**, en pleine fleur; **f. meal**, repas complet; **to pay f. fare**, payer place entière; **f. weight**, poids juste; **f. stop**, point final; *F:* **to come to a f. stop**, (i) s'arrêter brusquement; (ii) rester court (dans un discours); **roses in f. bloom**, roses épanouies; **in f. uniform**, en grande tenue; **I waited two f. hours**, j'ai attendu deux grandes heures. **5.** (*of face*) plein; (*of figure*) rond, replet, -ète. **II.** *s.* **1.** plein *m* (de la lune, etc.). **2.** (*a*) **in f.**, entièrement, complètement; en détail; **date in f.**, date en toutes lettres; **name in f.**, nom et prénoms; (*b*) **to the f.**, complètement; **f. in the face**, en pleine figure; **'full'blown**, *a.* (*a*) épanoui; en pleine fleur; (*b*) **he's a f. doctor**, il a tous ses diplômes (de médecin); **'full-dress**, *a.* (tenue *f*) de cérémonie; (débat) solennel; *Th:* **f.-d. rehearsal**, répétition générale; **'full-'length**, *a.* (portrait) en pied; (robe) longue; **'ful(l)ness**, *s.* **1.** plénitude *f*, totalité *f* (de qch.). **2.** ampleur *f* (d'un vêtement); abondance *f* (de détail); **'fulltime. 1.** *a.* (emploi) à plein temps, à temps complet. **2.** *adv.* (travailler) à pleines journées;

'fully, *adv.* **1.** pleinement, entièrement, complètement, amplement; **f. armed**, armé de toutes pièces; (*of stockings, etc.*) **f. fashioned**, entièrement diminué; **I'll write more f.**, j'écrirai plus longuement. **2.** **f. two hours**, deux bonnes heures. **3.** pleinement.

fulminate ['fʌlmineit], *v.i.* fulminer.

fulsome ['fulsəm], *a.* écœurant, excessif; **f. flattery**, flagornerie *f*, adulation *f*; **'fulsomeness**, *s.* bassesse *f*, platitude *f*.

fumble ['fʌmbl], *v.i.* fouiller; tâtonner; **to f. with sth.**, manier qch. maladroitement; **'fumbler**, *s.* maladroit, -oite; **'fumbling**, *a.* maladroit, gauche.

fume [fju:m]. **I.** *s.* fumée *f*, vapeur *f*, exhalaison *f*; **factory fumes**, fumée d'usine. **II.** *v.i.* (*a*) fumer, émettre de la fumée; (*b*) *F:* (*of pers.*) rager, fumer.

fumigate ['fju:migeit], *v.tr.* fumiger.

fun [fʌn], *s. F:* amusement *m*, gaieté *f*; plaisanterie *f*; **to make f. of, poke f. at, s.o.,** se moquer de qn; **for f., in f.,** pour rire; par plaisanterie; **it was great f.**, c'était très amusant; **to have f.**, s'amuser, se divertir; **f. fair**, (i) fête foraine; (ii) parc *m* d'attractions.

function ['fʌŋkʃ(ə)n]. **I.** *s.* **1.** fonction *f*. **2.** (*a*) fonction, charge *f*; **in his f. as a magistrate**, en sa qualité de magistrat; (*b*) *pl.* **to discharge one's functions**, s'acquitter de ses fonctions. **3.** (*a*) réception *f*, réunion *f*; (*b*) cérémonie publique. **II.** *v.i.* fonctionner, marcher; **this gadget won't f.**, ce truc ne marche pas; **'functional**, *a.* fonctionnel.

fund [fʌnd], *s.* **1.** fonds *m*. **2.** *Fin:* (*a*) fonds, caisse *f*; **to start a f.**, lancer une souscription; (*b*) *pl.* **funds**, fonds, masse *f*; ressources *f* pécuniaires; **to be in funds**, être en fonds.

fundamental [fʌndə'ment(ə)l]. **I.** *a* fondamental, -aux; essentiel; **-ally**, *adv.* fondamentalement, foncièrement. **II.** *s.pl.* **fundamentals**, principe *m*, partie essentielle (d'un système, etc.).

funeral ['fju:n(ə)rəl], *s.* (*a*) funérailles *fpl*; obsèques *fpl*; (*b*) convoi *m* funèbre; cortège *m* funèbre; **funereal** [fju:'niəriəl], *a.* lugubre, funèbre; (*of voice*) sépulcral, -aux.

fungus, *pl.* **fungi** ['fʌngəs, -gi:, -gai], *s.* champignon *m*; **edible f.**, champignon comestible.

funicular [fju'nikjulər], *a. & s.* funiculaire (*m*).

funk [fʌŋk]. **I.** *s. F:* **1.** frousse *f*, trac *m*, trouille *f*; **to be in a blue f.**, avoir la frousse, le trac, une peur bleue. **2.** (*pers.*) froussard, -arde. **II.** *v.tr. & i. F:* **to f. (it)**, caner, se dégonfler; **to f. doing sth.**, avoir peur de faire qch.; **'funky**, *a. F:* froussard.

funnel ['fʌn(ə)l], *s.* **1.** (*for pouring liquids*) entonnoir *m*. **2.** cheminée *f* (d'un bateau).

funny ['fʌni], *a.* drôle. **1.** comique, amusant, facétieux; **he's trying to be f.**, il veut faire de

l'esprit. **2.** curieux, bizarre; **a f. idea,** une drôle d'idée; *F:* **no f. business!** pas d'histoires! pas de blagues! **-ily,** *adv.* drôlement. **1.** comiquement. **2.** curieusement; **f. enough,** chose curieuse; ʹ**funnybone,** *s. F:* le petit juif.
fur [fəːr]. **I.** *s.* **1.** (*a*) fourrure *f,* pelleterie *f;* **f. coat,** manteau *m* de fourrure; (*b*) poil *m,* pelage *m* (de lapin); *F:* **to make the f. fly,** se battre avec acharnement; (*c*) *pl.* **furs,** peaux *fpl.* **2.** (*in kettle, etc.*) dépôt *m.* **II.** *v.tr.* (**furred**) entartrer, incruster; *Med:* **furred tongue,** langue chargée.
furbish [ʹfəːbiʃ], *v.tr.* **to f. (up). 1.** fourbir, polir. **2.** (re)mettre à neuf, retaper.
furious [ʹfjuːriəs], *a.* furieux; (*of look*) furibond; (*of battle*) acharné; **to be f. with s.o.,** être furieux contre qn; **f. driving,** (i) excès *m* de vitesse; (ii) train *m* d'enfer; **at a f. pace,** à une vitesse, une allure, folle; **-ly,** *adv.* furieusement; avec acharnement.
furl [fəːl], *v.tr.* serrer, ferler (une voile).
furnace [ʹfəːnis], *s.* (*a*) fourneau *m,* four *m;* **blast f.,** haut fourneau; (*b*) (*hot place*) fournaise *f.*
furnish [ʹfəːniʃ], *v.tr.* **1.** (*a*) fournir, donner; pourvoir; (*b*) **to f. s.o. with sth.,** fournir, pourvoir, munir, qn de qch. **2.** meubler, garnir; **to live in furnished apartments,** loger en garni, en meublé; ʹ**furnishings,** *s.pl.* (*a*) ameublement *m;* (*b*) *N.Am:* **men's f.,** lingerie *f* pour hommes, chemiserie *f.*
furniture [ʹfəːnitjər], *s.* meubles *mpl,* ameublement *m,* mobilier *m;* **piece of f.,** meuble; **antique f.,** meubles d'époque; **f. polish,** encaustique *f;* **f. shop,** magasin *m* d'ameublement; **f. remover,** déménageur *m.*
furrier [ʹfʌriər], *s.* pelletier, -ière; fourreur *m.*
furrow [ʹfʌrou]. **I.** *s.* **1.** *Agr:* sillon *m.* **2.** cannelure *f,* rainure *f.* **3.** ride profonde; sillon. **II.** *v.tr.* **1.** labourer (la terre). **2.** rider profondément, sillonner.
further [ʹfəːðər]. **I.** *adv.* **1.** = FARTHER **1. 2.** (*a*) davantage, plus; **until you hear f.,** jusqu'à nouvel avis; (*b*) **to go f. into sth.,** entrer plus avant dans qch.; (*c*) **f. back,** à une période plus reculée; (*d*) d'ailleurs, en outre, de plus. **II.** *a.* **1.** = FARTHER **2. 2.** nouveau, -el, -elle, -eaux, additionnel; **without f. loss of time, without f. ado,** sans plus de cérémonie; sans plus; **on f. consideration,** après plus ample réflexion. **III.** *v.tr.* avancer, favoriser (un projet, etc.); **furtherʹmore,** *adv.* en outre, de plus; ʹ**furthermost,** *a.* = FARTHEST **1;** ʹ**furthest,** *a. & adv.* = FARTHEST.

furtive [ʹfəːtiv], *a.* (*of glance*) furtif; (*of pers.*) sournois; **-ly,** *adv.* furtivement.
fury [ʹfjuːri], *s.* furie *f,* fureur *f,* emportement *m* acharnement *m* (d'un combat); *F:* **to work like f.,** travailler comme un fou; **to get into a f.,** s'emporter.
furze [fəːz], *s. Bot:* ajonc *m.*
fuse¹ [fjuːz], *s.* fusée *f* (d'obus); amorce *f;* **Min (safety) f.,** étoupille *f,* cordeau *m.*
fuse². **I.** *s. El:* fusible *m;* plomb *m;* **f. box,** boîte *f* fusibles; **f. wire,** (fil *m*) fusible; **the f. has gone,** le plomb a sauté. **II.** *v.* **1.** *v.tr.* (*a*) fondre (u métal, etc.); (*b*) fusionner, amalgamer (deu partis, etc.). **2.** *v.i.* (*a*) (*of metals*) fondre; **th lights have fused,** les plombs ont sauté; (*b*) s'amalgamer.
fuselage [ʹfjuːzəlɑːʒ], *s. Av:* fuselage *m.*
fusilier [fjuːzəʹliər], *s. Mil:* fusilier *m.*
fusillade [fjuːziʹleid], *s. Mil:* fusillade *f.*
fusion [ʹfjuːʒ(ə)n], *s.* fusion *f.* **1.** fondage *m,* font *f* (d'un métal, etc.); (*b*) *Atom.Ph:* fusion. fusionnement *m;* *Pol:* fusion (de deux parti etc.).
fuss [fʌs]. **I.** *s.* **1.** bruit exagéré; **a lot of f. (an bother) about nothing,** beaucoup de bruit po rien; **to make a f.,** faire un tas d'histoires; embarras *mpl;* façons *fpl;* **to make a f.,** fai des cérémonies; **to make a f. of s.o.,** être au petits soins pour qn. **II.** *v.* **1.** *v.i.* tatillonne faire des embarras; **to f. about,** faire l'affair **to f. over s.o.,** être aux petits soins pour qn. *v.tr.* tracasser, agiter (qn); ʹ**fussiness,** tatillonnage *m;* façons *fpl;* ʹ**fussy,** *a.* tatillo -onne; tracassier, méticuleux; **don't be so f.!** soyez pas si difficile! **-ily,** *adv.* (*a*) d'u manière tatillonne; (*b*) d'un air important.
fusty [ʹfʌsti], *a.* **f. smell,** odeur *f* de renferm ʹ**fustiness,** *s.* odeur de renfermé.
futile [ʹfjuːtail], *a.* **1.** futile, vain. **2.** puér **fuʹtility** [-ʹtil-], *s.* **1.** futilité *f.* **2.** puérilité *f.*
future [ʹfjuːtʃər]. **I.** *a.* (*a*) futur; (*of events*) venir; (*of prospects*) d'avenir; **there's no f. in** ça n'a pas d'avenir; **my f. wife,** ma future; (*Gram:* **f. tense,** temps futur. **2.** *s.* (*a*) avenir in (the) f.,** à l'avenir; **in the near f.,** dans avenir proche, peu éloigné; (*b*) *Gram:* (temp futur (*m*); **futuʹristic,** *a.* futuriste.
fuzz [fʌz], *s. coll. P:* **the f.,** la police, les flics
fuzzy [ʹfʌzi], *a.* **1.** (*of hair*) (i) bouffant, flou; (crépelu, crêpelé, frisotté. **2.** *Phot:* flou; ʹ**fu ziness,** *s.* **1.** crêpelure *f* (des cheveux). **2.** A flou *m;* manque *m* de netteté.

G

G, g [dʒiː], s. 1. (la lettre) G, g m. 2. Mus: sol m; G string, (i) corde f de sol; (ii) Cl: cache-sexe m inv.

[gæb], s. F: to have the gift of the g., avoir la langue bien pendue.

abardine, gaberdine [gæbə'diːn], s. gabardine f.

abble [gæbl]. I. s. 1. bredouillement m. 2. caquet m, jacasserie f. II. v. 1. v.i. (i) bredouiller; (ii) caqueter, jacasser; don't g., ne parlez pas si vite. 2. v.tr. to g. (out) a speech, débiter un discours à toute vitesse.

able [geibl], s. g. (end), pignon m.

abon ['gæbɔn]. Pr.n. Geog: le Gabon.

ad [gæd], v.i. (gadded) to g. about, être toujours sorti, en promenade, en voyage.

adget ['gædʒit], s. chose m, machin m, truc m, gadget m; 'gadgetry, s. F: accessoires mpl, trucs mpl.

aelic ['geilik]. 1. a. gaélique. 2. s. Ling: gaélique m.

aff¹ [gæf], Fish: I. s. gaffe f. II. v.tr. gaffer.

aff², s. F: to blow the g., vendre la mèche.

ag [gæg]. I. s. 1. bâillon m. 2. Th: interpolation faite par l'acteur; gag m. II. v. (gagged) 1. v.tr. bâillonner; mettre un bâillon à (qn). 2. v. i. Th: faire des gags; enchaîner.

aga ['gɑːgɑː], a. F: gaga; gâteux.

aiety ['geiəti], s. gaieté f.

aily ['geili], adv. gaiement, allègrement; g. coloured, aux couleurs vives.

ain [gein]. I. s. 1. gain m, profit m, avantage m, bénéfice m. 2. accroissement m, augmentation f. II. v. 1. v.tr. gagner, acquérir; you will g. nothing by it, vous n'y gagnerez rien; to g. weight, prendre du poids. 2. v.i. Sp: to g. on s.o., prendre de l'avance sur qn; a bad habit gains on one, une mauvaise habitude s'impose peu à peu; clock that gains (at the rate of) five minutes a day, pendule f qui avance de cinq minutes par jour.

ait [geit], s. façon f de marcher.

aiter ['geitər], s. guêtre f.

ala ['gɑːlə], s. fête f, gala m.

alaxy ['gæləksi], s. galaxie f; galactic [gə'læktik], a. galactique.

ale [geil], s. (a) Nau: coup m de vent; strong g., fort coup de vent; (b) it's blowing a g., le vent souffle en tempête, fait rage; (c) g. of laughter, accès m de rires.

alilee ['gælili:]. Pr.n. Geog: la Galilée.

gall¹ [gɔːl], s. (a) fiel m; (b) g. bladder, vésicule f biliaire; 'gallstone, s. calcul m biliaire.

gall², s. Bot: galle f; oak g., noix f de galle.

gall³, v.tr. irriter, exaspérer; froisser (qn); 'galling, a. irritant, exaspérant; blessant.

gallant ['gælənt], a. 1. courageux, vaillant. 2. (occ. [gə'lænt]) galant; -ly, adv. courageusement; galamment; 'gallantry, s. 1. vaillance f, courage m. 2. galanterie f.

gallery ['gæləri], s. 1. (a) galerie f; (b) Th: (troisième) galerie; to play to the g., jouer pour la galerie; (c) (in Parliament) press g., tribune f de la presse. 2. art g., musée m (d'art).

galley ['gæli], s. 1. Nau: (a) yole f (d'amiral); (b) Hist: galère f; g. slave, galérien m; I'm nothing but a g. slave, c'est à moi de faire toutes les sales besognes. 2. Nau: Av: cuisine f. 3. (of book) g. proof, (épreuve f en) placard m.

Gallic ['gælik], a. Hist: gaulois; 'Gallicism, s. Ling: gallicisme m.

gallon ['gælən], s. gallon m (= approx. 4.5 litres).

gallop ['gæləp]. I. s. galop m; to go for a g., faire une galopade. II. v. (a) v.i. galoper; aller au galop; to g. away, off, partir au galop; (b) v.tr. faire aller (un cheval) au galop.

gallows ['gælouz], s. potence f, gibet m; g. bird, gibier m de potence.

Gallup ['gæləp]. Pr.n. G. poll, sondage m Gallup.

galore [gə'lɔːr], adv. en abondance, à profusion, à gogo.

galvanize ['gælvənaiz], v.tr. galvaniser; galvanized iron, tôle galvanisée; galvani'zation, s. galvanisation f; galva'nometer, s. galvanomètre m.

Gambia (the) [ðə'gæmbiə]. Pr.n. Geog: la Gambie.

gambit ['gæmbit], s. (a) (at chess) gambit m; (b) manœuvre f.

gamble [gæmbl]. I. s. (a) jeu m de hasard; (b) spéculation f; affaire f de chance. II. v. 1. v.i. jouer de l'argent; to g. on the Stock Exchange, agioter. 2. v.ind.tr. to g. away a fortune, perdre une fortune au jeu; to g. on a rise in prices, jouer à la hausse; 'gambler, s. joueur, -euse; spéculateur, -trice; Stock Exchange g., joueur à la Bourse; 'gambling, s. le jeu.

gamboge [gæm'boudʒ], s. gomme-gutte f.

gambol ['gæmb(ə)l], v.i. (gambolled) gambader; s'ébattre.

game¹ [geim]. **I.** *s.* **1.** (*a*) amusement *m*, divertissement *m*; (*b*) jeu *m*; **g. of skill, of chance,** jeu d'adresse, de hasard; (*c*) **Olympic games,** jeux olympiques; *Sch:* **games,** sports *m*; (*d*) **to play the g.,** jouer franc jeu; **to beat s.o. at his own g.,** battre qn avec ses propres armes; **two can play at that g.,** à bon chat bon rat; (*e*) **what's his g.?** où veut-il en venir? **I can see your g.,** je vous vois venir; **to spoil s.o.'s g.,** déjouer les plans de qn; **the g.'s up,** l'affaire est dans l'eau, il n'y a plus rien à faire; (*f*) partie *f* (de cartes); manche *f* (d'une partie de cartes); **the odd g., the deciding g.,** la belle; **to have the g. in one's hands,** tenir le succès entre ses mains. **2.** (*a*) gibier *m*; **big g.,** les grands fauves; **g. bag,** carnassière *f*, gibecière *f*; **he's fair g.,** on a bien le droit de se moquer de lui; (*b*) *Cu:* gibier. **II.** *a.* courageux, résolu; **g. for anything,** prêt à tout; **to die g.,** mourir crânement; **'gamekeeper,** *s.* garde-chasse *m*, *pl.* gardes-chasse(s); **'gaming,** *s.* jeu *m*; **g. table,** table *f* de jeu.

game², *a.* **g. leg,** jambe boiteuse.

gamma ['gæmə], *s. Atom.Ph:* **g. rays,** rayons *m* gamma.

gammon ['gæmən], *s.* quartier *m* de lard fumé.

gamut ['gæmət], *s.* gamme *f*.

gander ['gændər], *s.* jars *m*.

gang [gæŋ]. **I.** *s.* (*a*) équipe *f* (d'ouvriers); (*b*) bande *f*, gang *m* (de voleurs); **the whole g.,** toute la bande; (*c*) *Tchn:* **g. saw,** scie *f* multiple. **II.** *v.i.* **to g. up with s.o.,** faire bande avec qn; **to g. up on s.o.,** attaquer qn, se liguer contre qn; **'ganger,** *s.* chef *m* d'équipe; *Civ.E:* chef cantonnier; **'gangster,** *s.* bandit *m*, gangster *m*; **'gangway,** *s.* (*a*) passage *m*; **g. please!** dégagez, s'il vous plaît! (*b*) *Nau:* passerelle *f* de service.

Ganges (the) [ðə'gæn(d)ʒiːz]. *Pr.n. Geog:* le Gange.

gangling ['gæŋgliŋ], *a.* dégingandé.

ganglion ['gæŋgliən], *s. Anat:* ganglion *m*.

gangrene ['gæŋgriːn], *s. Med:* gangrène *f*.

gannet ['gænit], *s. Orn:* fou *m* (de Bassan).

gaol [dʒeil]. **I.** *s.* prison *f*; *F:* taule *f*. **II.** *v.tr.* mettre (qn) en prison; **'gaoler,** *s.* gardien *m* de prison.

gap [gæp], *s.* (*a*) trou *m*; trouée *f*, ouverture *f*; **to stop a g.,** boucher un trou, combler un vide; **g. in a wall,** brèche *f* dans un mur; (*b*) *Geog:* **wind g.,** cluse sèche, morte; **the Belfort G.,** la Trouée de Belfort; (*c*) **g. between the planks,** jour *m* entre les planches; **g. in the curtains,** interstice *m* des rideaux; *El:* **g. between electrodes,** distance *f*, intervalle *m*, entre les électrodes; **g. between contacts,** écartement *m* des contacts; (*d*) **his death leaves a g.,** sa mort laisse un vide; **the gaps in his education,** les lacunes *f* de son

éducation; **trade g.,** déficit commercial ⏐ **credibility g.,** crise *f* de confiance; (*e*) **age g.** ⏐ écart *m* d'âge; **g. of 20 years,** intervalle de ⏐ vingt ans; **generation g.,** fossé *m* entre deux ⏐ générations.

gape [geip], *v.i.* **1.** (*a*) bâiller; (*b*) s'ouvrir (tou ⏐ grand); **boards that g.,** planches qui ne se ⏐ joignent pas. **2.** rester bouche bée; **to g. at s.o.** ⏐ regarder qn bouche bée; **'gaping,** *a.* béant.

garage ['gærɑːʒ, 'gæridʒ]. **I.** *s.* garage *m*; **g.** ⏐ **proprietor,** garagiste *m*. **II.** *v.tr.* garer; remise ⏐ (une voiture); **'garageman,** *pl.* **-men,** *s.* (i ⏐ mécanicien *m* de garage; (ii) garagiste.

garbage ['gɑːbidʒ], *s.* (*a*) immondices *fpl* ⏐ déchets *mpl*; (*b*) *esp. N.Am:* ordure ⏐ ménagères; **g. can,** poubelle *f*.

garble [gɑːbl], *v.tr.* tronquer (une citation) ⏐ dénaturer (des faits); **garbled account,** compt ⏐ rendu trompeur.

garden [gɑːdn]. **I.** *s.* (*a*) jardin *m*; **kitchen g** ⏐ **vegetable g.,** (jardin) potager (*m*); **g. of remem** ⏐ **brance** = cimetière *m* d'un crématorium ⏐ **zoological gardens,** jardin zoologique; *F:* t ⏐ **lead s.o. up the g. path,** duper qn; (*b*) **(public** ⏐ **garden(s),** jardin public, parc *m*; (*c*) *attrib.* ⏐ **party,** garden-party *f*, *pl.* garden-parties; ⏐ **produce,** produits maraîchers; **g. suburb,** ⏐ **city,** cité-jardin *f*, *pl.* cités-jardins; **g. tools,** o ⏐ tils *m* de jardinage. **II.** *v.i.* jardiner; **'gardene** ⏐ *s.* jardinier, -ière *m* (de jardin); **landscape g.,** (jardinie ⏐ paysagiste (*m*); **market g.,** *N.Am:* **truck g** ⏐ maraîcher, -ère; **'gardening,** *s.* jardinage *n* ⏐ horticulture *f*.

gargle [gɑːgl]. *Med:* **I.** *s.* gargarisme *m*. **II.** *v.i.* ⏐ gargariser.

gargoyle ['gɑːgɔil], *s.* gargouille *f*.

garish ['gɛəriʃ], *a.* voyant; (lumière) crue.

garland ['gɑːlənd], *s.* guirlande *f*; couronne *f* (¢ ⏐ fleurs).

garlic ['gɑːlik], *s.* ail *m*.

garment ['gɑːmənt], *s.* vêtement *m*.

garnet ['gɑːnit], *s.* grenat *m*.

garnish ['gɑːniʃ], *v.tr.* garnir (un plat); **'ga** ⏐ **nishing,** *s.* garniture *f*.

garret ['gærət], *s.* mansarde *f*, soupente ⏐ grenier *m*.

garrison ['gærisən]. **I.** *s.* garnison *f*; **g. tow** ⏐ ville *f* de garnison. **II.** *v.tr.* **to g. a town,** (i) me ⏐ tre une garnison, (ii) être en garnison, dans u ⏐ ville.

garrulous ['gærələs, -rjul-], *a.* loquace, bavar ⏐

garter ['gɑːtər], *s.* (*a*) jarretière *f*; (*b*) *N.A* ⏐ jarretelle *f*.

gas [gæs]. **I.** *s.* **1.** gaz *m*; (*a*) **natural g.,** g ⏐ naturel; **g. industry,** industrie gazière, du g ⏐ **g. cooker,** cuisinière *f* à gaz; **g. fire,** radiateu ⏐ à gaz; **g. lighter,** (i) allume-gaz *m inv*; ⏐ briquet *m* (à gaz); **g. meter,** compteur *m* à g

g. main, g. pipe, tuyau *m* à gaz; (*b*) *Dent:* to have g., se faire anesthésier (pour l'extraction d'une dent); (*c*) tear g., gaz lacrymogène. 2. *N.Am:* essence *f*; g. station, station-service *f*; to step on the g., marcher à plein gaz. 3. *F:* bavardage *m*. II. *v.* (gassed) 1. *v.tr.* asphyxier (qn); to g. oneself, s'asphyxier. 2. *v.i. F:* bavarder; 'gasbag, *s. F:* bavard, -arde; 'gasman, *pl.* -men, *s.* employé *m* de gaz; 'gasmask, *s.* masque *m* à gaz; 'gasoline, *s. N.Am:* essence *f*; gas'ometer, *s.* gazomètre *m*; 'gasworks, *s.pl.* usine *f* à gaz.

Gascony ['gæskəni]. *Pr.n. Geog:* la Gascogne.

ash [gæʃ]. I. *s.* coupure *f*, entaille *f*. II. *v.tr.* couper, entailler.

asket ['gæskit], *s. Mec.E:* joint *m* d'étanchéité; garniture *f* (de joint).

asp [gɑːsp]. I. *s.* hoquet *m* (de surprise); to be at one's last g., (i) être à la dernière extrémité; (ii) être à bout de souffle. II. *v.i.* (*a*) the news made me g., cette nouvelle m'a coupé le souffle; (*b*) to g. for breath, haleter, suffoquer.

astric ['gæstrik], *a.* gastrique; g. flu, grippe intestinale; g. ulcer, ulcère *m* d'estomac; gas-'tritis, *s.* gastrite *f*; 'gastro-ente'ritis, *s.* gastro-entérite *f*; gas'tronomy, *s.* gastronomie *f*.

ate [geit], *s.* 1. (*a*) porte *f* (de ville); portail *m*; (*b*) entrée *f*; *Sp:* the g., (i) le public (à un match); (ii) (*also* g. money) la recette. 2. (*wooden*) barrière *f*; (*iron*) garden g., grille *f* d'entrée; 'gatecrash, *v.tr.* resquiller; 'gatecrasher, *s.* resquilleur, -euse; 'gatepost, *s.* montant *m* de barrière; 'gateway, *s.* porte (monumentale); portail *m*.

ather ['gæðər]. I. *v.tr.* 1. (*a*) assembler (une foule); rassembler (ses forces); (*b*) to g. (up), ramasser (ses papiers); (*c*) cueillir (des fleurs), récolter (des fruits). 2. to g. speed, prendre de la vitesse. 3. conclure; I g. that . . ., je crois comprendre que . . . II. *v.i.* 1. (*a*) se réunir, s'assembler; (*b*) a crowd gathered, une foule s'est formée. 2. a storm is gathering, un orage se prépare; 'gathering, *s.* (*a*) assemblée *f*; family g., réunion *f* de famille; we were a large g., nous étions nombreux; (*b*) *Med:* abcès *m*; (*c*) *Needlew:* (*also* 'gathers) fronces *fpl.*

auche [gouʃ], *a.* gauche, maladroit.

udy ['gɔːdi], *a.* voyant, criard, éclatant; de mauvais goût; 'gaudily, *adv.* de manière voyante; (peint) en couleurs criardes.

uge [geidʒ]. I. *s.* 1. (*a*) calibre *m* (d'un écrou); fine g. stockings, bas fins; *Rail:* écartement *m* (de la voie); (*b*) *Rail:* standard g., voie normale. 2. *Tchn:* master g., calibre mère; rail g., gabarit *m* d'écartement. 3. *Aut:* oil (pressure) g., manomètre *m* de pression d'huile; petrol g., jauge *f* à essence; tyre g., vérificateur *m* de pres-

sion. II. *v.tr.* calibrer (un écrou); jauger, mesurer; to g. s.o.'s capacities, estimer, jauger, les capacités de qn.

Gaul [gɔːl]. 1. *Pr.n.* la Gaule. 2. *s.* Gaulois, -oise.

gaunt [gɔːnt], *a.* maigre, décharné.

gauntlet ['gɔːntlit], *s.* gant *m* à manchette.

gauze [gɔːz], *s.* gaze *f.*

gavel ['gævl], *s.* marteau *m* (de commissaire-priseur, etc.).

gawky ['gɔːki], *a.* dégingandé, gauche.

gay [gei], *a.* 1. (*a*) gai, réjoui; g. laugh, rire enjoué; (*b*) to lead a g. life, mener une vie de plaisir(s); s'amuser, sortir, beaucoup; (*c*) *F:* homosexuel. 2. gai, splendide, brillant; g. colours, couleurs vives, gaies.

gaze [geiz]. I. *s.* regard *m* fixe. II. *v.i.* regarder fixement; to g. at sth., contempler qch.

gazelle [gə'zel], *s. Z:* gazelle *f.*

gazetteer [gæzə'tiːər], *s.* répertoire *m* geographique.

gear ['giər]. I. *s.* 1. équipement *m*, appareil *m*; matériel *m* (de camping); attirail *m* (de pêche); *F:* my g., mes effets *m*, mes bagages *m*; mes vêtements. 2. (*a*) *E:* safety g., mécanisme *m* de sécurité; *Av:* landing g., train *m* d'atterrissage; (*b*) *E:* (driving, transmission) g., transmission *f*, commande *f*; engrenages *mpl* de transmission; in g., (i) en prise (ii) en marche; (*c*) *Aut:* first, bottom, g., première vitesse; top g., prise (directe); to change g., changer de vitesse; g. lever, levier *m* de changement. II. *v.tr.* to g. up, down (an engine), multiplier, démultiplier (un moteur); wages geared to the cost of living, salaires indexés au coût de la vie; 'gearbox, *s. Aut:* boîte *f* de vitesses; 'gearwheel, *s.* (roue *f* d')engrenage *m*; (on bicycle) pignon *m.*

Geiger ['gaigər]. *Pr.n. Atom.Ph:* G. counter, compteur *m* Geiger.

gelatine ['dʒelətiːn], *s.* gélatine *f*; gelatinous [dʒə'lætinəs], *a.* gélatineux.

gelding ['geldiŋ], *s.* (cheval *m*) hongre (*m*).

gelignite ['dʒelignait], *s.* gélignite *f.*

gem [dʒem], *s.* pierre précieuse; joyau *m.*

Gemini ['dʒeminai]. *Pr.n.pl. Astr:* les Gémeaux *m.*

gen [dʒen], *s. F:* renseignements *mpl*, tuyaux *mpl.*

gender ['dʒendər], *s.* genre *m.*

gene [dʒiːn], *s. Biol:* gène *m.*

genealogy [dʒiːni'ælədʒi], *s.* généalogie *f*; genea'logical, *a.* généalogique; gene'alogist, *s.* généalogiste *mf.*

general ['dʒen(ə)rəl]. I. *a.* général. 1. the rain has been pretty g., il a plu un peu partout. 2. (*a*) g. election, élections législatives; (*b*) in g. use, (d'usage) courant; the g. public, le grand public; (*c*) g. knowledge, connaissances générales; **g. store(s), g. shop,** magasin *m* de village. **3.** *adv.phr.* in g., en général, généralement. **II.** *s. Mil:* (i) (officier) général (*m*); (ii) (*rank*) général d'armée; **G. Martin,** le Général Martin; **generali′zation,** *s.* généralisation *f*; **′generalize,** *v.tr. & i.* généraliser; **′generally,** *adv.* généralement, en général; **′general-′purpose,** *a.* (à) toutes fins, (pour) tous usages.

generate [′dʒenəreit], *v.tr.* générer; produire (de la chaleur, etc.); **′generating,** *a. El:* g. station, centrale *f* électrique; **gene′ration,** *s.* **1.** *Z:* génération *f*, reproduction *f*. **2. from g. to g.,** de génération en génération; **′generator,** *s. El: etc:* génératrice *f*; générateur *m*.

generous [′dʒenərəs], *a.* généreux; **gene′rosity** [-′rɔsiti], *s.* générosité *f*; **′generously,** *adv.* généreusement.

genetics [dʒə′netiks], *s.pl.* (*usu. with sg. const.*) génétique *f*.

Geneva [dʒə′ni:və]. *Pr.n. Geog:* Genève *f*; **the Lake of G.,** le lac Léman.

genial [′dʒi:niəl], *a.* cordial; sympathique.

genitals [′dʒenitlz], *s.pl.* organes génitaux externes.

genitive [′dʒenitiv], *a. & s. Gram:* génitif (*m*).

genius [′dʒi:niəs], *s.* **1. to be s.o.'s evil g.,** être le mauvais génie de qn. **2. to have a g. for doing sth.,** avoir le don de faire qch.; **work of g.,** œuvre *f* de génie. **3. to be a g.,** être un génie.

Genoa [′dʒenouə]. *Pr.n. Geog:* Gênes *f*; **Geno′ese,** *a. & s.* génois, -oise.

genocide [′dʒenousaid], *s.* génocide *m*.

gent [dʒent], *s. F:* monsieur *m*; *Com:* **gents′ footwear,** chaussures *fpl* pour hommes; **where's the gents?** où sont les W.C.?

gentle [dʒentl], *a.* doux, *f.* douce; **′gentleness,** *s.* douceur *f*; **′gently,** *adv.* doucement; **g. does it!** allez-y doucement!

gentleman, *pl.* **-men** [′dʒentlmən], *s.m.* **1.** homme comme il faut. **2.** monsieur; (*to audience*) **ladies and gentlemen!** mesdames, mesdemoiselles, messieurs! *P.N:* (*public lavatory*) **gentlemen,** hommes, messieurs; **gentlemen's hairdresser,** coiffeur *m* pour hommes; **′gentlemanly,** *a.* bien élevé; **g. appearance,** air distingué.

genuine [′dʒenjuin], *a.* (*a*) authentique, véritable; (*b*) (*pers.*) sincère; **′genuinely,** *adv.* authentiquement; franchement; véritablement; sincèrement.

genus, *pl.* **genera** [′dʒi:nəs, ′dʒenərə], *s.* genre *m*.

geography [dʒi′ɔɡrəfi], *s.* géographie *f*; **geo′graphical** [dʒiə′ɡræfikl], *a.* géographique; **ge′ographer,** géographe *mf*.

geology [dʒi′ɔlədʒi], *s.* géologie *f*; **geo′logical** [dʒiə′lɔdʒikl], *a.* géologique; **ge′ologist,** *s.* géologue *mf*.

geometry [dʒi′ɔmətri], *s.* géométrie *f*; **geo′metrical** [dʒiə′metrikl], *a.* géométrique.

George [dʒɔ:dʒ]. *Pr.n.m.* Georges.

geranium [dʒə′reinijəm], *s.* géranium *m*.

geriatrics [dʒeri′ætriks], *s.pl.* (*usu. with sg const.*) *Med:* gériatrie *f*.

germ [dʒə:m], *s.* **1.** germe *m*; **wheat g.,** germe d blé. **2.** *Med:* germe, microbe *m*; **g. warfar** guerre *f* bactériologique; **′germicide,** *s.* ge micide *m*; **′germinate,** *v.tr. & i.* (faire) germe **germi′nation,** *s.* germination *f*.

Germany [′dʒə:məni]. *Pr.n. Geog:* l'Allemagn *f*; **West G.,** l'Allemagne de l'ouest; **East G** l'Allemagne de l'est; **′German. 1.** *a* allemand; **West-G., East-G.,** ouest-allemand est-allemand. **2.** *s.* Allemand, -ande. **3.** *s. Ling* allemand *m*.

gestation [dʒes′teiʃən], *s.* gestation *f*.

gesticulate [dʒes′tikjuleit], *v.i.* gesticule **gesticu′lation,** *s.* gesticulation *f*.

gesture [′dʒestʃər]. **I.** *s.* geste *m*. **II.** *v.i.* faire d gestes.

get [get], *v.* (**got** [gɔt]; *N.Am: also* **gotten**) **I.** *v.t* **1.** (*a*) procurer, obtenir; **where did you g. tha** où avez-vous trouvé, acheté, cela? (acquérir, gagner; **I'll see what I can g. for it,** verrai ce qu'on m'en donnera; **to g. nothing** it, out of it, n'y rien gagner; (*c*) **if I g. the time** j'ai le temps; **to g. one's own way,** faire val sa volonté. **2.** recevoir (une lettre); attraper (rhume); *F:* **to g. the sack,** être congédié; **to ten years,** attraper dix ans de prison. **3.** prendre, attraper (une bête, du gibier); **we'll them yet!** on les aura! (*b*) émouvoir (qn); t gets my goat, ça m'énerve; **what's got i** him? qu'est-ce qu'il a? (*c*) comprendre; **I do g. you,** je ne vous comprends pas; **you've** it! vous y êtes. **4. to (go and) g. sth., s.o.,** a chercher qch., qn. **5.** (*a*) faire parvenir; h **can I g. it to you?** comment vous le fa parvenir? (*b*) **it's getting me down,** ça décourage; (*c*) **to g. lunch (ready),** prépare déjeuner. **6.** (*a*) **to g. s.o. to do sth.,** faire f qch. à, par, qn; **to g. the house painted, f** repeindre la maison; (*b*) **to g. s.o. to ag** décider qn à consentir; (*c*) **to g. one's w** finished, finir son travail. **7. have got;** (*a*) **have you got there?** qu'avez-vous là? **I hav** got any, je n'en ai pas; (*b*) **you've got to do** faut absolument que vous le fassiez. **II.** *v.* (*a*) devenir (riche, vieux); (*b*) **to g. married** marier; **to g. dressed,** s'habiller; (*c*) **let'** going! allons-y! en route! **2.** (*a*) **he'll g. h** tomorrow, il arrivera demain; **we're not** ting anywhere, nous n'aboutissons à rien; **to g. within s.o.'s reach,** se mettre à la porté qn; (*c*) **when you g. to know him,** quand o connaît mieux; **′get a′cross,** *v.tr. F:*

couldn't g. it **across**, il n'a pas réussi à se faire comprendre; **'get at,** *v.tr.* **difficult to g. at,** difficile à atteindre; peu accessible; **to g. at the root of the trouble,** trouver la racine du mal; *F:* **what are you getting at?** (i) où voulez-vous en venir? (ii) qu'est-ce que vous voulez insinuer? *F:* **who are you getting at?** à qui en avez-vous? **get-'at-able,** *a. F:* d'accès facile; **'get a'way,** *v.i.* (a) partir; (b) s'échapper; (c) *Aut:* démarrer; (d) (*of burglar*) **to g. away with £1000,** rafler £1000; **to g. away with it,** s'en tirer à bon compte; **'getaway,** *s.* (a) fuite *f*, évasion *f*; (b) départ *m*; (c) démarrage *m*; **'get 'back.** 1. *v.i.* **to g. back (home),** rentrer chez soi. 2. *v.tr.* se faire rendre (qch.); retrouver (qch.); reprendre (ses forces); **to g. one's money back,** être remboursé; *F:* **to g. one's own back,** prendre sa revanche; **'get 'by,** *v.i. F:* se débrouiller; **'get 'down,** *v.i. & tr.* descendre; **to g. down to the facts,** en venir aux faits; *F:* **it gets him down,** ça le déprime; **'get 'in.** 1. *v.i.* entrer; monter (en voiture); *Pol:* être élu; **when the train gets in,** quand le train arrive. 2. *v.tr.* rentrer (la moisson); **to g. a man in to do sth.,** faire venir un ouvrier pour faire qch.; **to g. one's hand in,** se faire la main; **'get 'into,** *v.i.* monter dans (une voiture); **to g. into bad company,** faire de mauvaises connaissances; **'get 'off.** 1. *v.i.* (a) descendre (d'un autobus); *P:* **I told him where to g. off,** je lui ai dit ses vérités; (b) se faire exempter; **to g. off with a fine,** en être quitte pour une amende; **to g. off lightly,** s'en tirer facilement; (c) partir. 2. *v.tr.* (a) expédier (un colis); **to g. s.o. off on time,** faire partir qn à l'heure; **to g. sth. off one's hands,** se débarrasser de qch.; (b) tirer (qn) d'affaire; faire acquitter (un prévenu); **'get 'on.** 1. *v.tr.* mettre (ses chaussures). 2. *v.i.* **time's getting on,** l'heure avance; **to be getting on for forty,** friser la quarantaine; (b) réussir (dans la vie); faire des progrès; **I can't g. on without him,** je ne peux pas me passer de lui; (c) **to g. on with s.o.,** s'entendre avec qn; **'get 'out.** 1. *v.tr.* (a) arracher (un clou); tirer (un bouchon); **to g. nothing out of it,** n'y rien gagner; (b) **to g. out one's car,** sortir sa voiture; **to g. sth. out of the drawer,** prendre qch. dans le tiroir; **book that I got out of the library,** livre que j'ai emprunté à la bibliothèque. 2. *v.i.* (a) **to g. out of s.o.'s way,** faire place à qn; **g. out (of here)!** fiche-moi le camp! (b) **to g. out of a difficulty,** se tirer d'une position difficile; venir à bout d'une difficulté; **to g. out of doing sth.,** se faire exempter de faire qch.; **'getout,** *s. F:* échappatoire *f*; **'get 'over,** *v.tr.* (a) escalader, passer par-dessus (un mur); (b) **to g. sth. over,** en finir avec qch.; (c) se remettre d'(une maladie); surmonter (ses difficultés); **he can't g. over it,** il n'en revient pas; **'get 'round,**

v.tr. & i. (a) tourner (un coin); *F:* **if I can g. round him,** si je peux le persuader; (b) **to g. round to doing sth.,** trouver le temps de faire qch.; **'get 'through,** *v.tr.* être reçu à (un examen); venir à bout de (son travail); **to g. through to s.o.,** obtenir la communication avec qn; **'getting-'up,** *s.* lever *m*; **'get to'gether,** *v.i.* se réunir, se rassembler; **'get-together,** *s.* réunion *f*; rassemblement *m*; **'get'up.** 1. *v.i.* (a) se lever; se relever; (b) se lever (du lit). 2. *v.tr.* organiser (une fête); **to g. up speed,** prendre de la vitesse; **'getup,** *s. F:* (a) toilette *f*; (b) *Com:* présentation *f* (d'un livre, etc.).

geyser ['giːzər], *s.* 1. *Geol:* geyser *m*. 2. chauffe-bain *m*.

Ghana ['gɑːnə]. *Pr.n. Geog:* le Ghana.

ghastly ['gɑːstli], *a.* (a) horrible; (accident) affreux; (b) *F:* (temps) abominable.

Ghent [gent]. *Pr.n. Geog:* Gand *m*.

gherkin ['gəːkin], *s. Cu:* cornichon *m*.

ghetto, *pl.* -os ['getou, -ouz], *s.* ghetto *m*.

ghost [goust]. I. *s.* 1. **the Holy G.,** l'Esprit Saint. 2. (a) revenant *m*; **g. story,** histoire *f* de revenants; (b) **not the g. of a chance,** pas la moindre chance. 3. *F:* **g. (writer),** collaborateur, -trice, anonyme; hétéronyme *m*. II. *v.i. & tr.* **to g. for s.o.,** prêter sa plume à qn; **ghosted work,** hétéronyme; **'ghostly,** *a.* spectral.

ghoulish ['guːliʃ], *a.* macabre.

giant ['dʒaiənt], *a. & s.* géant (*m*); **gian'tess,** *s.f.* géante.

gibberish ['dʒib(ə)riʃ], *s.* baragouin *m*, charabia *m*, galimatias *m*.

gibe [dʒaib]. I. *s.* raillerie *f*; sarcasme *m*. II. *v.i.* **to g. at s.o.,** railler qn; se moquer de qn.

giblets ['dʒiblits], *s.pl.* abattis *m* (de volaille).

giddy ['gidi], *a.* étourdi; **I feel g.,** j'ai le vertige; la tête me tourne; **'giddiness,** *s.* étourdissement *m*; vertige *m*.

gift [gift], *s.* (a) don *m*; (b) cadeau *m*; **I wouldn't have it as a g.,** je n'en voudrais pas quand même on me le donnerait; (c) *Com:* (*on presentation of coupons*) prime *f*; (d) talent *m*; **to have a natural g. for mathematics,** être doué pour les mathématiques; **'gifted,** *a.* doué.

gigantic [dʒai'gæntik], *a.* géant, gigantesque; colossal, -aux.

giggle [gigl]. I. *s.* petit rire nerveux; rire bébête. II. *v.i.* rire nerveusement, bêtement.

gild [gild], *v.tr.* dorer; **'gilding,** *s.* dorure *f*; **gilt.** 1. *a.* doré; *Fin:* **g. edged securities,** fonds *mpl* d'État. 2. *s.* (a) doré *m*, dorure *f*; (b) *pl. Fin:* **gilts,** fonds *mpl* d'État.

gills [gilz], *s.pl.* ouïes *f*, branchies *f* (de poisson); lames *f*, lamelles *f* (d'un champignon).

gimlet ['gimlit], *s.* vrille *f*; foret *m*.

gimmick ['gimik], *s.* machin *m*; combine *f*;

advertising g., truc *m* publicitaire.
gin [dʒin], *s.* gin *m*.
ginger ['dʒindʒər]. **1.** *s.* gingembre *m*. **2.** *a. (of hair, pers.)* roux, *f.* rousse; **'gingerbread,** *s.* pain *m* d'épice; **'gingerly,** *a.* **in a g. fashion,** délicatement, avec précaution *f*; **'ginger'up,** *v.tr.* stimuler (qn).
gipsy ['dʒipsi], *s. (a)* bohémien, -ienne; *(b) Ent:* **g. moth,** zigzag *m*.
giraffe [dʒi'rɑːf, -'ræf], *s.* girafe *f*.
girder ['gəːdər], *s.* poutre *f*.
girdle [gəːdl], *s.* **1.** *Cl: (a)* ceinture *f*; *(b)* gaine *f*. **2.** *Anat:* **pelvic g.,** ceinture pelvienne.
girl [gəːl], *s.f.* jeune fille; **little g.,** petite fille, fillette; **girls' school,** école *f* de filles; **old g.,** (i) ancienne élève (d'un lycée, etc.); (ii) *F:* (petite) vieille; **a French g.,** une jeune Française; **chorus g.,** girl *f*; **his g. friend,** son amie; **my oldest g.,** ma fille aînée; **'girlish,** *a.* de petite fille, de jeune fille; *(of boy)* mou, efféminé.
Giro ['dʒairou], *s.* **Post Office G. system** = service *m* de chèques postaux.
girth [gəːθ], *s.* circonférence *f* (d'un arbre); tour *m* (de taille).
gist [dʒist], *s.* fond *m*, essence *f*; **the g. of the matter,** le vif de la question.
give [giv]. **I.** *v.* (gave [geiv]; given ['givən]) **1.** *v.tr. (a)* (i) **to g. sth. to s.o., to g. s.o. sth.,** donner qch. à qn; **to g. s.o. lunch,** offrir un déjeuner à qn; (ii) *(on telephone)* **g. me Mr X,** passez-moi, donnez-moi, M. X; (iii) **to g. and take,** faire des concessions mutuelles; *(b)* (i) **to g. s.o. sth. to eat,** donner à manger à qn; **to g. s.o. ten years,** condamner qn à dix ans de prison; (ii) **to g. sth. into s.o.'s hands,** remettre qch. entre les mains de qn; (iii) **g. him our congratulations,** félicitez-le de notre part; **to g. s.o. one's support,** prêter son appui à qn; (iv) **to g. one's word,** donner sa parole; *(c)* **to g. sth. in exchange for sth.,** donner qch. pour, contre, qch.; **what did you g. for it?** combien l'avez-vous payé? *(d) (of woman)* **to g. oneself,** se donner; *(e)* (i) **to g. a cry of astonishment,** pousser un cri d'étonnement; **to g. s.o. a smile,** adresser un sourire à qn; (ii) **to g. an answer,** faire, donner, une réponse; **to g. orders,** donner des ordres; *(at shop)* **to g. an order,** faire une commande; *(f)* **to g. s.o. one's attention,** faire attention à qn; *(g)* (i) **to g. particulars,** donner, fournir, des détails; (ii) **to g. an example,** donner un exemple; **given a triangle ABC,** soit un triangle ABC; (iii) **they're giving** *Macbeth,* on donne, on joue, *Macbeth;* (iv) **to g. a toast,** proposer un toast; *(h)* (i) **to g. pleasure,** faire plaisir; **to g. oneself trouble,** se donner du mal; (ii) **to g. s.o. to believe that . . .,** faire croire à qn que . . .; (iii) **lamp that gives a poor light,** lampe *f* qui éclaire mal; *(i) F:* **to g. as good as one gets,** ren-

dre coup pour coup; **g. it all you've got!** faites le maximum! *(j)* (i) **his strength is giving way,** les forces lui manquent; (ii) **to g. way to s.o.,** céder à qn; *P.N:* **g. way** = priorité *f* à droite. **2.** *v.i. (a)* (i) prêter, donner; **the springs don't g. enough,** les ressorts *m* manquent de souplesse; (ii) **the door will g. if you push,** la porte céder si vous la poussez; *(b)* **the door gives into th. yard,** la porte donne sur la cour. **II.** *s. (a)* élasticité *f*; *(b)* **g. and take,** concession mutuelles; **'give a'way,** *v.tr. (a)* donner; **to g. sth. away,** faire cadeau de qch.; *(b)* **to g. th. bride away,** conduire la mariée à l'autel; *(c)* **to g. s.o. away,** trahir, vendre, qn; **'giveaway,** *s. (a)* révélation *f* involontaire; *(b) Com:* **it's a g.,** c'est donné! **'give'back,** *v.tr.* rendre, restitue (qch. à qn); **'give'in,** *v.i.* se rendre; se soumettre; céder; **'given,** *a.* **1. at a g. time,** à une heu convenue; *N.Am:* **g. name,** prénom *m*. **2.** port enclin, à; **g. to drink,** adonné à la boisson; **'gi 'off,** *v.tr.* exhaler, dégager (un parfum); **'gi 'out. 1.** *v.tr.* distribuer (des livres); **to g. out notice,** lire une communication; **it was given o that . . .,** on a annoncé que . . . **2.** *v* manquer; faire défaut; *(of supplies)* s'épuise **my brakes gave out,** mes freins *m* ont lâch **'giver,** *s.* donneur, -euse; donateur, -tri **'give'up,** *v.tr. (a)* abandonner (ses biens); **t up one's seat,** céder sa place (à qn); *(b)* renonc à (un projet); *(of riddle)* **I g. up,** je donne langue au chat; **to g. sth. up as a bad job,** renoncer; *(c)* **I'd given you up!** je ne vous atte dais plus! *(d)* **to g. oneself up,** se constit prisonnier.
gizzard ['gizəd], *s.* gésier *m*.
glacier ['glæsiər], *s.* glacier *m*; **glaci** ['gleisiəl], *a. (a) Geog:* glaciaire; *(b)* (vent, cueil) glacial.
glad [glæd], *a.* heureux, content; **he is only too to help you,** il ne demande pas mieux que vous aider; **-ly,** *adv.* avec plaisir, volontiers
glade [gleid], *s.* clairière *f*.
gladiolus, *pl.* **-li** [glædi'ouləs, -lai], *s. Bot:* glaï *m*.
glamour ['glæmər], *s. (a)* **to lend a g. to s** prêter de l'éclat à qch.; *(b)* **g. girl,** ensorcele *f*; **'glamorous,** *a.* fascinateur; enchanteur
glance [glɑːns]. **I.** *s.* regard *m*, coup *m* d'œil; **g.,** d'un coup d'œil. **II.** *v.i. (a)* **to g. at s.o.,** j un regard sur qn; **to g. through,** parcou feuilleter (un livre); *(b)* **to g. off,** ricoch **'glancing,** *a. (of blow)* oblique.
gland [glænd], *s. Anat:* glande *f*; **'glandular** glandulaire.
glare ['glɛər]. **I.** *s. (a)* lumière éblouissante soleil); *(b)* regard fixe et irrité. **II.** *v.i. (a)* br d'un éclat éblouissant; *(b)* **to g. at s.o.,** lan un regard furieux à qn; **'glaring,** *a. (a)* (so

aveuglant; (*b*) manifeste; flagrant; **g. mistake,** faute grossière.

glass [glɑːs], *s.* **1.** verre *m*; **g. industry,** verrerie *f*; **g. fibre,** fibre *f* de verre; **stained g. window,** vitrail *m*; **safety g.,** verre de sûreté; **pane of g.,** vitre *f*, glace *f*, carreau *m*; **cut g.,** cristal taillé. **2.** verre (à boire); **g. of wine,** verre de vin; **table g.,** verrerie de table. **3.** lentille *f* (d'un instrument optique); **magnifying g.,** loupe *f*; **field glasses,** jumelles *fpl*; **to wear glasses,** porter des lunettes *fpl*. **4. looking g.,** glace, miroir *m*. **5. the g. is falling,** le baromètre baisse. **6. grown under g.,** cultivé sous verre, en serre *f*. **7. g. door,** porte vitrée, de, en, verre; **g. case,** vitrine *f*; **'glasshouse,** *s.* (*a*) serre *f*; (*b*) *F:* prison *f* militaire; **'glassware,** *s.* articles *mpl* de verre, verrerie *f*, cristaux *mpl*; **'glassy,** *a.* vitreux.

glaze [gleiz], *v.tr.* vitrer (une maison); *Cu:* glacer, dorer; **'glazier,** *s.* vitrier *m*; **'glazing,** *s.* vitrerie *f*; **double g.,** double vitrage *m*.

gleam [gliːm]. **I.** *s.* (*a*) rayon *m*, lueur *f*; **g. of hope,** lueur d'espoir; (*b*) reflet *m* (d'un couteau). **II.** *v.i.* luire, reluire; (*of water*) miroiter; **a cat's eyes g. in the dark,** les yeux du chat luisent dans l'obscurité.

glean [gliːn], *v.tr.* glaner (du blé, des renseignements); **'gleanings,** *s.pl.* glanure(s) *f(pl).*

glee [gliː], *s.* (*a*) joie *f*, gaieté *f*; (*b*) *Mus:* **g. club** = chorale *f*; **'gleeful,** *a.* joyeux; **-fully,** *adv.* avec joie, joyeusement; avec un air de triomphe.

glen [glen], *s. esp. Scot:* vallée étroite.

glib [glib], *a.* (*a*) (*of answer*) spécieux; (*b*) **g. tongue,** langue bien pendue; **-ly,** *adv.* (*a*) spécieusement; (*b*) (parler) avec aisance; (répondre) sans hésiter.

glide [glaid], *v.i.* (*a*) (se) glisser, couler; (*b*) *Av:* (i) planer; (ii) faire du vol à voile; **'glider,** *s.* planeur *m*; **'gliding,** *s. Av:* (i) (vol *m*) plané (*m*); (ii) vol à voile; **g. club,** club *m* de vol à voile.

glimmer ['glimər], *s.* faible lueur *f*.

glimpse [glimps]. **I.** *s.* vision momentanée; **to catch a g. of (s.o., sth.),** entrevoir (qn, qch.). **II.** *v.tr.* entrevoir (qch.).

glint [glint]. **I.** *s.* éclair *m* (de lumière); reflet *m*. **II.** *v.i.* étinceler.

glisten [glisn], *v.i.* reluire, scintiller.

glitter ['glitər]. **I.** *s.* étincellement *m*, scintillement *m*, éclat *m*. **II.** *v.i.* scintiller, étinceler.

gloat [glout], *v.i.* **to g. over (sth.),** savourer (un spectacle); se réjouir méchamment de (la nouvelle); triompher de (l'infortune d'autrui).

globe [gloub], *s.* globe *m*; sphère *f*; *Cu:* **g. artichoke,** artichaut *m*; **'global,** *a.* (*a*) global; (*b*) mondial; **g. warfare,** guerre mondiale; **'globe-trotter,** *s.* globe-trotter *m*, touriste *m* qui voyage partout dans le monde.

globule ['globjuːl], *s.* globule *m*, gouttelette *f*.

gloom [gluːm], *s.* mélancolie *f*, tristesse *f* pessimiste; **'gloomy,** *a.* lugubre, sombre; **to take a g. view of things,** voir tout en noir.

glory ['gloːri]. **I.** *s.* gloire *f*. **II.** *v.i.* **to g. in sth.,** se glorifier de qch.; se faire gloire de qch.; **glorifi'cation,** *s.* glorification *f*; **'glorious,** *a.* glorieux; **g. weather,** temps *m* superbe; **-ly,** *adv.* glorieusement, avec gloire; magnifiquement.

gloss [glos], *s.* vernis *m*, éclat *m*; **g. paint,** peinture *f* vernis; **'glossy,** *a.* lustré, glacé; **g. magazines,** *s.* **glossies,** revues *fpl* de luxe.

glossary ['glosəri], *s.* lexique *m*.

glove [glʌv], *s.* gant *m*; **the g. counter,** la ganterie; **rubber gloves,** gants de caoutchouc; **boxing gloves,** gants de boxe; **to handle s.o. with kid gloves,** ménager qn; *Aut:* **g. compartment,** boîte *f* à gants.

glow [glou]. **I.** *s.* (*a*) lueur *f* (rouge); incandescence *f*; **g. of the setting sun,** feux *mpl* du soleil couchant; (*b*) chaleur *f*; **the exercise had given me a g.,** l'exercice m'avait fouetté le sang; **g. of enthusiasm,** transport *m* d'enthousiasme. **II.** *v.i.* (*a*) (*of metal*) rougeoyer; (*of coal*) s'embraser; (*b*) **to g. with pleasure, with enthusiasm,** rayonner de plaisir, brûler d'enthousiasme; **to be glowing with health,** éclater de santé; **'glowing,** *a.* rougeoyant; embrasé; rayonnant; **to paint sth. in g. colours,** présenter qch. sous un jour des plus favorables; **'glow-worm,** *s.* ver luisant.

glucose ['gluːkouz], *s.* glucose *m*.

glue [gluː]. **I.** *s.* colle (forte). **II.** *v.tr.* (**glued, gluing**) coller; **he walked with his eyes glued to the road,** il marchait sans quitter la route des yeux.

glum [glʌm], *a.* renfrogné, maussade; (air) sombre.

glut [glʌt], *s.* surabondance *f* (d'une denrée); encombrement *m* (du marché).

glutton [glʌtn], *s.* glouton, -onne; **a g. for work,** un bourreau de travail; **'gluttonous,** *a.* glouton.

glycerine ['glisərin, -iːn], *s.* glycérine *f*.

gnarled [nɑːld], *a.* noueux.

gnash [næʃ], *v.tr.* **to g. one's teeth,** grincer des dents.

gnat [næt], *s.* moucheron *m*, moustique *m*, cousin *m*.

gnaw [noː], *v.tr. & i.* ronger.

gnome [noum], *s. Myth:* gnome *m*; *F:* **the gnomes of Zurich,** les banquiers internationaux suisses.

gnu [n(j)uː], *s. Z:* gnou *m*.

go [gou]. **I.** *v.i.* (**went; gone**) aller. **1.** (*a*) to come and go, aller et venir; **to go to Paris, to France**, aller à Paris, en France; **to go to a party**, aller à une réunion; **what shall I go in?** qu'est-ce que je vais mettre? **to go to prison**, être mis en prison; **to go for a walk**, faire une promenade; *F:* **to go places**, (i) sortir beaucoup; (ii) voyager; (iii) réussir; **to go by the shortest way**, prendre par le plus court; **you go first!** (i) partez le premier! (ii) à vous d'abord; (*b*) **to go up, down, across, a street**, monter, descendre, traverser, une rue; **to go into a room**, entrer dans une pièce; **to go behind s.o.'s back**, faire qch. derrière le dos de qn; (*c*) **to go to school**, aller à, fréquenter, l'école; **to go to sea, into the army**, se faire marin, soldat; (*d*) **to go hungry, thirsty**, souffrir de la faim, de la soif; **wine that goes to the head**, vin qui monte à la tête; (*e*) **to go one's own way**, faire à sa guise. **2.** (*a*) (*of machinery*) marcher; **my watch won't go**, ma montre ne marche pas; **to keep industry going**, faire marcher l'industrie; (*b*) **to go well, badly**, marcher bien, mal; (*c*) **the bell is going**, la cloche sonne; **it has just gone eight**, huit heures viennent de sonner; (*d*) *vendre* **goes like** *descendre*, *vendre* se conjugue comme *descendre*; (*e*) **these colours don't go (together)**, ces couleurs jurent. **3.** (*a*) (*of time*) passer; (*b*) **that's not dear as things go**, ce n'est pas cher au prix où sont les choses; **that goes without saying**, ça va sans dire. **4.** (*a*) partir; s'en aller; **after I've gone**, après mon départ; **from the word go**, dès le commencement; (*b*) disparaître; **it's all gone**, il n'y en a plus; **my strength is going**, mes forces s'affaiblissent; **her sight is going**, elle est en train de perdre la vue; *El:* **a fuse went**, un plomb a sauté; (*at auction*) **going! going! gone!** une fois! deux fois! adjugé! (*c*) mourir; **when I'm gone**, après ma mort. **5.** (*a*) **to go and see s.o.**, aller voir qn; **to go and fetch s.o., to go for s.o.**, aller chercher qn; (*b*) **I'm not going to be cheated**, je ne me laisserai pas abuser, jouer; **I was going to walk there**, j'avais l'intention d'y aller à pied; **I'm going to do it**, je vais le faire; (*c*) **to go fishing**, aller à la pêche; **you just go looking for trouble!** tu te cherches des ennuis! **6. to go to war**, se mettre en guerre; **to go to a lot of trouble**, se donner beaucoup de peine (pour faire qch.). **7.** (*a*) **it won't go into my case**, je ne peux pas le mettre dans ma valise; **the key won't go into the lock**, la clef n'entre pas dans la serrure; **where does this book go?** où est la place de ce livre? (*b*) **six goes into twelve**, douze se divise par six. **8. that just goes to show!** tu vois! **9. the garden goes down to the river**, le jardin s'étend jusqu'à la rivière. **10. to go mad**, devenir fou; **to go white, red**, pâlir, rougir; (*of pers.*) **to go to**

the bad, mal tourner. **11. to let go**, lâcher prise; **let me go!** lâchez-moi! **we'll let it go at that!** cela ira comme ça! **12. to go it**, aller grand train; **to go it alone**, agir tout seul; être seul contre tous. **II.** *s. F:* **1. to be always on the go**, être toujours à courir, à trotter. **2.** allant *m*; **to be full of go**, être plein d'entrain *m*. **3.** (*a*) cou[p] *m*, essai *m*; **to make a go of it**, réussir; **it's you[r] go**, à vous de jouer; **at one go**, d'un seul coup; (*b*) **a bad go of flu**, une forte attaque de gripp[e] **4. that was a near go!** nous l'avons, ils l'on[t] échappé belle! **no go!** rien à faire! **III.** *a. Space F:* **all systems are go**, tout est paré et en ord[re] de marche (pour le départ); **'go a'bout**, *v.i.* (a) circuler; (*b*) **to go about one's work**, se mettre [à] son travail; **how to go about it**, comment s'[y] prendre; **'go-ahead.** *F:* **1.** *a.* actif, en[tre]prenant; **go-a. signal**, feu vert. **2.** *s.* **to give s.[o.]** **the go-a.**, donner le feu vert à qn; **'go a'long** *v.i.* (a) suivre son chemin; **I check the figures as [I]** **go along**, je vérifie les chiffres à mesure; (*b*) **to g[o]** **along with s.o.**, être d'accord avec qn; **'g[o]** **a'way**, *v.i.* s'en aller; partir; **to go away for th[e]** **weekend**, s'absenter pour le week-end; **'g[o]** **'back**, *v.i.* (a) retourner; **to go back home**, re[n]trer chez soi; (*b*) **to go back to a subject**, reven[ir] sur un sujet; (*c*) **to go back on one's wor[d]**, revenir sur sa parole; **'go-between**, *s.* i[n]termédaire *mf*; **'go by**, *v.i.* (a) passer; (*b*) **to g[o]** **by appearances**, juger d'après les apparence[s] **that's nothing to go by**, on ne peut pas se fon[der] là-dessus; **'go 'down**, *v.i.* descendre; (*of sun*) coucher; (*of ship*) couler à fond; (*of win[d]* baisser; (*of neighbourhood*) déchoir; **t[he]** **suggestion went down well**, l'idée a été bi[en] reçue; **'go for**, *v.tr. F:* attaquer (qn); **'g[o-]** **getter**, *s. F:* arriviste *mf*; **'go 'in**, *v.i.* (a) entr[er] rentrer; (*b*) **to go in for painting**, faire de la pe[in]ture; **to go in for an exam**, préparer un exame[n] **'going.** I. *a.* (*a*) **g. concern**, affaire *f* qui march[e] (*b*) *N.Am:* **g. price**, prix courant. II. *s.* (*a*) [the] **good, heavy, g.**, terrain bon, lourd; **to go wh[ile]** **the going's good**, partir pendant que la voie [est] libre; (*b*) *F:* **goings on**, manège *m*; **'go 'in[to]** *v.tr.* (a) entrer dans; (*b*) étudier (une questio[n] **'go 'off**, *v.i.* (a) partir, s'en aller; (*b*) (*of gun*) [par]tir; (*c*) **everything went off well**, tout s'est b[ien] passé; (*d*) *F:* (*of food*) se détériorer; (*e*) *F:* [this] **gone off cheese**, je ne mange plus de froma[ge] **'go 'on**, *v.i.* (a) continuer; **I've enough to g[o]** **with**, j'en ai assez pour le moment; *P:* **g[o] on!** allons donc! à d'autres! (*b*) **what's gon[e] here?** qu'est-ce qui se passe ici? (*c*) *F:* **to go o[n at]** **s.o.**, gronder qn; **'go 'out**, *v.i.* (a) sortir; (*b*) passer de mode; (*c*) (*of fire*) s'éteindre; (*d*) (*of* *tide*) baisser; **go 'over. 1.** *v.tr.* vérifier (u[n] compte); relire (un document). **2.** *v.i.* **to go [over]** **to the enemy**, passer à l'ennemi; **'go 'rou[nd**

v.i. (*a*) faire un détour; (*b*) (*os wheel*) tourner; (*c*) (*of rumour*) circuler; (*d*) there isn't enough to go round, il n'y en a pas assez pour tout le monde; **'go 'through. 1.** *v.tr.* passer par (de rudes épreuves); examiner (des documents). **2.** *v.i.* the deal didn't go through, l'affaire a raté; **'go 'up,** *v.i.* monter; (*of prices*) hausser; **to go up in flames,** se mettre à flamber; **'go with'out,** *v.tr.* (*a*) se passer de (qch.); (*b*) manquer de (qch.).

goal [goul], *s.* but *m*; **'goalkeeper, F:'goalie,** *s.* *Fb:* goal *m*; gardien *m* (de but); **'goalpost,** *s.* montant *m* de but; **the goalposts,** le but.

goat [gout], *s.* chèvre *f*; **he g.,** bouc *m*; *F:* **he gets my g.,** il m'embête.

gob [gɔb], *s.* *P:* bouche *f*; **shut your g.!** ferme-la!

gobble [gɔbl], *v.tr.* avaler (qch.) goulûment; (*to child*) **don't g.!** mange plus lentement!

god [gɔd], *s.* **God,** Dieu *m*; (**pagan**) **g.,** dieu; *Th: F:* **the gods,** le poulailler, le paradis; **'godchild,** *pl.* **-children,** *s.* filleul, *f.* filleule; **'god-daughter,** *s.* filleule *f*; **'goddess,** *s.f.* déesse; **'godfather,** *s.m.* parrain; **'godmother,** *s.f.* marraine; **'godparents,** *s.pl.* le parrain et la marraine; **'godsend,** *s.* aubaine *f*; **'godson,** *s.m.* filleul.

goggle [gɔgl], *v.i.* **to g. at sth.,** fixer les yeux sur qch.; *F:* **the g. box,** la télé; **'goggles,** *s.pl.* lunettes (protectrices).

gold [gould], *s.* (*a*) or *m*; **g. leaf,** feuille *f* d'or, or en feuille; **g. plate,** vaisselle *f* d'or; (*b*) couleur *f* de l'or; **'gold-digger,** *s.* (*a*) chercheur *m* d'or; (*b*) (*woman*) exploiteuse *f* d'hommes riches; **'golden,** *a.* d'or; **g. wedding,** noces *fpl* d'or; **g. eagle,** aigle royal, doré; *F:* **g. handshake,** cadeau *m* d'adieu, indemnité *f* de départ; **'goldfinch,** *s.* chardonneret *m*; **'goldfish,** *s.* poisson *m* rouge; **'goldmine,** *s.* mine *f* d'or; *F:* **it's a g.,** c'est une affaire d'or; **'gold-'plated,** *a.* plaqué or; **'goldrush,** *s.* ruée *f* vers l'or; **'goldsmith,** *s.* orfèvre *m*.

golf [gɔlf], *s.* golf *m*; **g. club,** (i) crosse *f* de golf; (ii) club *m* de golf; **g. course,** terrain *m* de golf; **'golfer,** *s.* golfeur, -euse.

goner ['gɔnər], *s.* *F:* mort, *f.* morte; **I thought I was a g.,** je pensais que j'allais mourir.

gong [gɔŋ], *s.* **1.** gong *m*. **2.** *F:* décoration *f*, médaille *f*.

good [gud]. **I.** *a.* bon. **1.** (*a*) **g. handwriting,** belle écriture; **g. story,** bonne histoire; *F:* **that's a g. one!** en voilà une bonne! **g. to eat,** bon à manger; **to have g. sight,** avoir de bons yeux; (*b*) **is that meat still g.?** est-ce que la viande est encore bonne? (*c*) **g. reason,** raison *f* valable; (*d*) **g. opportunity,** bonne occasion; **people in a g. position,** gens bien placés; **I thought it a g. idea to do it,** il m'a semblé bon, avantageux, de le faire; **to make a g. thing out of sth.,** tirer bon parti de qch.; **to earn g. money,** gagner large-

ment sa vie; (*e*) **g. morning! g. afternoon!** bonjour! **g. evening!** bonsoir! (*f*) **g.! that's a g. thing!** tant mieux! bon! **very g.!** très bien! (*g*) **g. for nothing,** bon à rien; **g. with one's hands,** habile de ses mains; **g. at French,** fort, bon, en français; **he's g. at games,** c'est un sportif. **2.** (*a*) **g. man,** homme de bien; **g. conduct,** bonne conduite; **g. old John!** bravo Jean! (*b*) (*of child*) sage; (*c*) aimable; **that's very g. of you,** c'est bien aimable de votre part; **he's a g. sort,** c'est un bon garçon; (*d*) *F:* **g. Lord! g. heavens!** grand Dieu! **3. a g. time, a g. while,** pas mal de temps; **a g. hour,** une bonne heure; **a g. 10 kilometres,** dix bons kilomètres; **a g. deal,** beaucoup. **4. my family is as g. as his,** ma famille vaut bien la sienne; **to give as g. as one gets,** rendre coup pour coup; **it's as g. as new,** c'est comme neuf. **5. to make g.,** (i) se rattraper de (ses pertes); remédier à (l'usure); réparer (une injustice); (ii) justifier (une affirmation); remplir (sa promesse); (iii) effectuer (sa retraite); (iv) assurer (sa position); faire prévaloir (ses droits); (v) (*of pers.*) prospérer. **II.** *s.* **1.** bien *m*; (*a*) **to do g.,** faire du bien; **he's up to no g.,** il prépare quelque mauvais coup; (*b*) **I did it for your g.,** je l'ai fait pour votre bien; **much g. may it do you!** grand bien vous fasse! **that won't be much g.,** ça ne servira pas à grand-chose; **it's no g. talking about it,** inutile d'en parler; **he'll come to no g.,** il tournera mal; (*c*) **it's all to the g.,** autant de gagné; tant mieux; (*d*) *adv.phr.* **he's gone for g.,** il est parti pour (tout) de bon. **2.** *pl.* **goods,** (*a*) *Jur:* biens, effets *m*; (*b*) objets *m*, articles *m*; *Com:* marchandises *f*, denrées *f*; **manufactured goods,** produits fabriqués; **consumer goods,** biens de consommation; **to deliver the goods,** (i) livrer les marchandises; (ii) *F:* remplir ses engagements; (*c*) **goods train,** train *m* de marchandises; **good'bye,** *int. & s.* au revoir (*m inv*); adieu (*m*); *F:* **you can say g. to that,** tu peux en faire ton deuil; **'good-for-nothing,** (*a*) *a.* (*of pers.*) qui n'est bon à rien; (*b*) *s.* propre-à-rien *m*; vaurien, -ienne; **'good-'hearted,** *a.* (*of pers.*) qui a bon cœur; **'good-'humoured,** *a.* (*of pers.*) d'un caractère facile; facile à vivre; (sourire *m*) de bonne humeur; **'good-'looking,** *a.* beau; **'good-'natured,** *a.* (*of pers.*) au bon naturel; (sourire) bon enfant; **-ly,** *adv.* avec bonhomie *f*; **'goodness. 1.** *s.* (*a*) bonté *f*; (*b*) bonne qualité. **2.** *int.* **g.!** mon Dieu! **thank g.!** Dieu merci! **good'night,** *int. & s.* (i) bonsoir (*m*); (ii) bonne nuit; **'good-'tempered,** *a.* de caractère facile, égal; facile à vivre; **good'will,** *s.* **1.** bonne volonté; bienveillance *f*. **2.** *Com:* clientèle *f*; **to sell the g.,** vendre le pas de porte.

goose, *pl.* **geese** [guːs, giːs], *s.* **1.** oie *f*. **2.** *F:* niais,

f. niaise; **'gooseflesh, 'goose pimples,** *s.*
chair *f* de poule; **'goosestep,** *s. Mil:* pas *m* de
l'oie.

gooseberry ['guzbəri], *s.* (*a*) groseille *f* à
maquereau, groseille verte; (*b*) **g.(-bush),**
groseillier *m* (à maquereau).

gore [gɔ:r], *v.tr.* (*of bull*) blesser (qn) avec les
cornes; (en)corner (qn); **'goring,** *s.* cornade *f.*

gorge¹ [gɔ:dʒ], *s. Geog:* gorge *f.*

gorge², *v.i. & pr.* **to g.** (oneself), se gorger.

gorgeous ['gɔ:dʒəs], *a.* magnifique, splendide;
superbe; **-ly,** *adv.* magnifiquement,
splendidement.

gorilla [gə'rilə], *s. Z:* gorille *m.*

gormless ['gɔ:mlis], *a. F:* mollasse.

gorse [gɔ:s], *s. Bot:* ajonc(s) *m(pl).*

gory ['gɔ:ri], *a.* ensanglanté.

gosh [gɔʃ], *int.* mince (alors)!

go-slow ['gou'slou], *a. & s.* **go-s. (strike),** grève
perlée.

gospel ['gɔsp(ə)l], *s.* évangile *m;* **to take sth. for
g.,** accepter qch. comme parole d'évangile.

gossip ['gɔsip]. **I.** *s.* **1.** bavard, -arde. **2.** bavardage *m;* (*ill-natured*) cancans *mpl.* **II.** *v.i.*
bavarder.

gothic ['gɔθik], *a.* (architecture) gothique.

gouge [gaudʒ]. **I.** *s. Tls:* gouge *f.* **II.** *v.tr.* gouger
(le bois); creuser (une cannelure) à la gouge.

gourmand ['guəmənd], *s.* gourmand, -ande.

gourmet ['guəmei], *s.* gourmet *m.*

gout [gaut], *s. Med:* goutte *f.*

govern ['gʌvən], *v.tr. & i.* gouverner; **governing
body,** conseil *m* d'administration; **'government,** *s.* gouvernement *m;* **'governor,** *s.*
gouverneur *m.*

gown [gaun], *s.* toge *f,* robe *f* (d'universitaire,
d'avocat, etc.); **dressing g.,** robe de chambre.

grab [græb]. **I.** *v.tr.* **(grabbed) to g. (hold of)**
sth., saisir qch. **II.** *s. Civ.E:* excavateur *m,* pelle
f mécanique.

grace [greis], *s.* (*a*) grâce *f;* **to do sth. with a good
g.,** faire qch. de bonne grâce; **to be in s.o.'s
good graces,** être dans les bonnes grâces de
qn; (*b*) **to say g.,** dire le bénédicité; (*c*) (*also*
'gracefulness) grâce, élégance *f;* **'graceful,**
a. gracieux; **-fully,** *adv.* avec grâce, avec
élégance; **gracious** ['greiʃəs]. **1.** *a.* gracieux,
bienveillant. **2.** *int.* **(good) g.!** mon Dieu! **good
g. no!** jamais de la vie!

grade [greid]. **I.** *s.* **1.** (*a*) grade *m,* rang *m,* degré
m; Sch: N.Am: classe *f;* **g. school** = école *f*
primaire; (*b*) qualité *f;* **high-g.,** de qualité
supérieure. **2.** (*a*) *N.Am:* pente *f,* rampe *f;* (*b*) **to
make the g.,** réussir; (*c*) *N.Am:* **g. crossing,**
passage *m* à niveau. **II.** *v.tr.* classer (des
marchandises); graduer (des exercices);
dégrader (des couleurs); régulariser (une
pente).

gradient ['greidiənt], *s. Civ.E:* **upward g.,** rampe
f; **downward g.,** pente *f.*

gradual ['grædju(ə)l], *a.* graduel; progressif;
-ally, *adv.* graduellement; peu à peu.

graduate. I. *s.* ['grædjuət]. *Sch:* = licencié, -ée.
II. *v.* ['grædjueit]. **1.** *v.i. Sch:* = obtenir sa
licence. **2.** *v.tr.* graduer; **graduated income tax,**
impôt progressif.

graft [grɑ:ft]. **I.** *s.* **1.** *Bot: Med:* greffon *m,* greffe
f. **2.** *F:* gratte *f.* **II.** *v.tr.* greffer; **'grafting,** *s.*
greffe *f,* greffage *m;* **skin g.,** greffe épidermique.

grain [grein], *s.* **1.** grain *m* (de blé, de sel). **2.** fil *m*
(du bois); **against the g.,** à contre-fil; *F:* **it goes
against the g.,** c'est à contrecœur que le fais.

grammar ['græmər], *s.* grammaire *f;* **g. school**
= lycée *m;* **gra'mmatical,** *a.* grammatical;
-ally, *adv.* grammaticalement.

gram(me) [græm], *s. Meas:* gramme *m.*

gramophone ['græməfoun], *s.* phonographe *m.*

granary ['grænəri], *s.* entrepôt *m* de grain.

grand [grænd], *a.* **1.** (*a*) grand; principal; **g.
piano,** piano *m* à queue; *Geog:* **the G. Canyon,**
le Grand Canyon; (*b*) **g. total,** total global. **2.**
grandiose, magnifique. **3.** *F:* (*a*) excellent,
épatant; (*b*) **I'm not feeling too g.,** je ne suis pas
dans mon assiette; **-ly,** *adv.* (*a*) grandement,
magnifiquement, à merveille; (*b*) gran-
diosement; **'grandchild,** *pl.* **-children,** *s.*
petit-fils *m,* petite-fille *f,* petits-enfants *mpl;*
'grand-daughter, *s.f.* petite-fille; **grandeur**
['grændjər], *s.* grandeur *f;* **'grandfather,** *s.m.*
grand-père; **'grandiose,** *a.* grandiose;
'grandmother, *s.f.* grand-mère; **'grandparents,** *s.pl.* grands-parents *m;* **'grandson,**
s.m. petit-fils *m;* **'grandstand,** *s. Sp:* tribune *f.*

granite ['grænit], *s.* granit *m.*

granny ['græni], *s. F:* grand-maman *f, pl.* grand
mamans.

grant [grɑ:nt]. **I.** *s.* aide *f* pécuniaire; subventio⌐
f; Sch: allocation *f* d'études. **II.** *v.tr.* **1.** (*a*) ac
corder, concéder; **he was granted permissio⌐
to do it,** il a reçu la permission de le faire; (*b*) t⌐
take sth. for granted, considérer qch. comm⌐
allant de soi; **you take too much for granted**
vous présumez trop; (*c*) accéder à (un
requête). **2. granting, granted, that this story ⌐
true,** si l'on admet la vérité de cette histoire
'grant-'aided, *a.* subventionné.

granulate ['grænjuleit], *v.tr.* granule⌐
'granular, *a.* granulaire, granuleu⌐
'granulated, *a.* granulé; (sucre) cristallisé.

grape [greip], *s.* (grain *m* de) raisin *m;* **bunch ⌐
grapes,** grappe *f* de raisin; **dessert grape⌐**
raisin(s) de table; **g. harvest,** vendange *f;* **so⌐
grapes!** ils sont trop verts! **'grapefruit,**
pamplemousse *m;* **'grape-'hyacinth,** *s. B⌐*
muscari *m;* **'grapevine,** *s.* **1.** vigne *f.* **2,** *⌐*
téléphone *m* arabe.

graph [græf], s. *Mth:* graphique *m*; courbe *f*; **g. paper,** papier millimétré; '**graphic,** *a.* 1. *Mth:* graphique. 2. (*of description*) pittoresque; vivant.

graphite ['græfait], s. graphite *m*; mine *f* de plomb.

grapple [græpl], *v.i.* **to g. with s.o.,** en venir aux prises avec qn; **to g. with a difficulty,** s'attaquer à une difficulté.

grasp [grɑːsp]. **I.** *s.* (*a*) poigne *f*; **to have a strong g.,** avoir de la poigne; (*b*) prise *f*; étreinte *f*; **to lose one's g.,** lâcher prise; **within one's g.,** (avoir qch.) à sa portée; (*c*) compréhension *f*. **II.** *v.tr.* 1. (*a*) saisir; empoign,, serrer dans la main; étreindre; **to g. s.o.'s hand,** serrer la main à qn; (*b*) s'emparer de, se saisir de (qch.); **to g. the opportunity,** saisir l'occasion (de faire qch.). 2. comprendre; '**grasping,** *a.* âpre au gain.

grass [grɑːs], s. (*a*) herbe *f*; **blade of g.,** brin *m* d'herbe; (*b*) gazon *m*; *P.N:* **keep off the g.,** défense de marcher sur le gazon; '**grasshopper,** s. sauterelle *f*; '**grassland,** s. pré *m*; prairie *f*; '**grassroots,** *s.pl.* (*a*) **g. democracy,** le populisme; (*b*) **to tackle a problem at g. level,** remonter à la source d'un problème; '**grass-snake,** s. couleuvre *f* (à collier); '**grass-'widow, -'widower,** s. femme, homme, dont le mari, la femme, est absent(e); '**grassy,** *a.* herbeux.

grate[1] [greit], s. (*a*) grille *f* (de foyer); (*b*) foyer *m*, âtre *m*; **a fire in the g.,** un feu dans la cheminée; '**grating**[1], s. grille *f*, grillage *m*.

grate[2], *v.* 1. *v.tr.* (*a*) râper (du fromage); (*b*) **to g. one's teeth,** grincer des dents. 2. *v.i.* grincer, crisser; **to g. on the ear,** choquer, écorcher, l'oreille; **to g. on the nerves,** taper sur les nerfs; '**grater,** s. râpe *f*; '**grating**[2], *a.* grinçant; **g. sound,** grincement *m*.

grateful ['greitfəl], *a.* reconnaissant; **-ful'y,** *adv.* avec reconnaissance; '**gratefulness,** s., '**gratitude** ['græt-], s. gratitude *f*, reconnaissance *f* (**to,** envers).

gratify ['grætifai], *v.tr.* 1. faire plaisir, être agréable, à (qn). 2. satisfaire (le désir de qn); '**gratification,** s. satisfaction *f*; '**gratified,** *a.* satisfait, content; **g. smile,** sourire *m* de satisfaction; '**gratifying,** *a.* agréable; flatteur, satisfaisant.

gratis ['grætis]. 1. *a.* gratis, gratuit. 2. *adv.* gratis, gratuitement, à titre gratuit.

gratuity [grə'tjuiti], s. 1. prime *f* (de démobilisation, etc.). 2. *P.N:* **no gratuities,** défense de donner des pourboires *m*; **gra'tuitous,** *a.* (*a*) gratuit; (*b*) **g. insult,** insulte injustifiée, gratuite.

grave [greiv]. **I.** *s.* tombe *f*, tombeau *m*; **mass g.,** tombe collective; **to have one foot in the g.,** être au bord de la tombe. **II.** *a.* grave, sérieux;

to look g., avoir l'air *m* sévère; **g. mistake,** lourde erreur; **-ly,** *adv.* gravement, sérieusement; '**gravedigger,** s. fossoyeur *m*; '**gravestone,** s. pierre tombale; '**graveyard,** s. cimetière *m*.

gravel ['grævəl], s. gravier *m*; **g. path,** allée sablée.

gravity ['græviti], s. gravité *f*; *Ph:* **specific g.,** poids *m* spécifique; '**gravitate,** *v.i.* graviter (**towards,** vers, **round,** autour de); **gravi'tation,** s. gravitation *f*.

gravy ['greivi], s. *Cu:* (i) jus *m* (de la viande); (ii) sauce *f* (au jus).

gray [grei], *a. & s. See* GREY.

graze[1] [greiz]. 1. *v.i.* paître, brouter. 2. *v.tr.* paître, faire paître (un troupeau); paître (l'herbe); '**grazing,** s. pâturage *m*.

graze[2]. **I.** *s.* écorchure *f*, éraflure *f*. **II.** *v.tr.* 1. écorcher, érafler (ses genoux). 2. effleurer, raser, frôler (qn, qch.).

grease [griːs]. **I.** *s.* graisse *f*; **g. remover,** dégraisseur *m.* **II.** *v.tr.* graisser; '**greasing,** s. graissage *m*, lubrification *f*; '**greasepaint,** s. *Th:* fard *m*; '**greaseproof,** *a.* **g. paper,** papier *m* jambon, papier beurre; '**greasy,** *a.* (*a*) graisseux, huileux; taché de graisse, d'huile; (*b*) (chemin) gras, glissant.

great [greit], *a.* grand; **Greater London,** l'agglomération londonienne; **to grow greater,** grandir; **a g. deal of money,** beaucoup d'argent; **a g. many people,** beaucoup de gens; **the greater part of the day,** la plus grande partie de la journée; **the g. majority of women,** la plupart des femmes; **to a g. extent,** en grande partie; **to have no g. opinion of s.o.,** tenir qn en médiocre estime; **-ly,** *adv.* **g. displeased,** fort mécontent; très irrité; **to be g. mistaken,** se tromper grandement; **I would g. prefer,** je préférerais (de) beaucoup; '**great-'aunt,** s. grand-tante *f*; '**greatcoat,** s. pardessus *m*; *Mil:* capote *f*; '**great-'grandfather, -'grandmother,** s. arrière-grand-père *m*; arrière-grand-mère *f*; '**greatness,** s. grandeur *f*; '**great-uncle,** s. grand-oncle *m*.

Greece [griːs]. *Pr.n. Geog:* la Grèce; **Greek.** 1. *a.* grec. 2. *s.* Grec, *f.* Grecque. 3. *s. Ling:* grec *m*; *F:* **it's all G. to me,** c'est de l'hébreu pour moi.

greed [griːd], s. (*also* '**greediness**) (*a*) avidité *f*, cupidité *f*; (*b*) gourmandise *f*; gloutonnerie *f*; '**greedy,** *a.* (*a*) avide, cupide; âpre (au gain); (*b*) gourmand, glouton; **-ily,** *adv.* (*a*) avidement, cupidement; (*b*) avec gourmandise, gloutonnement.

green [griːn]. 1. *a.* vert; (*a*) **to grow g.,** verdir; (*b*) **a g. Christmas,** un Noël sans neige; (*c*) **to keep s.o.'s memory g.,** chérir la mémoire de qn; (*d*) **the plums are still g.,** les prunes sont encore

vertes; (e) **to turn g.**, blêmir; (f) (i) jeune, inexpérimenté; (ii) naïf; **he's not so g.**, il n'est pas né d'hier; (g) **she has g. fingers**, N.Am: **a g. thumb**, en jardinage, elle a le pouce vert. **2.** s. (a) vert m; (b) pl. **greens**, légumes verts; (c) pelouse f, gazon m; Golf: vert; **village g.**, pelouse communale, place f du village; **'greenback**, s. U.S: billet m de banque; **'greenery**, s. verdure f, feuillage m; **'greenfinch**, s. verdier m; **'greenfly**, s. puceron m, aphis m; coll. aphidés mpl; **'greengage**, s. Bot: reine-claude f; **'greengrocer**, s. marchand, -ande, de légumes; fruitier, -ière; **'greenhouse**, s. serre f; **'greenish**, a. verdâtre; **'greenness**, s. (a) verdeur f; (b) verdure f (du paysage); **'greenroom**, s. Th: foyer m des artistes.
Greenland ['gri:nlənd]. Pr.n. Geog: le Groenland.
greet [gri:t], v.tr. saluer, aborder, accueillir (qn); **'greeting**, s. salutation f, salut m; **greetings card**, carte f de vœux; **to send one's greetings**, envoyer le bonjour (à qn).
gregarious [gri'gɛəriəs], a. grégaire; **human beings are g.**, les hommes aiment à vivre en société.
grenade [grə'neid], s. grenade f; **grenadier** [grenə'diər], s. Mil: grenadier m.
grey [grei], a. & s. gris (m); **g. matter**, matière grise (du cerveau); **to go, turn, g.**, (i) (of hair) grisonner; (ii) (of face) blêmir; **g.-haired**, aux cheveux gris; **'greyish**, a. grisâtre.
greyhound ['greihaund], s. lévrier m; **g. racing**, courses fpl de lévriers; **g. track**, cynodrome m.
grid [grid], s. **1.** grille f, grillage m. **2.** El: réseau m électrique national; **'gridiron**, s. gril m.
grief [gri:f], s. chagrin m, douleur f, peine f; **to come to g.**, (i) faire de mauvaises affaires; (ii) avoir un accident; (iii) (of plan) échouer; **'grievance**, s. **1.** grief m; **to air one's grievances**, conter ses doléances f; **someone with a g.**, un aigri. **2.** injustice f; **grieve. 1.** v.tr. chagriner, affliger; **we are grieved to learn . . .**, nous apprenons avec peine . . . . **2.** v.i. se chagriner, s'affliger (**over sth.**, de qch.).
grill [gril]. **I.** s. Cu: **1.** grillade f; **g. (room)**, grillroom m (de restaurant). **2.** (appliance) gril m. **II.** v.tr. Cu: griller; F: **to g. a prisoner**, cuisiner un détenu.
grille [gril], s. grille f; judas m (de porte); Aut: **radiator g.**, calandre f.
grim [grim], a. sinistre; (humour m) macabre; (visage m) sévère; **it's a g. prospect**, ça s'annonce mal; **to hold on like g. death**, se cramponner avec acharnement; **g. determination**, volonté f inflexible; **-ly**, adv. sinistrement; sévèrement; (se battre) avec acharnement.
grime [graim], s. saleté f, poussière f de charbon;

'grimy, a. sale, encrassé, noirci.
grin [grin]. **I.** s. large sourire m; sourire épanoui; **to give a broad g.**, sourire à belles dents. **II.** v.i. (grinned) sourire à belles dents; **to g. and bear it**, (tâcher de) garder le sourire.
grind [graind]. **I.** s. labeur monotone et continu; **the daily g.**, le boulot journalier. **II.** v. (ground; ground) **1.** v.tr. (a) moudre; **to g. to dust**, réduire en poudre; **to g. sth. between one's teeth**, broyer qch. entre ses dents; **to g. sth. under one's heel**, écraser qch. sous ses pieds; **to g. (the faces of) the poor**, opprimer les pauvres; (b) affûter, repasser (un outil) (sur la meule); (c) **to g. one's teeth**, grincer des dents. **2.** v.i. grincer, crisser; **'grinder**, s. **coffee g.**, moulin m à café; **'grinding. I.** a. **1. g. sound**, grincement m, crissement m. **2. g. poverty**, misère écrasante. **II.** s. **1.** mouture (du blé); broyage m; **g. mill**, broyeur m. **2.** aiguisage m, affûtage m. **3.** grincement, crissement; **'grindstone**, s. meule f à aiguiser; **to keep s.o.'s nose to the g.**, faire travailler qn sans relâche, ne laisser à qn aucun répit.
grip [grip]. **I.** s. **1.** prise f; serrement m; étreinte f; **to have a strong g.**, avoir une bonne poigne; **to come to grips with s.o.**, en venir aux mains avec qn; **to get a g. on sth.**, trouver prise à qch.; **to keep a g. on oneself**, se contrôler, se maîtriser. **2.** poignée f. **II.** v.tr. (gripped) saisir empoigner; **'gripping**, a. (of book) passionnant.
grisly ['grizli], a. affreux, sinistre.
gristle [grisl], s. cartilage m, croquant m; **'gristly**, a. cartilagineux.
grit [grit]. **I.** s. **1.** grès m, sable m. **2.** F: courage m, cran m. **II.** v.tr. (gritted) **to g. one's teeth**, grincer des dents; **'gritty**, a. sablonneux, cendreux.
grizzle [grizl], v.i. F: **1.** ronchonner, grognonner. **2.** pleurnicher, geindre.
grizzly ['grizli], a. & s. **g. (bear)**, ours gris d'Amérique, grizzli m.
groan [groun]. **I.** s. gémissement m, plainte f. **II.** v.i. gémir.
grocer ['grousər], s. épicier, -ière; **the g.'s (shop)**, l'épicerie f, l'alimentation f; **'grocery**, s. épicerie f; pl. **groceries**, (articles m d')épicerie.
grog [grɔg], s. grog m; **'groggy**, a. chancelant, titubant; **to feel (a bit) g.**, (i) être peu solide sur ses jambes; (ii) ne pas être dans son assiette.
groin [grɔin], s. Anat: aine f.
groom [gru:m]. **I.** s. **1.** valet m d'écurie. **2.** (wedding) le marié. **II.** v.tr. panser (un cheval); **groomed**, a. **well-g.**, bien soigné.
groove [gru:v], s. **1.** rainure f; Rec: **sound g.**, sillon m sonore. **2. to get into a g.**, s'encroûter, devenir routinier.
grope [group], v.i. tâtonner; **to g. for sth.**

chercher qch. à tâtons; **to g. one's way,**
avancer à tâtons.

gross[1] [grous], *s.inv.* (= 144) grosse *f*; douze
douzaines *f*; **five g.,** cinq grosses.

gross[2], *a.* **1.** gras; gros. **2.** grossier; **g. ignorance,**
ignorance crasse, grossière; **g. injustice,** in-
justice flagrante. **3.** *Com: etc:* **g. weight,** poids
brut; **-ly,** *adv.* grossièrement; **g. exaggerated,**
exagéré outre mesure.

grotesque [grou'tesk], *a.* (*a*) grotesque; (*b*) absurde; saugrenu.

grotto, *pl.* -o(e)s ['grɔtou, -ouz], *s.* grotte *f.*

ground[1] [graund], *a.* moulu; broyé, pilé.

ground[2]. **I.** *s.* **1.** *Nau:* fond ṁ; **g. swell,** houle *f*,
lame *f*, de fond. **2. coffee grounds,** marc *m* de
café. **3.** (*a*) raison *f*, cause *f*, sujet *m*; **g. for complaint,** grief *m*; **on what grounds,** à quel titre;
on health grounds, pour raison de santé; (*b*)
Jur: **grounds for divorce,** motifs *m* de divorce.
4. (*a*) sol *m*, terre *f*; **g. floor,** rez-de-chaussée *m
inv*; **sitting on the g.,** assis par terre; **to fall to
the g.,** (i) tomber à, par, terre; (ii) (*of scheme*)
tomber à l'eau; **to get off the g.,** (i) (*of aircraft*)
décoller; (ii) (*of scheme*) démarrer; **to dash
s.o.'s hopes to the g.,** anéantir les espérances
f de qn; **above g.,** (i) sur terre; (ii) *F:* (*of pers.*)
pas encore enterré; **burnt to the g.,** brûlé de
fond en comble; **that suits me down to the g.,**
(i) cela me va à merveille; (ii) ça m'arrange le
mieux du monde; **to be on firm g.,** connaître le
terrain; être sûr de son fait; **to cut the g. from
under s.o.'s feet,** couper l'herbe sous les pieds
de qn; (*b*) *Av:* **g. crew,** personnel rampant;
(*c*) terrain *m*; *Mil:* **parade g.,** terrain de
manœuvre; **to shift one's g.,** changer ses
batteries, changer d'arguments; **to gain g.,**
gagner du terrain; (*of idea*) faire son chemin;
to stand one's g., tenir bon; (*d*) *pl.* **grounds,**
parc *m*, jardin *m* (d'une maison). **II.** *v.tr. Av:* interdire de vol; '**grounding,** *s.* connaissance *f*
solide (d'un sujet); '**groundless,** *a.* (soupçon)
mal fondé, sans fondement; '**groundsheet,** *s.*
tapis *m* de sol; '**groundsman,** *pl.* -men, *s.*
préposé d'un terrain de jeux.

group [gru:p]. **I.** *s.* groupe *m*; **blood g.,** groupe
sanguin; **in groups,** par groupes; **g. action,** action collective; **to form a g.,** se grouper; **pop g.,**
groupe pop; *Av:* **g. captain,** colonel *m.* **II.** *v.* **1.**
v.tr. grouper (des articles); disposer en
groupes. **2.** *v.i.* se grouper (**round,** autour de).

grouse[1] [graus], *s. inv. Orn:* tétras *m*; (**red**) **g.,**
lagopède *m* rouge d'Ecosse, grouse *m.*

grouse[2]. **I.** *s.* grogne *f.* **II.** *v.i.* ronchonner,
grogner, bougonner; '**grousing,** *s.*
ronchonnement *m.*

grovel ['grɔv(ə)l], *v.i.* ramper; se mettre à plat
ventre (devant qn); '**grovelling,** *a.* rampant.

grow [grou], *v.* (**grew** [gru:]; **grown** [groun]) **I.** *v.i.*

1. (*of plant*) pousser; (*of seeds*) germer; **olives
won't g. here,** l'olivier ne pousse pas ici. **2.** (*of
pers.*) grandir; **to g. up,** grandir, atteindre l'âge
adulte; **he'll g. out of it,** cela lui passera avec
l'âge. **3.** (*a*) s'accroître, croître, augmenter,
grandir; **the crowd grew,** la foule grossissait;
(*b*) **habit that grows on one,** habitude qui vous
gagne. **4.** devenir; **to g. old,** devenir vieux,
vieillir; **it's growing dark,** il commence à faire
nuit, le jour baisse. **II.** *v.tr.* (*a*) cultiver (des
roses); (*b*) laisser pousser (sa barbe); '**grower,**
s. cultivateur, -trice; '**growing,** *a.* **1.** croissant;
qui pousse; **g. crops,** récoltes sur pied. **2.** gran-
dissant; **g. child,** enfant *mf* en cours de
croissance; **g. debt,** dette croissante; **grown,**
a. **g. man,** homme fait; **when you are g. up,**
quand tu seras grand; '**grown-ups,** *s.pl.* les
grandes personnes; **growth,** *s.* **1.** croissance *f*;
to reach full g., arriver à maturité. **2.** accroissement *m*, augmentation *f*; **economic g.,**
développement *m* économique. **3.** (*a*) **yearly g.,**
pousse annuelle; (*b*) pousse (des cheveux). **4.**
Med: grosseur *f*, tumeur *f.*

growl [graul]. **I.** *s.* grondement *m*, grognement *m*
(d'un chien, etc.). **II.** *v.i.* grogner; gronder.

grub [grʌb]. **I.** *s.* **1.** (*a*) larve *f*; (*b*) ver (blanc);
asticot *m.* **2.** *P:* mangeaille *f*; **g.'s up!** à la
soupe! **II.** *v.i.* (**grubbed**) fouiller (dans la terre);
to g. up a plant, déraciner une plante; '**grub-
biness,** *s.* saleté *f*; '**grubby,** *a.* sale,
malpropre.

grudge [grʌdʒ]. **I.** *s.* rancune *f*; **to bear s.o. a g.,**
garder rancune à qn; en vouloir à qn. **II.** *v.tr.*
to g. s.o. his pleasures, voir d'un mauvais œil
les plaisirs de qn; '**grudging,** *a.*
(consentement) donné à contrecœur; **-ly,** *adv.*
(faire qch.) à contrecœur.

gruelling ['gru:əliŋ], *a.* éreintant, épuisant.

gruesome ['gru:səm], *a.* macabre, affreux.

gruff [grʌf], *a.* bourru, revêche, brusque; **g.
voice,** grosse voix; **-ly,** *adv.* d'un ton bourru.

grumble ['grʌmbl]. **I.** **without a g.,** (faire qch.)
sans murmurer; **to have a good g.,** donner libre
cours à sa mauvaise humeur. **II.** *v.i.*
grommeler, grogner, murmurer, rouspéter; **to
g. at s.o.,** rouspéter contre qn; '**grumbler,** *s.*
grognon *mf*; mécontent, -ente; rouspéteur,
-euse; '**grumbling.** **I.** *a.* grognon, grondeur.
II. *s.* grognonnerie *f*, rouspétance *f*;
mécontentement *m.*

grumpy ['grʌmpi], *a.* maussade, renfrogné,
grincheux; **-ily,** *adv.* maussadement.

grunt [grʌnt]. **I.** *s.* grognement *m.* **II.** *v.i.* grogner,
grognonner; pousser un grognement; '**grunt-
ing,** *s.* grognement(s) *m(pl).*

guarantee [gærən'ti:]. **I.** *s.* **1.** (*pers.*) garant,
-ante; caution *f*; **to go g. for s.o.,** se porter garant de, caution pour, qn. **2.** garantie *f.* **II.** *v.tr.*

garantir, cautionner; se porter garant de, caution pour (qn, qch.); **guaran'teed,** a. g. **hourly rate,** salaire minimum garanti.

guard [gɑːd]. I. s. 1. (a) garde f; **to be on one's g.,** être sur ses gardes; **to be caught off one's g.,** être pris au dépourvu; (b) **to be on g. (duty),** être en, de, faction; **to keep g.,** faire la garde. 2. coll. (a) Mil: garde f; **g. of honour,** garde d'honneur; (b) **to set a g. on a house,** faire surveiller une maison. 3. (a) chef m de train; (b) N.Am: gardien m de prison; (c) Mil: **the Guards,** les Gardes m du corps; les soldats de la Garde. 4. **g. rail,** garde-fou m; **fire g.,** garde-feu m inv. II. v. 1. v.tr. (a) garder; (b) Ind: protéger (un mécanisme). 2. v.i. **to g. against sth.,** se garder de qch.; parer à qch.; **'guarded,** a. prudent; **g. answer,** réponse qui n'engage à rien;**'guardhouse,**s.,**'guardroom,**s. Mil:(a) corps-de-garde m inv; (b) poste m de police; **'guardian,** s. 1. gardien, -ienne. 2. tuteur, -trice (d'un mineur). 3. **g. angel,** ange gardien; **'guardianship,** s. 1. garde f. 2. Jur: gestion f tutélaire; tutelle f;**'guardsman,**pl. **-men,**s.m. officier, soldat, de la Garde.

Guatemala [gwætə'mɑːlə]. Pr.n. Geog: le Guatémala.

Guernsey ['gəːnzi]. Pr.n. Geog: Guernesey m; **G. cow,** vache f de Guernesey.

guer(r)illa [gə'rilə], s. Mil: guérillero m; **band of guer(r)illas,** guérilla f; **g. warfare,** guerre f de guérillas.

guess [ges]. I. s. conjecture f, estimation f; **I give you three guesses,** (i) tu as droit à trois réponses; (ii) tu devines? **it's anybody's g.,** qui sait? II. v.tr. & i. 1. **to g. at sth.,** (tâcher de) deviner, conjecturer, qch.; **to g. the length of sth.,** estimer la longueur de qch.; **to keep s.o. guessing,** mystifier qn; **to g. right, wrong,** bien, mal, deviner; **to g. a riddle,** trouver le mot d'une énigme; **you've guessed it!** vous y êtes! 2. N.Am: croire, penser; **I g. you're right,** il me semble que vous avez raison; **I g. so!** sans doute! **'guesswork,** s. estime f, conjecture f; **by g.,** au jugé.

guest [gest], s. (a) invité, -ée; (b) client, -ente (d'un hôtel); **paying g.,** pensionnaire mf; **'guesthouse,** s. pension f de famille.

guffaw [gə'fɔː]. I. s. gros rire (bruyant). II. v.i. pouffer (de rire).

guide [gaid]. I. s. 1. (a) guide m; **to take sth. as a g.,** prendre qch. pour règle; (b) **(girl) g.,** éclaireuse f; guide f de France. 2. (book) **g. to Switzerland,** guide m de la Suisse; **g. to photography,** manuel m de la photographie. 3. indication f, exemple m; **as a g.,** à titre indicatif. II. v.tr. guider, conduire, diriger (qn); **they are guided by him,** ils se règlent sur lui; **'guidance,** s. direction f, conduite f; conseil

m; Sch: **vocational g.,** orientation professionnelle; **'guide book,** s. guide m; **'guided,** a. (a) (excursion) sous la conduite d'un guide; (b) (missile, etc.) (télé)guidé; **'guidelines,** s.pl. directives f;**'guiding,**a. qui sert de guide; **g. principle,** principe directeur; **g. star,** guide m.

guile [gail], s. artifice m, ruse f, astuce f; **'guileless,** a. (a) franc, sans malice; (b) candide, naïf.

guillotine [gilə'tiːn]. I. s. guillotine f. II. v.tr. guillotiner.

guilt [gilt], s. culpabilité f; **'guilty,** a. coupable; **g. conscience,** mauvaise conscience; **g. look,** regard confus; **-ily,** adv. comme un coupable; d'un air coupable.

Guinea ['gini]. Pr.n. Geog: la (République de) Guinée; **New G.,** la Nouvelle-Guinée; **'guinea-fowl,** s. pintade f; **'guinea-pig,** s. cobaye m, cochon m d'Inde; (of pers.) **to be a g.-p.,** servir de cobaye.

guitar [gi'tɑr], s. Mus: guitare f; **electric g.,** guitare électrique; **gui'tarist,** s. guitariste mf.

gulf [gʌlf], s. 1. Geog: golfe m; **the G. Stream,** le Courant du Golfe, le Gulfstream. 2. gouffre m, abîme m.

gull [gʌl], s. Orn: mouette f; goéland m.

gullet ['gʌlit], s. œsophage m; gosier m.

gullible ['gʌlibl], a. facile à duper; jobard **gulli'bility,** s. jobarderie f, jobardise f crédulité f.

gully ['gʌli], s. Geog: (petit) ravin; couloir m.

gulp [gʌlp]. I. s. coup m de gosier; **at one g.,** d'u (seul) coup, d'un (seul) trait. II. v.tr. **to g. sth down,** avaler qch. à grosses bouchées, n'e faire qu'une bouchée, (of drink) n'en fair qu'une gorgée, avaler à pleine gorge.

gum¹ [gʌm]. I. s. 1. (adhesive) gomme f, colle f. 2 **g. arabic,** gomme arabique; **g. resin,** gomme résine f. 3. (a) chewing-gum m; (b) (fruit) g boule f de gomme. 4. Bot: **g. (tree),** gommier m eucalyptus m; F: **to be up a g. tree,** être dans l pétrin. II. v.tr. (gummed) gommer; colle **'gumboot,** s. botte f de caoutchouc **gummed,** a. (of label) gommé.

gum², s. gencive f; **'gumboil,** s. abcès m à gencive.

gumption ['gʌm(p)ʃ(ə)n], s. F: jugeotte f, sens pratique.

gun [gʌn], s. 1. canon m; **naval g.,** canon, pièce de bord; **g. carriage,** affût m (de canon). 2. fus m (de chasse); **g. runner,** contrebandier d'armes. 3. revolver m; pistolet m. 4. **spray** pistolet (à peinture); **'gunboat,** s. (chaloupe canonnière (f); **'guncotton,** s. fulmicoton m coton-poudre m; **'gunfire,** s. canonnade f **'gunman,** pl. **-men,** s. voleur armé; terroris m; **'gunner,** s. artilleur m, canonnier '**gunnery,** artillerie *f*; tir *m* au canon;'**gun-powder,** *s.* poudre *f* (à canon); '**gunroom,** *s.* (*in Navy*) poste *m* des aspirants; '**gunshot,** *s.* coup *m* de fusil, de canon; coup de feu; **g. wound,** blessure *f* de balle; **gunwale** ['gʌn(ə)l], *s. Nau:* plat-bord *m.*

rgle [gəːgl]. I. *s.* (*a*) glouglou *m* (d'un liquide); (*b*) gloussement *m*, roucoulement *m* (de rire). II. *v.i.* (*a*) glouglouter; faire glouglou; (*b*) glousser, roucouler.

sh [gʌʃ]. I. *s.* jaillissement *m*; effusion *f* (de larmes); jet *m*, flot *m* (de sang). II. *v.i.* (*a*) **to g. (out),** jaillir, saillir, couler à flots; (*b*) faire de la sensiblerie; '**gushing,** *a.* (*a*) jaillissant; (*b*) (*pers.*) exubérant, expansif.

st [gʌst], *s.* **g. of rain,** ondée *f,* giboulée *f*; **g. of wind,** coup *m* de vent; rafale *f,* bourrasque *f, Nau:* grain *m*; '**gusty,** *a.* (vent) à rafales; (journée) de grand vent.

sto ['gʌstou], *s.* **to do sth. with g.,** faire qch. (i) avec plaisir; (ii) avec élan, avec entrain.

t [gʌt]. I. *s.* (*a*) *Anat:* boyau *m*; (*b*) *pl.* **guts,** boyaux, intestins *m*; *F:* **to have guts,** avoir du cran; *P:* **to sweat one's guts out,** se casser les reins. II. *v.tr.* (**gutted**) vider (un poisson, une volaille); **the fire gutted the house,** le feu n'a laissé que la carcasse de la maison.

tter ['gʌtər], *s.* 1. gouttière *f* (de toit); **g. pipe,** tuyau *m* de descente. 2. ruisseau *m* (de rue);

caniveau *m*; '**guttersnipe,** *s.* gamin, -ine, des rues.

guttural ['gʌt(ə)rəl]. 1. *a.* guttural. 2. *s. Ling:* gutturale *f*; **-ally,** *adv.* gutturalement.

guy¹ [gai]. I. *s.* (*a*) épouvantail *m*; (*b*) *F:* esp. *N.Am:* type *m*, individu *m*; **a tough g.,** un dur.

guy², *s.* (*a*) hauban *m*, étai *m*; (*b*) *Nau:* gui *m*, retenue *f*; '**guyrope,** *s.* cordon *m* (de tente).

Guyana [gai'ænə]. *Pr.n. Geog:* la Guyane.

guzzle [gʌzl], *v.tr. & i.* (*a*) bâfrer, bouffer (la nourriture); (*b*) boire avidement, lamper; '**guzzler,** *s.* (*a*) bâfreur, -euse; goinfre *m*; (*b*) pochard, -arde; sac *m* à vin.

gym [dʒim], *s. F:* 1. gymnase *m.* 2. gymnastique *f*; **g. shoes,** chaussures *f* (de) tennis.

gymnasium [dʒim'neiziəm], *s.* gymnase *m*; '**gymnast** [-næst], *s.* gymnaste *mf*; **gym'nastic,** *a.* gymnastique; **gym'nastics,** *s.pl.* gymnastique *f.*

gynaecology [gaini'kɔlədʒi], *s.* gynécologie *f*; **gynae'cologist,** *s.* gynécologue *mf.*

gyrate [dʒai'reit], *v.i.* tourner; tournoyer; **gy'ration,** *s.* giration *f.*

gyro ['dʒairou], *s. Av:* **g. control,** commande *f* gyroscopique; **gyro'compass,** *s. Nau:* gyrocompas *m*; '**gyroscope,** *s.* gyroscope *m*, gyro *m*; **gyro'scopic,** *a.* gyroscopique.

H

H, h [eitʃ], s. **1.** (la lettre) H, h *mf*; **to drop one's h's** ['eitʃiz], ne pas aspirer les h. **2.** *Mil:* **H-bomb,** bombe *f* H.

haberdashery ['hæbədæʃəri], s. **1.** mercerie *f*. **2.** *esp. N.Am:* chemiserie *f*.

habit ['hæbit], s. **1.** habitude *f*, coutume *f*; **to be in the h. of doing sth.,** avoir l'habitude de faire qch.; **I don't make a h. of it,** ce n'est pas une habitude chez moi; **from force of h.,** par habitude; **to get into bad habits,** prendre de mauvaises habitudes; **to get out of the h. (of doing sth.),** perdre l'habitude (de faire qch.). **2.** *Cl:* (*a*) habit *m* (de religieuse); (*b*) **riding h.,** amazone *f*; '**habit-forming,** *a.* (drogue) qui cause accoutumance; **ha'bitual** [-juəl], *a.* habituel, d'habitude; **-ally,** *adv.* habituellement, d'habitude; **ha'bituate,** *v.tr.* **to h. s.o. to (doing) sth.,** habituer, accoutumer, qn à (faire) qch.

habitat ['hæbitæt], s. *Z: Bot:* habitat *m*.

habitation [hæbi'teiʃ(ə)n], s. habitation *f*; **fit for h.,** en état d'être habité, habitable; '**habitable,** *a.* habitable.

hack[1] [hæk], *v.tr. & i.* hacher; **to h. sth. to pieces,** tailler qch. en morceaux; **to h. up the joint,** massacrer le rôti; '**hacking,** *a.* **h. cough,** toux sèche et pénible.

hack[2], s. **1.** cheval *m* de louage; cheval de selle. **2.** **literary h.,** écrivain *m* à la tâche; **to be a h. reporter,** *F:* faire la chronique des chiens écrasés.

hackneyed ['hæknid], *a.* (sujet) rebattu, usé; **h. phrase,** expression devenue banale; cliché *m*.

hacksaw ['hæksɔː], s. scie *f* à métaux.

haddock ['hædək], s. *Ich:* aiglefin *m*; **smoked h.,** haddock *m*.

haemoglobin [hiːmə'gloubin], s. hémoglobine *f*.

haemophilia [hiːmou'filiə], s. *Med:* hémophilie *f*.

haemorrhage ['heməridʒ], s. hémorragie *f*.

hag [hæg], s. (vieille) sorcière; *F:* **old h.,** vieille taupe; **h.-ridden,** tourmenté.

haggard ['hægəd], *a.* (*a*) hâve; (visage) décharné; (*b*) (visage) égaré, hagard.

haggle [hægl], *v.i.* marchander; **to h. about the price of sth.,** chicaner sur le prix de qch.

Hague (the) [ðə'heig]. *Pr.n.* la Haye.

hail[1] [heil]. **I.** s. grêle *f*. **II.** *v.i. & tr.* grêler; *impers.* **it's hailing,** il grêle; '**hailstone,** s. grêlon *m*; '**hailstorm,** s. orage accompagné de grêle.

hail[2]. **I.** **1.** s. *esp. Nau:* appel *m*; **within h.,** à portée *f* de voix; **to be h.-fellow-well-met with everyone,** être à tu et à toi avec tout le monde. **2.** *int:* salut! *Ecc:* **the H. Mary,** le Je vous salue Marie, la salutation angélique. **II.** *v.* **1.** *v.tr.* (*a*) saluer (qn); héler (qn, un navire); appeler, héler (un taxi). **2.** *v.i.* **ship hailing from London,** navire en provenance de Londres; **where does he h. from?** d'où vient-il?

hair ['hɛər], s. **1.** (*of head*) cheveu *m*; *coll.* **the h.,** les cheveux; **head of h.,** chevelure *f*; **to do one's h.,** se coiffer; **to wash one's h.,** se laver la tête; **h. dryer,** séchoir *m*; **to have one's h. set,** se faire faire une mise en plis; **to split hairs,** fendre, couper, les cheveux en quatre; *F:* **to let one's h. down,** (i) se mettre à son aise; (ii) s'amuser follement; **it was enough to make your h. stand on end,** c'était à faire dresser les cheveux sur la tête; *P:* **keep your h. on!** ne vous emballez pas! **2.** (*a*) (*of body*) poil *m*; (*b*) *coll.* (*of animal*) poil, pelage *m*; (*c*) crin *m* (de cheval); '**hair('s) breadth,** s. **to have a h. escape,** l'échapper belle; '**hairbrush,** s. brosse *f* à cheveux; '**haircut,** s. coupe *f* de cheveux; **to have a h.,** se faire couper les cheveux; '**hairdo,** s. coiffure *f*; '**hairdresser,** s. coiffeur, -euse; '**hairdressing,** s. coiffure *f*; '**hairless,** *a.* sans cheveux; (*of animal*) sans poils: '**hairnet,** s. filet *m* à cheveux; '**hairpin,** s. épingle *f*, pince *f*, à cheveux; (*in road*) **h. bend** (virage *m* en) épingle à cheveux, lacet *m*; '**hair raising,** *a.* effrayant; '**hairslide,** s. barrette *f* '**hairspring,** s. (ressort) spiral (*m*) (de montre); '**hairy,** *a.* velu, poilu.

hake [heik], s. *Ich:* colin *m*.

hale [heil], *a.* vigoureux; (*usu. in the expr.*) **to be h. and hearty,** se porter comme un charme.

half, *pl.* **halves** [hɑːf, hɑːvz]. **1.** s. (*a*) moitié *f*; **h the loaf,** la moitié du pain; **to cut sth. in h.,** couper qch. en deux; **to go halves with s.o.,** s[e] mettre de moitié avec qn; *F:* **he's too clever b[y] h.,** il est beaucoup trop malin; **to do things b[y] halves,** faire les choses à dèmi; (*b*) demi *m* demie *f*; **three and a h.,** trois et demi; **tw[o] hours and a h., two and a h. hours,** deux heure[s] et demie; (*c*) *Rail:* **return h.** (billet *m* de) retou[r] *m*; (*d*) *Sp:* **the first h.,** la première mi-temps. **2** *a.* demi; **h. an hour,** une demi-heure; **in h. a s[e] cond,** en moins de rien; **at h. price,** à moiti[é] prix. **3.** *adv.* (*a*) à moitié; **he only h. u[n] derstands,** il ne comprend qu'à moitié; (*[b]* *work, etc.*) **h. done,** à moitié fait; *P:* **not h.!,** un[...]

peu! (*b*) **it's h. past two,** il est deux heures et demie; (*c*) **h. as big,** moitié aussi grand; **h. as big again,** plus grand de moitié; **'half-and-'half,** *adv.* moitié-moitié; moitié l'un, moitié l'autre; **how shall I mix them?**—**h.-and-h.,** comment faut-il les mélanger?—à doses égales; **'half-back,** *s. Sp:* demi(-arrière) *m*; **'half-baked,** *a. F:* (*of pers.*) niais; (projet) bâclé, qui ne tient pas debout; **'half-breed,** *s.* 1. métis, -isse. 2. (cheval) demi-sang (*m inv*); **'half-brother,** *s.* demi-frère *m, pl.* demi-frères; **'half-caste,** *a. & s.* métis, -isse; **'half-'closed,** *a.* entrouvert; **'half'cock,** *a. F:* **to go off at h.,** mal démarrer; **'half-'dozen,** *s.* demi-douzaine *f*; **'half-'dressed,** *a.* à moitié vêtu; à demi vêtu; **'half-'empty,** *a.* à moitié vide; **'half-'fare,** *s. Rail: etc:* demi-place *f*; **'half-'hearted,** *a.* tiède; sans entrain; **-ly,** *adv.* avec tiédeur; **'half-'holiday,** *s.* après-midi *m inv* libre; **'half-'hourly,** *a. & adv.* (qui a lieu) toutes les demi-heures; **'half-'mast,** *s.* **at h.-m.,** en berne; **'half-'open,** *v.tr.* entrouvrir (une porte, etc.); **'half-'shaft,** *s. Aut:* demi-arbre *m*; **'half-'sister,** *s.* demi-sœur *f, pl.* demi-sœurs; **'half-'term,** *s. Sch:* congé *m* de mi-trimestre; **'half-'timbered,** *a.* (maison) en colombage, à poutres apparentes; **'half-'time,** *s.* 1. **to work h.-t.,** travailler à mi-temps. 2. *Fb: etc:* (la) mi-temps; **'half-tone,** *s. Phot:* simili *m*; **'half-track,** *s. Veh:* (auto)chenille *f*; **'half-'way,** *adv.* à moitié chemin; à mi-chemin; **to meet s.o. h.-w.,** faire la moitié des avances; composer avec qn; *F:* couper la poire en deux; **'halfwit,** *s.* idiot, -ote; **'half-'year,** *s.* semestre *m*; **-ly,** *a. & adv.* 1. *a.* semestriel. 2. *adv.* tous les six mois.

halibut ['hælibət], *s. Ich:* flétan *m*.

hall [hɔːl], *s.* 1. grande salle; (*a*) **dining h.,** réfectoire *m*; (*b*) **concert h.,** salle de concert; **music h.,** music-hall *m*. 2. **(entrance-)h.,** vestibule *m*, entrée *f*, hall *m*; **h. porter,** concierge *m*. 3. *Sch:* **h. (of residence)** = cité *f* universitaire; **'hallmark,** *s.* poinçon *m* (sur les objets d'orfèvrerie).

hallo [hə'lou], *int. & s.* (*a*) holà! ohé! (*b*) bonjour!

hallow ['hælou], *v.tr.* sanctifier, consacrer; *Ecc:* **hallowed be thy name,** que ton nom soit sanctifié; **hallowed ground,** terre sainte; **'Hallow'e'en** [-'iːn], *s.* veille *f* de la Toussaint.

hallucination [həljuːsi'neiʃ(ə)n], *s.* hallucination *f*.

halo, *pl.* **-oes** ['heilou, -ouz], *s.* 1. halo *m*. 2. auréole *f*; nimbe *m* (d'un saint).

halt [hɔlt]. I. *s.* 1. halte *f*, arrêt *m*; *P.N: Aut:* stop *m*; **to come to a h.,** faire halte; s'arrêter; **to call a h. to sth.,** arrêter qch. 2. *Rail:* halte. II. *v.i.* s'arrêter; **h.!** halte! **'halting,** *a.* hésitant.

halter ['hɔ(ː)ltər], *s.* licou *m*, licol *m*.

halve [hɑːv], *v.tr.* (*a*) diviser en deux; (*b*) réduire de moitié.

ham [hæm], *s.* 1. *Cu:* jambon *m*; **h. and eggs,** œufs au jambon. 2. (*a*) **h. (actor),** cabotin *m*; (*b*) **(radio) h.,** amateur *m* de radio; **'hamstring.** I. *s.* tendon *m* du jarret. II. *v.tr.* (hamstrung) 1. couper les jarrets à (une bête). 2. couper les moyens à (qn).

Hamburg ['hæmbəːg]. *Pr.n. Geog:* Hambourg; **'hamburger,** *s.* 1. Hambourgeois, -oise. 2. *Cu:* hamburger *m*.

hamlet ['hæmlit], *s.* hameau *m*.

hammer ['hæmər]. I. *s.* 1. *Tls:* marteau *m*; (*heavy*) masse *f*. 2. **to come, go, under the h.,** être mis aux enchères. II. 1. *v.tr.* marteler, battre (le fer). 2. *v.i.* **to h. at the door,** frapper à la porte à coups redoublés; **to h. away at sth.,** travailler d'arrache-pied à qch.; **to h. in a nail,** enfoncer un clou à coups de marteau; **'hammering,** *s.* **to give s.o. a good h.,** battre qn à plate couture.

hammock ['hæmək], *s.* hamac *m*.

hamper¹ ['hæmpər], *s.* manne *f*, banne *f*.

hamper², *v.tr.* embarrasser, gêner.

hamster ['hæmstər], *s. Z:* hamster *m*.

hand [hænd]. I. *s.* 1. main *f*; (*a*) **to go on one's hands and knees,** aller à quatre pattes; **to vote by show of hands,** voter à main levée; **to hold (sth.) in one's h.,** tenir (qch.) à la main; **to take s.o.'s h.,** donner la main à qn; **to lay hands on sth.,** mettre la main sur qch.; s'emparer de qch.; **hands up!** haut les mains! (*b*) **he can turn his h. to anything,** il sait faire n'importe quoi, il sait tout faire; **to have a h. in sth.,** se mêler de qch.; tremper dans (un crime); **I had no h. in it,** je n'y suis pour rien; **to give s.o. a h.,** donner un coup de main à qn; (*c*) **to have one's hands full,** avoir fort à faire; **to have sth. on one's hands,** avoir qch. à sa charge, sur les bras; *Com:* **goods left on our hands,** marchandises invendues; **to change hands,** changer de propriétaire; **to be in the hands of s.o.,** s'en remettre à qn. 2. *adv.phrs.* (*a*) **to be (near) at h.,** être sous la main, à portée de la main; **Christmas was (close) at h.,** Noël était tout proche; (*b*) **made by h.,** fait (à la) main; (*c*) **hat in h.,** chapeau bas; **revolver in h.,** revolver au poing; **to have some money in h.,** avoir de l'argent disponible; **the matter in h.,** la chose en question; **to take sth. in h.,** prendre qch. en main; se charger de qch.; **situation well in h.,** situation bien en main; (*d*) **work in h.,** travail en cours; (*e*) **on the right h. (side),** du côté droit; **on the one h.,** d'une part; **on the other h.,** d'autre part; par contre; (*f*) **to do sth. out of h.,** faire qch. immédiatement, sur-le-champ; **to get out of h.,** perdre toute discipline; (*g*) **your parcel has come to h.,** votre envoi m'est parvenu, est arrivé à destination; **the first excuse to h.,** le premier prétexte venu; (*h*) **to be h. in glove with s.o.,** être d'intelligence avec qn; (*i*) **h. in h.,** la main dans la main; (*j*) **to make money h. over fist,** faire des affaires d'or; (*k*) **h. to h. (combat),** corps *m* à corps; (*l*) **to live from h. to mouth,** vivre au jour le jour; (*m*) *Rac:* **to win hands down,** gagner haut la main. **3.** (*pers.*) (*a*) ouvrier, -ière; manœuvre *m*; *Nau:* **the hands,** l'équipage *m*; **all hands on deck!** tout le monde sur le pont! **to be lost with all hands,** périr corps et biens; (*b*) **to be a good h. at doing sth.,** être adroit à faire qch. **4.** *Cards:* jeu *m*. **5.** aiguille *f* (de montre). **6. horse 15 hands high,** cheval qui mesure 15 paumes. **5.** *attrib.* **h. luggage,** bagages à main. **II.** *v.tr.* **to h. (sth. to s.o.),** passer, remettre (qch. à qn); **'handbag,** *s.* sac *m* à main; **'handbook,** *s.* manuel *m*; guide *m*; **'handcuff,** *v.tr.* mettre des menottes à (qn); **handcuffs,** *s.pl.* menottes *f*; **'hand 'down,** *v.tr.* **1.** descendre (qch.) (et le remettre à qn). **2.** transmettre (une tradition); **'handful,** *s.* (*a*) poignée *f*; **a h. of people,** une poignée de gens; **by the h.,** par poignées; (*b*) (*of child*) enfant *mf* terrible; **'handicap. I.** *s.* (*a*) *Sp:* handicap *m*; (*b*) désavantage *m*. **II.** *v.tr.* **(handicapped)** (*a*) *Sp:* handicaper; (*b*) **to be handicapped,** être désavantagé; **'handicraft,** *s.* métier manuel; *pl.* **handicrafts,** l'artisanat *m*; (i) métiers; (ii) produits *m* de l'industrie artisanale; **'hand 'in,** *v.tr.* remettre (un paquet, une lettre, à qn); **'handiwork,** *s.* ouvrage *m*, œuvre *f*; **is that your h.?** c'est toi qui as fait cela? **'handkerchief** ['hæŋkətʃi(ː)f], *s.* mouchoir *m*; **'hand 'made,** *a.* fait, fabriqué, à la main; **'hand 'on,** *v.tr.* transmettre; **'hand 'out,** *v.tr.* distribuer (le courrier, etc.); **'hand-out,** *s.* **1.** *F:* communiqué (à la presse); prospectus *m* publicitaire. **2.** *N.Am:* aumône *f*; **to live on hand-outs,** vivre d'aumônes; **'hand 'over,** *v.tr.* (*a*) remettre (qch. à qn); (*b*) livrer (qn à la justice); (*c*) transmettre (ses pouvoirs) **(to,** à); céder (sa propriété); **'handrail,** *s.* main courante (d'escalier, etc.); **'hand 'round,** *v.tr.* passer, faire circuler (la bouteille, les gâteaux); **'handshake,** *s.* poignée *f* de main; **'handwork,** *s.* travail *m* à la main; travail manuel; **'handwriting,** *s.* écriture *f*; **'handwritten,** *a.* manuscrit; écrit à la main; **'handy,** *a.* **1.** (*of tool, etc.*) maniable. **2.** commode; **that would come in very h.,** cela ferait bien l'affaire. **3.** à portée de la main; **to keep sth. h.,** tenir qch. sous la main; **'handyman,** *pl.* -men, *s.* homme *m* à tout faire.

handle [hændl]. **I.** *s.* manche *m* (de couteau, etc.); poignée *f* (de porte); anse *f* (de seau, de panier); *Aut:* manivelle *f*; **to fly off the h.,** s'em-

porter, sortir de ses gonds. **II.** *v.tr.* (*a*) manier, manipuler (des marchandises); manutentionner (des pièces lourdes); (*b*) (*of pers.*) **he's hard to h.,** il n'est pas commode; **'handlebar,** *s.* guidon *m* (de vélo, de moto); **'handling,** *s.* maniement *m* (d'un outil); manœuvre *f* (d'une voiture, d'un bateau); traitement *m* (de qn); **rough h.,** traitement brutal.

handsome ['hænsəm], *a.* (*a*) beau; **h. young man,** beau jeune homme; **h. furniture,** meubles élégants; (*b*) (*of action, conduct*) gracieux, généreux; (*c*) **to make a h. profit,** réaliser de beaux bénéfices; **-ly,** *adv.* (*a*) élégamment, avec élégance; (*b*) généreusement.

hang [hæŋ]. **I.** *v.* (**hung**) **1.** *v.tr.* (*a*) pendre, accrocher, suspendre (qch.) **(on, from,** à); (*b*) **to h. (down) one's head,** baisser la tête; (*c*) (*of plan, etc.*) **to h. fire,** traîner (en longueur); (*d*) **to h. wallpaper,** poser un papier peint; (*e*) **(hanged) pendre** (un criminel). **2.** *v.i.* (*a*) pendre, être suspendu **(on, from,** à); (*b*) **a heavy silence hung over the meeting,** un silence pesait sur l'assemblée; (*c*) **her hair hangs down her back,** ses cheveux lui tombent dans le dos; (*d*) (*of criminal*) être pendu. **II.** *s.* *F:* **to get the h. of sth.,** (i) saisir le sens de qch.; (ii) saisir le truc de qch.; **'hang a'bout, a'round,** *v.i.* rôder, flâner; **'hang 'back,** *v.i.* **1.** rester en arrière. **2.** hésiter; **'hang 'down,** *v.i.* pendre; **'hanger,** *s.* **coat h.,** cintre *m*; porte-vêtements *m* inv; **'hanger-'on,** *pl.* **hangers-on,** *s.* (*pers.*) parasite *m*; **'hanging,** *s.* **1.** (*a*) suspension; (*b*) pendaison *f*; (*c*) **h. cupboard,** penderie *f*; *usu.pl.* tenture *f*; tapisserie *f*; **'hangman,** *pl.* -men, *s.* bourreau *m*; **'hang 'on,** *v.i.* se cramponner, s'accrocher **(to,** à qch.); **h. on to your job,** ne lâchez pas votre situation; *F:* **h. on a minute!** *P.T.T:* ne raccrochez pas! **'hang 'out 1.** *v.tr.* pendre (qch.) au dehors; étendre (le linge); arborer (un pavillon); (*of dog*) **to h. out its tongue,** tirer la langue. **2.** *v.i.* *F:* habiter; **where do you h. out?** où nichez-vous; **'hangover,** *s.* *F:* gueule *f* de bois; **'hang 'up,** *v.tr.* (*a*) accrocher, pendre (un tableau, etc.); *P.T.T:* **to h. up (the receiver),** raccrocher (l'appareil); *F:* **to h. up on s.o.,** couper la communication avec qn; (*b*) **to be hung up,** (i) être retardé; (ii) *F:* être obsédé, frustré.

hangar ['hæŋər], *s.* *Av:* hangar *m*.

hank [hæŋk], *s.* écheveau *m* (de laine).

hanker ['hæŋkər], *v.i.* **to h. after sth.,** désirer ardemment qch.; **'hankering,** *s.* vif désir (pour qch.); **to have a h. for sth.,** soupirer après qch.

hanky-panky ['hæŋki'pæŋki], *s.* *F:* supercherie *f*; finasseries *fpl*; **that's all h.-p.,** tout ça c'est du boniment.

haphazard [hæp'hæzəd], *a.* **h. arrangement**

disposition fortuite; -**ly**, *adv.* au petit bonheur.
happen ['hæp(ə)n], *v.i.* **1.** (*a*) arriver; se passer,
se produire; **don't let it h. again!** que cela
n'arrive plus! **just as if nothing had happened,**
comme si de rien n'était; **whatever happens,**
quoi qu'il arrive; **as it happens,** justement; *F:*
worse things h. at sea, il y a pire; (*b*) **what's**
happened to him? (i) qu'est-ce qui lui est
arrivé? (ii) qu'est-ce qu'il est devenu? **if**
anything happened to you, si vous veniez à
mourir; **something has happened to him,** il lui
est arrivé quelque malheur. **2.** **if I h. to forget,**
s'il m'arrive d'oublier; **the house happened to**
be empty, la maison se trouvait vide; **do you h.**
to know whether . . ., sauriez-vous par
hasard si . . .? **3. to h. upon sth.,** tomber sur
qch.; '**happening,** *s.* événement *m*; *Th:* spectacle improvisé.
happy ['hæpi], *a.* **1.** heureux, bien aise, content;
h. party of children, bande joyeuse d'enfants;
to be h. to do sth., être content de faire qch. **2.**
h. thought! bonne inspiration! -**ily**, *adv.*
heureusement; **to live h.,** vivre heureux; '**hap-**
piness, *s.* bonheur *m*, félicité *f*; '**happy-go-**
'**lucky,** *a.* (*of pers.*) sans souci; insouciant.
harangue [hə'ræŋ]. **I.** *s.* harangue *f*. **II.** *v.tr.*
haranguer (la foule).
harass ['hærəs], *v.tr.* harasser, tracasser,
tourmenter (qn); '**harassment,** *s.* **1.** harcèle-
ment *m* (de l'ennemi). **2.** tracasserie *f*.
harbour ['hɑːbər]. **I.** *s.* *Nau:* port *m*; **inner, outer,**
h., arrière-, avant-port *m*; **h. installations,** installations *f* portuaires; **h. master,** capitaine *m*
de port. **II.** *v.tr.* héberger (qn); receler (un
criminel); **to h. dirt,** retenir la saleté; **to h. a**
grudge against s.o., garder rancune à qn; **to h.**
suspicions, entretenir des soupçons;
'**harbour-station,** *s.* gare *f* maritime.
hard [hɑːd]. **I.** *a.* **1.** dur; **to get h.,** durcir; **to be as**
h. as nails, (i) être en bonne forme physique;
(ii) être impitoyable; **h. currency,** devise forte.
2. difficile; (tâche) pénible; **h. work,** (i) travail
difficile; (ii) travail assidu; (iii) travail ingrat; **to**
be h. to please, être exigeant, difficile; **to be h.**
of hearing, être dur d'oreille. **3.** (*a*) dur, sévère,
rigoureux (**to, towards,** envers); (*b*) **h. fact,** fait
brutal; **times are h.,** les temps sont rudes, durs;
to have a h. time of it, en voir de dures; **h. luck!**
pas de chance! **to try one's hardest,** faire tout
son possible. **4. h. frost,** forte gelée; **h. winter,**
hiver rigoureux. **II.** *adv.* **1.** (*a*) fort; **as h. as one**
can, de toutes ses forces; **to hit h.,** cogner dur;
to look h. at s.o., regarder fixement qn; **to think**
h., réfléchir profondément; **to be h. at work,**
être en plein travail; **it's raining h.,** il pleut à
verse; **to snow h.,** neiger dru; **to freeze h.,** geler
dur, à pierre fendre; (*b*) **to be h. up,** être à court
d'argent. **2.** difficilement; avec peine; **h.-**

earned wages, salaire péniblement gagné;
'**hard and 'fast,** *a.* **a h. and f. rule,** une règle
absolue; '**hardback,** *s.* livre cartonné; '**hard-**
board, *s.* Isorel *m* (*R.t.m.*); '**hard-'boiled,** *a.*
(œuf) dur; (*of pers.*) dur à cuire; '**hardcore,** *s.*
Const: blocaille *f*; '**harden,** *v.tr. & i.* durcir;
hardened criminal, criminel endurci; '**hard-**
'**fought,** *a.* (élection, etc.) chaudement con-
testé; âprement disputé; '**hard-'headed,** *a.*
(*of pers.*) positif, pratique; '**hard-'hearted,** *a.*
insensible, impitoyable, au cœur dur; '**hardly,**
adv. à peine; ne . . . guère; **I h. know,** je n'en
sais trop rien; **you'll h. believe it,** vous aurez
peine à le croire; **I need h. say . . .,** point besoin de dire . . .; **h. anyone,** presque per-
sonne; '**hardness,** *s.* **1.** dureté *f*. **2.** difficulté *f*.
3. sévérité *f*, rigueur *f*, dureté *f*; '**hardship,** *s.*
privation *f*, fatigue *f*; (dure) épreuve;
'**hardware,** *s.* (*a*) quincaillerie *f*; **h. dealer,**
quincaillier *m*; **builders' h.,** serrurerie *f* de
bâtiments; (*b*) les éléments matériels (d'un ordinateur, d'un système stéréophonique);
'**hard-'wearing,** *a.* (vêtement, etc.) durable;
'**hard-'working,** *a.* laborieux, travailleur,
assidu; '**hardy,** *a.* **1.** audacieux, intrépide. **2.**
robuste; endurci; *Bot:* rustique; vivace;
(plante) de pleine terre.
hare [hɛər]. **I.** *s.* *Z:* lièvre *m*; **buck h.,** bouquin *m*;
doe h., hase *f*; **young h.,** levraut *m*; *Cu:* **jugged**
h., civet *m* de lièvre. **II.** *v.i.* *F:* **to h. off,** se
sauver à toutes jambes; '**hare-brained,** *a.*
écervelé; étourdi; '**hare-lip,** *s.* bec-de-lièvre *m*.
haricot ['hærikou], *s.* (*a*) *Bot:* **h. (bean),** haricot
blanc; (*b*) *Cu:* **h. mutton,** haricot de mouton.
hark [hɑːk], *v.i.* **1. h.!** écoutez! **2. to h. back to**
sth., revenir à un sujet.
harm [hɑːm]. **I.** *s.* mal *m*, tort *m*; **to do s.o. h.,**
faire du tort à qn; nuire à qn; **to see no h. in**
sth., ne pas voir de mal à qch.; **you'll come to**
h., il vous arrivera malheur; **out of h.'s way,** à
l'abri du danger; **that won't do any h.,** cela ne
gâtera rien; **there's no h. in trying,** on peut
toujours essayer. **II.** *v.tr.* faire du mal, du tort,
à (qn); nuire à (qn); '**harmful,** *a.* malfaisant,
pernicieux; nuisible; '**harmless,** *a.* (animal)
inoffensif; (individu) sans malice, pas
méchant; (passe-temps) innocent.
harmony ['hɑːməni], *s.* **1.** *Mus:* harmonie *f*. **2.**
accord *m*; **to live in perfect h.,** vivre en parfaite
intelligence; **his tastes are in h. with mine,** ses
goûts sont conformes aux miens;
har'**monious,** *a.* **1.** harmonieux; mélodieux.
2. en bon accord; '**harmonize. 1.** *v.tr.* harmoniser (des idées); faire accorder (des textes);
Mus: harmoniser (une mélodie). **2.** *v.i.* (*of*
colours, etc.) s'harmoniser, s'assortir; (*of*
facts, pers.) s'accorder.
harness ['hɑːnis]. **I.** *s.* harnais *m*; **to get back**

into h., reprendre le collier; **to die in h.,** mourir
à la besogne; *Av:* **parachute h.,** ceinture *f* de
parachute. **II.** *v.tr.* **1.** harnacher (un cheval);
atteler (un cheval à une voiture). **2.** aménager
(une chute d'eau); domestiquer (l'énergie
atomique).
harp [hɑːp]. **I.** *s. Mus:* harpe *f*; **to play the h.,**
jouer de la harpe. **II.** *v.i. F:* **he's always harping
on about it,** c'est toujours la même ritournelle.
harpoon [hɑːˈpuːn]. **I.** *s.* harpon *m*. **II.** *v.tr.*
harponner.
harpsichord [ˈhɑːpsikɔːd], *s.* clavecin *m*.
harrow [ˈhærou]. **I.** *s. Agr:* herse *f*. **II.** *v.tr.*
herser; **to h. s.o.'s feelings,** déchirer le cœur à
qn; **'harrowing,** *a.* poignant; navrant.
Harry [ˈhæri]. *Pr.n.m.* **1.** Henri. **2. Old H.,** le
diable; **the climate has played Old H. with him,**
le climat l'a complètement détraqué.
harsh [hɑːʃ], *a.* **1.** dur, rêche, rude (au toucher);
strident (à l'oreille); **h. voice,** voix rude. **2.**
(caractère) dur, bourru; (maître) rude; **-ly,**
adv. avec dureté; **'harshness,** *s.* **1.** dureté *f,*
rudesse *f*; âpreté *f.* **2.** sévérité *f*; rigueur *f.*
harvest [ˈhɑːvist]. **I.** *s.* **1.** moisson *f*; récolte *f*; **to
get in the h.,** faire la moisson. **2.** (époque *f* de)
la moisson. **II.** (*a*) *v.tr.* moissonner (les blés);
récolter (les fruits); (*b*) *v.i.* rentrer, faire, la
moisson; **'harvester,** *s.* **1.** (*pers.*)
moissonneur, -euse. **2. (combine) h.,**
moissonneuse(-batteuse) *f.*
hash [hæʃ]. **I.** *s.* **1.** *Cu:* hachis *m.* **2.** *F:* **to make a
h. of it,** bousiller l'affaire. **II.** *v.tr.* **to h. (up)
meat,** hacher de la viande; *N.Am: F:* **to h. over
(a subject),** discuter (qch.).
haste [heist], *s.* hâte *f*; **to make h.,** se hâter, se
dépêcher; **hasten** [heisn]. **1.** *v.tr.* **to h. s.o.'s
death,** avancer la mort de qn. **2.** *v.i.* se
dépêcher (**to do sth.,** de faire qch.);
'hastiness, *s.* **1.** précipitation *f,* hâte *f.* **2.** (*of
temper*) emportement *m,* vivacité *f*; **'hasty,** *a.*
1. (départ) précipité; (repas *m*) sommaire. **2.**
(*of temper*) emporté; vif; **-ily,** *adv.* **1.** à la hâte;
précipitamment. **2.** (parler) sans réfléchir;
(juger) à la légère.
hat [hæt], *s.* chapeau *m*; **soft felt h.,** chapeau
mou; **to raise one's h. to s.o.,** saluer qn (d'un
coup de chapeau); **to pass the h. round (for
s.o.),** faire la quête (pour qn); *F:* **keep it under
your h.,** gardez ça pour vous; *F:* **old h.,** vieux
jeu; **to talk through one's h.,** dire, débiter, des
sottises; *Sp:* **h. trick,** trois réussites de suite;
'hat-shop, *s.* **1.** (*for men*) chapellerie *f.* **2.** (*for
women*) (boutique *f* de) modiste *f*; **at the h.-s.,**
chez la modiste.
hatch[1] [hætʃ], *s.* **1.** *Nau:* écoutille *f*; **under
hatches,** dans la cale; *H:* **service h.,** passe-plats
m.
hatch[2]. **1.** *v.tr.* faire éclore (des poussins); **to h.**

out eggs, (faire) couver des œufs; **to h. a plot,**
ourdir un complot. **2.** *v.i.* **to h. (out),** éclore.
hatchet [ˈhætʃit], *s.* hachette *f*, cognée *f*; hache *f*
à main; **to bury the h.,** faire la paix.
hate [heit]. **I.** *s.* (*a*) haine *f*; (*b*) *F:* (**pet) h.,** objet *m*
d'aversion. **II.** *v.tr.* **1.** haïr, détester (qn); avoir
(qn, qch.) en horreur. **2. to h. to do sth.,**
détester (de) faire qch.; **I h. to trouble you,** je
suis désolé de vous déranger; **'hateful,** *a.*
odieux; détestable; **'hatred,** *s.* haine *f* (**of,** de,
contre).
haughty [ˈhɔːti], *a.* hautain, altier; **-ily,** *adv.*
avec hauteur; **'haughtiness,** *s.* hauteur *f,*
arrogance *f.*
haul [hɔːl]. **I.** *v.tr.* tirer; traîner; remorquer; *Min:*
rouler (le charbon); hercher. **II.** *s.* **1.** *Fish:* (*a*)
coup *m* de filet; (*b*) prise *f*, pêche *f*; **to make a
good h.,** (i) faire une bonne pêche; (ii) *F:* (*of
burglar*) emporter un fameux butin. **2.** *Aut:
etc:* parcours *m*, trajet *m*; **a long h.,** un long
trajet; **'haulage,** *s.* **1.** (*a*) transport routier; **h.
contractor,** entrepreneur *m* de transports; (*b*)
traction *f,* remorquage *m*, halage *m.* **2.** frais
mpl de transport.
haunch [hɔːn(t)ʃ], *s.* (*a*) *Anat:* hanche *f*; (*b*) *Cu:*
cuissot *m*, quartier *m* (de chevreuil); (*c*) *pl.*
haunches, arrière-train *m* (d'un animal); **dog
sitting on its haunches,** chien assis sur son
derrière.
haunt [hɔːnt]. **I.** *s.* lieu fréquenté (par qn); repaire
m (d'un animal); **it's a favourite h. of mine,** (i)
c'est un de mes endroits favoris; (ii) c'est un
lieu où j'aime souvent aller. **II.** *v.tr.* (*a*) (*o
pers., animal*) fréquenter (un endroit); (*b*) (*o
ghost*) hanter; **this house is haunted,** il y a des
revenants dans cette maison; (*c*) **haunted by
memories,** obsédé par des souvenirs.
Havana [həˈvænə]. **1.** *Pr.n. Geog:* la Havane. **2**
s. **a H. (cigar),** un havane.
have [hæv] (**had;** *pr.* **he has**), *v.tr.* **1.** (*a*) avoir
posséder; **he has no friends,** il n'a pas d'amis
all I h., tout ce que je possède, tout mon avoir
I h. it! j'y suis! **my bag has no name on it,** m
valise ne porte pas de nom; (*b*) **we don't h
many visitors,** nous ne recevons pas beaucou
de visites. **2. to h. a child,** avoir, donne
naissance à, un enfant. **3.** (*a*) **there was m
work to be had,** on ne pouvait pas obtenir c
travail; (*b*) **to h. news from s.o.,** recevoir de
nouvelles de qn; **I h. it on good authority th**
. . ., je tiens de bonne source que . . .; (*c*
must h. them by tomorrow, il me les faut po
demain; **let me h. your keys,** donnez-moi v
clefs; **let me h. an early reply,** répondez-mo
sans retard; *P:* **I let him h. it,** (i) je lui ai dit s
fait; (ii) je lui ai réglé son compte; *P:* **you'**
had it! (i) tu es foutu! (ii) c'est loupé! **4. to h**
with s.o., prendre le thé avec qn; **to h. lunc**

déjeuner; **will you h. some wine?** voulez-vous prendre du vin? **I had some more,** j'en ai repris; **he is having his dinner,** il est en train de dîner; **to h. a cigar,** fumer un cigare; *F:* **I'm not having any!** on ne me la fait pas! ça ne prend pas! **5.** (*a*) **to h. an idea,** avoir une idée; **to h. a right to sth.,** avoir droit à qch.; (*b*) **to h. measles,** avoir la rougeole; **to h. a dream,** faire un rêve; **to h. a game,** faire une partie; (*c*) **to h. a lesson,** prendre une leçon; **to h. a bath, a shower,** prendre un bain, une douche; (*d*) **to h. a pleasant evening,** passer une soirée agréable; **I didn't h. any trouble at all,** cela ne m'a donné aucune peine; **we had a rather strange adventure,** il nous est arrivé une aventure assez étrange. **6.** (*a*) **he will not h. that she is delicate,** il n'admet pas qu'elle soit de santé délicate; (*b*) *F:* **you've been had!** on vous a eu! **7. to h. sth. done,** faire faire qch.; **to h. one's hair cut,** se faire couper les cheveux; **I had my watch stolen,** on m'a volé ma montre; **he had his leg broken,** il s'est cassé la jambe. **8.** (*a*) **which (one) will you h.?** lequel voulez-vous? (*b*) **what would you h. me do?** que voulez-vous que je fasse? (*c*) **I won't h. him teased,** je ne veux pas qu'on le taquine. **9. to h. to do sth.,** devoir faire qch.; être obligé de faire qch.; être forcé de faire qch.; **we shall h. to walk faster,** il nous faudra marcher plus vite. **10.** (*aux. use*) (*a*) **to h. been,** avoir été; **to h. come, to h. hurt oneself,** être venu, s'être blessé; **I h. lived in London for three years,** voilà trois ans que j'habite Londres; (*emphatic*) **well, you 'h. grown!** ce que tu as grandi! (*b*) **you h. forgotten your gloves—so I h.!** vous avez oublié vos gants—en effet! **you haven't swept the room—I h.!** vous n'avez pas balayé la pièce—si! mais si! **11. I had,** *F:* **I'd, better say nothing,** je ferais mieux de ne rien dire; **I had,** *F:* **I'd, as soon stay here,** j'aimerais autant rester ici; **'have 'in,** *v.tr.* **I had them in for a cup of tea,** je les ai fait entrer pour prendre une tasse de thé; **I had the doctor in,** j'ai fait venir le médecin; **'have 'on,** *v.tr.* **1.** (*a*) **to h. a coat on,** porter un manteau; **to h. nothing on,** être à poil, être nu; (*b*) **I h. a lecture on this evening,** ce soir, je dois (i) faire, (ii) assister à, une conférence. **2. to h. s.o. on,** duper, faire marcher, qn. **3. to h. something on (a horse),** faire un pari; **'have 'out,** *v.tr.* (*a*) **to h. a tooth out,** (se) faire arracher une dent; (*b*) *F:* **to h. it out with s.o.,** vider une querelle avec qn; **'have 'up,** *v.tr.* *F:* citer (qn) en justice; **to be had up,** être cité devant le tribunal.

ven [heivn], *s.* (*a*) port *m*; (*b*) abri *m*, asile *m*.

versack ['hævəsæk], *s.* sac *m* à dos.

voc ['hævək], *s.* ravage *m*, dégâts *mpl*; **to play h. (with sth.),** faire de grands dégâts (dans

qch.).

haw [hɔː], *s. Bot:* cenelle *f*.

Hawaii [hə'waiː]. *Pr.n. Geog:* Hawaï.

Hawaiian [hə'waiən], *a. & s.* hawaïen, -ïenne.

hawk [hɔːk], *s. Orn:* faucon *m*; **to have eyes like a h.,** avoir des yeux d'aigle.

hawker ['hɔːkər], *s.* (*a*) colporteur *m*; marchand ambulant; (*b*) (*of vegetables*) marchand des quatre saisons.

hawthorn ['hɔːθɔːn], *s.* aubépine *f*.

hay [hei], *s.* foin *m*; **to make h.,** faire les foins; faner; **'haycock,** *s.* tas *m*, meulon *m*, de foin; **'hay-fever,** *s. Med:* rhume *m* des foins; **'hay-fork,** *s.* fourche *f* à foin; **'hayloft,** *s.* fenil *m*; grenier *m* à foin; **'haymaker,** *s.* **1.** (*pers.*) faneur, -euse. **2.** (*machine*) faneuse *f*; **'haymaking,** *s.* fenaison *f*; **'hayrick,** *s.*, **'haystack,** *s.* meule *f* de foin; **'haywire,** *a. F:* **he's gone h.,** il déraille, il ne tourne plus rond.

hazard ['hæzəd]. **I.** *s.* **1.** (*a*) hasard *m*; (*b*) risque *m*; péril *m*. **2.** *Golf:* accident *m* de terrain. **II.** *v.tr.* hasarder, risquer (sa vie, etc.); hasarder (une opinion); **'hazardous,** *a.* chanceux, risqué.

haze [heiz], *s.* brume légère; **'hazy,** *a.* brumeux, embrumé; gris; (*of ideas*) nébuleux, vague; **I'm a bit h. about it,** je n'en ai qu'une connaissance vague, qu'un souvenir vague; **-ily,** *adv.* vaguement, indistinctement.

hazel ['heizl], *s.* **h.(-tree),** noisetier *m*, coudrier *m*; **hazel-nut,** noisette *f*.

he [hiː], *pers.pron.m.* **1.** (*unstressed*) il; (*a*) **what did he say?** qu'a-t-il dit? (*b*) **here he comes,** le voici qui vient; **he's an honest man,** c'est un honnête homme. **2.** (*a*) (*stressed*) lui; **he and I, I'm as tall as he,** je suis aussi grand que lui; **'he knows nothing about it,** il n'en sait rien, lui; (*b*) (i) celui; **he that believes,** celui qui croit; (ii) **it is he who said so,** c'est lui qui l'a dit. **3.** *s.* **he-,** mâle; **he-bear,** ours mâle; **he-goat,** bouc; **he-man,** *pl.* **-men,** homme viril, dominateur.

head [hed]. **I.** *s.* **1.** tête *f*; **from h. to foot,** de la tête aux pieds; **to walk with one's h. in the air,** marcher le front haut; **he gives orders over my h.,** il donne des ordres sans me consulter; **h. down,** (la) tête baissée; **h. downwards,** la tête en bas; **h. first, h. foremost,** la tête la première; *F:* **I could do it standing on my h.,** c'est simple comme bonjour; **to go, turn, h. over heels,** faire la culbute; *Rac:* **to win by a h.,** gagner d'une tête; *F:* **to talk s.o.'s h. off,** étourdir qn, rompre les oreilles à qn; **a fine h. of hair,** une belle chevelure. **2. to have a good h. for business,** s'entendre aux affaires; **what put that into your h.?** où avez-vous pris cette idée-là? **to take it into one's h. to do sth.,** s'aviser, se mettre en tête, de faire qch.; **to put ideas into s.o.'s h.,**

donner des idées à qn; **his name has gone out of my h.**, j'ai complètement oublié son nom; **to have a good h. for heights,** ne pas avoir le vertige; **we put our heads together,** nous nous sommes concertés; **to be over the heads of the audience,** dépasser (l'entendement de) l'auditoire; **to lose, to keep, one's h.**, perdre, conserver, son sang-froid; **to go off one's h.**, devenir fou; **weak in the h.**, faible d'esprit. **3.** tête (d'arbre); pointe *f* (d'asperge); pomme *f* (de chou); pied *m* (de céleri); tête (d'épingle); pomme (de canne); haut *m* (d'un escalier); tête, culasse *f*, fond *m* (de cylindre); chevet *m* (de lit); haut bout (de la table); **to bring a matter to a h.**, faire aboutir une affaire. **4. on this h.**, sur ce chapitre; **under separate heads**, sous des rubriques différentes. **5.** (*a*) **to be at the h. of the list, of a procession,** venir en tête de liste, d'un cortège; (*b*) (*pers.*) chef *m* (de famille, d'une entreprise); directeur, -trice (d'une école); **h. of a department,** chef de service; (*c*) **h. clerk,** chef de bureau; **h. gardener,** jardinier *m* en chef; **h. office,** siège social, bureau principal; **h. wind,** vent *m* contraire. **6.** *inv.* **thirty h. of oxen,** trente bœufs; **to pay so much per h.,** a h., payer tant par tête, par personne. **7.** (*of coin*) face *f*; **to toss heads or tails,** jouer à pile ou face; *F:* **I can't make h. or tail of this,** je n'y comprends rien. **8.** *Mch:* **h. of steam,** volant *m* de vapeur; *Civ.E:* **h. of water,** colonne *f* d'eau; (*of flood, discontent, etc.*) **to gather h.,** augmenter, gagner de la force. **II. v. 1.** *v.tr.* mener (un parti); **to h. a procession, the poll,** venir en tête d'un cortège, du scrutin; **to h. a letter,** mettre l'en-tête *m* à une lettre. **2.** *v.i.* s'avancer, se diriger (**for somewhere,** vers un endroit); **to be heading for ruin,** marcher tout droit vers la ruine; 'head**ache,** *s.* mal *m* de tête; *F:* (*of problem*) casse-tête *m* inv; 'head**dress,** *s.* coiffure *f*; 'head**er,** *s.* **1. to take a h.,** plonger (dans l'eau) la tête la première; faire un plongeon; piquer une tête (par terre). **2.** *Fb:* coup *m* de tête; 'head**ing,** *s.* rubrique *f*; entête *m*; 'head**lamp,** *s. Aut:* phare *f*; 'head**land,** *s.* cap *m*, promontoire *m*; 'head**light,** *s. Aut:* phare *f*; feu *m* de route; **dipped h.,** feu de croisement; **to dip the headlights,** se mettre en code; 'head**line,** *s. Journ:* titre *m* de rubrique; **banner headlines,** gros titres; **to hit the headlines,** défrayer la chronique; 'head**long. 1.** *adv.* **to fall h.,** tomber la tête la première; **to rush h. into a fight,** se jeter tête baissée dans une bagarre. **2.** *a.* **h. flight,** fuite précipitée, panique *f*; head'**master,** *s.m.* directeur (d'une école); proviseur (d'un lycée); head'**mistress,** *s.f.* directrice; 'head-**on,** *a.* **h.-on collision,** collision *f* de front; 'head**phones,** *s.pl.* casque *m* (téléphonique);

'head'**quarters,** *s.pl.* **1.** *Mil:* quartier général; **h. staff,** état-major *m.* **2.** centre *m*, siège social, bureau principal (d'une banque, d'une administration); 'head**rest,** *s.* appui-tête *m*; 'head**room,** *s.* hauteur *f* libre; 'head**set,** *s.* casque *m* (radio, téléphonique); 'head**ship,** *s.* direction *f* (d'une école); 'head**strong,** *a.* volontaire, têtu, obstiné; 'head**way,** *s.* **to make h.,** faire des progrès *m*; avancer; 'head**y,** *a.* (vin, etc.) capiteux.

heal [hi:l]. **1.** *v.tr.* guérir. **2.** *v.i.* (*of wound*) **to h. (up),** (se) guérir, se cicatriser, se refermer; 'heal**ing,** *s.* guérison *f*; cicatrisation *f*.

health [helθ], *s.* **1.** santé *f*; **good h.**, bonne santé; **ill, bad, poor, h.**, mauvaise santé; **the National H. Service,** le Service de la Santé (de la Sécurité sociale); **h. insurance,** assurance *f* maladie. **2. to drink (to) the h. of s.o.,** boire à la santé de qn; **'healthy,** *a.* **1.** (*of pers.*) sain; en bonne santé; bien portant; (*of climate, etc.*) salubre. **2. h. appetite,** appétit *m* robuste.

heap [hi:p]. **I.** *s.* (*a*) tas *m*, monceau *m*; **in a h.,** en tas; *F:* (*of pers.*) **to be struck all of a h.,** en rester abasourdi; (*b*) *F:* (*large number*) **heaps of times,** bien des fois, très souvent; **heaps of time,** grandement, largement, le temps; **to have heaps of money,** avoir beaucoup, des tas, d'argent. **II.** *v.tr.* **1. to h. (up),** entasser, amonceler; amasser; **to h. praises, insults, on s.o.,** combler qn d'éloges; accabler qn d'injures. **2. to h. one's plate with strawberries,** remplir son assiette de fraises; *Cu:* **heaped measure,** mesure *f* comble; **heaped spoonful,** cuillère bien pleine.

hear ['hiər], *v.tr.* (**heard** [hə:d]) **1.** entendre; **to h. s.o. speak,** entendre parler qn; **to h. s.o. say sth.,** entendre dire qch. à qn. **2.** (= *listen to*) écouter; **h. me out,** écoutez-moi jusqu'au bout; **h.! h.!** très bien! très bien! bravo! **3. to h. a piece of news,** apprendre une nouvelle. **4.** (*a*) **to h. from s.o.,** recevoir des nouvelles, une lettre de qn; *Com:* **hoping to h. from you,** dans l'attente de vous lire; (*b*) **to h. of, about, s.o.,** avoir des nouvelles de qn; entendre parler de qn; **I never heard of such a thing!** a-t-on jamais entendu une chose pareille! **father won't h. of it,** mon père ne veut pas en entendre parler; **mon père s'y oppose formellement;** 'hear**er,** *s.* auditeur, -trice; **'hearing,** *s.* **1.** audition *f*; audience *f*; **give me a h.!** veuillez m'entendre. **2.** ouïe *f*; **to be hard of h.,** avoir l'oreille dure; **within h.,** à portée de la voix; **it was said in my h.,** on l'a dit en ma présence; 'hear**say,** *s.* ouï dire *m* inv.

hearse [hə:s], *s.* corbillard *m*.

heart [ha:t], *s.* cœur *m.* **1.** *Med:* **to have a weak h.,** être cardiaque; **h. attack,** crise *f* cardiaque; *Surg:* **h. transplant,** greffe *f* du cœur; **open**

surgery, opération *f* à cœur ouvert; **h. failure,** défaillance *f* cardiaque; **to have one's h. in one's mouth,** avoir un serrement de cœur; être angoissé; **my h.** sank, j'ai eu un serrement de cœur; **to break s.o.'s h.,** briser le cœur à qn; **he died of a broken h.,** il est mort de chagrin. 2. (*a*) **set your h. at rest,** soyez tranquille; **with a heavy h.,** le cœur serré; **in my h. of hearts,** au plus profond de mon cœur; **from the bottom of my h.,** du fond de mon cœur; **he's a reactionary at h.,** au fond c'est un réactionnaire; **to learn sth. by h.,** apprendre qch. par cœur; (*b*) **to love s.o. with all one's h.,** aimer qn de tout son cœur; **with all my h.,** de tout mon cœur; (*c*) **to have one's h. on sth.,** avoir qch. à cœur; **to one's h.'s content,** à cœur joie; (*d*) **to have one's h. in one's work,** avoir le cœur à l'ouvrage; (*e*) **to lose h.,** perdre courage; **to take h.,** prendre courage. 3. cœur (de chou); fond *m* (d'artichaut); vif *m* (d'un arbre); **the h. of the matter,** le fond de l'affaire; **in the h. of (a town),** au cœur d'(une ville). 4. *Cards:* **queen of hearts,** dame *f* de cœur; **have you any hearts?** avez-vous du cœur? **'heart-breaking,** *a.* navrant; **'heart-broken,** *a.* **to be h.-b.,** être navré; **'heartburn,** *s. Med:* brûlures *fpl* d'estomac; **'hearten,** *v.tr.* **to h. s.o.,** ranimer le courage de qn; **'heartfelt,** *a.* sincère; qui vient du cœur; **'heartless,** *a.* sans cœur, sans pitié; dur; **'heart-rending,** *a.* à fendre le cœur; navrant; **h.-r. cries,** cris déchirants; **'heartsearching,** *s.* examen *m* de conscience; **'heart-to-'heart,** *a.* **h.-to-h. talk,** conversation *f* intime; **'hearty,** *a.* 1. (accueil) cordial. 2. (*a*) vigoureux, robuste; (*b*) (repas) copieux; **-ily,** *adv.* 1. cordialement; sincèrement; **to be h. sick of sth.,** être profondément dégoûté de qch. 2. (manger) de bon appétit.

hearth [hɑːθ], *s.* foyer *m*, âtre *m*; **'hearth-rug,** *s.* tapis *m* de foyer; devant *m* de foyer.

heat [hiːt], **I.** *s.* 1. (*a*) chaleur *f*; ardeur *f* (du soleil, d'un foyer); (*b*) *Ph: etc:* chaleur; **h. efficiency,** rendement *m* calorifique. 2. **to reply with some h.,** répondre avec une certaine vivacité; **in the h. of the moment,** dans la chaleur du moment. 3. *Sp:* épreuve *f*, manche *f*; **dead h.,** manche nulle; course nulle. 4. (*of animal*) rut *m*; chaleur. **II.** *v.tr. & i.* chauffer; s'échauffer; **'heater,** *s.* appareil *m* de chauffage; **(water) h.,** chauffe-eau *m inv*; **car h.,** chauffage *m* (de voiture); **electric h.,** radiateur *m* (électrique); **'heating,** *s.* chauffage *m*; **central h.,** chauffage central; **'heat-resisting,** *a.* calorifuge; thermorésistant; **'heatwave,** *s. Meteor:* vague *f* de chaleur.

heath [hiːθ], *s.* 1. bruyère *f*; lande *f*. 2. *Bot:* bruyère.

heathen ['hiːð(ə)n], *a. & s.* païen, -ïenne.

heather ['heðər], *s. Bot:* bruyère *f*, brande *f*.

heave [hiːv]. **I.** *v.* (**heaved** *or* (*esp. Nau:*) **hove** [houv]) 1. *v.tr.* (*a*) (*lift*) lever, soulever (un fardeau); *Nau:* **to h. (up) (the anchor),** lever l'ancre; (*b*) pousser (un soupir); (*c*) (*pull, haul*) **to h. coal,** porter le charbon; (*d*) lancer, jeter (sth. at s.o.), qch. contre qn). 2. *v.i.* (*a*) (se) gonfler, se soulever; (*b*) (*of pers.*) avoir des haut-le-cœur *m*; (*c*) *Nau:* **to h. to,** se mettre à la cape; **to h. at a rope,** haler sur une manœuvre; **to h. in sight,** paraître. **II.** *s.* 1. soulèvement *m*, effort *m* (pour soulever qch.). 2. haut-le-cœur *m inv.*

heaven ['hev(ə)n], *s.* ciel *m*, *pl.* cieux; **in h.,** au ciel; **good heavens!** juste ciel! **thank H.!** Dieu merci! **for H.'s sake!** pour l'amour de Dieu! **H. only knows!** Dieu seul le sait! **'heavenly,** *a.* (*a*) céleste; (*b*) *F:* **what h. peaches!** quelles pêches délicieuses! **'heaven-sent,** *a.* providentiel.

heavy ['hevi], *a.* 1. lourd; (*a*) **h. blow,** (i) coup violent; (ii) rude coup (du sort); (*b*) **h. tread,** pas pesant, lourd. 2. (*a*) **h. luggage,** gros bagages; **h. guns,** artillerie lourde; (*b*) **h. features,** gros traits; **h. beard,** forte barbe; (*c*) **h. shower,** grosse averse; **air h. with scent,** air chargé de parfums. 3. (*a*) (travail) pénible, laborieux; **h. day,** journée chargée; (*b*) **h. weather,** gros temps; **h. sea,** grosse mer. 4. **h. eater,** gros mangeur; **to be a h. sleeper,** avoir le sommeil dur; **-ily,** *adv.* 1. lourdement; **time hangs h. on his hands,** le temps lui pèse. 2. **h. underlined,** fortement souligné; **to lose h.,** perdre gros. 3. **to sleep h.,** dormir profondément; **'heaviness,** *s.* (*a*) lourdeur *f*, pesanteur *f*; (*b*) engourdissement *m*, lassitude *f*; **'heavy-duty,** *a.* (machine) à grand rendement; (appareil) soumis à un travail très dur; (pneu) tous-terrains; **'heavy-'handed,** *a.* à la main lourde; **'heavyweight,** *s. Box:* poids lourd.

Hebrew ['hiːbruː], (*a*) *a. & s.* hébraïque (*mf*); israélite (*mf*); (*b*) (**the**) **H. (language),** l'hébreu *m.*

heck [hek], *s. & int. F:* **what the h. are you doing?** que diable faites-vous? **h.!** zut! flûte!

heckle ['hekl], *v.tr.* (*at public meetings*) interpeller (l'orateur); **'heckler,** *s.* interpellateur, -trice; **'heckling,** *s.* interpellation *f.*

hectic ['hektik], *a.* agité, fiévreux; **to have a h. time,** ne pas savoir où donner de la tête.

hector ['hektər], *v.tr.* intimider, rudoyer (qn); **'hectoring,** *a.* (ton, etc.) autoritaire, impérieux.

hedge [hedʒ]. **I.** *s.* haie *f*; **quickset h.,** haie vive. **II.** *v.* 1. *v.tr.* enfermer, enclore (un terrain); **to be hedged in with difficulties,** être entouré de difficultés. 2. *v.i.* se réserver, chercher des

hedgehog H:9 her

hedgehog ['hedʒhɔg], s. hérisson m.

heed [hi:d]. I. v.tr. faire attention à, prendre garde à, tenir compte de (qn, qch.). II. s. **to take h. of sth.,** tenir compte de qch.; **'heedless,** a. étourdi, insouciant, imprudent; **-ly,** adv. étourdiment.

heel [hi:l], s. (a) talon m; **to tread on s.o.'s heels,** marcher sur les talons de qn; **to take to one's heels,** prendre la fuite; **to come to h.,** (of dog) venir au pied; (of pers.) se soumettre; (to dog) **h.!** au pied! (b) talon (d'un soulier); **to be down at h.,** être dans la dèche.

hefty ['hefti], a. F: (homme) fort, solide; costaud; (somme) importante.

heifer ['hefər], s. génisse f.

height [hait], s. 1. (a) hauteur f, élévation f; **wall six metres in h.,** mur haut de six mètres; **of average h.,** de taille moyenne; (b) taille f, grandeur f (de qn). 2. **h. above sea level,** altitude (absolue). 3. hauteur; éminence f (de terrain); colline f. 4. apogée m (de la fortune); comble m (de la folie); **at the h. of the storm,** au plus fort de l'orage; **in, at, the h. of summer,** en plein été; **in the h. of fashion,** à la (toute) dernière mode.

heighten ['haitn], v.tr. accroître, augmenter (un plaisir); accentuer (un contraste).

heinous ['heinəs], a. (crime) odieux.

heir ['ɛər], s. héritier m; Jur: **h. apparent,** héritier présomptif; **'heiress,** s. héritière f; **'heirloom,** s. meuble m, tableau m, bijou m, de famille.

Helen ['helin]. Pr.n. Hélène f.

helicopter ['helikɔptər], s. Av: hélicoptère m; **h. station,** héligare f; **transport by h.,** héliportage m; **transported by h., h.-borne,** héliporté.

helium ['hi:liəm], s. Ch: hélium m.

hell [hel], s. (a) l'enfer m; (b) F: **oh h.!** zut alors! **it's h. on earth!** c'est infernal! **to raise h.,** faire une scène; **to make a h. of a noise,** faire un bruit d'enfer, un bruit infernal; **to give s.o. h.,** passer un savon à qn; **to work like h.,** travailler avec acharnement; **what the h. do you want?** que diable désirez-vous? **'hellish,** a. infernal; diabolique.

hello [he'lou], int. (a) bonjour! (b) (on the telephone) allô! (c) **h., is that you?** tiens! c'est vous?

helm [helm], s. Nau: barre f (du gouvernail); gouvernail m, timon m; **'helmsman,** pl. **-men,** s. homme de barre; timonier m.

helmet ['helmit], s. casque m.

help [help]. I. s. 1. aide f, assistance f, secours m; **with the h. of a friend,** avec l'aide d'un ami; **mutual h.,** entraide f; **to call for h.,** crier au secours; **there's no h. for it,** il n'y a rien à faire. 2. (pers.) aide mf; **daily h.,** femme f de

ménage; **mother's h.,** aide familiale; aide mf. II. v.tr. 1. (a) aider, secourir, assister (qn); venir en aide à (qn); venir à l'aide de (qn); **that will not h. you,** cela ne vous servira à rien; **I got a friend to h. me,** je me suis fait aider par un ami; **h.!** au secours! à l'aide! (b) faciliter (le progrès); **to h. s.o. out,** dépanner qn. 2. (at table) servir (qn); **to h. s.o. to soup,** servir du potage à qn; **h. yourself,** servez-vous. 3. (with negation, expressed or implied) (a) **things we can't h.,** choses qu'on ne saurait empêcher; **I can't h. it,** je n'y peux rien; **it can't be helped,** tant pis! (b) s'empêcher (de faire qch.); **I can't h. laughing,** je ne peux m'empêcher de rire; **I can't h. it,** c'est plus fort que moi; **'helper,** s. aide mf; **'helpful,** a. (personne f) serviable; (chose f, objet m) utile; **'helping. I.** a. **to lend a h. hand,** apporter son aide. II. s. portion f (de nourriture); **'helpless,** a. 1. sans ressource, sans appui. 2. faible, impuissant; **'helplessness,** s. faiblesse f; manque m d'énergie, d'initiative.

helter-skelter ['heltə'skeltər]. 1. adv. (courir, fuir) pêle-mêle, à la débandade. 2. a. **h.-s. flight,** fuite désordonnée; sauve-qui-peut m inv.

hem [hem]. I. s. 1. bord m (d'un vêtement). 2. ourlet m (d'un mouchoir, etc.). II. v.tr. 1. ourler. 2. **to h. in,** cerner, entourer (l'ennemi); **hemmed in by mountains,** serré entre les montagnes.

hemisphere ['hemisfiər], s. hémisphère m; **hemi'spherical** [-'sferi-], a. hémisphérique.

hemoglobin [hi:mə'gloubin], s. hémoglobine f.

hemophilia [hi:mou'filiə], s. Med: hémophilie f.

hemorrhage ['heməridʒ], s. hémorragie f.

hemp [hemp], s. (a) Bot: chanvre m; (b) Tex: (toile f, corde f, de) chanvre.

hen [hen], s. 1. poule f. 2. femelle f (d'oiseau); **h. party,** réunion f de femmes; **'hen-coop,** cage f à poules; mue f; **'hen-house,** poulailler m; **'hen-pecked,** a. **h.-p. husband,** mari dont la femme porte la culotte.

hence [hens], adv. 1. (of time) dorénavant, désormais; **five years h.,** dans cinq ans (d'ici). 2. (consequence of action, etc.) **h. his anger,** de sa fureur; **hence'forth,** adv. désormais, dorénavant, à l'avenir.

henchman, pl. **-men** ['henʃmən], s. partisan, acolyte.

Henry ['henri]. Pr.n.m. Henri.

hepatitis [hepə'taitis], s. Med: hépatite f.

her [hər, hə:r]. I. pers. pron. object. 1. (a) (direct) la, (before vowel sound) l'; (indirect) lui; **have you seen h.?** l'avez-vous vue? **look at h.,** regardez-la; **tell h.,** dites-lui; (b) (refl.) she took h. luggage with h., elle a pris ses bagages avec elle. 2. (stressed, after prep.) elle; **I'm thinking of h.,** c'est à elle que je pense.

remember h., je me souviens d'elle; **I found him and h. at the station,** je les ai trouvés, lui et elle, à la gare. **3.** *F:* **it's h.,** c'est elle; **that's h.!** la voilà! **II.** *poss.a.* son,*f.* sa,*pl.* ses; **h. friend,** son ami, *f.* son amie; *pl.* ses amis, *fpl.* ses amies; **she hurt h. hand,** elle s'est blessée à la main.

herald ['herəld]. **I.** *s.* (*a*) héraut *m*; (*b*) précurseur *m*; messager *m*. **II.** *v.tr.* annoncer, proclamer; **he'raldic** [-'ræld-], *a.* héraldique; **'heraldry,** *s.* l'art *m*, la science, héraldique; le blason.

herb [hə:b], *s. Bot:* (*a*) herbe*f*; (*b*) *pl. Cu:* **herbs,** fines herbes; **her'baceous,** *a. Bot:* **h. border,** bordure herbacée;**'herbal. 1.** *s.* (*book*) herbier *m* **2.** *a.* (tisane, etc.) d'herbes; **her'bivorous,** *a. Z:* herbivore;**'herb-shop,** *s.* herboristerie*f.*

herd [hə:d]. **I.** *s.* (*a*) troupeau *m* (de bétail, de moutons); troupe*f*, bande*f*(d'animaux);**the h. instinct,** l'instinct *m* grégaire; (*b*) troupeau, foule *f* (de gens). **II.** *v.* **1.** *v.i.* **to h. together,** (i) (*of animals*) vivre, s'assembler, en troupeau; (*of people*) s'assembler en foule. **2.** *v.tr.* garder (le bétail, les oies, etc.);**'herdsman,** *pl.* -men, *s.* bouvier *m*, pâtre *m*.

here ['hiər], *adv.* **1.** (*a*) ici; **in h.,** ici; **come in h., please,** venez par ici, s'il vous plaît; **up to h., down to h.,** jusqu'ici; **between h. and London,** d'ici à Londres; **h. and now,** sur-le-champ; **h. goes!** allons-y! (*b*) (*at roll-call*) présent! **2. here's your hat,** voici votre chapeau; **h. you are!** (i) vous voici! (ii) tenez! (ceci est pour vous). **3. here's to you!** à votre santé! **4. my friend h. will tell you,** mon ami que voici vous le dira. **5.** *exclam.* **h.! I want you!** pst! venez ici! **6.** (*a*) **h. and there,** par-ci par-là; çà et là; (*b*) **h., there, and everywhere,** un peu partout; (*c*) **that's neither h. nor there,** cela ne fait rien, cela n'a rien à voir (à l'affaire); **'hereabout(s),** *adv,* près d'ici, par ici, dans ces parages, dans les environs; **here'with,** *adv.* avec ceci; ci-joint.

heredity [hi'rediti], *s.* hérédité *f*; **he'reditary,** *a.* héréditaire.

heresy ['herəsi], *s.* hérésie *f*; **'heretic,** *s.* hérétique *mf*; **he'retical,** *a.* hérétique.

heritage ['heritidʒ], *s.* héritage *m*, patrimoine *m*.

hermetic [hə:'metik], *a.* hermétique; **h. joint,** joint *m* hermétique, étanche; **-ally,** *adv.* (scellé) hermétiquement.

hermit ['hə:mit], *s.* ermite *m*;**'hermitage,** *s.* ermitage *m*.

hernia ['hə:niə], *s. Med:* hernie*f.*

hero, *pl.* -oes ['hiərou, -ouz], *s.* héros *m*; **h. worship,** culte *m* des héros; **he'roic,** *a.* héroïque; **-ally,** *adv.* héroïquement; **'heroine** ['her-], *s.f.* héroïne;**'heroism,** *s.* héroïsme *m.*

heroin ['herouin], *s. Ch:* héroïne*f.*

heron ['herən], *s. Orn:* héron *m*; **young h.,** héronneau *m.*

herring ['heriŋ], *s. Ich:* hareng *m*; **red h.,** (i) hareng saur; (ii) diversion*f.*

hers [hə:z], *poss.pron.* le sien, la sienne, les siens, les siennes; **she took my pen and h.,** elle a pris ma plume et la sienne; **this book is h.,** ce livre est à elle; **a friend of h.,** un(e) de ses ami(e)s.

herself [hə:'self], *pers.pron.* elle-même; **by h.,** (toute) seule; **I saw Louise h.,** j'ai vu Louise elle-même; (*refl.*) se; **she hurt h.,** elle s'est fait mal.

hesitate ['heziteit], *v.i.* hésiter; **to h. to do sth.,** hésiter à faire qch.; **'hesitant,** *a.* hésitant; irrésolu; **'hesitating,** *a.* hésitant, incertain; **-ly,** *adv.* avec hésitation; en hésitant; **hesi'tation,** *s.* hésitation*f.*

heterogeneous [hetərə'dʒi:niəs], *a.* hétérogène.

hew [hju:], *v.tr.* (**hewed; hewed, hewn**) couper, tailler; **to h. one's way,** se frayer, se tailler, un passage.

hexagon ['heksəgən], *s.* hexagone *m.*

heyday ['heidei], *s.* apogée *m.*

hi [hai], *int.* (i) hé! là-bas! (ii) *N.Am:* bonjour! salut!

hiatus, *pl.* -uses [hai'eitəs, -əsiz], *s.* interruption *f.*

hibernate ['haibəneit], *v.i.* (*of animal*) hiberner.

hiccup, hiccough ['hikʌp]. **I.** *s.* hoquet *m*; **to have the hiccups,** avoir le hoquet. **II.** *v.i.* hoqueter.

hide¹ [haid], *v.* (**hid; hidden** [hidn]) **1.** *v.tr.* (*a*) cacher (**from,** à); **to h. one's face,** se cacher la figure; **I did not know where to h. my head,** je ne savais où me mettre; **to h. (away) a treasure,** mettre un trésor dans une cache; (*b*) **to h. sth. from sight,** dérober, soustraire, qch. aux regards; **clouds hid the sun,** des nuages voilaient le soleil. **2.** *v.i.* se cacher;**'hide-and-seek,** *s. Games:* cache-cache *m*;**'hiding¹,** *s.* **to go into h.,** se cacher; **h. place,** cachette *f*; **'hide-out,** *s. F:* refuge *m*, *F:* planque*f.*

hide², *s.* peau *f*; *Com:* cuir *m*; **to save one's h.,** sauver sa peau;**'hidebound,** *a.* (*of pers.*) aux vues étroites;**'hiding²,** *s. F:* raclée*f.*

hideous ['hidiəs], *a.* **1.** hideux, affreux, effroyable. **2.** d'une laideur repoussante; **-ly,** *adv.* hideusement, affreusement; **'hideousness,** *s.* hideur*f*, laideur*f*; horreur*f.*

hierarchy ['haiəra:ki], *s.* hiérarchie*f.*

hi-fi ['hai'fai], *a. & s.* (de) haute fidélité.

higgledy-piggledy ['higldi'pigldi], *adv.* sans ordre, en pagaïe, pêle-mêle.

high [hai]. **I.** *a.* **1.** haut; **wall two metres h.,** mur haut de deux mètres; **how h. is that tree?** quelle est la hauteur de cet arbre? **2.** élevé; (*a*) **to hold one's head h.,** porter la tête haute; (*b*) **to be h. in office,** avoir un poste élevé; (*c*) **h. rate of interest,** taux élevé; **it fetches a h. price,** cela se vend cher; **to set a h. value on sth.,** estimer hautement qch.; **to play for h. stakes**, jouer gros (jeu); **h. speed**, grande vitesse; (*d*) **in the highest degree**, au plus haut degré; par excellence; **h. fever**, forte fièvre; **h. wind**, vent fort, violent. **3.** *Sch:* **the higher forms**, les classes supérieures. **4.** (*principal*) **the H. Street**, la Grand-rue, la Grande rue; *Ecc:* **h. mass**, la grand-messe. **5.** (*a*) **it's h. time he went to school**, il est grand temps qu'il aille à l'école; (*b*) *Cu:* (*of meat*) avancé, gâté; (*of game*) faisandé; *F:* (*of pers.*) ivre, parti, éméché. **6.** (i) (*of ship*) **h. and dry**, échoué; à sec; (ii) (*of pers.*) **to leave s.o. h. and dry**, abandonner qn, laisser qn en plan; **-ly**, *adv.* **1. to think h. of s.o.**, avoir une haute opinion de qn. **2. h. amusing**, fort, très, amusant. **3. h. paid**, (services) largement rétribués; (*of pers.*) **h. strung**, nerveux. **II.** *adv.* **1.** haut; en haut; **higher and higher**, de plus en plus haut; **to aim h.**, viser haut. **2. to go as h. as £2000**, aller jusqu'à 2000 livres. **3.** fort, fortement, très; **to run h.**, (i) (*of the sea*) être grosse, houleuse; (ii) (*of feelings*) s'échauffer; (iii) (*of prices*) être élevé. **III.** *s.* **1.** *Meteor:* zone *f* de haute pression. **2.** *F:* **all-time h.**, record le plus élevé; **'highball**, *s. N.Am:* (i) whisky *m* à l'eau; (ii) whisky-soda *m*; **'highbrow**, *s. F:* intellectuel, -elle; **'high-handed**, *a.* (action *f*) arbitraire; (autorité *f*) tyrannique; **'highland. 1.** *s.* pays montagneux. **2.** *attrib.* (*a*) des montagnes; montagnard; (*b*) des montagnes écossaises; **'highlander**, *s.* montagnard écossais; **'highlight. I.** *s.* clou *m* (de la fête). **II.** *v.tr.* mettre (qn, qch.) en vedette; **'high-'minded**, *a.* à l'esprit élevé; aux sentiments *m* nobles; **'Highness**, *s.* (*title*) Altesse *f*; **'high-pitched**, *a.* **1.** (*of sound*) aigu, *f.* aiguë. **2.** *h.-p.* **roof**, comble *m* à forte pente; **'high-'powered**, *a.* (machine *f*, avion *m*, etc.) de haute puissance; **'high-speed**, *a.* (voiture *f*, avion *m*) à grande vitesse; **'high-'spirited**, *a.* intrépide; plein d'ardeur; (cheval) fougueux; **'highway**, *s.* (*a*) grande route; (*b*) *Adm:* voie publique; **the H. Code**, le code de la route; (*c*) *N.Am:* **dual h.**, route à deux chaussées séparées; **h. patrolman**, *pl.* **-men**, motard *m*; **'highwayman**, *pl.* **-men**, *s.* voleur *m* de grand chemin.

hijack ['haidʒæk], *v.tr. F:* s'emparer de force d'(un véhicule, un avion); **'hijacker**, *s.* pirate *m* de l'air, de la route; **'hijacking**, *s.* vol armé d'un véhicule; déroutement *m* d'un avion.

hike [haik]. **I.** *s.* excursion *f* (à pied). **II.** *v.i.* faire une excursion (à pied); **'hiker**, *s.* excursionniste *mf*; **'hiking**, *s.* excursions *fpl*, tourisme *m*, à pied.

hilarious [hi'lɛəriəs], *a.* gai, joyeux, hilare; **-ly**, *adv.* gaiement, joyeusement; **hi'larity**, [-'lær-], *s.* hilarité *f*, gaieté *f*.

hill [hil], *s.* **1.** (*a*) colline *f*, coteau *m*; **up h. and down dale**, par monts et par vaux; (*b*) éminence *f*; monticule *m*. **2.** (*on road*) côte *f*, *P.N:* **h. 1 in 10**, pente 10%; **'hillock**, *s.* petite colline; butte *f*; tertre *m*; **'hillside**, *s.* coteau *m*; flanc *m* de coteau; **'hilly**, *a.* (terrain) accidenté; (route) à fortes pentes.

hilt [hilt], *s.* poignée *f*, garde *f* (d'épée); **to prove an assertion up to the h.**, démontrer surabondamment une assertion.

him [him], *pers. pron. object.* **1.** (*a*) (*direct*) le (*before a vowel*) l'; (*indirect, stressed*) lui; **do you love h.?** l'aimez-vous? **call h.**, appelez-le; **I am speaking to h.**, je lui parle; (*b*) (*refl.*) **he took his luggage with h.**, il a pris ses bagages avec lui. **2.** (*stressed, after prep.*) lui; **I'm thinking of h.**, je pense à lui; **I remember h.**, je me souviens de lui; **I found h. and her at the station**, je les ai trouvés, lui et elle, à la gare. **3.** *F:* **it's h.**, c'est lui; **that's h.!** le voilà! **him'self** *pers. pron.* lui-même; **I saw Louis h.**, j'ai vu Louis lui-même; (*refl.*) se; **he hurt h.**, il s'est fait mal.

hind [haind], *a.* (*of animal*) **h. legs**, jambes *f* de derrière; **h. quarters**, arrière-train *m*.

hinder ['hindər], *v.tr.* **1.** gêner, embarrasser (qn), retarder, entraver (qch.). **2.** empêcher, retenir, arrêter (**s.o. from doing sth.**, qn de faire qch.); **'hindrance**, *s.* empêchement *m*, obstacle *m*.

Hindi ['hindi:], *s. Ling:* le hindi.

hindsight ['haindsait], *s.* sagesse *f* après coup.

Hindu [hin'du:], *a. & s. Ethn:* hindou, -oue; **'Hinduism**, *s.* hindouisme *m*.

hinge [hindʒ]. **I.** *s.* **1.** gond *m* (de porte). **2.** charnière *f*. **II.** *v.i.* tourner, pivoter (**on**, autour de); **everything hinges on his reply**, tout dépend de sa réponse; **hinged**, *a.* (couvercle *m*) à charnière(s); (*of counter*) **h. flap**, battant *m*.

hint [hint]. **I.** *s.* **1.** (*a*) insinuation *f*; **broad h.**, allusion peu voilée; **to give s.o. a h.**, toucher un mot à qn; **to drop a h.**, donner à entendre; **to know how to take a h.**, savoir entendre (qn) à demi-mot; (*b*) signe *m*, indication *f*; **not the slightest h. of . . .**, pas le moindre soupçon de . . . . **2. hints for housewives**, conseils *m* aux ménagères. **II.** *v.i.* **to h.** (**at sth.**), insinuer (qch.).

hip [hip], *s. Anat:* hanche *f*; *Dressm:* **h. measurement**, tour *m* de hanches.

hippopotamus, *pl.* **-muses, -mi** [hipə'pɔtəmə -məsiz, -mai], *s. Z:* hippopotame *m*.

hire ['haiər]. **I.** *s.* louage *m* (d'une voiture); *N.Am:* location *f* (d'une maison); embauchage *m* (de main-d'œuvre); **cars for h.**, voitures en location; **h. purchase**, vente *f* à crédit. **II.** *v.tr.* **1.** louer (une voiture, *N.Am:* un ouvrier). **2. to h. out**, louer, donner en location (une voiture, etc.).

his [hiz]. **I.** *poss.a.* (*denoting a m. possessor*) son *f.* sa, *pl.* ses; **h. master,** son maître; **h. wife,** sa femme; **h. friends,** ses ami(e)s; **he fell on h. back,** il tomba sur le dos. **II.** *poss. pron.* (*denoting a m. possession*) le sien, la sienne, les siens, les siennes; **he took my pen and h.,** il prit ma plume et la sienne; **this book is h.,** ce livre est à lui; **a friend of h.,** un de ses amis.

hiss [his]. **I.** *s.* (*a*) sifflement *m* (du gaz, etc.); (*b*) *Th:* sifflet *m.* **II.** *v.* **1.** *v.i.* (*of snake, gas*) siffler. **2.** *v.tr. Th:* siffler (un acteur).

history ['hist(ə)ri], *s.* **1.** l'histoire *f*; **that's ancient h.,** c'est une vieille histoire; **h. book,** livre *m*, manuel *m*, d'histoire. **2.** **natural h.,** histoire naturelle; **historian** [his'tɔːriən], *s.* historien, -ienne; **historic** [his'tɔrik], *a.* (événement) historique, marquant; **place of h. interest,** monument historique; **his'torical,** *a.* (fait *m*) historique; **h. novel,** roman *m* historique; **-ally,** *adv.* historiquement.

hit [hit]. **I.** *v.* (**hit;** *pr.p.* **hitting**) **1.** *v.tr.* (*a*) frapper; **to h. s.o. a blow,** porter, donner, un coup à qn; (*b*) *v.i.* **to h. against sth.,** se cogner contre qch.; (*c*) atteindre; toucher; *F:* **he couldn't h. a haystack,** il raterait un éléphant dans un couloir; (*d*) *v.i.* **to h. or miss,** au hasard. **2.** *v.tr. & i.* **to h. (up)on sth.,** découvrir, trouver, qch.; **you've h. it!** vous y êtes! **II.** *s.* **1.** coup *m*; **that's a h. at you,** c'est vous qui êtes visé; c'est une pierre dans votre jardin. **2.** *Th:* etc: pièce *f*, roman *m*, chanson *f*, etc. à succès *m*; **'hit 'back,** *v.tr. & i.* se défendre; rendre coup pour coup (à qn); **'hit 'off,** *v.tr.* **to h. it off with s.o.,** s'accorder avec qn; **'hit 'out,** *v.i.* **to h. out at s.o.,** décocher un coup à qn.

hitch [hitʃ]. **I.** *s.* anicroche *f*, contretemps *m*; **there's a h. somewhere,** il y a quelque chose qui cloche; **it went off without a h.,** tout s'est passé sans à-coup; *Rad: T.V: etc:* **a technical h.,** une panne (d'émission), un incident technique. **II.** *v.tr.* accrocher, attacher, fixer (qch.); **to h. (up) one's trousers,** remonter son pantalon; *F:* **to h. a ride,** voyager en auto-stop; *P:* **to get hitched (up),** se marier; **'hitch-hike,** *v.i.* faire de l'auto-stop; **'hitch-hiker,** *s.* auto-stoppeur, -euse; **'hitch-hiking,** *s.* auto-stop *m.*

hive [haiv]. **I.** *s.* ruche *f.* **II.** *v. F:* **to h. sth. off,** séparer (qch.) (de la partie principale).

hoard [hɔːd]. **I.** *s.* amas *m*, accumulation (secrète); **h. of money,** trésor *m*, magot *m.* **II.** *v.tr.* amasser, accumuler (des vivres, de l'argent); **'hoarder,** *s.* personne qui accumule des vivres (en temps de disette).

hoarding ['hɔːdiŋ], *s.* **1.** palissade *f* (de chantier). **2.** panneau-réclame *m*, *pl.* panneaux-réclame.

hoarfrost ['hɔː'frɔst], *s.* gelée blanche; givre *m.*

hoarse [hɔːs], *a.* enroué, rauque; **-ly,** *adv.* d'une voix rauque, enrouée; **'hoarseness,** *s.* enrouement *m.*

hoax [houks]. **I.** *s.* mystification *f*, farce *f*, attrape *f.* **II.** *v.tr.* mystifier, attraper (qn); faire marcher (qn).

hobble ['hɔbl]. **1.** *v.i.* boitiller, clocher, clopiner; **to h. along,** avancer clopin-clopant. **2.** *v.tr.* entraver (un cheval).

hobby ['hɔbi], *s.* passe-temps (favori); **my h. is carpentry,** mon violon d'Ingres, c'est la menuiserie.

hobnailed ['hɔbneild], *a.* (soulier) ferré, à gros clous.

hobnob ['hɔbnɔb], *v.i.* (**hobnobbed**) **to h. with s.o.,** être à tu et à toi avec qn; **to h. with the great,** frayer avec les grands.

hobo, *pl.* **-os** ['houbou, -ouz], *s. N.Am: F:* clochard *m.*

hock[1] [hɔk], *s.* jarret *m* (de quadrupède).

hock[2], *s.* vin *m* du Rhin.

hockey ['hɔki], *s.* (jeu *m* de) hockey *m.*

hod [hɔd], *s.* hotte *f* (de maçon).

hoe [hou]. **I.** *s. Hort:* houe *f*, binette *f.* **II.** *v.tr.* (**hoed**) houer, biner (le sol); sarcler (les mauvaises herbes).

hog [hɔg]. **I.** *s.* **1.** cochon *m*; porc *m*; **to go the whole h.,** aller jusqu'au bout. **2.** (*pers.*) *F:* goinfre *m*, glouton *m.* **II.** *v.tr. & i.* (**hogged**) *F:* (*a*) manger, boire, goulûment; (*b*) monopoliser (qch.); **to h. the limelight,** accaparer la vedette; **'hoggish,** *a.* (*of pers.*) glouton, grossier; **'hoggishness,** *s.* gloutonnerie *f*; grossièreté *f.*

Hogmanay ['hɔgmənei], *s. Scot:* la Saint-Sylvestre.

hogshead ['hɔgzhed], *s.* tonneau *m*, barrique *f.*

hoist [hɔist]. **I.** *s.* **1.** **to give s.o. a h. (up),** aider qn à monter. **2.** (*a*) appareil *m* de levage, treuil *m*; (*b*) ascenseur *m* (de marchandises), monte-charge *m inv.* **II.** *v.tr.* **to h. (sth.) (up),** hisser (qch.).

hold[1] [hould]. **I.** *v.* (**held**) **1.** *v.tr.* (*a*) tenir (qch.); **to h. sth. tight,** serrer qch.; tenir qch. serré; **to h. s.o. fast,** tenir solidement qn; **to h. sth. in position,** tenir qch. en place; **to h. views,** professer des opinions; **to h. oneself in readiness,** se tenir prêt; **to h. s.o. to his promise,** contraindre qn à tenir sa promesse; (*b*) **to h. one's ground,** tenir bon, tenir ferme; **to h. one's own,** maintenir sa (propre) position; **to h. one's drink,** bien porter le vin; **car that holds the road well,** voiture *f* qui tient bien la route; *P.T.T:* **h. the line!** ne quittez pas! **to h. oneself upright,** se tenir droit; (*c*) contenir, renfermer; **car that holds six people,** voiture *f* à six places; **what the future holds,** ce que l'avenir nous réserve; (*d*) tenir (une séance); célébrer (une fête); avoir (une consultation); **the Motor Show is held in October,** le Salon de l'automobile se tient au mois d'octobre; (*e*) retenir, arrêter, empêcher; **to h. one's breath,**

retenir son souffle; **there was no holding him,** il n'y avait pas moyen de l'arrêter; **to h. water,** (i) être étanche; (ii) *F: (of theory)* tenir debout; (*f*) **to h. s.o. responsible,** tenir qn responsable; *F:* **to be left holding the baby,** être, se trouver, responsable (d'un événement, etc.); *F:* payer les pots cassés; **to h. s.o. in respect,** avoir du respect pour qn; **to h. an opinion,** avoir une opinion. **2.** *v.i.* (*a*) *(of rope, etc.)* tenir (bon); **to h. fast,** tenir ferme; (*b*) durer; continuer; *(of weather)* se maintenir; *(of promise)* **to h.** (**good**), être valable. **II.** *s.* prise *f*; **to have a h. over s.o.,** avoir prise sur qn; **to take h. of sth.,** saisir qch.; **to let go one's h.,** lâcher prise; *F:* **where did you get h. of that?** où avez-vous pêché ça? ʹ**hold-all,** *s.* fourre-tout *minv.*; ʹ**hold ʹback. 1.** *v.tr.* retenir (qn, ses larmes); cacher, dissimuler (la vérité). **2.** *v.i.* rester en arrière; hésiter; ʹ**holder,** *s.* **1.** (i) tenancier, -ière; (ii) propriétaire *mf* (d'une terre); **small-h.,** petit propriétaire; *(pers.)* titulaire *mf* (d'un droit). **2.** (*device*) support *m*; monture *f*. **3.** récipient *m;* ʹ**hold ʹforth,** *v.i.* disserter, pérorer; ʹ**hold ʹin,** *v.tr.* **to h. oneself in,** se contenir; ʹ**holding,** *s.* (*a*) *Fin:* avoir *m* (en actions); (*b*) petite propriété; terrain *m;* ʹ**hold ʹoff,** (*a*) *v.tr.* tenir (qn) à distance; (*b*) *v.i.* **the rain is holding off,** jusqu'ici il ne pleut pas; (*c*) *v.i.* s'abstenir; se réserver; ʹ**hold ʹon,** *v.i.* **1.** se maintenir. **2.** (*a*) **to h. on to sth.,** (i) s'accrocher à qch.; (ii) ne pas lâcher qch.; **h. on!** (i) tenez bon! (ii) *P.T.T:* ne quittez pas! (iii) (attendez) un instant! (*b*) *F:* **h. on (a bit)!** pas si vite! ʹ**hold ʹout. 1.** *v.tr.* tendre, offrir. **2.** *v.i.* durer; **how long can you h. out?** combien de temps pouvez-vous tenir? **to h. out to the end,** tenir jusqu'au bout; ʹ**hold ʹup. 1.** *v.tr.* (*a*) soutenir (qn, qch.); (*b*) lever (qch.) (en l'air); (*c*) **to h. s.o. up as a model,** citer qn comme modèle; **to h. s.o. up to ridicule,** tourner qn en ridicule; (*d*) arrêter; entraver, gêner (la circulation); (*e*) attaquer (qn). **2.** *v.i.* (*a*) se soutenir; (*b*) *(of weather)* se maintenir; ʹ**hold-up,** *s.* **1.** (*a*) arrêt *m*, suspension *f* (de la circulation, etc.); (*b*) panne *f* (du métro, etc.). **2.** attaque *f*, vol *m*, à main armée.

hold², *s. Nau:* cale *f*.
hole [houl]. **I.** *s.* **1.** trou *m*; creux *m*, cavité *f*; terrier *m* (de lapin); *F:* **to be in a h.,** être dans le pétrin; *(of place)* **what a rotten h.!** quel sale trou! **2.** orifice *m*, ouverture *f*; *Med: F:* **h. in the heart,** communication *f* (i) interventriculaire, (ii) interauriculaire; **holes in a strap,** points *m* d'une courroie; *Mec: etc:* **inspection h.,** regard *m;* **to bore a h.,** percer un trou; **to wear a h. in a garment,** trouer un vêtement. **II.** *v.* **1.** *v.tr.* trouer, percer. **2.** *v.i.* se trouer, se percer.
holiday [ʹhɔlidei], *s.* (*a*) (jour *m* de) fête *f*; jour

férié; **public h.,** fête légale; (*b*) **to take a h.,** prendre (un) congé; (*c*) **the holidays,** les vacances *f*; **a month's h.,** un mois de vacances; **where did you spend your h.?** où avez-vous passé vos vacances? **h.-maker,** vacancier, -ière.
Holland [ʹhɔlənd]. *Pr.n. Geog:* la Hollande.
hollow [ʹhɔlou]. **I.** *a.* **1.** creux, caverneux, évidé; **h.-eyed,** aux yeux caves; **h.-cheeked,** aux joues creuses. **2.** (son) sourd; **in a h. voice,** d'une voix caverneuse. **3.** *(of promise, etc.)* faux, *f.* fausse; trompeur, -euse. **II.** *adv.* **1. to sound h.,** sonner creux. **2. to beat s.o. h.,** battre qn à plate couture. **III.** *s.* (*a*) creux *m* (de la main); cavité *f* (d'une dent); excavation *f*; (*b*) dépression *f* (du sol); bas-fond *m.* **IV.** *v.tr.* **to h.** (**out**), creuser, évider.
holly [ʹhɔli], *s. Bot:* houx *m*.
hollyhock [ʹhɔlihɔk], *s. Bot:* rose trémière.
holster [ʹhoulstər], *s.* étui *m* de revolver.
holy [ʹhouli], *a.* (*a*) saint, sacré; **the H. Ghost, Spirit,** le Saint-Esprit; **h. water,** eau bénite; (*b*) *(of pers.)* saint, pieux; ʹ**holiness,** *s.* sainteté *f; Ecc:* **His H.,** Sa Sainteté.
homage [ʹhɔmidʒ], *s.* hommage *m*; **to pay h. to s.o.,** rendre hommage à qn.
home [houm]. **I.** *s.* **1.** (*a*) chez-soi *m inv*; foyer (paternel); **to have a h. of one's own,** avoir un chez-soi; **the Ideal H. Exhibition** = le Salon des arts ménagers; (*b*) **at h.,** à la maison, chez soi; **to stay at h.,** garder la maison; **is Mr X at h.?** M. X est-il chez lui? est-ce que je puis voir M. X? **to feel at h. with s.o.,** se sentir à l'aise avec qn; **to be 'not at h.' to anyone,** consigner sa porte à tout le monde; **to make oneself at h.,** faire comme chez soi. **2.** patrie *f*; pays (natal) *m.* **3. old people's h.,** maison *f* de retraite; **children's h.,** foyer, home *m*, de, pour, enfants; **convalescent h.,** maison de repos; **nursing h.,** clinique *f.* **II.** *adv.* **1.** à la maison; chez soi; **to go, come, h.,** (i) rentrer (à la maison); (ii) rentrer dans sa famille; **the train h.,** le train pour rentrer, le train du soir; **to go h.,** retourner au pays; **to send s.o. h. (from abroad),** rapatrier qn; *F:* **that's nothing to write h. about,** ce n'est pas bien extraordinaire. **2.** (*a*) **the reproach went h.,** le reproche le toucha au vif; **to strike h.,** frapper juste; **to bring sth. h. to s.o.,** faire sentir qch. à qn; **to bring a charge h. to s.o.,** prouver une accusation contre qn; (*b*) *Mec:* **to screw a piece h.,** visser une pièce à fond, à bloc. **III.** *a.* **1. h. circle,** cercle *m* de famille; **h. address,** adresse personnelle; **the h. counties,** les comtés *m* avoisinant Londres; *Sp:* **h. ground,** le terrain du club. **2. the H. Office** = le Ministère de l'Intérieur; **the H. Secretary** = le Ministre de l'Intérieur; **h. trade,** commerce intérieur. **IV.** *v.i.* **1.** *(of pigeon)* revenir au colom-

bier. **2.** (*of missile*) revenir par auto-guidage; **'homeless**, *a.* sans foyer; **'homely**, *a.* **1.** (*of food, people*) simple, modeste. **2.** *N.Am:* (*of pers.*) sans beauté; plutôt laid; **'home-'made**, *a.* fait à la maison; **'homesick**, *a.* nostalgique; **she's h.**, elle a le mal du pays; **'homesickness**, *s.* nostalgie *f*, mal *m* du pays; **'homewards**, *adv.* vers sa maison, vers sa demeure; **to hurry h.**, se presser de rentrer; *Nau:* **cargo h.**, cargaison *f* de retour; **'homework**, *s. Sch:* devoirs *mpl*, ètude *f* (du soir).

homeopathy [houmi'ɔpəθi], *s. Med:* homéopathie *f*; **'homeopath**, *s.* médecin *m* homéopathe; **homeo'pathic**, *a.* (traitement *m*) homéopathique.

homicide ['hɔmisaid], *s.* (*a*) (*crime*) homicide *m*; (*b*) (*pers.*) homicide *mf*; **homi'cidal**, *a.* homicide.

homogeneous [hɔmou'dʒi:niəs], *a.* homogène.

homogenize [hɔ'mɔdʒənaiz], *v.tr.* homogénéiser (le lait, etc.).

homosexual [hɔmou'seksjuəl, hou-], *a.* & *s.* homosexuel, -elle.

honest ['ɔnist], *a.* (*a*) honnête, probe; loyal; (*b*) vrai, sincère; **the h. truth**, la pure vérité; **-ly**, *adv.* (*a*) honnêtement, loyalement; (*b*) sincèrement; **'honesty**, *s.* (*a*) honnêteté *f*, probité *f*; (*b*) véracité *f*, sincérité *f*.

honey ['hʌni], *s.* **1.** miel *m*; **he was all h.**, il a été tout sucre et tout miel. **2.** *F:* chéri, *F:* chérie; **'honey-bee**, *s. Ent:* abeille *f* domestique; **'honeycomb**. **I.** *s.* rayon *m* de miel. **II.** *v.tr.* cribler (de petits trous); **'honeycombed**, *a.* alvéolé; **'honeyed**, *a.* (*a*) couvert de miel; (*b*) **h. words**, paroles doucereuses, mielleuses; **'honeymoon**, *s.* lune *f* de miel; **h. (trip)**, voyage *m* de noces; **'honeysuckle**, *s. Bot:* chèvrefeuille *m*.

honorary ['ɔnərəri], *a.* (*a*) honoraire; non rétribué, bénévole; (*b*) *Sch:* **h. degree**, grade *m* honorifique.

honour ['ɔnər]. **I.** *s.* honneur *m*. **1. the seat of h.**, la place d'honneur. **2. to make (it) a point of h. to do sth.**, se piquer d'honneur de faire qch.; **in h. bound**, obligé par l'honneur; **he's the soul of h.**, il est l'honneur personnifié, la probité même; **word of h.**, parole *f* d'honneur; **to be on one's h.**, être engagé d'honneur. **3.** distinction *f* honorifique; **to carry off the honours**, remporter la palme; *Sch:* **honours list**, tableau *m* d'honneur, palmarès *m*. **4. to do the honours**, faire les honneurs (de sa maison). **5. Your H., His H.**, Monsieur le juge, Monsieur le président. **II.** *v.tr.* **1. to h. s.o. with one's confidence**, honorer qn de sa confiance. **2.** *Com:* **to h. a bill**, faire honneur à, honorer, un effet; **'honourable**, *a.* (conduite *f*, famille *f*) honorable; (*title*) **the H. . . .** (*abbr.* **the Hon.**),

l'Honorable . . .; **-ably**, *adv.* honorablement.

hooch [hu:tʃ], *s. N.Am: F:* whisky *m* (de mauvaise qualité).

hood [hud], *s.* **1.** (*a*) *Cl:* capuchon *m*; (*b*) capuchon (de cobra). **2.** *Aut:* (*a*) capote *f*; (*b*) *N.Am:* capot *m*.

hoodwink ['hudwiŋk], *v.tr.* tromper, donner le change à (qn).

hoof, *pl.* **-s, hooves** [hu:f, -s, hu:vz], *s.* sabot *m* (de cheval, etc.); **hoofed**, *a. Z:* ongulé, à sabots.

hook [huk]. **I.** *s.* **1.** crochet *m*, croc *m*; (*a*) **chimney h.**, crémaillère *f*; **hat and coat h.**, patère *f*; (*b*) *Cost:* agrafe *f*; **h. and eye**, agrafe et œillet *m*. **2.** (fish-)**h.**, hameçon *m*; *F:* **swallow sth. h., line and sinker**, gober le morceau. **3.** *P:* **to sling one's h.**, décamper; plier bagage. **II.** *v.tr.* **1. to h. (sth. to sth.)**, accrocher (qch. à qch.). **2.** *Cl:* **to h. up**, agrafer. **3.** crocher, gaffer (un objet flottant); prendre (un poisson) à l'hameçon; **hooked**, *a.* **1.** crochu, recourbé. **2.** muni de crochets, d'hameçons.

hooligan ['hu:ligən], *s.* voyou *m*; **'hooliganism**, *s.* voyouterie *f*.

hoop [hu:p], *s.* **1.** cercle *m* (de tonneau); jante *f*, bandage *m* (de roue). **2.** cerceau *m* (d'enfant).

hoot [hu:t]. **I.** *v.* **1.** *v.i.* (*a*) (*of owl*) (h)ululer, huer; (*b*) (*of pers.*) **to h. with laughter**, rire aux éclats; (*c*) *Aut:* klaxonner; (*d*) (*of siren*) mugir. **2.** *v.tr.* huer, conspuer (qn); siffler (une pièce de théâtre); **to h. s.o. down**, faire taire qn (par des huées). **II.** *s.* (h)ululement *m* (de hibou); coup *m* de sirène, de klaxon; **'hooter**, *s.* sirène *f*; *Aut:* avertisseur *m*, klaxon *m*.

hoover ['hu:vər]. **I.** *s. R.t.m:* aspirateur *m* (de la marque Hoover). **II.** *v.tr. F:* passer l'aspirateur sur (qch.).

hop¹ [hɔp]. **I.** *s. Bot:* houblon *m*; **'hop-field**, *s.* houblonnière *f*; **'hop-picker**, *s.* cueilleur, -euse, de houblon; **'hop-picking**, *s.* cueillette *f* du houblon. **II.** *v.tr.* (**hopped** [hɔpt]) houblonner (la bière).

hop². **I.** *s.* **1.** (*a*) petit saut; sautillement *m*; (*b*) saut à cloche-pied; **to catch s.o. on the h.**, prendre qn au pied levé. **2.** *Av:* étape *f*. **II.** *v.* (**hopped** [hɔpt]) **1.** *v.i.* sauter, sautiller. **2.** *v.tr. F:* **to h. it**, filer, fiche(r) le camp; *P:* **to h. the twig**, (i) filer; (ii) mourir; *P:* casser sa pipe.

hope [houp]. **I.** *v.* **1.** *v.i.* espérer; **to h. for sth.**, espérer qch. **2.** *v.tr.* **I h. to see you again**, j'espère vous revoir; *Com:* **hoping to hear from you**, dans l'espoir de vous lire. **II.** *s.* espérance *f*; espoir *m*; **to be full of h.**, avoir bon espoir; *Geog:* **the Cape of Good H.**, le cap de Bonne Espérance; *F:* **what a h.!** si vous comptez là-dessus! **'hopeful**, *a.* plein d'espoir; (avenir) qui donne de belles espérances, qui promet; **the situation looks more h.**, la situation est plus

encourageante; -**fully**, *adv.* (travailler, etc.)
avec bon espoir, avec confiance; *F:* **h. the
snow will be gone by tomorrow,** espérons que
la neige aura fondu demain; '**hopefulness,**
s. (bon) espoir; confiance *f*; '**hopeless,** *a.*
sans espoir; désespéré; (maladie) incurable;
(enfant, etc.) incorrigible; **it's a h. job,** c'est
désespérant; -**ly,** *adv.* (vivre) sans espoir;
regarder (qn, qch.) avec désespoir; (être vaincu) irrémédiablement; '**hopelessness,** *s.* état
désespéré.
hopper ['hɔpər], *s.* trémie *f.*
hopscotch ['hɔpskɔtʃ], *s. Games:* la marelle.
horde [hɔːd], *s.* horde *f.*
horizon [hə'raiz(ə)n], *s.* horizon *m*; **on the h.,** à
l'horizon.
horizontal [hɔri'zɔnt(ə)l], *a.* horizontal; -**ally,**
adv. horizontalement.
hormone ['hɔːmoun], *s.* hormone *f.*
horn [hɔːn], *s.* **1.** (*a*) corne *f*; bois *m* (d'un cerf);
(*b*) (*of insects*) antenne *f*; *F:* **to draw in one's
horns,** en rabattre. **2.** *Mus:* cor *m*; **French h.,**
cor d'harmonie; **hunting h.,** cor, trompe *f*, de
chasse. **3.** *Aut:* klaxon *m*, avertisseur *m*;
horned, *a.* (animal) à cornes, cornu; '**horny,**
a. corné, en corne; **h.-handed,** aux mains
calleuses.
hornet ['hɔːnit], *s. Ent:* frelon *m.*
horoscope ['hɔrəskoup], *s.* horoscope *m.*
horrify ['hɔrifai], *v.tr.* (*a*) horrifier; faire horreur
à (qn); (*b*) scandaliser (qn); '**horrible,** *a.* horrible, affreux; -**ibly,** *adv.* horriblement,
affreusement; '**horrid,** *a.* horrible, affreux; (*of
pers.*) déplaisant, désagréable; méchant; **to be
h. to s.o.,** être méchant envers qn; **don't be h.!**
(i) ne dites pas des horreurs pareilles! (ii) ne
faites pas le, la, vilain(e)! **ho'rrific,** *a.*
horrifique, macabre, terrifiant.
horror ['hɔrər], *s.* **1.** horreur *f*; **to have a h. of
sth.,** **of doing sth.,** avoir horreur de qch., de
faire qch.; **h. film,** film *m* d'épouvante. **2.** (*a*)
chose horrible, affreuse; **it gives me the
horrors,** cela me donne le frisson; (*b*) (*of child*)
a little h., une petite peste; '**horror-stricken,**
-**struck,** *a.* saisi d'horreur.
horse [hɔːs], *s.* **1.** cheval, -aux *m*; (*a*) **draught h.,**
cheval de trait; **riding h.,** cheval de selle;
thoroughbred h., pur-sang *m inv*; *F:* **dark h.,**
cheval, personne, dont on ne sait rien; (*b*) **h.
racing,** courses *fpl* de chevaux; **h. show,** concours *m* hippique. **2.** (*a*) *Gym:* (**vaulting**) **h.,**
cheval d'arçons; (*b*) (**clothes**) **h.,** séchoir *m*;
'**horseback,** *s.* **on h.,** à cheval; '**horse-
'chestnut,** *s.* marron *m* d'Inde; **h.-c.** (**tree**),
marronnier *m* d'Inde; '**horse-dealer,** *s.*
maquignon *m*; '**Horse Guards,** *s.pl.* **the
(Royal) H. G.,** le régiment de la Garde du
corps à cheval; '**horsehair,** *s.* crin *m* (de

cheval); '**horseman,** *f.* -**woman,** *s.* cavalier,
-ière; (bon) écuyer, (bonne) écuyère;
'**horsemanship,** *s.* (l'art de) l'équitation *f*;
'**horseplay,** *s.* jeux brutaux; conduite brutale;
'**horse-power,** *s. Aut: Mec:* (*abbr.* **h.p.**)
cheval-vapeur *m*; '**horse-radish,** *s. Cu:*
raifort *m*; '**horseshoe,** *s.* fer *m* à cheval;
'**hors(e)y,** *a.* (*of pers.*) hippomane; qui affecte
le langage, le costume, des grooms et des
jockeys.
horticulture ['hɔːtikʌltʃər], *s.* horticulture *f.*
hose [houz], *s.* **1.** *Com:* bas *mpl.* **2.** manche *f* à
eau; tuyau *m* flexible. **II.** *v.tr.* **to h.** (**down**) **the
car,** laver la voiture; '**hosiery,** *s. Com:*
bonneterie *f.*
hospitable [hɔs'pitəbl], *a.* hospitalier; accueillant; -**ably,** *adv.* hospitalièrement; d'une
manière accueillante; **hospi'tality,** *s*
hospitalité *f.*
hospital ['hɔspitl], *s.* hôpital *m*; **h. nurse,** infirmière *f*; **patients in h.,** les hospitalisés, -ées.
host [houst], *s.* **1.** (*a*) hôte *m*; (*b*) hôtelier *m*,
aubergiste *m*. **2.** *Ecc:* hostie *f*; '**hostess,** *s.f*
(*a*) hôtesse; (*b*) hôtelière; (*c*) **air h.,** hôtesse de
l'air.
hostage ['hɔstidʒ], *s.* otage *m.*
hostel ['hɔstəl], *s.* (*a*) foyer *m* (sous la direction
d'une œuvre sociale); (*b*) **youth h.,** auberge *f* de
la jeunesse.
hostile ['hɔstail], *a.* (*a*) hostile, ennemi; (*b*)
hostile, opposé (**to,** à); ennemi (**to,** de);
hos'tility [-tiliti], *s.* **1.** hostilité *f* (**to,** contre);
animosité *f*. **2.** *pl.* **hostilities,** hostilités; état *m* de
guerre.
hot [hɔt]. **I.** *a.* **1.** (*a*) chaud; **boiling h.,** bouillant
to be (**very**) **h.,** (*of thg*) être (très) chaud; (*o
pers.*) avoir (très) chaud; (*of weather*) fair
(très) chaud; **to get into h. water,** se créer de
ennuis; (*b*) brûlant; (*c*) *Cu:* piquant
(assaisonnement) épicé. **2. to be h. on th**
scent, être sur la bonne piste; *Games:* **you'r**
getting h., tu brûles; *P.T.T: F:* **h. line,** ligne
rouge. **3.** (*a*) violent; **to have a h. temper,** s'em
porter facilement; (*b*) (*of struggle*) acharné; **b**
contest, chaude dispute; **to be h. on the trail, i**
h. pursuit, of s.o., presser qn de près; *adv.phi*
they went at it h. and strong, ils y allaient ave
acharnement; *Rac:* **h. favourite,** grand favori
h. tip, tuyau *m* increvable. **4. to make thing**
too h. for s.o., rendre la vie intolérable à qi
things are getting too h., la situation devient in
tenable; **we are going to have a h. time,** ça v
chauffer; *P:* **h. car,** voiture volée. **II.** *v.* (**hotte**
v.tr. F: **to h. sth. up,** (i) chauffer, (ii) fair
réchauffer, qch.; *Aut:* **hotted-up engine,** moteu
gonflé; '**hot-'blooded,** *a.* (*of pers.*) emporté
passionné; '**hot 'dog,** *s.* hot dog *m*, petit pai
fourré d'une saucisse chaude; '**hothead,** :

(*pers.*) tête chaude, impétueux, -euse; '**hothouse**, *s.* serre chaude; '**hot-'tempered**, *a.* (*of pers.*) emporté, vif; **hot-'water bottle**, *s.* bouillotte *f.*

hotchpotch ['hɔtʃpɔtʃ], *s.* mélange confus.

hotel [hou'tel], *s.* hôtel *m*; **private h.**, **residential h.**, pension *f* de famille; **h.-keeper**, hôtelier, -ière.

hound [haund]. I. *s.* chien courant; **the (pack of) hounds**, la meute; **master of hounds**, maître *m* d'équipage; **to ride to hounds**, chasser à courre. II. *v.tr.* **to h. s.o. down**, poursuivre qn avec acharnement, sans relâche; **to be hounded from place to place**, être pourchassé d'un lieu à l'autre.

hour ['auər], *s.* heure *f*; **an h. and a half**, une heure et demie; **half an h.**, une demi-heure; **a quarter of an h.**, un quart d'heure; **h. by h.**, d'une heure à l'autre; **to pay s.o. by the h.**, payer qn à l'heure; *F:* **to take hours over sth.**, mettre un temps interminable à faire qch.; **five kilometres an h.**, cinq kilomètres à l'heure; **office hours**, heures de bureau; **after hours**, après l'heure de fermeture; **in the small hours (of the morning)**, fort avant dans la nuit; au petit matin; *a.* **h. hand**, petite aiguille (de montre, de pendule); '**hourly**. I. *a.* de toutes les heures; (salaire) à l'heure. II. *adv.* toutes les heures; d'heure en heure.

house, *pl.* -**ses** [haus, 'hauziz]. I. *s.* 1. (*a*) maison *f*; **town h.**, (i) (*large*) hôtel (particulier); (ii) (*small*) pavillon *m*; (iii) (*in row*) une entre plusieurs pavillons groupés; **country h.**, (i) (*large*) château *m*; (ii) (*small*) maison de campagne; **small h.**, maisonnette *f*; pavillon; **at, to, in, my h.**, chez moi; **to keep h. for s.o.**, tenir le ménage de qn; **to set up h.**, se mettre en ménage; **to move h.**, déménager; **to keep open h.**, tenir table ouverte; **h. of cards**, château de cartes; **h. telephone**, téléphone intérieur; *Parl: F:* **the H.**, la Chambre (i) des Communes, (ii) des Lords; *Fin: F:* **the H.**, la Bourse; (*b*) **business h.**, maison de commerce, *F:* boîte *f*; (*c*) **public h.**, café *m*, débit *m* de boissons; **a drink on the h.**, consommation offerte aux frais de la maison. 2. famille *f*, maison, dynastie *f*; **the H. of Valois**, les Valois, la maison des Valois; *Cin:* **first h.**, première séance. II. *v.tr.* [hauz], loger, héberger (qn); pourvoir au logement de (la population); caser (des ustensiles, des livres); '**house-agent**, *s.* agent immobilier; '**house-arrest**, *s.* **under h.-a.**, sous résidence surveillée; '**houseboat**, *s.* péniche aménagée en habitation; '**housebreaker**, *s.* 1. cambrioleur *m*. 2. *Const:* démolisseur *m*; '**housebreaking**, *s.* 1. cambriolage *m*. 2. *Const:* démolition *f*; '**housecoat**, *s. Cl:* peignoir *m*; robe *f*

d'intérieur; **quilted h.**, douillette *f*; '**housefly**, *s.* mouche *f* domestique; '**houseful**, *s.* maisonnée *f*; pleine maison (d'invités, etc.); '**household**, *s.* la famille; le ménage; **h. expenses**, frais *mpl* de ménage; **h. word**, mot *m* d'usage courant; '**householder**, *s.* chef *m* de famille; '**housekeeper**, *s.* 1. concierge *mf*. 2. femme *f* de charge; gouvernante *f* (d'un prêtre, etc.). 3. **my wife's a good h.**, ma femme est bonne ménagère; '**housekeeping**, *s.* 1. le ménage. 2. économie *f* domestique; les soins *m* du ménage; **h. money**, argent *m* pour les dépenses de ménage; '**housemaid**, *s.* bonne *f*; femme *f* de chambre; '**housemaster**, *s.m.*, '**housemistress**, *s.f. Sch:* professeur chargé de la surveillance d'un internat; '**houseroom**, *s.* place *f* (pour loger qn, qch.); **I wouldn't give it h.**, je n'en voudrais pas quand même on me le donnerait; '**house-surgeon**, *s. Med:* interne *m* (d'un hôpital); '**house-warming**, *s.* **h.-w. party**, réunion *f* d'amis pour fêter la pendaison de la crémaillère; '**housewife**, *pl.* -**wives**, *s.f.* maîtresse de maison, ménagère femme d'intérieur; '**housework**, *s.* travaux *m* domestiques; **to do the h.**, faire le ménage; **housing** ['hauziŋ], *s.* 1. logement *m*; **the h. problem**, la crise du logement; **h. estate**, cité *f*, groupe *m* de HLM. 2. *E: etc:* logement; bâti *m*; cage *f*; carter *m*; boîte *f*.

hovel ['hɔvl], *s.* taudis *m*; masure *f*.

hover ['hɔvər], *v.i.* (*of bird*) planer; (*of pers.*) errer, rôder (autour de qn); '**hovercraft**, *s. Nau:* hovercraft *m*, aéroglisseur *m*.

how [hau], *adv.* 1. comment; **h. do you do?** enchanté (de faire votre connaissance); **h. are you?** comment allez-vous? **h. is it that?** comment se fait-il que? **h.'s that? h. come?** comment ça? **to learn h. to do sth.**, apprendre à faire qch. 2. (*a*) **h. much, h. many**, combien (de); **you see h. little he cares**, vous voyez combien peu il s'en soucie; **h. long is this room?** quelle est la longueur de cette pièce? **h. old are you?** quel âge avez-vous? (*b*) **h. pretty she is!** comme elle est jolie! **h. I wish I could!** si seulement je pouvais!

however [hau'evər], *adv.* 1. (*a*) **h. he may do it**, de quelque manière qu'il le fasse; **h. that may be**, quoi qu'il en soit; (*b*) **h. good his work is**, quelque excellent que soit son ouvrage; **h. little**, si peu que ce soit. 2. toutefois, cependant, pourtant.

howl [haul]. I. *v.i. & tr.* hurler; pousser des hurlements; (*of wind*) mugir, rugir. II. *s.* (*also* '**howling**) hurlement *m*, mugissement *m* (du vent, etc.); '**howler**, *s.* grosse gaffe; bévue *f*; impair *m*; *Sch:* perle *f*; '**howling**. 1. *s.* See **howl** II. 2. *a.* **h. tempest**, tempête furieuse; *F:* **a h. success**, un succès fou; **h. injustice**, in-

justice criante.
hub [hʌb], *s.* **1.** moyeu *m* (de roue). **2.** centre *m* d'activité; **'hub-cap,** *s. Aut:* enjoliveur *m*.
hubbub ['hʌbʌb], *s.* remue-ménage *m inv,* vacarme *m*; **h. of voices,** brouhaha *m* de voix.
huddle ['hʌdl]. **I.** *v.tr. & i.* **1.** entasser pêle-mêle, sans ordre; **to h. together,** se tasser; se serrer les uns contre les autres. **2. huddled (up) in a corner,** blotti dans un coin. **II.** *s.* tas confus; fouillis *m*, ramassis *m*; *F:* **to go into a h.,** tenir une séance secrète.
hue[1] [hju:], *s.* teint *m*, couleur *f.*
hue[2], *s.* **h. and cry,** clameur *f* publique.
huff [hʌf], *s.* **to be in a h.,** être froissé; **'huffiness,** *s.* **1.** susceptibilité *f.* **2.** mauvaise humeur; **'huffy,** *a.* **1.** susceptible; **in a h. tone of voice,** d'un ton pincé. **2.** vexé, fâché; **he was very h. about it,** il a très mal pris la chose.
hug [hʌg], *v.tr.* **(hugged) 1.** étreindre, embrasser (qn). **2.** *Nau:* **to h. the shore,** raser, longer, la côte; **to h. the wind,** serrer le vent; *Aut:* **to h. the kerb,** serrer le plus près possible du trottoir.
huge [hju:dʒ], *a.* énorme, vaste; (succès) immense, formidable; **-ly,** *adv.* énormément; immensément.
hulk [hʌlk], *s.* carcasse *f* de navire; **'hulking,** *a.* gros, lourd.
hull [hʌl], *s.* coque *f* (de navire).
hullo [hʌ'lou], *int.* (*a*) ohé! holà! **h. you!** hé, là-bas! (*b*) (*expressing surprise*) **h., old chap!** tiens, c'est toi, mon vieux! (*c*) **h. everybody!** salut à tous! (*d*) *P.T.T:* allô!
hum [hʌm]. **I.** *v.* **(hummed) 1.** *v.i.* (*of insect*) bourdonner; (*of machine*) ronfler. **2.** *v.tr.* fredonner (un air). **II.** *s.* bourdonnement *m*; ronflement *m*; ronron *m* (d'un moteur); **'humming-bird,** *s.* oiseau-mouche *m, pl.* oiseaux-mouches.
human ['hju:mən]. **1.** *a.* humain; **h. being,** être humain; **h. nature,** la nature humaine. **2.** *s.* être humain; **'humanly,** *adv.* **everything h. possible,** tout ce qui est humainement possible; **humanity** [hju:'mæniti], *s.* humanité *f.*
humane [hju:(')'mein], *a.* (*a*) humain, compatissant; (*b*) (*of pers.*) clément; qui évite de faire souffrir; **-ly,** *adv.* humainement; avec humanité; **humanitarian** [hju:mæni'tɛəriən], *a. & s.* humanitaire (*mf*).
humble ['hʌmbl]. **I.** *a.* humble; modeste. **II.** *v.tr.* humilier, mortifier (qn); **to h. oneself,** s'abaisser; **to h. s.o.'s pride,** (r)abattre l'orgueil de qn; **'humbleness,** *s.* humilité *f.*
humbug ['hʌmbʌg]. **I.** *s.* **1.** charlatanisme *m*; blagues *fpl*; **h.!** tout cela c'est de la blague! **2.** (*pers.*) (*a*) charlatan *m*; blagueur *m*; (*b*) enjôleur, -euse. **3.** = bêtise *f* de Cambrai. **II.** *v.tr.* **(humbugged) to h. s.o.,** (i) conter des blagues à (qn); (ii) enjôler (qn).
humdrum ['hʌmdrʌm], *a.* (travail, existence)

monotone; **my h. daily life,** mon train-train quotidien.
humerus, *pl.* **-i** ['hju:mərəs, -ai], *s. Anat:* humérus *m.*
humid ['hju:mid], *a.* humide; (*of heat, skin*) moite; **hu'midifier,** *s.* humidificateur *m*; **hu'midify,** *v.tr.* humidifier (l'air, etc.); **hu'midity,** *s.* humidité *f*; **h.-proof,** étanche à l'humidité.
humiliate [hju(:)'milieit], *v.tr.* humilier, mortifier (qn); **humili'ation,** *s.* humiliation *f*, affront *m*, mortification *f*; **hu'mility,** *s.* humilité *f*; **with all h.,** en toute humilité.
humour ['hju:mər]. **I.** *s.* **1.** humeur *f*, disposition *f*; **to be in a good, bad, h.,** être de bonne, de mauvaise, humeur; **to be out of h.,** être (d'humeur) maussade. **2.** (*a*) humour *m*; **to have a (good) sense of h.,** avoir (le sens) de l'humour; (*b*) **the h. of the situation,** le comique de la situation. **II.** *v.tr.* **to h. s.o.,** ménager qn; **to h. s.o.'s fancy,** passer une fantaisie à qn; **'humorist,** *s.* **1.** farceur *m.* **2.** *Th:* comique. **3.** écrivain humoristique; humoriste *m*; **'humorous,** *a.* (*of pers.*) plein d'humour; drôle; comique; (*of writer*) humoriste, humoristique.
hump [hʌmp]. **I.** *s.* bosse *f* (de bossu, de chameau). **II.** *v.tr.* **to h. the back,** arquer, bomber, le dos; **'humpbacked,** *a.* (*of pers.*) bossu; (pont *m*) en dos d'âne.
humus ['hju:məs], *s. Hort:* humus *m*; terreau *m*; terre végétale.
hunch [hʌn(t)ʃ]. **I.** *v.tr.* arrondir (le dos); voûter (les épaules). **II.** *s. F:* **to have a h. that . . .,** soupçonner que . . .; avoir sa petite idée que . . .; **'hunchback,** *s.* (*pers.*) bossu, -ue.
hundred ['hʌndrəd], *num. a. & s.* cent (*m*); **about a h. houses,** une centaine de maisons; **two h. apples,** deux cents pommes; **two h. and one pounds,** deux cent une livres; **in 1900,** en dix-neuf cent; **to live to be a h.,** atteindre la centaine; **'hundredth,** *num. a. & s.* centième (*m*); **'hundredweight,** *s.* (*a*) poids *m* de 112 livres; (*b*) *N.Am:* poids de 100 livres.
Hungarian [hʌŋ'gɛəriən], *a. & s.* hongrois, -oise.
Hungary ['hʌŋgəri]. *Pr.n. Geog:* la Hongrie.
hunger ['hʌŋgər], *s.* faim *f*; **h. strike,** grève *f* de la faim; **'hungry,** *a.* **1.** affamé; **to be h.,** avoir faim; **to be ravenously h.,** avoir une faim de loup. **2. a h. look,** l'œil *m* avide; **hungrily,** *adv.* avidement; voracement.
hunk [hʌŋk], *s.* gros morceau (de fromage); quignon *m* (de pain).
hunt [hʌnt]. **I.** *s.* (*a*) chasse *f*; *esp.* chasse à courre, aux fauves; (*b*) équipage *m* de chasse. **II.** *v.* **1.** *v.i.* (*a*) chasser à courre; (*b*) **to h. for sth.,** chercher qch. **2.** *v.tr.* (*a*) chasser

renard, etc.); (b) **to h. a thief,** poursuivre un voleur; (c) **to h. a horse,** monter un cheval à la chasse; **to h. the pack,** diriger la meute; **'hunt 'down,** v.tr. traquer, mettre aux abois (une bête); **'hunter,** s. 1. chasseur m; tueur m (de lions, etc.). 2. cheval m de chasse; **'hunting,** s. (a) chasse f (à courre); (b) **bargain h.,** la chasse aux soldes; **to go house h.,** se mettre à la recherche d'une maison, d'un logement; (c) **h. ground,** (i) terrain m de chasse; (ii) endroit m propice (aux collectionneurs, etc.); **'hunt 'out,** v.tr. 1. déterrer, dénicher (qch.) (à force de recherches). 2. aller relancer (qn); **'huntsman,** pl. -men, s. veneur m, piqueur m.

hurdle ['hə:dl], s. 1. claie f. 2. Sp: barrière f, obstacle m; (horse racing) haie f.

hurl [hə:l], v.tr. lancer (qch.) avec violence (**at,** contre); **to h. oneself at s.o.,** se ruer sur qn; **to h. reproaches at s.o.,** accabler qn de reproches.

hurrah [hu'rɑ:], **hurray** [hu'rei], int. & s. hourra (m).

hurricane ['hʌrikən], s. ouragan m.

hurry ['hʌri]. I. v. 1. v.tr. hâter, presser, bousculer (qn); **work that cannot be hurried,** travail m qui demande du temps. 2. v.i. (a) se hâter, se presser; se dépêcher; **h. up!** dépêchez-vous! (b) presser le pas; **to h. to a place,** se rendre en toute hâte à un endroit. II. s. hâte f; précipitation f; **to be in a h.,** être pressé; **'hurried,** a. (pas) précipité, pressé; (travail) fait à la hâte; -ly, adv. à la hâte, en toute hâte; précipitamment.

hurt [hə:t], v.tr. (hurt) 1. faire (du) mal à, blesser (qn); **to h. one's foot,** se blesser au pied; **to be, get, h.,** être blessé. 2. faire de la peine à (qn); **to h. s.o.'s feelings,** blesser, peiner, qn. 3. nuire à, abimer (qch.); **'hurtful,** a. nuisible, nocif; préjudiciable (à qn).

hurtle ['hə:tl], v.i. se précipiter, s'élancer (avec bruit, comme un bolide).

husband ['hʌzbənd], s. mari m, époux m; **h. and wife,** les (deux) époux.

hush [hʌʃ]. I. v. 1. v.tr. apaiser, faire taire (qn, un bébé); imposer silence à (qn). 2. v.i. se taire; faire silence. II. s. silence m, calme m. III. int. chut! silence! **'hush-'hush,** a. F: secret; **'hush 'up,** v.tr. étouffer (un scandale).

husk [hʌsk], s. cosse f, gousse f (de pois, etc.); écale f (de noix); balle f (de grain); **rice in the h.,** riz non décortiqué.

husky¹ ['hʌski], a. (of voice) (i) enroué, voilé; (ii) altéré (par l'émotion); **'huskiness,** s. enrouement m, empâtement m (de la voix).

husky², s. chien m esquimau.

hustle ['hʌsl]. I. v. 1. v.tr. bousculer, pousser, presser (qn); **to h. things on,** pousser le travail. 2. v.i. se dépêcher, se presser. II. s. 1. bousculade f. 2. activité f énergique; **'hustler,** s. (pers.) débrouillard m; brasseur m d'affaires; abatteur m de besogne.

hut [hʌt], s. hutte f, cabane f; **mountain h.,** refuge m.

hutch [hʌtʃ], s. (**rabbit-)h.,** clapier m.

hyacinth ['haiəsinθ], s. Bot: jacinthe f.

hybrid ['haibrid], a. & s. Biol: hybride (m).

hydrangea [hai'drein(d)ʒə], s. hortensia m.

hydrant ['haidrənt], s. prise f d'eau; **fire h.,** bouche f d'eau.

hydraulic [hai'drɔ:lik], a. hydraulique.

hydrochloric [haidrou'klɔrik], a. Ch: (acide) chlorhydrique.

hydroelectric ['haidroui'lektrik], a. hydro(-)électrique; **h. power,** énergie f hydraulique, houille blanche; **'hydroelec'tricity,** s. E: hydro(-)électricité.

hydrofoil ['haidroufɔil], s. hydrofoil m.

hydrogen ['haidrədʒən], s. Ch: hydrogène m.

hydrophobia [haidrə'foubiə], s. Med: hydrophobie f; F: la rage.

hydroplane ['haidrouplein], s. hydroglisseur m.

hyena [hai'i:nə], s. Z: hyène f.

hygiene ['haidʒi:n], s. hygiène f; **hy'gienic,** a. hygiénique; -ally, adv. hygiéniquement.

hymn [him], s. Ecc: hymne f, cantique m; **'hymn-book,** s recueil m de cantiques.

hymnal ['himnəl], s. recueil m de cantiques.

hypermarket ['haipəmɑ:kit], s. hypermarché m.

hypersensitive [haipə'sensitiv], a. hypersensible.

hyphen ['haif(ə)n], s. trait m d'union; **'hyphenate,** v.tr. mettre un trait d'union à (un mot); **hyphenated word,** mot m qui s'écrit avec un trait d'union.

hypnosis [hip'nousis], s. hypnose f; **hypnotism** ['hipnətizm], s. hypnotisme m; **hypnotic** [hip'nɔtik], a. hypnotique; **'hypnotist,** s. hypnotiste mf; **'hypnotize,** v.tr. hypnotiser.

hypochondria [haipou'kɔndriə], s. hypocondrie f; **hypo'chondriac,** a. & s. hypocondriaque (mf); malade mf imaginaire.

hypocrisy [hi'pɔkrisi], s. hypocrisie f; **hypocrite** ['hipəkrit], s. hypocrite mf; **hypo'critical,** a. hypocrite; -ally, adv. hypocritement.

hypodermic [haipə'də:mik], a. **h. syringe,** seringue f hypodermique.

hypotenuse [hai'pɔtinju:z], s. Mth: hypoténuse f.

hypothesis, pl. -ses [hai'pɔθisis, -si:z], s. hypothèse f.

hypothetical [haipə'θetikl], a. hypothétique, supposé; -ally, adv. par hypothèse.

hysteria [his'tiəriə], s. Med: hystérie f; **hysterical** [his'terikl], a. (a) Med: hystérique; (b) sujet à des crises de nerfs; **h. laugh,** rire nerveux, énervé; **h. sobs,** sanglots convulsifs; -ally, adv. **to laugh h.,** rire nerveusement; avoir le fou rire; **to weep h.,** avoir une crise de larmes; **hys'terics,** s.pl. (a) crise f de nerfs; (b) fou rire.

I

I¹, i [ai], *s.* (la lettre) I, i *m*; **to dot one's i's,** mettre les points sur les i.

I², pers. pron. (*a*) je (*before vowel sound*) j'; **I sing,** je chante; (*b*) moi; **it is I,** c'est moi; (*stressed*) **'I'll do it,** c'est moi qui le ferai; **'he and 'I are great friends,** lui et moi, nous sommes de grands amis.

ice [ais]. **I.** *s.* glace *f.* **1. my feet are like i.,** j'ai les pieds glacés; **to break the i.,** (i) rompre la glace; (ii) faire cesser la contrainte; (iii) entamer un sujet (délicat); **to skate on thin i.,** toucher à un sujet délicat; **to cut no i. with s.o.,** ne faire aucune impression sur qn; **to put a project on i.,** mettre un projet en suspens. **2.** (*a*) *Cu:* **strawberry i.,** glace à la fraise; (*b*) *Ind:* **dry i.,** neige *f* carbonique. **3.** *attrib.* **i. axe,** piolet *m*; **i. floe,** banquise *f*; banc *m* de glace; **i. hockey,** hockey *m* sur glace; **i. skating,** patinage *m* (sur glace). **II.** *v.* **1.** *v.tr.* geler, congeler. **2.** *v.tr.* rafraîchir, frapper (une boisson). **3.** *v.tr.* glacer (un gâteau). **4.** *v.i.* **to i. up,** se givrer; **'ice-age,** *s.* période *f* glaciaire; **'iceberg,** *s.* iceberg *m*; **'ice-breaker,** *s.* brise-glace(s) *m*; **'ice-'cream,** *s.* glace *f*; **'ice cube,** *s.* glaçon *m*; **'icehouse,** *s.* glacière *f*; **it's an i. in here,** on gèle ici; **'icicle,** *s.* glaçon *m*; **'iciness,** *s.* **1.** froid glacial. **2.** froideur glaciale (d'un accueil); **'icing,** *s.* glace *f* (sur un gâteau); **i. sugar,** sucre *m* à glacer; **'icy,** *a.* **1.** couvert de glace; glacial; **i. road,** route verglacée. **2.** (vent, accueil) glacial; **i. hands,** mains glacées; **'icily,** *adv.* glacialement, d'un air glacial.

Iceland ['aisland]. *Pr.n. Geog:* l'Islande *f*; **'Icelander,** *s.* Islandais, -aise; **Ice'landic,** (*a*) *a.* islandais, d'Islande; (*b*) *s. Ling:* l'islandais *m.*

idea [ai'diə], *s.* idée *f*; **what a funny i.!** quelle drôle d'idée! **to have some i. of chemistry,** avoir des notions de chimie; **I have an i. that . . .,** j'ai idée que . . .; **I had no i. that . . .,** I **hadn't the faintest i.** that . . ., j'ignorais absolument que . . .; j'étais loin de me douter que . . .; **I have an i. that I've already seen it,** j'ai l'impression de l'avoir déjà vu; **to get ideas into one's head,** se faire des idées; *F:* **what's the big i.?** qu'est-ce qui vous prend?

ideal [ai'di:əl], *a. & s.* idéal (*m*); **i'dealism,** *s.* idéalisme *m*; **i'dealist,** *s.* idéaliste *mf*; **i'dealize,** *v.tr.* idéaliser; **i'deally,** *adv.* idéalement.

identify [ai'dentifai], *v.tr.* **1.** identifier (**sth. with** sth., qch. avec qch.). **2. to i.** s.o., constater, établir, l'identité de qn; **i'dentical,** *a.* identique (**with, to, à**); **-ally,** *adv.* identiquement; **identifi'cation,** *s.* identification *f*; **i'dentikit.** *s.* **i. picture,** photo-robot *m*, *pl.* photos robots; **i'dentity,** *s.* identité *f*; **i. card,** carte *f* d'identité; **mistaken i.,** erreur *f* sur la personne.

ideology [aidi'ɔlədʒi], *s.* idéologie *f* **ideo'logical,** *a.* idéologique.

idiom ['idiəm], *s.* **1.** langue *f*, idiome *m* (d'un pays, d'une région). **2.** idiotisme *m*, locution *f* **idio'matic,** *a.* idiomatique; **i. phrase,** idiotisme *m*; **-ally,** *adv.* (parler, s'exprimer) d'une façon idiomatique.

idiosyncrasy [idiou'siŋkrəsi], *s.* **1.** idiosyncrasi *f.* **2.** petite manie; particularité *f* (de style).

idiot ['idiət], *s.* (*a*) *Med:* idiot, -ote; (*b*) imbécil *mf*; *F:* **you i.!** espèce d'imbécile! **'idiocy,** *s.* (*a* idiotie (congénitale); (*b*) stupidité *f*; **idioti** [idi'ɔtik], *a.* bête; **don't be i.!** ne fais pa l'imbécile! **that's i.,** ça, c'est stupide; **-ally** *adv.* bêtement, stupidement.

idle ['aidl]. **I.** *a.* **1.** (*a*) inoccupé, oisif; (*b*) (machine) au repos; **capital lying i.,** fonds do mants. **2.** paresseux, fainéant. **3.** inutile; futil **i. threats,** menaces en l'air; **out of i. curiosit** par simple curiosité; **'idly,** *adv.* **1.** sa travailler. **2.** paresseusement. **II.** *v.i.* **1.** (*de pers.*) fainéanter, paresser; flâner. **2.** (*engine*) tourner au ralenti; **'idleness,** *s.* **1.** oisiveté *f*, désœuvrement *m*. **2.** paresse fainéantise *f*; **'idler,** *s.* **1.** oisif, -ive; désœuvr -ée; flâneur, -euse. **2.** fainéant, -ant paresseux, -euse.

idol ['aidl], *s.* idole *f*; **idolatrous** [ai'dɔlətrəs]. idolâtre; **i'dolatry,** *s.* idolâtrie *f*; **'idolize,** *v.* idolâtrer, adorer (qn, qch.).

idyllic [i'dilik], *a.* idyllique.

if [if], *conj.* si. **1.** (*a*) **if I'm late I apologize,** si suis en retard, je fais mes excuses; **if I want** **him I rang,** si j'avais besoin de lui, je sonna (*b*) **if he does it he will be punished,** s'il le fai sera puni; **if I am free I shall go out,** si je s libre, je sortirai; **if I were free I would go o** si j'étais libre, je sortirais; **if they are to** **believed nobody was saved,** à les croire, p sonne n'aurait survécu; **you'll get five per** **for it, if that,** on vous en donnera cinq penc encore! **if not,** sinon; **go and see him, if only** **please me,** allez le voir, ne serait-ce que p me faire plaisir; (*c*) **if I were you,** si j'étais vo

I:1

à votre place; (*d*) (*exclamatory*) **if only I had known!** si seulement je l'avais su! **if only he comes in time!** pourvu qu'il vienne à temps! (*e*) **as if,** comme (si); **as if by chance,** comme par hasard. **2.** (*concessive*) **pleasant weather, if rather cold,** temps agréable, bien qu'un peu froid. **3.** (= *whether*) **do you know if he is at home?** savez-vous s'il est chez lui? **4.** *s.* **your ifs and buts,** vos si (*inv.*) et vos mais; **it's a very big if,** c'est une condition difficile à remplir.

igloo ['iglu:], *s.* igloo *m*.

ignite [ig'nait]. **1.** *v.tr.* mettre le feu à (qch.); enflammer (du bois). **2.** *v.i.* prendre feu; s'enflammer; **ignition** [ig'niʃən], *s.* **1.** ignition *f*. **2.** *Aut:* allumage *m*; **i. key,** clef *f* de contact.

ignoble [ig'noubl], *a.* ignoble; infâme, vil, indigne.

ignominious [ignə'miniəs], *a.* ignominieux; honteux; **-ly,** *adv.* avec ignominie; **'ignominy,** *s.* ignominie *f*, honte *f*.

ignore [ig'nɔ:r], *v.tr.* ne tenir aucun compte de (qch.); passer (qch.) sous silence; **to i. s.o.,** ne pas vouloir reconnaître qn; **to i. the facts,** méconnaître les faits; **to i. an invitation,** ne pas répondre à une invitation; **ignorance** ['ignərəns], *s.* ignorance *f*; **to keep s.o. in i. of sth.,** laisser ignorer qch. à qn; **i. of the law is no excuse,** nul n'est censé ignorer la loi; **'ignorant,** *a.* ignorant; **to be i. of a fact,** ignorer un fait.

ill [il]. **I.** *a.* **1.** (*a*) mauvais; **i. effects,** effets pernicieux; **of i. repute,** mal famé; (*b*) méchant, mauvais; **i. deed,** mauvaise action. **2.** malade, souffrant; **i. health,** mauvaise santé. **II.** *s.* **1.** mal *m*; **to speak i. of s.o.,** dire du mal de qn. **2.** dommage *m*, tort *m*. **III.** *adv.* mal; **i. informed,** (i) mal renseigné; (ii) ignorant; **to be i. at ease,** (i) être mal à l'aise; (ii) être inquiet; **'ill-ad'vised,** *a.* **1.** malavisé. **2.** (*of action*) peu judicieux; **'ill-'bred,** *a.* mal élevé; malappris; **'ill-dis'posed,** *a.* malintentionné, malveillant; **'ill-'fated,** *a.* (*of pers.*) infortuné; (*jour m*) néfaste; **'ill-'feeling,** *s.* ressentiment *m*, rancune *f*; **no i.-f.!** sans rancune! **ill-'gotten,** *a.* (bien) mal acquis; **'ill-'humoured,** *a.* de mauvaise humeur; maussade, grincheux; **'ill-'mannered,** *a.* grossier; impoli; **'ill-'natured,** *a.* méchant; désagréable; **-ly,** *adv.* méchamment; **'illness,** *s.* maladie *f*; **'ill-'timed,** *a.* mal à propos; **i.-t. arrival,** arrivée inopportune; **'ill-'treat,** *v.tr.* maltraiter, brutaliser (qn, un animal); **'ill-'treatment,** *s.* mauvais traitements; **'ill-'will,** *s.* malveillance *f*, rancune *f*.

illegal [i'li:g(ə)l], *a.* illégal; **-ally,** *adv.* illégalement.

illegible [i'ledʒibl], *a.* illisible; **-ibly,** *adv.* illisiblement.

illegitimate [ili'dʒitimət], *a.* illégitime.

illicit [i'lisit], *a.* illicite; clandestin; **i. betting,** paris clandestins.

illiteracy [i'lit(ə)rəsi], *s.* analphabétisme *m*; **i'lliterate,** *a. & s.* analphabète (*mf*); illettré (-ée).

illogical [i'lɔdʒik(ə)l], *a.* illogique; peu logique; **-ally,** *adv.* illogiquement.

illuminate [i'l(j)u:mineit], *v.tr.* **1.** éclairer (une salle, l'esprit de qn). **2.** illuminer (un bâtiment pour une fête). **3.** enluminer (un manúscrit); **illumi'nation,** *s.* **1.** (*a*) éclairage *m*; (*b*) illumination *f* (d'un édifice). **2.** (*usu.pl.*) enluminures *fpl* (d'un manuscrit); **i'lluminating,** *a.* **1.** éclairant. **2.** **i. talk,** entretien *m* qui apporte des éclaircissements.

illusion [i'l(j)u:ʒ(ə)n], *s.* illusion *f*; tromperie *f*; **he had no illusions on that point,** il ne se faisait aucune illusion à cet égard; **i'llusionist,** *s.* prestidigitateur *m*; illusionniste *mf*; **i'llusory,** *a.* illusoire.

illustrate ['iləstreit], *v.tr.* **1.** expliquer, démontrer par des exemples. **2.** illustrer; orner (un livre) de gravures; **illus'tration,** *s.* **1.** explication *f*, exemple *m*. **2.** illustration *f*, gravure *f*, image *f*; **'illustrator,** *s.* illustrateur *m*.

illustrious [i'lʌstriəs], *a.* illustre, célèbre.

image ['imidʒ], *s.* image *f*. **1.** image sculptée; représentation *f* (d'un dieu); idole *f*. **2.** **he's the living i. of his father,** c'est le portrait vivant de son père. **3.** (*public*) **i.,** image de marque.

imagine [i'mædʒin], *v.tr.* **1.** (*a*) imaginer, concevoir; se figurer, se représenter (qch.); **i. yourself in Paris,** supposez que vous êtes à Paris; **as may (well) be imagined,** comme on peut (se) l'imaginer; (*b*) **I i. them to be fairly rich,** je les crois assez riches. **2. to be always imagining things,** se faire des idées; **I imagined I heard a knock at the door,** j'ai cru entendre frapper à la porte; **i'maginable,** *a.* imaginable; **i'maginary,** *a.* imaginaire; **imagi'nation,** *s.* imagination *f*; **it's your i.!** vous avez rêvé! **i'maginative,** *a.* imaginatif.

imbalance [im'bæləns], *s.* déséquilibre *m*.

imbecile ['imbisil], *s.* imbécile *mf*; *F:* **you i.!** espèce d'idiot! **imbe'cility** [-'siliti], *s.* imbécillité *f*; faiblesse *f* d'esprit.

imbibe [im'baib], *v.tr.* (*a*) absorber, s'assimiler (des connaissances); (*b*) boire, avaler (une boisson); aspirer (l'air frais); (*c*) (*of thg*) imbiber (qch.); s'imprégner, se pénétrer, de (qch.).

imitate ['imiteit], *v.tr.* (*a*) imiter, copier; (*b*) mimer, singer (qn); contrefaire (la voix de qn); **imi'tation,** *s.* (*a*) imitation *f*; **beware of imitations,** méfiez-vous des contrefaçons *f*; (*b*) *attrib.* factice; **i. jewellery,** bijoux en simili; **'imitative** [-tətiv], *a.* imitatif; **'imitator,** *s.*

imitateur, -trice.

immaculate [i'mækjulət], *a.* 1. immaculé; sans tache; the I. Conception, l'Immaculée Conception. 2. (*of dress*) irréprochable, impeccable; -ly, *adv.* 1. sans défaut. 2. (vêtu) impeccablement.

immaterial [imə'tiəriəl], *a.* 1. (esprit) immatériel. 2. peu important; that's quite i. to me, cela m'est indifférent.

immature [imə'tjuər], *a.* pas mûr; (*of plan*) pas suffisamment mûri; (*of pers.*) très jeune (pour son âge).

immediate [i'mi:djət], *a.* immédiat. 1. sans intermédiaire; direct; my i. object, mon premier but; in the i. future, dans l'immédiat *m*; in the i. vicinity, dans le voisinage immédiat. 2. instantané; sans retard; -ly. I. *adv.* immédiatement; (*a*) it does not affect me i., cela ne me touche pas directement; (*b*) tout de suite; i. on his return, dès son retour; i. after, aussitôt après. II. *conj.* i. he received the money, dès qu'il eut reçu l'argent.

immemorial [imi'mɔːriəl], *a.* from time i., de toute antiquité.

immense [i'mens], *a.* (étendue) immense, vaste; (quantité) énorme; -ly, *adv.* immensément; *F:* to enjoy oneself i., s'amuser énormément; i'mmensity, *s.* immensité *f.*

immerse [i'mɜːs], *v.tr.* 1. immerger, submerger, plonger (qch.) (dans un liquide). 2. to be immersed in one's work, s'absorber dans son travail; i'mmersion, *s.* immersion *f*; i. heater, (i) chauffe-eau *m inv* électrique; (ii) élément chauffant.

immigrate ['imigreit], *v.i.* immigrer; 'immigrant, *a. & s.* immigrant, -ante; immigré, -ée; immi'gration, *s.* immigration *f.*

imminent ['iminənt], *a.* (danger, etc.) imminent; 'imminence, *s.* imminence *f*, proximité *f* (of, de).

immobile [i'moubail], *a.* fixe; immobile; immo'bility [-'bili-], *s.* immobilité *f*; immobili'zation [-bilai-], *s.* immobilisation *f* (i) *Med:* d'un membre fracturé, (ii) de la circulation, (iii) *Fin:* de capitaux; i'mmobilize [-bil-], *v.tr.* immobiliser.

immoderate [i'mɔdərət], *a.* immodéré, intempéré; extravagant; -ly, *adv.* immodérément.

immoral [i'mɔrəl], *a.* immoral; (*of pers.*) dissolu; immo'rality, *s.* immoralité *f.*

immortal [i'mɔːtl], *a. & s.* immortel (*m*); immor'tality, *s.* immortalité *f*; i'mmortalize, *v.tr.* immortaliser (qn, le nom de qn); perpétuer (la mémoire de qn).

immovable [i'muːvəbl], *a.* 1. fixe; à demeure. 2. (volonté) inébranlable. 3. (visage) impassible; -ably, *adv.* 1. sans bouger. 2. immuablement;

inébranlablement.

immune [i'mjuːn], *a. Med:* à l'abri (de la contagion); immunisé; i'mmunity, *s.* immunité *f*; immuni'zation, *s.* immunisation *f*; 'immunize, *v.tr.* immuniser (qn) (against, contre (une maladie).

immutable [i'mjuːtəbl], *a.* immuable; inaltérable; -ably, *adv.* immuablement.

imp [imp], *s.* (*a*) diablotin *m*, lutin *m*; (*b*) (child) petit diable.

impact ['impækt], *s.* choc *m*, impact *m*.

impair [im'pɛər], *v.tr.* affaiblir; altérer, abîmer (la santé); diminuer (les forces).

impart [im'pɑːt], *v.tr.* communiquer (des connaissances).

impartial [im'pɑːʃ(ə)l], *a.* (*of pers., conduct*) impartial; -ally, *adv.* impartialement; impar-ti'ality, *s.* impartialité *f.*

impassable [im'pɑːsəbl], *a.* infranchissable; (chemin) impraticable.

impassioned [im'pæʃ(ə)nd], *a.* (discours) passionné, exalté.

impassive [im'pæsiv], *a.* impassible; (visage) composé; -ly, *adv.* sans s'émouvoir.

impatient [im'peiʃ(ə)nt], *a.* impatient; to get s'impatienter; -ly, *adv.* avec impatience; i patiemment; im'patience, *s.* (*a*) impatience (*b*) intolérance *f.*

impeach [im'piːtʃ], *v.tr. Jur:* accuser (qn) haute trahison, etc.).

impeccable [im'pekəbl], *a.* impeccable; -ab *adv.* de façon irréprochable; impeccableme

impecunious [impi'kjuːniəs], *a.* impécunie besogneux.

impede [im'piːd], *v.tr.* mettre obstacle empêcher, entraver (qn, qch.); impedime [im'pedimənt], *s.* empêchement *m*, obstacle (to, à).

impel [im'pel], *v.tr.* (impelled) 1. pousser, for (s.o. to do sth., qn à faire qch.). 2. pousser avant); boat impelled by the wind, bat poussé par le vent.

impending [im'pendiŋ], *a.* (danger) immin menaçant; her i. arrival, son arrivée procha

impenetrable [im'penitrəbl], *a.* impénétra (to, à); i. mystery, mystère *m* insonda -ably, *adv.* impénétrablement; i penetra'bility, *s.* impénétrabilité *f.*

impenitent [im'penitənt], *a.* impénitent.

imperative [im'perətiv], 1. *a. & s. Gram:* pératif (*m*). 2. *a.* urgent, impérieux; discre is i., la discrétion s'impose; -ly, *a* impérativement.

imperceptible [impə'septibl], *a.* impercepti (bruit) insaisissable; an i. difference, différence insensible; -ibly, *adv.* imper tiblement, insensiblement.

imperfect [im'pɜːfikt], 1. *a.* imparfait,

complet, défectueux. **2.** *a. & s. Gram:* **i. (tense)**, (temps) imparfait (*m*); **-ly,** *adv.* imparfaitement; **imper′fection,** *s.* imperfection *f*, défectuosité *f*.

imperial [im′piəriəl], *a.* impérial; **-ally,** *adv.* impérialement; **im′perialism,** *s.* impérialisme *m*.

imperil [im′peril], *v.tr.* **(imperilled)** mettre en péril, en danger.

imperious [im′piəriəs], *a.* impérieux, arrogant; **-ly,** *adv.* impérieusement.

impermeable [im′pə:miəbl], *a.* imperméable, étanche.

impersonal [im′pə:sənəl], *a.* (style) impersonnel; *Gram:* **i. verb,** verbe impersonnel; **-ally,** *adv.* impersonnellement.

impersonate [im′pə:səneit], *v.tr.* se faire passer pour (qn); **imperso′nation,** *s.* imitation *f* (de qn); **im′personator,** *s.* (*a*) imitateur, -trice; (*b*) personne qui se fait passer pour une autre (en substitution frauduleuse).

impertinence [im′pə:tinəns], *s.* impertinence *f*, insolence *f*; **a piece of i.,** une impertinence; **im′pertinent,** *a.* impertinent, insolent; **-ly,** *adv.* avec impertinence; d′un ton insolent.

imperturbable [impə(:)′tə:bəbl], *a.* imperturbable; calme; impassible; **-ably,** *adv.* imperturbablement, avec sang-froid; **imperturba′bility,** *s.* imperturbabilité *f*; flegme *m*; sang-froid *m*.

impervious [im′pə:viəs], *a.* (*a*) impénétrable; **i. to water,** imperméable, étanche à l′eau; (*b*) (*of pers.*) **i. to humour, to reason,** fermé à la plaisanterie, à la raison; **im′perviousness,** *s.* (*a*) impénétrabilité; (*b*) imperméabilité *f*; étanchéité *f*.

impetigo [impi′taigou], *s. Med:* impétigo *m*; *F:* gourme *f*.

impetuous [im′petjuəs], *a.* impétueux; **-ly,** *adv.* impétueusement; **impetu′osity,** **im-′petuousness,** *s.* impétuosité *f*.

impetus [′impitəs], *s.* vitesse acquise; élan *m*; **to give an i. to sth.,** donner l′impulsion à qch.

implacable [im′plækəbl], *a.* implacable (towards s.o., à, pour, qn); **-ably,** *adv.* implacablement.

implement[1] [′implimənt], *s.* outil *m*, instrument *m*, ustensile *m*.

implement[2] [′impliment], *v.tr.* rendre effectif (un contrat); remplir (un engagement); accomplir une promesse).

implicate [′implikeit], *v.tr.* impliquer; **impli′cation,** *s.* **1.** implication *f* (in, dans); **the i. of his words,** la portée de ses paroles; **by i.,** implicitement. **2.** insinuation *f*.

implicit [im′plisit], *a.* (condition) implicite; **i. faith,** confiance aveugle (**in,** dans); **i. obedience,** obéissance absolue; **-ly,** *adv.* **to**

obey i., obéir aveuglément.

implore [im′plɔ:r], *v.tr.* implorer; **to i. s.o. to do sth.,** supplier qn de faire qch.

imply [im′plai], *v.tr.* **1.** impliquer; **the questions implied,** les questions en jeu. **2. you seem to i. that . . .,** ce que vous dites fait supposer que . . .; **im′plied,** *a.* (consentement) implicite, tacite.

impolite [impə′lait], *a.* impoli (**to, towards,** envers); **-ly,** *adv.* impoliment; **impo′liteness,** *s.* impolitesse *f*.

import. I. *s.* [′impɔ:t]. **1.** sens *m*, signification *f* (d′un mot). **2.** (*usu. pl.*) *Com:* **imports,** articles *m* d′importation; importations *f*; **i. duty,** droit *m* d′entrée. **II.** *v.tr.* [im′pɔ:t], *Com:* importer (des marchandises); **impor′tation,** *s.* importation *f*; **im′porter,** *s.* importateur, -trice.

importance [im′pɔ:təns], *s.* (*a*) importance *f*; **to give i. to a word,** mettre un mot en valeur; **to attach the greatest i. to a fact,** tenir le plus grand compte d′un fait; (*b*) importance, conséquence *f* (d′une personne); **people of i.,** personnages importants; **im′portant,** *a.* (*a*) important; (*b*) (*of pers.*) **to look i.,** prendre des airs d′importance.

importune [impɔ:′tju:n], *v.tr.* importuner (qn); **im′portunate,** *a.* importun; (visiteur) ennuyeux; **impor′tunity,** *s.* importunité *f*.

impose [im′pouz]. **1.** *v.tr.* (*a*) **to i. conditions on s.o.,** imposer des conditions à qn; (*b*) **to i. a tax on sugar,** imposer, taxer, le sucre; **to i. a penalty on s.o.,** infliger une peine à qn. **2.** *v.i.* **to i. (up)on s.o.,** en imposer à qn; abuser de l′amabilité de qn; **im′posing,** *a.* (air) imposant; (spectacle) grandiose; **impo′sition,** *s.* **1.** imposition *f* (i) de conditions, (ii) d′une tâche, (iii) d′une taxe, d′un impôt. **2.** abus *m* de la bonne volonté de qn.

impossible [im′pɔsəbl, -ibl], *a.* (*a*) impossible; (*b*) (histoire) invraisemblable; **i. person,** personne *f* difficile à vivre; **impossi′bility,** *s.* impossibilité *f*; chose *f* impossible.

impostor [im′pɔstər], *s.* imposteur *m*; **im-′posture,** *s.* imposture *f*.

impotence [′impətəns], *s.* (*a*) *Med:* impuissance (sexuelle); (*b*) impotence *f*; faiblesse *f*; ′**impotent,** *a.* (*a*) *Med:* impuissant; (*b*) impotent; décrépit; **-ly,** *adv.* sans force.

impound [im′paund], *v.tr.* confisquer, saisir (des marchandises).

impoverish [im′pɔvəriʃ], *v.tr.* appauvrir (qn, un pays); **im′poverishment,** *s.* appauvrissement *m* (d′un pays); dégradation *f* (du sol).

impracticable [im′præktikəbl], *a.* infaisable, impraticable.

impractical [im′præktikl], *a.* (projet) impraticable.

impregnable [im'pregnəbl], *a.* (forteresse) imprenable, inexpugnable.

impregnate ['impregneit], *v.tr.* imprégner (**sth. with sth.**, qch. de qch.).

impresario [impre'sa:riou], *s.* impresario *m.*

impress. **I.** *s.* ['impres], (*a*) impression *f,* empreinte *f;* (*b*) marque distinctive; cachet *m.* **II.** *v.tr.* [im'pres]. **1.** imprimer (un dessin sur du tissu). **2. to i. sth. upon s.o.,** faire bien comprendre qch. à qn. **3.** faire impression sur (qn); impressionner (qn); **he impressed me,** il m'a fait une impression favorable; **I'm not impressed,** cela me laisse froid; je ne m'emballe pas; **im'pression,** *s.* **1.** impression *f;* **to make a good i. on s.o.,** faire une bonne impression sur qn. **2.** tirage *m,* édition *f* (d'un livre); **im-'pressionable,** *a.* (*of pers.*) impressionnable; sensible; **im'pressionism,** *s. Art:* impressionnisme *m;* **im'pressionist,** *s. Art:* impressionniste *mf;* **impressio'nistic,** *a.* impressionniste; **im'pressive,** *a.* impressionnant; **-ly,** *adv.* d'une manière impressionnante.

imprint ['imprint], *s.* **1.** empreinte *f.* **2.** firme *f,* rubrique *f* (d'un éditeur).

imprison [im'prizn], *v.tr.* emprisonner (qn); **im-'prisonment,** *s.* emprisonnement *m.*

improbable [im'prɔbəbl], *a.* improbable; (histoire *f*) invraisemblable; **-ably,** *adv.* improbablement; **improba'bility,** *s.* improbabilité *f;* invraisemblance *f.*

impromptu [im'prɔm(p)tju:]. **I.** *adv.* (faire qch.) sans préparation; impromptu. **II.** *a.* (discours) impromptu *inv,* improvisé. **III.** *s. Lit: Mus:* impromptu *m.*

improper [im'prɔpər], *a.* **1.** (expression) impropre; (terme) inexact. **2.** choquant; inconvenant; **-ly,** *adv.* **1. word i. used,** mot employé abusivement. **2.** (se conduire) d'une façon inconvenante; **impropriety** [im-prə'praiəti], *s.* (*a*) impropriété *f* (de langage); (*b*) inconvenance *f* (de conduite).

improve [im'pru:v]. **1.** (*a*) *v.tr.* améliorer; perfectionner; **to i. the appearance of sth.,** embellir qch.; (*b*) *v.ind.tr.* **to i. (up)on sth.,** améliorer qch. **2.** *v.i.* s'améliorer; **he has greatly improved,** il a fait de grands progrès; **business is improving,** les affaires reprennent; **im'provement,** *s.* amélioration *f;* perfectionnement *m;* embellissement *m* (d'une maison); **to be an i. on sth.,** surpasser qch.; **my new car is a great i. on the old one,** ma nouvelle voiture est bien supérieure à l'ancienne.

improvident [im'prɔvidənt], *a.* (*a*) imprévoyant; (*b*) prodigue; **-ly,** *adv.* sans prévoyance; **im'providence,** *s.* imprévoyance *f.*

improvise ['imprəvaiz], *v.tr.* improviser (des vers, etc.); **improvi'sation,** *s.* improvisation *f.*

imprudent [im'pru:dənt], *a.* imprudent; **-ly** *adv.* imprudemment; **im'prudence,** *s.* imprudence *f.*

impudent ['impjudənt], *a.* effronté, insolent; **-ly** *adv.* effrontément, insolemment; **'impudence** *s.* impudence *f,* effronterie *f,* insolence audace *f;* **to have the i. to say . . .,** avo l'aplomb *m, F:* le culot, de dire . . . .

impugn [im'pju:n], *v.tr.* attaquer, contester (u proposition); mettre en doute (la véracité qch.).

impulse ['impʌls], *s.* **1.** impulsion *f;* pouss motrice. **2.** impulsion; mouvement spontan élan *m;* **im'pulsive,** *a.* (*of pers.*) impulsif; action, coup *m* de tête; **-ly,** *adv.* (agir) p impulsion.

impunity [im'pju:niti], *s.* impunité *f;* **with** impunément.

impure [im'pju:ər], *a.* impur; **im'purity,** **1.** impureté *f.* **2.** *pl.* saletés *f;* corps étra gers.

impute [im'pju:t], *v.tr.* imputer; **to i. a crime an innocent man,** imputer un crime à un nocent; **impu'tation,** *s.* imputation *f;* (*a*) tribution *f* (d'un crime à qn); (*b*) chose impu à qn.

in [in]. **I.** *prep.* **1.** (*of place*) (*a*) en, à, dans; Europe, en Europe; **in Japan,** au Japon; **Paris,** à Paris; **in the country,** à la campag (*of book*) **in the press,** sous presse; **in schoo** l'école; **in bed,** au lit; **in one's house,** chez **in the distance,** au loin; **in your place,** à vo place; (*b*) (*among*) **in the crowd,** dans la fou **he's in his sixties,** il a passé la soixantaine (*in respect of*) **blind in one eye,** aveugle d œil; **two metres in length,** long de deux mèt **3.** (*of ratio*) **one in ten,** un sur dix; **once in years,** une fois tous les dix ans. **4.** (*of time* **in 1927,** en 1927; **in those days,** en ce tem là; **at four o'clock in the afternoon,** à qu heures de l'après-midi; **in the evening,** le s pendant la soirée; **in summer, autumn, win** en été, en automne, en hiver; **in spring,** printemps; **in August,** au mois d'août; **in** future, à l'avenir; **in the past,** par le pa never in my life, jamais de ma vie; (*b*) **to do in three hours,** faire qch. en trois heures; **be here in three hours,** il sera là dans t heures; **in a little while,** sous peu. **5. in tears** larmes; **in despair,** au désespoir. **6.** (*clothe* **in his shirt,** en chemise; **dressed in** w habillé de blanc. **7. to go out in the rain,** s par la pluie; **to work in the rain,** travailler s la pluie; **in the sun,** au soleil. **8. in my opini** mon avis. **9.** (*a*) **in a gentle voice,** d'une douce; **to be in (the) fashion,** être à la mode **to write in French,** écrire en français; **to** w **in ink,** écrire à l'encre; **in writing,** par écri

in alphabetical order, par ordre alphabétique; (*d*) **in the form of,** sous forme de; (*e*) **I've nothing in your size,** je n'ai rien à votre taille. **10. in that,** parce que, vu que. **II.** *adv.* **1.** (*a*) à la maison, chez soi; **Mr Smith is in,** M. Smith y est, est ici, est à la maison; (*b*) **the harvest is in,** la moisson est rentrée; (*c*) **the train is in,** le train est en gare; (*d*) **is the fire still in?** est-ce que le feu brûle encore? **2.** (*a*) **strawberries are in,** c'est la saison des fraises; **stripes are in this year,** les rayures sont à la mode cette année; (*b*) **I've got my hand in,** je suis bien en train; (*c*) **to be (well) in with s.o.,** être en bons termes avec qn; **the Labour Party is in,** le parti travailliste est au pouvoir; (*d*) **my luck is in,** je suis en veine. **3. he is in for it!** le voilà dans de beaux draps! **4.** (*a*) **day in, day out,** jour *m* après jour, sans trêve; (*b*) **all in,** (i) (prix *m*) tout compris; (ii) *F:* **I'm all in,** je suis éreinté. **III.** *s.* **the ins and outs of a matter,** les coins *m* et recoins *m* d'une affaire.

ability [inə'biliti], *s.* incapacité *f* (de faire qch.); impuissance *f* (à faire qch.).

accessible [inæk'sesəbl], *a.* inaccessible (**to,** à); (*of pers.*) inabordable; **inaccessi'bility,** *s.* inaccessibilité *f.*

accurate [in'ækjurət], *a.* (calcul) inexact; (sens) incorrect; **-ly,** *adv.* inexactement; incorrectement; **in'accuracy,** *s.* inexactitude *f*; imprécision *f.*

active [in'æktiv], *a.* inactif; **in'action,** *s.* inaction *f*; **inac'tivity,** *s.* inactivité *f*; passivité *f*; **masterly i.,** (sage) politique *f* de laisser-faire.

adequate [in'ædikwət], *a.* inadéquat, insuffisant; **-ly,** *adv.* insuffisamment; **in-adequacy,** *s.* insuffisance *f.*

admissible [inəd'misəbl], *a.* inadmissible; irrecevable; **inadmissi'bility,** *s.* inadmissibilité *f.*

advertent [inəd'və:tənt], *a.* commis par inadvertance, par mégarde, par étourderie; **-ly,** *adv.* par inadvertance, par mégarde; **in-ad'vertence,** *s.* inadvertance *f*, étourderie *f.*

advisable [inəd'vaizəbl], *a.* peu sage; imprudent; à déconseiller.

ne [i'nein], *a.* inepte, stupide; bête; niais; **i.** **remark,** ineptie *f*; **-ly,** *adv.* bêtement, stupidement; **inanity** [i'næniti], *s.* inanité *f*, niaiserie *f.*

nimate [in'ænimət], *a.* inanimé.

pplicable [in'æplikəbl, inə'plik-], *a.* inapplicable (**to,** à).

ppropriate [inə'proupriət], *a.* qui ne convient pas (**to,** à); (*of words*) impropre; **-ly,** *adv.* d'une façon impropre.

pt [in'æpt], *a.* inapte. **1.** (*of pers.*) (*a*) incapable; (*b*) inhabile, inexpert. **2.** peu approprié (**to,** à); **in'aptitude,** *s.* inaptitude *f* (**for,** à).

rticulate [ina:'tikjulət], *a.* (son) inarticulé;

(*b*) muet, incapable de parler; **i. with rage,** bégayant de colère; **-ly,** *adv.* (parler, prononcer) indistinctement.

inartistic [ina:'tistik], *a.* sans valeur artistique; (*of pers.*) dépourvu de sens artistique.

inattentive [inə'tentiv], *a.* inattentif, distrait; *Sch:* (élève) dissipé; **-ly,** *adv.* distraitement; **ina'ttention,** *s.* inattention *f*, distraction *f.*

inaudible [in'ɔ:dibl], *a.* (son) imperceptible; (voix) faible; **-ibly,** *adv.* sans bruit; (parler, bouger) de manière à ne pas être entendu.

inaugurate [i'nɔ:gjureit], *v.tr.* inaugurer; **in-'augural,** *a. & s. i.* (**address**), discours *m* d'inauguration; **inaugu'ration,** *s.* inauguration *f.*

inauspicious [inɔ:s'piʃəs], *a.* peu propice; (jour) néfaste; **an i. moment,** un moment malencontreux.

inbred ['inbred], *a.* inné, naturel.

incalculable [in'kælkjuləbl], *a.* incalculable; **-ably,** *adv.* incalculablement.

incandescent [inkæn'des(ə)nt], *a.* incandescent; **incan'descence,** *s.* incandescence *f.*

incapable [in'keipəbl], *a.* **1.** incapable (**of,** de); **i. of speech,** incapable de parler; **i. of pity,** inaccessible à la pitié. **2.** (*of pers.*) incapable, incompétent; **incapa'bility,** *s.* incapacité *f.*

incapacity [inkə'pæsiti], *s.* incapacité *f*, incompétence *f*; **the i. of the staff,** la nullité du personnel; **inca'pacitate,** *v.tr.* rendre (qn) incapable (**from, for,** de).

incarcerate [in'ka:səreit], *v.tr.* incarcérer; emprisonner; mettre (qn) en prison; **incarce'ration,** emprisonnement *m.*

incarnation [inka:'neiʃ(ə)n], *s.* **1.** incarnation *f* (du Christ). **2. to be the i. of wisdom,** être la sagesse incarnée; **in'carnate,** *a.* fait de chair; (*of Christ*) **to become i.,** s'incarner.

incautious [in'kɔ:ʃəs], *a.* imprudent; inconsidéré; **-ly,** *adv.* imprudemment.

incendiary [in'sendjəri], *a. & s.* incendiaire (*m*); **i. bomb,** bombe *f* incendiaire.

incense¹ ['insens], *s.* encens *m.*

incense² [in'sens], *v.tr.* exaspérer (qn); **in-'censed,** *a.* exaspéré, en colère.

incentive [in'sentiv], *s.* stimulant *m*, encouragement *m.*

inception [in'sepʃ(ə)n], *s.* commencement *m*, début *m* (d'une entreprise, etc.).

incessant [in'sesnt], *a.* incessant, continuel; **-ly,** *adv.* sans cesse; incessamment.

incest ['insest], *s.* inceste *m*; **in'cestuous,** *a.* incestueux.

inch [in(t)ʃ], *s. Meas:* pouce *m* (= 2 cm 54); **he couldn't see an i. in front of him,** il ne voyait pas à deux pas devant lui; **by inches, i. by i.,** peu à peu, petit à petit; **not to give way an i.,** ne pas reculer d'une semelle.

incident ['insidənt], *s.* incident *m*; **'incidence,** *s.*
the high i. of traffic accidents, la fréquence des
accidents de la route; **inci'dental. I.** *a.*
(événement) fortuit, accidentel; **i. expenses,**
faux frais; **-ally,** *adv.* (*a*) accessoirement; (*b*)
(soit dit) en passant, entre parenthèses. **II.** *s.*
éventualité; *pl.* **the incidentals,** les faux frais.

incinerator [in'sinəreitər], *s.* incinérateur *m*;
domestic i., refuse i., incinérateur d'ordures.

incipient [in'sipiənt], *a.* naissant; qui commence; **i. beard,** barbe naissante.

incision [in'siʒ(ə)n], *s.* incision *f*, entaille *f*.

incisive [in'saisiv], *a.* incisif, tranchant; (ton)
mordant; (esprit) pénétrant; **-ly,** *adv.* in-
cisivement; d'un ton mordant.

incisor [in'saizər], *s.* (dent) incisive (*f*).

incite [in'sait], *v.tr.* inciter, stimuler, pousser
(s.o. to sth., qn à qch.); **to i. s.o. to revolt,**
exciter qn à la révolte; **in'citement,** *s.* incitation *f* (**to,** à).

incivility [insi'viliti], *s.* incivilité *f*.

incline. I. *v.i.* [in'klain], (*a*) incliner, pencher (**to,
towards,** à, vers); **inclined at an angle of 45°,**
incliné à un angle de 45°; (*b*) avoir un penchant
(**to,** pour qch., à faire qch.); être enclin, porté
(**to,** à); **to i. to pity,** incliner à la pitié. **II.** *s.*
['inklain], pente *f*, déclivité *f*; **incli'nation**
[-'kli-], *s.* 1. inclination *f* (de la tête). 2. pente *f*. 3.
inclination, penchant *m* (**to, for,** à, pour); **to
follow one's own i.,** en faire à sa tête; **to do sth.
from i.,** faire qch. par goût; **in'clined,** *a.* 1.
(plan) incliné. 2. enclin, porté (**to,** à); **to be i. to
do sth.,** avoir de l'inclination, une tendance, à
faire qch.

include [in'klu:d], *v.tr.* comprendre, renfermer,
embrasser, comporter; **we were six including
our host,** nous étions six y compris notre hôte;
up to and including 31st December, jusqu'au
31 décembre inclus; **inclusion** [in'klu:ʒən],
s. inclusion *f*; **inclusive** [in'klu:siv], *a.* qui
comprend, qui renferme; **i. sum,** somme
globale; (*at hotel*) **i. terms,** prix *m* tout compris; **-ly,** *adv.* inclusivement.

incognito [inkɔg'ni:tou], *s. & adv.* incognito (*m*).

incoherent [inkou'hiərənt], *a.* incohérent;
(style) décousu; **-ly,** *adv.* sans cohérence, sans
suite; **inco'herence,** *s.* incohérence *f*.

incombustible [inkəm'bʌstəbl], *a.*
incombustible.

income ['inkəm], *s.* revenu(s) *m(pl)*; **i. tax,** impôt
m sur le revenu.

incoming ['inkʌmiŋ]. **I.** *a.* qui arrive; (locataire)
entrant; **i. tide,** marée montante. **II.** *s.* 1. entrée
f, arrivée *f*. 2. *pl.* recettes *f*, revenus *m*.

incommunicable [inkə'mju:nikəbl], *a.*
incommunicable.

incommunicado [inkəmju:ni'ka:dou], *a.* (*of*
pers.) tenu au secret.

incomparable [in'kɔmprəbl], *a.* incomparable
(**to, with,** à); **i. artist,** artiste hors ligne; **-ably,**
adv. incomparablement.

incompatible [inkəm'pætibl], *a.* incompatible
inconciliable (**with,** avec); (*of ideas, etc.*)
inalliable; **-ibly,** *adv.* incompatiblement; **in
compati'bility,** *s.* incompatibilité *f*; incon
ciliabilité *f* (de deux théories, etc.); **i. of temper**
incompatibilité d'humeur.

incompetent [in'kɔmpitənt], *a.* incapable; in
compétent; **in'competence,** *s.* incompétence
f, incapacité *f* (d'une personne).

incomplete [inkəm'pli:t], *a.* incomplet; ina
chevé; **-ly,** *adv.* incomplètement.

incomprehensible [inkɔmpri'hensibl], *a.* in
compréhensible; **-ibly,** *adv.* incompréhen
siblement; **incompre'hension,** *s.* manque *r*
de compréhension, incompréhension *f*.

inconceivable [inkən'si:vəbl], *a.* inconcevable

inconclusive [inkən'klu:siv], *a.* peu concluan
-ly, *adv.* d'une manière peu concluante.

incongruous [in'kɔŋgruəs], *a.* 1. sans rappo
(**to, with,** avec). 2. (*of remark*) incongr
déplacé.

inconsequent [in'kɔnsikwənt], *a.* inconséquen
illogique; **in'consequence,** *s.* inconséquen
f.

inconsiderable [inkən'sid(ə)rəbl], *a.* peu co
sidérable; insignifiant.

inconsiderate [inkən'sid(ə)rət], *a.* (*of pers*
sans égards pour les autres; **-ly,** *adv.* **to beha**
i. to(wards) s.o., manquer d'égards envers q

inconsistent [inkən'sistənt], *a.* 1. incompatik
(**with,** avec); contradictoire (**with,** à). 2. (
pers.) inconsistant, inconséquent; **to be i.**
one's replies, varier dans ses réponses.
(histoire *f*) qui ne tient pas debout; **i
con'sistency,** *s.* 1. inconsistance *f*; cc
tradiction *f*. 2. inconséquence *f*, illogisme *m*

inconsolable [inkən'souləbl], *a.* inconsolab
-ably, *adv.* inconsolablement.

inconspicuous [inkən'spikjuəs], *a.* peu a
parent, peu frappant; effacé; **-ly,** *a*
discrètement.

inconstant [in'kɔnstənt], *a.* inconstant, vola
in'constancy, *s.* inconstance *f*.

incontestable [inkən'testəbl], *a.* incontestab
indéniable; **-ably,** *adv.* incontestablement.

inconvenience [inkən'vi:njəns]. **I.** *s.* inco
modité *f*, contretemps *m*; **I'm putting you t**
lot of i., je vous donne beaucoup de déran
ment *m*; **without the slightest i.,** sans le m
dre inconvénient. **II.** *v.tr.* déranger, gêner (o
incon'venient, *a.* malcommode; gênant;
time) inopportun; **if it's not i. for you,** si cela
vous dérange pas; **-ly,** *adv.* incommodéme
d'une façon gênante.

incorporate [in'kɔːpəreit], *v.tr.* incorporer, unir (with, à); *Com:* constituer (une association) en société commerciale; **in'corporated**, *a.* 1. faisant corps (**with others**, avec d'autres); incorporé. 2. *N.Am: Com:* (société *f*) anonyme.

incorrect [inkə'rekt], *a.* 1. inexact. 2. (*of behaviour*) incorrect; **-ly**, *adv.* 1. inexactement. 2. incorrectement.

incorrigible [in'kɔridʒəbl], *a.* incorrigible.

incorruptible [inkə'rʌptəbl], *a.* incorruptible.

increase. I. *s.* ['inkriːs], (*a*) augmentation *f* (de prix, de salaire); accroissement *m* (de vitesse); redoublement *m* (d'efforts); (*b*) *adv. phr.* **to be on the i.**, être en augmentation; augmenter. **II.** *v.* [in'kriːs]. 1. *v.i.* augmenter, s'agrandir; s'accroître; se multiplier. 2. *v.tr.* augmenter (la production); grossir (le nombre); accroître (sa fortune); **to i. the cost of goods**, renchérir des marchandises; **to i. speed**, forcer la vitesse; **increased cost of goods**, renchérissement *m* des marchandises; **in'creasing**, *a.* croissant; **-ly**, *adv.* de plus en plus (grand, difficile, etc.).

incredible [in'kredibl], *a.* incroyable; **-ibly**, *adv.* incroyablement.

incredulous [in'kredjuləs], *a.* incrédule; **i. smile**, sourire *m* d'incrédulité; **-ly**, *adv.* avec incrédulité; **incre'dulity**, *s.* incrédulité *f*.

increment ['inkrimənt], *s.* augmentation *f*.

incriminate [in'krimineit], *v.tr.* 1. incriminer (qn). 2. impliquer (qn) (dans une accusation); **incrimi'nation**, *s.* incrimination *f*, accusation *f* (de qn); **in'criminating**, *a.* **i. documents**, pièces *f* à conviction.

incubate ['inkjubeit], *v.tr.* couver (des œufs, une maladie); **incu'bation**, *s.* incubation *f*; *Med:* **i. period**, période *f* d'incubation (d'une maladie); **'incubator**, *s.* incubateur *m*; couveuse (artificielle).

incumbent [in'kʌmbənt]. 1. *s.* titulaire *m* (d'une fonction administrative). 2. *a.* **to be i. on s.o. to do sth.**, incomber, appartenir, à qn de faire qch.

incur [in'kəːr], *v.tr.* (**incurred**) courir (un risque); encourir (un blâme, des frais); s'attirer (la colère de qn); contracter (des dettes).

incurable [in'kjuərəbl], *a. & s.* incurable; **-ably**, *adv.* **to be i. lazy**, être d'une paresse incurable.

incursion [in'kəːʃən], *s.* incursion *f*.

indebted [in'detid], *a.* 1. endetté. 2. redevable (**to s.o. for sth.**, à qn de qch.).

indecent [in'diːs(ə)nt], *a.* peu décent, indécent; **-ly**, *adv.* indécemment; d'une manière indécente.

indecipherable [indi'saif(ə)rəbl], *a.* indéchiffrable.

indecision [indi'siʒ(ə)n], *s.* indécision *f*, irrésolution *f*.

indecisive [indi'saisiv], *a.* (*of argument, battle,*

etc.) indécis, incertain; **an i. sort of person**, une personne plutôt irrésolue.

indeed [in'diːd], *adv.* 1. (*a*) en effet; vraiment; (*b*) (*intensive*) **I'm very glad i.**, je suis très très content; **thank you very much i.**, merci infiniment. 2. même; à vrai dire. 3. **yes i.!** (i) mais certainement! (ii) (*contradicting*) si fait!

indefatigable [indi'fætigəbl], *a.* infatigable, inlassable; **-ably**, *adv.* infatigablement, inlassablement.

indefensible [indi'fensəbl], *a.* indéfendable; (argument) insoutenable; **-ibly**, *adv.* d'une manière inexcusable.

indefinable [indi'fainəbl], *a.* indéfinissable; **-ably**, *adv.* d'une manière indéfinissable; vaguement.

indefinite [in'definit], *a.* indéfini; (idée) vague; (nombre) indéterminé; **i. leave**, congé illimité; **-ly**, *adv.* vaguement; **to postpone sth. i.**, remettre qch. indéfiniment.

indelible [in'delibl], *a.* indélébile, ineffaçable; **-ibly**, *adv.* ineffaçablement.

indemnify [in'demnifai], *v.tr.* 1. garantir (**from, against**, contre). 2. indemniser, dédommager (**for a loss**, d'une perte); **in'demnity**, *s.* (*a*) garantie *f*, assurance *f* (contre une perte); (*b*) indemnité *f*, dédommagement *m*.

indent [in'dent]. 1. *v.tr.* denteler, découper (le bord de qch.); *Typ:* renfoncer, (faire) rentrer (une ligne). 2. *v.i.* **to i. for sth.**, (i) réquisitionner qch. (à qn); (ii) passer une commande (à qn) pour qch.; **inden'tation**, *s.* dentelure *f*, découpure *f*; empreinte creuse; **in'dented**, *a.* (bord) dentelé; (littoral) échancré; (ligne) en alinéa, en retrait.

indentures [in'dentʃəz], *s.pl.* contrat *m* d'apprentissage.

independent [indi'pendənt], *a.* indépendant; (état *m*) autonome; *Pol:* **i. candidate**, candidat indépendant; **to be i.**, être son propre maître; **to be (of) i. (means)**, vivre de ses rentes; **i. school** = école *f* libre; **-ly**, *adv.* (*a*) indépendamment (**of**, de); (*b*) avec indépendance; **inde'pendence**, *s.* indépendance *f*; **to show i.**, faire preuve d'indépendance; *U. S:* **I. Day**, le quatre juillet.

indescribable [indis'kraibəbl], *a.* indescriptible; (joie) indicible; **-ably**, *adv.* indescriptiblement, indiciblement.

indestructible [indis'trʌktəbl], *a.* indestructible.

index ['indeks]. **I.** *s.* 1. (*pl.* **indexes**) **i.** (**finger**), index *m*, premier doigt. 2. (*pl.* **indices** ['indisiːz]) indice *m*; signe (indicateur). 3. (*pl.* **indexes**) index; table *f* alphabétique, répertoire *m* (d'un livre); **card i.**, (i) fichier *m*, classeur *m*; (ii) catalogue *m* sur fiches; **cost of living i.**, index du coût de la vie; *Ecc:* **to put a book on the I.**, mettre un livre à l'Index. **II.** *v.tr.* faire l'index d'(un

livre); classer (un article).
India ['indjə]. *Pr.n.* l'Inde *f.*
Indian ['indjən]. **1.** (*a*) *a.* de l'Inde; des Indes; indien; (*b*) *s.* Indien, -ienne. **2.** *s.* (*a*) **Red Indians,** (les) Peaux-Rouges *m*; (*b*) **West I.,** Antillais, -aise.
indiarubber ['indjə'rʌbər], *s.* gomme *f* (à effacer).
indicate ['indikeit], *v.tr.* indiquer; **indi'cation,** *s.* indice *m*, signe *m*; **in'dicative,** *a.* & *s.* indicatif (*m*); **'indicator,** *s.* (tableau *m*) indicateur (*m*).
indict [in'dait], *v.tr. Jur:* accuser, inculper (qn) (**for,** de); traduire, poursuivre, (qn) en justice (**for,** pour); **in'dictable,** *a.* **i. offence,** délit *m*; **in'dictment,** *s.* accusation *f*; **i. for theft,** inculpation *f* de vol.
Indies (the) [ði'indiz]. *Pr.n.pl.* les Indes *f*; **the East I.,** les Indes (orientales); **the West I.,** les Antilles *f.*
indifferent [in'dif(ə)rənt], *a.* **1.** indifférent (**to,** à); **he's i. to everything,** tout lui est indifférent, égal. **2.** médiocre; **very i. quality,** qualité *f* très médiocre. **3. to converse on i. topics,** causer de choses sans importance; **-ly,** *adv.* **1.** indifféremment; avec indifférence. **2.** médiocrement; **in'difference,** *s.* **1.** indifférence *f*, manque *m* d'intérêt (**to, towards, sth., s.o.,** pour qch., à l'égard de qn). **2.** médiocrité *f* (de talent, etc.).
indigenous [in'didʒənəs], *a.* indignène (**to,** à).
indigestion [indi'dʒestʃ(ə)n], *s.* dyspepsie *f*; mauvaise digestion; **an attack of i.,** une indigestion; **indi'gestible,** *a.* indigeste.
indignant [in'dignənt], *a.* (air) indigné; (cri) d'indignation; **to feel i. at sth.,** s'indigner de qch.; **to make s.o. i.,** indigner qn; **-ly,** *adv.* avec indignation; **indig'nation,** *s.* indignation *f.*
indignity [in'digniti], *s.* indignité *f*, affront *m*; outrage *m.*
indigo ['indigou], *s.* indigo *m.*
indirect [indi'rekt, -dai-], *a.* **1.** indirect; *Gram:* **i. speech,** discours indirect. **2.** détourné, oblique; **-ly,** *adv.* indirectement.
indiscreet [indis'kri:t], *a.* **1.** indiscret. **2.** peu judicieux; imprudent; **-ly,** *adv.* (*a*) indiscrètement; (*b*) imprudemment; sans considération *f*; **indis'cretion,** *s.* (*a*) manque *m* de discrétion; (*b*) indiscrétion *f*; (*c*) action inconsidérée; imprudence *f.*
indiscriminate [indis'kriminət], *a.* **i. blows,** coups frappés à tort et à travers; **-ly,** *adv.* sans faire de distinction; au hasard; aveuglément.
indispensable [indis'pensəbl], *a.* indispensable, de première nécessité; **-ably,** *adv.* indispensablement.
indisposed [indis'pouzd], *a.* **1.** peu enclin, peu disposé (**to do sth.,** à faire qch.). **2. to be i.,** être

souffrant; ne pas être dans son assiette; **indispo'sition** [-pə'ziʃ(ə)n], *s.* malaise *m.*
indisputable [indis'pju:təbl], *a.* incontestable, indiscutable; **-ably,** *adv.* incontestablement, indiscutablement.
indissoluble [indi'sɔljubl], *a.* indissoluble.
indistinct [indis'tiŋkt], *a.* indistinct; (bruit) confus; (souvenir) vague; **-ly,** *adv.* indistinctement.
indistinguishable [indis'tiŋgwiʃəbl], *a.* indistinguible (**from,** de); **i. to the naked eye,** imperceptible à l'œil nu.
individual [indi'vidjuəl]. **1.** *a.* (*a*) individuel; (*b*) particulier. **2.** *s.* individu *m*; **a private i.,** un simple particulier; **-ally,** *adv.* individuellement, personnellement; **indi'vidualist,** *s.* individualiste *mf*; **individu'ality,** *s.* individualité *f*; **indi'vidualize,** *v.tr.* individualiser, distinguer, considérer (qn, qch.) à part, isolément.
indivisible [indi'vizibl], *a.* indivisible; **-ibly,** *adv.* indivisiblement; **indivisi'bility,** *s.* indivisibilité *f.*
indoctrinate [in'dɔktrineit], *v.tr.* endoctriner (qn); **indoctri'nation,** *s.* endoctrinement *m.*
indolence ['indələns], *s.* indolence *f*, paresse *f*; **'indolent,** *a.* indolent, paresseux.
Indonesia [ində'ni:zjə]. *Pr.n. Geog:* l'Indonésie *f*; **Indo'nesian,** *a.* & *s. Geog: Ethn:* indoné sien, -ienne.
indoor ['indɔ:r], *a.* (travail) d'intérieur; (plante) d'appartement; **i. swimming pool,** piscine couverte; **in'doors,** *adv.* à la maison; **to go i.,** entrer, rentrer (à la maison); **stay i.,** restez à la maison.
indubitable [in'dju:bitəbl], *a.* incontestable; **-ably,** *adv.* incontestablement.
induce [in'dju:s], *v.tr.* **1. to i. s.o. to do sth.,** persuader à qn de faire qch.; décider qn à faire qch. **2.** amener, produire, occasionner; **to sleep,** provoquer le sommeil; **in'ducement,** *s.* motif *m*, cause *f* (qui encourage qn à faire qch.); **the i. of a good salary,** les attraits *m* d'un bon salaire.
induction [in'dʌkʃ(ə)n], *s.* **1. i. course,** stage préparatoire. **2.** *El:* induction *f.*
indulge [in'dʌldʒ]. **1.** *v.tr.* (*a*) gâter (qn); (b) oneself, s'écouter; ne rien se refuser; **to i. s.o.'s fancies,** flatter les caprices de qn; (*b*) se laisser aller (à un penchant). **2.** *v.i.* **to i. in a practice,** s'adonner à une habitude; **to i. in a cigar,** se permettre un cigare; **in'dulgence,** *s.* indulgence *f*, complaisance *f* (**to, towards, s.o.,** envers qn); **in'dulgent,** *a.* indulgent (**to, envers, pour, qn**); **-ly,** *adv.* avec indulgence.
industry ['indəstri], *s.* **1.** application *f*; assiduité *f* au travail; diligence *f.* **2.** industrie *f*; **heavy light i.,** l'industrie lourde, légère; **the car i.,** l'in-

dustrie automobile; **in'dustrial**, *a.* industriel; **i. injuries**, accidents *m* du travail; **i. disputes, unrest**, conflits ouvriers, agitation ouvrière; **i. estate**, complexe industriel; **in'dustrialist**, *s.* industriel *m*; **industriali'zation**, *s.* industrialisation *f*; **in'dustrialize**, *v.tr.* industrialiser; **in'dustrious**, *a.* travailleur, assidu, industrieux; **-ly**, *adv.* assidûment; industrieusement; **in'dustriousness**, *s.* assiduité *f* (au travail).

inedible [in'edibl], *a.* 1. immangeable. 2. non comestible.

ineffective [ini'fektiv], *a.* inefficace, sans effet.

ineffectual [ini'fektjuəl], *a.* inefficace; **i. person**, personne incapable; **-ally**, *adv.* inefficacement; vainement; **ine'ffectualness**, *s.* **in'efficacy**, *s.* inefficacité *f.*

inefficient [ini'fiʃ(ə)nt], *a.* incapable, incompétent; **-ly**, *adv.* sans compétence; **ine'fficiency**, *s.* incapacité *f*; incompétence *f*, insuffisance *f.*

inelegant [in'eligənt], *a.* inélégant; **-ly**, *adv.* sans élégance.

ineligible [in'elidʒibl], *a.* (*a*) inéligible; inapte (au service militaire); (*b*) indigne d'être choisi, inacceptable.

inept [i'nept], *a.* 1. déplacé; mal à propos. 2. (*of remark*) inepte, absurde; **-ly**, *adv.* ineptement; stupidement; **i'neptitude**, *s.* 1. manque *m* d'à-propos (d'une observation). 2. ineptie *f*, sottise *f.*

inequality [ini(:)'kwɔliti], *s.* inégalité *f*; irrégularité *f.*

inequitable [in'ekwitəbl], *a.* inéquitable; **-ably**, *adv.* inéquitablement, injustement.

ineradicable [ini'rædikəbl], *a.* indéracinable; inextirpable.

inert [i'nəːt], *a.* inerte; **i'nertia** [-ʃ(i)ə], *s.* inertie *f*; *Ph: Mec:* force *f* d'inertie; (*of pers.*) inertie, paresse *f.*

inescapable [inis'keipəbl], *a.* inéluctable, inévitable.

inestimable [in'estiməbl], *a.* inestimable, incalculable.

inevitable [in'evitəbl], *a.* (*a*) inévitable; (*b*) fatal; **-ably**, *adv.* inévitablement; fatalement.

inexact [inig'zækt], *a.* inexact; **-ly**, *adv.* inexactement; **inex'actitude**, *s.* (*a*) inexactitude *f*; (*b*) erreur *f.*

inexcusable [iniks'kjuːzəbl], *a.* inexcusable; impardonnable; **-ably**, *adv.* inexcusablement.

inexhaustible [inig'zɔːstəbl], *a.* inépuisable; (source, etc.) intarissable.

inexpensive [iniks'pensiv], *a.* peu coûteux; bon marché; pas cher.

inexperienced [iniks'piəriənst], *a.* 1. inexpérimenté. 2. inaverti; **i. eye**, œil inexercé.

inexplicable [iniks'plikəbl], *a.* inexplicable; **-ably**, *adv.* inexplicablement.

inexpressible [iniks'presəbl], *a.* inexprimable; (charme) indicible; **-ibly**, *adv.* indiciblement; **inex'pressive**, *a.* (geste) inexpressif; sans expression; (visage) fermé.

inextricable [in'ekstrikəbl, iniks'trik-], *a.* inextricable; **-ably**, *adv.* inextricablement.

infallible [in'fæləbl], *a.* infaillible; **-ibly**, *adv.* infailliblement; **infalli'bility**, *s.* infaillibilité *f.*

infamous ['infəməs], *a.* infâme; (personne, conduite) abominable; **'infamy**, *s.* infamie *f.*

infant ['infənt], *s.* 1. enfant *mf* (en bas âge); nourrisson *m*; bébé *m*; **i. mortality**, mortalité *f* infantile; **i. school**, école *f* pour les enfants de cinq à huit ans. 2. *Jur:* mineur, -eure; **'infancy** [-si], *s.* 1. première enfance; bas âge. 2. *Jur:* minorité *f*; **'infantile**, *a.* 1. (esprit *m*) d'enfant; (raisonnement) enfantin. 2. (maladie *f*) infantile.

infantry ['infəntri], *s.* infanterie *f.*

infatuated [in'fætjueitid], *a.* **to be, to become, i. with s.o.**, s'enticher, s'éprendre, de qn; avoir un béguin pour qn; **infatu'ation**, *s.* engouement.

infect [in'fekt], *v.tr.* 1. infecter, corrompre, vicier (l'air, les mœurs). 2. *Med:* contaminer (qn); **in'fection**, *s. esp. Med:* infection *f*, contagion *f*; contamination *f*; **in'fectious**, *a.* (*a*) infectieux; (*b*) **i. laughter, i. good humour**, rire contagieux, bonne humeur contagieuse; **in'fectiousness**, *s.* nature infectieuse (d'une maladie); contagion *f* (du rire, etc.).

infer [in'fəːr], *v.tr.* (**inferred**) 1. **to i. sth. from sth.**, déduire, arguer, qch. de qch.; **it is inferred that . . .**, on suppose que . . . 2. impliquer; **inference** ['infərəns], *s.* déduction *f*, conclusion *f.*

inferior [in'fiəriər]. 1. *a.* inférieur; **i. piece of work**, ouvrage *m* de second ordre; **he's very i. to his brother**, il est bien au-dessous de son frère; **inferi'ority**, *s.* infériorité *f*; **i. complex**, complexe *m* d'infériorité; **to be in no way i. to s.o.**, ne le céder en rien à qn. 2. *s.* (*a*) inférieur; (*b*) *Adm:* subordonné, -ée; subalterne *mf.*

infernal [in'fəːn(ə)l], *a.* 1. infernal; des enfers. 2. *F:* (*a*) infernal, diabolique; (*b*) **i. row**, bruit infernal; **-ally**, *adv. F:* **it's i. hot**, il fait une chaleur d'enfer.

inferno, *pl.* **-os** [in'fəːnou, -ouz], *s.* enfer *m.*

infertile [in'fəːtail], *a.* infertile.

infest [in'fest], *v.tr.* (*of vermin, etc.*) infester (**with**, de).

infidelity [infi'deliti], *s.* infidélité *f.*

infighting ['infaitiŋ], *s.* guerre intestine (entre les membres d'un groupe).

infiltrate ['infiltreit]. 1. *v.tr.* infiltrer; pénétrer (dans qch.); *Pol:* noyauter. 2. *v.i.* s'infiltrer; **infil'tration**, *s.* infiltration *f*; *Pol:* noyautage *m.*

infinite ['infinit], *a.* infini; (*a*) illimité; sans bornes; (*b*) to have i. **trouble (in) doing sth.,** avoir une peine infinie à faire qch.; **-ly,** *adv.* infiniment; **infini'tesimal,** *a.* infinitésimal; **in-'finitive,** *a. & s. Gram:* infinitif (*m*); **in'finity,** *s.* 1. infinité *f.* 2. *Mth: etc:* infini *m*; **tò i.,** à l'infini.

infirm [in'fə:m], *a.* (*of pers.*) infirme, débile; **in-'firmary,** *s.* (*a*) infirmerie *f* (d'école, de caserne, etc.); (*b*) hôpital *m*; **in'firmity,** *s.* infirmité *f*; **the infirmities of age,** les ennuis *m*, les misères *f*, (physiques) de la vieillesse.

inflame [in'fleim]. 1. *v.tr.* enflammer (une plaie); allumer (l'ambition, etc.). 2. *v.i.* s'enflammer; prendre feu; *Med:* (*of wound*) s'enflammer, s'irriter; **inflamma'bility,** *s.* inflammabilité *f*; **in'flammable,** *a.* inflammable; *N.Am:* ignifuge; **infla'mmation,** *s.* 1. inflammation *f* (d'un combustible). 2. *Med:* inflammation; **i. of the lungs,** *F:* fluxion *f* de poitrine; **in'flammatory,** *a.* (discours *m*) incendiaire.

inflate [in'fleit], *v.tr.* 1. gonfler (un pneu). 2. hausser, faire monter (les prix); recourir à l'inflation *f*; **in'flatable,** *a.* gonflable; **in-'flated,** *a.* (*a*) gonflé; **i. with pride,** gonflé d'orgueil; (*b*) **i. prices,** prix exagérés; **in'flation,** *s.* (*a*) gonflement *m*; (*b*) *Pol.Ec:* inflation *f*; **galloping i.,** inflation galopante; **in-'flationary,** *a.* **i. policy,** politique *f* inflationniste.

inflexible [in'fleksəbl], *a.* inflexible; **-ibly,** *adv.* inflexiblement; **inflexi'bility,** *s.* inflexibilité *f.*

inflict [in'flikt], *v.tr.* to i. **suffering on s.o.,** occasionner, faire subir, du chagrin à qn; *Jur:* to **i. a punishment on s.o.,** infliger une punition à qn; to i. **oneself on s.o.,** imposer sa compagnie à qn.

influence ['influəns]. I. *s.* (*a*) influence *f* (**on s.o.,** sur qn); to have **great i. over s.o.,** avoir beaucoup d'influence sur qn; **to have an i. on sth.,** agir, influer, sur qch.; **under the i. of fear,** sous le coup de la peur; *Jur:* **undue i.,** intimidation *f*; (*b*) to have **i.,** avoir de l'influence, de l'autorité. II. *v.tr.* (*of pers.*) influencer (qn); (*of thg*) influer sur (qch.); **influ'ential,** *a.* influent; **to be i.,** avoir de l'influence; avoir le bras long; **to have i. friends,** avoir des amis en haut lieu, bien placés.

influenza [influ'enzə], *s. Med:* grippe *f.*

influx ['inflʌks], *s.* affluence *f*, afflux *m* (de gens); invasion *f* (d'idées nouvelles).

inform [in'fɔ:m]. 1. *v.tr.* (*a*) to i. **s.o. of sth.,** informer, avertir, qn de qch.; faire part de qch. à qn; **to keep s.o. informed,** tenir qn au courant; to i. **the police,** avertir la police; (*b*) to i. **s.o. about sth.,** renseigner qn sur qch.; **I regret to have to i. you that . . .,** j'ai le regret de vous annoncer que . . .. 2. *v.i.* to i. **against s.o.,**

dénoncer qn; **in'formant,** *s.* informateur, -trice; **information** [infə'meiʃən], *s.* 1. renseignements *mpl*; **for your i.,** à titre d'information *f*; **to get i. about sth.,** se renseigner sur qch.; **i. bureau,** (bureau *m* de) renseignements; **Ministry of I.,** le Ministère de l'Information; (*computers*) **i. processing,** informatique *f.* 2. savoir *m*, connaissances *fpl*; **in'formative,** *a.* instructif; **in'formed,** *a.* bien renseigné; bien au courant; **in'former,** *s.* dénonciateur, -trice; *Pej:* délateur, -trice; *F:* mouchard *m.*

informal [in'fɔ:ml], *a.* (dîner, etc.) sans cérémonie, en famille; (*of meeting*) non officiel; **-ally,** *adv.* à titre non officiel; sans cérémonie; sans formalités; **infor'mality,** *s.* absence *f* de cérémonie.

infra dig ['infrə'dig], *adj.phr. F:* au-dessous de la dignité de (qn); au-dessous de soi.

infra-red ['infrə'red], *a.* infrarouge.

infrasonic ['infrə'sɔnik], *a.* infrasonore; **i. vibration,** infra-son *m, pl.* infra-sons.

infrastructure ['infrəstrʌktʃər], *s.* infrastructure *f.*

infrequent [in'fri:kwənt], *a.* rare; peu fréquent; **-ly,** *adv.* rarement.

infringe [in'frindʒ]. 1. *v.tr.* enfreindre, violer (une loi). 2. *v.ind.tr.* to i. **upon s.o.'s rights,** empiéter sur les droits de qn; **in'fringement,** *s.* infraction *f* (d'un règlement); violation *f* (d'une loi); **i. of patent, of copyright,** contrefaçon *f.*

infuriate [in'fjuərieit], *v.tr.* rendre furieux; **in-'furiated,** *a.* furieux; en fureur.

infuse [in'fju:z], *v.tr.* 1. to i. **courage into s.o.,** infuser du courage à qn. 2. infuser, faire infuser (le thé, une tisane); **in'fusion,** *s.* (*a*) infusion *f* (d'une tisane); (*b*) tisane.

ingenious [in'dʒi:niəs], *a.* ingénieux; **-ly,** *adv.* ingénieusement; **ingenuity** [indʒi'nju:iti], *s.* ingéniosité *f.*

ingenuous [in'dʒenjuəs], *a.* ingénu, candide; naïf, *f.* naïve; **-ly,** *adv.* ingénument, naïvement; **in'genuousness,** *s.* ingénuité *f*, naïveté *f*, candeur *f.*

ingot ['ingət], *s.* lingot *m* (d'or); saumon *m* (d'étain).

ingrained ['in'greind], *a.* **i. dirt,** saleté encrassée; **i. prejudices,** préjugés enracinés; **i. habits,** habitudes invétérées.

ingratiate [in'greiʃieit], *v.pr.* to i. **oneself with s.o.,** s'insinuer dans les bonnes grâces de qn; **in'gratiating,** *a.* insinuant.

ingratitude [in'grætitju:d], *s.* ingratitude *f.*

ingredient [in'gri:diənt], *s.* ingrédient *m*, élément *m* (d'un médicament, d'une sauce).

ingrowing ['ingrouiŋ], *a.* (ongle) incarné.

inhabit [in'hæbit], *v.tr.* habiter (une maison, un endroit); **in'habitable,** *a.* habitable; **in'habitant,** *s.* habitant, -ante.

(d'un village, d'une maison).

inhale [in'heil], *v.tr.* aspirer, humer (un parfum); avaler (la fumée d'une cigarette).

inherent [in'hiərənt], *a.* inhérent, naturel (**in,** à); **i. defect,** vice propre; **-ly,** *adv.* par inhérence; **i. lazy,** né paresseux.

inherit [in'herit], *v.tr.* (*a*) hériter de (qch.); succéder à (une fortune); (*b*) **to i. sth. from s.o.,** hériter qch. de qn; **in'heritance,** *s.* succession *f*; héritage *m.*

inhibit [in'hibit], *v.tr.* inhiber (un sentiment); **inhi'bition,** *s.* inhibition *f.*

inhospitable [inhɔs'pitəbl], *a.* inhospitalier.

inhuman [in'hju:mən], *a.* inhumain; brutal; **-ly,** *adv.* inhumainement; **inhu'manity** [-'mæniti], *s.* inhumanité *f*, cruauté *f.*

inimical [i'nimik(ə)l], *a.* ennemi, hostile; **-ally,** *adv.* hostilement; en ennemi.

inimitable [i'nimitəbl], *a.* inimitable.

iniquitous [i'nikwitəs], *s.* inique; **-ly,** *adv.* iniquement; **i'niquity,** *s.* iniquité *f.*

initial [i'niʃ(ə)l]. **I.** *a. & s.* **1.** *a.* initial, premier. **2.** *s.* (*usu. pl.*) **initials,** initiales *f*; parafe *m*; **the UNESCO initials,** le sigle de l'UNESCO; **-ally,** *adv.* au commencement; au début; initialement. **II.** *v.tr.* (**initialled**) parafer (une correction); viser (un acte, etc.).

initiate. **I.** [i'niʃieit]. *v.tr.* **1.** commencer, ouvrir (des négociations); lancer (une mode); **to i. a reform,** prendre l'initiative d'une réforme. **2.** initier (qn à un secret). **II.** [i'niʃiət], *a. & s.* initié, -ée; **initi'ation,** *s.* **1.** début(s) *m* (d'une entreprise). **2.** initiation *f* (**into,** à); **i'nitiative,** *s.* initiative *f*; **to do sth. on one's own i.,** faire qch. par soi-même; **i'nitiator,** *s.* initiateur, -trice.

inject [in'dʒekt], *v.tr.* injecter; faire une piqûre à (qn); **in'jection,** *s.* injection *f*; piqûre *f*; **to have an i.,** se faire faire une piqûre; **intramuscular, intravenous, i.,** piqûre intramusculaire, intraveineuse.

injudicious [indʒu(:)'diʃəs], *a.* peu judicieux; malavisé.

injunction [in'dʒʌŋ(k)ʃ(ə)n], *s.* **1.** injonction *f*, ordre *m*; **to give s.o. strict injunctions to do sth.,** enjoindre strictement à qn de faire qch. **2.** *Jur:* arrêt *m* de suspension, de sursis.

injure ['indʒər], *v.tr.* **1.** nuire à, faire tort à (qn); **to i. s.o.'s interests,** compromettre, léser, les intérêts de qn. **2.** (*a*) blesser; faire mal à (qn); (*b*) endommager, gâter (qch.); **to i. one's eyes,** se gâter la vue; **'injured. I.** *a.* **1. the i. party,** l'offensé, -ée; **in an i. tone (of voice),** d'une voix offensée. **2.** (bras, etc.) blessé ou estropié. **II.** *s.* **the i.,** les blessés *m*; (*from accident*) les accidentés *m*; **in'jurious,** *a.* **1.** nuisible, pernicieux (**to, s.o., sth.,** à qn, qch.). **2.** (langage) offensif; **'injury,** *s.* tort *m*, mal *m*; **to do s.o. an i.,** faire du tort à qn. **2.** blessure *f*; **to do oneself**

an i., se blesser, se faire du mal; **industrial injuries,** accidents *mpl* du travail. **3.** *Com: etc:* dommage *m*, dégât *m*; avarie *f.*

injustice [in'dʒʌstis], *s.* **1.** injustice *f.* **2. you do him an i.,** vous êtes injuste envers lui.

ink [iŋk]. **I.** *s.* encre *f*; **Indian i.,** encre de Chine; **invisible i.,** encre sympathique; **written in i.,** écrit à l'encre. **II.** *v.tr.* **1.** noircir d'encre, tacher d'encre. **2. to i. in** (**letters**), encrer (les lettres); **to i. in, over, a drawing,** repasser un dessin à l'encre; **'inkpad,** *s.* tampon encreur; **'inkpot,** *s.*, **'inkstand,** *s.*, **'inkwell,** *s.* encrier *m*; **'inky,** *a.* taché d'encre; barbouillé d'encre; **i.-black,** noir comme de l'encre.

inkling ['iŋkliŋ], *s.* soupçon *m*; **he had an i. of the truth,** il entrevoyait la vérité.

inland ['inlænd, -lənd]. **1.** *s.* (l')intérieur *m* (d'un pays). **2.** *attrib.* intérieur; **i. trade,** commerce intérieur; **the I. Revenue,** le fisc. **3.** *adv.* **to go i.,** pénétrer dans les terres.

in-laws ['inlɔ:z], *s.pl. F:* les beaux-parents *m.*

inlay ['in'lei, in'lei], *v.tr.* (**inlaid**) incruster (**with,** de); marqueter (une table, etc.); *Metalw:* damasquiner; **'inlaid,** *a.* incrusté, marqueté; **i. work,** marqueterie *f.*

inlet ['inlet], *s.* (*a*) (orifice *m* d')admission *f* (d'eau, d'essence, etc.); (*b*) *Geog:* petit bras de mer.

inmate ['inmeit], *s.* (*a*) pensionnaire *mf* (d'une maison de retraite, etc.); (*b*) détenu, -ue (dans une prison).

inmost ['inmoust], *a.* le plus profond; **i. thoughts,** pensées les plus secrètes.

inn [in], *s.* auberge *f*; hôtellerie *f*; **'innkeeper,** *s.* aubergiste *mf*; hôtelier, -ière.

innards ['inədz], *s.pl. F:* intestins *m.*

innate ['in'eit], *a.* inné; naturel; **i. common sense,** bon sens foncier.

inner ['inər], *a.* intérieur; de dedans; **i. meaning,** sens intime; **to belong to the i. circle,** compter parmi les initiés; **i. harbour,** arrière-port *m*; *Aut:* **i. tube,** chambre *f* à air; *F:* **the i. man,** l'estomac *m.*

innings ['iniŋz], *s. inv.* (*at cricket*) tour *m* de batte; **he had a good i.,** il a vécu longtemps.

innocent ['inəs(ə)nt], *a.* **1.** innocent; pas coupable. **2.** (*a*) pur; innocent; (*b*) naïf, *f.* naïve; **to put on an i. air,** faire l'innocent; **-ly,** *adv.* innocemment; **'innocence,** *s.* (*a*) innocence *f* (d'un accusé); (*b*) innocence; candeur *f*, naïveté *f.*

innocuous [i'nɔkjuəs], *a.* inoffensif; **-ly,** *adv.* inoffensivement.

innovation [inou'veiʃ(ə)n], *s.* innovation *f*, changement *m*; **'innovator,** *s.* (in)novateur *m.*

innuendo, *pl.* **-oes** [inju(:)'endou, -ouz], *s.* allusion (malveillante), insinuation *f.*

innumerable [i'nju:m(ə)rəbl], *a.* innombrable;

sans nombre.

inoculate [i'nɔkjuleit], *v.tr. Med:* inoculer, vacciner (qn contre une maladie); **inocu'lation**, *s. Med:* inoculation (immunisante).

inoffensive [inə'fensiv], *a.* inoffensif.

inoperable [in'ɔp(ə)rəbl], *a. Med:* inopérable.

inopportune [in'ɔpətjuːn], *a.* inopportun; intempestif; hors de saison, hors de propos; **-ly**, *adv.* inopportunément; mal à propos.

inordinate [i'nɔːdinət], *a.* démesuré, excessif, immodéré; **-ly**, *adv.* démesurément.

inorganic [inɔː'gænik], *a.* inorganique.

input ['input], *s.* 1. *El:* tension *f* d'entrée. 2. i. data, données introduites.

inquest ['inkwest], *s.* enquête *f*; **(coroner's) i.**, enquête judiciaire (en cas de mort suspecte).

inquire [in'kwaiər], *v.tr. & i.* se renseigner (sur qch.); **to i. the price of sth.**, s'informer du prix de qch.; **to i. (of s.o.) how to get somewhere**, demander son chemin (à qn); *P.N:* **i. within**, s'adresser ici; **to i. after s.o.'s health**, s'informer de la santé de qn; **to i. about sth.**, se renseigner sur qch.; **to i. for s.o.**, demander qn; **to i. into sth.**, faire des recherches sur qch.; **in-'quiring**, *a.* curieux; **an i. glance**, un coup d'œil interrogateur; **-ly**, *adv.* d'un air, d'un ton, interrogateur; **to glance i. at s.o.**, interroger qn du regard; **in'quiry**, *s.* 1. enquête *f*; **to hold an i.**, procéder à une enquête. 2. demande *f* de renseignements; **to make inquiries about s.o.**, s'informer de, se renseigner sur, qn; **i. office, inquiries**, (bureau *m* de) renseignements.

inquisitive [in'kwizitiv], *a.* curieux; **-ly**, *adv.* avec curiosité; **in'quisitiveness**, *s.* curiosité (indiscrète).

inroads ['inroudz], *s.* **to make i. on sth.**, **on s.o.'s time**, entamer qch., prendre le temps de qn.

inrush ['inrʌʃ], *s.* irruption *f* (d'eau, de gens); entrée soudaine (d'air, de gaz).

insane [in'sein], *a.* 1. fou; (esprit) dérangé; **to become i.**, perdre la raison. 2. (désir) insensé, fou. 3. *s.pl.* **the i.**, les aliénés; **-ly**, *adv.* follement; **insanity** [in'sæniti], *s. Med:* folie *f*, démence *f*, aliénation mentale.

insanitary [in'sænit(ə)ri], *a.* insalubre; malsain; antihygiénique.

insatiable [in'seiʃəbl], *a.* insatiable; **-ably**, *adv.* insatiablement.

inscribe [in'skraib], *v.tr.* 1. inscrire, graver. 2. dédier (un livre à qn); **in'scription** [-ipʃ(ə)n], *s.* 1. inscription *f* (sur un monument, etc.); légende *f* (d'une pièce de monnaie). 2. dédicace *f* (d'un livre, etc.).

inscrutable [in'skruːtəbl], *a.* (dessein) impénétrable, incompréhensible; (visage) fermé.

insect ['insekt], *s.* insecte *m*; **in'secticide**, *s.* insecticide *m*.

insecure [insi'kjuər], *a.* 1. peu sûr; peu solide;

mal affermi. 2. exposé au danger; **-ly**, *adv.* peu solidement; sans sécurité; **inse'curity**, *s.* insécurité *f*.

insemination [insemi'neiʃn], *s.* **artificial i.**, insémination artificielle.

insensitive [in'sensitiv], *a.* insensible (**to**, à); **in-'sensitiveness**, *s.*, **insensi'tivity** [-'tiviti], *s.* insensibilité *f*.

inseparable [in'sep(ə)rəbl], *a.* inséparable (**from**, de); **-ably**, *adv.* inséparablement.

insert [in'səːt], *v.tr.* insérer, introduire (la clef dans la serrure); **in'sertion** [-'səː.ʃ(ə)n], *s.* insertion *f*, introduction *f* (de qch. dans qch.); *Typ:* **i. mark**, renvoi *m*.

inside [in'said]. 1. *s.* (*a*) dedans *m*, (côté) intérieur (*m*); **on the i.**, en dedans, au dedans; **to know the i. of an affair**, connaître les dessous d'une affaire; **to turn everything i. out**, mettre tout sens dessus dessous; **to know sth. i. out**, savoir qch. à fond; (*b*) intérieur (d'une maison, etc.); (*c*) *F:* l'estomac *m*, ventre *m*; **I've a pain in my i.**, j'ai mal à l'estomac, au ventre; (*d*) *Fb:* **i. left**, intérieur gauche. 2. *a.* intérieur, d'intérieur; **i. information**, renseignements privés. 3. *adv.* intérieurement; en dedans; **i. of three hours**, en moins de trois heures. 4. *prep.* à l'intérieur de; dans.

insidious [in'sidiəs], *a.* insidieux; (raisonnement) astucieux; **-ly**, *adv.* insidieusement.

insight ['insait], *s.* 1. perspicacité *f*; pénétration *f*. 2. aperçu *m*; **to get an i. into sth.**, avoir un aperçu de qch.

insignificant [insig'nifikənt], *a.* insignifiant; de peu d'importance; (personne) sans importance; **insig'nificance**, *s.* insignifiance *f*.

insincere [insin'siər], *a.* (*a*) peu sincère; de mauvaise foi; (*b*) (*of smile, etc.*) faux, *f.* fausse; **-ly**, *adv.* sans sincérité; **insin'cerity** [-'seriti], *s.* manque *m* de sincérité.

insinuate [in'sinjueit]. 1. *v.tr.* insinuer. 2. *v.pr.* **to i. oneself into s.o.'s favour**, s'insinuer (dans les bonnes grâces de qn). 3. *v.tr.* donner adroitement à entendre (que), insinuer (que); laisser (sous-)entendre (que); **insinu'ation**, *s.* insinuation *f*; sous-entendu *m*, *pl.* sous-entendus.

insipid [in'sipid], *a.* insipide, fade; **insi'pidity**, *s.* insipidité *f*; fadeur *f*.

insist [in'sist], *v.i.* insister; **he insisted that it was so**, il soutenait qu'il en était ainsi; **to i. on doing sth.**, insister pour faire qch.; **I i. (up)on it**, je le veux, j'y tiens, absolument; **in'sistence**, *s.* insistance *f*; **in'sistent**, *a.* qui insiste, insistant; (créancier) importun, pressant; **-ly**, *adv.* instamment; avec insistance.

insolent ['ins(ə)lənt], *a.* insolent (**to**, envers); **-ly**, *adv.* insolemment; avec insolence; **'insolence**, *s.* insolence *f* (**to**, envers).

insoluble [in'sɔljubl], a. 1. *Ch:* (sel, etc.) insoluble. 2. (problème) insoluble; **insolu'bility**, s. insolubilité *f* (d'un produit chimique, d'un problème).

insolvent [in'sɔlvənt], a. (débiteur *m*) insolvable; **to become i.**, faire faillite; **in'solvency**, s. (a) insolvabilité *f*; (b) faillite *f*.

insomnia [in'sɔmniə], s. insomnie *f*.

inspect [in'spekt], v.tr. examiner (qch.) de près; inspecter; contrôler (les livres d'un négociant); vérifier (un moteur); **in'spection** [-'spekʃ(ə)n], s. inspection *f*; vérification *f*; contrôle *m* (de billets); **i. chamber**, regard *m*; *Pub:* **i. copy**, spécimen *m*; **in'spector**, s. inspecteur, -trice; **in'spectorate**, s. corps *m* d'inspecteurs.

inspire [in'spaiər], v.tr. **to i. s.o. with confidence, with admiration, with hatred,** inspirer confiance, de l'admiration, de la haine, à qn; **in-spi'ration** [-spi-], s. inspiration *f*.

instability [instə'biliti], s. instabilité *f*.

install [in'stɔ:l], v.tr. installer (qn dans une fonction); installer, poser (une machine); **to i. oneself in a place,** s'installer dans un endroit; **to i. a workshop,** monter un atelier; **insta'llation** [instə-], s. installation *f*.

instalment [in'stɔ:lmənt], s. 1. acompte *m*; versement partiel; **to pay by instalments,** échelonner les paiements; **to buy sth. on the i. plan,** acheter qch. à crédit. 2. **i. of a book,** fascicule *m* d'un ouvrage; feuilleton *m*.

instance ['instəns], s. 1. exemple *m*, cas *m*. 2. **for i.,** par exemple. 3. **in the first i.,** en (tout) premier lieu; **in the present i., in this i.,** dans le cas actuel; dans cette circonstance.

instant ['instənt]. I. s. instant *m*, moment *m*; **come this i.,** venez sur-le-champ. II. a. 1. *Com:* (*abbr.* **inst.**) de ce mois; **the 5th inst.,** le 5 courant. 2. immédiat. 3. **i. coffee,** café instantané; **-ly,** adv. tout de suite; **instan'taneous,** a. instantané.

instead [in'sted]. 1. *prep.phr.* **i. of sth.,** au lieu de qch.; **i. of s.o.,** à la place de qn. 2. *adv.* au lieu de cela; **if he can't come, take me i.,** s'il ne peut pas venir, emmenez-moi à sa place.

instep ['instep], s. cou-de-pied *m*, pl. cous-de-pied.

instigate ['instigeit], v.tr. inciter, provoquer (qn) (**to do sth.,** à faire qch. de mal); **insti'gation,** s. instigation *f*, incitation *f*; **'instigator,** s. 1. instigateur, -trice. 2. fomentateur, -trice, auteur *m* (de troubles).

instil [in'stil], v.tr. (**instilled**) instiller (un liquide) (**into,** dans); **to i. an idea into s.o.,** faire pénétrer une idée dans l'esprit de qn.

instinct ['instiŋ(k)t], s. instinct *m*; **by i.,** d'instinct; **in'stinctive,** a. instinctif; **-ly,** adv. d'instinct; instinctivement.

institute ['institju:t]. I. v.tr. 1. instituer, établir.

2. *Jur:* ordonner, instituer (une enquête); **to i. (legal) proceedings against s.o.,** intenter un procès à qn. II. s. institut *m*; **insti'tution,** s. 1. institution *f*; établissement *m*. 2. institution; chose établie. 3. **charitable i.,** établissement d'intérêt public; **insti'tutional,** a. institutionnel.

instruct [in'strʌkt], v.tr. 1. instruire (qn en, dans, qch.); enseigner (qch. à qn). 2. **to i. s.o. to do sth.,** charger qn de faire qch.; **in'struction,** s. 1. instruction *f*, enseignement *m*. 2. usu. pl. indications *f*, instructions, ordres *m*; (*to sentry, etc.*) consigne *f*; **instructions for use,** mode *m* d'emploi; *Aut: etc:* **i. book,** manuel *m* d'entretien; *Adm:* **standing instructions,** règlement *m*; **to go beyond one's instructions,** aller au delà des ordres reçus; **in'structional,** a. (école *f*) d'application; (film) éducatif; **in'structive,** a. instructif; **-ly,** adv. d'une manière instructive; **in'structor,** s. maître (enseignant); instructeur *m*; *Sp:* moniteur *m*; **swimming i., fencing i.,** professeur *m* de natation, d'escrime.

instrument ['instrəmənt, -trum-], s. (a) instrument *m*, appareil *m*; (b) **musical i.,** instrument de musique; **wind, stringed, i.,** instrument à vent, à cordes; **instru'mental,** a. 1. **to be i. in doing sth.,** contribuer à faire qch. 2. **i. music,** musique instrumentale; **instru'mentalist,** s. *Mus:* instrumentiste *mf*; **instrumen'tation,** s. *Mus:* instrumentation *f*.

insubordinate [insə'bɔ:dinət], a. insubordonné; insoumis; **'insubordi'nation,** s. insubordination *f*.

insufferable [in'sʌf(ə)rəbl], a. insupportable, intolérable; **-ably,** adv. insupportablement.

insufficient [insə'fiʃ(ə)nt], a. insuffisant; **-ly,** adv. insuffisamment; **insu'fficiency,** s. insuffisance *f*.

insular ['insjulər], a. (a) (climat) insulaire; (b) (esprit) étroit, borné; **insu'larity,** s. étroitesse *f* (d'esprit).

insulate ['insjuleit], v.tr. isoler; calorifuger (une chaudière); *Const: Cin: etc:* insonoriser (une salle); **insu'lation,** s. isolation *f*; calorifugeage *m*; insonorisation *f*; **'insulator,** s. (a) (*material*) isolant *m*; (b) (*device*) isolateur *m*.

insulin ['insjulin]. s. insuline *f*.

insult. I. s. ['insʌlt], insulte *f*, affront *m*. II. v.tr. [in'sʌlt], insulter (qn); **in'sulting,** a. offensant, injurieux.

insuperable [in'sju:p(ə)rəbl], a. insurmontable.

insure [in'ʃuər], v.tr. 1. (i) assurer, (ii) faire assurer (sa maison, sa voiture); **to i. one's life,** s'assurer, se faire assurer, sur la vie. 2. garantir, assurer (le succès, etc.); **in'surance,** s. assurance *f*; **i. policy,** police *f* d'assurance; **life**

i., assurance-vie *f* ; *Aut:* **third party i.**, assurance aux tiers; **comprehensive i.**, assurance tous risques; *Adm:* **National I.**, assurances sociales; **(employer's) Social I. contributions,** charges sociales.

insurgent [in'sɔ:dʒ(ə)nt], *a. & s.* insurgé, -ée.

insurmountable [insə(:)'mauntəbl], *a.* insurmontable.

insurrection [insə'rekʃ(ə)n], *s.* insurrection *f,* soulèvement *m,* émeute *f.*

intact [in'tækt], *a.* intact.

intake ['inteik], *s.* (*a*) appel *m* (d'air); prise *f,* adduction *f* (d'eau); admission *f* (de vapeur); **i. valve,** soupape *f* ; (*b*) consommation *f* ; **food i.**, ration *f* alimentaire; (*c*) *Mil:* le contingent.

intangible [in'tændʒəbl], *a.* intangible, impalpable.

integral ['intigrəl], *a.* 1. (*a*) **to be an i. part of sth.**, faire corps avec qch.; (*b*) *Mth:* **i. calculus,** calcul intégral. 2. *s. Mth:* intégrale *f* ; **'integrate** [-eit]. 1. *v.tr.* intégrer (qch. dans qch.). 2. *v.i.* s'intégrer (dans un milieu social, racial); **inte'gration,** *s.* intégration *f.*

integrity [in'tegriti], *s.* intégrité *f,* honnêteté *f,* probité *f.*

intellect ['intəlekt], *s.* intelligence *f,* esprit *m* ; **inte'llectual,** *a. & s.* intellectuel, -elle; **-ally,** *adv.* intellectuellement.

intelligence [in'telidʒəns], *s.* 1. intelligence *f* ; entendement *m,* sagacité *f* ; **i. test,** test *m* de capacité intellectuelle; **i. quotient, I.Q.,** quotient intellectuel. 2. renseignement(s) *m*(*pl*); nouvelles *fpl*; informations *fpl*; *Mil:* **I. Branch** = Deuxième Bureau *m* ; **in'telligent,** *a.* intelligent; avisé; **-ly,** *adv.* intelligemment; avec intelligence.

intelligible [in'telidʒəbl], *a.* intelligible; **-ibly,** *adv.* intelligiblement.

intemperate [in'tempərət], *a.* 1. (*of pers.*) intempérant, immodéré. 2. adonné à la boisson; **-ly,** *adv.* (boire) immodérément, à l'excès.

intend [in'tend], *v.tr.* 1. **to i. to do sth.**, avoir l'intention de faire qch.; **was it intended?** était-ce fait avec intention? 2. **to i. sth. for s.o.**, destiner qch. à qn; **he intends to be a schoolmaster,** il se destine au professorat; **in'tended,** *a.* 1. (*a*) (voyage) projeté; (*b*) **the i. effect,** l'effet voulu. 2. intentionnel; fait avec intention.

intense [in'tens], *a.* (*a*) vif; fort, intense; (*b*) **i. expression,** expression d'intérêt profond; (*c*) d'un sérieux exagéré; **-ly,** *adv.* excessivement; avec intensité; **to hate s.o. i.**, haïr qn profondément; **in'tensify.** 1. *v.tr.* intensifier, augmenter; (*of sound*) rendre plus fort, plus vif; (*of colour*) renforcer. 2. *v.i.* devenir plus intense; **in'tensity,** *s.* intensité *f* ; force *f* ; violence *f* (d'une douleur); **in'tensive,** *a.* intensif; **-ly,** *adv.* intensivement.

intent [in'tent]. **I.** *a.* (*a*) **to be i. on sth.**, être absorbé par qch., être tout entier à qch.; **to be i. on doing sth.**, être résolu, déterminé, à faire qch.; (*b*) attentif; **i. gaze,** regard fixe, profond; **-ly,** *adv.* attentivement; (regarder) fixement. **II.** *s.* intention *f* ; dessein *m* ; **with i. to defraud,** dans le but de frauder; **to all intents and purposes,** virtuellement, en fait.

intention [in'tenʃ(ə)n], *s.* intention *f* ; (*a*) dessein *m* ; **to do sth. with the best (of) intentions,** faire qch. avec les meilleures intentions du monde; (*b*) but *m* ; **in'tentional,** *a.* intentionnel, voulu; **-ally,** *adv.* à dessein; exprès; intentionnellement.

inter [in'tə:r], *v.tr.* (**interred**), ensevelir (qch., un mort).

interact [intə'rækt], *v.i.* réagir réciproquement; **inte'raction,** *s.* action *f* réciproque.

interbreed [intə'bri:d] (**interbred**) 1. *v.tr.* croiser (des races). 2. *v.i.* se croiser.

intercede [intə'si:d], *v.i.* **to i. (with s.o.) for s.o.**, intercéder (auprès de qn) en faveur de qn.

intercept [intə'sept], *v.tr.* intercepter; arrêter (qn) au passage; **inter'ception,** *s.* interception *f.*

intercession [intə'seʃ(ə)n], *s.* intercession *f.*

interchange ['intətʃeindʒ], *s.* 1. échange *m,* communication *f* (d'idées). 2. *Civ.E:* échangeur *m* (d'autoroute).

interchangeable [intə'tʃeindʒəbl], *a.* interchangeable.

intercom ['intəkəm], *s.* intercom *m.*

intercontinental [intəkɔnti'nentl], *a.* (vol *m,* missile *m,* etc.) intercontinental.

intercourse ['intəkɔ:s], *s.* (*a*) **human i.**, commerce *m* du monde; relations humaines; (*b*) rapports (sexuels).

interest ['int(ə)rest]. **I.** *s.* intérêt *m.* 1. *Com:* (*a*) participation *f* ; **to have an i. in the profits,** participer aux bénéfices; **to have a financial i. in sth.**, avoir des capitaux, être intéressé, dans qch.; (*b*) **the shipping i.**, les armateurs *m* ; le commerce maritime. 2. avantage *m,* profit *m* ; **to act in one's own i.**, agir dans son propre intérêt. 3. **to take an i. in s.o.**, s'intéresser à qn; **questions of public i.**, questions d'intérêt public. 4. *Fin:* **to bear i. at 10%,** porter intérêt à dix pour cent. **II.** *v.tr.* 1. intéresser (qn à qch.). 2. éveiller l'intérêt de (qn); **to be interested in music,** s'intéresser à la musique; **'interested,** *a.* **the i. party,** l'intéressé *m* ; **'interesting,** *a.* intéressant.

interfere [intə'fi:ər], *v.i.* (*a*) intervenir (dans une affaire); s'interposer (dans une querelle); (*b*) **don't i. with it!** n'y touchez pas! (*c*) **to i. with (sth.),** gêner (la circulation, etc.); **it interferes with my plans,** cela dérange mes plans; (*d*) *Ph:*

interférer; *Rad:* brouiller; **inter′ference,** *s.* **1.** intervention *f,* intrusion *f* (**in s.o. else's business,** dans les affaires de qn). **2.** *Ph:* interférence *f*; *Rad:* parasites *mpl*; **inter′fering,** *a.* importun; qui se mêle de tout.

interim [′intərim]. **1.** *s.* **in the i.,** pendant, dans, l'intérim. **2.** *a.* (rapport *m*) intérimaire.

interior [in′tiəriər], *a. & s.* intérieur (*m*).

interjection [intə′dʒekʃ(ə)n], *s.* interjection *f.*

interloper [′intəloupər], *s.* intrus, -use.

interlude [′intəl(j)u:d], *s. Th: Mus:* intermède *m*; interlude *m.*

intermediary [intə′mi:djəri], *a. & s.* intermédiaire (*m*).

intermediate [intə′mi:diət], *a.* intermédiaire.

interminable [in′tə:minəbl], *a.* interminable; **sans fin;** **-ably,** *adv.* interminablement; sans fin.

intermingle [intə′miŋgl], *v.i.* s'entremêler.

intermission [intə′miʃ(ə)n], *s.* (*a*) entracte *m*; (*b*) interruption *f*; **without i.,** sans arrêt.

intermittent [intə′mitənt], *a.* intermittent; **-ly,** *adv.* par intervalles, par intermittence.

intern. **I.** *v.tr.* [in′tə:n], interner. **II.** *s.* [′intə:n], *N.Am:* interne *m* (d'un hôpital); **inter′nee,** *s.* interné, -ée; **in′ternment,** *s.* internement *m.*

internal [in′tə:nəl], *a.* **1.** intérieur; (angle, maladie) interne. **2.** **i. trade,** commerce *m* intérieur; *N.Am:* **i. revenue,** le fisc; **-ally,** *adv.* intérieurement; *Pharm:* **not to be taken i.,** pour usage *m* externe.

international [intə′næʃ(ə)nəl], *a.* international.

interphone [′intəfoun], *s.* interphone *m,* téléphone *m* intérieur.

interplanetary [intə′plænit(ə)ri], *a.* (exploration *f,* vol *m*) interplanétaire.

interplay [′intəplei], *s.* effet *m* réciproque; réaction *f*; interaction *f.*

interpolate [in′tə:pəleit], *v.tr.* interpoler, intercaler; **interpo′lation,** *s.* interpolation *f.*

interpose [intə′pouz]. **1.** *v.tr.* interposer. **2.** *v.i.* s'interposer, intervenir.

interpret [in′tə:prit], *v.tr.* **1.** interpréter, expliquer (un texte). **2.** interpréter, traduire; **interpre′tation,** *s.* interprétation *f*; **in′terpreter,** *s.* interprète *mf.*

interrogate [in′terəgeit], *v.tr.* interroger, questionner (qn); **interro′gation,** *s.* interrogation *f*; interrogatoire *m* (d'un prévenu); **inte′rrogative,** *a.* interrogateur; (pronom) interrogatif; **-ly,** *adv.* d'un air, d'un ton, interrogateur; **in′terrogator,** *s.* interrogateur, -trice; questionneur, -euse.

interrupt [intə′rʌpt], *v.tr.* interrompre; couper la parole à (qn); **inte′rruption,** *s.* interruption *f*; dérangement *m.*

intersect [intə(:)′sekt]. **1.** *v.tr.* entrecouper, intersecter, entrecroiser (**with, by, de**). **2.** *v.i.* (*of*

lines) se couper, s'intersecter, se croiser; **inter′section,** *s.* **1.** intersection *f* (de lignes). **2.** carrefour *m.*

intersperse [intə′spə:s], *v.tr.* entremêler, parsemer (**with, de**).

interval [′intəvəl], *s.* intervalle *m*; (*a*) **at intervals,** par intervalles; **meetings held at short intervals,** séances très rapprochées; (*b*) *Meteor:* **bright intervals,** belles éclaircies; (*c*) *Th:* entracte *m.*

intervene [intə(:)′vi:n], *v.i.* **1.** intervenir, s'interposer. **2.** (*of event*) survenir, arriver; (*of time*) **ten years intervened,** dix années se sont écoulées; **inter′vention,** *s.* intervention *f.*

interview [′intəvju:]. **I.** *s.* entrevue *f*; *Journ:* interview *f.* **II.** *v.tr.* (*a*) avoir une entrevue avec (qn); (*b*) *Journ:* interviewer (qn); **′interviewer,** *s.* interviewer *m.*

intestine [in′testin], *s. Anat:* intestin *m.*

intimate¹ [′intimət]. **1.** *a.* (ami) intime; **to become i. with s.o.,** se lier d'amitié (avec qn); **to be on i. terms with s.o.,** être à tu et à toi avec qn; **to have an i. knowledge of sth.,** avoir une connaissance approfondie de qch.; **i. connection,** rapport intime, étroit. **2.** *s.* **his intimates,** ses intimes *mf,* ses familiers *m*; **-ly,** *adv.* intimement; à fond; **′intimacy,** *s.* intimité *f.*

intimate² [′intimeit], *v.tr.* **to i. sth. to s.o.,** signifier, notifier, qch. à qn.

intimidate [in′timideit], *v.tr.* intimider (qn); **easily intimidated,** timide, peureux; **in′timidating,** *a.* intimidateur, -trice; intimidant; **intimi′dation,** *s.* intimidation *f.*

into [′intu, ′intə], *prep.* dans, en; **1. to go i. a house,** entrer dans une maison; **to fall i. the hands of the enemy,** tomber entre les mains de l'ennemi. **2. to change sth. i. sth.,** changer qch. en qch.; **to grow i. a man,** devenir un homme; **to burst i. tears,** fondre en larmes.

intolerable [in′tol(ə)rəbl], *a.* intolérable, insupportable; **-ably,** *adv.* insupportablement.

intolerant [in′tolərənt], *a.* intolérant (**of, de**); **-ly,** *adv.* avec intolérance; **in′tolerance,** *s.* intolérance *f.*

intonation [intə′neiʃ(ə)n], *s.* intonation *f.*

intoxicate [in′toksikeit], *v.tr.* enivrer, griser (qn); **in′toxicated,** *a.* ivre; pris de boisson; **i. with praise,** grisé d'éloges; **in′toxicating,** *a.* enivrant, grisant; **i. drink,** boisson alcoolisée; **intoxi′cation,** *s.* ivresse *f.*

intransigent [in′trænzidʒənt], *a.* intransigeant.

intransitive [in′tra:nsitiv, -′træns-], *a. Gram:* intransitif.

intrepid [in′trepid], *a.* intrépide.

intricate [′intrikət], *a.* compliqué; **′intricacy,** *s.* complexité *f.*

intrigue [in′tri:g]. **I.** *v.* **1.** *v.i.* intriguer; mener des intrigues. **2.** *v.tr.* intriguer; éveiller la curiosité de (qn). **II.** *s.* intrigue *f.*

intrinsic [in'trinsik], *a.* intrinsèque; **-ally,** *adv.* intrinsèquement.

introduce [intrə'dju:s], *v.tr.* **1.** introduire; (*a*) **to i. s.o. (into s.o.'s presence),** faire entrer (qn); introduire (qn auprès de qn); **to i. a subject,** amener un sujet; (*b*) **to i. a Bill (before Parliament),** déposer un projet de loi. **2. to i. s.o. to s.o.,** présenter qn à qn; **intro'duction,** *s.* **1.** introduction *f.* **2.** présentation *f* (de qn à qn). **3.** avant-propos *m inv* (d'un livre); *Mus:* introduction. **4.** manuel *m* élémentaire; **intro'ductory,** *a.* (mots) d'introduction.

introspective [intrə'spektiv], *a.* introspectif; **intro'spection,** *s.* introspection *f.*

introvert ['introuvə:t], *s.* introverti, -ie.

intrude [in'tru:d], *v.i.* faire intrusion (**on s.o.,** auprès de qn); **I'm afraid of intruding,** je crains d'être importun; **in'truder,** *s.* intrus, -use; **in'trusion,** *s.* intrusion *f*; **in'trusive,** *a.* importun, indiscret; **-ly,** *adv.* importunément, en importun.

intuition [intju(:)'iʃ(ə)n], *s.* intuition *f*; **in'tuitive,** *a.* intuitif; **-ly,** *adv.* intuitivement; par intuition *f.*

inundate ['inʌndeit], *v.tr.* inonder (**with,** de); **to be inundated with requests,** être débordé de requêtes; **inun'dation,** *s.* inondation *f.*

inure [i'njuər], *v.tr.* accoutumer, habituer, rompre, endurcir (qn à qch.); **inured to fatigue,** dur à la fatigue.

invade [in'veid], *v.tr.* **1.** envahir. **2.** empiéter sur (les droits de qn); **in'vader,** *s.* envahisseur *m.*

invalid¹ [in'vælid], *a. Jur:* (mariage) invalide; (arrêt) nul et non avenu; **-ly,** *adv.* sans validité; illégalement; **in'validate,** *v.tr. Jur:* invalider, rendre nul (un testament); vicier (un contrat); casser (un jugement).

invalid² ['invəlid, -li:d], *a. & s.* malade (*mf*); infirme (*mf*); invalide (*mf*).

invaluable [in'vælju(ə)bl], *a.* inestimable; d'un prix incalculable.

invariable [in'vɛəriəbl], *a.* invariable; **-ably,** *adv.* invariablement, immanquablement.

invasion [in'veiʒ(ə)n], *s.* invasion *f*, envahissement *m.*

invective [in'vektiv], *s.* invective *f*; **a torrent of i.,** un torrent d'injures *f.*

inveigle [in'vi:gl, -'veigl], *v.tr.* entraîner (qn à faire qch.).

invent [in'vent], *v.tr.* inventer; **newly invented process,** procédé *m* d'invention récente; **in'vention,** *s.* invention *f*; **a story of his own i.,** une histoire de son cru; **in'ventive,** *a.* inventif; **in'ventiveness,** *s.* fécondité *f* d'invention; don *m* d'invention; imagination *f*; **in'ventor,** *s.* inventeur, -trice.

inventory ['invəntri], *s.* inventaire *m.*

inverse ['in'və:s]. **1.** *a.* inverse; **in i. ratio, proportion,** en raison inverse (**to,** de). **2.** *s.* inverse *m*, contraire *m* (**of,** de); **-ly,** *adv.* inversement; **in'version,** *s.* renversement *m*; inversion *f.*

invert [in'və:t], *v.tr.* **1.** renverser, retourner (un objet) (le haut en bas). **2.** invertir, renverser (l'ordre, les positions). **3.** retourner, mettre à l'envers; **inverted commas,** guillemets *m.*

invertebrate [in'və:tibreit], *a. & s. Z:* invertébré (*m*).

invest [in'vest], *v.tr.* **1. to i. s.o. with an office,** investir qn d'une fonction. **2.** *Fin:* placer, investir; **to i. money,** engager des capitaux, faire des placements; **to i. in property,** faire des placements en immeubles; **to i. in a new piece of furniture,** se payer un nouveau meuble; **in'vestiture,** *s.* (*a*) investiture *f* (d'un évêque, etc.); (*b*) remise *f* de décorations; **in'vestment,** *s.* placement *m* (de fonds), mise *f* de fonds; **in'vestor,** *s.* actionnaire *mf*; **small investors,** petits épargnants.

investigate [in'vestigeit], *v.tr.* examiner, étudier (une question); **to i. a crime,** faire une enquête sur un crime; **investi'gation,** *s.* investigation *f*; enquête *f* (**of,** sur); **question under i.,** question à l'étude; **in'vestigator,** *s.* investigateur, -trice.

inveterate [in'vet(ə)rət], *a.* (*of smoker, etc.*) obstiné, acharné; (*of drunkard, criminal*) invétéré; **i. hatred,** haine implacable.

invidious [in'vidiəs], *a.* **1.** haïssable, odieux; **i task,** tâche ingrate. **2.** qui excite la jalousie; **i comparison,** comparaison désobligeante; **-ly** *adv.* odieusement, désobligeamment, de façon désobligeante.

invigorate [in'vigəreit], *v.tr.* (*a*) fortifier (qn); (*b of the air, etc.*) vivifier, tonifier.

invincible [in'vinsəbl], *a.* invincible; **-ibly,** *adv* invinciblement; **invinci'bility,** *s.* invincibilit *f.*

invisible [in'vizəbl], *a.* invisible; **i. mending stoppage** *m*; **invisi'bility,** invisibilité *f.*

invite [in'vait], *v.tr.* inviter; convier (qn à dîner **to i. s.o. in,** prier qn d'entrer; **invitation** [i vi'teiʃ(ə)n], *s.* invitation *f*; **in'viting,** *a.* inv tant, attrayant; (plat) appétissant.

invoice ['invɔis]. *Com:* **I.** *s.* facture *f*; **i. cler** facturier, -ière. **II.** *v.tr.* facturer (des marchandises; **in'voicing,** *s.* **i. of goods,** facturatior de marchandises.

invoke [in'vouk], *v.tr.* (*a*) invoquer (Dieu); (appeler (qn à son secours); (*c*) *Jur:* invoqu (les termes d'un contrat).

involuntary [in'vɔlənt(ə)ri], *a.* involontair **-ily,** *adv.* involontairement.

involve [in'vɔlv], *v.tr.* **1.** (*often passive*) **to i. s in a quarrel,** engager qn dans une querelle;

be **involved in a dispute, a plot,** etc., être engagé, impliqué, compromis, dans une dispute, un complot, etc.; **the car involved,** la voiture en cause (dans l'accident); **the forces involved,** les forces en jeu. 2. comporter, entraîner; **to i. much expense,** nécessiter de grands frais; **in′volved,** a. (style) embrouillé, compliqué; **in′volvement,** s. engagement m; participation f, collaboration f.

invulnerable [in′vʌlnərəbl], a. invulnérable.

inward [′inwəd]. **1.** a. intérieur; interne; vers l'intérieur. **2.** adv. **-ly** (also **inwards**), intérieurement; vers l'intérieur; en dedans.

iodine [′aiədi:n], s. iode m.

ion [′aiən], s. El: Ph: ion m.

Iran [i′rɑːn]. Pr.n. Geog: l'Iran m; **Iranian** [i′reinjən], a. & s. iranien, -ienne.

Iraq [i′rɑːk]. Pr.n. Geog: l'Irak m; **I′raqi,** a. & s. irakien, -ienne, iraquien, -ienne.

irate [ai′reit], a. furieux; en colère.

Ireland [′aiələnd]. Pr.n. Geog: l'Irlande f.

iridescent [iri′des(ə)nt], a. irisé, iridescent; **i. colours,** couleurs chatoyantes.

iris [′aiəris], s. **1.** Anat: (pl. **irides**) iris m (de l'œil). **2.** Bot: (pl. **irises**) iris m.

Irish [′aiəriʃ]. **1.** a. irlandais; d'Irlande. **2.** s. (a) Ling: l'irlandais m; (b) pl. **the I.,** les Irlandais m; **′Irishman,** pl. **-men,** s. Irlandais m; **′Irishwoman,** pl. **-women,** s. Irlandaise f.

irksome [′ə:ksəm], a. (travail) ennuyeux, ingrat.

iron [′aiən]. **I.** s. **1.** fer m; **cast i.,** fonte f; **corrugated i.,** tôle (ondulée); **old i.,** ferraille f; **i. ore,** minerai de fer; Med: **i. lung,** poumon m d'acier. **2.** H: fer à repasser. **3.** pl. **irons,** fers, chaînes f. **II.** v.tr. repasser (le linge); **to i. out difficulties,** aplanir des difficultés; **′ironing,** s. repassage m (du linge); **i. board,** planche f à repasser; **′ironmonger** [-mʌŋgər], s. quincaillier m; **′ironmongery,** s. quincaillerie f; **′ironwork,** s. **1.** serrurerie f; ferronnerie f (d'art). **2.** pl. **ironworks,** usine f sidérurgique; forges fpl; **′ironworker,** s. serrurier m; ferronnier m (d'art).

irony [′aiərəni], s. ironie f; **i′ronical,** a. ironique; **-ally,** adv. ironiquement.

irradiate [i′reidieit], v.tr. (of light, heat) irradier, rayonner; (of light rays) illuminer.

irrational [i′ræʃ(ə)n(ə)l], a. déraisonnable, absurde; **-ally,** adv. déraisonnablement.

irreconcilable [irekən′sailəbl], a. **1.** (ennemi) irréconciliable; (haine) implacable. **2.** (croyance) incompatible, inconciliable (**with,** avec).

irrecoverable [iri′kʌv(ə)rəbl], a. irrécouvrable.

irredeemable [iri′di:məbl], a. (of pers.) incorrigible; (perte) irrémédiable; Fin: (obligation) non amortissable.

irrefutable [iri′fjutəbl], a. irréfutable.

irregular [i′regjulər], a. irrégulier; (a) contraire aux règles; **i. life,** vie déréglée; (b) (of surface) inégal; **-ly,** adv. irrégulièrement; **irregu′larity,** s. irrégularité f (de conduite, etc.).

irrelevant [i′relivənt], a. non pertinent; hors de propos; **that's i.,** cela n'a rien à voir avec la question; **-ly,** adv. mal à propos; hors de propos; **i′rrelevance,** s. manque m d'à-propos.

irremediable [iri′mi:diəbl], a. irrémédiable; sans remède; **-ably,** adv. irrémédiablement.

irreparable [i′rep(ə)rəbl], a. irréparable; (perte) irrémédiable; **-ably,** adv. irréparablement.

irreplaceable [iri′pleisəbl], a. irremplaçable.

irrepressible [iri′presəbl], a. irrésistible, irréprimable; **-ibly,** adv. irrésistiblement.

irreproachable [iri′proutʃəbl], a. irréprochable; **-ably,** adv. irréprochablement.

irresistible [iri′zistəbl], a. irrésistible; **-ibly,** adv. irrésistiblement.

irresolute [i′rezəl(j)u:t], a. **1.** indécis. **2.** (caractère) irrésolu; **-ly,** adv. irrésolument.

irrespective [iri′spektiv]. **1.** a. indépendant (**of,** de). **2.** adv. **i. of sth.,** indépendamment, sans tenir compte, de qch.

irresponsible [iri′spɔnsəbl], a. (of pers.) étourdi; (of action) irréfléchi; **-ibly,** adv. étourdiment; **irresponsi′bility,** s. étourderie f; manque m de sérieux.

irretrievable [iri′tri:vəbl], a. irréparable, irrémédiable; **-ably,** adv. irréparablement, irrémédiablement.

irreverent [i′rev(ə)rənt], a. irrévérent; irrévérencieux; **-ly,** adv. irrévérencieusement; **i′reverence,** s. irrévérence f; manque m de respect (**towards s.o.,** envers, pour, qn).

irrevocable [i′revəkəbl], a. irrévocable; **-ably,** adv. irrévocablement.

irrigate [′irigeit], v.tr. irriguer (des champs); (of river) arroser (une région); **irri′gation,** s. irrigation f.

irritate [′iriteit], v.tr. **1.** irriter, agacer. **2.** Med: irriter; envenimer (une plaie); **′irritable,** a. irritable, irascible; **-ably,** adv. d'un ton de mauvaise humeur; **′irritant,** a. & s. irritant (m); **′irritating,** a. irritant; agaçant; **irri′tation,** s. irritation f; agacement m; **nervous i.,** énervement m.

irruption [i′rʌpʃ(ə)n], s. irruption f.

Islam [′izlɑːm], s. Islam m (religion ou peuple); **Islamic** [iz′læmik], a. islamique.

island [′ailənd], s. île f; (street) **i.,** refuge m (pour piétons); **′islander,** s. habitant, -ante, d'une île; **isle,** s. (esp. in Pr.n.) île f; **the British Isles,** les Iles Britanniques; **′islet,** s. îlot m.

isolate [′aisəleit], v.tr. isoler (**s.o., sth., from s.o., sth.,** qn qch., de, d'avec, qn, qch.); **iso′lation,** s. isolement m; solitude f; **iso′lationism,** s.

Pol: isolationnisme *m*; **iso'lationist**, *a. & s.* isolationniste *(mf)*.

Israel ['izrei(ə)l]. *Pr.n. Geog:* Israël *m*; **Is'raeli**, *a. & s.* israélien, -ienne.

ism ['iz(ə)m], *s. F:* doctrine *f,* théorie *f.*

issue ['isju:]. **I.** *s.* **1.** écoulement *m.* **2.** issue *f,* sortie *f,* débouché *m* (**out of,** de). **3.** issue, résultat *m*, dénouement *m*; **to bring a matter to an i.,** faire aboutir une question; **to await the i.,** attendre le résultat; **the point at i.,** la question en discussion; **to confuse the i.,** brouiller les cartes; **I don't want to make an i.** of it, je ne veux pas trop insister. **4.** progéniture *f,* descendance *f.* **5.** *(a) Fin:* émission *f* (de billets de banque, d'actions); *(b)* publication *f* (d'un livre); *(c) Mil:* distribution *f,* versement *m* (de vivres, etc.); **i. shirt,** chemise *f* réglementaire. **II.** *v.* **1.** *v.i.* *(a)* jaillir, s'écouler **(from,** de); *(b)* provenir, dériver **(from,** de). **2.** *v.tr.* *(a)* émettre, mettre en circulation (des billets de banque, etc.); *(b)* publier (un livre); lancer (un prospectus); *Mil:* **to i. an order,** publier, donner, un ordre; *(c)* verser, distribuer (des provisions, etc.); délivrer (des billets, des passeports).

isthmus, *pl.* **-uses** ['is(θ)məs, -iz], *s. Geog:* isthme *m*.

it [it], *pers.pron.* **1.** *(a)* *(subject)* il, *f.* elle; *(b)* *(object)* le, *f.* la; **he took her hand and pressed it,** il lui prit la main et la serra; **and my cake, have you tasted it?** et mon gâteau, y avez-vous goûté? *(c)* *(indirect object)*; **bring the cat and give it a drink,** amenez le chat et donnez-lui à boire; *(d) F:* **this book is absolutely it!** c'est un livre épatant! **he thinks he's it** [hi:z'it], il se croit sorti de la cuisse de Jupiter. **2.** *(impersonal use)* **now for it!** et maintenant allons-y! **there is nothing for it but to run,** il n'y a qu'une chose à faire, c'est de filer; **to have a bad time of it,** en voir de dures; **to face it,** faire front; **he hasn't got it in him to . . .,** il n'est pas capable de . . .; il n'a pas ce qu'il faut pour . . .; **the worst of it is that . . .,** le plus mauvais de la chose c'est que . . . **3.** ce, cela, il; **who is it?** qui est-ce? **that's it,** (i) c'est ça; (ii) ça y est! **it doesn't matter,** cela ne fait rien; **it's Monday,**

c'est aujourd'hui lundi; **it's raining,** il pleut. **4.** **it's nonsense talking like that,** c'est absurde de parler comme ça; **it makes you think,** cela (vous) fait réfléchir; **how is it that . . .?** d'où vient que . . .? **it's said that . . .,** on dit que . . .; **I thought it well to warn you,** j'ai jugé bon de vous avertir. **5.** **at it, in it, to it,** y; **to consent to it,** y consentir; **to fall in it,** y tomber; **above it, over it,** au-dessus; dessus; **for it,** en; pour lui, pour elle, pour cela; **I feel (the) better for it,** je m'en trouve mieux; **from it,** en; **far from it,** tant s'en faut, il s'en faut; **of it,** en; **on it,** y, dessus.

Italian [i'tæljən]. **1.** *a.* italien, d'Italie. **2.** *s.* *(a)* Italien, -ienne; *(b) Ling:* l'italien *m*.

italic [i'tælik], *a. & s.* italique *(m)*; **to print in i.,** imprimer en italique(s); **i'talics,** *s.pl.* italique *m*; **the i. are mine,** c'est moi qui souligne.

Italy ['itəli]. *Pr.n. Geog:* l'Italie *f.*

itch [itʃ]. **I.** *v.i.* démanger; *(of pers.)* éprouver des démangeaisons; **my hand itches,** la main me démange; **to be itching to do sth.,** brûler d'envie de faire qch. **II.** *s.* *(also* **'itching**), démangeaison *f.*

item ['aitəm], *s.* article *m*; détail *m*; **news items,** faits divers; **the last i. on the programme,** le dernier numéro du programme; **items on the agenda,** questions *f* à l'ordre du jour; **'itemize,** *v.tr.* détailler.

itinerary [i'tinərəri, ai-], *s.* itinéraire *m*; **i'tinerant,** *a.* (musicien) ambulant; (marchand) forain.

its [its], *poss.a.* son, *f.* sa, *(before vowel sound)* son; *pl.* ses; **I cut off its head,** je lui ai coupé la tête.

it's [its]. = **it is; it has.**

itself [it'self], *pers.pron.* lui-même, elle-même *(refl.)* se.

I've [aiv]. =**I have.**

ivory ['aiv(ə)ri], *s.* **1.** ivoire *m*; (objet *m* d')ivoire **2.** *attrib.* d'ivoire, en ivoire; *Geog:* **the I. Coas (Republic),** la (République de la) Côte d'Ivoire.

ivy ['aivi], *s. Bot:* lierre *m.*

J

J, j [dʒei], s. (la lettre) J, j m.

jab [dʒæb]. **I.** v.tr. & i. (jabbed) to j. (at) s.o. with sth., piquer qn du bout de qch.; Med: F: to j. s.o., faire une piqûre à qn. **II.** s. coup m (du bout de qch.); coup de pointe; Med: F: piqûre f.

jabber ['dʒæbər]. **1.** v.i. jacasser; jaser, bavarder. **2.** v.tr. baragouiner (le français).

Jack¹ [dʒæk]. **1.** Pr.n.m. (dim. of **John**) Jeannot. **2.** s. (pers.) j. of all trades, touche-à-tout m inv; j. tar, marin m; j.-in-the-box, boîte f à surprise. **3.** (at cards) valet m. **4.** Aut: etc: cric m. **5.** (indicating the male of a species) j. hare, bouquin m; 'jackass, s. âne m (mâle), baudet m; 'jack-knife, s. couteau pliant, de poche; 'jack 'up, v.tr. soulever (une voiture, etc.) avec un cric, un vérin.

jack², s. Nau: the Union J., le pavillon britannique.

jackal ['dʒækəl], s. chacal m, pl. -als.

jackdaw ['dʒækdɔ:], s. choucas m; corneille f d'église.

jacket ['dʒækit], s. **1.** (a) Cl: veston m (d'homme); jaquette f (de femme); dinner j., smoking m; bed j., liseuse f; lumber j., blouson m; (b) Cu: potatoes in their jackets, pommes f de terre en robe de chambre. **2.** chemise f (de documents); jaquette f (de livre).

jackpot ['dʒækpɔt], s. to hit the j., gagner le gros lot.

jade [dʒeid], s. Miner: jade m; j.(-green), vert m de jade.

jaded ['dʒeidid], a. (of pers., horse) surmené, éreinté, excédé; j. palate, goût blasé.

jagged ['dʒægid], a. déchiqueté, dentelé, ébréché; j. stone, pierre aux arêtes vives.

jaguar ['dʒægjuər], s. jaguar m.

jail [dʒeil], s. prison f, F: taule f; 'jailer, s. gardien m de prison.

jam¹ [dʒæm]. **I.** v. **1.** v.tr. (a) serrer, presser (qch. dans qch.); (b) to get one's finger jammed, avoir le doigt coincé; se (faire) coincer le doigt; (c) to j. on the brakes, freiner brusquement; (d) coincer, caler (une machine); (e) Rad: brouiller (un signal). **2.** v.i. (se) coincer, (se) caler; (of brake) se bloquer. **II.** s. (traffic) j., embouteillage m, bouchon m; F: to be in a j., être dans le pétrin; 'jamming, s. Rad: brouillage m.

jam², s. confiture f; strawberry j., confiture(s) de fraises; F: it's money for j., c'est donné; 'jam-

jar, s. pot m à confitures.

Jamaica [dʒə'meikə]. Pr.n. Geog: la Jamaïque; **Ja'maican**, a. & s. jamaïquain, -aine.

jamb [dʒæm], s. jambage m, montant m, chambranle m (de porte).

James [dʒeimz]. Pr.n.m. Jacques.

Jane [dʒein]. Pr.n.f. Jeanne.

Janet ['dʒænit]. Pr.n.f. Jeannette.

jangle ['dʒæŋgl]. **1.** v.i. cliqueter; s'entrechoquer. **2.** v.tr. faire entrechoquer (des clefs, etc.); jangled nerves, nerfs en pelote.

janitor ['dʒænitər], s. portier m; concierge m.

January ['dʒænjuəri], s. janvier m; in J., en janvier; on J. the first, the seventh, le premier, le sept, janvier.

Japan [dʒə'pæn]. Pr.n. Geog: le Japon; in J., au Japon; **Japa'nese**. **1.** a. & s. japonais, -aise. **2.** s. Ling: le japonais.

jar¹ [dʒɑ:r]. **I.** v. (jarred) **1.** v.i. (a) rendre un son discordant; (b) heurter, cogner; to j. on s.o.'s feelings, choquer les sentiments de qn; to j. on s.o.'s nerves, taper sur les nerfs de qn; (c) (of window, etc.) vibrer, trembler; (of colours) jurer (with, avec). **2.** v.tr. faire vibrer. **II.** s. choc m; secousse f; ébranlement m; 'jarring. **1.** a. (of sound) discordant, dur. **2.** s. j. of a machine, à-coups m, secousses f, d'une machine; j. of the nerves, agacement m des nerfs.

jar², s. récipient m; pot m.

jargon ['dʒɑ:gən], s. jargon m, langage m (technique, de métier).

jasmine ['dʒæzmin], s. Bot: jasmin m.

jaundice ['dʒɔ:ndis], s. Med: jaunisse f.

jaundiced ['dʒɔ:ndist], a. to take a j. view of things, voir tout en noir.

jaunt [dʒɔ:nt], s. petite excursion, randonnée f, sortie f, promenade f.

jaunty ['dʒɔ:nti], a. **1.** insouciant, désinvolte. **2.** enjoué, vif; j. gait, démarche vive; -ily, adv. avec insouciance; 'jauntiness, s. désinvolture f, insouciance f.

Java ['dʒɑ:və]. Pr.n. Geog: Java; **Java'nese**, a. & s. javanais, -aise.

javelin ['dʒævlin], s. javelot m.

jaw [dʒɔ:], s. mâchoire f; 'jaw-bone, s. os m maxillaire; mâchoire f; -'jawed, a. (with adj. or noun prefixed) heavy-j., à forte mâchoire; lantern-j., aux joues creuses.

jay [dʒei], s. Orn: geai m; 'jay-walker, s. piéton m qui se faufile à travers la circulation.

jazz [dʒæz]. **I.** s. jazz m. **II.** v.tr. **to j. sth. up,** rendre qch. plus vivant, plus voyant.

jealous ['dʒeləs], a. jaloux (**of,** de); **-ly,** adv. jalousement; **'jealousy,** s. jalousie f.

Jean [dʒiːn]. Pr.n.f. Jeanne.

jeans [dʒiːnz], s.pl. Cl: blue-jean m.

jeep [dʒiːp], s. Aut: jeep f.

jeer ['dʒiər]. **I.** v.i. **to j. at sth., s.o.,** se moquer de qch., de qn. **II.** s. raillerie f, moquerie f; **'jeering. I.** a. railleur, moqueur. **II.** s. raillerie f, moquerie f.

jelly ['dʒeli], s. Cu: gelée f; **'jellyfish,** s. méduse f.

Jenny ['dʒeni]. **1.** Pr.n.f. (dim. of **Jane**) Jeannette. **2.** s. Orn: **J. wren,** roitelet m.

jeopardize ['dʒepədaiz], v.tr. exposer au danger; mettre en péril; **'jeopardy,** s. danger m, péril m.

jerk [dʒəːk]. **I.** s. saccade f, secousse f; **to move by jerks,** avancer par à-coups; F: **physical jerks,** la gymnastique. **II.** v.tr. donner une secousse à (qch.); tirer (qch.) d'un coup sec; **he jerked himself free,** il se dégagea d'une secousse; **'jerky,** a. saccadé; **-ily,** adv. par saccades; par à-coups.

Jerry ['dʒeri]. **1.** Pr.n.m. Jérémie. **2.** s. F: pot m de chambre; **'jerrycan,** s. jerrycan m; **'jerry-builder,** s. constructeur m de maisons de camelote; **'jerry-built,** a. (maison) de camelote.

Jersey ['dʒəːzi]. **1.** Pr.n. Geog: (Ile de) Jersey. **2.** s. Cl: jersey m; **sailor's j.,** pull marin; **football j.,** maillot m. **3.** j. (**cloth**), jersey.

jester ['dʒestər], s. bouffon m (à la cour d'un roi).

Jesus ['dʒiːzəs]. Pr.n.m. Jésus; **J. Christ,** Jésus-Christ; **Jesuit** ['dʒezjuit], s.m. jésuite.

jet¹ [dʒet], s. jais m; **'jet 'black,** a. noir comme du jais.

jet², s. **1.** jet m (d'eau, etc.) **2.** (a) ajutage m, jet (de tuyau d'arrosage); (b) Aut: gicleur m; brûleur m (à gaz). **3.** Av: **j. engine,** moteur m à réaction; **j. fighter,** chasseur m à réaction; **j.(-propelled aircraft),** jet m.

jettison ['dʒetis(ə)n], v.tr. Nau: **to j. the cargo,** jeter la cargaison à la mer; Av: larguer (des bombes, etc.).

jetty ['dʒeti], s. jetée f, digue f.

Jew [dʒuː], s. juif m; **'Jewess,** s.f. juive; **'Jewish,** a. juif.

jewel ['dʒuːəl], s. **1.** (a) bijou m, joyau m; **she's a j.,** c'est une perle; (b) pl. pierres précieuses; pierreries f. **2.** (in watch) rubis m; **'jewel-case,** s. coffret m à bijoux; écrin m; **'jewelled,** a. **1.** orné de bijoux. **2.** (of watch) monté sur rubis; **'jeweller,** s. bijoutier m, joaillier m; **'jewel(le)ry,** s. bijouterie f, joaillerie f; **costume j.,** bijoux mpl de fantaisie.

jib [dʒib], v.i. (**jibbed**) (a) (of horse) refuser; se

dérober; (b) (of pers.) se regimber; **to j. at doing sth.,** rechigner à faire qch.

jiffy ['dʒifi], s. F: **in a j.,** en un instant, en moins de rien.

jig [dʒig], s. **1.** Danc: gigue f. **2.** Mec.E: calibre m, gabarit m; **'jigsaw,** s. **j.** (**puzzle**), puzzle m.

jilt [dʒilt], v.tr. laisser là, planter (un amoureux).

jingle ['dʒiŋgl]. **1.** v.i. (of bells) tinter; (of keys) cliqueter. **2.** v.tr. faire tinter; faire sonner; **'jingling,** s. tintement m (de clochettes); cliquetis m (de clefs).

jinx [dʒiŋks], s. F: porte-malheur m inv.

jitter ['dʒitər], s. F: **to have the jitters,** avoir la frousse; **'jittery,** a. **to be j.,** avoir la frousse.

job [dʒɔb], s. **1.** (a) tâche f, besogne f, travail m; **to do a j.,** exécuter un travail; **odd jobs,** petits travaux; **to do odd jobs,** bricoler; F: **odd j. man,** homme à tout faire; **to do j. work,** travailler à la tâche, à la pièce; F: **to make a good j. of sth.,** réussir qch., F: faire du bon boulot; **that's a good j.!** à la bonne heure! **it's a good j. that . . .,** il est fort heureux que . . .; **to give sth. up as a bad j.,** y renoncer; F: **that's a lovely j.,** c'est du beau travail; **that's just the j.,** cela fait juste l'affaire; (b) tâche difficile; corvée f; **I had a j. to do it,** j'ai eu du mal à le faire. **2.** emploi m; F: **to find a cushy j.,** trouver une bonne planque; F: **jobs for the boys,** la distribution des planques, l'assiette au beurre; **to be out of a j.,** être en chômage, chômer; **j. lot** (lot m de) soldes mpl; **he knows his j.,** il connaî son affaire. **3.** (a) intrigue f; (b) cambriolage m; **'jobber,** s. St.Exch: marchand m de titres; **'jobbing,** a. **j. workman,** ouvrier m à la tâche; **j. tailor,** tailleur m à façon; **j. gardener,** jardinier m à la journée.

jockey ['dʒɔki], s. jockey m.

jocular ['dʒɔkjulər], a. jovial; **-ly,** adv. jovialement; **jocu'larity,** s. jovialité f.

jodhpurs ['dʒɔdpəːz], s.pl. Cost: pantalon d'équitation.

jog [dʒɔg]. **I.** s. (a) coup m (de coude); (b) secousse f, cahot m. **II.** v.tr. & i. (**jogged**) pousser (le coude à qn); rafraîchir (la mémoire à qn); F: **we're jogging along,** les choses vont leur train; **'jog-trot,** s. **at a j.-t.,** au petit trot.

John [dʒɔn]. Pr.n.m. Jean; **'Johnny.** Pr.n.m. Jeannot.

join [dʒɔin]. **I.** s. joint m, jointure f; ligne f jonction. **II.** v.tr. **1.** (a) joindre, unir, réunir; **j. forces with s.o.,** se joindre à qn; (b) ajoute (c) **the neck joins the head to the body,** le cou relie la tête au corps. **2.** (a) se joindre à, s'unir (qn); rejoindre (qn); **will you j. us?** voulez-vous être des nôtres? (b) Mil: **to j. one's unit,** ralli son unité; (c) entrer dans (un club); P s'affilier à (un parti). **3.** se joindre, s'unir (qch.); **the footpath joins the road,** le sent rejoint la route; **'joiner,** s. menuisier m; **j.'s shop,** menuiserie f; **'joinery,** s. (trade) menuiserie f; **'join 'in,** v.i. se mettre de la partie; prendre part à (une querelle); **joint. I.** s. **1.** Const: joint m, jointure f; Carp: assemblage m. **2.** Anat: joint, jointure; **out of j.,** (bras, etc.) disloqué, déboîté. **3.** (a) partie f entre deux articulations; phalange f (du doigt); (b) Cu: morceau m de viande; rôti m. **4.** P: boîte f (louche); **gambling j.,** tripot m. **II.** v.tr. **1.** joindre, assembler (des pièces de bois). **2.** découper (une volaille). **3.** jointoyer (un mur). **III.** a. **1.** en commun; combiné; **j. action,** action collective; **j. commission,** commission f mixte; Fin: **j. shares,** actions indivises; **j. stock,** capital social. **2.** co-, associé; **j. author,** coauteur m; **j. heir,** co-héritier, -ière; **j. management,** codirection f; **j. owner,** copropriétaire mf; **j. ownership,** copropriété f; **j. tenant,** colocataire mf; **-ly,** adv. ensemble, conjointement; **to manage a business j.,** cogérer une affaire; **'jointed,** a. articulé; **'join 'up,** v.i. s'engager (dans l'armée).

joist [dʒɔist], s. Const: solive f, poutre f.

joke [dʒouk]. **I.** s. plaisanterie f, farce f; F: blague f; **I did it for a j.,** je l'ai fait histoire de rire; **practical j.,** mystification f, farce; **that's a good j.!** en voilà une bonne! **to play a j. on s.o.,** faire une farce à qn; **he knows how to take a j.,** il entend la plaisanterie; **he must have his little j.,** il aime à plaisanter. **II.** v.i. plaisanter; **to j. at, about, sth.,** plaisanter de qch.; **'joker,** s. **1.** farceur, -euse; **practical j.,** mauvais plaisant. **2.** Cards: joker m; **'joking,** a. (ton) moqueur, de plaisanterie; **-ly,** adv. en plaisantant; pour rire.

olly ['dʒɔli]. **1.** a. joyeux, gai. **2.** adv. F: rudement, drôlement; **j. glad,** rudement content; **I'll take j. good care,** je ferai drôlement attention.

olt [dʒoult]. **I.** s. cahot m, secousse f. **II.** v. **1.** v.tr. cahoter, secouer (qn, qch.). **2.** v.i. (of vehicle) cahoter; tressauter.

ordan ['dʒɔ:d(ə)n]. Pr.n. Geog: **1.** (country) la Jordanie. **2.** (river) le Jourdain.

ostle ['dʒɔsl]. **1.** v.i. jouer des coudes (dans une foule). **2.** v.tr. bousculer, coudoyer (qn); **'jostling,** s. bousculade f.

t [dʒɔt]. **I.** v.tr. (jotted) **to j. sth. down,** noter, prendre note de, qch. **II.** s. **not a j.,** pas un iota; **'jotting,** s. **1. j. down,** prise f (d'une note). **2.** pl. jottings, notes f.

urnal ['dʒə:nəl], s. journal m, pl. -aux; revue savante; Book-k: (livre) journal; **journa'lese,** s. F: style m journalistique; **'journalism,** s. journalisme m; **'journalist,** s. journaliste mf.

urney ['dʒə:ni], s. voyage m; trajet m; **j. there and back,** voyage aller (et) retour; **on a j.,** en voyage.

vial ['dʒouvjəl], a. jovial; **-ally,** adv.

jovialement; **jovi'ality,** s. jovialité f, gaieté f.

jowl [dʒaul], s. (a) mâchoire f; (b) joue f.

joy [dʒɔi], s. joie f, allégresse f; **'joyful,** a. joyeux, heureux, **-fully,** adv. joyeusement; **'joyfulness,** s. joie f, allégresse f; **'joyless,** a. sans joie; triste; **'joy-ride,** s. (a) balade f en voiture (faite à l'insu du propriétaire); (b) promenade f agréable; **'joy-stick,** s. Av: manche m à balai.

jubilant ['dʒu:bilənt], a. (a) réjoui (at sth., de qch.); (b) (cri) joyeux; **j. face,** visage épanoui; **-ly,** adv. avec joie; **jubi'lation,** s. joie f; jubilation f.

jubilee ['dʒu:bili:], s. jubilé m; **golden j.,** fête f du cinquantième anniversaire.

judge [dʒʌdʒ]. **I.** s. **1.** Jur: juge m; **presiding j.,** président m du tribunal. **2.** membre m du jury (d'une exposition). **3.** connaisseur, -euse; **to be a good j. of wine,** s'y connaître en vin. **II.** v.tr. **1.** juger (un accusé, une affaire); arbitrer (à un comice agricole). **2.** apprécier, estimer (une distance); **'judg(e)ment,** s. **1.** (a) jugement m; **the Last J.,** le jugement dernier; (b) décision f judiciaire; arrêt m, sentence f. **2.** opinion f, avis m. **3.** bon sens; discernement m; **to have good, sound, j.,** avoir du jugement; **judicial** [dʒu'diʃəl], a. juridique; **j. inquiry,** enquête judiciaire; **-ally,** adv. **1.** judiciairement. **2.** impartialement; **judicious** [dʒu'diʃəs], a. judicieux; **-ly,** adv. judicieusement; **ju'diciousness,** s. discernement m; bon sens.

jug [dʒʌg], s. **1.** cruche f, broc m; (for milk) pot m; **small j.,** cruchon m. **2.** P: prison f, taule f; **jugged,** a. Cu: **j. hare** = civet m de lièvre.

juggernaut ['dʒʌgənɔ:t], s. F: gros camion.

juggle ['dʒʌgl], v.i. (a) jongler; (b) faire des tours de passe-passe; **'juggler,** s. (a) jongleur, -euse; (b) prestidigitateur m; **'jugglery,** s. **1.** (a) jonglerie f; (b) tours mpl de passe-passe. **2.** fourberie f, mauvaise foi.

juice [dʒu:s], s. jus m, suc m (de la viande, d'un fruit); **to stew in one's own j.,** mijoter dans son (propre) jus; **'juiciness,** s. succulence f; **'juicy,** a. succulent, juteux; plein de jus.

jukebox ['dʒu:kbɔks], s. juke-box m.

July [dʒu'lai], s. juillet m; **in (the month of) J.,** en juillet, au mois de juillet; (on) **the seventh of J.,** le sept juillet.

jumble ['dʒʌmbl]. **I.** v.tr. brouiller, mêler; **to j. everything up,** F: tout mettre en salade. **II.** s. méli-mélo m; fouillis m; **j. sale,** vente f d'objets usagés (pour une œuvre de charité).

jumbo ['dʒʌmbou]. s. **1.** F: éléphant m. **2.** Av: **j. (jet),** (avion) gros porteur.

jump [dʒʌmp]. **I.** s. **1.** saut m, bond m; Sp: **high, long, j.,** saut en hauteur, en longueur. **2.** sursaut m, haut-le-corps m inv; **that gave me a j.,** cela m'a fait sursauter. **3.** Equit: obstacle m. **II.**

v. 1. *v.i.* (*a*) sauter, bondir; **to j. off a wall,** sauter à bas d'un mur; **to j. at an offer,** s'empresser d'accepter une offre; **to j. to a conclusion,** conclure à la légère; (*b*) sursauter, tressauter. 2. *v.tr.* (*a*) franchir, sauter (une haie); *Rail:* **to j. the rails,** sortir des rails; (*b*) **to j. the queue,** passer avant son tour; **to j. the gun,** (i) *Sp:* voler le départ; (ii) prendre les devants; **'jump a'bout,** *v.i.* sautiller; **'jump a'cross,** *v.tr.* franchir (qch.) d'un bond; **'jumped-'up,** *a. F:* (bourgeois) parvenu; **'jumper¹,** *s.* sauteur, -euse; **'jumper²,** *s. Cl:* 1. vareuse *f* (de marin). 2. tricot *m*, *F:* pull *m* (de femme). 3. *N.Am:* (*a*) robe *f* à bretelles; robe chasuble; (*b*) barboteuse *f* (pour enfant); **'jump 'in,** *v.i.* 1. entrer d'un bond; *Rail: Aut:* **j. in!** montez vite! 2. se jeter à l'eau; **'jump 'out,** *v.i.* sortir d'un bond; **to j. out of bed,** sauter à bas du lit; **I nearly jumped out of my skin,** cela m'a fait sursauter; **'jumping-'off,** *a.* j.-o. **place,** base avancée (d'une expédition, etc.); **'jumpy,** *a. F:* agité, nerveux; **to be j.,** avoir les nerfs à vif.

junction ['dʒʌŋ(k)ʃ(ə)n], *s.* 1. jonction *f*, confluent *m*; raccordement *m* (de tuyaux). 2. (*a*) (point *m* de) jonction; (em)branchement *m*, bifurcation *f*; (*b*) *Rail:* gare *f* de bifurcation, d'embranchement.

juncture ['dʒʌŋ(k)tʃər], *s.* conjoncture *f* (de circonstances); **at this j.,** dans les circonstances actuelles.

June [dʒuːn], *s.* juin *m*; **in (the month of) J.,** en juin, au mois de juin; **(on) the seventh of J.,** le sept juin.

jungle ['dʒʌŋgl], *s.* jungle *f*.

junior ['dʒuːnjər], *a. & s.* 1. (*in age*) cadet, -ette; plus jeune; **W. Smith J.** (*abbr:* jr, jnr, jun.), W. Smith (i) le jeune (*abbr:* je), (ii) fils; *Sp:* **j. event,** épreuve *f* des cadets. 2. (*in rank*) moins ancien; subalterne (*m*).

juniper ['dʒuːnipər], *s. Bot:* genévrier *m*, genièvre *m*.

junk¹ [dʒʌŋk], *s. Nau:* jonque *f*.

junk², *s.* matériaux *mpl* de rebut; *F:* camelote *f*; **j. dealer,** marchand *m* de ferraille, de chiffons; brocanteur *m*; **j. heap,** dépotoir *m*; décharge publique; **I got it at a j. shop,** je l'ai acheté chez un brocanteur.

junket ['dʒʌŋkit]. **I.** *s.* 1. *Cu:* lait caillé. 2. *F:* festin *m*. 3. *esp. N.Am:* voyage officiel aux frais de la princesse. **II.** *v.i. F:* 1. festoyer; *F:* faire la noce, la bombe. 2. *esp. N.Am:* voyager aux frais de la princesse.

jurisdiction [dʒuəris'dikʃ(ə)n], *s.* juridiction *f*; **this matter does not come within our j.,** cette matière n'est pas de notre compétence.

jury ['dʒuəri], *s.* jury *m*; jurés *mpl*; **to serve on the j.,** être du jury; **'juror,** *s.*, **'juryman,** *pl.*

-**men,** *s.* juré *m*, membre *m* du jury.

just [dʒʌst]. **I.** *a.* juste, équitable; **it's only j., ce** n'est que justice; **as was only j.,** comme de juste; -**ly,** *adv.* avec justice; **to deal j. with s.o.,** traiter qn équitablement; **j. famous,** célèbre à juste titre. **II.** *s.pl.* **to sleep the sleep of the j.,** dormir du sommeil du juste. **III.** *adv.* 1. (*a*) juste, justement, au juste; **j. by the door,** tout près de la porte; **not ready j. yet,** pas encore tout à fait prêt; **j. how many are there?** combien y en a-t-il au juste? **that's j. it,** (i) c'est bien cela; (ii) justement! **j. so!** c'est bien cela! parfaitement! **very j. so,** très correct; **it's j. the same,** c'est tout un; **he did it j. for a joke,** il l'a fait simplement histoire de rire; **it's j. the same,** c'est tout un; (*b*) **j. as:** (i) **I can do it j. as well as** he, je peux le faire tout aussi bien que lui; **j. as you please!** comme vous voudrez! **leave my things j. as they are,** laissez mes affaires telles quelles; (ii) **j. as he was starting out,** au moment où il partait; (*c*) **j. now,** (i) actuellement; en ce moment; (ii) **I can't do it j. now,** je ne peux pas le faire pour le moment; (iii) **I saw** him **j. now,** je l'ai vu tout à l'heure. 2. (*a*) **j. before I came,** immédiatement avant mor arrivée; (*b*) **he has j. written to you,** il vient de vous écrire; **he has j. come,** il ne fait que d'arriver; (*of book*) **j. out,** vient de paraître. 3 **I'm j. coming!** j'arrive! **he's j. going out,** il es sur le point de sortir. 4. **I was only j. save** **from drowning,** j'ai failli me noyer; **I've go** only **j. enough to live on,** j'ai tout juste de quo vivre; **you're j. in time to . . .,** vous arrive juste à temps pour . . .. 5. (*a*) seulement; **once,** rien qu'une fois; **j. one,** un seul; **j. a litt** **bit,** un tout petit peu; (*b*) **j. listen!** écoutez donc

justice ['dʒʌstis], *s.* 1. justice *f*; (*a*) **poetic j** justice idéale; **the portrait didn't do him j.,** portrait ne l'avantageait pas; **to do j. to a mea** faire honneur à un repas; (*b*) **to bring s.o. to j** traduire qn en justice. 2. magistrat *m*; juge *m*

justify ['dʒʌstifai], *v.tr.* justifier (qn, sa co duite); légitimer (une action); **justi'fiable,** (*action*) justifiable; (colère) légitim **justification** [dʒʌstifi'keiʃ(ə)n], justification *f*; **'justified,** *a.* justifié; **fully decision,** décision bien fondée; **to be j. (in doi** **sth.),** avoir raison (de faire qch.).

justness ['dʒʌstnis], *s.* 1. justice *f*. 2. justesse (d'une observation).

jut [dʒʌt], *v.i.* (jutted) **to j. (out),** être en saill faire saillie; **to j. out over sth.,** surplomber qc

juvenile ['dʒuːvənail], *a.* juvénile; **j. books, livr** pour la jeunesse; **j. delinquency,** délinquanc juvénile; **j. delinquent,** enfant délinqua jeune délinquant, -ante.

juxtaposition [dʒʌkstəpə'ziʃ(ə)n], *s.* juxtapo tion *f*; **to be in j.,** se juxtaposer.

K

K, k [kei], s. (la lettre) K, k m.
kale [keil], s. **curly k.,** chou frisé.
kangaroo [kæŋgə'ru:], s. Z: kangourou m.
kaolin ['keiɔlin], s. kaolin m.
kapok ['keipɔk], s. kapok m.
Kashmir [kæʃ'miər]. Pr.n. Geog: le Cachemire; **Kash'miri,** a. & s. Cachemirien, -ienne.
Kate [keit]. Pr.n.f. Catherine.
kayak ['kaiæk], s. kayak m.
keel [ki:l]. I. s. Nau: quille f. II. v.i. to k. over, chavirer.
keen [ki:n]. a. 1. (couteau) affilé, aiguisé; k. **edge,** fil tranchant. 2. (vent, froid) vif, perçant. 3. k. **appetite,** appétit vorace. 4. (a) ardent, zélé; k. **golfer,** enragé m de golf; F: to be k. on sth., être emballé pour qch.; **he isn't k. on it,** il n'y tient pas beaucoup; (b) k. **competition,** concurrence acharnée. 5. (œil) perçant, vif; to have a k. **ear,** avoir l'ouïe fine. 6. (esprit) fin, pénétrant; -ly, adv. âprement, vivement; **'keenness,** s. 1. finesse f, acuité f (du tranchant d'un outil). 2. âpreté f (du froid). 3. ardeur f, zèle m. 4. k. of **sight,** acuité de la vision.
keep [ki:p]. I. v. (kept) 1. v.tr. (a) observer, suivre (une règle); tenir (une promesse); to k. **an appointment,** ne pas manquer un rendez-vous; (b) célébrer (une fête); observer (le carême); (c) préserver (s.o. **from evil,** qn du mal); (d) tenir (un journal); avoir (une voiture); élever (de la volaille); tenir (un hôtel); **badly kept road,** route mal entretenue; **he has his parents to k.,** il a ses parents à sa charge; (in shop) **we don't k. cigars,** nous ne vendons pas de cigares; (e) maintenir (l'ordre); garder (le silence); (f) retenir (qn à dîner); cacher (qch. à qn); k. **this to yourself,** gardez cela pour vous; **don't let me k. you,** je ne vous retiens pas; **the noise keeps me from sleeping,** le bruit m'empêche de dormir; (g) **I'll k. a seat for you,** je vous réserverai une place; to k. **one's seat,** rester assis; (h) he can't k. **a thing in his head,** il ne retient rien; to k. **one's figure,** garder sa ligne; (i) to k. **warm,** (i) se tenir au chaud; (ii) se vêtir chaudement; to k. s.o. **waiting,** faire attendre qn. 2. v.i. (a) to k. **standing,** rester debout; to k. **smiling,** garder le sourire; to k. **straight on,** aller tout droit; F: to k. **at it,** travailler sans relâche; (b) (of food, etc.) se garder, se conserver. II. s. 1. donjon m. 2. nourriture f; frais mpl de subsistance; to **earn one's k.,** gagner de quoi vivre; F: gagner sa croûte; **fifty francs a day and his k.,**

cinquante francs par jour logé et nourri; **he isn't worth his k.,** il ne gagne pas sa nourriture. 3. F: for keeps, pour de bon; **'keep a'way.** 1. v.tr. éloigner; tenir éloigné. 2. v.i. se tenir à l'écart; **'keep 'back.** 1. v.tr. (a) arrêter (l'ennemi); retenir (la foule); (b) dissimuler (la vérité); (c) retenir (une somme sur un compte). 2. v.i. k. back! n'avancez pas! **'keep 'down.** 1. v.tr. (a) empêcher (qn, qch.) de monter; (b) she **kept her head down,** elle se tenait la tête baissée; to k. **prices down,** maintenir les prix bas. 2. v.i. se tapir; **'keeper,** s. gardien m; garde-chasse m; surveillant m; conservateur m (de musée); **'keep 'in.** 1. v.tr. (a) retenir (qn) à la maison; Sch: mettre en retenue; (b) contenir (sa colère); (c) entretenir (le feu); (d) to k. **one's hand in,** s'entretenir la main. 2. v.i. to k. **in with** s.o., cultiver qn; **'keeping,** s. 1. observation f (d'une règle); célébration f (d'une fête). 2. to be **in s.o.'s safe k.,** être sous la garde de qn. 3. tenue f (d'une comptabilité, etc.). 4. **in k. with . . .,** en accord, en rapport, avec . . .; **out of k. with . . .,** en désaccord avec . . .; **'keep 'off.** 1. v.tr. k. **off the grass,** défense de marcher sur le gazon; k. **your hands off!** n'y touchez pas! 2. v.i. se tenir éloigné; **if the rain keeps off,** s'il ne pleut pas; **'keep 'on.** 1. v.tr. (a) garder (son chapeau); k. **your hat on,** restez couvert; (b) ne pas congédier (un employé); **I hope I'll be kept on,** j'espère garder ma place. 2. v.i. to k. **on doing sth.,** continuer de, à, faire qch.; **he keeps on hoping,** il s'obstine à espérer; F: to k. **on at** s.o., être toujours sur le dos de qn; **'keep 'out.** 1. v.tr. empêcher (qn) d'entrer. 2. F: k. **out of this!** mêlez-vous de ce qui vous regarde! ne vous en mêlez pas! **'keep to,** (a) v.tr. to k. s.o. **to his promise,** obliger qn à tenir sa promesse; (b) v.i. to k. **to a resolution,** s'en tenir à une résolution; to k. **to one's bed,** garder le lit; to k. **to the left,** tenir la gauche; **keep to'gether.** v.i. (a) rester ensemble; (b) rester unis; **'keep 'up.** 1. v.tr. (a) entretenir (une route); maintenir (une maison) en bon état; (b) to k. **up the pace,** conserver l'allure; F: k. **it up!** allez toujours! continuez! (c) soutenir (l'intérêt); to k. **up appearances,** sauver les apparences; (d) **I mustn't k. you up,** je ne veux pas vous empêcher de vous coucher. 2. v.i. to k. **up with the Joneses,** rivaliser avec le voisin; to k. **up with the times,** être de son temps.
keg [keg], s. caque f (de harengs); barillet m

K:1

(d'eau-de-vie).

kelp [kelp], s. varech m.

kennel ['ken(ə)l], s. chenil m (de chiens de chasse); niche f (de chien de garde); pl. (i) établissement m d'élevage de chiens (de race); (ii) pension f pour chiens et chats.

Kenya ['ki:njə, 'kenjə]. Pr.n. Geog: le Kenya.

kerb [kə:b], s. 1. bord m, bordure f, du trottoir; Aut: to hit the k., heurter le trottoir. 2. H: garde-feu m inv.

kernel ['kə:n(ə)l], s. 1. amande f (de noix, de noisette). 2. the k. of the matter, l'essentiel m, le fond, de l'affaire.

kerosene ['kerəsi:n], s. kérosène m.

ketchup ['ketʃəp], s. sauce piquante à base de tomates.

kettle [ketl], s. bouilloire f.

key [ki:], s. 1. clef f, clé f; to leave the k. in the door, laisser la clef sur la porte; k. man, homme indispensable, pilier m (d'un établissement); k. money, pas m de porte; k. position, poste m, position f, clef; k. ring, porte-clefs m inv; k. word, mot-clé m, pl. mots-clés. 2. Mus: major k., ton majeur; the k. of C., le ton d'ut; to speak in a high k., parler sur un ton haut. 3. touche f (de piano, de machine à écrire, etc.); 'keyboard, s. 1. clavier m (de piano, de machine à écrire). 2. (in hotel) porte-clefs m inv; tableau m; 'keyhole, s. trou m de (la) serrure; 'key-note, s. Mus: tonique f; note dominante (d'un discours); 'key-'signature, s. Mus: armature f (de la clef); 'keystone, s. Const: clef f de voûte, claveau m.

khaki ['ka:ki], a. & s. kaki (m).

kick [kik]. I. v. 1. v.i. (a) (of animals) ruer; (b) (of pers.) to k. at, against, sth., regimber contre qch.; (c) (of gun) reculer, repousser. 2. v.tr. donner un coup de pied à (qn, qch.); (of horse) détacher un coup de sabot à (qn); I could have kicked myself, je me serais donné des claques; Fb: to k. a goal, marquer un but; to k. the ball, botter le ballon; to k. off, donner le coup d'envoi; to k. up a fuss, faire des embarras. II. s. 1. coup m de pied; ruade f (d'un cheval). 2. F: he has no k. left in him, il est à plat; a drink with a k. in it, une boisson qui vous remonte. 3. recul m (d'un fusil); 'kick-off, s. Fb: coup m d'envoi.

kid¹ [kid], s. 1. Z: chevreau m, f. chevrette; k. gloves, gants (en peau) de chevreau; to handle s.o. with k. gloves, ménager qn. 2. F: gosse mf; my k. brother, mon petit frère.

kid², v.tr. (kidded) F: en conter à (qn); faire marcher (qn); no kidding! sans blague! to k. oneself that . . ., se faire accroire que . . ..

kidnap ['kidnæp], v.tr. (kidnapped) enlever de vive force; voler (un enfant); kidnapper (qn);

'kidnapper, s. auteur m d'un enlèvement; voleur, -euse (d'enfant); kidnappeur, -euse; 'kidnapping, s. enlèvement m; Jur: rapt m, vol m (d'enfant); kidnapping m.

kidney ['kidni], s. 1. (a) Anat: rein m; (b) of the same k., du même acabit. 2. Cu: rognon m.

kill [kil]. I. v.tr. 1. (a) tuer, faire mourir (qn); to be hard to k., avoir la vie dure; he was laughing fit to k. himself, he was killing himself laughing, il crevait de rire; (b) abattre, tuer (une bête). 2. to k. time, tuer le temps. II. s. (a) mise f à mort (d'un renard, etc.); (b) le gibier tué, le tableau (de chasse); 'killer, s. tueur, -euse; meurtrier m; 'killing. I. a. 1. (travail) tuant, assommant, écrasant. 2. F: tordant, crevant. II. s. 1. tuerie f, massacre m; abattage m (d'animaux). 2. meurtre m; 'killjoy, s. rabat-joie m inv; 'kill 'off, v.tr. exterminer.

kiln [kiln], s. four m (à céramique, etc.).

kilogram(me) ['kiləgræm], s. kilogramme m, F: kilo m.

kilometre ['kiləmi:tər, ki'ləmitər], s. kilomètre m.

kilt [kilt], s. kilt m.

kimono, pl. -os [ki'mounou, -ouz], s. kimono m.

kin [kin], s. (a) parents mpl; (b) to inform the next of k., prévenir la famille.

kind¹ [kaind], s. 1. genre m, espèce f, sorte f; of what k. is it? de quelle sorte est-ce? what k. of man is he? quel genre d'homme est-ce? F: I k. of expected it, je m'en doutais presque; nothing of the k., rien de la sorte; in a k. of a way, en quelque façon. 2. payment in k., paiement en nature.

kind², a. bon, aimable, bienveillant; to be k. to s.o., se montrer bon pour, envers, qn; it's very k. of you, c'est bien aimable de votre part; 'kind-'hearted, a. bon, bienveillant; 'kindliness, s. bonté f, bienveillance f; 'kindly. 1. a. bon, bienveillant. 2. adv. avec bonté, avec douceur; to be k. disposed towards s.o., éprouver de la sympathie pour qn; Com: remit by cheque, prière de nous couvrir par chèque; not to take k. to sth., ne pas s'accommoder de qch.; 'kindness, s. 1. bonté f, amabilité f. 2. to do s.o. a k., rendre service à qn.

kindergarten ['kindəga:tn], s. école maternelle.

kindle ['kindl]. 1. v.tr. allumer; enflammer, embraser. 2. v.i. s'allumer, s'enflammer, prendre feu.

king [kiŋ], s. 1. (a) roi m; K. John, le roi Jean; (b) magnat (industriel, financier). 2. (a) (at chess, cards) roi; (b) (at draughts) dame; 'kingcup, s. Bot: bouton m d'or; 'kingdom, s. 1. royaume m; the United K., le Royaume-Uni. 2. règne (animal, végétal). 3. Ecc: Thy k. come, que ton règne arrive; 'kingfisher,

martin-pêcheur *m*; **'king-size(d)**, *a. Com:*
(format) géant.

kink [kiŋk], *s.* **1.** nœud *m* (dans une corde); faux
pli. **2.** *F:* lubie *f*, marotte *f*; manie *f*.

kinsman, *f.* **-woman** ['kinzmən, -wumən], *s.*
esp. Scot: parent *m*, parente *f*; **'kinsfolk**, *s. pl.*
esp. Scot: parents et alliés *mpl*; la famille.

kiosk ['ki:ɔsk], *s.* kiosque *m*.

kipper ['kipər], *s.* hareng salé et fumé; kipper *m*.

kirk [kə:k], *s. Scot:* église *f*.

kiss [kis]. **I.** *s.* baiser *m*; *F:* bise *f*. **II.** *v.tr.* embrasser (qn); donner un baiser à (qn); *F:*
donner une bise à (qn); **they kissed (each
other)**, ils se sont embrassés.

kit [kit], *s.* **1.** *(a) Mil: Nau:* petit équipement; *F:*
fourbi *m*; *(b)* sac *m* (de marin); *(c)* effets *mpl* (de
voyageur). **2.** *Tchn:* trousseau *m*, trousse *f*
(d'outils); **repair k.**, nécessaire *m* de réparation;
model k., boîte *f* de construction; **first aid k.**,
trousse de première urgence; **'kit-bag**, *s.* **1.**
sac *m* (de voyage). **2.** *Mil:* ballot *m*, musette *f*.

kitchen ['kitʃən], *s.* cuisine *f*; *attrib.* **k. table**,
table *f* de cuisine; **k. equipment, k. utensils**,
batterie *f* de cuisine; **k. unit**, bloc-cuisine *m*; **k.
garden**, potager *m*, jardin *m* potager; **k. maid**,
fille *f* de cuisine; **kitche'nette**, *s.* petite
cuisine.

kite [kait], *s.* **1.** *Orn:* milan *m*. **2.** cerf-volant *m*,
pl. cerfs-volants.

kitten [kitn], *s.* chaton *m*; petit(e) chat(te);
'kittenish, *a. (of woman)* coquette; enjouée;
to have a k. grace, avoir une grâce féline; **'kitty**[1], *s. F:* chaton *m*.

kitty[2] ['kiti], *s.* cagnotte *f*.

kiwi ['ki:wi:], *s. Orn:* aptéryx *m*; kiwi *m*.

kleptomania [kleptə'meiniə], *s.* kleptomanie *f*;
klepto'maniac, *a. & s.* kleptomane (*mf*).

knack [næk], *s.* tour *m* de main; *F:* truc *m*; **to
have the k. of doing sth.**, avoir le talent pour
faire qch.

knapsack ['næpsæk], *s.* havresac *m*; sac alpin,
sac à dos.

knave [neiv], *s.* **1.** fripon *m*, coquin *m*. **2.** *Cards:*
valet *m*.

knead [ni:d], *v.tr.* pétrir, malaxer, travailler (la
pâte, l'argile, les muscles d'un athlète);
'kneading-trough, *s.* pétrin *m*.

knee [ni:], *s.* genou *m*; **on one's knees**, à genoux;
to go down on one's knees, s'agenouiller; se
mettre à genoux; **'knee-cap**, *s. Anat:* rotule *f*;
'knee-'deep, *a.* jusqu'aux genoux; à hauteur
du genou.

kneel [ni:l], *v.i.* **(knelt** [nelt]) **to k. (down)**,
s'agenouiller; se mettre à genoux.

knell [nel], *s.* glas *m*; **to toll the k.**, sonner le glas.

knickers ['nikəz], *s. pl.* culotte *f* (de femme).

knick-knack ['niknæk], *s.* bibelot *m*.

knife, *pl.* **knives** [naif, naivz]. **I.** *s.* couteau *m*;

table, kitchen, k., couteau de table, de cuisine;
flick k., couteau automatique à cran d'arrêt; **to
get one's k. into s.o.**, s'acharner après, contre,
qn. **II.** *v.tr.* donner un coup de couteau à (qn);
poignarder (qn).

knight [nait]. **I.** *s.* **1.** chevalier *m*. **2.** *(at chess)*
cavalier *m*. **II.** *v.tr.* faire, créer, (qn) chevalier;
'knighthood, *s.* titre *m* de chevalier.

knit [nit], *v.tr.* **(knitted)** **1.** *(a)* tricoter; *(b)* **to k.
one's brows**, froncer les sourcils. **2.** *(a)* joindre,
unir; *(b) v.i. (of bones)* se souder; **'knitting**, *s.*
1. *(action)* tricotage *m*. **2.** tricot *m*; **plain k.**,
tricot en point mousse; **'knitting machine**, *s.*
tricoteuse *f*; **'knitting-needle**, *s.* aiguille *f* à
tricoter.

knob [nɔb], *s.* **1.** *(a)* bosse *f*, protubérance *f*; *(on
tree)* nœud *m*; *(b)* pomme *f* (de canne); bouton
m (de porte, de tiroir). **2.** morceau *m* (de
beurre, de charbon); **'knobbly**, *a.* plein de
bosses.

knock [nɔk]. **I.** *s.* coup *m*, heurt *m*, choc *m*; **to get
a nasty k.**, attraper un vilain coup; **there was a
k. (at the door)**, on a frappé à la porte. **II.** *v.* **1.**
v.tr. frapper, heurter, cogner; **to k. one's head
against sth.**, (i) se frapper la tête contre qch.;
(ii) se heurter à un obstacle. **2.** *v.i.* *(a)* **to k.
against sth.**, se heurter, se cogner, contre qch.;
(b) *Aut: (of engine)* cogner; *(c)* **to k. at the
door**, frapper à la porte; **'knock a'bout**,
a'round. **1.** *v.tr.* bousculer, malmener (qn);
maltraiter (qn, qch.). **2.** *v.i.* **to k. about (the
world)**, parcourir le monde; rouler sa bosse;
'knock 'back, *v.tr. F:* **to k. back a drink**, prendre un verre; *F:* s'enfiler un pot; **'knock 'down**,
v.tr. **1.** jeter (qch.), étendre (qn), par terre;
démolir (un mur, etc.); **to be knocked down by a
car**, être renversé par une voiture. **2.** *(at auction)*
to k. sth. down to s.o., adjuger qch. à qn. **3.**
baisser, faire baisser, considérablement (le prix
de qch.); **'knocker**, marteau *m*, heurtoir *m* (de
porte); **'knocking**, *s.* **1.** coups *mpl* (à la porte,
etc.). **2.** cognement *m* (d'un moteur); **'knock-
'kneed**, *a.* cagneux; **'knock 'off. 1.** *v.tr.* faire
tomber (qch.) (de la table, etc.); **to k. sth. off the
price**, rabattre qch. sur le prix. **2.** *v.i. F:* cesser le
travail; *F:* débrayer; **'knock 'out**, *v.tr.* faire
sortir, faire sauter (un clou, etc.); chasser,
repousser (un rivet); *Box:* knockouter, mettre
knock-out, *F:* mettre k.-o. (son adversaire); *Sp:*
(in tournament, etc.) **to be knocked out**, être
éliminé; **'knock 'over**, *v.tr.* faire tomber,
renverser (qch.); **'knock 'up. 1.** *v.tr. (a)*
réveiller, faire lever (qn); *(b)* **I'm completely
knocked up**, je suis complètement éreinté; *(c)*
construire (un batiment) à la hâte. **2.** *v.i.* **to k. up
against sth.**, s.o., (se) heurter contre qch.; rencontrer qn par hasard.

knoll [noul], *s.* tertre *m*, monticule *m*, butte *f*.

knot [nɔt]. **I.** *s.* **1.** (*a*) nœud *m*; **to tie a k.,** faire un nœud; (*b*) **k. of hair,** chignon *m*. **2.** *Nau:* **to make ten knots,** filer dix nœuds. **3.** nœud (du bois). **4.** groupe *m* (de personnes). **II.** *v.tr. & i.* (knotted) (se) nouer, faire des nœuds; **'knot-ty,** *a.* plein de nœuds; noueux; **a k. problem,** un problème difficile, délicat.

know [nou]. **I.** *v.tr. & i.* (knew; known) **1.** con-naître; **do you k. his son?** avez-vous fait la connaissance de son fils? **to be in surroundings one knows,** être en pays de connaissance. **2.** connaître, fréquenter (qn). **3.** savoir, connaître, posséder (un sujet); **to k. how to do sth.,** savoir faire qch.; **to k. sth. by heart,** savoir qch. par cœur; **I k. that only too well,** je ne le sais que trop; **as far as I k.,** autant que je sache; **not to k. sth.,** ne pas savoir qch., ignorer qch.; **I don't k.,** je ne sais pas; **as everyone knows,** comme tout le monde le sait; **he had never been known to laugh,** on ne l'avait jamais vu rire; **to get to k. sth.,** apprendre qch.; **everything gets known,** tout se sait; *F:* **he knows what's what,** il est sûr de son fait; *F:* **don't I k. it!** à qui le dites-vous! *F:* **not if I k. it!** pour rien au monde! **4. to k. better than to . . .,** bien se gar-der de . . .; **you k. best,** vous en êtes le meilleur juge. **5. to k. about sth.,** être au courant de qch.; **I don't k. about that,** je n'en suis pas bien sûr! **I k. nothing about it,** je n'en sais rien. **II.** *s.* *F:* **to be in the k.,** être au courant; être dans le secret; **'know-all,** *s.* *F:*

je-sais-tout *m*; **'know-how,** *s.* *F:* tour *m*, coup *m*, de main, méthode *f*, technique *f*, manière *f* (de s'y prendre); connaissances *f* techniques; **'knowing.** **I.** *a.* fin, malin, rusé; **a k. smile,** un sourire entendu; **-ly,** *adv.* **1.** sciemment. **2.** habilement; d'un air entendu; d'un air malin, rusé. **II.** *s.* **there's no k.** (how), il n'y a pas moyen de savoir (comment); **knowledge** ['nɔlidʒ], *s.* **1.** connaissance *f* (d'un fait, d'une personne); **lack of k.,** ignorance *f* (of, de); **I had no k. of it,** je ne le savais pas; je l'ignorais; **to the best of my k.,** à ma connaissance; **it's a matter of common k. that . . .,** il est notoire que . . .; **without my k.,** à mon insu *m*; **not to my k.,** pas que je sache. **2.** savoir *m*, con-naissances *fpl*; **to have a k. of several languages,** connaître plusieurs langues; **to have a thorough k. of a subject,** connaître, posséder, un sujet à fond; **'knowledgeable,** *a.* bien informé.

knuckle ['nʌkl]. **I.** *s.* **1.** articulation *f*, jointure *f* du doigt. **2.** *Cu:* souris *f* (d'un gigot); jarret *m* (de veau). **II.** *v.i.* **to k. down (to work, etc.),** s'y mettre sérieusement; **to k. under,** se soumettre, céder.

koala [kou'ɑ:lə], *s.* *Z:* koala *m*.

Korea [kə'riə]. *Pr.n.* *Geog:* la Corée; **Ko'rean** *a. & s.* coréen, -enne; **the K. War,** la Guerre de Corée.

kudos ['kju:dɔs], *s.* *F:* prestige *m*.

Kuwait [ku:'weit]. *Pr.n.* *Geog:* Koweït *m*.

L

,, l [el], *s.* (la lettre) L, l *m or f.*

a [lɑ:], *s. Mus:* la *m.*

ab [læb], *s. F:* labo *m.*

abel ['leibl]. **I.** *s.* **1.** étiquette *f.* **2.** *Com:* label *m.* **II.** *v.tr.* (**labelled**) étiqueter.

abial ['leibiəl]. **1.** *a.* labial. **2.** *s. Ling:* labiale *f.*

aboratory [lə'bɔrətri, 'læbrətri], *s.* laboratoire *m*; **l. assistant,** laborantin, -ine.

aborious [lə'bɔːriəs], *a.* laborieux; (*a*) travailleur; (*b*) pénible, fatigant; **-ly**, *adv.* laborieusement, péniblement.

abour ['leibər]. **I.** *s.* **1.** (*a*) travail *m*, labeur *m*, peine *f*; **material and l.,** matériel *m* et main-d'œuvre *f*; **manual l.,** travail manuel; (*b*) *Jur:* **hard l.,** travaux forcés; réclusion criminelle. **2.** (*a*) *Ind:* main-d'œuvre; travailleurs *mpl*; **skilled l.,** main-d'œuvre qualifiée; **l. troubles,** agitation ouvrière; (*b*) *coll. Pol:* les travaillistes *m*; **the L. Party,** le parti travailliste. **3. l. of love,** travail fait avec plaisir. **4.** *Med:* travail. **II.** *v.* **1.** *v.i.* (*a*) travailler, peiner; (*b*) **to l. under a delusion,** se faire illusion; (*c*) (*of car engine*) peiner. **2.** *v.tr.* **I will not l. the point,** je ne m'étendrai pas là-dessus; '**laboured**, *a.* **1.** (style) travaillé. **2.** (respiration) pénible; '**labourer**, *s.* (*a*) travailleur; (*b*) *Ind:* manœuvre *m*; homme *m* de peine; (*c*) **agricultural l.,** ouvrier *m* agricole; '**Labour Exchange,** *s.* bourse *f* du travail; '**labour-saving,** *a.* (appareil) électroménager.

burnum [lə'bɔːnəm], *s.* cytise *m.*

byrinth ['læbirinθ], *s.* labyrinthe *m.*

ce [leis]. **I.** *s.* **1.** lacet *m* (de soulier); cordon *m.* **2. gold l.,** galon *m*, passement *m* d'or. **3.** dentelle *f*; **Alençon l.,** point *m* d'Alençon. **II.** *v.tr.* **1. to l. (up) one's shoes,** lacer ses chaussures; **l.-up shoes,** chaussures *f* à lacets. **2. milk laced with rum,** lait *m* au rhum.

cerate ['læsəreit], *v.tr.* lacérer; déchirer (la chair, le cœur); **lace'ration,** *s.* **1.** lacération *f*, déchirement *m.* **2.** *Med:* déchirure *f.*

ck [læk]. **I.** *s.* manque *m*, absence *f*, défaut *m* (**of,** de); **for l. of sth.,** faute de qch. **II.** *v.tr.* manquer de (qch.); ne pas avoir (qch.); '**lacking,** *a.* qui manque; manquant; **l. in meaning,** dénué de sens; *F:* **he's a bit l.,** il est un peu simplet.

onic [lə'kɔnik], *a.* laconique; **-ally,** *adv.* laconiquement.

quer ['lækər]. **I.** *s.* **1.** vernis-laque *m inv*; laque *m.* **2.** laque *f*; *Aut:* **cellulose l.,** laque *f*

(cellulosique). **3.** (**hair**) l., laque *f.* **II.** *v.tr.* **1.** laquer. **2.** vernir (des meubles).

lacrosse [lə'krɔs], *s. Sp:* crosse canadienne.

lad [læd], *s.* (*a*) jeune homme *m*; (jeune) garçon *m*; (*b*) *Rac:* (**stable**) l., lad *m.*

ladder ['lædər]. **I.** *s.* **1.** échelle *f.* **2.** (*in stocking*) maille *f* qui file; **to mend a l.,** rem(m)ailler un bas. **II.** *v.i.* (*of stocking*) se démailler.

laden ['leidn], *a.* chargé; *Nau:* **fully l.,** (navire) en pleine charge; '**lading,** *s. Nau:* chargement *m.*

ladle ['leidl]. **I.** *s.* cuiller *f* à pot; **soup l.,** louche *f.* **II.** *v.tr.* **to l.** (**out**), servir (le potage).

lady ['leidi], *s.* dame *f.* **1.** (*a*) femme bien élevée; (*b*) **a l. and a gentleman,** un monsieur et une dame; **an old l.,** une vieille dame; (*at meeting*) **ladies and gentlemen!** mesdames, mesdemoiselles, messieurs! (*on W.C.*) **ladies,** dames; *F:* **where's the ladies?** où est la toilette? (*c*) **ladies' tailor,** tailleur *m* pour dames. **2.** (*a*) *Ecc:* **Our L.,** Notre-Dame; **L. day,** la fête de l'Annonciation; (*b*) **my l.,** madame *f* (la comtesse, etc.); '**ladybird,** *s. Ent:* coccinelle *f*, bête *f* à bon Dieu; '**ladyship,** *s.* **her l.,** madame (la comtesse, etc.).

lag¹ [læg]. **I.** *v.i.* (**lagged**) traîner, rester en arrière. **II.** *s.* (**time**) l., retard *m.*

lag², *v.tr.* (**lagged**) garnir, revêtir, (une chaudière) d'un calorifuge; '**lagging,** *s.* revêtement *m* calorifuge.

lager ['lɑːgər], *s.* bière blonde (de type allemand).

lagoon [lə'guːn], *s.* (*a*) lagune *f*; (*b*) lagon *m* (d'atoll).

lair ['lɛər], *s.* tanière *f*, repaire *m* (de bête fauve).

lake¹ [leik], *s.* lac *m.*

lake², *s. Paint:* **crimson l.,** laque carminée.

lama ['lɑːmə], *s. Rel:* lama *m.*

lamb [læm], *s.* agneau *m*; **ewe l.,** agnelle *f*; *F:* **he took it like a l.,** il s'est laissé faire.

lame [leim]. **I.** *a.* **1.** boiteux; (*through accident*) estropié; **to be l. in one leg,** boiter d'une jambe; **to go l.,** se mettre à boiter. **2.** (*of excuse*) pauvre, faible. **II.** *v.tr.* rendre (qn) boiteux; estropier (qn); '**lameness,** *s.* **1.** claudication *f*; boitement *m*; boiterie *f* (d'un cheval). **2.** faiblesse *f* (d'une excuse).

lament [lə'ment]. **I.** *s.* lamentation *f.* **II.** *v.tr. & i.* **to l. (for, over) s.o., sth.,** se lamenter sur qch.; pleurer qn, qch.; '**lamentable,** *a.* lamentable, déplorable; **-ably,** *adv.* lamentablement, déplorablement; **lamen'tation,** *s.* lamentation *f*; **la'mented**, *a*. **the late l. X**, le regretté X.

laminated ['læmineitid], *a*. (*of plastic, glass*) lamifié; (*of book*) **l. jacket**, jaquette plastifiée; **l. furniture**, meubles *mpl* en contre-plaqué *m*.

lamp [læmp], *s*. **1**. (*a*) lampe *f*; (*b*) *Aut:* **inspection l.**, baladeuse *f*; (*c*) *Min:* **safety l.**, lampe de sécurité. **2. table l.**, lampe de table; **standard l.**, lampadaire *m*; **street l.**, réverbère *m*. **3. arc l.**, lampe à arc; **neon l.**, lampe au néon; '**lamplight**, *s*. lumière *f* de la lampe; '**lamppost**, *s*. réverbère *m*; '**lampshade**, *s*. abat-jour *m inv*.

lance [lɑːns]. **I**. *s*. lance *f*. **II**. *v.tr*. *Med:* donner un coup de bistouri, de lancette, à (un abcès); '**lance-'corporal**, *s*. *Mil:* soldat *m* de première classe; '**lancet**, *s*. *Med:* lancette *f*; bistouri *m*.

land [lænd]. **I**. *s*. **1**. (*a*) terre *f*; **dry l.**, terre ferme; **by l. and sea**, sur terre et sur mer; **to see how the l. lies**, tâter le terrain; (*b*) terre, sol *m*; **waste l.**, terrain *m* vague. **2**. terre, pays *m*; **foreign lands**, terres étrangères. **3. come and shoot over my l.**, venez chasser sur mes terres. **II**. *v*. **1**. *v.tr*. (*a*) mettre (qn) à terre; débarquer (qn, qch.); décharger (qch.); (*b*) **to l. a fish**, amener un poisson à terre; *F:* **to l. a prize**, remporter un prix; (*c*) amener; *F:* **that will l. you in prison**, cela vous vaudra de la prison. **2**. *v.i*. (*a*) (*of pers.*) descendre à terre; débarquer; (*of aircraft*) atterrir; faire escale (at, à); **to l. on the moon**, atterrir sur la lune, alunir; (*b*) **he slipped and landed in a puddle**, il a glissé et est tombé dans une flaque d'eau; (*c*) *F:* **he always lands on his feet**, il retombe toujours sur ses pieds; '**landfall**, *s*. arrivée *f* en vue de terre; '**landing**, *s*. **1**. (*a*) débarquement *m*; mise *f* à terre; **l. stage**, débarcadère *m*, embarcadère *m* (flottant); (*b*) *Mil:* descente *f*; (*c*) *Av:* atterrissage *m*; **crash l.**, atterrissage brutal; *Space:* **soft l.**, atterrissage en douceur; **parachute l.**, parachutage *m*; **l. ground, field**, terrain *m* d'atterrissage; (*d*) *Fish:* **l. net**, épuisette *f*. **2**. palier *m* (d'un escalier); '**landlady**, *s.f*. **1**. logeuse (en garni). **2**. hôtelière; '**landlord**, *s*. **1**. propriétaire *mf* (d'un immeuble). **2**. aubergiste *m*, hôtelier *m*; '**landmark**, *s*. **1**. (point *m* de) repère *m*. **2**. point décisif, événement marquant; '**landowner**, *s*. propriétaire (foncier); '**landscape**, *s*. paysage *m*; **l. gardener**, jardinier *m* paysagiste; '**landslide**, *s*. **1**. éboulement *m*, glissement *m* (de terrain). **2**. *Pol:* débâcle *f*; **l. victory**, victoire écrasante.

lane [lein], *s*. **1**. chemin (vicinal, rural). **2**. *Nau:* (**shipping**) **l.**, route *f* (de navigation); *Aut:* (**traffic**) **l.**, voie *f*; **four l. highway**, route à quatre voies.

language ['læŋgwidʒ], *s*. **1**. langue *f*; **modern languages**, langues vivantes. **2**. langage *m*; **bad**

l., gros mots *mpl*, langage grossier.

languid ['læŋgwid], *a*. languissant; mou; **-ly** *adv*. avec langueur, mollement.

languish ['læŋgwiʃ], *v.i*. languir; '**languishing** *a*. languissant, langoureux; **languor** ['læŋgər], *s*. langueur *f*.

lank [læŋk], *a*. **1**. (*of pers.*) maigre; sec. **2**. **l. hair** cheveux . plats et gras; '**lanky**, *a*. grand e maigre, grand et sec.

lantern ['læntən], *s*. lanterne *f*, falot *m*; *Nau* fanal *m*; **Chinese l.**, lanterne vénitienne '**lantern-'jawed**, *a*. aux joues creuses.

lap¹ [læp], *s*. genoux *mpl*, giron *m*; **to sit on s.o.'** **l.**, s'asseoir sur les genoux de qn; '**lapdog**, *s* chien *m* de salon.

lap², *s*. *Sp:* tour *m* (de piste); boucle *f*, circuit *m* étape *f*.

lap³, *v*. (**lapped**) **1**. *v.tr*. (*of animal*) **to l.** (**u** **milk**, laper du lait. **2**. *v.i*. (*of waves*) clapoter.

lapel [lə'pel], *s*. revers *m* (d'un habit).

Lapland ['læplænd]. *Pr.n*. *Geog:* la Laponie '**Laplander**, *s*. Lapon, -one; **Lapp. 1**. lapon. **2**. *s*. Lapon, -one. **3**. *s*. *Ling:* le lapon.

lapse [læps]. **I**. *s*. **1**. (*a*) erreur *f*, faute *f*; **l.** **memory**, défaillance *f* de mémoire; (*b*) fau pas; **l. from duty**, manquement *m* au devoir. **2** cours *m*, marche *f* (du temps); laps *m* d temps; **after a l. of three months**, après un dél de trois mois; au bout de trois mois. **II**. *v.i*. **1** **l. from duty**, manquer au devoir. **2**. (*of la* *etc*.) (se) périmer; tomber en désuétude; cess d'être en vigueur; **lapsed**, *a*. **1**. déchu; **Catholic**, catholique non pratiquant. périmé; (*of contract*) caduc.

lapwing ['læpwiŋ], *s*. *Orn:* vanneau (huppé).

larceny ['lɑːsəni], *s*. larcin *m*.

larch [lɑːtʃ], *s*. *Bot:* mélèze *m*.

lard [lɑːd], *s*. saindoux *m*, graisse *f* de porc.

larder ['lɑːdər], *s*. garde-manger *m inv*.

large [lɑːdʒ]. **I**. *a*. (*a*) de grandes dimension grand; gros; fort; **to grow l.**, **larger**, gross grandir; (*b*) **a l. sum**, une forte somme, u somme considérable; **l. fortune**, belle fortun **l. family**, famille nombreuse; **l. meal**, rep copieux. **II**. *s*. (*a*) **to set a prisoner at l.**, élarg relaxer, un prisonnier; **at l.**, libre, en liberté; **people, the public, at l.**, le grand public; **-l** *adv*. en grande partie; pour une grande pa **very l.**, pour la plupart; '**large-'scale**, grosse (entreprise); (carte *f*) à grande échel

lariat ['læriət], *s*. **1**. corde *f* à piquet. **2**. lasso

lark¹ [lɑːk], *s*. *Orn:* alouette *f*; **to get up with** **l.**, se lever au chant du coq; '**larkspur**, *s*. *B* pied-d'alouette *m*.

lark². **I**. *s*. *F:* farce *f*, blague *f*, rigolade *f*; **for a** pour rire, histoire de rigoler. **II**. *v.i*. *F:* **to** (**about**), faire des farces; rigoler.

larrikin ['lærikin], *s*. *Austr:* *F:* gamin *m* (d rues).

arva, *pl.* -vae ['lɑ:və, -vi:], *s.* larve *f.*

arynx ['læriŋks], *s.* larynx *m*; **laryngitis** [lærin'dʒaitis], *s. Med:* laryngite *f.*

aser ['leizər], *s. Ph:* laser *m.*

ash¹ [læʃ]. I. *s.* 1. (*a*) coup *m* de fouet; (*b*) lanière *f* (de fouet). 2. cil *m.* II. *v.tr.* & *i.* (*a*) cingler (un cheval); fouetter (qn, un animal); (*b*) to l. oneself into a fury, entrer dans une violente colère; (*c*) (*of animal*) to l. its tail, se battre les flancs avec la queue;'**lashing**, *s.* 1. fouettée *f.* 2. *F:* **lashings of (sth.)**, des tas *mpl* de (qch.);'**lash 'out**, *v.i.* (*a*) (*of horse*) ruer; (*b*) (*of pers.*) to l. out at s.o., (i) invectiver qn; (ii) essayer de donner un coup de poing à qn; (*c*) se livrer à de folles dépenses.

ash², *v.tr.* lier, attacher; *Nau:* amarrer.

ass [læs], *s.f.* jeune fille.

assitude ['læsitjuːd], *s.* lassitude *f.*

asso, *pl.* -os [læ'suː, -uːz]. I. *s.* lasso *m.* II. *v.tr.* prendre (un cheval) au lasso.

ast¹ [lɑːst], *s.* forme *f* (à chaussure).

ast². I. *a.* dernier. 1. she was the l. to arrive, elle arriva la dernière; the l. but one, l'avant-dernier; l. but not least, le dernier, mais non le moindre; in the l. resort, as a l. resort, en dernier recours; l. thing at night, tard dans la soirée; *F:* the l. word in hats, chapeau dernier cri. 2. l. Monday, lundi dernier; l. week, la semaine dernière; l. night, (i) la nuit dernière; (ii) hier soir; this day l. week, il y a aujourd'hui huit jours; this day l. year, l'an dernier à pareil jour. II. *s.* (*a*) we shall never hear the l. of it, on ne nous le laissera pas oublier; we haven't heard the l. of it, tout n'est pas dit; that's the l. I saw of him, je ne l'ai pas revu depuis; this is the l. of it, c'est la fin; (*b*) to, till, the l., jusqu'au bout, jusqu'à la fin; (*c*) at (long) l., enfin, à la fin; (*d*) to look one's l. on (sth.), jeter un dernier regard sur (qch.); voir (qch.) pour la dernière fois. III. *adv.* (*a*) when I saw him l., l. saw him, la dernière fois que je l'ai vu; (*b*) he came l., il est arrivé le dernier; l. but not least, enfin et surtout; -ly, *adv.* pour finir; en dernier lieu.

ast³, *v.i.* durer, se maintenir; too good to l., trop beau pour durer; the supplies will not l. two months, les vivres ne feront pas deux mois; it will l. me a lifetime, j'en ai pour la vie; *F:* he won't l. long, il n'ira pas loin; '**lasting**, *a.* durable.

tch [lætʃ]. I. *s.* (*a*) loquet *m*; to leave the door on the l., fermer la porte au loquet; (*b*) serrure *f* de sûreté. II. *v.tr.* fermer (la porte) au loquet; '**latchkey**, *s.* clef *f* de maison.

e [leit]. I. *a.* 1. (*a*) I am l., je suis en retard; the train is l., le train a du retard; the train is ten minutes l., le train a dix minutes de retard; (*b*) (*delayed*) retardé. 2. tard; it's (getting) l., il est, il se fait, tard; I was too l., je suis arrivé trop tard, je ne suis pas arrivé à temps; *F:* it's a bit l.

in the day for changing your mind, il est un peu tard pour changer d'avis; to be l. going to bed, se coucher tard; he came in the l. afternoon, il est venu en fin d'après-midi; in l. summer, vers la fin de l'été; in later life, plus tard dans la vie. 3. (*of fruit*) tardif; l. frost, gelée tardive. 4. (*a*) ancien, ex-; the l. minister, l'ancien ministre, l'ex-ministre; (*b*) my l. father, feu mon père; the l. queen, feu la reine, la feue reine. 5. récent, dernier; of l., dernièrement; depuis peu; his latest novel, son dernier roman; is there any later news? a-t-on des nouvelles plus récentes? II. *adv.* l. en retard; to arrive too l., arriver trop tard; better l. than never, mieux vaut tard que jamais. 2. tard; sooner or later, tôt ou tard; to keep s.o. l., retenir, retarder, qn; to stay up l., se coucher tard; very l. at night, très tard dans la nuit; l. in life, à un âge avancé; a moment later, l'instant d'après; as l. as yesterday, no later than yesterday, hier encore; pas plus tard qu'hier; see you later! à plus tard! à tout à l'heure! -ly, *adv.* dernièrement; récemment; depuis peu; till l., jusqu'à ces derniers temps; '**latecomer**, *s.* retardataire *mf*; '**lateness**, *s.* 1. arrivée tardive. 2. the l. of the hour, l'heure avancée.

latent ['leitənt], *a.* latent; caché.

lateral ['lætərəl], *a.* latéral; -ally, *adv.* latéralement.

lath [lɑ:θ], *s.* latte *f.*

lathe [leið], *s. Tls:* tour *m.*

lather ['læðər]. I. *s.* 1. mousse *f* (de savon). 2. (*on horse*) écume *f.* II. *v.* 1. *v.tr.* (*a*) savonner; (*b*) *F:* rosser (qn). 2. *v.i.* (*a*) (*of soap*) mousser; (*b*) (*of horse*) jeter de l'écume; '**lathering**, *s.* 1. savonnage *m.* 2. *F:* rossée *f.*

Latin ['lætin]. 1. *a.* latin. 2. *s. Ling:* le latin.

latitude ['lætitjuːd], *s.* 1. to allow s.o. the greatest l., laisser à qn la plus grande latitude. 2. *Geog:* latitude *f*; in these latitudes, sous ces latitudes.

latter ['lætər], *a.* 1. dernier (des deux); the l., ce, le, dernier; celui-ci, ceux-ci. 2. the l. half of June, la seconde quinzaine de juin; -ly, *adv.* dans les derniers temps; dernièrement.

lattice ['lætis], *s.* treillis *m*, treillage *m*; l. window, (i) fenêtre treillagée; (ii) fenêtre à losanges.

laudable ['lɔːdəbl], *a.* louable; digne d'éloges; -ably, *adv.* louablement; '**laudatory**, *a.* élogieux.

laugh [lɑːf]. I. *s.* rire *m*; with a l., en riant; to raise a l., faire rire; to do sth. for a l., faire qch. histoire de rire. II. *v.* 1. *v.i.* (*a*) rire; to l. heartily, rire de bon cœur; to l. till one cries, rire (jusqu')aux larmes; to l. to oneself, rire tout bas; to l. up one's sleeve, rire sous cape; to l. in s.o.'s face, rire au nez de qn; (*b*) to l. at, over, sth., rire de qch.; there's nothing to l. at, il n'y a pas de quoi rire; **to l. at s.o.,** se moquer, (se) rire, de qn. **2.** *v.tr.* **we laughed him out of it,** nous nous sommes tellement moqués de lui qu'il y a renoncé; **he laughed the matter off,** il a tourné la chose en plaisanterie; **'laughable,** *a.* risible, ridicule; **'laughing. 1.** *a.* riant; rieur. **2.** *s.* rires *mpl*; **it's no l. matter,** il n'y a pas de quoi rire; **-ly,** *adv.* en riant; **'laughing-stock,** *s.* to be the l.-s. of the school, être la risée de l'école; **to make a l.-s. of oneself,** se faire moquer de soi; **'laughter,** *s.* rire(s) *m(pl)*; **to burst into l.,** éclater de rire; **to be convulsed with l.,** se tordre de rire; **to roar with l.,** rire aux éclats; *F:* **to die with l.,** crever de rire.

launch [lɔːntʃ]. **I.** *s.* chaloupe *f*; **motor l.,** vedette *f*; **police l.,** vedette de la police. **II.** *v.* **1.** *v.tr.* (*a*) lancer (un projectile, un coup); (*b*) mettre (une embarcation) à la mer; (*c*) lancer (une affaire); *Mil:* déclencher (une offensive). **2.** *v.i.* **to l. out (into expense),** se lancer dans la dépense; se mettre en frais; **'launching,** *s.* lancement *m* (d'un navire, d'une affaire, d'une fusée); mise *f* à l'eau (d'un navire); **l. pad,** rampe *f* de lancement.

laundry ['lɔːndri], *s.* **1.** blanchisserie *f*. **2.** linge (i) blanchi, (ii) à blanchir; **l. list,** liste *f* de blanchissage; **launde'rette,** *s.* laverie *f* automatique.

laurel ['lɔrəl], *s. Bot:* laurier *m*; **to rest on one's laurels,** se reposer sur ses lauriers.

lava ['lɑːvə], *s.* lave *f*.

lavatory ['lævətri], *s.* cabinets *mpl*; toilette *f*; **public l.,** W.C. public.

lavender ['lævindər]. **1.** *s.* lavande *f*; **l. water,** eau de lavande. **2.** *a.* (*colour*) lavande *inv*.

lavish ['læviʃ]. **I.** *a.* **1.** prodigue; **he is not l. with his praise,** il ne prodigue pas les éloges; **to be l. with one's apologies,** se confondre en excuses. **2.** somptueux; abondant; **l. expenditure,** dépenses folles. **II.** *v.tr.* prodiguer; **to l. sth. on s.o.,** prodiguer qch. à qn; **-ly,** *adv.* avec prodigalité; **'lavishness,** *s.* prodigalité *f*.

law [lɔː], *s.* **1.** loi *f*; **the laws in force,** la législation en vigueur. **2. the l.,** la loi; **his word is l.,** sa parole fait loi; **to lay down the l. to s.o.,** faire la loi à qn; **to be a l. unto oneself,** n'en faire qu'à sa tête. **3.** droit *m*; **to study l.,** faire son droit; **civil, criminal, l.,** le droit civil, criminel; **l. student,** étudiant en droit. **4. court of l.,** cour *f* de justice; tribunal *m*; **to go to l.,** avoir recours à la justice; **to go to l. with s.o.,** *F:* **to have the l. on s.o.,** citer, poursuivre, qn en justice; **to take the l. into one's own hands,** faire soi-même la justice; **'law-abiding,** *a.* respectueux des lois; ami de l'ordre; **'lawbreaker,** *s.* violateur *m* de la loi; **'lawful,** *a.* légal; licite; **-fully,** *adv.* légalement, légitimement; **'lawless,** *a.* sans loi; déréglé, désordonné; **'lawlessness,** *s.* dérèglement *m*, désordre *m*, anarchie *f*; **'law-**

suit, *s.* procès *m*; **'lawyer,** *s.* (*a*) homme d[e] loi, juriste *m*; (*b*) (i) avocat *m*; (ii) notaire *m*.

lawn [lɔːn], *s.* pelouse *f*; gazon *m*; **'lawnmower** *s.* tondeuse *f* (à gazon).

Lawrence ['lɔrəns]. *Pr.n.m.* Laurent; *Geog:* th[e] St L. (river), le (fleuve) Saint-Laurent.

lax [læks], *s.* (*of conduct*) relâché; (*of pers[.]* négligent; (*of government*) mou; **l. morals** morale facile; **'laxative,** *a.* & *s. Med:* laxati[f] (*m*); **'laxity,** *s.* relâchement *m* (des mœurs[)] négligence *f*, inexactitude *f*; mollesse *f*.

lay¹ [lei], *a.* laïque, lai; *Ecc:* **l. brother,** frère la[i] frère convers; **l. sister,** sœur converse; **to the [l.] mind,** aux yeux du profane; **'layman,** p[.] -men, *s.* (*a*) laïque *m*; (*b*) profane *m*.

lay², *v.tr.* (**laid** [leid]) **1.** coucher; **to l. s.o. low** terrasser qn, abattre qn. **2.** abattre (l[a] poussière). **3.** mettre, placer, poser (**sth. o**[n] **sth.,** qch. sur qch.); **to have nowhere to l. one'[s] head,** n'avoir pas où reposer la tête. **4.** pondr[e] (un œuf). **5.** faire (un pari); parier (un[e] somme); **to l. evens,** parier à égalité. **6. he lai[d]** **before me all the facts of the case,** il me prése[nta] ta tous les faits. **7.** (*a*) **to l. a tax on sth.,** mettr[e] un impôt sur qch.; frapper qch. d'un impôt; (b[)] *P:* **to l. into s.o.,** taper ferme sur qn; **don't y[ou]** **dare l. a finger on him,** je vous défends de [le] toucher. **8.** (*a*) poser, asseoir (des fondements[)] ranger (des briques); **to l. the table,** mettre [le] couvert; **to l. for three,** mettre trois couvert[s]; **to l. a carpet,** poser un tapis; **to l. the fir[e]** préparer le feu; (*b*) dresser, tendre (un piège[)]; (*c*) *Th:* **the scene is laid in Paris,** la scène [se] passe à Paris; **'lay a'side, 'lay 'by,** *v.tr.* me[t]tre (qch.) de côté; épargner (de l'argen[t]); **'layby,** *s.* (*on road*) terre-plein *m* [de] stationnement; **'lay 'down,** *v.tr.* **1.** [(a)] déposer, poser (qch.); **to l. d. one's arms,** me[t]tre bas les armes; (*b*) coucher, étendre (qn); [(c)] quitter (ses fonctions); (*d*) donner, sacrifier ([sa] vie). **2.** poser, établir (une règle); imposer (d[es] conditions); **to l. d. that . . .,** stipuler que . . [.] **'layer,** *s.* (*of hen*) **good l.,** bonne pondeus[e] **2.** couche *f* (de peinture); assise *f*, lit *m* ([de] béton); **'lay 'in,** *v.tr.* faire provision de, s'[a] provisionner de (qch.); **'lay 'off,** *v.tr.* co[n]gédier (des ouvriers); **'lay 'on,** *v.* **1.** *v*[.] appliquer (un enduit); *F:* **to l. it on with [a] trowel,** flatter qn grossièrement. **2.** *v.i.* **to l. [on]** **with a whip,** appliquer le fouet. **3.** *v.tr.* instal[ler] (le gaz); **with water laid on,** avec eau couran[te] **'lay 'out,** *v.tr.* **1.** arranger (des objets); éta[ler] (des marchandises). **2.** coucher (qn) par ter[re] étendre (qn) d'un coup. **3.** dépenser ([de] l'argent). **4.** dessiner (un jardin); faire le tr[acé] d'(une route). **5. to l. oneself o. to do sth.,** mettre en frais pour faire qch.; **'layout,** tracé *m*; dessin *m*; **'lay 'up,** *v.tr.* **1.** accumu[ler] (des provisions); **to l. up trouble for oneself,**

préparer bien des ennuis. **2.** remiser (une voiture). **3. to be laid up,** être alité, être obligé de garder le lit.

azy ['leizi], *a.* paresseux, fainéant; **laze,** *v.i.* **paresser, fainéanter; -ily,** *adv.* paresseusement; **'laziness,** *s.* paresse *f*, fainéantise *f*; **'lazybones,** *s.* paresseux, -euse; fainéant, -ante.

ad[1] [led], *s.* **1.** plomb *m*; **white l.,** blanc *m* de plomb; céruse *f*; **red l.,** minium *m*; **l. pipe,** tuyau de plomb. **2.** mine *f* (de crayon). **3.** *Nau:* (plomb de) sonde *f*; **'leaden,** *a.* (teint, ciel) de plomb.

ad[2] [li:d]. **I.** *v.* **(led** [led]) **1.** *v.tr.* (*a*) mener, conduire, guider; **to l. s.o. into temptation,** induire qn en tentation; **to l. the way,** (i) montrer le chemin; (ii) aller devant; (*b*) conduire; mener (un cheval); tenir (un chien) en laisse; **he is easily led,** il va comme on le mène; (*c*) mener (une vie heureuse, misérable); **to l. a dog's life,** mener une vie de chien; **to l. s.o. a dog's life,** faire une vie de chien à qn; (*d*) commander (une armée); diriger (un mouvement); (*e*) (*in race*) **to l. (the field),** tenir la tête; (*f*) *Cards:* **to l. the queen,** attaquer de la reine. **2.** *v.i.* (*a*) (*of road*) mener, conduire (**to,** à); (*b*) **to l. to a discovery,** mener à une découverte; **to l. to nothing,** n'aboutir, ne mener, à rien. **II.** *s.* **1.** (*a*) **to follow s.o.'s l.,** se laisser conduire par qn; suivre l'exemple de qn; **to give the l.,** donner le ton; (*b*) **to take the l.,** (i) prendre la tête; (ii) prendre la direction. **2.** *Cards:* **to have the l.,** jouer le premier; **your l.!** à vous de jouer! **3.** *Th:* premier rôle. **4.** (*for dog*) laisse *f*; **on a l.,** en laisse. **5.** *El:* câble *m*, branchement *m*; **'lead a'way,** *v.tr.* **1.** emmener. **2.** entraîner, détourner (qn); **to be led away,** se laisser entraîner; **'lead 'back,** *v.tr.* ramener, reconduire; **'leader,** *s.* **1.** (*a*) conducteur, -trice; guide *m*; (*b*) chef *m* (d'un parti); directeur *m*; meneur *m* (d'une émeute); (*c*) *Pol:* leader *m*. **2.** *Journ:* article de fond, de tête; *F:* leader; **leadership,** *s.* (*a*) conduite *f*; **under s.o.'s l.,** sous la conduite de qn; (*b*) commandement *m*, direction *f* (d'un parti), *F:* leadership *m*; **leading,** *a.* **1.** *Jur:* **l. question,** question tendancieuse. **2.** premier, principal; **a l. man,** une personnalité; *Journ:* **l. article,** article *m* de fond, de tête; *Th:* **l. part,** premier rôle; **l. man, lady,** vedette *f*; **'lead 'on,** *v.tr.* conduire, entraîner (qn); **l. on!** en avant! **to l. s.o. on to talk,** encourager qn à parler; **'lead 'up,** *v.i.* **to l. up to a subject,** amener un sujet.

f, *pl.* **leaves** [li:f, li:vz], *s.* **1.** feuille *f*; **in l.,** (arbre) en feuilles, couvert de feuilles. **2.** feuillet *m* (de livre); **to turn over the leaves of (a book),** feuilleter (un livre); *F:* **to turn over a new l.,** changer de conduite; **to take a l. out of s.o.'s book,** prendre exemple *m* sur qn. **3.** battant *m*

(de porte, de table); **'leaflet,** *s.* (*a*) *Bot:* foliole *f*; (*b*) feuillet *m*; papillon *m* (de publicité); **'leafy,** *a.* feuillu; couvert de feuilles.

league [li:g]. **I.** *s.* ligue *f*; **he was in l. with them,** il était de connivence avec eux; *Fb:* **l. match,** match *m* de championnat. **II.** *v.i.* **to l. (together),** se liguer.

leak [li:k]. **I.** *s.* (*a*) fuite *f*, écoulement *m* (d'un liquide); (*b*) *Nau:* voie *f* d'eau; **to spring a l.,** faire une voie d'eau; **to stop a l.,** (i) aveugler une voie d'eau; (ii) boucher une fuite. **II.** *v.* **1.** *v.i.* (*of tank*) avoir une fuite, fuir; (*of liquid*) fuir, couler; **to l. away,** se perdre; (*b*) (*of roof*) laisser entrer la pluie; (*of ship*) faire eau. **2.** *v.tr.* *F:* laisser filtrer (des nouvelles); **'leakage,** *s.* (*a*) fuite *f* (d'eau, de gaz); perte *f* (d'électricité); (*b*) fuite (de secrets officiels); **'leak 'out,** *v.i.* (*of news*) s'ébruiter, transpirer; **'leaky,** *a.* (*a*) (tonneau) qui coule, qui perd, qui fuit; (*b*) (bateau) qui fait eau; (souliers) qui prennent l'eau; (toit) qui laisse entrer la pluie.

lean[1] [li:n]. **1.** *a.* (*a*) maigre, amaigri, décharné; (*of animal*) efflanqué; (*b*) **l. meat,** viande *f* maigre. **2.** *s.* maigre *m* (de la viande); **'leanness,** *s.* maigreur *f*.

lean[2], *v.* **(leant** [lent] *or* **leaned) 1.** *v.i.* (*a*) s'appuyer (**against, on, sth.,** contre, sur, qch.); **to l. on one's elbow(s),** s'accouder; (*b*) se pencher (**over,** sur); (*of wall*) incliner, pencher; (*c*) **to l. over backwards to . . .,** (i) mettre tout en œuvre pour . . .; (ii) aller aux concessions extrêmes pour . . . . **2.** *v.tr.* **to l. a ladder against a wall,** appuyer une échelle contre un mur; **'leaning. 1.** *a.* penché. **2.** *s.* **l. towards,** inclination *f* pour (qch.); tendance *f* à (qch.); penchant *m* pour, vers (qch.); **'lean-to,** *s.* appentis *m*.

leap [li:p]. **I.** *s.* saut *m*, bond *m*; **a l. in the dark,** un saut dans l'inconnu; **to advance by leaps and bounds,** progresser par bonds, à pas de géant. **II.** *v.* **(leapt** [lept] *or* **leaped) 1.** *v.i.* (*a*) sauter, bondir; **to l. to one's feet,** se lever brusquement; **to l. over the ditch,** sauter le fossé; **to l. at an offer,** sauter sur une offre; **to l. up with indignation,** sursauter d'indignation; (*b*) (*of flame*) **to l. (up),** jaillir. **2.** *v.tr.* sauter (un fossé); franchir (qch.) d'un saut; **'leapfrog,** *s.* saute-mouton *m*; **'leap year,** *s.* année *f* bissextile.

learn [lə:n], *v.tr.* **(learnt** [lə:nt] *or* **learned** [lə:nd]) **1.** apprendre; **I have learnt better since then,** je sais à quoi m'en tenir maintenant; **live and l.,** on apprend à tout âge. **2.** apprendre (une nouvelle); **learnèd** ['lə:nid], *a.* savant, instruit; **'learner,** *s.* **1. to be a quick l.,** apprendre facilement. **2.** débutant, -ante; *Aut:* **l. driver,** apprenti conducteur; **'learning,** *s.* **1.** étude *f* (des leçons). **2.** science *f*, instruction *f*, érudition *f*.

lease [li:s]. **I.** *s. Jur:* bail *m*; **to give s.o. a new l. of life**, donner à qn un regain de vie. **II.** *v.tr.* **1.** louer; donner (une maison) à bail. **2.** prendre (une maison) à bail; louer; **'leasehold. 1.** *s.* (*a*) tenure *f* à bail; (*b*) immeuble loué à bail. **2.** *a.* tenu à bail; **'leaseholder**, *s.* locataire *mf* à bail; **'leasing**, *s.* location *f* à bail.

leash [li:ʃ], *s.* laisse *f*, attache *f*; **on the l.**, (chien) en laisse.

least [li:st]. **1.** *a.* (*a*) (**the**) **l.**, (le, la) moindre; (le, la) plus petit(e); **not the l. chance**, pas la moindre chance; (*b*) le moins important; **that's the l. of my worries**, c'est le dernier de mes soucis. **2.** *s.* (**the**) **l.**, (le) moins; **to say the l. (of it)**, pour ne pas dire plus; **at l.**, (tout) au moins; **I can at l. try**, je peux toujours essayer; **not in the l.**, pas le moins du monde; **it doesn't matter in the l.**, cela n'a aucune importance, pas la moindre importance. **3.** *adv.* (**the**) **l.**, (le) moins; **he deserves it l. of all**, il le mérite moins que personne; **last but not l.**, enfin et surtout.

leather ['leðər], *s.* cuir *m*; **l. shoes**, chaussures *f* en cuir; **fancy l. goods**, maroquinerie *f*.

leave [li:v]. **I.** *s.* **1.** permission *f*, autorisation *f*, permis *m*; **without asking anybody's l.**, sans demander la permission de personne. **2.** *Mil: etc:* **l. (of absence)**, (*in months*) congé *m*; (*in days*) permission; **absence without l.**, absence illégale. **3. to take one's l.**, prendre congé; faire ses adieux; **to take French l.**, filer à l'anglaise. **II.** *v.tr.* (**left** [left]) **1.** laisser; (*a*) **take it or l. it**, c'est à prendre ou à laisser; (*b*) **to be left badly off**, être laissé dans la gêne; (*c*) **to l. one's money to s.o.**, laisser, léguer, sa fortune à qn; (*d*) **to l. the door open**, laisser la porte ouverte; **left to oneself**, livré à soi-même; **let's l. it at that**, demeurons-en là; (*e*) **to l. go of sth.**, lâcher qch.; (*f*) déposer (qch. quelque part); confier (**sth. with s.o.**, qch. à qn); **left-luggage office**, consigne *f*; (*g*) **l. it to me**, remettez-vous-en à moi; laissez-moi faire; (*h*) **to be left**, rester; **I've none left**, il ne m'en reste plus. **2.** (*a*) quitter (un endroit, qn); **to l. the room**, sortir (de la salle); **to l. the table**, se lever de table; **we l. tomorrow**, nous partons demain; *Nau:* **to l. harbour**, sortir du port; (*b*) abandonner; quitter (sa femme); (*c*) (*of train*) **to l. the rails**, dérailler; **'leave a'bout**, *v.tr.* laisser traîner (des objets); **'leave be'hind**, *v.tr.* laisser, oublier (qch.); partir sans (qn); **'leave 'off. 1.** *v.tr.* cesser de porter, quitter (un vêtement); **to l. off smoking**, renoncer au tabac; **to l. off work**, cesser de travailler. **2.** *v.i.* cesser, s'arrêter; **where did we l. off?** où en sommes-nous restés? **'leave 'out**, *v.tr.* **1.** exclure (qn). **2.** (*a*) omettre (qch.); (*b*) oublier; **'leave 'over**, *v.tr.* **1.** remettre (une affaire) à plus tard. **2. to be left over**, rester; **'leaving**, *s.* **1.** départ *m*. **2.** *pl.* **leavings**, restes *m*.

leaven ['lev(ə)n], *s.* levain *m*.

Lebanon ['lebənən]. *Pr.n. Geog:* le Liban; **Leba'nese. 1.** *a.* libanais. **2.** *s.* Libanais, -aise.

lecture ['lektʃər]. **I.** *s.* **1.** conférence *f* (**on**, sur); *Sch:* cours *m* (**on**, sur); **to give a l.**, faire une conférence; **l. hall**, salle *f* de conférences. **2.** *F:* sermon *m*, semonce *f*. **II.** *v.* **1.** *v.i.* faire une, des conférence(s); faire un cours. **2.** *v.tr. F:* sermonner, semoncer, réprimander (qn); **'lecturer**, *s.* (*a*) conférencier, -ière; (*b*) *Sch:* maître *m* de conférences; chargé *m* de cours.

ledge [ledʒ], *s.* rebord *m*; saillie *f*; (*on building*) corniche *f*.

ledger ['ledʒər], *s. Com:* grand livre *m*.

lee [li:], *s.* (*a*) *Nau:* côté *m* sous le vent; **under the l. of the land**, sous le vent de la terre; **l. shore**, terre *f* sous le vent; (*b*) abri *m* (contre le vent); **in the l. of a rock**, abrité par un rocher; **the l. side**, le côté abrité; **'leeward**. *Nau:* **1.** *a. & ad.* sous le vent. **2.** *s.* côté *m* sous le vent; **'leeway**, *s. Nau:* dérive *f*; **he has a lot of l. to make up**, a un fort retard à rattraper.

leech [li:tʃ], *s.* sangsue *f*.

leek [li:k], *s.* poireau *m*.

leer ['liər]. **I.** *s.* (*a*) regard *m* de côté (malicieux mauvais); (*b*) regard polisson. **II.** *v.i.* **to l. at s.o.**, lorgner, guigner, qn d'un air méchant.

left [left]. **1.** *a.* gauche; **on the l. bank**, sur la rive gauche. **2.** *adv.* **turn l.**, tournez à gauche; **M eyes l.!** tête (à) gauche! **3.** *s.* (*a*) gauche *f*; **sitting on my l.**, assis à ma gauche; **on the l.**, **to the l.**, à gauche; (*b*) (poing) gauche *m*; **with the l.**, (frapper) du gauche; (*c*) *Pol:* **the L.**, Gauche; **'left-hand**, *a.* **on the l.-h. side**, gauche; **'left-'handed**, *a.* (*a*) (*of pers.*) gaucher; (*b*) **l.-h. compliment**, compliment douteux; **'left-'hander**, *s.* **1.** (*of pers.*) gaucher, -ère. **2.** coup *m* du gauche; **'leftist** *a. & s. Pol:* gauchiste (*mf*), de gauche; **'left wing**, *a. l.-w. politics**, politique *f* de gauche.

leftovers ['leftouvəz], *s.pl.* restes *m* (d'un repas).

leg [leg], *s.* **1.** jambe *f*; patte *f* (de chien, d'oiseau); **I ran as fast as my legs would carry me**, j'ai couru à toutes jambes; **to be on one's last legs**, tirer vers sa fin; être à bout de ressources; **to give s.o. a l. up**, (i) faire la courte échelle à qn; (ii) *F:* donner à qn un coup d'épaule; **to stand on one l.**, se tenir sur un pied; *F:* **to pull s.o.'s l.**, se payer la tête de qn. *Cu:* cuisse *f* (de volaille); **l. of mutton**, gigot *m*. **3.** jambe (de pantalon); tige *f* (de bas). **4.** pied *m* (de table). **5.** *Sp:* **the first l.**, la première manche; **legged** ['legid], *a.* **a four-l. animal**, un animal à quatre pattes; **'leggings**, *s.pl.* guêtres *f*; **'legpull**, *s.* mystification *f*; **'legpuller**, *s.* farceur *m*.

legacy ['legəsi], *s.* legs *m*; **to leave s.o. a l.**, faire un legs à qn; **lega'tee**, *s.* légataire *mf*.

legal ['li:g(ə)l], *a.* **1.** légal, licite. **2.** lé

judiciaire, juridique; l. **document,** acte *m* authentique; **to go into the l. profession,** se faire une carrière dans le droit; **to get a l. opinion** = consulter un avocat; **-ally,** *adv.* légalement; l. **responsible,** responsable en droit; **le′gality,** *s.* légalité *f*; **′legalize,** *v.tr.* rendre (un acte) légal; légaliser (un document).

egend [′ledʒənd], *s.* légende *f*; **′legendary,** *a.* légendaire.

eghorn [′legɔːn]. *Pr.n. Geog:* Livourne *f.*

gible [′ledʒibl], *a.* lisible, net; **-ibly,** *adv.* lisiblement; **legi′bility,** *s.* lisibilité *f*, netteté *f* (d'une écriture).

gion [′liːdʒ(ə)n], *s.* légion *f.*

gislate [′ledʒisleit], *v.i.* faire des lois; légiférer; **legis′lation,** *s.* législation *f*; **′legislative,** *a.* législatif; **′legislator,** *s.* législateur *m*; **′legislature,** *s.* législature *f.*

gitimacy [li′dʒitiməsi], *s.* légitimité *f*; **le′gitimate,** *a.* légitime; **-ly,** *adv.* légitimement.

isure [′leʒər], *s.* loisir(s) *m(pl)*; **to have l. for reading,** avoir le loisir, le temps, de lire; **to be at l.,** ne pas être occupé; **in my l. moments,** à mes moments perdus; **when I have a moment's l.,** quand j'ai un instant de libre; **to examine sth. at l.,** examiner qch. à loisir; **′leisured,** *a.* l. **people,** les désœuvrés *m*; **′leisurely,** *a. (of pers.)* qui n'est jamais pressé; l. **pace,** allure mesurée; **in a l. fashion,** sans se presser.

mon [′lemən]. 1. *s.* citron *m*; l. **(tree),** citronnier *m*; l. **squash,** citronnade *f*; l. **squeezer,** presse-citrons *m inv*; **fresh l. juice,** citron pressé. 2. *a.* jaune citron *inv*; **lemon′ade,** *s.* limonade *f*; *(still)* citronnade *f.*

nur [′liːmər], *s. Z:* lémur *m.*

d [lend], *v.tr.* **(lent)** 1. prêter. 2. **to l. s.o. a hand,** aider qn, porter, prêter, secours à qn. 3. **to l. oneself, itself, to sth.,** se prêter à qch.; **place that lends itself to meditation,** lieu propice à la méditation; **′lender,** *s.* prêteur, -euse; **′lending,** *s.* prêt *m*; *Fin:* prestation *f* (de capitaux); l. **library,** bibliothèque *f* de prêt.

gth [leŋθ], *s.* 1. longueur *f*; **to be two metres in l.,** avoir deux mètres de long, de longueur, être ong de deux mètres; *(of ship, etc.)* **to turn in its wn l.,** virer sur place; *Sp:* **by a l.,** (gagner) d'une longueur; **throughout the l. and breadth of the country,** dans toute l'étendue du pays; **I ell full l.,** je suis tombé de tout mon long. 2. **tay of some l.,** séjour assez prolongé; l. **of serice,** ancienneté *f*; **to speak at some l.,** parler assez longuement; **at l.,** enfin, à la fin. 3. **to go o the l. of asserting . . .,** aller jusqu'à prétendre . . .; **to go to great lengths,** faire tout son ossible. 4. morceau *m*, bout *m* (de ficelle); **ress l.,** coupon *m* de robe; **what l. of material o you require?** quel métrage vous faut-il?

lengthen, *v.* 1. *v.tr.* allonger, rallonger;

prolonger (la vie, etc.). 2. *v.i.* s'allonger, se rallonger; augmenter, croître; **his face lengthened,** son visage s'allongea; **′lengthening,** *s.* allongement *m*; rallongement *m*; prolongation *f* (d'un séjour); **′lengthiness,** *s.* longueurs *fpl*; prolixité *f* (d'un discours); **′lengthways, ′lengthwise,** *adv.* en longueur; en long; **′lengthy,** *a.* (discours) qui traine en longueur, prolixe; **-ily,** *adv.* (parler) longuement, avec prolixité.

leniency [′liːniənsi], *s.* clémence *f*; douceur *f*, indulgence *f* **(to, towards,** envers, pour); **′lenient,** *a.* clément; doux; indulgent; **-ly,** *adv.* avec clémence; avec douceur.

lens [lenz], *s.* (a) lentille *f*; verre *m* (de lunettes); **contact l.,** verre de contact; (b) *Phot:* objectif *m.*

Lent [lent], *s. Ecc:* le carême.

lentil [′lentil], *s. Bot:* lentille *f.*

Leo [′liːou]. *Pr.n. Astr:* le Lion.

leopard [′lepəd], *s.* léopard *m.*

leper [′lepər], *s. Med:* lépreux, -euse; **′leprosy,** *s.* lèpre *f*; **′leprous,** *a.* lépreux.

less [les]. 1. *a.* (a) moindre; **of l. value,** de, d'une, moindre valeur; **a sum l. than . . .,** une somme au-dessous de . . .; (b) **eat l. meat,** mangez moins de viande. 2. *prep.* **purchase price l. 10%,** prix d'achat moins 10%. 3. *s.* moins *m*; **in l. than an hour,** en moins d'une heure; **at l. than cost price,** à moins du prix de revient. 4. *adv.* l. **known,** moins connu; **one man l.,** un homme en, de, moins; l. **than six,** moins de six; l. **and l.,** de moins en moins; **even l.,** moins encore; **he's much l. intelligent than his sister,** il est beaucoup moins intelligent que sa sœur; **I'm l. afraid of it now,** je le crains moins maintenant; **′lessen,** *v.* 1. *v.i.* s'amoindrir, diminuer. 2. *v.tr.* amoindrir, diminuer; **′lesser,** *a.* **to choose the l. of two evils,** de deux maux choisir le moindre.

lessee [le′siː], *s.* locataire *mf* (à bail); **le′ssor,** *s. Jur:* bailleur, -eresse.

lesson [′les(ə)n], *s.* leçon *f*; **to take French lessons,** prendre des leçons de français; *Aut:* **driving lessons,** leçons de conduite; **let that be a l. to you!** que cela vous serve d'exemple, de leçon!

let [let], *v.* **(let)** I. *v.tr.* 1. (a) permettre; laisser; l. **me tell you that . . .,** permettez-moi de vous dire que . . .; **to l. s.o. do sth.,** laisser qn faire qch.; **to l. go of sth., to l. sth. go,** lâcher qch.; **when can you l. me have it?** quand pourrai-je l'avoir? (b) **to l. s.o. know sth. about sth.,** faire savoir qch. à qn, faire part à qn de qch.; l. **me hear the story,** racontez-moi l'histoire; (c) **to l. s.o. through,** laisser passer qn. 2. **house to l.,** maison à louer. II. *v.aux.* *(1st & 3rd pers. of imp.)* **let's hurry!** dépêchons-nous! **don't let's start yet,** ne partons pas encore; l. **there be no** mistake about it! qu'on ne s'y trompe pas! I. them all come! qu'ils viennent tous!! I. me see! voyons! attendez un peu! 'let 'down, v.tr. 1. (a) baisser (la glace); (b) allonger (une robe). 2. I won't I. you d., vous pouvez compter sur moi; 'letdown, s. désappointement m, déception f; 'let 'in, v.tr. I. laisser entrer (qn, qch.); I. him in! faites entrer! shoes that I. in the wet, souliers qui prennent l'eau. 2. F: I didn't know what I was letting myself in for, je ne savais pas à quoi je m'engageais; 'let 'into, v.tr. to I. s.o. i. the house, laisser entrer qn dans la maison; to I. s.o. i. a secret, mettre qn dans le secret; 'let 'off, v.tr. 1. tirer, faire partir (un feu d'artifice). 2. (a) to I. s.o. off from doing sth., dispenser qn de faire qch.; (b) to I. s.o. off, faire grâce à qn; to be I. off with a fine, en être quitte pour une amende; 'let 'on, v.i. & tr. don't I. on that I was there, n'allez pas dire que j'y étais; 'let 'out, v.tr. 1. laisser sortir (qn); élargir (un prisonnier); to I. out a yell, laisser échapper un cri. 2. louer (des canots); 'letting, s. louage m; 'let 'up, v.i. once started he never lets up, une fois lancé il ne s'arrête plus.

lethal ['li:θ(ə)l], a. mortel; I. **weapon**, arme meurtrière.

lethargy ['leθədʒi], s. léthargie f; torpeur f; **le'thargic**, a. léthargique.

letter ['letər]. I. s. 1. lettre f, caractère m; **to carry out an order to the I.**, exécuter un ordre à la lettre, au pied de la lettre. 2. lettre, missive f; **registered I.**, lettre recommandée; **to open the letters**, dépouiller le courrier; I. **box**, boîte f aux lettres. 3. **man, woman, of letters**, homme, femme, de lettres. II. v.tr. marquer (qch.) avec des lettres; 'lettercard, s. carte-lettre f, pl. cartes-lettres; 'letterhead, s. en-tête m, pl. entêtes; 'lettering, s. 1. lettrage m. 2. lettres f pl; inscription f; 'letterpress, s. 1. impression f typographique. 2. texte m (accompagnant une illustration).

lettuce ['letis], s. laitue f, F: salade f.

leukaemia [lu:'ki:miə], s. Med: leucémie f.

level ['lev(ə)l]. I. s. 1. niveau m (de la mer, de la société); **on a I. with (sth.)**, à la hauteur de (qch.); **at eye I.**, à la hauteur de l'œil; **room on a I. with the garden**, pièce f de plain-pied avec le jardin; **at ministerial I.**, à l'échelon ministériel. 2. terrain m, surface f, de niveau; Aut: Rail: palier m; **on the I.**, (i) à plat, sur le plat; (ii) F: (of pers.) loyal; de bonne foi; **speed on the I.**, vitesse en palier. II. a. 1. (a) de niveau, à niveau; (b) (flat) égal; uni; (c) I. **with**, de niveau avec (qch.); au niveau de (qch.); à (la) hauteur de (qch.); I. **with the water**, à fleur d'eau, au ras de l'eau; I. **crossing**, passage m à niveau; **to draw I. with**, arriver à la hauteur de (qn). 2. **to keep a I. head**, garder sa tête, son sang-froid; F: **to do one's I. best**, faire tout son possible.

III. v.tr. (levelled) 1. niveler; **to I. a house to th ground**, raser une maison. 2. pointer, braque (un fusil), diriger (une longue-vue) (at, sur); to **accusations against s.o.**, lancer des accusatio contre qn; **to I. a blow at s.o.**, porter un coup qn; 'level-'headed, a. qui a la tête bie équilibrée; 'levelling, s. 1. mise f à niveau. nivellement m; aplanissement m (d'un surface).

lever ['li:vər]. I. s. levier m; Aut: **gear I.**, levier d vitesses. II. v.tr. **to I. sth. up**, soulever qch. ≥ moyen d'un levier; 'leverage, s. 1. force puissance f, de levier. 2. système m de levie

leveret ['levərit], s. Z: levraut m.

levy ['levi]. I. s. 1. levée f (d'un impôt). 2. imp m, contribution f; **capital I.**, prélèvement m s le capital. II. v.tr. lever, percevoir (un impô imposer (une amende).

liable ['laiəbl], a. 1. Jur: responsable (**for, de**). I. **to a fine**, passible d'une amende; I. **military service**, astreint au service militaire sujet, exposé (**to, à**); **car I. to overturn**, voit sujette à verser. 4. **difficulties are I. to occ** des difficultés pourraient bien se présent **lia'bility**, s. 1. Jur: responsabilité f; **joint** responsabilité conjointe. 2. pl. Com: **liabiliti** ensemble m des dettes; engagements obligations f; **assets and liabilities**, actif m passif m; **to meet one's liabilities**, faire fac ses engagements. 3. (a) I. **to a fine**, risque d'(encourir une) amende; (b) I. **to sth.**, to sth., disposition f, tendance f, à qch., à f qch.; (c) I. **to explode**, danger m d'explosion F: **he's a I.**, c'est un poids mort.

liaison [li'eiz(ə)n], s. liaison f; **li'aise**, v.i. F: fa effectuer, la liaison (**with**, avec).

liar ['laiər], s. menteur, -euse.

libel ['laibl]. I. s. diffamation f (par écrit), cal nie f; **a I. action**, un procès en diffamation v.tr. (**libelled**) Jur: diffamer (qn) (par éc calomnier (qn); 'libellous, a. (éc diffamatoire, calomnieux; -ily, calomnieusement.

liberal ['lib(ə)rəl], a. 1. libéral; (of pers.) d'es large; sans préjugés; **in the most I. sense**, sens le plus large (du mot, etc.). 2. (a) libé généreux; I. **with one's money**, prodigue de argent; I. **offer**, offre généreuse; (b) abond I. **provision**, ample provision (de qch.). 3. s. Pol: libéral, -ale; -ally, adv. libéralem 'liberalism, s. Pol: libéralisme m; libe'ral s. libéralité f; largeur f (de vues); générosit

liberate ['libəreit], v.tr. libérer; mettre en lib libe'ration, s. libération f; mise f en lib 'liberator, s. libérateur, -trice.

Liberia [lai'bi:riə]. Pr.n. Geog: le Libéria.

liberty ['libəti], s. liberté f; (a) **to be at I. t** sth., être libre de faire qch.; (b) **to take the** doing sth., se permettre de faire qch.; (c take liberties, prendre des libertés; he takes a good many liberties, il se permet bien des choses.

Libra ['librə]. *Pr.n. Astr:* la Balance.

library ['laibrəri], *s.* bibliothèque *f*; **lending l.**, bibliothèque de prêt; **public l.**, bibliothèque municipale; **record l.**, discothèque *f*; **librarian** [lai'brɛəriən], *s.* bibliothécaire *mf*.

Libya ['libiə]. *Pr.n. Geog:* la Libye; **'Libyan. 1.** *a.* libyen; **the L. Desert**, le désert de Libye. **2.** *s.* Libyen, -enne.

ice [lais], *s. see* LOUSE.

licence ['lais(ə)ns], *s.* **1.** permis *m*, autorisation *f*, patente *f*; **l. to sell alcoholic drinks**, licence *f* de débit de boissons; **television l.**, autorisation d'avoir un poste de télévision; **marriage l.**, dispense *f* de bans; *Aut:* **driving l.**, permis de conduire. **2.** (*a*) licence; **poetic l.**, licence poétique; (*b*) licence, dérèglement *m*.

cense ['lais)ns], *v.tr.* accorder un permis, une patente, à (qn); patenter (qn); **licensed dealer**, patenté *m*; **licensed premises**, débit *m* de boissons; *Av:* **licensed pilot**, pilote breveté; **licen'see**, *s.* patenté, -ée; (*of public house*) gérant, -ante; propriétaire *mf*.

centious [lai'senʃəs], *a.* licencieux, dévergondé; **li'centiousness**, *s.* licence *f*, dérèglement *m*, dévergondage *m*.

chen ['laikən, 'litʃin], *s.* lichen *m*.

ck [lik]. **I.** *v.tr.* **1.** lécher; **to l. one's lips**, se (pour)lécher les babines; **the cat licks her kittens**, la chatte lèche ses petits; **to l. a recruit into shape**, dégrossir une recrue; **to l. s.o.'s boots**, lécher les bottes de, à, qn. **2.** *F:* battre, rosser (qn); rouler (un concurrent). **II.** *s.* **1.** coup *m* de langue; *F:* **to give oneself a l. and a promise**, se faire un brin de toilette. **2.** *F:* **at a great l.**, à toute vitesse; **'licking**, *s.* (*a*) **to give s.o. a good l.**, donner une volée de coups à qn; (*b*) défaite *f*.

l [lid], *s.* **1.** couvercle *m*; *F:* **that puts the l. on it!** il ne manquait plus que ça! **2.** *Anat:* paupière *f*.

¹ [lai]. **I.** *s.* (*a*) mensonge *m*; **it's a pack of lies**, pure invention tout cela; **to tell lies**, mentir; (*b*) **to give the l. to an assertion**, donner un démenti formel à une assertion. **II.** *v.i.* mentir; **'lying¹. 1.** *a.* menteur; faux. **2.** *s.* le mensonge.

². **I.** *v.i.* (lay [lei]; lain [lein]; **lying) 1.** (*a*) être couché (à plat); **he was lying on the floor**, il était couché sur le plancher; **to l. asleep**, être endormi; **to l. dead**, être (étendu) mort; (*on tombstone*) **here lies . . .,** ci-gît . . .; (*b*) être, rester, se tenir; **to l. in wait for s.o.**, se tenir à l'affût de qn; **to l. still**, rester tranquille; **to l. ow**, (i) se tapir; (ii) faire le mort. **2.** (*of thg*) être, se trouver; **his clothes were lying on the ground**, ses habits étaient éparpillés par terre; **he snow lies deep**, la neige est épaisse; **the now did not l.**, la neige n'est pas restée; **I find**

time lying heavy on my hands, le temps me pèse; **the onus of proof lies with them**, c'est à eux qu'incombe le soin de faire la preuve; **the difference lies in this**, c'est là que réside toute la différence; **we must see how the land lies**, il faut sonder, tâter, le terrain; **as far as in me lies**, autant qu'il m'est possible. **II.** *s.* disposition *f* (du terrain); *Golf:* assiette *f* (d'une balle); **'lie a'bout**, *v.i.* traîner; **'lie 'back**, *v.i.* se laisser retomber; se renverser (dans un fauteuil); **'lie 'down**, *v.i.* (*a*) se coucher, s'étendre; **l. down for a bit**, reposez-vous un peu; *F:* **he took it lying down**, il n'a pas dit mot; **he won't** take it lying down, il ne se laissera pas faire; **'lie 'down**, *s. F:* **to have a l. d.**, faire une sieste; **'lie 'in**. *F:* **1.** *v.i.* faire la grasse matinée. **2.** *s. F:* **to have a l. in**, faire la grasse matinée; **'lie 'up**, *v.i. F:* garder le lit; **'lying²**, *a.* couché, étendu.

lien ['li(:)ən], *s. Jur:* **l. on goods**, droit *m* de rétention de marchandises.

lieu [lju:], *s.* **in l. of**, au lieu de.

lieutenant [lef'tenənt, *N.Am:* lu:-], *s.* lieutenant *m*; *Navy:* lieutenant de vaisseau; **second l.**, sous-lieutenant *m*; *Av:* **flight-l.**, capitaine *m* (d'aviation); **l.-colonel**, lieutenant-colonel *m*; *Navy:* **l.-commander**, capitaine de corvette; **l.-general**, général *m* de corps d'armée; **l.-governor**, *Fr.C:* lieutenant-gouverneur *m*.

life, *pl.* **lives** [laif, laivz], *s.* **1.** vie *f*; **it's a matter of l. and death**, c'est une question de vie ou de mort; **l.-and-death struggle**, lutte désespérée; **to take s.o.'s l.**, tuer qn; **to take one's own l.**, se suicider; **to save s.o.'s l.**, sauver la vie de, à, qn; **to escape with one's l.**, s'en tirer la vie sauve; **to run for dear l.**, s'enfuir à toutes jambes; **run for your lives!** sauve qui peut! **I can't for the l. of me understand**, je ne comprends absolument pas; **not on your l.!** jamais de la vie! **to put new l. into s.o., sth.**, ranimer, galvaniser (qn, une entreprise); **he's the l. and soul of the party**, c'est le boute-en-train de la soirée; **animal l.**, la vie animale. **2.** (*a*) vie, vivant *m* (de qn); **never in (all) my l.**, jamais de la vie; **at my time of l.**, à mon âge; **early l.**, enfance *f*; **tired of l.**, las de vivre; **l. annuity**, rente *f* viagère; **appointed for l.**, nommé à vie; (*b*) biographie *f*; (*c*) durée *f* (d'une lampe). **3.** **to depart this l.**, quitter ce monde; mourir; *F:* **what a l.!** quelle vie! quel métier! **such is l.!** c'est la vie! **he's seen l.**, il a beaucoup vécu; **'lifebelt**, *s.* ceinture *f* de sauvetage; **'lifeboat**, *s.* canot *m* de sauvetage; **'lifeguard**, *s.* (*at seaside*) sauveteur *m*; maître-nageur *m*; **'lifejacket**, *s.* gilet *m* de sauvetage; **'lifeless**, *a.* sans vie; inanimé; sans vigueur; **'lifelike**, *a.* (portrait) vivant; **'lifelong**, *a.* (amitié) de toute la vie; (ami) de toujours; **'lifesaving**, *s.* sauvetage *m*; **'life-**

'size(d), a. (portrait) de grandeur naturelle, de grandeur nature; 'lifetime, s. vie f; in his l., de son vivant; it's the work of a l., c'est le travail de toute une vie; once in a l., une fois dans la vie.

lift [lift]. I. v. 1. v.tr. (a) lever, soulever (un poids); lever (les yeux); to l. up one's head, redresser la tête; to l. sth. down, descendre qch.; (b) Agr: arracher (les pommes de terre); (c) F: voler; (d) lever (un embargo). 2. v.i. (of fog) se lever, se dissiper. II. s. 1. Aut: may I give you a l.? puis-je vous conduire quelque part? a l. up in the world, une promotion sociale. 2. ascenseur m; l. attendant, liftier, -ière; goods l., montecharge m inv; service l., monte-plats m inv; 'lifting, s. levage m; l. power, puissance f de levage (d'une grue).

light¹ [lait]. I. s. 1. lumière f; (a) by the l. of the sun, à la lumière du soleil; (b) (of crime) to come to l., se découvrir; to bring (sth.) to l., révéler (un crime); déterrer, exhumer (des objets anciens); (c) éclairage m; the lamp gives a bad l., la lampe éclaire mal; sitting against the l., assis à contre-jour; to stand in s.o.'s l., cacher le jour, la lumière, à qn; to stand in one's own l., (i) tourner le dos à la lumière; (ii) ne pas se faire valoir; I don't look on it in that l., ce n'est pas ainsi que j'envisage la chose; (d) to throw l. on sth., jeter une lumière sur qch.; éclairer qch.; to act according to one's lights, agir selon ses lumières. 2. (a) lumière; Aut: dashboard l., lampe f du tableau de bord; (of pers.) one of the leading lights of the town, l'une des personnalités de la ville; (b) the l., the lights, la lumière, l'éclairage; electric l., lumière électrique; to turn off the l., éteindre la lumière; (c) feu m; traffic lights, feux de circulation, F: feu rouge; F: to see the red l., se rendre compte du danger; Nau: port l., starboard l., feu de bâbord, feu de tribord; Aut: tail, rear, lights, feux arrière; side lights, feux de stationnement; Av: boundary l., feu de balisage; (d) Nau: the Portland l., le phare de Portland; flashing l., phare, feu, à éclats. 3. have you got a l.? avez-vous du feu? 4. the lights in a painting, les clairs d'une peinture. II. v.tr. & i. (lit or lighted) 1. (a) allumer; to l. a fire, faire du feu; the fire won't l., le feu ne prend pas, ne s'allume pas; (b) éclairer, illuminer; house lit by electricity, maison éclairée à l'électricité; the moon lit up the road, la lune illuminait la route; (c) a smile lit up her face, un sourire lui illumina le visage. 2. (a) to l. up, allumer; (b) s'éclairer, s'illuminer; her face lit up, son visage s'éclaira. III. a. 1. clair; (bien) éclairé. 2. (of hair) blond; (of colour) clair; 'lighter¹, s. briquet m (à gaz, à essence); 'lighthouse, s. Nau: phare m; l. keeper, gardien m de phare; 'lighting, s. l. allumage m. 2. éclairage m; l.-up time, heure f

d'éclairage; 'lightship, s. Nau: bateau-feu m

light². I. a. 1. (a) léger; to be l. on one's feet, avoi le pas léger; (b) (deficient) l. weight, poids fai ble. 2. to travel l., voyager avec peu d bagages; to be a l. sleeper, avoir le somme léger. 3. (a) l. punishment, punition légère; (b l. task, tâche facile; travail peu fatigant. 4. reading, lecture(s) divertissante(s amusante(s); to make l. of sth., traiter qch. à l légère. II. v.i. (lighted) (a) (of bird) se poser; (b to l. on sth., trouver qch. par hasard; 'lightl adv. 1. l. dressed, vêtu légèrement; to touch l. o a delicate matter, couler sur un point délicat; h responsibilities sit l. on him, ses responsabilité ne lui pèsent pas. 2. to get off l., s'en tirer à bc compte. 3. to speak l. of sth., parler de qch. à légère; 'lighten, v.tr. alléger (un navire réduire le poids de (qch.); soulager (u douleur); 'lighter², s. Nau: péniche f, chalan m; 'light-'fingered, a. 1. aux doigts agiles. adonné au vol, esp. vol à la tire; 'ligh 'headed, a. to be l., avoir le délire; 'ligh 'hearted, a. au cœur léger; allègre; -ly, ac gaiement; de gaieté de cœur; 'lightness, légèreté f; 'lightweight. 1. s. Box: poids lég 2. a. l. trousers, pantalon léger.

light³, a. it is l., il fait jour; it's hardly l., il fai peine jour.

lightning ['laitniŋ], s. éclairs mpl, foudre f flash of l., un éclair; struck by l., frappé par foudre; like l., as quick as l., rapide com l'éclair; l. conductor, paratonnerre m; progress, progrès m foudroyants; Ind: strike, grève f surprise.

lights [laits], s.pl. Cu: mou m (de bœuf, etc.).

like¹ [laik]. I. a. semblable, pareil, tel. 1. l. fath l. son, tel père, tel fils; they are as l. as two pe ils se ressemblent comme deux gouttes d'e 2. (a) I want to find one l. it, je veux trouve pareil, la pareille; a critic l. you, un critique que vous; he's rather l. you, il a de votre what is he l.? comment est-il? what's weather l.? quel temps fait-il? she has been mother to him, elle lui a servi de mère; old p ple are l. that, les vieilles gens, les vieux, s ainsi faits; I never saw anything l. it, je jamais rien vu de pareil; it costs somethin ten pounds, cela coûte quelque dix li that's something l.! à la bonne heure! the nothing l. being frank, rien de tel que de pa franchement; she's nothing l. as pretty as elle est (bien) loin d'être aussi jolie que v (b) that's just l. a woman! voilà bien femmes! that's just l. me! c'est bien de mo prep. comme; just l. anybody else, tout cor un autre; he ran l. anything, l. mad, il co comme un dératé; don't talk l. that, ne pa pas comme ça; he stood l. a statue, il se te debout telle, comme, une statue; to hate te

poison, détester qn comme la peste. **III.** *adv. F:*
l. enough, as l. as not, probablement,
vraisemblablement. **IV.** *s.* semblable *mf*, pareil,
pareille; **I never saw the l.**, je n'ai jamais vu la
pareille; **he and his l.**, lui et ses pareils;
'**likelihood**, *s.* vraisemblance *f*; probabilité *f*;
in all l., selon toute probabilité;
vraisemblablement; '**likely. I.** *a.* **l.**
vraisemblable, probable; **it's very l. to happen,**
c'est très probable; **he's not very l. to succeed,**
il a peu de chances de réussir. **2. incident l. to
lead to a rupture,** incident susceptible d'entraîner une rupture; **the likeliest place for camping,** l'endroit le plus propre au camping. **II.**
adv. **most l., very l.,** vraisemblablement; très
probablement; **as l. as not,** (pour) autant que je
sache; *F:* **not l.!** pas de danger! '**likeness**, *s.*
ressemblance *f* (to, à); **portrait that is a good l.,**
portrait bien ressemblant; '**likewise,** *adv.* **l.**
(*moreover*) de plus, également; aussi. **2.**
(*similarly*) **to do l.,** faire de même.

ke². **I.** *v.tr.* **1.** aimer; **I l. him,** je l'aime bien; il me
plaît; **I've come to l. him,** il m'est devenu sympathique; **I don't l. his looks,** sa figure ne me
revient pas; **how do you l. him?** comment le
trouvez-vous? **as much as ever you l.,** tant que
vous voudrez; **your father won't l. it,** votre
père ne sera pas content; **whether he likes it or
not,** qu'il le veuille ou non; bon gré, mal gré; *F:*
I l. that! en voilà une bonne! par exemple! **2.**
(*a*) **I l. to see them,** j'aime les voir; **would you l.
some more?** vous en prendrez encore un peu?
I should have liked to go there, j'aurais bien
voulu y aller; (*b*) **as you l.,** comme vous
voudrez; **he is free to act as he likes,** il est libre
d'agir comme il lui plaira; **to do (just) as one
likes,** en faire à sa tête; **he thinks he can do
anything he likes,** il se croit tout permis; **people
can say what they l . . . .,** on a beau dire . . . .
l. *s.pl.* **likes and dislikes,** (i) sympathies *f* et an-
tipathies *f*; (ii) goûts *m*; '**likeable,** *a.* agréable,
sympathique; '**liking,** *s.* goût *m*, penchant *m*;
to one's l., à souhait; **I've taken a l. to it,** j'y ai
pris goût; **I've taken a l. to him,** il m'est devenu
sympathique.

ic ['lailək]. **1.** *s. Bot:* lilas *m*. **2.** *a.* lilas *inv.*

[lilt], *s.* rythme *m*, cadence *f* (des vers).

' ['lili], *s. Bot:* **1.** lis *m*. **2.** **l. of the valley,**
nuguet *m*.

ib [lim], *s.* **1.** membre *m*; **to tear an animal l.
rom l.,** mettre un animal en pièces. **2.** (grosse)
ranche (d'un arbre).

e¹ [laim], *s.* chaux *f*; **slaked l.,** chaux éteinte; **l.
iln,** four *m* à chaux; '**limestone,** *s.* pierre *f* à
haux; calcaire *m*.

e², *s.* citron doux; **l. juice,** jus *m* de citron
oux.

e³, *s.* **l.** (tree), tilleul *m*.

elight ['laimlait], *s.* **in the l.,** sous les feux de

---

la rampe; très en vue.

limit ['limit]. **I.** *s.* limite *f*, borne *f*; **within a three-
mile l.,** dans un rayon de trois milles; **age l.,**
limite d'âge; *F:* **that's the l.!** ça, c'est le comble!
you're the l.! vous êtes impayable! **II.** *v.tr.*
limiter, borner, restreindre; *Pub:* **limited edition,** édition *f* à tirage limité; **limited (liability)
company** = société à responsabilité limitée;
limi'tation, *s.* **1.** limitation *f*, restriction *f*. **2.**
he has his limitations, ses capacités, ses connaissances, sont bornées.

limp¹ [limp]. **I.** *s.* boitement *m*, clochement *m*,
claudication *f*; **to have a l.,** boiter. **II.** *v.i.*
boiter, clocher, clopiner; '**limping,** *a.* boiteux.

limp², *a.* mou; flasque; **-ly,** *adv.* **1.** mollement,
flasquement. **2.** sans énergie; '**limpness,** *s.*
mollesse *f*.

limpet ['limpit], *s. Moll:* patelle *f*.

limpid ['limpid], *a.* limpide, clair; **lim'pidity,** *s.*
limpidité *f*, clarté *f*.

line¹ [lain]. **I.** *s.* **1.** *Nau: Fish: P. T. T:* ligne *f*; **party l.,** ligne partagée; *F:* **it's hard lines,** c'est dur.
2. ligne, trait *m*; **straight l.,** ligne droite; **the
lines on his forehead,** les rides *f* de son front;
Geog: **the L.,** la Ligne (équatoriale); l'équateur
m; **the hard lines of his face,** ses traits durs; **to
be working on the right lines,** être en bonne
voie; **one must draw the l. somewhere,** il y a
limite à tout; **I draw the l. at that,** je ne vais pas
jusqu'à ce point-là. **3.** (*a*) ligne, rangée *f*; *F:* **to
fall into l.,** s'aligner (avec son parti); se conformer (aux idées de qn); (*b*) file *f*; queue *f*; **ten
cars in a l.,** dix voitures à la file; (*c*) *F:* **to drop
s.o. a l.,** envoyer un (petit) mot à qn; **l. of
poetry,** vers *m*. **4.** ligne, compagnie *f* de
navigation, de transports aériens. **5.** ligne de
descendants; **in direct l.,** en ligne directe. **6.**
Rail: voie *f*; ligne. **7. l. of argument,** raisonnement *m*; **the l. to be taken,** la conduite à tenir.
8. genre *m* d'affaires; métier *m*; **that's more in
his l.,** c'est plus dans son genre; *Com:* **l. (of
goods),** série *f* (d'articles); article *m*. **II.** *v.tr.* **1.**
(*a*) **lined paper,** papier réglé; (*b*) (*of face*) **to
become lined,** se rider. **2. the troops lined the
streets,** les troupes faisaient la haie; **the street
is lined with plane trees,** la rue est bordée de
platanes; '**line 'up,** *v.i.* s'aligner; se mettre en
ligne; faire la queue.

line², *v.tr.* doubler (un vêtement); **to l. a nest with
moss,** garnir un nid de mousse; **lined,** *a.*
doublé; **fur-l. gloves,** gants fourrés; '**lining,** *s.*
doublure *f* (de robe, etc.); *Aut:* **brake l.,** garniture *f* de frein.

linen ['linin], *s.* **1.** toile *f* (de lin); **l. sheets,** draps
en toile de fil. **2.** linge *m*, lingerie *f*; **table l.,** linge
de table; **l. department,** rayon *m* de la lingerie;
F: **don't wash your dirty l. in public,** il faut
laver son linge sale en famille.

liner ['lainər], *s. Nau:* paquebot *m*; **trans-**

Atlantic l., transatlantique *m*.

ling [liŋ], *s. Bot:* bruyère (commune).

linger ['liŋgər], *v.i. (a)* tarder, s'attarder; **to l.
over a meal,** prolonger un repas; **a doubt still
lingers in his mind,** un doute subsiste encore
dans son esprit; *(b) (of invalid)* **to l. (on),**
traîner; **'lingering,** *a. (a)* (regard) prolongé;
(doute) qui subsiste encore; *(b)* **l. death,** mort
lente.

linguist ['liŋgwist], *s.* linguiste *mf*; **lin'guistics,**
s.pl. (usu. with sg. const.) linguistique *f*.

liniment ['linimənt], *s.* liniment *m*.

link [liŋk]. **I.** *s.* **1.** *(a)* chaînon *m*, maillon *m*,
anneau *m* (d'une chaîne); *(b)* **cuff links,**
boutons de manchette. **2.** lien *m*, trait *m* d'u-
nion **(between,** entre); **missing l.,** (i) lacune *f*;
(ii) *Biol:* forme intermédiaire disparue; *F:* le
pithécanthrope; **air l.,** liaison aérienne. **II.** *v.* **1.**
v.tr. enchaîner, (re)lier, attacher **(with, to,** à);
closely linked facts, faits étroitement unis; **to l.
arms,** se donner le bras. **2.** *v.i.* **to l. on to sth., to
l. up with sth.,** s'attacher, s'unir, à qch.

links [liŋks], *s.pl.* terrain *m* de golf.

linnet ['linit], *s. Orn:* linotte *f*.

linoleum [li'nouliəm], *s.* linoléum *m*.

linotype ['lainoutaip], *s. Typ:* linotype *f*.

linseed ['linsi:d], *s.* graine *f* de lin; **l. oil,** huile *f* de
lin.

lint [lint], *s. Med:* tissu *m* de coton (pour
pansements).

lintel ['lint(ə)l], *s.* linteau *m*.

lion ['laiən], *s.* **1.** *(a)* lion *m*; **l. cub,** lionceau *m*; *F:*
the l.'s share, la part du lion; *(b)* **mountain l.,**
puma *m*, couguar *m*. **2.** *Geog:* **the Gulf of
Lions,** le golfe du Lion; **'lioness,** *s.* lionne *f*;
'lion'hearted, *a.* au cœur de lion.

lip [lip], *s.* **1.** *(a)* lèvre *f*; babine *f* (d'un animal); **to
keep a stiff upper l.,** ne pas broncher; serrer les
dents; **to bite one's lip(s),** se mordre les lèvres;
to smack one's lips over sth., se lécher les
babines; *(b) F:* insolence *f*; **none of your l.!** en
voilà assez! **2.** bord *m*, rebord *m*
(d'une tasse, etc.); **'lip-reading,** *s.* lecture *f*
sur les lèvres; **'lip-service,** *s.* **to pay l.-s. to
sth.,** rendre à qch. des hommages peu sincères;
'lipstick, *s.* rouge *m* à lèvres.

liquefy ['likwifai], *v.tr. & i.* (se) liquéfier;
lique'faction, *s.* liquéfaction *f*.

liqueur [li'kjuər], *s.* liqueur *f*; **l. brandy,** fine *f*.

liquid ['likwid]. **1.** *a. (a)* liquide; *(b) Fin:* **l. assets,**
valeurs *f* disponibles. **2.** *s.* liquide *m*;
'liquidate, *v.tr. Com:* liquider (une société,
une dette); *F:* **to l. s.o.,** liquider qn; **liqui'dation,** *s.* liquidation *f*; **li'quidity,** *s. Fin:*
liquidité *f*; **'liquidizer,** *s.* mixeur *m*.

liquor ['likər], *s.* boisson *f* alcoolique.

liquorice ['likəris], *s.* réglisse *f*.

Lisbon ['lizbən]. *Pr.n. Geog:* Lisbonne *f*.

lisp [lisp]. **I.** *s.* zézaiement *m*, blèsement *m*; **to**
have a l., zézayer. **II.** *v.i. & tr.* zézayer, blése
'lisping. **1.** *a.* blèse. **2.** *s.* blésité *f*.

list [list]. **I.** *s.* liste *f*, rôle *m*, tableau *m*, état *m*
alphabetical l., liste, répertoire *m*
alphabétique; **wine l.,** carte *f* des vins; *(of in
valid)* **on the danger l.,** dans un état grave; **th
black l.,** la liste noire; *Mil: etc:* **sick l.,** état de
malades; *F:* **to be on the sick l.,** être malade
Com: **l. price,** prix (de) catalogue. **II.** *v.t
cataloguer (des articles).

listen ['lisn], *v.ind.tr.* **1. to l. to s.o., sth.,** écoute
qn, qch.; **to l. attentively,** prêter une oreill
attentive. **2.** faire attention; écouter; **I
wouldn't l. (to us),** il a refusé de nous entendr
'listener, *s.* auditeur, -trice; **'listening,**
écoute *f*.

listless ['listlis], *a.* nonchalant; apathique; -l
adv. nonchalamment; **'listlessness,** *s.* no
chalance *f*, apathie *f*; indifférence *f*.

Litany ['litəni], *s. Ecc:* litanies *fpl*.

literacy ['litərəsi], *s.* fait *m* de savoir lire et écrir

literal ['litərəl], *a. (a)* littéral; **in the l. sense of t
word,** au sens propre du mot; *(of pers., min
positif, prosaïque; **-ally,** *adv.* littéraleme
(interpréter qch.) à la lettre.

literate ['litərət], *a.* lettré.

literature ['litrətʃər], *s. (a)* littérature *f*; **light
lectures amusantes; *(b) Com:* prospectus *m
literary ['litərəri], *a.* littéraire.

lithe [laið], *a.* souple, agile.

lithograph ['liθəgræf]. **I.** *s.* lithographie *f
v.tr. lithographier; **li'thographer,** *s.* lith
graphe *mf*; **litho'graphic** [-'græfik], *a.* lit
graphique; **li'thography,** *s.* lithographie *f*.

litigate ['litigeit]. **1.** *v.tr.* mettre (qch.) en litige
v.i. plaider; **'litigant,** *s.* plaideur, -eu
liti'gation, *s.* litige *m*; **li'tigious** [-'tidʒəs]
litigieux.

litmus ['litməs], *s.* tournesol *m*; **l. paper,** pa
m (de) tournesol.

litter ['litər]. **I.** *s.* **1.** litière *f*. **2.** *Agr:* litière
paille). **3.** *(a)* fouillis *m*, désordre *m*; *(b)* papi
etc., jetés par terre. **4.** portée *f* (d'un anim
II. *v.* **1.** *v.tr.* mettre (une chambre) en désor
table littered with papers, table encombré
papiers. **2.** *v.i. (of animal)* mettre bas.

little ['litl]. **I.** *a.* **1.** petit; **the l. finger,** le
doigt. **2.** peu (de); **l. money,** peu d'argen
l. money, un peu d'argent. **3.** (esprit) mesq
II. *s.* **1.** peu; **to eat l. or nothing,** manger pe
point; **he knows very l.,** il ne sait pas gr
chose; **I took very l. of it,** j'en ai pris très
moins que rien; **I see very l. of him,** je le
rarement; **to think l. of sth.,** faire peu de ca
qch.; **l. by l.,** petit à petit; peu à peu; **ev
helps,** tout fait nombre. **2. a l. more,** encor
peu; **for a l.,** pendant un certain temps;
adv. peu; **l. more than an hour ago,** il n
guère, il y a à peine, plus d'une he

'**littleness**, *s.* petitesse *f.*
live. I. *a.* [laiv]. **1.** (*a*) vivant; en vie; **a real l.
burglar,** un cambrioleur en chair et en os; (*b*) **l.
coals,** charbons ardents; (*c*) **l. broadcast,** émission en direct. **2.** *El:* **l. wire,** fil *m* en charge; *F:*
he's a real l. wire, il est dynamique. **II.** *v.* [liv].
1. *v.i.* vivre; (*a*) **while my father lives,** du vivant
de mon père; **he won't l. through the winter,** il
ne passera pas l'hiver; **l. and learn,** on apprend
à tout âge; **l. and let l.,** il faut que tout le monde
vive; (*b*) **to l. on vegetables,** se nourrir de
légumes; **I've enough to l. on,** j'ai de quoi vivre;
to l. on one's capital, manger son capital; **to l.
on one's reputation,** vivre sur, de, sa
réputation; (*c*) **to l. in style,** mener grand train;
to l. well, faire bonne chère; **to l. up to one's
reputation,** faire honneur à sa réputation; (*d*)
where do you l.? où habitez-vous? où
demeurez-vous? **he lives at No. 7 rue de
Rivoli,** il demeure rue de Rivoli, numéro 7;
house not fit to l. in, maison inhabitable; (*e*)
he's living with his grandparents, il habite chez
ses grands-parents. **2.** *v.tr.* **to l. a happy life,**
mener une vie heureuse; **'live 'down,** *v.tr.*
faire oublier (un scandale, etc.) à la longue;
'live 'in, *v.i.* (*of employee*) être logé et nourri;
'livelihood ['laiv-], *s.* vie *f;* moyens *mpl*
d'existence; gagne-pain *m;* **'liveliness** ['laiv-],
s. vivacité *f,* animation *f,* entrain *m,* vie *f;*
'livelong ['liv-], *a.* **the l. day,** toute la (sainte)
journée; tout le long du jour; **'lively** ['laiv-], *a.*
(*a*) vif, animé, plein d'entrain; **l. conversation,**
conversation animée; (*b*) *F:* **things are getting
l.,** ça chauffe; (*c*) **to take a l. interest in sth.,**
s'intéresser vivement à qch.; **'liven** ['laiv-],
v.tr. & i. **to l. up,** (s')animer; **'livestock** ['laiv-],
s. Agr: bétail *m,* bestiaux *mpl;* **'living** ['liv-]. **I.**
a. vivant, vif, en vie; **I didn't meet a l. soul,** je
n'ai pas rencontré âme qui vive; **no man l.
could do better,** personne au monde ne
pourrait mieux faire. **II.** *s.* **l.** vie *f;* **standard of l.,**
niveau *m* de vie; **l. space,** espace vital. **2. to earn,
get, make, one's l.,** gagner sa vie; **to work for
one's l.,** travailler pour vivre; **to write for a l.,**
vivre de sa plume; **to make a l.,** gagner de quoi
vivre. **3.** *Ecc:* bénéfice *m,* cure *f;* **'living-room,**
s. salle *f* de séjour, salon *m.* **4. the l.,** les vivants;
he's still in the land of the l., il est encore de ce
monde.
...er ['livər], *s. Anat:* foie *m;* **'liverish,** *a.* **to feel
l.,** se sentir mal en train; avoir une crise de foie.
...ery ['livəri], *s.* livrée *f.*
...id ['livid], *a.* (teint) livide, blême; **l. with anger,**
blême de colère; *F:* **to be absolutely l.,** être
dans une colère folle.
...ard ['lizəd], *s.* lézard *m.*
...ma ['lɑːmə], *s. Z:* lama *m.*
...d [loud]. **I.** *s.* **1.** (*a*) fardeau *m;* (*b*) charge *f*
d'un camion; *Av:* **commercial l.,** charge utile;

flight l., charge en vol; (*c*) **a (lorry-)l. of gravel,**
une charge, un camion, de gravier. **2.** charge
(d'une arme à feu). **3. to have a l. on one's conscience,** avoir un poids sur la conscience;
that's a l. off my mind! quel soulagement! **4.** *F:*
loads of . . ., des tas *m,* des quantités *f,* de
. . .. II. *v.* **1.** *v.tr.* (*a*) **to l. sth. with sth.,** charger
qch. de qch.; (*b*) **to l. s.o. with favours,** combler
qn de faveurs; (*c*) charger (un fusil). **2.** *v.i.* **to l.
(up),** charger; prendre charge; **'loading,** *s.*
chargement *m;* **bulk l.,** chargement en vrac.
loaf[1], *pl.* **loaves** [louf, louvz], *s.* pain *m;* miche *f*
(de pain); **cottage l.** = pain de ménage; **half a l.
is better than no bread,** faute de grives on
mange des merles.
loaf[2], *v.i.* **to l. (about),** flâner, fainéanter; **'loafer,**
s. flâneur *m;* **young l.,** voyou *m;* **'loafing,** *s.*
flânerie *f,* fainéantise *f.*
loam [loum], *s. Agr:* terre grasse.
loan [loun]. **I.** *s.* **1.** prêt *m;* **to offer s.o. sth. on l.,**
offrir qch. à qn à titre de prêt. **2.** emprunt *m;* **to
have the l. of sth.,** emprunter qch.; *Fin:* **to raise
a l.,** contracter un emprunt; **l. word,** mot d'emprunt (à une autre langue). **II.** *v.tr.* prêter.
loath [louθ], *a.* **to be l. to do sth.,** faire qch. à
contrecœur.
loathe [louð], *v.tr.* détester, exécrer; **I l. doing it,**
il me répugne de le faire; **'loathing,** *s.* dégoût
m, répugnance *f* (**for,** pour); **'loathsome,** *a.*
repoussant, écœurant, dégoûtant, répugnant;
-ly, *adv.* d'une manière répugnante; **l. ugly
man,** homme dégoûtant par sa laideur.
lobby ['lɔbi], *s.* vestibule *m.*
lobe [loub], *s. Biol:* lobe *m.*
lobster ['lɔbstər], *s.* homard *m;* **spiny l., rock l.,**
langouste *f;* **'lobster-pot,** *s.* casier *m* à
homards.
local ['louk(ə)l]. **1.** *a.* local, régional; de la
localité; **l. government** = administration
départementale, communale. **2.** *s.* (*a*) habitant,
-ante, de l'endroit; **the locals,** les gens du pays;
(*b*) *F:* **the l.** = le café du coin; **-ally,** *adv.*
localement; **staff engaged l.,** personnel engagé
sur place; **well known l.,** bien connu dans la
région; **lo'cality,** *s.* localité *f;* endroit *m,*
voisinage *m;* **in this l.,** dans cette région;
lo'cate, *v.tr.* **1.** localiser (qch.); découvrir; **to l.
a leak,** localiser, repérer, une fuite. **2. to be
located in the village,** être situé dans le village;
lo'cation, *s.* **1.** relève *f* (d'un défaut); repérage
m (d'une batterie, etc.). **2.** (*a*) situation *f,*
emplacement *m;* (*b*) *Cin:* extérieurs *mpl;* **on l.,**
sur les lieux.
lock[1] [lɔk], *s.* mèche *f,* boucle *f* (de cheveux).
lock[2]. **I.** *s.* **1.** serrure *f,* fermeture *f;* **under l. and
key,** (i) sous clef; (ii) (*of pers.*) sous les verrous.
2. platine *f* (de fusil); **l., stock and barrel,** tout
sans exception, tout le tremblement. **3.** *Aut:*
(steering) l., angle *m* de braquage. **4.** écluse *f;* **l.**

gate, porte ƒ d'écluse; l. **keeper**, gardien *m* d'écluse; éclusier *m*. **II.** *v.* **1.** *v.tr.* (*a*) fermer à clef; **to l. s.o. in a room**, enfermer qn dans une pièce; (*b*) **to l. the wheels**, bloquer, enrayer, les roues; **to be locked (together) in a struggle**, être engagés corps à corps dans une lutte; **to be locked in each other's arms**, se tenir étroitement embrassés; (*c*) **to l. a barge**, écluser un chaland. **2.** *v.i.* (*of wheels*) se bloquer, s'enrayer; **'locker**, *s.* armoire ƒ; coffre *m*; **'lock 'out**, *v.tr.* to be locked out, trouver porte close; **'lock-out**, *s.* *Ind:* lock-out *m inv*; **'locksmith**, *s.* serrurier *m*; **'lock 'up**, *v.tr.* mettre, enfermer, (qn, qch.) sous clef; fermer (une maison) à clef; **'lockup**, (*a*) *s.* cellule ƒ, cachot *m*; (*b*) *a.* fermant à clef.

locket ['lɔkit], *s.* médaillon (porté en parure).

locomotive [loukə'moutiv]. **1.** *a.* locomotif. **2.** *s.* locomotive ƒ; **loco'motion**, *s.* locomotion ƒ.

locum(-tenens) ['loukəm('tenenz)], *s.* remplaçant, -ante; suppléant, -ante (d'un médecin); **to act as a l.**, faire l'intérim; faire un remplacement.

locust ['loukəst], *s.* *Ent:* criquet *m* pèlerin, voyageur.

lode [loud], *s.* *Min:* filon *m*, veine ƒ, gisement *m*.

lodge [lɔdʒ]. **I.** *s.* **1.** loge ƒ (de concierge, etc.); pavillon *m* d'entrée (d'une propriété). **2.** **shooting l.**, pavillon de chasse. **3.** (*in freemasonry*) loge, atelier *m*. **II.** *v.* **1.** *v.tr.* (*a*) héberger (qn); (*b*) **to l. a complaint**, porter plainte. **2.** *v.i.* (*a*) être en pension (**with s.o.**, chez qn); (*b*) (*of thg*) rester, se loger; **'lodger**, *s.* locataire *mf* (en meublé); pensionnaire *mf*; **'lodging**, *s.* **1.** hébergement *m*. **2. a night's l.**, le logement pour la nuit. **3.** *pl.* **lodgings**, appartement meublé; chambre meublée; **to let lodgings**, louer des chambres, des appartements; **to let furnished lodgings**, louer en garni, tenir un meublé.

loft [lɔft], *s.* (*a*) grenier *m*, soupente ƒ; (*b*) (*in church*) **organ l.**, tribune ƒ (de l'orgue).

lofty ['lɔfti], *a.* **1.** haut, élevé. **2.** (*of pers.*) hautain; (air) condescendant; **'loftiness**, *s.* hauteur ƒ, élévation ƒ.

log[1] [lɔg]. **I.** *s.* **1.** bûche ƒ; tronçon *m* de bois; **to sleep like a l.**, dormir à poings fermés; **as easy as falling off a l.**, simple comme bonjour; **l. cabin**, cabane ƒ en rondins. **2.** *Nau:* loch *m*. **3.** **ship's l. (book)**, journal *m* de bord; **l. book**, (i) *Av:* carnet *m* de vol; (ii) *Aut: F:* = carte grise. **II.** *v.tr.* (**logged**) *Nau:* porter (un fait) au journal de bord.

logarithm ['lɔgeriθm], *F:* **log**², *s.* *Mth:* logarithme *m*; **log table**, table ƒ de logarithmes.

loggerheads ['lɔgəhedz], *s.* **to be at l. with s.o.**, être en brouille, être brouillé, avec qn.

logic ['lɔdʒik], *s.* logique ƒ; **'logical**, *a.* **1.** logique.

2. (*of pers.*) qui a de la logique; **-ally**, *adv.* logiquement; **logician** [lɔ'dʒiʃn], *s.* logicien -ienne.

loin [lɔin], *s.* **1.** *pl.* **loins**, reins *m*; **l. cloth**, pagne *m*. **2.** *Cu:* filet *m* (de mouton, de veau); aloyau *m* e faux-filet *m* (de bœuf); **l. chop**, côtelette ƒ de filet.

loiter ['lɔitər], *v.i.* flâner, traîner; *Jur:* rôde d'une manière suspecte; **'loiterer**, *s.* flân eur; -euse; rôdeur *m*; **'loitering. 1.** *a.* flân eur; traînard. **2.** *s.* flânerie ƒ; vagabondage *m*.

loll [lɔl], *v.i.* être étendu; **to l. in an armchair**, s prélasser dans un fauteuil; **to l. about**, flâner fainéanter.

lolly ['lɔli], *s.* *F:* **1.** sucette ƒ; **iced l.**, sucett glacée. **2.** argent *m*, *F:* pognon *m*.

London ['lʌndən]. *Pr.n. Geog:* Londres *m* **'Londoner**, *s.* Londonien, -ienne.

lone [loun], *a.* solitaire, seul.

lonely ['lounli], *a.* solitaire, isolé; **to feel very l** se sentir bien seul; **l. spot**, endroit désert, isole **'loneliness**, *s.* **1.** solitude ƒ, isolement *m*. sentiment *m* d'abandon.

long[1] [lɔŋ]. **I.** *a.* long, ƒ. longue. **1. to be te metres l.**, avoir dix mètres de long, d longueur, être long de dix mètres; **how l. is th room?** quelle est la longueur de la pièce? th **best by a l. way**, de beaucoup le meilleur; th **longest way round**, le chemin le plus long; t **make sth. longer**, (r)allonger qch.; **to pull a face**, faire la grimace. **2.** (*in time*) **how l. are th holidays?** quelle est la durée des vacances? t **days are getting longer**, les jours rallongent; **will take a l. time**, ce sera long; **they're a l. ti (in) coming**, ils se font attendre; **a l. time ago**, y a longtemps; **to wait for a l. time**, attend longtemps; **it won't happen for a l. time**, n'est pas pour demain; **three days at t longest**, trois jours (tout) au plus. **II.** *s.* **1. th and the short of it is that . . .**, le fin mot l'affaire c'est que . . .. **2. before l.**, avant pe sous peu; **for l.**, pendant longtemps; **it wo take l.**, cela ne sera pas long, ce sera l'affa d'une minute. **III.** *adv.* **1.** (*a*) longtemps; **he h been gone so l.**, il y a beau temps qu'il est par **l. live the King!** vive le roi! **as l. as I live**, ta que je vivrai; **do what you like so l. as y leave me alone**, faites tout ce que vous voud pourvu que vous me laissiez tranquille; **wasn't l. in putting things straight**, il eut bien fait de réparer le désordre; **you weren't l. ab it**, vous l'avez vite fait; **he won't be l.**, il tardera pas; **now we shan't be l.!** (i) nous n avons plus pour longtemps; (ii) *F:* voilà qui bien! *F:* **so l.!** au revoir! à bientôt! (*b*) **I hav been convinced of it**, j'en suis convain depuis longtemps; (*c*) **how l.?** combien temps? **how l. have you been here?** dep combien de temps êtes-vous ici? **how l. do t**

holidays last? quelle est la durée des vacances? **2. l. before, after,** longtemps avant, après; **not l. before,** peu de temps avant; **he died l. ago,** il est mort depuis longtemps; **not l. ago,** depuis peu. **3. all day l.,** pendant toute la journée. **4. I could no longer see him,** je ne pouvais plus le voir; **I couldn't wait any longer,** je ne pouvais pas attendre plus longtemps; **three months longer,** pendant trois mois encore; **how much longer?** combien de temps encore? **5. a l. felt want,** un besoin senti depuis longtemps; **'long-'distance,** a. Sp: l.-d. **runner,** coureur m de fond; P.T.T: l.-d. **call,** appel interurbain; **'long-drawn-'out,** a. prolongé; **'long-'lived,** a. qui a la vie longue; vivace; (erreur) persistante; **'long-'playing,** a. **l.-p. record,** microsillon m; **'long-'standing,** a. ancien; de longue date; **'long-'suffering,** a. patient, endurant; indulgent; **'long-'term,** a. (politique, opération) à longue échéance, à long terme; **'long-'winded,** a. (of pers.) verbeux, intarissable; (of speech) interminable.

long², v.i. **to l. for,** désirer (qch.) ardemment; avoir grande envie de (qch.); **to l. for home,** avoir la nostalgie du foyer; **'longing,** s. désir ardent, grande envie (**for,** de).

longitude ['lɔndʒitju:d, 'lɔŋgi-], s. longitude f.

loo (the) [ðə'lu:], s. F: les cabinets m.

look [luk]. **I.** s. **1.** regard m; **to have a l. at sth.,** jeter un coup d'œil sur qch.; regarder qch.; **to have a l. round the town,** faire un tour de ville. **2.** (a) aspect m, air m, apparence f (de qn, de qch.); mine f (de qn); **to judge by looks,** juger d'après les apparences; **I don't like the l. of him,** (i) sa figure ne me revient pas; (ii) il a l'air d'être malade; **I don't like the l. of it,** cela ne me dit rien de bon; **by the look(s) of it,** d'après l'apparence; (b) **(good) looks,** belle mine, bonne mine, beauté f. **II.** v.i. & tr. **1.** regarder; **to l. out of the window,** regarder par la fenêtre; **to l. down a list,** parcourir une liste; **to l. the other way,** (i) regarder de l'autre côté; (ii) détourner les yeux; **l. (and see) what time it is,** regardez quelle heure il est; **l. where you're going,** regardez où vous allez. **2. to l. s.o. (full) in the face,** regarder qn bien en face; dévisager qn; **I could never l. him in the face again,** je me sentirais toujours honteux devant lui; **to l. s.o. up and down,** toiser qn; **to l. one's last on sth.,** jeter un dernier regard sur qch. **3.** avoir l'air, paraître, sembler; **he looks young for his age,** il ne paraît pas son âge; **she looks her age,** elle paraît bien son âge; **things are looking bad,** les choses prennent une mauvaise tournure; **how does my hat l.?** comment trouvez-vous mon chapeau? **what does he l. like?** comment est-il? **he looks a rascal,** il a une mine de coquin; **he looks the part,** il a le physique de l'emploi; **it**

looks like it, cela en a l'air; on le dirait; **it looks like rain,** on dirait qu'il va pleuvoir. **4.** F: **l. here!** dites donc! écoutez donc! **'look 'after,** v.ind.tr. soigner, s'occuper de (qn, qch.); **to l. after oneself,** (i) se dorloter; (ii) se débrouiller; **to l. after one's interests,** veiller à ses intérêts; **I l. after my own car,** j'entretiens ma voiture moi-même; **'look at,** v.ind.tr. (a) regarder, considérer (qn, qch.); **just l. at this!** regardez-moi ça! **to l. at one's watch,** regarder sa montre; **to l. at him one would say . . .,** à le voir on dirait . . .; **the hotel is not much to l. at,** l'hôtel ne paie pas de mine; (b) **l. at the result,** voyez, considérez, le résultat; **way of looking at things,** manière f de voir les choses; **however you l. at it,** de n'importe quel point de vue; **'look a'way,** v.i. détourner les yeux; **'look 'back,** v.i. (a) regarder en arrière; se retourner, tourner la tête (**at sth.,** pour regarder qch.); (b) **what a day to l. back on!** quelle journée à se rappeler plus tard! **'look 'down,** v.i. regarder en bas, par terre; baisser les yeux; **to l. down on s.o.,** regarder qn de haut; dédaigner qn; **'looker,** s. **l. on,** spectateur, -trice; **'look for,** v.ind.tr. (a) chercher; **to go and l. for s.o.,** aller à la recherche de qn; (b) s'attendre à (qch.); **'look 'forward,** v.i. (i) s'attendre (à qch.); (ii) attendre, envisager (qch.) avec plaisir; **'look 'in,** v.i. **to l. in on s.o.,** entrer chez qn en passant; **I shall l. in again tomorrow,** je repasserai demain; **'look-in,** s. F: **he won't get a l.-in,** il n'a pas la moindre chance; **'looking-glass,** s. miroir m, glace f; **'look 'into,** v.ind.tr. examiner, étudier (une question); **I'll l. into it,** j'en prendrai connaissance; **look 'on,** (a) v.tr. **I don't l. on it in that light,** je n'envisage pas la chose ainsi; (b) v.i. être spectateur; **suppose you helped me instead of looking on,** si vous m'aidiez au lieu de me regarder faire; **'look 'out,** v.i. (a) regarder au dehors; (b) **room that looks out on the garden,** pièce qui donne sur le jardin; (c) veiller; **to l. out for s.o.,** être à la recherche de qn; guetter qn; (d) F: **l. out!** attention! prenez garde! **'look-out,** s. **1.** guet m, surveillance f; **to keep a sharp l.-out,** guetter d'un œil attentif; faire bonne garde; **to be on the l.-out for s.o.,** guetter qn. **2.** F: a poor **l.-out,** une triste perspective; **that's his l.-out,** ça c'est son affaire; **'look 'over,** v.tr. parcourir (qch.) des yeux; examiner (qch.); **to l. over a house,** visiter une maison; **'look 'round,** v.i. **1.** regarder autour de soi; **to l. round for s.o.,** chercher qn du regard. **2.** se retourner (pour voir), tourner la tête; **don't l. round!** ne regardez pas en arrière! **'look 'through,** v.tr. parcourir, examiner (des papiers); repasser (un compte, etc.) **'look to,** v.i. (a) **to l. to sth.,** s'occuper de qch., voir à qch.; (b) **to l. to s.o. to do sth.,** compter sur qn pour faire qch.; **'look 'up,** **1.** v.i. (a) regarder en haut; lever les yeux; (b) **to l.**

up to s.o., respecter, considérer, qn; (c) **business is looking up**, les affaires reprennent; **things are looking up with him**, ses affaires vont mieux. 2. *v.tr.* (a) **to l. up a train (in the timetable)**, consulter l'indicateur; **to l. up a word in the dictionary**, (re)chercher un mot dans le dictionaire; (b) F: **to l. s.o. up**, aller voir qn; **'look upon**, *v.ind.tr.* **to l. upon sth. as a crime**, regarder qch. comme un crime; **that is not the way I l. upon it**, ce n'est pas ainsi que j'envisage la chose.

loom[1] [lu:m], *s.* métier *m* (à tisser).

loom[2], *v.i.* apparaître indistinctement; **to l. up out of the fog**, surgir, sortir, du brouillard; (of *event*) **to l. large**, paraître imminent.

loop [lu:p]. I. *s.* boucle *f.* II. *v.tr.* boucler; **to l. back a curtain**, retenir un rideau avec une embrasse; **'loophole**, *s.* 1. *Mil:* meurtrière *f*, créneau *m.* 2. **to find a l.**, trouver une échappatoire.

loose [lu:s]. I. *a.* 1. (a) mal assujetti; branlant; (of *page*) détaché; (of *knot*) défait; **to come l.**, se dégager; (of *machine parts*) **to work l.**, prendre du jeu; (b) déchaîné, échappé, lâché; **to let a dog l.**, lâcher un chien; **it was hell let l.**, ils on fait un beau sabbat; (c) non assujetti; mobile; **l. sheets**, feuilles volantes; **to hang l.**, pendre, flotter; F: **to be at a l. end**, être, se trouver, désœuvré, sans occupation; (d) **l. cash**, petite, menue, monnaie. 2. (a) **l. rope**, câble détendu; **l. knot**, nœud lâche; (of *shoelace*) **to come l.**, se relâcher; **l. draperies**, draperies flottantes; (b) **man of l. build**, homme dégingandé. 3. **l. earth**, terre *f* meuble; terrain *m* sans consistance. 4. vague, peu exact; **l. translation**, traduction approximative. 5. dissolu; débauché; libertin; **l. living**, mauvaise vie. II. *v.tr.* délier; détacher; **to l. one's hold**, lâcher prise; **-ly**, *adv.* 1. (tenir qch.) sans serrer. 2. vaguement, inexactement; **'loose box**, *s.* box *m* (d'écurie); **'loose-fitting**, *a.* non ajusté; (vêtement) ample, large; **'loose-'leaf**, *a.* (of *album*) à feuilles mobiles; **'loose-limbed**, *a.* dégingandé; **'loosen**, *v.* 1. *v.tr.* relâcher (un nœud); desserrer (un écrou); **to l. one's grip**, relâcher son étreinte; **to l. s.o.'s tongue**, délier la langue à qn; faire parler qn. 2. *v.i.* se délier, se défaire; se desserrer; se relâcher; (of *machinery*) prendre du jeu; **'looseness**, *s.* 1. état branlant (d'une dent). 2. relâchement *m* (d'une corde); ampleur (d'un vêtement). 3. (a) imprécision *f*; (b) relâchement (de la discipline); (c) licence *f* (de conduite).

loot [lu:t]. I. *s.* butin *m.* II. *v.* 1. *v.tr.* piller, saccager (une ville). 2. *v.i.* se livrer au pillage · **'looter**, *s.* pillard *m*; **'looting**, *s.* pillage *m*; sac *m* (d'une ville, etc.).

lop[1] [lɔp], *v.tr.* (**lopped**) élaguer, tailler, émonder (un arbre); **to l. off a branch**, élaguer une branche.

lop[2]; **'lop-eared**, *a.* (lapin, etc.) aux oreilles pendantes; **'lop'sided**, *a.* qui penche d'un côté; déjeté, déversé; de guingois; **'lop'sided ness**, *s.* manque *m* de symétrie; déjettemen' *m.*

lope [loup]. I. *s.* pas de course allongé. II. *v.i.* **to l along**, aller bon train.

loquacious [lɔ'kweiʃəs], *a.* loquace; **-ly**, *adv* avec loquacité; **lo'quaciousness**, *s.* **lo'quacity** [-'kwæs-], *s.* loquacité *f.*

lord [lɔ:d]. I. *s.* 1. seigneur *m*, maître *m.* 2. **the L.** le Seigneur; Dieu *m*; **in the year of our L.** . . en l'an de grâce . . .. 3. (title) lord *m*; **to liv like a l.**, mener une vie de grand seigneur; **m** **l.**, (i) monsieur le baron, etc.; (ii) (to bishop monseigneur; (iii) monsieur le juge; mon sieur le président. II. *v.tr.* **to l. it over s.o** vouloir en imposer à qn; le prendre de hau avec qn; **'lordliness**, *s.* 1. (a) dignité *f*; (b magnificence *f* (d'un château, etc.). 2. hauteu *f*, orgueil *m*; **'lordly**, *a.* 1. de grand seigneu' noble, majestueux; magnifique. 2. hautai' altier; **'lordship**, *s.* 1. suzeraineté *f*, seigneuri *f* (**over**, de). 2. **your l.**, votre seigneuri monsieur le comte, etc.; (to bishop) monsei neur.

lorry ['lɔri], *s.* camion *m*; **heavy l.**, poids lourc **articulated l.**, véhicule articulé; **l. driver**, co' ducteur *m* de camion, routier *m.*

lose [lu:z], *v.tr.* (**lost** [lɔst]) 1. (a) perdre; **the inc dent did not l. in the telling**, en raconta' l'histoire on en a rajouté; **to l. in value**, perd' de sa valeur; (b) **he has lost an arm**, il a perc un bras; **to l. one's voice**, avoir une extincti' de voix; **to l. one's reputation**, perdre s réputation; **to l. strength**, s'affaiblir; **to weight**, perdre du poids; (c) **to be lost at se** périr en mer. 2. **to l. oneself, to get lost, to one's way**, perdre son chemin; s'égarer; **to sight of s.o.**, perdre qn de vue. 3. perdre (s temps, sa peine); **the joke was lost on him**, n'a pas saisi la plaisanterie. 4. **that clock los ten minutes a day**, cette pendule retarde de d minutes par jour. 5. manquer (le train, etc.) **lost most of his answer**, la plupart de réponse m'a échappé. 6. perdre (une partie, procès); **the motion was lost**, la motion a é rejetée. 7. faire perdre (qch. à qn); **that mista lost him the match**, cette faute lui coûta la p tie; **'loser**, *s.* 1. **I'm the l. by it**, j'y perds. 2. p dant, -ante; **to be a bad l.**, être mauvais joue' **'losing**, *a. Sp:* **the l. side**, l'équipe perdar **lost**, *a.* perdu; **l. property office**, service *m* c objets trouvés; **to give s.o., sth., up for l.**, aba donner tout espoir de retrouver qn, qch. **gave myself up for l.**, je me crus perdu; **looks l.**, il a l'air dépaysé; **to be l. to all sense shame**, avoir perdu tout sentiment de honte

loss [lɔs], *s.* 1. perte *f*; **l. of sight**, perte, privati *f*; de la vue; **l. of voice,** extinction *f* de voix; **without l. of time,** sans perte de temps; sans tarder. **2.** (*a*) **the widow and children cannot get over their l.,** la veuve et les enfants sont inconsolables de leur perte; (*b*) **to meet with a l.,** subir une perte; **dead l.,** perte sèche; **to sell at a l.,** vendre à perte; **the l. is hers,** c'est elle qui y perd; **he's no l.,** la perte n'est pas grande. **3.** déperdition *f* (de chaleur); écoulement *m* (de sang). **4. to be at a l.,** être embarrassé, désorienté; **to be at a l. what to do, what to say,** ne pas savoir que faire, que dire; **I am at a l. for words,** les mots me manquent.

lot [lɔt], *s.* **1. to draw lots for sth.,** tirer au sort pour qch.; tirer qch. au sort; **to throw in one's l. with s.o.,** partager le sort, la fortune, de qn. **2.** (*a*) sort, part *f*, partage *m*; **to fall to s.o.'s l.,** tomber en partage à qn; **it fell to my l. to decide,** c'était à moi de décider; (*b*) destin *m*, destinée *f*; **to envy s.o.'s l.,** envier la destinée de qn. **3.** (*a*) (*at auction*) lot *m*; (*b*) *N.Am:* lot (de terrain); **parking l.,** parking *m*; (*c*) *F:* **a bad l.,** un mauvais garnement; (*d*) *Com:* **to buy in one l.,** acheter en bloc; (*e*) *F:* **the l.,** le tout; **that's the l.,** c'est tout; **the whole l. of you,** tous tant que vous êtes. **4.** *F:* (*a*) beaucoup; **what a l.!** ce qu'il y en a! **what a l. of people!** que de monde! que de gens! **such a l.,** tellement; **I have quite a l.,** j'en ai une quantité considérable; **I see quite a l. of him,** je le vois assez souvent; **he knows quite a l. about you,** il en sait long sur votre compte; *adv. phr.* **times have changed a l.,** les temps ont bien changé; (*b*) **I've lots of things to do,** j'ai un tas de choses à faire; **'lottery,** *s.* loterie *f*.

lotion ['louʃ(ə)n], *s.* lotion *f*.

loud [laud]. **1.** *a.* (*a*) bruyant, retentissant; **l. laugh,** gros rire; **in a l. voice,** à haute voix; **l. cheers,** vifs applaudissements; (*b*) (*of colour*) criard, voyant; (*of dress*) tapageur. **2.** *adv.* haut, à haute voix; **those who shout loudest,** ceux qui crient le plus fort; **-ly,** *adv.* **1.** (crier) haut, fort, à voix haute; (rire) bruyamment; **to call l. for sth.,** réclamer qch. à grands cris. **2. l. dressed,** à toilette tapageuse; **'loud- 'mouthed,** *a. F:* fort en gueule, gueulard; **'loudness,** *s.* force *f* (d'un bruit, etc.); grand bruit; **'loud'speaker,** *s. Rad:* haut-parleur *m*, *pl.* haut-parleurs.

lounge [laundʒ]. **I.** *s.* promenoir *m*; (*in hotel*) hall *m*; (*in house*) salon *m*; **sun l.,** véranda *f*. **II.** *v.i.* flâner; **'lounger,** *s.* flâneur, -euse; **'lounge-'suit,** *s.* complet *m*.

louse, *pl.* **lice** [laus, lais], *s.* pou *m*, *pl.* poux; **infested with lice,** pouilleux; **'lousy** [-zi], *a.* **1.** pouilleux. **2.** *F:* sale; *P:* moche; **l. trick,** sale coup *m*, sale tour *m*.

lout [laut], *s.* rustre *m*, lourdaud *m*; voyou *m*; **'loutish,** *a.* rustre, lourdaud.

love [lʌv]. **I.** *s.* **1.** amour *m*; (*a*) affection *f*, tendresse *f*; **there's no l. lost between them,** ils ne peuvent pas se sentir; **for the l. of God,** pour l'amour de Dieu; **to play for l.,** jouer pour l'honneur; **to work for l.,** travailler pour rien; **give your parents my l.,** faites mes amitiés à vos parents; **it can't be had for l. or money,** on ne peut se le procurer à aucun prix; (*b*) **to fall in l. with s.o.,** s'éprendre, tomber amoureux, de qn; **to be in l.,** être amoureux; **to make l. to s.o.,** faire l'amour avec qn; **to marry for l.,** faire un mariage d'amour; **l. match,** mariage d'amour; **l. letter,** billet doux; **l. story,** histoire *f* d'amour; roman *m* d'amour; **l. affair,** affaire *f* de cœur, d'amour. **2.** (*pers.*) **my l.,** mon amour, mon ami, mon amie. **3.** (*at tennis*) zéro *m*, rien *m*. **II.** *v.tr.* **1.** (*a*) aimer, affectionner (qn); **l. me, l. my dog,** qui m'aime aime mon chien; (*b*) aimer d'amour. **2.** aimer (passionnément); **to l. doing sth.,** aimer, adorer, faire qch.; **will you do it?—I'd l. to,** voulez-vous le faire?—je ne demande pas mieux; très volontiers; **'lovable,** *a.* aimable; sympathique; **'loveliness,** *s.* beauté *f*, charme *m*; **'lovely,** *a.* **1.** beau, ravissant; (*of meal, etc.*) excellent, épatant. **2.** **it's been l. seeing you again,** j'ai été ravi de vous revoir; **'lover,** *s.* **1.** (*a*) amoureux *m*; (*b*) amant *m*; **to take a l.,** prendre un amant. **2.** amateur *m*, ami(e) (de qch.); **nature-l.,** ami de la nature; **'loving,** *a.* affectueux, affectionné, tendre; **-ly,** *adv.* affectueusement, tendrement, avec tendresse; **'lovesick,** *a.* féru d'amour.

low[1] [lou]. **I.** *a.* **1.** bas, basse; **l. tide,** marée basse; **l. ceiling,** plafond bas, peu élevé; **l. prices,** bas prix; **the lowest price,** le dernier prix; **a hundred pounds at the lowest,** cent livres pour le moins; **l. speed,** petite vitesse; **the lower jaw,** la mâchoire inférieure; *Mus:* **l. note,** note basse; **in a l. voice,** à voix basse, à mi-voix; *Ecc:* **l. mass,** messe basse; **to lie l.,** se tenir coi, *f.* coite. **2. the lower animals,** les animaux inférieurs; **l. trick,** un sale coup. **3. to be in l. spirits,** être abattu; *F:* avoir le cafard; (*of invalid*) **in a very l. state,** bien bas. **II.** *adv.* (*a*) bas; **to aim l.,** viser bas; (*b*) **the lowest paid workers,** les employés les moins payés. **III.** *s.* **all-time l.,** record le plus bas; **'lowbrow,** *a.* peu intellectuel; **'low- 'budget,** *a.* bon marché, peu coûteux; **'low- down. I.** *a.* bas, vil, ignoble; **l.-d. trick,** sale coup *m*. **II.** *s.* **to give s.o. the l.-d.,** tuyauter qn; **'lower,** *v.tr.* (*a*) descendre (qch.); **to l. a boat,** mettre une embarcation à la mer; (*b*) abaisser (qch.); diminuer la hauteur de (qch.); rabaisser, réduire (le prix de qch.); (*c*) baisser (la voix); (*d*) **to l. oneself, one's standards, so far as to . . .,** s'abaisser jusqu'à (faire qch.); **'lowering**[1], *s.* descente *f*; mise à la mer (d'une embarcation); abaissement *m*, diminution *f* de la hauteur (de qch.); réduction *f*, diminution (de prix); **'low-'grade,** *a.* de qualité inférieure; **'low-'lying,** *a.* situé en bas; (terrain) bas; **'low-'pitched,** *a.* 1. (son) grave. 2. *Const:* (comble *m*) à faible pente.

low², *v.i.* meugler.

lowering² ['lauəriŋ], *a.* (ciel) sombre, menaçant.

loyal ['lɔiəl], *a.* fidèle, dévoué **(to,** à); loyal **(to,** envers); **-ally,** *adv.* fidèlement; **'loyalty,** *s.* fidélité *f.*

lozenge ['lɔzindʒ], *s.* pastille *f,* tablette *f.*

lubricate ['lu:brikeit], *v.tr.* lubrifier; graisser; **lubricating oil,** huile *f* de graissage; **'lubricant,** *s.* lubrifiant *m*; **lubri'cation,** *s.* lubrification *f,* graissage *m*; **'lubricator,** *s.* graisseur *m.*

Lucerne [lu(:)'sə:n]. *Pr.n. Geog:* Lucerne *f*; **the Lake of L.,** le lac des Quatre-Cantons.

lucid ['lu:sid], *a.* (style, etc.) lucide; *Med:* **l. interval,** intervalle *m* de lucidité; **-ly,** *adv.* lucidement; **lu'cidity,** *s.* lucidité *f.*

luck [lʌk], *s.* 1. hasard *m,* chance *f,* fortune *f*; **good l.,** bonne chance, bonheur *m*; **to be down on one's l.,** avoir de la déveine; **to try one's l.,** tenter la fortune, la chance; **to bring s.o. good, bad, l.,** porter bonheur, malheur à qn; **better l. next time!** ça ira mieux une autre fois; **worse l.!** tant pis! **hard l.! tough l.!** pas de chance! **as l. would have it . . .,** le hasard fit que + *ind. or sub.* 2. bonheur, fortune, (bonne) chance; **to keep sth. for l.,** garder qch. comme porte-bonheur; **stroke of l.,** coup *m* de chance, coup de veine; **to be in l.,** avoir de la chance; **to be out of l.,** jouer de malheur; **as l. would have it,** par bonheur; **'lucky,** *a.* (*a*) (*of pers.*) heureux, fortuné, chanceux; **to be l.,** avoir de la chance; (*b*) **l. hit,** coup *m* de bonheur; **l. day,** jour de veine; **at a l. moment,** au bon moment; **how l.!** quelle chance! (*c*) (*of thg*) **to be l.,** porter bonheur; **l. charm,** porte-bonheur *m inv*; **-ily,** *adv.* heureusement; par bonheur.

lucrative ['lu:krətiv], *a.* lucratif.

ludicrous ['lu:dikrəs], *a.* risible, grotesque, ridicule; **-ly,** *adv.* risiblement, grotesquement, ridiculement.

lug [!ʌg], *v.tr.* (**lugged**) traîner, tirer (qch. de pesant).

luggage ['lʌgidʒ], *s.* bagage(s) *m(pl)*; **l. label,** étiquette *f* à bagages; **l. rack,** (i) *Rail:* portebagages *m inv*; *Aut:* galerie *f*; *Rail:* **l. van,** fourgon *m* (aux bagages).

lukewarm ['lu:kwɔ:m], *a.* tiède.

lull [lʌl]. I. *s.* moment *m* de calme; *Nau:* accalmie *f.* II. *v.tr.* bercer, endormir (qn); endormir (les soupçons); **lullaby** ['lʌləbai], *s. Mus:* berceuse *f.*

lumber¹ ['lʌmbər]. I. *s.* 1. vieux meubles; fatras *m*; **l. room,** chambre *f* de débarras. 2. *N.Am:* bois *m* en grume. II. *v.tr.* encombrer, embarrasser (un lieu); **'lumberjack,** *s.* bûcheron

m; **'lumberman,** *pl.* **-men,** *s. N.Am:* (*a*) exploitant forestier; (*b*) bûcheron *m*; **'lumber-yard,** *s. N.Am:* chantier *m* de bois.

lumber², *v.i.* **to l. along,** avancer à pas pesants; **'lumbering,** *a.* lourd, pesant.

luminous ['lu:minəs], *a.* lumineux; **l. watch,** watch with **l. hands,** with a **l. dial,** montre *f* à cadran lumineux.

lump¹ [lʌmp]. I. *s.* 1. (*a*) gros morceau, bloc *m* (de pierre); motte *f* (d'argile); morceau (de sucre); (*in porridge*) grumeau *m*; **l. sum,** (i) somme globale; (ii) prix *m* à forfait; **to have a l. in one's throat,** avoir un serrement de gorge; se sentir le cœur gros; (*b*) bosse *f* (au front, etc.). 2. *F:* (*of pers.*) empoté *m,* lourdaud *m*; **great l. of a woman,** grosse dondon. II. *v.tr.* **to l. everything together,** tout mettre ensemble; **'lumpy,** *a.* (*of sauce*) grumeleux.

lump², *v.tr. F:* **if he doesn't like it he can l. it,** si cela ne lui plaît pas, qu'il s'arrange.

lunacy ['lu:nəsi], *s.* aliénation mentale; folie *f*; *Jur:* démence *f*; **it's sheer l.,** c'est de la folie; **'lunatic,** *a. & s.* fou, *f.* folle; aliéné, -ée; dément, -ente.

lunar ['lu:nər], *a.* lunaire; de (la) lune.

lunch [lʌn(t)ʃ]. I. *s.* déjeuner *m.* II. *v.i.* déjeuner; **luncheon** ['lʌn(t)ʃən], *s.* déjeuner *m*; **l. voucher,** chèque-repas *m.*

lung [lʌŋ], *s.* poumon *m*; **iron l.,** poumon d'acier.

lunge [lʌndʒ]. I. *s.* mouvement (précipité) en avant. II. *v.i.* s'élancer, se précipiter.

lurch¹ [lə:tʃ], *s.* **to leave s.o. in the l.,** planter là qn.

lurch². I. *s.* 1. embardée *f* (d'un navire, d'une voiture); coup *m.* 2. pas titubant (d'un ivrogne). II. *v.i.* 1. (*of car, ship*) faire une embardée. 2. (*of pers.*) **to l. along,** marcher en titubant.

lure ['ljuər]. I. *s.* 1. *Fish:* leurre *m.* 2. (*a*) piège *m*; (*b*) attrait *m* (de la mer, etc.). II. *v.tr.* 1. leurrer (un poisson). 2. attirer, séduire, allécher; **to be lured into a trap,** être attiré, entraîné, dans un piège.

lurid ['ljuərid], *a.* 1. (*of light*) blafard, sinistre. 2. (*a*) **l. flames,** flammes rougeoyantes; (*b*) (film, etc.) corsé, à sensation.

lurk [lə:k], *v.i.* se cacher; rester tapi (dans un coin); **'lurking,** *a.* caché; **l. suspicion,** vague soupçon; **l. thought,** arrière-pensée *f,* pensée arrière-pensées.

luscious ['lʌʃəs], *a.* succulent, savoureux.

lush [lʌʃ], *a.* (végétation) luxuriante, abondante, riche.

lust [lʌst], *s.* (*a*) appétit *m* (coupable); convoitise *f*; (*b*) désir (libidineux).

lustre ['lʌstər], *s.* éclat *m,* brillant *m,* lustre *m.*

lusty ['lʌsti], *a.* vigoureux, fort, robuste; **-ily,** *adv.* vigoureusement; **'lustiness,** *s.* vigueur *f.*

lute [lu:t], *s. Mus:* luth *m.*

Luxemb(o)urg ['lʌksəmbɔ:g]. *Pr.n. Geog:* le Luxembourg; **'Luxemb(o)urger,** *s.* Luxembourgeois, -oise.

luxuriance [lʌg'zjuəriəns], *s.* luxuriance *f,* exubérance *f;* **lux'uriant,** *a.* exubérant, luxuriant; **-ly,** *adv.* avec exubérance; en abondance; **lux'uriate,** *v.i.* **to l. in idleness,** s'abandonner à la paresse.

luxury ['lʌkʃəri], *s.* **1.** luxe *m;* **to live in l.,** vivre dans le luxe. **2.** (objet *m* de) luxe; **it's quite a l. for us,** c'est du luxe pour nous; **luxurious** [lʌg'zjuəriəs], *a.* luxueux, somptueux; **-ly,** *adv.* luxueusement; dans le luxe;

lux'uriousness, *s.* luxe *m;* somptuosité *f.*

lying ['laiiŋ]. **I.** *a.* faux; (récit) mensonger. **II.** *s.* le mensonge.

lymphatic [lim'fætik], *a.* lymphatique.

lynch [lin(t)ʃ], *v.tr.* lyncher; **'lynching,** *s.* lynchage *m.*

lynx [liŋks], *s. Z:* lynx *m;* loup-cervier *m.*

lyre ['laiər], *s. Mus:* lyre *f;* **'lyre-bird,** *s.* oiseau-lyre *m, pl.* oiseaux-lyres.

lyric ['lirik]. **1.** *a.* lyrique. **2.** *s.* (*a*) poème *m* lyrique; (*b*) *Th:* **lyrics by . . .,** chansons du livret par . . .; **l. writer,** parolier *m;* **'lyrical,** *a.* lyrique; **lyricism** ['lirisizm], *s.* lyrisme *m.*

M

M, m [em], *s.* (la lettre) M, m *f.*
mac [mæk], *s. F:* imper *m.*
macaroni [mækə'rouni], *s. Cu:* macaroni *m;* **m. cheese,** macaroni au gratin.
macaroon [mækə'ruːn], *s.* macaron *m.*
Macedonia [mæsi'douniə]. *Pr.n. Geog:* la Macédoine; **Mace'donian,** *a. & s.* macédonien, -ienne.
macerate ['mæsəreit], *v.tr. & i.* macérer; **mace'ration,** *s.* macération *f.*
Mach [mæk, mætʃ], *s. Av:* **M. (number),** (nombre *m* de) Mach.
machination [mæki'neiʃ(ə)n, mæʃ-], *s.* machination *f;* complot *m.*
machine [mə'ʃiːn]. **I.** *s.* machine *f,* appareil *m;* **sewing m., washing m.,** machine à coudre, à laver; (*of pers.*) **to be a mere m.,** n'être qu'un automate; **the party m.,** l'organisation *f* politique du parti; **m. gun,** mitrailleuse *f;* **m. gunner,** mitrailleur *m;* **m. shop,** atelier *m* (i) de construction mécanique, (ii) d'usinage; **m. tool,** machine-outil *f.* **II.** *v.tr.* **1.** *Ind:* façonner (une pièce); usiner. **2.** *Dressm:* coudre, piquer, à la machine; **ma'chinery,** *s.* mécanisme *m;* machines *fpl;* machinerie *f;* **ma'chining,** *s.* **1.** usinage *m.* **2.** couture *f,* piquage *m,* à la machine.
mackerel ['mæk(ə)rəl], *s. Ich:* maquereau *m.*
mackintosh ['mækintɔʃ], *s.* imperméable *m.*
mad [mæd], *a.* **1.** fou, dément; **raving m.,** fou furieux; **as m. as a hatter,** fou à lier; **to drive s.o. m.,** rendre qn fou; **nationalism gone, run, m.,** nationalisme forcené; **m. gallop,** galop furieux, effréné; *F:* **like m.,** comme un enragé. **2. m. for revenge,** assoiffé de revanche; **to be m. about, on, s.o., sth.,** être fou, raffoler, de qn, qch. **3.** *F:* **to be m. with s.o.,** être furieux contre qn. **4. m. bull,** taureau furieux; **m. dog,** chien enragé; **-ly,** *adv.* **1.** follement; comme un fou. **2.** (aimer) à la folie, éperdument. **3.** furieusement; **'madden,** *v.tr.* rendre fou; exaspérer; **'maddening,** *a.* à rendre fou; exaspérant, enrageant; **'madhouse,** *s. F:* **the place is like a m.,** on se croirait dans une maison de fous; **'madman,** *pl.* **-men,** *s.* fou *m,* aliéné *m;* **like a m.,** (faire qch.) comme un forcené; **'madness,** *s.* folie *f.*
Madagascar [mædə'gæskər]. *Pr.n. Geog:* le Madagascar.
madam ['mædəm], *s.* madame *f,* mademoiselle *f;* (*in letter*) **Dear M.,** Madame, Mademoiselle.

madder ['mædər], *s. Bot:* garance *f.*
made [meid]. *See* MAKE.
Madeira [mə'diərə], (*a*) *Pr.n. Geog:* la Madère; **M. cake** = gâteau *m* de Savoie; (*b*) *s.* (*wine*) madère *m.*
madonna [mə'dɔnə], *s.* madone *f.*
madrigal ['mædrig(ə)l], *s. Mus:* madrigal *m.*
magazine [mægə'ziːn], *s.* **1.** magasin *m* (d'un fusil, d'une caméra). **2.** revue *f* périodique; périodique *m;* magazine *m.* **3.** *Mil:* magasin d'armes.
maggot ['mægət], *s.* ver *m,* asticot *m;* **'maggoty,** *a.* véreux, plein de vers.
magic ['mædʒik]. **1.** *s.* magie *f,* enchantement *m;* **like m.,** comme par enchantement, comme par magie. **2.** *a.* magique, enchanté; **'magical,** *a.* magique; **-ally,** *adv.* magiquement; comme par enchantement, comme par magie; **ma'gician,** *s.* magicien, -ienne.
magisterial [mædʒis'tiəriəl], *a.* magistral.
magistrate ['mædʒistreit], *s.* magistrat *m,* juge *m.*
magnanimous [mæg'næniməs], *a.* magnanime -**ly,** *adv.* magnanimement; **magna'nimity,** s. magnanimité *f.*
magnate ['mægneit], *s.* magnat *m; F:* gros bonnet (de l'industrie, etc.); **oil m.,** roi *m* magnat, du pétrole.
magnesia [mæg'niːʒə], *s. Ch:* magnésie *f.*
magnesium [mæg'niːziəm], *s. Ch:* magnésium *m.*
magnet ['mægnit], *s.* (*a*) aimant *m;* (*b*) électro aimant *m;* **mag'netic,** *a.* magnétique aimanté; **m. pole,** pôle *m* magnétique; **m. tape,** bande *f,* ruban *m,* magnétique; **-ally** *adv.* magnétiquement; **mag'netics,** *s.p.* magnétisme *m;* **'magnetism,** *s.* magnétism *m;* **'magnetize,** *v.tr.* (*a*) magnétiser, attirer (qn); (*b*) aimanter (une aiguille).
magneto, *pl.* **-os** [mæg'niːtou, -ouz], *s. Aut:* etc magnéto *f.*
magnificence [mæg'nifis(ə)ns], *s.* magnificenc *f;* **mag'nificent,** *a.* magnifique; (repas) somp tueux; **-ly,** *adv.* magnifiquement.
magnify ['mægnifai], *v.tr.* grossir, agrandir **magnifying glass,** loupe *f;* verre grossissan **magnifi'cation,** *s.* grossissement *n* amplification *f.*
magnitude ['mægnitjuːd], *s.* grandeur *f; Ast* magnitude *f.*
magnolia [mæg'nouliə], *s. Bot:* magnolia *m.*

magnum ['mægnəm], *s.* magnum *m* (de champagne, etc.).

magpie ['mægpai], *s. Orn:* pie *f.*

mahogany [mə'hɔgəni], *s.* acajou *m.*

maid [meid], *s.* **1.** old m., vieille fille. **2.** bonne *f,* domestique *f;* (*in hotel*) room m., femme *f* de chambre; **'maiden,** *s. attrib.* (*a*) **m. aunt,** tante non mariée; (*b*) **m. name,** nom *m* de jeune fille; (*c*) **m. voyage,** premier voyage (d'un navire); **m. flight,** premier vol (d'un avion); **m. speech,** discours *m* de début (d'un député); **'maidenhair,** *s. Bot:* **m. (fern),** capillaire *m;* cheveu *m* de Vénus.

mail [meil]. **I.** *s. P. T. T:* **1.** courrier *m.* **2.** la poste; *Com:* **m. order,** commande *f* par correspondance; vente *f,* achat *m,* sur catalogue. **II.** *v.tr.* envoyer, expédier, (une lettre) par la poste; mettre (une lettre) à la poste; **'mailbag,** *s.* sac postal; **'mailbox,** *s. N.Am:* boîte *f* à lettres; **mailman,** *pl.* **-men,** *s. N.Am:* facteur *m.*

maim [meim], *v.tr.* estropier, mutiler.

main [mein]. **I.** *s.* **1. with might and m.,** de toutes ses forces. **2. in the m.,** en général, en somme. **3.** (*a*) *Civ.E:* **water m., gas m.,** conduite *f* d'eau, de gaz; **m. drainage,** tout-à-l'égout *m;* (*b*) *El:* câble *m* de distribution; **the vacuum cleaner was plugged into the mains,** l'aspirateur était branché sur le secteur. **II.** *a.* **1. by m. force,** de vive force. **2.** principal; premier, essentiel; (*a*) **the m. body,** le gros; *Agr:* **m. crop,** culture principale; (*b*) **the m. point, the m. thing,** l'essentiel *m,* le principal; (*c*) **m. road,** grande route; *Rail:* **m. line,** voie principale, grande ligne; **-ly,** *adv.* **1.** principalement, surtout. **2.** en grande partie; **'mainland,** *s.* continent *m;* terre *f* ferme; **'mainspring,** *s.* **1.** grand ressort, ressort moteur. **2.** mobile essentiel, cheville ouvrière; **'mainstay,** *s.* point *m* d'appui; soutien principal.

maintain [mein'tein], *v.tr.* **1.** maintenir (l'ordre); conserver (la santé); **the improvement is maintained,** l'amélioration se maintient. **2.** entretenir, soutenir (une famille). **3.** entretenir (une armée). **4.** soutenir, défendre (une cause). **5.** garder (un avantage). **6. I m. that it's not true,** je maintiens que c'est faux; **'maintenance,** *s.* **1.** maintien *m* (de l'ordre). **2.** entretien *m* (d'une famille, des routes).

maison(n)ette [meizə'net], *s.* appartement *m* à un ou deux étages.

maize [meiz], *s.* maïs *m.*

majesty ['mædʒisti], *s.* majesté *f;* **His M., Her M.,** Sa Majesté le Roi, Sa Majesté la Reine; **ma'jestic,** *a.* majestueux; **-ally,** *adv.* majestueusement.

major[1] ['meidʒər], *s. Mil:* commandant *m;* **'major-'general,** *s.* général *m* de division.

major[2]. **1.** *a.* **the m. part,** la majeure partie, la plus grande partie; *Mus:* **m. key,** ton majeur;

Adm: **m. road,** route *f* à priorité. **2.** *s. Jur:* (*pers.*) majeur, -eure; **majority** [mə'dʒɔriti], *s.* **1.** (*a*) majorité *f;* **to be in a m.,** être en majorité; (*b*) la plus grande partie, le plus grand nombre, la plupart (des hommes, etc.). **2.** *Jur:* **to attain one's m.,** atteindre sa majorité, devenir majeur.

Majorca [mə'dʒɔːkə]. *Pr.n. Geog:* la Majorque.

make [meik]. **I.** *s.* **1.** (*a*) façon *f,* fabrication *f* (d'un objet); (*b*) *Com: Ind:* marque *f* (d'un produit). **2.** *F:* **to be on the m.,** chercher à faire fortune à tout prix. **II.** *v.* (**made** [meid]) **1.** *v.tr.* (*a*) faire; construire (une machine); fabriquer (du papier); confectionner (des vêtements); **you're made for this work,** vous êtes fait pour ce travail; **he's as sharp as they m. 'em,** c'est un malin s'il en est; **what's it made of?** c'est en quoi? **I don't know what to m. of it,** je n'y comprends rien; **what do you m. of it?** qu'en pensez-vous? **to show what one is made of,** donner sa mesure; **to m. a friend of s.o.,** faire de qn son ami; **to m. a bed, the tea,** faire un lit, le thé; **to m. trouble,** causer des désagréments; **to m. a noise,** faire du bruit; **to m. peace,** faire, conclure, la paix; **to m. a mistake,** faire une erreur, se tromper; **to m. one's escape,** s'échapper, se sauver; **we just made it,** nous sommes arrivés juste à temps; (*b*) établir, assurer (un raccordement); **two and two m. four,** deux et deux font quatre; **he made an excellent captain,** il s'est montré excellent chef d'équipe; (*c*) **to m. fifty pounds a week,** gagner, se faire, cinquante livres par semaine; **what will you m. out of it?** qu'est-ce que vous en tirerez? **to m. a bit on the side,** se faire de la gratte; **to m. a name,** se faire un nom; (*d*) **the book that made his name,** le livre qui lui a assuré la célébrité; (*e*) **to m. s.o. happy,** rendre qn heureux; **to m. s.o. hungry,** donner faim à qn; **to m. s.o. a judge,** nommer qn juge; **to m. sth. known,** faire connaître qch.; **to m. oneself comfortable,** se mettre à l'aise; **to m. oneself ill,** se rendre malade; (*f*) **what time do you m. it?** quelle heure avez-vous? (*g*) **you should m. him do it,** vous devriez le forcer à le faire; **what made you say that?** pourquoi avez-vous dit cela? **2.** *v.i.* (*a*) **to m. for,** se diriger vers (un endroit), *Nau:* mettre le cap sur . . .; **to m. for the open sea,** prendre le large; (*b*) **design which makes for easier maintenance,** construction qui facilite le maintien; (*c*) **to m. as if to do sth.,** faire semblant de faire qch.; **'make a'way,** *v.i.* **to m. away with sth.,** faire disparaître, enlever, qch.; **to m. away with oneself,** se suicider; **'make 'do,** *v.i.* **to m. do with sth.,** se contenter de qch.; **'make 'off,** *v.i.* se sauver; décamper, filer; **to m. off with the cash,** filer avec l'argent; **'make 'out. 1.** *v.tr.* (*a*) faire, dresser (une liste);

établir, relever (un compte); faire, tirer (un chèque); (*b*) **how do you m. that out?** comment arrivez-vous à ce résultat, à cette conclusion? **the climate's not so bad as you m.** out, le climat n'est pas si mauvais que vous le dites; **he's made out to be richer than he is,** on le fait plus riche qu'il ne l'est; (*c*) (i) comprendre (une énigme); déchiffrer (une écriture); **I can't m. it out,** je n'y comprends rien; (ii) **I can't m. out his features,** je ne peux pas distinguer se traits. 2. *v.i.* he's making out very well, il réussit dans son travail; il fait de bonnes affaires; **'make 'over,** *v.tr.* céder, transférer (sth. **to s.o.,** qch. à qn); **'maker,** *s.* 1. faiseur, -euse; *Com: Ind:* fabricant *m*; constructeur *m* (de machines). 2. **Our M.,** le Créateur; **'makeshift,** *s.* pis-aller *m inv*, expédient *m*, bouche-trou *m*; **a m. shelter,** un abri de fortune; **'make 'up,** *v.* I. *v.tr.* 1. compléter (une somme); combler (un déficit). 2. **to m. up lost ground,** regagner le terrain perdu; **to m. it up to s.o. for sth.,** dédommager qn de qch. 3. faire (un paquet); *Pharm:* exécuter (une ordonnance). 4. (*a*) faire, confectionner (des vêtements); (*b*) inventer, forger (une histoire, des excuses). 5. **to m. up the fire,** ajouter du combustible au feu. 6. former, composer (un ensemble). 7. **to m. (oneself) up,** se farder, se maquiller. 8. **to m. up one's mind,** se décider; prendre son parti. 9. arranger, accommoder (un différend); **to m. it up,** se réconcilier. II. *v.i.* 1. (*a*) **to m. up for lost time,** rattraper le temps perdu; **that makes up for it,** c'est une compensation; (*b*) **to m. up for the lack of sth.,** suppléer au manque de qch. 2. **to m. up to s.o.,** faire des avances à qn; **'make-up,** *s.* 1. composition *f* (de qch.). 2. maquillage *m*, fard *m*; **'makeweight,** *s.* complément *m* de poids; **'making,** *s.* (*a*) fabrication *f*; confection *f* (de vêtements); construction *f* (d'un pont); **this incident was the m. of him,** c'est à cet incident qu'il dut sa fortune; **history in the m.,** l'histoire en train de se faire; (*b*) **I haven't the makings of a hero,** je n'ai rien du héros.

maladjusted [mælə'dʒʌstid], *a.* inadapté.

maladroit [mælə'drɔit], *a.* maladroit.

Malagasy [mælə'gæsi], *a. Geog:* **the M. Republic,** la République malgache.

malaria [mə'lɛəriə], *s. Med:* malaria *f*.

Malawi [mə'lɑːwi]. *Pr.n. Geog:* le Malawi.

Malaya [mə'leiə]. *Pr.n. Geog:* la Malaisie; **Ma'lay,** *a. & s.* malais, -aise; **Ma'layan,** *a.* malais.

Malaysia [mə'leiʒə]. *Pr.n. Geog:* la Malaysia, la Malaisie.

male [meil]. 1. *a.* mâle; **m. sex,** sexe masculin; **m. child,** enfant mâle. 2. *s.* mâle *m*.

malevolence [mə'levələns], *s.* malveillance *f* (**towards,** envers); **ma'levolent,** *a.* malveillant; **-ly,** *adv.* avec malveillance.

Mali ['mɑːli]. *Pr.n. Geog:* (la République du) Mali.

malice ['mælis], *s.* 1. malice *f*, malveillance *f*; **out of m.,** par malice; **to bear s.o. m.,** en vouloir à qn. 2. *Jur:* intention criminelle; **ma'licious,** *a.* (*a*) méchant, malveillant; (*b*) rancunier; **-ly,** *adv.* (*a*) avec méchanceté, avec malveillance; (*b*) par rancune.

malign [mə'lain]. I. *a.* pernicieux, nuisible. II. *v.tr.* calomnier, diffamer; **malignancy** [mə'lignənsi], *s.,* **malignity** [mə'ligniti], *s.* malignité *f*; **ma'lignant,** *a.* (*a*) malin, *f.* maligne; méchant; (*b*) *Med:* **m. tumour,** tumeur maligne; **-ly,** *adv.* avec malignité, méchamment.

malinger [mə'lingər], *v.i.* faire le malade.

mallard ['mælɑːd], *s. Orn:* malard *m*, col-vert *m*.

malleable ['mæliəbl], *a.* malléable.

mallet ['mælit], *s.* maillet *m*, mailloche *f*.

mallow ['mælou], *s. Bot:* mauve *f*.

malnutrition [mælnju'triʃ(ə)n], *s.* malnutrition *f*.

malt [mɔːlt], *s.* malt *m*; **'malted,** *a. Com:* **m. milk,** lait malté.

Malta ['mɔːltə]. *Pr.n. Geog:* (l'île de) Malte *f* **'Maltese.** 1. *a.* maltais; **M. cross,** croix *f* de Malte. 2. *s.* Maltais, -aise; (*dog*) chien maltais.

maltreat [mæl'triːt], *v.tr.* maltraiter, malmener **mal'treatment,** *s.* mauvais traitement.

mammal ['mæm(ə)l], *s. Z:* mammifère *m*.

mammoth ['mæməθ]. 1. *s.* mammouth *m*. 2. *a* monstre; *Com:* **m. reduction,** rabais géant.

man, *pl.* **men** [mæn, men]. I. *s.* 1. (*a*) homme *m* **every m.,** tout le monde; chacun; **any m.,** n'im porte qui; **no m.,** personne; *Mil:* **no m.'s land** no man's land *m*, zone *f* neutre; **some mer** quelques personnes, quelques-uns, certains **few men,** peu de gens; **men say that . . .,** on d que . . .; (*b*) l'homme; **m. proposes, God di: poses,** l'homme propose et Dieu dispose; **th m. in the street,** l'homme de la rue. 2. (*a*) **t** speak to s.o. as m. to m.,** parler à qn d'homn à homme; **they were killed to a m.,** ils fure tués jusqu'au dernier; **to show oneself a m** montrer qu'on est un homme; **be a m.!** sois u homme! **to bear sth. like a m.,** supporter qc comme un homme; **he's not the m. to refuse,** n'est pas homme à refuser; **I'm your m.!** je su votre homme! cela me va! **a m.'s m.,** un vr homme; *F:* **come here, young m.!** venez i jeune homme! **good m.!** bravo! **goodbye, o m.!** adieu, mon vieux! (*b*) **an old m.,** vieillard; **the dead m.,** le mort; (*c*) **ice-crea m.,** marchand de glaces. 3. **m. and wife,** m et femme *f*; *F:* **her young m.,** son fiancé. (*a*) domestique *m*; (*b*) employé *m*; (**deliver m.,** livreur *m*; *Ind:* **the employers and the m** les patrons et les ouvriers; (*c*) *Mil:* office N.C.O.s **and men,** officiers, sous-officiers hommes de troupe; (*d*) *Sp:* joueur *m*. 5.

chess) pièce *f*; (*at draughts*) pion *m*. **II.** *v.tr.* (manned) garnir d'hommes; **we need s.o. to m. this stall,** nous avons besoin de qn pour garder, s'occuper de, ce comptoir; **fully manned boat,** canot *m* à armement complet; **'maneater,** *s*. (*of lion, etc*.) mangeur *m* d'hommes; **'manhandle,** *v.tr.* maltraiter, malmener (qn); **'manhole,** *s*. trou *m* de visite (d'égout, etc.), regard *m*; **'manhood,** *s*. âge *m* d'homme; âge viril; virilité *f*; **man'kind,** *s*. le genre humain; l'homme, les hommes; **'manliness,** *s*. caractère mâle, viril; virilité *f*; **'manly,** *a*. d'homme; mâle, viril; **'manpower,** *s. coll.* (*a*) *Ind:* main-d'œuvre *f*; (*b*) effectifs *mpl*; **'manservant,** *pl.* **menservants,** *s*. domestique *m*; **'manslaughter,** *s. Jur:* (*a*) homicide *m* involontaire, par imprudence; (*b*) homicide sans préméditation.

manacle ['mænəkl]. **I.** *s*. menotte *f*. **II.** *v.tr.* mettre les menottes à (qn).

manage ['mænidʒ], *v.tr.* **1.** diriger, gérer (une entreprise); mener (une affaire). **2.** gouverner; tenir (des enfants); maîtriser (un animal); **to know how to m. s.o.,** savoir prendre qn. **3.** arranger, conduire (une affaire); **to m. to do sth.,** trouver moyen de faire qch.; **I'll m. it,** j'en viendrai à bout; **if you can m. to see him,** si vous pouvez vous arranger pour le voir; **m. as best you can,** arrangez-vous comme vous pourrez; **he'll m. all right,** il se débrouillera; **'manageable,** *a*. **1.** (outil) maniable; (canot) manœuvrable. **2.** (*of pers*.) traitable. **3.** praticable, faisable; **'management,** *s*. **1.** (*a*) maniement *m* (d'un outil, des hommes); (*b*) direction *f*, conduite *f* (d'une affaire); gérance *f*, gestion *f* (d'une propriété); **under new m.,** changement de propriétaire. **2. by good m.,** par adresse *f*. **3. the m.,** l'administration *f*, la direction; **'manager,** *s*. **1.** directeur *m*, administrateur *m*, gérant *m*; *Th:* impresario *m*; *Cin: Sp:* manager *m*; **joint m.,** cogérant *m*; **sales m.,** directeur commercial; **department(al) m.,** chef *m* de service. **2. she's a good m.,** elle est bonne ménagère; **'manageress,** *s.f.* directrice, gérante; **'managing,** *a*. **1.** directeur; **m. director,** président directeur général *m*. **2. one of those m. women,** une maîtresse femme.

mandarin(e) ['mændərin], *s. Bot:* mandarine *f*.

mandate ['mændeit], *s.* mandat *m*.

mandatory ['mændətri], *a*. obligatoire.

mane [mein], *s.* crinière *f*.

manganese [mæŋgə'ni:z], *s. Ch:* manganèse *m*; **m. steel,** acier *m* au manganèse.

mange [mein(d)ʒ], *s.* gale *f*; **'mangy,** *a*. (*a*) galeux; (*b*) *F:* minable, miteux, moche.

manger ['mein(d)ʒər], *s.* mangeoire *f*, crèche *f*.

mangle ['mæŋgl]. **I.** *s.* essoreuse *f* (à rouleaux). **II.** *v.tr.* **1.** essorer (le linge). **2.** déchirer, lacérer,

mutiler (qn); charcuter (une volaille); déformer, estropier (une citation); **'mangling,** *s.* lacération *f*, mutilation *f*.

mango, *pl.* **-oes** ['mæŋgou, -ouz], *s. Bot:* mangue *f*; (*tree*) manguier *m*.

mangrove ['mæŋgrouv], *s.* palétuvier *m*; **m. swamp,** mangrove *f*.

mania ['meiniə], *s.* **1.** *Med:* manie *f*; folie *f*. **2. to have a m. for (doing) sth.,** avoir la passion de (faire) qch.; **'maniac,** *a. & s.* fou, folle; maniaque (*mf*).

manicure ['mænikjuər]. **I.** *s.* soin *m* des mains; **to give oneself a m.,** se faire les ongles; **m. set,** trousse *f* de manucure. **II.** *v.tr.* soigner les mains de (qn); **to m. one's nails,** se faire les ongles; **'manicurist,** *s.* manucure *mf*.

manifest ['mænifest]. **I.** *a.* manifeste, évident, clair. **II.** *v.tr.* manifester, témoigner (qch.); **to m. itself,** se manifester; **-ly,** *adv.* manifestement; **manifes'tation,** *s.* manifestation *f*; **mani'festo,** *pl.* **-os,** *s. Pol:* manifeste *m*.

manifold ['mænifould]. **1.** *a.* (*a*) divers, varié; de diverses sortes; (*b*) multiple, nombreux. **2.** *s. Aut: etc:* **exhaust m.,** tubulure *f* d'échappement.

manipulate [mə'nipjuleit], *v.tr.* **1.** manipuler (un objet). **2.** *F:* **to m. accounts,** cuisiner les comptes; **manipu'lation,** *s.* **1.** manipulation *f*. **2.** *F:* tripotage *m*.

mannequin ['mænikin], *s.* mannequin *m*.

manner ['mænər], *s.* **1.** manière *f*, façon *f* (de faire qch.); (*of doctor*) **a good bedside m.,** une bonne manière professionnelle; **in some m. or other,** de manière ou d'autre; **in a m. of speaking,** en quelque sorte; pour ainsi dire; **it's a m. of speaking,** c'est une façon de parler. **2.** maintien *m*, tenue *f*, air *m*; **in a solemn m.,** d'un air solennel. **3.** *pl.* (*a*) manières; **bad manners,** mauvaises manières; **it's very bad manners to do that,** c'est très mal élevé de faire ça; (*b*) (**good) manners,** bonnes manières, politesse *f*; **to teach s.o. manners,** donner à qn une leçon de politesse; **to forget one's manners,** oublier les convenances; s'oublier; *Aut:* **road manners,** politesse de la route. **4.** espèce *f*, sorte *f*; **all m. of things,** toutes sortes de choses; **no m. of doubt,** aucun doute.

manœuvre [mə'nu:vər]. **I.** *s.* manœuvre *f*. **II.** *v.tr. & i.* manœuvrer; **ma'nœuvrable,** *a.* maniable, manœuvrable.

manor ['mænər], *s.* **m. (house),** manoir *m*, gentilhommière *f*.

mansion ['mænʃən], *s.* (*in country*) château *m*; (*in town*) hôtel (particulier).

mantelpiece ['mæntlpi:s], *s.* (*a*) (manteau *m* de) cheminée *f*; (*b*) dessus *m* de cheminée.

manual ['mænjuəl]. **1.** *a.* manuel; **m. labour,** travail manuel, de manœuvre. **2.** *s.* (*a*) manuel *m*, aide-mémoire *m inv*; **teacher's m.**, livre *m* du maître; (*b*) *Mus:* clavier *m* (d'un orgue).

manufacture [mænju'fæktʃər]. **I.** *s.* **1.** fabrication *f*, élaboration *f* (d'un produit industriel); confection *f* (de vêtements). **2.** produit manufacturé. **II.** *v.tr.* (*a*) fabriquer, manufacturer; confectionner (des vêtements); **manufacturing town**, ville industrielle; (*b*) forger, fabriquer (des nouvelles); **manu'facturer**, *s.* fabricant *m*, industriel *m*.

manure [mə'njuər]. **I.** *s.* engrais *m*; **farmyard m.**, fumier *m* (d'étable); **m. heap**, (tas *m* de) fumier. **II.** *v.tr.* fumer, engraisser (la terre).

manuscript ['mænjuskript], *a. & s.* manuscrit (*m*).

Manx [mæŋks], *a. Geog:* mannois, manx(ois); **M. cat**, chat sans queue de l'île de Man.

many ['meni], *a. & s.* un grand nombre (de); beaucoup (de); bien des; plusieurs; **m. a time**, maintes fois; **a good m. times**, bien des fois; **ever so m. times**, je ne sais combien de fois; **before m. days have passed**, avant longtemps; **for m. years**, pendant longtemps, pendant plusieurs années; **m. of us**, beaucoup d'entre nous; **m. a man**, bien des gens; **there were so m. of them**, ils étaient si nombreux; **in so m. words**, en propres termes; **too m. people**, trop de monde; **a card too m.**, une carte de trop; **how m. horses?** combien de chevaux? **I've as m. books as you**, j'ai autant de livres que vous; **as m. again, twice as m.**, deux fois autant; **as m. as ten people saw it**, il y a bien dix personnes qui l'ont vu; **a good m. . . .**, bon nombre de . . ., un assez grand nombre de . . .; **a great m. tourists**, des quantités de touristes.

map [mæp]. **I.** *s.* carte *f*; **ordnance survey m.** = carte d'état-major; **town m.**, plan *m* d'une ville; **m. of the world**, mappemonde *f*; **our village is right off the m.**, notre village est vraiment au bout du monde. **II.** *v.tr.* (**mapped**) **1.** dresser une carte de (la région, etc.). **2. to m. out a route**, tracer un itinéraire; **'mapmaking**, *s.*, **mapping**, *s.* cartographie *f*.

maple ['meipl], *s.* érable *m*; **m. sugar, syrup**, sucre *m*, sirop *m*, d'érable.

maquis ['mæki:], *s. Geog: Pol:* maquis *m*; *Pol:* **to take to the m.**, prendre le maquis; **member of the m.**, maquisard *m*.

mar [mɑ:r], *v.tr.* (**marred**) gâter, gâcher (le plaisir de qn); **to make or m. s.o.**, faire la fortune ou la ruine de qn.

marathon ['mærəθən], *s. Sp:* marathon *m*.

maraud [mə'rɔ:d], *v.i.* marauder; **ma'rauding**, *s.* maraude *f*; **ma'rauder**, *s.* maraudeur, -euse.

marble ['mɑ:bl], *s.* **1.** marbre *m*; **m. pavement**, dallage *m* en marbre; **m. quarry**, marbrière *f*, carrière *f* de marbre. **2.** *Games:* bille *f*; **to play marbles**, jouer aux billes.

March¹ [mɑ:tʃ], *s.* mars *m*; **in M.**, au mois de mars; (**on**) **the fifth of M.**, le cinq mars.

march². **I.** *s.* **1.** *Mil:* (*a*) marche *f*; **on the m.**, en marche; **to do a day's m.**, faire une étape; **route m.**, marche d'entraînement; **m. past**, défilé *m* (de revue); (*b*) pas *m*, allure *f*; **slow m.**, pas de parade; **quick m.**, pas cadencé, accéléré. **2.** marche, progrès *m* (des événements). **3.** *Mus:* marche. **II.** *v.* **1.** *v.i. Mil: etc:* marcher; **quick m.!** en avant, marche! **m. at ease!** sans cadence, marche! **to m. past** (s.o.), défiler (devant qn). **2.** *v.tr.* **to m. s.o. off to gaol**, emmener qn en prison; **'marching**, *s. Mil:* marche *f*; **m. orders**, feuille *f* de route; *F:* **to give s.o. his m. orders**, signifier son congé à qn.

marchioness ['mɑ:ʃənes], *s.f.* marquise.

mare ['mɛər], *s.* jument *f*; *Meteor:* **m.'s tails**, (nuages *m* en) queue-de-chat *f*.

margarine [mɑ:dʒə'ri:n], *s. Com:* margarine *f*.

margin ['mɑ:dʒin], *s.* **1.** (*a*) marge *f*; lisière *f*; (*b*) marge, écart *m*; **to allow s.o. some m.**, accorder quelque marge à qn; **to allow a m. for error**, calculer large; (*c*) **safety m.**, marge de sécurité. **2.** marge, blanc *m* (d'une page) **'marginal**, *a.* marginal, en marge; *Pol:* **m. seat**, siège chaudement disputé.

marguerite [mɑ:gə'ri:t], *s. Bot:* (*a*) leucanthème *m*, (grande) marguerite; (*b*) anthémis *f*.

marigold ['mærigould], *s. Bot:* (*a*) souci *m*; (*b*) **French m.**, œillet *m* d'Inde; **African m.**, rose d'Inde; (*c*) **corn m.**, marguerite dorée.

marijuana [mæri'(h)wɑ:nə], *s.* marihuana, marijuana *f*.

marine [mə'ri:n]. **1.** *a.* marin; **m. engine**, moteur marin; **m. insurance**, assurance *f* maritime. **2.** *s.* (*a*) marine *f*; **merchant, mercantile, m.**, marine marchande; (*b*) *Mil:* = fusilier marin *F:* **tell that to the marines!** à d'autres!

marionette [mæriə'net], *s.* marionnette *f*.

maritime ['mæritaim], *a.* maritime; *Geog:* **the M. Provinces**, les (Provinces) Maritimes *fpl.*

marjoram ['mɑ:dʒ(ə)rəm], *s. Bot:* (**sweet**) **m.** marjolaine *f*.

mark [mɑ:k]. **I.** *s.* **1.** but *m*, cible *f*; **to hit the m** atteindre le but; frapper juste; **wide of the m** loin de la réalité. **2.** marque *f*, preuve *f*, signe *m* témoignage *m*; **as a m. of respect**, en signe c respect. **3.** (*a*) marque, tache *f*, signe *m*, empreinte *f*; **to make one's m.**, se faire u réputation; arriver; (*b*) **the m. of a foot**, marque, l'empreinte, d'un pied. **4.** (*a*) marqu signe; **punctuation m.**, signe de ponctuatio **exclamation m.**, point *m* d'exclamation; (*Sch:* point; note *f*. **5.** **guide-m., reference m** repère *m*; *F:* **to be up to the m.**, (i) (*in abilit* être à la hauteur; (ii) (*in health*) être dans s assiette. **II.** *v.tr.* marquer; *Sch:* corriger (devoir); **to m. time**, (i) *Mil:* marquer le pas; *F:* piétiner sur place; **m. my words!** croye

moi! écoutez-moi bien! **'mark 'down,** *v.tr.*
baisser le prix de (qch.); **marked,** *a.* marqué;
m. improvement, amélioration *f* sensible;
strongly m. features, traits fortement accusés; **markedly** [mɑ:kidli], *adv.* d'une façon
marquée;'**marking,** *s.* 1. marquage *m*; **m. ink,**
encre *f* à marquer. 2. *pl.* **markings,** marques *f*;
(*on animal*) taches *f*, rayures *f*; '**mark 'out,**
v.tr. 1. délimiter, tracer (une frontière). 2. **she
was marked out for promotion,** elle a été sélec-
tionnée pour un avancement; '**mark 'up,** *v.tr.*
augmenter, élever, le prix de (qch.).

market ['mɑ:kit]. I. *s.* (*a*) marché *m*; **covered m.,**
marché couvert, halle(s) *f(pl)*; **in the m.,** au
marché, à la halle; **m. day,** jour *m* de marché;
(*b*) **to be on the m., to come onto the m.,** être
mis en vente, être mis sur le marché; **to find a
m. for sth.,** trouver un débouché pour qch.; (*of
thg*) **to find a ready m.,** être d'un débit facile;
m. price, prix courant; (*c*) **black m.,** marché
noir; *Pol:* **the Common M.,** le Marché commun. II. *v.tr.* trouver des débouchés pour (ses
marchandises); lancer (un article) sur le
marché;'**marketable,** *a.* vendable; d'un débit
facile; '**market 'garden,** *s.* jardin *m*
maraîcher;'**market 'gardener,** *s.* maraîcher,
-ère; '**marketing,** *s.* *Com:* le marketing.

marksman, *pl.* -men ['mɑ:ksmən], *s.* bon tireur;
tireur *m* d'élite; '**marksmanship,** *s.* adresse *f*,
habileté *f*, au tir.

marmalade ['mɑ:məleid], *s.* *Cu:* confiture *f*
d'oranges.

marmoset [mɑ:mə'zet], *s.* *Z:* ouistiti *m*.

marmot ['mɑ:mət], *s.* *Z:* marmotte *f*.

maroon[1] [mə'ru:n]. 1. *a.* & *s.* (*colour*) marron
pourpré *inv.* 2. *s.* (*firework*) marron *m*, fusée *f*
à pétard.

maroon[2], *v.tr.* (*a*) abandonner (qn) dans une île
déserte; (*b*) **people marooned by the floods,**
gens isolés par les inondations.

marquee [mɑ:'ki:], *s.* grande tente.

marquess, marquis ['mɑ:kwis], *s.* marquis *m*.

marriage ['mærid3], *s.* mariage *m*; **relation by
m.,** parent *m* par alliance; **m. certificate,** acte *m*
de mariage; **the m. service,** la bénédiction nuptiale; '**married,** *a.* (*a*) **m. man,** homme marié;
m. couple, un ménage; (*b*) **m. name,** nom *m* de
mariage; '**marry,** *v.tr.* 1. (*of priest, parent*)
marier; **to m. (off) a daughter,** marier sa fille. 2.
(*a*) se marier avec, à (qn); épouser (qn); **to m.
money,** faire un mariage d'argent; (*b*) *abs.* **to m.,
to get married,** se marier; **to m. again,** se remarier; **to m. into a family,** s'allier à une famille.

marrow ['mærou], *s.* 1. moelle *f*. 2. (**vegetable)
m.,** courge *f*; courgette *f*.

marsh [mɑ:ʃ], *s.* marais *m*, marécage *m*; **m.
mallow,** (i) *Bot:* guimauve *f*; (ii) (pâte de)
guimauve; **m. marigold,** souci *m* d'eau;
'**marshy,** *a.* marécageux.

marshal ['mɑ:ʃəl]. I. *s.* 1. *Mil:* **field-m.,** maréchal
m; *Av:* **M. of the R.A.F.** = Commandant *m* en
Chef des Forces aériennes; **Air Chief M.,**
général *m* d'armée aérienne; **Air M.,** général
(de corps aérien). 2. maître *m* des cérémonies.
II. *v.tr.* (**marshalled**) placer (des personnes) en
ordre, en rang; *Rail:* classer, trier (des wagons);
'**marshalling,** *s.* 1. disposition *f* en ordre (de
personnes, de choses). 2. *Rail:* classement *m*,
triage *m*, manœuvre *f* (des wagons); **m.-yard,**
gare *f* de triage.

marsupial [mɑ:'su:piəl], *a.* & *s.* *Z:* marsupial
(*m*).

marten ['mɑ:tin], *s.* *Z:* mart(r)e *f*.

martial ['mɑ:ʃ(ə)l], *a.* martial; **m. law,** loi
martiale.

Martian ['mɑ:ʃən], *a.* & *s.* martien, -ienne.

martin ['mɑ:tin], *s.* *Orn:* (**house) m.,** martinet *m*;
hirondelle *f* de fenêtre; **sand m.,** hirondelle de
rivage.

martinet [mɑ:ti'net], *s.* (personne) à cheval sur la
discipline.

martyr ['mɑ:tər]. I. *s.* martyr, *f.* martyre; **to be a
m. to migraine,** être torturé par la migraine. II.
v.tr. martyriser; '**martyrdom,** *s.* martyre *m*.

marvel ['mɑ:v(ə)l]. I. *s.* merveille *f.* II. *v.i.*
(**marvelled**) s'émerveiller, s'étonner (**at, de**);
'**marvellous,** *a.* merveilleux, étonnant; **-ly,**
adv. à merveille; merveilleusement.

marzipan ['mɑ:zipæn], *s.* pâte *f* d'amandes,
massepain *m*.

mascot ['mæskət], *s.* mascotte *f*; porte-bonheur
m inv.

masculine ['mæskjulin]. 1. *a.* masculin, mâle. 2.
a. & *s.* (nom) masculin; **in the m.,** au masculin.

mash [mæʃ]. I. *v.tr.* broyer, écraser (qch.);
réduire (qch.) en purée; *Cu:* **mashed potatoes,**
purée *f* de pommes de terre; pommes *f*
mousseline. II. *s.* purée *f*; *F:* purée de pommes
de terre; '**masher,** *s.* broyeur *m*; **potato m.,**
presse-purée *m inv*.

mask [mɑ:sk]. I. *s.* masque *m*; (*silk or velvet*)
loup *m*; **to throw off the m.,** lever le masque; se
démasquer. II. *v.tr.* masquer; **to m. one's face,
oneself,** se masquer; **masked,** *a.* masqué; **m.
ball,** bal masqué.

masochist ['mæsəkist], *s.* masochiste *mf.*

mason ['meis(ə)n], *s.* 1. (*worker*) maçon *m*. 2.
(= *freemason*) franc-maçon *m*; **ma'sonic,**
a. maçonnique; de la franc-maçonnerie;
'**masonry,** *s.* 1. *Const:* maçonnerie *f.* 2. franc-
maçonnerie *f*.

masquerade [mæskə'reid]. I. *s.* mascarade *f.* II.
v.i. **to m. as . . .,** se déguiser en . . .; se faire
passer pour . . .; **masque'rader,** *s.* (*a*) personne déguisée, masquée; (*b*) imposteur *m*.

mass[1] [mæs, mɑ:s], *s.* *Ecc:* messe *f*; **high m.,**
grand-messe *f*; **low m.,** messe basse; **requiem
m.,** messe de requiem.

mass² [mæs]. **I.** *s.* **1.** masse *f,* amas *m*; *Atom. Ph:* **critical m.**, masse critique. **2.** (*a*) **a m. of people**, une foule, une multitude, de gens; **to gather in masses**, se masser; **he was a m. of bruises**, il était tout couvert de meurtrissures; **m. executions**, exécutions *f* en masse; (*b*) **the great m. of the people**, la plus grande partie de la population; **the masses**, les masses; la foule; **m. protest**, protestation *f* en masse; **m. meeting**, réunion *f* en masse; **m. production**, fabrication *f* en (grande) série. **II.** *v.tr.* & *i.* (se) masser; (*of clouds*) s'amonceler; **'massive**, *a.* massif.
massacre ['mæsəkər]. **I.** *s.* massacre *m*, tuerie *f.* **II.** *v.tr.* massacrer.
massage. **I.** *s.* ['mæsɑːʒ], massage *m.* **II.** *v.tr.* [mæ'sɑːʒ], masser (un muscle, etc.); **ma'sseur** *m*, **ma'sseuse**, *s.* masseur, -euse.
mast [mɑːst], *s.* **1.** *Nau:* mât *m*; **to sail before the m.**, servir comme simple matelot. **2.** pylône *m* (de radio, etc.); **'masthead**, *s.* tête *f* de mât.
master ['mɑːstər]. **I.** *s.* **1.** (*a*) maître *m*; **to be m. in one's own house**, être maître chez soi; **to be one's own m.**, s'appartenir; ne dépendre que de soi(-même); **to meet one's m.**, trouver son maître; (*b*) (*employer*) maître, patron *m*, chef *m*; (*c*) *Nau:* capitaine marchand, au long cours; patron (d'un bateau de pêche); (*d*) **m. of ceremonies**, maître des cérémonies. **2.** *Sch:* (*a*) professeur *m*, instituteur *m*; (*b*) **fencing m.**, maître d'armes; (*c*) **M. of Arts** = licencié ès lettres. **3. to be m. of a subject**, posséder un sujet à fond; *Art:* **an old m.**, (i) un maître; (ii) un tableau de maître. **4.** (*a*) **m. mariner**, capitaine au long cours; capitaine marchand; **m.'s certificate**, brevet *m* de capitaine; (*b*) **m. key**, passe-partout *m inv*; **m. mind**, esprit supérieur; esprit dirigeant; (*c*) **he's a m. hand at (doing sth.)**, il est passé maître dans l'art de (faire qch.). **II.** *v.tr.* maîtriser (un cheval, etc.); surmonter (une difficulté); apprendre (un sujet) à fond; **to have mastered a subject**, posséder un sujet à fond; **'master-at-'arms**, *s. Navy:* capitaine *m* d'armes; **'masterful**, *a.* impérieux, autoritaire; **-fully**, *adv.* impérieusement; **masterly**, *a.* de maître; magistral; **in a m. fashion**, magistralement; **'masterpiece**, *s.* chef-d'œuvre *m*, *pl.* chefs-d'œuvre; **'masterstroke**, *s.* coup *m* de maître; **'mastery**, *s.* (*a*) maîtrise *f* (of, de); domination *f* (over, sur); (*b*) connaissance approfondie (d'un sujet).
masticate ['mæstikeit], *v.tr.* mâcher, mastiquer; **masti'cation**, *s.* mastication *f.*
mastiff ['mæstif], *s.* mâtin *m*; dogue anglais.
mat [mæt]. **I.** *s.* (*a*) natte *f* (de paille); (*b*) paillasson *m*, essuie-pieds *m inv*; **wire m.**, essuie-pieds métallique; (*c*) carpette *f*; *F:* **he's been on the m.**, on lui a passé un savon. **II.** *v.tr.*

(*a*) natter, tresser (le jonc); (*b*) (*of hair*) **to be matted**, *v.i.* **to m.**, s'emmêler, se coller ensemble; **'matting**, *s.* natte(s) *f*(*pl*); **coconut m.**, tapis *m* de coco.
match¹ [mætʃ]. **I.** *s.* **1.** (*a*) égal, -ale; pareil, -eille; **to meet one's m.**, trouver à qui parler; **to be a m. for s.o.**, être de force à lutter avec qn; **he's more than a m. for me**, il est plus fort que moi; (*b*) (*of thgs*) **to be a good m.**, aller bien ensemble. **2.** *Sp:* **football m.**, match *m* de football; **tennis m.**, match, partie *f,* de tennis; **(ice) hockey m.**, *Fr. C:* joute *f* de hockey. **3.** mariage *m*, alliance *f*; **a good m.**, un beau mariage. **II.** *v.* **1.** *v.tr.* (*a*) égaler (qn); être l'égal de (qn); rivaliser avec (qn); **evenly matched**, de force égale; (*b*) apparier (des gants); appareiller; assortir (des couleurs). **2.** *v.i.* s'assortir, s'harmoniser; **dress with hat to m.**, robe avec chapeau assorti; **'matching**, *s.* assortiment *m* appariement *m*; **'matchless**, *a.* incomparable inimitable; sans égal; **'matchmaker**, *s* marieur, -euse; **'matchmaking**, *s.* arrangement *m* des mariages.
match², *s.* allumette *f*; **safety m.**, allumette de sûreté; **to strike a m.**, frotter, craquer, une allumette; **'matchbox**, *s.* boîte *f* à allumettes **'matchwood**, *s.* bois d'allumettes; **smashed to m.**, mis en miettes.
mate¹ [meit]. *Chess:* **I.** *s.* échec *m* et mat *m.* **II.** *v.tr.* **to m. s.o.**, donner le mat à qn; **to m. in three**, faire échec et mat en trois coups.
mate². **I.** *s.* **1.** (*of animals, birds*) mâle *m*, femelle *f.* **2.** *F:* compagnon *m*; camarade *m*. *Nau:* (*a*) (*merchant navy*) officier *m*; **first m** second *m*; **second m.**, lieutenant *m*; (*b*) *Navy* second *m*. **II.** *v.tr.* & *i.* (*of birds, animals*) (s')accoupler; (s')apparier.
material [mə'tiəriəl]. **I.** *a.* **1.** (*a*) matériel grossier; **to be too interested in m. things**, êt trop attaché à la matière; (*b*) **to have enou for one's m. needs**, avoir de quoi viv matériellement. **2.** (*a*) important, essentiel (t pour); **it was of m. service to me**, cela me re dait un réel service; (*b*) (fait) pertinent. **II.** *s.* *Tex:* tissu *m.* **2.** (*a*) matière *f*, matériaux *m* **raw materials**, matières premières; **buildi materials**, matériaux de construction; (*b*) **materials**, fournitures *f*, accessoires *m*; **writi materials**, de quoi écrire; **-ally**, *adv.* matériellement, essentiellement. **2.** se siblement; **ma'terialism**, *s.* matérialisme **ma'terialist**, *s.* matérialiste *m* **ma'terialize**, *v.i.* se matérialiser; se réalis (*of plan*) aboutir.
maternal [mə'təːnəl], *a.* maternel; **-ally**, *a* maternellement; **ma'ternity**, *s.* maternité **m. hospital**, maternité; **m. dress**, robe *f* grossesse.
mathematics [mæθə'mætiks], *s.*,

mathématiques *fpl*; **mathe'matical,** *a.*
mathématique; -**ally,** *adv.*
mathématiquement; **mathema'tician,** *s.*
mathématicien, -ienne; **maths,** *s.pl. F:*
math(s) *f* (*pl*).
matinee ['mætinei], *s. Th:* matinée *f.*
matins ['mætinz], *s.pl. Ecc:* matines *fpl.*
matrimony ['mætriməni], *s.* le mariage;
matri'monial, *a.* matrimonial; conjugal.
matrix ['meitriks, 'mætriks], *s.* matrice *f.*
matron ['meitrən], *s.* **1.** femme d'un certain âge;
F: matrone *f.* **2.** (*a*) intendante *f* (d'une école,
etc.); (*b*) infirmière-major *f* (d'un hôpital).
matt [mæt], *a.* mat, *f.* matte.
matter ['mætər]. **I.** *s.* **1.** matière *f*; substance *f*;
vegetable m., matières végétales. **2.** *Med:*
matière (purulente); pus *m.* **3.** matière, sujet *m*
(d'un discours); **reading m.,** choses *fpl* à lire. **4.**
no m.! it makes no m.! n'importe! cela ne fait
rien! **no m. how,** de n'importe quelle manière.
5. affaire *f*, chose, cas *m*; **it's an easy m.,** c'est
facile; **it's no great m.,** c'est peu de chose;
that's quite another m., c'est tout autre chose;
as matters stand, au point où en sont les
choses; **business matters,** affaires; **in this m.,** à
cet égard; **m. of taste,** affaire de goût; **for that
m.,** quant à cela; d'ailleurs; **as a m. of fact,** à
vrai dire; en réalité; **what's the m.?** qu'est-ce
qu'il y a? qu'y a-t-il? **something must be the
m.,** il doit y avoir quelque chose; **as if nothing
was the m.,** comme si de rien n'était. **II.** *v.i.* importer (**to s.o.,** à qn); avoir de l'importance; **it
doesn't m.,** n'importe; cela ne fait rien; **nothing
else matters,** cela mis à part, rien ne compte,
tout le reste n'est rien; **what does it m. to you?**
qu'est-ce que cela vous fait? '**matter-of-
'fact,** *a.* pratique, positif, prosaïque.
Matterhorn (the) [ðə'mætəhɔːn]. *Pr.n. Geog:* le
Mont Cervin.
Matthew ['mæθjuː]. *Pr.n.m.* Mat(t)hieu.
mattress ['mætris], *s.* matelas *m.*
mature [mə'tjuər]. **I.** *a.* mûr; mûri. **II.** *v.i. & tr.*
mûrir; **ma'turity,** *s.* maturité *f.*
maudlin ['mɔːdlin], *a.* larmoyant, pleurard.
maul [mɔːl], *v.tr.* meurtrir, malmener (qn); **to be
mauled by a tiger,** être écharpé par un tigre.
maunder ['mɔːndər], *v.i.* divaguer, radoter;
'**maunderings,** *s.pl.* radotage *m.*
Maundy Thursday ['mɔːndi'θəːzdi], *s.* le jeudi
saint.
Mauritania [mɔri'teinjə]. *Pr.n. Geog:* **the
Islamic Republic of M.,** la République
islamique de Mauritanie.
Mauritius [mə'riʃəs]. *Pr.n. Geog:* l'île *f* Maurice.
mausoleum [mɔːsə'liːəm], *s.* mausolée *m.*
mauve [mouv], *a. & s.* mauve (*m*).
maverick ['mævərik], *a. & s.* (politicien) non-
conformiste.
mawkish ['mɔːkiʃ], *a.* (*a*) fade, insipide; (*b*)

d'une sensiblerie outrée.
maxim ['mæksim], *s.* maxime *f*, dicton *m.*
maximize ['mæksimaiz], *v.tr.* exploiter au
maximum, tirer le plus grand profit de (qch.).
maximum ['mæksiməm], *a. & s.* maximum (*m*).
may[1] [mei], *v.aux.* (*p. t.* **might** [mait]) **1.** (*a*)
I m. do it with luck, avec de la chance je peux le
faire; **he m. not have been hungry,** il n'avait
peut-être pas faim; **he m. miss the train,** il se
peut qu'il manque le train; (*b*) **how old might
she be?** quel âge peut-elle bien avoir? **and who
might you be?** qui êtes-vous, sans indiscrétion? **mightn't it be as well to warn him?**
est-ce qu'on ne ferait pas bien de l'avertir? (*c*) **it
m. be, might be, that he'll come tomorrow,** il se
peut qu'il vienne demain; **be that as it m.,** quoi
qu'il en soit; **that's as m. be,** c'est selon; **as you
m. suppose,** comme vous (le) pensez bien; **run
as he might he couldn't overtake me,** il a eu
beau courir, il n'a pas pu me rattraper; (*d*) **we
m., might, as well stay where we are,** autant
vaut, vaudrait, rester où nous sommes; (*e*) **I
say, you might shut the door!** dites donc, vous
pourriez bien fermer la porte! **he might have
offered to help,** il aurait bien pu offrir son aide.
2. I only hope it m. last, pourvu que cela dure!
3. m. I? vous permettez? **m. I come in?** puis-je
entrer? **if I m. say so,** si j'ose (le) dire. **4. m. he
rest in peace!** qu'il repose en paix! **long m. you
live to enjoy it!** puissiez-vous vivre longtemps
pour en jouir! **much good m. it do you!** grand
bien vous fasse! '**maybe,** *adv.* peut-être.
May[2], *s.* **1.** mai *m*; **in M.,** en mai; au mois de mai;
(on) the seventh of M., le sept mai; **M. day,** le
premier mai. **2.** *Bot:* aubépine *f*; fleurs *fpl*
d'aubépine; '**mayfly,** *s. Ent:* éphémère *m*;
'**maypole,** *s.* **to set up a m.,** planter un mai.
mayday ['meidei], *s. W.Tel:* S.O.S. *m.*
mayonnaise [meiə'naiz], *s. Cu:* mayonnaise *f.*
mayor ['mɛər], *s.* maire *m*; **deputy m.,** adjoint *m*
au maire; '**mayoress,** *s.f.* femme du maire.
maze [meiz], *s.* labyrinthe *m*, dédale *m.*
me [mi, miː], *pers. pron.* **1.** (*a*) me, (*before a vowel
sound*) m'; moi; **he sees me,** il me voit; **they
hear me,** ils m'entendent; **listen to me!** écoutez-
moi! **give me some,** donnez-m'en! (*b*) **I'll take it
with me,** je le prendrai avec moi. **2.** (*stressed*)
moi; **come with me,** venez avec moi. **3.** *F:* **it's
me,** c'est moi; **he's younger than me,** il est plus
jeune que moi. **4. dear me!** mon Dieu!
vraiment! par exemple!
meadow ['medou], *s.* pré *m*, prairie *f*; *Bot:*
saffron, safran *m* des prés; '**meadowsweet,** *s.*
Bot: reine *f* des prés.
meagre ['miːgər], *a.* maigre; peu copieux; -**ly,**
adv. maigrement.
meal[1] [miːl], *s.* farine *f* (d'avoine, de seigle, etc.);
'**mealy,** *a.* (*a*) farineux; (*b*) **m.-mouthed,**
doucereux.

meal[2], *s.* repas *m*; **square m.**, repas copieux, substantiel; **to make a m. of it,** en faire son repas; '**mealtime,** *s.* heure *f* du repas.

mean[1] [mi:n]. **I.** *s.* **1.** (*a*) milieu *m*, moyen terme; **golden m.,** le juste milieu; (*b*) *Mth:* moyenne *f.* **2. means,** moyen(s) *m*(*pl*); **to find the means of doing sth.,** trouver moyen de faire qch.; **there's no means of doing it,** il n'y a pas moyen; **by all means!** mais certainement! mais faites donc! **by no means,** pas du tout, sûrement pas; **he's not a hero by any means,** il n'est rien moins qu'un héros; **by some means or other,** de manière ou d'autre; **by means of sth.,** au moyen, par le moyen, de qch. **3. means,** ressources *fpl*; **it is beyond my means,** c'est au-dessus de mes moyens; **he's a man of means,** il a une belle fortune; **means test,** enquête *f* sur la situation. **II.** *a.* moyen.

mean[2], *a.* **1.** (*a*) misérable, minable; **that should be clear to the meanest intelligence,** cela devrait être compris par l'esprit le plus borné; (*b*) **he has no m. opinion of himself,** il ne se croit pas peu de chose. **2.** bas, méprisable; **a m. trick,** un vilain tour; un sale coup; **to take a m. advantage of s.o.,** exploiter indignement qn; **how m. of him!** c'est très mesquin de sa part. **3.** avare, mesquin, chiche; **-ly,** *adv.* **1.** misérablement, pauvrement; **to think m. of s.o.,** avoir une piètre opinion de qn. **2.** (se conduire) bassement. **3.** (récompenser qn) mesquinement, chichement; '**meanness,** *s.* **1.** médiocrité *f*, pauvreté *f*; bassesse *f* (d'esprit). **2.** mesquinerie *f*, avarice *f*; '**mean-'spirited,** *a.* à l'âme basse; abject; mesquin.

mean[3], *v.tr.* (**meant** [ment]) **1.** (*a*) avoir l'intention (**to do sth.,** de faire qch.); se proposer (de faire qch.); **what do you m. to do?** que comptez-vous faire? **he means no harm,** il le fait très innocemment; **I m. him no harm,** je ne lui veux pas de mal; **he didn't m. (to do) it,** il n'a pas fait exprès; **without meaning it,** sans le vouloir; (*b*) **he means well,** il a de bonnes intentions; (*c*) **I m. to succeed,** je veux réussir (et je réussirai). **2.** (*a*) **I meant this purse for you,** je vous destinais ce porte-monnaie; (*b*) **the remark was meant for you,** la remarque s'adressait à vous; (*c*) **do you m. me?** est-ce de moi que vous parlez? est-ce de moi qu'il s'agit? **3.** (*a*) (*of words*) vouloir dire; signifier; **the name means nothing to me,** ce nom ne me dit rien; (*b*) **what do you m.?** que voulez-vous dire? **what do you m. by that?** qu'entendez-vous par là? **you don't m. it!** vous voulez rire! **I m. it,** c'est sérieux; (*c*) **twenty pounds means a lot to him!** vingt livres, c'est une somme importante pour lui! **you don't know what it means to live alone,** vous ne savez pas ce que c'est que de vivre seul; '**meaning. I.** *a.* (*a*) **well-m.,** bien intentionné;

(*b*) (regard) significatif; (sourire) d'intelligence. **II.** *s.* (*a*) signification *f*, sens *m*, acception *f* (d'un mot); **what's the m. of that word?** que veut dire ce mot? *F:* **what's the m. of this?** qu'est-ce que cela signifie? (*b*) **you mistake my m.,** vous me comprenez mal; (*c*) **look full of m.,** regard significatif; **-ly,** *adv.* d'un air significatif; '**meaningless,** *a.* dénué de sens, qui ne signifie rien.

meander [mi'ændər]. **I.** *s.* méandre *m*, repli *m*. **II.** *v.i.* (*of river*) faire des méandres, serpenter; **me'andering,** *a.* (*a*) (sentier, etc.) sinueux; (*b*) (discours) sans suite.

meantime ['mi:ntaim], **meanwhile** ['mi:n(h)wail], *s.* & *adv.* (**in the) m.,** dans l'intervalle *m*; en attendant, entre-temps.

measles ['mi:zlz], *s.pl.* (*usu. with sg. const.*) *Med:* rougeole *f*; **German m.,** rubéole *f.*

measly ['mi:zli], *a. F:* misérable, chiche.

measure ['meʒər]. **I.** *s.* mesure *f.* **1. cubic m.,** mesure de volume; **made to m.,** fait sur mesure. **2.** mesure (à grain, etc.); (**tape) m.,** mètre *m.* **3.** mesure, limite *f*; **beyond m.,** outre mesure; démesurément; **in some m.,** en partie, jusqu'à un certain point. **4.** (*a*) mesure, démarche *f*; **precautionary m.,** mesure de précaution; **to take extreme measures,** employer les grands moyens; (*b*) projet *m* de loi. **5. coal measures,** gisements houillers. **II.** *v.* **1.** *v.tr.* (*a*) mesurer; métrer; arpenter (un terrain); *F:* **to m. one's length (on the ground),** s'étaler par terre; (*b*) mesurer (qn); prendre mesure de (qn); (*c*) **to m. one's words,** peser ses paroles. **2.** *v.i.* **the paper measures 21 cm. by 15,** le papier a 21 cm. de long sur 15 (cm.). **-able,** large; '**measured,** *a.* **1.** mesuré, déterminé. (*a*) (pas) cadencé; (*b*) **with m. steps,** à pas comptés. **3. m. language,** langage modéré; '**measurement,** *s.* **1.** mesurage *m.* **2.** mesure, dimension *f*; **to take s.o.'s measurements,** prendre les mesures de qn; **hip m.,** tour *m* de hanches; '**measuring,** *s.* mesurage *m*; **m. glass,** verre gradué; **m. tape,** mètre *m* (ruban).

meat [mi:t], *s.* **1.** viande *f*; **m. ball,** boulette *f* (de viande); **m. extract,** concentré *m* de viande. **2.** **m. and drink,** le boire et le manger; *F:* **this was m. and drink to them,** ils en faisaient des gorges chaudes.

Mecca ['mekə]. *Pr.n. Geog:* la Mecque.

mechanic [mi'kænik], *s.* **1.** mécanicien *m*, mécano *m*; **motor m., car m.,** mécanicien auto; **radio m.,** mécanicien radio. **2.** *pl.* **mechanics,** la mécanique; **me'chanical,** *a.* **1.** mécanique. **2.** (*of personal actions*) machinal, automatique; **-ally,** *adv.* **1.** mécaniquement, machinalement; automatiquement. **mechanism** ['mekənizm], *s.* appareil *m*, dispositif *m*; mécanisme *m*; **mechani'zation,** mécanisation *f*; '**mechanize,** *v.tr.* mécani-

medal [medl], *s.* médaille *f*; **medallion** [me'dæljən], *s.* médaillon *m*.

meddle [medl], *v.i.* **to m. with sth.**, (i) se mêler de qch.; (ii) toucher à qch.; **don't m. in my affairs**, ne vous mêlez pas de mes affaires; '**meddler**, *s.* officieux, -euse; intrigant, -ante; touche-à-tout *m inv*; '**meddlesome**, *a.* intrigant; qui se mêle de tout; '**meddling. I.** *a.* intrigant. **II.** *s.* intervention *f*, ingérence *f* (dans une affaire); **no m. with my tools!** touche pas à mes outils!

media ['mi:diə], *see* MEDIUM.

medi(a)eval [medi'i:v(ə)l], *a.* du moyen âge; médiéval; *Pej:* moyenâgeux.

mediate ['mi:dieit], *v.i.* s'entremettre, s'interposer; servir de médiateur; **medi'ation**, *s.* médiation *f*; intervention (amicale); '**mediator**, *s.* médiateur, -trice.

medical ['medik(ə)l]. **1.** *a.* médical; **the m. profession**, (i) le corps médical; (ii) la profession de médecin; **m. student**, étudiant, -ante, en médecine; **m. man**, médecin *m*; **m. officer of health**, médecin du Service de Santé; **army m. officer**, médecin militaire. **2.** *s.* *F:* examen médical; **-ally**, *adv.* **m. speaking**, au point de vue médical; **to be m. examined**, subir un examen médical, une visite médicale.

medicine ['meds(i)n], *s.* **1.** la médecine; **to study m.**, faire sa médecine. **2.** médicament *m*; **m. chest**, (armoire *f* à) pharmacie *f*; **m. glass**, verre gradué; **me'dicinal** [-'disinl], *a.* médicinal; **-ally**, *adv.* médicinalement.

mediocre [mi:di'oukər], *a.* médiocre; **medi'ocrity** [-'okriti], *s.* médiocrité *f*.

meditate ['medieit]. **1.** *v.tr.* méditer; **to m. doing sth.**, méditer de faire qch. **2.** *v.i.* (*a*) **to m. on sth.**, méditer sur qch.; (*b*) se recueillir; **medi'tation**, *s.* méditation *f*; recueillement *m*; '**meditative**, *a.* méditatif; recueilli.

Mediterranean [medita'reiniən], *a.* *Geog:* (*a*) **the M. (Sea)**, la (mer) Méditerranée; (*b*) **M. climate**, climat méditerranéen.

medium, *pl.* **-iums, -ia** ['mi:diəm, -iə]. **I.** *s.* **1.** milieu *m*; moyen terme (**between**, entre); **happy m.**, juste milieu. **2.** milieu, véhicule *m*; **air is the m. of sound**, l'air est le véhicule du son. **3.** (*a*) intermédiaire *m*, entremise *f*; **advertising m.**, organe *m* de publicité; (*b*) *pl.* **the (mass) media**, les moyens de diffusion de l'information. **4.** (*spiritualism*) médium *m*. **II.** *a.* moyen; **m.-sized**, de grandeur moyenne, de taille moyenne.

medley ['medli], *s.* mélange *m*, bariolage *m*; *Mus:* pot-pourri *m*.

meek [mi:k], *a.* doux, humble; **-ly**, *adv.* avec douceur; humblement; '**meekness**, *s.* douceur *f*; soumission *f*, humilité *f*.

meet [mi:t]. **I.** *v.* (**met** [met]) **1.** *v.tr.* (*a*) rencontrer; se rencontrer avec; **to m. s.o. on the stairs**, croiser qn dans l'escalier; **he met his death**

there, il y trouva la mort; (*b*) faire face à (une difficulté); (*c*) rejoindre; **to go to m. s.o.**, aller au-devant de qn; aller à la recontre de qn; **to arrange to m. s.o.**, donner (un) rendez-vous à qn; **I'll m. you at the station**, je vous attendrai à la gare; (*d*) faire la connaissance de (qn); **I've already met him**, je l'ai déjà rencontré; (*e*) **the scene that met my eyes**, le spectacle qui s'offrait à mes yeux; **there's more in it than meets the eye**, on ne voit pas le dessous des cartes; **to m. s.o.'s eye**, regarder qn en face; (*f*) **to m. s.o.'s views**, se conformer aux vues de qn; **to m. s.o. (halfway)**, faire des concessions à qn; (*g*) satisfaire, répondre, à (un besoin); faire face à (une demande). **2.** *v.i.* (*a*) se rencontrer, se voir; **we have already met, have met before**, nous nous sommes déjà vus, rencontrés; **they met at the station**, ils se sont rencontrés à la gare; (*b*) se réunir (en session); **the society meets in London**, la société tient ses réunions à Londres; (*c*) se joindre; **extremes m.**, les extrêmes se touchent; **our eyes met**, nos regards se croisèrent; *F:* **to make (both) ends m.**, joindre les deux bouts; (*d*) **to m. with sth.**, rencontrer, trouver, qch.; **to m. with a warm welcome**, être accueilli chaleureusement; **to m. with difficulties**, éprouver des difficultés; rencontrer des obstacles; **to m. with a refusal**, essuyer un refus; **he met with an accident**, il lui est arrivé une accident. **II.** *s.* rendez-vous de chasse à courre; '**meeting**, *s.* **1.** rencontre *f*. **2.** assemblée *f*, réunion *f*; *Pol: Sp:* meeting *m*; **to address the m.**, prendre la parole; **m. place**, lieu *m* de réunion; rendez-vous *m inv*.

megaphone ['megəfoun], *s.* porte-voix *m inv*; *Sp:* mégaphone *m*.

melancholy ['melənkəli]. **1.** *s.* mélancolie *f*. **2.** *a.* (*a*) (*of pers.*) mélancolique; triste; (*b*) **m. news**, nouvelle attristante.

mellow ['melou]. **I.** *a.* **1.** (fruit) fondant, mûr; (vin) mœlleux. **2.** (*of voice*) mœlleux, doux. **3.** (*a*) (esprit) mûr; **to grow m.**, s'adoucir; (*b*) *F:* éméché. **II.** *v.* **1.** *v.tr.* (*a*) (faire) mûrir (des fruits); donner du mœlleux à (un vin); (*b*) mûrir, adoucir (le caractère de qn); (*c*) **church mellowed by time**, église patinée par le temps. **2.** *v.i.* (*a*) mûrir; (*b*) s'adoucir; (*c*) prendre de la patine; '**mellowness**, *s.* maturité *f* (des fruits); mœlleux *m* (du vin); douceur *f* (du caractère).

melodrama ['melədra:mə], *s.* mélodrame *m*; **melodra'matic**, *a.* mélodramatique; **-ally**, *adv.* d'un air mélodramatique.

melody ['melədi], *s.* mélodie *f*, air *m*, chant *m*; **me'lodious**, *a.* mélodieux; **-ly**, *adv.* mélodieusement.

melon ['melən], *s.* *Bot:* melon *m*; **water m.**, pastèque *f*.

melt [melt], *v.* (**melted**; *p.p.adj.* **molten** ['moult(ə)n]) **1.** *v.i.* (*a*) (se) fondre; **butter melts**

in the sun, le beurre fond au soleil; (*b*) **to m. into tears**, fondre en larmes; **my heart melted with pity**, mon cœur s'attendrit de pitié; (*c*) (*of sugar, etc.*) fondre, se dissoudre. **2.** *v.tr.* (*a*) (faire) fondre; (*b*) attendrir, émouvoir (qn); **'melting. 1.** *a.* (*a*) (i) (*of snow*) fondant; (ii) attendri; **m. mood**, attendrissement *m*; (*b*) (i) **m. sun**, soleil brûlant; (ii) attendrissant, émouvant. **2.** *s.* (*a*) fonte *f*, fusion *f*; **m. point**, point *m* de fusion; **m. pot**, creuset *m*; (*b*) attendrissement *m* (des cœurs).

member ['membər], *s.* membre *m.* **1.** *Nat. Hist:* organe *m.* **2.** (*a*) **he's a m. of the family**, il fait partie de la famille; **m. of the audience**, spectateur, -trice, auditeur, -trice, assistant, -ante; (*b*) **M. of Parliament** = député *m*; **'membership**, *s.* **1.** qualité *f* de membre; **m. card**, carte *f* de membre. **2.** (nombre *m* des) membres (d'une société).

membrane ['membrein], *s.* membrane *f.*

memento, *pl.* **-o(e)s** [mi'mentou, -ouz], *s.* mémento *m*, souvenir *m.*

memo, *pl.* **-os** ['memou, -ouz], *s. F:* note *f*; **m. pad**, bloc-notes *m.*

memoir ['memwɑ:r], *s.* (*a*) mémoire *m*, étude *f* (scientifique); (*b*) notice *f* biographique; (*c*) **memoirs**, mémoires.

memorandum, *pl.* **-da**, **-dums** [memə'rændəm, -də, -dəmz], *s.* mémorandum *m*, note *f.*

memory ['meməri], *s.* **1.** mémoire *f*; **m. like a sieve**, mémoire de lièvre; **I've no m. for names**, je n'ai pas la mémoire des noms; **loss of m.**, amnésie *f*; **if my m. serves me correctly**, autant que je m'en souviens, si j'ai bonne mémoire; **to play sth. from m.**, jouer qch. de mémoire. **2.** mémoire, souvenir *m*; **childhood memories**, souvenirs d'enfance; **in m. of s.o.**, en, à la, mémoire de qn; **'memorable**, *a.* mémorable; **-ably**, *adv.* mémorablement; **me'morial. 1.** *a.* commémoratif. **2.** *s.* monument *m*; **war m.**, monument aux morts; **'memorize**, *v.tr.* apprendre (qch.) par cœur, mémoriser (qch.).

menace ['menəs]. **I.** *s.* menace *f.* **II.** *v.tr.* menacer (qn); **'menacing**, *a.* menaçant.

menagerie [mə'nædʒəri], *s.* ménagerie *f.*

mend [mend]. **I.** *s.* **1.** (*in fabric*) reprise *f*, raccommodage *m.* **2. to be on the m.**, être en voie de guérison. **II.** *v.* **1.** *v.tr.* (*a*) raccommoder, repriser (un vêtement); réparer (une machine, etc.); (*b*) rectifier, corriger; **to m. one's ways**, changer de conduite; (*c*) réparer (une faute). **2.** *v.i.* (*of invalid*) se remettre; **the weather is mending**, le temps se remet (au beau), s'améliore; **'mending**, *s.* (*a*) raccommodage *m*; (*b*) vêtements *mpl* à raccommoder.

menial ['mi:niəl], *a.* (*of duties*) servile, bas.

meningitis [menin'dʒaitis], *s. Med:* méningite *f.*

menopause ['menoupɔ:z], *s. Med:* ménopause *f.*

menstruate ['menstrueit], *v.i.* (*of woman*) avoir ses règles; **menstru'ation**, *s.* menstruation *f*; règles *fpl.*

mental ['ment(ə)l], *a.* mental, de l'esprit; **m. reservation**, restriction mentale; **m. arithmetic**, calcul mental; **m. hospital, home**, clinique *f* psychiatrique; **m. patient**, malade mental, -ale; **m. specialist**, psychiatre *mf*; *P:* **he's m.!** il est fou! **m. defective**, débile (mental(e)); **-ally**, *adv.* mentalement; **m. defective, m. deficient**, débile (mental(e)); **men'tality**, *s.* mentalité *f.*

mention ['menʃən]. **I.** *s.* mention *f.* **II.** *v.tr.* mentionner, citer, faire mention de (qch.); **I'll m. it to him**, je lui en toucherai un mot; **it must never be mentioned again**, il ne faut plus jamais en reparler; **it's not worth mentioning**, cela est sans importance; **not to m. (s.o., sth.)**, sans parler de (qn, qch.); **I heard my name mentioned**, j'ai entendu prononcer mon nom; **he mentioned no names**, il n'a nommé personne; *F:* **don't m. it!** il n'y a pas de quoi!

menu ['menju:], *s.* menu *m*; carte *f.*

mercenary ['mə:sin(ə)ri], *a. & s.* mercenaire (*m*).

merchant ['mə:tʃənt]. **1.** *s.* négociant, -ante; commerçant, -ante; **wine m.**, négociant en vins. **2.** *a.* marchand; de commerce; **m. ship, vessel**, navire marchand, de commerce; **m. seaman**, marin *m* de la marine marchande; **m. navy, marine, service**, marine marchande; **'merchandise**, *s.* marchandise(s) *f*(*pl*); **'merchantman**, *pl.* **-men**, *s.* navire marchand, de commerce.

Mercury ['mə:kjuri]. **1.** *Pr.n.m. Astr: Myth:* Mercure. **2.** *s. Ch:* mercure *m*; **mer'curial**, *a.* d'esprit vif.

mercy ['mə:si], *s.* miséricorde *f*, grâce *f*, merci *f*; (*a*) **to have m. on s.o.**, avoir pitié de qn; **to beg for m.**, demander grâce; *Ecc:* **Lord have m.!** Seigneur aie pitié! (*b*) **at s.o.'s m.**, à la merci de qn; **at the m. of the waves**, au gré des flots; à la dérive; **left to the tender mercies of s.o.**, livré à la discrétion de qn; (*c*) **thankful for small mercies**, reconnaissant des moindres bienfaits *m*; **what a m.!** quel bonheur! quelle chance! (*d*) *Ecc:* **Sister of M.**, sœur *f* de la charité; **'merciful**, *a.* miséricordieux (to, pour); clément (to, envers); **-fully**, *adv.* miséricordieusement avec clémence; **'merciless**, *a.* impitoyable sans pitié; **-ly**, *adv.* impitoyablement; sans merci; **'mercilessness**, *s.* caractère *m* impitoyable; manque *m* de pitié.

mere¹ ['miər], *s.* lac *m*, étang *m.*

mere², *a.* simple, pur, seul; **the m. sight of her**, sa seule vue; **from m. spite**, par pure méchanceté; **by m. chance**, par pur hasard; **I shudder at the m. thought of it**, je frissonne rien que d'y penser; **he's a m. boy**, ce n'est qu'un enfant; **-ly**, *adv.* simplement, seulement; tout bonnement; **he m. smiled**, il se contenta de sourire; **I said it m. as a joke**, j'ai dit cela histoire de rire.

merge [məːdʒ], *v.tr. & i.* (se) fondre; (se) confondre; *Fin:* fusionner; **'merger,** *s. Fin:* fusion *f* (de plusieurs sociétés).

meridian [məˈridiən], *a. & s.* méridien (*m*); (point) culminant.

meringue [məˈræŋ], *s. Cu:* meringue *f.*

merino [məˈriːnou], *s. Agr: Tex:* mérinos *m*; **m. ewe,** brebis *f* mérinos.

merit [ˈmerit], **I.** *s.* **1.** (*a*) mérite *m*; **to treat s.o. according to his merits,** traiter qn selon ses mérites; (*b*) **to judge sth. on its merits,** juger qch. au fond; **to go into the merits of sth.,** discuter le pour et le contre de qch. **2.** valeur *f*, mérite; **novel of considerable m.,** roman *m* de grande valeur. **II.** *v.tr.* mériter.

mermaid [ˈməːmeid], *s.f.* sirène; **'merman,** *s.m.* triton.

merry [ˈmeri], *a.* joyeux, gai; **to make m.,** s'amuser; **m. Christmas!** joyeux Noël! **the more the merrier,** plus on est de fous plus on rit; **-ily,** *adv.* gaiement, joyeusement; **'merry-go-round,** *s.* (manège *m* de) chevaux *mpl* de bois; carrousel *m*; **'merrymaker,** *s.* fêtard *m*; **'merrymaking,** *s.* réjouissances *fpl*; partie *f* de plaisir.

mesh [meʃ], *s.* **1.** maille *f* (d'un filet). **2.** *Mec.E:* prise *f*, engrenage *m*; **in m. with,** en prise avec.

mesmerize [ˈmezməraiz], *v.tr.* hypnotiser (qn).

mess [mes]. **I.** *s.* saleté *f*; **to make a m. of the tablecloth,** salir la nappe. **2.** fouillis *m*, gâchis *m*; **everything's in a m.,** tout est en désordre; **what a m.!** voilà du propre! quel désordre! (*of pers.*) **to get into a m.,** se mettre dans de beaux draps; **to make a m. of it,** tout gâcher. **3.** (*for officers*) table *f*, mess *m*; (*for men*) *Mil:* ordinaire *m*; *Navy:* plat *m*. **II.** *v.* **1.** *v.tr.* (*a*) salir, souiller; **she has messed up her dress,** elle a sali sa robe; (*b*) gâcher; **to m. it (up),** tout gâcher. **2.** *v.i. Mil: Navy:* faire popote (avec qn); **'mess a'bout,** *v.i. F:* (*a*) patauger (dans la boue); (*b*) bricoler; perdre son temps; **'mess-up,** *s. F:* **1.** gâchis *m.* **2.** malentendu *m*; **'messy,** *a.* **1.** (*a*) sale, malpropre; (*b*) en désordre. **2.** qui salit; salissant; **m. job,** travail salissant.

message [ˈmesidʒ], *s.* **1.** (*a*) message *m*; **to leave a m. for s.o.,** laisser un mot pour qn; *F:* **has he got the m.?** est-ce qu'il a compris? (*b*) communication *f* (par téléphone). **2.** commission *f*, course *f*; **'messenger,** *s.* (*a*) messager, -ère; (*b*) commissionnaire *m*; garçon *m* de bureau; (*in hotel*) chasseur *m*; **telegraph m.,** télégraphiste *m*; (*c*) **King's, Queen's, m.,** courrier *m* diplomatique.

Messrs [ˈmesəz], *s.m.pl. Com: etc:* Messieurs, *abbr.* MM.

metabolism [meˈtæbəlizm], *s.* métabolisme *m.*

metal [metl], *s.* **1.** métal *m*; **sheet m.,** métal en feuilles. **2.** *Civ.E:* **road m.,** cailloutis *m*,

pierraille *f.* **3.** *Rail:* **the metals,** les rails *m*; **metallic** [miˈtælik], *a.* métallique; **me'tallurgist,** *s.* métallurgiste *m*; **me'tallurgy,** *s.* métallurgie *f*; **'metalwork,** *s.* **1.** travail *m* des métaux; serrurerie *f.* **2.** métal ouvré.

metamorphosis, *pl.* **-oses** [metəˈmɔːfəsis, -əsiːz], *s.* métamorphose *f*; **meta'morphose,** *v.tr.* métamorphoser, transformer (**to, into, en**).

metaphor [ˈmetəfər], *s.* métaphore *f*; **mixed m.,** métaphore incohérente; **meta'phorical,** *a.* métaphorique; **-ally,** *adv.* métaphoriquement.

metaphysics [metəˈfiziks], *s.pl.* (*usu. with sg. const.*) la métaphysique.

meteor [ˈmiːtiər], *s.* météore *m*; **mete'oric,** *a.* météorique; **'meteorite,** *s.* météorite *m* or *f.*

meteorology [miːtjəˈrɔlədʒi], *s.* météorologie *f*, *F:* météo *f*; **meteo'rologist,** *s.* météorologue *mf*, météorologiste *mf.*

meter [ˈmiːtər]. **1.** *s.* compteur *m*; (*in taxi*) taximètre *m*; **electric, electricity, gas, m.,** compteur d'électricité, de, à, gaz; **parking m.,** parcmètre *m.* **II.** *v.tr.* **to have one's water metered,** payer l'eau à la consommation.

methane [ˈmiːθein], *s. Ch:* méthane *m.*

method [ˈmeθəd], *s.* (*a*) méthode *f*; **m. of doing sth.,** manière *f* de faire qch.; procédé *m* pour faire qch.; (*b*) **man of m.,** homme *m* méthodique; **me'thodical,** *a.* méthodique; **m. life,** vie réglée, ordonnée; **-ally,** *adv.* méthodiquement, avec méthode.

methyl [ˈmeθil], *s. Ch:* méthyle *m*; **meths,** *s. F:* alcool *m* à brûler; **'methylate,** *v.tr.* méthyler; **methylated spirits,** alcool *m* à brûler.

meticulous [miˈtikjuləs], *a.* méticuleux; **-ly,** *adv.* méticuleusement; **me'ticulousness,** *s.* méticulosité *f.*

metre¹ [ˈmiːtər], *s. Lit:* mètre *m*, mesure *f*; **in m.,** en vers; **metric(al)** [ˈmetrik(l)], *a.* (poésie *f*) métrique.

metre², *s.* mètre *m*; **square m., cubic m.,** mètre carré, cube; **metric** [ˈmetrik], *a.* (système *m*) métrique; **metri'cation,** *s.* adoption *f* du système métrique.

metronome [ˈmetrənoum], *s.* métronome *m.*

metropolis [meˈtrɔpəlis], *s.* métropole *f*; **metro'politan,** *a.* métropolitain.

mettle [metl], *s.* **1.** (*of pers.*) ardeur *f*, courage *m*, feu *m*; (*of horse*) fougue *f*; **to put s.o. on his m.,** exciter l'émulation de qn. **2.** caractère *m*, tempérament *m*; **to show one's m.,** faire ses preuves.

mew [mjuː]. **I.** *s.* miaulement *m.* **II.** *v.i.* miauler; **'mewing. I.** *a.* miauleur. **II.** *s.* miaulement *m.*

mews [mjuːz], *s.* **1.** écuries *fpl.* **2.** **m. flat,** appartement aménagé dans une ancienne écurie.

Mexico [ˈmeksikou]. *Pr.n. Geog:* le Mexique; **M. (City),** Mexico; **'Mexican,** *a. & s.* mexicain, -aine.

mezzanine ['mezəni:n], *s.* **m.** (**floor**), entresol *m*.

miaow [mi(:)'au]. **I.** *s.* miaulement *m*, miaou *m*. **II.** *v.i.* miauler.

mica ['maikə], *s.* mica *m*.

mice [mais], *s. see* MOUSE.

Michael ['maikl]. *Pr.n.m.* Michel; **Michaelmas** ['miklməs], *s.* **1. M.** (**Day**), la Saint-Michel. **2.** *Bot:* **M. daisy,** aster *m* œil-du-Christ.

microbe ['maikroub], *s.* microbe *m*.

microcosm ['maikroukɔzm], *s.* microcosme *m*.

microfilm ['maikroufilm]. **I.** *s.* microfilm *m*. **II.** *v.tr.* microfilmer.

microphone ['maikrəfoun], *s.* microphone *m*, *F:* micro *m*.

microscope ['maikrəskoup], *s.* microscope *m*; **electron m.,** microscope électronique; **visible under the m.,** visible au microscope; **micro'scopic** [-'skɔpik], *a.* microscopique.

mid [mid], *a.* du milieu; mi-, moyen; **in m. air,** entre ciel et terre; en plein ciel; **m. June,** la mi-juin; **in m. Channel,** au milieu de la Manche; '**mid'day,** *s.* midi *m*; '**midland. 1.** *a.* du centre (de l'Angleterre). **2.** *s.* **the Midlands,** les comtés *m* du centre; '**midnight,** *s.* minuit *m*; '**midriff,** *s.* ventre *m*; '**midshipman,** *pl.* -**men,** *s.* aspirant *m* (de marine); **midst,** *s.* **in the m. of,** au milieu de, parmi (la foule, etc.); **in the m. of winter,** en plein hiver; **in the m. of all this,** sur ces entrefaites; **to be in the m. of doing sth.,** être en train de faire qch.; '**mid'stream,** *s.* **in m.,** au milieu du courant; '**midsummer,** *s.* (*a*) cœur *m* de l'été; (*b*) le solstice d'été; **M. day,** la Saint-Jean; '**mid'way,** *adv.* à mi-chemin, à moitié chemin; **m. between Paris and London,** à mi-distance entre Paris et Londres; '**mid'winter,** *s.* milieu *m*, fort *m*, de l'hiver.

midge [midʒ], *s. Ent:* moucheron *m*; cousin *m*.

midget ['midʒit], *s.* **1.** nain, *f.* naine. **2.** *a.* minuscule; **m. submarine,** sous-marin *m* de poche.

middle [midl]. **1.** *a.* du milieu; central; moyen, intermédiaire; **to take a m. course,** garder un juste milieu; **m. size,** grandeur moyenne; **the m. class(es),** la classe moyenne; la bourgeoisie; **m.-class values,** les valeurs bourgeoises; **m.-aged, of m. age,** entre deux âges; d'un certain âge; *Hist:* **the M. Ages,** le moyen âge. **2.** *s.* (*a*) milieu *m*, centre *m*; **in the m. of,** au milieu de; **in the m. of August,** à la mi-août; **right in the m. of sth.,** au beau milieu de qch.; **to be in the m. of doing sth.,** être en train de faire qch.; (*b*) taille *f*, ceinture *f*; **the water came up to his m.,** l'eau lui venait à micorps; '**middleman,** *pl.* -**men,** *s. Com:* revendeur *m*; '**middle-of-the-'road,** *a.* (politique) modérée, du centre; '**middling. 1.** *a.* médiocre; passable; comme ci comme ça; pas mal. **2.** *adv.* assez bien; passablement.

midwife, *pl.* -**wives** ['midwaif, -waivz], *s.* sage-femme *f*, *pl.* sages-femmes; **midwifery** ['midwifri], *s.* obstétrique *f*.

might[1] [mait], *s.* puissance *f*, force(s) *f(pl)*; **to work with all one's m.,** travailler de toutes ses forces; **m. is right,** la force prime le droit; '**mighty. I.** *a.* (*a*) puissant, fort; (*b*) grand, vaste, grandiose; (*c*) *F:* **you're in a m. hurry,** vous êtes diablement pressé. **II.** *adv. F:* fort, extrêmement, rudement (content, etc.); -**ily,** *adv.* (*a*) puissamment, fortement; (*b*) extrêmement, fameusement.

might[2], *v. aux. see* MAY[1].

mignonette [minjə'net], *s. Bot:* réséda odorant.

migraine ['mi:grein], *s. Med:* migraine *f*.

migrate [mai'greit], *v.i.* émigrer; '**migrant,** *a.* & *s.* (oiseau) migrateur (*m*); (ouvrier) migrant (*m*); **mi'gration,** *s.* migration *f*; '**migratory,** *a.* migrateur.

mike [maik], *s. F:* micro *m*.

mild [maild], *a.* (*a*) (*of pers.*) doux; (*b*) peu sévère; **m. punishment,** punition légère; (*c*) (climat) doux; (hiver) clément; **it's milder here,** il fait meilleur ici; (*d*) **m. form of measles,** forme bénigne de la rougeole; -**ly,** *adv.* **1.** doucement, avec douceur. **2. to put it m.,** pour ne pas dire plus; '**mildness,** *s.* (*a*) douceur *f*, clémence *f* (de qn, du temps); (*b*) bénignité *f* (d'une maladie), caractère bénin.

mildew ['mildju:]. **I.** *s.* **1.** moisissure *f*; (*on vine, etc.*) mildiou *m*. **2.** moisi *m*; taches *fpl* d'humidité. **II.** *v.i.* moisir.

mile [mail], *s. Meas:* mille *m*; *F:* **nobody comes within miles of him,** personne ne lui monte à la cheville; '**mileage,** *s.* distance en milles, *Fr.C:* millage *m*; **with low m.,** (voiture) qui a très peu roulé; **mile'ometer,** *s.* compteur *m* kilométrique; '**milestone,** *s.* **1.** borne *f* kilométrique. **2. milestones in s.o.'s life,** événements qui jalonnent la vie de qn.

militant ['militənt], *a.* & *s.* militant, -ante; activiste (*mf*); '**military. 1.** *a.* militaire; **m. service,** service *m* militaire. **2.** *s.pl. coll.* **the m.,** les militaires *m*, l'armée *f*; '**militate,** *v.i.* militer; **militia** [mi'liʃə], *s.* milice *f*; garde nationale.

milk [milk]. **I.** *s.* **1.** lait *m*; **homogenized m.,** lait homogénéisé; **m. diet,** régime lacté; **m. chocolate,** chocolat *m* au lait; **m. shake,** lait parfumé; **m. jug,** pot *m* à lait; **m. tooth,** dent *f* de lait; **it's no use crying over spilt m.,** inutile de pleurer, ça ne changera rien. **2. coconut m.,** lait de coco. **II.** *v.tr.* **1.** traire (une vache). **2.** *F:* dépouiller, exploiter (qn); '**milk bar,** *s.* milk-bar *m*; '**milker,** *s.* trayeur, -euse; '**milking,** *s.* traite *f*; **m. machine,** trayeuse *f*; '**milkman,** *pl.* -**men,** *s.* laitier *m*; '**milksop,** *s. F:* poule mouillée; '**milky,** *a.* laiteux; **the M. Way,** la Voie lactée.

mill [mil]. **I.** *s.* (*a*) moulin *m* (à blé); **to go through the m.,** passer par de dures épreuves; (*b*)

pepper m., moulin à poivre; (c) **rolling m.**, laminoir m; (d) usine f, manufacture f; **cotton m.**, filature f de coton. **II.** v. **1.** v.tr. moudre (le blé); broyer (du minerai); créneler (une pièce de monnaie); **milled edge**, grènetis m. **2.** v.i. (of crowd) **to m. (about)**, fourmiller; tourner en rond; '**millboard**, s. carton-pâte m inv; '**miller**, s. meunier m; '**millpond**, s. réservoir m de moulin; **sea like a m.**, mer f d'huile; '**millstone**. s. meule f (de moulin).

millennium [mi'leniəm], s. **1.** Rel. H: millénium m. **2.** millénaire m; mille ans m.

millet ['milit], s. Bot: millet m, mil m.

milligramme ['miligræm], s. Meas: milligramme m; '**millimetre**, s. Meas: millimètre m.

milliner ['milinər], s. modiste f; **m.'s (shop)**, magasin m de modes; '**millinery**, s. (articles mpl de) modes fpl.

million ['miljən], s. million m; **two m. men**, deux millions d'hommes; **millio'naire**, s. millionnaire mf; '**millionth**, a. & s. millionième (m).

mime [maim]. **I.** s. mime m. **II.** v.tr. mimer.

mimic ['mimik]. **I.** s. imitateur, -trice. **II.** v.tr. (mimicked) imiter, mimer, contrefaire (qn, la nature, etc.); '**mimicry**, s. mimique f, imitation f.

minaret [minə'ret], s. minaret m.

mince [mins]. **I.** s. Cu: hachis m. **II.** v.tr. **1.** hacher (menu); **minced meat**, hachis. **2.** **not to m. matters**, ne pas y aller par quatre chemins; **not to m. one's words**, parler carrément, franchement; **to m. along**, marcher à petits pas; '**mincemeat**, s. (sorte de) compote f de raisins secs et de pommes; F: **to make m. of s.o.**, réduire qn en chair à pâté; '**mincer**, s. hachoir m (à viande, etc.), hache-viande m inv; '**mincing. I.** a. affecté, minaudier; **to take m. steps**, marcher à petits pas. **II.** s. mise f en hachis; **m. machine**, hache-viande m inv, hachoir m.

mind [maind]. **I.** s. **1.** souvenir m, mémoire f; **to bear, keep, sth. in m.**, (i) se souvenir de qch.; ne pas oublier qch.; (ii) tenir compte de qch.; **bear him in m.**, songez à lui; **to bring sth. to s.o.'s m.**, rappeler qch.' à la mémoire de qn; **to call sth. to m.**, évoquer le souvenir de qch.; **he puts me in m. of his father**, il me rappelle son père; **it went (clean) out of my m.**, cela m'est sorti de l'esprit. **2.** (a) pensée f, avis m, idée f; **to give s.o. a piece of one's m.**, dire son fait à qn; **we're of the same m.**, nous sommes du même avis; (b) **to know one's own m.**, savoir ce qu'on veut; **to make up one's m.**, prendre (un) parti; se décider; **to make up one's m. about sth.**, prendre une décision au sujet de qch.; **to make up one's m. to sth.**, se résigner à qch.; **to be in two minds about sth.**, être indécis sur qch.; **I've a good m. to (do sth.)**, j'ai (grande) envie

de (faire qch.); (c) **to let one's m. run upon sth.**, songer à qch.; **to set one's m. on sth.**, désirer qch. ardemment, tenir à qch.; **to give one's m. to sth.**, s'adonner, s'appliquer, à qch.; **to have sth. in m.**, avoir qch. en vue. **3.** esprit m, âme f; **state of m.**, état m d'âme; **turn of m.**, mentalité f (de qn); **peace of m.**, tranquillité f d'esprit. **4.** (a) esprit, idée; **she has something on her m.**, il y a quelque chose qui la préoccupe; **to take s.o.'s m. off his sorrow**, distraire qn de son chagrin; **to be easy in one's m.**, avoir l'esprit tranquille; (b) **great minds think alike**, les grands esprits se rencontrent. **5.** **to be out of one's m.**, avoir perdu la raison; **to be in one's right m.**, avoir toute sa raison. **II.** v.tr. **1.** faire attention à (qn, qch.); **never m. that!** qu'à cela ne tienne! **never m. the money!** ne regardez pas à l'argent! **m. you!** remarquez bien! **2.** s'occuper de, se mêler de (qch.); **m. your own business!** occupez-vous, mêlez-vous, de ce qui vous regarde! **3.** (a) **would you m. shutting the door?** voudriez-vous bien fermer la porte? **you don't m. my smoking?** la fumée ne vous gêne pas? **you don't m. my mentioning it?** cela ne vous froisse pas que je vous le dise? **if you don't m.**, si cela vous est égal, ne vous fait rien; F: **I wouldn't m. a cup of tea**, je prendrais volontiers une tasse de thé; (b) **never m.!** (i) n'importe! tant pis! (ii) ne vous inquiétez pas! **who minds what he says?** qui s'occupe de ce qu'il dit? **he doesn't m. the cost**, il ne regarde pas à la dépense; **I don't m.**, cela m'est égal, peu (m')importe. **4.** **m. what you're doing!** prenez garde à ce que vous faites! **m. you don't fall!** prenez garde de tomber! **m. the step!** attention à la marche! **m. you're not late!** ayez soin de ne pas être en retard! **m. your backs!** dégagez! **5.** garder, avoir l'œil sur (des enfants); garder (des animaux); **to m. the house**, garder la maison; '**minded**, a. disposé, enclin (**to do sth.**, à faire qch.); commercially-m., à l'esprit commerçant; **food-m.**, intéressé par la nourriture.

mine[1] [main]. **I.** s. **1.** mine f (de houille, d'or); **to work a m.**, exploiter une mine; **m. shaft**, puits m de mine; **it's a m. of information**, c'est une mine de renseignements. **2.** Mil: Navy: mine; **to lay a m.**, poser, mouiller, une mine. **II.** v.tr. & i. **1.** **to m. (for) coal**, exploiter, extraire, le charbon. **2.** (a) Mil: miner, saper (une muraille); (b) Mil: Navy: miner, semer des mines dans, un port, un champ; '**minefield**, s. Mil: Navy: champ de mines; '**minelayer**, s. Navy: mouilleur m de mines; '**minelaying**, s. Mil: Navy: pose f, mouillage m, de mines; '**miner**, s. Min: mineur m; '**minesweeper**, s. Navy: dragueur m de mines; '**mining**, s. **1.** Min: exploitation minière; l'industrie minière; **m. village**, village minier; **m. engineer**, ingénieur *m* des mines. **2.** *Mil: Navy:* pose *f*, mouillage *m*, de mines.

mine², *poss.pron.* le mien, la mienne, les miens, les miennes; **your country and m.**, votre patrie et la mienne; **these gloves are m.**, ces gants sont à moi, m'appartiennent; **a friend of m.**, un(e) de mes ami(e)s; **it's no business of m.**, ce n'est pas mon affaire; **no effort of m.**, aucun effort de ma part.

mineral ['minərəl]. **1.** *a.* minéral; **m. waters**, (i) eaux minérales; (ii) boissons gazeuses. **2.** *s.* (*a*) minéral *m*; (*b*) *Min:* minerai *m*; **m. rights**, droits miniers; **mine'ralogist**, *s.* minéralogiste *mf*, minéralogue *mf*; **mine'ralogy**, *s.* minéralogie *f*.

mingle ['miŋgl]. **1.** *v.tr.* mêler, mélanger. **2.** *v.i.* (*a*) se mêler, se mélanger, se confondre (**with**, avec); (*b*) **to m. with the crowd**, se mêler à la foule.

mini ['mini]. **1.** *s.* (*a*) *Aut: R.t.m:* Mini *f*; (*b*) *Cost:* mini(jupe) *f*. **2.** *a.* **m. demonstration**, une petite manifestation; **'minibus**, *s.* minibus *m*; **'miniskirt**, *s.* minijupe *f*.

miniature ['mini(ə)tʃər]. **1.** *s.* miniature *f*; **in m.**, en miniature, en petit. **2.** *a.* en miniature; **m. model**, maquette *f*.

minimum ['miniməm], *a.* & *s.* minimum (*m*); **'minimize**, *v.tr.* réduire au minimum, minimiser.

minister ['ministər]. **I.** *s.* **1.** *Adm:* ministre *m*. **2.** *Ecc:* ministre, pasteur *m*. **II.** *v.i.* **to m. to s.o.'s needs**, soigner qn, pourvoir aux besoins de qn; **minis'terial**, *a.* **1.** *Pol:* ministériel; gouvernemental, du gouvernement. **2.** *Ecc:* de ministre; sacerdotal; **'ministering**, *a.* (ange) secourable; **minis'tration**, *s.* service *m*; ministère *m*, soins *mpl*; **to receive the ministrations of a priest**, être administré par un prêtre; **'ministry**, *s.* **1.** (*a*) *Pol:* ministère *m*, gouvernement *m*; (*b*) *Adm:* ministère, département *m*. **2.** *Ecc:* **the m.**, le saint ministère; **he was intended for the m.**, on le destinait à l'Église. **3.** ministère, entremise *f* (**of**, de).

mink [miŋk], *s. Z:* vison *m*.

minnow ['minou], *s. Ich:* vairon *m*.

minor ['mainər]. **1.** *a.* (*a*) petit, mineur; **Asia M.**, l'Asie mineure; (*b*) petit, menu, peu important; **m. poet**, petit poète; **of m. interest**, d'intérêt *m* secondaire; **to play a m. part**, jouer un rôle subalterne, secondaire; *Med:* **m. operation**, opération bénigne; (*c*) *Mus:* **in a m. key**, en mineur *m*. **2.** *s. Jur:* mineur, -eure; **mi'nority**, *s.* **1.** minorité *f*; **in a, the, m.**, en minorité; **m. party**, parti *m* minoritaire. **2.** *Jur:* minorité (d'âge).

Minorca [mi'nɔːkə]. *Pr.n. Geog:* Minorque *f*.

mint¹ [mint]. **I.** *s.* **the M.** = (l'Hôtel *m* de) la Monnaie; **in m. condition**, à l'état (de) neuf; **to be worth a m. of money**, (i) (*of pers.*) rouler sur l'or; (ii) (*of thg*) valoir une somme fabuleuse; **it costs a m. of money**, cela coûte les yeux de la tête. **II.** *v.tr.* (*a*) **to m. money**, (i) frapper de la monnaie; (ii) *F:* amasser de l'argent à la pelle; (*b*) monnayer (de l'or, etc.).

mint², *s. Bot:* menthe *f*; *Cu:* **m. sauce**, vinaigrette *f* à la menthe.

minus ['mainəs]. **1.** *prep.* moins; **ten m. two equals eight**, dix moins deux égale huit; **it's m. 10** (°C.), il fait moins 10 (degrés). **2.** *a.* & *s. Mth:* **m. (sign)**, moins *m*; **m. quantity**, quantité négative.

minute¹ ['minit], *s.* **1.** (*a*) minute *f*; **ten minutes past, to, three**, trois heures dix, trois heures moins dix; **m. hand**, grande aiguille (d'une montre); (*b*) **wait a m.!** attendez un instant! **I'll come in a m.**, j'arrive(rai) dans un instant; **I shan't be a m.**, j'en ai pour une seconde; je ne ferai qu'aller et (re)venir; **you're punctual to the m.**, vous êtes à la minute; **he'll be here any m.**, je l'attends d'un moment à l'autre. **2.** minute (de degré). **3.** (*a*) note *f*; (*b*) **minutes of a meeting**, procès-verbal *m* d'une séance.

minute² [mai'njuːt], *a.* **1.** tout petit; menu, minuscule, minime; **the minutest particulars**, les moindres détails *m*. **2.** minutieux, détaillé; **-ly**, *adv.* minutieusement, avec minutie; en détail, dans les moindres détails; **mi'nuteness**, *s.* **1.** petitesse *f*, exiguïté *f*. **2.** minutie *f*; exactitude minutieuse.

miracle ['mirəkl], *s.* miracle *m*; **by a m.**, par miracle; *F:* **it's a m. he's still alive**, c'est (un) miracle qu'il soit encore en vie; **mi'raculous** *a.* (*a*) miraculeux; **it's m.**, cela tient du miracle; (*b*) *F:* extraordinaire, merveilleux; **-ly**, *adv.* (*a*) miraculeusement, par miracle; (*b*) *F:* merveilleusement.

mirage ['mirɑːʒ], *s.* mirage *m*.

mirror ['mirər]. **I.** *s.* miroir *m*, glace *f*; **hand m.** glace à main; **shaving m.**, miroir à barbe; *Aut:* **driving m.**, rétroviseur *m*. **II.** *v.tr.* **the trees are mirrored in the water**, les arbres se reflètent dans l'eau.

mirth [məːθ], *s.* gaieté *f*.

misadventure [misəd'ventʃər], *s.* mésaventure *f*; contretemps *m*.

misanthrope ['misənθroup], **misanthropist** [mi'sænθrəpist], *s.* misanthrope *mf*; **misan'thropic** [-'θrɔpik], *a.* misanthrope; **mi'santhropy**, *s.* misanthropie *f*.

misapply [misə'plai], *v.tr.* **1.** mal appliquer (qch.); appliquer (qch.) mal à propos. **2.** détourner (des fonds).

misapprehension [misæpri'henʃ(ə)n], *s.* malentendu *m*; idée fausse (des faits); **to be under a m.**, se méprendre; **to do sth. under a m.**, faire qch. par méprise.

misappropriate ['misə'prouprieit], *v.t*

détourner (des fonds); **'misappropri'ation,** s. détournement m (de fonds).

misbehave [misbi'heiv], v.i. & pr. to m. (oneself), se mal conduire; **misbe'haviour,** s. mauvaise conduite; inconduite f; écart m de conduite.

miscalculate [mis'kælkjuleit]. 1. v.tr. mal calculer (une somme). 2. v.i. to m. about sth., se tromper sur qch.; **miscalcu'lation,** s. faux calcul; erreur f de calcul; mécompte m.

miscarriage [mis'kærid3], s. 1. (a) avortement m, insuccès m (d'un projet); (b) **m. of justice,** erreur f judiciaire. 2. Med: fausse couche; **mis'carry,** v.i. 1. (of scheme) avorter, échouer; rater, mal tourner. 2. Med: faire une fausse couche.

miscellaneous [misə'leiniəs], a. varié, mêlé, mélangé, divers; **miscellany** [mi'seləni], s. mélange m.

mischance [mis'tʃa:ns], s. by m., par malchance.

mischief ['mistʃif], s. 1. mal m; tort m, dommage m; to mean m., chercher à nuire; méditer un mauvais coup; to make m., apporter le trouble; to make m. between two people, brouiller deux personnes; m. maker, brandon m de discorde; mauvaise langue. 2. malice f; out of pure m., par pure malice; (of child) to get into m., faire des bêtises; **mischievous,** a. 1. méchant, malfaisant; (of thg) mauvais, nuisible; the m. effects of sth., les effets pernicieux de qch. 2. (enfant) espiègle, malicieux; -ly, adv. 1. (a) méchamment, par malveillance; (b) nuisiblement. 2. malicieusement, par espièglerie; **'mischievousness,** s. 1. (a) méchanceté f; (b) nature f nuisible (de qch.). 2. malice f, espièglerie f.

misconception ['miskən'sepʃ(ə)n], s. 1. idée fausse. 2. malentendu m.

misconduct. I. s. 1. [mis'kondʌkt], mauvaise administration, mauvaise gestion (d'une affaire). 2. mauvaise conduite. II. v.tr. [miskən'dʌkt], mal diriger, mal gérer (une affaire).

misconstrue ['miskən'stru:], v.tr. mal interpréter (qch.); **miscon'struction,** s. fausse, mauvaise, interprétation.

miscount [mis'kaunt], v.tr. mal compter.

misdemeanour ['misdi'mi:nər], s. Jur: délit m, contravention f.

misdirect [misdai'rekt], v.tr. mal diriger (une entreprise); mal renseigner (qn), mettre (qn) sur la mauvaise voie; Jur: (of judge) mal instruire (le jury).

miser ['maizər], s. avare mf; **'miserliness,** s. avarice f; **'miserly,** a. avare, avaricieux; pingre.

miserable ['miz(ə)rəbl], a. (a) (of pers.) malheureux, triste; to make s.o.'s life m., ren-

dre la vie dure à qn; (b) misérable, déplorable; what m. weather! quel temps abominable! (c) misérable, pauvre; m. wages, salaire m dérisoire; -ably, adv. (a) malheureusement, tristement; (b) misérablement; (c) pauvrement; **'misery,** s. 1. souffrance(s) f(pl), supplice m; his life was sheer m., sa vie fut un martyre; to make s.o.'s life a m., rendre la vie dure à qn; to put an animal out of its m., achever un animal. 2. misère f, détresse f.

misfire [mis'faiər]. I. s. (of gun, engine) raté m. II. v.i. (a) (of gun) rater; (b) Aut: avoir des ratés; (c) (of joke) manquer son effet; (of plan) échouer.

misfit ['misfit], s. (a) vêtement manqué; (b) (of pers.) inadapté(e).

misfortune [mis'fɔ:tʃ(ə)n, -tju:n], s. infortune f, malheur m, calamité f.

misgiving [mis'givíŋ], s. doute m, crainte f; not without misgivings, non sans hésitation.

misguided [mis'gaidid], a. peu judicieux; hors de propos; malencontreux.

mishap ['mishæp], s. mésaventure f, contretemps m.

misinform ['misin'fɔ:m], v.tr. mal renseigner (qn).

misinterpret ['misin'tə:prit], v.tr. mal interpréter; **'misinterpre'tation,** s. (a) fausse interprétation; (b) (in translating) contresens m.

misjudge [mis'dʒʌdʒ], v.tr. mal juger; méconnaître (qn); **mis'judged,** a. (of pers.) mal compris.

mislay [mis'lei], v.tr. (mislaid) égarer (ses clefs, etc.).

mislead [mis'li:d], v.tr. (misled [-'led]) (a) induire (qn) en erreur; tromper (qn); (b) égarer, fourvoyer (qn); **mis'leading,** a. trompeur; fallacieux.

mismanage [mis'mænidʒ], v.tr. mal conduire, mal administrer, mal gérer (une affaire); **mis'management,** s. mauvaise administration, mauvaise gestion.

misnomer [mis'noumər], s. fausse appellation; nom m, terme m, impropre.

misogynist [mi'sɔdʒinist, mai-], s. misogyne m.

misplace [mis'pleis], v.tr. (a) mal placer (sa confiance); (b) déplacer (un objet).

misprint ['misprint], s. faute f d'impression, F: coquille f.

mispronounce ['misprə'nauns], v.tr. mal prononcer; **'mispronunci'ation,** s. mauvaise prononciation, faute f de prononciation.

misquote ['mis'kwout], v.tr. citer (qch.) à faux, inexactement; **'misquo'tation,** s. citation inexacte.

misread ['mis'ri:d], v.tr. (misread ['mis'red]) mal lire, mal interpréter (qch.).

misrepresent ['misrepri'zent], v.tr. mal représenter; dénaturer, travestir (les faits);

'misrepresen'tation, *s.* faux rapport, présentation erronée des faits.

miss¹ [mis]. **I.** *s.* coup manqué; *F:* to give (s.o., sth.) a m., négliger de voir (qn, qch.), de visiter (qch.). **II.** *v.tr.* **1.** (*a*) manquer (le but); *abs.* he never misses, il ne manque jamais son coup; to m. the point, ne pas comprendre; (*b*) to m. one's way, se tromper de route; he missed his footing, le pied lui a manqué; (*c*) ne pas trouver, ne pas rencontrer (qn); (*d*) manquer (un train); (*e*) manquer, laisser échapper; an opportunity not to be missed, une occasion à saisir; *F:* you haven't missed much, vous n'avez rien manqué; (*f*) he just missed being killed, il a failli se faire tuer; (*g*) you can't m. the house, vous ne pouvez pas manquer de reconnaître la maison. **2.** to m. (out) a word, passer, sauter, un mot. **3.** (*a*) remarquer l'absence de (qn, qch.); it will never be missed, on ne se rendra jamais compte que ça manque; (*b*) regretter (qn); regretter l'absence de (qn); I m. you, vous me manquez; they'll m. one another, ils se manqueront; 'missing, *a.* absent; perdu; disparu, manquant; one man is m., il manque un homme; *s.pl. Mil: etc:* the m., les disparus.

miss², *s.f.* (*title*) mademoiselle; *pl.* the Misses Martin, *F:* the Miss Martins, les demoiselles Martin.

missal ['mis(ə)l], *s. Ecc:* missel *m.*

misshapen ['mis'ʃeip(ə)n], *a.* difforme, contrefait; (*of figure*) déformé.

missile ['misail, *N.Am:* 'mis(ə)l], *s.* projectile *m*; (guided) m., missile *m*; ground-to-air m., missile sol-air; anti-m. m., missile antimissile; homing m., engin autoguidé.

mission ['miʃ(ə)n], *s.* mission *f*; 'missionary, *a.* & *s.* missionnaire (*m*); m. work, œuvre *f* missionnaire.

missive ['misiv], *s.* lettre *f.*

misspell ['mis'spel], *v.tr.* (misspelt) mal épeler, mal orthographier; 'mis'spelling, *s.* faute *f* d'orthographe.

misstatement ['mis'steitmənt], *s.* rapport inexact; erreur *f* de fait.

mist [mist]. **I.** *s.* **1.** brume *f*; Scotch m., bruine *f*, crachin *m.* **2.** buée *f* (sur une glace); voile *m* (devant les yeux); to see things through a m., voir trouble. **II.** *v.i.* to m. over, (i) (*of landscape*) disparaître sous la brume; (ii) (*of windscreen*) se couvrir de buée; 'misty, *a.* brumeux, embrumé; (*of windscreen*) embué; it's m., le temps est brumeux; m. outlines, contours vagues; m. recollection, souvenir vague, confus.

mistake [mis'teik]. **I.** *s.* erreur *f*, méprise *f*, faute *f*; to make a m., faire une faute; être dans l'erreur; se méprendre, se tromper; to do sth. by m., faire qch. par erreur; there's some m.! il

y a erreur! there is, can be, no m. about that, i[l] n'y a pas à se tromper; *F:* I'm unlucky and no m.! décidément je n'ai pas de chance! **II.** *v.tr.* (mistook; mistaken) **1.** mal comprendre (les paroles de qn); se méprendre sur (les intentions de qn); to m. the time, se tromper d'heure. **2.** to m. s.o. for s.o. else, prendre une personne pour une autre; mis'taken, *a.* **1.** to be m., se tromper; if I'm not m., si je ne m'abuse. **2.** m. opinion, opinion erronée; m. zeal, zèle ma[l] entendu; -ly, *adv.* par erreur.

mister ['mistər], *s.* (*always abbreviated to* Mr) Mr Martin, Monsieur Martin.

mistime ['mis'taim], *v.tr.* **1.** faire (qch.) à con[tre]tretemps. **2.** mal calculer (un coup).

mistletoe ['misltou], *s. Bot:* gui *m.*

mistress ['mistris], *s.f.* **1.** (*a*) maîtresse; to b[e] one's own m., être indépendant; she is m. o[f] her subject, elle possède son sujet à fond; (*b*) m. of a household, maîtresse de maison; (*c*) in[s]stitutrice; professeur *m* (de lycée); the Frenc[h] m., le professeur de français. **2.** maîtresse amante.

mistrust [mis'trʌst]. **I.** *s.* méfiance *f*, défiance [f]. **II.** *v.tr.* se méfier de (qn, qch.); ne pas avoi[r] confiance en (qn).

misunderstand ['misʌndə'stænd], *v.t[r]* (misunderstood) [-'stud]) **1.** mal comprendre, s[e] méprendre sur (qch.); if I have not mi[s] understood, si j'ai bien compris; we mi[s] understood each other, il y a eu malentendu. [2] méconnaître (qn); se méprendre sur le comp[te] de (qn); 'misunder'standing, *s.* **1.** malente[r] du *m*, quiproquo *m.* **2.** mésintelligence [f] mésentente *f*; 'misunder'stood, *a.* **1.** m[al] compris. **2.** (*of pers.*) incompris.

misuse. **I.** *s.* ['mis'ju:s], abus *m*; mauvais usag[e] mauvais emploi. **II.** *v.tr.* ['mis'ju:z]. **1.** fai[re] (un) mauvais usage, (un) mauvais emploi, c (qch.); to m. a word, employer un mot i[n]correctement. **2.** maltraiter, malmener (qn).

mite [mait], *s.* **1.** the widow's m., le denier de [la] veuve. **2.** mioche *mf*; poor little m.! pauv[re] petit! **3.** *Arach:* acarien *m*; mite *f.*

mitigate ['mitigeit], *v.tr.* **1.** adoucir, atténuer ([la] souffrance); amoindrir (un mal). **2.** atténue[r] (une faute); mitigating circumstances, ci[r]constances atténuantes; miti'gation, [s.] adoucissement *m*; amoindrissement *m* (d'u[n] mal); atténuation *f* (d'une peine).

mitre ['maitər], *s. Ecc:* mitre *f.*

mitt [mit], *s.* gant *m* (de toilette).

mix [miks]. **1.** *v.tr.* (*a*) mêler, mélanger; (préparer, composer (un breuvage); (*c*) to [mix] the salad, retourner la salade; (*d*) confond[re] (des faits). **2.** *v.i.* se mêler, se mélanger (wi[th] avec); (*of colours*) to m. well, aller bi[en] ensemble; to m. in society, with peopl[e] fréquenter la société, les gens; mixed, *a.*

mêlé, mélangé, mixte; **m. sweets,** bonbons assortis; **m. ice,** glace panachée; **m. feelings,** sentiments mixtes; **m. motives,** motifs complexes; **m. company,** compagnie mêlée; milieu *m* hétéroclite; **m. marriage,** mariage *m* mixte. **2. m. school,** école *f* mixte; *Sp:* **m. doubles,** double *m* mixte. **3.** (*of pers.*) **to get m.,** s'embrouiller; ʹ**mixer,** *s.* **1.** (*machine*) *Ind:* malaxeur *m; Dom.Ec:* **(electric) m.,** batteur-broyeur *m,* batteur-mélangeur *m,* mixe(u)r *m.* **2.** (*of pers.*) **to be a good, bad, m.,** savoir, ne savoir, pas s'adapter à son entourage; être très sociable, peu sociable; **mixture** [ʹmikstʃər], *s.* **1.** mélange *m.* **2.** *Pharm:* mixtion *f,* mixture *f;* ʹ**mix** ʹ**up,** *v.tr.* **1.** mêler, mélanger; embrouiller (ses papiers). **2. I always m. him up with his brother,** je le confonds toujours avec son frère. **3. to be mixed up in** (sth.), être mêlé à (une affaire). **4.** embrouiller (qn); **I was getting all mixed up,** je ne savais plus où j'en étais; ʹ**mix-up,** *s.* confusion *f;* embrouillement *m,* pagaille *f.*

ʹoan [moun]. **I.** *s.* gémissement *m,* plainte *f.* **II.** *v.i.* gémir, se lamenter; pousser des gémissements; ʹ**moaning,** *s.* gémissement *m.*

ʹoat [mout], *s.* fossé *m,* douve *f;* ʹ**moated,** *a.* (château) entouré d'un fossé.

ʹob [mɔb]. **I.** *s.* **1. the m.,** la populace. **2.** foule *f,* cohue *f;* bande *f* d'émeutiers. **II.** *v.tr.* **(mobbed)** (*a*) (*of angry crowd*) molester, attaquer, malmener (qn); (*b*) (*of admiring crowd*) assiéger (qn); faire foule autour de (qn).

ʹobile [ʹmoubail], *a.* mobile; **mobility** [mouʹbiliti], *s.* mobilité *f;* **mobiliʹzation,** *s.* mobilisation *f;* ʹ**mobilize. 1.** *v.tr.* mobiliser (des troupes, le capital). **2.** *v.i.* (*of army*) se mobiliser.

ʹock [mɔk]. **I.** *a.* d'imitation; contrefait; faux; **m. turtle soup,** consommé *m* à la tête de veau. **II.** *v.tr. & i.* **to m. (at)** s.o., sth., se moquer de qn, qch.; railler qn, qch.; ʹ**mockery,** *s.* **1.** moquerie *f,* raillerie *f.* **2.** sujet *m* de moquerie; objet *m* de risée. **3.** semblant *m,* simulacre *m* (of, de); **the trial is a mere m.,** le procès n'est qu'un simulacre; ʹ**mocking. I.** *a.* moqueur, railleur; *Orn:* **m. bird,** moqueur *m.* **II.** *s.* moquerie *f,* raillerie *f;* **-ly,** *adv.* d'un ton moqueur, railleur; par dérision; ʹ**mock-up,** *s. Ind:* maquette *f.*

ʹode [moud], *s.* **1.** mode *m,* méthode *f,* manière *f;* **m. of life,** façon *f* de vivre; train *m* de vie. **2.** (*fashion*) mode *f.*

ʹodel [ʹmɔdl]. **I.** *s.* **1.** modèle *m;* **to make a m. of** sth., faire une maquette de qch. **2.** (*a*) **to take** s.o. as one's m.,** prendre modèle sur qn; (*b*) (*artist's*) m.,** modèle *mf.* **3.** *Dressm:* (*a*) modèle *m,* patron *m;* (*b*) mannequin *m.* **4. new m.,** modèle nouveau; **1975 m.,** modèle 1975. **II.** *a.* (*a*) **m. husband,** époux modèle; (*b*) modèle réduit; **m.**

aeroplane, modèle réduit d'avion. **III.** *v.tr.* modeler; **to m.** (fashions), être mannequin.

moderate. I. *a. & s.* [ʹmɔd(ə)rət]. **I.** *a.* modéré; moyen; médiocre; **m. language,** langage mesuré; **m. price,** prix modique; **m. size,** grandeur moyenne; **m.-sized room,** pièce de grandeur moyenne; **m. opinions,** opinions modérées; **m. meal,** repas *m* sobre. **2.** *s. Pol:* modéré(e). **II.** *v.* [ʹmɔdəreit]. **1.** *v.tr.* modérer, tempérer; **to m. one's claims,** rabattre de ses prétentions. **2.** *v.i.* (*of storm, etc.*) diminuer, s'apaiser; **-ly,** *adv.* modérément; avec modération; sobrement; médiocrement; **modeʹration,** *s.* modération *f,* mesure *f;* sobriété *f* (de langage); **with m.,** avec modération; **in m.,** modérément.

modern [ʹmɔd(ə)n], *a. & s.* moderne (*m*); **in the m. style,** à la moderne; **m. times,** le temps présent, les temps modernes; **m. languages,** langues vivantes; **moʹdernity,** *s.* modernité *f;* ʹ**modernize,** *v.tr.* moderniser; rénover.

modest [ʹmɔdist], *a.* modeste; (*a*) **to be m. about one's achievements,** avoir le succès modeste; (*b*) pudique, honnête; (*c*) **m. in one's requirements,** peu exigeant; **m. fortune,** fortune modeste; (*d*) sans prétentions; **-ly,** *adv.* (*a*) modestement, avec modestie; (*b*) pudiquement; (*c*) modérément; (*d*) sans prétentions; ʹ**modesty,** *s.* (*a*) modestie *f;* **with all m.,** soit dit sans vanité; (*b*) **offence against m.,** outrage *m* à la pudeur; (*c*) modération *f* (d'une demande); modicité (d'un prix); (*d*) absence *f* de prétention; simplicité *f.*

modicum [ʹmɔdikəm], *s.* **a m. of** sth., une petite portion, un peu, de qch.

modify [ʹmɔdifai], *v.tr.* (*a*) modifier, faire une modification à (qch.); (*b*) mitiger, atténuer (une peine); **to m. one's demands,** rabattre de ses prétentions; **modifiʹcation,** *s.* (*a*) modification *f;* (*b*) atténuation *f.*

modulate [ʹmɔdjuleit], *v.tr. & i.* moduler; **moduʹlation,** *s.* modulation *f; Rad:* **frequency m.,** modulation de fréquence.

Mohammedan [məʹhæmid(ə)n], *a. & s.* musulman, -ane.

moist [mɔist], *a.* (climat) humide; (peau) moite; **eyes m. with tears,** yeux mouillés de larmes; **moisten** [ʹmɔisən]. **1.** *v.tr.* (*a*) humecter, mouiller; arroser (la pâte); (*b*) **to m. a rag with water,** imbiber un chiffon d'eau. **2.** *v.i.* s'humecter, se mouiller; ʹ**moistness,** *s.* humidité *f;* moiteur *f* (de la peau); ʹ**moisture,** *s.* humidité *f;* buée *f* (sur une glace); ʹ**moisturizer,** *s.* (produit) hydratant (*m*); ʹ**moisturizing,** *a.* **m. cream,** crème hydratante.

molar [ʹmoulər], *a. & s.* molaire (*f*).

molasses [məʹlæsiz], *s. pl.* mélasse *f.*

mole[1] [moul], *s.* grain *m* de beauté.

mole², s. Z: taupe f; **m. catcher,** taupier m; preneur m de taupes; **'molehill,** s. taupinière f; **'moleskin,** s. (peau f de) taupe f.
mole³, s. môle m; brise-lames m inv.
molecule ['mɔlikju:l], s. molécule f; **mo'lecular** [mɔ'lekjulər], a. moléculaire.
molest [mə'lest], v.tr. (a) Jur: molester (qn); (b) rudoyer (qn); **moles'tation,** s. (a) molestation f; (b) voies fpl de fait.
mollify ['mɔlifai], v.tr. adoucir, apaiser (qn); **mollifi'cation,** s. adoucissement m, apaisement m.
mollusc ['mɔləsk], s. mollusque m.
molten [moult(ə)n], a. fondu; **m. lava,** lave f en fusion.
Molucca [mɔ'lʌkə]. Pr.n. Geog: **the Moluccas,** les Moluques f.
moment ['moumənt], s. 1. moment m, instant m; **just a m.!** un moment! **to expect s.o. (at) any m.,** attendre qn d'un moment à l'autre; **to interrupt at every m.,** interrompre à tout bout de champ; **I have just this m., only this m., heard of it,** je l'apprends à l'instant; **at this m., at the present m.,** en ce moment; actuellement; **I'll come in a m.,** je viendrai dans un instant; **for the m.,** pour le moment; **not for a m.!** jamais de la vie! 2. Mec: **m. of inertia,** moment d'inertie. 3. (of fact, etc.) **to be of m.,** être important; **'momentary,** a. momentané, passager; **-ily,** adv. momentanément, pour le moment; **mo'mentous,** a. important; **m. decision,** décision capitale; **mo'mentum,** s. 1. Mec: Ph: force vive. 2. (impetus) vitesse acquise; **to lose m.,** perdre son élan.
Monaco [mə'na:kou]. Pr.n. Geog: **Principality of M.,** Principauté f de Monaco.
monarch ['mɔnək], s. monarque m; **mo'narchic** [-'na:k-], a. monarchique; **'monarchist,** a. & s. monarchiste (mf); **'monarchy,** s. monarchie f.
monastery ['mɔnəstri], s. monastère m; **mo'nastic,** a. monastique; monacal; **mo'nasticism,** s. monachisme m.
Monday ['mʌndi], s. lundi m; **to take M. off,** prolonger le week-end jusqu'au mardi.
monetary ['mʌnit(ə)ri], a. monétaire.
money ['mʌni], s. (a) monnaie f; argent m; **paper m.,** papier-monnaie m; **to throw good m. after bad,** s'enfoncer davantage dans une mauvaise affaire; **ready m.,** argent comptant; **to pay in ready m.,** payer comptant; (b) F: **to be coining m. (hand over fist),** être en train de faire fortune; **to come into m.,** hériter d'une fortune; **to be made of m.,** être cousu d'or; **to be rolling in m.,** rouler sur l'or; **there's m. in it,** c'est une bonne affaire; **it will bring in big m.,** cela rapportera gros; **I want to get my m. back,** je voudrais rentrer dans mes fonds; **you've had your m.'s worth,** vous en avez eu pour votre argent; **'moneybox,** s. tirelire f; **'money-changer,** s. changeur m, cambiste m; **'moneyed,** a. 1. riche; qui a de l'argent; **the m. classes,** les classes possédantes. 2. **the m. interest,** les capitalistes m, les puissances d'argent; **'moneygrubber,** s. homme m d'argent; grippe-sou m, pl. grippe-sous; **'moneylender,** s. 1. prêteur m d'argent. 2. Com: bailleur m de fonds; **'money order,** s. mandat-poste m; **'money-spinner,** s. F:(livre etc.) qui rapporte beaucoup d'argent.
Mongolia [mɔŋ'goulia]. Pr.n. Geog: la Mongolie; **'Mongol,** a. & s. 1. Geog: mongol -ole. 2. Med: **m.** (child), enfant mongolien; **Mon'golian,** a. Geog: mongol, mongolien; **the M. People's Republic,** la République populaire de Mongolie; **'mongolism,** s. Med: mongolisme m.
mongoose ['mɔŋgu:s], s. Z: mangouste f.
mongrel ['mʌŋgrəl], a. & s. **m. (dog),** chien bâtard.
monitor ['mɔnitər]. I. s. (a) (pers.) opérateur d'interception; (b) appareil m de surveillance. II. v.tr. (a) Rad: surveiller (des émissions); (contrôler (des résultats); **'monitoring,** s. Rad: interception f des émissions, monitoring m; **m. station,** centre m d'écoute.
monk [mʌŋk], s.m. moine, religieux; **'monkshood,** s. Bot: aconit m (napel).
monkey ['mʌŋki]. I. s. Z: singe m; **female m., she-m.,** guenon f; F: **you little m.!** petit polisson! **to get s.o.'s m. up,** mettre qn en colère; **m. house,** singerie f; pavillon m des singes; **m. nut,** arachide f; Bot: **m. puzzle,** araucaria m; **I'm not having any m. business,** vous n'allez pas me la faire; **m. tricks,** singeries, chinoiseries f; **m. wrench,** clef anglaise, clef à molette. II. v.i. **to m. (about) with sth.,** tripoter qch.
mono ['mɔnou], a. Rec: F: mono.
monochrome ['mɔnəkroum], a. & monochrome (m).
monocotyledon [mɔnəkɔti'li:d(ə)n], s. Bot: monocotylédone f.
monoculture ['mɔnəkʌltʃər], s. monoculture.
monogamist [mə'nɔgəmist], s. monogame m; **mo'nogamous,** a. monogame; **mo'nogamy,** s. monogamie f.
monogram ['mɔnəgræm], s. monogramme chiffre m.
monolith ['mɔnəliθ], s. monolithe m.
monologue ['mɔnələg], s. monologue m.
monomania [mɔnə'meiniə], s. monomanie f; **mono'maniac,** s. monomane mf.
monopolist [mə'nɔpəlist], s. & monopolisateur (m); **monopoli'zation,** s. monopolisation f; **mo'nopolize,** v.tr. monopoliser, accaparer (une denrée); s'emparer de (la conversation); **mo'nopoly**

monopole *m*.

monorail [ˈmɔnəreil], *a. & s.* monorail (*m*).

monosyllable [mɔnəˈsiləbl], *s.* monosyllabe *m*.

monotonous [məˈnɔtənəs], *a.* monotone; fastidieux; **-ly**, *adv.* avec monotonie; fastidieusement; **moˈnotony**, *s.* monotonie *f*.

nonoxide [məˈnɔksaid], *s. Ch:* **carbon m.**, oxyde *m* de carbone.

nonsoon [mɔnˈsuːn], *s. Meteor:* mousson *f*.

nonster [ˈmɔnstər]. **1.** *s.* monstre *m*. **2.** *a. F:* monstre; colossal; énorme; **monstrosity** [mɔnˈstrɔsiti], *s.* monstruosité *f*; monstre *m*; **ˈmonstrous**, *a.* monstrueux; **ˈmonstrousness**, *s.* monstruosité *f*, énormité *f* (d'un crime, etc.).

nonth [mʌnθ], *s.* mois *m*; **calendar m.**, mois du calendrier; **on the 19th of this m.**, le 19 courant; **what day of the m. is it?** quel jour du mois, le combien, sommes-nous? **a m. today,** dans un mois, jour pour jour; **by the m.**, au mois; **once a m.**, une fois par mois; mensuellement; **ˈmonthly. I.** *a.* mensuel; **m. instalment,** mensualité *f*; *Med: F:* **m. period,** règles *fpl*. **II.** *s.* revue mensuelle; publication mensuelle. **III.** *adv.* mensuellement; une fois par mois; tous les mois.

Montreal [mɔntriˈɔːl]. *Pr.n. Geog:* Montréal *m*.

nonument [ˈmɔnjumənt], *s.* monument *m*; **scheduled as an ancient m.**, classé comme monument historique; **monuˈmental**, *a.* (*a*) monumental; *F:* **m. stupidity,** bêtise monumentale; (*b*) **m. mason,** entrepreneur *m* de monuments funéraires.

oo [muː]. **I.** *s.* meuglement *m*, beuglement *m*. **II.** *v.i.* (mooed) meugler, beugler; mugir.

ooch [muːtʃ], *v.i. F:* **to m. about,** flâner, traîner.

ood¹ [muːd], *s. Gram:* mode *m*.

ood², *s.* humeur *f*, disposition *f*; **to be in the m. for doing sth.**, être d'humeur à faire qch.; **he's in one of his bad moods**, il est de très mauvaise humeur; **ˈmoodiness**, *s.* humeur chagrine; morosité *f*; **ˈmoody**, *a.* **to be m.**, être maussade; **-ily**, *adv.* d'un air morose.

oon [muːn], *s.* lune *f*; **to land on the m.**, alunir; **once in a blue m.**, une fois par extraordinaire; **ˈmoonbeam**, *s.* rayon *m* de lune; **ˈmoonlight**, *s.* clair *m* de lune; **in the m.**, **by m.**, au clair de (la) lune; **ˈmoonlit**, *a.* éclairé par la lune; **ˈmoonshine**, *s.* (*a*) clair *m* de lune; (*b*) *F:* balivernes *fpl*; contes *mpl* en l'air; **ˈmoonstone**, *s.* pierre *f* de lune.

oor¹ [ˈmuər], *s.*, **moorland** [ˈmuələnd], *s.* lande *f*, bruyère *f*; **ˈmoorhen**, *s. Orn:* poule *f* d'eau.

oor², *v. Nau:* **1.** *v.tr.* amarrer (un navire); mouiller (une bouée). **2.** *v.i.* s'amarrer; **ˈmooring**, *s.* **1.** amarrage *m*, mouillage *m*; **m. rope**, amarre *f*. **2.** **ship at her moorings**, navire sur ses amarres.

moose [muːs], *s. Z:* élan *m*, *Fr.C:* orignal *m*.

moot [muːt]. **I.** *a.* **m. point**, point *m* discutable. **II.** *v.tr.* **the question was mooted**, la question fut soulevée.

mop [mɔp]. **I.** *s.* **1.** balai *m* à franges, *Fr.C:* vadrouille *f*; **dish m.**, lavette *f*. **2.** **m. of hair,** tignasse *f*. **II.** *v.tr.* (mopped) éponger, essuyer (le parquet); **ˈmop ˈup**, *v.tr.* (*a*) éponger, essuyer (de l'eau); (*b*) rafler, absorber (tous les bénéfices); (*c*) *Mil:* nettoyer; **ˈmopping ˈup**, *s. Mil:* nettoyage *m*.

mope [moup], *v.i.* être triste; s'ennuyer.

moped [ˈmouped], *s.* cyclomoteur *m*.

moraine [məˈrein], *s. Geol:* moraine *f*.

moral [ˈmɔrəl]. **I.** *a.* **1.** moral; **to raise m. standards,** relever les mœurs. **2.** conforme aux bonnes mœurs. **3.** **m. courage,** courage moral. **II.** *s.* **1.** morale *f*, moralité *f* (d'un conte). **2.** *pl.* **morals,** moralité, mœurs *fpl*; **-ally,** *adv.* moralement; **ˈmoralist**, *s.* moraliste *mf*; **moˈrality**, *s.* (*a*) moralité *f*; principes moraux; sens moral; (*b*) bonnes mœurs; **ˈmoralize,** *v.i.* moraliser; **ˈmoralizing**, *s.* **stop your m.!** pas de morale!

morale [mɔˈrɑːl], *s.* moral *m* (d'une armée, d'une personne).

morass [məˈræs], *s.* marais *m*; fondrière *f*.

morbid [ˈmɔːbid], *a.* morbide; **m. curiosity,** curiosité malsaine, maladive; **-ly,** *adv.* morbidement, maladivement; **morˈbidity,** *s.*, **ˈmorbidness,** *s.* (*a*) morbidité *f*; état maladif; (*b*) tristesse maladive (des pensées).

mordant [ˈmɔːd(ə)nt], *a.* mordant, caustique.

more [mɔːr]. **1.** *a.* plus (de); **m. than ten men,** plus de dix hommes; **some m. bread,** encore du pain. **2.** *s. or indef. pron.* **I can't give m.,** je ne peux donner davantage; **that's m. than enough,** c'est plus qu'il n'en faut (to, pour); **what is m.,** de plus, qui plus est. **3.** *adv.* (*a*) plus, davantage; **m. and m.,** de plus en plus; **he was m. surprised than annoyed,** il était plutôt surpris que fâché; **m. or less,** plus ou moins; (*b*) **once m.,** encore une fois, une fois de plus; **I don't want to go there any m.,** je ne veux jamais plus y aller. **4.** the **m.,** (*a*) *a.* **he only does the m. harm,** il n'en fait que plus de mal; (*b*) *s.* **the m. one has the m. one wants,** plus on en a, plus on en veut; (*c*) *adv.* **all the m. . . .,** à plus forte raison. . . **5.** (*a*) *a.* I've **no m. money,** je n'ai plus d'argent; **no m. soup, thank you,** plus de potage, merci; (*b*) *s.* I've no **m.,** je n'en ai plus; **to say no m.,** ne pas en dire davantage, **let us say no m. about it,** n'en parlons plus; **one m.,** un de plus; encore un; **one or m.,** un ou plusieurs; **is there any m.?** y en a-t-il encore? en reste-t-il? **many m.,** beaucoup d'autres; **as many m.,** encore autant; (*c*) *adv.* **the house doesn't exist any m.,** la maison d'existe plus; **I don't want to see him—no m. do I,** je ne veux pas le voir—ni moi non plus; **moreˈover,** *adv.* d'ailleurs; du reste; et qui plus est; bien plus.

morgue [mɔːg], *s.* morgue *f.*

moribund [ˈmɔribʌnd], *a.* moribond.

morning [ˈmɔːniŋ]. **1.** *s.* (*a*) matin *m*; **tomorrow m.**, demain matin; **(the) next m.**, le lendemain matin; **the previous m.**, la veille au matin; **every Monday m.**, tous les lundis matins; **at four in the m.**, à quatre heures du matin; **first thing in the m.**, dès le matin; **in the early m.**, **early in the m.**, de grand matin; matinalement; **what do you do in the m.?** que faites-vous le matin? **good m.!** bonjour! (*b*) matinée *f*; **in the course of the m.**, dans la matinée; **a m.'s work**, une matinée de travail. **2.** *a.* matinal; du matin; **m. coat**, frac *m*.

Morocco [məˈrɔkou]. **1.** *Pr.n. Geog:* le Maroc. **2.** *s.* (*leather*) maroquin *m*; **Mo'roccan**, *a. & s.* marocain, -aine.

moron [ˈmɔːrɔn], *s.* (homme, femme) faible d'esprit; *F:* idiot, -ote; **mo'ronic**, *a.* faible d'esprit; *F:* idiot, bête.

morose [məˈrous], *a.* chagrin, morose; **-ly**, *adv.* d'un air chagrin, morose; **mo'roseness**, *s.* morosité *f*; humeur chagrine.

morphia [ˈmɔːfiə], *s.*, **morphine** [ˈmɔːfiːn], *s.* morphine *f*.

morphology [mɔːˈfɔlədʒi], *s.* morphologie *f*.

morse [mɔːs], *s.* **m. code**, code *m* morse.

morsel [ˈmɔːs(ə)l], *s.* petit morceau; **not a m. of bread**, pas une bouchée de pain; **choice m.**, morceau friand, de choix.

mortal [ˈmɔːt(ə)l], *a.* mortel; (*a*) **m. remains**, dépouille mortelle; (*b*) funeste, fatal; **m. blow**, coup mortel; (*c*) **m. enemy**, ennemi mortel; (*d*) **to be in m. fear of sth.**, avoir une peur mortelle de qch.; *F:* **any m. thing**, n'importe quoi; **-ally**, *adv.* mortellement; **m. wounded**, blessé à mort; **m. offended**, mortellement offensé; **mor'tality**, *s.* mortalité *f*.

mortar [ˈmɔːtər], *s.* mortier *m*; **'mortarboard**, *s.* **1.** *Const:* planche *f* à mortier. **2.** *Sch:* toque universitaire anglaise.

mortgage [ˈmɔːgidʒ]. **I.** *s.* hypothèque *f*; **m. deed**, contrat *m* hypothécaire. **II.** *v.tr.* hypothéquer; **mortga'gee**, *s.* créancier *m* hypothécaire; **'mortgagor**, *s.* débiteur *m* hypothécaire.

mortician [mɔːˈtiʃ(ə)n], *s.* *N.Am:* entrepreneur *m* de pompes funèbres.

mortification [mɔːtifiˈkeiʃ(ə)n], *s.* **1.** mortification (corporelle). **2.** humiliation *f*, déconvenue *f*; **'mortify**, *v.tr.* mortifier; humilier (qn).

mortuary [ˈmɔːtjuəri]. **1.** *a.* mortuaire. **2.** *s.* morgue *f*.

mosaic[1] [məˈzeiik], *a.* mosaïque *f*; **m. flooring**, dallage *m* en mosaïque.

Moscow [ˈmɔskou]. *Pr.n. Geog:* Moscou *m*.

Moses [ˈmouziz]. *Pr.n.m.* Moïse; **Mo'saic** [mouˈzeiik], *a.* (loi) mosaïque, de Moïse.

Moslem [ˈmuzləm, ˈmɔ-], *a. & s.* musulmar -ane.

mosque [mɔsk], *s.* mosquée *f*.

mosquito, *pl.* **-oes** [mɔsˈkiːtou, -ouz], *s.* En moustique *m*; **m. net**, moustiquaire *f*.

moss [mɔs], *s.* *Bot:* mousse *f*; **m. rose**, ros moussue; *Knitting:* **m. stitch**, point *m* de ri **'mossy**, *a.* moussu.

most [moust]. **1.** *a.* (*a*) le plus (de); **who mad (the) m. mistakes?** qui a fait le plus de fautes (*b*) **m. men**, la plupart des hommes; **for the n part**, (i) pour la plupart; (ii) le plus souvent. *s. & indef. pron.* (*a*) **at m.**, at the (very) m., ; maximum; (tout) au plus; **to make the m. ‹ sth.**, tirer le meilleur parti possible de qch.; (**m. of them**, la plupart d'entre eux; **m. of tl work**, la plus grande partie du travail. **3.** *ac* (*comparison*) **what I desire m.**, ce que je désir le plus; **the m. beautiful woman**, la plus bel femme; **the m. intelligent child**, l'enfant le pl intelligent. **4.** *adv.* (*intensive*) très, fort, bien; displeased, fort mécontent; **m. probably**, tr probablement; **it's m. remarkable**, c'est tout qu'il y a de plus remarquable; **m. unhapp** bien malheureux; **he has been m. rude**, il a é on ne peut plus grossier; **-ly**, *adv.* **1.** pour plupart. **2.** le plus souvent, la plupart du temp

motel [mouˈtel], *s.* motel *m*.

moth [mɔθ], *s. Ent:* **1.** (clothes) **m.**, mite *f*; **ruin by moths**, abîmé par les mites. **2.** papillon *m* nuit; phalène *f*; **'mothballs**, *s.pl.* boules *f* naphtaline; **'motheaten**, *a.* mangé, rongé, les mites, mité.

mother [ˈmʌðər]. **I.** *s.* **1.** mère *f*; **unmarried i fille-mère** *f*; **m. country**, mère-patrie *f*; **tongue**, langue maternelle; **m.-in-law**, be mère *f*. **2.** **M. Goose stories**, contes de ma m l'Oie. **3.** *Ecc:* **M. Superior**, Mère supérieure. **m. of pearl**, nacre *f*. **II.** *v.tr.* (*a*) donner soins maternels à (qn); servir de mère à (q (*b*) dorloter (qn); **'motherhood**, *s.* materr *f*; **'motherless**, *a.* sans mère; orphelin mère); **'motherly**, *a.* maternel.

motion [ˈmouʃ(ə)n]. **I.** *s.* **1.** mouvement déplacement *m*; **in m.**, en mouvement; marche. **2.** signe *m*, geste *m*; **to go through** **motions**, faire semblant (de faire qch.). **3.** n tion *f*, proposition *f*; **to propose a m.**, faire ‹ motion, une proposition. **II.** *v.tr. & i.* **to m.** (**s.o. to do sth.**, faire signe à qn de faire qc **'motionless**, *a.* immobile; sans mouveme:

motive [ˈmoutiv]. **1.** *a.* moteur; **m. power**, fo motrice. **2.** *s.* (*a*) **m. (for doing sth.)**, moti (d'une action); (*b*) **m. of an action**, mobile d'une action; **'motivate**, *v.tr.* motiver (une tion); **moti'vation**, *s.* motivation *f*.

motley [ˈmɔtli], *a.* (*a*) bariolé, bigarré; (*b*) div

mêlé.

motor ['moutər]. **I. 1.** *a.* moteur. **2.** *s.* moteur *m*; **two-stroke m.**, moteur à deux temps; **outboard m.**, moteur hors-bord; **m. show**, salon *m* de l'automobile. **II.** *v.i.* aller, voyager, en voiture; '**motorboat**, *s.* canot *m* automobile; vedette *f* à moteur; '**motorcade**, *s. N.Am:* défilé *m* d'automobiles; '**motorcycle**, *F:* '**motorbike**, *s.* motocyclette *f*, *F:* moto *f*; '**motoring**, *s.* automobilisme *m*; **school of m.**, auto-école *f*; '**motorist**, *s.* automobiliste *mf*; '**motorize**, *v.tr.* motoriser; '**motorway**, *s.* autoroute *f*.

mottle ['mɔtl], *v.tr.* tacheter, marbrer.

motto, *pl.* -o(e)s ['mɔtou, -ouz], *s.* devise *f*.

nould[1] [mould], *s.* terre végétale; terreau *m*.

mould[2]. **I.** *s.* moule *m*; **casting m.**, moule à fonte. **II.** *v.tr.* mouler; former, pétrir (le caractère de qn); '**moulder**[1], *s.* mouleur *m*; '**moulding**, *s.* **1.** moulage *m*; formation *f* (du caractère). **2.** moulure *f*.

nould[3], *s.* moisi *m*, moisissure *f*; '**mouldiness**, *s.* moisissure *f*; '**mouldy**, *a.* moisi; **to go m.**, moisir.

noulder[2] ['mouldər], *v.i.* **to m. (away)**, tomber en poussière; s'effriter.

noult [moult]. **I.** *s.* mue *f*. **II.** *v.* **1.** *v.i.* muer. **2.** *v.tr.* perdre (ses plumes); '**moulting. 1.** *a.* en mue. **2.** *s.* mue *f*.

nound [maund], *s.* tertre *m*, monticule *m*, butte *f*; monceau *m*, tas *m* (de pierres, etc.).

nount[1] [maunt], *s.* mont *m*, montagne *f*; **M. Sinai**, le mont Sinaï.

nount[2]. **I.** *s.* **1.** (*a*) montage *m*, support *m*; monture *f* (d'objectif); (*b*) (*of photograph*) carton *m* de montage; (*c*) **stamp m.**, charnière *f*. **2.** monture (d'un cavalier). **II.** *v.* **1.** *v.i.* (*a*) monter (en haut d'une colline); (*b*) *Equit:* se mettre en selle; monter à cheval. **2.** *v.tr. & i.* (*a*) **to m. (on, upon) a chair**, monter sur une chaise; (*of car*) **to m. the pavement**, monter sur le trottoir; (*b*) **to m. a horse, a bicycle**, monter sur, enfourcher, un cheval, une bicyclette. **3.** *v.tr.* (*a*) **to m. a ladder**, monter à une échelle; (*b*) **to m. s.o.**, (i) hisser qn sur un cheval; (ii) pourvoir qn d'un cheval; **mounted police**, agents à cheval; (*c*) **to m. guard over sth.**, monter la garde auprès de qch.; (*d*) monter (un diamant); *Th:* mettre (une pièce) à la scène; '**mounting**, *s.* **1.** entoilage *m*, collage *m* (d'une photographie, etc.). **2.** monture *f*, garniture *f* (de fusil); '**mount up**, *v.i.* (*of costs*) croître, monter, augmenter.

nuntain ['mauntin], *s.* montagne *f*; **to make a n. out of a molehill**, se faire une montagne de **qch.**; **m. range**, chaîne *f* de montagnes; **m. scenery**, paysage montagneux; *Bot:* **m. ash**, orbier *m* sauvage, des oiseaux; **moun-ai'neer. I.** *s.* alpiniste *mf*. **II.** *v.i.* faire de 'alpinisme; **mountai'neering**, *s.* alpinisme

m; '**mountainous**, *a.* (pays) montagneux.

mountebank ['mauntibæŋk], *s.* charlatan *m*, *Pol: etc:* saltimbanque *m*.

mourn [mɔːn], *v.i. & tr.* pleurer, se lamenter, s'affliger; **to m. (for, over) sth.**, pleurer, déplorer, qch.; **to m. for s.o.**, pleurer (la mort de) qn; '**mourner**, *s.* **1.** affligé, -ée. **2. the mourners**, le cortège funèbre; '**mournful**, *a.* lugubre, mélancolique, (figure) d'enterrement; (voix) funèbre; **-fully**, *adv.* lugubrement; '**mourning**, *s.* **1.** affliction *f*, deuil *m*. **2.** (*a*) **house of m.**, maison endeuillée; (*b*) habits *mpl* de deuil; **to go into m.**, prendre le deuil.

mouse, *pl.* **mice** [maus, mais]. **I.** *s.* souris *f*. **II.** *v.i.* (*of cat*) chasser les souris; '**mousehole**, *s.* trou *m* de souris; '**mouser**, *s.* **good m.**, chat bon souricier; '**mousetrap**, *s.* souricière *f*; *F:* **m. (cheese)**, fromage *m* de qualité inférieure; '**mousy**, *a.* (*a*) timide; (*b*) gris (de) souris; (*of hair*) de couleur indéterminée.

moustache [məs'taːʃ], *s.* moustache(s) *f*(*pl*).

mouth. I. *s.* [mauθ]. **1.** bouche *f*; **to make s.o.'s m. water**, faire venir l'eau à la bouche de qn; **to put words into s.o.'s m.**, attribuer des paroles à qn. **2.** bouche (de cheval); gueule *f* (de chien, de carnivore). **3.** (*a*) bouche (de puits); goulot *m* (de bouteille); gueule (de four, de canon); ouverture *f*, entrée *f* (de tunnel); (*b*) embouchure *f* (de fleuve). **II.** *v.tr. & i.* [mauð], déclamer (des phrases); '**mouthful**, *s.* bouchée *f*; '**mouth-organ**, *s.* harmonica *m*; '**mouthpiece**, *s.* **1.** embouchure *f* (de clarinette, etc.). **2.** *Pol:* porte-parole *m inv* (d'un parti).

move [muːv]. **I.** *s.* (*a*) *Chess:* coup *m*; **to have first m.**, avoir le trait; **whose m. is it?** c'est à qui de jouer? (*b*) coup, démarche *f*; **what is the next m.?** qu'est-ce qu'il faut faire maintenant? **he must make the first m.**, c'est à lui de faire le premier pas; *F:* **he's up to every m.**, il sait parer à tous les coups. **2.** mouvement *m*; **always on the m.**, toujours en mouvement; *F:* **to get a m. on**, se dépêcher; **we must make a m.**, il faut partir. **3.** déménagement *m*. **II.** *v.* **1.** *v.tr.* (*a*) déplacer (qch.); **to m. one's chair**, changer sa chaise de place; *Chess:* **to m. a piece**, jouer une pièce; **to m. (house)**, déménager; (*b*) remuer, bouger (la tête); mouvoir, animer (qch.); mettre (qch.) en mouvement; mettre (une machine) en marche; **not to m. a muscle**, ne pas sourciller; **the wind was moving the trees**, le vent agitait les arbres; (*c*) (i) **he is not to be moved**, il est inébranlable; **to m. s.o. to do sth.**, pousser, inciter, qn à faire qch.; (ii) émouvoir, toucher (qn); **to m. s.o. to anger**, provoquer la colère de qn; **to m. s.o. to tears**, émouvoir qn jusqu'aux larmes; **tears won't m. him**, les larmes le laisseront insensible; (*d*) **to m. a resolution**, proposer une motion. **2.** *v.i.* (*a*) se

mouvoir, se déplacer; **keep moving!** circulez!
to m. in high society, fréquenter la haute
société; (b) **to m. (about),** bouger, (se) remuer;
don't m.! ne bougez pas! (c) marcher, aller,
s'avancer; F: **we must be moving,** il faut partir;
'**movable. 1.** a. mobile. **2.** s.pl. **movables,**
mobilier m; '**move a'bout. 1.** v.tr. déplacer
(qch.). **2.** v.i. aller et venir; '**move a'way,** v.i.
s'éloigner, s'en aller; '**move 'back,** v.i. (se)
reculer; revenir en arrière; '**move 'forward.**
1. v.tr. avancer, faire avancer (qn, qch.). **2.** v.i.
(s')avancer; '**move 'in,** v.i. emménager;
'**movement,** s. mouvement m; **m. of impatience,** geste m d'impatience; '**move 'off,**
v.i. s'éloigner, s'en aller; (of train) se mettre en
marche; '**move 'on,** v.i. avancer; continuer
son chemin; se remettre en route; '**move 'out,**
v.i. déménager; '**mover,** s. **1. prime m.,**
premier moteur, premier mobile. **2.** auteur m
(d'une motion). **3.** N.Am: déménageur m;
'**movie,** s. F: esp. N.Am: film m; **the movies,** le
cinéma; '**moving,** a. **1.** (a) en mouvement; en
marche; (b) mobile; **m. staircase,** escalier
roulant. **2.** moteur; **the m. spirit,** l'âme f (d'une
entreprise). **3.** émouvant, attendrissant.

mow [mou], v.tr. (**mowed; mown**) **1.** faucher (le
blé, un champ). **2.** tondre (le gazon); '**mower,**
s. **1.** (pers.) faucheur m. **2.** (machine) (a)
faucheuse f; (b) (**lawn) m.,** tondeuse f (à
gazon); **motor m.,** tondeuse à moteur.

much [mʌtʃ]. **1.** a. (a) beaucoup (de); bien (du, de
la, des); **with m. care,** avec beaucoup de soin;
(b) **how m. bread?** combien de pain? **how m. is
it?** c'est combien? **2.** adv. beaucoup, bien; **m.
better,** beaucoup mieux; **m. worse,** bien pis; **it
doesn't matter m.,** cela ne fait pas grand-
chose; **m. the biggest,** de beaucoup le plus
grand; **m. of an age,** à peu près du même âge;
m. to my surprise, à ma grande surprise. **3.** s.
(a) **m. remains to be done,** il reste encore
beaucoup à faire; **do you see m. of one
another?** vous voyez-vous souvent? **it's not up
to m.,** cela ne vaut pas grand-chose; **not m. of
a dinner,** un pauvre dîner; (b) **this m.,** autant
que ceci; **that m. too big,** trop grand de cela;
this m. is certain, il y a ceci de certain; (c) **to
make m. of s.o.,** faire fête à qn; **I don't think m.
of it,** ça ne me dit pas grand-chose. **4.** (a) **m. as
I like him . . .,** quelle que soit mon affection
pour lui . . .; (b) **as m.,** autant (de); **I thought
as m.,** je m'y attendais; je m'en doutais bien;
(c) **as m. as possible,** autant que possible; **do as
m. as you can,** faites autant que vous pourrez;
(d) **I haven't so m. as my fare,** je n'ai pas même
le prix de mon voyage; (e) **so m.,** tant (de), autant (de); **so m. money,** tant d'argent; **so m. the
better,** tant mieux; **it's so m. the less to pay,**
c'est autant de moins à payer; **so m. so that
. . .,** à ce point, à tel point, que . . .; **so m. for**

his friendship! et voilà ce qu'il appelle l'amitié!
so m. for that! voilà pour cela! (f) **so m. per
cent,** tant pour cent; (g) **too m.,** trop (de); **too
m. by half,** moitié de trop, la moitié en trop; **to
make too m. of sth.,** attacher trop d'importance à qch.; **they were too m. for him,** il n'était
pas de taille à leur résister.

muck [mʌk]. **I.** s. (a) fumier m; (b) fange f; ordures fpl; (c) choses dégoûtantes; saletés fpl;
to talk m., dire des ordures. **II.** v. **1.** F: v.tr. **to
m. (up) a job,** cochonner, gâcher, un travail. **2.**
v.i. **to m. about,** flâner, flânocher; '**mucky,** a
sale, crotté, malpropre.

mud [mʌd], s. boue f, bourbe f; (**river) m.,** vase f
to fling, throw, m. at s.o., déblatérer contre qn
'**muddy,** a. **1.** (a) boueux, fangeux, bourbeux
(cours d'eau) vaseux; (b) (vêtement) crotté
couvert de boue. **2.** (liquide) trouble; (couleur
sale; **m. complexion,** teint brouillé
'**mudguard,** s. garde-boue m inv.

muddle ['mʌdl]. **I.** s. confusion f, emmêlemen
m, fouillis m; (of thgs) **to be in a m.,** être e
désordre, en pagaille; **his business is getting i**
a m., ses affaires s'embrouillent. **II.** v.tr. (a) e
brouiller, brouiller (qch.); brouiller l'esprit d
(qn); embrouiller (qn); '**muddle'headed,** a
l'esprit confus; brouillon; '**muddler,**
brouillon, -onne; '**muddle 'through,** v.i. s
tirer d'affaires tant bien que mal.

muffle ['mʌfl], v.tr. **1.** emmitoufler (**in,** de); **to**
oneself up, s'emmitoufler. **2.** assourdir (un
cloche); étouffer (un son); **muffled drums,** tam
bours voilés; '**muffler,** s. **1.** cache-nez m inv.
Aut: N.Am: pot d'échappement; silencieux m

mufti ['mʌfti], s. Mil: tenue civile.

mug[1] [mʌg], s. (for beer) chope f; (grosse) tass

mug[2], s. P: jobard m, nigaud m; **that's a m.**
game, c'est de la jobardise.

mug[3], v.tr. (**mugged**) F: **1.** Sch: **to m. up,** bûch
(un sujet). **2.** attaquer (qn) à main armée.

mug[4], s. P: (face) binette f; **ugly m.,** vila
museau.

mugging ['mʌgiŋ], s. vol m avec agression.

muggy ['mʌgi], a. (temps) mou, lourd.

mulatto, pl. -os [mju'lætou, -ouz], s. mulât
-esse.

mulberry ['mʌlb(ə)ri], s. Bot: mûre f; (tr
mûrier m.

mule [mju:l], s. Z: (**he-)m.,** mulet m; (**she-)**
mule f; **m. driver,** muletier m; **m. track,** chen
muletier; '**muleteer,** s. muletier m; '**mulis**
a. entêté, têtu, comme un mulet; **-ly,** adv. a
entêtement.

mullet ['mʌlit], s. Ich: (a) muge m; **grey**
mulet m; (b) **red m.,** rouget m.

multicoloured ['mʌltikʌləd], a. multicolore.

multiple ['mʌltipl], a. & s. multiple (m); **m. sto**
maison f à succursales; **multipli'cation,**
multiplication f; **multi'plicity,** s. multiplic

ƒ; **'multiply,** v.tr. & i. (se) multiplier.
multistorey ['mʌlti'stɔ:ri], a. **m. car park,**
garage m à étages.
multitude ['mʌltitju:d], s. multitude ƒ; foule ƒ.
mum[1] [mʌm], int. & a. chut! **m.'s the word!**
motus! **to keep m.,** ne pas souffler mot (de
qch.).
mum[2], s. F: maman ƒ.
mumble ['mʌmbl], v.tr. marmotter, marmonner;
v.i. manger ses mots.
mummy[1] [mʌmi], s. momie ƒ; **'mummify,** v.tr.
& i. (se) momifier.
mummy[2], s. F: maman ƒ.
mumps [mʌmps], s.pl. Med: oreillons mpl.
munch [mʌntʃ], v.tr. mâcher, mâchonner.
mundane ['mʌn'dein], a. terrestre, terre à terre.
municipal [mju(:)'nisip(ə)l], a. municipal; **m.
buildings** = hôtel m de ville; **munici'pality,** s.
municipalité ƒ.
munificence [mju(:)'nifisəns], s. munificence ƒ;
mu'nificent, a. munificent, généreux.
munition [mju(:)'niʃ(ə)n], s. (i) pl. **munitions,**
munitions ƒ (de guerre); (ii) **m. factory,** usine ƒ de
guerre.
mural ['mjuərəl]. **1.** a. mural. **2.** s. peinture
murale.
murder ['mɔ:dər]. **I.** s. meurtre m; **m.!** au meurtre! à l'assassin! **II.** v.tr. **1.** assassiner (qn); v.i.
commettre un meurtre. **2.** F: massacrer (une
chanson, etc.); **'murderer,** s. meurtrier m,
assassin m; **'murderess,** s. meurtrière ƒ;
'murderous, a. meurtrier, assassin.
murky ['mɔ:ki], a. ténébreux; **'murkiness,** s.
obscurité ƒ.
murmur ['mɔ:mər]. **I.** s. murmure m; **m. of approval,** murmure d'approbation. **II.** v.tr. & i. **1.**
murmurer, susurrer. **2. to m. at sth., against
s.o.,** murmurer contre qch., qn.
muscle ['mʌsl], s. muscle m; **muscular**
['mʌskjulər], a. **1.** (force) musculaire. **2.**
(homme) musculeux, musclé.
muse[1] [mju:z], s. muse ƒ.
muse[2], v.i. méditer, rêver, rêvasser.
museum [mju(:)'zi:əm], s. musée m.
mushroom ['mʌʃrum]. **I.** s. champignon m
(comestible); F: **m. town,** ville ƒ champignon.
II. v.i. F: se développer rapidement.
music ['mju:zik], s. musique ƒ; **m. stand,** pupitre
m à musique; **'musical. 1.** a. musical; **m. instrument,** instrument m de musique. **2.** a. (of
pers.) (a) musicien; (b) amateur de bonne
musique. **3.** a. (of sound) harmonieux,
mélodieux, chantant. **4.** s. comédie musicale;
'music-hall, s. music-hall m; **mu'sician,** s.
musicien, -ienne.
musk [mʌsk], s. musc m; **m. ox,** bœuf musqué;
m. rat, rat musqué; **m. rose,** (i) rose musquée;
(ii) rosier musqué; **'musky,** a. musqué;
(odeur) de musc.

Muslim ['muzləm], a. & s. musulman, -ane.
muslin ['mʌzlin], s. mousseline ƒ.
musquash ['mʌskwɔʃ], s. Com: rat musqué.
mussel ['mʌsl], s. Moll: moule ƒ.
must [mʌst]. **I.** modal aux. v. **1.** (a) (obligation)
you m. hurry up, il faut vous dépêcher; **you
mustn't tell anyone,** il ne faut le dire à personne;
they m. have new clothes, il leur faut absolument de nouveaux vêtements; **do it if you m.,**
faites-le s'il le faut; **he's failing, I m. say,** il faut
avouer qu'il baisse; (b) (probability) **it m. be the
doctor,** ce droit être le médecin; **I m. have made
a mistake,** je me serais trompé. **2. I saw that he
m. have suspected something,** j'ai bien vu qu'il
avait dû se douter de quelque chose. **II.** s. F: **it's
a m.,** c'est une nécessité.
mustang ['mʌstæŋ], s. Z: mustang m.
mustard ['mʌstəd], s. moutarde ƒ; **m. pot,**
moutardier m.
muster ['mʌstər]. **I.** s. **1.** rassemblement m; Mil:
revue ƒ; F: **to pass m.,** passer; être passable;
être à la hauteur. **2.** assemblée ƒ, réunion ƒ. **II.** v.
1. v.tr. rassembler (ses partisans); Mil: passer
(des troupes) en revue. **2.** v.i. se réunir, se
rassembler.
musty ['mʌsti], a. **1.** (goût, odeur) de moisi; (of
room) **to smell m.,** sentir le renfermé. **2.** F:
suranné; **'mustiness,** s. goût m, odeur ƒ, de
moisi; relent m.
mutation [mju:'teiʃ(ə)n], s. mutation ƒ.
mute [mju:t]. **I.** a. muet; Ling: **'h' m.,** 'h' muet. **II.**
s. **1.** (of pers.) (a) muet, -ette; **deaf m.,** sourd-
muet, ƒ. sourde-muette; (b) employé m des
pompes funèbres; croque-mort m; (c) Th: personnage muet. **2.** Ling: consonne sourde. **3.**
Mus: sourdine ƒ.
mutilate ['mju:tileit], v.tr. mutiler, estropier
(qn); **muti'lation,** s. mutilation ƒ.
mutiny ['mju:tini]. **I.** s. révolte ƒ, mutinerie ƒ. **II.**
v.i. se révolter, se mutiner; **muti'neer,** s.
révolté m, mutiné m, mutin m; **'mutinous,** a.
rebelle, mutiné, mutin; (équipage) en révolte.
mutter ['mʌtər], v.tr. & i. marmonner, marmotter; **to m. an oath,** grommeler un juron;
'muttering, s. marmottage m; murmures
mpl; grondement m.
mutton ['mʌt(ə)n], s. Cu: mouton m; **leg of m.,**
gigot m; **m. chop,** côtelette ƒ de mouton.
mutual ['mju:tjuəl], a. **1.** réciproque. **2. m.
friend,** ami commun; **-ally,** adv. mutuellement, réciproquement.
muzzle [mʌzl]. **I.** s. **1.** museau m (d'un animal).
2. bouche ƒ, gueule ƒ (d'une arme à feu). **3.**
muselière ƒ (pour chien). **II.** v.tr. museler (un
chien, Fr: la presse).
my [mai], poss.a. mon, ƒ. ma, pl. mes; **I've
broken my arm,** je me suis cassé le bras; **my
idea would be to . . .,** mon idée à moi serait
de . . ..

myopia [mai'oupiə], s. Med: myopie f; **myopic** [mai'ɔpik], a. myope.
myrtle ['məːtl], s. Bot: myrte m.
myself [mai'self], pers.pron. (a) **I've hurt m.**, je me suis fait mal; (b) **I'm keeping it for m.**, je le garde pour moi(-même); (c) **I saw it m.**, je l'ai vu moi-même.
mystery ['mistəri], s. mystère m; **mysterious** [mis'tiəriəs], a. mystérieux; **-ly**, adv. mystérieusement.

mystic ['mistik], s. mystique mf; **'mystical**, a. mystique; **'mysticism**, s. mysticisme m.
mystify ['mistifai], v.tr. 1. mystifier, intriguer (qn). 2. embrouiller, désorienter, dérouter (qn); **mystifi'cation**, s. 1. mystification f. 2. désorientation f, embrouillement m.
myth [miθ], s. mythe m; **'mythical**, a. mythique; **mytho'logical**, a. mythologique; **my'thology**, s. mythologie f.
myxomatosis [miksəmə'tousis], myxomatose f.

N

N, n [en], s. (la lettre) N, n m or f.

nab [næb], v.tr. (nabbed) P: saisir, arrêter, pincer (qn); **to get nabbed**, se faire pincer.

nadir ['neidiər], s. nadir m.

nag¹ [næg], s. F: bidet m.

nag², v.tr. & i. (nagged) quereller (qn); gronder (qn) sans cesse; **to be always nagging (at) s.o.**, être toujours sur le dos de qn; **'nagging**, a. 1. (of pers.) querelleur; grondeur; hargneux. 2. (of pain) agaçant, énervant.

nail [neil]. I. s. 1. ongle m (de doigt); n. **file**, lime f à ongles; n. **scissors**, ciseaux mpl à ongles; ongliers mpl; n. **varnish**, vernis m à ongles. 2. clou m; **brass-headed n.**, clou doré; F: **to hit the n. on the head**, frapper juste; mettre le doigt dessus. 3. F: **to pay on the n.**, payer argent comptant, payer rubis sur l'ongle. II. v.tr. **to n.** (sth. **down**), clouer (qch.); **'nailbrush**, s. brosse f à ongles; **nailed**, a. (a) cloué; (b) clouté; garni de clous.

naïve [nai'i:v], a. naïf, ingénu; **-ly**, adv. naïvement, ingénument.

naked ['neikid], a. 1. (a) (of pers.) nu; **stark n.**, tout nu, nu comme un ver; (b) (pays) dénudé; (arbre) dépouillé de ses feuilles. 2. n. **sword**, épée nue; n. **light**, feu nu; **visible to the n. eye**, visible à l'œil nu; **the n. truth**, la vérité toute nue; **'nakedness**, s. nudité f.

name [neim]. I. s. 1. (a) nom m; **full n.**, nom et prénoms; **Christian n., first n.**, N.Am: **given n.**, prénom m; nom de baptême; **my n. is . . .**, je m'appelle . . .; n. **of a firm**, raison sociale (d'une maison); **to go by the n. of . . .**, être connu sous le nom de . . .; F: **to mention no names**, ne nommer personne; **to put one's n. down (for sth.)**, (i) poser sa candidature; (ii) s'inscrire (pour qch.); **by n., in n.**, de nom; **to be master in n. only**, n'être maître que de nom; (b) **to call s.o. names**, injurier qn. 2. réputation f, renommée f; **to have a n. for honesty**, passer pour honnête; **to make a n. for oneself, to make one's n.**, se faire un nom, une réputation. II. v.tr. 1. nommer; dénommer; **to n. s.o. after s.o.**, U.S: **for s.o.**, donner à qn le nom de qn. 2. désigner (qn, qch.) par son nom. 3. (a) citer (un exemple); (b) fixer (le jour); **'nameless**, a. 1. sans nom; inconnu. 2. anonyme; **someone who shall be n.**, quelqu'un dont je tairai le nom. 3. (of fear, etc.) indicible, inexprimable; (vice) innommable; **'namely**, adv. (à) savoir; c'est-à-dire; **'namesake**, s. homonyme m.

nanny ['næni], s.f. 1. bonne d'enfant, nurse. 2. n. **goat**, chèvre, F: bique.

nap¹ [næp]. I. s. petit somme; **afternoon n.**, sieste f. II. v.i. (napped) sommeiller; **to catch s.o. napping**, (i) prendre qn au dépourvu; (ii) prendre qn en faute.

nap², s. (of cloth) poil m; (of garment) **to have lost its n.**, être râpé.

nap³, s. 1. Cards: Napoléon m, nap m. 2. Turf: tuyau sûr.

napalm ['neipɑ:m], s. napalm m.

nape [neip], s. n. **of the neck**, nuque f.

naphtha ['næfθə], s. (huile f de) naphte m.

napkin ['næpkin], s. (table) n., serviette f (de table).

Napoleonic [næpouli'ɔnik], a. napoléonien.

nappy ['næpi], s. F: couche f.

narcissus [nɑ:'sisəs], s. Bot: narcisse m.

narcotic [nɑ:'kɔtik], a. & s. narcotique (m); stupéfiant (m).

narrate [nə'reit], v.tr. narrer, raconter (qch.); **na'rration**, s. narration f; **'narrative. 1.** a. narratif. 2. s. récit m, narration f; **na'rrator**, s. narrateur, -trice.

narrow ['nærou]. I. a. (a) (chemin) étroit; **to grow n.**, se rétrécir; (b) de faibles dimensions; (esprit) étroit, borné; n. **limits**, limites restreintes; **in the narrowest sense**, dans le sens le plus étroit; (c) n. **majority**, faible majorité f. II. v. 1. v.tr. (a) resserrer, rétrécir; (b) restreindre, limiter, borner; **to n. (down) an investigation**, limiter une enquête. 2. v.i. devenir plus étroit; se rétrécir; **-ly**, adv. 1. (a) (interpréter) étroitement, rigoureusement; (b) (examiner) minutieusement, de près. 2. tout juste; **he n. missed being run over**, il a failli être écrasé; **'narrow-'minded**, a. borné; à l'esprit étroit; **'narrow-'mindedness**, s. étroitesse f, petitesse f, d'esprit; **'narrowness**, s. 1. (a) étroitesse f; (b) petitesse f; limitation f; étroitesse (d'esprit). 2. minutie f (d'un examen).

nasal ['neiz(ə)l]. 1. a. nasal; n. **accent**, accent nasillard. 2. s. Ling: nasale f.

nasturtium [nə'stə:ʃəm], s. Hort: capucine f.

nasty ['nɑ:sti], a. 1. (a) désagréable, dégoûtant; **to smell n.**, sentir mauvais; (b) n. **weather**, sale, vilain, mauvais, temps; n. **job**, besogne difficile, dangereuse; n. **accident**, accident sérieux; n. **corner**, tournant dangereux. 2. (of pers.) méchant, désagréable; P: rosse; **to turn**

n., prendre un air méchant; **he's a n. piece of work,** c'est un sale type. **3.** (a) esp. N.Am: sale, malpropre; (b) (of film, etc.) ordurier; (c) **to have a n. mind,** avoir l'esprit mal tourné.

nation ['neiʃ(ə)n], s. **1.** nation f; **people of all nations,** des gens de toutes les nationalités; Pol: **United Nations Organization,** Organisation des Nations Unies. **2. the whole n. rose in arms,** tout le pays s'est soulevé; **national** ['næʃ(ə)nəl], a. national, de l'État; (costume) du pays; Mil: **n. service,** service m militaire; **-ally,** adv. nationalement; du point de vue national; **'nationalism,** s. nationalisme m; **'nationalist,** a. & s. nationaliste (mf); **natio'nality,** s. nationalité f; **nationali'zation,** s. nationalisation f; **'nationalize,** v.tr. nationaliser; **'nationwide,** a. répandu partout le pays.

native ['neitiv]. **1.** a. (a) (of qualities) naturel, inné; (b) (of place) natal, de naissance; **n. language,** langue maternelle; **n. land,** terre natale; patrie f. **2.** s. (a) natif, -ive (d'un pays, d'une ville); indigène mf (d'un pays); (b) (of plant, animal) indigène; **the tiger is a n. of Asia,** le tigre est originaire de l'Asie.

nativity [nə'tiviti], s. nativité f.

Nato ['neitou], s. Mil: l'Otan m.

natter ['nætər]. F: **I.** s. **to have a n.,** discuter le coup. **II.** v.i. bavarder.

natty ['næti], a. (a) (of pers., dress) pimpant, coquet; (b) (of gadget, etc.) bien imaginé.

natural ['nætʃərəl], a. naturel. **1. n. history,** histoire naturelle; **n. law,** loi naturelle; **n. size,** grandeur f nature. **2.** (a) natif, inné; (b) **it's n. he should go away,** il est (bien) naturel qu'il s'en aille; **as is n.,** comme de raison; **-ally,** adv. naturellement; **it comes n. to him,** c'est un don chez lui; **'naturalist,** s. naturaliste mf; **naturali'zation,** s. naturalisation f (d'un étranger); acclimatation f (d'une plante); **'naturalize,** v.tr. naturaliser (un étranger); acclimater (une plante, un animal); **'naturalness,** s. **1.** caractère naturel. **2.** naturel m; absence f d'affectation.

nature ['neitʃər], s. nature f. **1.** (a) (of thg) essence f, caractère m; **it is in the n. of things that . . .,** il est dans l'ordre des choses que . . .; (b) (of pers.) naturel m, caractère; **it is not in his n. to . . .,** il n'est pas de sa nature de . . .; **by n.,** par tempérament; naturellement. **2.** espèce f, sorte f, genre m; **something of that n.,** quelque chose de la sorte. **3.** (a) (la) nature; **n. study,** histoire naturelle; (b) **human n.,** la nature humaine.

naught [nɔːt], s. **1.** rien m, néant m; **to bring sth. to n.,** faire échouer qch. **2.** Mth: zéro m.

naughty ['nɔːti], a. (of child) vilain, méchant; **-ily,** adv. **to behave n.,** ne pas être sage; **'naughtiness,** s. mauvaise conduite (d'un enfant).

nausea ['nɔːziə], s. **1.** nausée f. **2.** F: dégoût m, nausée, écœurement m; **'nauseate,** v.tr. écœurer, dégoûter (qn); **'nauseating,** a. écœurant, dégoûtant.

nautical ['nɔːtik(ə)l], a. nautique, marin.

naval ['neiv(ə)l], a. naval; **n. engagement,** combat sur mer; **n. base,** base navale, port m de guerre; **n. officer,** officier m de marine; **n. college,** école navale.

nave [neiv], s. nef f (d'église).

navel ['neiv(ə)l], s. Anat: nombril m.

navigate ['nævigeit], v.tr. & i. Nau: Av: naviguer; **naviga'bility,** s. navigabilité f; **'navigable,** a. (fleuve) navigable; **navi'gation,** s. navigation f; **radio n.,** navigation pa radio; **n. officer,** officier de navigation; **'navigator,** s. navigateur m.

navvy ['nævi], s. terrassier m.

navy ['neivi], s. **1.** marine f de guerre; **the Royal N.** = la Marine nationale; **merchant n.,** marin marchande. **2. n. (blue),** bleu marine inv.

Nazi ['nɑːtsi], a. & s. nazi, -ie.

neap [niːp], a. & s. **n. (tide),** morte-eau f, p mortes-eaux; **marée f de quadrature.**

Neapolitan [niə'pɔlitən], a. & s. napolitai -aine; **N. ice-cream,** tranche napolitaine.

near ['niər]. **I.** adv. **1.** (a) près, proche; **to com n., draw n., to s.o., sth.,** s'approcher de q qch.; **n. at hand,** à proximité, tout près; (b **those n. and dear to him,** ceux qui le touche de près. **2. as n. as I can remember,** autant qu je puisse m'en souvenir; **I came n. to cryin** j'étais sur le point de pleurer. **II.** prep. **1.** pr de, auprès de; **bring your chair near(er) th fire,** (r)approchez votre chaise du feu. **2.** death, près de mourir; **to be n. the end,** touch à sa fin; **he came n. being run over,** il a fai être écrasé. **III.** a. **1.** (ami) intime, cher; **our relations,** nos proches (parents). **2.** Aut: **the side,** (in Eng.) le côté gauche, (in Fr., N.Am etc.) le côté droit. **3. the nearest hotel,** l'hôtel plus proche; **the hour is n.,** l'heure est proch **to the nearest metre,** à un mètre près. **4. to g by the nearest road,** prendre par le plus cou **5. it was a n. thing,** nous l'avons échappé bell P: il était moins cinq. **IV.** v.tr. (s')approcher (qch.); **the road is nearing completion,** la rou est presque terminée; **to be nearing one's go** toucher au but; **-ly,** adv. **1.** (de) près; **to resen ble s.o. n.,** ressembler beaucoup à qn. **2.** presque, à peu près, près de; **it's n. midnight** est bientôt minuit; **very n.,** peu s'en faut; **I fell,** j'ai failli tomber; (b) **she's not n. so pre as her sister,** elle est loin d'être aussi jolie q sa sœur; **'nearby,** a. voisin, proche; **near b** adv. tout près; tout proche; **'nearness,** proximité f.

neat [niːt], a. **1.** (of spirits) pur; sans eau;

whisky, whisky sec. 2. (*a*) simple et de bon goût; (*of room*) bien rangé, en ordre; **n. handwriting**, écriture nette; **as n. as a new pin**, tiré à quatre épingles; (*b*) (*of phrase*) bien tourné. 3. (*of pers.*) ordonné; qui a de l'ordre; **-ly**, *adv*. 1. avec ordre; **n. dressed**, habillé avec soin. 2. adroitement; **n. turned**, (compliment, etc.) bien tourné; **'neatness**, *s*. 1. simplicité *f*, bon goût (dans la mise); apparence soignée (d'un jardin); netteté *f* (d'écriture); bon ordre (d'un tiroir). 2. (*of pers.*) (*a*) ordre *m*; (*b*) adresse *f*, dextérité *f*.

nebulous ['nebjulǝs], *s*. nébuleux.

necessary ['nesǝsǝri]. 1. *a*. (*a*) nécessaire, indispensable (**to, for, à**); **it is n. to do it**, il est nécessaire de le faire, il faut le faire; **to make all n.** arrangements, prendre toutes dispositions utiles; **if n.**, s'il le faut; s'il y a lieu; au besoin; **to do no more than is strictly n.**, ne faire que le strict nécessaire; (*b*) (résultat) inévitable. 2. *s*. (*a*) **to go without necessaries**, se refuser le nécessaire; (*b*) *F*: **to do the n.**, faire le nécessaire; payer la note; **the n.**, de l'argent; **-ily**, *adv*. nécessairement; de (toute) nécessité; forcément; **ne'cessitate**, *v.tr*. nécessiter (qch.); rendre (qch.) nécessaire; **ne'cessity**, *s*. 1. (*a*) nécessité *f*, obligation *f*, contrainte *f*; **of n.**, de (toute) nécessité, nécessairement; **case of absolute n.**, cas de force majeure; (*b*) besoin *m*; **there's no n. for you to come**, vous n'avez pas besoin de venir. 2. **bare necessities**, le strict nécessaire; **for me a car is a n.**, une voiture m'est indispensable. 3. nécessité, indigence *f*.

neck [nek]. I. *s*. 1. (*a*) cou *m*; **to have a stiff n.**, avoir un, le, torticolis; **to be up to one's n. in work**, avoir du travail par-dessus la tête; **to throw one's arms round s.o.'s n.**, se jeter au cou de qn; *F*: **to breathe down s.o.'s n.**, talonner qn; *Rac*: **to win by a n.**, gagner par une encolure; **to finish n. and n.**, arriver à égalité; *F*: **n. and crop**, tout entier; à corps perdu; **it's n. or nothing**, il faut jouer le tout pour le tout; **he's a pain in the n.**, c'est un casse-pieds; (*b*) *Cu*: collet *m* (de mouton); (*c*) encolure *f* (de robe); **low n.**, décolleté *m*. 2. (*a*) goulot *m* (de bouteille); (*b*) langue *f* (de terre). II. *v.i. F*: se bécoter; **'necklace**, *s*. collier *m* (de diamants, etc.); **'necklet**, *s*. collier *m* (de perles, de fourrure, etc.); **'necktie**, *s*. cravate *f*.

necromancy ['nekrǝmænsi], *s*. nécromancie *f*.

nectar ['nektǝr], *s*. nectar *m*.

nectarine ['nektǝri(:)n], *s*. brugnon *m*.

need [ni:d]. I. *s*. 1. besoin *m*; (*a*) **if n. be, in case of n.**, en cas de besoin, au besoin; si besoin est; **there's no n. to go there**, il n'est pas nécessaire, il n'est pas besoin, d'y aller; **what n. is there to send for him?** à quoi bon le faire venir? **no n. to say that . . .**, inutile de dire que . . .; (*b*) **to have n., be in n., of sth.**, avoir besoin de qch.; **I**

have no n. of your help, je n'ai que faire de votre aide. 2. (*a*) adversité *f*; embarras *m*; **in times of n.**, aux moments difficiles; (*b*) besoin, indigence *f*; **to be in n.**, être dans le besoin. 3. **to supply s.o.'s needs**, pourvoir aux besoins de qn. II. *v*. 1. *v.tr*. (*a*) avoir besoin de (qn, qch.); (*of thg*) réclamer, exiger, demander (qch.); **this needs explaining**, ceci demande à être expliqué; **to n. a lot of asking**, se faire prier; (*b*) **to n. to do sth.**, être obligé, avoir besoin, de faire qch.; **they n. to be told everything**, il faut qu'on leur dise tout; **you only needed to ask**, vous n'aviez qu'à demander. 2. *modal aux*. **n. he go?** a-t-il besoin, est-il obligé, d'y aller? **he needn't go**, **n. he?** il n'est pas tenu d'y aller, n'est-ce pas? **you needn't wait**, inutile d'attendre; **I n. hardly tell you . . .**, point n'est besoin de vous dire . . .; **why n. he do it?** qu'a-t-il besoin de le faire? **'needful**, *a*. nécessaire (**to, for, à, pour**); *s. F*: **to do the n.**, faire le nécessaire; **'needless**, *a*. inutile, peu nécessaire, superflu; **she's very pleased n. to say**, il va sans dire qu'elle est très contente; **needs**, *adv*. **if n. must**, s'il le faut; **'needy**, *a*. nécessiteux.

needle ['ni:dl], *s*. aiguille *f*; **knitting n.**, aiguille à tricoter; *Med*: **hypodermic n.**, aiguille hypodermique; **'needlewoman**, *s*. **she's a good n.**, elle travaille adroitement à l'aiguille; **'needlework**, *s*. travaux *mpl* à l'aiguille; **bring your n.**, apportez votre ouvrage.

ne'er-do-well ['nɛǝdu:wel], *a*. & *s*. propre à rien (*mf*).

negative ['negǝtiv]. I. *a*. négatif. II. *s*. 1. négative *f*; *Gram*: négation *f*. 2. *Phot*: négatif *m*, cliché *m*. III. *v.tr*. 1. s'opposer à, rejeter (un projet). 2. contredire, nier (un rapport); **-ly**, *adv*. négativement; **ne'gation**, *s*. négation *f*.

neglect [ni'glekt]. I. *s*. 1. (*a*) manque *m* d'égards (**of, envers, pour**); (*b*) manque de soin(s); (*c*) mauvais entretien (d'une machine). 2. négligence *f*, inattention *f*; **from n.**, par négligence. II. *v.tr*. 1. (*a*) manquer d'égards envers (qn); (*b*) manquer de soins pour (qn); ne prendre aucun soin de (ses enfants). 2. négliger, oublier (ses devoirs); **to n. an opportunity**, laisser échapper une occasion; **to n. to do sth.**, négliger, omettre, de faire qch.; **ne'glected**, *a*. (*of appearance*) négligé; **n. garden**, jardin mal tenu, à l'abandon; **ne'glectful**, *a*. négligent.

negligence ['neglidʒǝns], *s*. négligence *f*, incurie *f*; **through n.**, par négligence; **'negligent**, *a*. 1. négligent. 2. (air, ton) nonchalant, insouciant; **-ly**, *adv*. négligemment; avec négligence; **'negligible**, *a*. négligeable.

negotiate [ni'gouʃieit]. 1. *v.tr*. (*a*) négocier (un emprunt, un traité, etc.); (*b*) *Aut*: **to n. a bend**, prendre un virage. 2. *v.i*. **to n. for peace**, entreprendre des pourparlers de paix; **they refuse to n.**, ils refusent de négocier; **ne'gotiable,** a. 1. *Fin:* (effet) négociable. 2. (barrière) franchissable; (chemin) praticable; **negoti'a-tion,** s. 1. négociation f (d'un emprunt, etc.); **price subject to n.**, prix à débattre; **to start negotiations**, engager des négociations (avec qn). 2. franchissement m (d'un obstacle); prise f (d'un virage); **ne'gotiator,** s. négociateur, -trice.

negro, pl. **-oes** ['niːgrou, -ouz], a. & s. nègre (m), noir (m); **n. race,** race nègre, noire; **'negress,** s.f. négresse, noire.

neigh [nei]. I. s. hennissement m. II. v.i. hennir; **'neighing,** s. hennissement m.

neighbour ['neibər], s. voisin, -ine; **'neighbourhood,** s. 1. voisinage m; **to live in the n. of . . .**, habiter à proximité de . . .; *F:* **something in the n. of £10**, environ dix livres. 2. (a) alentours mpl, environs mpl (d'un lieu); (b) voisinage, quartier m; **'neighbouring,** a. avoisinant, voisin; proche; **'neighbourly,** a. **in a n. fashion**, en bon voisin, amicalement.

neither ['naiðər, 'niːðər]. 1. adv. & conj. (a) **he will n. eat nor drink**, il ne veut ni boire ni manger; **n. here nor anywhere else**, ni ici ni ailleurs; (b) non plus; **if you don't go n. shall I**, si vous n'y allez pas, je n'irai pas non plus; (c) **n. does it seem that . . .**, il ne semble pas non plus que . . . 2. a. & pron. ni l'un(e) ni l'autre; aucun(e); **n. (of them) knows**, ils ne le savent ni l'un ni l'autre; **on n. side**, ni d'un côté ni de l'autre.

neolithic [niːou'liθik], a. & s. **the n. (age)**, l'époque f néolithique, le néolithique.

neon ['niːɔn], s. néon m; **n. sign**, enseigne f au néon.

nephew ['nevjuː, 'nef-], s. neveu m.

nerve [nəːv]. I. s. 1. (a) *Anat:* nerf m; **to be in a state of nerves**, être énervé; **to get on s.o.'s nerves**, porter, donner, sur les nerfs de qn; *Med:* **n. specialist**, neurologue mf; (b) courage m, assurance f; **to lose one's n.**, perdre son sang-froid; (c) *F:* audace f, aplomb m; **you've got a n.!** tu en as un toupet! 2. **to strain every n. to do sth.**, déployer tous ses efforts pour faire qch. II. v.tr. **to n. oneself to do sth.**, s'armer de courage pour faire qch.; **'nervelessness,** s. inertie f; manque m de force, d'énergie; **'nerve-racking,** a. énervant, horripilant; **'nervous,** a. 1. *Anat:* **the n. system**, le système nerveux. 2. (of pers.) (a) excitable, irritable; (b) inquiet; (c) timide, peureux; **it makes me n.**, cela m'intimide; **-ly,** adv. (a) timidement; (b) craintivement; **'nervousness,** s. (a) nervosité f, état nerveux; (b) timidité f; **'nervy,** a. *F:* énervé, irritable; **she's n. today**, elle est nerveuse aujourd'hui.

nest [nest]. I. s. 1. (a) nid m; (b) repaire m, nid (de brigands). 2. (nestful) nichée f (d'oiseaux). 3. **n. of tables**, table f gigogne. II. v.i. (se) nicher; faire son nid; **'nest-egg,** s. 1. nichet m; œuf m en faïence. 2. argent mis de côté.

nestle [nesl], v.i. se nicher; se blottir (dans un fauteuil); **to n. close (up) to s.o.**, se serrer contre qn; **'nestling,** s. oisillon m; petit oiseau.

net¹ [net]. I. s. filet m; **butterfly n.**, filet à papillons. II. v.tr. (netted) prendre (des poissons, etc.) au filet; **'netting,** s. **wire n.**, treillis m métallique; **'network,** s. réseau m (routier, etc.).

net², a. (of price, weight) net; **n. profit**, bénéfice net; **terms strictly n. cash**, sans déduction; payable au comptant.

nether ['neðər], a. inférieur, bas; **'Netherlands (the).** *Pr.n.pl.* les Pays-Bas m; **'nethermost,** a. le plus bas; le plus profond.

nettle ['netl]. I. s. *Bot:* ortie f; **stinging n.**, ortie brûlante. II. v.tr. piquer, irriter (qn); **'nettlerash,** s. *Med:* urticaire f.

neuralgia [njuə'rældʒə], s. *Med:* névralgie f.

neuritis [njuə'raitis], s. *Med:* névrite f.

neurology [njuə'rɔlədʒi], s. *Med:* neurologie f; **neu'rologist,** s. neurologue mf.

neurosis, pl. **-ses** [njuə'rousis, -siːz], s. *Med:* névrose f; **neurotic** [njuə'rɔtik], a. & s. névrosé, -ée; neurotique.

neuter ['njuːtər]. I. a. & s. (a) *Gram:* neutre (m); (b) animal châtré. II. v.tr. châtrer (un chat, etc.); **'neutral,** a. & s. neutre (m); **to remain n.**, rester neutre, garder la neutralité; *Aut:* **in n.**, au point mort; **neu'trality,** s. neutralité f; **'neutralize,** v.tr. neutraliser.

never ['nevər], adv. (a) (ne . . .) jamais; **I n. go there**, je n'y vais jamais; **he n. came back**, il n'est plus revenu; **I shall n. forget it**, jamais je ne l'oublierai; **n. in (all) my life**, jamais de la vie; (b) (emphatic) **I n. expected him to come**, je ne m'attendais aucunement à ce qu'il vînt; **he n. said a word about it**, il n'en a pas dit le moindre mot; *F:* **well I n.!** par exemple! c'est formidable! (c) **n. mind!** ne vous en faites pas; **'never-'ending,** a. perpétuel, éternel; qu'en finit plus; **'never-'never,** s. *F:* **to buy sth. on the n.-n.**, acheter qch. à crédit, à tempérament; **neverthe'less,** adv. néanmoins, quand même, toutefois, pourtant; **'never-to-be-for'gotten,** a. inoubliable.

new [njuː], a. 1. (a) nouveau; **n. ideas**, idées nouvelles, idées neuves; **n. ground**, terre vierge; **that has made a n. man of him**, cela a fait de lui un autre homme; (for torch, etc.) **n. battery**, pile f de rechange; *Sch:* **the n. boys**, les nouveaux; (b) (of pers.) **to be n. to business**, être nouveau, neuf, dans les affaires. 2. neuf, non usagé; *Com:* **as n.**, à l'état (de) neuf; **to make sth. like n.**, remettre qch. à neuf; **the subject is quite n.**, ce sujet est neuf. 3. (pain) frais (vin) nouveau, jeune; **n. potatoes,** pommes de terre nouvelles; **-ly,** *adv.* récemment, nouvellement; **n.-elected members,** nouveaux élus; **n.-painted wall,** mur fraîchement peint; **n.-married couple, n.-weds,** nouveaux mariés; **'newborn,** *a.* nouveau-né; **n. babies,** (enfants) nouveau-nés *(mpl);* **'New 'Brunswick.** *Pr.n. Geog:* le Nouveau-Brunswick; **'newcomer,** *s.* nouveau venu, nouvelle venue; **'New 'England.** *Pr.n. Geog:* la Nouvelle-Angleterre; **'new 'fangled,** *a.* d'une modernité outrée; **Newfoundland** ['nju:fəndlænd]. **1.** *Pr.n. Geog:* Terre-Neuve *f.* **2.** *s. (dog)* terre-neuve *m inv;* **'Newfoundlander,** *s.* Terre-neuvien, -ienne; **'New 'Guinea.** *Pr.n. Geog:* la Nouvelle-Guinée; **'new-'laid,** *a.* (œuf) du jour; **'newness,** *s.* **1.** *(a)* nouveauté *f* (d'une mode); *(b)* inexpérience *f* (d'un employé). **2.** état neuf (d'un objet); **'New Or'leans.** *Pr.n. Geog:* la Nouvelle-Orléans; **'New South 'Wales.** *Pr.n. Geog:* la Nouvelle-Galles du Sud; *attrib.* néo-gallois; **'New 'Year,** *s.* le nouvel an; la nouvelle année; **N.Y.'s Day,** le jour de l'an; **N.Y.'s Eve,** la Saint-Sylvestre; **to wish s.o. a happy N.Y.,** souhaiter la bonne année à qn; **'New 'York.** *Pr.n. Geog:* New York; *attrib.* new-yorkais; **'New 'Yorker,** *s.* New-yorkais, -aise; **'New 'Zealand.** *Pr.n. Geog:* la Nouvelle-Zélande; *attrib.* néo-zélandais; **'New 'Zealander,** *s.* Néo-Zélandais, -aise.

news [nju:z], *s.* **1.** nouvelle(s) *f(pl);* **what (is the) n.?** quelles nouvelles? **a sad piece of n.,** une triste, fâcheuse, nouvelle; **to break the n. to s.o.,** faire part d'une mauvaise nouvelle à qn; **no n. is good n.,** pas de nouvelles, bonnes nouvelles. **2.** *Rad: T.V:* **n. (bulletin),** informations *fpl,* journal parlé; **'newsagent,** *s.* marchand *m* de journaux; **'newscast,** *s. T.V:* bulletin *m* d'informations; **'newscaster,** *s. T.V:* speaker *m,* speakerine *f;* **'newspaper,** *s.* journal *m;* **n. man,** (i) marchand *m* de journaux; (ii) journaliste *m;* **'newsprint,** *s.* papier *m* journal; **'newsreel,** *s. Cin:* actualités *fpl;* **'news-stand,** *s.* kiosque *m* à journaux.

newt [nju:t], *s.* triton *m;* salamandre *f* aquatique.

next [nekst]. **I.** *a.* **1.** *(of place)* prochain; le plus proche; **the n. room,** la chambre voisine; **her room is n. to mine,** sa chambre est à côté de la mienne; **sitting n. to me,** assis à côté de moi. **2.** *(a) (of time)* prochain, suivant; **the n. day,** le lendemain; **the n. day but one,** le sur-lendemain; **the n. moment,** l'instant d'après; **n. year,** l'année prochaine; **by this time n. year,** dans un an d'ici; *(b)* **the n. chapter,** le chapitre suivant; **the n. time I see him,** la prochaine fois que je le reverrai; **the n. size** *(in shoes),* la pointure au-dessus; *F:* **what n.!** par exemple! **who's n.?** à qui le tour? *(c)* **the n. best thing would be**

to. . ., à défaut de cela le mieux serait de. . .; **I got it for n. to nothing,** je l'ai eu pour presque rien. **II.** *adv.* **1.** ensuite, après; **what shall we do n.?** qu'est-ce que nous allons faire maintenant, après cela? **2. when you are n. that way,** la prochaine fois que vous passerez par là; **when I n. saw him,** quand je l'ai revu. **III.** *prep.* **n. to,** auprès de, à côté de (qn, qch.); **'next 'door,** *adv. & a.* he lives **n. d.,** il habite à côté; **it's n. d. to madness,** cela frise, avoisine, la folie, **the people n. d., the n. d. neighbours,** les gens, les voisins, d'à côté.

nib [nib], *s.* (bec *m* de) plume *f.*

nibble ['nibl]. **I.** *s.* *(a)* grignotement; *(b)* *Fish:* touche *f.* **II.** *v.tr. & i.* grignoter; mordiller (qch.); *(of fish, F: of pers.)* **to n. (at the bait),** mordre à l'hameçon.

nice [nais], *a.* **1. n. distinction,** distinction délicate. **2.** *(a) (of pers.)* gentil; sympathique; **he was as n. as could be,** il s'est montré aimable au possible; **to be n. to s.o.,** se montrer gentil, aimable, avec qn; *(b) (of thg)* joli, bon; **a n. dress,** une jolie robe; **n. dinner,** bon dîner; **it's n. here,** il fait bon ici; *(c) (intensive)* **it's n. and cool,** le temps est d'une fraîcheur agréable; **n. and sweet,** bien sucré; *(d)* **n. people,** des gens bien; **not n.,** pas tout à fait convenable; *(e)* **this is a n. mess we're in!** nous voilà dans de beaux draps! **a n. way to behave!** une jolie conduite! **that will do n.,** cela fera très bien l'affaire; **he's getting on n.,** (i) *(of invalid)* il fait du progrès; (ii) ses affaires ne marchent pas mal; **'niceness,** *s.* gentillesse *f* (de qn); **'nicety,** *s.* **1. to a n.,** exactement, à la perfection, à merveille. **2.** *pl.* **niceties,** minuties *f,* finesses *f* (d'un métier).

niche [nitʃ, ni:ʃ], *s.* niche *f.*

Nicholas ['nikələs]. *Pr.n.m.* Nicolas; **Nick[1].** *Pr.n.m.* Nicolas; *F:* **Old N.,** le diable.

nick[2] [nik]. **I.** *s.* **1.** entaille *f,* encoche *f,* cran *m.* **2. in the n. of time,** à point nommé; juste à temps. **II.** *v.tr.* **1.** entailler, encocher. **2.** *F: (a)* arrêter; **to get nicked,** se faire pincer; *(b)* **to n. sth.,** chiper qch.

nickel ['nikl]. **I.** *s.* **1.** nickel *m.* **2.** *N.Am:* pièce *f* de cinq cents. **II.** *v.tr.* **(nickelled)** nickeler (qch.).

nickname ['nikneim]. **I.** *s.* surnom *m;* sobriquet *m.* **II.** *v.tr.* surnommer (qn).

nicotine [nikə'ti:n], *s.* nicotine *f.*

niece [ni:s], *s.* nièce *f.*

Niger ['naidʒər]. *Pr.n. Geog:* **the N. Republic,** la République du Niger.

Nigeria [nai'dʒiəriə]. *Pr.n. Geog:* le Nigeria.

niggardly ['nigədli], *a. (of pers.)* chiche, pingre; *(of sum, etc.)* mesquin.

nigger ['nigər], *a. & s. P: Pej:* nègre *(m); (colour)* **n. (brown),** tête-de-nègre *inv.*

niggle ['nigl], *v.i.* vétiller, tatillonner; **'niggler,**

s. (*of pers.*) tatillon, -onne; '**niggling**, *a.* (*of work*) fignolé; **n. details**, détails insignifiants.

night [nait], *s.* 1. (*a*) nuit *f*, soir *m*; **last n.**, hier soir; **the n. before**, la veille (au soir); **tomorrow n.**, demain soir; **ten o'clock at n.**, dix heures du soir; **good n.!** bonsoir! (*when retiring*) bonne nuit! **at n.**, la nuit; **in the n.**, (pendant) la nuit; **by n.**, de nuit; **n. watchman**, gardien *m* de nuit; **n. shift**, équipe *f* de nuit; **to be on n. shift**, *F:* **on nights**, être de nuit; **n. nurse**, infirmière *f* de nuit; (*b*) *Th:* **first n.**, première *f.* 2. obscurité *f*, ténèbres *fpl*; **n. is falling**, il commence à faire nuit, la nuit tombe; **n. driving is dangerous**, conduire la nuit est dangereux; '**nightcap**, *s.* boisson (alcoolique) (prise avant de se coucher); '**nightclothes**, *s.pl.* vêtements *m* de nuit; '**nightclub**, *s.* boîte *f* de nuit; '**night-dress**, *s.* chemise *f* de nuit; '**nightfall**, *s.* tombée *f* du jour, de la nuit; **at n.**, à la nuit tombante; '**nightie**, *s.* *F:* chemise *f* de nuit; '**nightingale**, *s.* *Orn:* rossignol *m*; '**nightjar**, *s.* *Orn:* engoulevent *m*; '**nightlight**, *s.* veilleuse *f*; '**nightly**. 1. *a.* (de) tous les soirs. 2. *adv.* tous les soirs, toutes les nuits; '**night-mare**, *s.* cauchemar *m*; '**nightshade**, *s.* *Bot:* **woody n.**, douce-amère *f*; **deadly n.**, belladone *f*; '**nightshirt**, *s.* chemise *f* de nuit (d'homme); '**night-time**, *s.* la nuit.

nil [nil], *s.* rien *m*; néant *m*; zéro *m*.

Nile (the) [ðə'nail]. *Pr.n. Geog:* le Nil.

nimble ['nimbl], *a.* (*of pers.*) agile, leste, preste; (*of mind*) délié, prompt; (*of old pers.*) **still n.**, encore ingambe, alerte; **-bly**, *adv.* agilement; lestement, prestement; '**nimble-'footed**, *a.* aux pieds agiles; '**nimble-'witted**, *a.* à l'esprit délié.

nincompoop ['niŋkəmpu:p], *s.* benêt *m*, nigaud *m*, niais *m*.

nine [nain], *num.a. & s.* neuf (*m*); **n. times out of ten**, neuf fois sur dix; en général; **to be dressed up to the nines**, être sur son trente et un; '**ninepins**, *s.pl.* (jeu *m* de) quilles *fpl*; *F:* **to go down like n.**, tomber comme des capucins de cartes, comme des quilles; **nine'teen**, *num.a. & s.* dix-neuf (*m*); **nine'teenth**, *num.a. & s.* dix-neuvième (*mf*); '**ninety**, *num.a. & s.* quatre-vingt-dix (*m*); **n.-one**, quatre-vingt-onze; **ninth**, *num.a. & s.* neuvième (*mf*).

nip [nip]. I. *s.* 1. pincement *m*; **to give s.o. a n.**, pincer qn. 2. morsure *f* (du froid); **there was a n. in the air**, l'air piquait. II. *v.* (**nipped**) 1. *v.tr.* (*a*) pincer; (*b*) to n. (sth.) **in the bud**, étouffer (qch.) dans l'œuf; (*c*) (*of cold*) pincer, piquer, mordre; brûler (les bourgeons). 2. *v.i.* *F:* **just n. round to the baker's**, cours vite chez le boulanger; '**nipper**, *s.* *F:* gamin *m*, gosse *m*; '**nippy**, *a.* *F:* 1. alerte, vif; **tell him to look n.**, dis-lui de se grouiller. 2. (vent) âpre.

nipple [nipl], *s.* *Anat:* mamelon *m*, bout *m* de sein.

nitrogen ['naitrədʒən], *s.* azote *m*; '**nitrate**, *s.* nitrate *m*; '**nitric**, *a.* **n. acid**, acide *m* nitrique; *Com:* eau-forte *f*; '**nitrous**, *a.* nitreux, azoteux.

nitwit ['nitwit], *s.* *F:* imbécile *mf*; andouille *f.*

no [nou]. I. *a.* 1. nul, pas de, point de, aucun; **to have no heart**, n'avoir pas de cœur; **he made no reply**, il ne fit aucune réponse; **it's no distance**, ce n'est pas loin; **no two men are alike**, il n'y a pas deux hommes qui se ressemblent; **of no interest**, sans intérêt; **no-man's land**, (i) terrains *m* vagues; (ii) *Mil:* no man's land *m*; **no surrender!** on ne se rend pas! **no nonsense!** pas de bêtises! **no admittance**, entrée interdite; **no smoking**, défense de fumer. 2. peu; **ne . . .** pas (du tout); (*a*) **it's no easy job**, ce n'est pas une tâche facile; (*b*) **he is no artist**, il n'est pas artiste; (*c*) **there's no pleasing him**, il n'y a pas moyen de le satisfaire; **there's no getting out of it**, impossible de s'en tirer. 3. **no one** = NOBODY 1. II. *adv.* 1. **whether or no**, que cela soit ou non; dans tous les cas. 2. **I'm no richer than he is**, je ne suis pas plus riche que lui; **he is no longer here**, il n'est plus ici. III. 1. *adv.* non; **have you seen him?—no**, l'avez-vous vu?—non; **no, no, you're mistaken**, mais non, vous vous trompez! 2. *s.* non *m inv*; **I won't take no for an answer**, je n'admettrai pas de refus; (*in voting*) **ayes and noes**, voix *[...]* pour et contre.

noble ['noubl], *a. & s.* noble (*m*); **-bly**, *adv.* (*a*) noblement; (*b*) magnifiquement; superbement *[...]*; **no'bility**, *s.* noblesse *f*; '**nobleman**, *pl.* -**men** *s.* noble *m*; gentilhomme *m*.

nobody ['noubədi]. 1. *pron.* personne *m*; nul *m*; aucun *m*; **who's there?—n.**, qui est là?—personne; **n. is perfect**, nul n'est parfait; **n. spoke to me**, personne ne m'a parlé; **there was n. else on board**, personne d'autre n'était à bord; **there was n. about**, il n'y avait pas âme qui vive. 2. *s.* (*of pers.*) nullité *f*, zéro *m*; **when he was still a n.**, quand il était encore inconnu.

nocturnal [nɔk'tə:n(ə)l], *a.* (oiseau, etc.) nocturne.

nod [nɔd]. I. *s.* inclination *f* de la tête; (*a*) signe *n* de tête affirmatif; (*b*) **he gave me a n.**, il me fi*[t]* un petit signe de la tête (en guise de salut). I*[I.]* *v.tr. & i.* (**nodded**) 1. **to n.** (one's head), faire u*[n]* signe de tête; incliner la tête. 2. dodeliner de l*[a]* tête; somnoler, sommeiller; '**nodding**, *s.* in*[...]* clination *f* de tête; **to have a n. acquaintance** **with s.o.**, connaître qn vaguement.

node [noud], *s.* *Bot: etc:* nœud *m.*

noise [nɔiz], *s.* 1. bruit *m*, tapage *m*, vacarme *m* fracas *m*; **to make a n.**, faire du bruit, d*[u]* tapage; **to make a n. in the world**, faire parl*[er]* de soi; *P:* **the big n.**, le grand manitou (d'un*[e]* entreprise). 2. bruit, son *m*; *Rad:* (**backgroun***[d]* n., bruit de fond; **noises in the ears,** bourdonnement *m* dans les oreilles; **'noiseless,** *a.* sans bruit; silencieux; **-ly,** *adv.* silencieusement; sans bruit; **'noisy,** *a.* bruyant, tapageur; (enfant) turbulent; (*of street*) tumultueux; **to be n.,** faire du bruit, du tapage; **-ily,** *adv.* bruyamment; à grand bruit.

nomad ['noumæd], *a.* & *s.* nomade (*mf*); **no'madic,** *a.* nomade.

nomenclature [nə'meŋklətʃər], *s.* nomenclature *f.*

nominal ['nɔmin(ə)l], *a.* nominal; **to be the n. head,** n'être chef que de nom; **n. rent,** loyer purement nominal, insignifiant; **-ally,** nominalement; de nom.

nominate ['nɔmineit], *v.tr.* (*a*) nommer, choisir, désigner (qn à un emploi); (*b*) proposer, présenter (un candidat); **nomi'nation,** *s.* (*a*) nomination *f*; (*b*) présentation *f*, investiture *f* (d'un candidat); **'nominative,** *a.* & *s. Gram:* nominatif (*m*); **nomi'nee,** *s.* candidat, -ate, désigné(e), choisi(e).

non-aggression ['nɔnə'greʃən], *s.* non-agression *f.*

non-alcoholic ['nɔnælkə'hɔlik], *a.* non alcoolisé.

non-aligned ['nɔnə'laind], *a.* non aligné.

nonchalant ['nɔnʃələnt], *a.* nonchalant; indifférent; **-ly,** *adv.* nonchalamment; avec nonchalance; **'nonchalance,** *s.* nonchalance *f.*

non-combatant ['nɔn'kɔmbətənt], *a.* & *s.* non-combatant (*m*).

non-commissioned ['nɔnkə'miʃ(ə)nd], *a. Mil:* **n.-c. officer,** sous-officier *m*; gradé *m.*

noncommittal ['nɔnkə'mit(ə)l], *a.* qui n'engage à rien; (réponse *f*) diplomatique.

non-committed ['nɔnkə'mitid], *a.* non aligné.

non-conductor ['nɔnkən'dʌktər], *s.* non-conducteur *m*; (*of heat*) calorifuge *m*; (*of electricity*) isolant *m*; **'non-con'ducting,** *a.* non conducteur.

nonconformist ['nɔnkən'fɔ:mist], *a.* & *s. Ecc:* dissident, -ente.

nondescript ['nɔndiskript], *a.* indéfinissable, inclassable; (style) quelconque.

none [nʌn]. **1.** *pron.* (*a*) aucun; **n. at all,** pas un(e) seul(e); **n. of this concerns me,** rien de ceci ne me regarde; **I know n. of them,** je n'en connais aucun; **strawberries! there are n.,** des fraises! il n'y en a pas; **n. of your impudence!** pas d'insolences de votre part! (*b*) **he knew, n. better, that . . .,** il savait mieux que personne que . . .; (*c*) (*in forms, etc.*) néant *m.* **2.** *adv.* (*a*) **I like him n. the worse for it,** je ne l'en aime pas moins; (*b*) **he was n. too soon,** il arriva juste à temps.

nonentity [nɔn'entiti], *s.* personne insignifiante, de peu d'importance; non-valeur *f*; nullité *f.*

nonexistent ['nɔnig'zist(ə)nt], *a.* non existant;

inexistant.

non-fiction ['nɔn'fikʃən], *s.* littérature générale.

non-iron ['nɔn'aiən], *a.* (tissu) n'exigeant aucun repassage.

non-payment ['nɔn'peimənt], *s.* non-paiement *m*; défaut *m* de paiement.

nonplus ['nɔn'plʌs], *v.tr.* (**nonplussed**) embarrasser, interdire, interloquer (qn); **to be nonplussed,** être désemparé.

non-resident ['nɔn'rezid(ə)nt], *a.* & *s.* non-résident (*m*); (*hotel*) **open to non-residents,** repas servis aux voyageurs de passage.

non-returnable ['nɔnri'tə:nəbl], *a.* (emballage) perdu, non repris, non consigné.

nonsense ['nɔnsəns], *s.* **1.** non-sens *m.* **2.** absurdité *f*; **piece of n.,** bêtise *f*; **to talk n.,** dire des bêtises; **n.!** pas possible! à d'autres! **no n.!** pas de bêtises! **non'sensical,** *a.* absurde.

non-skid ['nɔn'skid], *a.* antidérapant.

non-smoker ['nɔn'smoukər], *s.* (*a*) (*of pers.*) non-fumeur *m*; (*b*) *Rail: Av:* siège, wagon, compartiment, etc., dans lequel il est interdit de fumer.

nonstop ['nɔn'stɔp]. **1.** *a.* (train) direct; *Av:* (vol) sans escale. **2.** *adv.* sans arrêt; (voler) sans escale; **to talk n.,** parler sans arrêt.

non-union ['nɔn'ju:niən], *a.* (ouvrier) non syndiqué.

non-violence ['nɔn'vaiələns], *s.* non-violence *f.*

noodles ['nu:dlz], *s.pl. Cu:* nouilles *f.*

nook [nuk], *s.* coin *m*; recoin *m*; **in every n. and cranny,** dans tous les coins et recoins.

noon [nu:n], *s.* midi *m*; **'noonday,** **the n. sun,** le soleil de midi.

noose [nu:s], *s.* nœud coulant; (*to catch rabbits*) lacet *m*, collet *m.*

nor [nɔ:r], *conj.* **1.** (ne, ni . . .) ni; **he has neither father n. mother,** il n'a ni père ni mère; **neither you n. I know,** ni vous ni moi ne le savons; **he shan't go, n. you either,** il n'ira pas, ni vous non plus. **2. n. does it seem that . . .,** il ne semble pas non plus que . . .; **n. was this all,** et ce n'était pas tout.

norm [nɔ:m], *s.* norme *f*; **'normal. 1.** *a.* normal, régulier, ordinaire. **2.** *s.* normale *f*; **temperature above (the) n.,** température au-dessus de la normale; **-ly,** *adv.* normalement; **nor'mality,** *s.* normalité *f.*

Normandy ['nɔ:məndi]. *Pr.n. Geog:* la Normandie; **'Norman,** *a.* & *s.* normand, -ande; **N. architecture,** l'architecture romane (anglaise).

Norse [nɔ:s] *s. Ling:* le norrois.

north [nɔ:θ]. **1.** *s.* nord *m*; **on the n., to the n. (of),** au nord (de); **in the n. of England,** dans le nord de l'Angleterre. **2.** *adv.* au nord; **to travel n.,** voyager vers le nord. **3.** *a.* nord *inv*; **the n. coast,** la côte nord; **n. wall,** mur exposé au nord; **n. wind,** vent du nord; **the N. Sea,** la mer du Nord; **the N. Pole,** le Pôle nord; **'North-**

'**African**, *a. & s.* nord-africain, -aine; '**North-A'merican**, *a. & s.* nord-américain, -aine; '**north-'east.** **1.** *s.* nord-est *m.* **2.** *a.* (du) nord-est *inv.* **3.** *adv.* vers le nord-est; '**north'eastern**, *a.* (du) nord-est; '**northerly** [-ð-], *a.* du nord; vers le nord; **n. wind**, vent *m* du nord; '**northern** [-ð-], *a.* (du) nord; septentrional; **N. Ireland**, l'Irlande *f* du Nord; **n. lights**, aurore boréale; '**northward**. **1.** *a.* au, du, nord. **2.** *s.* **to the n.** (**of**), au nord (de); '**northwards**, *adv.* vers le nord; '**north-'west. 1.** *s.* nord-ouest *m.* **2.** *a.* (du) nord-ouest *inv.* **3.** *adv.* vers le nord-ouest; '**north'western**, *a.* (du) nord-ouest.

Norway ['nɔːwei]. *Pr.n. Geog:* la Norvège; **Norwegian** [nɔː'wiːdʒən]. **1.** *a. & s.* norvégien, -ienne. **2.** *s. Ling:* le norvégien.

nose [nouz]. **I.** *s.* **1.** (*of pers., dog, etc.*) nez *m*; (*of many animals*) museau *m*; **to blow one's n.**, se moucher; **to hold one's n.**, se boucher le nez; **to speak through one's n.**, nasiller; parler du nez; **I did it under his very n.**, je l'ai fait à son nez; **to poke one's n. into sth.**, fourrer son nez dans qch.; **to lead s.o. by the n.**, mener qn par le bout du nez. **2.** odorat *m*; **to have a n. for sth.**, avoir du flair pour qch. **3.** nez (d'un avion, etc.); *Aut:* **n. to tail**, pare-choc à pare-choc. **II.** *v.* **1.** *v.tr.* (*of dog*) **to n. out the game**, flairer le gibier; *F:* **to n. sth. out**, découvrir (qch.); flairer (qch.). **2.** *v.i.* **to n. about**, (a)**round**, fureter, fouiner; '**nosebag**, *s.* musette *f* (de cheval); '**nosebleed**, *s.* **to have a n.**, saigner du nez; '**nosedive. I.** *s.* piqué *m*, descente *f* en piqué. **II.** *v.i.* descendre en piqué; piquer de l'avant; '**nosegay**, *s.* bouquet *m*; '**nosy**, *a.* curieux, fouinard; fureteur; **a n.** parker, un indiscret, un fouinard.

nostalgia [nɔs'tældʒ(i)ə], *s.* nostalgie *f*; **nos'talgic**, *a.* nostalgique.

nostril ['nɔstril], *s.* (*of pers.*) narine *f*; (*of horse*) naseau *m*.

not [nɔt], *adv.* (ne) pas, (ne) point. **1.** (*a*) **he will n., won't, come**, il ne viendra pas; **she is n., isn't, there**, elle n'est pas là; **you understand, do you n., don't you?** vous comprenez, n'est-ce pas? (*b*) **n. at all**, pas du tout; **I think n.**, je crois que non; **why n.?** pourquoi pas? **n. negotiable**, non négociable. **2. n. including**, sans compter; **he begged me n. to move**, il me pria de ne pas me déranger; *F:* **n. to worry!** ne vous en faites pas! (*of party, etc.*) **we can't n. go**, impossible de s'en tirer. **3. n. that . . .**, ce n'est pas que . . .; **n. that I'm afraid of him**, non (pas) que je le craigne. **4. I was n. sorry to leave**, j'étais bien content de partir; **n. without reason**, non sans raison. **5. n. a murmur was heard**, on n'entendait pas un murmure.

notable ['noutəbl], *a.* notable, insigne; (*of pers.*) éminent; -**ably**, *adv.* **1.** notablement, remarquablement. **2.** notamment, particulièrement.

notation [nou'teiʃ(ə)n], *s.* notation *f*.

notch [nɔtʃ]. **I.** *s.* (*a*) entaille *f*, encoche *f*, cran *m*; (*b*) brèche *f* (dans une lame, etc.). **II.** *v.tr.* (*a*) entailler, encocher (un bâton, etc.); (*b*) ébrécher (une lame).

note [nout]. **I.** *s.* **1.** (*a*) note *f* (de musique); (*b*) touche *f* (d'un piano); (*c*) note, son *m*; **to sing a wrong n.**, chanter faux. **2.** marque *f*, signe *m*, indice *m*. **3.** (*a*) note, mémorandum *m*; **to make a n. of sth.**, noter qch.; prendre note de qch.; (*b*) billet *m*; petite lettre. **4.** (*a*) *Com:* **n. of hand**, reconnaissance *f* (de dette); **advice n.**, note, lettre, d'avis; (*b*) (**bank**) **n.**, billet *m* (de banque). **5. to take n. of sth.**, remarquer qch. **II.** *v.tr.* **1.** noter, constater, remarquer, prendre note de (qch.); **it's worth noting that . . .**, il convient de remarquer que . . . **2. to n. sth.** (**down**), écrire, inscrire (qch.); '**notebook**, *s.* carnet *m*, calepin *m*; **bloc-notes** *m*; '**notecase**, *s.* porte-billets *m inv*, portefeuille *m*; '**noted**, *a.* (*of pers.*) distingué, éminent; (*of thg*) célèbre (**for** sth., par qch.); '**notepaper**, *s.* papier *m* à lettres; '**noteworthy**, *a.* remarquable; digne d'attention, de remarque.

nothing ['nʌθiŋ]. **I.** *s. or pron.* rien (**with ne** expressed or understood); (*a*) **n. could be simpler**, rien de plus simple; **to say n. of . . .**, sans parler de . . .; **there's n. in these rumours**, ces bruits sont sans fondement; **to be n. if not discreet**, être discret avant tout; **to create sth. out of n.**, créer qch. de toutes pièces; (*b*) **n. new**, rien de nouveau; **n. much**, pas grand-chose; **there's n. more to be said**, n'y a plus rien à dire; (*c*) **I have n. to do with it**, je n'y suis pour rien; **that's n. to do with you**, cela ne vous regarde pas; **there's n. to cry about**, il n'y a pas de quoi pleurer; **n. doing!** rien à faire! (*d*) **he is n. of a scholar**, ce n'es pas du tout un savant; **n. of the kind**, rien de la sorte; (*e*) **n. else**, rien d'autre; **n. but the truth** rien que la vérité; **he does n. but complain**, il n' fait que se plaindre; **there was n. for it but t wait**, il ne nous restait plus qu'à attendre; (*f* **all that goes for n.**, tout cela ne compte pas; **got n. out of it**, j'en suis pour mes frais; (*g*) **h is n. to me**, il m'est indifférent; **it's n. to m either way**, cela m'est égal; (*h*) **to think n.** **sth.**, ne faire aucun cas de qch. **II.** *s.* **1.** *Mth* zéro *m.* **2.** néant *m*; rien *m*; **to come to n.**, n pas aboutir; (*of hopes, etc.*) s'anéantir; **a hur dred francs? a mere n.!** cent francs? une m sère! **III.** *adv.* aucunement, nullement; pas d tout; **n. like as big**, loin d'être aussi grand; **n. less than madness**, c'est de la folie ni plus moins; **n. daunted**, nullement intimidé.

notice ['noutis]. **I.** *s.* **1.** (*a*) avis *m*, notification (*b*) avertissement *m*; **to give s.o. n. of st**

prévenir qn de qch.; **to do sth. without n.,** faire qch. sans en aviser personne; **public n.,** avis au public; **until further n.,** jusqu'à nouvel avis; (c) avis formel, instructions formelles; **to give s.o. n. to do sth.,** aviser qn de faire qch.; (d) **ready to leave at short n., at a moment's n.,** prêt à partir à l'instant; (e) **n. to quit,** congé m; **to give n. to an employee,** donner son congé à un employé; **to give n. (to one's employer),** donner sa démission. 2. (a) affiche f; indication f, avis (au public); (b) (in newspaper) annonce f. 3. **to take n. of sth.,** tenir compte, prendre connaissance, de qch.; **to take no n. of sth.,** ne prêter aucune attention à qch.; **to bring sth. to s.o.'s n.,** faire observer qch. à qn; **to attract n.,** se faire remarquer; F: **to sit up and take n.,** dresser l'oreille. II. v.tr. observer, remarquer, s'apercevoir de, tenir compte de (qn, qch.); **I have never noticed it,** je ne l'ai jamais remarqué; **'noticeable,** a. perceptible, sensible; **it's not n.,** cela ne se voit pas; **-ably,** adv. perceptiblement, sensiblement; **'notice-board,** s. tableau m d'affichage.

notify ['noutifai], v.tr. annoncer, notifier (qch.); déclarer (une naissance); **to n. s.o. of sth.,** avertir, aviser, qn de qch.; **to n. the police of sth.,** signaler qch. à la police; **notifi'cation,** s. avis m, notification f, annonce f; déclaration f (de naissance).

notion ['nouʃ(ə)n], s. (a) notion f, idée f; **to have no n. of sth.,** n'avoir aucune notion de qch.; (b) opinion f, pensée f; **I have a n. that . . .,** j'ai dans l'idée que . . ..

notorious [nou'tɔːriəs], a. d'une triste notoriété; (menteur) insigne; (malfaiteur) reconnu comme notoire; (endroit) mal famé; **-ly,** adv. notoirement; **n. cruel,** connu pour sa cruauté; **notoriety** [noutə'raiəti], s. notoriété f.

notwithstanding [notwiθ'stændiŋ, -wið-], prep. malgré, en dépit de; **n. any clause to the contrary,** nonobstant toute clause contraire.

nought [nɔːt], s. Mth: zéro m.

noun [naun], s. Gram: substantif m, nom m.

nourish ['nʌriʃ], v.tr. nourrir, alimenter (qn); **'nourishing,** a. nourrissant, nutritif; **'nourishment,** s. 1. alimentation f, nourriture f. 2. aliments mpl, nourriture.

Nova Scotia ['nouvə'skouʃə]. Pr.n. Geog: la Nouvelle-Écosse.

novel[1] ['nɔv(ə)l], s. roman m; **'novelist,** s. romancier, -ière.

novel[2], a. nouveau; original; **that's a n. idea!** voilà qui est original! **'novelty,** s. 1. chose nouvelle; innovation f; Com: (article m de) nouveauté f. 2. nouveauté (de qch.).

november [nou'vembər], s. novembre m; **in N.,** au mois de novembre; (on) **the fifth of N.,** le cinq novembre.

novice ['novis], s. novice mf; apprenti, -ie; débu-

tant, -ante.

now [nau]. I. adv. 1. maintenant; (a) en ce moment, actuellement, à l'heure actuelle; **n. or never!** allons-y! (b) **he won't be long n.,** il ne tardera plus guère; (c) **it's going to begin n.,** ça va commencer tout de suite; (d) (in narrative) alors; à ce moment-là; **all was n. ready,** dès lors tout était prêt; **I saw him just n.,** je l'ai vu il y a un instant; (e) (every) **n. and then,** de temps en temps; **n. . . . . n. . . . .,** tantôt . . . tantôt . . .; **even n.,** même à cette heure tardive. 2. (a) or; déjà; **n. it happened that . . .,** or il advint que . . .; **n. this was little enough but . . .,** c'était déjà peu mais . . .; (b) **n. what's all this about?** qu'avez-vous donc? **come n.!** voyons, voyons! **well n.!** eh bien! **n. then!** (i) attention! (ii) voyons! allons! II. conj. maintenant que, à présent que; **n. I'm older I think differently,** maintenant que je suis plus âgé je pense autrement. III. s. **in three days from n.,** d'ici trois jours; **between n. and then,** d'ici là; **by n.,** à l'heure qu'il est; **he ought to be here by n.,** il devrait déjà être arrivé; **until n., up to n.,** jusqu'à présent, jusqu'ici; **from n. (on),** désormais, à partir de maintenant; **nowadays,** adv. aujourd'hui; de nos jours; à l'heure actuelle.

nowhere ['nouwɛər], adv. nulle part; en aucun lieu; Rac: **to be n.,** arriver dans les choux; **it's n. near big enough,** ce n'est pas assez grand à beaucoup près, c'est loin d'être assez grand.

noxious ['nokʃəs], a. nuisible, nocif; malfaisant; (gaz m) délétère.

nozzle ['nozl], s. ajutage m; jet m, lance f (de tuyau); bec m, tuyau m (de soufflet); Av: injecteur m; Aut: gicleur m.

nucleus ['njuːkliəs], s. noyau m (de cellule, etc.); **'nuclear,** a. nucléaire; **n. power,** énergie f atomique; **n. submarine,** sous-marin m nucléaire; **n. reaction,** réaction f nucléaire.

nude [njuːd], a. & s. nu (m); **to paint n. figures,** peindre des nus; **to draw from the n.,** dessiner d'après le nu; **in the n.,** nu; **'nudism,** s. nudisme m; **'nudist,** s. nudiste mf; **'nudity,** s. nudité f.

nudge [nʌdʒ]. I. s. coup m de coude. II. v.tr. pousser (qn) du coude.

nugget ['nʌgit], s. pépite f (d'or).

nuisance ['njuːs(ə)ns], s. (a) peste f, fléau m; **he's a perfect n.,** il est assommant; **go away, you n.!** va-t'en, tu m'embêtes! (b) **that's a n.,** voilà qui est bien ennuyeux! **what a n.!** quel ennui!

null [nʌl], a. Jur: **n. and void,** nul et de nul effet, nul et non avenu; **'nullify,** v.tr. annuler, Jur: infirmer (un acte); **'nullity,** s. 1. nullité f. 2. (of pers.) non-valeur f; homme nul.

numb [nʌm]. I. a. engourdi. II. v.tr. engourdir; **numbed with terror,** glacé d'effroi; **'numbness,** s. engourdissement m; torpeur f (de l'esprit).

number ['nʌmbər]. I. s. 1. (a) Mth: nombre m; (b) **they were six in n.**, ils étaient au nombre de six; **without n.**, sans nombre; (c) **a (large) n. of men, numbers of men, came,** un grand nombre d'hommes sont venus, les hommes sont venus nombreux; **a great n. are of this opinion,** beaucoup de gens sont de cet avis; **a n. of people,** plusieurs personnes; **any n. of . . .,** un grand nombre de . . .; (d) **in small numbers,** en petit nombre; **to be overcome by numbers,** succomber sous le nombre; (e) **one of their n.,** (l')un d'entre eux. 2. chiffre m; **to write the n. on a page,** numéroter une page. 3. numéro m (d'une maison, etc.); **I live at n. forty,** je demeure au numéro quarante; Aut: **registration n.,** numéro d'immatriculation; F: **his n.'s up,** son affaire est faite. 4. Gram: nombre. 5. numéro (d'un journal). II. v.tr. 1. compter, dénombrer; **his days are numbered,** ses jours sont comptés. 2. numéroter (les maisons, etc.); **'numbering,** s. numérotage m; **n. machine, stamp,** numéroteur m; **'numberless,** a. innombrable; sans nombre.

numeral ['nju:mərəl]. 1. a. numéral. 2. s. chiffre m, nombre m; **nu'merical,** a. numérique; **-ally,** adv. numériquement; **'numerous,** a. nombreux.

numismatics [nju:miz'mætiks], s.pl. (usu. with sg. const.) la numismatique.

nun [nʌn], s. Ecc: religieuse f; F: (bonne) sœur; **'nunnery,** s. couvent m (de religieuses).

nuptial ['nʌpʃəl], a. nuptial.

nurse [nə:s]. I. s. (a) infirmière f; **male n.,** infirmier m; (b) **children's n.,** bonne f d'enfants. II. v.tr. 1. soigner (un malade); **to n. a cold,** soigner un rhume. 2. (a) allaiter (un enfant); (b) nourrir, entretenir (un chagrin, un espoir); cultiver (une plante); Pol: **to n. a constituency,** cultiver, soigner, les électeurs. 3. bercer (un enfant); tenir (qn, qch.) dans ses bras; **'nursemaid,** s. bonne f d'enfants; **'nursery,** s. 1. (a) chambre f des enfants; nursery f; **n. rhyme,** poème m, chanson f, pour les petits; **n. story,** conte m de nourrice; (b) **day n.,** crèche f; garderie f; **n. school,** (école f) maternelle (f), jardin m d'enfants. 2. Hort: pépinière f; **n. gardener,** pépiniériste mf; **'nurseryman,** s. pépiniériste m; **'nursing.** I. a. 1. **n. mother,** mère qui allaite son enfant. 2. (in hospital) **n. staff,** personnel m infirmier. II. s. (a) soins mpl (d'une garde-malade); (b) profession f d'infirmière; (c) **n. home,** (i) (for mental cases) maison f de santé; (ii) (for surgical cases) clinique f; hôpital privé.

nut [nʌt], s. 1. (a) noix f; **hazel n.,** noisette f, aveline f; **cashew n.,** noix d'acajou; F: **tough, hard, n. to crack,** (i) problème m difficile à résoudre; (ii) personne difficile, peu commode: F: **he can't sing for nuts,** il ne sait pas chanter du tout; (b) P: tête; **off one's n.,** timbré, toqué; **he's nuts,** il est cinglé. 2. écrou m; **wing n., butterfly n.,** écrou à oreilles, à ailettes; **'nutcrackers** s.pl. casse-noisettes m inv, casse-noix m inv **'nutmeg,** s. (noix f) muscade (f); **'nutshell,** s coquille f de noix; **in a n.,** en un mot, en deux mots.

nutrient ['nju:triənt], s. nourriture f; **nu'trition,** s. nutrition f; **nu'tritious,** a., **nutritive** a. nutritif, nourrissant.

nuzzle ['nʌzl], v.i. fourrer son nez (contre l'épaul de qn).

nylon ['nailɔn], s. Tex: nylon m; **n. stocking nylons,** bas mpl (de) nylon.

nymph [nimf], s. nymphe f.

O

O¹, o [ou], s. 1. (la lettre) O, o *m*. 2. (*nought*) zéro *m*; 3103 ['θri:wʌnou'θri:], = 31.03 [trãteœzerotrwa].

O², *int.* ô! oh!

oaf [ouf], s. lourdaud *m*, ours mal léché; **'oafish**, *a.* lourdaud, stupide.

oak [ouk], s. (*a*) o. (**tree**), chêne *m*; **o. apple**, noix *f* de galle; (*b*) (bois *m* de) chêne; **o. furniture**, meubles *mpl* de, en, chêne.

oakum ['oukəm], s. étoupe *f*, filasse *f*.

oar [ɔːr], s. (*a*) pagaie *f*, aviron *m*, rame *f*; *F:* **to rest on one's oars**, s'accorder un moment de répit; *F:* **to stick one's o. in**, intervenir (mal à propos); (*b*) **good o.**, bon rameur; **'oarlock**, s. *N.Am:* dame *f* de nage; tolet *m*; **'oarsman**, *pl.* **-men**, s. rameur *m*; *Nau:* nageur *m*.

oasis, *pl.* **oases** [ou'eisis, ou'eisi:z], s. oasis *f*.

oath, *pl.* **oaths** [ouθ, ouðz], s. 1. serment *m*; *Jur:* **to take an o.**, prêter serment; **I'll take my o. on it**, j'en jurerais; **on o.**, sous serment. 2. juron *m*; gros mot.

oats [outs], *s.pl.* avoine *f*; **field of o.**, champ *m* d'avoine; **to sow one's wild o.**, faire des frasques; **'oatmeal**, s. farine *f* d'avoine.

obdurate ['ɔbdjurət], *a.* (*a*) endurci; têtu, opiniâtre; (*b*) inexorable, inflexible; **'obduracy**, s. (*a*) endurcissement *m* (de cœur); entêtement *m*, opiniâtreté *f*; (*b*) inflexibilité *f*.

obedience [ə'bi:djəns], s. obéissance *f*; **to secure o.**, se faire obéir; **o'bedient**, *a.* obéissant; soumis; docile; **-ly**, *adv.* avec obéissance, avec soumission.

obelisk ['ɔbilisk], s. obélisque *m*.

obese [ou'bi:s], *a.* obèse; **o'besity**, s. obésité *f*.

obey [ə'bei], *v.tr.* obéir à (qn, un ordre); **to make oneself obeyed**, se faire obéir.

obituary [ə'bitjuəri], *a. & s.* **o.** (**list**), nécrologe *m*; (registre *m*) obituaire (*m*); **o. notice**, notice *f* nécrologique; *Journ:* **the o. column, the obituaries**, nécrologie *f*.

object. I. s. ['ɔbdʒikt]. 1. (*a*) objet *m*, chose *f*; **o. lesson**, exemple *m*; (*b*) **o. of, for, pity**, objet, sujet *m*, de pitié. 2. (*a*) but *m*, objectif *m*, objet; **with this o.**, dans ce but, à cette fin; **there's no o. in doing that**, il ne sert à rien de faire cela; (*b*) **expense is no o.**, il ne faut pas regarder à la dépense. 3. *Gram:* complément *m*, objet; **direct o.**, complément direct. II. *v.i.* [əb'dʒekt], **to o. to sth.**, faire une objection, trouver à redire, à qch.; **to o. to s.o.**, soulever des objections contre qn; **to o. to doing sth.**, se refuser à faire qch.; **ob'jection**, s. 1. objection *f*; **to raise an o.**, soulever une objection; **the o. has been raised that . . .**, on a objecté que . . .; **to take o. to s.o., to sth.**, être mécontent de qn, se fâcher de qch.; **I've no o. to that**, je ne m'oppose pas à cela; **if you have no o.**, si cela ne vous fait rien. 2. obstacle *m*; **I see no o. (to it)**, je n'y vois pas d'inconvénient; **ob'jectionable**, *a.* 1. répréhensible, inacceptable, inadmissible. 2. désagréable; **idea that is most o. to me**, idée qui me répugne; **a most o. man**, un homme que personne ne peut souffrir; **ob'jective**. 1. *a. Gram:* **o. case**, accusatif *m*. 2. s. (*a*) but *m*; objectif *m*; (*b*) *Phot:* objectif; **objec'tivity**, s. objectivité *f*; **ob'jector**, s. protestataire *mf*.

oblige [ə'blaidʒ], *v.tr.* 1. obliger, astreindre (qn à faire qch.); **to be obliged to do sth.**, être obligé, tenu, de faire qch. 2. (*a*) **to o. a friend**, rendre service à un ami; **can you o. me with a light?** auriez-vous l'amabilité de me donner du feu? (**in order**) **to o. you**, pour vous être agréable; (*b*) **to be obliged to s.o.**, être obligé à qn; être reconnaissant à qn; **obligation** [ɔbli'geiʃ(ə)n], s. (*a*) obligation *f*; **I'm under no o.**, rien ne m'oblige (à faire qch.); *Ecc:* **day of o.**, fête *f* d'obligation; (*b*) dette *f* de reconnaissance; **to be under an o. to s.o.**, devoir de la reconnaissance à qn; **to put, lay, s.o. under an o. (to do sth.)**, obliger qn (à faire qch.); (*c*) *Com:* **to meet, fail to meet, one's obligations**, faire honneur, manquer, à ses engagements; **obligatory** [ə'bligətri], *a.* obligatoire; de rigueur; **to make it o. to do sth.**, imposer l'obligation de faire qch.; **o'bliging**, *a.* obligeant, complaisant, serviable; **-ly**, *adv.* obligeamment.

oblique [ə'bli:k], *a.* oblique; de biais; **-ly**, *adv.* obliquement, de biais, en biais.

obliterate [ə'blitəreit], *v.tr.* (*a*) faire disparaître, effacer; (*b*) oblitérer (un timbre); **oblite'ration**, s. 1. (*a*) effacement *m*; (*b*) rature *f*. 2. oblitération *f* (d'un timbre).

oblivion [ə'bliviən], s. (état *m* d')oubli *m*; **to sink into o.**, tomber dans l'oubli; **o'blivious**, *a.* oublieux (**of**, de); **o. of what is going on**, inconscient de ce qui se passe; **to be o. of the difficulties**, ignorer les difficultés.

oblong ['ɔblɔŋ]. 1. *a.* oblong, -ongue, rectangulaire. 2. s. rectangle *m*.

obnoxious [əb'nɔkʃəs], *a.* (*a*) odieux; antipathique (**to s.o.**, à qn); (*b*) repoussant, désagréable.

oboe ['oubou], *s. Mus:* hautbois *m*.

obscene [əb'si:n, ɔ-], *a.* obscène; **obscenity** [ɔb'seniti], *s.* obscénité *f.*

obscure [əb'skjuər]. **I.** *a.* **1.** obscur, ténébreux, sombre. **2.** (livre) obscur; (argument) peu clair. **3.** (auteur) peu connu. **II.** *v.tr.* obscurcir; **clouds obscured the sun,** des nuages voilaient le soleil; **-ly,** *adv.* obscurément; **ob'scurity,** *s.* obscurité *f.*

obsequies ['ɔbsikwiz], *s.pl.* obsèques *f,* funérailles *f.*

obsequious [əb'si:kwiəs], *a.* obséquieux; **-ly,** *adv.* obséquieusement; **ob'sequiousness,** *s.* servilité *f.*

observe [əb'zə:v], *v.tr.* **1.** observer (la loi); se conformer à (un ordre). **2.** observer, regarder (les étoiles). **3.** remarquer, noter (un fait); **at last I observed a dark stain,** enfin j'ai aperçu une tache foncée. **4.** dire, remarquer (que . . .); **ob'servable,** *a.* visible; perceptible; **ob'servance,** *s.* **1.** observation *f,* observance *f.* **2. religious observances,** pratiques religieuses; **ob'servant,** *a.* (*a*) observateur; (*b*) **he's very o.,** rien ne lui échappe; **obser'vation,** *s.* **1.** observation *f;* (*a*) **to keep, put, s.o. under o.,** mettre (un malade) en observation; surveiller qn; **to escape o.,** se dérober aux regards; (*b*) *Nau:* **to take an o.,** faire le point. **2.** remarque *f;* **ob'servatory,** *s.* observatoire *m;* **ob'server,** *s.* observateur, -trice.

obsess [əb'ses], *v.tr.* obséder; **to be obsessed with an idea,** être obsédé par une idée; **ob'session,** *s.* obsession *f;* **ob'sessive,** *a.* obsédant.

obsolete ['ɔbsəli:t], *a.* désuet; hors d'usage; tombé en désuétude; **obsolescent** [ɔbsə'lesənt], *a.* (mot) vieilli.

obstacle ['ɔbstəkl], *s.* obstacle *m,* empêchement *m; Sp:* **o. race,** course *f* d'obstacles.

obstetrics [ɔb'stetriks], *s.pl.* obstétrique *f.*

obstinate ['ɔbstinət], *a.* obstiné (**in doing sth.,** à faire qch.); opiniâtre; **o. as a mule,** entêté, têtu, comme un mulet, une mule; **-ly,** *adv.* obstinément, opiniâtrement; **'obstinacy,** *s.* obstination *f,* entêtement *m,* opiniâtreté *f;* **to show o.,** s'obstiner.

obstreperous [əb'strep(ə)rəs], *a.* bruyant, tapageur; turbulent.

obstruct [əb'strʌkt], *v.tr.* (*a*) obstruer, encombrer (la rue); **to o. the view,** incommoder, gêner, la vue; (*b*) gêner, entraver (les mouvements de qn); (*c*) embarrasser, entraver (la circulation); **ob'struction,** *s.* **1.** (*a*) engorgement *m* (d'un tuyau); (*b*) empêchement *m* (de qn). **2.** encombrement *m,* embarras *m* (dans la rue); *Rail:* **o. on the line,** obstacle *m* sur la voie; **ob'structionist,** *s. Pol:* obstructionniste *mf;* **ob'structive,** *a.* obstructif; **o.**

tactics, tactique *f* d'obstruction.

obtain [əb'tein], *v.tr.* obtenir; se procurer (qch.); **ob'tainable,** *a.* **where is that o.?** où peut-on se procurer cela?

obtrude [əb'tru:d], *v.tr. & i.* mettre (qch.) en avant; **to o. oneself on s.o.,** importuner qn; **ob'trusion,** *s.* intrusion *f;* importunité *f;* **ob'trusive,** *a.* importun, indiscret; (*of smell, etc.*) pénétrant; **ob'trusiveness,** *s.* importunité *f.*

obtuse [əb'tju:s], *a.* obtus; **ob'tuseness,** *s.* stupidité *f.*

obviate ['ɔbvieit], *v.tr.* éviter, parer à, obvier à (une difficulté, etc.).

obvious ['ɔbviəs], *a.* évident, clair, manifeste; **o. fact,** fait patent; **it's the o. thing to do,** c'est indiqué, cela s'impose; **-ly,** *adv.* évidemment, manifestement; **she's o. wrong,** il est clair qu'elle a tort.

occasion [ə'keiʒ(ə)n]. **I.** *s.* **1.** cause *f,* occasion *f;* **I've no o. for complaint,** je n'ai pas à me plaindre; **if the o. arises,** s'il y a lieu; le cas échéant. **2.** occasion, occurrence *f;* **on the o. of his marriage,** à l'occasion de son mariage; **on one o.,** une fois; **on several occasions,** à plusieurs reprises; **on such an o.,** en pareille occasion. **II.** *v.tr.* occasionner, donner lieu à (qch.); **o'ccasional,** *a.* **o. visitor,** visiteur *m* qui vient de temps en temps; **o. showers,** de rares averses; **-ally,** *adv.* de temps en temps.

occident ['ɔksidənt], *s.* occident *m;* **occi'dental,** *a.* occidental.

occult [ɔ'kʌlt], *a.* occulte; **'occultism,** *s.* occultisme *m.*

occupy ['ɔkjupai], *v.tr.* **1.** (*a*) occuper, habiter (une maison); (*b*) *Mil:* s'emparer de (la ville etc.); **occupied territory,** territoire occupé. **2.** remplir (un espace); occuper (une place, temps). **3.** occuper (qn); donner du travail (qn); **to o. one's mind,** s'occuper l'esprit; **'occupant,** *s.* occupant, -ante; locataire *m* (d'une maison); **occu'pation,** *s.* occupation *f.* **1. to be in o. of (a house),** occuper (une maison); **army of o.,** armée *f* d'occupation. (*a*) **to give s.o. o.,** occuper qn; (*b*) métier *m,* emploi *m;* **occu'pational,** *a.* **o. disease,** maladie *f* professionnelle; **o. therapy,** thérapie *f* rééducative; **o. hazards,** risques *mpl* du métier; **'occupier,** *s.* occupant, -ante; locataire *mf* (d'une maison).

occur [ə'kə:r], *v.i.* (**occurred**) **1.** (*of event*) avoir lieu; arriver; se produire; **if another opportunity occurs,** si une autre occasion se présente; **don't let it o. again!** que cela n'arrive plus! **2.** rencontrer, se trouver. **3. it occurs to me that . . .,** il me vient à l'idée que . . .; **o'ccurrence,** *s.* événement *m,* occurrence *f;* **everyday o.,** un fait journalier.

ocean ['ouʃ(ə)n], *s.* océan *m;* **o. curren**

courants *m* océaniques; **o.-going ship,** navire de
haute mer; **oceanic** [ousi'ænik], *a.* océanique;
ocean'ography, *s.* océanographie *f.*
Oceania [ouʃi'a:niə]. *Pr.n. Geog:* l'Océanie *f.*
ocelot ['ousilɔt], *s. Z:* ocelot *m.*
ochre ['oukər], *s.* ocre *f*; **yellow, red, o.,** ocre
jaune, rouge.
o'clock [ə'klɔk], *adv. phr.* **six o'c.,** six heures;
twelve o'c., (i) midi *m*; (ii) minuit *m.*
octagon ['ɔktəgən], *s.* octogone *m*; **octagonal**
[ɔk'tægənəl], *a.* octogonal.
octane ['ɔktein], *s.* **high o. petrol,** essence *f* à
haut indice d'octane *m.*
octave ['ɔktiv, 'ɔkteiv], *s.* octave *f.*
octet [ɔk'tet], *s. Mus:* octuor *m.*
October [ɔk'toubər], *s.* octobre *m*; **in O.,** au
mois d'octobre; **(on) the sixth of O.,** le six
octobre.
octogenarian [ɔktoudʒi'nɛəriən], *a. & s.* octogénaire *(mf).*
octopus, *pl.* **-uses** ['ɔktəpəs, -əsiz], *s.* poulpe *m*;
pieuvre *f.*
ocular ['ɔkjulər], *a.* oculaire; **'oculist,** *s.*
oculiste *mf.*
odd [ɔd], *a.* **1.** (*a*) (nombre) impair; (*b*) **£6 o.,** six
livres et un peu plus; **fifty o.,** cinquante et
quelques; **a hundred o. sheep,** une centaine de
moutons; **a thousand o. soldiers,** quelque mille
soldats; **to be o. man out,** rester en surnombre;
(*at cards, etc.*) **the o. game,** la belle. **2.** (*a*)
dépareillé; (*b*) **at o. times,** par-ci par-là; **o.
moments,** moments *m* de loisir, moments
perdus; **o. job man,** homme à tout faire; **to do
o. jobs,** bricoler; *Com:* **o. lot,** soldes *mpl.* **3.**
singulier, drôle; (*of pers.*) excentrique,
original; **that's o.!** c'est curieux, bizarre,
singulier! **-ly,** *adv.* bizarrement,
singulièrement; **o. enough nobody arrived,**
chose singulière, curieuse, personne n'est
arrivé; **'oddity,** *s.* **1.** singularité *f,* bizarrerie *f.*
2. (*a*) personne *f* excentrique, original, -ale; (*b*)
chose *f* bizarre; curiosité *f*; **'oddments,** *s.pl.*
1. *Com:* fonds *m* de boutique; fins *f* de série.
2. petits bouts; restes *m*; **'oddness,** *s.* **1.** im-
parité *f.* **2.** singularité *f,* bizarrerie *f*; **odds,**
s.pl. **1.** (*a*) avantage *m*; chances *f*; **the o. are
against him,** les chances sont contre lui; **to
fight against (great) o.,** lutter contre des forces
supérieures; (*b*) différence *f*; **what's the o.?**
qu'est-ce que ça fait? **it makes no o.,** ça ne fait
rien; (*c*) *Rac:* cote *f* (d'un cheval); **long, short,
o.,** forte, faible, cote; **the o. are that . . .,** **it's an
o. on chance that . . .,** il y a gros à parier que
. . . .. **2. to be at o. with s.o.,** ne pas être d'accord avec qn. **3. o. and ends,** petits bouts;
bribes *f* et morceaux *m*; restes *m.*
odious ['oudjəs], *a.* odieux (**to,** à); détestable;
-ly, *adv.* odieusement, détestablement;
'odiousness, *s.* caractère odieux, l'odieux *m*

(d'une action); **'odium,** *s.* réprobation *f.*
odour ['oudər], *s.* **1.** (*a*) odeur *f*; (*b*) parfum *m.* **2.
to be in bad o. with s.o.,** ne pas être en odeur de
sainteté auprès de qn; **'odourless,** *a.* inodore;
sans odeur.
of [*accented* ɔv, *unaccented* əv, v], *prep.* de. **1.** (*a*)
(*separation*) **south of,** au sud de; **free of,** libre
de; *N.Am:* **five (minutes) of one,** une heure
moins cinq; (*b*) (i) (*origin*) **the works of**
Shakespeare, les œuvres de Shakespeare; (ii)
(*cause*) **of necessity,** par nécessité; **to die (as
the result) of a wound,** mourir (des suites)
d'une blessure. **2. it's very kind of you,** c'est
bien aimable de votre part. **3. made of wood,**
fait de, en, bois. **4.** (*a*) **to think of s.o.,** penser à
qn; (*b*) **guilty of,** coupable de; (*c*) **doctor of
medicine,** docteur en médecine; **bachelor of
arts** = licencié(e) ès lettres; (*d*) **well, what of it?**
eh bien, et après? **5.** (*a*) (i) **the town of Rouen,**
la ville de Rouen; **trees of my planting,** arbres
que j'ai plantés moi-même; **child of ten,** enfant
(âgé) de dix ans; (ii) **hard of hearing,** (un peu)
sourd, dur d'oreille; (*b*) **that fool of a sergeant,**
cet imbécile de sergent; (*c*) **all of a sudden,** tout
d'un coup. **6.** (*a*) **how much of it do you want?**
combien en voulez-vous? **two of them,** deux
d'entre eux; **there are several of us,** nous
sommes plusieurs; **of the twenty only one was
bad,** sur les vingt un seul était mauvais; (*b*) **the
best of men,** le meilleur des hommes; **the one
he loved most of all,** celui qu'il aimait entre
tous; (*c*) **the one thing of all others that I want,**
ce que je désire par-dessus tout, avant tout. **7.**
(*a*) **the widow of a doctor,** la veuve d'un
médecin; **the first of June,** le premier juin; (*b*) **a
friend of mine,** un de mes amis; **it's no business
of yours,** ce n'est pas votre affaire; cela ne vous
regarde pas.
off [ɔf]. **I.** *adv.* **1.** (*a*) **house a kilometre o.,** maison
à un kilomètre de distance; **to keep s.o. o.,**
empêcher qn d'approcher; (*b*) **I'm o. to London,** je pars pour Londres; **be o. with you!**
allez-vous-en! filez! **they're o.!** les voilà partis!
o. we go! (i) en route! (ii) nous voilà partis! **to
go o. to sleep,** s'endormir. **2.** (*a*) **to take o. one's
shoes,** ôter ses souliers; (*b*) (*of gas, electric,
stove, etc.*) fermé; *Aut:* **the ignition is o.,**
l'allumage est coupé; (*in restaurant*) **chicken
is o.,** il n'y a plus de poulet; **the deal's o.,** le
marché ne se fera pas; (*c*) **meat that is slightly
o.,** viande un peu avancée; (*d*) **to finish o. a
piece of work,** (par)achever un travail. **3. badly
o.,** dans la gêne; **well o.,** riche, prospère; **he's
better o. where he is,** il est bien mieux où il est;
he's worse o., sa situation a empiré. **4. on and
o.,** par intervalles; **right o., straight o.,** immédiatement, tout de suite. **II.** *prep.* **1.** (*a*) de;
to fall o. a horse, tomber d'un cheval; **to take
sth. o. a table,** prendre qch. sur une table; **door**

o. its hinges, porte qui est hors de ses gonds; to take sth. o. the price, rabattre qch. du prix; adv. to allow 2½% for cash, faire une remise de 2½% pour paiement comptant; (b) écarté de, éloigné de; a few kilometres o. the coast, à quelques kilomètres de la côte; house o. the road, maison éloignée de la route; Sp: o. side, hors jeu; (c) F: to be o. one's food, ne pas avoir d'appétit; to be o. colour, ne pas être dans son assiette; to have a day o., avoir un jour de congé. 2. Nau: o. the Cape, au large du Cap; o. Calais, devant Calais. III. a. (a) Aut: o. side, côté droit; (in Fr., N.Am., etc.) côté gauche; (b) o. day, (i) jour de liberté; (ii) jour où l'on n'est pas en train; o. season, morte-saison f, saison morte; 'off-beat, a. F: original, pas ordinaire; 'off'hand. 1. adv. (a) sans préparation; to speak o., parler impromptu; (b) sans cérémonie; sans façon; d'un air dégagé. 2. a. (a) spontané; (b) brusque, cavalier; désinvolte, dégagé; 'off'handed, a. in an o. way, sans façon, avec désinvolture; -ly, adv. sans façon, avec désinvolture; 'off'handedness, s. brusquerie f, sans-façon m, désinvolture f; 'off-licence, s. (a) licence f permettant exclusivement la vente des boissons à emporter; (b) débit m où on vend des boissons à emporter; 'off-'peak, a. o.-p. hours, heures creuses; o.-p. tariff, tarif m de nuit; 'off-putting, a. F: déconcertant; 'offshore, a. o. wind, vent m de terre; o. islands, îles au large de la côte.

offal ['ɔfl], s. abats mpl; abattis mpl.

offend [ə'fend]. 1. v.i. to o. against, violer (la loi); pécher contre (la politesse, etc.). 2. v.tr. (a) offenser, froisser (qn); to be offended at, by, sth., se fâcher de qch.; easily offended, très susceptible; (b) (of thg) to o. the eye, choquer les regards; it offends our sense of justice, cela outrage notre sentiment de la justice; o'ffence, s. 1. to take o. at sth., se froisser de qch.; to give o. to s.o., blesser, froisser, qn; I mean no o., je ne veux offenser personne. 2. offense f, faute f; infraction f (à la loi); Jur: crime m, délit m; minor o., contravention f; o'ffender, s. 1. Jur: délinquant, -ante; the chief o., le grand coupable. 2. offenseur m; o'ffending, a. offensant, fautif; o'ffensive. 1. a. (a) Mil: offensif; (b) offensant, choquant; (odeur) nauséabonde; (c) to be o. to s.o., insulter qn. 2. s. Mil: to take the o., prendre l'offensive f; -ly, adv. 1. Mil: offensivement. 2. désagréablement; d'un ton injurieux.

offer ['ɔfər]. I. s. offre f; any offers? combien m'en offrez-vous? that's the best o. I can make, c'est le plus que je puis offrir; o. of marriage, demande f en mariage. II. v. 1. v.tr. (a) to o. s.o. sth., offrir qch. à qn; how much will you o. for it? combien m'en offrez-vous?

house offered for sale, maison mise en vente; to o. to do sth., offrir de, s'offrir à, faire qch.; (b) to o. a remark, an opinion, faire une remarque, avancer une opinion; (c) to o. resistance, offrir, opposer, une résistance. 2. v.i. s'offrir, se présenter; 'offering, s. offre f; 'offertory, s. Ecc: 1. offertoire m. 2. quête f.

office ['ɔfis], s. 1. office m, service m; through the good offices of s.o., par les bons offices de qn. 2. (a) fonctions fpl; it's my o. to . . ., il rentre dans mes fonctions de (faire qch.); (b) charge f, emploi m; (of government) to be in o., être au pouvoir; N.Am: o. holder, fonctionnaire mf. 3. (a) bureau m; (lawyer's) o., étude f; (of company) head o., registered offices, bureau central; siège social; o. work, travail m de bureau; o. boy, coursier m, garçon m de courses; (b) private o., cabinet particulier; (c) the Foreign O. = le ministère des Affaires Étrangères; (d) (of house) the usual offices, cuisine f, salle f de bains, etc.

officer ['ɔfisər], s. 1. fonctionnaire m, officier m, police o., agent m de police, de la sûreté. 2. Mil: officier; staff o., officier d'état-major; Av: pilot o., sous-lieutenant m; flying o., lieutenant m.

official [ə'fiʃ(ə)l]. 1. a. (a) officiel; to do sth. in one's o. capacity, faire qch. dans l'exercice de ses fonctions; (b) o. news, nouvelles authentiques, officielles; this news is not o., cette nouvelle est officieuse. 2. s. fonctionnaire m; railway o., employé(e) des chemins de fer; -ally, adv. officiellement; officia'lese, s. F: jargon administratif; o'fficiate, v.i. 1. Ecc: officier (à un office). 2. to o. as host, remplir les fonctions d'hôte; o'fficious, a. empressé; trop zélé; -ly, adv. to behave o., faire l'empressé; o'fficiousness, s. excès m de zèle.

offing ['ɔfiŋ], s. Nau: in the o., au large; F: I've got a job in the o., j'ai un emploi en perspective.

offset ['ɔfset]. I. s. 1. compensation f, dédommagement m; as an o. to my losses, en compensation de mes pertes. 2. Typ: offset m; o. printing, impression f offset. II. v.tr. (offset) compenser (une perte).

offshoot ['ɔfʃuːt], s. rejeton m.

offspring ['ɔfspriŋ], s. 1. coll. progéniture f, descendance f; descendants mpl. 2. descendant, rejeton m.

often [ɔfn, 'ɔftən], adv. souvent, fréquemment; how o.? combien de fois? as o. as not, more than not, le plus souvent; every so o., de temps en temps.

ogre, f. ogress ['ougər, 'ougris], s. ogre, ogresse.

oh [ou], int. oh!

oil [ɔil]. I. s. 1. huile f; olive o., huile d'olive; o.-painting, (i) une huile, un tableau peint l'huile; (ii) la peinture *f* à l'huile; o. **colours,** couleurs *f* à l'huile; to **burn the midnight-o.,** travailler fort avant dans la nuit. 2. **mineral o.,** pétrole *m,* huile minérale; **fuel o.,** mazout *m;* the o. **industry,** l'industrie pétrolière; o.(**-fired**) **heating,** chauffage *m* au mazout; o. **well,** puits *m* de pétrole. 3. **essential o.,** essence *f.* II. *v.* 1. *v.tr.* huiler, graisser, lubrifier (une machine); to o. **the wheels,** graisser les roues; F: faciliter les choses. 2. *v.i. Nau:* faire le plein de mazout; **'oil-bearing,** *a.* pétrolifère; **'oilcan,** *s.* (*a*) bidon *m* à huile; (*b*) burette *f* à huile; **oiled,** *a.* graissé, huilé; F: he's well o., il est un peu parti, (un peu) éméché; **'oilfield,** *s.* champ *m,* gisement *m,* pétrolifère; **'oiling,** *s.* graissage *m,* huilage *m,* lubrification *f;* **'oilskins,** *s.pl. Cl:* ciré *m;* **'oilstone,** *s. Tls:* pierre *f* à huile (pour affûter); **'oil-tanker,** *s.* pétrolier *m;* **'oily,** *a.* (*a*) huileux, gras, graisseux; (*b*) (*of manner*) onctueux.

ointment ['ɔintmənt], *s.* onguent *m,* pommade *f.*

O.K. (*also* **okay**) [ou'kei]. F: I. *int.* très bien! ça va! d'accord! II. *a.* that's O.K., d'accord! **everything's O.K.,** tout est en règle. III. *s.* approbation *f;* to **give the O.K.,** donner le feu vert. IV. *v.tr.* (O.K.'d, **okayed**) passer, approuver (un projet).

old [ould], *a.* 1. (*a*) vieux; âgé; to **grow o.,** vieillir; to **be getting o.,** se faire vieux; **an o. man,** un vieillard; **an o. woman,** une vieille; **an o. maid,** une vieille fille; o. **wives' tale,** conte de bonne femme; *s.pl.* o. **and young,** grands et petits; o. **age,** vieillesse *f;* to **die at a good o. age,** mourir à un âge avancé, à un bel âge; (*b*) o. **clothes,** vieux habits. 2. **how o. are you?** quel âge avez-vous? to **be five years o.,** avoir cinq ans; **he's older than I am,** il est plus âgé que moi; il est mon aîné; to **be o. enough to do sth.,** être d'âge à faire qch. 3. (*a*) vieux, ancien; (famille) de vieille souche; **an o. friend of mine,** un de mes vieux amis; **an o. dodge,** un coup classique; (*b*) o. **hand,** ouvrier expérimenté; he's **an o. hand** (**at it**), il a du métier. 4. (*a*) *Sch:* **an o. boy,** un ancien élève; (*b*) **the O. World,** l'ancien monde; **the O. Country,** la mère-patrie. 5. *F:* (*a*) **any o. thing,** la première chose venue; n'importe quoi; (*b*) **the o. man,** (i) papa; (ii) le patron; **'old-es'tablished,** *a.* ancien; établi depuis longtemps; **'old-'fashioned,** *a.* 1. (i) à l'ancienne mode; (ii) démodé. 2. (*of pers., ideas*) vieux jeu; **she is, it is, a bit o.-f.,** elle est, c'est, un peu vieux jeu. 3. *F:* **an o.-f. look,** un regard de travers; **'oldish,** *a.* vieillot; **'old-'time,** *a.* o.-t. **dances,** danses *f* du bon vieux temps; **'old-'timer,** *s.* vieux (de la vieille); **'old-'world,** *a.* du temps jadis.

oleaginous [ouli'ædʒinəs], *a.* oléagineux.

oleander [ouli'ændər], *s. Bot:* laurier-rose *m.*

oligarchy ['ɔligɑːki], *s.* oligarchie *f.*

olive ['ɔliv], *s.* 1. o. (**tree**), olivier *m;* o. **grove,** olivaie *f;* o. **branch,** rameau *m* d'olivier; to **hold out the o. branch,** faire les premières avances (pour une réconciliation). 2. olive *f;* o. **oil,** huile *f* d'olive. 3. *Cu:* (**meat**) o., paupiette *f.* 4. *a.* o.(**-green**) **dress,** robe *f* vert olive.

Olympic [ə'limpik], *a.* **the O. Games, the Olympics,** les Jeux Olympiques.

omelet(te) ['ɔmlit], *s. Cu:* omelette *f.*

omen ['oumen], *s.* présage *m,* augure *m;* to **take sth. as a good o.,** tirer un bon augure de qch.; **bird of ill o.,** oiseau de malheur, de mauvais augure; **'ominous** ['ɔm-], *a.* de mauvais augure; sinistre; inquiétant; **-ly,** *adv.* sinistrement.

omit [ou'mit], *v.tr.* (**omitted**) 1. omettre (qch.). 2. to o. to **do sth.,** omettre, oublier, de faire qch.; o'**mission,** *s.* 1. omission *f.* 2. négligence *f.*

omnibus, *pl.* **-buses** ['ɔmnibəs, -bəsiz], *a. & s. Pub:* o. (**volume**), gros recueil (de contes, etc.).

omnipotence [ɔm'nipətəns], *s.* omnipotence *f;* om'**nipotent,** *a.* omnipotent.

omnivorous [ɔm'nivərəs], *a.* omnivore.

on [ɔn]. I. *prep.* 1. (*a*) sur; to **tread on sth.,** marcher sur qch.; **don't tread on it,** ne marchez pas dessus; to **be on the telephone,** (i) être abonné au téléphone; (ii) parler au téléphone; **dinner on the train,** dîner dans le train; **on the high seas,** en haute mer; (*b*) **on shore,** à terre; **on foot,** à pied; **on horseback,** à cheval; (*c*) to **be on the committee,** être membre du comité; to **be on the staff,** faire partie du personnel. 2. (*a*) **hanging on the wall,** pendu au mur; **on the ceiling,** au plafond; **have you any money on you?** avez-vous de l'argent (sur vous)? **on page four,** à la page quatre; (*b*) **just on a year ago,** il y a près d'un an. 3. (*a*) **on the right, left,** à droite, à gauche; **on this side,** de ce côté; (*b*) to **turn one's back on s.o.,** tourner le dos à qn; (*c*) to **hit s.o. on the head,** frapper qn sur la tête. 4. to **have sth. on good authority,** savoir qch. de source certaine; **on pain of death,** sous peine de mort; **it all depends on circumstances,** tout dépend des circonstances; **on condition that . . .,** à condition que . . . 5. (*a*) **on Sundays,** le(s) dimanche(s); **on the following day,** le lendemain; **on April 3rd,** le trois avril; **on the evening of June the first,** le premier juin au soir; (*b*) **on a warm day like this,** par une chaleur comme celle-ci; **on and after Monday,** à partir de lundi; **on or about the twelfth,** vers le douze; **on that occasion,** à, en, cette occasion; **on my arrival,** à mon arrivée; **on application,** sur demande; **on examination,** après examen. 6. **on the cheap,** à bon marché; **on the sly,** en sourdine. 7. **on sale,** en vente. 8. to **congratulate s.o. on his success,** féliciter qn de son succès. 9. **I am here on business,** je suis ici pour affaires; **on holiday,**

en vacances. **10. to have pity on** s.o., avoir
pitié de qn; **attack on** s.o., attaque contre qn;
F: **the drinks are on me,** c'est moi qui paie cette
tournée; **the police have nothing on him,** les
flics n'ont rien contre lui. **11. many live on less
than that,** beaucoup vivent avec moins que ça.
12. to put money on a horse, parier sur un
cheval. **II.** *adv.* **1.** (*a*) **to put the kettle on,** mettre la bouilloire à chauffer; (*of actor*) **to be on,**
être en scène; *F:* **it's just not on,** il n'y a pas
moyen; (*b*) **to have one's shoes on,** être
chaussé; **what did he have on?** qu'est-ce qu'il
portait? **to have nothing on,** être tout(e) nu(e).
2. to fly on, work on, continuer son vol, son
travail; **to talk on,** continuer à parler; **go on!** (i)
continuez! allez toujours! (ii) *P:* pas vrai! **to
toil on and on,** peiner sans fin; **and so on,** et
ainsi de suite. **3. to be sideways on to sth.,**
présenter le côté à qch. **4.** (*a*) **later on,** plus
tard; **from that day on,** à dater de ce jour; **well
on in April,** bien avant dans le mois d'avril;
well on in years, d'un âge avancé; (*b*) *F:* **to
have** s.o. **on,** monter un bateau à qn. **5.** (*of gas,
etc.*) ouvert; (*of electric circuit*) fermé; **to turn
the tap on,** ouvrir le robinet; **the engine is on,** le
moteur est en marche; **the brakes are on,** les
freins sont serrés; **what's on (at the theatre)?**
qu'est-ce qu'on joue actuellement? **this film
was on last week,** ce film a passé la semaine
dernière; **have you anything on this evening?**
êtes-vous occupé ce soir? **6.** *F:* (*a*) **I'm on!** ça
me va! (*b*) **I was on to him on the phone yesterday,** je lui ai parlé au téléphone hier; **the police
are on to him,** la police est sur sa piste; (*c*) **he's
always on at me,** il s'en prend toujours à moi.
7. on and off, par intervalles; à différentes
reprises; **'oncoming,** *a.* **o. traffic,** véhicules
venant en sens inverse.

once [wʌns], *adv.* **1.** (*a*) une fois; **o. only,** une
seule fois; **o. a week,** tous les huit jours; **o.
more,** encore une fois; **o. in a while,** une fois en
passant; **o. and for all,** une (bonne) fois pour
toutes; (*b*) (**if**) **o. you hesitate it's all up with
you,** pour peu que vous hésitiez vous êtes
fichu. **2.** autrefois; **o. (upon a time) there was
. . .,** il était une fois . . .; **I knew him o.,** je l'ai
connu autrefois; **o. when I was young . . .,** un
jour, quand j'étais petit(e) . . .. **3.** (*a*) **at o.,**
tout de suite; à l'instant; sur-le-champ; (*b*) **all
at o.,** soudainement, subitement; **don't all
speak at o.,** ne parlez pas tous à la fois; **'once-
over,** *s. F:* **to give sth. the o.-o.,** jeter un coup
d'œil sur qch.

one [wʌn]. **I.** *num.a.* **1.** (*a*) un; **twenty-o.
apples,** vingt et une pommes; **a hundred and
o.,** cent un; (*b*) **that's o. way of doing it,** c'est
une manière comme une autre de le faire;
that's o. comfort, c'est déjà une consolation. **2.**
(*a*) seul, unique; **the o. way of doing it,** le seul

moyen de le faire; (*b*) **like o. man,** comme un
seul homme; (*c*) même; **it's all o.,** cela revient
au même; **it's all o. to me,** cela m'est égal. **II.** *s.*
1. the typist has left out a o., la dactylo a oublié
un un; **number o.,** (i) numéro un; *F:* soi-même;
to look after number o., mettre ses intérêts en
premier lieu. **2.** (*a*) **there's only o. left,** il n'en
reste qu'un; **the top step but o.,** l'avant-
dernière marche; **the last but o.,** l'avant-
dernier, -ière; **all in o.,** (vêtement) en une pièce;
to be at o., être d'accord (avec qn); (*b*) **o.
(pound) fifty,** une livre cinquante pence; **o.
(o'clock),** une heure; *F:* **to land** s.o. **o.,** flanquer
un marron à qn. **III.** *dem.pron.* (*a*) **this o.,**
celui-ci, *f.* celle-ci; **which o. do you like best?**
lequel, laquelle, préférez-vous? **the o. on the
table,** celui, celle, qui est sur la table; **she's the
o. who helped him,** c'est elle qui l'a aidé; (*b*)
our dear ones, ceux qui nous sont chers; **to
pick the ripe plums and leave the green ones,**
cueillir les prunes mûres et laisser les vertes; *F:*
that's a good o.! en voilà une bonne! **he's a
sharp o.,** c'est un malin. **IV.** *indef.a.* **o. day,** un
jour; **o. stormy evening,** (par) un soir de
tempête. **V.** *indef.pron.* **1.** (*pl.* **some, any**) **I
haven't a pencil, have you got o.?** je n'ai pas de
crayon, en avez-vous un? **o. of them,** (i) l'un
d'entre eux; l'un d'eux; (ii) *P:* un homosexuel;
he's o. of the family, il est de la famille; **except**
(**of them**), pas un; **o. and all,** tous sans exception; **o. after the other,** l'un après l'autre; **o. by
o.,** un(e) à un(e); **o. of the ladies will see to it,**
une de ces dames va s'en occuper. **2. I for o.
shall come,** quant à moi, je viendrai; **I'm not o.
to . . .,** je ne suis pas de ceux qui . . .; *F:* **I'm
not much of a o. for sweets,** je ne suis pas
grand amateur de bonbons. **3.** (*subject*) on;
(*object*) vous; **o. never knows,** on ne sait
jamais; **it's enough to kill o.,** il y a de quoi vous
faire mourir. **4.** **one's,** *poss.a.* sa, *pl.* ses; **votre,**
pl. vos; **to give one's opinion,** donner son avis;
to cut one's finger, se couper le doigt; **'one-
'armed,** *a.* (*of pers.*) manchot; *F:* **o.-a. bandit,**
tire-pognon *m*; **'one-'eyed,** *a.* borgne; **'one-
'horse,** *a. F:* **o.-h. town,** petit bourg de rie(n)
du tout; bled *m*; **'one-'legged** [-'legid], *a.* qui
n'a qu'une jambe; **one'self,** *pron.* (*a*) **to flatter
o.,** se flatter; **to talk to o.,** se parler à soi-même;
to speak of o., parler de soi; (*b*) **one must do
o.,** il faut le faire soi-même; **'one-'sided,** *a.* (*a*)
(*of bargain*) inégal; (*b*) (*of judgment*) partial;
'one-'storey(ed), *a.* (maison) sans étage;
'one-'time, *a.* **o.-t. major,** autrefois major;
'one-'track, *a.* (esprit) obsédé par une seule
idée; **'one-'way,** *a.* (rue) à sens *m* unique.

onerous [ˈɔnərəs], *a.* onéreux; (tâche) pénible.
onion [ˈʌnjən], *s.* oignon *m*; **spring o.,** ciboule.
onlooker [ˈɔnlukər], *s.* spectateur, -trice;
onlookers, l'assistance *f.*

only ['ounli]. **I.** *a.* seul, unique; **o. son,** fils unique; **his one and o. hope,** son seul et unique espoir; **his o. answer was to burst out laughing,** pour toute réponse il éclata de rire; **you're the o. one,** il n'y a que vous. **II.** *adv.* seulement; ne . . . que; **I've o. three,** je n'en ai que trois; **staff o.,** réservé au personnel; **o. he can say,** lui seul saurait le dire; **I o. touched it,** je n'ai fait que le toucher; **you've o. to ask for it,** vous n'avez qu'à le demander; **I will o. say . . .,** je me bornerai à dire . . .; **o. to think of it,** rien que d'y penser; **if o. I knew!** si seulement je le savais! **o. yesterday,** hier encore; pas plus tard qu'hier. **III.** *conj.* mais; **it's a beautiful dress o. it's rather dear,** c'est une belle robe, seulement elle coûte cher.

onrush ['ɔnrʌʃ], *s.* ruée *f,* attaque *f.*

onset ['ɔnset], *s.* assaut *m,* attaque *f.*

onslaught ['ɔnslɔːt], *s.* assaut *m,* attaque *f;* **to make an o. on s.o.,** attaquer qn (avec véhémence, vigoureusement).

Ontario [ɔn'tɛəriou]. *Pr.n. Geog:* l'Ontario *m;* **On'tarian,** *s.* Ontarien, -ienne.

onus ['ounəs], *s.* responsabilité *f,* charge *f.*

onward(s) ['ɔnwəd(z)], *adv.* (a) en avant; (b) **from tomorrow o.,** à partir de demain; **from this time o.,** désormais, dorénavant.

ooze [uːz]. **I.** *s.* vase *f,* limon *m.* **II.** *v.i.* suinter, dégoutter; **his courage oozed away,** son courage l'abandonnait; **'oozing,** *s.* suintement *m.*

op [ɔp], *s. F:* 1. *Med:* opération *f.* 2. *Mil:* **combined op(s),** opération (i) amphibie, (ii) inter-armées.

opal ['oup(ə)l], *s.* opale *f.*

opaque [ou'peik], *a.* opaque.

open ['oup(ə)n]. **I.** *a.* 1. ouvert; (a) **half o.,** entrouvert, entrebâillé; **to throw the door wide o.,** ouvrir la porte toute grande; (b) (of box) ouvert; (of bottle) débouché; (of parcel) défait; (c) **o. to the public,** ouvert, accessible, au public; (d) *Jur:* **in o. court,** en plein tribunal. 2. sans limites; sans bornes; **in the o. air,** *s.* **in the o.,** au grand air, en plein air; **o. country,** pays découvert; **in the o. country,** en pleine campagne; **the o. sea,** la haute mer; le large. 3. (a) **o. carriage,** voiture découverte; (b) **o. field,** champ *m* sans enclos; (c) **o. to every wind,** exposé à tous les vents; (d) **to lay oneself o. to criticism,** donner prise à la critique; (e) **o. to conviction,** accessible à la conviction; **o. to improvement,** susceptible d'amélioration. 4. (a) manifeste; public; **o. secret,** secret *m* de polichinelle; (b) franc; **o. admiration,** franche admiration; **o. enemy,** ennemi déclaré; **to be o. with s.o.,** parler franchement à qn; ne rien cacher à qn. 5. **o. wound,** plaie (i) béante, (ii) non cicatrisée; **o. at the neck,** (chemise) à col ouvert. 6. non serré. 7. (a) non obstrué; **o.**

road, chemin libre; **o. view,** vue dégagée; (b) **the job is still o.,** la place est toujours vacante; **two courses are o. to us,** deux moyens s'offrent à nous; **it's o. to you to object,** il vous est permis de faire des objections. 8. non résolu; **o. question,** question *f* discutable; **to keep an o. mind,** rester sans parti pris. 9. *Com:* **o. account,** compte ouvert; compte courant; **o. cheque,** chèque ouvert, non barré. **II.** *v.* 1. *v.tr.* (a) ouvrir (une porte); baisser (une glace); déboucher, entamer (une bouteille); décacheter (une lettre); défaire, ouvrir (un paquet); inaugurer (une fête); **to o. one's mail,** dépouiller son courrier; **to o. a new shop,** ouvrir un nouveau magasin; (b) ouvrir (la main); (c) **to o. a way, path, through sth.,** ouvrir, frayer, un chemin à travers qch.; (d) commencer; entamer, engager (une conversation); *Com:* ouvrir (un compte). 2. *v.i.* (a) s'ouvrir; **door that opens into the garden,** porte qui ouvre sur le jardin; **exit opening on to the street,** sortie qui donne accès à la rue; **the bank opens at ten,** la banque ouvre (ses portes) à dix heures; **as soon as the season opens,** dès l'ouverture de la saison; (b) (of flower) s'ouvrir, s'épanouir; (of view) s'étendre; (c) (of play, etc.) commencer; **-ly,** *adv.* ouvertement, franchement, en toute franchise; au vu et au su de tout le monde; **'open-'air,** *a.* (assemblée) en plein air; **'opencast,** *a.* (exploitation) à ciel ouvert; **'opener,** *s.* (a) (of pers.) ouvreur, -euse; (b) **can, tin, o.,** ouvre-boîte(s) *m;* **bottle o.,** décapsulateur *m;* **'open-'handed,** *a.* libéral, généreux; **'open-'hearted,** *a.* 1. franc, expansif. 2. au cœur tendre, compatissant; **'opening,** *s.* 1. (a) ouverture *f;* débouchage *m* (d'une bouteille); dépouillement *m* (du courrier); (b) formal o., inauguration *f;* (c) (at cards) attaque *f.* 2. trou *m,* ouverture, orifice *m;* clairière *f* (dans un bois). 3. occasion *f* favorable, opportunité *f; Com:* débouché *m* (pour une marchandise); **to give s.o. an o. against you,** prêter son flanc à un adversaire. 4. *attrib.* d'ouverture; inaugural; **o. sentence,** phrase de début; **'open-'minded,** *a.* qui a l'esprit ouvert, large; impartial; **to be o.-m. about sth.,** être sans préjugés sur qch.; **'open-'mouthed,** *a.* **to stand o.-m.,** rester bouche bée; **'open-'necked,** *a.* à col ouvert; **'openness,** *s.* franchise *f;* **'open'out,** *v.* 1. *v.tr.* ouvrir, déplier (une feuille de papier). 2. *v.i.* (of view) s'ouvrir, s'étendre; **'open 'up,** *v.* 1. *v.tr.* ouvrir (une mine); exposer, révéler (une perspective); frayer (un chemin); ouvrir (un pays au commerce). 2. *v.i. F:* **to make s.o. o. up,** délier la langue à qn.

opera ['ɔp(ə)rə], *s.* opéra *m;* **o. glasses,** jumelles *f* de théâtre; **o. house,** opéra; **ope'ratic,** *a.* d'opéra; **o. singer,** chanteur, -euse, d'opéra; cantatrice *f;* **ope'retta,** *s.* opérette *f.*

operate ['ɔpəreit]. **1.** *v.i.* (*a*) opérer; (*of machine*) fonctionner; (*b*) *Med:* **to o. on s.o.**, opérer qn; **to be operated on**, subir une opération. **2.** *v.tr.* faire manœuvrer (une machine); faire jouer (un mécanisme); **'operating**, *s. Med:* **o. table**, **o. theatre**, table *f*, salle *f*, d'opération; **ope'ration**, *s.* **1.** fonctionnement *m*, action *f*; **to be in o.**, fonctionner, jouer; (*of machine*) être en marche; (*of law*) **to come into o.**, entrer en vigueur. **2.** *Mil: etc:* opération *f.* **3.** *Med:* opération, intervention chirurgicale; **ope'rational**, *a.* opérationnel; **'operative. 1.** *a.* opératif, actif; (*of law*) **to become o.**, entrer en vigueur; **the o. word**, le mot qui compte. **2.** *s.* ouvrier, -ière; **'operator**, *s.* opérateur, -trice; **radio o.**, radio *m*; *St.Exch:* joueur, -euse; *F:* **a slick o.**, un commerçant, un escroc, habile.

ophthalmia [ɔf'θælmiə], *s. Med:* ophtalmie *f.*

opinion [ə'pinjən], *s.* (*a*) opinion *f*; avis *m*; **in my o.**, à mon avis; **to be entirely of s.o.'s o.**, abonder dans le sens de qn, être tout à fait de l'avis de qn; **matter of o.**, affaire d'opinion; **to give one's o.**, donner, exprimer, son opinion; **to ask s.o.'s o.**, se référer à qn; consulter qn; **what's your o. of him?** que pensez-vous de lui? **public o.**, l'opinion (publique); (*b*) consultation *f* (de médecin, etc.); **o'pinionated**, *a.* opiniâtre.

opium ['oupjəm], *s.* opium *m*; **o. addict**, opiomane *mf.*

Oporto [ə'pɔːtou]. *Pr.n. Geog:* Porto *m.*

opossum [ə'pɔsəm], *s. Z:* opossum *m.*

opponent [ə'pounənt], *s.* adversaire *mf*, antagoniste *mf.*

opportune ['ɔpətjuːn], *a.* opportun, convenable, commode; à propos; **the o. moment**, le moment opportun; **-ly**, *adv.* opportunément, en temps opportun, à propos; (arriver) à point (nommé), juste à point; **oppor'tunist**, *s.* opportuniste *mf*; **oppor'tunity**, *s.* occasion *f* (favorable); **when the o. occurs**, à l'occasion; **if I get an o.**, si l'occasion se présente; *Com:* **fantastic sales opportunities**, soldes et occasions exceptionnels.

oppose [ə'pouz], *v.tr.* s'opposer à (qn, qch.); résister à (qn, qch.); *Pol: etc:* **to o. the motion**, soutenir la contrepartie; **o'pposed**, *a.* **1.** opposé, hostile; **papers o. to the government**, journaux hostiles au gouvernement. **2. sth. as o. to sth.**, qch. par opposition à, par contraste avec, qch.; **o'pposing**, *a.* opposé; **the o. forces**, les forces qui s'opposent.

opposite ['ɔpəzit]. **1.** *a.* (*a*) opposé (**to**, à); vis-à-vis, en face; **see the diagram on the o. page**, voir la figure ci-contre; **the house o.**, la maison (d')en face; (*b*) contraire; **the o. sex**, l'autre sexe; **o. poles**, pôles *m* contraires; **in the o. direction**, en sens opposé, inverse. **2.** *s.* opposé

m; **le contre-pied**; **the o. of what he said**, le contraire de ce qu'il a dit. **3.** *adv.* vis-à-vis; en face. **4.** *prep.* en face de, vis-à-vis de; **oppo'sition**, *s.* opposition *f*; (*a*) **in o. to public opinion**, contrairement à l'opinion publique; (*b*) résistance *f*; **to meet with no o.**, ne rencontrer aucune résistance; (*c*) (le) camp adverse; *Pol:* **o. spokesman**, porte-parole *m* de l'opposition; (*d*) **to set up (shop) in o. to s.o.**, ouvrir un magasin en concurrence avec qn.

oppress [ə'pres], *v.tr.* (*a*) opprimer; (*b*) oppresser, accabler (l'esprit); **o'ppression**, *s.* (*a*) oppression *f*; abus *m* d'autorité; (*b*) accablement *m* (de l'esprit); **o'ppressive**, *a.* **1.** oppressif, opprimant, tyrannique. **2.** (*a*) (*of atmosphere*) lourd, étouffant; (*b*) (*of grief*) accablant; **-ly**, *adv.* **1.** oppressivement, tyranniquement. **2.** d'une manière accablante; **o'ppressiveness**, *s.* **1.** caractère oppressif (d'un gouvernement). **2.** lourdeur (du temps); **o'ppressor**, *s.* (*a*) oppresseur; (*b*) **the oppressors and the oppressed**, les opprimants *m* et les opprimés *m.*

opprobrium [ə'proubriəm], *s.* opprobre.

opt [ɔpt], *v.i.* opter (**for**, pour); **'opt 'out**, *v.i.* **o.o.** (**of sth.**), décider de ne pas participer (à qch.).

optical ['ɔptik(ə)l], *a.* **1.** optique. **2.** (instrument) d'optique; **o. illusion**, illusion *f* d'optique; **'optic**, *a. Anat:* **o. nerve**, nerf *m* optique; **op'tician**, *s.* opticien, -ienne; **'optics**, *s.pl.* l'optique *f.*

optimist ['ɔptimist], *s.* optimiste *mf*; **'optimism**, *s.* optimisme *m*; **opti'mistic**, *a.* optimiste; **-ally**, *adv.* avec optimisme.

option ['ɔpʃ(ə)n], *s.* option *f*, choix *m*; **I have no o.**, je ne peux pas faire autrement; **'optional**, *a.* facultatif.

optometrist [ɔp'tɔmətrist], *s. N.Am:* opticien, -ienne.

opulence ['ɔpjuləns], *s.* opulence *f*, richesse *f*; **'opulent**, *a.* opulent; **-ly**, *adv.* avec opulence.

or [ɔːr], *conj.* (*a*) ou; (*with neg.*) ni; **either one or the other**, soit l'un soit l'autre; l'un ou l'autre; **he can't read or write**, il ne sait ni lire ni écrire; **without money or luggage**, sans argent ni bagages; **in a day or two**, dans un jour ou deux; **ten kilometres or so**, environ dix kilomètres; (*b*) **keep still or I'll shoot!** ne bougez pas, sinon je tire!

oracle ['ɔrəkl], *s.* oracle *m.*

oral ['ɔːr(ə)l], *a.* **1.** oral; *Sch:* **o. examination**, *s. F:* **o.**, (examen) oral (*m*). **2.** *Med:* **o. vaccine**, vaccin buccal; **o. administration**, administration *f* par la bouche; **-ally**, *adv.* **1.** oralement; de vive voix. **2.** *Med:* par la bouche; par voie buccale.

orange ['ɔrin(d)ʒ], *s.* **1.** orange *f*; **blood o.**, sanguine *f.* **2. o. (tree)**, oranger *m*; **o. blossom**

fleurs *fpl* d'oranger; **o. grove**, orangeraie *f*. **3.** *a.*
& *s.* (*colour*) orangé (*m*); orange (*m*) *inv*; **o.
lily**, lis orangé.
orang-utan(g) ['ɔræŋ'uːtæŋ, ə'ræŋu:'tæn], *s.*
Z: orang-outan *m*, *pl.* orangs-outans.
oration [ə'reiʃ(ə)n, ɔ-], *s.* allocution *f*, discours
m; **funeral o.**, oraison *f* funèbre; **'orator,** *s.*
orateur *m*; **ora'torical,** *a.* (*a*) (style) oratoire;
(*b*) (discours) verbeux, ampoulé; **'oratory¹,** *s.*
l'art *m* oratoire; l'éloquence *f*.
oratorio, *pl.* **-os** [ɔrə'tɔːriou, -ouz], *s.* Mus:
oratorio *m*.
oratory² ['ɔrət(ə)ri], *s.* Ecc: oratoire *m*; chapelle
privée.
orb [ɔːb], *s.* orbe *m*; globe *m*, sphère *f*.
orbit ['ɔːbit]. **I.** *s.* (*a*) orbite *f*; **to put a satellite into
o.**, mettre un satellite sur son orbite, en orbite; **to
go into o.**, se mettre en orbite; (*b*) **the Russian o.**,
la sphère d'influence soviétique. **II.** *v.i.* & *tr.*
décrire une orbite (autour de la lune, etc.).
orchard ['ɔːtʃəd], *s.* verger *m*.
orchestra ['ɔːkistrə], *s.* orchestre *m*;
or'chestral [-'kes-], *a.* orchestral;
'orchestrate, *v.tr.* Mus: orchestrer;
orches'tration, *s.* orchestration *f*, instrumentation *f*.
orchid ['ɔːkid], *s.* Hort: orchidée *f*.
ordain [ɔː'dein], *v.tr.* **1.** Ecc: **to o. s.o. priest**, ordonner qn prêtre; **to be ordained**, recevoir les
ordres; être reçu, ordonné, prêtre. **2.** (*a*) **so fate
ordains**, ainsi le veut le sort; (*b*) (*of pers.*)
décréter (une mesure), prescrire, ordonner.
ordeal [ɔː'diːl], *s.* épreuve *f*.
order ['ɔːdər]. **I.** *s.* **1.** ordre *m*; (*a*) **workmanship
of the highest o.**, travail *m* de premier ordre, de
qualité supérieure; (*b*) Ecc: **holy orders**, ordres
sacrés; **to be in holy orders**, être prêtre; (*c*)
monastic o., ordre religieux; communauté *f*; **o.
of knighthood**, ordre de chevalerie; (*d*) **to wear
all one's orders**, porter toutes ses décorations.
2. ordre, succession *f*, suite *f*; **in alphabetical
o.**, par ordre alphabétique; **out of (its) o.**, hors
de son rang. **3.** Mil: (*a*) **close o., open o.**, ordre
serré, ouvert; (*b*) **in review o.**, en grande tenue;
heavy marching o., tenue de campagne. **4.** (*a*)
to set one's house in o., remettre de l'ordre
dans ses affaires; **is your passport in o.?** votre
passeport est-il en règle? **in good o.**, en bon
état; **out of o.**, en mauvais état; en panne; **to
get out of o.**, se dérégler, se détraquer; (*b*) Parl:
etc: **in o.**, dans les règles; **to call s.o. to o.**,
rappeler qn à l'ordre. **5.** **law and o.**, l'ordre
public. **6. in o. to do sth.**, afin de, pour, faire
qch.; **in o. to put you on your guard**, pour que
vous soyez sur vos gardes; **in o. that they may
see it**, afin qu'ils puissent le voir. **7.** (*a*) commandement *m*, instruction *f*, Mil: *etc:* consigne
f; **I have orders to do it**, j'ai ordre de le faire;
orders are orders, je ne connais que la con

signe; **until further orders**, jusqu'à nouvel ordre; (*b*) Com: commande *f*; **made to o.**, fait sur
commande; F: **that's a tall o.!** c'est demander
un peu trop! **8.** (*a*) arrêt *m*; Jur: **o. of the court**,
injonction *f* de la cour; **deportation o.**, arrêté *m*
d'expulsion; Mil: **mention in orders**, citation *f*
(à l'ordre du jour); (*b*) **money o., postal o.**,
mandat (postal), madat-poste *m*, *pl.*
mandats-poste. **II.** *v.tr.* (*a*) **to o. s.o. to do sth.**,
ordonner, commander, à qn de faire qch.; **to o.
s.o. about**, faire marcher, faire aller, qn;
donner des ordres à qn; (*b*) Med: prescrire, ordonner (un traitement); (*c*) Com: commander;
to o. a taxi, faire venir un taxi; **'orderliness,** *s.*
1. bon ordre; méthode *f*. **2.** habitudes *fpl* d'ordre. **3.** discipline *f*; calme *m*; **'orderly. 1.** *a.* (*a*)
ordonné, méthodique, (*of life*) réglé, rangé,
régulier; (*of pers.*) **to be very o.**, avoir
beaucoup de méthode; (*b*) (*of crowd*)
tranquille, discipliné. **2.** *s.* Mil: planton *m*; **to
be on o. duty**, être de planton; **medical o.**, infirmier *m*; **o. room**, salle *f* des rapports.
ordinal ['ɔːdin(ə)l], *a.* & *s.* ordinal (*m*).
ordinance ['ɔːdinəns], *s.* ordonnance *f*, décret
m, règlement *m*; **police o.**, arrêté *m*, ordonnance, de police.
ordinary ['ɔːdin(ə)ri]. **I.** *a.* **1.** ordinaire;
coutumier; normal; **the o. Englishman**,
l'Anglais moyen, typique. **2.** Pej: **a very o. kind
of man**, un homme très quelconque. **II.** *s.* ordinaire *m*; **out of the o.**, exceptionnel; peu ordinaire; **-ily,** *adv.* ordinairement, normalement; à l'ordinaire, d'ordinaire;
d'habitude.
ordination [ɔːdi'neiʃ(ə)n], *s.* Ecc: ordination *f*.
ordnance ['ɔːdnəns], *s.* **1.** artillerie *f*. **2.** Mil:
Royal Army O. Corps = Service *m* du
Matériel; **O. Survey**, service *m* topographique.
ore [ɔːr], *s.* minerai *m*; **iron o.**, minerai de fer.
organ ['ɔːgən], *s.* **1.** Mus: orgue *m*, orgues *fpl*;
street o., orgue de Barbarie. **2.** (*a*) organe *m*;
the vocal organs, l'appareil vocal; (*b*) journal
m, bulletin *m*, organe; **or'ganic,** *a.* **1.**
(maladie) organique. **2.** (*a*) **o. beings**, êtres
organisés; (*b*) **o. chemistry**, chimie *f*
organique; **-ally,** *adv.* **1.** organiquement. **2.**
foncièrement; **the system is o. wrong**, le
système est foncièrement mauvais;
'organism, *s.* organisme *m*; **'organist,** *s.*
Mus: organiste *mf*; **organi'zation,** *s.*
organisation *f*; organisme *m* (politique); **youth
o.**, mouvement *m* de jeunesse; **'organize,** *v.tr.*
organiser (qch.); arranger (un concert);
'organizer, *s.* organisateur, -trice.
orgy ['ɔːdʒi], *s.* orgie *f*; **o. of colour**, orgie de
couleurs.
orient ['ɔːriənt], *s.* Geog: **the O.**, l'Orient *m*;
ori'ental. 1. *a.* oriental; d'Orient. **2.** *s.* Oriental, -ale; **'orientate,** *v.tr.* orienter; **orien'ta-**

tion, s. orientation f.

origin ['ɔridʒin], s. origine f; **country of o.,** pays m de provenance; **o'riginal. 1.** a. (a) originaire, primordial, primitif; **o. meaning of a word,** sens premier d'un mot; (b) (ouvrage) original; **it's not an o.** scheme, le projet n'est pas inédit. **2.** s. original m (d'un tableau, etc.); **to read a French author in the o.,** lire un auteur français dans l'original; **-ally,** adv. **1.** (a) originairement; à l'origine; (b) originellement; dès l'origine. **2.** originalement; **origi'nality,** s. originalité f; **o'riginate. 1.** v.tr. faire naître, donner naissance à, être l'auteur de (qch.). **2.** v.i. tirer son origine, dériver, provenir (**from, in,** de); avoir son origine (dans); **o'riginator,** s. créateur, -trice; auteur m; initiateur, -trice; promoteur m (d'une industrie).

Orinoco (the) [ɔiːɔri'noukou]. Pr.n. Geog: l'Orénoque m.

oriole ['ɔːrioul], s. Orn: (European) loriot m; (American) troupiale m, Fr.C: oriole m.

Orkneys (the) [ɔːr'ɔːkniz]. Pr.n.pl. Geog: les Orcades f.

ornament. I. s.['ɔːnəmənt], ornement m. **II.** v.tr. ['ɔːnəment], orner, ornementer, décorer; **orna'mental,** a. ornemental; d'ornement; **ornamen'tation,** s. **1.** ornementation f, décoration f. **2.** les ornements m.

ornate [ɔː'neit], a. orné; surchargé d'ornements.

ornithology [ɔːni'θɔlədʒi], s. ornithologie f; **ornitho'logical,** a. ornithologique; **orni'thologist,** s. ornithologiste mf, ornithologue mf.

orphan ['ɔːf(ə)n]. **I.** s. & a. **an o. (child),** un(e) orphelin(e). **II.** v.tr. rendre orphelin(e); **he was orphaned by an earthquake,** il a perdu ses parents dans un tremblement de terre; **'orphanage,** s. orphelinat m.

orthodox ['ɔːθədɔks], a. orthodoxe; **'orthodoxy,** s. orthodoxie f.

orthography [ɔː'θɔgrəfi], s. orthographe f; **ortho'graphical,** a. orthographique.

orthopaedic [ɔːθə'piːdik], a. orthopédique.

oscillate ['ɔsileit], v.i. & tr. osciller; faire osciller; **osci'llation,** s. oscillation f.

osier ['ouziər], s. osier m; **o. bed,** oseraie f.

osseous ['ɔsiəs], a. osseux; **ossifi'cation,** s. ossification f; **'ossify,** v.tr. & i. (s')ossifier.

Ostend [ɔs'tend]. Pr.n. Geog: Ostende.

ostensible [ɔs'tensibl], a. prétendu; qui sert de prétexte; soi-disant; feint; **-ibly,** adv. en apparence; censément; **he went out o. to . . .,** il est sorti sous prétexte de . . ., soi-disant pour . . ..

ostentation [ɔsten'teiʃ(ə)n], s. ostentation f; **osten'tatious,** a. plein d'ostentation; fastueux; **-ly,** adv. avec ostentation.

osteopath ['ɔstiəpæθ], s. ostéopathe m.

ostracism ['ɔstrəsizm], s. ostracisme m;

'**ostracize,** v.tr. ostraciser (qn).

ostrich ['ɔstritʃ], s. autruche f; **o. feather,** plume f d'autruche.

other ['ʌðər]. **1.** a. autre; (a) **the o. one,** l'autre; **the o. day,** l'autre jour; (b) **the o. four,** les quatre autres; **o. things being equal,** toutes choses égales; (c) **o. people have seen it,** d'autres l'ont vu; **o. people's property,** le bien d'autrui. **2.** pron. autre; (a) **one after the o.,** l'un après l'autre; (b) **the others,** les autres, le reste; (c) **some . . . others . .,** les uns . . . les autres . . .; **I have no o.,** je n'en ai pas d'autre; **one or o. of us,** l'un de nous; **this day of all others,** ce jour entre tous; (d) (of pers.) **others,** d'autres; **the happiness of others,** le bonheur d'autrui; (e) **I could not do o. than . . .,** je n'ai pu faire autrement que . . .. **3.** adv. autrement; '**otherwise,** adv. **1.** autrement (**than, que**) **he couldn't do o.,** il n'a pu faire autrement; **should it be o.,** dans le cas contraire; **if. he's not o. engaged,** s'il n'est pas occupé à autre chose; **except where o. stated,** sauf indication contraire. **2.** autrement; sans quoi, sans cela; dans le cas contraire. **3.** sous d'autres rapports; par ailleurs; **o. he's quite sane,** à part ça il est complètement sain d'esprit.

otter ['ɔtər], s. Z: loutre f; **o. (skin),** loutre.

ought [ɔːt], v.aux. (with present and past meaning, inv.) (parts of) devoir, falloir. **1.** (obligation) **one o. never to be unkind,** il ne faut, on ne doit, jamais être malveillant; **I thought I o. to tell you,** j'ai cru devoir vous en faire part; **to behave as one o.,** se conduire comme il convient. **2.** (vague desirability) **you o. not to have waited,** vous n'auriez pas dû attendre; **you o. to see the exhibition,** vous devriez aller voir l'exposition; **you o. to have seen it!** il fallait voir ça! **3.** (probability) **your horse o. to win,** votre cheval a de grandes chances de gagner; **that o. to do,** je crois que cela suffira.

ounce [auns], s. Meas: once f; **he hasn't an o. of courage,** il n'a pas pour deux sous de courage.

our [ɑːr, 'auər], poss.a. notre, pl. nos; **o. house and garden,** notre maison et notre jardin; **o. friends,** nos ami(e)s; **it's one of o. books,** c'est un livre (i) à nous, (ii) que nous avons écrit, (iii) publié par notre maison; **ours,** poss.pron. le nôtre, la nôtre, les nôtres; **this is o.,** c'est le, la nôtre; ceci est à nous; ceci nous appartient; **a friend of o.,** un(e) de nos ami(e)s; **our'selves,** pers.pron.pl. (a) **we did it o.,** nous l'avons fait nous-mêmes; **we o. are to blame,** c'est nous qui sommes à blâmer; (b) (at meal) **we can help o.,** nous pouvons nous servir.

oust [aust], v.tr. **1. to o. s.o. from his post,** déloger qn de son poste. **2.** prendre la place de (qn); évincer, supplanter (qn).

out [aut]. **I.** adv. **1.** dehors; (a) **to go o.**

sortir; **o. you go!** sortez! **to throw sth. o.,** jeter qch. dehors; *Nau:* **the voyage o.,** l'aller *m*; (*b*) **my father is o.,** mon père est sorti; **he's o. and about again,** il est de nouveau sur pied; *Ind:* **the men are o.,** les ouvriers sont en grève; **a long way o.** (of the town), loin de la ville; **o. at sea,** en mer, au large; **o. there,** là-bas; **the tide is o.,** la marée est basse. **2. to lean o.,** se pencher au dehors; **to hang o. the washing,** étendre la lessive. **3.** (*a*) au clair; découvert, exposé; **the sun is o.,** il fait du soleil; **the book is just o.,** le livre vient de paraître; **the secret is o.,** le secret est connu, éventé; (*b*) **to pull o. a revolver,** tirer, sortir, un revolver; *F:* **o. with it!** achevez donc! allons, dites-le! expliquez-vous! (*c*) (*of flower*) épanoui; **the hawthorn is o.,** l'aubépine est en fleur; (*d*) **all o.,** (aller) à toute vitesse; (*e*) **o. loud,** tout haut, à haute voix; **to tell s.o. sth. straight o.,** dire qch. à qn carrément; (*f*) *F:* **I'm not o. to do that,** je n'ai pas entrepris de faire cela. **4. shoulder o.** (of joint), épaule luxée; **I'm (quite) o. of practice,** je n'ai plus la main; **the Conservatives are o.,** les Conservateurs ne sont plus au pouvoir; *Games:* **o.,** (déclaré) hors-jeu; *F:* **to be o. on one's feet,** tituber de fatigue. **5. to be o. in one's calculations,** être loin de, du, compte; **I'm five pounds o.,** j'ai une erreur de cinq livres dans mes comptes; **I wasn't far o.,** je ne me trompais pas de beaucoup; **you've put me o.,** vous m'avez dérouté. **6.** (*of fire, etc.*) éteint. **7.** (*a*) à bout; achevé; **before the week is o.,** avant la fin de la semaine; (*b*) **hear me o.,** écoutez-moi jusqu'au bout; **to have one's sleep o.,** finir de dormir; **to fight it o.,** se battre jusqu'à une décision; (*c*) **the plan is now definitely o.,** il n'est plus possible de considérer ce projet. **8. o. of,** (*a*) hors de, au dehors de, en dehors de; **it is o. of my power to . . .,** il n'est pas en mon pouvoir de . . .; **to be o. of things,** être laissé à l'écart; **to feel o. of it,** se sentir dépaysé, de trop; (*b*) **o. of season,** hors de saison; **times o. of number,** maintes et maintes fois; **to be o. of one's mind,** avoir perdu la raison; (*c*) **to throw sth. o. of the window,** jeter qch. par la fenêtre; **to turn s.o. o. of the house,** mettre qn à la porte; **to get money o. of s.o.,** obtenir de l'argent de qn; (*d*) dans, à, par; **to drink o. of a glass,** boire dans un verre; **to drink o. of the bottle,** boire à (même) la bouteille; **to look o. of the window,** regarder par la fenêtre; (*e*) parmi, d'entre; **choose one o. of these ten,** choisissez-en un parmi les dix; **one o. of (every) three,** un sur trois; (*f*) **hut made o. of a few old planks,** cabane faite de quelques vieilles planches; (*g*) **o. of respect,** par respect (pour qn); **o. of curiosity,** par curiosité; (*h*) **to be o. of, to have run o. of, tea,** ne plus avoir de thé; *Pub:* **o. of print,** épuisé. **II.** *s.* **to know the ins and outs of sth.,** connaître

qch. dans tous ses détails; *N.Am:* **to be at outs with s.o.,** être brouillé avec qn; **'out and 'out.** **1.** *adv.phr.* complètement, absolument. **2.** *a.* **an o. a. o. liar,** un menteur fieffé, achevé; **'outback,** *s. Austr:* l'intérieur *m*; **out'bid,** *v.tr.* (**outbid; outbid**) (*at auction*) renchérir sur (qn); **'outboard,** *a. Nau:* **o. motor,** moteur *m* hors-bord; **'outbreak,** *s.* **1.** éruption *f*; début *m*, ouverture *f* (des hostilités); *Med:* épidémie *f* (de la grippe, etc.). **2.** révolte *f*; émeute *f*; **'outbuilding,** *s.* bâtiment extérieur; annexe *f*; *pl.* **outbuildings,** communs *m*, dépendances *f*; **'outburst,** *s.* éruption *f*, explosion *f*; éclat *m* (de rire); élan *m* (de générosité); **'outcast,** *a.* & *s.* expulsé, -ée; proscrit, -ite; **'outcaste,** *a.* & *s.* hors-caste (*mf*); **out'class,** *v.tr. Sp:* surpasser; **'outcome,** *s.* issue *f*, résultat *m*, dénouement *m*; **'outcry,** *s.* réclamations indignées; **out'dated,** *a.* démodé; vieux jeu; **out'distance,** *v.tr.* distancer, dépasser (un concurrent); **out'do,** *v.tr.* (**outdid; outdone**) surpasser (qn); l'emporter sur (qn); **'outdoor,** *a.* extérieur; au dehors; (jeux) de plein air; **to put on one's o. clothes,** s'habiller pour sortir; **out'doors,** *adv.* dehors; hors de la maison; en plein air; (coucher) à la belle étoile; **'outer,** *a.* extérieur, externe; **o. space,** l'espace intersidéral; **o. garments,** vêtements de dessus; **'outfit,** *s.* **1.** équipement *m*, équipage *m*; attirail *m*; équipement *m*; **tool o.,** jeu *m* d'outils; **first aid o.,** trousse *f* de premiers secours. **2.** (*of clothes*) trousseau *m*; effets *mpl*; *Mil:* équipement. **3.** *F:* organisation *f*; **'outfitter,** *s. Com:* marchand *m* de confections, confectionneur *m*; **out'flank,** *v.tr.* (*a*) *Mil:* déborder (l'ennemi) (*b*) circonvenir (qn); **'outflow,** *s.* écoulement *m*, dépense *f* (d'eau, etc.); décharge *f* (d'un égout); **'outgoing,** *a.* sortant; **o. tide,** marée descendante; **o. mail,** courrier à expédier; **'outgoings,** *s.pl.* dépenses *f*; débours *m*; sorties *f* de fonds; **out'grow,** *v.tr.* (**outgrew; outgrown**) devenir trop grand pour (ses vêtements); perdre (une habitude, le goût de qch.); **'outhouse,** *s.* (*a*) dépendance *f*; (*b*) appentis *m*, hangar *m*; **'outing,** *s.* (*a*) promenade *f*; (*b*) excursion *f*, sortie *f*; **out'landish,** *a.* bizarre, étrange; **out'last,** *v.tr.* durer plus longtemps que (qch.); survivre à (qn); **'outlaw. I.** *s.* hors la loi *m inv.* **II.** *v.tr.* mettre (qn) hors-la-loi; **'outlay,** *s.* débours *mpl*, dépenses *fpl*, frais *mpl*; **capital o.,** dépenses d'établissement; **'outlet,** *s.* **1.** orifice *m* d'émission; issue *f.* **2.** *Com:* débouché *m* (pour marchandises); **'outline. I.** *s.* contour *m*, profil *m*; **general o. of a plan,** aperçu *m* d'un projet. **II.** *v.tr.* esquisser (qch.); **out'live,** *v.tr.* survivre à (qn); **'outlook,** *s.* vue *f*; **the o. is not very promising,** la perspective n'est pas des plus rassurantes; **to share s.o.'s o.,** entrer dans les idées, les vues, de qn;' **outlying,** *a.* éloigné, écarté; **out'moded,** *a.* démodé; **out-'number,** *v.tr.* l'emporter en nombre sur, être plus nombreux que (l'ennemi, etc.); **'out-of-'date,** *a.* (*a*) vieilli; démodé; vieux jeu; (*b*) (passeport) périmé; **'out-of-'doors,** *adv.* = OUTDOORS; **'out-of-the-'way,** *a.* **1.** (*of house*) écarté. **2.** peu ordinaire; (*of price*) **not o.-of-t.-w.,** pas exorbitant; **'out-patient,** *s.* malade *mf* externe; **out-patients' department,** service *m* de consultations externes; **'output,** *s.* rendement *m* (d'une machine); production *f* (d'une mine); débit *m* (d'un générateur).

outrage ['autreidʒ]. **I.** *s.* (*a*) outrage *m*, atteinte *f*; (*b*) (**bomb**) o., attentat *m*. **II.** *v.tr.* outrager, faire outrage à (la morale, etc.); **out'rageous,** *a.* (*a*) immodéré, indigne; (*of price*) excessif; (*b*) outrageant, outrageux; (conduite) atroce; -**ly,** *adv.* (*a*) immodérément; outre mesure; **o. dear,** horriblement cher; (*b*) d'une façon scandaleuse, indigne.

outright ['autrait]. **I.** *adv.* **1.** (*a*) complètement; **to buy sth. o.,** acheter qch. comptant, à forfait; (*b*) **to kill s.o. o.,** tuer qn raide. **2.** franchement, carrément; **to laugh o. (at s.o.),** partir d'un franc rire (au nez de qn); éclater de rire. **II.** *a.* **1. o. sale,** vente *f* à forfait; **o. purchase,** marché *m* forfaitaire. **2.** (*of manner*) franc, carré.

outset ['autset], *s.* commencement *m*; **at the o.,** au début; tout d'abord; **from the o.,** dès le début, dès l'origine, dès l'abord.

outside [aut'said]. **1.** *s.* (*a*) extérieur *m*, dehors *m*; **on the o. of sth.,** à l'extérieur de qch.; **to open a door from the o.,** ouvrir une porte du dehors; (*b*) **at the o.,** tout au plus; au maximum. **2.** *a.* (*a*) du dehors, extérieur; (*b*) **an o. opinion,** un avis du dehors, un avis étranger; (*c*) **it's an o. chance,** il y a tout juste une chance (de réussite). **3.** *adv.* dehors, à l'extérieur, en dehors; **I've left my dog o.,** j'ai laissé mon chien dehors, à la porte; **seen from o.,** vu de dehors. **4.** *prep.* en dehors de, hors de, à l'extérieur de; **o. the house,** en dehors de la maison; **out'sider,** *s.* (*a*) étranger, -ère; profane *mf*; intrus, -use; (*b*) Rac: outsider *m*.

outsize ['autsaiz], *s.* Com: dimension *f*, pointure *f*, hors série; taille exceptionnelle; **for outsizes,** pour les grandes tailles; *a.* **o. packet,** paquet géant.

outskirts ['autskə:ts], *s.pl.* abords *m*; lisière *f* (d'une forêt); faubourgs *mpl*, banlieue *f*, approches *fpl* (d'une ville).

outspoken [aut'spoukən], *a.* (*of pers.*) franc; carré, rond; **to be o.,** avoir son franc-parler; -**ly,** *adv.* carrément, rondement; **out-'spokenness,** *s.* franchise *f*; franc-parler *m*.

outstanding [aut'stændiŋ], *a.* **1.** (trait) saillant; (incident) marquant; (artiste, etc.) hors ligne, éminent. **2.** (affaire) en suspens; (compte) im-

payé, dû; (paiement) en retard, arriéré; -**ly,** *adv.* éminemment; **he's not o. talented,** son talent n'est pas hors ligne.

outstay [aut'stei], *v.tr.* **1.** rester plus longtemps que (qn). **2. to o. one's welcome,** lasser l'amabilité de ses hôtes.

outvote [aut'vout], *v.tr.* obtenir une majorité sur (qn); **to be outvoted,** être mis en minorité.

outward ['autwəd]. **1.** *a.* (*a*) en dehors; Nau: pour l'étranger; Rail: **o. half,** billet *m* d'aller; **the o. voyage,** l'aller *m*; (*b*) extérieur; de dehors. **2.** *adv.* au dehors; Nau: **o. bound** (navire) (i) en partance, sortant, (ii) faisant route pour l'étranger; -**ly,** *adv.* **1.** à l'extérieur, au dehors. **2.** en apparence; **'outwards,** *adv.* au dehors; vers l'extérieur.

outwit [aut'wit], *v.tr.* (**outwitted**) **1.** circonvenir (qn); déjouer les intentions de (qn); duper (qn). **2.** dépister (la police).

oval ['ouv(ə)l]. **1.** *a.* ovale; en ovale. **2.** *s.* ovale *m*.

ovary ['ouvəri], *s.* ovaire *m*.

ovation [ou'veiʃ(ə)n], *s.* ovation *f*.

oven ['ʌv(ə)n], *s.* four *m*; **in the o.,** au four; **to cook sth. in a very slow o.,** faire cuire qch. à four très doux; **this room's like an o.,** est une fournaise; **'ovenware,** *s.* vaisselle allant au four.

over ['ouvər]. **I.** *prep.* **1.** (*a*) **to spread a cloth o. sth.,** étendre une toile par-dessus, sur qch.; (*b*) **famous all o. the world,** célèbre par tout le monde; (*c*) **o. (the top of) sth.,** par-dessus qch.; **to throw sth. o. the wall,** jeter qch. par-dessus le mur; **to fall o. a cliff,** tomber du haut d'une falaise. **2.** (*a*) **jutting out o. the street,** faisant saillie sur la rue; **his name is o. the door,** il a son nom au-dessus de la porte; **with water o. one's ankles,** avec de l'eau par dessus la cheville; (*b*) **to have an advantage o. s.o.,** avoir un avantage sur qn; (*c*) **bending o. his work,** courbé sur son travail; **sitting o. the fire,** assis tout près du feu. **3.** (*a*) **the house o. the way,** la maison d'en face; **o. the border,** au delà de la frontière; (*b*) **the bridge o. the river,** le pont qui traverse la rivière. **4. o. fifty pounds,** plus de cinquante livres; **o. five (years old),** au dessus, de plus, de cinq ans; **he's o. fifty,** il dépassé la cinquantaine; **o. and above,** en plus de, en sus de. **5. o. the last three years,** au cours des trois dernières années. **II.** *adv.* **1.** (*a*) su toute la surface; **to be dusty all o.,** être tou couvert de poussière; **to ache all o.,** avoir ma partout; (*b*) **to read a letter o.,** lire une lettre e entier; **to do sth. all o. again,** refaire qch. d'u bout à l'autre; (*c*) **ten times o.,** dix fois de suite **twice o.,** à deux reprises; **o. and o. (again),** plusieurs reprises; maintes et maintes fois. (*a*) par-dessus (qch.); **to jump o.,** sauter pa dessus; **the milk boiled o.,** le lait s'est sauvé; (*b* **to lean o.,** (*of pers.*) se pencher (à la fenêtre etc.); (*of thg*) pencher. **3.** (*a*) **to fall o.**, (*of pers.*) tomber (par terre); (*of thg*) se renverser; être renversé; **to knock sth. o.**, renverser qch.; (*b*) **please turn o.**, voir au dos; tournez, s'il vous plaît; **to turn sth. o. and o.**, tourner et retourner qch.; **to bend sth. o.**, replier qch. **4. to cross o.**, traverser (la rue); faire la traversée (de la Manche); **o. there**, là-bas; **o. here**, ici; de ce côté. **5.** en plus, en excès; (*a*) **children of sixteen and o.**, les enfants qui ont seize ans et plus; (*b*) **keep what's left o.**, gardez le surplus; **I have a card o.**, j'ai une carte de, en, trop; **o. and above**, en outre; (*c*) **the question is held o.**, la question est différée; (*d*) (*in compounds*) (i) trop; à l'excès; **o.-abundant**, surabondant; **o.-particular**, trop exigeant; **o.-scrupulous**, scrupuleux à l'excès; (ii) **o.-confidence**, excès de confiance; (iii) **to overstretch a spring**, trop tendre, distendre, un ressort. **6.** fini, achevé; **the danger is o.**, le danger est passé; **it's all o.**, c'est fini; tout est fini; **it's all o. with me**, c'en est fait de moi; **'overall. 1.** *a.* total, global, d'ensemble; **o. length**, longueur hors tout. **2.** *s.* (*a*) blouse *f*; (*b*) *pl.* **overalls**, salopette *f*; combinaison *f*; **'overarm**, *a. Swimming:* (nage) indienne (*f*); *Cricket:* (service) par le haut; **over'awe**, *v.tr.* intimider (qn); en imposer à (qn); **over'balance. 1.** *v.tr.* renverser (qch.). **2.** *v.i.* (*of pers.*) perdre l'équilibre; (*of thg*) se renverser; tomber; **over'bearing**, *a.* arrogant, impérieux, autoritaire; **'overboard**, *adv. Nau:* par-dessus bord; **to fall o.**, tomber à la mer; **over'burden**, *v.tr.* surcharger, accabler (**with**, de); *F:* **he's not overburdened with work**, ce n'est pas le travail qui l'écrase; **'overcast**, *a.* (ciel) couvert, nuageux; **'over'charge. I.** *s.* prix excessif; prix surfait. **II.** *v.tr. & i.* **to o. s.o.**, faire payer trop cher un article à qn; **'overcoat**, *s.* pardessus *m*; **over'come. I.** *v.tr.* (**overcame**) triompher de, vaincre (ses ennemis); venir à bout de (ses difficultés); surmonter (son émotion). **II.** *a.* **to be o. with, by** (**sth.**), être accablé de (douleur); être gagné par (le sommeil); succomber à (la chaleur, l'émotion); **over'crowded**, *a.* (*a*) trop rempli (**with**, de); (train) bondé (**with people**, de monde); (*b*) (*of town, forest*) surpeuplé; **over'crowding**, *s.* encombrement *m*; surpeuplement *m*; **'overde'veloped**, *a.* développé à l'excès; *Phot:* **o. negative**, cliché trop poussé; **over'do**, *v.tr.* (**overdid**; **overdone**) **1. to o. things**, se surmener. **2.** *Cu:* trop cuire (qch.); **'overdose**, *s.* trop forte dose; dose (i) nuisible, (ii) mortelle; **'overdraft**, *s. Bank:* découvert *m*; solde débiteur; **over'draw**, *v.tr.* (**overdrew**; **overdrawn**) *Bank:* mettre (son compte) à découvert; **overdrawn account**, compte découvert; **'overdrive**, *s. Aut:* vitesse surmultipliée; **over'due**,

a. arriéré, en retard; **over'eat**, *v.i.* (**overate**; **overeaten**) trop manger; **over'eating**, *s.* excès *mpl* de table; **over'estimate. I.** *s.* surestimation *f.* **II.** *v.tr.* surestimer; exagérer (le danger, etc.); **'overex'ertion**, *s.* surmenage *m*; **'overex'pose**, *v.tr. Phot:* surexposer; **'overex'posure**, *s. Phot:* surexposition *f*; **over'fed**, *a.* (chien, etc.) qui mange trop; **over'filled**, *a.* (verre) plein à déborder; **overflow. I.** ['ouvə-], *s.* **1.** débordement *m*, épanchement *m* (d'un liquide); (*b*) inondation *f.* **2.** trop-plein *m inv*; **o. pipe**, (tuyau *m* de) trop-plein; déversoir. **3. o. meeting**, réunion *f* supplémentaire. **II.** [ouvə'flou]. **1.** *v.tr.* (*a*) déborder de (la coupe); (*b*) (*of river*) inonder (un champ); **to o. its banks**, sortir de son lit. **2.** *v.i.* déborder; **over'flowing**, *s.* **full to o.**, plein à déborder; **over'grown**, *a.* couvert (de qch.); **o. with weeds**, (jardin) envahi par les mauvaises herbes; **'over'hang**, *v.tr.* (**overhung**) surplomber; **'overhanging**, *a.* surplombant, en surplomb; **overhaul.1.** *s.* ['ouvəhɔ:l],(*a*) examen détaillé; révision (d'une machine); (*b*) remise en état. **II.** *v.tr.* [ouvə'hɔ:l]. **1.** examiner en détail; réviser; remettre en état, réparer. **2.** *Nau:* rattraper, dépasser (un autre navire); **overhead. 1.** *adv.* ['ouvə'hed], au-dessus (de la tête); en haut, en l'air. **2.** *a.* ['ouvəhed], (*a*) **o. cable**, câble aérien; (*b*) *Com:* **o. expenses**, *s.pl.* **overheads**, frais généraux; (*c*) *Aut:* (soupapes) en tête; **over'hear**, *v.tr.* (**overheard**) surprendre (une conversation); **over'heat. 1.** *v.tr.* surchauffer, trop chauffer. **2.** *v.i. Aut:* **the engine is overheating**, le moteur chauffe; **over'in'dulge. 1.** *v.tr.* gâter (ses enfants). **2.** *v.i.* **o.-i. in wine**, abuser du vin; **over'joyed**, *a.* transporté de joie; au comble de la joie; **to be o. to see s.o.**, être ravi de voir qn; **'overland. 1.** *adv.* par voie de terre. **2.** *a.* **o. route**, voie *f* de terre; **overlap. I.** [ouvə'læp], *v.tr. & i.* (**overlapped**) **1. to o.** (**one another**), chevaucher. **2.** dépasser (l'extrémité de qch.). **3.** faire double emploi. **II.** ['ouvə-], *s.* chevauchement *m*; **'over'leaf**, *adv.* au dos, au verso (de la page); **over'load**, *v.tr.* **1.** surcharger. **2.** surmener (une machine); **over'look**, *v.tr.* **1.** avoir vue sur (qch.); (*of building*) dominer, commander; (*of window*) donner sur (la rue). **2.** (*a*) oublier, négliger (qch.); **I overlooked the fact**, ce fait m'a échappé; (*b*) fermer les yeux sur (qch.); **we'll o. it**, passons; **o. it this time**, passez-le-moi cette fois; **'over'much**, *adv.* (par) trop; à l'excès; **overnight. 1.** *adv.* ['ouvə'nait], (*a*) la veille (au soir); (*b*) (pendant) la nuit; **to stay o.**, passer une nuit; (*of food*) **to keep o.**, se conserver jusqu'au lendemain. **2.** *a.* ['ouvənait], de la veille; **o. stay**, séjour *m* d'une seule nuit; **o. bag**, sac *m* de voyage; **overpass**, *s. Civ.E:* enjambement *m*; passage supérieur; **'over'payment**, *s.* surpaye

f; paiement *m* en trop; **over'play,** *v.tr.* **to o. one's hand,** viser trop haut; **over'power,** *v.tr.* maîtriser, dominer, vaincre, accabler; **over'powering,** *a.* accablant; (désir) irrésistible; (odeur) très forte; *F:* (femme) imposante; **'overpro'duction,** *s.* surproduction *f*; **over'rate,** *v.tr.* surestimer; faire trop de cas de (qch.); **overrated restaurant,** restaurant surfait; **over'reach,** *v.pr.* **to o. oneself,** (i) se donner un effort; (ii) être victime de sa propre fourberie; **over'ride,** *v.tr.* **(overrode; overridden)** (*a*) outrepasser (un ordre); (*b*) avoir plus d'importance que (qch.); **considerations that o. all others,** considérations qui l'emportent sur toutes les autres; **'overrider,** *s.* *Aut:* sabot *m* (de parechoc); **'over'ripe,** *a.* trop mûr; **over'rule,** *v.tr.* (*a*) décider contre (l'avis de qn); (*b*) *Jur:* annuler, casser (un arrêt); rejeter (une réclamation); (*c*) passer outre à (une difficulté); passer à l'ordre du jour sur (une objection); **over'run,** *v.* **(overran; overrun)** I. *v.tr.* 1. (*a*) (*of invaders*) se répandre sur, envahir (un pays); dévaster (un pays); (*b*) **house o. with mice,** maison infestée de souris. 2. dépasser (la limite). II. *v.i.* déborder; **over'seas.** 1. *adv.* outre-mer. 2. *a.* d'outremer; **'overseer,** *s.* surveillant, -ante; *Ind:* contremaître, -tresse; chef *m* d'atelier; **over'shadow,** *v.tr.* 1. couvrir de son ombre. 2. éclipser (qn); surpasser en éclat; **'over'shoot,** *v.tr.* **(overshot)** dépasser, aller plus loin que (ie point d'arrêt); *Av:* se présenter trop long sur (la piste); **to o. the mark,** dépasser le but; **'oversight,** *s.* oubli *m*, omission *f*; **through, by, an o.,** par mégarde, par inadvertance; **over'sleep,** *v.i.* **(overslept)** dormir trop tard, ne pas se réveiller à temps; **over'spend,** *v.i.* **(overspent)** dépenser trop; **over'state,** *v.tr.* exagérer (les faits); **over'statement,** *s.* exagération *f*; récit exagéré; **over'stay,** *v.tr.* dépasser (son congé); **to o. one's welcome,** lasser l'amabilité de ses hôtes; **over'step,** *v.tr.* **(overstepped)** outrepasser, dépasser (les bornes); **'over'stuffed,** *a.* rembourré, capitonné; **over'take,** *v.tr.* **(overtook, overtaken)** 1. (*a*) rattraper, atteindre (qn); (*b*) doubler, dépasser (une voiture). 2. (*of catastrophe*) frapper (qn); **over'taking,** *s.* *Aut:* dépassement *m*; **no o.,** défense de doubler; **'over'tax,** *v.tr.* (*a*) pressurer (le peuple); accabler (la nation) d'impôts; (*b*) trop exiger de (qn); **to o. one's strength,** se surmener; abuser de ses forces; **over'throw,** *v.tr.* **(overthrew; overthrown)** défaire, vaincre (qn); renverser (un ministère); ruiner (les projets de qn); **'overtime.** 1. *s.* *Ind:* heures *f* supplémentaires (de travail). 2. *adv.* **to work o.,** faire des heures supplémentaires; **'overtones,** *s.pl.* **sinister o.,** allusions *f* sinistres.
overture ['ouvətjuər], *s.* 1. ouverture *f*, offre *f*; **to**

make overtures to s.o., faire des ouvertures à qn. 2. *Mus:* ouverture.
overturn [ouvə'tə:n]. 1. *v.tr.* renverser; faire verser (une voiture); (faire) chavirer (un canot). 2. *v.i.* (*a*) se renverser; chavirer; (*b*) *Aut:* capoter.
overweight ['ouvəweit], *a.* (colis) qui excède, dépasse, le poids réglementaire; (*of pers.*) **to become o.,** prendre de l'embonpoint; engraisser; **I'm 10 pounds o.,** je pèse 5 kilos de trop.
overwhelm [ouvə'(h)welm], *v.tr.* 1. ensevelir (une ville dans la lave); submerger. 2. (*a*) écraser, accabler (l'ennemi); (*b*) **to be overwhelmed with work,** être débordé, accablé, de travail; (*c*) combler (qn de bontés); **over'whelmed,** *a.* confus, honteux; **o. with joy,** au comble de la joie; **over'whelming,** *a.* irrésistible; accablant; **o. majority,** majorité écrasante; **of o. importance,** de la première importance.
overwork ['ouvə'wə:k]. I. *s.* surmenage *m*. II. *v.* 1. *v.tr.* surmener; surcharger (qn) de travail. 2. *v.i.* se surmener; travailler outre mesure.
owe [ou], *v.tr.* 1. **to o. s.o. sth., to o. sth. to s.o.,** devoir qch. à qn; *v.i.* **I still o. you for the petrol,** je vous dois encore l'essence. 2. **I o. my life to you,** je vous dois la vie; **to what do I o. this honour?** qu'est-ce qui me vaut cet honneur? **'owing.** 1. *a.* dû; **the money o. to me,** l'argent qui m'est dû. 2. **o. to,** à cause de, par suite de; **o. to a recent bereavement . . .,** en raison d'un deuil récent . . . .
owl [aul], *s.* *Orn:* hibou *m*; **the o.,** le hibou; **tawny o.,** chouette *f* des bois; **'owlet,** *s.* jeune hibou.
own [oun]. I. *v.tr.* 1. posséder; **who owns this land?** qui est le propriétaire de cette terre? 2. reconnaître; (*a*) **dog that nobody will o.,** chien que personne ne réclame; (*b*) avouer (qch.). 3. convenir de (qch.). 3. *v.ind.tr.* **to o. up to a mistake,** reconnaître, avouer, une erreur; **to o. up to sth.,** faire l'aveu de qch.; *v.i.* *F:* **to o. up,** faire des aveux. II. *a.* (*a*) propre; **her o. money,** son propre argent; (*b*) le mien, le tien, etc.; à moi, toi, etc.; **the house is my o.,** la maison est à moi; **my time is my o.,** mon temps est à moi. III. *s.* **my o., his o.,** etc., (*a*) le mien, le sien, etc. **I have money of my o.,** j'ai de l'argent à moi; **he has a copy of his o.,** il a un exemplaire à lui en propre; **for reasons of his o.,** pour des raisons particulières; **to come into one's o.,** recevoir sa récompense; *F:* **to get one's o. back,** prendre sa revanche; **he can hold his o.,** il sait se défendre; (*b*) **to do sth. on one's o.,** faire qch. (i) de sa propre initiative, (ii) indépendamment, tout seul; **I'm (all) on my o. today,** je suis seul aujourd'hui; **'owner,** *s.* propriétaire *m*, possesseur *m*; patron, -onne (d'une maison de

commerce); **joint owners,** copropriétaires *mpl*;
cars parked here at o.'s risk, garage pour
voitures aux risques et périls de leurs
propriétaires; *Aut:* **o.-driver,** conducteur *m*
propriétaire; **'ownerless,** *a.* o. **dog,** chien *m*
sans maître; **'ownership,** *s.* (droit *m* de)
propriété *f*; possession *f*.

ox, *pl.* **oxen** [ɔks, 'ɔks(ə)n], *s.* bœuf *m*; **'oxtail,** *s.*
Cu: queue *f* de bœuf; **'ox-tongue,** *s. Cu:* langue
f de bœuf.

oxide ['ɔksaid], *s. Ch:* oxyde *m*; **oxidi'zation**
[ɔksidai'zeiʃ(ə)n], *s.* oxydation *f*; **'oxidize**
['ɔksidaiz], *v.tr.* & *i.* (s')oxyder.

oxyacetylene [ɔksiə'setilin], *a.* o. **torch,**
chalumeau *m* oxyacétylénique.

oxygen ['ɔksidʒən], *s. Ch:* oxygène *m*; *Med:* o.
tent, tente *f* à oxygène.

oyster ['ɔistər], *s.* huître *f*; **pearl o.,** huître
perlière; o. **bed,** huîtrière *f*; o. **breeding,** os-
tréiculture *f*; o. **farm,** parc *m* à huîtres; clayère
f; o. **shell,** écaille *f* d'huître.

ozone ['ouzoun], *s. Ch:* ozone *m*.

P

P, p [piː], s. (la lettre) P, p m; **to mind one's P's and Q's,** se surveiller.

pace [peis]. I. s. 1. pas m; **ten paces off,** à dix pas de distance. 2. vitesse f, train m, allure f; **at a walking p.,** au pas; **at a good, smart, p.,** à vive allure; *Sp:* **to set the p.,** mener le train; **to keep p. with** (s.o., sth.), marcher de pair avec (qn, qch.). II. v. 1. v.i. **to p. up and down,** faire les cent pas. 2. v.tr. (a) arpenter (une salle, etc.); (b) **to p. off a distance,** mesurer une distance au pas; (c) *Sp:* entraîner (un coureur cycliste, etc.).

pacify ['pæsifai], v.tr. pacifier; apaiser, calmer; **pacific** [pə'sifik]. *Geog:* 1. a. **the P. coast,** la côte pacifique. 2. a. & s.m. **the P. (Ocean),** l'océan m Pacifique, le Pacifique; **'pacifism,** s. pacifisme m; **'pacifist,** s. pacifiste mf.

pack [pæk]. I. v.tr. 1. (a) emballer, empaqueter (qch.); (b) abs. faire ses malles; (c) *F:* **the T.V. has packed up,** la télé ne marche plus. 2. tasser; entasser, serrer (des voyageurs dans une voiture). 3. remplir, bourrer (**sth. with sth.,** qch. de qch.); **the train was packed,** le train était bondé; **packed hall,** salle comble. 4. **to p. a child off to bed,** envoyer un enfant au lit; *F:* **to send s.o. packing,** envoyer promener qn. II. s. 1. paquet m; ballot m (de colporteur); **p. of lies,** tissu m de mensonges. 2. bande f (de loups); **p. (of hounds),** meute f; *Rugby Fb:* **the p.,** le pack, les avants m. 3. jeu m (de cartes). 4. (ice-)**p.,** embâcle m (de glaçons); **p. ice,** glace f de banquise; **'package. I.** s. 1. empaquetage m, emballage m. 2. paquet m, colis m. 3. attrib. **p. deal,** contrat global; **p. tour,** voyage organisé. II. v.tr. *Com:* conditionner (des marchandises); **'packaged,** a. *Com:* préconditionné; **'packaging,** s. *Com:* conditionnement m; **'packer,** s. emballeur, -euse; **'packet,** s. paquet m; colis m; **'packing,** s. 1. emballage m, empaquetage m; **to do one's p.,** faire ses malles; **p. case,** caisse f d'emballage; **p. paper,** papier m pour emballage. 2. (a) matière f pour emballage; (b) garniture f (d'un piston).

pact [pækt], s. pacte m, convention f.

pad [pæd]. I. s. 1. (a) bourrelet m, coussinet m; (b) tampon m; **inking p.,** tampon encreur. 2. bloc m (de papier). 3. *Tchn:* (a) tampon amortisseur; (b) **launching p.,** base f de lancement (pour engins spatiaux, etc.). II. v.tr. (**padded**) rembourrer (un coussin); capitonner (un

meuble); **to p. (out) a speech,** délayer un discours; **'padding,** s. (a) remplissage m, rem bourrage m; (b) délayage m (d'un discours); *F* bla-bla-bla m; (c) ouate f, bourre f.

paddle¹ ['pædl]. I. s. pagaie f. II. v.tr. & pagayer.

paddle², v.i. barboter, patauger (dans l'eau, l boue); **'paddling pool,** s. piscine f de jardin

paddock ['pædək], s. (a) enclos m (pou chevaux); (b) *Rac:* pesage m, paddock m.

paddy ['pædi], s. **p. field,** rizière f.

padlock ['pædlɔk]. I. s. cadenas m. II. v.t cadenasser.

pagan ['peigən], a. & s. païen, -ïenne.

page¹ [peidʒ], s. 1. page m. 2. **p.(-boy),** chasse m (d'hôtel).

page², s. page f; **on p. 6,** à la page 6.

pageant ['pædʒənt], s. grand spectac pompeux.

paid [peid], a. (emploi) rétribué; (*of bill*) pay réglé; (*on receipted bill*) pour acquit.

pail [peil], s. seau m; **'pailful,** s. (plein) seau (lait, etc.).

pain [pein], s. 1. douleur f, souffrance f; (*menta* peine f; **to be in great p.,** souffrir beaucou **shooting pains,** élancements m; *F:* **he's a in the neck,** c'est un casse-pieds. 2. pl. **to ta pains to do sth.,** se donner du mal pour fai qch. 3. **on p. of death,** sous peine de mo **pained,** a. **p. expression,** l'air (i) triste, peiné; souffrant; **'painful,** a. 1. douloureux; **my ha is p.,** la main me fait mal. 2. (*of spectacle, effo* pénible; **-fully,** adv. (a) douloureusement; (péniblement; **'painless,** a. sans douleu indolore; **'painstaking,** a. soigneu assidu; (élève) travailleur, appliqué; (trava soigné.

paint [peint]. I. s. (a) peinture f; **gloss(y) p.,** pe ture brillante; peinture laquée; **matt p.,** pe ture mate; **coat of p.,** couche f de peintu *P.N:* **wet p.!** attention à la peinture! **p. bru** pinceau m; **p. roller,** rouleau m à peinture **spray,** pistolet m à peinture; (b) **box of pai** boîte f de couleurs. II. v. 1. (a) v.tr. peindre (portrait); (b) v.i. faire de la peinture. 2. v.tr. **p. (in words),** dépeindre. 3. v.tr. enduire peinture; peindre (une porte, une cloison); *I* **to p. (the scenery),** brosser (les décor **'painter**¹, s. 1. (artiste) peintre m. 2. (hou **p.,** peintre en bâtiment, peintre décorate **'painting,** s. 1. **to study p.,** étudier la peintu

P:1

2. peinture, tableau *m*; **'paintwork,** *s. Const:* les peintures *f.*

painter², *s. Nau:* amarre *f.*

pair¹ ['pɛər]. **I.** *s.* (a) paire *f*; **p. of scissors,** paire de ciseaux; (b) (*husband and wife*) couple *m*; (c) **a p. of trousers,** un pantalon; (d) **these two pictures are a p.,** ces deux tableaux se font pendant. **II.** *v.tr.* appareiller, assortir (des gants, etc.); accoupler (des oiseaux, etc.).

pair², *used in phr.* **au p.** (**student**), un(e) étudiant(e) au pair.

pajamas [pə'dʒæməz], *s.pl. N.Am:* pyjama *m.*

Pakistan [pɑ:kis'tɑ:n, pæk-]. *Pr.n. Geog:* le Pakistan; **Pakis'tani,** *a. & s.* pakistanais, -aise.

pal [pæl], *s. F:* camarade *mf.*

palace ['pæləs], *s.* palais *m.*

palate ['pælət], *s. Anat:* palais *m*; **'palatable,** *a.* agréable au palais, au goût.

palatial [pə'leiʃ(ə)l], *a.* magnifique, grandiose.

palaver [pə'lɑ:vər], *s.* palabre *f.*

pale [peil], *a.* (a) pâle, blême; **ghastly p.,** pâle comme la mort; **to turn p.,** pâlir; (b) (*of colour*) clair; (*of moonlight, etc.*) blafard; **'paleness,** *s.* pâleur *f*; **'palish,** *a.* un peu pâle; pâlot; **she's p. this morning,** elle est pâlotte ce matin.

Palestine ['pæləstain]. *Pr.n. Geog:* la Palestine; **Pales'tinian,** *a. & s.* palestinien, -ienne.

palette ['pælit], *s. Art:* palette *f.*

paling ['peiliŋ], *s.* (*often pl.*) palissade *f.*

palisade [pæli'seid], *s.* palissade *f.*

pall [pɔ:l]. **I.** *s.* **1.** *Ecc:* drap *m* mortuaire. **2.** manteau·*m* (de neige); voile *m* (de fumée). **II.** *v.i.* s'affadir; devenir fade (**on s.o.,** pour qn); it never palls on you, on ne s'en dégoûte jamais.

palliate ['pælieit], *v.tr.* pallier (une faute); atténuer (un vice); **palli'ation,** *s.* atténuation *f*; **'palliative,** *a. & s.* palliatif (*m*), lénitif (*m*).

pallid ['pælid], *a.* (a) pâle, décoloré; (b) (*of light*) blafard; (c) (*of face*) blême.

pallor ['pælər], *s.* pâleur *f.*

palm¹ [pɑ:m], *s.* **1.** **p.**(-**tree**), palmier *m*; **p. grove,** palmeraie *f.* **2.** *Ecc:* **P. Sunday,** le dimanche des Rameaux.

palm², *s.* paume *f* (de la main); *F:* **to grease s.o.'s p.,** graisser la patte de, à, qn; **'palmist,** *s.* chiromancien, -ienne; **'palmistry,** *s.* chiromancie *f.*

palm³, *v.tr.* **to p. a card,** escamoter une carte; **'palm'off,** *v.tr.* faire passer; *P:* refiler (**a bad coin on s.o.,** une mauvaise pièce à qn).

palpable ['pælpəbl], *a.* **1.** palpable; que l'on peut toucher. **2.** palpable; manifeste, clair; **-ably,** *adv.* manifestement; sensiblement.

palpitate ['pælpiteit], *v.i.* palpiter; **palpi'tation,** *s.* palpitation *f.*

paltry ['pɔ:ltri], *a.* misérable, mesquin; **'paltriness,** *s.* mesquinerie *f.*

pamper ['pæmpər], *v.tr.* choyer, dorloter (un

enfant).

pamphlet ['pæmflit], *s.* brochure *f.*

pan¹ [pæn], *s.* **1.** *Cu:* casserole *f*, poêlon *m*; **frying p.,** poêle *f*; **baking p., roasting p.,** plat *m* à rôtir, lèchefrite *f*; **pots and pans,** batterie *f* de cuisine. **2.** plateau *m* (d'une balance); cuvette *f* (de W.C.); **'pancake,** *s.* crêpe *f*; **p. day,** mardi gras.

pan², *v.* (**panned**) *v.i. F:* **things did not p. out as he intended,** les choses ne se sont pas passées comme il l'aurait voulu.

panacea [pænə'si:ə], *s.* panacée ·

pan-African ['pæn'æfrikən], *a* panafricain.

pan-American ['pænə'merikən], *a.* panaméricain; **'pan-A'mericanism,** *s.* panaméricanisme *m.*

panchromatic ['pænkrou'mætik], *a. Phot:* panchromatique.

pancreas ['pænkriəs], *s. Anat:* pancréas *m.*

panda ['pændə], *s. Z:* panda *m*; *F:* **p. car,** voiture *f* de police.

pandemonium [pændi'mouniəm], *s.* pandémonium *m*, bruit infernal.

pander ['pændər], *v.i.* **to p. to a vice,** se prêter à un vice; **to p. to a taste,** flatter bassement un goût.

pane [pein], *s.* vitre *f*, carreau *m.*

panel ['pæn(ə)l]. **I.** *s.* **1.** panneau *m* (de porte); *Aut: Av:* **instrument p.,** tableau *m* de bord. **2.** tableau, liste *f*; *Jur: T.V: Sch: etc:* **the p.,** le jury. **3.** commission *f.* **II.** *v.tr.* (**panelled**) recouvrir (une cloison) de panneaux; lambrisser (une cloison); **'panelling,** *s.* lambris *m*, boiserie *f*; **oak p.,** panneaux *mpl* de chêne.

pang [pæŋ], *s.* angoisse subite; douleur *f*; **the pangs of death,** les affres *f* de la mort; **to feel a p.,** sentir (i) un serrement de cœur, (ii) une petite pointe au cœur; **pangs of jealousy,** tourments *m* de la jalousie; **to feel the pangs of hunger,** avoir l'estomac creux.

panic ['pænik]. **I.** *s.* panique *f*; affolement *m*; *Journ:* **p. press,** presse *f* alarmiste. **II.** *v.i.* (**panicked**) être pris de panique; s'affoler; **'panicky,** *a. F:* sujet à la panique; alarmiste; **'panic-stricken,** *a.* pris de panique; affolé.

panorama [pænə'rɑ:mə], *s.* panorama *m*; **pan'oramic** [-'ræm-], *a.* panoramique.

pansy ['pænzi], *s. Bot:* pensée *f.*

pant [pænt], *v.i.* haleter; **to p. for breath,** chercher à reprendre haleine; **'panting,** *s.* essoufflement *m.*

panther ['pænθər], *s. Z:* panthère *f.*

panties ['pæntiz], *s.pl. Cl:* slip *m* (de femme).

pantomime ['pæntəmaim], *s. Th:* revue-féerie *f.*

pantry ['pæntri], *s.* **1.** garde-manger *m inv.* **2.** butler's p., office *f.*

pants [pænts], *s.pl. Cl:* **(pair of) p.,** caleçon *m*; *F:* pantalon *m.*

papacy ['peipəsi], *s.* papauté *f*; **'papal,** *a.* papal.

paper ['peipər]. **I.** s. **1.** papier m; (a) **brown p.,** papier gris; **cigarette p.,** papier à cigarettes; **carbon p.,** papier carbone; (b) **it's a good scheme on p.,** c'est un bon projet en théorie; **p. profits,** profits fictifs. **2.** (morceau m de) papier; document m, pièce f; **to send in one's papers,** donner sa démission; **my private papers,** mes papiers; **old papers,** paperasse(s) f(pl); **voting p.,** bulletin m de vote; Sch: **examination p.,** épreuve écrite; **to correct papers,** corriger l'écrit. **3.** journal m; **weekly p.,** hebdomadaire m. **4. p. clip,** trombone m; **p. fastener,** attache f métallique; **p. knife,** coupe-papier m inv; **p. weight,** presse-papiers m inv. **II.** v.tr. tapisser (une salle); **'paperback,** s. livre m de poche.

par [pɑ:r], s. pair m, égalité f; (a) **to be on a p. with s.o.,** être au niveau de, aller de pair avec, qn; (b) F: **to feel below p.,** ne pas être dans son assiette.

parable ['pærəbl], s. parabole f.

parachute ['pærəʃuːt]. **I.** s. parachute m; **to land arms by p.,** parachuter des armes; **p. drop,** parachutage m; **p. regiment,** régiment m de parachutistes. **II.** v.tr. & i. parachuter; **to p. down,** descendre en parachute; **'parachutist,** s. parachutiste mf.

parade [pə'reid]. **I.** s. **1.** parade f. **2.** Mil: (a) rassemblement m; (b) exercice m; **on p.,** à l'exercice; **p.-ground,** terrain m de manœuvres; place f d'armes. **3.** défilé m (de troupes, etc.); **mannequin p.,** defilé m de mannequins; **fashion p.,** présentation f de collection. **4.** esplanade f; promenade f. **II.** v. **1.** v.tr. faire parade, étalage m, de (ses richesses, etc.); Mil: faire l'inspection f (des troupes). **2.** v.i. défiler (dans les rues).

paradise ['pærədais], s. paradis m; **bird of p.,** oiseau m de paradis; **an earthly p.,** un paradis sur terre.

paradox ['pærədɔks], s. paradoxe m; **para'doxical,** a. paradoxal; **-ally,** adv. paradoxalement.

paraffin ['pærəfin], s. **1.** Ch: paraffine f; Pharm: **liquid p.,** huile f de paraffine. **2.** Com: **p. (oil),** pétrole (lampant); kérosène m; **p. store,** réchaud m à pétrole.

paragon ['pærəgən], s. modèle m (de vertu, de beauté, etc.).

paragraph ['pærəgrɑːf, -græf], s. **1.** paragraphe m, alinéa m; (indication) **p.!** à la ligne! **2.** Journ: entrefilet m.

parakeet [pærə'kiːt], s. Orn: perruche f.

parallel ['pærəlel]. **I.** a. **1.** parallèle (**with, to, à**); **in a p. direction with sth.,** parallèlement à qch. **2.** semblable; (cas) analogue (**to, with, à**). **II.** s. **1.** (a) (ligne f) parallèle f; (b) Geog: parallèle m (de latitude). **2.** parallèle m, comparaison f; **to draw a p.,** établir un parallèle (entre deux

choses); **para'llelogram,** s. parallélogramme m.

paralyse ['pærəlaiz], v.tr. paralyser; **paralysed in one leg,** paralysé d'une jambe; **paralysed with fear,** transi de peur; **'paralysing,** a. paralysant; **pa'ralysis,** s. Med: paralysie f; **para'lytic,** a. & s. paralytique (mf).

paramilitary [pærə'militri], a. paramilitaire.

paramount ['pærəmaunt], a. éminent souverain; **of p. importance,** d'une suprême importance.

paranoia [pærə'nɔiə], s. Med: paranoïa f; **para'noiac,** a. paranoïaque.

parapet ['pærəpet], s. parapet m; garde-fou m.

paraphernalia [pærəfə'neiliə], s.pl. (a) effets m affaires f; (b) attirail m, appareil m (de pêche etc.).

paraphrase ['pærəfreiz]. **I.** s. paraphrase f. **II.** v.tr. paraphraser.

parasite ['pærəsait], s. parasite m; (of pers pique-assiette m inv; **parasitic** [pærə'sitik], a (of insect, etc.) parasite (**on, de**); **p. diseas** maladie f parasitaire.

parasol ['pærəsɔl], s. ombrelle f; parasol m.

paratrooper ['pærətruːpər], s. (soldat parachutiste (m); **'paratroops,** s.pl. (soldat parachutistes.

parcel ['pɑːs(ə)l]. **I.** s. paquet m, colis m; **parce office,** bureau m de(s) messageries; **p. post,** se vice m des colis postaux; service c messageries. **II.** v.tr. (**parcelled**) empaquete (du thé); Com: mettre (des marchandises) e colis, conditionner (des marchandises); **to up a consignment of books,** emballer un env de livres.

parch [pɑːtʃ], v.tr. (a) rôtir, griller (des céréales (b) **grass parched (up) by the wind,** her desséchée par le vent; **to be parched (wi thirst),** mourir de soif.

parchment ['pɑːtʃmənt], s. parchemin m.

pardon ['pɑːd(ə)n]. **I.** s. (a) pardon m; **I beg yo p.!** je vous demande pardon! (b) Jur: **free grâce f; general p.,** amnistie f. **II.** v.tr. (a) pa donner à (qn); (b) Jur: gracier, amnistier (q **'pardonable,** a. pardonnable, excusable.

parent ['pɛərənt], s. père m, mère f; pl. parer m, les père et mère; **'parentage,** s. origine naissance f; **parental** [pə'rentəl], a. (autori etc.) des parents, des père et mère; (pouvo paternel.

parenthesis, pl. **-ses** [pə'renθəsis, -siːz], parenthèse f; **in parentheses,** ent parenthèses.

Paris ['pæris]. Pr.n. Geog: Paris m; **plaster of** plâtre m de moulage; **Parisian** [pə'riziən], a s. parisien, -ienne.

parish ['pæriʃ], s. Ecc: paroisse f; **p. chur** église paroissiale; R.C.Ch: **p. priest,** curé **pa'rishioner,** s. paroissien, -ienne.

parity ['pæriti], *s.* égalité *f*; parité *f* (de rang, de valeur).

park [pɑːk]. **I.** *s.* **1.** parc (clôturé); (**public**) **p.**, jardin public; **national p.**, parc national; *N.Am:* **ball p.**, terrain *m* de jeux. **2. car p.**, stationnement autorisé; **parking** *m*; **underground car p.**, parking souterrain. **II.** *v.tr.* (*a*) *Aut:* garer (sa voiture); *abs.* stationner; (*b*) *F:* **p. it there!** mets-le là! **'parking,** *s.* parcage *m*; *P.N.:* '**no p.**,' 'défense de stationner'; *N.Am:* **p. lot,** parking *m*; **p. meter,** compteur *m* de stationnement, parcmètre *m*; **p. lights,** feux *mpl* de position.

arliament ['pɑːləmənt], *s.* le Parlement; **Member of P.,** membre *m* du Parlement; **the Houses of P.,** le palais du Parlement; **in p.,** au parlement; **parliamen'tarian. 1.** *a.* parlementaire. **2.** *s.* membre *m* du Parlement; **parlia'mentary,** *a.* parlementaire; **p. election,** élection législative.

arlour ['pɑːlər], *s.* **beauty p.,** institut *m* de beauté; *N.Am:* **funeral p.,** pompes *f* funèbres.

arochial [pə'roukiəl], *a. Ecc:* paroissial; *Pej:* (point de vue) provincial; **p. spirit,** esprit *m* de clocher.

arody ['pærədi]. **I.** *s.* parodie *f*, pastiche *m*. **II.** *v.tr.* parodier, pasticher.

arole [pə'roul]. **I.** *s.* **prisoner on p.,** prisonnier sur parole. **II.** *v.tr.* libérer (un prisonnier) (i) sur parole, (ii) conditionnellement.

arquet ['pɑːkei], *s.* **p.** (**floor**), parquet *m*; **p. flooring,** parquetage *m*.

arrot ['pærət], *s. Orn:* perroquet *m*.

arry ['pæri], *v.tr.* parer, détourner (un coup).

arsimony ['pɑːsiməni], *s.* parcimonie *f*; *F:* pingrerie *f*; **parsi'monious,** *a.* parcimonieux; *F:* pingre; **-ly,** *adv.* parcimonieusement.

arsley ['pɑːsli], *s. Bot:* persil *m*.

arsnip ['pɑːsnip], *s.* panais *m*.

arson ['pɑːs(ə)n], *s. Ecc:* **1.** titulaire *m* d'un bénéfice de l'église anglicane). **2.** *F:* pasteur *m*; **'parsonage,** *s.* = presbytère *m*, cure *f*.

art [pɑːt]. **I.** *s.* **1.** (*a*) partie *f*; **good in parts,** bon en partie; **the funny p. is . . .,** le comique de l'histoire, c'est . . .; **in my p. of the world . . .,** (par) chez moi . . .; (*b*) *Ind:* pièce *f*; **spare parts,** pièces de rechange, pièces détachées; (*c*) **parts of speech,** parties du discours; (*d*) fascicule *m* (d'une œuvre littéraire). **2.** (*a*) part *f*; **to take p. in sth.,** prendre part à qch.; (*b*) *Th:* rôle *m*, personnage *m*; **to play one's p.,** remplir son rôle; (*c*) **orchestral parts,** parties d'orchestre. **3.** (*a*) **to take s.o.'s p.,** prendre le parti de qn; (*b*) **an indiscretion on the p. of s.o.,** une indiscrétion de la part de qn; **for my p.,** quant à moi, pour ma part. **4. to take sth. in good p.,** prendre qch. en bonne part. **II.** *adv.* **p. eaten,** partiellement mangé; mangé en partie. **III.** *v.* **1.** *v.tr.* (*a*) séparer (**from,** de); **to p. one's**

hair, se faire une raie; (*b*) rompre (une amarre, etc.). **2.** *v.i.* (*a*) se diviser; (*b*) (*of two people*) se quitter, se séparer; (*of roads*) diverger; **to p. with one's money,** débourser; (*c*) (se) rompre; céder; **'parting,** *s.* **1.** (*a*) séparation *f*; (*b*) départ *m*; **a few p. directions,** quelques dernières recommandations. **2.** rupture *f* (d'un câble). **3.** (*of the hair*) raie *f*.

partial ['pɑːʃ(ə)l], *a.* **1.** (*a*) partial; injuste; (*b*) **to be p. to sth.**, avoir un faible pour qch.; **I'm p. to a pipe,** je fume volontiers une pipe. **2.** partiel; en partie; **p. board,** demi-pension *f*; **-ally,** *adv.* **1.** partialement; avec partialité. **2.** partiellement; en partie; **parti'ality,** *s.* partialité *f* (**for, to,** pour, envers); favoritisme *m*; **a p. for the bottle,** un penchant pour la boisson.

participate [pɑː'tisipeit], *v.i.* **to p. in sth.**, prendre part, participer, s'associer, à qch.; **par'ticipant,** *s.* participant, -ante; **partici'pation,** *s.* participation *f* (**in,** à).

participle ['pɑːtisipl], *s. Gram:* participe *m*.

particle ['pɑːtikl], *s.* particule *f*, parcelle *f* (de sable, etc.); *Atom.Ph:* particule; **not a p. of evidence,** pas la moindre preuve.

particular [pə'tikjulər]. **I.** *a.* **1.** particulier; spécial; **a p. object,** un objet déterminé; **my own p. feelings,** mes propres sentiments, mes sentiments personnels; **for no p. reason,** sans raison précise; **in p.,** en particulier; notamment. **2.** (*of pers.*) méticuleux, minutieux; pointilleux; **to be p. about one's food,** être difficile sur la nourriture; **to be p. about one's clothes,** soigner sa mise. **3. I'm not p. about it,** je n'y tiens pas plus que ça; **-ly,** *adv.* particulièrement; **I want it p. for tomorrow,** il me le faut absolument pour demain; **I p. asked him to be careful,** je lui ai recommandé avant tout d'être prudent. **II.** *s.* détail *m*, particularité *f*; **alike in every p.,** semblables en tout point; **for further particulars apply to . . .,** pour plus amples renseignements, s'adresser à . . ..

partisan [pɑːti'zæn], *s.* partisan, -ane.

partition [pɑː'tiʃ(ə)n]. **I.** *s.* **1.** partage *m* (d'un pays); morcellement *m* (d'une terre). **2.** (*a*) cloison *f*; **glass p.,** vitrage *m*; (*b*) compartiment *m* (de cale, etc.). **II.** *v.tr.* **1.** partager; morceler. **2. to p.** (**off**) **a room,** cloisonner une pièce.

partly ['pɑːtli], *adv.* partiellement; en partie.

partner ['pɑːtnər], *s.* (*a*) associé, -ée; **sleeping p.,** commanditaire *m*; (*b*) *Sp:* partenaire *mf*; (*c*) **dancing p.,** cavalier, -ière; **'partnership,** *s.* **1.** association *f*; *Com:* **to go into p. with s.o.,** s'associer avec qn; **to take s.o into p.,** prendre qn comme associé. **2.** *Com: Ind:* société *f*; **limited p.,** société en commandite *f*.

partridge ['pɑːtridʒ], *s.* perdrix *f*.

party ['pɑːti], *s.* **1.** *Pol:* parti *m* (politique); **to follow the p. line,** obéir aux directives du parti. **2. private p.,** réunion *f* intime; **evening p.,**

soirée *f*; **to give a p.,** recevoir du monde; **will you join our p.?** voulez-vous être des nôtres? **3.** (*a*) bande *f*, groupe *m* (de touristes, etc.); (*b*) **rescue p.,** équipe *f* de secours; (*c*) *Mil:* détachement *m.* **4.** (*a*) **a third p.,** un tiers, une tierce personne; **third-p. insurance,** assurance *f* au tiers; (*b*) **to be** (**a**) **p. to a crime,** être complice d'un crime; (*c*) *P.T.T:* **p. line,** ligne partagée.

pass [pɑːs]. **I.** *v.* **1.** *v.i.* passer; **everyone smiles as he passes,** chacun sourit à son passage; **the procession passed (by) slowly,** le cortège défilait lentement; **to let s.o. p.,** livrer passage à qn; (*of time*) **to p. (by),** (se) passer, s'écouler; **when five minutes had passed,** au bout de cinq minutes. **2.** *v.tr.* (*a*) passer devant, près de (qn, qch.); **to p. s.o. on the stairs,** croiser qn dans l'escalier; (*b*) passer, franchir (la frontière); passer devant (une fenêtre); dépasser, doubler (une autre voiture); (*c*) dépasser (le but); outrepasser (les bornes de qch.); **that passes my comprehension,** cela me dépasse; (*d*) **to p. an examination,** être reçu à un examen; réussir un examen; (*e*) **to p. a dividend,** approuver un dividende; (*f*) *Sch:* **to p. a candidate,** recevoir un candidat; (*g*) *Parl:* **to p. a bill,** voter, adopter, un projet de loi; (*h*) transmettre, donner; **p. me the salt,** passez-moi le sel; (*i*) **to p. the time,** passer le temps; (*j*) **to p. sentence,** prononcer le jugement; *F:* **to p. the buck,** se débrouiller sur le voisin. **II.** *s.* **1.** col *m*, défilé *m* (de montagne). **2.** *Sch:* **to obtain a p.,** être reçu. **3.** laisser-passer *m inv.* **4.** *Fb: etc:* passe *f*; *F:* **to make a p. at s.o.,** faire des avances (amoureuses) à qn; **'passable,** *a.* passable, assez bon; **-ably,** *adv.* passablement; **passage** [ˈpæsidʒ], *s.* **1.** passage *m.* **2.** couloir *m*, corridor *m.* **3. air, sea, p.,** voyage *m* par avion, par bateau. **4.** passage (d'un texte); **'passenger,** *s.* voyageur, -euse; **'passer-'by,** *s.* passant, -ante; **'passing. I.** *a.* (*a*) passant; **p. remark,** remarque en passant; (*b*) passager, éphémère. **II.** *s.* passage *m* (d'un train); dépassement *m* (d'une autre voiture); écoulement *m* (du temps); **'pass 'off. 1.** *v.i.* **everything passed off well,** tout s'est bien passé. **2.** *v.tr.* **to p. oneself off as an actor,** se faire passer pour comédien; **pass 'on,** *v.tr.* (*a*) remettre (qch. à qn); **read this and p. it on,** lisez ceci et faites circuler; (*b*) transmettre (une nouvelle); **'pass 'over. 1.** *v.i. passer* (qch.) sous silence; (*of storm*) se dissiper. **2.** *v.tr.* **to p. s.o. over (for promotion),** passer par-dessus le dos à qn; **'passport,** *s.* passeport *m*; **'pass 'round,** *v.tr.* **to p. round the wine,** faire circuler le vin; **'pass 'through,** *v.tr.* traverser; **past. I.** *a.* passé, ancien; **in times p.,** autrefois; **for some time p.,** depuis quelque temps. **II.** *s.* passé *m.* **III.** *prep.* (*a*) au delà de . . .; **to walk p. s.o.,** passer devant qn; (*b*) (*of time*) plus de; **a**

quarter p. four, quatre heures et quart, quatre heures un quart; **he's p. eighty,** il a quatre-vingts ans passés. **IV.** *adv.* **to walk, go, p.,** passer.

passion [ˈpæʃ(ə)n], *s.* **1.** passion *f*; **ruling p.,** passion dominante; **p. for work,** acharnement *m* au travail. **2.** colère *f*, emportement *m*; **fit of p.,** accès de colère; **to be in a p.,** être furieux. **3.** amour *m*, passion; **'passionate,** *a.* **1.** emporté; (discours) véhément. **2.** passionné; **-ly** *adv.* passionnément; (aimer qn) à la folie.

passive [ˈpæsiv], *a. & s.* passif (*m*); *Gram:* **the p** (**voice**), la voix passive; le passif; **-ly,** *adv* passivement.

paste [peist]. **I.** *s.* **1.** (*a*) **tooth p.,** (pâte *f*) den tifrice *m*; (*b*) **anchovy p.,** beurre *m* d'anchois (*c*) colle *f.* **2.** (*of jewellery*) faux brillants; **it'** only p.,** c'est du toc. **II.** *v.tr.* coller (une affiche etc.); *F:* **to p. s.o.,** flanquer une raclée à qn.

pastel [ˈpæst(ə)l], *s. Art:* pastel *m*; **p. drawing** dessin *m* au pastel; *Cl:* **p. shades,** couleurs tendres; tons *m* pastel.

pasteurize [ˈpɑːstjəraiz], *v.tr.* pasteuriser **pasteuri'zation,** *s.* pasteurisation *f.*

pastime [ˈpɑːstaim], *s.* passe-temps *m inv*, dive tissement *m.*

pastor [ˈpɑːstər], *s. Ecc:* pasteur *m*, ministre *n*

pastry [ˈpeistri], *s.* **1.** pâtisserie *f.* **2.** pâte *f* (c pâtisserie); **'pastry-cook,** *s.* pâtissier, -ière.

pasture [ˈpɑːstjər]. **I.** *s.* pâturage *m*, pacage *n* **II.** *v.i. & tr.* pacager; (faire) paître.

pasty[1] [ˈpeisti], *a.* pâteux; **p. face,** visage terreu:

pasty[2] [ˈpæsti], *s. Cu:* (petit) pâté (en croûte).

pat [pæt]. **I.** *s.* **1.** (*a*) coup léger; petite tape; (caresse *f*; **p. on the back,** éloge *m*; mot *m* d'e couragement. **2.** médaillon *m*, coquille *f* (beurre). **II.** *v.tr.* (**patted**) taper, tapote caresser; **to p. s.o. on the back,** encourager q **to p. oneself on the back,** s'applaudir; **to p. t dog,** flatter le chien.

patch [pætʃ]. **I.** *s.* **1.** pièce *f* (pour racco moder); **not to be a p. on s.o.,** ne pas arriver à cheville de qn. **2.** *Cy:* (**rubber**) **p.** (**for inn tube**), pastille *f.* **3.** tache *f* (de couleur); **p. blue sky,** échappée *f* de ciel bleu. **4.** (morceau *m*, parcelle *f* (de terre); (*b*) carré plant *m* (de légumes). **II.** *v.tr.* rapiécer, r commoder (un vêtement); *Cy:* poser u pastille à (une chambre à air); **to p. sth.** rapetasser, rafistoler, qch.; **'patchwork,** ouvrage fait de pièces et de morcea **'patchy,** *a.* inégal.

pâté [ˈpætei], *s. Cu:* pâté *m.*

patent [ˈpætənt, ˈpei-]. **I.** *a.* **1. letters p.,** lett patentes. **2.** breveté; **p. medicine,** spécia pharmaceutique; **p. leather,** cuir verni. **3.** (f etc.) patent, manifeste clair. **II.** *s.* **1. p. nobility,** lettres de noblesse. **2.** (*a*) brevet d'invention; **to take out a p. for an inventi**

faire breveter une invention; **infringement of a p.**, contrefaçon *f*; (*b*) invention brevetée. III. *v.tr.* faire breveter.

paternity [pə'tə:niti], *s.* (*a*) paternité *f*; (*b*) origine *f*; **he's of French p.**, il est d'origine française; **pa'ternal**, *a.* paternel; **-ally**, *adv.* paternellement.

path, *pl.* **paths** [pɑ:θ, pɑ:ðz], *s.* 1. chemin *m*; sentier *m*; (*in garden*) allée *f*. 2. course *f*, orbite *f* (d'une planète); route *f* (du soleil); trajectoire *f* (de l'orage, d'une fusée); **'pathway**, *s.* sentier *m*.

pathetic [pə'θetik], *a.* pathétique, attendrissant; **-ally**, *adv.* pathétiquement.

pathology [pə'θɔlədʒi], *s.* pathologie *f*; **patho'logical**, *a.* pathologique; **pa'thologist**, *s.* (*a*) pathologiste *mf*; (*b*) médecin *m* légiste.

pathos ['peiθɔs], *s.* pathétique *m*; **told with p.**, raconté d'une façon touchante.

patience ['peiʃ(ə)ns], *s.* 1. patience *f*; **to try s.o.'s p.**, exercer la patience de qn; **my p. is exhausted**, je suis à bout de patience; **I have no p. with him**, il m'impatiente. 2. *Cards:* réussite *f*; **'patient.** I. *a.* patient, endurant; **to be p.**, patienter; **-ly**, *adv.* patiemment. II. *s.* malade *mf*; patient *m*.

Patrick ['pætrik]. *Pr.n. m.* Patrice.

patrimony ['pætriməni], *s.* patrimoine *m*.

patriot ['peitriət, 'pæ-], *s.* patriote *mf*; **patri'otic**, *a.* (*of pers.*) patriote (discours) patriotique; **-ally**, *adv.* (agir) en patriote, patriotiquement; **'patriotism**, *s.* patriotisme *m*.

patrol [pə'troul]. I. *s.* patrouille *f*; **p. leader**, chef *m* de patrouille; **to go on p.**, faire la patrouille; *Scouting:* troupe *f*; **p. leader**, chef de troupe; **police p. car**, voiture *f* de liaison policière; *N.Am:* **p. wagon**, voiture cellulaire, F: panier *m* à salade. II. *v.* (**patrolled**) 1. *v.i.* patrouiller; faire une ronde. 2. *v.tr.* faire la patrouille dans (un quartier); **pa'trolman**, *pl.* **-men**, *s.* *N.Am:* 1. patrouilleur *m*. 2. agent *m* de police.

patron ['peitrən]. 1. *s.* (*a*) protecteur *m* (des arts); patron *m* (d'une œuvre de charité); (*b*) *Ecc:* **p. saint**, patron, -onne; (*c*) *Ecc:* patron (d'un bénéfice). 2. *s.m. & f. Com:* client, -ente (d'un magasin); **the patrons of a theatre**, le public, les habitués, d'un théâtre; **patronage** ['pætrən-], *s.* (*a*) patronage *m*; protection *f*, encouragement *m* (des arts, etc.); (*b*) air protecteur (envers qn); (*c*) clientèle *f* (d'un hôtel, etc.); **patronize** ['pæ-], *v.tr.* 1. protéger (un artiste); traiter (qn) avec condescendance. 2. accorder sa clientèle à (un magasin); fréquenter (un cinéma); **patronizing** ['pæ-], *a.* (*a*) protecteur; (*b*) **p. tone**, ton *m* de condescendance; **-ly**, *adv.* d'un air protecteur.

patter[1] ['pætər], *s.* 1. boniment *m* (de charlatan);

bagout *m*. 2. parlé *m* (dans une chansonnette).

patter[2]. I. *v.i.* (*of pers.*) trottiner, marcher à petits pas rapides et légers; (*of hail, rain*) grésiller, crépiter. II. *s.* petit bruit (de pas rapides); crépitement *m*, grésillement *m* (de la pluie); bruit de la pluie qui tombe.

pattern ['pætən], *s.* 1. modèle *m*, type *m*; **to take s.o. as a p.**, se modeler sur qn. 2. (*a*) modèle, dessin *m*; **dresses of different patterns**, robes *f* de coupes différentes; (*b*) *Dressm:* patron *m* (en papier); **to take a p.**, relever un patron. 3. échantillon *m*. 4. dessin, motif *m* (de papier peint, etc.).

patty ['pæti], *s. Cu:* = bouchée *f* à la reine.

Paul [pɔ:l]. *Pr.n.m.* Paul.

paunch [pɔ:n(t)ʃ], *s.* panse *f*, ventre *m*; *F:* bedaine *f*.

pause [pɔ:z]. I. *s.* pause *f*, arrêt *m*; **a p. (in the conversation)**, un silence. II. *v.i.* 1. faire une pause; s'arrêter un instant, marquer un temps. 2. hésiter.

pave [peiv], *v.tr.* paver (une rue); carreler (une cour); **to p. the way**, préparer le terrain; **'pavement**, *s.* trottoir *m*; *N.Am:* chaussée *f*; **'paving**, *s.* 1. pavage *m*, dallage *m*, carrelage *m*. 2. pavé *m*, dalles *fpl*; **'paving-stone**, *s.* pavé *m*.

pavilion [pə'viliən], *s. Sp: Arch:* pavillon *m*.

paw [pɔ:]. I. *s.* (*a*) patte *f* (d'animal à ongles); (*b*) *F:* main *f*, *F:* patte (de qn). II. *v.tr.* donner des coups de patte à (qn, qch.); *F:* (*of pers.*) tripoter (qn, qch.); (*of horse*) **to p. (the ground)**, piaffer.

pawn[1] [pɔ:n]. I. *s.* **in p.**, en gage; **to put one's watch in p.**, engager sa montre. II. *v.tr.* mettre (qch.) en gage; engager (qch.); **'pawnbroker**, *s.* prêteur, -euse, sur gages; commissionnaire *m* au crédit municipal; **'pawnshop**, *s.* crédit municipal; bureau *m* de prêt sur gages.

pawn[2], *s. Chess:* pion *m*; **to be s.o.'s p.**, être le jouet de qn.

pay [pei]. I. *v.tr.* (**paid**) 1. **to p. s.o. ten francs**, payer dix francs à qn; *abs.* **to p. cash down**, payer (argent) comptant; **to p. in advance**, payer d'avance; *F:* **to p. through the nose**, payer un prix excessif; *Adm:* **p. as you earn**, **P.A.Y.E.**, retenue *f* de l'impôt à la source; (*on receipted bill*) **paid**, pour acquit; **to p. a bill**, solder, régler, un compte; **to p. a debt**, payer une dette; **to p. for sth.**, payer qch.; **how much did you p. for it?** combien l'avez-vous payé? **to p. in a cheque**, donner un chèque à l'encaissement, encaisser un chèque; **to p. an employee**, rétribuer, payer, un employé; **to p. s.o. to do sth.**, payer qn pour faire qch. 2. **to p. s.o. a visit**, faire, rendre, (une) visite à qn; *F:* **to p. a visit**, aller faire pipi; **to p. s.o. back**, (i) rembourser qn; (ii) rendre la pareille à qn. 3. **it will p. you**, vous y gagnerez; **it doesn't p.**, on n'y

trouve pas son compte; ce n'est pas rentable.
II. *s.* paie *f*, salaire *m* (d'un ouvrier, d'un employé); traitement *m* (d'un fonctionnaire); **holidays with p.**, congés *m* payés; **to be in s.o.'s p.**, être à la solde, aux gages, de qn; **'payable**, *a.* payable, acquittable; **taxes p. by the tenant**, impôts à la charge du locataire; **'pay 'back**, *v.tr.* rendre, rembourser (de l'argent emprunté); **to p. s.o. back (in his own coin)**, rendre la pareille à qn; **'paying.** *I. a.* **1.** rémunérateur; qui rapporte; rentable. **2. p. guest**, pensionnaire *mf.* **II.** *s.* paiement *m*, versement *m* (d'argent); remboursement *m* (d'un créancier); règlement *m* (d'une dette); **'paymaster**, *s.* trésorier *m*; **'payment**, *s.* paiement *m*; versement *m*; règlement *m*; rémunération *f* (de services rendus); **on p. of ten francs**, moyennant paiement de dix francs; **p. on account**, acompte *m*; **'pay 'out**, *v.tr.* payer, débourser; **'payroll**, *s.* feuille *f* de paie; **to be on the p. (of a firm)**, être employé (d'une maison).

pea [pi:], *s.* Hort: pois *m*; Cu: **green peas**, petits pois; Cu: **p. soup**, soupe *f* aux pois; Bot: **sweet peas**, pois de senteur; **p.-green**, vert feuille (*m*) *inv.*

peace [pi:s], *s.* **1.** (*a*) paix *f*; **at p.**, en paix (with, avec); **to make (one's) p. with s.o.**, faire la paix avec qn; (*b*) traité *m* de paix. **2. to keep the p.**, (i) ne pas troubler l'ordre public; (ii) veiller à l'ordre public. **3.** tranquillité *f*; **to live in p.**, vivre en paix; **you may sleep in p.**, vous pouvez dormir tranquille.

peaceable ['pi:səbl], *a.* pacifique; qui aime la paix; **-ably**, *adv.* pacifiquement; en paix.

peaceful ['pi:sful], *a.* **1.** paisible, calme, tranquille. **2.** pacifique; **-fully**, *adv.* **1.** paisiblement, **2.** pacifiquement; **'peacefulness**, *s.* tranquillité *f*, calme *m*, paix *f*; **'peacemaker**, *s.* pacificateur, -trice; conciliateur, -trice.

peach [pi:tʃ], *s.* Hort: pêche *f*; **p.(-tree)**, pêcher *m*.

peacock ['pi:kɔk], *s.* Orn: paon *m*; **'peahen**, *s.* paonne *f*.

peak [pi:k], *s.* **1.** visière *f* (de casquette). **2.** (*a*) pic *m*, cime *f*, sommet *m* (de montagne); (*b*) El: **p. load**, charge *f* maximum (d'un générateur); Ind: **p. output**, record *m* (de production); Rail: etc: **p. hours**, heures de pointe, heures d'affluence; (*c*) Med: (of fever) pointe *f*; **peaked**, *a.* (casquette) à visière.

peal [pi:l]. *I. s.* **1. p. of bells**, carillon *m*; **to ring a p.**, carillonner; **full p. of (the) bells**, volée *f* de cloches. **2.** coup *m*, grondement *m* (de tonnerre). **3. p. of laughter**, éclat *m* de rire. **II.** *v.* **1.** *v.i.* (of bells) carillonner; (*b*) (of thunder) gronder. **2.** *v.tr.* sonner (les cloches) à toute volée.

peanut ['pi:nʌt], *s.* arachide *f*; **p. oil**, huile *f** d'arachide; Com: **roasted peanuts**, cacahuètes *f*; **p. butter**, beurre *m* d'arachide.

pear ['peər], *s.* poire *f*; **p.(-tree)**, poirier *m*.

pearl [pə:l], *s.* **1.** perle *f*; **string of pearls**, collier *m* de perles; **cultured pearls**, perles de culture; **p. oyster**, huître perlière. **2. mother of p.**, nacre *f*; **p. button**, bouton *m* de nacre. **3. p. barley**, orge perlé; **'pearl-diver**, *s.* pêcheur *m* de perles; **'pearly**, *a.* perlé, nacré.

peasant ['pez(ə)nt], *s.* paysan, -anne; campagnard, -arde.

peat [pi:t], *s.* tourbe *f*.

pebble ['pebl], *s.* **1.** caillou, -oux *m*; (on shore) galet *m*; F: **you're not the only p. on the beach**, vous n'êtes pas unique au monde. **2.** Opt: cristal *m* de roche; **'pebbly**, *a.* caillouteux (plage) à galets.

peck [pek]. *I. s.* coup *m* de bec. **II.** (*a*) *v.tr.* picorer, picoter, becqueter; donner un coup de bec à (qn, qch.); (*b*) *v.ind.tr.* **to p. at s.o., sth.**, donner des coups de bec à qn, qch.; **'peckish**, *a.* F: **to feel (a bit) p.**, se sentir le ventre creux.

peculiar [pi'kju:liər], *a.* (*a*) particulier; spécial; **of p. interest**, d'un intérêt tout particulier; (*b*) étrange; bizarre, singulier; **-ly**, *adv.* (*a*) particulièrement; (*b*) étrangement, singulièrement; **peculi'arity**, *s.* **1.** trait distinctif; particularité *f*; (on passport) special peculiarities, signes particuliers. **2.** bizarrerie *f*, singularité *f*.

pecuniary [pi'kju:niəri], *a.* pécuniaire; **difficulties**, ennuis *m* d'argent.

pedagogical [pedə'gɔdʒikl], *a.* pédagogique.

pedal ['ped(ə)l]. *I. s.* pédale *f*; Aut: **clutch p.**, pédale d'embrayage; (of piano) **soft, loud, p.**, petite, grande, pédale; (at the seaside) **p. craft**, pédalo *m*. **II.** *v.i.* (**pedalled**) **1.** Cy: pédaler. **2.** (piano, etc.) mettre la pédale.

pedant ['ped(ə)nt], *s.* pédant, -ante; **pe'dantic**, *a.* pédant, pédantesque; **-ally**, *adv.* de façon pédantesque; **'pedantry**, *s.* pédantisme *m*.

peddle ['pedl]. **1.** *v.i.* faire le colportage. **2.** *v.tr.* colporter (des marchandises); **to p. drugs**, faire le trafic des stupéfiants; **'peddler, 'pedlar**, **1.** colporteur *m*. **2.** (drug) **p.**, trafiquant *m* (de stupéfiants).

pedestal ['pedist(ə)l], *s.* piédestal, -aux *m*; socle *m*.

pedestrian [pi'destriən]. **1.** *a.* pédestre. **2.** piéton *m*; voyageur, -euse, à pied; **p. crossing**, passage clouté, pour piétons; **p. precinct**, zone piétonne.

pediatrician [pi:diə'triʃ(ə)n], *s.* pédiatre *mf*.

pedigree ['pedigri:], *s.* **1.** arbre *m* généalogique. **2.** (*a*) ascendance *f*, généalogie *f* (de qn); Breed: certificat *m* d'origine, pedigree *m* (d'un animal); **p. dog**, chien *m* de race.

peel [pi:l]. **I.** *s.* pelure *f*; écorce *f*, peau *f*; **orange p.**, zeste *m* d'orange; **candied p.**, zeste confit. **II.** v. **1.** v.tr. peler (un fruit); éplucher (des pommes de terre). **2.** v.i. to p. (off), (of paint) s'écailler; (of skin, nose, etc.) peler; **'peeler,** s. éplucheur m; **'peelings,** s.pl. épluchures f.

peep [pi:p]. **I.** s. coup d'œil (furtif); to get a p. at sth., entrevoir qch. **II.** v.i. **1.** to p. at sth., regarder qch. à la dérobée. **2.** to p. (out), se laisser entrevoir, se montrer; **'peep-hole,** s. **1.** judas m. **2.** Mec: etc: (trou m de) regard m.

peer¹ ['pi:ər], s. **p.** of the Realm, pair m du Royaume-Uni; **'peerage,** s. **1.** pairie f. **2.** coll. les pairs; la noblesse; **'peeress,** s.f. pairesse.

peer², v.i. (a) to p. at s.o., sth., scruter qn, qch., du regard; (b) to p. over the wall, risquer un coup d'œil par-dessus le mur.

peevish ['pi:viʃ], a. irritable, geignard; maussade; **-ly,** adv. maussadement; **peeved,** a. F: embêté; **'peevishness,** s. maussaderie f.

peewit ['pi:wit], s. Orn: vanneau (huppé).

peg [peg]. **I.** s. (a) cheville f (en bois); fiche f; (b) (hat, coat) p., patère f; he's a square p. in a round hole, il n'est pas dans son emploi; F: to take s.o. down a p. (or two), rabattre le caquet à qn; to buy a suit off the p., acheter un complet de confection. **II.** v.tr. **(pegged) 1.** cheviller (un assemblage). **2.** Fin: stabiliser (le cours du change); Com: indexer (les prix); Sp: it's still level pegging, ils sont encore à égalité. **3.** v.i. F: to p. out, mourir, F: casser sa pipe.

pejorative [pi'dʒɔrətiv], a. péjoratif.

Pekinese ['pi:ki'ni:z], F: **Peke** [pi:k], s. (chien) pékinois (m).

pelican ['pelikən], s. Orn: pélican m.

pellet ['pelit], s. (a) boulette f (de papier); pelote f (d'argile); (b) Sm.a: (lead) p., grain m de plomb; (c) Pharm: pilule f; granulé m.

pell-mell ['pel'mel]. **1.** adv. pêle-mêle. **2.** a. en désordre.

pellucid [pe'lju:sid], a. (a) translucide; (b) (style) lucide; (c) (esprit) clair.

pelt [pelt]. **1.** v.tr. to p. s.o. with stones, lancer une volée de pierres à qn. **2.** v.i. (of rain, etc.) to p. (down), tomber à verse; **pelting rain,** pluie battante.

pen¹ [pen], s. parc m, enclos m; **submarine p.,** abri m, nid m, de sous-marins.

pen², s. plume f (pour écrire); **fountain p.,** stylo m; **ball-point p.,** stylo à bille; to put p. to paper, mettre la main à la plume; **p.-and-ink drawing,** dessin à la plume; **p. friend,** correspondant, -ante; **p. name,** pseudonyme m.

penal ['pi:n(ə)l], a. (of laws) pénal; **p. servitude,** travaux forcés; **'penalize,** v.tr. **1.** sanctionner (un délit) d'une peine. **2.** (a) infliger une peine à (qn); (b) Sp: pénaliser (un joueur); (c) handicaper (un coureur, un cheval); **penalty** ['pen-], s. **1.** peine f, pénalité f; Adm: sanction (pénale); Jur: the death p., la peine de mort. **2.**

Sp: (a) pénalisation f, pénalité f; Fb: p. kick, penalty m, pl. penalties.

penance ['penəns], s. to do p. for one's sins, faire pénitence f de, pour, ses péchés.

pence [pens], s.pl. 100 p. = une livre sterling (£1); a book costing 50 p., un livre qui coûte cinquante pence, une demi-livre (sterling).

pencil ['pens(i)l], s. crayon m; **lead p.,** crayon à mine (de plomb); **coloured p.,** crayon de couleur; **written in p.,** écrit au crayon; **p. sharpener,** taille-crayon(s) m.

pendant ['pendənt], s. pendentif m (de collier).

pending ['pendiŋ]. **1.** a. Jur: (procès, etc.) pendant. **2.** prep. en attendant (qch.); **p. the negotiations,** en attendant la conclusion des négociations.

pendulum ['pendjuləm], s. pendule m, balancier m.

penetrate ['penitreit], v.tr. & i. pénétrer; **'penetrating,** a. (vent) pénétrant; (son) mordant; (esprit) pénétrant; **pene'tration,** s. (a) pénétration f; (b) perspicacité f.

penguin ['peŋgwin], s. Orn: manchot m; pingouin m.

penicillin [peni'silin], s. Med: pénicilline f.

peninsula [pe'ninsjulə], s. péninsule f; presqu'île f.

penitence ['penit(ə)ns], s. pénitence f, contrition f; **'penitent,** a. & s. pénitent, -ente; **-ly,** adv. d'un air contrit; **peni'tentiary,** s. esp. N.Am: prison f.

penknife, pl. -knives ['pennaif, -naivz], s. canif m.

penny ['peni], s., pl. pennies, pence. **1.** = 1/100 d'une livre sterling. **2.** that will cost a pretty p., cela coûtera cher; F: the p.'s dropped, on comprend, on y est; **'penniless,** a. to be p., être sans le sou, sans ressources; **'penny-'whistle,** s. flûteau m.

pension ['penʃ(ə)n]. **I.** s. pension f, retraite f; **Government p.,** pension sur l'État; **old age p.,** retraite de vieillesse; **retiring p.,** pension de retraite; to be discharged with a p., être mis à la retraite. **II.** v.tr. pensionner (qn); mettre (qn) à la retraite; **'pensionable,** a. **1.** (pers.) qui a droit à une retraite; (of job) qui donne droit à une pension, à une retraite; **p. age,** âge m de la mise à la retraite; **'pensioner,** s. retraité, -ée.

pensive ['pensiv], a. pensif, songeur; **-ly,** adv. pensivement; d'un air pensif.

pent [pent], a. **1.** p. (in, up), renfermé. **2.** p.-up emotion, émotion refoulée; to be p. up, avoir les nerfs tendus.

pentagon ['pentəgən], s. pentagone m.

pentathlon [pen'tæθlən], s. Sp: (Olympic Games) pentathlon m.

penthouse ['penthaus], s. (a) appentis m, hangar m; (b) appartement m, avec terrasse, construit sur le toit d'un immeuble.

penultimate [pen'ʌltimət], *a. & s.* pénultième (*mf*); avant-dernier, -ière.
penury ['penjuri], *s.* 1. pénurie *f*; indigence *f*; misère *f.* 2. manque *m*, pauvreté *f* (of, de); **pe'nurious**, *a.* pauvre; **-ly**, *adv.* pauvrement.
peony ['pi(:)əni], *s. Bot:* pivoine *f.*
people ['piːpl]. **I.** *s. coll.* (*with pl. const.*) 1. (*a*) peuple *m*; habitants *mpl* (d'une ville); **country p.**, les populations rurales; (*b*) **the King and his p.**, le roi et ses sujets; (*c*) *F:* parents *mpl*; **my p. are abroad**, mes parents sont à l'étranger. 2. (*a*) *Pol:* citoyens *mpl*; **government by the p.**, gouvernement par le peuple; *Pol:* **p.'s democracy**, démocratie *f* populaire; (*b*) **the (common) p.**, la populace; le (bas) peuple. 3. (*a*) gens *mpl*, monde *m*; **young p.**, jeunes gens; **old p.**, les vieux *m*, les vieilles gens; **society p.**, gens du monde; **what do you p. think?** qu'en pensez-vous, vous autres? (*b*) personnes *fpl*; **one thousand p.**, mille personnes; (*c*) (*impers.*) on; vous; **p. say**, on dit; **that's enough to alarm p.**, il y a de quoi vous alarmer. **II.** *v.tr.* peupler (with, de).
pep [pep]. **I.** *s. F:* entrain *m*, fougue *f*; **full of p.**, plein d'allant; **p. pill**, excitant *m*; **p. talk**, petit discours d'encouragement. **II.** *v.tr.* (**pepped**) *F:* **to p. s.o., sth., up**, ragaillardir qn, donner de l'entrain à qch.; *Th:* corser (une pièce).
pepper ['pepər]. **I.** *s.* 1. poivre *m.* 2. *Bot:* **p.(-tree)**, poivrier *m.* **II.** *v.tr.* poivrer; **'pepper-corn**, *s.* grain *m* de poivre; **'pepper(-)mill**, *s.* moulin *m* à poivre; **'peppermint**, *s.* 1. *Bot:* menthe anglaise. 2. pastille *f* de menthe; **'peppery**, *a.* 1. (trop) poivré. 2. (*of pers.*) irascible.
per [pəːr], *prep.* 1. (*a*) par; **sent p. carrier**, expédié par messageries; (*b*) **ten francs p. kilo**, dix francs le kilo; **as p. invoice**, suivant facture; **as p. sample**, conformément à l'échantillon; **sixty kilometres p. hour**, soixante kilomètres à l'heure. 2. **p. day**, par jour; **p. annum**, par an; **p. cent**, pour cent.
perambulator [pə'ræmbjuleitər], *s.* voiture *f* d'enfant; landau *m.*
perceive [pə'siːv], *v.tr.* 1. s'apercevoir de (qch.). 2. **to p. s.o.**, apercevoir qn; **per'ceptible**, *a.* perceptible (à l'oreille, à l'œil); **p. difference**, différence *f* sensible; **-ibly**, *adv.* sensiblement; **per'ception**, *s.* (*a*) perception *f*; sensibilité *f*; **per'ceptive**, *a.* (*of pers.*) perceptif; sensible.
percentage [pə'sentidʒ], *s.* pourcentage *m*; **a small p.**, une petite proportion.
perch¹ [pəːtʃ]. **I.** *s.* perchoir *m.* **II.** *v.i.* (se) percher (on, sur); (se) jucher.
perch², *s. Ich:* perche *f.*
percolate ['pəːkəleit], *v.i.* s'infiltrer; (*of coffee*) filtrer; **perco'lation**, *s.* infiltration *f*; filtration *f*; filtrage *m*; **'percolator**, *s.* filtre *m*; cafetière *f* automatique.

percussion [pə'kʌʃ(ə)n], *s.* percussion *f*; choc *m*; *Mus:* **p. instrument**, instrument *m* de, à, percussion; *Sm.a:* **p. cap**, amorce *f.* ·
peremptory [pə'rem(p)təri], *a.* péremptoire; (*a*) (*of refusal*) absolu; (*b*) (*of tone*) tranchant; **-ily**, *adv.* (*a*) péremptoirement, absolument; (*b*) impérieusement.
perennial [pə'renjəl]. 1. *a.* (*a*) éternel, perpétuel; (*b*) *Bot:* vivace. 2. *s.* plante *f* vivace; **-ally**, *adv.* à perpétuité.
perfect. I. *a.* ['pəːfikt] 1. (*a*) parfait; (ouvrage) achevé; **to have a p. knowledge of sth.**, savoir qch. à fond; **his English is p.**, son anglais est impeccable; (*b*) *F:* **p. idiot**, parfait imbécile; **he's a p. stranger to me**, il m'est parfaitement étranger. 2. *Gram:* **the p. tense**, *s.* **the p.**, le parfait; **-ly**, *adv.* parfaitement. **II.** *v.tr.* [pə'fekt] rendre (qch.) parfait; parfaire (qch.); mettre (une invention) au point; **per'fecting**, s perfectionnement *m*; **per'fection**, *s.* perfection *f.*
perfidy ['pəːfidi], *s.* perfidie *f*, traîtrise *f*; **per'fidious**, *a.* perfide, traître; **-ly**, adv perfidement, traîtreusement.
perforate ['pəːfəreit], *v.tr.* perforer, percer, transpercer; **perfo'ration**, *s.* 1. perforation *f*; perçage *m*; percement *m.* 2. (*a*) petit trou; (*b*) *coll.* trous *mpl.*
perform [pə'fɔːm], *v.tr.* 1. exécuter (un mouvement); accomplir (une tâche); s'acquitter de (son devoir). 2. (*a*) *Th:* jouer (une pièce); (*b*) **performing dogs**, chiens savants; **per'formance**, *s.* 1. fonctionnement *m* (d'une machine); *Aut: etc:* rendement *m*; *Sp:* performance *f.* 2. *Th:* représentation *f* (d'une pièce); séance *f* (de cinéma); **evening p.**, soirée *f*; **afternoon p.**, matinée *f*; **no p. tonight**, ce soir relâche; **per'former**, *s.* artiste *mf*; *Mus:* exécutant, -ante; acteur, -trice.
perfume. I. *s.* ['pəːfjuːm] parfum *m*; odeur agréable; **bottle of p.**, flacon *m* de parfum. **II.** *v.tr.* [pə'fjuːm] parfumer; **per'fumer**, *s.* parfumeur; **per'fumery**, *s.* parfumerie *f.*
perfunctory [pə'fʌŋkt(ə)ri], *a.* 1. **p. glance**, coup d'œil superficiel; **p. inquiry**, enquête peu poussée. 2. (*of pers.*) négligent; peu zélé; **-ily** *adv.* superficiellement; pour la forme.
perhaps [pə'hæps, præps], *adv.* peut-être; **p. so** **p. not**, peut-être (bien) que oui, que non; **p. I have it**, il se peut que je l'aie.
peril ['peril], *s.* péril *m*, danger *m*; **in p. of one's life**, en danger de mort; **perilous**, *a.* périlleux, dangereux; **-ly**, *adv.* périlleusement, dangereusement.
perimeter [pə'rimitər], *s.* périmètre *m*; *Sp:* **p. track**, piste *f* périphérique.
period ['piəriəd], *s.* 1. période *f*; durée *f*, délai *m*; *Sch:* heure *f* de cours; **within the agreed** dans le délai fixé. 2. époque *f*, âge *m*; **p. f**

niture, meubles *m* de style. **3.** *Gram:* point *m* (de ponctuation); *F: esp. NAm:* **he's no good, p.,** il est nul, tout court. **4.** *F:* règles *fpl* (d'une femme); **peri'odical. 1.** *a* périodique. **2.** *s.* (publication, etc.) périodique *m*; **-ally,** *adv.* périodiquement.

periscope ['periskoup], *s.* périscope *m*.

perish ['periʃ], *v.i.* (*a*) périr, mourir; (*b*) (*of rubber*) se détériorer; **'perishable. 1.** *a.* périssable; sujet à s'altérer; éphémère. **2.** *s.pl.* **perishables,** marchandises *f* périssables; **'perished,** *a.* (*a*) détérioré; (*b*) *F:* (*of pers.*) transi (de froid); **'perishing,** *a.* **it's p.,** il fait un froid de loup; **I'm p.,** je meurs de froid.

peritonitis [peritə'naitis], *s. Med:* péritonite *f.*

periwinkle[1] ['periwiŋkl], *s. Bot:* pervenche *f.*

periwinkle[2], *s. Moll:* bigorneau *m*.

perjure ['pəːdʒər], *v.pr.* **to p. oneself,** commettre un parjure; se parjurer; **'perjurer,** *s.* parjure *mf*; **'perjury,** *s. Jur:* faux témoignage.

perk [pəːk], *v.i.* **to p.** (**up**), se ranimer; **'perky,** *a.* éveillé; guilleret; (ton) désinvolte.

perks [pəːks], *s.pl. F:* gratte *f*, à-côtés *mpl.*

perm [pəːm]. *F:* **I.** *s.* permanente *f.* **II.** *v.tr.* permanenter; **to have one's hair permed,** se faire faire une permanente.

permanent ['pəːmənənt], *a.* permanent; **p. address,** résidence fixe; *Rail:* **the p. way,** la voie ferrée; **p. wave,** permanente *f*; **-ly,** *adv.* d'une façon permanente; **'permanence,** *s.* permanence *f*; **'permanency,** *s.* emploi permanent.

permeate ['pəːmieit], *v.tr. & i.* **to p.** (**through**) **sth.,** filtrer à travers qch.; **permea'bility,** *s.* perméabilité *f*, pénétrabilité *f*; **'permeable,** *a.* perméable, pénétrable; **perme'ation,** *s.* pénétration *f*, infiltration *f.*

permissible [pə'misibl], *a.* tolérable, permis; **per'mission,** *s.* permission *f*; autorisation *f*; **per'missive,** *a.* **p. society,** société permissive.

permit. I. *v.tr.* [pə'mit] (**permitted**) permettre; **to p. s.o. to do sth.,** permettre à qn de faire qch.; **p. me to tell you the truth,** souffrez que je vous dise la vérité; **I was permitted to visit the works,** on m'a autorisé à visiter l'usine. **II.** *s.* ['pəːmit], permis *m*; autorisation *f.*

pernicious [pə'niʃəs], *a.* pernicieux; **-ly,** *adv.* pernicieusement.

pernickety [pə'nikiti], *a. F:* (*a*) (*of pers.*) vétilleux, pointilleux; **p. old fool!** vieux tatillon! (*b*) **p. about one's food,** difficile au sujet de sa nourriture; (*c*) (*of job*) délicat, minutieux.

peroxide [pə'rɔksaid], *s. Ch:* peroxyde *m*; **hydrogen p.,** eau oxygénée.

perpendicular [pəːpən'dikjulər], *a. & s.* perpendiculaire (*f*); **-ly,** *adv.* perpendiculairement; verticalement.

perpetrate ['pəːpitreit], *v.tr.* commettre,

perpétrer (un crime); **'perpetrator,** *s.* auteur *m* (d'un crime, d'une farce).

perpetual [pə'petjuəl], *a.* (*a*) perpétuel, éternel; (*b*) sans fin; continuel; **-ally,** *adv.* (*a*) perpétuellement; (*b*) sans cesse; **per'petuate,** *v.tr.* perpétuer, éterniser; **perpetu'ation,** *s.* préservation *f* (de qch.) de l'oubli.

perpetuity [pəːpi'tjuːiti], *s.* perpétuité *f*; **in, for, p.,** à perpétuité.

perplex [pə'pleks], *v.tr.* embarrasser (qn); rendre (qn) perplexe; **per'plexed,** *a.* (*of pers.*) perplexe, embarrassé; **per'plexedly** [-idli], *adv.* d'un air perplexe; avec perplexité; **per'plexing,** *a.* embarrassant, troublant; **per'plexity,** *s.* perplexité *f*, embarras *m.*

perquisite ['pəːkwizit], *s.* (*a*) casuel *m*; (*b*) *pl.* **perquisites,** *F:* **perks,** *F:* gratte *f.*

persecute ['pəːsikjuːt], *v.tr.* **1.** persécuter (qn). **2.** tourmenter; harceler; **perse'cution,** *s.* persécution *f*; **p. mania,** délire *m*, manie *f*, de la persécution; **'persecutor,** *s.* persécuteur, -trice.

persevere [pəːsi'viər], *v.i.* persévérer (**with, in,** dans); **perse'verance,** *s.* persévérance *f*; **perse'vering,** *a.* persévérant, assidu (**in doing sth.,** à faire qch.); **-ly,** *adv.* avec persévérance.

Persia ['pəːʃə]. *Pr.n. Geog:* la Perse, l'Iran *m*; **'Persian. 1.** *a. & s.* persan, -ane, iranien, -ienne; **the P. Gulf,** le golfe persique; **P. carpet,** tapis *m* de Perse. **2.** *s. Ling:* le persan.

persist [pə'sist], *v.i.* **1.** persister; **to p. in doing sth.,** persister, s'obstiner, à faire qch. **2.** continuer; **the fever persists,** la fièvre persiste, continue; **per'sistence. 1.** *s.* persistance *f.* **2.** obstination *f.* **3.** continuité *f*; **per'sistent,** *a.* persistant; tenace; continu; **-ly,** *adv.* avec persistance; avec ténacité.

person ['pəːs(ə)n], *s.* personne *f*; individu *m*; *pl.* gens *m*; **'personable,** *a.* bien (fait) de sa personne; qui se présente bien; **'personage,** *s.* personnage *m*; personnalité *f*; **'personal,** *a.* personnel. **1.** (*a*) **p. liberty,** liberté individuelle; **p. rights,** droits *m* du citoyen; **to give a p. touch to sth.,** personnaliser qch.; *Journ:* **p. column,** petite correspondance; (*b*) **don't be p.,** ne faites pas de personnalités; (*c*) **to make a p. application,** se présenter en personne; (*d*) *Jur:* **p. property,** biens mobiliers. **2.** *Gram:* **p. pronoun,** pronom personnel; **-ally,** *adv.* personnellement; **p., I'm willing,** moi, je veux bien; **don't take that remark c.,** ne prenez pas cette remarque pour vous; **to deliver sth. to s.o. p.,** remettre qch. à qn en main(s) propre(s); **perso'nality,** *s.* personnalité *f*; caractère *m* propre (de qn); **to be lacking in p.,** manquer de personnalité; **he's quite a p.,** *F:* c'est vraiment quelqu'un; **'personalized,** *a.* personnalisé; **personifi'cation,** *s.* personnification *f*; **per'sonify,** *v.tr.* personnifier; **perso'nnel,** *s.*

coll. personnel *m*; **p. manager**, chef *m* du personnel.
perspective [pə'spektiv], *s.* perspective *f.*
perspicacious [pə:spi'keiʃəs], *a.* perspicace; **perspicacity** [-'kæsiti], *s.* perspicacité *f.*
perspire [pə'spaiər], *v.i.* transpirer, suer; **perspiration** [pə:spi'reiʃ(ə)n], *s.* (*a*) transpiration *f*; (*b*) sueur *f*; **bathed in p.**, trempé de sueur, *F:* en nage.
persuade [pə'sweid], *v.tr.* (*a*) **to p. s.o. of sth.**, persuader, convaincre, qn de qch.; (*b*) **to p. s.o. to do sth.**, persuader à qn de faire qch.; **p. your brother to come!** déterminez, décidez, votre frère à venir! (*c*) **he persuaded me not to,** il m'en a dissuadé; **per'suasion**, *s.* (*a*) persuasion *f*; (*b*) conviction *f*; **per'suasive**, *a.* persuasif; **-ly**, *adv.* d'un ton persuasif.
pert [pə:t], *a.* effronté, hardi; **-ly**, *adv.* d'un air effronté; **'pertness**, *s.* effronterie *f.*
pertinacious [pə:ti'neiʃəs], *a.* obstiné, entêté, opiniâtre; **-ly**, *adv.* obstinément, opiniâtrement; **perti'nacity** [-'næsiti], *s.* obstination *f*, opiniâtretê *f*, entêtement *m* (à faire qch.).
pertinent ['pə:tinənt], *a.* pertinent; à propos, juste; **-ly**, *adv.* d'une manière pertinente; à propos.
perturb [pə'tə:b], *v.tr.* troubler, inquiéter; **pertur'bation**, *s.* agitation *f*, inquiétude *f.*
Peru [pə'ru:]. *Pr.n. Geog:* le Pérou; **Pe'ruvian**, *a. & s.* péruvien, -ienne.
peruse [pə'ru:z], *v.tr.* lire (qch.) attentivement; **pe'rusal**, *s.* lecture attentive.
pervade [pə:'veid], *v.tr.* s'infiltrer dans; **the smell of garlic pervades the house,** l'odeur d'ail s'infiltre dans la maison; **to become pervaded,** se pénétrer (**with**, de); (**all-)pervading,** qui se répand partout; dominant; **per'vasive,** *a.* qui se répand partout; pénétrant.
perverse [pə'və:s], *a.* (*a*) pervers, méchant; (*b*) contrariant; **-ly,** *adv.* (*a*) avec perversité; (*b*) d'une manière contrariante; **per'verseness,** *s.,* **per'versity,** *s.* (*a*) perversité *f*; (*b*) esprit contraire; **per'version,** *s.* perversion *f*; **pervert. I.** *v.tr.* [pə'və:t] pervertir (qn); dépraver (le goût de qn); fausser (les faits). **II.** *s.* ['pə:və:t], perverti, -ie.
pessimism ['pesimizm], *s.* pessimisme *m*; **'pessimist,** *s.* pessimiste *mf*; **pessi'mistic,** *a.* pessimiste; **-ally,** *adv.* avec pessimisme.
pest [pest], *s.* peste *f*, fléau *m*; **'pester,** *v.tr.* tourmenter, importuner (qn); *F:* empoisonner (qn); **'pesticide,** *s.* pesticide *m*; **pesti'lential,** *a.* (*a*) pestilentiel; (*b*) *F:* assommant, empoisonnant.
pestle ['pesl], *s.* pilon *m.*
pet [pet]. **I.** *s.* (*a*) animal favori; **to make a p. of an animal,** choyer un animal; *P.N:* **no pets,** pas de bêtes; (*b*) enfant gâté; (*c*) **my p.!** mon

chou! **2.** *attrib.* favori; **he's on his p. subject again,** le revoilà sur son dada; **p. name,** diminutif *m*; nom *m* d'amitié. **II.** *v.tr.* (**petted**) choyer, chouchouter (qn, une bête).
petal ['pet(ə)l], *s. Bot:* pétale *m.*
Peter[1] ['pi:tər]. **1.** *Pr.n.m.* Pierre. **2.** *s. Nau:* **Blue P.,** pavillon *m* de partance.
peter[2], *v.i.* **to p. out,** (*a*) s'épuiser; disparaître, se perdre; **the path's petering out,** le sentier se perd; (*b*) (*of plan*) tomber à l'eau.
petition [pi'tiʃ(ə)n], *s.* pétition *f*, requête *f*; *Jur:* **p. for a reprieve,** recours *m* en grâce; **to file a p. for divorce,** demander le divorce.
petrify ['petrifai], *v.tr.* (*a*) pétrifier (le bois); (*b*) pétrifier, méduser (qn de peur); **I was petrified,** j'étais paralysé de terreur; *F:* j'ai eu une sacré frousse; **petri'faction,** *s.* pétrification *f.*
petrol ['petrəl], *s.* essence *f* (de pétrole); **high grade p.,** supercarburant *m*, *F:* super *m*; **pe'troleum,** *s.* pétrole *m*; **the p. industry,** l'industrie pétrolière; **'petrol-lorry,** *s.* camion citerne *m*; **'petrol-station,** *s.* poste d'essence.
petticoat ['petikout], *s.* (*a*) dessous *m* de robe; waist **p.,** jupon *m.*
petty ['peti], *a.* **1.** (*a*) petit, insignifiant, sans importance; (*b*) **p.(-minded),** mesquin. **2.** *Com:* **cash,** petite caisse. **3.** *Nau:* **p. officer,** officier marinier, *F:* gradé *m*; **'pettiness,** *s.* petitesse (d'esprit), mesquinerie *f.*
petulant ['petjulənt], *a.* irritable, susceptible, vif; **-ly,** *adv.* avec irritation; **'petulance,** irritabilité *f*, susceptibilité *f*; **outburst of p.** mouvement *m* d'humeur.
pew [pju:], *s.* banc *m* d'église.
pewter ['pju:tər], *s.* étain *m*; **p. ware,** vaisselle d'étain.
phantom ['fæntəm], *s.* fantôme *m*, spectre *m.*
pharmaceutical [fɑ:mə'sju:tik(ə)l], pharmaceutique.
pharmacopœia [fɑ:məkə'pi:ə], *s.* codex pharmaceutique.
pharmacy ['fɑ:məsi], *s.* pharmacie *f.*
phase [feiz]. **I.** *s.* phase *f.* **II.** *v.tr.* **to p. sth. out,** réduire, éliminer, qch. progressivement.
pheasant ['feznt], *s. Orn:* (**cock-)p.,** faisan *m*; **hen-p.,** faisane *f.*
phenobarbitone ['fi:nou'bɑ:bitoun], *s. Med:* barbiturique *m*, phénobarbital *m.*
phenomenon, *pl.* **-ena** [fi'nɔminən, -inə], phénomène *m*; chose *f* remarquable; (*of person*) prodige *m*; **phe'nomenal,** *a.* phénoménal, extraordinaire, prodigieux.
philanthropy [fi'lænθrəpi], *s.* philanthropie *f*; **philan'thropic(al),** *a.* philanthropique; **-ically,** *adv.* avec philanthropie; **phi'lanthropist,** *s.* philanthrope *mf.*
philately [fi'lætəli], *s.* philatélie *f*; **phi'latelist,** *s.* philatéliste *mf.*

Philip ['filip]. *Pr.n.m.* Philippe.
Philippines (the) [ðə'filipi:nz]. *Pr.n. Geog:* les Philippines *f.*
philology [fi'lɔlədʒi], *s.* philologie *f*; **philo'logical**, *a.* philologique; **-ally**, *adv.* philologiquement; **phi'lologist**, *s.* philologue *mf.*
philosophy [fi'lɔsəfi], *s.* philosophie *f*; **phi'losopher**, *s.* philosophe *mf*; **philo'sophical**, *a.* 1. philosophique. 2. (*of pers.*) philosophe, calme, modéré; **-ally**, *adv.* philosophiquement; calmement.
phlegm [flem], *s.* flegme *m*; **phlegmatic** [fleg'mætik], *a.* flegmatique; **-ally**, *adv.* flegmatiquement.
phone [foun]. I. *s.* téléphone *m*; **he's not on the p.,** il n'a pas le téléphone. II. *v.tr. & i.* téléphoner (à qn).
phonetic [fə'netik], *a.* phonétique; **-ally**, *adv.* phonétiquement; **pho'netics,** *s.pl.* (*usu. with sg. const.*) la phonétique.
phoney ['founi], *a. F:* faux; (*of jewellery*) en toc; **that's a p. story,** cette histoire, c'est de la blague.
phosphate ['fɔsfeit], *s. Ch:* phosphate *m.*
phosphorescent [fɔsfə'res(ə)nt], *a.* phosphorescent; **phospho'rescence,** *s.* phosphorescence *f.*
phosphorus ['fɔsf(ə)rəs], *s. Ch:* phosphore *m.*
photo- ['foutou-], *prefix used in combined forms;* photo-; **'photocopier,** *s.* photocopieur *m*; **'photocopy.** I. *s.* photocopie *f.* II. *v.tr.* photocopier (un document); **'photoe'lectric,** *a.* (cellule) photo-électrique; **'photo-finish,** *s. Sp:* décision *f* par photo; photo-finish *f inv*; **photo'genic** [-'dʒi:nik, -'dʒe-] *a.* photogénique; **'photograph.** I. *s. F:* 'photo, *s.* photographie *f, F:* photo *f.* II. *v.tr.* photographier; **pho'tographer** [fə'tɔ-], *s.* photographe *mf*; **photo'graphic,** *a.* photographique; **p. library,** photothèque *f*; **-ally**, *adv.* photographiquement; **pho'tography,** *s.* photographie *f*; prise *f* de vue(s); **colour p.,** photographie en couleurs; **'photo-re'connaissance,** *s. Av:* reconnaissance *f* photographique; **'photostat.** I. *s.* photocopie *f.* II. *v.tr.* (**photostatted**) photocopier.
phrase [freiz]. I. *s.* 1. locution *f,* expression *f,* tour *m* de phrase; **technical p.,** locution technique. 2. *Mus:* phrase *f,* période *f.* II. *v.tr.* 1. exprimer (sa pensée); **a well phrased letter,** une lettre bien tournée. 2. *Mus:* phraser; **phrase'ology** [-i'ɔlədʒi], phraséologie *f.*
physical ['fizik(ə)l], *a.* physique; **p. impossibility,** impossibilité matérielle; **p. force,** force physique; **-ally**, *adv.* physiquement; **thing p. impossible,** chose matériellement impossible; **a p. handicapped person,** un(e) handicapé(e)

physique.
physician [fi'ziʃ(ə)n], *s.* médecin *m.*
physics ['fiziks], *s.pl.* (*usu. with sg. const.*) la physique; **'physicist,** *s.* physicien, -ienne.
physiognomy [fizi'ɔnəmi], *s.* physionomie *f.*
physiology [fizi'ɔlədʒi], *s.* physiologie *f*; **physio'logical,** *a.* physiologique; **physi'ologist,** *s.* physiologiste *mf.*
physiotherapy ['fiziou'θerəpi], *s.* physiothérapie *f.*
physique [fi'zi:k], *s.* physique *m*; **to have a fine p.,** avoir un beau physique.
piano, *pl.* **-os** [pi'ænou, -ouz], *s. Mus:* piano *m*; (**concert) grand p.,** piano à queue; **pianist** ['pi:ənist], *s.* pianiste *mf.*
pick [pik]. I. *v.tr.* 1. (*a*) piocher (la terre); (*b*) to p. holes in sth., trouver à redire à qch.; **why p. on me?** pourquoi m'accuser, moi? 2. **to p. one's teeth,** se curer les dents. 3. **to have a bone to p. with s.o.,** avoir maille à partir avec qn. 4. picoter, becqueter; **to p. (at) one's food,** manger du bout des dents. 5. (*also* **to p. out**) choisir; **to p. one's steps,** marcher avec précaution; **to p. and choose,** se montrer difficile; *Games:* **to p. sides,** tirer les camps. 6. (*a*) cueillir (des fruits, etc.); (*b*) **to p. acquaintance with s.o.,** lier connaissance avec qn. 7. (*a*) **to p. pockets,** pratiquer le vol à la tire; (*b*) crocheter (une serrure); **to p. s.o.'s brains,** exploiter l'intelligence de qn. II. *s.* 1. pic *m,* pioche *f.* 2. choix *m,* élite *f*; **the p. of the bunch,** le dessus du panier; **the p. of the Armed Forces,** l'élite, la fine fleur, des Forces armées; **take your p.!** choisissez! **'pickaxe,** *s.* pioche *f*; **'pick 'over,** *v.tr.* trier; **'pickpocket,** *s.* pickpocket *m*; **'pick 'up.** 1. *v.tr.* (*a*) prendre, (*from off the ground*) ramasser; **to p. up a £,** (i) ramasser une livre (par terre); (ii) se faire, gagner, une livre; **to p. s.o. up on the way,** prendre qn en passant; *Knitting:* **to p. up a stitch,** relever une maille; (*b*) apprendre; **to p. up a language,** s'initier (rapidement) à une langue; (*c*) trouver; **to p. sth. up cheap,** acheter qch. à bon marché; **to p. up New York on the radio,** capter New York à la radio; (*d*) *Aut: etc:* **to p. up (speed),** reprendre. 2. *v.i.* (*a*) **he's picking up,** il reprend (ses forces); il se rétablit. **'pick-up,** *s.* 1. connaissance *f* de rencontre. 2. *Aut:* reprise *f* (du moteur). 3. *Rec:* pick-up *m.* 4. *Electronics:* capteur *m.*
picket ['pikit]. I. *s.* 1. piquet *m.* 2. *Mil:* piquet; poste *m* (d'hommes); **fire p.,** poste d'incendie; *Ind:* **strike p.,** piquet de grève. II. *v.tr.* (*a*) mettre en place des piquets; (*b*) *Ind:* **to p. a factory,** installer des piquets de grève aux portes d'une usine.
pickle ['pikl]. I. *s.* 1. marinade *f*; saumure *f.* 2. *pl. Cu:* **pickles,** conserves *f* au vinaigre. 3. *F:* **to be in a p.,** être dans de beaux draps. II. *v.tr. Cu:*

mariner; conserver (au vinaigre).
picnic ['piknik]. **I.** s. (a) pique-nique m, pl. pique-niques; (b) **the Vietnam war was no p.**, la guerre au Vietnam n'a pas été une partie de plaisir. **II.** v.i. (**picnicked**) pique-niquer; '**picnicker**, s. pique-niqueur, -euse.
picture ['piktʃər]. **I.** s. image f; tableau m; peinture f; gravure f; **he's the p.** of health, il respire la santé; **she's a perfect p.**, elle est à peindre; **to be in the p.**, être au courant. **II.** v.tr. **to p.** sth. (**to oneself**), se figurer, s'imaginer, qch.; **pic'torial**, a. & s. (périodique, magazine) illustré (m); **pictu'resque**, a. pittoresque.
pie [pai], s. (a) meat p. = pâté m en croûte; **p. crust**, croûte f de pâté; **shepherd's p.**, hachis m Parmentier; (b) **fruit pie**, tourte f; '**pie-dish**, s. (a) terrine f (à pâtés); (b) tourtière f.
piebald ['paibɔːld], a. & s. (cheval) pie (m).
piece [piːs]. **I.** s. **1.** pièce f; (a) morceau m (de pain); bout m (de ruban); (b) fragment m; **to come to pieces**, s'en aller en morceaux; **he went to pieces**, il s'est écroulé; **to fly into pieces**, voler en éclats m; **to pull s.o. to pieces**, critiquer qn sévèrement. **2.** partie f; **to take a machine to pieces**, démonter une machine. **3.** Com: pièce (de drap); rouleau m (de papier peint); **to pay by the p.**, payer à la pièce, à la tâche. **4. all in one p.**, tout d'une pièce. **5.** (a) a **p. of my work**, un échantillon de mon travail; (b) **p. of folly**, acte m de folie; (c) **a p. of advice**, un conseil; **a p. of news**, une nouvelle; **a p. of furniture**, un meuble; **a p. of clothing**, un vêtement. **6.** morceau (de musique, de poésie). **7.** Chess: pièce. **II.** v.tr. **1.** rapiécer, raccommoder (qch.); **to p. together**, joindre, unir; rassembler (des fragments); '**piecemeal**, adv. par morceaux.
pier ['piər], s. **1.** jetée f, digue f; (**landing**) p., quai m. **2.** Civ.E: pilier m.
pierce ['piəs], v.tr. percer, transpercer, pénétrer; **a thorn pierced his finger**, une épine lui est entrée dans le doigt; **to have one's ears pierced**, se faire percer les oreilles; '**piercing**, a. (cri) aigu, perçant; (froid) pénétrant.
piety ['paiəti], s. piété f.
pig [pig], s. **1.** (a) porc m, cochon m; **sucking p.**, cochon de lait; pl. **pigs** [pigz] (in general), les porcins m; **p. farm**, porcherie f; **p. breeding**, l'élevage m des porcs; **to buy a p. in a poke**, acheter chat en poche; (b) P: (i) grossier personnage; (ii) **to make a p. of oneself**, manger gloutonnement; **you (dirty) little p.!** petit sale! **2. p. (iron)**, fer m en fonte, en gueuse; '**piggish**, a. (a) sale, malpropre, grossier; (b) goinfre; (c) égoïste, désagréable; '**piggy-bank**, s. tirelire f (en forme de cochon); '**pig-headed**, a. F: obstiné, entêté; '**piglet**, s. porcelet m, cochonnet m; '**pigskin**, s. peau f de porc; '**pigsty**, s. porcherie f; '**pigtail**, s.

queue f, natte f (de cheveux).
pigeon ['pidʒin], s. **1.** pigeon m. **2.** F: pigeon, dupe f; '**pigeon-hole**. **I.** s. case f; alvéole m (de bureau). **II.** v.tr. classer (des papiers); '**pigeon-house**, s. colombier m, pigeonnier m.
pigment ['pigmənt], s. Art: matière colorante; colorant m.
pike [paik], s. Ich: brochet m.
pile¹ [pail], s. pieu m; **built on piles**, bâti sur pilotis; '**pile driver**, s. sonnette f.
pile². **I.** s. (a) tas m, monceau m; **atomic p.**, pile f atomique; (b) Mil: faisceau m (d'armes); (c) F: magot m; **to make one's p.**, faire fortune. **II.** v. **1.** v.tr. (a) **to p.** (**up**), entasser, amasser (une fortune); empiler (du bois); (b) **to p. on the agony**, accumuler les détails pénibles; F: **to p. it on**, exagérer. **2.** v.i. **to p. up**, s'amonceler, s'entasser; (of ship) **to p. up** (**on the rocks**), échouer; '**pile-up**, s. Aut: F: carambolage m.
pile³, s. poil m (d'un tapis).
piles [pailz], s.pl. Med: hémorroïdes f.
pilfer ['pilfər], v.tr. chiper (**sth. from s.o.**, qch. à qn); chaparder; '**pilferer**, s. chapardeur, -euse; '**pilfering**, s. chapardage m.
pilgrim ['pilgrim], s. pèlerin, -ine; '**pilgrimage**, s. pèlerinage m.
pill [pil], s. pilule f; Med: "**the p.**", "la pilule" **sugar-coated p.**, dragée f.
pillage ['pilidʒ]. **I.** s. pillage m. **II.** v.tr. piller saccager.
pillar ['pilər], s. pilier m; colonne f; **he's a p.** of the Church, c'est un pilier de l'Église; '**pillar box**, s. boîte f aux lettres; (colour) p.-b. red rouge drapeau (m).
pillion ['piliən], s. siège m arrière (de moto); t **ride p.**, monter derrière.
pillow ['pilou], s. oreiller m; **p.-case**, s. taie d'oreiller.
pilot ['pailət]. **I.** s. (a) Nau: Av: pilote m; (b guide m; (c) **p. lamp**, lampe f témoin. **II.** v.t. (a) piloter (un navire, un avion); (b) mene conduire (qn à travers des obstacles).
pimento [pi'mentou], s. Bot: Cu: piment n poivron m.
pimple ['pimpl], s. bouton m; **to come out** pimples, avoir une poussée de boutons.
pin [pin]. **I.** s. **1.** (a) épingle f; **he doesn't care tw pins**, il s'en moque, F: il s'en fiche; (b) **to hav pins and needles**, avoir des fourmillements **2.** goupille f, cheville f. **II.** v.tr. (**pinned**) épingler (qch.). **2.** fixer; **to p. s.o. down to tl facts**, obliger qn à accepter, à reconnaître, faits; '**pinpoint**, v.tr. indiquer exactemer '**pinprick**, s. piqûre f d'épingle; pl. **pinprick** tracasseries f.
pinafore ['pinəfɔːr], s. tablier m.
pincers ['pinsəz], s.pl. (pair of) p., pince tenaille(s) f (pl).
pinch [pin(t)ʃ]. **I.** v.tr. **1.** pincer. **2.** serrer, gên

3. *P:* (*a*) voler, chiper; (*b*) arrêter (un malfaiteur); **to get pinched,** se faire pincer. **II.** *s.* (*a*) action *f* de pincer (qn); pinçade *f*; **the p. of poverty,** la gêne; **at a p.,** au besoin; (*b*) **a p. (of salt, etc.),** une pincée (de sel, etc.); **pinched,** *a.* (*a*) (*of face*) tiré, hâve; (*b*) (*for money*) (être) à l'étroit, dans la gêne.

pine¹ [pain], *s.* **1. p.**(-tree), pin *m.* **2.** (bois *m* de) pin; **p. cone,** pomme *f* de pin; **pine-wood,** *s.* pinède *f*; (bois *m* de) pins.

pine², *v.i.* **1. to p.** (away), languir, dépérir. **2. to p. for s.o.,** languir pour, après, qn.

pineapple ['painæpl], *s.* ananas *m.*

pinion ['pinjən], *s.* **1.** aileron *m.* **2.** *Orn:* penne *f.* **3.** *E:* pignon *m;* **p. wheel,** roue *f* à pignon.

pink [piŋk]. **1.** *s.* (*a*) *Bot:* œillet *m;* **garden p.,** mignardise *f;* (*b*) *F:* **in the p.,** en excellente condition. **2.** *a. & s.* rose (*m*); couleur *f* de rose; **'pinkish,** *a.* rosé, rosâtre.

pinnacle ['pinəkl], *s.* **1.** (*a*) cime *f;* pic *m;* (*b*) **rock p.,** gendarme *m.* **2. the p. of glory,** le faîte, l'apogée *m,* de la gloire.

pint [paint], *s. Meas:* pinte *f* (= 0,568 litre); **a p. of beer** = une can(n)ette de bière.

pioneer [paiə'niər]. **I.** *s.* pionnier *m.* **II.** *v.tr.* être le premier à (faire qch.).

pious ['paiəs], *a.* pieux; **-ly,** *adv.* pieusement.

pip¹ [pip], *s.* **1.** *Mil: F:* = galon *m* d'officier, *F:* ficelle *f.* **2.** *Rad:* **the pips,** le signal horaire, *F:* les tops *m.*

pip², *s.* pépin *m* (de fruit).

pipe [paip]. **I.** *s.* **1.** tuyau *m,* tube *m,* conduit *m.* **2.** *Mus:* pipeau *m,* chalumeau *m; pl.* (**bag**)**pipes,** cornemuse *f.* **3.** pipe *f* (de fumeur). **II.** *v.tr.* canaliser (l'eau, le gaz, etc.); **'pipe'down,** *v.i. F:* cesser de parler, *F:* la boucler; **'pipe-line,** *s.* conduite *f,* canalisation *f;* (*for oil*) pipe-line *m,* oléoduc *m;* (*for gas*) gazoduc *m;* **'piper,** *s.* joueur *m* de cornemuse; **'piping,** *s. coll.* tuyauterie *f.*

pippin ['pipin], *s.* (pomme *f*) reinette (*f*).

piquant ['pi:kənt], *a.* (*a*) (*of flavour, etc.*) piquant; (*b*) **p. beauty,** beauté piquante, stimulante; (*c*) (style) mordant; **'piquancy,** *s.* **1.** goût piquant (d'un mets). **2.** sel *m,* piquant *m* (d'un conte, d'une situation).

pique [pi:k]. **I.** *s.* pique *f,* ressentiment *m;* **feeling of p.,** sentiment *m* de rancune. **II.** *v.tr.* **1.** piquer, dépiter (qn). **2.** piquer, exciter (la curiosité de qn). **3. to p. oneself on sth.,** se piquer de qch.

pirate ['paiərət], *s.* pirate *m; Rad: a.* **p. station,** émetteur pirate; **'piracy,** *s.* **1.** piraterie *f.* **2.** contrefaçon *f* (d'un livre); **pi'ratical,** *a.* **1.** de pirate. **2.** de contrefaçon.

Pisces ['paisi:z]. *Pr.n. Astr:* les Poissons *m.*

piss [pis]. **I.** *s. P:* urine *f.* **II.** *v.i. P:* uriner, pisser.

pistachio [pis'ta:ʃiou], *s.* pistache *f.*

pistil ['pistil], *s. Bot:* pistil *m.*

pistol ['pist(ə)l], *s.* pistolet *m;* **p. shot,** coup *m* de pistolet.

piston ['pistən], *s. E:* piston *m; Aut:* **p. ring,** segment *m* de piston; **p. stroke,** (i) coup *m,* (ii) course *f,* de piston.

pit¹ [pit], *s.* **1.** (*a*) fosse *f,* trou *m; Aut:* inspection **p.,** fosse (à réparations); *Mil:* **gun (etc.) p.,** emplacement *m* de pièce; (*b*) *F:* **to dig a p. for s.o.,** tendre un piège à qn; (*c*) (i) carrière *f* (à chaux); (ii) puits *m* (d'une mine de charbon). **2.** *Th:* parterre *m.* **3.** petite cavité, piqûre *f.* **4.** *Anat:* **the p. of the stomach,** le creux de l'estomac.

pit², *s. N.Am:* noyau *m* (de cerise, etc.).

pit-a-pat ['pitəpæt], *adv.* **to go p.-a-p.,** (*of rain*) crépiter; (*of feet*) trottiner; (*of the heart*) battre, palpiter.

pitch¹ [pitʃ], *s.* poix *f;* brai *m;* bitume *m;* **'pitch'dark,** *a.* **it is p. d.,** il fait nuit noire, il fait noir comme dans un four; **'pitch'pine,** *s.* faux sapin.

pitch². **I.** *v.* **1.** *v.tr.* (*a*) dresser (une tente); (*b*) *Mus:* **to p. one's voice higher,** hausser le ton de sa voix; (*c*) lancer; jeter (une balle). **2.** *v.i.* (*of ship*) tanguer; *F:* **to p. into s.o., sth.,** (i) s'attaquer à qn, qch.; (ii) passer une savon à qn; (iii) taper sur qn; **pitched battle,** bataille rangée. **II.** *s.* **1.** *Mus:* hauteur *f* (d'un son); diapason *m* (d'un instrument). **2.** *Nau:* tangage *m.* **3.** *Sp:* terrain *m* (de football, etc.); emplacement *m,* place *f* (dans un marché, etc.). **4.** degré *m* de pente (d'un toit); **'pitchfork,** *s.* fourche *f* (à foin).

pitcher ['pitʃər], *s.* cruche *f;* broc *m, N.Am: pot m* (à lait).

pitfall ['pitfɔ:l], *s.* trappe *f,* fosse *f;* piège *m.*

pith [piθ], *s.* **1.** (*a*) moelle *f;* (*b*) peau blanche (d'une orange). **2.** (*a*) vigueur *f,* sève *f,* ardeur *f;* (*b*) moelle, essence *f* (d'un livre); **'pithiness,** *s.* (*of style*) concision *f;* style nerveux; **'pithy,** *a.* **1.** (*of plant stem*) plein de moelle. **2.** (*of style*) (i) nerveux, concis, vigoureux; (ii) substantiel; **-ily,** *adv.* d'un style condensé.

pittance ['pit(ə)ns], *s.* maigre salaire *m.*

pity ['piti]. **I.** *s.* (*a*) pitié *f;* compassion *f;* **to take p. on s.o.,** prendre qn en pitié; **to feel p. for s.o.,** s'apitoyer sur qn; (*b*) **what a p.!** quel dommage! **II.** *v.tr.* plaindre (qn); avoir pitié de, s'apitoyer sur (qn); **'piteous,** *a.* pitoyable, piteux; **-ly,** *adv.* pitoyablement; **'pitiable,** *a.* pitoyable, piteux; **-ably,** *adv.* pitoyablement; **'pitiful,** *a.* **1.** compatissant; plein de pitié. **2.** (*a*) pitoyable, lamentable; **it's p. to see him,** il fait pitié; (*b*) *Pej:* **he's a p. speaker,** c'est un orateur lamentable; **-fully,** *adv.* **1.** avec compassion. **2.** (*a*) pitoyablement; **to cry p.,** pleurer à fendre l'âme; (*b*) *Pej:* lamentablement; **'pitiless,** *a.* impitoyable; sans pitié; **p. wind,**

vent cruel; **-ly,** *adv.* sans pitié; **'pitying,** *a.* compatissant; (regard) de pitié.

pivot ['pivət]. I. *s.* pivot *m*; axe *m* (de rotation). II. *v.i.* pivoter, tourner; **'pivot-bridge,** *s.* *Civ.E:* pont tournant.

placard ['plæka:d]. I. *s.* écriteau *m*; affiche *f.* II. *v.tr.* 1. couvrir (un mur) d'affiches. 2. afficher (une annonce).

placate [plə'keit], *v.tr.* apaiser, calmer (qn).

place ['pleis]. I. *s.* 1. (*a*) lieu *m*, endroit *m*, localité *f*; **to come to a p.,** arriver dans un lieu; **this is the p.,** c'est ici; **a native of the p.,** quelqu'un du pays; **to move from p. to p.,** se déplacer souvent; **books all over the p.,** des livres dans tous les coins; **in another p.,** autre part; ailleurs; **this is no p. for you,** vous n'avez que faire ici; *F:* **to go places,** (i) sortir; (ii) voyager; (iii) réussir; (*b*) **p. of business,** maison *f* de commerce; établissement *m*; **p. of residence,** demeure *f*; **at our p.,** chez nous; (*c*) **market p.,** place *f* du marché. 2. (*position*) place; **to lay a p.,** mettre un couvert; **to change places with s.o.,** changer de place avec qn; **in your p.,** à votre place; **in (the) p. of . . .,** au lieu de . . .; **remark out of p.,** observation hors de propos, déplacée; **to look out of p.,** avoir l'air dépaysé; **to take p.,** avoir lieu; se passer; arriver. 3. place, rang *m*; **to put s.o. in his p.,** remettre qn à sa place; *Rac:* **to back a horse for a p.,** jouer un cheval placé; *Mth:* **answer to three places of decimals,** solution *f* à trois décimales; **in the first p.,** d'abord; **in the second p.,** en second lieu; **in the next p.,** ensuite; puis. 4. poste *m*, emploi *m*, situation *f*; **it's not my p. to do it,** ce n'est pas à moi de le faire. II. *v.tr.* 1. placer, mettre, poser; (*a*) **to be awkwardly placed,** se trouver dans une situation difficile; (*b*) *Com:* **difficult to p.,** de vente difficile; **to p. an order,** passer une commande; (*c*) **to p. a matter in s.o.'s hands,** remettre une affaire entre les mains de qn. 2. donner un rang à (qn); **to be well placed,** avoir une bonne place; **to be placed third,** se classer troisième. 3. *F:* **I can't p. you,** je ne vous remets pas.

placid ['plæsid], *a.* placide, calme, tranquille; **-ly,** *adv.* avec calme; tranquillement; **pla'cidity,** *s.* placidité *f*, calme *m*, tranquillité *f*.

plagiarism ['pleidʒiərizm], *s.* plagiat *m*; **'plagiarist,** *s.* plagiaire *mf.*

plague [pleig]. I. *s.* 1. fléau *m*. 2. peste *f*; **'plague-spot,** *s.* foyer *m* d'infection. II. *v.tr.* tourmenter (qn); embêter, raser (qn); *F:* casser les piéds à (qn).

plaice [pleis], *s. Ich:* carrelet *m*; plie *f.*

plain [plein]. I. *a.* 1. clair, évident; **it's as p. as daylight,** cela saute aux yeux; **in p. English,** pour parler clairement; **goods marked in p. figures,** articles marqués en chiffres connus. 2.

(*a*) **soldier in p. clothes,** militaire en civil; *Knitting:* **p. (stitch),** maille *f* à l'endroit; (*b*) lisse; **p. material,** tissu uni; (*c*) **p. cooking,** cuisine simple; (*d*) **p. truth,** vérité pure, simple; **p. speaking,** franchise *f*, franc-parler *m*. 3. **to be p.,** manquer de beauté; **she looks plainer than ever,** elle a enlaidi; **-ly,** *adv.* 1. clairement, manifestement, évidemment; **I can see it p.,** cela saute aux yeux. 2. (*a*) simplement; (*b*) franchement, carrément; **to put it p.,** pour parler clair. II. *adv.* **I tell you p.,** je vous dis clairement, franchement, distinctement; **I can't put it any plainer,** je ne peux pas m'exprimer plus clairement. III. *s.* plaine *f*; **'plainness,** *s.* 1. clarté *f* (de langage); netteté *f* (d'un objet lointain). 2. (*a*) simplicité *f* (de vie); (*b*) franchise *f* (de langage). 3. manque *m* de beauté.

plaintiff ['pleintif], *s. Jur:* plaignant, -ante.

plaintive ['pleintiv], *a.* plaintif; **-ly,** *adv.* plaintivement; d'un ton plaintif.

plait [plæt]. I. *s.* natte *f*, tresse *f* (de cheveux). II. *v.tr.* natter, tresser.

plan [plæn]. I. *s.* 1. (*a*) plan *m* (d'une maison, d'un livre); **to draw a p.,** tracer un plan; (*b*) *Surv:* levé *m* (d'un terrain). 2. projet *m*, plan; **preliminary p.,** avant-projet *m*; **to draw up a p.,** dresser un plan; **to change one's plans,** prendre d'autres dispositions; **everything went according to p.,** tout a marché selon les prévisions. II. *v.tr.* (**planned**) 1. faire, tracer, le plan de (qch.). 2. projeter (un voyage); combiner (une attaque); **to p. to do sth.,** se proposer de faire qch.; **'planning,** *s.* dirigisme (gouvernemental, économique, etc.); **town p.,** urbanisme *m*; **family p.,** contrôle *m* des naissances, planning familial.

plane¹ [plein]. I. *s.* 1. plan *m*; **horizontal p.,** plan horizontal. 2. *Mec:* **inclined p.,** plan incliné. *Av:* avion *m*. II. *a* plan, uni; plat.

plane². I. *s. Tls:* rabot *m*. II. *v.tr.* raboter; aplanir

plane³, *s.* **p.(-tree),** platane *m.*

planet ['plænit], *s. Astr:* planète *f*; **plane'tarium,** *s.* planétarium *m*; **'planetary,** *a.* (système *m*) planétaire.

plank [plæŋk], *s.* planche *f*; madrier *m*; **'planking,** *s. coll.* planches *fpl.*

plant [pla:nt]. I. *s.* 1. plante *f*; **p. life,** (i) la vie végétale; (ii) flore *f* (d'une région); **house plant,** plante d'appartement. 2. *Ind:* (*a*) usine *f*; **automobile p.,** usine d'automobiles; (*b*) appareil(s) *m(pl)*; installation(s) *f(pl)*; matériel *m*, outillage *m* (d'une usine); **the p.,** machinerie *f*; **heavy p.,** grosses machines. II. *v.tr.* planter (un arbre); enterrer (des oignons); **to p. a bomb,** poser une bombe; *F:* **to p. oneself in front of s.o.,** se planter, se camper, devant qn; **to p. out some seedlings,** repiquer des semis; **plan'tation,** *s.* plantation *f*; **'planter,** *s.* planteur *m.*

plaque |plɑːk, plæk|, s. plaque f (de bronze, etc.).
plaster |'plɑːstər|. I. s. 1. Med: emplâtre m;
adhesive p., sparadrap m. 2. plâtre m; p. of
Paris, plâtre de moulage. II. v.tr. plâtrer (un
mur); to p. sth. over, enduire qch. de plâtre; to
be plastered with mud, être tout couvert de
boue; plastered with decorations, chamarré de
décorations; 'plasterer, s. plâtrier m.
plastic |'plæstik|, a. 1. (art) plastique; p. sur-
gery, chirurgie f plastique. 2. plastique; qui se
laisse mouler; p. mind, esprit malléable. 3. a. &
s. (matière f) plastique (m); a p. cup, une tasse
en (matière) plastique; laminated p., laminé m;
p. foam, mousse f plastique. 4. p. bomb, p.
explosive, plastic m; p. bomb attack,
plasticage m.
plate |pleit|, s. 1. plaque f, lame f, feuille f (de
métal). 2. (a) Cu: hot p., (i) plaque chauffante
(de cuisinière électrique); (ii) chauffe-assiettes
m; (b) Aut: number p., plaque d'immatriculation; clutch p., plateau m d'embrayage; (c) Dent: dentier m. 3. Phot: plaque.
4. (a) Engr: gravure f, estampe f; full-page p.,
gravure hors texte; (b) p. glass, glace f de
vitrage; verre m à glaces. 5. (a) orfèvrerie f;
vaisselle f d'or, d'argent; (b) Sp: coupe
(donnée en prix). 6. assiette f; dinner p.,
assiette plate; soup p., assiette creuse; F: to
have a lot on one's p., avoir du pain sur la
planche; Ecc: collection p., plateau de
quête; 'plateful, s. assiettée f; 'platelayer, s.
Rail: ouvrier m de la voie; 'plate-rack, s. H:
égouttoir m.
◄ateau, pl. -x, -s |'plætou, -z|, s. Ph. Geog:
plateau m.
◄atform |'plætfɔːm|, s. 1. terrasse f. 2. (a) plate-
forme f; oil-rig p., plate-forme de forage; (b)
Rail: quai m; departure p., (quai de) départ m;
arrival p., (quai d')arrivée f; from which p.
does the train start? de quel quai part le train?
3. estrade f, tribune f (de réunion publique).
◄atinum |'plætinəm|, s. platine m.
◄atitude |'plætitjuːd|, s. platitude f; lieu
commun.
◄atoon |plə'tuːn|, s. Mil: section f.
◄ausible |'plɔːzibl|, a. 1. (a) plausible; (b)
spécieux. 2. (of pers.) enjôleur; -ibly, adv.
plausiblement; plausi'bility, s. plausibilité f.
◄ay |plei|. I. s. 1. jeu m; activité f; in full p., en
pleine activité; to come into p., entrer en jeu; to
give full p. to sth., donner libre cours à qch.; it's
child's p., c'est la simplicité même. 2. jeu,
amusement m; to say sth. in p., dire qch. pour
plaisanter; p. on words, calembour m, jeu de
mots. 3. Games: p. began at one o'clock, la
partie a commencé à une heure; ball in p., out
of p., balle f en jeu; balle hors jeu. 4. pièce f de
théâtre; Shakespeare's plays, le théâtre de
Shakespeare. II. v. 1. v.i. (of fountains, music,

children, etc.) jouer. 2. v.tr. to p. a match, disputer un match; to p. tennis, jouer au tennis; to
p. chess, jouer aux échecs; Th: to p. Macbeth,
tenir le rôle de Macbeth; to p. the fool, faire des
sottises, faire l'idiot; F: to p. ball, coopérer;
'play 'back, v.tr. faire repasser (une bande au
magnétophone); 'play 'down, v.tr. minimiser
(l'importance de qch.); 'player, s. esp. Sp:
joueur, -euse; 'playful, a. enjoué, gai; folâtre;
-fully, adv. gaiement; avec enjouement; en
badinant; 'playground, s. Sch: etc: cour f,
terrain m, de récréation; covered p., préau m;
'play-pen, s. parc m pour enfants;
'plaything, s. jouet m; 'play time, s. Sch:
récréation; 'play 'up. 1. v.tr. to p. s.o. up,
agacer, chahuter, qn. 2. v.i. to p. up to s.o.,
flatter qn; my back's playing me up, mon dos
me donne du tracas; 'playwright, s. auteur m
dramatique; dramaturge m.
plea |pliː|, s. 1. Jur: défense f. 2. (a) excuse f,
prétexte m; (b) p. for mercy, appel m à la
clémence.
plead |pliːd|. 1. v.i. Jur: plaider (for, pour;
against, contre); to p. guilty, not guilty, plaider
coupable, non coupable. 2. v.tr. (a) plaider; to
p. s.o.'s cause with s.o., intercéder pour qn
auprès de qn; (b) to p. ignorance, prétexter
l'ignorance.
pleasant |'plez(ə)nt|, a. 1. agréable, charmant,
aimable. 2. (of pers.) affable; to make oneself
p. (to s.o.), se rendre agréable (à qn); -ly, adv.
1. agréablement. 2. avec affabilité.
please |pliːz|, v.tr. 1. (i) plaire à (qn); faire plaisir
à (qn); (ii) contenter (qn); to be easily pleased,
être facile à contenter; s'arranger de tout;
there is no pleasing him, il n'y a pas moyen de
lui plaire; he's hard to p., il est difficile; p.
yourself! (faites) à votre guise. 2. (if you) p., s'il
vous plaît; p. tell me . . ., veuillez me dire
. . .; may I?—p. do! vous permettez?—je
vous en prie. 3. to do as one pleases, agir à sa
guise; do as you p., faites comme vous
voudrez; he'll do just as he pleases, il n'en fera
qu'à sa tête; pleased, a. satisfait, content; to
be p. with sth., être satisfait de qch.; to be
anything but p., n'être pas du tout content;
'pleasing, a. agréable; p. expression, expres-
sion f sympathique; 'pleasure |'pleʒər|, s. 1.
plaisir m; with p., avec plaisir; volontiers. 2.
plaisir(s); jouissances fpl; p. trip, voyage m
d'agrément. 3. volonté f, bon plaisir; at p., à
volonté; at s.o.'s p., au gré de qn.
pleat |pliːt|. I. s. Dressm: etc: pli m; flat pleats,
plis couchés; box pleats, plis doubles, plis
creux. II. v.tr. plisser (une jupe); permanently
pleated skirt, jupe f indéplissable.
plebiscite |'plebisit, -sait|, s. plébiscite m.
pledge |pledʒ|. I. s. 1. gage m, nantissement m;
p. of good faith, garantie f de bonne foi. 2.

promesse f, vœu m; **I'm under a p. of secrecy,** j'ai fait vœu de garder le secret. **II.** v.tr. **1.** mettre (qch.) en gage. **2.** engager (sa parole).
plenary ['pli:nəri], a. complet; entier; **p. powers,** pleins pouvoirs; **p. assembly,** assemblée plénière.
plenipotentiary [plenipə'tenʃ(ə)ri], a. & s. plénipotentiaire (m).
plenty ['plenti], s. abondance f; **he has p. of everything,** il a de tout en suffisance; **you have p. of time,** vous avez largement le temps; **to have p. to live on,** avoir grandement de quoi vivre; **'plentiful,** a. abondant, copieux; **-fully,** adv. abondamment; copieusement.
plethora ['pleθərə], s. pléthore f, surabondance f.
pleurisy ['pluərisi], s. Med: pleurésie f.
pliable ['plaiəbl], a. **1.** flexible; souple. **2.** (caractère) docile, complaisant; **plia'bility,** s. (a) flexibilité f; (b) souplesse f (de caractère).
pliers ['plaiəz], s.pl. Tls: **(pair of) p.,** pince(s) f (pl), tenaille(s) f (pl).
plight [plait], s. condition f, état m.
plimsolls ['plimsoulz], s.pl. chaussures f de gymnastique.
plinth [plinθ], s. Arch: plinthe f; socle m.
plod [plɔd], v.i. **(plodded) 1.** marcher péniblement; **to p. along,** marcher d'un pas pesant; **to p. on,** persévérer; F: s'accrocher. **2. to p. (away),** travailler laborieusement **(at sth.,** à qch.); **'plodder,** s. travailleur persévérant (mais peu doué).
plonk¹ [plɔŋk]. F: **1.** s. bruit sourd. **II.** adv. avec un bruit sourd. **III.** v.tr. **to p. sth. down,** poser qch. bruyamment et sans façons; **to p. oneself down,** s'asseoir lourdement.
plonk², s. P: vin m ordinaire, pinard m.
plot [plɔt]. **I.** s. **1.** (parcelle f, lot m, de) terrain m; **building p.,** terrain à bâtir, lotissement m. **2.** intrigue f, action f (d'un roman, etc.). **3.** complot m, conspiration f. **II.** v.tr. **(plotted) 1.** relever (un terrain, etc.); tracer (un levé de terrain). **2.** abs. comploter, conspirer **(against s.o.,** contre qn); **'plotter,** s. conspirateur, -trice; **'plotting,** s. **1:** levé m (d'un terrain). **2.** tracé m, graphique m. **3.** complots mpl, machinations fpl.
plough [plau]. **I.** s. charrue f; **trenching p.,** défonceuse f. **II.** v.tr. **1.** labourer (la terre); tracer (un sillon). **2.** Com: **to p. back (the profits),** réinvestir (les bénéfices dans l'entreprise); **'ploughman,** pl. **-men,** s. laboureur m; **p.'s lunch,** pain et fromage.
plover ['plʌvər], s. Orn: pluvier m.
plow [plau], s. & v.tr. N.Am: = PLOUGH.
ploy [plɔi], s. démarche astucieuse.
pluck [plʌk]. **I.** v.tr. **1.** arracher (des plumes); épiler (les sourcils). **2.** plumer (une volaille). **II.** s. courage m, F: cran m; **'pluck 'up,** v.tr. **to p. up (one's) courage,** s'armer de courage;

'plucky, a. courageux; **to be p.,** avoir du cran; **-ily,** adv. courageusement.
plug [plʌg]. **I.** s. **1.** tampon m, bouchon m, bonde f. **2.** (a) cheville f; El: fiche f; **wall p.,** prise f de courant; (b) Aut: **sparking p.,** bougie f. **II.** v. **(plugged) 1.** v.tr. boucher, tamponner. **2.** v.tr. Com: faire une publicité à tout casser pour (qch.). **3.** v.i. **to p. away,** persévérer, s'acharner, F: s'accrocher, **'plug-hole,** s. trou m d'écoulement (de baignoire).
plum [plʌm], s. **1.** prune f; **p.(-tree),** prunier m. **2.** morceau de choix; **the plums,** les meilleurs postes; **that's a p. job,** F: c'est le filon; Cu: **p. cake,** cake m; **p. pudding,** pudding m (de Noël).
plumage ['plu:midʒ], s. plumage m.
plumb [plʌm]. **I.** s. **1.** plomb m (de fil à plomb); **p. line,** (i) fil m à plomb; (ii) Nau: ligne f de sonde. **2.** adv. **p. in the middle,** juste au milieu. **II.** v.tr. **1.** sonder (la mer); vérifier l'aplomb de (qch.). **2.** plomber (une canalisation); **'plumber,** s. plombier m; **'plumbing,** s. **1.** plomberie f. **2.** coll. tuyauterie f.
plump [plʌmp], a. rebondi, grassouillet, dodu (of chicken or pers.) bien en chair **'plumpness,** s. embonpoint m.
plunder ['plʌndər]. **I.** s. butin m. **II.** v.tr. piller.
plunge [plʌn(d)ʒ]. **I.** v. **1.** v.tr. plonger, immerger (qch. dans l'eau); **plunged in darkness,** plong dans l'obscurité. **2.** v.i. (a) plonger (dans l'eau), se jeter à corps perdu (dans une affaire); **to p. forward,** s'élancer en avant. **3.** v.i. (of horse) ruer; (of ship) tanguer. **II.** s. plongeon m; **take the p.,** sauter le pas.
pluperfect [plu:'pə:fikt], a. & s. Gram: plu que-parfait (m).
plural ['pluərəl], a. & s. Gram: pluriel (m).
plus [plʌs]. **1.** prep. plus. **2.** s. (pl. **pluse** ['plʌsiz]), plus m, signe m de l'addition.
plush [plʌʃ], s. Tex: peluche f.
plutocrat ['plu:təkræt], s. ploutocrate n **plu'tocracy,** s. ploutocratie f.
ply¹ [plai]. **1.** v.tr. (a) manier (qch vigoureusement; (b) **to p. s.o. with question** presser qn de questions. **2.** v.i. (a) faire le se vice, la navette **(between . . . and . . .,** ent . . . et . . .); (b) **to p. for hire,** faire un servi de taxi.
ply², s. **1.** pli f, épaisseur f (de contre-plaqué). fil m (de corde, de laine); **three p. wool,** lain trois fils; **'plywood,** s. contre-plaqué m.
p.m. ['pi:'em], adv. de l'après-midi, du soir; **four p.m.,** à quatre heures de l'après-midi.
pneumatic [nju:'mætik], a. pneumatique.
pneumonia [nju:'mouniə], s. Med: pneumonie
poach¹ [poutʃ], v.tr. Cu: pocher (des œufs).
poach² v.tr. & i. braconner (le gibier); **to p. s.o.'s preserves,** empiéter sur les prérogativ de qn; F: piquer dans l'assiette de c **'poacher,** s. braconnier m; **'poaching,**

braconnage *m*.
pocket |'pɔkit]. I. *s.* I. (*a*) poche *f*; **trouser p.**,
poche de pantalon; **hip p.**, poche revolver; **inside breast p.**, poche à portefeuille; **to go
through s.o.'s pockets**, faire les poches à qn; **p.
dictionary**, dictionnaire *m* de poche; (*b*) **he's
always dipping into his p.**, il est toujours à
débourser; **to be in p.**, être en bénéfice; **I'm out
of p. by it**, j'y suis de ma poche. 2. (*a*) *Bill:*
blouse *f*; (*b*) *Av:* (**air**) **p.**, trou *m* d'air; *Hyd.E:*
poche d'air; (*c*) **p. book**, calepin *m*; **p. knife**,
couteau *m* de poche; **p. money**, argent *m* de
poche. II. *v.tr.* I. (*a*) empocher; mettre (qch.)
dans sa poche; (*b*) *Pej:* soustraire (de l'argent);
F: chiper (qch.). 2. *Bill:* blouser (la bille). 3.
Min: poche, sac *m* (de minerai); **'pocketful**, *s.*
pleine poche (de qch.).
pod |pɔd], *s.* cosse *f*, gousse *f*.
poem |'pouim], *s.* poème *m*; poésie *f*; **'poet**, *s.*
poète *m*; **'poetess**, *s.* femme *f* poète;
po'etic(al), *a.* poétique; **'poetry**, *s.* poésie *f*;
to write p., écrire des vers; **a piece of p.**, une
poésie.
poignant ['pɔinjənt], *a.* (*of emotion*) poignant,
vif; (*of thought*) angoissant; **-ly**, *adv.* d'une
façon poignante; **'poignancy**, *s.* violence *f*
(d'une émotion); acuité *f* (d'une douleur).
poinsettia [pɔin'setiə], *s. Bot:* poinsettia *f*.
point [pɔint]. I. *s.* I. **point** *m*; (*a*) **decimal p.**,
virgule *f*; (*b*) **p. of departure**, point de départ;
p. of view, point de vue; **to consider sth. from
all points of view**, considérer qch. sous tous ses
aspects; (*c*) point, détail *m*; **figures that give p.
to his argument**, chiffres qui ajoutent du poids
à sa thèse; **to make a p.**, faire ressortir un
argument; **points to be remembered**, considérations *f* à se rappeler; **to make a p. of
doing sth.**, se faire un devoir de faire qch.; (*d*)
here's the p., voici ce dont il s'agit; **off the p.**,
hors de propos; **on this p.**, à cet égard; **your
remark is not to the p.**, votre observation
manque d'à-propos; **let's get back to the p.**,
revenons à nos moutons; (*e*) **what would be the
p. (of doing sth.)?** à quoi bon (faire qch.)? **p. of
interest**, détail intéressant; **to have one's good
points**, avoir ses qualités; (*f*) **to be on the p. of
doing sth.**, être sur le point de faire qch.; **I was
on the p. of going**, j'allais partir; **up to a certain
p.**, jusqu'à un certain point; **to come to the p.**,
arriver au fait; (*g*) *Games:* point; **to win on
points**, gagner aux points; (*h*) **policeman on p.
duty**, agent *m* de service; (*i*) **to refuse p. blank**,
refuser net. 2. (*a*) pointe *f* (d'une aiguille);
piquant *m* (d'une plaisanterie); (*b*) *pl. Rail:*
points, aiguillage *m*; (*c*) *Geog:* promontoire *m*;
(*d*) **the points of the compass**, les aires *f* du
vent. II. *v.* I. *v.tr.* braquer (un fusil, etc.) (**at**,
sur). 2. (*a*) *v.i.* **to p. at s.o., sth.**, montrer qn,
qch., du doigt; (*b*) *v.tr.* **to p. sth. out**, signaler

qch.; **'pointed**, *a.* I. pointu. 2. (*réplique*) mordante; (*allusion f*) peu équivoque; **-ly**, *adv.*
d'un ton mordant; **'pointer**, *s.* I. chien *m*
d'arrêt; pointer *m*. 2. renseignement *m*, *F:*
tuyau *m*; **'pointing**, *s.* jointoiement *m* (d'un
mur); **'pointless**, *a.* (plaisanterie *f*) fade;
(observation *f*) qui ne rime à rien;
'pointsman, *pl.* **-men**, *s. Rail:* aiguilleur *m*.
poise |pɔiz]. I. *s.* I. équilibre *m*, aplomb *m*. 2.
port *m* (du corps). II. *v.tr.* (*a*) équilibrer; (*b*)
balancer (qch.); **to p. sth. in the hand**, soupeser
qch.
poison ['pɔizn]. I. *s.* poison *m*; **to take p.**, s'empoisonner; *Bot:* *N.Am:* **p. ivy**, sumac
vénéneux. II. *v.tr.* (*a*) empoisonner (qn); (*b*)
corrompre, pervertir (l'esprit de qn); (*c*) *Med:*
(*esp. of food, etc.*) intoxiquer; **'poisoner**, *s.*
empoisonneur, -euse; **'poisoning**, *s.* empoisonnement *m*; *Med:* **food, etc., p.**, intoxication *f*; **'poisonous**, *a.* toxique; empoisonné;
(*of animal*) venimeux; (*of plant*) vénéneux; **p.
doctrine**, doctrine pernicieuse; **she has a p.
tongue**, elle a une langue de vipère; **p. slander**,
le poison de la calomnie; *F:* **she's a p. creature!**
c'est une vraie poison!
poke [pouk]. I. *v.* I. *v.tr.* (*a*) toucher (qn, qch., du
bout du doigt), pousser (qn du coude); (*b*)
tisonner (le feu); (*c*) **to p. fun at s.o.**, se moquer
de qn. 2. *v.i.* **to p. (about)**, fouiller, farfouiller
(dans tous les coins); **to p. into other people's
business**, fourrer son nez dans les affaires
d'autrui; **'poker**[1], *s.* tisonnier *m*.
poker[2] ['poukər], *s. Cards:* poker *m*.
poky ['pouki], *a.* (*of room*) exigu et triste; (*of job,
etc.*) mesquin.
Poland ['poulənd]. *Pr.n. Geog:* la Pologne.
polarize ['pouləraiz], *v.tr.* (*a*) polariser; (*b*) **to be
polarized**, se polariser; **polari'zation**, *s.*
polarisation *f*.
pole[1] [poul], *s.* (*a*) perche *f*; **tent p.**, mât *m*, montant *m*, de tente; **telegraph p.**, poteau *m*
télégraphique; *F:* **to be up the p.**, être fou; (*b*)
Sp: **p. vaulting**, saut *m* à la perche.
pole[2], *s. Geog:* pôle *m*; **South P.**, pôle sud; **the p.-
star**, l'étoile *f* polaire; **'polar**, *a.* polaire; **p.
bear**, ours blanc.
Pole[3], *s. Geog:* Polonais, -aise.
polemic [pə'lemik], *s.* polémique *f*.
police [pə'li:s], *s. inv.* **the p.**, la police; **p.
superintendent** = commissaire *m* central; **p. inspector** = (i) inspecteur *m* de police; (ii) (*in the
CID*) commissaire de police; **p. constable,
officer** = agent *m* de police; **p. station** = com-
missariat *m* (de police); (*in London*) **River p.**,
police fluviale; **the Royal Canadian Mounted
P.**, la Gendarmerie royale du Canada; *F:* **the p.
are after him**, la police est à ses trousses;
po'liceman, *pl.* **-men**, *s.* agent *m* de police;
po'licewoman, *pl.* **-women**, *s.f.* femme-

agent (de police).

policy ['pɔlisi], s. **1.** politique *f*; ligne *f* de conduite; **foreign p.**, politique extérieure; *Com: etc:* **our p. is to satisfy our customers,** notre but est de satisfaire nos clients. **2.** *Ins:* insurance p., police *f* (d'assurance).

poliomyelitis, *F:* **polio** ['poulioumaiə'laitis, 'pouliou], s. *Med:* poliomyélite *f, F:* polio *f.*

polish[1] ['pɔliʃ]. **I.** *s.* **1.** poli *m*, brillant *m*, lustre *m*; **high p.,** poli brillant; **to take the p. off sth.,** dépolir qch. **2.** *Com: Ind:* **household polishes,** produits *m* d'entretien; **floor p.,** encaustique *f*, cire *f* à parquet; **shoe p.,** cirage *m*; **nail n.,** vernis *m* à ongles. **3.** politesse *f*; belles manières. **II.** *v.tr.* polir; cirer (des chaussures, des meubles); astiquer, cirer, faire reluire (le parquet); **'polish 'off,** *v.tr.* terminer vite, expédier (un travail); vider (un verre); ne rien laisser d'(un plat); **'polish 'up,** *v.tr.* **1.** faire reluire (qch.). **2. to p. up one's French,** dérouiller son français; **'polished,** *a.* (*of manners*) poli; (*of furniture, etc.*) ciré.

Polish[2] ['pouliʃ]. **1.** *a. Geog:* polonais, -aise. **2.** *s. Ling:* le polonais.

polite [pə'lait], *a.* poli, courtois (**to s.o.,** envers, avec, qn); **-ly,** *adv.* poliment; avec politesse; **po'liteness,** s. politesse *f.*

politics ['pɔlitiks], *s.pl.* (*usu. with sg. const.*) la politique; **to go into p.,** se lancer dans la politique; **po'litical,** *a.* politique; **p. parties,** partis *m* politiques; **-ally,** *adv.* politiquement; **poli'tician,** s. homme *m*, femme *f*, politique.

poll [poul], s. **1.** vote *m* (par bulletins); scrutin *m*; **to go to the polls,** aller aux urnes *f*; **to declare the p.,** proclamer le résultat du scrutin; **to head the p.,** venir en tête de liste. **2.** sondage *m* (d'opinion publique); **Gallup p.,** (sondage) Gallup *m*; **'polling,** s. vote *m*; élections *fpl*; **p. booth,** isoloir *m*; **p. station,** bureau *m* de vote.

pollen ['pɔlən], s. *Bot:* pollen *m.*

pollute [pə'l(j)u:t], *v.tr.* polluer, souiller, corrompre (qch., un endroit); **po'llution,** s. pollution *f.*

polo ['poulou], s. **1.** *Sp:* polo *m*; **water p.,** polo nautique. **2.** *Cl:* **p. neck,** col roulé.

polonaise [pɔlə'neiz], s. *Mus:* polonaise *f.*

poltergeist ['pɔltəgaist], s. esprit frappeur.

polygamy [pə'ligəmi], s. polygamie *f*; **po'lygamist,** s. polygame *mf.*

polyglot ['pɔliglɔt], *a. & s.* polyglotte (*mf*).

polygon ['pɔligən], s. polygone *m*; **po'lygonal,** *a.* polygonal.

Polynesia [pɔli'ni:ziə]. *Pr.n. Geog:* la Polynésie; **Poly'nesian,** *a. & s.* polynésien, -ienne.

polyp ['pɔlip], s. polype *m.*

polytechnic [pɔli'teknik]. **!.** *a.* polytechnique. **2.** *s.* collège *m* d'enseignement technique.

polythene ['pɔliθi:n], s. polyéthylène *m*, polythène *m.*

pomegranate ['pɔmigrænit], s. *Bot:* grenade *f.*

pomp [pɔmp], s. pompe *f*, éclat *m*, splendeur *f*; **'pompous,** *a.* **a p. man,** un homme suffisant; **-ly,** *adv.* pompeusement, avec suffisance.

pond [pɔnd], s. étang *m*; mare *f.*

ponder ['pɔndər]. **1.** *v.tr.* réfléchir sur (une question); ruminer. **2.** *v.i.* méditer; **to p. over sth.,** réfléchir à, méditer sur, qch.; **'ponderous,** *a.* lourd, pesant.

pontiff ['pɔntif], s. pontife *m*; *Ecc:* **the sovereign p.,** le souverain pontife, le pape; **pon'tifical,** *a.* pontifical.

pontoon [pɔn'tu:n], s. ponton *m*; **p. bridge,** pont *m* de bateaux, pont flottant.

pony ['pouni], s. poney *m*; **'pony-carriage,** *s.* attelage *m* à poney.

poodle ['pu:dl], s. caniche *mf.*

pool[1] [pu:l], s. **1.** mare *f*; **swimming p.,** piscine *f.* **2.** *Pr.n.* **the P.** (of London), le port de Londres (en aval de London Bridge).

pool[2]. **I.** *s.* **1.** (*a*) poule *f*, cagnotte *f*; (*b*) **football pools,** concours *m* de pronostics de football. **2.** *Com:* (*a*) fonds communs; masse commune; (*b*) *Pol.Ec:* pool *m*; (*c*) **typing p.,** pool dactylographique, de dactylos. **II.** *v.tr.* mettre en commun (des capitaux, etc.).

poor ['puər, pɔ:r], *a.* pauvre. **1.** (*a*) besogneux, malheureux; (*b*) *s.pl.* **the p.,** les pauvres *m*, les malheureux, les indigents. **2.** de qualité médiocre; (*a*) **p. soil,** terre *f* maigre; **p. wine,** piquette *f*; (*b*) **p. excuse,** piètre excuse; **p. quality,** basse qualité; **p. health,** santé débile; **to have a p. opinion of s.o.,** avoir une pauvre opinion de qn. **3.** **p. fellow!** le pauvre homme! la pauvre garçon! **-ly. 1.** *adv.* pauvrement, médiocrement, piètrement. **2.** *a.* **to be p.,** être souffrant; **to look p.,** avoir mauvaise mine; **'poorness,** s. **1.** pauvreté *f*, insuffisance *f.* **2.** infériorité *f*; peu *m* de valeur.

pop[1] [pɔp]. **I.** *v.i.* (**popped**) **1.** éclater, péter; (*cork*) sauter. **2.** *F:* **to p. round to the grocer's,** faire un saut (jusque) chez l'épicier. **II.** *s.* **1.** bruit sec. **2.** *F:* boisson pétillante, gazeuse. **III.** *int.* **to go off p.,** éclater; **'pop-gun,** pistolet *m* d'enfant, pétoire *f*; **'pop 'off,** *v.i.* (*a*) filer, déguerpir; (*b*) mourir subitement.

pop[2], s. *F:* esp. *N.Am:* papa *m.*

pop[3], *a.* (= *popular*) **p. art,** pop'art *m*; **p. music,** la musique pop; **p. song,** chanson *f* pop; **p. singer,** chanteur, -euse, pop.

pope [poup], s. pape *m.*

poplar ['pɔplər], s. *Bot:* peuplier *m.*

poppy ['pɔpi], s. *Bot:* pavot *m*; **field poppy,** coquelicot *m.*

popular ['pɔpjulər], *a.* populaire; (*a*) du peuple; **p. uprising,** insurrection *f* populaire; *Pol:* **Front,** front *m* populaire, coalition *f* de gauche; (*b*) (opéra, livre) à la mode; (acteur) très couru; (*c*) compréhensible pour tout monde; **p. book on rockets,** ouvrage *m* de vulgarisation sur les fusées; (*d*) **p. error,** erreur courante; **-ly,** *adv.* **it is p. believed that . , .,** les gens croient que . . .; **popu'larity,** *s.* popularité *f*; **populari'zation,** *s.* vulgarisation *f*; **'popularize,** *v.tr.* populariser; vulgariser.

populate ['pɔpjuleit], *v.tr.* peupler; **thickly populated area,** région très peuplée; **popu'lation,** *s.* population *f*.

porcelain ['pɔːslin], *s.* porcelaine *f*.

porch [pɔːtʃ], *s.* (*a*) porche *m*, portique *m*; (*b*) **p. roof,** auvent *m*; (*c*) *N.Am:* véranda *f*; *Fr.C:* galerie *f*.

porcupine ['pɔːkjupain], *s.* *Z:* porc-épic *m*, *pl.* porcs-épics.

pore[1] [pɔːr], *s.* *Anat:* pore *m*.

pore[2], *v.i.* **to p. over a book,** être plongé dans un livre.

pork [pɔːk], *s.* *Cu:* (viande *f* de) porc *m*; **salt p.,** salé *m*; **p. chop,** côtelette *f*, côte *f*, de porc; **p. pie,** pâté *m* de porc (en croûte); **p. butcher,** charcutier, -ière.

pornography [pɔː'nɔgrəfi], *s.* pornographie *f*; **porno'graphic,** *a.* pornographique.

porous ['pɔːrəs], *a.* poreux, perméable; **po'rosity,** *s.* porosité *f*.

porpoise ['pɔːpəs], *s.* *Z:* marsouin *m*.

porridge ['pɔridʒ], *s.* bouillie *f* d'avoine; porridge *m*.

port[1] [pɔːt], *s.* port *m*; **naval p.,** port militaire; **trading p.,** port marchand; **free p.,** port franc; **home p.,** port d'attache; **p. of registry,** port d'armement; **p. charges,** droits *m* de port; **to reach p. safely,** arriver à bon port.

port[2], *s.* *Nau:* bâbord *m*.

port[3], *s.* vin *m* de Porto; porto *m*.

portable ['pɔːtəbl], *a.* portatif; mobile.

portal ['pɔːt(ə)l], *s.* (*a*) portail *m* (de cathédrale); (*b*) portique *m*.

porter[1] ['pɔːtər], *s.* portier *m*, concierge *m*; **p.'s lodge,** loge *f* de concierge.

porter[2], *s.* chasseur *m* (d'hôtel); *Rail:* porteur *m*; **'porterage,** *s.* frais *mpl* de transport.

portfolio, *pl.* -os [pɔːt'fouljou, -ouz], *s.* (*a*) serviette *f* (pour documents); (*b*) chemise *f* (de carton); (*c*) portefeuille *m* (de ministre); **Minister without p.,** ministre sans portefeuille; (*d*) *Com:* portefeuille (i) d'assurances, (ii) de valeurs.

porthole ['pɔːthoul], *s.* *Nau:* hublot *m*.

portion ['pɔːʃ(ə)n]. I. *s.* (*a*) partie *f*; part *f*; (*b*) portion *f*, ration *f*. II. *v.tr.* **to p. out,** partager (un bien, etc.); distribuer (les parts).

portly ['pɔːtli], *a.* corpulent, ventru; **'portliness,** *s.* corpulence *f*, embonpoint *m*.

portrait ['pɔːtrit], *s.* portrait *m*; **por'tray,** *v.tr.* dépeindre, décrire (des scènes, des personnages, des caractères); **por'trayal,** *s.* (i) peinture *f*, représentation *f*; (ii) description *f* (d'une

scène, d'un personnage).

Portugal ['pɔːtjug(ə)l]. *Pr.n. Geog:* le Portugal; **Portu'guese** [-'giːz]. 1. *a.* & *s.* portugais, -aise. 2. *s. Ling:* le portugais.

pose [pouz]. I. *s.* 1. pose *f*, attitude *f* (du corps). 2. pose, affectation *f*. II. *v.tr.* & *i.* poser (un problème); (faire) poser (un modèle); **to p. as a Frenchman,** se faire passer pour Français; **to p. as a scholar,** prétendre être un savant; **'poser,** *s.* question embarrassante; *F:* colle *f*.

posh [pɔʃ], *a. F:* chic.

position [pə'ziʃ(ə)n]. I. *s.* 1. posture *f*, position *f*, attitude *f* (du corps, etc.). 2. position; (*a*) place *f*; situation *f*; **in p.,** en place; (*b*) **to fix one's p.,** faire le point; (*c*) **to manœuvre for p.,** manœuvrer pour s'assurer l'avantage. 3. (*a*) état *m*, condition *f*, situation; **to be in a p. to do sth.,** être à même de faire qch.; **put yourself in my p.,** mettez-vous à ma place; (*b*) rang social; **in a high p.,** haut placé; (*c*) *Sch:* **p. in class,** place dans la classe. 4. emploi *m*, place, situation; **p. of trust,** poste *m* de confiance. II. *v.tr.* déterminer la position de (qch.); situer (un lieu sur la carte); **po'sitioning,** *s.* mise *f* en place; *T.V:* orientation *f* (de l'antenne).

positive ['pɔzitiv], *a.* 1. (*a*) positif, affirmatif; (*b*) **it's a p. fact!** c'est un fait authentique. 2. (*a*) convaincu, assuré, sûr, certain (**of, de**); (*b*) **p. tone of voice,** ton absolu, tranchant; **-ly,** *adv.* 1. positivement, affirmativement. 2. assurément; **I can't speak p.,** je ne puis rien affirmer.

possess [pə'zes], *v.tr.* 1. (*a*) posséder (un bien); **all I p.,** tout mon avoir; (*b*) avoir, posséder (une qualité, des facultés). 2. **what possessed you (to do that)?** qu'est-ce qui vous a pris (de faire cela)? **to be possessed with an idea,** être obsédé d'une idée; **po'ssession,** *s.* 1. possession *f*, jouissance *f* (d'un bien); **to take p. of sth.,** s'emparer de qch.; **to take p. of a house,** entrer en possession d'une maison; **vacant p.** (**of a house**), libre possession, jouissance immédiate (d'une maison). 2. objet possédé; possession; **po'ssessive,** *a.* & *s. Gram:* possessif (*m*); **po'ssessor,** *s.* possesseur *m*; propriétaire *mf*.

possible ['pɔsəbl, -ibl], *a.* (*a*) possible; **it's p.,** c'est possible; cela se peut bien; **as many details as p.,** le plus de détails possible; **as far as p.,** autant que possible; dans la mesure du possible; **as early as p.,** le plus tôt possible; (*b*) (*of candidate for job*), acceptable; **-ibly,** *adv.* 1. **I cannot p. do it,** il ne m'est pas possible de le faire; **it can't p. be!** pas possible! **I'll do all I p. can,** je ferai tout mon possible. 2. peut-être (bien); c'est possible; cela se peut; **possi'bility,** *s.* 1. possibilité *f*; **if, by any p., I'm not there,** si, par impossible, je n'y étais pas; **within the bounds of p.,** dans la limite du possible. 2. éventualité *f*.

post[1] [poust], s. **1.** poteau m, pieu m; **as deaf as a p.**, sourd comme un pot. **2.** *Rac:* **starting p., winning p.**, poteau de départ, d'arrivée.

post[2], *v.tr.* **to p. (up)**, afficher (un avis); coller (des affiches); *P.N:* **p. no bills**, défense d'afficher; **'poster**, s. affiche (murale).

post[3]. **I.** s. **1.** poste m (de sentinelle, etc.). **2.** poste, emploi m. **II.** *v.tr. Mil:* **1.** poster (une sentinelle). **2. to be posted**, être affecté (à un commandement, à une unité).

post[4], s. *Mil:* **the last p.**, (i) la retraite au clairon; (ii) la sonnerie aux morts.

post[5]. **I.** s. **1.** courrier m; **by return of p.**, par retour du courrier; **the p. has come**, le facteur est passé; **to miss the p.**, manquer la levée, le courrier. **2.** poste f; **to send sth. by p.**, envoyer qch. par la poste. **3. p. office**, bureau m de poste; **the P. Office**, l'Administration f des Postes, les PTT, les P. et T.; **to take a letter to the p.**, porter une lettre à la poste. **II.** *v.tr.* (*a*) **to p. a letter**, mettre une lettre à la poste; poster une lettre; (*b*) **to keep oneself posted**, se tenir au courant; **'postage**, s. affranchissement m (d'une lettre); **p. paid**, port payé; **'postal**, *a.* postal; (International) **P. Union**, Union postale universelle; **the p. service**, les Postes et Télécommunications f; **'postcard**, s. carte postale; **'postcode**, s. code postal; **'postman**, *pl.* -men, s. facteur m; **'postmark**, s. cachet m de la poste; **'postmaster, -mistress**, s. receveur, -euse, des Postes; **the Postmaster General** = le Ministre des Postes et Télécommunications.

post- [poust-], *prefix used in combined forms*; post-; **post'date**, *v.tr.* postdater (un chèque); **post'graduate**. *a. & s.* **p. (student)**, étudiant(e) licencié(e) qui continue ses études; **posthumous** ['pɔstjuməs], *a.* posthume; **'post-im'pressionism**, s. post-impressionnisme m; **'post'mortem**, s. autopsie f (cadavérique); *F:* **to conduct a p. on sth.**, examiner critiquement les résultats de qch.; **post'pone**, *v.tr.* remettre, ajourner, renvoyer à plus tard (une action, un départ); différer, arriérer (un paiement, etc.); **post'ponement**, s. remise f à plus tard; renvoi m; ajournement m; **'postscript**, s. (*abbr.* P.S.), post-scriptum m *inv*; **'post'war**, *a.* d'après-guerre.

posterior [pɔs'tiəriər]. **1.** *a.* postérieur (**to**, à). **2.** s. *F:* derrière (de qn); **pos'terity**, s. postérité f.

posture ['pɔstʃər]. **I.** s. **1.** (*a*) posture f, attitude f (du corps); (*b*) position f, situation f, état m (des affaires, etc.). **II.** *v.* **1.** *v.tr.* mettre (qn) dans une certaine posture; poser (un modèle). **2.** *v.i.* prendre une posture, une attitude.

pot [pɔt]. **I.** s. (*a*) pot m; (*b*) marmite f; **pots and pans**, batterie f de cuisine; (*c*) *F:* **to go to p.**, aller à la ruine; être fichu. **II.** *v.tr.* (**potted**) **1.** (*a*) mettre en pot, conserver (la viande, etc); (*b*)

mettre en pot, empoter (une plante). **2.** *Bill:* blouser (une bille); **'pot-hole**, s. **1.** nid m de poule (dans une route). **2.** *Geol:* marmite f de géants; **'pot-holer**, s. spéléologue mf; **'pot-holing**, s. spéléologie f; **'pot-'luck**, s. **to take p.-l.**, (i) manger à la fortune du pot; (ii) choisir au hasard; **'pot-shot**, s. **to take a p.-s. at sth.**, lâcher au petit bonheur un coup de fusil à qch.

potash ['pɔtæʃ], s. potasse f.

potassium [pə'tæsiəm], s. *Ch:* potassium m.

potato, *pl.* -oes [pə'teitou, -ouz], s. **1.** pomme f de terre; **boiled potatoes**, pommes (de terre) à l'eau; **baked potatoes**, pommes (de terre) au four; **mashed potatoes**, purée f de pommes (de terre); **chipped potatoes**, pommes (de terre) frites, *F:* frites f pl. **2. sweet p.**, patate f.

potency ['pout(ə)nsi], s. (*a*) force f, puissance f (d'un argument); (*b*) efficacité f (d'un médicament); (*c*) force (d'un alcool); **'potent**, *a.* (*of motive, etc.*) convaincant, plein de force; (*of drug, etc.*) efficace, puissant; **p. poison**, poison très fort, violent.

potential [pə'tenʃ(ə)l]. **1.** *a.* (*a*) en puissance; virtuel; (*of danger*) latent; (*b*) potentiel; **the p resources of Africa**, les ressources potentielles de l'Afrique. **2.** s. *El:* operating p., voltage m de régime. **3. the military p. of a country**, le poten tiel militaire d'un pays; **-ally**, *adv.* potentielle ment, virtuellement, en puissance; **poten ti'ality**, s. potentialité f.

potter[1] ['pɔtər], *v.i.* **1.** s'occuper de bagatelles s'amuser à des riens; **to p. about (at odd jobs** bricoler. **2.** trainer, flâner; **to p. about th house**, s'occuper à de petites tâches dans l maison; **he just potters (about)**, il bricole.

potter[2], s. potier m; **p.'s wheel**, tour m de potie

pottery ['pɔtəri], s. **1.** poterie f. **2.** *coll.* vaisselle de terre; **a piece of p.**, une poterie.

potty ['pɔti], *a. F:* toqué, timbré.

pouch [pautʃ], s. **1.** petit sac; bourse f. **2.** poche ventrale (des marsupiaux).

poultice ['poultis]. **I.** s. cataplasme m. **II.** *v.t* mettre un cataplasme sur (qch.).

poultry ['poultri], s. *coll.* volaille f; **p. yard**, basse-cour f; **'poulterer**, s. marchand, -and de volaille.

pounce [pauns], *v.i.* (*a*) **to p. on the prey**, fondr s'abattre, sur la proie; (*b*) se précipiter, se jet (**on sth.**, sur qch.).

pound[1] [paund], s. **1.** (*abbr.* lb.) livre f; **to s sugar by the p.**, vendre le sucre à la livre. (*symbol* £) **p. sterling**, livre sterling; **p. no** billet m (de banque) d'une livre.

pound[2], s. fourrière f (pour animaux erran pour autos).

pound[3]. **1.** *v.tr.* (*a*) broyer, piler, concasser; bourrer (qn) de coups de poing; (*c*) **to p. sth.** **pieces**, réduire qch. en miettes. **2.** *v.i.* **to p.** **at sth.**, cogner dur, frapper ferme, sur qch.

pour [pɔːr]. **1.** *v.tr.* verser (du vin, etc., dans un verre). **2.** *v.i.* (*of rain*) tomber à verse; **it's pouring (with rain)**, il pleut à verse; **'pouring**, *a*. **p. rain**, pluie torrentielle, pluie battante; **'pour 'out**. **1.** *v.tr.* verser (une tasse de thé, etc.). **2.** *v.i.* (*a*) (*of water, etc.*) sortir à flots; (*b*) **the people poured out of the cinema**, les gens sont sortis en foule du cinéma.

pout [paut]. **I.** *s.* moue *f*. **II.** *v.i.* (*a*) faire la moue; (*b*) (*sulk*) bouder.

poverty ['pɔvəti], *s*. **1.** pauvreté *f*, misère *f*, gêne *f*; **to live in p.**, vivre dans la misère; **p. of ideas**, dénuement *m* d'idées.

powder ['paudər]. **I.** *s.* poudre *f*; (*a*) **to reduce sth. to p.**, réduire qch. en poudre; pulvériser qch.; (*b*) (**gun-)p.**, poudre (à canon); (*c*) (**face-)p.**, poudre (de riz). **II.** *v.tr.* **1.** saupoudrer (**with**, de). **2.** se poudrer (le visage). **3.** pulvériser (qch.); **'powder-compact**, *s.* poudrier *m*; **'powder-magazine**, *s*. poudrière *f*; **'powdery**, *a*. (*a*) poudreux; (*b*) friable.

power ['pauər], *s*. **1.** pouvoir *m*; **I'll do all in my p.**, je ferai tout mon possible; **it is beyond my p.**, cela ne m'est pas possible. **2.** faculté *f*, capacité *f*; **p. of speech**, la parole; **mental powers**, facultés intellectuelles. **3.** vigueur *f*, force *f*; *F:* **more p. to your elbow!** puissiez-vous réussir! **4.** (*a*) puissance *f* (d'une machine); force (d'un aimant); (*b*) **motive p.**, force motrice; **p. station**, centrale *f* (électrique). **5.** (*a*) pouvoir, influence *f*, autorité *f*; **to fall into s.o.'s p.**, tomber au pouvoir de qn; **p. of life and death**, droit *m* de vie et de mort; (*b*) **to act with full powers**, agir de pleine autorité; (*c*) *Jur:* procuration *f*, mandat *m*, pouvoir. **6. the Great Powers**, les Grandes Puissances. **7.** *Mth:* puissance; **'powerful**, *a*. (*a*) puissant; (*b*) fort, vigoureux; **p. remedy**, remède *m* énergique; **-fully**, *adv.* puissamment, fortement; **'powerless**, *a*. impuissant; **they are p. in the matter**, ils n'y peuvent rien; **'powerlessness**, *s*. impuissance *f*.

practicable ['præktikəbl], *a*. praticable; **practica'bility**, *s*. praticabilité *f*.

practical ['præktik(ə)l], *a*. pratique; (*a*) **p. chemistry**, chimie appliquée; (*b*) **p. proposal**, proposition d'ordre pratique; **-ally**, *adv*. **1.** pratiquement, en pratique. **2.** pour ainsi dire; **there's been p. no snow**, il n'y a pas eu de neige, pour ainsi dire; **he's p. cured**, il est presque guéri; **p. the whole of the audience**, la quasi-totalité de l'assistance.

practice ['præktis], *s*. **1.** pratique *f*; **the p. of medicine**, l'exercice *m* de la médecine; **to put a principle into p.**, mettre un principe en action, en pratique. **2.** habitude *f*, coutume *f*, usage *m*; **to make a p. of doing sth.**, se faire une habitude de faire qch. **3.** exercice(s); **it can only be learnt by p.**, cela ne s'apprend que par l'usage; **to be**

in p., être en forme; out of p., rouillé; choir p., répétition *f*; *Mil:* target p., exercices de tir. **4.** pratique, clientèle *f* (de médecin); étude *f* (d'avocat). **5.** *esp. in pl.* pratiques, menées *fpl*.

practise ['præktis], *v.tr.* **1.** pratiquer (une vertu, etc.); mettre en pratique, en action (un principe, une règle); **to p. what one preaches**, prêcher d'exemple. **2.** pratiquer, exercer (une profession). **3.** *abs. Mus:* faire des exercices; **'practised**, *a*. exercé, expérimenté; (joueur) averti; **p. in sth.**, habile dans qch., rompu à qch.; **prac'titioner**, *s*. praticien, -ienne; **medical p.**, médecin *m*; **general p.** (*abbr.* **G.P.**), (médecin) généraliste (*m*).

pragmatic [præg'mætik], *a*. pragmatique.

prairie ['prɛəri], *s. usu. pl.* **the prairies**, la prairie (de l'Amérique du Nord).

praise [preiz]. **I.** *s.* (i) (*deserved*) éloge(s) *m*(*pl*); (ii) (*adulation*) louange(s) *f*(*pl*); **I've nothing but p. for him**, je n'ai qu'à me louer de lui; **beyond all p.**, au-dessus de tout éloge. **II.** louer (qn); faire l'éloge de (qn, qch.); **'praiseworthy**, *a*. digne d'éloges; (travail) méritoire.

pram [præm], *s*. *F:* voiture *f* d'enfant.

prance [prɑːns], *v.i.* **1.** (*of horse*) caracoler; piaffer. **2.** (*of pers.*) se pavaner.

prank [præŋk], *s*. **1.** escapade *f*, frasque *f*, fredaine *f*. **2.** tour *m*, farce *f*; **to play pranks on s.o.**, jouer des tours à qn.

prawn [prɔːn], *s*. crevette *f* rose, rouge; **Dublin Bay p.**, langoustine *f*.

pray [prei], *v.tr. & i.* **to p. (to) God**, prier Dieu; **to p. for s.o.**, prier à l'intention de qn; **he's past praying for**, il est incorrigible; **prayer** ['prɛər], *s*. prière *f* (à Dieu); **the Lord's P.**, l'oraison dominicale, le pater; **to say one's prayers**, faire ses dévotions; **the P. Book**, le rituel de l'Église anglicane; (*of Buddhists*) **p. wheel**, moulin *m*, cylindre *m*, à prières; **p. mat**, tapis *m* à prières.

preach [priːtʃ], *v. tr. & i.* prêcher; **to p. a sermon**, prononcer un sermon; **to p. the Gospel**, prêcher l'Évangile; **'preacher**, *s*. prédicateur *m*.

precarious [pri'kɛəriəs], *a*. précaire, incertain; **to make a p. living**, gagner précairement sa vie; **-ly**, *adv*. précairement.

precast ['priːkɑːst], *a*. **p. concrete block**, parpaing *m*.

precaution [pri'kɔːʃ(ə)n], *s*. précaution *f*; **pre'cautionary**, *adv*. (mesures) de précaution.

precede [pri(ː)'siːd], *v.tr.* **1.** précéder; **for a week preceding this match**, pendant une semaine avant ce match. **2.** avoir le pas, la préséance, sur (qn); **precedence** ['presidəns], *s*. (droit *m* de) priorité *f*; **to take p. over s.o.**, prendre le pas sur qn; **ladies take p.**, les dames passent avant; **precedent** ['presidənt], *s*. précédent *m*;

to create a p., créer un précédent; according to p., conformément à la tradition; pre'ceding, a. précédent; the p. day, la veille, le jour précédent.

precept |'pri:sept|, s. précepte m.

precinct |'pri:siŋkt|, s. (a) enceinte f, enclos m; (b) pl. precincts, pourtour m (d'une cathédrale); (c) shopping p., centre commercial (fermé à la circulation automobile).

precious |'preʃəs|. 1. a. (a) précieux; de grand prix; p. stones, pierres précieuses; (b) Iron: fameux, fier; a p. lot he cares about it! il s'en fout comme de l'an quarante! (c) (style) recherché, affecté. 2. s. my p.! mon trésor! mon amour! 3. adv. to take p. good care, prendre un soin particulier.

precipice |'presipis|, s. précipice m; to fall over a p., tomber dans un précipice; pre'cipitous, a. escarpé, abrupt; à pic; à pic.

precipitate |pri'sipiteit|, v.tr. (a) Ch: précipiter (une substance); (b) accélérer, hâter, précipiter (un événement); to p. matters, brusquer les choses; pre'cipitancy, s., precipi'tation, s. précipitation f; (i) empressement m; (ii) manque m de réflexion.

précis ['preisi, pl. -i:z|, s. précis m, résumé m.

precise |pri'sais|, a. 1. (a) précis; exact; (b) at the p. moment when . . ., au moment précis où . . .. 2. (of pers.) pointilleux; méticuleux; -ly, adv. 1. (a) avec précision; (b) at six (o'clock) p., à six heures précises. 2. p. (so)! précisément! parfaitement! pre'ciseness, s. méticulosité f; formalisme m; precision |pri'siʒ(ə)n|, s. précision f; p. instruments, instruments m de précision.

preclude |pri'klu:d|, v.tr. empêcher, écarter (qch.); to be precluded from doing sth., être dans l'impossibilité de faire qch.

precocious |pri'kouʃəs|, a. (of child, plant) précoce; (of plant) hâtif, -ive; -ly, adv. précocement; avec précocité; pre'cociousness, s., precocity [-'kositi], s. précocité f.

preconceive |pri:kən'si:v|, v.tr. préconcevoir; preconceived idea, idée préconçue; precon'ception, s. idée, opinion, préconçue; préjugé m.

preconcerted |pri:kən'sə:tid|, a. arrangé, concerté, d'avance.

precursor |pri(:)'kə:sər|, s. précurseur m.

predate |'pri:'deit|, v.tr. 1. antidater (un document, etc.). 2. venir avant (un fait historique, etc.).

predatory |'predət(ə)ri|, a. (a) rapace, pillard; (b) p. animals, bêtes de proie; 'predators, s.pl. bêtes f de proie.

predecease |'pri:di'si:s|, v.tr. mourir avant (qn).

predecessor |'pri:disesər|, s. prédécesseur m; devancier, -ière.

predicament |pri'dikəmənt|, s. situation difficile, fâcheuse; we're in a fine p.! nous voilà dans de beaux draps!

predict |pri'dikt|, v.tr. prédire (un événement); pre'dictable, a. qui peut être prédit; pre'diction, s. prédiction f.

predilection |pri:di'lekʃ(ə)n|, s. prédilection f (for, pour); to have a p. for sth., affectionner, affecter, qch.

predispose |pri:dis'pouz|, v.tr. prédisposer; to p. s.o. in favour of doing sth., prédisposer, incliner, qn à faire qch.; 'predispo'sition, s. prédisposition f (to, à).

predominate |pri:'domineit|, v.i. 1. prédominer. 2. l'emporter par le nombre, par la quantité; pre'dominant, a. prédominant; pre'dominating, a. prédominant.

preen |pri:n|, v.tr. 1. (of bird) lisser, nettoyer (ses plumes). 2. to p. oneself, (i) se bichonner; (ii) prendre un air avantageux.

prefabricate |pri:'fæbrikeit|, v.tr. préfabriquer; prefabri'cation, s. préfabrication f.

preface ['prefəs|. I. s. préface f; avant-propos m inv. II. v.tr. préfacer, écrire une préface pour (u. ouvrage).

prefect ['pri:fekt|, s. 1. Fr.Adm: préfet m. 2. Sch: élève choisi(e) pour aider à maintenir l. discipline.

prefer |pri'fə:r|, v.tr. (preferred) préférer, aime mieux; to p. sth. to sth., préférer qch. à qch.; would p. to go without, j'aimerais mieux m'e passer; preferable ['pref-], a. préférable (to à); -ably, adv. préférablement; de préférence preference ['pref-], s. préférence f (for, pour) p. clause, pacte de préférence; Fin: shares, actions privilégiées, de priorité; pre fe'rential [pref-], a. (traitement, etc.) préférer tiel; (tarif) de faveur.

prefix ['pri:fiks|. I. s. Gram: préfixe m. II. v. préfixer.

pregnancy ['pregnənsi|, s. grossesse f; (of animal) gestation f; 'pregnant, a. 1. (femm enceinte, grosse; (vache, jument) plein gravide. 2. p. with consequences, gros conséquences.

prehensile |pri'hensail|, a. préhensile.

prehistory |pri:'hist(ə)ri|, s. préhistoire f prehis'torian, s. préhistorien, -ienn prehis'toric, a. préhistorique.

prejudice ['predʒudis|. I. s. 1. préjudice m, t m, dommage m; without p., sous tou réserves. 2. préjugé m; to have a p. against st être prévenu contre qch. II. v.tr. 1. nu porter préjudice, à (une réputation, etc.). prévenir, prédisposer (s.o. against s.o., qn c tre qn); 'prejudiced, a. prévenu (contre qch.); to be p., avoir des préjug preju'dicial, a. préjudiciable, nuisible (to,

prelate ['prelət|, s. prélat m.

preliminary [pri'liminəri]. 1. *a.* préliminaire, préalable. 2. *s.* (*a*) prélude *m*; (*b*) *pl.* **preliminaries**, préliminaires *m*.

prelude ['prelju:d], *s.* 1. prélude *m* (**to**, de). 2. *Mus:* prélude.

premature ['premətjuər, premə'tjuər], *a.* prématuré; **-ly**, *adv.* prématurément.

premeditate [pri:'mediteit], *v.tr.* préméditer; **pre'meditated**, *a.* prémédité; (crime) réfléchi; **p. insolence**, insolence calculée; **premedi'tation**, *s.* préméditation *f.*

premier ['pri:miər, 'prem-]. 1: *a.* premier (en rang, en importance). 2. *s.* premier ministre.

première ['premiɛər], *s. Th:* première *f* (d'une pièce, d'un film).

premises ['premisiz], *s.pl.* le local, les locaux; **on the p.**, sur les lieux.

premium ['pri:miəm], *s.* 1. prix *m*, récompense *f*; prime *f.* 2. (*a*) prix convenu, indemnité *f*; (*b*) **insurance p.**, prime d'assurance. 3. **to be at a p.**, faire prime; être très recherché.

premonition [pri:mə'niʃ(ə)n], *s.* prémonition *f*; pressentiment *m* (de malheur, etc.); **pre'monitory**, *a.* prémonitoire; (signe) avant-coureur.

prenatal ['pri:'neit(ə)l], *a.* prénatal (*mpl.* prénatals *or* prénataux); **p. care**, soins prénatals; (*Fr. Health Service*) **p. allowances**, allocations prénatales.

preoccupation [pri:ɔkju'peiʃ(ə)n], *s.* préoccupation *f* (de l'esprit); **my greatest p.**, mon plus grand souci; **pre'occupied**, *a.* préoccupé; absorbé (par ses études, un souci).

prep [prep]. *Sch: F:* 1. *s.* étude *f*, devoirs *mpl* (du soir); **p. room**, salle *f* d'étude. 2. *a.* **p. school**, école préparatoire privée (pour élèves de 8 à 13 ans).

prepare [pri'pɛər]. 1. *v.tr.* préparer (un repas, etc.); accommoder (un mets, etc.); **to p. a surprise for s.o.**, ménager une surprise à qn; **to p. the way for negotiations**, amorcer des négociations. 2. *v.i.* se préparer, se disposer (**for sth.**, à qch.); **to p. for departure**, faire ses préparatifs de départ; **to p. for an examination**, préparer un examen; **prepa'ration**, *s.* 1. préparation *f* (de la nourriture, etc.). 2. (*usu. pl.*) préparatifs *mpl* (de voyage, etc.); **pre'paratory**, *a.* préparatoire, préalable (**to**, à); **p. school**, école préparatoire privée (pour élèves de 8 à 13 ans); **pre'pared**, *a.* **to be p. for anything**, être prêt, s'attendre, à toute éventualité; **be p. to be coolly received**, attendez-vous à être mal accueilli.

prepay ['pri:'pei], *v.tr.* (**prepaid**) payer d'avance; affranchir (une lettre); (*on telegram*) **answer prepaid**, réponse payée.

preponderate [pri'pɔndəreit], *v.i.* peser davantage; emporter la balance, l'emporter (**over**, sur); **pre'ponderance**, *s.* prépondérance *f*

(**over**, sur); **pre'ponderant**, *a.* prépondérant.

preposition [prepə'ziʃ(ə)n], *s. Gram:* préposition *f.*

prepossessing ['pri:pə'zesiŋ], *a.* (visage *m*) agréable; **p. appearance**, mine avantageuse, avenante; **p. person**, personne *f* sympathique.

preposterous [pri'pɔst(ə)rəs], *a.* contraire au bon sens; absurde; **pre'posterousness**, *s.* absurdité *f.*

prerequisite [pri:'rekwizit], *s.* nécessité *f* préalable.

prerogative [pri'rɔgətiv], *s.* prérogative *f*, privilège *m.*

prescribe [pri'skraib], *v.tr.* (*a*) prescrire, ordonner; **prescribed task**, tâche imposée; **in the prescribed time**, dans le délai prescrit; (*b*) *abs. Med:* **to p. for s.o.**, rédiger une ordonnance pour qn; **prescription** [-'skripʃ(ə)n], *s.* ordonnance *f.*

presence ['prez(ə)ns], *s.* présence *f.* 1. **in the p. of . . .**, en présence de . . . . 2. **p. of mind**, présence d'esprit; **to keep one's p. of mind**, garder son sang-froid; **to lose one's p. of mind**, perdre la tête; **'present**[1]. I. *a.* 1. présent; **to be p. at a ceremony**, assister à une cérémonie; **nobody else was p.**, personne d'autre n'était là. 2. (*a*) (*also* present-day) d'aujourd'hui, actuel; **at the p. time**, à présent; de nos jours; actuellement; (*b*) en question; que voici; **the p. volume**, le volume en question, ce volume; (*c*) *Gram:* **the p. tense**, *s.* **the p.**, le présent; **-ly**, *adv.* (*a*) tout à l'heure; dans un instant; (*b*) *N.Am:* & *Scot:* maintenant, actuellement. II. *s.* **the p.**, le présent; le temps présent; **up to the p.**, jusqu'à présent; **at p.**, à présent; actuellement; **for the p.**, pour le moment.

present[2]. I. *s.* ['prez(ə)nt], don *m*, cadeau *m*; **to make s.o. a p. of sth.**, faire cadeau de qch. à qn; **it's for a p.**, c'est pour offrir. II. *v.tr.* [pri'zent], présenter. 1. (*a*) *Th:* **to p. a play**, donner une pièce; (*b*) **matter that presents some difficulty**, affaire qui présente des difficultés; **a good opportunity presents itself**, une bonne occasion se présente (de faire qch.). 2. (*a*) **to p. sth. to s.o.**, donner qch. à qn; (*b*) **to p. one's compliments** (**to s.o.**), présenter ses compliments (à qn). 3. *Mil:* **to p. arms**, présenter les armes; **pre'sentable** [pri-], *a.* (*of pers.*) présentable; **he's quite p.**, il n'est pas mal; (*of garment*) portable, mettable; **presen'tation** [prez-], *s.* présentation *f.*

presentiment [pri'zentimənt], *s.* pressentiment *m.*

preserve [pri'zə:v]. I. *v.tr.* 1. préserver, garantir (**from**, de). 2. (*a*) conserver (un bâtiment); maintenir (la paix); garder (le silence); **to p. appearances**, sauver les apparences; (*b*) conserver, mettre en conserve (des aliments); confire (des fruits); (*c*) **she's well preserved**, elle ne marque pas son âge. 3. (*a*) élever (du gibier) dans une réserve; (*b*) garder (une chasse). **II.** *s.* **1.** réserve *f*; **game p.,** chasse gardée; **salmon p.,** vivier *m* à saumons; **to trespass on s.o.'s preserves,** *F:* marcher sur les plates-bandes de qn. **2.** *usu.pl.* (*a*) confiture(s) *f*(*pl*); (*b*) conserves *fpl*; **preser'vation** [prezə-], *s.* (*a*) conservation *f*; (*b*) maintien *m* (de la paix); **pre'servative,** *s.* (*a*) préservatif *m* (contre un danger, etc.); (*b*) antiseptique *m*; agent *m* de conservation; **pre'served,** *a.* conservé; (*of fruit, poultry, etc.*) confit; **p. food,** conserves *fpl*; **pre'serving(-)pan,** *s.* bassine *f* à confitures.

preside [pri'zaid], *v.i.* présider; **to p. at a meeting,** présider (à) une réunion; **presidency** ['prez-], *s.* présidence *f*; **'president,** *s.* président, -ente; **presi'dential,** *a.* présidentiel.

press [pres]. **I.** *s.* **1.** presse *f*; **hydraulic p.,** presse hydraulique. **2.** (*a*) **printing p.,** presse à imprimer, d'imprimerie; **rotary p.,** presse rotative; **to pass (a proof) for p.,** donner le bon à tirer; **in time for p.,** à temps pour l'impression; **ready for p.,** prêt à mettre sous presse; (*b*) la presse, les journaux *m*; **p. agency,** agence *f* de presse, d'informations; **to write for the p.,** faire du journalisme; **to have a good, bad, p.,** avoir une bonne, mauvaise, presse. **II.** *v.* **I.** *v.tr.* (*a*) presser; appuyer, peser, sur (qch.); **p. the button,** appuyez sur le bouton; (*b*) serrer; **to p. the juice out of a lemon,** exprimer le jus d'un citron; (*c*) **to p. a suit,** donner un coup de fer à un complet; (*d*) **pressed by one's creditors,** pressé, harcelé, par ses créanciers; (*e*) **he didn't need much pressing,** il ne s'est pas fait prier; **to p. for an answer,** insister pour avoir une réponse immédiate; (*f*) **to p. a point,** insister sur un point; **to p. one's advantage,** poursuivre son avantage; (*g*) **to p. a gift on s.o.,** forcer qn à accepter un cadeau; (*h*) **time presses,** le temps presse. **2.** *v.i.* (*a*) **to p. on sth.,** appuyer sur qch.; **to p. on,** forcer le pas; *F:* **p. on regardless!** allons-y quand même! **pressed,** *a.* **p. for time,** à court de temps; **to be hard p. to find the money,** avoir beaucoup de difficultés à trouver l'argent; **'pressing. I.** *a.* (danger) pressant; (travail) urgent; (invitation) pressante; **since you are so p. . . .,** puisque vous insistez . . .. **II.** *s.* calandrage *m* (du papier); repassage *m* (d'un vêtement), pressing *m* (d'un complet); *E:* emboutissage *m*; **'pressure** ['preʃər], *s.* **1.** (*a*) pression *f*; poussée *f*; (*b*) **blood p.,** tension artérielle. **2. to bring p. to bear,** exercer une pression; **p. of business,** pression des affaires; **'pressure-cooker,** *s. Cu:* autocuiseur *m*, cocotte *f* minute; **'pressurize,** *v.tr.* pressuriser.

prestige [pres'ti:ʒ], *s.* prestige *m*; **to lose p.,** perdre de son prestige.

presume [pri'zju:m]. **1.** *v.tr.* (*a*) présumer; supposer; **you are Mr X, I p.,** vous êtes M. X, je suppose; (*b*) **to p. to do sth.,** prendre la liberté, présumer, de faire qch.; **may I p. to advise you?** puis-je me permettre de vous conseiller? **2.** *v.i.* (*a*) **to p. too much,** trop présumer de soi; (*b*) se montrer présomptueux; (*c*) **to p. on s.o.'s friendship,** abuser de l'amitié de qn; **pre'sumably,** *adv.* probablement; **p. he'll come,** il est à croire qu'il viendra; **pre'suming,** *a.* (*of pers.*) (*a*) présomptueux; (*b*) indiscret; **pre'sumption,** *s.* **1.** présomption *f*; **the p. is that he's dead,** il est présumé mort, on présume qu'il est mort. **2.** présomption, arrogance *f*; **pre'sumptuous,** *a.* présomptueux.

pretend [pri'tend]. **1.** *v.tr.* (*a*) feindre, simuler; **to p. ignorance,** faire l'ignorant; **to p. to do sth.,** faire semblant de faire qch.; (*b*) prétendre; **he does not p. to be artistic,** il ne prétend pas être artiste; **I can't p. to advise you,** je n'ai pas la prétention de vous conseiller. **2.** *v.i.* faire semblant; jouer la comédie; **pre'tence,** *s.* **1.** (faux) semblant; simulation *f*; prétexte *m*; **under the p. of friendship,** sous prétexte, sous couleur, d'amitié; **to obtain sth. by false pretences,** obtenir qch. par fraude, par des moyens frauduleux. **2.** prétention *f*, vanité *f*; **pre'tender,** *s.* **1.** simulateur, -trice. **2.** prétendant *m* (**to,** à une couronne, etc.); *Hist:* **the Young P.,** le jeune Prétendant (Charles Stuart); **pre'tension,** *s.* prétention *f* (**to,** à); **to have pretensions to literary taste,** se piquer de littérature; **pre'tentious,** *a.* prétentieux; **-ly,** *adv.* prétentieusement.

preterite ['pretərit], *a. & s. Gram:* **p. (tense),** le passé; preterit *m*.

pretext ['pri:tekst], *s.* prétexte *m*; **to find a p. for refusing,** trouver prétexte à un refus; **on the p. of consulting me,** sous prétexte de me consulter.

pretty ['priti]. **1.** *a.* (*a*) joli; beau; (*of manner, etc.*) gentil; **p. as a picture,** gentil, joli, à croquer; *F:* **to be sitting p.,** avoir la bonne place; (*b*) *Iron:* **this is a p. state of affairs!** c'est du joli! **2.** *adv.* assez, passablement; **I'm p. well,** cela ne va pas trop mal; **p. much the same,** à peu près la même chose; **-ily,** *adv.* gentiment, délicatement; avec délicatesse; **'prettiness,** *s.* gentillesse *f*.

prevail [pri'veil], *v.i.* **1. to p. over s.o.,** prévaloir, l'emporter, sur qn. **2. to p. on s.o. to do sth.,** amener, décider, qn à faire qch.; **he was prevailed on by his friends,** il se laissa persuader par ses amis (**to,** de). **3.** prédominer; régner; **calm prevails,** le calme règne; **the conditions prevailing in France,** les conditions qui règnent en France; **pre'vailing,** *a.* **p. winds,** vents dominants; **p. fashion,** mode actuelle; **p.**

opinion, opinion courante; **prevalence** ['prevələns], s. prédominance *f*; **p. of corruption**, généralité *f* de la corruption; **p. of an epidemic**, fréquence *f* d'une épidémie; **'prevalent**, *a.* répandu, général.

prevaricate [pri'værikeit], *v.i.* 1. équivoquer, biaiser, tergiverser. 2. mentir; altérer la vérité; **prevari'cation**, *s.* 1. équivoques *fpl*; tergiversation *f*. 2. mensonge *m*.

prevent [pri'vent], *v.tr.* 1. empêcher, mettre obstacle à (qch.); **to be unavoidably prevented from doing sth.**, être dans l'impossibilité (matérielle) de faire qch. 2. (*a*) prévenir, détourner (un malheur); parer à (un accident); (*b*) éviter (que qch. se passe); **pre'ventable**, *a.* évitable; qui peut être évité; **pre'vention**, *s.* empêchement *m*; prévention *f*; **p. of accidents**, précautions *fpl* contre les accidents; **pre'ventive**. 1. *a.* (médicament) préventif; **p. medicine**, la médecine préventive. 2. *s.* empêchement *m*; mesure préventive; **rust p.**, antirouille *m*.

previous ['pri:viəs]. 1. *a.* préalable; antérieur, antécédent (to, à); **the p. day**, le jour précédent; la veille; **p. engagement**, engagement antérieur. 2. *adv.* **p. to my departure**, avant mon départ; **-ly**, *adv.* préalablement; auparavant.

prevision [pri:'viʒ(ə)n], *s.* prévision *f*.

pre-war ['pri:'wɔːr], *a.* d'avant-guerre.

prey [prei]. I. *s.* proie *f*; **birds of p.**, oiseaux de proie; **beasts of p.**, carnassiers *m*; **beasts (or birds) of p.**, les grands prédateurs. II. *v.i.* **to p. (up)on sth.**, faire sa proie de qch.; **sth. is preying on his mind**, il y a qch. qui le travaille.

price [prais]. I. *s.* prix *m*; **cost p.**, prix de revient, prix coûtant; **cash p.**, prix au comptant; **at a reduced p.**, au rabais; *Ind:* **contract p.**, prix forfaitaire; **p. ex works**, prix départ usine; **beyond p.**, sans prix; hors de prix; **this must be done at any p.**, il faut que cela se fasse à tout prix, coûte que coûte; **not at any p.**, pour rien au monde; **to set a high p. on sth.**, faire grand cas de qch. II. *v.tr.* 1. mettre un prix à (qch.). 2. estimer, évaluer (qch.). 3. s'informer du prix de (qch.); **'priceless**, *a.* (*a*) hors de prix; inestimable; (*b*) *F:* (*of joke, pers.*) impayable; marrant.

prick [prik]. I. *s.* piqûre *f* (d'aiguille, etc.); **pricks of conscience**, remords *m* de conscience. II. *v.tr.* 1. (*a*) piquer; dégonfler (un ballon); crever (une ampoule); **his conscience pricks him**, sa conscience l'aiguillonne, le tourmente; (*b*) **to p. a hole in sth.**, faire un trou dans qch. 2. **to p. up one's ears**, (i) (*of animal*) dresser les oreilles; (ii) (*of pers.*) dresser l'oreille; **'prickle**, *s.* piquant *m*; épine *f*, aiguillon *m*; **'prickly**, *a.* hérissé; armé de piquants; épineux.

pride [praid]. I. *s.* 1. orgueil *m*; (*a*) fierté *f*,

morgue *f*; **puffed up with p.**, bouffi d'orgueil; **false p.**, vanité *f*; (*b*) **proper p.**, orgueil légitime; amour-propre *m*; **to take (a) p. in sth.**, être fier de qch. 2. a p. of lions, une bande de lions. II. *v.pr.* **to p. oneself on (doing) sth.**, s'enorgueillir, se vanter, de (faire) qch.

priest [pri:st], *s.* prêtre *m*; **parish p.** = curé *m*; **assistant p.**, vicaire *m*; **'priesthood**, *s.* 1. *coll.* **the p.**, le clergé. 2. prêtrise *f*; **to enter the p.**, se faire prêtre.

prig [prig], *s.* poseur *m* (à la vertu); homme suffisant; **'priggish**, *a.* poseur, suffisant; **'priggishness**, *s.* pose *f* (à la vertu), suffisance *f*.

prim [prim], *a.* affecté; (*of manner*) guindé, compassé; **p. smile**, sourire pincé; **-ly**, *adv.* d'un air affecté.

prima facie ['praimə'feiʃii], *adv. & a.* de prime abord, à première vue; *Jur:* **p. f. case**, affaire qui paraît bien fondée.

primary ['praiməri], *a.* 1. premier, primitif, originel; **p. product**, produit *m* de base; **p. colours**, couleurs fondamentales; *Sch:* **p. education**, enseignement *m* primaire; *Geol:* **p. era**, ère *f* primaire; *U.S: Pol:* **p. election**, *s.* **primary**, élection *f* primaire. 2. premier, principal, essentiel; **p. cause**, cause première.

primate ['praimit, -meit], *s. Ecc:* (*a*) primat *m*; (*b*) archevêque *m*.

primates ['praimeits], *s.pl. Z:* primates *m*.

prime[1] [praim]. I. *a.* 1. premier; principal; de premier ordre; **P. Minister**, premier Ministre; **of p. importance**, de toute première importance. 2. de première qualité; **p. quality meat**, viande *f* de surchoix. 3. premier, originel, primitif; **p. cause**, cause première. II. *s.* (*a*) perfection *f*; **in the p. of life, in one's p.**, dans la force, la vigueur, de l'âge; **to be past one's p.**, *F:* être sur le retour; (*b*) le choix, le meilleur (de la viande, etc.).

prime[2], *v.tr.* 1. amorcer (une pompe); **to p. the boilers**, faire le plein des chaudières. 2. **to p. a witness, etc.**, faire la leçon à un témoin, etc.; **to be well primed with information**, être bien au courant.

primeval [prai'mi:v(ə)l], *a.* primordial; **p. forest**, forêt *f* vierge.

primitive ['primitiv], *a.* (*a*) primitif; (*b*) (*of method*) primitif, rude, grossier.

primrose ['primrouz], *s. Bot:* primevère *f* à grandes fleurs; **evening p.**, herbe *f* aux ânes.

primula ['primjulə], *s. Bot:* primevère *f*.

prince [prins], *s.* prince *m*; **'princely**, *a.* princier; royal; **a p. gift**, un cadeau royal, magnifique; **prin'cess**, *s.* princesse *f*; **princi-'pality**, *s.* principauté *f*.

principal ['prinsip(ə)l]. I. *a.* principal; **p. clerk**, premier commis; commis en chef; *Cu:* **p. dish**, pièce *f* de résistance; **-ally**, *adv.* principalement. **II.** *s.* **1.** (*a*) (*pers.*) directeur, -trice (de fabrique, d'école); chef *m*, patron, -onne (d'entreprise, de maison de commerce); (*b*) *Th:* premier rôle, rôle principal. **2.** *Com:* capital *m*, principal *m* (d'une dette).

principle ['prinsipl], *s.* principe *m*. **1. to lay sth. down as a p.**, poser qch. en principe. **2. man of high principles**, homme de haute moralité; **laxity of p.**, morale relâchée; **to do sth. on p.**, faire qch. par principe.

print [print]. **I.** *s.* **1.** empreinte (digitale, etc.), impression *f.* **2.** (*a*) matière imprimée; **he likes to see himself in p.**, il aime à se voir imprimé; (*of book*) **out of p.**, épuisé; (*b*) **large, small, p.**, gros, petits, caractères; (*c*) édition *f*, impression. **3.** estampe *f*, gravure *f*, image *f.* **4.** *Phot:* épreuve *f*; copie *f.* **5.** *Tex:* (tissu) imprimé (*m*). **II.** *v.tr.* **1.** imprimer; **to p.** (**off**) **a newspaper**, tirer un journal; **to have a book printed**, faire imprimer un livre; *P.T.T:* **printed matter**, imprimés *mpl*; (**hand-**)**printed letters**, lettres moulées. **2.** *Phot:* **to p.** (**off**) **a negative**, tirer une épreuve (d'un cliché); **negative that prints well**, cliché qui rend bien; '**printer**, *s.* imprimeur *m*; typographe *m*; **p.'s error**, faute *f* d'impression; coquille *f*; '**printing**, *s.* impression *f*; tirage *m* (d'un livre); (*art of printing*) imprimerie *f*; typographie *f*; **p. press**, presse *f* d'imprimerie.

prior[1] ['praiər]. **1.** *a.* préalable, précédent; antérieur (**to sth.**, à qch.); **to have a p. claim**, être le premier en date. **2.** *adv.* antérieurement; **p. to my departure**, avant mon départ; **priority** [prai'ɔriti], *s.* priorité *f.*

prior[2], *s. Ecc:* prieur *m*; '**prioress**, *s.* prieure *f*; '**priory**, *s.* prieuré *m.*

prise [praiz], *v.tr.* **to p. sth. up**, soulever qch. à l'aide d'un levier.

prism ['priz(ə)m], *s.* prisme *m*; **pris'matic**, *a.* prismatique.

prison ['priz(ə)n], *s.* prison *f*; maison *f* d'arrêt; **to send s.o. to p.**, mettre qn en prison; '**prisoner**, *s.* **1.** prisonnier, -ière. **2.** *Jur:* (*a*) **p. at the bar**, prévenu, -ue; accusé, -ée; (*b*) (*after sentence*) détenu, -ue; coupable *mf.*

private ['praivit]. **I.** *a.* privé, particulier. **1. p. persons**, (simples) particuliers; **in p. life**, dans le particulier, dans l'intimité *f.* **2.** secret; **to keep a matter p.**, tenir une affaire secrète; **p. entrance**, entrée (i) dérobée, (ii) particulière. **3. p. study**, études particulières; **in my p. opinion**, à mon avis personnel. **4. p. and confidential**, secret et confidentiel; **p. conversation**, conversation *f* intime; **p. interview**, entretien *m* à huis clos; **p. arrangement**, accord *m* à l'amiable. **5.** (*a*) **p. house**, maison particulière; (*b*) (*in hotel*) **p. room**, salon réservé; (*c*) **p. theatricals**, comédie de salon; **the funeral will be p.**, les obsèques auront lieu dans la plus stricte in-

timité. **6. p. property**, propriété privée; *P.N:* **p.**, défense d'entrer; entrée interdite au public; **p. income**, rentes *fpl*; fortune personnelle; **-ly**, *adv.* **1.** en (simple) particulier. **2. to speak to s.o. p.**, parler à qn en particulier. **II.** *s.* **1.** *adv.phr.* **in p.**, (i) en famille; (ii) dans l'intimité; (iii) sans témoins. **2.** *Mil:* simple soldat *m*; **privacy** ['prai-, 'priv-], *s.* intimité *f*; **to live in p.**, vivre retiré du monde; **there's no p. here**, on n'est jamais seul ici.

privation [prai'veiʃ(ə)n], *s.* privation *f.*

privet ['privit], *s. Bot:* troène *m.*

privilege ['privilidʒ]. **I.** *s.* **1.** privilège *m*, prérogative *f.* **2. parliamentary p.**, prérogative, immunité *f*, parlementaire. **II.** *v.tr.* **the privileged few**, les quelques privilégiés; **to be privileged to do sth.**, jouir du privilège de faire qch.

prize[1] [praiz]. **I.** *s.* **1.** prix *m*; **to win, carry off, the p.**, remporter le prix. **2.** (*in a lottery*) lot *m*; **to draw the first p.**, gagner le gros lot. **3. p. fighter**, boxeur professionnel; **p. fighting**, boxe professionnelle. **II.** *v.tr.* estimer, apprécier (qch.); **to p. sth. highly**, faire grand cas de qch.

prize[2], *v.tr.* **to p. sth. up**, soulever qch. à l'aide d'un levier.

pro[1] [prou]. *Lt.prep.* **1. p. forma**, pour la forme; **p. forma invoice**, facture fictive, de complaisance. **2. p. rata**, au prorata. **3. p. tempore**, *F:* **pro tem.**, *adv.phr.* temporairement. **4. p. and contra**, *F:* **the pros and cons**, le pour et le contre.

pro[2], *a. & s. Sp: F:* professionnel, -elle.

probable ['probabl], *a.* probable; **p. story**, histoire *f* vraisemblable; **-ably**, *adv.* probablement; vraisemblablement; **proba'bility**, *s.* probabilité *f*; vraisemblance *f.*

probate ['proubeit], *s. Jur:* validation *f*, homologation *f* (d'un testament); **pro'bation**, *s.* **1.** épreuve *f*, stage *m*; *Ecc:* probation *f* (d'un novice); **to be on p.**, être à l'épreuve; faire son stage; **period of p.**, période *f* stagiaire; stage. **2.** *Jur:* mise *f* en liberté sous surveillance; **p. officer**, délégué, -ée, à la liberté surveillée; **pro'bationary**, *a.* (période) d'épreuve, de stage; **pro'bationer**, *s.* **1.** stagiaire *mf.* **2.** *Ecc:* novice *mf.* **3.** condamné, -ée, qui bénéficie d'un sursis sous surveillance.

probe [proub]. **I.** *v.* **1.** *v.tr.* (*a*) *Med: etc:* sonder, explorer; (*b*) approfondir, fouiller (un mystère); scruter (des témoignages). **2.** *v.i.* **to p. into**, sonder, fouiller (le passé, etc.). **II.** *s.* **1.** *Med:* sonde *f.* **2.** *esp. N.Am:* enquête *f.* **3. space p.**, sonde spatiale.

problem ['problem], *s.* problème *m*; **the housing p.**, la crise du logement; **p. child**, enfant *m* difficile; *Th:* **p. play**, pièce *f* à thèse **proble'matic(al)**, *a.* problématique douteux, incertain; **p. gain**, profit *m* aléatoire.

proceed |prə'si:d|, *v.i.* 1. (*a*) to p. (on one's way), continuer son chemin; **before we p. any further**, avant d'aller plus loin; (*b*) to p. to a place, se rendre à un endroit; *Aut:* to p. at 50 m.p.h., filer à 80 km l'heure; (*c*) how shall we p.? quelle est la marche à suivre? to p. cautiously, agir avec prudence; (*d*) to p. to do sth., se mettre à faire qch.; I'll now p. to another matter, je passe maintenant à une autre question. 2. (*a*) (se) continuer, se poursuivre; (*b*) things are proceeding as usual, les choses vont leur train; (*c*) to p. with sth., poursuivre, continuer (ses études, etc.). 3. *Jur:* to p. against s.o., intenter un procès à qn. 4. sounds proceeding from a room, sons qui proviennent d'une pièce; pro'cedure, s. 1. procédé *m*; the correct p., la bonne méthode. 2. procédure *f* (du Parlement, etc.); pro'ceedings, s.pl. (*a*) débats *m* (d'une assemblée); (*b*) *Jur:* to take p. against s.o., procéder contre qn; 'proceeds, s.pl. produit *m*, montant *m* (d'une vente).

process |'prouses|. I. s. 1. (*a*) processus *m*; it's a slow p., c'est un travail long; (*b*) cours *m*, avancement *m*; marche *f* (des événements); building in p. of construction, immeuble *m* en cours, en voie, de construction; to be in p. of moving, être en train de déménager. 2. méthode *f*; procédé *m*. II. *v.tr. Ind: etc:* traiter, transformer (qch.); faire subir une opération à (une matière première); *Tex:* apprêter; 'processing, s. traitement *m* (d'une matière première); food p., l'industrie *f* alimentaire; p. industry, industrie de transformation; data p., l'informatique *f*; pro'cession |prə-|, s. cortège *m*; défilé *m*; (*religious*) procession *f*.

proclaim |prə'kleim|, *v.tr.* proclamer; déclarer (publiquement); his face proclaims his guilt, son visage crie sa culpabilité; procla'mation |prɔklə-|, s. proclamation *f*; déclaration (publique).

proclivity |prə'kliviti|, s. penchant *m*, tendance *f*, inclination *f* (to sth., à qch.).

procrastinate |prou'kræstineit|, *v.i.* remettre (les affaires) au lendemain, à plus tard; temporiser; procrasti'nation, s. remise *f* des affaires à plus tard; temporisation *f*; pro'crastinator, s. celui, celle, qui remet au lendemain; temporisateur, -trice.

procreate |'proukrieit|, *v.tr.* procréer, engendrer; procre'ation, s. procréation *f*; engendrement *m*; 'procreative, a. procréateur.

procure |prə'kjuər|, *v.tr.* obtenir, procurer; to p. sth. for s.o., procurer qch. à qn; pro'curable, a. procurable; procu'ration |prɔkjuə-|, s. 1. *Jur:* procuration *f*; to act by p., agir par procuration. 2. acquisition *f* (de qch. pour qn); pro'curer, s. 1. (i) acquéreur, -euse; (ii) personne *f* qui procure (qch. pour qn). 2. (with *f.* procuress) entremetteur, -euse, proxénète

mf; pro'curing, s. *Jur:* proxénétisme *m*.

prod |prɔd|. I. *v.tr.* (prodded) 1. to p. sth., pousser qch. (du bout d'un bâton). 2. aiguillonner, stimuler (qn à faire qch.). II. s. 1. coup (donné avec qch. de pointu). 2. give him a p., aiguillonnez-le un peu.

prodigal |'prɔdig(ə)l|, a. & s. prodigue (*mf*); gaspilleur; -ally, adv. avec prodigalité; prodi'gality, s. prodigalité *f*.

prodigy |'prɔdidʒi|, s. prodige *m*; merveille *f*; infant p., enfant *mf* prodige; pro'digious, a. prodigieux; merveilleux; -ly, adv. prodigieusement; merveilleusement, énormément.

produce. I. *v.tr.* |prə'dju:s|. 1. (*a*) présenter, exhiber (son passeport, des documents); (*b*) *Th:* to p. a play, mettre une pièce en scène. 2. (*a*) créer; *El:* to p. a spark, faire jaillir une étincelle; (*b*) *Ind:* fabriquer; (*c*) produire, éditer (un livre); (*d*) produire, causer, provoquer (un effet); to p. a sensation, faire sensation. 3. rapporter, rendre (un bénéfice). II. s. |'prɔdju:s|. 1. (*a*) rendement *m* (d'une mine, d'une exploitation); (*b*) produit *m* (de son travail). 2. *coll.* denrées *fpl*; produits (agricoles, etc.); pro'ducer, s. producteur, -trice; *Th:* metteur *m* en scène; *Cin:* directeur *m* de production; *Rad: T.V:* metteur en scène; 'product |'prɔdʌkt|, s. produit *m*; denrées *fpl*, produits (d'un pays); pro'duction, s. production *f*; fabrication *f* (de marchandises); *Th:* mise *f* en scène; *T.V: etc:* mise en ondes; pro'ductive, a. productif; (*of land*) fécond; (*of mine, etc.*) en rapport; produc'tivity, s. productivité *f*; rendement *m*.

profane |prə'fein|, a. profane; (langage) impie; p. word, juron *m*, blasphème *m*; pro'fanity |-'fæn-|, s. 1. impiété *f* (d'une action). 2. to utter profanities, proférer des blasphèmes, des jurons.

profess |prə'fes|, *v.tr.* (*a*) professer, faire profession de (sa foi, etc.); to p. oneself satisfied, se déclarer satisfait; I do not p. to be a scholar, je ne prétends pas être savant; pro'fessed, a. (*a*) (ennemi) déclaré; (*b*) prétendu (savant); self-p. (actor, etc.), soi-disant (acteur, etc.); professedly |prə'fesidli|, adv. de son propre aveu; ouvertement; he's p. ignorant, il avoue son ignorance; pro'fession, s. (*a*) profession *f*, métier *m*; the (learned) professions, les carrières libérales; (*b*) the p., les gens du métier; pro'fessional. I. a. professionnel; de métier; (*a*) p. practice, usages *m* du métier; (*b*) p. diplomat, diplomate *m* de carrière; (*c*) the p. classes, les membres *m* des professions libérales. II. s. (*a*) expert *m*; (*b*) *Sp:* professionnel, -elle; to turn p., passer professionnel; -ally, adv. professionnellement; to act p., agir dans l'exercice de sa profession; **pro′fessionalism,** s. 1. caractère professionnel (de qch.). 2. esp. Sp: professionnalisme m; **pro′fessor,** s. professeur m (de faculté); **pro′fessorship,** s. professorat m.

proficient [prə′fiʃənt], a. capable, compétent; **to be p. in maths,** être fort en math(s) f(pl); posséder à fond les mathématiques; **pro′ficiency,** s. capacité f, compétence f (in a subject, en une matière).

profile [′proufail], s. (i) profil m; (ii) silhouette f; Journ: portrait m.

profit [′prɔfit]. I. s. profit m, bénéfice m; (a) avantage m; **to turn sth. to p.,** tirer profit de qch.; (b) Com: net p., bénéfice net; **to sell at a p.,** vendre à profit; **to make huge profits,** réaliser de gros bénéfices; **p. and loss,** profits et pertes. II. v. 1. v.tr. to p. s.o., profiter à (qn); être avantageux à (qn). 2. v.i. to p. by sth., profiter, bénéficier, de qch.; **profita′bility,** s. rentabilité f; **′profitable,** a. profitable, avantageux; rentable; **-ably,** adv. profitablement, avantageusement; **profi′teer,** s. profiteur m, mercanti m; **profi′teering,** s. mercantilisme m; **′profitless,** a. sans bénéfice; pas rentable; sans intérêt.

profligate [′prɔfligət], a. & s. 1. débauché, -ée; libertin, -ine. 2. prodigue; **′profligacy,** s. 1. débauche f, libertinage m. 2. prodigalité f.

profound [prə′faund], a. profond; **p. secret,** secret absolu; **-ly,** adv. profondément; **profundity** [-′fʌnd-], s. profondeur f (de la pensée de qn).

profuse [prə′fju:s], a. 1. to be p. in one's apologies, se confondre en excuses. 2. profus, abondant, excessif; **-ly,** adv. profusément; **to perspire p.,** transpirer abondamment; **profusion** [-′fju:ʒ(ə)n], s. profusion f, abondance f; **flowers in p.,** des fleurs à foison.

progeny [′prɔdʒəni], s. 1. progéniture f. 2. descendants mpl, lignée f, postérité f.

prognosticate [prɔg′nɔstikeit], v.tr. pronostiquer, présager, prédire (qch.); **prog′nosis,** s. Med: pronostic m.

program(me) [′prougræm]. I. s. programme m; **to arrange a p.,** arrêter un programme; **what's the p. today?** que faisons-nous aujourd'hui? T.V: etc: p. editor, éditorialiste mf; **request p.,** programme des auditeurs. II. v.tr. Computers: T.V: etc: programmer; **programmed teaching,** enseignement programmé; **′programmer,** s. Computers: (a) (pers.) programmeur, -euse; (b) (machine) programmateur m; **′programming,** s. programmation f.

progress. I. s. [′prougres], (a) marche f en avant; avancement m (d'un travail, etc.); **the p. of events,** le cours des événements; **the work now in p.,** le travail en cours; **harvesting in full p.,** moisson qui bat son plein; (b) progrès m; to

make p. in one's studies, faire des progrès dans ses études; **to make slow p.,** n'avancer que lentement; Com: Ind: p. report, état m périodique. II. v.i. [prə′gres], (a) s'avancer; **as the year progresses,** au cours de l'année; (b) to p. with one's studies, faire des progrès dans ses études; **pro′gression,** s. progression f; **mode of p.,** mode m de locomotion; **pro′gressive,** a. progressif; (a) by p. stages, par degrés; (b) to be p., être ami du progrès; **-ly,** adv. progressivement; au fur et à mesure.

prohibit [prə′hibit], v.tr. prohiber, défendre, interdire (qch.); P.N: smoking prohibited, défense de fumer; **to p. s.o. from doing sth.,** défendre, interdire, à qn de faire qch.; **prohi′bition** [prouhi′biʃ(ə)n], s. prohibition f, interdiction f, défense f (de faire qch.); **pro′hibitive,** a. p. price, prix prohibitif, inabordable; **the price of peaches is p.,** les pêches sont hors de prix.

project. I. v. [prə′dʒekt]. 1. v.tr. (a) projeter (un voyage); **projected buildings,** édifices en projet; (b) projeter, lancer (un objet, etc.). 2. v.i. faire saillie. II. s. [′prɔdʒekt]. 1. projet m; to form, carry out, a p., former, réaliser, un projet. 2. Civ.E: ouvrage (réalisé); travaux (réalisés); **pro′jectile,** s. projectile m; **pro′jecting,** a. saillant, en saillie; **pro′jection,** s. 1. (a) lancement m (d'une fusée, etc.); Cin: p. room, cabine f de projection; (b) conception f (d'un projet, etc.). 2. saillie f; porte-à-faux m inv (d'un balcon); avant-corps m inv (de façade); **pro′jector,** s. projecteur m.

proletariat [prouli′tɛəriət], s. prolétariat m; **prole′tarian.** 1. a. prolétarien; prolétaire. 2. s. prolétaire mf.

prolific [prə′lifik], a. prolifique; fécond (in, of, en).

prologue [′prɔlɔg], s. prologue m (to, de).

prolong [prə′lɔŋ], v.tr. prolonger; **prolon′gation** [proulɔŋ′geiʃ(ə)n], s. prolongation f; délai accordé.

promenade [prɔmə′nɑ:d], F: prom [prɔm], s. (a) (lieu m de) promenade; (at seaside) esplanade f; (b) Th: promenoir m; pourtour m (du parterre); p. concert, concert m où une partie de l'auditoire reste debout; Nau: p. deck, pont-promenade m, promenoir m.

prominence [′prɔminəns], s. 1. (a) proéminence f; relief m; (b) saillie f, protubérance f. 2. éminence f; **to give sth. p.,** faire ressortir qch. **to come into p.,** (i) (of pers.) percer; (ii) (of thg) acquérir de l'importance; **′prominent,** a. 1. saillant; en saillie. 2. (a) remarquable; **in a p. position,** très en vue; **to play a p. part,** jouer un rôle important; (b) éminent; **a p. figure,** un personnage remarquable; **-ly,** adv. (a) éminemment; (b) goods p. displayed, marchandises fpl bien en vue.

promiscuous [prə'miskjuəs], *a.* casuel; **she's completely p.**, elle couche avec n'importe qui; **-ly**, *adv.* casuellement; **promis'cuity**, *s.* promiscuité *f.*

promise ['prɔmis]. I. *s.* promesse *f*; (*a*) **to release s.o. from his p.**, rendre sa parole à qn; **to break one's p.**, manquer de parole; (*b*) **to show great p.**, donner de belles espérances. II. *v.tr. & i.* (*a*) **to p. s.o. sth.**, promettre qch. à qn; (*b*) **action that promises trouble**, action qui laisse prévoir des ennuis; **the scheme promises well**, le projet s'annonce bien; **'promising**, *a.* plein de promesses; **p. young man**, jeune homme qui promet.

promontory ['prɔmənt(ə)ri], *s.* promontoire *m.*

promote [prə'mout], *v.tr.* 1. donner de l'avancement à (qn); **to be promoted**, être promu; monter en grade. 2. (*a*) encourager (les arts); favoriser (le succès); avancer (les intérêts de qn); **to p. a company**, lancer une société anonyme; **pro'moter**, *s.* promoteur *m*, fondateur *m* (d'une société anonyme); **pro'motion**, *s.* promotion *f*; **to gain p.**, obtenir de l'avancement.

prompt [prɔm(p)t]. I. *a.* prompt; (*a*) vif, rapide; (*b*) immédiat; **p. delivery**, livraison immédiate; **-ly**, *adv.* promptement; (*a*) avec empressement; (*b*) sur-le-champ, immédiatement; **to pay p.**, (i) payer comptant; (ii) payer ponctuellement. II. *v.tr.* 1. **to p. s.o. to do sth.**, inciter qn à faire qch.; **to be prompted by a feeling of pity**, être animé par un sentiment de pitié. 2. souffler (un acteur); **'prompter**, *s.* *Th:* souffleur, -euse; **'promptness**, *s.* promptitude *f*, empressement *m.*

prone [proun], *a.* 1. couché sur le ventre. 2. **to be p. to sth.**, être enclin à qch.; **accident p.**, prédisposé aux accidents; **'proneness**, *s.* **accident p.**, prédisposition *f* aux accidents.

prong [prɔŋ], *s.* fourchon *m* (de fourche); dent *f* (de fourchette); **pronged**, *a.* à fourchons; à dents.

pronoun ['prounaun], *s.* *Gram:* pronom *m.*

pronounce [prə'nauns], *v.tr.* 1. (*a*) déclarer; (*b*) *Jur:* prononcer (une sentence). 2. prononcer, articuler (un mot); **pro'nounced**, *a.* prononcé, marqué; **p. taste of garlic**, goût d'ail très fort; **p. accent**, accent marqué; **pro'nouncement**, *s.* déclaration *f*; **pronunci'ation** [-nʌn-], *s.* prononciation *f.*

proof [pru:f]. I. *s.* 1. preuve *f*; **positive p.**, preuve patente; **to give p. of one's gratitude**, témoigner sa reconnaissance; **this is p. that he is lying**, cela prouve qu'il ment; **to produce p. to the contrary**, fournir la preuve contraire. 2. (*a*) épreuve *f*; **to put sth. to the p.**, mettre qch. à l'épreuve; (*b*) teneur *f* en alcool (d'un spiritueux). 3. (**printer's**) **p.**, épreuve *f.* II. *a.* **p. against sth.**, résistant à qch.; **damp-p.**, étanche

à l'humidité; **to be p. against a disease**, être immunisé contre une maladie; **p. against flattery**, insensible à la flatterie.

prop [prɔp]. I. *s.* appui *m*, support *m*, soutien *m.* II. *v.tr.* (**propped**) **to p. (up)**, appuyer, soutenir.

propaganda [prɔpə'gændə], *s.* propagande *f.*

propagate ['prɔpəgeit]. 1. *v.tr.* (*a*) propager; (*b*) **to p. ideas**, propager, répandre, disséminer, des idées. 2. *v.pr. & i.* se propager, se reproduire; **propa'gation**, *s.* 1. propagation *f*, reproduction *f.* 2. dissémination *f* (d'une doctrine).

propel [prə'pel], *v.tr.* (**propelled**) propulser; pousser en avant; **propelled by steam**, mû par la vapeur; **pro'pellant**, *s.* combustible *m*, *Rockets:* propergol *m*; **pro'peller**, *s.* 1. propulseur *m*; *Aut:* **p. shaft**, arbre *m* de transmission. 2. *Nau: Av:* hélice *f*; **p. shaft**, arbre de l'hélice.

propensity [prə'pensiti], *s.* propension *f*, penchant *m*, inclination *f*, tendance *f* (**to, towards, sth.**, à, vers, qch.; **for doing sth.**, à faire qch.).

proper ['prɔpər], *a.* 1. propre; (*a*) **p. to sth.**, propre, particulier, à qch.; **to put sth. to its p. use**, utiliser rationnellement qch.; (*b*) **to paint s.o. in his p. colours**, dépeindre qn sous son vrai jour; (*c*) *Gram:* **p. noun**, nom propre. 2. (*a*) vrai, juste, approprié; **in a p. sense**, au sens propre; (*b*) *Mth:* **p. fraction**, fraction moindre que l'unité. 3. *F:* **to get a p. hiding**, recevoir une belle raclée; **we're in a p. mess**, nous voilà dans un joli pétrin. 4. (*a*) convenable; **at the p. time**, en temps opportun; en temps utile; **to think it p. to (do sth.)**, juger bon de (faire qch.); **do as you think p.**, faites comme bon vous semblera; **to do the p. thing by s.o.**, agir loyalement avec qn; **the p. way to do it**, la meilleure manière de le faire; **the p. tool**, le bon outil; **to keep sth. in p. condition**, tenir qch. en bon état; (*b*) comme il faut; (*of language*) bienséant, correct; **-ly**, *adv.* 1. (*a*) **p. so called**, proprement dit; (*b*) bien; de la bonne façon; **do it p. or not at all**, faites-le comme il faut ou pas du tout. 2. *F:* (*intensive*) **to tick s.o. off p.**, rembarrer vertement qn. 3. convenablement; **to behave p.**, se conduire comme il faut.

property ['prɔpəti], *s.* 1. (*a*) propriété *f*, biens *mpl*, avoir(s) *m(pl)*; **that's my p.**, cela m'appartient; **landed p.**, biens fonciers; **lost p.**, objets trouvés; **p. tax**, impôt foncier; (*b*) immeuble(s) *m(pl)*. 2. *Th: Cin:* accessoire *m*; **p. man**, accessoiriste *m.* 3. propriété; qualité *f* (*propre*); **inherent p.**, attribut *m.*

prophecy ['prɔfisi], *s.* prophétie *f.*

prophesy ['prɔfisai]. 1. *v.i.* parler en prophète; prophétiser. 2. *v.tr.* prophétiser, prédire (un événement).

prophet, *f*, **-ess** ['prɔfit, -is], *s.* prophète *m*, prophétesse *f*; **pro'phetic**, *a*. prophétique; **-ally**, *adv*. prophétiquement.

propitiate [prə'piʃieit], *v.tr*. apaiser (qn); se faire pardonner par (qn); **propiti'ation**, *s*. 1. propitiation *f*. 2. apaisement *m* (de qn). 3. expiation *f* (d'une faute); **pro'pitious**, *a*. propice; favorable; **-ly**, *adv*. d'une manière propice; favorablement.

proportion [prə'pɔ:ʃ(ə)n], *s*. 1. partie *f*; portion *f*; part *f*; **to divide expenses in equal proportions**, répartir équitablement les frais; **p. of an ingredient in a mixture**, dose *f* d'un ingrédient dans un mélange. 2. rapport *m*, proportion *f*; (*a*) **p. of the net load to the gross load**, rapport du poids utile au poids mort; (*b*) **in due p.**, en proportions raisonnables; (*c*) **in p. as . . .**, à mesure que . . .; (*d*) **out of p.**, mal proportionné; **to lose all sense of p.**, ne garder aucune mesure. 3. *pl*. **proportions**, proportions (d'un édifice); dimensions *f* (d'une machine); **pro'portional**, *a*. proportionnel; en proportion (**to**, de); proportionné (**to**, à); *Pol*: **p. representation**, représentation proportionnelle; **-ally**, *adv*. en proportion (**to**, de), proportionnellement (**to**, à); **pro'portionate**, *a*. proportionné (**to**, à).

propose [prə'pouz], *v.tr*. 1. (*a*) **to p. a course of action**, proposer une ligne de conduite; (*b*) **to p. a motion**, proposer une motion; **to p. a toast**, porter un toast; (*c*) **to p. to do sth.**, se proposer de faire qch.; **what do you p. to do now?** que comptez-vous faire maintenant? 2. *abs*. **to p. to a girl**, demander la main d'une jeune fille; **pro'posal** [-z(ə)l], *s*. 1. (*a*) proposition *f*, offre *f*; **to make a p.**, faire, formuler, une proposition; (*b*) demande *f* en mariage. 2. dessein *m*; projet *m*; **pro'poser**, *s*. proposeur, -euse; **proposition** [prɔpə'ziʃ(ə)n], *s*. proposition *f*, offre *f*; **paying p.**, affaire *f* qui rapporte; affaire intéressante, rentable; **it's a tough p.**, c'est une question difficile à résoudre; *F*: **he's a tough p.**, il n'est guère commode.

propound [prə'paund], *v.tr*. proposer (une énigme); émettre (une idée); poser (une question); exposer (un programme).

proprietor, *f*. **-tress** [prə'praiətər, -tres], *s*. propriétaire *mf*; **landed p.**, propriétaire foncier; **garage p.**, garagiste *m*; **pro'prietary**, *a*. (*a*) de propriété, de propriétaire; (*b*) *Com*: **p. article**, spécialité *f*; article, produit, breveté; **p. medicines**, spécialités pharmaceutiques.

propriety [prə'praiəti], *s*. 1. propriété *f*, justesse *f*: à-propos *m* (d'une expression, etc.); rectitude *f* (de conduite). 2. (*a*) bienséance *f*, décence *f*; **breach of p.**, manque *m* de savoir-vivre; (*b*) **to observe the proprieties**, observer les convenances.

propulsion [prə'pʌlʃ(ə)n], *s*. propulsion *f*; **pro'pulsive**, *a*. propulsif; (effort *m*) de propulsion.

prosaic [prou'zeiik], *a*. prosaïque; (esprit) positif, banal; **-ally**, *adv*. prosaïquement.

prose [prouz], *s*. 1. prose *f*. 2. *Sch*: **French p.**, thème français; **p. writer**, prosateur *m*; **'prosy**, *a*. (*of pers*.) verbeux; ennuyeux; (*of style*) prosaïque; **-ily**, *adv*. fastidieusement.

prosecute ['prɔsikju:t], *v.tr*. (*a*) poursuivre (qn) (en justice); engager des poursuites contre (qn); (*b*) **to p. a claim**, poursuivre une réclamation; **prose'cution**, *s*. *Jur*: poursuites *fpl* judiciaires; **the p.**, les plaignants; **witness for the p.**, témoin à charge; **'prosecutor**, *s*. *Jur*: 1. plaignant, -ante; demandeur, -eresse. 2. **the Public P.** = le procureur de la République.

prospect. I. *s*. ['prɔspekt]. 1. vue *f*; point *m* de vue; perspective *f*; **wide p.**, horizon très étendu. 2. (*a*) perspective, expectative *f*; **to have sth. in p.**, avoir qch. en perspective, en vue; (*b*) **no p. of agreement**, aucune perspective d'accord. 3. *pl*. **prospects**, avenir *m*, espérances *fpl*; **the prospects for the harvest are excellent**, la récolte s'annonce excellente; **his prospects are brilliant**, un brillant avenir s'ouvre devant lui. II. *v*. [prəs'pekt]. 1. *v.i*. *Min*: prospecter. 2. *v.tr*. prospecter (un terrain); **pros'pective**, *a*. en perspective; prospectif; **p. visit**, visite prochaine; **a p. buyer**, un acheteur éventuel; **pros'pector**, *s*. chercheur *m* (d'or, de minerais).

prospectus, *pl*. **-uses** [prə'spektəs, -təsiz], *s*. prospectus *m*.

prosper ['prɔspər], *v.i*. prospérer, réussir; **he'? p.**, il arrivera; **pros'perity**, *s*. prospérité *f*; **'prosperous**, *a*. prospère, florissant; **-ly**, *adv*. avec prospérité.

prostate ['prɔsteit], *s*. *Anat*: **p. (gland)**, prostate *f*.

prostitute ['prɔstitju:t], *s*. prostituée; **prosti'tution**, *s*. prostitution *f*.

prostrate. I. *v.tr*. [prɔs'treit], **to p. oneself before s.o.**, se prosterner devant qn; **prostrated by the heat**, accablé par la chaleur. II. *a*. ['prɔstreit] 1. prosterné; couché (à terre); étendu. 2. abattu; accablé; **pros'tration**, *s*. 1. prosternement *m*. 2. abattement *m*; *Med*: prostration *f*, affaissement *m*; **nervous p.**, dépression nerveuse.

protagonist [prou'tægənist], *s*. protagoniste *m*

protect [prə'tekt], *v.tr*. 1. (*a*) protéger (qn); **to p. s.o. from sth.**, protéger qn contre qch.; (*b*) sauvegarder (les intérêts de qn). 2. patronner (qn); tenir (qn) en tutelle; **pro'tection**, *s*. 1. (*a*) protection *f*, défense *f* (**against the weather** etc., contre les intempéries, etc.); sauvegarde (des intérêts de qn); (*b*) **under s.o.'s p.**, sous la sauvegarde de qn; (*c*) patronage *m*. 2. (*a*) abri *m*; (*b*) blindage *m*; **pro'tective**, *a*. protecteur; **pro'tector**, *s*. protecteur, -trice; patron

-onne; **pro′tectorate**, s. protectorat m.

protégé ['prɔteʒei], s. protégé, -ée.

protein ['prouti:n], s. protéine f.

protest. I. s. ['proutest], protestation f; **to make a p.**, protester; faire des représentations; **a day of p.**, une journée revendicative; **under p.**, (i) (signer, etc.) sous réserve; (ii) (faire qch.) à son corps défendant, en protestant. II. v. [prə'test]. 1. v.tr. protester; **to p. one's innocence**, protester de son innocence; N.Am: **to p. sth.**, protester contre qch. 2. v.i. **to p. against sth.**, protester contre qch.; **Protestant** ['prɔtistənt], a. & s. Ecc: protestant; **protes′tation**, s. protestation f.

protocol ['proutəkɔl], s. protocole m.

prototype ['proutətaip], s. prototype m.

protract [prə'trækt], v.tr. prolonger, allonger; traîner (une affaire) en longueur.

protrude [prə'tru:d], v.i. s'avancer, faire saillie, ressortir; **pro′truding**, a. en saillie; saillant; **p. forehead**, front bombé; **p. teeth**, dents saillantes; **pro′trusion**, s. saillie f; protubérance f.

protuberance [prə'tju:bərəns], s. protubérance f; **pro′tuberant**, a. protubérant.

proud [praud], a. (a) fier, orgueilleux; (b) **to be p. of sth.**, être fier de qch.; (c) F: **to do s.o. p.**, se mettre en frais pour qn; **to do oneself p.**, ne se priver de rien; **-ly**, adv. fièrement, orgueilleusement; avec fierté.

prove [pru:v]. 1. v.tr. (a) éprouver; mettre à l'épreuve; **proved remedy**, remède éprouvé; (b) Mth: vérifier (un calcul). 2. v.tr. (a) prouver, démontrer; **it remains to be proved**, cela n'est pas encore prouvé; (b) Jur: homologuer (un testament); (c) **to p. oneself**, faire ses preuves. 2. v.i. se montrer; **to p. useful**, se trouver utile; **the news proved false**, la nouvelle s'est avérée fausse; **their rashness proved fatal to them**, leur audace leur fut fatale.

provenance ['prɔv(ə)nəns], s. provenance f.

proverb ['prɔvə:b], s. proverbe m; **pro′verbial**, a. proverbial; passé en proverbe; **-ally**, adv. proverbialement.

provide [prə'vaid]. 1. (a) v.i. **to p. against sth.**, se pourvoir contre (une attaque); **expenses provided for in the budget**, dépenses prévues au budget; (b) v.tr. stipuler (that, que). 2. (a) v.tr. **to p. s.o. with sth.**, fournir qch. à qn; (b) v.i. **to p. for s.o.**, pourvoir à l'entretien de qn; **to p. for oneself**, se suffire; **to be provided for**, être à l'abri du besoin; (c) v.i. **he provided for everything**, il a subvenu à tout; **pro′vided.** 1. a. pourvu, muni (with, de). 2. conj. **p. (that)**, pourvu que + sub.; à condition que + ind. or sub.; **pro′vider**, s. pourvoyeur, -euse; fournisseur, -euse.

providence ['prɔvid(ə)ns], s. 1. prévoyance f, prudence f. 2. providence (divine); **provi′den-**

tial, a. providentiel; **-ally**, adv. providentiellement.

province ['prɔvins], s. 1. province f; **in the provinces**, en province. 2. **that is not (within) my p.**, ce n'est pas de mon ressort, de mon domaine, de ma compétence; **provincial** [prə'vinʃ(ə)l], a. & s. provincial, -ale, pl. -aux, -ales.

provision [prə'viʒ(ə)n]. I. s. 1. **to make p. for sth.**, pourvoir à qch.; **to make p. for one's family**, assurer l'avenir de sa famille. 2. (a) Com: provision f; (b) pl. **provisions**, provisions (de bouche); vivres m, comestibles m. 3. article m (d'un traité); clause f, stipulation f (d'un contrat); **there's no p. to the contrary**, il n'y a pas de clause contraire; **to come within the provisions of the law**, tomber sous le coup de la loi. II. v.tr. approvisionner; ravitailler (une armée, etc.); **pro′visional**, a. provisoire; **-ally**, adv. provisoirement.

proviso, pl. -os [prə'vaizou, -ouz], s. clause conditionnelle; **pro′visory**, a. (of clause) conditionnel; provisoire.

provoke [prə'vouk], v.tr. 1. (a) provoquer, pousser, inciter (s.o. to do sth., qn à faire qch.); **to p. s.o. to anger**, mettre qn en colère; (b) irriter, fâcher, agacer. 2. exciter (la curiosité); **to p. a smile**, faire naître un sourire; **provocation** [prɔvə'keiʃ(ə)n], s. provocation f; **pro′vocative** [-'vɔk-], a. (a) provocant, agaçant; (b) provocateur, -trice.

prow [prau], s. Nau: proue f.

prowl [praul]. I. v.i. rôder. II. s. **to be always on the p.**, être toujours à rôder; **′prowler**, s. rôdeur, -euse.

proximity [prɔk'simiti], s. proximité f; **in the p. of a town**, à proximité d'une ville.

proxy ['prɔksi], s. Jur: 1. procuration f; pouvoir m; mandat m. 2. mandataire mf; fondé m de pouvoir(s).

prude [pru:d], s.f. prude; bégueule; **′prudery**, s., **′prudishness**, s. pruderie f; pudibonderie f, bégueulerie f; **′prudish**, a. prude; pudibond, bégueule; **-ly**, adv. avec pruderie; en prude.

prudence ['pru:d(ə)ns], s. prudence f, sagesse f; **′prudent**, a. prudent, sage, judicieux; **-ly**, adv. prudemment, sagement.

prune[1] [pru:n], s. pruneau m.

prune[2], v.tr. (a) tailler (un rosier, etc.); (b) **to p. (off) a branch**, élaguer une branche; **′pruning**, s. taille f; **p.-knife**, s. serpette f.

Prussia ['prʌʃə]. Pr.n. la Prusse; **′Prussian**, a. & s. prussien, -ienne; **P. blue**, bleu m de Prusse.

pry[1] [prai], v.i. (**pried**) fureter; fouiller; F: fourrer le nez (**into sth.**, dans qch.); **′prying**, a. curieux, indiscret, fureteur.

pry[2], v.tr. (**pried**) soulever, mouvoir, à l'aide d'un levier; **to p. a door open**, exercer des pesées sur une porte.

psalm [sɑ:m], *s.* psaume *m*; **'psalmist,** *s.* psalmiste *m.*

pseudonym ['sju:dənim], *s.* pseudonyme *m.*

psychiatry [sai'kaiətri], *s.* psychiatrie *f*; **psy-'chiatrist,** *s.* psychiatre *mf.*

psychic ['saikik], *a.* psychique.

psychoanalysis [saikouə'nælisis], *s.* psychanalyse *f.*

psychology [sai'kɔlədʒi], *s.* psychologie *f*; **psycho'logical,** *a.* psychologique; **the p. moment,** le moment psychologique; **-ally,** *adv.* psychologiquement; **psy'chologist,** *s.* psychologue *mf.*

psychopath ['saikoupæθ], *s.* psychopathe *mf.*

psychosomatic [saikousə'mætik], *a. Med:* psychosomatique.

ptomaine ['toumein, tə'mein], *s. Ch:* ptomaïne *f*; **p. poisoning,** intoxication *f* alimentaire.

pub [pʌb], *s. F:* = bistro(t) *m*; **to go on a p. crawl,** faire la tournée des bistro(t)s; **'pub-crawler,** *s. F:* coureur *m* de bistro(t)s.

puberty ['pju:bəti], *s.* puberté *f.*

pubis ['pju:bis], *s. Anat:* pubis *m*; **'pubic,** *a.* pubien.

public ['pʌblik]. **I.** *a.* public, *f.* publique; **p. holiday,** fête légale; **p. utility service,** service public; **p. library,** bibliothèque municipale; **p. house** = débit *m* de boissons, café *m*, bistro(t) *m*; **to make a p. protest,** protester publiquement; **p. life,** vie publique; **p. spirit,** civisme *m*; **-ly,** *adv.* publiquement, en public. **II.** *s.* public *m*; **the general p.,** le grand public; **'publican,** *s.* = débitant *m* de boissons, patron, -onne, de café.

publicity [pʌb'lisiti], *s.* **1.** publicité *f.* **2.** *Com:* réclame *f*; **'publicize,** *v.tr.* faire connaître au public; faire de la réclame, de la publicité, pour (un article).

publish ['pʌbliʃ], *v.tr.* publier, faire paraître (un livre, etc.); **just published,** vient de paraître; **publi'cation,** *s.* **1.** publication *f*, parution *f* (d'un livre, etc.). **2.** ouvrage publié; publication; **'publisher,** *s.* éditeur *m*; **'publishing,** *s.* **1.** publication *f*; **p. house,** maison d'édition. **2.** l'édition *f.*

pucker ['pʌkər]. **I.** *s.* ride *f*, pli *m* (du visage); fronce *f*, faux pli (d'un tissu). **II.** *v.* **1.** *v.tr.* rider, plisser; froncer. **2.** *v.i.* se froncer.

pudding ['pudiŋ], *s. Cu:* (*a*) pudding *m*, pouding *m*; (*b*) **rice p.,** riz *m* au lait; **Christmas p.** = gâteau de Noël, (*in Eng.*) pudding, pouding; (*c*) **black p.,** boudin *m.*

puddle ['pʌdl], *s.* flaque *f* d'eau.

puerile ['pjuərail], *a.* puéril; **pue'rility** [-'ril-], *s.* puérilité *f.*

puff [pʌf]. **I.** *s.* **1.** souffle *m* (d'air); bouffée *f* (de tabac). **2. powder p.,** houppe *f*, houppette *f.* **3.** *Cu:* (*a*) **p. pastry,** pâte feuilletée; (*b*) gâteau feuilleté (fourré de confiture, etc.). **II.** *v.i.*

souffler; haleter; **to be puffed up with pride,** être gonflé d'orgueil; **puffed,** *a.* essoufflé; **'puffiness,** *s.* boursouflure *f*, enflure *f*; **'puffy,** *a.* bouffi; boursouflé.

pugnacious [pʌg'neiʃəs], *a.* querelleur, batailleur; **pug'nacity** [-'næs-], *s.* humeur querelleuse, batailleuse.

pull [pul]. **I.** *s.* **1.** (*a*) traction *f*, tirage *m*; **to give a p.,** tirer; (*b*) effort *m* de traction; **uphill p.,** effort à la montée; (*c*) *Row:* coup *m* (d'aviron). **2.** avantage *m*; **to have a great deal of p.,** *F:* avoir du piston (with s.o., chez qn). **II.** *v.tr.* **1.** (*a*) tirer; **to p. the trigger,** presser la détente; (*b*) *abs. Row:* ramer; (*c*) *v.i.* **to p. at a rope,** tirer sur un cordage. **2.** traîner, tirer (une charrette, etc.). **3. to p. a face,** faire une grimace. **4.** *F:* **to p. a fast one,** avoir qn; **'pull a'part,** *v.tr.* séparer (deux choses); déchirer (qch.) en deux; **'pull 'down,** *v.tr.* baisser (un store); démolir (une maison); (*of illness*) abattre, affaiblir (qn); **'pull 'in. 1.** *v.tr. F:* (*of police*) arrêter (un suspect), rafler (un gang). **2.** *v.i.* (*of train*) entrer en gare; *Aut:* **to p. in to the kerb,** se ranger près du trottoir; **'pull-in,** *s.* **1.** parking *m* (près d'un café, etc.). **2.** café *m* restaurant *m* (pour routiers); **'pull 'off,** *v.tr.* (*a*) retirer, ôter (un vêtement); (*b*) *Sp: F:* gagner, remporter, *F:* décrocher (un prix); (*c*) *F:* réussir à faire (qch.); venir à bout de (qch.); **'pull 'out. 1.** *v.tr.* (*a*) **to p. s.o. out of a hole,** tirer qn du pétrin; (*b*) arracher (une dent). **2.** *v.i. Rail:* (*of train*) sortir de la gare; démarrer (*c*) *Aut:* **to p. out from behind a vehicle,** sortir de la file pour doubler; **'pullover,** *s. Cost:* pull-over *m*, *F:* pull *m*; **'pull 'round, 'through,** *v.i.* guérir (d'une maladie), se remettre; **'pull to'gether,** *v.tr.* **1. to p. oneself together,** se reprendre, se ressaisir. **2.** *abs.* tirer ensemble; **they are not pulling together,** ils ne s'entendent pas; **'pull 'up. 1.** *v.tr.* (*a*) (re)monter, hisser (qn, qch.); (*b*) hausser, lever retrousser (sa jupe); *F:* **to p. one's socks up,** *F:* se dégourdir, s'activer; (*c*) arracher, extirper une mauvaise herbe; (*d*) **to be pulled up (by the police),** se faire siffler (par l'agent). **2.** *v.* s'arrêter.

pullet ['pulit], *s.* poulette *f*; **corn-fed p., roastin p.,** poulet *m* de grain.

pulley ['puli], *s.* poulie *f.*

Pullman ['pulmən]. *Pr.n. Rail:* **P. car,** voiture Pullman.

pulp [pʌlp], *s.* pulpe *f*; **to reduce sth. to a p** réduire qch. en pulpe; **'pulpy,** *a.* (*a*) pulpeu charnu; (*b*) mou, flasque.

pulpit ['pulpit], *s.* chaire *f* (de prédicateur).

pulse [pʌls], *s.* **1.** pouls *m*; **to feel s.o.'s p.,** tâte prendre, le pouls de qn. **2.** *El:* pulse *m*; **radar,** radar *m* à impulsions; **pul'sate,** *v.i.* ((*of heart*) battre; (*b*) palpiter, vibrer; **pul's**

tion, s. pulsation f, battement m.

pulverize ['pʌlvəraiz], v.tr. **1.** pulvériser; broyer (qch.). **2.** atomiser, vaporiser (un liquide); **pulveri'zation,** s. pulvérisation f; **'pulverizer,** s. pulvérisateur m, vaporisateur m, atomiseur m.

pumice ['pʌmis], s. **p.**(-**stone**), (pierre f) ponce f.

pummel ['pʌm(ə)l], v.tr. (**pummelled**) bourrer (qn) de coups de poing; **'pummelling,** s. volée f de coups (de poing).

pump [pʌmp]. **I.** s. pompe f; **hand p.,** pompe à bras; **bicycle p.,** pompe à bicyclette, à vélo; Aut: **petrol p.,** pompe à essence; **p. attendant,** pompiste mf; **pressure p.,** pompe foulante; **foot p.,** pompe à pied. **II.** v.tr. & i. pomper; **to p. a well dry,** assécher un puits; **to p. s.o.,** sonder qn.

pumpkin ['pʌm(p)kin], s. Hort: potiron m, citrouille f.

pun [pʌn], s. calembour m; jeu m de mots.

punch¹ [pʌntʃ]. **I.** s. **1.** Tls: (a) (**centre-**)p., pointeau m (de mécanicien); (b) chasse-clou(s) m; (c) perçoir m; découpoir m; (d) Rail: etc: poinçon m (de contrôleur); pince f de contrôle; **p. card,** carte perforée. **2.** (a) coup m de poing; (b) F: force f, énergie f. **II.** v.tr. **1.** percer; découper; poinçonner. **2.** donner un coup de poing à (qn); cogner sur (qn); **to p. s.o.'s face, to p. s.o. in the face,** casser la figure à qn.

punch², s. **1.** (beverage) punch m. **2.** p.-**bowl,** (i) bol m à punch; (ii) cuvette (entourée de collines).

punch³. Pr.n. = Polichinelle m, Guignol m; **P. and Judy show,** (théâtre m de) Guignol.

unctilious [pʌŋk'tiliəs], a. pointilleux, méticuleux; -**ly,** adv. pointilleusement; scrupuleusement; méticuleusement.

unctual ['pʌŋktju(ə)l], a. ponctuel, exact; **always p.,** toujours à l'heure; -**ally,** adv. ponctuellement; **punctu'ality,** s. ponctualité f, exactitude f.

unctuate ['pʌŋktjueit], v.tr. ponctuer (une phrase, etc.); **punctu'ation,** s. ponctuation f.

uncture ['pʌŋktʃər]. **I.** s. **1.** (of tyre, abscess, etc.) crevaison f. **2.** (hole) piqûre f, perforation f. **II.** v.tr. (a) crever, perforer (un pneu, un abcès); (b) (with passive force) (of tyre) crever.

ungent ['pʌndʒənt], a. **1.** (of style, etc.) mordant, caustique. **2.** âcre; (of smell, etc.) fort, piquant, irritant; -**ly,** adv. d'une manière piquante; âcrement f, aigreur f (de paroles).

unish ['pʌniʃ], v.tr. punir; corriger (un enfant); **to p. s.o. for sth.,** punir qn de qch.; Aut: **to p. the engine,** fatiguer le moteur; **'punishable,** a. punissable; **p. by a fine,** passible d'amende; **'punishment,** s. punition f, châtiment m; (for a child) correction f; **capital p.,** peine capitale; **as a p.,** en punition.

punt [pʌnt]. **I.** s. = bachot (conduit à la perche); **p. pole,** gaffe f, perche f. **II.** v.tr. conduire (un bateau plat, un bachot) à la perche.

puny ['pju:ni], a. **1.** (a) petit, menu; (b) mesquin. **2.** (of pers.) chétif, faible, débile.

pup [pʌp], s. petit chien, jeune chien; chiot m; (of bitch) **to be in p.,** être pleine; F: **to sell s.o. a p.,** tromper qn; **'puppy,** s. jeune chien m, chiot m; (of pers.) **p. fat,** adiposité f d'enfance, d'adolescence.

pupil¹ ['pju:p(i)l], s. Sch: élève mf; écolier, -ière.

pupil², s. pupille f (de l'œil).

puppet ['pʌpit], s. marionnette f; (of pers.) **mere p.,** pantin m; **p. government,** gouvernement m fantoche; Th: **p. show,** (i) spectacle m, (ii) théâtre m, de marionnettes; **puppe'teer,** s. marionnettiste mf, montreur, -euse, de marionnettes.

purchase ['pə:tʃəs]. **I.** s. **1.** achat m, acquisition f; **p. price,** prix m d'achat. **2.** prise f; point m d'appui; appui m; **to get a p. on sth.,** trouver prise à qch. **II.** v.tr. acheter, acquérir (qch.); **purchasing power,** pouvoir m d'achat; **'purchaser,** s. acheteur, -euse.

pure ['pjuər], a. pur; **p. gold,** or pur; **p. alcohol,** alcool rectifié; **p. silk,** soie naturelle; -**ly,** adv. purement; **'pure-bred,** a. (chien) de race.

purgatory ['pə:gət(ə)ri], s. le purgatoire; **it was p. to me,** j'étais au supplice.

purge [pə:dʒ]. **I.** s. (a) purgation f; purge f; purgatif m; (b) Pol: épuration f. **II.** v.tr. purger (un malade); purifier (le sang); assainir (les finances du pays); nettoyer (un égout); Pol: épurer (des adversaires); **'purgative** [-gə-], a. & s. purgatif (m).

purify ['pjuərifai], v.tr. purifier (l'air, etc.); épurer (le gaz, l'huile); **purifi'cation,** s. purification f; épuration f; **'purist,** s. puriste mf; **'purity,** s. pureté f.

Puritan ['pjuərit(ə)n], a. & s. puritain, -aine; **puri'tanical,** a. puritain.

purl [pə:l]. Knitting: **I.** s. **p. stitch,** maille f à l'envers. **II.** v.i. faire des mailles à l'envers.

purple ['pə:pl], a. & s. violet (m); pourpre (m); **to get p. in the face,** devenir cramoisi; **'purplish,** a. violacé; (of the face) cramoisi.

purpose ['pə:pəs], s. **1.** (a) dessein m, objet m; but m, fin f, intention f; **fixed p.,** dessein bien arrêté; **to do sth. on p.,** faire qch. exprès, à dessein; **of set p.,** de propos délibéré, de parti pris; (b) résolution f; **infirmity of p.,** manque m de volonté; **steadfastness of p.,** ténacité f de caractère; détermination f. **2.** destination f, fin; **to answer the p.,** répondre au but; **for this p.,** à cet effet; **for all necessary purposes,** à tous usages. **3.** **to speak to the p.,** parler à propos. **4.** **to work to good p., to some p.,** travailler utilement, efficacement; **'purposeful,** a. (of ac-

tion) prémédité; réfléchi; (*of pers.*) avisé; tenace; **-fully**, *adv.* dans un but réfléchi; **'purposeless**, *a.* sans but; inutile; **'purposely**, *adv.* à dessein; exprès.

purr [pə:r]. **I.** *s.* ronron *m* (de chat); ronron, ronflement *m*, vrombissement *m* (d'un moteur). **II.** *v.i.* (*of cat, engine*) ronronner; (*of engine*) ronfler, vrombir; **the cat's purring**, le chat fait ronron.

purse [pə:s]. **I.** *s.* bourse *f*, porte-monnaie *m inv*; **well-lined p.**, bourse bien garnie; **that car is beyond my p.**, cette voiture est au delà de mes moyens; *Adm:* **the public p.**, le Trésor. **II.** *v.tr.* **to p. (up) one's lips**, pincer les lèvres.

purser ['pə:sər], *s. Nau:* commissaire *m* (de la marine marchande).

pursue [pə'sju:], *v.tr.* **1. to p. s.o., sth.,** (i) poursuivre qn; (ii) rechercher (le plaisir); être à la poursuite (du bonheur). **2.** continuer, suivre (son chemin); poursuivre (une enquête); **to p. a line of conduct,** suivre une ligne de conduite; **pur'suer,** *s.* poursuivant, -ante; **pur'suit,** *s.* **1.** (*a*) poursuite *f*; **to set out in p. of s.o.,** se mettre à la poursuite de qn; (*b*) **in p. of happiness,** à la recherche du bonheur. **2.** (*a*) carrière *f*, profession *f*; **his literary pursuits,** ses travaux *m* littéraires; (*b*) occupation *f*; **his favourite p. is shooting,** son occupation favorite, c'est la chasse.

purveyor [pə:'veiər], *s.* fournisseur, -euse (de provisions).

push [pʌʃ]. **I.** *s.* **1.** poussée *f*, impulsion *f*; **to give sth. a p.,** pousser qch.; *F:* **to give s.o. the p.,** donner son congé à qn. **2.** (*a*) effort *m*; (*b*) **to have plenty of p.,** (i) être dynamique; (ii) *Pej:* être un arriviste. **3.** *F:* **at a p.,** dans une extrémité; au besoin; **when it comes to the p.,** quand on en vient au moment décisif. **II.** *v.* **1.** *v.tr.* pousser; (*a*) **to p. the button,** appuyer sur le bouton; **to p. one's finger into s.o.'s eye,** fourrer le doigt dans l'œil de qn; (*b*) **don't p. (me)!** ne (me) bousculez pas! (*c*) **to p. oneself (forward),** se mettre en avant; **to p. (s.o., sth.) aside,** écarter (qn, qch.); **to p. (s.o., sth.) back,** repousser (qn, qch.); faire reculer (qn); **to p. in a door,** enfoncer une porte; (*d*) pousser la vente de (ses marchandises); (*e*) **I'm pushed for time,** le temps me manque. **2.** *v.i.* (*a*) **to p. through the crowd,** se frayer un chemin à travers la foule; (*b*) pousser; exercer une pression; **'push 'back,** *v.tr.* repousser; faire reculer; **'pusher,** *s. F:* arriviste *mf*; **'pushing,** *a.* (*a*) débrouillard, entreprenant; (*b*) **a p. man,** un ambitieux; **'push 'off,** *v.i. F:* **it's time to p. off,** il est temps de se mettre en route.

pusillanimous [pju:si'læniməs], *a.* pusillanime, timide, craintif.

puss, pussy [pus, 'pusi], *s.* minet *m*, minette *f*; minou *m*.

put [put], *v.* (**put; put**) **1.** *v.tr.* mettre; (*a*) p. it on the table, mettez-le, posez-le, sur la table; **to p. milk in one's tea,** mettre du lait dans son thé; **to p. s.o. in his place,** remettre qn à sa place; **to p. one's signature to sth.,** apposer sa signature sur, à, qch.; **to p. the matter right**, arranger l'affaire; **to p. the law into operation**, appliquer la loi; **to p. money into an undertaking,** verser des fonds dans une affaire; **to p money on a horse,** miser sur un cheval; (*b*) **to p. a question to s.o.,** poser une question à qn; **to p. it to you whether . . .,** je vous demande un peu si . . .; **p. it to him nicely,** présentez-lui la chose gentiment; **to p. it bluntly,** pour parler franc; **if one may p. it that way,** si l'on peut s'exprimer ainsi; (*c*) **to p. the population a 10,000,** estimer, évaluer, la population à 10 000; (*d*) **to p. a stop to sth.,** mettre fin à qch.; (*e*) **to p. s.o. to bed,** mettre qn au lit, coucher (un enfant); *F:* **to p. s.o. through it** faire passer un mauvais quart d'heure à qn; t **p. s.o. to sleep,** endormir qn. **2.** *v.i. Nau:* **to p (out) to sea,** prendre le large; **to p. into port** faire relâche; **'put a'way,** *v.tr.* **1.** (*a*) serre (qch. dans une armoire remiser); (sa voiture); **to p away your books,** rangez vos livres; (*b*) mettr de côté (de l'argent); **to p. s.o. away,** mettre qu en prison; *F:* coffrer qn. **2.** écarter, chasse (une pensée); **'put 'back,** *v.tr.* (*a*) remettr (qch.) à sa place; (*b*) retarder (une horloge **'put 'by,** *v.tr.* mettre en réserve; *abs.* **to p. b for the future,** économiser pour l'avenir; **'p 'down,** *v.tr.* **1.** déposer, poser; **p. it dow** laissez cela! (*of bus*) **to p. down passenger** débarquer des voyageurs. **2.** supprimer (un révolte). **3.** noter (sur papier); **to p. down one name,** s'inscrire; se faire inscrire (**for,** pour); **it down to my account,** mettez-le à mo compte; **to p. sth. down to s.o.,** attribuer qch. qn. **4. to p. down an animal,** abattre, faire aba tre, un animal; **I had to have my old dog down,** j'ai dû faire piquer mon vieux chie **'put 'forward,** *v.tr.* **1.** (*a*) émettre, avance proposer (un projet); (*b*) **to p. oneself forwa** se mettre en avant, en évidence; (*c*) **to p. one best foot forward,** (i) presser le pas; (ii) se me tre en devoir de faire de son mieux. **2.** avanc (la pendule); **'put 'in. 1.** *v.tr.* (*a*) **to p. in (good) word for s.o.,** dire, placer, un mot faveur de qn; (*b*) **to p. in an hour's work, fa** une heure de travail. **2.** *v.i.* (*a*) **to p. in at a po** faire escale dans un port; (*b*) **to p. in for a po** poser sa candidature à un poste; **'put 'off.** *v.tr.* (*a*) remettre; différer (de faire qch.); **to off a case for a week,** ajourner une affaire huitaine; (*b*) **to p. s.o. off with an excuse,** débarrasser de qn avec une excuse; déconcerter (qn); **you p. me off,** vous m' timidez; **to p. s.o. off doing sth.,** décourager de faire qch. 2. *v.i. Nau:* pousser au large; démarrer; **'put 'on,** *v.tr.* 1. (*a*) **to p. the kettle on,** mettre chauffer de l'eau; **to p. on a dish,** servir un plat; **to p. on a record, a tape,** passer un disque, une bande; (*b*) **to p. a play on,** monter une pièce de théâtre; (*c*) *Aut:* **to p. the brake on,** freiner. 2. (*a*) mettre (ses vêtements); chausser (ses pantoufles); **p. on your hat,** couvrez-vous; **to p. on one's shoes,** se chausser; (*b*) **to p. on an innocent air,** prendre un air innocent; *F:* **to p. it on,** poser; afficher de grands airs. 3. **to p. on weight,** prendre du poids. 4. avancer (la pendule). 5. **to p. on the light,** mettre la lumière; allumer; **'put 'out,** *v.tr.* 1. avancer (la main); étendre (le bras). 2. (*a*) mettre (le chat) dehors; **to p. s.o. out (of the house),** mettre qn à la porte; **to p. the washing out to dry,** mettre du linge à sécher; (*b*) **to p. one's tongue out,** tirer la langue. 3. **to p. out (of joint),** démettre, déboîter (l'épaule, le genou, etc.). 4. éteindre (la lumière). 5. déconcerter; ennuyer, contrarier (qn); incommoder, gêner (qn); **he never gets p. out,** il ne s'émeut jamais; **to p. oneself out for s.o.,** se déranger pour qn; **'put to'gether,** *v.tr.* 1. joindre; monter; assembler (une robe, une machine). 2. rapprocher, comparer (des faits); **'put 'up,** *v.tr.* 1. (*a*) lever (une glace); ouvrir (un parapluie); dresser (une échelle); poser; **p. up your hands!** haut les mains! (*b*) coller (une affiche). 2. augmenter (les prix). 3. **to p. sth. up for sale,** mettre qch. en vente. 4. *Pol: etc:* **to p. up a candidate,** proposer un candidat. 5. **to p. up a stout resistance,** se défendre vaillamment. 6. héberger (qn); **to p. a friend up for the night,** offrir un lit à un ami pour une nuit; *v.i.* **to p. up**

at a hotel, loger à un hôtel. 7. *abs.* **to p. up with sth.,** s'accommoder de qch.; se résigner à (des inconvénients); souffrir, endurer (des railleries). 8. **to p. s.o. up to sth.,** pousser qn à qch. 9. construire (une maison); ériger (un monument); **'put-up,** *a. F:* **a p.-up job,** un coup monté; **'put upon,** *v.tr.* **to p. upon s.o.,** en imposer à qn.

putrefy ['pju:trifai], *v.i.* se putréfier, pourrir; **putre'faction,** *s.* putréfaction *f.*

putrid ['pju:trid], *a.* 1. putride; en putréfaction; infect. 2. *F:* moche.

putt [pʌt]. *Golf:* I. *s.* putt *m.* II. *v.tr. & i.* putter; jouer sur le putting; **'putting-green,** *s.* putting *m.*

putty ['pʌti], *s.* mastic *m,* enduit *m;* **p. knife,** spatule *f* de vitrier.

puzzle ['pʌzl]. I. *s.* 1. embarras *m;* perplexité *f.* 2. énigme *f;* problème *m;* devinette *f;* **crossword p.,** mots croisés. II. *v.* 1. *v.tr.* embarrasser, intriguer. 2. *v.i.* **to p. over sth.,** se creuser la tête pour comprendre qch.; **'puzzling,** *a.* embarrassant, intrigant.

pygmy ['pigmi]. 1. *s.* pygmée *mf.* 2. *a.* pygméen.

pyjamas [pi'dʒɑːməz], *s.pl.* pyjama *m.*

pylon ['pailən], *s.* pylône *m.*

pyramid ['pirəmid], *s.* pyramide *f.*

pyre ['paiər], *s.* bûcher *m* (funéraire).

Pyrenees (the) [ðəpirə'niːz]. *Pr.n. Geog:* les Pyrénées *f;* **Pyre'nean,** *a.* pyrénéen; des Pyrénées.

pyrites [paiə'raitiːz], *s.* pyrite *f.*

pyromaniac [paiərə'meiniæk], *s.* pyromane *mf.*

pyrotechnics [paiərə'tekniks], *s.pl.* (*usu. with sg. const.*) pyrotechnie *f.*

python ['paiθ(ə)n], *s. Rept:* python *m.*

Q

Q, q [kjuː], s. (la lettre) Q, q m; F: **on the strict q.t.** [ˈkjuːˈtiː], en secret.
quack[1] [kwæk]. I. s. & int. couin-couin (m). II. v.i. (of duck) crier; faire couin-couin.
quack[2]. F: (a) a. & s. q. (doctor), charlatan m; (b) s. the q., le toubib.
quad [kwɔd], s. Sch: F: cour (carrée).
Quadragesima [kwɔdrəˈdʒesimə], s. Ecc: la Quadragésime.
quadrangle [ˈkwɔdræŋgl], s. Sch: cour (carrée).
quadratic [kwɔdˈrætik], a. Mth: q. equation, équation f du second degré.
quadrilateral [kwɔdriˈlæt(ə)rəl], a. & s. quadrilatère (m).
quadruped [ˈkwɔdruped], s. quadrupède m.
quadruple [ˈkwɔdrupl]. I. a. & s. quadruple (m). II. v.tr. & i. quadrupler; 'quadruplets, F: quads, s.pl. quadruplé(e)s; qua'druplicate. I. a. quadruple; in q., en quatre exemplaires. II. v.tr. quadrupler; faire quatre exemplaires de (qch.).
quagmire [ˈkwægmaiər, ˈkwɔg-], s. fondrière f; marécage m.
quail [kweil], s. Orn: caille f.
quaint [kweint], a. pittoresque (à l'ancienne mode); q. ideas, idées f (i) bizarres, un peu vieux jeu, (ii) baroques; q. style, (i) style original; (ii) style d'un archaïsme piquant.
quake [kweik], v.i. trembler (with fear, de peur); to q. in one's shoes, trembler dans sa peau.
Quaker [ˈkweikər], s. Ecc: Quaker m.
qualify [ˈkwɔlifai]. 1. v.tr. (a) Gram: qualifier; (b) to q. oneself for a job, acquérir les titres nécessaires pour remplir un emploi; (c) apporter des réserves à (un consentement, etc.); modifier, atténuer (une affirmation). 2. v.i. acquérir les connaissances requises, se qualifier (for, pour); to q. as a doctor, être reçu médecin; Av: to q. as a pilot, réussir son brevet de pilote; qualifi'cation [-fi-], s. qualification f; qualifications for a job, titres m à un emploi; to accept without q., accepter (i) sans réserve, (ii) sans condition; 'qualified, a. 1. (a) to be q. to do sth., être qualifié pour faire qch.; q. teacher, instituteur, -trice, diplômé(e); (b) autorisé; to be q. to vote, avoir qualité d'électeur. 2. restreint, modéré; q. acceptance, acceptation conditionnelle.
quality [ˈkwɔliti], s. (a) qualité f; of good, poor, q., de bonne qualité; de qualité inférieure; Com: q. goods, marchandises f de qualité; q.

newspapers, journaux sérieux; of the best q., de premier choix; (b) he has many good qualities, bad qualities, il a beaucoup de qualités, de défauts.
qualm [kwɑːm, kwɔːm], s. scrupule m, remords m; to have no qualms about doing sth., ne pas se faire le moindre scrupule de faire qch.
quandary [ˈkwɔndəri], s. to be in a q., (i) se trouver dans une impasse; être dans l'embarras; (ii) ne trop savoir que faire.
quantity [ˈkwɔntiti], s. (a) quantité f; a small, a large, q. of . . ., une petite, une grande, quantité de . . .; in great quantities, en grande quantité, en abondance; (b) Mth: quantité; un known q., inconnue f; (c) Civ.E: q. surveying toisé m; métrage m; q. surveyor, métreu (vérificateur).
quarantine [ˈkwɔrəntiːn]. I. s. quarantaine f; t be in q., faire (la) quarantaine. II. v.tr. mettr (qn, un chien) en quarantaine.
quarrel [ˈkwɔrəl]. I. s. querelle f, dispute , brouille f; to try to pick a q. with s.o., cherche querelle à qn; I have no q. with him, je n'ai rie à lui reprocher. II. v.i. (quarrelled) 1. s quereller, se disputer (with s.o. over, abou sth., avec qn à propos de qch.); se brouille (avec qn). 2. to q. with s.o. for having done sth reprocher à qn d'avoir fait qch.; to q. with sth trouver à redire à qch.; 'quarrelling, . querelle(s) f(pl), dispute(s) f(pl 'quarrelsome, a. querelleur; he's a q. fellow, est mauvais coucheur.
quarry[1] [ˈkwɔri], s. Ven: proie f; gibier m.
quarry[2]. I. s. carrière f (de pierres, etc.). II. v.t extraire, tirer, (la pierre) de la carrière; ab exploiter une carrière; 'quarrying, s. exploit tion f de carrières; 'quarryman, pl. -men, (ouvrier m) carrier m.
quart [kwɔːt], s. Meas: approx. = 1 litre (U.I = 1 litre 136, U.S: = 0 litre 946).
quarter [ˈkwɔːtər]. I. s. 1. (a) quart m; bottle o q. full, bouteille au quart pleine; (b) Cu: qua tier m (de bœuf). 2. (a) trimestre m; terme (de loyer); (b) moon at the first q., lune à premier quartier; (c) a q. to six, six heur moins le quart; a q. past six, six heures quart. 3. (a) what q. is the wind in? de quel cô souffle le vent? (b) the four quarters of th globe, les quatre parties du globe; from quarters, de tous côtés; in high quarters,

Q:1

haut lieu. **4.** quartier (d'une ville). **5.** *pl.* (*a*) **to shift one's quarters,** changer de résidence *f*; (*b*) *Mil:* quartier, logement *m*. **II.** *v.tr.* **1.** diviser (une pomme, etc.) en quatre. **2.** *Mil:* cantonner, caserner (des troupes); **'quarter-'final,** *s. Sp:* quart *m* de finale; **'quarter-'hourly,** *adv.* tous les quarts d'heure; de quart d'heure en quart d'heure; **'quarterly. 1.** *a.* trimestriel. **2.** *s.* publication trimestrielle. **3.** *adv.* par trimestre; tous les trois mois.

quartet(te) [kwɔːˈtet], *s. Mus:* quatuor *m*.

quarto [ˈkwɔːtou], *a & s.* in-quarto (*m*) *inv.*

quartz [kwɔːts], *s. Miner:* quartz *m*.

quash [kwɔʃ], *v.tr. Jur:* casser, annuler (un jugement).

quasi [ˈkweisai], *pref.* quasi, presque; **q.-expert,** quasi-expert; **q.-public,** quasi-public; soi-disant public.

quaver [ˈkweivər]. **I.** *s.* **1.** *Mus:* croche *f*. **2.** (*a*) *Mus:* trille *m*, tremolo *m*; (*b*) tremblement *m*, chevrotement *m* (de la voix). **II.** *v.i.* chevroter, trembloter; **'quavering,** *a.* **q. voice,** voix chevrotante, tremblotante; **-ly,** *adv.* d'une voix mal assurée.

quay [kiː], *s.* quai *m*.

queasy [ˈkwiːzi], *a.* sujet à des nausées; **to feel q.,** *F:* avoir l'estomac barbouillé; **q. conscience,** conscience scrupuleuse à l'excès.

Quebec [kwiˈbek]. *Pr.n. Geog:* (*a*) (*town*) Québec; (*b*) (*province*) le Québec.

queen [ˈkwiːn], *s.* **1.** reine *f*; **the Q. Mother,** la reine mère. **2.** (*a*) *Cards:* dame *f*; (*b*) *Chess:* dame, reine. **3.** *Ent:* (*of bees, ants*) reine; **'queenly,** *a.* de reine; digne d'une reine.

queer [ˈkwiər]. **I.** *a.* **1.** (*a*) bizarre, étrange, singulier; **a q.-looking chap,** une drôle de tête; *F:* **to be in Q. Street,** être dans une situation (financière) embarrassée; (*b*) suspect; (*c*) *P:* homosexuel; *s.* **a q.,** un homosexuel. **2.** *F:* **I feel very q.,** je me sens patraque; **-ly,** *adv.* étrangement, bizarrement. **II.** *v.tr. F:* déranger, détraquer; **to q. s.o.'s pitch,** faire échouer les projets de qn; **'queerness,** *s.* étrangeté *f*, bizarrerie *f*.

quell [kwel], *v.tr.* calmer, apaiser (une émotion); dompter, étouffer (une passion); réprimer (une révolte).

quench [kwen(t)ʃ], *v.tr.* **to q. one's thirst,** apaiser sa soif; se désaltérer.

querulous [ˈkwerjuləs], *a.* plaintif et maussade.

query [ˈkwiəri]. **I.** *s.* (*a*) question *f*; (*b*) point *m* d'interrogation. **II.** *v.tr.* (*a*) mettre (une affirmation) en question, en doute; (*b*) marquer (qch.) d'un point d'interrogation.

quest [kwest], *s.* recherche *f*; **to go in q. of s.o.,** se mettre à la recherche de qn.

question [ˈkwestʃ(ə)n]. **I.** *s.* question *f*; **without q.,** sans aucun doute; **to obey without q.,** obéir aveuglément; **to call sth. in q.,** mettre qch. en question; **the matter in q.,** l'affaire en question, dont il s'agit; **that's not the q.,** il ne s'agit pas de cela; **it's out of the q.,** il ne faut pas y songer; **to ask s.o. a q.,** poser une question à qn; **q. mark,** point *m* d'interrogation; **a q. of time,** une question de temps. **II.** *v.tr.* **1.** questionner, interroger (qn). **2.** mettre (qch.) en question, en doute; **'questionable,** *a.* **1.** contestable, discutable. **2.** équivoque; **in q. taste,** d'un goût douteux; **'questioner,** *s.* interrogateur, -trice; **questio'nnaire,** *s.* questionnaire *m*.

queue [kjuː]. **I.** *s.* queue *f* (de personnes, de voitures); **to stand in a q.,** faire la queue; **to jump the q.,** passer avant son tour. **II.** *v.i.* **to q. (up),** faire la queue; (*of cars*) prendre la file.

quibble [ˈkwibl]. **I.** *s.* argutie *f*; chicane *f* de mots; faux-fuyant *m, pl.* faux-fuyants. **II.** *v.i.* chicaner sur les mots; user d'équivoque, vétiller; **'quibbler,** *s.* ergoteur, -euse; chicaneur, -euse.

quick [kwik]. **I.** *a.* (*a*) rapide; **the quickest way,** le chemin le plus court; **q. sale,** vente *f* facile; **to have a q. lunch,** déjeuner sur le pouce; **as q. as lightning,** comme un éclair; en un clin d'œil; **be q.!** faites vite! dépêchez-vous! (*b*) **q. child,** enfant vif, éveillé; **q. wit,** esprit prompt à la repartie; **q. ear,** oreille fine; **she has a q. temper,** elle s'emporte facilement; **q. to anger,** prompt, vif, à se fâcher; (*c*) *Mus:* animé; (*d*) **q. hedge,** haie vive; **-ly,** *adv.* vite; rapidement. **II.** *s.* vif *m*; chair vive; **to cut s.o. to the q.,** blesser qn au vif; **the q. and the dead,** les vivants et les morts; **'quick-'acting,** *a.* (mécanisme) à action immédiate; *Med:* (médicament) à réaction rapide; **'quicken,** *v.tr.* (*a*) exciter, stimuler (l'appétit); animer (la conversation); (*b*) hâter, presser, accélérer (le pas); **'quick-'freeze,** *v.tr.* surgeler; **'quicklime,** *s.* chaux vive; **'quickness,** *s.* **1.** vitesse *f*, rapidité *f*. **2.** acuité *f* (de vision); finesse *f* (d'oreille); vivacité *f* (d'esprit); **'quicksand,** *s.* sable(s) mouvant(s); **to get caught in a q.,** s'enliser; **'quicksilver,** *s.* vif-argent *m*, mercure *m*; **'quick-'tempered,** *a.* emporté; prompt à la colère; **'quick-'witted,** *a.* d'esprit vif, éveillé.

quid [kwid], *s. P:* livre *f* (sterling); **five q.,** cinq livres.

quiescent [kwaiˈes(ə)nt], *a.* en repos; tranquille; **qui'escence,** *s.* repos *m*; quiétude *f*, tranquillité *f*.

quiet [ˈkwaiət]. **I.** *s.* **1.** tranquillité *f*, repos *m*, calme *m*. **2.** *F:* **to do sth. on the q.,** faire qch. en cachette; **I'm telling you that on the q.,** je vous dis ça entre nous deux. **II.** *a.* **1.** tranquille, calme, silencieux; **to keep q.,** rester tranquille; **be q.!** (i) taisez-vous! (ii) laissez-moi tranquille! **2.** **q. disposition,** caractère doux, calme. **3.** simple; sobre; discret; **q. dinner,** dîner intime; **q. wedding,** mariage célébré dans l'intimité; **to have a q. dig at s.o.,** faire une allusion discrète à qn. **4.** calme, tranquille, paisible; **to lead a q. life,** mener une vie calme; **he's had a q. sleep,** il a dormi tranquillement; **you may be q. on that score,** quant à cela vous pouvez être tranquille; **-ly,** *adv.* (*a*) tranquillement, doucement; (*b*) silencieusement, sans bruit. **III.** *v.* (*also* **quieten**) **1.** *v.tr.* apaiser, calmer. **2.** *v.i.* **to q., to quieten, down,** s'apaiser, se calmer; **'quietness,** *s.* **1.** tranquillité *f,* repos *m,* calme *m.* **2.** sobriété *f* (de tenue, etc.).

quilt [kwilt]. **I.** *s.* couverture piquée; édredon piqué. **II.** *v.tr.* piquer, capitonner (un vêtement, un couvre-pied(s)).

quince [kwins], *s.* coing *m*; **q. tree,** cognassier *m.*

quinine ['kwini:n], *s. Med:* quinine *f.*

quinsy ['kwinzi], *s. Med:* angine *f* (laryngée).

quintet(te) [kwin'tet], *s. Mus:* quintette *m.*

quintuple ['kwintjupl], *a. & s.* quintuple (*m*); **quin'tuplet,** *s.* **1.** groupe *m* de cinq. **2.** *pl.* **quintuplets,** *F:* **quins,** quintuplé(e)s.

quip [kwip], *s.* sarcasme *m,* repartie *f*; raillerie *f,* mot piquant.

quire ['kwaiər], *s.* =main *f* (de papier).

quirk [kwə:k], *s.* bizarrerie *f.*

quit [kwit]. **I.** *a.* quitte; **to be q. of s.o.,** être débarrassé de qn. **II.** *v.tr.* (**quitted** *or* **quit**) (*a*) quitter (qn, un endroit); *abs.* vider les lieux; déménager; s'en aller; (*b*) **to q. one's job,** quitter son emploi; démissionner; *esp. N.Am:* **to q. doing sth.,** cesser de faire qch.

quite [kwait], *adv.* **1.** tout à fait; entièrement; **q. new,** tout nouveau; **q. recovered,** complètement rétabli; **it's q. five days ago,** il y a bien cinq jours de cela; **q. as much,** tout autant; **q. enough,** bien assez; **I q. understand,** j'ai bien compris; je me rends parfaitement compte; **q.**

right, très bien; **q. so!** *F:* **q.!** parfaitement! d'accord! **I don't q. know what he will do,** je ne sais pas trop ce qu'il fera. **2. his story is q. a romance,** son histoire est tout un roman; **it's q. interesting,** cela ne manque pas d'intérêt; **q. a surprise,** une véritable surprise; **I q. believe that . . .,** je veux bien croire que . . ..

quiver ['kwivər]. **I.** *s.* tremblement *m*; frisson *m*; **with a q. in his voice,** d'une voix frémissante; **q. of the eyelid,** battement *m* de paupière. **II.** *v.i* trembler; frémir, tressaillir, frissonner; (*o, voice*) trembloter; **to q. with fear,** frémir de crainte.

quixotic [kwik'sɔtik], *a.* exalté, visionnaire.

quiz, *pl.* **quizzes** [kwiz, 'kwiziz]. **I.** *s. Rad: T.V etc:* devinette *f*; jeu *m.* **II.** *v.tr.* (**quizzed**) poser des colles à (qn).

quizzical ['kwizik(ə)l], *a.* railleur; plaisant; **a smile,** un sourire moqueur.

quorum ['kwɔ:rəm], *s.* quorum *m*; nombre voulu; **not to have a q.,** ne pas être en nombre

quota ['kwoutə], *s.* quote-part *f, pl.* quotes-parts quotité *f*; quota *m*; *Com: Adm:* **to fix quota for imports of butter,** fixer les quotas d'impo tation pour le beurre, contingenter les impo tations du beurre.

quote [kwout]. **I.** *v.tr.* **1.** citer (un auteur); **to an instance of sth.,** fournir un exemple de qch *Com:* **in reply please q. this number,** prière rappeler ce numéro; **q. . . . unquote . . .** ouvrez les guillemets . . . fermez l guillemets . . .. **2.** *Com:* établir, faire (u prix). **II.** *s. F:* **1.** citation *f.* **2.** *pl.* **quote** guillemets *mpl*; **quo'tation,** *s.* **1.** citation **q. marks,** guillemets *mpl.* **2.** cote *f,* cours *r* prix *m.*

quotient ['kwouʃ(ə)nt], *s. Mth:* quotient *m.*

R

R, r [ɑːr], s. (la lettre) R, r m; **the three Rs,** l'enseignement m primaire.

abbi ['ræbai], s. *Jew.Rel:* rabbin m.

abbit ['ræbit], s. 1. lapin m; **buck r.,** lapin mâle; **doe r.,** lapine f; **wild r.,** lapin de garenne; **r. hole,** terrier m (de lapin); **r. hutch,** clapier m. 2. *Cu:* **Welsh r.,** fondue f au fromage sur canapé.

abble ['ræbl], s. *Pej:* 1. cohue f; foule f (en désordre). 2. **the r.,** la canaille.

abid ['ræbid], a. 1. (a) furieux; (ennemi) acharné; (b) outrancier. 2. *Vet:* (chien) enragé.

abies ['reibi(ː)z], s. *Med: Vet:* rage f.

accoon [rəˈkuːn], s. *Z:* raton laveur.

ace[1] [reis]. I. s. 1. *Sp:* course f; **to run a r.,** courir, disputer, une course; **long-distance r.,** course de fond; **to go to the races,** aller aux courses; **a r. against time,** une course contre la montre. 2. (*at sea*) raz m, ras m, de courant; (*in canal, river*) (**mill**) **r.,** canal m; bief m. II. v. 1. *v.i.* lutter de vitesse (**with,** avec); (*of engine*) s'emballer; (*of propeller*) s'affoler; (*of pulse*) battre rapidement; *Aut: etc:* courir. 2. *v.tr.* faire courir (un cheval); *Aut:* emballer (le moteur); **I'll r. you to school,** faisons une course jusqu'à l'école; **'racecourse,** s. champ m de courses; **'racehorse,** s. cheval m de course; **'racer,** s. 1. (*pers.*) coureur, -euse. 2. cheval m de course; vélo m, voiture, f, de course; **'racing,** s. courses fpl; **horse r.,** les courses (de chevaux); l'hippisme m; **r. stable,** écurie f de courses; **'racy,** a. vif, piquant; (*style*) plein de verve.

ace[2], s. race f. 1. **the human r.,** la race humaine; **r. hatred,** haine raciale; **r. relations,** rapports m entre les races (d'un même pays). 2. (a) descendance f; (b) lignée f; **racial** ['reiʃ(ə)l], a. racial, de (la) race; **r. discrimination,** discrimination raciale; **r. minorities,** les races en minorité; **'racialism,** s., **'racism,** s. racisme m; **'racialist, 'racist,** a. & s. raciste (mf).

ck[1] [ræk], s. (*only in the phr.*) **to go to r. and ruin,** aller à la ruine; (*of house*) se délabrer.

ck[2], s. (a) râtelier m (d'écurie); (b) *Av:* **bomb r.,** lance-bombes m inv; *Rail:* **luggage r.,** porte-bagages m inv; filet m (à bagages); *Aut:* **roof r.,** galerie f; **'rack-'railway,** s. chemin m de fer à crémaillère.

ck[3], v.tr. tourmenter, torturer (qn); **to r. one's brains,** se creuser la cervelle; **racked by remorse,** tenaillé par le remords.

cket[1], **racquet** ['rækit], s. raquette f.

racket[2], s. 1. tapage m, vacarme m; *F:* **to stand the r.,** (i) subvenir aux dépenses; (ii) subir les conséquences. 2. (a) racket m; **it's a r.,** c'est une escroquerie, c'est du vol; (b) entreprise f de gangsters; **is he in on this r.?** est-il dans le coup? **racke'teer,** s. gangster m; escroc m; trafiquant m.

radar ['reidɑːr], s. radar m; **navigation by r.,** navigation f au radar.

radiate ['reidieit]. 1. v.i. rayonner; irradier; (a) émettre des rayons; (b) (*of lines*) partir d'un même centre. 2. v.tr. émettre, dégager (de la chaleur, etc.); **'radial,** a. *Aut:* **r. tyre,** pneu radial; **'radiance,** s. 1. rayonnement m, splendeur f; éclat m (de la beauté, etc.). 2. *Ph:* rayonnement, radiation f; **'radiant,** a. radieux; **r. smile,** sourire radieux; **r. heat,** chaleur rayonnante; **-ly,** adv. radieusement; **r. happy,** rayonnant de joie; **radi'ation,** s. 1. irradiation f; rayonnement m. 2. radiation f (du radium, etc.); **nuclear r.,** rayonnement nucléaire; **'radiator,** s. (a) radiateur m (pour chauffage); (b) **fan-cooled r.,** radiateur refroidi par ventilateur; *Aut:* **r. cap,** bouchon m de radiateur.

radical ['rædik(ə)l]. 1. a. radical; **to make a r. change in sth.,** changer qch. radicalement. 2. s. *Ch: Ling: Mth:* radical m; *Pol:* **the Radicals,** les Radicaux; **-ally,** adv. radicalement, foncièrement.

radio ['reidiou]. I. s. 1. la radio; **I heard it on the r.,** je l'ai entendu à la radio; **r. station,** poste émetteur de radio; **r. (set),** poste (récepteur) de radio, une radio; **turn on the r.,** ouvrez le poste. 2. **r. operator,** radio m. 3. *Av:* **r. beacon,** radiobalise f; **r. control,** téléguidage m; **r. direction,** radioguidage m. II. v.tr. envoyer (un message) (par) radio; **'radio'active,** a. radio(-)actif; **'radioac'tivity,** s. radio(-)activité f; **'radiogram,** s. 1. radiogramme m. 2. combiné m (radiophone); **'radiograph. I. s.** *Med:* radiographie f, *F:* radio f. II. v.tr. radiographier; **radi'ographer,** s. assistant, -ante, d'un radiologue; **radi'ography,** s. *Med:* radiographie f; **radi'ologist,** s. radiologue mf; **radi'ology,** s. radiologie f; **'radio'sonde,** s. radiosonde f; **'radio'telephone,** s. radiotéléphone m; **'radio'therapy,** s. radiothérapie f.

radish ['rædiʃ], s. radis m.

radium ['reidiəm], s. radium m.

radius, pl. -ii ['reidiəs, -iai], s. Geom: rayon m (de cercle); Aut: steering r., rayon de braquage; **within a r. of three kilometres**, dans un rayon de trois kilomètres.

raffle ['ræfl]. I. s. tombola f; loterie f. II. v.tr. mettre (qch.) en loterie.

raft [rɑːft], s. radeau m.

rafter ['rɑːftər], s. Const: chevron m.

rag[1] [ræg], s. 1. chiffon m; lambeau m. 2. pl. **rags (and tatters)**, haillons m, guenilles f, loques f. 3. **the r. trade**, l'industrie f de l'habillement, du prêt-à-porter. 4. Pej: (of newspaper), feuille f de chou; '**ragged** [-gid], a. en lambeaux; en haillons; '**rag-picker**, s. chiffonnier, -ière.

rag[2]. I. s. Sch: F: brimade f; mauvais tour; farce f; chahut m. II. v. F: (**ragged**) 1. v.tr. (a) brimer (un camarade); (b) chahuter (un professeur); chambarder les effets d'(un étudiant). 2. v.i. chahuter; faire du chahut.

rage [reidʒ]. I. s. 1. rage f, fureur f, emportement m; **to be in a r. with s.o.**, être furieux contre qn; **to fly into a r.**, s'emporter. 2. manie f, toquade f; **to be all the r.**, faire fureur. II. v.i. être furieux; être dans une colère bleue (contre qn); (of wind) faire rage; (of epidemic) sévir; '**raging**, a. furieux; en fureur; **r. sea**, mer déchaînée; **r. fever**, fièvre f de cheval; **r. thirst**, soif ardente.

raid [reid]. I. s. (a) razzia f (de bandits); (b) (**police**) r., rafle f; (c) Mil: raid m; **air r.**, raid aérien. II. v. 1. v.i. faire (une) razzia, un raid. 2. v.tr. razzier (une tribu); (of police) faire une rafle dans (un quartier);'**raider**, s. maraudeur m, pillard m.

rail [reil], s. 1. (a) barre f, barreau m; bâton m (de chaise); (b) barre d'appui; garde-fou m, parapet m (de pont); rampe f (d'escalier). 2. pl. (iron) grille f; (wood) palissade f; clôture f. 3. Rail: (a) rail m; **live r.**, rail de contact; **to leave the rails**, dérailler; (of pers.) **to go off the rails**, dérailler, être détraqué; (b) **to travel by r.**, voyager en chemin de fer; '**rail-car**, s. automotrice f; autorail m; '**railhead**, s. tête f de ligne; '**railings**, s.pl. 1. grille f; parapet m (de pont); balustrade f (de balcon); rampe f (d'escalier); '**railway**, N.Am: '**railroad**, s. chemin m de fer; **r. line**, voie ferrée; **r. station**, N.Am: **railroad depot**, gare f; **r. cutting**, déblai m; **r. embankment**, remblai m;'**railwayman**, pl. -**men**, s. cheminot m.

rain [rein]. I. s. 1. pluie f; **driving r.**, pluie battante; **it looks like r.**, le temps est à la pluie. 2. pl. (in tropics) **the rains**, la saison des pluies. II. v.tr. & i. pleuvoir; **it's raining**, il pleut; '**rainbow**, s. arc-en-ciel m; '**raincheck**, s. N.Am: **I'll take a r. on that**, ce sera partie remise; '**raincoat**, s. imperméable m, F: imper m; '**rainfall**, s. précipitation f; **area of heavy r.**, région pluvieuse;'**rainproof**, a. imperméable.

'**rainwear**, s. coll. vêtements mpl de pluie
'**rainy**, a. pluvieux; **a r. day**, un jour de pluie; **to put sth. by for a r. day**, garder une poire pour la soif.

raise [reiz], v.tr. 1. (a) dresser, mettre debou (une échelle); relever (qch. qui est tombé); (b soulever (le peuple) (**against**, contre). 2. érige (une statue). 3. élever (une famille, du bétail) cultiver (des légumes). 4. (a) produire; **to r.** bump, faire une bosse; **to r. a smile**, provoque un sourire; (b) **to r. a hope**, faire naître une es pérance; (b) **to r. an objection**, soulever un objection. 5. (a) lever (le bras); soulever (u poids); (b) élever; **to r. s.o. to power**, élever q au pouvoir. 6. (a) hausser, relever (un store (b) **to r. one's voice**, élever, hausser, la voix; (c **to r. s.o.'s salary**, augmenter le salaire de qn. (a) **to r. an army**, lever, mettre sur pied, un armée; (b) **to r. money**, se procurer de l'argen (c) (of the State) **to r. a loan**, émettre u emprunt.

raisin ['reizn], s. raisin sec.

rake[1] [reik]. I. s. Tls: râteau m. II. v.tr. ratisse (les feuilles); râteler (le sol); gratter, racler (un surface); '**rake 'in**, v.tr. **to r. in the money** amasser de l'argent; '**rake-off**, s. F: gratte f '**rake 'out**, v.tr. **to r. out the fire**, enlever le cendres du feu; '**rake 'up**, v.tr. 1. rassemble attiser (le feu). 2. **to r. up s.o.'s past**, fouille dans le passé de qn.

rake[2], s. viveur m, roué m, noceur m; **old r.**, vieu marcheur; '**rakish**, a. libertin, dissolu; appearance, air m bravache; -**ly**, adv. 1. libertin. 2. crânement, effrontément; **hat tilte r.**, chapeau sur l'oreille.

rally ['ræli]. I. s. 1. (a) ralliement m (de pa tisans); (b) réunion f (de scouts); (c) Aut: (ca r., rallye m automobile. 2. reprise f (d forces); mieux momentané (d'un malade); S dernier effort (pour gagner le match); Cor reprise (des prix). II. v. 1. v.tr. rallier (ses pa tisans) (**round**, autour de). 2. v.i. (of troops) reformer; (of pers.) reprendre ses forces, remettre (d'une maladie); Pol: se rallier (à u parti).

ram [ræm]. I. s. 1. Z: bélier m. 2. (a) béli hydraulique; (b) mouton m, pilon m (d marteau-pilon. II. v.tr. (**rammed**) 1. battr damer, tasser (le sol); enfoncer (un pieu); Au **to r. a car**, tamponner une voiture.

ramble ['ræmbl]. I. s. promenade f (sa itinéraire bien arrêté); **to go for a r.**, F: fai une balade. II. v.i. 1. errer à l'aventure. parler sans suite; **to r. on**, dire mille conséquences; '**rambling**, a. 1. errant, vag bond. 2. (discours) décousu, sans suite. 3. **house**, maison pleine de coins et de recoins.

ramify ['ræmifai], v.i. se ramifier; **ramifi c tion**, s. ramification f.

ramjet ['ræmdʒet], s. *Av:* statoréacteur *m*.

ramp [ræmp], s. rampe *f*; pente *f*; *Aut:* **(repair) r.**, ponton *m* de visite, pont élévateur; *P.N: Aut:* **beware r.!** dénivellation! **unloading r.**, rampe de débarquement.

rampage [ræm'peidʒ]. I. s. *F:* **to be on the r.**, ne pas décolérer; se comporter comme un fou; **to go on a r.**, faire du tapage. II. *v.i.* **to r. (about)**, faire du tapage, chahuter (dans les rues, etc.).

rampant ['ræmpənt], *a.* **r. corruption**, la corruption omniprésente; **crime is r.**, le crime prolifère.

rampart ['ræmpɑ:t], s. *Fort:* rempart *m*.

ramshackle ['ræmʃækl], *a.* délabré.

ranch [rɑːn(t)ʃ], s. *N.Am:* ranch *m*.

rancid ['rænsid], *a.* rance.

rancour ['ræŋkər], s. rancune *f*; **'rancorous** ['ræŋkərəs], *a.* (of pers.) rancunier; haineux.

random ['rændəm]. 1. s. **at r.**, au hasard; **to speak at r.**, parler à tort et à travers; **to hit out at r.**, lancer des coups à l'aveuglette. 2. *a.* **r. shot**, coup tiré au hasard.

range [reindʒ]. I. s. 1. (a) rangée *f* (de bâtiments); (b) chaine *f* (de montagnes). 2. direction *f*, alignement *m*. 3. (a) champ *m* libre; *Com:* **free r. chickens**, poulets élevés en liberté; (b) *N.Am:* grand pâturage (non clôturé). 4. (a) étendue *f*, portée *f*; **r. of action**, champ d'activité; (b) **r. of colours**, gamme *f* de couleurs; **salary r.**, éventail *m* des salaires. 5. (ballistics) (a) distance *f*; (b) portée (d'une arme à feu); **within r.**, à portée de tir. 6. *H:* fourneau *m* de cuisine. II. *v.i.* 1. courir, errer; **researches ranging over a wide field**, recherches qui s'étendent sur un vaste terrain. 2. **temperatures ranging from ten to thirty degrees**, températures comprises entre dix et trente degrés. 3. **these guns r. over nine kilometres**, ces pièces ont une portée de neuf kilomètres.

rank[1] [ræŋk]. I. s. 1. *Mil:* (a) rang *m*; **to close the ranks**, serrer les rangs; (b) *pl.* **to rise from the ranks**, sortir du rang; (c) **the other ranks**, les hommes de troupe; **the r. and file**, (i) *Mil:* la troupe; (ii) le commun des mortels; **the r. and file of trade union members**, le commun des syndiqués. 2. (a) rang (social); (b) *Mil:* grade *m*; **to attain the r. of captain**, passer capitaine; **all ranks**, officiers et troupe. 3. **(taxi) r.**, station *f*, stationnement *m* (de taxis). II. *v.* 1. *v.tr.* ranger, compter (qn parmi les grands écrivains). 2. *v.i.* se ranger, être classé **(among**, parmi); **to r. above s.o.**, occuper un rang supérieur à qn.

rank[2], *a.* 1. (trop) luxuriant; exubérant. 2. (a) rance; fétide; (b) grossier, répugnant. 3. **r. poison**, poison violent; **r. lie**, mensonge grossier; **r. injustice**, injustice criante.

rankle ['ræŋkl], *v.i.* **to r. with s.o.**, rester sur le cœur de qn.

ransack ['rænsæk], *v.tr.* 1. fouiller (un tiroir). 2. saccager, piller (une ville).

ransom ['rænsəm]. I. s. rançon (demandée pour un captif, un otage). II. *v.tr.* 1. mettre (qn) à rançon. 2. payer la rançon de (qn); rançonner (qn).

rant [rænt], *v.i.* déclamer, tempêter, tonitruer; **'ranting**, s. déclamation(s) tonitruante(s).

rap [ræp]. I. s. petit coup sec et dur; **to give s.o. a r. on the knuckles**, remettre qn à sa place; *F:* **to take the r.**, payer les pots cassés. II. *v.tr. & i.* **(rapped)** frapper; **to r. s.o. on, over, the knuckles**, donner sur les doigts de qn; **to r. at the door**, frapper à la porte.

rapacious [rə'peiʃəs], *a.* rapace; **-ly**, *adv.* avec rapacité; **ra'pacity** [-'pæs-], s. rapacité *f*.

rape [reip]. I. s. viol *m*. II. *v.tr.* violer (une femme).

rapid ['ræpid], *a.* 1. rapide. 2. s. (usu. pl.) (in river) rapide(s) *m(pl)*; **-ly**, *adv.* rapidement; à grands pas; **ra'pidity**, s. rapidité *f*.

rapier ['reipiər], s. rapière *f*.

rapture ['ræptʃər], s. ravissement *m*, extase *f*; **to be in raptures**, être ravi **(with, over**, de); **to go into raptures**, s'extasier **(over**, sur); **'rapturous**, *a.* (cris) de ravissement, d'extase; **r. applause**, applaudissements *m* frénétiques; **-ly**, *adv.* avec ravissement; **to applaud r.**, applaudir avec frénésie.

rare ['rɛər], *a.* 1. (atmosphère) rare, peu dense. 2. **r. occurrence**, événement rare. 3. *F:* **you gave me a r. fright**, tu m'as fait une rude peur. 4. (of meat) **r. steak**, bifteck saignant; **-ly**, *adv.* rarement; **'rarefied**, *a.* (air) raréfié; **to become r.**, se raréfier; **'rarity**, s. 1. rareté *f* (d'un objet, d'un événement). 2. objet *m*, événement *m*, rare.

rarebit ['rɛəbit], s. *Cu:* **Welsh r.**, fondue *f* au fromage sur canapé.

rascal ['rɑ:sk(ə)l], s. coquin *m*, fripon *m*, mauvais sujet; (of child) polisson *m*; **'rascally**, *a.* (comportement) de canaille; **r. trick**, mauvais, vilain, tour.

rash[1] [ræʃ], s. *Med:* éruption *f*.

rash[2], *a.* (of pers.) téméraire; **r. words**, paroles *f* irréfléchies, imprudentes; **r. act**, coup *m* de tête; **-ly**, *adv.* témérairement; **to speak r.**, parler à la légère; **to act r.**, agir sans réflexion; **'rashness**, s. témérité *f*; étourderie *f*.

rasher ['ræʃər], s. *Cu:* tranche *f* (de bacon).

rasp [rɑːsp]. I. *v.* 1. *v.tr.* râper (le bois). 2. *v.i.* grincer, crisser. II. s. *Tls:* râpe *f*; **'rasping**, *a.* (son) grinçant; (voix *f*) âpre.

raspberry ['rɑːzb(ə)ri], s. framboise *f*; **r. bush**, framboisier *m*.

rat [ræt]. I. s. 1. *Z:* rat *m*; **sewer r.**, rat d'égout; **r. extermination**, dératisation *f*; **r. poison**, raticide *m*, mort *f* aux rats; **to smell a r.**, soupçonner anguille sous roche. 2. *Ind:* jaune *m*; renard *m*. II. *v.i.* (**ratted**) (*of dog, etc.*) **to go ratting**, faire la chasse aux rats. 2. *Ind:* faire le jaune, le renard; **to r. on a friend**, vendre un copain; '**rat-race**, *s. F:* la course au bifteck.

ratchet ['rætʃit], *s.* 1. encliquetage *m* à dents. 2. cliquet *m*, rochet *m*; **r. wheel**, roue *f* à cliquet.

rate [reit]. I. *s.* 1. nombre proportionnel, quantité proportionnelle; **r. per cent**, pourcentage *m*; **birth, death, r.**, (taux *m* de) natalité *f*, mortalité *f*. 2. (*a*) taux, raison *f*; **r. of growth**, taux de croissance, d'accroissement; (*b*) allure *f*, vitesse *f*, train *m*; **to go at a tremendous r.**, aller d'un train d'enfer; (*c*) taux, cours *m*; **r. of interest**, taux d'intérêt; **r. of exchange, exchange r.**, taux d'échange; **the minimum lending r.**, le taux d'escompte; *Com:* **market rates**, cours du marché; **advertising rates**, tarif *m* de publicité; **insurance r.**, prime *f* d'assurance; **r. of living**, train *m* de vie; (*d*) **at that r.**, sur ce pied-là; à ce compte-là; **at any r.**, dans tous les cas, en tout cas. 3. *Adm:* impôt foncier; **rates and taxes**, impôts et contributions. 4. estimation *f*, évaluation *f*; **to value sth. at a low r.**, (i) assigner une basse valeur à qch.; (ii) faire peu de cas de qch. II. *v.* 1. *v.tr.* (*a*) estimer, évaluer (qch.); **to r. sth. highly**, (i) assigner une haute valeur à qch.; (ii) faire grand cas de qch.; (*b*) considérer (**as**, comme); (*c*) *Nau:* classer (un navire, une voiture). 2. *v.i.* être classé (**as**, comme); '**rateable**, *a. Adm:* **r. value** (**of house, etc.**) = valeur locative imposable (d'un immeuble, etc.); '**ratepayer**, *s.* contribuable *mf*; '**rating**, *s.* 1. estimation *f*, évaluation *f*; *Adm:* répartition *f* des impôts locaux. 2. *Sp:* classe *f*, catégorie *f*. 3. *pl. Nau:* **the ratings**, les matelots et gradés.

rather ['rɑ:ðər], *adv.* 1. plutôt. 2. un peu; assez; **r. pretty**, assez joli; **r. plain**, plutôt laid; **r. a lot**, *F:* un peu trop; **I r. think you know him**, je crois bien que vous le connaissez. 3. plutôt (**than**, que); **I'd r. be liked than feared**, plutôt être aimé que craint; **I'd r. not**, veuillez m'excuser; *F:* **do you know him?—r.!** le connaissez-vous?—bien sûr que oui!

ratify ['rætifai], *v.tr.* ratifier, entériner (un décret, etc.); approuver (un contrat); **ratifi'cation**, *s.* ratification *f*.

ratio, *pl.* -**os** ['reiʃiou, -ouz], *s.* raison *f*, rapport *m*, proportion *f*; **in the r. of . . .**, dans le rapport de . . .; **in direct r. to . . .**, en raison directe de . . .

ration ['ræʃ(ə)n]. I. *s.* ration *f*; **to put s.o. on short rations**, rationner, limiter sévèrement, qn; **r. book**, carte *f* d'alimentation. II. *v.tr.* rationner (qn, les aliments, etc.); '**rationing**, *s.* rationnement *m*.

rational ['ræʃən(ə)l], *a.* (*a*) raisonnable; doué de raison; **to be quite r.**, avoir toute sa tête; (*b*) raisonné; conforme à la raison; **-ally**, *adv.*

raisonnablement.

rattle ['rætl]. I. *s.* 1. (*a*) hochet *m* (d'enfant) (hand) r., crécelle *f*; (*b*) *pl. Rept:* rattles sonnettes *f* (d'un crotale). 2. (*a*) bruit *m*, fraca *m* (d'une voiture, etc.); trictrac *m* (de dés) tapotis *m* (d'une machine à écrire); cliquetis *m* (de chaîne, etc.); (*b*) *Med:* (**death**) r., râle *m*. II. *v.* 1. *v.i.* (*a*) (*of arms*) cliqueter; (*of window* branler; **to make the windows r.**, faire tremble les vitres; (*b*) *Aut:* **to r. along**, rouler à tout vitesse, à grand bruit de ferraille; (*c*) *Mea* râler. 2. *v.tr.* (*a*) agiter (qch.) avec bruit; fair cliqueter (des clefs); (*b*) consterner boulverser (qn); **he never gets rattled**, il ne s laisse pas épater; il ne s'épate jamais '**rattlesnake**, *s. Rept:* crotale *m*, serpent *m* sonnettes.

raucous ['rɔ:kəs], *a.* (voix *f*) rauque; **-ly**, *ad*' d'une voix rauque, éraillée.

ravage ['rævidʒ], *v.tr.* ravager, dévaster (u pays, une ville); '**ravaging**, *a.* ravageur; **the** fire, l'incendie dévastateur.

rave [reiv], *v.i.* (*a*) être en délire; *F:* battre la can pagne; **you're raving mad!** tu es complètemen fou! (*b*) **to r. at s.o.**, pester contre qn; **ravin lunatic**, fou furieux; (*c*) (*of wind*) être en furi (*d*) *F:* **to r. about sth.**, s'extasier sur qch '**raving**, *s.* 1. délire *m*, divagation *f*. 2. *p* ravings, paroles incohérentes.

raven ['reiv(ə)n], *s. Orn:* (grand) corbeau; (*colour*) d'un noir de jais.

ravening ['ræv(ə)niŋ], *a.* (loup *m*, etc.) vorac rapace.

ravenous ['ræv(ə)nəs], *a.* 1. (animal *m*) vorac 2. (*a*) **r. appetite**, appétit vorace; (*b*) *F:* **to be** avoir une faim de loup; **-ly**, *adv.* voracemen **to eat r.**, manger gloutonnement.

ravine [rə'vi:n], *s.* ravin *m*.

ravish ['ræviʃ], *v.tr.* 1. ravir; enlever (qn) force. 2. ravir (d'admiration); enchanter (qn '**ravishing**, *a.* ravissant; **r. sight**, spectac enchanteur; **-ly**, *adv.* d'une manièr ravissante; **r. beautiful**, ravissant.

raw [rɔ:]. I. *a.* 1. cru; **r. meat**, viande crue. 2. *In* **r. materials**, matières premières; **r. hide**, cu vert; **r. silk**, soie grège; **r. metal**, métal brut. sans expérience; **a r. hand**, un novice; **troops**, troupes non aguerries. 4. à vif; **wound**, plaie vive; **her nerves are r.**, elle a l nerfs à fleur de peau. 5. **r. weather**, temps g et froid. II. *s.* **to touch s.o. on the r.**, piquer au vif; '**raw(-)'boned**, *a.* maigre; décharn '**rawness**, *s.* 1. crudité *f* (des fruits, etc.). inexpérience *f*. 3. froid *m* humide; âpreté *f* (temps).

ray [rei], *s. Ph:* rayon *m*; **X-rays**, rayons X; **X treatment**, radiothérapie *f*; **r. of light**, ray lumineux; **a r. of hope**, une lueur d'espoir.

rayon ['reiɔn], *s. Tex:* rayonne *f*.

raze [reiz], *v.tr.* raser; **to r. a building to the ground**, raser un édifice.

razor ['reizər], *s.* rasoir *m*; **safety r.**, rasoir de sûreté; **electric r.**, rasoir électrique; **r. blade**, lame *f* de rasoir.

re¹ [ri:], *prep.* 1. *Jur:* (in) re Smith v. Jones, (en) l'affaire Smith contre Jones. 2. **re your letter of June 10th**, au sujet de votre lettre du 10 juin.

re-², *pref.* re-; ré-; de nouveau; **to re-read**, relire; **to reprint**, réimprimer; **to revisit**, revisiter, visiter de nouveau; **reconquest**, reconquête *f*; **reaffirmation**, réaffirmation *f*; **to reaccustom**, réhabituer, *etc.*

reach [ri:tʃ]. **I.** *s.* 1. extension *f* (de la main); *Box:* allonge *f.* 2. (*a*) portée *f,* atteinte *f*; **within s.o.'s r.**, à la portée de qn; **out of r.**, hors de portée; **jobs within the r. of all**, emplois accessibles à tous; (*b*) **hotel within easy r. of the station**, hôtel à proximité de la gare. 3. partie droite (d'un fleuve) entre deux coudes; bief *m* (d'un canal). **II.** *v.tr.* 1. **to r. out**, étendre; tendre, avancer (la main). 2. atteindre (qch.). 3. (*a*) arriver à (un endroit); parvenir à (un but); **to r. perfection**, atteindre à la perfection; **your letter reached me today**, votre lettre m'est parvenue aujourd'hui; (*b*) arriver à (une conclusion); **to r. an agreement**, arriver à un accord. 4. **r. me my gloves**, passez-moi mes gants. **III.** *v.tr. & i.* arriver, s'élever, monter, descendre (jusqu'à . . .); **to r. the bottom**, atteindre le fond; descendre jusqu'au fond. **IV.** *v.i.* 1. s'étendre; **as far as the eye could r.**, à perte de vue. 2. **to r. out for sth.**, tendre la main pour prendre qch.

react [ri'ækt], *v.i.* réagir ((up)on, sur; **against**, contre); **re'action**, *s.* réaction *f*; **re'actionary**, *a. & s.* réactionnaire (*mf*); **re'actor**, *s. El.E:* réacteur *m*; *Atom.Ph:* **atomic r.**, réacteur atomique; **breeder r.**, pile *f* couveuse.

read [ri:d]. **I.** *v.tr.* (**read** [red]) 1. (*a*) lire; **to teach s.o. to r.**, apprendre à lire à qn; *Adm:* **read** [red] **and approved**, lu et approuvé; (*b*) *Typ:* **to r. proofs**, corriger des épreuves; (*c*) **to r. up a subject**, étudier un sujet; **he's reading for his exam**, il prépare son examen; (*at university*) **he's reading French**, il étudie le français; **to r. law**, faire son droit. 2. **to r. sth. aloud**, lire qch. à haute voix; **to r. to s.o.**, faire la lecture à qn. 3. (*a*) lire (la musique); (*b*) **to r. s.o.'s thoughts**, lire dans la pensée de qn; **to r. between the lines**, lire entre les lignes. 4. **the clause reads both ways**, l'article peut s'interpréter dans les deux sens; **to r. through an article**, (i) parcourir un article; (ii) lire un article en entier. **II.** *s.* action *f* de lire; **he was having a quiet r.**, il lisait tranquillement. **III.** *a.* [red] **well-r.**, instruit, savant, qui a beaucoup lu; **'readable**, *a.* (*of book or handwriting*) lisible; **'reader**, *s.* 1. (*a*) lecteur, -trice; **he's not much of a r.**, il n'aime pas beaucoup la lecture; (*b*) **publisher's r.**, lecteur, -trice, de manuscrits; **proof r.**, correcteur, -trice, d'épreuves. 2. *Sch:* = professeur *m* (de faculté). 3. *Sch:* livre *m*, manuel *m*, de lecture; **'reading. I.** *a.* **the r. public**, le public qui lit; **a r. man**, un grand liseur. **II.** *s.* 1. lecture(s) *f* (*pl*); **to be fond of r.**, aimer la lecture. 2. lecture (d'un instrument de précision); relevé *m* (d'un compteur à gaz); **barometric r.**, hauteur *f* barométrique; **'reading-lamp**, *s.* lampe *f* de travail; **'reading-room**, *s.* salle *f* de lecture (d'une bibliothèque).

readjust ['ri:ə'dʒʌst], *v.tr.* rajuster; **'rea'djustment**, *s.* rajustement *m*.

ready ['redi]. **I.** *a.* 1. (*a*) prêt; **to get r**, se préparer (**to**, à); (*of book*) **now r.**, sur le point de paraître; **to be r. to face s.o.**, attendre qn de pied ferme; (*b*) **r. to hand**, sous la main; **r. money**, argent comptant. 2. (*a*) prêt, disposé (à faire qch.); (*b*) **r. to die of hunger**, sur le point de mourir de faim. 3. prompt, facile; **to have a r. tongue**, avoir la langue bien pendue; **to be r. with an answer**, avoir la réplique prompte. **II.** *adv.* **r. dressed**, tout habillé; **table r. laid**, table toute préparée; **-ily**, *adv.* 1. (faire qch.) volontiers, avec empressement. 2. (imaginer qch.) aisément, facilement; **'readiness**, *s.* 1. empressement *m* (à faire qch.); bonne volonté. 2. facilité *f* (de parole); vivacité *f* (d'esprit). 3. **to be in r.**, être prêt; **'ready'cooked**, *a.* (*a*) (plat) tout cuit; (*b*) (mets) à emporter; **'ready 'made**, *a.* (article) tout fait; **'ready-'reckoner**, *s. Com:* barème *m* (de calculs tout faits); **'ready-to-'wear**, *a.* r.-to-w. clothes, le prêt-à-porter.

real ['riəl], *a.* 1. (*a*) vrai; **r. silk**, soie naturelle; **r. gold**, or *m* véritable; (*b*) véritable, réel; **a r. friend**, un vrai ami, un véritable ami; **it's the r. thing**, c'est authentique. 2. *Jur:* **r. estate**, propriété immobilière; **really**, *adv.* vraiment; réellement; en effet; **you r. must go there**, il faut absolument que vous y alliez; **is it r. true?** est-ce bien vrai? **not r.!** pas possible! **'realism**, *s.* réalisme *m*; **'realist**, *a. & s.* réaliste (*mf*); **rea'listic**, *a.* réaliste; **-ally**, *adv.* avec réalisme; **reality** [ri'æliti], *s.* la réalité; le réel; **in r.**, en réalité.

realize ['riəlaiz], *v.tr.* 1. (*a*) réaliser (un projet, etc.); (*b*) *Com:* convertir (des biens) en espèces, réaliser (des biens). 2. concevoir nettement, bien comprendre (qch.); se rendre compte de (qch.); **reali'zation**, *s.* (*a*) réalisation *f* (d'un projet); (*b*) *Com:* conversion en espèces; (*c*) conception nette, compréhension claire (d'un fait).

realm [relm], *s.* royaume *m*.

realtor ['riəltər], *s. N.Am:* agent immobilier.

ream [ri:m], *s.* = rame *f* (de papier).

reanimate ['ri:'ænimeit], *v.tr.* ranimer,

réanimer.

reap [riːp], *v.tr.* (*a*) moissonner (le blé, un champ); (*b*) recueillir (le fruit de son travail); **to r. profit from sth.**, tirer profit de qch.; **'reaper,** *s.* 1. (*pers.*) moissonneur, -euse. 2. (*machine*) moissonneuse *f*; **r. binder,** moissonneuse-lieuse *f*.

reappear ['riːə'piər], *v.i.* reparaître; **'rea'appearance,** *s.* réapparition *f*.

rear[1] ['riər]. I. *s.* 1. *Mil:* (*also* **rear-guard**) arrière-garde *f* (d'une armée). 2. (*a*) arrière *m* (d'une maison), derrière *m*; (*b*) dernier rang, queue *f*. II. *a.* d'arrière, de queue; postérieur; **'rear-'admiral,** *s.* contre-amiral *m*, *pl.* contre-amiraux; **'rearmost,** *a.* dernier; de queue.

rear[2]. 1. *v.tr.* élever (une famille, des animaux); cultiver (des plantes). 2. *v.i.* (*of horse*) **to r. (up),** se cabrer.

rearm ['riː'ɑːm], *v.tr.* réarmer; **'re'armament,** *s.* réarmement *m*.

re-arrange ['riːə'reindʒ], *v.tr.* arranger de nouveau; remettre en ordre; réarranger; **'rea'rrangement,** *s.* nouvel arrangement; remise *f* en ordre; réarrangement *m* (moléculaire).

reason ['riːz(ə)n]. I. *s.* 1. raison *f*, cause *f* (for, de); **for reasons best known to myself,** pour des raisons de moi seul connues; **for no r. at all,** sans motif; **the r. why,** le pourquoi; **you have r. to be glad,** vous avez sujet de vous réjouir; **I have r. to believe that. . .,** j'ai lieu de croire que . . .; **with (good) r.,** à bon droit; **all the more r. for going,** raison de plus pour y aller. 2. raison; faculté *f* de raisonner; **to lose one's r.,** perdre la raison. 3. raison; bon sens; **to listen to r.,** entendre raison; **it stands to r.,** c'est évident; cela va sans dire. II. *v.* 1. *v.i.* **to r. with s.o.,** raisonner qn, avec qn. 2. *v.tr.* (*a*) **to r. that . . .,** arguer que . . .; (*b*) **to r. s.o. out of doing sth.,** faire entendre raison à qn; **'reasonable,** *a.* 1. raisonnable; **you must be r.,** il faut vous raisonner. 2. **r. prices,** prix raisonnables, modérés; **-ably,** *adv.* raisonnablement; **'reasonableness,** *s.* caractère *m* raisonnable; raison *f*; modération *f*; **'reasoned,** *a.* 1. raisonné; motivé. 2. raisonnable; **'reasoning,** *s.* raisonnement *m*.

reassemble ['riːə'sembl]. 1. *v.tr.* (*a*) rassembler; assembler de nouveau; (*b*) remonter, remettre en état (une machine). 2. *v.i.* **school reassembles tomorrow,** c'est demain la rentrée (des classes); **'rea'ssembly,** *s.* remontage *m* (d'une machine, etc.).

reassure ['riːə'ʃuər], *v.tr.* rassurer, tranquilliser (qn) (**on, about,** sur); **to feel reassured,** se rassurer; **'rea'ssuring,** *a.* rassurant.

reawaken ['riːə'weikən]. 1. *v.tr.* réveiller (qn) de nouveau. 2. *v.i.* se réveiller de nouveau, encore.

rebate ['riːbeit], *s.* rabais *m*, escompte *m*; ristourne *f*.

rebel. I. ['reb(ə)l]. 1. *a.* insurgé. 2. *s.* rebelle *mf*; insurgé, -ée, révolté, -ée. II. *v.i.* [ri'bel], (**rebelled**) se rebeller, se soulever (**against,** contre); **re'bellion,** *s.* rébellion *f*, révolte *f* (**against,** contre); **re'bellious,** *a.* rebelle; **-ly,** *adv.* en rebelle; d'un ton de défi; **re'belliousness,** *s.* esprit *m* de rébellion.

rebound. I. *v.i.* [ri'baund], rebondir. II. *s.* ['riːbaund], rebondissement *m*; retour *m* brusque; ricochet *m* (d'une balle).

rebuff [ri'bʌf]. I. *s.* rebuffade *f*; échec *m*. II. *v.tr.* repousser, rebuter.

rebuild ['riː'bild], *v.tr.* (**rebuilt**) rebâtir, reconstruire.

rebuke [ri'bjuːk]. I. *s.* réprimande *f*, blâme *m*. II. *v.tr.* réprimander, blâmer (qn).

recall [ri'kɔːl]. I. *s.* 1. rappel *m* (de qn). 2. rétractation *f*, révocation *f*; **decision past r.,** décision *f* irrévocable; **lost beyond r.,** perdu irrévocablement. II. *v.tr.* 1. rappeler (un ambassadeur). 2. rappeler (qch. à qn); **I don't r. his name,** je ne me souviens pas de son nom. 3. annuler (un jugement); **re'calling,** *s.* 1. rappel *m*. 2. révocation *f*.

recapitulate ['riːkə'pitjuleit], *F:* **recap** ['riː'kæp] (**recapped**), (*a*) *v.tr.* récapituler; (*b*) *v.i.* faire le point; **'recapitu'lation,** *s.*, *F:* **'recap,** récapitulation *f*; **let's do a recap,** faisons le point.

recapture ['riː'kæptʃər]. I. *v.tr.* reprendre, recapturer. II. *s.* reprise *f*.

recast ['riː'kɑːst], *v.tr.* (**recast**) (*a*) refondre (une cloche, etc.); (*b*) faire (une pièce, un roman); (*c*) redistribuer les rôles d'(une pièce).

recede [ri'siːd], *v.i.* (*a*) s'éloigner, reculer; (*b*) (*of forehead*) fuir; **re'ceding,** *a.* (*a*) qui s'éloigne; **r. tide,** marée descendante; (*b*) **r. forehead,** front fuyant.

receipt [ri'siːt]. I. *s.* 1. (*a*) *Com:* recette *f*; (*b*) perception *f* (des impôts); (*c*) réception *f*; **on r. of this letter,** au reçu, dès réception, de cette lettre; **to acknowledge r. of a letter,** accuser réception d'une lettre; **to pay on r.,** payer à la réception. 2. reçu *m*, quittance *f*; **to give a r. for sth.,** donner acquit de qch, donner un reçu. II. *v.tr. Com:* acquitter (une facture).

receive [ri'siːv], *v.tr.* 1. (*a*) recevoir; **received with thanks,** pour acquit; (*b*) *Jur:* **to r. stolen goods,** receler des objets volés. 2. recevoir (des invités); **to r. s.o. with open arms,** accueillir qn à bras ouverts; **re'ceiver,** *s.* 1. (*a*) personne *f* qui reçoit (qch.); (*b*) destinataire *mf* (d'une lettre); (*c*) **r. in bankruptcy** = syndic *m* de faillite; (*d*) receleur *m* (d'objets volés). 2. récepteur *m* (de téléphone); **to lift the r.,** décrocher (le récepteur); **re'ceiving,** *s.* réception *f*; recel *m* (d'objets volés).

recent ['riːs(ə)nt], *a.* récent; **-ly,** *adv.*

récemment; tout dernièrement; **as r. as yester-day,** pas plus tard qu'hier; **until quite r.,** jusque dans ces derniers temps.

receptacle [ri'septəkl], *s.* récipient *m.*

reception [ri'sepʃ(ə)n], *s.* **1.** (*a*) réception *f*; (*b*) (*in hotel, etc.*) **r. desk,** la réception. **2.** accueil *m.* **3.** réception (officielle). **4.** *Rad: etc:* **the r. is poor in the evenings,** le soir, la réception est médiocre; **re'ceptionist,** *s.* hôtesse *f* (à la réception, dans un hôtel, à un aéroport, etc.); réceptionniste *mf* (dans un salon de beauté, chez un médicin, etc.).

receptive [ri'septiv], *a.* réceptif; **recep'tivity,** *s.* réceptivité *f.*

recess, *pl.* **-esses** [ri'ses, -esiz], *s.* **1.** vacances *fpl* (des tribunaux). **2.** (*a*) recoin *m*; (*b*) enfoncement *m* (de muraille); embrasure *f* (de fenêtre); niche *f*; **re'cession,** *s. Ind: Com: etc.* récession *f.*

recipe ['resipi], *s. Cu:* recette *f.*

recipient [ri'sipiənt], *s.* **1.** (*object*) récipient *m.* **2.** (*pers.*) donataire *mf*; destinataire *mf* (d'une lettre); bénéficiaire *mf* (d'un chèque).

reciprocate [ri'siprəkeit], *v.* **1.** *v.tr.* (*a*) se rendre mutuellement (des services); (*b*) payer de retour (un sentiment); **to r. s.o.'s good wishes,** souhaiter la pareille à qn. **2.** *v.i.* retourner le compliment; **re'ciprocal,** *a.* réciproque, mutuel; **-ally,** *adv.* réciproquement, mutuellement; **reciprocity** [resi'prɔsiti], *s.* réciprocité *f.*

recite [ri'sait], *v.tr.* **1.** (*a*) réciter, déclamer; (*b*) *v.i.* réciter une pièce. **2.** énumérer (des dates, des détails); **re'cital,** *s.* **1.** récit *m* (d'un incident). **2.** récitation *f* (d'une poésie). **3.** *Mus:* récital, **-als** *m*; **reci'tation,** *s.* récitation *f*; **recitative** [resitə'ti:v], *a. Mus:* récitatif *m.*

reckless ['reklis], *a.* insouciant (**of,** de); téméraire; *Aut:* **r. driving,** conduite téméraire; **-ly,** *adv.* témérairement; avec insouciance; **he spends r.,** il dépense sans compter; **'recklessness,** *s.* insouciance *f* (**of,** de); imprudence *f*, témérité *f.*

reckon ['rek(ə)n], (*a*) *v.tr. & i.* compter, calculer; (*b*) *v.tr.* estimer, juger; (*c*) *v.tr.* **to r. s.o. as . . .,** considérer qn comme . . .; (*d*) *v.i.* **to r. on sth.,** compter sur qch.; **to r. with s.o.,** avoir à compter avec qn; **a man to be reckoned with,** un homme avec qui il faut compter; **'reckoning,** *s.* (*a*) compte *m*, calcul *m*; (*b*) **to be out in one's r.,** s'être trompé dans son calcul; **to the best of my r.,** autant que j'en puis juger; **day of r.,** jour *m* d'expiation.

reclaim [ri'kleim], *v.tr.* (*a*) **to r. land,** détricher du terrain; mettre (un terrain) en valeur; (*b*) récupérer (un sous-produit); **recla'mation** [reklə-], *s.* (*a*) défrichement *m* (d'un terrain); mise *f* en valeur; assèchement *m* (des terres); (*b*) récupération *f* (des sous-produits).

recline [ri'klain]. **1.** *v.tr.* reposer, appuyer (sa tête sur qch.). **2.** *v.i.* être couché; (*of head*) reposer, être appuyé (**on,** sur); **reclining on a couch,** étendu sur un canapé.

recluse [ri'klu:s], *s:* reclus, -use; solitaire *mf.*

recognize ['rekəgnaiz], *v.tr.* reconnaître (qn, qch.); **to r. one's mistake,** reconnaître, admettre, son erreur; **I don't r. you,** je ne vous remets pas; **to r. s.o. by his walk,** reconnaître qn à sa démarche; **recog'nition,** *s.* reconnaissance *f*; **to alter sth. beyond r.,** changer qch. au point de le rendre méconnaissable; *Av:* **r. light,** feu *m* d'identification; **'recog'nizable,** *a.* reconnaissable; **not r.,** méconnaissable; **recognizance** [ri'kɔgnizəns], *s. Jur:* **1.** caution personnelle; engagement *m* (par-devant le tribunal). **2.** somme fournie à titre de cautionnement; **'recognized,** *a.* reconnu, admis, reçu; **the r. term,** le terme consacré; *Com:* **r. agent,** agent accrédité.

recoil. I. ['ri:kɔil], *s.* recul *m* (d'une arme à feu). **II.** *v.i.* [ri:'kɔil]. **1.** (*a*) (*of spring*) se détendre; (*b*) (*of firearm*) reculer. **2.** (*of pers.*) reculer (**from,** devant); se révolter (**from,** contre).

recollect [rekə'lekt], *v.tr.* se rappeler; se souvenir de (qch.); **I don't r. you,** je ne vous remets pas; **as far as I r.,** autant qu'il m'en souvienne; **reco'llection,** *s.* souvenir *m*, mémoire *f*; **to the best of my r.,** autant que je m'en souvienne.

recommend [rekə'mend], *v.tr.* recommander; conseiller (à qn de faire qch.); **she has little to r. her,** elle n'a pas grand-chose pour elle; **not to be recommended,** à déconseiller; **reco'mmendable,** *a.* (chose) à conseiller; **recommen'dation,** *s.* recommandation *f.*

recompense ['rekəmpens]. **I.** *s.* **1.** récompense *f* (**for,** de). **2.** dédommagement *m* (**for,** de). **II.** *v.tr.* **1.** récompenser (**s.o. for sth.,** qn de qch.). **2.** dédommager (**s.o. for sth.,** qn de qch.).

reconcile ['rekənsail], *v.tr.* **1.** réconcilier (deux personnes); **to become reconciled,** se réconcilier. **2. to r. oneself to sth.,** se résigner à qch. **3.** concilier, faire accorder (des faits); **recon'cilable,** *a.* conciliable, accordable (**with,** avec); **reconcili'ation** [-sili-], *s.* **1.** réconciliation *f*, rapprochement *m* (entre deux personnes). **2.** conciliation *f* (d'opinions contraires).

recondite ['rekəndait], *a.* (*of knowledge*) abstrus, profond; (*of style*) obscur.

recondition ['ri:kən'diʃ(ə)n], *v.tr.* rénover; remettre à neuf, en état; *Com:* reconditionner; *Aut: etc:* **reconditioned engine,** moteur révisé.

reconnaissance [ri'kɔnis(ə)ns], *s. Mil: etc:* reconnaissance *f*; **r. aircraft,** avion *m* de reconnaissance; **to make a r.,** explorer le terrain.

reconnoitre [rekə'nɔitər], *v.tr.* reconnaître (le

terrain); *v.i.* faire une reconnaissance; **reco'nnoitring,** *s.* reconnaissance *f.*

reconsider |'ri:kən'sidər|, *v.tr.* 1. considérer de nouveau, repenser (une question). 2. revenir sur (une décision).

reconstruct ['ri:kən'strʌkt], *v.tr.* 1. reconstruire (un édifice). 2. **to r. a crime,** reconstituer (un crime); **recon'struction,** *s.* 1. reconstruction *f.* 2. reconstitution *f* (d'un crime).

record. I. *s.* ['rekɔ:d]. 1. *Jur:* (a) enregistrement *m* (d'un fait); **to be on r.,** être enregistré; *F:* **off the r.,** en secret, entre nous; (b) minute *f* (d'un acte). 2. (a) note *f,* mention *f;* (b) registre *m;* **r. of attendances,** registre de présence; **to make, keep, a r. of** (sth.), noter (qch.). 3. *pl.* archives *f,* annales *f.* 4. monument *m,* document *m,* souvenir *m* (de qch.). 5. carrière *f,* dossier *m* (de qn); **service r.,** état *m* de service; **his past r.,** sa conduite passée; **police r.,** casier *m* judiciaire. 6. *Sp:* record *m;* **at r. speed,** à une vitesse record; **to break the r.,** battre le record. 7. disque *m;* **long-playing r.,** microsillon *m.* II. *v.tr.* [ri'kɔ:d]. 1. enregistrer (un fait); **to r. one's vote,** voter. 2. (*of instrument*) enregistrer (i) **on a record,** sur disque, (ii) **on tape,** sur bande; **re'corder,** *s.* 1. *Jur:* = juge *m.* 2. **tape r.,** magnétophone *m; Aut:* **trip r.,** enregistreur *m* de distance. 3. *Mus:* flûte *f* à bec; **re'cording.** 1. *a.* enregistreur, -euse. 2. *s.* (a) enregistrement *m;* (b) narration *f,* relation *f;* **'record-player,** *s.* tourne-disque *m.*

recount¹ [ri'kaunt], *v.tr.* raconter.

recount². I. *v.tr.* ['ri:'kaunt], recompter. II. *s.* ['ri:kaunt] *Pol:* nouveau dépouillement du scrutin.

recoup [ri'ku:p], *v.tr.* **to r. one's losses,** se dédommager de ses pertes.

recourse [ri'kɔ:s], *s.* 1. recours *m;* **to have r. to sth.,** recourir à qch. 2. expédient *m.*

recover¹ [ri'kʌvər], *v.tr.* 1. recouvrer, retrouver (un objet perdu); **to r. one's breath,** reprendre haleine. 2. regagner (de l'argent perdu); rentrer en possession de (ses biens); **to r. lost time,** rattraper le temps perdu; **to r. lost ground,** regagner le terrain perdu; se rattraper. 3. **to r. one's health,** *v.i.* **to r.,** guérir; **to r. from an illness,** se remettre d'une maladie; **to r. from one's astonishment,** revenir, se remettre, de son étonnement. 4. **to r. oneself,** *v.i.* **to r.,** se remettre, se ressaisir; **re'coverable,** *a.* récupérable; **re'covery,** *s.* 1. recouvrement *m* (d'un objet perdu); *Ind:* récupération *f* (de sous-produits). 2. (a) rétablissement *m,* guérison *f* (de qn); **to be past r.,** être dans un état désespéré (b) redressement *m* (économique).

recover² ['ri:'kʌvər], *v.tr.* recouvrir (le canapé).

recreation [rekri:'eiʃ(ə)n], *s.* récréation *f,* divertissement *m;* **r. ground,** *Sch:* terrain *m* de

jeux, de sports; **covered r. ground,** préau *m.*

recrimination [rikrimi'neiʃ(ə)n], *s. usu. pl.* récrimination(s) *f(pl);* contre-accusation(s) *f(pl);* **recriminatory** [ri'kriminət(ə)ri], *a.* récriminatoire.

recruit [ri'kru:t]. I. *s.* recrue *f; F:* un bleu. II. *v.tr.* recruter (une armée, des partisans); **re'cruiting,** *s. Mil:* recrutement *m.*

rectangle ['rektæŋgl], *s.* rectangle *m;* **rec'tangular,** *a.* rectangulaire.

rectify ['rektifai], *v.tr.* rectifier, corriger (une erreur); réparer (un oubli); **recti'fiable,** *a.* rectifiable; **rectifi'cation,** *s.* rectification *f.*

rector ['rektər], *s.* 1. *Ecc:* = curé *m.* 2. *Sch:* recteur *m* (d'une université); **'rectory,** *s.* = presbytère *m.*

recumbent [ri'kʌmbənt], *a.* couché, étendu; (*on tomb*) **r. figure,** gisant *m.*

recuperate [ri'kju:pəreit]. 1. *v.tr. Ind: etc:* récupérer (la chaleur perdue, etc.). 2. *v.i.* rétablir, se remettre (d'une maladie); **recupe'ration,** *s.* 1. *Ind:* récupération *f.* 2. *Med:* rétablissement *m.*

recur [ri'kə:r], *v.i.* (**recurred**) se reproduire, se renouveler; **re'currence** [-'kʌr-], *s.* réapparition *f,* renouvellement *m,* retour *m; Med:* récidive *f* (d'une maladie); **to be of frequent r.,** revenir fréquemment; **re'current** [-'kʌr-], *a.* périodique; qui revient souvent; *Mth:* **r. series,** série récurrente; **re'curring,** *a.* périodique.

recycle [ri:'saikl], *v.tr.* recycler (le papier de rebut).

red [red], *a. & s.* (a) rouge (*m*); (*of hair*) roux, *f.* rousse; **to turn, go, r.,** rougir; **to see r.,** voir rouge, se mettre en colère; **to be caught r.handed,** être pris en flagrant délit; *Adm:* **r. tape,** (i) bolduc *m* (rouge) (des documents officiels); (ii) *F:* bureaucratie *f,* paperasserie *f;* (b) *Pol:* rouge (*mf*); communiste (*mf*); **'redbrick,** *a. F: Sch:* **r. university,** université provinciale moderne; **'redden,** *v.i.* (*of pers.*) rougir; (*of sky*) rougeoyer; (*of leaves*) roussir; **'reddish,** *a.* rougeâtre; **'redness,** *s.* rougeur *f;* **'redwood,** *s. Bot:* séquoia *m.*

redeem [ri'di:m], *v.tr.* 1. racheter, rembourser (une obligation); amortir (une dette); purger (une hypothèque); **to r. one's watch** (from pawn), retirer sa montre. 2. tenir, accomplir (sa promesse). 3. libérer, racheter (qn, qch.); **his good points r. his faults,** ses qualités compensent ses défauts; **re'deemer,** *s.* **the R.,** le Rédempteur; **re'deeming,** *a.* rédempteur; qui fait compensation (pour un défaut); **re'demption,** *s.* 1. *Fin:* remboursement *m,* amortissement *m.* 2. rédemption *f* (du genre humain); **crime past r.,** crime irréparable.

redirect ['ri:dai'rekt, -di-], *v.tr.* faire suivre (une lettre, etc.).

redouble [riːˈdʌbl], *v.tr.* redoubler (ses efforts, etc.).

redoubt [riˈdaut], *s. Fort:* redoute *f*, réduit *m*.

redoubtable [riˈdautəbl], *a.* redoutable, formidable.

redound [riˈdaund], *v.i.* contribuer (**to**, à); **this will r. to your credit**, votre réputation y gagnera.

redress [riˈdres]. I. *s.* redressement *m*, réparation *f* (d'un tort); réforme *f* (d'un abus); **legal r.**, réparation légale. II. *v.tr.* 1. rétablir (l'équilibre). 2. redresser, réparer (un tort); corriger, réformer (un abus).

reduce [riˈdjuːs], *v.tr.* 1. (*a*) réduire, rapetisser; (*in length*) raccourcir; (*b*) réduire (la température); diminuer (le prix); **to r. speed**, ralentir la marche; *Ind:* **to r. (the) output**, ralentir, freiner, la production. 2. (*a*) **to r. sth. to ashes**, réduire qch. en cendres; (*b*) **to r. a fraction to its lowest terms**, ramener une fraction à sa plus simple expression. 3. **to r. s.o. to silence**, faire taire qn. 4. *Med:* **to r. a fracture, a dislocation**, réduire une fracture, une luxation; **reˈduced**, *a.* réduit; **at r. prices**, au rabais; en solde; **in r. circumstances**, dans la gêne; **reˈduction**, *s.* réduction *f*, diminution *f* (des prix); baisse *f* (de température); *Com:* rabais *m*; **to make a r. on an article**, faire une remise sur un article.

redundant [riˈdʌndənt], *a.* surabondant; (personnel) superflu; (ouvriers) en surnombre; **reˈdundancy**, *s.* surplus *m*; excédent *m*; (*of workers*) surnombre *m*.

re-echo [riː(ˈ)ekou]. 1. *v.tr.* répéter, renvoyer (un son). 2. *v.i.* retentir, résonner.

reed [riːd], *s.* 1. *Bot:* roseau *m*; jonc *m* à balais. 2. *Mus:* (*a*) pipeau *m*; (*b*) anche *f* (de hautbois, etc.); (*in orchestra*) **r. instruments, the reeds**, les instruments *m* à anche; **ˈreedy**, *a.* 1. couvert de roseaux. 2. **r. voice**, voix (i) flûtée, (ii) ténue.

reef¹ [riːf], *v.tr.* **to r. a sail**, prendre un ris dans une voile.

reef², *s.* 1. récif *m*; **coral r.**, récif de corail; **submerged r.**, récif sous-marin; écueil *m*, brisant *m*. 2. *Gold-min:* filon *m* de quartz aurifère.

reek [riːk]. I. *s.* odeur forte, âcre; **r. of tobacco**, relent *m* de tabac. II. *v.i.* exhaler une mauvaise odeur; **to r. of garlic**, puer, empester, l'ail.

reel [riːl]. I. *s.* 1. *Tex: etc:* (*for spinning, sewing-machines*) dévidoir *m*, bobine *f*. 2. moulinet *m* (de canne à pêche); (**straight**) **off the r.**, (tout) d'une traite; d'affilée. 3. bobine (de coton, etc.). 4. *Danc:* branle écossais. II. *v.* 1. *v.tr.* dévider, bobiner (le fil). 2. *v.i.* (*a*) tournoyer; **my head's reeling**, la tête me tourne; (*b*) chanceler; (*of drunken man*) tituber.

re-elect [ˈriːiˈlekt], *v.tr.* réélire; **ˈre-eˈlection**, *s.* réélection *f*.

re-eligible [ˈriːˈelidʒibl], *a.* rééligible.

re-embark [ˈriːimˈbɑːk], *v.tr. & i.* rembarquer; **ˈre-embarˈkation**, *s.* rembarquement *m*.

re-enter [ˈriːˈentər]. 1. *v.i.* (*a*) rentrer; (*b*) **to re-e. for an exam**, se présenter de nouveau à un examen. 2. *v.tr.* rentrer dans (un endroit); **ˈre-ˈentry**, *s.* rentrée *f*.

refectory [riˈfektəri], *s.* réfectoire *m*.

refer [riˈfəːr], *v.* (**referred**) 1. *v.tr.* (*a*) rapporter, rattacher (un fait à une cause); (*b*) **to r. a matter to s.o.**, s'en référer à qn d'une question; **to r. a matter to a tribunal**, soumettre une affaire à un tribunal; (*c*) **to r. s.o. to s.o.**, renvoyer qn à qn. 2. *v.i.* (*a*) se référer (à une autorité); (*b*) **to r. to sth.**, se rapporter, avoir rapport, à qch.; (*c*) faire allusion (à qn); **I'm not referring to you**, je ne parle pas de vous; (*of statement*) **to r. to sth.**, se rapporter, avoir rapport, à qch.; **to r. to a fact**, faire mention d'un fait; **let's not r. to it again**, n'en reparlons plus; **referee** [refəˈriː], *s.* (*a*) *Sp:* (*F:* **ref.**) arbitre *m*; (*b*) **to give s.o. as a r.**, se recommander de qn; **reference** [ˈref(ə)rəns], *s.* 1. (*a*) renvoi *m*, référence *f* (d'une question à une autorité); (*b*) compétence *f*, pouvoirs (d'un tribunal); **terms of r.**, mandat *m* (d'une commission, etc.). 2. **r. library**, bibliothèque *f* de référence; **r. book, work of r.**, livre *m*, ouvrage *m*, de référence; **with r. to my letter**, me référant à, comme suite à, ma lettre; **r. was made to this conversation**, on a fait allusion à cette conversation. 3. renvoi *m* (dans un livre); (*on map*) **r. point**, point coté. 4. **to give a r. about s.o.**, fournir des renseignements sur qn; **to have good references**, avoir de bonnes recommandations; **to give s.o. as a r.**, se recommander de qn; **refeˈrendum**, *pl.* **-ˈrenda**, **-ˈrendums**, *s. Pol: etc:* référendum *m*.

refill. I. *v.tr.* [ˈriːˈfil], remplir (qch.) (à nouveau). II. *s.* [ˈriːfil], objet *m* de remplacement, de rechange; recharge *f*, cartouche *f* (d'encre, etc.); pile *f* de rechange.

refine [riˈfain], *v.tr.* raffiner; affiner (les métaux); **reˈfined**, *a.* 1. (or) fin, affiné; (sucre) raffiné. 2. (goût) raffiné; (homme) cultivé, distingué; **reˈfinement**, *s.* raffinement *m* (d'une personne, des métaux); **reˈfining**, *s.* affinage *m* (des métaux); raffinage *m* (du sucre, du pétrole); **reˈfinery**, *s.* raffinerie *f*.

reflate [ˈriːˈfleit], *v.tr.* relancer (l'économie); **ˈreˈflation**, *s.* reflation *f*.

reflect [riˈflekt]. 1. *v.tr.* (*a*) (*of surface*) réfléchir, refléter (la lumière, une image); renvoyer (la chaleur, la lumière); (*b*) **action that reflects credit on s.o.**, action qui fait honneur à qn. 2. *v.i.* (*a*) méditer (**on, upon**, sur); réfléchir (à, sur); (*b*) (*of action*) faire du tort (**on s.o.**, à qn); nuire à la réputation de (qn); **reˈflection**, *s.* 1. réfléchissement *m*, réflexion *f* (de la lumière, etc.). **2.** réflexion, reflet *m*, image *f*. **3. to cast reflections on s.o.**, critiquer qn. **4. on r.**, (toute) réflexion faite; **to do sth. without due r.**, faire qch, sans avoir suffisamment réfléchi. **5.** *pl.* **reflections,** considérations *f*, pensées *f*; **re'flector,** *s.* réflecteur *m*; *Adm:* (*on highways*) (**cat's-eye**) **r.**, catadioptre *m*, cataphote *m*.

reflex ['ri:fleks]. **I.** *s. Med:* réflexe *m*. **II.** *a.* **1.** (*of movement*) réflexe. **2.** *Phot:* **single lens r.** (camera), (appareil *m*) reflex (*m*). **3.** *Mth:* **r. angle,** angle rentrant.

reflexive [ri'fleksiv], *a.* & *s. Gram:* (verbe) réfléchi, pronominal; **r. pronoun,** pronom personnel réfléchi.

refloat ['ri:'flout], *v.tr.* renflouer, (re)mettre à flot (un navire échoué).

reform [ri'fɔ:m]. **I.** *v.* **1.** *v.tr.* (*a*) réformer (un abus); apporter des réformes à (une administration); (*b*) réformer, corriger (qn). **2.** *v.i.* se réformer, se corriger. **II.** *s.* réforme *f*; **refor'mation** [refə-], *s.* réformation *f*, réforme *f*; *Ecc:* **the R.**, la Réforme; **re'formatory,** *s.* maison *f* de correction; **re'former,** *s.* réformateur, -trice.

refractory [ri'fræktəri], *a.* (*of pers.*) réfractaire, indocile, mutin, insoumis.

refrain¹ [ri'frein], *s. Mus:* refrain *m*.

refrain², *v.i.* se retenir, s'abstenir (**from, de**); **he could not r. from smiling,** il ne put s'empêcher de sourire.

refresh [ri'freʃ]. **1.** *v.tr.* (*a*) rafraîchir; (*of rest*) délasser (qn); **to awake refreshed,** s'éveiller bien reposé; (*b*) rafraîchir (la mémoire); (*c*) (*of rain, etc.*) rafraîchir (l'air). **2.** *v.pr.* **to r. oneself,** se rafraîchir, se reposer; se restaurer; **re'fresher,** *s.* **1.** *F:* **let's have a r.**, allons boire un pot. **2.** *Sch:* **course,** cours *m* de perfectionnement; **re'freshing,** *a.* rafraîchissant; (sommeil) reposant; **re'freshment,** *s.* rafraîchissement *m*; *Rail:* **r. room,** buffet *m*.

refrigerator [ri'fridʒəreitər], *s.* réfrigérateur *m*; Frigidaire *m* (*R.t.m*:), *F:* frigo *m*; **re'frigerate,** *v.tr.* réfrigérer; frigorifier; **refrige'ration,** *s.* réfrigération *f*.

refuel ['ri:'fjuəl], *v.i.* (**refuelled**) *Nau: Av: Aut:* se réapprovisionner, se ravitailler, en combustible; faire le plein d'essence.

refuge ['refju:dʒ], *s.* **1.** refuge *m*, abri *m* (**from,** contre); **to take r.**, se réfugier. **2.** lieu de refuge, d'asile; (**mountain**) **r.**, refuge; **refu'gee,** *s.* réfugié, -ée.

refund. I. *v.tr.* [ri:'fʌnd], (*a*) rembourser (de l'argent) (à qn); (*b*) ristourner (un paiement en trop); restituer (de l'argent). **II.** *s.* ['ri:fʌnd], (*a*) remboursement *m*; (*b*) ristourne *f*.

refurnish ['ri:'fə:niʃ], *v.tr.* meubler de neuf; remeubler (un appartement); remonter (sa maison).

refuse¹ ['refju:s], *s.* rebut *m* (de boucherie); déchets *mpl* (du marché, etc.); **household r.**, ordures ménagères; **town r.**, ordures; **garden r.**, détritus *m* de jardin; **r. bin,** poubelle *f*; **r. dump,** décharge publique.

refuse² [ri'fju:z], *v.tr.* **1.** refuser (une offre, un don). **2.** (*a*) rejeter, repousser (une requête); **to r. s.o. sth.**, refuser qch. à qn; (*b*) **to r. to do sth.**, refuser de faire qch.; se refuser à faire qch.; **re'fusal,** *s.* **1.** refus *m*; **to give a flat r.**, refuser (tout) net. **2.** droit *m* de refuser; **to have the first r. of sth.**, avoir la première offre de qch.

refute [ri'fju:t], *v.tr.* réfuter; **to r. a statement,** démontrer la fausseté d'une déclaration.

regain [ri(:)'gein], *v.tr.* regagner; recouvrer (la liberté); **to r. possession of sth.**, rentrer en possession de qch.; **to r. consciousness,** reprendre connaissance, revenir à soi.

regal ['ri:g(ə)l], *a.* royal; **-ally,** *adv.* royalement; en roi.

regale [ri'geil], *v.tr.* régaler (**s.o. with a good meal,** qn d'un bon repas).

regard [ri'gɑ:d]. **I.** *s.* **1. with r. to . . .**, quant à . . . . **2.** égard *m* (**to, for,** à, pour); attention *f* (**to, for,** à); **to have no r. for human life,** faire peu de cas de la vie humaine; **having r. to . . .**, si l'on tient compte de . . . . **3.** (*a*) égard, respect *m*, estime *f*; **to have (a) great r. for s.o.**, tenir qn en haute estime; **out of r. for s.o.**, par égard pour qn; (*b*) *pl.* **give my kind regards to your brother,** faites mes amitiés à votre frère. **II.** *v.tr.* **1. to r. sth. as a crime,** considérer qch comme un crime; **to r. sth. with suspicion,** avoir des soupçons *m* au sujet de qch. **2. con cerner; as regards . . .**, pour ce qui regarde . . ., en ce qui concerne . . .; **re'garding** *prep.* à l'égard de; concernant; quant à; **r. your enquiry,** en ce qui concerne votre demande; **re'gardless,** *a.* peu soigneux (**of,** de); **r. of expense,** sans regarder à la dépense; **re'gardlessly,** *adv.* avec insouciance.

regatta [ri'gætə], *s.* régates *fpl*.

regenerate [ri'dʒenəreit]. **1.** *v.tr.* régénérer. **2.** *v.i.* se régénérer; **regene'ration,** *s.* régénération *f*.

regent ['ri:dʒənt], *s.* régent, -ente; **'regency,** *s.* régence *f*.

regime [rei'ʒi:m], *s.* régime *m*; **the new industrial r.**, le nouveau régime industriel; *Pol:* **the parliamentary r.**, le régime parlementaire; **the present r.**, le régime actuel.

regiment ['redʒimənt], *s.* régiment *m*; **regi'mental,** *a.* du régiment, de régiment; régimentaire.

region ['ri:dʒ(ə)n], *s.* région *f*; **the Arctic regions,** les terres du grand Nord; **the car cost in the r. of £1000,** la voiture a coûté dans le mille livres sterling; **'regional,** *a.* régional; **'regionalism,** *s.* régionalisme *m*.

register [ˈredʒistər]. I. s. 1. registre m; matricule f. 2. Mus: registre (d'un instrument, de la voix); étendue f (de la voix). 3. compteur m (kilométrique, etc.); **cash r.**, caisse (enregistreuse, automatique). II. v. 1. v.tr. (a) enregistrer; inscrire (un nom); **to r. a birth,** déclarer une naissance; (b) **to r. luggage,** enregistrer des bagages; **to r. a letter,** recommander une lettre; (c) (of thermometer) marquer; F: **it didn't r.** (with her), elle n'a rien pigé. 2. v.i. s'inscrire sur le registre (d'un hôtel, etc.); ˈregistered, a. enregistré, immatriculé; Com: **r. pattern,** modèle déposé; P.T.T: **r. parcel, letter,** colis recommandé, lettre recommandée; **State r. nurse,** infirmière diplômée d'État; **regisˈtrar,** s. 1. Jur: greffier m. 2. officier m de l'état civil. 3. secrétaire m et archiviste m (d'une université); **regisˈtration,** s. enregistrement m, inscription f, immatriculation f (d'un véhicule, etc.); recommandation f (d'une lettre); **r. of a trade-mark,** dépôt m d'une marque de fabrique; **r. of luggage,** enregistrement des bagages; Aut: etc: **r. number,** numéro minéralogique; **r. plate,** plaque f d'immatriculation; **a car with r. number SPF 342,** une voiture immatriculée SPF 342; ˈregistry, s. **r.** (office), bureau m de l'état civil; **to be married at a r. office** = se marier civilement.

regret [riˈgret]. I. s. regret m; **to have no regrets,** n'avoir aucun regret; **I say so with r.,** je le dis à regret; **much to my r.,** à mon grand regret. II. v.tr. (regretted) regretter; **I r. to have to tell you . . .,** je regrette d'avoir à vous dire . . .; **I r. to have to inform you that . . .,** j'ai le regret d'avoir à vous annoncer que . . .; **we very much r. to hear . . .,** nous sommes désolés d'apprendre . . .; reˈgretful, a. (of pers.) plein de regrets; -fully, adv. avec regret, à regret; reˈgrettable, a. regrettable.

regular [ˈregjulər]. I. a. régulier. 1. **as r. as clockwork,** exact comme une horloge; **my r. time for going to bed,** l'heure habituelle à laquelle je me couche; **to do sth. as a r. thing,** faire qch. régulièrement; **r. staff,** employés permanents. 2. réglé, rangé; **man of r. habits,** homme rangé dans ses habitudes. 3. (a) dans les règles; réglementaire; **the r. expression,** l'expression consacrée; (b) ordinaire; normal; (c) Gram: (verbe) régulier; (d) **r. troops,** troupes régulières; **r. officer,** officier de carrière. 4. F: (intensive) vrai, véritable; **a r. hero,** un vrai héros; **a r. swindle,** une véritable escroquerie; -ly, adv. régulièrement. II. s. 1. militaire m de carrière. 2. F: habitué, -ée; bon(ne) client(e); (of pub) = pilier m de café; **reguˈlarity,** s. régularité f; **r. of attendance,** assiduité f; ˈregularize, v.tr. régulariser (un document, une situation); ˈregulate,

v.tr. régler, ajuster (une montre, une machine); **reguˈlation,** s. 1. réglage m (d'une machine, etc.). 2. (a) règlement m, arrêté m, ordonnance f; (b) attrib. réglementaire; Aut: etc: **r. lighting,** les feux m réglementaires; ˈregulator, s. régulateur m.

rehabilitate [riːhəˈbiliteit], v.tr. réhabiliter; réadapter (des mutilés, des réfugiés, des enfants inadaptés, etc.); **rehabiliˈtation,** s. réhabilitation f; rééducation f (des mutilés); réadaptation f.

rehash. I. s. [ˈriːhæʃ], réchauffé m. II. v.tr. [riːˈhæʃ], réchauffer (un vieux conte, etc.).

rehearse [riˈhəːs], v.tr. Th: répéter (une pièce); reˈhearsal, s. Th: répétition f; **the dress r.,** la (répétition) générale; l'avant-première f.

reign [rein]. I. s. règne m; **in the r. of George VI,** sous le règne de Georges VI. II. v.i. régner (over, sur).

reimburse [riːimˈbəːs], v.tr. rembourser; reimˈbursement, s. remboursement m.

rein [rein], s. rêne f; guide f.

reindeer [ˈreindiər], s. inv. Z: renne m.

reinforce [riːinˈfɔːs], v.tr. renforcer; consolider (un bâtiment); entretoiser (deux poutres); arc-bouter (un mur); **reinforced concrete,** béton armé; reinˈforcement, s. 1. renforcement m, renforçage m (d'un bâtiment); armature f (du béton). 2. Mil: usu. pl. **to await reinforcements,** attendre des renforts m.

reinstate [ˈriːinˈsteit], v.tr. 1. réintégrer (qn dans ses fonctions); rétablir (un fonctionnaire). 2. remettre, rétablir (qch.); reinˈstatement, s. 1. réintégration f (de qn). 2. rétablissement m (de qch.).

reiterate [riːˈitəreit], v.tr. réitérer, répéter; reiteˈration, s. réitération f, répétition f.

reject. I. v.tr. [riˈdʒekt], rejeter, repousser (qch.); refuser (qch., un candidat); Ind: **to r. a casting,** mettre une pièce au rebut. II. s. [ˈriːdʒekt], pièce f de rebut; **export r.,** article impropre, non destiné à l'exportation; reˈjection, s. rejet m; refus m (d'une offre).

rejoice [riˈdʒɔis], v.i. (a) se réjouir (at, over, de); (b) **to r. in sth.,** jouir de qch.; posséder qch.; reˈjoicing, s. réjouissance f, allégresse f.

rejoin[1] [riˈdʒɔin], v.i. répliquer, répondre.

rejoin[2] [ˈriːˈdʒɔin]. 1. v.tr. rejoindre (qn); **to r. one's ship,** rallier le bord. 2. v.i. (of lines, etc.) se réunir, se rejoindre.

rejuvenation [ridʒuːviˈneiʃ(ə)n], s. rajeunissement m.

rekindle [ˈriːˈkindl]. 1. v.tr. rallumer (le feu); ranimer (l'espoir). 2. v.i. se rallumer.

relapse [riˈlæps]. I. s. Med: rechute f. II. v.i. avoir une rechute.

relate [riˈleit]. 1. v.tr. raconter, conter; **to r. one's adventures,** faire le récit de ses aventures. 2. (a) v.tr. rapporter, rattacher (une espèce à une famille); établir un rapport entre (deux faits); (b) v.i. se rapporter, avoir rapport (to, à); re'lated, a. 1. ayant rapport (to, à); r. ideas, idées f connexes. 2. (of pers.) apparenté (to, à); parent (to, de); (by marriage) allié (to, à); he's r. to us, il est notre parent; they are closely r., ils sont proches parents; re'lation, s. 1. relation f, récit m (d'événements). 2. (a) relation, rapport m; in r. to . . ., relativement à . . .; par rapport à . . .; Adm: Com: public relations, service m des relations avec le public, des relations publiques; that bears no r. to the present situation, cela n'a rien à faire avec la situation actuelle; (b) pl. to enter into relations with s.o., entrer en rapport, en relations, avec qn. 3. parent, -ente; r. by marriage, parent, -ente, par alliance; is he a r. of yours? est-il de vos parents? re'lationship, s. 1. rapport m (entre deux personnes ou deux choses). 2. parenté f; lien m de parenté; blood r., proximité f de sang.

relative ['relətiv]. 1. a. (a) relatif, qui se rapporte (to, à); (b) (of terms) relatif; (c) Gram: r. pronoun, pronom relatif. 2. s. parent, -ente; -ly, adv. (a) relativement (to, à); par rapport (à); (b) she's r. happy, somme toute elle est assez heureuse; rela'tivity, s. relativité f; Ph: theory of r., théorie f de la relativité.

relax [ri'læks]. 1. v.tr. (a) relâcher (la discipline, les muscles); détendre (l'esprit); (b) mitiger (une loi, une peine). 2. v.i. (a) se relâcher, se détendre; his face relaxed into a smile, son visage se détendit et il sourit; (b) (of pers.) se détendre, se décontracter, se relaxer; to r. for an hour, prendre une heure de délassement; F: faire une heure de détente f; relax'ation, s. 1. (a) relâchement m (des muscles, de la discipline); (b) mitigation f (d'une peine). 2. délassement m, détente f, relaxation f, décontraction f; to take some r., se détendre, se délasser; re'laxed, a. to be quite r., être complètement décontracté; Med: r. throat, pharyngite subaiguë; re'laxing, a. (climat) débilitant, mou; (médicament) relâchant; (séjour) décontractant, relaxant, reposant.

relay. I. v.tr. [ri'lei], relayer; transmettre (un message) par relais; T.V: etc: the programme was relayed by the Peak radio relay station, on a diffusé le programme par la station hertzienne du Pic. II. s. ['ri:lei]. 1. relai m; relève f; to work in relays, se relayer; Sp: r. race, course f de, à, relais. 2. Rad: radiodiffusion relayée; r. station, relai hertzien.

release [ri'li:s]. I. s. 1. (a) délivrance f (from, de); décharge f, libération f (from an obligation, d'une obligation); (b) élargissement m, mise f en liberté (d'un prisonnier); order of r., (ordre de) levée f d'écrou; (c) Aut: mise en vente (d'un nouveau modèle); Cin: mise en circulation

(d'un film). 2. Av: lâchage m (d'une bombe); lancement m (d'un parachute); dégagement m (d'un frein). 3. Com: acquit m, quittance f. II. v.tr. 1. (a) décharger, acquitter, libérer; to r. s.o. from his promise, rendre sa parole à qn; (b) libérer, élargir (un prisonnier); (c) mettre en vente (une nouvelle voiture, etc.); mettre (un film) en circulation. 2. Av: lâcher (une bombe); lancer (un parachute); desserrer (le frein); to r. one's hold, lâcher prise; Phot: to r. the shutter, déclencher l'obturateur.

relegate ['religeit], v.tr. reléguer (un tableau au grenier, etc.).

relent [ri'lent], v.i. se laisser attendrir; revenir sur une décision (sévère); re'lentless, a. implacable, impitoyable; -ly, adv. implacablement, impitoyablement; re'lentlessness, s. inflexibilité f, implacabilité f; acharnement m.

relevant ['relivənt], a. qui a rapport (to, à); pertinent (to, à); à propos (to, de); all r. information, tous renseignements utiles; -ly, adv. pertinemment; 'relevance, s. pertinence f, à-propos m.

reliable [ri'laiəbl], a. sûr; (homme) sérieux; (machine f) d'un fonctionnement sûr; r. firm, maison de confiance; r. guarantee, garantie f solide; -ably, adv. sûrement; d'une manière digne de confiance; relia'bility, s. sûreté f; honnêteté f; sécurité f du fonctionnement, régularité f de marche, fiabilité f (d'une machine).

reliant [ri'laiənt], a. to be r. on s.o., dépendre de qn, compter sur qn; re'liance, s. confiance f.

relic ['relik], s. 1. Ecc: relique f. 2. pl. restes m; relics of the past, vestiges m du passé.

relief¹ [ri'li:f], s. 1. soulagement m; allégement m; to heave a sigh of r., pousser un soupir de soulagement. 2. to go to s.o.'s r., aller au secours de qn; r. fund, caisse f de secours; refugee r. (work), œuvre f de secours aux réfugiés; r. train, train m supplémentaire. 3. Jur: réparation f (d'un grief); redressement m (d'un tort). 4. Mec: etc: r. valve, soupape f de sûreté, de décompression; clapet m de décharge; re'lieve, v.tr. 1. soulager, alléger (les souffrances); tranquilliser (l'esprit de qn); to r. one's feelings, se décharger le cœur; to r. oneself, faire ses besoins, se soulager; to r. boredom, tromper, dissiper, l'ennui. 2. secourir, aider (qn); venir en aide à (qn). 3. to r. s.o. of sth., soulager, délester, qn d'(un fardeau); débarrasser qn d'(un manteau); dégager qn d'(une obligation). 4. Mil: dégager, débloquer (une ville).

relief² , s. Art: relief m; modelé m; to stand out in r., ressortir, se détacher (against, sur); r. map, carte en relief.

religion [ri'lidʒən], s. religion f; culte m; Adm:

confession *f*; **re′ligious**, *a.* (*a*) religieux, pieux, dévot; (*b*) (ordre) religieux; (*c*) (soin) religieux, scrupuleux; **-ly**, *adv.* religieusement; (*a*) pieusement; (*b*) scrupuleusement.

elinquish [ri′liŋkwiʃ], *v.tr.* abandonner (une habitude, tout espoir); renoncer à (un projet); *Jur:* délaisser (un droit, une succession); **re′- linquishment**, *s.* abandon *m*; renonciation *f.*

eliquary [′relikwəri], *s.* reliquaire *m.*

elish [′reliʃ]. **I.** *s.* **1.** (*a*) goût *m*, saveur *f*; (*b*) assaisonnement *m.* **2.** **to eat sth. with r.**, manger qch. de bon appétit; **he used to tell the story with great r.**, il se délectait à raconter cette histoire. **II.** *v.tr.* (*a*) relever le goût de (qch.); (*b*) goûter, savourer (un mets); **to r. doing sth.**, trouver (du) plaisir à faire qch.; **we didn't r. the idea**, l'idée *f* ne nous souriait pas.

:luctant [ri′lʌktənt], *a.* **1. to be r. to do sth.**, être peu disposé à faire qch. **2.** (consentement) accordé à contrecœur; **-ly**, *adv.* à contrecœur; **I say it r.**, il m'en coûte de le dire; **he paid up very r.**, il s'est fait tirer l'oreille pour payer; **re′luctance**, *s.* répugnance *f* (à faire qch.); **to do sth. with r.**, faire qch. à regret, à contrecœur; **to affect r.**, faire des manières *f.*

ly [ri′lai], *v.i.* **to r. (up)on s.o., sth.**, compter sur qn, qch.; se fier à qn.

main [ri′mein], *v.i.* **1.** rester; **the fact remains that . . .**, il n'en est pas moins vrai que . . .; **it remains to be seen whether . . .**, reste à savoir si . . .. **2.** demeurer, rester; (*a*) **to r. sitting**, demeurer assis; **to r. at home**, rester à la maison; **to r. behind**, rester, ne pas partir; (*b*) **let it r. as it is**, laissez-le comme cela. **3.** (*a*) **the weather remains fine**, le temps se maintient au beau; (*b*) *Corr:* **I r., Sir, yours truly**, agréez, Monsieur, mes salutations distinguées; **re′mainder. I.** *s.* **1.** reste *m*, restant *m*; **the r. of his life**, le reste, restant, de sa vie. **2.** (*a*) *coll.* **the r.**, les autres *mf*; (*b*) *pl. Com:* **remainders**, (i) invendus soldés; (ii) (*of books*) solde *m* d'édition. **II.** *v.tr. Com:* solder (une édition); **re′maining**, *a.* **I have four r.**, j'en ai quatre de reste; **the r. travellers**, le reste des voyageurs; **re′mains**, *s.pl.* restes *m*; vestiges *m* ((i) d'un repas, (ii) d'une civilisation, etc.).

nand [ri′mɑnd], *v.tr. Jur:* renvoyer (un prévenu) à une autre audience; **to r. s.o. for a week**, remettre le cas de qn à huitaine; **r. home** = maison *f* d'éducation surveillée.

1ark [ri′mɑ:k]. **I.** *s.* remarque *f*, observation *f*, commentaire *m*; **to make a r.**, (i) faire une observation; (ii) faire une réflexion; **to venture r.**, se permettre un mot; *F: usu. Pej:* **to pass emarks about s.o.**, faire des observations sur n. **II.** *v.* **1.** *v.tr.* remarquer, observer; **it may be emarked that . . .**, constatons que . . .. **2.** *v.i.* aire une remarque, des remarques (on, sur); **I emarked (up)on it to my neighbour**, j'en ai fait

l'observation à mon voisin; **re′markable**, *a.* remarquable; frappant; **our family has never been r.**, notre famille *f* n'a jamais marqué; **-ably**, *adv.* remarquablement.

remedy [′remidi]. **I.** *s.* remède *m.* **II.** *v.tr.* remédier à (qch.); **remedial** [ri′mi:djəl], *a.* (cours d'anglais) destinés à corriger les défauts de langage.

remember [ri′membər], *v.tr.* **1.** (*a*) se souvenir de (qch.); se rappeler (qch.); **if I r. rightly, si j'ai bonne mémoire; as far as I r.**, autant qu'il m'en souvient, qu'il m'en souvienne; **don't you r. me?** vous ne me remettez pas? **it will be something to r. you by**, ce sera un souvenir de vous; (*b*) **that's worth remembering**, cela est à noter; (*c*) **he remembered me in his will**, il ne m'a pas oublié dans son testament. **2. r. me (kindly) to them**, rappelez-moi à leur bon souvenir; **re′membrance**, *s.* souvenir *m*, mémoire *f*; **in r. of s.o.**, en souvenir de qn; **to the best of my r.**, autant qu'il m'en souvienne.

remind [ri′maind], *v.tr.* **to r. s.o. of sth.**, rappeler qch. à qn; **that reminds me!** à propos! **r. me to write to him**, faites-moi penser à lui écrire; **re′minder**, *s.* (*a*) mémento *m*; (*b*) *Com:* (letter of) r., lettre *f* de rappel; **I'll send him a r.**, je vais lui rafraîchir la mémoire; (*c*) *Com:* rappel *m* de compte; rappel d'échéance.

reminiscence [remi′nis(ə)ns], *s.* **1.** réminiscence *f*; souvenir *m.* **2. to write one's reminiscences**, écrire ses souvenirs; **remi′nisce**, *v.i.* raconter ses souvenirs; échanger des souvenirs (**with s.o.**, avec qn); **remi′niscent**, *a.* **r. of s.o., sth.**, qui rappelle, fait penser à, qn, qch.; **-ly**, *adv.* **he smiled r.**, il sourit à ce souvenir.

remiss [ri′mis], *a.* négligent, insouciant; **re′missness**, *s.* négligence *f.*

remission [ri′miʃ(ə)n], *s.* **1. r. of sins**, pardon *m*, rémission *f* des péchés. **2.** remise *f* (d'une peine); *Jur:* **with r. of sentence**, avec sursis *m.*

remit [ri′mit], *v.tr.* (**remitted**) **1.** (*a*) remettre, pardonner (les péchés); (*b*) remettre (une peine, une dette). **2.** *Com:* remettre, envoyer (de l'argent à qn); *abs.* **kindly r. by cheque**, prière de nous couvrir par chèque; **re′mittal**, *s.* **1.** remise *f* (d'une dette, d'une peine). **2.** *Jur:* renvoi *m* (d'un procès à un autre tribunal); **re′mittance**, *s. Com:* remise *f* (d'argent); envoi *m* de fonds.

remnant [′remnənt], *s.* **1.** reste *m*, restant *m.* **2.** coupon *m* (de tissu); **r. sale**, solde *m* de coupons.

remonstrate [′remənstreit], *v.i.* **to r. with s.o. about sth.**, faire des représentations *f* à qn au sujet de qch.; **to r. against sth.**, protester contre qch.; **re′monstrance**, *s.* protestation *f.*

remorse [ri′mɔ:s], *s.* **1.** remords *m*; **a feeling of r.**, un remords. **2. without r.**, sans remords; sans pitié; **re′morseful**, *a.* plein de remords;

repentant; **-fully,** adv. avec remords;
re'morseless, a. 1. sans remords. 2. sans pitié
f; impitoyable; **-ly,** adv. 1. sans remords. 2.
sans pitié; impitoyablement.

remote [ri'mout], a. 1. lointain; éloigné, écarté;
in the r. future, dans un avenir lointain; **r. con-**
trol, télécommande f; **to operate sth. by r. con-**
trol, télécommander qch. 2. **a r. resemblance,**
une vague ressemblance; **without the remotest**
chance of success, sans la moindre chance de
réussir; **I haven't the remotest idea,** je n'ai pas
la moindre idée; **r. prospect,** éventualité f peu
probable; **-ly,** adv. 1. loin; au loin; dans le lointain. 2. **we're r. related,** nous sommes parents
de loin. 3. vaguement.

remount ['ri:'maunt], v.tr. remonter (à vélo).

remove [ri'mu:v], v.tr. 1. (a) enlever, effacer, ôter
(une tache); écarter (un obstacle); supprimer
(un abus); enlever, retirer, son chapeau; **to r.**
make-up, (se) démaquiller; to r. s.o.'s name
from a list, rayer qn d'une liste; (b) révoquer
(un fonctionnaire); (c) assassiner, supprimer
(qn). 2. déplacer (qch.); déménager (ses
meubles); **re'movable,** a. détachable;
amovible; transportable; **re'moval,** s. 1.
enlèvement m (d'une tache, etc.); suppression f
(d'un abus). 2. déménagement m; **r. expenses,**
frais mpl de déplacement; **re'mover,** s. 1. (furniture) r., déménageur m. 2. (varnish, paint) r.,
décapant m (pour vernis, pour peinture);
make-up r., démaquillant m; **superfluous hair**
r., pâte f épilatoire; **(nail-varnish) r.,** dissolvant
m (pour ongles).

remunerate [ri'mju:nəreit], v.tr. rémunérer (qn
de ses services); **remune'ration,** s. rémunération f (for, de); **re'munerative,** a. (travail,
etc.) rémunérateur.

Renaissance [rə'neis(ə)ns, -sã:s], s. Hist: Art:
Lit: **the R.,** la Renaissance; **R. style,** style m
(de la) Renaissance.

renal ['ri:nəl], a. Anat: rénal; des reins.

render ['rendər], v.tr. rendre. 1. **to r. good for**
evil, rendre le bien pour le mal. 2. **to r. a service**
to s.o., rendre un service à qn; **to r. oneself**
liable to (legal) proceedings, s'exposer à des
poursuites (judiciaires). 3. **to r. an account of**
sth., rendre compte de qch.; Com: **as per ac-**
count rendered, to account rendered, suivant
notre compte, suivant compte remis. 4. interpréter; rendre; traduire. 5. Cu: fondre (de la
graisse); clarifier (de l'huile). 6. Const: **to r. a**
wall (with cement), enduire un mur de ciment;
cimenter un mur.

rendezvous ['rɔndivu:]. I. s. rendez-vous m inv.
II. v.i. **(rendezvoused** [-vu:d]) F: se rencontrer.

renew [ri'nju:], v.tr. (a) renouveler; **to r. one's**
youth, rajeunir; **to r. one's subscription,** se
réabonner **(to a paper,** à un journal); (b) **to r.**
one's acquaintance with s.o., renouer con-

naissance avec qn; (c) remplacer (une pièce
d'une machine, un vêtement); **re'newal,** s. (a)
renouvellement m; **r. of subscription,**
réabonnement m **(to, à);** (b) **r. of acquaintance,**
renouement m des relations; **r. of negotiations,**
reprise f de négociations.

renounce [ri'nauns], v.tr. 1. renoncer à, abandonner (un droit, un projet). 2. renier (son fils).
dénoncer (un traité); **to r. one's faith,** abjurer
sa foi; **re'nouncement,** s. renoncement m
abandon m; Jur: **r. of an inheritance,** répudiation f d'une succession.

renovate ['renəveit], v.tr. remettre à neuf
rénover; **reno'vation,** s. rénovation f
renouvellement m; remise f à neuf.

renown [ri'naun], s. renommée f, renom m
re'nowned, a. renommé **(for,** pour); célébr
(for, par).

rent[1] [rent], s. 1. déchirure f, accroc m (à un vête
ment, etc.). 2. fissure f (de terrain).

rent[2]. I. s. loyer m; (prix m de) location f (d'un
maison). II. v.tr. (a) (let) louer (une maison
(b) (hire) louer, prendre en location (un
maison); **'rental,** s. 1. loyer m; valeur locativ
(d'une maison); montant m du loyer; **yearl**
r., redevance annuelle. 2. **fixed r.,** redevance
d'abonnement (d'un téléphone, etc.); **'ren**
collector, s. receveur m de loyers; **'rent-da**
s. jour m du terme.

renunciation [rinʌnsi'eiʃ(ə)n], s. 1. renonc
ment m, renonciation f (of, de). 2. reniement
(of, de).

reopen ['ri:'oup(ə)n]. 1. v.tr. (a) rouvrir (
livre); **to r. an old sore,** raviver une plaie; (
reprendre (les hostilités); (c) **the question ca**
not be reopened, il n'y a pas à y revenir. 2.
(a) (of wound) se rouvrir; (b) (of theatr
rouvrir; (of school) rentrer.

reorganize ['ri:'ɔ:gənaiz]. 1. v.tr. réorganiser.
v.i. se réorganiser; **'reorgani'zation,**
réorganisation f; **'re'organizer,**
réorganisateur, -trice.

rep [rep], s. F: représentant m (d'une maison
commerce).

repair [ri'pɛər]. I. s. 1. réparation f (d'u
machine); **road repairs,** réfection f de route
emergency repairs, réparations d'urgen
dépannage m; **to be under r.,** subir c
réparations. 2. **to be in (good) r.,** être en b
état; **in poor r.,** mal entretenu; Ind: **r. sh**
atelier m de réparations; **r. kit,** trousse
réparations. II. v.tr. réparer, remettre en ét
raccommoder (un vêtement); **re'pairer,**
réparateur, -trice; **shoe r.,** cordonnier

reparable ['repərəbl], a. (machine f, faut
tort m) réparable; **repa'ration** [repə-],
réparation f.

repartee [repɑ:'ti:], s. repartie f.

repatriate [ri:'pætrieit], v.tr. rapatri

re'patriated. 1. *a.* rapatrié. 2. *s. coll.* the **r.,** les rapatriés; **repatri'ation,** *s.* rapatriement *m.*

repay [riː'pei], *v.tr.* **(repaid)** 1. rendre; **to r. an obligation,** s'acquitter d'une obligation. 2. (i) rembourser (de l'argent); (ii) récompenser (qn) (for, de); **to r. s.o. with ingratitude,** payer qn d'ingratitude; **how can I r. you?** comment pourrai-je m'acquitter envers vous? **to r. s.o. in full,** s'acquitter envers qn. 3. **book that repays study,** livre qui vaut la peine d'être étudié; **re'payment,** *s.* 1. remboursement *m.* 2. récompense *f* (d'un service).

epeal [ri'piːl]. I. *s.* abrogation *f* (d'une loi); rappel *m,* révocation *f* (d'un décret). II. *v.tr.* abroger, annuler (une loi); révoquer (un décret).

epeat [ri'piːt], *v.tr.* (*a*) répéter; réitérer; (*b*) rapporter (un méfait); (*c*) renouveler (ses efforts; *Com:* une commande); **re'peated,** *a.* répété, réitéré, redoublé; **-ly,** *adv.* à plusieurs reprises.

epel [ri'pel], *v.tr.* **(repelled)** repousser (qn); répugner à (qn); **re'pelling,** *a.* répulsif; **re'pellent.** 1. *a.* répulsif; répugnant, repoussant; **to have a r. manner,** avoir l'abord antipathique. 2. *a.* **water-r.,** (tissu *m,* surface *f*) imperméable. 3. *s.* **insect r.,** insectifuge *m.*

pent [ri'pent]. 1. *v.i.* se repentir (of, de). 2. *v.tr.* **he has bitterly repented it,** il s'en est repenti amèrement; **re'pentance,** *s.* repentir *m*; **re'pentant,** *a.* repentant, repenti.

percussion [riːpə'kʌʃ(ə)n], *s.* répercussion *f.*

pertoire ['repətwɑːr], *s. Th:* répertoire *m.*

pertory ['repət(ə)ri], *s. Th:* **r. theatre, company,** théâtre *m* à demeure.

petition [repi'tiʃ(ə)n], *s.* 1. (*a*) répétition *f* (d'un mot). 2. répétition, réitération *f* (d'une action); renouvellement *m* (d'un effort); **re'petitive,** *a.* (livre) plein de répétitions.

place [ri'pleis], *v.tr.* 1. replacer; remettre (qch.) en place; *P.T.T:* **to r. the receiver,** raccrocher (le récepteur, le combiné). 2. remplacer; substituer; **to r. coal by oil fuel,** remplacer le charbon par le mazout; **I shall ask to be replaced,** je demanderai à me faire remplacer; **re'placeable,** *a.* remplaçable; **re'placement,** *s.* 1. remise *f* en place (d'un objet). 2. (*a*) remplacement *m,* substitution *f*; (*b*) (*pers.*) remplaçant, -ante; (*c*) *Ind:* **r. parts, replacements,** pièces *f* de rechange.

play ['riːplei], *s. Sp:* match rejoué (après match nul).

plenish [ri'pleniʃ], *v.tr.* remplir (de nouveau) (with, de); **to r. one's supplies,** se réapprovisionner (with, de); **re'plenishment,** *s.* (*a*) (*of fuel, petrol, etc.*) remplissage *m*; (*b*) (*of food, household stores, etc.*) réapprovisionnement *m*; ravitaillement *m.*

pletion [ri'pliːʃ(ə)n], *s.* réplétion *f.*

replica ['replikə], *s.* réplique *f,* double *m* (d'une œuvre d'art).

reply [ri'plai]. I. *s.* réponse *f*; **what have you to say in r.?** qu'avez-vous à répondre? (*of telegram*) **r. paid,** réponse payée. II. *v.i. & tr.* **(replied)** répondre, répliquer (**to, à**).

report [ri'pɔːt]. I. *s.* 1. (*a*) rapport *m* (**on,** sur); compte rendu; exposé *m* (d'une affaire); **policeman's r.,** procés-verbal *m*; **expert's r.,** expertise *f*; (*b*) **weather r.,** bulletin *m* météorologique, *F:* météo *f.* 2. bruit *m* qui court; rumeur *f*; **to know of sth. by r.,** savoir qch. par ouï-dire. 3. détonation *f* (d'une arme à feu); coup *m* (de fusil). II. *v.* 1. *v.tr.* rapporter (un fait); rendre compte de (qch.); (*of journalist*) faire le reportage de (qch.); **to r. a meeting,** faire le compte rendu d'une séance; **to r. an accident to the police,** signaler un accident à la police; **to r. s.o. to the police,** dénoncer qn à la police; *abs.* **to r. to (s.o.),** se présenter devant (un supérieur); **reported missing,** porté manquant. 2. *v.i.* **to r. on sth.,** faire un rapport sur qch.; **re'porter,** *s.* reporter *m*; **re'porting,** *s.* reportage *m*; comptes rendus.

repose [ri'pouz]. I. *s.* repos *m*; (*a*) sommeil *m*; (*b*) calme *m,* tranquillité *f* (d'esprit). II. *v.i.* se reposer.

repository [ri'pɔzit(ə)ri], *s.* dépôt *m,* entrepôt *m*; **furniture r.,** garde-meuble *m, pl.* gardemeubles.

reprehensible [repri'hensibl], *a.* répréhensible, blâmable, condamnable; **-ibly,** *adv.* de façon répréhensible.

represent [repri'zent], *v.tr.* 1. (*a*) représenter (qch. à l'esprit); (*b*) *Th:* jouer (un personnage). 2. **he represents himself as a model of virtue,** il se donne pour un modèle de vertu; **exactly as represented,** conforme à la description. 3. représenter (une maison de commerce, une circonscription électorale, etc.); **represen'tation,** *s.* 1. représentation *f*; *Pol:* **proportional r.,** représentation proportionnelle. 2. *Pol:* (*diplomacy*) démarche *f*; **joint representations,** démarche collective; **repre'sentative.** I. *a.* représentatif; *Com:* **r. sample,** échantillon *m* type. II. *s.* (*a*) représentant, -ante, délégué, -ée; (*b*) représentant (d'une maison de commerce); (*c*) *Pol: esp. U.S:* = député *m.*

repress [ri'pres], *v.tr.* 1. réprimer (une sédition). 2. réprimer, retenir (ses désirs); refouler (ses sentiments); **re'pressed,** *a.* réprimé, contenu; **a r. young man,** un jeune homme renfermé; **re'pression,** *s.* 1. répression *f.* 2. **unconscious r.,** refoulement *m*; **re'pressive,** *a.* répressif, réprimant.

reprieve [ri'priːv]. I. *s.* 1. commutation *f* de la peine capitale. 2. répit *m,* délai *m.* II. *v.tr.* 1. *Jur:* accorder (à un condamné) une commutation de la peine capitale. 2. accorder un délai à (qn).

reprimand ['reprimɑ:nd]. I. *s.* réprimande *f.* II. *v.tr.* réprimander (qn).

reprint. I. *v.tr.* ['ri:'print], réimprimer. II. *s.* ['ri:print], réimpression *f*; nouveau tirage.

reprisal [ri'praiz(ə)l], *s.* as a r., en représailles; *pl.* reprisals, représailles *fpl.*

reproach [ri'proutʃ]. I. *s.* 1. to be a r. to (one's family), être la honte de (sa famille). 2. reproche *m*, blâme *m*; **beyond r.**, irréprochable. II. *v.tr.* to r. s.o. with sth., reprocher qch. à qn; to r. s.o. about sth., faire des reproches à qn au sujet de qch.; **re'proachful**, *a.* réprobateur; plein de reproches; **-fully**, d'un air de reproche.

reprobate ['reprəbeit], *s.* vaurien *m.*

reproduce ['ri:prə'dju:s]. 1. *v.tr.* reproduire; (*a*) copier; (*b*) multiplier (par génération). 2. *v.i.* se reproduire, se multiplier; **'repro'duction**, *s.* 1. reproduction *f* (d'un tableau, de la race humaine); *Cin: etc:* **sound r.**, reproduction sonore; *Art: etc:* **correct r. of colour**, rendu exact des couleurs. 2. copie *f*, imitation *f*; **'repro'ductive**, *a. Anat:* (organe) reproducteur.

reproof[1] [ri'pru:f], *s.* 1. reproche *m*, blâme *m.* 2. réprimande *f.*

reproof[2] ['ri:'pru:f], *v.tr.* réimperméabiliser.

reprove [ri'pru:v], *v.tr.* reprendre, réprimander (qn); **re'proving**, *a.* réprobateur; **-ly**, *adv.* d'un ton, d'un air, de reproche.

reptile ['reptail], *s.* reptile *m.*

republic [ri'pʌblik], *s.* république *f*; **re'publican**, *a.* & *s.* républicain, -aine; **re'publicanism**, *s.* républicanisme *m*; **re'publicanize**, *v.tr.* républicaniser.

repudiate [ri'pju:dieit], *v.tr.* répudier (ses dettes); désavouer (une opinion); *Com: Jur:* to r. (a contract), refuser d'honorer (un contrat); **repudi'ation**, *s.* répudiation *f*; désaveu *m* (d'une opinion).

repugnant [ri'pʌgnənt], *a.* répugnant (to s.o., à qn); to be r. to s.o., répugner à qn; **re'pugnance**, *s.* répugnance *f*; antipathie *f* (to, against, pour).

repulse [ri'pʌls], *v.tr.* repousser (un ennemi, une demande); **re'pulsion**, *s.* répulsion *f*, aversion *f*, répugnance *f* (to, for, s.o., sth., pour qn, qch.); **re'pulsive**, *a.* répulsif, repoussant; **-ly**, *adv.* r. ugly, d'une laideur repoussante.

repute [ri'pju:t], *s.* réputation *f*, renom *m*; to know s.o. by r., connaître qn de réputation; **doctor of r.**, médecin réputé; **a family of good r.**, une famille honorablement connue; **place of ill r.**, endroit mal famé; **reputable** ['repjutəbl], *a.* honorable, estimé, estimable; **-ably**, *adv.* honorablement; **repu'tation** [repju-], *s.* réputation *f*, renom *m*; to ruin s.o.'s r., perdre

qn de réputation; **re'puted**, *a.* réputé, censé supposé; **a r. Hogarth**, un tableau attribué à Hogarth; *Jur:* **r. father**, père putatif; **he's r** wealthy, il passe pour riche; **-ly**, *adv.* **he's r** the best heart specialist, il passe pour le meilleur cardiologue.

request [ri'kwest]. I. *s.* demande *f*, requête *f* **earnest r.**, sollicitation *f*; **samples sent on r.** échantillons *m* sur demande; *P.N:* **r. stop** arrêt facultatif; *Rad: etc:* **r. programme** programme *m* des auditeurs; **to make a r.**, fair une demande; **to grant a r.**, accéder à un demande. II. *v.tr.* demander (qch. à qn, à qn d faire qch.); *Com:* **as requested**, conformémer à vos instructions.

requiem ['rekwiem], *s.* 1. requiem *m*; messe *f* de morts. 2. musique *f*, chant *m*, funèbre.

require [ri'kwaiər], *v.tr.* 1. to r. sth. of s.o demander, réclamer, qch. à qn. 2. exige réclamer; **work that requires great precisio** travail qui nécessite une grande précisio **have you got all you r.?** avez-vous tout ce qu' vous faut? **you won't r. a coat**, vous n'aure pas besoin d'un manteau; **I'll do whatever required**, je ferai tout ce qu'il faudr **re'quired**, *a.* exigé, demandé, voulu; **in the time**, dans le délai prescrit; **the qualities r. f this post**, les qualités requises pour ce poste; **r.**, s'il le faut; au besoin; **re'quirement**, *s.* demande *f*, réclamation *f*. 2. exigence *f*, beso *m.* 3. condition requise.

requisition [rekwi'ziʃ(ə)n]. I. *v.tr. Mil: e* réquisitionner (des vivres, etc.); **to r. s.o.'s** vices, avoir recours aux services de qn. II demande *f*; *Mil:* réquisition *f*; **'requisite. 1** (objet) requis (to do sth., pour faire qch nécessaire (to, à); indispensable (to, pou condition requise (for, pour). 2. *s.* chos nécessaire; *esp. Com:* **toilet requisit** accessoires *m* de toilette; **office requisit** fournitures *f* de bureau; **travel requisites,** ticles *m* de voyage.

reredos ['riərədɔs], *s. Ecc:* retable *m.*

rescind [ri'sind], *v.tr. Jur: Adm:* rescinder acte); annuler (un vote); abroger (une loi).

rescue ['reskju:]. I. *s.* délivrance *f*; sauvetage **r. squad**, équipe *f* de sauvetage. II. *v.tr.* sauv délivrer, secourir (qn); **to r. a child fr drowning**, sauver un enfant de la noyade **the rescued (men)**, les rescapés.

research [ri'sə:tʃ]. 1. *s.* recherche *f* (for, **scientific r.**, recherche scientifique; **r. wc** recherches; **r. worker**, chercheur, -euse; *In* **department**, service *m* de recherches. II. *v.t.* *i.* to r. (into) sth., faire des recherches d qch.; **well researched**, bien étudié, étudi fond.

resemble [ri'zembl], *v.tr.* ressembler à (qch.); **re'semblance**, *s.* ressemblance *f* (t

avec; **between,** entre).
resent [ri'zent], *v.tr.* **1.** être offensé, irrité, de
(qch.); **you r. my being here,** ma présence vous
déplaît. **2.** s'offenser de (qch.); ressentir (une
critique); **re'sentful,** *a.* **1.** plein de ressentiment; rancunier. **2.** froissé, irrité (**of,** de);
-fully, *adv.* avec ressentiment; d'un ton, d'un
air, froissé; **re'sentment,** *s.* ressentiment *m*.
reserve [ri'zə:v]. **I.** *v.tr.* réserver (**sth. for s.o.,**
qch. pour qn); mettre (qch,) en réserve; **to r. a
seat for s.o.,** retenir une place pour qn; **to r. the
right to do sth.,** se réserver de faire qch. **II.** *s.*
(*a*) réserve *f* (d'argent, d'énergie); **cash r.,**
réserve de caisse; **r. fund,** fonds *m* de réserve;
(*b*) réserve (forestière); **nature r.,** réserve
naturelle; **reser'vation** [rezə-], *s.* **1.** *Jur:*
réservation *f* (d'un droit); **with reservations,**
avec certaines réserves. **2.** *Rail: etc:* **seat r.,** (i)
location *f* des places; (ii) place retenue. **3. to
accept sth. without r.,** accepter qch. sans
arrière-pensée. **4.** *esp. N.Am:* parc national;
réserve zoologique; **Indian r.,** réserve indienne; **re'served,** *a.* (*a*) **r. seats,** places
réservées; (*b*) (homme) réservé, renfermé, peu
communicatif; **'reservoir** [-wɑ:r], *s.* réservoir
m.
reshuffle [ri:'ʃʌfl]. **I.** *s.* remaniement *m* (du personnel). **II.** *v.tr.* remanier (le personnel).
reside [ri'zaid], *v.i.* résider; **residence**
['rezidəns], *s.* résidence *f,* demeure *f*; *Com:*
desirable r. for sale, belle propriété à vendre;
Sch: **(students') hall of r.** = cité *f* universitaire;
'resident. I. *a.* résidant; qui réside; **the r. population,** la population fixe; (*in hospital*) **r.
physician,** interne *m*; *Sch:* **r. master** = maître
m d'internat. **II.** *s.* habitant, -ante; (*in hotel,
etc.*) pensionnaire *mf*; **resi'dential,** *a.* (quartier) résidentiel.
residue ['rezidju:], *s.* **1.** *Ch:* résidu *m*. **2.** reste(s)
m(pl). **3.** *Jur:* reliquat *m* (d'une succession);
re'siduary [ri'zidjuəri], *a. Jur:* **r. legatee,**
légataire (à titre) universel.
resign [ri'zain], *v.tr.* **1.** résigner (une possession);
donner sa démission de (son emploi); *abs.*
démissionner. **2. to r. oneself to doing sth.,** se
résigner à faire qch.; **resignation**
[rezig'neiʃ(ə)n], *s.* **1.** (*a*) démission *f* (d'un
emploi); (*b*) abandon *m* (d'un droit). **2.** résignation *f,* soumission *f* (à son destin); **re'signed,**
a. résigné (**to,** à); **to become r. to sth.,** prendre
son parti de qch.; se résigner à qch.;
re'signedly [-idli], *adv.* avec résignation *f*;
d'un air, d'un ton, résigné.
resilient [ri'ziliənt], *a.* (*a*) rebondissant,
élastique; (*b*) (*of pers.*) **to be r.,** avoir du
ressort; **re'silience,** *s.* (*a*) élasticité *f*; (*b*) (*of
pers.*) élasticité (de tempérament).
resin ['rezin], *s.* résine *f*; **'resinous,** *a.*
résineux.

resist [ri'zist], *v.tr.* **1.** (*a*) résister à (la chaleur, la
tentation); (*b*) **I couldn't r. telling him . . .,** je
n'ai pas pu m'empêcher de lui dire . . .. **2.** (*a*)
résister à, s'opposer à (un projet); (*b*)
repousser (une suggestion); **re'sistance,** *s.* **1.**
résistance *f*; **she made no r.,** elle s'est laissé
faire; **weary of r.,** de guerre lasse; **the R.**
(movement), la Résistance; **r. fighter,** résistant,
-ante. **2. to take the line of least r.,** aller au plus
facile; *Mec:* **high-r. steel,** acier *m* à haute
résistance; *El:* **r. coil,** bobine *f* de résistance.
resolute ['rezəl(j)u:t], *a.* résolu, déterminé; **-ly,**
adv. résolument; **reso'lution,** *s.* **1.** résolution
f, délibération *f* (d'une assemblée); **to put a r. to
the meeting,** mettre une résolution aux voix. **2.**
résolution, détermination *f*. **3.** résolution,
fermeté *f,* décision *f*; **lack of r.,** manque *m* de
caractère. **4.** *Ch: Mth: etc:* **r.** (**of water into
steam, etc.**), résolution (de l'eau en vapeur,
etc.); *T.V:* **picture r.,** définition *f* (de l'image).
resolve [ri'zolv]. **I.** *s.* résolution *f*. **II.** *v.* **1.** *v.tr.*
résoudre (qch. en ses éléments); résoudre (un
problème); dissiper (un doute). **2.** (*of committee*) résoudre, décider (de faire qch.). **3.** *v.i.*
se résoudre ((**up**)**on** (**doing**) **sth.,** à (faire) qch.
resonant ['rezənənt], *a.* résonnant; **r. voice,** voix
sonore; **'resonance,** *s.* résonance *f*; *Mus:*
vibration *f* (de la voix).
resort [ri'zo:t]. **I.** *s.* **1.** (*a*) **the only r.,** la seule
ressource; (*b*) recours *m*; **without r. to compul-
sion,** sans avoir recours à la force; **last r.,** dernier ressort. **2.** lieu *m* de séjour, de rendez-
vous; **health r.,** station climatique, thermale;
holiday r., (centre *m* de) villégiature *f*; **seaside
r.,** station balnéaire, plage *f*. **II.** *v.i.* avoir
recours (**to,** à); user (**to,** de); **to r. to
blows,** en venir aux coups.
resound [ri'zaund], *v.i.* résonner; retentir (**with
cries,** de cris); **re'sounding,** *a.* résonnant,
retentissant; (rire) sonore; (*of voice*) sonore;
r. victory, victoire fracassante.
resource [ri'so:s, -'zo:s], *s.* **1.** ressource *f*. **2.** *pl.*
natural resources, ressources naturelles; **to be
at the end of one's resources,** être au bout de
ses ressources; **re'sourceful,** *a.* fertile en
ressources, *F:* débrouillard.
respect [ri'spekt]. **I.** *s.* **1.** rapport *m,* égard *m*;
with r. to . . ., en ce qui concerne . . .; **quant
à . . .; in some respects,** sous quelques rapports; **in this r.,** à cet égard. **2.** respect *m*; **to
have r. for s.o.,** avoir du respect pour qn;
worthy of r., respectable; digne d'estime; **with
(all) due r. (to you),** sans vouloir vous contredire. **3.** *pl.* **respects,** respects, hommages *m*;
to pay one's respects to s.o., présenter ses
respects à qn. **II.** *v.tr.* respecter; honorer (qn);
to r. s.o.'s opinion, respecter l'opinion de qn;
respecta'bility, *s.* respectabilité *f*; **re'spec-
table,** *a.* respectable; digne de respect,

honorable, convenable; **a r. family,** une famille honnête; **to put on some r. clothes,** mettre des vêtements convenables; **she's of a r. age,** elle n'est plus jeune; **a r. sum (of money),** une somme rondelette; **-ably,** *adv.* 1. respectablement; **r. dressed,** convenablement vêtu. 2. pas mal; passablement; **re′spectful,** *a.* respectueux **(to, envers, pour); -fully,** *adv.* respectueusement; avec respect; **re′spective,** *a.* respectif; **-ly,** *adv.* respectivement.

respiration [respi′reiʃ(ə)n], *s.* respiration *f*; **artificial r.,** respiration artificielle.

respite [′respait], *s.* 1. *Jur:* sursis *m*, délai *m.* 2. répit *m*, relâche *m*; **to work without r.,** travailler sans relâche.

resplendent [ri′splendənt], *a.* resplendissant; éblouissant (de beauté, de santé).

respond [ri′spɔnd], *v.i.* 1. répondre. 2. répondre, être sensible (à la bonté, à l'affection); **to r. to music,** apprécier la musique; *(of machine)* **to r. to the controls,** obéir aux contrôles; **re′sponse,** *s.* réponse *f*, réplique *f*; *Ecc:* répons *m*; **responsi′bility,** *s.* responsabilité*f*; **to do sth. on one's own r.,** faire qch. de son propre chef, de sa propre initiative; **re′sponsible,** *a.* 1. responsable; **to be r. to s.o.,** être responsable devant qn **(for sth.,** de qch.); **he's not r. for his actions,** il n'est pas maître de ses actes. 2. capable, compétent; **job for a r. man,** emploi *m* pour un homme sérieux; **she's a r. woman,** c'est une femme compétente; **re′sponsive,** *a.* impressionnable; sensible **(to,** à); *Mec: Aut:* (moteur) nerveux, souple; *Rad:* (détecteur *m*) sensible; **-ly,** *adv.* avec sympathie; **re′sponsiveness,** *s.* sensibilité *f*; flexibilité *f*, nervosité *f*, souplesse *f* (d'un moteur, etc.).

rest¹ [rest]. **I.** *s.* 1. *(a)* repos *m*; **to have a good night's r.,** passer une bonne nuit; **at r.,** en repos; **to set s.o.'s mind at r.,** calmer l'esprit de qn; *(b)* **to take a r.,** se reposer; *(c)* **to come to r.,** s'arrêter, s'immobiliser. 2. *Mus:* pause *f*, silence *m*; **crotchet r.,** soupir *m*; **quaver r.,** demi-soupir *m.* 3. support *m*; *(of chair)* **arm r.,** accoudoir *m*, bras *m*; **r. cure,** cure *f* de repos; *(in large shops, etc.)* **r. room,** toilettes *fpl*; *P.N:* Dames *fpl.* **II.** *v.* 1. *v.i.* *(a)* se reposer; *Th:* **to be resting,** se trouver sans engagement; *(b)* **there the matter rests,** les choses en sont là; l'affaire en reste là; *(c)* se poser, s'appuyer; **a heavy responsibility rests on them,** une lourde responsabilité pèse sur eux. 2. *v.tr.* appuyer (qch. sur qch.); déposer (un fardeau par terre); laisser reposer (qn); **′restful,** *a.* *(of place)* paisible, tranquille; reposant; **′resting,** *a.* au repos; **′restless,** *a.* agité; (enfant) remuant; **r. audience,** assistance impatiente, énervée; **′restlessness,** *s.* agitation *f*; turbulence *f*; nervosité *f*.

rest², *s.* 1. reste *m*, restant *m*; **to do the r.,** faire le reste; **for the r.,** quant au reste; d'ailleurs; **and all the r. of it,** et tout ce qui s'ensuit; *F:* et patati et patata. 2. *(coll., with pl. vb.)* **the r.,** les autres *mf*; **the r. of us,** nous autres.

restaurant [′restərɔnt], *s.* 1. restaurant *m*; *Rail:* **r. car,** wagon-restaurant *m*; **civic r.,** restaurant communautaire. 2. **r. owner, r. manager,** restaurateur, -trice.

restitution [resti′tjuːʃ(ə)n], *s.* restitution *f*; **to make r. of sth.,** restituer qch.

restive [′restiv], *a.* 1. (cheval) rétif. 2. *(of pers.)* *(a)* indocile; *(b)* nerveux, énervé; **′restiveness,** *s.* 1. humeur rétive; nature vicieuse (d'un cheval). 2. nervosité *f*; *Pol:* **a certain r. on the left,** une certaine effervescence parmi les gauchistes.

restore [ri′stɔːr], *v.tr.* 1. restituer (rendre (qch. à qn). 2. restaurer (un monument); réparer (un tableau); rénover (un meuble). 3. *(a)* **to r. sth. to its former condition,** remettre qch. en état; *(b)* rétablir, réintégrer (qn dans ses fonctions); *(c)* **to r. s.o. to health,** rétablir la santé de qn. 4. rétablir (la liberté); ramener (la confiance); **to r. s.o.'s strength,** redonner des forces à qn; **resto′ration** [restə-], *s.* 1. restitution*f*(de qch. à qn). 2. restauration *f* (d'un monument). 3. rétablissement *m* (de la santé). 4. restauration (d'un régime de gouvernement); **re′storative,** *a. & s. Med:* fortifiant (*m*); **re′storer,** *s.* restaurateur, -trice (d'un monument, d'un tableau); rénovateur, -trice (de meubles de style, etc.).

restrain [ri′strein], *v.tr.* retenir, empêcher **(s.o. from doing sth.,** qn de faire qch.); retenir (sa curiosité); **to r. one's laughter,** se retenir de rire; **to r. oneself,** se contraindre; **to r. s.o.'s activities,** freiner les activités de qn; **re′strained,** *a. (of anger)* contenu; (style) tempéré, sobre; **in r. terms,** en termes mesurés; **re′strainedly** [-idli], *adv.* avec retenue; **re′straint,** *s.* (a) contrainte*f*, entrave*f*, frein *m*; **wage r.,** blocage *m* des salaires; *(b)* contrainte, réserve*f*; **to put a r. on oneself,** se contenir; **lack of r.,** abandon *m*; manque *m* de réserve; **to speak without r.,** parler en toute liberté.

restrict [ri′strikt], *v.tr.* restreindre; réduire (les libertés publiques); limiter (le pouvoir de qn); **re′stricted,** *a.* restreint, limité; **r. diet,** régime *m* sévère; *Adm: Aut:* **r. area,** zone *f* à limitation de vitesse; **re′striction,** *s.* restriction *f*; **r. of expenditure,** limitation *f* de dépenses; **re′strictive,** *a.* restrictif.

result [ri′zʌlt]. **I.** *s.* résultat *m* **(of,** de); aboutissement *m* (des efforts de qn); **the r. is that . . .,** il en résulte que . . .; **without r.,** sans résultat. **II.** *v.i.* 1. résulter, provenir **(from,** de); **little will r. from all this,** il ne sortira pas grand-chose de tout cela. 2. aboutir **(in a discovery,** à une découverte); **it resulted in nothing,** cela n'a mené à rien.

resume [ri'zju:m], *v.tr.* 1. reprendre; **to r. one's seat,** se rasseoir. 2. reprendre (possession *f* de qch.); renouer (des relations); **to r. work,** se remettre au travail; *abs.* **the meeting will r. at 3 p.m.,** la séance est suspendue jusqu'à 15h. 3. reprendre, récapituler (les faits); **resumption** [ri'zʌmpʃən], *s.* reprise *f* (de négociations, des travaux).

résumé ['rezju:mei, 'reiz-], *s.* résumé *m.*

resurface ['ri:'sə:fis]. 1. *v.tr.* **to r. a road,** refaire le revêtement d'une route. 2. *v.i.* (*of submarine, etc.*) faire surface, remonter à la surface.

resurrection [rezə'rekʃ(ə)n], *s.* résurrection *f.*

resuscitate [ri'sʌsiteit], *v.tr. & i.* ressusciter; **resusci'tation,** *s.* ressuscitation *f.*

retail ['ri:teil]. I. *s. Com:* détail *m;* vente *f* au détail; **wholesale and r.,** en gros et au détail; **r. dealer,** détaillant *m;* **r. price,** prix *m* de détail. II. *v.tr.* 1. détailler, vendre au détail. 2. répéter (des commérages); **'retailer,** *s.* détaillant *m,* marchand *m* au détail.

retain [ri'tein], *v.tr.* 1. retenir. 2. conserver, garder (un bien); **to r. hold of sth.,** ne pas lâcher (prise de) qch.; **to r. control of the car,** rester maître de la voiture. 3. garder (qch.) en mémoire; **I can't r. anything,** j'oublie tout; **re'tainer,** *s. Com:* arrhes *fpl;* **Jur:** avance *f.*

retaliate [ri'tælieit], *v.i.* rendre la pareille (à qn); user de représailles (envers qn); **retali'ation,** *s.* revanche *f,* représailles *fpl;* **re'taliatory,** *a.* **r. measures,** représailles *fpl.*

retention [ri'tenʃ(ə)n], *s.* conservation *f* (d'un usage); **re'tentive,** *a.* (mémoire *f*) fidèle.

reticent ['retis(ə)nt], *a.* peu communicatif; réticent; réservé; **-ly,** *adv.* avec réticence; **'reticence,** *s.* caractère peu communicatif; réticence *f;* réserve *f.*

retina ['retinə], *s. Anat:* rétine *f* (de l'œil).

retinue ['retinju:], *s.* suite *f* (d'un prince).

retire [ri'taiər], *v.i.* 1. se retirer (**to a place,** dans un endroit); **to r. into oneself,** se replier sur soi-même; se recueillir. 2. se démettre (de ses fonctions); **to r. from business,** se retirer des affaires; **to r. (on a pension),** prendre sa retraite; **re'tired,** *a.* 1. (endroit) retiré, peu fréquenté. 2. en retraite, à la retraite, retraité; **r. civil servant,** fonctionnaire en retraite; **re'tirement,** *s.* la retraite; **re'tiring,** *a.* (*of pers.*) (*a*) réservé; farouche; (*b*) **r. chairman,** président sortant.

retort[1] [ri'tɔ:t]. I. *s.* réplique *f* (**to,** à); riposte *f.* II. *v.i.* répliquer; riposter.

retort[2], *s. Ch: Ind:* cornue *f.*

retrace ['ri:'treis], *v.tr.* (*a*) remonter à l'origine de (qch.); reconstituer (le passé); (*b*) **to r. one's steps,** revenir sur ses pas.

retract [ri'trækt], (*a*) *v.tr.* rétracter (qch.); *Av:* **to**

r. the undercarriage, escamoter, rentrer, le train d'atterrissage; (*b*) *v.i.* se rétracter; se dédire; **re'tractable,** *a.* (*of undercarriage*) escamotable.

retread. *Aut:* I. *v.tr.* ['ri:'tred], rechaper (un pneu). II. *s.* ['ri:tred]. F: pneu rechapé.

retreat [ri'tri:t]. I. *s.* 1. *Mil:* retraite *f.* 2. asile *m;* retraite. II. *v.i.* se retirer; *Mil:* battre en retraite.

retrench [ri'tren(t)ʃ], (*a*) *v.tr.* restreindre (ses dépenses); (*b*) *v.i.* faire des économies; **re'trenchment,** *s.* réduction *f* (des dépenses); **policy of r.,** politique *f* d'économies.

retribution [retri'bju:ʃ(ə)n], *s.* châtiment *m;* jugement *m.*

retrieve [ri'tri:v], *v.tr.* 1. (*a*) (*of dog*) rapporter (le gibier); (*b*) recouvrer (des biens); retrouver (un objet perdu). 2. relever, rétablir (la fortune de qn); **to r. oneself,** se racheter (après une faute commise). 3. réparer (une erreur); **re'trievable,** *a.* (somme *f*) recouvrable; (perte *f,* erreur *f*) réparable; **re'triever,** *s.* (*dog*) retriever *m.*

retrograde ['retrougreid], *a.* rétrograde.

retrospect ['retrouspekt], *s.* coup d'œil rétrospectif; vue rétrospective; **when I consider these events in r.,** quand je jette un coup d'œil rétrospectif sur ces événements; **retro'spective,** *a.* rétrospectif; (loi *f,* etc.) avec effet rétroactif.

return [ri'tə:n]. I. *s.* 1. retour *m;* **the r. to school,** la rentrée (des classes); (**immediately**) **on my r.,** dès mon retour, à mon retour; **on my r. home,** de retour à la maison; **many happy returns (of the day)!** mes meilleurs vœux pour votre anniversaire! *Rail:* **r. (ticket),** (billet d')aller et retour; **r. journey,** voyage de retour. 2. *Com:* (*a*) *pl.* **returns,** recettes *f;* **quick returns,** un prompt débit; (*b*) revenu *m,* profit *m;* rendement *m;* **to bring in a fair r.,** rapporter un bénéfice raisonnable. 3. (*a*) renvoi *m,* retour (de marchandises avariées, etc.); **on sale or r.,** (marchandises) en dépôt (avec reprise des invendus), à condition; (*b*) restitution *f* (d'un objet volé, etc.); ristourne *f* (d'une somme payée en trop); (*c*) **in r. for which,** moyennant quoi. 4. *Ten:* renvoi; riposte *f;* **r. match,** match *m* retour. 5. récompense *f;* **in r. for this service,** en retour de ce service. 6. (*a*) état *m,* exposé *m;* relevé *m;* **quarterly r.,** rapport trimestriel; (*b*) **income tax r.,** déclaration *f* de revenu. 7. *Pol:* élection *f* (d'un député); **to announce the election returns,** publier les résultats du scrutin. II. *v.* 1. *v.i.* (*come back*), revenir; (*go back*) retourner; **to r. home,** rentrer (chez soi); **they have returned,** ils sont de retour; **to r. to work,** reprendre le travail. 2. *v.tr.* (*a*) rendre (un objet emprunté); restituer (un objet volé); renvoyer (un cadeau); rembourser (un emprunt); (*b*) **to**

r. a book to its place, remettre un livre à sa place; (c) élire (un député).

reunion [ri:'ju:njən], s. (a) (reuniting) réunion f; (b) (meeting) réunion, assemblée f.

rev [rev]. F: I. s. Aut: etc: (abbr. of revolution) 4000 revs a minute, 4 000 tours m à la minute. II. v.tr. (revved) Aut: etc: to r. up the engine, faire emballer le moteur.

reveal [ri'vi:l], v.tr. (a) révéler, découvrir (son jeu); to r. one's identity, se faire connaître; (b) laisser voir; (c) révéler, découvrir (un objet caché); dévoiler (un mystère); re'vealing, a. révélateur; revelation [revə'leiʃ(ə)n], s. révélation f; (the Book of) Revelations, l'Apocalypse f.

reveille [ri'væli], s. Mil: le réveil; la diane.

revel ['rev(ə)l], v.i. (revelled) (a) to r. in sth., se délecter à qch., à faire qch.; (b) se réjouir, se divertir; (c) F: faire la bombe, la noce; 'reveller, s. joyeux convive; noceur, -euse; 'revelry, s. divertissements mpl, réjouissances fpl.

revenge [ri'vendʒ]. I. s. 1. vengeance f; to take r. on s.o. for sth., se venger de qch. sur qn; in r., par vengeance. 2. revanche f; in r., en revanche. II. v.tr. 1. venger (une injure); venger (qn). 2. v.pr. to r. oneself, to be revenged, se venger (for sth., de qch.; on s.o., de, sur, qn); re'vengeful, a. vindicatif.

revenue ['revənju:], s. 1. revenu m, rentes fpl; the Public R., (i) le Trésor public; (ii) Adm: le fisc.

reverberate [ri'və:bəreit]. 1. v.tr. renvoyer, répercuter (le son). 2. v.i. (of sound) retentir, résonner; the thunder reverberated, le tonnerre retentissait; reverbe'ration, s. renvoi m (d'un son).

revere [ri'viər], v.tr. révérer, vénérer; reverence ['rev(ə)rəns]. I. s. respect religieux; révérence f, vénération f; to pay r. to s.o., rendre hommage à qn. II. v.tr. révérer (qn); 'reverend, a. Ecc: (as title) révérend; the R. Father Brown, le révérend Père Brown; the R. Mother Superior, la révérende Mère supérieure; 'reverent, a. respectueux; plein de vénération; -ly, adv. avec respect; avec vénération.

reverie ['revəri], s. rêverie f; F: songerie f.

reversal [ri'və:s(ə)l], s. 1. Jur: réforme f, annulation f. 2. r. of opinion, revirement m d'opinion.

reverse [ri'və:s]. I. a. inverse, contraire, opposé (to, à); in the r. order, en ordre inverse; the r. side of a medal, le revers, l'envers m, d'une médaille; the r. side of a picture, le dos d'un tableau. II. s. 1. inverse m, contraire m, opposé m; quite the r. of s.o., sth., tout le contraire de qn, qch.; Aut: to get into r., se mettre en marche f arrière. 2. revers m (d'une médaille; de fortune); to suffer a r., essuyer une défaite. III. v.tr. renverser (un mouvement); invertir

(l'ordre de qch.); P.T.T: to r. the charge, demander une communication avec P.C.V.; Aut: to r. one's car, abs. to r., faire marche f arrière; Jur: to r. a sentence, révoquer une sentence; re'versible, a. (drap m) à deux endroits; (vêtement m) à double face; re'versing, s. 1. renversement m. 2. inversion f; Aut: marche f arrière; r. light, phare m de recul; El: r. switch, inverseur m de courant.

revert [ri'və:t], v.i. (a) Jur: (of property) revenir, retourner (to, à); (b) Biol: to r. to type, revenir au type primitif; (c) to r. to our subject, pour en revenir à notre sujet; re'version, s. (a) Jur: (of property) retour m; réversion f; (b) retour (à un état antérieur); Biol: r. to type, réversion (au type primitif).

review [ri'vju:]. I. s. 1. Mil: revue f. 2. examen m, revue (du passé). 3. critique f (d'un livre). 4. revue (périodique). II. v.tr. 1. passer (des faits, des troupes) en revue. 2. faire la critique d'(un livre). 3. N.Am: Sch: revoir, relire (une leçon); re'viewer, s. critique m littéraire.

revile [ri'vail], v.tr. injurier; insulter (qn).

revise [ri'vaiz], v.tr. revoir, relire (un travail, Sch: une leçon); corriger (des épreuves); réviser (des lois); re'vision [-'viʒ(ə)n], s. révision f.

revive [ri'vaiv]. 1. v.i. (a) ressusciter; reprendre ses sens; (b) (of courage) se ranimer; (c) (of arts, of feelings) renaître; (d) (of trade, customs) reprendre. 2. v.tr. (a) faire revivre; ressusciter; (b) ranimer (les espérances); renouveler (un usage); to r. s.o.'s courage, remonter le courage de qn; (c) remettre (une pièce) au théâtre; ressusciter (un journal, un parti politique); re'vival, s. 1. renaissance f (des arts, des lettres); reprise f (d'une pièce au théâtre, Com: des affaires). 2. retour m à la vie; retour des forces. 3. religious r., renouveau religieux.

revoke [ri'vouk]. 1. v.tr. révoquer (un ordre); rétracter (une promesse); to r. a driving licence, retirer un permis de conduire. 2. v.i. Cards: faire une fausse renonce; revocation [revə'keiʃ(ə)n], s. révocation f; abrogation f (d'un décret).

revolt [ri'voult]. I. s. révolte f. II. v. 1. v.i. se révolter, se soulever (against, contre). 2. v.tr. (of action) révolter, indigner (qn); re'volting, a. révoltant, dégoûtant, écœurant.

revolution [revə'l(j)u:ʃ(ə)n], s. 1. (a) rotation f (autour d'un axe); (b) tour m, révolution f; Aut: r. counter, compte-tours m inv. 2. Pol: révolution; revo'lutionary, a. & s. révolutionnaire (mf); revo'lutionize, v.tr. révolutionner (l'industrie, les mœurs, etc.).

revolve [ri'vɔlv]. 1. v.tr. (a) retourner, ruminer (une pensée); (b) faire tourner (des roues). 2. v.i. tourner, pivoter (sur un axe); re'volving, *a.* en rotation; *Ind:* **r. crane,** grue pivotante; *Th:* **r. stage,** scène tournante; **r. door,** porte tournante.

evolver [ri'vɔlvər], *s.* revolver *m.*

evue [ri'vju:], *s. Th:* revue *f.*

evulsion [ri'vʌlʃ(ə)n], *s.* **1.** revirement *m* (de sentiments); **r. from s.o.,** réaction *f* contre qn. **2.** *Med:* révulsion *f*; écœurement *m.*

eward [ri'wɔ:d]. **I.** *s.* récompense *f.* **II.** *v.tr.* récompenser, rémunérer **(s.o. for sth.,** qn de qch.).

hapsody ['ræpsədi], *s.* rapsodie *f*; **'rhapsodize,** *v.i. F:* **to r. over sth.,** s'extasier sur qch.

heims [ri:mz]. *Pr.n. Geog:* Reims *m.*

heostat ['ri:oustæt], *s. El:* rhéostat *m.*

hesus ['ri:səs]. **1.** *s. Z:* **r. (monkey),** (macaque) rhésus (m). **2.** *attrib. a. Med:* **r. factor,** facteur *m* rhésus (du sang); **r. positive, negative,** rhésus positif, négatif.

hetoric ['retərik], *s.* rhétorique *f*, éloquence *f*; *Pej:* discours creux; **rhe'torical** [-'tɔrikəl], *a.* (*a*) (terme) de rhétorique; (*b*) (style) ampoulé; **r. question,** question *f* pour la forme.

heumatism ['ru:mətizm], *s.* rhumatisme *m*; **rheu'matic** [-'mætik], *a.* (*of pain, etc.*) rhumatismal; **r. person,** *s.* **rheumatic,** rhumatisant, -ante; **'rheumatoid,** *a.* (*usu. in expr.*) **r. arthritis,** polyarthrite chronique évolutive.

hine (the) [ðə'rain]. *Pr.n. Geog:* le Rhin.

hinoceros [rai'nɔsərəs], *s. Z:* rhinocéros *m.*

hodesia [rou'di:ziə, -'di:ʒə]. *Pr.n. Geog:* la Rhodésie; **Rho'desian,** *a. & s.* rhodésien, -ienne.

hododendron [roudə'dendrən], *s. Bot:* rhododendron *m.*

hubarb ['ru:bɑ:b], *s. Bot:* rhubarbe *f.*

hyme [raim]. **I.** *s.* **1.** rime *f*; **without r. or reason,** sans rime ni raison. **2.** poésie *f*; **in r.,** en vers. **II.** *v.i.* (*a*) rimer (avec); (*b*) faire des vers.

hythm [rið(ə)m], *s.* rythme *m*, cadence *f*; **'rhythmic(al),** *a.* rythmique, cadencé; **r. tread,** marche scandée; **-ally,** *adv.* avec rythme; avec cadence.

ib [rib], *s.* **1.** *Anat:* côte *f.* **2.** nervure *f* (d'une feuille). **3.** baleine *f* (de parapluie).

ibald ['ribəld], *a.* licencieux, impudique; **r. song,** chanson grivoise; **'ribaldry,** *s.* grivoiserie *f.*

ibbon ['ribən], *s.* **1.** ruban *m.* **2.** ruban (d'une décoration); cordon *m* (d'un ordre). **3. to tear sth. to ribbons,** mettre qch. en lambeaux; *Adm:* **r. development,** extension urbaine en bordure de route.

ice [rais], *s.* riz *m*; **ground r.,** farine *f* de riz; **brown r.,** riz complet; **polished r.,** riz glacé; *Cu:* **r. pudding** = (i) riz au lait; (ii) gâteau *m* de riz; **'rice-grower,** *s.* riziculteur *m*; **'rice-growing,** *s.* riziculture *f*; **'rice-plan'tation,**

s. rizière *f.*

rich [ritʃ], *a.* **1.** riche; **r. people,** *s.* **the r.,** les riches; **the newly r.,** les nouveaux riches; **to grow r.,** s'enrichir. **2.** (*of soil*) fertile; **r. food,** (i) nourriture grasse, graisseuse; (ii) aliments *mpl* de choix; **-ly,** *adv.* **1.** richement. **2.** *F:* **he r. deserves it,** il l'a joliment bien mérité; **'riches,** *s.pl.* richesse(s) *f(pl)*; **'richness,** *s.* richesse *f*, abondance *f*; richesse, fertilité *f* (du sol); somptuosité *f*, luxe *m.*

rick [rik], *s.* meule *f* (de foin).

rickets ['rikits], *s. Med:* rachitisme *m.*

rickety ['rikiti], *a.* (*of furniture*) branlant; délabré; (fauteuil) bancal.

ricochet ['rikəʃei]. **I.** *s.* ricochet *m.* **II.** *v.i.* (**ricocheted** [-ʃeid]) ricocher.

rid [rid], *v.tr.* (**rid**) débarrasser, délivrer **(s.o. of sth.,** qn de qch.); **to get r. of sth.,** se débarrasser de qch.; *Com: etc:* **article hard to get r. of,** article *m* d'écoulement difficile; **'riddance,** *s.* **good r.!** bon débarras!

riddle¹ ['ridl], *s.* énigme *f*, devinette *f.*

riddle². **I.** *s.* crible *m.* **II.** *v.tr.* **1.** passer (qch.) au crible. **2. to r. s.o. with bullets,** cribler qn de balles.

ride [raid]. **I.** *s.* **1.** (*a*) promenade *f* (à cheval, à vélo); (*b*) promenade (en auto); **to go for a r. in the car,** faire un tour en voiture; **it's a short r. on the bus,** c'est un court trajet en autobus; *F:* **to take s.o. for a r.,** duper, escroquer, faire marcher, qn. **2.** (*in forest*) allée cavalière; piste *f.* **II.** *v.* (**rode; ridden**) **1.** *v.i.* (*a*) se promener, monter, à cheval; **he rides well,** il est bon cavalier; il monte bien; (*b*) aller, se promener, en voiture; aller en autobus; (*c*) (*of boat, ship*) **to r. at anchor,** mouiller. **2.** *v.tr.* (*a*) **to r. a race,** courir (une course); (*b*) **to r. a horse,** monter un cheval; **to r. a bicycle,** aller, se promener, monter, à bicyclette; (*c*) **to r. one's horse at a fence,** diriger son cheval sur une barrière; (*d*) **ridden by fear,** hanté par la peur; **'rider,** *s.* **1.** cavalier, -ière; (*horse-racing*) jockey *m*; **he's a good r.,** il monte bien (à cheval). **2.** ajouté *m*, annexe *f*, clause additionnelle (d'un document); **'riderless,** *a.* (cheval *m*) sans cavalier; **'riding,** *s.* équitation *f*; *attrib.* **r. habit,** amazone *f*; **r. breeches,** culotte *f* de cheval; **r. boots,** bottes *fpl*; **r. school,** (i) école *f* d'équitation; (ii) (*enclosed*) manège *m*; **'ride 'up,** *v.i.* (*of garment*) remonter.

ridge [ridʒ], *s.* **1.** (*a*) arête *f*, crête *f* (de montagne); (*b*) faîte *m*, crête *f* (d'un comble). **2.** chaîne *f* (de coteaux). **3.** *Agr:* billon *m*, butte *f.* **4.** ride *f* (sur le sable).

ridicule ['ridikju:l]. **I.** *s.* moquerie *f*, raillerie *f*, dérision *f*; **to hold s.o., sth., up to r.,** se moquer de qn, de qch. **II.** *v.tr.* se moquer de, ridiculiser (qn, qch.); **ri'diculous,** *a.* ridicule; **to make oneself r.,** se rendre ridicule; **to be perfectly r.,**

se montrer d'un ridicule achevé; **-ly,** *adv.* (se conduire) d'une façon ridicule; **ri′diculousness,** *s.* the r. of the situation, le ridicule de la situation.

rife [raif], *a.* (*of disease*) to be r., régner, sévir; (*of rumour*) courir les rues.

rifle[1] [′raifl], *v.tr.* piller (une armoire); to r. a tomb, violer, spolier, un tombeau.

rifle[2], *s.* carabine *f*, fusil *m*.

rift [rift], *s.* fente *f*; fissure *f*; r. in the clouds, éclaircie *f*.

rig [rig], *s. Ind:* tour *f* de forage; derrick *m*; ′**rigging,** *s.* gréement *m* (d'un navire); *Mec:* équipage *m*, montage *m* (d'une machine); ′**rig ′up,** *v.tr.* (**rigged up**) monter, installer (un appareil).

right [rait]. **I.** *a.* **1.** *Geom:* r. angle, angle droit; **to meet at r. angles,** se croiser à angle droit. **2.** bon, honnête, droit; **more than is r.,** plus que de raison; **it's only r.,** ce n'est que justice, c'est juste; **I thought it r. to . . .,** j'ai cru devoir . . .; **to take a r. view of things,** voir juste. **3.** (*a*) correct, juste, exact; **to give the r. answer,** répondre juste; **the sum is r.,** l'addition est exacte; **to put an error r.,** corriger, rectifier, une erreur; **my watch is r.,** ma montre est à l'heure, est juste; (*b*) **to be r.,** avoir raison; (*c*) **the r. word,** le mot juste; **the r. side of a material,** l'endroit *m* d'un tissu; **have you the r. amount?** avez-vous votre compte? **is that the r. house?** est-ce bien la maison? **the r. train,** le bon train; **r. side up,** à l'endroit; (*d*) **in the r. place,** (i) bien placé; (ii) à sa place; **you came at the r. moment,** vous êtes venu au bon moment; **the r. thing to do,** ce qu'il y a de mieux à faire; **that's r.!** c'est bien cela! à la bonne heure! **quite r.!** parfaitement! *F:* **r.!** bon! d'accord! (*e*) **to get on the r. side of s.o.,** s'insinuer dans les bonnes grâces de qn; **he's on the r. side of forty,** il a moins de quarante ans. **4.** (*a*) **to be in one's r. mind,** avoir toute sa raison; **to set things r.,** rétablir les choses; **things will come r. in the end,** les affaires s'arrangeront; (*b*) **everything's all r.,** tout est très bien; **all r.!** c'est bon! ça y est! **I'm all r. again now,** je suis tout à fait remis maintenant; **he's all r.!** c'est un bon type! **5.** (côté, etc.); droit; **on the r.(-hand) side,** à droite, sur la droite; **-ly,** *adv.* **1. to act r.,** bien agir. **2.** correctement; **r. speaking,** à bien prendre les choses; **I can't r. say,** je ne saurais dire au juste; **r. or wrongly,** à tort ou à raison; **if I remember r.,** si je me souviens bien. **II.** *s.* **1.** le droit; la justice; le bien; **r. and wrong,** le bien et le mal; **to be in the r.,** avoir raison; être dans son droit. **2.** (*a*) droit, titre *m*; **to have a r. to sth.,** avoir droit à qch.; **by what r.?** de quel droit? **in one's own r.,** de son chef; en propre; (*b*) *pl.* **rights,** droits; droit; **by rights,** en toute justice; **to be within one's rights,** être dans son

droit. **3.** (*a*) **to set things to rights,** rétablir les choses; (*b*) **I want to know the rights of it,** je voudrais en avoir le cœur net. **4.** droite *f*; côté droit; **on the r.,** à droite; *Aut: etc:* **to keep to the r.,** tenir la droite; *Pol:* **the R.,** la Droite. **III.** *adv.* **1.** (*a*) droit; **to go r. on,** continuer tout droit; (*b*) **to do sth. r. away,** faire qch. sur-le-champ, immédiatement. **2.** (*a*) **to sink r. to the bottom,** couler droit au fond; (*b*) **r. at the top,** tout en haut; **r. in the middle,** au beau milieu; **he threw it r. in my face,** il me le jeta en pleine figure. **3.** (*a*) **to do r.,** bien faire; bien agir; **it serves you r.!** c'est bien fait! vous ne l'avez pas volé! (*b*) (répondre) correctement; (deviner) juste; **nothing goes r. with me,** rien ne me réussit; **if I remember r.,** si je me souviens bien; **I got your letter all r.,** j'ai bien reçu votre lettre. **4.** à droite; **he owes money r. and left,** il doit de l'argent de tous les côtés. **IV.** *v.tr.* redresser; réparer (un tort); ′**right-angled,** *a.* à angle droit; **righteous** [′raitʃəs], *a.* juste, vertueux; ′**righteousness,** *s.* droiture *f*, vertu *f*; ′**right ful,** *a.* légitime, juste; **-fully,** *adv.* légitimement; à juste titre; ′**right-hand,** *a.* (*a*) (pouce, gant) de la main droite; (*b*) **the r.-hand drawer,** le tiroir de droite; (*c*) **he's my r.-hand man,** c'est (i) mon homme de confiance, (ii) mon bras droit; ′**right-′minded,** *a.* bien pensant; ′**rightness,** *s.* justesse *f* (d'une décision); exactitude *f* (d'une réponse).

rigid [′ridʒid], *a.* **1.** rigide, raide. **2.** (*of conduct*) sévère, strict; **-ly,** *adv.* **1.** rigidement. **2.** sévèrement; **ri′gidity,** *s.* **1.** rigidité *f*. **2.** sévérité *f*; intransigence *f*.

rigmarole [′rigməroul], *s.* discours sans suite, incohérent.

rigour [′rigər], *s.* rigueur *f*, sévérité *f* (de la loi etc.); austérité *f* (d'une doctrine); ′**rigorous,** *a.* rigoureux; **-ly,** *adv.* rigoureusement; avec rigueur.

rim [rim], *s.* **1.** jante *f* (d'une roue). **2.** bord *m* (d'un vase, etc.); **spectacle rims,** monture *f* de lunettes; ′**rimless,** *a.* (lunettes) sans monture.

rime [raim], *s.* givre *m*; gelée blanche.

rind [raind], *s.* peau *f*, pelure *f* (de fruit); couenne *f* (de lard); croûte *f*, pelure *f* (de fromage).

ring[1] [riŋ], *s.* **1.** (**finger-)r.,** anneau *m*; **bishop's r.,** anneau pastoral; (*for adornment*) bague *f*; **wedding r.,** alliance *f*. **2.** rond *m*, anneau; **napkin, serviette, r.,** rond de serviette; **split r.,** anneau brisé; *Mec:* segment *m* (de piston). **3.** anneau (d'une planète); cerne *m* (autour des yeux); auréole *f* (autour de la lune). **4.** cercle *m*; **sitting in a r.,** assis en rond. **5.** (*a*) groupe *m*; petite coterie (de personnes); (*b*) *Com:* syndicat *m*, cartel *m*; *Pej:* gang *m*. **6.** arène *f*, piste *f* (de cirque); *Box:* ring *m*; *Rac:* **the R.,** le pesage. **7. r. road,** route *f* de ceinture (autour d'une ville); ′**ring-dove,** *s.* (pigeon) ramier *m* palombe *f*; **'ringleader,** *s.* meneur *m* (de révolte); chef *m* (de gang, d'émeute); **'ringlet,** *s.* boucle *f* (de cheveux).

·ring². **I.** *s.* **1.** son (clair); sonnerie *f* (de cloches); tintement *m*; timbre *m* (de la voix). **2.** (*a*) coup *m* de sonnette; **there's a r. at the door,** on sonne (à la porte); (*b*) **r. on the telephone,** appel *m* téléphonique; **I'll give you a r.,** je vous téléphonerai; *F:* je vous passerai un coup de fil. **II.** *v.* **(rang; rung). 1.** *v.i.* (*a*) (*of bell*) sonner; (*b*) **his answer didn't r. true,** sa réponse a sonné faux; (*c*) résonner, retentir (**with,** de); (*d*) **my ears are ringing,** les oreilles me tintent. **2.** *v.tr.* sonner; *v.i.* **to r. for the lift,** appeler l'ascenseur; **r. the bell!** sonnez! **'ringing,** *a.* (son) sonore; retentissant; **in r. tones,** d'une voix vibrante; **'ring 'off,** *v.i. P.T.T:* raccrocher (l'appareil); **'ring 'up,** *v.tr.* **to r. s.o. up,** donner un coup de téléphone à qn; *F:* passer un coup de fil à qn.

·ink [riŋk], *s.* **(skating) r.,** patinoire *f*.

·inse [rins]. **I.** *v.tr.* rincer (le linge, une bouteille, ses cheveux). **II.** *s.* (*a*) (*of hair*) rinçage *m*; (*b*) **to give the washing a r.,** rincer le linge.

·iot ['raiət]. **I.** *s.* **1.** émeute *f.* **2.** orgie *f* (de couleurs, de fleurs, etc.). **3.** (*a*) **to run r.,** se déchaîner; (*of plants*) foisonner; (*b*) **it's, he's, a r.,** c'est rigolo; c'est un rigolo. **II.** *v.i.* se manifester de façon violente; **'rioter,** *s.* émeutier, -ière; **'rioting,** *s.* émeutes *fpl*, troubles *mpl*; **'riotous,** *a.* séditieux; tumultueux; turbulent.

·ip [rip]. **I.** *s.* déchirure *f*; fente *f*. **II.** *v.* **(ripped) 1.** *v.tr.* fendre; déchirer; **'rip(-)cord,** *s.* corde *f* d'ouverture (de parachute); **'rip 'off,** *v.tr.* arracher, déchirer (ce qui recouvre qch.); **'rip 'out,** *v.tr.* arracher (une page d'un livre).

·ipe [raip], *a.* (*a*) (*of fruit*) mûr; **a r. cheese,** un fromage (bien) fait; (*b*) **a r. old age,** un bel âge; **'ripen. 1.** *v.tr.* mûrir; faire mûrir. **2.** *v.i.* mûrir; venir à maturité; **'ripeness,** *s.* maturité *f.*

·ipple ['ripl], *s.* ride *f* (sur l'eau); ondulation *f.*

·ise [raiz]. **I.** *v.i.* **(rose; risen)** (*a*) (*of pers., sun, wind*) se lever; (*of pers.*) se mettre debout; (*b*) **Parliament will r. next week,** le Parlement doit s'ajourner la semaine prochaine; **to r. (in revolt),** se soulever (**against,** contre); (*c*) (*of ground*) s'élever, s'élever; (*d*) **the barometer is rising,** le baromètre est à la hausse; **prices have risen,** les prix ont augmenté; (*e*) **to r. to the occasion,** se montrer à la hauteur de la situation; (*f*) (*of river*) prendre sa source; (*g*) (*of pers.*) **to r. in the world,** faire son chemin dans le monde. **II.** *s.* (*a*) montée *f*, côte *f* (sur une route); rampe *f*; éminence *f* (de terrain); élévation *f* (de terrain, de température); hausse *f*, augmentation *f* (des prix); **r. in value of a possession,** appréciation *f* d'un bien; **to ask for a r.,** demander une augmentation (de salaire); (*b*) **to give r. to sth.,** engendrer, occasionner, qch.; (*c*) avancement *m* (dans sa carrière); (*d*) *F:* **to get, to take, a r.**

out of s.o., se payer la tête de qn; **'riser,** *s.* **early r.,** personne matinale; un(e) matinal(e); **'rising. I.** *a.* (soleil) levant; (route) qui monte; (prix, baromètre) en hausse; **r. tide,** marée montante; **the r. generation,** la nouvelle génération; (*of child*) **to be r. five,** aller sur ses cinq ans. **II** *s.* ameutement *m*, soulèvement *m* (de la population); lever *m* (du soleil); hausse *f* (du baromètre); crue *f* (des eaux); **r. and falling,** mouvement *m* de hausse et de baisse.

risk [risk]. **I.** *s.* risque *m*, péril *m*; **to take, run, a r.,** courir un risque; **the risks of an undertaking,** les aléas *m* d'une entreprise; **it isn't worth the r.,** *F:* ça ne vaut pas le coup. **II.** *v.tr.* risquer; hasarder (qch.); **I'll r. it,** je vais risquer, tenter, le coup; **'risky,** *a.* hasardeux, chanceux.

rissole ['risoul], *s. Cu:* croquette *f.*

rite [rait], *s.* rite *m*; **the last rites,** les derniers sacrements; **ritual** ['ritjuəl], (*a*) *a.* rituel; (*b*) *s.* rites *mpl*; **-ally,** *adv.* selon les rites.

rival ['raiv(ə)l]. **I.** *a.* & *s.* (*a*) rival, -ale; concurrent, -ente; (*b*) émule *mf.* **II.** *v.tr.* **(rivalled)** rivaliser avec (qn); être l'émule de (qn); **'rivalry,** *s.* rivalité *f*; émulation *f.*

river ['rivər], *s.* (*main*) fleuve *m*; (*tributary, smaller river*) rivière *f*; **r. port,** port fluvial; **r. bank,** rive *f* (d'un fleuve, d'une rivière); **'river-side,** *s.* **1.** bord *m* de l'eau; rive *f.* **2. r. inn,** auberge située au bord de la rivière.

rivet ['rivit]. **I.** *s.* rivet *m.* **II.** *v.tr.* (*a*) river, riveter; (*b*) **to r. s.o.'s attention,** fixer, capter, l'attention de qn; **'riveter,** *s.* riveteur *m*, riveur *m.*

Riviera (the) [ðərivi'eərə]. *Pr.n.* la Côte d'Azur.

road [roud], *s.* **1.** route *f*, chemin *m*, voie *f*; **'A' r.** = route nationale; **'B' r.** = route départementale; **r. transport,** transports routiers; **to take the r.,** se mettre en route; *Com:* **to be on the r.,** (i) être représentant (de commerce); (ii) (*of representative*) être en tournée; **r. sense,** sens pratique des dangers de la route; **he's on the right r.,** il est sur la bonne voie; **the r. to success,** la voie du succès. **2.** chaussée *f*; (*of car*) **to hold the r. well,** bien tenir la route; **r. test,** essai *m* (de voiture) sur route. **3.** *Nau: pl.* **roads** (*also* **roadstead**) rade *f*; **'roadblock,** *s.* barrage *m* (de police); **'roadman,** *pl.* **-men,** *s.* cantonnier *m*; **'roadside,** *s.* bord *m* de la route; **r. repairs,** dépannage *m*; **'road-user,** *s.* usager *m* (de la route); **'roadway,** *s.* chaussée *f*; **'roadworthy,** *a.* (*of car*) en état de marche.

roam [roum], *v.i.* errer, rôder; **'roaming,** *a.* errant, vagabond.

roar [rɔːr]. **I.** *s.* **1.** (*a*) hurlement *m*; rugissement *m*; **roars of laughter,** grands éclats de rire; (*b*) rugissement (du lion). **2.** grondement *m* (de canon); mugissement (de la mer). **II.** *v.i.* hurler, rugir; (*of sea*) mugir; (*of thunder*) gronder; (*of fire*) ronfler.

roast [roust]. **I.** *v.* **1.** *v.tr.* (*a*) rôtir, faire rôtir; (*b*) griller, torréfier (le café). **2.** *v.i.* (*of meat*) rôtir; (*of pers.*) se rôtir (devant le feu); **I'm roasting in the sun,** je (me) grille au soleil. **II.** *s.* *Cu:* rôti *m*; **a r. of beef,** un rosbif; **a r. of veal, of pork,** un rôti de veau, de porc. **III.** *a.* **r. meat,** viande rôtie; **r. beef,** rôti *m* de bœuf; rosbif *m*; **r. chicken,** poulet rôti; 'roaster, *s.* *Cu:* 1. rôtissoire *f*; brûloir *m*, torréfacteur *m* (à café). 2. volaille *f* à rôtir; 'roasting, *s.* 1. rôtissage *m*, cuisson *f* (de la viande); **r. chicken,** poulet *m* à rôtir. 2. torréfaction *f* (du café).

rob [rɔb], *v.tr.* (**robbed**) voler, dévaliser (qn); piller (un verger); **to r. s.o. of sth.,** voler qch. à qn; 'robber, *s.* voleur *m*; 'robbery, *s.* vol (qualifié); *F:* **it's highway, daylight, r.!** c'est de l'escroquerie!

robe [roub], *s.* **1.** robe *f* (d'office, de cérémonie); robe (de magistrat); toge *f* (universitaire). **2.** **bath r.,** peignoir *m* de bain.

robin ['rɔbin], *s.* (*a*) *Orn:* **r. (redbreast),** rouge-gorge *m*; (*b*) *Bot:* **ragged r.,** lychnide *f* des prés.

robot ['roubɔt], *s.* robot *m*.

robust [rou'bʌst], *a.* robuste, vigoureux, solide; ro'bustness, *s.* robustesse *f*, vigueur *f*.

rock[1] [rɔk], *s.* **1.** (*a*) rocher *m*, roc *m*; (*b*) *Geol:* roche *f*. **2.** **a r.,** un rocher, une roche; *Nau:* **to run on the rocks,** donner sur les écueils; **to see rocks ahead,** voir des obstacles devant soi; *F:* **to be on the rocks,** être dans la dèche. **3.** *Cu:* **r. cake,** petit gâteau aux raisins secs; (**Brighton, etc.**) **r.,** bâton *m* de sucrerie; **whisky on the rocks,** whisky frappé. **4.** *attrib.* **r. drawings,** dessins *m* rupestres; **r. plant,** plante alpine; 'rock-'bottom, *s.* **prices have touched r.-b.,** les prix sont au plus bas; 'rockery, *s.* jardin *m* de rocaille; 'rock 'salt, *s.* sel *m* gemme; 'rocky[1], *a.* rocheux; *Geog:* **the R. Mountains,** les (montagnes) Rocheuses.

rock[2]. **1.** *v.tr.* (*a*) bercer, balancer; basculer (un levier); **to r. a child on one's knees,** balancer un enfant sur ses genoux; (*b*) **the earthquake rocked the house,** le tremblement de terre a ébranlé la maison. **2.** *v.i.* **the cradle rocks,** le berceau balance; **rocking. I.** *a.* **1.** oscillant. **2.** branlant; **r. chair, horse,** fauteuil *m*, cheval *m*, à bascule. **II.** *s.* **1.** balancement *m*, bercement *m*; oscillation *f*. **2.** tremblement *m*, branlement *m*; **rocky**[2], *a.* *F:* instable, chancelant.

rocket ['rɔkit]. **I.** *s.* (*a*) fusée *f*; **r. launcher,** (i) lance-fusée *m*, *pl.* lance-fusées; (ii) rampe *f* de lancement de fusées; (*b*) *F:* savon *m*; **he's just had a r. from his father,** son père vient de lui passer un savon. **II.** *v.i.* *F:* **prices are rocketing,** les prix montent en flèche.

rod [rɔd], *s.* **1.** baguette *f*. **2.** verge *f*; **to make a r. for one's own back,** se préparer des ennuis; **to have a r. in pickle for s.o.,** la garder bonne à

qn; **to rule s.o. with a r. of iron,** mener qn à la baguette. **3.** (**fishing**) **r.,** canne *f* à pêche; **r. and line,** ligne *f* de pêche. **4.** **curtain, stair, r.,** tringle *f* de rideau, d'escalier.

rodent ['roud(ə)nt], *s.* *Z:* rongeur *m*.

roe[1] [rou], *s.* *Z:* **r.(-deer),** chevreuil *m*; 'roebuck *s.* chevreuil (mâle).

roe[2], *s.* (*a*) (**hard**) **r.,** œufs *mpl* (de poisson); (*b*) **soft r.,** laite *f*, laitance *f*.

roger ['rɔdʒər], *int.* *W.Tel:* (message) reçu e compris.

rogue [roug], *s.* **1.** coquin, -ine; fripon, -onne. 2 malin, -igne; espiègle *mf*. **3.** **r. elephant** éléphant *m* solitaire; 'roguish, *a.* coquin polisson; de coquin(e); malin, espiègle 'roguishness, *s.* **1.** coquinerie *f*, friponnerie *f* fourberie *f*. **2.** malice *f*, espièglerie *f*.

rôle [roul], *s.* *Th:* etc: rôle *m*.

roll [roul], *s.* **1.** (*a*) rouleau *m* (de papier, etc.) (*b*) **r.** (**of bread**), petit pain. **2.** *Adm:* rôle *m* contrôle *m*, liste *f*; **to call the r.,** faire l'appel; t enter a man on the rolls, porter un homme s les contrôles; **'R. of Honour',** (i) 'Morts pour l Patrie'; (ii) *Sch:* tableau *m* d'honneur; *Jur:* etc to strike s.o. off the rolls, rayer qn du tableau **3.** (*a*) *Nau:* coup *m* de roulis; *Av:* vol *m* e tonneau; (*b*) roulement *m* (de tambour, d tonnerre). **II.** *v.* **1.** *v.tr.* (*a*) rouler (une bille, se yeux); (*b*) **to r. one's r's,** rouler les r; grasseye (*c*) **to r. the lawn,** rouler le gazon, passer l gazon au rouleau; (*d*) laminer (les métaux); t rouler (une cigarette). **2.** *v.i.* rouler; **the tear rolled down his cheeks,** les larmes coulaie sur ses joues; **to be rolling in money,** rouler su l'or; (*of thunder*) gronder, rouler; 'roller, *s.* rouleau *m* (de pâtisserie); *Typ:* rouleau en creur; *Mec:* laminoir *m*; **road r.,** rouleau com presseur. 2. (*of the sea*) lame *f* de houle. 3. *attri* **r. skates,** patins *m* à roulettes; **r. towel,** serviett *f* sans fin; 'rolling. **I.** *a.* **to have a r. gait,** s balancer, se dandiner, en marchant; **r. countr** région *f* de coteaux, de collines. **II.** *s.* roulemen *m*; **r. pin,** rouleau *m* (à pâtisserie); **r. mill,** usin de laminage; laminoir *m*; *Rail:* **r. stoc** matériel roulant; 'roll 'over. **1.** *v.tr.* retourne culbuter (qch., qn). **2.** *v.i.* se retourner (e roulant); **dogs r. over to have their stomach scratched,** les chiens se roulent (sur le dos) pou se faire gratter le ventre; 'roll 'up, *v.tr.* roule enrouler (une carte); retrousser (ses manches enwrapper (qch.); **to r. oneself up in a blanke** s'enrouler dans une couverture.

Roman ['roumən], *a.* & *s.* romain, -aine; **numerals,** chiffres romains; **R. nose,** n busqué, aquilin; **R. Catholic,** *a.* & *s.* catholiqu (*mf*).

romance [rə'mæns, rou-]. **I.** *s.* **1.** **the** *f* **languages,** les langues romanes, néo-latines. : (*a*) histoire *f* romanesque; **it's quite a r.,** c'e tout un roman; **love of r.**, amour du romanesque; **the r. of the sea**, la poésie de la mer; (*b*) (*between two people*) idylle *f.* **II.** *v.i.* exagérer; inventer à plaisir; **ro'mantic**, *a.* (histoire *f*) romanesque; qui tient du roman; **r. landscape**, paysage *m* romantique; *Art: Lit: etc:* (école *f*, mouvement *m*) romantique; **ro'manticize.** **1.** *v.tr.* romancer (une idée, un incident); faire tout un roman d'(un incident). **2.** *v.i.* donner dans le romantique.

Rome [roum]. *Pr.n.* Rome *f*; *Ecc:* **the Church of R.**, l'Église romaine; le catholicisme.

romp [rɔmp], *v.i.* s'ébattre (bruyamment); *Rac: etc:* **to r. home**, gagner haut la main.

roof [ruːf]. **I.** *s.* **1.** toit *m*, toiture *f*, comble *m*; **to raise the r.**, faire beaucoup de bruit. **2. r. of the mouth**, dôme *m* du palais; le palais. **3.** *Aut:* **sunshine r.**, toit ouvrant; **r. rack**, galerie *f*; **r. light**, plafonnier *m.* **II.** *v.tr. Const:* couvrir (une maison); **'roofer**, *s.* (ouvrier *m*) couvreur *m*; **'roofing**, *s.* toiture *f*, couverture *f*; **corrugated r.**, couverture en plaques ondulées.

rook[1] [ruk], *s. Orn:* freux *m*; **'rookery**, *s.* colonie *f* de freux.

rook[2], *s. Chess:* tour *f*.

rook[3], *v.tr. F:* refaire, rouler (qn).

room [ruːm, rum]. **I.** *s.* **1.** place *f*, espace *m*; **to take up a lot of r.**, être très encombrant; **to be cramped for r.**, être à l'étroit; **to make r. for s.o.**, faire place à qn. **2. that leaves no r. for doubt**, le doute n'est plus permis; **there's r. for improvement**, cela laisse à désirer. **3.** (*a*) pièce *f*; salle *f*; (**bed**)**r.**, chambre *f* (à coucher); **double r.**, chambre à deux personnes; **single r.**, chambre à une personne; **living r.**, salle de séjour; (*b*) *pl.* (**set of**) **rooms**, appartement *m*; **furnished rooms to let**, chambres garnies à louer. **II.** *v.i. N.Am:* vivre en garni; partager un logement (**with s.o.**, avec qn); **'rooming-house**, *s. N.Am:* maison *f* de rapport; immeuble *m* à studios; **'room-mate**, *s.* personne avec qui on partage une chambre; **'roomy**, *a.* (appartement) spacieux; (vêtement *m*) ample.

roost [ruːst]. **I.** *s.* juchoir *m*, perchoir *m*; (*of crime*) **to come home to r.**, retourner sur son auteur; **to rule the r.**, faire la loi (chez soi). **II.** *v.i.* (*of hens*) se percher, se jucher; **'rooster**, *s.* coq *m*.

root [ruːt]. **I.** *s.* **1.** racine *f*; **to take r.**, prendre racine. **2.** source *f*, fondement *m*; **r. ideas**, idées fondamentales; **r. cause**, cause première. **3.** *Mth:* **square r.**, racine carrée. **4.** *Ling:* racine (d'un mot). **II.** *v.* **1.** *v.tr.* enraciner; **to remain rooted to the spot**, rester cloué sur place. **2.** *v.i.* (*of plant*) s'enraciner; prendre racine. **3.** *v.i. N.Am:* **to r. for a team**, applaudir une équipe; **'rooted**, *a.* (préjugé) enraciné, invétéré; **'root out**, **'up**, *v.tr.* déraciner (une plante); extirper

(un abus).

rope [roup]. **I.** *s.* corde *f*, cordage *m*; **to know the ropes**, connaitre son affaire; **to show s.o. the ropes**, mettre qn au courant. **II.** *v.tr.* corder (un paquet); (*of climbers*) s'encorder; **roped together**, en cordée; **'rope 'down**, *v.i.* faire une descente en rappel; **'rope 'off**, *v.tr.* réserver (un espace) au moyen d'une corde tendue.

rosary ['rouzəri], *s.* rosaire *m*; chapelet *m*.

rose [rouz], *s.* **1.** rose *f*; **r. bush**, rosier *m*. **2.** pomme *f* (d'arrosoir). **3.** (*colour*) rose *m*; *a.* rose, rosé; couleur de rose; **'rosebud**, *s.* bouton *m* de rose; **'rose leaf**, *s.* (i) feuille *f*, (ii) pétale *m*, de rose; **'rosemary**, *s. Bot:* romarin *m*; **'rosewood**, *s. Carp:* bois *m* de rose; **'rosy**, *a.* (couleur de) rose; rosé; **r. cheeks**, joues *f* vermeilles; **a r. prospect**, une perspective souriante.

rosette [rou'zet], *s.* cocarde *f*; rosette *f* (de ruban, d'une décoration).

rosin ['rɔzin], *s.* colophane *f.*

rostrum ['rɔstrəm], *s.* tribune *f*; (*at auction sale*) **to take the r.**, monter sur l'estrade *f.*

rot [rɔt]. **I.** *s.* **1.** pourriture *f*, carie *f*; *Vit:* **brown r.**, mildiou *m*; (*in timber*) **dry, wet, r.**, carie sèche, humide. **2. to stop the r.** parer à la démoralisation; **a r. set in**, le moral (de l'équipe) a flanché. **II.** *v.* (**rotted**) **1.** *v.i.* (se) pourrir; se décomposer, se carier; **r. away**, tomber en pourriture. **2.** *v.tr.* pourrir, faire pourrir; putréfier, carier; **'rotten**, *a.* pourri; décomposé; carié; *F:* **I feel r.**, je me sens patraque; **'rotter**, *s. F:* raté *m*; **he's a r.!** c'est un sale type!

rota ['routə], *s.* tableau *m* de service.

rotate [rou'teit]. **1.** *v.i.* tourner. **2.** *v.tr.* faire tourner (qch.); **'rotary**, *a.* rotatif, rotatoire; **r. motion**, mouvement *m* de rotation; **r. dryer, drier**, séchoir *m* sur pied; **r. (printing) press**, rotative *f*; **ro'tation**, *s.* **1.** (mouvement *m* de) rotation *f*; **in r.**, à tour de rôle; *Agr:* **r. of crops**, assolement *m*; *Mec:* **rotations per minute**, tours-minute *mpl*; **ro'tatory**, *a.* rotatoire; de rotation; **'rotor**, *s. E: Av:* rotor *m*; *Aut:* balai rotatif (du delco); (*on helicopter*) rotor.

rotund [rou'tʌnd], *a.* rond, arrondi; **ro'tundity**, *s.* rondeur *f.*

rouge [ruːʒ]. **I.** *s. Toil:* rouge *m*, fard *m*; **jeweller's r.**, rouge à polir. **II.** *v.tr.* **to r. one's cheeks**, se farder (les joues); mettre du rouge.

rough [rʌf]. **I.** *a.* **1.** (*a*) (*of surface*) rêche, rugueux, rude; (*b*) (*of road*) raboteux, rude; (*of ground*) inégal, accidenté; (*c*) **in the r. state**, l'état brut; **r. to the touch**, rude, âpre, au toucher. **2.** grossier; brutal; **r. sea**, mer agitée; *Nau:* **r. weather**, gros temps; **to have a r. crossing**, faire une mauvaise traversée; **r. play**, jeu brutal; **to be r. with s.o.**, brutaliser, rudoyer, qn; *F:* **a r. customer**, un sale type; **to**

give s.o. a r. **handling**, malmener, houspiller, qn. 3. (*of manners*) grossier; bourru, rude. 4. approximatif; r. **sketch**, ébauche *f*, esquisse *f*; r. **translation**, essai *m* de traduction, premier jet; r. **draft**, brouillon *m*; r. **estimate**, évaluation *f* en gros. 5. (*of voice*) rude, rauque; -**ly**, *adv.* 1. rudement, brutalement; **to treat s.o. r.**, malmener qn. 2. grossièrement. 3. approximativement; à peu près; en gros; r. **speaking**, en général. II. *s.* 1. *Golf:* **to be in the r.**, être, se trouver, dans l'herbe longue. 2. **one must take the r. with the smooth**, à la guerre comme à la guerre. 3. *F:* (*pers.*) voyou *m*, bandit *m*. III. *adv.* rudement, grossièrement; **to play r.**, jouer brutalement; *F:* **to cut up r.**, se mettre en colère. IV. *v.tr. F:* **to r. it**, vivre à la dure; **to r. down**, dégrossir (une pièce de forge); **to r. out a plan**, ébaucher un plan; *F:* **to r. (s.o.) up**, malmener (qn); '**rough-and-**'**ready**, *a.* exécuté grossièrement; r.-and-r. **installation**, installation *f* de fortune; '**rough-house**, *s. F:* chahut *m*, bousculade *f*; '**roughneck**, *s. F: esp. N.Am:* voyou *m*; '**roughness**, *s.* (*a*) rudesse *f*, rugosité *f*; (*b*) inégalité *f*, rugosité (du sol); (*c*) (*of pers.*) grossièreté *f*; manières bourrues (de qn); (*d*) agitation *f* (de la mer); rudesse (du temps); '**roughshod**, *a.* **to ride r. over s.o.**, traiter qn sans ménagement.

roulette [ru:'let], *s.* roulette *f*.

round [raund]. I. *a.* 1. rond, circulaire; r. **table conference**, table ronde, réunion *f* paritaire; r. **shoulders**, épaules voûtées; **to make sth. r.**, arrondir qch. 2. r. **dance**, ronde *f*; r. **trip**, voyage *m* aller-retour. 3. (*a*) r. **dozen**, bonne douzaine; **in r. figures**, en chiffres ronds; (*b*) **to go at a good r. pace**, aller bon train. II. *s.* 1. cercle *m*, rond *m*. 2. *Cu:* r. **of sandwiches**, sandwich fait de pain de mie et coupé en quatre; r. **of toast**, rôtie *f*. 3. **the daily r.**, le train-train quotidien; **one continual r. of pleasures**, une succession perpétuelle de plaisirs. 4. (*a*) tour *m*; **to stand a r. (of drinks)**, payer une tournée (générale); **to have a r. of golf**, faire une tournée de golf; **the story went the rounds**, l'histoire a passé de bouche en bouche; (*b*) tournée *f* (du facteur, d'un médecin); (*c*) *Mil:* ronde *f* (d'inspection). 5. *Box:* round *m*, reprise *f*. 6. (*a*) r. **of applause**, salve *f* d'applaudissements; (*b*) *Mil:* **a r. of ammunition**, une cartouche. 7. *Mus:* canon *m*. III. *adv.* 1. (*a*) **to go r.**, tourner, décrire un cercle, des cercles; **the wheels go r.**, les roues tournent; **to turn r.**, se retourner; (*b*) **all the year r.**, (pendant) toute l'année; **winter came r.**, l'hiver est revenu. 2. (*a*) **garden with a wall right r.**, all r., jardin avec un mur tout autour; **to be six feet r.**, avoir six pieds de tour; (*b*) **all the country r. about**, tout le pays à l'entour; **for**

a **mile r.**, à un mille à la ronde. 3. **to hand r. the cakes**, faire circuler les gâteaux; **there isn't enough to go r.**, il n'y en a pas pour tout le monde. 4. **it's a long way r.**, cela fait un grand détour; **to take the longest way r.**, prendre par le plus long; **to ask s.o. r.**, inviter qn chez soi; **you're r. this way, si vous passez par ici.** IV. *prep.* r. **(the table, etc.)**, autour de (la table, etc.); **to go r. the museum**, visiter le musée; **to go r. an obstacle**, contourner un obstacle; *F:* **to go r. the bend**, devenir fou, *F:* dingue. V. *v. tr.* arrondir (un angle); contourner (un obstacle); *Nau:* doubler, franchir (un cap). 2. *v.i.* s'arrondir; **to r. on s.o.**, s'en prendre à qn; '**roundabout**. I. *s.* 1. chevaux *mpl* de bois, manège *m*. 2. *Aut:* rond-point *m*. II. *a.* détourné; indirect; **to take a r. way**, faire un détour; '**rounded**, *a.* arrondi; '**roundish**, *a.* rondelet; '**roundness**, *s.* rondeur *f*; '**round-'shouldered**, *a.* voûté; '**round 'up**, *v.tr.* rassembler (le bétail); rafler (des malfaiteurs).

rouse [rauz], *v.tr.* 1. (*a*) **to r. s.o. (from sleep)**, réveiller qn; **to r. the neighbourhood**, alerter le voisinage; **to r. s.o.**, secouer la paresse de qn; **to r. oneself**, se secouer; **to r. s.o. to action**, inciter qn à agir; (*b*) mettre (qn) en colère. 2. soulever (l'indignation); susciter (l'admiration, l'opposition); '**rousing**, *a.* r. **cheer**, applaudissements chaleureux; r. **speech**, discours vibrant; r. **chorus**, refrain entraînant.

rout[1] [raut]. I. *s. Mil:* déroute *f*; débandade *f*. II. *v.tr. Mil:* mettre (une armée) en déroute; '**routed**, *a.* en déroute.

rout[2], *v.tr. & i.* fouiller (dans des papiers, etc.); '**rout 'out**, *v.tr.* dénicher (qn); tirer (qn) de son lit, etc.; faire déguerpir (un renard, etc.).

route [ru:t], *s.* (*a*) itinéraire *m*; route *f*; chemin *m*; **sea r.**, route maritime; **trade routes**, routes commerciales; **bus r.**, itinéraire, parcours *m* d'un autobus; (*b*) *Mil:* **column of r.**, colonne de route; r. **march**, marche *f* d'entraînement; r. **map**, carte routière.

routine [ru:'ti:n], *s.* routine *f*; r. **work**, affaires courantes; **daily r.**, le train-train journalier.

roving [ˈrouviŋ], *a.* vagabond, nomade; r. **instincts**, instincts *m* nomades; **to have a r. eye**, avoir l'œil gaillard.

row[1] [rou], *s.* 1. rang *m*, rangée *f*; ligne *f*; file *f* (de voitures); **in a r.**, en rang, en ligne; **in rows**, par rangs. 2. rang (de chaises); **in the front r.**, premier rang; r. **of houses**, ligne, rangée, de maisons.

row[2] [rou]. I. *v.* 1. *v.i.* (*a*) ramer; *Nau:* nager; **to row round the island**, faire le tour de l'île à la rame; (*b*) canoter; faire du canotage. 2. *v.tr.* conduire (un bateau) à l'aviron; **to r. a race**, faire une course d'aviron. II. *s.* promenade *f* en canot, partie *f* de canotage; **to go for a r.**, faire une promenade en canot; ʹ**rower**, *s.* rameur, -euse; ʹ**rowing**, *s.* canotage *m*; **r. boat,** canot *m* à l'aviron; **rowlocks** [ʹrɔləks], *s.pl.* dames *f* de nage; tolets *m*.

ʹow³ [rau], *s.* **1.** chahut *m*, tapage *m*, vacarme *m*; **to make a r.,** faire du chahut; faire du tapage. **2.** dispute *f*; scène *f*; bagarre *f*. **3. to get into a r.,** se faire attraper.

owan [ʹrouən], *s. Bot:* **r. (tree),** sorbier *m*.

owdy [ʹraudi]. **1.** *a.* tapageur, -euse. **2.** *s.* voyou *m*; ʹ**rowdiness,** *s.* turbulence *f*; tapage *m*; violence *f*; brutalité *f*; ʹ**rowdyism,** *s.* violence *f*; désordre public.

oyal [ʹrɔiəl], *a.* (*a*) royal; **the R. household,** la maison du roi, de la reine; (*b*) royal, princier; magnifique; **a r. feast,** un festin de roi; **-ally,** *adv.* royalement; ʹ**royalist,** *a. & s.* royaliste (*mf*); ʹ**royalty,** *s.* **1.** royauté *f*; *pl.* **royalties,** membres de la famille royale. **2.** *pl.* redevances *f*, droits *m* d'auteur; *Ind:* (*on patent, for use of oil pipeline*) royalties *f*.

ub [rʌb]. **I.** *v.* (**rubbed**) **1.** *v.tr.* (*a*) frotter; **to r. one's hands (together),** se frotter les mains; **to r. shoulders with other people,** frayer avec d'autres gens; **to r. s.o. (up) the wrong way,** contrarier qn; prendre qn à rebrousse -poil; (*b*) **to r. sth. dry,** sécher qch. en le frottant; (*c*) **to r. sth. over a surface,** enduire une surface de qch. **2.** *v.i.* frotter (**against,** contre); (*of pers.*) se frotter (contre). **II.** *s.* frottement *m*; friction *f*; ʹ**rub aʹlong,** *v.i. F:* se débrouiller; ʹ**rubber**¹, *s.* **1.** caoutchouc *m*; (**India**) **r.,** gomme *f*; **crepe r.,** crêpe *m* de latex; **foam r.,** caoutchouc mousse; **r. dinghy,** canot *m* pneumatique. **2.** *pl. esp. N.Am:* (**overshoes**) caoutchoucs; ʹ**rubber** ʹ**stamp,** *s.* tampon *m*; **rubber-stamp,** *v.tr.* entériner (automatiquement, sans délibérations); ʹ**rub** ʹ**down,** *v.tr.* (*a*) panser (un cheval); (*b*) frictionner (qn); ʹ**rub** ʹ**in,** *v.tr.* faire pénétrer (un liniment) par des frictions; **don't r. it in!** n'insistez pas davantage (sur ma gaffe, etc.)! ʹ**rub** ʹ**out,** *v.tr.* effacer; ʹ**rub** ʹ**up,** *v.tr.* astiquer, frotter, fourbir; **to r. s.o. up the wrong way,** prendre qn à rebrousse-poil.

ubber², *s.* (*at bridge*) robre *m*; **the r. game,** la belle.

ubbish [ʹrʌbiʃ], *s.* **1.** (*a*) immondices *fpl*, détritus *mpl*; **household r.,** ordures ménagères; *P.N:* **no r.!** défense de déposer des ordures; (*b*) choses *fpl* sans valeur; (*c*) camelote *f*. **2. to talk r.,** dire des bêtises *f*; (**what**) **r.!** quelle blague! ʹ**rubbish-bin,** *s.* poubelle *f*; ʹ**rubbish-dump,** *s.* décharge publique; ʹ**rubbish-shoot,** *s.* (*in flats*) vide-ordures *m inv*; ʹ**rubbishy,** *a.* sans valeur; (marchandises) de camelote.

ubble [ʹrʌbl], *s. Const:* **1.** blocaille *f*. **2.** décombres *mpl*.

ubicund [ʹru:bikənd], *a.* (*of s.o.'s face*) rougeaud.

ruby [ʹru:bi]. **1.** *s. Miner:* rubis *m*. **2.** *a. & s.* couleur de rubis; rouge (*m*).

rucksack [ʹrʌksæk], *s.* sac *m* à dos.

ructions [ʹrʌkʃ(ə)nz], *s.pl. F:* **there'll be r.,** il va y avoir du grabuge; **if you're late there'll be r.,** si tu es en retard, tu te feras engueuler.

rudder [ʹrʌdər], *s.* gouvernail *m*; ʹ**rudderless,** *a.* (vaisseau *m*) sans gouvernail, à la dérive.

ruddy [ʹrʌdi], *a.* **1.** (*a*) (teint) coloré, haut en couleur; **a large, r. man,** un gros rougeaud; (*b*) rougeâtre; **the r. glow (of the fire),** la lueur rouge (du feu). **2.** *P:* (= *bloody*) **all this r. work,** tout ce sacré travail; **he's a r. nuisance,** il est bigrement enquiquinant.

rude [ru:d], *a.* **1.** (*a*) primitif, rude; (*b*) grossier; **r. verses,** vers scabreux; **r. drawing,** dessin *m* obscène. **2.** violent, brusque; **r. shock,** choc violent. **3. r. health,** santé robuste. **4.** impoli; mal élevé; **to be r. to s.o.,** dire des grossièretés à qn; **-ly,** *adv.* **1.** primitivement; grossièrement. **2.** violemment; brusquement. **3.** impoliment, grossièrement; ʹ**rudeness,** *s.* impolitesse *f*, grossièreté *f*.

rudiment [ʹru:dimənt], *s.* **1.** *Biol:* rudiment *m*. **2.** *pl. Sch:* rudiments, éléments *m*, premières notions (d'une discipline); **rudiʹmentary,** *a.* rudimentaire.

ruffian [ʹrʌfjən], *s.* bandit *m*, brute *f*; ʹ**ruffianly,** *a.* (homme) brutal; (conduite *f*) de brute; **r. appearance,** allure *f* de brigand.

ruffle [ʹrʌfl], *v.tr.* ébouriffer (les cheveux); (*of bird*) hérisser (ses plumes); troubler, rider (la surface de l'eau); **to r. s.o.'s feelings,** froisser qn; **nothing ever ruffles him,** rien ne le trouble jamais.

rug [rʌg], *s.* **1.** couverture *f*. **2.** carpette *f*; descente *f* de lit.

rugby [ʹrʌgbi], *s.* **r. (football),** *F:* **rugger** [ʹrʌgər], le rugby; **R. Union,** rugby à quinze; **R. League,** rugby à treize; **r. player,** rugbyman *m*, *pl.* -men.

rugged [ʹrʌgid], *a.* (*of ground*) raboteux, accidenté, inégal; (*of tree bark*) rugueux. **2. r. features,** traits rudes, irréguliers. **3.** (*of character*) bourru, rude; **r. independence,** indépendance *f* farouche.

ruin [ʹru:in]. **I.** *s.* **1.** ruine *f*; **to go to r.,** tomber en ruine; **the r. of my hopes,** l'effondrement *m* de mes espoirs; **to bring (s.o.) to r.,** ruiner, perdre (qn). **2.** (*often pl.*) ruine(s); décombres *mpl*; **the building is a r.,** l'édifice est en ruines. **II.** *v.tr.* ruiner; (*a*) abîmer (son chapeau); (*b*) **to r. one's prospects,** gâcher son avenir; **to r. one's health,** démolir sa santé; **to r. s.o.'s reputation,** perdre qn de réputation. **2. her extravagance ruined him,** ses folles dépenses l'ont ruiné; **ruiʹnation,** *s.* ruine *f*, perte *f*; **it'll be the r. of him,** ce sera sa ruine; ʹ**ruined,** *a.* **1.** en ruines.

2. ruiné; **'ruinous**, *a*. 1. (tombé) en ruines; délabré. 2. ruineux; r. **expense**, dépenses ruineuses; -ly, *adv*. r. expensive, ruineux.

rule [ru:l]. I. *s*. 1. règle *f*; (*a*) **as a** (general) **r.**, en règle générale; **r. of thumb**, méthode *f* empirique; (*b*) **to make it a r. to . . .**, se faire une règle de . . .; r. **of conduct**, directive *f*; norme *f* de conduite; (*c*) **rules and regulations**, statuts *m* et règlements *m*; *Ind*: **work(ing) to r.**, grève *f* du zèle; **the rules of the game**, les règles du jeu; *Aut*: **the r. of the road**, le code de la route. 2. empire *m*, autorité *f*; administration *f*; domination *f*. 3. *Carp*: etc: règle graduée; mètre *m*. II. *v*. 1. *v.tr*. gouverner (un état); régner sur (une nation); **to r. one's passions**, contenir ses passions; **to be ruled by s.o.**, être sous la coupe de qn; subir la loi de qn. 2. régler, rayer (du papier); **to r. a line**, tracer une ligne à la règle. 2. *v.i*. **the prices ruling in London**, les prix *m* qui se pratiquent à Londres; **'ruler**, *s*. 1. souverain, -aine. 2. règle *f*, mètre *m*; **'ruling**. I. *a*. 1. souverain, dominant. 2. **r. price**, prix *m* pratique, prix du jour. II. *s*. ordonnance *f*; décision *f* (d'un juge); **to give a r. in favour of** s.o., décider en faveur de qn; **'rule'out**, *v.tr*. 1. **to r. o.** (s.o., sth.), écarter, éliminer (qn, qch.). 2. biffer, rayer (un mot).

rum [rʌm], *s*. rhum *m*; r. **distillery**, rhumerie *f*.
Rumania [ru(:)'meiniə]. *Pr.n. Geog:* la Roumanie; **Ru'manian**, *a. & s.* roumain, -aine.
rumble ['rʌmbl]. I. *s*. grondement *m*; roulement *m* (d'un train, d'un camion); *F:* **tummy rumbles**, borborygmes *mpl*. II. *v.i*. (*of thunder*, etc.) gronder (sourdement); rouler.
ruminate ['ru:mineit], *v.i*. 1. (*of cow*) ruminer. 2. *v.i. & tr.* (*of pers.*) ruminer; méditer; **'ruminant**, *a. & s. Z:* ruminant (*m*); **rumi-'nation**, *s*. rumination *f*; **'ruminative**, *a*. méditatif.
rummage ['rʌmidʒ]. I. *v.tr. & i.* fouiller (dans) (une armoire); **to r. about among old papers**, fouiller, fourrager, dans de vieux documents. II. *s*. 1. recherches *fpl*; fouille *f* (parmi de vieux objets). 2. vieilleries *fpl*; objets divers (sans utilité); objets de rebut.
rumour ['ru:mər], *s*. rumeur *f*, bruit *m* (qui court); on-dit *m inv*; **'rumoured**, *a*. **it's r. that . . .**, le bruit court que . . .
rump [rʌmp], *s*. croupe *f* (d'un quadrupède); croupion *m* (de volaille); *F:* (*of pers.*) postérieur *m*, derrière *m*; *Cu:* **r. steak**, rum(p)-steak *m*; romsteck *m*.
rumple ['rʌmpl], *v.tr*. chiffonner, froisser (une robe, etc.); ébouriffer (les cheveux).
rumpus ['rʌmpəs], *s. F:* chahut *m*, vacarme *m*; **to kick up a r.**, faire une scène, avoir une prise de bec (avec qn).
run [rʌn]. I. *v*. (**ran; run;** *pr.p.* **running**) 1. *v.i*.

(*a*) courir; **to r. upstairs**, monter l'escalie quatre à quatre; **to r. a race**, disputer un course; **to r. an errand**, faire une course; **up, down, the street**, monter, descendre, la r en courant; **to r. like the devil**, courir comm un dératé; (*b*) fuir, s'enfuir, se sauver; *Nau:* (*yacht*) **to r. before the wind**, aller vent arrièr **now we must r. for it!** maintenant sauvon nous! (*c*) *Pol:* **to r. for office**, se porter ca didat; (*d*) aller, marcher; circuler; **train ru ning at fifty kilometres an hour**, train q marche à cinquante kilomètres à l'heure; **tra running to Paris**, train à destination *f* de Par **this train is not running today**, ce train est su primé aujourd'hui; (*e*) **the thought keeps ru ning through my head**, cette idée me revie continuellement à l'esprit; (*f*) **the talk ran this subject**, la conversation a roulé sur sujet; (*g*) (*of amount, number*) **to r. to . . .**, monter, s'élever, à . . .; **I can't r. to that**, c'e au-dessus de mes moyens; (*h*) fonctionn marcher; **the engine's running**, le moteur est marche; *El:* **to r. off the mains**, se brancher s le secteur; (*i*) (*of colour*) déteindre (au lavag (*of paint*) couler; (*of nose*) couler; (*of ey* pleurer; (*j*) **a heavy sea was running**, la m était grosse; (*of mountain chain, etc.*) to **north and south**, s'étendre du nord au s **money runs through his fingers**, l'argent fond dans les mains. 2. *v.tr*. (*a*) **to r. s.o. clo age**, rentrer la voiture dans le garage; (*c*) t s.o. into town, conduire qn en ville (en voitur (*d*) **I can't afford to r. a car**, je n'ai pas moyens d'entretenir une auto; **my car is che to r.**, ma voiture est économique; (*e*) tenir hôtel, un commerce); éditer, gérer (un jo nal); **to r. one's house**, tenir sa maison; (*f*) **a thorn into one's finger**, s'enfoncer une ép dans le doigt; **to r. one's eye over sth.**, jeter coup d'œil sur qch., parcourir qch. des ye II. *s*. (*a*) at a **r.**, au pas de course; **to break** a r., se mettre à courir; **prices have come do with a r.**, les prix ont dégringolé, *F:* ont ch **she's always on the r.**, elle est tout le temp courir; **to have a r. for one's money**, en av pour son argent; *Cricket:* **to make, score, runs**, marquer dix points; (*b*) *Aut: etc:* **to go a r.**, faire une promenade; **trial r.**, course *f*, cours *m*, d'essai; *Av:* **take-off r.**, parcours décollage; **landing r.**, parcours à l'atterriss (*c*) **to have a r. of luck**, être en veine; **a r. of** luck, une suite de malheurs, une série no (*d*) **there's a r. on that novel**, ce roman es demandé, on demande beaucoup ce roman **to have free r. of s.o.'s house**, avoir libre ac à la maison de qn; **to give s.o. the r. of o library**, mettre sa bibliothèque à la disposi de qn; (*f*) **toboggan, ski, r.**, piste *f* de tobog de ski; **'run a'cross,** *v.tr.* (*a*) traverser en courant; (*b*) rencontrer (qn) par hasard; **'run a'long,** *v.i.* 1. **road that runs along the river,** chemin qui longe la rivière. 2. **r. along!** allez-vous-en! va-t-en! filez! *F:* fichez-moi le camp! **'run a'way,** *v.i.* (*a*) s'enfuir, se sauver; (*b*) (*of horse*) (*c*) **don't r. away with the idea that . . .,** n'allez pas vous imaginer que . . .; **that runs away with a lot of money,** cela mange beaucoup d'argent; **'runaway,** *s.* fugitif, -ive; **'run 'down.** 1. *v.i.* **the sweat ran down his forehead,** la sueur lui coulait sur le front. 2. *v.i.* **the clock is running down,** l'horloge a besoin d'être remontée. 3. *v.tr.* (*a*) dénigrer, déprécier (qn, qch.); (*b*) *Aut:* heurter, renverser (qn sur la route); **to get r. down,** se faire écraser (par une voiture). 4. **to r. down stocks,** laisser s'épuiser les stocks; (*of pers.*) **to get r. down,** se débiliter; **'run 'in,** *v.tr.* 1. *Aut:* roder (un moteur); **running in,** en rodage. 2. *F:* (*of police*) arrêter (qn); **'run 'into,** *v.i.* (*a*) **to r. into debt,** s'endetter; (*b*) **to r. into sth.,** entrer en collision avec qch.; **'runner,** *s.* 1. coureur, -euse. 2. *Hort:* (*a*) **r. bean, scarlet r.,** haricot *m* d'Espagne; (*b*) coulant *m*, stolon *m*, traînée *f* (d'une plante). 3. patin *m* (de traîneau). 4. chariot *m* de roulement; trolley *m*. 5. *H:* (carpet-)r., chemin *m* d'escalier, de couloir; (table-)r., chemin de table; **'runner-'up,** *s. Sp: etc:* second, -onde; celui qui est battu dans l'épreuve finale; **'running.** I. *a.* (*a*) (*before the noun*) **r. water,** eau courante; **r. cold,** rhume *m* de cerveau; **r. expenses,** dépenses courantes; **r. commentary,** reportage *m* en direct; (*b*) (*after the noun*) consécutif; de suite; **three days r.,** trois jours de suite. II. *s.* 1. *Sp:* course(s) *f(pl)* (à pied); **to be in the r.,** avoir des chances de réussir; **to be out of the r.,** ne plus avoir aucune chance. 2. (*a*) marche *f*, fonctionnement *m* (d'une machine); roulement *m* (d'une voiture); **smooth r.,** allure régulière; (*b*) **to modify the r. of the trains,** modifier la marche des trains; (*c*) direction (d'un hôtel, etc.); exploitation *f* (d'une mine, etc.); administration *f* (d'une industrie, d'une affaire commerciale, d'un bureau, etc.); **'run 'off.** 1. *v.i.* fuir, s'enfuir, se sauver; **to r. off with the cash,** filer avec l'argent. 2. *v.tr.* (*a*) faire écouler (un liquide); (*b*) photocopier (qch.) rapidement; **'run 'on,** *v.i.* (*a*) continuer sa course; (*b*) (*of time*) s'écouler; (*c*) continuer à parler; **'run 'out,** *v.i.* (*a*) sortir en courant; (*b*) (*of the tide is running out,** la mer se retire; (*c*) (*of liquid*) couler, fuir; (*d*) (*of time*) se terminer, expirer; (*e*) (*of supplies*) venir à manquer; faire défaut; **we are running out of food,** les vivres s'épuisent; **'run 'over,** *v.tr.* 1. parcourir (un document, etc.) du regard. 2. *Aut:* passer sur le corps de (qn); **he's been r. over,** il a été écrasé,

il s'est fait écraser; **'run 'through,** *v.tr.* (*a*) traverser (la salle) en courant; (*b*) parcourir (un document) du regard; (*c*) **to r. through a fortune,** dissiper une fortune; **'run 'up.** 1. *v.i.* (*a*) monter (les escaliers) en courant; (*b*) accourir; **to come running up,** arriver en courant; **to r. up against s.o.,** (i) rencontrer qn par hasard; (ii) se trouver en conflit avec qn. 2. *v.tr.* (*a*) laisser grossir (un compte); laisser accumuler (des dettes); (*b*) **to r. up a flag,** hisser un pavillon; **'runway,** *s. Av:* piste *f* d'envol.

rung [rʌŋ], *s.* échelon *m*, barreau *m*, (barre *f* de) traverse *f* (d'une échelle); bâton *m* (d'une chaise).

rupture ['rʌptʃər]. I. *s.* rupture *f* (de négociations); brouille *f* (entre amis); *Med:* rupture (d'une veine); hernie *f*. II. *v.* (*a*) *v.tr.* rompre (des relations); *Med:* se rompre, claquer (un tendon); (*b*) *v.i.* se rompre.

rural ['ruərəl], *a.* rural, -aux; champêtre; de (la) campagne.

ruse [ru:z], *s.* ruse *f*, stratagème *m*.

rush¹ [rʌʃ], *s.* jonc *m*.

rush². I. *s.* 1. (*a*) course précipitée; **to make a r. at s.o.,** se précipiter sur qn; **a general r.,** une ruée générale; une bousculade; (*b*) **the r. hours,** les heures d'affluence, de pointe. 2. hâte *f*; **r. order,** commande urgente; **the r. of modern life,** la vie fiévreuse d'aujourd'hui. 3. **r. of blood to the head,** (i) coup *m* de sang; (ii) accès *m* de colère. II. *v.* 1. *v.i.* (*a*) se précipiter; s'élancer; **to r. into the room,** faire irruption dans la salle; **to r. to the window,** se ruer à la fenêtre; (*b*) **the wind rushes up the chimney,** le vent s'engouffre dans la cheminée; **the blood rushed to his face,** le sang lui est monté au visage. 2. *v.tr.* (*a*) pousser, entraîner, violemment; **they were rushed to hospital,** on les a transportés d'urgence à l'hôpital; **I don't want to r. you,** je ne voudrais pas vous bousculer; **don't r. me,** laissez-moi le temps de souffler; (*b*) se dépêcher à faire (un travail); exécuter (une commande) d'urgence.

russet ['rʌsɪt]. 1. *s. Hort:* reinette grise. 2. *a. & s.* (couleur *f*) roussâtre.

Russia ['rʌʃə]. *Pr.n. Geog:* la Russie; **'Russian.** 1. *s.* (*a*) Russe *mf*; (*b*) *Ling:* le russe. 2. *a.* de Russie; russe.

rust [rʌst]. I. *s.* rouille *f*. II. *v.i.* (se) rouiller; **'rusty,** *a.* rouillé; **to get r.,** se rouiller.

rustic ['rʌstik]. 1. *a.* rustique; paysan. 2. *s.* paysan, -anne; campagnard, -arde.

rustle ['rʌsl]. I. *s.* bruissement *m*; frou-frou *m* (de la soie); froissement *m* (de papiers). II. *v.* 1. *v.i.* (*of wind, leaves, paper, etc.*) bruire; (*of silk*) faire frou-frou. 2. *v.tr.* faire bruire (des papiers); **'rustle 'up,** *v.tr.* **to r. up support,** rassembler des partisans; **'rustling,** *s.* vol *m* (de bétail).

rut [rʌt], *s.* ornière *f*; (*of pers.*) **to be in a r.,** s'encroûter; devenir routinier; **to get out of the r.,** sortir de son ornière; se désencroûter;'**rutted,** *a.* (chemin) coupé d'ornières.

ruthless ['ru:θlis], *a.* impitoyable; sans pitié; **-ly,** *adv.* sans pitié; '**ruthlessness,** *s.* nature *f* impitoyable (de qn).

rye [rai], *s.* (*a*) seigle *m*; (*b*) **r. bread,** pain *m* de seigle; (*c*) *N.Am:* whisky *m*.

S

S, s [es], s. (la lettre) S, s m or f.
Sabbath ['sæbəθ], s. (a) Jew: sabbat m; (b) Ecc: dimanche m; **sa'bbatical,** a. & s. **s.** (year), année de congé (accordée à un professeur).
sable ['seibl], s. zibeline f (animal ou fourrure).
sabotage ['sæbətɑ:ʒ]. I. s. sabotage m. II. v.tr. saboter (des appareils, une usine; un projet); **sabo'teur,** s. saboteur, -euse.
sabre ['seibər], s. Mil: sabre m; **s. cut,** (i) coup m de sabre; (ii) (scar) balafre f.
saccharin(e) ['sækərin, -i:n], s. saccharine f.
sachet ['sæʃei], s. sachet m.
sack¹ [sæk]. I. s. **1.** (grand) sac; **to put (sth.) into sacks,** ensacher (qch.). **2.** F: **to give s.o. the s.,** congédier (un employé); F: balancer, P: saquer (qn); **to get the s.,** recevoir son congé; P: être saqué. II. v.tr. F: **to s. s.o.,** congédier, P: saquer (qn); **'sackcloth,** s. toile f d'emballage; **'sackful,** s. plein sac (de qch.); **'sacking¹,** s. **1.** mise f en sac. **2.** F: congédiement m.
sack², v.tr. saccager, mettre à sac, au pillage (une ville); **'sacking²,** s. sac m.
sacrament ['sækrəmənt], s. Ecc: sacrement m; **to receive the s.,** communier.
sacred ['seikrid], a. (a) Ecc: sacré, saint; (b) s. **music,** musique religieuse; (c) sacré, inviolable; **nothing was s. to him,** il ne respectait rien; **'sacredness** [-idnis], s. (a) caractère sacré (**of a place,** d'un lieu); (b) inviolabilité f (d'une promesse).
sacrifice ['sækrifais]. I. s. **1.** (a) sacrifice m; **to offer sth. as a s.,** offrir qch. en sacrifice (**to,** à); (b) victime f; offrande f. **2.** (a) sacrifice (de qch.); renoncement m (à qch.); **he succeeded at the s. of his health,** il a réussi en sacrifiant sa santé; (b) Com: **to sell sth. at a s.,** vendre qch. à perte. II. v.tr. sacrifier; renoncer à (qch.); Com: vendre à perte.
sacrilege ['sækrilidʒ], s. sacrilège m; **sacri'legious,** a. sacrilège.
sacristy ['sækristi], s. Ecc: sacristie f; **'sacristan,** s. Ecc: sacristain m.
sacrosanct ['sækrousæŋkt], a. sacro-saint.
sad [sæd], a. **1.** (a) triste; **to make s.o. s.,** attrister qn; **to be s. at heart,** avoir le cœur gros; (b) (of news, etc.) affligeant; (of loss, etc.) cruel; **to come to a s. end,** faire une triste fin; **-ly,** adv. tristement; **'sadden,** v.tr. attrister; **'sadness,** s. tristesse f, mélancolie f.
saddle ['sædl]. I. s. **1.** selle f (de cheval, de vélo,

de moto); **hunting s.,** selle anglaise. **2.** col m (de montagne). **3.** Cu: selle (de mouton). II. v.tr. (a) seller (un cheval); (b) **to s. s.o. with sth.,** charger qn de qch.; **she's saddled with five children,** elle a cinq enfants sur le dos; **'saddlebag,** s. sacoche f (de selle); **'saddler,** s. sellier m; bourrelier m.
sadism ['seidizm], s. sadisme m; **'sadist,** s. sadique mf; **sa'distic** [sə'-], a. sadique.
safari [sə'fɑ:ri], s. safari m; **on s.,** en safari; **s. park,** réserve f d'animaux sauvages.
safe [seif]. I. a. **1.** (a) en sûreté; à l'abri; (b) **s. and sound,** sain et sauf. **2.** (a) sans danger; sûr; (of bridge, etc.) solide; **to put sth. in a s. place,** mettre qch. en lieu sûr; (b) **is it s. to leave him alone?** est-ce qu'il n'y a pas de danger à le laisser seul? (c) **to be on the s. side,** être du bon côté; **to play a s. game,** jouer serré; **it's s. to say that . . .,** on peut dire à coup sûr que . . .; **-ly,** adv. **1. to arrive s.,** arriver sans accident, à bon port. **2.** sans risque, sans danger. II. s. **1.** coffre-fort m. **2.** **meat-s.,** garde-manger m; **'safeguard.** I. s. sauvegarde f, garantie f (**against,** contre). II. v.tr. sauvegarder, protéger (les droits de qn); mettre (ses intérêts) à couvert; **'safety,** s. sûreté f, sécurité f; salut m; **in a place of s.,** en lieu sûr; **road s.,** la sécurité de la route; Ind: etc: **s. measures,** mesures de sécurité; **s. factor,** coefficient m de sécurité; Av: Aut: **s. belt,** ceinture f de sécurité; **s. catch,** (i) (on gun, etc.) cran m d'arrêt; (ii) Aut: etc: (on door) serrure f à condamnation; **s. pin,** épingle anglaise, de nourrice; épingle double; **s. valve,** soupape f de sûreté.
saffron ['sæfrən], s. **1.** safran m. **2.** a. & s. jaune safran inv.
sag [sæg], v.i. (**sagged**) s'affaisser, fléchir (sous un poids, etc.).
saga ['sɑ:gə], s. saga f; **s. novel,** roman-fleuve m.
sagacious [sə'geiʃəs], a. sagace, avisé; perspicace; **-ly,** adv. avec sagacité; **sa'gacity** [-'gæsiti], s. sagacité f; sagesse f (d'une remarque); intelligence f (d'un animal).
sage¹ [seidʒ]. **1.** a. sage, prudent. **2.** s. philosophe m, sage m.
sage², s. Bot: sauge f; a. & s. **s. green,** vert cendré inv.
Sagittarius [sædʒi'tɛəriəs]. Pr.n. Astr: le Sagittaire.
sago ['seigou], s. Cu: sagou m; **s. pudding,** sagou au lait; **'sago-'palm,** s. sagoutier m.

Sahara (the) [ðəsə'hɑːrə]. *Pr.n.* le Sahara; **Sa'haran**, *a.* saharien.

sail [seil]. **I.** *s.* **1.** *Nau:* (*a*) voile *f*; (*b*) *coll.* voile(s), voilure *f*, toile *f*; **to set s.**, prendre la mer. **2.** aile *f*, volant *m* (de moulin). **3. to go for a s.**, faire une promenade à la voile. **II.** *v.* **1.** *v.i.* (*a*) (*of sailing ship*) faire de la voile; (*of steamer*) naviguer, faire route; **to s. up the coast**, remonter la côte; (*b*) **to s. for New York**, partir, appareiller, pour New York; **the boat sails at 10 o'clock**, le bateau part, prend la mer, à dix heures; **to be about to s.**, être en partance. **2.** *v.tr.* **to s. the seas**, parcourir les mers. **3.** *v.i.* planer (dans l'air); **'sailcloth**, *s.* toile *f* (à voile); **'sailing. I.** *a.* **s. ship**, voilier *m*. **II.** *s.* (*a*) navigation *f*; **it's all plain s.**, cela marche (i) tout seul, (ii) comme sur des roulettes; (*b*) allure *f* (d'un navire); (*c*) **port of s.**, port *m* de départ; **'sailor**, *s.* marin *m*; **to be a good s.**, avoir le pied marin; **to be a bad s.**, être sujet au mal de mer.

saint [seint] (*before Pr.n.* [s(ə)nt]), *abbr.* **St., S.** (*a*) *s.* saint, -e; **All Saints' (Day)**, la Toussaint; (*b*) *attrib.a.* **St. Peter's**, (l'église *f*) Saint-Pierre; **St. Bernard**, *s.* (chien *m*) saint-bernard *inv*; *Geog:* **St. Helena.** *Pr.n.* Sainte-Hélène *f*; **St. Lawrence.** *Pr.n.* le (fleuve) Saint-Laurent; **the St. Lawrence Seaway**, la voie maritime du Saint-Laurent; **'saintliness**, *s.* sainteté *f*; **'saintly**, *a.* (de) saint.

sake [seik], *s. used only in the phr.* **for the s. of s.o., sth.**, à cause de, pour l'amour de, qn, qch.; **I forgive you for her s.**, je vous pardonne à cause d'elle; **do it for my s.**, faites-le pour moi, pour me faire plaisir; **for goodness s.**, pour l'amour de Dieu; **for old times' s.**, en souvenir du passé; **art for art's s.**, l'art pour l'art.

salad ['sæləd], *s.* salade *f*; **fruit s.**, macédoine *f* de fruits; **s. bowl**, saladier *m*; **s. dressing**, (i) vinaigrette *f*; (ii) sauce *f* mayonnaise (en bouteille); **s. oil**, huile *f* de table; **s. shaker**, panier *m* à salade.

salami [sə'lɑːmi], *s. Cu:* salami *m*; saucisson *m*.

salary ['sæləri], *s.* traitement *m*, appointements *mpl.*

sale [seil], *s.* **1.** vente *f*; (*a*) mise *f* en vente; (**retail**) **s.**, débit *m*; **cash s.**, vente au comptant; **hire-purchase s.**, vente à crédit; **house for s.**, maison à vendre; **on s.**, en vente; (*b*) **s. by auction**, vente aux enchères. **2.** *Com:* **s. price**, prix *m* de solde; **'saleable**, *a.* vendable; de vente facile; **'sale-room**, *s.* salle *f* de(s) vente(s); **'sales clerk**, *s. N.Am:* vendeur, -euse; **'salesman**, *pl.* **-men**, *s.* **1.** vendeur *m*. **2.** représentant *m* de commerce; **'salesmanship**, *s.* l'art *m* de vendre; **'saleswoman**, *pl.* **-women**, *s.* vendeuse *f*.

salient [seiliənt], *a.* **1.** (*of angle, etc.*) saillant; en saillie. **2.** (trait) saillant, frappant.

saliva [sə'laivə], *s.* salive *f*.

sallow ['sælou], *a.* (teint) jaunâtre, olivâtre; **'sallowness**, *s.* teint *m* jaunâtre.

Sally¹ ['sæli]. *Pr.n.f.* Sarah.

sally², *s.* boutade *f*, trait *m* d'esprit.

salmon ['sæmən]. **1.** *s. inv. Ich:* saumon *m*; **river full of s.**, rivière pleine de saumons; **s. trout**, truite saumonée. **2.** *a. & s.* (*colour*) saumon *inv.*

saloon [sə'luːn], *s.* salle *f*, salon *m*; (*a*) *Nau:* salon (de paquebot); **s. cabin**, cabine *f* de première classe; **s. deck**, pont *m* des premières; (*b*) *N.Am:* café *m*; débit *m* de boissons; (*in Eng.*) **s. bar** = bar *m*; (*c*) **billiard s.**, salle de billard; **hairdressing s.**, salon de coiffure (pour hommes); (*d*) *Aut:* **s. (car)**, conduite intérieure, berline *f*.

salt [sɔlt]. **I.** *s.* **1.** (*a*) *Cu:* sel (commun); **kitchen s.**, gros sel; **table s.**, sel de table, sel blanc; **s. cellar**, salière *f*; **to take a story with a pinch of s.**, prendre une histoire avec un grain de sel; **he isn't worth his s.**, il ne vaut pas le pain qu'il mange; (*b*) *F:* **old s.**, loup *m* de mer. **2.** *Ch:* sel; **spirit(s) of salts**, acide *m* chlorhydrique; **Epsom salts**, sulfate *m* de magnésie, *Com:* sels anglais. **II.** *a.* salé; **s. water**, eau salée; eau de mer. **III.** *v.tr.* saler; saupoudrer (qch.) de sel; **'salt-'free**, *a. Med:* **s.-f. diet**, régime *m* sans sel; **'saltings**, *s.pl.* (i) marais salants; (ii) prés salés; **'saltish**, *a.* légèrement salé; **'saltless**, *a.* sans sel; fade; **'saltness**, *s.* salinité *f*, **salt'petre**, *s.* salpêtre *m*; **'salty**, *a.* salé saumâtre; **s. deposit**, grumeaux de sel.

salubrious [sə'luːbriəs], *a.* salubre, sain **sa'lubrity**, *s.* salubrité *f*.

saluki [sə'luːki], *s.* (*dog*) sloughi *m*.

salute [sə'l(j)uːt]. **I.** *s.* (*a*) salut *m*, salutation *f* (*b*) *Mil:* **to give a s.**, faire un salut; **to take the s.**, passer les troupes en revue; (*c*) **to fire a s.** tirer une salve. **II.** *v.tr.* saluer (qn); *abs. Mil* faire le salut militaire; **salu'tation**, *s.* salutation *f*.

salvage ['sælvidʒ]. **I.** *s.* **1.** indemnité *f*, prime *f*, d sauvetage. **2.** sauvetage *m* (d'un navire, etc.) **s. company**, société *f* d sauvetage. **3.** objets sauvés (d'un navire, d'u incendie, etc.); récupération *f* (de matière pour l'industrie). **II.** *v.tr.* sauver, relever (u navire); sauver (des objets dans un incendie récupérer (des matières usagées).

salvation [sæl'veiʃ(ə)n], *s.* salut *m*; **to find s** faire son salut; **the S. Army**, l'Armée du Salu

salve [sælv], *s.* baume *m*, onguent *m*.

salvo, *pl.* **-oes** ['sælvou, -ouz], *s.* salve *f*; **s.** **applause**, salve d'applaudissements.

same [seim]. **1.** *a. & pron.* (le, la) même, (le mêmes; **he's the s. age as myself**, il a le mêm âge que moi; **they're sold the s. day as the come in**, ils sont vendus le jour même de le arrivée; **of the s. kind**, similaire; **in the s. way**, de même; **he got up and I did the s.**, il se leva et je fis de même; **the very s. thing**, exactement, tout à fait, la même chose; **at the s. time**, (i) en même temps; (ii) à la fois; **it all comes to the s. thing**, tout cela revient au même; **it's all the s.**, c'est tout un; **it's all the s. to me**, ça m'est égal; **he's much, about, the s.**, il va à peu près de même; *F:* **s. here!** et moi aussi! et moi de même! d'accord! **2.** *adv.* **to think the s.**, penser de même; **all the s.**, malgré tout; quand même; **all the s. it cost us a lot**, n'empêche que cela nous a coûté cher; **things go on just the s.**, tout marche comme d'habitude; **'sameness,** *s.* **1.** (*a*) identité *f* (**with s.o.**, sth., avec qn, qch.); (*b*) ressemblance *f* (**with**, à). **2.** monotonie *f,* uniformité *f* (d'un paysage, etc.).

sample ['sɑ:mpl]. **I.** *s.* échantillon *m*; prise *f,* prélèvement *m* (de minerai, de sang, etc.); **fair s.**, échantillon représentatif; **s. survey**, (enquête *f* par) sondage *m*; **up to s.**, conforme à l'échantillon. **II.** *v.tr.* (*a*) *Com:* prendre des échantillons de (qch.); (*b*) déguster (un vin); goûter (un plat); essayer (un nouveau restaurant).

sanatorium [sænə'tɔ:riəm], *s.* sanatorium *m, F:* sana *m*; *Sch:* infirmerie *f.*

sanctify ['sæŋ(k)tifai], *v.tr.* sanctifier; consacrer; **custom sanctified by time**, usage consacré par le temps; **'sanctified,** *a.* (*of pers.*) sanctifié, saint; (*of thg*) consacré; **'sanctity,** *s.* **1.** sainteté *f.* **2.** inviolabilité *f*; caractère sacré (de qch.).

sanctimonious [sæŋ(k)ti'mouniəs], *a.* béat; *F:* bondieusard.

sanction ['sæŋ(k)ʃ(ə)n]. **I.** *s.* **1.** *Jur:* sanction *f.* **2.** sanction, consentement *m*, approbation *f.* **II.** *v.tr.* **1.** *Jur:* imposer des sanctions pénales à (qn). **2.** (*a*) ratifier (une loi, etc.); (*b*) approuver, autoriser (qch.); **sanctioned by usage**, consacré par l'usage.

sanctuary ['sæŋktjuəri], *s.* **1.** sanctuaire *m.* **2. to take s.**, chercher asile. **3.** refuge *m* (de bêtes sauvages, d'oiseaux); **wild life s.**, réserve *f* zoologique.

sand [sænd], *s.* **1.** sable *m*; **choked (up) with s.**, ensablé. **2.** *pl.* **sands**, plage *f,* grève *f*; **'sand-bag. I.** *s.* sac *m* de sable. **II.** *v.tr.* (**sandbagged**) protéger (un bâtiment) avec des sacs de sable; **'sand-bank,** *s.* banc *m* de sable; **'sand-dune, -hill,** *s.* dune *f*; **'sandpaper. I.** *s.* papier *m* de verre. **II.** *v.tr.* **1.** frotter (qch.) au papier de verre. **2.** poncer, doucir (une surface); **'sandstone,** *s. Geol:* grès *m*; **s. quarry,** grésière *f*; **'sandy,** *a.* **1.** sableux, sablonneux; **s. stretches of coast**, longues grèves de sable. **2.** (*of hair*) roux pâle *inv*; blond roux *inv.*

sandal ['sænd(ə)l], *s.* sandale *f*; **rope-soled sandals**, espadrilles *f.*

sandwich ['sænwidʒ, -witʃ]. **I.** *s.* sandwich *m*; **ham sandwiches**, sandwichs au jambon. **II.** *v.tr.* serrer, intercaler (**between**, entre); **'sandwich-board,** *s.* double panneau *m* publicitaire (porté par un homme-sandwich); **'sandwich-man,** *pl.* **-men,** *s.* homme-sandwich *m, pl.* hommes-sandwichs.

sane [sein], *a.* sain d'esprit; raisonnable, sensé; **to be s.**, avoir toute sa raison; **-ly**, *adv.* raisonnablement; **sanity** ['sæniti], *s.* santé *f* d'esprit.

sanguinary ['sæŋgwinəri], *a.* (*a*) (*of battle*) sanguinaire, sanglant; (*b*) altéré de sang.

sanguine ['sæŋgwin], *a.* (*a*) (*of complexion*) d'un rouge sanguin; rubicond; (*b*) (*of temperament*) sanguin; (*c*) confiant, optimiste; **to feel s. about the future**, avoir confiance en l'avenir.

sanitation [sæni'teiʃ(ə)n], *s.* hygiène *f*; salubrité publique; système *m* sanitaire; aménagements *m* sanitaires; **'sanitary,** *a.* hygiénique; sanitaire.

Santa Claus ['sæntəklɔ:z]. *Pr.n.* le Père Noël.

sap[1] [sæp], *s.* sève *f*; **'sappy,** *a.* plein de sève; (*of timber*) vert.

sap[2]. **I.** *s. Mil:* sape *f.* **II.** *v.tr. & i.* (**sapped**) *Mil:* saper, miner; **'sapper,** *s. Mil:* sapeur *m*; *F:* **the Sappers**, le Génie.

sapling ['sæpliŋ], *s.* jeune arbre *m*; baliveau *m.*

sapphire ['sæfaiər], *s.* saphir *m.*

sarcasm ['sɑ:kæzm], *s.* **1.** ironie *f*; esprit *m* sarcastique. **2.** (**piece of**) **s.**, sarcasme *m*; **sar'castic,** *a.* sarcastique, mordant; **s. remark**, sarcasme *m*; **-ally**, *adv.* d'une manière sarcastique; ironiquement.

sarcoma [sɑ:'koumə], *s. Med:* sarcome *m.*

sarcophagus, *pl.* **-phagi** [sɑ:'kɔfəgəs, -fəgai], *s.* sarcophage *m.*

sardine [sɑ:'di:n], *s. Ich:* sardine *f*; **tinned sardines**, sardines à l'huile.

Sardinia [sɑ:'diniə]. *Pr.n. Geog:* la Sardaigne; **Sar'dinian,** *a. & s.* sarde (*mf*).

sardonic [sɑ:'dɔnik], *a.* (rire) sardonique; **-ally**, *adv.* sardoniquement; d'une manière sardonique.

Sark [sɑ:k]. *Pr.n. Geog:* Sercq *m.*

sash[1] [sæʃ], *s. Cl:* écharpe *f*; ceinture *f* (en tissu).

sash[2], *s. Const:* châssis *m*, cadre *m* (d'une fenêtre à guillotine); **s. window**, fenêtre *f* à guillotine.

Satan ['seit(ə)n]. *Pr.n.* Satan *m*; **satanic** [sə'tænik], *a.* diabolique.

satchel ['sætʃ(ə)l], *s. Sch:* cartable *m.*

satellite ['sætəlait], *s. Astr: Ph: Pol: etc:* satellite *m*; **s. state**, pays *m*, état *m*, satellite; (*town planning*) **s. town**, agglomération *f* satellite.

satiate ['seiʃieit], *v.tr.* rassasier (qn) (jusqu'au dégoût) (**with**, de); blaser (qn) (**with**, de); **'satiated,** *a.* rassasié; **sati'ation,** *s.* rassasiement *m*; satiété *f.*

satin ['sætin], *s. Tex:* satin *m.*

satire ['sætaiər], *s.* satire *f*, sarcasme *m*;

satirical [sə'tirik(ə)l], *a.* 1. satirique. 2. sarcastique, ironique; -**ally,** *adv.* satiriquement; avec sarcasme; d'un ton moqueur.
satisfaction [sætis'fækʃ(ə)n], *s.* 1. (*a*) acquittement *m*, paiement *m* (d'une dette); (*b*) **s. for an offence,** réparation *f*, expiation *f*, d'une offense; (*c*) assouvissement *m* (de la faim, d'un désir). 2. satisfaction *f*, contentement *m* (**at, with,** de); **to give s.o. s.,** satisfaire, contenter, qn; **the work will be done to your s.,** le travail sera fait de manière à vous satisfaire. 3. **that's a great s.,** c'est un grand motif de contentement; **satis'factoriness,** *s.* caractère satisfaisant (d'un travail, etc.); **satis'factory,** *a.* satisfaisant; **to bring negotiations to a s. conclusion,** mener à bien des négociations; **to give a s. account of one's movements,** justifier ses mouvements; -**ily,** *adv.* de façon satisfaisante.
satisfy ['sætisfai], *v.tr.* 1. (*a*) s'acquitter d'(une obligation); remplir (une condition); (*b*) satisfaire (qn); faire réparation à (qn); **to s. one's conscience,** par acquit de conscience. 2. (*a*) satisfaire, contenter (qn); (*b*) satisfaire, assouvir (un appétit, un désir); **to s. all requirements,** suffire à tous les besoins; *abs.* **food that satisfies,** nourriture rassasiante, *F:* bourrative. 3. convaincre, satisfaire (qn); **I have satisfied myself that . . .,** je me suis assuré que . . .; **'satisfied,** *a.* 1. content, satisfait (de qch.). 2. convaincu; **'satisfying,** *a.* satisfaisant; (*of food*) nourrissant; (*of argument, reasons*) convaincant.
saturate ['sætjureit], *v.tr.* 1. saturer, tremper, imbiber (**with,** de); **to become saturated with . . .,** s'imprégner de . . . . 2. *Ch: Ph:* saturer (une solution); **satu'ration,** *s.* imprégnation *f*; *Ph: Ch:* saturation *f*; *Com:* **the market has reached s. point,** le marché est saturé.
Saturday ['sætədi], *s.* samedi *m*; **she's coming on S.,** elle viendra samedi; **he comes on Saturdays,** il vient le samedi.
saturnine ['sætənain], *a.* taciturne, sombre.
sauce [sɔːs], *s.* 1. (*a*) sauce *f*; (*b*) assaisonnement *m*; condiment *m*. 2. *F:* (i) impertinence *f*, insolence *f*; (ii) culot *m*, toupet *m*; **'sauce-boat,** *s.* saucière *f*; **saucepan** ['sɔːspən], *s.* casserole *f*; **double s.** bain-marie *m, pl.* bains-marie; **'saucer,** *s.* soucoupe *f*; **'sauciness,** *s.* *F:* impertinence *f*; toupet *m*; **'saucy,** *a.* *F:* impertinent, effronté; -**ily,** *adv.* *F:* d'un ton impertinent.
Saudi Arabia [saudiə'reibiə]. *Pr.n. Geog:* l'Arabie *f* Saoudite.
sauerkraut ['sauəkraut], *s.* *Cu:* choucroute *f*.
sauna ['sɔːnə], *s.* sauna *m*.
saunter ['sɔːntər]. I. *v.i.* **to s. (along),** flâner; se promener à loisir. II. *s.* flânerie *f*; promenade faite à loisir.
sausage ['sɔsidʒ], *s.* *Cu:* (*a*) (*eaten hot*) saucisse

f; (*b*) (*hard, dry*) saucisson *m*; **s. meat,** chair *f* à saucisse; **s. roll** = friand *m*.
savage ['sævidʒ]. I. 1. *a.* (*a*) sauvage, barbare; non civilisé; (*b*) (animal, coup) féroce. 2. *s.* sauvage *mf*; -**ly,** *adv.* sauvagement, férocement. II. *v.tr.* (*of animals*) attaquer, mordre (qn, un autre animal); **the lion savaged his trainer,** le lion a attaqué et grièvement blessé son dompteur; **'savagery,** *s.* 1. sauvagerie *f*, barbarie *f* (d'une nation). 2. férocité *f*; brutalité *f* (d'un coup).
save [seiv], *v.tr.* 1. (*a*) sauver; **to s. s.o.'s life,** sauver la vie à qn; **to s. s.o. from death,** arracher qn à la mort; **to s. s.o. from falling,** empêcher qn de tomber; *Fb:* (*of goalkeeper*) **to s. the ball,** arrêter le ballon; (*b*) sauver, protéger; **to s. the situation,** se montrer à la hauteur (de l'occasion); **to s. appearances,** sauver, sauvegarder, les apparences. 2. (*a*) mettre de côté; **s. a dance for me,** réservez-moi une danse; (*b*) économiser, épargner; **I have money saved,** j'ai de l'argent de côté; *abs.* **to s. (up),** économiser (pour l'avenir). 3. ménager (ses vêtements); éviter (une dépense, de la peine); **to s. time,** gagner du temps; **I'm saving my strength,** je me ménage. 4. **to s. s.o. sth.,** éviter, épargner, qch. à qn; **'saving.** I. *a.* *Jur. Com:* **s. clause,** clause *f* de sauvegarde; réservation *f*. II. *prep. & conj.* sauf, excepté, hormis III. *s.* 1. (*a*) délivrance *f*, salut *m* (de qn); **this was the s. of him,** cela a été son salut; (*b*) sauvetage *m*; (*c*) protection *f*. 2. (*a*) économie *f*, épargne *f*; (*b*) *pl.* **savings,** économies *f*; **savings bank,** caisse *f* d'épargne.
saveloy ['sævəloi], *s.* *Cu:* cervelas *m*.
saviour ['seivjər], *s.* sauveur *m*; *Ecc:* **Our S.** Notre Sauveur.
savour ['seivər]. I. *s.* 1. saveur *f*, goût *m*, arome *m*. 2. trace *f*, soupçon *m*, pointe *f* (d'ail d'hérésie). II. *v.* 1. *v.tr.* savourer, déguster (u bon vin, des huitres). 2. *v.i.* (*of thg*) **to s. of sth.** sentir qch.; tenir de qch.; **doctrine that savour of heresy,** doctrine qui sent le fagot **'savouriness,** *s.* saveur *f*, succulence *f* **'savoury.** 1. *a.* (*a*) savoureux, appétissant succulent; (*b*) **s. herbs,** plantes aromatiques; s **omelette,** omelette aux fines herbes. 2. *s.* en tremets salé (de fin de repas).
Savoy [sə'voi]. 1. *Pr.n. Geog:* la Savoie. 2. s **s. (cabbage),** chou frisé de Milan.
saw [sɔː]. I. *s.* *Tls:* scie *f*; **hand-s.,** scie à main **power s.,** tronçonneuse *f*; **cross-cut s.** (scie passe-partout (*m inv*). II. *v.tr.* (**sawed; sawn** scier; **to s. up wood,** débiter du bois; **'saw dust,** *s.* sciure *f*; **'sawmill,** *s.* scierie *f*; **'saw pit,** *s.* fosse *f* de scieur de long.
Saxony ['sæksəni]. *Pr.n. Geog:* la Saxe.
saxophone ['sæksəfoun], *s.* *Mus:* saxophone *m* **saxophonist** [sæk'sɔfənist], *s.* (joueur *m* de

saxophone *m*.

say |sei|. **I.** *v.tr.* (**said** |sed|) dire. 1. (*a*) **to ask s.o.
to s. a few words,** prier qn de prendre la parole;
who shall I s.? qui dois-je annoncer? **to s.
again,** répéter; **it isn't said,** cela ne se dit pas;
he says |sez| **not,** il dit que non; **what did you
s.?** qu'avez-vous dit? **to s. yes,** dire (que) oui;
what do you s. to a drink? si on buvait un
verre? **so he says!** à l'en croire! (*b*) **all that can
be said in a couple of words,** tout ça tient en
deux mots; **so to s.,** pour ainsi dire; **as one
might s.,** comme qui dirait; **one might as well s.
...,** autant dire ...; **I must s.,** j'avoue
franchement; **that's to s.,** c'est-à-dire; à savoir;
have you said anything about it to him? lui en
avez-vous parlé? **the less said the better,** moins
nous parlerons, mieux cela vaudra; **s. no
more!** n'en dites pas davantage! **to s. nothing
of . . .,** sans parler de . . .; **there's something
to be said on both sides,** il y a du pour et du
contre; **you don't s. (so)!** allons donc! pas
possible! (*c*) **he's said to be rich,** on le dit riche;
(*d*) **anyone would s. that he was asleep,** on
dirait qu'il dort; **I should s. not,** je ne crois pas;
je crois que non; **didn't I s. so!** quand je vous le
disais! **come soon, Sunday,** venez bientôt,
disons dimanche; (*e*) **well, s. it were true, what
then?** eh bien, mettons que ce soit vrai, alors
quoi? (*f*) **I s.!** (i) dites donc! (ii) pas possible! 2.
dire, réciter; faire (ses prières); dire (la messe).
II. *s.* dire *m*, parole *f*, mot *m*; **to have one's s.,**
dire son mot; **I've no s. in the matter,** je n'ai pas
voix au chapitre; **'saying,** *s.* 1. (*a*) **it goes
without s. that . . .,** il va de soi, cela va sans
dire, que . . .; (*b*) **there's no s.,** (il est) impossible de dire. 2. (**common**) *s.,* dicton *m*; **as the s.
goes,** comme dit le proverbe.

scab |skæb|, *s.* 1. (*on wound*) croûte *f*. 2. *Ind: F:*
(*of pers.*) jaune *m*.

scaffold |'skæf(ə)ld|, *s.* échafaud *m* (pour
exécutions); **'scaffolding,** *s. Const:*
échafaudage *m*; **s. pole,** perche *f*
d'échafaudage.

scald |skɔːld|, *v.tr.* échauder, ébouillanter (qn,
qch.); **to s. one's foot,** s'échauder le pied;
'scalding. I. *adv.* **s. hot,** tout bouillant. **II.** *s.*
échaudage *m*, ébouillantage *m*; (*in slaughter-
house, etc.*) **s. room,** échaudoir *m*.

scale[1] |skeil|. **I.** *s.* 1. (*on fish, bud, etc.*) écaille *f*. 2.
incrustation *f*, dépôt *m*; tartre *m* (des dents);
Mec: Aut: etc: calamine *f*; **boiler s.,** incrustation; dépôt calcaire; **s. remover,** désin-
crustant *m*, détartrant *m*. **II.** *v.* 1. *v.tr.* (*a*)
écailler (un poisson); (*b*) détartrer, nettoyer
(ses dents); détartrer, désincruster (une
chaudière, etc.). 2. *v.i.* (*a*) **to s. (off),** s'écailler;
(*b*) (*of boiler, etc.*) s'entartrer, s'incruster;
'scaly, *a.* écailleux; squameux; tartreux.

scale[2], *s.* 1. échelle *f*; (*a*) graduation(s) *f(pl)*

(d'un thermomètre, etc.); série *f*, suite *f* (de
nombres); **s. of salaries,** échelle, barème *m*, des
traitements; (*b*) échelle (d'une carte); **to draw
sth. to s.,** dessiner qch. à l'échelle; **on a large s.,**
en grand; **s. model,** modèle réduit; (*c*) *Com:* **s. of
prices,** gamme *f* des prix; (*d*) envergure *f* (d'une
entreprise); étendue *f* (d'une catastrophe); **to
keep house on a small s.,** avoir un train de
maison très simple. 2. *Mus:* gamme *f*.

scale[3], *v.tr.* 1. escalader; **to s. a mountain,** faire
l'ascension d'une montagne. 2. **to s. a map,**
tracer une carte à l'échelle; **to s. a building,**
établir à l'échelle le dessin d'un bâtiment. 3. **to
s. wages up, down,** augmenter, réduire, les
salaires selon le barème.

scales |skeilz|, *s.pl.* (**pair of**) **s.,** balance *f*; **plat-
form s.,** bascule *f*; **steelyard s.,** balance
romaine; **bathroom s.,** pèse-personne *m*; **to
turn the s. at 150 lbs,** peser 68 kilos.

scallop |'skɔləp|, *s.* 1. (*a*) *Moll:* pétoncle *m*,
coquille *f* Saint-Jacques; (*b*) *Cu:* coquille (de
poisson au gratin). 2. *Needlew:* feston *m*,
dentelure *f*.

scalp |skælp|. **I.** *s.* 1. *Anat:* cuir chevelu. 2.
scalp(e) *m*. **II.** *v.tr.* scalper (un ennemi).

scalpel |'skælp(ə)l|, *s. Surg:* scalpel *m*.

scamp |skæmp|. **I.** *s.* vaurien *m*; mauvais sujet;
garnement *m*; **young s.,** petit galopin, petit
polisson. **II.** *v.tr. F:* bâcler (un travail).

scamper |'skæmpər|. **I.** *s.* (*a*) course *f* folâtre,
allègre; (*b*) course rapide; **to take the dog for
his morning s.,** emmener le chien faire sa
course matinale. **II.** *v.i.* courir joyeusement, en
gambadant; **to s. off,** se sauver à toutes
jambes.

scampi |'skæmpi|, *s.pl. Cu:* langoustines *f*.

scan |skæn|. **I.** *v.tr.* (**scanned**) 1. (*a*) scander,
mesurer (des vers); (*b*) *v.i.* (*of verse*) se scander.
2. examiner, scruter (l'horizon, la foule); **to s.
the paper,** parcourir le journal. 3. *T.V:*
balayer, explorer (l'image à transmettre). **II.** *s.*
T.V: Radar: balayage *m*; **s. axis,** axe *m* radioélectrique; **s.
frequency,** fréquence *f* de balayage; **'scanner,**
*s. radar s.,** déchiffreur *m* de radar; **'scanning,**
s. 1. scansion *f* (de vers). 2. *T.V: etc:* balayage
m; **s. apparatus,** appareil *m* explorateur.

scandal |'skænd(ə)l|, *s.* 1. scandale *m*; honte *f*;
to create a s., faire un scandale. 2. médisance
f; cancans *mpl*; **to talk s.,** cancaner; **'scandalize,** *v.tr.* scandaliser (qn); **'scandalous,** *a.*
1. scandaleux, infâme, honteux. 2. *Jur: (of
statement)* diffamatoire, calomnieux; **-ly,** *adv.*
scandaleusement.

Scandinavia |skændi'neivjə|. *Pr.n.* la Scan-
dinavie; **Scandi'navian,** *a. & s.* scandinave
(*mf*).

scant |skænt|, *a.* (*in certain phrases*) insuffisant,
peu abondant, limité; **s. weight,** poids *m* bien
juste; **to have s. regard for ...,** avoir peu

d'égard, de considération, pour …; **with s.
courtesy,** peu poliment; **'scantiness,** s. insuffisance f, rareté f; pauvreté f (de la végétation); **the s. of my resources,** l'exiguïté f de mes ressources; **the s. of her dress,** l'étroitesse f de sa jupe; **'scanty,** a. insuffisant; à peine suffisant; peu abondant; (of garment) étroit, étriqué; **s. hair,** cheveux rares; **s. meal,** repas sommaire; **-ily,** adv. insuffisamment; peu abondamment.

scapegoat ['skeipgout], s. bouc m émissaire.

scar [skɑːr]. I. s. cicatrice f. II. v. (scarred) 1. v.tr. laisser une cicatrice sur (la peau); marquer (qn) d'une cicatrice; balafrer. 2. v.i. (of wound) se cicatriser.

scarce ['skɛəs], a. rare; peu abondant; **good craftsmen are growing s.,** les bons artisans se font rares; **to make oneself s.,** décamper, filer; **-ly,** adv. 1. à peine; presque pas; **she could s. speak,** c'est à peine si elle pouvait parler; **you'll s. believe it,** vous aurez de la peine à le croire; **I s. know what to say,** je ne sais trop que dire. 2. (expressing incredulity) sûrement pas; **s.!** j'en doute! **'scarcity,** s., **'scarceness,** s. rareté f, manque m, pénurie f; **s. of rain,** rareté des pluies; **s. of labour,** manque de main-d'œuvre; **s. of water,** pénurie d'eau.

scare ['skɛər]. I. s. panique f, alarme f; **you did give me a s.,** vous m'avez fait rudement peur; **to raise a s.,** semer l'alarme, la panique. II. v. 1. v.tr. effrayer, alarmer (qn); faire peur à (qn); **to s. away,** effaroucher (le gibier, etc.). 2. v.i. s'effrayer, s'alarmer; **I don't s. easily,** je ne m'effraie pas facilement; **'scared,** a. (air) effaré, épouvanté; **to be s. to death,** avoir une peur bleue; **to be s. out of one's wits,** être affolé; **'scaremonger,** s. alarmiste mf; **'scaremongering,** s. **she loves s.,** elle adore semer la panique; **'scary,** a. effrayant.

scarecrow ['skɛəkrou], s. épouvantail m.

scarf, pl. **scarfs, scarves** [skɑːf(s), skɑːvz], s. 1. écharpe f, fichu m; cache-col m; (in silk) foulard m. 2. écharpe (de dignitaire, d'officier).

scarlet ['skɑːlət], a. & s. écarlate (f); **to blush s.,** devenir cramoisi; Med: **s. fever,** (fièvre f) scarlatine (f).

scathing ['skeiðiŋ], a. acerbe, cinglant; **-ly,** adv. d'une manière acerbe; d'un ton cinglant.

scatter ['skætər]. 1. v.tr. (a) disperser, mettre en fuite; (b) éparpiller; **to s. the floor with paper,** joncher le sol de papiers; **the region is scattered over with small towns,** la région est parsemée de petites villes. 2. v.i. (of crowd) se disperser; (of shot) s'éparpiller; **'scatterbrained,** a. F: étourdi, écervelé; **to be s.,** avoir une tête de linotte; **'scattered,** a. dispersé, éparpillé; épars; **thinly s. population,** population clairsemée.

scavenger ['skævindʒər], s. Z: insecte m, animal m, nécrophage, coprophage; Ent: **s. beetle,** nécrophore m.

scenario, pl. **-os** [si'nɑːriou, -ouz], s. scénario m.

scene [siːn], s. 1. Th: (i) scène f; **Act III, scene ii,** Acte III, scène ii; (ii) **the s. is laid in London,** l'action se passe à Londres; **to appear on the s.,** entrer en scène; (iii) **behind the scenes,** dans la coulisse; **s. shifter,** machiniste m. 2. théâtre m, lieu m (d'un événement); **a change of s. will do him good,** un changement d'air lui fera du bien; **at the s. of the disaster,** sur les lieux du sinistre; **the s. of operations,** le théâtre des opérations. 3. **the s. from my window,** la vue de ma fenêtre. 4. scène; scandale m; dispute bruyante; **to make a s.,** faire de l'esclandre, un scandale; **family scenes,** disputes de famille; **'scenery,** s. 1. Th: décors mpl; mise f en scène. 2. paysage m; vue f; **'scenic,** a. 1. esp. N.Am: **s. road,** route f touristique. 2. **s. railway,** montagnes f russes.

scent [sent]. I. s. 1. (a) parfum m, senteur f odeur f agréable; (b) **bottle of s.,** flacon m de parfum. 2. (of fox, etc.) (a) fumet m, vent m (de la bête); (b) (of hounds) **to be on the right s.,** être sur la piste. 3. odorat m, flair m (d'un chien). II. v.tr. 1. (of hounds) flairer, éventer (le gibier); (of pers.) **to s. trouble,** flairer des ennuis. 2. (of flowers, etc.) parfumer, embaumer (l'air); v.pr. **to s. oneself,** se parfumer; **'scented,** a. 1. parfumé (**with,** de); (of air) embaumé (**with,** de). 2. **keen-s. dog,** chien au nez fin.

sceptic ['skeptik], s. sceptique mf; **'sceptical** a. sceptique; **-ally,** adv. sceptiquement; avec scepticisme; **'scepticism,** s. scepticisme m.

sceptre ['septər], s. sceptre m (d'un roi).

schedule ['ʃedjuːl, N.Am: 'skedʒəl]. I. s. 1. (a) annexe f (à une loi); (b) bordereau m; note explicative. 2. (a) inventaire m; barème m (de prix); **s. of charges,** liste officielle des taux; tarif m; (b) Adm: cédule f (d'impôts). 3. plan r (d'exécution d'un travail); **testing s.,** tableau r d'épreuve; **everything went off according to s.,** tout a marché selon les prévisions; (of train etc.) **on s.,** à l'heure; **ahead of, behind, s.,** er avance, en retard. II. v.tr. 1. inscrire (qch.) su une liste, un inventaire; **scheduled as a place c historical interest,** classé comme monumer historique. 2. dresser le programme de (qch. **the mayor is scheduled to make a speech,** maire doit prononcer un discours; **the train i scheduled to arrive at noon,** selon l'horaire r l'indicateur m, le train arrive à midi; Rail: et **scheduled services,** services réguliers.

Scheldt (the) [ðə'skelt]. Pr.n. l'Escaut m.

scheme [skiːm]. I. s. 1. arrangement m; **colour s** combinaison f de couleurs. 2. résumé e exposé *m* (d'un sujet d'étude); plan *m* (d'un livre). **3.** (*a*) plan, projet *m*; **s. for a canal,** étude *f* d'un canal; (*b*) machination *f*, intrigue *f*; complot *m*; **shady s.,** combinaison louche, *F:* combine *f*. **II.** *v.* **1.** *v.i.* intriguer, ruser, comploter (**to do sth.,** pour faire qch.). **2.** *v.tr.* machiner, comploter, combiner (une prise d'otages); projeter (de faire qch.); **sche'matic,** *a.* schématique; **'schemer,** *s. Pej:* intrigant, -ante; **'scheming. 1.** *a.* intrigant. **II.** *s.* plans *mpl*, projets *mpl*; intrigues *fpl*, combinaisons *fpl*; *F:* combines *fpl*.

schism ['sizm], *s.* schisme *m*; **schis'matic,** *a. & s.* schismatique (*mf*).

schist [ʃist], *s. Geol:* schiste *m*.

schizophrenia [skitsou'fri:niə, skidzou-], *s. Psy:* schizophrénie *f*; **schizo'phrenic** [-'frenik], *a. & s.* schizophrène (*mf*).

schnorkel ['ʃnɔːkl], *s.* (*a*) schnorkel *m*; (*b*) masque sous-marin.

scholar ['skɔlər], *s.* **1.** élève *mf*; personne *f* qui apprend; **at 80 he was still a s.,** à quatre-vingts ans, il apprenait encore. **2.** savant, lettré, érudit; **he's no s.,** son éducation laisse à désirer; **'scholarly,** *a.* savant, érudit; **a very s. man,** un homme d'un grand savoir, d'une grande érudition; **'scholarship,** *s.* **1.** savoir *m*, science *f*; érudition *f*. **2.** *Sch:* bourse *f* (d'études); **scho'lastic,** *a.* (*a*) (philosophie *f*) scolastique; (*b*) (l'année *f*) scolaire; **the s. profession,** l'enseignement *m*.

school[1] [skuːl]. **I.** *s.* (*a*) école *f*; **to go to s.,** aller en classe; **s. leaving age,** âge *m* de fin de scolarité; **nursery s.,** école maternelle; **primary s.,** école primaire; **junior s.** = cours moyen; **grammar s., high s.** = lycée *m*; **comprehensive s.** = collège d'enseignement secondaire; **technical s.** = collège d'enseignement technique; **independent, private, s.,** école libre; **public s.,** (i) collège privé (avec internat); (ii) *N.Am:* école d'État; **preparatory s.,** école privée pour élèves de 8 à 13 ans; **what s. were you at?** où avez-vous fait vos études? **s. equipment,** matériel *m* scolaire; **the s. year,** l'année scolaire; **s. bus,** car *m* scolaire; **s. bus service,** service *m* de ramassage scolaire; *N.Am:* **to teach s.,** être dans l'enseignement; (*b*) *Art: etc:* **s. of art,** école des Beaux-Arts; **the Italian s.,** l'école italienne; **s. of dancing,** cours *m* de danse; **s. of music,** académie *f* de musique; conservatoire *m*; **summer s.,** cours de vacances, cours d'été; **s. of motoring,** auto-école *f*. **II.** *v.tr.* former (un enfant, l'esprit de qn); discipliner (sa voix, ses gestes); dresser (un cheval, un chien); **to s. oneself to patience,** apprendre à patienter; **'schoolbook,** *s.* livre *m* de classe; **'schoolboy,** *s.* écolier *m*, élève *m*; **s. slang,** argot *m* scolaire; **'schoolgirl,** *s.* écolière *f*, élève *f*; **'schooling,** *s.* instruction *f*, éducation

f; **'schoolma'am, -marm,** *s.* (*a*) *N.Am:* institutrice *f*; (*b*) *F:* **a real s.,** (i) une pédante; (ii) une vraie prude; **'schoolmaster,** *s.* professeur *m*; instituteur *m*; **'schoolmastering,** *s.* l'enseignement *m*; **'schoolmistress,** *s.* professeur *m*; institutrice *f*; **'schoolroom,** *s.* (salle *f* de) classe *f*; **'schoolteacher,** *s.* instituteur *m*, institutrice *f*.

school[2], *s.* banc *m* (de poissons); bande *f* (de marsouins).

schooner[1] ['skuːnər], *s.* schooner *m*; goélette *f*.

schooner[2], *s.* (*a*) *N.Am:* grande flûte (pour bière); (*b*) grand verre (à porto, à vin de xérès).

science ['saiəns], *s.* science *f*; **s. master, mistress,** professeur *m* de sciences; **s. fiction,** science-fiction *f*; **scien'tific,** *a.* scientifique; **s. instruments,** instruments de précision; **-ally,** *adv.* scientifiquement; **'scientist,** *s.* savant, -ante; scientifique *mf*.

Scilly ['sili]. *Pr.n. Geog:* **the S. Isles,** les Sorlingues *f*.

scintillate ['sintileit], *v.i.* scintiller, étinceler; **scinti'llation,** *s.* scintillation *f*, scintillement *m*.

scissors ['sizəz], *s.pl.* (**a pair of**) **s.,** (une paire de) ciseaux *mpl*; **cutting-out s.,** ciseaux de couturière; **nail s.,** ciseaux à ongles.

sclerosis, *pl.* **-es** [sklə'rousis, -iːz], *s. Med:* sclérose *f*.

scoff [skɔf], *v.i.* se moquer; **to s. at s.o.,** se moquer de qn; **to s. at dangers,** mépriser les dangers; **'scoffer,** *s.* moqueur, -euse; railleur, -euse; **'scoffing. I.** *a.* moqueur, -euse; **-ly,** *adv.* par moquerie. **II.** *s.* moquerie *f* raillerie *f*.

scold [skould], *v.tr.* gronder, réprimander (qn); **'scolding,** *s.* semonce *f*, réprimande *f*.

scone [skɔn, skoun], *s.* pain *m* au lait.

scoop [skuːp]. **I.** *v.tr.* **1. to s.** (**out**), excaver; évider (qch.); **to s. up,** ramasser à la pelle. **2.** *F: Journ: abs.* **to s.,** faire un scoop. **II.** *s.* **1.** (*a*) pelle *f* à main; (**coal**) **s.,** seau *m* à charbon (coupé en biseau). **2. at one s.,** d'un seul coup. **3.** *F: Journ:* scoop *m*, reportage sensationnel.

scooter ['skuːtər], *s.* (*a*) (*child's*) trottinette *f*, patinette *f*; (*b*) (*motorized*) scooter *m*.

scope [skoup], *s.* (*a*) portée *f*, étendue *f*; **that's outside my s.,** cela n'est pas de ma compétence; **to extend the s. of one's activities,** élargir le champ de son activité; (*b*) espace *m*, place *f*; **to give full s. to s.o.,** donner (libre) carrière à qn.

scorch [skɔːtʃ]. **I.** *v.* **1.** *v.tr.* roussir, brûler légèrement (du linge, etc.); (*of sun*) rôtir, flétrir, dessécher (l'herbe, etc.). **2.** *v.i.* roussir, brûler légèrement. **3.** *v.i. F:* **to s.** (**along**), brûler le pavé; aller un train d'enfer; **scorched,** *a.* roussi, légèrement brûlé; (*of grass*) desséché;

(visage) brûlé; s. **earth policy**, tactique *f* de la terre brûlée; '**scorcher**, *s*. *F:* (*a*) journée *f* torride; (*b*) riposte cinglante; '**scorching. I.** *a*. brûlant, ardent; s. **heat**, chaleur *f* torride. **II.** *adv*. s. **hot**, tout brûlant; **it's s.** (hot) **here**, on rôtit ici. **III.** *s*. roussissement *m*; dessèchement *m*.

score [skɔːr]. **I.** *s*. **1.** éraflure *f*, entaille *f*; (*on paint, etc.*) rayure *f*. **2. to pay off old scores**, régler de vieux comptes. **3.** (nombre *m* de) points *mpl*; *Fb: etc:* **what's the s.?** où en est le jeu? **4.** *Mus:* partition *f*. **5.** (*a*) (*inv. in pl.*) vingt; vingtaine *f* (de gens); (*b*) *pl*. *F:* **scores**, un grand nombre; **scores of people**, une masse de gens. **6.** point *m*, question *f*, sujet *m*; **have no fear on that s.**, n'ayez aucune crainte à cet égard; **on the s. of ill-health**, pour cause de santé. **II.** *v.tr*. **1.** (*a*) érafler; strier; rayer; **face scored with wrinkles**, visage haché de rides; (*b*) souligner (un passage). **2.** *Sp:* (*a*) compter, marquer (les points); (*b*) gagner (une partie); *Cr:* **to s. a century**, faire une centaine; *Fb:* **to s. a goal**, marquer un but; **to s.** (**a success**), remporter un succès; **that's where he scores**, c'est par là qu'il l'emporte. **3.** *Mus:* orchestrer (une composition); '**scoreboard**, *s. Sp:* tableau *m* (des points, des buts, etc.); '**scorer**, *s. Sp:* marqueur *m*; '**scoring**, *s*. **1.** éraflement *m*; striation *f*; rayage *m*. **2.** *Sp:* marque *f* des points; '**score 'off**, *v.i.* **to s. off s.o.**, *F:* river son clou à qn; '**score 'out**, *v.tr.* rayer, biffer (un mot).

scorn [skɔːn]. **I.** *s*. dédain *m*, mépris *m*. **II.** *v.tr*. dédaigner, mépriser (qn, qch.); '**scornful**, *a*. dédaigneux, méprisant; **-fully**, *adv*. dédaigneusement; avec mépris.

Scorpio ['skɔːpiou]. *Pr.n. Astr:* le Scorpion.

scorpion ['skɔːpjən], *s*. scorpion *m*.

Scot [skɔt], *s*. Écossais, -aise; **she's a S.**, c'est une Écossaise; **to get off s.**(-)**free**, s'en tirer indemne.

Scotch [skɔtʃ]. **I.** *a*. (*not used of pers. in Scotland; mainly used by the Eng. and other foreigners*) écossais; **S. terrier**, scotch-terrier *m*; **S. broth**, soupe *f* comprenant du mouton, des légumes et de l'orge; **S. mist**, bruine *f*; **S. woodcock**, œufs *m* aux anchois sur canapé; **S. egg**, œuf dur enrobé de chair de saucisse, cuit au poêle. **II.** *s*. (*a*) dialecte écossais (de l'anglais); (*b*) whisky écossais; **a** (**glass of**) **S.**, un whisky, un scotch; (*c*) *N.Am:* *R.t.m:* ruban adhésif. **III.** *v.tr.* (faire) avorter (un projet); '**Scotchman**, *pl*. **-men**, '**Scotchwoman**, *pl*. **-women**, *s.* (*not used in Scotland*) Écossais, -aise.

Scotland ['skɔtlənd]. *Pr.n. Geog:* l'Écosse *f*.

Scots [skɔts], *a. & s.* (*used in Scotland*) écossais, -aise; **to talk S.**, parler en dialecte écossais (en anglais); **S. law**, le droit écossais; *Mil:* **the S. Guards**, la Garde écossaise; '**Scotsman**, *pl*.

-men, *s.m*. Écossais; *Rail:* **the Flying S.**, le rapide de Londres à Edimbourg; '**Scotswoman**, *pl*. **-women**, *s.f*. Écossaise; '**Scottish**, *a. & s.* (*used in Scotland*) écossais, -aise; **the S. Border**, les marches *f* d'Écosse.

scoundrel ['skaundrəl], *s*. scélérat *m*; escroc *m*.

scour ['skauər]. **I.** *v.tr*. nettoyer, lessiver, frotter (le plancher, etc.); décaper (une surface métallique); **to s. out a saucepan**, récurer une casserole. **II.** *s*. nettoyage *m*, récurage *m*; **to give a saucepan a good s.**, récurer à fond une casserole; '**scourer**, *s*. **pot s.**, tampon *m* métallique; '**scouring**, *s*. **1.** bousculade *f* (pour avoir qch.); '**scrambler**, *s. P.T.T.:* *Rad*: brouilleur *m*; '**scrambling**, *s*. **1.** bousculade *f*. **2.** *P.T.T:* *Rad: etc:* brouillage *m*.

scout [skaut]. **I.** *s*. **1.** *Mil:* éclaireur *m*; **s. car**, **plane**, véhicule *m*, avion *m*, de reconnaissance. **2. boy s.**, (*Catholic*) boy-scout *m*; (*non-Catholic*) éclaireur *m*. **II.** *v.i.* **1.** *Mil: etc:* aller en reconnaissance. **2. to s. about, around, for sth.**, chercher qch. (partout); '**scouter**, '**scoutmaster**, *s*. chef *m* de troupe; '**scouting**, *s*. **1.** *Mil:* reconnaissance *f*. **2. s.** (**for boys**), scoutisme *m*.

scowl [skaul]. **I.** *s*. air menaçant, renfrogné; froncement *m* des sourcils. **II.** *v.i.* **to s. at s.o.**, regarder qn de travers, d'un air menaçant; '**scowling**, *a*. renfrogné, menaçant.

scraggy ['skrægi], *a*. (*of pers., animal*) décharné, maigre; '**scragginess**, *s*. décharnement *m*, maigreur *f*.

scramble ['skræmbl]. **I.** *v*. **1.** *v.i.* (*a*) **to s. up a mountain**, monter, escalader, une montagne; (*b*) **to s. for sth.**, se bousculer pour avoir qch. **2.** *v.tr*. (*a*) *P.T.T:* *Rad: etc:* **to s. a message, a broadcast**, brouiller un message, une radiodiffusion; (*b*) **scrambled eggs**, œufs brouillés. **II.** *s*. **1.** (*mountaineering, etc.*) ascension *f*, escalade *f*, difficile. **2.** bousculade *f*

scrap[1] [skræp]. **I.** *s*. **1.** petit morceau (de qch.); bout *m*, chiffon *m*; **s. book**, album *m* (de découpures, etc.); **not a s. of evidence**, pas une parcelle de preuve; **to catch scraps of conversation**, saisir des bribes de conversation; **s. of comfort**, brin *m* de consolation. **2.** *pl*. **scraps** (*a*) restes *m* (d'un repas); déchets *m* (de papeterie, d'usine, etc.); (*b*) **s. heap**, tas *m* de ferraille; **s. metal**, ferraille *f*; **to throw sth. on the s. heap**, jeter qch. au rebut. **II.** *v.tr.* (**scrapped**) **1.** mettre (qch.) au rebut; envoyer (une voiture) à la ferraille, à la casse. **2.** mettre (un projet) au rancart; '**scrappy**, *a*. **s. knowledge**, bribes *fpl* de connaissances; **s. dinner**, maigre repas (composé de restes).

scrap[2]. **I.** *v.i.* (**scrapped**) *F:* se bagarrer, se battre. **II.** *s*. bagarre *f*.

scrape [skreip]. **I.** *s*. **1.** coup *m* de grattoir, d racloir. 2. *F:* mauvaise affaire, mauvais pas; **to get out of a s.,** se tirer d'affaire. II. *v.* 1. *v.tr.* (*a*) érafler, écorcher (la peau, etc.); (*b*) racler, gratter (qch.); gratter (des carottes, des salsifis); **to s.** one's boots, s'essuyer les pieds; **to s. the barrel,** racler les fonds des tiroirs; (*c*) **to s. one's feet along the floor,** frotter les pieds sur le plancher; **to s. the fiddle,** gratter, racler, du violon; (*d*) **to s. acquaintance with s.o.,** trouver moyen de lier connaissance avec qn; **to s. together, up, a sum of money,** amasser petit à petit une somme d'argent. 2. *v.i.* (*a*) gratter; grincer; (*b*) **to s. against the wall,** raser le mur; (*c*) **to s. clear (of disaster),** échapper tout juste (à l'accident); friser (la catastrophe); 'scrape a'long, *v.i. F:* vivoter péniblement.

scratch [skrætʃ]. I. *s.* 1. (*a*) coup *m* d'ongle, de griffe, griffade *f*; (*b*) égratignure *f*, éraflure *f*; griffure (faite par un chat, etc.); **to escape without a s.,** en sortir indemne, sans une égratignure. 2. (*a*) grattement *m*; **to give one's head a s.,** se gratter la tête; (*b*) grincement *m* (d'un tourne-disques). 3. **to start from s.,** (i) *Sp:* partir scratch; (ii) partir de zéro; **to come up to s.,** se montrer à la hauteur (de l'occasion); **to bring s.o. up to s.,** amener qn à se décider, à s'exécuter. II. *v.* 1. *v.tr.* (*a*) égratigner, griffer; donner un coup de griffe à (qn); (*b*) **to s. one's head,** se gratter la tête; **to s. the surface,** ne pas aller au fond (du sujet, etc.); (*c*) (*of animal*) gratter (le sol); *v.i.* **to s. at the door,** gratter à la porte; (*d*) **to s. s.o. off a list,** rayer, biffer, qn d'une liste; *Sp:* (*of competitor*) **to s. the race,** *abs.* **to s.,** déclarer forfait. 2. *v.i.* (*of pen. etc.*) grincer, gratter. III. *a.* (repas, etc.) improvisé, sommaire; **a s. collection,** une collection hétérogène; *Sp:* **a s. team,** une équipe improvisée; 'scratch a'long, *v.i. F:* se débrouiller tant bien que mal; 'scratch 'out, *v.tr.* 1. rayer, biffer, raturer (un mot). 2. **to s. s.o.'s eyes out,** arracher les yeux à qn; 'scratchy, *a.* qui gratte; qui grince; (*of cloth*) rugueux, qui gratte la peau.

crawl [skrɔːl]. I. *v.tr.* griffonner, gribouiller. II. *s.* griffonnage *m*, gribouillage *m*.

crawny ['skrɔːni], *a.* décharné, maigre.

cream [skriːm]. I. *s.* 1. (*a*) cri perçant; (*b*) screams of laughter, de grands éclats de rire. 2. *F:* chose amusante, grotesque; **it was a perfect s.,** c'était tordant, *F:* marrant. II. *v.i.* (*a*) pousser un cri perçant; crier (de peur, de douleur); (*b*) *F:* **to s. with laughter,** rire aux éclats; **he made us s.,** il nous a fait tordre; 'screamingly, *adv. F:* **s. funny,** tordant, crevant.

cree [skriː], *s.* éboulis *m*, chaos *m* (en montagne).

creech [skriːtʃ]. I. *s.* cri perçant; cri rauque. II. *v.i.* pousser des cris perçants, des cris rauques;

'screech-owl, *s. Orn:* chouette *f* des clochers.

screen [skriːn]. I. *s.* 1. *H:* (draught) **s.,** paravent *m*; *Arch:* choir **s.,** jubé *m*; **s. of trees,** rideau *m* d'arbres; *Av:* blast **s.,** déflecteur *m* de souffle; *Mil: Navy:* **to form a s.,** former un écran (against, contre). 2. *Cin: T.V:* écran (de projection); **the s.** (*as a profession*), le cinéma; **s. star,** vedette *f* de l'écran; **television s.,** le petit écran. 3. **gravel s.,** crible *m* à gravier. II. *v.tr.* 1. (*a*) **to s. sth. from view,** cacher, masquer, dérober, qch. aux regards; **to s. oneself behind sth.,** se cacher derrière qch.; (*b*) abriter, protéger (qch. du vent). 2. tamiser, cribler (du gravier). 3. examiner et interroger (une personne suspecte). 4. *Cin:* mettre (un roman) à l'écran; projeter (un film); *T.V:* passer (une émission) sur l'écran; (*of pers.*) **to s. well,** être photogénique; 'screening, *s.* 1. protection *f* (from, contre); dissimulation *f* (d'un défaut). 2. examen *m* et interrogatoire *m* (d'une personne suspecte). 3. criblage *m* (de gravier, etc.); 'screenplay, *s. Cin:* scénario *m*; 'screenwriter, *s.* dialoguiste *mf*.

screw [skruː]. I. *s.* 1. vis *f*; **thumb s.,** vis à ailettes; papillon *m*; **s. joint,** joint vissé; **s. thread,** pas *m* de vis; **set s.,** vis d'arrêt; vis de réglage; *F:* **to have a s. loose,** être toqué, timbré; **there's a s. loose somewhere,** il y a quelque chose qui cloche. 2. *Av: Nau:* hélice *f*; **helicopter s.,** rotor *m.* 3. (*a*) coup *m* de tournevis; **to give it another s.,** serrez-le encore un peu; (*b*) *Sp:* **s. (on a ball),** effet *m*; *Ten:* **to put (a) s. on the ball,** couper la balle. 4. *F:* salaire *m.* II. *v.* 1. *v.tr.* visser; **to s. (sth.) down,** visser (un couvercle, etc.); **to s. sth. on,** visser, fixer, qch.; **to s. sth. tight,** visser qch. à fond, à bloc; **to s. up a nut,** serrer un écrou; *F:* **his head's screwed on the right way,** c'est un homme de tête; il a du bon sens; c'est une forte tête; **to s. up one's handkerchief,** tire-bouchonner son mouchoir; **to s. up one's eyes,** plisser les yeux; **to s. up one's courage,** prendre son courage à deux mains. 2. *v.i.* (*of tap, etc.*) tourner (à droite, à gauche); **the knob screws into the drawer,** le bouton se visse dans le tiroir; 'screwball, *a.* & *s. N.Am: F:* loufoque (*mf*), dingue (*mf*); 'screwdriver, *s.* tournevis *m*; 'screwy, *a. esp. N.Am: F:* dingue, cinglé, loufoque.

scribble ['skribl]. I. *v.tr.* griffonner (une note dans un carnet). II. *s.* 1. griffonnage *m.* 2. écriture *f* illisible; 'scribbler, *s.* 1. griffonneur, -euse. 2. écrivailleur, -euse; gratte-papier *m inv*; 'scribbling, *s.* griffonnage *m*; **s. paper,** papier à brouillon.

scrimmage ['skrimidʒ], *s.* mêlée *f*; bousculade *f*; bagarre *f*.

script [skript], *s.* (*a*) manuscrit *m*; *Sch:* copie *f* d'examen; (*b*) *Cin:* scénario *m*; **s. girl,** script-girl *f*; **s. writer,** scénariste *mf.*

scripture ['skriptʃər], *s.* **Holy S.,** l'Écriture sainte; *Sch:* **S. (lesson),** leçon *f* d'histoire sainte; **'scriptural,** *a.* biblique; des saintes Écritures.

scroll [skroul], *s.* rouleau *m* (de parchemin, de papier).

scrounge [skraundʒ], *v.tr. & i.* (*a*) (*steal*) chiper; (*b*) **to s. a meal,** écornifler un repas; **'scrounger,** *s.* écornifleur *m,* resquilleur *m.*

scrub¹ [skrʌb], *v.tr.* **(scrubbed)** récurer (une casserole); laver, frotter (le plancher) (avec une brosse dure); **'scrubbing,** *s.* récurage *m,* nettoyage *m* (avec une brosse dure); **'scrubbing-brush,** *s.* brosse *f* de chiendent, brosse dure.

scrub², *s.* broussailles *fpl,* brousse *f*; **'scrubby,** *a.* 1. (*of land*) couvert de broussailles *fpl.* 2. mal rasé; (*of moustache*) hérissé.

scruff [skrʌf], *s.* (peau *f* de la) nuque; **to seize an animal by the s. of the neck,** saisir un animal par la peau du cou; **'scruffy,** *a.* mal soigné; *F:* mal fichu.

scrum [skrʌm], *s.* (*a*) *Rugby Fb:* mêlée *f*; **s. half,** demi *m* de mêlée; (*b*) **what a s. in the Underground!** quelle bousculade dans le Métro!

scruple ['skru:pl]. **I.** *s.* scrupule *m*; **to have no scruples about doing sth.,** n'avoir aucun scrupule à faire qch. **II.** *v.i.* **to s. to do sth.,** avoir des scrupules à faire qch.; **'scrupulous,** *a.* scrupuleux **(about, over, as to,** sur); méticuleux; **-ly,** *adv.* scrupuleusement; méticuleusement; **'scrupulousness,** *s.* 1. scrupulosité *f*; méticulosité *f*. 2. esprit scrupuleux.

scrutinize ['skru:tinaiz], *v.tr.* scruter; examiner (qch.) minutieusement; **'scrutinizing,** *a.* (regard, etc.) scrutateur, inquisiteur; **'scrutiny,** *s.* examen minutieux.

scuffle ['skʌfl]. **I.** *s.* mêlée *f,* bousculade *f*; (*between crowd and police*) bagarre *f.* **II.** *v.i.* 1. (*a*) se bousculer; (*b*) se bagarrer. 2. (*of child*) traîner les pieds.

scull [skʌl]. **I.** *s.* aviron *m* de couple; rame *f.* **II.** *v.i.* ramer, nager, en couple; **'sculler,** *s.* rameur *m* de couple.

scullery ['skʌləri], *s.* arrière-cuisine *f,* souillarde *f.*

sculptor ['skʌlptər], *s.* sculpteur *m*; **'sculpture,** *s.* sculpture *f.*

scum [skʌm], *s.* écume *f*; mousse *f* (sur un liquide); **'scummy,** *a.* couvert d'écume, écumeux.

scurf [skə:f], *s.* pellicules *fpl* (sur la tête).

scurrilous ['skʌriləs], *a.* (*of language, etc.*) grossier, injurieux, ordurier; (*of pers.*) ignoble; **scu'rrility,** *s.* grossièreté *f* (de langage); bassesse *f* (d'une personne, d'une action).

scurry ['skʌri], *v.i.* courir à pas précipités; **to s.**

off, **away,** détaler, décamper; **to s. through one's work,** expédier son travail.

scuttle¹ ['skʌtl], *s.* **coal s.,** seau *m* à charbon.

scuttle², *v.tr. Nau:* saborder (un navire).

scuttle³, *v.i.* **to s. off,** déguerpir, filer.

scythe [saið], *s. Tls:* faux *f.*

sea [si:], *s.* 1. mer *f*; (*a*) **by the s.,** au bord de la mer; **s. bathing,** bains *mpl* de mer; **by s.,** par (voie de) mer; **beyond the sea(s),** outre-mer; **s. trip,** excursion *f* en mer; **s. battle,** bataille navale; (*b*) **the open s.,** le large; **to put (out) to s.,** prendre le large; **to be all at s.,** être tout désorienté. 2. (*a*) **heavy s.,** grosse mer; mer houleuse; (*b*) lame *f,* houle *f*; **to run before the s.,** fuir devant la lame; **head s.,** mer debout; **beam s.,** mer de travers; (*c*) coup *m* de mer; paquet *m* de mer; **to ship a (green) s.,** embarquer une lame, un paquet de mer. 3. océan *m,* multitude *f*; **a s. of faces,** un océan de visages; **'sea-a'nemone,** *s. Z:* actinie *f*; **'seabird,** *s.* oiseau *m* de mer; **'sea-'breeze,** *s.* vent *m,* brise *f,* du large; **'sea'coast,** *s.* littoral *m,* -aux; côte *f*; **'seafarer,** *s.* homme *m* de mer; marin *m*; **'seafood,** *s.* = fruits *mpl* de mer; **'seafront,** *s.* bord *m* de mer, esplanade *f*: **a house on the s.,** une maison qui donne sur la mer; **'seagull,** *s. Orn:* mouette *f*; goéland *m*; **'sea-legs,** *s.pl.* **to have one's s.-l.,** avoir le pied marin; **'seaman,** *pl.* **-men,** *s.* 1. marin *m,* matelot *m.* 2. **a good s.,** un bon navigateur **'seamanship,** *s.* (la technique de) la manœuvre et le matelotage en mer; la manœuvre; **'seaplane,** *s.* hydravion *m* **'seaport,** *s.* port *m* de mer; **'sea-shell,** *s* coquillage *m*; **'sea-shore,** *s.* (*a*) bord *m* de mer; (*b*) plage *f*; **'sea-sickness,** *s.* mal *m* de mer; **'seaside,** *s.* bord *m* de la mer; **s. resort** station *f* balnéaire; plage *f*; **'seaway,** *s.* 1. sillage *m* (d'un navire). 2. **the St. Lawrence S.** la voie maritime du Saint-Laurent; **'seaweed** *s.* algue *f*; goémon *m*; varech *m*; **'seaworthy** *a.* (*of ship*) en (bon) état de navigabilité.

seal¹ [si:l], *s. Z:* phoque *m*; **'sealer,** *s.* 1. navir armé pour la chasse au phoque. 2. (*pers* chasseur *m* de phoques; **'sealskin,** *s.* peau *f* de phoque.

seal². **I.** *s.* (*a*) (*on deed, etc.*) sceau *m*; (*on letter* cachet *m*; **to set one's s. to sth.,** autoriser qch donner son approbation à qch.; **book the bears the s. of genius,** livre *m* qui porte cachet du génie; (*b*) cachet (de bouteille de vi etc.); *Ind:* **s. of approval,** label *m*; *Jur:* offici **s. (on property, etc.),** scellé *m*; *Com:* **lead s** plomb *m* (pour sceller une caisse). **II.** *v.tr.* (*e* sceller (un acte); cacheter (une lettre, un bouteille); plomber (un colis); **his fate is seale** son sort est réglé; **'sealing-wax,** *s.* cire *f* cacheter.

seam [si:m], *s.* 1. couture *f*; **French s.,** coutu

double; **flat s.**, couture rabattue; **saddle-stitched s.**, couture piquée. **2.** fissure *f*, gerçure *f*; (*in metal pipe, etc.*) couture, joint *m*; **brazed s.**, brasure *f*; **welded s.**, joint soudé, soudure *f*. **3.** *Min:* couche *f*, gisement *m*, veine *f*; **'seamless**, *a.* sans couture *f*; sans soudure *f*; **'seamy**, *a.* qui montre les coutures; **the s. side of life**, les dessous *m* de la vie.

séance ['seiɑ̃:ns], *s.* séance *f* de spiritisme.

search [sə:tʃ]. **I.** *s.* **1.** recherche(s) *f*(*pl*); **in s. of . . .**, à la recherche de . . . **2.** (*a*) *Cust:* visite *f*; (*b*) *Jur:* perquisition *f*; **s. warrant**, mandat *m* de perquisition. **3.** fouille *f* (dans un tiroir). **II.** *v.* **1.** *v.tr.* inspecter; chercher dans (un endroit); fouiller (un suspect); scruter (un visage); *Cust:* visiter (les valises de qn); *Jur:* perquisitionner dans (une maison); *P:* **s. me!** je n'ai pas la moindre idée! **2.** *v.i.* **to s. for sth.**, (re)chercher qch.; **'searching**, *a.* (examen) minutieux; (regard) pénétrant, scrutateur; **'searchlight**, *s.* projecteur *m*; **'search-party**, *s.* expédition *f* de secours.

season¹ ['si:z(ə)n], *s.* **1.** saison *f*; **holiday s.**, saison des vacances; **close s., open s.**, chasse, pêche, fermée, ouverte; (*of fruit, etc.*) **to be in s.**, être de saison. **2.** période *f*, temps *m*; **s. ticket**, *F:* **s.**, carte *f* d'abonnement; **s. ticket holder**, abonné, -ée; **word in s.**, mot dit à propos; **'seasonable**, *a.* **1.** de (la) saison; **s. weather**, temps *m* de saison. **2.** (*of advice, etc.*) à propos, opportun; **-ably**, *adv.* opportunément, à propos; **'seasonal**, *a.* (commerce) saisonnier; **s. worker**, saisonnier, -ière.

season². **1.** *v.tr.* (*a*) assaisonner, relever (un mets); (*b*) dessécher, étuver, conditionner (le bois); mûrir, laisser se faire (le vin); (*c*) acclimater, endurcir (qn); (*d*) *F:* tempérer, modérer (une opinion). **2.** *v.i.* (*of wood, etc.*) se sécher; (*of wine*) mûrir, se faire; **'seasoned**, *a.* assaisonné; **highly s. dish**, plat relevé; (*of wine*) mûr, fait; (*of wood*) sec; (*of pers.*) **to become s.**, s'acclimater; s'aguerrir; **'seasoning**, *s.* *Cu:* assaisonnement *m*, condiment *m*.

seat [si:t]. **I.** *s.* **1.** (*a*) siège *m*; banquette *f* (de car, etc.); gradin *m* (d'amphithéâtre, etc.); selle *f* (de vélo, de moto); lunette *f* (de w.-c.); **folding s.**, pliant *m*; **flap s.**, strapontin *m*; (*b*) **to take a s.**, s'asseoir; **to keep one's s.**, rester assis; (*c*) *Rail: etc:* place (assise); (*d*) **he has a s. in the House**, il siège au Parlement. **2.** (*a*) siège, fond *m* (d'une chaise); (*b*) fond (de culotte); *F:* postérieur *m*; derrière *m*. **3.** siège, centre *m* (du gouvernement, etc.); **country s.**, château *m*. **4.** *Equit:* assiette *f*, assise *f*; **to have a good s.**, se tenir bien en selle; avoir de l'assiette. **II.** *v.tr.* **1.** placer (qn); trouver place pour (qn); **please be seated**, veuillez vous asseoir; (*of car, etc.*) **to s. six**, à six places (assises); **this table seats twelve**, cette table tient douze à cette table. **2.** (re)met-

tre, (re)faire, le siège à (une chaise); **'seating**, *s.* (*a*) allocation *f* de places; (*b*) **s. capacity**, nombre *m* de places (assises).

secateurs [sekə'tə:z], *s.pl.* *Hort:* sécateur *m*.

secede [si'si:d], *v.i.* faire sécession (**from**, de); se séparer (d'un parti politique); **se'ceding**, *a.* sécessionniste; **se'cession** [-'seʃ(ə)n], *s.* sécession *f*.

seclude [si'klu:d], *v.tr.* tenir (qn, qch.) retiré (**from**, de); **se'cluded**, *a.* (endroit) écarté, retiré; **se'clusion** [-'klu:ʒ(ə)n], *s.* solitude *f*, retraite *f*.

second¹ ['sekənd], *s.* **1.** seconde *f* (de temps); **I'll be back in a s.**, je reviens dans un instant; **in a split s.**, en un rien de temps; (*on watch*) **s. hand**, trotteuse *f*. **2.** seconde (de degré).

second². **I.** *a.* second, deuxième; (*a*) **the s. of January**, le deux janvier; **to live on the s. floor**, habiter au deuxième (étage); **every s. day**, tous les deux jours; (*b*) **the s. largest**, le plus grand sauf un; **to travel s. class**, voyager en deuxième (classe); *Aut:* **s. (gear)**, deuxième (vitesse); **to be s. in command**, commander en second; **s. sight**, clairvoyance *f*; **-ly**, *adv.* deuxièmement; **en second lieu**. **II.** *s.* **1.** (le) second, (la) seconde; (le, la) deuxième; **Charles the S.**, Charles Deux. **2.** *pl.* *Com:* **seconds**, articles *m* de deuxième qualité. **III.** *v.tr.* **1.** seconder (qn); appuyer (qn), soutenir (ses amis); **to s. a motion**, appuyer une proposition. **2.** *Mil: etc:* [sə'kɔnd], mettre (un officier) en disponibilité; **to be seconded for service with . . .**, être détaché auprès de . . .; **'secondary**, *a.* secondaire; *Sch:* **s. education**, enseignement *m* du second degré; **s. causes**, causes secondes; **s. road** = route départementale; **-arily**, *adv.* secondairement; en second; **'second(-)'hand**, *a.* & *adv.* d'occasion; **s.(-)h. dealer**, brocanteur, -euse; **'second-'rate**, *a.* médiocre, inférieur; de second ordre.

secret ['si:krit]. **I.** *a.* (*a*) secret; caché; **to keep sth. s.**, tenir qch. secret; garder le secret au sujet de qch.; **-ly**, *adv.* secrètement, en secret. **II.** *s.* (*also* **'secrecy**), *s.* discrétion *f*; **in s.**, en secret; **there's no s. about it**, il n'y a pas de mystère; **secrete** [si'kri:t], *v.tr.* cacher (qch.); receler (des objets volés); **'secretive**, *a.* (*of pers.*) réservé, dissimulé; *F:* cachottier.

secretary ['sekrətri], *s.* (*a*) secrétaire *mf*; *Adm:* **executive s.**, secrétaire de direction; *Med: Dent: etc:* secrétaire médical(e); (*b*) *Pol:* **S. of State**, (i) Ministre *m* (ii) Secrétaire d'État; **S. General to the United Nations**, Secrétaire général des Nations Unies; **secre'tarial** [-'teəriəl], *a.* (travail) de secrétaire.

sect [sekt], *s.* secte *f*; **sec'tarian**, *a.* sectaire.

section ['sekʃ(ə)n], *s.* **1.** sectionnement *m*, section *f*. **2.** (*a*) tranche *f*; (*b*) *Geom:* **conic sections**, sections coniques; (*c*) coupe *f*, profil *m*;

vertical s., coupe verticale. **3.** section; partie *f*, division *f*; **made in sections,** démontable; **'sectional,** *a.* **1.** (dessin *m*, etc.) en coupe, en profil. **2.** en sections; **s. bookcase,** bibliothèque démontable, par éléments.

sector ['sektər], *s.* secteur *m*.

secular ['sekjulər], *a.* séculier; laïque; **s. music,** musique profane.

secure [si'kjuər]. **I.** *a.* **1.** sûr; (avenir) assuré; **to feel s. of victory,** être certain de la victoire. **2.** en sûreté; sauf; **s. against attack,** à l'abri de toute attaque. **3.** (*of beam, etc.*) fixé, assujetti; solide; (*of foothold*) ferme, sûr; **-ly,** *adv.* **1.** (*a*) sûrement; avec sécurité; (*b*) avec confiance. **2.** fermement, solidement. **II.** *v.tr.* **1.** (*a*) mettre (qch.) en sûreté, à l'abri; (*b*) mettre en lieu sûr. **2.** fixer, retenir (qch. à sa place); verrouiller (la porte). **3.** obtenir, acquérir; se procurer (qch.); **to s. s.o.'s services,** s'assurer de l'aide de qn; **se'curity,** *s.* **1.** sécurité *f*, sûreté *f*; *Pol:* **S. Council** (**of U.N.O.**), Conseil *m* de sécurité (de l'O.N.U.); *Adm:* **social s.,** sécurité sociale. **2.** (moyen *m* de) sécurité; sauvegarde *f*. **3.** *Com:* (*a*) caution *f*; **s. for a debt,** garantie *f* d'une créance; **to pay (in) a sum as a s.,** verser une provision; **without s.,** à découvert; (*b*) (*pers.*) (donneur *m* de) caution; garant *m*; (*c*) *Fin:* usu. *pl.* **securities,** titres *mpl*, valeurs *fpl*.

sedate [si'deit], *a.* posé, reposé; (maintien) composé; **-ly,** *adv.* posément; **se'dateness,** *s.* maintien calme, posé.

sedative ['sedətiv], *a. & s.* sédatif (*m*); calmant (*m*).

sedentary ['sedəntri], *a.* sédentaire.

sediment ['sedimənt], *s.* sédiment *m*, dépôt *m*; boue *f* (d'un accu); lie *f* (du vin); **sedi'mentary,** *a.* sédimentaire; **sedimen'tation,** *s.* sédimentation *f*.

sedition [si'diʃ(ə)n], *s.* sédition *f*; **se'ditious,** *a.* séditieux; **-ly,** *adv.* séditieusement.

seduce [si'djuːs], *v.tr.* séduire, corrompre (qn); **se'ducer,** *s.* séducteur *m*; **se'duction** [-'dʌkʃ(ə)n], *s.* séduction *f*, corruption *f* (de qn); **se'ductive,** *a.* séduisant, attrayant; **-ly,** *adv.* d'une manière attrayante.

see[1] [siː], *v.tr.* (**saw; seen**) **1.** *voir;* (*a*) **to s. the sights of the town,** visiter les monuments de la ville; **to s. s.o. in the distance,** apercevoir qn dans le lointain; **he's not fit to be seen,** il n'est pas présentable; (*b*) *abs.* **as far as the eye can s.,** à perte de vue; **it was too dark to s. clearly,** il faisait trop noir pour bien distinguer; (*c*) **to s. s.o. coming,** voir venir qn; (*d*) **I'll s. you to the door,** je vais vous accompagner jusqu'à la porte. **2.** (*a*) comprendre, saisir; **I don't s. the point,** je ne saisis pas la nuance; **I s.!** je comprends! (*b*) observer, remarquer (qch.); s'apercevoir de (qch.); **I can s. no fault in him,** je ne lui connais pas de défaut; **s. for yourself,**

voyez par vous-même; **what *can* you s. in her?** que pouvez-vous trouver en elle? (*c*) voir, juger, apprécier; **this is how I s. it,** voici comment j'envisage la chose; **if you s. fit to . . .,** si vous trouvez bon de . . .. **3.** examiner; regarder avec attention; *abs.* **I'll go and s.,** je vais aller voir; **let me s.,** (i) attendez un peu; (ii) faites voir! **4. to s.** (**to it**) **that everything's in order,** s'assurer que tout est en ordre. **5.** (*a*) fréquenter, avoir des rapports avec (qn); **he sees a great deal of the Smiths,** il fréquente beaucoup les Smith; **s. you on Thursday!** à jeudi! **s. you soon!** à bientôt! (*b*) **to go and s. s.o.,** aller trouver qn; **to s. the doctor,** consulter le médecin; **to s. s.o. on business,** voir qn pour (parler) affaires; (*c*) recevoir (un visiteur); **'see about,** *v.ind.tr.* s'occuper de (qch.); se charger de (qch.); **I'll s. about it,** (i) je m'en occuperai (ii) j'y réfléchirai; **'seeing,** *s.* vue *f*; vision *f*; **s. is believing,** voir c'est croire; **it's worth s.,** cela vaut la peine d'être vu; *conj. phr.* **s. that** puisque, vu que; **'see'through. 1.** *v.i.* (*a*) voir à travers (qch.); (*b*) pénétrer les intentions de (qn); pénétrer (un mystère). **2.** *v.tr.* **to s. a business through,** mener une affaire à bonne fin; **to s. it through,** tenir jusqu'au bout; **'see to,** *v.ind.tr.* s'occuper de (qn, qch.); veiller à (qn. qch.); **to s. to everything,** avoir l'œil à tout.

see[2], *s. Ecc:* siège épiscopal.

seed [siːd], *s.* (*a*) graine *f* (de tomate, etc.); pépin *m* (de pomme, de raisin); (*b*) *coll.* semence *f*, graine(s); **to go to s.,** (i) monter en graine; (ii) *F:* (*of pers.*) se ramollir; **'seeded,** *a. Ten:* **players,** têtes *f* de série; **'seedling,** *s.* **Hor** (jeune) plant *m*; **'seedsman,** *pl.* **-men,** grainetier *m*; **'seedy,** *a.* **1.** monté en graine. **2.** (vêtement) râpé, usé, *F:* miteux; (*of pers.*) s **looking,** d'aspect *m* minable. **3.** (*of pers.*) m en train; *F:* patraque.

seek [siːk], *v.tr.* (**sought** [sɔːt]) **1.** chercher (u objet perdu); rechercher (de l'avancement, u emploi); **to s. shelter,** se réfugier (sous un a bre, etc.). **2.** (*a*) **to s. sth. from s.o.,** demand qch. à qn; **to s. advice,** demander conseil; (**much sought after,** très recherché, très cour

seem [siːm], *v.i.* sembler, paraître. **1.** (*a*) (*of per:* avoir l'air (fatigué, etc.); **how does it s. to yo** que vous en semble? **it seems like a dream,** dirait un rêve; (*b*) **I s. to have heard his name** me semble avoir entendu son nom. **2.** *imper* **seems to me that you are right,** il me semb que vous avez raison; **it seemed as though,** if . . ., il semblait que + *sub.*; on aurait dit q + *ind.*; **so it seems,** à ce qu'il paraît; **'seemin** *a.* apparent; soi-disant *inv*; **-ly,** *adv.* a parement; en apparence.

seep [siːp], *v.i.* (*of liquids, etc.*) suinter; s'infiltr **'seepage,** *s.* suintement *m*; infiltration *f*.

see-saw ['siːsɔː]. **I.** *s.* bascule *f*, balançoire *f*.

v.i. basculer; osciller; (*of pers.*) **to s.-s. be-tween two opinions,** balancer entre deux opinions.

seethe [si:ð], *v.i.* (*a*) bouillonner; (*b*) (*of crowd, etc.*) s'agiter, grouiller; **country seething with discontent,** pays en effervescence; **to be seething with anger,** bouillir de colère.

segment ['segmənt], *s.* segment *m*; **s. of an orange,** tranche *f* d'une orange.

segregate ['segrigeit], *v.tr.* isoler; mettre (qch.) à part; **segre'gation,** *s.* ségrégation *f*; isolement *m; Pol:* **racial s.,** ségrégation raciale; **segre'gationist,** *s.* ségrégationiste *mf*; partisan, -ane, de la ségrégation raciale.

seismology [saiz'mɔlədʒi], *s.* sismologie *f*; **'seismic,** *a.* sismique.

seize [si:z]. **1.** *v.tr.* saisir; (*a*) se saisir, s'emparer, de (qch.); (*b*) **to s. s.o. by the throat,** prendre qn à la gorge; **to s. the opportunity,** saisir l'occasion. **2.** *v.i. E:* **to s.** (**up**), gripper, coincer, (se) caler; (se) bloquer; **'seizure,** *s.* **1.** saisie *f* (de marchandises). **2.** *Med:* attaque *f.*

seldom ['seldəm], *adv.* rarement; peu souvent; **I s. see him now,** je ne le vois plus guère.

select [si'lekt]. **I.** *v.tr.* choisir (**from,** parmi); sélectionner. **II.** *a.* choisi; de (premier) choix; d'élite; **s. club,** club très fermé; **s. audience,** public choisi; **se'lection,** *s.* choix *m*, sélection *f*: **a good s. of wines,** un bon choix de vins fins; **to make a s.,** faire un choix; **selections from Byron,** morceaux choisis de Byron; **se'lective,** *a.* sélectif.

self, *pl.* **selves** [self, selvz]. **1.** *s.* le moi; **one's better s.,** son meilleur côté; **he's quite his old s. again,** il est complètement rétabli; **all by one's very s.,** absolument tout seul. **2.** *pron.* (*on cheque*) **pay s.,** payez à moi-même; (*in compound pronouns, for emphasis*) **I'm not (quite) myself today,** je ne suis pas dans mon assiette aujourd'hui; **she's kindness itself,** elle est la bonté même; **everyone for himself,** chacun pour soi; **to live by oneself,** vivre seul; **'self-a'ssertive,** *a.* autoritaire; **'self-a'ssurance,** *s.,* **'self-'confidence,** *s.* confiance *f* en soi; assurance *f*; aplomb *m*; **'self-a'ssured,** *a.,* **'self-'confident,** *a.* sûr de soi; plein d'assurance; **'self-'conscious,** *a.* embarrassé, gêné; intimidé; **'self-'consciousness,** *s.* contrainte *f*, embarras *m*, gêne *f*; timidité *f*; **'self-con'tained,** *a.* **1.** (*of pers.*) indépendant (d'esprit); peu communicatif. **2.** (*appareil m, industrie f*) autonome. **3. s.-c. flat,** appartement *m* avec entrée particulière; **'self-con'trol,** *s.* sang-froid *m*; maîtrise *f* de soi; **'self-de'fence,** *s.* défense personnelle; *Jur:* légitime défense; **'self-de'nial,** *s.* (*a*) abnégation *f* de soi; renoncement(s) *m(pl)*; (*b*) frugalité *f*; **'self-determi'nation,** *s. Pol:* auto-détermination

f: **right of peoples to s.-d.,** droit *m* des peuples de disposer d'eux-mêmes; **'self-'drive,** *a.* **s.-d. cars for hire,** location *f* de voitures sans chauffeur; **'self-'educated,** *a.* autodidacte; **'self-em'ployed,** *a.* (travailleur) indépendant; **'self-es'teem,** *s.* respect *m* de soi; amour-propre *m*; **'self-'evident,** *a.* (fait *m*) qui saute aux yeux; **'self-'governing,** *a.* (territoire) autonome; **'self-'government,** *s.* autonomie *f*; **'self-ig'nition,** *s. Aut:* auto-allumage *m*; **'self-im'portant,** *a.* suffisant, présomptueux; **'self-in'dulgent,** *a.* sybarite; qui se dorlote; qui ne se refuse rien; **'selfish,** *a.* égoïste, intéressé; **-ly,** *adv.* égoïstement, en égoïste; **'selfishness,** *s.* égoïsme *m*; **'self-po'ssessed,** *a.* maître de soi; qui a du sang-froid; **'self-po'ssession,** *s.* aplomb *m*, sang-froid *m*; **'self-pro'pelled,** *a.* (*of vehicle, etc.*) autopropulsé; **'self-'raising flour,** *s. Cu:* farine préparée à la levure chimique; **'self-re'liance,** *s.* indépendance *f*; **'self-re'liant,** *a.* indépendant; **'self-re'spect,** *s.* respect *m* de soi; amour-propre *m*; **'self-'service,** *a. & s. Com:* libre-service (*m*); **'self-'starter,** *s. Aut:* démarreur *m*; **'self-'willed,** *a.* opiniâtre, volontaire, obstiné; **'self-'winding,** *a.* (montre *f*, etc.) à remontage automatique.

sell [sel], *v.tr.* (**sold**) **1.** (*a*) vendre (**to,** à); **he sold it for fifty pence,** il l'a vendu cinquante pence; (*b*) **this book sells well,** ce livre se vend bien, se place facilement; **land to s.,** terrain à vendre. **2.** (*a*) vendre, trahir (un secret); (*b*) duper, tromper; *F:* **you've been sold a pup,** on vous a refait; **'seller,** *s.* vendeur, -euse; **'selling,** *s.* vente *f*; écoulement *m*, placement *m*; **s. price,** prix *m* de vente; **selling off,** *s.* liquidation *f*; **'sell 'off,** *v.tr.* solder; liquider (son stock); **'sell 'out,** *v.tr.* **1. we're sold out of this article,** nous sommes démunis de cet article; **the edition is sold out,** l'édition est épuisée. **2.** *Fin:* réaliser (des actions); **'sell 'up,** *v.tr.* vendre, faire saisir (un failli).

Sellotape ['selouteip], *s. R.t.m:* ruban adhésif.

selvedge ['selvidʒ], *s. Tex:* lisière *f.*

semaphore ['seməfɔːr], *s.* sémaphore *m.*

semblance ['semblans], *s.* apparence *f*; **to put on a s. of gaiety,** faire semblant d'être gai.

semester [sə'mestər], *s. Sch:* semestre *m.*

semi- ['semi], *pref.* semi-; demi-; **s.-automatic gun,** arme *f* (à feu) semi-automatique; **'semicircle,** *s.* demi-cercle *m*; **'semi'circular,** *a.* demi-circulaire; **'semi-'colon,** *s.* point-virgule *m*; **'semi-'conscious,** *a.* à demi conscient; **'semi-de'tached,** *a.* **s.-d. houses,** maisons jumelées; **'semi-'final,** *s. Sp:* demi-finale *f*; **'semi-o'fficial,** *a.* officieux.

seminar ['semɪnɑːr], *s. Sch:* séminaire *m.*

seminary ['semɪnəri], *s.* séminaire *m.*

semolina [semə'liːnə], *s. Cu:* semoule *f.*

senate ['senət], s. sénat m; '**senator**, s. sénateur m.

send [send], v.tr. (sent) 1. (a) envoyer; **to s. s.o. for sth.,** envoyer qn chercher qch.; (b) envoyer, expédier (un colis, etc.); **I'm sending you a present by post,** je vous fais parvenir un cadeau par la poste; **to s. clothes to the wash,** donner du linge à blanchir. 2. **it sent a shiver down my spine,** cela m'a fait passer un frisson dans le dos; **the blow sent him sprawling,** le coup l'a envoyé rouler; F: **to s. s.o. packing,** envoyer promener qn; flanquer qn à la porte. 3. abs. **to s. for s.o.,** envoyer chercher qn; **I shall s. for it,** je vais l'envoyer prendre; '**send a'way,** v.tr. (a) renvoyer, congédier (qn); (b) expédier (un colis); '**send 'back,** v.tr. renvoyer; '**sender,** s. expéditeur, -trice (d'une lettre, etc.); '**send 'in,** v.tr. 1. (a) faire (r)entrer (qn); (b) **to s. in one's name,** se faire annoncer. 2. (a) livrer, rendre (un compte); remettre (une demande); (b) **to s. in one's resignation,** donner sa démission; '**send 'off,** v.tr. (a) envoyer (qn) (en mission, etc.); (b) expédier (une lettre, etc.); (c) Sp: exclure (un joueur) du terrain; '**send 'on,** v.tr. (a) faire suivre (une lettre); (b) transmettre (un message); '**send 'out,** v.tr. (a) faire sortir (qn); (b) lancer (des circulaires, etc.); (c) émettre (des signaux, de la chaleur); '**send 'round,** v.tr. 1. faire circuler, faire passer (la bouteille, etc.). 2. envoyer (qn); **I'll s. s.o. round tomorrow,** j'enverrai qn demain; '**send 'up,** v.tr. 1. faire monter (qn, un ballon). 2. faire hausser, monter (les prix). 3. F: parodier (qn, qch.).

Senegal [seni'gɔ:l]. Pr.n. le Sénégal; '**Senega'lese,** a. & s. sénégalais, -aise.

senile ['si:nail], a. sénile; **senility** [si'niliti], s. sénilité f.

senior ['si:njər]. 1. a. (a) **William Jones senior,** William Jones aîné, père; **he's two years s. to me,** il est mon aîné de deux ans; (b) s. (**in rank**), (de grade) supérieur; **the s. officer,** le doyen des officiers; **s. clerk,** premier commis; Jur: premier clerc. 2. s. (a) aîné, -ée; doyen, -enne (d'âge); (b) (le plus) ancien, (la plus) ancienne; **to be s.o.'s s.,** être l'ancien, le doyen, de qn; **seni'ority** [-'ɔriti], s. 1. priorité f d'âge; supériorité f d'âge. 2. ancienneté f (de grade); **to be promoted by s.,** avancer à l'ancienneté.

sensation [sen'seiʃ(ə)n], s. 1. sensation f; sentiment m (de malaise, etc.); **I had a s. of falling,** j'avais l'impression que je tombais. 2. sensation; effet sensationnel; **sen'sational,** a. sensationnel; (roman m) à sensation; **s. happening,** sensation f; **s. writer,** auteur m à gros effets.

sense [sens]. I. s. 1. sens m; **to have a keen s. of smell,** avoir l'odorat fin. 2. pl. (a) **to be in one's senses,** être sain d'esprit; **any man in his senses,** tout homme jouissant de son bon sens; **to frighten s.o. out of his senses,** effrayer qn jusqu'à lui faire perdre la raison; **to come to one's senses,** revenir à la raison; (b) **to lose one's senses,** perdre connaissance f; **to come to one's senses,** revenir à soi. 3. (a) sensation f (de plaisir, etc.), sens; **to labour under a s. of injustice,** nourrir un sentiment d'injustice; (b) sentiment, conscience f; **to have a s. of time,** avoir le sentiment de l'heure; **keen s. of humour,** sentiment très vif de l'humour. 4. bon sens, intelligence f; **common s.,** sens commun; **to talk s.,** parler raison. 5. sens, signification f; **I can't make s. of this passage,** je n'arrive pas à comprendre ce passage; **in the full s. of the word,** dans toute l'acception du terme. II. v.tr. sentir (qch.) intuitivement; pressentir (qch.); '**senseless,** a. 1. stupide; déraisonnable; **a s. remark,** une bêtise. 2. **to knock s.o. s.,** assommer qn; **-ly,** adv. stupidement; bêtement; '**senselessness,** s. manque m de bon sens; stupidité f; **sensi'bility,** s. sensibilité f; '**sensible,** a. sensé, raisonnable; (choix) judicieux; **-ibly,** adv. raisonnablement; judicieusement.

sensitive ['sensitiv], a. (a) (of skin, tooth) sensible, sensitif; (of pers.) **to be s. to cold,** être frileux; (b) (of pers.) susceptible; impressionnable; (c) Ind: Fin: **s. market,** marché m instable; **-ly,** adv. d'une manière sensible; '**sensitiveness,** s., **sensi'tivity,** s. sensibilité f.

sensual ['sensjuəl], a. sensuel; voluptueux; **-ally,** adv. avec sensualité, sensuellement; **sensu'ality,** s. sensualité f.

sensuous ['sensjuəs], a. (of pleasure) sybaritique, voluptueux; (of charm) capiteux; **-ly,** adv. avec volupté.

sentence ['sentəns]. I. s. 1. Jur: (a) jugement m; sentence f, condamnation f; (b) (term of imprisonment) peine f. 2. Gram: phrase f. II. v.tr Jur: condamner (qn).

sententious [sen'tenʃəs], a. sentencieux pompeux; **-ly,** adv. sentencieusement.

sentiment ['sentimənt], s. 1. sentiment m; (a **noble sentiments,** sentiments nobles; (b) opinion f, avis m; **those are my sentiments,** voilà ce que je pense. 2. sentimentalité f; **sen ti'mental,** a. sentimental; (d'une sensiblerie romanesque; **-ally,** adv. sentimentalement **senti'mentalist,** s. **he's, she's, a s.,** c'est un(e sentimental(e); **sentimen'tality,** s. sentimentalité f; sensiblerie f.

sentry ['sentri], s. 1. (a) (guard) factionnaire m **to relieve a s.,** relever qn de faction; (b) (ou post) sentinelle f. 2. faction f; **to stand s.,** êtr de faction; monter la garde; '**sentry-box,** : Mil: guérite f.

sepal ['sep(ə)l], s. Bot: sépale m.

separate. I. a. ['sep(ə)rət], (a) séparé, détach (**from,** de); (b) distinct, indépendant; **entered i**

a s. **column,** inscrit dans une colonne à part; -**ly,** *adv.* séparément; à part. **II.** *v.tr. & i.* ['sepəreit], (se) séparer; (se) détacher (de qn, qch.); **sepa'ration,** *s.* 1. séparation *f* (d'avec qn); **judicial s.** (**of husband and wife**), séparation de corps (et de biens); séparation judiciaire. **2.** écart *m*, distance *f.*

sepia ['si:pjə], *s. Art:* sépia *f.*

September [sep'tembər], *s.* septembre *m*; **in S.,** au mois de septembre, en septembre.

septic ['septik], *a. Med:* septique; *P:* moche, infecte; **s. tank,** fosse *f* septique; **septi'caemia** [-'si:miə], *s. Med:* septicémie *f.*

septuagenarian [septjuədʒi'nɛəriən], *s. & a.* septuagénaire (*mf*).

sepulchral [si'pʌlkrəl], *a.* sépulcral; **s. vault,** caveau *m*; **s. stone,** pierre *f* tumulaire; **s. voice,** voix caverneuse.

sequel ['si:kwəl], *s.* suite *f* (d'un roman, etc.).

sequence ['si:kwəns], *s.* 1. (*a*) succession *f*; ordre naturel; **in s.,** en série; (*b*) suite *f*, série *f*; (*c*) *Gram:* **s. of tenses,** concordance *f* des temps. **2.** *Cards:* séquence *f.* **3.** *Cin:* (**film**) **s.,** scène *f.*

sequoia [se'kwɔiə], *s. Bot:* séquoia *m.*

serenade [serə'neid]. **I.** *s.* sérénade *f.* **II.** *v.tr.* faire la sérénade à (qn).

serene [sə'ri:n], *a.* serein, calme, tranquille; (ciel) clair; -**ly,** *adv.* tranquillement; avec sérénité; **se'renity** [-'reniti], *s.* sérénité *f*, calme *m*, tranquillité *f.*

serge [sə:dʒ], *s. Tex:* serge *f.*

sergeant ['sɑ:dʒənt], *s.* (*a*) *Mil:* (*infantry*) sergent *m*; (*mounted*) = maréchal *m* des logis; *Av:* **flight s.,** sergent-chef *m*; (*b*) **police s.,** brigadier *m* (de police); **'sergeant-'major,** *s. Mil:* 1. (*infantry*) sergent *m* major; adjudant *m*; (*mounted*) = maréchal *m* des logis chef. **2. regimental s.-m.** = adjudant chef.

serial ['siəriəl]. 1. *a.* **s. number,** numéro *m* de série. **2.** *s. & a.* **s.** (**story**), feuilleton *m.*

series ['siəri:z], *s.inv.* 1. série *f*, suite *f*; échelle *f*, gamme *f* (de couleurs, etc.); *Ch: etc:* **s. of reactions,** réactions *f* en chaîne. **2.** *adv.phr.* **in s.,** en série.

serious ['siəriəs], *a.* sérieux. 1. **s. injury,** blessure *f* grave; **s. mistake,** grosse faute. **2.** (*a*) **s. promise,** promesse sérieuse, sincère; (*b*) (*of pers.*) réfléchi; **I'm s.,** je ne plaisante pas; -**ly,** *adv.* sérieusement. 1. **s. ill,** gravement malade. **2. to take sth. s.,** prendre qch. au sérieux; **'seriousness,** *s.* 1. gravité *f* (d'une maladie, d'un événement). **2.** sérieux *m* (de maintien, etc.); **in all s.,** sérieusement.

sermon ['sə:mən], *s.* 1. *Ecc:* sermon *m.* **2.** *F:* sermon, semonce *f.*

serpent ['sə:p(ə)nt], *s.* serpent *m*; **'serpentine,** *a.* (cours d'eau, chemin) serpentin, sinueux.

serrated [sə'reitid], *a.* dentelé.

serum ['siərəm], *s.* sérum *m*; **protective s.,** im-

munisant *m.*

serve [sə:v]. 1. *v.tr.* (*a*) servir (un maître, un client, une cause, etc.); *abs.* **to s.** (**at table**), servir (à table); (*in shop*) **are you being served?** est-ce qu'on s'occupe de vous? *Jur:* **to s. on the jury,** être du jury; **to s. one's apprenticeship,** faire son apprentissage; (*b*) (*of thg*) être utile à (qn, qch.); **it will s. the purpose,** *abs.* it will s., cela fera l'affaire; **if my memory serves me right,** si j'ai bonne mémoire; (*c*) (*of bus route, railway*) **to s. a place,** desservir (une localité); (*d*) (*in shop, etc.*) **to s. s.o. with a pound of butter,** servir une livre de beurre à qn; (*at table*) **to s. a dish,** servir un mets; (*e*) *F:* **it serves you right!** c'est bien fait! vous ne l'avez pas volé! (*f*) (*of bull, etc.*) couvrir (une vache, etc.). **2.** *v.i.* (*a*) **to s. for sth.,** servir à qch.; **to s. as sth.,** servir de qch.; faire fonction de qch.; **to s. as an example,** servir d'exemple; **'servant,** *s.* 1. domestique *mf*; bonne *f.* **2. civil s.,** fonctionnaire *mf*; **'server,** *s.* 1. (*a*) serveur, -euse; (*b*) *Ecc:* acolyte *m*, répondant *m.* **2. salad, fish, servers,** service *m* à salade, à poisson; **'service. I.** *s.* 1. service *m*; **public services,** services publics; **military s.,** service militaire. **2. the civil s.,** l'administration *f*; **to go into the civil s.,** entrer dans le fonctionnariat, devenir fonctionnaire; **the foreign s.,** le service diplomatique; **he's in the diplomatic s.,** il est de la carrière; **the (armed) services,** les forces armées; **the Senior S.,** la Marine Royale; **s. families,** les familles de militaires. **3. s. flat,** appartement *m* avec service; (*in restaurant*) **s. charge,** service. **4. to do s.o. a s.,** rendre (un) service à qn; **I'm at your s.,** je suis à votre disposition *f*; **social services,** institutions sociales; **to be of s. to s.o.,** être utile à qn. **5.** *Ecc:* office *m*; culte *m.* **6.** *Ten:* service. **7. tea s.,** service à thé; **dinner s.,** service de table. **II.** *v.tr. Aut: Mec: etc:* entretenir et réparer (des moteurs, voitures et mécanique en général); **'serviceable,** *a.* (*a*) en état de fonctionner, utilisable; (*b*) pratique, commode; **'serviceman,** *pl.* -**men,** *s.* soldat mobilisé; **disabled ex-s.,** mutilé de guerre; **'service station,** *s. Aut:* station-service *f.*

serviette [sə:vi'et], *s.* serviette *f* de table.

servile ['sə:vail], *a.* (*of pers.*) servile; -**ly,** *adv.* servilement; **ser'vility** [-'viliti], *s.* servilité *f.*

servitude ['sə:vitju:d], *s.* servitude *f*, esclavage *m.*

session ['seʃ(ə)n], *s.* session *f*; séance *f*; (*of Parliament*) **the House is now in s.,** la Chambre siège actuellement.

set [set]. **I.** *s.* 1. ensemble *m*; (*a*) jeu *m* (d'outils); série *f* (de casseroles); batterie *f* (d'ustensiles de cuisine); collection complète (des œuvres de qn); service *m* (de porcelaine); train *m* (de pneus); (*b*) **wireless, television, s.,** poste *m* de radio, de télévision; (*c*) *Ten:* manche *f*, set *m*;

(d) groupe *m* (de personnes); **s. of thieves,** bande *f* de voleurs; (**literary**) s., coterie *f* (littéraire). **2.** (*a*) *F:* **to make a dead s. at s.o.,** attaquer furieusement qn; (*b*) (*of hair*) mise *f* en plis. **3.** direction *f* (du vent, du courant); assiette *f* (d'une poutre); voie *f*, chasse *f* (des dents d'une scie). **4.** *Th: Cin:* décor *m*; mise en scène. **II.** *v.* (**setting**; **set**) **1.** *v.tr.* (*a*) mettre, poser (un plat sur la table, etc.); **I haven't s. eyes on him,** je ne l'ai pas vu; (*b*) **to s. one's heart on doing sth.,** avoir, prendre, à cœur de faire qch.; (*c*) **to s. the table,** mettre le couvert, la table; (*d*) **to s. the alarm for 6 o'clock,** mettre le réveil sur six heures; *Aut:* **to s. the tripmeter to zero,** ramener le compteur à zéro; (*e*) **to have one's hair s.,** se faire faire une mise en plis; (*f*) *Th:* **to s. a scene,** monter un décor; (*g*) sertir une pierre (précieuse); **ring s. with rubies,** bague ornée de rubis; (*h*) **to s. words to music,** mettre des paroles en musique; (*i*) **to s. a trap,** dresser, tendre, un piège; (*j*) **to s. a chisel,** affûter un ciseau; (*k*) *Typ:* **to s. type,** composer; (*l*) **to s. the fashion,** fixer, mener, la mode; (*m*) **to s. a bone,** remettre un os; (*n*) **to s. one's teeth,** serrer les dents; (*o*) **to s. sth. going,** mettre qch. en train, en marche; **to s. s.o. to do sth.,** mettre qn à faire qch.; **to s. a man to work,** mettre un homme au travail; (*p*) **to s. a good example,** donner un bon exemple; **to s. a problem,** donner un problème à résoudre; *Sch:* **to s. a book,** mettre un livre au programme. **2.** *v.i.* (*a*) (*of sun*) se coucher; (*b*) (*of dress*) **to s. well, badly,** bien, mal, tomber; (*c*) (*of broken bone*) se ressouder; (*d*) (*of white of egg, etc.*) se coaguler; (*of blood*) se figer; (*of milk*) (se) cailler; (*of jelly*) prendre; (*of cement*) prendre, durcir; (*e*) **to s. to work,** se mettre au travail. **III.** *a.* **1. s. face,** smile, visage *m* rigide; sourire figé; *F:* **to be all s.,** être prêt à commencer, à partir. **2. s. price,** prix fixe; **s. phrase,** cliché *m*; **at s. hours,** à des heures réglées; **s. purpose,** ferme intention; **s. task,** tâche assignée. **3. to be s. on sth.,** être résolu, déterminé, à qch., à faire qch.; '**set a'bout,** *v.i.* **to s. about doing sth.,** se mettre à faire qch.; **I don't know how to s. about it,** je ne sais pas comment m'y prendre; '**set a'part,** *v.tr.,* '**set a'side,** *v.tr.* **1.** mettre (qch.) à part. **2.** (*esp.* **set aside**) rejeter, mettre de côté, écarter (une proposition); '**set 'back,** *s.* déconvenue *f*; revers *m* de fortune; '**set 'down,** *v.tr.* **1.** poser (qch.); déposer (qn); (*of public transport*) **to s. down passengers at . . .,** débarquer, déposer, des passagers à . . .. **2. to s. sth. down** (**in writing**), consigner, coucher, qch. par écrit; '**set 'in,** *v.i.* commencer; **before winter sets in,** avant le début de l'hiver; **it's setting in for rain,** le temps tourne, se met, à la pluie; **if no complications s. in,** s'il ne survient pas de complications; '**set 'off.**

1. *v.tr.* faire partir (une fusée). **2.** *v.i.* partir; se mettre en route; '**set 'out. 1.** *v.tr.* arranger, disposer (des livres, une exposition); **his work is well s. out,** son travail est bien présenté. **2.** *v.i.* partir (en voyage); se mettre en route; s'embarquer; '**set-square,** *s.* équerre *f*; '**setting,** *s.* cadre *m* (d'un récit, etc.); *Th:* mise *f* en scène; monture *f* (d'un diamant); aiguisage *m*, affûtage *m* (d'un outil); mise en plis (des cheveux); coucher *m* (du soleil); *Med:* réduction *f* (d'une fracture); **type s.,** composition *f*; '**set-'to,** *s. F:* lutte *f*; combat *m*; '**set 'up,** *v.tr.* monter (une machine); (*of printer*) composer (un manuscrit); établir (une agence, un record); fonder (une maison de commerce); monter (un magasin); **to s. up house,** établir son domicile; '**set-up,** *s. F:* organisation *f*.

settee [se'tiː], *s.* canapé *m*; **bed s.,** canapé-lit *m*, *pl.* canapés-lits.

setter ['setər], *s.* chien *m* d'arrêt; setter *m*.

settle ['setl]. **I.** *s. H:* banc *m* à dossier. **II.** *v. v.tr.* (*a*) établir, installer (qn); (*b*) **to s. one's affairs,** mettre ordre à ses affaires; (*c*) **to s. s.o.'s doubts,** dissiper les doutes de qn; (*d*) calmer (les nerfs); (*e*) fixer, déterminer; **it's all settled,** c'est une affaire faite; (*f*) résoudre, décider (une question); vider (une querelle); arranger, liquider (une affaire); **s. it among yourselves,** arrangez cela entre vous; **that settles it!** (i) voilà qui tranche la question! (ii) cela me décide! (*g*) conclure (une affaire); régler, solder (un compte); payer (une dette). *abs.* **to s. (up) with s.o.,** payer, régler, son compte avec qn; **I settled for £100,** j'ai décidé d'accepter £100. **2.** *v.i.* (*a*) **to s. (down) in a place,** s'établir dans un lieu; (*b*) (*of bird*) se percher; (*c*) **to s. (down) to work,** se mettre sérieusement au travail; (*d*) (*of snow*) prendre; ne pas fondre; (*e*) (*of liquid*) se clarifier; déposer; (*of sediment*) se précipiter; (*f*) (*of ground, soil*) se tasser; (*of foundations*) s'affaisser; (*g*) **the weather's settling,** le temps se calme, s'arrange; le temps se remet au beau; '**settled,** *a.* (*a*) invariable, sûr; (*of idea*) fixe enraciné; **s. policy,** politique continue; **s. intention,** intention bien arrêtée; **s. weather,** temps fait, fixe; (*of pers.*) rangé; *esp.* marié; (*b*) (*of question*) arrangé, décidé; (*of pers.*) domicilié établi; '**settle 'down,** *v.i.* (*of pers.*) se ranger devenir sérieux; **he's settled down since he married,** le mariage l'a rangé; **he's beginning to s. down at school,** il commence à s'habituer à l'école; '**settlement,** *s.* (*also* '**settling**). **1.** (*c* établissement *m*; installation *f*; (*b*) peuplement *m* (d'un pays). **2.** règlement *m* (d'une affaire d'un compte); *Com:* **in (full) settlement,** pou solde de tout compte; **they have reached settlement,** ils sont arrivés à un accord amica '**settler,** *s.* colon *m*.

seven ['sev(ə)n], *num. a. & s.* sept (*m*); **seven-**
'teen, *num. a. & s.* dix-sept (*m*); **seven'teenth,**
num. a. & s. dix-septième (*m*); **Louis the S.,**
Louis Dix-sept; **the s. of August, August the s.,**
le dix-sept août; **'seventh,** *num. a. & s.* septième (*m*); **the s. of July, July the s.,** le sept
juillet; **to be in the s.** heaven, être aux anges;
-ly, *adv.* en septième lieu; **'seventieth,** *num. a.*
& s. soixante-dixième (*m*); **'seventy,** *num. a.*
& s. soixante-dix (*m*); (*Belgium, Switzerland*)
septante (*m*); **s.-one, s.-nine,** soixante et onze,
soixante-dix-neuf; **to be in one's seventies,** être
septuagénaire.

sever ['sevər], *v.tr.* désunir, disjoindre; rompre
(une amitié); **to s. one's connection with s.o.,** se
désassocier d'avec qn; **'severance,** *s.* séparation *f* (**from,** de); rupture *f* (de relations); interruption *f* (de communications).

several ['sev(ə)rəl], *a.* plusieurs, divers;
quelques; **he and s. others,** lui et quelques
autres; **I have s.,** j'en ai plusieurs.

severe [si'viər], *a.* 1. sévère, strict, rigoureux
(**with s.o.,** envers qn). 2. (*a*) (temps) rigoureux,
dur; **the cold was s.,** le froid sévissait; (*b*)
vif; rude; **s. pain,** vive douleur; **-ly,** *adv.*
1. sévèrement; avec sévérité. 2. grièvement; gravement (blessé); **se'verity** [-'veriti],
s. 1. sévérité *f*, rigueur *f*. 2. (*a*) rigueur, in-
clémence *f* (du temps); (*b*) gravité *f* (d'une
maladie).

sew [sou], *v.tr.* (**sewed; sewn**) coudre; **to s. on a**
button, coudre, attacher, un bouton; **to s. (up)**
a seam, faire une couture; **'sewing,** *s.* 1.
couture *f*; **s. needle,** aiguille *f* à coudre; **s. cot-**
ton, fil *m* à coudre; **s. machine,** machine *f* à
coudre. 2. ouvrage *m* (à l'aiguille).

sewer ['s(j)u:ər], *s. Civ. E:* égout *m*; **main s.,** égout
collecteur; **'sewage,** *s.* eau(x) *f* (*pl*) d'égout; **s.**
farm, champs *mpl* d'épandage; **s. system,**
système *m* du tout-à-l'égout; **'sewerman,** *pl.*
-men, *s.* égoutier *m*.

sex [seks], *s.* sexe *m*; **s. appeal,** charme *m*, *F:* sex-
appeal *m*; **'sexless,** *a.* 1. asexué. 2. *F:* froid,
frigide; **'sexual,** *a.* sexuel; **s. intercourse,** rapports sexuels; **s. reproduction,** reproduction
sexuée; **'sexy,** *a. F:* excitant, aguichant; **to be**
s., avoir du tempérament.

sextet [seks'tet], *s. Mus:* sextuor *m*.

sexton ['sekstən], *s. Ecc:* (*a*) sacristain *m*; (*b*)
sonneur *m* (des cloches, du carillon, d'une
église); (*c*) fossoyeur *m*.

shabby ['ʃæbi], *a.* 1. (mobilier *m*, etc.) pauvre,
minable; **to look s.,** avoir l'air usé, râpé. 2.
mesquin; **to do s.o. a s. turn,** faire une
mesquinerie à qn; **-ily,** *adv.* 1. pauvrement; **s.**
dressed, miteux. 2. (se conduire) mesquinement; **'shabbiness,** *s.* 1. état râpé, usé
(d'un vêtement); état défraîchi (d'un meuble);
apparence pauvre, miteuse (de qn). 2. (*a*)

mesquinerie *f* (de conduite); (*b*) parcimonie *f*.

shack [ʃæk]. I. *s.* cabane *f*, hutte *f*. II. *v.i. F:* **to s.**
(**up**) **with s.o.,** vivre (en concubinage),
cohabiter, avec qn.

shade [ʃeid]. I. *s.* 1. ombre *f*; **s. temperature,**
température à l'ombre; **to put s.o. in(to) the s.,**
éclipser qn. 2. *Art:* (*a*) **light and s.,** l'ombre et la
lumière; (*b*) nuance *f*; teinte *f*. 3. (*a*) (**lamp-)s.,**
abat-jour *m inv*; (*b*) *N.Am:* store *m* (de
fenêtre). II. *v.* 1. *v.tr.* (*a*) ombrager; couvrir
(qch.) d'ombre; abriter (qch.) (du soleil);
voiler, masquer (une lumière); (*b*) ombrer (un
dessin); nuancer (une couleur); **to s. off a**
colour, dégrader une couleur. 2. *v.i.* **blue that**
shades off into green, bleu qui se fond en vert;
'shadiness, *s.* 1. ombre *f*, ombrage *m* (d'un
sentier, d'un arbre). 2. *F:* aspect *m* louche
(d'une affaire); **'shady,** *a.* 1. (*a*) qui donne de
l'ombre, ombreux; (*b*) ombragé, couvert d'ombre; **s. walk,** allée couverte. 2. (*of transaction*)
louche; **s. pub,** bistrot *m* louche; **the s. side of**
politics, les dessous de la politique.

shadow ['ʃædou]. I. *s.* 1. ombre *f*; obscurité *f*. 2.
to cast a s., projeter une ombre; faire ombre;
not the s. of a doubt, pas l'ombre d'un doute;
Pol: **s. cabinet,** conseil *m* des ministres
fantôme; **to wear oneself to a s.,** s'épuiser. 3.
(*a*) compagnon, *f.* compagne, inséparable. II.
v.tr. **to s. s.o.,** filer qn; **'shadower,** *s.* filateur,
-trice; **'shadowing,** *s.* filature *f* (d'une personne suspecte); **'shadowy,** *a.* vague, indécis;
a s. form in the dusk, une ombre dans la nuit
tombante.

shaft¹ [ʃɑːft], *s.* 1. hampe *f*, bois *m* (de hache,
etc.). 2. flèche *f*, trait *m.* 3. rayon *m* (de
lumière). 4. tige *f* ((i) de plume d'oiseau; (ii)
d'une colonne). 5. (*a*) *Mec:* arbre *m* (de
transmission, à cames); (*b*) (*of horse-drawn*
vehicle) brancard *m.*

shaft², *s. Min:* puits *m*; cage *f* (d'un ascenseur).

shaggy ['ʃægi], *a.* poilu; à longs poils; (sourcils)
en broussailles; (barbe) touffue.

shake [ʃeik]. I. *s.* 1. (*a*) secousse *f*; **to give sth. a**
good s., bien secouer, bien agiter, qch.; **a s. of**
the head, un hochement, un mouvement, de
tête; **I'll be there in a s.,** j'arrive en un rien de
temps; **to be all of a s.,** trembler de tous ses
membres. 2. **milk s.,** lait parfumé. 3. *F:* **to be no**
great shakes, ne pas valoir grand-chose. II. *v.*
(**shook; shaken**) 1. *v.tr.* (*a*) secouer; agiter
(qch.); **to s. one's head,** faire non de la tête; **to**
s. one's fist at s.o., menacer qn du poing; **to s.**
hands with s.o., serrer la main à qn; **s.! tope là!**
to s. oneself free, se dégager d'une secousse;
(*b*) ébranler; **to feel shaken after a fall,** se
ressentir d'une chute. 2. *v.i.* trembler; (*of*
building) chanceler, branler; (*of voice*)
trembloter; **to s. all over,** trembler de tout son
corps; **'shake'down,** *v.i.* se tasser; **the team is**

shaking down, l'équipe se forme; **'shake-down,** s. F: lit improvisé; **'shaken,** a. secoué; ébranlé; émotionné; **'shaking. I.** a. tremblant; branlant; **s. voice,** voix tremblante, chevrotante. **II.** s. secousse f; secouement m; ébranlement m; **to get a good s. up,** être pas mal secoué; **'shake 'off,** v.tr. **1.** se débarrasser, se défaire, de (qch.). **2.** venir à bout d'(un rhume); **'shake 'up.** v.tr. **1.** secouer, brasser; agiter (une bouteille). **2.** éveiller, secouer, stimuler (qn); **'shake-up,** s. **1. to get a good s.-up,** être pas mal secoué. **2.** a **big s.-up,** un grand changement, un grand remaniement (de l'administration, du personnel, etc.); **'shaky,** a. peu solide; (santé f) faible; **s. hand,** main tremblante; (voix) mal assurée.

shall [ʃæl, ʃ(ə)l], modal aux. v. def. (should [ʃud]) **I.** (implying command, insistence) **1.** (a) **ships s.** carry three lights, les navires sont tenus de porter trois feux; **all is as it should be,** tout est très bien; (b) **he s. not (shan't,** abbreviated neg. form) **do it,** je défends qu'il le fasse; **you s. do it!** vous le ferez, je le veux! (c) **you should do it at once,** vous devriez le faire tout de suite; **you should have seen him!** il fallait le voir! (d) **he should have arrived by this time,** il devrait être arrivé à l'heure qu'il est; **I should think so!** je crois bien! **2.** (polite request) **s. I open the window?** voulez-vous que j'ouvre la fenêtre? **3.** (a) (exclamative & rhetorical questions) **why should you suspect me?** pourquoi me soupçonner (,moi)? **whom should I meet but Jones!** voilà que je rencontre Jones! (b) **if he should come,** si par hasard il vient; **should I be free,** si je suis libre; **should the occasion arise,** le cas échéant; **in case he shouldn't be there,** au cas où il n'y soit pas. **II.** aux. verb forming the future & conditional tenses. **1. you shan't have any!** tu n'en auras pas! **2.** (a) **tomorrow I s. go and he'll arrive,** demain, moi je partirai et lui arrivera; **will you be there?—I s.,** y serez-vous?—oui (j'y serai); (b) **s. you come tomorrow?** vous viendrez demain? **3. if he comes I s. speak to him,** s'il vient je lui parlerai; **we should come if we were invited,** nous viendrions si on nous invitait. **4. I should like a drink,** je prendrais bien quelque chose.

shallot [ʃə'lɔt], s. échalote f.

shallow ['ʃælou]. **1.** a. (a) (of water) peu profond; (of dish) plat; (b) (of pers.) superficiel, frivole. **2.** s. (usu. pl.) bas-fond m, pl. basfonds, haut-fond m, pl. hauts-fonds; **'shallowness,** s. (le) peu de profondeur; (of pers., book, etc.) caractère superficiel.

sham [ʃæm]. **I.** a. simulé, feint; (of jewellery) faux, f. fausse, postiche, en toc. **II.** s. **1.** feinte f, trompe-l'œil m inv. **2. he's a s.,** c'est un imposteur. **III.** v.tr. (shammed) feindre, simuler; **to s. sleep,** faire semblant de dormir; **he's only**

shamming, tout ça c'est de la frime.

shamble [ʃæmbl], v.i. **to s. along,** s'avancer en traînant le pas.

shambles ['ʃæmblz], s.pl. (with sg. const.) désordre m, gâchis m; **what a s.!** quelle pagaille!

shame [ʃeim]. **I.** s. (a) honte f; **to put s.o. to s.,** faire honte à qn; (b) **it's a s.!** c'est honteux! **what a s.!** quel dommage! **II.** v.tr. **to s. s.o.,** faire honte à, humilier, qn; **to be shamed into doing sth.,** faire qch. par amour-propre; **'shamefaced,** a. honteux, penaud; embarrassé; **-ly,** adv. honteusement; d'un air penaud; **'shameful,** a. honteux, scandaleux; **-fully,** adv. honteusement, scandaleusement; **'shamefulness,** s. honte f, infamie f; **'shameless,** a. **1.** éhonté, effronté, cynique. **2.** honteux, scandaleux; **-ly,** adv. effrontément; **to lie s.,** mentir impudemment; **'shamelessness,** s. effronterie f, impudence f.

shampoo [ʃæm'pu:]. **I.** s. shampooing m. **II.** v.tr se laver (les cheveux).

shamrock ['ʃæmrɔk], s. trèfle m d'Irlande.

shandy ['ʃændi], s. bière panachée.

shan't [ʃɑ:nt], see SHALL.

shanty ['ʃænti], s. hutte f, cabane f, baraque f; **s. town,** bidonville m.

shape [ʃeip]. **I.** s. **1.** (a) forme f, configuration (du terrain, etc.); façon f, coupe f (d'un habit); **to get out of s.,** to lose (its) **s.,** se déformer; **to put, knock, (a book) into s.,** mettre (un livre au point; (b) taille f, tournure f. **2. to take s.** prendre forme. **3. no communication in any s or form,** aucune communication de n'import quelle sorte. **4.** Cu: moule m. **II.** v. **1.** v.tr façonner; tailler (la pierre); **to s. one's life** régler sa vie; **to s. a coat,** ajuster une veste. **2** v.i. se développer; **the affair is shaping well,** (i l'affaire prend bonne tournure; (ii) l'affair promet bien; **'shapeless,** a. inform difforme; **'shapelessness,** s. manque m d forme; **'shapely,** a. bien fait, bien tourné.

share [ʃɛər]. **I.** s. **1.** (a) part f, portion f; **equal shares,** par portions égales; **s. in profit** participation f aux bénéfices; **to go shares,** pa tager (with, avec); **s. and s. alike,** en partagea également; (b) **(fair) s.,** portion juste; lot m. contribution f, écot m; **to take a s. in the co versation,** contribuer à la conversation; **doesn't do his s.,** il n'y met pas du sien; **to ha a s. in an undertaking,** avoir un intérêt da une entreprise. **3.** Fin: action f, titre m. **II.** v. v.tr. partager. **2.** v.tr. & ind.tr. **to s. (in)** st prendre part à, participer à, qch.; **to s. (i s.o.'s grief,** partager la douleur de qn; **'shar cropper,** s. Agr: métayer, -ère; **'shar cropping,** s. Agr: métayage m; **shareholde** s. Fin: actionnaire mf; **'sharing,** s. **1.** parta m. **2.** participation f.

shark [ʃɑːk], *s.* **1.** requin *m.* **2.** (*pers.*) escroc *m*; requin.

sharp [ʃɑːp]. **I.** *a.* **1.** (*a*) tranchant, aiguisé, affilé; (*of point*) aigu, pointu; (*b*) (*of features*) anguleux; **s. turn,** tournant brusque; (*c*) (*of outline*) net; (*d*) **s. contrast,** contraste marqué. **2.** (*of pers.*) (*a*) fin, éveillé; (*of hearing*) fin, subtil; (*of sight*) perçant; (*of glance*) pénétrant; **a s. child,** un enfant vif, *Pej:* futé; (*b*) rusé, malin; peu scrupuleux; **s. practice,** procédés *m* peu honnêtes; **to be too s. for s.o.,** être trop malin pour qn. **3.** (*a*) (combat) vif, acharné; (*b*) (orage) violent; **s. shower,** forte averse; (*c*) (hiver) rigoureux; (vent) vif, perçant; (froid) pénétrant; **s. pain,** vive douleur; (*d*) **s. pace,** allure vive, rapide; (*e*) **s. tongue,** langue acérée; **in a s. tone,** d'un ton acerbe, cassant. **4.** (*of sauce*) piquant; (*of apple*) aigre, acide; (*of wine*) vert. **5.** (*of sound*) pénétrant, aigu. **II.** *s. Mus:* dièse *m.* **III.** *adv.* **1.** (tourner) brusquement; **turn s. right,** prenez à droite à angle droit. **2.** ponctuellement, exactement; **at four o'clock s.,** à quatre heures précises; à quatre heures sonnantes, *F:* pile. **3.** *F:* **look s.!** fais vite! dépêche-toi! *F:* grouille-toi! **'sharpen,** *v.tr.* **1.** (*a*) affiler, affûter, aiguiser; (*b*) tailler en pointe; **to s. a pencil,** tailler un crayon. **2. to s. s.o.'s wits,** dégourdir qn; **'sharply,** *adv.* **1. s. divided,** nettement divisé. **2. the road dips s.,** la route plonge brusquement. **3.** (*a*) **he looked s. at her,** il dirigea sur elle un regard pénétrant; (*b*) (réprimander) sévèrement; **to answer s.,** répondre avec brusquerie; **'sharpness,** *s.* **1.** (*a*) acuité *f*, finesse *f*; (*b*) netteté *f* (des contours); (*c*) caractère marqué (d'un contraste). **2.** (*a*) **s. of sight,** acuité de la vue; (*b*) intelligence *f.* **3.** sévérité *f*, acerbité *f*; **'sharpshooter,** *s. Mil:* tirailleur *m*; **'sharp-'witted,** *a.* éveillé; intelligent; dégourdi.

shatter ['ʃætər]. **1.** *v.tr.* fracasser; briser (en éclats). **2.** *v.i.* se briser (en éclats); se fracasser; **'shattering,** *a.* **s. blow,** un coup écrasant.

shave [ʃeiv]. **I.** *s.* **1. to have a s.,** (i) se faire raser; (ii) se raser. **2. to have a close, narrow, s.,** l'échapper belle. **II.** *v.tr.* (*a*) raser; faire la barbe à (qn); (*b*) **to s. (oneself),** se raser, se faire la barbe; **'shaven,** *a.* rasé; *only used in a few expressions, e.g.* **clean-s.,** (visage *m*) glabre; sans barbe ni moustache; **'shaver,** *s.* **electric s.,** rasoir *m* électrique; **'shaving,** *s.* **1.** action *f* de se raser; **s. brush,** blaireau *m*; **s. cream,** crème *f* à raser; **s. soap,** savon *m* à barbe. **2.** *usu. pl.* **shavings,** copeaux *mpl* (de bois, de métal).

shawl [ʃɔːl], *s.* châle *m.*

she [ʃi, ʃiː], *pers. pron. nom.* **1.** elle; (*a*) **what's s. doing?** que fait-elle? **here s. comes,** la voici qui vient; (*b*) (i) (*of female animals, motor*

cars, *etc.*) elle; (ii) (*of ships*) il; **s. sails tomorrow,** il appareille demain. **2.** (*a*) (*stressed*) elle; **she and I,** elle et moi; **she knows nothing about it,** elle n'en sait rien, elle; (*b*) (*antecedent to a rel. pron.*) (i) celle; **she who believes,** celle qui croit; (ii) **it's she who did it,** c'est elle qui l'a fait. **3.** (*used as a noun*) femelle *f*; **s.-ass,** ânesse *f*; **s.-bear,** ourse *f*; **s.-cat,** chatte *f*; **s.-monkey,** guenon *f.*

sheaf, *pl.* **sheaves** [ʃiːf, ʃiːvz], *s.* **1.** gerbe *f* (de blé, de fleurs). **2.** liasse *f* (de papiers).

shear ['ʃiər], *v.tr.* (**sheared; shorn**) **1. to s.** (**off**), couper (une branche); **to s. through sth.,** trancher qch.; *Metalw:* cisailler (une tôle). **2.** tondre (un mouton); **to be shorn of sth.,** être dépouillé, privé, de qch.; **'shearer,** *s.* tondeur *m* (de moutons); **'shearing,** *s.* taille *f* (d'une haie); cisaillement *m* (d'une tôle); tonte *f*, tondaison *f* (des moutons); **shears,** *s.pl.* (**pair of**) **s.,** cisaille(s) *f*(*pl*); grands ciseaux; **shorn,** *a.* (mouton) tondu; **s. of all his possessions,** dépouillé de tout ce qu'il possédait.

sheath [ʃiːθ], *s.* fourreau *m*; gaine *f*; **s.-knife,** couteau *m* à gaine.

sheathe [ʃiːð], *v.tr.* (re)mettre au fourreau, rengainer.

shed[1] [ʃed], *s.* hangar *m*; **lean-to s.,** appentis *m*; **open s.,** auvent *m*; **building s.,** atelier *m* de construction; **vehicle s.,** remise *f* de véhicules; **garden s.,** resserre *f* dans un jardin; **bicycle s.,** remise, resserre, de vélos.

shed[2], *v.tr.* (**shedding; shed**) **1.** (*a*) perdre (ses feuilles); (*b*) se défaire de (qn); (*c*) **to s. one's clothes,** se dévêtir. **2.** répandre, verser (des larmes, le sang); **to s. light on a matter,** éclairer une affaire; *El:* **to s. the load,** délester.

sheen [ʃiːn], *s.* luisant *m*, lustre *m*; chatoiement *m.*

sheep [ʃiːp], *s.inv.* mouton *m*; **'sheepdog,** *s.* chien *m* de berger; **'sheepfold,** *s.* parc *m* à moutons; bercail *m*; **'sheepish,** *a.* **1.** penaud; interdit. **2.** timide; gauche; **-ly,** *adv.* **1.** d'un air penaud. **2.** d'un air timide; **'sheepishness,** *s.* **1.** timidité *f*; fausse honte. **2.** air penaud; **'sheepskin,** *s.* peau *f* de mouton.

sheer[1] ['ʃiər], *v.i. Nau:* embarder; **'sheer 'off,** *v.i.* **1.** larguer les amarres. **2.** *F:* prendre le large.

sheer[2]. **1.** *a.* (*a*) pur, véritable, absolu; **a s. impossibility,** une impossibilité absolue; **a s. waste of time,** une pure perte de temps; (*b*) (rocher *m*) perpendiculaire; à pic; (*of silk, etc.*) léger, fin, diaphane; **s. nylon tights,** collant *m* en nylon extra-fin. **2.** *adv.* (*a*) tout à fait; **the tree was torn s. out by the roots,** l'arbre a été bel et bien déraciné; (*b*) à pic.

sheet [ʃiːt], *s.* **1.** drap *m* (de lit). **2.** feuille *f* (de papier); **loose s.,** feuille volante; *Com:* **order s.,** bulletin *m* de commande. **3.** feuille (de verre);

s. **iron,** tôle *f.* **4.** nappe *f* (d'eau); s. **lightning,** éclairs *m* diffus; éclairs en nappe(s).

shelf, *pl.* **shelves** [ʃelf, ʃelvz], *s.* **1.** planche *f* (d'armoire); rayon *m* (de bibliothèque); **set of shelves,** étagère *f*; *F:* **to be on the s.,** être au rancart. **2.** rebord *m,* corniche *f* (d'un rocher); *Geog:* **the continental s.,** le plateau, banc, continental.

shell [ʃel]. **I.** *s.* **1.** (*a*) coquille *f*; carapace *f* (de tortue); écaille *f* (d'huître); (**empty**) **shells,** coquillages *m*; **to retire into one's s.,** rentrer dans sa coquille; (*b*) coquille (d'œuf); coque *f* (d'œuf plein); (*c*) *F:* forme *f* vide; simple apparence *f.* **2.** carcasse *f,* coque (de navire). **3.** *Mil:* obus *m*; **high-explosive s.,** obus brisant. **II.** *v.tr.* **1.** écosser (des petits pois); écaler (des noix). **2.** *Mil:* bombarder; **'shellfish,** *s. coll.* mollusques *m* et crustacés *m*; fruits *m* de mer; **'shell 'out,** *v.tr. & i. F:* payer (la note); débourser.

shelter ['ʃeltər]. **I.** *s.* lieu *m* de refuge; abri *m*; asile *m*; **under s.,** à l'abri, à couvert; **to take s.,** s'abriter, se mettre à l'abri. **II.** *v.* **1.** *v.tr.* abriter (qn); donner asile à, recueillir (un malheureux). **2.** *v.i. & pr.* s'abriter; se mettre à l'abri, à couvert (**from,** contre); **'sheltered,** *a.* abrité (**against, from,** contre); **'sheltering,** *a.* protecteur, -trice.

shelve¹ [ʃelv], *v.tr.* ajourner, enterrer (une question); **my request has been shelved,** ma demande est restée dans les cartons; **'shelving¹,** *s.* **1.** enterrement *m,* ajournement *m* (d'une question). **2.** (ensemble *m* de) rayons *mpl*; rayonnage *m*; **adjustable s.,** rayons mobiles.

shelve², *v.i.* aller en pente; **'shelving²,** *a.* en pente; (*of shore, etc.*) incliné.

shepherd ['ʃepəd], *s.* berger *m*; pâtre *m*; *Ecc:* **the Good S.,** le bon Pasteur; *Cu:* **s.'s pie,** hâchis *m* aux pommes de terre; **'shepherdess,** *s.* bergère *f.*

sheriff ['ʃerif], *s. N.Am:* chef *m* de la police (d'un comté); shérif *m.*

sherry ['ʃeri], *s.* vin *m* de Xérès; xérès *m.*

Shetland ['ʃetlənd]. *Pr.n.* **the S. Islands,** les îles *f* Shetland; **S. pony,** *s.* poney shetlandais; **'Shetlander,** *s.* Shetlandais, -aise.

shield [ʃiːld]. **I.** *s.* **1.** bouclier *m.* **2.** *Tchn:* tôle protectrice. **II.** *v.tr.* protéger (qn, qch., **from, against,** contre); **to s. one's eyes,** se protéger les yeux.

shift [ʃift]. **I.** *s.* **1.** changement *m* de position; renverse *f* (de la marée); **to make a s.,** changer de place; **s. of the wind,** saute *f* du vent. **2.** *Ind:* équipe *f,* poste *m* (d'ouvriers); **to work in shifts,** se relayer; travailler par équipes; **day, night, s.,** équipe de jour, de nuit; **he's on day, night, s.,** il est de jour, de nuit; **s. work,** travail par équipes. **3.** expédient *m*; **to make s. to do sth.,** trouver

moyen de faire qch. **II.** *v.* **1.** *v.tr.* changer (qch.) de place; déplacer, bouger, remuer (les meubles, etc.); *Th:* **to s. the scenery,** changer le décor. **2.** *v.i.* (*a*) changer de place; se déplacer; (*b*) **the wind has shifted,** le vent a tourné; **to s. for oneself,** se débrouiller; **'shiftiness,** *s.* sournoiserie *f*; manque de franchise; **'shifting,** *a.* **1.** qui se déplace; **s. sands,** sables *m* mouvants. **2.** (*of scene*) changeant; (*of wind*) inégal; **'shiftless,** *a.* paresseux; peu débrouillard; (*of pers., action*) futile; **'shifty,** *a.* roublard, retors; sournois; **s. eyes,** yeux fuyants.

shilly-shally ['ʃiliʃæli], *v.i.* barguigner, vaciller.

shimmer ['ʃimər], *v.i.* miroiter, luire, chatoyer.

shin [ʃin]. **I.** *s. Anat:* le devant du tibia, de la jambe; *Cu:* jarret *m* (de bœuf). **II.** *v.i.* (**shinned**) *F:* **to s. up a tree,** grimper à un arbre.

shindy ['ʃindi], *s. F:* tapage *m,* chahut *m*; **to kick up a s.,** chahuter.

shine [ʃain]. **I.** *v.i.* (**shone** [ʃɔn]) **1.** briller; reluire; **the sun is shining,** il fait du soleil; **his face shone with happiness,** sa figure rayonnait de bonheur; **he doesn't s. in conversation,** il ne brille pas dans la conversation. **2.** **to s. on sth.,** illuminer qch. **II.** *s.* **1.** éclat *m,* lumière *f*; **rain or s.,** par tous les temps. **2.** brillant *m,* luisant *m*; **to give a s. to the brasses,** faire reluire les cuivres; **to take the s. off sth.,** défraîchir, délustrer, qch.; faire ternir qch.; **'shining,** *a.* brillant, (re)luisant; **s. example,** exemple brillant, insigne (**of,** de); **'shiny,** *a.* brillant; luisant; (vêtement) lustré par l'usage.

shingle ['ʃingl], *s.* (*a*) galets *mpl*; (gros) cailloux *mpl*; (*b*) *Const:* bardeau *m*; **'shingly,** *a.* couvert de galets; cailouteux.

shingles ['ʃinglz], *s.pl. Med:* zona *m.*

ship [ʃip]. **I.** *s.* (*usu. referred to as* **she, her**) navire (marchand); bâtiment *m*; bateau *m*; **His, Her, Majesty's ships,** les vaisseaux *m* de la Marine Royale; **the ship's company,** l'équipage *m*; **on board s.,** à bord; **to take s., to go on board a s.,** (s')embarquer. **II.** *v.* (**shipped**) **1.** *v.tr.* (*a*) embarquer (une cargaison, etc.); expédier (des marchandises); *Nau:* **to s. a sea,** embarquer une lame. **2.** *v.i.* s'embarquer; **'shipbuilder,** *s.* constructeur de navires; **'shipbuilding,** *s.* construction navale; **'shipment,** *s.* **1.** (*a*) embarquement *m*; (*b*) expédition *f* (de marchandises) par mer. **2.** chargement *m*; cargaison *f*; **'shipowner,** *s.* armateur *m*; **'shipper,** *s.* **1.** chargeur *m*; expéditeur *m.* **2.** affréteur *m*; **'shipping,** *s.* **1.** embarquement *m*; expédition *f* (de marchandises); **s. agent,** agent *m* maritime; **s. company,** compagnie *f* de navigation. **2.** *coll.* navires *mpl* (d'un pays, dans un port). **3.** **s. routes,** routes *f* de navigation; **'shipshape,** *a.* bien tenu; en bon ordre; **'shipwreck. I.** *s.* naufrage *m.* **II.** *v.tr.* **to be shipwrecked,** faire naufrage; **'shipyard,** *s.*

chantier *m* de constructions navales; chantier naval.

shire [ˈʃaiər, *as suffix usu.* ʃ(i)ər], *s.* comté *m*; **Ayrshire,** le comté d'Ayr; **Oxfordshire,** le comté d'Oxford.

shirk [ʃəːk], *v.tr.* manquer à, se dérober à (une obligation); *abs.* négliger son devoir; ˈ**shirker,** *s.* carotteur, -euse.

shirt [ʃəːt], *s.* chemise *f*; *F:* **to put one's s. on a horse,** parier tout ce qu'on possède sur un cheval; *F:* **keep your s. on!** ne vous emballez pas! ˈ**shirtsleeves,** *s.pl.* **to be in one's s.,** être en bras de chemise.

shiver[1] [ˈʃivər], *v.* (*esp. of glass*) 1. *v.tr.* fracasser; briser (une vitre) en éclats. 2. *v.i.* voler en éclats.

shiver[2]. I. *v.i.* **to s.** (**with cold, with fear, with fever**), frissonner, grelotter, trembler (de froid, de peur, de fièvre). II. *s.* frisson *m*, grelottement *m*, tremblement *m*; ˈ**shivery,** *a.* **to feel s.,** (i) avoir le frisson; (ii) se sentir fiévreux.

shoal[1] [ʃoul]. 1. *a.* **s. water,** eau peu profonde. 2. *s.* haut-fond *m, pl.* hauts-fonds, bas-fond *m, pl.* bas-fonds.

shoal[2], *s.* banc voyageur (de poissons).

shock[1] [ʃɔk], *s.* **s. of hair,** tignasse *f*; toison *f*.

shock[2], *s.* 1. choc *m*, heurt *m*. 2. (*a*) coup *m*, atteinte *f*; **it gave me a dreadful s.,** cela m'a porté un coup terrible; **the s. killed him,** il mourut de saisissement; (*b*) **electric s.,** secousse *f* électrique; (*c*) *Med:* choc; commotion *f*; **electric s. treatment,** traitement *m* par électrochocs; (*d*) **s. wave,** onde *f* de choc; ˈ**shock-absorber,** *s. Aut: etc:* amortisseur *m*; ˈ**shock-proof,** *a.* anti-choc *inv*; ˈ**shock troops,** *s.pl.* troupes *f* d'assaut, de choc.

shock[3], *v.tr.* (*a*) choquer, scandaliser (qn); **easily shocked,** pudibond; (*b*) bouleverser (qn); ˈ**shocking,** *a.* choquant; révoltant, affreux; **how s.!** quelle horreur!

shoddy [ˈʃɔdi], *a.* (article) de mauvaise qualité; de camelote; ˈ**shoddiness,** *s.* mauvaise qualité (d'un article fabriqué).

shoe [ʃuː], *s.* 1. soulier *m*; chaussure *f*; **to put one's shoes on,** se chausser; **I shouldn't like to be in his shoes,** je ne voudrais pas être à sa place. 2. fer *m* (de cheval); ˈ**shoebrush,** *s.* brosse *f* à cirer; brosse à chaussures; ˈ**shoehorn,** *s.* chausse-pied *m, pl.* chausse-pieds; ˈ**shoe-lace,** *s.* lacet *m*; ˈ**shoemaker,** *s.* (*a*) bottier *m*; fabricant *m* de chaussures; ˈ**shoestring,** *s. N.Am:* lacet *m*; **on a s.,** à peu de frais; **to set up business on a s.,** s'établir avec de minces capitaux.

shoo [ʃuː], *v.tr.* **to s.** (**away**) **chickens,** chasser des poules.

shoot [ʃuːt]. I. *v.* (**shot** [ʃɔt]) 1. *v.i.* (*a*) se précipiter, se lancer; **to s. ahead of s.o.,** devancer qn rapidement; (*b*) (*of pain*) lanciner,

élancer; (*of tree, bud*) pousser, bourgeonner; (*of plant*) germer. 2. *v.tr.* (*a*) franchir (un rapide); *Aut:* **to s. the lights,** brûler le feu rouge; (*b*) *F:* **to s. a line,** (i) exagérer sa propre importance; (ii) baratiner; (*c*) lancer, tirer (une balle); décharger (un fusil), *abs.* tirer; **to s. wide of the mark,** (i) mal viser; (ii) être loin de la vérité; (*d*) tuer (qn) d'un coup de fusil; (*e*) chasser (le gibier); (*f*) *Cin:* tourner (un film); (*g*) *Sp:* **to s. a goal,** marquer un but. II. *s.* 1. pousse *f* (d'une plante); (*of vine*) sarment *m*. 2. *Ind:* couloir *m*; glissière *f*; goulotte *f*; *H:* **rubbish s.,** vide-ordure *m inv.* 3. (*a*) partie *f* de chasse; (*b*) concours *m* de tir; (*c*) chasse gardée. 4. *F:* **the whole s.,** tout le bataclan, tout le tremblement; ˈ**shoot** ˈ**down,** *v.tr.* abattre, descendre (qn, un avion); ˈ**shooting.** I. *a.* 1. qui s'élance; jaillissant; **s. star,** étoile filante; **s. pains,** douleurs lancinantes. II. *s.* (*a*) tir *m* (au pistolet, etc.); (*b*) la chasse; *Aut:* **s. brake, break** *m* (de chasse), canadienne *f*; (*c*) **s. incident,** bagarre *f* avec coups de feu; **s. stick,** canne-siège *f*; ˈ**shoot** ˈ**up.** 1. *v.i.* (*a*) (*of flames*) jaillir; (*b*) (*of prices*) augmenter rapidement; (*c*) (*of plant*) pousser. 2. *v.tr. Mil:* mitrailler (un aérodrome, etc.).

shop [ʃɔp]. I. *s.* 1. magasin *m*; (*small*) boutique *f*; **s. assistant,** vendeur, -euse; employé(e) de magasin; **s. window,** vitrine *f*; devanture *f* (de magasin); étalage *m*; **wine s., tobacconist's s.,** débit *m* de vins, de tabac; **grocer's s.,** épicerie *f*, (magasin d')alimentation *f*; **baker's s.,** boulangerie *f*; **butcher's s.,** boucherie *f*; **mobile s.,** camionnette-boutique *f, pl.* camionnettes-boutiques; **to keep a s.,** tenir un commerce; **to go round the shops,** courir les magasins; *F:* **you've come to the wrong s.,** vous tombez mal; *F:* **everything was all over the s.,** tout était en confusion, en désordre. 2. *Ind:* atelier *m*; **closed s.,** atelier fermé aux (ouvriers) non-syndiqués. 3. **to talk s.,** parler métier. II. *v.i.* (**shopped**) faire des achats; faire ses courses; ˈ**shopkeeper,** *s.* commerçant, -ante; ˈ**shop-lifter,** *s.* voleur, -euse, à l'étalage; ˈ**shop-lifting,** vol *m* à l'étalage; ˈ**shopper,** *s.* acheteur, -euse; ˈ**shopping,** *s.* achats *mpl*; **to go s.,** faire ses courses *fpl*; **to go window s.,** faire du lèche-vitrines; **s. centre,** centre commercial; ˈ**shop-soiled,** *a.* défraîchi; ˈ**shop** ˈ**steward,** *s. Ind:* délégué syndical; ˈ**shopwalker,** *s.* 1. chef *m* de rayon. 2. *Ind:* inspecteur, -trice.

shore[1] [ʃɔːr], *s.* (*a*) rivage *m*, littoral *m*; bord *m* (de la mer, d'un lac); (*b*) *Nau:* **on s.,** à terre; **off s.,** au large; (*c*) *N.Am:* **s. dinner,** repas composé de fruits de mer.

shore[2]. I. *s. Const: etc:* étai *m*; étançon *m*; contre-boutant *m*. II. *v.tr.* **to s.** (**sth.**) **up,** étayer, étançonner (qch.); contre-bouter, arc-bouter (un mur).

short [ʃɔːt]. I. a. 1. court; **a s. way off**, à peu de distance; **s. steps**, petits pas; **a s. man**, un homme de petite taille. 2. court, bref; (a) de peu de durée; **the days are getting shorter**, les jours se raccourcissent; **for a s. time**, pour peu de temps; **in a s. time**, sous peu; bientôt; **a s. time ago**, il y a peu de temps; **a s. sleep**, un petit somme; (b) **s. story**, nouvelle f; **in s.**, bref; **he's called Bob for s.**, on l'appelle Bob pour abréger; (c) (of reply) brusque; sec; **to be s. with s.o.**, être sec, cassant, avec qn; **s. temper**, caractère brusque, vif. 3. (a) (of weight) insuffisant; **to give s. weight**, ne pas donner le poids; **I'm twenty francs s.**, il me manque vingt francs; (b) **to be s. of sth.**, être à court de qch.; **to be s. of hands**, manquer de main-d'œuvre; **to go s. of sth.**, se priver de qch. 4. Cu: **s. pastry**, pâte brisée; **-ly**, adv. 1. brièvement. 2. (répondre) brusquement, sèchement. 3. bientôt, prochainement; sous peu; **s. after(wards)**, peu (de temps) après. II. s. (a) **the long and the s. of it**, le fin mot de l'affaire; (b) pl. Cl: **shorts**, short m; (c) Cin: court métrage; (d) El: **s. (circuit)**, court circuit. III. adv. 1. **to stop s.**, s'arrêter court; **to cut s.o. s.**, couper la parole à qn. 2. **to fall s. of sth.**, être au-dessous de qch.; **s. of burning it . . .**, à moins de le brûler . . .; **to stop s. of crime**, s'arrêter au seuil du crime. IV. v.tr. El: F: court-circuiter; **'shortage**, s. 1. insuffisance f, manque m; **the housing s.**, la crise du logement. 2. pénurie f; **food s.**, disette f; **'short-bread**, s. Cu: = sablé m; **'shortcake**, s. gâteau m de pâte sablée, souvent fourré aux fruits et à la crème fraîche; **'shortcomings**, s.pl. défauts m, imperfections f (de qn, d'un plan, etc.); **'shorten**, v.i. & tr. raccourcir; **'shortening**, s. Cu: N.Am: graisse f de porc; **'shorthand**, s. sténo(graphie) f; **s. typist**, sténo(dactylo) mf; **'short-'handed**, a. à court de main-d'œuvre, de personnel; **'short list**, s. list choisie (d'aspirants à un poste); **'shortlist**, v.tr. mettre (un candidat) à la liste choisie pour un poste; **'short-'lived**, a. (of pers.) qui meurt jeune; (of joy) éphémère, de courte durée; **'shortness**, s. 1. (a) peu m de longueur; (b) brièveté f, courte durée (de la vie); **s. of memory**, manque m de mémoire; (c) brusquerie f (d'humeur). 2. manque, insuffisance f (de vivres); **'short-'sighted**, a. 1. myope. 2. imprévoyant; **'short-'sightedness**, s. 1. myopie f. 2. imprévoyance f; **'short-'tempered**, a. vif; d'un caractère emporté; **'short-term**, a. Fin: (placement, etc.) à court terme.

shot [ʃɔt]. I. a. chatoyant; **s. silk**, soie gorge-de-pigeon. II. s. 1. coll. projectiles mpl. 2. (a) plomb m; (b) Sp: **putting the s.**, lancement m du poids. 3. (a) coup m (de feu); (b) tireur, -euse; **he's a good s.**, il est bon chasseur. 4. coup; F: **I'll have a s. at it**, je vais tenter le coup. 5. F: **big s.**, gros bonnet; **'shotgun**, s. fusil m de chasse.

should [ʃud], see SHALL.

shoulder ['ʃouldər]. I. s. (a) épaule f; **breadth of shoulders**, carrure f; **slung across the s.**, en bandoulière; **s. strap**, bretelle f; épaulette f; (b) Cu: épaule (de mouton); (c) (of road), bas-côté m. II. v.tr. 1. pousser avec l'épaule; **to s. one's way through the crowd**, se frayer un chemin à travers la foule; **to s. s.o. out of the way**, écarter qn d'un coup d'épaule; **to s. the responsibility**, endosser la responsabilité; **'shoulderblade**, s. omoplate f.

shout [ʃaut]. I. s. (a) cri m (de joie, etc.); **shouts of laughter**, éclats m de rire; (b) clameur f; **shouts of applause**, acclamations f. II. v. 1. v.i. crier; pousser des cris; v.pr. **to s. oneself hoarse**, s'enrouer à force de crier. 2. v.tr. crier (qch.); vociférer (des injures); **to s. s.o. down**, huer qn; **'shouting**, s. cris mpl; acclamations fpl; **it's all over bar the s.**, c'est dans le sac, les applaudissements suivront.

shove [ʃʌv]. I. s. F: coup m (d'épaule); poussée f. II. v.tr. F: pousser (qn, qch.); **to s. s.o., sth., aside**, écarter qn, qch., d'une poussée; **to s. sth. into a drawer**, fourrer qch. dans un tiroir.

shovel ['ʃʌv(ə)l]. I. s. pelle f. II. v.tr. (**shovelled**) pelleter; prendre, ramasser, enlever, etc., (le charbon, etc.) à la pelle; **'shovelful**, s. pelletée f.

show [ʃou]. I. s. 1. étalage m; **s. of hands**, vote m à main(s) levée(s); **s. flat, house**, appartement m, maison f, témoin. 2. (a) exposition f (de tableaux, de marchandises); comices m agricoles; **motor s.**, salon m de l'automobile; **fashion s.**, présentation f de collection; **s. breeder, s. breeding**, éleveur m, élevage m, de bêtes à concours; (b) spectacle m (de théâtre); séance f (de cinéma); **s. business**, le monde des spectacles; **to steal the s.**, tirer la couverture à soi; **to make a s. of oneself**, se donner en spectacle; F: **good s.!** compliments! bravo! 3. (a) apparence f; semblant m; **with some s. of reason**, avec quelque apparence de raison; **s. of resistance**, simulacre m de résistance; **to make a great s. of friendship**, faire de grandes démonstrations d'amitié; (b) parade f, ostentation f; **to make a s. of learning**, faire parade d'érudition; **to do sth. for s.**, faire qch. pour la galerie. 4. F: affaire f; **to run the s.**, diriger l'affaire. II. v. (**showed; shown**) 1. v.tr. montrer; (a) faire voir, exhiber (qch.); **to s. s.o. sth.**, montrer, faire voir, qch. à qn; **we're going to s. some films this evening**, on va passer des films ce soir; **to have sth. to s. for one's money**, en avoir pour son argent; **he won't s. his face here again**, il ne se montrera plus ici; (of thg) **to s. itself**, devenir visible; se révéler; (b) représenter, figurer; **machine shown in section,**

machine figurée en coupe; (c) indiquer; (of watch) to s. the time, indiquer, marquer, l'heure; to s. a profit, faire ressortir un bénéfice; (d) to s. s.o. the way, indiquer le chemin à qn; to s. s.o. to his room, conduire qn à sa chambre; to s. s.o. into a room, faire entrer qn dans une pièce; to s. s.o. round, faire visiter (la maison, etc.) à qn; (e) to s. an interest in s.o., témoigner de l'intérêt à qn; he shows his age, il marque son âge; abs. time will s., qui vivra verra; F: I'll s. you, je vous apprendrai! 2. v.i. se montrer, (ap)paraître; se laisser voir; your slip's showing, votre combinaison f dépasse; to s. willing, faire preuve de bonne volonté; to s. to advantage, faire bonne figure; 'showcase, s. vitrine f; 'showdown, s. déballage m; if it comes to a s., s'il faut en venir au fait; 'showiness, s. prétention f, clinquant m, faste m; ostentation f; 'show-jumper, s. jumper m; 'show-jumping, s. jumping m; 'showman, pl. -men, s. (a) forain m; he's a great s., c'est un as pour la mise en scène; (b) montreur m de curiosités (à la foire); 'showmanship, s. art m de la mise en scène; 'show 'off. 1. v.tr. faire valoir (un bijou); mettre (un tableau) en valeur. 2. v.i. Pej: parader, poser; se pavaner; 'show-off, s. poseur, -euse; 'showpiece, s. article m d'exposition; monument m de grand intérêt; 'showroom, s. Com: salle f, magasin m, d'exposition; 'show 'up. 1. v.tr. démasquer (un imposteur); révéler (un défaut). 2. v.i. (a) se détacher, ressortir (sur un fond); (b) F: se présenter; faire acte de présence; 'showy, a. prétentieux; voyant; s. hat, chapeau m à effet.

shower ['ʃauər]. I. s. (a) averse f; heavy s., ondée f; (b) s. of stones, volée f de pierres; (c) to take a s., prendre une douche. II. v.tr. (a) verser, faire pleuvoir (de l'eau); (b) to s. blows (on s.o.), frapper dru (sur qn); to s. invitations on s.o., accabler qn d'invitations; 'showery, a. (temps) pluvieux.

shrapnel ['ʃræpnəl], s. éclats mpl d'obus.

shred [ʃred]. I. s. brin m; lambeau m, fragment m (de tissu); to tear sth. to shreds, mettre qch. en lambeaux; there isn't a s. of evidence, il n'y a pas la moindre évidence. II. v.tr. (shredded) couper (qch.) par languettes; effilocher, déchiqueter (qch.).

shrew¹ (-mouse, pl. -mice) ['ʃru:(maus, -mais)], s. Z: musaraigne f.

shrew², s. mégère f; 'shrewish, a.f. (femme) acariâtre; -ly, adv. en mégère.

shrewd [ʃru:d], a. 1. sagace, perspicace; qui a du flair; s. business man, homme d'affaires très entendu; s. reasoning, raisonnement judicieux. 2. (intensive) I have a s. idea that . . ., je suis porté à croire que . . .; -ly, adv. avec perspicacité; avec finesse; 'shrewdness, s.

sagacité f; perspicacité f, finesse f.

shriek [ʃri:k]. I. s. cri déchirant; cri perçant; shrieks of laughter, grands éclats de rire. II. v. 1. v.i. pousser des cris aigus; to s. with laughter, rire aux éclats; s'esclaffer de rire. 2. v.tr. to s. (out) a warning, avertir qn d'un cri.

shrill [ʃril], a. aigu, strident; -s. stridence f; 'shrilly, adv. d'un ton aigu, criard.

shrimp [ʃrimp]. I. s. crevette (grise). II. v.i. pêcher la crevette; 'shrimping, s. pêche f à la crevette.

shrine [ʃrain], s. 1. tombeau m (de saint). 2. chapelle f, autel m (consacré(e) à un saint).

shrink [ʃriŋk], v. (shrank [ʃræŋk]; shrunk [ʃrʌŋk]) 1. v.i. (a) se contracter; (se) rétrécir; my shirt has shrunk in the wash, ma chemise s'est rétrécie au lavage; (b) faire un mouvement de recul; to s. (back) from (danger, etc.), reculer devant (un danger, etc.); to s. from doing sth., répugner à faire qch.; (c) to s. into oneself, rentrer dans sa coquille. 2. v.tr. (r)étrécir, faire rétrécir (un tissu); 'shrinkage, s. contraction f (du métal); rétrécissement m (d'un tissu); 'shrinking, a. 1. qui se contracte. 2. (of pers.) timide, craintif; -ly, adv. timidement.

shrivel ['ʃriv(ə)l], v. (shrivelled) 1. v.tr. to s. (up), rider, ratatiner (la peau); (of sun, frost) brûler (les plantes). 2. v.i. to s. (up), se rider, se ratatiner.

shroud [ʃraud], s. linceul m, suaire m; 'shrouded, a. enveloppé, voilé (in mist, de brume).

shrove [ʃrouv], a. used in expr. S. Tuesday, (le) mardi gras.

shrub [ʃrʌb], s. arbrisseau m, arbuste m; 'shrubbery, s. plantation f, massif m, d'arbustes.

shrug [ʃrʌg]. I. v.tr. (shrugged) to s. (one's shoulders), hausser les épaules. II. s. haussement m d'épaules; a resigned s., un geste de résignation.

shrunken ['ʃrʌŋk(ə)n], a. contracté, rétréci; (of features) ratatiné.

shudder ['ʃʌdər]. I. s. frisson m, frémissement m (d'horreur). II. v.i. to s. with horror, frissonner, frémir, d'horreur.

shuffle ['ʃʌfl]. 1. v.tr. & i. to s. (one's feet), traîner les pieds. 2. v.tr. (a) (entre)mêler (des papiers); (b) (at cards) battre, mêler (les cartes). 3. v.i. équivoquer, tergiverser.

shun [ʃʌn], v.tr. (shunned) fuir, éviter (qn, qch.); to s. everybody, s'éloigner du monde.

shunt [ʃʌnt], v.tr. Rail: manœuvrer, garer (un train); 'shunting, s. 1. Rail: garage m, manœuvre f; aiguillage m; s. yard, gare f de manœuvre et de triage.

shush [ʃʌʃ, ʃuʃ], int. chut!

shut [ʃʌt], v. (shutting; shut) 1. v.tr. fermer (une

porte, une boîte); **to s. one's mouth,** (i) fermer la bouche; (ii) *F:* se taire. **2.** *v.i.* (se) fermer; **'shut 'down,** *v.tr.* (*a*) rabattre (un couvercle); (*b*) *Ind:* fermer (une usine); **'shutdown,** *s.* fermeture *f* (d'une usine); **'shut 'in,** *v.tr.* (*a*) enfermer; (*b*) (*of hills, etc.*) entourer, encercler (un endroit); **'shut 'off,** *v.tr.* **1.** couper (le courant, le moteur); fermer (l'eau). **2.** séparer, isoler (**from,** de); **'shut 'out,** *v.tr.* (*a*) exclure (qn); **the trees s. out the view,** les arbres bouchent la vue; (*b*) **to s. s.o. out (of doors),** fermer la porte à qn; **'shutter,** *s.* **1.** volet *m;* **outside s.,** contrevent *m; Venetian shutters,* persiennes *f.* **2.** *Phot:* obturateur *m;* **'shuttering,** *s. Const:* coffrage *m* (pour le béton armé); **'shutting,** *s.* fermeture *f;* **'shut 'up. 1.** *v.tr.* (*a*) enfermer; **to s. the dog up,** enfermer le chien; (*b*) fermer (une maison); **to s. up shop,** fermer boutique; (*c*) *F:* réduire (qn) au silence. **2.** *v.i. F:* se taire; **s. up!** *P:* ta gueule! la ferme!

shuttle ['ʃʌtl], *s.* navette *f;* **to run a s. service,** faire la navette; **'shuttlecock,** *s. Games:* volant *m.*

shy[1] [ʃai], *v.i.* (shying; shied) (*of horse*) faire un écart; broncher; **to s. at sth.,** prendre ombrage de qch.

shy[2], *a.* (*of pers.*) sauvage, farouche, timide; **to make s.o. s.,** intimider qn; **to fight s. of sth.,** se défier, se méfier, de qch.; **don't pretend to be s.,** ne faites pas le, la, timide; **the fish are s.,** les poissons ne mordent pas; **-ly,** *adv.* timidement; **'shyness,** *s.* timidité *f,* réserve *f;* sauvagerie *f.*

shy[3]. **I.** *v.tr.* (shying; shied) *F:* **to s. a stone, a ball,** lancer une pierre, une balle (**at,** à). **II.** *s. F:* jet *m,* lancement *m* (d'une pierre, d'une balle); (*at fair*) **three shies for six pence,** trois coups pour six pence.

Siamese [saiə'mi:z], *a. & s.* siamois, -oise; **S. twins,** frères siamois, sœurs siamoises; **S. cat,** (chat) siamois (*m*).

Siberia [sai'biəriə]. *Pr.n.* la Sibérie; **Si'berian,** *a. & s.* sibérien, -ienne.

Sicily ['sisili]. *Pr.n.* la Sicile; **Si'cilian,** *a. & s.* sicilien, -ienne.

sick [sik], *a.* **1.** malade; **she's still s.,** elle est toujours malade; *s.pl.* **the s.,** les malades. **2. to be s.,** vomir, rendre; **a s. feeling,** un malaise; **to feel s.,** avoir mal au cœur; **s. headache,** migraine *f.* **3. to be s. at heart,** être abattu; **he did look s.!** il en faisait une tête! *F:* **to be s. of sth.,** être dégoûté de qch.; *F:* **I'm s. of it!** j'en ai plein le dos! *F:* **I'm s. and tired of telling you,** je me tue à vous le dire; **'sicken. 1.** *v.i.* (*a*) tomber malade (**of, with,** de); **to be sickening for an illness,** couver une maladie; (*b*) **to s. of sth.,** se lasser de qch. **2.** *v.tr.* (*a*) **his methods s. me,** ses procédés me soulèvent le cœur; **he**

sickens me, il m'écœure; **'sickening,** *a.* écœurant; navrant; **-ly,** *adv.* d'une façon écœurante, à vous écœurer; **'sick leave,** *s.* congé *m* de maladie; **'sickliness,** *s.* état maladif (de qn); **'sickly,** *a.* maladif, souffreteux; **a s. smile,** un sourire pâle; **'sickness,** *s.* **1.** maladie *f;* **air, car, s.,** mal *m* de l'air, de voiture. **2.** mal de cœur, nausées *fpl.*

sickle ['sikl], *s. Agr:* faucille *f.*

side [said]. **I.** *s.* côté *m.* **1.** (*a*) flanc *m;* **by s.o.'s s.,** à côté de qn; **s. by s.,** côte à côte; **to split one's sides (with laughter),** se tenir les côtes de rire; (*b*) **s. of bacon,** flèche *f* de lard. **2.** côté (d'un triangle); versant *m,* flanc (d'une montagne); paroi *f* (d'un fossé). **3.** (*surface*) (*a*) **the right s.,** le bon côté; l'endroit *m* (d'un tissu); **wrong s. out,** à l'envers; (*b*) **the bright s. of things,** le bon côté des choses; **the other s. of the picture,** le revers de la médaille; **to get on the soft s. of s.o.,** prendre qn par son côté faible; **to hear both sides,** entendre le pour et le contre; **the weather's on the cool s.,** il fait plutôt froid. **4. on this s.,** de ce côté-ci; **on all sides,** de tous côtés; **to be on the right s. of forty,** avoir moins de quarante ans; **to move to one s.,** se ranger; **to put sth. on one s.,** mettre qch. de côté; **to make sth. on the s.,** faire de la gratte. **5.** (*a*) parti *m;* **he's on our s.,** il est de notre parti; **you have the law on your s.,** vous avez la loi pour vous; (*b*) section *f,* division *f;* (*c*) *Games:* équipe *f;* (*d*) (*family connections*) **on his mother's s.,** du côté maternel. **6.** *attrib.* latéral, de côté; **s. entrance,** entrée *f* de côté; **s. door,** porte latérale; **s. line,** (i) *Rail:* voie *f* secondaire; (ii) **as a s. line,** comme occupation secondaire; **s. issue,** question *f* d'intérêt secondaire; *Med:* **s. effect,** résultat *m* secondaire. **II.** *v.i.* **to s. with s.o.,** se ranger du parti de qn; se mettre du parti de qn; **'sideboard,** *s.* buffet *m;* **'sideboards,** *s.pl. N.Am:* **'sideburns,** *s.pl.* favoris *m;* **'side-face. 1.** *s.* profil *m.* **2.** *adv.* **to take s.o. s.-f.,** photographier qn de profil; **'sidelight,** *s.* **1.** *Phot: etc:* lumière *f* oblique; **to throw a s. on a subject,** donner un aperçu secondaire, indirect, sur un sujet. **2.** *Aut: etc:* feu *m* de position; **'sidestep,** *v.* (sidestepped) (*a*) *v.tr.* éviter (une question); (*b*) *v.i.* faire un pas de côté; **'sidetrack,** *v.tr.* détourner l'attention de (qn); **'sidewalk,** *s., N.Am:* trottoir *m;* **'sideways,** *adv.* de côté, latéralement; **'siding,** *s. Rail:* voie *f* de garage.

sidle ['saidl], *v.i.* **to s. along,** s'avancer de côté, en crabe; **to s. up to s.o.,** se couler auprès de qn.

siege [si:dʒ], *s. Mil:* siège *m;* **to lay s. to a town,** assiéger une ville.

sienna [si'enə], *s. Art:* terre *f* de Sienne; **raw, burnt, s.,** terre de Sienne naturelle, brûlée.

siesta [si'estə], *s.* sieste *f.*

sieve [siv]. **I.** *s.* crible *m;* tamis *m.* **II.** *v.tr.* passer au tamis; tamiser.

sift [sift], *v.tr.* (*a*) passer au tamis; tamiser; (*b*) examiner minutieusement (les témoignages dans une affaire); **'sifter,** *s.* **1.** appareil à cribler; cribleuse *f.* **2.** H: saupoudroir *m* (à sucre, à farine).

sigh [sai]. **I.** *s.* soupir *m.* **II.** *v.i.* soupirer; pousser un soupir; **to s. for sth.,** soupirer après qch.

sight [sait]. **I.** *s.* **1.** vue *f*; (*a*) **short s.,** myopie *f*; **to lose one's s.,** perdre la vue; devenir aveugle; (*b*) **to catch s. of s.o.,** apercevoir qn; **to lose s. of s.o.,** perdre qn de vue; **I can't bear the s.** of him, je ne peux pas le sentir; **to shoot s.o. at, on, s.,** faire feu sur qn à première vue; **at first s.,** au premier abord; **love at first s.,** le coup de foudre; **to know s.o. by s.,** connaître qn de vue. **2. to come into s.,** (ap)paraître; **to be within s.,** être à portée de la vue; être en vue; **out of s.,** caché aux regards. **3.** (*a*) spectacle *m*; **sad s.,** spectacle navrant; **it's a s. well worth seeing,** cela vaut la peine d'être vu; (*b*) F: **his face was a s.!,** si vous aviez vu son visage! **what a s. you are!** comme vous voilà fait! (*c*) *pl.* **the sights,** les monuments *m*, les curiosités *f* (de la ville). **II.** *v.tr.* **1. to s. land,** relever la terre. **2. to s. a gun,** pointer un fusil; **'sightless,** *a.* aveugle; **'sightseeing,** *s.* **to go s.,** visiter les monuments de la ville; **'sightseer,** *s.* touriste *mf.*

sign [sain]. **I.** *s.* **1.** signe *m*; **to make an affirmative s.,** faire signe que oui. **2.** (*a*) indice *m*, indication *f*; **sure s.,** indice certain; **s. of rain,** signe de pluie; **there's no s. of his coming,** rien n'annonce sa venue; (*b*) trace *f*; **no s. of . . .,** nulle, aucune, trace de . . .; **to show no s.** of life, ne donner aucun signe de vie; **there was no s. of him,** il restait invisible. **3.** (*a*) enseigne *f* (d'auberge, de magasin, etc.); **neon s.,** réclame *f* au néon; (*b*) *Aut: etc:* panneau indicateur; **international road signs,** signalisation routière internationale; **s. of the Zodiac,** signe du zodiaque. **4. s. of the cross,** signe de la croix. **II.** *v.tr.* signer (une lettre, etc.); signer (son nom); **'sign 'off,** *v.i.* (*of worker*) pointer au départ; **'sign 'on. 1.** *v.tr.* embaucher (un ouvrier); engager (un employé). **2.** *v.i.* (*of worker*) pointer à l'arrivée; **'signpost,** *s.* poteau indicateur. **II.** *v.tr.* signaliser (une route); **badly signposted road,** route mal signalisée.

signal[1] ['signəl]. **I.** *s.* signal *m*; **to give the s. (for departure),** donner le signal (du départ); *Rad: T.V:* **station s.,** indicatif *m* (de l'émetteur); *Aut:* **traffic signals,** feux *m* de circulation. **II.** *v.* **(signalled) 1.** *v.i.* signaler; *Aut:* **to s. before stopping,** avertir avant de stopper. **2.** *v.tr.* signaler (un train); *Aut:* **to s. a turn,** signaler un changement de direction; **to s. s.o. to stop,** faire signe à qn de s'arrêter; **'signal box,** *s. Rail:* poste *m* d'aiguillage; **'signalman,** *pl.* **-men,** *s. Rail:* aiguilleur *m.*

signal[2], *a.* insigne; (succès) éclatant, remarquable; **-ally,** *adv.* remarquablement.

signature ['signətʃər], *s.* signature *f*; **s. tune,** indicatif (musical).

signet ['signit], *s.* sceau *m*, cachet *m*; **s. ring,** (bague *f*) chevalière (*f*).

signify ['signifai]. **1.** *v.tr.* signifier; vouloir dire. **2.** *v.i.* importer; **it doesn't s.,** cela ne fait rien; cela n'importe guère; **sig'nificance** [-'nifikəns], *s.* **1.** signification *f.* **2.** importance *f* conséquence *f*; **sig'nificant,** *a.* **1.** (mot) significatif. **2.** (événement) important, de grande portée; **-ly,** *adv.* (regarder qn) d'une manière significative; **signifi'cation,** *s.* signification *f*, sens *m* (d'un mot, etc.).

silence ['sailəns]. **I.** *s.* silence *m*; (*a*) **dead s.,** silence absolu; **a breathless s.,** un silence ému, anxieux; (*b*) **to pass over sth. in s.,** passer qch. sous silence. **II.** *v.tr.* **1.** réduire (qn) au silence; faire taire (qn); étouffer (les plaintes); **to s. criticism,** fermer la bouche à la critique. **2.** étouffer, amortir (un bruit); *Aut:* **to s. the exhaust,** assourdir l'échappement *m*; **'silencer,** *s. Aut:* pot *m* d'échappement; silencieux *m*; (*on gun*) silencieux; **'silent,** *a.* silencieux; **to keep s.,** se taire (**about,** sur); **a s. man,** un homme silencieux, taciturne; **-ly,** *adv.* silencieusement; en silence.

silhouette [silu(:)'et]. **I.** *s.* silhouette *f.* **II.** *v.tr.* silhouetter.

silicone ['silikoun], *s. Ch:* silicone *f.*

silicosis [sili'kousis], *s. Med:* silicose *f*, chalicose *f.*

silk [silk], *s.* soie *f*; **raw s.,** soie grège; **sewing s.,** soie à coudre; *pl. Com:* **silks,** soierie *f*; **'silken,** *a.* soyeux; **'silkiness,** *s.* **1.** nature soyeuse (d'un tissu). **2.** moelleux *m* (d'une voix); **'silkscreen,** *s.* **s. printing,** sérigraphie *f*; **'silkworm,** *s.* ver *m* à soie; **'silky,** *a.* (*a*) soyeux; (*b*) **s. voice,** voix moelleuse.

sill [sil], *s.* **(window-)s.,** tablette *f*, appui *m*, de fenêtre; seuil *m* (de porte).

silly ['sili], *a.* **1.** sot, niais; **s. answer,** réponse *f* stupide, ridicule; **you s. boy!** petit nigaud! **s. ass!** imbécile! **to do a s. thing,** faire une bêtise; **to knock s.o. s.,** étourdir, assommer, qn; **'silliness,** *s.* sottise *f*, niaiserie *f*, bêtise *f.*

silo, *pl.* **-os** ['sailou, -ouz], *s. L Agr:* silo *m.* **2.** *Mil:* (*for guided missile*) **launching s.,** puits *m* de lancement.

silt [silt]. **I.** *s.* dépôt (vaseux); vase *f*; limon *m.* **II.** *v.tr. & i.* (*of harbour, river*) **to s. up,** (s')envaser; (s')ensabler.

silver ['silvər], *s.* **1.** argent *m.* **2.** *attrib.* (*a*) d'argent, en argent; **s. spoon,** cuiller *f* d'argent; **s.-mounted,** monté en argent; **s.-plated,** argenté; *coll.* **s. (plate),** argenterie *f*; vaisselle *f* d'argent; **s. paper,** papier *m* d'étain. **3.** argent monnayé; **s. coin,** pièce *f* d'argent;

'**silversmith**, *s.* orfèvre *m*; '**silvery**, *a.*
(nuage) argenté; (écailles, etc.) d'argent; (son)
argentin.

similar ['similər], *a.* semblable, pareil (**to**, à);
-ly, *adv.* pareillement, semblablement;
simi'larity, *s.* ressemblance *f*, similarité *f*.

simile ['simili], *s.* comparaison *f*, image *f*.

simmer ['simər]. **1.** *v.i.* (*a*) (*of liquid*) frémir; (*of
soup, stews*) mijoter, bouillotter; mitonner; (*b*)
(*of revolt, etc.*) fermenter; (*of pers.*) **to s. down**,
s'apaiser peu à peu. **2.** *v.tr.* (faire) mijoter (un
ragoût).

simper ['simpər]. **I.** *s.* sourire affecté, minauderie.
II. *v.i.* minauder; '**simpering**, *s.* minauderie(s)
f(*pl*); grimaces *fpl.*

simple ['simpl], *a.* (*a*) simple; naturel (de
caractère); sans affectation; (*b*) naïf; crédule;
niais; (*c*) **s. problem**, problème simple, peu
difficile; **as s. as shelling peas**, simple comme
bonjour; (*d*) *Com:* **s. interest**, intérêts *m*
simples; (*e*) **it's robbery, pure and s.!** c'est du
vol pur et simple! **sim'plicity**, *s.* simplicité *f*,
candeur *f* (d'esprit); absence *f* de recherche,
simplicité (dans la mise); '**simplify**, *v.tr.*
simplifier; **to become simplified**, se simplifier;
'**simply**, *adv.* **1.** (parler) simplement. **2.** (*a*) absolument; **you s. must**, il le faut absolument;
the weather's s. ghastly! il fait un temps de
chien; (*b*) uniquement; tout simplement; **he did
it s. to test you**, il l'a fait uniquement pour vous
éprouver; **I s. said that . . .**, je me suis borné à
dire que . . .

simulate ['simjuleit], *v.tr.* simuler, feindre (une
maladie); **simu'lation**, *s.* simulation *f*, feinte *f*.

simultaneous [sim(ə)l'teiniəs, saim-], *a.*
simultané; **-ly**, *adv.* (*a*) simultanément; (*b*) en
même temps (**with**, que).

sin [sin]. **I.** *s.* péché *m*; **to fall into s.**, tomber dans
le péché; **to live in s.**, vivre dans le collage. **II.**
v.i. (**sinned**) pécher; '**sinful**, *a.* **s. person**,
pécheur, *f.* pécheresse; **s. pleasure**, plaisir *m*
coupable; **s. waste**, gaspillage scandaleux;
-fully, *adv.* d'une façon coupable; '**sin-
fulness**, *s.* **1.** caractère *m* coupable (d'une action); culpabilité *f.* **2.** le péché; '**sinner**, *s.*
pécheur, *f.* pécheresse.

since [sins]. **1.** *adv.* depuis; (*a*) **ever s.**, depuis
(lors); (*b*) **many years s.**, il y a bien des années.
2. *prep.* depuis; **he's been up s. dawn**, il était
levé dès l'aurore; **s. when have you been here?**
depuis quand êtes-vous ici? **s. then**, depuis
lors. **3.** *conj.* (*a*) depuis que; que; **s. I've been
here**, depuis que je suis ici; **it's a week s. he
came**, il y a huit jours qu'il est arrivé; (*b*)
puisque; **s. he's not of age**, puisqu'il est
mineur.

sincere [sin'siər], *a.* (*a*) sincère; franc; (*b*) (sentiment) sincère; **-ly**, *adv.* sincèrement; **yours
s.**, cordialement à vous; **sin'cerity** [-'seriti], *s.*

sincérité *f*; bonne foi; **speaking in all s.**, en
toute bonne foi.

sinecure ['sainikjuər], *s.* sinécure *f*.

sinew ['sinju:], *s.* **1.** tendon *m.* **2.** *pl.* **sinews**, nerf
m, force *f*; '**sinewy**, *a.* (*of meat*) tendineux; **s.
arm**, bras musclé, nerveux.

sing [siŋ], *v.* (**sang** [sæŋ]; **sung** [sʌŋ]) **1.** *v.tr. & i.*
chanter. **2.** *v.i.* (*of the ears*) tinter, bourdonner;
(*of kettle*) chanter; '**singer**, *s.* chanteur, *f.*
-euse; (*operatic*) cantatrice *f*; *Ecc:* chantre *m*;
'**singing**. **I.** *a.* (oiseau) chanteur; chantant, qui
chante. **II.** *s.* **1.** chant *m.* **2.** bourdonnement *m*,
tintement *m* (d'oreilles); '**singsong**. **1.** *a.* (*of
voice, song*) monotone; **in a s. voice**, en
psalmodiant. **2.** *s.* concert improvisé.

Singapore [siŋgə'pɔːr]. *Pr.n.* Singapour *m.*

singe [sindʒ], *v.tr.* **1.** brûler (qch.) légèrement;
roussir. **2.** passer à la flamme.

single ['siŋgl]. **I.** *a.* **1.** (*a*) seul, unique; **not a s.
one**, pas un seul; pas un; **I haven't seen a s.
soul**, je n'ai pas vu âme qui vive; (*b*) individuel,
particulier. **2.** (*a*) **s. bed**, lit pour une personne;
s. bedroom, chambre à un lit; (*b*) célibataire;
non marié(e); **to lead a s. life**, vivre dans le
célibat; (*c*) *Rail:* **s. ticket**, (billet *m* d')aller *m.* **II.**
s. (*a*) *Ten: Golf:* (partie *f*) simple (*m*); *Ten:*
men's singles, simple messieurs; (*b*) *Rail:* (billet
d')aller *m.* **III.** *v.tr.* **to s.** (s.o., sth.) **out**, (i)
choisir (qn, qch.); (ii) remarquer, distinguer
(qn, qch.) (**for**, pour; **as**, comme); '**single-
'barrelled**, *a.* (fusil) à un coup; '**single-
'handed**, *a.* seul, sans aide; '**singleness**, *s.* **1.**
with s. of purpose, avec un seul but en vue. **2.**
célibat *m*; '**single-'track**, *a.* *Rail:* (ligne) à voie
unique; '**singly**, *adv.* **1.** séparément; un à un. **2.**
seul; sans aide.

singlet ['siŋglit], *s.* **1.** gilet *m* de corps (pour
homme). **2.** *Sp:* maillot fin.

singular ['siŋgjulər]. **1.** *a. & s. Gram:* singulier
(*m*). **2.** *a.* singulier, bizarre; **-ly**, *adv.*
singulièrement; (*a*) remarquablement; (*b*)
bizarrement; **singu'larity**, *s.* singularité *f*.

sinister ['sinistər], *a.* sinistre; **a s.-looking man**,
un homme de mauvaise mine.

sink[1] [siŋk], *s.* évier *m* (de cuisine); **to pour sth.
down the s.**, jeter qch. à l'égout.

sink[2], *v.* (**sank** [sæŋk]; **sunk** [sʌŋk]) **1.** *v.i.* (*a*)
tomber au fond; aller au fond; (*of ship*) couler
bas; sombrer; (*b*) s'enfoncer, pénétrer (**into**,
dans); (*of words*) **to s. into the memory**, se
graver dans la mémoire; **his words begin to s.
in**, ses paroles commencent à faire impression;
(*c*) tomber (dans le vice, dans l'oubli); **to s.
deep(er) into crime**, s'enfoncer dans le crime;
to s. into insignificance, devenir insignifiant;
(*d*) **to s. (down)**, s'affaisser; **the fire is sinking**,
le feu baisse; (*of pers.*) **to s. (down) into a chair**,
se laisser tomber, s'affaisser, dans un fauteuil;
his heart sank, le cœur lui manqua; (*e*) descen-

dre; aller en descendant; s'abaisser; **the sun is sinking,** le soleil baisse; (*f*) baisser (en valeur); diminuer; s'affaiblir; **he has sunk in my esteem,** il a baissé dans mon estime. **2.** *v.tr.* (*a*) couler, faire sombrer (un navire); (*b*) enfoncer (un pieu); (*c*) creuser (un puits); (*d*) supprimer (une objection, des différends).

sinuous ['sinjuəs], *a.* **1.** sinueux. **2.** (*of pers.*) souple, agile; **sinu'osity,** *s.* sinuosité *f*.

sinus ['sainəs], *s. Anat:* sinus *m*; **she has bad s. trouble,** elle a une mauvaise sinusite; **sinu'sitis,** *s. Med:* sinusite *f*.

sip [sip]. **I.** *s.* petit coup; petite gorgée. **II.** *v.tr.* (**sipped**) boire (qch.) à petits coups.

siphon ['saif(ə)n]. **I.** *s.* siphon *m*. **II.** *v.tr.* **to s.** (**off**), siphonner (un liquide).

sir [sə:r, sər], *s.* **1.** monsieur *m*; **yes, s.,** oui, monsieur; (*in letter*) (**Dear**) **Sir,** Monsieur. **2.** (*title*) Sir (*always used with Christian name*).

sire ['saiər], *s.* **1.** (*in addressing a King*) Sire. **2.** *Breed:* père *m*; (*of horses*) étalon *m*; (*of cattle*) taureau *m*; sire *m*.

siren ['saiərən], *s.* sirène *f*.

sirloin ['sə:lɔin], *s. Cu:* aloyau *m*.

sister ['sistər], *s.* **1:** sœur *f*. **2.** (*a*) *Ecc:* religieuse *f*; sœur; (*b*) *Med:* (**ward-**)**s.,** surveillante *f*; **'sister-in-law,** *s.* belle-sœur *f*, *pl.* belles-sœurs; **'sisterly,** *a.* de sœur; comme une sœur.

sit [sit], *v.* (**sitting; sat**) **1.** *v.i.* (*a*) (*of pers.*) s'asseoir; être assis; rester assis; **to s. still,** rester tranquille; **to s. tight,** ne pas céder; **to s. for an exam(ination),** se présenter pour un examen, passer un examen; **to s. for one's portrait,** poser pour son portrait; **sitting tenant,** locataire en possession des lieux; (*b*) **to s. in Parliament,** siéger au parlement; (*of assembly, etc.*) siéger; être en séance; **to s. on a project,** laisser dormir un projet; (*c*) (*of hen*) **to s.** (**on eggs**), couver (des œufs); (*of food*) **to s. heavy on the stomach,** peser sur l'estomac. **2.** *v.tr.* (*a*) **to s. a horse,** se tenir à cheval; **to s. a child on a chair,** asseoir un enfant sur une chaise; (*b*) **to s.** (**oneself**) **down,** s'asseoir; **'sit 'down,** *v.i.* s'asseoir; **please s. down,** veuillez vous asseoir; **to s. down to table,** s'attabler, se mettre à table; **'sit-down,** *a.* **s.-d. strike,** grève *f* sur le tas; **'sitter,** *s.* **1.** (*for painter*) (*a*) modèle *m*; (*b*) client, -ente. **2.** **baby-s.,** garde-bébé *mf*; **'sitting,** *s.* séance *f*, réunion *f* (d'une commission, etc.); **to paint a portrait in three sittings,** faire, compléter, un portrait en trois séances; **to serve 200 people at one s.,** servir 200 personnes à la fois; **to write two chapters at one s.,** écrire deux chapitres d'un seul jet, d'arrache-pied; *Agr:* **a s. of eggs,** une couvée d'œufs; **'sitting-room,** *s.* salle *f* de séjour, *F:* séjour *m*; living-room *m*, *F:* living *m*; **'sit 'up,** *v.i.* **1.** (*a*) se redresser (sur sa chaise); **to make s.o. s. up,** étonner qn. **2.** **to s. up late,** veiller tard; **to**

s. up for s.o., veiller à attendre qn; **to s. up with s.o.,** veiller qn, un malade.

site [sait], *s.* **1.** emplacement *m* (d'un édifice, d'une ville); **caravan, camping, s.,** camping *m*; **prehistoric s.,** gisement *m* préhistorique. **2.** chantier *m*; **building s.,** (i) terrain *m* à bâtir; (ii) chantier de construction.

situate ['sitjueit], *v.tr.* situer (une maison, etc.); **'situated,** *a.* **1.** **well s. house,** maison bien située. **2.** (*of pers.*) **this is how I am s.,** voici la situation dans laquelle je me trouve; **situ'ation,** *s.* **1.** situation *f*. **2.** emploi *m*, place *f*; **situations vacant,** offres *f* d'emplois.

six [siks], *num. a. & s.* six (*m*); **everything's at sixes and sevens,** tout est en désordre; **six'teen,** *num. a. & s.* seize (*m*); **she's s.,** elle a seize ans; **six'teenth,** *num. a. & s.* seizième (*m*); **Louis the S.,** Louis Seize; (**on**) **the s.** (**of August**), le seize (août); **sixth,** *num. a. & s.* sixième (*m*); (**on**) **the s. of June,** le six juin; *Sch:* **s. form** = classe *f* de première; **s. former** = élève de première; **'sixtieth,** *num. a. & s.* soixantième (*m*); **'sixty,** *num. a. & s.* soixante (*m*); **he is in his sixties,** il a passé la soixantaine.

size¹ [saiz]. **I.** *s.* **1.** grandeur *f*, dimension *f*, grosseur *f*; **to take the s. of sth.,** mesurer qch.; **all of a s.,** tous de même taille; **full s.,** grandeur naturelle. **2.** (*a*) taille *f*; (*b*) taille (de vêtements); encolure *f* (de chemise); pointure *f* (de chaussures). **II.** *v.tr.* classer (qn) par taille, par dimension; **to s. s.o. up,** classer, juger, qn; **'sizeable,** *a.* assez grand; d'une belle taille.

size², *s.* apprêt *m*; colle *f*.

sizzle ['sizl], *v.i.* grésiller.

skate¹ [skeit], *s. Ich:* raie *f*.

skate². **I.** *s.* patin *m*. **II.** *v.i.* patiner; **to s. over sth.,** effleurer un sujet (difficile); **to s. on thin ice,** toucher à un sujet délicat; **'skateboard,** *s.* planche *f* à roulettes; **'skater,** *s.* patineur, -euse; **'skating,** *s.* patinage *m*; **s. rink,** patinoire *f*.

skein [skein], *s.* écheveau *m* (de laine, etc.).

skeleton ['skelit(ə)n], *s.* **1.** squelette *m*, ossature *f* (de l'homme, d'un animal). **2.** charpente *f*, carcasse *f* (d'un navire, etc.); **s. key,** crochet *m* (de serrurier); clef *f* passe-partout, *F:* rossignol *m*. **3.** **s. staff,** personnel réduit; **s. staff of three,** permanence *f* de trois employés.

sketch [sketʃ]. **I.** *s.* croquis *m*, esquisse *f*; **s. book,** cahier *m*, album *m*, de croquis; **freehand s.,** dessin *m* à main levée. **II.** *v.tr.* esquisser; faire le croquis de; **'sketching,** *s.* (i) prise *f* de croquis; (ii) dessin *m* à main levée; **'sketch-map,** *s.* croquis *m* topographique, *F:* topo *m*; **'sketchy,** *a.* (ouvrage) qui manque de précision; **s. knowledge,** connaissances superficielles; **-ily,** *adv.* d'une manière incomplète, imprécise, vague.

skewer ['skju(:)ər]. **I.** *s. Cu:* brochette *f*. **II.** *v.tr.*

brocheter (une volaille).

ski [ski:]. **I.** *s.* ski *m*; **s. binding,** fixation *f*; **s. jump,** saut *m* de ski; **s. lift,** remonte-pente *m*, téléski *m*. **II.** *v.i.* faire du ski; skier; **'skier,** *s.* skieur, -euse; **'skiing,** *s.* le ski.

skid [skid], *v.i.* **(skidded)** *Aut:* déraper; glisser; *Av:* glisser sur l'aile; **'skidding,** *s.* dérapage *m*; **'skidpan,** *s. Aut:* piste savonnée.

skiff [skif], *s.* **1.** *Nau:* yole *f*. **2.** *Row:* skiff *m*.

skill [skil], *s.* habileté *f*, adresse *f*, dextérité *f*; **'skilful,** *a.* adroit, habile; **-fully,** *adv.* habilement, adroitement; avec adresse; **'skilfulness,** *s.* habileté *f*, adresse *f*, dextérité *f*; **skilled,** *a.* habile; **s. labour,** main-d'œuvre spécialisée; **to be s. in business,** se connaitre en affaires.

skillet ['skilit], *s. N.Am:* poêle *f*.

skim [skim], *v.tr. & i.* **(skimmed)** **1.** écumer (le bouillon); écrémer (le lait). **2.** effleurer, raser (une surface); **to s. through a book,** parcourir rapidement un livre.

skimp [skimp], *v.tr.* **1. to s. the food,** lésiner sur la nourriture; **to s. material,** être parcimonieux d'étoffe. **2. to s. one's work,** bâcler son ouvrage; **'skimpy,** *a.* **s. meal,** maigre repas; **s. garment,** vêtement étriqué.

skin [skin]. **I.** *s.* **1.** peau *f*; **to have a thin s.,** être susceptible; **next (to) one's s.,** à même, sur, la peau. **2.** dépouille *f*, peau (d'un animal). **3. orange s.,** peau d'orange; **banana s.,** pelure *f* de banane; *Cu:* **potatoes baked in their skins,** pommes de terre en robe de chambre. **II.** *v.tr.* **(skinned)** écorcher, dépouiller (un lapin, etc.); peler (un fruit); éplucher (des pommes de terre, des courgettes); **'skindiver,** *s.* plongeur sous-marin; **'skinflint,** *s.* avare *m*; **'skinny,** *a.* maigre, décharné.

skip [skip], *v.* **(skipped)** **1.** *v.i.* (*a*) sauter, sautiller, gambader; (*b*) sauter à la corde. **2.** *v.tr.* sauter, passer (un passage dans un livre); *F:* **s. it!** laisse courir! **'skipping,** *s.* saut *m* à la corde; **s. rope,** corde *f* à sauter.

skipper ['skipər], *s.* **1.** *Nau:* patron *m*. **2.** *Sp:* chef *m* d'équipe.

skirmish ['skə:miʃ], *s.* *Mil:* échauffourée *f*; **'skirmisher,** *s.* tirailleur *m*.

skirt [skə:t]. **I.** *s.* *Cl:* jupe *f*; **mini-s.,** mini-jupe. **II.** *v.tr.* contourner (un village); longer, serrer (le mur); **the path skirts the wood,** le sentier côtoie, contourne, le bois.

skit [skit], *s.* satire *f* **(on,** de).

skittle ['skitl], *s.* **1.** quille *f*. **2.** *pl.* **(game of) skittles,** jeu *m* de quilles.

skulk [skʌlk], *v.i.* **1.** se cacher. **2.** rôder furtivement.

skull [skʌl], *s.* crâne *m*.

skunk [skʌŋk], *s.* **1.** *Z:* mouffette *f*. **2.** (*fur*) skunks *m*, sconce *m*.

sky [skai], *s.* ciel *m*; **to praise s.o. to the skies,** élever qn aux nues; *Art:* **Turner's skies,** les ciels de Turner; **we live under other skies,** nous vivons dans un autre climat; **'sky-'blue,** *a. & s.* bleu ciel; **'sky-'high,** *adv.* **to blow sth. s.-h.,** faire sauter qch. jusqu'aux cieux; **'skylark,** *s.* *Orn:* alouette *f* des champs; **'skylight,** *s.* châssis vitré; lucarne *f*; **'skyline,** *s.* (ligne *f* d')horizon *m*; **'skyscraper,** *s.* gratte-ciel *m*; **'skyway,** *s.* **1.** route aérienne. **2.** *N.Am: Aut:* route surélevée.

slab [slæb], *s.* plaque *f*, tranche *f* (de marbre); dalle *f* (de pierre); **s. of gingerbread,** pavé *m* de pain d'épice; **s. of cake,** grosse tranche de gâteau; **s. of chocolate,** tablette *f* de chocolat.

slack [slæk]. **I.** *s.* **1.** mou *m*, ballant *m* (d'un câble); **to take up the s. in a cable,** mettre un câble au raide; *Mec:* jeu *m*; **to take up the s.,** reprendre le jeu. **2.** *s.pl. Cl:* **slacks,** (i) pantalon *m* (d'homme) (en flanelle grise); (ii) pantalon (de dame). **II.** *a.* **1.** (*a*) mou, lâche, flasque; dégonflé; (*b*) (main, prise) faible, sans force. **2.** (*of pers.*) négligent; **to be s. at one's work,** être mou au travail. **3.** peu vif; faible; **s. business,** affaires languissantes; **s. time,** accalmie *f*; **the s. season,** la morte-saison, *pl.* mortes-saisons; **-ly,** *adv.* **1.** (agir) négligemment; sans énergie. **2.** mollement, lâchement. **III.** *v.i.* **to s. (off),** (*a*) prendre du lâche, du mou; (*b*) se relâcher; **to s. (up),** ralentir; **'slacken. 1.** *v.tr.* (*a*) ralentir (le pas); diminuer (de vitesse); (*b*) détendre (un cordage); desserrer (un écrou). **2.** *v.i.* (*of pers.*) **to s. off,** se relâcher; devenir négligent; (*of rope*) prendre du mou; **'slacker,** *s.* paresseux, -euse; **'slackness,** *s.* **1.** manque *m* d'énergie; négligence *f*; fainéantise *f*. **2.** mou *m* (d'un cordage). **3.** *Com:* stagnation *f*, marasme *m* (des affaires).

slag [slæg], *s.* *Metall:* scories *fpl*, crasses *fpl*; **s. heap,** crassier *m*.

slake [sleik], *v.tr.* **1. to s. one's thirst,** étancher sa soif; se désaltérer. **2.** éteindre, amortir (la chaux).

slam[1] [slæm]. **I.** *s.* claquement *m* (d'une porte). **II.** *v.tr. & i.* **(slammed)** claquer.

slam[2], *s.* (*at bridge*) chelem *m*.

slander ['slɑ:ndər]. **I.** *s.* calomnie *f*; diffamation *f*. **II.** *v.tr.* calomnier; diffamer (qn); **'slanderer,** *s.* calomniateur, -trice; diffamateur, -trice; **'slanderous,** *a.* (propos) calomnieux, diffamatoire; **-ly,** *adv* calomnieusement.

slang [slæŋ], *s.* argot *m*.

slant [slɑ:nt]. **I.** *s.* **1.** pente *f*, inclinaison *f*. **2.** biais *m*, biseau *m*; **on the s.,** en écharpe. **3.** point *m* de vue; **he has an interesting s. on the question,** il envisage la question d'une manière intéressante. **II.** *v.* **1.** *v.i.* (*a*) être en pente, (s')incliner; (*b*) être oblique, être en biais. **2**

v.tr. incliner (qch.); mettre (qch.) en pente; **'slanting**, *a.* (*a*) (toit) en pente, incliné; (*b*) (direction) oblique; **'slantwise**, *adv.* obliquement; de biais; en écharpe.

slap [slæp]. **I.** *s.* claque *f*, tape *f*; **s. in the face**, (i) soufflet *m*, gifle *f*; (ii) affront *m*. **II.** *adv.* **to run s. into sth.**, se heurter en plein contre qch. **III.** *v.tr.* (**slapped**) frapper (qn) avec la main (ouverte); donner une fessée à (un enfant); **to s. s.o.'s face**, gifler, souffleter, qn; **'slapdash**, *a.* sans soin; **s. work**, travail bâclé; **'slap-'happy**, *a. F:* (*a*) (*of boxer*) sonné; (*b*) plein d'entrain, fougueux; **'slapstick**, *s.* **s. (comedy)**, farce bouffonne; **'slap-up**, *a. F:* fameux, chic, de premier ordre.

slash [slæʃ]. **I.** *s.* estafilade *f*, entaille *f*; balafre *f*. **II.** *v.tr.* (*a*) taillader; balafrer (le visage); (*b*) **to s. a speech**, faire des amputations dans un discours; (*c*) critiquer, *F:* esquinter (un ouvrage littéraire); (*d*) *Com:* **to s. the price of sth.**, vendre qch. à un prix sacrifié; **'slashing**, *a.* (*of criticism*) mordant, cinglant.

slate [sleit], *s. Const:* ardoise *f*; **s. industry**, ardoiserie *f*; **s. quarry**, ardoisière *f*.

slaughter ['slɔːtər]. **I.** *s.* 1. abattage *m* (de bétail). 2. carnage *m*, massacre *m*. **II.** *v.tr.* 1. abattre (des bêtes de boucherie). 2. tuer, massacrer (des gens); **'slaughterhouse**, *s.* abattoir *m*.

slav [slɑːv], *a. & s. Ethn:* slave (*mf*); **Sla'vonic** [sla'vɔnik], *a. & s. Ling:* slave (*m*).

slave [sleiv]. **I.** *s.* esclave *mf*. **II.** *v.i.* peiner; s'éreinter; bûcher (à un travail); **'slavery**, *s.* 1. esclavage *m*. 2. travail tuant; **'slavish**, *a.* (imitation *f*) servile; **-ly**, *adv.* (obéir) en esclave; (imiter) servilement.

slaver ['slævər]. **I.** *s.* bave *f*, salive *f*. **II.** *v.i.* baver (**over**, sur).

slaw [slɔː], *s.* **cole s.**, salade *f* de chou cru.

slay [slei], *v.tr.* (**slew** [sluː]; **slain** [slein]) tuer; mettre à mort; **'slaying**, *s.* tuerie *f*; massacre *m*.

sled, sledge [sled(ʒ)], *s.* traîneau *m*.

sledge-hammer ['sledʒhæmər], *s.* marteau *m* de forgeron; marteau à deux mains; masse *f*.

sleek [sliːk], *a.* lisse; luisant; **'sleekness**, *s.* (*of hair, skin*) luisant *m*.

sleep [sliːp]. **I.** *s.* 1. sommeil *m*; **sound s.**, sommeil profond; **short s.**, somme *m*; **to go to s.**, s'endormir; **to drop off to s.**, s'assoupir; **to send s.o. to s.**, endormir qn; **to have a good s.**, bien dormir, dormir profondément; **to put a dog to s.** (= *kill*), piquer un chien; **to rouse s.o. from s.**, réveiller qn. 2. **my foot has gone to s.**, j'ai le pied engourdi. **II.** *v.i. & tr.* (**slept**) 1. dormir; (*a*) **to s. like a log**, dormir à poings fermés; **I've not slept a wink all night**, je n'ai pas fermé l'œil de (toute) la nuit; **to s. on it**, prendre conseil de son oreiller; (*b*) **to s. the s. of the just**, dormir du sommeil du

juste. 2. coucher; **to s. at a hotel**, coucher à un hôtel; **to s. away from home**, découcher; **'sleeper**, *s.* 1. dormeur, -euse; **to be a light, a heavy, s.**, avoir le sommeil léger, profond. 2. *Rail:* traverse *f*. 3. *Rail:* wagon-lit *m*; **'sleep 'in**, *v.i.* 1. être logé dans la maison. 2. faire la grasse matinée; **'sleepiness**, *s.* 1. somnolence *f*. 2. indolence *f*, léthargie *f*; **'sleeping. I.** *a.* 1. dormant, endormi. 2. *Com:* **s. partner**, commanditaire *m*. **II.** *s.* sommeil *m*; **s. pill**, somnifère *m*; **s. bag**, sac *m* de couchage; *Rail:* **s. car**, wagon-lit *m*; **'sleepless**, *a.* sans sommeil; **s. night**, nuit blanche; **'sleeplessness**, *s.* insomnie *f*; **'sleepy**, *a.* 1. somnolent; **to feel s.**, avoir sommeil; **s. look**, air endormi; **s. little town**, petite ville endormie. 2. engourdi. 3. (*of over-ripe fruit*) blet; **s. pears**, des poires blettes; **-ily**, *adv.* d'un air endormi, somnolent.

sleet [sliːt]. **I.** *s.* grésil *m*. **II.** *v.impers.* grésiller; **it's sleeting**, il grésille.

sleeve [sliːv], *s.* 1. manche *f*; **to have a plan up one's s.**, avoir un expédient en réserve. 2. *E:* manchon *m*; douille *f*; bague *f* d'assemblage.

sleigh [slei], *s.* traîneau *m*.

sleight [slait]. *s.* **s. of hand**, prestidigitation *f*; tours *mpl* de passe-passe.

slender ['slendər], *a.* 1. mince, ténu; (*of figure*) svelte, élancé; (*of finger*) fuselé. 2. (*of hope*) faible; (*of income*) exigu, mince; **our s. means**, nos ressources exiguës; **'slenderness**, *s.* 1. minceur *f*, ténuité *f*; sveltesse *f*. 2. exiguïté *f* (d'une fortune, etc.); faiblesse *f* (des ressources).

slice [slais]. **I.** *s.* 1. tranche *f*; darne *f* (de gros poisson); rond *m*, rondelle *f* (de saucisson); **s. of bread and butter**, tartine *f* de beurre; **s. of (good) luck**, coup *m* de veine. 2. **fish-s.**, truelle *f* à poisson. **II.** *v.tr.* 1. découper (qch.) en tranches; **to s. thinly**, émincer (la viande, etc.). 2. *Sp:* (i) couper, (ii) faire dévier, la balle; **'slicer**, *s.* machine *f* à trancher le pain, etc.; **'slice 'off**, *v.tr.* trancher, couper (un morceau).

slick [slik]. **I.** *a.* habile, adroit; **a s. customer**, un fin matois. **II.** *s.* **oil s.**, traînée *f* de pétrole (échappée d'un pétrolier).

slide [slaid]. **I.** *s.* 1. glissade *f*, glissement *m*; (*on ice*) glissoire *f*, glissade. 2. (*a*) (*for microscope*) lamelle *f*; (*b*) *Phot:* diapositive *f*. 3. (**hair**) **s.**, barrette *f*. **II.** *v.* (**slid**) 1. *v.i.* (*a*) glisser; (*of door*) coulisser; (*b*) **to s. (on ice)**, faire des glissades; (*c*) **he slid on the floor**, il glissa sur le parquet; (*d*) **to let things s.**, se désintéresser de tout. 2. *v.tr.* (faire) glisser; **'sliding**, *a.* glissant; coulissant; **s. door**, porte à glissières, porte coulissante; **on a s. scale**, suivant une échelle mobile; **s. panel**, panneau *m* mobile; **s. seat**, siège *m* amovible.

slight [slait]. **I.** *a.* **1.** (*of pers.*) mince, ténu; frêle; menu. **2.** (*of pain*) léger; **to some s. extent**, quelque peu; **not the slightest danger**, pas le moindre danger; **not in the slightest (degree)**, pas le moins du monde; **-ly,** *adv.* **1. s. built**, à la taille mince, svelte. **2.** légèrement, faiblement; **s. better**, un petit peu mieux; **I know him s.**, je le connais un peu. **II.** *s.* manque *m* d'égards; affront *m*. **III.** *v.tr.* traiter (qn) sans considération; manquer d'égards envers (qn); **'slighting,** *a.* (air *m*) de mépris; -**ly,** *adv.* avec mépris, dédaigneusement.

slim [slim]. **I.** *a.* (*a*) svelte, élancé; mince; **s.- waisted**, à la taille svelte; (*b*) (*of chance, hope, etc.*) mince, léger. **II.** *v.i.* (**slimmed**) suivre un régime amaigrissant; **'slimness,** *s.* sveltesse *f*; taille *f* mince.

slime [slaim], *s.* **1.** limon *m*, vase *f*. **2.** bave *f* (de limace, etc.); **'sliminess,** *s.* (*a*) état vaseux; (*b*) viscosité *f*; **'slimy,** *a.* **1.** (*a*) limoneux, vaseux; (*b*) visqueux, gluant; (*c*) couvert de vase. **2.** (*of pers.*) servile, obséquieux.

sling [sliŋ]. **I.** *s.* **1.** fronde *f*. **2.** (*a*) *Med:* écharpe *f*; (*b*) bandoulière *f*; (*c*) (*for hoisting*) élingue *f*. **II.** *v.tr.* (**slung**) **1.** lancer, jeter. **2.** suspendre (un hamac, etc.). **3.** élinguer (un fardeau). **4.** *F:* **to s. s.o. out**, flanquer qn à la porte.

slink [sliŋk], *v.i.* (**slunk**) **to s. off**, partir furtivement; **'slinking,** *a.* furtif; **'slinky,** *a.* (forme) svelte; (vêtement) collant.

slip [slip]. **I.** *s.* **1.** (*a*) glissade *f*, glissement *m*, faux pas; (*b*) **to give s.o. the s.**, se dérober à qn; (*c*) faute *f*, erreur *f*, d'inattention; inadvertance *f*; **it was a s. of the tongue**, la langue lui a fourché; (*d*) écart *m* (de conduite); peccadille *f*. **2.** taie *f* d'oreiller. **3.** *Cl:* (*a*) combinaison *f* (de femme); (*b*) slip *m* (de bain, pour homme). **4.** *Nau:* cale *f*, chantier *m* de construction. **II.** *v.* (**slipped**) **1.** *v.i.* (*a*) glisser; (*b*) **to s. into the room**, se glisser dans la salle; *F:* **I slipped round to the baker's**, j'ai fait un saut jusqu'à la boulangerie. **2.** *v.tr.* (*a*) **your name has slipped my memory**, votre nom m'échappe; (*b*) *Aut:* **to s. the clutch**, laisser patiner l'embrayage; **to s. s.o.'s notice**, échapper à l'attention de qn; (*c*) *Rail:* **to s. a carriage**, décrocher un wagon en marche; (*d*) pousser (un verrou); **'slipper,** *s.* *Cl:* pantoufle *f*; *Fr.C:* chaussette *f*; **'slippery,** *a.* **1.** glissant; **he's as s. as an eel**, il est souple comme une anguille. **2.** (sujet) délicat. **3.** malin, rusé; **he's a s. customer**, on ne sait par où le prendre; **'slippy,** *a.* *F:* **to look s.**, se dépêcher; **look s.!** *P:* grouille-toi! **'slipshod,** *a.* (*of pers.*) mal soigné; (*of work*) négligé, bâclé; **'slip'up,** *v.i.* se tromper; faire une bourde; (*of plan*) échouer; tomber à l'eau; **'slip-up,** *s.* *F:* erreur *f*, bévue *f*; **'slipway,** *s.* *Nau:* cale *f*, chantier *m* de construction.

slit [slit]. **I.** *s.* fente *f*; fissure *f*. **II.** *v.tr.* (**slitting;**

slit) (*a*) fendre; **to s. s.o.'s throat**, couper l gorge à qn; égorger qn; **to s. open a sack**, éven trer un sac; (*b*) **the blow s. his cheek (open)**, l coup lui a déchiré la joue.

slither [ˈsliðər], *v.i.* glisser; manquer de tomber

sliver [ˈslivər], *s.* éclat *m* (de bois); (mince tranche *f* (de viande, etc.).

slobber [ˈslɔbər], *v.i.* (*a*) baver; (*b*) larmoyer; t **s. over s.o.**, témoigner une tendresse exagéré envers qn.

sloe [slou], *s.* *Bot:* **1.** prunelle *f*. **2.** prunellier *m*

slog [slɔg], *v.i.* (**slogged**) (*a*) **to s. away**, travaill avec acharnement (**at sth.**, à qch.); *F:* turbiner (*b*) **to s. along**, marcher d'un pas lourd **'slogger,** *s.* bûcheur, -euse.

slogan [ˈslougən], *s.* (*a*) slogan *m*; (*b*) *Com* devise *f*.

slop [slɔp]. **I.** *s.pl.* **slops**, (*a*) boissons renversées (*b*) aliments *m* liquides; **the patient is on slops** le malade est réduit au bouillon; (*c*) eau ménagères. **II.** *v.* (**slopped**) **1.** *v.tr.* répandre (u liquide). **2.** *v.i.* (*of liquid*) déborder; *F:* (*c pers.*) faire de la sensiblerie; **'sloppily,** *adv.* **'sloppily dressed**, débraillé; **'sloppy,** *a.* (*of pers.*) mou flasque; peu soigné; (travail) bâclé, négligé (vêtement) mal ajusté, trop grand; (roman film) larmoyant; **s. sentimentality**, sensiblerie

slope [sloup]. **I.** *s.* pente *f*, inclinaison *f*; **steep s** pente rapide; **s. down**, descente *f*; talus *m; s up**, montée *f*; **mountain slopes**, versants *m d* montagne. **II.** *v.i.* être en pente; incline pencher; aller en pente; **to s. down**, descendre **to s. up**, monter; **'sloping,** *a.* en pente, incliné (jardin) en talus; **s. shoulders**, épaule tombantes.

slot [slɔt], *s.* entaille *f*, encoche *f*, rainure *f*; **s machine**, (i) distributeur *m* automatique; (i appareil *m* à jetons (pour jeux, etc.); **s. mete** compteur *m* à paiement préalable.

slothful [ˈslouθfəl], *a.* paresseux, fainéant; ir dolent; **-fully,** *adv.* paresseusement.

slouch [slautʃ], *v.i.* se laisser aller en marchan manquer de tenue; **don't s.!** tenez-vous droit

slovenly [ˈslʌv(ə)nli], *a.* **1.** (*of pers.*) mal peign mal soigné. **2.** (*a*) négligent; sans soin; (travail) négligé, *F:* bousillé; **'slovenliness,** **1.** négligence *f* (de mise); manque *m* de tenu laisser-aller *m inv.* **2.** manque de soin.

slow [slou]. **I.** *a.* **1.** (*a*) lent; **s. speed**, peti vitesse; ralenti *m*; **it's s. work**, ça ne va p vite; *Cu:* **s. cooking**, la cuisine à feu dou *Rail:* **s. train**, train *m* omnibus; (*b*) **to be s.** **starting sth.**, être lent à commencer qch.; **s.** **anger**, lent à la colère; (*c*) **s. (of intellect)** l'esprit lourd; **s. child**, enfant retardé, arriér (*d*) qui manque d'entrain; **business is s., l** affaires traînent. **2.** (*of clock*) en retard; **yo** **watch is five minutes s.**, votre montre retard de cinq minutes; **-ly,** *adv.* lentement; **engi**

running s., moteur au ralenti; drive s.! ralentir!
II. *adv.* lentement; to go slower, ralentir sa
marche; *Ind:* to go s., faire la grève perlée; to
go s. with one's provisions, ménager ses
vivres; go s.! ralentir! III. *v.* 1. *v.i.* to s. down,
to s. up, ralentir (son allure); diminuer de
vitesse. 2. *v.tr.* to s. sth. down, ralentir qch.;
'slowcoach, *s.* lambin, -ine; 'slowness, *s.*
lenteur *f.*
sludge [slʌdʒ], *s.* vase *f*; fange *f*; *Ind:* tartres
boueux; (sewage) s., vidanges *fpl*; 'sludgy, *a.*
vaseux, fangeux; boueux.
slug [slʌg], *s.* limace *f.*
sluggish ['slʌgiʃ], *a.* paresseux, léthargique; *Aut:*
s. engine, moteur peu nerveux, léthargique;
-ly, *adv.* 1. paresseusement. 2.(*of river*) to flow
s., couler lentement; 'sluggishness, *s.* 1. (*a*)
paresse *f*; (*b*) lourdeur *f* (de l'esprit). 2. (*a*)
lenteur *f*(d'une rivière); (*b*) paresse (du foie, de
l'intestin).
sluice [sluːs]. I. *s.* 1. (*a*) écluse *f*; (*b*) canal *m*,
-aux, de décharge. 2. to give sth. a s. down,
laver qch. à grande eau. II. *v.tr.* laver (qch.) à
grande eau; débourber (un égout).
slum [slʌm], *s.* bas quartier (d'une ville); rue *f*
sordide; taudis *m*; s. clearance campaign, lutte
f contre les taudis.
slumber ['slʌmbər]. I. *s.* sommeil *m* (paisible); assoupissement *m*; somme *m.* II. *v.i.*
sommeiller; dormir (paisiblement);
'slumberwear, *s.* Com: vêtements *mpl* de
nuit.
slump [slʌmp]. I. *s.* Com: baisse soudaine; effondrement *m* (des cours); dégringolade *f* (de la
livre sterling); the s., la crise économique. II.
v.i. Ind: Com: etc: baisser tout à coup; s'effondrer, dégringoler.
slur¹ [sləːr], *s.* affront *m*; to cast a s. on s.o., infliger un affront à qn.
slur², *v.tr. & i.* (slurred) to s. (over) a word,
bredouiller, escamoter, un mot; to s. (over) a
fact, glisser sur un fait; slurred, *a.* brouillé, indistinct; (*of outline*) estompé.
slush [slʌʃ], *s.* (*a*) neige à demi fondue; (*b*) fange
f, bourbe *f*; 'slushy, *a.* boueux; fangeux.
slut [slʌt], *s.* souillon *f*; salope *f*; 'sluttish, *a.*
(femme) malpropre, sale.
sly [slai], *a.* 1. (*a*) matois, rusé; (*b*) sournois; (*c*) *s.*
to do sth. on the s., faire qch. furtivement. 2.
malin; -ly, *adv.* (*a*) avec finesse; (*b*) sour-
noisement; 'slyness, *s.* (*a*) finesse *f*; (*b*) sournoiserie *f*; (*c*) malice *f.*
smack¹ [smæk], *v.i.* to s. of sth., avoir un léger
goût de qch.; opinions that s. of heresy,
opinions *f* qui sentent le fagot.
smack². I. *s.* 1. claquement *m.* 2. claque *f*; s. in
the face, (i) gifle *f*; (ii) affront *m*; *F:* to have a s.
(at doing sth.), tenter le coup, tenter sa chance
(à faire qch.). II. *v.tr.* frapper, taper (qn); to s.

s.o.'s face, donner une gifle à qn; *F:* to s. one's
lips, se lécher les babines.
smack³, *s.* (fishing-)s., bateau pêcheur.
small [smɔːl]. I. *a.* 1. (*a*) petit, menu; s. stature,
petite taille; to make oneself s., se faire tout
petit; s. game, menu gibier; *Typ:* s. letters,
minuscules *f*; (*b*) in s. numbers, en petit nombre; (*c*) s. voice, voix fluette; (*d*) s. income,
mince revenu; s. harvest, maigre récolte; (*e*)
peu important; peu considérable; s. change,
menue monnaie; a s. cup of coffee, une petite
tasse de café; in a s. way, en petit; a s. matter,
une bagatelle; s. hotel, hôtel *m* modeste. 2.
mesquin; s. mind, petit esprit; to look s., avoir
l'air penaud; to make s.o. look s., humilier qn.
II. *s.* 1. s. of the back, creux *m* des reins. 2. *pl.*
F: smalls, sous-vêtements *m.* III. *adv.* (hacher)
menu, en petits morceaux; 'smallholding,
petite exploitation agricole; 'smallish, *a.*
plutôt petit; assez petit; 'smallness, *s.*
petitesse *f*; exiguïté *f* (de taille); faiblesse *f*
(d'une somme d'argent); 'smallpox, *s.* petite
vérole; variole *f*; 'small-scale, *a.* 1. s.-s.
model, modèle réduit. 2. s.-s. business, affaire
peu importante.
smart [smɑːt]. I. *s.* douleur cuisante (d'une
blessure). II. *v.i.* (*of wound*) (*a*) cuire, brûler;
my eyes are smarting, les yeux me picotent; (*b*)
to s. under an injustice, souffrir sous le coup
d'une injustice; he'll make you s. for it, il vous
le fera payer cher. III. *a.* 1. (coup) cinglant;
(coup) sec. 2. to walk at a s. pace, marcher à
une allure vive; look s. (about it)! dépêchez-
vous! 3. habile; débrouillard, dégourdi; s.
answer, réponse adroite; to try to be s., faire le
malin. 4. élégant, distingué, chic; to make
oneself s., se faire beau; -ly, *adv.* 1.
promptement; vivement. 2. habilement,
adroitement. 3. (s'habiller) élégamment;
'smarten. 1. *v.tr.* to s. s.o. up, dégourdir
qn; (*b*) to s. oneself up, se faire beau. 2. *v.i.* to s.
up, (*a*) s'animer; (*b*) se dégourdir;
'smartness, *s.* 1. (*a*) vivacité *f*; esprit
débrouillard; (*b*) à-propos *m* (d'une réponse).
2. habileté peu scrupuleuse. 3. élégance *f*; chic
m.
smash [smæʃ]. I. *s.* 1. coup écrasant. 2. désastre
m; car s., accident *m* (de la route). 3. *Fin:* débâcle *f*; faillite (commerciale). II. *v.* 1. *v.tr.* (*a*) to
s. sth. to pieces, briser qch. en morceaux; to s.
the door open, enfoncer la porte; *F:* to s. s.o.'s
face, abîmer le portrait de qn; s.-and-grab
raid, rafle *f* après bris de devanture; (*b*)
détruire (qch.); écraser (une armée). 2. *v.i.* (*a*)
se heurter violemment (contre qch.); (*b*) éclater
en morceaux; se briser. 3. *v.i.* faire faillite;
'smashing, *a.* 1. (coup) écrasant. 2. *F:* that's
s.! c'est formidable! c'est sensas! 'smash up,
v.tr. briser en morceaux; fracasser; 'smash-

up, *s.* destruction complète; *Rail: etc:* collision *f.*

smattering ['smæt(ə)riŋ], *s.* légère connaissance (d'une matière); **to have a s. of chemistry**, avoir des notions *f* de chimie.

smear ['smiːər]. **I.** *s.* tache *f*, souillure *f*; **s. campaign**, campagne *f* de diffamation. **II.** *v.tr.* 1. (*a*) barbouiller, salir (**with**, de); (*b*) enduire (**with**, de). 2. maculer (une page écrite).

smell [smel]. **I.** *s.* 1. (**sense of**) **s.**, odorat *m*; flair *m*; **to have a keen sense of s.**, avoir l'odorat fin. 2. (*a*) odeur *f*; parfum *m*; **musty s.**, **stale s.**, relent *m*; (*b*) mauvaise odeur. **II.** *v.* (**smelt**) 1. *v.tr. & ind.tr.* (*a*) flairer (qch.); sentir (une fleur); (*b*) sentir l'odeur de (qch.); sentir (une odeur); **the dog smelt at my shoes**, le chien a flairé mes souliers. 2. *v.i.* (*a*) **to s. nice**, sentir bon; (*b*) sentir (mauvais); avoir une forte odeur; '**smelly**, *a.* malodorant.

smelt [smelt], *v.tr. Metall:* 1. fondre; faire fondre (le minerai). 2. extraire (le métal) par fusion; '**smelting**, *s.* (*a*) fonte *f*; (*b*) extraction *f* (du métal); **s. works**, fonderie *f.*

smile [smail]. **I.** *s.* sourire *m*; **to be all smiles**, être tout souriant. **II.** *v.i.* sourire; **to s. at s.o.**, sourire à qn; **to keep smiling**, garder le sourire; '**smiling**, *a.* souriant; **-ly**, *adv.* en souriant.

smith [smiθ], *s.* 1. **shoeing s.**, maréchal ferrant; (**black**)**s.**, (**iron**)**s.**, forgeron *m.* 2. (**lock**)**s.**, **general s.**, serrurier *m*; **smithy** ['smiði], *s.* forge *f.*

smithereens [smiðə'riːnz], *s.pl. F:* morceaux *m*; miettes *f*; **to blow, smash, sth. to s.**, réduire qch. en éclats, en mille morceaux, atomiser qch.

smock [smɔk], *s.* blouse *f*, sarrau *m.*

smog [smɔg], *s.* brouillard enfumé.

smoke [smouk]. **I.** *s.* 1. fumée *f*; (*of project*) **to end up in s.**, s'en aller en fumée, n'aboutir à rien. 2. **do you want to have a s.?** voulez-vous fumer? **II.** *v.* 1. *v.i.* fumer. 2. *v.tr.* (*a*) fumer (un jambon); (*b*) fumer (du tabac); *abs.* **do you s.?** êtes-vous fumeur? **do you mind if I s.?** la fumée vous gêne-t-elle? '**smokeless**, *a.* (combustible) sans fumée; (zone) où la fumée est interdite; '**smoker**, *s.* fumeur, -euse; **heavy s.**, grand fumeur; '**smoking**, *s.* 1. fumage *m* (du jambon). 2. action *f*, habitude *f*, de fumer (le tabac); *P.N:* **no s.**, défense de fumer; '**smoky**, *a.* (*of atmosphere*) fumeux; enfumé; (*of room*) plein, rempli, de fumée.

smooth [smuːð]. **I.** *a.* 1. (*a*) lisse; uni, égal; **s. as glass**, poli comme la glace; **sea as s. as a millpond**, mer calme comme un lac; (*b*) (menton) glabre. 2. (*a*) doux, sans heurts; (*of machine*) **s. running**, marche douce; (*b*) **s. voice**, voix moelleuse; (*c*) doucereux, mielleux; **he has a s. tongue**, il est beau parleur; **-ly**, *adv.* 1. uniment; sans inégalités. 2. (marcher) doucement.

II. *v.tr.* lisser (ses cheveux); égaliser (le terrain); aplanir (une planche); **to s. the way for s.o.**, aplanir la voie pour qn; '**smoothness**, *s.* 1. (*a*) égalité *f* (d'une surface); satiné *m* (de la peau); (*b*) calme *m* (de la mer). 2. douceur *f* (de la marche d'une machine).

smother ['smʌðər], *v.tr.* (*a*) étouffer; suffoquer (qn); (*b*) recouvrir (i) un piéton de poussière, (ii) un gâteau de crème Chantilly.

smoulder ['smouldər], *v.i.* (*a*) brûler lentement; (*b*) couver (sous la cendre).

smudge [smʌdʒ]. **I.** *s.* tache *f*; noircissure *f*. **II.** *v.tr.* salir (la page), barbouiller (son écriture); '**smudgy**, *a.* taché, barbouillé; souillé; (contour) estompé.

smug [smʌg], *a.* (ton, air) suffisant; satisfait de soi-même; **-ly**, *adv.* d'un air suffisant; '**smugness**, *s.* suffisance *f*; fatuité *f.*

smuggle ['smʌgl], *v.tr.* (faire) passer en contrebande, en fraude; *abs.* faire de la contrebande; '**smuggler**, *s.* contrebandier, -ière; '**smuggling**, *s.* contrebande *f.*

smut [smʌt], *s.* 1. parcelle *f*, tache *f*, de suie. 2. *coll.* (*in conversation*) grivoiseries *fpl*, in décences *fpl*, ordures *fpl*; **to talk s.**, dire des cochonneries *f*; '**smuttiness**, *s.* 1. noirceur *f*, saleté *f.* 2. obscénité *f*, grivoiserie *f*; '**smutty**, *a.* 1. noirci, sali (de suie). 2. (*of conversation*) malpropre, ordurier, grivois.

snack [snæk], *s.* léger repas; casse-croûte *m inv*; **to have a s.**, manger sur le pouce; **s. bar**, snack bar *m.*

snag [snæg], *s.* (*a*) chicot *m* (d'arbre); souche au ras d'eau; (*b*) obstacle caché; **to find, strike a s.**, se heurter à un obstacle, *F:* rencontrer u pépin.

snail [sneil], *s.* limaçon *m*, escargot *m* colimaçon *m*; **edible s.**, escargot comestible.

snake [sneik], *s.* serpent *m*; (**common**) **grass s.**, couleuvre *f* à collier; serpent d'eau.

snap [snæp]. **I.** *s.* 1. (*a*) coup *m* de dents; bru sec, claquement *m* (de dents, de doigts). 2. cassure *f*; rupture soudaine. 3. **cold s.**, cour période de temps froid; coup de froid. **s.(-fastener)**, fermoir *m*; bouton *m* à pression 5. *Cu:* **ginger s.**, biscuit croquant au gingen bre. 6. *Phot:* **snap(shot)**, instantané *m*. **II.** *a.* instantané, imprévu; **s. decision**, décision pri sur le coup. **III.** *v.* (**snapped**) 1. *v.i.* (*a*) **to s. sth., s.o.**, chercher à mordre qch., qn; (*b*) (*sharp sound*) claquer; faire un bruit sec; (*break*) (se) casser net. 2. *v.tr.* (*a*) (*of do* happer (qch.); (*b*) **to s. one's fingers at s.** narguer qn, se moquer de qn; (*c*) casser, romp (un bâton); **snapped tendon**, tendon claqu (*d*) *v.i. F:* **to s. out of it**, se secouer; (*e*) *v.* **to s. up a bargain**, saisir une occasion; '**sna dragon**, *s. Bot:* muflier *m*; gueule-de-loup *pl.* gueules-de-loup; '**snappish**, *a.* hargneu de mauvaise humeur; **'snappy,** *a.* 1. irritable; hargneux. 2. *F:* **look s.! make it s.!** grouille-toi!

snare ['snεər], *s.* (*a*) lacet *m*, collet *m*; (*b*) piège *m*; **a s. and a delusion,** quelque chose de trompeur.

snarl¹ [snɑ:l]. I. *v.i.* (*of dog, etc.*) grogner, gronder. II. *s.* grondement *m*, grognement *m*; (*of tiger*) feulement *m*; **'snarling,** *a.* (*of pers., animal*) hargneux.

snarl², *v.tr.* (*of traffic*) **to be snarled up,** être pris dans un embouteillage; **'snarl-up,** *s.* embouteillage *m*, bouchon *m*.

snatch [snætʃ]. I. *v.tr.* 1. saisir, empoigner (qch.); **to s. a meal,** manger un morceau sur le pouce; **to s. some sleep,** faire un petit somme. 2. **to s. sth. out of s.o.'s hands,** arracher qch. des mains de qn. II. *s.* 1. **to make a s. at sth.,** chercher à saisir qch. 2. une courte période; **to work by snatches,** travailler à bâtons rompus; **snatches of song,** fragments *m* de chanson.

sneak [sni:k]. I. *v.* 1. *v.i.* (*a*) **to s. off,** partir furtivement; (*b*) *Sch:* moucharder, cafarder. 2. *v.tr. P:* chiper, chaparder. II. *s. Sch: F:* mouchard *m*; rapporteur, -euse; **'sneakers,** *s.pl.* souliers *m* basket, souliers tennis; **'sneaking,** *a.* 1. (*a*) furtif; (*b*) **to have a s. liking for sth.,** avoir un penchant inavoué pour qch. 2. rampant, servile.

sneer ['sniər]. I. *s.* 1. sourire *m* de mépris; ricanement *m*. 2. sarcasme *m*. II. *v.i.* ricaner; **to s. at s.o.,** (i) parler de qn d'un ton méprisant; (ii) lancer des sarcasmes à qn; **'sneering,** *a.* ricaneur; moqueur; **-ly,** *adv.* d'un air méprisant; en ricanant.

sneeze [sni:z]. I. *s.* éternuement *m*. II. *v.i.* éternuer; **that's not to be sneezed at,** cela n'est pas à dédaigner, *F:* ce n'est pas à cracher dessus.

sniff [snif]. I. *s.* reniflement *m*. II. *v.i. & tr.* renifler; *Med:* **to be sniffed up the nostrils,** aspirer par les narines.

sniffle ['snifl]. I. *s. F:* petit rhume (de cerveau). II. *v.i.* renifler; être légèrement enrhumé.

snigger ['snigər], *v.i.* rire sous cape; ricaner; **'sniggering,** *s.* rires *mpl* en dessous.

snip [snip]. I. *v.tr.* (**snipped**) couper avec des ciseaux. II. *s.* 1. (*a*) morceau coupé; petite entaille; (*b*) coup *m* de ciseaux. 2. *F:* (*a*) certitude *f*; *Rac:* gagnant sûr; (*b*) affaire avantageuse.

snipe [snaip], *s. Orn:* bécassine *f*.

sniper ['snaipər], *s. Mil:* tireur d'élite (caché); tireur isolé.

snivel ['snivl], *v.i.* (**snivelled**) pleurnicher, larmoyer; **'snivelling.** I. *a.* pleurnicheur; larmoyant. II. *s.* pleurnicherie *f*.

snob [snɔb], *s.* prétentieux, -euse; snob *mf*; **intellectual s.,** poseur, -euse; **'snobbery,** *s.*, **'snobbishness,** *s.* morgue *f*; snobisme *m*; **'snobbish,** *a.* poseur; snob.

snooker ['snu:kər], *s.* (sorte de) jeu *m* de billard.

snoop [snu:p], *v.i.* fureter, fouiner; **'snooper,** *s. F:* fureteur, -euse; fouineur, -euse.

snooze [snu:z]. I. *s. F:* petit somme, roupillon *m*. II. *v.i. F:* sommeiller; faire un petit somme; piquer un roupillon; **'snoozing,** *a.* endormi, assoupi.

snore [snɔ:r]. I. *v.i.* ronfler. II. *s.* (*also* **snoring**) ronflement *m*.

snorkel ['snɔ:kl], *s.* (*a*) schnorkel *m*; (*b*) masque sous-marin.

snort [snɔ:t]. I. *v.i.* renifler fortement; (*of horse*) s'ébrouer. II. *s.* (*also* **snorting**) reniflement *m*; ébrouement *m*; **'snorter,** *s. F:* problème difficile à résoudre.

snout [snaut], *s.* museau *m*; groin *m* (de porc).

snow [snou]. I. *s.* 1. neige *f*; **there's been a fall of s.,** il est tombé de la neige; **s. shower,** chute *f* de neige; **flurry of s.,** rafale *f* de neige; **s. gauge,** nivomètre *m*; *Ski:* **crusted s.,** (neige) tôlée (*f*); **powdered s.,** (neige) poudreuse (*f*). 2. *P:* (*drug*) cocaïne *f*, *P:* coco *f*. II. *v. impers.* neiger; **it's snowing,** il neige; **to be snowed up,** être bloqué par la neige; **I'm snowed under with work,** je suis submergé de besogne; **'snowball,** *s.* boule *f* de neige; **'snow-blindness,** *s.* cécité *f* des neiges; **'snowbound,** *a.* bloqué par la neige; **'snowdrift,** *s.* congère *f*; **'snowdrop,** *s. Bot:* perce-neige *m inv*; **'snowfall,** *s.* (*a*) chute *f* de neige; (*b*) (profondeur *f* d')enneigement *m*; **'snowflake,** *s.* flocon *m* de neige; **'snowline,** *s.* limite *f* des neiges perpétuelles; **'snowman,** *pl.* **-men,** *s.* 1. bonhomme *m* de neige. 2. **the abominable s.,** l'abominable homme des neiges; yéti *m*; **'snowmobile,** *s.* tracteur *m* automobile (pour expéditions polaires); **'snowplough,** *s., N.Am:* snowplow, *s.* chasse-neige *m inv*; **'snowshoes,** *s.pl.* raquettes *f*; **'snowstorm,** *s.* tempête *f* de neige; **'snowy,** *a.* neigeux; de neige.

snub¹ [snʌb]. I. *s.* mortification *f*, rebuffade *f*. II. *v.tr.* (**snubbed**) infliger un affront à (qn); remettre (qn) à sa place.

snub², *a.* (nez) camus, retroussé.

snuff [snʌf], *s.* tabac *m* à priser; **to take s.,** priser; **a pinch of s.,** une prise.

snug [snʌg], *a.* confortable; **to lie s. in bed,** être bien au chaud dans son lit; **it's very s. in here,** on est bien ici; il fait très bon ici; **-ly,** *adv.* confortablement, douillettement; **'snuggle,** *v.i.* **to s. up (to s.o.),** se pelotonner (contre qn); **to s. down in bed,** se blottir dans son lit.

so [sou]. I. *adv.* 1. si, tellement; tant, aussi; **he's so (very) kind,** s'il est si aimable; **I am not so sure of that,** je n'en suis pas bien sûr; **so true it is that . . .,** tant il est vrai que. . .; **he's not so feeble as he appears,** il n'en a l'air pas aussi faible qu'il n'en a l'air; **would you be so kind as to . . . ?** voudriez-vous avoir la bonté de. . .? **so**

much, tellement, tant; **we enjoyed ourselves so much,** on s'est joliment bien amusés. **2.** (*a*) ainsi; de cette manière; **why do you cry so?** pourquoi pleurez-vous ainsi? **it so happened that . . .,** le hasard a voulu que (+ *sub.*); **and so on,** et ainsi de suite; **so to speak,** pour ainsi dire; (*b*) **I think so,** je le crois; **I'm afraid so,** j'en ai bien peur; **so it seems,** à ce qu'il paraît; **I told you so!** je vous l'avais bien dit! **so much so that . . .,** le hasard a voulu que + *sub.*; **and so** bien plus encore; **is that so?** vraiment? **it's not so,** il n'en est rien; **so be it!** soit! (*c*) **how so?** comment cela? **perhaps so,** cela se peut; **not so,** pas du tout; **quite so!** parfaitement! **a week or so,** une semaine environ; (*d*) **he's right and so are you,** il a raison et vous aussi; (*e*) **you're late—so I am!** vous êtes en retard—c'est vrai! **3.** *conj.phr.* **so that,** (*a*) pour que + *sub.*; (*b*) de sorte que + *ind. or sub.* **4.** *conj.phr.* **so as to,** (*a*) **we hurried so as not to be late,** nous nous sommes dépêchés pour ne pas être en retard; (*b*) **speak so as to be understood,** parlez de sorte qu'on vous comprenne. **II.** *conj.* **1.** donc; c'est pourquoi. **2. so there you are!** vous voilà donc! **so you're not coming?** ainsi vous ne venez pas? **so what?** (i) et alors? (ii) et puis quoi? (iii) ça te regarde, toi? '**so-and-so,** *s. F:* (*a*) *Pej:* sale type *m*; (*b*) **Mr. So-and-So,** Monsieur Untel; '**so-called,** *a.* soi-disant; '**so so,** *a. & adv.* comme ci comme ça.

soak [souk]. **I.** *v.* **1.** *v.tr.* (*a*) tremper, détremper; (*b*) **to s. sth. in sth.,** tremper qch. dans qch.; (*c*) *F:* écorcher (un client); **to s. the rich,** faire payer les riches. **2.** *v.i.* (*a*) baigner, tremper (**in sth.,** dans qch.); (*b*) s'infiltrer, s'imbiber (**into,** dans); (*c*) *P:* boire comme une éponge, comme un trou. **II.** *s.* **1.** *Metalw: etc:* trempe *f*; **to put sth. in, to, s.,** (i) (faire) tremper (le linge); (ii) faire macérer (des cornichons, etc.); (faire) dessaler (la morue). **2.** *P:* ivrogne *m*, soûlard *m*; '**soaking,** *s.* (*a*) trempage *m* (du linge); (*b*) trempée *f*; (*of pers.*) **to get a (good) s.,** se faire tremper.

soap [soup]. **I.** *s.* savon *m*; **bar of s.,** savonnette *f*. **II.** *v.tr.* savonner; '**soapflakes,** *s.pl.* savon *m* en paillettes; '**soapy,** *a.* **1.** savonneux, couvert de savon. **2.** *Pej:* (*of pers.*) mielleux, doucereux.

soar [sɔ:r], *v.i.* prendre son essor; monter, s'élever (dans les airs); (*of prices*) monter (en flèche); '**soaring. I.** *a.* **1.** (*a*) qui monte dans les airs; (*b*) **s. flight,** vol plané. **2.** (ambition) sans bornes. **II.** *s.* **1.** (*a*) essor *m*; (*b*) hausse *f* (des prix). **2.** planement *m* (d'un oiseau).

sob [sɔb]. **I.** *s.* sanglot *m*. **II.** *v.i.* (**sobbed**) sangloter; '**sob-stuff,** *s. F:* littérature sentimentale.

sober ['soubər]. **I.** *a.* (*a*) sobre, modéré, tempéré; (*b*) calme, posé; **in s. earnest,** bien

sérieusement; (*c*) **he's never s.,** il est toujours ivre; **to sleep oneself s.,** cuver son vin; **-ly,** *adv.* (*a*) sobrement, modérément; (*b*) avec calme; tranquillement. **II.** *v.i.* (*a*) **to s. up,** se dégriser, se dessoûler; (*b*) **to s. down,** s'assagir; '**sober-'minded,** *a.* (*of pers.*) sérieux; pondéré; '**soberness,** *s.* (*a*) sobriété *f*, tempérance *f*; (*b*) calme *m*, tranquillité *f*, modération *f*; **so'briety** [-'braiəti], *s.* sobriété *f*, tempérance *f*.

soccer ['sɔkər], *s. F:* football *m*.

sociable ['souʃəbl], *a.* sociable; **-ably,** *adv.* sociablement, amicalement; **socia'bility,** *s.* sociabilité *f*.

social ['souʃ(ə)l], *a.* social; (*a*) **s. problems,** problèmes sociaux; **s. sciences,** sciences humaines; **s. security,** sécurité sociale; **s. worker,** assistante sociale; **s. system,** société *f*; **s. insurance,** assurances sociales; (*b*) **s. events,** mondanités *f*; **s. gathering,** (i) soirée *f*; (ii) réception *f*; **s. evening,** petite soirée intime.

socialism ['souʃəlizm], *s.* socialisme *m* '**socialist,** *a. & s.* socialiste (*mf*) **socia'listic,** *a.* socialiste.

society [sə'saiəti], *s.* **1.** société *f*. **2.** société association *f*.

sock [sɔk], *s.* **1.** chaussette *f*. **2.** semelle intérieur (d'une chaussure).

socket ['sɔkit], *s.* **1.** emboîture *f*, douille *f*; *El* **lamp s.,** douille de lampe. **2.** *Anat:* (*a*) alvéol *m or f* (de dent); (*b*) orbite *f* (de l'œil).

soda ['soudə], *s.* **1.** (*a*) *Ch:* soude *f*; **caustic s.** soude caustique; (*b*) **baking s.,** bicarbonate *m* de soude. **2. s. (water),** eau *f* de seltz; soda *m* '**soda-fountain,** *s.* bar *m* pour glaces e rafraîchissements.

sodden ['sɔdn], *a.* (*of field, lawn*) (dé)trempé.

sodium ['soudiəm], *s. Ch:* sodium *m*.

sofa ['soufə], *s. H:* canapé *m*.

soft [sɔft], *a.* **1.** mou; (*a*) **s. pencil,** crayon *m* ter dre; *Com:* **s. fruit,** fruits *m* rouges; *Fin:* **currency,** devise *f* faible; **s. landing** atterrissage *m* en douceur; (*b*) **s. to the touch** doux au toucher. **2.** doux; (*a*) **s. voice,** voi douce; *F:* **s. job,** emploi *m* pépère; (*b*) **s. hear** cœur *m* tendre. **3.** *a.* (*of pers.*) niais; **-l** *adv.* **1.** (*a*) doucement; **to tread s.,** marche sans bruit; (*b*) tendrement.. **2.** mollemen '**soft-boiled,** *a. Cu:* (œuf) mollet, à la coqu **soften** ['sɔfn]. **1.** *v.tr.* (*a*) amollir, ramolli assouplir (le cuir); (*b*) adoucir (la voix); (*(* attendrir, émouvoir (qn). **2.** *v.i.* (*a*) s'amollir, s ramollir; (*b*) s'attendrir; **softener** ['sɔfnər], **water s.,** adoucisseur *m* d'eau; **softenin** ['sɔfniŋ], *s.* (*a*) amollissement *m* (du beurre (*b*) attendrissement *m* (de qn); (*c*) assoupliss ment *m* (du cuir); (*d*) adoucissement *m* (d caractère); '**soft-'hearted,** *a.* au cœur tendr '**softness,** *s.* douceur *f*; '**software,** *s. Con**

puters: (ensemble *m* de) programmes *m*.
soggy ['sogi], *a.* **1.** détrempé; saturé d'eau. **2.** (*of bread, etc.*) pâteux; lourd.
soil [soil]. **I.** *s.* sol *m*, terrain *m*, terre *f*; **rich s.**, terre grasse; **light s.**, terre meuble. **II.** *v.tr.* souiller, salir; **soiled**, *a.* souillé, sali; **s. linen**, linge sale.
solar ['soulər], *a.* (système, etc.) solaire.
solder ['souldər]. **I.** *s.* soudure *f*; **soft s.**, sou dure tendre; **hard s.**, brasure *f*. **II.** *v.tr.* souder, ressouder; **'soldering iron,** *s.*, **soldering bit,** *s.* fer *m* à souder.
soldier ['souldʒər], *s.* soldat *m*; **three soldiers and two civilians**, trois militaires *m* et deux civils; **private s.**, simple soldat; **'soldierly,** *a.* (allure *f*) militaire, de militaire; martial.
sole[1] [soul]. **I.** *s.* **1.** plante *f* (du pied). **2.** semelle *f* (de chaussure). **II.** *v.tr.* ressemeler (des chaussures); **'soling,** *s.* ressemelage *m*.
sole[2], *s. Ich:* sole *f*.
sole[3], *a.* seul, unique; **s. agent**, agent exclusif; **-ly,** *adv.* uniquement.
solemn ['soləm], *a.* **1.** solennel; **s. fact**, réalité sérieuse; **s. duty**, devoir sacré; **s. ceremony,** solennité *f*. **2.** (*of pers.*) grave, sérieux; **to keep a s. face**, composer son visage; **-ly,** *adv.* **1.** solennellement. **2.** gravement, sérieusement; **so'lemnity** [-'lemniti], *s.* **1.** solennité *f*. **2.** gravité *f* (de maintien). **3.** fête solennelle; **solemni'zation** [-nai-], *s.* célébration *f* (d'un mariage, d'une fête religieuse); **'solemnize,** *v.tr.* célébrer (un mariage, une fête religieuse).
solicit [sə'lisit], *v.tr.* solliciter (une faveur); **to s. s.o. for sth.**, solliciter qch. de qn; **solici'tation,** *s.* sollicitation *f*, demande *f*.
solicitor [sə'lisitər], *s. Jur:* = notaire *m*.
solicitous [sə'lisitəs], *a.* soucieux, désireux (**of sth.**, de qch.); **s. about sth.**, préoccupé de qch.; **to be s. for s.o.'s comfort**, avoir à cœur le confort de qn; **-ly,** *adv.* avec sollicitude; **so'licitude,** *s.* sollicitude *f*, souci *m*, préoccupation *f*.
solid ['solid]. **1.** *a.* solide; (*a*) **s. food**, aliment solide; (*b*) **steps cut in the s. rock**, escalier taillé dans la pierre vive; (*c*) plein, massif; **s. mahogany table**, table *f* en acajou massif; **s. measures**, mesures de volume; **to sleep for nine s. hours**, dormir neuf heures d'affilée; **s. vote**, vote unanime; (*d*) en une seule pièce; **parts cast s.**, parties (coulées) en monobloc. **2.** *s.* solide *m*; **-ly,** *adv.* solidement; (voter) avec unanimité; **soli'darity,** *s.* solidarité *f*; **so'lidify. 1.** *v.tr.* solidifier. **2.** *v.i.* (i) se solidifier; (ii) se figer; **so'lidity,** *s.* solidité *f*; **'solid-'state,** *a.* (appareil) transistorisé.
soliloquy [sə'liləkwi], *s.* monologue *m*.
solitary ['solit(ə)ri], *a.* (*a*) solitaire; **not a s. one,** pas un seul; (**prisoner**) **in s. confinement,** (prisonnier) au secret; (*b*) (lieu) solitaire, retiré;

'solitude, s. (*a*) solitude *f*, isolement *m*; (*b*) lieu *m* solitaire; lieu inhabité.
solo, *pl.* **-os** ['soulou, -ouz], *s.* **1.** *Mus:* solo *m*; **to play s.**, jouer en solo; **violin s.**, solo de violon; **s. violin**, violon solo. **2.** *Cards:* **s. whist,** whist *m* de Gand. **3.** *Av:* **to make a s. flight,** voler seul; **'soloist,** *s. Mus:* soliste *mf*.
solstice ['solstis], *s. Astr:* solstice *m*.
soluble ['soljubl], *a.* **1.** (sel *m*) soluble. **2.** (problème) (ré)soluble; **solu'bility,** *s.* **1.** solubilité *f* (d'un sel). **2.** (ré)solution *f* (d'un problème).
solution [sə'lu:ʃ(ə)n], *s.* solution *f*. **1.** dissolution *f*. **2.** (*a*) (ré)solution *f* (d'une équation); (*b*) (*answer*) solution.
solve [solv], *v.tr.* résoudre (un problème); **to s. a riddle,** trouver le mot d'une énigme; **to s. an equation,** résoudre une équation; **'solvency,** *s. Com: etc:* solvabilité *f* (d'une affaire); **'solvent. 1.** *a. Com:* solvable. **2.** *a. & s.* dissolvant (*m*); *Ch:* solvant *m*.
Somalia [sə'mɑ:liə]. *Pr.n. Geog:* la (République démocratique de) Somalie.
sombre ['sombər], *a.* sombre, morne, **-ly,** *adv.* sombrement.
some [sʌm]. **I.** *a.* **1.** quelque, quelconque; (*a*) **he'll arrive s. day,** il arrivera un de ces jours; **I'll see you s. day this week,** je vous verrai dans le courant de la semaine; **s. other solution will have to be found,** il faudra trouver quelque autre solution; **s. way or another,** d'une manière ou d'une autre; **to make s. sort of reply,** répondre d'une façon quelconque; (*b*) **give it to s. lawyer or other,** remettez-le à n'importe quel notaire; **ask s. experienced person,** demandez l'avis de qn qui a de l'expérience. **2.** (*partitive*) de; **to drink s. water,** boire de l'eau; **to eat s. fruit,** manger des fruits. **3.** (*a*) quelque; **s. distance away,** à quelque distance; **after s. time,** après un, au bout d'un, certain temps; **s. days ago,** il y a quelques jours; **it takes s. time,** cela prend pas mal de temps; **at s. length,** assez longuement; (*b*) **there are s. others,** il y en a d'autres. **4.** *F:* (*intensive*) **it was s. dinner,** c'était un chic dîner; **he's s. doctor,** comme médecin, (i) c'est un as, (ii) *Pej:* il est plutôt quelconque. **II.** *pron.* **1.** (*pers.*) certains; **s. agree with us, and s. disagree,** les uns sont de notre avis, d'autres ne le sont pas. **2.** **I have s.,** j'en ai; **take s.!** prenez-en! **s. of them,** quelques-uns d'entre eux. **III.** *adv.* (*a*) environ, quelque *inv*; **s. twenty pounds,** une vingtaine de livres; (*b*) **I waited s. few minutes,** j'ai attendu quelques minutes.
somebody, someone ['sʌmbədi, 'sʌmwʌn], *s. or pron.* quelqu'un. **1.** **s.'s knocking,** on frappe. **2.** **he's (a) somebody,** c'est un personnage; **he thinks he's somebody,** il se croit quelqu'un.
somehow ['sʌmhau], *adv.* **1.** de façon ou

d'autre, d'une manière ou d'une autre. 2. I never liked him s., je ne sais pourquoi mais il ne m'a jamais été sympathique.

someplace ['sʌmpleis], adv. N.Am: quelque part; s. else, ailleurs.

somersault ['sʌməsɔ:lt], s. to turn a s., (i) Gym: faire le saut périlleux; (ii) (accidental) (of pers.) faire la culbute; (of car) capoter.

something ['sʌmθiŋ]. I. s. or pron. quelque chose m. 1. say s.! dites quelque chose! s. or other went wrong, je ne sais quoi a cloché; s. to drink, de quoi boire; to ask for s. to drink, demander à boire; I have s. else to do, j'ai autre chose à faire; the four s. train, le train de quatre heures quelque chose. 2. (a) perhaps we shall see s. of you now, peut-être que maintenant on vous verra un peu; (b) there's s. in what you say, il y a un fond de vérité dans ce que vous dites; there's s. in him, il a du fond; well, that's s.! bon, c'est toujours quelque chose! II. adv. quelque peu, tant soit peu; that's s. like a cigar! voilà un vrai cigare!

sometime ['sʌmtaim], adv. s. (or other), tôt ou tard; s. last year, au cours de l'année dernière; s. soon, bientôt, un de ces jours.

sometimes ['sʌmtaimz], adv. quelquefois, parfois; s. one, s. the other, tantôt l'un, tantôt l'autre.

somewhat ['sʌmwɔt]. 1. adv. quelque peu; un peu; tant soit peu; to be s. surprised, être passablement étonné. 2. s. he was s. of a coward, il était quelque peu poltron.

somewhere ['sʌmwɛər], adv. quelque part; s. else, ailleurs; autre part; s. or other, je ne sais où; s. in the world, de par le monde; he's s. about fifty, il a environ cinquante ans.

somnambulism [sɔm'næmbjulizm], s. somnambulisme m; **som'nambulist**, s. somnambule mf.

somnolence ['sɔmnələns], s. somnolence f; **'somnolent**, a. somnolent.

son [sʌn], s. fils m; **'son-in-law**, s. gendre m, beau-fils m.

sonar ['sounɑ:r], s. sonar m.

sonata [sə'nɑ:tə], s. Mus: sonate f.

song [sɔŋ], s. 1. chant m; to burst into s., se mettre tout à coup à chanter. 2. chanson f; **marching s.**, chanson de route; to buy sth. for a s., acheter qch. à vil prix; to make a s. (and dance) about sth., faire des histoires à propos de qch.; **'song bird**, s., **'songster**, s. (oiseau) chanteur (m); **'song thrush**, s. grive musicienne.

sonic ['sɔnik], a. sonique; Nau: s. depth-finder, sondeur m à écho; Av: s. barrier, mur m du son.

sonnet ['sɔnit], s. sonnet m.

sonorous ['sɔnərəs], a. sonore; **-ly**, adv. d'un ton sonore.

soon [su:n], adv. 1. (a) bientôt, tôt; s. after, bientôt après; tôt après; see you again s.! à bientôt! how s. can you be ready? en combien de temps serez-vous prêt? too s., trop tôt; avant l'heure; he escaped none too s., il s'est échappé juste à temps; (b) as s. as, aussitôt que, dès que; as s. as possible, le plus tôt possible; (c) I'd as s. stay, j'aime autant rester. 2. (a) the sooner the better, le plus tôt sera le mieux; sooner or later, tôt ou tard; no sooner said than done, aussitôt dit, aussitôt fait; (b) I'd sooner die, j'aimerais mieux mourir; plutôt mourir! I'd sooner come, j'aimerais mieux venir.

soot [sut], s. suie f; **'sooty**, a. couvert de suie; noir de suie.

soothe [su:ð], v.tr. calmer, apaiser (la douleur); tranquilliser (l'esprit de qn); **'soothing**, a. calmant, apaisant; **-ly**, adv. avec douceur.

sop [sɔp], v.tr. (**sopped** [sɔpt]) to s. up a liquid, éponger un liquide; **'sopping**, a. to be s. wet, être (tout) trempé; **'soppy**, a. F: (of pers.) mou; avachi.

sophistication [səfisti'keiʃ(ə)n], s. sophistication f; savoir-vivre m inv; usage m du monde; **so'phisticated**, a. (of pers.) aux goûts cultivés, Pej: compliqués; qui a du savoir-vivre, Pej: blasé.

sophomore ['sɔfəmɔ:r], s. N.Am: Sch: étudiant, -ante, de seconde année.

soporific [sɔpə'rifik], a. & s. soporifique (m); somnifère (m).

soprano, pl. -os [sə'prɑ:nou, -ouz], s. Mus: soprano mf.

sorcery ['sɔ:səri], s. sorcellerie f; **'sorcerer**, f. **'sorceress**, s. sorcier, -ière; magicien, -ienne.

sordid ['sɔ:did], a. sordide; sale, crasseux; **'sordidness**, s. sordidité f; saleté f; crasse f.

sore [sɔ:r]. I. a. 1. (a) douloureux, endolori; to be s. all over, avoir mal partout; (b) enflammé, irrité; s. throat, mal m de gorge; (c) that's his s. spot, c'est son endroit sensible. 2. chagriné; to be s. about sth., être fâché au sujet de qch. II. s. plaie f; blessure f; écorchure f; ulcère m; **'soreness**, s. 1. endolorissement m. 2. (a) chagrin m, peine f; (b) sentiment m de rancune.

sorrel¹ ['sɔrəl], s. Bot: oseille f; Cu: salts of s., sels m d'oseille; s. soup, soupe f à l'oseille.

sorrel², a. & s. (cheval) rouan roux.

sorrow ['sɔrou], s. peine f, chagrin m, tristesse f; to my s., à mon regret; **'sorrowful**, a. affligé, chagriné, triste; **-fully**, adv. tristement; **'sorry**, a. fâché, désolé, peiné; (I'm) s.! pardon! I'm so s. about it, j'en suis désolé; I'm extremely s., je regrette infiniment; I'm s. for him, je le plains.

sort [sɔ:t]. I. s. (a) sorte f, genre m, espèce f; a strange s. of fellow, un type bizarre; that's the

s. of man he is, il est comme ça; he looks a good s., il a l'air bon garçon; she's a (real) good s., c'est une brave fille; something of that s., quelque chose dans ce genre-là; nothing of the s.! pas du tout! I shall do nothing of the s., je n'en ferai rien; what s. of day is it? quel temps fait-il? I have a s. of idea that. . ., j'ai comme une idée, j'ai une sorte d'idée, que . . .; (b) Pej: we had coffee of a s., on nous a donné du soi-disant café; (c) to be out of sorts, être indisposé. II. v.tr. (a) trier, assortir; classer (des papiers); P.T.T: to s. the letters, trier les lettres; (b) to s. out the bad ones, trier les mauvais; 'sorter, s. (a) (pers.) trieur, -euse; classeur, -euse; (b) (machine) trieuse f; 'sorting, s. triage m, tri m; classement m; P.T.T: s. office, s. centre, centre m de tri.

sortie ['sɔ:ti], s. Mil: Av: sortie f, mission f.

soul [soul], s. âme f. 1. (a) with all my s., de tout mon cœur, de toute mon âme; (b) he's the s. of honour, il est l'honneur personnifié, la probité même; he's the life and s. of the party, c'est le boute-en-train de la soirée; he's the s. of the enterprise, c'est lui qui mène, fait marcher, l'affaire. 2. All Souls' Day, la fête des Morts. 3. (a) ship lost with all souls, navire perdu corps et biens; without meeting a living s., sans rencontrer âme qui vive; (b) poor s.! pauvre créature f! 'soul-destroying, a. (emploi) abrutissant; 'soulful, a. (a) plein d'âme; s. eyes, yeux expressifs; (b) sentimental; -fully, adv. (chanter) (i) avec expression, (ii) sentimentalement; 'soulless, a. sans âme; terre à terre; s. work, travail abrutissant, dégradant; 'soul-stirring, a. (discours, etc.) émouvant.

sound[1] [saund]. I. s. (a) son m, bruit m; (b) Av: the s. barrier, le mur du son; Cin: s. track, bande f sonore; s. wave, onde f sonore; s. engineer, ingénieur m du son; (c) (the science of) s., l'acoustique f; (d) to catch the s. of sth., entendre qch. à demi; I don't like the s. of it, cela ne me dit rien qui vaille. II. v. 1. v.i. (a) sonner; résonner; retentir; to s. hollow, sonner creux; (b) that sounds well in a speech, cela fait bon effet dans un discours; it sounded a long way off, on aurait dit que cela venait de loin; it sounds like Mozart, on dirait du Mozart. 2. v.tr. (a) sonner (la cloche, le tocsin); Aut: to s. the horn, klaxonner; (b) prononcer (une lettre); (c) Med: ausculter (un malade); 'sounding[1], s. résonnement m, retentissement m (du tambour, etc.); Med: auscultation f; 'soundless, a. silencieux; muet; -ly, adv. sans bruit; silencieusement; 'soundproof. I. a. isolant; insonore. II. v.tr. insonoriser.

sound[2], v.tr. Nau: sonder; abs. prendre le fond; 'sounding[2], s. Nau: sondage m; to take soundings, sonder, prendre le fond; s. balloon, ballon-sonde m.

sound[3], s. détroit m; goulet m.

sound[4], a. 1. (a) sain; of s. mind, sain d'esprit; (of pers.) to be s. in wind and limb = avoir bon pied bon œil; (b) en bon état; pas endommagé; s. timber, bois sans tare; s. fruit, fruits sains. 2. (a) s. financial position, situation financière solide; s. statesman, homme d'état au jugement sain; (b) (argument) valide; (raisonnement m) juste; it isn't s. finance, ce n'est pas de la finance sérieuse. 3. s. sleep, sommeil profond; -ly, adv. 1. sainement; judicieusement. 2. to sleep s., dormir profondément; dormir à poings fermés; 'soundness, s. 1. état sain (d'esprit); bon état (des marchandises). 2. solidité f (d'une maison de commerce); solidité (d'un argument); justesse f (d'un jugement).

soup [su:p], s. soupe f, potage m; thick s., crème f, purée f; clear s., consommé m; F: to be in the s., être dans le pétrin; s. ladle, louche f; s. plate, assiette creuse; s. tureen, soupière f; 'soup 'up, v.tr. F: gonfler, agrandir (la puissance de qch.); Aut: souped-up engine, moteur gonflé; souped-up publicity campaign, publicité exagérée, mensongère.

sour ['sauər], a. 1. (a) (fruit m) aigre, acide; (b) to turn s., tourner à l'aigre; to turn sth. s., (faire) aigrir qch.; to smell s., sentir l'aigre. 2. (of pers.) revêche; aigre; -ly, adv. avec aigreur; 'sourish, a. aigrelet; 'sourness, s. 1. aigreur f, acidité f (d'un fruit). 2. (of pers.) aigreur; humeur f revêche.

source [sɔ:s], s. source f; to trace a tradition back to its s., remonter aux sources, à l'origine, d'une tradition.

souse [saus], v.tr. (a) Cu: faire mariner (un aliment); (b) plonger, immerger (in, dans); (c) tremper, noyer (qch., qn) (with water, d'eau).

south [sauθ]. 1. a. & s. sud (m); on the s. (of), au sud (de); the S. of France, le Midi (de la France). 2. adv. au sud; to travel s., voyager vers le sud; South 'Africa. Pr.n. la République de l'Afrique du Sud, la République sud-africaine; South-'African, a. & s. sud-africain, -aine; south-'east. 1. s. sud-est m. 2. adv. vers le sud-est. 3. a. du sud-est; south-'easterly, a., south-'eastern, a. du sud-est; 'southerly ['sʌð-], a. (a) (vent) du sud; (b) s. aspect, exposition f au midi; 'southern ['sʌð-], a. (du) sud; méridional; s. lights, aurore australe; the S. Cross, la Croix du Sud; 'southerner ['sʌð-], s. habitant, -ante, du sud; méridional, -ale; U.S: Hist: sudiste mf; 'southwards, adv. vers le sud; south-'west. 1. s. sud-ouest m. 2. adv. vers le sud-ouest. 3. a. du sud-ouest; south-'wester [sau'westər], s. vent m du sud-ouest; south-'westerly, a., south-'western, a. du sud-ouest.

souvenir [su:və'ni(:)ər], s. souvenir m.

sou'wester [sau'westər], s. Cl: chapeau m im-

perméable; suroît *m*.
sovereign ['sɔvrin]. **1.** *s.* souverain, -aine. **2.** souverain *m* (ancienne pièce en or, valeur £1); **'sovereignty,** *s.* souveraineté *f*.
Soviet ['souvjǝt, 'sɔv-], *s.* soviet *m*; **S. Union,** Union *f* soviétique; **Union of S. Socialist Republics (USSR),** Union des Républiques socialistes soviétiques (URSS).
sow¹ [sou], *v.tr.* (sowed; sown) semer; **to s. land with wheat,** ensemencer une terre en blé; **to s. discord,** semer, répandre, la discorde; **'sowing,** *s.* semailles *fpl,* semis *m*; **s. machine,** semoir *m*; **s. season,** semaison *f*; **'sower,** *s.* semeur, -euse.
sow² [sau], *s.* truie *f*.
sow-thistle ['sauθisl], *s. Bot:* laiteron *m*.
soya ['sɔiǝ], *s.* soja *m*; **s. bean,** soja, soya *m*; **s. sauce,** sauce *f* soja.
spa [spɑ:], *s.* ville *f* d'eau; station thermale.
space [speis]. **I.** *s.* **1.** espace *m*, intervalle *m* (de temps). **2.** (*a*) l'espace; *attrib.* spatial; **s. flight,** voyage spatial; **s. port,** base *f* de lancement de fusées spatiales; **s. station,** station spatiale; **s. suit,** scaphandre *m* d'astronaute; vêtement *m* anti-g.; **s. travel,** l'astronautique *f*; **s. race,** course *f* interplanétaire; (*b*) **in a confined s.,** dans un espace restreint; **to take up a lot of s.,** occuper beaucoup de place. **3.** espace libre; espacement *m,* intervalle; **s. between two things,** écartement *m* de deux choses; **blank s.,** blanc *m*; **sign in the s. indicated,** signez dans la case indiquée. **II.** *v.tr.* **to s.** (**out**), espacer; échelonner (des paiements); **'spacecraft,** *s.* vaisseau spatial; **spaceman,** *pl.* **-men,** *s.* (*a*) habitant *m* de l'espace; (*b*) cosmonaute *m*; **'space-saving,** *a.* compact; **'spaceship,** *s.* vaisseau spatial; **'spacing,** *s.* (*a*) espacement *m,* écartement *m*; échelonnement *m*; *Typ:* espacement; *Typew:* **in single, double, s.,** à interligne simple, double; **'spacious,** *a.* vaste, spacieux; (*of garment*) ample; **'spaciousness,** *s.* (*a*) vaste étendue *f*; proportions spacieuses (d'une salle).
spade¹ [speid], *s. Tls:* bêche *f*; (*child's*) pelle *f*; **to call a s. a s.,** appeler les choses par leur nom; **s.-work,** *s.* travaux *m* préliminaires (en vue d'une enquête, etc.).
spade², *s. Cards:* pique *m*.
spaghetti [spǝ'geti], *s. Cu:* spaghetti *mpl*.
Spain [spein]. *Pr.n.* l'Espagne *f*.
span [spæn]. **I.** *s.* **1.** (*of bird, aircraft*) **wing s.,** envergure *f*. **2.** ouverture *f,* largeur *f* (d'une voûte, d'une arche); écartement *m* (de deux piliers); travée *f* (d'un pont). **II.** *v.tr.* (spanned) (*of bridge, etc.*) franchir, enjamber (un ravin, etc.).
Spaniard ['spænjǝd], *s.* Espagnol, -ole.
spaniel ['spænjǝl], *s.* épagneul *m*.
Spanish ['spæniʃ]. **1.** *a.* espagnol; **S. onion,**

oignon d'Espagne. **2.** *s. Ling:* l'espagnol *m*; **'Spanish-A'merican,** *a.* hispano-américain; ibéro-américain.
spank [spæŋk], *v.tr.* fesser (un enfant); **'spanking,** *s.* fessée *f*.
spanner ['spænǝr], *s.* clef *f* (à écrous); **adjustable s.,** clef anglaise, clef à molette; **to throw a s. in the works,** mettre des bâtons dans les roues.
spar¹ [spɑ:r], *s. Nau:* (*a*) espar *m*; (*b*) *pl.* **the spars,** la mâture.
spar². **I.** *s. Box:* combat *m* d'entraînement. **II.** *v.i.* (sparred) **to s. up to s.o.,** se mettre en posture de combat; **sparring match,** combat d'entraînement; **sparring partner,** partenaire *m* (d'un boxeur).
spare ['spɛǝr]. **I.** *a.* **1.** **in my s. time,** à mes moments perdus; **s.-time activities,** les loisirs *m*; **s. capital,** fonds *m* disponibles; **s. room,** chambre *f* d'ami(s). **2.** *Aut: etc:* **s. parts, s. spares,** pièces *f* de rechange, pièces détachées; **s. engine,** moteur *m* de remplacement; **s. wheel,** roue *f* de secours. **II.** *v.tr.* **1.** épargner, ménager; **to s. no expense,** ne pas regarder à la dépense; **to s. no pains,** ne pas ménager, marchander, sa peine. **2.** (*a*) se passer de (qch.); **can you s. it?** pouvez-vous vous en passer? **we can s. him,** nous n'avons pas besoin de lui; **to have nothing to s.,** n'avoir que le strict nécessaire; **to have enough and to s.,** avoir plus qu'il ne faut (de qch.); (*b*) **I can't s. the time,** je n'ai pas le temps; le temps me fait défaut; **can you s. me a few moments?** pouvez vous m'accorder quelques moments? **3.** faire grâce à (qn); **to s. s.o.'s life,** épargner la vie à qn; **to s. s.o.'s feelings,** ménager qn; **'sparing,** *a.* **to be s. with the butter,** épargner, ménager le beurre; **he's s. of praise,** il est avare de louanges; **s. of words,** sobre de paroles; **-ly** *adv.* frugalement; (manger) sobrement; **to use sth. s.,** ménager qch.
spark [spɑ:k]. **I.** *s.* (*a*) étincelle *f*; (*from fire*) flammèche *f*; (*b*) *El:* étincelle; *Aut: etc:* **s. ignition,** allumage *m* par étincelle. **II.** *v.i.* émettre des étincelles; **'sparking,** *s. El:* (i) émission, (ii) (*accidental*) jaillissement *m,* d'étincelles; *Aut: etc:* **s. plug,** bougie *f*.
sparkle ['spɑ:kl]. **I.** *s.* **1.** brève lueur. **2.** étincellement *m*; éclat *m* (des yeux); feux *mpl* (d'un diamant). **II.** *v.i.* (*a*) étinceler, scintiller; (*of jewel*) chatoyer; (*b*) (*of wine*) pétiller; **'sparkling,** *a.* (*a*) étincelant, brillant; (*b*) (*of wine*) mousseux.
sparrow ['spærou], *s. Orn:* moineau *m,* passereau *m*; **hedge s.,** fauvette *f* d'hiver; **'sparrowhawk,** *s. Orn:* épervier *m*.
sparse [spɑ:s], *a.* clairsemé, épars; **s. population,** population clairsemée; **-ly,** *adv.* peu abondamment; **s. populated,** peu peuplé.
spartan ['spɑ:tǝn], *a.* spartiate; **s. life,** vie

austère; **s. meal,** repas *m* spartiate.
spasm ['spæz(ə)m], *s.* accès *m* (de toux, de jalousie); **to work in spasms,** travailler par à-coups; **spas'modic,** *a.* **1.** *Med:* spasmodique; convulsif; (saut) involontaire. **2.** (travail) fait par à-coups; **-ally,** *adv.* (travailler) par à-coups.
spastic ['spæstik]. *Med:* **1.** *a.* (paralysie *f*) spasmodique, spastique. **2.** *s.* personne atteinte de paralysie spasmodique.
spate [speit], *s.* crue *f*; **river in s.,** rivière *f* en crue; **to have a s. of work,** être débordé de travail.
spatial ['speiʃ(ə)l], *a.* spatial; dans l'espace; concernant l'espace.
spatter ['spætər], *v.tr.* **to s. s.o. with mud,** éclabousser qn de boue.
spatula ['spætjulə], *s.* spatule *f*.
spawn [spɔːn]. **I.** *s.* frai *m*; œufs *mpl* (de poisson); **mushroom s.,** blanc *m* de champignon. **II.** *v.i.* (*of fish*) frayer.
speak [spiːk], *v.* (spoke [spouk]; spoken) **1.** *v.i.* (*a*) parler; **without speaking,** sans rien dire; (*b*) **to s. to s.o.,** parler à qn; s'adresser à qn; **I'll s. to him about it,** je lui en toucherai un mot; **I know him to s. to,** je le connais assez pour lui dire bonjour; **to s. to s.o.,** causer avec qn; **speaking for myself,** pour ma part; **roughly speaking,** approximativement; *P.T.T:* **who's speaking?** qui est à l'appareil? c'est de la part de qui? (*c*) **the facts s. for themselves,** ces faits se passent de commentaire; (*d*) faire un discours; prendre la parole. **2.** *v.tr.* (*a*) dire (un mot, sa pensée); **to s. the truth,** dire la vérité; (*b*) parler; **do you s. French?** parlez-vous français? **'speaker,** *s.* **1.** parleur, -euse; orateur *m*; **to be a fluent s.,** avoir la parole facile. **2.** *Pol:* **the S.** = le Président (des Communes); **'speak 'for,** *v.i.* (*a*) **to s. for s.o.,** parler, plaider, pour qn; (*b*) **that speaks well for your courage,** cela en dit long sur votre courage; **'speaking,** *a. & s.* **1.** *a.* **a s. likeness,** un portrait très ressemblant, vivant; **English-s.,** anglophone. **2.** *s.* parler *m*; parole *f*; **plain s.,** franchise *f*, franc-parler *m*; **not to be on s. terms (with s.o.),** s'être brouillé (avec qn); **public s.,** l'art *m* oratoire; **'speak of,** *v.i.* parler de (qn, qch.); **she has no voice to s. of,** elle n'a pour ainsi dire pas de voix; **to s. well of s.o.,** dire du bien de qn; **'speak 'out,** *v.i.* parler franchement; trancher le mot; **'speak 'up,** *v.i.* **1.** parler plus haut. **2. to s. up for s.o.,** parler en faveur de qn.
spear ['spiər], *s.* **1.** (*a*) lance *f*; (*b*) (*for throwing*) javelot *m*, javeline *f*. **2.** *Fish:* foëne *f*; harpon *m*; **'spearmint,** *s.* menthe verte.
special ['speʃ(ə)l]. **I.** *a.* (*a*) spécial; particulier; **s. feature,** particularité *f*; *Journ:* **s. correspondent,** envoyé spécial; **to make a s. study of sth.,**

se spécialiser en qch.; *Com:* **s. price,** prix de faveur, d'ami; (*b*) **s. friend,** ami(e) intime; **I've nothing s. to tell you,** je n'ai rien de particulier à vous dire; **-ally,** *adv.* spécialement, particulièrement; surtout. **II.** *s.* (*a*) édition spéciale (d'un journal); (*b*) *F:* citoyen *m* faisant fonction d'agent de police; (*c*) (*in restaurant*) **today's s.,** plat *m* du jour; **'specialist,** *s.* spécialiste *mf*; **heart s.,** cardiologue *mf*; **speciality** [speʃi'æliti], *s.* **1.** spécialité *f*; **that's my s.,** c'est mon fort. **2.** qualité particulière; particularité *f*; **speciali'zation,** *s.* spécialisation *f*; **'specialize,** *v.i.* se spécialiser (**in,** dans).
species ['spiːʃiːz], *s. inv.* **1.** *Nat.Hist:* espèce *f*; **closely related s.,** espèces voisines. **2.** espèce, sorte *f*.
specify ['spesifai], *v.tr.* spécifier, déterminer; **specified load,** charge prévue; **unless otherwise specified,** sauf indication contraire; **spe'cific,** *a.* (*a*) spécifique; *Ph:* **s. gravity,** poids *m* spécifique; (*b*) (*of statement*) précis; (*of order*) explicite; **s. aim,** but déterminé; **-ally,** *adv.* **1.** spécifiquement. **2.** précisément; **specifi'cation,** *s.* (*a*) spécification *f* (des détails); (*b*) (*usu. pl.*) devis descriptif; **specifications of a car,** caractéristiques *f* d'une voiture.
specimen ['spesimin], *s.* (*a*) spécimen *m*; (*b*) exemple *m*, échantillon *m*; (*c*) *F:* (*of pers.*) **queer s.,** drôle *m* de type.
specious ['spiːʃəs], *a.* spécieux; trompeur; captieux; **'speciousness,** *s.* apparence trompeuse (de qch., qn).
speck [spek], *s.* **1.** petite tache; point *m*; moucheture *f*. **2.** grain *m*, atome *m*; **s. on the horizon,** point noir à l'horizon. **3.** (*on fruit, etc.*) défaut *m*; tavelure *f*; **'speckled,** *a.* tacheté, moucheté; (*of plumage*) grivelé.
specs [speks], *s.pl. F:* lunettes *f*.
spectacle ['spektəkl], *s.* **1.** spectacle *m*. **2.** *pl.* lunettes *f*; **s. case,** étui *m* à lunettes; **spec'tacular** [-'tæk-], *a.* spectaculaire; **spec'tator** [-'teit-], *s.* spectateur, -trice; assistant, -ante; **the spectators,** l'assistance *f*.
spectre ['spektər], *s.* spectre *m*, fantôme *m*.
spectrum, *pl.* **-tra** ['spektrəm, -trə], *s. Ph:* spectre *m*; **the colours of the s.,** les couleurs spectrales.
speculate ['spekjuleit], *v.i.* **1. to s. about sth.,** faire des conjectures sur qch. **2.** *Fin:* spéculer (**in,** sur); **specu'lation,** *s.* **1.** (*a*) spéculation *f*, méditation *f* (**on,** sur); (*b*) conjecture *f*. **2.** (*a*) *Fin:* spéculation; (*b*) entreprise spéculative; **good s.,** bonne affaire; **'speculative,** *a.* **1.** (*a*) spéculatif, contemplatif; (*b*) conjectural. **2.** *Fin:* spéculatif; **'speculator,** *s. Fin:* spéculateur, -trice; joueur *m* à la Bourse; agioteur, -euse.
speech [spiːtʃ], *s.* **1.** (*a*) (**faculty of**) **s.,** la parole; **to lose the power of s.,** perdre la parole; (*b*) **to**

be slow of s., parler lentement; (c) *Gram:* **parts of s.,** parties *f* du discours. **2.** langue *f* (d'un peuple); parler *m.* **3.** discours *m;* **to make a s.,** faire, prononcer, un discours. **4.** *Sch:* **s. day,** distribution *f* des prix; **'speechless,** *a.* **1.** incapable de parler. **2.** interdit, interloqué; muet (de surprise).

speed [spi:d]. **I.** *s.* vitesse *f;* rapidité *f;* **at full s.,** **at top s.,** au plus vite; (*of car*) à toute vitesse, à toute allure, à fond de train; **maximum s.,** vitesse limite, pleine allure; *Aut: etc:* (vitesse) plafond (*m*); *F:* **s. merchant,** chauffard *m; F:* **s. cop,** motard *m; Av:* **ground s.,** vitesse vraie; **air s.,** vitesse propre; **to pick up s.,** prendre de la vitesse. **II.** *v.* (**speeded,** *occ.* **sped**) **1.** *v.tr.* **to s. up the work,** activer, accélérer, les travaux. **2.** *v.i. Aut:* faire de la vitesse, foncer; **'speedboat,** *s.* canot-automobile *m;* hors-bord *m;* **'speeding,** *s. Aut:* excès *m* de vitesse; **spee'dometer,** *s.* indicateur *m* de vitesse; **'speedway,** *s. Aut:* **1.** *N.Am:* autoroute *f.* **2.** piste *f* (d'autodrome); **'speedy,** *a.* rapide, prompt.

speleology [spi:li'ɔlədʒi], *s.* spéléologie *f;* **spele'ologist,** *s.* spéléologue *mf.*

spell[1] [spel], *s.* **1.** incantation *f;* formule *f* magique. **2.** charme *m,* maléfice *m;* **to cast a s. over s.o.,** jeter un sort sur qn; ensorceler qn; **'spellbound,** *a.* ensorcelé, magnétisé; figé sur place; **to hold one's audience s.,** tenir ses auditeurs sous le charme.

spell[2], *v.tr.* (**spelled** *or* **spelt**) **1.** épeler; (*in writing*) orthographier (un mot); **he can't s.,** il ne sait pas l'orthographe; **to s. out sth.,** déchiffrer, lire, qch. péniblement; **how is it spelt?** comment cela s'écrit-il? **2.** **what do these letters s.?** quel mot forment ces lettres? **3.** signifier; **that would s. disaster!** ce serait le désastre! **'spelling,** *s.* orthographe *f.*

spell[3], *s.* **1.** tour *m* (de travail, etc.); **to do a s. of duty,** faire un tour de service; **to take spells at the pumps,** se relayer aux pompes; **three hours at a s.,** trois heures de suite. **2.** (courte) période; **a. s. of cold weather,** une période de froid; **during the cold s.,** pendant le coup de froid; **a new s. of cold,** une reprise du froid.

spend [spend], *v.tr.* (**spent**) **1.** dépenser; **to s. money on s.o.,** faire des dépenses pour qn; **without spending a penny,** sans bourse délier, sans rien débourser; *F:* **to s. a penny,** aller faire pipi. **2.** **to s. care, time, on sth.,** consacrer du soin, du temps, à qch. **3.** passer, employer (son temps); **to s. Monday working,** passer lundi à travailler. **4.** **to s. oneself,** s'épuiser; **'spending,** *s.* dépense *f;* **s. power,** pouvoir *m* d'achat; **'spendthrift,** *a.* & *s.* dépensier, -ière; gaspilleur, -euse; **s. habits,** habitudes dépensières.

sperm [spə:m], *s.* **1.** sperme *m.* **2.** *Z:* **s.-whale,** cachalot *m;* **sperm 'oil,** *s.* huile *f* de baleine.

sphere ['sfi(:)ər], *s.* **1.** sphère *f.* **2.** (*a*) milieu *m,*

sphère; (*b*) limited s., cadre restreint; **that doesn't come within my s.,** cela ne rentre pas dans ma compétence; **s. of influence,** sphère, zone *f,* d'influence; **in the political s.,** sur le plan politique; **spherical** ['sfe-], *a.* sphérique.

sphinx [sfiŋks], *s.* sphinx *m;* **'sphinx-like,** *a.* (sourire) de sphinx.

spice [spais]. **I.** *s.* (*coll. sg. usu. preferred to pl.*) épice *f,* aromate *m;* **mixed spice(s),** épices mélangées; **to give s. to a story,** pimenter un récit; **the s. of adventure,** le piment de l'aventure. **II.** *v.tr.* épicer (un mets); pimenter (un récit); **'spiciness,** *s.* (*a*) goût épicé; (*b*) piquant *m,* sel *m* (d'un récit); **'spicy,** *a.* **1.** (*of food*) épicé; (goût) relevé. **2.** (*of story, etc.*) (i) piquant; (ii) salé, épicé.

spick and span ['spikən(d)'spæn], *adj.phr.* reluisant de propreté; (*of pers.*) tiré à quatre épingles.

spider ['spaidər], *s.* araignée *f;* **'spidery,** *a.* **1. s. handwriting,** pattes *fpl* d'araignée. **2. a s. attic,** un grenier infesté d'araignées.

spiel [spi:l], *s. F:* boniment *m, F:* baratin *m.*

spigot ['spigət], *s.* **1.** fausset *m,* broche *f* (de tonneau). **2.** *N.Am:* robinet *m.*

spike [spaik], *s.* pointe *f;* piquant *m* (de fil barbelé); pointe (de chaussures de course).

spill [spil]. **I.** *v.* (**spilt** *or* **spilled**) **1.** *v.tr.* répandre, renverser (du vin, de l'eau); verser (du sang); *F:* **to s. the beans,** avouer, *F:* vendre la mèche. **2.** *v.i.* (*of liquid*) se répandre; **to s. (away),** s'écouler. **II.** *s.* **to have a s.,** culbuter; (*from bicycle, etc.*) *F:* ramasser une pelle, une bûche.

spin [spin]. **I.** *v.* (**span; spun**) **1.** *v.tr.* (*a*) filer (la laine); (*b*) **to s. a coin,** jouer à pile ou face; (*c*) *Fish:* pêcher à la cuiller. **2.** *v.i.* (*of wheel, etc.*) tourner; (*of aircraft*) descendre en vrille; (*of compass*) s'affoler; **to s. round and round,** tournoyer; **my head's spinning,** la tête me tourne; **blow that sent him spinning,** coup qui l'a envoyé rouler. **II.** *s.* tournoiement *m;* Av: **(tail) s.,** vrille *f;* **flat s.** (i) *Av:* tonneau *m;* (ii) *F:* panique *f;* **to get into a flat s.,** ne (pas) savoir où donner de la tête; **'spin drier,** *s.* essoreuse *f;* **'spinner,** *s.* fileur, -euse; **'spinning,** *s.* (*a*) filage *m;* (*b*) *Ind:* filature *f;* **s. wheel,** rouet *m;* **'spin 'out,** *v.tr.* faire traîner (une affaire) en longueur; délayer (un discours).

spinach ['spinidʒ], *s. Cu:* épinards *mpl.*

spindle [spindl], *s.* **1.** *Tex:* fuseau *m.* **2.** *E:* mandrin *m;* axe *m* (de pompe); arbre *m* (de tour).

spindrift ['spindrift], *s.* embrun *m;* poudrin *m.*

spine [spain], *s.* **1.** *Anat:* épine dorsale; colonne vertébrale. **2.** dos *m* (d'un livre); **'spinal,** *a.* spinal; **s. column,** colonne vertébrale; **s. complaint,** maladie *f* de la moelle épinière; **'spineless,** *a.* (*of pers.*) mou; qui manque de caractère; **'spiny,** *a.* épineux; couvert de piquants *mpl.*

spinney ['spini], s. petit bois; bosquet m.

spinster ['spinstər], s. (a) Adm: célibataire f; (b) vieille fille.

spiraea [spai'ri:ə], s. Bot: spirée f.

spiral ['spaiərəl]. I. s. (a) spirale f, hélice f; (b) Av: montée f, descente f, en spirale; (c) **wage-price s.**, montée en flèche des prix et des salaires. II. a. spiral; en spiral; vrillé; s. **spring**, ressort m en boudin; s. **staircase**, escalier m en colimaçon. III. v.i. (**spiralled**) tourner en spirale; (of smoke) tire(-)bouchonner; (of rocket, etc.) **to s. up**, vriller.

spire ['spaiər], s. aiguille f, flèche f (d'église).

spirit ['spirit]. I. s. 1. esprit m, âme f; **the Holy S.**, le Saint-Esprit. 2. **the leading s.**, l'âme, le chef, le meneur (d'une entreprise). 3. esprit, disposition f; **party s.**, l'esprit du parti; **to enter into the s. of sth.**, entrer de bon cœur dans (la partie); **to take sth. in the wrong s.**, prendre qch. en mauvaise part, de travers; **that's the s.!** à la bonne heure! **to show s.**, montrer du caractère, du courage; **to be in high spirits**, être en train, en forme; **to be in low spirits**, être abattu, accablé; **to keep up one's spirits**, ne pas perdre courage; **their spirits rose**, ils reprenaient courage. 4. usu. pl. (a) spiritueux mpl; alcool m; (b) **surgical s.** = alcool à 90°. II. v.tr. **to s. sth. away**, subtiliser, escamoter, qch.; '**spirited**, a. (of pers.) (**high-)s.**, vif, animé; **he gave a s. performance**, il a joué avec verve; '**spirit-level**, s. Tls: niveau m à bulle d'air; '**spiritual**, a. (a) de l'esprit; (b) immatériel.

piritualism ['spiritjuəlizm], s. Psychics: spiritisme m; '**spiritualist**, a. & s. spirite (mf).

pit[1] [spit]. I. s. 1. Cu: broche f. 2. Geog: flèche littorale. II. v.tr. (**spitted**) embrocher, brocheter, mettre à la broche (un rôti).

pit[2]. I. v. (**spat**) 1. v.i. cracher; **it's spitting (with rain)**, il tombe quelques gouttes; (of engine) **to s. back**, avoir des retours m de flamme (au carburateur). 2. v.tr. cracher (du sang); **to s. sth. out**, cracher qch. II. s. crachat m; F: **he's the dead s. of his father**, c'est son père tout craché; F: **s. and polish**, astiquage m; '**spitting**. I. s. crachement m. II. a. F: **he's the s. image of his father**, c'est son père tout craché; '**spittle**, s. salive f, crachat m.

pite [spait]. I. s. 1. rancune f; malveillance f; dépit m; **to have a s. against s.o.**, en vouloir à qn. 2. prep.phr. **in s. of**, en dépit de; malgré. II. v.tr. **to do sth. to s. s.o.**, faire qch. pour contrarier, vexer, qn; '**spiteful**, a. rancunier, vindicatif, méchant, malveillant; s. **tongue**, langue f de vipère; **-fully**, adv. par dépit, par rancune, par méchanceté; méchamment; '**spitefulness**, s. méchanceté f; rancœur f; malveillance f.

plash [splæʃ]. I. s. 1. éclaboussement m;

clapotis m (des vagues); **to make a s.**, (i) faire sensation; (ii) jeter l'argent par la fenêtre; Journ: **s. headline**, grosse manchette. 2. (a) éclaboussure f (de boue, etc.); (b) tache f (de couleur, de lumière); (c) flaque f (d'eau). II. v. 1. v.tr. (a) éclabousser (**with**, de); (b) **to s. one's money about**, prodiguer son argent, jeter son argent par la fenêtre. 2. v.i. (of liquid) rejaillir en éclaboussures; (of waves) clapoter; (of tap) cracher; **to s. up**, gicler; barboter, patauger (dans l'eau); **to s. about in the water**, s'agiter dans l'eau; '**splash 'down**, v.i. (of spacecraft) amerrir; '**splash-down**, s. amerrissage m (d'un engin spatial).

splendid ['splendid], a. splendide; superbe; magnifique; **that's s.!** à la bonne heure! **-ly**, adv. splendidement; magnifiquement; '**splendour**, s. splendeur f, magnificence f, éclat m.

splint [splint], s. Surg: éclisse f, attelle f; **to put a limb in splints**, éclisser un membre.

splinter ['splintər]. I. s. 1. éclat m (de bois, etc.); écharde (logée sous la peau). 2. Pol: **s. group**, groupe m fractionnaire. II. v.i. voler en éclats; éclater; '**splintered**, a. (bois m) en éclats; (os m) en esquilles.

split [split]. I. s. 1. fente f; fissure f; crevasse f (dans une roche). 2. division f; rupture f (dans un parti politique, etc.). 3. **banana s.**, banane fourrée à la crème et à la glace; **cream s.**, brioche fourrée à la crème. 4. Gym: **to do the splits**, faire le grand écart. II. v. (**split**) 1. v.tr. fendre (du bois); **to s. a hide**, dédoubler une peau; Ph: **to s. the atom**, diviser l'atome. 2. v.i. (a) se fendre; (b) (of cloth) so déchirer; (c) F: **my head's splitting**, j'ai un mal de tête fou; (d) F: **to s. on s.o.**, dénoncer qn; vendre (un complice). III. a. 1. fendu; F: **s. peas**, pois cassés; **in a s. second**, en un rien de temps. 2. **s. personality**, dédoublement m de la personnalité; '**split 'up**, v.tr. & i. (se) fractionner, (se) diviser; **the party s. up into three groups**, le parti s'est divisé en trois groupes.

splodge, splotch [splɔdʒ, splɔtʃ], s. F: tache f (de couleur).

splutter ['splʌtər], v.i. (a) (of pers.) lancer de la salive (en parlant), F: postillonner; (b) (of pers.) bredouiller, bafouiller; (c) Aut: (of engine) bafouiller.

spoil [spɔil], v. (**spoiled** or **spoilt**) 1. v.tr. (a) gâter, endommager, abîmer, gâcher (qch.); **to s. a piece of work**, gâcher un travail; (b) gâter (un enfant). 2. v.i. (of fruit, etc.) se gâter, s'abîmer; s'avarier, s'altérer; **spoils**, s.pl. (a) butin m; **to claim one's share of the s.**, demander sa part du gâteau; (b) Min: etc: déblai(s) m(pl); '**spoilsport**, s. trouble-fête m inv; gâte-tout m inv; **spoilt**, a. gâté, abîmé, avarié; **s. child**, enfant gâté.

spoke [spouk], s. 1. rayon m (de roue). 2.

échelon *m* (d'échelle); **to put a s. in the wheel,** mettre des bâtons dans les roues.

spokesman, *pl.* **-men** ['spouksmən], *s.* porte-parole *m inv.*

sponge [spʌn(d)ʒ]. **I.** *s.* **1.** éponge *f*; **to throw up the s.,** s'avouer vaincu; quitter la partie. **2. s. cake,** (i) gâteau *m* de Savoie; (ii) = madeleine; **s. finger,** biscuit *m* à la cuiller. **II.** *v.* **1.** *v.tr.* éponger (qch.). **2.** *v.i. F:* **to s. on s.o.,** vivre aux crochets de qn; **to s. on s.o. for drinks,** se faire payer des tournées par qn; **'sponger,** *s.* parasite *m*; écornifleur, -euse; *F:* pique-assiette *m inv*; **'spongy,** *a.* spongieux.

sponsor ['spɒnsər]. **I.** *s.* **1.** garant *m*, caution *f* (**for s.o.,** de qn). **2.** (*at baptism*) parrain *m*, marraine *f.* **II.** *v.tr.* être le garant de, répondre pour (qn); parrainer (qn); *Rad: etc:* offrir (un programme); **'sponsorship,** *s.* parrainage *m.*

spontaneous [spɒn'teinjəs], *a.* spontané; -ly, *adv.* **spontanément; spontaneity** [spɒntə'niːiti], *s.*, **spon'taneousness,** *s.* spontanéité *f.*

spool [spuːl], *s.* bobine *f* (de coton); (*of sewing machine, loom*) cannette *f*; *Typew:* **ribbon spools,** bobines du ruban.

spoon [spuːn], *s.* cuiller *f*, cuillère *f*; **s. and fork,** couvert *m*; **dessert s.,** cuiller à dessert; **soup s.,** cuiller à potage; **tea s.** = cuiller à café; **'spoon-feed,** *v.tr.* (-fed) nourrir (un enfant) à la cuiller; *F:* mâcher les morceaux à (un élève); subventionner (une industrie); **'spoonful,** *s.* cuillerée *f.*

spoor ['spuər], *s.* foulées *fpl*, erre *f* (d'un cerf, etc.).

sporadic [spɒ'rædik], *a.* sporadique; -ally, *adv.* sporadiquement.

sport [spɔːt], *s.* **1.** (*a*) jeu *m*, divertissement *m*; **to make s. of s.o.,** se moquer de qn; (*b*) (*of fox-hunting, fishing, shooting*) **to have good s.,** faire bonne chasse, bonne pêche. **2.** sport *m*; **school sports,** fête (annuelle) d'athlétisme; *attrib. Aut:* **sports car, model,** voiture *f*, modèle *m*, grand sport; **sports ground,** terrain *m* de jeux; stade *m*; **sports jacket,** veston *m* sport; **sports equipment,** accessoires *mpl*, fournitures *fpl*, articles *mpl*, de sport. **3.** *F:* **he's a good s.,** (i) c'est un beau joueur; (ii) c'est un chic type; **'sporting,** *a.* **s. man,** amateur *m* de sport; **in a s. spirit,** sportivement; **you've a s. chance,** ça vaut la peine d'essayer le coup; **'sportsman,** *pl.* **-men,** *f.* **-woman,** *pl.* **-women,** *s.* **1.** chasseur, -euse; pêcheur, -euse. **2.** amateur *m* de sport; sportif, -ive; **a real s.,** un beau joueur; un vrai sportif; **'sportsmanlike,** *a.* (conduite *f*) digne d'un beau joueur, d'un vrai sportif; **'sportsmanship,** *s.* **1.** qualités *fpl* d'un vrai sportif; pratique *f* des sports. **2.** sportivité *f*, esprit sportif.

spot [spɒt]. **I.** *s.* **1.** (*a*) endroit *m*, lieu *m*; **you should always be on the s.,** vous devez toujours être là; (*b*) *adv.phr.* **on the s.,** sur-le-champ; immédiatement; **to be killed on the s.,** être tué raide; *F:* **to be on the s.,** être dans une situation dangereuse; *F:* **to put s.o. on the s.,** mettre qn dans une situation difficile; (*c*) *Com:* **s. cash,** argent comptant; (*d*) **to put one's finger on a weak s.,** mettre le doigt sur un point faible. **2.** tache *f*; (*on face*) bouton *m*. **3.** pois *m*; **blue tie with red spots,** cravate bleue à pois rouges; **a leopard's spots,** la moucheture d'un léopard; **the blind s.,** (i) *Anat:* la papille optique; (ii) *Aut:* angle *m* aveugle; (*radar*) **scanning s.,** spot explorateur; *F:* **to knock spots off s.o.,** battre qn à plate(s) couture(s). **4.** (*a*) goutte *f* (de pluie); (*b*) *F:* **a s. of whisky,** deux doigts de whisky; **what about a s. of lunch?** si nous allions déjeuner? **a s. of trouble,** un petit ennui, un pépin. **II.** *v.tr.* (**spotted**) **1.** tacher, souiller; **it's spotting with rain,** il se met à pleuvoir. **2.** *F:* (*a*) repérer; apercevoir (qn, qch.); (*b*) reconnaître; *Turf:* **to s. the winner,** prédire le gagnant; **'spot'check,** *s.* contrôle-surprise *m*; **'spotless,** *a.* sans tache; immaculé; pur; -ly, *adv.* **s. clean,** d'une propreté irréprochable; **'spotlight,** *s.* projecteur *m*; **to put the s. on sth.,** mettre qch. en vedette; **'spot-'on,** *F:* **1.** *a.* exact, au point. **2.** *adv.* au poil; **'spotted,** *a.* (*a*) tacheté, moucheté; (*b*) *Tex:* à pois; **'spotter,** *s.* **aircraft, train, s.,** personne qui regarde passer les avions, les trains (pour repérer les différents modèles); **'spotty,** *a.* (*a*) tacheté, moucheté; (*b*) (visage) couvert de boutons.

spout [spaut]. **I.** *s.* (*a*) **rain-water s.,** tuyau *m* (de décharge); (*b*) bec *m* (de théière); jet *m* (de pompe). **II.** *v.* **1.** *v.i.* (*of liquid*) jaillir; (*of whale*) souffler. **2.** *v.tr.* (*a*) faire jaillir, faire lancer (de l'eau, etc.); (*b*) *F: abs.* parler à jet continu.

sprain [sprein]. **I.** *s.* entorse *f*, foulure *f.* **II.** *v.tr.* **to s. one's wrist,** se fouler le poignet; **to s. one's ankle,** se donner une entorse (à la cheville).

sprat [spræt], *s. Ich:* sprat *m*, harenguet *m.*

sprawl [sprɔːl], *v.i.* (*a*) s'étendre, s'étaler; (*b*) **to go sprawling,** s'étaler par terre; (*c*) (*on grass, on a sofa*) se vautrer.

spray¹ [sprei], *s.* **s. of flowers,** rameau fleuri.

spray². **I.** *s.* **1.** embrun *m.* **2.** (*a*) poussière *f* d'eau (*b*) jet pulvérisé (de parfum). **3.** gicleur *m* vaporisateur *m*; **s. gun,** pulvérisateur *m* pistolet *m* (à peinture, aux insecticides, etc.) **II.** *v.tr.* **1.** pulvériser, atomiser, vaporiser (un liquide). **2.** asperger, arroser; **to s. the vines,** passer les vignes au vaporisateur; **'sprayer,** *s.* **1.** vaporisateur *m*, atomiseur *m*; (*for fuel oil*) brûleur *m* (de mazout). **2.** (*for fire-fighting*) **foam s.,** extincteur *m* à mousse.

spread [spred]. **I.** *s.* **1.** (*a*) étendue *f* (de pays

etc.); (*b*) (*of bird's wings, aircraft*) envergure
f; **middle-age s.**, l'embonpoint *m* de l'âge mûr.
2. diffusion *f* (de l'éducation); propagation *f*
(d'une doctrine); expansion *f*. **3.** régal *m*, festin
m. **4.** fromage *m*, pâté *m*, etc., à tartiner. **5.**
Journ: **double-page s.**, annonce *f* sur deux
pages. **II.** *v.* (spread) **1.** *v.tr.* étendre; **to s. a net**,
tendre un filet; **to s. out goods for sale**, étaler
des marchandises; **to s. oneself on a subject**, se
répandre sur un sujet. **2.** *v.tr.* (*a*) répandre; (*b*)
instalments s. over several months, versements
échelonnés sur plusieurs mois. **3.** *v.tr.* **to s.**
butter (on a bit of bread), tartiner du beurre. **4.**
v.i. (*a*) s'étendre, s'étaler; (*b*) (*of news*) se disséminer; se répandre; (*of disease*) se propager;
the fire is spreading, le feu gagne;
'spread'eagled, *a.* vautré (sur le gazon, la
plage).
spree [spri:], *s. F:* partie *f* de plaisir; **to go on a**
spending s., faire des achats extravagants.
sprig [sprig], *s.* brin *m*, brindille *f*; petite
branche.
sprightly ['spraitli], *a.* sémillant, fringant.
spring [spriŋ], *s.* **1.** source *f* (d'eau). **2.** printemps
m; **in (the) s.**, au printemps; **s. flowers**, fleurs
printanières; **s. tide**, marée *f* de syzygie;
grande marée. **3.** saut *m*, bond *m*; **to take a s.**,
prendre son élan; faire un bond. **4.** élasticité *f*.
5. (*a*) ressort *m*; **spiral s.**, ressort en boudin; (*b*)
pl. (*of car, etc.*) suspension *f*. **II.** *v.* (**sprang**
[spræŋ]; **sprung** [sprʌŋ]) **1.** *v.i.* (*a*) bondir,
sauter; **to s. out of bed**, sauter du lit; **where did**
you s. from? d'où sortez-vous? **the lid sprang**
open, le couvercle se releva instantanément;
(*b*) (*of water*) jaillir. **2.** *v.tr.* (*a*) *Nau:* (*of ship*) **to**
s. a leak, (se) faire une voie d'eau; (*b*) **to s. a**
surprise on s.o., prendre qn à l'improviste; **to s.**
a question on s.o., poser à qn une question im-
prévue; **'springboard**, *s.* tremplin *m*;
'springbok, *s. Z:* springbok *m*; **'spring-**
'clean, *v.tr.* nettoyer à fond (une maison),
Fr.C: faire le grand ménage; **'springiness**, *s.*
élasticité *f* (d'un ressort, d'un tremplin);
'springlike, *a.* (temps *m*, etc.) printanier;
'springy, *a.* élastique; flexible; (pas *m*) alerte;
s. carpet, tapis moelleux.
'prinkle ['spriŋkl], *v.tr.* (*a*) répandre, jeter (de
l'eau, du sel, du sable, etc.); (*b*) asperger (**with**
water, d'eau); saupoudrer (**with salt**, de sel);
'sprinkler, *s.* **1.** arroseur automatique rotatif;
arroseur à jet tournant. **2.** *Ecc:* goupillon *m*,
aspergès *m*. **3.** (*for sugar, flour*) saupoudroir
m; **'sprinkling**, *s.* **1.** aspersion *f*, arrosage
m; saupoudrage *m*. **2. a s. of sugar**, un
(léger) saupoudrage de sucre; **a s. of**
knowledge, quelques connaissances *f* (d'une
matière).
'print [sprint]. *Sp:* **I.** *s.* pointe *f* de vitesse; sprint
m. **II.** *v.i.* sprinter; **'sprinter**, *s.* sprinter *m*

[sprintœːr].
sprout [spraut]. **I.** *v.* **1.** *v.i. Bot:* (*a*) pousser,
pointer; (*b*) (*of seed*) germer. **2.** *v.tr.* (*of*
animal) **to s. horns**, pousser des cornes. **II.** *s.*
Bot: (*a*) jet *m*, rejeton *m*, pousse *f*; (*b*)
bourgeon *m*; **Brussels sprouts**, choux *m* de
Bruxelles.
spruce[1] [spru:s]. **I.** *a.* pimpant; soigné; tiré à
quatre épingles. **II.** *v.pr.* **to s. oneself up**, se faire
beau; se pomponner; **'spruceness**, *s.* mise
pimpante.
spruce[2], *s. Bot:* sapin *m*, épinette *f*; **white s.**,
sapinette *f*.
spry [sprai], *a.* (*esp. of elderly people*) *a.* vif, actif; plein d'entrain; **he's very s. for his age**, il est
plein d'allant pour (un homme de) son âge.
spud [spʌd], *s. F:* pomme *f* de terre.
spur [spəːr]. **I.** *s.* **1.** éperon *m*. **2.** coup *m*
d'éperon; stimulant *m*; **the s. of necessity**,
l'aiguillon *m* de la nécessité; **on the s. of the**
moment, sous l'impulsion du moment. **3.**
Geog: éperon, contrefort *m* (d'une chaîne de
montagnes). **II.** *v.tr.* (**spurred**) **1.** éperonner (un
cheval). **2. to s. s.o. on**, aiguillonner, stimuler,
qn.
spurious ['spjuəriəs], *a.* faux; contrefait;
'spuriousness, *s.* fausseté *f*; nature falsifiée
(de qch.).
spurn [spəːn], *v.tr.* rejeter (une offre) avec
mépris; traiter (qn) avec mépris.
spurt [spəːt]. **I.** *s.* **1.** jaillissement *m*; jet *m*; **s. of**
petrol, giclée *f* d'essence. **2.** (*a*) effort soudain;
coup *m* de collier; (*b*) *Sp:* **to put on a s.**,
démarrer; **final s.**, pointe finale. **II.** *v.i.* **1.** (*of oil*
well, etc.) **to s. up**, jaillir; **to s. out**, saillir, gicler.
2. *Sp:* démarrer, faire un effort de vitesse, un
sprint.
spy [spai]. **I.** *s.* espion, -onne; **police s.**, *F:*
mouchard *m*. **II.** *v.i.* (**spied**) espionner;
F: moucharder; **'spying**, *s.* espionnage *m*.
squabble ['skwɔbl]. **I.** *s.* querelle *f*, chamaillerie
f; prise *f* de bec. **II.** *v.i.* se chamailler, se
quereller; **'squabbling**, *s.* chamaillerie *f*;
querelles *f pl*.
squad [skwɔd], *s.* **1.** *Mil: etc:* escouade *f*; **firing**
s., peloton *m* d'exécution. **2.** brigade *f* (de
cheminots); **the flying s.**, la brigade mobile (de
la police); **rescue s.**, équipe *f* de secours; **s. car**,
voiture *f* de police.
squadron ['skwɔdrən], *s.* (*a*) *Mil:* escadron *m*;
(*b*) *Av:* escadrille *f*, groupe *m*; **s. leader**, commandant *m* de groupe; (*c*) *Nau:* escadrille *f*;
escadre *f*.
squalid ['skwɔlid], *a.* sale; misérable; sordide;
'squalor, *s.* saleté *f*; misère *f*; aspect *m* sordide; **born in s.**, né dans la crasse.
squall[1] [skwɔːl], *v.i.* (*of child, etc.*) crier, brailler,
piailler; **'squalling**, *a.* criard, braillard.
squall[2], *s. Nau:* grain *m*; coup *m* de vent;

bourrasque *f*; rafale *f*; **'squally**, *a.* (temps) à
grains, à rafaleş.

squander ['skwɔndər], *v.tr.* gaspiller (l'argent);
dissiper, dilapider (sa fortune); **'squanderer,**
s. gaspilleur, -euse; **'squandering,** *s.* gaspillage *m.*

square [skwɛər]. **I.** *s.* **1.** carré *m*; *Mil:* terrain *m*
de manœuvre; *F:* **s. bashing** = l'exercice *m.* **2.**
(*a*) carreau *m* (de carte quadrillée); case *f*
(d'échiquier); **to divide a map into squares,**
quadriller une carte; (*b*) *Cl:* **silk s.,** foulard *m.*
3. (*of town*) place *f*; (*with garden*) square *m.* **4.**
set s., équerre *f* (à dessin); **T s.,** équerre en T. **5.**
Mth: carré (d'une expression). **6.** *F:* **he's a s.,** il
est un peu vieux jeu. **II.** *a.* **1.** carré; (*a*) **s.**
measure, mesure de surface; (*b*) **s. shoulders,**
épaules carrées. **2.** *Mth:* **s. root,** racine carrée.
3. to get things s., mettre en ordre; **he**
always gives you a s. deal, il est toujours loyal
en affaires; **to be s. with s.o.,** être quitte envers
qn. **4.** *F:* **to be s.,** être vieux jeu; **-ly,** *adv.* carrément. **III.** *adv.* **1.** à angles droits (**to, with,**
avec). **2. set s. on its base,** d'aplomb sur sa
base; **fair and s.,** loyalement, carrément. **IV.** *v.*
1. *v.tr.* (*a*) carrer, équarrir (la pierre, etc.); (*b*)
balancer, régler (un compte); arranger (qch.);
F: **to s. s.o.,** acheter qn; suborner qn; *F:*
graisser la patte à qn; (*c*) *Mth:* élever (une
expression) au carré; carrer (un chiffre); (*d*)
quadriller (une carte). **2.** *v.i.* **his actions don't s.**
with his principles, ses actions ne s'accordent
pas, ne cadrent pas, avec ses principes;
'squared, *a.* (papier) quadrillé.

squash¹ [skwɔʃ]. **I.** *v.* **1.** *v.tr.* écraser, aplatir
(qch., qn); *F:* remettre (qn) à sa place. **2.** *v.i.* (*a*)
(*of fruit, etc.*) s'écraser; (*b*) (*of people*) se
serrer, se presser. **II.** *s.* **1.** cohue *f*, presse *f*,
bousculade *f.* **2.** pulpe *f* (de fruit, etc.); **lemon,**
orange, s., citronnade *f*, orangeade *f.* **3.** *Sp:*
squash *m*; **'squash-court,** *s.* *Sp:* terrain *m* de
squash; **'squashy,** *a.* mou (et humide);
détrempé.

squash², *s.* *Bot:* (*a*) gourde *f*; (*b*) *esp.* *N.Am:*
courge *f*; courgette *f.*

squat [skwɔt]. **I.** *v.i.* (**squatted**) **1.** (*a*) **to s.**
(**down**), s'accroupir; (*b*) (*of animals*) se tapir.
2. s'approprier un terrain, un logement
(inhabité). **II.** *a.* ramassé, trapu; **'squatter,** *s.*
squatter *m.*

squaw [skwɔ:], *s.* femme *f* Peau-Rouge.

squawk [skwɔ:k]. **I.** *s.* cri *m* rauque; couac *m.* **II.**
v.i. pousser des cris rauques; couaquer.

squeak [skwi:k]. **I.** *s.* cri aigu (d'oiseau, de
souris); crissement *m*; grincement *m*; **to have a**
narrow s., l'échapper belle. **II.** *v.i.* pousser des
cris aigus; (*of shoes*) crier.

squeal [skwi:l]. **I.** *s.* cri aigu; cri perçant. **II.** *v.i.*
(*a*) pousser des cris aigus; (*b*) protester;
pousser de hauts cris; (*c*) **to s. on s.o.,** dénoncer
qn.

squeamish ['skwi:miʃ], *a.* **1.** sujet aux nausées *f*;
to feel s., avoir mal au cœur. **2.** difficile, délicat;
dégoûté; **don't be so s.,** ne faites pas tant de
façons; **'squeamishness,** *s.* **1.** disposition *f*
aux nausées. **2.** délicatesse exagérée.

squeegee ['skwi:'dʒi:], *s.* balai *m* éponge.

squeeze [skwi:z]. **I.** *s.* **1.** (*a*) compression *f*; (*b*)
étreinte *f.* **2.** presse *f*, cohue *f*; **it was a tight s.,**
on tenait tout juste. **3. a s. of lemon,** quelques
gouttes *f* de citron. **4.** *Fin:* **the credit s.,** la
restriction du crédit. **II.** *v.tr.* **1.** (*a*) presser; **to s.**
s.o.'s hand, serrer la main à qn; (*b*) étreindre
(qn). **2.** se faufiler (par un trou, etc.); **to s. up,** se
serrer, se tasser; **to s. a lemon,** exprimer le jus
d'un citron. **3.** (*a*) exercer une pression sur
(qn); (*b*) **to s. money out of s.o.,** extorquer de
l'argent à qn.

squelch [skweltʃ], *v.i.* (*of water*) gargouiller,
gicler; (*of pers.*) patauger (dans la boue, etc.).

squib [skwib], *s.* pétard *m*; **damp s.,** affaire ratée.

squid [skwid], *s.* *Moll:* calmar *m.*

squiggle ['skwigl], *s.* (*a*) fioriture *f*; (*b*) écriture
illisible.

squint [skwint]. **I.** *s.* strabisme *m.* **II.** *v.i.* loucher.

squire ['skwaiər], *s.* **the s.** = le châtelain (de
l'endroit).

squirm [skwə:m], *v.i.* (*a*) (*of worm*) se tordre, se
tortiller; (*b*) ne pas savoir comment se tenir,
être au supplice; **to make s.o. s.,** mettre qn au
supplice.

squirrel ['skwirəl], *s.* écureuil *m.*

squirt [skwə:t]. **I.** *v.* **1.** *v.tr.* lancer en jet, faire
jaillir (un liquide); **to s. in oil,** injecter de l'huile.
2. *v.i.* (*of liquid*) jaillir, gicler. **II.** *s.* jet *m*; giclée
f (de liquide).

Sri Lanka ['sri:'læŋkə]. *Pr.n.* le Sri Lanka.

stab [stæb]. **I.** *v.tr.* (**stabbed**) poignarder (qn); **to**
s. s.o. in the back, attaquer qn déloyalement.
II. *s.* coup *m* de poignard, de couteau; **s. in the**
back, attaque déloyale.

stable¹ ['steibl]. **I.** *s.* écurie *f*; **racing s.,** écurie de
course; **s. boy,** valet *m*, garçon *m*, d'écurie. **II.**
v.tr. loger (un cheval); **'stabling,** *s.* (*a*) logement *m* (pour chevaux); (*b*) *coll.* écuries *fpl.*

stable², *a.* **1.** stable; solide, fixe. **2.** (*of pers.*) constant, ferme; **sta'bility** [stə-], *s.* stabilité *f*;
solidité *f* (d'une construction); constance *f*,
fermeté *f* (d'une personne); **stabili'zation,**
stabilisation *f*; **'stabilize,** *v.tr.* stabilise
'stabilizer, *s.* stabilisateur *m*, équilibreur *m*

stack [stæk]. **I.** *s.* **1.** (*a*) meule *f* (de foin); (*b*) pil
f, tas *m* (de bois); **I've stacks of work,** j'ai d
pain sur la planche. **2.** souche *f* (de cheminée
II. *v.tr.* **1.** mettre (le foin) en meule. **2. to s. (up**
empiler, entasser.

stadium, *pl.* **-ia, -iums** ['steidiəm, -iə, -iəmz],
stade *m.*

staff [stɑ:f], *s.* **1.** bâton *m*; mât *m* (de pav

lon). 2. (a) coll. personnel m; (b) Mil: état-major m; **teaching s.,** personnel enseignant; Journ: **editorial s.,** la rédaction; s. **officer,** officier m d'état-major. II. v.tr. pourvoir (un bureau, etc.) de personnel; **'staffwork,** s. travail m d'organisation.

stag [stæg], s. 1. Z: cerf m. 2. St. Exch: F: loup m. 3. F: s. **party,** réunion f entre hommes; **'stag-beetle,** s. Ent: lucane m, cerf-volant m.

stage [steidʒ]. I. s. 1. (a) estrade f; (b) platine f (d'un microscope); (c) étage m (d'une fusée à exploration spatiale). 2. (a) Th: scène f; F: les planches f; s. **play,** pièce f de théâtre; **front of the s.,** avant-scène f; **to come on s.,** entrer en scène; **to go on the s.,** se faire acteur, actrice; s. **directions,** indications f scéniques; s. **door,** entrée f des artistes; s. **fright,** trac m; s. **hand,** machiniste m; s. **manager,** régisseur m; s. **rights,** droits m de production; s. **whisper,** aparté m; (b) champ m d'action. 3. phase f, période f, stade m; **the stages of an evolution,** les étapes f d'une évolution; **to rise by successive stages,** monter par échelons. 4. étape f; (on bus route) **fare s.,** section f; **to travel by easy stages,** voyager à petites étapes. II. v.tr. monter (une pièce); organiser (une démonstration); monter (un coup); **'stagecraft,** s. Th: technique f de la scène; **'stager,** s. F: **old s.,** vieux routier; **'staging,** s. 1. Th: mise f en scène. 2. Const: échafaudage m; **'stagy,** a. usu. Pej: (a) théâtral, histrionique; (b) peu sincère.

stagger ['stægər]. 1. v.i. chanceler, tituber; **to s. along,** avancer en titubant; **to s. to one's feet,** se lever en chancelant. 2. v.tr. (a) confondre, consterner (qn); frapper (qn) de stupeur; (b) Av: décaler (les ailes); E: disposer (des rivets) en chicane; El: échelonner (les balais); étaler, échelonner (les vacances); **'staggered,** a. s. **holidays,** congés échelonnés; **'staggering,** a. s. **blow,** coup m d'assommoir; (of news) renversant, atterrant.

staghound ['stæghaund], s. lévrier m d'Écosse.

stagnant ['stægnənt], s. (of water) stagnant; croupi; (of trade, etc.) (être) en stagnation f, dans le marasme; **stag'nate,** v.i. (of water, etc.) stagner, croupir; **stag'nation,** s. stagnation f (de l'eau, dans les affaires); marasme m (du commerce).

staid [steid], a. posé, sérieux, sage; **'staidness,** s. caractère posé, sérieux m.

stain [stein]. I. s. 1. (a) tache f, souillure f; (b) **he came out of the affair without a s. on his character,** il est sorti de l'affaire sans atteinte à sa réputation. 2. couleur f, colorant m; **wood s.,** colorant pour bois; s. **remover,** détachant m. II. v.tr. 1. tacher; souiller (**with,** de); ternir (une réputation, etc.). 2. teindre, teinter (le bois); **'stainless,** a. sans tache; immaculé; s.

steel, (acier m) inoxydable (m), F: inox (m).

stair ['stɛər], s. 1. marche f, degré m (d'un escalier). 2. usu. pl. (also **'staircase**) escalier; **'stair-rod,** s. tringle f d'escalier; **'stairwell,** s. cage f d'escalier.

stake [steik]. I. s. 1. pieu m, poteau m; Hort: tuteur m. 2. Gaming: mise f, enjeu m; **the interests at s.,** les intérêts m en jeu; **to have a s. in sth.,** avoir des intérêts dans une affaire. II. v.tr. 1. **to s.** (off, out), jalonner. 2. ramer (des haricots); tuteurer (des tomates, etc.). 3. mettre (une somme) en jeu; jouer (une somme); miser (sur un cheval).

stalactite ['stæləktait], s. stalactite f.

stalagmite ['stæləgmait], s. stalagmite f.

stale [steil], a. 1. (a) (pain) rassis; (b) (œuf) qui n'est pas frais; (c) (air) vicié; s. **smell,** odeur f de renfermé; remugle m. 2. vieux, passé; s. **goods,** articles défraîchis; s. **joke,** vieille plaisanterie. 3. fatigué, éreinté; (of athlete) **to go s.,** se surentraîner; **'stalemate,** s. (at chess) pat m; **'staleness,** s. état rassis (du pain); manque m de fraîcheur (d'un article, d'une nouvelle); odeur f de renfermé.

stalk¹ [stɔ:k]. 1. v.i. **to s.** (along), marcher d'un pas majestueux; marcher à grands pas. 2. v.tr. (a) traquer (une bête) à l'approche; (b) filer (qn); **'stalker,** s. chasseur m à l'approche; **'stalking,** s. (deer, etc.) s., chasse f à l'approche.

stalk² [stɔ:k], s. tige f (de plante); queue f (de fruit); trognon m (de chou).

stall [stɔ:l]. I. s. 1. stalle f (d'écurie, d'étable). 2. étalage m (en plein vent); (at exhibition) stand m; **newspaper s.,** kiosque m. 3. Ecc: stalle; Th: (orchestra) **stalls,** fauteuils m d'orchestre. II. v. 1. v.tr. Aut: caler (le moteur); Av: mettre (l'appareil) en perte de vitesse. 2. v.i. (a) (of engine) caler; (b) (of pers.) **to s. (for time),** chercher à gagner du temps; **'stall-holder,** s. marchand, -ande, aux halles, aux foires; (at exhibition, etc.) vendeur, -euse.

stallion ['stæljən], s. étalon m; cheval entier.

stalwart ['stɔ:lwət]. 1. a. (a) robuste, vigoureux; (b) vaillant, résolu. 2. s. **one of the old stalwarts,** un vieux de la vieille.

stamen ['steimen], s. Bot: étamine f.

stamina ['stæminə], s. vigueur f, résistance f.

stammer ['stæmər]. I. s. (a) (stutter) bégaiement m; (b) (mumble) balbutiement m. II. v. 1. v.i. (a) bégayer; (b) balbutier. 2. v.tr. **to s. (out) sth.,** bégayer, balbutier, qch.; **'stammerer,** s. bègue mf; balbutieur, -euse; **'stammering.** 1. a. (personne) bègue. 2. s. bégaiement m; balbutiement m; **-ly,** adv. en bégayant.

stamp [stæmp]. I. s. 1. battement m de pied; trépignement m; **with a s. (of the foot),** en frappant du pied. 2. (a) timbre m, empreinte f; **date s.,** timbre à date; **rubber s.,** tampon m; (b)

découpoir *m* (à emporte-pièce); (*c*) étampe *f*,
poinçon *m*. **3.** timbre; marque (apposée). **4.**
revenue s., timbre du fisc; **adhesive s.**, timbre
mobile; **embossed s.**, timbre à empreinte;
(**postage**) **s.**, timbre(-poste) *m*; **used s.**, timbre
oblitéré; **National Insurance s.** = cotisation *f*
de la sécurité sociale; *Com:* **trading s.**, timbre-
prime *m*; **s. collector**, philatéliste *mf*; **s. album**,
album *m* de timbres; **s. machine**, distributeur
m automatique de timbres-poste; *Adm:* **s.
duty**, droit *m* de timbre. **5.** *Min:* bocard *m*
(pour écraser les minerais); pilon *m*; broyeuse
f. **II.** *v.tr.* **1.** (*a*) **to s. one's foot**, frapper du pied;
trépigner; (*b*) *v.i.* **to s.** (**about**), piétiner; **to s. on
sth.**, fouler qch. aux pieds. **2.** frapper, imprimer, une marque sur (qch.); frapper, es-
tamper (la monnaie, le cuir); contrôler,
poinçonner (l'or, l'argent). **3.** timbrer (un
document); viser (un passeport); estampiller
(un document); timbrer, affranchir (une lettre);
the letter is insufficiently stamped,
l'affranchissement est insuffisant. **4.** *Min:*
broyer, bocarder (le minerai). **5.** étamper,
matricer (des objets en métal). **6. to s. out the
fire**, piétiner sur le feu pour l'éteindre; **to s. out
an epidemic**, étouffer, juguler, une épidémie;
stamped, *a.* **s. paper**, papier timbré; **s. addressed envelope**, enveloppe timbrée; **'stamp-
ing**, *s.* **1.** timbrage *m* (de documents). **2.**
piétinement *m*; *F:* **s. ground**, terrain *m* d'élection, lieu favori.
stampede [stæm′piːd]. **I.** *s.* (*a*) fuite précipitée;
panique *f*; (*b*) ruée *f*. **II.** *v.* **1.** *v.i.* (*a*) fuir en
désordre, à la débandade; (*b*) se ruer, se
précipiter (**for, towards**, vers, sur). **2.** *v.tr.* jeter
la panique parmi (des animaux).
stance [stæns, stɑːns], *s.* position *f* des pieds;
posture *f*; **to take one's s.**, se mettre en posture
(pour jouer).
stanch [stɔːn(t)ʃ, stɑːn(t)ʃ], *v.tr.* étancher (le
sang); étancher le sang de (la blessure).
stand [stænd]. **I.** *s.* **1.** (*a*) **to take a firm s.**,
(i) se planter, se camper solidement, sur ses
jambes; (ii) se montrer résolu; (*b*) arrêt *m*, halte
f; **to be brought to a s.**, être forcé de s'arrêter.
2. résistance *f*; **to make a s. against s.o., sth.**,
résister à qn, qch. **3.** situation *f*, position *f*; **to
take one's s. near the door**, se placer près de la
porte; **to take one's s. on a principle**, se fonder
sur un principe. **4.** support *m*, pied *m* (de
lampe); dessous *m* (de carafe). **5.** étalage *m*; (*at
exhibition*) stand *m*. **6.** *Sp:* tribune *f*; stand. **7.**
N.Am: Jur: (*witness*) **s.** = barre *f* des témoins.
II. *v.* (**stood** [stud]) **1.** *v.i.* (*a*) être debout;
se tenir debout; rester debout; **I could hardly
s.**, je pouvais à peine me tenir; **to s. on one's
own feet**, ne dépendre que de soi; **I didn't leave
him a leg to s. on**, j'ai détruit ses arguments de
fond en comble; **to s. six feet high**, avoir six

pieds de haut; **to s.** (**up**), se lever; (*b*) se trouver,
être; **the chapel stands on a hill**, la chapelle se
dresse sur une hauteur; **the tears stood in his
eyes**, il avait les larmes aux yeux; **to let sth. s. in
the sun**, laisser qch. exposé au soleil; **to buy the
house as it stands**, acheter la maison telle
quelle; **nothing stands between you and
success**, rien ne s'oppose à votre succès; **he
stood in the doorway**, il se tenait à la porte; **to
s. talking**, rester causer; *F:* **don't leave her
standing there**, ne la laissez pas plantée là; (*c*)
rester, durer; **to s. fast**, tenir (pied); tenir bon;
(*d*) **the contract stands**, le contrat tient; **the
objection stands**, cette objection subsiste; (*e*)
(i) **to s. convicted of lying**, être convaincu d'un
mensonge; **to s. in need of sth.**, avoir besoin de
qch.; **you s. in danger of being killed**, vous
vous exposez à vous faire tuer; **I don't s. to lose
anything**, je n'ai rien à perdre; (ii) **to s. as candidate, as surety**, se porter candidat, caution;
(iii) **he stands first on the list**, il vient en tête de
la liste; **the thermometer stands at 30°**, le thermomètre marque 30°; (iv) **the amount standing to your credit**, votre solde créditeur; **how
do we s.?** où en sont nos comptes? **as things s.**,
as it stands, au point où en sont les choses; **I
don't know where I s.**, j'ignore quelle est ma
position; **to s. well with s.o.**, être estimé de qn;
(v) **the house stands in her husband's name**, la
maison est portée au nom de son mari; (*f*) **I'll
s. by the window**, je me mettrai à la fenêtre; (*g*)
to let a liquid s., laisser reposer un liquide; **to let
the tea s.**, laisser infuser le thé; **taxis may s.
here**, les taxis peuvent stationner ici. **2.** *v.tr.* (*a*)
mettre, poser; **to s. sth. against the wall**,
dresser qch. contre le mur; (*b*) **to s. one's
ground**, tenir bon, ferme; (*c*) supporter, subir;
to s. the cold, supporter le froid; **to s. rough
handling**, résister à des manipulations
brutales; **we had to s. the loss**, la perte a porté
sur nous; *F:* **I can't s. him**, je ne peux pas le
sentir; **I can't s. it any longer**, je n'y tiens plus,
j'en ai assez; **I won't s.** (**for**) **any more of that**,
je ne supporterai plus de cela; (*d*) *F:* payer,
offrir; **to s. s.o. a drink**, payer à boire à qn; **I'm
standing this one**, c'est ma tournée; **'stand
a′side**, *v.i.* s'écarter, se ranger; **to s. aside in
favour of s.o.**, se désister en faveur de qn;
'stand 'back, *v.i.* se tenir en arrière; reculer;
house standing back from the road, maison en
retrait (de la route); **'stand 'by**, *v.i.* **1.** (*a*) se
tenir prêt; (*b*) se tenir là (sans intervenir). **2.** (*a*)
se tenir près de (qn); (*b*) soutenir, défendre
(qn); rester fidèle à (sa promesse); **I s. by what
I said**, j'en tiens à ce que j'ai dit; **'standby**,
(*a*) (*pers.*) appui *m*, soutien *m*; (*b*) ressource *f*;
s. engine, locomotive de réserve; **'stand
′down**, *v.i.* **to s. down in favour of s.o.**, retirer
sa candidature en faveur de qn; **'stand for**

v.ind.tr. **1.** signifier, vouloir dire (qch.). **2.** supporter, tolérer (qch.); ' **stand-in**, *s.* remplaçant *m* (temporaire); *Th: etc:* doublure *f*; **to be s.o.'s s.-in**, doubler qn; ' **standing.** **I.** *a.* **1.** *(a)* (qui se tient) debout; *Rac: F:* **to leave the rest s.**, brûler ses concurrents; **to be left s.**, être laissé sur place; *(b)* **s. crops**, récoltes sur pied. **2.** **s. water**, eau stagnante, dormante; *Typ:* **s. type**, conservation *f.* **3.** *Com:* **s. expenses**, frais généraux; **s. rule**, règle *f* fixe; **s. joke**, plaisanterie courante, traditionnelle. **II.** *s.* **1.** station *f* debout; **s. room, place(s)** *f(pl)* debout; **there wasn't even s. room**, il n'y avait pas où mettre le pied. **2.** durée *f*; **friend of long s.**, ami de longue main, de longue date. **3.** rang *m*, position *f*; standing *m*; **s. of a firm**, importance *f* d'une maison; **it would mean a loss of s.**, ce serait déchoir; ' **stand 'off**, *v.tr. Ind:* **to be stood off**, être congédié; ' **stand 'offish**, *a. F: (of pers.)* peu accessible, distant, réservé; ' **stand 'offishness**, *s. F:* raideur *f*, réserve *f*, morgue *f*; ' **stand 'out**, *v.i.* **1.** **to s. out against sth.**, résister à qch., tenir bon contre qch. **2.** **to s. out for sth.**, s'obstiner à demander qch. **3.** faire saillie; **to s. out against sth.**, se détacher sur qch.; **to make a figure s. out**, détacher une figure; **the qualities that s. out in his work**, les qualités marquantes de son œuvre. **4.** *Nau:* **to s. out to sea**, gagner le large; ' **stand 'over**, *v.i.* **1.** rester en suspens; **to let a question s. over**, remettre une question à plus tard. **2.** **if I don't s. over him he does nothing**, si je ne suis pas toujours sur son dos il ne fait rien; ' **standpoint**, *s.* point *m* de vue; ' **standstill**, *s.* arrêt *m*, immobilisation *f*; **to come to a s.**, s'arrêter; *(of car)* rester en panne; **business is at a s.**, le commerce ne va plus; *Mil: etc:* alerte *f*; ' **stand 'up**, *v.i.* **1.** *(a)* se lever, se mettre debout; *(b)* se dresser, se tenir droit. **2.** **to s. up for s.o., sth.**, défendre qn, soutenir (une cause); **to s. up to s.o.**, affronter bravement qn; tenir pied à qn; *F:* **to s. s.o. up**, planter là qn; ' **stand-up**, *a.* **s.-up collar**, col droit, montant; **s.-up fight**, combat en règle; **s.-up buffet**, réception où les invités mangent debout au buffet. **andard** ['stændəd], *s.* **1.** bannière *f*; *Mil:* étendard *m*; *Nau:* pavillon *m.* **2.** étalon *m* (de poids); *Fin:* **the gold s.**, l'étalon (d')or. **3.** modèle *m*, type *m*; **s. of living**, niveau *m* de vie; **judged by that s.**, à cette mesure. **4.** degré *m* (d'excellence); qualité *f*; **to aim at a high s.**, viser à un haut degré d'excellence; **up to s.**, à la hauteur; *Com:* conforme à l'échantillon. **5.** pylône *m* d'éclairage **6.** *attrib.* **of s. size**, de taille courante; **s. model** (voiture, etc.) de série; **the s. authors**, les auteurs classiques; **s. English**, l'anglais des gens cultivés; **s. joke**, plaisanterie *f* classique; *Rail:* **s. gauge**, voie normale; **standardi'zation**, *s.* étalonnage *m*,

étalonnement *m* (des poids); unification *f* (des méthodes); standardisation *f* (d'une machine); ' **standardize**, *v.tr.* étalonner, unifier (des méthodes); *Ind:* standardiser (des produits). **stanza** ['stænzə], *s.* stance *f*, strophe *f*. **staple**[1] ['steipl]. **I.** *s.* crampon *m* (à deux pointes); **wire s.**, clou *m* à deux pointes; broche *f*, agrafe *f*. **II.** *v.tr.* agrafer, cramponner (qch.); brocher (un livre); ' **stapler**, *s.* agrafeuse *f*; ' **stapling**, *s.* agrafage *m*; fixage *m* à l'aide de crampons; brochage *m* (d'un livre). **staple**[2], *s.* *(a)* produit principal (d'un pays); **s. diet**, nourriture *f* de base; **s. industry**, industrie principale; *(b)* matière première, matière brute. **star** [staːr]. **I.** *s.* **1.** étoile *f*; astre *m*; **I thank my lucky stars that . . .**, je bénis mon étoile de ce que + *ind.*; **to see stars**, voir trente-six chandelles. **2.** *(a)* **the stars and stripes, the s.-spangled banner**, la bannière étoilée (des États-Unis); *(b)* **s., s.-shaped crack**, étoile, étoilement *m*; *(c)* *Typ: F:* astérisque *m*; **four s. hotel**, hôtel *m* de grand luxe, palace *m*. **3.** *Cin: Th:* étoile, vedette *f*, star *f*; **s. part**, rôle *m* de vedette. **II.** *v.* **(starred)** **1.** *v.tr.* étoiler, fêler (une glace). **2.** *v.i.* *(a)* *(of glass)* s'étoiler; se fêler; *(b)* *Th: Cin:* être en vedette; avoir un rôle de star, d'étoile; ' **stardom**, *s. Cin: etc:* **to rise to s.**, devenir une vedette; ' **starfish**, *s.* astérie *f*; étoile *f* de mer; ' **starless**, *a.* (nuit) sans étoiles; ' **starlet**, *s. Cin:* starlette *f*; ' **starlight**, *s.* lumière *f* des étoiles; **by s.**, à la lueur des étoiles; **a s. night**, une nuit étoilée; ' **starlit**, *a.* (ciel) étoilé; **starred**, *a. (a)* *(also* **starry***)* étoilé; (par)semé d'étoiles; *(b)* *F:* marqué d'un astérisque. **starboard** ['staːbəd], *s. Nau:* tribord *m*. **starch** [staːtʃ]. **1.** amidon *m*; *(of food)* **s.-reduced**, débarrassé de matières féculentes. **II.** *v.tr.* empeser, amidonner; ' **starchy**, *a.* **s. foods**, féculents *m*. **stare** [stɛər]. **1.** *s.* **(set) s.**, regard *m* fixe; **stony s.**, regard dur; **vacant s.**, regard vague; **with a s. of horror**, les yeux grands ouverts d'horreur. **II.** *v.* **1.** *v.i.* *(a)* regarder fixement; **to s. into the distance**, regarder au loin; **to s. in s.o.'s face**, dévisager qn; *(b)* écarquiller les yeux; ouvrir de grands yeux. **2.** *v.ind.tr.* **to s. at s.o.**, (i) regarder qn fixement; (ii) dévisager qn; (iii) regarder qn d'un air hébété. **3.** *v.tr.* **to s. s.o. in the face**, dévisager qn; **ruin is staring us in the face**, notre ruine est imminente; *F:* **it's staring you in the face**, ça vous saute aux yeux; **to s. s.o. out of countenance**, faire perdre contenance à qn; ' **staring.** **1.** *a.* **s. eyes**, (i) yeux fixes; (ii) yeux grands ouverts; regard ébahi. **2.** *adv.* **stark s. mad**, complètement fou. **stark** [staːk]. **1.** *a.* **s. nonsense**, pure bêtise. **2.** *adv.* **s. naked**, tout nu; nu comme un ver; **s.**

staring mad, complètement fou.
starling ['stɑ:liŋ], *s. Orn:* étourneau *m.*
start [stɑ:t]. **I.** *s.* **1.** (*a*) tressaillement *m*, sursaut *m*; **to wake with a s.,** se réveiller en sursaut; **he gave a s.,** il tressaillit, sursauta; **to give s.o. a s.,** faire tressaillir qn; (*b*) saut *m*; mouvement *m* brusque; **to work by fits and starts,** travailler par à-coups. **2.** (*a*) commencement *m*, début *m*; **to make a good s.,** bien commencer; **to make an early s.,** commencer de bonne heure; **at the s.,** au début; **from s. to finish,** du commencement à la fin; **to give s.o. a s.,** lancer qn (dans les affaires, etc.); **to make a fresh s. (in life),** recommencer (sa vie); (*b*) départ *m*; **to make an early s.,** partir de bonne heure; *Sp:* **false s.,** faux départ; (*c*) **to give s.o. a two second s.,** donner à qn deux secondes d'avance, une avance de deux secondes. **II.** *v.* **1.** *v.i.* (*a*) tressaillir, tressauter, sursauter; **to s. with surprise,** avoir un mouvement de surprise; **tears started from his eyes,** les larmes jaillirent de ses yeux; (*b*) (*of rivets*) se détacher; sauter; (*c*) commencer, débuter; **to s. in life,** débuter dans la vie; **to s. in business,** se lancer dans les affaires; **to s. with,** d'abord; en premier lieu; **to s. by doing sth.,** commencer par faire qch.; **to s. out,** partir, se mettre en route; **to s. back,** reprendre le chemin (de la maison); (*d*) (*of car*) démarrer; **I can't get it to s.,** je ne peux pas la faire marcher. **2.** *v.tr.* (*a*) commencer (un travail); **to s. a fresh loaf,** entamer un nouveau pain; **to s. life afresh,** recommencer sa vie; **to s. doing sth.,** commencer à, de, faire qch.; (*b*) *Sp:* donner le signal de départ à (des coureurs); (*c*) lancer (une entreprise); fonder (un commerce); ouvrir (une école); **to s. a fire,** provoquer un incendie; (*d*) mettre (une machine, etc.) en marche; *Aut:* démarrer; (*e*) **to s. s.o. on a career,** lancer qn dans une carrière; **once you s. him talking,** quand on le met à causer; **'starter,** *s.* **1.** (*a*) **you're an early s.,** vous partez de bonne heure; (*b*) *Sp:* partant *m.* **2.** starter *m* (qui donne le signal de départ). **3.** *Aut:* self-s., démarreur *m.* **4. to have sth. as a s.,** prendre qch. pour commencer (le repas); **'starting,** *s.* **s. point,** point *m* de départ; *Sp:* **s. post,** poteau *m* de départ; barrière *f*; **s. pistol,** pistolet *m* de starter; **s. price,** (i) *Com:* prix initial; (ii) *Rac:* dernière cote (d'un cheval) avant le départ; **'startle,** *v.tr.* effrayer, alarmer (qn); faire tressaillir, faire sursauter (qn); **to s. s.o. out of his sleep,** éveiller qn en sursaut; **'startling,** *a.* effrayant, saisissant; (événement) sensationnel; **s. get-up,** toilette ébouriffante; **s. likeness,** ressemblance saisissante.
starve [stɑ:v]. **1.** *v.i.* (*a*) **to s. to death,** mourir de faim; (*b*) manquer de nourriture; **I'm starving,** je meurs de faim. **2.** *v.tr.* (*a*) faire mourir (qn) de faim; (*b*) priver (qn) de nourriture; **star'vation,** *s.* privation *f*, manque *m* de nourriture; **to die of s.,** mourir de faim; **s. wages,** salaire *m* de famine; **starved,** *a.* affamé; **s. of affection,** privé d'affection; **'starving,** *a.* mourant de faim.
stash [stæʃ], *v.tr.* **to s. (sth.) away,** cacher (un trésor); mettre (son argent) en sécurité.
state [steit]. **I.** *s.* **1.** (*a*) état *m*, condition *f*; **in a good s.,** en bon état; **here's a nice s. of things!** nous voilà bien! c'est du joli! (*b*) **s. of health,** état de santé; **s. of mind,** disposition *f* d'esprit; *F:* **to get into a terrible s.,** (i) se mettre dans tous ses états; (ii) se trouver dans un état lamentable. **2.** (*a*) rang *m*, dignité *f*; (*b*) pompe *f*, parade *f*; apparat *m*; **to live in s.,** mener grand train; **to dine in s.,** dîner en grand gala; (*of body*) **to lie in s.,** être exposé (sur un lit de parade); **lying in s.,** exposition (d'un corps); **robes of s.,** costume *m* d'apparat; (*c*) **s. coach,** voiture *f* d'apparat; **s. ball,** grand bal officiel; **s. reception,** réception solennelle (d'un prince, etc.); **s. apartments,** salons *m* d'apparat. **3.** état *m*, nation *f*; **Secretary of S.,** (i) secrétaire *m* d'État; (ii) *U.S:* = Ministre *m* des Affaires étrangères; **head of s.,** chef *m* d'état; **affairs of s.,** affaires d'État; **s.-aided,** subventionné par l'État; **s.-controlled,** étatisé; **the United States of America,** les États-Unis d'Amérique. **II.** *v.tr.* (*a*) énoncer, déclarer, faire connaître (qch.); **condition stated in the contract,** condition énoncée dans le contrat; **as stated above,** ainsi qu'il est dit plus haut; **I have seen it stated that . . .,** j'ai lu quelque part que . . .; **he is stated to have been in Paris,** on affirme l'avoir vu à Paris; (*b*) **to s. a claim,** exposer une réclamation; *Jur:* **to s. the case,** exposer les faits; **'stated,** *a.* **at s. intervals,** à des époques fixées; à intervalles réglés; **on s. days,** à jours fixes; **'stateless,** *a. Adm:* **s. person,** apatride *mf*; **'stateliness,** *s.* majesté *f*; aspect imposant; dignité *f*; **'stately,** *a.* majestueux, imposant, plein de dignité; noble, élevé; **state ment,** *s.* exposition *f*, exposé *m* (des faits); rapport *m*, compte rendu; **official s. (to the press)** communiqué *m*; **according to his own s.,** suivant sa propre déclaration; **to contradict a s.,** nier une affirmation; *Com:* **s. of account,** état *m* de compte; **'statesman,** *pl.* -men, *s.* homme *m* d'état; **'statesmanlike,** *a.* **to act in a s. way,** se conduire en homme d'état; **'statesmanship,** *s.* science *f* du gouvernement.
static ['stætik], *a.* statique.
station ['steiʃ(ə)n]. **I.** *s.* **1.** (*a*) position *f*, place *f*, poste *m*; (*b*) station *f*, poste *m*; *Av:* base (aérienne); *Austr:* **sheep s.,** élevage *m* de moutons; **lifeboat s.,** station de sauvetage; *El:* **power s.,** centrale *f* électrique; **transformer s.,**

transformateur *m*; *Aut:* **service s.,** station-service *f*, *pl.* stations-service. **2.** position *f*, condition *f*; rang *m*; **s. in life,** situation sociale. **3.** (railway) **s.,** gare *f*; **passenger s., goods s.,** gare de voyageurs, de marchandises; **coach, bus, s.,** gare routière; **underground, tube, s.,** station *f* de métro. **4.** *Ecc:* **the Stations of the Cross,** le chemin de (la) Croix. **II.** *v.tr.* (a) placer, mettre (qn dans un endroit); (b) **to s. troops,** poster des troupes; (c) **to be stationed at . . .,** *Mil:* être en garnison à . . .; *Navy:* être en station à . . .; **'stationary,** *a.* stationnaire; immobile; **s. car,** voiture en stationnement; **'stationmaster,** *s.* chef *m* de gare; **'stationwagon,** *s. Aut:* break *m*, familiale *f*.

stationer ['steiʃənər], *s.* papetier *m*; **s.'s shop,** papeterie *f*; **'stationery,** *s.* papeterie *f*; **office s.,** fournitures *fpl* de bureau.

statistics [stə'tistiks], *s.pl.* (a) (*usu. with sg. const.*) la statistique; (b) **s. for 1977,** statistiques pour 1977; **sta'tistical,** *a.* statistique; **s. tables,** statistiques *fpl*; **statis'tician,** *s.* statisticien, -ienne.

statue ['stætjuː], *s.* statue *f*; **'statuary,** *s.* statues *fpl*; **statu'ette,** *s.* statuette *f*.

stature ['stætjər], *s.* stature *f*; taille *f*.

status ['steitəs], *s.* (a) statut légal (de qn); (b) *Adm:* **civil s.,** état civil; (c) condition *f*, position *f*, rang *m*; **social s.,** rang social; **s. symbol,** marque *f* de standing; **without any official s.,** sans titre officiel; (d) **s. quo,** statu quo *m inv.*

statute ['stætjuːt], *s.* **1.** acte *m* du Parlement; loi *f*; **s. book,** code *m* (des lois); **s. law,** droit écrit; jurisprudence *f*; **the S. of Limitations,** la loi de prescription. **2.** *pl.* statuts *m*, règlements *m* (d'une société); **'statutory,** *a.* **1.** établi, imposé, par la loi; réglementaire; **s. holiday,** fête légale. **2.** statutaire; conforme aux statuts.

staunch¹ [stɔːn(t)ʃ], *a.* sûr, dévoué; ferme; **s. friend,** ami à toute épreuve; **-ly,** *adv.* avec fermeté; avec résolution; avec dévouement; **'staunchness,** *s.* fermeté *f*; dévouement *m*.

staunch², *v.tr.* étancher (le sang); étancher le sang de (la blessure).

stave [steiv]. **I.** *s.* **barrel s.,** douve *f* (d'un tonneau). **II.** *v.tr.* (**staved; staved,** *Nau:* **stove**) (a) **to s. in,** défoncer, enfoncer (un bateau, une barrique); (b) **to s. off,** détourner, écarter (un ennui); prévenir (un danger); conjurer (un désastre); **to s. off hunger,** tromper la faim.

stay¹ [stei]. **I.** *s.* **1.** séjour *m*; visite *f* (chez un ami); **fortnight's s.,** séjour de quinze jours. **2.** *Jur:* **s. of proceedings,** suspension *f* d'instance. **II.** *v.i.* (a) rester; demeurer sur les lieux; *F:* **to s. put,** rester sur place; **to s. at home,** rester à la maison; **to s. in bed,** garder le lit; **to s. to dinner, for dinner,** rester à dîner; (b) séjourner (dans un endroit); **he's staying with us for a few days,** il est venu passer quelques jours

chez nous; **to s. at a hotel,** (i) descendre à, (ii) s'installer à, un hôtel; (c) **horse that can s. three miles,** cheval qui peut fournir une course de trois milles; **'stay-at-home,** *a. & s.* casanier, -ière; **'stay a'way,** *v.i.* ne pas venir; s'absenter; **'stayer,** *s. Sp:* coureur *m* de fond; cheval *m* qui a du fond; stayer *m*; **'stay 'in,** *v.i.* (a) ne pas sortir; rester à la maison; (b) **s.-in strike,** grève *f* sur le tas; **'staying,** *s.* **s. power,** résistance *f*; endurance *f*; **horse with good s. power,** cheval qui a du fond; **'stay 'out,** *v.i.* rester dehors; ne pas rentrer; **to s. out all night,** découcher; ne pas rentrer; *Ind:* **the men are staying out,** la grève continue toujours; **'stay 'up,** *v.i.* ne pas se coucher; **to s. up late,** veiller tard; (*of child*) coucher plus tard que d'habitude.

stay², *s.* support *m*; soutien *m*; appui *m*, étai *m*.

stead [sted], *s.* **1. to stand s.o. in good s.,** être fort utile à qn. **2. to act in s.o.'s s.,** remplacer qn.

steadfast ['stedfɑːst], *a.* ferme; constant; **-ly,** *adv.* fermement; avec constance; **'steadfastness,** *s.* fermeté *f* (d'esprit); constance *f*; ténacité *f*.

steady ['stedi]. **I.** *a.* (a) ferme, solide; fixe, rigide; **to keep s.,** rester en place; ne pas bouger; **to have a s. hand,** avoir la main sûre; **with a s. hand,** d'une main assurée; (b) continu, soutenu; persistant; régulier; **s. progress,** progrès soutenus; **s. pace,** allure réglée; **s. downpour,** pluie persistante; **s. barometer,** baromètre *m* stationnaire; *Com:* **s. demand for sth.,** demande suivie pour qch.; (c) **s. worker,** travailleur assidu, régulier; (d) (*of pers.*) rangé, posé; sérieux. **II.** *adv. & int.* **s.!** ne bougez pas! **s. (on)!** (i) doucement! du calme! (ii) attention (de ne pas tomber)! **III.** *v.* **1.** *v.tr.* (a) (r)affermir; **to s. oneself against sth.,** s'étayer contre qch.; **to s. the nerves,** raffermir les nerfs; (b) **to s. a young man (down),** assagir un jeune homme. **2.** *v.i.* **the market has steadied (down),** le marché a repris son aplomb; **young man who has steadied down,** jeune homme qui s'est rangé; **prices are steadying,** les prix se raffermissent; **-ily,** *adv.* **1.** fermement; **to walk s.,** marcher d'un pas ferme. **2.** (a) régulièrement; sans arrêt; **his health gets s. worse,** sa santé va (en) empirant; (b) uniment; sans à-coups; **horse that gallops s.,** cheval qui galope uniment. **3. to work s. at sth.,** travailler assidûment à qch. **4.** (se conduire) d'une manière rangée; avec sagesse; **'steadiness,** *s.* **1.** fermeté *f*. **2.** assiduité *f*, persévérance *f*, application *f*. **3.** stabilité *f* (des prix, etc.). **4.** (*of pers.*) conduite rangée; sagesse *f*.

steak [steik], *s. Cu:* (a) tranche *f* (de viande, de poisson); (b) bifteck *m*, steak *m*; (*cut from the ribs*) entrecôte *f*; **fillet s.,** tournedos *m*.

steal [stiːl], *v.* (**stole** [stoul]; **stolen** ['stoulən]) **1.** *v.tr.* (a) voler, dérober, soustraire (**sth. from**

s.o., qch. à qn); (*b*) to **s. a glance** at s.o., regarder qn à la dérobée; (*c*) to **s. a march on** s.o., devancer qn; circonvenir qn. **2.** *v.i.* to **s. away**, s'en aller à la dérobée, furtivement; to **s. into the room**, se glisser dans la pièce; to **s. off**, s'esquiver; **'stealer**, *s.* **sheep s.**, voleur *m* de moutons; **'stealing**, *s.* vol *m*.

stealth [stelθ], *s.* **by s.**, à la dérobée; furtivement; **'stealthily**, *adv.* à la dérobée, furtivement; (entrer) à pas de loup; **'stealthiness**, *s.* caractère furtif (d'une action); **'stealthy**, *a.* furtif; **s. glance**, regard dérobé.

steam [sti:m]. **I.** *s.* (*a*) vapeur *f* (d'eau); buée *f*; **room full of s.**, salle remplie de buée; (*b*) **heated by s., s.-heated**, chauffé à la vapeur; to **get up s.**, mettre (la chaudière) sous pression; to **let off s.**, (i) lâcher la vapeur; (ii) *F:* dépenser son superflu d'énergie; (iii) *F:* épancher sa bile; **at full s.**, à toute vapeur; *Nau:* **full s. ahead**, en avant (à) toute (vitesse); **s. engine**, (i) machine *f* à vapeur; (ii) *F:* locomotive *f*; **s. roller**, (i) *Civ.E:* cylindre *m* compresseur; rouleau *m* compresseur; (ii) force *f* irrésistible. **II.** *v.* **1.** *v.tr.* (*a*) cuire à la vapeur; (*b*) to **s. open a letter**, décacheter une lettre à la vapeur. **2.** *v.i.* (*a*) jeter, exhaler, de la vapeur; fumer; (*b*) marcher (à la vapeur); *Nau:* to **s. at ten knots**, filer dix nœuds; (*c*) (*of windscreen, etc.*) to **s. (up)**, s'embuer; **'steamer**, *s.* **1.** *Nau:* paquebot *m.* **2.** *Cu:* marmite *f* à vapeur; **'steaming**, *a.* fumant; **s. hot**, tout chaud; **'steamy**, *a.* plein de vapeur, de buée; (*of atmosphere*) humide.

steel [sti:l]. **I.** *s.* **1.** acier *m*; **the iron and s. industry**, l'industrie *f* sidérurgique; **stainless s.**, acier inoxydable; **sheet s.**, tôle *f* d'acier; **heart of s.**, cœur *m* de fer, d'acier; **muscles of s.**, muscles *m* d'acier. **2.** to **fight with cold s.**, battre à l'arme blanche. **3.** (*for sharpening knives*) affiloir *m.* **II.** *v.tr.* to **s. oneself to do sth.**, (i) s'endurcir à faire qch.; (ii) s'armer de courage pour faire qch.; to **s. oneself, one's heart, against sth.**, se cuirasser contre qch.; **'steelworks**, *s.pl.* (*usu. with sg. const.*) aciérie *f*; **'steely**, *a.* d'acier; to **flash a s. look at s.o.**, jeter un regard dur à qn.

steep¹ [sti:p], *a.* (*a*) escarpé; à pic; raide; **s. climb**, rude montée *f*; (*b*) *F:* **that's a bit s.!** c'est un peu fort! **s. price**, prix exorbitant; **-ly**, *adv.* en pente rapide; à pic; **'steepen**, *v.i.* (*of road*) s'escarper; devenir plus raide; (*of prices*) augmenter; **'steepness**, *s.* raideur *f*, escarpement *m* (d'une pente).

steep², *v.tr.* (*a*) baigner, tremper; mettre (qch.) à tremper; (*b*) to **s. sth. in sth.**, saturer, imbiber, qch. de qch.; **steeped in prejudice**, imbibé de préjugés; **'steeping**, *s.* trempage *m*, macération *f*.

steeple ['sti:pl], *s.* (*a*) clocher *m*; (*b*) flèche *f* (de clocher); **'steeplechase**, *s.* steeple-chase *m*,

steeple *m*; **'steeplechaser**, *s.* cheval *m*, jockey *m*, de steeple; **'steeplejack**, *s.* réparateur *m* de clochers, de cheminées d'usines.

steer¹ ['sti:ər], *v.tr. & i.* gouverner; diriger; conduire (une voiture); barrer (un yacht); to **s. clear of sth.**, éviter qch.; **'steering**, *s.* (*a*) *Nau:* manœuvre *f* de la barre; (*b*) *Aut:* direction *f*; **power(-assisted) s.**, direction assistée; **s. wheel**, volant *m*; **s. column**, colonne *f* de direction; (*c*) *Pol: etc:* **s. committee**, comité *m* d'organisation.

steer², *s.* (*a*) jeune bœuf *m*; bouvillon *m*; (*b*) *N.Am:* bœuf.

stem¹ [stem]. **I.** *s.* **1.** *Bot:* tige *f* (de plante, de fleur); queue *f* (de fruit, de feuille); tronc *m*, souche *f* (d'arbre); régime *m* (de bananes). **2.** pied *m*, patte *f* (de verre à boire); tuyau *m* (de pipe de fumeur). **3.** souche (de famille); *Ling:* thème *m*, radical *m* (d'un mot). **4.** *Nau:* étrave *f*, avant *m*; **from s. to stern**, de l'avant à l'arrière. **II.** *v.i.* (**stemmed**) to **s. from**, être issu de, être le résultat de (qch.); **'stembogen**, *s. Ski:* stembogen *m*.

stem², *v.tr.* (**stemmed**) **1.** contenir, arrêter, endiguer (un cours d'eau). **2.** aller contre, lutter contre (la marée); refouler, remonter (le courant); (*of ship*) étaler (le courant); refouler, résister à (une attaque).

stench [sten(t)ʃ], *s.* odeur *f* infecte; puanteur *f*.

stencil ['stensl]. **I.** *s.* **1.** patron (ajouré); **s. (plate)**, pochoir. **2.** peinture *f* au pochoir. **3.** (*typing*) stencil *m.* **II.** *v.tr.* (**stencilled**) **1.** peindre (qch.) au pochoir; *Ind:* marquer (une caisse). **2.** polycopier (un document).

sten gun ['stengʌn], *s.* = fusil-mitrailleur *m*, *pl.* fusils-mitrailleurs.

stenographer [stə'nɔgrəfər], *s.* sténographe *m*; sténo *mf*; **steno'typist** [stenou-], *s.* sténotypiste *mf*.

stentorian [sten'tɔ:riən], *a.* (voix) de Stentor.

step [step]. **I.** *s.* **1.** pas *m*; to **take a s.**, faire un pas; to **turn one's steps towards . . .**, se diriger, diriger ses pas, vers . . .; **s. by s.**, pas à pas; petit à petit; to **retrace one's steps**, revenir sur ses pas; to **tread in the steps of s.o.**, marcher sur les traces de qn. **2.** pas, cadence *f*; to **keep s., to be in s.**, marcher au pas; être au pas; **waltz s.**, pas de valse. **3.** démarche *f*; to **take the necessary steps**, faire les démarches nécessaires; prendre toutes dispositions utiles; to **take steps to do sth.**, se préparer à faire qch.; **a s. in the right direction**, un pas dans la bonne voie. **4.** marche *f*, degré *m*, pas (d'un escalier); **top s.** (of a stair), palière *f*; (**flight of**) **steps**, (i) escalier *m*; (ii) (*stone*) perron *m.* **5.** (**pair of**) **steps, s. ladder**, escabeau *m*; échelle *f* double; **folding steps**, échelle brisée. **II.** *v.i.* (**stepped**) faire un pas, des pas; marcher pas à pas; **s. this way**, venez par ici; to **s. aside to let s.o. pass**

s'écarter pour laisser passer qn; **the car drew up
and he stepped in, out,** la voiture s'est arrêtée et
il y est monté, descendu; **s. in(side) for a moment,** entrez pour un moment; **s. over to my
place,** venez chez moi; **to s. out briskly,** allonger
le pas; marcher avec entrain; **somebody
stepped on my foot,** on m'a marché sur le pied;
Aut: F: **to s. on the gas,** mettre tous les gaz; **to s.
on the brakes,** donner un coup de frein; **to s. up
to s.o.,** s'approcher de qn; **'stepbrother,** *s.m.*
frère consanguin; demi-frère; **'stepchild,** *s.* enfant né d'un mariage antérieur; **'step-
daughter,** *s.f.* belle-fille, *pl.* belles-filles; **'stepfather,** *s.m.* beau-père, *pl.* beaux-pères; **'stepmother,** *s.f.* belle-mère, *pl.* belles-mères;
'stepsister, *s.f.* sœur consanguine; demi-
sœur; **'stepson,** *s.m.* beau-fils, *pl.* beaux-fils;
'step'up, *v.tr.* augmenter (la production); *El:*
survolter (le courant).
steppe [step], *s. Geog:* steppe *f*.
stereo ['stiəriou, 'steriou], *s. & a. F:* **1.** (*printing*)
cliché *m.* **2.** stéréoscopique. **3.**
stéréo(phonique); **stereo'graphic,** *a.*
stéréographique; **stereo'phonic,** *a.*
stéréophonique; **'stereoscope,** *s.* stéréoscope
m; **stereo'scopic,** *a.* stéréoscopique;
'stereotype. I. *s.* cliché *m.* II. *v.tr.* stéréotyper,
clicher; **'stereotyped,** *a.* **s. phrase,** cliché *m.*
sterile ['sterail], *a.* stérile; **sterility** [stə'riliti], *s.*
stérilité *f;* **sterili'zation** [sterilai-], *s.* stérilisa-
tion *f;* **'sterilize,** *v.tr.* stériliser; **'sterilizer,** *s.*
stérilisateur *m.*
sterling ['stə:liŋ]. **1.** *a.* (monnaie) de bon aloi,
d'aloi. **2.** *s.* **pound s.,** livre *f* sterling; **s. area,** zone
f sterling. **3.** *a.* de bon aloi, vrai, véritable; **s.
qualities,** qualités *f* solides.
stern[1] [stə:n], *a.* sévère, dur, rigide; **s. face,**
visage austère; **-ly,** *adv.* sévèrement,
durement; **'sternness,** *s.* sévérité *f;* austérité
f; dureté *f.*
stern[2] *s. Nau:* arrière *m;* poupe *f;* **s. light,** feu *m*
d'arrière, feu de poupe; **to go out s. first,** appareiller en culant; **'sternmost,** *a.* le plus à
l'arrière.
sternum ['stə:nəm], *s. Anat:* sternum *m.*
stet [stet]. *Typ:* **I.** *Lt.imp.* bon; à maintenir. **II.**
v.tr. (**stetted**) **to s. a word,** maintenir un mot (sur
l'épreuve, sur le MS).
stethoscope ['steθəskoup], *s. Med:* stéthoscope
m.
stevedore ['sti:vdɔ:r], *s.* arrimeur *m;* déchargeur
m.
stew [stju:]. **I.** *s.* (*a*) *Cu:* ragoût *m;* civet *m* (de
chevreuil, etc.); (*b*) *F:* **to be in a s.,** être dans
tous ses états. **II.** *v.* **1.** *v.tr. Cu:* faire cuire (la
viande) en ragoût, à la casserole; **to s. a rabbit,**
fricasser un lapin; **to s. fruit,** faire cuire des
fruits en compote. **2.** *v.i.* (*a*) *Cu:* cuire à la
casserole; mijoter; *F:* **to let s.o. s. in his own

juice,** laisser qn mijoter (dans son jus); (*b*) *F:*
étouffer; manquer d'air; **stewed,** *a.* **s. mutton,**
ragoût *m* de mouton; **s. beef,** bœuf (à la) mode;
bœuf en daube; **s. fruit,** compote *f* de fruits; **s.
apples,** marmelade *f* de pommes.
steward ['stju:əd], *s.* **1.** (*a*) maître *m* d'hôtel (d'un
cercle); (*b*) *Nau:* (i) commis *m* aux vivres; (ii)
garçon *m* de cabine; steward *m;* *Av:* steward;
chief s., maître d'hôtel. **2.** commissaire *m*
(d'une réunion sportive). **3.** *Ind:* **shop s.,**
délégué *m* d'atelier, d'usine, du personnel;
délégué syndical; **stewar'dess,** *s. Nau:*
femme *f* de chambre; *Av:* hôtesse *f* de l'air.
stick[1] [stik], *s.* **1.** (*a*) bâton *m;* (**walking**) **s.,** canne
f; **hockey s.,** crosse *f* de hockey; (*b*) morceau
m de bois; **to gather sticks,** ramasser du bois
sec, du petit bois; **without a s. of furniture,** sans
un meuble. **2.** *F:* (*of pers.*) **queer s.,** drôle de
type. **3.** bâton (de sucre d'orge, de cire à
cacheter). **4. s. of celery,** branche *f* de céleri; **s.
of rhubarb,** tige *f* de rhubarbe. **5.** *Av:* **s. of
bombs,** chapelet *m* de bombes.
stick[2], *v.* (**stuck** [stʌk]) **1.** *v.tr.* (*a*) piquer, enfoncer (**into,** dans); **to s. a knife into s.o.,** percer
qn d'un couteau; **to s. a pin through sth.,**
passer une épingle à travers qch.; (*b*) *F:* **to s. a
rose in one's buttonhole,** mettre une rose à sa
boutonnière; **to s. one's hat on one's head,**
planter son chapeau sur sa tête; **s. it in your
pocket,** fourrez-le dans votre poche; (*c*) coller;
to s. a stamp on a letter, timbrer une lettre; **to s.
down an envelope,** fermer, coller, une
enveloppe; (*d*) *F:* supporter, souffrir (qn,
qch.); **to s. it,** tenir le coup; tenir; **to s. it out,**
tenir jusqu'au bout; **I can't s. him,** je ne peux
pas le sentir. **2.** *v.i.* (*a*) se piquer, s'enfoncer, se
ficher, se planter; (*b*) (se) coller, s'attacher,
tenir, adhérer (**to,** à); **the envelope won't s.,**
l'enveloppe ne veut pas (se) coller; **the
vegetables have stuck to the pan,** les légumes
ont attaché; **the name stuck to him,** ce nom lui
(en) est resté; **to s. to a friend,** ne pas abandonner un ami; **to s. together,** faire preuve de
solidarité; **to s. (to s.o.) like glue,** se cramponner (à qn); **to s. to one's post,** rester à son
poste; **s. to it!** persévérez! ne lâchez pas! **to s.
to one's guns,** ne pas en démordre; **to s. to the
facts,** s'en tenir aux faits; *F:* **to s. to sth.,** garder
qch. pour soi; **he sticks in his room,** il ne sort
pas de sa chambre; (*c*) **to s., to be stuck,** être
pris, engagé; (*in mud*) s'embourber, être em-
bourbé; (*of machine parts, etc.*) coincer; **it
sticks in my throat,** je ne peux pas avaler ça;
the lift has stuck, l'ascenseur est en panne; **the
switch was stuck,** le contact était collé; **'stick
at,** *v.i.* **1.** **to s. at nothing,** ne reculer devant
rien. **2. to s. at a job for six hours,** travailler à
qch. pendant six heures d'arrache-pied;
'sticker, *s.* étiquette gommée, adhésive;

'**stickiness,** s. viscosité f; adhésivité f; '**sticking. 1.** a. adhésif; **s. plaster,** taffetas gommé, sparadrap m. **2.** s. (a) adhésion f; (b) arrêt m, coincement m; '**stick-in-the-mud,** s. F: **an old s.-in-t.-m.,** un vieux routinier; '**stick-on,** a. **s.-on label,** étiquette adhésive; '**stick 'out. 1.** v.tr. **to s. out one's tongue,** tirer sa langue; F: **to s. out one's neck,** prendre des risques. **2.** v.i. (a) faire saillie; **to s. out beyond sth.,** dépasser qch.; (b) F: **to s. out for sth.,** s'obstiner à demander qch.; '**stick 'up. 1.** v.tr. (a) F: **s. 'em up!** haut les mains, les pattes! (b) **to s. up a notice,** afficher un avis. **2.** v.i. (a) se dresser; (b) F: **to s. up for s.o.,** prendre la défense de qn; '**sticky,** a. **1.** collant, gluant, visqueux, adhésif; **to get one's hands s.,** s'engluer les mains; F: **to be on a s. wicket,** être dans une situation difficile. **2.** F: (a) **he's s. about these things,** il est peu accommodant, il fait le difficile, sur ces choses; (b) **to come to a s. end,** finir mal.

stickleback ['stiklbæk], s. Ich: épinoche f.

stickler ['stiklər], s. **s. for sth.,** rigoriste mf à l'égard de qch.; **to be a s. for etiquette,** être à cheval sur l'étiquette.

stiff [stif]. I. a. **1.** (a) raide, rigide, dur, inflexible; **s. shirt,** chemise empesée, de soirée; **s. brush,** brosse f rude; (b) **s. joint,** articulation ankylosée; (of pers.) **s. as a post,** droit comme un piquet; **the body was already s.,** le cadavre était déjà raide; (c) (of pers.) raide, guindé; **s. bow,** salut contraint; (d) inflexible, obstiné; **to offer s. resistance,** résister opiniâtrement. **2.** (a) **s. control lever,** commande dure; (b) **s. lubricant,** graisse consistante; **s. jelly,** gelée f ferme; (c) Nau: **s. breeze,** forte brise. **3.** (a) **s. climb,** montée f rude, pénible; (b) **s. examination,** examen m difficile; (b) **s. price,** prix salé; (c) **a s. whisky,** un whisky bien tassé. II. s. P: **1.** cadavre m; mac(c)habée m. **2. big s.,** gros bêta; **-ly,** adv. **1.** raidement; avec raideur. **2.** d'un air guindé; '**stiffen. 1.** v.tr. (a) raidir, renforcer; Aut: **to s. the suspension,** durcir la suspension; (b) **age has stiffened his joints,** l'âge lui a raidi les membres; (c) raidir, rendre obstiné (qn); (d) **the exam has stiffened,** l'examen est maintenant plus difficile. **2.** v.i. (a) (se) raidir; devenir raide; (b) (of pers.) se raidir, se guinder; (c) prendre de la consistance; (d) Nau: (of wind) fraîchir; '**stiff-'necked,** a. obstiné, entêté; '**stiffness,** s. (a) raideur f, rigidité f; **s. of manner,** raideur, contrainte f; air guindé; (b) fermeté f, consistance f; (c) raideur (d'une pente); difficulté f (d'un examen).

stifle ['staifl]. **1.** v.tr. (a) étouffer, suffoquer; **stifled by the smoke,** asphyxié par la fumée; (b) réprimer (une émotion). **2.** v.i. suffoquer, étouffer; '**stifling,** a. étouffant, suffocant; **it's**

s. here, on étouffe ici.

stigma ['stigmə], s. **1.** stigmate m, tache f. **2.** pl. **stigmata,** stigmates (d'un saint). **3.** Bot: stigmate; '**stigmatize,** v.tr. stigmatiser (qn).

stile [stail], s. échalier m.

stiletto, pl. -o(e)s [sti'letou, -ouz], s. stylet m; **s. heel,** talon m aiguille.

still[1] [stil], a. tranquille, immobile; **to keep s.,** ne pas bouger; se tenir tranquille; **his heart stood s.,** son cœur cessa de battre; **s. night,** nuit calme, silencieuse; **s. water,** eau tranquille; **s. wine,** vin non mousseux; Art: **s. life,** nature morte; '**stillborn,** a. mort-né; '**stillness,** s. tranquillité f, calme m, silence m.

still[2]. **1.** adv. (a) encore; **he's s. here,** il est toujours ici; **I s. have five francs,** il me reste cinq francs; **they are s. playing,** ils jouent encore; (b) **s. more, s. less,** encore plus, encore moins. **2.** conj. cependant, pourtant, encore, toutefois, malgré cela; **s. I did see her,** toujours est-il que je l'ai vue.

still[3], s. alambic m, cornue f.

stilt [stilt], s. (a) **(pair of) stilts,** échasses f; (b) Orn: échasse; '**stilted,** a. (style) guindé, tendu.

stimulate ['stimjuleit], v.tr. stimuler; aiguillonner, activer, exciter (**to,** à); aiguiser (l'appétit); encourager (la production); Med: stimuler (le foie, etc.); '**stimulant,** s. stimulant m; '**stimulating,** a. stimulant, encourageant; **stimu'lation,** s. stimulation f; '**stimulus,** pl. -i, s. stimulant m, aiguillon m; **to give trade a s.,** donner de l'impulsion au commerce.

sting [stiŋ]. I. s. **1.** dard m, aiguillon m (d'abeille). **2.** piqûre f (de guêpe, etc.); douleur cuisante (d'une blessure). II. v. (stung [stʌŋ]) **1.** v.tr. (a) (of bee, nettle) piquer; (of smoke) **to s. the eyes,** picoter les yeux; **that reply stung him (to the quick),** cette réponse l'a piqué (au vif); (b) F: **to be stung,** attraper le coup de fusil. **2.** v.i. **my eyes were stinging,** les yeux me cuisaient; '**stinging,** a. piquant, cuisant; **s. nettle,** ortie brûlante; **s. blow,** coup cinglant, coup raide.

stingy ['stin(d)ʒi], a. mesquin, chiche, ladre; **-ily,** adv. chichement, mesquinement; '**stinginess,** s. mesquinerie f, ladrerie f; pingrerie f.

stink [stiŋk]. I. s. (a) puanteur f; odeur infecte; (b) **to raise a s. (about sth.),** faire de l'esclandre; crier au scandale; rouspéter (à propos de qch.). II. v. (stank [stæŋk]; stunk [stʌŋk]) **1.** v.i. puer; sentir mauvais; empester; **to s. of garlic,** puer l'ail; P: **he (positively) stinks,** c'est un type infect! **2.** v.tr. **to s. s.o. out,** chasser qn par la mauvaise odeur; **to s. the room out,** empester la pièce; '**stinker,** s. P: **1.** (of pers.) sale type m. **2. to write s.o. a s.,** écrire une lettre carabinée à qn; '**stinking,** a. puant, empesté, infect.

stint [stint], v.tr. **1. to s. oneself,** se refuser le nécessaire; **to s. oneself for one's children,** se priver pour ses enfants; **to s. s.o. of sth.,** refuser qch. à qn; priver qn de qch. **2.** lésiner sur (qch.).

stipend ['staipend], *s.* traitement *m*, appointements *mpl* (d'un ecclésiastique, d'un magistrat).

stipple ['stipl], *v.tr.* pointiller; **stippled design,** dessin au pointillé; **'stippling,** *s.* pointillage *m*.

stipulate ['stipjuleit], *v.tr. & i.* **to s. for a reward of a thousand pounds,** stipuler une récompense de mille livres; **to s. that the tenant shall pay for repairs,** stipuler que toutes les réparations seront à la charge du locataire; **within the time stipulated,** dans le délai prescrit; **stipu'lation,** *s.* stipulation *f*; **with the s. that . . .,** à condition que . . ..

stir [stə:r]. **I.** *s.* **1.** remuement *m*; **to give one's coffee a s.,** remuer son café. **2.** (*a*) **the s. of a great town,** le mouvement d'une grande ville; **a great s.,** un grand remue-ménage; (*b*) agitation *f*, émoi *m*; **to make a s.,** faire du bruit, de l'éclat; faire sensation. **II.** *v.* (**stirred**) **1.** *v.tr.* (*a*) remuer, mouvoir; **I won't s. a foot,** je ne bougerai pas d'ici; (*b*) activer, agiter; **to s. one's tea,** remuer son thé; **to s. up trouble,** fomenter la dissension; (*c*) émouvoir, troubler (qn); **to s. s.o. to pity,** émouvoir la compassion de qn. **2.** *v.i.* bouger, remuer; **he didn't s. out of the house,** il n'est pas sorti de la maison; **there's not a breath of air stirring,** on ne sent pas un souffle d'air; **'stirring,** *a.* **1.** actif, remuant; **s. times,** époque mouvementée. **2.** émouvant; **s. speech,** discours entraînant.

stirrup ['stirəp], *s.* étrier *m*; **to lose one's stirrups,** perdre ses étriers; **s. cup,** coup *m* de l'étrier.

stitch [stitʃ]. **I.** *s.* **1.** (*a*) *Needlew:* point *m*, piqûre *f*; **to put a few stitches in a garment,** faire un point à un vêtement; **he hasn't a dry s. on him,** il est complètement trempé; (*b*) *Knitting:* maille *f*; **to drop a s.,** sauter, laisser échapper, une maille; (*c*) *Med:* (point de) suture *f*; **to put stitches in a wound,** suturer, faire une suture à, une plaie. **2.** *Med:* **s. (in the side),** point de côté. **II.** *v.tr.* (*a*) coudre (un vêtement); **to s. sth. on,** coudre qch. en place; **to s. up a tear,** recoudre une déchirure; (*b*) *Med:* **to s. (up) a wound,** suturer une plaie; (*c*) brocher (un livre).

stoat [stout], *s. Z:* hermine *f*.

stock [stɔk]. **I.** *s.* **1.** (*a*) *Hort:* sujet *m*; portegreffe(s) *m*; (*b*) race *f*, famille *f*, lignée *f*. **2.** fût *m*, bois *m* (de fusil). **3.** *Nau:* pl. **stocks,** chantier *m*; cale *f* de construction; **ship on the stocks,** navire en construction. **4.** (*a*) provision *f*, approvisionnement *m*; **to lay in a s. of wood,** faire (une) provision de bois; (*b*) *Com:* marchandises *fpl*; stock *m*; **surplus s.,** soldes *mpl*; **in s.,** en magasin, en stock, en dépôt; **to**

take s., faire l'inventaire; *F:* **to take s. of s.o.,** scruter, toiser, qn; (*c*) *Agr:* bétail *m*; **fat s.,** bétail de boucherie; **s. farming,** élevage *m* (de bétail). **5.** *Cu:* bouillon *m*. **6.** *Fin:* fonds *mpl*, valeurs *fpl*; **Government s.,** fonds d'état; **stocks and shares,** valeurs mobilières; **the S. Exchange,** la Bourse (de Londres). **7.** *Bot:* matthiole *f*; giroflée *f* des jardins; **Virginia s.,** julienne *f* de Mahon. **8.** *attrib.* **s. size,** taille courante; **s. argument,** argument habituel, bien connu; **s. phrase,** phrase toute faite; cliché *m*; *Sp:* **s. car,** stock-car *m*. **II.** *v.tr.* (*a*) monter (une ferme) en bétail; approvisionner (une maison) (**with,** de); **well stocked,** (magasin) bien monté, bien approvisionné. **2.** tenir, garder, (qch.) en magasin; stocker (des marchandises); **'stockbroker,** *s.* agent *m* de change; **'stockist,** *s. Com:* stockiste *mf*; **'stockman,** *pl.* **-men,** *s. Austr:* bouvier *m*; **'stockpile. I.** *s.* stocks *mpl* de réserve. **II.** *v.tr. & i.* stocker; constituer des stocks de réserve; **'stockpiling,** *s.* stockage *m*; constitution *f* de réserves; **'stockpot,** *s. Cu:* pot *m* à bouillon; pot-au-feu *m inv*; **'stock-'still,** *a.* **to stand s.-s.,** rester, complètement immobile; **'stocktaking,** *s. Com:* inventaire *m*; **'stocky,** *a.* trapu; (cheval) goussaut, ragot.

stockade [stɔ'keid], *s.* **1.** palissade *f*, palanque *f*. **2.** *Fort:* estacade *f*.

stocking ['stɔkiŋ], *s. Cl:* bas *m*; **fully-fashioned s.,** bas diminué; *Med:* **elastic stockings,** bas pour varices; *Knitting:* **s. stitch,** point *m* (de) jersey; **to stand six feet in one's stockings,** mesurer six pieds sans chaussures.

stodge [stɔdʒ], *s. F:* aliment bourrant, *esp.* pudding *m*; **'stodgy,** *a.* (repas) lourd; (livre) indigeste; *F:* (of pers.) lourd, rasoir.

stoical ['stouik(ə)l], *a.* stoïque; **-ally,** *adv.* stoïquement; **'stoicism** [-sizm], *s.* stoïcisme *m*.

stoke [stouk], *v.tr.* charger (un foyer); chauffer (un four); entretenir le feu d'(un four); **'stoker,** *s. Nau:* chauffeur *m*.

stole [stoul], *s.* étole *f*.

stolen ['stoulən], *a.* (argent) volé.

stolid ['stɔlid], *a.* lourd, lent, impassible; **-ly,** *adv.* avec flegme; **sto'lidity,** *s.* flegme *m*.

stomach ['stʌmək]. **I.** *s.* **1.** estomac *m*; **s. ache,** douleurs *fpl* d'estomac. **2. to crawl on one's s.,** ramper à plat ventre. **3.** envie *f*, goût *m* (**for,** de); cœur *m*, courage *m* (pour faire qch.). **II.** *v.tr. F:* endurer, supporter, tolérer (qch.); digérer (une insulte); **I can't s. it any longer,** j'en ai plein le dos.

stone [stoun]. **I.** *s.* **1.** (*a*) pierre *f*; **to leave no s. unturned (in order to do sth.),** ne rien négliger (pour faire qch.); **to throw stones at s.o.,** (i) lancer des pierres à qn; (ii) *F:* jeter des pierres dans le jardin de qn; **s.'s throw,** jet *m* de pierre;

within a s.'s throw, à quelques pas, à deux pas; (b) moellon m; pierre de taille; not to leave a s. standing, ne pas laisser pierre sur pierre; (c) meule f (à repasser, de moulin); honing s., oil-s., pierre à huile. 2. precious stones, pierres précieuses; pierreries f. 3. (material) pierre (à bâtir, etc.); s. quarry, carrière f (de pierre); broken s., pierraille f, cailloutis m; s. wall, mur m de pierre. 4. Med: calcul m, pierre (du rein). 5. noyau m (de fruit); s. fruit, fruit m à noyau. 6. inv. Meas: 6 kg 348; to weigh 12 s. = peser 76 kilos. 7. attrib. de, en, pierre; de grès; s. cold, froid comme (le) marbre, complètement froid; F: I've got him s. cold! je le tiens! s. dead, raide mort; s. deaf, complètement sourd; s. blind, complètement aveugle. II. v.tr. 1. to s. s.o. (to death), lapider qn. 2. to s. fruit, enlever les noyaux des fruits; énoyauter, dénoyauter, les fruits, épépiner (des raisins secs); 'stonecrop, s. Bot: orpin m; 'stonemason, s. maçon m; 'stoneware, s. poterie f de grès; 'stonework, s. (a) maçonnage m; maçonnerie f; (b) ouvrage m en pierre; 'stoniness, s. 1. nature pierreuse (du sol). 2. dureté f (de cœur); 'stony, a. 1. pierreux; couvert, rempli, de pierres. 2. dur comme la pierre. 3. s. heart, cœur de roche, de marbre; s.-hearted, dur, insensible; s. look, regard glacial. 4. F: s. (broke), dans la dèche; à sec; I'm s. (broke), je n'ai pas le sou; -ily, adv. (regarder) d'un air glacial.

stooge [stu:dʒ]. I. s. F: (a) Th: faire-valoir m inv; (b) subalterne m, nègre m; (c) police s., P: casserole f. II. v.i. F: (a) Th: servir de faire-valoir (à un acteur); (b) to s. (for s.o.), faire le nègre.

stool [stu:l], s. 1. tabouret m; folding s., pliant m; wooden s., escabeau m; to fall between two stools, demeurer entre deux selles. 2. pl. Med: selles f.

stoop [stu:p]. I. s. inclination f en avant; to walk with a s., marcher le dos voûté; marcher penché. II. v.i. (a) se pencher, se baisser; to s. to go through the door, se baisser pour passer par la porte; (b) s'abaisser, descendre (à (faire) qch.); I won't s. to (doing) that, je ne veux pas déroger jusqu'à faire cela; (c) avoir le dos rond; être voûté; 'stooping, a. penché, courbé; voûté.

stop [stɔp]. I. s. 1. (a) arrêt m, interruption f; to put a s. to sth., arrêter, faire cesser, qch.; it ought to be put a s. to, il faudrait y mettre fin; (b) arrêt, halte f; to come to a s., s'arrêter, faire halte; (c) bus s., arrêt d'autobus; request s., arrêt facultatif; (d) Av: scheduled s., escale prévue. 2. full s., point m. 3. Mus: jeu m, registre m (d'orgue). 4. dispositif m de blocage; arrêt, taquet m, butée f; door s., heurtoir m. II. v. (stopped) 1. v.tr. (a) boucher, aveugler (une

voie d'eau); plomber, obturer (une dent); to s. (up), boucher, fermer (un trou); obstruer (un tuyau); (of pipe) to get stopped (up), se boucher, s'obstruer; to s. one's ears, se boucher les oreilles; to s. a gap, (i) boucher un trou; (ii) combler une lacune; (b) arrêter (un cheval, etc.); s. thief! au voleur! to s. the traffic, interrompre la circulation; to s. s.o.'s breath, couper la respiration à qn; to s. a blow, parer un coup; Box: bloquer; to s. s.o. from doing sth., empêcher qn de faire qch.; I can't s. it happening, je ne peux pas l'empêcher; to s. a cheque, bloquer, stopper, un chèque; to s. a clock, a machine, arrêter une pendule, une machine; (of abuse) it ought to be stopped, il faudrait y mettre fin; (c) cesser (ses efforts); arrêter (de parler); s. it! assez! finissez! it's stopped raining, la pluie a cessé; (d) to s. the supply of electricity, couper l'électricité; to s. s.o.'s wages, retenir le salaire de qn; to s. s.o.'s allowance, couper les vivres à qn; Mil: all leave is stopped, toutes les permissions sont suspendues. 2. v.i. (a) s'arrêter; (of car, etc.) stopper; (of pers.) to s. short, dead, s'arrêter net; P.N: all buses s. here, arrêt m fixe; P.N: Aut: s., stop; s. light, le (feu) stop; Rail: how long do we s. at Aix? combien d'arrêt à Aix? to pass a station without stopping, brûler une gare; Nau: to s. at a port, faire escale à un port; (b) cesser; my watch has stopped, ma montre (s')est arrêtée; without stopping, (parler) sans cesse; (travailler) d'arrache-pied; he didn't s. at that, il ne s'en tint pas là; to s. for s.o., attendre qn; the matter won't s. there, l'affaire n'en demeurera pas là; the rain's stopped, la pluie a cessé; (c) to s. at home, rester à la maison; he's stopping with us a few days, il est venu passer quelques jours chez nous; to s. at a hotel, descendre, séjourner, à un hôtel; 'stopcock, s. robinet m d'arrêt; 'stopgap, s. bouche-trou m; it'll do as a s., cela servira à boucher un trou; 'stop 'off, v.i. s'arrêter, faire étape; 'stopover, s. Av: escale f; 'stoppage, s. 1. arrêt m; mise f au repos; suspension f (du travail, etc.). 2. obstruction f, engorgement m; s. of the bowels, occlusion intestinale. 3. arrêt, halte f; interruption f (du travail); 'stopper. I. s. (a) bouchon m; screw s., fermeture f à vis; (b) F: to put a s. on s.o.'s activities, enrayer les activités de qn. II. v.tr. boucher (un flacon); 'stopping, s. (a) plombage m (d'une dent); (b) s. place, (point m d')arrêt m; escale f; 'stop-'press, a. Journ: s.-p. news, (informations fpl de) dernière heure; interruption f (du travail); 'stopwatch, s. compte-secondes m inv; chronomètre m.

store [stɔːr]. I. s. 1. (a) provision f, approvisionnement m; (b) abondance f; to lay in a s. of sth., s'approvisionner de qch.; what the future holds in s., ce que l'avenir nous réserve;

that's a treat in s., c'est un plaisir à venir; **to set great s. by sth.**, faire grand cas de qch. **2.** *pl.* **stores**, provisions, approvisionnements, vivres *m.* **3.** (*a*) entrepôt *m*, magasin *m*; (*b*) **village s.**, alimentation *f*, épicerie *f*, du village; **(department) s.**, grand magasin. **II.** *v.tr.* **1. to s. (up)**, amasser, accumuler (qch.); emmagasiner (l'électricité, la chaleur). **2.** (*a*) emmagasiner, mettre en dépôt (des meubles); mettre en grange (le foin); (*b*) prendre en dépôt; **stored furniture**, mobilier *m* au garde-meuble; **'storage,** *s.* **1.** emmagasinage *m*, emmagasinement *m*; accumulation *f* (de pouvoir); **s. heating,** chauffage *m* par accumulation; **to take goods out of s.**, sortir des marchandises. **2.** caves *fpl*, greniers *mpl*; entrepôts *mpl*, magasins *mpl* (d'une maison de commerce); **s. unit,** (meuble *m* de) rangement *m.* **3.** frais *mpl* d'entrepôt; **'storehouse,** *s.* magasin *m*, entrepôt *m*; **'storekeeper,** *s.* **1.** magasinier *m.* **2.** *N.Am:* boutiquier, -ière.

storey ['stɔːri], *s.* étage *m* (d'une maison); **on the third s.**, *N.Am:* **on the fourth s.**, au troisième (étage).

stork [stɔːk], *s. Orn:* cigogne *f.*

storm [stɔːm]. **I.** *s.* **1.** orage *m*; **s. cloud,** (i) nuée *f* (d'orage); (ii) nuage *m* à l'horizon, nuage menaçant; **a s. in a teacup,** une tempête dans un verre d'eau; **to raise a s.,** soulever une tempête. **2. s. of abuse, of applause,** tempête d'injures, d'applaudissements. **3. to take by s.,** prendre d'assaut, emporter (un fort); emporter (un auditoire); **s. troops,** troupes *f* d'assaut. **II.** *v.* **1.** *v.i.* (*of pers.*) tempêter. **2.** *v.tr.* prendre d'assaut, livrer l'assaut à (une place forte); **storming party,** troupes d'assaut; **'stormy,** *a.* (vent) tempétueux; (temps, ciel) orageux, d'orage; **s. sea,** mer démontée; **s. discussion,** discussion orageuse.

story[1] ['stɔːri], *s.* **1.** histoire *f*, récit *m*, conte *m*; **according to his own s.,** d'après lui; **that's quite another s.,** ça c'est une autre paire de manches; **it's the (same) old s.,** c'est toujours la même rengaine, la même chanson; **it's a long s.,** c'est toute une histoire; **these bruises tell their own s.,** ces meurtrissures en disent long. **2. short s.,** nouvelle *f*; **detective s.,** (roman *m*) policier (*m*). **3.** intrigue *f* (d'un roman). **4. cock-and-bull s.,** conte à dormir debout; **idle s.,** conte fait à plaisir; **'storyteller,** *s.* conteur, -euse.

story[2], *s. N.Am:* = STOREY.

stout[1] [staut], *a.* **1.** (i) fort, vigoureux; (ii) brave, vaillant; (iii) ferme, résolu; **to put up a s. resistance,** se défendre vaillamment; **s. heart,** cœur vaillant; **s.-hearted,** intrépide, vaillant. **2.** (*of thg*) fort, solide; (*of cloth*) résistant. **3.** gros, corpulent; **-ly,** *adv.* **1.** fortement, vigoureusement, vaillamment; **to maintain sth. s.,** affirmer qch. énergiquement; **to deny sth. s.,**

nier qch. fort et ferme. **2. s. built,** solidement bâti; **'stoutness,** *s.* **1.** solidité *f.* **2.** embonpoint *m*, corpulence *f.*

stout[2], *s.* stout *m*; bière brune forte.

stove [stouv], *s.* (*a*) poêle *m*, fourneau *m*; **slow-combustion s.,** calorifère *m*; *Dom.Ec:* **oil s.,** poêle à mazout; (*b*) **gas s., electric s.,** cuisinière *f* à gaz, électrique; **'stovepipe,** *s.* tuyau *m* de poêle.

stow [stou], *v.tr.* **1. to s. (away),** mettre en place, ranger, serrer (des objets). **2.** *Nau:* arrimer (des marchandises); **to s. the cargo,** faire l'arrimage *m.* **3.** *v.i.* **to s. away,** s'embarquer clandestinement (à bord d'un navire); **'stowage,** *s. Nau:* arrimage *m*; **'stowaway,** *s.* passager clandestin.

straggle ['strægl], *v.i.* **to s. (along),** marcher sans ordre, à la débandade; **'straggler,** *s.* celui, celle, qui reste en arrière; traînard, -arde; **'straggling,** *a.* disséminé; **s. village,** village aux maisons éparses.

straight [streit]. **I.** *a.* **1.** (*a*) droit, rectiligne; **s. line,** ligne droite; droite *f*; **s. hair,** cheveux plats; (*b*) (mouvement) en ligne droite. **2.** juste, honnête; loyal; **s. answer,** réponse franche, sans équivoque. **3.** net; tout simple; *Pol:* **s. fight,** campagne électorale à deux candidats; **s. whisky,** whisky sec. **4.** (*a*) droit; d'aplomb; **to put sth. s.,** redresser, ajuster, qch.; **your tie isn't s.,** votre cravate est de travers; (*b*) en ordre; **to put the room s.,** remettre de l'ordre dans la pièce; **to put things s.,** arranger les choses; débrouiller l'affaire. **II.** *s.* **1. to be out of the s.,** n'être pas d'aplomb; être de travers; (*of pers.*) **to be on the s.,** agir loyalement; **material cut on the s.,** tissu coupé de droit fil. **2.** *Rac:* **the s.,** la ligne droite. **III.** *adv.* **1.** droit; **to shoot s.,** tirer juste; **keep s. on,** continuez tout droit; **to go s.,** (i) aller droit; (ii) vivre honnêtement; **to read a book s. through,** lire un livre d'un bout à l'autre. **2.** directement; **I'll come s. back,** je ne ferai qu'aller et (re)venir; **to go s. to the point,** aller droit au fait; **to drink s. from the bottle,** boire à même la bouteille; **to walk s. in,** entrer sans frapper; **s. away,** tout de suite; immédiatement, aussitôt; (deviner qch.) du premier coup; **s. off,** sur-le-champ; tout de suite; d'emblée. **3. to look s.o. s. in the face,** regarder qn bien en face; **I tell you s.,** je vous le dis tout net; **s. out,** franchement; sans détours, sans ambages. **4. to play s.,** jouer beau jeu; **'straighten,** *v.* **1.** *v.tr.* (*a*) rendre (qch.) droit; (re)dresser (qch.); défausser, dégauchir (une barre de fer); (*b*) **to s. (up),** ranger (qch.); mettre (qch.) en ordre; **to s. (out) one's affairs,** mettre ses affaires en ordre; **to s. one's tie,** arranger sa cravate. **2.** *v.i.* se redresser, devenir droit; (*of pers.*) **to s. up,** se redresser; **straight'forward,** *a.* loyal; franc; **to give a s.**

answer, répondre sans détours; **-ly,** *adv.*
(agir) avec droiture, loyalement; (parler)
carrément, franchement, sans détours;
straight'forwardness, *s.* droiture *f,*
honnêteté *f,* franchise *f;* **'straightness,** *s.* 1.
rectitude *f* (d'une ligne). 2. droiture *f,* rectitude
(de conduite).
strain[1] [strein]. **I.** *s.* 1. tension *f;* **s. on the rope,**
tension de la corde; **breaking s.,** effort *m* de
rupture; **it would be too great a s. on my purse,**
ce serait trop demander à ma bourse; **the s. of
modern life,** la tension de la vie moderne; **mental s.,** surmenage intellectuel. 2. *Med:* entorse *f,*
foulure *f; Mec. E:* déformation *f* (d'une pièce).
3. ton *m,* sens *m* (d'un discours); **he went on in
the same s.,** il s'est étendu dans ce sens. **II.** *v.* 1.
v.tr. (a) tendre, surtendre (un câble); **to s. one's
ears,** tendre l'oreille; **to s. one's eyes doing sth.,**
se fatiguer, s'abîmer, les yeux à faire qch.; **to s.
s.o.'s friendship,** exiger trop de l'amitié de qn;
(b) (i) *Med:* se forcer (le cœur); se fouler
(l'épaule); **to s. oneself doing sth.,** se surmener,
s'éreinter, à faire qch.; (ii) forcer (une poutre);
Mec. E: déformer (une pièce); (c) filtrer, passer
(un liquide); **to s. the vegetables,** faire égoutter
les légumes. 2. *v.i.* faire un grand effort; **to s.
after sth.,** faire tous ses efforts pour atteindre
qch.; **strained,** *a.* 1. **s. relations,** rapports tendus; **s. ankle,** cheville foulée; **s. heart,** cœur
fatigué. 2. filtré, tamisé; **'strainer,** *s.* filtre *m,*
tamis *m; Cu:* passoire *f.*
strain[2], *s.* 1. qualité héritée, inhérente; tendance
f; **a s. of weakness,** un héritage, un fond, de
faiblesse. 2. race *f,* lignée *f;* (*of virus*) souche *f.*
strait [streit]. 1. *a.* **s. waistcoat,** camisole *f* de
force. 2. *s.* (a) détroit *m;* **the Straits of Dover,** le
Pas de Calais; (b) **to be in great, dire, straits,**
être dans l'embarras; **'straitened,** *a.* **to be in s.
circumstances,** être dans la gêne, dans l'embarras; **'straitjacket,** *s.* camisole *f* de force;
'strait'laced, *a.* prude; collet monté *inv.*
strand[1] [strænd], *s.* (a) brin *m* (de cordage, de fil
à coudre); (b) fil *m* (de perles); tresse *f* (de
cheveux).
strand[2], *v.tr. & i.* échouer; **'stranded,** *a.* (*of
ship*) échoué; (*of pers.*) **to be s.,** être en panne;
to leave s.o. s., laisser qn en plan.
strange [strein(d)ʒ], *a.* 1. **s. faces,** visages in-
connus; **this writing is s. to me,** je ne connais
pas cette écriture. 2. singulier, bizarre, étrange;
s. to say . . ., chose étrange (à dire) . . .; **-ly,**
adv. étrangement, singulièrement; **s. enough
. . .,** chose étrange . . .; **'strangeness,** *s.* 1.
étrangeté *f,* singularité *f.* 2. **the s. of the work,** la
nouveauté du travail; **'stranger,** *s.* étranger,
-ère; inconnu, -ue; **I'm a s. here,** je ne suis pas
d'ici; **you're quite a s.!** on ne vous voit plus!
vous vous faites rare!
strangle ['stræŋgl], *v.tr.* étrangler (qn); **to s.**

oneself, s'étrangler; **strangled voice,** voix
étranglée; **'stranglehold,** *s.* **to have a s. on
s.o.,** tenir qn à la gorge; **strangu'lation,** *s.*
strangulation *f.*
strap [stræp]. **I.** *s.* 1. courroie *f;* **watch s.,**
bracelet *m* pour montre. 2. bande *f,* sangle *f* (de
cuir, de toile); barrette *f* (de soulier). **II.** *v.tr.*
(strapped) 1. **to s. sth. (up),** attacher, lier, qch.
avec une courroie; sangler (un paquet). 2.
Med: mettre de l'emplâtre adhésif à (une)
blessure); **'straphanger,** *s.* voyageur *m*
debout (dans le métro); **'strapping,** *a. s.*
fellow, grand gaillard.
stratagem ['strætədʒəm], *s.* ruse *f* (de guerre);
stratagème *m;* **stra'tegic(al)** [-'ti:dʒik-], *a.*
stratégique; **-ally,** *adv.* stratégiquement;
'strategist, *s.* stratégiste *m;* **'strategy,** *s.*
stratégie *f.*
stratify ['strætifai], *v.tr.* stratifier; **stratifi'cation,** *s.* stratification *f;* **'stratosphere,** *s.*
stratosphère *f.*
stratum, *pl.* **-a** ['strɑːtəm, 'streitəm, -ə], *s. Geog:*
couche *f;* **social strata,** couches sociales.
straw [strɔː]. 1. *s.* paille *f;* **s. hat,** chapeau *m* de
paille; **s. mat,** paillasson *m;* **s. mattress,**
paillasse *f.* 2. *s.* paille; chalumeau *m;* **to drink
through a s.,** boire (qch.) avec une paille; **s. in
the wind,** indication *f* de l'opinion publique; **it's
the last s.!** c'est le comble! il ne manquait plus
que cela! 3. *a.* **s.(-coloured),** paille *inv;* **'straw-
board,** *s.* carton *m* paille.
strawberry ['strɔːb(ə)ri], *s.* (i) fraise *f;* (ii)
(*plant*) fraisier *m;* **wild s.,** fraise des bois; **s.
jam,** confiture *f* de fraises; **s. ice,** glace *f* à la
fraise.
stray [strei]. **I.** *a.* 1. (animal) égaré, errant. 2. **s.
bullets,** balles perdues; **s. thoughts,** pensées
détachées; **a few s. houses,** quelques maisons
isolées. **II.** *s.* animal égaré; bête perdue. **III.** *v.i.*
s'égarer, errer; s'écarter (de qch.); **to let one's
thoughts s.,** laisser vaguer ses pensées.
streak [striːk]. **I.** *s.* 1. raie *f;* bande *f,* strie *f;* trait
m, filet *m;* **the first s. of dawn,** la première lueur
du jour; **like a s. of lightning,** comme un éclair.
2. **he had a s. of cowardice,** il avait de la lâcheté
dans sa nature. **II.** *v.i.* **to s. past,** passer comme
un éclair; **to s. off,** se sauver à toutes jambes;
streaked, *a.* rayé, strié; **'streaking,** *s. T.V:*
traînage *m;* **'streaky,** *a.* (a) en raies; (b) rayé,
strié; (c) (*of bacon*) entrelardé.
stream [striːm]. **I.** *s.* 1. cours *m* d'eau; ruisseau
m; flot *m* d'eau; **in a thin s.,** en mince filet. 2.
coulée *f* (de lave); **s. of abuse,** torrent *m*
d'injures; **people entered in streams,** les gens
entraient à flots; **s. of cars,** défilé ininterrompu
de voitures; **in one continuous s.,** à jet continu.
3. courant *m;* **with the s.,** au fil de l'eau; **against
the s.,** à contre-courant. **II.** *v.i.* (a) (*of liquid*)
couler (à flots); ruisseler; **people were**

streaming over the bridge, les gens traversaient le pont à flot continu; **they streamed in, out,** ils entraient, sortaient, à flots; (b) (*of hair, banner*) flotter (au vent); 'streamer, s. banderole f; **paper streamers,** serpentins m; 'streaming, a. ruisselant; **face s. with tears,** visage baigné de larmes; **to be s. with perspiration,** être en nage; **I've got a s. cold,** j'ai attrapé un fort rhume de cerveau; 'streamline, v.tr. caréner (une voiture); moderniser, rationaliser (des méthodes); 'streamlined, a. caréné, fuselé, profilé; aux formes élancées; **s. economy,** économie réduite à l'essentiel; 'streamlining, s. (a) carénage m, profilage m; (b) modernisation f (des méthodes, etc.).

street [stri:t], s. rue f; **to turn a family into the s.,** mettre une famille sur le pavé; **the man in the s.,** l'homme moyen; **they're not in the same s. with him,** ils ne sont pas de taille avec lui; **s. level,** rez-de-chaussée m inv; **s. accidents,** accidents de la circulation; **s. door,** porte f sur la rue; porte d'entrée; **s. lighting,** éclairage m des rues; **s. sweeper,** (i) (*pers.*) balayeur m des rues; (ii) (*machine*) balayeuse f (de rues); **s. musician,** musicien de carrefour; 'streetcar, s. N.Am: tramway m.

strength [streŋθ], s. 1. (a) force(s) f(pl); **with all one's s.,** de toutes ses forces; **s. of mind,** fermeté f d'esprit; **s. of will,** résolution f; **by sheer s.,** de vive force; **on the s. of his letter,** sur la foi de sa lettre; (b) solidité f. 2. **to be present in great s.,** être présents en grand nombre. 3. Mil: effectif(s) m(pl) (d'une unité); **at full s.,** à effectif complet; **to be on the s.,** figurer sur les effectifs; 'strengthen, v.tr. consolider (un mur); renforcer (une poutre); remonter, fortifier (qn); (r)affermir (l'autorité de qn); 'strengthening. 1. a. fortifiant; (*of drink*) remontant. 2. s. renforcement m; consolidation f; armement m (d'une poutre).

strenuous ['strenjuəs], a. 1. (*of pers.*) actif, énergique. 2. (travail) acharné, ardu; (effort) tendu; **s. life,** vie toute d'effort; **to offer s. opposition to sth.,** faire une opposition vigoureuse à qch.; -ly, adv. vigoureusement; avec acharnement; énergiquement; 'strenuousness, s. ardeur f, vigueur f; acharnement m.

stress [stres]. I. s. 1. force f, contrainte f. 2. (a) Mec: effort (subi); tension f, travail m; (b) **period of storm and s.,** période f de trouble et d'agitation. 3. (a) insistance f; **to lay s. on a fact,** insister sur un fait; (b) Ling: (accent) accent m; **s. mark,** accent écrit. II. v.tr. 1. Mec: charger, faire travailler (une poutre). 2. appuyer, insister, sur (qch.); souligner, peser sur (un mot); accentuer (une syllabe, un mot).

stretch [stretʃ]. I. s. 1. (a) allongement m, extension f; Rac: **at full s.,** à toute allure; (b) allongement; tension f; **by a s. of the imagination,** par un effort d'imagination; (c) élasticité f; **s. nylons,** bas extensibles. 2. (a) étendue f (de pays); **level s.** (of road), palier m; (b) **for a long s. of time,** longtemps; **at a s.,** tout d'un trait; d'affilée; F: **to do a s.,** faire de la prison, de la taule. II. v. 1. v.tr. (a) tendre (de l'élastique); élargir (ses chaussures); (b) **to s.** (oneself), s'étirer; **to s. one's legs,** se dégourdir les jambes; **stretched (out) on the ground,** étendu de tout son long par terre; (c) forcer (le sens d'un mot, etc.); **to s. a point,** faire une concession. 2. v.i. (a) s'élargir; s'allonger; (*of elastic*) s'étendre; (*of gloves*) s'élargir; **material that stretches,** tissu m qui prête; (*of meal*) **it will s. for four,** on en fera quand même quatre portions; (b) (*of landscape*) s'étendre; (c) **I can s. for it,** c'est à portée de ma main; 'stretcher, s. brancard m; **s. bearer,** brancardier m.

strew [stru:], v.tr. (strewed; strewn) **to s. the floor with sand, to s. sand over the floor,** jeter du sable sur le plancher; **to s. the pavement with flowers,** parsemer le pavé de fleurs.

strict [strikt], a. 1. exact; strict; **in the strictest sense of the word,** au sens précis du mot; **s. neutrality,** neutralité rigoureuse. 2. **s. orders,** ordres formels; **s. discipline,** discipline f sévère. 3. (*of pers.*) sévère; **to be s. with s.o.,** traiter qn avec beaucoup de rigueur; -ly, adv. 1. exactement, rigoureusement; **s. speaking,** à proprement parler; **s. in confidence,** à titre tout à fait confidentiel. 2. étroitement; strictement; **smoking (is) s. prohibited,** défense formelle, défense expresse, de fumer; **it is s. forbidden,** c'est absolument défendu. 3. sévèrement; (élevé) avec rigueur; 'strictness, s. 1. exactitude rigoureuse, précision f (d'une traduction). 2. rigueur f (des règles); sévérité f (de la discipline); 'stricture, s. **to pass strictures on s.o., sth.,** diriger des critiques f contre qn; trouver à redire à qch.

stride [straid]. I. s. (grand) pas; enjambée f; **to make great strides,** faire de grands progrès; **to take sth. in one's s.,** faire qch. sans le moindre effort; **to get into one's s.,** prendre son allure normale; attraper la cadence (d'un travail). II. v.i. (strode |stroud|; stridden |'strid(ə)n|) **to s. along,** avancer à grands pas; **to s. away,** s'éloigner à grands pas; **to s. over,** enjamber (un obstacle).

strident ['straidənt], a. strident.

strife [straif], s. lutte f.

strike [straik]. I. s. 1. Ind: grève f; **to come out on s.,** se mettre en grève; **token s.,** grève d'avertissement, grève symbolique; **sympathetic s.,** grève de solidarité; **lightning s.,** grève surprise; **sit-down s.,** grève sur le tas; **go-slow s.,** grève perlée. 2. rencontre f (de pétrole, etc.); **lucky s.,** coup m de veine. II. v. (struck [strʌk]) 1. v.tr. &

ind.tr. (*a*) frapper; **to s. at s.o.**, porter un coup à qn; **to s. home**, frapper juste; **to s. a medal**, frapper une médaille; **to s. a chord**, plaquer un accord; (*b*) **to s. a bargain**, faire, conclure, un marché; (*c*) **to s. a match, a light**, frotter une allumette; (*c*) (*of snake*) **to s.** (s.o.), foncer (sur qn); **to s. terror into s.o.**, frapper qn de terreur; (*of plant*) **to s.** (**root**), prendre (racine); *Fish:* **to s. the fish**, ferrer le poisson; (*d*) **struck with terror**, saisi d'effroi; (*e*) **to s.** (**against**) **sth.**, heurter contre qch.; **his head struck the pavement**, sa tête a porté sur le trottoir; (*of ship*) **to s.** (**on**) **the rocks**, donner, toucher, sur les écueils; **to s. a mine**, heurter une mine; **a sound struck my ear**, un bruit me frappa l'oreille; **the thought strikes me that . . .**, l'idée me vient que . . .; **how did she s. you?** quelle impression vous a-t-elle faite? **he strikes me as** (**being**) **sincere**, il me paraît sincère; **that's how it struck me**, voilà l'effet que cela m'a fait; **it strikes me that . . .**, il me semble que . . .; **what struck me was . . .**, ce qui m'a frappé, c'est . . .; **I was greatly struck**, j'ai été très impressionné; (*f*) tomber sur, découvrir (une piste, etc.); **to s. oil**, (i) rencontrer le pétrole; (ii) trouver le filon; **I've struck on an idea**, j'ai eu une idée; (*g*) **to s. one's flag**, amener, baisser, son pavillon; **to s. tents**, abattre, plier, les tentes; **to s. camp**, lever le camp; (*h*) **to s. an attitude**, poser; (*i*) **to s. an average**, établir, prendre, une moyenne. 2. *v.i.* (*a*) (*of clock*) sonner; **it's just struck ten**, dix heures viennent de sonner; **the clock struck six**, six heures sonnèrent; (*b*) **to s. across country**, prendre à travers champs; **to s. into the jungle**, s'enfoncer, pénétrer, dans la jungle; **the road strikes off to the right**, la route tourne à droite; **to s.** (**out**) **for the shore**, se mettre à nager dans la direction du rivage; **to s. out for oneself**, voler de ses propres ailes; (*c*) *Ind:* se mettre en grève; **'striker**, *s. Ind:* gréviste *mf*; **'striking**. I. *a.* 1. **s. clock**, pendule à sonnerie. 2. (spectacle) remarquable, frappant, saisissant. II. *s.* **within s. distance**, à portée; **-ly**, *adv.* **s. beautiful**, d'une beauté frappante; **'strike 'up**, *v.tr. & i.* (*a*) **to s. up an acquaintance, a friendship, with s.o.**, lier connaissance avec qn; se lier d'amitié avec qn; (*b*) (*of musicians*) attaquer un morceau.

string [striŋ]. I. *s.* 1. ficelle *f*; corde *f*, cordon *m*; **ball of s.**, pelote *f* de ficelle; **to pull the strings**, tirer les fils, les ficelles; **s. bag**, filet *m* à provisions. 2. *Mus:* **the strings**, les instruments *m* à cordes; **s. orchestra**, orchestre *m* à cordes. 3. **s. of beads**, collier *m*; **s. of onions**, chapelet *m* d'oignons; **s. of cars**, file *f* de voitures; **long s. of tourists**, longue procession de touristes. II. *v.tr.* (**strung** [strʌŋ]) 1. bander (un arc); **highly strung**, nerveux; impressionnable. 2.

enfiler (des perles). 3. *Cu:* effiler (des haricots). 4. *F:* **to s. s.o. along**, faire marcher qn; *v.i.* **to s. along with s.o.**, suivre qn, être copain avec qn; **'string 'up**, *v.tr.* pendre (qn) haut et court; **s. him up!** à la lanterne! **'stringy**, *a.* fibreux; **s. meat**, viande tendineuse, filandreuse.

stringent ['strin(d)ʒ(ə)nt], *a.* rigoureux, strict; **'stringency**, *s.* rigueur *f*, sévérité *f* (des règles).

strip [strip]. I. *s.* bande *f*; **s. of land**, bande, langue *f*, de terre; **s. cartoon, comic s.**, bande illustrée; **s. lighting**, éclairage fluorescent, par fluorescence; *F:* **to tear s.o. off a s.**, laver la tête à qn. II. *v.* (**stripped**) 1. *v.tr.* (*a*) mettre (qn) tout nu; **stripped to the waist**, nu jusqu'à la ceinture; (*b*) **to s. s.o. of sth.**, dépouiller qn de qch.; **trees stripped of their leaves**, arbres dépouillés de leurs feuilles; (*c*) dégarnir (un lit, une maison); défaire (un lit); démeubler (une maison); (*d*) **to s. sth. off, from, sth.**, ôter, enlever, qch. de qch. 2. *v.i.* (*a*) (*of pers.*) dépouiller de ses vêtements; se dévêtir; (*b*) (*of bark, etc.*) **to s.** (**off**), s'enlever, se détacher; **'striptease**, *s.* striptease *m*; **s. artiste**, strippeuse *f*, stripteaseuse *f*.

stripe [straip], *s.* (*a*) raie *f*, barre *f* (d'un tissu); raie, rayure *f*, zébrure *f* (sur le pelage); (*b*) bande *f* (de pantalon); (*c*) *Mil:* galon *m*; **to lose one's stripes**, être dégradé; **striped**, *a.* (chaussettes) à raies, à barres; (pelage) rayé, tigré; *Nat. Hist:* zébré, rubané.

stripling ['stripliŋ], *s.* tout jeune homme; adolescent *m*.

strive [straiv], *v.i.* (**strove** [strouv]; **striven** ['strivn]) tâcher, s'efforcer (de faire qch.); **to s. for sth.**, essayer d'obtenir qch.; **to s. after effect**, rechercher l'effet; **to s. against**, lutter, combattre, contre (qn, qch.).

stroke [strouk]. I. *s.* 1. coup *m*; (*a*) **with one s., at a s.**, d'un seul coup; **finishing s.**, coup de grâce; (*b*) (i) coup (d'aviron); **to lengthen the s.**, allonger la nage; (ii) *Swimming:* brassée *f*; (*c*) *Aut:* mouvement *m*, course *f* (du piston); **two-s.**, (moteur à) deux temps *m*; (*d*) **he hasn't done a s. of work**, il n'a rien fait de ses dix doigts; (*e*) **s. of** (**good**) **luck**, coup de chance; **s. of genius**, trait *m* de génie; **a good s. of business**, une bonne affaire; (*f*) coup (d'horloge); **on the s. of nine**, à neuf heures sonnant(es); (*g*) *Med:* **to have a s.**, avoir une attaque (d'apoplexie); (*h*) coup de crayon, de pinceau; **with a s. of the pen**, d'un trait de plume. 2. *Row:* (*a*) (*pers.*) chef *m* de nage; (*b*) **to row s.**, donner la nage. 3. caresse *f* de la main. II. *v.tr.* 1. *Row:* **to s. a boat**, donner la nage. 2. passer la main sur, caresser de la main; **to s. the cat the wrong way**, caresser le chat à contre-poil.

stroll [stroul]. I. *s.* petit tour; **to go for a s.**, faire un tour. II. *v.i.* errer à l'aventure; flâner; se balader; **'stroller,** *s.* flâneur, -euse; promeneur, -euse.

strong [strɔŋ], *a.* **(stronger** ['strɔŋɡər]) fort. **1.** (*a*) solide; **s. conviction,** ferme conviction; (*b*) **he's not very s.,** il est peu robuste. **2.** (*a*) **s. voice,** voix forte, puissante; **to be s. in the arm,** avoir le bras fort; **s. measures,** mesures *f* énergiques; **manners aren't his s. point,** la politesse n'est pas son fort; **s. in numbers,** en grand nombre; **s. argument,** argument puissant; **s. reasons,** fortes raisons; **s. wind,** grand vent; (*b*) **s. drink,** boissons fortes; **s. light,** vive lumière; (*c*) **s. cheese,** fromage qui pique; **s. butter,** beurre rance. **3.** *adv. F:* **it's still going s.,** ça marche toujours à merveille; **-ly,** *adv.* fortement. **1.** solidement, fermement. **2.** vigoureusement, énergiquement; **s. worded letter,** lettre en termes énergiques; **I don't feel very s. about it,** je n'y attache pas une grande importance; **'strongbox,** *s.* coffre-fort *m*; **'stronghold,** *s.* forteresse *f*; place forte; **'strong-'minded,** *a.* à l'esprit décidé; **'strongroom,** *s.* cave *f* des coffres-forts.

structure ['strʌktʃər], *s.* **1.** structure *f.* **2.** édifice *m*, structure, bâtiment *m*; *Civ.E:* ouvrage *m* d'art; **the social s.,** l'édifice social; **'structural,** *s.* **1.** de construction; **s. steel, iron,** acier *m*, fer *m*, de construction, charpentes *f* métalliques; **s. engineer,** ingénieur-constructeur *m.* **2.** structural.

struggle ['strʌɡl]. **I.** *s.* lutte *f*; **desperate s.,** lutte désespérée; combat acharné; **he gave in without a s.,** il n'a fait aucune résistance. **II.** *v.i.* lutter (**with, against,** avec, contre); se débattre; **to s. hard to succeed,** faire tous ses efforts pour réussir; **they struggled for the prize,** ils se disputaient le prix; **we struggled through,** nous avons surmonté tous les obstacles; **he struggled to his feet,** il réussit à se relever; **'struggler,** *s.* lutteur, -euse; **'struggling,** *a.* (artiste) qui vit péniblement.

strum [strʌm], *v.tr. & i.* **(strummed) to s. (on) the piano, the guitar,** taper sur le piano, pianoter; gratter de la guitare.

strut¹ [strʌt]. **I.** démarche orgueilleuse, affectée; pas mesuré. **II.** *v.i.* **(strutted) to s. (about),** se pavaner, se rengorger; **to s. in, out,** entrer, sortir, d'un air important.

strut², *s.* entretoise *f*; support *m*, étai *m.*

strychnine ['strikni:n], *s.* strychnine *f.*

stub [stʌb]. **I.** *s.* **1.** souche *f* (d'arbre); bout *m* (de crayon, de cigare). **2.** souche, talon *m* (de chèque). **II.** *v.tr.* **(stubbed) 1. to s. up roots,** extirper des racines. **2. to s. one's toe against sth.,** se cogner, se heurter, le pied contre qch. **3. to s. out a cigarette,** éteindre une cigarette (en écrasant le bout).

stubble ['stʌbl], *s.* **1.** chaume *m.* **2.** *F:* barbe *f* de trois jours; **'stubbly,** *a.* **s. beard,** (i) barbe de

trois jours; (ii) barbe courte et raide.

stubborn ['stʌbən], *a.* obstiné, opiniâtre, entêté, têtu; (cheval) rétif; **-ly,** *adv.* obstinément, opiniâtrement; **'stubbornness,** *s.* entêtement *m*; obstination *f*, opiniâtreté *f*; ténacité *f* (de volonté).

stucco ['stʌkou], *s.* stuc *m*; **s. work,** stucage *m.*

stuck [stʌk], *a.* (*a*) **s. pig,** porc égorgé; (*b*) immobilisé; en panne; **'stuck-'up,** *a.* prétentieux, guindé.

stud¹ [stʌd]. **I.** *s.* **1.** clou *m* à grosse tête; clou (de passage clouté). **2.** bouton *m* (de chemise). **II.** *v.tr.* **(studded)** garnir de clous; clouter; **'studded,** *a.* **1.** garni de clous; clouté. **2.** parsemé (**with,** de); **sky s. with stars,** ciel piqué d'étoiles.

stud², *s.* (*a*) écurie *f* (de chasse); (*b*) **breeding s., s. farm,** haras *m*; **s. horse,** étalon *m*; **s. book,** registre *m* (des chevaux, etc.); stud-book *m.*

student ['stju:d(ə)nt], *s.* étudiant, -ante; **medical s.,** étudiant en médecine; **s. organization,** organisation étudiante.

studio, *pl.* **-os** ['stju:diou, -ouz], *s.* (*a*) **(artist's) s.,** atelier *m*; (*b*) *Cin: Rad: T.V:* studio *m.*

studious ['stju:diəs], *a.* studieux, appliqué; **with s. politeness,** avec une politesse étudiée; **-ly,** *adv.* **1.** studieusement. **2.** avec empressement; **he s. avoided me,** il s'étudiait à m'éviter.

study ['stʌdi]. **I.** *s.* **1. brown s.,** rêverie *f.* **2.** étude *f*; **to make a s. of sth.,** étudier qch.; **to finish one's studies,** achever ses études; **his face was a s.,** il fallait voir son visage! **3.** *Art: Mus:* étude. **4.** (*a*) cabinet *m* de travail; (*b*) *Sch:* salle *f* d'étude; **s. bedroom,** chambre *f* d'étudiant(e). **II.** *v.tr. & i.* **1.** étudier; observer (les astres); **to s. under Professor Martin,** suivre les cours du professeur Martin; **to s. economics,** faire des études des sciences économiques; **to s. for an examination,** préparer un examen; **to s. hard,** travailler ferme. **2.** s'occuper de, se préoccuper de (qn, qch.); **to s. economy,** viser à l'économie; **'studied,** *a.* étudié, recherché; prémédité, calculé; **s. carelessness,** négligence voulue.

stuff [stʌf]. **I.** *s.* **1.** (*a*) matière *f*, substance *f*, étoffe *f*; **he's the s. heroes are made of,** il est du bois dont on fait les héros; **there's good s. in him,** il a de l'étoffe; *F:* **that's the s.!** c'est du bon! **that's the s. to give them!** c'est comme ça qu'il faut les traiter; **come on, do your s.!** allons! montre-nous ce que tu sais faire! **he knows his s.,** il s'y connaît; (*b*) **silly s.,** sottises *fpl*; **s. and nonsense!** quelle bêtise! allons donc! **2.** *Tex:* étoffe, tissu *m* (de laine). **II.** *v.tr.* **1.** (*a*) bourrer (**with,** de); rembourrer (un meuble); **to s. (oneself),** se bourrer; bâfrer; (*b*) *Cu:* farcir (une volaille); (*c*) empailler (un animal). **2. to s. up a hole,** boucher un trou; **my nose is all stuffed up,** je suis enchifrené. **3. to s.**

sth. into sth., fourrer qch. dans qch.; 'stuffing, *s.* bourrage *m*, rembourrage *m*; empaillage *m*; *Cu:* farce *f*; *F:* to knock the s. out of s.o., flanquer une tripotée à qn.

stuffy ['stʌfi], *a.* 1. mal ventilé; mal aéré; room that smells s., pièce *f* qui sent le renfermé. 2. *F:* (*of pers.*) collet monté *inv*; don't be s.! il n'y a pas de quoi te scandaliser! 'stuffiness, *s.* manque *m* d'air; odeur *f* de renfermé.

stumble ['stʌmbl]. I. *s.* trébuchement *m*; faux pas; bronchement *m* (de cheval). II. *v.i.* trébucher; faire un faux pas; (*of horse*) broncher; to s. over sth., buter contre qch. 2. to s. in one's speech, in speaking, hésiter en parlant. 3. to s. across s.o., sth., rencontrer qn, qch., par hasard; 'stumbling. 1. *a.* qui trébuche; (cheval) qui bronche; (*of speech*) hésitant. 2. *s.* (*a*) trébuchement *m*; faux pas; s. block, pierre *f* d'achoppement; (*b*) hésitation *f*.

stump [stʌmp]. I. *s.* 1. souche *f* (d'arbre); chicot *m* (de dent); moignon *m* (de bras, de jambe); bout *m* (de cigare, de crayon); mégot *m* (de cigare, de cigarette). 2. s. orator, harangueur *m*. 3. *Cricket:* piquet *m* (du guichet); to draw stumps, cesser la partie. II. *v.* *v.i.* to s. along, clopiner; to s. in, out, entrer, sortir, clopin-clopant. 2. *v.tr.* (*a*) *F:* coller (un candidat); réduire (qn) à quia; this stumped me, sur le coup je n'ai su que répondre; (*b*) *Cricket:* mettre hors jeu (un batteur); 'stump 'up, *v.i.* *F:* payer, casquer, s'exécuter; 'stumpy, *a.* (*of pers.*) trapu, ramassé.

stun [stʌn], *v.tr.* (stunned) 1. étourdir, assommer. 2. renverser, abasourdir; the news stunned me, ce fut un coup de massue; 'stunning, *a.* 1. (coup) étourdissant, d'assommoir; (malheur) accablant. 2. *F:* épatant.

stunt¹ [stʌnt], *v.tr.* rabougrir; 'stunted, *a.* rabougri, chétif.

stunt². I. *s.* 1. coup *m*, affaire *f*, de publicité. 2. tour *m* de force. II. *v.i.* *Av:* faire des acrobaties (en vol); 'stunt man, s. *Cin:* cascadeur *m*.

stupefy ['stju:pifai], *v.tr.* 1. (*a*) *Med:* stupéfier, engourdir; (*b*) stupefied with grief, hébété par la douleur. 2. abasourdir, stupéfier; I'm absolutely stupefied, je n'en reviens pas; les bras m'en tombent; stupe'faction, *s.* stupéfaction *f*; stupeur *f*, ahurissement *m*.

stupendous [stju:'pendəs], *a.* prodigieux; *F:* formidable; -ly, *adv.* prodigieusement.

stupid ['stju:pid], *a.* stupide; sot; *F:* bête; how s. of me! que je suis bête! don't be s.! ne faites pas la bête! -ly, *adv.* stupidement, sottement, bêtement; stu'pidity, *s.* stupidité *f*; lourdeur *f* d'esprit; sottise *f*, niaiserie *f*, bêtise *f*.

stupor ['stju:pər], *s.* stupeur *f*.

sturdy ['stə:di], *a.* (*a*) vigoureux, robuste; (*b*) (*of opposition, etc.*) hardi, résolu, ferme; -ily, *adv.* 1. fortement; avec robustesse. 2. hardiment,

vigoureusement; 'sturdiness, *s.* 1. vigueur *f*, robustesse *f*. 2. résolution *f*, fermeté *f*.

sturgeon ['stə:dʒ(ə)n], *s.* *Ich:* esturgeon *m*.

stutter ['stʌtər]. I. *s.* bégaiement *m*. II. *v.i. & tr.* bégayer, bredouiller; 'stutterer, *s.* bègue *mf*; 'stuttering. 1. *a.* bègue. 2. *s.* bégaiement *m*; -ly, *adv.* en bégayant.

sty, *pl.* -ies [stai, -aiz], *s.* étable *f* à porcs; porcherie *f.*

stye [stai], *s.* *Med:* orgelet *m.*

style [stail]. I. *s.* 1. style *m*, manière *f*; s. of living, manière de vivre; to live in s., mener grand train; to win in fine s., gagner haut la main; furniture in Empire s., meubles style Empire; *Com:* made in three styles, fabriqué en trois genres, sur trois modèles; something in that s., quelque chose de ce genre; the latest s., la dernière mode. 2. style, manière d'écrire; in a humorous s., sur un ton de plaisanterie. 3. ton *m*, chic *m*, cachet *m*; there's no s. about her, elle manque de chic. II. *v.tr.* 1. dénommer, appeler. 2. *Com:* créer; 'stylish, *a.* élégant, chic; -ly, *adv.* élégamment; avec chic; 'stylishness, *s.* élégance *f*, chic *m*; 'stylist, *s.* styliste *mf*; styli'zation, *s.* stylisation *f*; 'stylize, *v.tr.* styliser; 'stylized, *a.* s. flowers, fleurs stylisées.

stylus, *pl.* -uses ['stailəs, -əsiz], *s.* (*a*) *Engr:* style *m*; (*b*) *Rec:* aiguille *f.*

suave [swɑːv], *a.* suave; *Pej:* doucereux, mielleux; -ly, *adv.* suavement; *Pej:* doucereusement, mielleusement; 'suaveness, *s.*, 'suavity, *s.* suavité *f.*

sub [sʌb]. I. *pref.* (*used in compounds*) sous-. II. *s.* *F:* *abbr.* *for* (i) SUBSCRIPTION, (ii) SUB-EDITOR, (iii) SUBSTITUTION, (iv) SUBMARINE. III. *v.* (subbed) *F:* *abbr. for* (i) *v.tr.* SUB-EDIT, (ii) *v.i.* SUBSTITUTE; to s. for s.o., remplacer qn, se substituer à qn.

subacute [sʌbə'kju:t], *a.* *Med:* subaigu.

subaltern ['sʌbltən]. 1. *a.* subalterne. 2. *s.* *Mil:* lieutenant *m*; sous-lieutenant *m.*

subcommittee [sʌbkə'miti:], *s.* sous-comité *m.*

subconscious [sʌb'kɔnʃəs]. 1. *a.* subconscient. 2. *s.* the s., le subconscient; -ly, *adv.* subconsciemment.

subcontinent ['sʌb'kɔntinənt], *s.* the Indian s., la péninsule indienne.

subcontract. I. [sʌb'kɔntrækt], *s.* sous-traité *m.* II. [sʌbkən'trækt], *v.i.* to s. for (sth.), sous-traiter (une affaire); subcon'tractor, *s.* sous-entrepreneur *m*, sous-traitant *m.*

subdivide [sʌbdi'vaid], *v.tr. & i.* (se) subdiviser; subdi'vision, *s.* subdivision *f*; sous-division *f.*

subdue [səb'dju:], *v.tr.* 1. assujettir; maîtriser, dompter; vaincre. 2. adoucir (la lumière, la voix); sub'dued, *a.* 1. (peuple) vaincu. 2. (*of pers.*) déprimé. 3. (*of light*) tamisé, atténué; (conversation) à voix basse; s. colours, couleurs sobres, peu voyantes.

sub-edit [sʌb'edit], v.tr. corriger, mettre au point (un article); **sub-'editor,** s. secrétaire mf de la rédaction.

subheading [sʌb'hediŋ], s. sous-titre m.

subject. I. ['sʌbdʒikt], s. **1.** (pers.) sujet, -ette; British s., sujet britannique. **2.** Gram: sujet (du verbe). **3.** (a) sujet (de conversation); s. (matter), sujet (d'un livre); **to hark back to a s.,** revenir sur un sujet; **while we are on this s.,** pendant que nous sommes sur ce sujet; **to change the s.,** parler d'autre chose; changer de sujet; (b) Sch: **what subjects do you teach?** quelles matières enseignez-vous? **II.** ['sʌbdʒikt], a. **1.** (pays) assujetti, soumis (to, à). **2.** sujet, exposé (à qch.); **prices s. to 5% discount,** prix qui comportent 5% d'escompte; **s. to stamp duty,** passible du droit de timbre; **plan s. to modifications,** projet qui pourra subir des modifications. **3.** (conditional) s. **to ratification,** sous réserve de ratification; **s. to correction,** sauf correction. **III.** [səb'dʒekt], v.tr. **1.** assujettir, subjuguer (un peuple). **2.** soumettre (qn, qch., à qch.); **to be subjected to much criticism,** être en butte à de nombreuses critiques; **sub'jection,** s. sujétion f, soumission f, assujettissement m (to, à); **to be in s.,** être soumis (à qn); être sous la dépendance (de qn); **sub'jective,** a. subjectif.

subjunctive [səb'dʒʌŋ(k)tiv], a. & s. subjonctif (m); **in the s.,** au subjonctif.

sublease [sʌb'li:s]. **I.** s. sous-bail m, sous-location f. **II.** v.tr. (also **sublet**) sous-louer.

sublieutenant [sʌblef'tenənt], s. Navy: enseigne m (de vaisseau) de première classe.

sublime [sə'blaim], a. (a) sublime; (b) s. indifference, suprême indifférence; **-ly,** adv. (a) sublimement; (b) s. **unconscious of sth.,** dans une ignorance absolue de qch.

subliminal [sʌb'liminəl], a. subliminal; **s. advertising,** publicité subliminale.

submarine [sʌbmə'ri:n], a. & s. sous-marin (m).

submerge [səb'mə:dʒ]. **1.** v.tr. (a) submerger, immerger; (b) inonder, noyer (un champ). **2.** v.i. (of submarine) plonger; effectuer sa plongée, se mettre en plongée; **sub'merged,** a. (a) submergé; (b) **speed s.,** vitesse f en plongée (d'un sous-marin); (c) **s. reef,** écueil sous-marin; **sub'mergence,** s., **sub'mersion,** s. submersion f; plongée f (d'un sous-marin).

submission [səb'miʃ(ə)n], s. **1.** (a) soumission f, résignation f; **to starve into s.,** réduire (qn) par la famine; (b) docilité f, humilité f. **2.** soumission (d'une question à un arbitre); **sub'missive,** a. soumis, humble, résigné; **-ly,** adv. d'un ton soumis; avec docilité; humblement; avec résignation; **sub'missiveness,** s. soumission f, docilité f; **sub'mit,** v. (**submitted**) **1.** v.i. & pr. se soumettre

(to, à); se plier (à une nécessité); se résigner (à un malheur). **2.** v.tr. (a) soumettre; **to s. sth. to s.o.'s inspection,** soumettre, présenter, qch. à l'inspection de qn; **to s. proofs of identity,** présenter des pièces d'identité; (b) **to s. that . . .,** représenter, alléguer, que . . .

subnormal [sʌb'nɔ:m(ə)l], a. au-dessous de la normale; (of pers.) faible d'esprit.

subordinate. 1. [sə'bɔ:dinət], a. & s. **1.** a. (a) (rang) inférieur, subalterne; (rôle) secondaire; (b) Gram: etc: subordonné (to, à). **2.** s. subordonné, -ée. **II.** [sə'bɔ:dineit], v.tr. subordonner (to, à); **subordi'nation,** s. **1.** subordination f (to, à). **2.** soumission f (to, à).

subpoena [sʌb'pi:nə]. Jur: **I.** s. citation f, assignation f (de témoin, sous peine d'amende). **II.** v.tr. citer (qn) à comparaître; signifier une assignation à (qn).

subscribe [səb'skraib], v.tr. & i. **1.** **to s. to an opinion,** souscrire à une opinion. **2.** (a) **to s. ten pounds,** souscrire pour (la somme de) dix livres; **to s. to a charity,** verser sa cotisation à une œuvre de charité; Fin: **subscribed capital,** capital souscrit; **to s. to a loan,** souscrire à un emprunt; (b) **to s. to a newspaper,** (i) s'abonner, prendre un abonnement, à un journal; (ii) être abonné à un journal; **sub'scriber,** s. **1.** s. **to a charity, for shares,** cotisant, -ante, souscripteur, à une œuvre de charité; souscripteur à des actions. **2.** abonné, -ée (à un journal); **sub'scription** [-'skripʃ(ə)n], s. **1.** s. to (**an opinion, etc.**), adhésion f à, approbation f de (qch.). **2.** **to pay a s.,** verser une cotisation; **to get up a s.,** se cotiser; demander des cotisations (à une œuvre de charité, etc.); Fin: **s. to a loan,** souscription f à un emprunt; **s. list,** liste des souscripteurs. **3.** abonnement m (à un journal); **to take out a s. to a newspaper,** s'abonner à un journal; **s. to a club,** cotisation (annuelle) à un cercle.

subsequent ['sʌbsikwənt], a. (chapitre, etc.) subséquent, qui suit; **at a s. meeting,** dans une séance ultérieure; **at our s. meeting,** quand je l'ai rencontré plus tard; **-ly,** adv. plus tard; dans la suite; postérieurement (to, à).

subservient [səb'sə:viənt], a. **1.** **to make sth. s. to sth.,** faire servir qch. à qch. **2.** obséquieux, servile; **sub'servience,** s. soumission f, servilité f.

subside [səb'said], v.i. **1.** (of ground) s'affaisser, se tasser, s'enfoncer; **to s. into an armchair,** s'affaler, s'effondrer, dans un fauteuil. **2.** (of water) baisser; **the flood is subsiding,** la crue diminue. **3.** (a) (of storm, anger) s'apaiser, se calmer, tomber; (b) (of pers.) se taire; **'subsidence,** s. affaissement m; effondrement m.

subsidiary [səb'sidjəri], a. & s. subsidiaire, auxiliaire; **s. (company),** filiale f.

subsidy ['sʌbsidi], s. subvention f; Ind: prime f

'**subsidize**, *v.tr.* subventionner; primer (une industrie); **to be subsidized by the state,** recevoir une subvention de l'état.

subsistence [səb'sistəns], *s.* 1. existence *f.* 2. **means of s.,** moyens *mpl* de subsistance, de subsister; **a bare s. wage,** un salaire à peine suffisant pour vivre.

subsoil ['sʌbsɔil], *s. Geol:* sous-sol *m.*

subsonic ['sʌbsɔnik], *a. Av:* subsonique.

substance ['sʌbstəns], *s.* 1. substance *f,* matière *f.* 2. substance, fond *m,* essentiel *m* (d'un argument). 3. solidité *f*; **argument that has little s.,** argument qui n'a rien de solide. 4. avoir *m,* bien *m,* fortune *f*; **he's a man of s.,** il a du bien; **sub'stantial,** *a.* 1. substantiel, réel. 2. important; **s. reasons,** raisons sérieuses; **a s. difference,** une différence appréciable, sensible. 3. (*a*) **s. meal,** repas copieux, solide; (*b*) solide; (drap) résistant; **of s. build,** (homme) bien taillé. 4. (bourgeois) aisé; **s. firm,** maison de commerce bien assise; **-ally,** *adv.* substantiellement; (*a*) réellement; en substance; (*b*) solidement; **s. built,** (homme) bien taillé, (ameublement) solide; (*c*) fortement; **this contributed s. to our success,** cela a contribué pour une grande part à notre succès; **sub'stantiate,** *v.tr.* établir, justifier (une affirmation); établir le bien-fondé d'(une réclamation).

substandard ['sʌbstændəd], *a.* inférieur (à la norme).

substantive ['sʌbstəntiv], *s. Gram:* substantif *m,* nom *m.*

substitute ['sʌbstitjuːt]. I. *s.* (*pers.*) (*a*) suppléant, -ante; remplaçant, -ante; **to act as a s. for s.o.,** remplacer qn, se substituer à qn; **to find a s.** (**for oneself**), se faire suppléer; (*b*) mandataire *mf,* représentant, -ante. 2. (*a*) (*of foodstuffs*) succédané *m* (**for,** de); **coffee s.,** café ersatz; (*b*) **beware of substitutes,** se méfier des contrefaçons *f.* II. *v.* 1. *v.tr.* substituer; **to s. steel for stone,** substituer l'acier à la pierre; remplacer la pierre par l'acier. 2. *v.i.* **to s. for s.o.,** remplacer, suppléer, qn; **substi'tution,** *s.* substitution *f,* remplacement *m.*

substratum, *pl.* -**ta** [sʌb'strɑːtəm, -tə], *s.* couche inférieure; sous-couche *f*; **a s. of truth,** un fond de vérité.

subtenancy [sʌb'tenənsi], *s.* sous-location *f*; **sub'tenant,** *s.* sous-locataire *mf.*

subterfuge ['sʌbtəfjuːdʒ], *s.* subterfuge *m.*

subterranean [sʌbtə'reiniən], *a.* souterrain.

subtitle ['sʌbtaitl]. I. *s.* sous-titre *m.* II. *v.tr. Cin:* sous-titrer; '**subtitling,** *s.* sous-titrage *m.*

subtle ['sʌtl], *a.* subtil. 1. (parfum) délicat; (charme) qui échappe à l'analyse; **s. distinction,** distinction subtile. 2. (*a*) (esprit) fin, raffiné; (*b*) rusé, astucieux; **-tly,** *adv.* subtilement; avec finesse; '**subtlety,** *s.* 1. subtilité

f; raffinement *m,* finesse *f*; distinction subtile. 2. ruse *f,* astuce *f.*

subtract [səb'trækt], *v.tr. Mth:* soustraire, retrancher (**from,** de); **sub'traction,** *s. Mth:* soustraction *f.*

suburb ['sʌbəːb], *s.* banlieue *f*; **the suburbs,** la banlieue; **garden s.,** cité-jardin *f*; **su'burban** [sə-], *a.* suburbain; de banlieue; **su'burbanite,** *s. F: Pej:* banlieusard, -arde; **su'burbia,** *s. Pej:* la banlieue.

subvention [sʌb'venʃ(ə)n], *s.* subvention *f.*

subversion [səb'vəːʃ(ə)n], *s.* subversion *f*; **sub'versive,** *a.* subversif; **sub'vert,** *v.tr.* subvertir.

subway ['sʌbwei], *s.* (*a*) passage souterrain; (*b*) *N.Am:* métro *m.*

succeed [sək'siːd], *v.tr. & i.* 1. (*a*) succéder à (qn qch.); **to s. to the throne,** succéder à la couronne; (*b*) **day succeeds day,** les jours se suivent. 2. *v.i.* réussir; venir à bien; **how to s.,** le moyen de parvenir; **to s. in doing sth.,** réussir à faire qch.; **suc'ceeding,** *a.* 1. suivant, subséquent. 2. à venir; futur. 3. successif.

suc'cess, *s.* (*a*) succès *m,* réussite *f*; **without s.,** sans succès; sans y parvenir; (*b*) **to be a s.** (*of venture*) réussir, (*of play*) avoir du succès; **the evening was a great s.,** la soirée a été très réussie; **to make a s. of sth.,** réussir qch.; **suc'cessful,** *a.* (projet) couronné de succès (résultat) heureux; (portrait) réussi; **s. play,** pièce qui a du succès; **to be s. in doing sth.,** réussir à faire qch.; **he's s. in everything,** tout lui réussit; **s. candidates,** (i) candidats élus; (ii) *Sch:* candidats reçus; **-fully,** *adv.* avec succès; **suc'cession,** *s.* succession *f.* 1. (*a*) suite *f*; **in s.,** successivement; à la file; **for two years in s.,** pendant deux années successives, consécutives; **in rapid s.,** coup sur coup; (*b*) série *f,* suite (*f*); **after a s. of losses,** après de pertes successives. 2. (*a*) succession (à la couronne, etc.); **in s. to s.o.,** en remplacement de qn; **suc'cessive,** *a.* successif, consécutif; **-ly,** *adv.* successivement; **suc'cessor,** *s.* successeur *m* (**to, of,** de); **to appoint a s. to s.o.,** remplacer qn.

succinct [sʌk'siŋ(k)t], *a.* succinct, concis.

succulence ['sʌkjuləns], *s.* succulence *f*; '**succulent.** 1. *a.* succulent. 2. *s. Bot:* plante grasse.

succumb [sə'kʌm], *v.i.* succomber; céder; **to s. to one's injuries,** succomber à, mourir de, ses blessures.

such [sʌtʃ]. I. *a.* tel, pareil, semblable. 1. (*a*) **s. as you, s. men as you,** des gens comme vous; **s. a man,** un tel homme; **s. things,** de telles choses; **did you ever see s. a thing!** a-t-on jamais vu chose pareille! **in s. cases,** en pareil cas; **some s. plan,** un projet de ce genre; **nobody exists,** il n'existe aucun corps de cette

nature; **I said no s. thing,** je n'ai rien dit de la
sorte; **no s. thing!** il n'en est rien! pas du tout!
(b) **here it is, s. as it is,** le voici mais il ne vaut
pas grand-chose. **2. in s. (and s.) a place,** en tel
endroit; **on s. and s. a date,** à une certaine date;
s. a one, un tel, une telle. **3. in s. a way that. . .,**
de telle sorte que. . .; de manière, de façon, que
. . .; **to take s. steps as (shall) appear
necessary,** prendre telles mesures qui
paraîtront nécessaires; **until s. time as . . .,**
jusqu'à ce que + sub. **4.** (intensive) **s. big
houses,** de si grandes maisons; **s. a clever man,**
un homme si habile; **s. courage,** un tel courage; **I
had s. a fright!** j'ai eu une de ces peurs! **II.** pron.
1. down with traitors and all s.! à bas les traîtres
et tous ceux qui leur ressemblent. **2. I'll send you
s. as I have,** ce que j'en ai je vous les enverrai. **3.
history as s.,** l'histoire en tant que telle;
'suchlike. 1. a. F: semblable, pareil; de ce
genre. **2.** pron. usu. pl. **tramps and s.,** clochards
et autres gens de la sorte, de cette espèce.

suck [sʌk]. **I.** s. action f de sucer; **to take a s. at a
sweet,** sucer un bonbon. **II.** v.tr. & i. sucer; **to s.
(at) sth.,** sucer qch.; **to s. s.o.'s brains,** exploiter
les connaissances, l'intelligence, de qn; **to s.
s.o. dry,** sucer qn jusqu'au dernier sou; **'suck
'down,** v.tr. engloutir; entraîner au fond;
'sucker, s. **1.** Bot: rejeton m; drageon m (d'arbre). **2.** F: (of pers.) poire f; **'suck 'in,** v.tr. **1.**
(a) sucer, absorber; (b) engloutir. **2.** F: duper,
rouler, refaire (qn); **'sucking,** a. (animal) qui
tette; **s. pig,** cochon m de lait; **'suckle,** v.tr.
allaiter (un enfant); **'suck 'up. 1.** v.tr. sucer,
aspirer, pomper (un liquide, de l'air); (of
sponge) absorber, boire (l'eau). **2.** v.i. F: **to s.
up to s.o.,** faire (de) la lèche à qn; **'suction,** s.
succion f, aspiration f; appel m (d'air); **s.
pump,** pompe aspirante; **s. fan,** aspirateur m;
s. valve, clapet m d'aspiration.

Sudan (the) [ðəsuː'dæn]. Pr.n. Geog: le Soudan;
Suda'nese [suːdə'niːz], a. & s. soudanais,
-aise.

sudden ['sʌdn], a. (a) soudain, subit; **s. shower,**
averse soudaine; (b) (mouvement) brusque; **s.
turning,** tournant brusque; (c) adv.phr. **all of a
s.,** soudain, soudainement; tout à coup; **-ly,** adv.
soudain, soudainement; subitement; tout à
coup; **'suddenness,** s. (a) soudaineté f; **with
startling s.,** en coup de théâtre; (b) brusquerie f
(d'un départ).

suds [sʌdz], s.pl. **(soap-)s.,** eau f de savon;
mousse f (de savon).

sue [suː], v.tr. poursuivre (qn) en justice; **to s. s.o.
for damages,** poursuivre qn en dommages-
intérêts.

suede [sweid], s. (a) (for shoes) daim m; (b) (for
gloves) peau f de suède; suède m.

suet ['suːit], s. Cu: graisse f de rognon.

Suez ['suːiz]. Pr.n. Geog: Suez; **the S. Canal,** le
canal de Suez.

suffer ['sʌfər]. **1.** v.tr. (a) éprouver, souffrir (une
perte); subir (une peine); **to s. defeat,** essuyer,
subir, une défaite; (b) **he doesn't s. fools gladly,**
il ne supporte pas les imbéciles. **2.** v.i. (a)
souffrir; **to s. for one's rashness,** supporter la
conséquence de ses imprudences; (b) **to s. from
neglect,** souffrir d'un manque de soins; **country suffering from labour troubles,** pays en
proie à l'agitation ouvrière; (c) subir une perte,
un dommage; **the vines have suffered from the
frost,** les vignes ont souffert de la gelée;
'sufferance, s. **on s.,** (faire qch.) par
tolérance; **'sufferer,** s. (from calamity) victime f, sinistré, -ée; (from accident) accidenté,
-ée; (from illness) malade mf; **fellow-s.,** compagnon m d'infortune; **'suffering. 1.** a.
souffrant, qui souffre. **2.** s. souffrances fpl;
douleurs fpl.

suffice [sə'fais], v.tr. & i. suffire; **that will s. (for)
him,** cela lui suffira; **s. it to say that I got
nothing,** suffit que je n'ai rien obtenu;
su'fficiency [-'fiʃənsi], s. (a) suffisance f;
(b) fortune suffisante; **to have a bare s.,** avoir
tout juste de quoi vivre; **su'fficient,** a.
assez; suffisant; **one lamp is s.,** il suffit d'une
lampe; **a hundred francs will be s.,** j'aurai
assez de cent francs; **-ly,** suffisamment;
assez.

suffix ['sʌfiks], s. Gram: suffixe m.

suffocate ['sʌfəkeit], v.tr. & i. étouffer,
suffoquer; **'suffocating,** a. suffocant,
étouffant, asphyxiant; **it's s. in this room,** on
suffoque dans cette pièce; **suffo'cation,** s.
suffocation f; étouffement m, asphyxie f.

suffrage ['sʌfridʒ], s. suffrage m; **universal s.,**
suffrage universel.

sugar ['ʃugər]. **I.** s. sucre m; **the s. industry,** l'industrie sucrière; **granulated s.,** sucre
cristallisé; **castor, caster, s.,** sucre en poudre;
sucre semoule; **lump s.,** sucre en morceaux;
brown s., cassonade f; **s. beet,** betterave f à
sucre; **s. cane,** canne f à sucre; **s. refinery,**
raffinerie f (de sucre); **s. almond,** dragée f; **s.
basin,** sucrier m; **s. tongs,** pince f à sucre; Bot:
s. maple, érable m à sucre; F: **s. daddy,** vieux
protecteur; papa-gâteau m; **she's got (herself)
a s. daddy,** elle s'est trouvé un vieux. **II.** v.tr.
sucrer; saupoudrer (un gâteau) de sucre; lisser
(des amandes); **to s. the pill,** dorer la pilule;
'sugary, a. (a) (trop) sucré; (b) (sourire)
mielleux, sucré; (ton) doucereux.

suggest [sə'dʒest], v.tr. **1.** suggérer, proposer
(qch. à qn); **a solution suggested itself to me,**
une solution me vint à l'esprit. **2.** inspirer, faire
naître (une idée); **prudence suggests a retreat,**
la prudence conseille la retraite. **3.** insinuer; **do
you s. I'm lying?** est-ce que vous insinuez que
je mens? **4.** évoquer; **his nose suggests a rab-**

bit, son nez donne, évoque, l'idée d'un lapin; **suggesti'bility,** *s.* suggestibilité *f*; **su'ggestible,** *a.* (*of pers.*) influençable par la suggestion; suggestible; **su'ggestion,** *s.* suggestion *f*; **to make a s.,** faire une suggestion, une proposition; **su'ggestive,** *a.* (*a*) suggestif, évocateur; (*b*) qui frise l'obscénité; **s. joke,** plaisanterie suggestive.

suicide ['su(:)isaid], *s.* 1. (*pers.*) suicidé, -ée. 2. (*act*) suicide *m*; **to commit s.,** se suicider; **attempted s.,** tentative *f* de suicide; **sui'cidal,** *a.* **s. tendencies,** tendances au suicide; **this would be s.,** ce serait un véritable suicide que d'agir de la sorte.

suit [su:t]. I. *s.* 1. *Jur:* **to bring a s. against s.o.,** intenter un procès à qn. 2. *Cl:* complet *m* (pour homme); tailleur *m* (pour femme); **lounge s.,** complet veston. 3. *Cards:* couleur *f*; **to follow s.,** (i) donner de la couleur; (ii) en faire autant, faire de même. II. *v.tr.* 1. **to be suited to sth.,** être adapté, apte, à qch.; **they are suited to each other,** ils sont faits l'un pour l'autre; *Th:* **he is not suited to the part,** le rôle ne lui convient pas. 2. convenir à, aller à, accommoder (qn); **that just suits me,** ça me va à merveille; c'est juste mon affaire; **I shall do it when it suits me,** je le ferai quand cela me conviendra; **s. yourself,** arrangez cela à votre gré; faites comme vous voudrez; **this hat suits you,** ce chapeau vous va bien; **suita'bility,** *s.* convenance *f*; à-propos *m* (d'une remarque); **s. of s.o. for a job,** aptitude *f* de qn à un poste; **'suitable,** *a.* 1. convenable, qui convient; (exemple) approprié; **I've found nothing s.,** je n'ai rien trouvé qui me convient; **the most s. date,** la date qui conviendrait le mieux. 2. **s. to, for, sth.,** bon à qch.; propre, approprié, adapté, à qch.; **s. to the occasion,** qui convient à la circonstance; **-ably,** *adv.* convenablement; (répondre) à propos; (agir) comme il convient; **'suitcase,** *s.* mallette *f*, valise *f*; **'suitor,** *s.* prétendant *m*, soupirant *m*.

suite [swi:t], *s.* 1. suite *f* (d'un prince). 2. (*a*) **s. (of rooms),** appartement *m*; (*b*) **s. of furniture,** ameublement *m*; **dining-room s.,** salle *f* à manger; **bathroom s.,** salle de bains. 3. *Mus:* suite (d'orchestre).

sulk [sʌlk]. I. *s.* **to have a s., (a fit of) the sulks,** bouder; faire la mine. II. *v.i.* bouder; faire la mine; être maussade; **'sulkiness,** *s.* bouderie *f*, maussaderie *f*; **'sulky,** *a.* boudeur, maussade; **to be s.,** bouder; **to look s.,** faire la mine; **-ily,** *adv.* en boudant; d'un air boudeur, maussade.

sullen ['sʌlən], *a.* maussade, renfrogné, morose; sombre; **s. silence,** silence obstiné; **-ly,** *adv.* d'un air maussade, renfrogné; (obéir) de mauvaise grâce; **'sullenness,** *s.* maussaderie *f*; air renfrogné; obstination *f* à ne pas parler.

sully ['sʌli], *v.tr.* souiller, ternir; flétrir (la réputation de qn).

sulphur ['sʌlfər], *s.* soufre *m*; **s. mine,** soufrière *f*; **'sulphate,** *s.* sulfate *m*; **copper s.,** sulfate de cuivre; **'sulphide,** *s.* sulfure *m*; **'sulphite,** *s.* sulfite *m*; **sul'phonamide,** *s. Ch:* sulfamide *m*; **sul'phuric** [-'fju:rik], *a.* sulfurique; **'sulphuring,** *s.* soufrage *m*; **'sulphurous,** *a.* sulfureux.

sultan ['sʌltən], *s.* sultan *m*; **sul'tana,** *s.* 1. sultane *f*. 2. raisin sec de Smyrne.

sultry ['sʌltri], *a.* (*of heat*) étouffant, suffocant; (*of weather*) très lourd; **'sultriness,** *s.* chaleur étouffante; lourdeur *f* (de l'atmosphère).

sum [sʌm]. I. *s.* 1. (*a*) somme *f*, total *m*; montant *m*; **s. total,** somme totale, globale; (*b*) **s. of money,** somme d'argent; **to spend vast sums,** dépenser des sommes folles. 2. problème *m* exercice *m* (d'arithmétique); **to do a s. in one's head,** faire un calcul de tête; **to do sums,** faire du calcul, des problèmes. II. *v.tr.* (**summed**) **s. up,** résumer, faire un résumé de (qch.) récapituler; **to s. up the situation at a glance,** évaluer, se rendre compte de, la situation d'un coup d'œil; **to s. s.o. up,** juger, classer, qn **'summarize,** *v.tr.* résumer sommairement **'summarized,** *a.* (*of report, etc.*) compendieux; en résumé; **'summary.** 1. *a.* sommaire 2. *s.* sommaire *m*, résumé *m*; **-ily,** *adv.* sommairement; **'summing,** *s.* **s. up,** (*a*) *Jur* résumé *m* des débats; (*b*) évaluation *f* (de la situation).

summer ['sʌmər], *s.* été *m*; **in s.,** en été; **last s.** l'été dernier; **a summer('s) day,** un jour d'été; **s. clothes,** habits d'été; **s. visitor,** estivant, -ante the s. holidays,** les grandes vacances **'summerhouse,** *s.* pavillon *m*, kiosque *m* **'summertime,** *s.* l'été *m*; **'summer time,** s l'heure *f* d'été.

summit ['sʌmit], *s.* sommet *m*, cime *f*, faîte *m* (d'une montagne); *Pol:* **s. meeting,** conférence *f* au sommet.

summon ['sʌmən], *v.tr.* 1. (*a*) appeler, faire venir (qn); convoquer (une assemblée); (*b*) *Jur* sommer (qn) de comparaître; **to s. a witness to attend,** citer, assigner, un témoin. 2. **to s. up one's courage,** faire appel à tout son courage **'summons.** I. *s.* 1. appel (fait d'autorité); convocation urgente. 2. *Jur:* citation *f* (à comparaître); assignation *f*; procès-verbal *m*, *pl* procès-verbaux; **to take out a s. against s.o** faire assigner qn. II. *v.tr. Jur:* citer (qn) à comparaître; assigner (qn); appeler (qn) en justice

sump [sʌmp], *s. Aut:* fond *m* de carter; cuvette *f* d'égouttage.

sumptuous ['sʌm(p)tjuəs], *a.* somptueux fastueux; **-ly,** *adv.* somptueusement; **'sumptuousness,** *s.* somptuosité *f*, faste *m*; richesse *f* (du mobilier).

sun [sʌn]. **I.** s. (a) soleil m; **the sun's shining,** il fait du soleil; (b) **s. glasses,** lunettes f de soleil; **s. lounge,** solarium m; **full in the s.,** au grand soleil; **to get a touch of the s.,** prendre un coup de soleil; Aut: **s. visor,** pare-soleil m inv. **II.** v.tr. (sunned) exposer (qch.) au soleil; insoler (qch.); **to s. oneself,** prendre le soleil; se chauffer au soleil; **'sunbathe,** v.i. prendre des bains de soleil; s'insoler; **'sunbather,** s. personne f qui prend des bains de soleil; **'sunbathing,** s. bains mpl de soleil; **'sunbeam,** s. rayon m de soleil; **'sunburn,** s. Med: coup m de soleil; **'sunburnt,** a. hâlé, basané; brûlé par le soleil; **'Sunday,** s. dimanche m; **in one's S. best,** dans ses habits du dimanche; **'sundial,** s. cadran m solaire; **'sundown,** s. coucher m du soleil; **'sunflower,** s. tournesol m, soleil; **s. seed oil,** huile f de tournesol; **'sunless,** a. sans soleil; **'sunlight,** s. lumière f du soleil; **in the s.,** au (grand) soleil; **'sunlit,** a. ensoleillé; **'sunny,** a. **1.** (journée) de soleil; (endroit) ensoleillé; (côté) exposé au soleil; **it's s.,** il fait (du) soleil. **2.** (visage) radieux, rayonnant; (caractère) heureux; **'sunrise,** s. lever m du soleil; **'sunroof,** s. Aut: toit ouvrant; **'sunset,** s. coucher m du soleil; **at s.,** au soleil couchant; **'sunshade,** s. ombrelle f; **'sunshine,** s. (clarté f, lumière f, du) soleil; **in the s.,** au soleil; Aut: **s. roof,** toit ouvrant; **'sunspot,** s. Astr: tache f solaire; **'sunstroke,** s. Med: insolation f; coup m de soleil; **to get s.,** attraper un coup de soleil; **'suntan,** s. hâle m; **s. oil,** huile f solaire; **'suntanned,** a. hâlé, basané; **'suntrap,** s. endroit très ensoleillé; **'sun-up,** s. lever m du soleil.

'undry ['sʌndri]. **1.** a. pl. divers; **s. expenses,** frais divers; **on s. occasions,** à différentes occasions. **2.** s. (a) **all and s.,** tous sans exception; **he told all and s. about it,** il le racontait à tout venant; (b) pl. **sundries,** (i) articles divers; (ii) frais divers.

'unk [sʌŋk], a. F: perdu, ruiné; **we're s.,** nous sommes perdus; **'sunken,** a. (a) (rocher) noyé, submergé; (navire) sombré, coulé; **s. wreck,** épave sous-marine; (b) affaissé, enfoncé; **s. cheeks,** joues creuses; (c) **s. garden,** jardin m en contrebas; **s. road,** chemin creux.

'uper ['su:pər]. **I.** s. F: (a) abbr. for SUPERINTENDENT; (b) Aut: (petrol) super m. **II.** a. F: superbe; sensas. **III.** pref. (used in compounds) super-, sur-.

'uperabundance [su:pərə'bʌndəns], s. surabondance f (of, de); **supera'bundant,** a. surabondant; **-ly,** adv. surabondamment.

'uperannuate [su:pə'rænjueit], v.tr. mettre (qn) à la retraite; retraiter (qn); **super'annuated,** a. (a) suranné, démodé; (b) retraité, en retraite; **superannu'ation,** s. retraite f par limite d'âge; **s. fund,** caisse f des retraites; **s. con-**

tribution, retenue f pour la retraite.
superb [su:'pə:b], a. superbe, magnifique; **-ly,** adv. superbement, magnifiquement.
supercharged ['su:pətʃɑ:dʒd], a. Aut: (moteur) suralimenté, surcomprimé, à compresseur; **'supercharger,** s. Aut: (sur)compresseur m.
supercilious [su:pə'siliəs], a. sourcilleux, hautain; (air) pincé, dédaigneux; **-ly,** adv. avec une nuance de dédain; **super'ciliousness,** s. hauteur f; air dédaigneux.
superficial [su:pə'fiʃ(ə)l], a. superficiel; **to have a s. knowledge of sth.,** avoir des connaissances superficielles de qch.; **his knowledge is entirely s.,** son savoir est tout en surface, tout en superficie; **she has a s. mind,** elle manque de profondeur; **-ally,** adv. superficiellement.
superfine ['su:pəfain], a. superfin; Com: surfin.
superfluous [su:'pə:fluəs], a. superflu; **-ly,** adv. d'une manière superflue; inutilement; **super'fluity** [-'flu:iti], s. superfluité f; superflu m.
superhighway [su:pə'haiwei], s. N.Am: autoroute f.
superhuman [su:pə'hju:mən], a. surhumain.
superimpose [su:pərim'pouz], v.tr. superposer; surimposer; Cin: etc: surimprimer.
superintend [su:pərin'tend], v.tr. diriger, surveiller; **superin'tendence,** s. direction f, surveillance f, contrôle m; conduite f (des travaux); **superin'tendent,** s. directeur, -trice; surveillant, -ante; chef m (des travaux); **police s.** = commissaire m de police.
superior [su:'piəriər]. **1.** a. (a) supérieur; d'une classe supérieure; **to be s. in numbers,** être supérieur en nombre; **to be s. to flattery,** être au-dessus de la flatterie; (b) (of pers.) sourcilleux; **with a s. smile,** avec un sourire suffisant, condescendant. **2.** s. supérieur, -eure; Ecc: **the Father S., Mother S.,** le père supérieur, la mère supérieure; **superi'ority** [-'ɔriti], s. supériorité f.
superlative [su:'pə:lətiv]. **1.** a. suprême; d'une excellence suprême. **2.** a. & s. Gram: superlatif (m); **-ly,** adv. au suprême degré; **s. ugly,** d'une laideur sans pareille.
superman, pl. **-men** ['su:pəmæn, -men], s. surhomme m.
supermarket ['su:pəmɑ:kit], s. supermarché m.
supernatural [su:pə'nætʃ(ə)rəl], a. surnaturel; s. **the s.,** le surnaturel; **-ally,** adv. surnaturellement.
supernumerary [su:pə'nju:mərəri], a. & s. surnuméraire (mf).
supersede [su:pə'si:d], v.tr. (a) remplacer; **method now superseded,** méthode périmée; (b) prendre la place de (qn); supplanter (qn).
supersonic [su:pə'sɔnik], a. Av: supersonique.
superstition [su:pə'stiʃ(ə)n], s. superstition f;

super′stitious, *a*. superstitieux; **-ly**, *adv.* superstitieusement.

superstructure [′su:pəstrʌktʃər], *s.* superstructure *f*; tablier *m* (d'un pont).

supertax [′su:pətæks], *s.* surtaxe *f*.

supervene [su:pə′vi:n], *v.i.* survenir; **if no complications s.**, s'il ne survient pas de complications.

supervise [′su:pəvaiz], *v.tr.* 1. surveiller, avoir l'œil sur (qn, qch.). 2. diriger, conduire (une entreprise); **super′vision** [-′viʒ(ə)n], *s.* 1. surveillance *f*; **under police s.**, sous la surveillance de la police. 2. direction *f* (d'une entreprise); **′supervisor**, *s.* surveillant, -ante; directeur, -trice; **to act as s.**, exercer la surveillance.

supine [′su:pain], *a.* 1. (*of pers.*) couché, étendu, sur le dos. 2. mou; indolent, inerte.

supper [′sʌpər], *s.* souper *m*; **to have s.**, souper; **the Last S.**, la (Sainte) Cène; **′suppertime**, *s.* heure *f* du souper.

supplant [sə′plɑ:nt], *v.tr.* supplanter; prendre la place de (qn); évincer (qn); **su′pplanter**, *s.* supplanteur, -euse.

supple [′sʌpl], *a.* souple, flexible; **to become s.**, s'assouplir; **supply**[1] [′sʌpli], *adv.* souplement; avec souplesse; **′suppleness**, *s.* souplesse *f*, flexibilité *f*.

supplement. I. [′sʌplimənt], *s.* supplément *m*; *Journ:* **literary s.**, supplément littéraire. **II.** [′sʌpliment], *v.tr.* ajouter à (un livre, etc.); **to s. one's income by sth.**, augmenter ses revenus en faisant qch.; **supple′mentary**, *a.* supplémentaire.

supplication [sʌpli′keiʃ(ə)n], *s.* supplication *f*; supplique *f*.

supply[2] [sə′plai]. **I.** *s.* 1. approvisionnement *m*, fourniture *f*; *Mil: etc:* ravitaillement *m*; **food s.**, ravitaillement en vivres. 2. (*a*) provision *f*; **to lay in a s. of sth.**, se faire une provision, s'approvisionner, de qch.; *Pol.Ec:* **s. and demand**, l'offre *f* et la demande; **in short s.**, (marchandises) en manque; (*b*) *pl.* **supplies**, (i) fournitures; (ii) approvisionnements; réserves *f*; stocks *m*; **food supplies**, vivres *m*; **to get in supplies of sth.**, s'approvisionner en qch.; (*c*) **s. teacher**, remplaçant, -ante (d'un professeur). **II.** *v.tr.* 1. (*a*) **to s. s.o. with sth.**, fournir, pourvoir, approvisionner, qn de qch.; **to s. s.o. with food**, alimenter qn; (*b*) **to s. sth.**, fournir, apporter, qch.; amener (l'eau, le gaz, etc.). 2. réparer (une omission); combler (un déficit); répondre à (un besoin); **to s. s.o.'s needs**, subvenir aux besoins de qn; **su′pplier**, *s.* fournisseur, -euse; pourvoyeur, -euse (**of**, de); approvisionneur, -euse (**of**, en de).

support [sə′pɔ:t]. **I.** *s.* 1. (*a*) appui *m*, soutien *m*; **moral s.**, appui moral; **collection in s. of a charity**, quête *f* au profit d'une œuvre; (*b*) **to be without means of s.**, être sans ressources; *Jur:*

without visible means of s., sans moyens d'existence connus. 2. (*a*) **the sole s. of his old age**, son seul soutien dans sa vieillesse; (*b*) appui, support *m*, soutien *m*, soutien (d'une voûte, etc.); *Hort:* tuteur *m*. **II.** *v.tr.* 1. supporter, soutenir, appuyer, maintenir (une voûte, etc.); tuteurer (un arbuste). 2. appuyer (qn); soutenir, corroborer (une théorie); faire une donation à (une œuvre de charité); **thanks to the team that supported me**, grâce à l'équipe qui me secondait. 3. entretenir (la vie); **to s. a family**, faire vivre, faire subsister, maintenir, une famille; **to s. oneself**, gagner sa vie. 4. supporter, tolérer (une injure); **su′pporter**, *s.* défenseur *m*; adhérent *m* (d'une cause); partisan *m* (de qn); *Sp:* supporter *m*; **su′pporting**, *a.* (mur) d'appui, de soutènement; *Th:* **s. cast**, la troupe qui seconde les premiers rôles.

suppose [sə′pouz], *v.tr.* (*a*) supposer; **s. you are right, supposing (that) you are right**, supposons, supposé, que vous ayez raison; **supposing he came back**, si par supposition il revenait; **s. we change the subject**, si nous changions de sujet; (*b*) s'imaginer; croire, penser; **you'll do it, I s.**, je suppose que vous le ferez; **you mustn't s. that . . .**, il ne faut pas vous imaginer que . . .; **he's supposed to have a chance**, on lui croit des chances; **so I supposed**, je le pensais bien; **I s. so**, probablement, sans doute; **I don't s. he'll do it**, je ne suppose pas qu'il le fasse; **he's supposed to be rich**, il est censé être riche; **I'm not supposed to know**, je suis censé ne pas le savoir; **su′pposed**, *a.* supposé, prétendu; soi-disant; **the s. culprit**, présumé coupable; **supposedly** [sə′pouzidli], *adv.* censément; soi-disant; **he went away, s. with the intention of coming back**, il est part soi-disant pour revenir; **suppo′sition**, *s.* supposition *f*, hypothèse *f*.

suppress [sə′pres], *v.tr.* 1. (*a*) réprimer (une révolte); (*b*) supprimer (un journal); interdire (une publication); faire disparaître (un abus). 2. étouffer (un scandale, un bâillement); **to s. one's feelings**, se contenir. 3. cacher, dissimuler (qch.); supprimer (un fait). 4. *T.V: etc:* antiparasiter; **su′ppressed**, *a.* **s. anger**, colère réprimée, refoulée; **s. excitement**, agitation contenue; **in a s. voice**, en baissant la voix; **su′ppression**, *s.* 1. répression *f* (d'une émeute); suppression *f* (d'un livre). 2. étouffement *m* (d'un scandale); refoulement *m* (de émotions). 3. dissimulation *f* (de la vérité). 4. *T.V: etc:* antiparasitage *m*; **su′ppressor**, *s.* *T.V: etc:* (dispositif) antiparasite (*m*); **s. grid**, grille *f* de freinage.

supranational [′s(j)u:prə′næʃən(ə)l], *a.* supranational.

supreme [su(:)′pri:m], *a.* suprême; **s. contempt**, mépris souverain; **s. court**, cour souveraine

-ly, *adv.* au suprême degré; suprêmement; **su'premacy** [-'preməsi], *s.* suprématie *f* (over, sur).

urcharge ['sɔ:tʃɑ:dʒ]. I. *s.* 1. droit *m* supplémentaire; surtaxe *f.* 2. surcharge *f* (sur un timbre-poste). II. *v.tr.* 1. (sur)taxer (une lettre, etc.). 2. surcharger (un timbre-poste).

ure ['ʃuər]. 1. *a.* sûr, certain; (*a*) to be **s. of sth.**, être sûr, certain, de qch.; **I'm s. of it,** j'en suis convaincu; j'en ai la certitude; **I'm not so s. of that,** je n'en suis pas bien sûr; **I'm s. I don't know,** ma foi, je ne sais pas; **to make s. of a fact,** s'assurer d'un fait; (*b*) **with a s. hand,** d'une main assurée; **in s. hands,** en mains sûres; **to be s.-footed,** avoir le pied sûr; **a s.-footed pony,** un poney au pied sûr; (*c*) indubitable; **a s. thing,** une affaire sûre; une chose certaine; *Rac:* certitude *f*; *N.Am:* **s. thing!** bien sûr! **I don't know for s.,** je n'en suis pas bien sûr; **tomorrow for s.,** demain sans faute; **he'll be killed for s.,** à coup sûr il sera tué; (*d*) **it's s. to be fine,** il fera sûrement beau; **he's s. to come,** il viendra à coup sûr; il viendra sûrement; **be s. to come early,** ne manquez pas d'arriver de bonne heure; **be s. not to lose it,** prenez garde de le perdre; **(yes) to be s.!** certainement! bien sûr! 2. *adv.* (*a*) *N.Am:* certainement; **it s. is cold,** il fait vraiment froid; (*b*) **as s. as death, as s. as eggs is eggs,** aussi sûr que deux et deux font quatre; **s. enough he was there,** il était bien là; **he'll come s. enough,** il viendra à coup sûr; **s. enough!** *esp. N.Am:* **s.!** bien sûr! -ly, *adv.* 1. sûrement; **to work slowly but s.,** travailler lentement mais sûrement. 2. **s. you don't believe that!** vous ne croyez pas cela, voyons! **'sureness,** *s.* 1. sûreté *f* (de pied). 2. certitude *f*; **'surety,** *s.* (*pers.*) caution *f*; garant, -ante; **to stand s. for s.o.,** se porter caution, garant, pour qn.

rf [sə:f]. I. *s.* barre *f* (de plage); ressac *m*; brisants *mpl* sur la plage; **s. riding,** surf *m*, surfing *m.* II. *v.i.* (*a*) se baigner dans le ressac; (*b*) faire du surfing; **'surfboard,** *s.* planche *f* de surfing; **'surfboat,** *s.* surf-boat *m*; pirogue *f* de barre; **'surfing,** *s.* surf *m*, surfing *m.*

rface ['sə:fis]. I. *s.* 1. (*a*) surface *f*; **to send a letter by s. mail,** envoyer une lettre par voie *f* de terre, de mer; (*b*) extérieur *m*, dehors *m*; **on the s. everything was well,** tout allait bien en apparence; **he doesn't probe beneath the s.** (of things), il s'arrête à la superficie. 2. aire *f*, étendue *f*; **the earth's s.,** la superficie de la terre. II. *v.* 1. *v.tr.* (*a*) apprêter, polir, la surface de (qch.); (*b*) *Civ.E:* revêtir (une route) (with, de). 2. *v.i.* (*of submarine*) faire surface, revenir en surface.

rfeit ['sə:fit], *s.* 1. surabondance *f.* 2. réplétion *f*; satiété *f.*

surge [sə:dʒ]. I. *s. Nau:* levée *f* de la lame; houle *f*; **s. of anger, of enthusiasm,** vague *f* de colère, d'enthousiasme. II. *v.i.* (*of sea*) être houleux; (*of crowd*) se répandre en flots (dans la rue, etc.); **the blood surged to her cheeks,** le sang lui reflua au visage.

surgeon ['sə:dʒən], *s.* (*a*) chirurgien, -ienne; **house s.,** interne *mf* en chirurgie; **dental s.,** chirurgien dentiste; **veterinary s.,** vétérinaire *mf*; (*b*) *Mil: etc:* médecin *m*; **'surgery,** *s.* 1. chirurgie *f*; **plastic s.,** chirurgie esthétique. 2. cabinet *m* de consultation (d'un médecin); **s. hours,** heures de consultation; **'surgical,** *a.* chirurgical; **s. instruments,** instruments de chirurgie; **s. appliances,** (i) appareils chirurgicaux; (ii) appareils orthopédiques.

surly ['sə:li], *a.* (*a*) bourru; (*b*) hargneux, maussade; **'surliness,** *s.* air bourru; maussaderie *f.*

surmise [sə(:)'maiz]. I. *s.* conjecture *f*, supposition *f.* II. *v.tr.* conjecturer, deviner; **as I surmised,** comme je m'en doutais (bien).

surmount [sə(:)'maunt], *v.tr.* surmonter.

surname ['sə:neim], *s.* nom *m* de famille.

surpass [sə(:)'pɑ:s], *v.tr.* (*a*) surpasser; **you've surpassed yourself,** vous vous êtes surpassé; (*b*) **the result surpasses our hopes,** le résultat a excédé nos espérances.

surplice ['sə:plis], surplis *m*; **'surpliced,** *a.* en surplis.

surplus ['sə:pləs], (*a*) *s.* surplus *m*, excédent *m*; **to have a s. of sth.,** avoir qch. en exces; (*b*) *attrib.* de surplus; **s. provisions,** vivres de surplus, en surplus; **s. population,** surplus de la population; *Com:* **sale of s. stock,** vente *f* de soldes *m*; **government s.** (stock), les surplus du gouvernement.

surprise [sə'praiz]. I. *s.* surprise *f*; (*a*) **to take s.o. by s.,** prendre qn à l'improviste, au dépourvu; **s. visit,** visite *f* à l'improviste; (*b*) **to give s.o. a s.,** faire une surprise à qn; **it was a great s. to me,** j'en ai été grandement surpris; (*c*) **to my great s., much to my s.,** à ma grande surprise; **to recover from one's s.,** revenir de son étonnement; **to pause in s.,** s'arrêter surpris. II. *v.tr.* surprendre; (*a*) **to s. s.o. in the act,** prendre qn sur le fait, en flagrant délit; (*b*) **to be surprised at sth.,** être surpris de qch.; **I'm surprised to see you,** je m'étonne de vous voir; **I shouldn't be surprised if . . .,** cela ne me surprendrait pas si . . .; **I'm surprised at you!** vous m'étonnez! **sur'prising,** *a.* surprenant, étonnant; **that's s.,** cela me surprend; -ly, *adv.* étonnamment; **I found him looking s. young,** j'ai été surpris de lui trouver l'air si jeune.

surrealism [sə'ri:əlizm], *s.* surréalisme *m*; **su'rrealist,** *a. & s.* surréaliste (*mf*).

surrender [sə'rendər]. I. *s.* 1. (*a*) reddition *f* (d'une forteresse); (*b*) **no s.!** on ne se rend pas!

2. abandon *m*, cession *f* (de biens); remise *f* (des armes à feu). **3.** *Ins:* rachat *m* (d'une police). **II.** *v.* **1.** *v.tr.* (*a*) rendre, livrer (une forteresse); (*b*) abandonner, céder (un droit, ses biens); **to s. sth. to s.o.**, faire (l')abandon de qch. à qn; (*c*) *Ins:* racheter (une police). **2.** *v.pr.* & *i.* **to s. (oneself)**, se rendre; **to s. (oneself) to justice**, se livrer à la justice.

surreptitious [sʌrəp'tiʃəs], *a.* subreptice, clandestin; **-ly**, *adv.* subrepticement, clandestinement, furtivement.

surround [sə'raund]. **I.** *s.* encadrement *m*, bordure *f.* **II.** *v.tr.* entourer; **the walls that s. the town**, les murailles qui entourent la ville; **to be surrounded with, by, dangers**, être entouré de dangers; **su'rrounding**, *a.* entourant, environnant; **the s. countryside**, le pays d'alentour; **su'rroundings**, *s.pl.* **1.** entourage *m*, milieu *m*, ambiance *f.* **2.** environs *mpl*, alentours *mpl* (d'une ville).

surtax ['sə:tæks]. **I.** *s.* surtaxe (progressive sur le revenu). **II.** *v.tr.* surtaxer.

surveillance [sə(:)'veiləns], *s.* surveillance *f*, contrôle *m*.

survey. I. ['sə:vei], *s.* **1.** (*a*) aperçu *m*; vue générale (d'un sujet); (*b*) examen attentif; étude *f* (de la situation); enquête *f*; (*c*) inventaire *m* (de monuments historiques). **2.** *Surv:* (*a*) levé *m* des plans; relevé *m*; (*b*) plan *m*, levé (du terrain); **air s., aerial s.**, levé aérien; **to make a s.**, lever un plan. **3.** inspection *f*, visite *f*; expertise *f.* **II.** [sə(:)'vei], *v.tr.* **1.** (*a*) regarder, contempler (un paysage, etc.); (*b*) mettre (une question) à l'étude; passer (la situation) en revue. **2.** *Surv;* relever; faire le levé de, lever le(s) plan(s) de (la ville, etc.); arpenter (un champ); **to s. for quantities**, métrer, toiser. **3.** inspecter, visiter; faire l'expertise de l'état de, expertiser (un navire); **sur'veying**, *s.* levé *m* de plans; **(land) s.**, géodésie *f*; topographie *f*; **sur'veyor**, *s.* (architecte) expert (*m*); **(land) s.**, géomètre expert; arpenteur *m* (géomètre); **quantity s.**, métreur (vérificateur).

survive [sə'vaiv]. **1.** *v.i.* survivre; (*of custom*) subsister. **2.** *v.tr.* (*a*) survivre à (qn); (*b*) **to s. an injury**, survivre à une blessure; **to s. a shipwreck**, réchapper d'un naufrage; **sur'vival**, *s.* (*a*) survivance *f*; **s. of the fittest**, survivance des mieux adaptés, du plus apte; (*b*) *Jur:* survie *f*; **sur'vivor**, *s.* survivant, -ante; rescapé(e) (d'une catastrophe).

susceptible [sə'septibl], *a.* **1.** (*a*) **s. of proof**, susceptible d'être prouvé; (*b*) **s. to a disease**, prédisposé à une maladie. **2.** (*a*) sensible, impressionnable; **to be s.**, avoir la fibre sensible; (*b*) qui se froisse facilement; susceptible; **suscepti'bility**, *s.* **1.** susceptibilité *f*; prédisposition *f* (à une maladie); **s. to impressions**, suggestibilité *f.* **2.** sensibilité *f*,

susceptibilité; **to avoid wounding anyone's susceptibilities**, éviter tout froissement.

suspect. I. ['sʌspekt], *a.* & *s.* suspect, -e; **t** **regard s.o. as s.**, tenir qn pour suspect. **II** [səs'pekt], *v.tr.* **1.** soupçonner (qn de qch.); **t** **be suspected**, être suspect; **I s. him of running into debt**, je le suspecte de faire des dettes. **2** soupçonner, s'imaginer; **to s. danger**, flairer l **danger**; **I suspected as much**, je m'en doutai **he suspects nothing**, il ne se doute de rien.

suspend [səs'pend], *v.tr.* **1. to s. sth. from th** **ceiling**, suspendre, pendre, qch. au plafond. **2** suspendre (son jugement, les paiements, l **travail); *Jur:* to s. judgement**, surseoir au juge ment. **3.** suspendre (un fonctionnaire); *Aut:* **t** **s. a driving licence**, suspendre un permis d **conduire; sus'pended**, *a.* suspendu; (*a*) *Ch* (particules) en suspension; (*b*) (*of services*) in **terrompu; *Jur:* (*of proceedings*) en suspens** *Med:* **s. animation**, arrêt momentané des fonc tions vitales; **sus'penders**, *s.pl.* (*a*) jarretelle *f*; **sock s.**, fixe-chaussettes *m inv*; (*b*) *N.Am* bretelles *f*; **sus'pense**, *s.* (*a*) suspens *m*; **t** **keep s.o. in s.**, tenir qn en suspens; (*b*) **s. nove** roman *m* à suspense; **sus'pension**, *s.* **1** suspension *f*; **s. bridge**, pont suspendu; *Ch:* i **s.**, en suspension. **2.** suspension (de la ci culation). **3.** suspension (d'un fonctionnaire) *Pol:* exclusion *f* temporaire (d'un député); **s. c** **a driving licence**, retrait *m* temporaire d'u permis de conduire.

suspicion [səs'spiʃ(ə)n], *s.* **1.** soupçon *m*; **to loo** **at s.o. with s.**, regarder qn avec défiance; **t** **have suspicions about s.o.**, avoir des dout sur qn; soupçonner qn; **to arouse s.**, éveiller l soupçons; **to arouse s.o.'s suspicions**, éveill la défiance de qn; **above s.**, au-dessus de to soupçon; **evidence not above s.**, témoignag sujets à caution; *Jur:* **to arrest s.o. on** arrêter qn préventivement. **2. I had m suspicions about it**, je m'en doutais. **3.** tr petite quantité, soupçon (de qch.).

su'spicious, *a.* **1.** soupçonnable, suspect; (*conduct*) louche, équivoque; **it looks s. to m** cela me paraît louche; **s.-looking customer**, i dividu *m* aux allures louches. **2.** méfiar soupçonneux; **to be s. about s.o.**, avoir d soupçons à l'égard de qn; **-ly**, *adv.* **1.** d'un manière suspecte, équivoque, louche; **it loo to me s. like measles**, ça m'a tout l'air d'êt la rougeole. **2.** d'un air méfian soupçonneusement; **su'spiciousness**, *s.* caractère suspect, louche, équivoque (de q qch.). **2.** caractère soupçonneux; méfiance *f*.

sustain [sə'stein], *v.tr.* **1.** soutenir, support **enough to s. life**, de quoi entretenir la vie; quoi vivre; *Mus:* **to s. a note**, souteni prolonger, une note; *Jur:* **objection sustaine** réclamation admise. **2. to s. an injury**, recevo

une blessure; être blessé; **su'stained,** *a.* (*of effort, etc.*) soutenu; **s. applause,** applaudissements prolongés, nourris; **su'staining,** *a.* soutenant; **s. food,** nourriture fortifiante; **s. wall,** mur *m* de soutènement.
sustenance ['sʌstinəns], *s.* (*a*) *Med:* **means of s.,** moyens de subsistance; moyens de vivre; (*b*) aliments *mpl,* nourriture *f.*
suzerain, *f.* **-aine** ['su:zərein], *s.* suzerain, -aine; **'suzerainty,** *s.* suzeraineté *f.*
swab [swɔb]. **I.** *s.* (*a*) torchon *m;* serpillière *f;* (*b*) *Med:* tampon *m* (d'ouate); (*c*) *Nau:* (deck) s., fauber(t) *m.* **II.** *v.tr.* (**swabbed**) nettoyer, essuyer (avec un torchon, etc.); *Nau:* fauberder (le pont).
swag [swæg], *s. F:* (*a*) rafle *f,* butin *m* (d'un cambrioleur); (*b*) *Austr:* baluchon *m,* paquet *m* (de clochard); **'swagman,** *pl.* **-men,** *s. Austr:* clochard *m.*
swagger ['swægər]. **I.** *s.* **1.** (*a*) air important; **to walk with a s.,** faire la roue; (*b*) air cavalier, désinvolte. **2.** rodomontades *fpl;* crâneries *fpl.* **II.** *v.i.* (*a*) crâner, se pavaner; faire la roue; (*b*) fanfaronner; faire le glorieux; (*c*) **to s. in, out,** entrer, sortir, d'un air important; **'swaggering,** *a.* (air) important, crâneur, glorieux.
wallow¹ ['swɔlou]. **I.** *s.* gorgée *f* (d'eau, etc.); **to drink sth. at one s.,** boire qch. d'un seul coup; *Geol:* **s. hole,** aven *m,* gouffre *m.* **II.** *v.tr.* **to s. sth. (down),** avaler qch.; gober (une huître); **to s. one's tears,** dévorer ses larmes; **to s. an insult,** dévorer une injure; **to s. one's pride,** mettre son orgueil dans sa poche; **you'll have a job to make them s. that story,** tu auras mal à leur faire avaler ça; **to s. up a fortune,** engloutir, engouffrer, une fortune; **swallowed up by the waves,** (navire) englouti par les flots.
wallow², *s. Orn:* hirondelle *f; Sp:* **s. dive,** saut *m* de l'ange; **'swallowtail,** *s. Ent:* **s. (butterfly),** machaon *m.*
wamp [swɔmp]. **I.** *s.* marais *m,* marécage *m.* **II.** *v.tr.* **1.** inonder, submerger. **2.** remplir (un bateau) d'eau; **to be swamped with work,** être débordé de travail; **'swampy,** *a.* marécageux.
wan [swɔn], *s.* cygne *m; Sp: N.Am:* **s. dive,** saut *m* de l'ange; **'swan-necked,** *a. Tls: etc:* en col de cygne; **'swansong,** *s.* chant *m* du cygne.
wank [swæŋk]. **I.** *s.* **1.** prétention *f,* gloriole *f,* épate *f.* **2.** (*pers.*) crâneur, -euse; épateur *m.* **II.** *v.i.* se donner des airs; crâner; faire de l'épate.
wap [swɔp]. **I.** *s. F:* (*a*) troc *m,* échange *m;* **to get sth. as a s. for sth.,** recevoir qch. en échange de qch.; **to do a s.,** faire un troc; (*b*) (*in stamp collecting, etc.*) **swaps,** doubles *m.* **II.** *v.tr.* (**swapped**) **to s. sth. for sth.,** échanger, troquer, qch. contre, pour, qch.; **shall we s.?** si nous faisions un échange? **to s. places with s.o.,** changer de place avec qn; **'swapping,** *s.*

échange *m,* troc *m.*
swarm¹ [swɔ:m]. **I.** *s.* essaim *m,* jetée *f* (d'abeilles); **s. of locusts,** vol *m* de sauterelles; **s. of children,** essaim, troupe *f,* d'enfants. **II.** *v.i.* **1.** (*a*) (*of bees*) essaimer; faire l'essaim; (*b*) (*of pers.*) accourir en foule, se presser (autour de, dans, qch.); (*c*) pulluler, grouiller. **2. to s. with . . .,** fourmiller, grouiller, de . . .; **street swarming with people,** rue qui grouille, regorge, de monde.
swarm², *v.tr. & i.* **to s. (up) a tree,** monter, grimper, à un arbre.
swarthy ['swɔ:ði], *a.* (teint) basané, bistré, boucané; **'swarthiness,** *s.* teint basané, bistré.
swastika ['swɔstikə], *s.* svastika *m;* croix gammée.
swat [swɔt], *v.tr.* (**swatted**) écraser (une mouche, etc.); **'swatter,** *s.* **(fly) s.,** tue-mouches *m inv,* tapette *f* (à mouches).
swathe [sweið], *v.tr.* emmailloter; envelopper; **head swathed in bandages,** tête enveloppée de linges.
sway [swei]. **I.** *s.* empire *m,* domination *f;* **under his s.,** sous son influence *f.* **II.** *v.* **1.** *v.i.* se balancer; osciller; **tree that sways in the wind,** arbre qui se balance au vent. **2.** *v.tr.* (*a*) faire osciller; balancer, agiter (les arbres, etc.); (*b*) gouverner, diriger; **papers that s. public opinion,** journaux qui influencent l'opinion; **'swaying. 1.** *a.* oscillant; **s. crowd,** foule ondoyante. **2.** *s.* balancement *m,* oscillation *f; Rail:* mouvement *m* de lacet (des voitures).
swear [swɛər]. **I.** *s. F:* (*a*) jurons *mpl;* **to have a good s.,** lâcher une bordée de jurons; (*b*) **s. (word),** juron, gros mot. **II.** *v.* (**swore** [swɔ:r]; **sworn** [swɔ:n]) **1.** *v.tr.* jurer; **to s. to do sth.,** jurer de faire qch.; **I could have sworn I heard footsteps,** j'aurais juré entendre des pas; **to be sworn (in),** prêter serment; **to s. s.o. to secrecy,** faire jurer le secret à qn; **to s. at s.o.,** maudire qn; **to s. (to) sth.,** attester qch. sous serment; **I'd s. to it,** j'en jurerais; **to s. sth. on one's honour,** jurer qch. sur l'honneur. **2.** *v.i.* jurer; proférer un juron; **to s. like a trooper,** jurer comme un charretier; **to s. by s.o., sth.,** vanter qn, qch.; s'enthousiasmer pour, de, sur, qn, qch.; **'swearing,** *s.* **1.** (*a*) attestation *f* sous serment; (*b*) prestation *f* de serment. **2. s. (in) of the jury,** assermentation *f* du jury. **3.** jurons *mpl;* gros mots.
sweat [swet]. **I.** *s.* sueur *f,* transpiration *f;* **by the s. of one's brow,** à la sueur de son front; *F:* **to be in a s. about sth.,** s'inquiéter de qch. **II.** *v.* **1.** *v.i. & tr.* (*a*) suer, transpirer; **to s. blood,** suer du sang; (*b*) (*of worker*) peiner; **to s. workers,** exploiter la main-d'œuvre. **2.** *v.i.* (*of walls, etc.*) suer, suinter; **'sweated,** *a.* (travail) mal rétribué; **'sweater,** *s. Cl:* chandail *m,* tricot *m,*

sweater *m*; **'sweating,** *s.* (*a*) transpiration *f*;
suintement *m* (d'un mur); (*b*) exploitation *f* (de
la main-d'œuvre); **'sweaty,** *a.* en sueur; **s.
hands,** mains moites.
Sweden ['swi:d(ə)n]. *Pr.n. Geog:* la Suède;
Swede, *s.* 1. (*pers.*) Suédois, -oise. 2. *Agr:*
rutabaga *m*; navet *m* de Suède; **'Swedish.** 1.
a. suédois. 2. *s. Ling:* le suédois.
sweep [swi:p]. I. *s.* 1. (*a*) coup *m* de balai, de
faux; **at one s.,** d'un seul coup; (*b*) **to give the
room a s.,** balayer la pièce; **to make a clean s.,**
faire table rase; **to make a clean s. of the staff,**
balayer tout le personnel. 2. mouvement *m* circulaire (du bras, etc.); **with a wide s. of the
arm,** d'un geste large. 3. (*a*) boucle *f* (d'une
rivière); (*b*) **fine s. of grass,** belle étendue de
gazon; (*c*) *T. V: etc:* balayage *m.* 4. (**chimney**)
s., ramoneur *m.* 5. *F:* sweepstake *m.* II. *v.*
(**swept** |swept|) 1. *v.tr.* (*a*) balayer (une cham-
bre); ramoner (une cheminée); **to s. the
horizon with a telescope,** parcourir l'horizon
avec une lunette; **to s. the board,** faire table
rase; *abs.* **to s. for mines,** draguer des mines;
(*b*) balayer (la poussière); **to s. away the snow,**
balayer la neige; (*of current*) **to s. sth. along,**
entraîner, emporter, qch.; **bridge swept away
by the torrent,** pont emporté par le torrent; **to
s. up the dead leaves,** balayer, ramasser, les
feuilles mortes. 2. *v.i.* **to s. (along),** avancer
d'un mouvement rapide et uni; **to s. into a
room,** entrer dans une pièce d'un air
majestueux; **the enemy swept down on us,**
l'ennemi s'abattit sur nous; **hills sweeping
down to the sea,** collines qui dévalent vers la
mer; **to s. on,** continuer d'avancer
(irrésistiblement); **to s. out,** sortir d'un air
majestueux; **'sweeper,** *s.* 1. (*pers.*) balayeur,
-euse. 2. (*machine*) balayeuse *f* (mécanique);
'sweeping. 1. *a.* **s. gesture,** geste large; **s.
statement,** déclaration par trop générale; **s.
reform,** réforme complète; **s. changes,** changement *m* de fond en comble. 2. *s.* (*a*) balayage
m; (**chimney**) **s.,** ramonage *m*; (*b*) *pl.*
sweepings, balayures *f,* ordures *f*;
'sweepstake, *s.* sweepstake *m.*
sweet [swi:t]. I. *a.* 1. doux, sucré; **as s. as honey,**
doux comme le miel; **to have a s. tooth,** aimer
les douceurs; être friand de sucreries; **my tea is
too s.,** mon thé est trop sucré. 2. **s.(-scented,
-smelling),** qui sent bon, qui embaume; au parfum délicieux; **s. pea,** pois *m* de senteur. 3. (*of
food*) frais; **s. breath,** haleine saine, fraîche. 4.
(son) doux, mélodieux. 5. (*a*) **s. temper,**
caractère doux, aimable; **s.-tempered,** au
caractère doux; **revenge is s.,** la vengeance est
douce; (*b*) (*of pers.*) charmant, gentil; **a s. little
kitten,** un petit chat adorable; **to keep s.o.
s.,** cultiver la bienveillance de qn. 6. *F:* **to be s.
on s.o.,** être amoureux de qn. II. *s.* (*a*) bonbon

m; *pl.* **sweets,** sucreries *f,* confiseries *f*; (*b*) (*a
dinner*) entremets sucré; **-ly,** *adv.* 1.
doucement; avec douceur; (chanter)
mélodieusement. 2. agréablement, gentiment
3. (*of machine*) **to run s.,** fonctionner sans à
coups; avoir une allure douce; **'sweetbread,**
s. Cu: ris *m* de veau, d'agneau; **'sweeten,** *v.tr*
(*a*) sucrer (un plat); (*b*) purifier (l'air); (*c*)
adoucir (la vie); (*d*) *F:* graisser la patte à (qn)
'sweetening, *s.* 1. adoucissement *m*; sucrag
m. 2. substance *f* pour sucrer; **'sweetish,** c
douceâtre; **'sweetness,** *s.* 1. douceur *f.* 2. gen
tillesse *f,* charme *m*; **'sweetshop,** *s.* confiseri
f; **'sweet-'william,** *s. Bot:* œillet *m* de poète
swell [swel]. I. *s.* 1. *Nau:* houle *f*; levée *f* (de l
lame); **heavy s.,** forte houle. 2. *Mus:* (*of orga*
soufflet *m*; **s. box,** boîte *f* d'expression. II. c
esp. N.Am: F: épatant; **he's a s. guy,** c'est u
chic type. III. *v.* (**swelled** [sweld]; **swolle**
['swoulən]) 1. *v.tr.* (r)enfler, gonfler; ey
swollen with tears, yeux gonflés de larmes; t
s. the crowd, augmenter la foule. 2. *v.i.* **to
(up),** (s')enfler, se gonfler; (*of debt*) augmente
grossir; (*of sea*) se soulever; houler; **to s. (ou**
être bombé; bomber; **'swelling,** *s.* 1. enfl
ment *m,* gonflement *m.* 2. *Med:* tuméfaction *f*
boursouflement *m* (du visage). 3. bosse
enflure *f* (au front); fluxion *f* (à la joue); tume
f; grosseur *f.*
swelter ['sweltər], *v.i.* étouffer de chaleu
'sweltering, *a.* **s. heat,** chaleur étouffant
accablante.
swerve [swə:v]. I. *s.* écart *m,* déviation *f*; *Au*
embardée *f.* II. *v.i.* faire un écart, un croche
(*of horse*) se dérober; (*of car*) **to s. (across th
road),** faire une embardée.
swift [swift]. I. *a.* (*a*) rapide; (*b*) (*of repl*
prompt; **s. to act,** prompt à agir. II. *s. Orr*
martinet *m*; **-ly,** *adv.* rapidement, vite
promptement; **'swiftness,** *s.* 1. rapidité
vitesse *f.* 2. promptitude *f.*
swig [swig]. *F:* I. *s.* grand trait, lampée *f* (c
bière). II. *v.tr.* (**swigged**) boire (un verre)
grands traits; lamper (qch.).
swill [swil]. I. *s.* 1. lavage *m* à grande eau; **to gi
a glass s. (out),** rincer un verre. 2. (*a*) (**pig**)
pâtée *f* pour les porcs; eaux grasses; (*b*)
mauvaise boisson. II. *v.* 1. *v.tr.* laver (
plancher) à grande eau; rincer (un verre). 2. *l*
(*a*) *v.tr.* boire avidement (qch.); (*b*) *v.i.* ribote
swim [swim]. I. *s.* 1. **to have a s.,** faire un peu c
nage, nager un peu; **to go for a s.,** aller nage
2. *F:* **to be in the s.,** être dans le mouvement. I
v. (**swam** |swæm|; **swum** [swʌm]) *v.i. & tr.*
(*a*) nager; **to s. (across) the river,** traverser l
rivière à la nage; (*b*) **he can't s. a stroke,** il na
comme un chien de plomb; (*c*) **meat swimmir
in gravy,** viande noyée dans la sauce. 2. ey
swimming with tears, yeux inondés de larme

3. (*a*) **my head's swimming,** la tête me tourne; (*b*) **everything swam before my eyes,** tout semblait tourner autour de moi; **'swimmer,** *s.* nageur, -euse; **'swimming. 1.** *a.* **s. eyes,** yeux noyés de larmes; **s. head,** tête qui tourne. **2.** *s.* nage *f*, natation *f*; **s. bath, pool,** piscine *f*; **-ly,** *adv.* *F:* comme sur des roulettes; à merveille; **'swimsuit,** *s.* costume *m*, maillot *m*, de bain.

swindle ['swindl]. **I.** *s.* escroquerie *f*, filouterie *f*; duperie *f*; déception *f*. **II.** *v.tr.* escroquer, filouter (qn); *F:* rouler (qn); **to s. s.o. out of sth.,** escroquer qch. à qn; **'swindler,** *s.* escroc *m*.

swine [swain], *s.inv.* **1.** cochon *m*, porc *m*; pourceau *m*. **2.** *F:* **dirty s.!** sale cochon! **he's a s.,** c'est un salaud.

swing [swiŋ]. **I.** *s.* **1.** (*a*) balancement *m*; (*b*) tour *m*, pivotement *m*. **2.** (*a*) oscillation *f* (d'un pendule); **to be in full s.,** (i) (*of dance, etc.*) battre son plein; (ii) (*of factory*) être en plein travail; **s. of public opinion,** revirement *m* de l'opinion publique; **s.-to of the door,** rabattement *m* de la porte; (*b*) **to give a child a s.,** balancer un enfant. **3.** (*a*) amplitude *f* (d'une oscillation) (*b*) *Nau:* évitage *m* (d'un navire à l'ancre). **4. to walk with a s.,** marcher d'un pas rythmé; **song that goes with a s.,** chanson entraînante; *F:* **everything went with a s.,** tout a très bien marché; **when you've got into the s. of things,** quand vous serez au courant. **5.** escarpolette *f*, balançoire *f*. **II.** *v.* (**swung** [swʌŋ]) **1.** *v.i.* (*a*) (i) **to s. to and fro,** se balancer; (*of bell*) branler; (*of pendulum*) osciller; (ii) tourner, pivoter; basculer; (*of door*) **to s. open,** s'ouvrir; **to s. on its hinges,** tourner sur ses gonds; (iii) *Nau:* (*of ship*) **to s. at anchor,** éviter sur l'ancre; (iv) *Games:* se balancer; (*b*) **to s. round,** faire volte-face; **the car swung right round,** la voiture a fait un tête-à-queue; (*c*) **to s. along,** marcher d'un pas rythmé. **2.** *v.tr.* (*a*) (faire) balancer (qch.); faire osciller (un pendule); **to s. one's arms,** balancer les bras (en marchant); *F:* **to s. it on s.o.,** duper qn; (*b*) faire tourner (qch.); *Nau:* **boat swung out,** embarcation parée au dehors; *Aut:* **to s. a car round,** faire faire un brusque virage à une voiture; **to s. it right round,** la faire faire un tête-à-queue; (*c*) **to s. a hammock,** pendre, (ac)crocher, un hamac; (*d*) *v.pr. & i.* **to s. (oneself) into the saddle,** monter vivement à cheval; **'swingback,** *s.* retour *m* en arrière; revirement *m* (d'opinion); **'swingbridge,** *s.* pont tournant, pivotant; **'swingdoor,** *s.* porte battante; **'swinging. 1.** *a.* balançant, oscillant; **s. arms,** bras ballants; **s. stride,** allure rythmée. **2.** *s.* balancement *m*, oscillation *f*; mouvement *m* de bascule, de rotation; *Nau:* évitage *m*; **'swing-round,** *s. Aut:* tête-à-queue *m inv.*

swingeing ['swindʒiŋ], *a.* (*of tax*) excessif,

extrêmement onéreux.

swipe [swaip]. **I.** *s.* **1.** *Sp:* coup *m* à toute volée. **2.** *F:* taloche *f*. **II.** *v.tr.* **1.** *Sp:* frapper (la balle) à toute volée. **2.** *F:* donner une taloche à (qn). **3.** *F:* chiper, chaparder (qch. à qn).

swirl [swə:l]. **I.** *s.* remous *m* (de l'eau); **s. of dust,** tourbillon *m* de poussière. **II.** *v.i.* tournoyer, tourbillonner; (*of dust*) **to s. up,** monter en tourbillons.

swish [swiʃ]. **I.** *s.* bruissement *m* (de l'eau); froufrou *m* (d'une robe); sifflement *m* (d'un fouet); crissement *m* (d'une faux). **II.** *v.tr.* faire siffler (sa canne); (*of animal*) **to s. its tail,** battre l'air de sa queue.

Swiss [swis]. **1.** *a.* suisse; **the S. government,** le gouvernement helvétique. **2.** *s.* Suisse, -esse; **the S.,** les Suisses.

switch [switʃ]. **I.** *s.* (*a*) *Rail:* aiguille *f*; changement *m* de voie; (*b*) *El:* interrupteur *m*; commutateur *m*; *Aut:* **starting s.,** contact *m.* **II.** *v.tr.* **1. to s. a train on to a branch line,** aiguiller, dériver, un train sur un embranchement. **2. to s. on the light,** allumer (l'électricité); *Aut:* **to s. on the ignition,** mettre le contact; *T.V: etc:* **to s. on,** ouvrir le poste; **to s. off the light, the engine,** couper la lumière, l'allumage; *T.V:* **to s. off,** fermer le poste; *v.i. Mil: etc:* **to s. over to the offensive,** passer à l'offensive; **'switchback,** *s.* montagnes *f* russes; **s. road,** route qui monte et descend; **'switchboard,** *s. El: Tp:* tableau *m* de distribution; *Tp:* **office s.,** standard *m*; **s. operator,** standardiste *mf*.

Switzerland ['switsələnd]. *Pr.n. Geog:* la Suisse; **French-speaking, German-speaking, Italian-speaking, S.,** la Suisse romande, alémanique, italienne.

swivel ['swiv(ə)l]. **I.** *s.* (*a*) émerillon *m*; maillon tournant; (*b*) pivot *m*; tourillon *m.* **II.** *v.i.* (**swivelled**) pivoter, tourner.

swollen ['swoulən], *a.* **1.** enflé, gonflé; **s. river,** rivière en crue; **to have a s. face,** (i) avoir le visage bouffi; (ii) avoir une fluxion à la joue. **2.** *F:* **to have a s. head,** être pénétré de sa propre importance; **s.-headed,** vaniteux, suffisant.

swoop [swu:p]. **I.** *s.* descente *f* (d'un faucon sur sa proie, de police); attaque brusquée; *F:* **at one fell s.,** d'un seul coup (fatal). **II.** *v.i.* (*of police*) faire une descente; **to s. (down) on sth.,** s'abattre, foncer, sur qch.

swop [swɔp], *s. & v.tr.* (**swopped**) = SWAP.

sword [sɔ:d], *s.* (*a*) épée *f*; **to cross swords with s.o.,** (i) croiser le fer avec qn; (ii) mesurer ses forces avec qn; **s. arm,** bras droit; **s. thrust,** coup *m* de pointe; coup d'épée; (*b*) sabre *m*; **with drawn s.,** sabre au clair; **s. cut,** coup de sabre; (*on face*) balafre *f*; **'swordbelt,** *s.* ceinturon *m*; **'swordfish,** *s. Ich:* espadon *m*; **'swordplay,** *s.* maniement *m* de l'épée; escrime *f*; **'swordsman,** *pl.* **-men,** *s.* escrimeur *m*; **fine s.**, fine lame; **'swordsmanship,** *s.* habileté *f* au maniement de l'épée; escrime *f*; **'swordstick,** *s.* canne *f* à épée.

sworn [swɔːn], *a.* 1. assermenté; **s. enemies,** ennemis jurés, acharnés. 2. **s. statement,** déclaration *f* sous serment.

swot [swɔt]. *F:* I. *s. Sch:* 1. (*a*) travail *m* intense; (*b*) corvée *f.* 2. (*of pers.*) bûcheur, -euse. II. *v.tr.* & *i.* (swotted) bûcher, piocher; **to s. for an exam,** potasser un examen.

sycamore ['sikəmɔːr], *s.* sycomore *m.*

sycophant ['sikəfənt], *s.* flagorneur, -euse.

syllable ['siləbl], *s.* syllabe *f*; **sy'llabic** [-'læbik], *a.* syllabique.

syllabus, *pl.* **-uses** ['siləbəs, -esiz], *s.* programme *m*, sommaire *m* (d'un cours).

symbiosis [simbi'ousis, -bai-], *s. Nat. Hist:* symbiose *f.*

symbol ['simb(ə)l], *s.* symbole *m*, emblème *m*; **sym'bolic** [-'bɔlik], *a.* symbolique; **-ally,** *adv.* symboliquement; **'symbolism,** *s.* symbolisme *m*; **symboli'zation,** *s.* symbolisation *f*; **'symbolize,** *v.tr.* symboliser.

symmetry ['simitri], *s.* symétrie *f*; **sy'mmetrical** [-'metrikl], *a.* symétrique; **-ally,** *adv.* symétriquement.

sympathize ['simpəθaiz], *v.i.* 1. **to s. with s.o.,** avoir de la compassion pour qn; **they called to s.,** ils sont venus exprimer leurs condoléances. 2. **I don't agree with him but I s. with his point of view,** je ne suis pas d'accord avec lui mais je comprends son point de vue; **sympa'thetic,** *a.* (*a*) compatissant; **he's always very s.,** il est toujours prêt à vous écouter; (*b*) **s. audience,** auditoire bien disposé; **s. words,** paroles de condoléance; (*c*) **s. strike,** grève *f* de solidarité; **-ally,** *adv.* d'une manière compatissante; **'sympathizer,** *s.* 1. **to be a s. with s.o.** (in his grief), compatir au chagrin de qn. 2. partisan, -ane (d'une cause); sympathisant, -ante; **'sympathy,** *s.* 1. compassion *f*; **accept my deep s.,** agréez mes condoléances. 2. (*a*) sympathie *f*, solidarité *f* (**for s.o.,** à l'égard de qn); **popular s. is on his side,** il a l'opinion pour lui; **I know you're in s. with them,** je sais que vous êtes de leur côté; **to strike in s.,** se mettre en grève par solidarité; (*b*) **prices went up in s.,** les prix sont montés par contrecoup.

symphony ['simfəni], *s.* symphonie *f*; **s. concert,** concert *m* symphonique; **sym'phonic,** *a.* symphonique.

symposium, *pl.* **-ia** [sim'pouziəm, -iə], *s.* (*a*) discussion *f* (académique); (*b*) recueil *m* d'articles.

symptom ['simptəm], *s.* symptôme *m*; **to show symptoms of sth.,** présenter des indices *m* de qch.

synagogue ['sinəgɔg], *s.* synagogue *f.*

synchronize ['siŋkrənaiz]. 1. *v.tr.* synchroniser. 2. *v.i.* (*of events*) arriver, avoir lieu, simultanément; **synchroni'zation,** *s.* synchronisation *f.*

syncopate ['siŋkəpeit], *v.tr. Mus:* syncoper; **synco'pation,** *s.* syncope *f.*

syndicalism ['sindikəliz(ə)m], *s.* syndicalisme *m*; **'syndicalist,** *s.* syndicaliste *mf.*

syndicate. I. ['sindikət], *s.* syndicat *m.* II. ['sindikeit], *v.tr.* syndiquer (des ouvriers, une industrie).

syndrome ['sindroum], *s. Med:* syndrome *m.*

synod ['sinəd], *s. Ecc:* synode *m*, concile *m.*

synonym ['sinənim], *s.* synonyme *m*; **sy'nonymous,** *a.* synonyme (**with,** de).

synopsis, *pl.* **-ses** [si'nɔpsis, -siːz], *s.* résumé *m*, sommaire *m.*

syntax ['sintæks], *s.* syntaxe *f.*

synthesis, *pl.* **-ses** ['sinθisis, -siːz], *s.* synthèse *f*; **'synthesize,** *v.tr.* synthétiser.

synthetic [sin'θetik], *a.* synthétique; **-ally,** *adv.* synthétiquement.

syphilis ['sifilis], *s. Med:* syphilis *f*; **syphi'litic,** *a.* syphilitique.

Syria ['siriə]. *Pr.n. Geog:* la Syrie; **'Syrian,** *a.* & *s.* syrien, -ienne.

syringe [si'rindʒ]. I. *s.* seringue *f.* II. *v.tr.* seringuer.

syrup ['sirəp], *s.* 1. sirop *m.* 2. **golden s.,** mélasse raffinée; sirop de sucre; **'syrupy,** *a.* sirupeux.

system ['sistəm], *s.* 1. (*a*) système *m*; organisme *m*; **digestive s.,** appareil digestif; (*b*) réseau (routier, etc.). 2. méthode *f*; **to lack s.,** manquer de méthode, d'organisation; **syste'matic,** *a.* systématique, méthodique; **he's s.,** il a de l'ordre; **-ally,** *adv.* systématiquement; (travailler) avec méthode; **system(at)i'zation,** *s.* systématisation *f*; **'systematize,** *v.tr.* systématiser.

T

T, t [tiː], s. (a) (la lettre) T, t m; **to (dot one's i's and) cross one's t's,** mettre les points sur les i; **to a T,** exactement; **it suits me to a T,** cela me va à merveille; (b) Cl: **T-shirt,** tee-shirt m.

ta [tɑː], int. F: merci.

tab [tæb], s. **1.** (a) patte f (de vêtement); (b) écusson m, insigne m (d'officier d'état-major); (c) (for hanging up coat) attache f; (d) onglet m (de fichier). **2.** étiquette f (pour bagages); F: **to keep tabs on s.o.,** tenir qn à l'œil.

tabby ['tæbi], s. t. (**cat**), chat tigré.

tabernacle ['tæbənækl], s. tabernacle m.

table ['teibl], s. table f. **1.** (a) **occasional t.,** petite table; **nest of tables,** table gigogne; **picnic t.,** table pliante, de camping; (b) **to lay the t.,** mettre la table; dresser le couvert; **to clear the t.,** desservir; **to sit down to t.,** se mettre à table; **t. knife,** couteau m de table; **t. fork,** fourchette f; **t. linen,** linge m de table; **t. mat,** dessous m d'assiette; **t. wine,** vin m de table; (c) Ecc: **the Communion T.,** la Sainte Table; (d) **t. tennis,** tennis m de table; ping-pong m. **2. to turn the tables on s.o.,** renverser les rôles; retourner la situation. **3.** table, tableau m; **multiplication t.,** table de multiplication; **tide tables,** annuaire m des marées; '**tablecloth,** s. nappe f; '**tableland,** s. Geog: plateau m; '**tablespoon,** s. cuiller f à servir; '**tablespoonful,** s. cuillerée f (à servir).

tablet ['tæblit], s. **1.** plaque commémorative. **2.** (a) Pharm: comprimé m; (b) **t. of soap,** savonnette f. **3.** N.Am: bloc-correspondance m.

tabloid ['tæbloid], s. journal m populaire (de petit format).

taboo [tə'buː]. **I.** s. tabou m. **II.** a. interdit, proscrit; **it's t.,** c'est une chose qui ne se fait pas. **III.** v.tr. déclarer tabou; F: proscrire, interdire (qch.).

tabular ['tæbjulər], a. tabulaire; **appendix in t. form,** appendice m en forme de tableau.

tabulate ['tæbjuleit], v.tr. classifier (des résultats); disposer (des chiffres) en forme de table(s).

tacit ['tæsit], a. (consentement) tacite, implicite; **-ly,** adv. tacitement; '**taciturn,** a. taciturne; **taci'turnity,** s. taciturnité f.

tack [tæk]. **I.** s. **1.** petit clou; broquette f; semence f; F: **to get down to brass tacks,** en venir au fait. **2.** Needlew: point m de faufilage, de bâti. **3.** Nau: **to make a t.,** tirer une bordée;

to be on the right t., être sur la bonne voie. **II.** v. **1.** v.tr. (a) **to t. sth. (down),** clouer qch. (avec des semences); **to t. sth. on to sth.,** attacher qch. à qch.; (b) Needlew: faufiler, bâtir. **2.** v.i. Nau: **to t. (about),** (i) virer (de bord); (ii) tirer des bordées; louvoyer; '**tacking,** s. (a) clouage m; (b) Needlew: bâtissage m; faufilure f; **to take out the t.,** défaufiler; (c) Nau: virement m de bord.

tackle ['tækl]. **I.** s. **1.** attirail m, appareil m, engins mpl; **fishing t.,** articles mpl de pêche. **2.** appareil de levage. **3.** Sp: placage m. **II.** v.tr. (a) empoigner; saisir (qn) à bras-le-corps; (b) s'attaquer à, aborder (un problème); (c) Sp: plaquer (qn).

tacky ['tæki], a. collant; (vernis) qui n'est pas encore sec.

tact [tækt], s. tact m, savoir-faire m; '**tactful,** a. (homme) de tact; délicat; **to be t.,** avoir du tact; **-fully,** adv. avec tact; **to deal t. with s.o.,** ménager qn; '**tactless,** a. (a) dépourvu de tact; maladroit; (b) **t. question,** question indiscrète; **-ly,** adv. sans tact; '**tactlessness,** s. manque m de tact; maladresse f.

tactics ['tæktiks], s.pl. tactique f; '**tactical,** a. tactique; **t. error,** erreur f, faute f, de tactique; **tac'tician,** s. tacticien, -ienne.

tadpole ['tædpoul], s. têtard m.

taffeta ['tæfitə], s. taffetas m.

tag [tæg]. **I.** s. **1.** (a) morceau m (de tissu) qui pend; (b) attache f; (c) ferret m (de lacet); (d) étiquette f. **2.** citation banale; cliché m. **3.** (jeu m du) chat; **to play t.,** jouer au chat. **II.** v.tr. & i. (**tagged**) **to t. on to s.o.,** s'attacher à qn; **to t. along behind s.o.,** traîner derrière qn.

Tahiti [tɑː'hiːti]. Pr.n. Geog: Tahiti m.

tail [teil]. **I.** s. **1.** (a) queue f (d'animal); (of peacock) **to spread his t.,** faire la roue; **with his t. between his legs,** (i) (of dog) la queue entre les jambes; (ii) F: (of pers.) l'oreille basse; **to keep one's t. up,** ne pas se laisser abattre; **to turn t.,** s'enfuir; (b) (of shirt, coat) pan m; **to grab s.o. by the coat tails,** saisir qn par le pan de son habit; **to wear tails,** mettre sa queue-de-morue; (c) Av: **t. unit,** empennage m; (d) **t. end,** fin f (d'un orage); queue (d'un défilé); **at the t. (end),** en queue; Aut: **there's a car on my t.,** une voiture me suit de près; (of cars) **nose to t.,** à la queue leu leu. **2.** (of coin) pile f, revers m; **heads or tails,** pile ou face. **II.** v.tr. & i. **1.** équeuter, enlever les queues (des groseilles,

T:1

etc.). 2. to t. s.o., suivre qn de près;'**tailboard**, s. (*of lorry*) layon *m*; '**tailless,** *a.* sans queue; '**tail** '**off,** *v.i.* (*a*) (*of sound*) s'éteindre; (*b*) (*of novel, etc.*) finir en queue de poisson.

tailor ['teilər]. **I.** *s.* tailleur *m* (d'habits); **t.-made costume,** (costume *m*) tailleur. **II.** *v.tr.* faire, façonner (un complet); **well tailored,** de facture soignée;'**tailoring,** *s.* 1. métier *m* de tailleur. 2. ouvrage *m* de tailleur.

taint [teint]. **I.** *s.* 1. corruption *f,* infection *f.* 2. tare *f* héréditaire. 3. trace *f* (d'infection). **II.** *v.tr.* infecter, vicier (l'air); corrompre, gâter (la nourriture); '**tainted,** *a.* infecté, corrompu; t. meat, viande gâtée.

take [teik], *v.* (**took** |tuk|; **taken** ['teik(ə)n]) prendre. **I.** *v.tr.* 1. (*a*) to t. sth. on one's back, prendre, charger, qch. sur son dos; (*b*) to t. sth. from s.o., enlever, prendre, qch. à qn; to t. sth. from the table, prendre qch. sur la table; (*c*) to t. (hold of) s.o., sth., saisir, empoigner, qn, qch.; to t. sth. with both arms, prendre qch. à pleins bras; she took my arm, elle me prit le bras; to t. an opportunity, saisir une occasion; (*d*) *Mil:* prendre (une ville); to t. s.o. prisoner, faire qn prisonnier; to be taken ill, tomber malade; he was very much taken with the idea, l'idée lui souriait beaucoup; I wasn't taken with him, il ne m'a pas fait bonne impression; (*e*) to t. a passage from a book, emprunter un passage à un livre. 2. (*a*) louer, prendre (une maison); (*b*) to t. tickets, prendre des billets; (*of seat, table*) taken, occupé; to t. a paper, s'abonner à un journal; (*c*) prendre (le train); t. your seats! prenez vos places! *Rail:* en voiture! (*d*) t. the turning on the left, prenez à gauche; to t. the wrong road, se tromper de chemin; (*e*) to t. legal advice = consulter un avocat; (*f*) *Ecc:* to t. (holy) orders, recevoir les ordres. 3. (*a*) gagner, remporter (un prix); *Cards:* to t. a trick, faire une levée; (*b*) she's taking a degree in law, elle fait son droit; to t. an examination, se présenter à un examen; (*c*) *Com:* to t. so much per week, se faire tant par semaine. 4. prendre (de la nourriture); I can't t. gin, je ne supporte pas le gin. 5. (*a*) to t. a walk, faire une promenade; to t. a bath, prendre un bain; *Sch:* she is taking our form, elle prend notre classe; to t. breath, reprendre haleine; to t. effect, produire son effet; (*b*) to t. a photograph, faire une photographie; to have one's photograph taken, se faire photographier; (*c*) to t. sth. apart, to pieces, démonter qch. 6. (*a*) prendre, recevoir; to t. no denial, ne pas accepter de refus; what will you t. for it? combien en voulez-vous? to t. a bet, tenir un pari; to t. all responsibility, assumer toute la responsabilité; to t. things as one finds them, prendre les choses comme elles sont; t. it from me! croyez-m'en! I wonder how he'll t. it,

je me demande quelle tête il fera; (*b*) car that takes six people, voiture qui tient six personnes. 7. to t. a dislike to s.o., prendre qn en grippe; to t. exception to sth., (i) trouver à redire à qch.; (ii) se froisser de qch. 8. (*a*) how old do you t. him to be? quel âge lui donnez-vous? I t. it that . . ., je suppose que . . .; (*b*) I took him for an Englishman, je le croyais anglais; *F:* what do you t. me for? pour qui me prenez-vous? 9. (*require*) (*a*) that will t. some explaining, voilà qui va demander des explications; the work takes some doing, le travail est difficile, dur; the journey takes five days, le voyage prend cinq jours; it won't t. long, ce sera tôt fait; it took four men to hold him, il a fallu le tenir à quatre; (*b*) verb that takes a preposition, verbe qui veut une préposition; (*c*) I t. size six, j'ai six de pointure. 10. (*a*) to t. s.o. somewhere, mener, conduire, qn dans un endroit; to t. s.o. out of his way, écarter qn de sa route; (*b*) to t. sth. to s.o., porter qch. à qn; to t. s.o. to hospital, transporter qn à l'hôpital. **II.** *v.i.* (*a*) avoir du succès; the play has taken, la pièce a pris, a réussi; the fire has taken, le feu a pris; (*b*) *Med:* (*of vaccine*) prendre;'take 'after, *v.i.* tenir de (qn); she doesn't t. after her father, elle n'a rien de son père;'take a'way, *v.tr.* 1. enlever, emporter (qch.); emmener (qn). 2. (*a*) to t. a knife away from a child, ôter un couteau à un enfant; (*b*) to t. a child away from school, retirer un enfant de l'école; 'take 'back, *v.tr.* 1. reconduire (qn); reporter (qch. à qn). 2. reprendre (un employé); retirer (ce qu'on a dit); 'take 'down, *v.tr.* 1. descendre (qch.); démolir (un mur); démonter (une machine); *F:* to t. s.o. down a peg, remettre qn à sa place. 2. to t. down a few notes, prendre quelques notes; to t. sth. down in shorthand, sténographier qch., prendre qch. en sténo(graphie); 'take 'in, *v.tr.* 1. (*a*) faire entrer (qn); (*b*) to t. in the washing, rentrer la lessive; *Nau:* to t. in (a supply of) water, faire de l'eau; (*of boat*) to t. in water, faire eau; prendre l'eau; (*c*) to t. in lodgers, prendre des locataires. 2. to t. in a dress at the waist, reprendre une robe à la taille. 3. comprendre, inclure. 4. (*a*) comprendre; to t. in the situation, se rendre compte de la situation; to t. in everything at a glance, tout embrasser d'un coup d'œil; (*b*) *F:* mettre (qn) dedans; rouler (qn); to be taken in, se laisser attraper; 'take 'into, *v.tr.* 1. to t. s.o. into one's confidence, se confier à qn. 2. to t. into one's head to do sth., se mettre dans la tête de faire qch.; 'take 'off, *v.* **I.** *v.tr.* 1. not to t. one's eyes off sth., ne pas quitter qch. des yeux. 2. (*a*) enlever, ôter; to t. off one's clothes, quitter ses vêtements; se déshabiller; (*b*) emmener (qn); *F:* to t. oneself off, s'en aller, s'éloigner; (*c*) to t.

so much off (the price of sth.), rabattre tant (sur le prix de qch.); (*d*) *F:* imiter, singer (qn). **II.** *v.i. Av:* décoller; **'takeoff,** *s.* (*a*) *Av:* décollage *m*; (*b*) caricature *f*, imitation *f*; **'take 'on,** *v.* **1.** *v.tr.* (*a*) se charger de, entreprendre (un travail); (*b*) accepter le défi de (qn); (*c*) engager, embaucher (un ouvrier); (*d*) prendre, revêtir (une qualité); (*e*) mener (qn) plus loin. **2.** *v.i. F:* **don't t. on so!** ne vous désolez pas comme ça! **'take 'out,** *v.tr.* **1.** (*a*) sortir (qch. de sa poche); **to t. out a stain,** enlever une tache; **to t. out a tooth,** arracher une dent; (*b*) *F:* **the heat takes it out of me,** la chaleur m'épuise; **don't t. it out on me,** ne vous en prenez pas à moi. **2.** faire sortir (qn); sortir (un enfant); **he's taking me out to dinner,** il va m'emmener dîner. **3.** prendre, obtenir (un brevet); **to t. out an insurance (policy),** contracter une assurance; **'take 'over,** *v.tr.* **1. to t. over a business,** prendre la suite des affaires; acheter une entreprise commerciale; **to t. over the liabilities,** prendre les dettes à sa charge; *v.i.* **to t. over from s.o.,** remplacer qn (dans ses fonctions); relever qn. **2.** transporter (qn, qch.); **'takeover,** *s.* reprise *f* (d'une maison de commerce); prise *f* de possession (du pouvoir); **t. bid,** offre *f* de rachat; **'taker,** *s.* preneur, -euse (d'un bail); **at that price there were no takers,** à ce prix on n'a pas pu trouver d'acheteurs; **'take to,** *v.i.* **1.** to **t. to flight,** to **t. to one's heels,** prendre la fuite; **to t. to the woods,** se réfugier dans les bois; **to t. to one's bed,** s'aliter. **2. to t. to drink,** s'adonner à la boisson, se mettre à boire. **3.** (*a*) **to t. to s.o.,** prendre qn en amitié; (*b*) **I don't t. to the idea,** cette idée ne me dit rien; **I shall never t. to it,** je ne m'y ferai jamais; **'take 'up,** *v.* **1.** *v.tr.* **1.** (*a*) relever, ramasser (qch.); (*b*) enlever (un tapis); dépaver (une rue); (*c*) *Rail:* **to stop to t. up passengers,** s'arrêter pour prendre des voyageurs; (*d*) raccourcir (une jupe, etc.). **2.** absorber (de l'eau). **3.** (*a*) **to t. up shares (in a company),** souscrire à des actions; (*b*) **to t. up a challenge,** relever un défi; (*c*) **to t. up an idea,** adopter une idée. **4.** (*a*) **to t. up a question,** prendre une question en main; (*b*) embrasser (une carrière); s'adonner à (une occupation); épouser (une querelle); **to t. up one's duties again,** reprendre ses fonctions; (*c*) prendre (qn) sous sa protection. **5. to be taken up (by the police),** être arrêté. **6. to t. s.o. up sharply,** reprendre qn vertement; **to t. s.o. up short,** couper la parole à qn. **7. to t. s.o. up wrongly,** mal comprendre les paroles de qn. **8.** (*a*) **to t. up too much room,** occuper trop de place; (*b*) **to t. up all s.o.'s attention,** absorber l'attention de qn; (*c*) **he's very much taken up with her,** il ne pense plus qu'à elle. **II.** *v.i.* **to t. up with s.o.,** (i) se lier d'amitié avec qn; (ii) se mettre à fréquenter (des vauriens); (iii) se mettre (en

ménage) avec qn; **'take u'pon,** *v.tr.* **to t. it upon oneself to do sth.,** prendre sur soi de faire qch.; **'taking,** *a.* attrayant; (visage) séduisant; **t. ways, manners,** manières engageantes; **'takings,** *s.pl. Com:* recette *f*, produit *m*.
talcum ['tælkəm], *s.* **t. powder,** (poudre *f* de) talc *m*.
tale [teil], *s.* **1.** conte *m*; récit *m*, histoire *f*; **old wives' t.,** conte de bonne femme; **I've heard that t. before,** je connais des paroles sur cet air-là. **2.** (*a*) racontar *m*; **I've heard a fine t. about you,** j'en ai appris de belles sur votre compte; (*b*) rapport *m*; **to tell tales,** rapporter; **'talebearer,** *s.* rapporteur, -euse.
talent ['tælənt], *s.* **1.** (*a*) talent *m*, capacité (naturelle); aptitude *f*; don *m* (de faire qch.); (*b*) **man of t.,** homme de talent. **2.** *coll.* gens *mpl* de talent; **exhibition of local t.,** exposition des œuvres d'artistes régionaux; *Cin: etc:* **t. scout,** dénicheur *m* de vedettes; **'talented,** *a.* doué.
talisman ['tælizmən], *s.* talisman *m*.
talk [tɔːk]. **I.** *s.* **1.** (*a*) paroles *fpl*; **he's all t.,** ce n'est qu'un bavard; (*b*) bruit *m*, dires *mpl*, racontages *mpl*; **there's some t. of his returning,** il est question qu'il revienne; **it's all t.,** ce ne sont que des on-dit; (*c*) propos *mpl*; bavardage *m*; **idle t.,** paroles en l'air; **small t.,** menus propos; **double t.,** propos nègre blanc. **2.** (*a*) entretien *m*; causerie *f*; **to have a t. with s.o.,** causer, s'entretenir, avec qn; (*b*) **to give a t. on, about, sth.,** faire une causerie sur qch. **3.** **it's the t. of the town,** on ne parle que de cela. **II.** *v.* **1.** *v.i.* (*a*) parler; **to learn to t.,** apprendre à parler; **to t. big,** se vanter; **to t. through one's hat,** débiter des sottises; **it's easy to t.!** cela vous plaît à dire! *F:* **now you're talking!** voilà qui s'appelle parler! **talking of that . . .,** à propos de cela . . .; **he knows what he's talking about,** il sait ce qu'il dit; **t. about luck!** tu parles d'une chance! **to t. of doing sth.,** parler de faire qch.; (*b*) **to t. to s.o.,** causer, s'entretenir, avec qn; **to t. freely,** s'ouvrir (à qn); **to t. to oneself,** se parler à soi-même; *F:* **who do you think you're talking to?** à qui croyez-vous donc parler? *F:* **I'll t. to him!** je vais lui dire son fait! (*c*) jaser, bavarder; **to get oneself talked about,** faire parler de soi; défrayer la conversation. **2.** *v.tr.* (*a*) **to t. French,** parler français; **to t. (common) sense,** parler raison; (*b*) **to t. oneself hoarse,** s'enrouer à force de parler; **to t. s.o. into doing sth.,** amener qn à faire qch.; **to t. s.o. round, over,** amener qn à changer d'avis; **to t. sth. over,** discuter qch.; **'talkative,** *a.* causeur; jaseur; bavard, loquace; **'talkativeness,** *s.* loquacité *f*; **'talker,** *s.* **1.** causeur, -euse; parleur, -euse. **2. he's a great t.,** il est bien bavard; **'talking,** *s.* **1.** discours *mpl*, propos *mpl*; **it's no use my t.,**

je perds mes paroles. 2. (a) conversation f; (b) bavardage m; **to do all the t.**, faire tous les frais de la conversation; **no t. please!** pas de bavardage! 3. **to give s.o. a good t.**-to, semoncer qn.

tall [tɔːl], a. 1. (of pers.) (a) grand; de haute taille; (b) **how t. are you?** combien mesurez-vous? **she is getting t.**, elle se fait grande. 2. (of thg) haut, élevé; **tree ten metres t.**, arbre haut de dix mètres. 3. (histoire) incroyable; **that's a t. story!** celle-là est raide! F: **that's a t. order!** c'est demander un peu trop!

tally ['tæli]. I. s. pointage m; **to keep t. of goods,** pointer des marchandises (sur une liste); **t. clerk,** pointeur m. II. v. 1. v.tr. pointer, contrôler (des marchandises). 2. v.i. **to t. with sth.,** correspondre à, s'accorder avec, qch.; **they don't t.,** ils ne s'accordent pas.

talon ['tælən], s. serre f (d'aigle).

tamarisk ['tæmərisk], s. Bot: tamaris m.

tambourine [tæmbə'riːn], s. Mus: tambour m de basque.

tame [teim]. I. a. 1. (animal) apprivoisé, domestiqué. 2. (a) (of pers.) soumis, docile; (b) (style) monotone, terne. II. v.tr. (a) apprivoiser; (b) domestiquer (une bête); (c) mater (qn, une passion); dompter (un lion); **-ly,** adv. (a) docilement; **to submit t.,** n'offrir aucune résistance; (b) fadement; platement; **'tameness,** s. 1. (a) nature douce (d'un animal); (b) caractère soumis, docilité f (de qn). 2. monotonie f, fadeur f (du style); insipidité f, banalité f (d'un conte); **'tamer,** s. dresseur, -euse, dompteur, -euse (de fauves); **'taming,** s. (a) apprivoisement m; (b) domestication f.

tamper ['tæmpər], v.i. (a) **to t. with,** toucher à (un mécanisme); altérer (un document); falsifier (un registre); fausser (une serrure); (b) **to t. with a witness,** suborner un témoin.

tan [tæn]. I. 1. s. (a) tan m; (b) hâle m (du teint). 2. a. tanné; tan inv: **black and t. dog,** chien noir et feu inv. II. v. (tanned) 1. v.tr. (a) tanner (les peaux); F: **to t. s.o.'s hide,** tanner le cuir à qn; (b) (of sun) hâler, bronzer (la peau). 2. v.i. se hâler, se bronzer; **'tanner,** s. tanneur m; **'tannery,** s. tannerie f; **'tanning,** s. 1. tannage m. 2. F: tannée f, raclée f.

tang [tæŋ], s. goût vif; saveur f; **the t. of the sea,** la senteur de l'air marin.

tangent ['tæn(d)ʒənt], s. tangente f; **to fly off at a t.,** prendre la tangente.

tangerine [tæn(d)ʒə'riːn], s. mandarine f.

tangible ['tæn(d)ʒibl], a. 1. tangible; **t. assets,** valeurs matérielles. 2. réel; **t. difference,** différence f sensible; **-ibly,** adv. 1. tangiblement. 2. sensiblement, manifestement; **tangi'bility,** s. tangibilité f.

Tangier(s) [tæn'(d)ʒiər, -iəz]. Pr.n. Geog: Tanger m.

tangle ['tæŋgl]. I. s. embrouillement m; emmêle-

ment m (de cheveux); F: **to be in a t.,** ne plus savoir où on en est; **to get into a t.,** (i) s'embrouiller; (ii) se mettre dans le pétrin. II. v.tr. **to t. sth.** (up), embrouiller, (em)mêler (des fils); embrouiller (une affaire); **to get tangled (up),** (of thgs) s'emmêler; (of thgs, pers.) s'embrouiller; (of pers.) se mettre dans le pétrin; **tangled web,** trame compliquée.

tank [tæŋk], s. 1. réservoir m; **water t.,** réservoir à eau; **hot water t.,** réservoir d'eau chaude; Aut: (petrol) t., réservoir à essence; **to fill up one's t.,** faire le plein. 2. (a) Mil: char m (de combat); (b) Rail: **t. wagon,** N.Am: **t. car,** wagon-citerne m; **'tanker,** s. Nau: bateau-citerne m; Aut: camion-citerne m.

tankard ['tæŋkəd], s. pot m, chope f (en étain).

tantalize ['tæntəlaiz], v.tr. taquiner (qn); mettre (qn) au supplice; **'tantalizing,** a. tentant; (sourire) provocant; **-ly,** adv. (a) cruellement; (b) d'un air provocant.

tantamount ['tæntəmaunt], a. **t. to,** équivalent à; **that is t. to a refusal,** cela équivaut à un refus.

tantrum ['tæntrəm], s. accès m de mauvaise humeur; **to get into a t.,** se mettre en colère; sortir de ses gonds.

Tanzania [tænzə'niːə]. Pr.n. Geog: la Tanzanie.

tap¹ [tæp]. I. s. (a) fausset m (de fût); (b) robinet m; **to turn the t. on, off,** ouvrir, fermer, le robinet; **t. water,** eau f du robinet, eau de la ville. II. v.tr. (tapped) (a) percer (un fût); (b) **to t. a tree (for resin),** inciser, gemmer, un arbre; Metall: **to t. the furnace,** percer le haut fourneau; (c) **to t. wine,** tirer du vin; (d) **to t. a telephone,** brancher un téléphone sur la table d'écoute; (e) Com: **to t. new markets,** créer de nouveaux débouchés; **'tapping¹,** s. (a) mise f en perce, perçage m (d'un tonneau); incision f, gemmage m (d'un arbre); (b) tirage m (du vin); **'taproot,** s. Bot: racine pivotante; pivot m.

tap². I. s. tape f; petit coup; **there was a t. at the door,** on frappa doucement à la porte; **t. dancing,** danse f à claquettes. II. v. (tapped) 1. v.tr. frapper légèrement; taper, tapoter. 2. v.ind.tr. **to t. at, on, the door,** frapper doucement à la porte; **'tapping²,** s. tapement m, tapotement m.

tape [teip]. I. s. 1. (a) ruban m; ganse f; F: **red t.,** fonctionnarisme m; (b) Sp: bande f d'arrivée; (c) Med: **adhesive t.,** bande adhésive; sparadrap m; El: **insulating t.,** chatterton m. 2. **t. measure,** mètre m à ruban; centimètre m (de couturière); **steel t.,** ruban d'acier. 3. **ticker t.,** bande de téléimprimeur; **recording t.,** bande magnétique; **t. recording,** enregistrement m sur bande magnétique. II. v.tr. (a) F: **I've got him taped,** j'ai pris sa mesure; (b) enregistrer sur bande; **'tape-recorder,** s. magnétophone m; **'tapeworm,** s. ver m solitaire.

taper ['teipər]. I. *s. Ecc:* cierge *m.* II. *v.* 1. *v.tr.* effiler; tailler en cône. 2. *v.i.* **to t.** (**off**), s'effiler; aller en diminuant; **'tapering,** *a.* en pointe; effilé, fuselé.

tapestry ['tæpistri], *s.* tapisserie *f.*

tapioca [tæpi'oukə], *s.* tapioca *m.*

tar [tɑ:r]. I. *s.* goudron *m*; **coal t.,** goudron de houille; (*on road*) **t. spraying,** goudronnage *m*; **to spoil the ship for a ha'p'orth of t.,** faire des économies de bouts de chandelle. II. *v.tr.* (**tarred**) goudronner; **tarred felt,** feutre bitumé; **'tarring,** *s.* goudronnage *m*; bitumage *m*; **'tarry,** *a.* goudronneux, bitumeux.

tarantula [tə'ræntjulə], *s.* tarentule *f.*

target ['tɑ:git], *s.* cible *f*; but *m*, objectif *m*; **to hit the t.,** atteindre le but; **an obvious t. for caricaturists,** une cible facile pour les caricaturistes; **his t. is to reform the world,** il a pour but de, son but est de, réformer le monde.

tariff ['tærif], *s.* 1. tarif *m*; **t. walls,** barrières douanières. 2. tableau *m*, liste *f*, des prix.

tarmac ['tɑ:mæk], *s.* 1. *Civ.E:* goudron *m*, bitume *m.* 2. *Av:* (*a*) aire *f* de stationnement; (*b*) aire d'embarquement; (*c*) piste *f* d'envol.

tarnish ['tɑ:niʃ]. I. *s.* ternissure *f.* II. *v.tr. & i.* (se) ternir.

tarpaulin [tɑ:'pɔ:lin], *s.* toile, bâche, goudronnée.

tarragon ['tærəgən], *s.* estragon *m.*

tart[1] [tɑ:t]. I. *s.* 1. *Cu:* tarte *f*; (*small*) tartelette *f*; (*covered*) tourte *f.* 2. *P:* fille *f*, poule *f.* II. *v.tr. F:* **to t. sth., oneself, up,** attifer qch.; s'attifer.

tart[2], *a.* (*a*) acerbe, aigrelet; (*of wine*) vert; (*b*) (*of answer*) mordant; acrimonieux; acerbe; **-ly,** *adv.* acrimonieusement; avec acerbité, d'un ton acerbe; d'une manière mordante; **'tartness,** *s.* verdeur *f* (d'un vin); acidité *f*, aigreur *f*, causticité *f* (du ton).

tartan ['tɑ:t(ə)n], *s. Tex: Cl:* tartan *m.*

Tartar[1] ['tɑ:tər]. 1. *a. & s. Geog:* tartare. 2. *s. F:* homme *m* intraitable; (*of woman*) mégère *f.*

tartar[2], *s. Ch:* tartre *m*; **tar'taric** [-'tærik], *a. Ch:* tartrique.

task [tɑ:sk], *s.* 1. tâche *f*; travail *m*; ouvrage *m*; **a hard t.,** une grosse besogne; **to carry out one's t.,** remplir sa tâche. 2. **to take s.o. to t. for sth.,** prendre qn à partie, réprimander qn, pour avoir fait qch. 3. *Mil:* **t. force,** corps *m* expéditionnaire; **'taskmaster,** *s.* chef *m* de corvée; surveillant *m*; **hard t.,** véritable tyran *m.*

Tasmania [tæz'meiniə]. *Pr.n. Geog:* la Tasmanie; **Tas'manian,** *a. & s.* tasmanien, -ienne.

tassel ['tæs(ə)l], *s.* 1. *Furn: Cl:* gland *m*, pompon *m*, houppe *f.* 2. *Bot:* (*of maize*) aigrette *f*; **'tasselled,** *a.* à glands; à houppes.

taste [teist]. I. *s.* 1. (*a*) (**sense of**) **t.,** goût *m*; (*b*) saveur *f*, goût *m*; **it has no t.,** cela n'a pas de goût,

est insipide; **it has a burnt t.,** cela a un goût de brûlé; (*c*) **a t. of sth.,** un petit peu (de fromage); une petite gorgée (de vin); (*d*) *F:* **he's already had a t. of prison,** il a déjà tâté de la prison. 2. goût, penchant (particulier), prédilection *f* (**for,** pour); **to have a t. for sth.,** avoir du goût pour qch.; **to find sth. to one's t.,** trouver qch. à son goût; **everyone to his t.,** chacun (à) son goût. 3. **to have (good) t.,** avoir du goût; **it's (in) bad t.,** c'est de mauvais goût. II. *v.* 1. *v.tr.* (*a*) percevoir la saveur de (qch.); goûter (qch.); (*b*) déguster (des vins); (*c*) goûter à (qch.); manger un petit morceau d'(un mets); tâter de (qch.); **to t. happiness, misfortune,** connaître, goûter, le bonheur, la malchance. 2. *v.i.* **to t. of sth.,** avoir un goût de qch.; **'tasteful,** *a.* de bon goût; **-fully,** *adv.* avec goût; **'tasteless,** *a.* 1. sans saveur; fade, insipide. 2. (ameublement) qui manque de goût, de mauvais goût; laid; **-ly,** *adv.* sans goût; **'tastelessness,** *s.* 1. insipidité *f*, fadeur *f.* 2. manque *m* de goût; **'taster,** *s.* dégustateur, -trice (de vins); **'tastiness,** *s.* saveur *f*, goût *m* agréable (d'un mets); **'tasting,** *s.* dégustation *f* (du vin); **'tasty,** *a.* (mets) savoureux; (morceau) succulent.

ta-ta [tæ'tɑ:], *int. P:* au revoir!

tatters ['tætəz], *s.pl.* **in t.,** (vêtement) en lambeaux *m*, en loques *f*; **'tattered,** *a.* (vêtement) dépenaillé, en loques.

tattle ['tætl]. I. *s.* 1. bavardage *m*, commérage *m.* 2. cancans *mpl*; commérages. II. *v.i.* 1. bavarder; jaser. 2. cancaner; faire des cancans; **'tattler,** *s.* 1. bavard, -arde. 2. cancanier, -ière.

tattoo[1] [tə'tu:], *s. Mil:* 1. retraite *f* (du soir); **to beat a t. on the table,** tambouriner sur la table. 2. **torchlight t.,** retraite aux flambeaux.

tattoo[2]. I. *s.* tatouage *m.* II. *v.tr.* tatouer (le corps); **ta'ttooing,** *s.* tatouage *m.*

tatty ['tæti], *a. F:* défraîchi.

taunt [tɔ:nt]. I. *s.* reproche méprisant; sarcasme *m.* II. *v.tr.* (*a*) accabler (qn) de sarcasmes; (*b*) **to t. s.o. with sth.,** reprocher qch. à qn (avec mépris); **'taunting,** *a.* (ton) de sarcasme.

Taurus ['tɔ:rəs]. *Pr.n. Astr:* le Taureau.

taut [tɔ:t], *a.* tendu, raidi; **'tauten,** *v.tr.* raidir (un câble); **'tautness,** *s.* raideur *f.*

tawdry ['tɔ:dri], *a.* d'un mauvais goût criard; **'tawdriness,** *s.* clinquant *m*; faux brillant.

tawny ['tɔ:ni], *a.* fauve; tirant sur le roux; **t. owl,** (i) *Orn:* chat-huant *m*; (ii) *Scouting:* assistante *f* (de Jeannettes).

tax [tæks]. I. *s.* 1. impôt *m*, contribution *f*, taxe *f*; **income t.,** impôt sur le revenu; **t. free,** exempt d'impôts; **t. collector,** percepteur *m* (des contributions directes); receveur *m* (des contributions indirectes); **t. evasion,** fraude fiscale. 2. charge *f*; fardeau *m*; **to be a t. on s.o.,** être une charge pour qn. II. *v.tr.* 1. (*a*) taxer (qch.); frapper (qch.) d'un impôt; (b) imposer (qn); (c) mettre à l'épreuve (la patience de qn). **2. to t. s.o. with doing sth.**, accuser qn d'avoir fait qch.; **'taxable**, a. imposable; **tax'ation**, s. (a) imposition f (de la propriété, etc.); (b) charges fiscales; (c) revenu réalisé par les impôts; les impôts m; **'taxpayer**, s. contribuable mf.

taxi ['tæksi]. **I.** s. taxi m; **t. driver**, chauffeur m de taxi; **t. rank**, station f de taxis. **II.** v.i. (**taxied, taxying**) (of aircraft) rouler au sol; **'taximeter**, s. taximètre m.

taxidermy ['tæksidə:mi], s. taxidermie f; **'taxidermist**, s. naturaliste m, taxidermiste m, empailleur m (d'animaux).

tea [ti:], s. **1.** (a) thé m; **t. bag**, sachet m de thé; **t. service, t. set**, F: **t. things**, service m à thé; **t. plant**, arbre m à thé; **t. rose**, rose f thé; (b) (i) Austr: dîner m; (ii) (**afternoon**) **t.**, thé; **to give a t. party**, donner un thé. **2. camomile t.**, infusion f, tisane f, de camomille; **beef t.**, bouillon gras; **'teacloth**, s. torchon m; essuie-verres m; **'teacup**, s. tasse f à thé; **'tealeaf**, s. feuille f de thé; **'teapot**, s. théière f; **'teashop**, s. salon m de thé; **'teaspoon**, s. cuiller f à thé; **'teaspoonful**, s. cuiller(ée) f à thé; **'teatime**, s. l'heure f du thé; **'tea towel**, s. torchon m, essuie-verres m.

teach [ti:tʃ], v.tr. (**taught** [tɔ:t]) enseigner, instruire (qn); enseigner (qch.); **to t. s.o. sth.**, enseigner, apprendre, qch. à qn; **she teaches French**, elle enseigne le français; **she teaches, N.Am: she teaches school**, elle est dans l'enseignement; **to t. s.o. (how) to do sth.**, apprendre à qn à faire qch.; **to t. oneself sth.**, apprendre qch. tout seul; **that will t. him!** ça lui apprendra! **to t. s.o. a thing or two**, dégourdir qn; **'teachable**, a. **1. not t.**, (enfant) à qui on ne peut rien enseigner. **2.** (sujet) enseignable; **'teacher**, s. (i) instituteur, -trice; maître, maîtresse, d'école; (ii) (in general sense) maître; **he's a good t.**, c'est un bon professeur; **'teaching**, s. **1.** enseignement m, instruction f; **to go in for t.**, entrer dans l'enseignement. **2.** doctrine f.

teak [ti:k], s. teck m.

team [ti:m]. **I.** s. **1.** attelage m (de chevaux). **2.** équipe f; **football t.**, équipe de football. **II.** v.i. **to t. up with s.o.**, se joindre à qn (pour faire un travail); **'teamwork**, s. travail m d'équipe.

tear[1] ['tiər], s. larme f; **to burst into tears**, fondre en larmes; **to shed tears of joy**, verser des larmes de joie; **'teardrop**, s. larme f; **'tearful**, a. éploré, tout en pleurs; Pej: larmoyant; **in a t. voice**, (i) avec les larmes dans la voix; (ii) Pej: en pleurnichant; **-fully**, adv. en pleurant; les larmes aux yeux; **'tear-gas**, s. gaz m lacrymogène; **'tear-stained**, a. (visage) barbouillé de larmes.

tear[2] [tɛər]. **I.** s. **1. wear and t.**, usure f, dégradation f (d'un immeuble). **2.** déchirure f, accroc m (dans un vêtement). **II.** v. (**tore; torn**) **1.** v.tr. (a) déchirer; **to t. sth. to pieces**, déchirer qch. en morceaux; **to t. a hole in sth.**, faire un trou dans, un accroc à, qch.; **torn between two opposing feelings**, tiraillé entre deux émotions; (b) **to t. sth. out of s.o.'s hands**, arracher qch. des mains de qn; **to t. one's hair**, s'arracher les cheveux. **2.** v.i. **to t. along**, aller à toute vitesse; **he was tearing along the road**, il dévorait la route; **'tear a'way**, v.tr. arracher (qch.); **to t. s.o. away from his work**, arracher qn à son travail; **I could not t. myself away**, je ne pouvais me décider à partir; **'tear 'down**, v.tr. arracher (une affiche); démolir (une maison); **'tearing. I.** a. **1.** déchirant. **2. in a t. hurry**, (être) terriblement pressé. **II.** s. **1.** déchirement m. **2. t. away, off, out**, arrachement m; **'tear 'off**, v.tr. **a** shell tore off his arm, un obus lui arracha le bras; **'tear 'out**, v.tr. **to t. out s.o.'s eyes**, arracher les yeux à qn; **'tear 'up**, v.tr. **1.** déchirer (une lettre); mettre (qch.) en pièces. **2. to t. up a tree by the roots**, déraciner, arracher, un arbre.

tease [ti:z], v.tr. taquiner, tourmenter, faire enrager (qn); **'teaser**, s. F: problème m difficile; **'teasing. I.** a. taquin. **II.** s. taquinerie f, taquinage m.

technique [tek'ni:k], s. technique f; **technical** ['teknik(ə)l], a. technique; **t. terms**, termes m techniques; termes de métier; **-ally**, adv. techniquement; **techni'cality**, s. détail m technique; considération f d'ordre technique; **tech'nician** [-'niʃ(ə)n], s. technicien, -ienne; **tech'nologist**, s. technologue mf, technologiste mf; **tech'nology**, s. technologie f.

Teddy ['tedi]. Pr.n.m. (diminutive) Édouard, Théodore; **t. (bear)**, ours m, ourson m, en peluche.

tedious ['ti:diəs], a. fatigant; ennuyeux; pénible; **-ly**, ennuyeusement; **'tediousness, 'tedium**, s. ennui m; manque m d'intérêt (d'un travail).

tee [ti:], s. Golf: tee m.

teem [ti:m], v.i. **to t. with**, foisonner de (gibier); fourmiller d'(insectes); abonder en (poisson); **teeming rain**, pluie torrentielle.

teens [ti:nz], s.pl. l'âge m entre treize et vingt ans; **to be in one's t.**, être adolescent(e); **'teenage**, a. adolescent; de l'adolescence; **'teenager**, s. adolescent, -ente.

teeny(-weeny) ['ti:ni('wi:ni)], a. F: minuscule.

tee-shirt ['ti:ʃət], s. tee-shirt m.

teeter-totter ['ti:tətɔtər], s. N.Am: bascule f, balançoire f.

teeth [ti:θ], see TOOTH.

teethe [ti:ð], v.i. faire ses (premières) dents; **'teething**, s. dentition f; **t. troubles**, difficultés initiales (d'une industrie, etc.).

teetotal [tiː'toutl], a. antialcoolique; qui s'abstient de boissons alcooliques; **tee'totalism**, s. abstention f de boissons alcooliques; **tee'totaller**, s. abstinent, -ente.

telecommunications ['telikəmjuːni'keiʃ(ə)nz], s.pl. télécommunications f; **t. specialist**, télémécanicien m.

teleferic [teli'ferik], s. téléphérique m.

telegram ['teligræm], s. télégramme m, dépêche f; **radio t.**, radiotélégramme m.

telegraph ['teligrɑːf]. I. s. télégraphe m; **t. pole**, poteau m télégraphique; **t. operator**, télégraphiste mf; **t. messenger**, facteur m télégraphiste. II. v.i. & tr. télégraphier; **tele'graphic** [-'græfik], a. télégraphique; **telegraphist** [te'legrəfist], s. télégraphiste mf; **te'legraphy**, s. télégraphie f.

telepathy [te'lepəθi], s. télépathie f; **telepathic** [teli'pæθik], a. télépathique.

telephone ['telifoun]. I. s. téléphone m; **automatic t.**, automatique m; **are you on the t.?** avez-vous le téléphone? **you're wanted on the t.**, on vous demande au téléphone; **t. number**, numéro m de téléphone; **t. box**, cabine f téléphonique; **t. directory**, annuaire m du téléphone; **t. operator**, standardiste mf. II. v. 1. v.i. téléphoner. 2. v.tr. téléphoner (un message); téléphoner à (qn); **tele'phonic** [-'fɔnik], a. téléphonique; **telephonist** [te'lefənist], s. standardiste mf; **te'lephony**, s. téléphonie f.

telephoto [teli'foutou], s. **t. lens**, téléobjectif m.

teleprinter ['teliprintər], s. (appareil) télétype m; **t. operator**, télétypiste mf.

telescope ['teliskoup]. I. s. (a) (refracting) t., lunette f d'approche, longue-vue f; (b) **reflecting t.**, télescope m (à miroir, à réflexion); **electron t.**, télescope électronique. II. v.tr. & i. (se) télescoper; **cars that telescoped**, voitures qui se sont télescopées; **parts made to t.**, pièces assemblées en télescope; **tele'scopic** [-'skɔpik], a. télescopique; **telescoping**, s. (of trains) télescopage m.

television ['telivi3(ə)n, teli'vi3(ə)n], s. télévision f; **colour t.**, télévision en couleur; **on (the) t.**, à la télévision; **t. (set)**, téléviseur m, F: télévision; **televise**, v.tr. téléviser.

telex ['teleks], s. télex m.

tell [tel], v. (told [tould]). I. v.tr. 1. (a) dire; **to t. the truth**, (i) dire la vérité; (ii) à dire vrai; (b) **to t. s.o. sth.**, dire, apprendre, qch. à qn; faire savoir qch. à qn; **I have been told that . . .**, on m'a dit que . . .; **I don't want to have to t. you that again**, tenez-vous cela pour dit; **I told you so!** je vous l'avais (bien) dit! F: **you're telling me!** (i) allons donc! (ii) tu parles! (c) raconter, conter (une histoire); **I'll t. you what happened**, je vais vous raconter ce qui est arrivé; F: **t. me**

another! à d'autres! **more than words can t.**, plus qu'on ne saurait dire; (d) annoncer, proclamer (un fait); révéler (un secret); **the postman will t. you the way**, le facteur va vous indiquer le chemin; (of clock) **to t. the time**, marquer l'heure. 2. (a) **to t. s.o. about s.o., sth.**, parler de qn, de qch., à qn; (b) **it's not so easy, let me t. you**, ce n'est pas si facile, je vous assure; **he'll be furious, I (can) t. you!** il va être furieux, je vous en réponds! 3. **to t. s.o. to do sth.**, ordonner, dire, à qn de faire qch.; **do as you're told**, faites ce qu'on vous dit; **I told him not to . . .**, je lui ai défendu de . . .. 4. (a) discerner, distinguer, reconnaître; **to t. right from wrong**, discerner le bien du mal; **you can't t. her from her sister**, elle ressemble à sa sœur à s'y tromper; **one can t. him by his voice**, on le reconnaît à sa voix; **one can t. she's intelligent**, on sent qu'elle est intelligente; (b) savoir; **who can t.?** qui sait? **you never can t.**, on ne sait jamais; **I can't t.**, je n'en sais rien. 5. **to t. (over)**, compter; **all told**, tout compris; somme toute. II. v.i. (a) produire son effet; porter; **every shot tells**, chaque coup porte; **these drugs t. on one**, l'effet de ces drogues se fait sentir; (b) **his face told of suffering**, son visage révélait ses souffrances; **everything told against him**, tout témoignait contre lui; **'teller**, s. 1. (ra)conteur, -euse; narrateur, -trice. 2. (a) caissier, -ière; (b) Pol: scrutateur m; recenseur m; **'telling.** I. a. efficace; **t. blow, style, coup, style, qui porte.** II. s. 1. récit m; narration f (d'une histoire). 2. divulgation f (d'un secret). 3. **there's no t.**, on ne sait pas; qui sait? 4. **t. (over)**, dénombrement m; énumération f (des votes); **'telling-off**, s. F: engueulade f; **'tell 'off**, v.tr. F: réprimander (qn); dire son fait à (qn); **'telltale**, s. (a) (of pers.) rapporteur, -euse; (b) **t. signs**, signes révélateurs.

telly (the) [ðə'teli], s. F: la télé.

temerity [ti'meriti], s. témérité f, audace f.

temper ['tempər]. I. s. 1. (of steel) trempe f; **to lose its t.**, se détremper. 2. (of pers.) sang-froid m; **to lose one's t.**, se fâcher; perdre son sang-froid; s'emporter; **to keep one's t.**, rester calme. 3. humeur f; (a) caractère m, tempérament m; **to have a bad t.**, avoir (un) mauvais caractère; (b) **in a vile t.**, d'une humeur massacrante; **to be in a good, a bad, t.**, être de bonne, de mauvaise, humeur; (c) mauvaise humeur f; **fit of t.**, mouvement m d'humeur; **to be in a t.**, être en colère; **to get into a t.**, se fâcher; **to put s.o. in a t.**, mettre qn en colère; fâcher qn. II. v.tr. 1. tremper (l'acier). 2. tempérer, modérer (son ardeur); **'temperament**, s. tempérament m, humeur f; **tempera'mental**, a. (a) capricieux, fantasque; (b) qui s'emballe ou se déprime facilement.

temperance ['temp(ə)rəns], s. (a) tempérance f; modération f; sobriété f; (b) abstention f des boissons alcooliques; **'temperate**, a. **1.** (of pers.) tempérant, sobre; (of language) modéré, mesuré; **t. habits**, habitudes de sobriété. **2.** (of climate) tempéré; **-ly**, adv. sobrement; avec modération.

temperature ['tempritʃər], s. température f; Med: **to have a t.**, avoir de la fièvre.

tempest ['tempist], s. tempête f; **tem'pestuous**, a. (a) tempétueux; de tempête; (b) (of meeting) orageux.

temple¹ ['templ], s. temple m.

temple², s. Anat: tempe f; **'temporal**¹, a. & s. (os) temporal m.

tempo ['tempou], s. (a) Mus: (pl. tempi ['tempi]) tempo m; (b) rythme m; **to upset the t. of production**, interrompre le rythme de production.

temporal² ['tempərəl], a. temporel.

temporary ['temp(ə)rəri], a. (a) temporaire, provisoire; **t. measures**, mesures f transitoires; **t. post**, situation f intérimaire; (b) momentané; **the improvement is only t.**, l'amélioration n'est que passagère; **-ily**, adv. (a) temporairement, provisoirement; intérimairement; (b) momentanément; pour le moment; **tempori'zation**, s. temporisation f; **'temporize**, v.i. temporiser; chercher à gagner du temps.

tempt [tem(p)t], v.tr. **1. to t. s.o. to do sth.**, induire qn à faire qch.; **to let oneself be tempted**, se laisser tenter; céder à la tentation; **I was greatly tempted**, l'occasion était bien tentante; **I am tempted to accept**, j'ai bien envie d'accepter. **2. to t. providence**, tenter la providence; **temp'tation**, s. tentation f; **'tempter**, s. tentateur, -trice; **'tempting**, a. tentant, alléchant; (of offer) séduisant, attrayant; (of food) appétissant.

ten [ten], num.a. & s. dix (m); **about t. years ago**, il y a une dizaine d'années; **to bet t. to one**, parier à dix contre un; F: **t. to one he finds out**, je vous parie qu'il le découvrira.

tenable ['tenəbl], a. (opinion) soutenable.

tenacious [tə'neiʃəs], a. tenace; **to be t.**, tenir à son opinion; s'opiniâtrer (dans un projet); **-ly**, adv. obstinément; avec ténacité; **tenacity** [tə'næsiti], s. ténacité f.

tenant ['tenənt], s. locataire mf; **t.'s repairs**, réparations locatives; **'tenancy**, s. location f; **during my t.**, pendant que j'étais locataire.

tend¹ [tend], v.tr. soigner (un malade); surveiller (des enfants, une machine); garder (des moutons); entretenir (un jardin); **'tender**¹, s. Nau: bateau ravitailleur; Rail: tender m; **bar t.**, barman m.

tend² , v.i. **1.** tendre, se diriger (**towards**, vers); **that tends to annoy him**, cela tend à le fâcher. **2. to t. to do sth.**, être porté, enclin, à faire qch.;

he tends to forget, il est porté à oublier; **to t. to shrink**, avoir tendance à rétrécir; **'tendency**, s. tendance f; inclination f; disposition f (**to**, à); penchant m (à qch.).

tender² ['tendər], a. **1.** (viande) tendre. **2.** (cœur) tendre, sensible; **t. to the touch**, sensible au toucher. **3.** (a) (of plant) délicat, fragile; peu résistant (au froid); (b) **of t. years**, (enfant) d'âge tendre, en bas âge. **4.** (of pers.) tendre, affectueux; **-ly**, adv. **1.** (toucher qch.) doucement. **2.** tendrement; avec tendresse; **'tender-'hearted**, a. compatissant; au cœur tendre, sensible; **'tender-'heartedness**, s. sensibilité f; **'tenderness**, s. **1.** sensibilité f (de la peau). **2.** délicatesse f, fragilité f (d'une plante). **3.** tendresse f (des sentiments); affection f (**for**, pour). **4.** tendreté f (de la viande).

tender³. **I.** s. **1.** Com: soumission f, offre f; **to invite tenders for a piece of work**, mettre un travail en adjudication. **2. legal t.**, cours légal. (of money) **to be legal t.**, avoir cours. **II.** v. **1.** v.tr. offrir (ses services); **to t. one's resignation** offrir de démissionner. **2.** v.i. Com: **to t. for** faire une soumission pour, soumissionner (un travail).

tenderloin ['tendəlɔin], s. Cu: filet m (de bœuf de porc).

tendon ['tendən], s. Anat: tendon m.

tendril ['tendril], s. Bot: vrille f; crampon m.

tenement ['tenimənt], s. esp. Scot: **t. house** maison f de rapport.

tenfold ['tenfould]. **1.** a. décuple. **2.** adv. dix foi autant; au décuple; **to increase t.**, décupler.

tennis ['tenis], s. tennis m; **to play t.**, jouer au tennis; **table t.**, tennis de table; ping-pong m; **ball**, balle f de tennis; **t. court,** (i) court m (d tennis); (ii) (terrain m de) tennis; **t. player** joueur, -euse, de tennis.

tenor ['tenər], s. **1.** teneur f; contenu m, sen général (d'un document); cours m, marche (de la vie). **2.** Mus: ténor m; **t. sax(ophone** saxophone m ténor.

tense¹ [tens], s. Gram: temps m.

tense², a. tendu, rigide, raide; **t. moment**, mc ment angoissant; **t. silence**, silence impression nant; **t. voice**, voix étranglée (par l'émotion **'tenseness**, s. rigidité f; tension f (de muscles, des relations); **tension** ['tenʃ(ə)n],. (a) tension f, raideur f, rigidité f (des muscles (b) tension (nerveuse); (c) pression f (d'un gaz (d) El: tension, voltage m; **high t. circuit,** ci cuit m de haute tension.

tent [tent], s. tente f; **t. peg**, piquet m de tente; **pitch a t.**, monter une tente; Med: **oxygen** tente à oxygène.

tentacle ['tentəkl], s. Z: tentacule m.

tentative ['tentətiv], a. expérimental, d'essai; **offer**, ouverture f; **-ly**, adv. à titre d'essai; av une certaine hésitation.

tenterhooks ['tentəhuks], *s. pl.* **to be on t.**, être au supplice, sur des charbons ardents; **to keep s.o. on t.**, faire languir qn.

tenth [tenθ], *num.a. & s.* dixième (*m*); **(on) the t. of March**, le dix mars.

tenuous ['tenjuəs], *a.* ténu; délié; mince.

tenure ['tenjər], *s. Jur:* jouissance *f*; occupation *f*.

tepid ['tepid], *a.* tiède; **-ly**, *adv.* tièdement; sans ardeur.

erm [tə:m]. **I.** *s.* **1.** terme *m*, fin *f*, limite *f*. **2.** (*a*) terme, période *f*, durée *f*; **during his t. of office**, lorsqu'il était en fonctions; **long-t.**, **short-t.**, **transaction**, opération à long, à court, terme; (*b*) *Sch:* trimestre *m*; (*c*) *Jur:* session *f*. **3.** *pl.* (*a*) conditions *f*; clauses *f*, termes, teneur *f* (d'un contrat); **name your own terms**, faites vos conditions vous-même; **to dictate terms**, imposer des conditions; **to come to terms**, arriver à un accord, parvenir à une entente; **to come to terms with death**, accepter la mort; (*b*) **terms of payment**, conditions de paiement; **inclusive terms**, tout compris; **to buy sth. on easy terms**, acheter qch. avec facilités de paiement; **not on any terms**, à aucun prix. **4.** *pl.* relations *f*, termes, rapports *m*; **to be on friendly, on good, terms with s.o.**, vivre en bonne intelligence, en bons termes, avec qn; **to be on bad terms with s.o.**, être en mauvais termes avec qn; **we are on the best of terms**, nous sommes au mieux ensemble. **5.** *pl. Mth:* **terms of an equation**, termes d'une équation; **contradiction in terms**, termes contradictoires. **6.** (*a*) terme, mot *m*, expression *f*; **legal, medical, t.**, terme de droit, de médecine; (*b*) **to speak in disparaging terms of s.o.**, tenir des propos désobligeants envers qn; **how dare you speak to me in such terms?** c'est à moi que vous osez tenir un pareil langage? **II.** *v.tr.* appeler, désigner, nommer; **'terminable**, *a.* terminable; (contrat) résiliable; **'terminal. I.** *a. Med:* **t. cancer**, cancer *m* inguérissable. **II.** *s.* **1.** *Rail:* (gare *f*) terminus (*m*); *Av:* **air t.**, aérogare *f*. **2.** *El:* borne *f* (de prise de courant); **'terminate**, *v.* **1.** *v.tr.* terminer; mettre fin à (un engagement); résoudre, résilier (un contrat); être à la fin de (qch.). **2.** *v.i.* se terminer, finir (**in**, en, par); aboutir (**in, at,** à); **termi'nation**, *s.* (*a*) terminaison *f*, fin *f* (d'un procès, etc.); cessation *f* (de relations); (*b*) *Gram:* terminaison, désinence *f*; **terminus**, *pl.* **-i, -uses** ['tə:minəs, -i:, -əsiz], *s.* (gare *f*) terminus (*m*).

rmite ['tə:mait], *s. Ent:* termite *m*; fourmi blanche.

rn [tə:n], *s. Orn:* sterne *m*; hirondelle *f* de mer.

rrace ['terəs]. **I.** *s.* **1.** terrasse *f*; terre-plein *m*. **2.** rangée *f* de maisons de style uniforme. **II.** *v.tr.* **1.** disposer (un flanc de coteau) en terrasses. **2. terraced houses**, maisons de style uniforme en rangée.

terracotta ['terə'kɔtə], *s.* terre cuite.

terrain [tə'rein], *s.* terrain *m*.

terrestrial [te'restriəl], *a.* terrestre.

terrible ['teribl], *a.* terrible, affreux, épouvantable; atroce; *F:* **t. price**, prix *m* formidable; **-ibly**, *adv.* (*a*) terriblement, affreusement, atrocement; (*b*) *F:* **t. dangerous**, terriblement dangereux; **t. rich**, diablement riche; **t. expensive**, hors de prix.

terrier ['teriər], *s.* (chien *m*) terrier (*m*); **fox t.**, fox-terrier *m*; **bull t.**, bull-terrier *m*.

terrific [tə'rifik], *a. F:* terrible; énorme; **t. speed**, vitesse vertigineuse; **-ally**, *adv. F:* terriblement.

terrify ['terifai], *v.tr.* terrifier, effrayer, terroriser, épouvanter; **to t. s.o. out of his wits**, rendre qn fou de terreur; **to be terrified of s.o.**, avoir une peur bleue de qn; **'terrifying**, *a.* terrifiant, terrible, épouvantable.

territory ['terit(ə)ri], *s.* territoire *m*; **terri'torial**, *a.* territorial.

terror ['terər], *s.* **1.** terreur *f*, effroi *m*, épouvante *f*; **to be in a state of t.**, être dans la terreur; **to go in t. of s.o.**, avoir une peur bleue de qn; **to be in t. of one's life**, craindre pour sa vie. **2. to be the t. of the village**, être la terreur du village; *F:* **he's a little t.**, c'est un enfant terrible; **'terrorism**, *s.* terrorisme *m*; **'terrorist**, *s.* terroriste *mf*; **'terrorize**, *v.tr.* terroriser; **'terror-stricken, -struck**, *a.* saisi de terreur; épouvanté.

terse [tə:s], *a.* **1.** (style) concis, net. **2.** (réponse) brusque; **-ly**, *adv.* **1.** avec concision. **2.** brusquement; **'terseness**, *s.* **1.** concision *f*, netteté *f* (de style). **2.** brusquerie *f* (d'une réponse).

terylene ['terili:n], *s. R.t.m:* tergal *m*.

test [test]. **I.** *s.* **1.** (*a*) épreuve *f*; **to put s.o. to the t.**, mettre qn à l'épreuve; **to be equal to, to stand, the t.**, supporter l'épreuve; (*b*) essai *m*, épreuve; **endurance t.**, épreuve d'endurance; **the acid t.**, l'épreuve concluante; **blood t.**, analyse *f* du sang; **t. bench**, banc *m* d'essai; *Aut:* **t. run**, course *f* d'essai; *Av:* **t. pilot**, pilote *m* d'essai; **t. tube**, éprouvette *f*; *Sp:* **t. (match)**, rencontre internationale (de cricket). **2.** (*a*) examen *m*; *Aut:* **driving t.**, examen pour permis de conduire; (*b*) **intelligence t.**, test *m* de capacité intellectuelle. **II.** *v.tr.* (*a*) éprouver; mettre (qn, qch.) à l'épreuve, à l'essai; (*b*) essayer (une machine); contrôler, vérifier (des poids et mesures); expérimenter (un procédé); analyser (le sang); (*c*) *Sch:* **to t. s.o. in algebra**, examiner qn en algèbre; (*d*) *Ch:* **to t. with litmus paper**, faire la réaction au papier (de) tournesol.

testament ['testəmənt], *s.* **1.** testament *m*; dernières volontés. **2.** *Rel:* **Old T., New T.,** Ancien, Nouveau, Testament; **testa′mentary,** *a.* testamentaire; **tes′tator,** *f.* **tes′tatrix,** *s.* testateur, -trice.

testify [′testifai], *v. Jur:* (*a*) *v.tr.* **to t. sth. on oath,** déclarer, affirmer, qch. sous serment; (*b*) *v.i.* **to t. in s.o.'s favour, against s.o.,** témoigner en faveur de qn, contre qn; déposer en faveur de qn, contre qn; (*c*) *v.ind.tr.* **to t. to sth.,** témoigner de qch., attester qch.; **testi′monial** [-′mouniəl], *s.* **1.** certificat *m*; (lettre *f* de) recommandation *f*; attestation *f*. **2.** témoignage *m* d'estime; **′testimony** [-məni], *s.* témoignage *m*; *Jur:* attestation *f*; déposition *f* (d'un témoin); **to bear t. to sth.,** rendre témoignage de qch.

testy [′testi], *a.* (*a*) irritable, irascible; peu endurant; (*b*) susceptible; **-ily,** *adv.* d'un air irrité; **′testiness,** *s.* (*a*) irritabilité *f*, irascibilité *f*; (*b*) susceptibilité *f*.

tether [′teðər]. **I.** *s.* longe *f*, attache *f* (d'un cheval); **to be at the end of one's t.,** être à bout (i) de forces, (ii) de ressources, (iii) de patience. **II.** *v.tr.* attacher (un animal).

text [tekst], *s.* **1.** texte *m* (d'un manuscrit, etc.). **2.** (**scripture**) **t.,** citation tirée de l'Écriture sainte; **to stick to one's t.,** ne pas s'éloigner du sujet; **′textbook,** *s. Sch:* manuel *m*; **′textual,** *a.* **t. error,** erreur *f* de texte.

textile [′tekstail]. **1.** *a.* textile. **2.** *s.* (*a*) tissu *m*; (*b*) textile *m*; **the t. industries,** le textile; **strike in the t. trades,** grève *f* du textile.

texture [′tekstʃər], *s.* texture *f*; grain *m* (du bois).

Thailand [′tailænd]. *Pr.n. Geog:* la Thaïlande.

Thames (the) [ðə′temz]. *Pr.n. Geog:* la Tamise; **he'll never set the T. on fire,** il n'a pas inventé la poudre.

than [ðæn, ðən], *conj.* (*a*) que; (*with numbers*) de; **I have more, less, t. you,** j'en ai plus, moins, que vous; **more t. twenty,** plus de vingt; **more t. once,** plus d'une fois; **better t. anyone,** mieux que personne; **I'd rather phone him t. write,** j'aimerais mieux lui téléphoner que de lui écrire; **she would do anything rather t. let him suffer,** elle ferait n'importe quoi plutôt que de le laisser souffrir; **no sooner had we arrived t. the music began,** nous étions à peine arrivés que la musique a commencé; (*b*) **any person other t. himself,** tout autre que lui.

thank [θæŋk]. **I.** *s.pl.* **thanks,** remerciement(s) *m*; **give him my best thanks,** remerciez-le bien de ma part; **thanks!** je vous remercie; merci; **to pass a vote of thanks to s.o.,** voter des remerciements à qn; **thanks to your help,** grâce à votre aide; *F:* **that's all the thanks I get!** voilà comment on me remercie! **II.** *v.tr.* **1.** (*a*) remercier (qn), dire merci à (qn); **to t. s.o. for sth.,** remercier qn de qch.; **to t. s.o. effusively,** se confondre en remerciements; **t. goodness!** Dieu merci! (*b*) **t. you,** je vous remercie; merci;

no t. you, merci! **2. I'll t. you to mind your own business!** occupez-vous donc de ce qui vous regarde! **3. to have s.o. to t. for sth.,** devoir qch. à qn; **you've only yourself to t.,** c'est à vous seul qu'il faut vous en prendre; **′thankful,** *a.* reconnaissant; **that's something to be t. for,** il y a de quoi nous féliciter; **-fully,** *adv.* avec reconnaissance; **′thankfulness,** *s.* reconnaissance *f*, gratitude *f*; **′thankless,** *a.* (travail) ingrat, peu profitable; **a t. job,** une corvée; **thanks′giving,** *s.* action *f* de grâce(s); **T. Day,** fête célébrée (i) *U.S:* le 4ᵉ jeudi de novembre; (ii) *Can:* le 2ᵉ lundi d'octobre; *Fr.C:* le jour de l'action de grâces.

that[1] [ðæt]. **I.** *dem.pron., pl.* **those** [ðouz]. **1.** cel **F:** ça; ce; (*a*) **give me t.,** donnez-moi cela **what's t.?** qu'est-ce que c'est que ça? **who's t.** qui est-ce? **t.'s Mr Martin,** c'est M. Martin; **t.'** **my opinion,** voilà mon avis; **after t.,** après cela **with t. she took out her handkerchief,** là dessus elle a sorti son mouchoir; **what do yo** **mean by t.?** qu'entendez-vous par là? **they a** **think t.,** c'est ce qu'ils pensent tous; **hav** **things come to t.?** les choses en sont-elle arrivées là? **t. is (to say) . . .,** c'est-à-dire; (*b* (*stressed*) **and so t.'s settled,** quant à cela, c'es décidé; **he's a hack writer and a poor one at t** c'est un écrivain à la tâche, et qui ne vaut pa grand-chose; **will you help me?—t. I wil** voulez-vous m'aider?—volontiers! **t.'s righ** **t.'s it!** c'est cela! **t.'s odd!** voilà qui est curieu **and t.'s t.!** et voilà! **and t. was t.,** plus rien dire; **t.'s all,** voilà tout. **2.** (*opposed to* **thi** **these**) celui-là, *f.* celle-là; *pl.* ceux-là, *f.* celle là; **this is new, t. is old,** celui-ci est neuf et cel là est vieux. **3.** celui, *f.* celle; *pl.* ceux, *f.* celle **all those I saw,** tous ceux que j'ai vus; **those** **whom I speak,** ceux dont je parle; **there a** **those who maintain it,** certains l'affirment. **I** **dem.a.,** *pl.* **those;** (*a*) ce, (*before vowel or* '**mute**') cet; *f.* cette; *pl.* ces; (*for emphasis an* **in opposition to this, these**) ce . . . -là; **t. boo** **those books,** ce livre(-là), ces livres(-là); **t. on** celui-là, celle-là; **everyone agrees on t. poin** tout le monde est d'accord là-dessus; **I on** **saw him t. once,** je ne l'ai vu que cette fois-l (*b*) *F:* **well, how's t. leg of yours?** eh bien, cette jambe? (*c*) **I'm not one of those peop** **who take an interest in such things,** je ne s pas de ceux qui s'intéressent à ces choses- **III.** *dem. adv.* **t. high,** aussi haut que ça; **cut o** **t. much,** coupez-en grand comme ça.

that[2] [ðət, ðæt], *rel. pron. sg. & pl.* **1.** (*for su* ject) qui; (*for object*) que; **the house t. stan** **at the corner,** la maison qui se trouve au co **the letter t. I sent you,** la lettre que je vous envoyée; *F:* **idiot t. I am!** idiot que je suis! (*governed by prep.*) lequel, *f.* laquelle; lesquels, *f.* lesquelles; **the envelope t. I put it i**

l'enveloppe dans laquelle je l'ai mis; **nobody has come t. I know of,** personne n'est venu que je sache. 3. où; que; **the night t. we went to the theatre,** le soir où nous sommes allés au théâtre; **during the years t.** he had been in **prison,** pendant les années qu'il avait été en prison.

that³ [ðæt, ðət], *conj.* 1. (*introducing subordinate clause*) que; (*a*) **it was for her t.** they fought, c'est pour elle qu'ils se sont battus; **not t. I admire him,** non (pas) que je l'admire; (*b*) **I hope t. you'll have good luck,** j'espère que vous aurez de la chance; (*c*) **so t. . . .,** afin que, pour que + *sub.*; **come nearer so t. I can see you,** approchez, que je vous voie; **I'm telling you so t. you'll know,** je vous préviens pour que vous soyez au courant. 2. **t. he should behave like this!** dire qu'il se conduit comme cela!

thatch [θætʃ]. I. *s.* chaume *m* (de toiture); *F:* **good t. of hair,** belle chevelure. II. *v.tr.* couvrir (un toit) de, en, chaume; **thatched roof,** toit *m* de chaume; **thatched cottage,** chaumière *f*; **'thatcher,** *s.* chaumeur *m*, couvreur *m* en chaume.

thaw [θɔ:]. I. *s.* dégel *m*; fonte *f* des neiges. II. *v.* 1. *v.tr.* dégeler; décongeler (la viande, etc.). 2. *v.i.* (*a*) (*of snow*) fondre; (*of frozen meat*) se décongeler; (*b*) **it's thawing,** il dégèle; (*c*) (*of pers.*) se dégeler; (*d*) *F:* (*of pers.*) s'humaniser; **'thawing,** *s.* 1. dégèlement *m* (des conduites d'eau); décongélation *f* (de la viande). 2. dégel *m*; fonte *f* (des neiges).

the [ðə], *before vowel or when stressed* [ði:]. I. *def. art.* 1. le, *f.* la; (*before vowel or h 'mute'*) l'; *pl.* les; (*a*) **t. father and (t.) mother,** le père et la mère; **on t. other side,** de l'autre côté; **t. Alps,** les Alpes; **I spoke to t. postman,** j'ai parlé au facteur; **give it to t. woman,** donnez-le à la femme; **he has gone to t. fields,** il est allé aux champs; **t. voice of t. people,** la voix du peuple; **t. roof of t. house,** le toit de la maison; **t. arrival of t. guests,** l'arrivée des invités; **t. Martins,** les Martin; **George t. Sixth,** Georges Six; (*b*) **he's not t. person to do that,** ce n'est pas une personne à faire cela; **t. impudence of it!** quelle audace! **he hasn't t. patience to wait,** il n'a pas la patience d'attendre; (*c*) **t. beautiful,** le beau; **translated from t. Russian,** traduit du russe; *coll.* **t. poor,** les pauvres; (*d*) **to have t. measles,** avoir la rougeole; (*e*) **to work by t. day,** travailler à la journée. 2. (*demonstrative force*) ce, cet, *f.* cette; *pl.* ces; **I was away at t. time,** j'étais absent à cette époque; **I shall see him in t. spring,** je le verrai ce printemps; (*in café*) **and what will t. ladies have?** et ces dames, que prendront-elles? 3. (*stressed*) [ði:] **he's the surgeon here,** c'est lui le grand chirurgien ici; **Long's is the shop for furniture,** la maison

Long est la meilleure pour les meubles. II. *adv.* (*a*) **it will be all t. easier for you as you are young,** cela vous sera d'autant plus facile que vous êtes jeune; (*b*) **t. sooner t. better,** le plus tôt sera le mieux; **t. less said t. better,** moins on en parlera mieux cela vaudra; **t. more t. merrier,** plus on est de fous plus on rit.

theatre ['θi:ətər], *s.* 1. (*a*) théâtre *m*; (*b*) **the t.,** l'art *m* dramatique; le théâtre. 2. *Med:* (**operating**) **t.,** salle *f* d'opération. 3. **t. of war,** théâtre de la guerre; **theatregoer,** *s.* amateur *m* de théâtre; **theatrical** [θi:'ætrik(ə)l], *a.* 1. théâtral; **t. company,** troupe *f* d'acteurs. 2. (*of behaviour*) théâtral, histrionique; **-ally,** *adv.* 1. théâtralement (parlant). 2. de façon théâtrale; **the'atricals,** *s.pl.* **amateur t.,** spectacle *m* d'amateurs.

thee [ði:], *pers. pron., objective case; A: Ecc:* (*also poetic & dialect*) te; (*before vowel sound*) t'; (*stressed*) toi.

theft [θeft], *s.* (*a*) vol *m*; (*b*) **petty t.,** larcin *m*.

their ['ðɛər], *poss.a.* 1. (*a*) leur, *pl.* leurs; **t. father and mother,** leur père et leur mère, leurs père et mère; (*b*) **T. Majesties,** leurs Majestés. 2. *F:* **nobody in t. senses,** personne jouissant de son bon sens.

theirs ['ðɛəz], *poss.pron.* 1. le leur, la leur, les leurs; **this house is t.,** cette maison est la leur, est à eux, est à elles, leur appartient; **he's a friend of t.,** c'est un de leurs amis.

them [ðem], *pers.pron.pl., objective case.* 1. (*a*) (*direct*) les *mf*; (*indirect*) leur *mf*; **I like t.,** je les aime; **I shall tell t. so,** je le leur dirai; **speak to t.,** parlez-leur; (*b*) **they took the keys away with t.,** ils ont emporté les clefs avec eux; **walk in front of t.,** marchez devant eux. 2. (*stressed*) eux, *f.* elles; **it's t.!** ce sont eux, elles! **I don't like t.,** je ne les aime pas, eux. 3. **many of t.,** nombre, beaucoup, d'entre eux; **both of t., the two of t.,** tous les deux; **all of t., every one of t.,** eux tous; **every one of t. was killed,** ils furent tous tués; **give me half of t.,** donnez-m'en la moitié; **neither of t.,** ni l'un ni l'autre; **none of t.,** aucun d'eux; **most of t.,** la plupart d'entre eux; **lay the tables and put some flowers on t.,** préparez les tables et mettez-y des fleurs: **them'selves,** *pers. pron.* **they whispered among t.,** ils chuchotaient entre eux; **they think of nobody but t.,** ils ne pensent qu'à eux; **these questions crop up of t.,** ces questions se posent d'elles-mêmes; (*of women*) **all of them work for t.,** chacune d'elles travaille pour elle-même; **they work t. to death,** ils, elles, se tuent au travail.

theme [θi:m], *s.* 1. sujet *m*, thème *m* (d'un livre). 2. *Mus:* thème, motif *m*; **t. and variations,** air *m* avec variations; **t. song,** leitmotiv *m*.

then [ðen]. I. *adv.* 1. alors; en ce temps-là; **t. and there,** séance tenante; **now and t.,** de temps en temps. **2.** puis, ensuite, alors; **they travelled in France and t. in Spain,** ils voyagérent en France et ensuite en Espagne; **what t.?** et puis? et (puis) après? **3.** d'ailleurs; aussi (bien); et puis; **you weren't there, but t., neither was I,** tu n'y étais pas, moi non plus d'ailleurs; **I haven't the time, and t. it isn't my business,** je n'ai pas le temps, d'ailleurs, ce n'est pas mon affaire. **II.** *conj.* en ce cas, donc, alors; **go, t.,** soit, partez; **but t. . . .,** mais c'est que . . .; **you knew all the time t.?** vous le saviez donc d'avance? **now t.!** (i) attention! (ii) voyons! allons! **III.** *s.* ce temps-là; cette époque-là; **before t.,** avant cela; **by t. they had gone,** ils étaient déjà partis; **till t.,** (i) jusqu'alors; (ii) jusque-là; **(ever) since t.,** dès lors; depuis lors; depuis ce temps-là; **between now and t.,** d'ici là.

theodolite [θi'ɔdəlait], *s.* théodolite *m.*

theology [θi'ɔlədʒi], *s.* théologie *f;* **theologian** [θiə'loudʒiən], *s.* théologien, -ienne; **theo'logical,** *a.* théologique.

theorem ['θiərəm], *s.* théorème *m.*

theory ['θiəri], *s.* théorie *f;* **in t.,** en théorie; **the plan is all right in t.,** ce projet est beau sur le papier; **theo'retic(al),** *a.* théorique; **-ally,** *adv.* théoriquement; **theore'tician, 'theorist, 'theorizer,** *s.* théoricien, -ienne; **'theorize,** *v.i.* faire de la théorie; bâtir, construire, des théories.

therapy ['θerəpi], *s. Med:* thérapie *f;* **occupational t.,** thérapie rééducative; **'therapist,** *s.* **occupational t.,** spécialiste *mf* de la thérapie rééducative.

there ['ðɛər]. **I.** *adv.* **1.** (*stressed*) (*a*) là, y; **put it t.,** mettez-le là; **he's still t.,** il y est toujours; **we're t.,** nous voilà arrivés; *F:* **he's not all t.,** il n'a pas toute sa tête; **here and t.,** çà et là; **here, t. and everywhere,** un peu partout; (*b*) **I'm going t.,** j'y vais; **a hundred kilometres t. and back,** cent kilomètres aller et retour; (*c*) (*emphatic*) **that man t.,** cet homme-là; **hurry up t.!** dépêchez-vous là-bas! (*d*) **t. is, are. . .,** voilà. . .; **t.'s the bell ringing,** voilà la cloche qui sonne; **t. they are!** les voilà! **2.** (*unstressed*) (*a*) **t. is, are. . .,** il y a. . .; **t. was once a king,** il y avait une fois un roi; **t.'s a page missing,** il manque une page; (*b*) **t. comes a time when. . .,** il arrive un moment où . . .. **3.** (*stressed*) quant à cela; en cela; **t. you are mistaken,** quant à cela vous vous trompez; **t.'s the difficulty,** c'est là qu'est la difficulté; *F:* **t. you have me!** ça, ça me dépasse. **II.** *int.* (*stressed*) voilà! **t. now!** (i) voilà! (ii) allons bon! **t., I told you so!** là! je vous l'avais bien dit! **t., take this book,** tenez! prenez ce livre; **t.! t.! don't worry!** là, là, ne vous inquiétez pas! **but t., what's the good of talking?** mais à quoi bon en parler? **I shall do as I like, so t.!** je ferai comme il me plaira, voilà! **III.** *s.* **he left t. last night,** il est parti (de là) hier soir; **in t.,** là-dedans; là;

'thereabouts, *adv.* **1.** près de là; dans le voisinage; **somewhere t.,** quelque part par là. **2.** [ðɛərə'bauts] à peu près; environ; **it's four o'clock or t.,** il est à peu près quatre heures, il est quatre heures environ; **there'by,** *adv.* par ce moyen; de ce fait; de cette façon; **I hope t. to get him to consent,** j'espère par ce moyen de le faire consentir; **'therefore,** *adv.* donc; par conséquent; **it's probable, t., that he will consent,** par conséquent, il est à croire qu'il va consentir; **thereu'pon,** *adv.* **t.** he left us, sur ce il nous a quittés.

thermal ['θə:m(ə)l], *a.* **1.** thermal; **t. baths,** thermes *m.* **2.** *Ph:* thermal, thermique; **t. efficiency,** rendement *m* thermique. **3.** *a. & s. Av:* **t.** (current), courant *m* thermique.

thermometer [θə'mɔmitər], *s.* thermomètre *m;* **to take the t. reading,** regarder le thermomètre.

thermonuclear [θə:mou'nju:kliər], *a.* thermonucléaire.

Thermos ['θə:mɔs], *a. & s. R.t.m:* **T.** (flask), bouteille *f* Thermos.

thermostat ['θə:məstæt], *s.* thermostat *m.*

thesis, *pl.* **theses** ['θi:sis, 'θi:si:z], *s.* thèse *f.*

they [ðei]. **1.** *pers. pron. nom. pl.* (*a*) ils, *f.* elles; **t. are dancing,** ils, elles, dansent; **here t. come,** les voici (qui viennent); **t. are rich people,** ce sont des gens riches; (*b*) (*stressed*) eux, *f.* elles; **t. alone,** eux seuls; **it is t.,** ce sont eux; **it is t. who told me so, t. told me so themselves,** ce sont eux-mêmes qui me l'ont dit; **t. know nothing about it,** quant à eux, ils n'en savent rien; (*c*) ceux, *f.* celles (qui font qch.). **2.** *indef. pron.* on; **t. say that . . .,** on dit que . . .; **that's what t. say,** voilà ce qu'on raconte; *F:* **nobody ever admits t. are to blame,** on ne veut jamais reconnaître ses torts.

thick [θik]. **I.** *a.* **1.** épais; (*of book, thread*) gros; **wall two metres t.,** mur qui a deux mètres d'épaisseur; *F:* **to have a t. skin,** être peu sensible, peu susceptible; **t.-skinned,** (i) à la peau épaisse; *Z:* pachyderme; (ii) (*of pers.*) peu sensible, peu susceptible; **t.-lipped,** lippu; à grosses lèvres. **2.** (*of forest*) épais, serré, touffu, dru; **t. beard,** barbe fournie. **3.** (*of liquid*) épais, consistant; **t. mud,** boue grasse; **t. soup,** (potage *m*) crème (*f*); (*b*) (*of voice*) pâteux; (*c*) *F:* **t., t.-headed,** obtus. **4.** *F:* **to be very t. with s.o.,** être très lié avec qn; **they're as t. as thieves,** ils s'accordent comme larrons en foire. **5.** *F:* **that's a bit t.!** ça c'est un peu raide, un peu fort! **II.** *s.* **1.** (*a*) (la) partie charnue, le gras (de la jambe); (*b*) **the t. of the fight,** le (plus) fort de la mêlée. **2.** **to stick to s.o. through t. and thin,** rester fidèle à qn à travers toutes les épreuves. **III.** *adv.* **1.** en couche épaisse; **you're spreading the butter too t.,** vous mettez trop de beurre sur les tartines; **to cut the bread t.,** couper le pain en tranches épaisses; **to lay it on t.,** (i) flatter qn grossièrement; (ii) exagérer, y aller fort. **2. his blows fell t. and fast,** les coups tombaient dru; **-ly,** *adv.* **1.** en couche épaisse. **2. snow fell t.,** la neige tombait dru. **3.** (parler) d'une voix empâtée; ʹ**thicken,** *v.* **1.** *v.tr.* épaissir; lier (une sauce). **2.** *v.i.* (*a*) (s')épaissir; (*b*) (*of sauce*) se lier; **the crowd was thickening,** la foule augmentait; (*c*) (*of plot*) se compliquer, se corser; ʹ**thicket,** *s.* hallier *m*, fourré *m*; ʹ**thickness,** *s.* **1.** (*a*) épaisseur *f* (d'un mur); grosseur *f* (des lèvres); (*b*) épaisseur (d'une forêt); abondance *f* (de la chevelure); (*c*) consistance *f* (d'un liquide); épaisseur (du brouillard); (*d*) empâtement *m* (de la voix). **2.** couche *f* (de papier, etc.); ʹ**thickʹset,** *a.* **1.** (*of hedge*) épais; dru. **2.** (*of pers.*) trapu.

thief, *pl.* **thieves** [θiːf, θiːvz], *s.* voleur, -euse; **thieves** (*as a class*), la pègre; **stop t.!** au voleur! **set a t. to catch a t.,** à voleur, voleur et demi; **there's honour among thieves,** les loups ne se mangent pas entre eux; **thieve,** *v.* (*a*) *v.tr.* voler (qch.); (*b*) *v.i.* être voleur; voler; ʹ**thieving. 1.** *a.* voleur. **2.** *s.* vol *m*; **petty t.,** larcin(s) *m(pl).*

thigh [θai], *s.* cuisse *f*; **t. bone,** fémur *m*.

thimble [ˈθimbl], *s.* dé *m* (à coudre); ʹ**thimbleful,** *s.* doigt *m* (de cognac, etc.).

thin [θin]. **I.** *a.* (**thinner, thinnest**) **1.** (*a*) peu épais; (*of paper*) mince; (*of thread*) ténu; (*of fabric*) léger; **to cut the bread in t. slices,** couper le pain en tranches minces; **to have a t. skin, to be t.-skinned,** avoir l'épiderme sensible, être susceptible; se froisser facilement; (*b*) (*of pers.*) maigre, mince; **to get thinner,** maigrir, s'amaigrir; **t.-lipped,** aux lèvres minces. **2.** (*of hair, population*) clairsemé, rare; *Th:* **there was a t. house,** le théâtre était presque vide. **3.** (*of liquid*) fluide, clair; (*of voice*) fluet, grêle. **4.** *F:* (*a*) **t. excuse,** pauvre excuse; (*b*) **to have a t. time (of it),** passer un temps peu agréable. **II.** *s.* **through thick and t.,** à travers toutes les épreuves. **III.** *adv.* **to cut (bread, etc.) t.,** couper (le pain, etc.) en tranches minces; **to spread the paint t.,** peindre mince; **to butter the bread too t.,** mettre trop peu de beurre sur les tartines. **IV.** *v.* (**thinned**) **1.** *v.tr.* (*a*) **to t. (down),** amincir, alléger (une planche); (*b*) **to t. (down),** délayer (la peinture); allonger (une sauce); (*c*) éclaircir (les arbres); **to t. (out) seedlings,** éclaircir les jeunes plants. **2.** *v.i.* (*a*) maigrir; (*b*) s'amincir, s'effiler; (*c*) (*of crowd*) s'éclaircir; **-ly,** *adv.* **1.** en couche mince; **to paint t.,** peindre mince. **2.** à peine; **t. dressed,** vêtu insuffisamment; **t. veiled allusion,** allusion à peine voilée. **3.** d'une manière éparse; **to sow t.,** semer clair; **t. populated,** peu peuplé; ʹ**thinness,** *s.* **1.** (*a*) peu *m* d'épaisseur; minceur *f*; légèreté *f* (d'une voile); (*b*) maigreur *f*. **2.** rareté *f* (des cheveux). **3.** fluidité *f* (d'un

liquide); manque *m* de corps (d'un vin). **4.** *F:* faiblesse *f* (d'une excuse); ʹ**thinning,** *s.* **t.** (**down**), amincissement *m*, amaigrissement *m*; **t.** (**out**), éclaircissage *m*.

thine [ðain], *poss.pron. A: Ecc:* (*also poetic & dialect*) le tien, la tienne; **what is mine is t.,** ce qui est à moi est à toi.

thing [θiŋ], *s.* **1.** chose *f*; (*a*) objet *m*, article *m*; (*b*) *F:* **what's that t.?** qu'est-ce que c'est que ce machin-là? (*c*) **tea things,** service *m* à thé; **to clear (away) the things,** desservir; **to wash up the tea things, the dinner things,** faire la vaisselle; (*d*) *pl.* vêtements *m*, effets *m*; **to take off one's things,** (i) se déshabiller; (ii) enlever son manteau, etc.; (*e*) *pl.* affaires *f*, effets; **to pack up one's things,** faire ses malles; **to put one's things away,** ranger ses affaires. **2.** être *m*, créature *f*; **poor little things!** pauvres petits! **she's a nice old t.,** c'est une bonne vieille bien sympathique. **3.** (*a*) **you take the t. too seriously,** vous prenez la chose trop au sérieux; **he expects great things of the new treatment,** il attend grand bien du nouveau traitement; **of all things to do!** comme si vous ne pouviez pas faire autre chose! **to talk of one t. and another,** parler de choses et d'autres; **that's the very t.!** c'est juste ce qu'il faut! **that's the t. for me!** voilà mon affaire! **the t. is this,** voici ce dont il s'agit; **neither one t. nor the other,** ni l'un ni l'autre; **what with one t. and another,** tant et si bien que . . ., entre une chose et l'autre; **for one t.,** en premier lieu; **for another t.,** d'autre part; **that's quite another t.,** c'est tout autre chose; **it's just one of those things,** ce sont de ces choses qui arrivent! **to know a t. or two,** être malin; **I could tell you a t. or two,** je pourrais en conter; **first t. in the morning,** très tôt dans la matinée; **last t. at night,** très tard dans la soirée; (*b*) **things are going badly,** les affaires vont mal; **as things are,** dans l'état actuel des choses; **since that is how things are,** puisqu'il en est ainsi; *F:* **how's things?** comment ça va? **4. the latest t. in ties,** cravate(s) dernier cri. **5.** *F:* **it's not the t.,** cela ne se fait pas; **it's quite the t.,** c'est tout à fait correct; c'est la mode; ʹ**thingamy(bob),** ʹ**thingummy,** ʹ**thingumajig,** *s.* *F:* chose *m*, machin *m*, truc *m*.

think [θiŋk]. **I.** *s.* **to have a quiet t.,** réfléchir; *F:* **you've got another t. coming!** tu peux toujours courir! **II.** *v.* (**thought** [θɔːt]) **1.** *v.tr. & i.* (*a*) penser, réfléchir; **he thinks for himself,** il pense par lui-même; **I can't t. why,** je me demande pourquoi; **I know what you're thinking,** je connais vos pensées; **to act without thinking,** agir sans réflexion; **t. before you speak,** pesez vos paroles; **give me time to t.,** laissez-moi réfléchir; **his name was—let me t. . . .,** il s'appelait—voyons . . .; *F:* **t. again!**

réfléchissez! **to t. twice before doing sth.,** y regarder à deux fois avant de faire qch.; (*b*) songer, s'imaginer; **one would have thought that . . .,** c'était à croire que . . .; **anyone would t. that . . .,** on dirait que . . .; **who'd have thought it!** qui l'aurait dit! **just t.!** songez donc! (*c*) **I've been thinking that . . .,** l'idée m'est venue que . . .; **thinking to . . .,** dans l'intention de . . .; **did you t. to bring any money?** avez-vous pensé à apporter de l'argent? (*d*) **then you t. that . . .,** il vous semble donc que . . .; **it's better, don't you t., to get it over?** n'est-ce pas qu'il vaut mieux en finir? **what do you t. I ought to do?** que pensez-vous que je doive faire? **I thought it was all over,** je me disais que tout était fini; **I t. she's pretty,** je la trouve jolie; **everyone thought he was mad,** on le pensait fou; **I t. so,** je pense que oui; **I t. not,** je pense que non; **I should hardly t. so,** c'est peu probable; **I should (just) t. so!** je crois bien! *P:* **I don't t.!** jamais de la vie! **I hardly t. it likely that . . .,** il n'est guère probable que + *sub.*; **they are thought to be rich,** ils passent pour (être) riches; **do as you t. best,** faites comme bon vous semble(ra); (*e*) **I little thought to see him again,** je ne m'attendais guère à le revoir; **I thought as much, I thought so,** je m'y attendais; je m'en doutais; je m'en doutais. **2.** *v.ind.tr.* (*a*) **to t. of, about,** penser à (qch.); songer à (qch.); **one can't t. of everything,** on ne saurait penser à tout; **I've so much to t. about,** il y a tant de choses auxquelles il faut que je pense; **I can't t. of the right word,** le mot juste m'échappe; **the best thing I can t. of,** ce que je vois de mieux; **that's worth thinking about,** cela mérite réflexion; **what am I thinking of, about?** où ai-je la tête? (*b*) s'imaginer, se figurer, songer; **t. of that!** (i) ça, c'est pas banal! (ii) songez donc! **t. of it, I'm in love with him,** je l'aime, figure-toi; **t. of the pleasure it gave me,** imaginez (-vous) le plaisir que cela m'a fait; (*c*) **it's not to be thought of,** ce n'est pas à considérer; **to t. of the expense,** regarder à la dépense; **to t. of s.o.'s feelings,** avoir égard aux sentiments de qn; (*d*) **to t. of, about, doing sth.,** méditer, projeter, de faire qch.; penser à faire qch.; **I couldn't t. of it!** il n'y a pas à y songer! (*e*) *v.tr.* **what do you t. of it, about it?** qu'en pensez-vous? **to t. a great deal of oneself,** avoir une haute idée de sa personne; **to t. too much of sth.,** attacher trop d'importance à qch.; **I told him what I thought of him,** je lui ai dit son fait; **to t. well of s.o.,** estimer qn; **people t. well of him,** il est bien vu; **to t. better of it,** changer d'opinion; **I don't t. much of it,** ça ne me dit pas grand-chose; '**thinkable,** *a.* concevable, imaginable; '**thinker,** *s.* penseur, -euse; '**thinking. 1.** *a.* pensant; qui pense. **2.** *s.*

pensée(s) *f*(*pl*), réflexion(s) *f*(*pl*); **to my (way of) t.,** à mon avis; '**think 'out,** *v.tr.* **1.** imaginer, méditer (qch.); **to t. out a plan,** élaborer un plan; **carefully thought out answer,** réponse bien pesée; **that wants thinking out,** cela demande mûre réflexion. **2. he thinks things out for himself,** il juge des choses par lui-même; '**think 'over,** *v.tr.* réfléchir sur, aviser à (une question); **t. it over,** réfléchissez-y bien; **this wants thinking over,** cela mérite réflexion; '**think 'up,** *v.tr.* imaginer (une méthode, un projet); *F:* **what have you been thinking up?** qu'est-ce que tu as combiné?

third [θə:d]. **1.** *num.a.* troisième; **t. person,** (i) *Jur:* tierce personne, tiers *m*; (ii) *Gram:* troisième personne; **t. party insurance,** assurance *f* au tiers; **George the T.,** Georges Trois; **(on) the t. of March,** le trois mars. **2.** *s.* (*a*) *Mus:* tierce *f*; (*b*) *Aut:* troisième vitesse *f*. **3.** *s.* (*fraction*) tiers *m*; **a t. of the inhabitants were killed,** un tiers des habitants a été tué, ont été tués; **-ly,** *adv.* troisièmement; en troisième lieu *m*; '**third-'class, 'third-'rate,** *a.* de qualité inférieure; très inférieur; '**third-'hand,** *a.* & *adv.* de troisième main.

thirst [θə:st]. **I.** *s.* soif *f*; **to quench one's t.,** se désaltérer; **t. for knowledge,** soif de savoir. **II.** *v.i.* **to t. for blood,** être altéré de sang; '**thirsting,** *a.* altéré, assoiffé; **t. for blood, for riches,** assoiffé, avide, de sang, de richesses; '**thirsty,** *a.* altéré; **to be t.,** avoir soif; *F:* **this is t. work,** cela donne soif; **-ily,** *adv.* avidement.

thirteen [θə:'ti:n], *num.a.* & *s.* treize (*m*); **thir'teenth,** *num.a.* & *s.* treizième (*m*); **(on) the t. of May,** le treize mai.

thirty ['θə:ti], *num.a.* & *s.,* trente (*m*); **t.-one,** trente et un; **t.-first,** trente et unième; **about t. people,** une trentaine de personnes; '**thirtieth,** *num.a.* & *s.* trentième (*m*); **(on) the t. of June,** le trente juin.

this [ðis]. **I.** *dem.pron.,* *pl.* **these** [ði:z]. **1.** ceci; ce; **t. I already knew,** ceci, je le savais déjà; **who is t.?** qui est cette personne? qui est-ce? **you'll be sorry for t.,** vous le regretterez; **what good is t.?** à quoi cela est-il bon? **after t.,** après cela, ensuite, désormais; **it ought to have come before t.,** cela devrait être déjà arrivé; **t. is odd,** voilà qui est curieux; **t. is a free country,** nous sommes dans un pays libre; **t. is Mr Martin,** je vous présente M. Martin; **t. is where he lives,** c'est ici qu'il habite; **it was like t.,** voici comment les choses se sont passées; **the thing is t.,** voici ce dont il s'agit. **2. will you have t. or that?** voulez-vous ceci ou cela? **to talk of t. and that,** parler de choses et d'autres. **3.** celui-ci, *f.* celle-ci, *pl.* ceux-ci, *f.* celles-ci; **I prefer these to those,** je préfère ceux-ci à ceux-là. **II.** *dem.a.,* *pl.* **these;** (*a*) ce, (*before vowel or h 'mute'*) cet, *f.* cette, *pl.* ces; (*for emphasis*) ce (*etc.*). . . .-ci;

t. **book, these books,** ce livre(-ci), ces livres
(-ci); **in these days,** de nos jours; t. **day last
year,** l'an dernier à pareil jour; **to run t. way
and that,** courir de-ci, de-là; (*b*) **I've been
waiting for you t.** half hour, voilà une demi-
heure que je vous attends. III. *dem.adv.* t. **high,**
aussi haut que ceci, que ça; t. **far,** jusqu'ici.

histle ['θisl], *s. Bot:* chardon *m*; '**thistledown,**
s. duvet *m* de chardon.

hither ['ðiðər], *adv.* **to run hither and t.,** courir
çà et là.

nong [θɒŋ], *s.* lanière *f* de cuir.

orax ['θɔːræks], *s. Anat:* thorax *m*.

norn [θɔːn], *s.* (*a*) épine *f*; **a t. in the flesh,** une
épine au pied; (*b*) arbrisseau épineux; épine;
'**thorny,** *a.* épineux.

norough ['θʌrə], *a.* (*a*) (*of search*) minutieux;
(*of knowledge*) profond; (*of work*) consciencieux; t. **inquiry,** enquête approfondie; **to give
a room a t.** clean(ing), nettoyer une chambre à
fond; (*b*) a t. **Frenchman,** un vrai Français; a t.
republican, un républicain convaincu; **a t.
scoundrel,** un coquin achevé; -**ly,** *adv.* tout à
fait; (comprendre) parfaitement; (renouveler)
complètement; (nettoyer) à fond;
'**thoroughbred. 1.** *a.* (cheval) pur sang *inv*;
(chien) de (pure) race. **2.** *s.* cheval pur sang;
animal de race; '**thoroughfare,** *s.* voie *f* de
communication; **public t.,** voie publique; **a
main t.,** une des principales artères (d'une
ville); *P.N:* **no t.,** passage interdit; route
barrée; '**thoroughgoing,** *a.* (*of rascal*) accompli, fieffé; (*of socialist*) enragé, à tous
crins; '**thoroughness,** *s.* caractère approfondi (des recherches); perfection *f* (du travail).

nou [ðau], *pers.pron. A:Ecc:* (*also poetic &
dialect*) tu; (*stressed*) toi.

nough [ðou]. **I.** *conj.* **1.** quoique, bien que, encore que + *sub.*; **I am sorry for him t. he is
nothing to me,** je le plains encore qu'il ne me
soit rien; t. **I am a father . . .**, tout père que je
suis . . .; t. **small, he is none the less brave,**
pour être petit il n'en est pas moins brave. **2.
strange t. it may seem,** si étrange que cela pa-
raisse. **3.** **as t.,** comme si; **it looks as t. he's gone,**
il semble qu'il soit parti. **II.** *adv.* (*a*) cependant,
pourtant; (*b*) **did he t.!** vraiment! il a dit, fait,
cela?

nought [θɔːt], *s.* **1.** (la) pensée; **capable of t.,**
capable de penser. **2.** (*a*) idée *f*; **happy t.,**
heureuse idée; (*b*) **gloomy thoughts,** pensées
sombres; **a penny for your thoughts,** à quoi
pensez-vous? **to read s.o.'s thoughts,** lire dans
la pensée de qn; (*c*) **the mere t. of it,** rien que
d'y penser; **I didn't give it another t.,** je n'y ai
pas repensé; (*d*) *pl.* esprit *m*, pensée; **to collect
one's thoughts,** rassembler ses idées, ses esprits; **her thoughts were elsewhere,** son esprit
était ailleurs. **3.** (*a*) réflexion *f*, considération *f*;

lack of t., irréflexion *f*; **after much t.,** après
mûre réflexion; **he has no t. for others,** il est
peu soucieux des autres, il n'a pas de considération pour les autres; **on second thoughts,**
(toute) réflexion faite; (*b*) pensées, rêverie *f*,
méditation *f*; **lost in t.,** perdu dans ses pensées.
4. (*a*) intention *f*, dessein *m*; **to have thoughts,
some t., of doing sth.,** songer à faire qch.; **with
the t. of warning him,** dans le dessein de l'avertir; (*b*) **I had no t. of meeting you here,** je ne
m'attendais pas à vous rencontrer ici;
'**thoughtful,** *a.* **1.** (*a*) pensif, méditatif, rêveur;
(*b*) réfléchi, prudent. **2.** prévenant (of, pour); t.
of others, plein d'égards pour les autres; **he
was t. enough to warn me,** il a eu la prévenance
de m'avertir; -**fully,** *adv.* **1.** (*a*) pensivement;
(*b*) d'une manière réfléchie. **2.** avec
prévenance; '**thoughtfulness,** *s.* **1.** (*a*)
méditation *f*, recueillement *m*; (*b*) réflexion *f*,
prudence *f*. **2.** prévenance *f*, égards *mpl* (of,
pour, envers); '**thoughtless,** *a.* **1.** irréfléchi,
mal avisé; étourdi; t. **action,** étourderie *f*. **2.**
of others, peu soucieux des autres; -**ly,** *adv.* **1.**
étourdiment; (agir) sans réflexion, à la légère.
2. to treat s.o. t., manquer d'égards envers qn;
'**thoughtlessness,** *s.* **1.** irréflexion *f*;
étourderie *f*. **2.** manque *m* d'égards (of, pour,
envers); '**thought-reader,** *s.* liseur, -euse, de
pensées; '**thought-reading,** *s.* lecture *f* de la
pensée; télépathie *f*.

thousand ['θauz(ə)nd], *num.a. & s.* mille (*m*)
inv; *s.* millier *m*; **a t. men,** mille hommes; **about
a t. men,** un millier d'hommes; quelque mille
hommes; **I paid five t. for it,** je l'ai payé cinq
mille (livres, dollars); **the year 4000 B.C.,** l'an
quatre mille avant J.-C.; **a t. years,** un
millénaire; **thousands of people,** des milliers de
gens; **he's one in a t.,** c'est un homme entre
mille; **a t. apologies!** mille pardons!
'**thousandth,** *num.a. & s.* millième (*m*).

thrash [θræʃ], *v.tr.* (*a*) battre (qn); *F:* rosser (qn);
(*b*) *Sp:* etc: battre (qn) à plates coutures;
'**thrashing,** *s.* (*a*) rossée *f*, correction *f*; **to give
s.o. a t.,** flanquer une raclée à qn; (*b*) *Sp:*
défaite *f*; '**thrash 'out,** *v.tr.* débattre, creuser
(une question).

thread [θred]. **I.** *s.* **1.** filament *m*, fil *m* (de soie);
to hang by a t., ne tenir qu'à un fil. **2.** (*a*) **sewing
t.,** fil à coudre; **packing t.,** fil d'emballage; **gold
t.,** fil d'or; (*b*) *Tex:* fil (de trame, de chaine); **the
t. of life,** la trame de la vie; **to lose the t. of one's
discourse,** perdre le fil de son discours; (*c*)
(length of) t., brin *m*, bout *m* (de coton). **3.**
Tchn: filet *m*, filetage *m*, pas *m* (de vis); t.
cutter, tour *m* à fileter. **II.** *v.tr.* **1.** enfiler (une
aiguille). **2. to t. one's way,** se faufiler. **3.** fileter
(une vis); '**threadbare,** *a.* (*of clothes*) râpé; (*of
argument*) usé (jusqu'à la corde);
'**threadlike,** *a.* filiforme.

threat [θret], *s.* menace *f*; **to be under the t. of sth.**, être menacé de qch.; **there is a t. of rain**, la pluie menace; '**threaten**, (*a*) *v.tr.* menacer; **to t. s.o. with sth.**, menacer qn de qch.; **to t. to do sth.**, menacer de faire qch.; (*b*) *v.i.* **a storm is threatening**, la tempête, l'orage, menace; '**threatening**, *a.* (ton) menaçant; **t. letter**, lettre de menaces; **the weather looks t.**, le temps menace; **-ly**, *adv.* d'un air menaçant.

three [θri:], *num.a. & s.* trois (*m*); **to come in in threes, t. by t.**, **t. at a time**, entrer par trois; **t.-act play**, pièce en trois actes; **t.-cornered**, triangulaire; **t.-electrode lamp**, (lampe *f*) triode (*f*); *Mus:* **t.-four time**, trois-quatre *m*; **t.-legged**, (tabouret) à trois pieds; **t.-piece suit**, complet *m* (avec gilet); **t.-ply wood**, contre-plaqué *m* à trois épaisseurs; **t.-ply wool**, laine *f* trois fils; **t.-quarter-length coat**, trois-quarts *m inv*; *Aut:* **t.-wheeler**, trois-roues *m inv*; '**threefold. 1.** *a.* triple. **2.** *adv.* trois fois autant; **to increase t.**, tripler.

thresh [θreʃ], *v.tr.* battre (le blé); '**thresher**, *s.* batteuse *f*; '**threshing**, *s.* battage *m* (des blés); **t. machine**, batteuse *f*.

threshold ['θreʃ(h)ould], *s.* seuil *m*, pas *m*; **to cross the t.**, franchir le seuil; **t. of perception**, seuil de la perception.

thrift [θrift], *s.* **1.** économie *f*, épargne *f*. **2.** *Bot:* armérie (commune, maritime); '**thriftiness**, *s.* économie *f*; '**thriftless**, *a.* dépensier, prodigue; imprévoyant; '**thriftlessness**, *s.* prodigalité *f*; imprévoyance *f*; '**thrifty**, *a.* économe, ménager; *N.Am:* (*of plant*) vigoureux; **-ily**, *adv.* avec économie; (vivre) frugalement.

thrill [θril], **I.** *s.* (*a*) frisson *m*, tressaillement *m*; (*b*) (vive) émotion; **it gave me quite a t.**, ça m'a fait quelque chose. **II.** *v.* **1.** *v.tr.* (*a*) faire frissonner, faire frémir (qn); (*b*) émouvoir, empoigner (qn); électriser (un auditoire); **to be thrilled**, ressentir une vive émotion (à la vue de qch.). **2.** *v.i.* tressaillir, frissonner, frémir; '**thriller**, *s.* roman *m*, film *m*, pièce *f*, à sensation; *occ.* roman policier; '**thrilling**, *a.* excitant, (spectacle) empoignant, émouvant, passionnant; (roman) sensationnel.

thrive [θraiv], *v.i.* (**throve** [θrouv], **thrived**; **thrived**) (*a*) (*of child, plant*) se (bien) développer; (*of business*) bien marcher; (*of plant*) **thrives in all soils**, s'accommode à tous les sols; **he thrives on it**, il s'en trouve bien; (*b*) (*of pers.*) prospérer; **to t. on other people's misfortunes**, profiter, s'engraisser, des misères d'autrui; '**thriving**, *a.* vigoureux, (*of pers., business*) prospère, florissant.

throat [θrout], *s.* (*a*) gorge *f*; **to take s.o. by the t.**, empoigner qn à la gorge; **to cut s.o.'s t.**, couper la gorge à qn; *F:* **to cut one's own t.**, travailler à sa propre ruine; (*b*) gorge, gosier *m*; **to have a sore t.**, avoir mal à la gorge; **to clear one's t.**, s'éclaircir le gosier; *F:* **he's always ramming it down my t.**, il m'en raba toujours les oreilles; **to jump down s.o.'s t.**, rembarrer, rabrouer, qn; **it sticks in my t.**, je ne peux pas avaler ça; '**throaty**, *a.* (*of voice*) d'arrière-gorge; guttural; **-ily**, *adv* gutturalement.

throb [θrɔb]. **I.** *s.* pulsation *f*, battement *m* (du cœur); vrombissement *m* (d'une machine). **II.** *v.i.* (**throbbed**) (*a*) (*of heart*) battre fort, palpiter; (*of engine*) vrombir; **his hear throbbed with joy**, son cœur tressaillit de joie; (*b*) **my finger is throbbing**, le doigt me lancine; '**throbbing**, *s.* (*a*) battement *m*, pulsation *f*, palpitation *f* (du cœur); vrombissement *m* (d'une machine); (*b*) lancination *f*.

throes [θrouz], *s.pl.* douleurs *fpl*, angoisse *f* agonie *f*; **death t.**, affres *f* de la mort; agonie **we're in the t. of a general election**, nous sommes au beau milieu des élections.

thrombosis [θrɔm'bousis], *s. Med:* **coronary t.**, infarctus *m* du myocarde.

throne [θroun], *s.* trône *m*.

throng [θrɔŋ]. **I.** *s.* (*a*) foule *f*; (*b*) (*disorderly*) cohue *f*. **II.** *v.* **1.** *v.i.* s'assembler en foule affluer (à, dans, un endroit). **2.** *v.tr.* encombre (les rues); **street thronged with people**, ru pleine de gens.

throttle ['θrɔtl]. **I.** *s.* **1.** *F:* gosier *m*. **2.** *Mch I.C.E:* papillon *m*; **to open (out) the t.**, mettr les gaz. **II.** *v.tr.* **1.** étrangler (qn); serrer (qn) la gorge. **2.** étrangler (le moteur); **to t. down** mettre le moteur au ralenti; fermer le(s) gaz '**throttling**, *s.* étranglement *m*.

through [θru:]. **I.** *prep.* **1.** (*a*) à travers; par; **t.** hedge, au travers d'une haie; **to look t. the win dow**, regarder par la fenêtre; **to look t.** telescope, regarder dans un télescope; **to go t s.o.'s pockets**, fouiller qn; **he's been t. it**, il en vu de dures; **to talk t. one's nose**, parler du nez **he's t. his examination**, il a été reçu à son examen; **I'm halfway t. this book**, j'ai lu l moitié de ce livre; (*b*) pendant, durant; **all t. hi life**, sa vie durant; (*c*) *N.Am:* **Monday t Friday**, de lundi à vendredi; du lundi au ven dredi. **2. t. s.o.**, par qn; **to send sth. t.**, envoyer qch. par la poste. **3.** (*a*) en con séquence de, à cause de (qch.); **t. ignorance** par ignorance; **absent t. illness**, absent pa suite, pour cause, de maladie; **to do sth. t. fea** faire qch. sous le coup de la peur; (*b*) par l'ac tion de (qn, qch.); **it all happened t. him**, il es cause de tout. **II.** *adv.* **1.** (*a*) à travers; **the wate poured t.**, l'eau coulait à travers; **to let s.o. t.** laisser passer qn; (*b*) **t. (and t.)**, de bout e bout; de part en part; **to run s.o. t. (with** **sword)**, transpercer qn; **wet t.**, tremp jusqu'aux os; (*c*) d'un bout à l'autre; jusqu'a bout; **to see sth. t.**, mener qch. à bonne fin; **I'm t. with him**, j'en ai fini avec lui. 2. (*a*) **the train runs t. to Paris**, le train va directement à Paris, est direct jusqu'à Paris; (*b*) *P.T. T:* **I can't get t. to him**, je ne peux pas le joindre; **you're t.**, vous avez la communication; **to get t. to s.o.**, obtenir la communication avec qn. III. *a. Rail:* **t. carriage for Geneva**, voiture directe pour Genève; **t. traffic**, transit *m*; **through'out.** 1. *prep.* (*a*) **t. the country**, dans tout le pays; (*b*) **t. the year**, pendant toute l'année. 2. *adv.* (*a*) **central heating t.**, chauffage (central) partout, dans toutes les pièces; (*b*) tout le temps; **'throughway**, *s. U.S.* autoroute *f*.

throw [θrou]. I. *s.* (*a*) jet *m*, lancement *m*, lancer *m* (de qch.); **within a stone's t.**, à quelques pas; (*b*) *Wr:* mise *f* à terre (de l'adversaire). II. *v.tr.* (**threw** [θru:]; **thrown** [θroun]) 1. (*a*) jeter, lancer; *v.i.* **he can t. a hundred metres**, il est capable de lancer à cent mètres; **to t. oneself backwards**, se rejeter en arrière; **to t. temptation in s.o.'s way**, exposer qn à la tentation; **to t. the blame on s.o.**, rejeter la faute sur qn; (*b*) **to t. a sheet over sth.**, couvrir qch. d'un drap; **to be thrown back on one's own resources**, n'avoir plus à compter que sur soi-même; **to t. open the door**, ouvrir la porte toute grande. 2. projeter; **to t. a picture on the screen**, projeter une image sur l'écran; **to t. some light on the matter**, jeter de la lumière sur la question. 3. *F:* **to t. a fit**, tomber en convulsions; piquer une attaque de nerfs; **to t. a party**, inviter des amis à une réunion. 4. *Wr:* terrasser (son adversaire); (*of horse*) démonter (son cavalier); (*of rider*) **to be thrown**, être désarçonné; **'throw a'bout**, *v.tr.* 1. jeter (des objets) çà et là; gaspiller (son argent). 2. **to t. one's arms about**, faire de grands gestes; **to t. oneself about**, se démener; **to be thrown about**, être ballotté; **'throw a'way**, *v.tr.* 1. jeter (son cigare); rejeter (qch.); mettre (qch.) au rebut. 2. donner (qch.) inutilement; gaspiller (son argent); **to t. away a chance**, laisser passer une occasion; **to t. away one's life**, se sacrifier inutilement; **'throw 'down**, *v.tr.* jeter (qch.) (de haut en bas); jeter (qch.) à terre; **'throw 'in**, *v.tr.* 1. jeter (qch.) dedans, dans (qch.). 2. (*a*) ajouter (qch.); donner (qch.) par-dessus le marché; (*b*) placer (un mot). 3. **to t. in one's lot with s.o.**, partager le sort de qn. 4. (*a*) **to t. in one's hand, one's cards**, abandonner la partie; (*b*) *Fb: v.i.* remettre le ballon en jeu; **'throw 'off**, *v.tr.* 1. (*a*) enlever, quitter (ses vêtements); se débarrasser de (qn, qch.); abandonner (un déguisement); **to t. off a fever**, guérir de la fièvre. 2. **to t. the dogs off the scent**, dépister les chiens; **'throw 'out**, *v.tr.* 1. jeter (qch.) dehors; se débarrasser de (qch.); expulser (qn); mettre (qn) à la porte. 2. répandre, émettre (de

la chaleur). 3. rejeter (un projet de loi). 4. **to t. out one's chest**, bomber la poitrine. 5. lancer, laisser entendre (des insinuations); **'throwouts**, *s.pl. Com:* rebuts *m*; **'throw 'up**, *v.tr.* 1. jeter (qch.) en l'air. 2. *v.tr. & i.* vomir. 3. lever haut, mettre haut (les mains). 4. construire (une maison) à la hâte. 5. renoncer à, abandonner (un projet); **to t. everything up**, tout plaquer; **to t. up one's job**, se démettre de son poste.

thru [θru:]. *N.Am:* = THROUGH; **'thruway**, *s.* autoroute *f*.

thrush [θrʌʃ], *s. Orn:* grive *f*.

thrust [θrʌst]. I. *s.* (*a*) poussée *f*; (*b*) coup *m* de pointe; *Fenc:* coup d'estoc; **shrewd t.**, trait *m* qui frappe juste. II. *v.* (**thrust; thrust**) 1. *v.tr.* (*a*) pousser (avec force); **to t. one's hands into one's pockets**, fourrer les mains dans ses poches; **to t. a knife into s.o.'s back**, enfoncer un couteau dans le dos de qn; (*b*) **to t. oneself upon s.o.**, s'imposer à qn, chez qn; (*c*) **to t. (one's way) through the crowd**, se frayer un chemin à travers la foule. 2. *v.i.* **to t. at s.o.**, porter un coup de pointe à qn.

thud [θʌd]. I. *s.* bruit sourd; son mat; floc *m*. II. *v.i.* (**thudded**) tomber avec un bruit sourd; émettre un bruit mat.

thug [θʌg], *s.* bandit *m*.

thumb [θʌm]. I. *s.* pouce *m*; **his fingers are all thumbs**, il est maladroit de ses mains; **to be under s.o.'s t.**, être sous la domination de qn. II. *v.tr.* 1. **well-thumbed book**, livre fatigué; livre souvent feuilleté. 2. *F:* **to t. a lift**, faire de l'auto-stop; **'thumb-nail**, *s.* ongle *m* du pouce; *t.-n.* **sketch**, croquis *m* minuscule, hâtif; **'thumbprint**, *s.* empreinte *f* de pouce; **'thumbscrew**, *s.* vis *f* à ailettes; papillon *m*; **'thumbtack**, *s. N.Am:* punaise *f*.

thump [θʌmp]. I. *s.* 1. coup sourd; cognement *m*. 2. coup de poing; bourrade *f*. II. *v.tr. & i.* bourrer (qn) de coups; **to t. (on) the table**, frapper du poing sur la table; (*of heart*) battre fort.

thunder ['θʌndər]. I. *s.* (*a*) tonnerre *m*; **there's t. in the air**, (i) le temps est à l'orage; (ii) l'atmosphère (d'une réunion) est orageuse; (*b*) **t. of applause**, tonnerre d'applaudissements. II. *v.tr. & i.* 1. tonner; **it's thundering**, il tonne. 2. **to t. (out) threats**, fulminer des menaces; **'thunderbolt**, *s.* 1. (coup *m* de) foudre *f*. 2. nouvelle foudroyante; **'thunderclap**, *s.* coup *m* de tonnerre; **'thundercloud**, *s.* nuage orageux; **'thundering**, *a.* 1. tonnant; fulminant. 2. *F:* **in a t. rage**, dans une rage à tout casser; **'thunderstorm**, *s.* orage *m*; **'thunderstruck**, *a.* confondu, abasourdi, sidéré; atterré; **'thundery**, *a.* orageux.

Thursday ['θə:zdi], *s.* jeudi *m*; **Maundy T.**, le jeudi saint.

thus [ðʌs], *adv.* 1. ainsi; de cette façon. 2. ainsi, donc. 3. **t. far**, jusqu'ici; jusque-là.

thwart[1] [θwɔːt], *s.* banc *m* de nage (d'une embarcation).

thwart[2], *v.tr.* contrecarrer (qn); déjouer les menées de (qn); **to t. s.o.'s plans**, se mettre en travers des projets de qn; **to be thwarted**, essuyer un échec.

thy [ðai], *poss.a. A: Ecc:* (*also poetic & dialect*) ton, *f.* ta, *pl.* tes.

thyme [taim], *s. Bot:* thym *m.*

thyroid ['θairɔid], *a.* (glande) thyroïde.

tiara [ti'ɑːrə], *s.* tiare *f.*

Tiber (the) [ðə'taibər]. *Pr.n. Geog:* le Tibre.

Tibet [ti'bet]. *Pr.n. Geog:* le Tibet; **Ti'betan**, *a. & s.* tibétain, -aine.

tibia ['tibiə], *s. Anat:* tibia *m.*

tick[1] [tik]. I. *s.* 1. (*a*) tic(-)tac *m*; (*b*) *F:* moment *m*, instant *m*; **half a t.!** un instant! **he'll do it in two ticks**, il feraça en moins de rien. 2. marque *f*, pointage *m*, trait *m*; **to put a t. against a name**, pointer, cocher, un nom. II. *v.* 1. *v.i.* faire tic(-)tac; *F:* **I'd like to know what makes him t.**, je voudrais bien savoir ce qui le pousse. 2. *v.tr.* pointer (une liste); cocher (un nom); **'ticker**, *s.* 1. *F:* (*a*) montre *f*; (*b*) cœur *m*. 2. **t. tape**, bande *f* de téléimprimeur; **'ticking**, *s.* tic(-)tac *m*; **'tick 'off**, *v.tr.* 1. cocher (un nom). 2. *F:* rembarrer (qn); **'tick 'over**, *v.i. Aut:* (*of engine*) tourner au ralenti; **'tick-'tock**, *s.* tic(-)tac *m.*

tick[2], *s. Arach:* tique *f.*

tick[3], *s. F:* crédit *m*; **to buy sth. on t.**, acheter qch. à crédit.

ticket ['tikit]. I. *s.* 1. billet *m* (de chemin de fer); ticket *m* (d'autobus); **left-luggage t.**, **cloakroom t.**, bulletin *m* de consigne; **platform t.**, billet de quai; **t. collector**, contrôleur *m* (de billets); **season t. holder**, abonné(e); **single t.**, aller *m*; **return t.**, aller et retour. 2. étiquette *f*; *Aut: F:* **to get a t.**, attraper une contravention, se faire coller un papillon. II. *v.tr.* étiqueter, marquer (des marchandises); **'ticketing**, *s.* étiquetage *m.*

tickle ['tikl]. I. *s.* chatouillement *m.* II. *v.* 1. *v.tr.* (*a*) chatouiller; (*of food*) **to t. the palate**, chatouiller le palais; **to t. s.o.'s fancy**, amuser qn; (*b*) *F:* amuser; **to be tickled to death (over sth.)**, (i) se tordre de rire (à l'idée de qch.); (ii) *esp. N.Am:* être transporté de joie; (*c*) *Aut:* **to t. the carburettor**, amorcer le carburateur. 2. *v.i.* **my hand tickles**, la main me démange; **'tickling**, *s.* chatouillement *m*; **'ticklish**, *a.* 1. chatouilleux. 2. (*of pers.*) susceptible; (*of task*) délicat; **a t. subject**, un sujet brûlant; **'ticklishness**, *s.* 1. sensibilité *f* au chatouillement. 2. susceptibilité *f*; délicatesse *f* (d'une tâche).

tide [taid], *s.* marée *f*; **high, low, t.**, marée haute,

basse; **against the t.**, à contre-marée; **to g** with the t., suivre le courant; **'tidal**, *a.* 1. **t wave**, raz *m* de marée; vague *f* de fond. 2. **river**, fleuve *m* à marée; **'tideless**, *a.* san marée; **'tide 'over**, *v.tr.* **that will t. us ove** cela nous permettra de tenir le coup, *F:* v nous dépanner; **'tideway**, *s.* lit *m* de la maré

tidy ['taidi]. I. *a.* 1. (*a*) (*of room*) bien rangé, e bon ordre; (*of dress*) bien tenu; **make yoursel t.**, faites-vous propre; (*b*) (*of pers.*) ordonné qui a de l'ordre. 2. *F:* assez bon; passable; **a** sum, une somme rondelette. II. *s.* **sink t.**, coi *m* d'évier. III. *v.tr.* ranger; mettre de l'ordr dans (qch.); **to t. oneself (up)**, faire un brin d toilette; **to t. away**, ranger (qch.); *v.i.* **to t. up** tout remettre en place; **-ily**, *adv.* proprement avec ordre; **t. dressed**, mis avec soin **'tidiness**, *s.* bon ordre; (*in dress*) bonne tenue (*of pers.*) le goût de l'ordre.

tie [tai]. I. *s.* 1. (*a*) lien *m*; attache *f*; **ties o friendship**, liens d'amitié; (*b*) **she finds he children a t.**, ses enfants sont pour elle une en trave continuelle. 2. *Cl:* bow t., nœud *r* papillon; (*on invitation*) **black t.** = smoking *n* 3. *Mus:* liaison *f.* 4. (*a*) *Sp:* match nul; *Fb:* **cup t.**, match éliminatoire du champion nat; (*c*) **the election has ended in a t.**, les can didats sont à égalité de voix. II. *v.* (**tied; tying** 1. *v.tr.* (*a*) attacher; lier (qn à qch.); **to t. s.o.' hands**, enlever à qn toute liberté d'action, lie les mains à qn; **to be tied to one's work**, êt toujours à l'attache; (*b*) lier, nouer (un lacet faire (un nœud, sa cravate); (*c*) *Mus:* lier (deu notes). 2. *v.i. Sp: etc:* être, arriver, à égalit (**with**, avec); **'tie 'down**, *v.tr.* 1. immobilise (qn); assujettir (qch.). 2. **tied down to one' duties**, assujetti à ses fonctions; **'tie 'on**, *v.t* attacher (avec une ficelle); **t.-on label**, étiquett *f* à œillet(s); **'tiepin**, *s.* épingle *f* de cravate; **'ti 'up**, *v.tr.* 1. attacher, ficeler (un paquet bander, panser (un bras blessé). 2. attacher (u chien); ligoter (qn). 3. rendre (un legs) in aliénable; immobiliser (ses capitaux). 4. *F:* **w get tied up**, s'embrouiller; **just now I'm tied u** pour l'instant je suis très occupé. 5. **we are tie up with another firm**, nous avons des accor avec une autre maison; **'tie-up**, *s.* associatio *f*, rapport *m*, lien *m* (entre deux maisons d commerce, etc.).

tier ['tiər], *s.* rangée *f* (de sièges); étage *m*; **tiers**, en amphithéâtre; **to rise in tiers**, s'étage **four-t. cake**, gâteau *m* à quatre étages.

tiff [tif], *s.* petite querelle; fâcherie *f.*

tiger ['taigər], *s.* tigre *m*; **t. cub**, petit *m* du tigr *Bot:* **t. lily**, lis tigré; *Ent:* **t. moth**, arctia **'tigress**, *s.* tigresse *f.*

tight [tait]. I. *a.* 1. hermétique; étanche. 2. (raide, tendu; **to draw a cord t.**, serrer un co don; **to keep a t. hold over s.o.**, tenir qn serr

(b) (of clothes) **skin-t.**, collant; **(too) t.**, trop juste; **to be in a t. corner**, être en mauvaise passe. **3.** *(of money)* resserré, rare. **4.** *F:* ivre, gris; **to get t.**, prendre une cuite. **II.** *adv.* **1. shut t.**, (porte) hermétiquement close; (yeux) bien fermés. **2.** *(a)* fortement, fermement; **to hold sth. t.**, tenir qch. serré; **to screw a nut t.**, serrer un écrou à bloc, à refus; *(b)* étroitement; **to fit t.**, être bien ajusté; **-ly**, *adv.* **1. eyes t. shut**, yeux bien fermés. **2.** *(a)* (tendre, etc.) fortement; **to hold sth. t.**, tenir qch. serré; serrer qch. dans ses mains; *(b)* étroitement; **to fit t.**, être bien ajusté; **'tighten**, *v.* **1.** *v.tr.* *(a)* serrer, resserrer (une vis, un nœud); retendre (une courroie); raidir (un cordage); *Aut:* **to t. (up) the steering**, rattraper le jeu de la direction; *F:* **to t. one's belt**, se serrer la ceinture; *(b)* **to t. (up) restrictions**, renforcer des restrictions. **2.** *v.i.* *(a)* se (res)serrer; *(b) (of cable)* se tendre; raidir; **'tightness**, *s.* *(a)* tension *f*, raideur *f*; *(b)* étroitesse *f* (d'un vêtement); **'tightrope**, *s.* corde tendue; corde raide; **t. walker**, danseur, -euse, de corde; **tights**, *s.pl. Cl:* collant *m*.

le [tail]. **I.** *s.* **1.** tuile *f* (de toiture). **2. (paving) t.**, carreau *m* (de carrelage). **II.** *v.tr.* **1.** couvrir (un comble) de tuiles, en tuiles. **2.** carreler; **tiled**, *a.* **1.** (toit) de, en, tuiles. **2.** (pavage) carrelé, en carreaux; (paroi) à carreaux vernissés; **'tiling**, *s.* **1.** *(a)* pose *f* des tuiles; *(b)* carrelage *m*. **2.** *coll.* *(a)* couverture *f* en tuiles; *(b)* carreaux *mpl*, carrelage.

l¹ [til], *v.tr.* labourer, cultiver; **'tillage**, **'tilling**, *s.* labour *m*, labourage *m*, culture *f*.

l², *s.* tiroir-caisse *m*; *F:* **to be caught with one's hand in the t.**, être pris en flagrant délit.

l³. **1.** *prep.* *(a)* jusqu'à; **t. now**, **t. then**, jusqu'ici, jusque-là; **from morning t. night**, du matin au soir; *(b)* **not t. . . .**, pas avant . . .; **he won't come t. after dinner**, il ne viendra qu'après le dîner. **2.** *conj.* *(a)* jusqu'à ce que + *sub.*; **t. the doors are shut**, jusqu'à ce que les portes soient fermées; **I laughed t. I cried**, j'ai ri (jusqu')aux larmes; *(b)* **not t. . . .**, pas avant que + *sub.*; **he won't come t. he's invited**, il ne viendra pas avant d'être invité.

ler ['tilər], *s. Nau:* barre franche (de direction).

t [tilt]. **I.** *s.* **1.** inclinaison *f*, pente *f*; **to give a cask a t.**, incliner un tonneau. **2. (at) full t.**, à fond de train; **to run full t. into sth.**, se jeter tête baissée contre qch. **II.** *v.* **1.** *v.i.* *(a)* **to t. (up)**, s'incliner; pencher; **to t. over**, se renverser; *(b)* **to t. at s.o.**, attaquer qn, critiquer qn. **2.** *v.tr.* pencher, incliner; **to t. one's chair back**, se balancer sur sa chaise.

mber ['timbər], *s.* **1.** *(a)* bois *m* d'œuvre; **t. merchant**, marchand *m* de bois; *(b)* **standing t.**, bois en état, bois debout; **t. tree**, arbre *m* de haute futaie. **2. (piece of) t.**, poutre *f*, madrier

m; **'timbered**, *a.* (maison) en bois; **'timberyard**, *s.* chantier *m* de bois.

time [taim]. **I.** *s.* **1.** temps *m*; **t. will show**, qui vivra verra; **in (the course of) t.**, **as t. goes on, by**, avec le temps. **2. in a short t.**, en peu de temps; sous peu; **in three weeks' t.**, dans trois semaines; **to do sth. in no t.**, faire qch. en un rien de temps, en moins de rien; **within the required t.**, dans les délais voulus; **to take a long t. over sth.**, mettre un temps interminable à faire qch.; **for a long t. to come**, d'ici (à) longtemps; **I haven't seen him for a long t.**, voilà longtemps que je ne l'ai vu; **for some t. (past)**, depuis quelque temps; **for some t. (to come)**, pendant quelque temps; **all the t.**, (i) pendant tout ce temps; (ii) continuellement. **3.** *(a)* **my t. is my own**, je suis libre de mon temps; **to have t. on one's hands**, avoir du temps de reste; *F:* **I've no t. for him**, il m'embête; **you've heaps of t.**, vous avez tout le temps voulu; **to lose t., to waste t.**, perdre du temps; **to make up for lost t.**, rattraper le temps perdu; **to lose no t. in doing sth.**, s'empresser de faire qch.; **to take one's t. over sth.**, mettre le temps qu'il faut à faire qch.; *F:* **it will take you all your t. to . . .**, vous aurez fort à faire pour . . .; **t.'s up!** c'est l'heure! *(b)* *F:* **to do t.**, faire de la prison; **to serve one's t.**, faire son apprentissage; **the house will last our t.**, la maison durera autant que nous. **4.** *usu. pl.* époque *f*; *(a)* **a sign of the times**, un signe des temps; **in time(s) to come**, à l'avenir; **in our t.**, de nos jours; *(b)* **to be behind the times**, ne plus être de son siècle; être arriéré. **5.** *(a)* **I was away at the t.**, j'étais absent alors, à ce moment; **at that t.**, en ce temps-là; **at the present t.**, à l'heure qu'il est; actuellement; **at a given t.**, à un moment donné; **at the t. fixed**, à l'heure dite; **at one t . . . ., at another t . . . .**, tantôt . . ., tantôt . . .; **at any other t.**, en d'autres temps; **at one t.**, autrefois, dans le temps; **at no t.**, jamais; à aucun moment; **at times**, parfois; **at various times**, à diverses reprises; **(at) any t. (you like)**, n'importe quand; **he may turn up at any t.**, il peut arriver d'un moment à l'autre; **some t. or other**, un jour ou l'autre; **by the t. (that) I got there . . .**, (i) lorsque je suis arrivé . . .; (ii) lorsque je serais arrivé . . .; **from t. to t.**, de temps en temps; **from that t. (on)**, dès lors; depuis lors; **to do sth. when the t. comes**, faire qch. en son temps; **now's the t. to . . .**, voilà le moment de . . .; **to choose one's t.**, choisir son heure; *(b)* **in due t. and place**, en temps et lieu; **you'll hear from me at the proper t.**, je vous écrirai le moment venu. **6.** heure *f*; *(a)* **summer t.**, l'heure d'été, *Fr.C:* l'heure avancée; **Greenwich mean t.**, l'heure de Greenwich; **(standard) t. belt**, fuseau *m* horaire; *(b)* **what's the t.?** quelle heure est-il? **what t. do you make it?** quelle heure avez-vous? **watch that keeps (good) t.,** montre qui est exacte; F: **to pass the t. of day with s.o.,** échanger quelques mots avec qn; **at this t. of day,** à cette heure du jour; (c) **dinner t.,** l'heure du dîner; **to be ahead of t.,** être en avance; **to arrive on t.,** arriver à l'heure; **I was just in t.,** je suis arrivé juste à temps; **in good t.,** de bonne heure; F: c'est que **t. too!** c'est pas trop tôt! (d) **t. of the year,** époque f de l'année; saison f; **at my t. of life,** à mon âge; (e) **to die before one's t.,** mourir avant l'âge, mourir jeune. **7. we had a good t.,** on s'est bien amusé; **to have a bad t., a rough t. (of it),** en voir de dures. **8.** fois f; **next t.,** la prochaine fois; **several times over,** (faire qch.) à plusieurs, à différentes, reprises; plusieurs fois; **t. and t. again, t. after t.,** à maintes reprises; maintes et maintes fois; **for weeks at a t.,** des semaines durant; **three times running,** trois fois de suite, à trois reprises; **four times as big,** quatre fois plus grand. **9.** adv.phr. **at the same t.;** (a) en même temps; (b) **at the same t. you mustn't forget that . . .,** d'autre part il ne faut pas oublier que . . .. **10.** (a) Cin: **running t.,** durée f de projection; (b) Mus: mesure f; **to beat t.,** battre la mesure; **in strict t.,** en mesure; **to keep t.,** aller en mesure. **11.** v.tr. **1.** (a) fixer l'heure de (qch.); (b) **to t. a blow,** mesurer un coup; **well-timed remark,** observation f à propos; (c) Aut: etc: régler, ajuster (l'allumage). **2.** calculer la durée de (qch.). **3.** Sp: chronométrer (une course); '**time-bomb,** s. bombe f à retardement; '**timekeeper,** s. **1.** Sp: chronométreur m. **2. good t.,** (i) montre f, (ii) personne f, qui est toujours à l'heure; '**time-lag,** s. retard m; '**time-limit,** s. **1.** limite f de temps. **2.** délai m (de paiement); '**timely,** a. opportun, à propos; '**timepiece,** s. pendule f; montre f; '**timeserver,** s. opportuniste mf; '**time-signal,** s. Rad: signal m horaire; '**time-switch,** s. minuterie f (d'escalier, etc.); '**timetable,** s. **1.** horaire m; indicateur m (des chemins de fer). **2.** Sch: emploi m du temps; '**time-work,** s. Ind: travail m à l'heure; '**timing,** s. **1.** Aut: etc: réglage m (de l'allumage). **2.** Sp: chronométrage m.

timid ['timid], a. timide, timoré, peureux; **-ly,** adv. timidement; **ti'midity,** s. timidité f.

tin [tin]. I. s. **1.** étain m. **2.** (a) **t. whistle,** flageolet m; (b) boîte f (en métal); **cake t.,** moule m à gâteaux; **t. loaf,** pain moulé; **t. opener,** ouvre-boîte(s) m inv. II. v.tr. (**tinned**) **1.** étamer. **2.** mettre (des sardines, etc.) en conserve; **tinned food,** aliments m en conserve, conserves f alimentaires; **to live on tinned food,** se nourrir de conserves; '**tinfoil,** s. **1.** feuille f d'étain. **2.** papier m d'étain.

ting-a-ling ['tiŋəliŋ], s. drelin drelin m.

tinge [tin(d)ʒ]. I. s. teinte f, nuance f. II. v.tr.

teinter, nuancer.

tingle ['tiŋgl], v.i. **1.** (of ears) tinter. **2.** picote her cheeks tingled, les joues lui picotaient, l cuisaient; **my legs are tingling,** j'ai des fourmi dans les jambes; '**tingling,** s. **1.** tintement n (d'oreilles). **2.** picotement m, fourmillement n (de la peau).

tinker ['tiŋkər]. I. s. chaudronnier ambulant rétameur m. II. v.i. **to t. with (sth.),** retape rafistoler (une machine); replâtrer (un contra etc.); **to t. about,** bricoler; '**tinkering,** s. (a) (about), petites besognes d'entretien, d réparation; (b) rafistolage m.

tinkle ['tiŋkl]. I. s. (also **tinkling**) tintement m drelin m. II. v. **1.** v.i. tinter. **2.** v.tr. faire tinter

tinny ['tini], a. **to sound t.,** sonner grêle; rendr un son fêlé.

tinplate ['tin'pleit], s. fer-blanc m; ferblanterie,

tinsel ['tins(ə)l], s. (a) (decoration) lamé n paillettes fpl; (b) (false brilliance) clinquant m

tint [tint]. I. s. teinte f, nuance f. II. v.tr. teinte colorer.

tintack ['tintæk], s. broquette f; clou m d tapisserie.

tiny ['taini], a. minuscule; **a t. bit,** un tout pet morceau.

tip¹ [tip]. I. s. **1.** bout m, extrémité f, pointe artist to his finger-tips, artiste jusqu'au bo des ongles; **to have sth. on the t. of one' tongue,** avoir qch. sur le bout de la langu **asparagus tips,** pointes d'asperges. **2.** (walking-stick) bout ferré, embout m; (o billiard cue) procédé m. II. v.tr. (**tipped**) mettr un bout, un embout, à (qch.); '**tiptoe. I.** s. + adv. (on) **t.,** sur la pointe des pieds. **II.** v marcher sur la pointe des pieds; **to t. in, ou** entrer, sortir, sur la pointe des pieds; '**tip'to** a. F: de premier ordre; excellent, extra.

tip². I. s. **1.** pente f, inclinaison f. **2.** pourboire n gratification f; **the t. is included,** le service e compris. **3.** Rac: etc: tuyau m; **if you take my . . .,** si vous m'en croyez . . .. **4. rubbish** décharge f publique. II. v. (**tipped**) **1.** v.tr. faire pencher, faire incliner; **to t. (over** renverser (qch.); chavirer, verser (un canot); **t. (up),** soulever (un strapontin); faire bascul (une charrette); **to t. (out),** déverse décharger; (b) donner un pourboire à (qn); (Rac: tuyauter (qn). **2.** v.i. (a) **to t. (over** renverser, basculer; (of boat) chavirer, verse (b) **to t. (up),** se soulever, basculer; '**tip-lorr** s. camion m à benne; '**tipping,** s. **1.** (a) i clinaison f; (b) **t. (over),** renversement r chavirement m (d'un canot); (c) basculage n versage m; **t. (of rubbish) prohibited,** déchar interdite. **2.** (système m des) pourboires m; di tribution f de pourboires. **3.** Rac: tuyautage r '**tipster,** s. Rac: tuyauteur, -euse; '**tip-up,** (charrette) à bascule, à renversement; **t.-**

seat, strapontin *m*.

ipple ['tipl]. I. *s.* boisson *f* (alcoolique). II. *v.i.* se livrer à la boisson; **'tippler**, *s.* ivrogne *m*.

ipsy ['tipsi], *a.* gris, éméché, *F:* pompette; **to get t.**, se griser; **'tipsiness**, *s.* ivresse *f*.

irade [tai'reid], *s.* tirade *f*; **violent t. against s.o.**, diatribe *f* contre qn.

re¹ ['taiər]. 1. *v.tr.* (*a*) fatiguer, lasser; (*b*) **to t. s.o. out**, (i) épuiser, rompre, qn de fatigue; (ii) excéder qn. 2. *v.i.* se fatiguer, se lasser; **to t. of sth.**, se fatiguer, se lasser, de qch.; **'tired**, *a.* fatigué; (*a*) las; **t. out, t. to death**, rompu de fatigue; (*b*) **to be t.**, avoir sommeil, être fatigué; *F:* **you make me t.**, tu m'embêtes; (*c*) **to be t. of sth.**, être las de qch.; *F:* **I'm t. of you**, tu m'embêtes; **'tiredness**, *s.* lassitude *f*, fatigue *f*; **'tireless**, *a.* inlassable, infatigable; **-ly**, *adv.* inlassablement, infatigablement; **'tiresome**, *a.* 1. fatigant; (discours) ennuyeux. 2. exaspérant; (*of child*) fatigant, assommant; **how t.!** que c'est assommant! **'tiring**, *a.* 1. fatigant. 2. ennuyeux.

re², *s.* *N.Am:* = TYRE.

ssue ['tisju:], *s.* 1. (*a*) tissu *m*, étoffe *f*; (*b*) mouchoir *m* de papier; **t. paper**, papier *m* de soie; papier pelure; **toilet t.**, papier hygiénique; (*c*) **t. of lies**, tissu de mensonges. 2. *Biol:* tissu.

t¹ [tit], *s.* *Orn:* (*also* **titmouse**) mésange *f*.

t², *s.* **t. for tat**, à bon chat bon rat; **to give s.o. t. for tat**, rendre à qn la pareille.

tanic [tai'tænik], *a.* titanique, titanesque.

tbit ['titbit], *s.* friandise *f*.

tillate ['titileit], *v.tr.* titiller, chatouiller; **titi'llation**, *s.* titillation *f*, chatouillement *m*.

tivate ['titiveit]. 1. *v.tr.* faire (qn) beau. 2. *v.i. & pr.* se faire beau; faire un brin de toilette.

tle ['taitl], *s.* 1. (*a*) titre *m*; (*b*) titre de noblesse; **people with titles**, personnes titrées. 2. titre (d'un livre); **t. page**, (page *f* de) titre; *Th:* **t. part, rôle**, rôle *m* qui donne le titre à la pièce; *Cin:* **credit titles**, générique *m*. 3. titre, droit *m*; **t. to property**, droit de propriété; **to have a t. to sth.**, avoir droit, avoir des titres, à qch.; **t. deed**, titre (constitutif) de propriété; **'titled**, *a.* titré.

tter ['titər]. I. *s.* 1. rire étouffé. 2. petit rire bête, nerveux. II. *v.i.* 1. avoir un petit rire étouffé. 2. rire nerveusement, bêtement; **'tittering**, *s.* petits rires.

ttle-tattle ['titltætl], *s.* potins *mpl*, cancans *mpl*.

· [tu:]. I. *prep.* à. 1. (*a*) **what school do you go to?** à quelle école allez-vous? **he went to France, to Japan, to the U.S.A.**, il est allé en France, au Japon, aux États-Unis; **she came home to her family**, elle est rentrée auprès de sa famille; **I'm going to the grocer's**, je vais chez l'épicier; **from town to town**, de ville en ville; **airlines to and from America**, lignes aériennes à destination ou en provenance de l'Amérique; (*b*) **the road to London**, la route de Londres; **the road to ruin**, le chemin de la ruine; **it's thirty kilometres to London**, il y a trente kilomètres d'ici Londres. 2. **vers, à**; **to the east**, vers l'est; **to the right**, à droite. 3. **to clasp s.o. to one's heart**, serrer qn sur son cœur. 4. (*a*) **from morning to night**, du matin au soir; **from day to day**, de jour en jour; (*b*) **ten (minutes) to six**, six heures moins dix. 5. (*a*) **wet to the skin**, trempé jusqu'aux os; **to this day**, jusqu'à ce jour; (*b*) **accurate to a millimetre**, exact à un millimètre près; **a year to the day**, un an jour pour jour. 6. (*a*) **to this end**, à cet effet, dans ce but; **to come to s.o.'s help**, venir à l'aide de qn; (*b*) **to my despair**, à mon grand désespoir; **to everyone's surprise**, à la surprise de tous. 7. **en**; **to run to seed**, monter en graine; **to go to ruin**, tomber en ruine; **to put to flight**, mettre en fuite. 8. **to sing sth. to the tune of . . .**, chanter qch. sur l'air de . . .. 9. **heir to an estate**, héritier d'une propriété; **secretary to the manager**, secrétaire du directeur. 10. (*a*) **that's nothing to what I've seen**, cela n'est rien auprès de, à côté de, ce que j'ai vu; (*b*) **six votes to four**, six voix contre quatre; **to bet ten to one**, parier dix contre un; **one house to the square kilometre**, une maison par kilomètre carré. 11. **to all appearances**, selon toute apparence; **to write to s.o.'s dictation**, écrire sous la dictée de qn; **to the best of my recollection**, autant qu'il m'en souvienne. 12. **to drink to s.o.**, boire à la santé de qn. 13. **what did he say to my suggestion?** qu'est-ce qu'il a dit de ma proposition? **that's all there is to it**, c'est tout ce qu'il y a à dire; **there's nothing to it**, ce n'est rien. 14. (*a*) **what's that to you?** qu'est-ce que cela vous fait? (*b*) **envers, pour**; **good to all**, bon pour tous, envers tous; **kind to me**, aimable à mon égard; aimable pour, envers, moi; (*c*) **known to the ancients**, connu des anciens. II. (*with the infin.*) 1. (*a*) **pour**; **he came to help me**, il est venu (pour) m'aider; **so to speak**, pour ainsi dire; (*b*) **happy to do it**, heureux de le faire; **ready to listen**, prêt à écouter; **good to eat**, bon à manger; **too hot to drink**, trop chaud pour qu'on puisse le boire; (*c*) **to look at her you wouldn't imagine that . . .**, à la voir on ne s'imaginerait pas que . . .; **he woke to find the lamp still burning**, en s'éveillant il trouva la lampe encore allumée. 2. (*a*) **to have a great deal to do**, avoir beaucoup à faire; **nothing to speak of**, rien qui vaille la peine d'en parler; pour ainsi dire rien; **the first to complain**, le premier à se plaindre; (*b*) **tendency to do sth.**, tendance à faire qch.; **this is the time to do it**, c'est le moment de le faire. 3. (*infin. used as noun*) **to lie is shameful**, il est honteux de mentir. 4. (*infin.= finite clause*) **I want him to do it**, je veux qu'il le fasse; **you'd**

like it to be true, vous voudriez bien que cela soit vrai. **5. fifty employees are to go,** cinquante employés vont recevoir leur congé. **6. I didn't want to go but I had to,** je ne voulais pas y aller mais il a bien fallu; **you ought to,** vous le devriez; **I want to,** je voudrais bien. **III.** adv. (stressed) **1. to put the horses to,** atteler les chevaux; **to come to,** reprendre connaissance. **2. to go to and fro,** aller et venir; **movement to and fro,** va-et-vient m inv; **to-'do,** s. remue-ménage m; **to make a to-do,** faire des histoires; **what a to-do!** quelle affaire!

toad [toud], s. (a) crapaud m; (b) F: sale type m; **'toadstool,** s. champignon m, esp. champignon vénéneux.

toast [toust]. **I.** s. **1.** pain grillé, toast m; **piece of t.,** toast, rôtie f; **anchovies on t.,** anchois sur canapé. **2.** toast; **to give a t.,** boire à la santé de qn. **II.** v. (a) v.tr. & i. rôtir, griller; (b) v.tr. porter un toast à (qn); boire à la santé de (qn); **'toaster,** s. grille-pain m inv.

tobacco [tə'bækou], s. tabac m; **t. pouch,** blague f à tabac; **to'bacconist,** s. marchand m de tabac; **t.'s (shop),** débit m, bureau m, de tabac.

toboggan [tə'bɔgən]. **I.** s. toboggan m, luge f; **t. run,** piste f de toboggan. **II.** v.i. faire du toboggan; luger.

today [tə'dei], adv. & s. aujourd'hui (m); **t. week,** d'aujourd'hui en huit; **t.'s paper,** le journal d'aujourd'hui, du jour.

toddle ['tɔdl]. **I.** s. allure chancelante (d'un enfant). **II.** v.i. marcher à petits pas (chancelants); trottiner; F: **I must be toddling,** il faut que je me trotte; **'toddler,** s. enfant mf qui commence à marcher; **the toddlers,** les tout petits.

toddy ['tɔdi], s. grog chaud.

toe [tou]. **I.** s. **1.** orteil m; doigt m de pied; **big t.,** gros orteil; **from top to t.,** de la tête aux pieds; **to be on one's toes,** être alerte; **to tread on s.o.'s toes,** marcher sur les pieds de qn. **2.** bout m, pointe f (de chaussure, etc.). **II.** v.tr. F: **to t. the line,** se conformer au mot d'ordre; **'toecap,** s. bout rapporté (de chaussure); **'toeclip,** s. Cy: cale-pied m; **'toenail,** s. ongle m de pied.

toffee ['tɔfi], s. caramel m au beurre; F: **he can't sing for t.,** il ne sait pas chanter du tout.

together [tə'geðər], adv. ensemble; (a) **to go t.,** **to belong t.,** aller ensemble; **t. with,** avec; en même temps que; (b) **to bring t.,** rassembler, réunir; (c) **to act t.,** agir de concert; **all t.,** tout le monde ensemble; tous à la fois; (d) **for months t.,** pendant des mois entiers; **for hours t.,** des heures durant; (e) **a great get-t.,** une grande réunion.

Togo ['tougou]. Pr.n. Geog: **the Republic of T.,** la République du Togo.

toil [tɔil]. **I.** s. travail dur, pénible; labeur m,

peine f. **II.** v.i. travailler, peiner; se donner d[u] mal; **to t. up a hill,** gravir péniblement un[e] colline.

toilet ['tɔilit], s. **1.** (= washing, make-up) toilet[te] f; **t. soap,** savon m de toilette; **t. case,** nécessaire m de toilette. **2.** (in hotel, etc.) l[es] toilettes, les cabinets m; **t. paper,** papier [h]ygiénique; **t. roll,** rouleau m de papi[er] hygiénique.

token ['touk(ə)n], s. **1.** signe m, marque [,] témoignage m; **as a t. of respect,** en signe, e[n] témoignage, comme marque, de respect. **2.** (a[)] jeton m; (b) **book t.,** bon m pour l'achat d'u[n] livre; **flower t.,** chèque-fleurs m. **3. t. paymen[t]** paiement m symbolique; **t. strike,** grève [d']avertissement.

Toledo [tɔ'leidou]. Pr.n. Geog: Tolède.

tolerate ['tɔləreit], v.tr. tolérer, supporter ([la] douleur); **I can't t. noise,** je ne peux pas su[p]porter le bruit; **'tolerable,** a. (a) toléra[ble] supportable; (b) passable; assez bon; **-ab[ly]** adv. (a) tolérablement; (b) passablement; **it's [ ]certain,** il est à peu près certain; **'tolerance,** tolérance f; **'tolerant,** a. tolérant (of, à l'égar[d] de); **-ly,** adv. avec tolérance; **tole'ration,** tolérance (religieuse).

toll[1] [toul], s. **1.** péage m; **t. bridge, t. motorwa[y]** pont m, autoroute f, à péage; Aut: **at 20[ ]metres,** péage à 200 mètres. **2. rent tak[es]** **heavy t. of one's income,** le loyer mange u[ne] grande partie des revenus; **the t. of the road[,]** les accidents m de la route.

toll[2]. **1.** (a) v.tr. tinter, sonner (une cloche); (b) v[.i.] **to t. for the dead,** sonner le glas. **2.** v.i. (of bel[l]) (a) tinter, sonner; (b) sonner le glas; **'tollin[g]** s. (a) tintement m (de cloche); (b) glas m.

Tom [tɔm]. **1.** Pr.n.m. Thomas; **any T., Dick [&]** **Harry,** le premier venu; n'importe qui. **2.** s. **(cat),** matou m.

tomahawk ['tɔməhɔːk]. **I.** s. hache f de guer[re] (des Amérindiens); tomahawk m. **II.** v.[t.] frapper (qn) avec un tomahawk.

tomato, pl. -oes [tə'maːtou, -ouz, N.Am: -'mei[ ]] s. tomate f; **t. sauce,** sauce f tomate.

tomb [tuːm], s. tombe f; tombeau [m] **'tombstone,** s. pierre tombale.

tombola [tɔm'boulə], s. tombola f.

tome [toum], s. tome m; gros volume.

tomfool ['tɔm'fuːl], a. & s. F: **t. scheme,** pro[jet] insensé; **tom'foolery,** s. F: bêtise(s) f(p[l]) niaiserie(s) f(pl).

tommy-gun ['tɔmigʌn], s. mitraillette f.

tomorrow [tə'mɔrou], adv. & s. demain (m); **t. night,** demain soir; **t. week,** de demain en hu[it] **the day after t.,** après-demain (m).

tomtom ['tɔmtɔm], s. tam-tam m.

ton [tʌn], s. **1.** tonne f; **metric t.,** tonne métriqu[e] F: **there's tons of it,** il y en a des tas. **2.** Na[ut:] tonne, tonneau m; **ship of 500 tons,** navire [de] jauge 500 tonneaux; ' **tonnage,** s. Nau: (of ship) jauge f, tonnage m; (of port) tonnage.

tone [toun]. I. s. son m, accent m; timbre m (de la voix, d'une cloche). 2. (a) ton m, voix f; **in a gentle t.,** d'un ton doux; **to change one's t.,** changer de ton, de note; (b) Fin: **the t. of the market,** l'allure f du marché; (c) Med: tonicité f (des muscles); (of pers.) **to lose t.,** faiblir; **to recover t.,** se retremper. 3. ton, nuance f (d'une couleur); Mus: ton. II. v.i. **to t. with sth.,** s'harmoniser avec qch.; ' **tone 'down,** v.tr. adoucir, atténuer (une expression, etc.); ' **toneless,** a. **t. voice,** voix blanche.

Tonga ['tɔŋgə]. Pr.n. Geog: l'archipel m de Tonga, les îles des Amis.

tongs [tɔŋz], s.pl. 1. (fire) t., pincettes f. 2. pince(s) f, tenailles f.

tongue [tʌŋ], s. 1. langue f; (a) **to put one's t. out at s.o.,** tirer la langue à qn; (b) **to have a glib t.,** avoir la langue bien pendue; **to hold one's t.,** tenir sa langue; **to find one's t. again,** retrouver la parole; **to keep a civil t. in one's head,** rester courtois; **he's always got his t. in his cheek,** il ne fait que blaguer; (of hounds) **to give t.,** donner de la voix. 2. langue, idiome m (d'un peuple). 3. langue (de terre, de feu); patte f, languette f (de soulier); battant m (de cloche); ' **tongue-tied,** a. muet; interdit.

tonic ['tɔnik]. 1. a. tonique. 2. s. (a) Med: tonique m, fortifiant m; (b) Mus: tonique f.

tonight [tə'nait], adv. & s. cette nuit; ce soir.

tonsil ['tɔns(i)l], s. amygdale f; **tonsi'llitis,** s. Med: angine f; amygdalite f.

tonsure ['tɔnʃər]. I. s. tonsure f. II. v.tr. tonsurer.

too [tu:], adv. 1. trop, par trop; **t. much money,** trop d'argent; **ten pounds t. much,** dix livres de trop; **the job is t. much for me,** la tâche est au-dessus de mes forces; **he was t. much for me,** il était trop fort pour moi; **I know him all t. well,** je ne le connais que trop. 2. aussi; également; **I want some t.,** il m'en faut également; moi aussi il m'en faut. 3. d'ailleurs; de plus; en outre; **he, t. . . .,** lui aussi, d'ailleurs . . ..

tool [tu:l]. I. s. 1. outil m; instrument m, ustensile m; **garden(ing) tools,** outils, matériel m, de jardinage. 2. instrument; **to make a t. of s.o.,** se servir de qn; **he was a mere t. in his hands,** il était son instrument. II. v.tr. ciseler (de l'argent); travailler (le cuir); usiner (une pièce en acier); ' **toolbag,** s. sac m à outils; ' **tooling,** s. ciselage m; usinage m.

tooth, pl. **teeth** [tu:θ, ti:θ], s. 1. dent f; **milk t.,** dent de lait; **second teeth,** dentition définitive; **set of teeth,** denture f; (set of) **false teeth,** dentier m; **to cut one's teeth,** faire, percer, ses dents; **to have a t. out,** se faire arracher une dent; **in the teeth of all opposition,** en dépit de toute opposition; **to show one's teeth,** montrer les dents; **to fight t. and nail,** se battre avec

acharnement; **to set one's teeth,** serrer les dents; F: **to be long in the t.,** n'être plus jeune. 2. dent (de scie); **teeth,** denture (d'une roue); ' **toothache,** s. mal m de dents; ' **toothbrush,** s. brosse f à dents; **toothed,** a. **t. wheel,** roue dentée; ' **toothless,** a. sans dent(s); édenté; ' **toothpaste,** s. (pâte f) dentifrice (m); ' **toothpick,** s. cure-dents m inv; ' **toothsome,** a. savoureux; **t. morsel,** morceau friand.

top[1] [tɔp]. I. s. 1. haut m, sommet m, cime f, faîte m (d'une montagne, d'un arbre); **at the t. of the tree,** (i) en haut de l'arbre; (ii) au premier rang de sa profession; **from t. to bottom,** de haut en bas; de fond en comble; **from t. to toe,** de la tête aux pieds; **to come out on t.,** avoir le dessus; **on t. of it all he wanted . . .,** pour comble il a voulu . . .. 2. surface f; dessus m (d'une table); impériale f (d'un autobus). 3. tête f (de page); **gilt t.,** tête dorée. 4. haut bout (de la table). 5. **to shout at the t. of one's voice,** crier à tue-tête; **to be on t. of one's form,** être en pleine forme; Aut: **to climb a hill in t.,** prendre une montée en prise (directe). II. a. 1. supérieur; du dessus, du haut, d'en haut; **t. floor, t. storey,** dernier étage, étage du haut; **t. coat,** (i) pardessus m; (ii) couche f de finition (de peinture); F: **to be t. dog,** avoir le dessus; Mus: **the t. notes,** les notes hautes; Aut: **t. gear,** prise directe; Adm: **t. secret,** très secret, ultra-secret. 2. premier, principal; **t. people,** personnalités fpl, gens éminents; Sch: **t. pupil,** premier, -ière, de la classe. III. v.tr. (topped) 1. écimer (un arbre); **to t. and tail gooseberries,** équeuter des groseilles à maquereau. 2. surmonter, couronner, coiffer (with, de); **and to t. it all . . .,** et pour comble . . .. 3. dépasser, surpasser (qch.); **to. t. s.o. by a head,** dépasser qn de la tête. 4. **to t. a list,** être à la tête d'une liste. 5. Golf: calotter (la balle); ' **top-'hat,** s. chapeau m haut de forme; ' **top 'heavy,** a. trop lourd du haut; peu stable; ' **topmost,** a. le plus haut; le plus élevé; **topped,** a. gilt-t., (livre) doré en tête; ' **top 'up,** v.tr. remplir (complètement); Aut: faire le plein (d'essence).

top[2], s. toupie f; **to spin a t.,** faire aller une toupie.

topaz ['toupæz], s. topaze f.

topic ['tɔpik], s. matière f (d'une discussion); sujet m, thème m (d'une conversation); **topics of the day,** questions f d'actualité; ' **topical,** a. **t. allusion,** allusion f aux événements du jour; **t. song,** chanson f d'actualités.

topple ['tɔpl]. 1. v.i. (a) **to t. (down, over),** tomber, s'écrouler, culbuter; (b) chanceler, vaciller, branler. 2. v.tr. **to t. sth. over,** faire tomber qch.; jeter qch. à bas.

topsy-turvy ['tɔpsi'tə:vi], a. & adv. sens dessus dessous; **to turn everything t.-t.,** tout bouleverser; **everything is t.-t.,** tout est en désarroi.

torch [tɔːtʃ], *s.* **1.** torche *f,* flambeau *m.* **2.** (**electric**) **t.,** torche électrique, lampe *f* de poche; **'torchlight,** *s.* lueur *f* de(s) flambeaux; **t. procession, tattoo,** retraite *f* aux flambeaux.

torment. I. ['tɔːment], *s.* tourment *m,* torture *f,* supplice *m;* **he suffered torments,** il souffrait le martyre; **to be in t.,** être au supplice; *F:* **that child is a positive t.,** cet enfant est assommant. **II.** [tɔː'ment], *v.tr.* tourmenter, torturer (qn); **to be tormented by hunger,** éprouver les tourments de la faim.

tornado, *pl.* **-oes** [tɔː'neidou, -ouz], *s.* tornade *f.*

torpedo [tɔː'piːdou]. **I.** *s.* (*pl.* **-oes** [-ouz]) torpille *f;* **to carry out a t. attack,** attaquer à la torpille; **t. officer,** officier *m* torpilleur; **t. boom,** porte-torpille(s) *m inv;* **t. tube,** (tube *m*) lance-torpilles (*m*); **motor t. boat,** vedette *f* lance-torpilles; *Av:* **aerial t.,** torpille d'avion; **t. aircraft,** avion *m* torpilleur. **II.** *v.tr.* torpiller.

torpid ['tɔːpid], *a.* (*a*) engourdi, inerte, torpide; (*b*) endormi; léthargique; **tor'pidity,** *s.* engourdissement *m,* inertie *f,* torpeur *f;* léthargie *f.*

torrent ['tɔrənt], *s.* torrent *m;* (*of rain*) **to fall in torrents,** tomber à torrents, à verse; **t. of abuse,** torrent d'injures; **to'rrential,** *a.* torrentiel.

torrid ['tɔrid], *a.* torride.

torso, *pl.* **-os** ['tɔːsou, -ouz], *s.* torse *m.*

tortoise ['tɔːtəs], *s.* tortue *f;* **'tortoiseshell,** *s.* écaille *f* de tortue; **t. butterfly,** tortue *f.*

tortuous ['tɔːtjuəs], *a.* tortueux.

torture ['tɔːtʃər]. **I.** *s.* torture *f,* tourment *m,* supplice *m.* **II.** *v.tr.* torturer (qn); **tortured by remorse,** tenaillé par le remords.

toss [tɔs]. **I.** *s.* **1.** action *f* de jeter (qch.) en l'air; (*a*) lancement *m* (d'une balle); (*b*) coup *m* de pile ou face; *Sp:* tirage *m* au sort. **2. t. of the head,** mouvement de tête impatient, dédaigneux. **3. to take a t.,** faire une chute de cheval. **II.** *v.* **1.** *v.tr.* (*a*) lancer, jeter, (une balle, etc.) en l'air; (*of bull*) lancer (qn) en l'air; (*of horse*) démonter (son cavalier); **to t. sth. to s.o.,** jeter qch. à qn; (*b*) **to t.** (**up**) **a coin,** jouer à pile ou face; *v.i. Sp:* **to t.** (**up**), tirer au sort; **to t. for sth.,** jouer qch. à pile ou face; (*c*) **to t. one's head,** relever la tête d'un air dédaigneux; (*of horse*) **to t. its head,** hocher la tête; (*d*) agiter, secouer, ballotter; **tossed by the waves,** ballotté par les flots. **2.** *v.i.* (*a*) **to t.** (**about**) **in bed,** se tourner et se retourner dans son lit; **to t. in one's sleep,** s'agiter dans son sommeil; (*b*) (*of ship*) **to pitch and t.,** tanguer; (*c*) (*of waves*) s'agiter; **'tossing,** *s.* **1.** lancement *m* en l'air. **2.** agitation *f,* ballottement *m;* **'toss 'off,** *v.tr.* avaler d'un trait (un verre de vin); écrire (un article) au pied levé; **'toss-up,** *s.* **1.** coup *m* de pile ou face. **2.** affaire *f* à issue douteuse.

tot¹ [tɔt], *s.* **1.** tout(e) petit(e) enfant; **tiny t.,** bambin, -ine. **2.** goutte *f,* petit verre (de whisky, etc.).

tot², *v.* (**totted**) **1.** *v.tr.* **to t. up,** additionner (une colonne de chiffres); **to t. up expenses,** faire le compte des dépenses. **2.** *v.i.* (*of expenses, etc.*) **to t. up to . . .,** s'élever, se monter, à . . ..

total ['tout(ə)l]. **I.** *a. & s.* **1.** *a.* total, complet, global; **t. amount,** somme totale, globale; **they were in t. ignorance of it,** ils l'ignoraient complètement; **t. failure,** échec complet. **2.** *s.* total *m;* montant *m;* tout *m;* **grand t.,** total global. **II.** *v.tr. & i.* (**totalled**) **1.** totaliser, additionner (les dépenses). **2. to t.** (**up to**) **. . .,** s'élever, se monter, à . . .; **-ally,** *adv.* totalement, entièrement, complètement; **to'tality** [-'tæliti], *s.* totalité *f.*

totalitarian [toutæli'tɛəriən], *a.* totalitaire; **totali'tarianism,** *s.* totalitarisme *m.*

totalizator ['toutəlaizeitər], *s.* (*F:* **tote** [tout]) totalisateur *m* (des paris).

totem ['toutəm], *s.* **t. pole,** totem *m.*

totter ['tɔtər], *v.i.* **1.** (*of pers.*) chanceler; **to t. in,** entrer d'un pas chancelant. **2.** (*of building*) menacer ruine; chanceler, branler; **'tottering,** *a.* chancelant; **t. steps,** pas mal assurés; **t. empire,** empire qui menace ruine, qui croule; **'tottery,** *a.* chancelant.

toucan ['tuːkæn], *s. Orn:* toucan *m.*

touch [tʌtʃ]. **I.** *s.* **1.** attouchement *m;* **I felt a t. on my arm,** je sentis qu'on me touchait le bras. **2.** (le sens du) toucher; **rough to the t.,** rude au toucher; **to know sth. by the t.,** reconnaître qch. au toucher. **3.** (*a*) léger coup; (*b*) touche *f* (de pinceau); **to give the finishing t.,** mettre la dernière main (à qch.); **to add a few touches,** faire quelques retouches *f* (à un tableau). **4.** *Mus:* toucher; *Typew:* frappe *f;* **the pianist's delicate t.,** le toucher délicat du pianiste. **5. t. of garlic,** pointe *f* d'ail; **t. of rouge,** soupçon *m* de rouge; **with a t. of bitterness,** (parler) avec une nuance d'amertume; **t. of fever,** soupçon de fièvre. **6.** contact *m;* **to be in t. with s.o.,** être en contact avec qn; être en rapport avec qn; **to get in t. with the police,** se mettre en communication avec la police; **the personal t.,** les rapports personnels (avec les clients, etc.). **7.** *Fb:* **kick into t.,** envoi *m* en touche; **t. line,** ligne *f* de touche. **II.** *v.* **1.** *v.tr.* (*a*) toucher; effleurer; **to t. sth. with one's finger,** toucher qch. du doigt; **to t. s.o. on the shoulder,** toucher l'épaule à qn; **to t. one's hat,** porter, mettre, la main à son chapeau; *F:* **t. wood!** touche du bois! **don't t. those eggs,** ne touchez pas à ces œufs; **to t. a spring,** faire jouer un ressort; **to t. on a subject,** toucher, effleurer, un sujet; **the law can't t. him,** la loi ne peut rien contre lui; **nobody can t. him in comedy,** personne ne l'approche dans la comédie; **I never t. wine,** jamais je ne bois de vin; (*b*) toucher, émouvoir (qn); **to be touched by s.o.'s kindness,** être touché de la bonté de qn; (c) **flowers touched by the frost,** fleurs atteintes, touchées, par la gelée. **2.** *v.i.* (*of persons, thgs*) se toucher; être, venir, en contact; **'touch and 'go,** *s.* **it was t. and go whether we caught the train,** nous courions grand risque de manquer le train; **'touch 'down,** *v.i. Av:* faire escale; *Rugby Fb:* toucher dans les buts; **touched,** *a. F:* toqué, timbré; **'touchiness,** *s.* susceptibilité *f,* irascibilité *f;* **'touching. 1.** *a.* touchant, émouvant. **2.** *prep.* touchant, concernant; **'touch 'up,** *v.tr.* faire des retouches à (un tableau); badigeonner (un vieux meuble); **to t. up the paintwork,** faire des raccords de peinture; **'touchy,** *a.* susceptible, ombrageux.

tough [tʌf]. **I.** *a.* **1.** dur, résistant; **t. meat,** viande *f* coriace. **2.** (*of pers.*) fort, solide. **3.** (*of pers.*) raide, inflexible; *F:* **he's a t. customer!** il est peu commode! **4.** *F:* (*a*) **t. job,** tâche rude, difficile; (*b*) **that's t.!** c'est dur pour vous. **II.** *s. F:* voyou *m,* bandit *m,* dur *m;* **-ly,** *adv.* **1.** avec ténacité. **2.** vigoureusement. **3.** avec opiniâtreté; **'toughen. 1.** *v.tr.* (*a*) durcir (le verre, etc.); (*b*) endurcir (qn). **2.** *v.i.* (*a*) durcir; (*b*) (*of pers.*) s'endurcir; **'toughness,** *s.* **1.** dureté *f;* résistance *f.* **2.** (*a*) force *f,* solidité *f;* (*b*) résistance à la fatigue. **3.** caractère *m* peu commode (de qn). **4.** difficulté *f* (d'un travail).

tour ['tuər]. **I.** *s.* **1.** tour *m;* voyage *m* circulaire; **package t.,** voyage organisé; **conducted t.,** visite guidée; **walking t.,** excursion *f* à pied. **2. t. of inspection,** tournée *f* de visite; *Th:* **on t.,** en tournée. **II.** *v.tr. & i.* **to t. a country,** faire le tour d'un pays; voyager dans un pays; *Th:* **to t. the provinces,** faire une tournée en province; **touring company,** troupe *f* en tournée; **'tourist,** *s.* touriste *mf;* **t. agency,** bureau *m* de tourisme; **t. centre,** centre *m,* ville *f,* de tourisme; **the t. trade,** le tourisme; **t. class,** classe *f* touriste; (**special**) **t. menu,** menu touristique.

tournament ['tuənəmənt], *s.* **tennis t., bridge t.,** tournoi *m* de tennis, de bridge.

tourniquet ['tuənikei], *s. Med:* tourniquet *m.*

tousle ['tauzl], *v.tr.* ébouriffer (les cheveux).

tout [taut]. **I.** *s.* racoleur *m;* (*for hotels*) rabatteur *m,* pisteur *m.* **II.** *v.i. & tr.* **to t. for customers,** courir après la clientèle; racoler des clients; **to t. a product,** faire l'article d'un produit.

tow[1] [tou]. **I.** *s.* **1. to take a ship, a car, in t.,** prendre un navire, une voiture, en remorque; *F:* **he always has his family in t.,** il trimbale toujours sa famille avec lui. **2.** (*vessel towed*) remorque *f;* **a t. of barges,** une rame de péniches. **3.** *Aut:* **we can give you a t.,** nous pouvons remorquer votre voiture. **II.** *v.tr.* remorquer (un navire, une voiture); touer (un chaland); (*from towpath*) haler (un chaland); **'towboat,** *s.*

remorqueur *m;* toueur *m;* **'towing,** *s.* remorque *f,* remorquage *m;* touage *m;* (*from towpath*) halage *m;* **'towline, 'tow-rope,** *s.* (câble *m* de) remorque *f;* corde *f* de halage; **'towpath,** *s.* chemin *m* de halage.

tow[2], *s.* étoupe (blanche); filasse *f;* **'tow-'headed,** *a.* aux cheveux blond filasse.

towards [tə'wɔ:dz], *prep.* **1.** vers; du côté de. **2.** envers, pour, à l'égard de (qn); **his feelings t. me,** ses sentiments envers, pour, moi. **3.** pour; **to save t. sth.,** économiser pour qch. **4.** vers, sur; **t. noon,** vers midi; **t. the end of the week,** en fin de semaine; **t. the end of his life,** sur la fin de sa vie.

towel ['tauəl], *s.* **1.** serviette *f* (de toilette); essuie-mains *m inv;* **roller t.,** serviette sans fin; **t. horse,** chevalet *m;* **t. rail,** porte-serviettes *m inv.* **2. sanitary t.,** serviette hygiénique; **'towelling,** *s.* **1.** friction *f* avec une serviette. **2.** tissu-éponge *m.*

tower ['tauər]. **I.** *s.* (*a*) tour *f;* (*b*) **church t.,** clocher *m;* **water t.,** château *m* d'eau; (*c*) *Av:* **control t.,** tour de contrôle; (*d*) **he's a t. of strength,** c'est un puissant appui. **II.** *v.i.* **to t. over, above** (sth.), dominer (qch.); **he towers above the others,** il domine les autres par sa taille; **'towering,** *a.* **1.** (*a*) très haut; **a t. height,** une très grande hauteur; (*b*) **t. ambition,** ambition *f* sans borne. **2. in a t. rage,** au paroxysme de la colère.

town [taun], *s.* **1.** ville *f;* **county t.** = chef-lieu *m* (de département). **2.** (*a*) **he works in T.,** il travaille à Londres; (*b*) **to go into t.,** aller, se rendre, à la ville; **to go into t. to shop,** faire ses courses en ville; (*c*) *F:* **to go to t.,** (i) bien s'amuser; (ii) dépenser sans compter, à pleines mains. **3. t. life,** vie urbaine; **t. council, councillor,** conseil, conseiller, municipal; **t. hall,** hôtel *m* de ville; mairie *f;* **t. planning,** urbanisme *m;* **'township,** *s. esp. N.Am:* commune *f;* (*in Canada*) **Eastern Townships,** Cantons de l'Est; **'townsman, -men,** *f.* **-woman, -women,** *s.* **1.** habitant, -ante, de la ville; citadin, -ine. **2.** concitoyen, -enne; **'townspeople,** *s.pl.* **1.** (*also* **'townsfolk**) habitants *m* de la ville; citadins *m.* **2.** concitoyens *m.*

toxic ['tɔksik], *a. Med:* toxique; **toxi'cologist,** *s.* toxicologue *mf,* toxicologiste *mf;* **toxi'cology,** *s.* toxicologie *f;* **'toxin,** *s.* toxine *f.*

toy [tɔi]. **I.** *s.* **1.** jouet *m, F:* joujou *m.* **2. t. trumpet,** trompette *f* d'enfant. **II.** *v.i.* **to t. with sth.,** s'amuser, jouer, avec qch.; **to t. with one's food,** manger du bout des dents; **to t. with an idea,** caresser une idée; **'toyshop,** *s.* magasin *m* de jouets.

trace[1] [treis]. **I.** *s.* **1.** (*usu. pl.*) trace(s) *f* (*pl*) (de qn, d'un animal). **2.** trace, vestige *m;* **there's no**

t. of it, il n'en reste pas trace. II. *v.tr.* 1. tracer
(un plan); esquisser (un projet). 2. faire le tracé
de (qch.); calquer (un dessin). 3. **he has been
traced to Paris,** on a suivi sa piste jusqu'à
Paris; **to t. lost goods,** recouvrer des objets
perdus. 4. **I can't t. any reference to the accident,** je ne trouve aucune mention de l'accident; **he traces his family (back) to the
Crusades,** il fait remonter sa famille aux
croisades; **to t. an event (back) to its source,**
remonter à l'origine d'un événement; **'tracer,**
s. 1. traceur *m* (radio-actif). 2. *Mil:* **t. bullet,**
traçante *f*; **'tracery,** *s.* (**window**) *t.*,
remplissage *m*; **'tracing,** *s.* 1. (*a*) (*drawing*)
tracé *m*; (*b*) (*copying*) calquage *m*; **t. paper,**
papier *m* à calquer. 2. dessin calqué; calque
m.

trace², *s. Harn:* trait *m*; **the horse got tangled in
the traces,** le cheval s'empêtra dans les traits;
(*of pers.*) **to kick over the traces,** (i) s'insurger;
(ii) s'émanciper.

track [træk]. I. *s.* 1. trace(s) *f*(*pl*), piste *f* (de qn,
d'une bête); **to follow in s.o.'s tracks,** suivre,
marcher sur, les traces de qn; **to be on s.o.'s t.,**
être sur la piste de qn; **to keep t. of s.o.,** ne pas
perdre qn de vue; **to throw s.o. off the t.,**
dépister qn; *F:* **to make tracks,** filer, s'éclipser.
2. **mule t.,** chemin *m* muletier. 3. route *f*,
chemin; **to put s.o. on the right t.,** mettre qn sur
la voie; **to be on the wrong t.,** faire fausse
route. 4. *Rac:* piste *f*; **motor-racing t.,**
autodrome *m*; **t. racing,** courses *fpl* sur piste; **t.
suit,** survêtement *m.* 5. *Rail:* voie (ferrée);
single t., voie unique; (*of train*) **to leave the
tracks,** dérailler. 6. chenille *f* (de tracteur). II.
v.tr. suivre (une bête) à la piste; traquer (un
malfaiteur); **'track 'down,** *v.tr.* dépister (le
gibier, un malfaiteur); **tracked,** *a.* (véhicule) à
chenilles, chenillé; **'tracker,** *s.* traqueur *m* (de
gibier); **'trackless,** *a.* sans chemins.

tract¹ [trækt], *s.* étendue *f* (de pays).

tract², *s.* brochure *f* (de piété); tract *m.*

tractable ['træktəbl], *a.* docile; traitable; **trac-
ta'bility,** *s.* docilité *f.*

traction ['trækʃ(ə)n], *s.* traction *f*; **electric t.,
motor t.,** traction électrique; traction par
moteur; **t. engine,** tracteur *m*; *Rail:* **t. wheels,**
roues tractives; **'tractor,** *s.* tracteur *m.*

trade [treid]. I. *s.* 1. état *m*, emploi *m*; commerce
m; métier *m*; **to carry on a t.,** exercer un métier,
un commerce; **he's a carpenter by t.,** il est
charpentier de métier; **everyone to his t.,**
chacun son métier. 2. commerce, négoce *m*,
affaires *fpl*; **foreign t.,** commerce étranger;
Nau: **coastal t.,** cabotage *m*; **it's good for t.,**
cela fait marcher le commerce. 3. **t. name,**
marque déposée; **t. price,** prix marchand. II.
v. 1. *v.i.* (*a*) faire le commerce, le négoce (**in,**
de); (*b*) **to t. on s.o.'s ignorance,** exploiter

l'ignorance de qn. 2. *v.tr.* **to t. sth. for sth.,**
troquer qch. contre qch.; **'trade 'in,** *v.tr.*
donner (qch.) en reprise; **I'm trading in my
old car for a new one,** je vais échanger ma
vieille voiture contre une neuve; **'trademark,**
s. marque *f* de fabrique; **registered t.,** marque
déposée; **'trader,** *s.* négociant, -ante; commerçant, -ante; marchand, -ande;
'tradesman, *pl.* **-men,** *s.* fournisseur *m*;
'trade-'union, *s.* syndicat (ouvrier);
'trade-'unionism, syndicalisme (ouvrier);
'trade-'unionist, *s.* syndiqué, -ée; syndicaliste *mf*; **'tradewind,** *s.* (vent) alizé *m*;
'trading, *s.* commerce *m*, négoce *m*; **t. stamp,**
timbre-prime *m.*

tradition [trə'diʃ(ə)n], *s.* tradition *f*;
tra'ditional, *a.* traditionnel; **-ally,** *adv.*
traditionnellement.

traffic ['træfik]. I. *s.* 1. trafic *m*, négoce *m*, commerce *m* (**in,** de); *Pej:* **drug t.,** trafic des
stupéfiants; **t. in arms,** trafic des armes. 2.
mouvement *m*, circulation *f*; **heavy t.,** circulation intense; **t. jam,** embouteillage *m*, bouchon
m; **t. island,** refuge *m*; **t. accident,** accident de
la circulation; **t. lights,** feux *mpl* de circulation;
Aut: **t. indicator,** clignotant *m.* 3. **rail, road, air,
t.,** trafic ferroviaire, routier, aérien. II. *v.i. Pej:*
to t. in sth., trafiquer de, en, qch.; **'trafficator,**
s. Aut: indicateur *m*, clignotant *m*; **'trafficker,**
s. Pej: trafiquant, -ante (**in,** de, en).

tragedy ['trædʒidi], *s.* tragédie *f*; **'tragic,** *a.*
tragique; **t. actor, actress,** tragédien, -ienne; *F:*
to put on a t. act, jouer la tragédie; **-ally,** *adv.*
tragiquement; **to take things t.,** prendre les
choses au tragique.

trail [treil]. I. *s.* 1. traînée *f* (de fumée). 2. (*a*) piste
f, trace *f*, voie *f* (d'une bête); **to pick up the t.,**
retrouver la piste; (*b*) sentier (battu); piste. II.
v. 1. *v.tr.* (*a*) **to t. sth. (along),** traîner qch. après
soi; (*b*) traquer (une bête). 2. *v.i.* (*a*) traîner; **to
have sth. trailing behind one,** avoir qch. à la
traîne; (*b*) (*of pers.*) **to t. along,** se traîner; (*c*)
(*of plant*) ramper; grimper; **'trailer,** *s.* 1. *Aut:*
remorque *f*; *N.Am:* caravane *f* (de camping).
2. *Cin:* film *m* annonce.

train [trein]. I. *s.* 1. traîne *f*, queue *f* (d'une robe).
2. train *m*, convoi *m* (de wagons); succession *f*,
série *f* (d'événements); **t. of thought,** enchaîne-
ment *m* d'idées. 3. *Rail:* (*a*) train; **main-line t.,**
train de grande ligne; **through t.,** train direct;
slow t., train omnibus; **to travel by t.,** voyager
en train, par le train; **to board the t.,** monter
dans le train; (*b*) rame *f* (du Métro); (*c*) **t. ferry,**
ferry(-boat) *m.* II. *v.* 1. *v.tr.* (*a*) former, instruire (qn); dresser (un animal); exercer
(l'oreille, les yeux); *Sp:* entraîner (qn); *Hort:*
diriger, conduire (une plante); palisser (un arbre
fruitier); (*b*) pointer (un canon); braquer (une
lunette) (**on,** sur). 2. *v.i.* (*a*) s'exercer, se préparer

(for sth., à qch.); (b) Sp: s'entraîner; **trained,** a.
1. (soldat) instruit; (chien) dressé; (œil) exercé;
Sp: (coureur) entraîné. 2. **espalier-t.,** (arbre)
palissé; **trai'nee,** s. élève mf; stagiaire mf;
'**trainer,** s. 1. dresseur m (d'animaux). 2. Sp:
entraîneur m; '**training,** s. 1. (a) éducation f, instruction f; **professional t.,** formation
professionnelle; **to acquire a business t.,** se
former aux affaires; **military t.,** instruction
militaire; Av: **t. of pilots,** formation des pilotes;
(b) Sp: entraînement m; **to go into t.,** s'entraîner; (c) dressage m (d'un animal). 2.
palissage m (d'un arbre).

traipse [treips], v.i. traîner çà et là; se balader.

trait [trei], s. trait m (de caractère).

traitor ['treitər], s. traître m; **to turn t.,** passer à
l'ennemi; se vendre; **to be a t. to (one's country),** trahir (sa patrie); (of woman) t. (or
traitress), traîtresse f.

trajectory [trə'dʒektəri], s. trajectoire f.

tramp [træmp]. I. s. 1. bruit m de pas marqués.
2. marche f; promenade f à pied. 3. (pers.) (a)
clochard m; chemineau m, vagabond m; (b)
N.Am: prostituée f. 4. Nau: t. **(steamer),** cargo
m, tramp m. II. v. 1. v.i. marcher à pas
marqués; marcher lourdement. 2. v.i. & tr. (a)
marcher, voyager à pied; **to t. the country,** parcourir le pays à pied; (b) vagabonder; **to t. the
streets,** battre le pavé.

trample ['træmpl]. 1. v.i. **to t. on s.o., sth.,**
piétiner, écraser, qn, qch.; **to t. on s.o.'s
feelings,** choquer, blesser, la susceptibilité de
qn. 2. v.tr. **to t. sth. under foot,** fouler qch. aux
pieds; **to t. down the grass,** fouler, piétiner,
l'herbe; '**trampling,** s. piétinement m; bruit m
de pas.

trance [trɑːns], s. 1. Med: extase f; **state of t.,**
état m extatique. 2. **(hypnotic) t.,** transe f.

tranquil ['træŋkwil], a. tranquille; serein; calme,
paisible; **-illy,** adv. tranquillement,
paisiblement; avec sérénité; **tran'quillity,** s.
tranquillité f, calme m, sérénité f;
'**tranquillize,** v.tr. tranquilliser, calmer,
apaiser; '**tranquillizer,** s. Med: tranquillisant
m, calmant m.

trans- [træns, trænz], pref. trans-; **tran'sact,**
v.tr. **to t. business with s.o.,** faire des affaires,
traiter une affaire, avec qn; **tran'saction,** s.
1. conduite f (d'une affaire). 2. opération
(commerciale); **cash t.,** opération au comptant; **trans'alpine,** a. transalpin; **transat'lantic,** a. transatlantique; **tran'scend,**
v.tr. 1. dépasser les bornes de (la raison). 2.
surpasser (qn); '**transconti'nental,** a.
transcontinental; **tran'scribe,** v.tr. transcrire;
'**transcript, tran'scription,** s. transcription
f; '**transept,** s. Arch: transept m; '**transfer. I.**
s. 1. (a) transport m, renvoi m (de qch. à un
autre endroit); déplacement m (d'un fonction-

naire); (b) Jur: transfert m (d'un droit); Fin:
virement m (de fonds). 2. Jur: **(deed of) t.,** acte
m de cession. 3. Needlew: etc: décalque m. II.
v.tr. **(transferred)** 1. transférer; déplacer (un
fonctionnaire); Rail: transborder (des
voyageurs); Jur: céder (une propriété); Fin:
virer (une somme). 2. calquer; **trans'ferable,**
a. transmissible; Jur: (droit) cessible; (of
ticket, etc.) **not t.,** strictement personnel;
trans'figure, v.tr. transfigurer; **trans'form,**
v.tr. 1. transformer; métamorphoser. 2. Ch:
etc: convertir (into, en); El: transformer (le
courant); **transfor'mation,** s. 1. transformation f; métamorphose f. 2. conversion f;
trans'former, s. El: transformateur m (de
tension); **trans'fuse,** v.tr. Med: transfuser (du
sang); **trans'fusion,** s. Med: **blood t.,** transfusion f de sang; **tran'ship,** v.tr. transborder (du
fret, des voyageurs); '**transient,** a. transitoire;
(bonheur) passager, éphémère; (plaisir) de
passage; s.pl. N.Am: (in hotel) **transients,**
clientèle f de passage; **tran'sistor,** s. Rad:
transistor m; **tran'sistorize,** v.tr. tran-
sistoriser; '**transit,** s. 1. transit m; **passengers,
goods, in t.,** passagers, marchandises, en transit. 2. transport m (de marchandises); **damage
in t.,** avarie(s) f(pl) en cours de route; **loss in t.,**
freinte f de route; **tran'sition,** s. 1. transition
f; passage m (du jour à la nuit); **t. period,**
période f de transition. 2. Mus: modulation f;
'**transitive,** a. **t. verb,** verbe m transitif; '**transitory,** a. transitoire; fugitif; **trans'late,** v.tr.
traduire; **it can't really be translated,** ce, il,
n'est guère traduisable; **trans'lation,** s.
traduction f; **trans'lator,** s. traducteur m,
-trice; **translite'ration,** s. translit(t)ération f;
trans'lucence, s. translucidité f; **trans'lu-
cent,** a. translucide; **trans'missible,** a.
transmissible; **trans'mission,** s. transmission
f; El: **power t.,** transport m d'énergie; **high-
voltage power t.,** transport de force; Mec.E:
the t. (gear), la transmission; **trans'mit,** v.tr.
(transmitted) transmettre; **trans'mitter,** s.
P.T.T: transmetteur m; Rad: émetteur m,
poste m d'émission; '**transom,** s. Const: (a)
traverse f, linteau m (de fenêtre, de porte); (b)
meneau horizontal; **trans'parency,** s. 1.
transparence f (du verre); limpidité f (de l'eau).
2. Phot: diapositive f; **trans'parent,** a. 1.
transparent; (eau) limpide. 2. évident, clair; **t.
malice,** malices cousues de fil blanc; **-ly,** adv.
d'une manière transparente; clairement;
transpi'ration, s. transpiration f;
tran'spire, v.i. (a) Bot: transpirer; (b) (of
news) transpirer, s'ébruiter; (c) **his account of
what transpired,** sa version de ce qui s'est
passé; **transplant. I.** [træns'plɑːnt], v.tr. (a)
transplanter, repiquer (des plants); (b)
transplanter (une population); (c) Med: greffer

(un rein). **II.** ['trænsplɑːnt], *s. Med:* **kidney t.**, greffe ƒ du rein; **transport. I.** ['trænspɔːt], *s.* **1.** transport *m* (de marchandises); **t. café**, restaurant *m* de routiers. **2. t.(-ship)**, transport; **t. aircraft**, avion *m* de transport. **3.** transport (de joie); **to be in transports**, être ravi de joie. **II.** [træns'pɔːt], *v.tr.* **1.** transporter. **2. to be transported with joy**, être transporté de joie; être ravi; **transpor'tation**, *s.* transport *m*; **trans'porter**, *s.* **t. bridge**, (pont) transbordeur *m*; *Mil:* **tank t.**, porte-chars *m inv*; **trans'pose**, *v.tr.* transposer; **trans'posing, transpo'sition**, *s.* transposition ƒ; **'transubstanti'ation**, *s. Ecc:* transsubstantiation ƒ; **trans'versal**, *a.* transversal; **'transverse**, *a.* transversal; en travers; -**ly**, *adv.* transversalement; en travers.

trap [træp]. **I.** *s.* **1.** (*a*) piège *m*; **to set a t.**, dresser, tendre, un piège; **to catch in a t.**, prendre (une bête) au piège; (*b*) piège, ruse ƒ; *Aut:* **police t.**, zone ƒ de contrôle de vitesse. **2. t. (door)**, trappe ƒ. **II.** *v.tr.* **(trapped)** (*a*) prendre (une bête) au piège, piéger; **trapped by the flames**, cerné par les flammes; (*b*) tendre des pièges dans (un bois); (*c*) *v.i.* trapper; **'trapper**, *s.* trappeur *m*; **'trap-shooting**, *s. Sp:* ball-trap *m*.

trapeze [trə'piːz], *s.* trapèze *m*; **t. artist**, trapéziste *mf.*

trappist ['træpist], *s.m. Ecc:* trappiste; **t. monastery**, trappe ƒ.

trapse [treips], *v.i.* traîner çà et là; se balader.

trash [træʃ], *s.* (*a*) chose(s) ƒ(*pl*) sans valeur; camelote ƒ; (*b*) littérature ƒ de camelote; (*c*) **to talk a lot of t.**, dire des sottises; **'trashy**, *a.* sans valeur; (littérature) de camelote.

travel ['træv(ə)l]. **I.** *s.* (*a*) voyages *mpl*; **to be fond of t.**, aimer à voyager; **t. agency**, agence ƒ de voyage, bureau *m* de tourisme; (*b*) **is he still on his travels?** est-il toujours en voyage? **II.** *v.i.* **(travelled) 1.** (*a*) voyager; faire des voyages; **he is travelling**, il est en voyage; **to t. through (a region)**, parcourir (une région); **distance travelled**, distance parcourue; (*b*) aller, marcher; (*of news*) circuler. **2.** être représentant (de commerce); **'traveller**, *s.* **1.** voyageur, -euse; **fellow-t.**, compagnon de voyage, de route; *Pol:* communisant, -ante; **t.'s cheque**, chèque *m* de voyage. **2. (commercial) t.**, représentant *m* (de commerce); **'travelling. 1.** *a.* **t. crane**, grue ƒ mobile. **2.** *s.* voyages *mpl*; **t. bag**, sac *m* de voyage; **t. expenses**, frais *mpl* de voyage, de route, de déplacement.

traverse ['trævəs, trə'vəːs], *v.tr.* traverser, passer à travers (une région); passer (la mer).

travesty ['trævisti]. **I.** *s.* parodie ƒ; travestissement *m*. **II.** *v.tr.* parodier, travestir.

trawl [trɔːl]. **I.** *s.* **t. (net)**, chalut *m*, traille ƒ. **II.** *v.* **1.** *v.i.* pêcher au chalut; chaluter. **2.** *v.tr.* pren-

dre (le poisson) au chalut; **'trawler**, *s.* chalutier *m*; **'trawling**, *s.* pêche ƒ au chalut, chalutage *m*.

tray [trei], *s.* (*a*) plateau *m*; **t. cloth**, dessus *m* de plateau; (*b*) corbeille ƒ à correspondance.

treachery ['tretʃəri], *s.* trahison ƒ, perfidie ƒ; **'treacherous**, *a.* (*of pers. thg*) traître; infidèle; (action) perfide; -**ly**, *adv.* (agir) en traître, perfidement.

treacle ['triːkl], *s.* mélasse ƒ.

tread [tred]. **I.** *s.* **1.** (*a*) pas *m*; **to walk with measured t.**, marcher à pas comptés; (*b*) bruit *m* de pas. **2.** (*a*) **t. of a stair**, giron *m* d'une marche; (*b*) *Aut:* bande ƒ de roulement (d'un pneu); **non-skid t.**, roulement antidérapant. **II.** *v.* **(trod** [trɔd]; **trodden** ['trɔdn]) **1.** *v.i.* marcher; poser les pieds; **to t. softly**, marcher doucement, à pas feutrés; **to t. on sth.**, marcher, mettre le pied, sur qch. **2.** *v.tr.* (*a*) **to t. sth. under foot**, écraser qch. du pied; fouler qch. aux pieds; opprimer (un peuple); (*b*) **to t. water**, nager debout; **to t. pedale** ƒ; **to t. sewing machine**, machine ƒ à coudre à pédale.

treason ['triːz(ə)n], *s. Jur:* trahison ƒ; **high t.**, haute trahison; lèse-majesté ƒ; **'treasonable**, *a.* (*a*) de trahison; (*b*) traître, perfide; -**ably**, *adv.* traîtreusement.

treasure ['treʒər]. **I.** *s.* trésor *m*; **t. house**, trésor; **t. hunt**, chasse ƒ au(x) trésor(s); *Jur:* **t. trove**, trésor (découvert par hasard). **II.** *v.tr.* **1.** priser, tenir beaucoup à (qch.). **2.** garder (qch.) soigneusement; **'treasurer**, *s.* trésorier, -ière; **'treasury**, *s.* trésor (public); trésorerie ƒ; *Adm:* **the T.** = le Ministère des Finances; **t. bill**, bon *m* du Trésor.

treat [triːt]. **I.** *s.* **1.** (*a*) régal *m*; festin *m*; fête ƒ; (*b*) *F:* **to stand t. (all round)**, payer une tournée. **2.** plaisir *m*; **to give oneself a t.**, faire un petit extra; **a t. in store**, un plaisir à venir. **II.** *v.* **1.** *v.i.* (*a*) **to t. with s.o.**, traiter, négocier, avec qn; (*b*) **to t. of a subject**, traiter d'un sujet. **2.** *v.tr.* (*a*) traiter; **to t. s.o. like a dog**, traiter qn comme un chien; **to t. sth. as a joke**, considérer qch. comme une plaisanterie; (*b*) régaler (qn); payer à boire à (qn); **to t. oneself to sth.**, s'offrir, se payer, qch.; (*c*) *Med:* traiter (un malade); (*d*) traiter (un thème); **treatise** ['triːtiz], *s.* traité *m* **(on**, de); **'treatment**, *s.* **1.** (*a*) traitement *m* (de qn); **his t. of his friends**, sa manière d'agir envers ses amis; (*b*) traitement (d'un sujet). **2.** *Med:* **patient undergoing t.**, malade en traitement; **(course of) t.**, cure ƒ; **'treaty**, *s.* **1.** traité *m* (de paix); convention ƒ; **t. obligations**, obligations conventionnelles. **2.** accord *m*, contrat *m*; **to sell by private t.**, vendre (qch.) à l'amiable.

treble ['trebl]. **I.** *a.* **1.** triple. **2.** *Mus:* **t. voice**, (voix ƒ de) soprano *m*; **t. clef**, clef ƒ de sol. **II.** *adv.* trois fois autant. **III.** *s.* **1.** triple *m*. **2.** *Mus:*

(*pers., voice*) soprano *m*; **to sing the t.,** chanter le dessus. **IV.** *v.tr. & i.* (se) tripler; **'trebly,** *adv.* triplement; trois fois autant.

tree [tri:], *s.* arbre *m*; **apple-t.,** pommier *m*; **to climb a t.,** grimper sur, monter à, un arbre; **to be at the top of the t.,** être au haut de l'échelle; **to get to the top of the t.,** arriver; **'treeless,** *a.* dépourvu d'arbres; sans arbres; **'treetop,** *s.* cime *f* (d'un arbre).

trefoil ['tri:fɔil], *s.* trèfle *m*.

trek [trek]. **I.** *s.* voyage (long et difficile); **it's quite a t.,** c'est bien loin; **day's t.,** étape *f*. **II.** *v.i.* (**trekked**) faire un voyage long et difficile.

trellis ['trelis], *s.* **t.** (**work**), treillis *m*, treillage *m*.

tremble ['trembl]. **I.** *s.* frisson *m*; (*in voice*) tremblotement *m*; **F:** **to be all of a t.,** être tout tremblant, avoir la tremblote. **II.** *v.i.* (*a*) trembler, vibrer; (*b*) trembler, frissonner; **'trembling.** **1.** *a.* tremblant, tremblotant; **t. all over,** tout tremblant. **2.** *s.* tremblement *m*; tremblotement *m*; **in fear and t.,** tout tremblant; **tremolo,** *pl.* -os ['tremǝlou, -ouz], *s. Mus:* trémolo *m*; **'tremor,** *s.* **1.** tremblement *m*, frémissement *m*. **2.** tremblement (de terre); **'tremulous,** *a.* tremblotant, frémissant; **t. voice,** voix chevrotante; **-ly,** *adv.* en tremblant; **'tremulousness,** *s.* chevrotement *m* (de la voix); tremblement *m*.

tremendous [tri'mendǝs], *a.* immense, énorme; **a t. crowd,** un monde fou; **t. success,** succès fou; **-ly,** *adv.* énormément; démesurément; formidablement.

tremor ['tremǝr], *s.* tremblement *m*.

trench [tren(t)ʃ]. **I.** *s.* tranchée *f*, fossé *m*. **II.** *v.tr.* creuser un fossé, une tranchée, dans (le sol); **'trenchant,** *a.* (ton) tranchant, incisif; (réponse) caustique.

trend [trend], *s.* direction *f*; tendance *f* (de l'opinion, de la mode); **'trendy,** *a.* à la page; dans le vent; (personne) qui suit la mode.

trepidation [trepi'deiʃ(ǝ)n], *s.* trépidation *f*.

trespass ['trespǝs], *v.i.* s'introduire sans autorisation sur la propriété de qn; **'trespasser,** *s.* intrus, -use; **trespassers will be prosecuted,** défense d'entrer sous peine d'amende.

trestle ['tresl], *s.* tréteau *m*, chevalet *m*; **t. table,** table *f* à tréteaux.

trial ['traiǝl], *s.* **1.** *Jur:* (*a*) jugement *m*; **to stand one's t.,** passer en jugement; **t. by jury,** jugement par jury; (*b*) procès *m*; **famous trials,** causes *f* célèbres. **2.** essai *m*; (*a*) épreuve *f*; *Sp:* **t. game,** match *m* de sélection; (*b*) **to give sth. a t.,** faire l'essai de qch.; **on t.,** à l'essai; *Com:* **t. order,** commande d'essai; *Aut:* **t. run,** course d'essai; (*c*) **sheep-dog trials,** concours *m* de chiens de berger. **3.** épreuve douloureuse; **he's a great t. to his parents,** il fait le martyre de ses parents.

triangle ['traiæŋgl], *s.* triangle *m*; **tri'angular,** *a.* triangulaire; en triangle.

tribe [traib], *s.* tribu *f*; **'tribal,** *a.* de tribu; (système) tribal; **'tribesman,** *pl.* -men, *s.* membre *m* de la tribu.

tribunal [tr(a)i'bju:n(ǝ)l], *s.* tribunal *m*; cour *f* de justice; la cour.

tribute ['tribju:t], *s.* **1.** tribut *m*; **to pay t.,** payer tribut (**to,** à). **2.** tribut, hommage *m*; **to pay t. to s.o.,** rendre hommage à qn; **floral tributes,** (i) bouquets *m* de fleurs (offerts à une actrice); (ii) gerbes *f* et couronnes *f* (à un enterrement); **'tributary.** **1.** *a.* tributaire. **2.** *s.* affluent *m* (d'un fleuve).

trice [trais], *s.* **in a t.,** en un clin d'œil, en moins de rien.

trick [trik]. **I.** *s.* **1.** (*a*) tour *m*, ruse *f*; (*dishonest*) supercherie *f*; **to play a t. on s.o.,** jouer un tour à qn; (*b*) truc *m*; **the tricks of the trade,** les trucs, les astuces, du métier; **he knows a t. or two, all the tricks,** il est roublard; **to know the t. of it,** avoir le truc, le chic; **that'll do the t.,** ça fera l'affaire. **2.** farce *f*, tour; **to play a t. on s.o.,** faire une farce à qn; **you've been up to your old tricks,** vous avez encore fait des vôtres. **3.** tour d'adresse; **card t.,** tour de cartes; **conjuring t.,** tour de passe-passe; *F:* **the whole bag of tricks,** toute la boutique; tout le bataclan; *F:* **to do the t.,** réussir le coup. **4.** *Cards:* levée *f*; **the odd t.,** le trick, le tri; **to take a t.,** faire une levée. **II.** *v.tr.* attraper, duper (qn); *Fb:* mystifier (un adversaire); **I've been tricked out of (sth.),** je suis refait de (qch.); **to t. s.o. out of sth.,** escroquer qch. à qn; **'trickery,** *s.* fourberie *f*, tricherie *f*; **piece of t.,** fraude *f*, supercherie *f*; **'trickiness,** *s.* **1.** fourberie *f*. **2.** complication *f*, délicatesse *f* (d'un mécanisme); **'trickster,** *s.* fourbe *m*, escroc *m*; **'tricky,** *a.* **1.** rusé, astucieux, fin. **2.** (mécanisme) d'un maniement délicat; compliqué; **a t. situation,** une situation délicate.

trickle ['trikl]. **I.** *s.* filet *m* (d'eau); *El:* **t. charger,** chargeur *m* à régime lent. **II.** *v.i.* couler (goutte à goutte); **'trickling,** *s.* dégouttement *m*; écoulement *m* goutte à goutte.

tricolour ['trikǝlǝr], *s.* **the T.,** le drapeau tricolore (français).

tricycle ['traisikl], *s.* tricycle *m*.

trident ['traidǝnt], *s.* trident *m*.

tried [traid], *a.* (**well**) **t.,** éprouvé.

trier ['traiǝr], *s. F:* **he's a t.,** il fait toujours de son mieux; il ne se décourage jamais.

trifle ['traifl]. **I.** *s.* **1.** (*a*) bagatelle *f*, vétille *f*; (*b*) **a t.,** un tout petit peu; un soupçon; **he's a t. over forty,** il a un peu plus de quarante ans. **2.** *Cu:* = diplomate *m*. **II.** *v.i.* (*a*) jouer, badiner (**with,** avec); **to t. with s.o.,** se jouer de qn; **to t. with one's health,** jouer avec sa santé; (*b*) vétiller; s'occuper à des riens; **'trifler,** *s.* personne *f* frivole; **'trifling. 1.** *a.* insignifiant; peu important; **t. incidents,** menus incidents; **of t. value,** d'une valeur minime. **2.** *s.* (a) légèreté *f* d'esprit; manque *m* de sérieux; badinage *m*; (b) futilités *fpl.*

trigger ['trigər]. **I.** *s.* (a) poussoir *m* à ressort; (b) (*of firearm*) détente *f*; gâchette *f*; *F:* **to be t.- happy,** avoir la gâchette facile. **II.** *v.tr.* **to t.** (**off**), déclencher (qch.).

trigonometry [trigə'nɔmitri], *s.* trigonométrie *f.*

trill [tril]. **I.** *s.* (a) *Mus:* trille *m*; (b) **trills of laughter,** rires perlés; (c) consonne roulée. **II.** *v.* **1.** *v.i. Mus:* faire des trilles. **2.** *v.tr.* (a) *Mus:* triller (une note); (b) rouler (les r).

trillion ['triliən], *s.* (i) trillion *m* (10^{18}); (ii) *U.S:* billion *m* (10^{12}).

trilogy ['trilədʒi], *s.* trilogie *f.*

trim [trim]. **I.** *s.* **1.** bon ordre; **everything was in perfect t.,** tout était en parfait état; (*of pers.*) **to be in good t.,** être gaillard; *Sp:* être en forme. **2.** *Nau:* assiette *f,* arrimage *m*; *Av:* équilibrage *m*; (*of ship*) **to be in good t.,** avoir une bonne assiette. **3.** coupe *f* (de cheveux). **II.** *a.* soigné; en bon état; **a t. figure,** une tournure élégante. **III.** *v.tr.* (**trimmed**) **1.** tailler (une haie); dresser (une planche); rafraîchir (la barbe); couper (les cheveux); **to t. one's nails,** se faire les ongles. **2.** *Cl:* orner, parer (**with,** de); **trimmed with lace,** garni de dentelles; **'trimming,** *s.* **1.** taille *f* (d'une haie); dressage *m* (du bois). **2.** *Cl:* (a) garnissage *m*; (b) garniture *f,* ornement *m.* **3.** *Cu: F:* **with (the usual) trimmings,** (plat) garni.

Trinidad ['trinidæd]. *Pr.n. Geog:* (île *f* de) la Trinité.

Trinity ['triniti], *s.* la (sainte) Trinité; **T. Sunday,** (fête *f* de) la Trinité.

trinket ['triŋkit], *s.* (a) petit objet de parure; breloque *f*; (b) bibelot *m.*

trio, *pl.* -**os** ['tri:ou, -ouz], *s.* trio *m.*

triode ['traioud], *s. El:* (lampe *f*) triode (*f*).

trip [trip]. **I.** *s.* excursion *f*; voyage *m* d'agrément; *Aut:* **t. meter, recorder,** compteur *m* de trajet. **II.** *v.* (**tripped**) **1.** *v.i.* (a) **to t.** (**along**), aller d'un pas léger; (b) trébucher; faire un faux pas; (c) se tromper; commettre une faute. **2.** *v.tr.* **to t. s.o.** (**up**), (i) donner un croc-en-jambe à qn; (*of thg*) faire trébucher qn; (ii) prendre qn en défaut; **'tripper,** *s.* excursionniste *mf.*

tripe [traip], *s.* (a) *Cu:* tripe(s) *f*(*pl*); (b) *F:* fatras *m,* bêtises *fpl*; **to publish (a load of) t.,** publier des ouvrages sans valeur; **this is t.!** c'est un navet!

triple ['tripl]. **I.** *a.* triple; *Mus:* **t. time,** mesure *f* ternaire, à trois temps. **II.** *v.tr. & i.* (se) tripler; **'triplets,** *s.pl.* triplés, -ées; **'triplicate. I.** *s.* triple *m*; triplicata *m*; **in t.,** en triple exemplaire, en triple expédition. **II.** *v.tr.* rédiger (un document) en triple expédition; **'triply,** *adv.*

triplement.

tripod ['traipɔd], *s.* trépied *m.*

triptych ['triptik], *s. Art:* triptyque *m.*

trite [trait], *a.* banal; **t. subject,** sujet usé, rebattu; **-ly,** *adv.* banalement; **'triteness,** *s.* banalité *f.*

triumph ['traiəmf]. **I.** *s.* (a) triomphe *m,* succès *m*; (b) air *m* de triomphe; jubilation *f.* **II.** *v.i.* triompher; remporter un succès éclatant; **to t. over s.o.,** triompher de qn; l'emporter sur qn; **tri'umphal** [-'ʌmf(ə)l], *a.* triomphal; **t. arch,** arc *m* de triomphe; **tri'umphant,** *a.* triomphant; **-ly,** *adv.* triomphalement; d'un air, d'un ton, de triomphe.

trivial ['triviəl], *a.* insignifiant; sans importance; (incident) futile; **t. loss,** perte légère; **triviality,** *s.* (a) insignifiance *f*; (b) banalité *f* (d'une observation); (c) **to talk polite trivialities,** parler pour ne rien dire; dire des futilités *f.*

trolley ['trɔli], *s.* (a) chariot *m*; (*2-wheeled*) diable *m*; *Rail:* **luggage t.,** chariot à bagages; (b) **dinner t.,** table desserte, table roulante.

trombone [trɔm'boun], *s. Mus:* trombone *m.*

troop [tru:p]. **I.** *s.* **1.** troupe *f,* bande *f* (de personnes); **in troops,** par bandes. **2.** *Mil:* (a) *pl.* **troops,** troupes; **t. ship,** transport *m* (de troupes); **t. train,** train *m* militaire; (b) escadron *m* (de cavalerie). **3.** *Scouting:* troupe. **II.** *v.i.* (a) **to t. together, to t. up,** s'assembler, s'attrouper; (b) **to t. in, out, off,** entrer, sortir, partir, en troupe, en bande; **'trooper,** *s. Mil:* cavalier *m*; **'trooping,** *s.* **1. t.** (**together**), attroupement *m,* assemblement *m.* **2.** *Mil:* **t. the colour** = présentation *f* du drapeau.

trophy ['troufi], *s.* trophée *m.*

tropic ['trɔpik], *s. Geog:* (a) tropique *m*; **the T. of Capricorn,** le Tropique du Capricorne; (b) **the tropics,** les tropiques; **in the tropics,** sous les tropiques; **'tropical,** *a.* (climat) tropical; des tropiques; **'tropicalize,** *v.tr.* tropicaliser.

trot [trɔt]. **I.** *s.* trot *m*; **to go at a t.,** aller au trot; **to break into a t.,** prendre le trot; *F:* **to keep s.o. on the t.,** faire trotter qn. **II.** *v.i.* (**trotted**) (*of horse*) trotter, aller au trot; *F:* **she's always trotting about,** elle est toujours à trotter; **'trot out,** *v.tr. F:* exhiber, étaler, faire étalage de (son savoir); déterrer (de vieux griefs); **'trotter,** *s.* **1.** (*horse*) trotteur, -euse. **2.** *Cu:* **sheep's, pigs', trotters,** pieds *m* de mouton, de cochon; **'trotting,** *s.* **t. race,** course attelée.

trouble ['trʌbl]. **I.** *s.* **1.** peine *f,* chagrin *m*; malheur *m*; **to be in t.,** être dans la peine; avoir du chagrin; **his troubles are over,** il est au bout de ses peines. **2.** ennui *m,* difficulté *f*; **money troubles,** soucis *m* d'argent; **the t. is that . . .,** l'ennui, la difficulté, c'est que . . .; **you'll have t. with him,** il vous donnera du fil à retordre; **to get into t.,** s'attirer une mauvaise affaire; **to get s.o. out of t.,** tirer qn d'affaire; **to be in t.,** avoir des ennuis (avec la police, etc.); **he's asking for t.**, il se prépare des ennuis; **to make t.**, semer la discorde; **there's going to be t.**, il y aura du grabuge. **3.** peine; **to take the t.** to do sth., to go to the **t.** of doing sth., prendre, se donner, la peine de faire qch.; **it's not worth the t.**, ce n'est pas la peine; **to give s.o. t.**, déranger qn; **to give oneself a lot of t.**, se donner beaucoup de mal, de peine; **he thinks nothing too much t.**, rien ne lui coûte; **it's no t.!** ce n'est rien! **4.** (a) Med: dérangement m, troubles m; **eye t.**, troubles de vision; **to have heart t.**, souffrir du cœur; (b) Aut: **engine t.**, panne f du moteur; (c) Ind: **labour troubles**, conflits ouvriers. **II.** v. **1.** v.tr. (a) affliger, tourmenter, chagriner (qn); inquiéter, préoccuper (qn); **to be troubled about s.o.**, se tourmenter au sujet de qn; **that doesn't t. him much**, cela ne le préoccupe guère; ça lui donne fort peu de soucis; (b) (of disease) affliger; **my arm troubles me**, mon bras me fait souffrir; (c) déranger, incommoder, gêner (qn); **I'm sorry to t. you**, excusez-moi de vous déranger; **I won't t. you with the details**, je vous fais grâce de tous les détails; **to t. oneself about sth.**, se mettre en peine de qch.; **to t. oneself to do sth.**, se donner la peine de faire qch. **2.** v.i. (a) s'inquiéter (**about**, de, au sujet de); **don't t. about it**, ne vous inquiétez pas de cela; que cela ne vous inquiète pas; **without troubling about the consequences**, sans s'inquiéter des conséquences; (b) se déranger; se mettre en peine; **don't t. to write**, ne vous donnez pas la peine d'écrire; **don't t. to change your dress**, ce n'est pas la peine de changer de robe; **'troubled**, a. **1.** (of liquid) trouble; **to fish in t. waters**, pêcher en eau trouble. **2.** (a) (sommeil) inquiet, agité; (b) **t. period** (of history), époque f de troubles; **'troublemaker**, s. foment(at)eur, -trice, de troubles; factieux, -ieuse; **'troubleshooter**, s. dépanneur m; **'troublesome**, a. **1.** ennuyeux, gênant; **t. child**, enfant fatigant, énervant; **t. asthma**, asthme pénible. **2.** (tâche) difficile, pénible.

trough [trɔf], s. **1.** auge f; Husb: **drinking t.**, abreuvoir m; **feeding t.**, auge, mangeoire f. **2.** **t. of the wave**, creux m de la lame. **3.** Meteor: **t. of low pressure**, zone f de dépression.

trounce [trauns], v.tr. Sp: écraser (qn); battre (qn) à plate(s) couture(s); **'trouncing**, s. Sp: **to give s.o. a t.**, battre qn à plate(s) couture(s).

troupe [truːp], s. troupe f (de comédiens, etc.).

trousers ['trauzəz], s.pl. (**pair of**) t., pantalon m.

trousseau, pl. **-s** ['truːsou, -z], s. trousseau m.

trout [traut], s.inv. Ich: truite f; **river full of t.**, rivière pleine de truites; **salmon t.**, truite saumonée; **t. fishing**, pêche f à la truite; **t. stream**, ruisseau à truites.

trowel ['trau(ə)l], s. **1.** truelle f (à mortier); F: **to lay it on with a t.**, (i) flatter qn grossièrement; (ii) exagérer. **2.** Hort: déplantoir m.

truant ['truːənt], a. & s. (élève) absent de l'école sans permission; **to play t.**, faire l'école buissonnière; **'truancy**, s. absence f (de l'école) sans permission.

truce [truːs], s. trêve f.

truck¹ [trʌk], s. **1.** **I have no t. with him**, (i) je n'ai pas affaire à lui; (ii) je n'ai rien à faire avec lui. **2.** N.Am: produits m maraîchers; **t. farmer**, maraîcher m; **t. farming**, culture maraîchère.

truck², s. (a) Aut: camion m; **delivery t.**, camionnette f; (b) **luggage t.**, chariot m à bagages; (2-wheeled) diable m; (c) Rail: wagon m à marchandises (ouvert); **'truckdriver**, s. camionneur m; **'trucking**, s. N.Am: camionnage m.

truculence ['trʌkjuləns], s. férocité f; truculence f; **'truculent**, a. féroce; brutal; truculent; **-ly**, adv. avec truculence.

trudge [trʌdʒ]. **I.** s. marche f pénible. **II.** v.i. marcher lourdement, péniblement.

true [truː]. **I.** a. **1.** vrai; exact; **that's t.!** c'est juste! c'est bien vrai! **to come t.**, se réaliser; se vérifier. **2.** véritable; vrai; réel, authentique; **a t. friend**, un véritable ami. **3.** Mec.E: etc: juste, droit; **to make a piece t.**, ajuster une pièce. **4.** fidèle, loyal (**to**, à); **to be t. to one's promise**, rester fidèle à une promesse. **II.** adv. (a) **to sing t.**, chanter juste; (of wheel) **to run t.**, tourner rond; (b) **to breed t.**, se reproduire suivant un type invariable. **III.** s. **out of t.**, hors d'aplomb; (of cylinder) ovalisé; **to run out of t.**, tourner à faux; ne pas tourner rond. **IV.** v.tr. (**up**), ajuster (les pièces d'une machine); dresser (une surface); dégauchir (une planche); **'truly**, adv. **1.** (a) vraiment, véritablement; **I am t. grateful**, je vous suis sincèrement reconnaissant; (b) Corr: **yours t.**, veuillez agréer l'expression de mes sentiments distingués. **2.** en vérité; F: **really and t.?** vrai de vrai? **3.** (servir qn) fidèlement, loyalement. **4.** avec vérité; justement.

truffle ['trʌfl], s. truffe f.

truism ['truːizm], s. truisme m.

trump [trʌmp]. **I.** s. Cards: atout m; **to play trumps**, jouer atout; F: **he always turns up trumps**, (i) il a toujours la chance; tout lui réussit; (ii) il est toujours là pour donner un coup de main; **to play one's t. card**, jouer son atout. **II.** v.tr. **1.** Cards: couper (une carte); v.i. jouer atout. **2.** **to t. up an excuse**, inventer une excuse; **to t. up an accusation**, forger une accusation (contre qn).

trumpet ['trʌmpit]. **I.** s. (a) trompette f; **flourish of trumpets**, fanfare f de trompettes; (b) (pers.) (i) Mil: (also **trumpeter**) trompette f; (ii) (in orchestra) **t. (player)**, trompettiste mf. **II.** v.i. (a) sonner de la trompette; (b) (of elephant) barrir; **'trumpeting,** s. (a) sonnerie f de trompette; (b) (of elephant) barrit m, barrissement m.

truncheon ['trʌn(t)ʃ(ə)n], s. bâton m (d'agent de police); **rubber t.,** matraque f en caoutchouc.

trundle ['trʌndl], v.tr. pousser (une brouette).

trunk [trʌŋk], s. **1.** (a) tronc m (d'arbre); (b) tronc (du corps); (c) **t. road,** route nationale; (d) Tp: **t. call,** appel interurbain. **2.** malle f, coffre m; **to pack one's t.,** faire sa malle. **3.** trompe f (d'éléphant). **4.** Cl: **bathing trunks,** maillot m de bain.

truss [trʌs]. **I.** s. **1.** botte f (de foin). **2.** ferme f (de comble, de pont); armature f (de poutre). **3.** Med: bandage m herniaire. **II.** v.tr. **1.** botteler (le foin). **2. trussed roof,** comble m sur fermes; **trussed girder,** poutre armée. **3.** Cu: trousser, brider (une volaille); F: ligoter (qn).

trust [trʌst]. **I.** s. **1.** confiance f (in, en); **to take sth. on t.,** ajouter foi à qch. sans examen. **2.** espérance f, espoir m; **to put one's t. in sth.,** mettre ses espérances, son espoir, en qch. **3.** responsabilité f; **position of t.,** poste m de confiance; **breach of t.,** abus m de confiance; Jur: fait m de charge. **4.** Jur: fidéicommis m, fiducie f; **t. deed,** acte m de fidéicommis. **5.** Fin: trust m, syndicat m. **II.** v. **1.** v.tr. (a) se fier à (qn, qch.); mettre sa confiance en (qn); **he's not to be trusted,** on ne peut pas se fier à lui; **to t. s.o. with sth.,** confier qch. à qn; **to t. s.o. to do sth.,** se fier à qn, compter sur qn, pour faire qch.; F: **she won't t. him out of her sight,** elle ne le perd jamais de vue; (b) **to t. sth. to s.o.,** confier qch. à qn, aux soins de qn; (c) Com: F: faire crédit à (qn); (d) espérer; **I t. he will come,** j'espère qu'il viendra. **2.** v.i. (a) se confier (in, en); se fier (in, à); mettre sa confiance (in, en); (b) **to t. to sth.,** mettre ses espérances, son espoir, en qch.; **to t. to luck,** s'en remettre au hasard; **trus'tee,** s. Jur: fidéicommissaire m; mandataire mf; **public t. (in bankruptcy),** syndic m de faillite; **'trustful, 'trusting,** a. plein de confiance; confiant; **-fully, -ingly,** adv. avec confiance; **'trustworthiness,** s. **1.** (of pers.) fidélité f, loyauté f. **2.** crédibilité f, exactitude f (d'un témoignage); **'trustworthy,** a. **1.** (of pers.) (digne) de confiance, digne de foi; honnête, fidèle; **t. witness,** témoin irrécusable. **2.** (renseignement) digne de foi, exact.

truth [tru:θ], s. (a) vérité f; **the t. is, to tell the t.,** I forgot, pour dire la vérité, à dire vrai, j'ai oublié; F: **the honest t.,** la vérité vraie; **there's some t. in what you say,** il y a du vrai dans ce que vous dites; Jur: **the t., the whole t., and nothing but the t.,** la vérité, toute la vérité, rien que la vérité; (b) vérité; chose vraie; **to tell s.o. a few home truths,** dire ses quatre vérités à qn; **'truthful,** a. **1.** (of pers.) véridique. **2.** (témoignage) vrai; (portrait) fidèle; **-fully,**

adv. **1.** véridiquement; sans mentir. **2.** fidèlement; **'truthfulness,** s. véracité f; fidélité f (d'un portrait).

try [trai]. **I.** s. (a) essai m, tentative f; **to have a t. at (doing) sth.,** s'essayer à qch.; essayer de faire qch.; **let's have a t.!** essayons toujours! **at the first t.,** du premier coup; (b) Rugby Fb: essai; **to score, to convert, a t.,** marquer, transformer, un essai. **II.** v. **1.** v.tr. (a) éprouver (qn); mettre (qn, qch.) à l'épreuve; (b) affliger (qn); **sorely tried,** durement éprouvé; **to t. one's eyes,** se fatiguer les yeux; (c) essayer, expérimenter (qch.); faire l'essai de (qch.); **to t. a dish,** goûter, essayer, un mets; (d) Jur: juger (une cause, un accusé); (e) essayer, tenter; **to t. one's hand at sth.,** s'essayer à qch.; (f) **to t. to do, t. and do, sth.,** tenter, tâcher, essayer, de faire qch.; **he tried his hardest to save them,** il a fait tout son possible pour les sauver; **to t. again,** essayer de nouveau. **2.** v.i. **to t. for sth.,** tâcher d'obtenir qch.; **'trying,** a. **1.** difficile, dur, pénible. **2.** vexant; contrariant; **he's very t.,** il est insupportable; **'try 'on,** v.tr. **1.** essayer (un vêtement). **2. to t. it on with s.o.,** chercher à mettre qn dedans; bluffer qn; **'try-on,** s. F: **1.** tentative f de déception; bluff m. **2.** ballon m d'essai; **'try 'out,** v.tr. faire l'essai de (qch.); **'try-out,** s. essai m.

tsetse ['tsetsi], s. Ent: **t. (fly),** (mouche) tsétsé f.

tub [tʌb], s. **1.** baquet m, bac m; **to plant trees in tubs,** encaisser des arbres. **2.** bath **t.,** baignoire f, tub m. **3.** Nau: F: **old t.,** vieux rafiau, rafiot; **'tubby,** a. F: (of pers.) boulot; gros et rond; **'tub-thumper,** s. F: orateur m de carrefour.

tube [tju:b], s. **1.** (a) tube m, tuyau m; (b) tube (de pâte dentifrice, etc.); (c) T.V: **cathode-ray t.,** tube cathodique; (d) (of bicycle) **inner t.,** chambre f à air. **2.** Anat: tube (bronchique, etc.). **3.** F: **the t. =** le métro; **t. station =** station f du métro; **'tubing,** s. (a) coll. tuyautage m, tuyauterie f; (b) tube m, tuyau m; **rubber t.,** tuyau en caoutchouc; **'tubular,** a. tubulaire.

tuber ['tju:bər], s. Bot: tubercule m; **'tubercle,** s. Med: tubercule m; **tu'bercular,** a. Bot: tuberculeux; **tu'berculin,** s. Med: tuberculine f; **t. tested milk =** lait cru certifié; **tuber-cu'losis,** s. Med: tuberculose f; **tu'berculous,** a. Med: tuberculeux; **'tuberous,** a. Bot: tubéreux, tubérisé; **t. root,** racine tubérisée.

tuck [tʌk]. **I.** s. **1.** (petit) pli; rempli m, plissé m; **to make, take up, a t. in (a skirt),** faire un rempli à (une jupe). **2.** Sch: F: mangeaille f. **II.** v.tr. **1.** faire des plis à (une jupe); plisser, froncer (un tissu). **2.** replier, rentrer, serrer, mettre; **to t. a blanket round s.o.,** envelopper qn d'une couverture; **little tucked-away village,** petit village caché; **'tuck 'in.** v.tr. (a) serrer, rentrer; replier (le bord d'une jupe, etc.); **to t. in**

the bedclothes, border le lit; (b) **to t. s.o. in**, border qn (dans son lit). 2. *v.i. F:* manger à belles dents; **t. in!** allez-y! **'tuck-in**, *s. F:* bombance *f*, ripaille *f*; **'tuck'into**, *v.tr. F:* **to t. into a good square meal**, attaquer un repas copieux; **'tuck'up**, *v.tr.* (a) relever, retrousser (sa jupe); (b) border (qn) (dans son lit).

Tuesday ['tjuːzdi], *s.* mardi *m*; **Shrove T.**, (le) mardi gras.

tuft [tʌft], *s.* touffe *f* (d'herbe); houppe *f* (de plumes); mèche *f* (de laine, de cheveux); toupet *m* (de cheveux); **little t. of beard**, barbiche *f*; **'tufted**, *a.* houppé; en houppe, en touffe; *Orn:* huppé, à huppe.

tug [tʌg]. I. *s.* 1. traction (subite); saccade *f*, **to give a good t.**, tirer fort; **t. of war**, (i) *Sp:* lutte *f* de traction (à la corde); (ii) lutte acharnée et prolongée. 2. *Nau:* remorqueur *m*. II. *v.tr. & i.* **(tugged)** tirer avec effort; **to t. sth. along**, traîner qch.; **to t. at sth.**, tirer sur qch.

tuition [tjuː(ː)'iʃ(ə)n], *s.* instruction *f*, enseignement *m*; **private t.**, leçons particulières.

tulip ['tjuːlip], *s. Bot:* tulipe *f*.

tulle [tjuːl], *s. Tex:* tulle *m*.

tumble ['tʌmbl]. I. *s.* culbute *f*, chute *f*, dégringolade *f*. II. *v.* 1. *v.i.* (a) **to t. (down, over)**, tomber (par terre); dégringoler; faire la culbute; **building that is tumbling down**, édifice qui s'écroule, qui tombe en ruine; (b) **to t. about in the water**, s'agiter dans l'eau; (c) **to t. into bed**, se jeter dans son lit; **to t. out**, tomber (de la voiture, par la fenêtre); (d) **to t. to an idea**, comprendre, saisir, une idée. 2. *v.tr.* (a) **to t. sth. down, over**, culbuter, jeter à bas, renverser, qch.; (b) bouleverser, déranger; mettre en désordre; **tumbled heap of sth.**, masse confuse de qch.; **'tumbledown**, *a.* croulant, délabré; **t. old house**, maison qui tombe en ruine; **'tumbler**, *s.* verre *m* (à boire) sans pied; gobelet *m*.

tummy ['tʌmi], *s. F:* estomac *m*, ventre *m*; **he has a t. ache**, il a mal *m* au ventre.

tumour ['tjuːmər], *s. Med:* tumeur *f*.

tumult ['tjuːmʌlt], *s.* tumulte *m*; **tu'multuous**, *a.* tumultueux.

tumulus, *pl.* -li ['tjuːmjuləs, -lai], *s.* tumulus *m*.

tun [tʌn], *s.* tonneau *m*, fût *m*.

tuna ['tjuːnə], *s. Ich:* thon *m*.

tundra ['tʌndrə], *s. Geog:* toundra *f*.

tune [tjuːn]. I. *s.* 1. air *m* (de musique); *F:* **to call the t.**, donner la note; **to change one's t.**, changer de note, de ton. 2. (a) accord *m*; **the piano is in t., out of t.**, le piano est accordé, désaccordé; **to be, sing, play, out of t.**, détonner; **to sing in t., out of t.**, chanter juste, faux. 3. accord, harmonie *f*; **to be in t. with one's surroundings**, être en bon accord avec son milieu. II. *v.* 1. *v.tr.* accorder, mettre d'accord (un instrument). 2. *v.i. Rad:* **to t. in to a**

station, accrocher, capter, un poste. 3. *v.tr. Aut:* **to t. (up) the engine**, caler, régler, le moteur; **'tuneful**, *a.* mélodieux, harmonieux; **-fully**, *adv.* mélodieusement, harmonieusement; **'tuneless**, *a.* discordant, inharmonieux; **'tuner**, *s.* **piano t.**, accordeur *m* de pianos; **'tune'up**, *v.i.* (*of orchestra*) s'accorder; **'tuning**, *s.* 1. *Mus:* accordage *m*, accord *m*; **t. fork**, diapason *m*. 2. *Aut:* **t. (up)**, calage *m*, réglage *m* (du moteur). 3. *Rad:* **t. (in)**, réglage.

tungsten ['tʌŋstən], *s.* tungstène *m*; **t. steel**, acier *m* au tungstène.

tunic ['tjuːnik], *s.* tunique *f*.

Tunisia [tjuːˈnizjə]. *Pr.n. Geog:* la Tunisie.

tunnel ['tʌn(ə)l]. I. *s.* tunnel *m*; **road, rail, t., through a mountain**, percer un tunnel sous une montagne. II. *v.tr. & i.* **(tunnelled) to t. (through) a mountain**, percer un tunnel sous une montagne; **'tunnelling**, *s.* percement *m* d'un tunnel; percement (d'une montagne).

tunny(-fish) ['tʌni(fiʃ)], *s. Ich:* thon *m*.

turban ['təːbən], *s. Cl:* turban *m*.

turbid ['təːbid], *a.* (liquide) trouble, bourbeux; **tur'bidity**, *s.* turbidité *f*.

turbine ['təːbain], *s.* turbine *f*.

turbot ['təːbət], *s. Ich:* turbot *m*.

turbulent ['təːbjulənt], *a.* (a) turbulent, tumultueux; (b) insubordonné; **'turbulence**, *s.* turbulence *f*.

tureen [təˈriːn], *s.* soupière *f*.

turf, *pl.* **turves** [təːf, təːvz]. I. *s.* 1. (a) gazon *m*; (b) motte *f* de gazon. 2. (*in Ireland*) tourbe *f*. 3. *Rac:* **the t.**, le turf; le monde des courses; **t. accountant**, bookmaker *m*. II. *v.tr.* 1. gazonner (un terrain). 2. *F:* **to t. s.o. out**, flanquer qn dehors.

Turkey¹ ['təːki]. *Pr.n. Geog:* la Turquie; **Turk**, *s.* Turc, *f.* Turque; **'Turkish**. 1. *a.* truc; de Turquie; **T. bath**, bain turc; **T. cigarettes**, cigarettes d'Orient; **T. delight**, rahat lo(u)koum *m*. 2. *s. Ling:* le turc.

turkey², *s.* 1. *Orn:* dindon *m*; **hen t.**, dinde *f*; **young t.**, dindonneau *m*. 2. *Cu:* dinde, dindonneau; **'turkeycock**, *s.* dindon *m*.

turmoil ['təːmɔil], *s.* trouble *m*, tumulte *m*, agitation *f*.

turn [təːn]. I. *s.* 1. tour *m*, révolution *f* (d'une roue); **meat done to a t.**, viande cuite à point. 2. (a) changement *m* de direction; *Aut:* virage *m*; **at every t.**, à tout bout de champ; (b) tournure *f* (des affaires); **to take a tragic t.**, tourner au tragique; **to take a t. for the better**, prendre meilleure tournure; (c) renversement *m* (de la marée); **the tide is on the t.**, la mer est en étale, la marée change; **t. of the scale**, trait *m* de balance; (d) *F:* **the sight gave me quite a t.**, ce spectacle m'a donné un (vrai) coup; (e) *F:* **she**

had one of her (bad) **turns yesterday,** elle a eu une de ses crises, une de ses attaques, hier. **3. to take a t. in the garden,** faire un tour dans le jardin. **4.** (*a*) tour (de rôle); **it's your t.,** c'est votre tour; **it's your t.** (**to play**), (c'est) à vous (de jouer); **in t.,** tour à tour; à tour de rôle; **t. and t. about,** chacun son tour; **to play out of one's t.,** jouer avant son tour; **to take turns with s.o.,** relayer qn; **they take it in turns,** ils se relayent; (*b*) *Th:* numéro *m*. **5. to do s.o. a good t.,** rendre (un) service à qn; **to do s.o. a bad t.,** jouer un mauvais tour à qn; desservir qn. **6.** (*a*) **his t. of mind,** sa tournure d'esprit; (*b*) **t. of phrase,** tournure de phrase; (*c*) **car with a good t. of speed,** voiture rapide, qui roule bien. **7.** (*a*) tournant *m*, coude *m* (d'un chemin); **sudden t., sharp t.,** crochet *m*, virage brusque; (*b*) tour (d'une corde). **II.** *v.* **1.** *v.tr.* (*a*) tourner, faire tourner (une roue); **to t. the key in the lock,** donner un tour de clef à la porte; (*b*) **to t.** (**over**) **a page,** tourner une page; **to t. a garment inside out,** retourner un vêtement; **without turning a hair,** sans sourciller, sans broncher; (*c*) **to t. a blow,** détourner un coup; **to t. the conversation,** détourner la conversation; (*d*) (re)tourner (la tête); diriger (les yeux) (**towards,** vers); (*e*) **to t. everyone against one,** se mettre tout le monde à dos; (*f*) **to t. the corner,** tourner le coin; **he has turned forty,** il a passé la quarantaine; **it's turned seven,** il est sept heures passées; (*g*) changer, convertir, transformer (**into,** en); **to t. a field into a golf course,** convertir un champ en terrain de golf; **this weather has turned the milk** (**sour**), ce temps a fait tourner le lait; **success has turned his head,** le succès lui a tourné la tête; (*h*) tourner, façonner au tour (un pied de table); **well-turned sentence,** phrase bien tournée. **2.** *v.i.* (*a*) tourner; **the wheels t.,** les roues tournent; **everything turns on your answer,** tout dépend de votre réponse; **the talk turned on sport,** la conversation roulait sur le sport; (*b*) **to toss and t. in bed,** se tourner et se retourner dans son lit; **to t. upside down,** (i) (*of boat*) chavirer; (ii) (*of car*) capoter, se retourner; (*c*) se tourner, se retourner; *Mil:* **right t.!** à droite, marche! (*d*) tourner, se diriger; s'adresser (à qn); **to t. to the left,** tourner, prendre, à gauche; **the wind is turning,** le vent change; **I don't know which way to t.,** je ne sais de quel côté (me) tourner; **to t. to s.o.,** recourir à qn, avoir recours à qn; (*e*) **the tide is turning,** la marée change; **his luck has turned,** sa chance a tourné; **to t. against s.o.,** se retourner contre qn; **to t. on s.o.,** attaquer qn, s'en prendre à qn; (*f*) se changer, se convertir, se transformer (**into,** en); **it's turning to rain,** le temps se met à la pluie; **everything he touches turns to gold,** tout ce qu'il touche se change en or; **the milk has**

turned (**sour**), le lait a tourné; **the leaves are beginning to t.,** les feuilles commencent à tourner, à jaunir; **to t. socialist,** devenir socialiste; **'turn a'side,** *v.tr.* & *i.* (se) détourner, (s')écarter; **'turn a'way. 1.** *v.tr.* (*a*) détourner (les yeux); (*b*) renvoyer, congédier (qn). **2.** *v.i.* se détourner; **'turn 'back. 1.** (*a*) faire revenir, faire retourner, (qn) sur ses pas; barrer le passage à (qn); (*b*) rabattre (qch.). **2.** *v.i.* s'en retourner; rebrousser chemin; **'turncoat,** *s.* renégat, -ate; apostat, -ate; **'turn 'down,** *v.tr.* **1.** (*a*) rabattre; **to t. down the bed(clothes),** faire la couverture; ouvrir le lit; (*b*) faire un pli, une corne, à (une page). **2.** baisser (le gaz). **3. to t. down a candidate,** refuser un candidat; **to t. down an offer,** repousser une offre; **'turn 'in. 1.** *v.tr.* (*a*) rentrer (les bouts de qch.); replier (le bord d'un vêtement); (*b*) **to t. one's toes in,** tourner les pieds en dedans; (*c*) **to t. in one's equipment,** rendre son équipement. **2.** *v.i. F:* (aller) se coucher; **'turning. 1.** *a.* tournant; qui tourne. **2.** *s.* (*a*) virage *m* (d'une voiture); changement *m* de direction; renversement *m* (de la marée); (*b*) tournant *m* (d'une route); coude *m*; *Aut:* virage; **take the first t. to the right,** prenez la première (rue, route) à droite; **'turning-point,** *s.* point décisif; moment *m* critique; tournant *m* (de la carrière de qn); **'turn 'off. 1.** *v.tr.* (*a*) fermer, couper (l'eau, le gaz); fermer (un robinet); (*b*) *F:* **he turns me off,** il me dégoûte. **2.** *v.i.* (*a*) changer de route; tourner (à droite, à gauche); (*b*) **to t. off the main road,** quitter la grande route; **'turn 'on,** *v.tr.* ouvrir (l'eau, le gaz); allumer (l'électricité, le gaz); **'turn 'out. 1.** *v.tr.* (*a*) mettre (qn) dehors, à la porte; évincer, déloger (un locataire); renverser (le gouvernement); mettre (le bétail) au vert; *Cu:* démouler (une crème); *Mil:* **to t. out the guard,** faire sortir la garde; (*b*) vider (un tiroir); nettoyer, faire (une chambre) à fond; (*c*) produire, fabriquer (des marchandises); (*d*) (*of pers.*) **well turned out,** élégant; (*e*) **to t. out the light,** éteindre; fermer l'électricité, la lumière. **2.** *v.i.* (*a*) sortir; paraître en public; (*b*) **things have turned out well,** les choses ont bien tourné; **the weather has turned out fine,** le temps s'est mis au beau; **it turns out that . . .,** il se trouve que . . .; **'turn-out,** *s.* concours *m*, assemblée *f* (de gens); **there was a great t.-o.,** il y avait foule; **'turn 'over. 1.** *v.tr.* (*a*) retourner (qch.); tourner (une page); **to t. over the pages of a book,** feuilleter un livre; **to t. over an idea in one's mind,** ruminer une idée; (*b*) **he turns over £500 a week,** son chiffre d'affaires est de 500 livres par semaine; (*c*) **to t. sth. over to s.o.,** transférer, référer, remettre, qch. à qn. **2.** *v.i.* se tourner, se retourner; (*of car*) verser, capoter; **to t. right over,** faire panache; **'turnover,** *s.* (*a*)

Pol: **t. of four votes,** déplacement *m* de quatre voix; (*b*) *Com:* chiffre *m* d'affaires; **quick t. of goods,** écoulement *m* rapide de marchandises; (*c*) *Cu:* **apple t.,** chausson *m* aux pommes; **'turnpike,** *s. U.S:* autoroute *f* à péage; **'turn 'round. 1.** *v.tr.* retourner. **2.** *v.i.* (*a*) tourner; **to t. round and round,** tournoyer; (*b*) se retourner; faire volte-face; (*c*) (*of ship in port*) se retourner (pour repartir); **'turn-round,** *s. Com:* rotation *f* (de navires, de camions); **'turnstile,** *s.* tourniquet(-compteur) *m* (pour entrées); **'turntable,** *s.* **1.** *Rail:* plaque tournante. **2.** *Rec:* plateau *m* tourne-disques; **'turn 'to,** *v.i. F:* se mettre au travail; s'y mettre; **'turn 'up. I.** *v.tr.* **1.** (*a*) relever (son col); retrousser (ses manches); **turned-up nose,** nez *m* retroussé; **to t. up one's nose at sth.,** renifler sur qch.; (*b*) déterrer (un trésor, etc.); (*c*) trouver, se reporter à (une citation); (*d*) *F:* écœurer (qn). **2. to t. up the gas,** monter le gaz. **II.** *v.i.* **1.** se replier; **her nose turns up,** elle a le nez retroussé. **2.** (*a*) **the ace of clubs turned up,** l'as de trèfle est sorti; (*b*) arriver; faire son apparition; **something is sure to t. up,** il se présentera sûrement une occasion; **till something better turns up,** en attendant mieux; **'turnup,** *s.* (*a*) revers *m* (d'un pantalon); (*b*) (*at cards*) retourne *f.*

turnip ['tə:nip], *s.* navet *m.*

turpentine ['tə:p(ə)ntain], *s.* térébenthine *f*; **turps,** *s. Com: F:* (essence *f* de) térébenthine *f.*

turquoise ['tə:kwɑ:z, -kwɔiz]. **1.** *s.* turquoise *f.* **2.** *a. & s.* **t. (blue),** turquoise (*m*) *inv.*

turret ['tʌrit], *s.* tourelle *f.*

turtle ['tə:tl], *s.* tortue *f* de mer; **t. soup,** consommé *m* à la tortue; (*of boat*) **to turn t.,** chavirer; capoter.

turtledove ['tə:tldʌv], *s. Orn:* tourterelle *f.*

Tuscany ['tʌskəni]. *Pr.n. Geog:* la Toscane.

tusk [tʌsk], *s.* défense *f* (d'un éléphant, d'un sanglier, d'un morse); **'tusker,** *s.* éléphant *m,* sanglier *m,* adulte.

tussle ['tʌsl]. **I.** *s.* lutte *f,* bagarre *f,* mêlée *f,* corps-à-corps *m inv*; **to have a t.,** en venir aux mains (avec qn). **II.** *v.i.* lutter (avec qn); **to t. over sth.,** se disputer qch.

tussock ['tʌsək], *s.* touffe *f* d'herbe.

tutor ['tju:tər]. **I.** *s.* **1.** *Sch:* directeur *m* des études d'un groupe d'étudiants. **2. private t.,** précepteur *m.* **II.** *v.tr.* instruire (qn); donner (à qn) des leçons particulières.

tuxedo, *pl.* -os [tʌk'si:dou, -ouz], *s. Cl: N.Am:* smoking *m.*

twaddle ['twɔdl], *s. F:* fadaises *fpl,* futilités *fpl*; **to talk t.,** débiter des balivernes, des sottises.

twang [twæŋ]. **I.** *s.* **1.** son vibrant (d'une harpe). **2. nasal t.,** ton nasillard; **to speak with a t.,** parler du nez; nasiller. **II.** *v.* **1.** *v.tr.* **to t. a guitar,** pincer, *F:* gratter, de la guitare. **2.** *v.i.*

Mus: (*of string*) vibrer, résonner.

tweak [twi:k], *v.tr.* pincer; **to t. a boy's ears,** tirer les oreilles à un gamin.

tweed [twi:d], *s.* **1.** tweed *m,* cheviotte écossaise. **2.** *pl. Cl:* **tweeds,** complet *m,* tailleur *m,* de cheviotte.

tweet [twi:t]. **I.** *s.* pépiement *m*; gazouillement *m.* **II.** *v.i.* (*of bird*) pépier; gazouiller.

tweezers ['twi:zəz], *s.pl.* petite pince; brucelles *fpl.*

twelve [twelv], *num.a. & s.* douze (*m*); **t. o'clock,** (i) midi *m*; *Rail:* douze heures; (ii) minuit *m*; *Rail:* zéro heure; **half past t.,** midi, minuit, et demi; **twelfth,** *num. a. & s.* douzième (*mf*); **Louis the T.,** Louis Douze; **T. Night,** le jour des Rois.

twenty ['twenti], *num.a. & s.* vingt (*m*); **t.-one,** vingt et un; **t.-two,** vingt-deux; **t.-first,** vingt et unième; **(on) the t.-first of May,** le vingt et un mai; **about t. people,** une vingtaine de gens; **'twentieth,** *num.a. & s.* vingtième (*m*); **(on) the t. of June,** le vingt juin.

twerp [twə:p], *s. P:* nouille *f,* pauvre type *m.*

twice [twais], *adv.* deux fois; **t. as big,** deux fois plus grand (que qch.); **he's t. as old as I am, t. my age,** il a deux fois mon âge; **t. over,** (faire qch.) à deux reprises; **to think t. about doing sth.,** y regarder à deux fois avant de faire qch.; **he didn't have to be asked t.,** il ne se fit pas prier.

twiddle ['twidl], *v.tr. & i.* tourner (ses pouces); tortiller (sa moustache); jouer avec (qch.).

twig[1] [twig], *s.* brindille *f* (de branche); ramille *f.*

twig[2], *v.tr.* (**twigged**) *F:* comprendre, saisir, piger.

twilight ['twailait], (*a*) *s.* crépuscule *m*; (**morning) t.,** demi-jour *m*; **in the (evening) t.,** au crépuscule; **entre chien et loup;** (*b*) *a.* crépusculaire.

twin [twin]. **I.** *a. & s.* **1.** jumeau, jumelle; **t. brother, t. sister,** frère jumeau, sœur jumelle; **Siamese twins,** frères siamois, sœurs siamoises. **2.** *a.* **t. beds,** lits jumeaux; **t. tyres,** pneus jumelés; **t.-engine aircraft,** bimoteur *m.* **II.** *v.tr.* (**twinned**) jumeler; **twinned towns,** villes jumelées; **'twinning,** *s.* jumelage *m* (de villes).

twine [twain]. **I.** *s.* ficelle *f.* **II.** *v.* **1.** *v.tr.* tordre, tortiller (des fils); entrelacer (des branches); **to t. sth. round sth.,** (en)rouler qch. autour de qch.; entourer qch. de qch. **2.** *v.i.* se tordre, se tortiller; **to t. round sth.,** s'enrouler autour de qch.; (*of ivy*) **to t. round a tree,** s'enlacer autour d'un arbre, enlacer un arbre.

twinge [twin(d)ʒ], *s.* (*a*) élancement *m* (de douleur); (*b*) **t. of conscience,** remords *m* (de conscience).

twinkle ['twiŋkl]. **I.** *s.* **1.** scintillement *m,* clignotement *m* (des étoiles). **2.** pétillement *m* (du regard). **II.** *v.i.* **1.** scintiller, papilloter, clignoter. **2.** (*of eyes*) **to t. with mischief,** pétiller de malice; **'twinkling,** *s.* scintillement *m*, clignotement *m*; **in the t. of an eye, in a t.,** en un clin d'œil.

twirl [twə:l]. **I.** *s.* **1.** tournoiement *m*; (*of dancer*) pirouette *f*. **2.** volute *f* (de fumée). **II.** *v.* **1.** *v.tr.* (*a*) faire tournoyer; faire des moulinets avec (sa canne); (*b*) tortiller, friser (sa moustache). **2.** *v.i.* tournoyer; (*of dancer*) pirouetter.

twirp [twə:p], *s.* *P:* nouille *f*, pauvre type *m*.

twist [twist]. **I.** *s.* **1.** (*a*) fil *m* retors; cordon *m*; cordonnet *m*; (*b*) **t. of hair,** torsade *f* de cheveux; **t. of paper,** tortillon *m*, cornet *m*, de papier; papillote *f*. **2. to give sth. a t.,** exercer une torsion sur qch.; **to give one's ankle a t.,** se fouler la cheville; **a t. in the back,** un tour de reins. **3. twists and turns,** tours et retours. **II.** *v.* **1.** *v.tr.* (*a*) tordre, tortiller; **to t. together,** torsader, câbler (des fils); **to t. sth. round sth.,** rouler, entortiller, qch. autour de qch.; *F:* **she can t. him round her little finger,** elle lui fait faire ses quatre volontés; (*b*) **to t. one's ankle,** se fouler la cheville; **to t. s.o.'s arm,** tordre le bras à qn; (*c*) dénaturer (les paroles de qn); fausser (le sens de qch.); donner une entorse à (la vérité). **2.** *v.i.* (*a*) (*of worm*) se tordre, se tortiller; (*b*) (*of smoke*) former des volutes; (*c*) (*of road*) tourner; faire des détours, des lacets; **to t. and turn,** serpenter; **'twisted,** *a.* tordu, tors; **t. mind,** esprit tordu, faussé; **'twister,** *s.* *F:* filou *m*; **'twisting,** *a.* (sentier) en lacets.

twitch [twitʃ]. **I.** *s.* **1.** saccade *f*; petit coup sec. **2.** crispation nerveuse (des mains); mouvement convulsif; (*facial*) tic *m*. **II.** *v.* **1.** *v.tr.* (*a*) tirer vivement; donner une saccade à (qch.); (*b*) contracter (ses traits); crisper (les mains); (*of cat*) **to t. its tail,** avoir de petits mouvements de la queue. **2.** *v.i.* se contracter nerveusement; (*of hands*) se crisper nerveusement; **his face twitches,** il a un tic.

twitter ['twitər]. **I.** *s.* **1.** gazouillement *m*, gazouillis *m*. **2.** *F:* **to be all of a t., in a t.,** être tout en émoi. **II.** *v.i.* gazouiller; **'twittering,** *s.* gazouillement *m*.

two [tu:], *num. a. & s.* deux (*m*); **the t. of us, we t.,** nous deux; **to come in t. by t., t. and t., in twos,** entrer deux par deux; **to put t. and t. together,** tirer ses conclusions (après avoir rapproché les faits); **to have t. of everything,** avoir tout en double; **to be in t. minds about sth.,** être indécis sur qch.; **'two-'legged** [-'legid], *a.* bipède;

'two-piece, *a. & s. Cl:* (lady's) **t.-p.** (suit), deux-pièces *m inv*; **'two-ply,** *a.* (laine *f*) deux fils; **'two-'seater,** *s.* avion *m*, voiture *f*, à deux places; **'two-stroke,** *a.* (moteur) (à) deux-temps; **t.-s. mixture,** deux-temps *m*; **'two-'time,** *v.tr. esp. N.Am:* duper, tromper (qn); **'two-'timer,** *s. esp. N.Am:* (associé, etc.) malhonnête; trompeur, -euse; **'two-way,** *a.* (rue) à deux sens.

tycoon [tai'ku:n], *s. Com: Ind:* magnat *m*, grand manitou.

type [taip]. **I.** *s.* **1.** type *m*; **people of every t.,** monde *m* de tous les genres; gens de toute espèce. **2.** *Typ:* (*a*) caractère *m*, type; (*b*) *coll.* caractères. **II.** *v.tr. & i.* taper à la machine; dactylographier; **to t. well,** être bon à la dactylo; **'typescript,** *s.* manuscrit dactylographié; **'type-setter,** *s.* compositeur *m*; **'typewriter,** *s.* machine *f* à écrire; **'typewritten,** *a.* (document) dactylographié, tapé à la machine; **'typing,** *s.* **1.** dactylographie *f*, *F:* dactylo *f*; **t. paper,** papier *m* (pour) machine (à écrire). **2.** identification *f*, détermination *f*, des types; **blood t.,** détermination du groupe sanguin; **'typist,** *s.* dactylographe *mf*, dactylo *mf*; **t.'s error,** erreur *f* de frappe; **ty'pography,** *s.* typographie *f*.

typhoid ['taifɔid], *a. & s. Med:* typhoïde (*f*).

typhoon [tai'fu:n], *s.* typhon *m*.

typhus ['taifəs], *s. Med:* typhus *m*.

typical ['tipik(ə)l], *a.* typique; **the t. Frenchman,** le Français typique; **that's t. of him,** c'est bien de lui; **-ally,** *adv.* d'une manière typique; typiquement; **'typify,** *v.tr.* (*a*) symboliser (qch.); (*b*) être caractéristique de (qch.).

tyranny ['tirəni], *s.* tyrannie *f*; **tyrannical** [ti'rænik(ə)l], **'tyrannous,** *a.* tyrannique; **-ally, -ously,** *adv.* tyranniquement; **'tyrannize,** *v.i.* faire le tyran; **to t. over s.o.,** tyranniser qn.

tyrant ['taiərənt], *s.* tyran *m*.

tyre ['taiər], *s. Aut:* pneu *m*; **radial t.,** pneu à carcasse radiale; **non-skid t.,** (pneu) antidérapant (*m*); **checking of t. pressures,** vérification du gonflage des pneus; **t. lever,** démonte-pneus *m inv*.

tyro, *pl.* **-os** ['taiərou, -ouz], *s.* novice *mf*; néophyte *m*.

Tyrol (the) [ðə'tirɔl]. *Pr.n. Geog:* le Tyrol; **Tyrolean** [tirə'li:ən], *a. & s.,* **Tyrolese** [tirə'li:z], *a. & s.* tyrolien, -ienne.

U

U, u [juː], s. (la lettre) U, u *m*; U and non-U, ce qui est bien, comme il faut, et ce qui ne l'est pas; *Aut:* U-turn, demi-tour *m*; no U-turns, demi-tour interdit.

ubiquitous [juː'bikwitəs], a. qui se trouve partout; que l'on rencontre partout; u'**biquity,** s. ubiquité *f*.

udder ['ʌdər], s. mamelle *f*, pis *m* (de vache).

Uganda [juː'gændə]. *Pr.n.* l'Ouganda *m*.

ugh [uh, əː], *int.* 1. pouah! 2. u., it's cold! brrr, il fait froid!

ugly ['ʌgli], a. laid; disgracieux; to grow u., enlaidir; **u. piece of furniture,** vilain meuble; *F:* **u. customer,** vilain type; '**ugliness,** s. laideur *f*.

ulcer ['ʌlsər], s. ulcère *m*; '**ulcerate,** v.tr. & i. (s')ulcérer; '**ulcerated,** '**ulcerous,** a. ulcéré, ulcéreux; **ulce'ration,** s. ulcération *f*.

ulna ['ʌlnə], s. *Anat:* cubitus *m*.

ulterior [ʌl'tiəriər], a. 1. ultérieur. 2. **u. motive,** motif secret, caché; **without u. motive,** sans arrière-pensée.

ultimate ['ʌltimət], a. final; **u. purpose,** but final; **u. decision,** décision définitive; -ly, adv. à la fin; en fin de compte.

ultimatum [ʌlti'meitəm], s. ultimatum *m*.

ultra ['ʌltrə]. 1. a. extrême; **u.-short waves,** ondes ultra-courtes. 2. s. *Pol:* ultra *m*; **ultra-'fashionable,** a. tout dernier cri, ultra-chic; **ultrama'rine,** a. & s. (bleu *m* d')outremer *m* *inv*; **ultra'violet,** a. & s. ultraviolet (*m*).

umbelliferous [ʌmbe'lifərəs], a. *Bot:* ombellifère.

umber ['ʌmbər], s. (terre *f* d')ombre *f*.

umbrage ['ʌmbridʒ], s. ombrage *m*; ressentiment *m*; **to take u.,** s'offenser (**at sth.,** de qch.).

umbrella [ʌm'brelə], s. parapluie *m*; (*of jellyfish*) ombrelle *f*; **beach u.,** parasol *m*; *Bot:* **u. pine,** pin *m* parasol; *Av:* **air u.,** ombrelle de protection aérienne, parapluie aérien; **u. stand,** porte-parapluies *m inv*.

umpire ['ʌmpaiər]. I. s. arbitre *m*, juge *m*. II. v.tr. arbitrer (un match, etc.); '**umpiring,** s. arbitrage *m*.

umpteen [ʌm(p)'tiːn], a. & s. *F:* je ne sais combien.

unabashed [ʌnə'bæʃt], a. 1. sans perdre contenance. 2. aucunement ébranlé.

unabated [ʌnə'beitid], a. non diminué.

unable [ʌn'eibl], a. incapable, hors d'état (de faire qch.); **u. to speak,** incapable de parler; **we are u. to help you,** nous ne pouvons pas vous

aider; **u. to attend,** empêché.

unabridged [ʌnə'bridʒd], a. non abrégé; **u. edition,** édition intégrale.

unacceptable [ʌnək'septəbl], a. inacceptable; (théorie) irrecevable.

unaccommodating [ʌnə'kɔmədeitiŋ], a. peu accommodant; désobligeant.

unaccompanied [ʌnə'kʌmpənid], a. 1. non accompagné, seul; sans escorte. 2. *Mus:* sans accompagnement; **sonata for u. violin,** sonate *f* pour violon seul.

unaccountable [ʌnə'kauntəbl], a. (a) (phénomène) inexplicable; **it's u.,** explique cela qui pourra; (b) (conduite) bizarre; -**ably,** adv. inexplicablement; sans qu'on sache pourquoi; **una'ccounted, a. five passengers are still u. for,** on reste sans nouvelles de cinq voyageurs.

unaccustomed [ʌnə'kʌstəmd], a. (*of pers.*) **u. to sth.,** peu habitué à qch.

unacquainted [ʌnə'kweintid], a. **to be u. with** (s.o., sth.), ne pas connaître (qn); ignorer (un fait).

unadulterated [ʌnə'dʌltəreitid], a. pur; *Com:* sans mélange, non frelaté; *F:* **pure u. laziness,** paresse pure et simple; **he's an u. idiot,** c'est un sot en trois lettres.

unaffected [ʌnə'fektid], a. 1. sans affectation; (joie, douleur) sincère; (*of pers.*) sans pose; (style) sans recherche. 2. inaltérable (**by air, by water,** à l'air, à l'eau); -**ly,** adv. sans affectation; sincèrement; simplement; sans pose.

unaided [ʌn'eidid], a. sans aide; **he can walk u. now,** il peut marcher tout seul maintenant.

unalloyed [ʌnə'lɔid], a. (métal) pur, sans alliage; (bonheur) parfait, sans nuage.

unalterable [ʌn'ɔːltərəbl], a. immuable, invariable; **un'altered,** a. toujours le même; inchangé; sans changement; tel quel, *f*. telle quelle.

unambiguous [ʌnæm'bigjuəs], a. non équivoque.

unambitious [ʌnæm'biʃəs], a. 1. sans ambition. 2. (projet) sans prétention(s).

unanimous [juː(ː)'næniməs], a. unanime; -**ly,** adv. à l'unanimité; unanimement.

unannounced [ʌnə'naunst], a. **he came in u.,** il est entré sans se faire annoncer.

unanswerable [ʌn'ɑːnsərəbl], a. qui n'admet pas de réponse; (argument) sans réplique, sans réponse; **un'answered,** a. 1. (*of letter*) (i) sans réponse; (ii) à répondre. 2. irréfuté. 3. (*of* *prayer*) inexaucé.

unappetizing [ʌnˈæpitaiziŋ], *a.* peu appétissant.

unappreciated [ʌnəˈpriːʃieitid], *a.* inapprécié; peu estimé; (talent) méconnu.

unapproachable [ʌnəˈproutʃəbl], *a.* 1. inaccessible; (*of pers.*) inabordable, distant. 2. sans pareil.

unarmed [ʌnˈɑːmd], *a.* sans armes.

unashamed [ʌnəˈʃeimd], *a.* sans honte; éhonté.

unasked [ʌnˈɑːskt], *a.* (faire qch.) spontanément, sans y être invité.

unassuming [ʌnəˈsjuːmiŋ], *a.* sans prétention(s); simple, modeste.

unattached [ʌnəˈtætʃt], *a.* 1. libre (**to,** de); indépendant (**to,** de). 2. célibataire.

unattainable [ʌnəˈteinəbl], *a.* inaccessible (**by,** à); hors de la portée (**by,** de); impossible.

unattended [ʌnəˈtendid], *a.* (*a*) seul; sans escorte; (*b*) **u. to,** négligé; sans soins; (*c*) (paquet) qui traîne, abandonné.

unattractive [ʌnəˈtræktiv], *a.* peu attrayant; (*of pers.*) peu sympathique.

unauthorized [ʌnˈɔːθəraizd], *a.* non autorisé, sans autorisation; (commerce) illicite.

unavoidable [ʌnəˈvɔidəbl], *a.* inévitable; (événement) qu'on ne peut prévenir; **-ably,** *adv.* inévitablement; **u. absent,** empêché.

unaware [ʌnəˈwɛər], *a.* ignorant, pas au courant (**of sth.,** de qch.); **to be u. of sth.,** ignorer qch.; **unaˈwares,** *adv.* (faire qch.) inconsciemment, par inadvertance; **to take s.o. u.,** prendre qn au dépourvu.

unbalanced [ʌnˈbælənst], *a.* en équilibre instable; (esprit) déséquilibré.

unbearable [ʌnˈbɛərəbl], *a.* insupportable, intolérable; **u. pain,** douleur atroce; *F:* **to make oneself u.,** se rendre odieux; **-ably,** *adv.* insupportablement.

unbeatable [ʌnˈbiːtəbl], *a.* imbattable.

unbeaten [ʌnˈbiːtən], *a.* *Sp:* (record) qui n'a pas été battu.

unbecoming [ʌnbiˈkʌmiŋ], *a.* 1. peu convenable; déplacé. 2. (*of garment*) peu seyant.

unbeknown [ʌnbiˈnoun], *adv.* **u. to anyone,** (faire qch.) à l'insu de tous.

unbelievable [ʌnbiˈliːvəbl], *a.* incroyable; **-ably,** *a.* incroyablement.

unbend [ʌnˈbend], *v.i.* (**unbent**) se détendre; **unˈbending,** *a.* inflexible, ferme, raide; intransigeant.

unbias(s)ed [ʌnˈbaiəst], *a.* impartial; sans parti pris.

unbleached [ʌnˈbliːtʃt], *a.* *Com:* **u. (linen) sheet,** drap *m* écru.

unblemished [ʌnˈblemiʃt], *a.* sans défaut, immaculé; (réputation) sans tache.

unblushing [ʌnˈblʌʃiŋ], *a.* sans vergogne; éhonté; **-ly,** *adv.* (*a*) sans rougir; (*b*) sans vergogne; (mentir) impudemment.

unbounded [ʌnˈbaundid], *a.* sans borne; illimité; **u. ambition,** ambition démesurée.

unbreakable [ʌnˈbreikəbl], *a.* incassable.

unbridled [ʌnˈbraidld], *a.* (*of passion*) débridé; effréné.

unbroken [ʌnˈbrouk(ə)n], *a.* 1. (*a*) non brisé, non cassé; (*b*) intact; (*c*) *Sp:* **u. record,** record qui n'a pas été battu; (*d*) (*of silence*) ininterrompu, continu; **u. sheet of ice,** nappe de glace continue. 2. (cheval) non rompu, non dressé.

unburden [ʌnˈbəːd(ə)n], *v.pr.* **to u. oneself,** s'épancher.

unbusinesslike [ʌnˈbiznislaik], *a.* (*a*) peu commerçant; (*b*) (procédé) irrégulier; **to be u.,** manquer de méthode.

unbutton [ʌnˈbʌt(ə)n], *v.tr.* déboutonner.

uncalled for [ʌnˈkɔːldfɔːr], *a.* (*of remark*) déplacé; (*of rebuke*) immérité.

uncanny [ʌnˈkæni], *a.* mystérieux; (bruit) inquiétant; (lueur) sinistre.

uncared for [ʌnˈkɛədfɔːr], *a.* peu soigné; (enfant) délaissé; (jardin) à l'abandon.

unceasing [ʌnˈsiːsiŋ], *a.* (*a*) incessant, continu; (*b*) (travail) assidu; (effort) soutenu; **-ly,** *adv.* sans cesse.

unceremonious [ˈʌnseriˈmouniəs], *a.* (*of pers.*) sans façon, sans gêne; **-ly,** *adv.* 1. sans cérémonie. 2. sans façons; brusquement.

uncertain [ʌnˈsəːt(ə)n], *a.* incertain. 1. (*a*) (*of time, amount*) indéterminé; (*b*) (résultat) douteux; (*c*) (contour) mal défini. 2. (*a*) **u. steps,** pas mal assurés; **u. health,** santé vacillante; **u. temper,** humeur inégale; (*b*) **to be u. of, about, sth.,** être incertain de qch.; **to be u. whether . . .,** ne pas savoir au juste si . . .; **-ly,** *adv.* d'une façon incertaine; **unˈcertainty,** *s.* 1. incertitude *f*; **in order to remove any u.,** pour dissiper toute équivoque. 2. **to prefer a certainty to an u.,** préférer le certain à l'incertain.

unchallenged [ʌnˈtʃælin(d)ʒd], *a.* (droit, etc.) incontesté; **to let (sth.) pass u.,** ne pas relever (une affirmation).

unchangeable [ʌnˈtʃein(d)ʒəbl], *a.* immuable, inchangeable; **unˈchanged,** *a.* inchangé; toujours le même; **unˈchanging,** *a.* invariable, immuable.

uncharitable [ʌnˈtʃæritəbl], *a.* peu charitable.

unchecked [ʌnˈtʃekt], *a.* 1. sans frein; **u. advance,** avance qui ne rencontre pas d'obstacles. 2. non vérifié.

uncivilized [ʌnˈsivilaizd], *a.* peu civilisé, barbare.

unclaimed [ʌnˈkleimd], *a.* non réclamé; **u. right,** droit non revendiqué.

unclassified [ʌnˈklæsifaid], *a.* non classé.

uncle [ˈʌŋkl], *s.* oncle *m*; **yes, u.!** oui, mon oncle!

unclouded [ʌnˈklaudid], *a.* (*of sky*) sans nuage,

serein; (*of vision*) clair; (*of liquid*) limpide.
uncoil [ʌn'kɔil]. **1.** *v.tr.* dérouler. **2.** *v.i.* (*of snake*) se dérouler.
uncoloured [ʌn'kʌləd], *a.* (*a*) non coloré; (**plain**) **u. account,** rapport fidèle (de qch.); (*b*) incolore.
uncombed [ʌn'koumd], *a.* (*of hair*) non peigné, mal peigné, ébouriffé.
uncomfortable [ʌn'kʌmf(ə)təbl], *a.* **1.** inconfortable, peu confortable; incommode, incommodant; **this is a very u. bed,** on est très mal dans ce lit. **2.** désagréable; **to make things u. for s.o.,** créer des ennuis à qn; faire des histoires à qn; **it makes things u.,** c'est très gênant. **3. to feel u.,** être mal à l'aise; **to be, feel, u. about sth.,** se sentir inquiet au sujet de qch.; **-ably,** *adv.* **1.** peu confortablement; incommodément. **2.** désagréablement; **to be u. placed,** se trouver dans une situation embarrassante.
uncommitted [ʌnkə'mitid], *a.* libre, indépendant; *Pol:* **the u. countries,** les pays neutralistes.
uncommon [ʌn'kɔmən], *a.* peu commun; rare; (mot) peu usité; peu ordinaire; singulier; **-ly,** *adv.* singulièrement; **u. good,** excellent.
uncommunicative [ʌnkə'mju:nikətiv], *a.* renfermé, taciturne.
uncomplaining [ʌnkəm'pleiniŋ], *a.* patient, résigné.
uncomplimentary ['ʌnkɔmpli'ment(ə)ri], *a.* peu flatteur.
uncompromising [ʌn'kɔmprəmaiziŋ], *a.* intransigeant; intraitable; **u. sincerity,** sincérité absolue.
unconcealed [ʌnkən'si:ld], *a.* qui n'est pas caché; fait à découvert; **to give one's u. opinion,** dire franchement ce qu'on pense.
unconcern [ʌnkən'sə:n], *s.* insouciance *f*; indifférence *f*; **uncon'cerned,** *a.* (*a*) insouciant, indifférent; (*b*) **to be u. about sth.,** être sans inquiétude au sujet de qch.; **-edly** [-idli], *adv.* d'un air indifférent, dégagé; avec insouciance.
unconditional [ʌnkən'diʃənəl], *a.* inconditionnel; absolu; (offre *f*) sans condition; (refus *m*) catégorique; **-ally,** *adv.* (accepter) sans réserve; **to surrender u.,** se rendre sans condition.
unconfirmed [ʌnkən'fə:md], *a.* non confirmé; (*of news*) sujet à caution.
uncongenial [ʌnkən'dʒi:niəl], *a.* (*of pers.*) peu sympathique; (travail) ingrat.
unconnected [ʌnkə'nektid], *a.* sans rapport, sans lien; **the two events are quite u.,** les deux événements n'ont aucun rapport entre eux.
unconscious [ʌn'kɔnʃəs]. **1.** *a.* inconscient; **to be u. of sth.,** (i) ne pas avoir conscience de qch.; (ii) ignorer qch. **2.** *a.* sans connaissance; évanoui; **to become u.,** perdre connaissance. **3.**

s. **the u.,** l'inconscient *m*; **-ly,** *adv.* inconsciemment; **un'consciousness,** *s.* **1.** inconscience (**of,** de). **2.** évanouissement *m*, état *m* d'inconscience.
unconsidered [ʌnkən'sidəd], *a.* **1.** (*of remark*) inconsidéré, irréfléchi. **2.** (objet) auquel on n'attache aucune valeur.
uncontested [ʌnkən'testid], *a.* (droit) incontesté; *Pol:* **u. seat,** siège qui n'est pas disputé.
uncontrollable [ʌnkən'trouləbl], *a.* (enfant) ingouvernable; (désir) irrésistible; **u. laughter,** fou rire; **-ably,** *adv.* irrésistiblement; **uncon'trolled,** *a.* (*of passion*) effréné.
unconventional [ʌnkən'venʃən(ə)l], *a.* original, non-conformiste; **-ally,** à l'encontre des conventions; **'unconventio'nality,** *s.* originalité *f*; indépendance *f* (à l'égard des conventions).
unconvinced [ʌnkən'vinst], *a.* **u. of sth.,** sceptique à l'égard de qch.; **uncon'vincing,** *a.* peu convaincant; (excuse) peu vraisemblable.
uncooked [ʌn'kukt], *a.* (aliment) non cuit, cru.
uncork [ʌn'kɔ:k], *v.tr.* déboucher (une bouteille).
uncorrected [ʌnkə'rektid], *a.* (*a*) (*of proof*) non corrigé; (*b*) (*of error*) non rectifié; (*in science*) **u. result,** résultat brut; *Sp:* **u. time,** temps réel.
uncouth [ʌn'ku:θ], *a.* (*a*) grossier, rude; (*b*) malappris, gauche.
uncover [ʌn'kʌvər], *v.tr.* découvrir (qch.); mettre (qch.) à découvert; **un'covered,** *a.* (*a*) mis à découvert; découvert; (*b*) (chèque) sans provision.
uncritical [ʌn'kritik(ə)l], *a.* sans discernement; (auditoire) peu exigeant.
uncrossed [ʌn'krɔst], *a.* (chèque) non barré.
uncrushable [ʌn'krʌʃəbl], *a.* *Tex:* infroissable.
unction ['ʌŋkʃ(ə)n], *s.* *Ecc:* **extreme u.,** extrême-onction *f*.
uncultivated [ʌn'kʌltiveitid], *a.* (terrain) inculte; (personne) sans culture.
uncut [ʌn'kʌt], *a.* (*of hedge*) non taillé; (diamant) brut.
undamaged [ʌn'dæmidʒd], *a.* non endommagé; indemne; (*of reputation*) intact.
undated [ʌn'deitid], *a.* non daté; sans date.
undaunted [ʌn'dɔ:ntid], *a.* aucunement intimidé.
undeceive [ʌndi'si:v], *v.tr.* désabuser, détromper (qn).
undecided [ʌndi'saidid], *a.* indécis; (*of pers.*) irrésolu, hésitant; **to be u. how to act,** être indécis, être dans l'indécision, ne pas savoir quel parti à prendre.
undecipherable [ʌndi'saif(ə)rəbl], *a.* (écriture) indéchiffrable.
undefeated [ʌndi'fi:tid], *a.* invaincu.
undefended [ʌndi'fendid], *a.* (*a*) sans défense; (*b*) *Jur:* **u. divorce,** action *f* en divorce où le

défendeur s'abstient de plaider.
undefinable [ʌndi'fainəbl], *a.* indéfinissable; indéterminable; **unde'fined,** *a.* (*a*) non défini; (*b*) indéterminé; vague.
undelivered [ʌndi'livəd], *a.* non délivré; **u. letter,** lettre *f* au rebut; **if u. please return to sender,** en cas de non-délivrance prière de retourner à l'expéditeur.
undemonstrative [ʌndi'mɔnstrətiv], *a.* peu expansif, peu démonstratif; réservé.
undeniable [ʌndi'naiəbl], *a.* indéniable, incontestable; **-ably,** *adv.* incontestablement; indiscutablement.
under ['ʌndər]. I. *prep.* **1.** (*a*) sous; au-dessous de; **to swim u. water,** nager sous l'eau; **put it u. the table,** mettez-le sous la table; **to speak u. one's breath,** parler à mi-voix; (*b*) **he's u. thirty,** il a moins de trente ans; **the u.-thirties,** les moins de trente ans; (*c*) **to be u. s.o.,** être sous les ordres de qn; être inférieur à qn; *F:* **to be u. the doctor,** être entre les mains du médecin. **2. u. lock and key,** sous clef; **visible u. the microscope,** visible au microscope; **to be u. sentence of death,** être condamné à mort; **u. these circumstances,** dans ces conditions; **u. his father's will,** d'après le testament de son père; **to be u. the necessity of doing sth.,** être dans la nécessité de faire qch.; **I'm u. no obligation to do it,** rien ne m'oblige à le faire. **3. u. repair,** en (voie de) réparation; **u. treatment,** (malade) en traitement. II. *adv.* **1.** (au-)dessous; **as u.,** comme ci-dessous; *F:* **down u.,** aux antipodes. **2. to keep u.,** opprimer, écraser (qn); maîtriser (un incendie). III. *a.* subalterne; **u. gardener,** aide-jardinier *m*; **U. Secretary of State,** Sous-secrétaire *mf* d'État; **Permanent U. Secretary,** directeur général (d'un Ministère); **'undercarriage,** *s. Av:* train *m* d'atterrissage; **under'charge,** *v.tr.* ne pas faire payer assez à (qn); **'underclothes** *s.pl.,* **'underclothing,** *s.* sous-vêtements *mpl*; lingerie (féminine); **'undercoat,** *s.* première couche (de peinture), couche de fond; **'undercurrent,** *s.* (*a*) courant *m* de fond; (*in sea*) courant sous-marin; (*in air*) courant inférieur; (*b*) **u. of discontent,** secret courant de mécontentement; **'undercut,** *s. Cu:* filet *m* (de bœuf); **under'cut,** *v.tr.* (**under'cut; under'cutting**) vendre moins cher que (qn); **'underde'veloped,** *a. Phot:* (cliché) insuffisamment développé; **u. countries,** pays sous-développés; **'underdog,** *s.* **the u.,** l'opprimé *m*; **under'done,** *a.* (*a*) pas assez cuit; (*b*) pas trop cuit; (bœuf) saignant; **underestimate.** I. *s.* [ʌndər'estimət], sous-évaluation *f.* II. *v.tr.* [ʌndər'estimeit], sous-estimer; **'underex'pose,** *v.tr.* sous-exposer (un film); **under'fed,** *a.* mal nourri, sous-alimenté; **under'foot,** *adv.* **the snow was crunching u.,** la neige craquait sous les pieds; **to trample sth. u.,** fouler qch. aux pieds; **der'go,** *v.tr.* (**under'went; under'gone**) subir (un changement, une épreuve); **under'graduate,** *s.* étudiant, -ante (d'université); **'underground. 1.** *adv.* (*a*) sous terre; (*b*) secrètement; sous main. **2.** *a.* (*a*) souterrain; (*b*) clandestin. **3.** *s.* **the U.** = le métro; **'undergrowth,** *s.* broussailles *fpl*; sous-bois *m*; **'underhand,** *a.* secret; clandestin; (*of pers.*) sournois; **under'line,** *v.tr.* souligner; **'underling,** *s.* subalterne *m*; subordonné, -ée; **'underlying,** *s.* lèvre inférieure; **under'lying,** *a.* **1.** au-dessous; (*of rock*) sous-jacent. **2.** (principe) fondamental; **u. causes,** raisons profondes (d'un événement); **under'manned,** *a.* à court de personnel; *Nau:* à court d'équipage; **under'mentioned,** *a.* mentionné ci-dessous; sous-mentionné; **under'mine,** *v.tr.* miner, saper (une muraille); **his health was being undermined,** sa santé détériorait; **'undermost,** *a.* le plus bas, *f.* la plus basse; **under'neath. 1.** *prep.* au-dessous de; sous; **from u. sth.,** de dessous qch. **2.** *adv.* au-dessous; dessous; par-dessous. **3.** *a.* de dessous; inférieur; **under'nourished,** *a.* mal nourri, sous-alimenté; **under'paid,** *a.* mal rétribué; **'underpass,** *s.* passage souterrain (sous une route); **under'privileged,** *a.* déshérité; économiquement faible; **under'rate,** *v.tr.* mésestimer, sous-estimer; **under-'ripe,** *a.* pas assez mûr; **under'sell,** *v.tr.* (**under'sold**) vendre à meilleur marché, moins cher, que (qn); **'undersigned,** *a. & s.* soussigné, -ée; **'undersized,** *a.* d'une taille au-dessous de la moyenne; **'underskirt,** *s.* jupon *m*; sous-jupe *f, pl.* sous-jupes; **'underslung,** *a. Aut:* surbaissé; **under'staffed,** *a.* **to be u.,** manquer de personnel, ne pas avoir tout son personnel; **under'stand,** *v.* (**under'stood**) **1.** *v.tr.* comprendre; (*a*) **I don't u. French,** je ne comprends pas le français; **to u. business,** s'entendre aux affaires; **to u. horses,** se, s'y, connaître en chevaux; **to u. sth.,** se rendre compte de qch.; **I can't u. it,** je n'y comprends rien; **that's easily understood,** cela se comprend facilement; *v.i.* **now I u.!** je comprends, j'y suis, maintenant! (*b*) **to give s.o. to u. sth.,** donner à entendre qch. à qn; **am I to u. that . . .?** ai-je bien compris que . . .? **I u. he'll consent,** je crois savoir qu'il consentira; **now by me, I am determined to . . .,** sachez-le bien, je suis résolu à . . . **2.** *v.tr. Gram:* sous-entendre (un mot). **3.** *v.i.* **to u. about sth.,** savoir ce qu'il faut faire à propos de qch.; **under'standable,** *a.* compréhensible; **that's u.,** cela se comprend; **under'standing.** I. *s.* **1.** entendement *m*, compréhension *f*; **it's beyond u.,** c'est à n'y rien comprendre. **2.** (*a*) accord *m*, entente *f*; (*b*)

arrangement *m*; **to have an u.**, avoir un arrangement (avec qn); **there's an u. between them**, ils sont d'intelligence; **to come to an u.**, s'accorder, s'entendre (avec qn); (*c*) **on the u. that . . .**, à condition que, + *ind. or sub.* II. *a.* (*of pers.*) qui comprend, compréhensif; **'under'state**, *v.tr.* minimiser (les faits); **'un-der'statement**, *s.* 1. amoindrissement *m*, atténuation *f* (des faits). 2. affirmation *f* qui reste au-dessous de la vérité, de la réalité; **un-der'stood**, *a.* 1. compris. 2. convenu; **that's u.**, cela va sans dire; **'understudy.** I. *s. Th:* doublure *f.* II. *v.tr.* doubler (un rôle); **un-der'take**, *v.tr.* (**under'took; under'taken**) 1. entreprendre (un voyage). 2. se charger de, assumer (une tâche); **to u. to do sth.**, se charger de faire qch.; **'undertaker**, *s.* entrepreneur *m* de pompes funèbres; **'undertaking**, *s.* 1. (*a*) entreprise *f* (de qch.); (*b*) métier *m* d'en-trepreneur de pompes funèbres. 2. entreprise (commerciale); **it's quite an u.**, c'est toute une affaire. 3. engagement *m*, promesse *f*; **'under-tone**, *s.* **to talk in an u.**, parler bas; parler à mi-voix; **under'value**, *v.tr.* 1. sous-estimer, sous-évaluer. 2. mésestimer, faire trop peu de cas de (qn); **'underwater**, *a.* sous-marin; **u. fishing**, pêche sous-marine; **'underwear**, *s.* sous-vêtements *mpl*; lingerie *f*; **'underworld**, *s.* **the (criminal) u.**, le milieu, les gens du milieu; **'underwrite**, *v.tr. Ins:* souscrire (un risque); **'underwriter**, *s. Ins:* assureur *m*.

undeserved [ʌndi'zəːvd], *a.* immérité; **-edly** [-idli], *adv.* à tort; injustement; sans le mériter; **unde'serving**, *a.* peu méritant; sans mérite; (cas) peu intéressant.

undesirable [ʌndi'zaiərəbl], *a. & s.* indésirable (*mf*), peu désirable; inopportun.

undetected [ʌndi'tektid], *a.* 1. qui a échappé à l'attention; (*of mistake*) **to pass u.**, passer inaperçu. 2. (malfaiteur) insoupçonné.

undetermined [ʌndi'təːmind], *a.* indéterminé, incertain.

undeveloped [ʌndi'veləpt], *a.* non développé; **u. land**, terrains inexploités.

undies ['ʌndiz], *s.pl. F:* lingerie *f*, dessous *mpl* (de femme).

undigested [ʌnd(a)i'dʒestid], *a.* mal digéré; **u. knowledge**, connaissances confuses, mal assimilées.

undignified [ʌn'dignifaid], *a.* (*a*) peu digne; (*b*) **to be u.**, manquer de dignité, de tenue.

undiluted [ʌnd(a)i'l(j)uːtid], *a.* non dilué; non étendu (d'eau); (vin) pur; **to talk u. nonsense**, divaguer; débiter des sottises.

undiplomatic ['ʌndiplə'mætik], *a.* peu diplomatique; peu politique, peu adroit.

undischarged ['ʌndis'tʃɑːdʒd], *a.* (*a*) *Jur:* **u. bankrupt**, failli non réhabilité; (*b*) **u. debt**, dette non acquittée.

undisciplined [ʌn'disiplind], *a.* indiscipliné.

undiscriminating [ʌndis'krimineitiŋ], *a.* (*of pers.*) sans discernement; (*of taste*) peu averti.

undisputed [ʌndis'pjuːtid], *a.* incontesté.

undistinguished [ʌndis'tiŋgwiʃt], *a.* médiocre; banal; tout à fait quelconque.

undisturbed [ʌndis'təːbd], *a.* 1. (*of pers.*) tranquille; (*of sleep*) paisible. 2. (*of peace*) que rien ne vient troubler; **we found everything u.**, rien n'avait été dérangé.

undivided [ʌndi'vaidid], *a.* 1. complet; entier. 2. non partagé; **to give one's u. attention**, donner toute son attention.

undo [ʌn'duː], *v.tr.* (**undid** [-'did]; **undone** [-'dʌn]) 1. détruire (une œuvre); **to u. the mis-chief**, réparer le mal; **what's done cannot be undone** ['ʌndʌn], ce qui est fait est fait. 2. défaire, dénouer (un nœud); dégrafer, défaire (sa robe); **un'doing**, *s.* perte *f*; **gambling will be his u.**, le jeu sera sa ruine; **un'done**, *a.* 1. défait; **to come u.**, se défaire. 2. inaccompli; non accompli; **to leave some work u.**, laisser du travail inachevé; **to leave nothing u. that might help**, ne rien négliger qui puisse être utile.

undoubted [ʌn'dautid], *a.* (fait) indubitable, in-contestable; **-ly**, *adv.* indubitablement, assurément; **u. he's wrong**, sans aucun doute il a tort.

undress [ʌn'dres], *v.* 1. *v.i. & pr.* se déshabiller, se dévêtir. 2. *v.tr.* déshabiller, dévêtir; **un-'dressed**, *a.* déshabillé, dévêtu.

undrinkable [ʌn'driŋkəbl], *a.* (*a*) (*unpleasant*) imbuvable; (*b*) (*dangerous*) non potable.

undue ['ʌndjuː], *a.* (*a*) **to exert u. influence over s.o.**, faire pression sur qn; (*b*) (*of haste*) exagéré; **u. optimism**, optimisme excessif, peu justifié; **un'duly**, *adv.* 1. (*a*) (réclamer) in-dûment; (*b*) sans raison. 2. à l'excès, outre mesure; **u. high price**, prix exagéré.

undulate ['ʌndjuleit], *v.tr. & i.* onduler; **'un-dulating**, *a.* onduleux; (terrain) vallonné, on-dulé; **undu'lation**, *s.* ondulation *f*; accident *m* de terrain.

undying [ʌn'daiiŋ], *a.* immortel; impérissable.

unearned ['ʌn'əːnd], *a.* 1. immérité. 2. **u. income**, rente(s) *f*(*pl*).

unearth [ʌn'əːθ], *v.tr.* déterrer.

unearthly [ʌn'əːθli], *a.* (*a*) qui n'est pas de ce monde; surnaturel; (*b*) **u. pallor**, pâleur mortelle; **u. light**, lueur sinistre, blafarde; (*c*) *F:* **at an u. hour**, à une heure indue; **u. din**, vacarme de tous les diables.

uneasy [ʌn'iːzi], *a.* (*a*) mal à l'aise; gêné; **u. feeling**, sentiment de malaise; (*b*) inquiet, anxieux; **to be u. in one's mind**, avoir l'esprit inquiet; **u. sleep**, sommeil agité; (*c*) (*of situation*) incommode, gênant; **-ily**, *adv.* (*a*) d'un air gêné; (*b*) avec inquiétude; **un-**

'**easiness,** s. 1. gêne f, malaise m. 2. in-quiétude f.

uneatable [ʌn'i:təbl], a. immangeable.

uneconomic [ʌni:kə'nɔmik, ʌnek-], a. 1. non économique. 2. (travail, loyer) peu rémunérateur, non rentable; **uneco'nomical,** a. (méthode) peu économique.

uneducated [ʌn'edjukeitid], a. (a) sans instruc-tion, ignorant; (b) (prononciation) vulgaire.

unemployed [ʌnim'plɔid], a. (a) désœuvré; (b) sans travail; **the u.,** les chômeurs m; **un-em'ployable,** a. inemployable; **unem'ploy-ment,** s. chômage m.

unending [ʌn'endiŋ], a. 1. interminable; **u. com-plaints,** plaintes sans fin. 2. éternel.

unendurable [ʌnin'djuərəbl], a. insupportable, intolérable.

unenterprising [ʌn'entəpraiziŋ], a. peu en-treprenant; (homme) mou.

unenviable [ʌn'enviəbl], a. peu enviable.

unequal [ʌn'i:kwəl], a. (a) inégal; (b) **to be u. to the task,** ne pas être à la hauteur de sa tâche; **to be u. to doing sth.,** ne pas être de force à faire qch.; **-ally,** adv. inégalement; **un'equalled,** a. inégalé; sans égal.

Unesco [ju:'neskou]. Pr.n. Unesco f.

uneven [ʌn'i:v(ə)n], a. 1. inégal; rugueux; (terrain) accidenté; **u. temper,** humeur inégale. 2. (nombre) impair; **-ly,** adv. 1. inégalement. 2. irrégulièrement; **un'evenness,** s. inégalité f; irrégularité f (du pouls).

uneventful [ʌni'ventful], a. sans incident; **u. life,** vie calme, peu mouvementée.

unexceptionable [ʌnik'sepʃ(ə)nəbl], a. irréprochable; (conduite) inattaquable; (témoignage) irrécusable; (personne) tout à fait bien.

unexciting [ʌnik'saitiŋ], a. insipide; peu passionnant; (vie) monotone.

unexpected [ʌnik'spektid], a. (visiteur) inatten-du; (résultat) imprévu; (secours) inespéré; **u. meeting,** rencontre inopinée; **the expected and the u.,** le prévu et l'imprévu; **-ly,** adv. de manière inattendue; inopinément.

unexplained [ʌnik'spleind], a. inexpliqué; (fait, etc.) qui reste un mystère, une énigme.

unexplored [ʌnik'splɔ:d], a. (pays) inexploré, encore inconnu.

unexposed [ʌniks'pouzd], a. (film) vierge.

unexpurgated [ʌn'ekspəgeitid], a. (livre) non expurgé; **u. edition,** édition intégrale.

unfailing [ʌn'feiliŋ], a. 1. (moyen) infaillible, sûr; (bonne humeur) inaltérable. 2. (source) in-tarissable, inépuisable (of, de); **-ly,** adv. 1. in-failliblement. 2. intarissablement.

unfair [ʌn'fɛər], a. 1. (of pers.) injuste; peu équitable; **to be u. to s.o.,** défavoriser qn; **it's u.!** ce n'est pas juste! 2. inéquitable; **u. com-petition,** concurrence déloyale; **-ly,** adv. 1.

injustement; inéquitablement. 2. **to act u.,** commettre une déloyauté; **un'fairness,** s. 1. injustice f (envers qn); partialité f. 2. déloyauté f; mauvaise foi.

unfaithful [ʌn'feiθfəl], a. infidèle.

unfamiliar [ʌnfə'miljər], a. 1. peu familier; (visage) étranger, inconnu. 2. (of pers.) **to be u. with sth.,** être peu familier avec qch.

unfashionable [ʌn'fæʃ(ə)nəbl], a. (vêtement) démodé, qui n'est pas de mode.

unfasten [ʌn'fɑ:sn], v.tr. détacher (qch. de qch.); défaire (un vêtement); ouvrir, déverrouiller (la porte).

unfavourable [ʌn'feiv(ə)rəbl], a. défavorable, peu favorable; (of terms) désavantageux **(to,** à); **to show oneself in an u. light,** se montrer sous un jour désavantageux; **u. criticism,** critique f adverse; **-ably,** adv. défavorablement; **to affect (s.o.) u.,** désavan-tager (qn).

unfeeling [ʌn'fi:liŋ], a. insensible, impitoyable; **-ly,** adv. sans pitié; froidement.

unfeigned ['ʌn'feind], a. sincère.

unfinished [ʌn'finiʃt], a. (a) inachevé; (ouvrage) imparfait; (b) Ind: non façonné.

unfit [ʌn'fit], a. 1. impropre, peu propre **(for,** à); **u. for human consumption,** impropre à la con-sommation; Aut: **u. for vehicles,** (chemin) im-praticable pour les voitures; Mil: **u. for military service,** inapte au service (militaire). 2. (of pers.) en mauvaise santé; faible de con-stitution; **un'fitness,** s. 1. **u. for sth.,** inap-titude f à qch. 2. mauvaise santé.

unflattering [ʌn'flæt(ə)riŋ], a. peu flatteur.

unflinchingly [ʌn'flin(t)ʃiŋli], adv. sans reculer; sans broncher.

unfold [ʌn'fould], v. 1. v.tr. déplier (un journal); déployer (qch.); dérouler (un projet). 2. v.i. & pr. se déployer, se dérouler.

unforeseeable [ʌnfɔ:'si:əbl], a. imprévisible; **unfore'seen,** a. imprévu, inattendu; inopiné; **unless something u. happens,** sauf imprévu, à moins d'imprévu.

unforgettable [ʌnfə'getəbl], a. inoubliable; **un-for'gotten,** a. inoublié.

unforgivable [ʌnfə'givəbl], a. impardonnable; **unfor'giving,** a. implacable; rancunier.

unfortunate [ʌn'fɔ:tʃənət], a. (a) malheureux, infortuné; **to be u.,** avoir de la malchance; (b) (événement) malencontreux; (erreur) regret-table; **it is u. that . . .,** il est fâcheux, malheureux, que + sub.; **how u.!** quel malheur! quel dommage! **-ly,** adv. malheureusement; par malheur.

unfounded [ʌn'faundid], a. (accusation) sans fondement, sans base; (bruit) dénué de fondement.

unfrequented [ʌnfri'kwentid], a. peu fréquenté; (lieu) solitaire, écarté.

unfriendly [ʌn'frendli], *a.* peu amical; (acte) hostile; **u. towards s.o.**, mal disposé pour, envers, qn; **un'friendliness**, *s.* **u. towards s.o.**, inimitié *f* pour qn; hostilité *f* contre qn.

unfulfilled [ʌnful'fild], *a.* **u. prophecy**, prophétie irréalisée; **u. promise**, promesse non tenue.

unfurl [ʌn'fə:l], *v.tr.* déployer (un drapeau).

unfurnished [ʌn'fə:niʃt], *a.* (appartement) non meublé.

ungainly [ʌn'geinli], *a.* gauche, lourd; dégingandé.

un-get-at-able ['ʌnget'ætəbl], *a.* F: inaccessible.

ungovernable [ʌn'gʌv(ə)nəbl], *a.* ingouvernable; (*of emotions*) effréné, déréglé.

ungracious [ʌn'greiʃəs], *a.* malgracieux; peu aimable; **it would be u. to refuse**, il serait de mauvaise grâce de refuser; **-ly**, *adv.* de mauvaise grâce; **un'graciousness**, *s.* mauvaise grâce; manque *m* d'amabilité.

ungrammatical [ʌngrə'mætik(ə)l], *a.* peu grammatical; incorrect; **-ally**, *adv.* incorrectement.

ungrateful [ʌn'greitful], *a.* ingrat; peu reconnaissant; **-fully**, *adv.* avec ingratitude.

ungrudging [ʌn'grʌdʒiŋ], *a.* donné de bon cœur; **to give u. praise**, ne pas ménager ses louanges; **-ly**, *adv.* de bonne grâce; libéralement.

unguarded [ʌn'gɑ:did], *a.* 1. non gardé. 2. (*of pers.*) qui n'est pas sur ses gardes; (*of speech*) inconsidéré; **in an u. moment**, dans un moment d'inattention; **-ly**, *adv.* inconsidérément.

unhampered [ʌn'hæmpəd], *a.* libre (de ses mouvements); **u. by rules**, (faire qch.) sans être gêné par des règlements.

unhappy [ʌn'hæpi], *a.* 1. malheureux, triste; infortuné; **to make s.o. u.**, causer du chagrin à qn. 2. mal inspiré; peu heureux; **-ily**, *adv.* (*a*) malheureusement; par malchance; (*b*) tristement; **to live u. together**, faire mauvais ménage; **un'happiness**, *s.* chagrin *m*; peine *f*; soucis *mpl*.

unharmed [ʌn'hɑ:md], *a.* sain et sauf; indemne.

unhealthy [ʌn'helθi], *a.* 1. malsain, insalubre. 2. (*a*) (*of pers.*) maladif; **u. complexion**, visage terreux; (*b*) **u. influence**, influence malsaine; **u. curiosity**, curiosité *f* morbide; **un'healthiness**, *s.* 1. insalubrité (du climat). 2. mauvaise santé; **u. of mind**, morbidité *f* d'esprit.

unheard [ʌn'hə:d], *a.* 1. **to condemn s.o. u.**, condamner qn sans l'entendre. 2. **u. of**, inouï.

unheeded [ʌn'hi:did], *a.* (avertissement) négligé.

unhelpful [ʌn'helpfəl], *a.* (critique) peu utile; (conseil) vain; (personne) peu secourable; **don't be so u.!** tâche donc un peu de nous aider!

unhesitating [ʌn'heziteitiŋ], *a.* qui n'hésite pas;

ferme, résolu; (réponse) prompte; **-ly**, *adv.* sans hésiter; (répondre) d'un ton ferme.

unhinged [ʌn'hindʒd], *a.* **he, his mind, is u.**, il a le cerveau détraqué.

unholy [ʌn'houli], *a.* F: **u. muddle**, désordre affreux, invraisemblable.

unhook [ʌn'huk], *v.tr.* décrocher.

unhoped for [ʌn'houptfɔ:r], *a.* inespéré.

unhurt [ʌn'hə:t], *a.* sans mal; indemne; **to escape u.**, s'en tirer sain et sauf; s'en tirer sans aucun mal.

unicorn ['ju:nikɔ:n], *s.* licorne *f*.

unidentified [ʌnai'dentifaid], *a.* non identifié.

unification [ju:nifi'keiʃ(ə)n], *s.* unification *f*.

uniform ['ju:nifɔ:m], *a. & s.* uniforme (*m*); **-ly**, *adv.* uniformément; **uni'formity**, *s.* uniformité *f*, unité *f* (de style); régularité *f* (de fonctionnement).

unify ['ju:nifai], *v.tr. & i.* (s')unifier.

unilateral [ju:ni'læt(ə)rəl], *a.* unilatéral.

unimaginable [ʌni'mædʒinəbl], *a.* inimaginable; **uni'maginative**, *a.* dénué d'imagination; peu imaginatif.

unimportant [ʌnim'pɔ:t(ə)nt], *a.* sans importance; **it's quite u.**, cela n'a pas d'importance.

uninhabitable [ʌnin'hæbitəbl], *a.* inhabitable; **unin'habited**, *a.* inhabité, désert.

uninitiated [ʌni'niʃieitid], *s.pl.* **the u.**, les profanes *m*.

uninjured [ʌn'indʒəd], *a.* (*a*) (*of pers.*) sain et sauf; sans mal; indemne; (*b*) (*of thg*) intact; sans dommage.

uninspired [ʌnin'spaiəd], *a.* sans inspiration; (style) banal.

uninsured ['ʌnin'ʃuəd], *a.* non assuré (**against**, contre).

unintelligent [ʌnin'telidʒənt], *a.* inintelligent; à l'esprit borné; **unin'telligence**, *s.* inintelligence *f*; manque *m* d'intelligence.

unintelligible [ʌnin'telidʒibl], *a.* inintelligible; **-ibly**, *adv.* d'une manière peu intelligible.

unintentional [ʌnin'tenʃ(ə)nəl], *a.* involontaire; fait sans intention; **-ally**, *adv.* involontairement; sans le vouloir; sans intention.

uninterested [ʌn'intristid], *a.* non intéressé; indifférent; **un'interesting**, *a.* peu intéressant; sans intérêt; inintéressant.

uninterrupted ['ʌnintə'rʌptid], *a.* 1. ininterrompu. 2. continu; **u. correspondence**, correspondance suivie; **-ly**, *adv.* sans interruption.

uninvited [ʌnin'vaitid], *a.* **to come u.**, venir sans invitation; **u. guest**, visiteur inattendu; **unin'viting**, *a.* (*of appearance*) peu attrayant, peu engageant; (*of food*) peu appétissant.

union ['ju:njən], *s.* 1. union *f*; concorde *f*, harmonie *f*. 2. **the American U.**, les États-Unis; **customs u.**, union douanière; (**trade**) **u.**, syndicat *m*; **non-u. men**, ouvriers non syndiqués; **'unionist**, *s.* (**trade**) **u.**, syndicaliste *mf*; syndiqué, -ée; **'Union 'Jack,** *s.* le pavillon britannique.

unique [juːˈniːk], *a.* unique.

unisex [ˈjuːniseks], *a.* (pantalon, etc.) unisexe.

unison [ˈjuːnisən], *s.* **1.** *Mus:* unisson *m*; **in u.,** à l'unisson (**with,** de). **2. to act in u. with s.o.,** agir de concert avec qn.

unit [ˈjuːnit], *s.* **1.** unité *f*; *Com:* **u. price,** prix unitaire; *Fin:* **u. trust,** société *f* d'investissement à capital variable. **2.** (*a*) unité (de longueur, etc.); (*b*) *Mil:* **self-contained u.,** unité organique; (*c*) **kitchen u.,** bloc *m* cuisine; **u. furniture,** mobilier formé d'éléments.

unite [juːˈnait]. **1.** *v.tr.* (*a*) unir; (*b*) mettre (les gens) d'accord; unifier (un parti). **2.** *v.i.* (*a*) s'unir, se joindre (**with,** à); (*b*) (*of companies*) s'amalgamer; (*of states*) se confédérer; (*of party*) s'unifier; (*of parties*) faire bloc; **u'nited,** *a.* uni, réuni; **u. efforts,** efforts conjugués; **to present a u. front,** faire front unique; **the U. Kingdom,** le Royaume-Uni; **the U. States (of America),** les États-Unis (d'Amérique).

unity [ˈjuːniti], *s.* unité *f*; concorde *f*, accord *m*; **u. is strength,** l'union fait la force.

universe [ˈjuːnivəːs], *s.* univers *m*; **uni'versal,** *a.* universel; **he's a u. favourite,** tout le monde l'aime; **-ally,** *adv.* universellement.

university [juːniˈvəːsiti], *s.* université *f*; **u. education,** enseignement supérieur; **u. professor,** professeur de faculté; **u. town,** ville universitaire.

unjust [ʌnˈdʒʌst], *a.* injuste (**to,** envers, avec, pour); **u. suspicions,** soupçons mal fondés; **-ly,** injustement; **unjusti'fiable,** *a.* injustifiable, inexcusable; **un'justified,** *a.* injustifié.

unkempt [ʌnˈkem(p)t], *a.* **1.** (*of hair*) mal peigné; (*of appearance*) dépeigné, hirsute. **2.** (*of garden*) peu soigné; mal tenu.

unkind [ʌnˈkaind], *a.* (i) dur; cruel; (ii) peu aimable; **that's u. of him,** c'est peu aimable de sa part; **her aunt is u. to her,** sa tante la traite mal; **he was u. enough to . . .,** il a eu la méchanceté de . . .; **-ly,** *adv.* (i) méchamment, durement; (ii) sans bienveillance; **don't take it u. if . . .,** ne le prenez pas en mauvaise part si . . .; **un'kindness,** *s.* **1.** méchanceté *f*; **she had the u. to . . .,** elle a eu la méchanceté de . . .. **2.** manque *m* de bienveillance.

unknown [ʌnˈnoun]. **1.** *a.* inconnu (**to,** à, de); ignoré (**to,** de); **u. writer,** écrivain obscur; *adv.* **u. to anyone,** (faire qch.) à l'insu de tout le monde. **2.** *s.* (*a*) (*pers.*) inconnu, -ue; (*b*) *a. & s. Mth:* **u. (quantity),** inconnue *f*; (*c*) **the u.,** l'inconnu.

unleavened [ʌnˈlev(ə)nd], *a.* (pain) azyme, sans levain.

unless [ʌnˈles], *conj.* à moins que + *sub.*; **you'll be late u. you start at once,** vous arriverez trop tard à moins de partir immédiatement; **u. I am mistaken,** si je ne me trompe (pas); **u. I hear to the contrary,** à moins d'avis contraire.

unlicensed [ʌnˈlaisənst], *a.* non autorisé; illicite; **u. hotel,** hôtel *m* où la vente de boissons alcooliques n'est pas autorisée.

unlike [ʌnˈlaik], *a.* différent, dissemblable; **u. sth.,** différent de qch.; **not u. s.o.,** assez ressemblant à qn; **he, u. his father . . .,** lui, à la différence de son père . . .; **that was very u. him!** je ne le reconnais pas là!

unlik(e)able [ʌnˈlaikəbl], *a.* peu sympathique.

unlikely [ʌnˈlaikli], *a.* **1.** (*a*) invraisemblable; peu probable; **most u.,** très peu probable; **it's not at all u. that . . .,** il se pourrait bien que + *sub.*; (*b*) **he's u. to come,** il est peu probable qu'il vienne. **2. the most u. man to do such a thing,** l'homme le moins fait pour agir de la sorte; **un'likelihood,** *s.* invraisemblance *f*, improbabilité *f*.

unlimited [ʌnˈlimitid], *a.* illimité; sans borne.

unload [ʌnˈloud], *v.tr. & i.* décharger (un bateau, des marchandises, un fusil); enlever la charge (d'un fusil); **un'loaded,** *a.* **1.** déchargé; (fusil) désarmé. **2.** non chargé; (fusil) sans charge; **un'loading,** *s.* déchargement *m*.

unlock [ʌnˈlɔk], *v.tr.* **1.** ouvrir (la porte); faire jouer la serrure de (la porte). **2.** débloquer (une roue).

unlucky [ʌnˈlʌki], *a.* **1.** (*a*) malheureux, infortuné; **to be u.,** ne pas avoir de chance; jouer de malheur; (*b*) (*of thg*) malheureux, malencontreux; **how u. that he came!** quelle malchance qu'il soit venu! **2. u. star,** étoile *f* maléfique; **u. day,** jour néfaste; **it's u.,** cela porte malheur; **-ily,** *adv.* malheureusement.

unmanageable [ʌnˈmænidʒəbl], *a.* **1.** intraitable; (*of child*) intenable; (*of ship*) difficile à manœuvrer. **2.** difficile à manier.

unmarketable [ʌnˈmɑːkitəbl], *a.* invendable; d'un placement difficile.

unmarried [ʌnˈmærid], *a.* célibataire; non marié; **u. mother,** fille-mère *f*, mère célibataire.

unmentionable [ʌnˈmenʃ(ə)nəbl], *a.* (chose) dont il ne faut pas parler.

unmerciful [ʌnˈməːsiful], *a.* impitoyable; sans pitié.

unmethodical [ʌnmiˈθɔdik(ə)l], *a.* **1.** peu méthodique; (travail) décousu. **2.** (*of pers.*) brouillon.

unmistakable [ʌnmisˈteikəbl], *a.* (*a*) clair; évident; (*b*) facilement reconnaissable; **-ably,** *adv.* nettement, évidemment; à ne pas s'y méprendre.

unmitigated [ʌnˈmitigeitid], *a.* (*a*) (mal) non mitigé; **u. disaster,** désastre complet; (*b*) dans toute la force du terme; **u. lie,** pur mensonge.

unmixed [ʌnˈmikst], *a.* sans mélange; pur; it'

not an u. **blessing,** cela ne va pas sans quelques inconvénients.

unmounted [ʌn'mauntid], *a.* non monté; (*of gem*) non serti.

unmoved [ʌn'muːvd], *a.* impassible; **u. by sth.,** aucunement ému, touché, de, par, qch.; **u. by their entreaties,** insensible à leurs prières.

unmusical [ʌn'mjuːzik(ə)l], *a.* **1.** peu mélodieux. **2. she's quite u.,** elle n'est pas du tout musicienne; elle n'aime pas la musique.

unnatural [ʌn'nætʃrəl], *a.* qui n'est pas naturel; anormal; (crime) contre nature.

unnecessary [ʌn'nesis(ə)ri], *a.* peu, pas, nécessaire; inutile, superflu; (**it is**) **u. to say that . . .,** inutile de dire que . . .; **-ily,** *adv.* **1.** sans nécessité; inutilement. **2.** plus que de raison.

unnerve [ʌn'nəːv], *v.tr.* faire perdre son courage, son sang-froid, à (qn); effrayer (qn); **entirely unnerved,** tout à fait démonté.

unnoticed [ʌn'noutist], *a.* inaperçu, inobservé; **to pass u.,** passer inaperçu.

unnumbered [ʌn'nʌmbəd], *a.* non numéroté.

unobjectionable [ʌnəb'dʒekʃnəbl], *a.* (personne) à qui on ne peut rien reprocher; (chose) à laquelle on ne peut trouver à redire.

unobservant [ʌnəb'zəːvənt], *a.* peu observateur; **unob'served,** *a.* inobservé, inaperçu; **to go out u.,** sortir sans être vu.

unobstructed [ʌnəb'strʌktid], *a.* **1.** non obstrué; (*of street*) non encombré; (*of view*) libre. **2.** (avancer) sans obstacle; (faire qch.) sans rencontrer d'obstacles.

unobtainable [ʌnəb'teinəbl], *a.* impossible à obtenir, à se procurer.

unobtrusive [ʌnəb'truːsiv], *a.* discret; (rôle) effacé, modeste; **-ly,** *adv.* discrètement.

unoccupied [ʌn'ɔkjupaid], *a.* inoccupé; (*a*) sans occupation; (*b*) inhabité; (*c*) (*of seat*) libre, disponible.

unoffending [ʌnə'fendiŋ], *a.* innocent.

unofficial [ʌnə'fiʃ(ə)l], *a.* non officiel; non confirmé; (renseignement) officieux; **-ally,** *adv.* à titre officieux.

unopened [ʌn'oupənd], *a.* qui n'a pas été ouvert; **u. letter,** lettre non décachetée.

unopposed [ʌnə'pouzd], *a.* sans opposition.

unorthodox [ʌn'ɔːθədɔks], *a.* peu orthodoxe.

unostentatious ['ʌnɔsten'teiʃəs], *a.* **1.** peu fastueux; simple. **2.** fait sans ostentation; **-ly,** *adv.* sans ostentation, sans faste.

unpack [ʌn'pæk]. **1.** *v.tr.* déballer, dépaqueter (des objets). **2.** *v.tr.* défaire (une malle). **3.** *v.i.* défaire sa malle, sa valise; **un'packing,** *s.* déballage *m,* dépaquetage *m;* **my u. won't take long,** il me faudra peu de temps pour défaire mes valises.

unpaid [ʌn'peid], *a.* **1.** non payé; (*of post*) non rétribué; (magistrat) sans traitement. **2.** (*of bill*) impayé; **u. debt,** dette non acquittée.

unpalatable [ʌn'pælətəbl], *a.* (*a*) d'un goût désagréable; (*b*) (*of truth*) désagréable.

unpardonable [ʌn'paːdnəbl], *a.* impardonnable; **it's u. of her to have forgotten,** elle est impardonnable d'avoir oublié.

unpatriotic ['ʌnpætri'ɔtik], *a.* (*of pers.*) peu patriote; (*of action*) peu patriotique.

unperturbed [ʌnpə'təːbd], *a.* impassible; imperturbable.

unpick [ʌn'pik], *v.tr.* défaire (une couture).

unplaced [ʌn'pleist], *a.* (cheval) non placé.

unpleasant [ʌn'plez(ə)nt], *a.* désagréable, déplaisant; fâcheux; **-ly,** *adv.* désagréablement; fâcheusement; **un'pleasantness,** *s.* **1.** caractère *m* désagréable (de qch.). **2.** désagrément *m,* ennui *m;* **there'll be some u.,** il y aura de la brouille, du grabuge.

unpolished [ʌn'pɔliʃt], *a.* **1.** non poli; mat; (*of stone*) brut. **2.** rude, grossier.

unpolluted [ʌnpə'l(j)uːtid], *a.* non pollué; pur.

unpopular [ʌn'pɔpjulər], *a.* impopulaire; **to be generally u.,** être mal vu de tous; **'unpopu'larity** [-'læriti], *s.* impopularité *f.*

unpractical [ʌn'præktik(ə)l], *a.* (*of pers.*) peu pratique.

unprecedented [ʌn'presidentid], *a.* (i) sans précédent; (ii) sans exemple, inouï, inédit.

unprejudiced [ʌn'predʒudist], *a.* sans préjugé, sans prévention; impartial; désintéressé.

unprepared [ʌnpri'pɛəd], *a.* **1.** (discours) improvisé. **2. to catch s.o. u.,** prendre qn au dépourvu. **3.** sans préparatifs; **to go into (sth.) u.,** se lancer sans préparation dans (une affaire).

unprepossessing ['ʌnpriːpə'zesiŋ], *a.* peu engageant.

unpretentious [ʌnpri'tenʃəs], *a.* sans prétention; modeste; **-ly,** *adv.* modestement.

unprincipled [ʌn'prinsipld], *a.* sans principe; sans scrupule; **he is completely u.,** il ne s'embarrasse d'aucun scrupule.

unprintable [ʌn'printəbl], *a.* que l'on rougirait d'imprimer; (livre) inéditable.

unprocurable [ʌnprə'kjuərəbl], *a.* impossible à obtenir; que l'on ne peut se procurer; introuvable.

unproductive [ʌnprə'dʌktiv], *a.* (*of land, conversation, etc.*) improductif, stérile.

unprofessional [ʌnprə'feʃ(ə)n(ə)l], *a.* (*a*) **u. conduct,** manquement *m* aux devoirs de la profession; (*b*) **he's a very u. sort of architect,** comme architecte il est plutôt amateur.

unprofitable [ʌn'prɔfitəbl], *a.* peu lucratif; sans profit; peu rentable; (travail) inutile, stérile; **-ably,** *adv.* sans profit; inutilement, stérilement.

unpromising [ʌn'prɔmisiŋ], *a.* peu prometteur; **the weather looks u.,** le temps s'annonce mal.

unpronounceable [ʌnprə'naunsəbl], a. imprononçable.

unprotected [ʌnprə'tektid], a. inabrité; sans protection, sans défense.

unproved [ʌn'pru:vd], a. qui n'est pas prouvé.

unprovided for [ʌnprə'vaididfɔ:r], a. (laisser qn) sans ressources.

unprovoked [ʌnprə'voukt], a. non provoqué; fait sans provocation; **u. assault**, agression f.

unpublished [ʌn'pʌbliʃt], a. inédit; non publié; **un'publishable**, a. inéditable; impubliable.

unpunctual [ʌn'pʌŋ(k)tjuəl], a. (a) inexact; peu ponctuel; (b) en retard; pas à l'heure; **'unpunc- tu'ality** [-'æliti], s. inexactitude f; manque m de ponctualité.

unpunished [ʌn'pʌniʃt], a. impuni; (faire qch.) impunément.

unqualified [ʌn'kwɔlifaid], a. 1. (a) in- compétent; **u. to vote**, qui n'a pas le droit de vote; **I am u. to speak of it**, je ne suis pas qualifié pour en parler; (b) sans diplômes. 2. **u. statement**, déclaration générale; **u. praise**, éloges sans réserve.

unquestionable [ʌn'kwestʃənəbl], a. in- discutable, indubitable; (fait) hors de doute; **-ably**, adv. indubitablement, incontestable- ment, sans aucun doute; **un'questioned**, a. 1. (droit) indisputé, incontesté. 2. **to let a state- ment pass u.**, laisser passer une affirmation sans la relever; **un'questioning**, a. (obéissance) aveugle; inconditionnel; **-ly**, adv. aveuglément; sans question; sans hésitation ni murmure.

unquote ['ʌnkwout], v.i. fermer les guillemets; **quote . . . u.**, début m de citation . . . fin f de citation.

unravel [ʌn'ræv(ə)l], v.tr. (**unravelled**) effiler; effilocher (un tissu); débrouiller, démêler (des fils); éclaircir (un mystère).

unreadable [ʌn'ri:dəbl], a. illisible.

unreal [ʌn'ri:əl], a. irréel; imaginaire; **'unrea'listic**, a. qui n'est pas réaliste, utopique; **unre'ality**, s. irréalité f.

unreasonable [ʌn'ri:znəbl], a. déraisonnable; **don't be u.**, soyez raisonnable; **u. demands**, demandes exorbitantes; **at an u. hour**, à une heure indue; **-ably**, adv. déraisonnablement; d'une manière peu raisonnable; **un- 'reasoning**, a. **u. hatred**, haine irraisonnée.

unrecognizable [ʌn'rekəgnaizəbl], a. mécon- naissable; **un'recognized**, a. (of talent) méconnu.

unreconciled [ʌn'rekənsaild], a. irréconcilié.

unrecorded [ʌnri'kɔ:did], a. non enregistré; dont on ne trouve aucune mention.

unrefined [ʌnri'faind], a. 1. brut; (sucre) non raffiné. 2. (homme) peu raffiné, grossier.

unreformable [ʌnri'fɔ:məbl], a. irréformable; incorrigible; **unre'formed**, a. non réformé;

an u. character, un incorrigible.

unrehearsed [ʌnri'hə:st], a. (discours) im promptu; (effet) non préparé; **to put on a play u.**, jouer une pièce sans répétitions préalables.

unrelated [ʌnri'leitid], a. (of phenomena) **u. to each other**, sans rapport l'un avec l'autre; (o pers.) **they are entirely u.**, il n'y a aucun lien de parenté entre eux.

unrelenting [ʌnri'lentiŋ], a. (of pers.) im placable, impitoyable (**towards**, à, pour, à l'égard de); (of persecution) acharné.

unreliable [ʌnri'laiəbl], a. (homme) sur leque on ne peut pas compter; (renseignement) suje à caution; (machine) d'un fonctionnement in certain; **u. map**, carte peu fidèle; **'unrelia'bili ty**, s. (a) inexactitude f (des résultats d'un expérience); (b) instabilité f (de qn).

unremunerative [ʌnri'mju:nərətiv], a. pe rémunérateur; peu lucratif.

unrequited [ʌnri'kwaitid], a. (amour) nor partagé.

unreserved [ʌnri'zə:vd], a. 1. sans réserve franc; (of approval) complet, entier. 2. **u. seats** places non réservées; **-edly** [-idli], adv. san: réserve; franchement; entièrement; san restriction.

unresponsive [ʌnris'pɔnsiv], a. difficile émouvoir; froid; Aut: **u. engine**, moteur pet sensible, mou, plat.

unrest [ʌn'rest], s. **industrial u.**, agitatior ouvrière; **u. among the inhabitants**, malais chez les habitants.

unrewarded [ʌnri'wɔ:did], a. sans récompense

unripe [ʌn'raip], a. **u. fruit**, fruits verts, qui n sont pas mûrs.

unroll [ʌn'roul], v.tr., pr. & i. (se) dérouler.

unruffled [ʌn'rʌfld], a. (of sea, temper) calme **an u. composure**, un calme imperturbable.

unruly [ʌn'ru:li], a. indiscipliné.

unsaddle [ʌn'sædl], v.tr. desseller (un cheval).

unsafe [ʌn'seif], a. 1. (of action) dangereux; (o ice) peu sûr; (of undertaking) hasardeux. 2 exposé au danger.

unsaid [ʌn'sed], a. **to leave u.**, passer (qch.) sou: silence.

unsaleable [ʌn'seiləbl], a. invendable.

unsalted [ʌn'sɔltəd], a. (beurre) doux, non salé

unsatisfactory ['ʌnsætis'fækt(ə)ri], a. pe satisfaisant; qui laisse à désirer; (o explanation) peu convaincant.

unsatisfied [ʌn'sætisfaid], a. 1. mécontent, pet satisfait (**with**, de). 2. **I'm still u. about it**, j n'en suis pas encore convaincu. 3. (of appetite inassouvi; **un'satisfying**, a. 1. pet satisfaisant; peu convaincant. 2. (of meal) pet rassasiant.

unsavoury [ʌn'seiv(ə)ri], a. 1. (plat) d'un goû désagréable; **u. smell**, mauvaise odeur. 2 (scandale) répugnant; **u. business**, vilaine affaire: **u. reputation,** réputation *f* équivoque.

unscientific ['ʌnsaiən'tifik], *a.* non scientifique: peu scientifique: **u. name,** nom courant (d'une plante).

unscrew [ʌn'skru:], *v.tr.* dévisser.

unscrupulous [ʌn'skru:pjuləs], *a.* indélicat; sans scrupules; **-ly,** *adv.* peu scrupuleusement; sans scrupules.

unseasonable [ʌn'si:z(ə)nəbl], *a.* 1. (*of fruit*) hors de saison: **u. weather,** temps qui n'est pas de saison. 2. (*of action*) inopportun; intempestif: déplacé; **-ably,** *adv.* 1. hors de saison: **u. warm,** chaud pour la saison. 2. mal à propos: **un'seasoned,** *a.* 1. (*of food*) non assaisonné. 2. (bois) vert.

unseat [ʌn'si:t], *v.tr.* (*of horse*) désarçonner (son cavalier).

unselfish [ʌn'selfiʃ], *a.* (*of pers.*) généreux; sans égoïsme: **u. motive,** motif désintéressé; **-ly,** *adv.* généreusement: **un'selfishness,** *s.* générosité *f*; désintéressement *m*.

unserviceable [ʌn'sə:visəbl], *a.* (*a*) (cadeau) inutilisable; (*b*) (vêtement) de mauvais service, peu pratique: (*c*) hors d'état de servir.

unsettle [ʌn'setl], *v.tr.* ébranler (les convictions); troubler le repos de (qn); **un'settled,** *a.* 1. (pays) troublé; (temps) variable; **the u. state of the weather,** l'incertitude *f* du temps. 2. (*a*) (*of question*) indécis, en suspens; (*b*) (*of bill*) impayé, non réglé.

unsightly [ʌn'saitli], *a.* peu agréable à la vue; laid, vilain.

unskilled [ʌn'skild], *a.* inexpert, inexpérimenté; *Ind:* **u. worker,** manœuvre *m*; **u. work,** travail *m* de manœuvre; **unskilful,** *a.* maladroit; malhabile (à qch.).

unsociable [ʌn'souʃəbl], *a.* insociable; farouche.

unsold [ʌn'sould], *a.* invendu; *Journ:* **u. copies,** invendus *m*, bouillons *m*.

unsolicited [ʌnsə'lisitid], *a.* non sollicité; (*of action*) volontaire, spontané: (faire qch.) spontanément.

unsolved [ʌn'sɔlvd], *a.* (problème) non résolu; inexpliqué; mystérieux.

unsophisticated [ʌnsə'fistikeitid], *a.* 1. non frelaté, naturel. 2. (*of pers.*) ingénu, naïf, simple, candide.

unsound [ʌn'saund], *a.* 1. (*a*) of u. mind, qui n'est pas sain d'esprit; qui a le cerveau dérangé: **u. horse,** cheval taré; (*b*) gâté; en mauvais état. 2. (*of ice*) peu solide; (*of position*) mal affermi; (*of business*) qui périclite: **u. argument,** raisonnement *m* qui pèche.

unsparing [ʌn'spɛəriŋ], *a.* 1. prodigue (of, de); **u. in one's efforts,** infatigable; **to be u. of one's strength,** ne pas ménager ses forces. 2. **u. of others,** impitoyable, sans pitié, pour les autres.

unspeakable [ʌn'spi:kəbl], *a.* 1. (douleur) inexprimable: **u. muddle,** désordre sans nom. 2. *F:* détestable, inqualifiable: **it's u.!** ça n'a pas de nom!

unspecified [ʌn'spesifaid], *a.* non spécifié.

unspoilt ['ʌn'spɔilt], *a.* (paysage) non touché par l'industrialisation.

unstable [ʌn'steibl], *a.* 1. instable: (*of position*) peu sûr: **u. equilibrium,** équilibre *m* instable. 2. (*of pers.*) (i) peu consistant; (ii) qui n'est pas sain d'esprit: (*of character*) changeant, inconstant.

unsteady [ʌn'stedi], *a.* 1. (*of table*) peu stable, peu solide, branlant; (*of footsteps*) chancelant; (*of voice*) mal assuré, chevrotant; **to be u. on one's feet,** vaciller; tituber. 2. (*a*) (*of purpose*) vacillant: irrésolu: (*b*) (*of pers.*) dissipé; déréglé. 3. irrégulier; **un'steadiness,** *s.* 1. instabilité *f*; manque *m* d'aplomb (d'une table); manque de sûreté (de la main). 2. (*a*) irrésolution *f*, indécision *f*; (*b*) manque de conduite. 3. irrégularité *f*, variabilité *f* (du vent, des prix).

unstick [ʌn'stik], *v.tr.* (**unstuck** [-'stʌk]) **to come unstuck,** (i) se décoller; (ii) (*of plan*) s'effondrer.

unstitch [ʌn'stitʃ], *v.tr.* dépiquer, découdre (un vêtement); **to come unstitched,** se découdre.

unsuccessful [ʌnsək'sesful], *a.* 1. non réussi; **u. attempt,** tentative *f* sans succès; coup manqué. 2. (*of pers.*) qui n'a pas réussi; qui a échoué; (*of candidate*) refusé, (*at election*) non élu; **-fully,** *adv.* sans succès; vainement.

unsuitable [ʌn's(j)u:təbl], *a.* 1. (*of pers.*) peu fait (**to, for,** pour); inapte (à). 2. (*of thg*) impropre, mal adapté (à); (*of remark*) inconvenant, déplacé; inopportun; (*of marriage*) mal assorti: **u. for the occasion,** qui ne convient pas à la circonstance; **-ably,** *adv.* d'une manière qui ne convient pas; **'unsuita'bility,** *s.* 1. inaptitude *f* (de qn à qch.); incapacité *f*. 2. disconvenance *f* (du climat); inopportunité *f* (d'une observation); impropriété *f* (d'une locution); **un'suited,** *a.* **u. to, for, sth.,** (*of pers.*) peu fait pour qch.; inapte à qch.; (*of thg*) impropre, mal adapté, mal approprié à qch.; **u. to the occasion,** qui ne convient pas à la circonstance.

unsure [ʌn'ʃuər], *a.* peu sûr, incertain (**about,** de); **to be u. of oneself,** se défier, douter, de soi-même, manquer de confiance en soi.

unsuspected [ʌnsəs'pektid], *a.* insoupçonné (**by,** de); (i) non suspect; (ii) dont on ne soupçonnait pas l'existence; **unsus'pecting,** *a.* 1. qui ne se doute de rien; sans soupçons; sans défiance. 2. **naturally u.,** peu soupçonneux; **-ly,** *adv.* sans rien soupçonner.

unsuspicious [ʌnsəs'piʃəs], *a.* 1. peu soupçonneux. 2. sans soupçons; sans défiance; **to be u. of sth.,** ne pas se douter de qch.

unsympathetic [ˈʌnsimpəˈθetik], a. peu compatissant; froid; indifférent; **-ally**, adv. sans compassion; froidement.

unsystematic [ˈʌnsistəˈmætik], a. non systématique; sans méthode; **-ally**, adv. sans méthode; au petit bonheur.

unteachable [ʌnˈtiːtʃəbl], a. incapable d'apprendre; à qui l'on ne peut rien apprendre.

untenable [ʌnˈtenəbl], a. (of theory) insoutenable; (of position) intenable.

untested [ʌnˈtestid], a. pas encore essayé, inéprouvé; qui n'a pas encore été mis à l'épreuve.

unthinkable [ʌnˈθiŋkəbl], a. inimaginable; impensable; **it's u. that he should be acquitted**, il est inconcevable qu'il soit acquitté.

untidy [ʌnˈtaidi], a. (a) (of room) en désordre; mal tenu; (of hair) ébouriffé, mal peigné; **u. dress**, tenue négligée, débraillée; (b) (of pers.) désordonné; **-ily**, adv. sans ordre; sans soin; **un'tidiness**, s. désordre m; manque m d'ordre, de soin.

untie [ʌnˈtai], v.tr. **(untied; untying)** dénouer (sa ceinture); défaire, délier (un nœud, un paquet); détacher (un chien); déficeler (un paquet); **to come untied**, se défaire, se déficeler.

until [ʌnˈtil]. **1.** prep. (a) jusqu'à; **u. evening**, jusqu'au soir; (b) **not u.**, pas avant; **he won't come u. after dinner**, il ne viendra qu'après le dîner. **2.** conj. (a) jusqu'à ce que + sub.; **I'll wait u. he comes**, j'attendrai jusqu'à ce qu'il vienne; (b) **not u.**, pas avant que + sub.; **he won't come u. you invite him**, il ne viendra pas avant que vous (ne) l'invitiez, avant d'être invité.

untold [ˈʌnˈtould], a. **1.** (richesse) immense, énorme, incalculable; **u. losses**, pertes incalculables. **2. to leave u.**, passer (une histoire) sous silence.

untouched [ʌnˈtʌtʃt], a. **1.** (a) non touché; (of food) **u. by hand**, non manié; (b) **he had left the food u.**, il n'avait pas touché à la nourriture. **2.** (a) **to leave u.**, laisser (qch.) intact; (b) (se tirer de qch.) sain et sauf.

untranslatable [ˈʌntrænsˈleitəbl], a. intraduisible.

untried [ʌnˈtraid], a. **1.** non essayé; **we left nothing u.**, il n'y a rien qu'on n'ait essayé. **2.** qui n'a pas été mis à l'épreuve.

untrue [ʌnˈtruː], a. (of statement) faux; mensonger; erroné.

untrustworthy [ʌnˈtrʌstwəːði], a. **1.** (of pers.) indigne de confiance; (témoin) récusable; **u. memory**, mauvaise mémoire, mémoire peu sûre. **2.** (renseignement) douteux, peu sûr, sujet à caution.

untruthful [ʌnˈtruːθful], a. **1.** (of pers.) menteur. **2.** (of news) mensonger, faux; **-fully**, adv. menteusement, mensongèrement; **un'truthfulness**, s. **1.** (of pers.) caractère menteur. **2.** fausseté f, caractère mensonger (d'une histoire).

untuned [ʌnˈtjuːnd], a. Mus: non accordé.

unusable [ʌnˈjuːzəbl], a. inutilisable.

unused, a. **1.** [ʌnˈjuːzd] (a) inutilisé; non employé; (b) qui n'a pas encore servi; neuf; à l'état de neuf. **2.** [ʌnˈjuːst] peu habitué (**to**, à); **to get u. to sth.**, se déshabituer, perdre l'habitude, de qch.

unusual [ʌnˈjuːʒu(ə)l], a. (a) peu commun; exceptionnel; insolite; inhabituel; peu ordinaire; **that's u.**, (i) cela se fait peu; ce n'est pas l'usage; (ii) cela se voit rarement; cela sort de l'ordinaire; **nothing u.**, rien d'anormal; (b) (mot) peu usité; **-ally**, adv. **u. tall**, d'une taille exceptionnelle; **he was u. attentive**, il s'est montré plus attentif que d'habitude.

unvarying [ʌnˈvɛəriiŋ], a. invariable.

unwanted [ʌnˈwɔntid], a. **1.** non désiré, non voulu. **2.** superflu.

unwarrantable [ʌnˈwɔrəntəbl], a. (action) injustifiable, inexcusable; (assertion) insoutenable; **un'warranted**, a. **1.** sans garantie. **2.** injustifié; peu justifié; **u. remark**, observation déplacée; **u. interference**, ingérence f, immixtion f (dans une affaire).

unwashed [ʌnˈwɔʃt], a. non lavé; malpropre, sale.

unwelcome [ʌnˈwelkəm], a. (a) (visiteur) mal venu, inopportun; importun; (b) (of news) fâcheux, désagréable.

unwell [ʌnˈwel], a. indisposé; souffrant.

unwieldy [ʌnˈwiːldi], a. **1.** (of pers.) lourd, gauche; à la démarche lourde. **2.** (outil, colis) difficile à porter, à manier; peu maniable.

unwilling [ʌnˈwiliŋ], a. **1.** peu serviable; de mauvaise volonté. **2. u. to do sth.**, peu disposé à faire qch.; **u. acquiescence**, assentiment donné à contrecœur; **I was u. for my wife to know**, je ne voulais pas que ma femme le sache; **-ly**, adv. à contrecœur; de mauvaise grâce; à regret; **un'willingness**, s. **1.** mauvaise volonté; mauvaise grâce. **2.** répugnance f (à faire qch.).

unwise [ʌnˈwaiz], a. imprudent; peu prudent, peu sage; malavisé.

unworkable [ʌnˈwəːkəbl], a. (projet) inexécutable, impraticable; Min: (gisement) inexploitable.

unworthy [ʌnˈwəːði], a. **1. u. of sth., to do sth.**, indigne de qch., de faire qch. **2.** (conduite) indigne, méprisable. **3.** (travail) peu méritoire, indigne (de qn).

unwrap [ʌnˈræp], v.tr. **(unwrapped)** défaire, développer (un paquet); enlever l'enveloppe de (qch.).

unwritten [ʌnˈrit(ə)n], a. qui n'est pas écrit; (of tradition) oral; **u. law**, droit coutumier.

unyielding [ʌnˈjiːldiŋ], a. qui ne cède pas; raide,

ferme; (*of pers.*) inébranlable, opiniâtre; inflexible; **of u. principles,** inflexible dans ses principes.

up [ʌp]. **I.** *adv.* **1.** (*a*) en montant; vers le haut; **to go up,** monter; **my room is three flights up,** ma chambre est au troisième; **to throw sth. up,** jeter qch. en l'air; **right up (to the top),** (monter) jusqu'au haut (de la colline), jusqu'en haut (de l'escalier); **halfway up,** jusqu'à mi-hauteur; **hands up!** haut les mains! (*b*) **to walk up and down,** se promener de long en large; **to go up north,** aller dans le nord; **to go up to town,** aller à Londres; **to go up to (the) university,** aller à l'université; **to go up for an examination,** se présenter à un examen; (*c*) **from five pounds up,** à partir de cinq livres. **2.** (*a*) haut, en haut; **what are you doing up there?** que faites-vous là-haut? **up above,** en haut; **up above sth.,** au-dessus de qch.; **the moon is up,** la lune est levée; **game of a hundred up,** partie en cent; **the blinds are up,** on a relevé les stores; **the shops had their shutters up,** les magasins avaient leurs volets mis; **the new building is up,** le nouveau bâtiment est fini; **road up,** route en réfection; travaux; **halfway up,** à mi-hauteur; (*b*) en dessus; **face up,** face en dessus; (*on packing case*) **this side up,** haut; dessus; ne pas renverser; (*c*) **up in London,** à Londres; **up in Yorkshire,** au nord, dans le Yorkshire; **relations up from the country,** parents de province en visite à la ville; (*d*) *Sp:* **to be one goal up,** mener par un but. **3.** (*a*) **to go up,** (i) (*of prices*) monter; (ii) (*of commodity*) subir une hausse; **the thermometer has gone up,** le thermomètre a monté; **things are looking up,** les affaires *f* sont à la hausse; (*b*) **to screw up,** visser, serrer (un écrou); **to get up steam,** mettre (la chaudière) sous pression, faire monter la pression; **his blood was up,** il était monté; le sang lui bouillait; (*c*) **to be well up in a subject,** connaître un sujet à fond; être versé dans une matière; (*d*) **to praise s.o. up,** vanter, prôner, qn; **to speak up,** parler plus haut. **4. put it up against the other one,** mettez-le tout près de l'autre; **to follow s.o. up,** suivre qn de près; **to be up with s.o., sth.,** être au niveau de qn, de qch.; **he came up with me,** il m'a rejoint. **5.** (*a*) debout, levé; **to get up,** se lever; **to be up and about,** être sur pied; **hold yourself up!** tenez-vous droit! (*b*) **to be up all night,** ne pas se coucher de la nuit; **to stay up,** veiller; **to be up late,** (i) se coucher tard; (ii) se lever tard; (*c*) **to be up against s.o.,** avoir affaire à qn; **to be up against difficulties,** se heurter à, être aux prises avec, des difficultés; **to be up against it,** être dans la déveine, avoir la guigne. **6.** (*a*) **to be up in arms,** se révolter, s'insurger; **she was up in arms over what he had done,** elle s'indignait de ce qu'il avait fait; (*b*) **what's up?** qu'est-ce qui

se passe? **there's something up,** il y a quelque chose; **what's up with him (now)?** qu'est-ce qui lui prend? **7. time's up,** il est l'heure (de finir, de fermer); c'est l'heure; **his leave's up,** sa permission est expirée; *F:* **the game's up,** tout est perdu; **it's all up with him,** son affaire est faite; il est fichu; **I thought it was all up with me,** j'ai cru que ma dernière heure était venue. **8. up to;** (*a*) jusqu'à; **to come, go, up to s.o.,** s'approcher de, s'avancer vers, qn; (*b*) **up to now, to here,** jusqu'ici; (*c*) **to be up to a job,** être à la hauteur d'une tâche; **I don't feel up to it,** je ne m'en sens pas le courage, la force; (*d*) **what are you up to?** qu'est-ce que vous faites? **he's up to something,** il a quelque chose en tête; (*e*) **it's up to him to decide,** c'est à lui de décider. **II.** *prep.* **1. to go up the stairs, a hill,** monter l'escalier, une côte; **the cat is up the tree,** le chat est en haut de l'arbre. **2.** (*a*) **up the river,** en amont; **further up the street,** plus loin dans la rue; **to walk up and down the platform,** faire les cent pas sur le quai; **to walk up and down the room,** se promener de long en large dans la pièce; (*b*) **up the yard,** au fond de, dans, la cour. **III.** *a. Rail:* **up line,** voie descendante; **up train,** train descendant, de retour. **IV.** *s.pl.* **ups and downs,** ondulations *f* (du terrain); **the ups and downs of life,** les péripéties *f* de la vie; **'up-and-'coming,** *a.* (jeune homme) d'avenir; **'up-and-'up,** *s. F:* **to be on the up-and-up,** prospérer; **'upbringing,** *s.* éducation *f* (d'un enfant); **what sort of (an) u. did he have?** comment a-t-il été élevé? **'up-'end,** *v.tr.* dresser (qch.) debout; mettre (un tonneau) à cul; **'upgrade,** *s.* pente ascendante; rampe *f*, montée *f* (d'une route); **to be on the u.,** (i) (*of prices*) monter; être à la hausse; (ii) (*of business, of invalid*) reprendre; **up'grade,** *v.tr.* améliorer (un produit); **up'heaval,** *s.* **1.** soulèvement *m*; commotion *f*, bouleversement *m*. **2.** agitation *f*, convulsion *f* (politique); **'up'hill. 1.** *a.* (*of road*) montant; en rampe; (*of task*) ardu, rude. **2.** *adv.* **to go u.,** monter; aller en montant; **up'hold,** *v.tr.* (**up'held**) supporter, soutenir, maintenir; **to u. s.o.,** prêter son appui à qn; **to u. a decision,** confirmer une décision; **up'holstery,** *s.* (i) tapisserie *f* d'ameublement; (ii) garniture *f* d'intérieur (d'une voiture); **'upkeep,** *s.* (frais *mpl* d')entretien *m*; **'uplift,** *s.* **moral u.,** élévation morale; **up'lift,** *v.tr.* élever (l'âme); **u'pon** [ə'pɔn], *prep.* sur; **'upper. I.** *a.* **1.** (*a*) supérieur; (plus) haut; (plus) élevé; de dessus; d'au-dessus; **u. jaw,** mâchoire supérieure; **u. storey,** étage supérieur; **u. part,** dessus *m* (de qch.); (*b*) **u. reaches,** amont *m* (d'une rivière). **2.** supérieur (en rang); **the u. classes,** la haute société; **to get the u. hand,** prendre le dessus; **to let s.o. get the u. hand,** se laisser tyranniser, mener, par qn; *Sch:* **the u.**

forms, les hautes classes, les classes supérieures. **II.** *s.* empeigne *f* (d'une chaussure); **'uppermost. 1.** *a.* (*a*) le plus haut, le plus élevé; (*b*) de la plus grande importance; premier; **to be u.,** prédominer. **2.** *adv.* (*a*) (le plus) en dessus; **face u.,** face en dessus; (*b*) **the problem which is u. in our minds,** le problème qui nous préoccupe le plus; **'uppish,** *a. F:* présomptueux, arrogant; suffisant; **'upright. I.** *a.* **1.** vertical; perpendiculaire; droit; **to set sth. u.,** mettre qch. debout; (*on packing case*) **to be kept u.,** tenir debout; **to hold oneself u.,** se tenir droit. **2.** (*of conduct*) droit, intègre, honnête, probe. **II.** *s.* montant *m* (d'une échelle, etc.); *Fb:* **the uprights,** les montants du but; **'uprising,** *s.* soulèvement *m*, insurrection *f*; **'uproar,** *s.* vacarme *m*, tapage *m*; **the town is in an u.,** la ville est en rumeur; **up'roarious,** *a.* tumultueux, tapageur; **to burst into u. laughter,** partir d'un grand éclat de rire; **-ly,** *adv.* tumultueusement; (rire) à gorge déployée; **up'root,** *v.tr.* déraciner (qn, une plante, un mal); arracher (une plante); **upset. I.** [ˈʌpset], *s.* **1.** renversement *m* (d'une voiture); chavirement *m* (d'un bateau). **2.** (*a*) désorganisation *f,* bouleversement *m,* désordre *m;* (*b*) anicroche *f,* ennui *m;* (*c*) bouleversement (d'esprit); **it was such an u. for me!** cela m'en a donné un coup! (*d*) dérangement *m;* **I have a stomach u.,** j'ai l'estomac dérangé. **II.** [ʌpˈset], *v.* (**upset; upset;** *pr.p.* **upsetting**) **1.** *v.tr.* (*a*) renverser (un vase); (faire) verser (une voiture); (faire) chavirer (un bateau); culbuter (qn); (*b*) désorganiser, bouleverser, déranger (les plans de qn); tromper (les calculs de qn); (*c*) troubler, bouleverser, démonter (qn); mettre (qn) en émoi; **he's easily u.,** il s'émeut d'un rien; (*d*) indisposer (qn); dérégler; déranger (l'estomac); troubler (la digestion). **2.** *v.i.* (*of cup*) se renverser; (*of vehicle*) verser; (*of boat*) chavirer. **III.** [ʌpˈset], *a.* (*a*) bouleversé, ému; **don't be so u.,** ne vous désolez pas comme ça; **to get u.,** se laisser démonter; (*b*) **my digestion is u.,** j'ai l'estomac dérangé; **'upshot,** *s.* résultat *m,* issue *f,* dénouement *m* (d'une affaire); **'upside 'down,** *adv. phr.* (*a*) sens dessus dessous; la tête en bas; **to hold sth. u.down,** tenir qch. renversé, à l'envers; (*b*) en désordre, bouleversé; **to turn everything u.down,** tout bouleverser; tout mettre sens dessus dessous; **'up'stairs. 1.** *adv.* en haut (de l'escalier); **to go u.,** monter (l'escalier); aller en haut. **2.** *a.* (*of room*) d'en haut; situé à l'étage supérieur; **up'standing,** *a.* **a fine u. young man,** un jeune homme bien campé; **'upstart,** *s.* parvenu, -ue; **'uptake,** *s.* **to be slow in the u.,** avoir la compréhension lente; **quick in the u.,** à l'esprit vif, éveillé; **'upward,** *a.* **u. movement,** mouvement ascendant; (*of prices*) **to have an**

u. tendency, être à la hausse; **'upwards,** *adv.* **1.** de bas en haut; vers le haut; en montant; **the road runs u.,** la route va en montant. **2.** en dessus; **to lay sth. down face u.,** mettre qch. à l'endroit (sur qch.); **the knife fell with the edge u.,** le couteau est tombé le tranchant en dessus; **to look u.,** regarder en haut, en l'air. **3.** au-dessus; **a hundred pounds and u.,** cent livres et au-dessus, et au delà; **u. of fifty cows, from ten years old u.,** à partir de dix ans.

Ural [ˈjuərəl]. *Pr.n. Geog:* **the U.** (river), l'Oural *m;* **the U. mountains, the Urals,** les monts Oural.

uranium [juˈreiniəm], *s.* uranium *m;* **u.-bearing,** (roche) uranifère.

urban [ˈəːbən], *a.* urbain; **urbani'zation,** *s.* urbanisation *f;* **'urbanize,** *v.tr.* urbaniser.

urbane [əːˈbein], *a.* courtois, poli, civil; **-ly,** *adv.* courtoisement; avec urbanité.

urbanity [əːˈbæniti], *s.* urbanité *f;* courtoisie *f.*

urchin [ˈəːtʃin], *s.* (*a*) galopin *m,* gamin *m;* petit polisson; (*b*) gosse *mf;* marmot *m.*

Urdu [ˈəːduː], *s. Ling:* l'ourdou *m.*

urge [əːdʒ]. **I.** *s.* incitation *f,* impulsion *f;* poussée *f;* **to feel an u. to do sth.,** se sentir poussé à faire qch. **II.** *v.tr.* **1.** **to u. s.o.** (**on**), encourager, exhorter, exciter, qn; **to u. a horse forward, on,** pousser, enlever, un cheval; **to u. s.o. to do sth.,** pousser, exhorter, qn à faire qch.; **to u. forward a piece of work,** hâter, activer, un ouvrage. **2.** mettre en avant, alléguer (une raison*)*; faire valoir (une excuse); insister sur (un point). **3.** conseiller fortement, recommander; **to u. that sth. should be done,** insister pour que qch. se fasse.

urgent [ˈəːdʒ(ə)nt], *a.* urgent, pressant; **it's u.,** c'est urgent; **u. need,** besoin pressant; **the matter is u.,** l'affaire presse; **u. request,** prière instante; **-ly,** *adv.* avec instance; avec insistance; **a doctor is u. required,** on demande d'urgence un médecin; **'urgency,** *s.* **1.** urgence *f;* extrémité *f* (d'un besoin); **it's a matter of u.,** il y a urgence. **2.** besoin pressant; nécessité urgente.

urine [ˈjuərin], *s.* urine *f;* **u'rinal** [-ˈrainəl], *s.* urinoir *m;* **'urinate,** *v.i.* uriner.

urn [əːn], *s.* urne *f.*

Uruguay [ˈjuːrəgwai]. *Pr.n.* l'Uruguay *m.*

us, *pers.pron., objective case.* **1.** [əs] (*a*) nous; **he sees us,** il nous voit; **give us some,** donnez-nous-en; **there are three of us,** nous sommes trois; (*b*) **we'll take him with us,** nous l'amènerons avec nous. **2.** (*stressed*) [ʌs] nous; **between you and us,** entre vous et nous; **they can't deceive us women,** on ne peut pas nous tromper, nous autres femmes. **3.** (*stressed* [ʌs] *as a nominative*) **he wouldn't believe it was us,**

il ne voulait pas croire que c'était nous. **4.** [əs] (*with sg. meaning* = **me**) *F:* **let us, let's, have a look**, laissez-moi regarder. **use. I.** [ju:s], *s.* **1.** (*a*) emploi *m*, usage *m*; **a new u. for radio**, une nouvelle utilisation de la radio; **I'll find a u. for it**, je trouverai bien à l'employer; **to make u. of sth.**, se servir de qch.; tirer parti de qch.; **to make good u. of sth., to put sth. to good u.**, faire bon usage de qch.; **article in everyday u.**, article d'usage courant; **word in everyday u.**, mot très usité; **not in u.**, (i) hors d'usage; (ii) disponible; **it has been in u. for ten years**, il sert depuis dix ans; **fit for u.**, en état de servir; **ready for u.**, prêt à servir; **directions for u.**, mode *m* d'emploi; (*b*) **to improve with u.**, s'améliorer à l'usage. **2.** jouissance *f*, usage; (*of tenancy*) **with u. of kitchen**, avec jouissance de la cuisine; **he has lost the u. of his left leg**, il est impotent de la jambe gauche; **I'd like to have the u. of it**, je voudrais pouvoir en disposer. **3.** utilité *f*; **can I be of any u. (to you)?** puis-je vous être utile à quelque chose? **it's of no u.**, cela ne sert à rien; **to have no u. for sth.**, n'avoir que faire de qch.; *F:* **I've no u. for him**, je ne peux pas le voir; **it's no u. discussing the matter**, inutile de discuter la question; **what's the u. of making plans?** à quoi bon faire des projets? **II.** [ju:z], *v.tr.* **1.** (*a*) employer, se servir de; **are you using this knife?** vous servez-vous de ce couteau? (*of thg*) **to be used for sth.**, servir à qch.; être employé à qch.; **I used the money to rebuild my house**, j'ai utilisé l'argent à rebâtir ma maison; **word no longer used**, mot désuet; **to reserve the right to u. sth.**, se réserver l'usage de qch.; **I u. that as a hammer**, cela me sert de marteau; **you may u. my name (as a reference)**, vous pouvez vous réclamer de moi; (*b*) **to u. force**, employer la force; **to u. every means**, mettre en œuvre tous les moyens; **to u. one's influence**, user de son influence; **to u. discretion**, agir avec discrétion. **2. ill-used**, maltraité. **3. to u. sth. up**, épuiser, consommer, qch.; **it's all used up**, il n'en reste plus; **to u. up the scraps**, tirer parti des restes. **4.** (*aux. past tense*) **as children we used** [ju:st] **to play together**, quand nous étions petits nous jouions ensemble; **I used to do it**, j'avais l'habitude de le faire; **things aren't what they used to be**, ce n'est plus comme autrefois; **she used not to like him**, autrefois elle ne l'aimait pas; **'usable** ['ju:z-], *a.* utilisable; **'usage** ['ju:z-, 'ju:s-], *s.* **1.** traitement *m*. **2.** usage *m*, coutume *f*. **3.** emploi *m*, usage (d'un mot); **used**, *a.* **1.** [ju:zd], usagé; (timbre-poste) oblitéré; **u. cars**, voitures *f* d'occasion; **hardly u.**, à l'état de neuf; **u. up**, (*of supplies*) épuisé, fini. **2.** [ju:st] **to be u. to sth., to doing sth.**, être habitué, accoutumé, à qch., à faire qch.; **to get**

u. to sth., s'habituer, s'accoutumer, à qch.; **you'll get u. to it in time**, vous vous y ferez à la longue; **'useful** ['ju:s-], *a.* utile; (vêtement) pratique; **the book was very u. to me**, ce livre m'a été d'une grande utilité; **to make oneself u.**, se rendre utile; **-fully**, *adv.* utilement; **'usefulness**, *s.* utilité *f*; **'useless** ['ju:s-], *a.* inutile; bon à rien; (effort) vain; **to be u.**, ne servir à rien; **u. regrets**, regrets superflus; **-ly**, *adv.* inutilement; en vain, en pure perte; **'uselessness**, *s.* inutilité *f*; **user** ['ju:zər], *s.* usager, -ère; **road users**, les usagers de la route; **'usual** ['ju:ʒu(ə)l], *a.* usuel, habituel; **at the u. time**, à l'heure accoutumée; **the u. terms**, les conditions d'usage; **it's u. to pay in advance**, il est d'usage de payer d'avance; **it's the u. practice**, c'est la pratique courante; **earlier than u.**, plus tôt que d'habitude; **as u.**, comme à l'ordinaire; comme d'habitude; **-ally**, *adv.* ordinairement, habituellement; d'ordinaire; **he was more than u. polite**, il s'est montré encore plus poli que d'habitude.

Ushant ['ʌʃ(ə)nt]. *Pr.n. Geog:* Ouessant *m*.

usher ['ʌʃər]. **I.** *s.* (*at wedding*) garçon *m* d'honneur. **II.** *v.tr.* **u. (s.o.) in**, introduire (qn), faire entrer (qn); **to u. s.o. out**, reconduire qn (jusqu'à la porte); **ushe'rette**, *s.f. Cin:* ouvreuse.

usurer ['ju:ʒərər], *s.* usurier, -ière; **u'surious**, *a.* (intérêt) usuraire; (banquier) usurier; **'usury** ['ju:ʒuri], *s.* usure *f*.

usurp [ju:'zɜ:p], *v.tr.* **to u. s.o.'s rights**, usurper sur les droits de qn; **usur'pation**, *s.* usurpation *f*; **u'surper**, *s.* usurpateur, -trice; **u'surping**, *a.* usurpateur.

utensil [ju(:)'tens(i)l], *s.* (*a*) ustensile *m*; **household utensils**, ustensiles de ménage; **set of kitchen utensils**, batterie de cuisine; (*b*) outil *m*, instrument *m*.

uterus ['ju:tərəs], *s. Anat:* utérus *m*.

utility [ju:'tiliti], *s.* (*a*) utilité *f*; **of great u.**, d'une grande utilité; **u. van**, (i) camionnette *f* de livraison; (ii) break *m*; (*b*) (**public**) **u.**, entreprise *f* de service public, de service de ville; **utili'tarian**, *a.* utilitaire; **'utilizable** [-aizəbl], *a.* utilisable; **utili'zation** [-ai'zeiʃ(ə)n], *s.* utilisation *f*; mise *f* en valeur; exploitation *f* (d'une invention); **'utilize** [-aiz], *v.tr.* utiliser, se servir de (qch.); tirer parti de, tirer profit de, mettre en valeur (qch.).

Utopia [ju:'toupiə], *s.* l'utopie *f*; **u'topian**, *a.* utopique.

utter[1] ['ʌtər], *a.* complet; absolu; **he's an u. stranger to me**, il m'est complètement étranger; **u. fool**, parfait imbécile; **-ly**, *adv.* complètement, absolument, tout à fait; **'utmost**. **I.** *a.* (*also* **'uttermost**) extrême; dernier; **the u. ends of the earth**, les (derniers) confins, les extrémités *f*, de la terre; **it's of the u.**

importance that . . ., il est de toute importance, de la dernière importance, que + *sub*. **II.**
s. dernière limite: dernier degré: **to the u.**, le
plus possible: au suprême degré: **to the u. of
my ability,** dans toute la mesure de mes
moyens: **fifty at the u.,** cinquante (tout) au

plus: **to do one's u. to . . .,** faire tout son possible, faire l'impossible, pour . . ..
utter[2], *v.tr.* **1.** pousser, faire entendre (un cri):
prononcer, proférer (un mot): **not to u. a word,**
ne pas souffler mot. **2.** émettre (de la fausse
monnaie).

V

V, v |viː|, s. (la lettre) V, v m; Cl: **V neck,** décolleté m en pointe.

vacant |'veikənt|, a. 1. vacant, vide, libre; **v. space,** place f vide; **there are two seats v.,** il y a deux places de libres; **v. room,** chambre libre, inoccupée; **v. possession,** libre possession; **situations v.,** offres f pl d'emploi(s). **2.** (esprit) inoccupé; (regard) distrait, vague, sans expression; **v. expression,** air hébété; **-ly,** adv. d'un air distrait, hébété; le regard perdu; **'vacancy,** s. **1.** vide m, vacuité f; **to stare into v.,** regarder dans le vide, dans le vague. **2.** vacance f; poste vacant; (on boarding house) **no vacancies!** complet! **v. exists for a secretary,** on recherche secrétaire; **vacate** |və'keit|, v.tr. (a) quitter (un emploi); **to v. office,** donner sa démission; (b) quitter (une chambre d'hôtel); évacuer (une maison); Jur: **to v. the premises,** vider les lieux; **va'cation,** s. **1.** vacances f pl. **2.** (also **va'cating**) évacuation f (d'une maison).

vaccinate |'væksineit|, v.tr. vacciner; **vacci'nation,** s. vaccination f; **'vaccine,** s. vaccin m.

vacillate |'væsileit|, v.i. vaciller; hésiter (entre deux opinions); **'vacillating,** a. vacillant, irrésolu; **vaci'llation,** s. vacillation f, hésitation f.

vacuous |'vækjuəs|, a. vide de pensée, d'expression; **v. remark,** observation dénuée de bon sens; **v. laugh,** rire niais, bête; **v. expression,** air hébété; **-ly,** adv. (sourire) bêtement; **va'cuity, 'vacuousness,** s. vacuité f, vide m (de la pensée).

vacuum |'vækjuəm|, I. s. Ph: vide m; **v. packed,** emballé sous vide; **v. cleaner,** aspirateur m; **v. flask,** bouteille isolante. II. v.tr. F: passer (une pièce) à l'aspirateur.

vagabond |'vægəbɔnd|, **1.** a. vagabond, errant. **2.** s. vagabond, -onde; chemineau m.

vagary |'veigəri|, s. caprice m, fantaisie f, lubie f.

vagrant |'veigrənt|, s. Jur: vagabond, -onde; **'vagrancy,** s. vagabondage m.

vague |veig|, a. vague; imprécis; (of outline) estompé, flou, indécis; **to leave a point v.,** laisser un point dans l'imprécision; **I haven't the vaguest idea,** je n'en ai pas la moindre idée; **-ly,** adv. vaguement; **'vagueness,** s. vague m, imprécision f.

vain |vein|, a. **1.** vain; (espoir) mensonger. **2.** (effort) inutile, vain, futile, stérile. **3.** vaniteux.

4. in v., en vain; vainement; **we protested in v., it was in v. that we protested, the tree was cut down,** nous avons eu beau protester, l'arbre a été abattu; **to labour in v.,** travailler inutilement; perdre sa peine; **-ly,** adv. **1.** vainement, en vain; inutilement. **2.** vaniteusement; avec vanité; **'vainness,** s. vanité f.

valentine |'væləntain|, s. carte envoyée à son ami(e) le jour de la Saint-Valentin.

valet |'vælei|, s. valet m de chambre.

valiant |'væljənt|, a. vaillant, valeureux, courageux; **-ly,** adv. vaillamment.

valid |'vælid|, a. (contrat) valide, valable; (passeport) valide; (argument) solide; **v. for three months,** bon pour trois mois; **no longer v.,** périmé; **va'lidity,** s. validité f (d'un document); force f (d'un argument).

valise |və'liːz|, s. sac m de voyage.

valley |'væli|, s. vallée f; (small) vallon m; **the Rhone V.,** la vallée du Rhône.

valour |'vælər|, s. courage m.

value |'væljuː|, I. s. **1.** valeur f; **to be of v.,** avoir de la valeur; **of no v.,** sans valeur; **to set a high v. on sth.,** faire grand cas de qch.; Com: **market v.,** valeur marchande; **increase in v.,** plus-value f; **decrease in v.,** moins-value f; **v. added tax,** taxe à la valeur ajoutée. **2.** Com: for **v. received,** valeur reçue; **to get good v. for one's money,** en avoir pour son argent; **this article is very good v.,** cet article est à un prix très avantageux. II. v.tr. **1.** Com: évaluer, estimer, priser (des marchandises); **to get sth. valued,** faire expertiser qch. **2.** estimer, faire grand cas de (qn, qch.); tenir à (sa vie); **'valuable. 1.** a. (objet) précieux, de valeur, de prix; Jur: **for a v. consideration,** à titre onéreux. **2.** s. pl. **valuables,** objets m de valeur, de prix; **valu'ation,** s. **1.** évaluation f, estimation f, Jur: expertise f; **to make a v.,** faire une expertise; **to get a v. of sth.,** faire expertiser qch. **2.** valeur estimée; **to take s.o. at his own v.,** estimer qn selon l'opinion qu'il a de lui-même; **'valued,** a. estimé, précieux; **'valueless,** a. sans valeur; **'valuer,** s. estimateur m, commissaire-priseur m, expert m.

valve |vælv|, s. **1.** soupape f; clapet m; valve f (de pneu); **safety v.,** soupape de sûreté. **2.** Anat: valvule f. **3.** Rad: lampe f; tube m. **4.** Moll: valve; **'valvular,** a. valvulaire.

vampire |'væmpaiər|, s. **1.** Myth: vampire m. **2.** Z: **v. (bat),** vampire.

V:1

van[1] [væn], s. in the v., (gens) d'avant-garde.

van[2], s. 1. Aut: camionnette f; fourgon m, camion m (de déménagement). 2. Rail: wagon m, fourgon; guard's v., fourgon de queue; 'vanman, pl. -men, s. livreur m.

vandal ['vænd(ə)l], s. vandale m; 'vandalism, s. vandalisme m.

vane [vein], s. (weather) v., girouette f.

vanilla [və'nilə], s. vanille f; v. ice-cream, glace f à la vanille.

vanish ['væniʃ], v.i. disparaître; (of suspicions) se dissiper, s'évanouir; F: (of pers.) s'éclipser; to v. into thin air, se volatiliser; 'vanishing, s. disparition f; profits have dwindled to v. point, les bénéfices se sont réduits à néant; Toil: v. cream, crème f de jour.

vanity ['væniti], s. 1. vanité f, vide m. 2. vanité; orgueil m; to do sth. out of v., faire qch. par vanité.

vanquish ['væŋkwiʃ], v.tr. vaincre.

vantage ['vɑ:ntidʒ], s. v. point, position avantageuse.

vapid ['væpid], a. plat, insipide; (conversation) fade.

vaporize ['veipəraiz], v.tr. & i. (se) vaporiser; vapori'zation, s. vaporisation f; pulvérisation f (d'un liquide); 'vaporizer, s. vaporisateur m; pulvérisateur m; atomiseur m; 'vapour, s. vapeur f.

varicose ['værikous], a. Med: v. vein, varice f.

varnish ['vɑ:niʃ]. I. s. vernis m; Toil: nail v., vernis à ongles; v. remover, (i) Ind: décapant m; (ii) Toil: dissolvant m. II. v.tr. vernir; vernisser (la poterie); 'varnishing, s. vernissage m.

vary ['vɛəri]. 1. v.tr. varier, diversifier; faire varier; to v. one's diet, one's reading, diversifier son régime, ses lectures. 2. v.i. (a) varier, changer; être variable; (b) différer (d'avis); on this point historians v., sur ce point les historiens ne sont pas d'accord; varia'bility, s. variabilité f; 'variable, a. variable; changeant, inconstant; 'variance, s. to be at v. with s.o., être en désaccord avec qn; authors are at v. about the date, les auteurs varient sur la date (de qch.); theory at v. with the facts, théorie incompatible avec les faits; 'variant, s. variante f; vari'ation, s. 1. variation f, changement m. 2. différence f (entre qch. et qch.). 3. Mus: theme with variations, air m avec variations, air varié; 'varied, a. varié; divers; 'variegate, v.tr. 1. varier, diversifier (les couleurs). 2. bigarrer, barioler; diaprer; 'variegated, a. 1. varié; divers. 2. bigarré, bariolé; diapré; versicolore; Nat.Hist: panaché; to become v., (se) panacher; varie'gation, s. diversité f de couleurs; bigarrure f; Bot: panachure f, diaprure f; va'riety, s. 1.

variété f, diversité f; to give v. to the menu, donner de la variété au menu; for a v. of reasons, pour toutes sortes de raisons. 2. (a) Nat.Hist: variété; (b) Th: v. show, spectacle m de variétés; v. turns, numéros m de music-hall; 'various, a. 1. varié, divers; of v. kinds, de diverses sortes; in v. ways, diversement; to talk about v. things, parler de chose(s) et d'autre(s). 2. différent; plusieurs; for v. reasons, pour plusieurs raisons; at v. times, à différentes reprises; on v. occasions, en diverses occasions; 'varying, a. variable, changeant; varié, divers.

vase [vɑːz], s. vase m; flower v., vase à fleurs.

vast [vɑːst], a. vaste, immense; to spend v. sums, dépenser énormément d'argent; 'vastness, s. immensité f (de l'océan); amplitude f (d'une catastrophe).

vat [væt], s. cuve f; bac m; bain m; 'vatful, s. cuvée f.

Vatican ['vætikən]. Pr.n. the V., le Vatican; V. Council, Concile m du Vatican.

vault[1] [vɔ(ː)lt]. I. s. 1. voûte f. 2. (a) souterrain m; (of bank) safety v., chambre forte; (b) wine v., cave f; (c) family v., caveau m de famille. II. v.tr. voûter (une cave); 'vaulted, a. voûté; en voûte; 'vaulting, s. 1. construction f de voûtes. 2. coll. voûte(s) f(pl); fan v., voûte(s) en éventail.

vault[2]. I. s. saut m. II. v.i. & tr. to v. (over) sth. sauter (un obstacle).

veal [viːl], s. Cu: veau m; v. cutlet, côtelette f de veau.

veer ['viər], v.i. (a) (of wind) tourner, sauter; (b) (of ship) virer (vent arrière); changer de bord; (c) (of pers.) to v. round, changer d'opinion.

vegetable ['vedʒ(i)təbl]. 1. a. & s. Bot: végétal (m). 2. s. légume m; early vegetables, primeurs f; v. garden, potager m; vege'tarian, a. & s. végétarien, -ienne; vege'tarianism, s. végétarisme m; 'vegetate, v.i. végéter; vege'tation, s. végétation f.

vehemence ['viːəməns], s. véhémence f; 'vehement, a. véhément; -ly, adv. avec véhémence; passionnément.

vehicle ['viːikl], s. véhicule m, voiture f; Aut: commercial v., véhicule utilitaire; speech is the v. of thought, le langage est le véhicule de la pensée; vehicular [vi'hikjulər], a. Adm: v. traffic, circulation f des voitures.

veil [veil]. I. s. voile m (de religieuse, de mariée); (on hat) voilette f; Ecc: to take the v., prendre le voile; F: to draw a v. over sth., jeter un voile sur qch. II. v.tr. voiler; cacher, dissimuler (ses sentiments); 'veiled, a. voilé; couvert d'un voile; caché, dissimulé; in thinly v. terms, en termes peu voilés.

vein [vein], s. 1. Anat: veine f. 2. Bot: Ent: nervure f (de feuille, d'aile). 3. Min: veine, filon m.

4. (*in wood, marble*) veine. **5. in melancholy v.,** d'humeur mélancolique; **the poetic v.,** la veine poétique; **veined,** *a.* **1.** veiné, à veines. **2.** *Bot: Ent:* nervuré. **3.** marbré; (marbre) veiné.

veldt [velt], *s.* veld(t) *m.*

vellum ['veləm], *s.* vélin *m.*

velocity [vi'lɔsiti], *s.* vitesse *f.*

velour(s) [və'luər], *s. Tex:* velours *m* de laine.

velvet ['velvit], *s.* velours *m*; **v. coat,** habit de velours; **velve'teen,** *s.* velours *m* de coton; **'velvety,** *a.* velouté, velouteux.

venal ['vi:n(ə)l], *a.* vénal; mercenaire; **-ally,** *adv.* vénalement; **ve'nality,** *s.* vénalité *f.*

vendetta [ven'detə], *s.* vendetta *f.*

vendor ['vendər, -dɔ:r], *s.* vendeur, -euse; **'vending,** *s.* vente *f*; **automatic v.,** vente par distributeur(s) automatique(s); **v. machine,** distributeur *m* automatique.

veneer [və'ni(:)ər]. **I.** *s.* **1.** (*a*) placage *m*, revêtement *m* (de bois mince); (*b*) bois *m* de placage. **2.** masque *m*; apparence extérieure; vernis *m* (de connaissances); **a v. of politeness,** une politesse toute en surface. **II.** *v.tr.* plaquer (le bois).

venerate ['venəreit], *v.tr.* vénérer; **'venerable,** *a.* vénérable; (coutume *f*) séculaire; **vene'ration,** *s.* vénération *f* (**for,** pour); **to hold s.o. in v.,** avoir de la vénération pour qn.

venereal [vi'niəriəl], *a. Med:* **v. disease,** maladie vénérienne.

Venetian [vi'ni:ʃ(ə)n], *a. & s. Geog:* vénitien, -ienne; **V. blind,** jalousie *f*; store vénitien.

Venezuela [vene'zweilə]. *Pr.n. Geog:* le Vénézuéla; **Vene'zuelan,** *a. & s.* vénézuélien, -ienne.

vengeance ['ven(d)ʒəns], *s.* vengeance *f*; **to take v. on s.o.,** se venger sur qn; *F:* **with a v.,** furieusement; pour de bon; **it's raining with a v.,** voilà qui s'appelle pleuvoir.

venial ['vi:niəl], *a.* (péché) véniel; (*of fault*) léger, pardonnable.

Venice ['venis]. *Pr.n.* Venise *f.*

venison ['venizn], *s.* venaison *f*; cerf *m*, chevreuil *m.*

venom ['venəm], *s.* venin *m*; **'venomous,** *a.* **1.** venimeux. **2. v. tongue,** langue de vipère; mauvaise langue; **-ly,** *adv.* d'une manière venimeuse; méchamment; **'venomousness,** *s.* nature venimeuse (d'un serpent); méchanceté *f* (de langue).

venous ['vi:nəs], *a.* (sang) veineux.

vent [vent]. **I.** *s.* **1.** trou *m*, orifice *m*; évent *m*; **v. of a volcano,** cheminée volcanique. **2. to give v. to one's anger,** donner libre cours à sa colère. **II.** *v.tr.* **to v. one's anger on s.o.,** passer sa colère sur qn.

ventilate ['ventileit], *v.tr.* **1.** aérer (une chambre); ventiler (un tunnel). **2. question that needs to be ventilated,** question qui demande à

être ventilée; **venti'lation,** *s.* **1.** aération *f,* aérage *m,* ventilation *f*; **v. shaft,** puits *m* de ventilation. **2.** mise *f* en discussion publique (d'une question); **'ventilator,** *s.* ventilateur *m*; soupirail *m* (d'une cave); (*over door*) vasistas *m*; *Aut:* déflecteur *m.*

Ventimiglia [venti'mi:ljə]. *Pr.n. Geog:* Vintimille.

ventricle ['ventrikl], *s.* ventricule *m* (du cœur).

ventriloquist [ven'triləkwist], *s.* ventriloque *mf*; **ven'triloquism, ven'triloquy,** *s.* ventriloquie *f.*

venture ['ventʃər]. **I.** *s.* **1.** entreprise risquée. **2.** *Com:* entreprise, spéculation *f.* **3. at a v.,** à l'aventure, au hasard; **to answer at a v.,** répondre au petit bonheur. **II.** *v.* **1.** *v.tr.* (*a*) oser (faire qch.); se risquer à (faire qch.); (*b*) hasarder (une conjecture); (*c*) hasarder, aventurer, risquer (sa vie, son argent). **2.** *v.i.* (*a*) **to v. on (doing) sth.,** se risquer à faire qch.; (*b*) **to v. into an unknown country,** s'aventurer en pays inconnu; **to v. out of doors,** se risquer à sortir; **'venturesome,** *a.* **1.** aventureux, osé. **2.** (*of action*) aventuré, risqué.

venue ['venju:], *s.* lieu *m* de réunion.

Venus ['vi:nəs]. *Pr.n.f.* Vénus.

veracious [və'reiʃəs], *a.* véridique; **-ly,** *adv.* véridiquement; avec véracité; **ve'raciousness, ve'racity,** *s.* véracité *f.*

veranda(h) [və'rændə], *s.* véranda *f.*

verb [və:b], *s.* verbe *m*; **'verbal,** *a.* verbal; oral; **v. agreement,** convention verbale; **-ally,** *adv.* verbalement; de vive voix.

verbatim [və:'beitim], *a. & adv.* mot pour moi; (rapport, etc.) textuel.

verbena [və(:)'bi:nə], *s. Bot:* verveine *f.*

verbiage ['və:biidʒ], *s.* verbiage *m*; **ver'bose** [-'bous], *a.* verbeux; diffus, prolixe; **-ly,** *adv.* avec verbosité; **ver'boseness, ver'bosity** [-'bɔsiti], *s.* verbosité *f,* prolixité *f.*

verdict ['və:dikt], *s.* **1.** *Jur:* verdict *m*; **to bring in a v.,** prononcer, rendre, un verdict. **2.** jugement *m,* décision *f*; **to stick to one's v.,** maintenir le bien-fondé de son jugement.

verge [və:dʒ]. **I.** *s.* (*a*) bord *m* (d'un fleuve); orée *f* (d'une forêt); accotement *m* (d'une route); *Aut: P.N:* **soft v.,** accotement non stabilisé; (*b*) **on the v. of ruin,** à deux doigts de la ruine; **on the v. of tears,** au bord des larmes. **II.** *v.i.* (*a*) **to v. on,** toucher à, être contigu à (qch.); (*b*) **he's verging on forty,** il frise la quarantaine.

verger ['və:dʒər], *s. Ecc:* bedeau *m.*

verify ['verifai], *v.tr.* **1.** confirmer (un fait). **2.** vérifier, contrôler (des renseignements, des comptes); **verifi'cation** [-fi'keiʃ(ə)n], *s.* vérification *f,* contrôle *m.*

vermicelli [və:mi'seli, -'tʃeli], *s.* vermicelle *m.*

vermilion [və:'miljən]. **1.** *s.* vermillon *m,* cinabre *m.* **2.** *a.* (de) vermillon; vermeil.

vermin ['və:min], *s.* **1.** (*body parasites; Pej: of people*) vermine *f.* **2.** (*rats, etc.*) nuisibles *mpl*; **'verminous,** *a.* couvert, grouillant, de vermine.

vermouth ['və:məθ], *s.* vermout(h) *m.*

vernacular [və'nækjulər], *a. & s. Ling:* vernaculaire (*m*).

versatile ['və:sətail], *a.* (*a*) aux talents variés; (*b*) (esprit) souple; **versa'tility** [-'til-], *s.* souplesse *f,* universalité *f* (d'esprit); faculté *f* d'adaptation.

verse [və:s], *s.* (*a*) vers *m* (de poésie); (*b*) couplet *m* (d'une chanson); strophe *f* (d'un poème); (*c*) verset *m* (de la Bible); (*d*) *coll.* vers *mpl*; **free v.,** vers libres; **versifi'cation,** *s.* versification *f*; **'versify,** *v.tr. & i.* versifier; écrire des vers; mettre (qch.) en vers.

versed [və:st], *a.* versé (**in,** en, dans).

version ['və:ʃ(ə)n], *s.* **1.** version *f,* traduction *f.* **2.** version (des faits); interprétation *f* (d'un fait); **according to his v.,** selon son dire; d'après lui. **3. military v. of an aircraft,** version militaire d'un avion.

versus ['və:səs]. *Lt.prep. Jur: Sp:* contre; **Martin v. Thomas,** Martin contre Thomas.

vertebra, *pl.* **-ae** ['və:tibrə, -i:], *s.* vertèbre *f*; **'vertebrate,** *a. & s.* vertébré (*m*).

vertex, *pl.* **-tices** ['və:teks, -tisi:z], *s. Astr:* vertex *m*; sommet *m* (d'une courbe).

vertical ['və:tik(ə)l]. **1.** *a.* vertical; (falaise) à pic. **2.** *s.* verticale *f*; **-ally,** *adv.* verticalement; d'aplomb.

vertigo ['və:tigou], *s. Med:* vertige *m.*

verve [və:v], *s.* verve *f.*

very ['veri]. **I.** *a.* **1.** vrai, véritable. **2.** (*a*) même; **you're the v. man I wanted to see,** vous êtes justement l'homme que je voulais voir; **he's the v. man,** il est tout indiqué (pour un emploi); **at that v. moment,** à cet instant même; **a year ago to the v. day,** il y a un an jour pour jour; **these are his v. words,** ce sont là ses propres paroles; (*b*) **at the v. beginning,** tout au commencement; (*c*) **I shudder at the v. thought of it,** je frémis rien que d'y penser. **II.** *adv.* **1.** très, fort, bien; **v. good,** (i) très bon; (ii) très bien, fort bien; **you're not v. polite,** vous êtes peu poli; **it's v. kind of you,** c'est gentil de votre part; **it's not so v. difficult,** ce n'est pas tellement difficile; **v. much,** beaucoup; **I was v. (much) surprised,** j'en ai été très surpris. **2.** the **v. first,** le tout premier; **the v. best,** tout ce qu'il y a de meilleur, de mieux; **the v. next day,** dès le lendemain; **at the v. most,** tout au plus; at the **v. latest,** au plus tard; **the v. same,** absolument le même; **for your v. own,** pour vous seul.

vespers ['vespəz], *s.pl. Ecc:* vêpres *fpl.*

vessel ['vesl], *s.* **1.** récipient *m.* **2.** navire *m,* bâtiment *m.* **3.** *Anat:* **blood v.,** vaisseau sanguin.

vest[1] [vest], *s.* **1.** *Com: & N.Am:* gilet *m.* **2.** (*for man*) gilet (athlétique); (*for woman*) chemis[e] américaine; *Fr.C:* camisole *f.*

vest[2], *v.tr.* **to v. s.o. with a property,** saisir q[n] d'un bien; **right vested in the Crown,** dro[it] dévolu à la Couronne; **'vested,** *a.* **v. interests** droits acquis.

vestibule ['vestibju:l], *s.* vestibule *m.*

vestige ['vestidʒ], *s.* vestige *m,* trace *f*; **not a** [v.] **of . . .,** pas la moindre trace de . . ..

vestment ['vestmənt], *s. usu.pl. Ecc:* vêtement[s] ornements, sacerdotaux; **'vestry,** *s.* sacristie[.]

Vesuvius [vi's(j)u:viəs]. *Pr.n. Geog:* le Vésuve.

vet [vet]. **I.** *s. F:* vétérinaire *mf.* **II.** *v.tr.* (vette[d] (*a*) examiner (qn, une bête); (*b*) revoir, corrige[r] (l'œuvre de qn).

vetch [vetʃ], *s. Bot:* vesce *f.*

veteran ['vetərən]. **1.** *s.* vétéran *m; N.Am:* ancie[n] combattant. **2.** *a.* de vétéran; **v. car,** vieill[e] voiture d'avant 1914.

veterinary ['vetrənri], *a.* vétérinaire; **v. surgeo[n]** vétérinaire *mf.*

veto ['vi:tou]. **I.** *s.* veto *m*; **to have a v., the righ[t]** **of v.,** avoir le droit de veto. **II.** *v.tr.* interdi[re] (qch.); mettre son veto à (qch.).

vex [veks], *v.tr.* vexer, fâcher, chagriner; **vex'**[a-] **tion,** *s.* (*a*) contrariété *f,* ennui *m*; (*b*) chagr[in] *m.* dépit *m*; **vex'atious, 'vexing,** *a.* fâcheu[x] ennuyeux, contrariant; chagrinant; **vexed,** *a.* **1.** vexé, contrarié, chagrin; **v. at sth.,** vex[é] fâché, de qch.; **v. with s.o.,** fâché contre qn; **t[o] be v. with oneself,** s'en vouloir. **2. v. questio[n]** question souvent débattue, non résolue.

via ['vaiə], *prep.* via; par la voie de; **to travel** [via] **Calais,** passer par Calais.

viable ['vaiəbl], *a.* (projet) viable; **via'bility,** faisabilité *f* (d'un projet).

viaduct ['vaiədʌkt], *s.* viaduc *m.*

vibrate [vai'breit]. **1.** *v.i.* vibrer; trépider. **2.** *v.[t]* faire vibrer; **'vibrant,** *a.* vibrant; **vi'bratin[g]** *a.* vibrant; (mouvement) vibratoire; **vi'br[a-]** **tion,** *s.* (*a*) vibration *f*; oscillation *f*; (*[b]*) trépidation *f*; **vi'bratory,** *a.* vibratoire.

viburnum [vai'bə:nəm], *s. Bot:* viorne *f.*

vicar ['vikər], *s. Ecc:* = curé *m*; **'vicarage,** *Ecc:* = presbytère *m*; cure *f.*

vicarious [vi'keəriəs], *a.* **v. punishment,** châ[ti-] ment souffert (i) par un autre, (ii) pour un autr[e] **-ly,** *adv.* à la place d'un autre.

vice[1] [vais], *s.* **1.** vice *m; Adm:* **v. squad,** brigad[e] des mœurs. **2.** défaut *m.* **3.** vice (d'un cheva[l])

vice[2] [vais], *s. Tls:* étau *m*; **bench-v.,** étau d'étab[li]

vice[3] ['vaisi], *prep.* à la place de (qn); **Mr Mar[tin]** **v. Mr Thomas,** M. Martin qui succède à [Mr] Thomas, démissionnaire.

vice- [vais], *pref.* vice-; **'vice-'admiral,** *s.* vic[e-] amiral *m*; **'vice-'chairman,** *s.* vice-préside[nt] *m*; **'vice-'chairmanship,** *s.* vice-présiden[ce] *f*; **'vice-'chancellor,** *s.* **1.** vice-chancelier *[m].* **2.** recteur *m* (d'une université); **'vice-'cons[ul]**

s. vice-consul *m*; **'vice-'marshal,** *s.* air v.-m., général *m* de division aérienne; **'vice-'president,** *s.* vice-président *m*; **'vice'regal,** *a.* du vice-roi; vice-royal; **'viceroy,** *s.* vice-roi *m.*

ice versa ['vais'vəːsə]. *Lt.adv.phr.* vice versa; réciproquement.

icinity [vi'siniti], *s.* voisinage *m*, proximité *f*; abords *mpl*, alentours *mpl* (d'un lieu); **in the v.,** dans le voisinage; **to live in the v. of sth.,** demeurer à proximité de qch.

icious ['viʃəs], *a.* 1. vicieux. 2. (*a*) méchant, haineux; **v. criticism,** critique méchante; (*b*) **to give a v. tug at the bell,** tirer rageusement la sonnette; (*c*) **it's a v. circle,** c'est un cercle vicieux; **-ly,** *adv.* 1. vicieusement. 2. méchamment; rageusement; **'viciousness,** *s.* 1. nature vicieuse; vice *m*. 2. méchanceté *f*.

icissitude [vi'sisitjuːd], *s.* vicissitude *f*; **the vicissitudes of fortune,** les retours *m* de la fortune.

ictim ['viktim], *s.* victime *f*; **v. of an accident,** accidenté, -ée; **victimi'zation,** *s.* oppression *f*; (*after strike*) **no v.!** point de représailles! **'victimize,** *v.tr.* (*a*) prendre (qn) comme victime; exercer des représailles contre (les meneurs d'une grève); (*b*) tromper, escroquer (qn).

ictoria [vik'tɔːriə]. *Pr.n.f.* Victoire; **Queen V.,** la reine Victoria; **Vic'toria 'Cross,** *s.* (*abbr.* **V. C.** ['viː'siː]) Croix *f* de Victoria; **Vic'torian,** *a. & s.* victorien, -ienne; du règne de la reine Victoria.

ictorious [vik'tɔːriəs], *a.* victorieux; **to be v. over s.o.,** être victorieux de qn; vaincre qn; **-ly,** *adv.* victorieusement; en vainqueur; **'victor,** *s.* vainqueur *m*; **'victory,** *s.* victoire *f*.

ictual [vitl], *v.tr.* (**victualled**) ravitailler (un navire).

ideo ['vidiou], *s.* **v. tape,** bande *f* vidéo; **'video-ca'ssette,** *s.* vidéocassette *f*.

ie [vai], *v.i.* **to v. with s.o.,** le disputer à qn; rivaliser avec qn.

ienna [vi:'enə]. *Pr.n. Geog:* Vienne *f*; **Viennese** [viːəˈniːz], *a. & s.* viennois, -oise.

ietnam [vjet'næm, -'naːm]. *Pr.n. Geog:* le Viêt-nam; **Vietna'mese,** *a. & s.* vietnamien, -ienne.

iew [vjuː]. I. *s.* 1. vue *f*; regard *m*; coup *m* d'œil; **I should like a closer v. of it,** je voudrais l'examiner de plus près; **the collection is on v.,** la collection est ouverte au public. 2. **in v.,** en vue; (*of telescope*) **field of v.,** champ *m* de vision; **angle of v.,** angle *m* de champ. 3. (*prospect*) vue, perspective *f*; **front v. of the hotel,** l'hôtel vu de face; **you'll get a better v. from here,** vous verrez mieux d'ici; **it's worth while climbing up for the v.,** le panorama vaut le déplacement; **point of v.,** point *m* de vue; **to keep sth. in v.,** ne pas perdre qch. de vue. 4.

manière *f* de voir; opinion *f*; **to take the right v. of sth.,** voir juste; **to hold extreme views,** avoir des idées extrémistes; **in my v.,** à mon avis *m*; **to share s.o.'s views,** partager les sentiments de qn. 5. **in v. of . . .,** en considération de . . .; étant donné . . .; **in v. of the distance . . .,** vu l'éloignement . . . 6. vue, intention *f*; **to fall in with s.o.'s views,** entrer dans les vues de qn; **will this meet your views?** cela vous conviendra-t-il? **to have sth. in v.,** avoir qch. en vue; méditer (un voyage); **whom have you in v.?** à qui pensez-vous? vous avez un candidat (à proposer)? **what is the object in v.?** à quoi vise tout cela? **negotiations with a v. to an alliance,** négociations visant une alliance. II. *v.* 1. *v.tr.* (*a*) regarder (qn, qch.); examiner (qn, qch.); visiter (une maison à vendre); (*b*) envisager; **I don't v. the thing in that light,** je n'envisage pas la chose ainsi. 2. *v.i. T.V:* regarder; **'viewer,** *s.* 1. spectateur, -trice; *T.V:* téléspectateur, -trice. 2. *Phot:* visionneuse *f*; **'view-finder,** *s. Phot:* viseur *m*; **'viewpoint,** *s.* point *m* de vue.

vigilance ['vidʒiləns], *s.* vigilance *f*; **'vigilant,** *a.* vigilant, éveillé, alerte; **-ly,** *adv.* avec vigilance.

vigour ['vigər], *s.* vigueur *f*, énergie *f*; **'vigorous,** *a.* vigoureux, robuste; **-ly,** *adv.* vigoureusement, avec énergie; **he maintained v. that . . .,** il a affirmé énergiquement que . . .

vile [vail], *a.* 1. vil, bas, infâme. 2. abominable, exécrable; **v. weather,** un sale temps; **v. temper,** humeur massacrante; **-ly,** *adv.* 1. vilement; bassement. 2. abominablement; **'vileness,** *s.* 1. bassesse *f*, caractère *m* ignoble (de qn, d'un sentiment). 2. **the v. of the weather,** le temps abominable.

vilify ['vilifai], *v.tr.* vilipender; **vilifi'cation** [-fi'keiʃ(ə)n], *s.* dénigrement *m*.

villa ['vilə], *s.* villa *f*.

village ['vilidʒ], *s.* village *m*; **at the v. grocer's,** chez l'épicier du village; **v. inn,** auberge *f* de campagne; **'villager,** *s.* villageois, -oise.

villain ['vilən], *s.* scélérat *m*; gredin *m*; bandit *m*; *F:* **you little v.!** oh, le vilain! la vilaine! *Th: etc:* **the v.,** le traître; **'villainous,** *a.* 1. vil, infâme; (de) scélérat. 2. *F:* **v. weather,** un sale temps; **v. handwriting,** écriture *f* exécrable; **-ly,** *adv.* 1. d'une manière infâme; en scélérat. 2. *F:* exécrablement, abominablement.

vim [vim], *s. F:* vigueur *f*, énergie *f*.

vindicate ['vindikeit], *v.tr.* défendre, soutenir (qn); justifier (qn, sa conduite); prouver, maintenir (son dire); **to v. one's rights,** faire valoir son bon droit; **vindi'cation,** *s.* défense *f*, apologie *f*; **in v. of sth.,** pour justifier qch.

vindictive [vin'diktiv], *a.* vindicatif; rancunier; **-ly,** *adv.* par rancune; par esprit de vengeance;

vin'dictiveness, s. esprit *m* de vengeance; esprit rancunier.

vine [vain], s. (a) vigne *f*; v. **grower,** viticulteur *m*; vigneron *m*; v. **growing,** viticulture *f*; v.-**growing district,** pays vinicole; v. **stock,** cep *m* de vigne; (b) *N.Am:* plante grimpante.

vinegar ['vinigər], s. vinaigre *m*.

vineyard ['vinjəd], s. clos *m* (de vigne); vigne *f*, vignoble *m*; **the best vineyards,** les meilleurs crus.

vino ['vi:nou], s. *F:* vin *m* ordinaire.

vintage ['vintidʒ], s. 1. vendages *fpl*; récolte *f* du raisin. 2. année *f* (de belle récolte); **of the 1973 v.,** de l'année 1973; v. **wine,** vin de marque; grand vin. 3. v. **car,** vieille voiture (1914–1930).

vinyl ['vinil, 'vainil], s. *Ch:* vinyle *m*.

viola[1] [vi'oulə], s. *Mus:* alto *m*; v. **(player),** altiste *mf*.

viola[2] ['vaiələ], s. *Bot:* pensée *f*.

violate ['vaiəleit], v.tr. violer; manquer à (une règle); enfreindre (la loi); **vio'lation,** s. violation *f*; infraction *f* (à un ordre); v. **of s.o.'s privacy,** intrusion *f* auprès de, chez, qn.

violence ['vaiələns], s. 1. (a) violence *f*, intensité *f* (du vent); (b) **to die by v.,** mourir de mort violente; **to do v. to one's feelings,** se faire violence. 2. *Jur:* robbery **with v.,** vol *m* avec violence, avec agression; **acts of v.,** voies *f* de fait; **'violent,** a. 1. violent; *Aut:* v. **braking,** freinage brutal; **to become v.,** s'emporter; **to die a v. death,** mourir de mort violente. 2. (a) violent, aigu, fort; v. **dislike,** vive aversion; **in a v. hurry,** extrêmement pressé; v. **cold,** gros rhume; (b) v. **colours,** couleurs criardes; **-ly,** *adv.* 1. violemment; avec violence. 2. vivement; extrêmement; **to fall v. in love with s.o.,** tomber follement amoureux, -euse, de qn.

violet ['vaiələt]. 1. s. *Bot:* violette *f.* 2. a. & s. (*colour*) violet (*m*); **ultra-v. rays,** rayons ultra-violets.

violin [vaiə'lin], s. violon *m*; **vio'linist,** s. violoniste *mf.*

viper ['vaipər], s. vipère *f.*

virgin ['və:dʒin]. 1. s. vierge *f*; **the Blessed V.,** la Sainte Vierge. 2. a. de vierge; virginal; v. **forest,** forêt *f* vierge; **'virginal,** a. virginal; **vir'ginity,** s. virginité *f.*

Virginia [və:'dʒiniə]. *Pr.n. Geog:* la Virginie; *Bot:* **V. creeper,** vigne *f* vierge; **V. tobacco,** (tabac de) Virginie *m.*

Virgo ['və:gou]. *Pr.n. Astr:* la Vierge.

virile ['virail], a. viril, mâle; **vi'rility,** s. virilité *f.*

virtual ['və:tjuəl], a. de fait; en fait; **he's the v. head of the business,** c'est lui le vrai chef de la maison; **this was a v. confession,** de fait, c'était un aveu; **-ally,** *adv.* virtuellement; de fait; **I'm v. certain of it,** j'en ai la quasi-certitude.

virtue ['və:tju:], s. 1. vertu *f*; **to make a v. of**

necessity, faire de nécessité vertu. 2. **he ha[s] many virtues,** il a beaucoup de qualités; **th[e] great v. of the scheme is . . .,** le grand avan[tage] du projet, c'est . . . . 3. *prep.phr.* **by v. of** en vertu de; en raison de; **'virtuous,** a. ver[tueux]; **-ly,** *adv.* vertueusement.

virtuoso, pl. -os [və:tju'ouzou, -ouz], s. *Mus[:]* virtuose *mf*; **virtu'osity,** s. virtuosité *f.*

virulence ['vir(j)uləns], s. virulence *f*; **'virulent** a. virulent; **-ly,** *adv.* avec virulence.

virus ['vaiərəs], s. *Med:* virus *m*; v. **disease[,]** maladie virale, à virus.

visa ['vi:zə]. I. s. visa *m.* II. *v.tr.* viser; apposer u[n] visa à (un passeport).

viscera ['visərə], s.pl. viscères *m.*

viscosity [vis'kɔsiti], s. viscosité *f*; **'viscous, a[.]** visqueux.

viscount ['vaikaunt], s. vicomte *m*; **'viscountess,** s. vicomtesse *f.*

visible ['vizəbl, -ibl], a. visible; **to become v.,** ap[paraître]; **-ibly,** *adv.* visiblement manifestement; à vue d'œil; **visi'bility,** s[.] **good v.,** (i) *Nau: Av:* bonn[e] visibilité *f*; (ii) (*in car*) vue dégagée; **visio[n]** ['viʒ(ə)n], s. 1. (a) vision *f*, vue *f*; **field of v[.]** champ visuel; (b) **man of v.,** homme d'un[e] grande perspicacité, qui voit loin dans l'avenir[.] 2. (a) imagination *f*, vision; **visions of wealth[,]** visions de richesses; (b) apparition *f*, fantôm[e] *m*; **to see visions,** avoir des visions[;] **'visionary,** a. & s. visionnaire (*mf*).

visit ['vizit]. I. s. 1. (**social) v.,** visite *f*; **to pay s.o[.]** a v., faire une visite à qn; *F:* **to pay a v.,** alle[r] faire pipi. 2. visite, séjour *m*; **to be on a v. t[o] friends,** être en visite chez des amis. 3. **inspec[tion] v.,** visite de surveillance; *Ecc:* **pastoral v[.]** visite pastorale. II. *v.tr.* 1. rendre visite à (qn[)] aller voir (qn, qch.); visiter (un malade, un en[droit]. 2. (*of official*) visiter, inspecter; **visi'ta[tion],** s. (*by bishop*) visite pastorale; **'visiting[,]** 1. a. en visite; *Sp:* v. **team,** les visiteurs m[.] 2.[.] visites *fpl*; **they are not on v. terms,** ils ne s[e] voient pas; (*at hospital*) v. **hours,** heures d[e] visite; v. **card,** carte *f* de visite; **'visitor,** s. (a[)] visiteur, -euse; **she's got visitors,** elle a d[u] monde; (b) **summer visitors, winter visitors,** es[tivants] *m*, hivernants *m.*

vista ['vistə], s. 1. échappée *f* (de vue). 2. **to ope[n] up new vistas,** ouvrir de nouvelle[s] perspectives.

visual ['vizju(ə)l], a. visuel; perceptible à l'œil; v[.] **memory,** mémoire visuelle; **to keep within v[.] range,** garder le contact visuel; v. **distance,** dis[tance] de visibilité; **-ally,** *adv.* visuellemen[t]; **'visualize,** v.tr. se représenter (qch.); évoque[r] l'image de (qch.); **I can't v. . . .,** je n'arrive pa[s] à me représenter . . .

vital ['vait(ə)l], a. 1. vital; essentiel à la vie. 2. es[sentiel]; capital; **question of v. importance[,]**

question d'importance capitale. **3. v. statistics,** (i) statistiques _f_ démographiques; (ii) _F:_ mensurations _f_ (d'une femme); **'vitally,** _adv._ d'une manière vitale; **vi'tality,** _s._ vitalité _f_; vigueur _f_; **she's bubbling over with v.,** elle déborde de vie.

vitamin ['vitəmin, 'vait-], _s._ vitamine _f_; **v. deficiency,** carence _f_ vitaminique, avitaminose _f_; **'vitaminized,** _a._ vitaminé.

vitiate ['viʃieit], _v.tr._ vicier.

vitrify ['vitrifai], _v.tr. & i._ (se) vitrifier.

vituperation [vitju:pə'reiʃ(ə)n], _s._ injures _fpl_, insultes _fpl_, invectives _fpl_.

vivacious [vi'veiʃəs], _a._ vif, animé, enjoué; -ly, _adv._ avec enjouement; avec verve; **vi'vaciousness, vi'vacity** [-'væs-], _s._ vivacité _f_; animation _f_; enjouement _m_.

vivid ['vivid], _a._ 1. vif, éclatant; **v. flash of lightning,** éclair aveuglant. 2. **v. imagination,** imagination vive; **v. description,** description vivante; **v. recollection,** souvenir très net; -ly, _adv._ 1. vivement; avec éclat. 2. (décrire qch.) d'une manière vivante; **'vividness,** _s._ vivacité _f_, éclat _m_ (des couleurs).

viviparous [vi'vipərəs], _a._ _Z:_ vivipare.

vivisection [vivi'sekʃ(ə)n], _s._ vivisection _f_.

vixen [viksn], _s._ 1. _Z:_ renarde _f_. 2. mégère _f_; femme acariâtre.

viz [viz], _adv._ à savoir . . .; c'est-à-dire . . ..

vocabulary [və'kæbjuləri], _s._ vocabulaire _m_.

vocal ['vouk(ə)l], _a._ vocal; **v. cords,** cordes vocales; -ally, _adv._ vocalement, oralement; **'vocalist,** _s._ chanteur, -euse; cantatrice _f_.

vocation [və'keiʃ(ə)n, vou-], _s._ vocation _f_; **vo'cational,** _a._ **v. training,** enseignement professionnel.

vocative ['vɔkətiv], _a. & s._ vocatif (_m_).

vociferate [və'sifəreit], _v.i. & tr._ vociférer, crier (**against,** contre); pousser des vociférations; **vo'ciferous,** _a._ vociférant, bruyant, criard, braillard; -ly, _adv._ bruyamment; en vociférant.

vogue [voug], _s._ vogue _f_, mode _f_; **in v.,** en vogue, à la mode.

voice [vɔis]. I. _s._ 1. voix _f_; **to raise one's v.,** hausser la voix; **to lose one's v.,** attraper une extinction de voix; **in a low v.,** à voix basse; à demi-voix; **he likes the sound of his own v.,** il aime à s'entendre parler. 2. voix, suffrage _m_; **we have no v. in the matter,** nous n'avons pas voix au chapitre. II. _v.tr._ exprimer, énoncer (une opinion); **'voiceless,** _a._ sans voix; muet.

void [vɔid]. I. _a._ 1. vide. 2. (_of office_) vacant, inoccupé. 3. _Jur:_ nul; **null and v.,** nul et de nul effet, nul et non avenu. 4. dépourvu, dénué (**of,** de); **v. of sense,** (projet) dénué de sens. II. _s._ vide _m_; **to fill the v.,** combler le vide.

volatile ['vɔlətail], _a._ 1. _Ch:_ volatil. 2. volage, inconstant.

volcano, _pl._ -oes [vɔl'keinou, -ouz], _s._ volcan _m_; **active, dormant, extinct, v.,** volcan actif, dormant, éteint; **vol'canic** [-'kæn-], _a._ volcanique; **by v. action,** volcaniquement; -ally, _adv._ volcaniquement.

vole [voul], _s._ _Z:_ (**field**) **v.,** campagnol _m_ (des champs); **water v.,** rat _m_ d'eau.

volition [və'liʃ(ə)n], _s._ volonté _f_; **of one's own v.,** (faire qch.) de son propre gré.

volley ['vɔli]. I. _s._ (_a_) volée _f_, salve _f_ (d'armes à feu); grêle _f_ (de pierres); (_b_) volée, bordée _f_ (d'injures); (_c_) _Ten:_ (balle prise de) volée. II. _v._ 1. _v.tr. & i._ _Ten:_ **to v. (a return),** reprendre une balle de volée; **to half-v. a ball,** prendre une balle entre bond et volée. 2. _v.i._ (_of guns_) partir ensemble; **'volley-ball,** _s._ _Sp:_ volley-ball _m_; **v.-b. player,** volleyeur, -euse.

volt [voult], _s._ _El:_ volt _m_; **'voltage,** _s._ tension _f_ (en volts); **high v.,** haute tension.

voluble ['vɔljubl], _a._ (_of speech_) facile, aisé; (_of pers._) **to be v.,** avoir la langue bien pendue; parler avec volubilité; **'volubly,** _adv._ avec volubilité; **volu'bility,** _s._ volubilité _f_.

volume ['vɔlju:m], _s._ 1. volume _m_, livre _m_; **v. one,** tome premier; _F:_ **it speaks volumes for him,** cela en dit long en sa faveur. 2. **volumes of smoke, of water,** nuages _m_ de fumée, torrents _m_ d'eau. 3. _Ph:_ _Tec:_ volume; **v. of a reservoir,** cubage _m_ d'un réservoir. 4. volume (d'un son); ampleur _f_ (de la voix); **vo'luminous** [-'l(j)u:m-], _a._ volumineux.

volunteer [vɔlən'ti:ər]. I. _s._ (_a_) _Mil:_ volontaire _m_; **v. army,** armée _f_ de volontaires; (_b_) (_for dangerous enterprise_) homme de bonne volonté. II. _v._ 1. _v.tr._ offrir volontairement, spontanément, ses services; **to v. information,** donner spontanément des renseignements. 2. _v.i._ s'offrir; se proposer volontairement (pour qch.); _Mil:_ s'engager comme volontaire; **'voluntary,** _a._ (_a_) volontaire, spontané; (_b_) **v. work,** travail _m_ bénévole; **v. organization,** organisation bénévole; -ily, _adv._ volontairement, spontanément; de (son) plein gré.

voluptuous [və'lʌptjuəs], _a._ voluptueux.

vomit ['vɔmit]. I. _s._ vomissure _f_; vomissement _m_. II. _v.tr. & i._ vomir, rendre; **'vomiting,** _s._ vomissement _m_.

voracious [və'reiʃəs], _a._ vorace, dévorant; **v. appetite,** appétit _m_ de loup; **v. reader,** lecteur, lectrice, vorace; -ly, _adv._ avec voracité; **vo'raciousness, voracity** [vɔ'ræsiti], _s._ voracité _f_.

vortex, _pl._ -texes, -tices ['vɔ:teks, -teksiz, -tisi:z], _s._ (_a_) tourbillonnement _m_ (d'air); tourbillon _m_ (de fumée); (_b_) (_whirlpool_) tourbillon.

votary ['voutəri], _s._ fervent, -ente (**of,** de); adorateur, -trice (de); sectateur, -trice; partisan(e) zélé(e).

vote |vout|. **I.** *s.* **1.** (*a*) vote *m*, scrutin *m*; **to put a question to the v.**, mettre une question aux voix; (*b*) (**individual**) **v.**, voix *f*, suffrage *m*; **to have a v.**, avoir le droit de vote; **to record one's v.**, voter. **2. v. of censure**, motion *f* de censure; **to pass a v. of thanks**, voter des remerciements (à qn). **II.** *v.i. & tr.* voter; **to v. for a candidate**, voter pour un candidat; **to v. communist**, voter communiste; **v. for Martin!** votez Martin! **to v. a sum**, voter une somme; *F:* **I v. we go**, je propose que nous y allions; '**voter**, *s.* électeur, -trice; '**voting**, *s.* (participation *f* au) vote; scrutin *m*; **v. paper**, bulletin *m* de vote.

votive |'voutiv|, *a.* votif; **v. offering**, offrande votive; ex-voto *m*.

vouch |vautʃ|, *v.i.* **to v. for the truth of sth.**, témoigner de, répondre de, la vérité de qch.; **to v. for a fact**, garantir un fait; **to v. for s.o.**, répondre de qn; se porter garant de qn; '**voucher**, *s. Com:* fiche *f*; reçu *m*, bon *m*; **gift v.**, bon d'achat; **luncheon v.**, chèque-repas *m*.

vow |vau|. **I.** *s.* vœu *m*, serment *m*; **monastic vows**, vœux monastiques; **to have made a v. to do sth.**, avoir fait le vœu de faire qch. **II.** *v.tr.* vouer, jurer.

vowel |'vauəl|, *s.* voyelle *f*; **v. sound**, son *m* vocalique.

voyage |'vɔiidʒ|. **I.** *s.* voyage *m* sur mer; **on the v. out, home**, à l'aller, au retour. **II.** *v.i.* voyager sur mer; naviguer; '**voyager**, *s.* voyageur, -euse, par mer; passager, -ère; navigateur *m*.

vulcanize |'vʌlkənaiz|, *v.tr.* vulcaniser (le caoutchouc); **vulcani'zation**, '**vulcanizing**, *s.* vulcanisation *f*.

vulgar |'vʌlgər|, *a.* **1.** vulgaire, commun; **v. display of wealth**, gros luxe de mauvais goût; **v. expressions**, expressions vulgaires, triviales; **to make v. remarks**, dire des vulgarités *f*. **2.** (*a*) vulgaire; communément reçu; **v. error**, erreur très répandue; (*b*) **the v. tongue**, la langue commune, la langue vulgaire; (*c*) *Mth:* **v. fraction**, fraction *f* ordinaire; **-ly**, *adv.* **1.** vulgairement, grossièrement. **2.** vulgairement, communément; '**vulgarism**, *s.* expression *f* vulgaire, vulgarisme *m*; **vul'garity**, vulgarité *f*, trivialité *f*; **to lapse into v.**, tomber dans le trivial; **vulgari'zation**, *s.* vulgarisation *f*; '**vulgarize**, *v.tr.* vulgariser; trivialiser (son style).

vulnerable |'vʌln(ə)rəbl|, *a.* vulnérable; **vulnera'bility**, *s.* vulnérabilité *f*.

vulture |'vʌltʃər|, *s.* vautour *m*.

W

W, w |'dʌblju:|, s. (la lettre) W, w m.
wad |wɔd|. I. s. 1. (a) tampon m, bouchon m (d'ouate, etc.); (b) liasse f (de billets de banque). 2. bourre f (de cartouche). II. v.tr. (wadded) ouater, capitonner (un vêtement); 'wadding, s. 1. ouatage m; rembourrage m. 2. (a) ouate f; (b) tampon d'ouate.
waddle |wɔdl|. I. s. dandinement m; démarche f de canard. II. v.i. se dandiner; marcher en canard.
wade |weid|, v.i. marcher dans l'eau; to w. across a stream, passer un ruisseau à gué; to w. in, (i) entrer dans l'eau; (ii) F: intervenir, s'interposer; F: to w. through a book, venir péniblement à bout d'un livre; 'wader, s. 1. Orn: échassier m. 2. personne f qui marche dans l'eau. 3. pl. waders, bottes f d'égoutier, de pêcheur.
wafer |'weifər|, s. 1. Cu: gaufrette f. 2. Ecc: hostie f.
waffle¹ |'wɔfl|, s. Cu: gaufre f; w. iron, gaufrier m.
waffle². I. s. F: verbosité f; verbiage m. II. v.i. F: débiter dans le vague; parler, écrire, sans rien dire.
wag |wæg|. I. s. agitation f, frétillement m (de la queue); hochement m (de la tête); (of dog) with a w. of his tail, en remuant la queue. II. v. (wagged) 1. v.tr. (of dog) agiter, remuer (la queue). 2. v.i. s'agiter, se remuer; his tongue was beginning to w., sa langue se déliait; that'll set people's tongues wagging, cela va faire parler les gens.
wage¹ |weidʒ|, s. salaire m, paie f; to earn good wages, être bien payé; toucher un bon salaire; w. earner, (i) salarié, -iée; (ii) le soutien de la famille; minimum w., (i) salaire minimum interprofessionnel garanti; (ii) minimum vital.
wage², v.tr. to w. war, faire la guerre.
wager |'weidʒər|. I. s. pari m; gageure f. II. v.tr. parier; gager.
waggle |'wægl|, v.tr. (of dog, etc.) agiter, remuer (la queue).
wag(g)on |'wæg(ə)n|, s. 1. charrette f; chariot m. 2. Rail: wagon découvert (à marchandises); covered goods w., fourgon m; w. load, (charge f de) wagon. 3. F: to be on the (water) w., s'abstenir de boissons alcooliques; to come off the w., se remettre à boire; 'wag(g)oner, s. charretier m, voiturier m.
wagtail |'wægteil|, s. Orn: bergeronnette f,

hochequeue m.
waif |weif|, s. (a) Jur: épave f; (b) waifs and strays, (enfants) abandonnés.
wail |weil|. I. s. (a) cri plaintif; plainte f, gémissement m; (b) vagissement m (de nouveau-né). II. v.i. (a) gémir; se plaindre; (b) to w. about sth., se lamenter sur qch.; 'wailing. I. a. (cri) plaintif; (enfant) qui gémit. II. s. plaintes fpl; gémissements mpl.
wainscot |'weinskət|. I. s. lambris m; boiseries fpl (d'une pièce). II. v.tr. (wainscot(t)ed) lambrisser; 'wainscot(t)ing, s. 1. lambrissage m. 2. boiseries fpl.
waist |weist|, s. 1. (of pers.) taille f; w. measurement, tour m de taille; to put one's arm round s.o.'s w., prendre qn par la taille. 2. Dressm: dress with a short w., robe f à taille courte; 'waistband, s. ceinture f (de jupe, etc.); 'waistcoat, s. gilet m; 'waistline, s. taille f; to watch one's w., soigner sa ligne.
wait |weit|. I. v. 1. v.i. (a) attendre; w. a moment! attendez un moment! to w. for s.o., attendre qn; to keep s.o. waiting, faire attendre qn; he didn't w. to be told twice, on n'a pas dû le lui dire deux fois; we shall lose nothing if we w., by waiting, on ne perdra rien pour attendre; Com: repairs while you w., réparations f à la minute; w. and see! attendez voir! everything comes to him who waits, tout vient à point à qui sait attendre; (b) to w. up for s.o., veiller pour attendre qn; (c) to w. (at table), servir (à table). 2. (a) v.tr. don't w. dinner for me, ne m'attendez pas pour vous mettre à table; (b) v.ind.tr. to w. on s.o., servir qn; to w. on s.o. hand and foot, être aux petits soins pour qn. II. s. (a) attente f; it was a long w., nous avons dû attendre longtemps; twenty minutes' w. between the two trains, battement m de vingt minutes entre les deux trains; (b) to lie in w., être à l'affût. 2. pl. waits, chanteurs m de noëls; 'waiter, s. garçon m (de restaurant); head w., maître m d'hôtel; 'waiting, s. 1. attente f; Aut: no w., stationnement interdit; w. room, salle f d'attente; w. list, liste f d'attente. 2. (in restaurant) service m; lady in w., dame f d'honneur; 'waitress, s. serveuse f.
waive |weiv|, v.tr. renoncer à, abandonner (ses prétentions); déroger à (un principe); ne pas insister sur (une condition); 'waiver, s. abandon m (d'un droit); dérogation f.
wake¹ |weik|, s. (a) Nau: sillage m; to be in the w.

of a ship, être dans les eaux d'un navire; (b) **in the w. of the storm**, à la suite de la tempête; **to follow in s.o.'s w.**, marcher sur les traces de qn.

wake², s. 1. (*Ireland*) veillée f mortuaire. 2. (*N. of Eng.*) **wakes week**, la semaine de congé annuel.

wake³, v. (p.t. **woke** [wouk]; p.p. **woken** ['wouk(ə)n]) 1. v.i. (a) **waking or sleeping**, éveillé ou endormi; (b) **to w. (up)**, se réveiller; **w. up!** (i) réveillez-vous! (ii) F: secoue-toi! **he's waking up to the truth**, la vérité commence à lui apparaître; **to w. up to find oneself famous**, se réveiller célèbre. 2. v.tr. **to w. s.o. (up)**, réveiller qn; F: **he needs something to w. him up**, il lui faut quelque chose pour le secouer; F: **it's enough to w. the dead**, c'est (un bruit) à réveiller les morts; **'wakeful**, a. 1. (a) éveillé; peu disposé à dormir; (b) sans sommeil. 2. vigilant; **'wakefulness**, s. 1. insomnie f. 2. vigilance f; **'waken**. 1. v.tr. (a) réveiller (qn); (b) éveiller (une émotion). 2. v.i. se réveiller; **'wakening**, s. réveil m; **'waker**, s. **to be an early w.**, se réveiller de bonne heure; **'waking**. I. a. **w. hours**, heures f de veille. II. s. 1. **between sleeping and w.**, entre la veille et le sommeil. 2. réveil m.

Wales [weilz]. Pr.n. le pays de Galles; **North W.**, **South W.**, la Galles du Nord, du Sud; **New South W.**, la Nouvelle-Galles du Sud; **the Prince of W.**, le Prince de Galles.

walk [wɔ:k]. I. v. 1. v.i. (a) marcher; **to w. in one's sleep**, être somnambule; **I'll w. with you**, je vais vous accompagner; **he was walking along slowly**, il s'avançait lentement; (b) (as opposed to drive, etc.) aller à pied; **to w. home**, rentrer à pied; **to w. round the town**, faire le tour de la ville (à pied); **you can w. it in ten minutes**, vous en avez pour dix minutes à pied; (c) (for pleasure) se promener, faire des promenades (à pied); **I like walking**, j'aime bien me promener (à pied). 2. v.tr. (a) **to w. the streets**, courir les rues; (of prostitute) faire le trottoir; (b) **to w. s.o. off his legs, feet**, épuiser qn à force de le faire marcher; (c) **to w. a horse**, conduire, promener, un cheval. II. s. 1. marche f; **it's an hour's w. from here**, c'est à une heure de marche d'ici. 2. promenade f (à pied); **to go for a w.**, aller se promener, faire une promenade; **to take the dog for a w.**, promener le chien. 3. démarche f; **I recognize him by his w.**, je le reconnais à sa démarche. 4. allée f (de jardin); avenue f; **covered w.**, allée couverte. 5. **w. of life**, (i) position sociale; (ii) métier m, carrière f; **'walker**, s. marcheur, -euse; promeneur, -euse; piéton m; **he's a fast w.**, il marche vite; **'walkie-'talkie**, s. F: émetteur-récepteur m; poste m de radio portatif; **'walk 'in**, v.i. entrer; (please) **w. in**, entrez sans frapper; **'walking**, s. la marche; promenades f pl (à pied); **to like**

w., aimer la marche; **w. shoes**, chaussures f de marche; **w. stick**, canne f; **it's (with)in w. distance**, on peut s'y rendre à pied; **'walk 'into**, v.i. entrer (dans une pièce); **to w. into a wall**, se heurter contre un mur; **I walked into him in the street**, je l'ai rencontré par hasard dans la rue; **'walk 'off**. 1. v.i. (a) s'en aller, partir; (b) F: **to w. off with the silver**, décamper avec l'argenterie (volée); **he walked off with the first prize**, il a gagné facilement le premier prix. 2. v.tr. **to w. off one's lunch**, faire une promenade de digestion; **'walk 'on**, v.i. Th: remplir un rôle de figurant(e); **'walk 'out**, (a) sortir; F: **to w. out on s.o.**, (i) abandonner qn; (ii) quitter qn en colère; (b) Ind: F: se mettre en grève; **'walkout**, s. Ind: F: grève f; **'walk 'over**, v.i. **to w. over to s.o.**, s'avancer vers qn; **'walkover**, s. F: victoire f facile, dans un fauteuil; **'walk 'up**, v.i. **to w. up to s.o.**, s'avancer vers qn; s'approcher de qn; **to w. up to the fifth floor**, monter (à pied) jusqu'au cinquième (étage), N.Am: jusqu'au quatrième.

wall [wɔ:l]. I. s. 1. (a) mur m; **main walls**, gros murs; **surrounding w.**, mur d'enceinte; **blank w.**, mur plein; **to come up against a blank w.**, se heurter à un mur; **you might just as well talk to a brick w.**, autant vaut parler à un sourd; **walls have ears**, les murs ont des oreilles; **to go to the w.**, (i) succomber, perdre la partie; (ii) faire faillite; **to leave only the bare walls standing**, ne laisser que les quatre murs; **w. painting**, peinture murale; **w. map**, carte murale; **w. clock**, pendule murale; (b) muraille f; **the Great W. of China**, la muraille de Chine; **tariff walls**, barrières douanières. 2. paroi f (de la poitrine, d'une cellule, Min: d'une galerie); joue f (d'un pneu). II. v.tr. **to w. (in)**, murer, entourer de murs; **walled garden**, jardin entouré de murs; **'wallflower**, s. Bot: giroflée f des murailles; F: (at dance) **to be a w.**, faire tapisserie; **'wallpaper**, s. papier peint.

wallaby ['wɔləbi], s. Z: wallaby m.

wallet ['wɔlit], s. portefeuille m.

Walloon [wə'lu:n]. 1. a. wallon, -onne. 2. s. (a) (pers.) Wallon, -onne; (b) Ling: le wallon.

wallop ['wɔləp]. F: I. s. 1. gros coup, torgn(i)ole f. 2. **down he went with a w.**, et patatras, le voilà par terre! II. v.tr. rosser (qn), flanquer une tournée à (qn); **'walloping**. F: 1. a. énorme; **a w. (great) lie**, un mensonge phénoménal. II. s. volée f (de coups); rossée f, raclée f.

wallow ['wɔlou]. I. v.i. (of animal) se vautrer, rouler dans la boue; (of pers.) **to w. in blood**, se rouler dans le sang; F: **to be wallowing in money**, rouler sur l'or. II. s. trou bourbeux.

walnut ['wɔ:lnʌt], s. (a) noix f; (b) **w. (tree)**, noyer m; (c) (bois m de) noyer.

walrus ['wɔ:lrəs], s. Z: morse m; F: **w.**

moustache, moustache *f* à la gauloise.
Walter ['wɔːltər]. *Pr.n.m.* Gauthier.
waltz [wɔːls]. **I.** *s.* **1.** valse *f.* **2.** air *m* de valse. **II.** *v.i.* valser.
wan [wɔn], *a.* pâlot, -otte; blême; (*of light*) blafard; **a w. smile,** un pâle sourire.
wand [wɔnd], *s.* **1.** baguette *f* magique, de fée. **2.** bâton *m* (de commandement); verge *f* (d'huissier).
wander ['wɔndər], *v.i.* (*a*) errer (sans but); se promener au hasard; aller à l'aventure; **to let one's thoughts w.,** laisser vaguer ses pensées; (*b*) **to w. away from the subject,** s'écarter du sujet; **his mind wanders at times,** il a des absences; (*c*) (*of pers.*) divaguer; '**wanderer,** *s.* vagabond, -onde; **the w. has returned,** notre voyageur nous est revenu; '**wandering. I.** *a.* (*a*) errant, vagabond; **the w. Jew,** le Juif errant; (*b*) (esprit) distrait; (*c*) (discours) incohérent. **II.** *s.* (*a*) vagabondage *m*; **in his wanderings,** pendant son voyage; pendant qu'il voyageait; (*b*) rêverie *f*; (*c*) *Med:* égarement *m* (de l'esprit); divagation *f*; '**wanderlust,** *s.* la passion des voyages; l'esprit *m* d'aventure.
wane [wein]. **I.** *v.i.* (*of moon, power*) décroître, décliner; (*of beauty*) être sur le retour; (*of enthusiasm*) s'attiédir. **II.** *s.* déclin *m*; **moon on the w.,** lune à son décours, qui décroît; '**waning,** *s.* décours *m* (de la lune); déclin *m*.
wangle ['wæŋgl]. *F:* **I.** *v.tr.* obtenir (qch.) par subterfuge; resquiller; **to w. a week's leave,** carotter huit jours de congé. **II.** *s.* moyen détourné; truc *m*; **the whole thing's a w.,** tout ça, c'est de la resquille, c'est fricoté; '**wangler,** *s. F:* resquilleur, -euse; '**wangling,** *s. F:* fricotage *m*; resquille *f*; le système D.
want [wɔnt]. **I.** *v.* **1.** *v.i.* manquer (de qch.); être dépourvu (de qch.); **to w. for nothing,** ne manquer de rien. **2.** *v.tr.* (*a*) manquer de, ne pas avoir (qch.); (*b*) (*of pers.*) avoir besoin de (qch.); (*of thg*) exiger, réclamer (qch.); **he wants rest,** il a besoin de repos; **this work wants a lot of patience,** ce travail exige beaucoup de patience; **have you everything you w.?** avez-vous tout ce qu'il vous faut? **I've (got) all I w.,** j'en ai assez; **that's just what I w.,** voilà juste ce qu'il me faut, juste mon affaire; **do you w. a job?** (i) est-ce que tu cherches un emploi? (ii) ça ne te gênerait pas de m'aider? **wanted, a good cook,** on demande une bonne cuisinière; (*c*) **your hair wants cutting,** vous avez besoin de vous faire couper les cheveux; *F:* **that wants a bit of doing,** ce n'est pas si facile que ça; (*d*) désirer, vouloir; **he knows what he wants,** il sait ce qu'il veut; **how much do you w. for it?** c'est combien? *Iron:* **you don't w. much!** tu n'es pas difficile! **you're wanted,** on vous demande; **we're not wanted here,** nous sommes de trop ici; **I don't w. him,**

je n'ai pas besoin de lui; **what does he w. with me?** que me veut-il? **I w. to tell you about it,** je voudrais vous en parler; **I w. to see him,** j'ai envie de le voir; **I don't w. it known,** je ne veux pas que cela se sache. **II.** *s.* **1.** manque *m*, défaut *m*; **for w. of something better,** faute de mieux; **for w. of something (better) to do,** par désœuvrement. **2.** indigence *f*, misère *f.* **3.** besoin *m*; **a long-felt w.,** une lacune à combler; '**wanted,** *a.* **1.** désiré, voulu. **2.** recherché par la police; '**wanting,** *a.* **w. in intelligence,** dépourvu d'intelligence; '**wanton,** *a.* **w. cruelty,** cruauté gratuite; **w. destruction,** destruction voulue, pour le simple plaisir de détruire.
war [wɔːr]. **I.** *s.* guerre *f*; **total w.,** guerre totale; **cold w.,** guerre froide; **world w.,** guerre mondiale; **to make w. on s.o.,** faire la guerre à, contre, qn; **to go to w.,** se mettre en guerre; **w. of words,** dispute *f* de mots; *F:* **you look as if you've been in the wars,** vous avez l'air de vous être battu; **w. clouds were gathering,** il y avait des menaces de guerre; **w. correspondent,** correspondant *m* de guerre; **w. cry,** cri *m* de guerre; **w. dance,** danse guerrière; *Fin:* **w. loan,** emprunt *m* de guerre. **II.** *v.i.* (**warred**) faire la guerre (**against sth.,** à qch.); '**warfare,** *s.* la guerre; **class w.,** la lutte des classes; '**warhead,** *s.* (*a*) cône *m* de charge (d'une torpille); (*b*) tête *f*, ogive *f* (de fusée); **nuclear w.,** tête nucléaire; '**warhorse,** *s.* (*a*) cheval *m* de bataille; (*b*) *F:* **an old w.,** (i) un vieux militaire; (ii) un vétéran de la politique; '**warpaint,** *s.* **1.** peinture *f* de guerre (des Peaux-Rouges, etc.). **2.** *F:* (*of woman*) **to put on the w.,** se maquiller; '**warpath,** *s. F:* **to be on the w.,** chercher noise; être d'une humeur massacrante; '**warship,** *s.* navire *m* de guerre; '**wartime,** *s.* temps *m* de guerre; **on a w. footing, under w. conditions,** sur le pied de guerre.
warble ['wɔːbl]. **I.** *v.i.* (*of bird*) gazouiller. **II.** *s.* gazouillement *m* (d'un oiseau); '**warbler,** *s. Orn:* (*a*) bec-fin *m*; (*b*) fauvette *f*; '**warbling,** *s.* gazouillement *m*.
ward [wɔːd]. **I.** *s.* **1.** pupille *mf*; *Jur:* **w. in Chancery,** pupille sous tutelle judiciaire. **2.** (*a*) salle *f* (d'hôpital); **emergency w.,** salle d'urgence; (*b*) quartier *m* (d'une prison). **3.** circonscription électorale. **4.** **wards of a lock,** gardes *f* d'une serrure. **II.** *v.tr.* **to w. off a blow,** parer un coup; **to w. off an illness,** prévenir une maladie; '**warden,** *s.* (*a*) directeur *m* (d'une institution); (*b*) gardien *m* (d'un parc, etc.); (*c*) **traffic w.,** contractuel, -elle (qui surveille le stationnement des voitures); '**warder,** '**wardress,** *s.* gardien, -ienne, de prison; '**wardrobe,** *s.* (*a*) (*furniture*) armoire *f*; penderie *f*; (*b*) (= *clothes*) garde-robe *f*; '**wardroom,** *s. Navy:* carré *m* des officiers.
ware ['weər], *s.* (*a*) *coll.* articles fabriqués; usten-

siles *mpl* (en aluminium, etc.); (*b*) **to boost one's wares,** vanter ses marchandises *f*; **'warehouse. I.** *s.* entrepôt *m*; magasin *m*; **bonded w.,** entrepôt en douane. **II.** *v.tr.* emmagasiner; mettre en magasin; **'warehouseman,** *pl.* **-men,** *m*, (*a*) entrepositaire *mf*; magasinier *m*; (*b*) garde-magasin *m*.

warily ['wɛərili], *adv.* prudemment; avec circonspection.

wariness ['wɛərinəs], *s.* prudence *f*; circonspection *f*.

warm [wɔːm]. **I.** *a. & s.* **1.** *a.* (*a*) chaud; **to be w.,** (i) (*of water*) être chaud; (ii) (*of pers.*) avoir chaud; **I can't get w.,** je ne peux pas me réchauffer; (*in game*) **you're getting w.,** vous brûlez; **to keep oneself w.,** se tenir au chaud; porter des vêtements chauds; **w. coat,** manteau chaud; (*of weather*) **it's w.,** il fait chaud; (*b*) chaleureux, -euse; **w. welcome,** accueil chaleureux; **w. heart,** cœur généreux, chaud; **it's w. work,** c'est une rude besogne; *F:* **to make it w. for s.o.,** en faire voir de dures à qn. **2.** *s.* **in the w.,** au chaud; **come and have a w.,** venez vous réchauffer; **-ly,** *adv.* **1.** (vêtu) chaudement. **2.** (*a*) (applaudir) chaudement; (remercier qn) chaleureusement; (*b*) (répondre) vivement, avec chaleur. **II.** *v.* **1.** *v.tr.* chauffer; **to w. oneself by the fire,** s'asseoir auprès du feu pour se réchauffer. **2.** *v.i.* (se) chauffer; se réchauffer; **to w. to s.o.,** trouver qn de plus en plus sympathique; **'warm-'blooded,** *a.* *Z:* à sang chaud; **'warm-'hearted,** *a.* au cœur chaud, généreux; **'warming,** *a.* chauffage *m*; **w. pan,** bassinoire *f*; **warmth,** *s.* **1.** chaleur *f*. **2.** (*a*) cordialité *f*, chaleur (d'un accueil); (*b*) emportement *m*, vivacité *f*; **'warm 'up,** *v.* **1.** *v.tr.* chauffer; réchauffer; faire réchauffer (un plat). **2.** *v.i.* s'échauffer, s'animer; (*of pers.*) devenir plus cordial; **the lecturer was warming up to his subject,** le conférencier s'animait peu à peu.

warn [wɔːn], *v.tr.* avertir; **to w. s.o. of a danger,** avertir qn d'un danger; **to w. s.o. against sth.,** mettre qn en garde contre qch.; **he warned her not to go,** il lui a conseillé fortement de ne pas y aller; **you have been warned!** vous voilà prévenu! **'warning. I.** *a.* (geste, etc.) avertisseur, d'avertissement. **II.** *s.* **1.** avertissement *m*; **air-raid w.,** alerte *f*; **w. device,** avertisseur *m*. **2.** (*a*) avertissement, avis *m*, préavis *m*; **without w.,** sans préavis; (*b*) **to give s.o. fair w.,** donner à qn un avertissement formel; (*c*) **let this be a w. to you,** que cela vous serve de leçon, d'exemple.

warp [wɔːp]. **I.** *v.* **1.** *v.tr.* (*a*) déjeter, voiler (le bois, une tôle); fausser, pervertir (l'esprit); (*b*) *Tex:* ourdir; (*c*) *Nau:* touer (un navire). **2.** *v.i.* (*a*) se déformer; (se) gondoler; (*of timber*) se déjeter, gauchir; (*of wheel*) se voiler; **wood**

that **warps,** bois *m* qui joue, qui travaille. **II.** *s.* **1.** *Tex:* chaîne *f*. **2.** *Nau:* amarre *f*; touée *f*. **3.** voilure *f*, courbure *f*, gauchissement *m* (d'une planche, etc.); **warped** [wɔːpt], *a.* (*a*) (bois) déjeté, gauchi; (*of wheel*) voilé; (*b*) (esprit) perverti, faussé; **'warping,** *s.* **1.** (*a*) gauchissement *m* (du bois, etc.); gondolage *m* (de la tôle); (*b*) perversion *f* (de l'esprit). **2.** *Tex:* ourdissage *m*.

warrant ['wɔrənt]. **I.** *s.* **1.** garantie *f*; justification *f.* **2.** (*a*) mandat *m* (d'arrêt, de perquisition); (*b*) **w. for payment,** ordonnance *f* de paiement; **travel w.,** feuille *f* de route. **3.** **w. officer,** (i) *Mil:* = adjudant-chef *m*; (ii) *Nau:* = maître principal. **II.** *v.tr.* **1.** garantir (qch.); **it won't happen again, I w. you!** cela n'arrivera pas deux fois, je vous en réponds! **2.** justifier; **nothing can w. such behaviour,** rien ne justifie une pareille conduite; **'warranted,** *a.* *Com:* garanti; **'warranty,** *s.* **1.** autorisation *f*; justification *f.* **2.** garantie *f.*

warren ['wɔrən], *s.* (**rabbit**) **w.,** garenne *f.*

warrior ['wɔriər], *s.* guerrier *m*, soldat *m*; **the Unknown W.,** le Soldat inconnu.

Warsaw ['wɔːsɔː]. *Pr.n.* Varsovie *f.*

wart [wɔːt], *s.* verrue *f*; **'warthog,** *s.* *Z:* phacochère *m*.

wary ['wɛəri], *a.* (*a*) prudent, circonspect; (*b*) **to be w. of sth., s.o.,** se méfier de qch., qn; **-ily,** *adv.* prudemment, avec circonspection.

wash [wɔʃ]. **I.** *v.* **1.** *v.tr.* (*a*) laver; **to w. oneself,** se laver; **to w. one's hands, one's hair,** se laver les mains, la tête; **to w. one's hands of sth.,** se laver les mains de qch.; (*b*) blanchir, lessiver, laver (le linge); **material that won't w.,** tissu *m* qui ne se lave pas; *F:* **that (story) won't w.!** ça ne prend pas! (*c*) (*of sea*) **to w. sth. ashore,** rejeter qch. sur le rivage; **washed away by the tide,** emporté par la mer; **he was washed overboard,** il a été enlevé par une vague. **2.** *v.i.* **the waves were washing over the deck,** les vagues balayaient le pont. **II.** *s.* **1.** (*a*) lavage *m*; **to give sth. a w.,** laver qch.; (*of pers.*) **to have a w.,** se laver; faire un brin de toilette; (*b*) **I send the sheets to the w.,** j'envoie les draps à la blanchisserie; *F:* **it'll all come out in the w.,** ça se tassera. **2. colour w.,** badigeon *m*. **3.** *Nau:* sillage *m*, remous *m* (d'un navire); **'washable,** *a.* lavable; **'washbasin,** *s.* lavabo *m*; **'washbowl,** *s.* cuvette *f*; bassine *f*; **'washcloth,** *s.* *N.Am:* = gant *m* de toilette; **'washday,** *s.* jour *m* de lessive; **'wash'down,** *v.tr.* (*a*) laver à grande eau; (*b*) *F:* **to w. down one's dinner with a glass of beer,** faire descendre son dîner avec un verre de bière; **'wash'down,** *s.* toilette *f* rapide; **I'll give the car a w.,** je vais rapidement laver la voiture; (*b*) *Av:* aire *f* de lavage; **'washer¹,** *s.* (*pers.*) (*a*) laveur, -euse; (*b*) **w. up,** laveur, -euse, de vaisselle; (*in restaurant*) plongeur *m*. 2. (*a*) machine *f* à laver; (*b*) *Aut:* windscreen, *N.Am:* **windshield, w., lave-glace** *m*; **'washerwoman,** *s.* blanchisseuse *f*; **'washhouse,** *s.* (*a*) buanderie *f*; (*b*) laverie *f*; **'washing,** *s.* 1. lavage *m*; ablutions *fpl*. 2. (*a*) lessive *f* (du linge); **w. day,** jour *m* de lessive; **w. machine,** machine *f* à laver; *Aut:* **w. bay,** installation *f* de lavage; (*b*) linge *m* (à blanchir); *F:* **to take in one another's w.,** se rendre mutuellement service. 3. **w. up,** la vaisselle; (*in restaurant*) la plonge; **to do the w. up,** faire la vaisselle; **w.-up machine,** lave-vaisselle *m*; **w.-up bowl,** bassine *f* (à vaisselle); **'washleather,** *s.* (peau *f* de) chamois *m*; **'wash 'off,** *v.tr.* enlever, effacer, (qch.) par le lavage, à l'eau; **'wash 'out,** *v.tr.* (*a*) enlever (une tache) (par le lavage); (*with passive force*) **stain that won't w. out,** tache qui ne part pas à l'eau; *F:* **you can w. that right out!** inutile de compter là-dessus! (*b*) laver; **to w. out a few handkerchiefs,** laver (rapidement) quelques mouchoirs; *F:* **I'm completely washed out,** je suis complètement vanné, à plat; **'washout,** *s.* *F:* (*a*) fiasco *m*; four *m*; (*b*) **he's a w.,** c'est un raté; **'washrag,** *s. N.Am:* = gant *m* de toilette; **'washroom,** *s.* (*a*) cabinet *m* de toilette; (*b*) la toilette, les cabinets; (**where is**) **the w. please?** la toilette, s'il vous plaît? **'washstand,** *s.* (*a*) table *f* de toilette; (*b*) *N.Am:* lavabo *m*; **'wash 'up,** *v.tr. & i.* (*a*) **to w. up** (**the dishes**), faire la vaisselle; (*b*) (*of sea*) rejeter (qn, qch.) sur le rivage; (*c*) *F:* **to be washed up,** (i) être ruiné, fichu; (ii) être complètement à plat. **washer²** ['wɔʃər], *s. E:* rondelle *f*.

wasp [wɔsp], *s.* guêpe *f*; **wasps' nest,** guêpier *m*; **'waspish,** *a. F:* irritable; méchant; **w. tone,** ton aigre, irrité.

waste [weist]. I. *v.* 1. *v.tr.* (*a*) consumer, user; **wasted by disease,** miné, amaigri, par la maladie; (*b*) gaspiller (son argent, etc.); **to w. one's time,** perdre son temps; **it's just wasting one's words!** c'est parler en pure perte! **wasted life,** vie manquée; **w. not, want not,** qui épargne gagne. 2. *v.i.* **to w. (away),** dépérir. II. *a.* 1. **w. land, w. ground,** (i) terre *f* inculte; (ii) (*in town*) terrain *m* vague; (*of ground*) **to lie w.,** rester en friche; **to lay w.,** dévaster, ravager (un pays). 2. (matière) de rebut; **w. paper,** papier *m* de rebut; vieux papiers; **w. paper basket,** corbeille *f* à papier(s). III. *s.* 1. région *f* inculte; désert *m*. 2. gaspillage *m* (d'argent, etc.); **w. of time,** perte *f* de temps. 3. déchets *mpl*, rebut *m*; **radioactive w.,** déchets radioactifs; *H:* **w. disposal unit,** broyeur *m* à ordures; **'wastage,** *s.* (*a*) perte *f* (de chaleur, etc.); (*b*) gaspillage *m*; **'wasted,** *a.* (argent) gaspillé; (temps) perdu; **w. effort,** peine perdue; **'wasteful,** *a.* gaspilleur, -euse; prodigue; **w.**

habits, habitudes *f* de gaspillage; **-fully,** *adv.* avec prodigalité; en pure perte; **'wastefulness,** *s.* prodigalité *f*; gaspillage *m*; **'waster,** *s.* 1. gaspilleur, -euse; **time w.,** (i) personne qui perd son temps; (ii) travail, etc., qui vous fait perdre votre temps. 2. vaurien *m*, propre *m* à rien; **'wasting,** *s.* 1. gaspillage *m*. 2. **w. (away),** dépérissement *m*; **'wastrel,** *s.* = WASTER 2.

watch [wɔtʃ]. I. *s.* 1. garde *f*; surveillance *f*; **to be on the w.,** (i) être en observation; se tenir aux aguets; (ii) être sur ses gardes; **to be on the w. for s.o.,** guetter qn; **to keep a w. on s.o.,** surveiller qn; **w. committee,** comité *m* qui veille à l'ordre public (de la commune); **w. tower,** tour *f* d'observation, de guet. 2. *Hist:* **the w.,** la ronde de nuit. 3. *Nau:* (*a*) quart *m*; **to be on w.,** être de quart; **officer of the w.,** officier *m* de quart; (*b*) (**men**) bordée *f*. 4. montre *f*; **it's six o'clock by my w.,** il est six heures à ma montre. II. *v.* 1. *v.tr.* (*a*) observer; regarder attentivement; surveiller (qn); **we are being watched,** on nous observe, nous regarde; **to w. the expenses,** regarder à la dépense; **to w. one's step,** (i) prendre garde de ne pas tomber; (ii) éviter de faire un faux pas; (*b*) regarder; voir; **I watched her working,** je la regardais travailler; **to w. television,** regarder une émission de télévision; **to w. a football match,** (i) assister à un match de football; (ii) regarder un match de football à la télévision; (*c*) **to w. s.o.'s interests,** veiller aux intérêts de qn. 2. *v.i.* (*a*) **to w. for s.o.,** attendre qn; guetter qn; (*b*) **w. out!** prenez garde! attention! **'watchdog,** *s.* chien *m* de garde; **'watcher,** *s.* **bird w.,** observateur, -trice, (des mœurs) des oiseaux; **'watchful,** *a.* vigilant; alerte; attentif; **-fully,** *adv.* avec vigilance; **'watchfulness,** *s.* vigilance *f*; **'watching,** *s.* (*a*) surveillance *f*; (*b*) **bird w.,** observation *f* (des mœurs) des oiseaux; **'watchmaker,** *s.* horloger *m*; **'watchmaking,** *s.* horlogerie *f*; **'watchman,** *pl.* **-men,** *s.* gardien *m*; *Nau:* homme *m* de garde; *Ind:* **night w.,** veilleur *m* de nuit; **'watchnight,** *s. Ecc:* **w. service,** office *m* de minuit (la veille du jour de l'an); **'watchword,** *s.* mot *m* d'ordre.

water ['wɔːtər]. I. *s.* 1. eau *f*; (*a*) **salt w.,** eau salée; eau de mer; **fresh w.,** (i) eau douce; (ii) (*for drinking*) eau fraîche; **drinking w.,** eau potable; **hot, cold, w.,** eau chaude, froide; **hot w. bottle,** bouillotte *f*; **to throw cold w. on a scheme,** décourager un projet; (*b*) *H:* **to have w. laid on,** (i) faire installer; (ii) avoir, l'eau courante; (*in hotel*) **hot and cold w. in all rooms,** eau courante (chaude et froide) dans toutes les chambres; **to turn on the w.,** ouvrir l'eau; **w. supply,** service *m* des eaux, distribution *f* d'eau (de la ville); **w. main,** conduite principale d'eau; **w. softener,** adoucisseur *m* d'eau; (*c*) (*at spa*) **to take the waters,** prendre les eaux; faire une cure. **2.** (*a*) **the waters of a river, of a lake,** les eaux d'une rivière, d'un lac; (*b*) **on land and w.,** sur terre et sur eau; **by w.,** par mer; par bateau; **to be under w.,** être inondé, submergé; **to swim under w.,** nager sous l'eau, entre deux eaux; **above w.,** à flot; surnageant; **to keep one's head above w.,** (i) se maintenir à la surface; (ii) faire face à ses engagements; (*c*) **high, low, w.,** marée haute, basse; *F:* **to be in low w.,** être dans la dèche; être bien bas. **3.** (*a*) *Med:* **w. on the brain,** hydrocéphalie *f*; **w. on the knee,** hydarthrose *f* du genou; épanchement *m* de synovie; (*b*) **to make, pass, w.,** uriner. **4.** transparence *f*, eau (d'un diamant); orient *m* (d'une perle); **of the first w.,** de la plus belle eau. **5. w. ice,** sorbet *m*; **w. lily,** nénuphar *m*; **w. melon,** pastèque *f*; **w. polo,** water-polo *m*; **w. power,** force *f* hydraulique; **w. rat,** rat *m* d'eau; campagnol nageur; **w. skiing,** ski *m* nautique; *Geol:* **w. table,** nappe *f* aquifère; **w. tower,** château *m* d'eau. **II.** *v.* **1.** *v.tr.* (*a*) arroser (son jardin; (*of river*) une région); (*b*) couper (son vin); *Fin:* **to w. the capital,** diluer le capital (d'une société); (*c*) faire boire, abreuver (des bêtes); (*d*) *Tex:* moirer (la soie). **2.** *v.i.* (*a*) (*of eyes*) pleurer, larmoyer; (*b*) (*of ship*) faire de l'eau; **'watercourse,** *s.* cours *m* d'eau; **'watercress,** *s.* cresson *m* de fontaine; **'waterfall,** *s.* chute *f* d'eau; cascade *f*; **'waterfowl,** *s.* (*a*) oiseau *m* aquatique; (*b*) *coll.* gibier *m* d'eau; sauvagine *f*; **'waterfront,** *s.* bord *m* de l'eau, de mer; les quais *m*; *N.Am:* **on the w.,** chez les dockers; **'watering,** *s.* (*a*) arrosage *m* (du jardin); **w. can,** arrosoir *m*; (*b*) dilution *f* (d'une boisson); *Fin:* dilution (du capital); (*c*) abreuvage *m* (des bêtes); (*d*) larmoiement *m* (des yeux); **'waterless,** *a.* sans eau; **'waterlogged,** *a.* (terrain) imbibé d'eau, détrempé; **'watermark,** *s.* filigrane *m*; **'waterproof. I.** *a.* & *s. Cost:* imperméable (*m*). **II.** *v.tr.* imperméabiliser; hydrofuger (un mur, etc.); **'watershed,** *s. Geog:* ligne *f* de partage des eaux; **'waterside,** *s.* = WATERFRONT; **'waterspout,** *s.* **1.** tuyau *m*, descente *f*, d'eau. **2.** gouttière *f*, gargouille *f*. **3.** *Meteor:* trombe *f*; **'watertight,** *a.* étanche (à l'eau); **w. regulations,** règlement *m* qui a prévu tous les cas; **'waterway,** *s.* voie *f* d'eau; voie navigable; **'waterworks,** *s.pl.* **1.** usine *f* de distribution d'eau. **2.** *F:* (*a*) **to turn on the w.,** se mettre à pleurer; (*b*) **there's something wrong with my w.,** j'ai des ennuis avec mes voies urinaires; **'watery,** *a.* (*a*) aqueux, -euse; qui contient de l'eau; noyé d'eau; (yeux) larmoyants; (*b*) **w. soup,** potage clair, peu consistant.

Waterloo [wɔ:tə'lu:]. *Pr.n.* **the Battle of W.,** la bataille de Waterloo; **to meet one's W.,** arriver au désastre.

watt [wɔt], *s. El:* watt *m*.

wave [weiv]. **I.** *s.* **1.** (*in sea*) vague *f*; **w. of enthusiasm,** vague d'enthousiasme. **2.** *Ph:* onde *f*; **long waves,** grandes ondes; **short waves,** petites ondes, ondes courtes. **3.** ondulation *f* (des cheveux); **permanent w.,** (ondulation) permanente *f*. **4.** balancement *m*, ondoiement *m*; **with a w. of his hand,** d'un geste, d'un signe, de la main. **II.** *v.* **1.** *v.i.* (*a*) s'agiter; flotter (au vent); (*b*) **to w. to s.o.,** faire signe à qn (en agitant le bras); (*c*) **my hair waves naturally,** mes cheveux ondulent naturellement. **2.** *v.tr.* (*a*) agiter (le bras, un mouchoir); **to w. one's hand,** faire signe de la main; (*b*) **to w. s.o. aside,** écarter qn d'un geste; **to w. s.o. on,** faire signe à qn de continuer, d'avancer; **to w. aside an objection,** écarter une objection; (*c*) **to have one's hair waved,** se faire faire une permanente; **waved,** *a.* ondulé; **'wavelength,** *s. Ph:* longueur *f* d'onde; *F:* **we're not on the same w.,** on n'est pas sur la même longueur d'onde; **'waver,** *v.i.* (*a*) (*of flame, etc.*) vaciller, trembloter; (*b*) (*of pers.*) vaciller, hésiter; (*of courage*) défaillir; **'waverer,** *s.* indécis, -ise; irrésolu, -ue; **'wavering. I.** *a.* (*a*) (*of flame*) vacillant, tremblotant; (*b*) (*of pers.*) irrésolu, hésitant; (*of voice*) défaillant. **II.** *s.* (*a*) tremblement *m*, vacillement *m* (d'une flamme); (*b*) vacillation *f*, irrésolution *f*; **'wavy,** *a.* onduleux, -euse; (*of hair*) ondulé; **w. line,** ligne qui tremble, ligne hésitante; *F:* **the W. Navy,** les réservistes *m* de la Marine.

wax¹ [wæks]. **I.** *s.* **1.** (*a*) cire *f*; (*b*) (*in ear*) cérumen *m*. **2.** fart *m* (pour skis). **II.** *v.tr.* **1.** cirer, encaustiquer (un meuble, etc.). **2.** farter (des skis); **'waxbill,** *s. Orn:* bec-de-cire *m*; **'waxing,** *s.* **1.** encaustiquage *m*. **2.** fartage *m* (des skis); **'waxwing,** *s. Orn:* jaseur *m*; **'waxwork,** *s.* figure *f* de cire; **waxworks,** (musée *m* de) figures de cire; **'waxy,** *a.* cireux, -euse.

wax², *v.i.* (*of moon*) croître; **to w. and wane,** croître et décroître.

way¹ [wei], *s.* **1.** (*a*) chemin *m*, route *f*; voie *f*; *Rail:* **the permanent w.,** la voie ferrée; *N.Am:* **w. train,** (train *m*) omnibus (*m*); **over, across, the w.,** de l'autre côté de la route, de la rue; en face; *P.N: Aut:* **give w.** = priorité à droite; **to make w. for s.o.,** se ranger, céder le pas à qn; (*b*) **by the w.,** (i) incidemment, en passant; (ii) à (ce) propos; pendant que j'y pense; dis donc; **by w. of a warning,** en guise d'avertissement; **he's by w. of being a socialist,** il est vaguement socialiste. **2.** (*a*) **to show s.o. the w.,** montrer la route à qn; **which is the w. to the station?** où est le chemin de la gare? **to ask one's w.,** demander son chemin; **to lose one's w.,** se perdre; se tromper de chemin; s'égarer; **to go the wrong w.,** faire fausse route; **to go the shortest w.,** prendre par le plus court; **to know one's w. about,** savoir se débrouiller; **on the w.,** en cours de route; chemin faisant; **on the w. home,** en rentrant; en revenant chez moi; **to go one's own w.,** (i) faire à sa guise; (ii) faire bande à part; **to go out of one's w. to help s.o.,** se déranger pour aider qn; **to go out of one's w. to look for difficulties,** rechercher la difficulté; **the village is completely out of the w.,** ce village est complètement écarté, isolé, au bout du monde; *F:* **that's nothing out of the w.!** ça n'a rien d'extraordinaire! (b) **w. in,** entrée *f;* **w. out,** sortie *f;* **to find a w. out of a difficulty,** trouver la solution d'une difficulté, trouver une solution; (c) **to find one's w. to a place,** parvenir à un endroit; **to make one's w. through a crowd,** se frayer un chemin à travers la foule; **to make one's w. (in the world),** réussir; arriver; **to work one's w. up,** s'élever à force de travailler; **to pay one's w.,** se suffire; **I can't see my w. to doing it now,** je ne vois pas, pour le moment, comment le faire; (d) **to stand, be, in s.o.'s w.,** (i) barrer le passage à qn; (ii) faire obstacle à qn; gêner, embarrasser, qn; **he's always getting in my w.,** il est toujours à me gêner; **get out of the, my, w.!** rangez-vous! **I'm trying to keep out of his w.,** j'essaie de l'éviter; **to make w. for s.o.,** faire place à qn. 3. **I'll go part of the w. with you,** je ferai un bout de chemin, une partie du trajet, avec vous; **all the w.,** jusqu'au bout; tout le long du chemin; **it's a long w. from here,** c'est (bien) loin d'ici; **I've a long w. to go,** j'ai beaucoup de chemin à faire; **he'll go a long w.,** il ira loin; il fera son chemin; il réussira; **to know how to make a little go a long w.,** savoir ménager ses sous. 4. (a) côté *m,* direction *f;* **which w. is the wind blowing?** d'où vient le vent? **this w. out,** par ici la sortie; **this w. and that,** de-ci, de-là; **he looked the other w.,** il a détourné les yeux; **I don't know which w. to turn,** je ne sais pas de quel côté me tourner, me mettre; **if the opportunity comes your w.,** si vous en avez l'occasion; *F:* **down our w.,** chez nous; (b) sens *m;* **the wrong w.,** à contre-sens; **the wrong w. up,** à l'envers; sens dessus dessous; **the right w. up,** dans le bon sens; **one w. street,** rue *f* à sens unique. 5. moyen *m;* **to find a w. to do sth.,** trouver le moyen de faire qch.; *Pol:* **Committee of Ways and Means** = la Commission du Budget. 6. (a) façon *f,* manière *f;* **in this w.,** de cette façon; **in no w.,** en aucune façon; **in a friendly w.,** en ami; amicalement; **without wishing to criticize it in any w.,** sans vouloir aucunement le critiquer; **to go the right w. to work,** s'y prendre bien; **in one w. or another,** d'une façon ou d'une autre; **there are no two**

ways about it, il n'y a pas à discuter; **the w. things are going,** du train où vont les choses; **well, it's this w.,** voici ce que c'est; **that's his w.,** il est comme ça; **our w. of living,** notre façon de vivre; notre genre *m* de vie; **the American w. of life,** la vie américaine; **that's always the w. with him,** il est toujours comme ça; **to do things (in) one's own w.,** faire les choses à sa guise; **to get into the w. of doing sth.,** (i) prendre l'habitude de faire qch.; (ii) apprendre à faire qch.; (b) **he's got a w. with him,** il est insinuant; on le suit (en dépit de tout); **he has a w. with children,** il sait prendre les enfants; **I know his little ways,** je connais ses petites manies; (c) **to get one's (own) w.,** arriver à ses fins; **he wants it all his own w.,** il veut n'en faire qu'à sa tête; **he had it all his own w.,** il n'a pas rencontré de résistance; **you can't have it both ways,** on ne peut pas être et avoir été; (d) **in many ways,** à bien des égards, à bien des points de vue. 7. cours *m;* **in the ordinary w.,** d'habitude; **in the ordinary w. of business,** au cours des affaires; **things are in a bad w.,** les choses vont mal; **he's in a bad w.,** (i) ses affaires vont mal; (ii) il est bien malade. 8. (a) **the flood is making w.,** l'inondation fait des progrès; (b) erre *f* (d'un navire); **ship under w.,** navire en marche, faisant route; **we must get the work under w.,** il nous faut attaquer, nous mettre à, ce travail; **'wayfarer,** *s.* voyageur, -euse; passant, -ante; **way'lay,** *v.tr.* (**way'laid**) (a) attirer (qn) dans une embuscade; (b) arrêter (qn) au passage; **'wayside,** *s.* bord *m* de la route; **to fall by the w.,** rester en chemin; **'wayward,** *a.* (a) volontaire, rebelle; (b) capricieux, fantasque.

way², *adv. F:* (= AWAY) **it was w. back in 1900,** cela remonte à 1900; **w. up the mountainside,** en haut sur la pente de la montagne; **w. down in the valley,** en bas dans la vallée.

we [wiː], *pers. pron., nom. pl.* (a) nous; **we were playing,** nous jouions; **here we are!** nous voilà! **we had a wonderful time,** on s'est bien amusé(s); (b) *(stressed)* **we are English, they are French,** nous, nous sommes anglais, eux, ils sont français; **you don't think that we did it?** vous ne pensez pas que c'est nous qui l'avons fait? **we English,** nous autres Anglais; (c) *(indefinite)* on; nous; **as we say in England,** comme on dit en Angleterre; **we are living in difficult times,** nous vivons dans une période difficile; **we all make mistakes sometimes,** tout le monde peut se tromper.

weak [wiːk], *a.* 1. faible; *(of health)* débile; **to grow w.,** weaker, s'affaiblir; **to have a w. stomach,** avoir l'estomac fragile, peu solide. 2. **w. character,** caractère *m* faible; **that's his w. side,** c'est son côté faible. 3. *(of solution, etc.)* dilué; *(of petrol, etc.)* **w. mixture,** mélange *m*

pauvre: **w. tea,** thé léger, faible. **4.** *s.* **the w.,** (i)
les faibles *m*: (ii) les infirmes *m*, les débiles *m*:
-ly[1], *adv.* (a) faiblement, sans force: (b) sans
résolution: **'weaken. 1.** *v.tr.* affaiblir: amollir
(l'esprit). **2.** *v.i.* s'affaiblir: faiblir:
'weakening. I. *a.* **1.** affaiblissant. **2.**
faiblissant: qui faiblit. **II.** *s.* affaiblissement *m*;
'weak-'kneed, *a. F:* sans caractère: mou, *f.*
molle: **'weakling,** *s.* (a) être *m* faible, débile:
(b) homme faible de caractère: **'weakly**[2], *a.*
débile, faible (de santé): **'weak-'minded,** *a.*
(a) faible d'esprit: (b) indécis, qui manque de
résolution: **'weakness,** *s.* (a) faiblesse *f*: (b) **to
have a w. for sth., for s.o.,** avoir un faible pour
qch., pour qn.
weal [wi:l], *s.* marque *f*, trace *f* (d'un coup de
fouet).
wealth [welθ], *s.* **1.** richesse(s) *f(pl)*. **2.** abondance *f*, profusion *f* (de détails, etc.):
'wealthy, *a.* riche: **w. heiress,** grosse héritière:
s. **the w.,** les riches *m.*
wean [wi:n], *v.tr.* sevrer (un nourrisson).
weapon ['wepən], *s.* arme *f.*
wear [wɛər]. **I.** *v.* (wore [wɔ:r], worn [wɔ:n]) **1.**
v.tr. porter (un vêtement): **he was wearing a
hat,** il portait un chapeau: **to w. black,** porter
du noir: **what shall I w.?** qu'est-ce que je vais
mettre? **I've nothing fit to w.,** je n'ai rien de
mettable. **2.** *v.tr.* user: **to w. sth. into holes, to
w. holes in sth.,** trouer qch. (par usure): **to w.
oneself to death,** se tuer à force de travail. **3.**
(*with passive force*) (*of garment*) **to w. into
holes,** se trouer: **to w. well,** (i) (*of material, etc.*)
faire bon usage: (ii) (*of pers.*) être bien conservé. **II.** *s.* **1.** usage *m*; (a) **men's w.,** vêtements
mpl pour hommes: **dresses for evening w.,**
robes *f* de soirée: (b) **material that will stand
hard w.,** tissu *m* d'un bon usage: **to be the
worse for w.,** (i) (*of garment*) être usé,
défraîchi: (ii) *F:* (*of pers.*) avoir trop bu, avoir
la gueule de bois. **2.** usure *f*; fatigue *f* (d'une
machine): **w. and tear,** (i) usure (normale): (ii)
frais *mpl* d'entretien: **'wearable,** *a.* (vêtement)
mettable: **'wear a'way. 1.** *v.tr.* (a) user,
ronger: **he's worn away to a shadow,** il n'est
plus que l'ombre de lui-même: (b) effacer (une
inscription, etc.). **2.** *v.i.* (a) s'user: (b) s'effacer:
'wearer, *s.* personne qui porte un vêtement:
this new style does not suit many wearers, ce
nouveau style est difficile à porter: **'wearing.
I.** *a.* fatigant, épuisant: **good w. material,** tissu
m de bon usage. **II.** *s.* **1. w. apparel,** vêtements
mpl. **2.** usure *f*; **'wear 'off. 1.** *v.tr.* faire disparaître (par l'usure). **2.** *v.i.* s'effacer, disparaître: (*of pain*) se calmer: **when the novelty
has worn off,** quand la nouveauté aura passé:
'wear 'on, *v.i.* **as the evening wore on,** à
mesure que la soirée s'avançait: **'wear 'out. 1.**
v.tr. (a) user (un vêtement, etc.): **to w. oneself**

out, s'user, s'épuiser: **to be worn out,** (i) (*of
garment*) être usé: (ii) (*of pers.*) être épuisé: (b)
épuiser, lasser (la patience de qn). **2.** *v.i.* s'user.
weary ['wiəri]. **I.** *a.* **1.** fatigué: las, *f.* lasse. **2.**
las, dégoûté (**of,** de). **II.** *v.* (**wearied**) **1.** *v.i.* (a)
se lasser, se fatiguer: (b) trouver le temps long.
2. *v.tr.* lasser, fatiguer (qn): **'wearily,** *adv.* **1.**
d'un air, d'un ton, las, fatigué. **2.** (marcher)
péniblement: **'weariness,** *s.* lassitude *f*,
fatigue *f*: **'wearisome, 'wearying,** *a.* ennuyeux: fastidieux: *F:* assommant.
weasel ['wi:z(ə)l], *s. Z:* belette *f.*
weather ['weðər]. **I.** *s.* temps *m* (qu'il fait): **in all
weathers,** par tous les temps: **in this, such, w.,**
par le temps qu'il fait: **do you like this very hot
w.?** aimez-vous ces grandes chaleurs? **w. permitting,** si le temps le permet: **what's the w.
like?** quel temps fait-il? *F:* **to make heavy w. of
a job,** compliquer les choses: *F:* (*of pers.*) **to be
under the w.,** être indisposé: ne pas être dans
son assiette: **w. bureau, centre,** bureau *m*
météorologique: **w. forecast, report,** bulletin *m*
météorologique. *F:* météo *f*: *F:* **w. man,** météo
m. **II.** *v.* **1.** *v.tr.* (a) *Geog:* désagréger, altérer:
(b) *Nau:* **to w. a headland,** doubler un cap (à la
voile): **to w. a storm,** (i) survivre à une tempête:
(ii) (*of pers.*) se tirer d'affaire. **2.** *v.i.* (a) (*of rock*)
se désagréger, s'altérer: (b) (*of building, etc.*)
prendre de la patine: **'weatherbeaten,** *a.* **1.**
battu des vents, par la tempête. **2.** (*pers.*)
bronzé, hâlé, basané: **'weatherboard,** *s.* (a)
(*for roofs*) planche *f* à recouvrement: (b) (*for
window*) jet *m* d'eau: (c) (*rowing*) hiloire *f*:
'weathercock, *s.* (a) girouette *f*: (b) girouette,
personne inconstante: **'weathering,** *s.* (a)
altération *f*, désagrégation *f* (des roches): (b)
patine *f.*
weave [wi:v]. **I.** *v.* (**wove** [wouv]: **woven**
['wouv(ə)n]) **1.** *v.tr.* (a) *Tex:* tisser: (b) tresser
(une guirlande, un panier): (c) **to w. one's way
through the crowd,** se frayer un chemin à
travers la foule. **2.** *v.i. F:* **to get weaving,** s'y
mettre: **get weaving!** vas-y! grouille-toi! **II.** *s.*
Tex: (a) armure *f*: (b) tissage *m*: **'weaver,** *s.* **1.**
Tex: tisserand, -ande. **2. w.** (**bird**), tisserin *m*:
'weaving, *s.* tissage *m.*
web [web], *s.* **1.** *Tex:* tissu *m.* **2. spider's w.,** toile *f*
d'araignée. **3.** palmure *f*, membrane *f* (d'un
palmipède): **webbed,** *a.* palmé, membrané, **w.
feet,** pieds palmés: **'web-'footed,** *a.*
palmipède, aux pieds palmés.
wed [wed], *v.* (*p.t. & p.p.* **wed(ded)**) **1.** *v.tr.* (a)
épouser (qn): se marier avec (qn): (b) (*of
priest*) marier (un couple): (c) **to be wedded to
an idea,** être obstinément attaché à une idée. **2.**
v.i. se marier: **'wedding,** *s.* (a) mariage *m*,
noce(s) *f(pl)*: **church w.,** mariage à l'église:
silver, golden, w., noces d'argent, d'or: (b) *attrib.* **w. day,** jour *m* des noces: **w. breakfast,**

repas *m* de noces; **w. cake,** gâteau *m* de mariage; **w. dress,** robe *f* de mariée; **w. guest,** invité, -ée (à un mariage); **w. march,** marche nuptiale; **w. present,** cadeau *m* de mariage; **w. ring,** alliance *f.*

wedge |wedʒ|. **I.** *s.* **1.** coin *m* (de serrage); cale *f* (de fixation); **to drive in a w.,** enfoncer un coin; **it's the thin end of the w.,** c'est un premier empiétement. **2. w. of cake,** morceau *m* (triangulaire) de gâteau. **II.** *v.tr.* **1.** coincer, assujettir. **2.** caler (un meuble); **to w. a door open,** maintenir une porte ouverte avec une cale. **3.** enclaver, enfoncer, serrer (qch. dans qch.); **wedged in between two fat women,** coincé, serré, entre deux grosses femmes.

Wednesday |'wenzdi|, *s.* mercredi *m*; **Ash W.,** le mercredi des Cendres.

wee |wi:|, *a.* tout petit; minuscule.

weed |wi:d|. **I.** *s.* **1.** mauvaise herbe. **2.** *F:* personne malingre, chétive. **3.** *F:* (cigarette *f* de) marijuana *f.* **II.** *v.tr.* sarcler; désherber; **'weeder,** *s.* **1.** (*pers.*) sarcleur, -euse. **2.** (*tool*) sarcloir *m*; **'weediness,** *s.* *F:* maigreur *f*; apparence *f* malingre; **'weeding,** *s.* sarclage *m*; désherbage *m*; **'weedkiller,** *s.* herbicide *m*, désherbant *m*; **'weedy,** *a.* **1.** couvert de mauvaises herbes. **2.** *F:* (*of pers.*) malingre.

week |wi:k|, *s.* semaine *f*; (*a*) **what day of the w. is it?** quel jour de la semaine sommes-nous? **twice a w.,** deux fois par semaine; *P:* **to knock s.o. into the middle of next w.,** donner à qn un fameux coup; (*b*) huit jours; **once a w.,** une fois par semaine; tous les huit jours; **he stayed a w. with us,** il a passé huit jours chez nous; **a w. from now, today w.,** d'aujourd'hui en huit; **yesterday w.,** il y a eu hier huit jours; **within the w.,** dans la huitaine; **in a w. or so,** dans une huitaine; *Ind:* **forty-hour w.,** semaine de quarante heures; (*c*) **what I can't do in the w. I do on Sundays,** ce que je n'arrive pas à faire en semaine je le fais le dimanche; **'weekday,** *s.* jour *m* ouvrable; jour de semaine; **on weekdays,** en semaine; **week'end,** *s. fin f* de semaine; week-end *m*; **'weekly. 1.** *a.* (salaire) de la semaine; (visite, publication, etc.) hebdomadaire. **2.** *s.* journal *m*, revue *f*, hebdomadaire. **3.** *adv.* tous les huit jours; **twice w.,** deux fois par semaine.

weep |wi:p|. **I.** *v.i.* (wept |wept|) pleurer; **to w. bitterly,** pleurer à chaudes larmes; **to w. for joy,** pleurer de joie. **II.** *s.* crise *f* de larmes; **'weeping. I.** *a.* **1.** (enfant) qui pleure. **2. w. willow,** saule pleureur. **II.** *s.* pleurs *mpl*; larmes *fpl*; **'weepy,** *a.* *F:* larmoyant.

weevil |'wi:vil|, *s.* *Ent:* charançon *m*.

wee-wee |'wi:wi:|, *F:* **I.** *s.* pipi *m*. **II.** *v.i.* faire pipi.

weft |weft|, *s.* *Tex:* trame *f.*

weigh |wei|. **1.** *v.tr.* (*a*) peser (qch.); **to w. the pros and cons,** peser le pour et le contre; (*b*) *Nau:* **to w. anchor,** lever l'ancre; appareiller. **2.** *v.i.* peser, avoir du poids; **to w. heavy, light,** peser lourd, peu; **'weighbridge,** *s.* pontbascule *m*, bascule *f*; **'weigh 'down,** *v.tr.* surcharger; **branch weighed down with fruit,** branche surchargée de fruits; **weighed down with sorrow,** accablé de chagrin, de tristesse; **'weigh 'in,** *v.i.* (*of jockey, boxer*) se faire peser avant la course, le match; *Turf:* **weighing-in room,** le pesage; **'weighing,** *s.* **1.** pesée *f* (de qch.); *Turf:* pesage *m*; **w. enclosure,** (enceinte *f* du) pesage. **2.** *Nau:* levage *m* (de l'ancre); appareillage *m*; **weight,** *s.* **1.** (*a*) poids *m*; **to sell by w.,** vendre au poids; **it's worth its w. in gold,** cela vaut son pesant d'or; (*of pers.*) **to lose, gain, w.,** perdre, prendre, du poids; **to pull one's w.,** y mettre du sien; (*b*) poids, pesanteur *f*, lourdeur *f*; **to try the w. of sth.,** soupeser qch.; **specific w.,** poids spécifique, volumique; **atomic w.,** poids atomique. **2.** (*a*) set of weights,** série *f* de poids; **weights and measures,** poids et mesures; (*b*) **letter w., paper w.,** presse-papiers *m inv*; *Sp:* **putting the w.,** lancement *m* du poids; (*c*) charge *f*; **that's a w. off my mind,** voilà qui me soulage. **3.** force *f* (d'un coup). **4.** importance *f*; **his word carries w.,** sa parole a du poids, de l'autorité; **'weightiness,** *s.* **1.** pesanteur *f*, lourdeur *f* (de qch.). **2.** importance *f*, force *f* (d'une opinion); **'weightlessness,** *s.* apesanteur *f*; **'weighty,** *a.* **1.** pesant, lourd. **2.** (motif, etc.) grave, important; (argument) puissant.

weir |'wiər|, *s.* **1.** barrage *m* (dans un cours d'eau). **2.** déversoir *m* (d'un étang, etc.).

weird |'wiəd|, *a.* (*a*) surnaturel; mystérieux; (*b*) étrange, singulier; **-ly,** *adv.* étrangement; **'weirdie,** *s.* *F:* excentrique *mf*, drôle *m* de type; **'weirdness,** *s.* **1.** étrangeté inquiétante. **2.** caractère singulier; **'weirdo** [-dou], *s.* *F:* excentrique *mf.*

welcome |'welkəm|. **I.** *v.tr.* **1.** souhaiter la bienvenue à (qn); faire bon accueil à (qn). **2.** **to w. a piece of news,** se réjouir d'une nouvelle. **II.** *s.* (*a*) bienvenue *f*; **to outstay one's w.,** lasser l'amabilité de ses hôtes; (*b*) accueil *m*; **hearty w.,** bon accueil; **to have a cold w.,** être reçu froidement. **III.** *a.* **1. to make s.o. w.,** faire bon accueil à qn; *int.* **w.!** soyez le bienvenu, la bienvenue! **2. a w. change,** un changement bienvenu; **this cheque is most w.,** ce chèque tombe à merveille. **3. you're w. to try,** libre à vous d'essayer; **you're w. to it,** c'est à votre disposition; *esp. N.Am:* (*thanking s.o.*) **you're w.!** je vous en prie.

weld |weld|. **I.** *v.tr.* souder (au blanc); unir (à chaud). **II.** *s.* soudure *f*; **'welder,** *s.* **1.** (*pers.*) soudeur *m*. **2.** machine *f* à souder; **'welding,** *s.* soudage *m*, soudure *f*; **oxyacetylene w.,** soudure autogène.

welfare ['welfɛər], s. bien-être m; prospérité f; **social w.**, sécurité sociale; **child w.**, protection f de l'enfance; **the W. State**, l'État m providence.

well¹ [wel]. I. s. 1. puits m; **oil w.**, puits de pétrole. 2. puits, cage f (d'un ascenseur). II. v.i. **to w. up**, jaillir; (of spring) sourdre.

well². 1. adv. bien. 1. (a) **to work w.**, bien travailler; **he'll do w.**, il fera son chemin, il ira loin; **to do as w. as one can**, faire de son mieux; **w. done!** bravo! F: **we did ourselves w.!** on s'est bien soigné(s). bien nourri(s)! **he accepted, as w. he might**, il a accepté et rien d'étonnant; **you might just as w. say that . . .**, autant dire que . . .; **you could just as w. have stayed**, vous auriez tout aussi bien pu rester; **very w.!** très bien! entendu! (b) **we were very w. received**, on nous a fait un bon accueil; **it speaks w. for him**, cela lui fait honneur; **she deserves w. of you**, elle mérite bien votre reconnaissance; **it was w. intended**, c'était fait avec une bonne intention; (c) **you're w. out of it!** soyez heureux d'en être quitte! **it went off w.**, cela s'est bien passé; **you've come off w.**, vous avez eu de la chance. 2. (intensive) **it's w. worth trying**, cela vaut vraiment la peine d'essayer, cela vaut le coup; **w. after six (o'clock)**, six heures bien sonnées; **we went on w. into the small hours**, nous avons continué bien avant dans la nuit; **he's w. over fifty**, il a bien dépassé la cinquantaine; **to be w. up in history, in French**, être calé en histoire, en français. 3. **pretty w. all of them**, presque tous; F: **it serves him jolly w., damn w., right**, il l'a bien mérité. 4. (a) **as w.**, aussi; **take me as w.**, emmenez-moi aussi, également; (b) **as w. as**, de même que; comme; non moins que. 5. (a) **w., as I was telling you**, donc, eh bien, comme je vous disais; **w., and what of it?** eh bien, et après? (b) (expressing astonishment, etc.) **w.!** ça alors! pas possible! **w., it can't be helped!** tant pis! on n'y peut rien; **w. w.!** que voulez-vous? (c) **w. then, why worry?** eh bien alors, pourquoi vous faire de la bile? II. a. 1. **to be w.**, être bien portant, en bonne santé; **to look w.**, avoir bonne mine; **I'm not w.**, je ne vais pas bien, ne me sens pas bien. 2. (a) **it would be just as w. to do it**, il serait bon de le faire; **it would be just as w. if you came**, il y aurait avantage à ce que vous veniez; (b) **it was just as w. that you were there**, il est bien heureux que vous vous soyez trouvé là; (c) **all's w. that ends w.**, tout est bien qui finit bien; **all's w.**, tout va bien; (d) **that's all very w. but . . .**, tout cela est bel et bon mais . . .; **it's all very w. for you to say that**, libre à vous de le dire; vous avez beau le dire (mais . . .); **he's all very w. in his way, but . . .**, il n'y a rien à dire contre lui, mais . . .; **w. and good!** soit! bon! III. s. 1. pl. **the w. and the sick**, les bien portants et les malades. 2. **to wish s.o. w.**, vouloir du bien à qn; **I wish him w.**, je lui souhaite bonne chance; '**well ad'vised**, a. 1. (of pers.) (a) bien avisé; (b) bien conseillé. 2. (of action) sage, prudent; '**well-be'haved**, a. (enfant) sage; (chien, etc.) bien dressé; '**wellbeing**, s. bien-être m; '**well dis'posed**, a. 1. bien arrangé, bien disposé. 2. (of pers.) bien disposé (**to(wards)**, envers); '**well 'educated**, a. instruit; '**well in'formed**, a. bien renseigné; bien documenté; **to be w. i. on a subject**, bien connaître un sujet; **in w. i. quarters**, en lieu compétent; '**well 'known**, a. bien connu; célèbre; réputé; '**well 'made**, a. (article) bien fini; '**well-'meaning**, a. bien intentionné; '**well-'meant**, a. fait avec une bonne intention; '**well 'off**, a. (a) **to be w. o.**, être riche, dans l'aisance, à l'aise; (b) **you don't know when you're w. o.**, vous ne connaissez pas votre bonheur, quand vous êtes bien; '**well 'read**, a. (pers.) cultivé, qui a de la culture; '**well-to-'do**, a. riche, dans l'aisance, '**well-wisher**, s. ami(e), partisan(e) (de qn, d'une cause); '**well-'worn**, a. (a) (vêtement) fortement usagé; (b) (argument) rebattu, usé jusqu'à la corde.

Wellington ['weliŋtən]. Pr.n. **W. boots**, s. **wellingtons**, F: **wellies** ['weliz], bottes f en caoutchouc.

Welsh [welʃ]. I. a. & s. 1. a. gallois, du Pays de Galles. 2. s. (a) pl. **the W.**, les Gallois; (b) Ling: le gallois. II. v.i. décamper; filer; lever le pied; partir sans payer; **to w. on s.o.**, partir sans payer ses dettes à qn, sans remplir ses obligations; '**welsher**, s. tire-au-flanc m; '**Welshman**, pl. -**men**, s. Gallois m; '**Welshwoman**, pl. -**women**, s. Galloise f.

werewolf, pl. -**wolves** ['wiəwulf, -wulvz], s. loup-garou m, pl. loups-garous.

west [west]. 1. s. (a) ouest m; occident m; couchant m; **house facing the w.**, maison exposée à l'ouest; (b) Pol: **the W.**, l'Occident, l'Ouest; **the Far W.**, les États de l'ouest (des États-Unis). 2. a. ouest inv; occidental, -aux; **w. wind**, vent m d'ouest; **the W. Country**, les comtés de l'ouest (de l'Angleterre); **the W. End (of London)**, le quartier (chic) du centre-ouest (de Londres); **W. Africa**, l'Afrique occidentale; **the W. Indies**, les Antilles f; **W. Indian**, antillais; des Antilles. 3. adv. à l'ouest; **to travel w.**, voyager vers l'ouest; F: **that's another plate gone w.!** encore une assiette de cassée! '**westbound**, a. (of traffic) qui se dirige vers l'ouest; '**westerly**. 1. a. (vent) d'ouest; (courant) qui se dirige vers l'ouest; '**western**. 1. a. ouest inv; de l'ouest; occidental, -aux; **W. Europe**, l'Europe occidentale; **the w. world**, le monde occidental. 2. s. Cin: western m; '**westerner**, s. occidental, -ale, -aux; '**westernize**, v.tr. occidentaliser; '**westward**. 1. s. to

w., vers l'ouest. 2. *a.* à l'ouest, de l'ouest; **'westwards,** *adv.* vers l'ouest, à l'ouest.
wet [wet]. **I.** *a.* (*a*) mouillé; humide; imbibé d'eau; **to get one's feet w.,** se mouiller les pieds; (*of pers.*) **to be w. through, soaking w.,** être trempé (jusqu'aux os); (*of garment*) **wringing w., soaking w.,** mouillé à tordre; *F:* (*pers.*) w. **blanket,** rabat-joie *m inv*; **the ink is still w.,** l'encre n'est pas encore sèche; (*b*) w. **weather,** temps humide, pluvieux; **it's going to be w.,** il va pleuvoir; **three w. days,** trois jours de pluie; **the w. season,** la saison des pluies. **3.** *F:* **he's a bit w.,** c'est une nouille, une andouille. **II.** *s.* **1.** humidité *f.* **2.** pluie *f*; **to go out in the w.,** sortir sous la pluie. **3.** *P:* **to have a w.,** boire un coup, se rincer la dalle. **4.** *F:* **he's a w.,** c'est une nouille, une andouille. **III.** *v.tr.* (**wetted**) mouiller; **'wetness,** *s.* humidité *f*; **'wetting,** *s.* **to get a w.,** se faire tremper.
wether ['weðər], *s.* bélier châtré; mouton *m.*
whack [(h)wæk]. *F:* **I.** *v.tr.* (*a*) battre, rosser (qn); fesser (un enfant); (*b*) battre (ses adversaires) à plates coutures; (*c*) **I'm completely whacked,** je suis complètement épuisé, éreinté, à plat. **II.** *s.* (*a*) coup (de bâton) bien appliqué; (*b*) **let's have a w. at it,** essayons le coup; (*c*) part *f*, portion *f*, (gros) morceau; **'whacker,** *s. F:* (*a*) chose énorme, colossale; (*b*) mensonge *m* de taille; **'whacking.** *F:* **I.** *a.* énorme, colossal, -aux; w. **great lie,** mensonge *m* de taille. **II.** *s.* rossée *f*; raclée *f*; fessée *f.*
whale [(h)weil]. **I.** *s.* **1.** *Z:* baleine *f*; w. **calf,** baleineau *m.* **2.** *F:* **we had a w. of a time,** on s'est drôlement bien amusés. **II.** *v.i.* faire la pêche à la baleine; **'whaleboat,** *s.* baleinier *m*; **'whalebone,** *s.* baleine *f* (d'un corset, etc.); **'whaler,** *s.* **1.** (*pers.*) baleinier *m*, pêcheur *m* de baleines. **2.** (*ship*) baleinier; baleinière *f.*
wharf [(h)wɔ:f], *s.* appontement *m*; débarcadère *m*, embarcadère *m*; quai *m*; **'wharfage,** *s.* droit *m* de quai.
what [(h)wɔt]. **I.** *a.* **1.** (*relative*) (ce) que, (ce) qui; **he took away from me w. little I had,** il m'a pris le peu qui me restait; **with w. capital he had,** avec ce qu'il possédait de capital. **2.** (*interrogative*) **quel,** *f.* quelle; w. **time is it?** quelle heure est-il? w. **right has he to do that?** quel droit a-t-il de faire ça? de quel droit fait-il cela? w. **good is this?** à quoi cela est-il bon? à quoi cela sert-il? w. **day of the month is it?** nous sommes le combien? **3.** (*exclamatory*) w. **an idea!** quelle idée! w. **an idiot he is!** qu'il est bête! w. **a lot of people!** que de gens! **II.** *pron.* **1.** (*relative*) **what's done cannot be undone,** ce qui est fait est fait; w. **I like most,** ce que j'aime le plus; **and w. is more,** et qui plus est; **this is w. it's all about,** voilà ce dont il s'agit; **come w. may,** advienne que pourra; **say w. he will,** quoi qu'il dise; il a beau dire; w. **with this and with**

that **I haven't much free time,** entre toutes les choses que j'ai à faire j'ai peu de temps libre; *P:* **to give s.o. w. for,** donner une bonne raclée à qn; laver la tête à qn. **2.** (*interrogative*) (*a*) (*direct*) qu'est-ce qui? qu'est-ce? qu'est-ce que c'est? quoi? w. **are you doing here?** qu'est-ce que vous faites ici? w. **is it?** (i) qu'est-ce que c'est? (ii) qu'est-ce qu'il y a? **what's the matter?** qu'y a-t-il? de quoi s'agit-il? qu'est-ce que vous avez? **what's his name?** comment s'appelle-t-il? **what's that to you?** qu'est-ce que cela vous fait? **what's the good, the use?** à quoi bon? w. **can we do?** que faire? **what's the French for *dog*?** comment dit-on *dog* en français? **what's he like?** comment est-il? w. **about a game of bridge?** si on faisait une partie de bridge? w. **do you take me for?** pour qui me prenez-vous? w. **about you?** et vous? **well, w. about it?** (i) eh bien, quoi? et puis après? (ii) eh bien, qu'en dites-vous? **what's that for?** à quoi cela sert-il? *F:* à quoi ça sert? w. **on earth for?** mais pourquoi donc? *F:* **so w.?** et puis après? alors? w. **did you say?** pardon? (*b*) (*indirect*) ce qui, ce que; **tell me what's happening,** dites-moi ce qui se passe; **I don't know w. to do,** je ne sais que faire; **I wonder w. he's doing,** je me demande ce qu'il fait; *F:* **he knows what's w.,** s'y connaît; c'est un malin, un rusé. **3.** (*exclamatory*) w. **next!** par exemple! w. **he must have suffered!** ce qu'il a dû souffrir! **w.! can't you come?** comment! vous ne pouvez pas venir? **what'ever. 1.** *pron.* (*a*) w. **you like,** tout ce que vous voudrez; n'importe quoi; (*b*) w. **it may, might, be,** quoi que ce soit. **2.** *a.* (*a*) w. **price they are asking,** quel que soit le prix qu'on demande; **at w. time,** quelle que soit l'heure; à n'importe quelle heure; **under any pretext w.,** sous quelque prétexte que ce soit; (*b*) **no hope w.,** pas le moindre espoir; **is there any hope w.?** y a-t-il un espoir quelconque? y a-t-il quelque espoir? **nothing w.,** absolument rien; **none w.,** pas un seul; **'whatnot,** *s.* **1.** *Furn:* étagère *f.* **2.** *F:* machin *m*, truc *m*; **'what's-it, 'what's-its** (-his, -her)-name, **'what-d'you-call-it** (-him, -her), *s. F:* machin *m*, truc *m*; **old Mr W.,** le père Machin; **whatso'ever,** *a.* nothing w., absolument rien.
wheat [(h)wi:t], *s.* blé *m*, froment *m*; **'wheatsheaf,** *s.* gerbe *f* de blé.
wheedle ['(h)wi:dl], *v.tr.* enjôler, cajoler (qn); **to w. money out of s.o.,** soutirer de l'argent à qn; **'wheedler,** *s.* enjôleur, -euse; **'wheedling,** *s.* enjôleur, -euse; câlin.
wheel [(h)wi:l]. **I.** *s.* roue *f*; (*a*) **there are wheels within wheels,** c'est une affaire compliquée; il y a toutes sortes de forces en jeu; **the wheels of government,** les rouages *m* de l'administration; (*b*) *Aut:* **steering w.,** volant *m*; **to take the w.,** (i) *Aut:* prendre le volant; (ii) *Nau:*

prendre la barre; *Aut:* **w. disk,** enjoliveur *m;* (*c*) **potter's w.,** tour *m* de potier. **II.** *v.* **1.** *v.tr.* (*a*) tourner; faire pivoter; (*b*) rouler (une brouette); pousser (une bicyclette) à la main. **2.** *v.i.* (*a*) tourner en rond; tournoyer; (*b*) *Mil:* **left w.!** à gauche, marche! (*c*) **to w. round,** faire demi-tour; se retourner (brusquement); **'wheelbarrow,** *s.* brouette *f;* **'wheelbase,** *s. Aut: etc:* empattement *m;* **'wheelspin,** *s. Aut:* patinage *m;* **'wheelwright,** *s.* charron *m.*

wheeze [(h)wiːz]. **I.** *v.i.* respirer péniblement. **II.** *s.* **1.** respiration *f* asthmatique. **2.** *F:* truc *m;* **good w.,** idée géniale; **'wheezy,** *a.* asthmatique, *F:* poussif.

whelk [welk], *s. Moll:* buccin *m.*

whelp [(h)welp]. **I.** *s.* petit *m* d'un fauve; **lion's w.,** lionceau *m.* **II.** *v.i. & tr.* (*of lion, dog, etc.*) mettre bas.

when [(h)wen]. **I.** *interr. adv.* quand? **w. will you go?** quand partirez-vous? **w. is the meeting?** c'est pour quand la réunion? **w. on earth is he going to arrive?** quand donc, quand diable, va-t-il arriver? *F:* (*when pouring drink*) say **w.!** comme ça? **II.** *conj.* **1.** quand, lorsque; **w. I was young,** quand j'étais jeune; **w. he was born,** lors de sa naissance; **I'll come w. I've finished this work,** je viendrai quand j'aurai terminé ce travail. **2.** **one day w. I was on duty,** un jour que j'étais de service; **the time w. . . .,** le moment où . . .; **when'ever,** *adv.* toutes les fois que; chaque fois que; **I go w. I can,** j'y vais aussi souvent que possible; **come w. you like,** venez quand vous voudrez; venez n'importe quand.

where [(h)wɛər], *adv.* **1.** (*interr.*) où? **w. am I?** où suis-je? **w. have we got to? w. are we up to?** où en sommes-nous? **where's the way out?** où est la sortie? **w. do you come from?** (i) d'où venez-vous? (ii) de quel pays êtes-vous? **2.** (*relative*) **I shall stay w. I am,** je resterai (là) où je suis; **that's w. you are mistaken,** voilà où vous vous trompez; **w. you are mistaken is . . .,** ce en quoi vous vous trompez c'est . . .; **the house w. he was born,** la maison où, dans laquelle, il est né; sa maison natale; **'whereabouts,** *s.pl.* lieu *m* où se trouve qn, qch.; **nobody knows his w.,** personne ne sait où il est; **'whereas,** *conj.* **1.** (*introducing formal statement*) attendu que, vu que, puisque. **2.** alors que, tandis que; **'wherefore,** *s.* **the whys and wherefores,** les pourquoi et les comment; **wher'ever,** *adv.* **1. w. I go,** partout où je vais; n'importe où je vais; **I'll go w. you want me to,** j'irai où vous voudrez. **2. w. you are,** où que vous soyez; **w. they come from,** d'où qu'ils viennent; **'wherewithal** [-wiðɔːl], *s. F:* **the w.,** l'argent *m,* le nécessaire; les moyens *m.*

whet [(h)wet], *v.tr.* (**whetted**) **1.** aiguiser, affûter, affiler, repasser (un outil). **2.** stimuler, aiguiser

(l'appétit, etc.); *F:* **to w. one's whistle,** boire un coup; se rincer la dalle; **'whetstone,** *s.* pierre *f* à aiguiser.

whether [' (h)weðər], *conj.* **1.** si; **I don't know w. it is true,** je ne sais pas si c'est vrai; **it depends on w. you're in a hurry or not,** cela dépend de si vous êtes pressé ou non. **2. w. he comes or not we'll leave,** qu'il vienne ou non nous allons partir.

whey [(h)wei], *s.* petit lait.

which [(h)witʃ]. **I.** *a.* (*a*) quel, *f.* quelle, *pl.* quels, quelles; **w. colour do you like best?** quelle couleur aimez-vous le mieux? **w. way shall we go?** par où irons-nous? quelle route est-ce que nous allons prendre? **w. one?** lequel? laquelle? **I'm going with friends—w. friends?** j'y vais avec des amis—lesquels? (*b*) **they are coming on June 4th, by w. date we shall be in London,** ils viendront le 4 juin, date à laquelle nous serons à Londres. **II.** *pron.* **1.** lequel, *f.* laquelle, *pl.* lesquels, lesquelles; **w. have you chosen?** lequel avez-vous choisi? **w. of the dresses did you buy?** laquelle des robes avez-vous achetée? **w. of you can answer?** lequel d'entre vous peut répondre? **of w. is he speaking?** duquel parle-t-il? **tell me w. is w.,** dites-moi comment les distinguer; **I don't mind w.,** cela m'est égal. **2.** (*a*) que; qui; **the house w. is to be sold,** la maison qui est à vendre; **books w. I have read,** des livres que j'ai lus; **things w. I need,** des choses dont j'ai besoin; (*b*) ce qui; ce que; **he looked like a retired colonel, w. indeed he was,** il avait l'air d'un colonel en retraite, ce qu'il était en effet; **he told me of many things that happened, all of w. were true,** il m'a raconté beaucoup d'incidents qui étaient tous exacts. **3.** (*with prep.*) **the house of w. I was speaking,** la maison dont, de laquelle, je parlais; **the countries to w. we are going,** les pays où nous irons, que nous allons visiter; **the hotels at w. we stayed,** les hôtels où nous sommes descendus; **I have nothing with w. to write,** je n'ai pas de quoi écrire; **after w. he went out,** après quoi il est sorti; **which'ever,** *rel. pron. & a.* **1.** (*a*) *pron.* celui qui, celui que, n'importe lequel; **take w. you like,** prenez celui, celle, que vous voudrez, n'importe lequel, laquelle; (*b*) *a.* le . . . que; n'importe quel; **take w. book you like,** prenez le livre que vous voudrez; prenez n'importe quel livre. **2.** *a.* n'importe quel; quelque . . . que; **w. way I turn,** de quelque côté que je me tourne.

whiff [(h)wif]. **I.** *s.* (*a*) bouffée *f* (de fumée, etc.); (*b*) *F:* mauvaise odeur. **II.** *v.i.* (*a*) souffler par bouffées; (*b*) *F:* puer.

while [(h)wail]. **I.** *s.* **1.** (espace *m* de) temps *m;* **after a w.,** après quelque temps; **in a little w.,** sous peu; avant peu; **a little w. ago,** il y a peu de temps; **a long w.,** longtemps; **a good w.,**

quite a w., pas mal de temps; **it will take me quite a long w.** to do that, cela me prendra pas mal de temps, assez longtemps. **2. to be worth one's w.,** valoir la peine; **I'll make it worth your w.,** vous serez bien payé de votre peine; **it is perhaps worth w.** saying that . . ., il vaut peut-être la peine de dire que . . .. **II.** *v.tr.* **to w. away the time,** faire passer le temps. **III.** *conj.* **1.** (*a*) pendant que, tandis que; **w.** he was here, pendant qu'il était ici; **w.** (he was) reading he fell asleep, tout en lisant, il s'est endormi; **w.** this was going on, sur ces entrefaites; (*b*) tant que; **w. I live you will not go without anything,** tant que je vivrai vous ne manquerez de rien. **2.** quoique, bien que, tout en . . .; **w. I admit that it is difficult,** quoique j'admette, tout en admettant, que c'est difficile. **3.** tandis que; **I was dressed in white, w.** my sister wore grey, j'étais habillée de blanc, tandis que ma sœur portait du gris.

whim |(h)wim|, *s.* caprice *m*, fantaisie *f*; **'whim-sical,** *a.* (*a*) capricieux; fantasque; (*b*) bizarre.

whimper |'(h)wimpər|. **I.** *v.i.* pleurnicher, geindre; (*of dog*) pousser des petits cris plaintifs. **II.** *s.* (*a*) pleurnicherie *f*, pleurnichement *m*; (*b*) geignement *m*, plainte *f*; (*c*) (*of dog*) petit cri plaintif.

whine |(h)wain|. **I.** *v.i.* se plaindre; (*of child*) pleurnicher; (*of dog*) geindre. **II.** *s.* plainte *f*; geignement *m*; **'whining. I.** *a.* geignant; pleurnicheur, -euse; (ton) plaintif. **II.** *s.* plaintes *fpl*; geignement *m*.

whinny |'(h)wini|. **I.** *v.i.* (*of horse*) hennir. **II.** *s.* hennissement *m* (de cheval).

whip |(h)wip|. **I.** *v.* (whipped) **1.** *v.tr.* (*a*) fouetter; donner le fouet à (un cheval); **whipped cream,** crème fouettée; (*b*) **he whipped the revolver out of his pocket,** il a sorti vivement le revolver de sa poche. **2.** *v.i.* (*a*) **the rain was whipping against the window panes,** la pluie fouettait, cinglait, les vitres; (*b*) **he whipped behind the door,** il s'est jeté derrière la porte; **to w. round the corner,** tourner vivement le coin. **II.** *s.* **1.** fouet *m*. **2.** *Parl:* (*a*) chef *m* de file, whip *m*; (*b*) appel *m* (aux membres d'un parti). **3.** *Cu:* (lemon) w. = mousse *f* (au citron); **'whip'hand,** *s.* to have the w., avoir l'avantage; **'whiplash,** *s.* mèche *f* de fouet; **tongue like a w.,** langue cinglante; **'whip 'off,** *v.tr.* enlever vivement (son chapeau, etc.); **'whipping,** *s.* to give a child a w., donner le fouet à un enfant; **'whip 'round,** *v.i.* **1.** inviter les gens à souscrire. **2.** se retourner vivement; **'whip-round,** *s.* invitation *f* à souscrire.

whirl |(h)wə:l|. **I.** *v.* **1.** *v.i.* (*a*) to w. (round), tourbillonner, tournoyer; (*of dancer*) pirouetter; **my head's whirling,** la tête me tourne; (*b*) to w. along, rouler, filer, à toute vitesse. **2.** *v.tr.* (*a*) (*of wind*) faire tournoyer (les feuilles mortes,

etc.); (*b*) **the train whirled us along,** le train nous emportait à toute vitesse. **II.** *s.* (*a*) mouvement *m* giratoire, giration *f*; (*b*) tourbillonnement *m*, tournoiement *m*; **my head's in a w.,** la tête me tourne; **'whirlpool,** *s.* tourbillon *m* (d'eau); remous *m*; gouffre *m*; **'whirlwind,** *s.* tourbillon *m* (de vent); trombe *f*; **to come in like a w.,** entrer en trombe, en coup d vent.

whirr |(h)wə:r|. **I.** *s.* bruissement *m* (d'ailes); ronflement *m*, ronronnement *m* (de machines); vrombissement *m* (d'une hélice d'avion). **II.** *v.i.* (*of machinery, etc.*) tourner à toute vitesse; ronfler, ronronner; (*of propeller, etc.*) vrombir.

whisk |(h)wisk|. **I.** *v.tr.* (*a*) (*of cow*) agiter (sa queue); (*b*) **to w. sth. away,** enlever qch. d'un geste rapide; (*c*) *Cu:* battre (des œufs); fouetter (la crème). **II.** *s.* **1.** coup *m* (de queue). **2.** *H:* (*a*) (*for dusting*) époussette *f*; (*b*) batteur *m*, fouet *m* (à œufs).

whiskers |'(h)wiskəz|, *s.pl.* moustache(s) *f* (de chat, etc.); *F:* (i) (*side-whiskers*) favoris *m*; (ii) (*beard*) barbe *f* (d'homme).

whisk(e)y |'(h)wiski|, *s.* whisky *m*.

whisper |'(h)wispər|. **I.** *s.* chuchotement *m*; **to speak in a w.,** parler tout bas; *Th:* stage w., aparté *m*. **II.** *v.* **1.** *v.i.* chuchoter; parler bas; **to w. to s.o.,** chuchoter à l'oreille de qn. **2.** *v.tr.* to w. a word to s.o., dire, glisser, un mot à l'oreille de qn; **whispered conversation,** conversation *f* à voix basse; **'whisperer,** *s.* chuchoteur, -euse; **'whispering,** *s.* chuchotement *m*; **w. gallery,** galerie *f* à écho; voûte *f* acoustique.

whist |(h)wist|, *s.* *Cards:* whist *m*; **w. drive,** tournoi *m* de whist.

whistle |'(h)wisl|. **I.** *s.* **1.** sifflement *m*; coup *m* de sifflet. **2.** sifflet *m*; **to blow a w.,** donner un coup de sifflet. **3.** *U.S:* w. stop tour, tournée électorale faite par train spécial. **II.** *v.* **1.** *v.i.* (*a*) siffler; **to w. for one's dog,** siffler son chien; *F:* **he can w. for his money!** il peut courir après son argent! (*b*) donner un coup de sifflet; *Rail:* **to w. for the road,** demander la voie. **2.** *v.tr.* siffler (un air); **'whistler,** *s.* **1.** siffleur, -euse. **2.** oiseau siffleur. **3.** marmotte canadienne.

whit[1] |(h)wit|, *s.* brin *m*, iota *m*; **he's not a w. the better for it,** il ne s'en porte aucunement mieux.

Whit[2], *a.* W. Sunday, (le dimanche de) la Pentecôte; W. Monday, le lundi de la Pentecôte.

white |'(h)wait|. **I.** *a.* **1.** blanc, *f.* blanche; **he's going w.,** il commence à blanchir. **2.** (*a*) w. bread, pain blanc; **w. wine,** vin blanc; (*b*) **the w. races,** les races blanches; **a w. man,** un blanc; (*c*) **as w. as a sheet, as a ghost,** pâle comme un linge, comme un mort. **II.** *s.* **1.** blanc *m*, couleur blanche; **dressed in w.,** habillé en, de, blanc. **2.** (*pers.*) blanc, blanche; homme, femme, de la race blanche. **3.** (*a*) w. of egg, blanc d'œuf; (*b*)

w. of the eye, blanc de l'œil; ′**whitebait,** s. blanchaille f; **a dish of w.,** une friture; ′**white-**′**collar,** a. **w.-c.** worker, employé de bureau; ′**white-**′**haired,** a. aux cheveux blancs; ′**whiten,** v.tr. blanchir; ′**whiteness,** s. (a) blancheur f; (b) pâleur f; ′**whitethorn,** s. aubépine f; ′**whitewash.** I. s. blanc m de chaux; badigeon blanc. II. v.tr. (a) blanchir à la chaux; badigeonner en blanc; (b) blanchir, disculper (qn); ′**whitewashing,** s.(a) peinture f à la chaux; badigeonnage m en blanc; (b) réhabilitation f (de qn); ′**whitewood,** s. bois blanc.

whiting [′(h)waitiŋ], s. Ich: merlan m.

Whitsun(tide) [′(h)witsən(taid)], s. la Pentecôte.

whittle [′(h)witl], v.tr. **to w. down,** amenuiser (qch.); rogner (la pension de qn, etc.).

whizz [(h)wiz], v.i. (of bullet, etc.) siffler; **to w. past,** passer en sifflant; passer à toute vitesse.

who [hu:], pron.nom. **1.** (interr.) (a) qui? qui est-ce qui? **w. is that man?** qui, quel, est cet homme? **w. on earth is it?** qui cela peut-il bien être? **w. found it?** qui l'a trouvé? **F: w. does he think he is?** pour qui se prend-il? (b) **F: w. are you looking for?** qui cherchez-vous? **2.** (relative) (a) qui; **my friend w. came yesterday,** mon ami qui est venu hier; **those w. don't work,** ceux qui ne travaillent pas; (b) lequel, f. laquelle, pl. lesquel(le)s; **this girl's father, w. is very rich,** le père de cette fille, lequel est très riche; **who**′**dunit,** s. **F:** roman policier; **who**′**ever,** pron. **1.** celui qui; quiconque; **w. finds it may keep it,** celui qui le trouvera, quiconque le trouvera, peut le garder. **2.** qui que + sub.; **w. you are, speak!** qui que vous soyez, parlez! **3. w. she marries will be lucky,** celui qu'elle épousera sera heureux.

whoa [wou], int. (to horse) ho! **F:** (to pers.) doucement! attendez!

whole [houl]. **I.** a. (a) intégral, -aux, entier; complet; **roasted w.,** rôti entier; **he swallowed it w.,** (i) il l'a avalé tout rond; (ii) **F:** il a pris ça pour de l'argent comptant; **w. number,** nombre entier; **w. length,** longueur totale; (b) **to tell the w. truth,** dire toute la vérité; **to last a w. week,** durer toute une semaine; **the w. world,** le monde entier; **the w. lot of you,** vous tous. **II.** s. tout m, totalité f, ensemble m; **the w. of the school,** l'école entière; toute l'école; **the w. of our resources,** la totalité de nos ressources; **as a w.,** dans son ensemble; en totalité; **on the w.,** à tout prendre; en somme; dans l'ensemble; **whole**′**hoggism,** s. **F:** jusqu'au-boutisme m; ′**wholemeal,** a. (pain) complet; ′**wholesale.** **1.** s. (vente f en) gros m; **w. and retail,** gros et détail. **2.** a. (a) **w. trade, firm,** commerce, maison, de gros; **w. price,** prix m de gros; (b) **w. slaughter,** tuerie f en masse, massacre m. **3.**

adv. (vendre, acheter) en gros; ′**wholesaler,** s. grossiste mf; ′**wholly,** adv. **1.** tout à fait; complètement, entièrement. **2.** intégralement; en totalité; **w. or partly,** en tout ou en partie.

wholesome [′houlsəm], a. sain; (air, etc.) salubre; ′**wholesomeness,** s. nature saine; salubrité f (du climat, etc.).

whom [hu:m], pron. (object) **1.** (interrogative) qui? **w. did you see?** qui avez-vous vu? **of w. are you speaking?** de qui parlez-vous? **2.** (relative) (a) (direct) que; **the man w. you saw,** l'homme que vous avez vu; (b) (indirect and after prep.) **the friend to w. I lent the book,** l'ami à qui j'ai prêté le livre; **the man of w. I was speaking,** l'homme dont je parlais; **the two officers between w. she was sitting,** les deux officiers entre lesquels elle était assise.

whoop [hu:p]. **I.** int. houp! **II.** s. quinte f (de la coqueluche). **III.** v.i. faire la quinte convulsive de la coqueluche; ′**whooping cough,** coqueluche f.

whoopee [′wupi:], s. **F: to make w.,** (i) faire la noce, la bombe; (ii) s'amuser, se régaler.

whose [hu:z], poss.pron. **1.** (interr.) de qui? (ownership) à qui? **w. are these gloves? w. gloves are these?** à qui sont ces gants? **w. daughter are you?** de qui êtes-vous la fille? **2.** (relative) dont; **the pupil w. work I showed you,** l'élève dont je vous ai montré le travail.

why [(h)wai]. **1.** adv. (a) (interr.) pourquoi? pour quelle raison? **w. didn't you say so?** pourquoi ne l'avez-vous pas dit? il fallait le dire! **w. not?** pourquoi pas? (b) **that's (the reason) w.,** voilà pourquoi. **2.** s. pourquoi m. **3.** int. **w., it's David!** tiens, c'est David! **w. of course!** mais bien sûr! **w., you're not afraid, are you?** voyons, vous n'avez pas peur? **w., what's the matter?** mais qu'avez-vous donc?

wick [wik], s. mèche f (d'une lampe, etc.).

wicked [′wikid], a. **1.** mauvais, méchant. **2.** malicieux; **-ly,** adv. **1.** méchamment. **2.** malicieusement; ′**wickedness,** s. méchanceté f, perversité f.

wicker [′wikər], s. **1. w.(work),** vannerie f; osier tressé. **2.** attrib. d'osier, en osier; **w. chair,** fauteuil m en osier.

wicket [′wikit], s. **1.** guichet m (d'une porte, etc.). **2.** (a) (in large door) porte à piétons; (b) **w. (gate),** (i) petite porte à claire-voie, (ii) portillon m (de passage à niveau, etc.). **3.** N.Am: (in post office, etc.) guichet. **4.** Cr: guichet; **w. keeper,** gardien m de guichet.

wide [waid]. **I.** a. **1.** large; **to be 10 metres w.,** avoir 10 mètres de large; **how w. is the room?** quelle est la largeur de la pièce? **2.** étendu, vaste, ample; **the w. world,** le vaste monde. **3.** (vêtement) ample, large. **4.** éloigné, loin; **to be w. of the mark,** être loin du compte. **5.** **F:** malin, retors; **a w. boy,** un affranchi, un débrouillard; -**ly**, *adv.* largement; **w. read paper,** journal *m* à grande circulation; **to be w. read,** (i) (*of author*) avoir un public très étendu; (ii) (*of reader*) avoir de la lecture; **w. known,** très connu; **he has travelled w.,** il a beaucoup voyagé. **II.** *adv.* **1.** loin; **w. apart,** espacé. **2.** (ouvrir, etc.) largement; **to fling the door w. open,** ouvrir la porte toute grande; '**widen. 1.** *v.tr.* (*a*) élargir; (*b*) évaser (un trou); (*c*) étendre (les limites de qch.). **2.** *v.i.* s'élargir; s'agrandir (en large); **the breach is widening,** la rupture s'accentue; '**widespread,** *a.* **1.** étendu. **2.** répandu; universel; **w. opinion,** opinion largement répandue; **width** [widθ], *s.* largeur *f*; **to be 10 metres in w.,** avoir 10 mètres de largeur.

widow ['widou], *s.* veuve *f*; '**widowed,** *a.* (homme) veuf; (femme) veuve; **he lives with his w. mother,** il habite avec sa mère qui est veuve; '**widower,** *s.* veuf *m*; '**widowhood,** *s.* veuvage *m*.

wield [wi:ld], *v.tr.* manier (une épée, etc.); exercer (le pouvoir).

wife, *pl.* **wives** [waif, waivz], *s.* femme *f*, épouse *f*; **she was his second w.,** il l'avait épousée en secondes noces; **the farmer's w.,** la fermière; *P:* **the w.,** la ménagère, la bourgeoise; '**wifely,** *a.* (qualités, devoirs) d'épouse, de femme mariée.

wig [wig], *s.* perruque *f*; postiche *m*.

wiggle [wigl], *v.i. & tr. F:* (*a*) (se) tortiller; (se) remuer; (*b*) **to w. one's toes,** remuer, agiter, les orteils.

wigwam ['wigwæm], *s.* wigwam *m*.

wild [waild], *a.* **1.** sauvage; **w. country,** pays inculte; (*of plants*) **to run w.,** retourner à l'état sauvage; **w. life,** la nature; **w.-life sanctuary,** réserve naturelle. **2.** (*a*) (vent) furieux, violent; **a w. night,** une nuit de tempête; (*b*) (*of animal*) farouche, sauvage; **w. beast,** bête *f* sauvage; **w. horses wouldn't drag it out of me,** rien au monde ne me le ferait dire; (*c*) (*pers.*) dissipé, dissolu; **w. life,** vie déréglée, de bâton de chaise. **3.** (*a*) (*pers.*) affolé; **w. eyes,** yeux égarés; **w. with joy,** fou, *f.* folle, éperdu, de joie; *F:* **to be w. with s.o.,** être furieux contre qn; **it makes me w.,** ça me met en rage, me rend furieux; (*b*) (*of idea, etc.*) fantasque; insensé; **w. talk,** propos *mpl* en l'air. **4.** *s.pl.* **the wilds,** région sauvage; régions inexplorées; la brousse; -**ly,** *adv.* **1.** d'une manière extravagante; **to talk w.,** dire des folies; **w. inaccurate,** complètement inexact. **2.** (répondre) au hasard, au petit bonheur; '**wildcat,** *a. F:* **w. scheme,** projet dénué de bon sens; **w. strike,** grève non officielle; **wilderness** ['wildənis], *s.* désert *m*; lieu *m* sauvage; pays *m* inculte; '**wildfire,** *s.* **to spread like w.,** se répandre comme une traînée de poudre; '**wildfowl,** *s.*

coll. gibier *m* à plume; gibier d'eau; '**wildness,** *s.* **1.** état *m* sauvage (d'un pays, d'un animal). **2.** (*a*) fureur *f* (du vent); (*b*) dérèglement *m* (des mœurs). **3.** extravagance *f* (d'idées, de paroles).

wildebeest ['wildibi:st], *s. Z:* gnou *m*.

wile [wail], *v.tr.* séduire, charmer (qn); **wiles,** *s.pl.* ruses *f*, artifices *m*.

will [wil]. **I.** *s.* **1.** (*a*) volonté *f*; **to have a w. of one's own,** être volontaire; **to lack strength of w.,** manquer de caractère; **to take the w. for the deed,** accepter l'intention pour le fait; **where there's a w. there's a way,** vouloir c'est pouvoir; (*b*) **to work with a w.,** travailler de bon cœur, avec courage. **2.** (*a*) décision *f*; volonté; *Ecc:* **Thy w. be done,** que ta volonté soit faite; (*b*) bon plaisir; gré *m*; **at w.,** à volonté; **of one's own free w.,** de son plein gré; **I did it against my w.,** je l'ai fait malgré moi, à contrecœur; **with the best w. in the world,** avec la meilleure volonté du monde. **3.** *Jur:* testament *m*; **the last w. and testament of X,** les dernières volontés de X; **to make one's w.,** faire son testament; **to leave s.o. sth. in one's w.,** léguer qch. à qn. **II.** *v.tr.* **1.** (*a*) **as fate willed,** comme le sort l'a voulu; (*b*) **to w. s.o. into doing sth.,** faire faire qch. à qn (par un acte de volonté); (*in hypnotism*) suggestionner qn. **2.** léguer (qch. à qn); disposer de (qch.) par testament. **III.** *modal aux.v.def.* (*pres.* **will;** *p.t. & condit.* **would; w. not** *often contracted to* **won't**) **1.** vouloir; (*a*) **what would you expect me to do?** que voulez-vous que je fasse? **say what you w.,** quoi que vous disiez; **look which way you w.,** de quelque côté que vous regardiez; **would to heaven I were free!** si seulement j'étais libre! (*b*) **he could if he would,** il le pourrait s'il le voulait; **the engine won't start,** le moteur ne veut pas démarrer; **just wait a moment, w. you?** voulez-vous attendre un instant? **he won't have any of it,** il refuse d'en entendre parler; **I *won't* have it!** je ne le veux pas! **won't you sit down,** asseyez-vous, je vous en prie; (*c*) (*emphatic*) **accidents w. happen,** on ne peut pas éviter les accidents; **he w. have his little joke,** il aime à plaisanter; **I quite forgot!—you *would*!** je l'ai complètement oublié!—c'est bien de vous! (*d*) (*habit*) **this hen w. lay up to six eggs a week,** cette poule pond jusqu'à six œufs par semaine; **she would often come home tired out,** elle rentrait souvent très fatiguée; (*e*) (*conjecture*) **would this be your cousin?** c'est là sans doute votre cousin? **2.** (*auxiliary forming future tenses:* **I will, I will not, you will,** *often* **I'll, I won't, you'll** *in conversational style*) (*a*) (*emphatic*) **I won't be caught again,** on ne m'y reprendra plus; (*b*) **w. he be there?—he w.,** y sera-t-il?—oui (, bien sûr); **I'll starve!—no, you**

won't, je mourrai de faim!—pas du tout! **you won't forget, will you?** vous ne l'oublierez pas, hein? **you w. write to me, won't you?** vous m'écrirez, n'est-ce pas? **I think he'll come,** je crois qu'il viendra; **I'll dictate and you'll write,** moi je vais dicter et vous, vous allez écrire; (c) (*command*) **you w. be here at three o'clock,** soyez ici à trois heures; (d) (*conditional*) **he would come if you invited him,** il viendrait si vous l'invitiez; **'willing,** a. 1. (a) de bonne volonté; bien disposé; serviable; **a few w. men,** quelques hommes de bonne volonté; **w. hands,** mains empressées; (b) **to be w.,** consentir, être consentant. 2. **w. to do sth.,** prêt à faire qch.; **w. to help,** prêt à rendre service; **to be able and w.,** avoir à la fois le pouvoir et la volonté; F: **to show w.,** faire preuve de bonne volonté; **w. or not,** bon gré, mal gré; **-ly,** adv. 1. de plein gré. 2. de bon cœur; volontiers; **'willingness,** s. 1. bonne volonté; **with the utmost w.,** de très bon cœur. 2. consentement m; **'willpower,** s. volonté f; **to have no w.,** manquer de volonté.

William ['wiliəm]. Pr.n.m. Guillaume; **W. the Conqueror,** Guillaume le Conquérant.

will o' the wisp ['wiləðəwisp], s. feu follet.

willow ['wilou], s. **w. (tree),** saule m; **weeping w.,** saule pleureur; **'willowy,** a. souple, svelte, élancé.

willy-nilly ['wili'nili], adv. bon gré, mal gré; de gré ou de force.

wilt [wilt], v.i. (a) (*of plant*) se flétrir, faner; (b) (*of pers.*) dépérir, languir.

wily ['waili], a. rusé; astucieux; malin.

win [win], v.tr. & i. (p.t. & p.p. won [wʌn]) 1. gagner; remporter (une victoire, le prix); **to w. by a short head,** gagner de justesse. 2. acquérir (de la popularité); captiver (l'attention); **to w. a reputation,** se faire une réputation; **this action won him a decoration,** cette action lui a valu une décoration; **to w. s.o.'s love,** se faire aimer de qn; **'win'back,** v.tr. 1. reconquérir. 2. regagner (son argent); **'winning. I.** a. 1. **w. number,** numéro gagnant; (*in lottery*) numéro sortant; **w. stroke,** coup décisif. 2. **w. ways,** manières avenantes; **w. smile,** sourire engageant, attrayant, séduisant. **II.** s. 1. victoire f; **w. post,** poteau m d'arrivée; **the w. of the war,** le fait d'avoir gagné la guerre; **the w. of the war is the prime objective,** gagner la guerre est notre objectif principal. 2. **winnings,** gains m (au jeu); **'win'over,** v.tr. gagner (qn); **to w. over one's audience,** se concilier ses auditeurs; **'win'through,** v.i. parvenir à bout de ses difficultés.

wince [wins]. **I.** v.i. faire une grimace de douleur; tressaillir de douleur; **without wincing,** sans sourciller, sans broncher. **II.** s. crispation (nerveuse, de douleur); **without a w.,** sans sourciller, sans broncher.

winch [wintʃ], s. treuil m (de hissage).

wind¹ [wind]. **I.** s. 1. vent m; (a) **the north w., the west w.,** le vent du nord, de l'ouest; **high w.,** vent fort, violent; **to see which way the w. blows,** regarder de quel côté vient le vent; **to go like the w.,** aller comme le vent; F: **to raise the w.,** se procurer de l'argent; F: **to have, get, the w. up,** avoir le trac, la frousse; F: **to put the w. up s.o.,** faire une peur bleue, donner la frousse, à qn; (b) Nau: **head w.,** vent debout; **to sail, run, before the w.,** courir vent arrière; **in the teeth of the w.,** contre le vent; F: **to sail close to the w.,** friser (i) la malhonnêteté, (ii) l'insolence, (iii) l'indécence; **to take the w. out of s.o.'s sails,** déjouer les plans de qn; couper l'herbe sous le pied de qn; (c) attrib. **w. gauge,** anémomètre m; **w. tunnel,** tunnel m aérodynamique; soufflerie f. 2. **to have the w. of one's game,** avoir le vent de son gibier; F: **to get w. of sth.,** avoir vent de qch. 3. flatuosité f; F: **to have the w.,** (i) lâcher un vent; (ii) roter. 4. souffle m, respiration f, haleine f; **to get one's second w.,** reprendre haleine. 5. Mus: **w. instrument,** instrument m à vent; **the w.,** les instruments à vent. **II.** v.tr. (a) flairer, avoir vent (du gibier); (b) **it completely winded me,** ça m'a complètement essoufflé, m'a mis à bout de souffle; **'windbag,** s. 1. outre f (d'une cornemuse). 2. F: orateur verbeux; **he's just a w.,** il parle pour ne rien dire; **'windbreak,** s. brisevent m; **'windcheater,** s. blouson m; **'windfall,** s. 1. fruit tombé, abattu par le vent. 2. aubaine f; **'windmill,** s. moulin m à vent; **'windpipe,** s. Anat: gosier m; **'windproof,** a. à l'épreuve du vent; **'windscreen,** N.Am: **'windshield,** s. Aut: pare-brise m inv; **'windsock,** s. Av: manche f à vent; **'windswept,** a. balayé par le vent; venteux; **'windward. 1.** a. & adv. au vent; **the W. Islands,** les Iles f du Vent. 2. s. côté m du vent; **'windy,** a. 1. venteux, -euse; **w. day,** journée de grand vent. 2. balayé par le vent; exposé aux quatre vents. 3. F: **to be w.,** avoir le trac, la frousse.

wind² [waind], v. (p.t. & p.p. wound [waund]) 1. v.i. tourner; faire des détours; (*of path, river*) serpenter; **road that winds up, down, the hill,** route qui monte, descend, en serpentant; **the river winds across the plain,** la rivière traverse la plaine en serpentant. 2. v.tr. (a) enrouler; Tex: dévider (le fil); **to w. wool into a ball,** enrouler la laine en pelote; (b) remonter (sa montre); **'winding. I.** a. (*chemin*) sinueux, qui serpente; (route) en lacets; (rue) tortueuse. **II.** s. 1. mouvement sinueux; cours sinueux; replis mpl. 2. Tex: etc: bobinage m; **w. machine,** bobineuse f. 3. remontage m (d'une horloge); **'wind'up. 1.** v.tr. (a) enrouler (un cordage); (b) F: (*of pers.*) **to be all wound up,** avoir les nerfs en pelote; (c) terminer (qch.); Com:

liquider (une société); régler, clôturer (un compte). **2.** *v.i.* finir, terminer; **the company wound up**, la société s'est mise en liquidation.
windlass ['windlæs], *s.* treuil *m*.
window ['windou], *s.* (*a*) fenêtre *f*; **to look out of the w.**, regarder par la fenêtre; **w. pane**, carreau *m*; **I've broken a w.** (**pane**), j'ai cassé un carreau; **w. seat**, banquette *f* (dans l'embrasure d'une fenêtre); **w. box**, caisse *f*, bac *m*, à fleurs (sur le rebord d'une fenêtre); (*b*) **stained-glass w.**, vitrail, -aux *m* (d'église); (*c*) *Veh:* glace *f*; *Aut:* **rear w.**, lunette *f* arrière; *Rail:* **it is dangerous to lean out of the w.**, il est dangereux de se pencher dehors; (*d*) *Com:* vitrine *f*, devanture *f*; *F:* **w. shopping**, lèche-vitrines *m*; **to go w. shopping**, lécher les vitrines, faire du lèche-vitrines; **w. dressing**, (i) art *m* de l'étalage; (ii) *F:* camouflage *m*, trompe-l'œil *m*; (*e*) fenêtre (d'une enveloppe); **'window-ledge, 'window-sill**, *s.* rebord *m*, appui *m*, de fenêtre.
wine [wain]. **I.** *s.* vin *m*; **dry, sweet, w.**, vin sec, doux; **w. production, producing**, viticulture *f*; **w.-producing region**, région *f* viticole; **w. merchant**, négociant *m* en vins; (*in restaurant*) **w. list**, carte *f* des vins; **w. cellar**, cave *f* à vins; **w. waiter**, sommelier *m*. **II.** *v.tr.* **to w. and dine s.o.**, offrir à qn un repas soigné; fêter qn; **'wineglass**, *s.* verre *m* à vin.
wing [wiŋ], *s.* **1.** aile *f* (d'oiseau). **2.** (*a*) aile (d'un bâtiment); (*b*) *Mil:* escadre (aérienne); **w. commander**, lieutenant-colonel *m*. **3.** aile (d'un avion); **the wings**, la voilure; **w. area**, surface *f* alaire. **4. the wings**, (i) *Th:* les coulisses *f*; (ii) *Sp:* (*pers.*) les ailiers *m*; **winged**, *a.* ailé; **'wingless**, *a.* sans ailes.
wink [wiŋk]. **I.** *s.* clignement *m* d'œil; clin *m* d'œil; **with a w.**, en clignant de l'œil; *F:* **to tip s.o.**, **the w.**, avertir qn, faire signe de l'œil à qn; **to have forty winks**, faire un petit somme, une petite sieste. **II.** *v.i.* (*a*) cligner des yeux; **to w. at s.o.**, cligner de l'œil, faire un clin d'œil, à qn; (*b*) (*of light*) vaciller, clignoter; **'winking**, *s.* clignement *m* de l'œil; **like w.**, en un clin d'œil; **as easy as w.**, simple comme bonjour.
winkle ['wiŋkl], *s. Moll:* bigorneau *m*.
winner ['winər], *s.* gagnant, -ante; **the w. of the race**, le vainqueur de l'épreuve; **to back the w.**, parier sur le gagnant.
winter ['wintər]. **I.** *s.* hiver; *m*; **in w.**, en hiver; **w. clothes**, vêtements *m* d'hiver; **w. sports**, sports *m* d'hiver; **w. resort**, station *f* d'hiver. **II.** *v.i.* hiverner; passer l'hiver (at, à); **'wintry**, *a.* d'hiver; **w. weather**, temps *m* d'hiver; temps rigoureux; **w. smile**, sourire glacial; sourire décourageant.
wipe [waip]. **I.** *v.tr.* essuyer (qch.); **to w. one's eyes**, s'essuyer les yeux; **to w. one's nose**, se moucher; **to w. (up)**, essuyer la vaisselle; **to w.**

sth. **dry**, bien essuyer qch. **II.** *s.* coup *m* de torchon, de mouchoir, d'éponge; **give it a w.!** essuyez-le un peu! **'wipe a'way**, *v.tr.* essuyer (ses larmes); **'wiper**, *s.* (*a*) **windscreen**, *N.Am:* **windshield**, **w.**, essuie-glace *m*; (*b*) *P:* **nose w.**, mouchoir *m*; **'wipe 'out**, *v.tr.* (*a*) liquider, amortir (une dette); (*b*) effacer, exterminer (une armée, etc.); (*c*) *F:* tuer, assassiner (qn).
wire ['waiər]. **I.** *s.* **1.** (*a*) fil *m* métallique; fil de fer; **copper w.**, fil de laiton; **w. netting**, treillage *m* en fil de fer; **barbed w.**, (fil de fer) barbelé (*m*); **w. mattress**, sommier *m* métallique; (*b*) **telegraph wires**, fils télégraphiques; **w. tapping**, écoute *f* téléphonique; *F:* **to get one's wires crossed**, se tromper; *F:* (*pers.*) **a live w.**, un dégourdi, un débrouillard. **2.** télégramme *m*. **II.** *v.tr.* **1.** faire l'installation électrique, poser l'électricité, dans (une maison). **2.** télégraphier; **'wired**, *a.* monté sur fil de fer; (*of enclosure*) grillagé; **'wireless. I.** *a.* sans fil. **2.** *a. & s.* **w. (set)**, (poste *m* de) radio *f*; **'wirepulling**, *s. F:* intrigues *fpl*; **'wiring**, *s.* pose *f* de fils électriques; canalisation *f*; **'wiry**, *a.* (*of hair*) raide, rude; (*of pers.*) sec et nerveux.
wise [waiz], *a.* **1.** sage; prudent; **the W. Men**, les Rois Mages. **2.** (*a*) **to look w.**, prendre un (petit) air entendu; (*b*) **he's none the wiser for it**, il n'en est pas plus avancé; **to do sth. without anyone being any the wiser**, faire qch. à l'insu de tout le monde; **say nothing and nobody will be any the wiser**, si tu te tais, ni vu ni connu; **-ly**, *adv.* sagement; prudemment; **wisdom** ['wizdəm], *s.* sagesse *f*; **w. tooth**, dent *f* de sagesse.
wish [wiʃ]. **I.** *v.* **1.** *v.ind.tr.* **to w. for sth.**, désirer, souhaiter, qch.; **to have everything one could w. for**, avoir tout à souhait; **what more could you w. for?** que voudriez-vous de plus? (*to pers. pulling wishbone*) **w.!** faites un souhait! **2.** *v.tr.* vouloir; **to w. to do sth.**, désirer, vouloir, faire qch. **I don't w. you to do it**, je ne veux pas que vous le fassiez; **I w. I were in your place**, je voudrais être à votre place; **I w. I had seen it, him**, j'aurais bien voulu le voir; **I w. he would come!** pourvu qu'il vienne! *F:* **don't you w. you could (get it)!** je vous en souhaite! *F:* **it's been wished on me**, c'est une chose que je n'ai pas pu refuser; **to w. s.o. well**, (i) être bien disposé envers qn; (ii) souhaiter bonne chance à qn; **to w. s.o. goodnight**, dire bonsoir à qn; souhaiter une bonne nuit à qn. **II.** *s.* (*a*) désir *m*; vœu *m*; **I haven't the slightest w. to go**, je n'ai aucune envie d'y aller; **everything seems to go according to his wishes**, tout semble lui réussir à souhait; **you shall have your w.**, votre désir sera exaucé; (*b*) souhait *m*, vœu *m*; **my best wishes to your mother**, présentez mon meilleur souvenir à votre mère; **'wishbone**, *s.* lunette *f*,

fourchette *f* (d'un poulet); **'wishful,** *a.* *F:* **that's w. thinking,** c'est prendre ses désirs pour des réalités.

wishy-washy ['wiʃiwɔʃi], *a.* *F:* fade, insipide.

wisteria [wis'tiəriə], *s.* *Bot:* glycine *f.*

wistful ['wistful], *a.* (regard) plein d'un vague désir, d'un vague regret; **w. smile,** sourire (i) désenchanté, (ii) pensif; **-fully,** *adv.* d'un air songeur et triste; d'un air de regret.

wit [wit], *s.* 1. (*usu.pl.*) esprit *m,* entendement *m;* intelligence *f;* **to have lost one's wits,** avoir perdu la raison; **to collect one's wits,** se ressaisir; **to have one's wits about one,** avoir toute sa présence d'esprit; **that will sharpen your wits,** cela va vous aiguiser l'intelligence; **to be at one's wits' end,** ne plus savoir de quel côté se tourner; **to live by one's wits,** vivre d'expédients. 2. vivacité *f* d'esprit; **flash of w.,** trait *m* d'esprit. 3. (*pers.*) homme, femme, d'esprit.

witch [witʃ], *s.* (*a*) sorcière *f;* **w. doctor,** sorcier guérisseur; (*b*) *F:* **old w.,** vieille toupie; (*c*) *F:* **you little w.!** petite ensorceleuse! **'witchcraft,** *s.* sorcellerie *f;* magie noire.

with [wið], *prep.* avec. 1. (*a*) **to work w. s.o.,** travailler avec qn; **he's staying w. friends,** il est chez des amis; **is there someone w. you?** êtes-vous accompagné? **I'll be w. you in a moment,** je serai à vous dans un moment; (*b*) **girl w. blue eyes,** jeune fille aux yeux bleus; **child w. a cold,** enfant enrhumé; **he came w. his overcoat on,** il est venu en pardessus; **have you a pencil w. you?** avez-vous un crayon sur vous? **w. your intelligence,** intelligent comme vous l'êtes; (*c*) **to leave a child w. s.o.,** laisser un enfant à la garde de qn; **this decision rests w. you,** c'est à vous de décider; (*d*) **w, all his faults,** malgré tous ses défauts. 2. (*a*) **to trade w. France,** faire du commerce avec la France; **I have nothing to do w. him,** je n'ai rien à faire avec lui; **I can do nothing w. him,** je ne peux en faire; **to be sincere w. oneself,** être sincère avec soi-même; **it's a habit w. me,** c'est une habitude chez moi; (*b*) **I sympathize w. you,** je vous plains sincèrement; **I don't agree w. you,** je ne suis pas de votre avis; **I'm w. you there!** j'en conviens! d'accord! *F:* **to be w. it,** être dans le vent, dans le mouvement, à la page; (*c*) **w. these words he left me,** là-dessus, alors, sur ce, il m'a quitté; (*d*) **to wrestle w. s.o.,** lutter avec qn; **to fight w. s.o.,** se battre contre qn. 3. **to part w. sth.,** se défaire de qch. 4. (*a*) **to cut sth. w. a knife,** couper qch. avec un couteau, au couteau; **to walk w. a stick,** marcher avec une canne; **to take sth. w. both hands,** prendre qch. à deux mains; **to strike w. all one's might,** frapper de toutes ses forces; (*b*) **to tremble w. rage,** trembler de rage; **to be stiff w. cold,** être engourdi par le froid; **to be ill w. measles,** avoir

la rougeole; (*c*) **to fill a vase w. water,** remplir un vase d'eau; **it's pouring w. rain,** il pleut à verse. 5. **to work w. courage,** travailler avec courage; **to receive s.o. w. open arms,** recevoir qn à bras ouverts; **w. all due respect, I . . .,** si vous permettez, je . . .; **w. the object of . . .,** dans l'intention de . . .; **I say it w. regret,** je le dis à regret; **w. a few exceptions,** à part quelques exceptions. 6. **down w. the President!** à bas le Président!

withdraw [wið'drɔː], *v.* (**with'drew; with-'drawn**) 1. *v.tr.* (*a*) retirer; (*b*) ramener (des troupes) en arrière; (*c*) **to w. coins from circulation,** retirer des pièces de la circulation; **to w. money from the bank,** retirer une somme d'argent de la banque; (*d*) retirer (une offre, une promesse); *Com:* **to w. an order,** annuler une commande; *Jur:* **to w. an action,** abandonner un procès. 2. *v.i.* se retirer; s'éloigner; *Mil:* se replier; (*of candidate*) **to w. in favour of s.o.,** se désister en faveur de qn; **with'drawal,** *s.* 1. (*a*) retrait *m* (de troupes, d'une somme d'argent); (*b*) rétraction *f* (d'une offre, etc.); retrait (d'une plainte). 2. (*a*) retraite *f; Mil:* repli *m,* repliement *m* (des troupes); (*b*) désistement *m* (d'un candidat).

wither ['wiðər]. 1. *v.i.* (*of plant*) se dessécher, se faner. 2. *v.tr.* (*a*) dessécher, flétrir, faner (une plante, etc.); (*b*) **to w. s.o. with a look,** foudroyer qn du regard; **'withered,** *a.* (*a*) (*plant, etc.*) desséché, fané; (*b*) **w. arm,** bras atrophié; **'withering. I.** *a.* (regard) foudroyant; **-ly,** *adv.* d'un regard foudroyant; d'un ton de mépris. **II.** *s.* dessèchement *m;* flétrissement *m.*

withold [wið'hould], *v.tr.* (**with'held; with-'held**) (*a*) refuser (son consentement); (*b*) cacher (la vérité).

within [wið'in], *prep.* (*a*) à l'intérieur de; **w. four walls,** entre quatre murs; **w. these four walls,** (soit dit) entre nous; (*b*) **to keep w. the law,** rester dans la légalité; **w. the meaning of the act,** selon les prévisions de la loi; **to live w. one's income,** vivre dans les limites de ses moyens; **w. reason,** dans les limites du possible; **weight w. a kilo,** poids à un kilo près; (*c*) **w. sight,** en vue; **w. call,** à (la) portée de la voix; **situated w. five kilometres of the town,** situé à moins de cinq kilomètres de la ville; **w. a radius of ten kilometres,** dans un rayon de dix kilomètres; **w. an inch of death,** à deux doigts de la mort; (*d*) **w. an hour,** dans, avant, une heure; **w. the week,** avant la fin de la semaine; **w. the next five years,** d'ici cinq ans; **w. a short time,** (i) à court délai; (ii) peu de temps après; **w. living memory,** de mémoire d'homme.

without [wið'aut], *prep.* sans; **w. friends,** sans amis; **to be w. food,** manquer de nourriture; **he arrived w. money or luggage,** il est arrivé sans argent ni bagages; **not w. difficulty,** non sans difficulté; **w. seeing me,** sans me voir; **that goes w. saying,** cela va sans dire; **to go w. sth.,** se passer de qch.; *Ecc:* **world w. end,** pour les siècles des siècles.

withstand [wið'stænd], *v.tr.* (**with'stood;** **with'stood**) résister à (la douleur); *Mil:* soutenir (une attaque).

witness ['witnis]. **I.** *s.* **1.** témoignage *m.* **2.** témoin *m* (**of an incident,** d'un incident, **to an act,** à un acte); **to call s.o. as a w.,** citer qn comme témoin; **w. box** = barre *f* des témoins. **II.** *v.* **1.** *v.tr.* (*a*) être témoin d'(un incident); (*b*) attester (un acte); certifier (une signature). **2.** *v.i.* **to w. to sth.,** témoigner de qch.; **to w. against s.o.,** témoigner contre qn.

witty ['witi], *a.* spirituel; **'witticism,** *s.* trait *m* d'esprit; **'wittily,** *adv.* spirituellement; avec esprit; **'wittiness,** *s.* esprit *m.*

wizard ['wizəd], *s.* sorcier *m*; magicien *m.*

wizened ['wizənd], *a.* desséché, ratatiné; (visage) parcheminé.

wobble [wɔbl]. **I.** *v.i.* ballotter; branler. **II.** *s.* branlement *m*, oscillation *f*; tremblement *m*; *Aut:* **front wheel w.,** shimmy *m*; **'wobbly,** *a.* branlant, vacillant; hors d'aplomb; (chaise) bancale; **my legs feel w.,** j'ai les jambes en coton.

wodge [wɔdʒ], *s. F:* gros morceau.

woe [wou], *s.* malheur *m*, chagrin *m*, peine *f*; **to tell a tale of w.,** faire le récit de ses malheurs; **'woebegone,** *a.* triste, désolé, abattu.

wolf, *pl.* **wolves** [wulf, wulvz]. **I.** *s.* **1.** loup *m*; **she w.,** louve *f*; **w. cub,** louveteau *m*; **prairie w.,** coyote *m*; **that will keep the w. from the door,** cela vous mettra à l'abri du besoin. **2.** *F:* tombeur *m* (de femmes); **w. whistle,** sifflement admiratif (au passage d'une jolie femme). **II.** *v.tr.* **to w. one's food,** avaler sa nourriture à grosses bouchées; bâfrer; **'wolfhound,** *s.* lévrier *m* d'Irlande; **'wolfish,** *a.* rapace, vorace.

wolfram ['wulfrəm], *s.* wolfram *m.*

woman, *pl.* **women** ['wumən, 'wimin], *s.* (*a*) femme *f*; **a young w.,** une jeune femme; **an old w.,** une vieille (femme); *P:* **the old w.,** ma femme, la bourgeoise; (*b*) *attrib.* **w. doctor,** femme médecin; **w. friend,** amie *f*; **w. hater,** misogyne *m*; **'womanhood,** *s.* **to grow to w.,** devenir femme; **'womanly,** *a.* féminin; **she's so w.,** elle est tellement femme; **'womenfolk,** *s.pl.* **my w.,** les femmes de la famille.

womb [wu:m], *s. Anat:* matrice *f.*

wombat ['wɔmbæt], *s. Z:* phascolome *m.*

wonder ['wʌndər]. **I.** *s.* **1.** merveille *f*, prodige *m*; **to promise wonders,** promettre monts et merveilles; **the seven wonders of the world,** les sept merveilles du monde; **a nine days' w.,** la merveille d'un jour; **it's a w. he hasn't lost it,** il

est étonnant qu'il ne l'ait pas perdu; **for a w.,** chose remarquable; par extraordinaire; **and no w.,** et rien d'étonnant. **2.** (*a*) étonnement *m*, surprise *f*; (*b*) émerveillement *m.* **II.** *v.* **1.** *v.i.* s'étonner, s'émerveiller (**at,** de); **I don't w. at it,** cela ne m'étonne pas; **it's not to be wondered at,** cela n'est pas étonnant; **it makes me w.,** cela m'intrigue. **2.** *v.tr.* (*a*) s'étonner; **I w. he didn't buy it,** je m'étonne qu'il ne l'ait pas acheté; (*b*) se demander; **I w. whether he will come,** je me demande s'il viendra; **I w. why,** je voudrais bien savoir pourquoi; **I w. who invented that,** je suis curieux de savoir qui a inventé cela; **'wonderful,** *a.* merveilleux, prodigieux; **w. to relate,** chose étonnante, remarquable; **we had a w. time,** nous nous sommes très bien amusés; **it was w.!** c'était magnifique! **-fully,** *adv.* merveilleusement; **w. well,** à merveille; **'wonderment,** *s.* étonnement *m.*

wonky ['wɔŋki], *a. F:* (*a*) branlant; (*b*) patraque.

wood [wud], *s.* **1.** (*a*) (*small forest*) bois; **you can't see the w. for the trees,** les arbres empêchent de voir la forêt; on se perd dans les détails; **we're not out of the w. yet,** nous ne sommes pas encore tirés d'affaire; (*b*) *attrib.* **w. anemone,** anémone *f* des bois; **w. pigeon,** (pigeon *m*) ramier (*m*); colombe *f.* **2.** (*material*) bois; **w. shavings,** copeaux *m*; **touch w.!** *N.Am:* **knock on w.!** touchons du bois! *F:* **he's w. from the neck up,** il est bête comme ses pieds; **w. carving, engraving,** sculpture *f*, gravure *f*, sur bois; **w. pulp,** pâte *f* de bois; **'woodchuck,** *s. Z:* marmotte *f* d'Amérique; **'woodcock,** *s. Orn:* bécasse *f*; **'woodcraft,** *s.* connaissance *f* de la forêt; **'woodcut,** *s.* gravure *f* sur bois; **'wooded,** *a.* boisé; **'wooden,** *a.* **1.** de bois, en bois. **2.** (*a*) (*of movement, etc.*) raide, gauche; (*b*) sans intelligence; **'woodland,** *s.* pays boisé; bois *m*; **'woodlouse,** *s.* cloporte *m*; **'woodpecker,** *s. Orn:* pic *m*; **green w.,** pivert *m*; **'woodshed,** *s.* bûcher *m*; hangar *m* à bois; **'woodsman,** *pl.* **-men,** *s.* chasseur *m* (en forêt); trappeur *m*; **'woodwork,** *s.* **1.** travail *m* du bois; charpenterie *f*; menuiserie *f.* **2.** bois travaillé; boiseries *fpl*; charpente *f*; menuiserie.

wool [wul], *s.* **1.** laine *f*; **the w. trade,** le commerce des laines; **knitting w.,** laine à tricoter; *F:* **to pull the w. over s.o.'s eyes,** donner le change à qn. **2.** pelage *m* (d'animal). **3.** **steel w.,** paille *f* de fer; **glass w.,** laine de verre; **'woolgathering,** *s.* (*a*) *F:* rêvasserie *f*; (*b*) **to be w.,** être dans la lune; **'woollen,** *a.* de laine; **w. goods,** *s.* **woollens,** lainages *m*; **'woolliness,** *s.* manque *m* de netteté; imprécision *f* (de raisonnement, etc.); **'woolly.** **1.** *a.* (*a*) laineux, de laine; (*b*) flou, peu net, *f.* nette. **2.** *s.* (vêtement *m* en) tricot *m*; **put on your w.!** mets ton tricot!

word [wəːd]. I. *s.* **1.** mot *m*; (*a*) w. for w., (répéter qch.) mot pour mot; (traduire qch.) mot à mot; **in a w.**, en un mot; bref; **in other words**, en d'autres termes; autrement dit; **I told him in so many words that . . .**, je lui ai dit expressément que . . .; **bad isn't the w. for it**, mauvais n'est pas assez dire; (*b*) **spoken words**, paroles *f*; **in the words of the poet**, selon le poète; **a man of few words**, un homme qui parle peu; **to call on s.o.** to say a few words, prier qn de prendre la parole; **he didn't say a w.**, il n'a pas soufflé mot; **I can't get a w. out of him**, je ne peux pas le faire parler; **to put one's w. in**, intervenir; placer son mot; **without a w.**, sans mot dire; **you've taken the words out of my mouth**, c'est justement ce que j'allais dire; **he's too stupid for words**, il est d'une bêtise indicible; (*c*) **I'd like a w. with you**, j'ai un mot à vous dire; **I'll have a w. with him about it**, je lui en parlerai; **to say a good w. for s.o.**, dire un mot en faveur de qn; (*d*) *F:* **to have words with s.o.**, se disputer avec qn. **2.** **by w. of mouth**, de vive voix; verbalement. **3.** **to send s.o. w. of sth.**, faire dire, faire savoir, qch. à qn; prévenir qn de qch.; **w. came that . . .**, on nous a rapporté que . . .. **4.** **to keep one's w.**, tenir (sa) parole; **to break one's w.**, manquer à sa parole; **to take s.o. at his w.**, croire qn sur parole; **you can take my w. for it**, croyez-m'en; je vous en réponds; **I'll take your w. for it**, j'en crois votre parole; vous êtes bien placé pour le savoir; **my w.!** tiens! qui l'aurait cru? **5.** **w. of command**, ordre *m*; commandement *m*; **sharp's the w.!** vite! dépêchez-vous! II. *v.tr.* formuler (qch.) par écrit; rédiger (un document, un télégramme); **it might have been differently worded**, on aurait pu l'exprimer en d'autres termes; **well worded**, bien exprimé; 'wordiness, *s.* verbosité *f*; 'wording, *s.* mots *mpl*; termes *mpl* (d'un document); langage *m*; **your w. is not clear**, vous ne vous exprimez pas clairement; 'wordy, *a.* verbeux; prolixe, diffus.

work [wəːk]. I. *s.* **1.** travail, -aux *m*; **to be at w.**, travailler; **he was hard at w.**, il était en plein travail; **the forces at w.**, les forces en jeu; **to go the right way to w.**, s'y prendre bien. **2.** (*a*) travail, ouvrage *m*, besogne *f*, tâche *f*; **a piece of w.**, un travail, un ouvrage, une œuvre; *F:* (*pers.*) **a nasty piece of w.**, un sale type; **I've so much w. to do**, j'ai tellement (de travail) à faire; **the brandy had done its w.**, l'eau-de-vie avait fait son effet; **to do s.o.'s dirty w.**, faire les sales besognes de qn; **a day's w.**, (le travail d')une journée; **that's a good day's w.**, (i) j'ai, vous avez, etc., bien travaillé aujourd'hui; (ii) j'ai, vous avez, etc., été bien inspiré de faire ça; **it's all in a day's w.**, c'est l'ordinaire de mon

existence; ça ne me dérange pas de le faire (, j'en ai l'habitude); (*b*) **it was thirsty w.**, c'était un travail qui donnait soif. **3.** (*a*) **good works**, les bonnes œuvres; (*b*) ouvrage, œuvre (d'un auteur); **the works of Shakespeare**, l'œuvre de Shakespeare; **a w. of art**, une œuvre d'art. **4.** **to be out of w.**, être sans travail, chômer. **5.** (*a*) *Mil:* **defensive works**, ouvrages défensifs; (*b*) **public works**, travaux publics; *P.N:* **road works ahead!** travaux! **6.** *pl.* rouages *mpl*, mécanisme *m*, mouvement *m* (d'une horloge). **7.** *pl.* (*often with sg. const.*) usine *f*; atelier *m*; **steel works**, aciérie *f*; **works committee**, comité *m* d'entreprise; **price ex works**, prix sortie d'usine. **8.** *attrib.* **w. bag**, sac *m* à ouvrage; **w. basket**, corbeille *f*, nécessaire *m*, à ouvrage; **w. bench**, établi *m*; **w. table**, table *f* à ouvrage. II. *v.* **1.** *v.i.* (*a*) travailler; **to w. hard**, travailler dur, ferme; **he is working on a history of the war**, il travaille à une histoire de la guerre; **to w. to rule**, faire la grève du zèle; **to w. with an end in view**, travailler pour atteindre un but; (*b*) (*of machine, etc.*) fonctionner, aller, marcher; **system that works well**, système qui fonctionne bien; **the pump isn't working**, la pompe ne marche pas; (*c*) **medicine that works**, médicament qui produit son effet, qui agit; **his plan didn't w.**, son projet n'a pas réussi; *F:* **that won't w. with me!** ça ne prend pas avec moi! **2.** *v.tr.* (*a*) faire travailler (qn); **he works his men too hard**, il surmène ses hommes; **to w. oneself to death**, se tuer au, de, travail, à travailler; (*b*) faire fonctionner, faire marcher (une machine, etc.); faire jouer (un ressort); **to be worked by electricity**, marcher à l'électricité; (*c*) faire (un miracle); (*d*) **his keys worked a hole in his pocket**, ses clefs ont fini par faire un trou dans sa poche; (*e*) broder (un dessin); **worked with silver**, lamé d'argent; (*f*) **to w. one's hands free**, parvenir à se dégager les mains; **to w. one's way through the crowd**, se frayer un chemin à travers la foule; **he was working his way through college**, il travaillait pour payer ses études; *Nau:* **to w. one's passage**, gagner son passage en travaillant; (*g*) **to w. oneself into a rage**, se mettre peu à peu en colère; (*h*) exploiter (une mine); *Com:* (*of representative*) **to w. the south-eastern area**, faire le sud-est; 'workable, *a.* **1.** (mine) exploitable. **2.** (projet) réalisable; 'worker, *s.* **1.** (*a*) travailleur, -euse; **heavy w.**, travailleur de force; **to be a hard w.**, travailleur dur; (*b*) ouvrier, -ière; **white-collar w.**, employé *m* (de bureau); **w. priest**, prêtre-ouvrier *m*. **2.** **w.** (bee), abeille ouvrière. **3.** **w. of miracles**, faiseur *m* de miracles; 'working. I. *a.* **1.** (*a*) qui travaille; ouvrier; **the w. class**, la classe ouvrière; (*b*) **w. party**, équipe *f.* **2.** qui fonctionne; (*a*) **w. parts (of a machine)**, parties *f* (d'une machine) qui travaillent; (*b*) **w. agree-**

ment, modus vivendi *m*; **w. majority,** majorité suffisante. **II.** *s.* **1.** travail *m*; **w. clothes,** vêtements *m* de travail; **w. day,** jour *m* ouvrable. **2.** (*a*) manœuvre *f* (d'une machine); (*b*) mise *f* en œuvre (d'un procédé); exploitation *f* (d'une mine); **w. expenses,** frais *m* d'exploitation; **w. capital,** fonds *m* de roulement. **3.** marche *f*, fonctionnement *m* (d'un mécanisme); **in w. order,** en état de marche. **4. the workings of the mind,** le travail de l'esprit; **'workman,** *pl.* **-men,** *s.* ouvrier *m*; **'workmanlike,** *a.* **1.** bien fait, bien travaillé. **2. in a w. manner,** avec compétence; **'workmanship,** *s.* exécution *f*; façon *f*; **sound w.,** construction soignée; **a fine piece of w.,** un beau travail; **'work 'off,** *v.* **1.** *v.tr.* se dégager de (qch.); cuver (sa colère); **to w. off one's bad temper on s.o.,** passer sa mauvaise humeur sur qn. **2.** *v.i.* (*of nut, etc.*) se détacher; **work on,** *v.i.* **1.** ['wəːk'ɔn] continuer à travailler. **2.** ['wəːkɔn] (*a*) **we have no data to w. on,** nous n'avons pas de données sur lesquelles nous baser; (*b*) **to w. on s.o.,** agir sur qn; **'work 'out,** *v.* **1.** *v.tr.* (*a*) mener à bien; **to w. out one's salvation,** faire son salut; (*b*) développer (une idée); résoudre (un problème); **the plan is being worked out,** le projet est à l'étude. **2.** *v.i.* (*a*) **how will things w. out?** à quoi tout cela aboutira-t-il? **it worked out very well for me,** ça a bien marché pour moi; (*b*) **how much does it w. out at?** par combien cela chiffre-t-il? **it works out at £100,** le total s'élève à £100; **'workroom,** *s.* atelier *m*; **'workshop,** *s.* atelier *m*; **mobile w.,** camion-atelier *m*, *pl.* camions-ateliers; **'workshy,** *a. F:* qui boude à la besogne; flemmard; **'work 'up,** *v.* **1.** *v.tr.* (*a*) développer (une situation); *Com:* **to w. up a connection,** se faire une clientèle; (*b*) préparer (un sujet); (*c*) exciter, émouvoir (qn); **to be worked up,** être emballé. **2.** *v.i.* **what are you working up to?** à quoi voulez-vous en venir?

world [wəːld], *s.* monde *m.* **1.** (*a*) **in this w.,** en ce bas monde; ici-bas; **he's not long for this w.,** il n'a pas longtemps à vivre; (*b*) **to be alone in the w.,** être seul au monde; **what in the w. is the matter with you?** mais qu'avez-vous donc? **2. to go round the w.,** faire le tour du monde; **the Old W.,** le vieux monde, le vieux continent; **the New W.,** le nouveau monde; **the ancient w.,** l'antiquité *f*; **all the w. over,** dans le monde entier; **it's a small w.!** que le monde est petit! **w. politics,** politique mondiale; **w. power,** puissance mondiale; **w. war,** guerre mondiale. **3. it's the way of the w.,** ainsi va le monde; **man of the w.,** homme qui connaît la vie; **he has gone down in the w.,** il a connu des jours meilleurs; *F:* **it's something out of this w.,** c'est quelque chose d'extraordinaire. **4.** (*a*) **the theatrical w.,** le monde, le milieu, du théâtre;

the sporting w., le monde du sport; (*b*) **that will do you a w. of good,** cela vous fera énormément de bien; **to think the w. of s.o.,** avoir une très haute opinion de qn; **'world-'famous,** *a.* de renommée mondiale; **'worldliness,** *s.* mondanité *f*; **'worldly,** *a.* **1.** du monde, de ce monde; **all his w. goods,** toute sa fortune. **2.** mondain; **'worldwide,** *a.* universel; répandu partout; mondial, -aux.

worm [wəːm]. **I.** *s.* **1.** (*a*) (**earth**)**w.,** ver *m* (de terre); *F:* **the w. has turned,** il en a assez de laisser mener par le bout du nez; (*b*) *Ent:* (i) larve *f*; (ii) mite *f*; (*c*) *Med: Vet:* **to have worms,** avoir des vers. **2.** (*a*) filet *m* (de vis); (*b*) vis *f* sans fin. **II.** *v.tr.* (*a*) **to w. one's way,** se glisser, se faufiler; **to w. oneself into s.o.'s favour,** s'insinuer dans les bonnes grâces de qn; (*b*) **to w. a secret out of s.o.,** tirer les vers du nez à qn; **'wormeaten,** *a.* vermoulu; piqué des vers; **'wormwood,** *s.* armoise amère; absinthe *f*.

worn [wəːn], *a.* usé; **w. out,** (i) (complètement) usé; (ii) (*pers.*) épuisé, éreinté.

worry ['wʌri]. **I.** *v.* (**worried**) **1.** *v.tr.* (*a*) (*of dog*) harceler (des moutons); secouer (un rat); (*b*) tourmenter, tracasser (qn); **it worries me,** cela m'inquiète; **to w. oneself,** se tourmenter; se faire du mauvais sang. **2.** *v.i.* se tourmenter, se tracasser, s'inquiéter; **don't w.!** soyez tranquille! ne vous en faites pas! *F:* **we'll w. along somehow,** on se débrouillera. **II.** *s.* ennui *m*, souci *m*; **financial worries,** soucis d'argent; **he's always been a w. to me,** il a été le tourment de ma vie; *F:* **what's your w.?** qu'est-ce qu'il y a qui cloche? **'worried,** *a.* soucieux, inquiet.

worse [wəːs]. **1.** *a. & s.* pire; plus mauvais; **in w. condition,** en plus mauvais état; **it gets w. and w.,** cela va de mal en pis; **to make matters w.,** pour comble de malheur; **it might have been w.,** ce n'est qu'un demi-mal; **I'm none the w. for it,** je ne m'en porte pas plus mal; **he escaped with nothing w. than a fright,** il en a été quitte pour la peur; **he escaped none the w.,** il s'en est tiré sans aucun mal; **so much the w. for him,** tant pis pour lui. **2.** *s.* (*a*) **there was w. to come,** le pire était à venir; **I have been through w. than that,** j'en ai vu d'autres; (*b*) **to change for the w.,** s'altérer; **he has taken a turn for the w.,** son état s'est aggravé. **3.** *adv.* (*a*) pis; plus mal; **he behaves w. than ever,** il se conduit plus mal que jamais; **you might do w.,** vous pourriez faire pis; **he's w. off than before,** sa situation s'est détériorée; il a moins d'argent qu'avant; (*b*) **the noise went on w. than ever,** le vacarme a recommencé de plus belle; **'worsen. 1.** *v.tr.* empirer; aggraver. **2.** *v.i.* empirer; s'aggraver; se détériorer; se gâter.

worship ['wəːʃip]. **I.** *v.tr.* (**worshipped**) **1.** adorer

(Dieu). **2.** adorer (qn); avoir un culte pour (qn); **to w. money,** faire de l'argent son idole; **he worships the ground she treads on,** il baise la trace de ses pas. **II.** *s.* **1.** (*a*) culte *m*; **place of w.,** église *f*; temple *m*; **times of w.,** heures *f* des offices; (*b*) **to be an object of w.,** être un objet d'adoration. **2. his W. the Mayor,** Monsieur le maire; **yes, your W.,** oui, (i) Monsieur le maire, (ii) Monsieur le juge; '**worshipful,** *a.* (*a*) honorable; (*b*) (*freemasonry*) vénérable; '**worshipper,** *s.* adorateur, -trice; (*in church*) the worshippers, les fidèles *m*.

worst [wɔːst]. **1.** *a.* (le) pire, (le) plus mauvais; **his w. mistake,** sa plus grave erreur; **his w. enemy,** son pire ennemi. **2.** *s.* **the w. of the storm is over,** le plus fort de la tempête est passé; **that's the w. of cheap shoes,** c'est là l'inconvénient des chaussures bon marché; **when things are at their w.,** quand les choses sont au pire; (*in a fight*) **to get the w. of it,** avoir le dessous; **at the w.,** au pis aller; **if the w. comes to the w.,** en mettant les choses au pire; **the w. has happened,** c'est la catastrophe; **do your w.!** allez-y! **3.** *adv.* (le) pis, (le) plus mal; **that frightened me w. of all,** c'est cela qui m'a effrayé le plus.

worsted ['wustid], *s.* laine peignée.

worth [wɔːθ]. **1.** *a.* (*a*) **to be w. so much,** valoir tant; **that's w. something,** cela a de la valeur; **whatever it may be w.,** vaille que vaille; **it's not w. the money,** cela ne vaut pas le prix, n'est pas avantageux; **I'm telling you this for what it's w.,** je vous dis cela sans y attribuer grande valeur; (*b*) **it's not w. the trouble, w. it,** cela ne vaut pas la peine; **book w. reading,** livre qui mérite d'être lu; **a thing w. having,** une chose précieuse, utile; **it's w. thinking about,** cela mérite réflexion; **it's w. knowing,** c'est bon à savoir; (*c*) **he's w. millions,** il est riche à millions; c'est un millionnaire; **to die w. a million,** mourir en laissant un million; **that's all I'm w.,** voilà tout mon avoir; **to run for all one is w.,** courir de toutes ses forces, à toute vitesse. **2.** *s.* valeur *f*; **give me a pound's w.,** donnez-m'en pour une livre; **to want one's money's w.,** en vouloir pour son argent; '**worthless,** *a.* sans valeur; mauvais; '**worthlessness,** *s.* peu *m* de valeur; nature *f* méprisable; '**worth'while,** *a.* qui en vaut l'effort, la peine, *F:* le coup.

worthy ['wɔːði], *a.* digne; estimable; **to be w. of sth.,** être digne de qch.; **the town has no museum w. of the name,** la ville n'a aucun musée digne de ce nom; '**worthily,** *adv.* **1.** dignement. **2.** à juste titre; '**worthiness,** *s.* mérite *m*.

wound [wuːnd]. **1.** *s.* (*a*) blessure *f*; (*b*) plaie *f*. **II.** *v.tr.* blesser; faire une blessure à (qn); **to w. s.o.'s feelings,** froisser qn; **the wounded,** les blessés.

woven ['wouv(ə)n], *a.* tissé.

wrap [ræp]. **I.** *v.tr.* (**wrapped**) **1.** (*a*) envelopper; **to w. sth. (up) in paper,** envelopper qch. dans du papier; (*b*) **to w. (oneself) up,** se couvrir (de vêtements chauds), s'emmitoufler; (*c*) **to be wrapped up in one's work,** être entièrement absorbé par son travail; **to be wrapped in mystery,** être entouré de mystère; **wrapped up in one's thoughts,** plongé dans ses pensées. **2. to w. sth. round sth.,** enrouler qch. autour de qch.; *F:* **he wrapped his car round a tree,** il a encadré un arbre. **II.** *s.* châle *m*; *pl.* **wraps,** couvertures *f*; '**wrapper,** *s.* couverture *f* (d'un livre); bande *f* (de journal); '**wrapping,** *s.* **1.** emballage *m*; mise *f* en paquet(s). **2.** (*a*) enveloppe *f*, couverture *f*; (*b*) papier *m*, toile *f*, d'emballage; **w. paper,** papier d'emballage; '**wrap-round,** *a.* **w.-r. rear window,** lunette *f* arrière panoramique.

wreath [riːθ], *s.* **1.** couronne *f*, guirlande *f* (de fleurs); (*for funeral*) couronne mortuaire. **2.** volute *f*, panache *m* (de fumée); **wreathe** [riːð], *v.tr.* enguirlander; couronner de fleurs; **face wreathed in smiles,** visage rayonnant; **mountain wreathed in mist,** montagne couronnée de brouillard.

wreck [rek]. **I.** *s.* **1.** (*a*) épave *f*; navire naufragé; (*b*) **the building is a total w.,** le bâtiment n'est qu'une ruine; **my car's a complete w.,** ma voiture est bonne pour la casse; (*c*) **human w.,** épave humaine; **to be a nervous w.,** avoir les nerfs détraqués. **2.** (*a*) naufrage *m* (d'un navire); **to be saved from the w.,** échapper au naufrage; (*b*) *Rail: N.Am:* **w. train,** convoi *m* de secours. **II.** *v.tr.* (*a*) causer le naufrage d'(un navire); **to be wrecked,** faire naufrage; (*b*) faire dérailler (un train); démolir, détruire (un bâtiment); (*c*) faire échouer, saboter (une entreprise); détruire, ruiner (les espérances de qn); '**wreckage,** *s.* épaves éparses; débris *mpl*; **wrecked,** *a.* naufragé; **w. life,** existence brisée; '**wrecker,** *s.* **1.** naufrageur *m*; pilleur *m* d'épaves. **2.** destructeur *m*; démolisseur *m*; dérailleur *m* (de trains). **3.** *N.Am:* (*a*) membre *m* d'une équipe de secours; (*b*) *Aut:* camion *m* de dépannage; dépanneuse *f*; *Rail:* convoi *m* de secours; *Nau:* navire qui va au secours d'un navire naufragé; '**wrecking,** *s.* (*a*) destruction *f* (d'un navire, etc.); déraillement *m* (d'un train); (*b*) *N.Am:* **w. crew,** équipe *f* de secours.

wren [ren], *s.* **1.** *Orn:* troglodyte mignon, *F:* roitelet *m*; **golden-crested w.,** roitelet huppé. **2.** *F:* membre *m* du *Women's Royal Naval Service* (WRNS).

wrench [rentʃ]. **I.** *s.* **1.** (*a*) mouvement violent de torsion; **to pull sth. off with a w.,** arracher qch. d'un effort violent; (*b*) **he gave his ankle a w.,** il s'est donné une entorse; **it will be a w. to leave,** il m'en coûtera de partir. **2.** clef *f* (à écrous);

tourne-à-gauche *m inv*; **adjustable w., monkey w.,** clef anglaise, clef à molette. **II.** *v.tr.* (*a*) tordre; tourner violemment; **to w. a lid off,** arracher un couvercle (avec un effort violent); (*b*) **to w. oneself free,** se dégager d'une secousse; (*c*) **to w. one's ankle,** se fouler la cheville; **to w. one's shoulder,** se démettre l'épaule.

wrestle [resl], *v.i.* (*a*) **to w. with s.o.,** lutter avec, contre, qn; (*b*) **to w. with (sth.),** lutter contre (les difficultés); résister à (la tentation); s'attaquer à (un problème); **'wrestler,** *s.* lutteur *m*; **'wrestling,** *s.* lutte *f* (corps à corps); **all-in w.,** catch *m*.

wretch [retʃ], *s.* **1.** malheureux, -euse; infortuné, -ée; **poor w.,** pauvre diable *m*. **2.** (*a*) scélérat, -ate; (*b*) **you little w.!** petit fripon! petite friponne! **wretched** ['retʃid], *a.* **1.** (*of pers.*) misérable; malheureux; infortuné; **to feel w.,** (i) être mal en train; ne pas être dans son assiette; (ii) avoir le cafard; **to look w.,** avoir l'air malheureux. **2.** (*a*) pitoyale; lamentable; **what w. weather!** quel temps de chien! (*b*) pauvre, minable; (*c*) **where's my w. umbrella?** où est ce diable de parapluie? **what's that w. boy doing?** qu'est-ce qu'il fait, ce sacré garçon? **-ly,** *adv.* **1.** misérablement. **2.** de façon pitoyable, lamentable; **to be w. poor,** être dans la misère; **w. ill,** malade comme un chien.

wrick [rik]. **I.** *s.* **to have a w. in the neck,** avoir le torticolis. **II.** *v.tr.* **to w. one's neck,** se donner un torticolis; **to w. one's ankle,** se fouler la cheville, se donner une entorse.

wriggle [rigl]. **I.** *v.* **1.** *v.i.* se tortiller; **to w. out of a difficulty,** se tirer d'une position difficile; **to try to w. out of it,** chercher une échappatoire. **2.** *v.tr.* **to w. one's toes,** remuer, agiter, les orteils; **to w. one's way into . . .,** se faufiler, s'insinuer, dans . . .; **'wriggler,** *s.* enfant *mf* qui ne sait pas se tenir tranquille; **'wriggling,** *s.* tortillement *m*.

wring [riŋ], *v.tr.* (**wrung** [rʌŋ]; **wrung**) **1.** tordre; **to w. (out) the washing,** tordre, essorer, le linge; **to w. the neck of a chicken,** tordre le cou à un poulet; *F:* **I'd like to w. your neck!** tu m'exaspères, à la fin! **2.** arracher (un secret à qn); extorquer (de l'argent à qn); **'wringing,** *a.* **w. wet,** (i) (*of clothes*) mouillé à tordre; (ii) (*of pers.*) trempé jusqu'aux os.

wrinkle [riŋkl]. **I.** *s.* (*a*) (*on face*) ride *f*; (*b*) rugosité *f*; (*on water*) ondulation *f*, ride; (*c*) (*in garment*) faux pli. **II.** *v.* **1.** *v.tr.* rider, plisser; **to w. one's forehead,** froncer les sourcils; **her stockings were wrinkled,** ses bas' tirebouchonnaient. **2.** *v.i.* se rider; faire des plis.

wrist [rist], *s.* poignet *m*; **w. bone,** os *m* du carpe, le carpe; **w. watch,** montre-bracelet *f*.

writ [rit], *s. Jur:* acte *m* judiciaire; mandat *m*; **to**

serve a **w. on s.o.,** assigner qn en justice.

write [rait], *v.tr.* (**wrote** [rout]; **written** ['rit(ə)n]) **1.** écrire; **how is it written?** comment cela s'écrit-il? **to w. sth. down,** inscrire qch., noter qch.; **his guilt was written in his eyes,** on lisait dans ses yeux qu'il était coupable. **2.** écrire (une lettre, un roman); rédiger (un article); **he writes for the papers,** il fait du journalisme; **he writes,** il est écrivain; **he wrote to me yesterday,** il m'a écrit hier; *F:* **that's nothing to w. home about,** ça n'a rien d'extraordinaire; ça c'est plutôt moche! **'writer,** *s.* **1. to be a good, bad, w.,** avoir une belle, une mauvaise, écriture. **2.** écrivain *m*; auteur *m*; **woman w.,** (femme) auteur; **'writing,** *s.* **1.** écriture *f*; **good, bad, w.,** bonne, mauvaise, écriture; **to answer in w.,** répondre par écrit; **w. desk,** secrétaire *m*, bureau *m*; **w. paper,** papier *m* à lettres. **2. the w. profession,** le métier d'écrivain; **the art of w.,** l'art d'écrire; *pl.* **writings,** ouvrages *m* littéraires; œuvre *m* (d'un auteur); **'write 'off,** *v.tr.* (*a*) *Fin:* **to w. off capital,** réduire le capital; amortir du capital; (*b*) *Com:* défalquer (une mauvaise créance); **to w. off so much for wear and tear,** déduire tant pour l'usure; **three machines were written off,** il y a eu trois appareils de détruits; **'write-off,** *s.* perte totale; **the car's a w.-o.,** la voiture est bonne pour la casse; **'write 'up,** *v.tr.* **1.** *Journ:* écrire, rédiger (un fait-divers). **2.** mettre (son agenda) à jour; *Sch:* **w. up your notes,** recopiez vos notes; **'write-up,** *s. Journ:* article *m*; **a good w.-up,** un article élogieux; **'written,** *a.* écrit; **w. consent,** consentement *m* par écrit.

wrong [rɔŋ]. **I.** *a.* **1.** mauvais; mal *inv*; **stealing is w., it is w. to steal,** c'est mal de voler. **2.** (*a*) incorrect, inexact; faux, *f.* fausse; **w. calculation,** calcul faux; **my watch is w.,** ma montre n'est pas à l'heure; (*b*) (*of pers.*) **to be w.,** avoir tort; se tromper. **3.** (*a*) **to be in the w. place,** ne pas être à sa place; **to drive on the w. side of the road,** circuler à contre-voie; *F:* **to get out of bed on the w. side,** se lever du pied gauche; **your shirt's w. side out,** votre chemise est à l'envers; **to stroke a cat the w. way,** caresser un chat à rebrousse-poil; **you're doing it the w. way,** vous vous y prenez mal; (*of food*) **it went down the w. way,** je l'ai avalé de travers; *F:* **to be on the w. side of forty,** avoir (dé)passé la quarantaine; (*b*) **I went to the w. house,** je me suis trompé de maison; **that's the w. book,** ce n'est pas là le livre qu'il faut; **to be on the w. track,** suivre une mauvaise piste; **to do, say, the w. thing,** commettre un impair; *Tp:* **w. number,** erreur *f* de numéro; *Mus:* **w. note,** fausse note. **4. what's w. with you?** qu'avez-vous? **what do you find w. with this book?** qu'est-ce que vous reprochez à ce livre?

something's w. (somewhere), il y a quelque
chose qui ne va pas, qui cloche; **I hope
nothing's w.**, j'espère qu'il n'est rien arrivé (de
malheureux); -**ly,** *adv.* **1.** à tort, à faux; **rightly
or w.**, à tort ou à raison. **2.** mal. **II.** *s.* **1.** mal *m*;
to know right from w., distinguer le bien et le
mal; **two wrongs do not make a right**, deux
noirs ne font pas un blanc. **2.** (*a*) tort *m*, injustice *f*; (*b*) *Jur:* dommage *m*, préjudice *m*. **3.**
to be in the w., avoir tort; être dans son tort.
III. *adv.* **1.** mal; (*a*) inexactement, incorrectement; (*b*) à tort, à faux; *F:* **you've got**
me w.**, vous m'avez mal compris. **2. to go w.**,
(i) faire fausse route; (ii) se tromper; (iii) mal
tourner; (iv) (*of machinery*) se détraquer; être
en panne; **everything's going w.**, tout va mal.
IV. *v.tr.* (*a*) faire (du) tort à (qn); faire injure à
(qn); (*b*) être injuste pour, envers (qn);
'**wrongful,** *a.* injuste; **w. dismissal**, renvoi injustifié (d'un employé); -**fully,** *adv.* injustement; à tort.

wrought [rɔːt], *a.* **w. iron**, fer forgé.

wry |rai|, *a.* tordu; de travers; **a w. smile**, un petit
sourire forcé.

X

X, x |eks|, *s.* **1.** (la lettre) X, x *m*; *Cin:* **X certificate** = interdit aux moins de 18 ans. **2. X-rays,** rayons *m* X; **deep X-rays,** rayons X pénétrants: **X-ray examination,** examen *m* radiographique: **X-ray treatment,** radiothérapie *f*; **X-ray,** *v.tr.* radiographier (qn).

Xmas |'krismǝs|, *s. F:* Noël *m.*
xylophone |'zailǝfoun|, *s. Mus:* xylophone *m*; **xy'lophonist** [-'lɔf-], *s.* joueur, -euse, de xylophone.

Y

Y, y [wai], s. (la lettre) Y, y *m*; i grec.
yacht [jɔt]. **I.** s. yacht *m*; **y. club,** yacht-club *m, pl.* yacht-clubs. **II.** *v.i.* faire du yachting; **'yachting,** s. yachting *m*; **'yachtsman,** *pl.* -men, s. yachtman *m, pl.* yachtmen.
yak [jæk], s. *Z:* ya(c)k *m.*
yam [jæm], s. *Bot:* igname *f.*
yank¹ [jæŋk]. *F:* **I.** *v.tr.* tirer (d'un coup sec); **to y. out a tooth,** arracher une dent d'un seul coup. **II.** s. secousse *f,* saccade *f*; **give it a y.!** tirez bien fort!
Yank², Yankee ['jæŋki], s. *F:* (a) *U.S:* habitant, -ante, des États du Nord; (b) Américain, -aine (des États-Unis); Yankee *m.*
yap [jæp]. **I.** *v.i.* **(yapped)** japper. **II.** s. jappement *m,* glapissement *m* (d'un chien); **'yapping. I.** *a.* jappeur, -euse; glapissant. **II.** s. = YAP II.
yard¹ [jɑːd], s. **1.** *Meas:* yard *m* (0 m. 914). **2.** *Nau:* vergue *f*; **'yardage,** s. = métrage *m*; **'yardarm,** s. *Nau:* bout *m* de vergue.
yard², s. (a) cour *f* (d'une maison); (b) **New Scotland Y.,** *F:* **the Y.** = la Sûreté; (c) chantier *m*; dépôt *m*; **builder's, contractor's, y.,** dépôt de matériaux; *Rail:* **goods y.,** dépôt de marchandises; **marshalling y.,** gare *f* de triage.
yarn [jɑːn], s. **1.** *Tex:* fil *m*; filé *m* (de coton). **2.** histoire *f,* conte *m*; **he can tell a good y.,** c'est un bon raconteur; **to spin a y.,** mentir, en conter.
yawn [jɔːn]. **I.** *v.* **1.** *v.i.* bâiller. **2.** *v.tr.* **to y. one's head off,** bâiller à se décrocher la mâchoire. **II.** s. bâillement *m*; **to stifle a y.,** étouffer un bâillement; **'yawning,** s. bâillement *m.*
year [jəːr, jiər], s. an *m*; année *f*; (a) **in the y. 1850,** en l'an 1850; **last y.,** l'an dernier; l'année dernière; **a y. last March,** il y a eu un an au mois de mars; **to have ten thousand a y.,** avoir dix mille livres de revenu; **to be ten years old,** avoir dix ans; (b) **the New Y.,** le nouvel an; **New Year's Day,** le jour de l'an; **New Year's Eve,** la Saint-Sylvestre; **to see the New Y. in,** faire la veillée, le réveillon, de la Saint-Sylvestre; **to wish s.o. a happy New Y.,** souhaiter la bonne année à qn; (c) **calendar y.,** année civile; **leap y.,** année bissextile; **school y.,** année scolaire; **he's in my y.,** il est de ma promotion, c'est un camarade de classe; *Com:* **financial y.,** exercice *m*; **to rent sth. by the y.,** louer qch. à l'année; **from one y. to the next,** d'un bout de l'année à l'autre; **all the y.**

round, tout au long de l'année; **y. in y. out, y. after y.,** une année après l'autre; **years ago,** il y a bien des années; (d) **from his earliest years,** dès son enfance; **old for his years,** (i) plus vieux que son âge; (ii) (*of child*) précoce; **he's getting on in years,** il prend de l'âge; il n'est plus jeune; (e) *F:* **I haven't seen you for (donkey's) years,** voilà une éternité que je ne vous ai pas vu; **it's enough to put years on one,** c'est à vous donner des cheveux blancs; **'yearbook,** s. annuaire *m*; **'yearling,** s. animal d'une an; **y. colt,** poulain *m* d'un an; **'yearly. 1.** *a.* annuel; (location) à l'année. **2.** *adv.* annuellement.
yearn [jəːn], *v.i.* **to y. for sth.,** mourir d'envie de qch.; **'yearning,** s. désir ardent, envie *f* (**for, de**).
yeast [jiːst], s. levure *f.*
yell [jel]. **I.** *v.i.* hurler; crier à tue-tête. **II.** s. hurlement *m*; cri aigu.
yellow ['jelou]. **1.** *a.* (a) jaune; **the y. races,** les races jaunes; **y. fever,** fièvre *f* jaune; (b) *F:* (*of pers.*) poltron, lâche. **2.** s. jaune *m*; **chrome y.,** jaune de chrome; **'yellowhammer,** s. *Orn:* bruant *m* jaune; **'yellowish,** *a.* jaunâtre; **'yellowness,** s. teinte *f* jaune (de qch.); teint *m* jaune (de qn).
yelp [jelp]. **I.** *v.i.* japper, glapir. **II.** s. (*also* **yelping**) jappement *m,* glapissement *m.*
Yemen (the) [ðə 'jemən]. *Pr.n.* le Yémen.
yen [jen], s. *F:* **to have a y. for sth.,** avoir un désir obsédant de qch., une envie folle de qch.
yes [jes], *adv.* (a) oui; (*contradicting*) si; **to answer y. or no,** répondre par oui ou non; **y., of course,** mais oui, bien sûr; (b) (*interrogatively*) (i) vraiment? (ii) et puis après? (c) *F:* **y. man,** beni-oui-oui *m inv.*
yesterday ['jestədi], *adv. & s.* hier (*m*); **the day before y.,** avant-hier (*m*); **y. week,** il y a eu hier huit jours; **y. morning,** hier (au) matin; **y. was the tenth,** c'était hier le dix.
yet [jet]. **1.** *adv.* (a) déjà; jusqu'ici; **not y.,** pas encore; **it won't happen just y.,** nous n'en sommes pas encore là; **nothing has been done (as) y.,** jusqu'ici, jusqu'à présent, on n'a rien fait; (b) malgré tout; **he'll win y.,** malgré tout il gagnera. **2.** *conj.* néanmoins, cependant, tout de même; **y. I like him,** cependant, malgré tout, tout de même, il me plaît.
yew [juː], s. **y. (tree),** if *m.*
Yid [jid], s. *P: Pej:* youpin, -ine; **'Yiddish,** *a. & s. Ling:* judéo-allemand (*m*), yiddish (*m*).

yield [ji:ld]. **I.** *s.* production *f*; rapport *m*; rendement *m*; récolte *f*; **a good y.** of wheat, une bonne récolte de blé; **these shares give a poor y.**, ces actions rapportent mal; **net y.**, revenu net. **II.** *v.* **1.** *v.tr.* (*a*) rendre, donner; (*b*) rapporter, produire; **money that yields interest,** argent qui rapporte; (*c*) céder (du terrain, un droit). **2.** *v.i.* (*a*) se rendre; céder (**to,** à); (*b*) s'affaisser, fléchir, plier; **the plank yielded under our weight,** la planche a cédé sous notre poids; **'yielding,** *s.* **1.** rendement *m.* **2.** soumission *f.* **3.** affaissement *m*, fléchissement *m*.

yodel [joudl], *v.i.* (**yodel(l)ed**) iouler, jodler.

yoke [jouk]. **I.** *s.* **1.** joug *m*; **y. oxen,** bœufs *m* d'attelage. **2.** empiècement *m* (d'une robe). **II.** *v.tr.* accoupler (des bœufs).

yolk [jouk], *s.* jaune *m* d'œuf.

you [ju:], *pers.pron.* (i) vous; (ii) *sg.* (*to relative, child, animal*) tu, te, toi; (*a*) (*subject*) vous; tu; **y. are very kind,** vous êtes bien aimable(s); tu es bien aimable; **there y. are,** vous voilà; te voila; (*b*) (*object*) vous; te; **I'll see y. tomorrow,** je vous, te, reverrai demain; (*c*) (*after prep.*) **between y. and me,** (i) entre vous et moi; entre toi et moi; (ii) entre nous soit dit; **there's a fine apple for y.!** regardez-moi ça, si ce n'est pas une belle pomme! *F:* **go on with y.!** à d'autres! pour qui me prends-tu? (*d*) **y. and I will go by train,** vous et moi, nous prendrons le train; **if I were y.,** (si j'étais) à votre place; **is it y.?** est-ce (bien) vous, toi? *F:* **hi! y. there!** eh! dites donc, là-bas! (*e*) **y. Frenchmen,** vous autres Français; **y. idiot (y.)!** espèce d'imbécile! (*f*) (*indefinite*) on; **y. never can tell,** on ne sait jamais.

young [jʌŋ]. **1.** *a.* (*a*) jeune; **younger son, daughter,** fils cadet, fille cadette; **the youngest,** le, la, plus jeune; le cadet, la cadette; **when I was twenty years younger,** quand j'avais vingt ans de moins; **you're looking years younger!** comme vous avez rajeuni! **I'm not as y. as I was,** je n'ai plus mes jambes de vingt ans; **we are only y. once,** la jeunesse n'a qu'un temps; **y. Mr Thomas,** (i) M. Thomas fils; (ii) le jeune M. Thomas; (*b*) **the night is still y.,** la nuit n'est que peu avancée; (*c*) *F:* **lake like a y. sea,** lac

grand comme une petite mer. **2.** *s.pl. inv.* (*a*) **the y.,** les jeunes; la jeunesse; **the y. and the not so y.,** les jeunes et les moins jeunes; **books for the y.,** livres pour la jeunesse; (*b*) **animal and its y.,** animal et ses petits; **'youngster,** *s.* un, une, jeune; **the youngsters,** (i) les jeunes; (ii) les enfants, les gosses.

your [jɔːr], *poss. a.* **1.** (i) votre, *pl.* vos; (ii) *sg.*(*of relative, child, animal*) ton, ta, *pl.* tes; **y. house,** votre maison; ta maison; **y. friends,** vos ami(e)s; tes ami(e)s; **have you hurt y. hand?** vous vous êtes fait mal à la main? **y. turn!** à vous, à toi (de jouer)! **2.** (*indefinite*) son, sa, *pl.* ses; **you cannot alter y. nature,** on ne peut pas changer son caractère; **y. true reformer,** le vrai réformateur; **yours,** *poss.pron.* (i) le vôtre, la vôtre, les vôtres; (ii) *sg.* (*of relative, child, animal*) le tien, la tienne, les tiens, les tiennes; **this book is y.,** ce livre est à vous, à toi; **is it really y.?** c'est bien le vôtre, le tien? **he's a friend of y.,** c'est un de vos, de tes, amis; *F:* **what's y.?** qu'est-ce que tu prends? **y our'self,** *pl.* **your'selves,** *pers.pron.* vous-même; toi-même; (*a*) **do you do the cooking y.?** est-ce que vous faites la cuisine vous-même? *F:* **he's a do it y. enthusiast,** c'est un bricoleur passionné; (*b*) **have you hurt y.?** est-ce que vous vous êtes fait mal? est-ce que tu t'es fait mal? **are you enjoying y.?** vous amusez-vous? (*c*) **are you living by y.?** est-ce que vous vivez seul? **see for yourselves,** voyez vous-mêmes.

youth, *pl.* **-s** [ju:θ, ju:ðz], *s.* **1.** (*a*) jeunesse *f*; adolescence *f*; **from y. upwards,** dès sa jeunesse; (*b*) **y. club,** club *m* des jeunes; **y. hostel,** auberge *f* de la jeunesse; **y. hosteller,** ajiste *mf*; **y. hostelling,** ajisme *m.* **2.** jeune homme; adolescent *m.* **3.** *coll.* les jeunes; **'youthful,** *a.* (*a*) jeune; juvénile; **to look y.,** avoir l'air jeune; (*b*) **y. indiscretions,** erreurs *f* de jeunesse; **'youthfulness,** *s.* jeunesse *f*; air *m* de jeunesse.

yowl [jaul], *v.i.* (*of dog*) hurler; (*of cat*) miauler; *F:* (*of child*) pleurnicher.

Yugoslavia [ju:gou'slɑ:viə]. *Pr.n.* la Yougoslavie; **'Yugoslav,** *a. & s.* yougoslave (*mf*).

Yule [ju:l], *s.* **Y. log,** bûche *f* de Noël.

Z

Z, z [zed, *N.Am:* zi:], *s.* (la lettre) Z, z *m.*
Zaire [zaii:ər]. *Pr.n.* le Zaïre.
Zambezi [zæm'bi:zi]. *Pr.n.* the (river) Z., le Zambèze.
Zambia ['zæmbiə]. *Pr.n.* la Zambie.
zeal [zi:l], *s.* zèle *m*; empressement *m*; **zealot** ['zelət], *s.* fanatique *mf*; **'zealous** ['zel-], *a.* zélé; empressé; **-ly**, *adv.* avec zèle.
zebra ['zebrə, 'zi:brə], *s. Z:* zèbre *m*; **z. crossing** = passage *m* pour piétons, passage clouté.
zenith ['zeniθ], *s. Astr:* zénith *m.*
zephyr ['zefər], *s.* zéphyr *m.*
zero, *pl.* **-os** ['ziərou, -ouz], *s.* zéro *m*; *Mil: etc:* **z. hour,** l'heure *f* de l'attaque; l'heure H: **his enthusiasm had sunk to z.,** son enthousiasme était à zéro.
zest [zest], *s.* (*a*) enthousiasme *m*, entrain *m*; **to eat with z.,** manger avec appétit; (*b*) saveur *f,* goût *m*; **this added a bit of z. to the adventure,** cela a donné du piquant à l'aventure.
Zeus [zju:s]. *Pr.n.* Zeus.
zigzag ['zigzæg]. **I.** *s.* zigzag *m*; **in zigzags,** en zigzag. **II.** *v.i.* zigzaguer; faire des zigzags.
zinc [ziŋk], *s.* zinc *m*; **z. plating,** zingage *m.*
zing [ziŋ], *s. N.Am: F:* vitalité *f.*
zinnia ['ziniə], *s. Bot:* zinnia *m.*
Zion ['zaiən]. *Pr.n.* Sion *m*; **'Zionism,** *s. Pol:* sionisme *m*; **'Zionist,** *a. & s. Pol:* sioniste (*mf*).
zip [zip]. **I.** *s.* **1.** sifflement *m* (d'une balle). **2.** *F:* énergie *f*; **put a bit of z. into it,** mettez-y du nerf. **3. z. fastener,** fermeture *f* éclair (*R.t.m.*);

Belg: tirette-éclair *f.* **4.** *N.Am:* **z. code,** code postal. **II.** *v.* (zipped) **1.** *v.i.* siffler (comme une balle); **to z. past,** passer comme un éclair. **2.** *v.tr. F:* **can you z. me up?** peux-tu m'aider avec ma fermeture éclair? **'zippy,** *a. F:* plein d'entrain; **look z.!** grouille-toi!
zircon ['zə:kən], *s.* zircon *m.*
zither ['ziθər, 'ziδ-], *s. Mus:* cithare *f.*
zodiac ['zoudiæk], *s.* zodiaque *m.*
zombie ['zɔmbi], *s.* zombi *m.*
zone [zoun]. **I.** *s.* zone *f*; **time z.,** fuseau *m* horaire; *Geog:* **torrid z.,** zone torride; **the Canal Z.,** la Zone du Canal (de Panama); **frontier z.,** zone frontière; *Mil:* **war z.,** zone des armées; **danger z.,** zone dangereuse; *Rad:* **skip, silent, z.,** zone de silence. **II.** *v.tr.* répartir (une ville, etc.) en zones; **'zonal,** *a.* zonal, -aux; **'zoning,** *s.* zonage *m*, répartition *f* en zones.
zoo [zu:], *s.* zoo *m.*
zoology [zu:'ɔlədʒi, zou-], *s.* zoologie *f.* **zoo'logical** [zu:(ə)-], *a.* zoologique; **z. gardens,** jardin *m* zoologique; **zo'ologist,** *s.* zoologiste *mf.*
zoom [zu:m]. **I.** *s.* **1.** bourdonnement *m*, vrombissement *m.* **2.** *Av:* montée *f* en chandelle. **II.** *v.i.* **1.** bourdonner; vrombir. **2.** *Av:* monter en chandelle; *F:* **he suddenly zoomed up,** il est arrivé en trombe; **he zoomed past,** il est passé comme une flèche.
Zulu ['zu:lu:], *a. & s.* zoulou, -oue; du Zoulouland; **'Zululand.** *Pr.n.* le Zoulouland

Common Abbreviations

Abbreviations read as initials unless the phonetic spelling is shown.

Abréviations courantes

Les abréviations se lisent comme lettres initiales à moins que la prononciation phonétique ne soit donnée.

AA, *Automobile Association.*
AC, *El: alternating current,* courant alternatif, c.a.
acc., *Com: account,* compte, cpte.
AD, *anno Domini,* après Jésus-Christ, ap(r)., J.-C.
ag., *agriculture,* agriculture, agr.
AGM, *Annual General Meeting.*
agr(ic)., *agriculture,* agriculture, agr.
a.m., *ante meridiem,* a.m.
amp., *El: ampere,* ampère, amp.
&, *ampersand,* et commercial.
anon, *anonymous.*
appro., *approval;* **on a.,** à l'essai.
approx., *approximately.*
Apr., *April,* avril.
ASAP, *as soon as possible.*
ass(oc)., *association,* association, A.
asst., *assistant.*
Aug., *August,* août.
AV, *audio-visual.*
Av., *avenue,* avenue, av.
avdp., *Meas: avoirdupois,* avoirdupois, avdp.
avoir., *Meas: avoirdupois,* avoirdupois, avdp.
AWOL, *Mil: absent without leave,* absent sans permission.

b., *born,* né(e).
BA, 1. *Bachelor of Arts.* 2. *British Airways.*
b. & b., *bed and breakfast.*
BBC, *British Broadcasting Corporation.*
BC, *before Christ,* avant Jésus-Christ, av. J.-C.
BCG, (vaccin) bilié (de) Calmette et Guérin, BCG.
bldg, *building.*
BM, *British Museum.*
Boul., *Boulevard,* boulevard, b(l)d, boul.

Br., *Ecc: Brother,* Frère, Fr.
br., *branch,* succursale, succ(le).
BR, *British Rail(ways).*
BRS, *British Road Services.*
BSc., *Bachelor of Science.*
BST, *British Summer Time,* heure légale d'été (en Grande-Bretagne).

C. 1. *Ph: Celsius, centigrade,* Celsius, centigrade, C. 2. *El: coulomb,* coulomb, coul., C.
c. 1. *hundred,* cent, c. 2. *Num: centime,* centime, c., cent. 3. *circa, about,* vers.
cap. 1. *Fin: capital,* capital, cap. 2. *Geog: capital,* capitale, cap. 3. *Typ: capital (letter),* majuscule.
Capt., *Mil: Captain,* capitaine, Cap.
CAT, *College of Advanced Technology.*
cc., *cubic centimetre(s),* centimètre(s) cube(s), cc.
c.c., *cubic centimetre(s),* centimètre(s) cube(s), cc.
Cdr., *Navy: Commander.*
cent. 1. *hundred,* cent, c. 2. *Num: centime,* centime, c., cent.
cert., *Sch: certificate,* certificat, certif.
cf., *confer,* cf.
cg., *Meas: centigramme,* centigramme, cg.
chw., *constant hot water.*
CIA, *U.S: Central Intelligence Agency.*
CID, *Criminal Investigation Department* = police judiciaire, PJ.
CIF, *Com: cost, insurance, and freight,* coût, assurance, fret, CAF.
C.-in-C., *Mil: Commander-in-Chief,* commandant en chef.
cl., *Meas: centilitre,* centilitre, cl.
cm., *Meas: centimetre,* centimètre, cm.; **cm²,**

square centimetre(s), centimètre(s) carré(s), cm²; **cm³**, *cubic centimetre(s)*, centimètre(s) cube(s), cm³.

CO, *Mil: Commanding Officer*, officier commandant.

c/o., *care of*, aux (bons) soins de.

Co., *Com: Company*, Compagnie, Cie, Société, Sté.

COD, *cash on delivery*, contre remboursement.

C. of E., *Church of England*.

Col., *Mil: Colonel*, colonel, Col.

com(m)., *Com: commission*, commission, com.

Co-op, *Co-operative Society*.

Corp., *Corporation*.

CP, *Com: carriage paid*, port payé, p.p.

cp., *compare*.

c.p.s., *El.E: cycles per second*, hertz, Hz.

cr., *Book-k: credit*, crédit, cr., avoir, Av.

cu., *cubic*.

CV, *curriculum vitae*, CV.

cwt., *Meas: hundredweight*.

d. 1. *day*, jour, jr. **2.** *deceased, died*, mort, m. **3.** *Num: A: denarius*, penny. **4.** *Book-k: debit*, débit, déb.

db., dB., *decibel*, décibel, dB.

DC, 1. *El: direct current*, courant continu, c.c. **2.** *Mus: da capo*, DC. **3.** *U.S: Geog: District of Columbia*.

DDT, *Ch:* dichloro-diphényl-trichloréthane, DDT.

deb., *Book-k: debit*, débit, déb.

Dec., *December*, décembre, déc., Xbre.

dec., *deceased*, mort, m.

deg., *degree*, degré.

Dept., *department*.

Dip.Ed., *Diploma of Education* = Certificat d'aptitude au professorat de l'enseignement secondaire, CAPES.

dist., *Adm: district*, arrondissement, arr.

div. 1. *St.Exch: dividend*, dividende, div. **2.** *Mil: division*, division, div.

DJ, 1. *dinner jacket*, smoking. **2.** *disc jockey*, présentateur de disques.

DNA, *desoxyribonucleic acid*, acide désoxyribonucléique, ADN.

do, *ditto*, dito, do, d°.

dol., *dollar*, dollar, dol(l), $.

doz., *dozen*, douzaine, douz., dz.

Dr, *Doctor*, docteur, Dr.

E., *east*, est, E.

E. & O. E., *Com: errors and omissions excepted*, erreur ou omission exceptée, e.o.o.e., e. & o.e., sauf erreur ou omission, s.e. & o., s.e. ou o.

ECG, *electrocardiogram*, électrocardiogramme, ECG.

ECSC, *European Coal and Steel Community*,

Communauté européenne du charbon et de l'acier, CECA.

EDC, *European Defence Community*, Communauté européenne de défense, CED.

ed(it). 1. *edition*, édition, éd. **2.** *editor*, rédacteur.

EEC, *European Economic Community*, Communauté économique européenne, CEE.

EEG, *electroencephalogram*, électroencéphalogramme, EEG.

e.g., *for example*, par exemple, p. ex.

encl., *enclosure(s)*, pièce(s) jointe(s), P.J.

ENE, *east-north-east*, est-nord-est, E.-N.-E.

eng(r), *engineer*, ingénieur, ing(én).

ESE, *east-south-east*, est-sud-est, E.-S.-E.

Esq., *Esquire*.

est., *establishment*, établissement, établ., étabt.

ETA, *estimated time of arrival*.

et al., *et alia*, et caetera, etc.

etc., *etcetera*, et caetera, etc.

Euratom, Communauté européenne de l'énergie atomique, CEEA, Euratom.

ex., *example*, exemple, ex.

Exc., *Excellency*, Excellence, Exc.

F., *Fahrenheit*, Fahrenheit, F.

FBI, *U.S: Federal Bureau of Investigation*.

FC, *football club*.

Feb., *February*, février, fév.

fem., *feminine*, féminin, f.

FF, *French franc(s)*, franc(s) français, FF.

fig. 1. *figure*, illustration, figure, fig. **2.** *figurative*, figuré, fig.

fl., *florin*, florin, fl.

FM, *frequency modulation*, modulation de fréquence.

FO, *Foreign Office* = Ministère des Affaires Étrangères.

f.o.b., *Com: free on board*, franco à bord, f. à b.

f.o.c., *Com: free of charge*, franco, fco.

fol., *following*, suivant, suiv.

Fr. 1. *Ecc: Father*, Père. **2.** *franc*.

Fri., *Friday*, vendredi, vend.

ft, *Meas: foot, feet*.

fwd, *forward*.

gal., *Meas: gallon(s)*.

GB, *Great Britain*, Grande-Bretagne, G.-B.

GC, *George Cross*.

GDR, *German Democratic Republic*, République démocratique allemande, RDA.

Gen., *Mil: General*, Général, Gal.

gen., *general*, Général, gal.

GHQ, *Mil: General Headquarters*, Grand quartier général, GQG.

GI, *U.S: General* (or *Government*) *issue*, mobilisé américain.

GLC, *Greater London Council*.

GMT, *Greenwich Mean Time,* heure de Greenwich.

GNP, *Gross National Product,* produit national brut, PNB.

govt, *government.*

GPO, *the Post Office,* Postes et Télécommunications, P et T, Postes, télégraphes et téléphones, PTT.

gr. 1. *Meas: gramme(s),* gramme(s), g., **gr. 2.** *Ph: gravity,* gravité, g.

h., *hour,* heure, h.

h. & c., *hot and cold.*

HCF, *Mth: highest common factor,* plus grand commun diviseur, p.g.c.d.

hect., *Meas: hectolitre,* hectolitre, hl.

hectog., *Meas: hectogramme,* hectogramme, hg.

HF, 1. *high frequency,* haute fréquence, HF. **2.** *Ecc: Holy Father,* Saint-Père, S.-P.

HH, *His Holiness,* Sa Sainteté, SS.

HM, *His, Her, Majesty.*

HMSO, *His, Her, Majesty's Stationery Office.*

Hon. 1. *Honourable.* **2. Hon. Sec.,** *Honorary Secretary.*

HP, *hire purchase.*

h.p., *Mec: horse-power,* cheval, ch., cheval-vapeur, c.-v.

HQ, *Mil: headquarters,* état-major, E.-M., quartier général, QG.

HRH, *His, Her, Royal Highness.*

ibid., *ibidem,* ibidem, ibid.

i/c., *in command.*

i.e., *that is to say,* c'est-à-dire, c.-à-d.

ILO, *International Labour Organization,* Organisation internationale du travail, OIT, Bureau international du travail, BIT.

IMF, *International Monetary Fund,* Fonds monétaire international, FMI.

incl., *including.*

ind., *industry,* industrie, ind.

inf., *Mil: infantry,* infanterie, inf.

inst., *Corr: instant,* courant, ct.

IOC, *International Olympic Committee,* Comité international olympique, CIO.

IOU, *"I owe you"*

i.p.s., *Rec: inches per second* = centimètres par seconde, cm/s.

IQ, *intelligence quotient,* quotient d'intelligence, QI.

IRA, *Irish Republican Army.*

Is, *island(s).*

ITV, *Independent Television.*

j., *El: joule,* joule, J., j.

Jan., *January,* janvier, janv.

J.C., *Jesus Christ,* Jésus-Christ, J.-C.

JP, *Justice of the Peace.* .

Jr., *Junior.*

Jul., *July,* juillet, juil.

Jun. 1. *Junior.* **2.** *June,* juin.

k., *kilo,* kilo, k.

kc., *El: kilocycle,* kilocycle, kc., kilohertz, kHz.

kg., *Meas: kilogramme,* kilogramme, kg(r).

kilo, *Meas: kilogramme,* kilogramme, kilo.

km., *Meas: kilometre(s),* kilomètre(s), km; **k.p.h.,** *kilometres per hour,* kilomètres (à l')heure, km/h.

K.O., *Box: knockout,* knock-out, k.o.; **he was K.O'd.,** il a été mis k.o.

kva., *El: kilovolt-ampere(s),* kilovoltampère, kVA.

kw., *El: kilowatt,* kilowatt, kW.

kwhr., *El: kilowatt-hour(s),* kilowatt(s)-heure, kWh.

l. 1. *Meas: litre,* litre, l. **2.** *left,* gauche, g.

lat., *Geog: latitude,* latitude, lat.

lb., *Meas: pound,* livre, lb.

LF, *low frequency,* basse fréquence, BF.

l.h., *left hand*

Lieut., *Mil: Lieutenant,* lieutenant, Lieut.

Lieut.-Col., *Mil: Lieutenant-Colonel,* lieutenant-colonel, Lieut-Col.

loc. cit., *at the place cited,* loco citato, loc.cit.

log., *Mth: logarithm,* logarithme, log.

long., *Geog: longitude,* longitude, long.

LP, *longplaying record,* microsillon.

LSD, *Pharm: lysergic acid diethylamide,* lysergique synthétique diéthylamine, LSD.

Lt, *Mil: Lieutenant,* lieutenant, Lt.

Ltd., *Com: Limited (Company),* limitée, Ltée.

m. 1. *masculine,* masculin, m. **2.** *Meas: metre,* mètre, m; **m²,** *square metre,* mètre carré, m²; **m³,** *cubic metre,* mètre cube, m³.

MA, *Master of Arts.*

Mar., *March,* mars.

math., *N.Am: mathematics.*

maths, *mathematics.*

max., *maximum,* maximum, max.

Med., *Geog: the Mediterranean,* la Méditerranée.

Messrs, *Messieurs,* MM.

mg., *Meas: milligramme,* milligramme, mg.

Mgr, *Ecc: Monsignor,* Monseigneur, Mgr.

min., *minimum,* minimum, min.

mm., *Meas: millimetre(s),* millimètre(s), mm; **mm²,** *square millimetre(s),* millimètre(s) carré(s), mm²; **mm³,** *cubic millimetre(s),* millimètre(s) cube(s), mm³.

mod. cons, *modern conveniences.*

Mon., *Monday,* lundi, lun.

MP, 1. *Member of Parliament.* **2.** *Military Police(man).*

m.p.g., *miles per gallon.*

m.p.h., *miles per hour.*

MS., *manuscript,* manuscrit, MS; **MSS,** *manuscripts,* manuscrits, MSS.

N., *north,* nord, N.

NATO, *North Atlantic Treaty Organization,* Organisation du traité de l'Atlantique, OTAN.

NB, 1. *nota bene.* **2.** *New Brunswick.*

NCO, *Mil: non-commissioned officer.*

NE, *north-east,* nord-est, N.-E.

NHS, *Adm: National Health Service,* Sécurité Sociale, SS.

NNE, *north-north-east,* nord-nord-est, N.-N.-E.

NNW, *north-north-west,* nord-nord-ouest, N.-N.-O.

No., no., *number,* numéro, No, N°, n°.

Nov., *November,* novembre, nov.

nr, *near.*

NS, *Nova Scotia.*

NT, *New Testament,* Nouveau Testament, NT.

NW, *north-west,* nord-ouest, N.-O., N.-W.

NY, *New York.*

NZ, *New Zealand,* la Nouvelle-Zélande.

OAS, *Organization of American States,* Organisation des États américains, OEA.

ob., *obit,* décédé.

Oct., *October,* octobre, oct.

OECD, *Organization for Economic Co-operation and Development,* Organisation de coopération et de développement économique, OCDE.

OEEC, *Organization for European Economic Co-operation,* Organisation européenne de coopération économique, OECE.

o.n.o., *or nearest offer.*

op., *Mus: opus,* opus, op.

op.cit., *in the work quoted,* opere citato, op.cit.

ord., *ordinary,* ordinaire, ord.

oz., *Meas: ounce(s).*

p. 1. *page,* page, p. **2.** *per,* par, pour, p. **3.** *Num: penny, pence;* **this book costs 50p** ['fifti'piː], ce livre se vend cinquante pence.

PAYE, *Pay as you earn* = impôt retenu à la source.

PC, 1. *Police Constable.* **2.** *postcard,* carte postale.

PE, *Physical Education,* éducation physique.

PG, *paying guest.*

PhD, *Doctor of Philosophy.*

PM, *Prime Minister,* premier ministre.

p.m., *post meridiem,* p.m.

PO, 1. *post office* = bureau de poste. **2.** *postal order,* mandat.

poss., *possible.*

pp., *pages.*

Prof., *Professor,* professeur, Prof.

PS, *postscript,* post-scriptum, PS.

PT, *Physical Training,* éducation physique.

PTO, *please turn over,* tournez s'il vous plaît, TSVP.

PVC, *polyvinyl chloride.*

QC, *Jur: Queen's Counsel.*

QED, *Geom: quod erat demonstrandum,* ce qu'il fallait démontrer, CQFD.

q.v., *which see,* quod vide, q.v.

RA, *Royal Academy.*

RAF, *Royal Air Force.*

RC, *Roman Catholic.*

Rd., *road,* rue, r.

ref., *reference,* référence, Réf.

retd, *retired.*

Rev., *Ecc: Reverend,* Révérend, Rd.

rev., *revolution,* tour, t.

Rgt., *Mil: regiment,* régiment, rég.

r.h., *right hand.*

Rh., *Med: rhesus,* rhésus, Rh.

riv., *river,* fleuve, fl.

rly., *railway,* chemin de fer, c(h). de f.

RN, *Royal Navy.*

ro, *recto,* recto, ro.

rpm, r.p.m., *Mec.E: revolutions per minute,* tours par minute, t.p.m., t/mn.

RSFSR, *Russian Socialist Federated Soviet Republic,* République soviétique fédérative socialiste de Russie, RSFSR.

RSPCA, *Royal Society for the Prevention of Cruelty to Animals* = Société protectrice des animaux, SPA.

RSVP, *the favour of an answer is requested,* réponse s'il vous plaît, RSVP.

S., *south,* sud, S.

s.a.e., *stamped addressed envelope.*

SAYE, *Save as you earn.*

SE, *south-east,* sud-est, S.-E.

SEATO, *South-East Asia Treaty Organization,* Organisation du traité de l'Asie du sud-est, OTASE.

sec. 1. *second (of time),* seconde, sec. **2.** *secretary.*

Sen. 1. *Senior.* **2.** *U.S: Senator.*

Sept., *September,* septembre, sept.

SF, *science fiction.*

Sgt., *Mil: sergeant.*

SJ, *Ecc: of the Society of Jesus,* Societatis Jesu, SJ.

s.o., *someone,* quelqu'un, qn.

Soc., *Society.*

SOS, *W.Tel: Nau:* SOS.

Sq., *Square.*

Sr, *Senior.*

SRN, *State Registered Nurse,* infirmière diplômée.

SSE, *south-south-east,* sud-sud-est, S.-S.-E.

SSW, *south-south-west,* sud-sud-ouest, S.-S.-O.
St. 1. *Ecc: Saint:* Saint(e), St(e). 2. *Street,* rue.
STD, *Subscriber Trunk Dialling.*
sub. 1. *suburb,* faubourg, faub. 2. *submarine,* sous-marin.
Sun., *Sunday,* dimanche, dm.
Supt., *Superintendent.*
SW, *south-west,* sud-ouest, S.-O., S.-W.

T., *Meas: tesla,* tesla, T.
t., *Com: tare,* tare, T.
TB, *Med: tuberculosis.*
Tech., *Technical College.*
tel., *telephone,* téléphone, tél.
temp. 1. *temperature.* 2. *temporary (secretary).*
Th(ur)., *Thursday.*
TNT, *Exp: trinitrotoluene,* trinitrotoluène, TNT.
TUC, *Trades Union Congress.*
Tu(es)., *Tuesday,* mardi, M.
TV, *television,* télévision, TV.

UDI, *unilateral declaration of independence.*
UFO, *unidentified flying object,* objet volant non identifié, OVNI.
UHF, *ultra high frequency.*
UK, *Geog: United Kingdom,* Royaume-Uni.
UN, *United Nations,* Nations Unies.
UNESCO, *United Nations Educational, Scientific and Cultural Organization,* Organisation des Nations Unies pour l'éducation, la science et la culture, UNESCO.
UNICEF, *United Nations International Children's Emergency Fund,* Fonds international pour secours à l'enfance, FISE.
UNO, *United Nations Organization,* Organisation des Nations Unies, ONU.
unpub., *unpublished,* inédit, inéd.
UNRRA, *United Nations Relief and Rehabilitation Administration,* UNRRA.
UPU., *Universal Postal Union,* Union postale universelle, UPU.

US, *United States,* États-Unis, E.-U.
USA, *(the) United States,* (les) États-Unis, USA.
USSR, *Union of Socialist Soviet Republics,* Union des républiques socialistes soviétiques, URSS.

v. 1. *El: volt,* volt, V. 2. *Jur: versus,* contre, c.
VAT, *value added tax,* taxe à la valeur ajoutée, TVA.
VC, 1. *Vice-Chancellor.* 2. *Victoria Cross.*
VD, *venereal disease,* maladie vénérienne.
VHF, *very high frequency,* très haute fréquence.
VIP, *Very Important Person; to give s.o. VIP treatment,* recevoir qn avec grande cérémonie.
viz., *videlicet.*
vo, *back of page,* verso, vo.
vocab., *vocabulary,* vocabulaire.
vol. 1. *volume,* volume, vol. 2. *volume,* tome, tom., t.

W., *west,* ouest, O.
w., *El: watt,* watt, W.
WC, *water-closet,* water-closet, WC, w.c.
Wed., *Wednesday,* mercredi, M., Me.
wh., *El: watt-hour(s),* watt(s)-heure, wh.
WHO, *World Health Organization,* Organisation mondiale de la santé, OMS.
WNW, *west-north-west,* ouest-nord-ouest, O.-N.-O.
WSW, *west-south-west,* ouest-sud-ouest, O.-S.-O.

Xmas, *Christmas.*

yr, *your,* votre, v.

%, *per cent,* pour cent, %
‰, *per thousand,* pour mille, ‰
£, *pound sterling,* livre sterling, L.
£.s.d., *Num: A: librae, solidi, denarii, pounds, shillings, pence.*

Harrap's
French
and
English
Dictionaries

The famous Harrap family of bilingual dictionaries:

1. The **New Standard** (French-English) and **Standard** (English-French) for advanced students, translators and others needing a really comprehensive dictionary which can satisfy the highest demands.

2. The **New Shorter** for undergraduates, senior school students, executives and others who require a handy, modern work full enough for all normal needs.

3. The **New Pocket**, a really modern, useful little dictionary which contains a remarkable amount of material, for use in schools, by the tourist and in the office as a quick reference.

4. The **Mini**, an unabridged version of the *New Pocket* reduced in size and price, to fit all pockets.

Write for full details to: Harrap Books, 182-184 High Holborn, London WC1V 7AX.

Harrap's NEW STANDARD French and English Dictionary

Part One: French-English
Volume 1 (A-I), 597 pages
Volume 2 (J-Z), 556 pages
11¼" x 8¾"   286 x 222mm

Harrap's STANDARD French and English Dictionary

Part Two: English-French
Complete in one volume,
1551 pages
11¼" x 8¼"   286 x 210mm

"Reviewing **Harrap's New Standard French and English Dictionary** can probably be compared to road-testing the latest Rolls-Royce. In each case one knows that there is nothing better, that the product is unique, and that it is built on the experience of decades of thought and research. Equally important one knows that the purchase will have to give faithful service for many years."
The Times Higher Education Supplement

"The incomparable Standard bilingual dictionary"
Daily Telegraph

Harrap's NEW SHORTER French and English Dictionary

Part 1: French-English,
664 pages
Part 2: English-French,
872 pages
Complete in one volume
1524 pages
(The Complete dictionary is
also available in thumb indexed
and leather bound editions).
9½" x 6½"   242 x 166mm

"Use is the test of a dictionary and use over a period of some six months has proved to this reviewer that the New Shorter is almost impossible to fault. The definitions are exact and illuminating and they are lavishly illustrated by examples."
The Times Literary Supplement

"As welcome in the home as in the library."
Daily Telegraph

Harrap's NEW POCKET French and English Dictionary

Complete in one volume,
525 pages
$7\frac{3}{8}''$ x $4\frac{5}{8}''$ 188 x 117mm

Harrap's MINI POCKET French and English Dictionary

Complete in one volume,
544 pages
$5\frac{1}{4}''$ x $3\frac{3}{8}''$ 133 x 92mm

"This volume has the qualities one always finds in Harrap dictionaries."
The Times Educational Supplement

"Remarkably good value."
Daily Telegraph

"The **Mini** is the answer for those who could not get the *New Pocket* into their pockets. It is an unabridged version of the *New Pocket* which has simply been reduced in size although without any sacrifice to clarity. At the price it provides the best value for all pockets."